THE EUROPA DIRECTORY OF INTERNATIONAL ORGANIZATIONS 2012

THE EUROPA DIRECTORY OF INTERNATIONAL ORGANIZATIONS 2012

14TH EDITION

Routledge
Taylor & Francis Group

LONDON AND NEW YORK

14th edition published 2012
by Routledge
2 Park Square, Milton Park, Abingdon, Oxon, OX14 4RN

Simultaneously published in the USA and Canada
by Routledge
711 Third Avenue, New York, NY 10017

Routledge is an imprint of the Taylor & Francis Group, an Informa business

First published 1999

ISBN: 978-1-85743-648-8
ISSN: 1465-4628

Editor: Helen Canton

Contributing Editors: Robert Elster (Who's Who), Imogen Gladman (EU), Catriona Holman

Directory Editorial Researchers: Arijit Khasnobis (Team Manager), Sakshi Mathur

Editorial Director: Paul Kelly

Typeset in Helvetica and Plantin
by Data Standards Limited, Frome, Somerset

Printed and bound in Great Britain by
TJ International Ltd, Padstow, Cornwall

FOREWORD

The 14th edition of THE EUROPA DIRECTORY OF INTERNATIONAL ORGANIZATIONS offers readers a comprehensive guide to international organizations and an essential understanding of the framework of international affairs. It provides, in a single volume, detailed coverage of the most important intergovernmental groupings, as well as more concise details of almost 2,000 other entities.

Part One provides general background information to the complex architecture of international arrangements that has developed over the years. It includes a description of the history and basic structure of the international system, and indepth observations of international co-operation with respect to humanitarian and environmental challenges. A newly-commissioned essay details the efforts of the international community to effect a global security policy, and demonstrates the complexity of the institutional arrangements and operations of key international and regional organizations. An essay on the governance of the world economy has been given a new focus for this edition in light of the ongoing global financial and economic crisis. Important milestones in the development of today's international system are listed in a unique chronology.

The United Nations is covered in depth, in Part Two, reflecting its status as the world's largest intergovernmental body. Detailed information on the structure, membership and activities of all major offices, programmes and agencies is given. Similar information is provided, in Part Three, for other major international organizations. While these bodies do not operate in isolation, and there is an increasing level of collaboration between them, the structured approach of these principal sections is intended to provide the reader with an accessible overview of each organization as accurately and clearly as possible. Briefer details of other international organizations appear in Part Four, where, for ease of reference, they are listed according to subject. An index to all organizations appearing in Parts Two, Three and Four is to be found at the back of the volume.

Several articles incorporate the text of an organization's founding treaty or other significant document that shaped its future structure and objectives. Other important international treaties are positioned so as to be of most interest or use to the reader; usually this is where an organization has been actively involved in its formulation, even if not bearing any legal responsibility for its implementation or supervision. Separately documented are lists of key resolutions adopted by the UN General Assembly and Security Council, which aim to place the activities and development of these bodies, in particular the UN's peace-keeping and peace-building role, within a broader context.

The book concludes, in Part Five, with a Who's Who section, providing biographical information on the principal officers and other key personalities in international organizations.

All the information in this publication has been extensively researched and verified. The editors are most grateful to those organizations and individuals that have provided information for this edition, and to the contributors for their articles and advice.

June 2012

ACKNOWLEDGEMENTS

The reproduction of texts, and summaries of texts, of international treaties, founding documents and intergovernmental declarations is gratefully acknowledged.

The editors also wish to thank the many individuals and organizations whose interest and co-operation helped in the preparation of this publication, and all those who have replied to Europa's questionnaires. Their generous assistance is recognized as being invaluable in presenting consistently accurate and up-to-date material.

CONTENTS

PART FOUR

Other International Organizations

Listed by subject

PART FIVE

Who's Who in International Organizations

ABBREVIATIONS

Abog.	Abogado (Lawyer)
Acad.	Academician; Academy
ACP	African, Caribbean and Pacific (countries)
ADB	Asian Development Bank
Adm.	Admiral
admin.	administration
AEC	African Economic Community; African Economic Conference
AfDB	African Development Bank
AFESD	Arab Fund for Economic and Social Development
AFTA	ASEAN Free Trade Area
AU	African Union
AH	anno Hegirae
a.i.	ad interim
AIA	ASEAN Investment Area
AIDS	acquired immunodeficiency syndrome
Al.	Aleja (Alley, Avenue)
ALADI	Asociación Latinoamericana de Integración
Alt.	Alternate
amalg.	amalgamated
Apdo	Apartado (Post Box)
APEC	Asia-Pacific Economic Cooperation
approx.	approximately
Apt	Apartment
ARV	advanced retroviral
ASEAN	Association of Southeast Asian Nations
ASEM	Asia-Europe Meeting
asscn	association
assoc.	associate
asst	assistant
Aug.	August
auth.	authorized
av., Ave	Avenija, Avenue
Avda	Avenida (Avenue)
Avv.	Avvocato (Lawyer)
BA	Bachelor of Arts
Bd	Board
Bd, Bld, Blv., Blvd	Boulevard
b/d	barrels per day
BINUB	United Nations Integrated Office in Burundi
BIS	Bank for International Settlements
Bldg	Building
BINUCA	United Nations Integrated Peace-building Office in the Central African Republic
Bn	battallion
BNUB	United Nations Office in Burundi
BP	Boîte postale (Post Box)
br.(s)	branch(es)
Brig.	Brigadier
BSE	bovine spongiform encephalopathy
bte	boîte (box)
BSEC	(Organization of the) Black Sea Economic Cooperation
bul.	bulvar (boulevard)
c.	circa; cuadra(s) (block(s)); child, children
CACM	Central American Common Market
Cad.	Caddesi (Street)
CAN	Comunidad Andina de Naciones
CAP	Common Agricultural Policy; Consolidated Inter-agency Appeal Process
cap.	capital
Capt.	Captain
CAR	Central African Republic
CARICOM	Caribbean Community and Common Market
CBSS	Council of Baltic Sea States
Cdre	Commodore
Cen.	Central
CEO	Chief Executive Officer
CET	common external tariff
CFA	Communauté Financiére Africaine; Co-opération Financiére en Afrique centrale
CFE	Treaty on Conventional Armed Forces in Europe
CFP	Common Fisheries Policy; Communauté française du Pacifique; Comptoirs français du Pacifique
CFSP	Common Foreign and Security Policy
CGAP	Consultative Group to Assist the Poorest
CGIAR	Consultative Group on International Agricultural Research
Chair.	Chairman/person/woman
Cia	Companhia
Cía	Compañia
Cie	Compagnie
c.i.f.	cost, insurance and freight
C-in-C	Commander-in-Chief
circ.	circulation
CIS	Commonwealth of Independent States
CJTF	Combined Joint Task Force
cm	centimetre(s)
CMAG	Commonwealth Ministerial Action Goup on the Harare Declaration
Cnr	Corner
c/o	care of
Co	Company; County
Col	Colonel
Col.	Colonia
Coll.	College
COMESA	Common Market for Eastern and Southern Africa
Comm.	Commission; Commendatore
Commdr	Commander
Commdt	Commandant
Commr	Commissioner
Confed.	Confederation
Confs	conferences
Cont.	Contador (Accountant)
COO	Chief Operating Officer
COP	Conference of (the) Parties
Corpn	Corporation
CP	Case Postale; Caixa Postal; Casella Postale (Post Box)
Cres.	Crescent
CSCE	Conference on Security and Co-operation in Europe
CSDP	Common Security and Defence Policy
CTBT	Comprehensive (Nuclear) Test Ban Treaty
Cttee	Committee
cu	cubic
cwt	hundredweight
d.	daughter(s)
DC	District of Columbia; Distrito Central
DDC	UNDP Drylands Development Centre
Dec.	December
Del.	Delegación; Delegate
Dem.	Democratic; Democrat
Dep.	Deputy
dep.	deposits
Dept	Department
devt	development
DF	Distrito Federal
Diag.	Diagonal
Dir	Director
Div.	Division(al)
DN	Distrito Nacional
Doc.	Docent
DOMREP	Mission of the Representative of the Secretary-General in the Dominican Republic
DOTS	direct observation treatment; short-course
Dott.	Dottore
DPRK	Democratic People's Republic of Korea
Dr	Doctor
Dr.	Drive
Dra	Doctora
DRC	Democratic Republic of the Congo
DR-CAFTA	Dominican Republic-Central American Free Trade Agreement
Drs	Doctorandus
dwt	dead weight tons
E	East; Eastern
EAC	East African Community
EBRD	European Bank for Reconstruction and Development
EC	European Community
ECA	(United Nations) Economic Commission for Africa
ECE	(United Nations) Economic Commission for Europe
ECLAC	(United Nations) Economic Commission for Latin America and the Caribbean
ECO	Economic Co-operation Organization
Econ.	Economic; Economics; Economist

ECOSOC (United Nations) Economic and Social Council
ECOWAS Economic Community of West African States
ECU European Currency Unit
ed. educated
EDI Economic Development Institute
Edif. Edificio (Building)
edn edition
EEA European Economic Area
EEC European Economic Community
EFTA European Free Trade Association
e.g. exempli gratia (for example)
EIB European Investment Bank
EMS European Monetary System
EMU Economic and Monetary Union
Eng. Engineer; Engineering
ERM exchange rate mechanism
ESA European Space Agency
Esc. Escuela; Escudos; Escritorio
ESCAP (United Nations) Economic and Social Commission for Asia and the Pacific
ESCWA (United Nations) Economic and Social Commission for Western Asia
ESDI European Security and Defence Identity
ESDP European Security and Defence Policy
esq. esquina (corner)
est. established; estimate; estimated
etc. et cetera
EU European Union
excl. excluding
exec. executive
Ext. Extension

f. founded
fax facsimile
FAO Food and Agriculture Organization
FATF Financial Action Task Force on Money Laundering
FDI foreign direct investment
Feb. February
Fed. Federation; Federal
feds federations
FM frequency modulation
fmrly formerly
f.o.b. free on board
Fr Father
Fr. Franc
FRY Federal Republic of Yugoslavia
ft foot (feet)
FTA free trade agreement/area
FTAA Free Trade Area of the Americas
FYRM former Yugoslav republic of Macedonia

g gram(s)
GAFTA Greater Arab Free Trade Area
GATT General Agreement on Tariffs and Trade
GCC Gulf Cooperation Council
GDP gross domestic product
Gdns Gardens
GEF Global Environment Facility
Gen. General
GIEWS Global Information and Early Warning System
GM genetically modified
GMT Greenwich Mean Time
GNP gross national product
Gov. Governor
Govt Government
GPML Global Programme Against Money Laundering
grt gross registered tons
GSM Global System for Mobile Communications
GWh gigawatt hours

ha hectares
HE His/Her Eminence; His/Her Excellency
HEWS Humanitarian Early Warning System
HIPC heavily indebted poor country
HIV human immunodeficiency virus
HLTF High Level Task Force
HPAI highly pathogenic avian influenza
hl hectolitre(s)
HM His/Her Majesty
Hon. Honorary; Honourable
HQ Headquarters
HRH His/Her Royal Highness

IAEA International Atomic Energy Agency
IASC Inter-Agency Standing Committee
IBRD International Bank for Reconstruction and Development (World Bank)
ICAO International Civil Aviation Organization
ICC International Chamber of Commerce; International Criminal Court
ICJ International Court of Justice
ICRC International Committee of the Red Cross
ICSID International Centre for Settlement of Investment Disputes
ICT information and communication technology
ICTR International Criminal Tribunal for Rwanda
ICTY International Criminal Tribunal for the former Yugoslavia
IDA International Development Association
IDB Inter-American Development Bank
IDP internally displaced person
i.e. id est (that is to say)
IFAD International Fund for Agricultural Development
IFC International Finance Corporation
IFI international financial institution
IGAD Intergovernmental Authority on Development
IHL International Humanitarian Law
IML International Migration Law
ILO International Labour Organization/Office
IML International Migration Law
IMF International Monetary Fund
IMO International Maritime Organization
in (ins) inch (inches)
Inc, Incorp., Incd Incorporated
incl. including
Ind. Independent
Ing. Engineer
INSAG International Nuclear Safety Advisory Group
Insp. Inspector
Inst. Institute
Int. International
IOC International Olympic Committee
IOM International Organization for Migration
IP Intellectual Property
IPM Integrated Pest Management
IPU Inter-Parliamentary Union
irreg. irregular
Is Islands
ISIC International Standard Industrial Classification
IT information technology
ITU International Telecommunication Union
ITUC International Trade Union Confederation
IUU illegal, unreported and unregulated

Jan. January
Jnr Junior
Jr Jonkheer (Netherlands); Junior
Jt Joint

kg kilogram(s)
kHz kilohertz
km kilometre(s)
kv. kvartal (apartment block); kvartira (apartment)
kW kilowatt(s)
kWh kilowatt hours

LAC Latin America and Caribbean
LAIA Latin American Integration Association
lb pound(s)
LDCs Least Developed Countries
Lic. Licenciado
Licda Licenciada
Lt, Lieut Lieutenant
Ltd Limited

m metre(s)
m. married; million
MAFTA Mediterranean Arab Free Trade Area
Maj. Major
Man. Manager; managing
MDG Millennium Development Goal
MDG-F MDG Achievement Fund
MDRI multilateral debt relief initiative
mem. member
MEP Member of the European Parliament
Mercosul Mercado Comun do Sul (Southern Common Market)
Mercosur Mercado Común del Sur (Southern Common Market)

MFN	most favoured nation
mfrs	manufacturers
Mgr	Monseigneur; Monsignor
MHz	megahertz
MIGA	Multilateral Investment Guarantee Agency
Mil.	Military
Min.	Minister; Ministry
MINUCI	United Nations Mission in Côte d'Ivoire
MINUGUA	United Nations Verification Mission in Guatemala
MINURCA	United Nations Mission in the Central African Republic
MINURCAT	United Nations Mission in the Central African Republic and Chad
MINURSO	United Nations Mission for the Referendum in Western Sahara
MINUSTAH	United Nations Stabilization Mission in Haiti
MIPONUH	United Nations Civilian Police Mission in Haiti
Mlle	Mademoiselle
mm	millimetre(s)
Mme	Madame
MONUA	United Nations Observer Mission in Angola
MONUC	United Nations Mission in the Democratic Republic of the Congo
MONUSCO	United Nations Organization Stabilization Mission in the Democratic Republic of the Congo
MOU	Memorandum of Understanding
MP	Member of Parliament
MSS	Manuscripts
MW	megawatt(s); medium wave
MWh	megawatt hour(s)

N	North; Northern
n.a.	not available
nab.	naberezhnaya (embankment, quai)
NAFTA	North American Free Trade Agreement
nám.	námestí (square)
Nat.	National
NATO	North Atlantic Treaty Organization
NCO	Non-Commissioned Officer
NEPAD	New Partnership for Africa's Development
NGO	non-governmental organization
no	número (number)
no.	number
Nov.	November
NPT	(Nuclear) Non-Proliferation Treaty
NPV	net present value
nr	near
nrt	net registered tons
NSW	New South Wales
NY	New York
NZ	New Zealand

OAPEC	Organization of Arab Petroleum Exporting Countries
OAS	Organization of American States
OAU	Organization of African Unity
OCHA	Office for the Co-ordination of Humanitarian Affairs
Oct.	October
OECD	Organisation for Economic Co-operation and Development
OECS	Organisation of East Caribbean States
Of.	Oficina (Office)
OHCHR	Office of the United Nations High Commissioner for Human Rights
OIC	Organization of Islamic Cooperation
ONUB	United Nations Operation in Burundi
ONUC	United Nations Operation in the Congo
ONUCA	United Nations Observer Group in Central America
ONUMOZ	United Nations Operation in Mozambique
ONUSAL	United Nations Observer Mission in El Salvador
OPEC	Organization of the Petroleum Exporting Countries
opp.	opposite
ORB	OPEC Reference Basket
Org.	Organization
OSCE	Organization for Security and Co-operation in Europe

p.	page
p.a.	per annum
PA	Palestinian Authority
PACER	Pacific Agreement on Closer Economic Relations
PAPP	Programme of Assistance to the Palestinian People
Parl.	Parliament(ary)
pas.	passazh (passage)
per.	pereulok (lane, alley)
Perm. Rep.	Permanent Representative
PF	Postfach (Post Box)
PIC	Prior Informed Consent
PICTs	Pacific Island countries and territories
PICTA	Pacific Island Countries Trade Agreement
PK	Post Box (Turkish)
PKO	peace-keeping operation
pl.	platz; place; ploshchad (square)
PLC	Public Limited Company
PLO	Palestine Liberation Organization
PMB	Private Mail Bag
PNA	Palestinian National Authority
POB	Post Office Box
PoW	Prisoner of War
pr.	prospekt (avenue)
Pres.	President
PRSP	Poverty Reduction Strategy Paper(s)
Prin.	Principal
Prof.	Professor
Propr	Proprietor
Prov.	Province; Provincial; Provinciale (Dutch)
PRT	Provincial Reconstruction Team
Pte	Private
Pty	Proprietary
p.u.	paid up
publ.	publication; published
Publr	Publisher
Pvt.	Private

QIP	Quick Impact Project
q.v.	quod vide (to which refer)

Rd	Road
REC	regional economic community
reg., regd	register; registered
reorg.	reorganized
Rep.	Republic; Republican; Representative
Repub.	Republic
res	reserve(s)
retd	retired
Rev.	Reverend
Rm	Room
Rt	Right

S	South; Southern; San
s.	son(s)
SA	Société Anonyme, Sociedad Anónima (Limited Company); South Australia
SAARC	South Asian Association for Regional Cooperation
SACN	South American Community of Nations
SADC	Southern African Development Community
SAFTA	South Asian Free Trade Area
SAR	Special Administrative Region
SARS	Severe Acute Respiratory Syndrome
SDR(s)	Special Drawing Right(s)
Sec.	Secretary
Secr.	Secretariat
Sen.	Senior; Senator
Sept.	September
SICA	Sistema de la Integración Centroamericana
SIS	Small(er) Island States
SITC	Standard International Trade Classification
SJ	Society of Jesus
SMEs	small and medium-sized enterprises
Soc.	Society
Sok.	Sokak (Street)
SPARTECA	South Pacific Regional Trade and Economic Co-operation Agreement
Sq.	Square
sq	square (in measurements)
Sr	Senior; Señor
Sra	Señora
SRSG	Special Representative of the Secretary-General
St	Saint; Street
Sta	Santa
Ste	Sainte
STI(s)	sexually transmitted infections(s)
Str., str.	Strasse, strada, stradă, strasse (street)
subs.	subscriptions; subscribed
Supt	Superintendent

tech., techn.	technical
tel.	telephone
Treas.	Treasurer
TV	television

u.	utca (street)
u/a	unit of account
UAE	United Arab Emirates
UDEAC	Union Douanière et Economique de l'Afrique Centrale
UEE	Unidade Econónica Estatal
UEMOA	Union économique et monétaire ouest-africaine
UK	United Kingdom
ul.	ulitsa (street)
UN	United Nations
UNAMA	United Nations Assistance Mission in Afghanistan
UNAMI	United Nations Assistance Mission for Iraq
UNAMIC	United Nations Advance Mission in Cambodia
UNAMID	African Union/United Nations Hybrid Operation in Darfur
UNAMIR	United Nations Assistance Mission for Rwanda
UNAMSIL	United Nations Mission in Sierra Leone
UNASOG	United Nations Aouzou Strip Observer Group
UNASUR	Union of South American Nations
UNAVEM	United Nations Angola Verification Mission
UNCDF	United Nations Capital Development Fund
UNCED	United Nations Conference on Environment and Development
UNCRO	United Nations Confidence Restoration Operation in Croatia
UNCTAD	United Nations Conference on Trade and Development
UNDOF	United Nations Disengagement Observer Force
UNDP	United Nations Development Programme
UNEF	United Nations Emergency Force
UNEP	United Nations Environment Programme
UNESCO	United Nations Educational, Scientific and Cultural Organization
UNFICYP	United Nations Peace-keeping Force in Cyprus
UNGOMAP	United Nations Good Offices Mission in Afghanistan and Pakistan
UNHCHR	United Nations High Commissioner for Human Rights
UNHCR	United Nations High Commissioner for Refugees
UNICEF	United Nations Children's Fund
UNIDO	United Nations Industrial Development Organization
UNIFEM	United Nations Development Fund for Women
UNIFIL	United Nations Interim Force in Lebanon
UNIIMOG	United Nations Iran-Iraq Military Observer Group
UNIKOM	United Nations Iraq-Kuwait Observation Mission
UNIOGBIS	United Nations Integrated Peace-building Office in Guinea-Bissau
UNIOSIL	United Nations Integrated Office in Sierra Leone
UNIPOM	United Nations India-Pakistan Observation Mission
UNIPSIL	United Nations Integrated Peace-building Office in Sierra Leone
UNISFA	United Nations Interim Security Force for Abyei
UNITA	Uniâo Nacional para a Independência Total de Angola
Univ.	University
UNMEE	United Nations Mission in Ethiopia and Eritrea
UNMIBH	United Nations Mission in Bosnia and Herzegovina
UNMIH	United Nations Mission in Haiti
UNMIK	United Nations Interim Administration Mission in Kosovo
UNMIL	United Nations Mission in Liberia
UNMIN	United Nations Mission in Nepal
UNMIS	United Nations Mission in Sudan
UNMISET	United Nations Mission of Support in East Timor
UNMISS	United Nations Mission in South Sudan
UNMIT	United Nations Integrated Mission in East Timor
UNMOGIP	United Nations Military Observer Group in India and Pakistan
UNMOP	United Nations Mission of Observers in Prevlaka
UNMOT	United Nations Mission of Observers in Tajikistan
UNMOVIC	United Nations Monitoring,Verification and Inspection Commission
UNOCA	United Nations Regional Office for Central Africa
UNOCI	United Nations Operation in Côte d'Ivoire
UNODC	United Nations Office on Drugs and Crime
UNOGBIS	United Nations Peace-building Support Office in Guinea-Bissau
UNOGIL	United Nations Observation Group in Lebanon
UNOMIG	United Nations Observer Mission in Georgia
UNOMIL	United Nations Observer Mission in Liberia
UNOMSIL	United Nations Observer Mission in Sierra Leone
UNOMUR	United Nations Observer Mission Uganda-Rwanda
UNOPS	United Nations Office for Project Services
UNOSOM	United Nations Operation in Somalia
UNOWA	Office of the Special Representative of the UN Secretary-General for West Africa
UNPA	United Nations Protected Area
UNPEI	UNDP-UNEP Poverty-Environment Initiative
UNPOS	United Nations Political Office for Somalia
UNPREDEP	United Nations Preventive Deployment Force
UNPROFOR	United Nations Protection Force
UNRCCA	United Nations Regional Centre for Preventive Diplomacy for Central Asia
UNRWA	United Nations Relief and Works Agency for Palestine Refugees in the Near East
UNSCO	Office of the United Nations Special Co-ordinator for the Middle East Peace Process
UNSCOL	Office of the United Nations Special Co-ordinator for Lebanon
UNSCOM	United Nations Special Commission
UNSF	United Nations Security Force in West New Guinea (New Irian)
UNSMIH	United Nations Support Mission in Haiti
UNSMIL	United Nations Support Mission in Libya
UNSMIS	United Nations Supervision Mission in Syria
UNTAC	United Nations Transitional Authority in Cambodia
UNTAES	United Nations Transitional Administration for Eastern Slavonia, Baranja and Western Sirmium
UNTAET	United Nations Transitional Administration in East Timor
UNTAG	United Nations Transition Group
UNTMIH	United Nations Transition Mission in Haiti
UNTSO	United Nations Truce Supervision Organization
UNV	United Nations Volunteers
UNWTO	World Tourism Organization
UNYOM	United Nations Yemen Observation Mission
UPU	Universal Postal Union
US	United States
USA	United States of America
USAID	United States Agency for International Development
USSR	Union of Soviet Socialist Republics
VAT	value-added tax
Ven.	Venerable
VI	(US) Virgin Islands
viz.	videlicet (namely)
Vn	Veien (Street)
vol.(s)	volume(s)
vul.	vulitsa, vulytsa (street)
W	West; Western
WA	Western Australia; Washington (State)
WEU	Western European Union
WFP	World Food Programme
WFTU	World Federation of Trade Unions
WHO	World Health Organization
WIPO	World Intellectual Property Organization
WMD	weapons of mass destruction
WMO	World Meteorological Organization
WSSD	World Summit on Sustainable Development
WTO	World Trade Organization
yr	year

INTERNATIONAL TELEPHONE CODES

To make international calls to telephone and fax numbers listed in *The Europa Directory of International Organizations*, dial the international access code of the country from which you are calling, followed by the appropriate country code for the organization you wish to call (listed below), followed by the area code (if applicable) and telephone or fax number listed in the entry.

	Country code	+ or – GMT*
Abkhazia	7	+4
Afghanistan	93	+4½
Åland Islands	358	+2
Albania	355	+1
Algeria	213	+1
American Samoa	1 684	–11
Andorra	376	+1
Angola	244	+1
Anguilla	1 264	–4
Antigua and Barbuda	1 268	–4
Argentina	54	–3
Armenia	374	+4
Aruba	297	–4
Ascension Island	247	0
Australia	61	+8 to +10
Austria	43	+1
Azerbaijan	994	+5
Bahamas	1 242	–5
Bahrain	973	+3
Bangladesh	880	+6
Barbados	1 246	–4
Belarus	375	+2
Belgium	32	+1
Belize	501	–6
Benin	229	+1
Bermuda	1 441	–4
Bhutan	975	+6
Bolivia	591	–4
Bonaire	599	–4
Bosnia and Herzegovina	387	+1
Botswana	267	+2
Brazil	55	–3 to –4
British Indian Ocean Territory (Diego Garcia)	246	+5
British Virgin Islands	1 284	–4
Brunei	673	+8
Bulgaria	359	+2
Burkina Faso	226	0
Burundi	257	+2
Cambodia	855	+7
Cameroon	237	+1
Canada	1	–3 to –8
Cape Verde	238	–1
Cayman Islands	1 345	–5
Central African Republic	236	+1
Ceuta	34	+1
Chad	235	+1
Chile	56	–4
China, People's Republic	86	+8
Christmas Island	61	+7
Cocos (Keeling) Islands	61	+6½
Colombia	57	–5
Comoros	269	+3
Congo, Democratic Republic	243	+1
Congo, Republic	242	+1
Cook Islands	682	–10
Costa Rica	506	–6
Côte d'Ivoire	225	0
Croatia	385	+1
Cuba	53	–5
Curaçao	599	–4
Cyprus	357	+2
Czech Republic	420	+1
Denmark	45	+1
Djibouti	253	+3
Dominica	1 767	–4
Dominican Republic	1 809	–4
Ecuador	593	–5
Egypt	20	+2
El Salvador	503	–6
Equatorial Guinea	240	+1
Eritrea	291	+3
Estonia	372	+2
Ethiopia	251	+3
Falkland Islands	500	–4
Faroe Islands	298	0
Fiji	679	+12
Finland	358	+2
France	33	+1
French Guiana	594	–3
French Polynesia	689	–9 to –10
Gabon	241	+1
Gambia	220	0
Georgia	995	+4
Germany	49	+1
Ghana	233	0
Gibraltar	350	+1
Greece	30	+2
Greenland	299	–1 to –4
Grenada	1 473	–4
Guadeloupe	590	–4
Guam	1 671	+10
Guatemala	502	–6
Guernsey	44	0
Guinea	224	0
Guinea-Bissau	245	0
Guyana	592	–4
Haiti	509	–5
Honduras	504	–6
Hong Kong	852	+8
Hungary	36	+1
Iceland	354	0
India	91	+5½
Indonesia	62	+7 to +9
Iran	98	+3½
Iraq	964	+3
Ireland	353	0
Isle of Man	44	0
Israel	972	+2
Italy	39	+1
Jamaica	1 876	–5
Japan	81	+9
Jersey	44	0
Jordan	962	+2
Kazakhstan	7	+6
Kenya	254	+3
Kiribati	686	+12 to +13
Korea, Democratic People's Republic (North Korea)	850	+9
Korea, Republic (South Korea)	82	+9
Kosovo	381†	+3
Kuwait	965	+3
Kyrgyzstan	996	+5
Laos	856	+7
Latvia	371	+2
Lebanon	961	+2
Lesotho	266	+2
Liberia	231	0
Libya	218	+1
Liechtenstein	423	+1

	Country code	+ or – GMT*
Lithuania	370	+2
Luxembourg	352	+1
Macao	853	+8
Macedonia, former Yugoslav republic	389	+1
Madagascar	261	+3
Malawi	265	+2
Malaysia	60	+8
Maldives	960	+5
Mali	223	0
Malta	356	+1
Marshall Islands	692	+12
Martinique	596	–4
Mauritania	222	0
Mauritius	230	+4
Mayotte	262	+3
Melilla	34	+1
Mexico	52	–6 to –7
Micronesia, Federated States	691	+10 to +11
Moldova	373	+2
Monaco	377	+1
Mongolia	976	+7 to +9
Montenegro	382	+1
Montserrat	1 664	–4
Morocco	212	0
Mozambique	258	+2
Myanmar	95	+6½
Nagornyi Karabakh	374	+4
Namibia	264	+2
Nauru	674	+12
Nepal	977	+5¾
Netherlands	31	+1
New Caledonia	687	+11
New Zealand	64	+12
Nicaragua	505	–6
Niger	227	+1
Nigeria	234	+1
Niue	683	–11
Norfolk Island	672	+11½
Northern Mariana Islands	1 670	+10
Norway	47	+1
Oman	968	+4
Pakistan	92	+5
Palau	680	+9
Palestinian Autonomous Areas	970 or 972	+2
Panama	507	–5
Papua New Guinea	675	+10
Paraguay	595	–4
Peru	51	–5
Philippines	63	+8
Pitcairn Islands	872	–8
Poland	48	+1
Portugal	351	0
Puerto Rico	1 787	–4
Qatar	974	+3
Réunion	262	+4
Romania	40	+2
Russian Federation	7	+3 to +12
Rwanda	250	+2
Saba	599	–4
Saint-Barthélemy	590	–4
Saint Christopher and Nevis	1 869	–4
Saint Helena	290	0
Saint Lucia	1 758	–4
Saint-Martin	590	–4
Saint Pierre and Miquelon	508	–3
Saint Vincent and the Grenadines	1 784	–4
Samoa	685	+13
San Marino	378	+1
São Tomé and Príncipe	239	0
Saudi Arabia	966	+3
Senegal	221	0
Serbia	381	+1
Seychelles	248	+4
Sierra Leone	232	0
Singapore	65	+8
Sint Eustatius	1721	–4
Sint Maarten	599	–4
Slovakia	421	+1
Slovenia	386	+1
Solomon Islands	677	+11
Somalia	252	+3
South Africa	27	+2
South Ossetia	7	+4
South Sudan	211‡	+2
Spain	34	+1
Sri Lanka	94	+5½
Sudan	249	+2
Suriname	597	–3
Svalbard	47	+1
Swaziland	268	+2
Sweden	46	+1
Switzerland	41	+1
Syria	963	+2
Taiwan	886	+8
Tajikistan	992	+5
Tanzania	255	+3
Thailand	66	+7
Timor-Leste	670	+9
Togo	228	0
Tokelau	690	+15
Tonga	676	+13
Transnistria	373	+2
Trinidad and Tobago	1 868	–4
Tristan da Cunha	290	0
Tunisia	216	+1
Turkey	90	+2
'Turkish Republic of Northern Cyprus'	90 392	+2
Turkmenistan	993	+5
Turks and Caicos Islands	1 649	–5
Tuvalu	688	+12
Uganda	256	+3
Ukraine	380	+2
United Arab Emirates	971	+4
United Kingdom	44	0
United States of America	1	–5 to –10
United States Virgin Islands	1 340	–4
Uruguay	598	–3
Uzbekistan	998	+5
Vanuatu	678	+11
Vatican City	39	+1
Venezuela	58	–4½
Viet Nam	84	+7
Wallis and Futuna Islands	681	+12
Yemen	967	+3
Zambia	260	+2
Zimbabwe	263	+2

* The times listed compare the standard (winter) times in the various countries. Some countries adopt Summer (Daylight Saving) Time—i.e. +1 hour—for part of the year.

† Mobile telephone numbers for Kosovo use either the country code for Monaco (377) or the country code for Slovenia (386).

‡ Although South Sudan was assigned the international telephone code 211 by the International Telecommunication Union in July 2011, many mobile and fixed line telephone services continue to use either Sudanese (249) or Ugandan (256) networks. Therefore, all telephone numbers given for South Sudan include the full international dialling code.

Note: Telephone and fax numbers using the Inmarsat ocean region code 870 are listed in full. No country or area code is required, but it is necessary to precede the number with the international access code of the country from which the call is made.

PART ONE

Background Information

AN INTRODUCTION TO INTERNATIONAL ORGANIZATIONS

CLIVE ARCHER*

The international organizations most often seen in the media, such as the United Nations (UN), the European Union (EU) or the International Olympic Committee, have a wide range of activities and are also quite different in their history, size and nature. Yet they have in common the name 'international organization'. An international organization can be defined as *a formal, continuous structure established by agreement between members (governmental and/or non-governmental) from two or more sovereign states with the aim of pursuing the common interest of the membership.* This definition places an emphasis on membership, which does not have to be that of governments, the structure, i.e. it should be more permanent than a conference, and the pursuit of the members' interests, meaning that the organization should not just exist for the convenience of one member. The wide range of international organizations have become an integral part of the international system since they first appeared on the scene some 200 years ago.

HISTORY

The Beginnings

The first international organizations were established in the 19th century. The earliest was probably the commission established by the Convention of Octroi in 1804 to administer the navigation of the River Rhine, but this became a victim of the Napoleonic wars. It was re-established in 1831, 10 years after a similar international commission for the Elbe was set up. The European Danube Commission was established in 1856, the International Telegraph Union (which became the International Telecommunication Union—ITU) in 1865, with a formal secretariat established in 1868, and the General Postal Union (later the Universal Postal Union—UPU) in 1874. Before such organizations could exist, four preconditions needed to be fulfilled: a number of states functioning as independent political units had to exist; they had to have a substantial measure of contact between themselves; there had to be an awareness of problems that could arise from their co-existence and of the possibilities from co-operation; and there had to be a recognition that relations could be regulated by such institutions as international organizations. Greater ease of travel in the 19th century brought more frequent contact between states. The growth of internationalized commerce prompted the rise of international agencies to help manage it, such as the river commissions. Public organizations were joined by private ones, for example the International Institute of Agriculture, the World Anti-Slavery Convention and the Universal Peace Congress. According to the Union of International Associations (UIA), the number of intergovernmental organizations increased from seven in the 1870s to 37 by 1909, but the number of international non-governmental organizations was already 176 by that date.

The Paris Conference of 1856, at the end of the Crimean War, included a number of declarations covering free trade, naval warfare, the abolition of privateering, blockades and flags of neutrality in wartime. These were agreed not just by the European Great Powers but also by a number of smaller states and non-European countries such as China, Turkey, Japan and Mexico. Many of these states also attended a conference in 1889 in The Hague called to discuss disarmament; 44 states were present at the second Hague Conference, held in 1907. These gatherings established a panel of arbitrators to help settle disputes between states. However, these meetings and organizations did little to ameliorate tension between the main powers in Europe which led to the slide towards war in August 1914.

The First World War and the League of Nations

The First World War of 1914–18 saw immense slaughter and destruction in Europe and the collapse of four empires—the German, Austro-Hungarian, Turkish and Russian. However, the conduct of the war from the French and British, and later American, side involved close co-operation between these states. Several institutions were established, such as the Supreme War Council, served by a secretariat, as well as a range of inter-Allied councils covering economic, military and political aspects of the war. After the USA entered the war, President Woodrow Wilson issued his 'Fourteen Points', one of which was a commitment to 'a general association of nations' to be set up after the war. The British and French administrations had their own schemes for such an organization that would try to prevent a major war from occurring. These ideas were discussed at the Versailles Peace Conference in 1919.

The League of Nations, the main international organization that emerged from Versailles, drew on these plans as well as the wartime and 19th century experience. The Assembly of the League was similar to the Hague gatherings, with each state having one vote. Its Council was more like the Supreme War Council, including the major powers, though it also had some representation from other states, while the secretariat was also similar to that which served the Supreme War Council.

The League has often been seen as an institutionalization of the pre-war diplomacy. However, its founding document, the Covenant, attempted something more advanced. Under Article 11 any threat of war was declared a matter of concern for the whole League, with the League taking 'any action that may be deemed wise and effectual to safeguard the peace of nations'. Furthermore, Articles 12–16 outlined how states might conduct their relations by taking any disputes to the newly-established Permanent Court of International Justice, arbitration, conciliation or mediation, and by allowing a breathing space before resorting to war, unlike in August 1914. States resorting to war in contravention of these articles would be deemed to have committed an act of war against all other League members and would be subject to sanctions. Other parts of the Covenant dealt with matters such as open diplomacy, disarmament, former German colonies, and economic and social issues.

Though President Wilson was one of the founding fathers of the League, he was unable to get US membership accepted by the Senate, and the USA never joined the League, compromising its effectiveness from the start.

The Inter-war Period

At first, it seemed that the League of Nations was a useful, though modest, addition to international diplomacy. It helped solve disputes between Finland and Sweden in 1920, Greece and Bulgaria in 1925 and between Turkey and Iraq. It also brought the questions of refugees and the treatment of minorities to international attention. By the end of the 1920s it was turning its attention to the issue of disarmament.

Nevertheless, the League had two major structural deficiencies. The first was that of membership. As well as the absence of the USA, the Soviet Union only joined in 1935, by which time Germany, Italy and Japan had left. The second was that the Covenant was part of the Versailles Peace Conference and was seen as a victors' charter. It was thus a source of discontent for Germany, especially after Hitler came to power in 1933 with a determination to unravel both the Peace Treaty and the works of the League. Two other powers that had been on the winning side in 1919 felt that the settlement had not given them enough: both Italy and Japan had not received the overseas possessions they expected. In 1931 Japan occupied the northern part of China, Manchuria, and in 1935 Italy invaded Abyssinia (Ethiopia), then one of the few independent states in Africa. In the first case, the

* Clive Archer is Emeritus Professor in International Relations, Manchester Metropolitan University, United Kingdom.

League did little, and in the second it imposed sanctions against Italy, but these were ineffective. As Hitler expanded Germany's power over its neighbours, the League proved unable to act. Only in September 1939 were the British and the French ready to challenge Germany over its invasion of Poland, and this led to the start of the Second World War and the demise of the League of Nations.

The Second World War and the United Nations

The Second World War saw the effective end of the League of Nations and many other international organizations (although the International Committee of the Red Cross undertook important work between the belligerents in Europe overseeing the rules regarding prisoners of war and aiding the treatment and repatriation of injured combatants). The war was also the crucible for the formation of the post-war political structure, when, in a series of meetings, the Allies (the Soviet Union, United Kingdom and the USA, later joined by China and France) decided on the creation of a United Nations Organization (UNO).

The UNO (later shortened to UN) was established in June 1945, at an international conference held in San Francisco, USA, with 50 founding members. After the experience of the League of Nations, the new organization was negotiated during the war and was not tied to any specific peace treaty. Superficially the structure of the UN resembled that of the League. There was a Security Council, of which the Allied Powers had permanent membership; a General Assembly, with all states being allowed membership; a secretariat; and the International Court of Justice, which took over from the Permanent Court of International Justice. There was also an Economic and Social Council and a Trusteeship Council, which oversaw the administration of the colonies of the defeated states. A key difference from the League system was that the Security Council had the prime responsibility for matters of peace and security, something that was not clear about the League Council. Furthermore, the UN Secretary-General had the right to bring security matters to the notice of the Security Council and had wider political powers than his League predecessor.

The UN Security Council was empowered to act when it was agreed that there had been an act of aggression, a breach of the peace or a threat to the peace, a question that was to be settled by a majority of the Council members, but with no Permanent Member voting against (exercising a veto). The Security Council could then resolve, under Chapter Seven of the UN Charter, what sanctions, diplomatic action or armed action should be taken, and all member states were obliged to follow such resolutions. Unlike the fairly legalistic process of the League, the UN peace and security system rested more on political decisions, wherein lay both its strength and weakness.

The Cold War Period

In the post-Second World War period, the UN survived and expanded, especially after the increase in sovereign states resulting from decolonization in the 1960s and 1970s and the fragmentation of the Soviet Union after 1991. By 1955 there were 76 members, 100 by the end of the 1960s, 157 by 1982 and 193 by mid-2012. During the period 1945–89 the UN reflected the major political and economic conditions in the wider world. First, the division between the market-oriented West, led by the USA, and the state-controlled economies of the Soviet Union-led Eastern bloc affected the workings of the UN. By 1947 efforts by the Western states to pass resolutions through the Security Council were vetoed by the Soviet Union, a trend that continued until well into the 1980s. The main exception was in June 1950 after the invasion of the Republic of Korea (South Korea) by communist forces from North Korea. The USA, as the protector of South Korea, brought the matter before the Security Council while the Soviet Union was absent, owing to a dispute regarding the new communist government in Beijing which had not been seated as the representative of China. The Security Council declared the North Korean action to be aggression and instituted military action against the aggressors. However, many of the disputes between East and West, such as those over Berlin in the 1950s and 1960s, Viet Nam in the 1960s and 1970s, or Cuba in 1962, have been directly negotiated between the USA and its allies and the Soviet Union, and only incidentally involved the Security Council.

The other main development during this period was the growth of the southern hemisphere as a political presence. Decolonization in Asia in the late 1940s and 1950s, was followed by a similar process in Africa and the Caribbean in the 1960s and 1970s. These new countries formed a so-called Third World bloc between the East and West, and used their numbers in the UN General Assembly to place issues reflecting their own interests on the agenda. These questions mainly reflected the economic and social disparities between the richer Western nations and the Third World. During the late 1960s and 1970s the developing countries of the Third World used organizations such as the UN Conference on Trade and Development (UNCTAD) to advance their concerns in the face of the domination of world economic co-operation by the Bretton Woods institutions. These institutions—the International Bank for Reconstruction and Development (IBRD, or the World Bank), the International Monetary Fund (IMF) and the General Agreement on Tariffs and Trade, and their associated agencies—were established immediately after the Second World War and were dominated by Western states, especially the USA. The Third World states felt excluded from institutions in which they had little say, and turned to the UN and UNCTAD to press for greater control of their own natural resources, better trade conditions and a reduction in Third World debts. They had some success during the 1970s when their proposals were backed by the Organization of Petroleum Exporting Countries (OPEC), the membership of which was sympathetic to the general political aims of the Third World and which had some economic clout because of the rising oil prices.

By the 1980s much of this momentum had been lost and the Third World ('the South') had to wait until the end of the millennium for debt relief to be placed on the agendas of organizations dominated by 'the North', such as the Bretton Woods institutions, EU and the Group of Seven (G7) meetings of seven of the most wealthy industrialized states (the USA, United Kingdom, Canada, France, Germany, Italy and Japan). Many non-governmental organizations such as Caritas, Oxfam and Save the Children played a key role in campaigning for these countries and organizations to consider debt cancellations.

After the Cold War

By the mid-1980s the Soviet Union, under the leadership of Mikhail Gorbachev, had decided that 'the arms race' with the West that was central to the Cold War could no longer be afforded, let alone won. This led to a number of co-operative agreements between East and West and, eventually, the emergence of new political structures, for example the transformation of the Conference on Security and Co-operation in Europe into a permanent organization, the OSCE. From 1989 to 1991, the Soviet bloc in Eastern Europe and then the Soviet Union itself collapsed, ending the Cold War. The deadlock in the Security Council of the UN had already been ended with Gorbachev's new approach and the UN took on a new lease of life, establishing peace-keeping operations in the Middle East, Africa, Central America and the Far East. When Iraq invaded Kuwait in August 1990, the Security Council united in opposition, imposed sanctions against Iraq and supported the establishment of a coalition of forces, led by the USA, to expel Iraqi troops from Kuwait and establish an observation mission between the two states from April 1991. After Yugoslavia collapsed into conflict in 1991, the UN joined with the European Communities (later the EU) to broker peace between the new states and various factions within these states, but with little success. US-led intervention in the mid-1990s led to a settlement and the establishment of a number of UN peace missions in the region. After the US-led action in Kosovo and Metohija in 1999, a UN administration was established for that province.

While the end of the Cold War provided many opportunities for the UN to be involved in peace operations, and the Security Council showed some willingness in providing the mandate for such activities, the UN has not become as dominant in peace and security matters as some have wished. Many of the conflicts (such as those in former Yugoslavia) have been within, rather than between, states, and the permanent members of the Security Council have sometimes been reluctant to sanction UN action in civil wars. Furthermore, the UN has lacked resources, especially as a number of key countries, notably Russia and the USA, have not always paid their full dues. Finally, the most powerful state, the USA, has refused to place its military forces under UN control, and action in a number of areas has therefore depended on the willingness of US administrations to be involved. Action against terrorist networks and against the Taliban government of Afghanistan at the end of 2001 was another demonstration of a US-led operation that acted with the consent of the Security Council. The US-led invasion of Iraq initiated in March 2003 without the specific consent of the Security Council divided international opinion and seemed to undermine the UN.

A further phenomenon in the 1990s was the rise of regional international organizations. Some new ones, such as the Council of the Baltic Sea States and the Arctic Council, covered geographically defined areas. Existing regional agencies, such as the Economic Community of West African States (ECOWAS) and the Association of Southeast Asian Nations (ASEAN) became more active. A whole range of organizations, such as the Committee of the Regions, the European Community Humanitarian Office and the European Bank for Reconstruction and Development (EBRD), were in one form or another associated with the EU, which in itself forms a system of governance that includes a number of international organizations.

More generally, there has been in recent years a fluctuation in the number of international organizations, reflecting a closer questioning of costs and benefits of international organizations by governments from the 1990s. However the growth in the number of international non-governmental organizations continued apace. It had already risen from 1,470 in 1964 to 4,676 in 1985, and by 2012 the total was around 7,450.

TYPES OF INTERNATIONAL ORGANIZATIONS

International organizations can be classified in a number of ways. The three main methods of dividing them are by types of membership, aims and activities, and by structure.

Membership

Though the rise of international organizations had to wait until the establishment of a system of sovereign states that had frequent contact with each other, the membership of international organizations is not limited to states represented by their governments. An important distinction is between the kinds of international organizations that are interstate, or intergovernmental, and those whose membership is non-governmental. A further category has mixed membership.

Intergovernmental organizations (IGOs). According to the UN Economic and Social Council (ECOSOC), there is a distinction between intergovernmental organizations (IGOs) and international non-governmental organizations (INGOs—sometimes shortened to NGOs). IGOs are created by intergovernmental agreement and their members are governments or their agents. The terms 'intergovernmental organization' and 'interstate organization' are interchangeable.

International non-governmental organizations (INGOs). What are often called 'international organizations' sometimes contain members that are not states or governmental representatives but are drawn from groups, associations, organizations or individuals from within the state. These non-governmental actors are performing on the international stage and their activities give rise to transnational interaction.

Transnational organizations (TNOs). These are established when such relationships between more than two participants become institutionalized by agreement into a formal, continuous structure in order to pursue the common interests of the participants, one of which is not an agent of government or an international organization. In contrast to an intergovernmental organization, a TNO must have a non-state actor for at least one of its members.

Three sorts of TNOs can be identified. The genuine INGO is an organization with only non-governmental members. These bring together the representatives of like-minded groups from more than two countries, examples of which are the International Olympic Committee, the World Council of Churches, the Soroptimist International, the Salvation Army and the Universal Esperanto Association. A hybrid INGO has some governmental and some non-governmental representation. If established by a treaty between governments, it is an IGO, for example the International Labour Organization (ILO) which has trade union and management (i.e. non-governmental) membership as well as governmental representatives. However, some INGOs have a mixed membership and are not the result of a purely intergovernmental agreement, for example the International Council of Scientific Unions. The transgovernmental organization is set up by governmental actors not controlled by the central foreign policy organs of their governments. Examples include the International Union of Local Authorities (IULA), the International Council for the Exploration of the Sea (ICES), the International Criminal Police Organization (INTERPOL), and the Inter-Parliamentary Union.

A fourth category of TNOs is sometimes mentioned: that of the business international non-governmental organizations (BINGOs), alternatively called multinational enterprises or corporations. However these are normally excluded from the term 'international organization' on the following grounds: that ECOSOC does so; that they reflect the workings, albeit across frontiers, of one corporation domiciled in one state; and that they are profit-making organizations.

Aims and Activities

A common way of classifying international organizations is by examining what they do. The aims of most international organizations can be seen in the basic document that establishes them, such as a treaty or agreement. The record of the international organization can also be examined to see whether the organization has lived up to its aims. International organizations are quite often divided into those that have general aims—the UN being the most obvious example—and specialized organizations, including many members of the UN family such as the World Health Organization (WHO), the Food and Agriculture Organization (FAO) and the UN Children's Fund (UNICEF). Also, international organizations may have aims and activities that encourage co-operative behaviour, such as the Nordic Council, and/or they may aim at reducing conflict between members, as in the case of the UN, the African Union and the League of Arab States.

Structure

An easy way to distinguish between the variety of international organizations is to look at the structure of their institutions. The early international organizations in the 19th century had simple structures. The UPU and the International Telegraph Union (see above) both had permanent administrative offices and policy-making meetings of the representatives of member states every few years. The League of Nations, with its secretariat, council, assembly and court was more complicated and this institutional edifice was built on by the UN which added a Trusteeship Council and an Economic and Social Council as well as a host of committees and agencies. A number of organizations have judicial bodies attached to them—such as the European Court of Human Rights of the Council of Europe—and a few have parliamentary organs, such as the Consultative Assembly of the Council of Europe and the directly-elected European Parliament of the EU.

Power within the various organs of an international organizations may be divided unequally. In IGOs, the member states often try to retain the greatest power for the organ within which they are represented. However, not all members carry the same clout. In the UN there are the five permanent members of the Security Council—the USA, Russia, the People's Republic of China, the United Kingdom and France, in effect the main powers at the end of the Second World War—who have the privileged position of being able to veto any Security Council resolution by casting a negative vote. Those providing large capital subscriptions to the IMF and the IBRD have the most votes on their governing bodies, which are thus controlled by the industrialized states. Power may also fluctuate between the institutions of an international organization that represent the interests of the member states (especially the more powerful ones) and those that represent the wider interests of the organization. There has thus been a tension within the UN between the Security Council, in which Great Power interests dominate, and the Secretary-General's office. When the Security Council was paralysed by power divisions during the Cold War, the Secretaries-General tried to develop their powers and influence. Dag Hammarskjöld, who served as Secretary-General from 1953 to 1961, played an important role in developing the office, though both the Soviet Union and the USA attempted to prevent successive Secretaries-General from taking too much power.

ROLES OF INTERNATIONAL ORGANIZATIONS

Instrument of the Membership

The most common role played by international organizations in the global system is that of being used by the membership for their own ends. In the case of IGOs, the member states not only may try to limit the power of independent action by the institutions of international organizations but will also vie with other members to get the most out of any particular international organization. However, multilateral co-operation offers possibilities that individual states would not have if they acted separately. This means that there is often an ambiguity in states' policies towards international organizations. While membership offers new opportunities, it also brings responsibilities and restraints. Furthermore, the ability of a state to use an organization for its own ends may change over time. For example, the USA was able to use the UN for its own diplomatic needs during the first eight years of its existence as it had a Secretary-General sympathetic to its aims and a General Assembly on which it could normally rely. Only in the Security Council could the Soviet Union veto US resolutions. Later in the 1960s and 1970s, the majority of the General Assembly, consisting of developing states, were critical of US policies, and the Secretaries-General—U Thant and Kurt Waldheim—were more even-handed in their dealings with the power blocs. Consequently US administrations became less able and willing to use the UN as a diplomatic instrument during the Cold War.

Forums for Activity

A second role for international organizations is that of an arena within which the members meet, debate and act. Especially during the Cold War the UN was often used as an 'arena for combat' between East and West and also between North and South in the late 1960s and 1970s. This was aided by the arrangement of states into blocs—the West consisting of the NATO states and countries such as Australia and New Zealand, the East consisting of the Soviet bloc, and the South covering most of the states of Asia, Africa and Latin America. Other organizations were established to act as platforms for particular interests: OPEC being the forum for petroleum exporting states.

International Actors

International organizations are sometimes seen as independent actors on the world scene. Thus the organization as a whole is seen as separate from its membership. The media often talk about the 'UN taking action' or 'OPEC increasing prices' thus confirming the image of international organizations acting apart from their membership. Though all international organizations are dependent on their membership, not least for finance and other resources, they have institutional frameworks that allow them to achieve more than if their members acted separately or, indeed, just co-operated on an ad hoc basis. Depending on the strength of the institutions of the organization, such as a secretariat or a court, international organizations can sometimes act contrary to the wishes of at least some of their members, though they would be risking their very existence by doing this for any length of time. Even some INGOs are seen as effective independent actors on the world scene. The International Committee of the Red Cross and Red Crescent is a good example, and it has now been joined by a number of humanitarian organizations such as Médecins sans Frontières, Oxfam and Caritas.

FUNCTIONS OF INTERNATIONAL ORGANIZATIONS

Recruitment

On the whole, the functions that international organizations perform help to maintain the international system within which they exist. One task that they aid is that of recruitment of participants in the international political system. By consisting of the representatives of sovereign states, the very existence of IGOs has encouraged non-self-governing territories to achieve independence. This has allowed them to gain access to organizations where they can promote their state's interests. Thus many small territories have pressed for independence and membership of the UN. Furthermore, INGOs have recruited groups and individuals so that they may act more effectively at the international level, and their effectiveness is recognized by a number of leading IGOs such as ECOSOC, the ILO, UNESCO and UNCTAD, in which they are provided with consultative status.

Aggregation of Views

Organizations such as trade unions, charities, interest groups and political parties within national political systems help to aggregate viewpoints on a wide range of subjects from the national minimum wage and aid for the developing world to the moral aspects of genetic research and the benefits of privatization or nationalization. Most often this aggregation of interests is aimed at national (or regional) governments. Such interests aggregated at the international level by international organizations are faced with the lack of a central body that allocates values and resources, a government. However, values and resources are allocated internationally but by a diffuse system consisting of more than 190 states, international organizations themselves and the international markets. International organizations in all three roles mentioned above—instruments for members, forums and actors—can aggregate opinion and articulate it more or less effectively. Shipowners put forward their views to governments and agencies through the International Chamber of Shipping, religious groups have the forum of the World Council of Churches to express their opinions, and the labour movement attempts to advance workers' rights through the ILO.

Norms and Socialization

International organizations have played an important role in spreading certain norms and values throughout the world. The UN Charter in its Preamble expresses particular values such as 'faith in fundamental human rights' and in 'the equal rights of men and women and of nations large and small'. The Universal Declaration of Human Rights adopted by the UN General Assembly in 1948 'as a common standard of achievement for all peoples and all nations' has references to personal, social and economic rights. Furthermore, the UN helped to de-legitimize European colonialism and to outlaw white-ruled South Africa for its policy of apartheid or separate treatment of whites and blacks. The role of socialization by which societies decide what is acceptable and inculcate beliefs and behaviour into their members is often undertaken within states by families, voluntary groups and even governments. Internationally, it is quite often religions or multinational companies that can act as agents of socialization. International organizations can contribute to the process, but are often in competition with more powerful state and commercial forces. The International Olympic Committee tries to further the values of competitive sport world-wide, and the various Nordic associations, as well as the Nordic Council, have helped to produce a common feeling among the citizens of the five Nordic states. Also international organizations have helped to socialize governments. Organizations such as the League of Nations and UN have tried, with mixed success, to persuade some governments—often those with revolutionary credentials such as the Soviet Union, China, or Iran after 1979—to behave in a way more acceptable to the rest of the international community. The former Federal Republic of Yugoslavia under President Milošović was not allowed UN membership until the downfall of its turbulent leader in 2000. Some commentators view the World Trade Organization as an effective socializing instrument by which the former-Soviet bloc states and Third World countries are persuaded to accept the rigours of freer trade and the market economy.

Rules

At the national level, rule-making is the task of governments and parliaments. Though the UN is far from being either a world government or parliament, this does not mean that rules are not made, implemented and adjudicated internationally. This may be seen within the UN system when the General Assembly adopts a convention relating to the rules of diplomatic practice or the Third UN Conference on the Law of the Sea concludes a comprehensive agreement affecting the world's oceans. Organizations such as the International Bureau of Weights and Measures, the UPU and the Metric Union have had over a hundred years of experience of making international rules in their functional areas. Many of their rules, concerning the implementation of common standards, have been accepted because of their usefulness in international trade, for example. However, there are other international organizations that have wider rule-application capabilities. The International Committee of the Red Cross and Red Crescent has helped to supervise the rules of war and conflict across the globe. Amnesty International and a host of other INGOs have tried to make sure that human rights are respected. The International Atomic Energy Agency has wide powers to monitor the spread of fissionable material. International organizations also have rule-adjudication functions. The International Court of Justice makes judgments about claims between states. The International Criminal Court, the European Court of Human Rights (of the Council of Europe) and the European Court of Justice (of the EU) can make rulings that directly affect individuals in the member states.

Operations

International organizations undertake a number of functional activities. These includes banking (the Bank for International Settlements, the EBRD), providing aid (the humanitarian INGOs and several UN specialized agencies), helping refugees (the UN High Commissioner for Refugees) and running technical services (INTELSAT, the World Weather Watch of the World Meteorological Organization). A number of INGOs also run operations, especially in developing countries where they help clear landmines, feed refugees or encourage rural development.

CONCLUSIONS

International organizations have grown considerably since their inception in the early 19th century. The most rapid and continuous growth has been in international non-governmental organizations, with the number of inter-governmental organizations seeming to have peaked in the early 1990s. These organizations, ranging from the UN network down to the humblest of INGOs, can be instruments for their members, meeting-places and actors. They cover a wide role of functions in the international system including making and applying rules and carrying out a number of activities often associated with governments. International organizations have attempted, with mixed success, to tackle the wide range of global problems such as conflict, poverty, illness, environmental degradation and ignorance. Their effectiveness is constrained not just by the enormity of their tasks but also because of their own organizational shortcomings and the reluctance of member states to give them resources. The UN continues to be tested by regional and internal conflicts. Furthermore, a continued US preference for pursuing its foreign policy goals by using coalitions of like-minded states may adversely affect international organizations more generally. Nevertheless, international organizations play a part in the way that the world is run and are likely to continue to develop into the 21st century.

INTERNATIONAL ORGANIZATIONS AND 'GLOBAL' SECURITY POLICY: NOT EVERYTHING HANGS TOGETHER

STEPHANIE C. HOFMANN*

British politician Lord Hailsham said in his 1987 Granada Guildhall Lecture, 'Nations begin by forming their institutions, but, in the end, are continuously formed by them or under their influence'. This can be said of national and international institutions alike. The last decades have brought changes that challenge national sovereignty. International organizations have developed procedures that infringe on the principle of non-intervention. National governments are not the sole foreign policy-making institutions any longer—if they ever have been.

The number of international organizations of any kind, be they governmental or non-governmental, formal or informal, has increased, especially since the 1990s. Not all of these organizations have the same material and political resources available to them. Instead, they vary in power and authority. Some organizations are driving forces in setting, interpreting, implementing and enforcing rules and norms, others are epiphenomenal to powerful member states. In addition, in this myriad of organizations, some are more global in scope and function than others.

This observation not only implies that international politics has become more specialized, but it also indicates the complexity in which international politics is conducted these days. This complexity constrains most states' political range of action. However, it also increases opportunities of (institutionally) empowered states. Neither national governments nor international organizations are alike in terms of political clout. This holds for many policy domains, not least of all for international security policy.

THE UNITED NATIONS DOES NOT ALWAYS UNITE NATIONS

Violent conflict has always been a major attribute of international politics. However, its characteristics have changed over the centuries. Ever since the end of the tensions between the USA and the Soviet Union—also known as the Cold War—the superficial and relative stability that was guaranteed through the division of international politics into two spheres of influence, made room for a more diverse threat and risk scenario. Latest with these changes in the security environment, it became clear that the conflict intensity around the globe is not uniform.

International responses, especially in the form of peace operations, have not looked (or should look) the same. Peace operations involve the dispatch of expeditionary forces to implement an agreement between warring states or factions, which can include enforcing the agreement in the face of deliberate non-co-operation. They occur with or without a United Nations (UN) mandate. Peace operations can have military and/or civilian components—such as humanitarian and rescue operations, peace-keeping, and peace-making operations. These different components can be on the ground at the same time. In 2009 the Secretary-General of the North Atlantic Treaty Organization (NATO), Anders Rasmussen, observed: 'The days when the military could win the war, and then hand the baton to the civilians, are finished. In today's peace operations, we need to work together, from beginning to end, if we are to succeed.'

The UN, as the only global security institution, was one of the frontrunners in defining and implementing such a new peace and security policy. However, this process met with resistance from some of its member states, challenged old doctrines and asked for new assets and capacities that needed to be created first.

THE UN: DOCTRINAL CHANGE, MEMBER STATE POWER, AND REGIONAL ORGANIZATIONS

Renewed activism, doctrinal change, and overstretch are the major processes that the most prominent international organizations experienced with the end of the Cold War. The impact might have been largest on the UN. The UN is the only international organization with (almost) global membership in the realm of security policy, though it is not the sole forum in which issues on international peace and security are debated—and arguably not even the primary one. Many factors contribute to this. Initial UN activism after the end of the Cold War in combination with a lack of resources, the US government's occasional choice of conducting (disguised) unilateral policy and an increased activism of regional organizations were the most important drivers.

Renewed Activism, Doctrinal Change and Overstretch

The rapid and, by many, unforeseen disintegration of the Soviet Union, the retreat of the Soviet armies, and the disintegration of Yugoslavia, secessionist claims and civil wars in South-east Asia, Africa, the Caucasus and Central Asia changed the international security environment by emphasizing and bringing to the fore 'new' security issues. The sort of systemic change brought about by the end of the Cold War increased strategic uncertainty, and in particular uncertainty about how to tackle the new challenges. While the full implications of the eclipse of bipolar competition between rival ideological camps might not have been realized at the start of the 1990s, governments agreed that military capabilities for the purpose of deterring threats were ill-suited to solving the myriad of new security problems.

The UN Charter has given the Security Council primary responsibility for the maintenance of international peace and security. As a result, the UN concentrated on peace operations, which, although not explicitly provided for in the Charter, have evolved into one of the main tools used by the UN to maintain peace and stability around the world. And with the Cold War paralysis of the Security Council coming to an end, the UN responded with an increase in the number of interventions. UN peace-keeping operations have traditionally been associated with Chapter VI of the Charter concerned with the Pacific Settlement of Disputes. In recent years, the Council has adopted the practice of invoking Chapter VII, relating to Action with Respect to the Peace, Breaches of the Peace and Acts of Aggression, when authorizing the deployment of UN peace-keeping operations into volatile post-conflict settings where the government is unable to maintain security.

Over the years, the range of tasks assigned to UN peace operations has expanded in response to shifting patterns of conflict. The main tasks include the deployment of troops to prevent the outbreak of conflict or the spill-over of conflict across borders; stabilization of conflict situations after a ceasefire, to create an environment for the parties to reach a lasting peace agreement; assistance in implementing comprehensive peace agreements; and guiding states or territories through a transition to stable government, based on democratic principles, good governance and economic development.

Overextension of UN-led forces became a problem. The UN was understaffed for such operations, not enough governments committed a sufficient number of forces, money and materiel to the operations and there was a general lack of expertise in the beginning of the 1990s. One has to keep in mind that the UN has

* Stephanie Hofmann is Assistant Professor in the Department of Political Science, Graduate Institute of International and Development Studies, in Geneva, Switzerland, and is Deputy Director of the Center on Conflict, Development and Peacebuilding, Geneva.

no military equipment of its own and only a very small staff in its headquarters to oversee peace operations—force headquarters in the field are the main co-ordination nexus.

These actions on-the-ground were accompanied by a political debate over the terms and scope of UN peace operations. Various actors have tried to readjust and transform the role of the UN. The UN, especially under the leadership of Secretaries-General Boutros Boutros-Ghali and Kofi Annan, initiated—but also responded to input from countries such as Canada and Norway—a reconceptualization of the appropriate components of an effective security policy. Boutros-Ghali's *An Agenda for Peace*, published in 1992, is one document among many that have since tried to tackle the issue of maintaining peace and security worldwide. Boutros-Ghali was the first to present a reinterpretation of peace operations acknowledging that the role of the UN consists of conflict prevention, peace-keeping, peace-making, and post-conflict peace-building.

Later on, concepts such as 'human security' and the 'responsibility to protect' have seen the light of day. The UN shifted from human security to responsibility to protect because of the ambiguity of the concept (the nexus between development and human security as well as human rights and human security remained underspecified, for example, leading to conceptual overstretch). These normative changes, despite the fact that they have not become a positive obligation of the international community to intervene in other states' affairs, are also reflected in new institutional creations such as the UN Peace-building Commission, created in 2006.

US Power: The Fear of the End of Multilateralism

With the end of the Cold War, maintaining peace and security was increasingly seen in the light of multilateral policy; the bigger the coalition, the better. Organizations such as NATO expanded their membership, and various other multilateral forums were created and transformed. While multilateralism has become a dominant form of organizing international politics, it is far from being the sole option that states have at their disposal. Especially one state has the luxury of deciding when and how it wants to use force: the USA.

Since the end of the Cold War, consecutive US governments have formulated their foreign and security policy in light of unmatched American military power. As a result of the power differential, but also based on ideological texture of various governments in power, the US sometimes opts for unilateral foreign and security policies—or chooses to disguise its unilateral policies under the mantle of ad hoc coalitions. UN consent, while not unimportant, has not been the primary concern of US governments. While the justification for the various cases might be different, the administration of President Bill Clinton intervened in Kosovo in 1999 with its NATO allies, and the George W. Bush administration intervened in Iraq in 2003 without a UN Security Council mandate. The UN cannot count on the unconditional support of the strongest power in the international system.

Regional Delegation and Lack of UN Leadership

Many international organizations are committed to maintaining international peace. Regional organizations can ask the Security Council for authorization for a peace operation—as we have witnessed recently with the League of Arab States in the cases of Libya and Syria—or the UN Security Council approaches them. Chapter VIII of the UN Charter provides for the involvement of regional arrangements in the maintenance of international peace and security, provided such activities are consistent with the purposes and principles outlined in Chapter I. UN Security Council Resolution 1631, authorized in 2005, identified priority areas for collaboration between the UN and regional organizations. But there have also been instances when organizations acted not on behalf of the Security Council but instead justified their intervention with a set of moral principles or based on the invitation of the host government.

In the case of Libya regional organizations each acted upon difference interests and ambitions. It was the League of Arab States that adopted decisions paving the way for Security Council Resolutions 1970 and 1973 and was instrumental in advocating the use of 'responsibility to protect' vocabulary in the resolutions. The African Union (AU), on the other hand, had more difficulties in taking a unanimous stand towards Libya as many African governments had ties to the al-Qaddafi regime. When its leadership took action, pushing for a negotiated outcome, it did so on the basis of organizational turf. The AU wanted to act in its own geographical area and was disturbed that the UN seemed to rely on the League of Arab States instead.

Regional organizations have become active either among their membership or beyond and either through their own peace operations, a hybrid operation or supporting another international organization's operation providing it with technical and logistical support. However, not all regions have permanent regional security organizations at their disposal. Europe, the transatlantic region and Africa have experienced the transformation or development of such institutions for many decades. In Asia, the Middle East or Latin America, regional organizations such as the Association of Southeast Asian Nations, the Shanghai Cooperation Organization, the League of Arab States, the Union of South American States, and the Organization of American States, to name just a few, all have included the maintenance of (regional) peace and security in their institutional mandates but have only recently been created or are in the process of developing such mechanisms. Focusing on the most institutionalized security organizations in Europe and Africa, therefore, will clarify the roles regional organizations can play in maintaining peace and security.

European Security Organizations

The conflict in and subsequent disintegration of Yugoslavia in the early 1990s highlighted the persistence of threats to the security and stability of Europe. As NATO Secretary-General at the time, Manfred Wörner, observed: 'The risk is in uncertainty—about the future political structure of the Soviet Union, the bad economic situation, and all its consequences, in a country which still has more than three million people under arms and tens of thousands of nuclear weapons.' Instead of relying on the UN for their security and regional peace, European Union (EU) states set out to reform NATO and to create a Common Security and Defence Policy (CSDP).

Changes in the post-Cold War world made it possible for European governments to present proposals for a new security institution outside of NATO. As French President François Mitterrand observed at the time: 'There is no longer an imposed order. Europe is now master of its choices, or it can be.' What Mitterrand and others perceived as a new window of political opportunity for restructuring European security confronted European governments with several choices: they could renationalize security, relying less on their transatlantic allies; transform NATO into a security institution geared towards a new set of threats and challenges; or European governments could create a new multilateral institution outside the institutional framework of NATO.

At the end of the 1990s, the EU member states agreed on creating the European Security and Defence Policy (ESDP)—known as CSDP since the ratification of the Lisbon Treaty in December 2009. The reasons why EU member states have created CSDP are manifold. Some see the EU as a global actor that has to take on responsibilities beyond the realm of economic policy. Others insist more on the mere fact that the EU needed capabilities in the realm of security; capabilities that can be put to use in other multilateral forums as well. Either way, from its inception CSDP encompassed not only military but also civilian components. This comprehensive approach to security resembles the one of the UN.

Most EU member states (Denmark being the lonely exception) perceive the EU as an appropriate actor in peace operations today, sidelining the UN, Organization for Security and Co-operation in Europe (OSCE) or NATO at times. Granted, the institutional blueprint is still being drawn and redrawn, however, the EU has been rather active. It has conducted more than 20 military operations and civilian missions since 2003, some of them lasting over six years, with up to 4,000 personnel on the ground, in places such as Africa, Asia, the Middle East, and the Balkans. As with the UN, most times doctrine succeeds rather then precedes action.

To some at the end of the 1980s, NATO's posture of deterrence and its military structure seemed poorly adaptable to tackling new security challenges. None the less, the USA and some European governments pushed for reforms that would add a political dimension to NATO's longstanding military mandate.

These reforms were premised on the notion that NATO had to transform not just its military structure but also its political outlook—especially in order to manage relations with Eastern European states. In the new international system, approaching states as a purely military alliance would send the wrong signals. Instead, NATO had to develop political forums for discussion and consultation.

An initial shift from the Cold War posture led to possibilities for transforming NATO's command structure and forces. As the Clinton administration's first NATO initiative, the US government undertook to reform NATO's integrated structure. The intention was to provide flexible command arrangements within which allied forces could be organized on a task-specific basis. Through this link, the Petersberg Declaration, which lists possible operations that encompass virtually all military operations that are not result of a collective defence commitment, became part of NATO. At the NATO summit in Brussels in January 1994, NATO leaders informally endorsed this initiative. Further reforms of the command structure and doctrine followed.

The NATO summit held in Washington, DC, USA, in April 1999 confirmed that NATO was moving towards peace operations, reconfirming this in a change to its mandate. In the Strategic Concept of 1999, NATO members recognized that 'the appearance of complex new risks to Euro-Atlantic peace and stability, including oppression, ethnic conflict, economic distress, the collapse of political order, and the proliferation of weapons of mass destruction' had changed the Euro-Atlantic security. The Washington Summit also gave a legal cover to NATO to enter the peace operation arena and, thus, go beyond its traditional role of collective defence: 'To stand ready, case-by-case and by consensus, in conformity with Article 7 of the Washington Treaty, to contribute to effective conflict prevention and to engage actively in crisis management, including crisis response operations.' Article 7 of the Washington Treaty contains a vague reference to 'the maintenance of international peace and security'. Since then, NATO has conducted humanitarian relief operations in Pakistan, intervened—without a UN Security Council mandate—in Kosovo, supported the AU in Darfur, and is engaged in its biggest operation to date in Afghanistan.

Threats require tangible mechanisms for managing crisis and conflict. The process known as the Conference for Security and Co-operation in Europe (CSCE), which helped foster dialogue between the 'East' and the 'West' in the 1970s, was transformed into the OSCE with a permanent institutional framework. The reasoning behind this adaptation was to help its membership to meet unanticipated security problems. The OSCE counts 56 member states (as of 2012) ranging from the USA to the Russian Federation and focuses on preventive diplomacy, promotion of human rights and the peaceful settlement of disputes—democracy has thereby been conceived as vital to security. Its normative framework outlined in the Charter of Paris of 1990 legitimates international action. It is another witness to the reexamination and reinterpretation of the basic norms of international relations. While the OSCE has at times managed to bring Russia and 'Western' states to one table, more often than not, the institution falls prey to its diverse membership that uses the organization for its own national agendas.

African Regional and Sub-regional Organizations

The case in Africa is different in many ways. While the European and transatlantic security organizations are relatively well equipped, funded, staffed and can look back to operational experiences, African organizations lack funds and capacities. Furthermore, instead of several regional organizations with almost identical membership but no formal hierarchy between them, the AU is seen as the defining regional organization to such sub-regional organizations as the Economic Community of West African States (ECOWAS), Southern African Development Community (SADC) and the Intergovernmental Authority on Development (IGAD). In principle, a relationship of subsidiarity exists among these organizations. In addition, the geographic scope of African security institutions is constrained to their membership while the EU and NATO concentrate on security action outside their membership. This potentially impairs their effectiveness as states involved in conflicts can have leading roles in the organizations.

The AU was launched in 1999 and succeeded the Organization of African Unity in 2002—the latter, created in 1963, was an organization that had been criticized for being a talking shop only. Morocco is the only African state not to have joined the AU whose membership counts 54 states. Like its predecessor, the AU is based on five regions as constituent units. Its institutional structure has been loosely modelled on the EU, from which experts had been invited to help with the blueprint. Within the AU, the Peace and Security Council, set up in 2004, has the mandate to maintain peace and security.

Since its inception, the AU has sent troops to such places as Burundi, Darfur, Côte d'Ivoire, Comoros and Somalia. While in the previous cases, doctrine often followed action, the AU translated experiences made in the UN, EU and NATO to formulate a broad legal basis of action. Article 4 (h) of the AU's Constitutive Act recognizes the right of the AU to intervene in the internal affairs of member states in the case of war crimes, genocide, and crimes against humanity on a case-by-case basis. However, in stark contrast, the AU also upholds defending sovereign and territorial integrity of its member states (Article 3). As a result, the comprehensiveness of African security has been contested. The extraordinary AU summit meeting, held in Sirte, Libya, in 2004 adopted a framework agreement on a common African security and defence policy, including elements of human security (mimicking the UN). However, putting such a broad agreement into operation has proven to be difficult. In addition, the AU's military capacities are still not up to task.

ECOWAS represents the Western regional group with 15 member states. It also was the first African initiative on peace operations. It was created in 1975 with the primary aim of economic integration in West Africa. Civil wars in Sierra Leone and Liberia triggered a shift from economic to political and security priorities based on the realization that political stability precedes economic integration. Since then, ECOWAS has intervened in Sierra Leone, Liberia, Guinea and Côte d'Ivoire. While not all interventions were uncontroversial, through these actions, ECOWAS has gradually developed institutional capacities for peace operations.

In 1981 ECOWAS members agreed on the Protocol on Mutual Defence Assistance. The organization formally reformed in 1993 against the backdrop of a changed international environment and regime change in many member states. The fundamental principles of maintenance of regional peace, stability and security through the promotion and strengthening of good neighborliness, and promotion and consolidation of a democratic system of governance in each member state, have been repeated in several protocols, of which the 1999 Protocol Relating to the Mechanism for Conflict Prevention, Management, Resolution, Peacekeeping and Security is arguably the most important one. Furthermore, ECOWAS established new organs such as the Mediation and Security Council in 2001 to curb Nigerian hegemony within the grouping.

On the outset, creating SADC has been marked by various understandings of the purpose of security institutions. Some future member states wanted SADC to become a defence pact; others again favoured a comprehensive security policy. This and other political divisions, such as the political tensions between South Africa and Zimbabwe, have hampered the formulation of a common policy. Despite violent conflicts within its member states, SADC only became active on rare occasions as in the Democratic Republic of the Congo or in Lesotho in 1998.

NEW TRENDS AND CHALLENGES: ONE GLOBAL ORGANIZATION IS NOT ENOUGH

Chapter VIII of the UN Charter leaves open an array of interpretations as to the co-ordination, co-operation and competition among regional organizations. The UN neither has a monopoly on maintaining peace and security in the world nor is it the only legitimizing force. There is no assurance of the complementarity of roles. The argument often is that regional organizations are better placed to react to regional crises. They suffer more from the conflicts within their membership or in their region. Regional organizations in some cases have different needs than the UN. The UN machinery can be slow and regional organizations have to wait if they want to act with the Security Council's authorization. In addition, all these organizations have a different tolerance towards casualties: Western organizations are the least tolerant and African organizations the most tolerant —the UN is somewhere in-between. As a result, at times international organizations compete with each other and other times co-operate.

Opportunities and Constraints

Not all international organizations that conduct peace operations constrain themselves functionally or geographically. At times several international organizations operate in the same theatre. For example, five international organizations operate in Kosovo to create and maintain peace and security by establishing the rule of law, democracy and human rights within the territory: the UN (UNMIK), the EU (EULEX), NATO (KFOR), OSCE, and the International Civilian Office. This duplication arguably has led to a waste of resources and ultimately has put soldiers' and civilians' lives at risk.

The UN could theoretically manage this increased regional activity. After all, most regional security organizations refer to the UN as the authorizing power of their activities in their treaties and resolutions. However, this formal hierarchy at times is inconsequential or simply not acted upon. As the continued multilateral security efforts in the Balkans, but also in Afghanistan or sub-Saharan Africa have shown, inter-institutional interactions among international organizations are a hot political issue. Tensions exist despite the fact that troop-contributing states are strained by the combined demands of the UN, NATO, AU, EU and other multinational operations.

To be sure, co-operation among organizations happens. While the task of maintaining peace is hard to divide, international organizations differ in their troop strength, training, and institutional 'equipment' available. To conduct a wide array of operations, international institutions need planning structures (such as headquarters), a functioning bureaucracy that is large enough to oversee several operations at the same time, management structures, forces and joint training of forces, and a sizable budget to launch and continue the operation. Some international security institutions are still young (e.g. AU), others such as NATO have mainly military resources (though they aspire to a greater role in civilian crisis management) and others again, such as the OSCE, are more focused on civilian crisis management but are aware that they often need military backing. As a result, the empirical realities open up the door for burden sharing between international organizations in the form of a division of labour. Some international organizations can provide others with training, information, expertise, specialization, and niche capabilities.

Competition is another modus of interaction. Some organizations are nested within each other, that is, one organization's membership can be completely absorbed by another organization while no formal hierarchy between the two institutions need exist: all regional organizations are nested within the UN, or SADC and ECOWAS are nested within the AU. The EU and NATO, on the other hand, overlap. Because there exist nested and overlapping organizations, some member states are in the position to play off different institutions against each other. More often than not the UN is only a spectator to these dynamics instead of serving as arbiter. As a result, at times international organizations waste resources, do not diffuse knowledge, do not co-ordinate their actions on the ground, and do not agree to one common strategy, which can put a peace operation's success at risk. These complex institutional constellations are a reality that is hard to circumvent. Not all multilateralism is effective, and not all partnerships are strategic. Examples from the European and African experience will illuminate this point.

European and Transatlantic Security

Much has been said about the transatlantic relationship, its ups and downs, calling it in a perpetual or fundamental crisis, or declaring Europe from Venus and the USA from Mars. Though the EU and NATO vary in structure, they share principles and values as well as responsibilities in conflict prevention, crisis management and post-conflict peace-building. Instead of looking at the EU and NATO as separate entities, it is better to examine disagreements that exist both within each institution and across them. Too often analysts look at NATO and the EU as two separate and internally cohesive entities, but member states disagree over the function of the institutions as well as over the inter-institutional alignment. There is no one EU-way to look at the European security dialogue and neither is there one NATO-way. Instead, Greece, Cyprus, France and the United Kingdom all have different interests when it comes to the two institutions.

While there are some EU member states, such as the United Kingdom, which are working hard towards co-operation between EU and NATO, others again (such as France) use the institutional set up to their own advantage and to push for other national agendas than multilateral security policy-making. States such as Cyprus, Turkey or the USA, are left outside parts of the overall architecture (as they are only members of NATO or the EU). They either have to look for bilateral ways, go it alone if they can, or block inter-institutional dialogue and co-operation to demonstrate their preferences and leverage in the policy field. Overall, the establishment of overlapping institutions created a complex institutional chessboard where not all players have the same amount and types of pieces at their disposal. As a result, strategic consensus is sometimes difficult to find within any one institution.

Member states of various international institutions can use their membership(s) to push for policies closest to their national preferences. For example, NATO and the EU met in 2000 and 2001, right after CSDP was created, to try to come up with agreements that would manage the overlap between the two institutions and to co-ordinate their co-existence. Turkey more or less hijacked the negotiations, asking for concessions from the EU before agreeing to anything that would be permanent between the two institutions. France, on the other hand, was very reluctant to concede anything, as it did not want CSDP's autonomy being circumscribed in any way. In the end, a weak compromise was formalized in the form of the Berlin Plus agreements which have haunted the EU–NATO institutional interplay ever since.

Today, there are formalized meetings and various arrangements through which NATO and the EU try to cope with their coexistence. However, the agenda that binds both institutions is narrowly defined as some member states on either side of the institutions block wider strategic discussions. These tensions continue on-the-ground. Both EU and NATO have personnel in Afghanistan and Kosovo, for example, but they have no ways of communicating with one another directly and through formal channels as both operations are not linked through a common strategy or common security agreements. The latter have been blocked by some NATO member states. Former Director-General of the EU Military Staff Lt. Gen. David Leaky points out: 'the issue of co-operation between the EU and NATO is not just one of theoretical or academic importance, but rather one of life and death significance. Intelligence sharing, mutual security, medical and life support arrangements in Afghanistan and Kosovo are not just 'nice to have'; they are essential. Soldiers' lives and those of policemen and civilian actors depend on them.'

African Security

Co-operation and competition are also two dynamics that we can observe among African regional security organizations. While the UN does not play a major role in disputes and competition among NATO and the EU, UN capacities at times have changed the course of action within Africa. Other times, African organizations have challenged UN authority.

As the case of Madagascar showed, the UN, the AU and SADC can be in competition with one another. After political protests in 2009, the Madagascar government asked the UN for mediation support. However, soon after the president was removed from power. International organizations reacted to this differently: UN and SADC both condemned the ousting of the government but SADC threatened military intervention to reinstate the president while the UN did not. As a result, the UN was seen as more neutral. While the UN and SADC reacted first, other organizations wanted to stay involved and reconfirm their power. The AU initiated an international contact group to act as mediators, thereby presenting itself as the de facto agenda-setter. In the meantime, the UN lobbied SADC to change its position. SADC agreed to meditation and appointed the former president of Mozambique as mediator. SADC thereby made sure that its mediator was higher ranked than the AU's.

In the end, not only the fighting factions in Madagascar were in need of mediation but also the mediators. SADC and AU member states chose international organizations according to their needs and interest. As a result of so many mediators, structures were created that delayed decisions as to who should be responsible in the end (SADC under the auspices of the AU). The mediated power-sharing agreement collapsed eventually; would there have been better mediation, the situation on the ground would have arguably been different. With so many mediators, the parties called on the ones that were on their side and the mediators could not agree among themselves.

Another instance of competition refers not so much to dynamics among regional organizations but instead to a regional organization's relationship to the UN. It has already been mentioned that regional organizations have intervened in conflicts without prior UN approval. This is for instance the case when ECOWAS intervened in Liberia and Sierra Leone in the beginning of the 1990s. ECOWAS intervened in these conflict situations without a peace agreement in place, contrary to one of the major principles of the UN. In the end, however, ECOWAS lacked the resources to continue the operations and needed to ask the UN for assistance. The UN reluctantly complied and in the case of Liberia it provided a peace operation.

There are also examples of fruitful co-operation among the UN and African organizations. This co-operation can mainly be explained through one important asset: UN regional institutional capacities. In instances where the UN has a regional office in place, urgent matters can be handled much more efficiently because the UN representative in these offices is of the level of Assistant Secretary General and hence recognized as counterpart to national governments. While Southern Africa lacks such an office, West Africa has one, the UN Office for West Africa established in 2001.

This office became crucial in the case of Guinea and Côte d'Ivoire. After contested elections in Guinea in 2010 concerted efforts by the AU, ECOWAS and UN kept erupting violence at bay. The UN office was the bedrock for institutional co-operation on the ground and managed the relations between the AU and ECOWAS. This led to a common intervention; however, it could not prevent the military coup in 2012. In the case of Côte d'Ivoire in 2010, contested elections resulted in a four-month long civil war. ECOWAS wanted to send in military forces while the AU was against such an intervention. The UN helped overcome the different views. The regional office mediated between ECOWAS and the AU, which led to a common (non-military) intervention in which the AU, ECOWAS and the UN mediated among the fighting factions. In both cases, ECOWAS and the AU referred to the UN as the final arbiter with more institutional and political clout.

CONCLUSION

International organizations are not simply state constructs that respond to member state preferences or changed external circumstances. Instead, the international organizations' international staff contributes to the transformation of their organizations. With the end of the Cold War, the international staff was able to build more room of manoeuvre for itself. Secretaries-General have initiated processes of norm reformulation that have had major repercussions on the workings of regional organizations and member states. Both national governments and international staff have to live with a plethora of preferences when formulating policies.

The normative changes, however, had not an even impact on regional organizations or member states. A new feature of international politics has been the increasing number of international organizations that occupy the same policy domain. To judge the effectiveness or legitimacy of international organizations, we cannot look at them in isolation. The institutional complexities have opened up new possibilities of pushing for international and national agendas and many governments make use of them.

When it comes to international security, the complex interplay of national and international preferences has impacted the effectiveness and legitimacy not only of the UN but also regional organizations. At times, the UN has managed to play an independent role in fostering global peace and security. Most often, however, the UN relies on member states or is relegated to an observer role. Inter-institutional relations are far from being smooth, and competition between different international organizations, rather then leading to the establishment of a comparative advantage, has led to delays in sending out troops or in mediation. In the end, the potential for damage to ongoing peace processes has increased.

CRISIS MANAGEMENT AND GLOBAL GOVERNANCE IN THE WORLD ECONOMY

ANDRÉ BROOME*

The contemporary era is dominated by economic crises. Taking a short-term view, the subprime mortgage crisis in the USA in 2007 stimulated a sharp reduction in the availability of both retail and wholesale credit with the collapse of 'property bubbles' in the USA, the United Kingdom, and other industrialized economies, which prompted a slowdown in world economic output and a rapid contraction in the volume of world trade in 2008 and 2009. The subsequent full-blown global financial crisis resulted in the introduction of fiscal austerity programs in many developed economies, as public sector balance sheets strained under the added weight of government support for ailing banking sectors and earlier fiscal stimulus packages to ward off a new global depression. From 2010 a sovereign debt crisis has engulfed the euro zone and imperilled the future of the single currency project, with economies such as Greece, Ireland, Portugal, Italy, and Spain facing significant increases in interest rates on government bonds. When these events are taken as a series in the same causal chain, the crisis in developed economies which began in 2007 is now of five years duration, with few signs of the crisis abating and even less prospect of a return to the economic good times many countries enjoyed in the 1990s and early 2000s.

While this phenomenon of continuing crisis is relatively new for developed economies, the experience of overheated economies, rampant financial speculation amid increasing debt-servicing costs, fiscal austerity programs, and the need for financial assistance for fragile economies from the International Monetary Fund (IMF) and other international lenders, is an all too familiar experience for many of the world's developing economies. When the current crisis is situated in a longer-term perspective, the contemporary era of economic crisis stretches back over many years and includes the 1970s economic crisis prompted by the oil shocks and the breakdown of the Bretton Woods exchange rate regime, the 1980s sovereign debt crises in Latin America, the ongoing debt crisis in what are now termed heavily indebted poor countries, the transition crises in former centrally planned economies in the early 1990s, the 1995 'Tequila Crisis' in Mexico, the 1997-98 Asian financial crisis, the Argentine debt crisis in 1999-2002, and the list goes on.

The core challenge at the heart of the contemporary architecture of global economic governance is the problem of co-ordination. With the growth and evolution of economic governance responsibilities across multiple levels, from states to regional institutions such as the European Union (EU) to global governance institutions, and across different actor types, including formal organizations, transnational policy networks, and clubs such as the Group of Seven (G7) and Group of Twenty (G20), the sites of regulatory authority in the world economy have multiplied at the same time as lines of accountability for exercising authority—and responsibility for policy errors—have blurred. As a consequence, well before the onset of the global financial crisis, existing global economic governance institutions were already struggling to match their expanding public mandates with policy effectiveness. The difficulties inherent in global economic governance have become increasingly complex over the last four decades as a consequence of the international integration of national markets for trade in goods, services, and capital. During this period several of the major international economic organizations—such as the IMF, the World Bank, and the World Trade Organization (WTO)—have faced growing political challenges to their legitimacy amid claims of a 'democratic deficit' in the contemporary architecture of global economic governance.

This essay puts these broad trends in context through examining the dynamics of global governance and crisis management in the world economy, with a focus on the governance of trade, monetary relations, and economic development. The first section provides a brief history of international economic co-operation in the post-World War Two (WWII) era. The second section outlines the shape and institutional structure of the contemporary international economic order, with specific reference to the current respective roles of the IMF, the World Bank, and the WTO. The third section examines the principal challenges to these three pillars of contemporary global economic governance as they have struggled to achieve crisis management on a global scale in recent years. Finally, the essay concludes by considering the potential future evolution of global economic governance as the aftershocks of the financial crisis prompt further calls for far-reaching changes in the multi-level governance of the world economy.

LIBERAL MULTILATERALISM AFTER 1945

Created at the same time following complex negotiations at the United Nations Monetary and Financial Conference in Bretton Woods, New Hampshire, USA, in 1944, the IMF and the World Bank—the two 'Bretton Woods institutions'—formed the heart of the postwar compromise of 'embedded liberalism'. The new international economic order agreed at Bretton Woods centred on achieving the difficult task of balancing multilateralism and international openness with sufficient domestic policy autonomy to enable states to establish, rebuild, or expand national welfare states. This was to be realized through international co-operation to reduce national tariff levels and foreign exchange restrictions on trade in goods and services, combined with national controls on capital flows to guard against financial speculation and instability, while supplying external sources of credit to support postwar reconstruction and economic development.

Until the 1970s, the post-war era was characterized by national capital controls to allow for variation in domestic policy settings, combined with open current accounts and exchange rate co-ordination to provide a hospitable international environment for the expansion of world trade and economic growth. After a period of growing economic pressure on the USA, including expanding balance of payments deficits combined with rising inflation, US President Richard Nixon unilaterally suspended the convertibility of the US dollar into gold at the official exchange rate in 1971. Despite a series of subsequent efforts to re-establish a rules-based system of semi-fixed exchange rates during the early 1970s, the 1971 'Nixon Shocks' had effectively ended this component of the post-war international economic order, which quickly led to the emergence of 'floating' exchange rates among the major industrial economies and a shift towards capital mobility. With the onset of severe sovereign debt crises in the early 1980s, especially in Latin American economies, the IMF gained a new international crisis management role as an enforcer of policy reforms in borrowing member states, and as a mediator between debtor governments and external creditors. The expansion of IMF 'conditionality' (i.e. explicit policy reforms agreed between member states and the IMF in exchange for access to IMF loans) generated heated controversy about the organization's crisis management role for two main reasons. First, conditionality necessarily infringes upon national economic sovereignty, thereby diminishing the policy discretion available to governments to chart their own developmental trajectories. Second, 'Washington consensus'-style loan conditions were directed towards the liberalization and international integration

* André Broome is Senior Lecturer in International Political Economy in the Department of Political Science and International Studies, University of Birmingham, United Kingdom, and is Principal Research Fellow on the European Commission FP7 project Global Re-ordering: Evolution through European Networks (GR:EEN) in the Centre for the Study of Globalisation and Regionalisation at the University of Warwick, United Kingdom.

of national economies. This involved structural economic reforms that were often associated with negative economic and social consequences, such as increasing income inequality and slower economic growth.

To complement the IMF's role in fostering global economic stability, the World Bank was designed to provide support for countries undergoing post-conflict reconstruction and economic development through the promotion of trade, private investment, and equilibrium in national flows of trade and finance. With the inter-war international organizations widely perceived as failed experiments in international co-operation, the new organizations set up in the aftermath of WWII were intended to remedy the design flaws of earlier schemes. The World Bank's two lending arms are the International Bank for Reconstruction and Development (IBRD), which opened its doors in 1945 and now lends to middle-income developing economies, and the International Development Association (IDA), established in 1960, which provides concessional interest-free loans and grants to the world's poorest 79 economies. While the IMF is funded by member states' 'quotas', interest earned from loan repayments, and bilateral funding, and is not permitted to borrow on capital markets, the World Bank's loans through the IBRD to governments and public enterprises are funded through top-rated World Bank bonds issued on international capital markets, backed by sovereign guarantees. Following post-war reconstruction in Europe and Japan, the World Bank's lending became concentrated in developing countries (and later the 'transition' economies of East and Central Europe and the former Soviet Union), with World Bank credit comparatively cheaper for developing countries than private sources of credit because of the World Bank's top credit rating. In contrast, the World Bank's IDA lending is financed through the income earned from IBRD loan repayments and contributions from donor states.

The original third institutional pillar of the post-WWII international economic order, the International Trade Organization (ITO), was designed to institutionalize universal trade rules in order both to help liberalize trade flows and to guard against a return to the 'beggar-thy-neighbour' policies of the 1930s. However, the ITO failed to be established after it was rejected by the US Congress. Consequently, this third pillar of the new international economic order was supported by the General Agreement on Tariffs and Trade (GATT), which was established in 1947 and lasted until the end of 1994, when it was succeeded by the WTO. The GATT was designed both to set common rules for world trade and to keep trade rules up-to-date, but without the establishment of a permanent and independent international organization that could exercise enforcement powers. In contrast to the proposed ITO charter, the GATT was a voluntary system that relied on reciprocity and the willingness of participating states to abide by agreed rules. The three basic rules of the GATT included the 'most favoured nation principle' (which prevented discrimination between GATT members), the restriction of trade protections to tariffs (rather than import quotas, licenses, or new foreign exchange restrictions), and agreement that tariff rates would remain negotiable without any 'free riding' by GATT members.

THE CONTEMPORARY GOVERNANCE ARCHITECTURE FOR THE WORLD ECONOMY

The main business of decision making in the IMF is conducted through the Executive Board, which is chaired by the IMF Managing Director and currently consists of 24 directors who represent either individual countries or groups of countries. The IMF's system of representation has been a growing source of controversy in recent years, in particular because the IMF Managing Director is traditionally chosen by European governments, while the distribution of voting rights concentrates influence in the hands of a small number of large developed economies. For example, eight executive directors currently represent individual countries: the USA, Japan, the United Kingdom, Germany, France, Saudi Arabia, the People's Republic of China, and Russia. The remaining 180 member states of the IMF are organized into country groups that are represented on the Executive Board by 16 executive directors, which effectively dilutes the collective influence that developing economies are able to wield in the IMF.

The World Bank's governance architecture resembles that of the IMF. However, the World Bank's internal accountability mechanisms are more complicated due to the larger size of the organization, as well as the institutional differences between the five component parts of the World Bank Group, in contrast to the more centralized hierarchy of the IMF. In addition to the IBRD and the IDA, the World Bank Group also includes three additional bodies: the International Finance Corporation (IFC); the Multilateral Investment Guarantee Agency (MIGA); and the International Centre for Settlement of Investment Disputes (ICSID). Most of the day-to-day decision making in the World Bank takes place through the organization's Board of Directors, which has 24 executive directors. Like the IMF, member state influence in the World Bank is also concentrated in the hands of developed economies. Five executive directors represent individual countries that are the World Bank's largest shareholders: Germany, France, Japan, the United Kingdom, and the USA. The remaining 183 members are represented in multiple-country constituencies by 19 executive directors, while the Board of Directors is chaired by the World Bank President, who is traditionally nominated by the USA. The overall governance structure of the two Bretton Woods institutions is therefore heavily weighted towards developed economies with respect to both state representation and leadership selection (although the April 2009 G20 summit meeting agreed in principle to switch to an open, merit-based selection process for the heads of both organizations).

Since the third pillar of the postwar international economic order lacked a formal independent international organization until the WTO was established in 1995, the multilateral governance of international trade has evolved in a very different fashion to the two Bretton Woods institutions. There were eight rounds of trade negotiations held under the GATT, which achieved substantial progress in liberalizing trade through tariff reductions prior to the establishment of the WTO in 1995. Compared with both the IMF and the World Bank, the WTO has a relatively small professional staff, has no lending facility, and has limited financial resources under its control, which makes the organization more dependent on the support from, and voluntary acceptance of its authority by, member states. Furthermore, the WTO takes decisions by consensus among its members on the basis of 'one country, one vote'. This provides a striking contrast with the weighted voting system of the IMF and the World Bank, where authority is largely delegated to their respective governing boards and the heads of the organizations. While the formal process stipulates equal representation between all members, in practice the outcomes of official WTO trade negotiations continue to be shaped by informal negotiations between a small group of wealthy countries (including, for example, the 'Quad' of the USA, Canada, Japan, and the EU), which exercise a disproportionate influence over wider negotiations due to the size of their domestic markets and the economic power this implies.

A further difference with the Bretton Woods institutions is the WTO's Dispute Settlement Body (DSB), which represents one of the most powerful courts in international law, with mandatory jurisdiction, quasi-automatic procedures, binding rulings, and powers of retaliation. Rather than taking unilateral action when a member state of the WTO considers that another state is violating its international trade commitments, governments can refer alleged trade violations to the DSB, which has clearly defined procedural stages and agreed timetables for the completion of cases. Compared with the weaker and less transparent dispute settlement procedures under the GATT, under WTO rules it is not possible for losing countries in a case to block adoption of the ruling (unless there is a consensus among all WTO members to reject a ruling). The primary aim of the WTO's procedures for settling trade disputes via a formal rules-based process is to reduce instability and uncertainty in multilateral trading relations.

GLOBAL ECONOMIC GOVERNANCE AND CRISIS MANAGEMENT

The contemporary architecture of global governance in the world economy is charged with three core functions related to economic crises: pre-crisis prevention; in-crisis management; and post-crisis solutions. As the events of recent years have starkly demonstrated, the various actors and institutions which make up the global economic governance architecture struggle, at the best of times, to effectively prevent crises from emerging. The reasons for this are manifold, and include many factors that are out of the control of global governance institutions, such as inter-state rivalries and economic competition, insufficient resources and authority to tackle transnational problems in private sector markets, as well as the role of domestic politics in shaping the art of the possible in international economic co-operation. Other reasons include a status quo bias, the difficulties involved with convincing national economic decision makers to take policy decisions that may cut across their political interests, as well as a segmented analysis of the nature and drivers of emerging economic problems, which can make it hard for those actors charged with preventing economic crises at a global level to 'connect the dots' in time.

Global governance institutions such as the IMF and the World Bank can potentially exercise more influence over the dynamics of managing an economic crisis, compared with crisis prevention, through their ability to persuade national decision makers to choose one policy strategy over another, which is often reinforced by the opportunity to use loan policy conditions (or 'prior actions' that must be implemented before loans will be approved) as leverage for shifting the national policy agenda. Here, however, three further problems remain. First is the continuing ability of states to ignore the policy preferences and advice of global governance institutions, even if this comes with a high cost. Second is the persistent question of whether institutions such as the IMF and the World Bank indeed offer national decision makers the best advice for managing an economic crisis, or whether following their advice may in some cases make a bad situation worse (as is widely recognized was the case with the IMF in the Asian financial crisis). Third, is the fact that global governance institutions seldom have a free hand in their dealings with national governments, due to the interests of other actors as well as their own limited resources. In Europe, for example, the IMF must also negotiate with the European Commission as well as borrower governments, while the bilateral influence of creditor states such as Germany is of particular importance for euro zone economies, as well as others such as the role played by the United Kingdom in providing additional financial assistance to Ireland to support its IMF bailout programme.

When it comes to the gradual development of post-crisis regulatory and policy solutions aimed at structural changes that might prevent future global economic crises, so far the jury remains out on how effective institutions such as the IMF and others will be in proposing new ideas for global economic governance reforms. On the one hand, there is a potential conflict of interest in asking an organization to propose designs for its own reforms, as resulting reforms may be tilted towards the best interests of the organization itself rather the needs of its members (a problem that is equally relevant at the national and regional governance levels as well as the global level). On the other hand, existing global governance institutions may have a unique advantage over many national governments with respect to technocratic expertise, institutional memory, and comparative policy knowledge when it comes to the design of new global regulatory regimes and policy solutions.

With each of these three core crisis-related functions, global governance institutions face the issue of resource constraints. While this is perhaps less pertinent in the case of a crisis located in one particular economy, or limited to a small number of economies, when it comes to a global economic crisis or a more limited crisis in large developed economies the resource constraints within which organizations such as the IMF must operate shape the range of policy options on the table, and may determine the level of effectiveness of global governance responses to crises. The decline of the IMF's own financial resources relative to world trade and capital flows and international currency reserves has been a continuing problem for the organization over many years. In short, the IMF on its own has lacked the volume of funds required to support developed or middle-income developing economies experiencing a financial crisis. When faced with major financial crises such as in Mexico in 1994 or Asia in 1997-98, the organization has been forced to depend more heavily upon supplementary finance provided by major bilateral donors, other multilateral donors such as the World Bank, the Bank for International Settlements (BIS) or the EU, and large commercial banks. This has weakened the IMF's institutional legitimacy, due to widespread claims that the IMF's policy conditions in its rescue packages have often been geared towards the interests of creditors such as the US Treasury or private banks rather than the interests of country borrowers.

A high-profile early effort to alleviate the relative decline of the IMF's financial resources in the current crisis was the agreement at the G20 summit meeting, held in London, United Kingdom, in April 2009, effectively to triple the size of the IMF's resources (from US $250,000m. to $750,000m., with $100,000m. each provided by Japan and the EU), in addition to an extra $100,000m. of annual lending by the multilateral development banks up to $300,000m. over the following three years (including, for example, a 200% capital increase for the Asian Development Bank). While this represented an unprecedented increase in the IMF's lending capacity, IMF loan programmes are likely to continue to depend upon supplementary financing in the future, while even such a large increase in lending power may not be sufficient to support systemically-important countries undergoing a severe financial crisis due to the volume of global capital flows. While the IMF's broader institutional legitimacy problems are not yet resolved, the organization has recently found its services in much greater demand once again as countries around the world have struggled to cope with the economic distress caused by the global financial crisis, with the organization extending its first loans to 'western' economies in over three decades, such as the IMF's multi-year financial assistance packages for Iceland ($2,100m., 2008-2011), Greece (€30,000m., 2010-13), Ireland (€45,000m., 2010-13), and Portugal (€26,000m., 2011-14). At the same time, recent IMF bailouts have been associated with riots, large-scale public protests, and political instability, while borrowing governments facing voters at the ballot box (such as the Independence Party in Iceland in April 2009, and the Fianna Fáil Party in Ireland in February 2011) have quickly been shown the door.

Because of the problem of co-ordination in global governance with respect to crisis management, additional resources alone do not necessarily lead to improved outcomes. However, the substantial increases in IMF resources in recent years have put paid to earlier predictions of the institution's gradual demise as a key institution in global economic governance. From the start of the crisis in 2007 to 2012, the IMF has lent more than $300,000m. in new financial assistance to its member states. In June 2012, the G20 leaders' summit in Los Cabos, Mexico, agreed a further emergency boost to the IMF's lending resources of an additional $456,000m. through bilateral loans from 37 member states to the organization.

A key dynamic of recent international crisis management strategies has been the evolving relationship between national, regional, and global economic governance institutions. On the one hand, the IMF's system of governance continues to face political challenges given the under-representation of emerging market economies (despite recent and ongoing moves to increase the voting rights of major emerging economies), many of which became increasingly sceptical of the value of existing forms of international economic governance such as the IMF in the wake of the Asian financial crisis. This lead to an increasing reliance on regional forms of economic co-operation in Asia and Latin America, either through the creation of new regional economic institutions and agreements or the strengthening of existing regional forums, a process which has often been directly aimed at reducing the future dependence of emerging market economies on the IMF. On the other hand, leading euro zone economies such as France and, in particular, Germany have welcomed the IMF's involvement in developing crisis management strategies for euro zone and other EU member states over the past two years, in order to take advantage of the IMF's ability to act as a tough external enforcer of budget discipline without the need for the EU—or individual EU states, such as Germany—to become more directly involved in a country's domestic politics in the midst of an ongoing crisis. Even so, the experience of joint IMF-EU bailouts in euro zone economies so far illustrates the high-risk political gamble associated with the attempt to use an international organization as a scapegoat, with the European Commission and major creditor states bogged down in protracted horse-trading over the design, role and purposes of newly established regional financial assistance mechanisms such as the European Financial Stability Facility and the European Financial Stability Mechanism.

For its part, the World Bank has faced a difficult set of policy challenges in recent years, at the same time as the organization has signed up to support 'good governance' reforms in borrowing countries. Good governance reforms generally include the following main aims: empowering the poor; improving basic services; enhancing market access; and providing greater security. The World Bank's adoption of a good governance agenda from the early 1990s onwards has been promoted by the research, experience, and advocacy of major donors and non-governmental organizations (NGOs), based on the understanding that 'poor governance' contributes to continued under-development in many countries. One major problem for the World Bank is that its promotion of good governance reforms has enabled an expansion of the scope of its policy interventions in borrowing countries, which has generated significant controversy given the World Bank's formal status as an apolitical organization and the sovereignty costs that such interventions entail. Furthermore, the World Bank, which has also been castigated for its support of Washington consensus reforms, has been strongly criticized for using its good governance agenda to downsize the public sector in borrowing countries because the private sector is assumed to be more efficient and less prone to corruption than governments. While many actors in the international development community view the World Bank's support for good governance as a positive step, this expansion of the World Bank's role in many of the world's poorest societies raises important and unresolved questions about the appropriate balance of authority between international economic organizations and national governments, and also with respect to the World Bank's influential role in shaping the global development agenda. While the World Bank has been relatively more successful than the IMF at overcoming the legitimacy crisis associated with the Washington consensus agenda during the mid- and late-1990s, by empowering further extensions to the scope and style of policy interventions in developing economies the World Bank's 'post-Washington consensus' has generated a new set of policy problems and new challenges to its legitimacy.

The primary policy challenge facing the WTO in recent years is the failure to realize a new international trade agreement on the liberalization of trade in agriculture. The 'Doha Round' of trade negotiations, launched in 2001, aimed to achieve significant progress in the world-wide reduction of barriers to agricultural trade among WTO members. Yet despite the continuing support that key national policymakers voice for concluding the Doha Round, progress has proven to be painstakingly slow at best. The three main issues that are seen as crucial for the Doha Round to make substantial progress include the following important changes: the USA would have to agree to make further cuts in subsidies; the EU would have to agree to expand agricultural market access; and major emerging market economies, such as Brazil and India, would need to agree to lower tariffs on manufactured goods. One of the key problems stalling progress is that each main negotiating group wants the others to move first. A new effort to reach agreement in mid-2008 quickly collapsed when negotiators failed to achieve a compromise between the positions of the USA and India over the threshold for a measure to allow countries to impose special tariffs on specific agricultural goods to protect poor farmers when commodity prices fall rapidly or in the event of an import surge, and little tangible progress has been made on the talks in the three years since. Despite the recent report from the current Director-General, Pascal Lamy, to the WTO's General Council in May 2012 that members wished to make 'tangible progress' in the near future, 11 years after it was first launched a final deal on the Doha Round continues to elude the organization.

In the wake of the failure to conclude the Doha Round, many countries have turned to the creation of bilateral and regional free trade arrangements. The Trans-Pacific Strategic Economic Partnership Agreement (the P4), for example, between Brunei, Chile, New Zealand, and Singapore, eliminated 90% of all trade tariffs between participating countries when it came into force in 2006. Negotiations were continuing in 2012 to expand this regional free trade arrangement to include Australia, Malaysia, Peru, Japan, the USA, and Viet Nam. Other examples of recently concluded or proposed regional free trade agreements include the Commonwealth of Independent States Free Trade Agreement (CISFTA), signed in 2011 between eight of the former Soviet republics, and the creation of the Union of South American Nations (UNASUR), which is modelled on the EU and aims to eliminate tariffs among 12 countries between 2014 (for non-sensitive products) and 2019 (for sensitive products). The recent growth of regional economic agreements on trade and investment can be understood in part as resulting from a desire among some countries to balance the impact of economic blocs such as the North American Free Trade Agreement (NAFTA, established in 1994 between the USA, Canada, and Mexico) and the EU. However, many observers view the expanding number of bilateral preferential trade agreements and the creation of trading blocs as potentially weakening the multilateral trade regime of the WTO.

A further political challenge to the effectiveness and fairness of the WTO's structure centres on participation in the organization's dispute settlement procedures. Poorer developing countries face a significant disadvantage compared with wealthier emerging market economies or developed economies, because they may lack the level of expertise or resources required to mount a successful legal challenge to potential trade violations. Notably, while developing economies comprise two-thirds of the WTO membership, they only initiate around one-third of trade disputes. Most developing economy cases are initiated by a small number of active countries such as India and Thailand, while the overall number of filings is disproportionately dominated by developed economies such as the USA and the EU. WTO rules do make special provision for the challenges faced by developing countries in initiating dispute settlement procedures, although inequities still remain due to the substantial procedural costs that developing countries may face as a consequence of their greater capacity constraints. Rather than establishing a level playing field, therefore, the WTO's dispute settlement mechanisms require further fine-tuning in order to tilt the rules governing multilateral trade disputes away from the implicit bias in favour of developed economies.

ECONOMIC CRISES AND THE EVOLUTION OF GLOBAL ECONOMIC GOVERNANCE

In the last three decades the location of key decision-making processes has tended to migrate away from more traditional and formal international economic organizations toward more ad hoc and informal forums for economic governance such as the various 'G' summit meetings—in particular, the G7 and the G20—as well as technocratic forums such as the Basel Committee on Banking Supervision (an informal institution for co-operation among central bankers, based at the BIS, which sets standards on financial supervision). The G7 succeeded the Group of Five meetings, initiated in the early 1970s, for key national policymakers to deliberate informally over the redesign of the international monetary system, and brings together the finance ministers and central bank governors of the USA, Germany, France, the United Kingdom, Japan, Canada, and Italy. In contrast, the G20 was created more recently in the aftermath of the Asian financial crisis, and was endorsed by the G7 as a forum to promote dialogue on global financial and economic governance among a more inclusive group of countries that could help to bridge the North-South divide. In addition to the EU and other developed economies, the G20 includes major emerging market and developing economies such as Brazil, Mexico, South Africa, Indonesia, India, Russia, Turkey, Argentina, the Republic of Korea, Saudi Arabia, and the People's Republic of China.

Compared with the G7, the G20 is more representative on several measures. Collectively the G20 members represent two-thirds of the world's population, and account for 85% of the world's gross domestic product, as well as 80% of global trade. In September 2009, G20 leaders, meeting in Pittsburgh, USA, agreed to establish the forum as the primary 'steering committee' for the world economy—effectively substituting the G20 for the older, smaller, and less-representative G7. Despite the fanfare that surrounded the emergence of the G20 leaders' summits, subsequent meetings have yielded relatively little in the way of major policy initiatives, or even concrete multilateral agreement on core issues.

Another important addition to the series of informal forums of international economic governance in the post-WWII era has been the World Economic Forum (first established in the early 1970s as the European Management Forum), which meets annually in Davos, Switzerland, and brings together over 2,000 people including participants from business, politics, NGOs, media, international organizations, and academia. As a 'knowledge institution', the World Economic Forum potentially exercises an important influence on international economic governance through defining new policy ideas and shaping regulatory reform agendas. Despite its size and reputation among critics as an elite network, it has an advantage over the various 'G' forums because it provides an opportunity for world leaders to deliberate and exchange ideas in the absence of public pressure to produce a clear summit outcome such as a communiqué or treaty.

Unlike the cataclysmic effects of the Great Depression in the 1930s and WWII, the recent global financial crisis has not wholly swept away previous institutional forms of international policy co-ordination, which in some cases have been strongly reinforced (such as the boost to the IMF's lending resources). However, many conventional assumptions about 'best practice' economic governance have been severely challenged. In the continuing crises that have followed the peak of the global financial crisis three main dynamics can be identified that point to likely trends in the future evolution of global economic governance. These centre on the renewed importance of and relationship between: national institutions and intergovernmental clubs; regional economic agreements and institutions; and the role of global economic governance institutions.

First, the global financial crisis has shown that the nature, effectiveness, and respective roles of national institutions of economic governance remain crucially important. For example, the 'light touch' financial regulation models of the United Kingdom and the USA have been de-legitimated by both the emergence of the crisis and the way it has been managed at a national level, while current policy debates in many industrialized countries are prompting a rethink of the respective roles of central banks, finance ministries, and other national regulatory institutions to achieve a better balance between growth and stability. In addition, the role of intergovernmental 'G' summit meetings of a select group of national leaders and policy officials are likely to continue to remain the principal forums for proposing, approving, or vetoing major changes in the architecture of global economic governance. Indeed, with many of the world's largest developed economies preoccupied either with managing a fragile recovery, implementing domestic austerity programmes to trim public spending and sovereign debt ratios, or responding to ongoing sovereign debt crises, much of the initial appetite from national governments for a substantive overhaul of the entire architecture of global economic governance in the wake of the global financial crisis appears to have dissipated. Indeed, it is perhaps at the regional level that economic governance architectures are more likely to be reformed substantially in the next few years, especially in the case of the EU and the system for economic governance in the euro zone.

Second, with regulatory authority in the world economy split unevenly between multiple levels of governance, the evolving relationship between regional economic institutions and global economic governance institutions, such as the co-operation between the EU and the IMF in the euro zone sovereign debt crisis, is likely to prove an important motor of long-term change in global economic governance across the board. For example, despite widespread fears that the proliferation of regional and bilateral preferential trade agreements might weaken the effectiveness of the WTO as the global arbiter of international trade rules, it is also possible that the strengthening of regional trade ties can provide an important stepping stone for the WTO to move forward through further increasing the density of international trade legalization at a level where it is more politically feasible for governments to achieve multilateral agreement.

Third, the global financial crisis has reaffirmed the importance of the main global economic governance institutions. This is most obvious in the case of the IMF, with a large number of countries drawing on the organization's financial resources to plug sharp balance of payments shortfalls, compared with the stigma many countries associated with borrowing from the IMF in the decade following the Asian financial crisis. In addition, formal global economic governance institutions such as the World Bank, the IMF, and the WTO remain more suited than informal intergovernmental forums to the task of filling in the concrete technical details, definitions, and procedures of international regulatory regimes, and are better able effectively to diffuse, monitor, and enforce compliance with new rules and policy norms.

This suggests that, for the foreseeable future, both the mature international economic organizations such as the IMF and the World Bank, as well as more recent auxiliary institutions like the WTO, will continue to play the following major roles with respect to the governance of the world economy. Lending organizations such as the Bretton Woods institutions will continue to be important sources of credit for developing economies, especially the heavily indebted poor countries that do not have recourse to alternative sources of external finance, as well as industrialized economies suffering a severe sovereign debt crisis. Despite the stronger spotlight that is now focused on finalizing long-overdue reforms to IMF and World Bank lending practices, both organizations will continue to apply some form of policy conditionality before agreeing to extend credit, which means that they will have an ongoing role in domestic processes of policy reform and institutional change in borrowing countries.

Global economic governance institutions will continue to play an important, and expanded, role in global policy surveillance and economic forecasting. In the wake of the global financial crisis the need for more comprehensive oversight of the world economy and policy surveillance to enhance the potential for advance notification of future financial crises has become more urgent. This led G20 leaders in April 2009 to call for increased collaboration between the IMF and the new Financial Stability Board (the successor to the Financial Stability Forum, which had been set up in 1999 in the aftermath of the Asian financial crisis) to report on macroeconomic risks and the potential actions needed to address them, as well as sanctioning a clampdown on the activities of tax havens (with oversight from the Organisation for Economic Co-operation and Development).

Moreover, the continued existence of global economic governance institutions, such as the IMF, the World Bank, and the WTO, can help to diminish the potential for economic disagreements to spillover into strategic conflicts. In this respect, the formal mechanisms of the Bretton Woods institutions and the WTO's dispute settlement procedures remain a source of strength. While major powers can of course choose to violate these international rules and principles, the existence of codified principles for governing international co-operation and economic interactions helps to stabilize other actors' expectations of a state's behaviour, which raises the political and economic costs associated with unilaterally breaking the rules of the status quo. On the other side of the coin, the Bretton Woods institutions and the WTO continue to provide useful mechanisms for achieving policy compliance with international norms, which can potentially serve to reduce the more blatant unilateral exercise of economic power by one government over another.

Finally, the above roles suggest that formal international economic organizations will continue to perform a series of important intellectual tasks with respect to global economic governance. Among other things, these are likely to include collectively supplying national governments with the following functions:

a. Templates for crisis management options and short-term policy solutions to restore stability in fragile economies;

b. A source of new ideas for changes to existing international regulatory regimes;

c. A source of comparative policy knowledge on national economic reforms;

d. The capacity to model the effects of both national and international policy changes, as well as to monitor spillover effects between economies;

e. The promotion of global compliance with agreed rules and principles;

f. A source of comparable cross-country economic data and economic forecasting;

g. A storing house for institutional memory of what has worked, and what has not worked, with respect to international economic governance in the past.

Taken together, these functions can help to resolve collective problems at the global level that both national governments and market actors would struggle to address effectively in the absence of a formal institutional architecture for international economic governance.

In short, many of the familiar features of global economic governance in the contemporary era are unlikely to disappear anytime soon, and the future of global economic governance remains in large part a story of continuity in the principles that guide the governance of the world economy. Yet the roles that mature organizations play in governing the world economy have also changed markedly since their creation and are continuing to do so in the wake of the financial crisis. In addition, a plethora of new institutional forums have been established in recent years at the regional and global level to tackle issues that may be beyond the remit of traditional organizations, or because national governments have wished to retain a greater degree of direct influence over the development and implementation of new regulatory solutions. This has contributed to increasing both the complexity and the diversity of contemporary mechanisms of global economic governance. Whether these changes are sufficient to address the ongoing policy challenges of economic globalization, as well as the persistent political challenges of improving the legitimacy of the architecture for governing the world economy in the aftermath of the world's worst financial crisis for more than 70 years, remains to be seen.

INTERNATIONAL HUMANITARIAN CO-OPERATION

Dr Peter Walker*

INTRODUCTION

Humanitarian aid is assistance given in times of crisis to alleviate immediate suffering. It has evolved in form and scale tremendously over the past 150 years, but throughout that time there have been two features which distinguish it. Firstly, its prime purpose has not changed: the alleviation, or prevention of suffering in the here and now. Thus it deals with symptoms, not causes. It does this based on a strong ethical belief that all peoples in the world are of equal worth: that humanity is one family. Secondly, aid is given impartially, i.e. regardless of race, creed or colour and irrespective of which side of a conflict the sufferers are on. The only criteria of importance are need and urgency. This notion of impartiality, usually referred to as the 'principle of impartiality', has also led aid agencies to espouse the principle of neutrality as a way of ensuring access to those in need. The logic being that in a violent environment (a war, civil unrest and suchlike) to get access to all those suffering requires gaining the trust of all the warring parties. If they detect bias and believe that one side is being favoured over the other, then trust breaks down and aid agencies will only get access to victims on one side of the conflict: in such a situation assistance fails to be impartial. Neutrality for aid agencies, therefore, is not a political stance; it is a pragmatic and principled approach that maximizes the probability of gaining trust and thereby enhances access to crisis victims in order to alleviate suffering.

To make matters more complicated, there have never been enough resources available to address all the suffering generated in conflicts, famines, floods and suchlike, so aid agencies also have to practice triage, using the limited resources at their disposal to target the most urgent needs. Agencies may act impartially, provide aid proportionately, and think that they are neutral in their actions, but what matters is how those with power on the ground perceive them. Ironically, in order to be neutral, aid workers must have a deep understanding of the politics of any crisis they are thrown into, not just at the overview level, but right down to the local nuances needed to negotiate access with local commanders, or with each group of armed men (and they are almost always men) that they encounter. The repeated and complex negotiations needed in 2012 for aid agencies to gain access to southern Somalia at the height of the famine provide a perfect demonstration of the tremendous difficulty of cultivating trust and access in these environments.

The practice of humanitarian assistance is therefore both very local in its application and global in its interpretation. Factors such as who funds an operation, where the people come from that staff it, and where the operational agency is headquartered, can all affect how people on the ground perceive it, and thus whether the agency is able to access all populations in order to provide timely, proportional, and impartial life-saving aid.

Aid flows from the resources of the richer nations, through a handful of operational aid agencies, directly or else via local operational partners, to those in need.

In 2010 some US $18,200m. was provided in international humanitarian assistance. Some $12,400m. of this came from governments, and $5,800m. from private donations via aid agencies. These figures do not include aid disbursed via agencies that fail to publish annual reports, or aid in the form of increased diaspora remittances in times of crisis. Whilst the bulk of the governmental contributions (from 90%–99% of annual government humanitarian aid over the past decade) comes from the 34 member states of the Organisation for Economic Co-operation and Development (OECD), a total of 112 countries have at one time or another in the past decade made contributions to international aid appeals. Thus many states are both humanitarian aid donors and recipients (Development Initiatives: *Private Funding, an emerging trend in humanitarian donorship, 2011*).

TOP 10 STATE HUMANITARIAN DONORS IN 2010*

	Amount (US $m.)
USA	4,806
European Union	1,604
United Kingdom	951
Germany	685
Japan	537
Spain	501
Canada	452
Sweden	393
France	374
Norway	339

* Preliminary estimates.

TOP 10 STATES RECEIVING HUMANITARIAN AID IN 2010*

	Amount (US $m.)
Haiti	3,384.3
Pakistan	2,874.5
Sudan	1.159.3
Ethiopia	587.6
Afghanistan	574.2
Democratic Republic of the Congo	497.3
Palestinian Territories	322.0
Niger	304.7
Somalia	277.7
Zimbabwe	252.6

* Preliminary estimates.

Source: Development Initiatives, *Global Humanitarian Assistance Report*, 2011.

The 10 top state humanitarian donors in 2010 provided an estimated 85% of all state donations, while the top 10 recipient states were allocated some 52% of all international government donations. We are therefore dealing with two very skewed populations here: 85% of government aid flows *from* just 5% of the countries in the world, and more than 50% of aid flows *into* 5% of countries in the world.

Humanitarian aid made up about 10.0% of all government sponsored aid flows in 2010; this figure has risen gradually since the beginning of the decade when it accounted for around 6.9% of aid flows. When compared with the resources spent on defence, trade promotion, or through tourism, it is a very small amount of money, but of course it has high public profile and thus, from a political point of view, is a very tempting activity to be associated with. This dance between humanitarian agencies trying to keep to their principles of impartiality and neutrality on the one side, and governments seeking to use, benignly or coercively, aid to promote their own causes, has been a constant aspect of aid work from the beginning.

A BRIEF HISTORY OF INTERNATIONAL ACTION AND CO-OPERATION

There is no obvious starting point in history for the first aid programme. Clay tablets on display in the British Museum in

*Dr Peter Walker is the Irwin H. Rosenberg Professor of Nutrition and Human Security and Director of the Feinstein International Center, Friedman School of Nutrition Science and Policy, at Tufts University, Medford, MA, USA.

London, excavated from land now in Iraq, show, in the cuneiform script of 5,000 years ago, that local town accountants were worrying about the balance of food grown and food needed over the year, and how the gap could be filled to avoid famine and rioting. Roman history records many periods of famine and associated civil unrest, and the measures the state took to avoid suffering, including the fixing of grain prices, the rationing of food, and free handouts to the host needy—techniques still used today (Garnsey 1988).

In 1755 Lisbon, the Portuguese capital, was hit by a major earthquake which was comparable in its destructive force to that which hit Port-au-Prince in Haiti in 2010. Portugal's then First Minister, the Marquês de Pombal, organized what amounted to a massive humanitarian relief operation. He ordered the burial of the dead the day after the quake, the prompt distribution of food, and the freezing of grain prices. Within a week he was planning the rebuilding of the city (Khedouri 2007). Both Spain and Britain sent aid. Writing a few years after the event, the Swiss philosopher Emmerich de Vattel noted that 'the calamities of Portugal have given England an opportunity of fulfilling the duties of humanity'. De Vattel continued: 'if a nation is afflicted with famine, all those who have provisions to spare ought to relieve her distress, without, however, exposing themselves to want' (de Vattel 1757). Humanitarian action, thought de Vattel, was an intrinsic property of sovereignty.

But it was really not until the 19th century that humanitarian aid became sufficiently well-organized to the point where one could speak of systems. Over the period from the early 1800s to the end of the Second World War one can see maybe four different forces shaping the evolution of the global aid system.

Firstly: containment. In the wake of famine, floods and economic meltdown, states fear insurrection. The response organized by the then ruling East India Company to the famine of 1837–38 in India involved the provision of food or cash in return for work, coupled with free food distribution for the most destitute. It was a massive operation. But the language used to describe those seeking relief at the time is instructive. They were referred to as destitute, paupers, vagrants, and the 'labouring poor'—terminology which essentially depicted them as a threat to law and order (Alamgir 1980). Relief work was driven more by the fear of insurrection than by any notion of charity. It was essentially an agenda of containment. It is an agenda that we still see operating today, in the 'hearts and minds' relief operations mounted by foreign forces in Afghanistan.

To find our second agenda we need to fast forward to 1859 and a Swiss trader, Henry Dunant, witnessing the battle of Solferino in northern Italy. The armies of France and the Austro-Hungarian Empire were fighting, during daylight hours, in the fields outside the village. One could go along and stand on a hillside and watch, and, when the fighting finished for the day, the dead and wounded were just left on the battlefield. Dunant was so appalled by what he saw that, in the evening after the fighting, he organized the women of the village to accompany him onto the battlefield and to try to alleviate the suffering of the wounded. He had to negotiate with the commanders of both armies to gain access, assuring them that he would not favour one side's soldiers over the others. Upon his return to Geneva he wrote up his experiences in *A Memory of Solferino*. This passionate plea for the creation of an international body solely devoted to the alleviation of suffering on the battlefield, regardless of which side the wounded were on, was taken up by a group of Swiss philanthropists and rapidly evolved into the International Committee of the Red Cross (ICRC), which is still today one of the major humanitarian organizations in the world. Dunant's agenda, however, was not one of containment, but one of compassion, very different from that of the East India Company.

The end of the First World War saw the Allies blockading the Austrian capital of Vienna, starving the city. Those who suffered most were children. This suffering, reported in the newspapers, so appalled the British social activist Eglantine Jebb that she started organizing a fund to 'save the children' of Vienna. Colleagues in Sweden also took up the cause. Between them they bought food for the Red Cross to ship to Vienna. Jebb went further, beyond compassion, arguing that children should never be treated as disposable collateral in a war. She worked through the newly formed League of Nations to help draft a Declaration on the Rights of the Child, which in 1989 was eventually adopted by the League's successor, the United Nations (UN), as the Convention on the Rights of the Child. So, Jebb was going beyond compassion and actually had an agenda of change, seeking to address some of the root causes of suffering, and in so doing also gave birth to the Save the Children family of agencies, still active today. An agenda of change was the third force that shaped the global humanitarian system.

World War Two also saw the birth of major aid agencies (Oxfam and CARE, see below), and, at its end, the establishment of the UN system. As the war wound down, US NGOS were keen to support government efforts to alleviate suffering in Europe. Some 22 of them got together and formed the Co-operative for American Remittances to Europe (CARE). Jointly they raised funds to purchase surplus US army rations stockpiled in the Pacific, and organized to ship these to individual families in Europe, thereby bringing the first CARE Parcels into existence. It was a people-to-people equivalent of the Marshal Plan. CARE went on to provide similar aid during the Berlin Blockade. Their actions were certainly focused on the alleviation of suffering, but they never sought to be neutral and in many ways their aid activities were more akin to the provision of social warfare at a distance. This was essentially an agenda of comfort.

These four agendas—Containment, Compassion, Change and Comfort—interweave throughout the history of humanitarianism and compete today to guide agencies and operations. Most would identify the Henry Dunant (Red Cross) agenda, of principled compassion, as the core history of humanitarianism, but the competing agendas of containment, change and comfort are always there shaping the real-politic on the ground.

A TYPOLOGY OF THE KEY ACTORS

That real-politic, driven by the need caused in war, governance collapse and natural disasters, is played out amongst the main groups of actors that respond to crises. Broadly speaking there are five key groupings: states, the Red Cross and Red Crescent Movement, the UN system, international NGOs, and local NGOs.

States

The prime duty and responsibility to respond to a disaster and address the needs of those who are suffering rests with the affected state. Where states accept this duty and have the resources to deal with it, and the scale of the disaster does not overwhelm, things work well. We see this in the USA's response to flooding on the Mississippi for instance, in the People's Republic of China's response to earthquakes, and in India's response to drought. Problems arise either where states cannot cope, i.e. the disaster overwhelms them, or where they choose not to cope, i.e. they either do not want to meet the needs of their citizens or are sufficiently suspicious of external aid that they try to exclude it.

Through the 1970s external donor states used to supply the bulk of their aid directly to the affected host state; now, however, less than 14% flows that way. The rest goes via the UN, Red Cross and NGOs. Increasingly in the last decade external states, where they have a foreign policy interest in a crisis and support that interest with military involvement, are seeking to use those military forces also to supply humanitarian aid. In Afghanistan in 2010 US forces, through a new mechanism called the Commanders Emergency Response Fund, had access to upwards of US $1,000m. to spend on humanitarian-like projects. By definition, humanitarian aid in pursuit of a foreign policy objective is no longer neutral, and, some aid agencies would argue, the military do not have the skills to carry it out in a way that is impartial, and appropriate, sensitive to culture, etc.

Most donor aid though flows via the big operational agencies.

UN Bodies

As with the NGOs there is a plethora of UN bodies that can play a role in humanitarian response. Five bodies account for the lion's share of the work.

Firstly the Office for the Co-ordination of Humanitarian Assistance (OCHA). OCHA is a part of the UN Secretariat. Its mandate is to lead and co-ordinate, to provide information services, and to help shape the overall approach to crisis response. In most crises the UN will appoint a Humanitarian Co-ordinator on the ground: their lead person. OCHA also chairs the Inter-Agency Steering Committee (IASC), the prime global body that brings together the UN and non-UN operational actors to agree on policy, systems for better co-ordination and training, etc. OCHA runs ReliefWeb, the main web portal which supplies background and real time information on how a crisis is unfolding.

Secondly, the World Food Programme (WFP). In cash terms WFP is now the biggest humanitarian agency in the world, with more people and offices around the world than any other. In the past much of its attention was focused on the supply of food, usually western surpluses, as food-for-work programmes or for direct support to governments. Today it mostly buys food on the open market, often locally to a crisis, and supplies it as humanitarian assistance to the Red Cross and NGOs, which then distribute it.

Thirdly, the UN High Commissioner for Refugees (UNHCR). UNHCR is mandated to assist and protect refugees, and people in refugee-like situations. This means ensuring that refugee camps are operated fairly and that refugees are separated from the forces that may have compelled them to flee in the first place. It often means working closely with the host state to supply aid to refugees living with local families, and refugees seeking to return home or to repatriate to a third country.

Fourthly, the UN Children's Fund (UNICEF), which seeks to protect children and their families in times of crisis. UNICEF is often directly operational, running vaccination and feeding programmes on the ground.

Finally, the UN Development Programme (UNDP) which takes the lead in rehabilitation and reconstruction after a disaster.

The UN agencies are there at the request, and in support of, the host government. Their role is at times constrained, when the host government is reticent to act, and at times they effectively take over the role of the host government were it cannot act, as we saw after the January 2010 Haiti earthquake.

The Red Cross and Red Crescent

The Red Cross/Red Crescent Movement consists of three component bodies. Firstly the International Committee of the Red Cross (ICRC). This is the Swiss-based body that defends the Geneva Conventions and has a direct mandate, from states who have signed the Conventions, to provide aid in times of war and similar crises. It acts independently and is seen by most people as the most neutral and impartial of agencies. The ICRC also has a duty to visit prisoners of war, on all sides, and to seek to reunite families divided by war. It is supported by the staff and volunteers of the National Red Cross and Red Crescent Societies (the second component). Just about every country in the world has a Red Cross or Red Crescent Society. In times of war these Societies act under the direction of ICRC. In times of natural disasters, refugee flows, and suchlike, they act on their own or are supported by their sister societies. This support comes via the third body, the International Federation of Red Cross and Red Crescent Societies (IFRC). This is the Federation of all the National Societies, with a secretariat in Geneva.

NGOs

In any one crisis there can be hundreds of NGOs operating, often formed spontaneously by people who see suffering and want to act. Around 60% of all international humanitarian aid flows through NGOs, and in most disasters the vast majority of it flows through a small number of large international NGOs, most of which now have global, often federated, structures, and are better thought of as NGO families. Prime amongst these families are: World Vision International (WVI), CARE, the Save the Children Alliance (SCF), Caritas Internationalis (including its American member Catholic Relief Services—CRS), Oxfam International, and Médecins Sans Frontières (MSF); and there are many more. NGOs tend to have the highest media profile in crises, and often drive some of the most innovative solutions to improving the way aid works. Their more maverick and less experienced members also commit some of the most publicized mistakes.

Local Groups

Finally there are the local NGOs and aid groups. Often international NGOs will work with local NGOs, or other community bodies, to distribute aid. Increasingly, because of the way aid is passed down to the external NGOs, this co-operation is in the form of a formal sub-contact. Local bodies have the knowledge of context to help ensure that the right aid flows to the right people, to help negotiate access, and to do so at local rates of pay. But they also have the best chance, in a conflict, of being part of that conflict and acting in a non-neutral fashion. Increasingly, particularly in south and southeast Asia, we are seeing local NGOs grow to play a role on the international stage, Mercy Malaysia being an example.

THE STATE OF PLAY TODAY: EXISTING STRUCTURE FOR CO-OPERATION

With all these agencies it would be more accurate to talk about a humanitarian ecosystem, with individual actors, connected in different ways, seeking their own roles. There are governing principles for the ecosystem which the actors, to greater or lesser degrees, try to work to. Most agencies try to be impartial, and to use their resources effectively. Most try to meet the most urgent needs first. But there is no command and control. Co-ordination occurs via nudging, and facilitating the forming of groupings to agree self-policed standards. All this unfolds in the often chaotic and information-poor environment of a crisis in a foreign country.

Three key types of mechanism are used to nudge this ecosystem towards order, efficiency and effectiveness: quality assurance initiatives, funding initiatives, and associative structures.

Quality Assurance Initiatives

From the late 1980s onwards groupings of operational agencies, usually supported by the main donors, have come together to create common standards for their work. These standards are for the most part self policed. The Sphere Standards, established in the mid-1990s, and now used by just about every operational agency, lay down minimum benchmarks for the most urgent aid (food, water, sanitation, health care, shelter). Sphere Standards include carefully designed benchmarks, indicators to measure those standards, and best practice in achieving them. Companion Sphere Standards have now been developed relating to the supply of education in emergencies and to the care of animal livestock (see www.sphereproject.org).

The Active Learning Network for Accountability and Performance in Humanitarian Action (ALNAP) brings together agencies, donors, academics and consultants with a focus on improving the evaluation of, and learning from, humanitarian response. It has developed common agreed criteria for evaluations. Though meta-evaluations and a bi-annual *State of the World's Humanitarian System* report, it seeks also to evaluate the system at a global level (see www.alnap.org).

People In Aid brings aid agencies together to help improve the way they use and support their field staff, and promotes best practice in personal management (see www.peopleinaid.org).

Finally the Humanitarian Accountability Project (HAP-International) is a grouping of agencies concerned to improve their accountability towards the crisis affected populations. They have developed global standards for accountability and employ their own staff to review the effectiveness of their members in meeting these standards (see www.hapinternational.org).

In the past few years there has also been a move to promote quality though the individual rather than the agency. This is taking the form of a slowly growing movement amongst aid workers towards establishing a sense of profession, with the agreeing of common core competencies, skill and experience levels for certification, and ultimately the creation of an international professional association (see www.elrha.org/professionalisation).

Funding Initiatives

Increasingly, and via the mechanisms of the UN, donors are seeking to pool their funding, thus outsourcing some of their administration and decision-making. The act of managing these funds and being able to allocate funding from them, against set criteria, to operational agencies, acts as a strong co-ordination mechanism. Four mechanisms, all created in the last few years, now account for some 18% of all humanitarian funding.

The Central Emergency Response Fund (CERF) allows donor governments and the private sector to pool their financing on a global level to enable more timely and reliable humanitarian assistance to those affected by natural disasters and armed conflicts;

Country Humanitarian Funds (CHFs) are in-country pooled mechanisms; funding received is not earmarked, allowing money to be allocated on the basis of needs (as defined in the specific humanitarian action plan for the emergency);

Emergency Response Funds (ERFs) are also country-level mechanisms; these vary from CHFs in that they have the facility to provide finance to small-scale projects, allowing more national NGOs to access resources;

The Disaster Relief Emergency Fund (DREF) is a mechanism set up by the IFRC to provide immediate funding to Red Cross and Red Crescent societies responding to a humanitarian emergency; donors to this Fund include OECD Development Assistance Committee governments but also a range of smaller governments, Red Cross and Red Crescent National Societies, and private donors;

In addition, in every major crisis the UN seeks to pull together all its funding needs, as well as those of some of the larger non-UN bodies, into a Consolidated Appeals Process (CAP), representing an overview of requirements, rather than a set of agency by agency wish lists. The CAP is often backed up by joint agency assessment-missions on the ground.

Associative Structures

Many of the initiatives mentioned so far, all of which help agencies co-ordinate in times of crisis, are derived from the various committees, groups and other formal structures that have been established over the years. A few of these structures have genuine co-ordinating power.

The IASC (see above) is now the main forum for bringing together all the big operational agencies in the UN, and the Red Cross and the NGOs. Chaired by OCHA's Humanitarian Co-ordinator it meets twice a year at the head-of-agency level, and many more times via ad hoc working groups. It is the only forum that brings all the agencies together.

In 2005 in response to a major review of how the UN functioned in emergencies, the IASC initiated the Cluster System. Each of the 11 'clusters' brings together agencies around the specialization of a service provision. There is a cluster on water and sanitation, one on nutrition, etc. They meet at the global level to agree on common standards and approaches, and are also now replicated at the field operational level, thereby allowing for local sharing of information, agreeing on overall needs in that sector, and the planning of joint operations. Membership is voluntary and decisions are not binding, but, since their inauguration, the clusters have made a real difference to the timeliness and quality of disaster response.

There are numerous groupings of NGOs. For example, in the USA InterAction brings together more than 190 NGOs to promote standards, to lobby Congress and to seek better ways of co-ordinating their work. The Steering Committee for Humanitarian Response (SCRH) brings together the main transnational NGOs which work both in development and disaster relief. InterAction and the SCHR co-operated in developing the Sphere Standards.

Donor nations have formed their own grouping, the Good Humanitarian Donorship Group (GHD), which now includes 37 states, uniting the heads of each donor nation's department of humanitarian assistance funding. They have derived a set of common and public standards to which they hold themselves accountable, and periodically they carry out peer reviews of each others' work.

CHALLENGES TO THE CURRENT SYSTEM

All of these mechanisms: quality assurance initiatives, funding control and consolidation initiatives, peer groupings, technical committees, cluster committees, and so forth, act to nudge the ever changing population of donor states, UN agencies, Red Cross/Crescent structures, international NGOs and local community groups to act with more coherence, effectiveness and efficiency in times of crisis. Of course there are challenges.

Principal among these is non-compliance. Everything in this system is voluntary, from the funding, to the decisions to be operational, to co-ordination. Within individual agencies rules may be enforced, but very little is enforceable between agencies, outside of specific contracting arrangements. Although the bulk of the relief work will be carried out by a handful of large well known agencies, each crisis will see its own unique flowering of smaller organizations, usually highly motivated and often hopelessly inexperienced, trying to provide assistance, often from the best of intentions. Like static on a bad radio signal they can often severely degrade the overall quality of the work being carried out.

Even within the main, experienced agencies, keeping to best practice and previously agreed standards is not always easy. There is tremendous pressure to act, and be seen to act quickly, often at the expense of quality of assistance. Since agencies are driven by voluntary funding, most of which comes from government contracts they compete for, the system is biased to favour competition, not co-operation. The pooled funds discussed earlier try to counter this, but they still represent only a small fraction of the total resources.

In some crises one or more donors, or indeed an agency, may have a strong political agenda which at times seems to trump the humanitarian imperative. And on the ground the local host government may have the will to co-ordinate, but not the means.

Finally, as the international humanitarian system evolves, new important actors emerge from the many new organizations appearing in each crisis. China and India are becoming more significant donors. NGOs are starting to emerge from the South, not just from the North. High-tech highly networked groupings, providing mapping services or mobile phone services, are starting to surface. The old club comprising a small number of donors and agencies is being challenged. Will the new actors stick to the old rules, or make up rules of their own?

TRENDS TOWARDS MORE EFFICIENTLY CO-ORDINATING ACTION AND POSSIBLE FUTURE DEVELOPMENTS

What of the future then? The most certain prediction is that humanitarian agencies are not going to go out of business. Globalization and the gradual shift, country by country, from totalitarian to more democratic forms of government, are bringing huge increases in wealth and freedom, but not without crisis along the way. Globalization also causes great inequities in wealth, rendering many people more susceptible to the effects of flood and drought, particularly in the growing shanty towns around cities. Political change can often be violent in its process.

As climate change starts to stress society we may also see more crises, some direct, from crop failure or unexpected extreme weather events, some indirect, as stressed communities become more violent and states react by becoming more repressive.

International humanitarian response is here to stay. Many states are now recognizing this, and there are increasing calls for more formal systems to be put in place to improve the efficiency and equity of the system. Many states are now investing in disaster risk reduction programmes, which include legislation to govern how they interact with external agencies in times of crisis. Donor states are starting to talk about creating international systems to certify the competence of operational agencies, and within the operational community there is a growing movement to certify the competence of individuals via professional accreditation systems.

Like all ecosystems the international humanitarian community will continue to evolve, to provide service to those in need, and to seek more effective ways to act. Of course there will always be pressure from states wanting humanitarian aid to support their particular cause and not that of the opposition, and from warlords wanting to control the resources brought in by aid agencies, and from local criminals looking to make a quick profit, and from the agencies themselves, concerned for their own financial survival. Despite these pressures the basic trajectory of the system is towards one that is more effective, efficient, fairer and accountable. The maverick agency or corruption scandal, which become highlighted by the media, are more conspicuous because they are atypical. In truth the vast majority of states, agencies and individuals in the humanitarian aid community are there because they are committed to the notion that humanity is one family and that the acute suffering we see in times of crisis is something we can, and should, act to alleviate.

REFERENCES AND FURTHER READING

P. Garnsey. *Famine and Food Supply in the Graeco-Roman World.* New York: Cambridge University Press, 1988:229.

Adam Khedouri. *Bury the Dead and Feed the Living: Lessons from Lisbon: An Opinion.* Revista: Harvard Review of Latin America (Winter 2007):19.

E. de Vattel. *The Law of Nations, Book II.* Luke White, 1757:136.

M. Alamgir. *Famine in South Asia.* Westport, CT: Greenwood Press. 1980:68.

GLOBAL ENVIRONMENTAL GOVERNANCE

Kate O'Neill*

THE RISE IN AWARENESS OF AND ACTION AROUND GLOBAL ENVIRONMENTAL PROBLEMS

Environmental degradation, through resource depletion and emission of pollutants into the air, ground and water, is hardly a new phenomenon. It has accompanied economic growth since the early days of the Industrial Revolution. Water pollution, urban sanitation crises and land degradation through over-use actually predate industrialization. However, until the late 1960s, public awareness of environmental problems was most keen at the local level, where their effects were most visible. Smoke stacks, dead rivers, and waste dumps became focal points for early environmental activism in urban and industrial areas. Preservation of wilderness or countryside essentially focused on the land itself, not necessarily on broader causes, connections or ecosystems.

By 1970 a different perspective had pervaded environmental activism and policymaking: that environmental problems were not restricted to local or even national impacts. They crossed borders, even affecting the global commons, i.e. the atmosphere and the oceans, in ways unimagined years earlier. It had become abundantly clear that the unparalleled economic growth the world had experienced in the previous 25 years carried with it a huge ecological cost. Forests in Germany and Norway were being destroyed by acid rain which resulted from sulphur dioxide emissions in the United Kingdom and blown across by prevailing winds. Ocean fish stocks were starting rapidly to be depleted. Distinct and important (so-called 'charismatic') species, for example whales or pandas, were high on the list of those threatened with extinction, and the Amazon Rainforest became a symbol of the threats facing many whole ecosystems world-wide as a result of resource depletion to fulfil growing demand for timber products and agricultural goods, primarily from industrialized nations. In 1960 the world's population reached 3,000m., and was heading towards 4,000m. by the end of that decade. Scientists, too, were starting to identify and draw causal linkages with human behaviour around two problems that threatened the earth's atmosphere and climate. The first was stratospheric ozone layer depletion as a result of the production and use of a very widely applied chemical, chlorofluorocarbons (CFCs), and second was the very real potential for the alteration of the world's entire climate through the accumulation of greenhouse gases, such as carbon dioxide, in the atmosphere, the phenomenon we now call climate change, or global warming.

Even with this mounting evidence that environmental problems could be global in nature, it took concerted effort to persuade nation states to start working together to address these problems in a systematic way, utilizing international law and international institutions. Scientists and environmental activists worked hard to raise concern among the public and policy elites, with a good degree of success. Events such as the first 'Earth Day' in 1970 and the wide dissemination of the first pictures of the earth from space, depicting a fragile green and blue sphere hanging alone in the dark vacuum, helped to heighten public concern, and to create symbols that could stand in the absence of visible impacts. Economists and ecologists started to publish works that were critical of untrammelled economic and population growth, painting dire future scenarios in the absence of action: concepts such as 'limits to growth' or 'small is beautiful', and the slogan 'act local, think global', were all products of this time. At the same time that a global environmental movement was starting to emerge, scientific communities, which had been working across national and disciplinary boundaries for some time, began to take their findings about climate change, ozone layer and biodiversity depletion and other global problems to a wider audience.

The decisive step towards concerted international political action to combat global environmental problems was taken by the United Nations (UN). In 1972 the UN convened the first global 'earth summit', the UN Conference on Humans and the Environment (UNCHE), in Stockholm, Sweden. UNCHE brought together representatives from over 100 countries to discuss how to address the newly recognized global scope of environmental problems. The resulting agreements accomplished several goals. Delegates agreed that the most effective way forward would be through multilateral diplomacy: the negotiation of binding legal agreements among nation states on an issue by issue basis. This decision essentially ratified existing practices, as by then a number of international environmental agreements were already in existence—the 1946 International Whaling Convention, for example, although cases exist as far back as the 19th century. In order to reinforce this somewhat piecemeal system, the Stockholm Declaration codified 26 principles of international environmental law, including the rights of states to use their own resources but also their obligations not to harm the environments of other states. The Declaration placed strong emphasis on the importance of science in informing global environmental policymaking and laid out a number of priorities for the international community.

UNCHE delegates agreed to establish a new UN Environment Programme (UNEP), whose job it would be to co-ordinate global environmental governance through identifying important problems, convening and enabling international negotiations, and monitoring the resulting agreements. It now also houses convention secretariats. UNEP, although relatively small and underfunded given its mandate, has remained the most important international institution in the area of global environmental governance.

Since Stockholm, there have been three further global earth summits: the UN Conference on Environment and Development, convened in Rio de Janeiro, Brazil, in 1992, the World Summit on Sustainable Development (WSSD), held in Johannesburg, South Africa, in 2002, and the 'Rio+20' UN Conference on Sustainable Development, convened on the theme of a 'Green Economy', in June 2012, again in Rio. The 1992 Rio Summit marked the high point of international environmental diplomacy, with the opening for signature of two major conventions, on biological diversity and climate change. WSSD was a far more subdued event (at least in terms of output), reflecting some of the disillusionment with multilateral diplomacy as the primary global environmental governance tool. Likewise, initial reaction of the Rio+20 meeting is that it failed to produce substantive results. The titles of these conferences demonstrate how the language of sustainable development has been incorporated into global environmental governance, a recognition that environmental and development goals can not only be made compatible, they should be reconciled to achieve effective results. It is true, however, that the global summits have been sidelined to a great extent by the contentious politics characterizing climate governance, which have become the focal point for global environmental governance. None the less, while climate governance remains unresolved there have been moderate successes in addressing other, less high-profile issue areas.

EXISTING STRUCTURES OF GLOBAL ENVIRONMENTAL GOVERNANCE

The 1972 Stockholm conference essentially set the stage for the ensuing four decades of global environmental governance. The most important actors on this stage are, of course, nation states and their representatives, all with different and often conflicting interests about what, and how much, to do about specific environmental problems. The most important divide among states has been between the industrialized countries (the 'North') and the poorer 'South', largely around issues of responsibility for global environmental problems, and thus how adjustment costs

* Kate O'Neill is Associate Professor in the Department of Environmental Science, Policy and Management, University of California, Berkeley, USA.

should be distributed. International environmental politics (unlike some other global policy arenas) has, however, been remarkably open to participation by other sorts of actors. Environmental non-governmental organizations (NGOs) have been very active at this level, attending negotiations, lobbying for particular solutions, and helping to monitor resulting commitments. The scientific community, too, has played a central role in demonstrating cause and effect, generating new knowledge, and working towards consensus, in order to ameliorate two of the biggest obstacles to effective environmental policies: uncertainty and complexity. The most well known international scientific body at this level is the Intergovernmental Panel on Climate Change (IPCC), though other advisory groups, both ad hoc and permanent, advise other negotiating processes. The private sector was somewhat slower to get involved directly at the level of international negotiations, preferring instead to work through government representatives. Now, however, business coalitions represent their members' interests at many sets of negotiations, from climate change to hazardous waste trading. In some cases, they can obstruct effective measures, but in others they have been key partners in forging solutions.

Of the international organizations active in this policy arena, UNEP, as already mentioned, plays the leading role as an 'anchor' institution for global environmental governance (Ivanova 2007). Based in Nairobi, Kenya, it is relatively weak compared with other UN organizations such as the World Health Organization, lacking their budget and political autonomy. None the less, it has helped usher in dozens of environmental agreements and measures since its founding. Probably the second most important international organization in this area has in fact been the World Bank, which has worked hard to correct its negative environmental record in funding large-scale development projects, such as dams, in the absence of social and environmental assessments. The World Bank co-ordinates funding for the Global Environment Facility (GEF), established in 1991 as a partnership between UNEP, the Bank and the UN Development Programme (UNDP), to fund projects in developing countries with specific global environmental benefits. In addition, the UN Commission for Sustainable Development (CSD), established in 1992 at the Rio Summit, oversees progress towards world goals on sustainable development. Finally, in recent years the World Trade Organization (WTO) has come to have its own place on this stage, in part to address potential conflicts between global trade rules and environmental regulations (both national and international), and in part to examine how trade liberalization might be harnessed to sustainable development goals. This shift is not without opposition, as many civil society representatives have pointed out that economic liberalization has been a major driver of environmental problems, from resource extraction to waste generation.

The past 40 years have witnessed the introduction of dozens of major multilateral environmental agreements (MEAs). Taking into account the protocols and amendments associated with major treaties and framework conventions, as well as environmental components of other international agreements (notably around trade), this number runs well into the hundreds. Table 1 lists some of the major MEAs and, where applicable, their major associated legal protocols and amendments.

Table 1 illustrates some important points about the process of global environmental diplomacy. First, negotiations proceed in stages. In many cases, states initially negotiate a framework convention which outlines the parameters of a problem and an agenda for action without imposing strict obligations on signatory states. At subsequent Conferences of the Parties (COPs), states negotiate amendments and protocols that do require action, in the form of emissions limits, for example. The rationale for this approach is that to ensure as much participation as possible it is best to work gradually: if states commit themselves to a framework convention, they are more likely to take the next steps towards stricter measures. Second, as the table shows, for many agreements, there is a lengthy gap between the date they are open for signature and their entry into force in international law. This has to do with ratification requirements: a certain number of parties to the treaty need to enact the treaty into domestic law for it to enter into force. In some cases, requirements are simple (e.g. 50% of parties). In others, it is more complex: the 1997 Kyoto Protocol on climate change required 55% of parties to ratify, which had to include 'Annex 1' (developed) countries responsible for at least 55% of global emissions. Given that some of the leading opponents of the Protocol, such as the USA and Australia, fell into this category, it is not surprising that eight years elapsed between signature and entry into force. Third, Table 1 demonstrates how broad the membership of many conventions is, in some cases, approaching a near universal set of nation states. For most MEAs, membership has grown over the years, particularly as new states, or states newly re-engaging in global affairs, such as Iraq and Afghanistan, sign on.

Table 1: Major Multilateral Environmental Agreements

Agreement and major associated legal instruments	Date adopted/ entry into force	Number of parties (at mid-2012)
International Whaling Convention	1946/1946	89
Convention on International Trade in Endangered Species (CITES)	1973/1975	175
International Convention for the Prevention of Pollution from Ships (MARPOL)	1973/1983	151
Protocol Related to MARPOL	1978/1983	151
UN Convention on the Law of the Seas (UNCLOS)	1982/1994	162
Agreement for the Implementation of UNCLOS related to the Conservation and Management of Straddling and Highly Migratory Fish Stocks	1995/2001	78
Vienna Convention for the Protection of the Ozone Layer	1985/1988	197
Montreal Protocol	1987/1989	197
Basel Convention on the Control and Transboundary Movements of Hazardous Wastes and Their Disposal	1989	179
Basel Ban Amendment (Decision III/1, COP 3)	1995/n.a.	73
UN Framework Convention on Climate Change (UNFCCC)	1992/1994	194
Kyoto Protocol	1997/2005	192
Convention on Biological Diversity (CBD)	1992/1993	193
Cartagena Biosafety Protocol	2000/2004	163
UN Convention to Combat Desertification (UNCCD)	1994/1996	194
Stockholm Convention on Persistent Organic Pollutants (POPs)	2001/2004	177

Source: Adapted from O'Neill 2009, Table 4.1.

The table does not, however, show the organizational complexity of these MEAs. Typically, framework conventions establish a Convention Secretariat, which is responsible for day-to-day management of the convention's activities and subsequent negotiations. Many also include permanent advisory bodies, often on scientific and technical affairs. Although much environmental funding is channeled through the GEF, some conventions have been established with their own funding mechanisms.

One of the biggest success stories of international environmental diplomacy has been the effort to end the production of chemicals, notably CFCs, which threaten the stratospheric ozone layer. The 1985 Vienna Convention laid the groundwork for the 1987 Montreal Protocol which enacted a phased-in ban of CFC production world-wide. The reasons for this success have a lot to do with the nature of the issue area with relative certainty about the causes and impacts of ozone layer depletion, and a concentrated chemicals industry willing to manufacture safer substitutes. By contrast, negotiations over climate change have been far more contentious. Climate change is an inherently complex problem. Combating greenhouse gas (GHG) emissions requires action across industrial sectors, and would particularly affect fossil fuel producers, i.e. oil, gas and coal companies. It also requires significant behavioural change by individual consumers.

At the same time, climate change is an issue long plagued by a lack of scientific consensus over the causes, impacts and timeframe, a lack of consensus that fuelled opposition to strong global action. Only in 2007 did the IPCC report 'with 90% confidence' that climate change, resulting from human activity in the 20th century, would have a likely devastating impact on vulnerable communities, and a real world-wide impact in the coming century. Further complicating international negotiations was a lack of consensus over which countries should bear the burden of adjustment costs. The USA, for example, objected to the fact that under the Kyoto Protocol only developed ('Annex 1') countries had to meet emissions targets. The architects of the Kyoto Protocol were extremely creative in designing measures that would bring reluctant 'Annex 1' nations on board, for example the opportunity for those countries to meet targets through funding emissions reductions projects in developing countries, but the resulting agreement pleased no one in the environmental community. In 2001 the USA took the unusual step of withdrawing from the protocol. With the Kyoto Protocol commitments scheduled to expire in 2012, negotiations to create a successor agreement, too, have been hampered by conflicting national interests. Between 2007–11 five successive COPs have inched towards new obligations, even as the negotiations teetered on the edge of complete failure. In December 2011, at COP 17, held in Durban, South Africa, parties finally agreed to seek new binding obligations to be negotiated over succeeding years. Durban also marked the formal emergence of the so-called BASIC countries, i.e. Brazil, South Africa, India and the People's Republic of China, as a negotiating group. Regardless of whether this alliance continues, these countries are starting to wield real power in climate governance. The perceived failure of the UN process around climate change has in turn led to a search for governance alternatives, which will be considered in the final section of this essay.

Beyond the atmosphere, MEAs are clustered around a number of other issue areas, including conservation and biodiversity loss, oceans, and chemicals and hazardous waste production. In the conservation arena, some of the earlier, more specific, agreements are considered the most successful. The Convention on International Trade in Endangered Species (CITES, 1973), for example, commands a good deal of international support and action to combat trade in endangered species, despite recent conflicts about adding or removing specific species to trade-restricted lists. The 1992 Convention on Biological Diversity (CBD), a framework agreement designed to address biodiversity loss at species and ecosystem levels world-wide has been more contentious. Conservation biologists criticise its generality and lack of specific targets. Less developed nations, during negotiations, objected to language that would restrict their ability to exploit their own natural resources, resulting in a convention that emphasized state sovereignty and responsible national management over the protection of biodiversity as the 'common heritage of humanity'. Its first protocol, the Catagena Protocol (2000), deals not with specific targets, but with international trade in genetically modified organisms, politically important given moves in the trade regime to liberalize such trade, but a move some consider tangential, at best, to the primary challenges of biodiversity conservation. Its second protocol, adopted at the so-called Nagoya Biodiversity Summit, held in October 2010, addresses access and benefit sharing around biodiversity resources. The summit meeting also led to countries setting specific biodiversity goals.

The failure of negotiators at the 1992 Rio Summit to overcome divergent national interests and enact a framework convention to protect the world's forests left an important gap in the framework of global environmental governance. However, as an example of how issues are being increasingly linked in global politics, the issue of forest protection has emerged in discussions of climate funding, given the value of forests for carbon storage. This idea underlies the REDD+ (Reducing Emissions from Deforestation and Degradation) programme, a collaborative initiative launched in 2008 by the UN, which provides funding to developing countries to maintain and rehabilitate their forests.

The production of hazardous chemicals and wastes poses another set of challenges for global governance. Early negotiations focused on the trade in hazardous wastes from industrialized nations to less developed countries, a practice considered particularly appropriate for global action and which led to the 1989 Basel Convention. Later conventions, notably the 2001 Stockholm Convention on Persistent Organic Pollutants (POPs), address the production of and trade in particularly dangerous chemicals. In June 2010 intergovernmental negotiations were opened towards a new global mercury treaty, one of the first new treaty processes in many years. The Basel Convention has, in particular, faced criticism, first for failing to enact, and subsequently for failing to implement, a ban on waste trading: as at mid-2012 the 1995 Ban Amendment had not yet entered into force, although finally the secretariat, working at the initiative of Indonesia and Switzerland, is looking for ways to break this deadlock. One ongoing debate in global chemicals regulation is the possibility of bringing these disparate agreements under a common global framework, in order to regulate the entire chemicals life-cycle from production to transportation and trade to final disposal. These discussions mirror more general debates about the possibility of centralizing and strengthening the very fragmented architecture of international environmental law and diplomacy.

CHALLENGES

In many ways the existing framework of global environmental governance has led to some significant political accomplishments. International co-operation has been broader and more durable than international relations theory would predict. It has led to the establishment of important international organizations, and the participation of others in environmental affairs, as well as encouraging NGO and private sector engagement at the international level. International environmental negotiators have pioneered ways to incorporate scientific insights into diplomatic processes and the use of market mechanisms in global governance. However, it is clear that the system has faults, and political progress has failed to outstrip rates of global environmental degradation. Some have even labelled this system a 'failed experiment' (Speth 2004).

Successful global environmental governance has always faced significant political obstacles. Collective action problems have long plagued efforts towards international co-operation among nation states. As has been demonstrated, the system established at Stockholm contained measures specifically designed to overcome such problems and encourage national participation and commitments, including a practice of negotiating agreements in successively stronger stages, a process that can also allow parties to incorporate new information or correct earlier mistakes. On the other hand, the focus on universal membership has the potential to lead to 'lowest common denominator' outcomes that satisfy those parties least interested in changing the status quo but do little to address the actual problem. In addition, the process of negotiating in this iterated fashion can lead to years between when the time processes are set in motion, and when final agreements enter into force.

Another challenge to international legal approaches is that UNEP and associated agencies have very few enforcement powers, or the ability to sanction member states who violate an agreement. Results of existing arrangements are often monitored primarily through national reporting, and there are few penalties imposed on states if they fail to meet obligations. On the other hand, agreements do often contain transparency, or so-called 'sunshine', mechanisms, and secretariats publish national performance data online. Interested actors, often NGOs, are able to use this data to 'name and shame' violators. It is also debatable whether sanction mechanisms in environmental agreements would be politically acceptable to signatory states. Even where they exist in more powerful governance arenas, such as global trade, they are divisive.

With multiple separate treaty negotiation processes under way, or ongoing indefinitely, negotiators and observers have in recent years developed a distinct sense of fatigue. At any given time there are multiple meetings taking place all over the world, to which countries have to send representatives (Depledge and Chasek 2012). For many poorer countries, finding the people to attend, and the resources to send them to ensure adequate representation, is a real challenge. Further, functional and institutional overlap and conflict across policy domains have created challenges and opportunities that should be addressed by international policy actors. To address this problem, various plans have been put forward to rationalize or centralize global environmental governance at this level, as discussed in the following section.

A second, related, set of challenges to global environmental diplomacy concerns how to reconcile diverse and often conflicting national interests. Powerful states will frequently use their leverage to alter agreements in their favour, for better or worse. In the case of climate change, the USA has been one of the lead 'laggard' states, though counterbalanced to some extent by the European Union (EU). In CBD negotiations, less developed nations, whose territory contains most of the world's biodiversity hotspots, had the upper hand. Again, certain characteristics of MEAs and other negotiating processes are designed to overcome some of these problems: the incorporation of scientific evidence, for example, as a way of galvanizing serious action, or utilizing particularly skillful negotiation leaders. Smaller states, such as the Scandinavian countries, have been able to use moral suasion as a way of exhorting other nations to take stronger measures than they otherwise would have done: negotiations over transboundary air pollution in the late 1970s are a case in point. The North–South split has been a major challenge for negotiations to overcome (Najam 2005). Countries of the global South, the Group of 77 (G77) nations, have insisted that industrialized countries of the North bear the bulk of the responsibility for addressing global environmental degradation, and that any obligations they have should not prevent their ability to develop and meet the needs of their populations. In addition, many G77 countries lack the capacity, financial or otherwise, to meet treaty obligations. As a result, several environmental negotiations have incorporated the principle of 'common but differentiated responsibility', which allows for differential obligations to be placed on those countries, from the absence of fixed emissions targets under the Kyoto Protocol, to an additional 10 years to implement the CFC ban under the Montreal Protocol. The relevance of the G77 grouping, especially in climate change, is, however (and as seen above), coming increasingly under question by the countries themselves as well as non-G77 states.

To foster capacity in developing countries, many treaties also contain provisions for monetary aid and technology transfer. Much of this activity is overseen by the GEF, which, since its founding, has funded more than 2,700 projects in some 165 developing and transitional countries that help to meet global environmental goals concerning climate change, biodiversity, POPs, desertification, ozone depletion and international waters. Such aid is of course a drop in the ocean compared with annual (or even daily) global expenditures on military actions, but with major lending institutions such as the World Bank and regional development banks turning their attention explicitly to sustainable development goals, environmental concerns are starting to be at the forefront of development financing.

Third, a governance system focused primarily on resolving political collective action problems between nation states can omit or downplay other important global drivers of environmental change. In this case, many have argued that environmental problems should instead be framed as a result of global economic forces, most notably the processes of neoliberal globalization in recent decades associated most closely with the World Bank, the International Monetary Fund (IMF) and the WTO. Trade liberalization, privatization not only of industry but of what had been public goods such as fresh water, and structural adjustment programmes aimed at minimizing the role of the state and maximizing resource extraction in developing countries have all taken a serious environmental toll. To that end, global environmental governance needs to take economic globalization into account. This argument has been, to some extent, taken on board by international institutions. The WTO and UNEP have committed to a shared agenda around sustainable development, and steps have been taken to minimize the potential for conflict between global trade and environmental rules. A key development is the way that many multinational corporations are starting to design transboundary environmental governance measures, either on their own or in partnership with NGOs. Whether these actions constitute real and effective change, or whether they amount to 'rearranging the deckchairs on the Titanic', remains to be seen, and many civil society organizations remain sceptical, especially as economic inequalities continue to widen world-wide and a global recession pushes environmental issues to the backburner for many countries.

Finally, global environmental governance institutions face the critical challenge of continued, and accelerating, rates of environmental change. Problems such as climate change, biodiversity and even chemicals regulation are complex and ever-changing, particularly as new scientific information comes to light. At the same time, the international community continues to struggle with how to incorporate scientific uncertainty and complexity into institutional arrangements, in particular over the standard of certainty needed to take decisive action. While the EU and its allies favour the use of the precautionary principle in international agreements, which allows for action in advance of full certainty, the USA and like-minded countries strongly oppose this standard, arguing for waiting for greater certainty before taking costly and possibly misguided action. These debates over the use of science and expertise are quite fundamental to the practice of global environmental policy, but, as scientists have learned to their cost in the continued popularity of climate 'denial', cannot easily be resolved through factual arguments alone.

POSSIBLE FUTURE DEVELOPMENTS

One thing is certain in the contested field of global environmental governance: it continues to evolve as new challenges emerge, and as new actors and new ideas filter into existing processes. In recent years, the system has come to be characterized by 'fragmentation', whereby issue areas are characterized by a patchwork of governance institutions, state-led, non-state and hybrid (Biermann et al 2009). Climate governance is a case in point. As the formal UNFCCC process drags on without reaching new agreements, other institutional forms and venues have emerged to address the problem. These include non-binding governmental arrangements such as the Asia-Pacific Partnership on Clean Development and Climate Change, privately run carbon markets, NGOs working to change consumer behaviour, and global networks of local and municipal governments committed to reducing GHG emissions. Some issue areas where no intergovernmental agreement exists, such as forest degradation, are almost wholly dominated by non-state actors and forest certification schemes, such as the Forest Stewardship Council (FSC). Other issue areas, such as chemicals and biodiversity, remain anchored in intergovernmental arrangements, although with more outreach to private sector and civil society actors, and a greater emphasis on market mechanisms rather than direct regulation.

These changes, plus the realization that more urgent and effective action is required to combat global environmental change, suggest two possible (and, in fact, not necessarily mutually exclusive) directions in global environmental governance. The first is centralization and rationalization of existing and future MEAs. Such centralization could occur in a number of ways. One option is more formal issue-area clustering, already being considered for chemicals-related agreements, perhaps through the negotiation of umbrella conventions. Another could be functional: the creation, for example, of a global scientific agency that could supply expert advice across issue areas. At a higher level, some advocate the creation of a World Environment Organization with a legal and enforcement capacity that could match that of the WTO. Although political will for a new international bureaucracy is low, other options, such as strengthening UNEP by elevating it to agency status within the UN system, remain possibilities.

Second, global environmental governance functions could be devolved to a variety of non-state or hybrid governance initiatives, many of which already exist. Regional organizations, such as the EU, the Association for Southeast Asian Nations (ASEAN) and others, are formulating and implementing regional environmental agreements. Non-state governance initiatives are developed and conducted by actors outside government institutions. Hybrid initiatives have some state and/or international organization involvement. The most high profile form of non-state governance at the global level involves NGOs and private sector actors, working in partnership to develop, enforce and monitor environmental standards within a particular sector. Such certification schemes are emerging in areas as diverse and important as forestry (notably the FSC), fisheries, agriculture and the electronics sector. Other non-state or hybrid governance forms include harnessing or creating markets, such as insurance or carbon markets, or partnership arrangements, such as the 'Type 2' partnerships launched at the Johannesburg summit to foster particular sustainable development outcomes on the ground.

These sorts of initiatives are popular, as they are often more nimble and efficient than international agreements, and less vulnerable to dilution to satisfy national interests. They do, however, suffer some shortcomings. They are voluntary, thus failing to capture some of the worst corporate offenders. They are disparate, and sometimes confusing. Finally, they do not automatically have the legitimacy or authority associated with governmental institutions. Where, therefore, these two different trends, of potential centralization and the encouragement of diverse non-state and hybrid initiatives, can be compatible is that a re-engineered UN-led system could supply norms, principles and expertise that could support both state-led and non-state global environmental governance. The early decades of the 21st century are proving to be a time of experimentation and tentative moves forward in combating environmental change. International organizations and institutions continue to have a strong role in steering this process, efforts that will be critical in determining whether or not the international community can effectively combat the severity and complexity of global environmental problems such as climate change.

REFERENCES AND FURTHER READING

Biermann, Frank, Philipp Pattberg, Harro van Asselt, and Fariborz Zelli. 2009. The Fragmentation of Global Governance Architectures: A Framework for Analysis. *Global Environmental Politics*.

Depledge, Joanna, and Pamela S. Chasek. 2012. Raising the Tempo: The Escalating Pace and Intensity of Environmental Negotiations. *The Roads from Rio: Lessons Learned from Twenty Years of Multilateral Environmental Negotiations*. Routledge.

Ivanova, Maria. 2010. UNEP in Global Environmental Governance: Design, Leadership, Location. *Global Environmental Politics*.

Najam, Adil. 2005. Developing Countries and Global Environmental Governance: From Contestation to Participation to Engagement. *International Environmental Agreements*.

O'Neill, Kate. 2009. *The Environment and International Relations*. Cambridge University Press.

Speth, James Gustave. 2004. *Red Sky at Morning: America and the Crisis of the Global Environment*. Yale University Press.

THE DEVELOPMENT OF INTERNATIONAL ORGANIZATIONS: A CHRONOLOGY

1863

17 Feb. First meeting of the International Committee of the Red Cross (ICRC), as the International Committee for the Relief of Wounded Soldiers.

26 Oct. First international conference organized by the ICRC.

1864

22 Aug. Geneva Convention for the Amelioration of the Condition of Soldiers Wounded in Armies in the Field signed.

1865

17 May International Telegraph Convention signed in Paris, establishing the International Telegraph Union; present name—International Telecommunication Union—adopted in 1934 (became a specialized agency of the UN on 15 Oct. 1947).

1874

9 Oct. General Postal Union established (name changed to Universal Postal Union in 1878; became a specialized agency of the UN on 1 July 1948).

1889

31 Oct. Inter-Parliamentary Union established (initially as the Inter-Parliamentary Conference for International Arbitration).

1890

14 April International Union of American Republics founded, at first International American Conference, held in Washington, DC, USA.

1894

23 June International Olympic Committee established.

1899

18 May–29 July International Peace Conference held in The Hague (Convention for the Pacific Settlement of International Disputes signed).

1906

6 July Geneva Convention signed, extending the provisions of the first Convention to naval warfare.

1907

18 Oct. Convention respecting laws and customs of war on land (Hague Rules) signed at second Hague Peace Conference.

1914

Aug. Outbreak of World War I.

1918

18 Jan. US President Wilson outlined the objectives of a peace settlement, which included provisions for the establishment of an association of nations to strengthen international relations and help maintain peace.

11 Nov. Armistice declared, ending World War I.

1919

5 May League of Red Cross Societies established (became League of Red Cross and Red Crescent Societies in 1983; current name—International Federation of the Red Cross and Red Crescent Societies—adopted in 1991).

28 June Versailles Peace Treaty signed, incorporating the Covenant establishing a League of Nations.
International Labour Organization established by Part XIII of the Treaty of Versailles, to assume the functions of the International Labour Office (became a specialized agency of the UN on 14 Dec. 1946).

1920

10 Jan. Covenant establishing the League of Nations entered into force.

13 Dec. Statute of the Permanent Court of International Justice adopted (formally operational 15 Dec. 1922–31 Dec. 1945).

1921

19 June International Federation of Christian Trade Unions established (renamed World Confederation of Labour Oct. 1968 and merged with other organizations to form the International Trade Union Confederation in Nov. 2006).

20 Aug. First High Commissioner for Refugees appointed, by League of Nations.

21 Nov–6 Feb. 1922 Washington Conference, during which treaties were concluded relating to China's territorial integrity, the use of chemical weapons and limitations on naval armaments.

1925

4-5 May First International Congress of Official Tourism Traffic Associations convened in The Hague (renamed the International Union of Official Travel Organisations in 1947).

18 Dec. International Bureau of Education established (became an intergovernmental org. on 25 July 1929; incorporated into UNESCO in 1961).

1926

26 Sept. Slavery Convention signed by representatives of 36 nations, in Geneva.

1928

27 Aug. Kellogg-Briand Pact, renouncing war as an instrument of national policy, signed (based on the initiative of the US and French ministers of foreign affairs; entered into effect 24 July 1929).

26 Sept. General Act for the Pacific Settlement of International Disputes adopted by the General Assembly of the League of Nations.

1929

27 July Geneva Convention relating to the Treatment of Prisoners of War signed.

1930

13 March–12 April (Second) Conference on Codification of International Law held in The Hague.

17 May Bank for International Settlements established.

1939

1 Sept. German invasion of Poland, marking the start of World War II.

1941

14 Aug. Atlantic Charter signed by the US President Roosevelt and British Prime Minister Winston Churchill, proposing a set of principles for international collaboration in maintaining peace and security.

1942

1 Jan. Declaration by United Nations (UN) signed by representatives of 26 nations (pledged to continue fighting together against the Axis powers).

1943

18 May–3 June UN Conference on Food and Agriculture held in Hot Springs, Virginia, USA; proposed a world programme and creation of a Food and Agriculture Organization.

9 Nov. Agreement on establishment of an interim UN Relief and Rehabilitation Administration to extend emergency assistance to liberated countries.

1944

1–22 July UN Monetary and Financial Conference held in Bretton Woods, New Hampshire, USA: representatives of 45 countries formulated proposals relating to post-war international payment problems, and endorsed establishment of the International Monetary Fund (IMF) and International Bank for Reconstruction and Development (IBRD).

21 Sept–7 Oct. Dumbarton Oaks Conference Washington, DC, USA: China, United Kingdom, USA and USSR agreed on aims, structure and functioning of a world organization.

1945

22 March Pact of League of Arab States signed (entered into force 10 May 1945).

8 May Unconditional surrender of Germany, ending war in Europe.

26 June Charter of the United Nations signed by representatives of 50 nations.

6 Aug. First use of atomic bomb during warfare, on Hiroshima, Japan.

2 Sept. Unconditional surrender of Japan.

3 Oct. World Federation of Trade Unions established.

16 Oct. Food and Agriculture Organization established (incorporating the International Institute of Agriculture, an intergovernmental body established 7 June 1905).

24 Oct. UN Charter entered into force, formally establishing the United Nations.

16 Nov. Constitution adopted establishing a UN Educational, Scientific and Cultural Organization (UNESCO) (entered into force 4 Nov. 1946).

20 Nov. International Military Tribunal initiated trial proceedings in Nuremberg, Germany, against principal military officers in the former Nazi regime (continued functioning until 1 Oct. 1946).

27 Dec. Articles of Agreement establishing the IMF and IBRD adopted.

1946

10 Jan. First meeting of the UN General Assembly, held in London, United Kingdom.

13 Jan. UN Economic and Social Council (ECOSOC) formally constituted.

17 Jan. First meeting of the UN Security Council.

24 Jan. UN Atomic Energy Commission established (suspended 22 June 1948 after differences between the USA and USSR).

1 Feb. First Secretary-General of the UN, Trygve Lie, took office.

6 Feb. International Court of Justice inaugurated.

25 June IBRD commenced operations.

11 Dec. UN International Children's Emergency Fund (UNICEF) established (mandate extended in 1950; name and mandate amended in 1953 to become UN Children's Fund, retaining the same acronym).

15 Dec. International Refugees Organization (IRO) established (assumed responsibility from the UN Relief and Rehabilitation Administration).

1947

1 March IMF commenced operations.

28 March UN Economic Commission for Europe established by ECOSOC as the first regional commission of the UN (commenced operations in May 1947; became a permanent organ of the UN in 1951).

UN Economic Commission for Asia and the Far East (ECAFE) established (commenced operations in June 1948; name changed to UN Economic Commission for Asia and the Pacific—ESCAP in Aug. 1974).

4 April International Civil Aviation Organization established, following ratification of the Chicago Convention on International Civil Aviation, signed 7 Dec. 1944.

11 Oct. Convention on establishment of World Meteorological Organization signed, assuming functions of the International Meteorological Organization (f. 1873) (convention entered into force 23 March 1950; became a specialized agency of the UN on 20 Dec. 1951).

30 Oct. General Agreement on Tariffs and Trade signed (entered into force on 1 Jan. 1948, establishing multilateral rules for trade).

1948

25 Feb. UN Economic Commission for Latin America established (redesignated Economic Commission for Latin America and the Caribbean—ECLAC in July 1984).

6 March Inter-governmental Maritime Consultative Organization established at the conclusion of a UN Maritime Conference.

17 March Treaty of Economic, Social and Cultural Collaboration and Collective Self-Defence (The Brussels Treaty) signed by France, Belgium, Luxembourg, the Netherlands and the United Kingdom.

24 March Charter for an International Trade Organization (ITO) signed at the end of the International Conference on Trade and Employment, held in Havana, Cuba. (The establishment of the ITO was subsequently postponed indefinitely).

7 April Constitution establishing World Health Organization entered into force (signed July 1946).

16 April Organisation for European Economic Co-operation (OEEC) established, in connection with the post-war Marshall Plan for economic reconstruction.

2 May Organization of American States established, as a successor to the International Union of American Republics.

29 May UN Security Council resolved to deploy first group of UN military observers in order to supervise a halt in the hostilities between Palestinian Arabs and the newly-proclaimed state of Israel. (The UN Truce Supervision Organization was deployed in June).

25 June European and US commands began collaboration to deliver by air humanitarian provisions to Berlin,

Germany, which had been isolated by a Soviet blockade (the so-called 'Berlin Airlift'; continued to 30 Sept. 1949).

22 Aug. World Council of Churches established.

1 Dec. UN Relief for Palestinian Refugees established.

9 Dec. Convention on the Prevention and Punishment of the Crime of Genocide adopted by the UN General Assembly.

10 Dec. Universal Declaration of Human Rights adopted by the UN General Assembly.

1949

25 Jan. Council for Mutual Economic Assistance (CMEA or Comecon) established to support economic development of the USSR and countries of Eastern Europe.

4 April North Atlantic Treaty signed in Washington, DC, USA, institutionalizing the Atlantic Alliance and providing a legal basis for the establishment of the North Atlantic Treaty Organization (NATO).

5 May Statute establishing Council of Europe signed (entered into force 3 Aug. 1949).

12 Aug. Convention on the Protection of Civilian Populations in Time of War (Fourth Geneva Convention), together with revisions of previous Geneva Conventions, adopted at the conclusion of a Diplomatic Conference (initiated 21 April 1949).

8 Dec. UN Relief and Works Agency for Palestine Refugees (UNRWA) established to succeed earlier programme (began operations in May 1950).

1950

7 July UN Security Council authorized the establishment of a unified multinational force to restore peace in Korea, under the command of the USA.

4 Nov. Convention for the Protection of Human Rights and Fundamental Freedoms (European Convention on Human Rights) adopted by the Council of Europe; entered into force on 3 Nov. 1953.

1951

1 Jan. Office of the UN High Commissioner for Refugees began operations, assuming the functions of the IRO.

18 April Treaty of Paris signed, establishing a European Coal and Steel Community.

28 July Convention relating to the Status of Refugees adopted.

5 Dec. Provisional Intergovernmental Committee for Movement and Migrants from Europe established (mandate extended and name changed to become Intergovernmental Committee for European Migration in Nov. 1952, later Intergovernmental Committee for Migration; constitution changing name to International Organization for Migration entered into force in Nov. 1989).

1952

March Nordic Council inaugurated.

1954

23 Oct. Treaty of Brussels modified, providing for establishment of a Western European Union.

1955

6 May Western European Union formally established.

14 May Warsaw Treaty of Friendship, Co-operation and Mutual Assistance (the Warsaw Pact) signed by USSR and six Eastern European countries.

1956

24 July International Finance Corporation (IFC) established as an affiliate of the IBRD.

1957

25 March Treaty of Rome establishing a European Economic Community and a European Atomic Energy Community signed (entered into force 1 Jan. 1958).

3 June Council of Arab Economic Unity established (first meeting held in 1964).

29 July Statute establishing International Atomic Energy Agency (IAEA) entered into force (approved 23 Oct. 1956).

1958

17 March Convention establishing Inter-Governmental Maritime Consultative Organization entered into force (became a specialized agency of the UN on 13 Jan. 1959; present name, International Maritime Organization, adopted in May 1982).

1959

8 April Agreement to establish an Inter-American Development Bank adopted (entered into force 30 Dec. 1959).

20 Nov. Declaration on the Rights of the Child adopted by UN General Assembly.

1 Dec. Antarctic Treaty signed by 12 countries, banning weapons testing on the continent and guaranteeing its use solely for peaceful purposes (entered into force 23 June 1961).

1960

18 Feb. Montevideo Treaty signed, constituting Latin American Free Trade Association (LAFTA).

3 May Convention establishing European Free Trade Association entered into force (signed in Jan. 1960).

10–14 Sept. Conference held in Baghdad, Iraq, established Organization of the Petroleum Exporting Countries (OPEC).

24 Sept. International Development Association established.

1 Oct. Inter-American Development Bank commenced operations.

14 Dec. Convention on the establishment of an Organisation for Economic Co-operation and Development, to supersede the OEEC, signed.

15 Dec. General Treaty of Central American Economic Integration signed (ratified Sept. 1963, creating Central American Common Market).

1961

24 Nov. World Food Programme established (commenced operations 1 Jan. 1963).

1962

23 March Treaty of Nordic Co-operation (Helsinki Treaty) signed.

1963

25 May Charter establishing Organization of African Unity (OAU) adopted.

4 Aug. Agreement establishing African Development Bank signed (entered into force 10 Sept. 1964; Bank commenced operations on 1 July 1966).

1964

30 Dec. UN Conference on Trade and Development established as a permanent organ of the General Assembly.

1965

23 June First Secretary-General of the Commonwealth appointed (following decision in 1964 by Com-

monwealth heads of government to establish a permanent secretariat).

22 Nov. UN General Assembly approved the establishment of a UN Development Programme, by merger of the UN Special Fund and the Expanded Programme of Technical Assistance (created in 1949), effective from 1 Jan. 1966.

21 Dec. International Convention on the Elimination of All Forms of Racial Discrimination adopted (entered into force 4 Jan. 1969).

1966

14 Oct. International Centre for the Settlement of Investment Disputes established.

24 Nov. Asian Development Bank established (commenced operations 19 Dec. 1966).

16 Dec. International Covenants on Economic, Social and Cultural Rights and on Civil and Political Rights adopted by UN General Assembly.

1967

1 Jan. UN Industrial Development Organization established, on the basis of a resolution of the General Assembly adopted on 17 Nov. 1966 (became a specialized agency of the UN on 1 Jan. 1986).

14 Feb. Treaty for the Prohibition of Nuclear Weapons in Latin America (the Tlatelolco Treaty) signed (entered into force on 22 April 1968, establishing the first nuclear-free zone in a populated region).

14 July Convention establishing the World Intellectual Property Organization (WIPO) adopted; entered into force on 26 April 1970. (WIPO became a specialized agency of the UN in Dec. 1974).

8 Aug. Declaration establishing the Association of Southeast Asian Nations (ASEAN) signed in Bangkok, Thailand.

1968

9 Jan. Organization of Arab Petroleum Exporting Countries established.

1 May Caribbean Free Trade Area (CARIFTA) established (on basis of agreement signed between Antigua, Barbados and Guyana on 15 Dec. 1965).

12 June Treaty on the Non-Proliferation of Nuclear Weapons (NPT) adopted by UN General Assembly (entered into force 1970).

1969

26 May Agreement signed by Bolivia, Chile, Colombia, Ecuador and Peru to establish a common market (Andean Pact).

10 Sept. OAU Convention on Refugees signed.

22 Nov. American Convention on Human Rights adopted.

5 Dec. UN General Assembly resolution adopted determining that the International Union of Official Travel Organisations (IUOTO) be transformed into an intergovernmental body.

1970

27 Sept. An Extraordinary General Assembly of IUOTO adopted the Statutes of the World Tourism Organization (entered into force on 2 Jan. 1975).

1971

25 May Organization of the Islamic Conference (renamed in 2011 Organization of Islamic Cooperation) formally inaugurated.

5 Aug. First South Pacific Forum, held in Wellington, New Zealand.

25 Oct. People's Republic of China assumed a permanent seat on the UN Security Council, following recognition by the General Assembly of it being a permanent member of the UN (in place of the Republic of China, which had held the seat in the Security Council since 1949).

1972

10 April Convention on the Prohibition of the Development, Production and Stockpiling of Bacteriological (biological) and Toxin Weapons and on their Destruction (Biological Weapons Convention) opened for signature (entered into force 26 March 1975).

15 Dec. UN Environment Programme established.

18 Dec. UN Fund for Population Activities (UNFPA, established as the Trust Fund for Population Activities in 1967) designated a fund of the UN General Assembly; name changed to UN Population Fund in 1987, retaining the same acronym.

1973

17 April South Pacific Trade Bureau established to service South Pacific Forum meetings (changed name to South Pacific Forum Secretariat in 1988, and to Pacific Islands Forum Secretariat in 2000—when the annual South Pacific Forum was renamed Pacific Islands Forum).

4 July Treaty of Chaguaramas signed, establishing a Caribbean Community and Common Market (CARICOM) to supersede CARIFTA.

9 Aug. UN Economic Commission for Western Asia established (commenced operations 1 Jan. 1974; renamed Economic and Social Commission for Western Asia—ESCWA in 1985).

1974

12 Aug. Agreement establishing Islamic Development Bank signed.

17 Dec. World Food Council established.

1975

28 Feb. First Lomé Convention signed between EC and 46 African, Caribbean and Pacific (ACP) countries (replacing Yaoundé Conventions 1965/70 and Arusha Convention 1968).

28 May Treaty establishing Economic Community of West African States (ECOWAS) signed in Lagos, Nigeria.

31 May European Space Agency established (succeeding European Launcher Development Organization and the European Space Research Organization, established in 1962).

3 July–2 Aug. Conference on Security and Co-operation in Europe, held in Helsinki, Finland. Concluded the Helsinki Final Act on East-West Relations, signed by representatives of 35 nations.

1976

1 Jan. OPEC Fund for International Development began operations.

1977

2 Feb. Agreement establishing Arab Monetary Fund entered into force.

8 June Additional Protocols to the 1949 Geneva Conventions adopted, relating to the protection of victims of international and non-international conflicts.

30 Nov. Agreement establishing International Fund for Agricultural Development entered into force.

1978

Oct. UN Centre for Human Settlements (Habitat) established (renamed UN Human Settlements Programme in Jan. 2002).

1980

1 April — Southern African Development Co-ordination Conference (SADCC) established (succeeded by Southern African Development Community in 1992).

8 May — Eradication of smallpox declared by the 33rd World Health Assembly.

13 Aug. — Latin American Integration Association established (succeeding LAFTA).

1981

25 May — Cooperation Council for Arab States of the Gulf (GCC) inaugurated.

27 June — African Charter on Human and People's Rights signed (entered into force 21 Oct. 1986).

22 Dec. — Preferential Trade Area for Eastern and Southern African States (PTA) established.

1982

22 May — IMCO transformed into International Maritime Organization.

10 Dec. — UN Convention on the Law of the Sea signed in Montego Bay, Jamaica.

1984

10 Dec. — Convention against Torture and other Cruel, Inhuman or Degrading Treatment or Punishment adopted by UN General Assembly.

1985

6 Aug. — South Pacific Nuclear Free Zone Treaty (Rarotonga Treaty) signed in Cook Islands (entered into force 11 Dec. 1986).

1988

12 April — Convention establishing Multilateral Investment Guarantee Agency entered into force.

1989

7 Nov. — Inaugural meeting of Asia-Pacific Economic Cooperation (APEC), in Canberra, Australia.

20 Nov. — Convention on the Rights of the Child adopted by the UN General Assembly.

1990

Aug. — First multinational forces of the Economic Community of West African States (ECOMOG) dispatched, to Liberia.

1991

26 March — Treaty of Asunción signed establishing the Southern Common Market (Mercosur).

15 April — European Bank for Reconstruction and Development inaugurated.

1 July — Warsaw Pact countries agreed to end political functions of the Pact (its military institutions having already been abandoned).

30 Sept. — Council for Mutual Economic Assistance formally dissolved.

8 Dec. — Commonwealth of Independent States established by signature of the Minsk Agreement by Russia, Belarus and Ukraine; other republics joined on 21 Dec. giving formal recognition that the USSR had ceased to exist.

24 Dec. — Russia assumed USSR's permanent seat in the Security Council and in all other UN organs.

1992

21 Feb. — UN Security Council authorized initial mandate for UN peace-keepers in the former Yugoslavia.

3 July — UNHCR initiated an emergency airlift to provide humanitarian assistance to Sarajevo, Bosnia and Herzegovina (had become the longest humanitarian airlift in history by the time it ended on 9 Jan. 1996).

17 Aug. — Members of SADCC signed a treaty establishing a successor organization, the South African Development Community (treaty entered into effect 5 Oct. 1993).

1993

13 Jan. — Convention on the Prohibition of the Development, Production, Stockpiling and Use of Chemical Weapons and on their Destruction signed (entered into force 29 April 1997).

25 May — UN Security Council adopted statute of an International Tribunal for the Prosecution of Persons Responsible for Serious Violations of International Humanitarian Law Committed in the Territory of the Former Yugoslavia (the International Criminal Tribunal for the former Yugoslavia—ICTY).

1 Nov. — Treaty on European Union (Maastricht Treaty) entered into force.

20 Dec. — Position of UN High Commissioner for Human Rights established by the UN General Assembly.

1994

1 Jan. — North American Free Trade Agreement (NAFTA) entered into force.

11 Jan. — Partnership for Peace initiative launched by NATO.

9 Feb. — NATO endorsed the principle of air strikes against artillery positions responsible for attacks on civilian targets in the former Yugoslavia, to be activated at the request of the UN Secretary-General.

12 May — Treaty Establishing the African Economic Community entered into force.

1 Nov. — Trusteeship Council suspended.

8 Nov. — International Criminal Tribunal for Rwanda established.

16 Nov. — UN Convention on the Law of the Sea entered into force, providing for the establishment of the International Seabed Authority.

6 Dec. — CSCE transformed into Organization for Security and Co-operation in Europe (OSCE); authorized the grouping's first peace-keeping operation, to supervise a cease-fire in Nagorny-Karabakh.

8 Dec. — Common Market for Eastern and Southern African (COMESA) established, succeeding the PTA.

1995

1 Jan. — World Trade Organization formally established. Mercosur became fully operational.

11 May — States party to the 1968 Nuclear Non-Proliferation Treaty agreed to extend its provisions indefinitely.

15 Dec. — South-East Asia Nuclear Weapons Free Zone treaty signed (entered into force 27 March 1997).

20 Dec. — Responsibility for maintaining peace and stability in Bosnia and Herzegovina transferred from the UN Protection Force (UNPROFOR) to a NATO-led Implementation Force (later Stabilization Force).

1996

1 Jan. — Joint UN Programme on HIV/AIDS (UNAIDS) became operational.

10 March — Protocol to the Cartagena Agreement signed in Trujillo, Peru, establishing a Community of Andean Nations.

21 March — Charter of the Intergovernmental Authority on Development—IGAD adopted; IGAD superseded the Intergovernmental Authority on Drought and Development, established in 1986.

11 April — African Nuclear Weapons Free Zone Treaty (Pelindaba Treaty) signed in Cairo, Egypt.
24 Sept. — Comprehensive Test Ban Treaty signed.

1997

27 May — Founding Act on Mutual Relations, Co-operation and Security signed between Russia and NATO (provided for the establishment of a Permanent Joint Council).
18 Sept. — Convention on the Prohibition of the Use, Stockpiling, Production and Transfer of Anti-Personnel Land Mines and on their Destruction (Ottawa Convention) concluded; opened for signature 3 Dec.

1998

17 July — Statute for an International Criminal Court adopted, in Rome, Italy.
2 Sept. — First judgment by an international court for the crime of genocide passed by the International Criminal Tribunal for Rwanda.

1999

1 Jan. — Single currency ('euro') adopted by 11 EU states.
1 March — Ottawa Convention entered into force.
12 March — Czech Republic, Hungary and Poland admitted as full members of NATO.
24 March — NATO initiated its first military offensive against a sovereign state (the Federal Republic of Yugoslavia).
1 May — Treaty of Amsterdam, signed by EU ministers of foreign affairs on 2 Oct. 1997, entered into force.
10 June — UN Security Council authorized the deployment of an international security presence in Kosovo and Metohija (with NATO participation under unified command) and the establishment of an international civilian presence, the UN Interim Administration Mission in Kosovo (UNMIK). For the first time other organizations (the OSCE and EU) were mandated to co-ordinate aspects of a mission under the UN's overall jurisdiction.
17 Dec. — UN Monitoring, Verification and Inspection Commission (UNMOVIC) established in Iraq.

2000

23 June — Cotonou Agreement concluded between the EU and 78 African, Caribbean and Pacific (ACP) states, replacing the fourth Lomé Convention.
7 July — Treaty re-establishing the East African Community (signed by the heads of state of Kenya, Tanzania and Uganda on 30 Nov. 1999) entered into force.
14 Aug. — Special Court for Sierra Leone established by Resolution 1315 of the UN Security Council.
6–8 Sept. — Millennium Summit of UN heads of state or government convened to review challenges confronting the UN in the 21st century; adopted a series of Millennium Development Goals, incorporating targets to be achieved by 2015.
1 Nov. — Federal Republic of Yugoslavia assumed the seat in the UN General Assembly previously occupied by the former Yugoslavia.

2001

26 May — Constitutive Act of the African Union (signed 11 July 2000 in Lomé, Togo, by OAU heads of state and government) entered into force.
22 July — The G8 group of states endorsed the creation of the Global Fund to Fight AIDS, TB and Malaria.
12 Sept. — Following major terrorist attacks against targets in the USA, NATO's North Atlantic Council invoked for the first time Article 5 of the organization's founding treaty, concerning collective self-defence, which stipulates that an armed attack against one NATO member on European or North American territory is considered as an attack against all the allies.
23 Oct. — New Partnership for Africa's Development (NEPAD) launched by 15 OAU heads of state.
9–14 Nov. — Fourth WTO ministerial conference, convened in Doha, Qatar: Doha Declaration adopted, incorporating new negotiating agenda and work programme; China and Taiwan admitted as WTO members.
10 Dec. — Centennial Nobel Peace Prize awarded, in two equal portions, to the UN and to its then Secretary-General, Kofi Annan.

2002

1 Jan. — 'Euro' banknotes and coins entered into circulation in the then 12 'Euro Area' countries of the EU.
UN System Staff College became operational.
10 Jan. — International Security Assistance Force (authorized by the UN Security Council on 20 Dec. 2001) formally established to aid the Afghan Interim Authority with the maintanence of security in and around Kabul.
1 July — Rome Statute of the International Criminal Court (adopted on 17 July 1998) entered into force.
10 July — African Union (AU) formally inaugurated, succeeding the OAU.
10 Sept. — Switzerland admitted to the UN.
27 Sept. — Timor-Leste (East Timor) admitted to the UN.
1 Oct. — UN Office for Drug Control and Crime Prevention renamed the UN Office on Drugs and Crime.
8 Nov. — The UN Security Council adopted Resolution 1441 stipulating a detailed schedule under which Iraq was to comply with previous UN resolutions relating to the elimination of weapons of mass destruction, and providing for an enhanced inspection mandate.

2003

1 Jan. — Customs union of the Gulf Cooperation Council entered into force.
1 Feb. — Treaty of Nice, signed by EU ministers of foreign affairs on 26 Feb. 2001, entered into force.
1 April — Cotonou Agreement entered into force.
23 Dec. — World Tourism Organization became a specialized agency of the UN.

2004

29 March — Bulgaria, Estonia, Latvia, Lithuania, Romania, Slovakia and Slovenia admitted as full members of NATO.
1 May — Cyprus, the Czech Republic, Estonia, Hungary, Latvia, Lithuania, Malta, Poland, Slovakia and Slovenia admitted to the EU.
28 May — US-Central America Free Trade Agreement on the establishment of a Central American Free Trade Area (CAFTA) signed by the USA and CACM member countries.
29 Oct. — EU heads of state and government signed the Treaty establishing a Constitution for Europe.
9 Dec. — Leaders attending a pan-South American summit determined in principle to establish a South American Community of Nations (SACN).

2005

1 Jan. — Greater Arab Free Trade Area (GAFTA) came into effect.
East African Community customs union launched.
16 Feb. — The Kyoto Protocol of the UN Framework Convention on Climate Change entered into force.
21 March — The UN Secretary-General presented a report entitled *In Larger Freedom*, detailing proposals for extensive reforms to the UN.

14–16 Sept. UN General Assembly convened its 60th summit of heads of state and government.

2006

1 Jan. Single market component of the CARICOM Single Market and Economy (CSME) became operational.
South Asian Free Trade Area (SAFTA) came into effect.

19 June UN Human Rights Council inaugurated, replacing the former UN Human Rights Commission.

23 June UN Peace-building Commission inaugurated.

28 June Montenegro admitted to the UN, following its declaration of independence on 3 June; Serbia retained the UN seat hitherto occupied by Serbia and Montenegro.

24 July Negotiations on the Doha Development Round of multilateral negotiations on the liberation of international trade stalled across all sectors and all related deadlines postponed.

1 Nov. International Trade Union Confederation established by merger of the International Confederation of Free Trade Unions, the World Confederation of Labour and eight national trade union confederations.

19 Dec. South-Eastern European countries and territories signed the new Central European Free Trade Agreement (CEFTA).

2007

1 Jan. Ban Ki-Moon superseded Kofi Annan as UN Secretary-General.
Bulgaria and Romania admitted to the EU.

17 April South American heads of state endorsed the establishment of a Union of South American Nations (UNASUR), in place of the SACN.

31 July AU/UN Hybrid Operation in Darfur (UNAMID) established.

20 Nov. A new Charter of the Association of Southeast Asian Nations (ASEAN) signed by the heads of state of its 10 member countries.

2008

1 Jan. Gulf Cooperation Council Common Market inaugurated.
Cyprus and Malta admitted to the euro area.

24 May South American heads of state signed a constitutive treaty to establish UNASUR.

13 July Mediterranean Union launched by European Union and non-European Union Mediterranean states.

17 Aug. SADC Free Trade Area entered into effect.

15 Nov. Group of 20 (G20) major developed and emerging economies met for the first time at the level of heads of state and government, in Washington, DC, USA.

15 Dec. ASEAN Charter entered into effect.

2009

1 Jan. Slovakia admitted to the euro area.

1 March Special Tribunal for Lebanon became operational.

1 April Albania and Croatia admitted as members of NATO.

24–26 June UN Conference on the World Financial and Economic Crisis and its Impact on Development attended by high-level representatives of the 192 UN member states.

22–23 Oct. AU Special Summit on Refugees, Returnees and IDPs in Africa was convened, at which AU member states adopted the AU Convention for the Protection and Assistance of IDPs in Africa.

1 Dec. Treaty of Lisbon Treaty amending the Treaty on European Union and the Treaty establishing the European Community entered into force.

18 Dec. Copenhagen Accord agreed by participants at the UN Climate Change Conference held in Copenhagen, Denmark.

2010

2 Feb. AU heads of state approved the establishment of the NEPAD Planning and Co-ordination Agency (NPCA), formally integrating NEPAD (launched in Oct. 2001) into the AU's structures.

1 Aug. Entry into force of the Convention on Cluster Munitions (adopted on 30 May 2008).

23 Dec. International Convention for the Protection of All Persons from Enforced Disappearance entered into force.

11 Dec. Cancun Agreements adopted at the UN Climate Change Conference held in Cancun, Mexico.

2011

1 Jan. Estonia admitted as the 17th member of the euro area.
The UN Entity for Gender Equality and the Empowerment of Women (UN Women) became operational.

31 March NATO assumed full command of military operations under Operation Unified Protector to enforce a UN-sanctioned arms embargo and no-fly zone and to conduct air strikes against the armed forces in Libya in order to protect civilians and populated areas in that country.

9–13 May Istanbul Political Declaration and Programme of Action for the Least Developed Countries (LDCs) adopted by the Fourth UN Conference on the LDCs.

10 May The Gulf Cooperation Council invited Jordan and Morocco to submit membership applications.

21 June The UN General Assembly appointed Ban Ki-Moon for a second five-year term as UN Secretary-General, to cover the period 1 Jan. 2012–31 Dec. 2016.

28 June Organization of the Islamic Conference renamed Organization of Islamic Cooperation.

14 July South Sudan admitted as the 193rd member of the UN.

2–3 Dec. Inaugural summit of the Community of Latin American and Caribbean States.

11 Dec. Durban Platform for Enhanced Action adopted by the UN Climate Change Conference convened in Durban, South Africa.

2012

2 Feb. Treaty establishing the European Stability Mechanism signed by member states of the euro area.

22–23 March First Global Human Development Forum convened in İstanbul, Turkey.

26 April First guilty verdict imposed by a world court against a former head of state (Special Court for Sierra Leone v. Charles Taylor, the former President of Liberia).

6 June An agreement establishing the Pacific Alliance signed by the Presidents of Chile, Colombia, Mexico and Peru.

20–22 June UN Conference on Sustainable Development (UNCSD) convened, in Rio de Janeiro, Brazil.

1 July Residual workload of the ICTR assumed by the International Residual Mechanism for Criminal Tribunals.

INTERNATIONAL OBSERVANCES

(Mainly sponsored by the UN and its specialized agencies; other sponsoring organizations are indicated in parentheses)

Days and Weeks

January

27	International Holocaust Remembrance Day.
30	World Leprosy Day.

February

2	World Wetlands Day (Ramsar Convention on Wetlands).
4	World Cancer Day.
(1st week)	World Interfaith Harmony Week.
10	Safer Internet Day (European Commission and ITU).
13	World Radio Day (UNESCO).
21	International Mother Language Day.
22	International Day for the Eradication of Female Genital Mutilation/Cutting (UNFPA).
25	SADC Healthy Lifestyles Day.

March

3	Africa Environment Day (AU).
8	UN Day for Women's Rights and International Peace.
(2nd Monday)	Commonwealth Day (Commonwealth Secretariat).
15	World Consumer Rights Day (Consumers International).
16–20	World Forest Week (FAO).
20	UN French Language Day.
21	International Day for the Elimination of Racial Discrimination.
	International Day of Nowruz.
	World Poetry Day.
	World Forestry Day.
21–27	Week of Solidarity with the Peoples Struggling against Racism and Racial Discrimination.
22	World Day for Water.
22–26	EU Sustainable Energy Week.
23	World Meteorological Day.
25	International Day of Remembrance of the Victims of Slavery and the Transatlantic Slave Trade.
24	World Tuberculosis Day.
26	UN Social Work Day.
27	World Theatre Day (International Theatre Institute and UNESCO).

April

2	International Children's Book Day (International Board on Books for Young People).
4	International Day for Mine Awareness and Assistance in Mine Action.
6	World Autism Awareness Day.
7	Commemoration of the Rwanda Genocide (AU).
	World Health Day.
12	International Day for Street Children.
14	Pan-American Day (OAS).
20	UN Chinese Language Day.
22	International Mother Earth Day.
23	UN English Language Day.
	World Book and Copyright Day.
23–29	UN Global Road Safety Week.
24–30	Education for All Week.
25	Africa Malaria Control Day.
	World Malaria Day (WHO).
26	International Day of Remembrance for Victims of Radiation (CIS).
	World Intellectual Property Day (WIPO).
28	World Day for Safety and Health at Work (ILO).

May

3	World Press Freedom Day.
5	Europe Day (Council of Europe).
6	World Asthma Day.
8	World Red Cross Red Crescent Day (ICRC).
	International Day of the Midwife.
10	World Migratory Bird Day.
15	International Day of Families.
17	International Day Against Homophobia.
	World Telecommunication and Information Society Day.
21	World Day for Cultural Diversity for Dialogue and Development.
22	International Day for Biological Diversity.
25	Africa Day (AU).
	International Missing Children's Day.
25–31	Week of Solidarity with the Peoples of Non-Self-Governing Territories.
27	Multiple Sclerosis Day.
29	International Day of UN Peacekeepers.
30–2 June	Green Week (European Union).
31	World No Tobacco Day.

June

4	International Day of Innocent Children Victims of Aggression.
5	World Environment Day.
6	UN Russian Language Day.
7	UN Volunteers Family Day.
8	World Anti-Counterfeiting Day.
	World Oceans Day.
12	World Day against Child Labour (ILO).
14	World Blood Donor Day.
16	Day of the African Child (AU).
17	World Day to Combat Desertification and Drought.
19	Sickle-cell Anaemia Awareness Day.
20	Africa Refugee Day (AU).
	World Refugee Day.
23	UN Public Service Day.
	Olympic Day (International Olympic Committee).
25	BSEC Day.
	Day of the Seafarer (IMO).
26	UN International Day in Support of Victims of Torture.
	International Day against Drug Abuse and Illicit Trafficking.

July

(1st Saturday)	International Day of Co-operatives.
4–8	European Forest and Water Week (UN Economic Commission for Europe).
11	World Population Day.
17	International Criminal Justice Day (International Criminal Court).
18	Nelson Mandela International Day.
28	World Hepatitis Day (WHO).
30	International Day of Friendship.

August

1–7	World Breastfeeding Week.
3	World Friendship Day.
9	International Day of the World's Indigenous People.
10	Africa Day of Decentralization and Local Development (AU).
12	International Youth Day.
17	SADC Day (Southern African Development Community).
19	World Humanitarian Day.

- 23 International Day for the Remembrance of the Slave Trade and its Abolition (UNESCO).
- 29 International Day against Nuclear Tests.
- 30 International Day for Victims of Enforced Disappearance.

September

- 8 International Literacy Day.
- 9 African Union Day.
- 10 World Suicide Prevention Day (WHO).
- 15 International Day of Democracy.
- 16 International Day for the Preservation of the Ozone Layer ('International Ozone Day').
- 21 International Day of Peace.
- 25 Pan-African Women's Day.
- 27 World Tourism Day.
- 28 World Rabies Day.
- 29 World Heart Day (World Heart Federation and WHO).
- (Final week) World Maritime Day.

October

- 1 International Day of Older Persons.
  International Music Day (International Music Council).
- 2 International Day of Non-Violence.
- 3 International Action Day (WFTU).
- 4–10 World Space Week.
- 5 Conference on Interaction and Confidence Building Measures in Asia Day.
  World Teachers' Day.
- (1st Monday) World Habitat Day.
- (2nd Wednesday) International Day for Natural Disaster Reduction.
- (2nd week) European Week Against Pain (European Union).
- 7 World Day for Decent Work (International Confederation of Trade Unions).
- 9 World Post Day.
- 10 World Mental Health Day.
  World Standards Day (International Organization for Standardization).
- 11 Global Day Against Pain (International Association for the Study of Pain and WHO).
- 11–17 European Local Democracy Week (Council of Europe).
- 12 UN Spanish Language Day.
- 13 International Day for Disaster Reduction.
  World Sight Day (WHO).
- 15 Global Handwashing Day (Global Public-Private Partnership for Handwashing with Soap).
  World Rural Women's Day.
- (3rd week) European Local Democracy Week (Council of Europe).
- (3rd week) European Week for Safety and Health at Work (European Union).
- 16 World Food Day.
- 17 International Day for the Eradication of Poverty.
- 20 World Statistics Day.
- 21 African Human Rights Day (AU).
- 22 European Day for Organ Donation & Transplantation (Council of Europe).
- 24 United Nations Day.
  World Development Information Day.
  World Polio Day.
- 24–30 Disarmament Week.
- 27 World Day for Audiovisual Heritage.
- 29 Cybersecurity Awareness Day (APEC).
- 30 Africa Food and Nutrition Security Day (AU).
- 31 International Black Sea Day (BSEC).

November

- 1 African Youth Day (AU).
- 3 International Day for Biosphere Reserves (UNESCO).
- 6 International Day for Preventing the Exploitation of the Environment in War and Armed Conflict.
- (2nd week) International Week of Science and Peace.
- 10 World Science Day for Peace and Development.
- 14 World Diabetes Day (International Diabetes Federation and WHO).
- 15 World Philosophy Day.
- 16 International Day for Tolerance.
  World Chronic Obstructive Pulmonary Disease Day (WHO).
- 20 Africa Industrialization Day.
  Universal Children's Day.
- 21 European Cystic Fibrosis Awareness Day (Cystic Fibrosis Europe).
  World Television Day.
- 22 World Humanitarian Day.
- (3rd Sunday) World Day of Remembrance for Road Traffic Victims.
- 25 International Day for the Elimination of Violence against Women.
- 28 ECO Day (Economic Cooperation Organization).
- 29 International Day of Solidarity with the Palestinian People.

December

- 1 Antarctica Day.
  World Aids Day.
- 2 International Day for the Abolition of Slavery.
- 3 International Day of Disabled Persons.
  European Day of Disabled People (European Union).
- 5 International Volunteer Day for Economic and Social Development.
- 7 International Civil Aviation Day.
- 8 International Migrants Day.
  SAARC Day (South Asian Association for Regional Cooperation).
- 9 International Anti-corruption Day.
- 10 Human Rights Day.
- 11 World Asthma Day (Global Initiative for Asthma).
  International Mountain Day.
- (2nd Sunday) International Children's Day of Broadcasting.
- 18 International Migrants' Day.
  UN Arabic Language Day.
- 19 UN Day for South-South Co-operation.
  International Human Solidarity Day.
- 29 International Day for Biological Diversity.

Years

- 2012 Year of Shared Values (AU).
  International Year of Co-operatives.
  International Year of Sustainable Energy for All.
  Year of Sport and Healthy Life in the CIS.
- 2013 International Year of Quinoa.
  International Year of Water Co-operation.
- 2014 International Year of Family Farming.

Decades

- 2003–12 Asian and Pacific Decade of Disabled Persons (ESCAP).
  UN Literacy Decade: Education For All.
- 2005–14 UN Decade of Education for Sustainable Development.
  Second International Decade of the World's Indigenous People.
- 2005–15 Decade of Roma Inclusion.
  International Decade for Action, 'Water for Life' (from 22 March 2005).

2006–15	Decade of Recovery and Sustainable Development of the Affected Regions (relating to the Chornobyl disaster). Health Workforce Decade (WHO). SAARC Decade on Poverty Alleviation. Second Decade for Education in Africa (AU).
2006–16	Decade of the Americas for the Rights and Dignity of Persons with Disabilities (OAS).
2008–17	Second UN Decade for the Eradication of Poverty.
2010–20	African Women's Decade (AU). UN Decade for Deserts and the Fight against Desertification.
2011–20	Decade of Action for Road Safety. Third International Decade for the Eradication of Colonialism. UN Decade on Biodiversity.

PART TWO

The United Nations

UNITED NATIONS

Address: United Nations, New York, NY 10017, USA.

Telephone: (212) 963-1234; **fax:** (212) 963-4879; **internet:** www.un.org.

The United Nations (UN) was founded in 1945 to maintain international peace and security and to develop international co-operation in addressing economic, social, cultural and humanitarian problems.

The 'United Nations' was a name devised by President Franklin D. Roosevelt of the USA. It was first used in the Declaration by United Nations of 1 January 1942, when representatives of 26 nations pledged their governments to continue fighting together against the Axis powers.

The UN Charter was drawn up by the representatives of 50 countries at the UN Conference on International Organization, which met at San Francisco from 25 April to 26 June 1945. The representatives deliberated on the basis of proposals put forward by representatives of China, the USSR, the United Kingdom and the USA at Dumbarton Oaks in August–October 1944. The Charter was signed on 26 June 1945. Poland, not represented at the Conference, signed it later but nevertheless became one of the original 51 members.

The UN officially came into existence on 24 October 1945, when the Charter had been ratified by China, France, the USSR, the United Kingdom and the USA, and by a majority of other signatories. United Nations Day is celebrated annually on 24 October.

The UN's chief administrative officer is the Secretary-General, elected for a five-year term by the General Assembly on the recommendation of the Security Council. He acts in that capacity at all meetings of the General Assembly, the Security Council, the Economic and Social Council, and the Trusteeship Council, and performs such other functions as are entrusted to him by those organs. He is required to submit an annual report to the General Assembly and may bring to the attention of the Security Council any matter which, in his opinion, may threaten international peace.

Secretary-General: BAN KI-MOON (Republic of Korea) (2007–15).

Membership

MEMBERS OF THE UNITED NATIONS

(with assessments for percentage contributions to the UN budget for 2010–12, and year of admission)

Afghanistan	0.004	1946
Albania	0.010	1955
Algeria	0.128	1962
Andorra	0.008	1993
Angola	0.010	1976
Antigua and Barbuda	0.002	1981
Argentina	0.287	1945
Armenia	0.005	1992
Australia	1.933	1945
Austria	0.851	1955
Azerbaijan	0.015	1992
Bahamas	0.018	1973
Bahrain	0.039	1971
Bangladesh	0.010	1974
Barbados	0.008	1966
Belarus[1]	0.042	1945
Belgium	1.075	1945
Belize	0.001	1981
Benin	0.003	1960
Bhutan	0.001	1971
Bolivia	0.007	1945
Bosnia and Herzegovina	0.014	1992
Botswana	0.018	1966
Brazil	0.611	1945
Brunei	0.028	1984
Bulgaria	0.038	1955
Burkina Faso	0.003	1960
Burundi	0.001	1962
Cambodia	0.003	1955
Cameroon	0.011	1960
Canada	3.207	1945
Cape Verde	0.001	1975
Central African Republic	0.001	1960
Chad	0.002	1960
Chile	0.236	1945
China, People's Republic	3.189	1945
Colombia	0.105	1945
Comoros	0.001	1975
Congo, Democratic Republic	0.003	1960
Congo, Republic	0.003	1960
Costa Rica	0.034	1945
Côte d'Ivoire	0.010	1960
Croatia	0.097	1992
Cuba	0.071	1945
Cyprus	0.046	1960
Czech Republic[2]	0.349	1993
Denmark	0.736	1945
Djibouti	0.001	1977
Dominica	0.001	1978
Dominican Republic	0.042	1945
Ecuador	0.040	1945
Egypt	0.094	1945
El Salvador	0.019	1945
Equatorial Guinea	0.008	1968
Eritrea	0.001	1993
Estonia	0.040	1991
Ethiopia	0.008	1945
Fiji	0.004	1970
Finland	0.566	1955
France	6.123	1945
Gabon	0.014	1960
The Gambia	0.001	1965
Georgia	0.006	1992
Germany	8.018	1973
Ghana	0.006	1957
Greece	0.691	1945
Grenada	0.001	1974
Guatemala	0.028	1945
Guinea	0.002	1958
Guinea-Bissau	0.001	1974
Guyana	0.001	1966
Haiti	0.003	1945
Honduras	0.008	1945
Hungary	0.291	1955
Iceland	0.042	1946
India	0.534	1945
Indonesia	0.238	1950
Iran	0.233	1945
Iraq	0.020	1945
Ireland	0.498	1955
Israel	0.384	1949
Italy	4.999	1955
Jamaica	0.014	1962
Japan	12.530	1956
Jordan	0.014	1955
Kazakhstan	0.076	1992
Kenya	0.012	1963
Kiribati	0.001	1999
Korea, Democratic People's Republic	0.263	1991
Korea, Republic	2.260	1991
Kuwait	0.263	1963
Kyrgyzstan	0.001	1992
Laos	0.001	1955
Latvia	0.038	1991
Lebanon	0.033	1945
Lesotho	0.001	1966
Liberia	0.001	1945
Libya	0.129	1955
Liechtenstein	0.009	1990

Lithuania	0.065	1991
Luxembourg	0.090	1945
Macedonia, former Yugoslav republic	0.007	1993
Madagascar	0.003	1960
Malawi	0.001	1964
Malaysia	0.253	1957
Maldives	0.001	1965
Mali	0.003	1960
Malta	0.017	1964
Marshall Islands	0.001	1991
Mauritania	0.001	1961
Mauritius	0.011	1968
Mexico	2.356	1945
Micronesia, Federated States	0.001	1991
Moldova	0.002	1992
Monaco	0.003	1993
Mongolia	0.002	1961
Montenegro[3]	0.004	2006
Morocco	0.058	1956
Mozambique	0.003	1975
Myanmar	0.006	1948
Namibia	0.008	1990
Nauru	0.001	1999
Nepal	0.006	1955
Netherlands	1.873	1945
New Zealand	0.273	1945
Nicaragua	0.003	1945
Niger	0.002	1960
Nigeria	0.078	1960
Norway	0.871	1945
Oman	0.086	1971
Pakistan	0.082	1947
Palau	0.001	1994
Panama	0.022	1945
Papua New Guinea	0.002	1975
Paraguay	0.007	1945
Peru	0.090	1945
Philippines	0.090	1945
Poland	0.828	1945
Portugal	0.511	1955
Qatar	0.135	1971
Romania	0.177	1955
Russia[4]	1.602	1945
Rwanda	0.001	1962
Saint Christopher and Nevis	0.001	1983
Saint Lucia	0.001	1979
Saint Vincent and the Grenadines	0.001	1980
Samoa	0.001	1976
San Marino	0.003	1992
São Tomé and Príncipe	0.001	1975
Saudi Arabia	0.830	1945
Senegal	0.006	1960
Serbia[3]	0.037	2000
Seychelles	0.002	1976
Sierra Leone	0.001	1961
Singapore	0.335	1965
Slovakia[2]	0.142	1993
Slovenia	0.103	1992
Solomon Islands	0.001	1978
Somalia	0.001	1960
South Africa	0.385	1945
South Sudan[5]	—	2011
Spain	3.177	1955
Sri Lanka	0.019	1955
Sudan	0.010	1956
Suriname	0.003	1975
Swaziland	0.003	1968
Sweden	1.064	1946
Switzerland	1.130	2002
Syria	0.025	1945
Tajikistan	0.002	1992
Tanzania	0.008	1961
Thailand	0.209	1946
Timor-Leste	0.001	2002
Togo	0.001	1960
Tonga	0.001	1999
Trinidad and Tobago	0.044	1962
Tunisia	0.030	1956
Turkey	0.617	1945
Turkmenistan	0.026	1992
Tuvalu	0.001	2000
Uganda	0.006	1962
Ukraine[1]	0.087	1945
United Arab Emirates	0.391	1971
United Kingdom	6.604	1945
USA	22.000	1945
Uruguay	0.027	1945
Uzbekistan	0.010	1992
Vanuatu	0.001	1981
Venezuela	0.314	1945
Viet Nam	0.033	1977
Yemen[6]	0.010	1947/67
Zambia	0.004	1964
Zimbabwe	0.003	1980

Total Membership: 193 (June 2012)

[1] Until December 1991 both Belarus and Ukraine were integral parts of the USSR and not independent countries, but had separate UN membership.

[2] Czechoslovakia, which had been a member of the UN since 1945, ceased to exist as a single state on 31 December 1992. In January 1993, as Czechoslovakia's legal successors, the Czech Republic and Slovakia were granted UN membership, and seats on subsidiary bodies that had previously been held by Czechoslovakia were divided between the two successor states.

[3] Montenegro was admitted as a member of the UN on 28 June 2006, following its declaration of independence on 3 June; Serbia retained the seat formerly held by Serbia and Montenegro.

[4] Russia assumed the USSR's seat in the General Assembly and its permanent seat on the Security Council in December 1991, following the USSR's dissolution.

[5] South Sudan's percentage contribution to the UN budget was to be determined in mid-2012.

[6] The Yemen Arab Republic (admitted to the UN as Yemen in 1947) and the People's Democratic Republic of Yemen (admitted as Southern Yemen in 1967) merged to form the Republic of Yemen in May 1990.

Note: In September 2011 the Executive President of the Palestinian Authority submitted a formal application for the admission to the UN of Palestine as an independent member state; this remained under consideration in mid-2012.

SOVEREIGN STATES NOT IN THE UNITED NATIONS

(June 2012)

Taiwan (Republic of China) Vatican City (Holy See)

Diplomatic Representation

PERMANENT MISSIONS TO THE UNITED NATIONS

(June 2012)

Afghanistan: 633 Third Ave, 27th Floor New York, NY 10017; tel. (212) 972-1212; fax (212) 972-1216; e-mail info@afghanistan-un.org; Permanent Representative Dr ZAHIR TANIN.

Albania: 320 East 79th St, New York, NY 10075; tel. (212) 249-2059; fax (212) 535-2917; e-mail albania.un@albania-un.org; Permanent Representative FERIT HOXHA.

Algeria: 326 East 48th St, New York, NY 10017; tel. (212) 750-1960; fax (212) 759-5274; e-mail mission@algeria-un.org; internet www.algeria-un.org; Permanent Representative MOURAD BENMEHIDI.

Andorra: Two United Nations Plaza, 27th Floor, New York, NY 10017; tel. (212) 750-8064; fax (212) 750-6630; e-mail contact@andorraun.org; internet www.mae.ad; Permanent Representative NARCIS CASAL DE FONSDEVIELA.

Angola: 820 Second Ave, 12th Floor, New York, NY 10017; tel. (212) 861-5656; fax (212) 861-9295; e-mail themission@angolaun.org; internet www.angolamissionun.org; Permanent Representative ISMAEL ABRAÃO GASPAR MARTINS.

Antigua and Barbuda: 305 East 47th St, 6th Floor, New York, NY 10017; tel. (212) 541-4117; fax (212) 757-1607; e-mail unmission@abgov.org; internet www.abgov.org; Permanent Representative JOHN W. ASHE.

Argentina: One United Nations Plaza, 25th Floor, New York, NY 10017; tel. (212) 688-6300; fax (212) 980-8395; e-mail enaun@mrecic.gov.ar; internet enaun.mrecic.gov.ar; Chargé d'affaires a. i. MATEO ESTRÉMÉ.

Armenia: 119 East 36th St, New York, NY 10016; tel. (212) 686-9079; fax (212) 686-3934; e-mail armenia@un.int; internet www.un.mfa.am; Permanent Representative GAREN A. NAZARIAN.

Australia: 150 East 42nd St, 33rd Floor, New York, NY 10017; tel. (212) 351-6600; fax (212) 351-6610; e-mail australia@un.int; Permanent Representative GARY QUINLAN.

Austria: 600 Third Ave, 31st Floor, New York, NY 10016; tel. (212) 542-8400; fax (212) 949-1840; e-mail new-york-ov@bmeia.gv.at; internet www.un.int/austria; Permanent Representative MARTIN SAJDIK.

Azerbaijan: 866 United Nations Plaza, Suite 560, New York, NY 10017; tel. (212) 371-2559; fax (212) 371-2784; e-mail azerbaijan@un.int; Permanent Representative AGSHIN MEHDIYEV.

Bahamas: 231 East 46th St, New York, NY 10017; tel. (212) 421-6925; fax (212) 759-2135; e-mail mission@bahamasny.com; Permanent Representative PAULETTE A. BETHEL.

Bahrain: 866 Second Ave, 14th/15th Floor, New York, NY 10017; tel. (212) 223-6200; fax (212) 319-0687; e-mail bahrain1@un.int; Permanent Representative JAMAL FARES ALROWAIEI.

Bangladesh: 227 East 45th St, 14th Floor, New York, NY 10017; tel. (212) 867-3434; fax (212) 972-4038; e-mail bangladesh@un.int; internet www.un.int/bangladesh; Permanent Representative ABULKALAM ABDUL MOMEN.

Barbados: 820 Second Ave, 9th Floor, New York, NY 10017; tel. (212) 551-4300; fax (212) 986-1030; e-mail prun@foreign.gov.bb; Permanent Representative JOSEPH E. GODDARD.

Belarus: 136 East 67th St, 4th Floor, New York, NY 10065; tel. (212) 535-3420; fax (212) 734-4810; e-mail usa.un@mfa.gov.by; internet www.un.int/belarus; Permanent Representative ANDREI DAPKIUNAS.

Belgium: One Dag Hammarskjöld Plaza, 885 Second Ave, 41st Floor, New York, NY 10017; tel. (212) 378-6300; fax (212) 681-7618; e-mail newyorkun@diplobel.fed.be; internet www.diplomatie.be/newyorkun; Permanent Representative JAN GRAULS.

Belize: 675 Third Ave, Suite 1911, New York, NY 10017; tel. (212) 986-1240; fax (212) 593-0932; e-mail blzun@aol.com; Chargé d'affaires a. i. JANINE ELIZABETH COYE-FELSON.

Benin: 125 East 38th St, New York, NY 10016; tel. (212) 684-1339; fax (212) 684-2058; e-mail beninewyork@gmail.com; Permanent Representative JEAN-FRANCIS RÉGIS ZINSOU.

Bhutan: 343 43rd St, New York, NY 10017; tel. (212) 682-2268; fax (212) 661-0551; e-mail bhutan@un.int; Permanent Representative LHATU WANGCHUK.

Bolivia: 801 Second Ave, 4th Floor, Suite 402, New York, NY 10017; tel. (212) 682-8132; fax (212) 687-4642; e-mail delgaliviaonu@hotmail.com; Chargé d'affaires a. i. RAFAEL ARCHONDO.

Bosnia and Herzegovina: 420 Lexington Ave, Suites 607–608, New York, NY 10170; tel. (212) 751-9015; fax (212) 751-9019; e-mail bihun@mfa.gov.ba; internet www.bhmisijaun.org; Chargé d'affaires a. i. MILOŠ VUKAŠINOVIĆ.

Botswana: 154 East 46th St, New York, NY 10017; tel. (212) 889-2277; fax (212) 725-5061; e-mail botswana@un.int; Permanent Representative CHARLES THEMBANI NTWAAGAE.

Brazil: 747 Third Ave, 9th Floor, New York, NY 10017; tel. (212) 372-2600; fax (212) 371-5716; e-mail delbrasonu@delbrasonu.org; internet www.un.int/brazil; Permanent Representative MARIA LUIZA RIBEIRO VIOTTI.

Brunei: 771 United Nations Plaza, New York, NY 10017; tel. (212) 697-3465; fax (212) 697-9889; e-mail brunei@un.int; Permanent Representative LATIF BIN TUAH.

Bulgaria: 11 East 84th St, New York, NY 10028; tel. (212) 737-4790; fax (212) 472-9865; e-mail bulgaria@un.int; internet www.un.int/bulgaria; Permanent Representative STEFAN TAVROV.

Burkina Faso: 866 United Nations Plaza, Suite 326, New York, NY 10017; tel. (212) 308-4720; fax (212) 308-4690; e-mail bfapm@un.int; internet www.burkina-onu.org; Permanent Representative DER KOGDA.

Burundi: 336 East 45th St, 12th Floor, New York, NY 10017; tel. (212) 499-0001; fax (212) 499-0006; e-mail ambabunewyork@yahoo.fr; Permanent Representative HERMÉNÉGILDE NIYONZIMA.

Cambodia: 327 East 58th St, New York, NY 10022; tel. (212) 336-0777; fax (212) 759-7672; e-mail cambodia@un.int; internet www.un.int/cambodia; Permanent Representative SEA KOSAL.

Cameroon: 22 East 73rd St, New York, NY 10021; tel. (212) 794-2295; fax (212) 249-0533; e-mail cameroon.mission@yahoo.com; Permanent Representative TOMMO MONTHE.

Canada: One Dag Hammarskjöld Plaza, 885 Second Ave, 14th Floor, New York, NY 10017; tel. (212) 848-1100; fax (212) 848-1195; e-mail canada.un@international.gc.ca; internet www.un.int/canada; Permanent Representative GUILLERMO E. RISHCHYNSKI.

Cape Verde: 27 East 69th St, New York, NY 10021; tel. (212) 472-0333; fax (212) 794-1398; e-mail capeverde@un.int; Permanent Representative ANTONIO PEDRO MONTEIRO LIMA.

Central African Republic: 866 United Nations Plaza, Suite 444, New York, NY 10017; tel. (646) 415-9122; fax (646) 415-9149; e-mail repercaf.ny@gmail.com; internet www.pmcar.org; Permanent Representative CHARLES-ARMEL DOUBANE.

Chad: 129 East 36th St, New York, NY 10017; tel. (212) 986-0980; fax (212) 986-0152; e-mail chadmission@gmail.com; Permanent Representative AHMAD ALLAM-MI.

Chile: One Dag Hammarskjöld Plaza, 885 Second Ave, 40th Floor, New York, NY 10017; tel. (917) 322-6800; fax (917) 322-6890; e-mail chile.un@minrel.gov.cl; internet chileabroad.gov.cl/onu/en; Permanent Representative OCTAVIO ERRÁZURIZ.

China, People's Republic: 350 East 35th St, New York, NY 10016; tel. (212) 655-6100; fax (212) 634-7626; e-mail chinesemission@yahoo.com; internet www.china-un.org; Permanent Representative LI BAODONG.

Colombia: 140 East 57th St, 5th Floor, New York, NY 10022; tel. (212) 355-7776; fax (212) 371-2813; e-mail colombia@colombiaun.org; internet www.colombia.un.org; Permanent Representative NÉSTOR OSORIO.

Comoros: 866 United Nations Plaza, Suite 418, New York, NY 10017; tel. (212) 750-1637; fax (212) 750-1657; e-mail comoros@un.int; Permanent Representative MOHAMED TOIHIRI.

Congo, Democratic Republic: 866 United Nations Plaza, Suite 511, New York, NY 10017; tel. (212) 319-8061; fax (212) 319-8232; e-mail drcongo@un.int; internet www.un.int/drcongo; Chargé d'affaires a.i. CHARLOTTE OMOY MALENGA.

Congo, Republic: 14 East 65th St, New York, NY 10065; tel. (212) 744-7840; fax (212) 744-7975; e-mail congo@un.int; Permanent Representative RAYMOND SERGE BALÉ.

Costa Rica: 211 East 43rd St, Rm 903, New York, NY 10017; tel. (212) 986-6373; fax (212) 986-6842; e-mail contact costaricamission@gmail.com; Permanent Representative EDUARDO ULIBARRI-BILBAO.

Côte d'Ivoire: 800 Second Ave, 5th Floor, New York, NY 10017; tel. (646) 649-5061; fax (646) 781-9974; e-mail cotedivoiremission@yahoo.com; internet www.un.int/cotedivoire; Permanent Representative YOUSSOUFOU BAMBA.

Croatia: 820 Second Ave, 19th Floor, New York, NY 10017; tel. (212) 986-1585; fax (212) 986-2011; e-mail cromiss.un@mvp.hr; internet www.un.mfa.hr; Permanent Representative RANKO VILOVIĆ.

Cuba: 315 Lexington Ave and 38th St, New York, NY 10016; tel. (212) 689-7215; fax (212) 779-1697; e-mail cuba_onu@cubanmission.com; Permanent Representative PEDRO NÚNEZ MOSQUERA.

Cyprus: 13 East 40th St, New York, NY 10016; tel. (212) 481-6023; fax (212) 685-7316; e-mail mission@cyprusun.org; internet www.un.int/cyprus; Permanent Representative NICHOLAS EMILIOU.

Czech Republic: 1109–1111 Madison Ave, New York, NY 10028; tel. (646) 981-4001; fax (646) 981-4099; e-mail un.newyork@embassy.mzv.cz; internet www.mfa.cz; Permanent Representative EDITA HRDÁ.

Denmark: One Dag Hammarskjöld Plaza, 885 Second Ave, 18th Floor, New York, NY 10017; tel. (212) 308-7009; fax (212) 308-3384; e-mail nycmis@um.dk; internet www.missionfnnewyork.um.dk/en/; Permanent Representative CARSTEN STAUR.

Djibouti: 866 United Nations Plaza, Suite 4011, New York, NY 10017; tel. (212) 753-3163; fax (212) 223-1276; e-mail djibouti@nyct.net; Permanent Representative ROBLE OLHAYE.

Dominica: 800 Second Ave, Suite 400H, New York, NY 10017; tel. (212) 949-0853; fax (212) 808-4975; e-mail dominicaun@gmail.com; Permanent Representative VINCE HENDERSON.

Dominican Republic: 144 East 44th St, 4th Floor, New York, NY 10017; tel. (212) 867-0833; fax (212) 986-4694; e-mail drun@un.int; internet www.un.int/dr; Permanent Representative HÉCTOR VIRGILIO ALCÁNTARA MEJIA.

Ecuador: 866 United Nations Plaza, Rm 516, New York, NY 10017; tel. (212) 935-1680; fax (212) 935-1835; e-mail ecuador@un.int; internet www.ecuadoronu.com; Chargé d'affaires a.i. DIEGO MOREJÓN.

Egypt: 304 East 44th St, New York, NY 10017; tel. (212) 503-0300; fax (212) 725-3467; e-mail egypt@un.int; Permanent Representative MOOTAZ AHMADEIN KHALIL.

El Salvador: 46 Park Ave, New York, NY 10016; tel. (212) 679-1616; fax (212) 725-7831; e-mail elsalvador@un.int; Permanent Representative JOAQUÍN ALEXANDER MAZA MARTELLI.

Equatorial Guinea: 242 East 51st St, New York, NY 10022; tel. (212) 223-2324; fax (212) 223-2366; e-mail equatorialguineamission@yahoo.com; Permanent Representative ANATOLIO NDONG MBA.

Eritrea: 800 Second Ave, 18th Floor, New York, NY 10017; tel. (212) 687-3390; fax (212) 687-3138; e-mail general@eritrea-unmission.org; internet www.eritrea-unmission.org; Permanent Representative ARAYA DESTA.

Estonia: 3 Dag Hammarskjöld Plaza, 305 East 47th St, Unit 6B, New York, NY 10017; tel. (212) 883-0640; fax (646) 514-0099; e-mail mission.newyork@mfa.ee; Permanent Representative MARGUS KOLGA.

Ethiopia: 866 Second Ave, 3rd Floor, New York, NY 10017; tel. (212) 421-1830; fax (212) 756-4690; e-mail ethiopia@un.int; Permanent Representative TEKEDA ALEMU.

Fiji: 801 Second Ave, 10th Floor, New York, NY 10017; tel. (212) 687-4130; fax (212) 687-3963; e-mail mission@fijiprun.org; Permanent Representative PETER THOMSON.

Finland: 866 United Nations Plaza, Suite 222, New York, NY 10017; tel. (212) 355-2100; fax (212) 759-6156; e-mail sanomat.yke@formin.fi; Permanent Representative JARMO VIINANEN.

France: One Dag Hammarskjöld Plaza, 245 East 47th St, 44th Floor, New York, NY 10017; tel. (212) 702-4900; fax (212) 421-6889; e-mail france@un.int; Permanent Representative GÉRARD ARAUD.

Gabon: 18 East 41st St, 9th Floor, New York, NY 10017; tel. (212) 686-9720; fax (212) 689-5769; e-mail info@gabon-un.org; Permanent Representative NELSON MESSONE.

The Gambia: 800 Second Ave, Suite 400F, New York, NY 10017; tel. (212) 949-6640; fax (212) 856-9820; e-mail gambia_un@hotmail.com; internet gambia.un.int; Permanent Representative SUSAN WAFFA-OGOO.

Georgia: One United Nations Plaza, 26th Floor, New York, NY 10021; tel. (212) 759-1949; fax (212) 759-1832; e-mail geomission.un@mfa.gov.ge; internet www.un.int/georgia; Permanent Representative ALEXANDER LOMAIA.

Germany: 871 United Nations Plaza, New York, NY 10017; tel. (212) 940-0400; fax (212) 940-0402; e-mail info@new-york-un.diplo.de; internet www.germany-info.org/un; Permanent Representative HANS PETER WITTIG.

Ghana: 19 East 47th St, New York, NY 10017; tel. (212) 832-1300; fax (212) 751-6743; e-mail ghanaperm@aol.com; Permanent Representative KEN KANDA.

Greece: 866 Second Ave, 13th Floor, New York, NY 10017; tel. (212) 888-6900; fax (212) 888-4440; e-mail grdel.un@mfa.gr; internet www.greeceun.org; Permanent Representative ANASTASSIS MITSIALIS.

Grenada: 800 Second Ave, Suite 400K, New York, NY 10017; tel. (212) 599-0301; fax (212) 599-1540; e-mail grenada@un.int; Permanent Representative DESSIMA M. WILLIAMS.

Guatemala: 57 Park Ave, New York, NY 10016; tel. (212) 679-4760; fax (212) 685-8741; e-mail guatemala@un.int; internet www.guatemalaun.org; Permanent Representative GERT ROSENTHAL.

Guinea: 140 East 39th St, New York, NY 10016; tel. (212) 687-8115; fax (212) 687-8248; e-mail missionofguinea@aol.com; Permanent Representative MAMADOU TOURÉ.

Guinea-Bissau: 866 United Nations Plaza, Suite 481, New York, NY 10017; tel. (212) 896-8311; fax (212) 896-8313; e-mail guinea-bissau@un.int; Permanent Representative JOÃO SOARES DA GAMA.

Guyana: 801 Second Ave, 5th Floor, New York, NY 10017; tel. (212) 573-5828; fax (212) 573-6225; e-mail guyana@un.int; Permanent Representative GEORGE WILFRIED TALBOT.

Haiti: 801 Second Ave, Rm 600, New York, NY 10017; tel. (212) 370-4840; fax (212) 661-8698; e-mail haiti@un.int; Chargé d'affaires a.i. JEAN WESLEY CAZEAU.

Honduras: 866 United Nations Plaza, Suite 417, New York, NY 10017; tel. (212) 752-3370; fax (212) 223-0498; e-mail honduras_un@hotmail.com; internet www.un.int/honduras; Permanent Representative MARY ELIZABETH FLORES FLAKE.

Hungary: 227 East 52nd St, New York, NY 10022; tel. (212) 752-0209; fax (212) 755-5395; e-mail hungary@un.int; Permanent Representative CSABA KÖRÖSI.

Iceland: 800 Third Ave, 36th Floor, New York, NY 10022; tel. (212) 593-2700; fax (212) 593-6269; e-mail unmission@mfa.is; Permanent Representative GRÉTA GUNNARSDÓTTIR.

India: 235 East 43rd St, New York, NY 10017; tel. (212) 490-9660; fax (212) 490-9656; e-mail india@un.int; internet www.un.int/india; Permanent Representative HARDEEP SINGH PURI.

Indonesia: 325 East 38th St, New York, NY 10016; tel. (212) 972-8333; fax (212) 972-9780; e-mail ptri@indonesiamission-ny.org; internet www.indonesiamission-ny.org; Permanent Representative DESRA PERCAYA.

Iran: 622 Third Ave, 34th Floor, New York, NY 10017; tel. (212) 687-2020; fax (212) 867-7086; e-mail iran@un.int; internet www.un.int/iran; Permanent Representative MOHAMMAD KHAZAEE.

Iraq: 14 East 79th St, New York, NY 10075; tel. (212) 737-4433; fax (212) 772-1794; e-mail iraqny@un.int; Permanent Representative HAMID AL-BAYATI.

Ireland: 885 Second Ave, 19th Floor, New York, NY 10017; tel. (212) 421-6934; fax (212) 752-4726; e-mail newyorkpmun@dfa.ie; internet www.irelandunnewyork.org; Permanent Representative ANNE ANDERSON.

Israel: 800 Second Ave, New York, NY 10017; tel. (212) 499-5510; fax (212) 499-5516; e-mail info-un@newyork.mfa.gov.il; internet www.israel-un.org; Permanent Representative RON PROSOR.

Italy: One Dag Hammarskjöld Plaza, 885 Second Ave, 49th Floor, New York, NY 10017; tel. (212) 486-9191; fax (212) 486-1036; e-mail info.italyun@esteri.it; internet www.italyun.esteri.it; Permanent Representative CESARE MARIA RAGAGLINI.

Jamaica: 767 Third Ave, 9th Floor, New York, NY 10017; tel. (212) 935-7509; fax (212) 935-7607; e-mail jamaica@un.int; internet www.un.int/jamaica; Permanent Representative RAYMOND OSBOURNE WOLFE.

Japan: 866 United Nations Plaza, 2nd Floor, New York, NY 10017; tel. (212) 223-4300; fax (212) 751-1966; e-mail p-m-j@dn.mofa.go.jp; Permanent Representative TSUNEO NISHIDA.

Jordan: 866 Second Ave, 4th Floor, New York, NY 10017; tel. (212) 832-9553; fax (212) 832-5346; e-mail missionun@jordanmissionun.com; Permanent Representative Prince ZEID RA'AD ZEID AL-HUSSEIN.

Kazakhstan: 3 Dag Hammarskjöld Plaza, 305 East 47th St, 3rd Floor, New York, NY 10017; tel. (212) 230-1900; fax (212) 230-

1172; e-mail kazakhstan@un.int; internet www.kazakhstanun.org; Permanent Representative BYRGANYM AITIMOVA.

Kenya: 866 United Nations Plaza, Rm 304, New York, NY 10017; tel. (212) 421-4740; fax (212) 486-1985; e-mail info@kenyaun.org; Permanent Representative MACHARIA KAMAU.

Korea, Democratic People's Republic: 820 Second Ave, 13th Floor, New York, NY 10017; tel. (212) 972-3105; fax (212) 972-3154; e-mail dpr.korea@verizon.net; Permanent Representative SIN SON HO.

Korea, Republic: 335 East 45th St, New York, NY 10017; tel. (212) 439-4000; fax (212) 986-1083; e-mail korea@un.int; internet un.mofat.go.kr; Permanent Representative KIM SOOK.

Kuwait: 321 East 44th St, New York, NY 10017; tel. (212) 973-4300; fax (212) 370-1733; e-mail kuwaitmission@msn.com; internet www.kuwaitmission.com; Permanent Representative MANSOUR AYYAD AL-OTAIBI.

Kyrgyzstan: 866 United Nations Plaza, Suite 477, New York, NY 10017; tel. (212) 486-4214; fax (212) 486-5259; e-mail kyrgyzstan@un.int; internet www.un.int/kyrgyzstan; Permanent Representative TALAIBEK KYDYROV.

Laos: 317 East 51st St, New York, NY 10022; tel. (212) 832-2734; fax (212) 750-0039; e-mail lao@un.int; Permanent Representative SALEUMXAY KOMMASITH.

Latvia: 333 East 50th St, New York, NY 10022; tel. (212) 838-8877; fax (212) 838-8920; e-mail mission.un-ny@mfa.gov.lv; Permanent Representative NORMANS PENKE.

Lebanon: 866 United Nations Plaza, Rm 531–533, New York, NY 10017; tel. (212) 355-5460; fax (212) 838-2819; e-mail contact@lebanonun.org; internet www.un.int/lebanon; Permanent Representative NAWAF A. SALAM.

Lesotho: 204 East 39th St, New York, NY 10016; tel. (212) 661-1690; fax (212) 682-4388; e-mail lesotho@un.int; Chargé d'affaires a.i. MAFIROANE EDMOND MOTANYANE.

Liberia: 866 United Nations Plaza, Suite 480, New York, NY 10017; tel. (212) 687-1033; fax (212) 687-1035; e-mail liberia@un.int; Permanent Representative MARJON V. KAMARA.

Libya: 309–315 East 48th St, New York, NY 10017; tel. (212) 752-5775; fax (212) 593-4787; e-mail libyanmis2011@yahoo.com; internet www.libyanmission-un.org; Permanent Representative ABDURRAHMAN MOHAMED SHALGHAM.

Liechtenstein: 633 Third Ave, 27th Floor, New York, NY 10017; tel. (212) 599-0220; fax (212) 599-0064; e-mail mission@nyc.llv.li; internet www.un.int/liechtenstein; Permanent Representative CHRISTIAN WENAWESER.

Lithuania: 708 Third Ave, 10th Floor, New York, NY 10018; tel. (212) 983-9474; fax (212) 983-9473; e-mail lithuania@un.int; internet mission-un-ny.mfa.lt; Permanent Representative DALIUS ČEKUOLIS.

Luxembourg: 17 Beekman Pl., New York, NY 10022; tel. (212) 935-3589; fax (212) 935-5896; e-mail newyork.rp@mae.etat.lu; internet www.un.int/luxembourg; Permanent Representative SYLVIE LUCAS.

Macedonia, former Yugoslav republic: 866 United Nations Plaza, Suite 517, New York, NY 10017; tel. (212) 308-8504; fax (212) 308-8724; e-mail newyork@mfa.gov.mk; Permanent Representative PAJO AVIROVIKJ.

Madagascar: 820 Second Ave, Suite 800, New York, NY 10017; tel. (212) 986-9491; fax (212) 986-6271; e-mail repermad@verizon.net; Permanent Representative ZINA ANDRIANARIVELO-RAZAFY.

Malawi: 866 United Nations Plaza, Suite 486, New York, NY 10017; tel. (212) 317-8738; fax (212) 317-8729; e-mail malawinewyork@aol.com; Permanent Representative BRIAN G. BOWLER.

Malaysia: 313 East 43rd St, New York, NY 10017; tel. (212) 986-6310; fax (212) 490-8576; e-mail malnyun@kln.gov.my; internet www.un.int/malaysia; Permanent Representative HANIFF HUSSEIN.

Maldives: 800 Second Ave, Suite 400E, New York, NY 10017; tel. (212) 599-6195; fax (212) 661-6405; e-mail info@maldivesmission.com; internet www.maldivesmission.com; Chargé d'affaires a.i. AHMED SAREER.

Mali: 111 East 69th St, New York, NY 10021; tel. (212) 737-4150; fax (212) 472-3778; e-mail malionu@aol.com; internet www.un.int/mali; Permanent Representative OUMAR DAOU.

Malta: 249 East 35th St, New York, NY 10016; tel. (212) 725-2345; fax (212) 779-7097; e-mail malta-un.newyork@gov.mt; Permanent Representative CHRISTOPHER GRIMA.

Marshall Islands: 800 Second Ave, 18th Floor, New York, NY 10017; tel. (212) 983-3040; fax (212) 983-3202; e-mail marshallislands@un.int; internet marshallislands.un.int; Chargé d'affaires a.i. RINA M.L TAREO.

Mauritania: 116 East 38th St, New York, NY 10016; tel. (212) 252-0113; fax (212) 252-0175; e-mail mauritaniamission@gmail.com; Permanent Representative AHMED OULD TEGUEDI.

Mauritius: 211 East 43rd St, 15th Floor, Suite 1502, New York, NY 10017; tel. (212) 949-0190; fax (212) 697-3829; e-mail onuusr1@sre.gob.mx; internet www.sre.gob.mx/onu; Permanent Representative MILAN JAYA NYAMRAJSINGH MEETARBHAN.

Mexico: Two United Nations Plaza, 28th Floor, New York, NY 10017; tel. (212) 752-0220; fax (212) 688-8862; e-mail mexico@un.int; internet www.sre.gob.mx/onu; Permanent Representative LUIS ALFONSO DE ALBA GÓNGORA.

Micronesia, Federated States: 820 Second Ave, Suite 17A, New York, NY 10017; tel. (212) 697-8370; fax (212) 697-8295; e-mail fsmun@fsmgov.org; internet www.fsmgov.org/fsmun; Permanent Representative JANE JIMMY CHIGIYAL.

Moldova: 35 East 29th St, New York, NY 10016; tel. (212) 447-1867; fax (212) 447-4067; e-mail unmoldova@aol.com; internet www.onu.mfa.md; Permanent Representative VLADIMIR LUPAN.

Monaco: 866 United Nations Plaza, Suite 520, New York, NY 10017; tel. (212) 832-0721; fax (212) 832-5358; e-mail monaco@un.int; Permanent Representative ISABELLE F. PICCO.

Mongolia: 6 East 77th St, New York, NY 10075; tel. (212) 737-3874; fax (212) 861-9464; e-mail mongolia@un.int; internet www.un.int/mongolia; Permanent Representative OCHIR ENKHTSETSEG.

Montenegro: 801 Second Ave, 7th Floor, New York, NY 10017; tel. (212) 661-3700; fax (212) 661-3755; e-mail un.newyork@mfa.gov.me; Permanent Representative MILORAD ŠĆEPANOVIĆ.

Morocco: 866 Second Ave, 6th and 7th Floors, New York, NY 10017; tel. (212) 421-1580; fax (212) 980-1512; e-mail info@morocco-un.org; Permanent Representative MOHAMMED LOULICHKI.

Mozambique: 420 East 50th St, New York, NY 10022; tel. (212) 644-5965; fax (212) 644-5972; e-mail mozambique@un.int; Permanent Representative ANTÓNIO GUMENDE.

Myanmar: 10 East 77th St, New York, NY 10075; tel. (212) 744-1271; fax (212) 744-1290; e-mail myanmarmission@verizon.net; Permanent Representative U THAN SWE.

Namibia: 360 Lexington Ave, Suite 1502, New York, NY 10017; tel. (212) 685-2003; fax (212) 685-1561; e-mail namibia@un.int; Permanent Representative WILFRIED INOTIRA EMVULA.

Nauru: 801 Second Ave, Third Floor, New York, NY 10017; tel. (212) 937-0074; fax (212) 937-0079; e-mail nauru@un.int; internet www.un.int/nauru; Permanent Representative MARLENE INEMWIN MOSES.

Nepal: 820 Second Ave, Suite 17B, New York, NY 10017; tel. (212) 370-3988; fax (212) 953-2038; e-mail nepal@un.int; internet www.un.int/nepal; Permanent Representative GYAN CHANDRA ACHARYA.

Netherlands: 235 East 45th St, 16th Floor, New York, NY 10017; tel. (212) 519-9500; fax (212) 370-1954; e-mail nyv@minbuza.nl; internet www.netherlandsmission.org; Permanent Representative HERMAN SCHAPER.

New Zealand: 600 Third Ave, 14th Floor, New York, NY 10016; tel. (212) 826-1960; fax (212) 758-0827; e-mail nzmissionny@earthlink.net; internet www.nzmissionny.org; Permanent Representative JIM MCLAY.

Nicaragua: 820 Second Ave, 8th Floor, New York, NY 10017; tel. (212) 490-7997; fax (212) 286-0815; e-mail nicaragua@un.int; internet www.un.int/nicaragua; Permanent Representative MARÍA RUBIALES DE CHAMORRO.

Niger: 417 East 50th St, New York, NY 10022; tel. (212) 421-3260; fax (212) 753-6931; e-mail niger@ymail.com; Permanent Representative BOUBACAR BOUREIMA.

Nigeria: 828 Second Ave, New York, NY 10017; tel. (212) 953-9130; fax (212) 697-1970; e-mail permny@nigeriaunmission.org; internet nigeriaunmission.org; Permanent Representative U. JOY OGWU.

Norway: 825 Third Ave, 39th Floor, New York, NY 10022; tel. (646) 430-7510; fax (646) 430-7591; e-mail delun@mfa.no; internet www.un.norway-un.org; Permanent Representative MORTEN WETLAND.

Oman: 3 Dag Hammarskjöld Plaza, 305 East 47th St, 12th Floor, New York, NY 10017; tel. (212) 355-3505; fax (212) 644-0070; e-mail oman@un.int; Permanent Representative LYUTHA S. AL-MUGHAIRY.

Pakistan: 8 East 65th St, New York, NY 10021; tel. (212) 879-8600; fax (212) 744-7348; e-mail pakistan@un.int; internet www.pakun.org; Permanent Representative ABDULLAH HUSSAIN HAROON.

Palau: 866 United Nations Plaza, Suite 575, New York, NY 10017; tel. (212) 813-0310; fax (212) 813-0317; e-mail mission@palauun.org; internet www.palauun.org; Permanent Representative STUART BECK.

Panama: 866 United Nations Plaza, Suite 4030, New York, NY 10017; tel. (212) 421-5420; fax (212) 421-2694; e-mail emb@panama-un.org; internet www.panama-un.org; Permanent Representative PABLO ANTONIO THALASSINÓS.

Papua New Guinea: 201 East 42nd St, Suite 405, New York, NY 10017; tel. (212) 557-5001; fax (212) 557-5009; e-mail pngmission@pngun.org; Permanent Representative ROBERT GUBA AISI.

Paraguay: 801 Second Ave, Suite 702, New York, NY 10017; tel. (212) 687-3490; fax (212) 818-1282; e-mail paraguay@un.int; Permanent Representative JOSÉ ANTONIO DOS SANTOS.

Peru: 820 Second Ave, Suite 1600, New York, NY 10017; tel. (212) 687-3336; fax (212) 972-6975; e-mail onuper@unperu.org; internet www.un.int/peru; Permanent Representative ENRIQUE ROMÁN-MOREY.

Philippines: 556 Fifth Ave, 5th Floor, New York, NY 10036; tel. (212) 764-1300; fax (212) 840-8602; e-mail newyorkpm@gmail.com; internet www.un.int/philippines; Permanent Representative LIBRAN N. CABACTULAN.

Poland: 750 Third Ave, 30th Floor New York, NY 10017; tel. (212) 744-2506; fax (212) 517-6771; e-mail nowyjork.onz.sekretariat@msz.gov.pl; internet www.un.polemb.net; Permanent Representative WITOLD SOBKÓW.

Portugal: 866 Second Ave, 9th Floor, New York, NY 10017; tel. (212) 759-9444; fax (212) 355-1124; e-mail portugal@missionofportugal.org; internet www.un.int/portugal; Permanent Representative JOSÉ FILIPE MENDES MORAES CABRAL.

Qatar: 809 United Nations Plaza, 4th Floor, New York, NY 10017; tel. (212) 486-9335; fax (212) 758-4952; e-mail pmun@mofa.gov.qa; Permanent Representative MESHAL HAMAD MOHAMED JABR AL-THANI.

Romania: 573–577 Third Ave, New York, NY 10016; tel. (212) 682-3273; fax (212) 682-9746; e-mail misiune@romaniaun.org; internet www.mpnewyork.mae.ro; Permanent Representative SIMONA MIRELA MICULESCU.

Russia: 136 East 67th St, New York, NY 10065; tel. (212) 861-4900; fax (212) 628-0252; e-mail rusun@un.int; internet www.russiaun.ru; Permanent Representative VITALII I. CHURKIN.

Rwanda: 370 Lexington Ave, Suite 401, New York, NY 10017; tel. (212) 679-9010; fax (212) 679-9133; e-mail ambanewyork@minaffet.gov.rw; Permanent Representative EUGÈNE-RICHARD GASANA.

Saint Christopher and Nevis: 414 East 75th St, 5th Floor, New York, NY 10021; tel. (212) 535-1234; fax (212) 535-6854; e-mail sknmission@aol.com; Permanent Representative DELANO FRANK BART.

Saint Lucia: 800 Second Ave, 9th Floor, New York, NY 10017; tel. (212) 697-9360; fax (212) 697-4993; e-mail info@stluciamission.org; Permanent Representative MENISSA RAMBALLY.

Saint Vincent and the Grenadines: 800 Second Ave, Suite 400G, New York, NY 10017; tel. (212) 599-0950; fax (212) 599-1020; e-mail mission@svg-un.org; Permanent Representative CAMILLO M. GONSALVES.

Samoa: 800 Second Ave, Suite 400J, New York, NY 10017; tel. (212) 599-6196; fax (212) 599-0797; e-mail www.samoa@un.int; Permanent Representative ALI'IOAIGA FETURI ELISAIA.

San Marino: 327 East 50th St, New York, NY 10022; tel. (212) 751-1234; fax (212) 751-1436; e-mail sanmarinoun@hotmail.com; Permanent Representative DANIELE BODINI.

São Tomé and Príncipe: (temporarily closed); tel. (202) 415-7606; fax (202) 775-2077; e-mail embstpusa1@verizon.net; Permanent Representative OVIDIO MANUEL BARBOSA PEQUENO.

Saudi Arabia: 809 United Nations Plaza, 10th and 11th Floors, New York, NY 10017; tel. (212) 557-1525; fax (212) 983-4895; e-mail saudi-mission@un.int; Permanent Representative ABDULLAH YAHYA AL-MOUALLIMI.

Senegal: 747 Third Ave, 21st Floor (46th & 47th St), New York, NY 10017; tel. (212) 517-9030; fax (212) 517-3032; e-mail senegal.mission@yahoo.fr; Permanent Representative ABDOU SALAM DIALLO.

Serbia: 854 Fifth Ave, New York, NY 10065; tel. (212) 879-8700; fax (212) 879-8705; e-mail info@serbiamissionun.org; internet www.un.int/serbia; Permanent Representative FEODOR STARČEVIĆ.

Seychelles: 800 Second Ave, Suite 400C, New York, NY 10017; tel. (212) 972-1785; fax (212) 972-1786; e-mail seychelles@un.int; Permanent Representative RONALD JEAN JUMEAU.

Sierra Leone: 245 East 49th St, New York, NY 10017; tel. (212) 688-1656; fax (212) 688-4924; e-mail sierraleone@un.int; Permanent Representative SHEKOU MOMODOU TOURAY.

Singapore: 231 East 51st St, New York, NY 10022; tel. (212) 826-0840; fax (212) 826-2964; e-mail singapore@un.int; internet www.mfa.gov.sg/newyork; Permanent Representative ALBERT CHUA.

Slovakia: 801 Second Ave, 12th Floor, New York, NY 10017; tel. (212) 286-8418; fax (212) 286-8419; e-mail un.newyork@mzv.sk; internet www.msv.sk/unnewyork; Chargé d'affaires a.i. MANUEL KORČEK.

Slovenia: 600 Third Ave, 24th Floor, New York, NY 10016; tel. (212) 370-3007; fax (212) 370-1824; e-mail slovenia@un.int; internet www.un.int/slovenia; Permanent Representative SANJA ŠTIGLIC.

Solomon Islands: 800 Second Ave, Suite 400L, New York, NY 10017; tel. (212) 599-6193; fax (212) 661-8925; e-mail simun@solomons.com; Permanent Representative COLLIN D. BECK.

Somalia: 425 East 61st St, Suite 702, New York, NY 10065; tel. (212) 688-9410; fax (212) 759-0651; e-mail somalia@un.int; Permanent Representative ELMI AHMED DUALE.

South Africa: 333 East 38th St, 9th Floor, New York, NY 10016; tel. (212) 213-5583; fax (212) 692-2498; e-mail pmun.newyork@foreign.gov.za; Permanent Representative BASU SANGQU.

South Sudan: 336 East 45th St, 5th Floor, New York, NY 10017; tel. (917) 601-2376; fax (202) 293-7941; e-mail elgatkuoth@gossmission.org; Chargé d'affaires a.i. FRANCIS GEORGE NAZARIO.

Spain: One Dag Hammarskjöld Plaza, 245 East 47th St, 36th Floor, New York, NY 10017; tel. (212) 661-1050; fax (212) 949-7247; e-mail rep.nuevayorkonu@maec.es; internet www.spainun.org; Permanent Representative FERNANDO ARIAS.

Sri Lanka: 630 Third Ave, 20th Floor, New York, NY 10017; tel. (212) 986-7040; fax (212) 986-1838; e-mail mail@slmission.com; internet www.slmission.com; Permanent Representative PALITHA T. B. KOHONA.

Sudan: 305 East 47th St, 3 Dag Hammarskjöld Plaza, 4th Floor, New York, NY 10017; tel. (212) 573-6033; fax (212) 573-6160; e-mail sudan@sudanmission.org; Permanent Representative DAFFA-ALLA ELHAG ALI OSMAN.

Suriname: 866 United Nations Plaza, Suite 320, New York, NY 10017; tel. (212) 826-0660; fax (212) 980-7029; e-mail suriname@un.int; Permanent Representative HENRY LEONARD MACDONALD.

Swaziland: 408 East 50th St, New York, NY 10022; tel. (212) 371-8910; fax (212) 754-2755; e-mail swazinymission@yahoo.com; Permanent Representative ZWELETHU MNISI.

Sweden: One Dag Hammarskjöld Plaza, 885 Second Ave, 46th Floor, New York, NY 10017; tel. (212) 583-2500; fax (212) 583-2549; e-mail sweden@un.int; internet www.un.int/sweden; Permanent Representative MÅRTEN GRUNDITZ.

Switzerland: 633 Third Ave, 29th Floor, New York, NY 10017; tel. (212) 286-1540; fax (212) 286-1555; e-mail vertretung-un@nyc.rep.admin.ch; internet www.eda.admin.ch/missny; Permanent Representative PAUL R. SEGER.

Syria: 820 Second Ave, 15th Floor, New York, NY 10017; tel. (212) 661-1313; fax (212) 983-4439; e-mail exesec.syria@gmail.com; internet www.syria-un.org; Permanent Representative BASHAR JA'AFARI.

Tajikistan: 216 East 49th St, 4th Floor, New York, NY 10017; tel. (212) 207-3315; fax (212) 207-3855; e-mail tajikistan@un.int; Permanent Representative SIRODJIDIN MUKHRIDINOVICH ASLOV.

Tanzania: 201 East 42nd St, Suite 425, New York, NY 10017; tel. (212) 697-3612; fax (212) 697-3618; e-mail tzrepny@aol.com; Chargé d'affaires a.i. JUSTIN N. SERUHERE.

Thailand: 351 East 52nd St, New York, NY 10022; tel. (212) 754-2230; fax (212) 688-3029; e-mail thailand@un.int; Permanent Representative NORACHIT SINHASENI.

Timor-Leste: 866 Second Ave, Suite 441, New York, NY 10017; tel. (212) 759-3675; fax (212) 759-4196; e-mail timor-leste@un.int; Permanent Representative SOFIA MESQUÍTA BORGES.

Togo: 336 East 45th St, New York, NY 10017; tel. (212) 490-3455; fax (212) 983-6684; e-mail togo@un.int; Permanent Representative KODJO MENAN.

Tonga: 250 East 51st St, New York, NY 10022; tel. (917) 369-1025; fax (917) 369-1024; e-mail tongaunmission@gmail.com; Permanent Representative SONATANE TU'AKINAMOLAHI TAUMOEPEAU-TUPOU.

Trinidad and Tobago: 122 East 42nd St, 39th Floor, New York, NY 10017; tel. (212) 697-7620; fax (212) 682-3580; e-mail tto@un.int; internet www.un.int/trinidadandtobago; Permanent Representative RODNEY CHARLES.

Tunisia: 31 Beekman Pl., New York, NY 10022; tel. (212) 751-7503; fax (212) 751-0569; e-mail tunisnyc@nyc.rr.com; Permanent Representative OTHMAN JERANDI.

Turkey: 821 United Nations Plaza, 10th Floor, New York, NY 10017; tel. (212) 949-0150; fax (212) 949-0086; e-mail tr-delegation.newyork@mfa.gov.tr; internet www.turkuno.dt.mfa.gov.tr; Permanent Representative ERTUĞRUL APAKAN.

Turkmenistan: 866 United Nations Plaza, Suite 424, New York, NY 10017; tel. (212) 486-8908; fax (212) 486-2521; e-mail turkmenistan@un.int; Permanent Representative Dr AKSOLTAN T. ATAYEVA.

Tuvalu: 800 Second Ave, Suite 400D, New York, NY 10017; tel. (212) 490-0534; fax (212) 808-4975; e-mail tuvalu@onecommonwealth.org; Permanent Representative AFELEE F. PITA.

Uganda: 336 East 45th St, New York, NY 10017; tel. (212) 949-0110; fax (212) 687-4517; e-mail ugandaunny@un.int; internet ugandamissionunny.net; Chargé d'affaires a.i. ADONIA AYEBARE.

Ukraine: 220 East 51st St, New York, NY 10022; tel. (212) 759-7003; fax (212) 355-9455; e-mail uno_us@mfa.gov.ua; internet www.mfa.gov.ua/uno; Permanent Representative YURIY A. SERGEYEV.

United Arab Emirates: 3 Dag Hammarskjöld Plaza, 305 East 47th St, 7th Floor, New York, NY 10017; tel. (212) 371-0480; fax (212) 371-4923; e-mail uae@uaemission.com; Permanent Representative AHMED ABDULRAHMAN AL-JERMAN.

United Kingdom: One Dag Hammarskjöld Plaza, 885 Second Ave, New York, NY 10017; tel. (212) 745-9200; fax (212) 745-9316; e-mail uk@un.int; internet ukun.fco.gov.uk/en; Permanent Representative Sir MARK LYALL GRANT.

USA: 799 United Nations Plaza, New York, NY 10017; tel. (212) 415-4000; fax (212) 415-4443; e-mail usunpublicaffairs@state.gov; internet www.usunnewyork.usmission.gov; Permanent Representative SUSAN RICE.

Uruguay: 866 United Nations Plaza, Suite 322, New York, NY 10017; tel. (212) 752-8240; fax (212) 593-0935; e-mail uruguay@un.int; internet www.un.int/uruguay; Permanent Representative JOSÉ LUIS CANCELA GÓMEZ.

Uzbekistan: 801 Second Ave, 20th Floor, New York, NY 10017; tel. (212) 486-4242; fax (212) 486-7998; e-mail uzbekistan.un@gmail.com; Permanent Representative MURAD ASKAROV.

Vanuatu: 800 Second Ave, Suite 400B, New York, NY 10017; tel. (212) 661-4303; fax (212) 661-5544; e-mail vanunmis@aol.com; Permanent Representative DONALD KALPOKAS.

Venezuela: 335 East 46th St, New York, NY 10017; tel. (212) 557-2055; fax (212) 557-3528; e-mail missionvene@venezuela.gob.ve; Permanent Representative JORGE VALERO BRICEÑO.

Viet Nam: 866 United Nations Plaza, Suite 435, New York, NY 10017; tel. (212) 644-0594; fax (212) 644-5732; e-mail info@vietnam-un.org; internet www.un.int/vietnam; Permanent Representative LE HOAI TRUNG.

Yemen: 413 East 51st St, New York, NY 10022; tel. (212) 355-1730; fax (212) 750-9613; e-mail ymiss-newyork@mofa.gov.ye; Permanent Representative JAMAL ABDULLAH AL-SALLAL.

Zambia: 237 East 52nd St, New York, NY 10022; tel. (212) 888-5770; fax (212) 888-5213; e-mail zambia@un.int; internet www.un.int/zambia; Permanent Representative MWABA PATRICIA KASESE-BOTA.

Zimbabwe: 128 East 56th St, New York, NY 10022; tel. (212) 980-9511; fax (212) 308-6705; e-mail zimnewyork@gmail.com; Permanent Representative CHITSAKA CHIPAZIWA.

OBSERVERS

Intergovernmental organizations, etc., which have received an invitation to participate in the sessions and the work of the General Assembly as Observers, maintaining permanent offices at the UN:

African Union: 305 East 47th St, 5th Floor, 3 Dag Hammarskjöld Plaza, New York, NY 10017; tel. (212) 319-5490; fax (212) 319-7135; e-mail aumission_ny@yahoo.com; internet www.africa-union.org; Permanent Observer TÉTE ANTÓNIO.

Asian-African Legal Consultative Organization: 188 East 76th St, Apt 26B, New York, NY 10021; tel. (917) 623-2861; fax (206) 426-5442; e-mail aalco@un.int; Permanent Observer ROY LEE.

Caribbean Community (CARICOM): 88 Burnett Ave, Maplewood, NJ 07040; tel. (973) 378-9333; fax (973) 327-2671; e-mail caripoun@gmail.com; Permanent Observer NOEL SINCLAIR.

Central American Integration System: 320 West 75th St, Suite 1A, New York, NY 10023; tel. (212) 682-1550; fax (212) 877-9021; e-mail ccampos@sgsica-ny.org; Permanent Observer CARLOS CAMPOS.

Commonwealth Secretariat: 800 Second Ave, 4th Floor, New York, NY 10017; tel. (212) 599-6190; fax (212) 808-4975; e-mail comsec@thecommonwealth.org.

Cooperation Council for the Arab States of the Gulf: One Dag Hammarskjöld Plaza, 885 Second Ave, 40th Floor, New York, NY 10017; tel. (212) 319-3088; fax (212) 319-3434; Permanent Observer ADNAN AHMED ABDULLAH AL-ANSARI.

European Union: 222 East 41st St, 20th Floor, New York, NY 10017; tel. (212) 371-3804; fax (212) 758-2718; e-mail delegation-new-york@ec.europa.eu; internet www.europa-eu-un.org; the Observer is the Permanent Representative to the UN of the country currently exercising the Presidency of the Council of Ministers of the European Union; Head of Delegation THOMAS MAYR-HARTING.

Holy See: 25 East 39th St, New York, NY 10016; tel. (212) 370-7885; fax (212) 370-9622; e-mail office@holyseemission.org; internet www.holyseemission.org; Permanent Observer Most Rev. FRANCIS ASSISI CHULLIKATT (Titular Archbishop of Ostra).

International Committee of the Red Cross: 801 Second Ave, 18th Floor, New York, NY 10017; tel. (212) 599-6021; fax (212)

599-6009; e-mail newyork@icrc.org; Head of Delegation WALTER A. FÜLLEMANN.

International Criminal Court: 866 United Nations Plaza, Suite 476, New York, NY 10017; tel. (212) 486-1362; fax (212) 486-1361; e-mail liaisonofficeny@icc-cpi.int; Head of Liaison Office KAREN ODABA MOSOTI.

International Criminal Police Organization (INTERPOL): One United Nations Plaza, Suite 2610, New York, NY 10017; tel. (917) 367-3463; fax (917) 367-3476; e-mail c.perrin@interpol.int; Special Representative WILLIAM J. S. ELLIOTT (Canada).

International Development Law Organization: 336 East 45th St, 11th Floor, New York, NY 10017; tel. (212) 867-9707; fax (212) 867-9717; e-mail pcivili@idlo.int; Permanent Observer PATRIZIO M. CIVILI.

International Federation of Red Cross and Red Crescent Societies: 420 Lexington Ave, Suite 2811, New York, NY 10017; tel. (212) 338-0161; fax (212) 338-9832; e-mail ifrcny@un.int; Head of Delegation and Permanent Observer MARWAN JILANI.

International Institute for Democracy and Electoral Assistance: 336 East 45th St, 14th Floor, New York, NY 10017; tel. (212) 286-1084; fax (212) 286-0260; e-mail unobserver@idea.int; Permanent Observer MASSIMO TOMMASOLI.

International Olympic Committee: 708 Third Ave, 6th Floor, New York, NY 10017; tel. (212) 209-3952; fax (212) 209-7100; e-mail IOC-UNObserver@olympic.org; Permanent Observer MARIO PESCANTE.

International Organization for Migration: 122 East 42nd St, Suite 1610, New York, NY 10168; tel. (212) 681-7000; fax (212) 867-5887; e-mail unobserver@iom.int; internet www.un.int/iom; Permanent Observer MICHELE KLEIN-SOLOMON.

International Organization of La Francophonie (Organisation Internationale de la Francophonie): 801 Second Ave, Suite 605, New York, NY 10017; tel. (212) 867-6771; fax (212) 867-3840; e-mail francophonie@un.int; Permanent Observer FILIPE SAVADOGO.

International Renewable Energy Agency: 336 East 45th St, 11th Floor, New York, NY 10017; tel. (212) 867-9707; fax (212) 867-9719; internet www.irena.org.

International Seabed Authority: One United Nations Plaza, Rm 1140, New York, NY 10017; tel. (212) 963-6470; fax (212) 963-0908; e-mail seaun@un.org; Permanent Observer NII ALLOTEY ODUNTON.

International Tribunal for the Law of the Sea: Two United Nations Plaza, Rm 438, New York, NY 10017; tel. (212) 963-6140; fax (212) 963-5847; Permanent Observer SHUNJI YANAI (Pres. of the Tribunal).

Inter-Parliamentary Union: 336 East 45th St, 10th Floor, New York, NY 10017; tel. (212) 557-5880; fax (212) 557-3954; e-mail ny-office@mail.ipu.org; Permanent Observer ANDA FILIP.

International Union for Conservation of Nature (IUCN): 551 Fifth Ave, Suites 800 A-B, New York, NY 10176; tel. (212) 346-1163; fax (212) 346-1046; e-mail iucn@un.int; internet www.iucn.org; Permanent Observer NARINDER KAKAR (India).

League of Arab States: 866 United Nations Plaza, Suite 494, New York, NY 10017; tel. (212) 838-8700; fax (212) 355-3909; e-mail arableague@un.int; Permanent Observer (vacant).

Organization of Islamic Cooperation: 320 East 51st St, New York, NY 10022; tel. (212) 883-0140; fax (212) 883-0143; e-mail oicny@un.int; internet www.oicun.org; Permanent Observer UFUK GOKCEN.

Palestine: 115 East 65th St, New York, NY 10021; tel. (212) 288-8500; fax (212) 517-2377; e-mail palestine@un.int; internet www.un.int/palestine; Permanent Observer RIYAD H. MANSOUR.

Partners in Population and Development: 336 East 45th St, 14th Floor, New York, NY 10017; tel. (212) 286-1082; fax (212) 286-0260; e-mail srao@ppdsec.org; internet www.partners-popdev.org; Permanent Observer SETHURAMIAH L.N. RAO.

Sovereign Military Order of Malta: 216 East 47th St, 8th Floor, New York, NY 10017; tel. (212) 355-6213; fax (212) 355-4014; e-mail orderofmalta@un.int; Permanent Observer ROBERT L. SHAFER.

University for Peace: 551 Fifth Ave, Suites 800 A-B, New York, NY 10176; tel. (212) 346-1163; fax (212) 346-1046; e-mail nyinfo@upeace.org; internet www.upeace.org; Permanent Observer NARINDER KAKAR (India).

The following intergovernmental organizations have a standing invitation to participate as Observers, but do not maintain permanent offices at the United Nations: African, Caribbean and Pacific Group of States; African Development Bank; Agency for the Prohibition of Nuclear Weapons in Latin America and the Caribbean; Andean Community; Asian Development Bank; Association of Caribbean States; Association of Southeast Asian Nations; Collective Security Treaty Organization; Common Fund for Commodities; Commonwealth of Independent States; Communauté économique des états de l'Afrique centrale; Community of Sahel-Saharan States; Comunidade dos Países de Língua Portuguesa; Conference on Interaction and Confidence-building Measures in Asia; Council of Europe; East African Community; Economic Community of West African States; Economic Cooperation Organization; Energy Charter Conference; Eurasian Development Bank; Eurasian Economic Community; GUAM: Organization for Democracy and Economic Development; Hague Conference on Private International Law; Ibero-American General Secretariat; Global fund to Fight AIDS, Tuberculosis and Malaria; Indian Ocean Commission; Inter-American Development Bank; Intergovernmental Authority on Development; International Centre for Migration Policy Development; International Conference on the Great Lakes Region of Africa; International Fund for Saving the Aral Sea; International Humanitarian Fact-Finding Commission; International Hydrographic Organization; International Trade Union Confederation, Islamic Development Bank; Italian-Latin American Institute; Latin American Economic System; Latin American Integration Association; Latin American Parliament; OPEC Fund for International Development; Organisation for Economic Co-operation and Development; Organisation of Eastern Caribbean States; Organization for Security and Co-operation in Europe; Organization of American States; Organization of the Black Sea Economic Cooperation; Pacific Islands Forum; Parliamentary Assembly of the Mediterranean; Permanent Court of Arbitration; Regional Centre on Small Arms and Light Weapons in the Great Lakes Region, the Horn of Africa and Bordering States; Shanghai Cooperation Organization; South Asian Association for Regional Cooperation; South Centre; Southern African Development Community; Union of South American Nations; World Customs Organization.

United Nations Information Centres/Services

Algeria: POB 444, Hydre, Algiers; tel. and fax (21) 92 54 42; e-mail unic.dz@undp.org; internet algiers.unic.org.

Argentina: Junín 1940, 1°, 1113 Buenos Aires; tel. (11) 4803-7671; fax (11) 4804-7545; e-mail unic.buenosaires@unic.org; internet www.unic.org.ar; also covers Uruguay.

Armenia: 375010 Yerevan, 14 Petros Adamian St; tel. (10) 56-02-12; fax (10) 56-14-06; e-mail armineh.haladjian@unic.org; internet www.un.am.

Australia: POB 5366, Kingston, ACT 2604; tel. (2) 6270-9200; fax (2) 6273-8206; e-mail unic.canberra@unic.org; internet www.un.org.au; also covers Fiji, Kiribati, Nauru, New Zealand, Samoa, Tonga, Tuvalu and Vanuatu.

Austria: POB 500, Vienna International Centre, Wagramerstr. 5, 1400 Vienna; tel. (1) 26060-0; fax (1) 26060-5899; e-mail unis@unvienna.org; internet www.unis.unvienna.org; also covers Hungary, Slovakia and Slovenia.

Azerbaijan: 1001 Baku, UN 50th Anniversary St 3; tel. (12) 498-98-88; fax (12) 498-32-35; e-mail dpi@un-az.org; internet azerbaijan.unic.org.

Bahrain: POB 26814, UN House, Bldg 69, Rd 1901, Manama 319; tel. 17311676; fax 17311600; e-mail unic.manama@unic

.org; internet www.manama.unic.org; also covers Qatar and the United Arab Emirates.

Bangladesh: IDB Bhahan, 8th Floor, Rokeya Sharani Sher-e-Bangla Nagar, Dhaka 1207; tel. (2) 8117868; fax (2) 8129047; e-mail unic.dhaka@undp.org; internet www.unicdhaka.org.

Belarus: 220030 Minsk, vul. Kirova 17, 6th Floor; tel. (17) 227-38-17; fax (17) 226-03-40; e-mail dpi.staff.by@undp.org; internet www.un.by.

Bolivia: Calle 14 esq. Sánchez Bustamante, Ed. Metrobol II, Calacoto, La Paz; tel. (2) 2624512; fax (2) 2795820; e-mail unic.lapaz@unic.org; internet www.nu.org.bo.

Brazil: Palacio Itamaraty, Avda Marechal Floriano 196, 20080-002 Rio de Janeiro; tel. (21) 2253-2211; fax (21) 2233-5753; e-mail unic.brazil@unic.org; internet unicrio.org.br.

Burkina Faso: BP 135, 14 ave de la Grande Chancellerie, Secteur 4, Ouagadougou; tel. 50-30-60-76; fax 50-31-13-22; e-mail unic.ouagadougou@unic.org; internet ouagadougou.unic.org; also covers Chad, Mali and Niger.

Burundi: BP 2160, ave de la Révolution 117, Bujumbura; tel. (2) 225018; fax (2) 241798; e-mail unic.bujumbura@unic.org; internet bujumbura.unic.org.

Cameroon: PB 836, Immeuble Tchinda, rue 2044, Yaoundé; tel. 221-23-67; fax 221-23-68; e-mail unic.yaounde@unic.org; internet yaounde.unic.org; also covers the Central African Republic and Gabon.

Colombia: Calle 100, No. 8A-55, 10°, Edificio World Trade Center, Torre C, Bogotá 2; tel. (1) 257-6044; fax (1) 257-6244; e-mail unic.bogota@unic.org; internet www.nacionesunidas.org.co; also covers Ecuador and Venezuela.

Congo, Republic: POB 13210, ave Foch, Case ORTF 15, Brazzaville; tel. 661-20-68; e-mail unic.brazzaville@unic.org; internet brazzaville.unic.org.

Czech Republic: nam. Kinských 6, 150 00 Prague 5; tel. 257199831; fax 257316761; e-mail info@osn.cz; internet www.osn.cz.

Egypt: 1 Osiris St, Garden City, Cairo; tel. (2) 7900022; fax (2) 7953705; e-mail info@unic-eg.org; internet www.unic-eg.org; also covers Saudi Arabia.

Eritrea: Hiday St, Airport Rd, Asmara; tel. (1) 151166; fax (1) 151081; e-mail info.asmara@unic.org; internet asmara.unic.org.

Georgia: 0179 Tbilisi, Eristavi St 9; tel. (32) 25-11-26; fax (32) 25-02-71; e-mail uno.tbilisi@unic.org; internet www.ungeorgia.ge.

Ghana: POB GP 2339, Gamel Abdul Nassar/Liberia Rds, Accra; tel. (21) 665511; fax (21) 7010943; e-mail unic.accra@unic.org; internet accra.unic.org; also covers Sierra Leone.

India: 55 Lodi Estate, New Delhi 110 003; tel. (11) 46532242; fax (11) 24620293; e-mail unicindia@unicindia.org; internet www.unic.org.in; also covers Bhutan.

Indonesia: Gedung Surya, 14th Floor, 9 Jalan M. H. Thamrin Kavling, Jakarta 10350; tel. (21) 3983-1011; fax (21) 3983-1014; e-mail unic-jakarta@unic-jakarta.org; internet www.unic-jakarta.org.

Iran: POB 15875-4557; 8 Shahrzad Blvd, Darrous, Tehran; tel. (21) 2287-3837; fax (21) 2287-3395; e-mail unic.tehran@unic.org; internet www.unic-ir.org.

Japan: UNU Bldg, 8th Floor, 53–70 Jingumae 5-chome, Shibuya-ku, Tokyo 150 0001; tel. (3) 5467-4451; fax (3) 5467-4455; e-mail unic.tokyo@unic.org; internet www.unic.or.jp.

Kazakhstan: 67 Tole Bi Street, 050000 Almatı; tel. (727) 258-26-43; fax (727) 258-26-45; e-mail kazakhstan@unic.org; internet kazakhstan.unic.org.

Kenya: POB 30552, United Nations Office, Gigiri, Nairobi; tel. (20) 76225421; fax (20) 7624349; e-mail nairobi.unic@unon.org; internet www.unicnairobi.org; also covers Seychelles and Uganda.

Lebanon: UN House, Riad es-Solh Sq., POB 11-8575, Beirut; tel. (1) 981301; fax (1) 970424; e-mail unic-beirut@un.org; internet www.unicbeirut.org; also covers Jordan, Kuwait and Syria.

Lesotho: POB 301, Maseru 100; tel. (22) 313790; fax (22) 310042; e-mail unic.maseru@unic.org; internet maseru.unic.org.

Libya: POB 286, Khair Aldeen Baybers St, Hay al-Andalous, Tripoli; tel. (21) 4770251; fax (21) 4777343; e-mail tripoli@un.org; internet tripoli.unic.org.

Madagascar: 159 rue Damantsoa Ankorahotra, Antananarivo; tel. (20) 2233050; fax (20) 2236794; e-mail unic.ant@moov.mg; internet antananarivo.unic.org.

Mexico: Presidente Masaryk 29, 2°, Col. Chapultepec Morales, México 11 570, DF; tel. (55) 4000-9717; fax (55) 5203-8638; e-mail infounic@un.org.mx; internet www.cinu.mx; also covers Cuba and the Dominican Republic.

Morocco: BP 601; rue Tarik ibn Zyad 6, Rabat; tel. (3) 7768633; fax (3) 7768377; e-mail unicmor@unicmor.ma; internet www.unicmor.ma.

Myanmar: 6 Natmauk Rd, Tamwe P.O., Yangon; tel. (1) 546933; fax (1) 542634; e-mail unic.myanmar@undp.org; internet yangon.unic.org.

Namibia: Private Bag 13351, 38-44 Stein St, Windhoek; tel. (61) 2046111; fax (61) 2046521; e-mail unic.windhoek@unic.org; internet windhoek.unic.org.

Nepal: POB 107, UN House, Kathmandu; tel. (1) 5523200; fax (1) 5523991; e-mail unic.np@undp.org; internet kathmandu.unic.org.

Nigeria: 17 Alfred Rewane (formerly Kingsway) Rd, Ikoyi, Lagos; tel. (1) 7755989; fax (1) 4630916; e-mail lagos@unic.org; internet lagos.unic.org.

Pakistan: POB 1107, Serena Business Complex, G-5/1, Islamabad; tel. (51) 8355719; fax (51) 2271856; e-mail unic.islamabad@unic.org; internet www.unic.org.pk.

Panama: UN House Bldg 128, Ciudad del Saber, Clayton, Panama City; tel. (7) 301-0035; fax (7) 301-0037; e-mail unic.panama@unic.org; internet www.cinup.org.

Paraguay: Casilla de Correo 1107; Edif. Naciones Unidas, Avda Mariscal López, Asunción; tel. (21) 614443; fax (21) 611988; e-mail unic.py@undp.org; internet asuncion.unic.org.

Peru: POB 14-0199, Av. Perez Aranibar 750, Magdalena, Lima 17; tel. (1) 625-9140; fax (1) 625-9100; e-mail unic.lima@unic.org; internet www.uniclima.org.pe.

Philippines: POB 7285 ADC (DAPO), 1300 Domestic Rd, Pasay City, Metro Manila; tel. (2) 338-5520; fax (2) 338-0177; e-mail unic.manila@unic.org; internet www.unicmanila.org; also covers Papua New Guinea and Solomon Islands.

Poland: Al. Niepodległości 186; 00-608 Warsaw; tel. (22) 8255784; fax (22) 8257706; e-mail unic.poland@unic.org; internet www.unic.un.org.pl.

Romania: 011975 Bucharest, Bd. Primaverii 48A; tel. (21) 201-78-77; fax (21) 201-78-80; e-mail unic.romania@unic.org; internet www.onuinfo.ro.

Russia: 119002 Moscow, per. Glazovskii 4/16; tel. (499) 241-28-94; fax (495) 695-21-38; e-mail dpi-moscow@unic.ru; internet www.unic.ru.

Senegal: Immeuble SOUMEX, 3rd Floor, Mamelles, Almadies, Dakar; tel. 869-99-11; fax 860-51-48; e-mail unic.dakar@unic.org; internet dakar.unic.org; also covers Cape Verde, Côte d'Ivoire, The Gambia, Guinea-Bissau and Mauritania.

South Africa: Metro Park Bldg, 351 Schoeman St, POB 12677, Pretoria 0126; tel. (12) 354-8506; fax (12) 354-8501; e-mail unic.pretoria@unic.org; internet pretoria.unic.org.

Sri Lanka: POB 1505, 202/204 Bauddhaloka Mawatha, Colombo 7; tel. (11) 2580691; fax (11) 2501396; e-mail unic.colombo@unic.org; internet colombo.unic.org.

Sudan: POB 1992, UN Compound, House No. 7, Blk 5, Gamma'a Ave, Khartoum; tel. (183) 783755; fax (183) 773772; e-mail unic.sd@undp.org; internet khartoum.unic.org; also covers Somalia.

Switzerland: Palais des Nations, 1211 Geneva 10; tel. 229172302; fax 229170030; e-mail press_geneva@unog.ch; internet www.unog.ch.

Tanzania: POB 9224, International House, 6th Floor, Garden Ave/Shaaban Robert St, Dar es Salaam; tel. (22) 2199326; fax (22) 2667633; e-mail unic.daressalaam@unic.org; internet daressalaam.unic.org.

Thailand: ESCAP, United Nations Bldg, Rajadamnern Nok Ave, Bangkok 10200; tel. (2) 288-1865; fax (2) 288-1052; e-mail unisbkk.unescap@un.org; internet www.unescap.org/unis; also covers Cambodia, Laos, Malaysia, Singapore and Viet Nam.

Togo: 468 angle rue Atimé et ave de la Libération, Lomé; tel. and fax 221-23-06; e-mail unic.lome@unic.org; internet lome .unic.org; also covers Benin.

Trinidad and Tobago: 2nd Floor, Bretton Hall, 16 Victoria Ave, Port of Spain; tel. 623-4813; fax 623-4332; e-mail unic .portofspain@unic.org; internet portofspain.unic.org; also covers Antigua and Barbuda, Aruba, the Bahamas, Barbados, Belize, Dominica, Grenada, Guyana, Jamaica, the Netherlands Antilles, Saint Christopher and Nevis, Saint Lucia, Saint Vincent and the Grenadines, and Suriname.

Tunisia: BP 863, 41 ave Louis Braille, Tunis; tel. (71) 902-203; fax (71) 906-811; e-mail unic.tunis@unic.org; internet www .unictunis.org.tn.

Turkey: PK 407, Birlik Mahallesi, 2 Cad. No. 11, 06610 Cankaya, Ankara; tel. (312) 4541052; fax (312) 4961499; e-mail unic.ankara@unic.org; internet www.unicankara.org.tr.

Ukraine: 01021 Kyiv, Klovsky uzviz, 1; tel. (44) 253-93-63; fax (44) 253-26-07; e-mail registry@un.org.ua; internet www.un.org .ua.

USA: 1775 K St, NW, Suite 400, Washington, DC 20006; tel. (202) 331-8670; fax (202) 331-9191; e-mail unicdc@unicwash .org; internet www.unicwash.org.

Uzbekistan: 100029 Tashkent, Shevchenko ko'ch 4; tel. (71) 120-34-50; fax (71) 120-34-85; e-mail registry@undp.org; internet www.un.uz.

Western Europe: United Nations Regional Information Centre, Residence Palace, Bloc C, Level 7, 155 rue de la Loi/Wetstraat, 1040 Brussels, Belgium; tel. (2) 788-84-84; fax (2) 788-84-85; e-mail info@unric.org; internet www.unric.org; serves Belgium, Cyprus, Denmark, Finland, France, Germany, Greece, The Holy See, Iceland, Ireland, Italy, Luxembourg, Malta, Monaco, the Netherlands, Norway, Portugal, San Marino, Spain, Sweden, United Kingdom; also provides liaison with the institutions of the European Union.

Yemen: POB 237; St 5, off Al-Boniya St, Handhal Zone, San'a; tel. (1) 274000; fax (1) 274043; e-mail unicyem@y.net.ye; internet www.unic-yem.org.

Zambia: POB 32905, Revenue House, Ground Floor, Cairo Rd (Northend), Lusaka; tel. (21) 1228487; fax (21) 1222958; e-mail unic.lusaka@unic.org; internet lusaka.unic.org; also covers Botswana, Malawi and Swaziland.

Zimbabwe: POB 4408, Sanders House, 2nd Floor, First St/ Jason Moyo Ave, Harare; tel. (4) 777060; fax (4) 750476; e-mail unic.harare@unic.org; internet harare.unic.org.

Conferences

Global conferences are convened regularly by the United Nations. Special sessions of the General Assembly assess progress achieved in the implementation of conference action plans. The following global conferences were scheduled for 2012:

Conference on Disarmament (Jan.–March, May–June, July–Sept.: Geneva, Switzerland);

High-level Dialogue on Financing for Development (March: New York, USA);

UN Conference on Sustainable Development (UNCSD) (Rio+20) (June: Rio de Janeiro, Brazil);

UN Conference on the Arms Trade Treaty (July: New York, USA);

World Urban Forum-6 (Sept.: Naples, Italy);

ICAO high-level global aviation security conference (Sept.: Montreal, Canada);

UN Climate Change Conference (Nov.–Dec.: Qatar, with support from the Republic of Korea).

System-wide Coherence

The Senior Management Group, a committee of senior UN personnel established in 1997, acts as the Secretary-General's cabinet and as the central policy-planning body of the United Nations. The 28-member UN System Chief Executives Board for Co-ordination—CEB, convenes at least twice a year under the chairmanship of the Secretary-General to co-ordinate UN system-wide policies, activities and management issues. The UN Development Group (UNDG) unites, under the chairmanship of the Administrator of UNDP, the heads of some 32 UN funds, programmes and departments concerned with sustainable development, in order to promote coherent policy at country level. The UNDG is supported by the UN Development Operations Coordination Office (DOCO). Several inter-agency mechanisms, including UN-Energy, UN-Oceans and UN-Water, facilitate UN system-wide inter-agency co-operation and coherence. Project management services are provided throughout the UN system of entities and organizations, as well as to certain bilateral donors, international financial institutions and governments, by the UN Office for Project Services—UNOPS. UNOPS, founded in 1995 and a member of the UNDG, is self-financing, funded by fees earned from the services that it provides. The Inter-Agency Standing Committee—IASC, founded in 1992, comprises the executive heads of 17 leading UN and other agencies and NGO consortia, who convene at least twice a year under the leadership of the Emergency Relief Co-ordinator (see OCHA). It co-ordinates and administers the international response to complex and major humanitarian disasters, and the development of relevant policies.

In February 2005 the Secretary-General appointed a High-level Panel on UN System-wide Coherence in the Areas of Development, Humanitarian Assistance and the Environment, to study means of strengthening UN performance; in November the Panel published a report entitled *Ten ways for the UN to 'deliver as one'*, outlining the following 10 recommendations for future inter-agency co-operation: (i) the UN should 'deliver as one' at country level, with one leader, one programme, one budget and, where appropriate, one office; (ii) a UN Sustainable Development Board should be established to oversee the One UN Country Programme; (iii) a Global Leaders' Forum should be established within ECOSOC to upgrade its policy co-ordination role in economic, social and related issues; (iv) the UN Secretary-General, the President of the World Bank and the Managing Director of the IMF should initiate a process to review, update and conclude formal agreements on their respective roles and relations at the global and country levels; (v) a Millennium Development Goal (MDG) funding mechanism should be established to provide multi-year funding for the One UN Country Programme; (vi) the UN's leading role in humanitarian disasters and transition from relief to development should be enhanced; (vii) international environmental governance should be strengthened and made more coherent in order to improve effectiveness and targeted action of environmental activities in the UN system; (viii) a dynamic UN entity focused on gender equality and women's empowerment should be established; (ix) a UN common evaluation system should be established, while other business practices, such as human resource polices, planning and results-based management, should be upgraded and harmonized across the UN system to stimulate improved performance; and (x) the Secretary-General should establish an independent task force to eliminate further duplication within the UN system and, where necessary, to consolidate UN entities. In 2007 a *Delivering as One* pilot initiative was launched to test enhanced co-ordination in the provision of development assistance, based on the principles of one leader, one budget, one programme, and one office, in eight volunteer countries: Albania, Cape Verde, Mozambique, Pakistan, Rwanda, Tanzania, Uruguay, and Viet Nam. The CEB has established an action framework for co-ordinating system-wide activities to address climate change under the *Delivering as One* commitment. An Evaluation Management Group (EMG) was appointed by the Secretary-General in February 2011 to assess lessons learnt hitherto from *Delivering as One*. In January 2012 the Secretary-General announced a second generation of inter-agency *Delivering as One* co-operation, with a focus on enhanced monitoring of results and accountability.

In April 2009, having undertaken—under the chairmanship of the Director-General of the ILO—a comprehensive review of the challenges confronting the international community in view of the then developing global economic crisis, the CEB endorsed nine Joint Crisis Initiatives (JCIs), built upon the *Delivering as One* commitment and aimed at alleviating the impact of the economic situation and building a fair and inclusive globalization, allowing for sustainable economic, social and environmental development. The initiatives—led by one or more CEB participating agency, with the voluntary participation of others as co-operating organizations—were as follows: i) additional financing for the most vulnerable, to be implemented through the development of a joint World Bank-UN system mechanism, including through the Vulnerability Fund proposed in early 2009 by the World Bank; led by UNDP and the World Bank; ii) ensuring food security by strengthening feeding programmes and expanding support to farmers in developing countries; led by FAO, WFP and IFAD; iii) promoting trade, through combating protectionism, including through the conclusion of the Doha round, and through strengthening aid-for-trade financing-for-trade initiatives; led by UNCTAD and WTO; iv) a new Green Economy Initiative aimed at promoting investment in long-term environmental sustainability; led by UNEP; v) a new Global Jobs Pact; led by ILO; vi) a new Social Protection Floor, ensuring access to basic social services, shelter, and empowerment and protection of the most vulnerable; led by ILO and WHO; vii) emergency activities to meet humanitarian needs and promote security; led by WFP; viii) technology and innovation; led by ITU, UNIDO and WIPO; and ix) strengthening monitoring and analysis surveillance, and implementing an effective early warning system; led by IMF and the UN Department of Social and Economic Affairs.

CO-ORDINATING AND INTER-AGENCY BODIES

UN System Chief Executives Board for Co-ordination (CEB): CEB Secretariat (Geneva), Rm c551, UN Geneva Office, Palais des Nations, 1211 Geneva 10, Switzerland; tel. 2291071234; fax 229170123; CEB Secretariat (New York), United Nations, New York, NY 10017, USA; tel. (212) 963-1234; fax (212) 963-4879; internet www.unsceb.org; f. 1946 as the Administrative Committee on Co-ordination, present name adopted in 2001; meets at least twice a year under the chairmanship of the UN Secretary-General to co-ordinate UN system-wide policies, management issues and activities; supported by the High-Level Committee on Programmes (HLCP), concerned with global policy and issues; by the High-Level Committee on Management (HLCM), concerned with co-ordinating activities across the UN system; and by the UN Development Group (UNDG) (see below); thematic areas of interest in 2012 include: Africa; business practices; climate change; conflict prevention; gender mainstreaming; the global financial and economic crisis, and related Joint Crisis Initiatives; International Public Sector Accounting Standards (IPSAs), which are being adopted system-wide; knowledge-sharing; the MDGs; science and technology; security and safety of staff; and system-wide coherence; mems: heads of 27 UN agencies and of the WTO; Sec. THOMAS STELZER (Austria).

UN Development Operations Co-ordination Office (DOCO): One United Nations Plaza, DC1-1600, New York, NY 10017, USA; tel. (212) 906-5500; fax (212) 906-3609; tel. www.undg.org; f. 1997, to support the UNDG, which unites, under the chairmanship of the Administrator of UNDP, the heads of some 32 UN funds, programmes and departments concerned with sustainable development, in order to promote coherent policy at country level; the DOCO supports UN orgs in delivering coherent, efficient support at country level; the Office supports and strengthens the Resident Co-ordinator system, through funding, policy guidance and training; administers the UN Country Co-ordination Fund, which provides resources to Resident Co-ordinators; assists the UNDG with developing simplified and harmonized policies in areas such as ICT, human resources, procurement, and financial affairs; targets tailored support to Resident Co-ordinator offices and UN country teams (UNCTs) operating in transition countries; sends specialist help teams to conduct post-conflict needs assessments; and provides technical support for the work of the UNDG; Dir DEBBIE LANDEY (Canada).

UN Collaborative Programme on Reducing Emissions from Deforestation and Forest Degradation in Developing Countries (UN-REDD): UN-REDD Inter-agency Secretariat, International Environment House, 11–13 Chemin des Anémones, 1219 Châtelaine, Geneva, Switzerland; tel. 229178946; e-mail rosa.andolfato@un-redd.org; internet www.un-redd.org; f. 2008 to support developing countries in preparing and implementing national REDD+ strategies, involving investment in low-carbon routes to sustainable development, reversal of deforestation and the promotion of conservation, sustainable management of forests, and enhancement of forest carbon stocks; utilizes expertise from UNEP, UNDP and FAO; provides assistance to 42 partner countries in Africa, Asia, the Pacific, and Latin America; extends support to national programme activities aimed at developing and implementing REDD+ strategies in 16 of the partner countries, having (by 2012) approved funding totalling US $59.3m. in this respect, channelled through a Multi-Partner Trust Fund (MPTF), established in July 2008; governed by a Policy Board comprising representatives from UNEP, UNDP and FAO and from partner countries, donors to the MPTF, civil society, and indigenous peoples; in Aug. 2011 the Policy Board endorsed a Global Programme Framework for 2011–15 with the following areas of focus: measurement, reporting and verification; national REDD+ governance support; transparent, equitable and accountable management of REDD+ funds; engagement of indigenous peoples, civil society and other stakeholders; ensuring multiple benefits of forests and REDD+; and positioning REDD+ as a catalyst for transformations to a Green Economy; Head of the Secretariat YEMI KATERERE (Zimbabwe).

UN-Energy: UN Energy Secretariat, c/o UN Department of Economic and Social Affairs, Two United Nations Plaza, New York, NY 10017, USA; Internet: www.un-energy.org; f. 2002; established following the 2002 World Summit on Sustainable Development (WSSD), held in Johannesburg, South Africa, as a mechanism to promote coherence among UN agencies in energy matters, and to develop increased collective engagement between UN agencies and key external stakeholders; it aims to increase information-sharing, to promote and facilitate joint programming, and to develop action-oriented approaches to co-ordination; focal areas of activity include energy access, renewable energy, and energy efficiency; the sub-programme UN-Energy Africa (UNEA) was established in May 2004, by a meeting of African ministers responsible for energy affairs; UNEA is the principal inter-agency mechanism in the field of energy within Africa; Chair. KANDEH K. YUMKELLA (Sierra Leone).

UN-Oceans: UN-Oceans Secretariat, c/o UNDP Water and Ocean Governance Programme, One United Nations Plaza, New York, NY 10017, USA; tel. (212) 906-5300; e-mail Andrew .Hudson@undp.org; internet www.unoceans.org; f. 2003; has task forces on Marine Biodiversity beyond National Jurisdiction; on Establishing a Regular Process for Global Assessment of the Marine Environment; on Global Partnership for Climate, Fisheries and Aquaculture; and on Marine Protected Areas and Other Area-Based Management Tools; inter-agency activities in 2012 include updating the *UN Atlas of the Oceans*, an internet-based information system for policy makers and scientists, accessible at www.oceansatlas.org/index.jsp; implementing the Programme of Action for the Protection of the Marine Environment; undertaking the 'Assessment of Assessments' (AoA), under the co-leadership of UNEP and UNESCO/IOC; the International Coral Reef Initiative (ICRI); the Joint Group of Experts on the Scientific Aspects of Marine Environmental Protection (GESAMP); the Global Ocean Observing System (led by UNESCO/IOC); the Global Climate Observing System (led by WMO); organizing World Oceans Day, held annually on 8 June; and developing the International Waters focal area under the Global Environment Facility; UN-Ocean's Secretariat rotates between hosts, 2010–12: UNDP; Co-ordinator Dr ANDREW HUDSON.

UN-Water: UN-Water Secretariat, Rm 2250, c/o UN Department of Economic and Social Affairs, Two United Nations Plaza, New York, NY 10017, USA; Fax: (212) 963-4340; e-mail unwater@un.org; internet www.unwater.org; f. 2003 as an inter-agency mechanism to foster greater co-operation and information-sharing among UN agencies and other partners on water-related issues; specific agencies host activities and programmes on behalf of UN-Water, which is not itself an implementing body; senior programme managers from UN-Water member agencies meet twice a year, and an elected Exec. Head (upgraded from Chairperson in Feb. 2012), who, assisted by a deputy, oversees the larger work programme and represents UN-Water at international conferences and at other fora; a permanent Secretariat, hosted by the UN Department for Economic and Social Affairs in New York, provides administrative, technical and logistical support; UN-Water collaborates closely with the UN Secretary-General's Advisory Board on Water and Sanitation; UN-Water aims to strengthen co-ordination and coherence among UN entities concerned with all aspects of freshwater and sanitation, including surface and groundwater resources, the interface between freshwater and seawater, and water-related disasters; UN-Water is mandated to promote regional inter-agency networking arrangements (in 2012 UN-Water Africa was operational); appoints task forces with a focus on specific areas of interest, such as transboundary waters, and climate change and water; conducts four specific programmes: the World Water Assessment Programme, which is hosted and led by UNESCO, and synthesizes data and information, and issues triennial *World Water Development Reports*, comprehensively reviewing the state of the world's freshwater resources; the WHO/UNICEF Joint Monitoring Programme on Water Supply and Sanitation, established by WHO and UNICEF in 1990, and acting as the official mechanism of the UN mandated to monitor global progress towards achieving the MDG targets for drinking-water and sanitation, issuing regular *Joint Monitoring Programme on Water Supply and Sanitation* reports; and—both initiated in 2007 in support of the International Decade for Action Water for Life 2005–15—the UN-Water Decade Programme on Capacity Development, hosted by the UN University, in Bonn, Germany, and the UN-Water Decade Programme on Advocacy and Communication, based in Zaragoza, Spain; UN-Water monitors and reports on progress achieved towards reaching internationally agreed water and sanitation targets; Exec. Head MICHEL JARRAUD (France) (Sec.-Gen. of WMO); Sec. KENZA KAOUAKIB-ROBINSON.

Finance

UN member states pay assessed contributions towards the regular budget, towards peace-keeping operations, to international tribunals, and to the Capital Master Plan (which manages renovation works at UN headquarters in New York, USA).

Since the late 1990s the UN has suffered financial difficulties, owing to an expansion of the organization's political and humanitarian activities and delay on the part of member states in paying their contributions. In December 1997 a UN Development Account was established to channel administrative savings achieved as a result of reforms to the UN's administrative structure towards financing development projects. In December 2000 the General Assembly approved a restructuring of scale of assessment calculations, the methodology and accuracy of which had been contested, particularly by the USA. From 2001 the level of US contributions to the regular annual budget was reduced from 25% to 22%, while annual contributions were raised for several nations with rapidly developing economies. Some 27% of the UN peace-keeping budget is contributed by the USA. As at 11 May 2012 38 member states had paid in full their assessed contributions for 2012, with 96 having paid their assessed regular budget contributions, 68 having paid their contributions to the international tribunals budget, 41 having met their peace-keeping assessment obligations, and 144 having paid their contributions to the Capital Master Plan. Outstanding unpaid assessments to the regular budget stood, at that time, at US $1,180m., while at 1 January 2012 unpaid assessments to the peace-keeping budget exceeded $2,480m.

In 1997 a US business executive, Ted Turner, announced a donation of US $1,000m. to finance UN humanitarian and environmental causes until 2014. The donation has been paid in instalments and administered through his 'UN Foundation', and a UN Fund for International Partnerships (UNFIP) was established by the UN Secretary-General in 1998 to facilitate relations between the UN system and the UN Foundation. The Foundation, which is also sustained by resources from other partners and by grassroots donors, supports the UN through advocacy, grant-making, and the implementation of public-private partnerships.

In December 2011 the UN Secretary-General approved a proposed regular budget of US $5,152.3m. for the two-year period 2012–13. Initiatives provided for under the 2012–13 budget, with the aim of reducing organizational costs, included the introduction of salary freezes for administrative staff; the initiation of reforms to the 'recosting' process (whereby, hitherto, additional funding had been sought after the announcement of budgeted expenditure, in order to offset variances caused by exchange rates and inflation); the development of advanced transparency efforts, including public coverage (via webcast) of all formal committee meetings; and the strengthening of oversight and accountability capabilities.

PROPOSED TWO-YEAR BUDGET OF THE UNITED NATIONS
(US $'000)

	2012–13
Overall policy-making, direction and co-ordination	721,788.3
Political affairs	1,333,849.3
International justice and law	93,155.1
International co-operation for development	436,635.7
Regional co-operation for development	532,892.3
Human rights and humanitarian affairs	326,574.2
Public information	176,092.1
Common support services	600,210.0
Internal oversight	38,254.2
Jointly financed activities and special expenses	131,219.1
Capital expenditures	64,886.9
Safety and security	213,412.4
Development Account	29,243.2
Staff Assessment	451,086.8
Total	5,152,299.6

United Nations Publications

Demographic Yearbook.

Index to Proceedings (of the General Assembly; the Security Council; the Economic and Social Council; the Trusteeship Council).

International Law Catalogue.

Monthly Bulletin of Statistics.

Population and Vital Statistics Report (quarterly).

Statement of Treaties and International Agreements (monthly).

Statistical Yearbook.

UN Chronicle (quarterly).

United Nations Disarmament Yearbook.

United Nations Juridical Yearbook.

World Economic and Social Survey.

World Situation and Prospects.

World Statistics Pocketbook.

Yearbook of the United Nations.

Other UN publications are listed in the chapters dealing with the agencies concerned.

Secretariat

According to the UN Charter the Secretary-General is the chief administrative officer of the organization, and he/she may appoint further Secretariat staff as required. The principal departments and officers of the Secretariat are listed below. The chief administrative staff of the UN Regional Commissions and of all the subsidiary organs of the UN are also members of the Secretariat staff and are listed in the appropriate chapters. The Secretariat staff also includes a number of special missions and special appointments, including some of senior rank.

The Secretary-General chairs the Senior Management Group (SMG), a committee of senior UN personnel that acts as a cabinet and as the central policy-planning body of the UN. Two subsidiary committees of the SMG, the Policy Committee and the Management Committee, were inaugurated in 2005 to enhance the efficiency of high-level decision-making.

The Secretariat comprises about 15,000 staff holding appointments continuing for a year or more, but excluding staff working for the UN specialized agencies and subsidiary organs.

In July 1997 the Secretary-General initiated a comprehensive reform of the administration of the UN and abolished some 1,000 Secretariat posts. The reforms aimed to restructure the Secretariat's substantive work programme around the UN's five core missions, i.e. peace and security, economic and social affairs, development co-operation, humanitarian affairs and human rights. During 1997 the Centre for Human Rights and the Office of the High Commissioner for Human Rights were consolidated into a single office under the reform process, while an Office for Drug Control and Crime Prevention was established, within the framework of the UN Office in Vienna, to integrate efforts to combat crime, drug abuse and terrorism; this was subsequently renamed the UN Office on Drugs and Crime. In December a new post of Deputy Secretary-General was created to assist in the management of Secretariat operations, in particular the ongoing reform process, and represent the Secretary-General as required.

In July 2000 the UN Secretary-General launched the Global Compact, a voluntary initiative comprising leaders in the fields of business, labour and civil society who have undertaken to promote human rights, the fundamental principles of the ILO, and protection of the environment; the Global Compact is administered from the Global Compact Office, in the Executive Office of the Secretary-General. In December 2001, on the recommendation of the Secretary-General, the General Assembly established the Office of the High Representative for the Least Developed Countries, Landlocked Developing Countries and Small Island Developing States. In May 2002 the Secretary-General appointed the first United Nations Security Co-ordinator. A new Department for Safety and Security, headed by an Under-Secretary-General for Safety and Security and replacing the Office of the United Nations Security Co-ordinator, was established in February 2005, taking over responsibility for the safety of UN personnel.

In June 2004 a Panel of Eminent Persons on Civil Society and UN Relationships—appointed by the Secretary-General in February 2003, as part of the ongoing UN reform process, with a mandate to explore and make recommendations on the interaction between civil society, private sector enterprise, parliaments and the UN—issued its final report. A High-Level Panel on Threats, Challenges and Change was appointed by the Secretary-General in November 2003 (in the aftermath of the deaths in August of 21 UN staff members, including Sergio Vieira de Mello, UN High Commissioner for Human Rights, in a terrorist attack in Baghdad, Iraq): it was to evaluate the ability of the UN to address threats to the peace and security of the international community, and to recommend relevant policy and institutional changes, including reforms to the Security Council; the Panel published its findings in December 2004. The report of the Secretary-General entitled 'In Larger Freedom: Towards Development, Security and Human Rights for All', issued in March 2005 after consideration of the High-Level Panel's report, proposed a realignment of the Secretariat's structure, entailing the establishment of a peace-building support office and strengthening support within the body for mediation by the Secretary-General (his 'good offices'), democracy, and the rule of law. He also determined to establish a cabinet-style decision-making executive within the Secretariat, supported by a small subsidiary cabinet secretariat, and proposed a higher level of managerial authority for the role of Secretary-General. Further proposals included the appointment of a Scientific Adviser to the Secretary-General, mandated to supply strategic scientific advice on policy matters, and a comprehensive review of the functioning of the Office of Internal Oversight Services. The Secretary-General's reform proposals were reviewed by the World Summit of UN heads of state held in September (see General Assembly). In December an Ethics Office responsible for applying a uniform set of ethical standards was established within the Secretariat. From January 2008 the UN ethical code was extended to cover employees of all UN funds and programmes. In March 2006 the Secretary-General issued a report entitled 'Investing in the United Nations' in which he outlined proposals to strengthen the role of the Secretariat through a realignment of staff skills, involving relocating personnel and core practices away from headquarters; increasing management accountability and introducing a single comprehensive annual report of the Secretariat's activities; upgrading information technology capabilities; and streamlining the budget. In July 2007 a new Department of Field Support was established within the Secretariat to provide expert administrative and logistical support for UN peace-keeping operations in the field.

In February 2005 the Secretary-General appointed a High-level Panel on United Nations System-wide Coherence in the Areas of Development, Humanitarian Assistance and the Environment, to study means of strengthening UN performance, and, in November, the Panel published a report entitled *Ten ways for the UN to 'deliver as one'*, outlining 10 recommendations for future inter-agency co-operation. In February 2011 the Secretary-General appointed an Evaluation Management Group (EMG) to assess lessons learnt from the *Delivering as One* initiative.

In February 2006 the Secretary-General inaugurated an Internet Governance Forum, with a secretariat hosted by the UN Geneva Office, to pursue the objectives of the World Summit on the Information Society. The Forum incorporates a Multi-stakeholder Advisory Group which meets three times a year.

In 2007 the UN Secretary-General established a Millennium Development Goal Gap Task Force, which was to track, systematically and at both international and country level, existing international commitments in the areas of official development assistance, market access, debt relief, access to essential medicines and technology. The Task Force, led by the UN Department of Economic and Social Affairs and by UNDP, includes more than 20 UN agencies, and also OECD and the WTO. In June 2012 the Secretary-General appointed a new Special Adviser on Post-2015 Development Planning.

The UN Secretariat and the Iraqi Government jointly chair the International Compact for Iraq, a five-year framework for co-operation between Iraq and the international community that was launched in May 2007.

In April 2008 the Secretary-General announced that he was to chair a new High Level Task Force (HLTF) on the Global Food Security Crisis, comprising the heads of UN bodies and experts from the UN and the wider international community. The HLTF was to address the impact of soaring global levels of food and fuel prices and formulate a comprehensive framework for action, with a view to preventing the escalation of widespread hunger, malnutrition and related social unrest. The Department of Economic and Social Affairs, with the IMF, leads an initiative to strengthen monitoring and analysis surveillance, and to implement an effective warning system, one of nine Joint Crisis Initiatives that were endorsed in April 2009 by the UN System Chief Executives Board for Co-ordination (CEB), with the aim of alleviating the impact of the global economic and financial crisis on poor and vulnerable populations.

In May 2011 the UN Secretary-General established a Change Management Team (CMT), with a mandate to guide an agenda for further reform of the UN. The initial task of the CMT was to formulate a comprehensive plan to streamline processes, increase accountability and improve the efficiency of the delivery of its mandates.

In September 2011, at the annual Private Sector Forum, organized by the UN Global Compact, with UNIDO and UN-Energy, at the start of the 66th UN General Assembly, the UN Secretary-General launched a new initiative, Sustainable Energy for All by 2030, and a high-level group responsible for its implementation. The initiative aimed to meet three interlinked global targets: universal access to modern energy services; doubling energy efficiency; and doubling the share of renewable energy in world's energy supply. The year 2012 was designated by the General Assembly as International Year of Sustainable Energy for All.

In January 2012, at the commencement of his second five-year term of office, covering the period 2012–16, Ban Ki-Moon announced a five-year agenda for action with the following priority areas of activity: sustainable development; prevention in the areas of natural disaster risk reduction, violent conflict, and human rights abuses; building a more secure world; supporting nations in transition; working with and for women and young people; enhancing system-wide partnership; and strengthening the UN. The agenda envisaged a second generation of inter-agency *Delivering as One* co-operation, focusing on enhanced monitoring of results and accountability.

Secretary-General: BAN KI-MOON (Republic of Korea).

Deputy Secretary-General: JAN ELIASSON (Sweden) (from 1 July 2012).

OFFICES AND DEPARTMENTS OF THE SECRETARIAT

Executive Office of the Secretary-General

Under-Secretary-General, Chef de Cabinet: SUSANA MALCORRA (Argentina).

Deputy Chef de Cabinet, Assistant Secretary-General: (vacant).

Spokesperson for the Secretary-General: MARTIN NESIRKY (France).

Executive Director of the Global Compact: GEORG KELL (Germany).

Assistant Secretary-General for Planning and Policy Co-ordination: (vacant).

Assistant Secretary-General, Chief Information Technology Officer: CHOI SOON-HONG.

Department for Safety and Security

Under-Secretary-General: GREGORY B. STARR (USA).

Assistant Under-Secretary-General: MBARANGA GASARABWE (Rwanda).

Department of Economic and Social Affairs

Under-Secretary-General: SHA ZUKANG (People's Republic of China), WU HONGBO (People's Republic of China) (designate).

Under-Secretary-General for Gender Equality and the Advancement of Women: MICHELLE BACHELET (Chile).

Assistant Secretary-General for Intergovernmental Support and Strategic Partnerships at UN Women: LAKSHMI PURI (India).

Assistant Secretary-General for Policy and Programmes at UN Women: JOHN HENDRA (Canada).

Assistant Secretary-General, Senior Adviser on Economic Development and Finance: SHAMSHAD AKHTAR (Pakistan) (designate).

Assistant Secretary-General, Economic Development and and Group of 24 Research Co-ordinator: KWAME SUNDARAM JOMO (Malaysia).

Assistant Secretary-General, Policy Co-ordination and Inter-Agency Affairs: THOMAS STELZER (Austria).

Department of Field Support

Under-Secretary-General: AMEERAH HAQ (Bangladesh).

Assistant Secretary-General: ANTHONY BANBURY (USA).

Department of General Assembly and Conference Management

Under-Secretary-General: MUHAMMAD SHAABAN (Egypt), YUKIO TAKASU (Japan) (designate).

Assistant Secretary-General for General Assembly Affairs and Conference Management: FRANZ BAUMANN (Germany).

Assistant Secretary-General for Programme Planning, Budget and Accounts: MARIA EUGENIA CASAR PEREZ (Mexico).

Department of Management

Under-Secretary-General: ANGELA KANE (Germany).

Assistant Secretary-General, Central Support Services: WARREN SACH (United Kingdom).

Assistance Secretary-General, Controller: MARÍA EUGENIA CASAR (Mexico).

Assistant Secretary-General, Human Resources Management: CATHERINE POLLARD (Guyana).

Department of Peace-keeping Operations

Under-Secretary-General: HERVÉ LADSOUS (France).

Assistant Secretary-General: EDMOND MULET (Guatemala).

Assistant Secretary-General, Military Adviser for Peace-keeping Operations: Lt-Gen. BABACAR GAYE (Senegal).

Assistant Secretary-General, Rule of Law and Security Institutions: DMITRY TITOV (Russia).

Department of Political Affairs

Under-Secretary-General: B. LYNN PASCOE (USA), JEFFREY D. FELTMAN (USA) (designate).

Assistant Secretary-General: TAYÉ-BROOK ZERIHOUN (Ethiopia).

Assistant Secretary-General: OSCAR FERNANDEZ-TARANCO (Argentina).

Department of Communications and Public Information

Under-Secretary-General: KIYOTAKA AKASAKA (Japan), PETER LAUNSKY-TIEFFENTHAL (Austria) (designate).

Office for Disarmament Affairs

Under-Secretary-General, High Representative for Disarmament Affairs: ANGELA KANE (Germany).

Office for the Co-ordination of Humanitarian Affairs

Under-Secretary-General for Humanitarian Affairs and Emergency Relief Co-ordinator: VALERIE AMOS (United Kingdom).

Deputy Emergency Relief Co-ordinator and Assistant Secretary-General for Humanitarian Affairs: CATHERINE BRAGG (Canada).

Office of Internal Oversight Services

Under-Secretary-General: CARMEN L. LAPOINTE (Canada).

Assistant Secretary-General: DAVID MUCHOKO KANJA (Kenya) (designate).

Office of Legal Affairs

Under-Secretary-General, The Legal Counsel: PATRICIA O'BRIEN (Ireland).

Assistant Secretary-General, Legal Affairs: D. STEPHEN MATHIAS (USA).

Office of the Capital Master Plan

Assistant Secretary-General, Executive Director of the Office of the Capital Master Plan: MICHAEL ADLERSTEIN (USA).

Assistant Secretary-General, Legal Affairs: D. STEPHEN MATHIAS (USA).

Office of the High Representative for the Least Developed Countries, Landlocked Developing Countries and Small Island Developing States

Under-Secretary-General and High Representative, and Special Adviser on Africa: CHEICK SIDI DIARRA (Mali).

Office of the Special Representative of the Secretary-General for Children and Armed Conflict

Under-Secretary-General and Special Representative: RADHIKA COOMARASWAMY (Sri Lanka).

Office of the United Nations High Commissioner for Human Rights

Palais des Nations, 1211 Geneva 10, Switzerland; tel. 229179000; fax 229179010; internet www.unhchr.ch.

High Commissioner: NAVANETHEM PILLAY (South Africa).

Deputy High Commissioner: KYUNG-WHA KANG (Republic of Korea).

Assistant Secretary-General: IVAN ŠIMONOVIC (Croatia).

Office on Drugs and Crime

Under-Secretary-General: YURI FEDOTOV (Russia).

Peace-building Support Office

Assistant Secretary-General: JUDY CHENG-HOPKINS (Malaysia).

UN Ombudsperson and Mediation Services

Assistant Secretary-General, UN Ombudsman: JOHNSTONE BARKAT (USA).

Geneva Office

Palais des Nations, 1211 Geneva 10, Switzerland; tel. 2291071234; fax 229170123; internet www.unog.ch.

Director-General: KASSYM-JOMART TOKAYEV (Kazakhstan).

Nairobi Office

POB 30552, Nairobi, Kenya; tel. (20) 7621234.

Director-General and Under-Secretary-General: SAHLE-WORK ZEWDE (Ethiopia).

Vienna Office

Vienna International Centre, POB 500, 1400 Vienna, Austria; tel. (1) 26060; fax (1) 263-3389; internet www.unvienna.org.

Director-General: YURI FEDOTOV (Russia).

SPECIAL HIGH LEVEL APPOINTMENTS OF THE UN SECRETARY-GENERAL

Special Advisers

Special Adviser: JOSEPH V. REED (USA).

Special Adviser: RIZA IQBAL (Pakistan).

Special Adviser: EDWARD LUCK (USA).

Special Adviser and Mediator in the Border Dispute between Equatorial Guinea and Gabon: NICOLAS MICHEL (Switzerland).

Special Adviser on Africa: MAGED ABDELAZIZ (Egypt).

Special Adviser on Cyprus: ALEXANDER DOWNER (Australia).

Special Adviser on Innovative Financing for Development: PHILIPPE DOUSTE-BLAZY (France).

Special Adviser on Internet Governance: NITIN DESAI (India).

Special Adviser on Legal Issues related to Piracy off the Coast of Somalia: JACK LANG (France).

Special Adviser on Myanmar: VIJAY NAMBIAR (India).

Special Adviser on the International Compact with Iraq and Other Political Issues: IBRAHIM GAMBARI (Nigeria).

Special Adviser on Sport for Development and Peace: WIFRIED LEMKE (Germany).

Special Adviser on the Global Compact: KLAUS M. LEISINGER (Germany).

Special Adviser on the Millennium Development Goals: JEFFREY D. SACHS (USA).

Special Adviser on Post-2015 Development Planning: AMINA J. MOHAMMED (Nigeria).

Special Adviser on the Prevention of Genocide: FRANCIS DENG (Sudan).

Special Adviser on Yemen: JAMAL BENOMAR (Morocco).

Special Envoys

Joint Special Envoy of the UN and the League of Arab States on the Syrian Crisis: KOFI ANNAN (Ghana).

Special Envoy for Assistance to Pakistan: RAUF ENGIN SOYSAL (Turkey).

Special Envoy for the Implementation of UN Security Council Resolution 1559 (on Lebanon): TERJE ROED-LARSEN (Norway).

Special Envoy for HIV/AIDS in Africa: ELIZABETH MATAKA (Botswana).

Special Envoy for HIV/AIDS in Asia and in the Pacific: J. V. R. PRASADA RAO (India) (from 1 July 2012).

Special Envoy for HIV/AIDS in the Caribbean Region: Dr EDWARD GREENE (Guyana).

Special Envoy for HIV/AIDS in Eastern Europe: (vacant).

Special Envoy for Malaria: RAY CHAMBERS (USA).

Special Envoy for Sudan and South Sudan: HAILE MENKERIOS (South Africa).

Special Envoy on the Great Lakes Region: OLUSEGUN OBASANJO (Nigeria).

Special Envoy to Stop Tuberculosis: JORGE SAMPAIO (Portugal).

Special Envoys on Climate Change: GRO HARLEM BRUNDTLAND (Norway), RICARDO LAGOS ESCOBAR (Chile), FESTUS MOGAE (Botswana), SRGJAN KERIM (FYRM).

Special Representatives

UN Representative to the Georgia Joint Incident Prevention and Response Mechanism and to the international discussions in Geneva on security and stability and the return of IDPs: ANTII TURUNEN (Finland).

Special Representative to the AU: ZACHARY MUBURI-MUITA (Kenya).

Special Representative for Migration: PETER SUTHERLAND (Ireland).

Special Representative for the Implementation of the International Strategy for Disaster Reduction: MARGARETA WAHLSTRÖM (Sweden).

Special Representative for the United Nations International School: MICHAEL ADLERSTEIN (USA).

Special Representative on Food Security and Nutrition; and on Avian and Human Influenza: Dr DAVID NABARRO (United Kingdom).

Special Representative on the Issue of Human Rights and Transnational Corporations and other Business Enterprises: JOHN RUGGIE (USA).

Special Representative on Sexual Violence in Conflict: ZAINAB HAWA BANGURA (Sierra Leone).

Special Representative on Violence against Children: MARTA SANTOS PAIS (Portugal).

Other Special High Level Appointments

Head of the International Commission against Impunity in Guatemala: CARLOS CASTRESANA FERNÁNDEZ (Spain).

High-level Co-ordinator for Compliance by Iraq with its Obligations Regarding the Repatriation or Return of all Kuwaiti and Third Country Nationals or their Remains, as well as the Return of all Kuwaiti Property, including Archives seized by Iraq: GENNADY P. TARASOV (Russia).

High Representative for the Alliance of Civilizations: JORGE SAMPAIO (Portugal).

Joint UN-AU Chief Mediator for Darfur, a.i.: IBRAHIM GAMBARI (Nigeria).

Personal Envoy for Haiti: BILL (WILLIAM JEFFERSON) CLINTON (USA).

Personal Envoy for the Greece-FYRM Talks: MATTHEW NIMETZ (USA).

Personal Envoy for Western Sahara: CHRISTOPHER ROSS (USA).

Personal Representative on the Border Controversy between Guyana and Venezuela: NORMAN GIRVAN (Jamaica).

Representative for Human Rights of IDPs: WALTER KÄLIN (Switzerland).

Special Co-ordinator for Lebanon: MICHAEL C. WILLIAMS (United Kingdom).

Special Co-ordinator for the Middle East Peace Process, Personal Representative to the Palestine Liberation Organization and the Palestinian Authority, and the Secretary-General's Envoy to the Quartet: ROBERT H. SERRY (Netherlands).

Further Special Representatives and other high-level appointees of the UN Secretary-General are listed in entries on UN peace-keeping and peace-building missions and under Offices and Departments of the UN Secretariat. The Secretary-General also appoints distinguished figures in the worlds of arts and sports as Messengers of Peace, as a means of focusing global attention to the UN's activities.

General Assembly

The General Assembly was established as a principal organ of the United Nations under the UN Charter. It first met on 10 January 1946. It is the main deliberative organ of the United Nations, and the only one composed of representatives of all the UN member states. Each delegation consists of not more than five representatives and five alternates, with as many advisers as may be required. The Assembly meets regularly for three months each year, and special sessions may also be held. It has specific responsibility for electing the Secretary-General and members of other UN councils and organs, and for approving the UN budget and the assessments for financial contributions by member states. It is also empowered to make recommendations (but not binding decisions) on questions of international security and co-operation.

The regular session of the General Assembly commences in mid-September. After the election of its President and other officers, the Assembly opens its general debate, a two-week period during which the head of each delegation makes a formal statement of his or her government's views on major world issues. Since 1997 the Secretary-General has presented his report on the work of the UN at the start of the general debate. The Assembly then begins examination of the principal items on its agenda: it acts directly on some agenda items, but most business is handled by the six Main Committees (listed below), which study and debate each item and present draft resolutions to the Assembly. After a review of the report of each Main Committee, the Assembly formally approves or rejects the Committee's recommendations. On designated 'important questions', such as recommendations on international peace and security, the admission of new members to the United Nations, or budgetary questions, a two-thirds majority is needed for adoption of a resolution. Other questions may be decided by a simple majority. In the Assembly, each member has one vote. Voting in the Assembly is sometimes replaced by an effort to find consensus among member states, in order to strengthen support for the Assembly's decisions: the President consults delegations in private to find out whether they are willing to agree to adoption of a resolution without a vote; if they are, the President can declare that a resolution has been so adopted.

Special sessions of the Assembly may be held to discuss issues which require particular attention (e.g. illicit drugs) and 'emergency special sessions' may also be convened to discuss situations on which the UN Security Council has been unable to reach a decision. The Assembly's 10th emergency special session, concerning Illegal Israeli Actions in Occupied East Jerusalem and the rest of the Occupied Palestinian Territory, commenced in April 1997 and has been subsequently reconvened intermittently. The 23rd meeting of the session, called in December 2003 by Arab and non-aligned countries, requested that the International Court of Justice (ICJ) render an advisory opinion on the legal consequences arising from the construction of a wall by Israel in the Occupied Palestinian Territory including in and around East Jerusalem; this action was taken by the General Assembly following two failures by the Security Council to adopt resolutions on the matter. The 24th meeting of the session was convened in July 2004 to discuss the ICJ's ruling on this matter, which had been delivered earlier in that month. A special session on children, reviewing progress made since the World Summit for Children, held in 1990, and the adoption in 1989 of the Convention on the Rights of the Child, was convened in May 2002. In January 2005 a special session took place to commemorate the 60th anniversary of the liberation of the Nazi concentration camps.

The Assembly's 55th session (from September 2000) was designated as the Millennium Assembly. In early September a Millennium Summit of UN heads of state or government was convened to debate 'The Role of the United Nations in the 21st Century'. The Millennium Summit issued the UN Millennium Declaration, identifying the values and principles that should guide the organization in key areas including peace, development, environment, human rights, protection of the vulnerable, and the special needs of the African continent; and specified six fundamental values underlying international relations: freedom; equality; solidarity; tolerance; respect for nature; and a sense of shared responsibility for the global economy and social development. The summit adopted the following so-called Millennium Development Goals (MDGs), each incorporating specific targets to be attained by 2015: the eradication of extreme poverty and hunger; attainment of universal primary education; promotion of gender equality and empowerment of women; reduction of child mortality rates; improvement in maternal health rates; combating HIV/AIDS, malaria and other diseases; ensuring environmental sustainability; and the development of a global partnership for development. Reform of the Security Council and the need for increased UN co-operation with the private sector, non-governmental organizations and civil society in pursuing its goals were also addressed by the summit. Progress in attaining the MDGs was to be reviewed on a regular basis. A five-year review conference of the Millennium Declaration was convened in September 2005 at the level of heads of state and of government.

In October 2003 the President of the Assembly appointed six facilitators to oversee discussions on means of revitalizing the Assembly, and in mid-December the Assembly adopted a landmark resolution that, while reaffirming relevant provisions of the UN Charter and the UN Millennium Declaration, outlined a number of reforms to the Assembly's operations. The changes, aimed at enhancing the Assembly's authority, role, efficiency and impact, were to take effect following broad consultations over the next two years. The resolution provided for a regular meeting of the Presidents of the Assembly, Security Council and ECOSOC, with a view to strengthening co-operation and complementarity in the respective work programmes of the three bodies. In July 2004 the Assembly adopted a resolution on further revitalization of its work, with provisions for streamlining its agenda, sharpening the focus of the six Main Committees, and reducing paperwork.

In March 2005 the Secretary-General presented to the General Assembly a report entitled 'In Larger Freedom: Towards Development, Security and Human Rights for All'. Building on the September 2000 Millennium Declaration, the report focused on three main pillars, defined as: 'Freedom from Want', urging developing countries to improve governance and combat corruption, and industrialized nations to increase funds for development assistance and debt relief and to provide immediate free market access to all exports from least developed countries; 'Freedom from Fear', urging states to agree a new consensus on security matters and adopting a definition of an act of terrorism as one 'intended to cause death or serious bodily harm to civilians or non-combatants with the purpose of intimidating a population or compelling a government or an international organization to do or abstain from doing any act'; and 'Freedom to Live in Dignity', urging the international community to support the principle of 'responsibility to protect'. The report also detailed a number of recommendations for strengthening the UN, which were subsequently considered by the September 2005 World Summit of UN heads of state. These included: rationalizing the work of the Assembly (see above) and focusing its agenda on substantive topical issues, such as international migration and the conclusion of a new comprehensive international strategy against terrorism; restructuring the Secretariat; expanding the membership of the Security Council; and establishing a new UN Human Rights Council to replace the Commission on Human Rights. In December the General Assembly, acting concurrently with the Security Council, authorized the establishment of an intergovernmental advisory Peace-building Commission, which had been recommended in September by the World Summit. The Assembly and Council also authorized at that time the creation of a Peace-building Fund. In March 2006 the Assembly authorized the establishment of the new Human Rights Council. Both the Peace-building Commission and Human Rights Council were inaugurated in June. In February 2007 the Assembly appointed five ambassadors to host negotiations aimed at advancing the process of Security Council reform.

In early October 2008 the General Assembly voted to ask the ICJ for an Advisory Opinion on the legal status of the unilateral declaration of independence, in February of that year, of the Provincial Institutions of Self-Government of Kosovo. Later in October, in view of the ongoing international financial crisis, the President of the General Assembly announced that a body would be established to review the global financial system, including the role of the World Bank and the IMF. The first plenary meeting of the resulting Commission of Experts of the President of the UN General Assembly on Reforms of the International Monetary and Financial System was held in January 2009, and, in September, the Commission issued a report addressing the origins of, and outlining recommendations for the future global response to, the ongoing crisis; the latter included proposals to establish a new global reserve system, a new global credit facility to complement the IMF, a new global co-ordination council, and an International Debt Restructuring Court. In late June the General Assembly convened a UN Conference on the World Financial and Economic Crisis and its Impact on Development.

In September 2009 the General Assembly adopted, by consensus, its first resolution on the 'Responsibility to Protect', promoting efforts to protect the world's population from genocide, war crimes, ethnic cleansing and other crimes against humanity.

World leaders participating in the 65th session of the General Assembly, commencing in September 2010, adopted a document entitled 'Keeping the Promise: United to Achieve the MDGs'; the document called on the President of the Assembly's 68th session, in 2013, to organize a special event to follow up progress on attaining the MDGs. Meanwhile, the UN Secretary-General was requested to report annually on progress until 2015, and to recommend means of advancing the UN development agenda thereafter.

The UN Conference on Sustainable Development, convened in Rio de Janeiro, Brazil, in June 2012, determined to establish a new high-level intergovernmental forum to promote system-wide co-ordination and coherence of sustainable development policies, and to follow up the implementation of sustainable development objectives; this was to meet for the first time at the start of the 68th General Assembly, in September 2013.

President of 66th Session: (from Sept. 2011) NASSIR ABDULAZIZ AL-NASSER (Qatar).

President elect of 67th Session: (from Sept. 2012) VUK JEREMIĆ (Serbia).

MAIN COMMITTEES

There are six Main Committees, on which all members have a right to be represented. Each Committee includes an elected Chairperson and two Vice-Chairs.

First Committee: Disarmament and International Security.

Second Committee: Economic and Financial.

Third Committee: Social, Humanitarian and Cultural.

Fourth Committee: Special Political and Decolonization.

Fifth Committee: Administrative and Budgetary.

Sixth Committee: Legal.

OTHER SESSIONAL COMMITTEES

General Committee: f. 1946; composed of 28 members, including the Assembly President, the 21 Vice-Presidents of the Assembly and the Chairs of the six Main Committees.

Credentials Committee: f. 1946; composed of nine members appointed at each Assembly session.

POLITICAL AND SECURITY MATTERS

Special Committee on Peace-keeping Operations: f. 1965; 34 appointed members.

Disarmament Commission: f. 1978 (replacing body f. 1952); 61 members.

UN Scientific Committee on the Effects of Atomic Radiation: f. 1955; 21 members.

Committee on the Peaceful Uses of Outer Space: f. 1959; 61 members; has a Legal Sub-Committee and a Scientific and Technical Sub-Committee.

Ad Hoc Committee on the Indian Ocean: f. 1972; 44 members.

Committee on the Exercise of the Inalienable Rights of the Palestinian People: f. 1975; 25 members.

Special Committee on the Implementation of the Declaration on Decolonization: f. 1961; 24 members.

Ad Hoc Committee on Terrorism: f. 1996.

DEVELOPMENT

Commission on Science and Technology for Development: f. 1992; 33 members.

Committee on Energy and Natural Resources Development: f. 1998; 24 members.

United Nations Environment Programme (UNEP) Governing Council: f. 1972; 58 members.

LEGAL QUESTIONS

International Law Commission: f. 1947; 34 members elected for a five-year term; originally established in 1946 as the Committee on the Progressive Development of International Law and its Codification.

Advisory Committee on the UN Programme of Assistance in Teaching, Study, Dissemination and Wider Appreciation of International Law: f. 1965; 25 members.

UN Commission on International Trade Law: f. 1966; 36 members.

Special Committee on the Charter of the United Nations and on the Strengthening of the Role of the Organization: f. 1975; composed of all UN members.

There is also a UN Administrative Tribunal and a Committee on Applications for Review of Administrative Tribunal Judgments.

ADMINISTRATIVE AND FINANCIAL QUESTIONS

Advisory Committee on Administrative and Budgetary Questions: f. 1946; 16 members appointed for three-year terms.

Committee on Contributions: f. 1946; 18 members appointed for three-year terms.

International Civil Service Commission: f. 1972; 15 members appointed for four-year terms.

Committee on Information: f. 1978, formerly the Committee to review UN Policies and Activities; 95 members.

There is also a Board of Auditors, Investments Committee, UN Joint Staff Pension Board, Joint Inspection Unit, UN Staff Pension Committee, Committee on Conferences, and Committee for Programme and Co-ordination.

SUBSIDIARY BODIES

Human Rights Council: f. 2006, replacing the fmr Commission on Human Rights (f. 1946); inaugural meeting held in June

2006; mandated to promote universal respect for the protection of all human rights and fundamental freedoms for all; addresses and makes recommendations on situations of violations of human rights; promotes the effective co-ordination and mainstreaming of human rights within the UN system; supports human rights education and learning and provides advisory services, technical assistance and capacity-building support; serves as a forum for dialogue on thematic issues connected with human rights; makes recommendations to the General Assembly for the advancement of international human rights law; promotes the full implementation of human rights obligations undertaken by states; aims to contribute, through dialogue and co-operation, towards the prevention of human rights violations, and to ensure prompt responses to human rights emergencies; the Human Rights Council Advisory Committee functions as a think-tank under the direction of the Council; in March 2011 the Council established an independent International Commission of Inquiry on Syria to address the human rights situation in that country; the commission's first report was published in November, and an update issued was in March 2012; an emergency meeting convened at the beginning of June 2012 on the deteriorating situation in Syria—following the shelling, in late May, allegedly by Syrian government forces, of a residential neighbourhood, which resulted in the deaths of an estimated 108 men, women and children—adopted a resolution condemning the use of force against civilians as 'outrageous', condemning the Syrian authorities for failure to protect, and to promote the rights of, all Syrians, and calling for the International Commission of Inquiry on Syria to conduct a special investigation into the massacre, with a view to holding to account those responsible for 'violations that may amount to crimes against humanity'; in Feb. 2012 the Advisory Committee adopted seven recommendations for approval by the Council, concerning: the rights of peasants; the right to food; human rights and international solidarity; the right of peoples to peace; human rights and issues related to terrorist hostage-taking; traditional values of humankind; and enhancement of international co-operation in the field of human rights; the agenda of the 19th session of the Council, undertaken during Feb.–March 2012, included the right to adequate housing; social and cultural rights; sexual orientation and gender identity; the right to food; juvenile justice; and alleged violations of human rights in countries including Côte d'Ivoire, Iran, Libya, Myanmar and Syria; the first cycle of the Universal Periodic Review (UPR), an assessment of the human rights situation in all mem. states, was undertaken during 2006–11; the second cycle, to cover 2012–16, was launched in May 2012; 47 mems; Pres. LAURA DUPUY LASSERRE (Uruguay).

Peace-building Commission: f. 2006; inaugural meeting held in June 2006; an intergovernmental advisory body, subsidiary simultaneously to both the General Assembly and the Security Council; mandated to focus international attention on reconstruction, institution-building and sustainable development in countries emerging from conflict and to advise on and propose integrated strategies for post-conflict recovery; in December 2009 the President of the General Assembly appointed three co-facilitators: the Permanent Representatives of Ireland, Mexico and South Africa, to undertake, during 2010, a review of the Peace-building Commission's activities; in July 2010 the co-facilitators published a report entitled 'Review of the United Nations Peacebuilding Architecture', based upon extensive consultations with UN member states and with other stakeholders; 31 mem. states; Chair. Dr A. K. ABDUL MOMEN (Bangladesh).

Peace-building Fund: f. 2006; finances (through two funding facilities, the Immediate Response Facility and the Peace-building Recovery Facility) projects in countries that are on the agenda of the Peace-building Commisson, or that have been declared eligible for assistance by the Secretary-General; initiatives in receipt of funding must fulfil at least one of the following criteria: they respond to imminent threats to a peace process, build or strengthen national capacities to promote coexistence and peaceful resolution of conflict, stimulate economic revitalization facilitating peace, or re-establish essential administrative services; the Fund is replenished by voluntary contributions; its guidelines were revised in 2009; during 2007–11 the Fund allocated US $327.8m. in 22 countries.

General Assembly Resolutions

(Adoption of Agreements, Conventions, Declarations, Protocols and other instruments)

Note: Until 1976 resolutions of the General Assembly were numbered consecutively, with the session of the Assembly indicated in parentheses. Since that date (i.e. from the 31st regular session of the Assembly) a new numbering sequence has been established at the beginning of each session. Thus each resolution is numbered according to the session in which it was adopted, followed by its chronological position within that session. Resolutions adopted in special or emergency session are identified with an 'S' or 'ES', respectively.

Resolution 22 (I): Adopted 13 Feb. 1946. General Convention on Privileges and Immunities of the UN.

Resolution 54 (I): Adopted 19 Nov. 1946. Transfer to the UN of power exercised by the League of Nations under the International Agreements, Conventions and Protocols on Narcotic Drugs, including a Protocol amending the Agreements, Conventions and Protocols on Narcotic Drugs.

Resolution 84 (I): Adopted 11 Dec. 1946. Agreement between the UN and the Carnegie Foundation concerning the use of the premises of the Peace Palace at The Hague by the International Court of Justice.

Resolution 169 (II): Adopted 31 Oct. 1947. Agreement between the UN and the USA regarding the headquarters of the UN.

Resolution 179 (II): Adopted 21 Nov. 1947. Co-ordination of the privileges and immunities of the UN and of the specialized agencies of the UN, including the General Convention on Privileges and Immunities of the UN.

Resolution 211 (III): Adopted 8 Oct. 1948. International provisions for the control of certain drugs including a protocol bringing under international control drugs outside the scope of the Convention of 13 July 1931 for Limiting the Manufacture and Regulating the Distribution of Narcotic Drugs, as amended by the Protocol contained in Resolution 54 (I).

Resolution 217 (III): Adopted 10 Dec. 1948. International Bill of Human Rights, including the Universal Declaration of Human Rights.

Resolution 260 (III): Adopted 9 Dec. 1948. Convention on the Prevention and Punishment of the Crime of Genocide.

Resolution 317 (IV): Adopted 2 Dec. 1949. Convention for the Suppression of the Traffic in Persons and of the Exploitation of the Prostitution of others.

Resolution 428 (V): Adopted 14 Dec. 1950. Statute of the Office of the UN High Commissioner for Refugees.

Resolution 630 (VII): Adopted 16 Dec. 1952. Convention on the International Right of Correction.

Resolution 640 (VII): Adopted 20 Dec. 1952. Convention on the Political Rights of Women.

Resolution 1040 (XI): Adopted 29 Jan. 1957. Convention on the Nationality of Married Women.

Resolution 1386 (XIV): Adopted 20 Nov. 1959. Declaration of the Rights of the Child.

Resolution 1514 (XV): Adopted 14 Dec. 1960. Declaration on the Granting of Independence to Colonial Countries and Peoples.

Resolution 1541 (XV): Adopted 15 Dec. 1960. Principles which should guide members in determining whether or not an obligation exists to transmit the information called for under Article 73e of the Charter, in respect of such territories whose people have not yet attained a full measure of independence.

Resolution 1653 (XVI): Adopted 24 Nov. 1961. Declaration on the Prohibition of the Use of Nuclear and Thermonuclear Weapons.

Resolution 1763 (XVII): Adopted 7 Nov. 1962. Draft Convention and draft Recommendation on Consent to Marriage, Minimum Age for Marriages and Registration of Marriages.

Resolution 1904 (XVIII): Adopted 20 Nov. 1963. UN Declaration on the Elimination of all forms of Racial Discrimination.

Resolution 1962 (XVIII): Adopted 13 Dec. 1963. Declaration of Legal Principles governing the Activities of States in the Exploration and Use of Outer Space.

Resolution 2018 (XX): Adopted 1 Nov. 1965. Recommendation on Consent to Marriage, Minimum Age for Marriage and Registration of Marriages.

Resolution 2037 (XX): Adopted 7 Dec. 1965. Declaration on the Promotion among Youth of the Ideals of Peace, Mutual Respect and Understanding between Peoples.

Resolution 2106 (XX): Adopted 21 Dec. 1965. International Convention on the Elimination of all forms of Racial Discrimination.

Resolution 2131 (XX): Adopted 21 Dec. 1965. Declaration on the Inadmissibility of Intervention in the Domestic Affairs of States and the Protection of their Independence and Sovereignty.

Resolution 2200 (XXI): Adopted 16 Dec. 1966. International Covenant on Economic, Social and Cultural Rights, Civil and Political Rights and Optional Protocol to the International Covenant on Civil and Political Rights.

Resolution 2222 (XXI): Adopted 19 Dec. 1966. Treaty on Principles governing the Activities of States in the Exploration and Use of Outer Space, including the Moon and other Celestial Bodies.

Resolution 2263 (XXII): Adopted 7 Nov. 1967. Declaration on the Elimination of Discrimination against Women.

Resolution 2312 (XXII): Adopted 14 Dec. 1967. Declaration on Territorial Asylum.

Resolution 2345 (XXII): Adopted 19 Dec. 1967. Agreement on the Rescue of Astronauts, the Return of Astronauts and the Return of Objects launched into Outer Space.

Resolution 2373 (XXII): Adopted 12 June 1968. Treaty on the Non-proliferation of Nuclear Weapons.

Resolution 2391 (XXIII): Adopted 26 Nov. 1968. Convention on the Non-applicability of Statutory Limitations to War Crimes and Crimes against Humanity.

Resolution 2530 (XXIV): Adopted 8 Dec. 1969. Convention on Special Missions and Optional Protocol concerning the Compulsory Settlement of Disputes.

Resolution 2542 (XXIV): Adopted 11 Dec. 1969. Declaration on Social Progress and Development.

Resolution 2625 (XXV): Adopted 24 Oct. 1970. Declaration on Principles of International Law concerning Friendly Relations and Co-operation among States in accordance with the Charter of the UN.

Resolution 2626 (XXV): Adopted 24 Oct. 1970. International Development Strategy for the Second UN Development Decade.

Resolution 2627 (XXV): Adopted 24 Oct. 1970. Declaration on the Occasion of the 25th Anniversary of the UN.

Resolution 2660 (XXV): Adopted 7 Dec. 1970. Treaty on the Prohibition of the Emplacement of Nuclear Weapons and other Weapons of Mass Destruction on the Seabed and the Ocean Floor and in the Subsoil thereof.

Resolution 2734 (XXV): Adopted 16 Dec. 1970. Declaration on the Strengthening of International Security.

Resolution 2749 (XXV): Adopted 17 Dec. 1970. Declaration of Principles governing the Seabed and the Ocean Floor, and the Subsoil thereof, beyond the Limits of National Jurisdiction.

Resolution 2777 (XXVI): Adopted 29 Nov. 1971. Convention on International Liability for Damage caused by Space Objects.

Resolution 2826 (XXVI): Adopted 16 Dec. 1971. Convention on the Prohibition of the Development, Production and Stockpiling of Bacteriological (Biological) and Toxin Weapons and on their Destruction.

Resolution 2832 (XXVI): Adopted 16 Dec. 1971. Declaration of the Indian Ocean as a Zone of Peace.

Resolution 2856 (XXVI): Adopted 20 Dec. 1971. Declaration on the Rights of Mentally Retarded Persons.

Resolution 2902 (XXVI): Adopted 22 December 1971. Supplementary Agreement between the UN and the Carnegie Foundation concerning the use of the premises of the Peace Palace at The Hague by the International Court of Justice.

Resolution 3068 (XXVIII): Adopted 30 Nov. 1973. International Convention on the Suppression and Punishment of the Crime of Apartheid.

Resolution 3074 (XXVIII): Adopted 3 Dec. 1973. Principles of international co-operation in the detection, arrest, extradition and punishment of persons guilty of war crimes and crimes against humanity.

Resolution 3166 (XXVIII): Adopted 14 Dec. 1973. Convention on the Prevention and Punishment of Crimes against Internationally Protected Persons, including Diplomatic Agents.

Resolution 3201 (S-VI): Adopted 1 May 1974. Declaration on the Establishment of a New International Economic Order.

Resolution 3235 (XXIX): Adopted 12 Nov. 1974. Convention on the Registration of Objects launched into Outer Space.

Resolution 3281 (XXIX): Adopted 12 Dec. 1974. Charter of Economic Rights and Duties of States.

Resolution 3314 (XXIX): Adopted 14 Dec. 1974. Definition of Aggression.

Resolution 3318 (XXIX): Adopted 14 Dec. 1974. Declaration on the Protection of Women and Children in Emergency and Armed Conflict.

Resolution 3346 (XXIX): Adopted 17 Dec. 1974. Agreement between the UN and the World Intellectual Property Organization (WIPO).

Resolution 3384 (XXX): Adopted 10 Nov. 1975. Declaration on the Use of Scientific and Technological Progress in the Interests of Peace and for the Benefit of Mankind.

Resolution 3447 (XXX): Adopted 9 Dec. 1975. Declaration on the Rights of Disabled Persons.

Resolution 3452 (XXX): Adopted 9 Dec. 1975. Declaration on the Protection of all Persons from being subjected to Torture and other Cruel, Inhuman or Degrading Treatment or Punishment.

Resolution 31/72: Adopted 10 Dec. 1976. Convention on the Prohibition of Military or any other Hostile Use of Environmental Modification Techniques.

Resolution 32/105: Adopted 14 Dec. 1977. International Declaration against Apartheid in Sports.

Resolution 32/107: Adopted 15 Dec. 1977. Agreement between the UN and the International Fund for Agricultural Development (IFAD).

Resolution 32/155: Adopted 19 Dec. 1977. Declaration on the Deepening and Consolidation of International *Détente*.

Resolution 32/156: Adopted 19 Dec. 1977. Agreement on Co-operation and Relationships between the UN and the World Tourism Organization.

Resolution S-9/2: Adopted 3 May 1978. Declaration on Namibia.

Resolution 33/73: Adopted 15 Dec. 1978. Declaration on the Preparation of Societies for Life in Peace.

Resolution 33/162: Adopted 20 Dec. 1978. Charter of Rights for Migrant Workers in Southern Africa.

Resolution 34/68: Adopted 5 Dec. 1979. Agreement governing the Activities of States on the Moon and other Celestial Bodies.

Resolution 34/88: Adopted 11 Dec. 1979. Declaration on International Co-operation for Disarmament.

Resolution 34/93: Adopted 12 Dec. 1979. Declaration on South Africa.

Resolution 34/146: Adopted 17 Dec. 1979. International Convention against the Taking of Hostages.

Resolution 34/169: Adopted 17 Dec. 1979. Code of Conduct for law-enforcement officials.

Resolution 34/180: Adopted 18 Dec. 1979. Convention on the Elimination of all forms of Discrimination against Women.

Resolution 35/46: Adopted 3 Dec. 1980. Declaration of the 1980s as the Second Disarmament Decade.

Resolution 35/55: Adopted 5 Dec. 1980. International Agreement for the Establishment of the University for Peace and Charter of the University of Peace.

Resolution 35/56: Adopted 5 Dec. 1980. International Development Strategy for the Third UN Development Decade.

Resolution 36/55: Adopted 25 Nov. 1981. Declaration on the Elimination of all forms of Intolerance and of Discrimination based on Religion or Belief.

Resolution 36/100: Adopted 9 Dec. 1981. Declaration on the Prevention of Nuclear Catastrophe.

Resolution 36/103: Adopted 9 Dec. 1981. Declaration on the Inadmissibility of Intervention and Interference in the Internal Affairs of States.

Resolution 37/7: Adopted 28 Oct. 1982. World Charter for Nature.

Resolution 37/10: Adopted 15 Nov. 1982. Manila Declaration on the Peaceful Settlement of International Disputes.

Resolution 37/63: Adopted 3 Dec. 1982. Declaration on the Participation of Women in Promoting International Peace and Co-operation.

Resolution 37/92: Adopted 10 Dec. 1982. Principles governing the use by states of artificial earth satellites for international direct television broadcasting.

Resolution 37/194: Adopted 18 Dec. 1982. Principles of medical ethics relevant to the role of health personnel, particularly physicians, in the protection of prisoners and detainees against torture and other cruel, inhuman or degrading treatment or punishment.

Resolution 39/11: Adopted 12 Nov. 1984. Declaration on the Right of Peoples to Peace.

Resolution 39/29: Adopted 3 Dec. 1984. Declaration on the Critical Economic Situation in Africa.

Resolution 39/46: Adopted 10 Dec. 1984. Convention against Torture and other Cruel, Inhuman or Degrading Treatment or Punishment.

Resolution 39/142: Adopted 14 Dec. 1984. Declaration on the Control of Drugs-trafficking and Drug Abuse.

Resolution 40/33: Adopted 29 Nov. 1985. UN standard minimum rules for the administration of juvenile justice (The Beijing Rules).

Resolution 40/34: Adopted 29 Nov. 1985. Declaration of Basic Principles of Justice for Victims of Crime and Abuse of Power.

Resolution 40/64: Adopted 10 Dec. 1985. International Convention against Apartheid in Sports.

Resolution 40/144: Adopted 13 Dec. 1985. Declaration on the Human Rights of Individuals who are not Nationals of the Country in which they live.

Resolution 40/180: Adopted 17 Dec. 1985. Agreement between the UN and the UN Industrial Development Organization (UNIDO).

Resolution 41/65: Adopted 3 Dec. 1986. Principles relating to remote sensing of the earth from outer space.

Resolution 41/85: Adopted 3 Dec. 1986. Declaration on Social and Legal Principles Relating to the Protection and Welfare of Children, with special reference to Foster Placement and Adoption Nationally and Internationally.

Resolution 41/128: Adopted 4 Dec. 1986. Declaration on the Right to Development.

Resolution 42/22: Adopted 18 Nov. 1987. Declaration on the Enhancement of the Effectiveness of the Principle of Refraining from the Threat or Use of Force in International Relations.

Resolution 42/186: Adopted 11 Dec. 1987. Environmental perspective to 2000 and beyond.

Resolution 43/51: Adopted 5 Dec. 1988. Declaration on the Prevention and Removal of Disputes and Situations which may threaten International Peace and Security and on the Role of the UN in this Field.

Resolution 43/165: Adopted 9 Dec. 1988. UN Convention on International Bills of Exchange and International Promissory Notes.

Resolution 43/173: Adopted 9 Dec. 1988. Body of principles for the protection of all persons under any form of detention or imprisonment.

Resolution 44/25: Adopted 20 Nov. 1989. Convention on the Rights of the Child.

Resolution 44/34: Adopted 4 Dec. 1989. International Convention against the Recruitment, Use, Financing and Training of Mercenaries.

Resolution S-16/1: Adopted 14 Dec. 1989. Declaration on Apartheid and its Destructive Consequences in Southern Africa.

Resolution 44/114: Adopted 15 Dec. 1989. Principles that should govern further actions of states in the field of the 'freezing' and reduction of military budgets.

Resolution 44/128: Adopted 15 Dec. 1989. International Covenant on Civil and Political Rights: Second Optional Protocol aiming at the Abolition of the Death Penalty.

Resolution S-18/3: Adopted 1 May 1990. Declaration on International Economic Co-operation, in particular the Revitalization of Economic Growth and Development of the Developing Countries.

Resolution 45/62: Adopted 4 Dec. 1990. Declaration of the 1990s as the Third Disarmament Decade.

Resolution 45/95: Adopted 14 Dec. 1990. Guidelines for the regulation of computerized data files.

Resolution 45/110: Adopted 14 Dec. 1990. UN standard minimum rules for non-custodial measures (The Tokyo Rules).

Resolution 45/111: Adopted 14 Dec. 1990. Basic principles for the treatment of prisoners.

Resolution 45/112: Adopted 14 Dec. 1990. UN guidelines for the prevention of juvenile delinquency.

Resolution 45/113: Adopted 14 Dec. 1990. UN rules for the protection of juveniles deprived of their liberty.

Resolution 45/116: Adopted 14 Dec. 1990. Model Treaty on Extradition.

Resolution 45/117: Adopted 14 Dec. 1990. Model Treaty on Mutual Assistance in Criminal Matters and Optional Protocol concerning the Proceeds of Crime.

Resolution 45/118: Adopted 14 Dec. 1990. Model Treaty on the Transfer of Proceedings in Criminal Matters.

Resolution 45/119: Adopted 14 Dec. 1990. Model Treaty on the Transfer of Supervision of Offenders Conditionally Sentenced or Conditionally Released.

Resolution 45/158: Adopted 18 Dec. 1990. International Convention on the Protection of the Rights of All Migrant Workers and Members of their Families.

Resolution 45/199: Adopted 21 Dec. 1990. International Development Strategy for the Fourth UN Development Decade.

Resolution 46/59: Adopted 9 Dec. 1991. Declaration on Fact-finding by the UN in the Field of the Maintenance of International Peace and Security.

Resolution 46/91: Adopted 16 Dec. 1991. UN principles for older persons.

Resolution 46/119: Adopted 17 Dec. 1991. Principles for the protection of persons with mental illness and for the improvement of mental health care.

Resolution 46/151: Adopted 18 Dec. 1991. UN new agenda for the development of Africa in the 1990s.

Resolution 46/152: Adopted 18 Dec. 1991. Statement of Principles and Programme of Action of the UN Crime Prevention and Criminal Justice Programme.

Resolution 47/5: Adopted 16 Oct. 1992. Proclamation on Ageing.

Resolution 47/68: Adopted 14 Dec. 1992. Principles relevant to the use of nuclear power sources in outer space.

Resolution 47/133: Adopted 18 Dec. 1992. Declaration on the Protection of all Persons from Enforced Disappearance.

Resolution 47/135: Adopted 18 Dec. 1992. Declaration on the Rights of Persons belonging to National or Ethnic, Religious and Linguistic Minorities.

Resolution 48/96: Adopted 20 Dec. 1993. Standard rules on the equalization of opportunities for persons with disabilities.

Resolution 48/104: Adopted 20 Dec. 1993. Declaration on the Elimination of Violence against Women.

Resolution 48/134: Adopted 20 Dec. 1993. Principles relating to the status of national institutions for the promotion and protection of human rights (Paris Principles).

Resolution 48/263: Adopted 28 July 1994. Agreement relating to the implementation of part XI of the UN Convention on the Law of the Sea.

Resolution 49/57: Adopted 9 Dec. 1994. Declaration on the Enhancement of Co-operation between the UN and Regional Arrangements or Agencies in the Maintenance of International Peace and Security.

Resolution 49/59: Adopted 9 Dec. 1994. Convention on the Safety of UN and associated Personnel.

Resolution 49/60: Adopted 9 Dec. 1994. Declaration on Measures to Eliminate International Terrorism.

Resolution 50/5: Adopted 18 Oct. 1995. Declaration in Commemoration of the 50th Anniversary of the end of the Second World War.

Resolution 50/6: Adopted 24 Oct. 1995. Declaration on the Occasion of the 50th Anniversary of the UN.

Resolution 50/48: Adopted 11 Dec. 1995. UN Convention on Independent Guarantees and Stand-by Letters of Credit.

Resolution 50/50: Adopted 11 Dec. 1995. UN model rules for the conciliation of disputes between states.

Resolution 51/59: Adopted 12 Dec. 1996. International Code of Conduct for public officials.

Resolution 51/60: Adopted 12 Dec. 1996. UN Declaration on Crime and Public Security.

Resolution 51/122: Adopted 13 Dec. 1996. Declaration on International Co-operation in the Exploration and Use of Outer Space for the Benefit and in the Interest of all States, taking into Particular Account the Needs of Developing Countries.

Resolution 51/162: Adopted 16 Dec. 1996. Model law on electronic commerce.

Resolution 51/191: Adopted 16 Dec. 1996. UN Declaration against Corruption and Bribery in International Commercial Transactions.

Resolution 51/210: Adopted 17 Dec. 1996. Declaration to supplement the Declaration on Measures to Eliminate International Terrorism of 1994.

Resolution 51/229: Adopted 21 May 1997. Convention on the Law of the Non-navigational Uses of International Watercourses.

Resolution 51/240: Adopted 20 June 1997. Agenda for Development.

Resolution 52/27: Adopted 26 Nov. 1997. Agreement concerning the Relationship between the UN and the International Seabed Authority.

Resolution 52/86: Adopted 12 Dec. 1997. Model strategies and practical measures on the elimination of violence against women in the field of crime prevention and criminal justice.

Resolution 52/158: Adopted 15 Dec. 1997. Model law on cross-border insolvency.

Resolution 52/164: Adopted 15 Dec. 1997. International Convention for the Suppression of Terrorist Bombings.

Resolution S-20/3: Adopted 10 June 1998. Declaration on the Guiding Principles of Drug Demand Reduction.

Resolution 52/251: Adopted 8 Sept. 1998. Agreement on Co-operation and the Relationship between the UN and the International Tribunal for the Law of the Sea.

Resolution 53/2: Adopted 6 Oct. 1998. Declaration on the Occasion of the 50th Anniversary of UN Peace-keeping.

Resolution 53/101: Adopted 8 Dec. 1998. Principles and guidelines for international negotiations.

Resolution 53/144: Adopted 9 Dec. 1998. Declaration on the Right and Responsibility of Individuals, Groups and Organs of Society to Promote and Protect Universally Recognized Human Rights and Fundamental Freedoms.

Resolution 54/4: Adopted 6 Oct. 1999. Optional Protocol to the Convention on the Elimination of All Forms of Discrimination against Women (Resolution 34/180).

Resolution 54/109: Adopted 9 Dec. 1999. International Convention for the Suppression of the Financing of Terrorism.

Resolution 54/263: Adopted 16 May 2000. Optional Protocol to the Convention on the Rights of the Child concerning the involvement of children in armed conflict, and Optional Protocol on the sale of children, child prostitution and child pornography.

Resolution S-22/2: Adopted 12 June 2000. Declaration on state of progress of and initiatives for the future implementation of the Programme of Action for the Sustainable Development of Small Island Developing States.

Resolution 54/280: Adopted 30 June 2000. Agreement to regulate the relationship between the United Nations and the Preparatory Commission for the Comprehensive Nuclear Test Ban Treaty Organization.

Resolution 55/2: Adopted 8 Sept. 2000. UN Millennium Declaration.

Resolution 55/25: Adopted 15 Nov. 2000. UN Convention against Transnational Organized Crime; two additional Protocols.

Resolution 55/59: Adopted 4 Dec. 2000. Vienna Declaration on Crime and Justice: Meeting the Challenges of the Twenty-first Century.

Resolution 55/153: Adopted 12 Dec. 2000. Articles on nationality of natural persons in relation to the succession of states.

Resolution 55/255: Adopted 31 May 2001. Protocol against the Illicit Manufacturing of and Trafficking in Firearms, their Parts and Components and Ammunition, supplementing the UN Convention against Transnational Organized Crime.

Resolution S-25/2: Adopted 9 June 2001. Declaration on Cities and other Human Settlements in the New Millennium.

Resolution S-26/2: Adopted 27 June 2001. Declaration of Commitment on HIV/AIDS.

Resolution 55/278: Adopted 12 July 2001. Statute of the UN System Staff College in Turin, Italy.

Resolution 55/283: Adopted 7 Sept. 2001. Agreement concerning the relationship between the UN and the Organization for the Prohibition of Chemical Weapons.

Resolution 56/6: Adopted 9 Nov. 2001. Global Agenda for Dialogue among Civilizations.

Resolution 57/2: Adopted 16 Sept. 2002. UN Declaration on the New Partnership for Africa's Development.

Resolution 57/18: Adopted 19 Nov. 2002. Model Law of the UN Nations Commisson on International Trade Law on International Commercial Conciliation.

Resolution 57/199: Adopted 18 Dec. 2002. Convention against Torture and Other Cruel, Inhuman or Degrading Treatment or Punishment: Optional Protocol.

Resolution 58/4: Adopted 31 Oct. 2003. UN Convention against Corruption.

Resolution 58/232: Adopted 23 Dec. 2003. Agreement between the United Nations and the World Tourism Organization.

Resolution 59/38: Adopted 2 Dec. 2004. Convention on Jurisdictional Immunities of States and their Property.

Resolution 59/280: Adopted 8 March 2005. UN Declaration on Human Cloning.

Resolution 59/290: Adopted 13 April 2005. International Convention for the Suppression of Acts of Nuclear Terrorism.

Resolution 60/21: Adopted 23 Nov. 2005. UN Convention on the Use of Electronic Communications in International Contracts.

Resolution 60/42: Adopted 8 Dec. 2005. Convention on the Safety of UN and Associated Personnel: Optional Protocol.

Resolution 60/147: Adopted 16 Dec. 2005. Basic Principles and Guidelines on the Right to a Remedy and Reparation for Victims of Gross Violations of International Human Rights Law and Serious Violations of International Humanitarian Law.

Resolution 60/262: Adopted 2 June 2006. Political Declaration on HIV/AIDS.

Resolution 61/1: Adopted 19 Sept. 2006. Declaration of the High-Level Meeting of the 61st session of the General Assembly on the mid-term comprehensive global review of the implementation of the Programme of Action for the Least Developed Countries for the Decade 2001–10.

Resolution 61/106: Adopted 13 Dec. 2006. Convention on the Rights of Persons with Disabilities.

Resolution 61/177: Adopted 20 Dec. 2006. International Convention for the Protection of All Persons from Enforced Disappearance.

Resolution 61/295: Adopted 13 Sept. 2007. UN Declaration on the Rights of Indigenous Peoples.

Resolution 62/88: Adopted 13 Dec. 2007. Declaration of the Commemorative High-Level Plenary Meeting devoted to the follow-up to the outcome of the Special Session on Children.

Resolution 63/1: Adopted 22 Sept. 2008. Political Declaration on Africa's Development Needs.

Resolution 63/2: Adopted 3 Oct. 2008. Declaration of the High-Level Meeting of the sixty-third session of the General Assembly on the mid-term review of the Almaty Programme of Action.

Resolution 63/177: Adopted 10 Dec. 2008. Optional Protocol to the International Covenant on Economic, Social and Cultural Rights.

Resolution 63/122: Adopted 11 Dec. 2008. UN Convention on Contracts for the International Carriage of Goods Wholly or Partly by Sea.

Resolution 63/303: Adopted 9 July 2009. Outcome of the Conference on the World Financial and Economic Crisis and its Impact on Development.

Resolution 64/257: Adopted 9 April 2010. Observation of 65th Anniversary of the End of the Second World War.

Resolution 64/293: Adopted 30 July 2010. UN Global Plan of Action to Combat Trafficking in Persons.

Resolution 65/230: Adopted 21 Dec. 2010. Salvador Declaration on Comprehensive Strategies for Global Challenges: Crime Prevention and Criminal Justice Systems and Their Development in a Changing World.

Resolution 65/277: Adopted 10 June 2011. Political Declaration on HIV and AIDS: Intensifying Our Efforts to Eliminate HIV and AIDS.

Resolution 66/2: Adopted 19 Sept. 2011. Political Declaration of the High-Level Meeting of the General Assembly on the Prevention and Control of Non-communicable Diseases.

Resolution 66/3: Adopted 22 Sept. 2011. Political Declaration of the High-Level Meeting of the General Assembly to commemorate the 10th anniversary of the adoption of the Durban Declaration and Programme of Action 'United against racism, racial discrimination, xenophobia and related intolerance'.

Resolution 66/136: Adopted 9 Dec. 2011. Declaration on the 50th Anniversary of Human Space Flight and the 50th Anniversary of the Committee on the Peaceful Uses of Outer Space.

Resolution 66/137: Adopted 19 Dec. 2011. UN Declaration on Human Rights Education and Training.

Resolution 66/138: Adopted 19 Dec. 2011. 66th Optional Protocol to the Convention on the Rights of the Child on a Communications Procedure.

Security Council

The Security Council was established as a principal organ under the United Nations Charter; its first meeting was held on 17 January 1946. Its task is to promote international peace and security in all parts of the world.

MEMBERS

Permanent members: People's Republic of China, France, Russia, United Kingdom, USA, known as the P-5. The remaining 10 members are normally elected (five each year) by the General Assembly for two-year periods (five countries from Africa and Asia, two from Latin America, one from eastern Europe, and two from western Europe and others).

Non-permanent members in 2012: Colombia, Germany, India, Portugal and South Africa (term expires 31 December 2012); and Azerbaijan, Guatemala, Morocco, Pakistan and Togo (term expires 31 December 2013).

Rotation of the Presidency in 2012: South Africa (January); Togo (February); United Kingdom (March); USA (April); Azerbaijan (May); People's Republic of China (June); Colombia (July); France (August); Germany (September); Guatemala (October); India (November); Morocco (December).

Organization

The Security Council has the right to investigate any dispute or situation which might lead to friction between two or more countries, and such disputes or situations may be brought to the Council's attention either by one of its members, by any member state, by the General Assembly, by the Secretary-General or even, under certain conditions, by a state which is not a member of the UN.

The Council has the right to recommend ways and means of peaceful settlement and, in certain circumstances, the actual terms of settlement. In the event of a threat to or breach of international peace or an act of aggression, the Council has powers to take 'enforcement' measures in order to restore international peace and security. These include severance of communications and of economic and diplomatic relations and, if required, action by air, land and sea forces.

All members of the UN are pledged by the Charter to make available to the Security Council, on its call and in accordance with special agreements, the armed forces, assistance and facilities necessary to maintain international peace and security. These agreements, however, have not yet been concluded.

The Council is organized to be able to function continuously. The Presidency of the Council is held monthly in turn by the member states in English alphabetical order. Each member of the Council has one vote. On procedural matters decisions are made by the affirmative vote of any nine members. For decisions on other matters the required nine affirmative votes must include the votes of the five permanent members. This is the rule of 'great power unanimity' popularly known as the 'veto' privilege. In practice, an abstention by one of the permanent members is not regarded as a veto. Any member, whether permanent or non-permanent, must abstain from voting in any decision concerning the pacific settlement of a dispute to which it is a party. Any member of the UN that is party to a dispute under consideration by the Council may participate in the Council's discussions without a vote.

The allocation of the Security Council's permanent seats reflects the post-Second World War international situation. It is envisaged that reforms to the Council should be implemented aimed at establishing a more equitable regional representation and recognizing the current global balance of power. Consideration of such reform commenced in 1993 at the 48th Session of the General Assembly, which established a Working Group to assess the issue. Agreement on the size and composition of an expanded Security Council has been hindered by conflicting national and regional demands. Brazil, India, Japan and Germany (the 'Group of Four—G4') have requested the status of permanent members without veto rights; while Italy, Pakistan and other middle-ranking countries (known as 'Uniting for Consensus') have requested a 25-member Council with 10 new non-permanent seats; and the African Union (AU) has contended that African states should receive two permanent seats with veto power, and that there should be four further new permanent seats and five non-permanent seats. In September 2000 the UN Millennium Summit declared support for continued discussions on reform of the Council. The report of the High-Level Panel on Threats, Challenges and Change (see Secretariat), issued in December 2004, stated that the role of the developed countries that contribute most to the UN financially (in terms of contributions to assessed budgets), militarily (through participation in peace-keeping operations), and diplomatically should be reflected in the Council's decision-making processes, as well as the interests of the broader membership (particularly those of developing countries). The report proposed two models for the expansion of the Council. The first entailed the provision of six new permanent seats (broadening the current regional representation on the Council), with no veto, and of three non-permanent seats with a two-year term; while the second entailed the establishment of a new category of eight 'semi-permanent' seats to be occupied for periods of four years. In his report entitled 'In Larger Freedom: Towards Development, Security and Human Rights for All', issued in March 2005 (see General Assembly), the Secretary-General supported the High-Level Panel's proposals on Security Council reform. The proposals were reviewed by the World Summit of UN heads of state convened by the General Assembly in September. In February 2007 the General Assembly appointed five ambassadors to advance the process of Security Council reform by hosting negotiations on the following five key issues: categories of membership; veto power; regional representation; the size of an enlarged Council; and the working methods of the Council and its relationship with the General Assembly. In February 2009 a phase of intergovernmental negotiations on Security Council reform was launched, with three rounds of negotiations held during February–September. Prior to the commencement, in December, of the fourth round, some 138 member states jointly sent a letter to the chairperson of the negotiations requesting that a text should be prepared detailing the options under discussion. Consequently, the fifth round of intergovernmental negotiations, which opened in June 2010, were based on a prepared text. The first meeting of the eighth round of negotiations took place in November 2011.

Activities

As the UN organ primarily responsible for maintaining peace and security, the Security Council is empowered to deploy UN forces in the event that a dispute leads to fighting. It may also authorize the use of military force by a coalition of member states or a regional organization. A summit meeting of the Council convened during the Millennium Summit in September 2000 issued a declaration on ensuring an effective role for the Council in maintaining international peace and security, with particular reference to Africa. In June 2006 an intergovernmental advisory UN Peace-building Commission (see below) was inaugurated as a subsidiary advisory body of both the Security Council and the General Assembly, its establishment having been authorized by the Security Council and General Assembly, acting concurrently, in December 2005. The annual reports of the Commission were to be submitted to the Security Council for debate. During 2011 the Security Council continued to monitor closely all existing peace-keeping and political missions and the situations in countries where missions were being undertaken, and to authorize extensions of their mandates accordingly. The Council authorized the establishment of two new peace-keeping missions in that year: the UN Interim Security Force for Abyei (UNISFA)—concerning the disputed Abyei border area between Sudan and South Sudan—in June, and the UN Mission in South Sudan (UNMISS) in July.

In 2011 major priorities of the Council's formal agenda included consideration of African issues (such as ongoing crises in Côte d'Ivoire, Somalia and Sudan); of mass protests and political upheaval in several North African and Arab states (including Libya, Syria and Yemen); and of post-conflict situations (particularly Burundi, CAR, Guinea-Bissau and Sierra Leone). The Council focused also on the January 2011 referendum on independence for South Sudan, and the ensuing admission in July of the newly independent South Sudan as a UN member state (pursuant to the Council's recommendation to that effect made on 13 July to the General Assembly); and on the application by Palestine in September for membership of the organization. During 2011 the Security Council adopted 66 resolutions, 40 of which related to Africa; issued 22 presidential statements; and convened some 213 public meetings. Numerous meetings and debates were held to consider African matters, with a focus on peace and security, conflict prevention and resolution, peace-building, the humanitarian situation, return of refugees and IDPs, and development strategies. A Council special mission to Africa was undertaken in May 2011, covering Khartoum, Sudan; Juba, in the then soon-to-be independent South Sudan; Addis Ababa, Ethiopia; and Nairobi, Kenya.

On 12 September 2001 the Security Council expressed its unequivocal condemnation of the terrorist attacks against targets in the USA, which had occurred on the previous day. It expressed its readiness to combat terrorism and reiterated the right to individual or collective self-defence in accordance with the UN Charter. At the end of September the Council adopted Resolution 1373, establishing a Counter-Terrorism Committee (CTC) to monitor a range of measures to combat international terrorism, including greater international co-operation and information exchange and suppressing the financing of terrorist groups. A special session of the Council at ministerial level was convened on the issue of terrorism in November. The Council continued to review the work of the CTC and to urge all states to submit reports on efforts to implement Resolution 1373, as well as to ratify relevant international conventions and protocols. In January 2003 the Council met at ministerial level to discuss international terrorism, including the issue of particular states maintaining stocks of weapons of mass destruction. The meeting adopted a resolution urging intensified efforts to combat terrorism and full co-operation with the CTC. The CTC has made efforts to strengthen contacts with international, regional and sub-regional organizations, and in March 2003 it convened a meeting of 57 such groupings and agreed on a co-ordinated approach to the suppression of terrorism. A follow-up meeting was convened in March 2004. In that month the Council adopted a resolution to strengthen the CTC by classifying it as a special subsidiary body of the Council, headed by a Bureau and assisted by an Executive Directorate (the Counter-Terrorism Committee Executive Directorate—CTED). In December 2010 the Council extended the mandate of the CTED until 31 December 2013. In April 2004 the Council adopted Resolution 1540—which considered the threat posed by the possible acquisition and use by non-state actors, particularly terrorists, of weapons of mass destruction, and urged all states to establish controls to prevent the proliferation of such weapons—and established the '1540 Committee' to monitor its implementation. In April 2006 and August 2008 the 1540 Committee reported to the Security Council on the status of implementation of Resolution 1540. The December 2004 report of the High-Level Panel on Threats, Challenges and Change stated that, confronted by a terrorism 'nightmare scenario', the Council would need to take earlier, more pro-active and more decisive action than hitherto.

The imposition of sanctions by the Security Council as a means of targeting regimes and groupings that are deemed to threaten international peace and security has increased significantly in recent years and has been subjected to widespread scrutiny regarding enforceability and the potential adverse humanitarian consequences for general populations. In the latter respect the Council has, since 1999, incorporated clauses on humanitarian assessment in its resolutions; the sanctions that took effect against the Taliban regime in Afghanistan and al-Qa'ida in January 2001 were the first to entail mandatory monitoring of the humanitarian impact. In 2000 a proposal was submitted to the Council regarding the establishment of a permanent body to monitor sanctions violations. The UN Secretary-General established an informal working group in April 2000 to evaluate sanctions policy. During 2006 the group submitted a report to the Security Council recommending that resolutions enforcing sanctions should clearly specify intended goals and targets, include incentives to reward partial compliance, and focus in particular on the finances and movements of leaders (so-called 'smart sanctions'). In April 2000 the Council authorized the establishment of a temporary monitoring mechanism to investigate alleged violations of the sanctions imposed against União Nacional para a Independência Total de Angola (UNITA) rebels in Angola, owing to their failure to implement earlier Council resolutions demanding compliance with the obligations of the peace process in that country. In July 2000 the Council voted to prohibit the exportation of all rough diamonds from Sierra Leone that had not been officially certified by that country's Government. (It had become evident that the ongoing conflicts in Sierra Leone and Angola were fuelled by rebel groups' illegal exploitation of diamond resources and use of the proceeds derived therefrom to purchase armaments.) In December a panel of experts appointed by the Council issued a report on the connections between the illicit exportation of diamonds from Sierra Leone and the international trade in armaments. In March 2001 the Council banned the purchase of diamonds exported from Liberia, and demanded that the Liberian authorities refrain from purchasing so-called 'conflict diamonds' from illegal sources and cease providing support to rebel organizations, with particular reference to the main rebel grouping active in Sierra Leone. The Council also re-imposed an embargo on the sale or supply of armaments to Liberia and imposed diplomatic restrictions on senior Liberian government officials, with effect from May. In January 2003 the Council endorsed the Kimberley Process Certification Scheme, which had entered into effect on 1 January following an agreement reached by some 30 governments to regulate the trade in rough diamonds and eliminate the illegal sale of diamonds to fund conflicts. In May the Council imposed, additionally, a ban on the sale of timber products originating in Liberia. In December the Council endorsed the imposition against Liberia of a revised sanctions regime, to complement developments in the peace process there. The sale or supply of arms and related materiels to Liberia (except for use by the UN Mission in Liberia—UNMIL) and the purchase of rough diamonds and timber products from that country remained prohibited, and restrictions remained in force on travel by designated Liberian individuals. In June 2006 the Council terminated the sanctions on the purchase of timber products from Liberia, and in April 2007 the sanctions on the purchase of rough diamonds from that country were withdrawn. In May 2002 the Council suspended the travel restrictions on senior officials of the UNITA movement in Angola, following the signing of a cease-fire agreement ending hostilities in that country. All sanctions against UNITA were removed in December and the relevant Sanctions Committee, established pursuant to a resolution adopted in 1993, was dissolved. In September 2003 the Council voted to end punitive measures imposed against Libya in 1992 and 1993 relating to the destruction of a commercial airline flight over Lockerbie, United Kingdom, in December 1988. In July 2003 the Council banned the sale or supply of armaments and other military assistance to militias in the Democratic Republic of the Congo (DRC), and in November an arms embargo, travel restrictions and an assets freeze were imposed on designated individuals and entities in Côte d'Ivoire.

In February 2011 the Security Council, in reaction to violent measures recently taken by the regime of the Libyan leader Col Muammar al-Qaddafi against opposition groupings, imposed a new arms embargo against the Libyan regime. In March the Security Council adopted Resolution 1973, which imposed a no-fly zone in Libya's airspace, strengthened the sanctions against the Qaddafi regime (including freezing financial assets), demanded an immediate cease-fire, and authorized member states to take 'all necessary measures to protect civilians and civilian populated areas under threat of attack' by forces loyal to Qaddafi, 'while excluding a foreign occupation force of any form on any part of Libyan territory'. Later in that month NATO members determined to enforce the UN sanctioned no-fly zone over Libya, alongside a military operation to prevent further attacks on civilians and civilian-populated areas, undertaken by a multinational coalition under British, French and US command; at the end of March NATO assumed full command of the operation to protect civilians in Libya. The NATO operation was terminated at the end of October, following the overthrow of the Qaddafi regime. At the beginning of November the Security Council urged the new authorities in Libya to ensure the security of the former Qaddafi regime's large weapons stockpile, expressing concern that the proliferation of such armaments might fuel terrorist activities, including those of al-Qaida. The Council also demanded that the Libyan authorities, in co-ordination with international bodies, destroy any stockpiled chemical weaponry. In December the Council removed financial sanctions against the Libyan banking sector.

In July 2004 the Security Council imposed an arms embargo against non-governmental entities and individuals—including the Janjaweed militias—in Darfur, Sudan, and demanded that the Sudanese Government disarm the militias. In July 2007 the Security Council authorized the deployment of the AU/UN Hybrid Operation in Darfur (UNAMID), and during 2011 the Council continued to consult closely on the Darfur situation with the UN Secretariat, the AU and the Sudanese Government. In April 2012 the Council, concerned at escalating tensions between Sudan and recently independent South Sudan, demanded that the two states redeploy their forces from Abyei (Sudan); that they withdraw forces from their joint border and immediately end mounting cross-border violence; that Sudanese rebels should vacate oilfields in Heglig (Sudan); that Sudan should cease aerial bombardments of South Sudan; and that a summit should be convened between the two states to resolve outstanding concerns.

In February 2007 the UN Security Council endorsed the deployment of the AU Mission in Somalia (AMISOM), which had been established by the AU in January, with a mandate to contribute to the political stabilization of Somalia; the Security Council proposed that the mission should eventually be superseded by a UN operation focusing on the post-conflict restoration of Somalia. AMISOM became operational in May 2007. In December 2010 the UN Security Council, concerned at continuing unrest and terrorist attacks in Somalia, extended AMISOM's mandate until 30 September 2011 and requested the AU to increase the mission's numbers to 12,000. AMISOM's mandate was extended further, in September 2011, until 31 October 2012. In so doing, the UN Security Council requested the AU to 'urgently increase' the mission's strength to the then mandated level of 12,000. In late February 2012 the Security Council voted unanimously to strengthen the mission further, to comprise 17,700 troops, and to expand its areas of operation. The resolution also banned trade in charcoal with Somalia, having identified that commodity as a significant source of revenue for militants.

In June, October and December 2008, November 2009, April and November 2010, and April and November 2011, the Security Council adopted, respectively, Resolutions 1816, 1838, 1846, 1897, 1918, 1950, 1976, and 2015, on combating piracy being perpetrated against ships off the coast of Somalia and in the Gulf of Aden. A Contact Group on Piracy off the Coast of Somalia (CGPCS), established in January 2009 to facilitate discussion and the co-ordination of actions among states and organizations engaged in suppressing piracy off the coast of Somalia, reports periodically on its progress to the Security Council. In January 2011 the then Special Adviser to the UN Secretary-General on Legal Issues Related to Piracy off the Coast of Somalia, in a briefing to the Security Council, proposed 25 comprehensive measures to address the issue, including the establishment of specialized piracy courts in the region, and the promotion of regional economic development programmes, with a view to finding solutions on land, also, to the ongoing criminal activities at sea. In October 2011 and February 2012 the Council adopted, respectively, Resolutions 2018 and 2039 concerning acts of piracy committed in the Gulf of Guinea.

In December 2009, adopting Resolution 1907, the Council imposed an arms embargo, travel restrictions and assets freeze against the Eritrean political and military leadership, who were found to have provided political, financial and logistical support to armed groups engaged in undermining the reconciliation process in Somalia, and to have acted aggressively towards Djibouti.

In May 2012 the Council imposed a travel ban against five military officers implicated in a coup in April against the legitimately elected Guinea-Bissau authorities. The Council demanded that the Guinea-Bissau military leadership take immediate steps to restore constitutional order and relinquish authority.

In April 2005 the Council authorized the establishment of an independent commission to assist the Lebanese authorities with their investigation into a terrorist attack perpetrated in February that had killed 23 people, including the former Prime Minister of that country, Rafik Hariri. In October the investigating commission reported that it suspected officials and other individuals from both Lebanon and Syria of involvement in the fatal attack. Consequently, in that month the Security Council adopted a resolution imposing travel and economic sanctions against such suspected individuals, and requiring the Syrian authorities to detain named Syrian suspects and to co-operate fully and unconditionally with the commission. In March 2006 the Council adopted a resolution requesting the UN Secretary-General to negotiate an agreement with the Lebanese Government on the establishment of an international tribunal to try those suspected of involvement in the February 2005 terrorist attack. The resulting agreement on the Special Tribunal for Lebanon was endorsed by the Security Council in May 2007. The Tribunal, based in The Hague, Netherlands, comprises both international and Lebanese judges and was to apply Lebanese (not international) law. In February 2012 the UN Secretary-General extended the mandate of the Special Tribunal for a further three years, with effect from 1 March. In August 2006, following eruption in the previous month of full-scale conflict in southern Lebanon between the Israeli armed forces and the militant Shi'a organization, Hezbollah, the Security Council adopted a resolution calling for a full cessation of hostilities and the immediate withdrawal of all Israeli forces.

In early February 2012 the People's Republic of China and Russia vetoed a Security Council resolution to endorse a proposed peace plan that had been agreed in late January by ministers of the League of Arab States to end the ongoing and escalating conflict in Syria. In mid-February League ministers proposed the creation of a joint Arab-UN peace-keeping mission to Syria. Towards the end of that month the Secretaries-General of the UN and of the League appointed Kofi Annan—formerly the UN Secretary-General—as their Joint Special Envoy on the Syrian Crisis. A six-point peace plan proposed in March by Annan was accepted, towards the end of that month, by the Syrian Government. In mid-April the Security Council adopted, unanimously, a resolution authorizing an advance team of up to 30 unarmed military observers to monitor a cease-fire by all parties to the Syrian violence, pending the deployment of a full cease-fire supervision mission. Soon afterwards the UN Secretary-General reported to the Security Council that, as violence had escalated since the attempt to impose a cease-fire, and Syrian forces had not withdrawn from urban areas, a full team of 300 unarmed observers should be promptly deployed. Consequently, on 21 April, the Security Council unanimously authorized the establishment of the UN Supervision Mission in Syria (UNSMIS), initially for a 90-day period. Repeated violations of the terms of the peace plan continued, however, to be reported. In late May the Security Council issued a statement unanimously condemning—as an 'outrageous use of force against the civilian population' constituting a violation of applicable international law—the indiscriminate massacre (confirmed by UNSMIS observers), of an estimated 108 men, women and children, and the wounding of many more, resulting from the shelling of a residential neighbourhood—the rebel-controlled village of El-Houleh, near Homs—allegedly by forces loyal to the Syrian regime. The Council also condemned the killing of civilians in El-Houleh by shooting at close range and by severe physical abuse. Reiterating its full support to the efforts of the UN-Arab League Joint Special Envoy for the implementation of his six-point plan, the Council demanded that the Syrian Government immediately cease the use of heavy weapons in population centres, and immediately return its troops to their barracks. In early June at least an estimated further 78 people, again including women and children, were reported to have been killed in the western village of Qbeir, by pro-government militants, following the shelling of the area by government forces; UNSMIS observers en route to the site of the atrocity were reported to have been shot at. A meeting of the Security Council held soon afterwards, with participation by the UN and Arab League Secretaries-General and the Joint Special Envoy, requested the UN Secretary-General to put forward a range of options for resolving the Syrian crisis. The Council, while united behind the six-point plan, remained divided in its approach to the situation, with Russia and China refusing to countenance any external actions aimed at influencing regime change in Syria.

In October 2006 the Security Council adopted a resolution demanding that the Democratic People's Republic of Korea (North Korea) abandon all programmes related to nuclear weapons, ballistic missiles and other weapons of mass destruction in a complete, verifiable and irreversible manner; an embargo was imposed by the Council on the supply of arms, military technology and luxury goods to that country, and the foreign assets of personnel connected to its weapons programme were frozen. In April 2009 the Council strongly condemned a long-range missile test conducted by North Korea, in violation of the October 2006 resolution. In June 2009 the Council adopted a resolution that deplored a further nuclear test conducted by North Korea, in late May, imposed a total embargo on arms exports from, and strengthened the prohibition on the importation of armaments into, that country.

In December 2006 the Security Council imposed sanctions against Iran, including an embargo related to that country's nuclear and ballistic missile programmes and punitive measures targeted at individuals and entities connected to the programmes. In March 2007 the Council adopted a further resolution imposing a ban on the export of arms from Iran, and, in March 2008, an additional resolution was adopted authorizing inspections of any cargo to and from Iran suspected of concealing prohibited equipment; strengthening the monitoring of Iranian financial institutions; and adding names to the existing list of individuals and companies subject to asset and travel restrictions. A resolution adopted in June 2010 strengthened the sanctions further.

In September 2002 the then US President, George W. Bush, expressed concern that Iraq was challenging international security owing to its non-compliance with previous UN resolutions relating to the elimination of weapons of mass destruction. Subsequently, diplomatic discussions intensified regarding the need for a new UN resolution on Iraq, amidst increasing pressure from the US administration to initiate military action. An open debate was held in the Security Council in October, at the request of the Non-aligned Movement. On 8 November the Council adopted Resolution 1441 providing for an enhanced inspection mission and a detailed timetable according to which Iraq would have a final opportunity to comply with its disarmament obligations. Following Iraq's acceptance of the resolution, inspectors from the UN Monitoring, Verification and Inspection Commission (UNMOVIC, established in 1999 by the Council) and the IAEA arrived in Iraq in late November 2002, with Council authorization to have unrestricted access to all areas and the right to interview Iraqi scientists and weapons experts. In early December Iraq submitted a declaration of all aspects of its weapons programmes, as required under Resolution 1441. In early January 2003 UNMOVIC's then Executive Chairman, Dr Hans Blix, briefed the Council on Iraq's declaration and the inspection activities. A full update was presented to the Council on 27 January, as required by Resolution 1441, 60 days after the resumption of inspections. The then Director-General of the IAEA, Dr Mohammad el-Baradei, called for an ongoing mandate for his inspectors to clarify the situation regarding nuclear weapons. However, Blix declared that Iraq had potentially misled the UN on aspects of its chemical and biological weapons programmes and urged more active and substantive co-operation on the part of the Iraqi authorities to determine the existence or otherwise of proscribed items and activities. On 14 February Blix reported to the Council that the Iraqi authorities had recently become more active in proposing and undertaking measures to co-operate with UNMOVIC, and on 7 March he noted that Iraq had started to destroy, under UNMOVIC supervision, its Al Samoud 2 missiles and associated items, having accepted the conclusion of an international panel that these exceeded the permissible range decreed by the Council. Blix declared that the destruction to date of 34 Al Samoud 2 missiles and other items represented a 'substantial measure of disarmament', and that a significant Iraqi effort was under way to clarify a major source of uncertainty regarding quantities of biological and chemical weapons that had been unilaterally destroyed in 1991. Blix stated that UNMOVIC inspectors would require a number of further months in which to verify sites and items, analyse documents, interview relevant persons and draw conclusions, with a view to verifying Iraq's compliance with Resolution 1441. Meanwhile, extensive debate was conducted in the Council regarding Iraq's acceptance of its disarmament obligations and appropriate consequent measures, including the need for a new Council resolution to enforce Resolution 1441. On 24 February 2003 the USA, the United Kingdom and Spain submitted a draft resolution to the Council stating that Iraq had failed to co-operate 'immediately, unconditionally and actively' with UNMOVIC, as required by Resolution 1441, and insisting upon immediate full co-operation, failing which military force should be used to remove the incumbent regime; France, Germany and Russia, however, demanded that UNMOVIC should be given more time to fulfil its mandate. On 18 March UNMOVIC personnel were withdrawn from Iraq in view of the abandonment by the USA, the United Kingdom and Spain of efforts to win the Council's support for their draft resolution and a consequent ultimatum by the USA that the Iraqi leadership should leave the country immediately or face a military invasion. Unilateral military action by US, British and allied forces commenced on 19 March. On that day, presenting to the Council UNMOVIC's draft work programme (required under Resolution 1284 to be formulated within a fixed period after the commencement of inspection activities), Blix stated that the Commission's experts had found that the Iraqi authorities had hitherto supplied only limited new information that would be of substantial assistance in resolving outstanding issues of concern. Upon the initiation of military action Iraq's petroleum exports under an existing oil-for-food programme were suspended immediately. On 28 March the Security Council adopted a resolution enabling technical adjustments to the oil-for-food programme and authorizing the UN Secretary-General to facilitate the delivery and receipt of goods contracted by the Iraqi Government for the humanitarian needs of its people.

On 22 May 2003, following the overthrow of Saddam Hussain in April, the Security Council adopted Resolution 1483, withdrawing economic sanctions against Iraq, and providing for the resumption of petroleum exports and the phasing-out, by November, of the oil-for-food programme. The resolution also supported the formation by the Iraqi people, assisted by the 'Coalition Provisional Authority' (the occupying powers under unified command) and a new Special Representative of the Secretary-General, of an Iraqi-run interim administration, pending the establishment by the Iraqi people of an internationally recognized, representative government that would assume the responsibilities of the Authority. On the same day an open meeting of the Council was briefed on the post-conflict situation in Iraq by several UN agencies conducting humanitarian operations there and also by the International Committee of the Red Cross. The Council reaffirmed in Resolution 1483 that Iraq must meet its disarmament obligations and declared that the Council would revisit the mandates of UNMOVIC and the IAEA in this regard. Reporting on UNMOVIC's activities in June, shortly before retiring as the Commission's Executive Chairman, Blix stated that, although responsibility for weapons inspections in Iraq had been taken over by a US-led Iraq Survey Group, UNMOVIC remained available to continue its work in the field. Blix declared that while significant quantities of proscribed items remained unaccounted for in Iraq and might exist, it was not justifiable to assume that they must exist. In mid-August the Council authorized the establishment of the UN Assistance Mission for Iraq (UNAMI), which was mandated to support the Secretary-General in fulfilling his responsibilities under Resolution 1483. Shortly afterwards the newly appointed Special Representative of the Secretary-General for Iraq (and UN High Commissioner for Human Rights), Sergio Vieira de Mello, and 21 other UN staff were killed in a terrorist attack on the UNAMI headquarters in Baghdad. In response the Council adopted a resolution strongly condemning all forms of violence against participants in humanitarian operations and urging that perpetrators thereof should be brought to justice. Subsequently, until the formation of the Iraqi Interim Government at the end of June 2004 (see below), UNAMI operated primarily from outside Iraq. In mid-October 2003 the Council authorized a multinational peace-keeping force, under unified command, to help maintain security in Iraq and to support UNAMI and the institutions of the Iraqi interim administration. (The mandate of the multinational force was most recently extended to 31 July 2012.) In November 2003 the Council adopted a resolution that stressed the importance of continuing to enforce the ban on trade in armaments with Iraq and authorized the establishment of a sanctions committee to identify those individuals and entities holding the outstanding financial assets of the former Saddam Hussain regime. In April 2004 the Council adopted a resolution welcoming the decision of the Secretary-General in the previous month to appoint a high-level panel to investigate allegations of fraud and corruption in the administration of the oil-for-food programme. The panel's final report, released in October 2005, found that there had been serious manipulation of the humanitarian aims of the programme: the Saddam Hussain regime was accused of having diverted US $1,800m. in illicit surcharges and bribes from the scheme, and more than 2,000 companies were reported to have received illicit payments. Resolution 1546, adopted by the Council in June 2004, endorsed the newly formed Iraq Interim Government and outlined a timetable for Iraq's transition to democratic government. The resolution was approved after several weeks of discussions mainly concerned with the extent of Iraqi sovereignty and the continued presence of multinational forces in that country. The Council welcomed the elections held in January 2005 to the new Iraq Transitional National Assembly, while reaffirming the role of the Special Representative of the Secretary-General and UNAMI in support of Iraqi efforts to promote national dialogue, and urging the international community to continue to provide advisers and technical support towards UN activities in Iraq. The Council has reiterated demands for the repatriation of all Kuwaiti and third country nationals who had been missing since the 1990 Gulf War and for the return of their property. In June 2007 the Security Council voted to terminate UNMOVIC's mandate, noting testimonials that all of Iraq's known weapons of mass destruction had been deactivated and that the Iraqi Government had declared its support for international non-proliferation regimes. The Council also terminated the mandate of the IAEA weapons inspectors in Iraq.

The Council provides a forum for discussion of the situation in the Middle East and violence in the West Bank and Gaza and in Israel and to support a comprehensive and just settlement to the situation based on relevant Council resolutions, the outcome (including the principle of 'land for peace') of the Madrid Conference held in October–November 1991; agreements previously reached by the parties (including the 'statement of joint understanding' made in November 2007, see below); and the peace initiative of Saudi Crown Prince Abdullah that was endorsed by the Arab League summit in March 2002. In the latter month the Council adopted Resolution 1397, which envisaged two separate states of Israel and Palestine existing within secure and recognized borders. In November 2003 the Council endorsed the adoption in April by the so-called 'Quartet' comprising envoys from the UN, EU, Russia and USA of a 'performance-based roadmap to a permanent two-state solution to the Israeli-Palestinian conflict'. The Council welcomed the summit meeting held in February 2005, in Sharm el-Sheikh, Egypt, between the Palestinian and Israeli leaders, at which they reaffirmed commitment to the stalled roadmap initiative, and the Council also welcomed conciliatory actions subsequently taken by both sides. In July the Council convened an open debate on the situation in the Middle East, at the request of Arab member states of the UN. In December 2006 the Council endorsed a presidential statement expressing deep concern over the continuing insecurity in the Middle East and restating the key role of the Quartet. The UN Secretary-General attended a conference held in Annapolis, Maryland, USA, in November 2007, at which participants agreed to implement their respective obligations under the 2003 roadmap to achieving a two-state solution to the Israeli-Palestinian conflict, and a statement of 'joint understanding' was made by the Israeli and Palestinian leaders. Addressing an open debate on the Middle East situation in March 2008, the Secretary-General reaffirmed commitment to the ongoing framework for resolving the conflict and, noting that the Israeli and Palestinian leaders had in the previous month made a commitment to reaching a settlement promptly, urged that momentum towards a resolution of the conflict be maintained. In September, however, the Special Co-ordinator for the Middle East Peace Process reported to the Security Council that no agreement had yet been reached on core issues. In mid-December the Security Council adopted a resolution reaffirming its support for the agreements and negotiations resulting from the November 2007 Annapolis summit, and urging an intensification of efforts to achieve a peaceful two-state outcome. Direct talks been the two sides have, however, stalled since 2008. In January 2009, in response to the intensive bombardment of the Gaza Strip by Israeli forces that commenced in late December 2008 with the stated aim of ending rocket attacks launched by Hamas and other militant groups on Israeli targets, the Security Council adopted Resolution 1860, in which it expressed grave concern at the escalation of violence and stressed that Palestinian and Israeli civilian populations must be protected. In May 2009 the Council convened an open debate on the Middle East, at the level of ministers for foreign affairs, and expressed support for an initiative of the Quartet, and other interested parties, to hold a conference in Moscow; this was subsequently held in March 2010. An open debate on the Middle East situation, convened by the Council in July 2011, noted progress achieved in Palestinian state-building and urged the prompt resumption of negotiations on a two-state outcome. In September 2011 the Council met to consider Palestine's application in that month for full UN membership. An attempt in that month by Quartet diplomats to instigate new Israeli–Palestinian direct negotiations was unsuccessful.

In February 2008 the Council met in emergency session in reaction to Kosovo's unilateral declaration of independence from Serbia. Pending new guidance from the Council, Resolution 1244 governing the UN Interim Administration in Kosovo and Metohija (UNMIK) was to remain in force; following the enactment of a new Kosovan Constitution in June, providing for the transfer of executive powers from the UN to the elected Kosovan authorities and for an EU police and justice mission to assume supervisory responsibilities from the UN, the Council met to discuss a proposal of the UN Secretary-General for the reconfiguration of UNMIK. Discussions on the future status of Kosovo remained a priority for the Security Council in 2011.

The Security Council monitored and considered the situation in Haiti during 2011, and stressed the importance of the activities of the UN Stabilization Mission in Haiti (MINUSTAH) in supporting the presidential elections held in March of that year, and in continuing to restore stability following the devastating earthquake of January 2010.

In February 2006 the Security Council endorsed the Afghanistan Compact, which had been adopted in the previous month as a framework for the partnership between Afghanistan and the international community. In June 2008 the Council adopted a resolution in which it expressed concern at the smuggling into Afghanistan of chemicals used for refining heroin. The Security Council addressed the situation in Afghanistan at regular intervals during 2011, and in March held a public meeting on Afghanistan at which it was briefed by the SSRG and Head of the UN Assistance Mission in Afghanistan (UNAMA, established in March 2002) on the situation in the country. The SSRG urged full international support for the transition to Afghan responsibility and ownership of its own governance, security and development efforts, and confirmed that the UN would continue to support Afghanistan after that transition. In March 2012 the Council extended UNAMA's mandate until March 2013. It has also successively extended the mandate of the International Security Assistance Force in Afghanistan (most recently to October 2012).

In recent years the Council has made statements, adopted resolutions and held open debates on a number of other ongoing themes, including the protection of children from the effects of armed conflict; the protection of civilians in armed conflict situations; curbing the proliferation of small arms and light weapons; women; the role of the UN in supporting justice and the rule of law; security sector reform; non-proliferation of weapons of mass destruction; the relationship between the Council and regional organizations; the role of the Council in addressing humanitarian crises; and the role of the UN in post-conflict national reconciliation.

SPECIAL SUBSIDIARY BODIES

Counter-Terrorism Committee (CTC): f. 2001, pursuant to Security Council Resolution 1373 (2001) and, in March 2004, in accordance with Resolution 1535 (2004), elevated to a special subsidiary body; comprises a Plenary (composed of the Council member states) and a Bureau; assisted by an Executive Directorate (the Counter-Terrorism Committee Executive Directorate—CTED, which became operational in Dec. 2005); since Sept. 2005 the CTC has also been mandated to monitor member states' implementation of Resolution 1624 (2005), concerning incitement to commit acts of terrorism; Chair. HARDEEP SINGH PURI (India); Exec. Dir, Counter-Terrorism Exec. Directorate MICHAEL PETER FFLOYD SMITH (Australia).

The UN Peace-building Commission, which was inaugurated in June 2006, its establishment having been authorized by the Security Council and General Assembly in December 2005, is a subsidiary advisory body of both the Council and Assembly.

COMMITTEES

In June 2012 there were three **Standing Committees**, each composed of representatives of all Council member states:

Committee of Experts on Rules of Procedure (studies and advises on rules of procedure and other technical matters);

Committee on the Admission of New Members;

Committee on Council Meetings away from Headquarters.

Ad hoc Committees, which are established as needed, comprise all Council members and meet in closed session:

Governing Council of the UN Compensation Commission established by Security Council Resolution 692 (1991);

1540 Committee established pursuant to Security Council Resolution 1540 (2004).

Within this category are the Sanctions Committees, which may be established to oversee economic or political enforcement measures, imposed by the Security Council to maintain or restore international peace and security. At June 2012 the following committees were operational:

Security Council Committee established pursuant to Resolution 2048 (2012) concerning Guinea-Bissau;

Security Council Committee established pursuant to Resolution 1988 (2011) concerning the Taliban in Afghanistan;

Security Council Committee established pursuant to Resolution 1970 (2011) concerning the Libyan Arab Jamahiriya;

Security Council Committee established pursuant to Resolution 1737 (2006) concerning Iran;

Security Council Committee established pursuant to Resolution 1718 (2006) concerning the Democratic People's Republic of Korea;

Security Council Committee established pursuant to Resolution 1636 (2005) concerning Syria;

Security Council Committee established pursuant to Resolution 1591 (2005) concerning Sudan;

Security Council Committee established pursuant to Resolution 1572 (2004) concerning Côte d'Ivoire;

Security Council Committee established pursuant to Resolution 1533 (2004) concerning the Democratic Republic of the Congo;

Security Council Committee established pursuant to Resolution 1521 (2003) concerning Liberia;

Security Council Committee established pursuant to Resolution 1518 (2003) concerning the financial assets of the former Iraqi regime;

Security Council Committee established pursuant to Resolutions 1267 (1999) and 1989 (2011) concerning al-Qa'ida and the Taliban and associated individuals and entities;

Security Council Committee established pursuant to Resolution 751 (1992) concerning Somalia and Resolution 1907 (2009) concerning Eritrea.

Office of the Ombudsperson of the 1267 Committee: Rm TB-08041D, UN Plaza, New York, NY 10017, USA; f. Dec. 2009; reviews requests from individuals, groups, undertakings or entities seeking to be removed from the al-Qa'ida Sanctions List; Ombudsperson KIMBERLY PROST.

In June 1993 an Informal Working Group on Documentation and other procedural questions was established. An Informal Working Group on General Issues on Sanctions was established in 2000 to consider ways of improving the effectiveness of UN sanctions and a Working Group on Peace-keeping Operations was established in January 2001. In March 2002 an Ad Hoc Working Group on Conflict Prevention and Resolution in Africa was established. A Working Group established (in October 2004) pursuant to Resolution 1566 was mandated to consider practical measures to be imposed upon individuals, groups or entities involved in or associated with terrorist activities, other than those designated by the Committee on al-Qa'ida and the Taliban; and the possibility of establishing an international fund to compensate victims of terrorist acts and their families. A Working Group on Children and Armed Conflict was established in July 2005.

AD HOC INTERNATIONAL TRIBUNALS

INTERNATIONAL RESIDUAL MECHANISM FOR CRIMINAL TRIBUNALS

The Residual Mechanism was established by Security Council Resolution 1966 (December 2010) to undertake some essential functions of the International Tribunal for the Former Yugoslavia (ICTY) and of the International Criminal Tribunal for Rwanda (ICTR) upon their planned closure. The Residual Mechanism was to comprise two branches, based in Arusha, Tanzania (due to commence operations on 1 July 2012), and in The Hague, Netherlands (to be operational from 1 July 2013). In January 2012 the UN Secretary-General appointed John Hocking, the ICTY Registrar, to be concurrently Registrar of the Mechanism, and in February Theodor Meron, the ICTY President, and Hassan Bubacar Jallow, the ICTR Prosecutor, were appointed to be, respectively, President and Prosecutor of the Residual Mechanism. The Mechanism was to operate for an initial period of four years from the first commencement date (1 July 2012). It was to conduct any appeals against Tribunal judgements filed following its entry into operation.

President of the Residual Mechanism: THEODOR MERON (Poland).

Prosecutor of the Residual Mechanism: HASSAN BUBACAR JALLOW (The Gambia).

Registrar of the Residual Mechanism: JOHN HOCKING (Australia).

INTERNATIONAL CRIMINAL TRIBUNAL FOR THE FORMER YUGOSLAVIA—ICTY

Address: Registry: Public Information Unit, POB 13888, 2501 EW The Hague, Netherlands.

Telephone: (70) 512-5343; **fax:** (70) 512-5355; **internet:** www.icty.org.

In May 1993 the Security Council, acting under Article VII of the UN Charter, adopted Resolution 827, which established an ad hoc 'war crimes' tribunal. The so-called International Tribunal for the Prosecution of Persons Responsible for Serious Violations of International Humanitarian Law Committed in the Territory of the Former Yugoslavia (also referred to as the International Criminal Tribunal for the former Yugoslavia—ICTY) was inaugurated in The Hague, Netherlands, in November. The ICTY consists of a Chief Prosecutor's office, and 16 permanent judges, of whom 11 sit in three trial chambers and five sit in a seven-member appeals chamber (with the remaining two appeals chamber members representing the ICTR, see below). In addition, a maximum at any one time of nine *ad litem* judges, drawn from a pool of 27, serve as required. Public hearings were initiated in November 1994. The first trial proceedings commenced in May 1996, and the first sentence was imposed by the Tribunal in November. In July and November 1995 the Tribunal formally charged the Bosnian Serb political and military leaders Radovan Karadžić and Gen. Ratko Mladić, on two separate indictments, with genocide, crimes against humanity, violation of the laws and customs of war and serious breaches of the Geneva Conventions. In July 1996 the Tribunal issued international warrants for their arrest. Amended indictments, confirmed in May 2000, and announced in October and November, respectively, included the withdrawal of the fourth charge against Mladić. Karadžić was eventually detained in July 2008, and Mladić was captured in May 2011. In April 2000 Momčilo Krajišnik, a senior associate of Karadžić, was detained by the ICTY, charged with genocide, war crimes and crimes against humanity. Biljana Plavšić, another former Bosnian Serb political leader, surrendered to the Tribunal in January 2001, also indicted on charges of genocide, war crimes and crimes against humanity. In the following month three Bosnian Serb former soldiers were convicted by the ICTY of utilizing mass rape and the sexual enslavement of women as instruments of terror in wartime. In February 2003 Plavšić was sentenced to 11 years' imprisonment, having pleaded guilty in October 2002 to one of the charges against her (persecutions: a crime against humanity). (Under a plea agreement reached with the Tribunal the remaining charges had been withdrawn.) In mid-1998 the ICTY began investigating reported acts of violence against civilians committed by both sides in the conflict in the southern Serbian province of Kosovo and Metohija. In early 1999 there were reports of large-scale organized killings, rape and expulsion of the local Albanian population by Serbian forces. In April ICTY personnel visited refugee camps in neighbouring countries in order to compile evidence of the atrocities, and obtained intelligence information from NATO members regarding those responsible for the incidents. In May the then President of the then Federal Republic of Yugoslavia (FRY, which was renamed Serbia and Montenegro in February 2003, and divided into separate states of Montenegro and Serbia in 2006), Slobodan Milošević, was indicted, along with three senior government ministers and the chief-of-staff of the army, charged with crimes against humanity and violations of the customs of war committed in Kosovo since 1 January 1999; international warrants were issued for their arrests. In June, following the establishment of an international force to secure peace in Kosovo, the ICTY established teams of experts to investigate alleged atrocities at 529 identified grave sites. The new FRY administration, which had assumed power following legislative and presidential elections in late 2000, contested the impartiality of the ICTY, proposing that Milošević and other members of the former regime should be tried before a national court. In April 2001 Milošević was arrested by the local authorities in Belgrade. Under increasing international pressure, the Federal Government approved his extradition in June, and he was immediately transferred to the ICTY, where he was formally charged with crimes against humanity committed in Kosovo in 1999. A further indictment of crimes against humanity committed in Croatia during 1991–92 was confirmed in October 2001, and a third indictment, which included charges of genocide committed in Bosnia and Herzegovina in 1991–95, was confirmed in November 2001. In February 2002 the Appeals Chamber ordered that the three indictments be considered in a single trial. The trial commenced later in that month. Milošević, however, continued to protest at the alleged illegality of his arrest and refused to recognize the jurisdiction of the Court. The case was delayed repeatedly owing to the ill health of the defendant, and in March 2006 he died in captivity. In August 2001 the ICTY passed its first sentence of genocide, convicting a former Bosnian Serb military commander, Gen. Radislav Kristić, for his role in the deaths of up to 8,000 Bosnian Muslim men and boys in Srebrenica in July 1995. In January 2003 Fatmir Limaj, an ethnic Albanian deputy in the Kosovo parliament and former commander of the Kosovo Liberation Army (KLA), was indicted by the ICTY on several counts of crimes against humanity and war crimes that were allegedly committed in mid-1998 against Serb and Albanian detainees at the KLA's Lapusnik prison camp. Limaj was arrested in Slovenia in February 2003 and transferred to ICTY custody in early March. In July 2011 Serbian authorities arrested Goran Hadžic, who had been the last remaining indictee at large. At June 2012 the ICTY had indicted a total of 161 people. Of those who had appeared in proceedings before the Tribunal, 13 had been acquitted, 64 had received a final guilty sentence, and 13 had been referred to national jurisdictions. Some 36 people had completed their sentences. At that time proceedings were ongoing against 35 people accused by the Tribunal, including 17 who were on trial, and 17 at the appeals stage; one person (Goran Hadžic) was awaiting trial. The ICTY's completion strategy envisaged that the Tribunal's activities would be terminated on 30 June 2013, and that from 1 July 2013 outstanding essential functions of the Tribunal would be taken over by the International Residual Mechanism for Criminal Tribunals. Appeals procedures were expected to be finalized by the end of 2014, apart from any appeal in the Radovan Karadžić case, which was expected to be finalized subsequently, and any appeals relating to Gen. Ratko Mladić (who went on trial in May 2012) or Goran Hadžic. The ICTY was to complete all appellate proceedings for which the notice of appeal against the judgement or sentence was filed before the start date of the Mechanism. The ICTY assisted with the establishment of the War Crimes Chamber within the Bosnia and Herzegovina state court, which became operational in March 2005, and also helped Croatia to strengthen its national judicial capacity to enable war crimes to be prosecuted within that country

President of the ICTY: THEODOR MERON (Poland).

ICTY Prosecutor: SERGE BRAMMERTZ (Belgium).

ICTY Registrar: JOHN HOCKING (Australia).

INTERNATIONAL CRIMINAL TRIBUNAL FOR RWANDA—ICTR

Address: Registry: Arusha International Conference Centre, POB 6016, Arusha, Tanzania.

Telephone: (212) 963-2850; **fax:** (212) 963-2848; **e-mail:** ictr-press@un.org; **internet:** www.ictr.org.

In November 1994 the Security Council adopted Resolution 955, establishing the ICTR to prosecute persons responsible for genocide and other serious violations of humanitarian law that had been committed in Rwanda and by Rwandans in neighbouring states. Its temporal jurisdiction was limited to the period 1 January to 31 December 1994. UN Secretary Council Resolution 977, adopted in February 1995, determined that the seat of the Tribunal would be located in Arusha, Tanzania. The Tribunal consists of 11 permanent judges, of whom nine sit in four trial chambers and two sit in the seven-member appeals chamber that is shared with the ICTY and based at The Hague. A high security UN Detention Facility, the first of its kind, was constructed within the compound of the prison in Arusha and opened in 1996. In August 2002 the UN Security Council endorsed a proposal by the ICTR President to elect a pool of 18 *ad litem* judges to the Tribunal with a view to accelerating its activities. In October 2003 the Security Council increased the number of *ad litem* judges who may serve on the Tribunal at any one time from four to nine. The first plenary session of the Tribunal was held in The Hague in June 1995; formal proceedings at its permanent headquarters in Arusha were initiated in November. The first trial of persons charged by the Tribunal commenced in January 1997, and sentences were imposed in July. In September 1998 the former Rwandan Prime Minister, Jean Kambanda, and a former mayor of Taba, Jean-Paul Akayesu, both Hutu extremists, were found guilty of genocide and crimes against humanity; Kambanda subsequently became the first person ever to be sentenced under the 1948 Convention on the Prevention and Punishment of the Crime of Genocide. In October 2000 the Tribunal rejected an appeal by Kambanda. In November 1999 the Rwandan Government temporarily suspended co-operation with the Tribunal in protest at a decision of the appeals chamber to release an indicted former government official owing to procedural delays. (The appeals chamber subsequently reversed this decision.) In 2001 two ICTR investigators employed on defence teams were arrested and charged with genocide, having been found to be working at the Tribunal under assumed identities. Relations between the Rwandan Government and the ICTR deteriorated again in 2002, with the then Chief Prosecutor accusing the Rwandan authorities of failing to facilitate the travel of witnesses to the Tribunal and withholding access to documentary materials, and counter-accusations by the Rwandan Government that the Tribunal's progress was too slow, that further suspected perpetrators of genocide had been inadvertently employed by the Tribunal and that Rwandan witnesses attending the Tribunal had not received sufficient protection. Reporting to the UN Security Council in July, the then Chief Prosecutor alleged that the Rwandan refusal to co-operate ensued from her recent decision to indict former members of the Tutsi-dominated Rwanda Patriotic Army for human rights violations committed against Hutus in 1994. In January 2004 a former minister of culture and education, Jean de Dieu Kamuhanda, was found guilty on two counts of genocide and extermination as a crime against humanity. In the following month Samuel Imanishimwe, a former military commander, was convicted on seven counts of genocide, crimes against humanity and serious violations of the Geneva Conventions. In December 2008 Théoneste Bagosora, Aloys Ntabakuze and Anatole Nsengiyumva, former high-ranking military commanders, were found guilty of genocide, crimes against humanity and war crimes, and were each sentenced to life imprisonment. In May 2012 Callixte Nzabonimana, a former Minister of Youth, was convicted of genocide, conspiracy and incitement to commit genocide, and extermination as a crime against humanity, and sentenced to life imprisonment. By June 2012 the Tribunal had delivered judgments against 72 accused, of whom 10 were acquitted, and 17 were appealing their convictions. Trial proceedings relating to two cases were ongoing at that time, while one indictee was awaiting trial; two cases were being tried in France under French national jurisdiction and a further case was referred in June for the first time to be tried in the Rwandan national court system. Nine fugitives wanted by the Tribunal remained at large. In late March the ICTR ordered the case of one of the suspects at large, Charles Sikubwabo, to be referred to the Rwandan High Court for trial. It was envisaged that from 1 July 2012 the International Residual Mechanism for Criminal Tribunals would take over outstanding essential functions of the Tribunal.

Both the ICTY and ICTR have been supported by teams of investigators and human rights experts working in the field to collect forensic and other evidence in order to uphold indictments. Evidence of mass graves resulting from large-scale unlawful killings has been uncovered in both regions.

President of the ICTR: VAGN JOENSEN (Denmark).

ICTR Prosecutor: HASSAN BUBACAR JALLOW (The Gambia).

ICTR Registrar: ADAMA DIENG (Senegal).

Security Council Resolutions

Resolution 1: Adopted 25 Jan. 1946. Agreed to convene the Military Staff Committee established by the UN to provide advice and assistance to the Security Council and comprising the Chiefs of Staff of permanent members of the Security Council or their representatives.

Resolution 8: Adopted 29 Aug. 1946. Endorsed the admission of Afghanistan, Iceland and Sweden to the UN.

Resolution 13: Adopted 12 Dec. 1946. Endorsed the admission of Thailand to the UN.

Resolution 16: Adopted 10 Jan. 1947. Constituted a Free Territory of Trieste (in Italy).

Resolution 21: Adopted 2 April 1947. Designated the Pacific Islands, formerly held under a Japanese mandate, as a strategic area and placed them under the International Trusteeship System, with the USA as administering authority.

Resolution 27: Adopted 1 Aug. 1947. Requested that Indonesia and the Netherlands observe an immediate cease-fire and resolve their conflict peacefully.

Resolution 29: Adopted 12 Aug. 1947. Endorsed the admission of Pakistan and Yemen to the UN.

Resolution 30: Adopted 25 Aug. 1947. Recognized measures taken by the Governments of Indonesia and the Netherlands to comply with Resolution 27, a statement by the Netherlands of its intention to request career consuls in Batavia (Jakarta) to report on the situation in Indonesia and to organize a sovereign, democratic United States of Indonesia, and a request by Indonesia for the deployment of a Commission of Observers.

Resolution 35: Adopted 3 Oct. 1947. Requested that the UN Secretary-General deploy a three-member Committee of Good Offices to facilitate a settlement between Indonesia and the Netherlands.

Resolution 38: Adopted 17 Jan. 1948. Requested the Governments of India and Pakistan to implement measures to improve the situation in the disputed Indian state of Jammu and Kashmir.

Resolution 39: Adopted 20 Jan. 1948. Established a three-member investigatory and mediatory Commission for India and Pakistan, with one member to be selected by the Government of India and one by the Government of Pakistan, for deployment to the disputed state of Jammu and Kashmir.

Resolution 41: Adopted 28 Feb. 1948. Welcomed the Truce Agreement signed by the Governments of Indonesia and the Netherlands.

Resolution 43: Adopted 1 April 1948. Requested the Arab and Jewish communities to halt the violent disorder in Palestine. Requested the Jewish Agency for Palestine and the Arab Higher Committee to make available a representative to facilitate a truce.

Resolution 45: Adopted 10 April 1948. Endorsed the admission of Burma (Myanmar) to the UN.

Resolution 46: Adopted 17 April 1948. Requested all parties involved in the situation in Palestine and the governments of member states to facilitate a truce by means of the cessation of military activity, co-operation with the United Kingdom in its role as the administering authority, and the avoidance of actions likely to obstruct or damage Holy Places in Palestine.

Resolution 47: Adopted 21 April 1948. Increased membership of the Commission for India and Pakistan to five, and requested its immediate deployment. Made recommendations for the restoration of peace to the disputed state of Jammu and Kashmir, and requested that the Indian Government establish a Plebiscite Administration to hold a popular vote on the accession of the state to India or Pakistan. Authorized the Commission to establish a military observer group in Jammu and Kashmir.

Resolution 48: Adopted 23 April 1948. Established a Security Council Truce Commission for Palestine, to monitor the implementation of Resolution 46.

Resolution 49: Adopted 22 May 1948. Demanded that a cease-fire be observed in Palestine. Requested all parties to facilitate the work of a UN Mediator appointed by the General Assembly.

Resolution 50: Adopted 29 May 1948. Requested all those involved in the situation in Palestine to observe a cease-fire for a four-week period. Urged governments to refrain from sending troops or weapons to the area. Stated that any violation of the cease-fire could lead to action under the provisions of the Charter of the UN. Agreed to dispatch a number of military observers to Palestine to assist the UN Mediator and the Security Council Truce Commission.

Resolution 54: Adopted 15 July 1948. Determined that the situation in Palestine constituted a threat to peace under Article 39 of the UN Charter. Requested all those involved to co-operate with the UN Mediator in Palestine and to observe an immediate cease-fire, which was to remain in force pending a transition to peace. Requested the UN Mediator in Palestine to monitor the truce and investigate alleged breaches of the cease-fire.

Resolution 56: Adopted 19 Aug. 1948. Declared the authorities involved in the situation in Palestine to be responsible for preventing all violations of the truce and obliged them to convict any person acting in breach of it.

Resolution 57: Adopted 18 Sept. 1948. Expressed shock at the assassination of the UN Mediator in Palestine.

Resolution 61: Adopted 4 Nov. 1948. Requested governments involved in the situation in Palestine to withdraw any forces which had advanced beyond demarcation lines fixed by the Acting Mediator in Palestine, and to establish demilitarized, neutral zones to ensure the full observance of the cease-fire. Appointed a five-member Committee to advise the Acting Mediator.

Resolution 62: Adopted 16 Nov. 1948. Imposed an armistice in Palestine, with the establishment of permanent demarcation lines.

Resolution 63: Adopted 24 Dec. 1948. Expressed concern at the resumption of hostilities in Indonesia, and requested the Governments of Indonesia and the Netherlands to observe an immediate cease-fire. Demanded the release of the President of Indonesia and other political detainees.

Resolution 66: Adopted 29 Dec. 1948. Ordered the observation of an immediate cease-fire in Palestine and the implementation of Resolution 61, following an outbreak of hostilities on 22 Dec.

Resolution 67: Adopted 28 Jan. 1949. Demanded the cessation of military operations by Indonesia and the Netherlands and the release of all political prisoners. Recommended the establishment of an interim federal government by 15 March, the holding of elections to select representatives to an Indonesian constituent assembly by 1 Oct. and the transfer of sovereignty from the Netherlands to the United States of Indonesia by 1 July 1950. Decided that the Committee of Good Offices was to become the UN Commission for Indonesia, to be assisted by the Consular Committee.

Resolution 69: Adopted 4 March 1949. Endorsed the admission of Israel to the UN.

Resolution 73: Adopted 11 Aug. 1949. Requested all those involved in the conflict in Palestine to support the work of the Conciliation Commission for Palestine. Concluded that the Armistice Agreements reached superseded Resolutions 50 and 54. Reaffirmed a request for an unconditional cease-fire to be observed. Relieved the Acting Mediator in Palestine from further duties and confirmed that the implementation of each agreement was to be monitored by a Mixed Armistice Commission, the chairman of which was to be the Chief of Staff of the UN Truce Supervision Organization (UNTSO) in Palestine, or his representative.

Resolution 80: Adopted 14 March 1950. Commended the Governments of India and Pakistan for effecting a cessation of hostilities, establishing a cease-fire line and agreeing upon the appointment of a Plebiscite Administrator for the disputed state of Jammu and Kashmir, and requested the two sides to undertake a demilitarization programme and to appoint a UN Representative to assume the duties of the UN Commission for India and Pakistan.

Resolution 82: Adopted 25 June 1950. Condemned the invasion of the Republic of Korea (South Korea) and demanded an immediate cease-fire and the withdrawal of troops from the Democratic People's Republic of Korea (North Korea). Requested the UN Commission on Korea to monitor the situation.

Resolution 83: Adopted 27 June 1950. Appealed for assistance to enable South Korea to repel North Korean forces, and to restore peace and stability to the region.

Resolution 84: Adopted 7 July 1950. Welcomed the prompt military and other assistance provided to South Korea by member states. Recommended that the military forces provided form a unified command under the USA.

Resolution 85: Adopted 31 July 1950. Requested the unified force (officially entitled the UN Command) to determine the humanitarian needs of the population of North Korea.

Resolution 86: Adopted 26 Sept. 1950. Endorsed the admission of Indonesia to the UN.

Resolution 89: Adopted 17 Nov. 1950. Reminded all parties to the situation in Palestine to resolve disputes according to the procedures established by the Armistice Agreements, which envisaged permanent peace for Palestine.

Resolution 91: Adopted 30 March 1951. Instructed the UN Representative for India and Pakistan to effect the demilitarization of the disputed state of Jammu and Kashmir, on the basis of resolutions made by the UN Commission for India and Pakistan in Aug. 1948 and Jan. 1949.

Resolution 92: Adopted 8 May 1951. Expressed concern at the resumption of violence in the demilitarized zone established by the Israel–Syria Armistice Agreement of 20 July 1949, and demanded that an immediate cease-fire be observed.

Resolution 93: Adopted 18 May 1951. Instructed the Governments of Israel and Syria strictly to observe their Armistice Agreement and to inform the Mixed Armistice Commission of any grievances.

Resolution 95: Adopted 1 Sept. 1951. Requested the Egyptian Government to remove restrictions imposed on the movement of commercial ships through the Suez Canal to Israeli and other ports in contravention of the Egypt–Israel Armistice Agreement.

Resolution 96: Adopted 10 Nov. 1951. Welcomed an agreement by India and Pakistan to determine the accession of the disputed state of Jammu and Kashmir by means of a plebiscite and urged both parties to resolve the issues remaining.

Resolution 101: Adopted 24 Nov. 1953. Condemned retaliatory action taken by Israel against Jordan as constituting a violation of the cease-fire provisions of Resolution 54 and of the Israeli–Jordan Armistice Agreement.

Resolution 106: Adopted 29 March 1955. Condemned an attack by Israel against Egypt on 6 March as constituting a threat to the Egypt–Israel Armistice Agreement.

Resolution 108: Adopted 8 Sept. 1955. Expressed concern at the cessation of negotiations between Egypt and Israel, and deplored the resumption of violence along the armistice demarcation line established between the two countries in Feb. 1949.

Resolution 109: Adopted 14 Dec. 1955. Endorsed the admission of Albania, Austria, Bulgaria, Cambodia, Ceylon (now Sri Lanka), Finland, Hungary, Ireland, Italy, Jordan, Laos, Libya, Nepal, Portugal, Romania and Spain to the UN.

Resolution 111: Adopted 19 Jan. 1956. Condemned an attack by Israel against Syria in Dec. as constituting a violation of the cease-fire provisions of Resolution 54 and the Israel-Syria Armistice Agreement.

Resolution 112: Adopted 6 Feb. 1956. Endorsed the admission of Sudan to the UN.

Resolution 113: Adopted 4 April 1956. Concluded that the situation in the Middle East constituted a threat to peace in the region and requested the UN Secretary-General to arrange for the implementation of measures to reduce tension, including the withdrawal of forces from armistice demarcation lines, freedom of movement for UN observers and arrangements for the detection of violation of the Armistice Agreements.

Resolution 115: Adopted 20 July 1956. Endorsed the admission of Morocco to the UN.

Resolution 116: Adopted 26 July 1956. Endorsed the admission of Tunisia to the UN.

Resolution 118: Adopted 13 Oct. 1956. Agreed that a settlement of the dispute concerning the Suez Canal should ensure free movement through the Canal, be unrelated to political issues, and respect the sovereignty of Egypt, with tolls and charges to be decided between Egypt and the users of the Canal.

Resolution 121: Adopted 12 Dec. 1956. Endorsed the admission of Japan to the UN.

Resolution 123: Adopted 21 Feb. 1957. Requested the President of the Security Council to examine with the Governments of India and Pakistan proposals for resolving the dispute over the state of Jammu and Kashmir.

Resolution 124: Adopted 7 March 1957. Endorsed the admission of Ghana to the UN.

Resolution 125: Adopted 5 Sept. 1957. Endorsed the admission of Malaya (now Malaysia) to the UN.

Resolution 127: Adopted 22 Jan. 1958. Instructed the Chief of Staff of the Truce Supervision Organization in Palestine to regulate civilian activity between the demarcation lines of Israel and Jordan and to perform a survey of property ownership in the zone, in order to ensure that one party's property was not used by another without permission.

Resolution 128: Adopted 11 June 1958. Agreed to deploy a UN Observation Group in Lebanon (UNOGIL) to ensure that no illegal penetration of weapons or military personnel from the United Arab Republic (Egypt and Syria) was taking place.

Resolution 131: Adopted 9 Dec. 1958. Endorsed the admission of Guinea to the UN.

Resolution 133: Adopted 26 Jan. 1960. Endorsed the admission of Cameroon to the UN.

Resolution 134: Adopted 1 April 1960. Condemned the violent repression of demonstrators against racial discrimination in South Africa, and requested that South Africa abandon its policy of apartheid and seek to promote racial equality.

Resolution 135: Adopted 27 May 1960. Requested the Governments of France, the United Kingdom, the USA and the USSR to resume negotiations for a peaceful solution to existing problems, including nuclear disarmament and the cessation of nuclear weapons tests.

Resolution 136: Adopted 31 May 1960. Endorsed the admission of Togo to the UN.

Resolution 139: Adopted 28 June 1960. Endorsed the admission of Mali to the UN.

Resolution 140: Adopted 29 June 1960. Endorsed the admission of Malagasy (now Madagascar) to the UN.

Resolution 141: Adopted 5 July 1960. Endorsed the admission of Somalia to the UN.

Resolution 142: Adopted 7 July 1960. Endorsed the admission of the Republic of the Congo (now the Democratic Republic of the Congo (DRC, previously Zaire) to the UN.

Resolution 143: Adopted 14 July 1960. Demanded that the Belgian Government withdraw its troops from the newly independent territory of the (Democratic) Republic of the Congo and authorized the UN Secretary-General to dispatch UN troops to the region to maintain order.

Resolution 146: Adopted 9 Aug. 1960. Demanded that the Belgian Government withdraw its troops from the province of Katanga in the (Democratic) Republic of the Congo and allow the UN force to gain access to it.

Resolution 147: Adopted 23 Aug. 1960. Endorsed the admission of Dahomey (now Benin) to the UN.

Resolution 148: Adopted 23 Aug. 1960. Endorsed the admission of Niger to the UN.

Resolution 149: Adopted 23 Aug. 1960. Endorsed the admission of Upper Volta (now Burkina Faso) to the UN.

Resolution 150: Adopted 23 Aug. 1960. Endorsed the admission of Côte d'Ivoire to the UN.

Resolution 151: Adopted 23 Aug. 1960. Endorsed the admission of Chad to the UN.

Resolution 152: Adopted 23 Aug. 1960. Endorsed the admission of the Republic of the Congo (Brazzaville) to the UN.

Resolution 153: Adopted 23 Aug. 1960. Endorsed the admission of Gabon to the UN.

Resolution 154: Adopted 23 Aug. 1960. Endorsed the admission of the Central African Republic to the UN.

Resolution 155: Adopted 24 Aug. 1960. Endorsed the admission of Cyprus to the UN.

Resolution 158: Adopted 28 Sept. 1960. Endorsed the admission of Senegal to the UN.

Resolution 159: Adopted 28 Sept. 1960. Endorsed the admission of Mali to the UN.

Resolution 160: Adopted 7 Oct. 1960. Endorsed the admission of Nigeria to the UN.

Resolution 161: Adopted 21 Feb. 1961. Following the killing of the leaders of the (Democratic) Republic of the Congo, urged that measures be implemented to prevent the re-occurrence of civil war, that all troops, other than those under UN command, be withdrawn, and that an investigation into the assassinations be undertaken. Urged that Parliament be convened and that the Congolese forces be brought under control to prevent any further deterioration of the situation in the (Democratic) Republic of the Congo.

Resolution 163: Adopted 9 June 1961. Deplored the violent repression by Portuguese forces of a nationalist rebellion in Angola. Requested a Sub-committee on the Situation in Angola to implement its mandate promptly.

Resolution 165: Adopted 26 Sept. 1961. Endorsed the admission of Sierra Leone to the UN.

Resolution 166: Adopted 25 Oct. 1961. Endorsed the admission of the Mongolian People's Republic (Mongolia) to the UN.

Resolution 167: Adopted 25 Oct. 1961. Endorsed the admission of Mauritania to the UN.

Resolution 168: Adopted 3 Nov. 1961. Endorsed the appointment of U Thant as acting Secretary-General of the UN (following the death, in an aircraft accident, of Dag Hammarskjöld).

Resolution 169: Adopted 24 Nov. 1961. Condemned the Belgian Government's support for the secession of the Katanga region in the (Democratic) Republic of the Congo, and all armed attacks against UN forces, and demanded their immediate cessation.

Resolution 170: Adopted 14 Dec. 1961. Endorsed the admission of Tanganyika (now part of Tanzania) to the UN.

Resolution 171: Adopted 9 April 1962. Condemned an outbreak of hostilities between Israel and Syria in March. Requested that both parties co-operate with the Chief of Staff and abide by the new cease-fire agreement and the provisions of the Israel–Syria Armistice Agreement.

Resolution 172: Adopted 26 July 1962. Endorsed the admission of Rwanda to the UN.

Resolution 173: Adopted 26 July 1962. Endorsed the admission of Burundi to the UN.

Resolution 174: Adopted 12 Sept. 1962. Endorsed the admission of Jamaica to the UN.

Resolution 175: Adopted 12 Sept. 1962. Endorsed the admission of Trinidad and Tobago to the UN.

Resolution 176: Adopted 4 Oct. 1962. Endorsed the admission of Algeria to the UN.

Resolution 177: Adopted 15 Oct. 1962. Endorsed the admission of Uganda to the UN.

Resolution 179: Adopted 11 June 1963. Authorized the establishment of the UN Yemen Observation Mission.

Resolution 180: Adopted 31 July 1963. Confirmed General Assembly Resolution 1514 (XV). Declared Portugal's policy of claiming the territories administered by it to be 'inalienable' overseas possessions to be in contravention of the Charter of the UN. Demanded that Portugal recognize the right of the people under its administration to self-determination and independence, that it cease all acts of repression and evacuate its forces from the territories concerned, that it introduce an unconditional political amnesty, that it commence negotiations with the aim of transferring power to elected political institutions and that it, ultimately, grant independence to its overseas possessions. Requested all member states to refrain from providing the Portuguese Government with assistance that might enable it to continue to repress territories under its administration.

Resolution 181: Adopted 7 Aug. 1963. Declared South Africa's racial policy to be in contravention of the Charter of the UN and requested that it abandon the apartheid regime in compliance with Resolution 134. Established an arms embargo against South Africa.

Resolution 182: Adopted 4 Dec. 1963. Condemned South Africa's refusal to comply with previous resolutions and requested the Government to abolish discriminatory and repressive measures and release all political prisoners.

Resolution 184: Adopted 16 Dec. 1963. Endorsed the admission of Zanzibar (now part of Tanzania) to the UN.

Resolution 185: Adopted 16 Dec. 1963. Endorsed the admission of Kenya to the UN.

Resolution 186: Adopted 4 March 1964. Established a UN Peace-keeping Force in Cyprus (UNFICYP) and appointed a UN Mediator to promote a peaceful settlement to the dispute between the Greek and Turkish Cypriot communities.

Resolution 189: Adopted 4 June 1964. Condemned armed incursions into Cambodia by units of the Vietnamese army. Deployed three observers to Cambodia and Viet Nam to consider measures to prevent further hostilities.

Resolution 191: Adopted 18 June 1964. Reiterated its condemnation of apartheid and appealed to the South African Government to release opponents of the apartheid regime and abolish all charges brought against them.

Resolution 193: Adopted 9 Aug. 1964. Appealed for an immediate cease-fire to be observed in Cyprus, and requested the Government of Turkey to halt its use of military force.

Resolution 195: Adopted 9 Oct. 1964. Endorsed the admission of Malawi to the UN.

Resolution 196: Adopted 30 Oct. 1964. Endorsed the admission of Malta to the UN.

Resolution 197: Adopted 30 Oct. 1964. Endorsed the admission of Zambia to the UN.

Resolution 200: Adopted 15 March 1965. Endorsed the admission of Gambia to the UN.

Resolution 202: Adopted 6 May 1965. Expressed concern at the situation in Southern Rhodesia, following elections at which the white-supremacist party, the Rhodesian Front (RF), which sought full independence from the United Kingdom and the retention of a minority-rule constitution, won all seats.

Resolution 203: Adopted 14 May 1965. Authorized a mission of the representative of the UN Secretary-General in the Dominican Republic (DOMREP) to report on the conflict in that country.

Resolution 209: Adopted 4 Sept. 1965. Requested the Governments of India and Pakistan to observe a cease-fire and to co-operate with the UN Military Observer Group in India and Pakistan (UNMOGIP), following a deterioration in the situation along the cease-fire line in the disputed state of Jammu and Kashmir.

Resolution 211: Adopted 20 Sept. 1965. Demanded that India and Pakistan observe a cease-fire agreement over the disputed state of Jammu and Kashmir. Requested the UN Secretary-General to dispatch an Observation Mission to supervise the cease-fire and the withdrawal of military forces.

Resolution 212: Adopted 20 Sept. 1965. Endorsed the admission of the Maldives to the UN.

Resolution 213: Adopted 20 Sept. 1965. Endorsed the admission of Singapore to the UN.

Resolution 215: Adopted 5 Nov. 1965. Requested the Governments of India and Pakistan to instruct their armed forces to halt military activity and violations of the cease-fire agreement in Jammu and Kashmir and to meet a representative of the UN Secretary-General to establish a plan for the withdrawal of troops.

Resolution 216: Adopted 12 Nov. 1965. Condemned the unilateral declaration of independence made by the white minority party, the Rhodesian Front (RF), in Southern Rhodesia, and requested member states to refrain from recognizing the new regime.

Resolution 217: Adopted 20 Nov. 1965. Declared the declaration of independence in Rhodesia to be legally invalid. Requested the United Kingdom to resolve the situation in Rhodesia and to allow the population to determine its own future, in compliance with General Assembly Resolution 1514 (XV). Urged member states to avoid establishing economic links with Rhodesia.

Resolution 223: Adopted 21 June 1966. Endorsed the admission of Guyana to the UN.

Resolution 224: Adopted 14 Oct. 1966. Endorsed the admission of Botswana to the UN.

Resolution 225: Adopted 14 Oct. 1966. Endorsed the admission of Lesotho to the UN.

Resolution 229: Adopted 2 Dec. 1966. Endorsed the appointment of U Thant as Secretary-General of the UN.

Resolution 230: Adopted 7 Dec. 1966. Endorsed the admission of Barbados to the UN.

Resolution 232: Adopted 16 Dec. 1966. Determined that the rebellion in Rhodesia constituted a threat to international peace and security and imposed mandatory economic sanctions against that country.

Resolution 233: Adopted 6 June 1967. Requested a cease-fire to be observed by Israeli forces and Egypt, Iraq, Jordan and Syria (following the initiation by Israel of what came to be known as the 'Six-Day War').

Resolution 237: Adopted 14 June 1967. Demanded the Government of Israel to treat humanely prisoners of war, to ensure the security and welfare of the inhabitants of areas affected by the recent military operations and to facilitate the return of those displaced by the hostilities.

Resolution 239: Adopted 10 July 1967. Condemned all member states permitting or tolerating the recruitment of mercenaries and the provision of facilities to them, with the objective of overthrowing the governments of member states. In particular, requested governments to ensure that their territories were not used for the recruitment, training and transit of mercenaries seeking to overthrow the Government of the Democratic Republic of the Congo.

Resolution 242: Adopted 22 Nov. 1967. Refined principles for peace in the Middle East by means of the withdrawal of Israeli forces from the Occupied Territories and acknowledgement of the sovereignty, territorial integrity and political independence of all countries in the region. Established that the problem of refugees had to be resolved and requested a Special Representative to be deployed to the Middle East to promote a peaceful settlement.

Resolution 243: Adopted 12 Dec. 1967. Endorsed the admission of Southern Yemen to the UN.

Resolution 248: Adopted 24 March 1968. Condemned military action taken against Jordan by Israeli forces, in contravention of UN resolutions and the Charter of the UN, and reaffirmed Resolution 237.

Resolution 249: Adopted 18 April 1968. Endorsed the admission of Mauritius to the UN.

Resolution 252: Adopted 21 May 1968. Condemned Israel's refusal to comply with UN resolutions and declared invalid all legislative and administrative measures taken by Israel in Jerusalem, including the expropriation of land and property. Urgently requested Israel to rescind those measures and to refrain from taking further action of that kind.

Resolution 253: Adopted 29 May 1968. Condemned acts of political oppression undertaken by the Rhodesian regime and demanded the United Kingdom, as administering authority, to end the rebellion. Strengthened economic sanctions against Rhodesia and prohibited member states from permitting those connected with the regime to enter their territories. Established a Committee to monitor the implementation of sanctions.

Resolution 255: Adopted 19 June 1968. Welcomed the intention of a number of member states with nuclear weapons to assist non-nuclear-weapon states party to the Treaty on the Non-proliferation of Nuclear Weapons (adopted by General Assembly Resolution 2373 (XXII)) should they be subjected to a threat of aggression by a nuclear state.

Resolution 257: Adopted 11 Sept. 1968. Endorsed the admission of Swaziland to the UN.

Resolution 260: Adopted 6 Nov. 1968. Endorsed the admission of Equatorial Guinea to the UN.

Resolution 262: Adopted 31 Dec. 1968. Condemned Israel for a raid on Beirut airport in Lebanon, which destroyed 13 Lebanese aircraft.

Resolution 264: Adopted 20 March 1969. Recognized that the General Assembly had terminated South Africa's mandate over Namibia and assumed responsibility for the territory until it gained independence. Declared South Africa's continued presence in Namibia to be illegal and demanded its withdrawal.

Resolution 267: Adopted 3 July 1969. Reaffirmed Resolution 252 and deplored Israel's refusal to comply with UN resolutions. Requested Israel to rescind all measures purporting to alter the status of Jerusalem.

Resolution 277: Adopted 18 March 1970. Condemned Rhodesia for declaring itself a republic and demanded member states to withhold recognition of the Rhodesian regime. Reiterated the United Kingdom's responsibility for Rhodesia and demanded that member states sever all relations with Rhodesia and terminate transport services to and from that country.

Resolution 282: Adopted 23 July 1970. Reasserted its opposition to the apartheid regime of South Africa. Strengthened the arms embargo imposed against South Africa and condemned all violations of it.

Resolution 283: Adopted 29 July 1970. Requested member states formally to withdraw recognition of South Africa's authority over Namibia and to end all commercial and industrial investments in Namibia. Requested the General Assembly to establish a UN fund for Namibia.

Resolution 284: Adopted 29 July 1970. Requested the International Court of Justice to provide an advisory opinion on the legal consequences of South Africa's continued presence in Namibia.

Resolution 286: Adopted 9 Sept. 1970. Demanded the immediate release of all hijacked passengers and crews and requested that member states take all possible legal measures to prevent terrorist interference with international civil air travel.

Resolution 287: Adopted 10 Oct. 1970. Endorsed the admission of Fiji to the UN.

Resolution 292: Adopted 10 Feb. 1971. Endorsed the admission of Bhutan to the UN.

Resolution 294: Adopted 15 July 1971. Condemned acts of hostility perpetrated by the army of Portuguese Guinea (now Guinea-Bissau) against Senegal from 1967. Approved the establishment of a special mission to monitor the situation along the border between the two countries.

Resolution 296: Adopted 18 Aug. 1971. Endorsed the admission of Bahrain to the UN.

Resolution 297: Adopted 15 Sept. 1971. Endorsed the admission of Qatar to the UN.

Resolution 298: Adopted 25 Sept. 1971. Reaffirmed Resolutions 252 and 267 and condemned Israel's refusal to comply with UN resolutions. Confirmed all administrative and legislative actions by Israel which altered the status of Jerusalem to be invalid.

Resolution 299: Adopted 30 Sept. 1971. Endorsed the admission of Oman to the UN.

Resolution 301: Adopted 20 Oct. 1971. Condemned actions taken by the Government of South Africa to destroy the unity and territorial integrity of Namibia, including the establishment of 'Bantustans'. Supported the advisory opinion of the International Court of Justice (ICJ), which ruled that South Africa's presence in Namibia was illegal and that it should withdraw immediately. Requested all states to refrain from observing treaties or from entering into diplomatic relations with South Africa.

Resolution 304: Adopted 8 Dec. 1971. Endorsed the admission of the United Arab Emirates to the UN.

Resolution 306: Adopted 21 Dec. 1971. Endorsed the appointment of Kurt Waldheim as Secretary-General of the UN.

Resolution 307: Adopted 21 Dec. 1971. Demanded the strict observation of the cease-fire agreement for the disputed Indian state of Jammu and Kashmir, while troops were withdrawn. Appealed for international humanitarian aid.

Resolution 310: Adopted 4 Feb. 1972. Condemned South Africa's refusal to comply with Security Council resolutions and its repression of labourers in Namibia. Reaffirmed the illegality of South Africa's continued occupation of Namibia. Requested all member states with business interests in Namibia to ensure that they complied with the provisions of the Universal Declaration of Human Rights.

Resolution 312: Adopted 4 Feb. 1972. Requested Portugal to recognize the right of its territories to self-determination and independence, in accordance with General Assembly Resolution 1514 (XV). Demanded that Portugal end its colonial wars and its repression of Angola, Portuguese Guinea (now Guinea-Bissau) and Mozambique.

Resolution 313: Adopted 28 Feb. 1972. Demanded that Israel withdraw from Lebanese territory.

Resolution 320: Adopted 29 Sept. 1972. Expressed concern that a number of member states were ignoring the sanctions imposed against Rhodesia by Resolution 253, and urged the USA in particular to comply with its provisions.

Resolution 321: Adopted 23 Oct. 1972. Condemned a border attack on Senegal by the Portuguese army, and warned that the Security Council would consider taking further action if Portugal refused to comply with its resolutions.

Resolution 323: Adopted 6 Dec. 1972. Noted that the majority of Namibian people consulted voiced their support for national independence through the withdrawal of the South African administration and the abolition of its 'homelands' policy.

Resolution 326: Adopted 2 Feb. 1973. Condemned the acts of hostility perpetrated against Zambia by the regime of Rhodesia, in collaboration with the regime of South Africa, and condemned Rhodesia's acts of internal political repression. Demanded that the United Kingdom, as administrator of Rhodesia, implement measures to prevent further such actions. Agreed to deploy a special mission to assess the situation in the region.

Resolution 328: Adopted 10 March 1973. Endorsed the conclusions of the special mission established by Resolution 326. Affirmed that the Zimbabwean people should be permitted to exercise their right to self-determination in accordance with General Assembly Resolution 1514 (XV) and reiterated demands for the withdrawal of South African troops from Rhodesia.

Resolution 333: Adopted 22 May 1973. Strengthened sanctions imposed against Rhodesia.

Resolution 335: Adopted 22 June 1973. Endorsed the admission of the German Democratic Republic and the Federal Republic of Germany to the UN.

Resolution 336: Adopted 18 July 1973. Endorsed the admission of the Bahamas to the UN.

Resolution 338: Adopted 22 Oct. 1973. Demanded a cease-fire agreement between Israel and the Arab states. Reaffirmed the principles of Resolution 242.

Resolution 340: Adopted 25 Oct. 1973. Approved the establishment of a second UN Emergency Force (UNEF II) in the Middle East to assist in efforts for the establishment of peace.

Resolution 341: Adopted 27 Oct. 1973. Approved UNEF's mandate in the Middle East.

Resolution 347: Adopted 24 April 1974. Condemned the Israeli invasion of Lebanon and asked Israel to refrain from further acts of violence and to release all abducted Lebanese civilians.

Resolution 350: Adopted 31 May 1974. Welcomed the Agreement on Disengagement negotiated between Israeli and Syrian forces in the context of Resolution 338, and established a UN Disengagement Observer Force (UNDOF).

Resolution 351: Adopted 10 June 1974. Endorsed the admission of Bangladesh to the UN.

Resolution 352: Adopted 21 June 1974. Endorsed the admission of Grenada to the UN.

Resolution 353: Adopted 20 July 1974. Requested all states to recognize the sovereignty, independence and territorial integrity of Cyprus. Demanded an immediate cease-fire and the cessation of foreign military intervention in that country, and requested that Greece, Turkey and the United Kingdom commence negotiations for the restoration of peace and constitutional government to Cyprus. Requested that all parties co-operate fully with the UN Peace-keeping Force in Cyprus.

Resolution 356: Adopted 12 Aug. 1974. Endorsed the admission of Guinea-Bissau to the UN.

Resolution 360: Adopted 16 Aug. 1974. Expressed regret at the unilateral military action taken against Cyprus by Turkey, urged compliance with the provisions of previous resolutions, and requested the resumption of negotiations, as described in Resolution 353.

Resolution 361: Adopted 30 Aug. 1974. Commended the negotiations between the two community leaders in Cyprus. Expressed concern for persons displaced as a result of the situation and requested the provision of emergency humanitarian assistance to Cyprus.

Resolution 366: Adopted 17 Dec. 1974. Demanded that South Africa comply with the ruling of the International Court of Justice that confirmed its presence in Namibia to be illegal, that it withdraw its administration and transfer power to the Namibian people, and that it release all Namibian political prisoners, abolish the application of all racially and politically discriminatory practices, and allow the return of exiled Namibians to their country.

Resolution 367: Adopted 12 March 1975. Expressed concern that the unilateral declaration of a 'Federated Turkish State' in Cyprus could compromise continued negotiations, and requested that the UN Secretary-General undertake efforts to resume negotiations.

Resolution 372: Adopted 18 Aug. 1975. Endorsed the admission of Cape Verde to the UN.

Resolution 373: Adopted 18 Aug. 1975. Endorsed the admission of São Tomé and Príncipe to the UN.

Resolution 374: Adopted 18 Aug. 1975. Endorsed the admission of Mozambique to the UN.

Resolution 375: Adopted 18 Aug. 1975. Endorsed the admission of Papua New Guinea to the UN.

Resolution 376: Adopted 17 Oct. 1975. Endorsed the admission of the Comoros to the UN.

Resolution 377: Adopted 22 Oct. 1975. Requested that the UN Secretary-General enter into consultations with the parties involved with the situation in Spanish (Western) Sahara.

Resolution 379: Adopted 2 Nov. 1975. Advised all parties concerned with the situation in Spanish (Western) Sahara to avoid action that could increase tension in the area and requested the UN Secretary-General to intensify consultations with the parties involved.

Resolution 380: Adopted 6 Nov. 1975. Expressed disapproval of the Moroccan 'Green March' on Spanish (Western) Sahara, and demanded that Morocco withdraw all participants from the territory. Urged all parties involved to co-operate fully with the UN Secretary-General.

Resolution 382: Adopted 1 Dec. 1975. Endorsed the admission of Suriname to the UN.

Resolution 384: Adopted 22 Dec. 1975. Demanded that the territorial integrity and right to self-determination of East Timor be respected, and that the Government of Indonesia withdraw its troops from the territory. Requested that the UN Secretary-General deploy a Special Representative to East Timor.

Resolution 385: Adopted 30 Jan. 1976. Condemned South Africa's failure to comply with Resolutions 264, 269 and 366 and reaffirmed their terms. Condemned the country's illegal use of Namibia as a military base. Demanded that South Africa end its policy of 'Bantustans' and 'homelands'. Condemned South Africa's evasion of UN demands for free elections in Namibia and demanded that it make a formal declaration accepting provisions for elections to be held.

Resolution 386: Adopted 17 March 1976. Praised Mozambique's decision to impose economic sanctions on Rhodesia, condemned the aggression by the illegal regime in Rhodesia against Mozambique, and appealed to member states and UN bodies to assist Mozambique in its economic situation.

Resolution 387: Adopted 31 March 1976. Condemned aggression against Angola by South African forces and the use of Namibia as a military base. Demanded that South Africa respect Angola's independence, sovereignty and territorial integrity, and compensate Angola for losses incurred by its invasion.

Resolution 388: Adopted 6 April 1976. Resolved that member states should make sure not to insure any products in Rhodesia, or exported from or intended for importation to Rhodesia, in contravention of Resolution 253. Compelled member states to ensure that no trade marks or franchise agreements were entered into with Rhodesian enterprises.

Resolution 389: Adopted 22 April 1976. Reiterated Resolution 384 and requested that the UN Secretary-General's Special Representative continue the mission assigned to him.

Resolution 392: Adopted 19 June 1976. Condemned the South African regime for the violent repression of demonstrators against racial discrimination, including school children, on 16 June, and expressed its sympathy to the victims of this violence. Reaffirmed that the doctrine of apartheid constituted a crime against humanity, and requested the Government to end violence against African people and eliminate racial discrimination.

Resolution 393: Adopted 30 July 1976. Condemned South Africa for an attack on Zambia on 11 July and demanded that it respect Zambia's independence, sovereignty, territorial integrity and air space. Reiterated the demand that South Africa end its use of Namibia as a military base. Commended Zambia for its support of Namibia and declared that the liberation of Namibia and Rhodesia and the elimination of apartheid in South Africa were necessary for peace in the region.

Resolution 394: Adopted 16 Aug. 1976. Endorsed the admission of the Seychelles to the UN.

Resolution 395: Adopted 25 Aug. 1976. Requested that Greece and Turkey seek to reduce tensions and resume direct negotiations concerning the dispute over the extent of each country's jurisdiction of the Aegean Sea.

Resolution 397: Adopted 22 Nov. 1976. Endorsed the admission of Angola to the UN.

Resolution 399: Adopted 1 Dec. 1976. Endorsed the admission of (Western) Samoa to the UN.

Resolution 400: Adopted 7 Dec. 1976. Endorsed the appointment of Kurt Waldheim as Secretary-General of the UN for a second term of office.

Resolution 402: Adopted 22 Dec. 1976. Commended Lesotho for its refusal to recognize South Africa's proclamation of an 'independent' Transkei 'Bantustan'. Demanded the immediate reopening of border posts with Lesotho by the Transkeian authorities and condemned all actions intended to compel Lesotho to recognize the Transkei. Appealed to member states and UN bodies to provide assistance to Lesotho.

Resolution 403: Adopted 14 Jan. 1977. Condemned all provocation, harassment and political repression by the illegal regime in Rhodesia against Botswana, and demanded the immediate cessation of all hostilities. Deplored all acts of collaboration and collusion sustaining the illegal regime in Rhodesia. Agreed to dispatch a Mission to Botswana to establish the assistance required and to arrange for the provision of financial assistance.

Resolution 404: Adopted 8 Feb. 1977. Affirmed that the territorial integrity and political independence of Benin must be respected. Agreed to deploy a three-member Special Mission to Benin to investigate the invasion of the capital on 16 Jan.

Resolution 405: Adopted 14 April 1977. Acknowledged the work of the Special Mission to Benin. Condemned the act of aggression perpetrated against Benin on 16 Jan. and agreed to gather more information on the mercenaries. Reaffirmed Resolution 239. Requested member states to be alert to the danger posed by mercenaries, and to consider implementing measures to prohibit the domestic recruitment, training and transit of mercenaries.

Resolution 406: Adopted 25 May 1977. Expressed support for the Government of Botswana and endorsed the recommendations of the Mission to Botswana.

Resolution 407: Adopted 25 May 1977. Expressed appreciation to the UN Secretary-General for his arrangement of a Mission to Lesotho to establish the assistance required, and endorsed the recommendations of that Mission.

Resolution 409: Adopted 27 May 1977. Agreed that Member States should forbid the use or transfer of funds by the illegal regime in Rhodesia.

Resolution 411: Adopted 30 June 1977. Reiterated Resolution 386 and condemned the continued aggression carried out by Rhodesia against Mozambique. Condemned South Africa for its support of Rhodesia, reaffirmed that its regime constituted a source of instability in the region and requested that member states cease the provision of support to the regime. Reaffirmed the right of the people of Zimbabwe to self-determination and independence. Appealed to member states to provide assistance to Mozambique to allow it to increase its defence capabilities.

Resolution 412: Adopted 7 July 1977. Endorsed the admission of Djibouti to the UN.

Resolution 413: Adopted 20 July 1977. Endorsed the admission of Viet Nam to the UN.

Resolution 414: Adopted 15 Sept. 1977. Expressed concern at developments in the new Famagusta area of Cyprus and requested that the two communities in Cyprus resume negotiations under the auspices of the UN Secretary-General.

Resolution 415: Adopted 29 Sept. 1977. Requested the appointment of a representative to undertake discussions with the British Resident Commissioner, and other parties, concerning military and other arrangements required to enable a transition to majority rule in Rhodesia.

Resolution 417: Adopted 31 Oct. 1977. Condemned the South African authorities for the violent repression of black people and opponents of racial discrimination. Demanded that the Government release those imprisoned under arbitrary security laws, remove bans on organizations and media opposed to apartheid and abolish the policies of apartheid and 'Bantustans' and the 'Bantu' education system.

Resolution 418: Adopted 4 Nov. 1977. Imposed a mandatory arms embargo against South Africa.

Resolution 419: Adopted 24 Nov. 1977. Reaffirmed Resolution 405 and requested that member states gather information concerning the mercenaries involved in the attack on Benin of 16 Jan. and appealed for the provision of assistance to that country. Acknowledged the Government of Benin's wish to bring the mercenaries to justice.

Resolution 421: Adopted 9 Dec. 1977. Established a Security Council Committee to monitor and strengthen the implementation of the mandatory arms embargo against South Africa.

Resolution 423: Adopted 14 March 1978. Condemned the attempts of the minority regime in Rhodesia to maintain power and declared unacceptable any internal agreement concluded under that regime. Requested that the United Kingdom Government take the necessary measures to end the regime. Declared that the replacement of the police and military forces and the holding of free and fair elections under the auspices of the UN were required to restore legality to the country.

Resolution 424: Adopted 17 March 1978. Condemned the invasion of Zambia on 6 March by Rhodesian troops. Reiterated that the freedom of Namibia and Zimbabwe, and the elimination of the apartheid regime in South Africa were required to attain peace in the region. Demanded that the United Kingdom act promptly to end the illegal regime in Rhodesia.

Resolution 425: Adopted 19 March 1978. Demanded that Israel respect Lebanese territorial integrity, sovereignty and independence and withdraw its troops following an invasion of southern Lebanon. Established a UN Interim Force in Lebanon (UNIFIL) to assist in the restoration of peace.

Resolution 427: Adopted 3 May 1978. Criticized attacks carried out against UN troops in Lebanon.

Resolution 428: Adopted 6 May 1978. Condemned the invasion of Angola on 4 May by South African troops and their use of Namibia as a military base. Demanded that South Africa respect Angola's integrity, sovereignty and independence and withdrawal unconditionally from both Angola and Namibia.

Resolution 431: Adopted 27 July 1978. Requested the appointment by the UN Secretary-General of a Special Representative for Namibia, to facilitate its independence.

Resolution 432: Adopted 27 July 1978. Voiced support for the reintegration of Walvis Bay by Namibia, in order to ensure the territory's integrity and unity. Demanded that South Africa refrain from using Walvis Bay in a way likely to threaten Namibia's economy or independence.

Resolution 433: Adopted 17 Aug. 1978. Endorsed the admission of the Solomon Islands to the UN.

Resolution 435: Adopted 28 Sept. 1978. Endorsed proposals for the evacuation of South African forces from Namibia and for the election of a constituent assembly in Namibia under UN supervision. Established a UN Transition Assistance Group (UNTAG).

Resolution 436: Adopted 6 Oct. 1978. Requested all those involved in the conflict in Lebanon to implement an immediate cease-fire and to permit the International Committee of the Red Cross to gain access to the area of conflict.

Resolution 437: Adopted 10 Oct. 1978. Expressed regret at the decision by the US Government to permit members of the Rhodesian regime, including its leader, Ian Smith, to enter the USA in contravention of Resolution 253, and requested that the USA observe the provisions of Security Council resolutions.

Resolution 439: Adopted 13 Nov. 1978. Condemned South Africa for holding unilateral elections in Namibia and declared the results to be invalid. Requested South Africa to cancel further elections scheduled to take place in Dec. and to comply with Security Council resolutions.

Resolution 442: Adopted 6 Dec. 1978. Endorsed the admission of Dominica to the UN.

Resolution 445: Adopted 8 March 1979. Condemned Rhodesian regime for invasions of Angola, Mozambique and Zambia and requested that member states provide assistance to those three countries in order to increase their defence capabilities. Requested that the UK Government take action to prevent illegal executions in Rhodesia. Criticized the elections scheduled to be held in the territory in April and declared them invalid.

Resolution 446: Adopted 22 March 1979. Declared invalid the settlements established by Israel in Palestine and other Arab territories from 1967, and deplored Israel's contravention of Security Council resolutions. Established a three-member Commission to examine the situation in the Occupied Territories.

Resolution 447: Adopted 28 March 1979. Condemned the sustained invasions of Angola by South African troops and their continued use of Namibia as a military base. Demanded that South Africa respect Angola's integrity, sovereignty and independence and abandon its armed invasions. Requested that member states provide assistance to Angola to strengthen its defence capabilities.

Resolution 448: Adopted 30 April 1979. Condemned elections held in Rhodesia and declared the results to be invalid.

Resolution 452: Adopted 14 June 1979. Accepted the recommendations of the Commission established by Resolution 446 and requested that Israel halt the establishment of settlements in those territories, including Jerusalem.

Resolution 453: Adopted 12 Sept. 1979. Endorsed the admission of St Lucia to the UN.

Resolution 455: Adopted 23 Nov. 1979. Condemned Rhodesia's continued invasions of Zambia and condemned South Africa for its collaboration. Demanded that the United Kingdom

Government act promptly to dissolve the Rhodesian regime. Requested compensation for Zambia, and assistance from member states.

Resolution 457: Adopted 4 Dec. 1979. Demanded that the Government of Iran release hostages held in the US embassy in Tehran and requested that the Governments of Iran and the USA peacefully resolve their differences.

Resolution 460: Adopted 21 Dec. 1979. Agreed to remove sanctions implemented against Rhodesia by previous resolutions and to dissolve the Committee established by Resolution 253. Requested all parties to respect the provisions of agreements reached and requested the United Kingdom to ensure that troops remained in Rhodesia, other than those agreed upon by the Lancaster House Conference.

Resolution 463: Adopted 2 Feb. 1980. Requested that the United Kingdom effect the immediate withdrawal of all South African forces from Rhodesia, and condemned the South African regime for its interference. Demanded that the UK Government ensure full participation in the forthcoming elections by Zimbabweans, through the return of exiles and refugees, the release of political prisoners, compliance with the provisions of the Lancaster House Agreement, equal treatment of all parties and the termination of inappropriate emergency measures.

Resolution 464: Adopted 19 Feb. 1980. Endorsed the admission of St Vincent and the Grenadines to the UN.

Resolution 465: Adopted 1 March 1980. Deplored Israel's refusal to co-operate with the Security Council Commission, its formal rejection of Resolutions 446 and 452 and its refusal to allow the Mayor of Hebron to appear before the Security Council. Declared invalid the settlements established by Israel in Palestine and other Arab territories from 1967, and deplored Israel's continuing settlement policy.

Resolution 466: Adopted 11 April 1980. Condemned South Africa's intensified invasions of Zambia and demanded that it evacuate its troops. Warned South Africa that continued aggression would provoke further action by the Security Council.

Resolution 467: Adopted 24 April 1980. Condemned Israel's contravention of resolutions concerning its invasion of Lebanon (including Resolution 425) and all acts of hostility in Lebanon and towards UNIFIL, including an attack on UNIFIL headquarters. Requested that a meeting of the Israel–Lebanon Mixed Armistice Commission (ILMAC) be convened in the hope of reaffirming the General Armistice Agreement.

Resolution 468: Adopted 8 May 1980. Demanded that Israel allow the return of illegally expelled Palestinian leaders, the Mayors of Hebron and Halhoul and the Judge of Hebron.

Resolution 473: Adopted 13 June 1980. Condemned the South African regime for the continued violent repression of black people and opponents of apartheid. Expressed support for the victims of racial discrimination. Demanded that the Government release those imprisoned for their opposition to apartheid, including Nelson Mandela, remove bans on political parties, organizations and the media opposed to apartheid, halt all political trials, abolish the policy of apartheid and introduce equal opportunities for all South Africans.

Resolution 476: Adopted 30 June 1980. Reaffirmed the need for Israel to end its continued occupation of Arab territories, including Jerusalem, and reiterated that all changes made to Jerusalem were invalid. Deplored Israel's contravention of UN resolutions and requested that, henceforth, it comply with them.

Resolution 477: Adopted 30 July 1980. Endorsed the admission of Zimbabwe to the UN.

Resolution 478: Adopted 20 Aug. 1980. Announced its refusal to recognize a 'basic law' by Israel, which made East Jerusalem part of an undivided Jerusalem, and requested that member states withdraw all diplomatic missions established in Jerusalem.

Resolution 479: Adopted 28 Sept. 1980. Requested that Iran and Iraq halt the use of force and resolve their differences by peaceful means.

Resolution 487: Adopted 19 June 1981. Condemned an air attack by Israel on the Iraqi nuclear research centre on 7 June as representing a serious threat to the International Atomic Energy Agency (IAEA) safeguards regime and requested that Israel adhere to IAEA safeguards.

Resolution 489: Adopted 8 July 1981. Endorsed the admission of Vanuatu to the UN.

Resolution 490: Adopted 21 July 1981. Requested an immediate cease-fire in Lebanon.

Resolution 491: Adopted 23 Sept. 1981. Endorsed the admission of Belize to the UN.

Resolution 492: Adopted 10 Nov. 1981. Endorsed the admission of Antigua and Barbuda to the UN.

Resolution 494: Adopted 11 Dec. 1981. Endorsed the appointment of Javier Pérez de Cuéllar as Secretary-General of the UN.

Resolution 496: Adopted 15 Dec. 1981. Condemned an attempt by mercenaries on 25 Nov. to overthrow the Government of the Seychelles and agreed to send a three-member Commission of Inquiry to investigate the events.

Resolution 497: Adopted 17 Dec. 1981. Declared invalid Israel's formal annexation of the occupied Syrian Golan Heights.

Resolution 502: Adopted 3 April 1982. Demanded an immediate cease-fire in the Falkland (Malvinas) Islands, the withdrawal of all Argentine troops and a diplomatic solution to the dispute between the United Kingdom and Argentina concerning the islands.

Resolution 504: Adopted 30 April 1982. Requested that a fund be established to aid the peace-keeping force of the Organization of African Unity (OAU) in Chad.

Resolution 505: Adopted 26 May 1982. Requested the UN Secretary-General to seek to negotiate a cease-fire agreement for the Falkland (Malvinas) Islands.

Resolution 509: Adopted 6 June 1982. Demanded that Israel immediately evacuate its military troops from Lebanon and requested all parties to observe an immediate cease-fire in Lebanon, following the escalation of hostilities.

Resolution 512: Adopted 19 June 1982. Expressed concern at the suffering of both Lebanese and Palestinian refugees and appealed for the provision of humanitarian assistance and for those involved in the conflict to respect the rights of civilians and to facilitate the distribution of aid.

Resolution 513: Adopted 4 July 1982. Reaffirmed Resolution 512, and requested that access be restored to vital facilities, including water, electricity, food and medicine, in South Lebanon and West Beirut.

Resolution 514: Adopted 12 July 1982. Recalled Resolution 479, requesting a cease-fire in the war between Iran and Iraq. Agreed to deploy a group of observers to the region to monitor the cease-fire and the withdrawal of troops.

Resolution 515: Adopted 29 July 1982. Requested that the Israeli Government remove restrictions preventing the distribution of humanitarian supplies to the civilian population of Beirut, Lebanon.

Resolution 516: Adopted 1 Aug. 1982. Reaffirmed previous resolutions regarding military activity in Lebanon and at the Israel–Lebanon border and demanded a cease-fire. Authorized the deployment of UN observers to monitor the situation in the Beirut area.

Resolution 517: Adopted 4 Aug. 1982. Following the invasion of Beirut by Israeli troops on 3 Aug., reconfirmed demands for an immediate cease-fire and the evacuation of Israeli forces.

Resolution 518: Adopted 12 Aug. 1982. Reiterated demands for the cessation of hostilities in Lebanon and the removal of restrictions preventing the distribution of humanitarian supplies in Beirut.

Resolution 520: Adopted 17 Sept. 1982. Condemned the assassination of the elected President of Lebanon, and demanded the evacuation of Israeli troops from Beirut, following an invasion on 15 Sept.

Resolution 521: Adopted 19 Sept. 1982. Condemned the massacre of Palestinian refugees in Beirut, Lebanon. Authorized an increase in the number of UN observers in the vicinity of Beirut, from 10 to 50. Established a Commission of Investigation to Lebanon.

Resolution 527: Adopted 15 Dec. 1982. Condemned armed hostilities perpetrated by South African troops against Lesotho, and demanded that it provide compensation for damage caused. Affirmed the right of Lesotho to shelter victims of apartheid.

Resolution 532: Adopted 31 May 1983. Mandated the UN Secretary-General to undertake consultations in Namibia with the aim of implementing Resolution 435.

Resolution 537: Adopted 22 Sept. 1983. Endorsed the admission of St Vincent and the Grenadines to the UN.

Resolution 539: Adopted 28 Oct. 1983. Condemned South Africa's continued occupation of Namibia and its obstruction of Resolution 435 through its support for the policy of 'linkage' (whereby South Africa insisted on the withdrawal of Cuban troops from Angola prior to the implementation of Resolution 435).

Resolution 541: Adopted 18 Nov. 1983. Condemned the unilateral declaration of an independent 'Turkish Republic of Northern Cyprus' ('TRNC') by the Turkish Cypriot authorities and demanded its withdrawal. Requested that member states withhold recognition of the 'TRNC'.

Resolution 548: Adopted 24 Feb. 1984. Endorsed the admission of Brunei to the UN.

Resolution 550: Adopted 11 May 1984. Reaffirmed Resolution 541. Condemned the establishment of diplomatic links between the 'TRNC' and Turkey, and plans for a referendum to approve a new constitution and elections to a constituent assembly.

Resolution 552: Adopted 1 June 1984. Condemned attacks by Iran against Saudi Arabian and Kuwaiti commercial ships in the Gulf and reaffirmed their right to free navigation.

Resolution 554: Adopted 17 Aug. 1984. Declared the new Constitution of South Africa, which provided for the election of people of mixed race and of Asian origin, to be invalid and contrary to the principles of the UN Charter. Reiterated that the elimination of apartheid and the holding of elections under universal adult suffrage were required to resolve the situation in that country. Requested governments not to recognize the results of elections to be held under the apartheid regime.

Resolution 558: Adopted 13 Dec. 1984. Requested member states to refrain from importing arms and military vehicles manufactured in South Africa.

Resolution 560: Adopted 12 March 1985. Condemned the South African apartheid regime for the killing of those protesting against their forced removal from certain areas and the arbitrary arrest of members of opposition organizations and demanded the release of all political prisoners.

Resolution 566: Adopted 19 June 1985. Declared illegal the establishment of a 'Transnational Government of National Unity' by the South African regime in Windhoek, Namibia, and condemned South Africa's continued obstruction of Resolution 435. Mandated the UN Secretary-General to resume discussions with South Africa, with the aim of implementing the Resolution. Proposed that member states impose voluntary sanctions against South Africa.

Resolution 567: Adopted 20 June 1985. Condemned South Africa for the resumption of violence against Angola. Demanded that in evacuate its troops and refrain from using Namibia as a military base.

Resolution 568: Adopted 21 June 1985. Condemned a military attack on the capital of Botswana by South African forces. Requested the UN Secretary-General to dispatch an investigatory mission to Botswana to assess the damage caused and to propose measures to increase Botswana's capacity to assist South African refugees.

Resolution 569: Adopted 26 July 1985. Condemned the mass arrest of opponents of apartheid and the declaration of a state of emergency in 36 magisterial districts by the South African Government. Reaffirmed the need to eliminate apartheid and reiterated the proposal that member states adopt sanctions against South Africa.

Resolution 573: Adopted 4 Oct. 1985. Condemned Israel for an attack against the headquarters of the Palestine Liberation Organization (PLO) in Tunisia.

Resolution 574: Adopted 7 Oct. 1985. Condemned South Africa for an armed incursion into Angola, its continued occupation of parts of Angola and its continued use of Namibia as a military base. Demanded that South Africa halt all hostilities and evacuate its troops from Angolan territory. Affirmed Angola's right to defend its sovereignty, territorial integrity and independence. Requested all member states fully to implement Resolution 418.

Resolution 579: Adopted 18 Dec. 1985. Condemned abduction and the taking of hostages. Emphasized the obligation of member states to secure the release of those abducted or taken hostage on their territory. Urged all member states to become party to the relevant conventions.

Resolution 580: Adopted 30 Dec. 1985. Condemned South Africa for the deaths of nine people (including six South African refugees) in Lesotho. Affirmed the right of Lesotho to shelter victims of apartheid and appealed for economic assistance for Lesotho. Demanded that South Africa abolish the apartheid regime.

Resolution 581: Adopted 13 Feb. 1986. Condemned South Africa for threats made to other southern African countries and the escalation of violence in the region. Reiterated demands for the abolishment of apartheid.

Resolution 582: Adopted 24 Feb. 1986. Implicity blamed Iraq for initiating the conflict with Iran and condemned the continuance and escalation of the conflict. Demanded that both parties observe an immediate cease-fire.

Resolution 587: Adopted 23 Sept. 1986. Condemned attacks made against the UN Interim Force in Lebanon.

Resolution 589: Adopted 10 Oct. 1986. Endorsed the appointment of Javier Pérez de Cuéllar as Secretary-General of the UN for a second term of office.

Resolution 591: Adopted 28 Nov. 1986. Strengthened the arms embargo against South Africa.

Resolution 592: Adopted 8 Dec. 1986. Requested Israel to abide by the Geneva Convention relative to the Protection of Civilian Persons in Time of War, following an attack on university students by the Israeli armed forces.

Resolution 598: Adopted 20 July 1987. In response to the escalating tensions between Iran and Iraq, including the bombing of neutral shipping and the use of chemical weapons, urged an immediate cease-fire, the withdrawal of military forces to international boundaries, and the co-operation of both parties in mediation efforts to achieve a peace settlement.

Resolution 601: Adopted 30 Oct. 1987. Condemned South Africa's continued occupation of Namibia and its refusal to comply with Security Council resolutions, in particular resolutions 385 and 435. Welcomed the professed willingness of the Namibian nationalist organization, the South West Africa People's Organization (SWAPO), to observe a cease-fire with South Africa.

Resolution 602: Adopted 25 Nov. 1987. Reiterated condemnation of South Africa's continued attacks on Angola and its occupation of parts of Angola and Namibia, and the entry into Angola of the South African President. Repeated demands for a cease-fire and mandated the UN Secretary-General to monitor the evacuation of South African forces from Angola.

Resolution 605: Adopted 22 Dec. 1987. Deplored the killing of Palestinian civilians by the Israeli armed forces.

Resolution 607: Adopted 5 Jan 1988. Appealed to Israel to refrain from deporting Palestinian civilians from the Occupied Territories.

Resolution 608: Adopted 14 Jan. 1988. Demanded that Israel withdraw the order to deport Palestinian civilians and to ensure the safe return to the Occupied Territories of those already deported.

Resolution 611: Adopted 25 April 1988. Condemned the assassination by Israel of the military commander of the Palestine Liberation Organization (PLO) in Tunisia.

Resolution 612: Adopted 9 May 1988. Emphasized the need for Iran and Iraq urgently to observe the Protocol for the Prohibition of the Use in War of Asphyxiating, Poisonous or Other Gases, and of Bacteriological Methods of Warfare.

Resolution 616: Adopted 20 July 1988. Expressed distress and regret at the shooting down of an Iranian civilian aircraft mistakenly identified as an attacking fighter aircraft by US forces.

Resolution 619: Adopted 9 Aug. 1988. Established a UN Iran–Iraq Military Observer Group (UNIIMOG) to monitor the cease-fire between the two countries.

Resolution 620: Adopted 26 Aug. 1988. Condemned the continued use of chemical weapons by Iran and Iraq, in contravention of Resolution 612.

Resolution 621: Adopted 20 Sept. 1988. Authorized the appointment of a special representative for Western Sahara, following the provisional acceptance in Aug. by Morocco and a national liberation movement, the Polisario Front, of a peace plan proposed by the UN Secretary-General.

Resolution 622: Adopted 31 Oct. 1988. Agreed to deploy military officers from existing UN operations to assist in a UN Good Offices Mission in Afghanistan and Pakistan (UNGOMAP).

Resolution 626: Adopted 20 Dec. 1988. Established a UN Angola Verification Mission (UNAVEM) to monitor the withdrawal of Cuban troops from Angola.

Resolution 628: Adopted 16 Jan. 1989. Welcomed a bilateral agreement between Angola and Cuba for the withdrawal of Cuban troops from Angola, and a tripartite accord between Angola, Cuba and South Africa for the implementation of Resolution 435 from 1 April.

Resolution 635: Adopted 14 June 1989. Condemned all illegal and terrorist acts affecting civil aviation and requested all member states to co-operate to devise and implement measures to prevent terrorist acts, including the use of explosives.

Resolution 644: Adopted 7 Nov. 1989. Established a UN Observer Group in Central America (UNOCA) to monitor compliance with the 'Tela' peace accord in Nicaragua, to prevent cross-border incursions by rebel groups and to assist in supervising the forthcoming Nicaraguan elections.

Resolution 650: Adopted 27 March 1990. Increased the strength of UNOCA, in order to facilitate the demobilization of the Nicaraguan resistance forces.

Resolution 652: Adopted 17 April 1990. Endorsed the admission of Namibia to the UN.

Resolution 660: Adopted 2 Aug. 1990. Demanded the immediate and unconditional withdrawal of Iraqi forces from Kuwait.

Resolution 661: Adopted 6 Aug. 1990. Imposed mandatory economic sanctions against Iraq and the occupied areas of Kuwait, with exemptions for food and medical supplies, owing to Iraq's refusal to comply with Resolution 660. Established a Security Council Committee to monitor the implementation of sanctions.

Resolution 662: Adopted 9 Aug. 1990. Declared Iraq's annexation of Kuwait to be 'null and void'.

Resolution 663: Adopted 14 Aug. 1990. Endorsed the admission of Liechtenstein to the UN.

Resolution 664: Adopted 18 Aug. 1990. Demanded that Iraq allow the safe evacuation of foreign nationals from Iraq and Kuwait, and permit consular officials to gain access to those nationals.

Resolution 667: Adopted 16 Sept. 1990. Condemned acts of aggression perpetrated by Iraq against diplomatic premises and staff in Kuwait, including the abduction of foreign nationals. Stated Iraq's decision to close diplomatic and consular missions in Kuwait and to withdraw their immunity and privileges to be in contravention of international law.

Resolution 668: Adopted 20 Sept. 1990. Endorsed the framework for a comprehensive settlement in Cambodia.

Resolution 672: Adopted 12 Oct. 1990. Condemned the killing of Palestinians by Israeli police in Jerusalem, following clashes with Jewish worshippers. Voted to dispatch a mission of observers to Israel to investigate the killings.

Resolution 673: Adopted 24 Oct. 1990. Deplored Israel's refusal to co-operate with the mission of observers established by Resolution 672.

Resolution 677: Adopted 28 Nov. 1990. Condemned Iraqi attempts to alter the demographic character of Kuwait and to destroy Kuwait's civil records.

Resolution 678: Adopted 29 Nov. 1990. Authorized member states to use all necessary means to enforce the withdrawal of Iraqi forces from Kuwait after 15 Jan. 1991.

Resolution 681: Adopted 20 Dec. 1990. Deplored the Israeli Government's decision to resume the deportation of Palestinian civilians in the Occupied Territories. Requested the UN Secretary-General, in co-operation with the International Committee of the Red Cross, to consider convening a conference to examine the enforcement of the Geneva Convention in relation to the protection of Palestinian civilians under Israeli occupation.

Resolution 683: Adopted 22 Dec. 1990. Terminated the trusteeship agreements for the Pacific Islands of the Marshall Islands, the Federated States of Micronesia, and the Northern Mariana Islands, as established by Resolution 21.

Resolution 686: Adopted 2 March 1991. Required Iraq to repeal all laws and decrees concerning the annexation of Kuwait. Dictated terms for a permanent cease-fire in Kuwait, including the release of all prisoners of war.

Resolution 687: Adopted 3 April 1991. Extended the terms for a cease-fire in Kuwait. Demanded that both Iraq and Kuwait recognize the inviolability of the Iraq–Kuwait border and established an Iraq–Kuwait Boundary Demarcation Commission. Requested the deployment of UN observers to the area. Linked the removal of sanctions against Iraq to the elimination of its non-conventional weaponry, as certified by the UN Special Commission. Required Iraq to renounce international terrorism, and to accept proposals for the establishment of a war reparation fund to be derived from Iraqi petroleum revenues.

Resolution 688: Adopted 5 April 1991. Condemned the repression of the Iraqi civilian population in Iraq, particularly in the Kurdish populated areas.

Resolution 689: Adopted 9 April 1991. Established an Observation Mission (UNIKOM) to monitor the demilitarized zone between Iraq and Kuwait.

Resolution 690: Adopted 29 April 1991. Approved the establishment of a UN Mission for the Referendum in Western Sahara (MINURSO) to verify a cease-fire in the territory and to organize a plan for a referendum on self-determination.

Resolution 692: Adopted 20 May 1991. Decided to establish a UN Compensation Commission to administer a fund for victims of Iraqi aggression, which was to be financed by a levy on Iraqi petroleum revenues, as detailed in Resolution 687.

Resolution 693: Adopted 20 May 1991. Approved the establishment of a UN Observer Mission in El Salvador (ONUSAL) to verify accords reached between the Government of El Salvador and the guerrilla organization, the Frente Farabundo Martí para la Liberación Nacional (FMLN).

Resolution 696: Adopted 30 May 1991. Agreed to prolong the presence of the UN Angola Verification Mission (UNAVEM), as UNAVEM II, with a mandate to ensure the implementation of the peace accords concluded in Angola.

Resolution 702: Adopted 8 Aug. 1991. Endorsed the admission of North Korea and of South Korea to the UN.

Resolution 703: Adopted 9 Aug. 1991. Endorsed the admission of the Federated States of Micronesia to the UN.

Resolution 704: Adopted 9 Aug. 1991. Endorsed the admission of the Marshall Islands to the UN.

Resolution 705: Adopted 15 Aug. 1991. Agreed that war reparations to be paid by Iraq should not exceed 30% of the annual value of its exports of petroleum and petroleum products.

Resolution 706: Adopted 15 Aug. 1991. Proposed authorizing member states to allow the import of Iraqi petroleum worth up to US $1,600m. over a six-month period, to be paid into an escrow account controlled by the UN and to be used for humanitarian needs and war reparations.

Resolution 707: Adopted 15 Aug. 1991. Condemned Iraq's failure to comply with UN weapons inspectors and its safeguards agreement with the IAEA. Demanded that Iraq disclose details of all non-conventional weaponry, that it allow members of the UN Special Commission UNSCOM and the IAEA to gain unrestricted access to all the necessary areas and records, and that it halt all its nuclear activities.

Resolution 709: Adopted 12 Sept. 1991. Endorsed the admission of Estonia to the UN.

Resolution 710: Adopted 12 Sept. 1991. Endorsed the admission of Latvia to the UN.

Resolution 711: Adopted 12 Sept. 1991. Endorsed the admission of Lithuania to the UN.

Resolution 712: Adopted 19 Sept. 1991. Approved Resolution 706.

Resolution 713: Adopted 25 Sept. 1991. Imposed an arms embargo against Yugoslavia and demanded that all hostilities in that country end immediately.

Resolution 714: Adopted 30 Sept. 1991. Commended a framework peace agreement between the Government of El Salvador and the opposition FMLN movement, reached in New York, under the auspices of the UN.

Resolution 715: Adopted 11 Oct. 1991. Established the terms under which the UN Special Commission was to inspect Iraqi weapons.

Resolution 717: Adopted 16 Oct. 1991. Agreed to establish the UN Advance Mission in Cambodia (UNAMIC).

Resolution 718: Adopted 31 Oct. 1991. Welcomed the agreements signed in Paris for a comprehensive settlement of the conflict in Cambodia. Authorized the UN Secretary-General to dispatch a special representative to Cambodia.

Resolution 720: Adopted 21 Nov. 1991. Endorsed the appointment of Dr Boutros Boutros-Ghali as Secretary-General of the UN.

Resolution 724: Adopted 15 Dec. 1991. Endorsed a proposal by the UN Secretary-General to dispatch to Yugoslavia an advance contingent of peace-keeping troops, as part of the mission of his Personal Envoy. Established a Committee to supervise implementation of the arms embargo against Yugoslavia.

Resolution 727: Adopted 8 Jan. 1992. Deplored the deaths in Yugoslavia of five members of the European Community Monitoring Mission. Endorsed a proposal by the UN Secretary-General to dispatch to Yugoslavia up to 50 military liaison officers to help maintain the cease-fire.

Resolution 728: Adopted 8 Jan. 1992. Endorsed a proposal by the UN Secretary-General for the mandate of the UN Advance Mission in Cambodia to be extended to include mine-clearing operations.

Resolution 729: Adopted 14 Jan. 1992. Agreed to extend the mandate of the UN Observer Mission in El Salvador (ONUSAL) to include the verification and monitoring of the formal cease-fire agreement to be signed between the Government of El Salvador and the FMLN. Requested the UN Secretary-General to increase the strength of ONUSAL.

Resolution 731: Adopted 21 Jan. 1992. Demanded Libya's compliance with requests for the extradition of two Libyan nationals alleged to be responsible for the bombing of a civilian aircraft over Scotland in 1988, and its co-operation with a French inquiry into an aircraft bombing over Niger in 1989.

Resolution 732: Adopted 23 Jan. 1992. Endorsed the admission of Kazakhstan to the UN.

Resolution 733: Adopted 23 Jan. 1992. Urged all those involved in the conflict in Somalia to observe an immediate cease-fire and imposed an arms embargo against Somalia.

Resolution 735: Adopted 29 Jan. 1992. Endorsed the admission of Armenia to the UN.

Resolution 736: Adopted 29 Jan. 1992. Endorsed the admission of Kyrgyzstan to the UN.

Resolution 737: Adopted 29 Jan. 1992. Endorsed the admission of Uzbekistan to the UN.

Resolution 738: Adopted 29 Jan. 1992. Endorsed the admission of Tajikistan to the UN.

Resolution 739: Adopted 29 Jan. 1992. Endorsed the admission of Moldova to the UN.

Resolution 741: Adopted 7 Feb. 1992. Endorsed the admission of Turkmenistan to the UN.

Resolution 742: Adopted 14 Feb. 1992. Endorsed the admission of Azerbaijan to the UN.

Resolution 743: Adopted 21 Feb. 1992. Approved the establishment of a UN Protection Force (UNPROFOR) in response to the escalating conflict in Yugoslavia.

Resolution 744: Adopted 25 Feb. 1992. Endorsed the admission of San Marino to the UN.

Resolution 745: Adopted 28 Feb. 1992. Authorized the dispatch of a peace-keeping force to Cambodia to establish a UN Transitional Authority in Cambodia (UNTAC), replacing the UN Advance Mission in Cambodia. Requested that an election be held in Cambodia by May 1993.

Resolution 746: Adopted 17 March 1992. Urged all Somali factions to observe the cease-fire agreements signed, including an agreement to permit the presence of an observer mission to monitor the implementation of the cease-fire. Endorsed the decision of the UN Secretary-General urgently to dispatch a technical mission to Somalia to survey the situation.

Resolution 748: Adopted 31 March 1992. Agreed to impose economic sanctions against Libya, including an international air embargo, the prohibition of trade in arms and a reduction in its diplomatic personnel, if it refused to comply with the provisions of Resolution 731 and commit itself to the renunciation of terrorism by 15 April. Established a Security Council Committee to monitor the implementation of sanctions.

Resolution 750: Adopted 10 April 1992. Endorsed a 'set of ideas' on Cyprus compiled by the UN Secretary-General, which advocated uninterrupted negotiations until a settlement was reached.

Resolution 751: Adopted 24 April 1992. Established a UN Operation in Somalia (UNOSOM) to monitor the cease-fire in Somalia. Agreed in principle to establish a UN security force for deployment to that country, and welcomed the UN Secretary-General's intention to appoint a Special Representative. Established a Security Council Committee to monitor the implementation of the arms embargo against Somalia.

Resolution 752: Adopted 15 May 1992. Demanded an immediate cease-fire in Bosnia and Herzegovina and the cessation of all forms of external interference. Requested the withdrawal and the disarming of the Yugoslav People's Army and all irregular forces in Bosnia and Herzegovina. Emphasized the need for humanitarian assistance to the country.

Resolution 753: Adopted 18 May 1992. Endorsed the admission of Croatia to the UN.

Resolution 754: Adopted 18 May 1992. Endorsed the admission of Slovenia to the UN.

Resolution 755: Adopted 20 May 1992. Endorsed the admission of Bosnia and Herzegovina to the UN.

Resolution 757: Adopted 30 May 1992. Imposed economic sanctions against the Federal Republic of Yugoslavia for its continuing involvement in the conflict in Bosnia and Herzegovina, in contravention of Resolution 752.

Resolution 761: Adopted 29 June 1992. Authorized the immediate deployment of additional troops of the UN Protection Force (UNPROFOR) in order to protect Sarajevo airport in Bosnia and Herzegovina, following its surrender to UN authority for humanitarian purposes. Requested all parties involved in the conflict to observe an unconditional cease-fire.

Resolution 762: Adopted 30 June 1992. Required Croatian forces to end all hostilities and to withdraw to the positions held prior to 21 June and to refrain from entering Serbian areas, following the launch of a series of offensives in those areas. Authorized an increase in the number of military observers and civilian police-forces affiliated to UNPROFOR.

Resolution 763: Adopted 6 July 1992. Endorsed the admission of Georgia to the UN.

Resolution 764: Adopted 13 July 1992. Authorized the deployment to Sarajevo, Bosnia and Herzegovina, of additional UN troops.

Resolution 765: Adopted 16 July 1992. Endorsed the appointment of a special representative to facilitate mediation in South Africa, owing to the escalation of violence.

Resolution 766: Adopted 21 July 1992. Deplored violations of the cease-fire agreement in Cambodia and the lack of co-operation experienced by the UN Transitional Authority in Cambodia.

Resolution 767: Adopted 27 July 1992. Requested that an urgent airlift operation be organized to facilitate the provision of humanitarian assistance to the population of Somalia and urged all those involved in the conflict to co-operate with the UN in order to aid the distribution of humanitarian supplies. Reaffirmed the arms embargo against Somalia.

Resolution 769: Adopted 7 Aug. 1992. Authorized an increase in the number of the troops of the UN Protection Force. Condemned the abuses of human rights taking place in the Federal Republic of Yugoslavia.

Resolution 770: Adopted 13 Aug. 1992. Reaffirmed the demand for a cease-fire in Bosnia and Herzegovina. Demanded unimpeded access to detention camps in Bosnia and Herzegovina for the International Committee of the Red Cross and authorized member states to take all necessary measures to ensure the delivery of humanitarian aid. Expressed concern at the conditions of civilians imprisoned in camps, prisons and detention centres in that country.

Resolution 771: Adopted 13 Aug. 1992. Emphasized that those responsible for abusing human rights in the Federal Republic of Yugoslavia (FRY) would be held personally responsible. Strongly condemned all violations of international humanitarian law, including 'ethnic cleansing' (the expulsion of an ethnic group or groups in an attempt to create a homogenous population). Requested member states and appropriate organizations to gather substantiated evidence of human rights violations carried out in the FRY.

Resolution 772: Adopted 17 Aug. 1992. Authorized the deployment of a UN Observer Mission in South Africa.

Resolution 775: Adopted 28 Aug. 1992. Authorized the deployment of an additional 3,500 troops for the UN Operation in Somalia (UNOSOM).

Resolution 777: Adopted 19 Sept. 1992. Prohibited the Federal Republic of Yugoslavia from continuing the membership of the former Socialist Federal Republic of Yugoslavia in the UN, and demanded that it apply for membership and discontinue its participation at the General Assembly.

Resolution 778: Adopted 2 Oct. 1992. Permitted the confiscation of oil-related Iraqi assets in member states.

Resolution 779: Adopted 6 Oct. 1992. Authorized the UN Protection Force to monitor the withdrawal of the Yugoslav army from Croatia, the demilitarization of the Prevlaka peninsula and the removal of weapons from adjacent areas of Croatia and Montenegro.

Resolution 780: Adopted 6 Oct. 1992. Requested the UN Secretary-General to establish a Committee of Experts to investigate the evidence of human rights abuses in the Federal Republic of Yugoslavia received as a result of Resolution 771.

Resolution 781: Adopted 9 Oct. 1992. Imposed a ban on military flights in Bosnia and Herzegovina's airspace in order to facilitate the provision of humanitarian assistance and the cessation of hostilities.

Resolution 788: Adopted 19 Nov. 1992. Imposed a mandatory embargo on the supply of armaments to Liberia, owing to the civil war, and authorized the UN Secretary-General to dispatch a special representative to that country.

Resolution 789: Adopted 25 Nov. 1992. Following the suspension of negotiations over Cyprus, requested that the Turkish Cypriots adopt a position consistent with the 'set of ideas' proposed by the UN Secretary-General.

Resolution 790: Adopted 30 Nov. 1992. Condemned the non-co-operation of the Party of Democratic Kampuchea (PDK) with the UN Transitional Authority in Cambodia. Approved an embargo on petroleum supplies to the PDK and endorsed a ban on the export of timber (the party's principal source of income).

Resolution 794: Adopted 3 Dec. 1992. Reiterated demands for a cease-fire in Somalia and condemned those impeding the distribution of humanitarian assistance. Endorsed a US proposal to lead a Unified Task Force to restore security to Somalia.

Resolution 795: Adopted 11 Dec. 1992. Approved the deployment of a UN Protection Force contingent to the former Yugoslav republic of Macedonia to monitor its borders with the Federal Republic of Yugoslavia.

Resolution 797: Adopted 16 Dec. 1992. Established a UN Operation in Mozambique (ONUMOZ) to monitor demobilization and the creation of a new national defence force, and to supervise elections.

Resolution 798: Adopted 18 Dec. 1992. Condemned acts of 'unspeakable brutality' in Bosnia and Herzegovina, following allegations of the large-scale organized rape of Muslim women detained by Serb forces, and demanded access to and the closure of the detention camps.

Resolution 799: Adopted 18 Dec. 1992. Condemned Israel for the large-scale deportation of Palestinian civilians and demanded the return of the deportees to Israel.

Resolution 800: Adopted 8 Jan. 1993. Endorsed the admission of Slovakia to the UN.

Resolution 801: Adopted 8 Jan. 1993. Endorsed the admission of the Czech Republic to the UN.

Resolution 802: Adopted 25 Jan. 1993. Ordered Croatian forces to withdraw from areas protected by the UN Protection Force (UNPROFOR), following an offensive across UN peace-keeping lines, and ordered Serbian forces to return weapons reclaimed from UNPROFOR storage areas for defence purposes.

Resolution 808: Adopted 22 Feb. 1993. Provided for the establishment of an international tribunal to prosecute persons responsible for serious violations of international humanitarian law committed in the former Yugoslavia since 1991.

Resolution 809: Adopted 2 March 1993. Outlined a new plan for a resolution to the dispute with the Moroccan Government over Western Sahara, providing for a referendum on self-determination to take place by the end of the year.

Resolution 811: Adopted 12 March 1993. Condemned the continued violations of peace accords in Angola by the African nationalist group União Nacional para a Independência Total de Angola (UNITA). Demanded that UNITA recognize the results of elections held in Sept. 1992 and demanded that a cease-fire be observed throughout Angola. Condemned attacks on members of the UN Angola Verification Mission (UNAVEM II).

Resolution 813: Adopted 26 March 1993. Condemned attacks upon the forces of the Economic Community of West African States (ECOWAS) in Liberia. Declared its willingness to take action against factions failing to comply with the 'Yamoussoukro' peace accord of Oct. 1991.

Resolution 814: Adopted 26 March 1993. Requested the UN Secretary-General to arrange the provision of humanitarian assistance to Somalia, to assist in the repatriation of refugees, to promote the re-establishment of national and regional institutions and the police force and to help to develop a mine-clearance programme. Approved the establishment of the UN Operation in Somalia II (UNOSOM II) to replace the Unified Task Force, established by Resolution 794 to enforce peace in Somalia.

Resolution 816: Adopted 31 March 1993. Extended the ban on flights imposed by Resolution 781. Authorized member states to take all necessary measures to enforce the 'no-fly zone' applying to Bosnian airspace.

Resolution 817: Adopted 7 April 1993. Endorsed the admission of Macedonia to the UN, as 'The former Yugoslav Republic of Macedonia', owing to a dispute with Greece regarding the use of the name 'Macedonia'.

Resolution 818: Adopted 14 April 1993. Expressed concern at the delays in the implementation of the peace process in Mozambique, and urged the Government of Mozambique and the opposition guerrilla group, Resistência Nacional Moçambicana (RENAMO), to finalize a timetable for the implementation of the General Peace Agreement. Requested both sides to guarantee freedom of movement for members of the UN Operation in Mozambique.

Resolution 820: Adopted 17 April 1993. Commended the acceptance of a peace plan for Bosnia and Herzegovina by two parties. Expressed concern at the refusal of the Bosnian Serb Assembly to accept the plan and provided for the strengthening of sanctions.

Resolution 822: Adopted 30 April 1993. Demanded the withdrawal of Armenian forces from Azerbaijan and demanded that a cease-fire between the two parties be observed. Requested that negotiations to resolve the conflict be resumed and requested unrestricted access for humanitarian supplies.

Resolution 824: Adopted 6 May 1993. Established six 'safe areas' in Bosnia and Herzegovina (Sarajevo, Bihać, Tuzla, Goražde, Srebrenića and Žepa) to protect the civilian population from Serb attack, and demanded an immediate cease-fire to be observed in and around those areas.

Resolution 825: Adopted 11 May 1993. Urged North Korea to reconsider its decision to withdraw from the Treaty on the Non-Proliferation of Nuclear Weapons and requested it to allow an inspection of its nuclear facilities to be carried out by the International Atomic Energy Agency.

Resolution 827: Adopted 25 May 1993. Approved the statute of the International Criminal Tribunal for the former Republic of Yugoslavia (ICTY).

Resolution 828: Adopted 26 May 1993. Endorsed the admission of Eritrea to the UN.

Resolution 829: Adopted 26 May 1993. Endorsed the admission of Monaco to the UN.

Resolution 832: Adopted 27 May 1993. Extended the mandate of the UN Observer Mission in El Salvador (ONUSAL) to include the observation of elections in that country.

Resolution 836: Adopted 4 June 1993. Extended the mandate of the UN Protection Force (UNPROFOR) to allow it to use force in response to attacks on 'safe areas' in Bosnia and Herzegovina. Authorized member states to act nationally or through regional organizations to use air power to assist UNPROFOR to carry out its mandate.

Resolution 837: Adopted 6 June 1993. Condemned an armed attack which killed 24 members of the UN Operation in Somalia (UNOSOM II) and sought to bring to justice those responsible. Reiterated the need for all Somali parties to disarm and to comply with agreements.

Resolution 840: Adopted 15 June 1993. Endorsed the results of elections held in Cambodia and certified that they were free and fair.

Resolution 841: Adopted 16 June 1993. Imposed a mandatory world-wide arms and petroleum embargo against Haiti, in response to the continuing political crisis in that country.

Resolution 846: Adopted 22 June 1993. Approved the establishment of a UN Observer Mission Uganda–Rwanda (UNOMUR) to be deployed on the Ugandan side of the border in order to prevent military supplies reaching Rwandan rebels.

Resolution 848: Adopted 8 July 1993. Endorsed the admission of Andorra to the UN.

Resolution 851: Adopted 15 July 1993. Reiterated demands for the African nationalist group UNITA to cease military activity and to recognize the results of the elections held in Angola in Sept. 1992, and warned that an economic embargo would be imposed against UNITA if a cease-fire were not observed by 15 Sept.

Resolution 858: Adopted 24 Aug. 1993. Approved the establishment of a UN Observer Mission in Georgia (UNOMIG) to monitor and verify compliance with a cease-fire agreement.

Resolution 860: Adopted 27 Aug. 1993. Confirmed that the mandate of the UN Transition Authority in Cambodia (UNTAC) would be terminated upon the creation of a new government in Cambodia in Sept.

Resolution 861: Adopted 27 Aug. 1993. Suspended the arms and petroleum embargo against Haiti, owing to the reinstatement of the elected President.

Resolution 864: Adopted 15 Sept. 1993. Listed economic sanctions to be imposed against the nationalist UNITA movement in Angola, unless a cease-fire was established within 10 days, and established a Security Council Committee to monitor their implementation.

Resolution 866: Adopted 22 Sept. 1993. Approved the establishment of a UN Observer Mission in Liberia (UNOMIL), to co-operate with the military observers of the ECOWAS in monitoring the transition to peace.

Resolution 867: Adopted 23 Sept. 1993. Approved the establishment of a UN Mission in Haiti (UNMIH), to advise in the creation of a new police force and the modernization of the army.

Resolution 868: Adopted 29 Sept. 1993. Condemned the increasing number of attacks against UN personnel, and determined that for the purposes of future missions the Security Council would require host countries to ensure the security of all UN personnel.

Resolution 871: Adopted 4 Oct. 1993. Acknowledged the UN Secretary-General's decision to create three subordinate commands for Bosnia and Herzegovina, Croatia and the 'former Yugoslav republic of Macedonia' within the UN Protection Force (UNPROFOR). Condemned continuing armed hostilities in Bosnia and Herzegovina and Croatia and authorized UNPROFOR to use force if necessary.

Resolution 872: Adopted 5 Oct. 1993. Provided for the establishment of a UN Assistance Mission to Rwanda (UNAMIR), with a mandate to monitor observance of the cease-fire agreement, to contribute to the safety of the capital, to assist with mine-clearance, and to facilitate the repatriation of refugees, into which the UN Observer Mission Uganda–Rwanda was to be integrated.

Resolution 873: Adopted 13 Oct. 1993. Agreed to re-impose an arms and petroleum embargo against Haiti, owing to violations of the 'Governors' Island' peace accord signed in July.

Resolution 875: Adopted 16 Oct. 1993. Condemned the assassination of government officials in Haiti and appealed to member states to ensure full implementation of the embargo imposed against that country, in particular by monitoring the cargoes of incoming ships.

Resolution 876: Adopted 19 Oct. 1993. Affirmed the territorial integrity and sovereignty of Georgia, and condemned the violation of the cease-fire agreement by Abkhazia in July and the murder of the Chairman of the Defence Council and Council of Ministers of the Autonomous Republic of Abkhazia.

Resolution 880: Adopted 4 Nov. 1993. Welcomed the accession of the King of Cambodia and new Royal Government and confirmed that the withdrawal of the UN Transition Authority in Cambodia (UNTAC) would be completed by mid-Nov., with exceptions for the mine-clearance and training units, medical personnel and military police.

Resolution 883: Adopted 11 Nov. 1993. Provided for economic sanctions against Libya to be strengthened in the event of Libya's non-compliance with Resolutions 731 and 748 by 1 Dec., including the closure of Libyan Arab Airlines' offices abroad, a ban on the sale of equipment and services for the civil aviation sector, the sequestration of financial resources held overseas, a ban on the sale to Libya of specified items for use in the petroleum and gas industries, and a reduction in personnel levels at Libyan diplomatic missions.

Resolution 897: Adopted 4 Feb. 1994. Revised the mandate of the UN Operation in Somalia (UNOSOM II) to include assisting the implementation of the 'Addis Ababa' peace accords, protecting ports and airports and assisting the reorganization of the police and judicial services. Reduced the strength of UNOSOM II to a maximum of 22,000 troops.

Resolution 912: Adopted 21 April 1994. Expressed regret at the deaths of the Presidents of Burundi and Rwanda on 6 April, following the shooting down of the Rwandan presidential aircraft, and at the subsequent violence and political assassinations. Condemned the continuing violence and attacks against the UN Assistance Mission in Rwanda (UNAMIR) and altered UNAMIR's mandate to enable it to facilitate negotiations towards an immediate cease-fire and to assist in the resumption of humanitarian assistance.

Resolution 913: Adopted 22 April 1994. Condemned the continued shelling of the 'safe area' of Goražde by Serb forces in Bosnia and Herzegovina and demanded the observation of an immediate cease-fire.

Resolution 914: Adopted 27 April 1994. Authorized the strength of the UN Protection Force (UNPROFOR) to be increased by up to 6,500 troops.

Resolution 917: Adopted 6 May 1994. Imposed extended sanctions against Haiti from 21 May, including a ban on international trade (with exemptions for food and medicine), reduced air links, visa restrictions for certain officials, and a provision preventing members of the regime from gaining access to assets held outside Haiti.

Resolution 918: Adopted 17 May 1994. Imposed an arms embargo against Rwanda and established a Security Council Committee to monitor its implementation. Revised the mandate of the UN Assistance Mission in Rwanda (UNAMIR) to include the protection of refugees and displaced persons and the provision of security for the distribution of humanitarian supplies.

Resolution 919: Adopted 25 May 1994. Removed the mandatory arms embargo and other restrictions imposed against South Africa by Resolution 418 and other resolutions, and dissolved the Committee established by Resolution 421.

Resolution 924: Adopted 1 June 1994. Demanded a cease-fire and the resumption of negotiations to end the conflict in the Yemen and ordered a UN commission of inquiry to be dispatched to the region.

Resolution 925: Adopted 8 June 1994. Endorsed proposals for the deployment of additional battalions of UNAMIR and the establishment of a Trust Fund for Rwanda.

Resolution 929: Adopted 22 June 1994. Authorized the establishment of a multinational force in Rwanda for humanitarian purposes, pending the arrival of the necessary forces for UNAMIR.

Resolution 935: Adopted 1 July 1994. Requested the UN Secretary-General to establish a Commission of Experts to investigate evidence of violations of international humanitarian law in Rwanda and urged member states and humanitarian organizations to make available all relevant substantiated information.

Resolution 937: Adopted 21 July 1994. Authorized the UN Observer Mission in Georgia to be increased in strength, with an extended mandate to include monitoring the cease-fire agreement and the withdrawal of Georgian troops beyond the boundaries of Abkhazia.

Resolution 939: Adopted 29 July 1994. Reiterated that the status quo in Cyprus was unacceptable and advocated a new initiative by the UN Secretary-General for a solution to the conflict, based on a single nationality, international identity and sovereignty.

Resolution 940: Adopted 31 July 1994. Authorized the establishment in Haiti of a multinational force, under unified command, to restore the legitimately elected President and government authorities by 'all necessary means'. Approved the deployment of a UN Mission in Haiti (UNMIH), once stability had been achieved, to maintain security, facilitate the electoral process and to provide training for the Haitian army and police force.

Resolution 941: Adopted 23 Sept. 1994. Emphasized the policy of 'ethnic cleansing' to be a violation of international humanitarian law (with particular regard to the activities of Bosnian Serb forces).

Resolution 942: Adopted 23 Sept. 1994. Imposed sanctions on those areas of Bosnia and Herzegovina controlled by Serb forces, owing to the refusal of the Bosnian Serb party to accept a proposal for a territorial settlement.

Resolution 943: Adopted 23 Sept. 1994. Partially suspended sanctions imposed against the Federal Republic of Yugoslavia (FRY), with the border between the FRY and Bosnia and Herzegovina to remain closed, with exceptions for food, medical supplies and essential clothing.

Resolution 944: Adopted 29 Sept. 1994. Ordered the deployment of the UN Mission in Haiti established by Resolution 940. Agreed to remove all the sanctions imposed against Haiti upon the return of its exiled President, who was to resume his duties.

Resolution 948: Adopted 15 Oct. 1994. Welcomed the return from exile of the President of Haiti.

Resolution 949: Adopted 15 Oct. 1994. Demanded that the evacuation of Iraqi forces recently transferred to southern Iraq be completed immediately and stipulated that Iraq must not employ its forces in a manner that could constitute a threat to its neighbours or to UN operations in Iraq.

Resolution 955: Adopted 8 Nov. 1994. Approved the establishment of an international tribunal for the prosecution of persons responsible for serious violations of international humanitarian law in Rwanda or in neighbouring states during 1994 (the so-called International Criminal Tribunal for Rwanda—ICTR).

Resolution 956: Adopted 10 Nov. 1994. Terminated the trusteeship agreement for the Pacific Island of Palau, as established by Resolution 21.

Resolution 958: Adopted 19 Nov. 1994. Extended the provisions of Resolution 836 to Croatia.

Resolution 960: Adopted 21 Nov. 1994. Welcomed and endorsed as free and fair elections held in Mozambique in Oct.

Resolution 963: Adopted 29 Nov. 1994. Endorsed the admission of Palau to the UN.

Resolution 965: Adopted 30 Nov. 1994. Expanded the mandate of the UN Assistance Mission for Rwanda to include responsibility for the safety of personnel of the ICTR and human rights officers, including full-time protection for the Prosecutor's Office, and for the establishment and training of a new national police force.

Resolution 968: Adopted 16 Dec. 1994. Approved the establishment of a UN Mission of Observers in Tajikistan (UNMOT) to monitor a cease-fire agreement.

Resolution 975: Adopted 30 Jan. 1995. Approved the deployment of the UN Mission in Haiti (UNMIH) to succeed the incumbent multinational force by 31 March and the creation of a trust fund to support the Haitian national police.

Resolution 976: Adopted 8 Feb. 1995. Approved the establishment of a new Angola Verification Mission (UNAVEM III), with some 7,000 military troops, to assist in the restoration of peace to Angola upon the cessation of hostilities.

Resolution 977: Adopted 22 Feb. 1995. Designated Arusha, Tanzania, as the seat for the ICTR.

Resolution 981: Adopted 31 March 1995. Approved the establishment of a peace-keeping force, in Croatia, the UN Confidence Restoration Operation in Croatia (UNCRO).

Resolution 983: Adopted 31 March 1995. Resolved that the UN operation in the former Yugoslav republic of Macedonia would, henceforth, be known as the UN Preventive Deployment Force (UNPREDEP).

Resolution 985: Adopted 13 April 1995. Decided to establish a Security Council Committee to verify compliance with the arms embargo imposed on Liberia by Resolution 788.

Resolution 986: Adopted 14 April 1995. Approved the partial resumption of Iraqi petroleum exports, to generate funds for necessary humanitarian supplies, under an 'oil-for-food' agreement which provided for the export of petroleum valued at up to US $1,000m. every 90 days.

Resolution 990: Adopted 28 April 1995. Authorized the deployment of the UN Confidence Restoration Operation in Croatia (UNCRO).

Resolution 991: Adopted 28 April 1995. Affirmed that the mandate of the UN Observer Mission in El Salvador (ONUSAL) was to terminate on 30 April.

Resolution 994: Adopted 17 May 1995. Condemned the unacceptable treatment of the UN Confidence Restoration Operation in Croatia (UNCRO) and stressed the need for an early restoration of its authority.

Resolution 997: Adopted 9 June 1995. Reduced the strength of the UN Assistance Mission for Rwanda (UNAMIR) from 5,586 troops to 2,200.

Resolution 1001: Adopted 30 June 1995. Renewed the mandate of the UN Observer Mission in Liberia (UNOMIL) and urged parties to install a Council of State, to re-establish a comprehensive cease-fire and to create a timetable for the implementation of the Akosombo and Accra peace accords.

Resolution 1004: Adopted 12 July 1995. Demanded the immediate withdrawal of Bosnian Serbs from the designated 'safe area' of Srebreniča and the release of members of the UN Protection Force who had been taken hostage.

Resolution 1009: Adopted 10 Aug. 1995. Demanded a cease-fire, full compliance with UN resolutions and respect for the Serb population in Croatia and requested that international humanitarian organizations be allowed access to it.

Resolution 1011: Adopted 16 Aug. 1995. Authorized the removal of restrictions imposed by Resolution 918, to allow the sale and supply of arms to the Government of Rwanda through specified points of entry, until Sept. 1996.

Resolution 1012: Adopted 28 Aug. 1995. Authorized the establishment of a commission of inquiry to investigate the assassination of the President of Burundi in Oct. 1993 and subsequent acts of violence, and to recommend measures to bring to justice the perpetrators.

Resolution 1013: Adopted 7 Sept. 1995. Authorized the establishment of an international commission of inquiry to gather information concerning the provision of arms and military training to former Rwandan government forces in the Great Lakes region, in contravention of Security Council resolutions, and to recommend measures to prevent the illegal flow of arms.

Resolution 1020: Adopted 10 Nov. 1995. Adjusted the mandate of the UN Observer Mission in Liberia to comprise support for ECOWAS troops, the Liberian National Transitional Government (LNTG) and humanitarian assistance, the investigation of violations of cease-fire agreements and human rights, the monitoring of compliance with peace accords, the provision of assistance for the maintenance of assembly sites and the observation of elections.

Resolution 1021: Adopted 22 Nov. 1995. Authorized the phased removal of the arms embargo imposed against the Federal Republic of Yugoslavia (FRY) by Resolution 713, upon confirmation that the General Framework Agreement for Peace in Bosnia and Herzegovina in Dayton, Ohio, USA, had been signed by Bosnia and Herzegovina, Croatia and the FRY.

Resolution 1022: Adopted 22 Nov. 1995. Suspended indefinitely all measures imposed against the Federal Republic of Yugoslavia, owing to the signature of the General Framework Agreement for Peace in Bosnia and Herzegovina in Dayton, Ohio, USA. Measures imposed against the Bosnian Serb party were to be removed following confirmation by the commander of the international force to be deployed to the region of the withdrawal of Bosnian Serb forces beyond specified zones of separation.

Resolution 1023: Adopted 22 Nov. 1995. Welcomed the signature of the Basic Agreement on the Region of Eastern Slavonia, Baranja and Western Sirmium, by representatives of the Croatian Government and Eastern Slavonian Serbs, whereby Eastern Slavonia was to be administered by a transitional administration appointed by the UN prior to its re-integration into Croatia.

Resolution 1025: Adopted 30 Nov. 1995. Decided to terminate the mandate of the UN Confidence Restoration Operation on 15 Jan. 1996, or upon the deployment of a transitional peace-keeping force to Eastern Slavonia, as required by the Basic Agreement on the Region of Eastern Slavonia, Baranja and Western Sirmium.

Resolution 1026: Adopted 30 Nov. 1995. Established a deadline of 31 Jan. 1996 for the withdrawal of the UN Protection Force from Bosnia and Herzegovina.

Resolution 1029: Adopted 12 Dec. 1995. Adjusted the mandate of the UN Assistance Mission for Rwanda to include the repatriation of Rwandan refugees and the protection of members of the ICTR pending the implementation of alternative measures and approved a reduction in strength to 1,200 troops.

Resolution 1035: Adopted 21 Dec. 1995. Approved the establishment of a UN civilian police force, the International Police Task Force (IPTF), to assist with the implementation of the General Framework Agreement for Peace in Bosnia and Herzegovina after the replacement of the UN Protection Force by a multinational 'implementation force' (IFOR).

Resolution 1037: Adopted 15 Jan. 1996. Established a UN Transitional Administration for Eastern Slavonia, Baranja and Western Sirmium (UNTAES) to replace the UN Confidence Restoration Operation in Croatia.

Resolution 1044: Adopted 31 Jan. 1996. Condemned an attempt to assassinate the President of Egypt in Addis Ababa, Ethiopia, in June 1995, and demanded that the Government of Sudan comply with a request by the OAU for the extradition of the three individuals implicated in the attack.

Resolution 1048: Adopted 29 Feb. 1996. Welcomed the democratic election of a new president in Haiti and decided to reduce the strength of the UN Mission in Haiti to 1,200 troops and 300 civil police.

Resolution 1049: Adopted 5 March 1996. Condemned hostilities in Burundi and appealed for negotiations to take place. Requested states to help to identify and close radio stations encouraging violence and suggested that a UN radio station be established. Urged the OAU to increase the strength of the Observer Mission in Burundi.

Resolution 1050: Adopted 8 March 1996. Endorsed plans for the withdrawal of the UN Assistance Mission in Rwanda and requested a UN office to be maintained in Rwanda to support the Government with national reconciliation, to assist the strengthening of the judicial system and to facilitate the return of refugees.

Resolution 1051: Adopted 27 March 1996. Approved a monitoring mechanism for Iraqi exports and imports.

Resolution 1052: Adopted 18 April 1996. Condemned the shelling by Israeli forces of a base of the UN Interim Force in Lebanon, which resulted in the deaths of a large number of Lebanese civilians, and demanded an immediate cease-fire.

Resolution 1053: Adopted 23 April 1996. Demanded countries in the Great Lakes region to ensure that their territories were not used as military bases by armed groups, and to prevent the sale of arms to former Rwandan government forces or militia groups.

Resolution 1054: Adopted 26 April 1996. Imposed a range of diplomatic sanctions against Sudan, owing to the failure of the Sudanese Government to comply with the provisions of Resolution 1044.

Resolution 1060: Adopted 12 June 1996. Deplored Iraq's refusal to allow weapons inspectors of the UN Special Commission to gain access to specified sites.

Resolution 1063: Adopted 28 June 1996. Established a UN Support Mission in Haiti (UNSMIH) to replace and reduce the strength of the existing UN mission.

Resolution 1065: Adopted 12 July 1996. Expressed concern at the lack of progress towards a political settlement to the conflict in Abkhazia, Georgia, and voiced support for Georgia's territorial integrity.

Resolution 1070: Adopted 16 Aug. 1996. Imposed a further air embargo against Sudan.

Resolution 1072: Adopted 30 Aug. 1996. Condemned the overthrow of the Government of Burundi and appealed for a cessation of hostilities and a return to constitutional order in that country.

Resolution 1073: Adopted 28 Sept. 1996. Demanded the cessation of hostilities between members of the Palestinian security forces, Palestinian civilians and the Israeli army and urged the resumption of negotiations within the Middle East peace process, following the Israeli Government's decision to open a tunnel running under a mosque in East Jerusalem.

Resolution 1074: Adopted 1 Oct. 1996. Definitively removed the sanctions regime imposed against the Federal Republic of Yugoslavia and the Serb Republic by Resolution 1022, following the holding of elections in Bosnia and Herzegovina in Sept.

Resolution 1076: Adopted 22 Oct. 1996. Demanded the cessation of armed hostilities in Afghanistan and appealed to member states to refrain from supplying arms to parties to the conflict. Denounced discrimination against the female population and other violations of human rights in that country.

Resolution 1078: Adopted 9 Nov. 1996. Approved the establishment of a multinational humanitarian task force in eastern Zaire.

Resolution 1090: Adopted 13 Dec. 1996. Endorsed the appointment of Kofi Annan as Secretary-General of the UN.

Resolution 1097: Adopted 18 Feb. 1997. Endorsed a peace plan for eastern Zaire, which advocated an immediate cease-fire, the evacuation of external forces, respect for the sovereignty and territorial integrity of Zaire and other states in the Great Lakes region, security for refugees and displaced people and negotiations towards a peaceful settlement.

Resolution 1101: Adopted 28 March 1997. Condemned escalating hostilities in Albania, between insurgents and government troops, and endorsed a European Union initiative for the establishment of a multinational force to supervise humanitarian aid operations.

Resolution 1106: Adopted 16 April 1997. Welcomed the inauguration of the new Government of National Unity and Reconciliation in Angola on 11 April and urged the prompt completion of the remaining military aspects of the peace process and the full reinstatement of a state administration.

Resolution 1115: Adopted 21 June 1997. Condemned Iraq's repeated obstruction of the UN Special Commission (UNSCOM) weapons inspectors and demanded that they be allowed unconditional and unrestricted access to all requested areas, equipment, facilities, records and transport.

Resolution 1118: Adopted 30 June 1997. Approved the establishment of a UN Observer Mission in Angola (MONUA), to succeed the UN Angola Verification Mission, to oversee the implementation of the remaining provisions of the peace accord.

Resolution 1121: Adopted 22 July 1997. Established a Dag Hammarskjöld Medal to pay tribute to those killed while in the service of UN peace-keeping operations.

Resolution 1123: Adopted 30 July 1997. Approved the establishment of a UN Transition Mission in Haiti (UNTMIH), to replace the UN Support Mission in Haiti.

Resolution 1125: Adopted 6 Aug. 1997. Authorized the activities of the Inter-African Mission to Monitor the Implementation of the Bangui Agreements (MISAB) in the Central African Republic.

Resolution 1130: Adopted 29 Sept. 1997. Postponed the implementation of sanctions against UNITA militants in Angola, adopted in Aug., owing to the partial restoration of the state administration in several districts in Angola.

Resolution 1132: Adopted 8 Oct. 1997. Demanded the restoration of the democratically elected Government in Sierra Leone and the cessation of violence by the military junta. Imposed sanctions against Sierra Leone, including an embargo on the import of armaments and petroleum products, and established a Security Council Committee to monitor those sanctions.

Resolution 1134: Adopted 23 Oct. 1997. Condemned Iraq's refusal to comply with the UN Special Commission (UNSCOM) and warned that non-co-operation with UNSCOM would lead to the imposition of travel restrictions on Iraqi officials.

Resolution 1137: Adopted 12 Nov. 1997. Activated the measures proposed by Resolution 1134. Stipulated that Iraq should retract its decision to expel US weapons inspectors and warned that further intransigence could provoke possible military action.

Resolution 1141: Adopted 28 Nov. 1997. Established a UN Civilian Police Mission in Haiti (MIPONUH) of some 300 police to succeed the UN Transition Mission in Haiti.

Resolution 1145: Adopted 19 Dec. 1997. Established a UN Police Support Group to oversee the work of the Croatian police in the Danube region, in particular with regard to the return of displaced persons, following the withdrawal of the UN Transitional Administration for Eastern Slavonia, Baranja and Western Sirmium (UNTAES).

Resolution 1153: Adopted 20 Feb. 1998. Increased the maximum permitted revenue from Iraqi exports of petroleum under the 'oil-for-food' programme to US $5,256m. over a six-month period.

Resolution 1154: Adopted 2 March 1998. Endorsed the Memorandum of Understanding between the UN Secretary-General and Iraq concerning co-operation with UNSCOM and IAEA experts and threatened extreme consequences if the agreement were reneged upon by Iraq.

Resolution 1156: Adopted 16 March 1998. Welcomed the return from exile and reinstatement of the President of Sierra Leone and voted to end the embargo on imports of petroleum products to that country.

Resolution 1157: Adopted 20 March 1998. Endorsed a gradual reduction in the strength of the UN Observer Mission in Angola.

Resolution 1158: Adopted 25 March 1998. Authorized additional exports of Iraqi petroleum of up to a total of US $1,400m. over a 90-day period.

Resolution 1159: Adopted 27 March 1998. Approved the establishment of a UN Mission in Central African Republic (MINURCA) to assume responsibility from the Inter-African Mission to Monitor the Implementation of the Bangui Agreements (MISAB).

Resolution 1160: Adopted 31 March 1998. Demanded that the Federal Republic of Yugoslavia (FRY) undertake measures to resolve the conflict between Serbs and the ethnic Albanian majority in the Serbian province of Kosovo and Metohija. Imposed a ban on the sale or supply of armsto the FRY and established a Security Council Committee to monitor its implementation.

Resolution 1161: Adopted 9 April 1998. Re-established the international commission of inquiry created by Resolution 1013 to gather information concerning arms sales to former Rwandan government forces in the Great Lakes region and to recommend measures to prevent the illegal flow of arms.

Resolution 1162: Adopted 17 April 1998. Authorized the deployment of military and security personnel to Sierra Leone.

Resolution 1165: Adopted 30 April 1998. Approved the establishment of a third three-member trial chamber for the ICTR.

Resolution 1166: Adopted 13 May 1998. Approved the establishment of a third three-member trial chamber of the ICTY.

Resolution 1171: Adopted 5 June 1998. Removed the arms embargo imposed against the Government of Sierra Leone. Decided to prohibit the sale and supply of arms and related matériel to non-governmental forces in that country.

Resolution 1172: Adopted 6 June 1998. Condemned nuclear tests undertaken by India and Pakistan in May. Encouraged states to refrain from exporting equipment, materials and technology that could assist the nuclear weapon and ballistic missile programmes of those two countries.

Resolution 1173: Adopted 12 June 1998. Condemned UNITA militants in Angola for failure to comply with the provisions of the Lusaka Protocol and Security Council resolutions. Decided to impose sanctions against UNITA, including 'freezing' its funds in other countries, halting official contacts with its leaders and preventing the export from Angola of all diamonds not controlled by the Government's Certificate of Origin regime.

Resolution 1175: Adopted 19 June 1998. Authorized the export to Iraq of oil-production parts and equipment to enable Iraq to export sufficient quantities of petroleum to fulfil Resolution 1153.

Resolution 1177: Adopted 26 June 1998. Condemned the use of force in the border dispute between Ethiopia and Eritrea.

Resolution 1181: Adopted 13 July 1998. Approved the establishment of a UN Observer Mission in Sierra Leone (UNOMSIL) to monitor the security situation and the disarmament of former combatants.

Resolution 1189: Adopted 13 Aug. 1998. Condemned terrorist attacks carried out against the US embassies in Nairobi, Kenya, and in Dar es Salaam, Tanzania, on 7 Aug.

Resolution 1192: Adopted 27 Aug. 1998. Welcomed an initiative for the trial before a Scottish court convened in the Netherlands of the two Libyan nationals alleged to be responsible for the bombing of civilian aircraft Pan Am flight 103 over Scotland in 1988.

Resolution 1193: Adopted 28 Aug. 1998. Expressed concern at the continued conflict in Afghanistan and demanded the cessation of armed hostilities and the resumption of direct negotiations. Condemned attacks on UN personnel in the territories occupied by the Taliban.

Resolution 1194: Adopted 9 Sept. 1998. Condemned the decision by Iraq to suspend co-operation with the UN Special Commission and the IAEA, in contravention of Security Council resolutions and the Memorandum of Understanding signed in Feb. between the UN Secretary-General and Iraq.

Resolution 1197: Adopted 18 Sept. 1998. Appealed for measures to improve peace-keeping mechanisms within the OAU through the establishment of an early warning system in Africa and a UN Preventative Action Liaison Office.

Resolution 1199: Adopted 23 Sept. 1998. Demanded the observation and maintenance of an immediate cease-fire in the province of Kosovo and Metohija, the withdrawal of Serbian security forces, unrestricted access for humanitarian agencies and negotiations to end the conflict in the Federal Republic of Yugoslavia.

Resolution 1201: Adopted 15 Oct. 1998. Endorsed the decision by the authorities of the Central African Republic to conduct legislative elections and agreed to expand the mandate of the UN

Mission in the Central African Republic to include support for the conduct of elections.

Resolution 1203: Adopted 24 Oct. 1998. Endorsed two agreements signed with the North Atlantic Treaty Organization (NATO) and the Organization for Security and Co-operation in Europe (OSCE) by the Yugoslav authorities, providing for the establishment of NATO and OSCE verification missions in the province of Kosovo and Metohija.

Resolution 1205: Adopted 5 Nov. 1998. Condemned the decision made by Iraq on 31 Oct. to cease co-operation with the UN Special Commission and demanded that it reverse it immediately.

Resolution 1208: Adopted 19 Nov. 1998. Urged the international community to support host African states to enhance their protection and treatment of refugees in camps.

Resolution 1209: Adopted 19 Nov. 1998. Considered the problem of the illicit flow of armaments in Africa.

Resolution 1214: Adopted 8 Dec. 1998. Condemned violence perpetrated by the Taliban in Afghanistan and reiterated demands for a cease-fire and for the resumption of negotiations. Approved the establishment of a civil affairs unit within the UN Special Mission to Afghanistan to deter human rights violations in Afghanistan.

Resolution 1216: Adopted 21 Dec. 1998. Expressed appreciation for the accords reached in Aug. and Nov. 1998 between the Government of Guinea-Bissau and the self-proclaimed 'military junta for the consolidation of democracy, peace and justice' and demanded that they be implemented fully.

Resolution 1219: Adopted 31 Dec. 1998. Expressed concern at the crash of UN flight 806 in Angola and at the increased number of aircraft disappearing over territory controlled by the UNITA. Deplored UNITA's lack of co-operation with crash investigators and demanded that the UN be allowed access to the territory where the crash took place.

Resolution 1221: Adopted 12 Jan. 1999. Condemned the shooting down of a second UN aircraft over territory controlled by UNITA in Angola. Affirmed its determination to carry out an investigation of the circumstances of the two crashes and demanded that UNITA comply with Resolution 1219. Emphasized the member states' obligation to comply with sanctions imposed against UNITA.

Resolution 1227: Adopted 10 Feb. 1999. Condemned the use of force in the border dispute between Eritrea and Ethiopia and demanded a cease-fire and the resumption of negotiations. Urged member states to refrain from providing arms to either of the countries.

Resolution 1233: Adopted 6 April 1999. Approved establishment of a Post-Conflict Peace Building Support Office in Guinea-Bissau, headed by a Representative of the UN Secretary-General, to help consolidate peace, following the inauguration of a new Government of National Unity in that country.

Resolution 1239: Adopted 14 May 1999. Urged safe and unrestricted access for all humanitarian personnel throughout the Federal Republic of Yugoslavia in order to guarantee refugees and displaced persons the right to return home.

Resolution 1244: Adopted 10 June 1999. Authorized the deployment of international civilian and security personnel to Kosovo and Metohija, under UN auspices, and outlined the terms of a political settlement for the province based on the general principles agreed by ministers of foreign affairs of the Group of Eight (G-8) industrialized nations on 6 May. The authorized force, comprising mainly NATO personnel, was to be responsible for ensuring the withdrawal of all Serbian military, police and paramilitary forces, and preventing their return and any new hostilities, and for demobilizing Kosovo Albanian groups. The civilian operation (the UN Interim Administration in Kosovo and Metohija—UNMIK), under the control of a Special Representative of the UN Secretary-General, was to provide an interim administration to supervise the development of democratic, self-governing institutions.

Resolution 1246: Adopted 11 June 1999. Established a UN Mission in East Timor (UNAMET) to organize and conduct a popular poll on the political future of the territory, following agreements concluded between Indonesia, Portugal and the UN on 5 May.

Resolution 1248: Adopted 25 June 1999. Endorsed the admission of Kiribati to the UN.

Resolution 1249: Adopted 25 June 1999. Endorsed the admission of Nauru to the UN.

Resolution 1253: Adopted 28 July 1999. Endorsed the admission of Tonga to the UN.

Resolution 1261: Adopted 25 Aug. 1999. Expressed concern at the impact of armed conflict on children and the long-term consequences of this for durable peace and stability. Condemned the targeting of children in situations of armed conflict, including killing, maiming, sexual violence, abduction and forced displacement, the recruitment and use of child soldiers and attacks on places such as hospitals and schools.

Resolution 1265: Adopted 17 Sept. 1999. Condemned the deliberate targeting of civilians in situations of armed conflict as well as attacks on objects protected under international law. Called upon all parties to put an end to such practices. Decided to establish immediately a mechanism to review further the recommendations contained in the report by the UN Secretary-General on the protection of civilians in armed conflict.

Resolution 1267: Adopted 15 Oct. 1999. Demanded that the Taliban in Afghanistan deliver Osama bin Laden and his associates, accused of co-ordinating the 1998 terrorist bombings of the US embassies in Kenya and Tanzania, to appropriate authorities in order that they might be brought to justice in one of the countries where they had been indicted. Decided that, if this demand were not met within one month, all member states should 'freeze' funds owned or controlled by the Taliban and prohibit the take-off and landing on their territory of Taliban-owned aircraft.

Resolution 1270: Adopted 22 Oct. 1999. Authorized the establishment of the UN Mission in Sierra Leone (UNAMSIL), mandated to co-operate with all parties to the peace agreement signed in July at Lomé, Togo, to assist with the disarmament, demobilization and reintegration of former combatants, and to establish a presence at key locations.

Resolution 1272: Adopted 25 Oct. 1999. Authorized the establishment of the UN Transitional Administration in East Timor (UNTAET), empowered to exercise all legislative and executive authority over the territory, including the administration of justice.

Resolution 1279: Adopted 30 Nov. 1999. Authorized the establishment of the UN Mission in the Democratic Republic of the Congo (MONUC), mandated to establish contacts with the signatories to the Lusaka cease-fire agreement (concluded in Aug. 1999 by the parties to the conflict in the DRC) and to liaise with the Joint Military Commission, established under the agreement to enforce the cessation of hostilities. Also mandated to provide information on security conditions and to facilitate the delivery of humanitarian aid.

Resolution 1284: Adopted 17 Dec. 1999. Authorized the formation of the UN Monitoring, Verification and Inspection Commission (UNMOVIC) to establish and operate a reinforced system for overseeing the elimination of weapons of mass destruction in Iraq. Authorized member states to permit the importation of any volume of petroleum and petroleum products originating in Iraq and to permit financial and other essential transactions relating thereto. Stipulated conditions relating to the eventual suspension of sanctions against Iraq.

Resolution 1286: Adopted 19 Jan. 2000. Condemned continuing violence in Burundi, emphasizing attacks against civilians, in particular the murder of UN personnel and Burundi civilians in Oct. 1999. Urged that the perpetrators be brought to justice swiftly. Urged all parties to end the ongoing armed conflict.

Resolution 1289: Adopted 7 Feb. 2000. Approved the expansion of the military component of the UN Mission in Sierra Leone (UNAMSIL). Revised UNAMSIL's mandate to provide security at key locations in Sierra Leone.

Resolution 1290: Adopted 17 Feb. 2000. Endorsed the admission of Tuvalu to the UN.

Resolution 1293: Adopted 31 March 2000. Doubled the maximum permitted revenue that Iraq might use to purchase oil industry spare parts and equipment under the 'oil-for-food' programme.

Resolution 1295: Adopted 18 April 2000. Reiterated the demand that UNITA militants in Angola comply with obligations under the Lusaka Protocol and with previous Security Council resolutions. Emphasized concern at violations of sanctions imposed against UNITA and stressed the obligation of all member states to comply fully with these. Authorized the establishment of a temporary mechanism to monitor the sanctions violations.

Resolution 1298: Adopted 17 May 2000. Condemned the continuing conflict between Eritrea and Ethiopia. Demanded the immediate cessation of all military actions and avoidance of further use of force. Demanded the resumption of peace talks under the auspices of the OAU. Imposed an embargo on the sale or supply of arms and related materiel to Eritrea or Ethiopia.

Resolution 1299: Adopted 19 May 2000. Authorized the rapid reinforcement of the military component of UNAMSIL, providing for a total of 13,000 personnel.

Resolution 1306: Adopted 5 July 2000. Prohibited the exportation from Sierra Leone of rough diamonds not officially certified by that country's Government.

Resolution 1308: Adopted 17 July 2000. Expressed concern at the potentially damaging impact of HIV and AIDS on the health of personnel deployed to UN peace-keeping operations. Requested the Secretary-General to facilitate the provision of education on disease prevention to such personnel. Urged support from member states and encouraged UNAIDS to strengthen co-operation with member states.

Resolution 1310: Adopted 27 July 2000. Welcomed verification by the UN Secretary-General of Israel's removal of violations of the troop withdrawal line at its border with Lebanon. Welcomed the establishment by the Lebanon Government of checkpoints in the area vacated by the Israeli forces.

Resolution 1312: Adopted 31 July 2000. Authorized the establishment of the UN Mission in Ethiopia and Eritrea (UNMEE) to liaise with the parties to, and facilitate and verify compliance with, the cease-fire agreement signed in Algiers in mid-June.

Resolution 1315: Adopted 14 Aug. 2000. Requested the UN Secretary-General to negotiate an agreement with the Sierra Leone Government on the establishment of an independent special court to try those accused of perpetrating crimes against humanity, war crimes and other serious violations of international law within the territory of that country since 30 Nov. 1996.

Resolution 1318: Adopted 7 Sept. 2000. Declaration of the Millennium Summit Meeting of the Security Council on ensuring an effective role for the Council in the maintenance of international peace and security, with particular reference to promoting peace and sustainable development in Africa. Addressed the root causes of conflicts and the contributory effects of the illicit exploitation and sale of commodities and the illegal trade in armaments; welcomed the report issued in Aug. by the Panel on UN Peace Operations.

Resolution 1322: Adopted 7 Oct. 2000. Deplored the provocation at holy sites in Jerusalem and the subsequent fatal violent incidents. Condemned the escalation of violence and, in particular, the excessive use of force against Palestinians. Called upon Israel to abide by the obligations of the Geneva Conventions and urged a cessation of violence and an immediate resumption of the peace process. Stressed the importance of establishing a mechanism for an objective inquiry into the recent events.

Resolution 1325: Adopted 31 Oct. 2000. Invited the UN Secretary-General to report to the Security Council on the impact of armed conflict on women and girls, the role of women in peace-building, and on gender dimensions in peace processes and conflict resolution. Urged the improved protection of women and girls in armed conflict situations. Recommended more female appointments at all levels of UN peace-keeping activities, and increased participation by women in decision-making processes at national, regional and international level.

Resolution 1326: Adopted 31 Oct. 2000. Endorsed the admission of the Federal Republic of Yugoslavia to the UN.

Resolution 1327: Adopted 13 Nov. 2000. Agreed, having considered the report of the Panel on UN Peace Operations, to adopt several guidelines aimed at improving the Council's management of UN peace-keeping activities. Requested the Secretary-General, in consultation with UN member states, to prepare a comprehensive operational doctrine for the military component of peace-keeping operations.

Resolution 1329: Adopted 30 Nov. 2000. Authorized the expansion of the appeals chambers at both the ICTR and the ICTY. Approved the appointment of two further judges to the ICTR and the establishment of a pool of 27 *ad litem* judges at the ICTY.

Resolution 1333: Adopted 19 Dec. 2000. Demanded that the Taliban in Afghanistan comply with Resolution 1267. Imposed an embargo on the direct or indirect supply, sale or transfer of arms and related materiel to that part of the territory of Afghanistan under Taliban control. Decided that all member states should refrain from providing technical advice, assistance or training relating to Taliban military activities, close all Taliban offices and offices of Ariana Afghan Airlines in their territories, and that all states must 'freeze' the funds and assets of Osama bin Laden (believed to be responsible for the 1998 attacks on US embassies in Kenya and Tanzania) and of all associated individuals and entities. Also prohibited the supply to the Taliban-controlled area of a specific chemical believed to be used there in the production of illegal narcotic drugs.

Resolution 1338: Adopted 31 Jan. 2001. Urged the international community to provide financial and technical assistance to East Timor for institution-building and the establishment of a Defence Force.

Resolution 1341: Adopted 22 Feb. 2001. Required the full disengagement of foreign troops from the Democratic Republic of the Congo. Expressed the intention to send a Council mission to that country in order to monitor the situation and the implementation of the peace accord.

Resolution 1343: Adopted 7 March 2001. Demanded that Liberia cease to support the members or activities of the Revolutionary United Front of Sierra Leone, or of other armed rebel groups in the region, and that all neighbouring countries undertake efforts to maintain the security of border areas. Demanded that the Liberian Government comply with Resolution 1306. Terminated the existing arms embargo against Liberia (under the terms of Resolution 788), but imposed a further embargo on the sale of armaments and related materiel to Liberia and on the export of diamonds from that country, and travel restrictions on senior Liberian officials and their spouses, to be effective from 7 May 2001 if the above demands had not been met.

Resolution 1346: Adopted 30 March 2001. Approved an increase in the military component of the UN Mission in Sierra Leone (UNAMSIL) to 17,500, and a revised concept of operations, in order to implement the process of disarmament, demobilization and reintegration. Urged UNAMSIL to maintain its support for returning refugees and displaced persons.

Resolution 1353: Adopted 13 June 2001. Adopted decisions and recommendations of the Statement of principles on co-operation with troop-contributing countries, which aimed to strengthen relations between the UN and those countries and to enhance the effectiveness of peace-keeping operations.

Resolution 1355: Adopted 15 June 2001. Reiterated demands for all sides in the Democratic Republic of the Congo to respect the Lusaka cease-fire agreement, including the withdrawal of foreign troops, the cessation of aid to or co-operation with armed groups, and the end to the training and use of child soldiers. Urged neighbouring countries to co-operate in support of peace in the region. Approved the establishment of a civilian police component of the UN Mission in the DRC (MONUC) and for an increase in the number of human rights personnel.

Resolution 1358: Adopted 27 June 2001. Recommended to the General Assembly the appointment of Kofi Annan for a second term of office as UN Secretary-General, from 1 Jan. 2002 to 31 Dec. 2006.

Resolution 1363: Adopted 30 July 2001. Established a mechanism to monitor implementation of Council-imposed sanctions against the Taliban regime in Afghanistan and to assist neighbouring countries to increase their capacity to implement the measures. The mechanism was to comprise a five-member Monitoring Group, and a Sanctions Enforcement Support Team, of up to 15 members, to be located in bordering countries.

Resolution 1366: Adopted 30 Aug. 2001. Considered current and future aspects of the role of the Security Council in the prevention of armed conflict, on the basis of a report by the UN Secretary-General. Expressed support for the development of a comprehensive conflict prevention strategy, and the Council's willingness to consider preventive deployment missions.

Resolution 1367: Adopted 10 Sept. 2001. Terminated the measures against the Federal Republic of Yugoslavia, established by Resolution 1160.

Resolution 1368: Adopted 12 Sept. 2001. Unequivocally condemned the terrorist attacks of 11 Sept. against targets in the USA. Called upon all states to co-operate in bringing the perpetrators, organizers and sponsors of the attacks to justice, and expressed readiness to respond to the events as necessary and to combat all forms of terrorism. Reiterated the inherent right of individual or collective self-defence as recognized by the UN Charter.

Resolution 1372: Adopted 28 Sept. 2001. Terminated the sanctions imposed against Sudan by Resolutions 1054 and 1070 in 1996, in response to the efforts of the Government of Sudan to comply with the provisions of Security Council resolutions and its accession to international conventions for the elimination of international terrorism.

Resolution 1373: Adopted 28 Sept. 2001. Approved measures and strategies to combat the threat of international terrorism, including obligations on states to freeze the assets of any individual or group involved in terrorist activities, to deny them safe haven, to co-operate in the exchange of information and in criminal investigations, and to impose stricter border controls. Established a Counter-Terrorism Committee to monitor implementation of the resolution.

Resolution 1376: Adopted 9 Nov. 2001. Outlined the progress of the peace process in the Democratic Republic of the Congo. Expressed support for the new phase in deployment of the UN mission in that country in order to oversee the process of disarmament, demobilization, repatriation, resettlement and reintegration, although emphasized that this required the demilitarization of Kisangani as well as freedom of movement throughout the country.

Resolution 1377: Adopted 12 Nov. 2001. Adopted a ministerial declaration on the global effort to combat terrorism. Urged all states to intensify co-operation and all efforts to eliminate international terrorism and to become parties to international conventions relating to terrorism.

Resolution 1378: Adopted 14 Nov. 2001. Determined that the UN should play a central role in supporting the efforts of Afghanistan to establish a transitional administration prior to the formation of a new, multi-ethnic government. Expressed support for the activities of the Secretary-General's Special Representative on Afghanistan with overall authority for the humanitarian, human rights and political efforts of the UN in that country. Urged all states to provide humanitarian and longer-term assistance to Afghanistan.

Resolution 1379: Adopted 20 Nov. 2001. Considered all means to support children affected by armed conflict, and to extend protection wherever possible.

Resolution 1383: Adopted 6 Dec. 2001. Endorsed the Bonn Agreement on provisional arrangements in Afghanistan reached between representatives of the Northern Alliance and other Afghan groups meeting in Bonn, Germany. Declared willingness to take any necessary action to support the interim institutions and to support the full implementation of the agreement.

Resolution 1386: Adopted 20 Dec. 2001. Authorized the establishment of an International Security Assistance Force (ISAF), as envisaged in the Bonn Agreement, to assist the Interim Authority in Afghanistan to maintain a security in the capital, Kabul, and in the surrounding areas. Requested Afghan groupings to implement their commitment to withdraw all military units from Kabul.

Resolution 1388: Adopted 15 Jan. 2002. Decided that the air embargo and the freezing of assets controlled by the Taliban no longer applied to Ariana Afghan Airlines, and terminated measures to close all overseas offices of the airline (imposed by Resolution 1333).

Resolution 1389: Adopted 16 Jan. 2002. Mandated the UN Mission in Sierra Leone to assist with the conduct of elections, and authorized an expansion of the UN civilian police component to support the national police in undertaking election-related activities.

Resolution 1390: Adopted 16 Jan. 2002. Determined that all states adopt certain measures against the terrorist network led by Osama bin Laden, members of the Taliban and any individual or groups associated with them, including the freezing of all assets, preventing their entry or transit, and preventing the sale or supply of arms-related materiel. Measures to be overseen by the Monitoring Group established under Resolution 1363.

Resolution 1397: Adopted 12 March 2002. Envisaged separate states of Israel and Palestine, based on secure and internationally recognized borders. Expressed grave concern at the continued, escalating hostilities in the Middle East region and demanded an immediate end to all acts of violence. Urged both sides to co-operate in the implementation of the Tenet work plan and the Mitchell Report recommendations, with the aim of resuming negotiations for a political settlement.

Resolution 1401: Adopted 28 March 2002. Established a UN Assistance Mission in Afghanistan (UNAMA), on the basis of a report of the Secretary-General. It was to have a two-pillar mandate relating to political affairs and to relief and assistance. Reaffirmed support for the Secretary-General's Special Representative to Afghanistan, and endorsed his full authority over planning and conduct of UN activities in that country.

Resolution 1402: Adopted 1 April 2002. Called upon Israel and the Palestinian (National) Authority (PA) to implement a cease-fire, following further violent attacks by both sides, and to co-operate with the US Special Envoy and other diplomatic efforts to implement the Tenet work plan and, ultimately, to resume peace negotiations. Called for the withdrawal of Israeli troops from Palestinian cities, including Ramallah.

Resolution 1405: Adopted 19 April 2002. Expressed concern at the humanitarian situation in Palestine, and in particular in the Jenin refugee camp. Urged the removal of all restrictions on operations of humanitarian organizations and endorsed the dispatch of a UN fact-finding team to investigate recent events in Jenin.

Resolution 1410: Adopted 17 May 2002. Authorized the establishment of the UN Mission of Support in East Timor (UNMISET) as a successor mission to UNTAET, mandated to support East Timorese core administrative structures, to provide interim law enforcement and assist with the development of the East Timor Police Service, and to contribute to the maintenance of external and internal national security. Determined that UNMISET would fully devolve all operational responsibilities to the East Timorese authorities over a period of two years.

Resolution 1412: Adopted 17 May 2002. Welcomed the adoption by the Angolan Government and UNITA during the previous month of the Memorandum of Understanding Addendum to the Lusaka Protocol and also welcomed the Government's efforts to restore peaceful and secure conditions in the country and to re-establish an effective administration. Decided to suspend certain measures imposed against UNITA under Resolution 1127.

Resolution 1414: Adopted 23 May 2002. Endorsed the admission of Timor-Leste (East Timor) to the UN.

Resolution 1419: Adopted 26 June 2002. Welcomed the successful and peaceful staging during that month of the Emergency Loya Jirga in Afghanistan. Welcomed the election by the Emergency Loya Jirga of the Head of State and the establishment of the Transitional Authority. Urged significantly greater international assistance with the reintegration of Afghan refugees and internally displaced persons in order to promote stability, and urged all Afghan groups to support full access for and to ensure the safety of humanitarian personnel.

Resolution 1422: Adopted 12 July 2002. Requested that, for an initial 12-month period commencing 1 July 2002 (later extended), current or former peace-keeping personnel from states not party to the Rome Statute of the International Criminal

Court should be exempted from prosecution at the Court over acts or omissions relating to any operation established or authorized by the UN.

Resolution 1426: Adopted 24 July 2002. Endorsed the admission of the Switzerland to the UN.

Resolution 1430: Adopted 14 Aug. 2002. Adjusted the mandate of UNMEE in order to assist the Boundary Commission in the implementation of its Delimitation Decision. Endorsed technical steps for territorial transfers, recommended by the Secretary-General, as a broad framework for the process. Demanded that Eritrea and Ethiopia permit UNMEE personnel full freedom of movement.

Resolution 1431: Adopted 14 Aug. 2002. Decided to establish a pool of 18 *ad litem* judges at the ICTR.

Resolution 1433: Adopted 15 Aug. 2002. Authorized the establishment of the UN Mission in Angola (UNMA).

Resolution 1435: Adopted 24 Sept. 2002. Condemned recent terrorist attacks perpetrated in Israel and Hebron. Expressed concern at the reoccupation of the headquarters of the President of the Palestinian (National) Authority (PA) and of Palestinian cities, at the severe restrictions imposed on the freedom of movement of persons and goods in the Palestinian territories, and at the humanitarian crisis confronting the Palestinian people. Demanded that Israel immediately cease measures in and around Ramallah, including the destruction of Palestinian civilian and security infrastructure, and also demanded the expeditious withdrawal of Israeli occupying forces. Called on the PA to ensure that those responsible for terrorist acts were brought to justice.

Resolution 1441: Adopted 8 Nov. 2002. Deplored the fact that Iraq had not provided a complete disclosure of all aspects of its programmes to develop, and holdings of, weapons of mass destruction and long-range ballistic missiles, including their components, and production facilities and locations; also deplored the non-disclosure of all other nuclear programmes. Furthermore deplored the repeated obstruction of UNSCOM, UNMOVIC and IAEA weapons inspectors. Also deplored the Iraqi Government's failure to end repression of its civilian population and to provide access by international humanitarian organizations to those in need of assistance. Decided that Iraq had been and remained in material breach of its obligations under relevant Resolutions. Decided to afford Iraq a final opportunity to comply with its disarmament obligations and to establish an enhanced inspection regime aimed at bringing to full and verified completion the disarmament process established by Resolution 687 and subsequent Resolutions. Decided that the Iraqi Government should provide to UNMOVIC, IAEA and the Security Council, within 30 days, a complete declaration of all aspects of its programmes to develop chemical, biological and nuclear weapons, and that the Iraqi administration should co-operate immediately, unconditionally and actively with UNMOVIC and the IAEA.

Resolution 1445: Adopted 4 Dec. 2002. Endorsed a new concept of operations and ceiling for the UN Mission in the Democratic Republic of the Congo (MONUC).

Resolution 1448: Adopted 9 Dec. 2002. Decided to end punitive measures imposed against UNITA under Resolutions 864, 1127 and 1173, and to dissolve the Security Council Committee on Angola established under Resolution 864.

Resolution 1456: Adopted 20 Jan. 2003. Adopted a declaration on combating terrorism, issued following a meeting of the Council at the level of ministers for foreign affairs.

Resolution 1459: Adopted 28 Jan. 2003. Declared support for the Kimberley Process Certification Scheme for rough diamonds, which became effective on 1 Jan. as a means of combating the illicit trade in so-called 'conflict diamonds'.

Resolution 1460: Adopted 30 Jan. 2003. Further declaration identifying means of protecting children affected by armed conflict, preventing their recruitment or use in conflict and ensuring that their rights are integrated into peace agreements and the post-conflict reconstruction process.

Resolution 1467: Adopted 18 March 2003. Declaration on the proliferation of small arms and light weapons and mercenary activities: threat to peace and security in West Africa.

Resolution 1468: Adopted 20 March 2003. Welcomed the agreement on transitional arrangements reached earlier in the month in Pretoria, South Africa, by the parties to the ongoing conflict in the Democratic Republic of the Congo (DRC), and urged its full implementation. Demanded that all governments in the Great Lake region immediately cease military and financial support to all parties engaged in armed conflict in the Ituri region.

Resolution 1473: Adopted 4 April 2003. Strengthened the police component of the UN Mission of Support in East Timor. Decided that the downsizing of the military component would be effected more gradually than had been previously scheduled.

Resolution 1478: Adopted 6 May 2003. Determined that the Liberian Government had not complied fully with Resolution 1343. Reiterated the existing sanctions against the regime and decided, additionally, that states should take necessary measures to prevent the import into their territories of round logs and timber products originating in Liberia.

Resolution 1479: Adopted 13 May 2003. Established a UN Mission in Côte d'Ivoire (MINUCI) mandated to facilitate the implementation of the Linas-Marcoussis Agreement, which was concluded in Jan. providing for a government of national reconciliation. MINUCI was to include a military component to complement the operations of the French and ECOWAS forces deployed in that country and a military liaison group.

Resolution 1481: Adopted 19 May 2003. Amended the Statute of the ICTY, empowering *ad litem* judges to adjudicate in pre-trial proceedings.

Resolution 1483: Adopted 22 May 2003. Emphasized the right of the Iraqi people freely to determine their own political future and control their own natural resources. Resolved that the UN should play a vital role in humanitarian relief, the reconstruction of Iraq, and the restoration and establishment of national and local institutions for representative governance. Called upon member states immediately to provide food and medical supplies to Iraq, as well as the resources necessary for reconstruction and rehabilitation of its economic infrastructure. Also appealed to member states to support actions to bring to justice members of the former Iraqi regime alleged to be responsible for perpetrating crimes and atrocities. Decided that all member states should take appropriate steps to facilitate the safe return to Iraqi institutions of illegally-removed cultural property. Supported the formation by the people of Iraq, with the help of the 'Authority' (the occupying powers—the USA and United Kingdom—under unified command) and working with a Special Representative of the Secretary-General, of an Iraqi interim administration, pending the establishment by the Iraqi people of an internationally-recognized, representative government. Decided to remove all prohibitions related to trade with Iraq, with the exception of trade in armaments and related materiel. Determined that all outstanding financial assets or economic resources of the former Saddam Hussain regime should be frozen with immediate effect and transferred to a Development Fund, to be held by the Central Bank of Iraq and to be disbursed at the direction of the Authority. Requested that the UN Secretary-General terminate within a six-month period the ongoing operations of the oil-for-food programme and decided to disband after six months the Security Council Committee established pursuant to Resolution 661. Decided that export sales of petroleum, petroleum products and natural gas from Iraq should be made consistent with prevailing international market best practices and that all proceeds therefrom should be deposited into the Development Fund for Iraq, pending the introduction of a representative government. Decided further that five per cent of these proceeds be deposited into the Compensation Fund established under Resolution 687. Reaffirmed that Iraq must abide by its disarmament obligations and stated that the Council would revisit the mandates of UNMOVIC and the IAEA in this regard.

Resolution 1484: Adopted 30 May 2003. Authorized the deployment, until 1 Sept. 2003, of a reinforced UN Mission in the Democratic Republic of the Congo (MONUC) presence in Bunia and authorized the deployment in the town of an Interim Emergency Multinational Force to contribute to the stabilization of the security and humanitarian situation in close co-ordination with MONUC, pending the expansion of the Mission.

Resolution 1490: Adopted 3 July 2003. Decided to terminate the mandate of the UN Iraq–Kuwait Observation Mission and to end the demilitarized zone in force at the Iraq–Kuwait border with effect from 6 Oct.

Resolution 1493: Adopted 28 July 2003. Authorized an increase in the strength of MONUC to some 10,800 military personnel to support a new government of national unity and transition, which was formed on 30 June. Imposed an arms embargo on rebel militia groups and foreign troops operating in the Kivu and Itari regions of eastern DRC.

Resolution 1497: Adopted 1 Aug. 2003. Authorized the establishment of an ECOWAS-led multinational force in Liberia to support implementation of a cease-fire agreement, concluded in June, and declared willingness to authorize a follow-on UN stabilization force to be deployed no later than 1 Oct. 2003.

Resolution 1500: Adopted 14 Aug. 2003. Determined to establish the UN Assistance Mission for Iraq (UNAMI) with a mandate to support the Secretary-General in fulfilling his responsibilities under Resolution 1483, for an initial 12-month period.

Resolution 1502: Adopted 26 Aug. 2003. Expressed strong condemnation of all forms of violence against personnel participating in humanitarian operations and urged that the perpetrators thereof should be brought to justice. Requested that key provisions of the Convention on the Safety of UN and Associated Personnel (adopted by the General Assembly in Dec. 1994) should be included in all status-of-forces, status-of-missions and host country agreements negotiated between the UN and countries accommodating humanitarian operations.

Resolution 1503: Adopted 28 Aug. 2003. Amended the Statute of the International Criminal Tribunal for Rwanda to provide for the appointment of a Prosecutor separate to that of the ICTY.

Resolution 1506: Adopted 12 Sept. 2003. Removed punitive measures imposed against Libya under Resolutions 748 and 883 and determined to dissolve the Security Council Committee on Libya established pursuant to Resolution 748.

Resolution 1509: Adopted 19 Sept. 2003. Established the UN Mission in Liberia (UNMIL), consisting of up to 15,000 military personnel, to support the implementation of the cease-fire accord agreed in June and Comprehensive Peace Agreement concluded in mid-Aug. by the parties to the conflict in Liberia. UNMIL was mandated to assist with the development of an action plan for the disarmament, demobilization, reintegration and, where appropriate, repatriation of all armed groups and to undertake a programme of voluntary disarmament, to protect civilians and UN personnel, equipment and facilities, to support humanitarian and human rights activities, to support the implementation of national security reforms, and, in co-operation with ECOWAS and other partners, to assist with the training of a national police force and the restructuring of the military.

Resolution 1510: Adopted 13 Oct. 2003. Expanded the mandate of the ISAF in Afghanistan to support efforts to maintain security in areas outside of the capital, Kabul.

Resolution 1511: Adopted 16 Oct. 2003. Authorized a multinational force under unified command to help maintain security in Iraq and to support the UN Assistance Mission in Iraq and the institutions of the Iraqi interim administration. Resolved that the UN should strengthen its role in Iraq, including the provision of humanitarian relief, promoting economic reconstruction and advancing efforts to restore and establish institutions for representative government.

Resolution 1512: Adopted 27 Oct. 2003. Amended the Statute of the ICTR to provide for 16 permanent judges and nine *ad litem* judges. Up to six *ad litem* judges were to be members of a Trial Chamber and were to be permitted to adjudicate in pre-trial proceedings.

Resolution 1515: Adopted 19 Nov. 2003. Endorsed the adoption by the so-called 'Quartet' comprising envoys from the UN, European Union, Russia and USA of a 'performance-based roadmap to a permanent two-state solution to the Israeli-Palestinian conflict'.

Resolution 1518: Adopted 24 Nov. 2003. Emphasized the importance of enforcing prohibitions relating to trade in armaments and related materiel with Iraq originally imposed under Resolution 661 and reinforced under Resolution 1483. Established a sanctions committee to continue to identify individuals and entities holding the outstanding financial assets of the former Iraqi regime.

Resolution 1519: Adopted 16 Dec. 2003. Requested the UN Secretary-General to establish a Monitoring Group, composed of up to four experts, to investigate the ongoing violations of the arms embargo against Somalia (imposed under Resolution 733).

Resolution 1521: Adopted 22 Dec. 2003. Revised the sanctions regime imposed against Liberia under Resolution 1343 in recognition of the Aug. 2003 Comprehensive Peace Agreement and the inauguration in Oct. of a new transitional government. Imposed for an initial period of 12 months revised prohibitions relating to the sale or supply to Liberia of arms and related materiel, the importation from Liberia of rough diamonds (pending the introduction of a reliable certification of origin regime in the country) and timber products, and to travel by designated individuals. Established a Panel of Experts to monitor implementation of the measures and to maintain a list of individuals deemed to be a threat to the peace process in Liberia.

Resolution 1526: Adopted 30 Jan. 2004. Established an Analytical Support and Sanctions Monitoring Team to strengthen the implementation of the sanctions regime imposed against individuals or entities connected with the al-Qa'ida organization under Resolutions 1267, 1333 and 1390.

Resolution 1528: Adopted 27 Feb. 2004. Authorized the establishment (in April) of the UN Operation in Côte d'Ivoire (UNOCI), with a mandate to support the implementation of the Linas-Marcoussis cease-fire agreement concluded in Côte d'Ivoire in Jan. 2003, to assist with the disarmament, demobilization and reintegration of rebel groups, to protect civilians and UN personnel, institutions and equipment, and to support humanitarian and human rights activities.

Resolution 1529: Adopted 29 Feb. 2004. Authorized the deployment of a Multinational Interim Force to Haiti, for a period of no more than three months, to help to restore a secure and safe environment, to facilitate the provision of humanitarian assistance, and to enable international and regional organizations to continue their efforts in support of a new constitutional and political process.

Resolution 1532: Adopted 12 March 2004. Urged member states to freeze all misappropriated funds and assets of the former Liberian President Charles Taylor and his close family and associates, as identified by the Committee established pursuant to Resolution 1521.

Resolution 1533: Adopted 12 March 2004. Established a Committee of the Council to monitor implementation of Resolution 1493.

Resolution 1535: Adopted 26 March 2004. Reinforced the Counter-Terrorism Committee as a subsidiary body of the Council. An Executive Directorate of the Committee was to be established as a special political mission to assist the Bureau (Chair and Vice-Chairs) of the Committee in efforts to monitor implementation of Resolution 1373.

Resolution 1539: Adopted 22 April 2004. Strongly condemned the recruitment and use of child soldiers by parties to armed conflict and all other violations and abuses committed against children in situations of armed conflict. Requested the UN Secretary-General to devise an action plan for the establishment of a systematic and comprehensive monitoring mechanism to provide information on children affected by armed conflict.

Resolution 1540: Adopted 28 April 2004. Concerned with the non-proliferation of nuclear, chemical or biological weapons. Required states to adopt and enforce legislation to ensure that non-state actors are unable to obtain weapons of mass destruction, including their components or means of delivery. Established a committee, with a two-year mandate, to monitor compliance with the resolution.

Resolution 1542: Adopted 30 April 2004. Authorized the establishment of a UN Stabilization Mission in Haiti (MINUSTAH), with an initial six-month mandate, to assume control from the Multinational Interim Force on 1 June. The new mission had an authorized strength of 6,700 troops and 1,600 police officers. It was to work with the transitional government to restore law and order, investigate human rights abuses and assist preparations for new elections.

Resolution 1544: Adopted 19 May 2004. Condemned the killing of Palestinian civilians through Israeli action in the Rafah area. Urged Israel to cease further demolition of homes, in accordance with international humanitarian obligations, and called for emergency assistance to Palestinians made homeless.

Resolution 1545: Adopted 21 May 2004. Authorized the establishment of a UN Operation in Burundi (ONUB), with effect from 1 June, to help create stable conditions necessary for the implementation of the Arusha Agreement.

Resolution 1546: Adopted 8 June 2004. Endorsed the Interim Government of Iraq, as presented on 1 June, as the sovereign power of that country to which full responsibility and authority for governing Iraq was to be transferred when the Coalition Provisional Authority was dissolved on 30 June. Endorsed a timetable for Iraq's political transition to democratic government, including convening a national conference to select a Consultative Council, conducting direct elections to a Transitional National Assembly no later than Jan. 2005, and drafting a new constitution, leading to the formation of a constitutionally elected government by 31 Dec. 2005. Outlined the role of the Special Representative of the Secretary-General in that process as well as the duties of the UN Assistance Mission for Iraq. Reaffirmed authorization of the multinational force under unified command, mandated 'to take all necessary measures' to contribute to the maintenance of security and stability of Iraq, and noted that its continued presence was to be at the request of the Interim Government. Welcomed the security partnership under discussion between the Iraqi Government and the multinational force. Determined that, upon dissolution of the Coalition Provisional Authority, the Interim Government should direct the disbursement of the Development Fund and, additionally, assume the responsibilities and obligations relating to the oil-for-food programme. Urged member states, international and regional organizations and other financial institutions to support Iraq's reconstruction and to extend other financial assistance, including consideration of ways of reducing Iraq's sovereign debt.

Resolution 1547: Adopted 11 June 2004. Endorsed proposals of the UN Secretary-General to establish a UN advance team in Sudan, as a special political mission to facilitate political negotiations and to prepare for international monitoring and the introduction of a peace support operation following the signing of a Comprehensive Peace Agreement.

Resolution 1556: Adopted 30 July 2004. Endorsed the deployment of international monitors, under leadership of the AU, to the Darfur region of Sudan, in view of the ongoing humanitarian crisis, violence and violations of human rights in that region. Urged the Government of Sudan to implement the commitments made in a Joint Communiqué (3 July) with the UN Secretary-General, including facilitating international relief efforts, establishing secure conditions, and pursuing political dialogue with dissident groups. In addition, demanded the government to disarm the Janjaweed militias, identified as the main perpetrators of violence against the civilian population, and bring to justice those responsible for human rights violations. Required all sates to prevent the sale or supply of arms and related materiel or technical or training assistance, to all non-governmental entities operating in Darfur. Urged the international community and the UN Secretary-General to meet the urgent humanitarian needs of an estimated 1m. people.

Resolution 1559: Adopted 2 Sept. 2004. Called upon all foreign forces remaining in Lebanon to withdraw and for all militia to disband and disarm.

Resolution 1564: Adopted 18 Sept. 2004. Declared grave concern at the failure of the Government of Sudan to meet fully obligations under Resolution 1556 and the earlier Joint Communiqué to improve the security of the civilian population of Darfur. Expressed support for the efforts of the AU to enhance and augment its monitoring mission and urged member states to provide all necessary support to the AU. Urged the conclusion of a comprehensive peace accord, and for all parties and armed groups to cease violence and to address any violations reported by the Cease-Fire Commission. Requested the UN Secretary-General to establish an international commission of inquiry to investigate reports of violations of international humanitarian law in Darfur and to identify the perpetrators.

Resolution 1565: Adopted 1 Oct. 2004. Authorized an increase in the strength of the UN Mission in the Democratic Republic of the Congo (MONUC) by 5,900 personnel to reinforce security, particularly in the eastern provinces, with an additional mandate to support the Government of National Unity and Transition by assisting operations to disarm and repatriate foreign combatants, contributing to security arrangements for institutions and officials, and establishing a secure environment for the holding of free and peaceful elections.

Resolution 1566: Adopted 8 Oct. 2004. Reiterated the obligations of states to combat international terrorism. Requested the Counter-Terrorism Committee Executive Directorate to become fully operational. Established a new working group, consisting of all members of the Security Council, to consider recommendations of practical measures to be imposed on participants in terrorist activities, and more effective procedures to prevent their activities and to bring them to justice. Directed the working group to consider the establishment of an international fund to compensate victims of terrorist acts.

Resolution 1572: Adopted 15 Nov. 2004. Condemned renewed hostilities in Côte d'Ivoire and violations of the 2003 Linas-Marcoussis cease-fire agreement. Outlined measures to prevent the supply, sale or transfer (with certain exceptions) of arms or related materiel to that country, or any assistance, technical advice or training. Also requested states to prevent the entry into or transit through their territories of persons designated as constituting a threat to peace and national reconciliation in Côte d'Ivoire, and to freeze all funds and assets owned or controlled by those persons. Established a Committee of the Council to designate individuals and entities to be subject to those measures, to consider requests for exemptions, and to facilitate implementation of the measures. The measures were to enter into force on 15 Dec., initially for a period of 12 months.

Resolution 1574: Adopted 19 Nov. 2004. Welcomed the signing by the Government of Sudan and the Sudan People's Liberation Movement/Army of a *Declaration on the conclusion of IGAD negotiations on peace in the Sudan* and the agreement of six protocols constituting a core peace accord. Urged the international community to anticipate a comprehensive peace agreement to be signed by 31 Dec. 2004 and to prepare to support its implementation. Demanded the immediate cessation of violence by all government and rebel forces and co-operation with humanitarian relief personnel. Supported the decision of the AU to increase its mission in Darfur to 3,320 personnel.

Resolution 1575: Adopted 22 Nov. 2004. Endorsed the establishment of an EU stabilization force in Bosnia and Herzegovina from Dec. 2004, as a legal successor to NATO's military operation (SFOR), and authorized member states to assist both organizations to carry out their missions.

Resolution 1580: Adopted 22 Dec. 2004. Extended, for one year, and revised the mandate of the UN Peace-building Support Office in Guinea-Bissau (UNOGBIS), in support of efforts to achieve peace and stability in that country.

Resolution 1584: Adopted 1 Feb. 2005. Reaffirmed the decisions of Resolution 1572 and authorized the UN Operation in Côte d'Ivoire and supporting French forces to monitor implementation of the measures and collect and dispose of arms and related materiel brought into Côte d'Ivoire in violation of the imposed measures. Requested the UN Secretary-General to establish a Group of Experts mandated, *inter alia*, to examine and analyse information gathered by the forces in monitoring implementation of the measures, to communicate information to the Security Council about the supply of arms and related materiel to Côte d'Ivoire, and to consider more effective implementation of the measures.

Resolution 1590: Adopted 24 March 2005. Established a UN Mission in Sudan (UNMIS) to support and monitor implementation of a Comprehensive Peace Agreement signed by the Government of Sudan and the Sudan People's Liberation Movement/Army in Jan. Requirements of the accord included the establishment of a disarmament, demobilization and reintegration programme, restructuring of the police service, measures to enhance national reconciliation and preparations for elections. UNMIS was also mandated to facilitate the return of displaced persons, contribute to international efforts to protect and promote human rights and to provide assistance to de-mining programmes. It was to provide logistical and technical support to the AU Mission in Sudan, and assume the functions of the existing UN special political mission in that country.

Resolution 1591: Adopted 29 March 2005. Established a Committee of the Security Council to monitor implementation of the measures imposed in Resolution 1556 and to designate individuals, deemed to impede the peace process in Sudan or who have violated humanitarian law, to be subject to additional measures, including restrictions on their movement and freezing of all owned or controlled funds and financial assets. Demanded that all parties to the conflict comply with their commitments under cease-fire and peace agreements and demands of the Security Council and that the Government of Sudan cease offensive military flights in and over the Darfur region.

Resolution 1593: Adopted 31 March 2005. Decided to refer the situation in Darfur since 1 July 2002 to the Prosecutor of the International Criminal Court.

Resolution 1595: Adopted 7 April 2005. Established, with the consent of the Government of Lebanon, an International Independent Investigation Commission to assist the Lebanese authorities to investigate the terrorist attack of 14 Feb. in which former Prime Minister Rafiq Hariri was killed.

Resolution 1596: Adopted 18 April 2005. Defined further the application of measures imposed against the Democratic Republic of the Congo. Outlined measures to strengthen the control of the Government of National Unity and Transition over the country's border and airspace. Demanded that all parties with military capabilities in the provinces of North Kivu and South Kivu and the Ituri district assist the Government in the disarmament, demobilization and reintegration of foreign and national combatants.

Resolution 1599: Adopted 28 April 2005. Established a special political mission to maintain a UN presence in Timor-Leste upon the termination, in May, of the mandate of the UN Mission of Support in Timor-Leste. The UN Office in Timor-Leste was to support the development of state institutions, the national police force and a Border Patrol Unit, and to provide training in the observance of democratic governance and human rights.

Resolution 1603: Adopted 3 June 2005. Endorsed the adoption on 6 April by parties to the conflict in Côte d'Ivoire of the Pretoria Agreement peace accord and demanded that all concerned parties fully and immediately implement the Agreement; commended the ongoing mediation role of South African President Thabo Mbeki; and requested that the UN Secretary-General designate a High Representative to oversee the forthcoming legislative and presidential elections in that country.

Resolution 1609: Adopted 24 June 2005. Authorized the deployment of up to 850 additional military personnel to the UN Operation in Côte d'Ivoire. Authorized the operation to observe and monitor the implementation of the Pretoria Agreement adopted in April and a subsequent comprehensive cease-fire agreement; to monitor the movements of armed groups; to support the Côte d'Ivoire Government of National Reconciliation with the disarmament, demobilization, reintegration, repatriation and resettlement of former combatants; to provide protection to UN personnel, institutions and civilians; to monitor the arms embargo; to facilitate the flow of humanitarian assistance; to support the organization of the planned elections; and to assist the Government of National Reconciliation and regional organizations with the restoration of a civilian police force and imposition of the authority of the judiciary throughout the country.

Resolution 1610: Adopted 30 June 2005. Extended the mandate of the UN Mission in Sierra Leone (UNAMSIL) for a final period until 31 Dec. 2005. Requested the UN Secretary-General to finalize the necessary planning for an integrated UN system presence in Sierra Leone to co-ordinate UN activities and support that country's Government with the peace-building process following the withdrawal of UNAMSIL.

Resolution 1612: Adopted 26 July 2005. Requested the UN Secretary-General to implement without delay the mechanism for monitoring and reporting on children in armed conflict that was envisaged in Resolution 1539. Decided to establish a Security Council working group to review the progress of the action plan referred to in Resolution 1539 and to consider the reports of the planned monitoring mechanism.

Resolution 1620: Adopted 31 Aug. 2005. Requested the UN Secretary-General to establish the UN Integrated Office in Sierra Leone (UNIOSIL), following the termination of UNAMSIL, with a mandate to assist the Sierra Leone Government with peace-building activities; to monitor the security situation; to co-ordinate with UN bodies and regional organizations in monitoring cross-border trafficking activities; and to liaise with the Special Court for Sierra Leone.

Resolution 1621: Adopted 6 Sept. 2005. Authorized an increase by 841 personnel in the strength of MONUC, and an amended concept of the Mission's operations.

Resolution 1622: Adopted 13 Sept. 2005. Authorized the reconfiguration of the military component of UNMEE, including an increase in the number of military observers, within its existing overall mandated strength.

Resolution 1626: Adopted 19 Sept. 2005. Authorized the UN Mission in Liberia (UNMIL) to deploy, from Nov. 2005, up to 250 military personnel to provide security for the Special Court in Sierra Leone, and authorized a temporary increase (from Nov. 2005–March 2006) in UNMIL personnel to 15,250, to enable this deployment. Further authorized UNMIL to deploy troops to Sierra Leone to evacuate the above-mentioned personnel and Special Court officials in the case of a serious security crisis in that country.

Resolution 1631: Adopted 17 Oct. 2005. Welcomed the adoption of the 2005 World Summit Outcome (including the decision to establish a Peace-building Commission); acknowledged the Summit's resolve to expand the involvement of regional organizations in the work of the Security Council. Expressed determination to ensure the further development of co-operation between the UN and regional and sub-regional organizations in maintaining international peace and security.

Resolution 1635: Adopted 28 Oct. 2005. Authorized the temporary expansion of MONUC by 300 personnel, to enable the deployment of an infantry batallion in Katanga, with the additional strength to be downsized by 1 July 2006 (subsequently extended).

Resolution 1636: Adopted 31 Oct. 2005. Having examined the report of the commission established by Resolution 1595 to investigate the 14 Feb. terrorist attack in Beirut, noted with extreme concern allegations of involvement in this act by Lebanese and Syrian officials. Imposed travel and financial sanctions on all individuals suspected by the commission or Lebanese Government of such involvement. Established a Security Council Committee to undertake tasks connected with this resolution. Noted with extreme concern the commission's finding of non-co-operation by some Syrian officials. Decided that Syria must detain and make available to the commission suspected officials, demanded full and unconditional co-operation by Syria, and insisted that Syria must not interfere in Lebanese affairs.

Resolution 1640: Adopted 23 Nov. 2005. Deeply deplored Eritrea's continued restrictions on the freedom of movement of UNMEE personnel and demanded that Ethiopia accept fully the final and binding decision of the Eritrea-Ethiopia Boundary Commission.

Resolution 1645: Adopted 20 Dec. 2005. Decided, acting concurrently with the General Assembly, to establish an advisory, intergovernmental Peace-building Commission.

Resolution 1649: Adopted 21 Dec. 2005. Deplored the continuing presence of foreign armed groups in eastern regions of the Democratic Republic of the Congo (DRC). Extended, until 1 July 2006, punitive measures imposed under Resolution 1596 to leaders of foreign military groups operating in the DRC who were impeding the ongoing disarmament and repatriation process, and to externally-supported political and military leaders of Congolese militias, with a particular focus on those in Ituri.

Resolution 1657: Adopted 6 Feb. 2006. Authorized the immediate deployment of one infantry company from UNMIL to UNOCI, until 31 March 2006, to provide extra security for UN personnel and property in Côte d'Ivoire.

Resolution 1659: Adopted 15 Feb. 2006. Endorsed the 'Afghanistan Compact', agreed by the London Conference on

Afghanistan convened on 31 Jan.–1 Feb., as providing for the framework for partnership between the Afghan Government and the international community until end-2010, following the termination in Sept. 2005 of the interim process determined by the Dec. 2001 Bonn Agreement (see Resolution 1383).

Resolution 1663: Adopted 24 March 2006. Requested the UN Secretary-General, jointly with the AU, and in close co-operation with the Security Council and concerned parties, to expedite planning for the transition from the AU Mission in Sudan to a UN peace-keeping operation for Darfur.

Resolution 1664: Adopted 29 March 2006. Requested the UN Secretary-General to negotiate an agreement with the Lebanese Government on the establishment of an international tribunal to try those suspected of participation in the Feb. 2005 terrorist attack in that country.

Resolution 1667: Adopted 31 March 2006. Welcomed the transfer of former Liberian President Charles Taylor to the custody of the Special Court for Sierra Leone.

Resolution 1671: Adopted 25 April 2006. Authorized, for a period ending four months after the forthcoming elections in the DRC, the deployment by the European Union of EUFOR RD Congo, in support of MONUC.

Resolution 1673: Adopted 27 April 2006. Extended, by a further two-year period, the mandate of the Committee established pursuant to Resolution 1540. Urged all states to submit their reports on measures taken to implement efforts to contain proliferation of nuclear chemical and biological weapons.

Resolution 1674: Adopted 28 April 2006. Endorsed the conclusions of the UN Secretary-General's report concerning the protection of civilians in armed conflict. Demanded that all states comply with their obligations under international law and reaffirmed the commitment of UN missions and other bodies to upholding human rights and facilitating all humanitarian efforts.

Resolution 1682: Adopted 2 June 2006. Authorized the expansion of UNOCI, until 15 Dec., by 1,500 additional personnel.

Resolution 1688: Adopted 16 June 2006. Detailed the terms for the detention and trial of former Liberian President Taylor in the Netherlands, under the jurisdiction of the Special Court for Sierra Leone.

Resolution 1689: Adopted 20 June 2006. Determined not to renew the prohibition on the import of timber products from Liberia, imposed under Resolution 1521, in support of efforts by the Liberian Government to develop a transparent forestry management regime.

Resolution 1691: Adopted 22 June 2006. Endorsed the admission of Montenegro to the UN.

Resolution 1695: Adopted 15 July 2006. Condemned the launching of ballistic missiles by North Korea and demanded that the authorities in that country suspend all activities relating to its ballistic mission programme. Urged North Korea to resume international negotiations to ensure nuclear safeguards and non-proliferation.

Resolution 1696: Adopted 31 July 2006. Demanded that Iran suspend all nuclear enrichment and processing activities to be verified by the IAEA, in support of a negotiated international solution to Iran's intention to develop its nuclear programme. Requested a report from the Director-General of the IAEA on Iran's compliance by 31 Aug.

Resolution 1701: Adopted 11 Aug. 2006. Called for a full cessation of hostilities in Lebanon, the immediate withdrawal of all Israeli forces and the deployment of Lebanese and UN troops throughout the south of the country. Authorized an expansion of the UN Interim Force in Lebanon to up to 15,000 troops to be responsible for monitoring the cessation of hostilities, supporting the Lebanese forces to secure the Blue Line and international borders, and facilitating humanitarian activities. Prohibited the sale or supply of armaments and related materiel or training assistance to individuals or entities within Lebanon, except those authorized by the Lebanese Government.

Resolution 1702: Adopted 15 Aug. 2006. Increased the strength of the UN Stabilization Mission in Haiti to 7,200 military personnel and 1,951 police officers. Supported a strengthening of the mission's role in crime reduction and prevention, in particular with regard to gang violence and kidnapping.

Resolution 1704: Adopted 28 Aug. 2006. Established a UN Integrated Mission in Timor-Leste, for an initial six-month period, as a successor to the UN Office in Timor-Leste. The mission, consisting of up to 1,608 police personnel and 34 military officers, was mandated to support and facilitate the development of democratic governance, including the provision of technical assistance for the presidential and parliamentary electoral processes, and the restoration of public security and human rights mechanisms.

Resolution 1706: Adopted 31 Aug. 2006. Authorized the expansion of the mandate of the UN Mission in Sudan to include its deployment in Darfur with an increased mission strength of up to 17,300 military personnel and 3,300 civilian police officers. The operation was to support and monitor implementation of the Darfur Peace Agreement (signed in May) and a separate comprehensive cease-fire agreement. Additionally, it was mandated to contribute to international efforts to protect civilians in the region, to establish a secure environment for the return of refugees and internally displaced persons, and the provision of humanitarian assistance, to undertake mine awareness and de-mining activities, and to uphold regional security through the deployment of officers in neighbouring countries.

Resolution 1715: Adopted 9 Oct. 2006. Recommended the appointment of Ban Ki-Moon as Secretary-General of the UN for the period 1 Jan. 2007–31 Dec. 2011.

Resolution 1718: Adopted 14 Oct. 2006. Condemned the nuclear test conducted by North Korea on 9 Oct. Demanded that North Korea not conduct any further nuclear test or launch of a ballistic missile and that it retract its announcement of withdrawal from the Treaty on Non-proliferation of Nuclear Weapons (NPT). Decided that North Korea must suspend all activities related to its ballistic missile programme, abandon all nuclear weapons and existing nuclear programmes, and abandon all other existing weapons of mass destruction and ballistic missile programmes in a complete, verifiable and irreversible manner. Imposed an embargo on the supply of arms, military technology and luxury goods to that country and froze the foreign assets of personnel connected to the weapons programme. Demanded that North Korea return to the international six-party talks on its contravention of the NPT.

Resolution 1719: Adopted 25 Oct. 2006. Authorized the establishment of a UN Integrated Office in Burundi to support implementation of a comprehensive cease-fire agreement signed in Sept.

Resolution 1725: Adopted 6 Dec. 2006. Authorized the establishment, in Somalia, of a protection and training mission, under the auspices of IGAD and members of the AU, to help secure the process of national reconciliation and to support the Transitional Federal Charter and Institutions.

Resolution 1730: Adopted 19 Dec. 2006. Adopted a procedure to provide for the removal or exemption of an individual or entity from sanctions lists. Requested the establishment, within the UN Secretariat, of a focal point to administer the de-listing procedure and liaise with the Sanctions Committee.

Resolution 1735: Adopted 22 Dec. 2006. Reviewed the measures imposed against individuals and groups associated with al-Qa'ida and the Taliban. Encouraged member states to review and update the so-called Consolidated List of those against whom sanctions apply and to ensure that the measures are fully implemented.

Resolution 1737: Adopted 23 Dec. 2006. Required Iran to suspend all nuclear enrichment-related and reprocessing activities and to provide access to and co-operation with the IAEA to verify the suspension. Imposed an embargo on the supply, sale or transfer of all items, materials, equipment or technology which could contribute to those activities or to the development of nuclear weapon delivery systems. Requested that states monitor the movement of specific individuals and entities engaged in or associated with Iran's nuclear activities and freeze all funds and financial assets owned or controlled by them. Established a Committee of the Security Council to monitor implementation of the measures.

Resolution 1739: Adopted 10 Jan. 2007. Defined further the mandate of the UN Operation in Côte d'Ivoire (UNOCI), to be implemented in co-operation with French forces stationed in that country. The mandate included monitoring the cessation of hostilities and movement of armed groups; supporting implementation of all disarmament, demobilization, reintegration, repatriation and resettlement activities; undertaking the disarmament and dismantling of militias; participating in operations of population identification and voter registration; monitoring the arms embargo; facilitating provision of humanitarian assistance; and supporting the organization of open, free, fair and transparent elections. Authorized the French forces to use all necessary means to support UNOCI.

Resolution 1740: Adopted 23 Jan. 2007. Welcomed the signing on 21 Nov. 2006 by the Government of Nepal and the Communist Party of Nepal (Maoist) of a Comprehensive Peace Agreement, and authorized the establishment of the UN Mission in Nepal (UNMIN) to support the Agreement by monitoring the management of arms and armed personnel; assisting with monitoring cease-fire arrangements; providing technical support for the staging of elections to a Constituent Assembly; and providing a team of electoral monitors to review the electoral process.

Resolution 1741: Adopted 30 Jan. 2007. Approved a reconfiguration of the military component of UNMEE from 2,300 to 1,700 military personnel; maintained the current authorized force level.

Resolution 1744: Adopted 20 Feb. 2007. Endorsed the establishment of the AU Mission in Somalia (AMISOM) to support national dialogue and reconciliation and help to create a secure environment for the provision of humanitarian assistance.

Resolution 1745: Adopted 22 Feb. 2007. Increased UNMEE's authorized strength by up to 140 police personnel.

Resolution 1747: Adopted 24 March 2007. Called for states to refrain from new financial transactions with Iran, expect for humanitarian or development purposes, and to be vigilant in the movement of certain individuals given ongoing concern at Iran's nuclear programme and its failure to meet requirements of the IAEA and previous Security Council resolutions. Decided that Iran shall not supply, sell or transfer any arms or related materiel, and that states prohibit the procurement of these by their nationals.

Resolution 1753: Adopted 27 April 2007. Terminated measures against trade in Liberian rough diamonds, given that country's admission as a participant in the Kimberley Process Certification Scheme.

Resolution 1756: Adopted 15 May 2007. Determined that the mandate of MONUC was to assist the Government of the DRC to establish a stable security environment and thus, in particular, to undertake the following tasks: to ensure the protection and freedom of movement of civilians and UN and humanitarian personnel in the DRC; to monitor the territorial security of that country; to assist with the disarmament and demobilization of foreign and Congolese armed groups; and to support the strengthening of democratic institutions.

Resolution 1757: Adopted 30 May 2007. Authorized the provisions for the establishment of a Special Tribunal for Lebanon, on the basis of an agreement between the UN and the Lebanese Government, to prosecute those responsible for the terrorist attack in Feb. 2005.

Resolution 1760: Adopted 20 June 2007. Established a Panel of Experts to assess the Liberian Government's compliance with the Kimberley Process Certification Scheme; the impact and effectiveness of the measures imposed against the assets of former President Taylor; and the implementation of new forestry legislation, given the removal of the ban on exports of timber.

Resolution 1762: Adopted 29 June 2007. Terminated the mandates of the UN Monitoring, Verification and Inspection Commission (UNMOVIC) and the IAEA Iraq Nuclear Verification Office. Reiterated Iraq's disarmament obligations under international conventions.

Resolution 1769: Adopted 31 July 2007. Authorized the establishment of an African Union (AU)/UN Hybrid Operation in Darfur (UNAMID), comprising up to 19,555 military personnel, to help to facilitate humanitarian activities in that region of Sudan and to enforce the provisions of the Darfur Peace Agreement. Determined that UNAMID establish by the end of Oct. initial operational capabilities for its HQ and command structures and complete its preparations to assume authority from the existing AU Mission in Sudan by the end of Dec. Called for an immediate cessation of hostilities by all parties to the conflict.

Resolution 1771: Adopted 10 Aug. 2007. Amended, and extended until 15 Feb. 2008, arms embargo against militia groups and other troops operating in the DRC.

Resolution 1772: Adopted 20 Aug. 2007. Authorized an extension of the AU Mission in Somalia with a mandate to support the process of dialogue and reconciliation. Emphasized the need for all parties in Somalia and regional organizations to support the transitional federal institutions and pursue efforts to achieve a comprehensive peace. Requested that the UN Secretary-General continue to plan for the possible deployment of a UN peace-keeping force.

Resolution 1777: Adopted 20 Sept. 2007. Authorized a reduction in the military component of the UN Mission in Liberia by 2,450 during the period Oct. 2007–Sept. 2008.

Resolution 1778: Adopted 25 Sept. 2007. Approved the establishment of a multi-dimensional presence in Chad and the CAR to improve security, in particular for returning refugees and internally displaced persons, and the distribution of humanitarian assistance in eastern Chad and north-eastern CAR. The presence was to include a UN Mission in the Central African Republic and Chad (MINURCAT), mandated to support local police, army and regional forces in improving security and the protection of civilians and to assist both governments to uphold human rights and the rule of law. Its authorized strength was 300 police officers and 50 military liaison officers. Also authorized the deployment of an EU operation (EUFOR Chad/CAR) to contribute to the protection of civilians and to facilitate the delivery of humanitarian aid and the free movement of humanitarian personnel.

Resolution 1780: Adopted 15 Oct. 2007. Adjusted the composition of the UN Stabilization Mission in Haiti (MINUSTAH) to reflect the changing circumstances within that country. Determined that the operation should consist of a military component of up to 7,060 troops and 2,091 police officers. Recognized the need for MINUSTAH's continued assistance in reforming the national police force and upholding security, in particular in border regions.

Resolution 1790: Adopted 18 Dec. 2007. Extended the mandate of the multinational force in Iraq, until 31 Dec. 2008, given the agreement of the Government of Iraq for its continued presence in the country.

Resolution 1793: Adopted 21 Dec. 2007. Requested that the UN Secretary-General formulate a strategy to reduce the authorized strength of the UN Integrated Office in Sierra Leone, with a view to terminating its mandate by 30 Sept. 2008, and ensure its capacity to assist local elections, scheduled for June 2008, and peace-building activities.

Resolution 1797: Adopted 30 Jan. 2008. Authorized the UN Mission in the DRC (MONUC) to assist the authorities in that country, including the independent electoral commission, in the organization, preparation and conduct of local elections.

Resolution 1802: Adopted 25 Feb. 2008. Condemned the attacks, earlier in that month, against the President and Prime Minister of Timor-Leste and urged all parties to co-operate in bringing those responsible to justice and in maintaining stability in the country.

Resolution 1803: Adopted 3 March 2008. Imposed additional measures against Iran owing to that country's failure to comply with nuclear non-proliferation requirements of the IAEA and previous Security Council resolutions. Decided that all states must prevent the entry into or transit through their territories of certain individuals identified as being engaged in or associated with proliferation activities or the development of a nuclear weapons delivery system, unless granted an exemption by the Security Council Committee establish pursuant to Resolution 1737. Also decided that all states shall prevent the supply, sale or transfer to Iran of certain items, equipment or other technical goods detailed in Resolution 1737. Called upon states to inspect cargoes being transported by Iran's national air cargo and shipping line (in instances where there were grounds for believing prohibited goods were being transported). Also for states to monitor the activities of Iran's financial institutions and other financial arrangements made with the authorities or companies in that country.

Resolution 1806: Adopted 20 March 2008. Extended the mandate of the UN Assistance Mission in Afghanistan, specifying that its main areas of activity were to promote more coherent support by the international community to the Afghan Government, to strengthen co-operation with the ISAF, to promote implementation of the Afghanistan Compact and other national strategies at local level, as well as promoting efforts to improve governance and the rule of law and to monitor human rights, to provide good offices for reconciliation programmes, to facilitate the delivery of humanitarian assistance and to provide technical assistance in support of the electoral process. Condemned all attacks targeting civilians and international forces in Afghanistan, the recruitment and use of children by Taliban forces, and continuing forms of discrimination and violence against women and girls.

Resolution 1807: Adopted 31 March 2008. Detailed the terms for continued measures against the Democratic Republic of the Congo. Requested that all countries in the region strengthen their border controls, and monitor use of their airfields, in order to ensure the measures are enforced.

Resolution 1809: Adopted 16 April 2008. Determined to enhance the relationship and practical co-operation between the UN and regional and sub-regional organizations, in particular with regard to peace-keeping operations and the maintenance of international peace and security.

Resolution 1810: Adopted 25 April 2008. Extended, by a further three-year period, the mandate of the Committee established pursuant to Resolution 1540. Decided that the 1540 Committee should continue to intensify efforts to promote the full implementation by all states of Resolution 1540 relating to containing proliferation of nuclear, chemical and biological weapons.

Resolution 1814: Adopted 15 May 2008. Supported proposals of the UN Secretary-General to provide an updated comprehensive, integrated UN strategy for peace and stability in Somalia, including the relocation of the UN Political Office for Somalia from Nairobi, Kenya, to a location in Somalia in order to enhance its capacity to implement the strategy. Requested the Secretary-General to continue contingency planning for a future UN peace-keeping mission in Somalia to succeed the AU operation.

Resolution 1816: Adopted 2 June 2008. Condemned acts of piracy and armed robbery against vessels off the coast of Somalia. Urged co-operation among states and with other organizations, in particular the International Maritime Organization (IMO), to deter and exchange information regarding such acts and to assist the Transitional Federal Government of Somalia and neighbouring states to strengthen their coastal and maritime security. Decided that, for a period of six months, member states, with due notification, might enter Somalian territorial waters and use all permitted means necessary to repress acts of piracy and armed robbery.

Resolution 1817: Adopted 11 June 2008. Concerned with the high levels of production and trafficking of narcotic drugs in Afghanistan. Urged greater co-operation by all member states in monitoring the export of and trade in chemical precursors, and in providing financial and technical assistance to Afghanistan and neighbouring countries to combat the manufacture of and trade in chemical precursors, and to strengthen border control.

Resolution 1820: Adopted 19 June 2008. Demanded the immediate and complete cessation by all parties to armed conflicts of all acts of sexual violence against civilians. Demanded that all parties to armed conflict immediately take appropriate measures to protect civilians from all forms of sexual violence. Noted that rape and other forms of sexual violence can constitute a war crime, a crime against humanity, or a constitutive act with respect to genocide. Requested the UN Secretary-General and relevant UN agencies to develop mechanisms for providing protection from violence to women and girls in and around UN-managed refugee and IDP camps.

Resolution 1822: Adopted 30 June 2008. Expressed concern at criminal misuse of the internet by al-Qa'ida, Osama bin Laden and the Taliban. Urged the enforcement without delay of financial, economic and travel sanctions, and the prohibition on supplying arms and related materiel, against individuals, groups, undertakings and entities associated with al-Qa'ida, Osama bin Laden and the Taliban. Noted that means of financing the activities of al-Qa'ida, Osama bin Laden and the Taliban include but are not limited to the use of proceeds derived from illicit cultivation, production and trafficking of narcotic drugs originating in Afghanistan. Encouraged member states to submit names for entering on the Consolidated List.

Resolution 1823: Adopted 10 July 2008. Removed the prohibition relating to trade in armaments and related materiel with Rwanda. Decided to dissolve the Security Council Committee established pursuant to Resolution 918 concerning Rwanda.

Resolution 1827: Adopted 30 July 2008. Terminated the mandate of the UN Mission in Ethiopia and Eritrea. Demanded that Ethiopia and Eritrea comply fully with their obligations under the peace agreement concluded in Algiers, Algeria, in Dec. 2000.

Resolution 1829: Adopted 4 Aug. 2008. Established a UN Integrated Peace-building Office in Sierra Leone (UNIPSIL) for a 12-month period from 1 Oct. 2008, as a successor to the existing UN Integrated Office in Sierra Leone.

Resolution 1831: Adopted 19 Aug. 2008. Welcomed the signature on 19 Aug. of an agreement between the Transitional Federal Government of Somalia and the Alliance of the Re-Liberation of Somalia and noted that the agreement called for the UN to authorize and deploy an international stabilization force in Somalia; further noted a communiqué issued by the AU in June calling for the UN to deploy a peace-keeping operation to that country; and recalled its willingness to consider, at an appropriate time, a peace-keeping operation to take over from the AU Mission to Somalia. Renewed the AU's authorization to appoint the AU Mission to Somalia.

Resolution 1833: Adopted 22 Sept. 2008. Expressed strong concern about the security situation in Afghanistan, including an increase in violent and terrorist activities by al-Qa'ida, the Taliban, illegally armed groups, criminals and people involved in the narcotics trade, and expressed concern at the strengthening links between terrorist activities and illicit drugs. Encouraged the ISAF further to support Afghan-led sustained efforts to address the illicit production of and trafficking in drugs. Encouraged the Force to train, mentor and empower the Afghan national security forces. Extended the authorization of the Force.

Resolution 1835: Adopted 27 Sept. 2008. Called upon Iran to comply fully and without delay with its obligations under previous UN Security Council Resolutions and to meet the requirements of the IAEA Board of Governors.

Resolution 1836: Adopted 29 Sept. 2008. Endorsed a recommendation by the UN Secretary-General to reduce the overall strength of the UN Mission in Liberia, to be implemented during Oct. 2008–March 2009. Also endorsed, with immediate effect, the Secretary-General's recommendation for an increase by 240 in the authorized number of personnel deployed as part of UNMIL's police component.

Resolution 1838: Adopted 7 Oct. 2008. Called upon states interested in the security of maritime activities to take part actively in the fight against piracy on the high seas off the coast of Somalia, in particular by deploying naval vessels and military aircraft, in accordance with international law. Urged states and regional organizations to co-ordinate their actions, and to continue actively to protect WFP convoys carrying humanitarian assistance to Somalia.

Resolution 1843: Adopted 20 Nov. 2008. Authorized the immediate deployment of a temporary increase in MONUC's military strength by up to 2,785 military personnel, and an increase in its police unit by up to 300 personnel.

Resolution 1844: Adopted 20 Nov. 2008. Decided that all member states should freeze without delay the funds, other financial assets and economic resources owned or controlled, directly or indirectly, by individuals and designated entities engaging in or providing support for acts that threaten the peace, security or stability of Somalia, including acts that threaten the Djibouti Agreement of 18 Aug. 2008 or the political process, or that threaten by force the transitional federal institutions or the AU Mission in Somalia.

Resolution 1846: Adopted 2 Dec. 2008. Reiterated condemnation of all acts of piracy and armed robbery against vessels in waters off the coast of Somalia, and expressed concern over reports that escalating ransom payments are fuelling the growth of piracy in that region. Welcomed EU and NATO actions against piracy. Requested the Secretary-General of the IMO to brief the Council on the cases brought to his attention by the agreement of all affected coastal states.

Resolution 1850: Adopted 16 Dec. 2008. Welcomed the statement made on 9 Nov. 2008 by the Quartet and the Israeli-Palestinian Joint Understanding, including in relation to the implementation of the Performance-Based Roadmap to a Permanent Two-State Solution to the Israeli-Palestinian Conflict. Declared its support for and commitment to the irreversibility of the bilateral negotiations initiated at the Nov. 2007 Annapolis Conference. Called on the relevant parties to fulfil their obligations under the Roadmap. Urged the intensification of diplomatic efforts to foster mutual recognition and peaceful coexistence between all states in the region.

Resolution 1851: Adopted 16 Dec. 2008. Called on member states to assist the Somali transitional federal government, at its request, and with notification to the UN Secretary-General, to strengthen its operational capacity to bring to justice those who are using Somali territory to plan, facilitate or undertake criminal acts of piracy and armed robbery at sea.

Resolution 1856: Adopted 22 Dec. 2008. Decided that MONUC would also have the mandate, in close co-operation with the DRC authorities, the UN country team and donors, to support the strengthening of democratic institutions and the rule of law.

Resolution 1860: Adopted 8 Jan. 2009. Expressed grave concern at the escalation of violence and deepening humanitarian crisis in the Gaza Strip and the resulting heavy civilian casualties, and emphasized that Palestinian and Israeli civilian populations must be protected in the ongoing conflict between Israel Defence Forces and armed Hamas militants. Called for, and stressed the urgency of, an 'immediate, durable and fully respected cease-fire, leading to the full withdrawal of Israeli forces from Gaza'. Called for the unimpeded provision and distribution throughout Gaza of humanitarian assistance, including of food, fuel and medical treatment. Encouraged tangible steps towards intra-Palestinian resolution, and called for renewed and urgent efforts by the parties to the conflict and the international community towards achieving a comprehensive peace.

Resolution 1861: Adopted 14 Jan. 2009. Authorized the deployment of a military component of MINURCAT to follow on from EUFOR Chad/CAR upon the expiry of the latter's mandate; the transfer of authority between EUFOR and the military component of MINURCAT was to take place on 15 March 2009. Decided that MINURCAT should include a maximum of 300 police officers, 25 military liaison officers, 5,200 military personnel and an appropriate number of civilian personnel. Decided that MINURCAT should have the mandate to ensure the security and protection of civilians; to promote human rights and the rule of law; and to support regional peace.

Resolution 1862: Adopted 14 Jan. 2009. Demanded that Eritrea withdraw its forces and all their equipment to the positions of the *status quo ante*, and ensure that no military presence or activity was being pursued in the area where conflict erupted in Ras Doumeira and Doumeira Island in June 2008.

Resolution 1863: Adopted 16 Jan. 2009. Renewed authorization allowing the member states of the AU to maintain a mission in Somalia. Expressed intent to establish a peace-keeping operation in Somalia as a future follow-on from the AU Mission in Somalia, to facilitate humanitarian assistance and improve humanitarian access; to assist with the free movement, safe passage and protection of those involved in the political process; to monitor the Djibouti Peace Agreement; to support UN personnel; and to assist with the training of Somalian security personnel.

Resolution 1865: Adopted 27 Jan. 2009. Took note, with deep concern, of the postponement of presidential elections in Côte d'Ivoire, and urged Ivorian political actors to establish a new time frame for elections.

Resolution 1866: Adopted 13 Feb. 2009. Determined to outline by 15 June 2009 the elements of a future UN presence in Georgia.

Resolution 1868: Adopted 23 March 2009. Extended the mandate of the UN Assistance Mission in Afghanistan. Strongly condemned all attacks on civilians and on Afghan and international forces, as well as the use by the Taliban, and other extremist groups, of civilians as human shields and children as soldiers. Decided that the Mission and the UN Secretary-General's Special Representative in Afghanistan, within their mandate and guided by the principle of reinforcing Afghan ownership and leadership, would continue to lead international civilian efforts, in accordance with priorities outlined in Resolution 1806. Called on the Afghan Government and international organizations fully to implement the Afghanistan Compact.

Resolution 1874: Adopted 12 June 2009. Expressed grave concern at the nuclear test conducted by North Korea on 25 May 2009, in violation of Resolution 1718, and at the challenge constituted by such a test to the Treaty on the Non-proliferation of Nuclear Weapons. Deplored North Korea's pursuit of nuclear weapons, and demanded that North Korea retract its announcement of withdrawal from the Treaty. Imposed a total embargo on arms exports from North Korea and strengthened the prohibition on arms imports.

Resolution 1876: Adopted 26 June 2009. Requested the Secretary-General to establish a UN Integrated Peace-building Office in Guinea-Bissau (UNIOGBIS), to succeed UNOGBIS, to commence operations on 1 Jan. 2010, and to be tasked with assisting the Peace-building Commission in addressing critical peace-building needs in that country.

Resolution 1879: Adopted 23 July 2009. Welcomed the commitment of the Nepalese Government towards preparing an action plan whose implementation would facilitate the withdrawal of UNMIN from Nepal, and called upon all political parties in that country to work together to expedite the peace process.

Resolution 1882: Adopted 4 Aug. 2009. Requested the Secretary-General to name in the annexes to his reports on children and armed conflict those parties to armed conflict that engage—in contravention of applicable international law—in patterns of killing and maiming of children and/or rape and other sexual violence against children, in situations of armed conflict.

Resolution 1885: Adopted 15 Sept. 2009. Extended the mandate of UNMIL and authorized the mission to assist the Liberian Government with preparation for the 2011 presidential and legislative elections, through the provision of logistical support, with particular emphasis on facilitating access to remote areas; co-ordinating international electoral assistance; and supporting Liberian institutions and political parties in creating an atmosphere conducive to the conduct of peaceful elections.

Resolution 1887: Adopted 24 Sept. 2009. Welcomed the decision of Russia and the USA to conduct negotiations aimed at concluding a new comprehensive, legally binding agreement to replace the Treaty on the Reduction and Limitation of Strategic Offensive Arms, to expire in Dec. 2009. Called upon the Conference on Disarmament to negotiate as soon as possible a treaty banning the production of fissile material for nuclear weapons or other nuclear explosive devices. Urged states to adopt stricter national controls for the export of sensitive goods and technologies of the nuclear fuel cycle. Encouraged states to require as a condition of nuclear exports that the recipient state agree that, in the event that it should withdraw from, or be found by the IAEA Board of Governors to be in non-compliance with, its IAEA safeguards agreement, the supplier state would have a right to require the return of nuclear material and equipment provided prior to such withdrawal or non-compliance, and that safeguards should continue with respect to any nuclear material and equipment provided prior to such withdrawal or non-compliance.

Resolution 1888: Adopted 30 Sept. 2009. Demanded that all parties to armed conflict immediately take appropriate measures to protect civilians, including women and children, from all forms of sexual violence. Requested that the Secretary-General appoint a Special Representative to provide coherent and strategic leadership, to strengthen existing UN co-ordination mechanisms, and to engage in advocacy efforts, in order to address, at both headquarters and country level, sexual violence in armed conflict. Decided to include specific provisions, as appropriate, for the protection of women and children from sexual violence in the mandates of UN peace-keeping operations, including, on a case-by-case basis, the identification of women's protection advisers (WPAs) among gender advisers and human rights protection units. Requested the Secretary-General to ensure that the provision of WPAs is systematically assessed during the preparation of each UN peace-keeping operation; to work with member states to develop joint government/UN comprehensive strategies to combat sexual violence; and to ensure more systematic reporting on the use of sexual violence in armed conflict in all relevant reports to the Council.

Resolution 1889: Adopted 5 Oct. 2009. Requested the Secretary-General to submit a report to the Security Council within 12 months addressing the participation and inclusion of women in peace-building and planning in the aftermath of conflict.

Resolution 1890: Adopted 8 Oct. 2009. Extended the mandate of the UN Assistance Mission in Afghanistan, and called upon member states to contribute personnel, equipment and other resources further to strengthen the ISAF in all its operational requirements. Stressed the importance of increasing, in a comprehensive framework, the functionality, professionalism and accountability of the Afghan security sector.

Resolution 1894: Adopted 11 Nov. 2009. Requested the Secretary-General to include in his reports to the Security Council on country-specific situations more comprehensive information relating to the protection of civilians in armed conflict; and requested the Secretary-General to develop guidance for UN peace-keeping and other relevant missions on reporting on the protection of civilians in armed conflict, with a view to streamlining such reporting and to enhancing the Council's monitoring of the protection mandates of the UN's peace-keeping and other missions. Stressed the importance of consultation and co-operation between the UN, the International Committee of the Red Cross, and other relevant organizations, to improve the protection of civilians in armed conflict.

Resolution 1897: Adopted 30 Nov. 2009. Invited all states and regional organizations engaged in combating piracy and armed robbery at sea off the coast of Somalia to conclude special agreements or arrangements with countries willing to take custody of pirates, in order to embark law enforcement officials (known as 'shipriders') from the latter countries to facilitate the investigation and prosecution of persons detained for perpetrating acts of piracy. Called on member states to assist with strengthening capacity in Somalia for bringing to justice those using Somali territory to plan, facilitate, or undertake acts of piracy. Called upon all states, and in particular flag, port, and coastal states, states of the nationality of victims and perpetrators of piracy and armed robbery, and other states with relevant jurisdiction under international law and national legislation, to co-operate in determining jurisdiction, and in the investigation and prosecution of persons responsible for acts of piracy and armed robbery off the coast of Somalia, to ensure that all pirates handed over to judicial authorities are subject to a judicial process, and to provide further support, including disposition and logistics assistance. Commended the decision by the Contact Group on Piracy off the Coast of Somalia to establish an International Trust Fund in support of its activities.

Resolution 1904: Adopted 17 Dec. 2009. Decided that, when considering requests to remove names from the Consolidated List of those against whom sanctions apply, the Security Council Committee established pursuant to Resolution 1267 (1999), concerning al-Qa'ida and the Taliban and associated individuals and entities, should be assisted by an Office of the Ombudsperson, to be established for an initial period of 18 months with immediate effect.

Resolution 1905: Adopted 21 Dec. 2009. Called upon the Iraqi Government to put in place, by 1 April 2010, the necessary action plan and timeline to ensure the timely and effective transition, by 31 Dec. 2010, to a mechanism to succeed the Development Fund for Iraq, established under Resolution 1483.

Resolution 1907: Adopted 23 Dec. 2009. Called upon all member states, including Eritrea, to support the Djibouti Peace Process and to support reconciliation efforts by the Transitional Federal Government of Somalia, and demanded that Eritrea cease all efforts to destabilize or overthrow, directly or indirectly, the Transitional Federal Government of Somalia. Decided that all member states should immediately take measures to prevent the sale or supply of arms and related materiel to Eritrea, and of technical assistance, training, financial and other assistance related to that country's military activities.

Resolution 1908: Adopted 19 Jan. 2010. Expressed deepest sympathy and solidarity to those affected by the devastating earthquake of 12 Jan. in Haiti, and endorsed a recommendation of the Secretary-General to increase the overall force levels of the UN Stabilization Mission in Haiti to support the immediate recovery, reconstruction and stability efforts.

Resolution 1910: 28 Jan. 2010. Authorized the AU member states to maintain the AU Mission in Somalia for a further year, and to increase the Mission's force strength with a view to achieving its originally mandated strength.

Resolution 1916: Adopted 19 March 2010. Extended the mandate of the Monitoring Group on Somalia, established by Resolution 1519, to carry out additionally tasks relating to Resolution 1907: to investigate, in co-ordination with relevant international agencies, all activities, including in the financial and maritime sectors, which generate revenues used to commit violations of the arms embargoes on Eritrea and Somalia; to investigate any routes and means of transport used in connection with violations of those arms embargoes; and to compile a draft list of individuals and entities engaging in the acts of destabilization addressed by Resolution 1907.

Resolution 1917: 22 March 2010. Extended the mandate of the UN Assistance Mission in Afghanistan, and decided that the Mission should promote more coherent support by the international community to the Afghan Government's development and governance priorities; should strengthen, at all levels and throughout the country, co-operation with the ISAF and the NATO Senior Civilian Representative; and should provide political outreach, as well as good offices, to support, where requested by the Afghan Government, the implementation of Afghan-led reconciliation and reintegration programmes.

Resolution 1918: Adopted 27 April 2010. Requested the Secretary-General to present to the Security Council within three months a report on possible options to further the aim of prosecuting and imprisoning persons responsible for acts of piracy and armed robbery at sea off the coast of Somalia.

Resolution 1923: Adopted 25 May 2010. Decided that, by 15 July 2010, the military component of the UN Mission in the CAR and Chad (MINURCAT) should be reduced to 2,200 military personnel (1,900 in Chad and 300 in the CAR), alongside 25 military liaison officers, and 300 police personnel, and that from 15 Oct. 2010 the final withdrawal of MINURCAT's remaining troops should commence, with the complete withdrawal of all uniformed and civilian MINURCAT components, other than those required for the mission's subsequent liquidation, to be achieved by 31 Dec. Decided that, pending its withdrawal, MINURCAT should continue to provide assistance to Chad's security forces, and continue to contribute to the protection of civil rights and the rule of law.

Resolution 1925: Adopted 28 May 2010. Emphasized that the Government of the DRC had primary responsibility for security, peace-building and development in that country. Extended the mandate of MONUC until 30 June 2010. Authorized the redeployment of the mission as the UN Organization Stabilization Mission in the DRC (MONUSCO), with effect from 1 July 2010. Authorized that MONUSCO should comprise a maximum strength of 19,815 military personnel.

Resolution 1929: Adopted 9 June 2010. Strengthened the sanctions regime against Iran. Established a panel of experts to assist with monitoring and enforcing the implementation of the Iran sanctions.

Resolution 1940: Adopted 29 Sept. 2010. Decided to terminate, with immediate effect, the prohibition on the sale and supply of arms and related materiel to non-governmental forces in Sierra Leone (imposed by Resolution 1171).

Resolution 1942: Adopted 29 Sept. 2010. Authorized a temporary increase of UNOCI's military and police personnel from 8,650 to 9,150, and authorized their immediate deployment.

Resolution 1943: Adopted 13 Oct. 2010. Emphasized the need to strengthen, within a comprehensive framework, the functionality and accountability of the Afghan security sector, and stressed the importance of supporting the planned expansion of the Afghan National Army and the Afghan National Police. Extended the mandate of the ISAF.

Resolution 1944: Adopted 14 Oct. 2010. Urged the Haiti Government, with the support of MINUSTAH, to develop a new phase of the ongoing Haiti National Police (HNP) reform plan. Requested MINUSTAH to continue to pursue its expanded community violence reduction approach, adapting the programme to include a particular focus on the displaced and those living in violence-affected neighbourhoods in the aftermath of the Jan. 2010 Haiti earthquake. Requested the mission to continue to support the Haitian authorities in their efforts to control the flow of small arms.

Resolution 1947: Adopted 29 Oct. 2010. Welcomed the July 2010 *Review of the UN Peacebuilding Architecture*, based upon extensive consultations with UN member states and with other stakeholders, and compiled by the UN Peace-building Commission's 'co-facilitators' (i.e. the Permanent Representatives of Ireland, Mexico and South Africa, appointed to this task by the General Assembly President in Dec. 2009).

Resolution 1956: Adopted 15 Dec. 2010. Recognized positive developments and the strengthening of institutions in Iraq and welcomed a letter from the Prime Minister of Iraq reaffirming commitments by the Iraqi Government not to request any further extensions of the arrangements for the Development Fund for Iraq (established under Resolution 1483), and to ensure that oil revenue would continue to be used fairly and for the benefit of the Iraqi people. Decided to terminate, on 30 June 2011, the arrangements for depositing into the Development Fund proceeds from export sales of petroleum, petroleum products and natural gas. Called upon the Government of Iraq to work closely with the UN Secretary-General to finalize the full and effective transition to a post-Development Fund mechanism by or before 30 June 2011. Directed the transfer of the full proceeds from the Development Fund for Iraq to the Government of Iraq's successor arrangements account or accounts, and the termination of the Development Fund, no later than 30 June 2011.

Resolution 1958: Adopted 15 Dec. 2010. Requested the UN Secretary-General to take all actions necessary to terminate all residual activities under the former Iraq oil-for-food programme.

Resolution 1962: Adopted 20 Dec. 2010. Urged all parties and stakeholders in Côte d'Ivoire to respect the outcome of the presidential election held in Oct.–Nov. 2010, in view of recognition by ECOWAS and the AU of Alassane Dramane Ouattara as the legitimate President-elect of that country.

Resolution 1966: Adopted 22 Dec. 2010. Established the International Residual Mechanism for Criminal Tribunals to undertake some essential functions of the International Tribunal for the Former Yugoslavia and the International Criminal Tribunal for Rwanda after their closure.

Resolution 1967: Adopted 19 Jan. 2011. Authorized the deployment of an additional 2,000 military personnel to UNOCI, until 30 June 2011; and extended, up to 30 June 2011, the temporary additional military and police capabilities authorized by Resolution 1942.

Resolution 1970: Adopted 26 Feb. 2011. Expressed grave concern at the ongoing situation in Libya and condemned the use of force against civilians. Deplored the gross and systematic violation of human rights, including the repression of peaceful demonstrators, expressed deep concern at the deaths of civilians, and rejected unequivocally the incitement to hostility and violence against the civilian population made from the highest level of the Libyan Government. Demanded an immediate end to the violence and urged the Libyan authorities to respect human rights and international humanitarian law and to ensure the safe passage of humanitarian assistance, and immediately to lift restrictions on all forms of media. Decided to refer the situation in Libya since 15 Feb. 2011 to the Prosecutor of the International Criminal Court. Imposed an embargo on the direct or indirect supply, sale, or transfer to Libya, of arms and related materiel; a ban on travel by designated individuals associated with the Libyan regime; and the immediate freezing of financial assets and economic resources controlled, directly or indirectly, by designated individuals or entities associated with the Libyan regime.

Resolution 1973: Adopted 17 March 2011. Recalled the condemnation by the League of Arab States, the AU, and the Secretary General of the OIC of the serious violations of human rights and international humanitarian law that had been and were being committed in Libya. Authorized member states, acting in co-operation with the UN Secretary-General, nationally or through regional organizations or arrangements, to take all necessary measures to protect civilians and civilian populated areas under threat of attack in Libya, while excluding a foreign occupation force of any form on any part of Libyan territory. Decided to establish a ban on all flights in Libyan airspace, excepting those with a purpose that was humanitarian or otherwise aimed at protected civilians. Strengthened the sanctions imposed against Libya in Resolution 1970, including demanding that all states should deny permission to any aircraft registered in Libya, or owned or operated by Libyan nationals or companies, to take off from, land in or overfly their territory, unless a particular flight had been approved in advance by the Committee, or in the case of an emergency landing. Requested that the UN Secretary-General establish a Panel of (eight) Experts to assist with the implementation of the measures decided in Resolution 1970, and in particular with incidents of non-compliance.

Resolution 1974: Adopted 22 March 2011. Welcomed agreement reached at NATO's Lisbon Summit, held in Nov. 2010, by the Government of Afghanistan and the nations contributing to the ISAF, on transferring lead responsibility for country-wide security in Afghanistan to the Afghan National Security Forces by end-2014. Decided to extend UNAMA's mandate until 23 March 2012. Requested that the Secretary-General conduct, by the end of 2011, a comprehensive review of UNAMA's activities, with the aim of strengthening national ownership and leadership and informing the Council's review of UNAMA's mandate in March 2012.

Resolution 1980: Adopted 28 April 2011. Decided to renew until 30 April 2012 punitive measures relating to arms, finances and travel previously imposed on designated persons from Côte d'Ivoire; and further decided to renew until 30 April 2012 existing measures preventing the importation by any state of rough diamonds from Côte d'Ivoire.

Resolution 1987: Adopted 17 June 2011. Recommended to the General Assembly that Ban Ki-Moon be reappointed UN Secretary-General for a second term of office, covering the period 1 Jan. 2012 to 31 Dec. 2016.

Resolution 1988: Adopted 17 June 2011. Imposed against individuals and entities designated as the 'Taliban', and other individuals, groups, undertakings and entities associated with them, who were deemed to constitute a threat to the peace, stability and security of Afghanistan, an immediate freeze on funds and other financial assets or economic resources; a ban on travel; and a ban on the direct or indirect supply, sale and transfer of arms and related materiel of all types, spare parts, and technical advice, assistance, or training related to military activities.

Resolution 1989: Adopted 17 June 2011. Renamed the list of al-Qa'ida followers against whom sanctions apply (hitherto known as the Consolidated List) as the al-Qa'ida Sanctions List. Extended the term of the Office of the Ombudsperson (established in accordance with Resolution 1904) by a further 18 months.

Resolution 1990: Adopted 27 June 2011. Established the UN Interim Security Force for Abyei (UNISFA), deciding that UNISFA should comprise a maximum of 4,200 military personnel, 50 police personnel, and appropriate civilian support. Mandated UNISFA to monitor and verify the redeployment of Sudanese government troops and rebel forces from the Abyei Area; to facilitate the delivery of humanitarian supplies to Abyei; to strengthen the capacity of the Abyei police force; to support de-mining activities; and to protect civilians and ensure security in Abyei.

Resolution 1992: Adopted 29 June 2011. Extended until 31 July 2011 the deployment of an additional 2,000 military personnel to UNOCI and the temporary additional military and police capabilities authorized by Resolution 1967.

Resolution 1996: Adopted 8 July 2011. Established the UN Mission in South Sudan (UNMISS), with an authorized strength of up to 7,000 military personnel, and with a mandate to consolidate peace and security in South Sudan (which gained independence on 9 July 2011).

Resolution 1997: Adopted 11 July 2011. Determined to withdraw UNMIS from Sudan with immediate effect.

Resolution 1999: Adopted 13 July 2011. Recommended to the UN General Assembly that South Sudan be admitted to UN membership.

Resolution 2002: Adopted 29 July 2011. Extended the mandate of the Monitoring Group on Somalia mentioned in Resolution 1916, requesting the UN Secretary-General to re-establish the Group, with eight experts, for a period of 12 months.

Resolution 2009: Adopted 16 Sept. 2011. Established the UN Support Mission in Libya (UNSMIL), mandated to assist and support Libyan national efforts to restore public order and promote the rule of law; to promote inclusive political dialogue and national reconciliation; to embark upon a constitution-making and electoral process; to help extend the authority of the state; to protect human rights, with a particular focus on vulnerable groups; and to help promote economic recovery. Modified the provisions of the arms embargo imposed by Resolution 1970 to terminate the asset freeze on certain entities associated with the former Libyan regime, namely the Libyan National Oil Corporation, Zueitina Oil Company, the Central Bank of Libya, the Libyan Arab Foreign Bank, the Libyan Investment Authority, and the Libyan Africa Investment Portfolio.

Resolution 2014: Adopted 21 Oct. 2011. Expressed serious concern over the worsening security situation in Yemen, and profound regret at hundreds of—mainly civilian—deaths there. Strongly condemned continued human rights violations by the Yemeni authorities, including the excessive use of force against peaceful protesters, and condemned also acts of violence, use of force and human rights abuses perpetrated by other actors. Demanded that all sides immediately reject the use of violence to achieve political goals. Called on all parties to sign a peace initiative of the Gulf Cooperation Council.

Resolution 2015: Adopted 24 Oct. 2011. Urged the Somali authorities, UNODC, UNDP and other international partners to support the construction and reasonable operation of prisons in Somalia, in accordance with international law, recognizing that any increase in prosecution capacity in relation to those accused of acts of piracy must necessarily be accompanied by a related increase in prison capacity. Called upon member states, regional organizations and other appropriate partners to support efforts to establish specialized anti-piracy courts in the region by facilitating arrangements for the provision of relevant international experts,

Resolution 2016: Adopted 27 Oct. 2011. Took note of the Libyan National Transitional Council's recent 'Declaration of Liberation'; expressed concern at the proliferation of arms in Libya and declared the Council's intention to address that issue further; and expressed grave concern about reports of continuing reprisals against opponents of the new Libyan regime. Called on the Libyan authorities to promote and protect human rights and fundamental freedoms, and strongly urged that they desist from reprisals including wrongful imprisonment and extrajudicial executions. Emphasized the Libyan authorities' responsibility for the protection of its population, including foreign nationals and African migrants.

Resolution 2017: Adopted 27 Oct. 2011. Called upon the Libyan authorities to take all necessary steps to ensure the proper custody of and prevent the proliferation of all arms and related materiel, in particular man-portable surface-to-air missiles; and called upon the Libyan authorities to continue to pursue co-ordination with the Organization for the Prohibition of Chemical Weapons, with the aim of destroying chemical weapons stockpiles.

Resolution 2018: Adopted 31 Oct. 2011. Expressed deep concern at piracy in the Gulf and Guinea and the threat it posed to international navigation, security, and the economic development of states in the region. Welcomed plans by Gulf of Guinea area heads of states to convene a summit to address these matters, and encouraged ECOWAS, the Communauté économique des états de l'Afrique centrale (CEEAC) and the Gulf of Guinea Commission (GGC) to develop a comprehensive anti-piracy strategy. Encouraged member states of those organizations, through concerted action, to conduct bilateral or regional maritime patrols in the Gulf of Guinea, consistent with relevant international law; to give to vessels appropriate guidance on avoidance and on defensive measures to take if threatened by attack; and to co-operate in the prosecution of alleged perpetrators of acts of marine piracy, including facilitators and financiers. Urged the international community to assist states and organizations in the region to strengthen their anti-piracy efforts. Welcomed the intention of the UN Secretary-General to deploy a UN assessment mission to examine the threat of, and seek solutions to, piracy and armed robbery in the Gulf of Guinea.

Resolution 2022: Adopted 2 Dec. 2011. Decided to extend the mandate of UNSMIL until 16 March 2012 and to expand the mission's mandate to include, in co-ordination and consultation with the Transitional Government of Libya, supporting the efforts of Libya to address the threat of proliferation of all arms and related materiel of all types, in particular man-portable surface-to-air missiles.

Resolution 2023: Adopted 5 Dec. 2011. Condemned violations by Eritrea of Security Council Resolutions 1844, 1862 and 1907, through the continued provision of support to armed opposition groupings—including the al-Shabaab militia—engaged in undermining peace in Somalia and the wider region. Supported the AU's demand that Eritrea resolve its border disputes; demanded that Eritrea cease all direct or indirect efforts to destabilize states; and expressed the intention of applying targeted sanctions against individuals and entities identified in relation to the arms embargo imposed by Resolution 1907. Condemned the use by the Eritrean Government of a 'Diaspora tax' for purposes such as procuring arms and related materiel for transfer to armed opposition groups in other countries in the region. Expanded the mandate of the Monitoring Group on Somalia re-established by resolution 2002 (2011), to monitor and report on implementation of the measures imposed in this resolution and to further assist the Sanctions Committee on Eritrea.

Resolution 2024: Adopted 14 Dec. 2011. Welcomed the Agreement on Border Security and the Joint Political and Security Mechanism—JBVMM concluded on 29 June 2011 between the governments of Sudan and South Sudan, taking note of the commitment therein to create a Safe Demilitarized Border Zone. Welcomed also the two governments' Agreement on the Border Monitoring Support Mission (30 June), which elaborated on the establishment of the JBVMM, and of a Joint Political and Security Mechanism (JPSM). Decided to expand UNISFA's mandate to include assisting all parties in ensuring the observance of the Safe Demilitarized Border Zone; advising, and supporting the operational activities of, the JBVMM; facilitating liaison between the parties; and supporting the parties, when requested, in developing effective bilateral management mechanisms along the border. Called on member states, in particular Sudan and South Sudan, to ensure the free, unhindered and expeditious movement to and from Abyei, and throughout the Safe Demilitarized Border Zone, of all UNISFA personnel, and also of equipment, supplies and other goods intended for use by the mission.

Resolution 2036: Adopted 22 Feb. 2012. Tasked AMISOM with establishing a presence in four sectors (including areas beyond the Somali capital, Mogadishu) set out in the AMISOM Strategic Concept adopted on 5 Jan. by the AU Peace and Security Council, and authorized the mission to take all necessary measures in those sectors, in co-ordination with the Somali security forces, to reduce the threat posed by al-Shabaab and other armed opposition groups. Requested the AU to increase AMISOM's strength from 12,000 to a maximum of 17,731 uniformed personnel, and determined to expand the logistical support package for the mission. Decided that the Somali authorities should adopt necessary measures to prevent the export of charcoal from Somalia, and that all member states should take necessary measures to prevent the direct or indirect import of charcoal from that country. Directed that all member states should report, within 120 days, to the Security Council Committee on Somalia on steps taken towards the effective implementation of this instruction.

Resolution 2039: Adopted 29 Feb. 2012. Welcomed the report of the UN Secretary-General's assessment mission on piracy undertaken in Nov. 2011 in the Gulf of Guinea. Requested the UN Secretary-General to support—through UNOCA and UNOWA—states and sub-regional organizations in convening the joint Summit on combating maritime piracy in the Gulf of Guinea that was referenced in Resolution 2018. Encouraged the states of the Gulf of Guinea, ECOWAS, CEEAC, and the GGC to develop and implement transnational and transregional maritime security co-ordination centres covering the whole region of the Gulf of Guinea, building on existing initiatives, such as those under the auspices of the International Maritime Organization (IMO).

Resolution 2040: Adopted 12 March 2012. Extended, for 12 months, the mandate of UNSMIL, and modified it to include: assisting the Libyan authorities to define national needs and priorities; managing the process of democratic transition; promoting the rule of law and monitoring and protecting human rights, particularly those of women and vulnerable groups, such as children, minorities and migrants; restoring public security; countering illicit proliferation of all arms and related materiel of all types, in particular man-portable surface-to-air missiles; co-ordinating international assistance; and building government capacity across all relevant sectors. Extended the mandate of the Panel of Experts on Libya.

Resolution 2041: Adopted 27 March 2012. Welcomed the International Afghanistan Conference, convened in Bonn, Germany, in Dec. 2011, and its declaration that the Process of Transition in Afghanistan, to be completed by the end of 2014, should be followed by a Decade of Transformation (2015–24). Extended UNAMA's mandate until 23 March 2013, emphasizing that the renewed mandate should take into full account the transition process and should support Afghanistan's assumption of leadership, and ownership, in the areas of security, governance and development.

Resolution 2042: Adopted 14 April 2012. Condemned widespread violations of human rights perpetrated by the Syrian authorities, and any human rights abuses by armed groups, and expressed profound regret at the deaths of many thousands of people in Syria. Noted the Syrian Government's commitment made on 25 March 2012 to implement a six-point peace plan proposed by the Joint Special Envoy of the UN and the League of Arab States. Noted the assessment of the Envoy that, as of 12 April 2012, the parties appeared to be observing a cessation of fire and that the Syrian government had started to implement its commitments. Expressed the intention to establish a UN supervision mission to monitor the cessation of armed violence in all its forms by all parties and relevant aspects of the Envoy's six-point proposal, on the basis of a formal proposal from the Secretary-General, to be received no later than 18 April 2012. Called upon the Syrian government to ensure the effective operation of the mission. Authorized an advance team of up to 30 unarmed military observers to be deployed to liaise with the parties and to report on the implementation of a full cessation of armed violence.

Resolution 2043: Adopted 21 April 2012. Expressed concern over the violence in Syria that had escalated in recent days. Reaffirmed full support for and called for the urgent, comprehensive, and immediate implementation of all elements of the Joint UN/Arab League Envoy's six-point peace plan. Established for an initial period of 90 days a UN Supervision Mission in Syria (UNSMIS), under the command of a Chief Military Observer, comprising an initial deployment of up to 300 unarmed military observers as well as an appropriate civilian component. Decided that UNSMIS should be deployed expeditiously.

Resolution 2045: Adopted 29 April 2012. Decided that measures imposed against Côte d'Ivoire in connection with arms and related materiel should be modified and should no longer apply to the provision of training, advice and expertise related to security and military activities.

Resolution 2046: Adopted 2 May 2012. Decided that Sudan and South Sudan should, with immediate effect, cease all mutual hostilities, including aerial bombardments, and withdraw, unconditionally, all of their armed forces to their side of the border; and should, within one week, activate the Joint Border Verification and Monitoring Mechanism and the Safe Demilitarized Border Zone. Demanded that both sides cease harbouring or supporting rebel groups inimical to the other side, and cease making inflammatory statements through the media. Determined that both sides should unconditionally resume negotiations, under the auspices of the AU High Level Implementation Panel and with the support of the Chairman of IGAD.

Resolution 2048: Adopted 18 May 2012. Demanded that the Guinea-Bissau Military Command—having usurped power on 12 April from the legitimate Guinea-Bissau Government—take immediate steps to restore and respect constitutional order, by ensuring that all soldiers return to barracks, and that members of the Command relinquish their positions of authority. Encouraged ECOWAS to continue to pursue its mediation efforts, in close co-ordination with the UN, AU and CPLP, and requested the UN Secretary-General to be actively engaged in this process. Decided that all member states should take the necessary measures to prevent the entry into or transit through their territories of designated individuals deemed to be seeking to prevent the restoration of constitutional order, or to be taking action deemed to be undermining stability in Guinea-Bissau, in particular those who played a leading role in the coup d'état of 12 April. Established a Sanctions Committee to supervise the implementation of these measures.

Resolution 2051: Adopted 12 June 2012. Expressed grave concern at the political, security, economic and humanitarian situation in Yemen and condemned terrorist, and other, attacks conducted against civilians, against the oil, gas and electricity infrastructure, and against the Yemeni authorities. Reaffirmed the need for the full and timely implementation of the Gulf Cooperation Council peace initiative, in accordance with Resolution 2014. Demanded the cessation of all actions aimed at undermining the Yemeni Government of National Unity and political transition process, stressing that all those responsible for human rights violations and abuses must be held accountable. Urged continued national efforts to discourage the recruitment of child soldiers. Called on the Yemeni authorities to adopt, without further delay, legislation on transitional justice to support reconciliation. Encouraged the international community to provide humanitarian assistance to Yemen. Expressed concern over increasing attacks undertaken or sponsored by al-Qa'ida in the Arabian Peninsula.

Trusteeship Council

The Trusteeship Council (comprising the People's Republic of China—a non-active member until May 1989, France, Russia, the United Kingdom and the USA) was established to supervise United Nations Trust Territories through their administering authorities and to promote the political, economic, social and educational advancement of their inhabitants towards self-government or independence (see Charter). On 1 October 1994 the last territory remaining under UN trusteeship, the Republic of Palau (part of the archipelago of the Caroline Islands), declared its independence under a compact of free association with the USA, its administering authority. The Security Council terminated the Trusteeship Agreement on 10 November, having determined that the objectives of the agreement had been fully attained. On 1 November the

Trusteeship Council formally suspended its operations; thereafter it was to be convened on an extraordinary basis as required. The report of the UN Secretary-General entitled 'In Larger Freedom: Towards Development, Security and Human Rights for All', issued in March 2005, proposed that the Trusteeship Council should be terminated.

Economic and Social Council—ECOSOC

ECOSOC promotes world co-operation on economic, social, cultural and humanitarian problems. (See Charter of the United Nations.)

MEMBERS

Fifty-four members are elected by the General Assembly for three-year terms: 18 are elected each year. Membership is allotted by regions as follows: Africa 14 members, Western Europe and other developed countries 13, Asia 11, Latin America 10, Eastern Europe 6.

BUREAU

The Bureau, with responsibility for formulating the agenda and programme of work for the Council, is elected by the Council at its first meeting of the year. It comprises a President and four Vice-Presidents, each representing different regions.

President: MILOŠ KOTEREC (Slovakia) (2012).

ACTIVITIES

The Council, which meets annually for a four-week substantive session in July, alternately in New York and Geneva, is mainly a central policy-making and co-ordinating organ. It has a co-ordinating function between the UN and the specialized agencies, and also makes consultative arrangements with approved voluntary or non-governmental organizations which work within the sphere of its activities (around 3,400 organizations had consultative status in mid-2012). The Council has functional and regional commissions to carry out much of its detailed work. ECOSOC's purview extends to more than 70% of the human and financial resources of the UN system. The Council was given a leading role in following up the implementation of the Monterrey Consensus, adopted by the March 2002 International Conference on Financing for Development.

The report of the UN Secretary-General entitled 'In Larger Freedom: Towards Development, Security and Human Rights for All', issued in March 2005, outlined a number of proposed changes to ECOSOC aimed at improving its effectiveness. These included: the organization by the Council of annual ministerial-level progress reviews (AMRs) of agreed development goals, in particular the Millennium Development Goals (MDGs) pledged by UN heads of state and government in September 2000; the inauguration of a regular high-level Development Co-operation Forum (see below); the organization by the Council, whenever required, of meetings to assess and promote co-ordinated responses to threats to development, such as famines, epidemics and major natural disasters; and the development of a permanent structure within the Council for monitoring the economic and social dimensions of conflicts, with the aim of improving prospects for long-term recovery, reconstruction and reconciliation, and working in co-operation with the proposed new Peacebuilding Commission. The AMR process was initiated in 2007, comprising a series of global and regional preparatory meetings prior to the main review held during the annual session of the Council in July. As part of the review several countries each year prepare National Voluntary Presentations to demonstrate challenges, best practices and progress in implementing development goals. The theme of the 2012 AMR was 'promoting productive capacity, employment and decent work to eradicate poverty in the context of inclusive, sustainable and equitable economic growth at all levels for achieving the MDGs'.

Every year, normally in March or April, ECOSOC holds high-level consultations with the IMF, World Bank, WTO and UNCTAD. The 2012 consultations were held in March, in New York, USA, on the theme 'coherence, co-ordination and co-operation in the context of financing for development'.

DEVELOPMENT CO-OPERATION FORUM—DCF

The biennial high-level Development Co-operation Forum (DCF), held in New York, was inaugurated in July 2007. The Forum is mandated to advance the implementation of all internationally agreed development goals, including the MDGs, and to promote dialogue to find effective ways of supporting international development. The first Forum was convened in June–July 2008, with participation by UN bodies, bilateral development agencies, regional development banks, civil society and private sector representatives. The second DCF was held in June 2010. During 2011 two High-Level Symposia were held (in May, in Mali, and in October, in Luxembourg) in preparation for the third DCF, to be convened in July 2012.

YOUTH FORUM

The first ECOSOC Youth Forum was convened in early May 2012, with participation by young delegates including business people, students and representatives of youth organizations, on the theme 'Empowering Youth with Better Opportunities'. The Forum emphasised the importance of addressing youth unemployment and was conducted through two interactive dialogues, on education and training; and creating green jobs to ensure a sustainable future.

FUNCTIONAL COMMISSIONS

Commission on Crime Prevention and Criminal Justice: f. 1992; aims to formulate an international convention on crime prevention and criminal justice; 40 members.

Commission on Narcotic Drugs: f. 1946; mainly concerned in combating illicit traffic; 53 members; there is a Sub-Commission on Illicit Drug Traffic and Related Matters in the Near and Middle East.

Commission on Population and Development: f. 1946; advises the Council on population matters and their relation to socio-economic conditions; 47 members.

Commission on Science and Technology for Development: f. 1992; works on the restructuring of the UN in the economic, social and related fields; administration of the Commission undertaken by UNCTAD; 43 members.

Commission for Social Development: f. 1946 as the Social Commission; advises ECOSOC on issues of social and community development; 46 members.

Commission on the Status of Women: f. 1946; aims at equality of political, economic and social rights for women, and supports the right of women to live free of violence; 45 members.

Commission on Sustainable Development: f. 1993 to oversee integration into the UN's work of the objectives set out in 'Agenda 21', the programme of action agreed by the UN Conference on Environment and Development in June 1992; the UN Conference on Sustainable Development, convened in June 2012, determined to establish a high-level intergovernmental forum—to follow up its objectives—that would eventually replace the Commission on Sustainable Development; 53 members.

Statistical Commission: Standardizes terminology and procedure in statistics and promotes the development of national statistics; 24 members.

United Nations Forum on Forests: f. 2000; composed of all states members of the United Nations and its specialized agencies.

REGIONAL COMMISSIONS

(see United Nations Regional Commissions)

Economic Commission for Africa (ECA).

Economic Commission for Europe (ECE).

Economic Commission for Latin America and the Caribbean (ECLAC).

Economic and Social Commission for Asia and the Pacific (ESCAP).

Economic and Social Commission for Western Asia (ESCWA).

STANDING COMMITTEES

Committee on Negotiations with Intergovernmental Agencies: f. 1946.

Committee on Non-Governmental Organizations: f. 1946; 19 members.

Committee for Programme and Co-ordination: f. 1962; 34 members.

EXPERT BODIES

Committee for Development Policy: f. 1965 (as Cttee for Devt Planning), renamed in 1988; 24 members serving in a personal capacity for three-year terms.

Committee of Experts on International Co-operation in Tax Matters: f. 2004; 25 members serving in a personal capacity.

Committee of Experts on Public Administration: f. 1967 (as Group of Experts in Public Admin. and Finance), renamed 2002; 24 members serving in a personal capacity.

Committee of Experts on the Transport of Dangerous Goods and on the Globally Harmonized System of Classification and Labelling of Chemicals: 37 members serving as governmental experts.

Committee on Economic, Social and Cultural Rights: f. 1985; 18 members serving in a personal capacity.

Permanent Forum on Indigenous Issues: f. 2000; 16 members serving in a personal capacity.

United Nations Group of Experts on Geographical Names: f. 1972; 23 members serving as governmental experts.

In addition there are two ad hoc bodies: the open-ended working group on informatics and the open-ended intergovernmental group of experts on energy and sustainable development. Other ad hoc mechanisms in mid-2012 were advisory groups on African countries emerging from conflict, an ad hoc advisory group on Haiti, and the UN Public-Private Alliance for Rural Development.

RELATED BODIES

International Narcotics Control Board: f. 1964; 13 members.

Programme Co-ordination Board for the Joint UN Programme on HIV/AIDS (UNAIDS): f. 1995; 22 members.

UNDP/UNFPA Executive Board: 36 members, elected by ECOSOC.

UN-Habitat Governing Council: 58 members, elected by ECOSOC.

UNHCR Executive Committee: 53 members, elected by ECOSOC.

UNICEF Executive Board: 36 members, elected by ECOSOC.

WFP Executive Board: one-half of the 36 members are elected by ECOSOC, one-half by FAO; governing body of the World Food Programme.

International Court of Justice

Address: Peace Palace, Carnegieplein 2, 2517 KJ The Hague, Netherlands.

Telephone: (70) 3022323; **fax:** (70) 3649928; **e-mail:** information@icj-cij.org; **internet:** www.icj-cij.org.

Established in 1945, the Court (sometimes referred to as the World Court) is the principal judicial organ of the UN. All members of the UN are parties to the Statute of the Court. (See Charter.)

THE JUDGES

(June 2012; in order of precedence)

	Term Ends*
President: PETER TOMKA (Slovakia)	2021
Vice-President: BERNARDO SEPÚLVEDA-AMOR (Mexico)	2015
Judges:	
HISASHI OWADA (Japan)	2021
RONNY ABRAHAM (France)	2015
KENNETH KEITH (New Zealand)	2015
MOHAMED BENNOUNA (Morocco)	2015
LEONID SKOTNIKOV (Russia)	2015
ANTÔNIO AUGUSTO CANÇADO TRINDADE (Brazil)	2018
ABDULQAWI AHMED YUSUF (Somalia)	2018
CHRISTOPHER GREENWOOD (United Kingdom)	2018
XUE HANQIN (People's Republic of China)	2021
JOAN E. DONOGHUE (USA)	2015
GIORGIO GAJA (Italy)	2021
JULIA SEBUTINDE (Uganda)	2021
DALVEER BHANDARI (India)	2018

* Each term ends on 5 February of the year indicated.

Registrar: PHILIPPE COUVREUR (Belgium).

The Court is composed of 15 judges, each of a different nationality, elected with an absolute majority by both the General Assembly and the Security Council. Representation of the main forms of civilization and the different legal systems of the world are borne in mind in their election. Candidates are nominated by national panels of jurists.

The judges are elected for nine years and may be re-elected; elections for five seats are held every three years. The Court elects its President and Vice-President for each three-year period. Members may not have any political, administrative, or other professional occupation, and may not sit in any case with which they have been otherwise connected than as a judge of the Court. For the purposes of a case, each side—consisting of one or more states—may, unless the Bench already includes a judge with a corresponding nationality, choose a person from outside the Court to sit as a judge on terms of equality with the Members. Judicial decisions are taken by a majority of the judges present, subject to a quorum of nine Members. The President has a casting vote.

FUNCTIONS

The International Court of Justice operates in accordance with a Statute which is an integral part of the UN Charter. Only states may be parties in cases before the Court; those not parties to the Statute may have access in certain circumstances and under conditions laid down by the Security Council.

The Jurisdiction of the Court comprises:

1. All cases which the parties refer to it jointly by special agreement (indicated in the list below by a stroke between the names of the parties);

2. All matters concerning which a treaty or convention in force provides for reference to the Court through the inclusion of a jurisdictional clause. Some 300 agreements, both bilateral and multilateral, have been notified to the Court's Registry, for example: Treaty of Peace with Japan (1951); European Convention for Peaceful Settlement of Disputes (1957); Single Convention on Narcotic Drugs (1961); International Convention on the Elimination of All Forms of Racial Discrimination (1966); Protocol relating to the Status of Refugees (1967); Convention on the Suppression of the Unlawful Seizure of

Aircraft (1970); Convention on the Elimination of All Forms of Discrimination against Women (1979); Convention against Torture and Other Cruel, Inhuman or Degrading Treatment or Punishment (1984); International Convention for the Suppression of the Financing of Terrorism (1999);

3. Legal disputes between states which have recognized the jurisdiction of the Court as compulsory for specified classes of dispute. Declarations by the following 66 states accepting the compulsory jurisdiction of the Court are in force (although many with reservations): Australia, Austria, Barbados, Belgium, Botswana, Bulgaria, Cambodia, Cameroon, Canada, the Democratic Republic of the Congo (DRC), Costa Rica, Côte d'Ivoire, Cyprus, Denmark, Djibouti, Dominica, the Dominican Republic, Egypt, Estonia, Finland, The Gambia, Germany, Georgia, Greece, Guinea, Guinea-Bissau, Haiti, Honduras, Hungary, India, Japan, Kenya, Lesotho, Liberia, Liechtenstein, Luxembourg, Madagascar, Malawi, Malta, Mauritius, Mexico, the Netherlands, New Zealand, Nicaragua, Nigeria, Norway, Pakistan, Panama, Paraguay, Peru, the Philippines, Poland, Portugal, Senegal, Slovakia, Somalia, Spain, Sudan, Suriname, Swaziland, Sweden, Switzerland, Togo, Uganda, the United Kingdom and Uruguay.

Disputes as to whether the Court has jurisdiction are settled by the Court.

Judgments are without appeal, but are binding only for the particular case and between the parties. States appearing before the Court undertake to comply with its Judgment. If a party to a case fails to do so, the other party may apply to the Security Council, which may make recommendations or decide upon measures to give effect to the Judgment.

Advisory opinions on legal questions may be requested by the General Assembly, the Security Council or, if so authorized by the Assembly, other United Nations organs or specialized agencies.

Rules of Court governing procedure are made by the Court under a power conferred by the Statute.

CASES

JUDGMENTS

Since 1946 some 152 cases have been referred to the Court relating to legal disputes or legal questions. Some were removed from the list as a result of settlement or discontinuance, or on the grounds of a lack of basis for jurisdiction. Cases which have been the subject of a Judgment by the Court include: Monetary Gold Removed from Rome in 1943 (Italy *v.* France, United Kingdom and USA); Sovereignty over Certain Frontier Land (Belgium/ Netherlands); Arbitral Award made by the King of Spain on 23 December 1906 (Honduras *v.* Nicaragua); Temple of Preah Vihear (Cambodia *v.* Thailand); South West Africa (Ethiopia and Liberia *v.* South Africa); Northern Cameroons (Cameroon *v.* United Kingdom); North Sea Continental Shelf (Federal Republic of Germany/Denmark and Netherlands); Appeal relating to the Jurisdiction of the ICAO Council (India *v.* Pakistan); Fisheries Jurisdiction (United Kingdom *v.* Iceland; Federal Republic of Germany *v.* Iceland); Nuclear Tests (Australia *v.* France; New Zealand *v.* France); Aegean Sea Continental Shelf (Greece *v.* Turkey); United States of America Diplomatic and Consular Staff in Tehran (USA *v.* Iran); Continental Shelf (Tunisia/Libya); Delimitation of the Maritime Boundary in the Gulf of Maine Area (Canada/USA); Continental Shelf (Libya/ Malta); Application for revision and interpretation of the Judgment of 24 February 1982 in the case concerning the Continental Shelf (Tunisia *v.* Libya); Military and Paramilitary Activities in and against Nicaragua (Nicaragua *v.* USA); Frontier Dispute (Burkina Faso/Mali); Delimitation of Maritime Boundary (Denmark *v.* Norway); Maritime Boundaries (Guinea-Bissau *v.* Senegal); Elettronica Sicula SpA (USA *v.* Italy); Land, Island and Maritime Frontier Dispute (El Salvador/Honduras, in one aspect of which Nicaragua was permitted to intervene) (also, in 2003, Application for Revision of the 1992 Judgment in the Case concerning the Land, Island and Maritime Frontier Dispute, requested by El Salvador); Delimitation of Maritime Boundary in the area between Greenland and Jan Mayen island (Denmark *v.* Norway); Maritime Delimitation and Territorial Questions between Qatar and Bahrain (Qatar *v.* Bahrain); Territorial Dispute (Libya/Chad); East Timor (Portugal *v.* Australia); the Gabčíkovo–Nagymaros Hydroelectric Project (Hungary *v.* Slovakia); Fisheries Jurisdiction (Spain *v.* Canada); Delimitation of the Boundary around Kasikili Sedudu Island (Botswana *v.* Namibia); La Grand case (Germany *v.* USA); Arrest Warrant of 11 April 2000 (DRC *v.* Belgium); Land and Maritime Boundary between Cameroon and Nigeria (Cameroon *v.* Nigeria, with Equatorial Guinea intervening); Sovereignty over Pulau Ligatan and Pulau Sipadan (Indonesia/Malaysia); Destruction of Oil Platforms (Iran *v.* USA); Avena and other Mexican Nationals (Mexico *v.* USA); Legality of Use of Force (Serbia and Montenegro *v.* Belgium; Canada; France; Germany; Italy; the Netherlands; Portugal; and the United Kingdom); Certain Property (Liechtenstein *v.* Germany); Frontier Dispute (Benin/ Niger); Armed Activities on the Territory of the Congo (DRC *v.* Burundi; Rwanda; and Uganda); Application of the Convention on the Prevention and Punishment of the Crime of Genocide (Bosnia and Herzegovina *v.* Serbia and Montenegro); Territorial and Maritime Dispute in the Caribbean Sea (Nicaragua *v.* Honduras); a Case Concerning the Sovereignty of Pedra Branca/ Pulau Batu Puteh, Middle Rocks and South Ledge (Malaysia/ Singapore); Certain Questions of Mutual Assistance in Criminal Matters (Djibouti *v.* France); Request for Interpretation of the Judgment of 31 March 2004 in the Case concerning Avena and Other Mexican Nationals (Mexico *v.* USA); Maritime Delimitation in the Black Sea (Romania *v.* Ukraine); a Dispute regarding Navigational and Related Rights (Costa Rica *v.* Nicaragua); Pulp Mills on the River Uruguay (Argentina *v.* Uruguay); Application of the International Convention on the Elimination of All Forms of Racial Discrimination (Georgia *v.* Russia); Application of the Interim Accord of 13 September 1995 (former Yugoslav Republic of Macedonia *v.* Greece); Jurisdictional Immunities of the State (Germany *v.* Italy: Greece intervening); and Ahmadou Sadio Diallo—Compensation owed by the DRC to the Republic of Guinea (Republic of Guinea *v.* DRC).

PENDING CASES

In 2012 the following contentious cases were under consideration, or pending before the Court: a request by Slovakia for an additional judgment in the dispute with Hungary concerning the Gabčíkovo–Nagymaros Hydroelectric Project (initial Judgment having been delivered in Sept. 1997); further deliberation of the case brought by the DRC against Uganda concerning armed activities on its territory (initial Judgment having been delivered in Dec. 2005); a case brought by Croatia against Serbia concerning the application of the 1948 Convention on the Prevention and Punishment of the Crime of Genocide (Judgment on the preliminary objections regarding jurisdiction and admissibility having been delivered in Nov. 2008); a case brought by Peru against Chile on maritime delimitation in the Pacific ocean; a case brought by Ecuador concerning alleged aerial spraying by Colombia of toxic herbicides over Ecuadorian territory; a territorial and maritime dispute brought by Nicaragua against Colombia; proceedings brought by Belgium against Senegal concerning its obligation to prosecute, or extradite for prosecution, the former President of Chad; proceedings instituted by Australia against Japan for alleged breach of its obligations under the International Convention for the Regulation of Whaling; a joint application by Burkina Faso and Niger regarding a frontier dispute; a case brought by Costa Rica against Nicaragua for allegedly violating Costa Rica's territorial integrity during the construction of a canal and through interference in the San Juan River; a case brought by Nicaragua against Costa Rica concerning alleged violations of Nicaraguan sovereignty and major environmental damages to its territory through the construction of a road in Costa Rica alongside the San Juan River; and an application by Cambodia requesting interpretation of a 1962 Judgment in the case concerning the Temple of Preah Vihear (Cambodia *v.* Thailand).

ADVISORY OPINIONS

Matters on which the Court has delivered an Advisory Opinion at the request of the United Nations General Assembly include the following: Condition of Admission of a State to Membership in the United Nations; Competence of the General Assembly for the Admission of a State to the United Nations; Interpretation of the Peace Treaties with Bulgaria, Hungary and Romania; International Status of South West Africa; Reservations to the

Convention on the Prevention and Punishment of the Crime of Genocide; Effect of Awards of Compensation Made by the United Nations Administrative Tribunal (UNAT); Western Sahara; Application for Review of UNAT Judgment No. 333; Applicability of the Obligation to Arbitrate under Section 21 of the United Nations Headquarters Agreement of 26 June 1947 (relating to the closure of the Observer Mission to the United Nations maintained by the Palestine Liberation Organization); Legality of the Use or Threat of Nuclear Weapons; and Legal Consequences of the Construction of a Wall by Israel in the Occupied Palestinian Territory (delivered in July 2004); and the legality of a unilateral declaration of independence by the Provisional Institutions of Self-Government of Kosovo (delivered in July 2010).

An Advisory Opinion has been given at the request of the Security Council: Legal Consequences for States of the continued presence of South Africa in Namibia (South West Africa) notwithstanding Security Council resolution 276 (1970).

In 1989 (at the request of the UN Economic and Social Council—ECOSOC) the Court gave an Advisory Opinion on the Applicability of Article 6, Section 22, of the Convention on the Privileges and Immunities of the United Nations. The Court has also, at the request of UNESCO, given an Advisory Opinion on Judgments of the Administrative Tribunal of the ILO upon Complaints made against UNESCO, and on the Constitution of the Maritime Safety Committee of the Inter-Governmental Maritime Consultative Organization (IMCO), at the request of IMCO. In July 1996 the Court delivered an Advisory Opinion on the Legality of the Use by a State of Nuclear Weapons in Armed Conflict, requested by WHO. In April 1999 the Court delivered an Advisory Opinion, requested by ECOSOC, on the Difference Relating to Immunity from Legal Process of a Special Rapporteur of the Commission on Human Rights. In February 2012 the Court delivered an Advisory Opinion, requested by the International Fund for Agricultural Development, relating to a judgment rendered by the Administrative Tribunal of the International Labour Organization.

Finance

The UN budget appropriation for the Court for the two-year period 2012–13 amounted to US $47.8m.

Publications

Acts and Documents, No. 6 (contains Statute and Rules of the Court, the Resolution concerning its internal judicial practice and other documents).

Bibliography (annually).

Pleadings (Written Pleadings and Statements, Oral Proceedings, Correspondence).

Reports (Judgments, Opinions and Orders).

Yearbook.

UNITED NATIONS FUNDAMENTAL TREATIES

Charter of the United Nations

(Signed 26 June 1945)

(Note: The report of the UN Secretary-General entitled 'In Larger Freedom: Towards Development, Security and Human Rights for All', issued in March 2005, proposed the following amendments to the Charter: the elimination of the 'enemy' clauses in Articles 53 and 107; the deletion from the Charter of Chapter XIII, 'The Trusteeship Council'; and the deletion of Article 47 on The Military Staff Committee and related references.)

WE THE PEOPLES OF THE UNITED NATIONS DETERMINED

to save succeeding generations from the scourge of war, which twice in our lifetime has brought untold sorrow to mankind, and to reaffirm faith in fundamental human rights, in the dignity and worth of the human person, in the equal rights of men and women and of nations large and small, and

to establish conditions under which justice and respect for the obligations arising from treaties and other sources of international law can be maintained, and

to promote social progress and better standards of life in larger freedom,

AND FOR THESE ENDS

to practise tolerance and live together in peace with one another as good neighbours, and

to unite our strength to maintain international peace and security, and

to ensure, by the acceptance of principles and the institution of methods, that armed force shall not be used, save in the common interest, and

to employ international machinery for the promotion of the economic and social advancement of all peoples,

HAVE RESOLVED TO COMBINE OUR EFFORTS TO ACCOMPLISH THESE AIMS.

Accordingly, our respective Governments, through representatives assembled in the city of San Francisco, who have exhibited their full powers found to be in good and due form, have agreed to the present Charter of the United Nations and do hereby establish an international organization to be known as the United Nations.

I. PURPOSES AND PRINCIPLES

Article 1

The Purposes of the United Nations are:

1. To maintain international peace and security, and to that end: to take effective collective measures for the prevention and removal of threats to the peace, and for the suppression of acts of aggression or other breaches of the peace, and to bring about by peaceful means, and in conformity with the principles of justice and international law, adjustment or settlement of international disputes or situations which might lead to a breach of the peace;

2. To develop friendly relations among nations based on respect for the principle of equal rights and self-determination of peoples, and to take other appropriate measures to strengthen universal peace;

3. To achieve international co-operation in solving international problems of an economic, social, cultural, or humanitarian character, and in promoting and encouraging respect for human rights and for fundamental freedoms for all without distinction as to race, sex, language, or religion; and

4. To be a centre for harmonizing the accusations of nations in the attainment of these common ends.

Article 2

The Organization and its Members, in pursuit of the Purposes stated in Article 1, shall act in accordance with the following Principles.

1. The Organization is based on the principle of the sovereign equality of all its Members;

2. All Members, in order to ensure to all of them the rights and benefits resulting from membership, shall fulfil in good faith the obligations assumed by them in accordance with the present Charter;

3. All Members shall settle their international disputes by peaceful means in such a manner that international peace and security, and justice, are not endangered;

4. All Members shall refrain in their international relations from the threat or use of force against the territorial integrity or political independence of any state, or in any manner inconsistent with the Purposes of the United Nations;

5. All Members shall give the United Nations every assistance in any action it takes in accordance with the present Charter, and shall refrain from giving assistance to any state against which the United Nations is taking preventive or enforcement action;

6. The Organization shall ensure that states which are not Members of the United Nations act in accordance with these Principles so far as may be necessary for the maintenance of international peace and security;

7. Nothing contained in the present Charter shall authorize the United Nations to intervene in matters which are essentially within the domestic jurisdiction of any state or shall require the Members to submit such matters to settlement under the present Charter; but this principle shall not prejudice the application of enforcement measures under Chapter VII.

II. MEMBERSHIP

Article 3

The original Members of the United Nations shall be the states which, having participated in the United Nations Conference on International Organization at San Francisco, or having previously signed the Declaration by United Nations of January 1, 1942, sign the present Charter and ratify it in accordance with Article 110.

Article 4

1. Membership in the United Nations is open to all other peace-loving states which accept the obligations contained in the present Charter and, in the judgement of the Organization, are able and willing to carry out these obligations.

2. The admission of any such state to membership in the United Nations will be effected by a decision of the General Assembly upon the recommendation of the Security Council.

Article 5

A member of the United Nations against which preventive or enforcement action has been taken by the Security Council may be suspended from the exercise of the rights and privileges of membership by the General Assembly upon the recommendation of the Security Council. The exercise of these rights and privileges may be restored by the Security Council.

Article 6

A Member of the United Nations which has persistently violated the Principles contained in the present Charter may be expelled from the Organization by the General Assembly upon the recommendation of the Security Council.

III. ORGANS

Article 7

1. There are established as the principal organs of the United Nations: a General Assembly, a Security Council, an Economic and Social Council, a Trusteeship Council, an International Court of Justice, and a Secretariat.

2. Such subsidiary organs as may be found necessary may be established in accordance with the present Charter.

Article 8

The United Nations shall place no restrictions on the eligibility of men and women to participate in any capacity and under conditions of equality in its principal and subsidiary organs.

IV. THE GENERAL ASSEMBLY

Composition

Article 9

1. The General Assembly shall consist of all the Members of the United Nations.

2. Each Member shall have not more than five representatives in the General Assembly.

Functions and Powers

Article 10

The General Assembly may discuss any questions or any matters within the scope of the present Charter or relating to the powers and functions of any organs provided for in the present Charter, and, except as provided in Article 12, may make recommendations to the Members of the United Nations or to the Security Council or to both on any such questions or matters.

Article 11

1. The General Assembly may consider the general principles of co-operation in the maintenance of international peace and security, including the principles governing disarmament and the regulation of armaments, and may make recommendations with regard to such principles to the Members or to the Security Council or to both.

2. The General Assembly may discuss any questions relating to the maintenance of international peace and security brought before it by any Member of the United Nations, or by the Security Council, or by a state which is not a Member of the United Nations in accordance with Article 35, paragraph 2, and, except as provided in Article 12, may make recommendations with regard to any such question to the state or states concerned or to the Security Council or both. Any such question on which action is necessary shall be referred to the Security Council by the General Assembly either before or after discussion.

3. The General Assembly may call the attention of the Security Council to situations which are likely to endanger international peace and security.

4. The powers of the General Assembly set forth in this Article shall not limit the general scope of Article 10.

Article 12

1. While the Security Council is exercising in respect of any dispute or situation the functions assigned to it in the present Charter, the General Assembly shall not make any recommendations with regard to that dispute or situation unless the Security Council so requests. 2.

2. The Secretary-General, with the consent of the Security Council, shall notify the General Assembly at each session of any matters relative to the maintenance of international peace and security which are being dealt with by the Security Council and shall similarly notify the General Assembly, or the Members of the United Nations if the General Assembly is not in session, immediately the Security Council ceases to deal with such matters.

Article 13

1. The General Assembly shall initiate studies and make recommendations for the purpose of:

(a) promoting international co-operation in the political field and encouraging the progressive development of international law and its codification;

(b) promoting international co-operation in the economic, social, cultural, educational, and health fields, and assisting in the realization of human rights and fundamental freedoms for all without distinction as to race, sex, language, or religion.

2. The further responsibilities, functions and powers of the General Assembly with respect to matters mentioned in paragraph 1(b) above are set forth in Chapters IX and X.

Article 14

Subject to the provision of Article 12, the General Assembly may recommend measures for the peaceful adjustment of any situation, regardless of origin, which it deems likely to impair the general welfare or friendly relations among nations, including situations resulting from a violation of the provisions of the present Charter setting forth the Purposes and Principles of the United Nations.

Article 15

1. The General Assembly shall receive and consider annual and special reports from the Security Council; these reports shall include an account of the measures that the Security Council has decided upon or taken to maintain international peace and security.

2. The General Assembly shall receive and consider reports from the other organs of the United Nations.

Article 16

The General Assembly shall perform such functions with respect to the international trusteeship system as are assigned to it under Chapters XII and XIII, including the approval of the trusteeship agreements for areas not designated as strategic.

Article 17

1. The General Assembly shall consider and approve the budget of the Organization.

2. The expenses of the Organization shall be borne by the Members as apportioned by the General Assembly

3. The General Assembly shall consider and approve any financial and budgetary arrangements with specialized agencies referred to in Article 57 and shall examine the administrative budgets of such specialized agencies with a view to making recommendations to the agencies concerned.

Voting

Article 18

1. Each Member of the General Assembly shall have one vote.

2. Decisions of the General Assembly on important questions shall be made by a two-thirds majority of the members present and voting. These questions shall include: recommendations with respect to the maintenance of international peace and security, the election of the non-permanent Members of the Security Council, the election of the Members of the Economic and Social Council, the election of Members of the Trusteeship Council in accordance with paragraph 1(c) of Article 86, the admission of new Members to the United Nations, the suspension of the rights and privileges of membership, the expulsion of Members, questions relating to the operation of the trusteeship system, and budgetary questions.

3. Decisions on other questions, including the determination of additional categories of questions to be decided by a two-thirds majority, shall be made by a majority of the members present and voting.

Article 19

A Member of the United Nations which is in arrears in the payment of its financial contributions to the Organization shall have no vote in the General Assembly if the amount of its arrears equals or exceeds the amount of the contributions due from it for the preceding two full years. The General Assembly may, nevertheless, permit such a Member to vote if it is satisfied that the failure to pay is due to conditions beyond the control of the Member.

Procedure

Article 20

The General Assembly shall meet in regular annual sessions and in such special sessions as occasion may require. Special sessions shall be convoked by the Secretary-General at the request of the Security Council or of a majority of the members of the United Nations.

Article 21

The General Assembly shall adopt its own rules of procedure. It shall elect its President for each session.

Article 22

The General Assembly may establish such subsidiary organs as it deems necessary for the performance of its functions.

V. THE SECURITY COUNCIL

Composition

Article 23

1. The Security Council shall consist of 11 Members of the United Nations. The Republic of China, France, the Union of Soviet Socialist Republics, the United Kingdom of Great Britain and Northern Ireland, and the United States of America shall be permanent members of the Security Council. The General Assembly shall elect six other Members of the United Nations to be non-permanent members of the Security Council, due regard being specially paid, in the first instance to the contribution of Members of the United Nations to the maintenance of international peace and security and to the other purposes of the Organization, and also to equitable geographical distribution.

2. The non-permanent members of the Security Council shall be elected for a term of two years. In the first election of the non-permanent members, however, three shall be chosen for a term of one year. A retiring member shall not be eligible for immediate re-election.

3. Each member of the Security Council shall have one representative.

Note: From 1971 the Chinese seat in the UN General Assembly and its permanent seat in the Security Council were occupied by the People's Republic of China. In December 1991 Russia assumed the former USSR's seat in the UN General Assembly and its permanent seat in the Security Council.

Functions and Powers

Article 24

1. In order to ensure prompt and effective action by the United Nations, its Members confer on the Security Council primary responsibility for the maintenance of international peace and security, and agree that in carrying out its duties under this responsibility the Security Council acts on their behalf.

2. In discharging these duties the Security Council shall act in accordance with the Purposes and Principles of the United Nations. The specific powers granted to the Security Council for the discharge of these duties are laid down in Chapters VI, VII, VIII and XII.

3. The Security Council shall submit annual and, when necessary, special reports to the General Assembly for its consideration.

Article 25

The Members of the United Nations agree to accept and carry out the decisions of the Security Council in accordance with the present Charter.

Article 26

In order to promote the establishment and maintenance of international peace and security with the least diversion for armaments of the world's human and economic resources, the Security Council shall be responsible for formulating, with the assistance of the Military Staff Committee referred to in Article 47, plans to be submitted to the Members of the United Nations for the establishment of a system for the regulation of armaments.

Voting

Article 27

1. Each member of the Security Council shall have one vote.

2. Decisions of the Security Council on procedural matters shall be made by an affirmative vote of seven members.

3. Decisions of the Security Council on all other matters shall be made by an affirmative vote of seven members including the concurring votes of the permanent members; provided that, in decisions under Chapter VI, and under paragraph 3 of Article 52, a party to a dispute shall abstain from voting.

Procedure

Article 28

1. The Security Council shall be so organized as to be able to function continuously. Each member of the Security Council shall for this purpose be represented at all times at the seat of the Organization.

2. The Security Council shall hold periodic meetings at which each of its members may, if it so desires, be represented by a member of the government or by some other specially designated representative.

3. The Security Council may hold meetings at such places other than the seat of the Organization as in its judgment will best facilitate its work.

Article 29

The Security Council may establish such subsidiary organs as it deems necessary for the performance of its functions.

Article 30

The Security Council shall adopt its own rules of procedure, including the method of selecting its President.

Article 31

Any Member of the United Nations which is not a member of the Security Council may participate, without vote, in the discussion of any question brought before the Security Council whenever the latter considers that the interests of that Member are specially affected.

Article 32

Any Member of the United Nations which is not a member of the Security Council or any state which is not a Member of the United Nations, if it is a party to a dispute under consideration by the Security Council, shall be invited to participate, without vote, in the discussion relating to the dispute. The Security Council shall lay down such conditions as it deems just for the participation of a state which is not a Member of the United Nations.

VI. PACIFIC SETTLEMENT OF DISPUTES

Article 33

1. The parties to any dispute, the continuance of which is likely to endanger the maintenance of international peace and security, shall, first of all, seek a solution by negotiation, enquiry, mediation, conciliation, arbitration, judicial settlement, resort to regional agencies or arrangements, or other peaceful means of their own choice.

2. The Security Council shall, when it deems necessary, call upon the parties to settle their disputes by such means.

Article 34

The Security Council may investigate any dispute, or any situation which might lead to international friction or give rise to a dispute, in order to determine whether the continuance of the dispute or situation is likely to endanger the maintenance of international peace and security.

Article 35

1. Any Member of the United Nations may bring any dispute, or any situation of the nature referred to in Article 34, to the attention of the Security Council or of the General Assembly.

2. A state which is not a Member of the United Nations may bring to the attention of the Security Council or of the General

Assembly any dispute to which it is a party if it accepts in advance, for the purposes of the dispute, the obligations of pacific settlement provided in the present Charter.

3. The proceedings of the General Assembly in respect of matters brought to its attention under this Article will be subject to the provisions of Articles 11 and 12.

Article 36

1. The Security Council may, at any stage of a dispute of the nature referred to in Article 33 or of a situation of like nature, recommend appropriate procedures or methods of adjustment.

2. The Security Council should take into consideration any procedures for the settlement of the dispute which have already been adopted by the parties.

3. In making recommendations under this Article the Security Council should also take into consideration that legal disputes should as a general rule be referred by the parties to the International Court of Justice in accordance with the provisions of the statute of the Court.

Article 37

1. Should the parties to a dispute of the nature referred to in Article 33, fail to settle it by the means indicated in that Article, they shall refer it to the Security Council.

2. If the Security Council deems that the continuance of the dispute is in fact likely to endanger the maintenance of international peace and security, it shall decide whether to take action under Article 36 or to recommend such terms of settlement as it may consider appropriate.

Article 38

Without prejudice to the provisions of Articles 33 to 37, the Security Council may, if all the parties to any dispute so request, make recommendations to the parties with a view to a pacific settlement of the dispute.

VII. ACTION WITH RESPECT TO THREATS TO THE PEACE, BREACHES OF THE PEACE, AND ACTS OF AGGRESSION

Article 39

The Security Council shall determine the existence of any threat to the peace, breach of the peace, or act of aggression and shall make recommendations, or decide what measures shall be taken in accordance with Articles 41 and 42, to maintain or restore international peace and security.

Article 40

In order to prevent an aggravation of the situation, the Security Council may, before making the recommendations or deciding upon the measures provided for in Article 39, call upon the parties concerned to comply with such provisional measures as it deems necessary or desirable. Such provisional measures shall be without prejudice to the rights, claims, or position of the parties concerned. The Security Council shall duly take account of failure to comply with such provisional measures.

Article 41

The Security Council may decide what measures not involving the use of armed force are to be employed to give effect to its decisions, and it may call upon the Members of the United Nations to apply such measures. These may include complete or partial interruption of economic relations and of rail, sea, air, postal, telegraphic, radio, and other means of communication, and the severance of diplomatic relations.

Article 42

Should the Security Council consider that measures provided for in Article 41 would be inadequate or have proved to be inadequate, it may take such action by air, sea, or land forces as may be necessary to maintain or restore international peace and security. Such action may include demonstrations, blockade, and other operations by air, sea, or land forces of Members of the United Nations.

Article 43

1. All Members of the United Nations, in order to contribute to the maintenance of international peace and security, undertake to make available to the Security Council, on its call and in accordance with a special agreement or agreements, armed forces, assistance, and facilities, including rights of passage, necessary for the purpose of maintaining international peace and security.

2. Such agreement or agreements shall govern the numbers and types of forces, their degree of readiness and general location, and the nature of the facilities and assistance to be provided.

3. The agreement or agreements shall be negotiated as soon as possible on the initiative of the Security Council. They shall be concluded between the Security Council and Members or between the Security Council and groups of Members and shall be subject to ratification by the signatory states in accordance with their respective constitutional processes.

Article 44

When the Security Council has decided to use force it shall, before calling upon a Member not represented on it to provide armed forces in fulfilment of the obligations assumed under Article 43, invite that Member, if the Member so desires, to participate in the decisions of the Security Council concerning the employment of contingents of that Member's armed forces.

Article 45

In order to enable the United Nations to take urgent military measures, Members shall hold immediately available national airforce contingents for combined international enforcement action. The strength and degree of readiness of these contingents and plans for their combined action shall be determined, within the limits laid down in the special agreement and agreements referred to in Article 43, by the Security Council with the assistance of the Military Staff Committee.

Article 46

Plans for the application of armed force shall be made by the Security Council with the assistance of the Military Staff Committee.

Article 47

1. There shall be established a Military Staff Committee to advise and assist the Security Council on all questions relating to the Security Council's military requirements for the maintenance of international peace and security, the employment and command of forces placed at its disposal, the regulation of armaments, and possible disarmament.

2. The Military Staff Committee shall consist of the Chiefs of Staff of the permanent members of the Security Council or their representatives. Any Member of the United Nations not permanently represented on the Committee shall be invited by the Committee to be associated with it when the efficient discharge of the Committee's responsibilities requires the participation of that Member in its work.

3. The Military Staff Committee shall be responsible under the Security Council for the strategic direction of any armed forces placed at the disposal of the Security Council. Questions relating to the command of such forces shall be worked out subsequently.

4. The Military Staff Committee, with the authorization of the Security Council and after consultation with appropriate regional agencies, may establish regional sub-committees.

Article 48

1. The action required to carry out the decisions of the Security Council for the maintenance of international peace and security shall be taken by all the Members of the United Nations or by some of them, as the Security Council may determine.

2. Such decisions shall be carried out by the Members of the United Nations directly and through their action in the appropriate international agencies of which they are members.

Article 49

The Members of the United Nations shall join in affording mutual assistance in carrying out the measures decided upon by the Security Council.

Article 50

If preventive or enforcement measures against any state are taken by the Security Council, any other state, whether a Member of the United Nations or not, which finds itself confronted with special economic problems arising from the carrying out of those measures shall have the right to consult the Security Council with regard to a solution of those problems.

Article 51

Nothing in the present Charter shall impair the inherent right of individual or collective self-defence if an armed attack occurs against a Member of the United Nations, until the Security Council has taken measures necessary to maintain international peace and security. Measures taken by Members in the exercise of this right of self-defence shall be immediately reported to the Security Council and shall not in any way affect the authority and responsibility of the Security Council under the present Charter to take at any time such action as it deems necessary in order to maintain or restore international peace and security.

VIII. REGIONAL ARRANGEMENTS

Article 52

1. Nothing in the present Charter precludes the existence of regional arrangements or agencies for dealing with such matters relating to the maintenance of international peace and security as are appropriate for regional action, provided that such arrangements or agencies and their activities are consistent with the Purposes and Principles of the United Nations.

2. The Members of the United Nations entering into such arrangements or constituting such agencies shall make every effort to achieve pacific settlement of local disputes through such regional agencies before referring them to the Security Council.

3. The Security Council shall encourage the development of pacific settlement of local disputes through such regional arrangements or by such regional agencies either on the initiative of the states concerned or by reference from the Security Council.

4. This Article in no way impairs the application of Articles 34 and 35.

Article 53

1. The Security Council shall, where appropriate, utilize such regional arrangements or agencies for enforcement action under its authority. But no enforcement action shall be taken under regional arrangements or by regional agencies without the authorization of the Security Council, with the exception of measures against any enemy state, as defined in paragraph 2 of this Article, provided for pursuant to Article 107 or in regional arrangements directed against renewal of aggressive policy on the part of any such state, until such time as the Organization may, on request of the Governments concerned, be charged with the responsibility for preventing further aggression by such a state.

2. The term enemy state as used in paragraph I of this Article applies to any state which during the Second World War has been an enemy of any signatory of the present Charter.

Article 54

The Security Council shall at all times be kept fully informed of activities undertaken or in contemplation under regional arrangements or by regional agencies for the maintenance of international peace and security.

IX. INTERNATIONAL ECONOMIC AND SOCIAL CO-OPERATION

Article 55

With a view to the creation of conditions of stability and well-being which are necessary for peaceful and friendly relations among nations based on respect for the principle of equal rights and self-determination of peoples, the United Nations shall promote:

(a) higher standards of living, full employment, and conditions of economic and social progress and development;

(b) solutions of international economic, social, health, and related problems; and international cultural and educational co-operation; and

(c) universal respect for, and observance of, human rights and fundamental freedoms for all without distinction as to race, sex, language, or religion.

Article 56

All Members pledge themselves to take joint and separate action in co-operation with the Organization for the achievement of the purposes set forth in Article 55.

Article 57

1. The various specialized agencies, established by intergovernmental agreement and having wide international responsibilities, as defined in their basic instruments, in economic, social, cultural, educational, health, and related fields, shall be brought into relationship with the United Nations in accordance with the provisions of Article 63.

2. Such agencies thus brought into relationship with the United Nations are hereinafter referred to as specialized agencies.

Article 58

The Organization shall make recommendations for the co-ordination of the policies and activities of the specialized agencies.

Article 59

The Organization shall, where appropriate, initiate negotiations among the states concerned for the creation of any new specialized agencies required for the accomplishment of the purposes set forth in Article 55.

Article 60

Responsibility for the discharge of the functions of the Organization set forth in this Chapter shall be vested in the General Assembly and, under the authority of the General Assembly, in the Economic and Social Council, which shall have for this purpose the powers set forth in Chapter X.

X. THE ECONOMIC AND SOCIAL COUNCIL

Composition

Article 61

1. The Economic and Social Council shall consist of 18 Members of the United Nations elected by the General Assembly.

2. Subject to the provisions of paragraph 3, six members of the Economic and Social Council shall be elected each year for a term of three years. A retiring member shall be eligible for immediate re-election.

3. At the first election, 18 members of the Economic and Social Council shall be chosen. The term of office of six members so chosen shall expire at the end of one year, and of six other members at the end of two years, in accordance with arrangements made by the General Assembly.

4. Each member of the Economic and Social Council shall have one representative.

Functions and Powers

Article 62

1. The Economic and Social Council may make or initiate studies and reports with respect to international economic, social, cultural, educational, health, and related matters and may make recommendations with respect to any such matters to the General Assembly, to the Members of the United Nations, and to the specialized agencies concerned.

2. It may make recommendations for the purpose of promoting respect for, and observance of, human rights and fundamental freedoms for all.

3. It may prepare draft conventions for submission to the General Assembly, with respect to matters falling within its competence.

4. It may call, in accordance with the rules prescribed by the United Nations, international conferences on matters falling within its competence.

Article 63

1. The Economic and Social Council may enter into agreements with any of the agencies referred to in Article 57, defining the

terms on which the agency concerned shall be brought into relationship with the United Nations. Such agreements shall be subject to approval by the General Assembly.

2. It may co-ordinate the activities of the specialized agencies through consultation with and recommendations to such agencies and through recommendations to the General Assembly and to the Members of the United Nations.

Article 64

1. The Economic and Social Council may take appropriate steps to obtain regular reports from the specialized agencies. It may make arrangements with the Members of the United Nations and with specialized agencies to obtain reports on the steps taken to give effect to its own recommendations and to recommendations on matters falling within its competence made by the General Assembly.

2. It may communicate its observations on these reports to the General Assembly.

Article 65

The Economic and Social Council may furnish information to the Security Council and shall assist the Security Council upon its request.

Article 66

1. The Economic and Social Council shall perform such functions as fall within its competence in connection with the carrying out of the recommendations of the General Assembly.

2. It may, with the approval of the General Assembly, perform services at the request of Members of the United Nations and at the request of specialized agencies.

3. It shall perform such other functions as are specified elsewhere in the present Charter or as may be assigned to it by the General Assembly.

Voting

Article 67

1. Each member of the Economic and Social Council shall have one vote.

2. Decisions of the Economic and Social Council shall be made by a majority of the members present and voting.

Procedure

Article 68

The Economic and Social Council shall set up commissions in economic and social fields and for the promotion of human rights, and such other commissions as may be required for the performance of its functions.

Article 69

The Economic and Social Council shall invite any Member of the United Nations to participate, without vote, in its deliberations on any matter of particular concern to that Member.

Article 70

The Economic and Social Council may make arrangements for representatives of the specialized agencies to participate, without vote, in its deliberations and in those of the commissions established by it, and for its representatives to participate in the deliberations of the specialized agencies.

Article 71

The Economic and Social Council may make suitable arrangements for consultation with non-governmental organizations which are concerned with matters within its competence. Such arrangements may be made with international organizations and, where appropriate, with national organizations after consultation with the Member of the United Nations concerned.

Article 72

1. The Economic and Social Council shall adopt its own rules of procedure, including the method of selecting its President.

2. The Economic and Social Council shall meet as required in accordance with its rules, which shall include provision for the convening of meetings on the request of a majority of its members.

XI. NON-SELF-GOVERNING TERRITORIES

Article 73

Members of the United Nations which have or assume responsibilities for the administration of territories whose peoples have not yet attained a full measure of self-government recognize the principle that the interests of the inhabitants of these territories are paramount, and accept as a sacred trust the obligation to promote to the utmost, within the system of international peace and security established by the present Charter, the well-being of the inhabitants of these territories, and, to this end:

(a) to ensure, with due respect for the culture of the peoples concerned, their political, economic, social, and educational advancement, their just treatment, and their protection against abuses;

(b) to develop self-government, to take due account of the political aspirations of the peoples, and to assist them in the progressive development of their free political institutions, according to the particular circumstances of each territory and its peoples and their varying stages of advancement;

(c) to further international peace and security;

(d) to promote constructive measures of development, to encourage research, and to co-operate with one another and, when and where appropriate, with specialized international bodies with a view to the practical achievement of the social, economic, and scientific purposes set forth in this Article; and

(e) to transmit regularly to the Secretary-General for information purposes, subject to such limitations as security and constitutional considerations may require, statistical and other information, of a technical nature relating to economic, social, and educational conditions in the territories for which they are respectively responsible other than those territories to which Chapters XII and XIII apply.

Article 74

Members of the United Nations also agree that their policy in respect of the territories to which this Chapter applies, no less than in respect of their metropolitan areas, must be based on the general principles of good-neighbourliness, due account being taken of the interests and well-being of the rest of the world, in social, economic, and commercial matters.

XII. INTERNATIONAL TRUSTEESHIP SYSTEM

Article 75

The United Nations shall establish under its authority an international trusteeship system for the administration and supervision of such territories as may be placed thereunder by subsequent individual agreements. These territories are hereinafter referred to as trust territories.

Article 76

The basic objectives of the trusteeship system, in accordance with the Purposes of the United Nations laid down in Article 1 of the present Charter, shall be:

(a) to further international peace and security;

(b) to promote the political, economic, social, and educational advancement of the inhabitants of the trust territories, and their progressive development towards self-government or independence as may be appropriate to the particular circumstances of each territory and its peoples and the freely expressed wishes of the peoples concerned, and as may be provided by the terms of each trusteeship agreement;

(c) to encourage respect for human rights and for fundamental freedoms for all without distinction as to race, sex, language, or religion, and to encourage recognition of the interdependence of the peoples of the world; and

(d) to ensure equal treatment in social, economic, and commercial matters for all Members of the United Nations and their nationals, and also equal treatment for the latter in the administration of justice, without prejudice to the attainment of the foregoing objectives and subject to the provisions of Article 80.

Article 77

1. The trusteeship system shall apply to such territories in the following categories as may be placed thereunder by means of trusteeship agreements.

(a) territories now held under mandate;

(b) territories which may be detached from enemy states as a result of the Second World War; and

(c) territories voluntarily placed under the system by states responsible for their administration.

2. It will be a matter for subsequent agreement as to which territories in the foregoing categories will be brought under the trusteeship system and upon what terms.

Article 78

The trusteeship system shall not apply to territories which have become Members of the United Nations, relationship among which shall be based on respect for the principle of sovereign equality.

Article 79

The terms of trusteeship for each territory to be placed under the trusteeship system, including any alteration or amendment, shall be agreed upon by the states directly concerned, including the mandatory power in the case of territories held under mandate by a Member of the United Nations, and shall be approved as provided for in Articles 83 and 85.

Article 80

1. Except as may be agreed upon in individual trusteeship agreements, made under Articles 77, 79, and 81, placing each territory under the trusteeship system, and until such agreements have been concluded, nothing in this Chapter shall be construed in or of itself to alter in any manner the rights whatsoever of any states or any peoples or the terms of existing international instruments to which Members of the United Nations may respectively be parties.

2. Paragraph 1 of this Article shall not be interpreted as giving grounds for delay or postponement of the negotiation and conclusion of agreements for placing mandated and other territories under the trusteeship system as provided for in Article 77.

Article 81

The trusteeship agreement shall in each case include the terms under which the trust territory will be administered and designate the authority which will exercise the administration of the trust territory. Such authority, hereinafter called the administering authority, may be one or more states or the Organization itself.

Article 82

There may be designated, in any trusteeship agreement, a strategic area or areas which may include part or all of the trust territory to which the agreement applies, without prejudice to any special agreement or agreements made under Article 43.

Article 83

1. All functions of the United Nations relating to strategic areas, including the approval of the terms of the trusteeship agreements and of their alteration or amendment, shall be exercised by the Security Council.

2. The basic objectives set forth in Article 76 shall be applicable to the people of each strategic area.

3. The Security Council shall, subject to the provisions of the trusteeship agreements and without prejudice to security considerations, avail itself of the assistance of the Trusteeship Council to perform those functions of the United Nations under the trusteeship system relating to political, economic, social, and educational matters in the strategic areas.

Article 84

It shall be the duty of the administering authority to ensure that the trust territory shall play its part in the maintenance of international peace and security. To this end the administering authority may make use of volunteer forces, facilities, and assistance from the trust territory in carrying out the obligations towards the Security Council undertaken in this regard by the administering authority, as well as for local defence and the maintenance of law and order within the trust territory.

Article 85

1. The functions of the United Nations with regard to trusteeship agreements for all areas not designated as strategic, including the approval of the terms of the trusteeship agreements and of their alteration or amendment, shall be exercised by the General Assembly.

2. The Trusteeship Council, operating under the authority of the General Assembly, shall assist the General Assembly in carrying out these functions.

XIII. THE TRUSTEESHIP COUNCIL

Composition

Article 86

1. The Trusteeship Council shall consist of the following Members of the United Nations:

(a) those Members administering trust territories;

(b) such of those Members mentioned by name in Article 23 as are not administering trust territories; and

(c) as many other Members elected for three-year terms by the General Assembly as may be necessary to ensure that the total number of members of the Trusteeship Council is equally divided between those Members of the United Nations which administer trust territories and those which do not.

2. Each member of the Trusteeship Council shall designate one specially qualified person to represent it therein.

Note: On 1 October 1994 the Republic of Palau, the last remaining territory under UN trusteeship, became independent. The Trusteeship Council formally suspended operations on 1 November; subsequently it was to be convened, as required, on an extraordinary basis.

Functions and Powers

Article 87

The General Assembly and, under its authority, the Trusteeship Council, in carrying out their functions, may:

(a) consider reports submitted by the administering authority

(b) accept petitions and examine them in consultation with the administering authority

(c) provide for periodic visits to the respective trust territories at times agreed upon with the administering authority; and

(d) take these and other actions in conformity with the terms of the trusteeship agreements.

Article 88

The Trusteeship Council shall formulate a questionnaire on the political, economic, social, and educational advancement of the inhabitants of each trust territory, and the administering authority for each trust territory within the competence of the General Assembly shall make an annual report to the General Assembly upon the basis of such questionnaire.

Voting

Article 89

1. Each member of the Trusteeship Council shall have one vote.

2. Decisions of the Trusteeship Council shall be made by a majority of the members present and voting.

Procedure

Article 90

1. The Trusteeship Council shall adopt its own rules of procedure, including the method of selecting its President.

2. The Trusteeship Council shall meet as required in accordance with its rules, which shall include provision for the convening of meetings on the request of a majority of its members.

Article 91

The Trusteeship Council shall, when appropriate, avail itself of the assistance of the Economic and Social Council and of the specialized agencies in regard to matters with which they are respectively concerned.

XIV. THE INTERNATIONAL COURT OF JUSTICE

Article 92

The International Court of Justice shall be the principal judicial organ of the United Nations. It shall function in accordance with the annexed Statute, which is based upon the Statute of the Permanent Court of International Justice and forms an integral part of the present Charter.

Article 93

1. All Members of the United Nations are *ipso facto* parties to the Statute of the International Court of Justice.

2. A state which is not a Member of the United Nations may become a party to the Statute of the International Court of Justice on condition to be determined in each case by the General Assembly upon the recommendation of the Security Council.

Article 94

1. Each Member of the United Nations undertakes to comply with the decision of the International Court of Justice in any case to which it is a party.

2. If any party to a case fails to perform the obligations incumbent upon it under a judgment rendered by the Court, the other party may have recourse to the Security Council, which may, if it deems necessary, make recommendations or decide upon measures to be taken to give effect to the judgment.

Article 95

Nothing in the present Charter shall prevent Members of the United Nations from entrusting the solution of their differences to other tribunals by virtue of agreements already in existence or which may be concluded in the future.

Article 96

1. The General Assembly or the Security Council may request the International Court of Justice to give an advisory opinion on any legal question.

2. Other organs of the United Nations and specialized agencies, which may at any time be so authorized by the General Assembly, may also request advisory opinions of the Court on legal questions arising within the scope of their activities.

XV. THE SECRETARIAT

Article 97

The Secretariat shall comprise a Secretary-General and such staff as the Organization may require. The Secretary-General shall be appointed by the General Assembly upon the recommendation of the Security Council. He shall be the chief administrative officer of the Organization.

Article 98

The Secretary-General shall act in that capacity in all meetings of the General Assembly, of the Security Council, of the Economic and Social Council, and of the Trusteeship Council, and shall perform such other functions as are entrusted to him by these organs. The Secretary-General shall make an annual report to the General Assembly on the work of the Organization.

Article 99

The Secretary-General may bring to the attention of the Security Council any matter which in his opinion may threaten the maintenance of international peace and security.

Article 100

1. In the performance of their duties the Secretary-General and the staff shall not seek or receive instructions from any government or from any other authority external to the Organization. They shall refrain from any action which might reflect on their position as international officials responsible only to the Organization.

2. Each Member of the United Nations undertakes to respect the exclusively international character of the responsibilities of the Secretary-General and the staff and not to seek to influence them in the discharge of their responsibilities.

Article 101

1. The staff shall be appointed by the Secretary-General under regulations established by the General Assembly.

2. Appropriate staffs shall be permanently assigned to the Economic and Social Council, the Trusteeship Council, and, as required, to other organs of the United Nations. These staffs shall form a part of the Secretariat.

3. The paramount consideration in the employment of the staff and in the determination of the conditions of service shall be the necessity of securing the highest standards of efficiency, competence, and integrity. Due regard shall be paid to the importance of recruiting the staff on as wide a geographical basis as possible.

XVI. MISCELLANEOUS PROVISIONS

Article 102

1. Every treaty and every international agreement entered into by any Member of the United Nations after the present Charter comes into force shall as soon as possible be registered with the Secretariat and published by it.

2. No party to any such treaty or international agreement which has not been registered in accordance with the provisions of paragraph 1 of this Article may invoke that treaty or agreement before any organ of the United Nations.

Article 103

In the event of a conflict between the obligations of the Members of the United Nations under the present Charter and their obligations under any other international agreement, their obligations under the present Charter shall prevail.

Article 104

The Organization shall enjoy in the territory of each of its Members such legal capacity as may be necessary for the exercise of its functions and the fulfilment of its purposes.

Article 105

1. The Organization shall enjoy in the territory of each of its Members such privileges and immunities as are necessary for the fulfilment of its purposes.

2. Representatives of the Members of the United Nations and officials of the Organization shall similarly enjoy such privileges and immunities as are necessary for the independent exercise of their functions in connection with the Organization.

3. The General Assembly may make recommendations with a view to determining the details of the application of paragraphs 1 and 2 of this Article or may propose conventions to the Members of the United Nations for this purpose.

XVII. TRANSITIONAL SECURITY ARRANGEMENTS

Article 106

Pending the coming into force of such special agreements referred to in Article 43 as in the opinion of the Security Council enable it to begin the exercise of its responsibilities under Article 42, the parties to the Four-Nation Declaration signed at Moscow, October 30, 1943, and France, shall, in accordance with the provisions of paragraph 5 of that Declaration, consult with one another and as occasion requires with other Members of the United Nations with a view to such joint action on behalf of the Organization as may be necessary for the purpose of maintaining international peace and security.

Article 107

Nothing in the present Charter shall invalidate or preclude action, in relation to any state which during the Second World War has been an enemy of any signatory to the present Charter, taken or authorized as a result of that war by the Governments having responsibility for such action.

XVIII. AMENDMENTS

Article 108

Amendments to the present Charter shall come into force for all Members of the United Nations when they have been adopted by a vote of two-thirds of the members of the General Assembly and ratified in accordance with their respective constitutional processes by two-thirds of the Members of the United Nations, including all the permanent members of the Security Council.

Article 109

1. A General Conference of the Members of the United Nations for the purpose of reviewing the present Charter may be held at a date and place to be fixed by a two-thirds vote of the members of the General Assembly and by a vote of any seven members of the Security Council. Each Member of the United Nations shall have one vote in the conference.

2. Any alteration of the present Charter recommended by a two-thirds vote of the conference shall take effect when ratified in accordance with their respective constitutional processes by two-thirds of the Members of the United Nations including all the permanent members of the Security Council.

3. If such a conference has not been held before the tenth annual session of the General Assembly following the coming into force of the present Charter, the proposal to call such a conference shall be placed on the agenda of that session of the General Assembly, and the conference shall be held if so decided by a majority vote of the members of the General Assembly and by a vote of any seven members of the Security Council.

XIX. RATIFICATION AND SIGNATURE

Article 110

1. The present Charter shall be ratified by the signatory states in accordance with their respective constitutional processes.

2. The ratifications shall be deposited with the Government of the United States of America, which shall notify all the signatory states of each deposit as well as the Secretary-General of the Organization when he has been appointed.

3. The present Charter shall come into force upon the deposit of ratifications by the Republic of China, France, the Union of Soviet Socialist Republics, the United Kingdom of Great Britain and Northern Ireland, and the United States of America, and by a majority of the other signatory states. A protocol of the ratifications deposited shall thereupon be drawn up by the Government of the United States of America which shall communicate copies thereof to all the signatory states.

4. The states signatory to the present Charter which ratify it after it has come into force will become original Members of the United Nations on the date of the deposit of their respective ratifications.

Article 111

The present Charter, of which the Chinese, French, Russian, English, and Spanish texts are equally authentic, shall remain deposited in the archives of the Government of the United States of America. Duly certified copies thereof shall be transmitted by that Government to the Governments of the other signatory states.

IN FAITH WHEREOF the representatives of the Governments of the United Nations have signed the present Charter.

DONE at the city of San Francisco the twenty-sixth day of June, one thousand nine hundred and forty-five.

AMENDMENTS

The following amendments to Articles 23 and 27 of the Charter came into force in August 1965.

Article 23

1. The Security Council shall consist of 15 Members of the United Nations. The Republic of China, France, the Union of Soviet Socialist Republics, the United Kingdom of Great Britain and Northern Ireland, and the United States of America shall be permanent members of the Security Council. The General Assembly shall elect 10 other Members of the United Nations to be non-permanent members of the Security Council, due regard being specially paid, in the first instance to the contribution of Members of the United Nations to the maintenance of international peace and security and to the other purposes of the Organization, and also to equitable geographical distribution.

2. The non-permanent members of the Security Council shall be elected for a term of two years. In the first election of the non-permanent members after the increase of the membership of the Security Council from 11 to 15, two of the four additional members shall be chosen for a term of one year. A retiring member shall not be eligible for immediate re-election.

3. Each member of the Security Council shall have one representative.

Article 27

1. Each member of the Security Council shall have one vote.

2. Decisions of the Security Council on procedural matters shall be made by an affirmative vote of nine members.

3. Decisions of the Security Council on all other matters shall be made by an affirmative vote of nine members including the concurring votes of the permanent members; provided that, in decisions under Chapter VI and under paragraph 3 of Article 52, a party to a dispute shall abstain from voting.

The following amendments to Article 61 of the Charter came into force in September 1973.

Article 61

1. The Economic and Social Council shall consist of 54 Members of the United Nations elected by the General Assembly.

2. Subject to the provisions of paragraph 3, 18 members of the Economic and Social Council shall be elected each year for a term of three years. A retiring member shall be eligible for immediate re-election.

3. At the first election after the increase in the membership of the Economic and Social Council from 27 to 54 members, in addition to the members elected in place of the nine members whose term of office expires at the end of that year, 27 additional members shall be elected. Of these 27 additional members, the term of office of nine members so elected shall expire at the end of one year, and of nine other members at the end of two years, in accordance with arrangements made by the General Assembly.

4. Each member of the Economic and Social Council shall have one representative.

The following amendment to Paragraph 1 of Article 109 of the Charter came into force in June 1968.

Article 109

1. A General Conference of the Members of the United Nations for the purpose of reviewing the present Charter may be held at a date and place to be fixed by a two-thirds vote of the members of the General Assembly and by a vote of any nine members of the Security Council. Each Member of the United Nations shall have one vote in the conference.

Universal Declaration of Human Rights

(Adopted 10 December 1948)

Whereas recognition of the inherent dignity and of the equal and inalienable rights of all members of the human family is the foundation of freedom, justice and peace in the world,

Whereas disregard and contempt for human rights have resulted in barbarous acts which have outraged the conscience of mankind, and the advent of a world in which human beings shall enjoy freedom of speech and belief and freedom from fear and want has been proclaimed as the highest aspiration of the common people,

Whereas it is essential, if man is not to be compelled to have recourse, as a last resort, to rebellion against tyranny and oppression, that human rights should be protected by the rule of law,

Whereas it is essential to promote the development of friendly relations between nations,

Whereas the peoples of the United Nations have in the Charter reaffirmed their faith in fundamental human rights, in the dignity and worth of the human person and in the equal rights of men and women and have determined to promote social progress and better standards of life in larger freedom,

Whereas Member States have pledged themselves to achieve, in co-operation with the United Nations, the promotion of universal respect for and observance of human rights and fundamental freedoms,

Whereas a common understanding of these rights and freedoms is of the greatest importance for the full realization of this pledge,

Now, therefore,

The General Assembly

Proclaims this Universal Declaration of Human Rights as a common standard of achievement for all peoples and all nations, to the end that every individual and every organ of society, keeping this Declaration constantly in mind, shall strive by teaching and education to promote respect for these rights and freedoms and by progressive measures, national and international, to secure their universal and effective recognition and observance, both among the peoples of Member States themselves and among the peoples of territories under their jurisdiction.

Article 1

All human beings are born free and equal in dignity and rights. They are endowed with reason and conscience and should act towards one another in a spirit of brotherhood.

Article 2

Everyone is entitled to all the rights and freedoms set forth in this Declaration, without distinction of any kind, such as race, colour, sex, language, religion, political or other opinion, national or social origin, property, birth or other status.

Furthermore, no distinction shall be made on the basis of the political, jurisdictional or international status of the country or territory to which a person belongs, whether it be independent, trust, non-self-governing or under any other limitation of sovereignty.

Article 3

Everyone has the right to life, liberty and security of person.

Article 4

No one shall be held in slavery or servitude; slavery and the slave trade shall be prohibited in all their forms.

Article 5

No one shall be subjected to torture or to cruel, inhuman or degrading treatment or punishment.

Article 6

Everyone has the right to recognition everywhere as a person before the law.

Article 7

All are equal before the law and are entitled without any discrimination to equal protection of the law. All are entitled to equal protection against any discrimination in violation of this Declaration and against any incitement to such discrimination.

Article 8

Everyone has the right to an effective remedy by the competent national tribunals for acts violating the fundamental rights granted him by the constitution or by law.

Article 9

No one shall be subjected to arbitrary arrest, detention or exile.

Article 10

Everyone is entitled in full equality to a fair and public hearing by an independent and impartial tribunal, in a determination of his rights and obligations and of any criminal charge against him.

Article 11

1. Everyone charged with a penal offence has the right to be presumed innocent until proved guilty according to law in a public trial at which he has had all the guarantees necessary for his defence.

2. No one shall be held guilty of any penal offence on account of any act or omission which did not constitute a penal offence, under national or international law, at the time when it was committed. Nor shall a heavier penalty be imposed than the one that was applicable at the time the penal offence was committed.

Article 12

No one shall be subjected to arbitrary interference with his privacy, family, home or correspondence, nor to attacks upon his honour and reputation. Everyone has the right to the protection of the law against such interference or attacks.

Article 13

1. Everyone has the right to freedom of movement and residence within the borders of each state.

2. Everyone has the right to leave any country, including his own, and to return to his country.

Article 14

1. Everyone has the right to seek and to enjoy in other countries asylum from persecution.

2. This right may not be invoked in the case of prosecutions genuinely arising from non-political crimes or from acts contrary to the purposes and principles of the United Nations.

Article 15

1. Everyone has the right to a nationality.

2. No one shall be arbitrarily deprived of his nationality nor denied the right to change his nationality.

Article 16

1. Men and women of full age, without any limitation due to race, nationality or religion, have the right to marry and to found a family. They are entitled to equal rights as to marriage, during marriage and at its dissolution.

2. Marriage shall be entered into only with the free and full consent of the intending spouses.

3. The family is the natural and fundamental group unit of society and is entitled to protection by society and the State.

Article 17

1. Everyone has the right to own property alone as well as in association with others.

2. No one shall be arbitrarily deprived of his property.

Article 18

Everyone has the right to freedom of thought, conscience and religion; this right includes freedom to change his religion or belief, and freedom, either alone or in community with others and in public or private, to manifest his religion or belief in teaching, practice, worship and observance.

Article 19

Everyone has the right to freedom of opinion and expression; this right includes freedom to hold opinions without interference and to seek, receive and impart information and ideas through any media and regardless of frontiers.

Article 20

1. Everyone has the right to freedom of peaceful assembly and association.

2. No one may be compelled to belong to an association.

Article 21

1. Everyone has the right to take part in the government of his country, directly or through freely chosen representatives.

2. Everyone has the right of equal access to public service in his country.

3. The will of the people shall be the basis of the authority of government; this will shall be expressed in periodic and genuine elections which shall be by universal and equal suffrage and shall be held by secret vote or by equivalent free voting procedures.

Article 22

Everyone, as a member of society, has the right to social security and is entitled to realization, through national effort and international co-operation and in accordance with the organization and resources of each state, of the economic, social and cultural rights indispensable for his dignity and the free development of his personality.

Article 23

1. Everyone has the right to work, to free choice of employment, to just and favourable conditions of work and to protection against unemployment.

2. Everyone, without any discrimination, has the right to equal pay for equal work.

3. Everyone who works has the right to just and favourable remuneration ensuring for himself and his family an existence worthy of human dignity, and supplemented, if necessary, by other means of social protection.

4. Everyone has the right to form and to join trade unions for the protection of his interests.

Article 24

Everyone has the right to rest and leisure, including reasonable limitation of working hours and periodic holidays with pay.

Article 25

1. Everyone has the right to a standard of living adequate for the health and well-being of himself and of his family, including food, clothing, housing and medical care and necessary social services, and the right to security in the event of unemployment, sickness, disability, widowhood, old age or other lack of livelihood in circumstances beyond his control.

2. Motherhood and childhood are entitled to special care and assistance. All children, whether born in or out of wedlock, shall enjoy the same social protection.

Article 26

1. Everyone has the right to education. Education shall be free, at least in the elementary and fundamental stages. Elementary education shall be compulsory. Technical and professional education shall be made generally available and higher education shall be equally accessible to all on the basis of merit.

2. Education shall be directed to the full development of the human personality and to the strengthening of respect for human rights and fundamental freedoms. It shall promote understanding, tolerance and friendship among all nations, racial or religious groups, and shall further the activities of the United Nations for the maintenance of peace.

3. Parents have a prior right to choose the kind of education that shall be given to their children.

Article 27

1. Everyone has the right freely to participate in the cultural life of the community, to enjoy the arts and to share in scientific advancement and its benefits.

2. Everyone has the right to the protection of the moral and material interests resulting from any scientific, literary or artistic production of which he is the author.

Article 28

Everyone is entitled to a social and international order in which the rights and freedoms set forth in this Declaration can be fully realized.

Article 29

1. Everyone has duties to the community in which alone the free and full development of his personality is possible.

2. In the exercise of his rights and freedoms, everyone shall be subject only to such limitations as are determined by law solely for the purpose of securing due recognition and respect for the rights and freedoms of others and of meeting the just requirements of morality, public order and the general welfare in a democratic society.

3. These rights and freedoms may in no case be exercised contrary to the purposes and principles of the United Nations.

Article 30

Nothing in this Declaration may be interpreted as implying for any state, group or person any right to engage in any activity or to perform any act aimed at the destruction of any of the rights and freedoms set forth herein.

UNITED NATIONS REGIONAL COMMISSIONS

Economic Commission for Europe—ECE

Address: Palais des Nations, 1211 Geneva 10, Switzerland.

Telephone: 229174444; **fax:** 229170505; **e-mail:** info.ece@unece.org; **internet:** www.unece.org.

The UN Economic Commission for Europe (ECE) was established in 1947 and was, with ECAFE (now ESCAP), the earliest of the five regional economic commissions set up by the UN Economic and Social Council (ECOSOC). The Commission promotes pan-European and transatlantic economic integration. It provides a multilateral forum for dialogue and co-operation on economic and sectoral issues for governments from European countries, as well as central Asian republics, the USA, Canada and Israel. It provides analysis, policy advice and assistance to governments, gives focus to UN global mandates on economic issues, and establishes norms, standards and conventions to facilitate international co-operation within and outside the region.

MEMBERS

Albania
Andorra
Armenia
Austria
Azerbaijan
Belarus
Belgium
Bosnia and Herzegovina
Bulgaria
Canada
Croatia
Cyprus
Czech Republic
Denmark
Estonia
Finland
France
Georgia
Germany
Greece
Hungary
Iceland
Ireland
Israel
Italy
Kazakhstan
Kyrgyzstan
Latvia
Liechtenstein
Lithuania
Luxembourg
Macedonia, former Yugoslav republic
Malta
Moldova
Monaco
Montenegro
Netherlands
Norway
Poland
Portugal
Romania
Russia
San Marino
Serbia
Slovakia
Slovenia
Spain
Sweden
Switzerland
Tajikistan
Turkey
Turkmenistan
Ukraine
United Kingdom
USA
Uzbekistan

Organization

(June 2012)

COMMISSION

The Commission, the highest decision-making body of the organization, holds biennial formal sessions in Geneva to review the economic situation and decide on activities for the coming two years. The 64th session was held in March 2011. As well as taking strategic decisions the Commission provides a forum for senior-level dialogue on regional economic development policy.

EXECUTIVE COMMITTEE

The Executive Committee prepares the formal sessions of the Commission, implements the decisions of the Commission, and acts on behalf of the Commission between the sessions of that body. The Executive Committee also reviews and approves the programmes of work of the sectoral committees, which report at least once a year to the Executive Committee.

SECRETARIAT

The Secretariat services the meetings of the Commission and its sectoral committees and publishes periodic surveys and reviews, including a number of specialized statistical bulletins (see list of publications below). The Executive Secretary carries out secretarial functions for the executive bodies of several regional conventions and their protocols (see below).

Executive Secretary: SVEN ALKALAJ (Bosnia and Herzegovina).

SECTORAL COMMITTEES

Committee on Economic Co-operation and Integration;
Committee on Environmental Policy;
Committee on Housing and Land Management;
Committee on Inland Transport;
Committee on Sustainable Energy;
Committee on Timber;
Committee on Trade;
Conference of European Statisticians.

Activities

ECE's original purpose, when it was established by ECOSOC in 1947, was to give effective aid to the countries devastated by the Second World War. It was granted permanent status in 1951. During the 'cold war' period it served as the only major instrument of economic dialogue and co-operation linking the communist countries of central and eastern Europe with the countries of western Europe, and achieved the harmonization of a number of aspects of transport and trade, such as road signs, safety and anti-pollution standards for motor vehicles, standards for the transport of perishable or dangerous goods, and agreements on customs procedures. During the 1990s, when political changes in central and eastern Europe had allowed countries there to undergo transition from a centrally planned economy to a market economy, ECE adopted the role of assisting these countries, including the newly independent countries that had formerly been part of the USSR and Yugoslavia, and it extended its activities to the central Asian countries, which became members of both ECE and ESCAP.

The guiding principle of ECE activities is the promotion of sustainable economic growth among its member countries. To this end it provides a forum for communication among states; negotiates international legal instruments concerning trade, transport and the environment; and supplies statistics and economic and environmental analysis. The implications for ECE of the enlargement of the European Union (EU) and ongoing developments in member states with economies in transition, generated significant debate during the mid-2000s on the future direction of the Commission's work. The 59th session of ECE, convened in February 2004, commissioned a comprehensive, external evaluation of the state of ECE. The report, which was published in June 2005, included the following recommendations: more effective governance and management of the Commission, including restructuring work divisions and sub-programmes and identifying specialized areas of competence; raising the political profile of the Commission; co-ordinating the regional implementation of the UN Millennium Development Goals (MDGs); improving co-operation with other organizations, in particular a partnership with UNDP and with other regional commissions; and strengthening the participation of the private sector and non-governmental organizations in the Commission. Greater priority was to be given to the environment and transport, and to the specific problems affecting countries with economies in transition. The 61st session of ECE, convened in December 2005, adopted the resulting Work Plan on ECE Reform. The reform process was reviewed by the Commission in 2009. The 64th session of ECE, held in March 2011, focused on the Commission's role in promoting pan-European economic integration, addressing in particular the regional transport and trade infrastructure, and energy co-operation.

Economic Co-operation and Integration: The programme on Economic Co-operation and Integration, which is implemented by the Committee on Economic Co-operation and Integration, has the following thematic focuses: strengthening the competitiveness of member states' economies by promoting the knowledge-based economy and innovation; facilitating the development of entrepreneurship and the emergence of new enterprises; facilitating effective regulatory policies and corporate governance, including those in the financial sector; promoting public-private partnerships for domestic and foreign investment; maintaining intellectual property rights; and other relevant aspects of international economic co-operation and integration. At its inaugural session in September 2006 the Committee adopted a programme of work and established three teams of specialists, on innovation and competitiveness policies, on intellectual property, and on public-private partnerships (PPPs), which support programme implementation in these thematic areas. The third session of the Committee, held in December 2008, determined to enhance the practical dimension of its work, in particular the capacity-building activities in transition economies. In April 2011 it was announced that an International Centre of Excellence on PPPs was to be established in Geneva, under the aegis of ECE. Since 2006 ECE has hosted, jointly with the World Bank Institute and the Asian Development Bank, an annual global meeting, 'PPP Days', of PPP practitioners and experts. The theme of the 2012 meeting, held in February, in Geneva, was 'Strengthening institutions and frameworks for better PPP delivery'.

The UN Special Programme for the Economies of Central Asia (SPECA), begun in 1998, is implemented jointly by ECE and ESCAP: SPECA helps the participating countries to strengthen regional co-operation, particularly in the areas of water resources, energy and transport, and creates incentives for economic development and integration into the economies of Asia and Europe. The establishment of a joint UNECE-ESCAP SPECA Regional Office in Central Asia is under consideration. ECE also provides technical assistance to the Southeast European Co-operative Initiative.

Environment: ECE facilitates and promotes co-operation among member governments in developing and implementing policies for environmental protection, the rational use of natural resources, and sustainable development. It supports the integration of environmental policy into sectoral policies, seeks solutions to environmental problems, particularly those of a transboundary nature, and assists in strengthening environmental management capabilities, particularly in countries in transition. A programme of Environmental Performance Review helps individual countries to improve the effectiveness of environmental management and policies. The Committee on Environmental Policy brings governments together to formulate policy and provides a forum for the exchange of experience and good practices. It facilitates and prepares the Environment for Europe process, the focus of which is a ministerial-level conference normally held every four years (the 2011 meeting was held in September, in Astana, Kazakhstan, addressing two main themes: 'Sustainable Management of Water and Water-related Ecosystems' and 'Greening the Economy: Mainstreaming the Environment into Economic Development'). ECE also supports a Pan-European Programme (PEP) on transport, health and the environment, and sponsors a programme co-ordinating efforts to develop education for sustainable development in the ECE region. ECE has negotiated five environmental conventions, for which it serves as the secretariat: the Convention on Long-range Transboundary Air Pollution (the LRTAP, which entered into force in 1983 and has been extended by eight protocols); the Convention on the Protection and Use of Transboundary Watercourses and International Lakes (also known as the Water Convention, 1996, two protocols); the Convention on Environmental Impact Assessment in a Transboundary Context (Espoo Convention, 1997, one protocol, which entered into force in July 2010); the Convention on the Transboundary Effects of Industrial Accidents (2000, one protocol) and the Convention on Access to Information, Public Participation in Decision-making and Access to Justice in Environmental Matters (Aarhus Convention, 2001). A Protocol (to the Aarhus Convention) on Pollutant Release and Transfer Registers (PRTRs), which was adopted in May 2003, entered into force in October 2009. All UN member states are encouraged to accede to the Protocol. In July 2011 the meeting of the parties to the Aarhus Convention determined to encourage accession to the Convention, also, by states outside the ECE region. An amendment to extend the Water Convention to extra-regional members, adopted in 2003, was reviewed by a strategic workshop in February 2012, and had, by June, been ratified by 22 parties. Within the context of the amendment, in December 2011 ECE organized a high-level conference to promote greater co-operation between European and Asian countries in the management and protection of transboundary waters. In February 2012 the legal board of the Water Convention agreed proposals to establish an implementation committee, which would be presented to the meeting of parties to the Convention, scheduled to convene in November. In May 2012 amendments were adopted to the LRTAP's Gothenburg Protocol to Abate Acidification, Eutrophication and Ground-level Ozone that incorporated national emission reduction commitments to be attained by 2020 for main air pollutants, including 'fine particulate matter'.

In June 2011 parties to the Espoo Convention issued a caution against Ukraine—the first ever such caution—for non-compliance with its obligations under the Convention, in relation to alleged environmental damage caused to the ecosystem of the Danube delta (a UNESCO World Heritage Site) by the ongoing Bystroe (Bâstroe) channel project, which aims to provide a deep-water route linking the Danube and the Black Sea.

Forestry and Timber: ECE's Timber Committee works closely, through an integrated programme, with the European Forestry Commission of the FAO to promote sustainable forest management. It compiles data and analyses long-term trends and prospects for forestry and timber; keeps under review developments in the forest industries, including environmental and energy-related aspects; and publishes an annual market review of forest products. The Committee meets annually to review the programme, as well as to discuss policy and market trends and outlook. Assistance in the form of workshops and expert advice is provided to help countries that are undergoing economic transition to develop their forestry sectors. A strategic plan for the period 2008–13 was approved at a joint meeting of the Committee and the FAO Commission in October 2008, convened to coincide with events organized within the framework of European Forest Week. In March 2010 ECE and FAO launched a study of the state of forests and forestry management in Europe; the results were collated in the 2011 edition of the *State of Europe's Forests*, which was issued in June of that year.

Housing, Land Management and Population: The Committee organizes sub-regional workshops and seminars, and provides policy advice in the form of country profiles on the housing sector and land administration reviews, undertaken by experts. The Committee works to improve housing conditions as well as spatial planning and land administration policy. In particular, it promotes the provision of adequate housing, both in the Eastern European countries undergoing socio-economic transition and in deprived neighbourhoods in Western Europe. The Committee and its Working Party on Land Administration prepare guidance on urban renewal, condominium management, housing finance, land administration, social housing and energy efficiency in housing. The Committee organizes sub-regional workshops and seminars, and provides policy advice, through its country profiles on the housing sector and land administration reviews, which are prepared by teams of experts. In 2008 the Real Estate Market Advisory Group was established to support the Working Party on Land Administration's activities and to help structure a sustainable housing market. In April 2011 ECE published an Action Plan for Energy Efficient Housing in the UNECE Region, aimed at introducing institutional, technological and cultural changes needed to improve energy efficiency in the housing sector.

ECE tracks demographic and societal change through its Population Unit. The Generations and Gender Programme, initiated in 2000, works to improve the knowledge base for policy-making in ECE countries. In November 2007 ECE organized a Conference on Ageing to discuss the implications of regional fertility rates that had fallen below replacement level. A conference of experts and policy-makers, held in Geneva, in May 2008, examined the causes and consequences of demographic change. A new Working Group on Ageing was established, and convened for its inaugural meeting in December, to undertake a programme of action to counter the challenges of ageing societies. A Ministerial Conference on Ageing, on the theme of 'Ensuring a society for all ages' was scheduled to be held, in Vienna, Austria, in September 2012.

Statistics: The Conference of European Statisticians (CES) and ECE's Statistical Division have the task of co-ordinating international statistical activities in the region, by reviewing the most topical statistical areas, identifying gaps and duplication, and looking for issues not hitherto addressed. The CES plenary sessions and seminars offer a forum for senior statisticians, often leading to work in new areas and the preparation of new standards and recommendations. The CES and the Statistical Division work to develop methodology in compiling and disseminating economic, social and demographic statistics, for example in harmonizing methods of compiling gross domestic product, national accounts and other economic indicators; measuring the distorting effect of globalization on national statistical systems; and finding sound methods of measuring sustainable development. The Division helps countries, especially those undergoing economic transition, to improve their statistical systems in accordance with the UN Fundamental Principles of Official Statistics, by advising on legislation and institutions and on how to ensure the independence and impartiality of official statistics. It maintains an online statistical database, allowing comparison of major economic and social indicators, and publishes guidelines on the editing of statistical data.

Sustainable Energy: Through its Committee on Sustainable Energy, subsidiary bodies and projects, ECE's sub-programme on sustainable energy works to promote a sustainable energy development strategy for the region, with the following objectives: sustained access to high quality energy services for all individuals in the ECE region; security of energy supplies in the short, medium and long term; facilitating the transition to a more sustainable energy future and reducing health and environmental impacts resulting from the production, transport and use of energy; promoting well-balanced energy network systems across the region, tailored to optimize operating efficiencies and overall regional co-operation; ensuring sustained improvements in energy efficiency, in production and use, particularly in countries with economies in transition; and, in the context of post-EU enlargement, integrating energy restructuring, legal, regulatory and energy pricing reforms, as well as the social dimension, into energy policy making. Activities include labelling classification systems and related legal and policy frameworks; liberalization of energy markets, pricing policies and supply security; harmonization of energy policies and practices; rational use of energy, efficiency and conservation; energy infrastructure, including interconnection of gas networks; cleaner electricity production from coal and other fossil fuels; the Energy Efficiency 21 Project (GEE21, the first meeting of which was convened in July 2009); the promotion and development—through the UNECE Gas Centre programme—of a market-based gas industry in countries with economies in transition; and providing technical assistance and operational activities in energy to countries with economies in transition. In December 2011 ECE convened a regional preparatory meeting for the United Nations Conference on Sustainable Development (the so-called 'Rio+20' conference), which was held in June 2012.

Trade: ECE's Committee on Trade aims to focus on the facilitation of international trade by means of simpler and better-integrated trade procedures, electronic business methods, common agricultural quality standards, and the harmonization of technical regulations. The Committee works closely with other organizations, and provides a forum for dialogue between the public and the private sector. The UN Centre for Trade Facilitation and Electronic Business (UN/CEFACT, established in 2002 as part of ECE) works to reduce delays and costs in international transactions by simplifying procedures. ECE's Working Party on Agricultural Quality Standards develops and updates commercial quality standards for fruit, vegetables and other agricultural products, in co-operation with OECD, and promotes the application of these standards through regional seminars and workshops. The Working Party on Regulatory Co-operation and Standardization Policies aims to harmonize product regulations and standards, the diversity of which can seriously impede trade. It has developed an international model for technical harmonization to assist countries wishing to standardize their rules on specific products or sectors. In December 2011 the ECE Executive Committee established a new group of experts, within the Working Party, to develop a set of recommendations on the application of risk management to regulatory work. ECE's Advisory Group on Market Surveillance aims to combat the proliferation of counterfeit and pirated goods.

In December 2011 ECE hosted a Global Trade Facilitation Conference, organized by the five UN regional commissions, which requested the commissions prepare a roadmap to develop and enhance 'Single Window' facilities and information exchange in global supply chains.

Transport: ECE aims to promote a coherent, efficient, safe and sustainable transport system through the development of international agreements, conventions, norms and standards relating to road, rail, inland water and combined transport. These international legal instruments, which are developed by specialized intergovernmental working parties with participation from, among others, transport equipment manufacturers, consumers and road users, include measures for improving vehicle safety and limiting vehicle emissions, simplifying border crossing procedures, improving road traffic safety, setting the conditions for developing coherent infrastructure networks, and providing for the safe transport of dangerous goods. One of the working groups, the World Forum for Harmonization of Vehicle Regulations, has global participation. In January 2012 ECE's Working Party on Pollution and Energy adopted proposals to amend regulations on the emissions requirements of heavy duty vehicles. The proposals were to be presented to the World Forum for Harmonization of Vehicle Regulations in June for final approval. ECE addresses transport trends and economics and compiles transport statistics, and provides a forum for the exchange of technical and legal expertise in the field of inland transport. In 2005, a Master Plan was elaborated for investment in the Trans-European Motorway (TEM) and the Trans-European Railway (TER) projects, with the aim of improving the road and rail networks in 21 central, eastern and south-eastern European countries. A revision of the Master Plan was adopted in 2007. In July 2009 ECE signed an agreement with Slovakia to host the central project office of the TER initiative. In April 2010 the national co-ordinators for the TEM and TER projects in 13 countries adopted a new Innsbruck Initiative for safe, secure, prosperous and environmentally friendly transport. Objectives of the Innsbruck Initiative, which were to be incorporated into the TEM and TER work plans for 2011–15, included: the development of transport infrastructure to improve safety, environmental performance and security; encouraging measures conducive to secure and safe transport, and promoting the proper design of transport infrastructure; supporting interoperability between transport modes, intermodal connections and combined transport systems; and promoting the introduction of Intelligent Transport Systems, with a particular focus on increasing transport safety and security, and minimizing traffic congestion and air pollution. Another project, undertaken jointly with ESCAP, aims to develop Euro-Asian transport links. In February 2008 ECE established a Group of Experts on Hinterland Connections of Seaports to study the effectiveness of existing container management and inland transport connections with seaports, and to compile a set of recommendations. In conjunction with the European Office of WHO ECE administers a Transport, Health and Environment Pan-European Programme, which aims to promote sustainable transport policies and systems. A Conference on Improving Road Safety in South-Eastern Europe, organized by ECE, was held in Halkida, Greece, in June 2009. ECE and the other UN regional commissions were to play a key role in implementing the UN Decade of Action for Road Safety, covering 2011–20, which aimed to reduce the rate of road fatalities.

Finance

The proposed appropriation for ECE's regular budget in 2012–13 was US $65.2m.

Publications

UNECE Report (annually).

UNECE Weekly.

UNECE Compendium of Legal Instruments, Norms and Standards.

UNECE Countries in Figures.

Report of the Conference of European Statisticians (annually).

Trade Promotion Directory (annually).

For its different areas of activity ECE produces statistical bulletins, reports, performance reviews, country profiles, standards, agreements, recommendations, discussion papers, guidelines and manuals.

Economic and Social Commission for Asia and the Pacific—ESCAP

Address: United Nations Bldg, Rajadamnern Nok Ave, Bangkok 10200, Thailand.

Telephone: (2) 288-1234; **fax:** (2) 288-1000; **e-mail:** unisbkk .unescap@un.org; **internet:** www.unescap.org.

The Commission was founded in 1947, at first to assist in post-war reconstruction, and subsequently to encourage the economic and social development of Asia and the Far East; it was originally known as the Economic Commission for Asia and the Far East (ECAFE). The title ESCAP, which replaced ECAFE, was adopted after a reorganization in 1974. ESCAP's main objectives are to promote inclusive and sustainable economic and social development in Asia and the Pacific, and to help member countries to achieve internationally agreed development goals.

MEMBERS

Afghanistan
Armenia
Australia
Azerbaijan
Bangladesh
Bhutan
Brunei
Cambodia
China, People's Republic
Fiji
France
Georgia
India
Indonesia
Iran
Japan
Kazakhstan
Kiribati
Korea, Democratic People's Republic
Korea, Republic
Kyrgyzstan
Laos
Malaysia
The Maldives
Marshall Islands
Micronesia, Federated States
Mongolia
Myanmar
Nauru
Nepal
Netherlands
New Zealand
Pakistan
Palau
Papua New Guinea
Philippines
Russia
Samoa
Singapore
Solomon Islands
Sri Lanka
Tajikistan
Thailand
Timor-Leste
Tonga
Turkey
Turkmenistan
Tuvalu
United Kingdom
USA
Uzbekistan
Vanuatu
Viet Nam

ASSOCIATE MEMBERS

American Samoa
Cook Islands
French Polynesia
Guam
Hong Kong
Macao
New Caledonia
Niue
Northern Mariana Islands

Organization

(June 2012)

COMMISSION

The main legislative organ of ESCAP is the Commission, which meets annually at ministerial level to examine the region's problems, to review progress, to establish priorities and to decide upon the recommendations of the Executive Secretary or the subsidiary bodies of the Commission. It reports to the UN Economic and Social Council (ECOSOC). Ministerial and intergovernmental conferences on specific issues may be held on an ad hoc basis with the approval of the Commission, although no more than one ministerial conference and five intergovernmental conferences may be held during one year.

COMMITTEES AND SPECIAL BODIES

Specialized committees and special bodies have been established to advise the Commission and help to oversee the work of the Secretariat. They meet every two years, while any sub-committees meet in the intervening years. There are Committees on Macroeconomic Policy, Poverty Reduction and Inclusive Development; Trade and Investment; Transport; Environment and Development; Information and Communications Technology; Disaster Risk Reduction; Social Development; and Statistics. The two special bodies cover Least Developed and Landlocked Developing Countries; and Pacific Island Developing Countries.

In addition, an Advisory Committee of permanent representatives and other representatives designated by members of the Commission functions as an advisory body; it generally meets every month.

SECRETARIAT

The Secretariat operates under the guidance of the Commission and its subsidiary bodies. It consists of the Office of the Executive Secretary and two servicing divisions, covering administration and programme management, in addition to the following substantive divisions: Environment and Development; Information and Communications Technology and Disaster Risk Reduction; Macroeconomic Policy and Development; Social Development; Statistics; Trade and Investment; and Transport.

Executive Secretary: Noeleen Heyzer (Singapore).

SUB-REGIONAL OFFICES

ESCAP Pacific Operations Centre (EPOC): Private Mail Bag, Suva, Fiji; tel. 3319669; fax 3319671; e-mail epoc@un.org; internet www.unescap.org/epoc; f. 1984, relocated to Fiji 2005; responsible for ESCAP's sub-programme on Development of Pacific Island Countries and Territories; assists Pacific island governments in forming and implementing national sustainable development strategies, particularly poverty reduction programmes that create access to services by socially vulnerable groups; conducts research, promotes regional co-operation and knowledge-sharing, and provides advisory services, training and pilot projects; Dir Iosefa Maiava (Samoa).

Sub-Regional Office for East and North-East Asia: Meet-you-all Tower, 17th Floor, Techno Park, 7-50 Songdo-dong, Yeonsu-gu, Incheon, Republic of Korea; tel. (32) 458-6601; fax (32) 458-6699; e-mail vanlaere@un.org; f. 2010; covers activities in the People's Republic of China, Japan, the Democratic People's Republic of Korea, the Republic of Korea, Mongolia and Russia; Dir Kilaparti Ramakrishna.

Sub-regional Office for South and South-West Asia: Qutab Institutional Area, C-2, POB 4575, New Delhi 110 016, India; tel. (11) 309737100; f. 2011; serves Afghanistan, Bangladesh, Bhutan, India, Iran, Maldives, Nepal, Pakistan, Sri Lanka and Turkey; Dir Dr Nagesh Kumar (Samoa).

In May 2011 an agreement was signed to establish a Sub-Regional Office for North and Central Asia, in Almatı, Kazakhstan.

Activities

ESCAP acts as a UN regional centre, providing the only intergovernmental forum that includes the whole of Asia and the Pacific, and executing a wide range of development programmes through technical assistance, advisory services to governments, research, training and information. In May 2002, having considered the recommendations of an intergovernmental review meeting held in March, ESCAP determined to implement a restructuring of its structures and thematic priorities. Three main thematic programmes were identified: poverty reduction; managing globalization; and emerging social issues. In May 2007 the Commission, meeting in Almatı, Kazakhstan, commemorated the 60th anniversary of ESCAP and reaffirmed its central role in fostering regional and sub-regional co-operation. In April 2008 the Commission approved a new conference structure and requested a reorganization of the Secretariat in order to reflect the new structure and programme of work for the two years 2010–11.

Social Development: ESCAP's Social Development Division, formerly the Emerging Social Issues Division, comprises three sections: Social Protection and Integration; Social Policy and Population; and Gender Equality. The Division's main objective is to assess and respond to regional trends and challenges in social development, and to help member countries to build more inclusive societies, through social and financial policies and measures promoting social protection, social inclusion, gender equality and development. The Social Protection and Integration Section aims to strengthen the capacity of public and non-government institutions to address the problems of marginalized social groups and to promote initiatives to provide income to the poor. The Gender Equality Section promotes the advancement of women by helping to improve their access to education, economic resources, information and communication technologies and decision-making; it is also committed to combating violence against women, including trafficking. The Social Policy and Population Section focuses on issues concerning ageing, youth, disability, migration and population. Activities include providing technical assistance to national population programmes, promoting the rights of people with disabilities, supporting improvement of access to social services by poor people, and helping governments to form policies that take into account the increasing proportion of older people in the population. ESCAP chairs the UN Interagency Group on Youth, which was established to promote implementation of the World Programme of Action on Youth, UN Millennium Development Goals (MDGs) relating to young people, and events concerning the International Year of Youth (2010–11).

The Division implements global and regional mandates, such as the Programme of Action of the World Summit for Social Development and the Jakarta Plan of Action on Human Resources Development. The Biwako Millennium Framework for Action towards an Inclusive, Barrier-free and Rights-based Society for Persons with Disabilities in Asia and the Pacific was adopted by ESCAP as a regional guideline underpinning the Asian and Pacific Decade of Disabled Persons (2003–12). In 1998 ESCAP initiated a programme of assistance in establishing a regional network of Social Development Management Information Systems (SOMIS). ESCAP collaborated with other agencies towards the adoption, in November 2001, of a Regional Platform on Sustainable Development for Asia and the Pacific. The Commission undertook regional preparations for the World Summit on Sustainable Development, which was held in Johannesburg, South Africa, in August–September 2002. In following up the summit ESCAP undertook to develop a biodiversity park, which was officially inaugurated in Rawalpindi, Pakistan, in January 2005. The Commission also prepares specific publications relating to population and implements the Programme of Action of the International Conference on Population and Development. The Secretariat co-ordinates the Asia-Pacific Population Information Network (POPIN). The fifth Asia and Pacific Population Conference, sponsored by ESCAP, was held in Bangkok, Thailand, in December 2002. Expert group meetings to assess implementation of the Plan of Action on Population and Poverty adopted at the Conference were held in November 2005 and in February 2009. In September 2004 ESCAP convened a senior-level intergovernmental meeting on the regional review and implementation of the Beijing Platform for Action (Beijing + 10), relating to gender equality. A further intergovernmental review meeting, Beijing + 15, was hosted by ESCAP in November 2009. In September 2011 ESCAP hosted the inaugural meeting of an Asia-Pacific Regional Advisory Group on Women, Peace and Security, which was established in the previous year to support the effective implementation throughout the region of UN Security Council Resolution 1325 relating to the impact of conflict on women and girls and their role in peace-building. The 67th Commission, meeting in Bangkok, in May 2011, pledged commitment to protecting the poor and vulnerable sectors of the region's population from the aftershocks of economic and natural crises. In February 2012 ESCAP hosted a high-level intergovernmental meeting which endorsed an action plan towards greater regional co-operation in achieving global commitments to address and eliminate HIV/AIDS.

Environment and Development: ESCAP is concerned with strengthening national capabilities to achieve environmentally sound and sustainable development by integrating economic concerns, such as the sustainable management of natural resources, into economic planning and policies. The Environment and Development Division comprises sections on Energy Security, Environment and Development Policy, and Water Security. Activities include the promotion of integrated water resources development and management, including water quality and conservation and a reduction in water-related natural disasters; strengthening the formulation of policies in the sustainable development of land and mineral resources; and the consideration of energy resource options, such as rural energy supply, energy conservation and the planning of power networks. The Division administers a North-East Asia Sub-regional Programme for Environmental Co-operation (NEASPEC). Through the Division ESCAP prepares a report entitled *State of the Environment in Asia and the Pacific* which is published at five-yearly intervals. ESCAP helps to organize a ministerial conference on environment and development, also convened every five years. The Division received a mandate from the ministerial commission held in 2005 to work on issues related to climate change caused by global warming: it collates information, conducts regional seminars on adapting to climate change, and provides training in clean technology and guidance on reduction of harmful gas emissions. In March 2008 ESCAP organized an inaugural meeting of the Asia-Pacific Regional Platform on Climate Change and Development. In the following month ESCAP organized the first Asia-Pacific Mayors' Forum on Environmentally Sustainable Urban Infrastructure Development, convened in Ulsan, Republic of Korea (South Korea). In June 2011 ESCAP hosted an Asia-Pacific Urban Forum, in Bangkok, which was convened on the theme 'Cities of opportunity: Partnerships for an inclusive and sustainable future'. In September an expert group meeting on sustainable energy development in Asia and the Pacific, organized by ESCAP, UNDP, UNIDO and FAO, focused on the need for developing national policies in the region aimed at ensuring universal access to clean and efficient energy services, as a means of advancing poverty reduction and improving health and well-being.

In May 2010 the 66th Commission, convened in Incheon, South Korea, adopted a Declaration urging countries to strengthen and adopt 'green growth' strategies, in order to support recovery from the global economic and financial crisis and to achieve sustainable economic and social development. The sixth ministerial conference on environment and development, convened in Astana, Kazakhstan, in September–October, adopted a Ministerial Declaration on Green Growth, committing member countries to promoting environmentally sustainable economic growth and development. The conference also adopted a Regional Implementation Plan for Sustainable Development in Asia and the Pacific, covering the period 2011–15, and a Green Bridge Initiative to promote environmental partnerships and co-operation between Europe and Asia. In February 2012 ESCAP's Committee on Environment and Development endorsed the so-called 'Seoul Outcome', which was concluded in October 2011 by the Asia-Pacific Regional Preparatory Meeting, held in South Korea, for the UN Conference on Sustainable Development ('Rio+20'—convened in June 2012, in Rio de Janeiro, Brazil). The Committee also undertook to review regional priorities and commitments to sustainable growth in advance of Rio+20. In late May 2012 ESCAP's Executive Secretary proposed a 'Call for Action on Sustainable Development' to media organizations, urging these to generate greater impact for sustainable development issues.

Information and Communications Technology and Disaster Risk Reduction: ESCAP's Information and Communications Technology (ICT) and Disaster Risk Reduction Division comprises the following sections: ICT and Development; Disaster Risk Reduction; and Space Technology Applications. The Division aims to strengthen capacity for access to and the application of ICT and space technology, in order to enhance socio-economic development and maximize the benefits of globalization. It supports the development of cross-sectoral policies and strategies, and also supports regional co-operation aimed at sharing knowledge between advanced and developing economies and in areas such as cyber-crime and information security. In May 2005 the Commission approved the establishment, in South Korea, of the Asian and Pacific Training Centre for ICT for Development (APCICT); APCICT was inaugurated in June 2006 (see below). In June 2005 the Division convened a senior-level meeting of experts to consider technical issues relating to disaster management and mitigation in Asia and the Pacific. The Division organized several conferences in preparation for the second phase of the World Summit on the Information Society (WSIS), which took place in November, and co-ordinates regional activities aimed at achieving WSIS targets for the widespread use of ICT by 2015. It helps members to include space technology in their development planning, for example the use of satellites in meteorology, disaster prevention, remote sensing and distance learning. In August 2007 the Division hosted an international meeting on the use of space technology to combat avian influenza and other infectious diseases. A meeting of national policy-makers on disaster management was convened in March 2008 to discuss access to satellite information as a means of predicting and managing natural disasters. In September 2010 an agreement was reached to establish a Regional Co-operative Mechanism on Disaster Monitoring and Early Warning, Particularly Drought. An expert group meeting to consider priority areas for the mechanism was convened in Beijing, People's Republic of China, in March 2011.

The Division's policy with relation to disaster risk reduction is guided by the Hyogo Framework for Action, covering the period 2005–15, which was adopted by the World Conference on Disaster Reduction, held in Kobe, Hyogo, Japan, in January 2005. The accompanying Declaration, adopted by the Conference, emphasized the need to develop and strengthen regional strategies and operational mechanisms in order to ensure rapid and effective disaster response. A new Committee on Disaster Risk Reduction convened for an inaugural session in March 2009; participants agreed to strengthen information and knowledge-sharing in relation to risk reduction. During 2010 ESCAP worked with the International Strategy for Disaster Reduction to produce an *Asia and Pacific Disaster Report*, which was published in October. Following the massive earthquake and consequent devastating sea movements (tsunami) that occurred in late December 2004 in the Indian Ocean, ESCAP assisted other UN and international agencies with an initial emergency response and undertook early reviews of the impact of the event. In January 2005 the Executive Secretary appointed a Task Force on Tsunami Disaster Management to assist countries to address issues relating to natural disaster management, and to raise those issues at a regional level. The chairman of the Task Force was also appointed co-chair of an Inter-Agency Regional Task Force on Tsunami Relief and Rehabilitation that was established at a heads of agency meeting, convened by ESCAP later in that month, with particular responsibility to exchange information relating to rehabilitation and reconstruction in the aftermath of the tsunami disaster and to more general capacity-building on disaster preparedness. ESCAP administers the voluntary, multi-donor trust fund that was inaugurated in late 2005 to assist reconstruction, and to support national and regional efforts to develop a tsunami early-warning system: the Regional Integrated Multi-Hazard Early Warning System for Africa and Asia (RIMES). In March 2011 ESCAP and the government of Thailand, the founding donor of the Fund, signed an agreement to expand the mandate of the Fund and rename it as the Multi-Donor Trust Fund for Tsunami, Disaster and Climate Preparedness in Indian Ocean and Southeast Asian Countries. In June 2012 the first ministerial conference on RIMES, meeting in New Delhi, India, determined to develop a financial mechanism to finance the System. In 2011, in May and December, ESCAP helped to organise expert meetings to consider the experiences of the tsunami and earthquake in Japan, in March of that year, and observe lessons for regional disaster preparedness. In February 2012 ESCAP hosted a forum to reflect on the experiences of the extensive flooding which caused large-scale economic and humanitarian devastation in parts of Southeast Asia in 2011.

Macroeconomic Policy and Development: The work of the Division, formerly the Poverty and Development Division, is undertaken by the following sections: Development Policy, and Macroeconomic Policy and Analysis. The Division aims to increase the understanding of the economic and social development situation in the region, with particular attention given to the attainment of the MDGs, sustainable economic growth, poverty alleviation, the integration of environmental concerns into macroeconomic decisions and policy-making processes, and enhancing the position of the region's disadvantaged economies, including those Central Asian countries undergoing transition from a centrally-planned economy to a market economy. The Division is responsible for the provision of technical assistance, and the production of relevant documents and publications. It publishes the *Economic and Social Survey of Asia and the Pacific*. The 63rd Commission, meeting in Almatı, Kazakhstan, in May 2007, endorsed a regional plan, developed by ESCAP, UNDP and the Asian Development Bank, to help poorer member countries to achieve the MDGs. Assistance was to be provided in the following areas: knowledge and capacity-building; expertise; resources; advocacy; and regional co-operation in delivering public goods (including infrastructure and energy security). The Commission also approved a resolution urging greater investment in health care in all member countries. In 2009 the Macroeconomic Policy and Development Division co-ordinated the preparation of a joint report of all five UN Regional Commissions, entitled *The Global Economic and Financial Crisis: Regional Impacts, Responses and Solutions*, which was published in May. In February 2010 a regional report on achieving the MDGs acknowledged the impact of the crisis and highlighted the need to strengthen social protection throughout the region. In December 2011 ESCAP hosted a meeting of senior officials to address the implementation of the Istanbul Programme of Action for the Least Developed Countries for the Decade 2011–20 in the Asia-Pacific region.

Statistics: ESCAP's Statistics Division provides training and advice in priority areas, including national accounts statistics, poverty indicators, gender statistics, population censuses and surveys, and the strengthening and management of statistical systems. It supports co-ordination throughout the region of the development, implementation and revision of selected international statistical standards, and, in particular, co-ordinates the International Comparison Programme (ICP) for Asia and the Pacific (part of a global ICP initiative). The Division disseminates comparable socio-economic statistics, with increased use of the electronic media, promotes the use of modern technology in the public sector and trains senior-level officials in the effective management of ICT. Training is provided by the Statistical Institute for Asia and the Pacific (see below).

Trade and Investment: ESCAP aims to help members to benefit from globalization by increasing global and regional flows of trade and investment. Its Trade and Investment Division provides technical assistance and advisory services. It aims to enhance institutional capacity-building; gives special emphasis to the needs of least-developed, land-locked and island developing countries, and to Central Asian countries that are in transition to a market economy, in accelerating their industrial and technological advancement, promoting their exports, and furthering their integration into the region's economy; supports the development of electronic commerce and other information technologies in the region; and promotes the intra-regional and inter-subregional exchange of trade, investment and technology through the strengthening of institutional support services such as regional information networks.

The Division functions as the secretariat of the Asia-Pacific Trade Agreement (APTA), concluded in 1975 to promote regional trade through mutually agreed concessions by the participating states (in 2012 they comprised Bangladesh, China, India, South Korea, Laos and Sri Lanka; accession proceedings for Mongolia were ongoing). Since 2004 the Division has organized an annual Asia-Pacific Business Forum, involving representatives of governments, the private sector and civil society. It operates the Asia-Pacific Trade and Investment Agreements Database, the Trade and Transport Facilitation Online Database and an online *Directory of Trade and Investment-Related Organizations*, and publishes the *Asia-Pacific Trade and Investment Review* twice a year. The Division acts as the Secretariat of the Asia-Pacific Research and Training Network on Trade (ARTNeT), established in 2004, which aims to enhance the region's research capacity. ESCAP, with the World Trade Organization (WTO), implements a technical assistance programme, helping member states to implement WTO agreements and to participate in ongoing multilateral trade negotiations. In March 2009 ESCAP launched the UN Network of Experts for Paperless Trade in Asia and the Pacific (UN NExT).

Transport: ESCAP's Transport Division aims to improve the regional movement of goods and people, and to assist member states to manage and to benefit from globalization. The Division has three sections: Transport Infrastructure; Transport Facilitation and Logistics; and Transport Policy and Development (incorporating a sub-programme on Tourism). In April 2008 the ESCAP Commission determined to establish a Forum of Asian Ministers of Transport to provide strategic guidance for the development of efficient, reliable and cost-effective transport services throughout the region. The inaugural meeting of the Forum was held in December 2009, in Bangkok, Thailand. Principal infrastructure projects undertaken by the Transport Division have been the development of the Trans-Asian Railway and of the Asian Highway road network (see below). Other activities are aimed at improving the planning process in developing infrastructure facilities and services, in accordance with the Regional Action Programme of the New Delhi Action Plan on Infrastructure Development in Asia and the Pacific (which was adopted at a ministerial conference held in October 1996), and at enhancing private sector involvement in national infrastructure development through financing, management, operations and risk-sharing. The Division aims to reduce the adverse environmental impact of the provision of infrastructure facilities and to promote more equitable and easier access to social amenities. An Intergovernmental Agreement on the Asian Highway Network (adopted in 2003, identifying some 141,000 km of roads in 32 countries) came into effect in July 2005. By September 2011 the working group on the highway network estimated that more than 10,000 km of the highway network had been upgraded to meet the minimum standards set by the Agreement. In November 2005 ESCAP organized an intergovernmental meeting to conclude a draft agreement on the establishment of a Trans-Asian Railway Network. The intergovernmental accord was adopted in April 2006, and entered into force in June 2009, at which time it had received 22 signatures and been ratified by eight member states. The network was to comprise some 114,000 km of rail routes over 28 countries. The first meeting of a working group on the Trans-Asian Railway Network was held in December, in Bangkok, Thailand. ESCAP supports the development of dry ports along the Asian Highway and Trans-Asian Railway networks as part of an integrated regional transport and logistical system. In 2004 ESCAP and the UN Economic Commission for Europe (ECE) initiated a project for developing Euro-Asian transport linkages, aiming to identify and overcome the principal obstacles (physical and otherwise) along the main transport routes linking Asia and Europe. In November 2003 ESCAP approved a new initiative, the Asia-Pacific Network for Transport and Logistics Education and Research (ANTLER), to comprise education, training and research centres throughout the region. In November 2006 the Ministerial Conference on Transport, held in Busan, South Korea, adopted the Busan Declaration, which outlined a long-term development strategy for regional transport and identified investment priorities. The meeting also adopted a Ministerial Declaration on Road Safety which pledged to implement safety measures to save some 600,000 lives in the region in the period 2007–15. In May 2012 the 68th session of the Commission endorsed phase II of a Regional Action Programme for Transport Development in Asia and the Pacific, covering 2012–16 (phase I having been implemented during 2007–11), and a Regional Strategic Framework for the Facilitation of International Road Transport.

ESCAP's tourism concerns include the development of human resources, improved policy planning for tourism development, greater investment in the industry, and minimizing the environmental impact of tourism. A Plan of Action for Sustainable Tourism in the Asia and Pacific Region (1999–2005) was adopted in April 1999; a second phase of the Plan, to cover the period 2006–12, was adopted at an intergovernmental meeting held in Bali, Indonesia, in December 2005. A Network of Asia-Pacific Education and Training Institutes in Tourism, established in 1997, comprised 261 institutes and organizations in 45 countries and states in 2012.

CO-OPERATION WITH OTHER ORGANIZATIONS

ESCAP works with other UN agencies and non-UN international organizations, non-governmental organizations, academic institutions and the private sector; such co-operation includes joint planning of programmes, preparation of studies and reports, participating in meetings, and sharing information and technical expertise. In July 1993 a Memorandum of Understanding (MOU) was signed by ESCAP and the Asian Development Bank, outlining priority areas of co-operation between the two organizations. These were: regional and sub-regional co-operation; issues concerning the least-developed, land-locked and island developing member countries; poverty alleviation; women in development; population; human resource development; the environment and natural resource management; statistics and data bases; economic analysis; transport and communications; and industrial restructuring and privatization. The two organizations were to co-operate in organizing workshops, seminars and conferences, in implementing joint projects, and in exchanging information and data on a regular basis. A new MOU between the two organizations was signed in May 2004 with an emphasis on achieving poverty reduction throughout the region. In 2001 ESCAP, with the Bank and UNDP, established a tripartite regional partnership to promote the MDGs (see above); a joint report on implementation of the goals was prepared by the partnership and published in June 2005 prior to a global review, conducted at the UN General Assembly in September. In May 2007 ESCAP endorsed a regional plan developed by the partnership with the aim of addressing regional challenges (in particular those faced by poorer countries) to the achievement of the MDGs. A High-level Subregional Forum on Accelerating Achievement of the Millennium Development Goals in South Asia was organized by the partnership in February 2012. The annual regional review on progress towards achieving the MDGs was released at the meeting. The UN Special Programme for the Economies of Central Asia (SPECA), begun in 1998, is implemented jointly by ESCAP and ECE (see below). In May 2007 ESCAP signed an MOU with ECE and the Eurasian Economic Community to strengthen co-operation in sustainable development, in support of the MDGs. In the following month ESCAP signed an MOU with the International Organization for Migration (IOM) to provide for greater co-operation and co-ordination on international migration issues. In September 2008 ESCAP and the IOM organized an Asia-Pacific high-level meeting on international migration and development.

Special Programme for the Economies of Central Asia (SPECA): launched in 1998 by the presidents of central Asian states, SPECA is supported jointly by ESCAP and ECE. It aims to strengthen sub-regional co-operation by enabling the discussion of regional issues and offering technical assistance. Six project working groups cover: transport and border crossing; water and energy resources; trade; knowledge-based development; statistics; and gender and economy. The SPECA Economic Forum meets annually in conjunction with the sessions of the SPECA Governing Council, composed of the national co-ordinators of member countries. The 2011 Forum was convened in Aşgabat, Turkmenistan, in November, on the theme '20 Years of Regional Economic Cooperation in Central Asia: Successes, Challenges and Prospects'. During 2009, in response to requests by SPECA member countries for the further strengthening of the Special Programme, ESCAP and ECE determined to establish a SPECA Regional Office in Central Asia, with the aim of improving liaison with governments, the business and academic communities, and of supporting project implementation. Participating countries: Afghanistan, Azerbaijan, Kazakhstan, Kyrgyzstan, Tajikistan, Turkmenistan and Uzbekistan.

REGIONAL INSTITUTIONS

Asian and Pacific Centre for Agricultural Engineering and Machinery (APCAEM): A-7/F, China International Science and Technology Convention Centre, 12 Yumin Rd, Chaoyang District, Beijing 100029, People's Republic of China; tel. (10) 8225-3581; fax (10) 8225-3584; e-mail info@unapcaem.org; internet www.unapcaem.org; f. 1977 as Regional Network for Agricultural Engineering and Machinery, elevated to regional centre in 2002; aims to reduce poverty by enhancing environmentally sustainable agriculture and food production, and applying 'green' and modern agro-technology for the well-being of producers and consumers; work programmes comprise agricultural engineering, food chain management, and agro-enterprise development and trade; undertakes research, training, technical assistance and the exchange of information. Active mems: Bangladesh, People's Republic of China, Fiji, India, Indonesia, Iran, Democratic People's Republic of Korea, Republic of Korea, Mongolia, Nepal, Pakistan, Philippines, Sri Lanka, Thailand, Viet Nam; Dir LeRoy Hollenbeck (USA); publ. *APCAEM Policy Brief* (quarterly).

Asian and Pacific Centre for Transfer of Technology: APCTT Bldg, POB 4575, C-2 Qutab Institutional Area, New Delhi 110 016, India; tel. (11) 26966509; fax (11) 26856274; e-mail postmaster@apctt.org; internet www.apctt.org; f. 1977 to assist countries of the ESCAP region by strengthening their capacity to develop, transfer and adopt technologies relevant to the region, and to identify and promote regional technology development and transfer; operates Business Asia Network (www.business-asia.net) to promote technology-based co-operation, particularly between small and medium-sized enterprises; Dir Dr Krishnamurthy Ramanathan; publs *Asia Pacific Tech Monitor*, *VATIS Updates on Biotechnology*, *Food Processing*, *Ozone Layer Protection*, *Non-Conventional Energy*, and *Waste Management* (each every 2 months).

Asian and Pacific Training Centre for ICT for Development (APCICT): Bonbudong, 3rd Floor Songdo Techno Park, 7-50 Songdo-dong, Yeonsu-gu, Incheon City, Republic of Korea; tel. 245-1700; fax 245-7712; e-mail info@unapcict.org; internet www.unapcict.org; f. 2006 to provide training to ICT policy-makers and professionals, advisory services and analytical studies, to promote best practices in the field of ICT, and to contribute to narrowing the digital divide in the region; developed an Academy of ICT Essentials for Government Leaders, a virtual Academy, and an e-Collaborative hub; Dir Hyuen-Suk Rhee.

Centre for Alleviation of Poverty through Sustainable Agriculture (CAPSA): Jalan Merdeka 145, Bogor 16111, Indonesia; tel. (251) 343277; fax (251) 336290; e-mail capsa@uncapsa.org; internet www.uncapsa.org; f. 1981 as CGPRT Centre, current name adopted 2010; initiates and promotes socio-economic and policy research, training, dissemination of information and advisory services to enhance food security in Asia and the Pacific; Dir Dr Katinka Weinberger (Germany).

Statistical Institute for Asia and the Pacific (SIAP): JETRO-IDE Building, 2–2 Wakaba 3-chome, Mihama-ku, Chiba-shi, Chiba 2618787, Japan; tel. (43) 2999782; fax (43) 2999780; e-mail staff@unsiap.or.jp; internet www.unsiap.or.jp; f. 1970 as Asian Statistical Institute, present name adopted 1977; became a subsidiary body of ESCAP in 1995; trains government statisticians at the Institute and in various co-operating countries in Asia and the Pacific; prepares teaching materials, assists in the development of training on official statistics in national and sub-regional centres; Dir Margarita Guerrero (Philippines).

ASSOCIATED BODIES

ESCAP/WMO Typhoon Committee: Av. de 5 de Outubro, Coloane, Macao, SAR, People's Republic of China; tel. 88010531; fax 88010530; e-mail info@typhooncommittee.org; internet www.typhooncommittee.org; f. 1968; an intergovernmental body affiliated to ESCAP and regional body of the Tropical Cyclone Programme of the World Meteorological Organization; promotes disaster preparedness, trains personnel on meteorology, hydrology and disaster risk reduction and co-ordinates research. The committee's programme is supported by national resources and also by other international and bilateral assistance; Mems: Cambodia, People's Republic of China, Democratic People's Republic of Korea, Republic of Korea, Hong Kong SAR, Japan, Laos, Macao SAR, Malaysia, Philippines, Singapore, Thailand, USA, Viet Nam; Sec. Olavo Rasquinho.

WMO/ESCAP Panel on Tropical Cyclones: PTC Secretariat, Meteorological Complex, Pitras Buk. Rd, Sector H-8/2, Islamabad 44000, Pakistan; tel. (51) 9250365; fax (51) 9250368; e-mail PTC.Sectt@ptc-wmoescap.org; internet www.ptc-wmoescap.org; f. 1972 to mitigate damage caused by tropical cyclones in the Bay of Bengal and the Arabian Sea; mems: Bangladesh, India, Maldives, Myanmar, Oman, Pakistan, Sri Lanka, Thailand; Sec. Dr Qamar-uz-Zaman Chaudhry.

Finance

For the two-year period 2012–13 ESCAP's programme budget, an appropriation from the UN budget, was US $98.6m. The regular budget is supplemented annually by funds from various sources for technical assistance.

Publications

Annual Report.

Asia-Pacific Development Journal (2 a year).

Asia-Pacific in Figures (annually).

Asia-Pacific Population Journal (3 a year).

Asia-Pacific Trade and Investment Report (annually).

Asia and Pacific Disaster Report.

Bulletin on Asia-Pacific Perspectives (annually).

Economic and Social Survey of Asia and the Pacific (annually).

Environment and Sustainable Development News (quarterly).

ESCAP Energy News (2 a year).

ESCAP Human Resources Development Newsletter (2 a year).

ESCAP Population Data Sheet (annually).

ESCAP Tourism Review (annually).

Foreign Trade Statistics of Asia and the Pacific (every 2 years).

Key Economic Developments and Prospects in the Asia-Pacific Region (annually).

Population Headliners (several a year).

Poverty Alleviation Initiatives (quarterly).

Socio-Economic Policy Brief (several a year).

State of the Environment in Asia and the Pacific (every 5 years).

Statistical Indicators for Asia and the Pacific (quarterly).

Statistical Newsletter (quarterly).

Statistical Yearbook for Asia and the Pacific.

Technical Co-operation Yearbook.

Transport and Communications Bulletin for Asia and the Pacific (annually).

Water Resources Journal (annually).

Manuals; country and trade profiles; commodity prices; statistics; Atlas of Mineral Resources of the ESCAP Region (country by country).

Economic Commission for Latin America and the Caribbean—ECLAC

Address: Edif. Naciones Unidas, Avda Dag Hammarskjöld 3477, Vitacura, Casilla 179-D, Santiago, Chile.

Telephone: (2) 2102000; **fax:** (2) 2080252; **e-mail:** dpisantiago@eclac.cl; **internet:** www.eclac.cl.

The UN Economic Commission for Latin America was founded by the UN Economic and Social Council (ECOSOC) in 1948 to co-ordinate policies for the promotion of economic development in the Latin American region. The current name of the Commission was adopted in 1984.

MEMBERS

Antigua and Barbuda	El Salvador	Paraguay
Argentina	France	Peru
Bahamas	Germany	Portugal
Barbados	Grenada	Saint Christopher and Nevis
Belize	Guatemala	Saint Lucia
Bolivia	Guyana	Saint Vincent and the Grenadines
Brazil	Haiti	Spain
Canada	Honduras	Suriname
Chile	Italy	Trinidad and Tobago
Colombia	Jamaica	United Kingdom
Costa Rica	Japan	USA
Cuba	Korea, Republic	Uruguay
Dominica	Mexico	Venezuela
Dominican Republic	Netherlands	
Ecuador	Nicaragua	
	Panama	

ASSOCIATE MEMBERS

Anguilla	Cayman Islands	Puerto Rico
Aruba	Montserrat	Turks and Caicos
British Virgin Islands	Netherlands Antilles	United States Virgin Islands

Organization

(June 2012)

COMMISSION

The Commission, comprising representatives of every member state, normally meets every two years at ministerial level. It considers matters relating to the economic and social development of the region, reviews activities of the organization, and adopts programmes of work. The 33rd session was held in Brasilía, Brazil, in May–June 2010; the 34th session was scheduled to be convened in El Salvador, in August 2012. Member states may meet between Commission meetings in an ad hoc Committee of the Whole. The Commission has established the following ad hoc and permanent bodies:

Caribbean Development and Co-operation Committee;

Committee of High-level Government Experts;

Committee on Central American Economic Co-operation;

Committee on South-South Co-operation;

Regional Conference on Women;

Regional Council for Planning of ILPES;

Statistical Conference of the Americas.

SECRETARIAT

The Secretariat employs more than 500 staff and is headed by the Offices of the Executive Secretary and of the Secretary of the Commission. ECLAC's work programme is carried out by the following divisions: Economic Development (including a Development Studies Unit); Economic and Social Planning (ILPES, see below); International Trade and Integration; Natural Resources and Infrastructure (including a Transport Unit); Population (CELADE, see below); Production, Productivity and Management (including an Agricultural Development Unit, a joint ECLAC/UNIDO Industrial and Technological Development Unit and a Unit on Investment and Corporate Strategies); Social Development; Statistics; Programme Planning and Operations; Sustainable Development and Human Settlements; and Gender Affairs. There are also a Development Studies Unit and a Public Information and Web Services Section.

Executive Secretary: ALICIA BÁRCENA IBARRA (Mexico).

SUB-REGIONAL OFFICES

Caribbean: 1 Chancery Lane, POB 1113, Port of Spain, Trinidad and Tobago; tel. 224-8000; fax 623-8485; e-mail registry@eclacpos.org; internet www.eclacpos.org; f. 1956; covers non-Spanish-speaking Caribbean countries; functions as the secretariat for the Caribbean Development and Co-operation Committee; Dir DIANE QUARLESS.

Central America and Spanish-speaking Caribbean: Edif. Corporativo MCS, Av. Miguel de Cervantes Saavedra 193, piso 12, Col. Granada. Del. Miguel Hidalgo, CP11520, México, DF; tel. (55) 4170-5600; fax (55) 5531-1151; e-mail registromexico@cepal.org; internet www.cepal.org.mx; f. 1951; covers Central America and Spanish-speaking Caribbean countries; Dir HUGO E. BETETA.

There are also national offices, in Buenos Aires, Argentina; Brasilía, Brazil; Bogotá, Colombia; and Montevideo, Uruguay; and a liaison office in Washington, DC, USA.

Activities

ECLAC collaborates with regional governments in the investigation and analysis of regional and national economic problems, and provides guidance in the formulation of development plans. The activities of its different divisions include research, monitoring of trends and policies, and comparative studies; analysis; publication of information; provision of technical assistance; organizing and participating in workshops, seminars and conferences; training courses; and co-operation with national, regional and international organizations, including non-governmental organizations and the private sector. ECLAC's 29th session, held in Brasilía, Brazil, in May 2002, adopted the Brasilía Resolution, which outlined a strategic agenda to meet the challenges of globalization. Proposed action included the consolidation of democracy, strengthening social protection, the formulation of policies to reduce macroeconomic and financial vulnerability, and the development of sustainable and systemic competitiveness in order to build, gradually, an international social agenda based on rights.

The 32nd session of the Commission was convened in June 2008 in Santo Domingo, Dominican Republic. It considered a report, prepared by the Secretariat, entitled 'Structural Change and Productivity Growth—20 years later. Old problems, new opportunities'. The meeting endorsed its conclusions and voted to pursue further study of productive development and innovation policies and best practices. The Commission also requested that the Secretariat research challenges facing the region caused by escalating fuel and food costs at that time. The meeting approved a new programme of work for the period 2010–11, which aimed to promote policies to reduce vulnerability, to foster long-term production development strategies, to improve sustainable development policies, to improve the management of global issues at a regional level, and to strengthen social cohesion, reduce social risks and reinforce gender mainstreaming. In June 2009 ECLAC hosted a meeting of experts and officials from the region's ministries of finance to pursue discussions on structural reform and other measures to counter the impact of the global financial and economic crisis.

In June 2010 the 33rd session of the Commission, held in Brasilía, Brazil, adopted a new work programme for the two-year period 2012–13. The programme's main areas of activity aimed: to strengthen the region's access to financing for development; to contribute to improving the global, regional and national financial architecture; to heighten the productive potential of the region and reduce productivity gaps, with special emphasis on innovation and new technologies; to improve the region's position in the global economy through trade, co-operation and regional integration; to promote a social covenant through greater social equality, lower social risks and further inclusion of a gender perspective in public policies; to improve policies for sustainable development and energy efficiency and address the effects of climate change; and to improve the development of institutions that deal with the management of global and cross-border issues and the provision of public goods at a regional level. The focus of the Commission meeting was a report entitled 'Time for Equality: Closing gaps, opening trails', which identified economic, social and structural disparities throughout the region. Representatives of member states determined to pursue development efforts with a stronger equality agenda.

ECLAC works closely with other agencies within the UN system and with other regional and multinational organizations. In January 2010 ECLAC offered its total co-operation in the immediate humanitarian tasks resulting from the earthquake that caused extensive damage and loss of life in Haiti and in any future reconstruction process. In March, following a massive earthquake in Chile, ECLAC established a joint working group, with UNDP, OCHA and the Chilean authorities, to define priority areas for emergency funding. In February 2011 ECLAC hosted a meeting of representatives of UN agencies in order to initiate production of an inter-agency document in preparation for the UN Conference on Sustainable Development (which was convened in Rio de Janeiro, Brazil, in June 2012, 20 years after the first so-called Earth Summit); the resulting document was discussed at a meeting convened at ECLAC headquarters in September 2011.

ECLAC supports member countries in negotiations of bilateral or sub-regional free trade agreements, in particular with the USA. In January 2002 ECLAC hosted an Interregional Conference on Financing for Development, held in Mexico City, which it had organized as part of the negotiating process prior to the World Summit on Financing for Development, held in March. In June senior representatives of ECLAC, UNDP, the World Bank and the Inter-American Development Bank agreed to co-ordinate activities in pursuit of the development goals proclaimed by the Millennium Summit meeting of the UN General Assembly in September 2000. ECLAC was to adapt the objectives of the so-called Millennium Development Goals (MDGs) to the reality of countries in the region. In July 2004 the 30th session of the Commission approved the establishment of an intergovernmental forum to monitor the implementation of decisions emerging from the World Summit on Sustainable Development, held in Johannesburg, South Africa, in September 2002. In January 2006 ECLAC organized the first Regional Implementation Forum on Sustainable Development, as mandated by the UN Commission on Sustainable Development. In January 2003 a regional conference was convened, in the Dominican Republic, in preparation for the World Summit on the Information Society (WSIS), the first phase of which was held in December, in Geneva, Switzerland. In July 2004 delegates to the 30th session of the Commission requested that ECLAC co-ordinate a regional preparatory meeting to define objectives and proposals for the second phase of the Summit in 2005. The regional ministerial meeting was convened in Rio de Janeiro, Brazil, in June 2005, and a Regional Action Plan, eLAC 2007, was approved to support national and regional projects that incorporate information and communications technology for use in economic and social development in the region. A second plan, eLAC2010, was adopted by ministers in February 2008, to assist countries to attain the global targets identified by the WSIS. The first Follow-up Meeting of eLAC2010 was convened in April 2009. A third Ministerial Conference on the Information Society in Latin America and the Caribbean was convened in Lima, Peru, in November 2010, at which a new action plan, eLAC2015, was approved. ECLAC serves as the technical secretariat for a regional dialogue on the costs of international connections, broadband services and digital inclusion, which was inaugurated in August 2010. In May 2011 ECLAC launched a new Regional Broadband Observatory (ORBA), which was to facilitate public policy decision-making with regard to the provision of broadband services and in October ECLAC organized its first so-called 'School for broadband policymakers'. In that month, the fourth meeting of the regional dialogue on broadband endorsed ORBA proposals relating to minimum download speeds and connectivity.

In November 2003 a Regional Intergovernmental Conference on Ageing was convened, in Santiago, Chile, to further the objectives of a World Assembly on Ageing that had been held in Madrid, Spain, in April 2002. A second Regional Intergovernmental Conference on Ageing was held in Brasília, Brazil, in December 2007. In November 2003 ECLAC launched REDESA, a web-based network of institutions and experts in social and environmental statistics. The first phase of a Macroeconomic Dialogue Network (REDIMA I) was established in 2003, to assist communication on macroeconomic issues between economists from the region's central banks and ministries of finance: a second phase, REDIMA II, was initiated in 2005. In June 2012 ECLAC released the first annual Macroeconomic Report on Latin America and the Caribbean. In July 2007 ECLAC organized the fourth Statistical Conference of the Americas (SCA), which is convened every two years to promote the development and improvement of national statistics (in particular their comparability), and to encourage co-operation between national statistical offices and regional and international organizations. The fifth SCA was held in Bogotá, Colombia, in August 2009, and the sixth in Bávaro, Dominican Republic, in November 2011. ECLAC organizes an annual competition to encourage small-scale innovative social projects in local communities. In June 2008 ECLAC signed an agreement with the UN's International Research and Training Institute for the Advancement of Women (INSTRAW) to establish an observatory on gender equality in Latin America and the Caribbean. In July 2009 ECLAC signed a further agreement with the UN World Tourism Organization to strengthen co-operation in measuring and analysing tourism statistics and indicators. In January 2010 ECLAC initiated a joint project with the Inter-American Development Bank to conduct an economic analysis of the impact of climate change on the region. In January 2012 ECLAC and the Union of Universities of Latin America and the Caribbean signed a five-year co-operation agreement providing a frame work for collaboration between officials and consultants in the shared goal of improving research, debate and training of professionals.

In July 2006 Japan became the first Asian nation to be granted full membership of ECLAC. The membership of the Republic of Korea was formally approved in July 2007.

Latin American and Caribbean Institute for Economic and Social Planning (Instituto Latinoamericano y del Caribe de Planificacion Economica y Social—ILPES): Edif. Naciones Unidas, Avda Dag Hammarskjöld 3477, Vitacura, Casilla 179-D, Santiago, Chile; tel. (2) 2102507; fax (2) 2066104; e-mail ilpes@cepal.org; internet www.eclac.cl/ilpes/; f. 1962; supports regional governments through the provision of training, advisory services and research in the field of public planning policy and co-ordination; Dir JORGE MATTAR MÁRQUEZ (Mexico).

Latin American Demographic Centre (Centro Latinoamericano y Caribeno de Demografia—CELADE): Edif. Naciones Unidas, Avda Dag Hammarskjöld 3477, Casilla 179-D, Santiago, Chile; tel. (2) 2102021; fax (2) 2080196; e-mail celade@eclac.cl; internet www.eclac.cl/celade; f. 1957, became an autonomous entity within ECLAC in 1971 and was fully incorporated into ECLAC as its Population Division in 1997; provides technical assistance to governments, universities and research centres in demographic analysis, population policies, integration of population factors in development planning, and data processing; conducts courses on demographic analysis for development and various national and regional seminars; provides demographic estimates and projections, documentation, data processing, computer packages and training; Dir DIRK JASPERS-FAIJER.

Finance

For the two-year period 2012–13 ECLAC's proposed regular budget, an appropriation from the UN, amounted to US $110.3m. In addition, extra-budgetary activities are financed by governments, other organizations, and UN agencies.

Publications

(in English and Spanish)

CEPAL Review (3 a year).

Challenges/Desafíos (2–3 a year, with UNICEF).

Demographic Observatory (2 a year).

ECLAC Notes (quarterly).

Economic Survey of Latin America and the Caribbean (annually).

FAL Bulletin (Trade Facilitation and Transport in Latin America) (monthly).

Foreign Investment in Latin America and the Caribbean (annually).

Latin America and the Caribbean in the World Economy (annually).

Latin American Economic Outlook (annually).

Macroeconomic Report on Latin America and the Caribbean (annually).

Notas de Población (2 a year).

Preliminary Overview of the Economies of Latin America and the Caribbean (annually).

Social Panorama of Latin America (annually).

Statistical Yearbook for Latin America and the Caribbean.

Water Resources Newsletter (2 a year).

Studies, reports, bibliographical bulletins.

Economic Commission for Africa—ECA

Address: Menelik II Ave, POB 3001, Addis Ababa, Ethiopia.

Telephone: (11) 5517200; **fax:** (11) 5514416; **e-mail:** ecainfo@uneca.org; **internet:** www.uneca.org.

The UN Economic Commission for Africa (ECA) was founded in 1958 by a resolution of the UN Economic and Social Council (ECOSOC) to initiate and take part in measures for facilitating Africa's economic development.

MEMBERS

Algeria	Eritrea	Niger
Angola	Ethiopia	Nigeria
Benin	Gabon	Rwanda
Botswana	The Gambia	São Tomé and Príncipe
Burkina Faso	Ghana	Senegal
Burundi	Guinea	Seychelles
Cameroon	Guinea-Bissau	Sierra Leone
Cape Verde	Kenya	Somalia
Central African Republic	Lesotho	South Africa
Chad	Liberia	South Sudan
Comoros	Libya	Sudan
Congo, Democratic Republic	Madagascar	Swaziland
Congo, Republic	Malawi	Tanzania
Côte d'Ivoire	Mali	Togo
Djibouti	Mauritania	Tunisia
Egypt	Mauritius	Uganda
Equatorial Guinea	Morocco	Zambia
	Mozambique	Zimbabwe
	Namibia	

Organization

(June 2012)

COMMISSION

The Commission may only act with the agreement of the government of the country concerned. It is also empowered to make recommendations on any matter within its competence directly to the government of the member or associate member concerned, to governments admitted in a consultative capacity, and to the UN Specialized Agencies. The Commission is required to submit for prior consideration by ECOSOC any of its proposals for actions that would be likely to have important effects on the international economy.

CONFERENCE OF AFRICAN MINISTERS

The Conference, which meets every year, is attended by ministers responsible for finance, planning and economic development, representing the governments of member states, and is the main deliberative body of the Commission. The Commission's responsibility to promote concerted action for the economic and social development of Africa is vested primarily in the Conference, which considers matters of general policy and the priorities to be assigned to the Commission's programmes, considers inter-African and international economic policy, and makes recommendations to member states in connection with such matters.

OTHER POLICY-MAKING BODIES

Five intergovernmental committees of experts attached to the Sub-regional Offices (see below) meet annually and report to the Commission through a Technical Preparatory Committee of the Whole, which was established in 1979 to deal with matters submitted for the consideration of the Conference.

Seven other committees meet regularly to consider issues relating to the following policy areas: women and development; development information; sustainable development; human development and civil society; industry and private sector development; natural resources and science and technology; and regional co-operation, infrastructure and integration.

SECRETARIAT

The Secretariat provides the services necessary for the meeting of the Conference of Ministers and the meetings of the Commission's subsidiary bodies, carries out the resolutions and implements the programmes adopted there. It comprises the Office of the Executive Secretary and the following divisions: Food Security and Sustainable Development; Governance and Public Administration; ICT, Science and Technology; Economic Development and New Partnership for Africa's Development (NEPAD); Regional Integration and Trade; the African Centre for Gender and Social Development; and the African Centre for Statistics.

Executive Secretary: CARLOS LOPES (Guinea-Bissau) (designate).

SUB-REGIONAL OFFICES

The Sub-regional Offices (SROs) aim to enable member states to play a more effective role in the process of African integration and to facilitate the integration efforts of the other UN agencies active in the sub-regions. In addition, the SROs act as the operational arms of ECA at national and sub-regional levels with a view to: ensuring harmony between the objectives of sub-regional and regional programmes and those defined by the Commission; providing advisory services; facilitating sub-regional economic co-operation, integration and development; collecting and disseminating information; stimulating policy dialogue; and promoting gender issues. Under the radical restructuring of the ECA, completed in 2006, the SROs were given an enhanced role in shaping the Commission's agenda and programme implementation, and were also designated as privileged partners of the regional economic communities. (The following five of Africa's regional economic communities are regarded as the pillars of the envisaged African Economic Community: the Common Market for Eastern and Southern Africa—COMESA, the Communauté économique des états de l'Afrique centrale—CEEAC, the Economic Community of West African States—ECOWAS, the Southern African Development Community—SADC, and the Union of the Arab Maghreb.)

Central Africa: POB 14935, Yaoundé, Cameroon; tel. 2222-0861; fax 2223-3185; e-mail sroca@uneca.org; Dir EMILE AHOHE.

East Africa: POB 4654, Kigali, Rwanda; tel. 586549; fax 586546; e-mail APedro@uneca.org; Dir ANTONIO M. A. PEDRO.

North Africa: BP 2062 Rabat Ryad, Morocco; tel. (3) 771-78-29; fax (3) 771-27-02; e-mail srdc-na@uneca.org; Dir KARIMA BOUNEMRA BEN SOLTANE.

Southern Africa: POB 30647, Lusaka, Zambia; tel. (1) 228502; fax (1) 236949; e-mail srdcsa.uneca@uneca.org; Dir BEATRICE KIRASO (Uganda).

West Africa: POB 744, Niamey, Niger; tel. 72-29-61; fax 72-28-94; e-mail srdcwest@eca.ne; Dir FATOUMATA BA.

Activities

The Commission's activities are designed to encourage sustainable socio-economic development in Africa and to increase economic co-operation among African countries and between Africa and other parts of the world. The Secretariat has been guided in its efforts by major regional strategies, including the Abuja Treaty on the establishment of an African Economic Community, signed under the aegis of the Organization of African Unity (OAU, now African Union—AU) in 1991, the UN System-wide Support to the AU and NEPAD (approved in 2006, see below, replacing the UN System-wide Special Initiative on Africa that covered 1996–2005), and the UN New Agenda for the Development of Africa, which covered the period 1991–2000. In 2006 ECA initiated a major reform process in order to strengthen its capacity to promote regional integration and to help Africa to meet its particular needs. Greater emphasis to be placed on knowledge generation and networking, advocacy, advisory services and technical co-operation, as well as co-operation with other regional organizations. A high-level review of the reforms was undertaken in 2009, resulting in further restructuring of some programmes and divisions.

ICT, SCIENCE AND TECHNOLOGY

The ICT (Information and Communications Technology), Science and Technology Division has responsibility for co-ordinating the implementation of the Harnessing Information Technology for Africa project and for implementing the African Information Society Initiative (AISI), which was started in 1996 to support the creation of an African information and communications infrastructure. ECA is responsible for overseeing quality enhancement and dissemination of statistical databases; for improving access to information by means of enhanced library and documentation services and output; and for strengthening geo-information systems for sustainable development. In addition, ECA encourages member governments to liberalize the telecommunications sector and stimulate imports of computers in order to enable the expansion of information technology throughout Africa. ECA manages the Information Technology Centre for Africa (see below). The Commission administers the Partnership for Information and Communication Technologies in Africa (PICTA), which was established in 1999 as an informal grouping of donors and agencies concerned with developing an information society in Africa. In 1999 ECA's Committee on Development Information established the African Virtual Library and Information Network (AVLIN) as a hub for the exchange of data among African researchers and policy-makers. In August 2000 ECA launched the Africa Knowledge Networks Forum (AKNF). The Forum, to be convened on an annual basis under ECA auspices, was to facilitate co-operation in information-sharing and research between professional research and development networks, and also between these and policy-makers, educators, civil society organizations and the private sector. It was to provide technical support to the African Development Forum (see below). In May 2003 ECA launched the e-Policy Resource Network for Africa, under the Global e-Policy Resource Network initiative aimed at expanding the use and benefits of information and communication technologies. ECA provided institutional and logistical support to an African Ministerial Committee which was established in April 2004 to consider proposals of the first phase of the World Summit on Information Society (WSIS), convened in December 2003. ECA co-ordinated preparations for the African Regional Preparatory Conference in February 2005 for the second phase of the WSIS, which was convened in Tunis, Tunisia, in November of the same year. ECA was awarded responsibility for the Task Force on e-Government, following the summit meeting. The ECA Science and Technology Network (ESTNET) provides an information service on science and technology for African policy-makers and others. In March 2008 ECA organized a conference entitled Science with Africa to link African science-based organizations and businesses with their global counterparts; the second Science with Africa conference, held in June 2010, adopted a set of recommendations on how African countries might leverage science and technology to carry forwards their development agenda. In February 2009 representatives of UN agencies, NEPAD, the AU, and media executives, convened the first Regional Media Dialogue, in The Vaal, South Africa, at the end of which they adopted a Consensus Declaration and series of recommendations relating to the increasing role of the media in Africa's development. In July the first International Conference on African Digital Libraries and Archives, held under ECA auspices, urged the establishment of an ECA African Digital Library and Archives Programme. In October 2011 ECA organized, with the AU, a regional conference which approved the establishment of an Africa Internet Governance Forum (IGF), in accordance with the recommendations of the WSIS. ECA was to provide the secretariat for new body.

GOVERNANCE AND PUBLIC ADMINISTRATION

The role of ECA's Governance and Public Administration Division is to improve member states' capacity for good governance and development management. The Division provides support for the African Peer Review Mechanism, a NEPAD initiative whereby participating member governments mutually assess compliance with a number of codes, standards and commitments that uphold good governance and sustainable development. The Division also helps civil society organizations to participate in governance; supports the development of private sector enterprises; and helps to improve public administration in member states. To achieve these aims the Division provides technical assistance and advisory services, conducts studies, and organizes training workshops, seminars and conferences at national, sub-regional and regional levels for ministers, public administrators and senior policy-makers, as well as for private and non-governmental organizations. In October 1999 the first African Development Forum (ADF)—initiated by ECA as a process to formulate an agenda for effective sustainable development in African countries—was held in Addis Ababa, Ethiopia. It was intended that regular ADF meetings would consider a specific development issue. ADF VII was convened in October 2010, on the theme 'Acting on Climate Change for Sustainable Development in Africa'. In March 2011 the ECA launched the Africa Platform for Development Effectiveness (APDEv, accessible at www.africa-platform.org), a multi-stakeholder platform and organizing mechanism for policy-makers in the continent. The first African Governance Forum (AGF) was hosted by ECA, in Addis Ababa, in July 1997. AGF VIII, addressing the theme 'Democracy, Elections, and the Management of Diversity in Africa', was to be held in Johannesburg, South Africa, in November 2012. In 2005 the first *African Governance Report (AGR-1)* was published by ECA, monitoring progress towards good governance in 27 countries. A second Report, issued in August 2009, found improvements over the past few years in the observance of human rights and the rule of law, as well as in competitive electoral politics and the scope of political representation, although party and electoral systems were deemed to be weak and poorly structured. Advances were judged to have been made in economic governance, public sector management, private sector development and corporate governance, while weaknesses were highlighted in the management of the tax system and in service delivery, and corruption was cited as a major challenge to achieving sustainable economic progress and development in Africa. *AGR-3*, addressing elections and diversity management in Africa, was to be issued in 2013. A *Mutual Review of Development Effectiveness in Africa Report (MRDE)*, jointly compiled by the ECA's Governance and Public Administration Division and OECD, is issued annually; the Review considers progress achieved hitherto in delivering commitments made by African countries and their development partners, and outlines future key priorities. The 2012 edition was issued in May.

AFRICAN CENTRE FOR GENDER AND SOCIAL DEVELOPMENT

ECA aims to improve the socio-economic prospects of women through the promotion of equal access to resources and opportunities, and equal participation in decision-making. An African Centre for Gender and Development (renamed as above in 2006) was established in 1975 to service all national, sub-regional and regional bodies involved in development issues relating to gender and the advancement of women. The Centre manages the African Women's Development Fund, which was established in June 2000. An African Women's Rights Observatory, launched in 1995, monitors gender equality and the advancement of women. The preliminary results of a new African Gender and Development Index were presented in January 2005, measuring how far member states had met their commitments towards international agreements on gender equality and women's advancement. The African Women's Decade, covering 2010–20, was launched in October 2010 under the theme 'Grassroots approach to gender equality and women's empowerment'. A Commission on HIV/AIDS and Governance in Africa, with its secretariat based at ECA headquarters, was launched in September 2003. The Commission, an initiative of the UN Secretary-General, was mandated to assess the impact of the HIV/AIDS pandemic on national structures and African economic development and to incorporate its findings in a Final Report; this was issued in October 2005.

FOOD SECURITY AND SUSTAINABLE DEVELOPMENT

ECA's Food Security and Sustainable Development Division aims to strengthen the capacity of member countries to design institutional structures and implement policies and programmes, in areas such as food production, population, environment and human settlements, to achieve sustainable development. It also promotes the use of science and technology in achieving sustainable development. ECA promotes food security in African countries through raising awareness of the relationship between population, food security, the environment and sustainable development; encouraging the advancement of science and technology in member states; and providing policy analysis support and technical advisory services aimed at strengthening national population policies. In March 2010 ECA issued a report urging member countries to build upon the outcomes of the Abuja Food Security Summit, organized by the AU in December 2006, by establishing a common market of strategic food and agricultural commodities. From 2005 ECA increased its work devoted to the changes in climate caused by global warming, and the resulting threat posed by drought, floods and other extreme events. In 2006, with the AU and the African Development Bank (AfDB), it established a 10-year Climate for Development in Africa Programme (Clim-Dev Africa) to improve the collection of climate-related data and assist in forecasting and risk management. ECA provides the technical secretariat for Clim-Dev Africa. In December 2007 ECA announced the establishment of an African Climate Policy Centre (ACPC), to help member states to incorporate climate-related concerns in their development policies so as to counter the impact of climate change. The first Climate Change and Development in Africa Conference (CCDA-I) was held in Addis Ababa, Ethiopia, in October 2011. Members were encouraged, inter alia, to incorporate climate change data and analysis in their policy-making decisions, to identify means of increasing agricultural productivity, including water management and soil enrichment, and to develop strategies for low carbon development.

ECA assists member states in the assessment and use of water resources and the development of river and lake basins common to more than one country. ECA encourages co-operation between countries with regard to water issues and collaborates with other UN agencies and regional organizations to promote technical and economic co-operation in this area. In 1992, on the initiative of ECA, the Interagency Group for Water in Africa (now UN-Water/Africa) was established to co-ordinate and harmonize the water-related activities of the UN and other organizations on the continent. ECA has been particularly active in efforts to promote the integrated development of the water resources of the Zambezi river basin and of Lake Victoria. In December 2003 ECA hosted the Pan-African Implementation and Partnership Conference on Water (PANAFCON). In October 2011—following an invitation by the 17th regular summit of AU heads of state and government, held in late June–early July 2011, inviting African states to work on a common continental position for the UN Conference on Sustainable Development—UNCSD, which took place in Rio de Janeiro, Brazil, in June 2012—ECA organized a UNCSD Africa Regional Preparatory Conference. The October 2011 Conference noted emerging challenges to sustainable development in Africa, including low adaptive capacity to the effects of climate change; increasing severe biodiversity loss, desertification and land degradation, aggravated by the effects of climate change; and rapid urbanization. The conference urged the international community to meet its commitments to the continent in terms of transfer of financial and technological resources, and committed African states to enhancing efforts to improve national governance and development effectiveness, and to formulating national strategies for sustainable development.

STATISTICS

The African Centre for Statistics was established in 2006 as a new division of ECA, to encourage the use of statistics in national planning, to provide training and technical assistance for the compilation, analysis and dissemination of statistics, and to prepare members for the 2010 round of population censuses. An Advisory Board on Statistics in Africa, comprising 15 experts from national statistical offices, sub-regional bodies and training institutes, meets annually to advise ECA on statistical developments in Africa and guide its activities. The Statistical Commission for Africa (StatCom-Africa), comprising representatives of national statistical offices, regional and international institutions and development partners, meets every two years as the principal body overseeing statistical development in Africa, with annual working groups monitoring progress and deciding on activities. In January 2012 StatCom-Africa, meeting in Cape Town, South Africa, adopted the Robben Island Declaration on Statistical Development, which aimed to strengthen methods of data collection and analysis, of harmonizing statistics in Africa and upgrading the system of national accounts. ECA assists its member states in population data collection and data processing; analysis of demographic data obtained from censuses or surveys; training demographers; formulation of population policies and integrating population variables in development planning, through advisory missions and through the organization of national seminars on population and development; and in dissemination of demographic information.

REGIONAL INTEGRATION, INFRASTRUCTURE AND TRADE

ECA's Regional Integration, Infrastructure and Trade Division comprises sections concerning regional integration; infrastructure and natural resources development; and trade and international negotiations. ECA supports the implementation of the AU's regional integration agenda, through research; policy analysis; strengthening capacity and the provision of technical assistance to the regional economic communities; and working on trans-boundary initiatives and activities across a variety of sectors. In October 2008 ECA launched an Observatory on Regional Integration in Africa, an internet-based repository of knowledge and information aimed at supporting the activities of policy-makers, member states, regional economic communities, and other stakeholders. The Trade and International Negotiations Section conducts research and outreach activities aimed at ensuring best practice in trade policy development and undertakes research and dissemination activities on bilateral and international trade negotiations (such as the ongoing multilateral trade negotiations under the World Trade Organization) with a view to helping African countries to benefit from globalization through trade. In April 2003 ECA and the AfDB synchronized their annual meetings in an effort to find a common position on addressing the principal challenges confronting the continent. They concluded that development was constrained by national debt, a persistent decline in exports, and weak economic growth rates. They also urged a thorough review of development strategies to determine whether poor outcomes were the result of bad policy, poor implementation or external factors. The African Trade Policy Centre (ATPC), established in 2003, aims to strengthen the human, institutional and policy capacities of African governments to formulate and implement sound trade policies and participate more effectively in international trade negotiations. The Centre takes both a national and regional perspective, and provides a rapid response to technical needs arising from ongoing trade negotiations.

ECA and the World Bank jointly co-ordinate the sub-Saharan Africa Transport Programme (SSATP), established in 1987, which aims to facilitate policy development and related capacity-building in the continent's transport sector. A meeting of all participants in the programme is held annually. The regional Road Management Initiative (RMI) under the SSATP seeks to encourage a partnership between the public and private sectors to manage and maintain road infrastructure more efficiently and thus to improve country-wide communications and transportation activities. An Urban Mobility component of the SSATP aims to improve sub-Saharan African urban transport services, while a Trade and Transport component aims to enhance the international competitiveness of regional economies through the establishment of more cost-effective services for shippers. The Railway Restructuring element focuses on the provision of financially sustainable railway enterprises. In December 2003 the first Central African Forum on Transport Infrastructure and Regional Integration was convened by ECA. In November 2005 a meeting of sub-Saharan African ministers of transport, convened in Bamako, Mali, on the fringes of the SSATP Annual General Meeting, adopted a resolution aimed at developing Africa's transport infrastructure, focusing on the importance of incorporating transport issues into poverty reduction strategies, ensuring sustainable financing for Africa's road programmes, and prioritizing road safety issues. The African Road Safety Conference, convened in Accra, Ghana, in February 2007, by African ministers responsible for transport and health, reaffirmed road safety as a key development priority and pledged to set and achieve measurable national targets for road safety and the prevention of traffic injuries in all member states. A meeting of experts convened in September 2011 to review the development of interconnected Trans-African Highways (TAH) reported that by that time the TAH comprised some nine principal axes of roads across the continent, but that about one-quarter of an envisaged final network was yet to be constructed. The meeting recommended the adoption of an intergovernmental agreement on the TAH, and adopted a series of 10 recommendations aimed at accelerating the development of the highways interconnection initiative. In November 2011 the second African Road Safety Conference, convened by ECA within the framework of the SSATP, approved an Action Plan, which aimed to halve the number of road crash fatalities by 2020.

The Division supports efforts to advance the development of Africa's extensive mineral and energy resources, focusing on promoting co-operation, integration and public-private sector partnerships; facilitating policy decisions and dissemination of best practices; and supporting capacity building. The Southern and Eastern African Mineral Centre, established by ECA in Dar-es-Salaam, Tanzania, in 1977, opened its membership to all African states in 2007. The Centre provides data-processing, training, analytical services and research on mineral applications. An international study group to review African mining was convened by ECA for the first time in October 2007. ECA's Energy Programme provides assistance to member states in the development of indigenous energy resources and the formulation of energy policies to extricate member states from continued energy crises. In May 2004 ECA was appointed as the secretariat of a new UN-Energy/Africa initiative which aimed to facilitate the exchange of information, good practices and knowledge-sharing among UN organizations and with private sector companies, non-governmental organizations, power utilities and other research and academic institutions. In December 2011 ECA and the AU organized a second conference of African ministers responsible for mineral resources development.

ECONOMIC DEVELOPMENT AND NEPAD

ECA provides guidance to the policy-making organs of the UN and the AU on the formulation of policies supporting the achievement of Africa's development objectives. It contributes to the work of the General Assembly and of specialized agencies by providing an African perspective in the preparation of development strategies. The former UN System-wide Special Initiative on Africa, covering the decade 1995–2006, aimed to mobilize resources and to implement a series of political and economic development objectives; the Initiative was followed by the UN System-wide Support to the AU and NEPAD, launched in 2006. NEPAD was established by the AU in 2001, and ECA was assigned the task of co-ordinating UN support for NEPAD at the regional level. In February 2010 a new NEPAD Planning and Co-ordination Committee (NPCC) was established as a technical body of the AU, to replace the former NEPAD Secretariat, with the aim of improving the implementation of NEPAD projects at country level. In April 2010 ECA and the NPCC concluded a Memorandum of Understanding strengthening collaboration between the two bodies. In the following month ECA, the AU and the AfDB issued their fourth joint *Assessing Regional Integration in Africa* report (ARIA IV), urging enhanced action to lower business costs in order to help facilitate intra-African trade.

Within the Economic Development and NEPAD Division, a Finance, Industry and Investment Section supports members to analyse the challenges of mobilizing domestic and external resources for promoting investment and industrial development. Principal focus areas are foreign aid, debt, private capital flows, and savings and remittances. It also assists member states to implement effective policies and strategies to enhance their investment prospects and competitiveness in the global production system. A Macroeconomic Analysis Section assists member states to improve their capacity to formulate, implement and monitor sound macroeconomic policies and better institutional frameworks, with a view to achieving sustainable development. The Section also focuses on policy advocacy and collaboration with development organizations and institutions, produces publications and provides training, conferences and workshops. It undertakes macroeconomic research and policy analysis in the following areas: macroeconomic modelling and planning; growth strategies; fiscal and monetary policies; and debt management. The Section also prepares background documents for the annual Conference of African Ministers of Finance, Planning, and Economic Development. A separate Section serves to support members reviewing their progress towards and in implementing internationally agreed development objectives, including the Millennium Development Goals (MDGs) and those defined by the 2001 Brussels Programme of Action for least developed countries. The Section prepares annual reviews and supports capacity building and the sharing of knowledge among African countries.

In March 2009 the Coalition for Dialogue on Africa (CoDA) was launched, by ECA, the AU and the AfDB, as an independent African forum to serve as an umbrella for all existing forums on Africa. ECA hosts its secretariat. CoDA meetings, including a multi-stakeholder dialogue forum, were convened in Tunis, in November, to consider Africa's recovery from the global economic and financial crisis, and regional integration. In February 2010 CoDA met, again in Tunis, to discuss transforming the Coalition into a fully independent, non-governmental African initiative, with a chief executive; and to develop a work programme. A CoDA policy forum was held in Abidjan, Côte d'Ivoire, in May, on 'Financing Regional Integration in Africa'. Meeting in October 2010, on the sidelines of ADF VII, CoDA urged African leaders to continue to pursue participation multinational negotiations on climate change. A CoDA policy forum on foreign direct investments in land in Africa was convened in Lisbon, Portugal, in June 2011.

In June 2009 ECA and the AU hosted, in Cairo, Egypt, a joint meeting of African ministers of finance and economic affairs, which considered the impact on the region of the global crisis. During that month a joint report of all five UN Regional Commissions, entitled *The Global Economic and Financial Crisis: Regional Impacts, Responses and Solutions*, was launched. In October 2010 the ECA, AU and AfDB established a Joint Secretariat (based at ECA headquarters) to enhance coherence and collaboration in support of Africa's development agenda. In May 2011 ECA launched the *ECA LDC Monitor*, an internet-based tool aimed at assessing economic progress in member Least-Developed Countries. The theme of the 2011 *Economic Report on Africa*, released in September of that year, was 'Development in Africa: The Role of the State in Economic

Transformation'. Since 2006 ECA and AfDB have organized an annual African Economic Conference (AEC), aimed at enabling an exchange of ideas among economists and policy-makers on development policy. The sixth AEC was held in Addis Ababa, Ethiopia, in October 2011, on the theme 'Green Economy and Structural Transformation in Africa'.

ASSOCIATED BODY

Information Technology Centre for Africa (ITCA): POB 3001, Addis Ababa, Ethiopia; tel. (11) 551-4534; fax (11) 551-0512; e-mail itca@uneca.org; internet www.uneca.org/itca; f. 1999 to strengthen the continent's communications infrastructure and promote the use of information and communications technologies in planning and policy-making; stages exhibitions and provides training facilities; Man MAKANE FAYE.

Finance

ECA's proposed regular budget for the two-year period 2012–13, an appropriation from the UN budget, was US $138.3m.

Publications

African Governance Report.
African Statistical Yearbook.
Africa's Sustainable Development Bulletin.
African Women's Report.
Africa Youth Report.
ATPC News.
The ECA Echo (2 a month).
Economic Report on Africa.
ESTNET Newsletter (annually).
GenderNet (2 a year).
Insight (quarterly Southern Africa Office newsletter).
One Africa.
PICTA Bulletin (monthly).
Sustainable Development Report on Africa (every 2 years).
Assessing Regional Integration in Africa (ARIA) report series, country reports, policy and discussion papers, reports of conferences and meetings, training series, working paper series.

Economic and Social Commission for Western Asia—ESCWA

Address: Riad el-Solh Sq., POB 11-8575, Beirut, Lebanon.

Telephone: (1) 981301; **fax:** (1) 981510; **e-mail:** webmaster-escwa@un.org; **internet:** www.escwa.un.org.

The UN Economic Commission for Western Asia was established in 1974 by a resolution of the UN Economic and Social Council (ECOSOC), to provide facilities of a wider scope for those countries previously served by the UN Economic and Social Office in Beirut (UNESOB). The name 'Economic and Social Commission for Western Asia' (ESCWA) was adopted in 1985.

MEMBERS

Bahrain	Palestine
Egypt	Qatar
Iraq	Saudi Arabia
Jordan	Sudan
Kuwait	Syria
Lebanon	United Arab Emirates
Oman	Yemen

Note: Requests by Libya, Morocco and Tunisia to join ESCWA were welcomed by the 27th ministerial session held in May 2012; the applications were to be passed to ECOSOC for further consideration.

Organization

(June 2012)

COMMISSION

The Commission meets every two years in ministerial session to determine policy and establish work directives. Representatives of UN bodies and specialized agencies, regional organizations, other UN member states, and non-governmental organizations having consultative status with ECOSOC may attend as observers. The 27th ministerial session of the Commission was convened in May 2012.

PREPARATORY COMMITTEE

The Committee has the task of reviewing programming issues and presenting recommendations in that regard to the sessions of the Commission. It is the principal subsidiary body of the Commission and functions as its policy-making structure. Seven specialized inter-governmental committees have been established (see below) to consider specific areas of activity, to report on these to the Preparatory Committee and to assist the Committee in formulating ESCWA's medium-term work programmes: they meet every two years, except for the Committee on Transport, which meets annually.

SUBSIDIARY COMMITTEES

Statistical Committee: established in 1992;
Committee on Social Development: established in 1994;
Committee on Energy: established in 1995;
Committee on Water Resources: established in 1995;
Committee on Transport: established in 1997;
Committee on Liberalization of Foreign Trade and Economic Globalization: established in 1997;
Committee on Women: established in 2003.

In addition, an Advisory Committee meets every four months at ESCWA headquarters: it comprises the heads of diplomatic missions in the host country, and a senior representative of the host country, and fulfils a consultative role, while providing a means of communication between member governments and the ESCWA Secretariat. A further Technical Committee, made up of senior officials from member countries, was established pursuant to a decision of the 24th ministerial session of the Commission held in May 2006. The Committee held its inaugural meeting in January 2008 and was to convene every six months, with a mandate to advise and assist the Secretariat in formulating strategy and future priorities and implementing programmes of work. The Consultative Committee on Scientific Technological Development and Technological Innovation was established in 2001 and meets every two years. It comprises experts from public institutions, the private sector, civil society and research centres.

SECRETARIAT

The Secretariat comprises an Executive Secretary, a Deputy Executive Secretary, and the following administrative and programme divisions: Administrative Services; Economic Development and Globalization; Information and Communications Technology; Programme Planning and Technical Co-operation; Social Development; Statistics; and Sustainable Development and Productivity. Each division is headed by a Chief, who is accountable to the Executive Secretary. In addition, there is an ESCWA Centre for Women (established in 2003, formerly part of the Social Development Division), and a Unit for Emerging and Conflict Related Issues, established in 2006.

Executive Secretary: RIMA KHALAF (Jordan).

Activities

ESCWA aims to support development and to further economic co-operation and integration in western Asia. ESCWA undertakes or sponsors studies of economic, social and development issues of the region, collects and disseminates information, and provides advisory services to member states in various fields of economic and social development. It also organizes conferences and intergovernmental and expert group meetings and sponsors training workshops and seminars. ESCWA adopts biennial strategic frameworks as the basis for its programme planning.

Much of ESCWA's work is carried out in co-operation with other UN bodies, as well as with other international and regional organizations, for example the League of Arab States, the Cooperation Council for the Arab States of the Gulf (GCC) and the Organization of Islamic Cooperation (OIC). In May 2009 ESCWA co-hosted, with the International Labour Organization and the Syrian Government, a Regional High-Level Consultative Forum on the Impacts of the International Financial Crisis on the ESCWA Member Countries. The meeting adopted the Damascus Declaration, comprising a set of proposals for member countries to respond more effectively to the crisis, including support for greater investment in the region by ESCWA's sovereign wealth funds, adopting fiscal stimulus policies, and strengthening the efficiency of their regulatory frameworks. The Forum identified ESCWA as being key to enhancing the participation of Arab and Islamic financial institutions in member countries' efforts to counter the effects of the crisis. ESCWA's 26th ministerial session was convened, in May 2010, on the theme 'The Role of Youth and their Empowerment'.

In June 2011 ESCWA hosted the 15th meeting of a Regional Co-ordination Mechanism for Arab States, at which regional directors and officials from more than 20 UN agencies and other international and regional organizations considered the recent political and social reforms in several Arab countries. The grouping reaffirmed its commitment to strengthening co-operation in order to support more inclusive and sustainable development in the region. It also resolved to establish a new thematic working group to achieve greater regional integration. In mid-2011 ESCWA undertook an internal review of its work programmes in order to enhance its capacity to address the emerging needs of societies in transition. In January 2012 the UN Secretary-General addressed a High-level Meeting on Reform and Transition to Democracy, organized by ESCWA. The meeting emphasized the need to incorporate human rights and principles of social justice as essential elements of future economic strategies in countries in the region in order to secure democracy, as well as to protect and promote the empowerment of women and to stimulate youth employment opportunities.

ECONOMIC DEVELOPMENT AND GLOBALIZATION

Through its Economic Development and Globalization Division ESCWA aims to assist member states to achieve sustainable economic development in the region and to integrate more fully into the world economy. A Financing for Development Team aims to assist member countries to implement the recommendations of the Monterrey Consensus, adopted at the International Conference on Financing for Development, held in Monterrey, Mexico, in March 2002. Other concerns are to encourage domestic, intra-regional and foreign investment, to facilitate transboundary flows of goods, services, people and capital, by integrating regional markets (for example through the Greater Arab Free Trade Area) and to support member countries with debt management. The Division's Trade Team works to advance regional trading integration, as well as greater participation of the region in the multilateral trading system. It acts as a forum for member countries in preparation for multilateral trade negotiations, such as those within the Doha Round of negotiations under the World Trade Organization. An Economic Analysis Team aims to increase the capacity of member countries to co-ordinate economic policies. It makes continuous assessments of the region's macroeconomic performances; conducts economic research, modelling and forecasting; monitors the region's progress towards the UN Millennium Development Goals (MDGs); and disseminates its findings to support dialogue at various regional meetings. The Division aims to help member countries to increase their exports and to encourage domestic and foreign investment. The work of the Division's Transport Team includes the development of an integrated transport system in the Arab Mashreq region; development of a regional transport information system; formation of national and regional transport and trade committees, representing both the private and public sectors; simplification of cross-border trading procedures; and the use of electronic data exchange for more efficient transport and trade. In May 2008 the 25th ministerial session of the Commission adopted a Convention on International Multimodal Transport of Goods in the Arab Mashreq.

EMERGING AND CONFLICT-RELATED ISSUES

In January 2006 a Unit for Emerging and Conflict-related Issues (ECRI) was established to consolidate and develop ESCWA's activities in conflict and post-conflict countries and areas, including Iraq, the Palestinian territories and, initially, southern Lebanon. Following the Israeli military strikes that targeted the Lebanese bases of the militant Shi'a organization Hezbollah in July–August of that year, the mandate of ECRI was expanded to cover all of Lebanon. ECRI's priority areas include analysis and policy formulation for reducing the causes of conflict; capacity-building to improve the effectiveness of public administration and the rule of law; forging partnerships among civic entities at local and regional level; and working with other ESCWA divisions to meet the special needs of countries affected by conflicts. ESCWA administers an E-Caravan mobile computer school programme, to provide ICT training to communities in southern Lebanon. Other projects include: provision of regional and local 'networking academies' in Iraq, to give training in information technology; the Smart Communities Project, providing modern technology for villages in Iraq; improvement of statistics related to gender in Iraq; and support of the Coalition of Arab-Palestinian Civil Society Organizations. Regional expert group meetings organized by ECRI have included 'Strengthening Good Governance Practices in Conflict Affected Countries: Current Priorities and Future Interventions', and 'Policies for Peace-building and Conflict Prevention in Western Asia'. In September 2011 ESCWA hosted an expert group meeting, in part chaired by ECRI, to consider the impact of conflict on progress towards achieving the MDGs in countries in the region. In the following month ECRI contributed to a seminar on participatory governance in crisis-affected Arab countries.

ESCWA CENTRE FOR WOMEN

The ESCWA Centre for Women was established in October 2003. Its main focus of activities is the empowerment and advancement of women. It also aims to incorporate issues relating to gender in regional projects and programmes. The Centre monitors developments, compiles country profiles on the status of women, provides support for formulating relevant legislation, raises awareness by publishing reports and studies, and organizes conferences. In December 2003 ESCWA issued its first *Status of Arab Women* report; this was to assess the situation of Arab women at two-yearly intervals. The 2011 edition focused on equal participation in decision-making. In September 2008 the ESCWA Secretary-General launched a guide entitled *Gender in the Millennium Development Goals*, which summarized the key regional gender issues in the context of each MDG and provided a statistical framework for evaluating and following up adherence to international agreements relating to gender equality, in the context of reporting progress in achieving (by 2015) the Arab MDGs. During 2011 the Centre's activities included organizing training workshops relating to implementation of the Convention on the Elimination of All Forms of Discrimination against Women (CEDAW) and the protection of women in conflict situations.

INFORMATION AND COMMUNICATIONS TECHNOLOGY

The Information and Communications Technology Division works to increase the capabilities of ESCWA member countries in harnessing information and communications technology (ICT) in support of sustainable development and regional integration. It aims to narrow the so-called digital gap between Arab countries and other regions, and, consequently, to improve the competitiveness of local industries and the effectiveness of local services. It supports the formation of ICT policies and infrastructure, by providing technical assistance, pilot projects, studies and meetings of experts. ESCWA was responsible for advising member countries on the implementation of recommendations issued by the first phase of the World Summit on the Information Society, held in December 2003, and on preparations for the second phase of the Summit, which was convened in Tunis, Tunisia, in November 2005. As a follow-up to the Summit, ESCWA undertook to collate a profile of the region's information society based on national profile reports. A Regional Follow-up to the Outcome of the World Summit on the Information Society was held in Damascus, Syria, in June 2009. In November ESCWA organized a regional workshop on Arabic domain names and internet governance, held in Sharm el-Sheikh, Egypt. In July 2011 ESCWA co-organized, with the League of Arab States and International Telecommunication Union, a Partnership Building Forum for the Implementation of the Arab Top Level Domains. Consultations to establish an Arab Internet Governance Forum (AIGF) were formally initiated in February 2012; the inaugural meeting of the AIGF was to be convened in Kuwait, in October 2012. The 26th session of the Commission, held in May 2010, resolved to establish an ESCWA Technology Centre, in order to strengthen member states' ICT capabilities. An agreement was signed with the Government of Jordan, in December, to host the Centre in that country's capital, Amman. In May 2012 the 27th Commission session launched a set of directives on Cyber Legislation.

SOCIAL DEVELOPMENT

ESCWA's Social Development Division encourages regional co-operation in promoting comprehensive and integrated social policies, so as to achieve greater social equality and well-being, and to alleviate poverty, social exclusion, gender imbalances and social tension. It advises governments on the importance of integrating social analysis into policy-making, identifies methods for the effective formulation, implementation and monitoring of social policy, and assists national and regional research on social development. ESCWA's objectives with regard to population are to increase awareness and understanding of links between population factors and poverty, human rights and the environment, and to strengthen the capacities of member states to analyse and assess demographic trends and migration. In the area of social participatory development ESCWA aims to further the alleviation of poverty and to generate a sustainable approach to development through greater involvement of community groups, institutions and users of public services in decision-making. The Division's work on social policy in the city analyses urban problems, such as poverty, unemployment, violence, and failure to integrate vulnerable and marginal groups, and aims to assist policy-makers in ensuring that all city-dwellers have equal access to public services. ESCWA provides a forum for preparatory and follow-up meetings to global conferences. In December 2011 ESCWA organized a second regional review meeting of the International Plan of Action on Ageing, which resulted from the World Assembly, held in Madrid, Spain in 2002. In May 2010 ESCWA's 26th ministerial session emphasized the need to secure employment opportunities for young people. Efforts to increase the involvement of young people, and of women, in development programmes were also promoted, in particular at a time when the region was attempting to recover from the effects of the global financial and economic crisis. At early 2010 an estimated 60% of the region's population were under 25 years of age. In November 2011 ESCWA organized an inter-regional seminar on 'Participatory Development and Conflict Resolution: Path of Democratic Transition and Social Justice', to address aspects of the political and social changes taking place in several countries in the region.

STATISTICS

ESCWA helps to develop the statistical systems of member states in accordance with the UN Fundamental Principles of Official Statistics, in order to improve the accuracy and comparability of economic and social data, and to make the information more accessible to planners and researchers. It aims to improve human and institutional capacities, in particular in the use of statistical tools for data analysis, to expand the adoption and implementation of international statistical methods, and to promote co-operation to further the regional harmonization of statistics. ESCWA assists members in preparing for population and housing censuses, in accordance with the UN 2010 World Population and Housing Census Programme. In December 2011 ESCWA hosted a workshop on Population Census Preparedness. A Trade and Transport Statistics Team compiles, processes and disseminates statistics on international trade and transport within the region, and assists member countries to develop their statistical capacity in this sector.

SUSTAINABLE DEVELOPMENT AND PRODUCTIVITY

The work of ESCWA's Sustainable Development and Productivity Division is undertaken by four teams, covering: energy for sustainable development; water and environment; technology and enterprise development; and sustainable agriculture and rural development. ESCWA aims to counter the problem of an increasing shortage of freshwater resources and deterioration in water quality resulting from population growth, agricultural land use and socio-economic development, by supporting measures for more rational use and conservation of water resources, and by promoting public awareness of and community participation in water and environmental protection projects. The Division assists governments in the formulation and implementation of capacity-building programmes and the development of surface and groundwater resources. ESCWA promotes greater co-operation among member and non-member countries in the management and use of shared water resources, and supports the Arab Integrated Water Resources Management Network (AWARE-NET, comprising some 120 research and training institutes). ESCWA supports co-operation in the establishment of electricity distribution and supply networks throughout the region and promotes the use of alternative sources of energy and the development of new and renewable energy technologies. It places a special emphasis on increasing the access of poor people to cheap energy and water, and on the creation of new jobs. The Division promotes the application of environmentally sound technologies in order to achieve sustainable development, as well as measures to recycle resources, minimize waste and reduce the environmental impact of transport operations and energy use. ESCWA collaborates with national, regional and international organizations in monitoring and reporting on emerging environmental issues and to pursue implementation of Agenda 21, which was adopted at the June 1992 UN Conference on Environment and Development, with particular regard to land and water resource management and conservation. In July 2011 ESCWA hosted a regional meeting concerned with 'Economic Policies Supporting the Transition to a Green Economy in the Arab Region'. In September ESCWA hosted a conference on 'The Role of Green Industries in Promoting Socio-Economic Development in the Arab Countries'. In February 2012 ESCWA organized, jointly with the International Food Policy Research Institute, an international conference on food security in the Arab region.

ESCWA, in co-operation with the League of Arab States and UNEP's Office for West Asia, organized a series of preparatory meetings to formulate a regional strategy for the UN Conference on Sustainable Development (Rio+20), which was held in Rio de Janeiro, Brazil, in June 2012. In May 2012 the 27th ministerial session requested the Commission's Secretariat to report back to the membership on the outcomes of Rio+20, and to support member states in building capacity to address these.

Finance

ESCWA's proposed regular budget allocation from the UN budget for the two years 2012–13 was US $62.6m.

Publications

ESCWA Annual Report.

UN-ESCWA Weekly News.

Analysis of Performance and Assessment of Growth and Productivity in the ESCWA Region.

Annual Review of Developments in Globalization and Regional Integration.

Compendium of Environment Statistics.

Compendium of Social Statistics and Indicators.

Country and Regional Profiles for Sustainable Development Indicators.

ESCWA Centre for Women Newsletter (monthly).

Estimates and Forecasts for GDP Growth in the ESCWA Region.

External Trade Bulletin of the ESCWA Region (annually).

International Comparison Program Newsletter.

Review of Industry in ESCWA Member Countries.

Review of Information and Communications Technology and Development.

Status of Arab Women Report (every 2 years).

Survey of Economic and Social Developments in the ESCWA Region.

Transport Bulletin.

Weekly News.

ESCWA publishes reports, case studies, assessments, guides and manuals on the subjects covered by its various Divisions.

OTHER UNITED NATIONS BODIES

Office for the Co-ordination of Humanitarian Affairs—OCHA

Address: United Nations Plaza, New York, NY 10017, USA.

Telephone: (212) 963-1234; **fax:** (212) 963-1312; **e-mail:** ochany@un.org; **internet:** www.unocha.org.

OCHA was established in January 1998 as part of the UN Secretariat, and has a mandate to mobilize and co-ordinate international humanitarian assistance and to provide policy and other advice on humanitarian issues. It replaced the Department of Humanitarian Affairs, established in 1992.

Organization

(June 2012)

OCHA has headquarters in New York, and in Geneva, Switzerland. It maintains regional support offices in Dakar, Senegal (for west Africa), Johannesburg, South Africa (southern Africa) and Nairobi, Kenya (central and east Africa); and deploys regional disaster response advisers in Panama (for Latin America and the Caribbean), Kobe, Japan (Asia), and Suva, Fiji (the Pacific). OCHA also maintains field presences in Africa, Europe, Asia and Latin America. In 2012 there were 2,005 staff posts, of which one-third were based at the headquarters.

Under-Secretary-General for Humanitarian Affairs and Emergency Relief Co-ordinator: VALERIE AMOS (United Kingdom).

Activities

OCHA's mandate is to work with UN agencies, governments, inter-governmental humanitarian organizations and non-governmental organizations to ensure that a prompt, co-ordinated and effective response is provided to complex emergencies and natural disasters. OCHA monitors developments throughout the world and undertakes contingency planning. It liaises with UN Resident Co-ordinators, Humanitarian Co-ordinators and country teams, and reaches agreement with other UN bodies regarding the division of responsibilities, which may include field missions to assess requirements, organizing inter-agency Consolidated Appeals for financial assistance (see below), and mobilizing other resources. The Emergency Relief Co-ordinator is the principal adviser to the UN Secretary-General on humanitarian issues. He chairs the Inter-Agency Standing Committee (IASC), which co-ordinates and administers the international response to humanitarian disasters and the development of relevant policies. The Co-ordinator also acts as Convener of the Executive Committee for Humanitarian Affairs, which provides a forum for humanitarian agencies, as well as the political and peace-keeping departments of the UN Secretariat, to exchange information on emergency situations and humanitarian issues. In view of the serious challenges posed by the increasing frequency and intensity of extreme natural hazard events, combined with other developing 'mega-trends', such as the ongoing global crisis in food price levels, OCHA aims (in co-operation with governments and development agencies) to place a stronger focus on disaster risk reduction and preparedness and on increasing national disaster management capacities; and also on enabling the international emergency response system to respond successfully to these greater requirements. OCHA's strategic framework for 2010–13 aimed (through the Office's functions of co-ordination, advocacy, policy, information management and humanitarian financing) to promote an effective international response to humanitarian requirements; and to support, when emergencies arise, national efforts to co-ordinate the system-wide response. The framework incorporated the three principal goals of providing a more enabling environment for humanitarian action; establishing a more effective humanitarian co-ordination system; and strengthening OCHA management and administration.

OCHA participates in the High Level Task Force (HLTF) on the Global Food Crisis, which was established in April 2008 by the UN Secretary-General to promote a unified response to soaring food and fuel prices and other factors adversely affecting the supply and accessibility of food, and to formulate a Comprehensive Framework for Action.

OCHA's Early Warning Unit identifies and monitors potentially emerging humanitarian crises, as well as humanitarian emergencies at risk of deterioration and potentially resurgent humanitarian emergencies. Analysis by the Unit determines the at-risk areas to which inter-agency contingency planning missions should be directed.

OCHA maintains internet-based Integrated Regional Information Networks (IRINs). The first IRIN was created in 1995 in Nairobi, Kenya, to disseminate information on the humanitarian situation in central and east Africa. Additional IRINs have since been established in Abidjan, Côte d'Ivoire (covering west Africa), Johannesburg, South Africa (for southern Africa) and Islamabad, Pakistan (for central Asia). The IRINs provide news coverage of a total of 46 countries in sub-Saharan Africa and eight countries in central Asia. A complementary service, ReliefWeb, launched in 1996, monitors crises and publishes information on the internet.

OCHA's Humanitarian Emergency and Response Co-ordination branches (based, respectively, at the New York and Geneva headquarters) co-operate in mobilizing and co-ordinating international emergency assistance. The Response Co-ordination branch facilitates and participates in situation assessment missions; prepares briefings and issues Situation Reports to inform the international community on ongoing humanitarian crises, the type and level of assistance required and action being undertaken; and provides administrative support to OCHA field offices. The Emergency Services branch, based at the Geneva headquarters, undertakes disaster-preparedness activities and manages international rapid response missions in the field. UN Disaster Assessment and Co-ordination (UNDAC) teams, established by OCHA with the aid of donor governments, are available for immediate deployment to help to determine requirements and to co-ordinate assistance in those countries affected by disasters, for example by establishing reliable telecommunications and securing other logistical support. OCHA maintains a Central Register of Disaster Management Capacities, which may be available for international assistance. In addition, a stockpile of emergency equipment and supplies is maintained at the UN Humanitarian Response Depot in Brindisi, Italy, ready for immediate dispatch. The Field Co-ordination Support Section of the Emergency Services Branch acts as the secretariat of INSARAG, an inter-governmental network dealing with urban search and rescue (USAR) issues. INSARAG facilitates information exchange, defines standards for international USAR assistance, and develops methodology for international co-ordination in earthquake response. A joint OCHA/UNEP Environment Unit mobilizes and co-ordinates international assistance in environmental emergency situations. A UN inter-agency Displacement and Protection Support Section (DPSS), reporting to the Emergency Relief Co-ordinator, was established in 2007 to strengthen and co-ordinate the inter-agency collaborative response to the plight of people displaced from their homes by civil conflict and natural disasters.

The focal point within the UN system for co-ordinating disaster reduction activities in the socio-economic, humanitarian and development fields is the International Strategy for Disaster Reduction (ISDR), which has an Inter-Agency Secretariat (UN/ISDR) based in Geneva (see below). In January 2005 the UN/ISDR organized a World Conference on Disaster Reduction, held in Kobe, Japan, which launched the International Early Warning Programme (IEWP), comprising UN bodies and agencies including the ISDR, UNEP, WFP and WMO. The IEWP was to improve global resilience to natural disasters (such as droughts, wildland fires, volcanic eruptions, earthquakes, tsunamis—tidal waves, floods and hurricanes) by improving the exchange of observational data, promoting education on disaster preparedness, and ensuring an effective response mechanism to be activated on the issue of warnings. The Kobe Conference also adopted the Hyogo Declaration and the Hyogo Framework of Action (HFA) covering the period 2005–15, which had the following strategic goals: integrating disaster risk reduction into sustainable development policies and planning; development and strengthening of institutions, mechanisms and capacities to build resilience to hazards; and the systematic incorporation of risk reduction approaches into the implementation of emergency preparedness, response and recovery programmes. In July 2008 OCHA, in collaboration with UN/ISDR, issued guidelines for governments, local authorities and other stakeholders on the implementation of Priority Five of the HFA: 'Disaster Preparedness for Effective Response at all Levels'. OCHA has joint responsibility, with UNICEF and WFP, for managing emergency telecommunications assistance under the co-ordinated Cluster Approach to providing humanitarian assistance to IDPs developed by the IASC in 2005 (see below). In 2010 the ISDR recorded 373 natural disasters, which resulted in the deaths of some 297,000 people.

OCHA facilitates the inter-agency Consolidated Appeals Process (CAP), which aims to organize a co-ordinated response to resource mobilization following humanitarian crises. Participants in the process include UN bodies and agencies and other international governmental and non-governmental organizations (including the International Red Cross and Red Crescent Movement). Under guidelines adopted by the IASC in 1994, the CAP was clearly defined as a programming mechanism rather than simply an appeal process. Technical guidelines adopted in 1999 established a framework for developing a Common Humanitarian Action Plan (CHAP) to address a crisis, co-ordinating the relevant inter-agency appeal (on the basis of the CHAP), and preparing strategic monitoring reports. CAP appeals for 2012, seeking an estimated US $7,700m., were issued in December 2011; they contained action plans relating to complex humanitarian crises affecting some 51m. people in 16 countries and involving most globally active humanitarian organizations. The largest appeals were for Somalia ($1,522m.), Sudan (1,066m.), Kenya (764m.), South Sudan ($763m.) and the Democratic Republic of the Congo—DRC ($719m.).

In December 2005 the UN General Assembly adopted a resolution establishing a new Central Emergency Response Fund (CERF), expanding the former Central Emergency Revolving Fund (founded in 1991) to comprise a US $450m. grant facility, in addition to the existing $50m. revolving element, with a view to ensuring a more predictable and timely response to humanitarian crises. Both the grant and revolving facilities are financed by voluntary contributions from member states. Up to two-thirds of the grant facility can be allocated to life-saving rapid response initiatives. The upgraded Fund, administered on behalf of the UN Secretary-General by the Emergency Relief Co-ordinator in consultation with humanitarian agencies and relevant humanitarian co-ordinators, had three principle objectives: promotion of early action and response to save lives in the case of newly emerging crises or deterioration of existing complex crises, through an initial injection of funds before further donor contributions become available; enhanced response to time-crucial requirements based on demonstrable needs; and strengthening core elements of humanitarian response in underfunded crises. UN agencies and their implementing partners were to be able to access the Fund within 72 hours of the onset of a crisis. The new CERF became operational in March 2006, and by 2012 had raised more than $2,400m. from 124 donor states. During January–June 2012 the CERF allocated $167.3m. towards rapid response projects tackling emergency situations in 24 countries (9.9% of which was allocated to Pakistan; 7.7% to Niger; 7.7% to Syria; and 7.4% to South Sudan). OCHA organizes Emergency Response Funds (ERFs) to respond to unforeseen humanitarian planning requirements; and Common Humanitarian Funds (CHFs) to provide a predictable pool of funding for critical humanitarian situations. Some 13 ERFs and five CHFs (for the Central African Republic, DRC, Somalia, South Sudan and Sudan) were operational in the first half of 2012.

In December 2011, in response to severe food insecurity and malnutrition in the Sahel region of West Africa—caused by drought, poor harvests, rising food prices, and eroded resilience to repeated adverse conditions—OCHA and other UN agencies, chaired by the IASC, launched a 'Response Plan for a Food Security and Nutrition Crisis in the Sahel'; a revised version of the Plan was issued in February 2012. Some US $724m. was requested in funding for the Plan, including $480m. to address food security requirements, and $243m. in support of nutrition interventions.

GLOBAL CLUSTER LEADS

IASC co-ordinates agency assistance to IDPs through a 'Cluster Approach' (initiated in 2005); this currently comprises 11 core areas of humanitarian activity, with designated global cluster lead agencies, as follows:

Camp Co-ordination/Management: UNHCR (conflict situations), IOM (natural disasters).

Early Recovery: UNDP.

Education: UNICEF, Save The Children.

Emergency Shelter: UNHCR (conflict situations), International Federation of Red Cross and Red Crescent Societies (natural disasters).

Emergency Telecommunications: OCHA, WFP.

Food Security: FAO, WFP.

Health: WHO.

Logistics: WFP.

Nutrition: UNICEF.

Protection: UNHCR.

Water, Sanitation and Hygiene: UNICEF.

Finance

OCHA's budgetary requirements for 2012 were estimated at US $285.4m.

Publications

Annual Report.

OCHA in 2012–2013.

OCHA News (weekly).

Associated Body

Inter-Agency Secretariat of the International Strategy for Disaster Reduction—UN/ISDR: International Environment House II, 7–9 Chemin de Balexert, 1219 Châtelaine, Geneva 10, Switzerland; tel. 229178908; fax 229178964; e-mail isdr@un.org; internet www.unisdr.org; operates as secretariat of the International Strategy for Disaster Reduction (ISDR), adopted by UN member states in 2000 as a strategic framework aimed at guiding and co-ordinating the efforts of humanitarian organizations, states, intergovernmental and non-governmental organizations, financial institutions, technical bodies and civil society representatives towards achieving substantive reduction in disaster losses, and building resilient communities and nations as the foundation for sustainable development activities; UN/ISDR promotes information sharing to reduce disaster risk, and serves as the focal point providing guidance for the implementation of the Hyogo Framework for Action (HFA), adopted in 2005 as a 10-year plan of action for protecting lives and livelihoods against disasters; Head, Special Representative of the UN Secretary-General for Disaster Risk Reduction MARGARETA WAHLSTRÖM.

Office of the United Nations High Commissioner for Human Rights—OHCHR

Address: Palais des Nations, 1211 Geneva 10, Switzerland.

Telephone: 229179000; **fax:** 229179022; **e-mail:** infodesk@ohchr.org; **internet:** www.ohchr.org.

The Office is a body of the UN Secretariat and is the focal point for UN human rights activities. Since 1997 it has incorporated the Centre for Human Rights. OHCHR is guided by relevant resolutions of the General Assembly, the Charter of the United Nations, the Universal Declaration of Human Rights and subsequent human rights instruments, the Vienna Declaration and programme of action adopted by the 1993 World Conference on Human Rights (see below), and the outcome document of the 2005 World Summit of the General Assembly.

Organization

(June 2012)

HIGH COMMISSIONER

In December 1993 the UN General Assembly decided to establish the position of a United Nations High Commissioner for Human Rights (UNHCHR) following a recommendation of the World Conference on Human Rights, held in Vienna, Austria, in June of that year. The High Commissioner, who is the UN official with principal responsibility for UN human rights activities, is appointed by the UN Secretary-General, with the approval of the General Assembly, for a four-year term in office, renewable for one term. The High Commissioner is assisted by a Deputy High Commissioner for Human Rights.

High Commissioner: NAVANETHEM PILLAY (South Africa).

Deputy High Commissioner: KYUNG-WHA KHANG (Republic of Korea).

ADMINISTRATION

OHCHR's Executive Direction and Management comprises the following units: the Executive Office of the High Commissioner; the Policy, Planning, Monitoring, and Evaluation Section; the Communications Section; the Civil Society Unit; the Field Safety and Security Section; and the Donor and External Relations Section. OHCHR's headquarters contains the following four substantive Divisions: Field Operations and Technical Co-operation; Research and Right to Development; Special Procedures; and the Human Rights Council and Treaties Division. There is also a Programme Support and Management Services unit, and a branch office in New York, USA, that aims to ensure that human rights issues are fully integrated into the broader UN development and security agenda.

FIELD PRESENCES

As the Office's involvement in field work has expanded, in support of UN peace-making, peace-keeping and peace-building activities, a substantial structure of field presences has developed. In 2012 there were OHCHR regional offices in Addis Ababa, Ethiopia (covering East Africa); Bangkok, Thailand (South-east Asia); Beirut, Lebanon (the Middle East); Bishkek, Kyrgyzstan (Central Asia); Panama City, Panama (Central America); Santiago, Chile (South America); Pretoria, South Africa (Southern Africa); and Suva, Fiji (the Pacific); as well as an OHCHR Regional Centre for Human Rights and Democracy for Central Africa, based in Yaoundé, Cameroon. OHCHR country offices with human rights promotion and protection mandates were being maintained in Angola, Bolivia, Cambodia, Colombia, Guatemala, Mexico, Nepal, the Palestinian territories, Serbia (including Kosovo), Togo and Uganda. At 30 September 2011 some 532 OHCHR staff members (48%) were based in the field. At that time the Office was supporting 884 human rights officers serving in the human rights components of 15 peace missions, as well as 18 human rights officers who were participating in UN country teams. The Office was also undertaking a number of technical co-operation projects.

Activities

The mandate of OHCHR incorporates the following functions and responsibilities: the promotion and protection of human rights throughout the world; the reinforcement of international co-operation in the field of human rights; the promotion of universal ratification and implementation of international standards; the establishment of a dialogue with governments to ensure respect for human rights; and co-ordination of efforts by other UN programmes and organs to promote respect for human rights. Upon request OHCHR undertakes assessments of national human rights needs, in consultation with governments. Through the provision of guidance and training it supports the establishment of independent national human rights institutions. The Office may also study and react to cases of serious violations of human rights, and may undertake diplomatic efforts to prevent violations. It also produces educational and other information material to enhance understanding of human rights. OHCHR co-operates with academic bodies and non-governmental organizations working in the area of human rights.

The Office offers support and expertise to the UN system's human rights monitoring mechanisms, including the Human Rights Council (established in 2006) and the Universal Periodic Review (UPR, also established in 2006, to assess, cyclically, the human rights situation in all UN member states). OHCHR supports the committees that observe implementation of the following core international human rights treaties: the International Covenant on Civil and Political Rights, which entered into force in 1976; the International Covenant on Economic, Social and Cultural Rights (1976); the Convention against Torture and Other Cruel, Inhuman or Degrading Treatment or Punishment (1987); the Optional Protocol of the Convention against Torture (2006); the Convention on the Rights of the Child (1990) and its optional Protocols on Involvement of Children in Armed Conflict, on Sale of Children, Child Prostitution and Child Pornography, and on a Communications Procedure—allowing individual children to submit complaints about specific violations of their human rights under the Convention; the International Convention on the Protection of the Rights of All Migrant Workers and Members of Their Families (1990); the Convention on the Rights of Persons with Disabilities (2008); and the International Convention for the Protection of All Persons from Enforced Disappearance (2010).

In 2005 the High Commissioner published a Plan of Action for the future development of the Office and the development of the UN's human rights agenda. The Plan proposed greater involvement of the Office in both setting and ensuring—through improved monitoring and public reporting of violations and the provision of sustained technical assistance and advice at country level—the implementation of human rights norms. The World Summit of heads of state and government convened by the General Assembly in December 2005 noted the Plan of Action and made a commitment to the expansion of the UN human rights programme and to increasing the Office's funding. The High Commissioner subsequently issued consecutive biennial strategic management plans for the Office. The most recent plan, covering 2012–13, focused on the following six thematic priorities and strategies: countering discrimination, in particular racial discrimination, discrimination on the grounds of sex, religion, and discrimination against others who are marginalized; combating impunity and strengthening accountability, the rule of law and democratic society; pursuing economic, social and cultural rights, and combating inequalities and poverty, including in the context of the economic, food and climate crises; protecting human rights in the context of migration; protecting human rights in situations of armed conflict, violence and insecurity; and strengthening human rights mechanisms and the progressive development of international human rights law.

OHCHR was the lead agency in undertaking preparations for the World Conference against Racism, Racial Discrimination, Xenophobia and Related Intolerance, convened in Durban, South Africa, in August–September 2001, and attended by representatives of 168 governments. The following five core themes were addressed at Durban: sources, causes, forms and contemporary manifestations of racism; victims; prevention, education and protection measures; provision of remedies and redress (i.e. compensation); and future strategies to achieve full and effective equality. The Conference adopted the 'Durban Declaration' and a Programme of Action, in accordance with which national plans of action were to be implemented by participating states: universal ratification of the International Convention on the Elimination of all Forms of Racism (ICERD) was to be prioritized, with the broadest possible ratification of other human rights instruments, and national legislation was to be improved in line with the ICERD. On the recommendation of the Conference an interim Anti-discrimination Unit was established within OHCHR to enable the Office to play a leading role in following up the implementation of the Programme of Action. OHCHR also participated in preparations for the follow-up Durban Review Conference, which was convened in Geneva, Switzerland, in April 2009, to evaluate progress towards the achievement of the objectives set by the 2001 World Conference, and to address current major issues. The latter included the concept of defamation of religions within the existing framework of international human rights law, as a matter of incitement to religious hatred; improving understanding of different legislative patterns and judicial practices world-wide; ongoing challenges impeding the implementation of the Durban Programme of Action, such as slow progress towards eradicating extreme poverty and hunger and the effects of the global financial and food crises and of climate change, all deemed to have disproportionately severe effects on already vulnerable population groups; growing diversification of societies—resulting from globalization—exacerbated by competition for scarce resources, placing migrants at increased risk of racism; and attitudes engendered by increasing implementation of counter-terrorism measures (particularly in view of the international terrorist attacks that occurred on 11 September 2001, shortly after the end of the Durban World Conference). The 2009 Review Conference issued an Outcome Document which identified further measures and initiatives aimed at combating and eliminating, with OHCHR involvement, manifestations of racism, racial discrimination, xenophobia and related intolerance.

OHCHR assisted with the preparation of the International Convention for the Protection of All Persons from Enforced Disappearance, which was opened for signature in February 2007 and entered into force in December 2010; by June 2012 the Convention had been ratified by 33 states.

The Office promotes adherence to the Second Optional Protocol to the International Covenant on Civil and Political Rights, Aiming at the Abolition of the Death Penalty, which had been ratified by 74 states by June 2012; states where the Protocol is binding are obliged not to conduct executions or extradite individuals to a country where the death penalty is enforced, to take all necessary steps towards definitively abolishing the death penalty, and to report on their efforts in this respect.

The Office acts as the secretariat for three grant-making humanitarian funds: the UN Voluntary Fund for Victims of Torture, which was established in 1981; the Voluntary Fund for Indigenous Populations (established in 1985); and the Voluntary Fund on Contemporary Forms of Slavery (established in 1991).

OHCHR field offices and operations ('field presences'—see above) undertake a variety of activities, such as training and other technical assistance, support for Special Rapporteurs (usually appointed by the Commission on Human Rights to investigate human rights emergencies), monitoring and fact-finding. Increasingly they provide support to conflict prevention, peace-making, peace-keeping and peace-building activities. OHCHR co-operates with the UN Department of Peace-keeping Operations and Department of Political Affairs in developing the human rights component of peace-keeping and peace-building missions. In 2012 OHCHR was concerned with 35 thematic mandates, and with the following 10 country mandates (serviced by the Field Operations and Technical Co-operation Division): Burundi (mandate established in 2004; and most recently extended in 2008), Cambodia (1993; 2011), Côte d'Ivoire (2011), Democratic Republic of Korea (2004; 2011), Haiti (1995; 2011), Iran (2011), Myanmar (1992; 2011), Palestinian Territories (1993), Somalia (1993; 2011), Syria (2011), and Sudan (2009; 2011).

The OHCHR quick response desk co-ordinates urgent appeals for assistance in addressing human rights emergencies. The High Commissioner issues reports on human rights emergencies to the Commission on Human Rights.

TECHNICAL CO-OPERATION PROGRAMME

The UN Technical Co-operation Programme in the Field of Human Rights was established in 1955 to assist states, at their request, to strengthen their capacities in the observance of democracy, human rights, and the rule of law. Examples of work undertaken within the framework of the programme include training courses and workshops on good governance and the observance of human rights, expert advisory services on the incorporation of international human rights standards into national legislation and policies and on the formulation of national plans of action for the promotion and protection of human rights, fellowships, the provision of information and documentation, and consideration of promoting a human rights culture. In recent years the Programme, one of the key components of OHCHR's activities, has expanded to undertake UN system-wide human rights support activities, for example in the area of peace-keeping (see above).

Finance

OHCHR's activities are financed from the regular budget of the UN, as well as by voluntary contributions (which are channelled through the Trust Fund for the Support of the Activities of the UNHCHR and the Voluntary Fund for Technical Co-operation in the Field of Human Rights), and the three humanitarian trust funds administered by the Office. For the two years 2012–13 the projected regular budget appropriation for OHCHR amounted to US $156.5m. In addition, to cover expenditure over that period, the Office was to appeal to the international community for voluntary contributions of $291.6m. Voluntary contributions in support of OHCHR's activities are channelled through two main humanitarian funds: the Trust Fund for the Support of the Activities of the High Commissioner for Human Rights, and the Voluntary Fund for Technical Co-operation in the Field of Human Rights; there is also a small special fund supporting human rights education activities in Cambodia.

Publications

A Handbook for Civil Society.

Annual Report.

Fact sheet series.

Human Rights Quarterly.

Human rights study series.

Professional training series.

Other reference material, reports, proceedings of conferences, workshops, etc.

UN Women—United Nations Entity for Gender Equality and the Empowerment of Women

Address: 304 East 45th St, 15th Floor, New York, NY 10017, USA.

Telephone: (212) 906-6400; **fax:** (212) 906-6705; **internet:** www.unwomen.org.

The UN Entity for Gender Equality and the Empowerment of Women, referred to most commonly as UN Women, was established by the UN General Assembly in July 2010 in order to strengthen the UN's capacity to promote gender equality, the empowerment of women, and the elimination of discrimination against women and girls. It commenced operations on 1 January 2011. It has a universal mandate covering all countries.

Organization

(June 2012)

EXECUTIVE BOARD

The Executive Board comprises representatives from 41 countries around the world who serve on a rotating basis. The first Board was elected, by ECOSOC, in November 2010 for an initial three-year term. A five-member Bureau was elected by the Board in December.

SECRETARIAT

Executive Director and Under-Secretary-General: MICHELLE BACHELET (Chile).

REGIONAL OFFICES

Egypt: 1113 Corniche en-Nil, Tahrir, Cairo, Egypt; tel. (202) 574-8494; fax (202) 223-3990; e-mail mohammad.naciri@unwomen.org; Regional Programme Dir MOHAMMAD NACIRI.

Panama: City of Knowledge, Bldg 128, POB 0816-1914, Panama City, Panama; tel. (507) 302-4507; fax (507) 6747-6224; e-mail moni.pizani@unwomen.org; Regional Programme Dir MONI PINAZI.

There are also UN Women Liaison Offices in Brussels, Belgium; Osaka, Japan; Addis Ababa, Ethiopia (for the African Union); and Madrid, Spain; 15 Sub-regional Offices; and Country Offices and Programme Presences world-wide.

Activities

UN Women was established in order to consolidate the resources and mandates of existing UN bodies working to promote gender equality. It incorporated the functions of the Office of the Special Adviser on Gender Issues and Advancement of Women, the Division for the Advancement of Women of the Secretariat, the United Nations Development Fund for Women (UNIFEM) and the International Research and Training Institute for the Advancement of Women (INSTRAW).

UN Women supports deliberations on international policy, standards and norms by UN member states in intergovernmental bodies such as the Commission on the Status of Women. It also co-ordinates UN system-wide efforts to achieve gender equality; and assists countries with putting international standards into practice.

In June 2012 UN Women—maintaining that the most effective strategy in addressing HIV/AIDS is the empowerment of women and the guaranteeing of women's rights—became the 11th co-sponsor of the Joint United Nations Programme on HIV/AIDS (UNAIDS).

The core areas of activity of UN Women are identified as: Violence against Women; Peace and Security; Leadership and Participation; Economic Empowerment; Making National Plans and Budgets Gender-Responsive; Human Rights; and the Millennium Development Goals. The organization aims to work with national partners, regional organizations and UN country teams to extend the necessary expert technical, practical and advocacy assistance to further gender equality efforts. Civil society organizations are actively encouraged to collaborate with UN Women. In May 2012 UN Women launched a Global Civil Society Advisory Group, comprising advocates for women's rights and experts on gender issues, which was to facilitate UN Women-civil society dialogue. By mid-2012 UN Women was active in more than 50 countries.

In all areas of activity UN Women aims to promote implementation of internationally agreed standards as incorporated, for example, in the Convention on the Elimination of All Forms of Discrimination against Women (1979); the Beijing Declaration and Platform for Action (approved at the Fourth World Conference on Women, held in 1995); the Millennium Declaration (2000); and UN Security Council commitments such as Resolution 1325 (2000) on women, peace and security.

UN Women's first Strategic Plan, covering the period 2011–13, envisaged combating gender-based discrimination, to create equal opportunities and to ensure the comprehensive development of women and girls to enable them to be active agents of change; and upholding the rights of women in all efforts to further development, human rights, peace and security.

VIOLENCE AGAINST WOMEN

By the end of 2011 the UN Women's Trust Fund to End Violence Against Women, established in 1997, maintained a portfolio of 96 active grants covering 86 countries. Under its 14th grant-making cycle, covering 2009–10, the Fund allocated US $20.5m. to 26 initiatives in 33 countries and territories.

In November 2010 UNIFEM, operating as part of UN Women, inaugurated a new initiative, the Global Safe Cities Free of Violence Against Women and Girls Programme. Pilot projects were to be implemented in the poorest areas of five cities: Quito (Ecuador), Cairo (Egypt), New Delhi (India), Port Moresby (Papua New Guinea) and Kigali (Rwanda).

UN Women supports a public campaign ('Say NO—UNiTE'), which was launched in 1998 by the UN Secretary-General's initiative to end violence against women. The UN Entity maintains the Virtual Knowledge Centre to End Violence against Women and Girls (accessible at www.endvawnow.org), envisaged as a global one-stop resource for formulating and implementing anti-violence programmes.

PEACE AND SECURITY

UN Women has played a leading role in the development of an inter-agency framework for implementing and monitoring UN Security Council Resolution 1325 (adopted in October 2000), which urged the full and equal participation of women in peace-building efforts, and consideration of the protection needs of women and girls during conflict, and in post-conflict rehabilitation and recovery initiatives. In 2011 UN Women reported that fewer than 6% of national reconstruction budgets made specific provision for the particular needs of women and girls, and that, since 1992, fewer than 10% of peace negotiators had been female.

LEADERSHIP AND PARTICIPATION

With the Inter-Parliamentary Union, UN Women reported in the 2012 *Women in Politics* situation summary that, at 1 January of that year, only 27 countries world-wide had achieved female parliamentary representation of 30% or more, and that there were at that time only 17 female elected heads of state or government. UN Women supports national efforts to advance women's political leadership, including through constitutional reforms and through special temporary measures to raise the number of women in political positions. It supports women in acquiring the skills needed to be effective politicians, and by ensuring that election management bodies respond to women's concerns. In March 2012 the Executive Director of UN Women urged the broader use of quotas to expand participation by women in parliaments.

In 2011 UN Women deployed experts to Tunisia to support that country's newly formed electoral subcommission in its work to ensure gender parity, and also to assist with transitional justice and reconciliation processes. During that year UN Women helped Tunisian women's groups with refreshing advocacy skills. In 2011 UN Women also provided support to a coalition of 500 women's groups in Egypt.

ECONOMIC EMPOWERMENT

UN Women advocates for economic empowerment as a women's right, promoting it as a significant benefit for societies and economies. The Entity supports countries with enacting legislation and implementing policies aimed at increasing women's access to economic resources, and at establishing services that support sustainable livelihoods.

UN Women's multi-donor Fund for Gender Equality (established in 2009) aims to support women in attaining political and economic empowerment. The Fund's first cycle, covering 2009–10, allocated US $37.5m. in grants to 40 programmes in 35 countries. The Fund focuses its support on women's organizations, civil society groups, and governments, and distributes two types of grant: catalytic grants, aimed at accelerating progress in advancing gender equality; and implementation grants, aimed at consolidating existing gender equality infrastructures.

In October 2011 a Social Protection Floor Advisory Group, launched in August 2010 by ILO and WHO, and chaired by UN-Women's Executive Director, issued a report entitled *Social Protection Floor for a Fair and Inclusive Globalization.*

In September 2011 UN Women and WFP announced a joint initiative to provide income generating opportunities for women in rural areas.

NATIONAL PLANNING AND BUDGETING

UN Women advocates for provisions on gender equality to be integrated into national and local policies, plans, budgets and statistical data, and for gender equality to be a priority in channelling development assistance. UN Women provides support to national institutions that aim to make advancements for women.

MILLENNIUM DEVELOPMENT GOALS

UN Women supports the 'Global Strategy for Women's and Children's Health', launched by heads of state and government participating in the September 2010 UN Summit on the MDGs; some US $40,000m. has been pledged towards women's and child's health and achieving goals (iv) Reducing Child Mortality and (v) Improving Maternal Health.

Finance

The General Assembly estimated that the organization required a minimum annual budget of US $500m., which was to be financed by voluntary contributions and from the regular UN budget. Donor contributions to UN Women in 2011 totalled $235m, and were forecast to increase to $400m. in 2012 and to $500m. in 2013. UN Women was allocated an appropriation of $14.5m. from the UN regular budget for 2012–13.

Publications

Annual Report.

Progress of the World's Women (every 2 years).

Words to Action (quarterly).

World Survey on the Role of Women in Development (every 5 years).

Women in Parliament (with the IPU, annually).

United Nations Children's Fund—UNICEF

Address: 3 United Nations Plaza, New York, NY 10017, USA.

Telephone: (212) 326-7000; **fax:** (212) 887-7465; **e-mail:** info@unicef.org; **internet:** www.unicef.org.

UNICEF was established in 1946 by the UN General Assembly as the UN International Children's Emergency Fund, to meet the emergency needs of children in post-war Europe. In 1950 its mandate was expanded to respond to the needs of children in developing countries. In 1953 the General Assembly decided that UNICEF should become a permanent branch of the UN system, with an emphasis on programmes giving long-term benefits to children everywhere, particularly those in developing countries. In 1965 UNICEF was awarded the Nobel Peace Prize.

Organization

(June 2012)

EXECUTIVE BOARD

The Executive Board, as the governing body of UNICEF, comprises 36 member governments from all regions, elected in rotation for a three-year term by ECOSOC. The Board establishes policy, reviews programmes and approves expenditure. It reports to the General Assembly through ECOSOC.

SECRETARIAT

The Executive Director of UNICEF is appointed by the UN Secretary-General in consultation with the Executive Board. The administration of UNICEF and the appointment and direction of staff are the responsibility of the Executive Director, under policy directives laid down by the Executive Board, and under a broad authority delegated to the Executive Director by the Secretary-General. Around 85% of UNICEF staff positions are based in field offices.

Executive Director: ANTHONY LAKE (USA).

UNICEF OFFICES

UNICEF has a network of eight regional and 127 field offices serving 155 countries and territories. Its offices in Tokyo, Japan, and Brussels, Belgium, support fund-raising activities; UNICEF's supply division is administered from the office in Copenhagen, Denmark. A research centre concerned with advocacy for child rights and development is based in Florence, Italy.

Belgium: Keizerinlaan 66, 1000 Brussels, 1000 Brussels; tel. (2) 230-59-70; fax (2) 230-34-62; e-mail brussels@unicef.org; internet unicef.be.

Japan: UNICEF House, 4-6-12 Takanawa, Minato-ku, Tokyo 108-8607, Japan; tel. (3) 5467-4431; fax (3) 5467-4437; e-mail tokyo@unicef.org; internet www.unicef.or.jp.

Regional Office for the Americas and the Caribbean: Apdo 0843-03045, Panamá, Panama; tel. (507) 301-7400; e-mail thahn@unicef.org; internet www.uniceflac.org.

Regional Office for Central and Eastern Europe and the Commonwealth of Independent States: Palais des Nations, 1211 Geneva 10, Switzerland; tel. 229095433; fax 229095909; e-mail ceecis@unicef.org; internet www.unicef.org/ceecis.

Regional Office for East Asia and the Pacific: POB 2-154, Bangkok 10200, Thailand; tel. (2) 2805931; fax (2) 2803563; e-mail eapro@unicef.org; internet www.unicef.org/eapro.

Regional Office for Eastern and Southern Africa: POB 44145, Nairobi, Kenya 00100; tel. (20) 7621234; fax (20) 7622678; e-mail unicefesaro@unicef.org; internet www.unicef.org/esaro.

Regional Office for the Middle East and North Africa: POB 1551, 11821 Amman, Jordan; tel. (6) 5502400; fax (6) 5531112; e-mail amman@unicef.org.jo; internet www.unicef.org/jordan.

Regional Office for South Asia: POB 5815, Leknath Marg, Kathmandu, Nepal; tel. (1) 4419082; fax (1) 4419479; e-mail rosa@unicef.org; internet www.unicef.org/rosa.

Regional Office for West and Central Africa: POB 29720, Dakar-Yoff, Senegal; tel. 33-869-58-58; fax 33-820-89-65; e-mail wcaro@unicef.org; internet www.unicef.org/wcaro/index.html.

UNICEF Innocenti Research Centre: Piazza SS. Annunziata 12, 50122 Florence, Italy; tel. (055) 20330; fax (055) 2033220; e-mail florence@unicef.org; internet www.unicef-irc.org; f. 1988; undertakes research in two thematic areas: Social and economic policies and children; and Child protection and implementation of international standards for children; Dir GORDON ALEXANDER.

UNICEF Supply Division: Oceanvej 10–12, 2100 Copenhagen, Denmark; tel. 35-27-35-27; fax 35-26-94-21; e-mail supply@unicef.org; internet www.unicef.org/supply; responsible for overseeing UNICEF's global procurement and logistics operations.

UNICEF New York Supply Centre (USA): UNICEF House, 3 UN Plaza, New York, NY 10017 USA; tel. (212) 35-67-490; fax (212) 35-67-477.

Further strategic supply hubs are located in Dubai, United Arab Emirates; Douala, Cameroon; Colón, Panama; and Shanghai, People's Republic of China.

NATIONAL COMMITTEES

UNICEF is supported by 36 National Committees, mostly in industrialized countries, whose volunteer members raise money through various specific campaigns and activities, including the sale of greetings cards and collection of foreign coins. The Committees also undertake advocacy and awareness campaigns on a number of issues and provide an important link with the general public.

Activities

UNICEF is dedicated to the well-being of children, adolescents and women and works for the realization and protection of their rights within the frameworks of the Convention on the Rights of the Child, which was adopted by the UN General Assembly in 1989, and by 2012 was almost universally ratified, and of the Convention on the Elimination of All Forms of Discrimination Against Women, adopted by the UN General Assembly in 1979. Promoting the full implementation of the Conventions, UNICEF aims to ensure that children world-wide are given the best possible start in life and attain a good level of basic education, and that adolescents are given every opportunity to develop their capabilities and participate successfully in society. The Fund also continues to provide relief and rehabilitation assistance in emergencies. Through its extensive field network in more than 150 developing countries and territories, UNICEF undertakes, in co-ordination with governments, local communities and other aid organizations, programmes in health, nutrition, education, water and sanitation, the environment, gender issues and development, and other fields of importance to children. Emphasis is placed on low-cost, community-based programmes. UNICEF programmes are increasingly focused on supporting children and women during critical periods of their life, when intervention can make a lasting difference. Since the 1950s UNICEF has engaged the services of prominent individuals as Goodwill Ambassadors and Advocates, who can use their status to attract attention to particular causes and support UNICEF's objectives. During 2011 UNICEF advocated for increased focus on children in national development plans and budgets in 102 countries.

The principal themes of UNICEF's medium-term strategic plan for the period 2006–13 are: young child survival and development; basic education and gender equality (including the Fund's continued leadership of the UN Girls' Education Initiative, see below); HIV/AIDS and children (including participation in the Joint UN Programme on HIV/AIDS—UNAIDS—see below); child protection from violence, exploitation and abuse; and policy advocacy and partnerships for children's rights. These priority areas are guided by the relevant UN Millennium Development Goals (MDGs) adopted by world leaders in 2000, and by the 'A World Fit for Children' declaration and plan of action endorsed by the UN General Assembly Special Session on Children in 2002. The 'A World Fit for Children' declaration reaffirmed commitment to the agenda of the 1990 World Summit for Children. The plan of action resolved to work towards the attainment by 2015 of 21 new goals and targets supporting the MDGs in the areas of education, health and the protection of children; these included: a reduction of mortality rates for infants and children under five by two-thirds; a reduction of maternal mortality rates by three-quarters; a reduction by one-third in the rate of severe malnutrition among children under the age of five; and enrolment in primary education by 90% of children. UNICEF issues regular reports that monitor progress in achieving the MDGs. The ninth in the series, entitled *Progress for Children: Achieving the MDGs with Equity (No. 9)*, was published in September 2010. UNICEF supports the 'Global Strategy for Women's and Children's Health', launched by heads of state and government participating in the September 2010 UN Summit on the MDGs; some US $40,000m. has been pledged towards women's and child's health and achieving goals (iv) Reducing Child Mortality and (v) Improving Maternal Health. In 2012 a roadmap was being developed towards the Fund's next medium-term strategic plan, which was to cover the period 2014–17; the new plan was to be passed to the Executive Board for approval in late 2013.

UNICEF estimates that more than 500,000 women die every year during pregnancy or childbirth, largely because of inadequate maternal healthcare, and nearly 4m. newborns die within 28 days of birth. For every maternal death, approximately 30 further women suffer permanent injuries or chronic disabilities as a result of complications during pregnancy or childbirth. Under the Global Partnership for Maternal, Newborn and Child Health, UNICEF works with WHO, UNFPA and other partners in countries with high maternal mortality to improve maternal health and prevent maternal and newborn death through the integration of a continuum of home, community, outreach and facility-based care, embracing every stage of maternal, newborn and child health. UNICEF and partners work with governments and policy-makers to ensure that ante-natal and obstetric care is a priority in national health plans. UNICEF's recent activities in this area have included support for obstetric facilities and training in, and advocacy of, women's health issues, such as ending child marriage, eliminating female genital mutilation/cutting (FGM/C), preventing malaria and promoting the uptake of tetanus toxoid vaccinations and iron and folic acid supplements among pregnant women.

YOUNG CHILD SURVIVAL AND DEVELOPMENT

In 2011 UNICEF allocated some 52% of total programme assistance to young child survival and development. In 2009 UNICEF estimated that around 8.1m. children under five years of age died (compared with some 20m. child mortalities in 1960 and some 13m. in 1990)—mainly in developing countries (three-quarters occurring in the People's Republic of China, the Democratic Republic of the Congo, India, Nigeria, and Pakistan), and the majority from largely preventable causes. UNICEF has worked with WHO and other partners to increase global immunization coverage against the following six diseases: measles, poliomyelitis, tuberculosis, diphtheria, whooping cough and tetanus. In 2003 UNICEF, WHO, the World Bank and other partners established a new Child Survival Partnership, which acts as a forum for the promotion of co-ordinated action in support of efforts to save children's lives in 68 targeted developing countries. UNICEF, WHO, the World Bank and the UN Population Division established an Inter-agency Group for Child Mortality Estimation (IGME) in 2004, to advance work on monitoring progress towards meeting the MDG on reducing child mortality. In September 2005 UNICEF, WHO and other partners launched the Partnership for Maternal, Newborn and Child Health, which aimed to accelerate progress towards the attainment of the MDGs to reduce child and maternal mortality. In 2000 UNICEF, WHO, the World Bank and a number of public- and private-sector partners launched the Global Alliance for Vaccines and Immunization (GAVI), subsequently renamed the GAVI Alliance, which aims to protect children of all nationalities and socio-economic groups against vaccine-preventable diseases. GAVI's strategy includes improving access to sustainable immunization services, expanding the use of existing vaccines, accelerating the development and introduction of new vaccines and technologies and promoting immunization coverage as a focus of international development efforts. In 2006 UNICEF, WHO and other partners launched the Global Immunization Vision and Strategy (GIVS), a global 10-year framework, covering 2006–15, aimed at reducing deaths due to vaccine-preventable diseases by at least two-thirds compared to 2000 levels, by 2015; and increasing national vaccination coverage levels to at least 90%. (In 2009 the global child vaccination coverage rate was estimated at 82%.) From 2006 a Global Immunization Meeting was convened annually by UNICEF, WHO and GAVI Alliance partners; the fifth Meeting, held in February 2010, addressed issues including means of improving routine vaccination and supporting accelerated disease control initiatives; the introduction of new vaccines; and vaccine supply, including the status of pandemic influenza vaccines.

UNICEF works to improve safe water supply, sanitation and hygiene, and thereby reduce the risk of diarrhoea and other water-borne diseases. In partnership with other organizations the Fund supports initiatives to make schools in more than 90 developing countries safer through school-based water, sanitation and hygiene programmes. UNICEF places great emphasis on increasing the testing and protection of drinking water at its source as well as in the home. UNICEF, the World Bank and other partners participate in the Global Public-Private Partnership for Handwashing with Soap, which was established in 2001 with the aim of empowering communities in developing countries to prevent diarrhoea and respiratory infections through the promotion of the practice of thorough hand-washing with soap. In 2006 UNICEF and partners established the Global Task Force on Water and Sanitation with the aim of providing all children with access to safe water, and accelerating progress towards MDG targets on safe drinking water and basic sanitation.

UNICEF-assisted programmes for the control of diarrhoeal diseases promote the low-cost manufacture and distribution of prepackaged salts or home-made solutions. The use of 'oral rehydration therapy' has risen significantly in recent years, and is believed to prevent more than 1m. child deaths annually. During 1990–2000 diarrhoea-related deaths were reduced by one-half. UNICEF also promotes the need to improve sanitation and access to safe water supplies in developing nations in order to reduce the risk of diarrhoea and other water-borne diseases (see 20/20 initiative, below). To control acute respiratory infections, another leading cause of death in children under five in developing countries, UNICEF works with WHO in training health workers to diagnose and treat the associated diseases. At the UN General Assembly Special Session on Children, in 2002, goals were set to reduce measles deaths by 50%. Expanded efforts by UNICEF, WHO and other partners led to a reduction in world-wide measles deaths by 78% between 2000 and 2008. Around 1m. children die from malaria every year, mainly in sub-Saharan Africa. In October 1998 UNICEF, together with WHO, UNDP and the World Bank, inaugurated a new global campaign, Roll Back Malaria, to fight the disease. UNICEF is actively engaged in developing innovative and effective ways to distribute highly-subsidized insecticide-treated mosquito nets at local level, thereby increasing the proportion of children and pregnant women who use them.

According to UNICEF estimates, around 25% of children under five years of age are underweight, while each year malnutrition contributes to more than one-third of the child deaths in that age group and leaves millions of others with physical and mental disabilities. UNICEF supports national efforts to reduce malnutrition, for example, fortifying staple foods with micronutrients, widening women's access to education, improving the nutritional status of pregnant women, strengthening household food security and basic health services, providing food supplies in emergencies, and promoting sound childcare and feeding practices. Since 1991 more than 19,000 hospitals in about 130 countries have been designated 'baby-friendly', having implemented a set of UNICEF and WHO recommendations entitled '10 steps to successful breast-feeding'. The Executive Director of UNICEF chairs the Lead Group of the Scaling Up Nutrition (SUN) initiative, which convened its first meeting in April 2012, and comprises 27 national leaders and agencies jointly providing strategic guidance with a view to improving child and maternal nutrition. SUN, initiated in 2009, and co-ordinated by the UN Secretary-General's Special Representative for Food Security and Nutrition, aims to increase the coverage of interventions that improve nutrition during the first 1,000 days of a child's life (such as exclusive breastfeeding, optimal complementary feeding practices, and provision of essential vitamins and minerals); and to ensure that national nutrition plans are implemented and that government programmes take nutrition into account. The activities of SUN are guided by the Framework for Scaling up Nutrition, which was published in April 2010 and subsequently endorsed by more than 100 partners, including UN agencies, governments, research institutions, and representatives of civil society and of the private sector; and by the SUN Roadmap, finalized in September 2010.

The results of integrated approaches to child health, such as the Accelerated Child Survival and Development (ACSD) strategy and community-based Integrated Management of Childhood Illnesses (IMCI) programme, have demonstrated new potential to reduce child mortality. The ACSD strategy, implemented by UNICEF since 2002, is an intensive combination of life-saving interventions including the promotion of antenatal care, vaccination and breast-feeding, volunteer health-worker follow-up of newborns, and the distribution of insecticide-treated mosquito nets. Focused in 97 high-mortality districts in 11 mainly West African countries, ACSD has reached around 16m. people, including 2.8m. children under the age of five.

BASIC EDUCATION AND GENDER EQUALITY

In 2011 UNICEF allocated some 21% of total programme assistance to basic education and gender equality. UNICEF considers education to be a fundamental human right, and works to ensure all children receive equal access to quality education. UNICEF participated in and fully supports the objectives and framework for action adopted by the World Education Forum in Dakar, Senegal, in April 2000, including the Education for All initiative. UNICEF was assigned formal responsibility within the initiative for education in emergencies, early childhood care and technical and policy support. UNICEF leads and acts as the secretariat of the United Nations Girls' Education Initiative (UNGEI), which aims to increase the enrolment of girls in primary schools in more than 100 countries. It is estimated that more than 100m. school-age children world-wide, of whom more than one-half are girls, remain deprived of basic education. In May 2010 UNGEI convened the first ever international conference on 'Engendering Empowerment: Education and Equality' ('E4'), in Dakar, Senegal. The E4 conference unanimously adopted the Dakar Declaration on Accelerating Girls' Education and Gender Equality, in which it urged that increased focus should be placed on accelerating access to education for the most socially deprived girls, deemed to be the most disadvantaged group in education.

UNICEF advocates the implementation of the Child Friendly School model, designed to facilitate the delivery of safe, quality education. UNICEF, in partnership with UNESCO, has developed an Essential Learning Package to support countries to reduce disparities in the provision of basic education. The initiative was implemented for the first time by Burkina Faso in 2003, and has since been adopted by a further 11 countries in West and Central Africa.

It was reported in 2011 that the literacy rate for young women aged between 15–24 in Afghanistan was 18%, compared with 50% for young men. In 2005 approximately 500,000 girls in Afghanistan were enrolled in schools for the first time, and in March 2007 an UNGEI project (the Afghanistan Girls' Education Initiative—AGEI) was launched in that country.

Major 'back-to-school' campaigns and enrolment drives were launched in countries struck by the December 2004 Indian Ocean tsunamis; within three months of the disaster 90% of affected children had returned to school. Similar campaigns have been undertaken in countries emerging from civil conflict, for example Kyrgyzstan, Somalia and South Sudan, and include advocacy efforts as well as the distribution of essential educational supplies, often in the form of specially designed 'school-in-a-box' kits.

HIV/AIDS AND CHILDREN

In 2011 UNICEF allocated some 4% of total programme assistance to combating HIV/AIDS. UNICEF is concerned at the danger posed by HIV/AIDS to the realization of children's rights and aims to provide expertise, support, logistical co-ordination and innovation towards ending the epidemic and limiting its impact on children and their mothers. At the end of 2009 it was estimated that 2.5m. children under the age of 15 were living with HIV/AIDS world-wide. During that year some 370,000 children under the age of 15 were estimated to have been newly infected with HIV, while 260,000 died as a result of AIDS and AIDS-related illnesses. Some 16.6m. children world-wide have lost one or both parents to AIDS since the start of the pandemic, and as a result of HIV/AIDS many children have suffered poverty, homelessness, discrimination, and loss of education and other life opportunities. UNICEF's priorities in this area include prevention of infection among young people (through, for example, support for education programmes and dissemination of information through the media), reduction in mother-to-child transmission, care and protection of orphans and other vulnerable children, and care and support for children, young people and parents living with HIV/AIDS. UNICEF works closely in this field with governments and co-operates with other UN agencies in the Joint UN Programme on HIV/AIDS (UNAIDS), which became operational on 1 January 1996. Young people aged 15–24 are reported to account for around 45% of new HIV infections world-wide. In July 2002 UNICEF, UNAIDS and WHO jointly produced a study entitled *Young People and HIV/AIDS: Opportunity in Crisis*, examining young people's sexual behaviour patterns and knowledge of HIV/AIDS. UNICEF advocates Life Skills-Based Education as a means of empowering young people to cope with challenging situations and of encouraging them to adopt healthy patterns of behaviour. In July 2004 UNICEF and other partners produced a *Framework for the Protection, Care and Support of Orphans and Vulnerable Children Living in a World with HIV and AIDS*. In October 2005 UNICEF launched Unite for Children, Unite against AIDS, a campaign that was to provide a platform for child-focused advocacy aimed at reversing the spread of HIV/AIDS amongst children, adolescents and young people; and to provide a child-focused framework for national programmes based on the following four pillars (known as the 'Four Ps'): the prevention of mother-to-child HIV transmission, improved provision of paediatric treatment, prevention of infection among adolescents and young people, and protection and support of children affected by HIV/AIDS. In December 2009 UNICEF issued its fourth *Children and AIDS: A Stocktaking Report*, detailing ongoing progress and challenges. In October 2010 UNICEF issued its first Mother-Baby Pack, containing drugs to prevent mother-to-child transmission of HIV in the poorest households. In June 2011 a high-level meeting on HIV/AIDs convened at UN headquarters launched a global plan towards eliminating new HIV infections among children by 2015. UNICEF supports the Global Plan towards the Elimination of New HIV Infections among Children by 2015 and Keeping Their Mothers Alive, which was endorsed in June 2011 by a UN High Level Meeting on HIV/AIDS.

At December 2009 it was estimated that of the total cases of children aged 0–14 living with HIV/AIDS 2.3m. were in sub-Saharan Africa, 150,000 in South and South-East Asia, 53,000 in Latin America and the Caribbean, 21,000 in the Middle East and North Africa, 19,400 in Europe and Central Asia, 8,000 in East Asia, 4,500 in North America and 3,100 in the Pacific region.

CHILD PROTECTION FROM VIOLENCE, EXPLOITATION AND ABUSE

In 2011 some 10% of total programme resources were allocated to child protection. UNICEF is actively involved in global-level partnerships for child protection, including the Inter-Agency Co-ordination Panel on Juvenile Justice; the Inter-Agency Working Group on Unaccompanied and Separated Children; the Donors' Working Group on Female FGM/C (see above); the Better Care Network; the Study on Violence Against Children; the Inter-Agency Standing Committee (IASC) Task Force on Protection from Sexual Exploitation and Abuse in Humanitarian Crises; and the IASC Task Force on Mental Health and Psychological Support in Emergency Settings.

UNICEF estimates that the births of around 48m. children annually (about 36% of all births) are not registered, and that some 63% of births occuring in South Asia, and 55% of births in sub-Saharan Africa, are unregistered. UNICEF promotes universal registration in order to prevent the abuse of children without proof of age and nationality, for example through trafficking, forced labour, early marriage and military recruitment.

UNICEF estimates that some 158m. children aged from five–14 are engaged in child labour, while around 1.2m. children world-wide are trafficked each year. The Fund, which vigorously opposes the exploitation of children as a violation of their basic human rights, works with the ILO and other partners to promote an end to exploitative and hazardous child labour, and supports special projects to provide education, counselling and care in developing countries. UNICEF co-sponsored and actively participated in the Third Congress Against Commercial Sexual Exploitation of Children, held in Rio de Janeiro, Brazil, in November 2008.

More than 250,000 children are involved in armed conflicts as soldiers, porters and forced labourers. UNICEF encourages ratification of the Optional Protocol to the Convention on the Rights of the Child on the involvement of children in armed conflict, which was adopted by the General Assembly in May 2000 and entered into force in February 2002, and bans the compulsory recruitment of combatants below the age of 18. The Fund also urges states to make unequivocal statements endorsing 18 as the minimum age of voluntary recruitment to the armed forces. UNICEF, with Save the Children, co-chairs the Steering Group of the Paris Principles, which aims to support the implementation of a series of 'Commitments', first endorsed in 2007, to end the recruitment of children, support the release of children from the armed forces and facilitate their reintegration into civilian life. By the end of 2010 95 countries had voluntarily signed up to the Paris Commitments. It is estimated that landmines kill and maim between 8,000 and 10,000 children every year. UNICEF supports mine awareness campaigns, and promotes the full ratification of the Convention on the Prohibition of the Use, Stockpiling, Production and Transfer of Anti-Personnel Mines and on their Destruction, which was adopted in December 1997 and entered into force in March 1999. By June 2012 the Convention had been ratified by 160 countries (most recently by Somalia, in April).

POLICY AND ADVOCACY AND PARTNERSHIPS FOR CHILDREN'S RIGHTS

In 2011 UNICEF allocated some 11% of total programme assistance to policy and advocacy and partnerships for children's rights. UNICEF's annual publication *The State of the World's Children* includes social and economic data relevant to the well-being of children; the theme of the 2012 report, issued in March, was 'Children in an Urban World'. UNICEF's Multiple Indicator Cluster Survey (MICS) method of data collection, initiated in 1995, is a main tool used in measuring progress towards the achievement of the UN MDGs.

The UNICEF Regional Monitoring Project (MONEE) was undertaken during 1992–2001 to monitor the effects of economic and social transition on children in Central and South-Eastern Europe and the former USSR. Since 2003 the UNICEF Innocenti Research Centre has published an annual social monitoring report, addressing the state of child wellbeing in Eastern European and Central Asian states with economies in transition. The *Innocenti Social Monitor 2009* reviewed the effects of the global economic crisis on children in the region.

Since 2005 young people from the Group of Eight (G8) nations (Canada, France, Germany, Italy, Japan, Russia, the United Kingdom and the USA) and selected emerging countries (including Brazil, People's Republic of China, Egypt, India, Mexico and South Africa) have participated in a Junior 8 (J8) summit, which is organized with support from UNICEF on the fringes of the annual G8 summit. The J8 summits address issues including education, energy, climate change, HIV/AIDS, the global financial crisis, and tolerance. Since 2010 G(irls)20 summits have been convened alongside summits of G20 leaders; the participants represent the G20 countries, and include, also, young female representatives of the African Union and European Union.

UNICEF aims to break the cycle of poverty by advocating for the provision of increased development aid to developing countries, and aims to help poor countries obtain debt relief and to ensure access to basic social services. UNICEF was the leading agency in promoting the 20/20 initiative, which was endorsed at the World Summit for Social Development, held in Copenhagen, Denmark, in March 1995. The initiative encouraged the governments of developing and donor countries to allocate at least 20% of their domestic budgets and official development aid to healthcare, primary education, and low-cost safe water and sanitation.

Through this focus area, UNICEF seeks to work with partners to strengthen capacities to design and implement cross-sectoral social and economic policies, child-focused legislative measures and budgetary allocations that enable countries to meet their obligations under the Convention on the Rights of the Child and the Convention on the Elimination of All Forms of Discrimination against Women. UNICEF has identified the following priority areas of support to 'upstream' policy work: child poverty and disparities; social budgeting; decentralization; social security and social protection; holistic legislative reform for the two Conventions; and the impact of migration on children.

HUMANITARIAN RESPONSE

UNICEF provides emergency relief assistance to children and young people affected by conflict, natural disasters and food crises. In situations of violence and social disintegration the Fund provides support in the areas of education, health, mine-awareness and psychosocial assistance, and helps to demobilize and rehabilitate child soldiers. In 2011 UNICEF responded to 292 humanitarian challenges in 80 countries. The largest humanitarian crisis addressed in that year was the outbreak of severe famine in the Horn of Africa, where some 13m. people were suffering acute hunger, with 750,000 children deemed to be at risk of death. UNICEF, with local partners, provided assistance to more than 241,000 acutely malnourished children in the region; and, in co-ordinated actvities with other international agencies, supported a further 263,000 children. Furthermore, UNICEF facilitated the provision of measles vaccinations to more than 1m. children under 16; provided access to safe water for 3m. Somalis; and supported more than 800,000 people in maintaining good hygiene.

In 1999 UNICEF adopted a Peace and Security Agenda to help guide international efforts in this field. Emergency education assistance includes the provision of 'Edukits' in refugee camps and the reconstruction of school buildings. In the area of health the Fund co-operates with WHO to arrange 'days of tranquillity' in order to facilitate the immunization of children in conflict zones. Psychosocial assistance activities include special programmes to support traumatized children and help unaccompanied children to be reunited with parents or extended families.

In July 2011 UNICEF estimated that more than 2m. malnourished young children required urgent assistance owing to severe and prolonged drought conditions, compounded by high food prices, in Somalia (where famine was formally declared in two regions), Djibouti, Ethiopia and Kenya; around 500,000 of affected children in the Horn of Africa were deemed to be acutely undernourished and in a life-threatening situation. UNICEF undertook immunization campaigns, airlifted supplies—including therapeutic food and medicine, and equipment to supply clean water to IDPs—into Somalia (which was also destabilized by violent unrest), and, with other humanitarian agencies, established emergency feeding centres in countries neighbouring Somalia. During that month UNICEF requested some US $31.8m. in donor funding to provide support to children and their mothers in the region at that time. Families in Somalia were provided with food vouchers that could be exchanged for essential items at local markets.

In 2012 UNICEF assisted refugee children in Jordan and Lebanon, whose families had fled from escalating violence in Syria, by facilitating immunization, supporting programmes in the areas of education and psychosocial support, and through the provision of child-friendly spaces.

In the mid-2000s UNICEF country offices prepared contingency plans for a possible future avian influenza pandemic among humans, with a particular focus on children, as part of the inter-agency response to the threat.

Since 1998 UNICEF's humanitarian response has been structured within a framework of identified Core Commitments for Children in Humanitarian Action (CCCs). Revised CCCs were issued in April 2010 to reflect new humanitarian structures and best practices. The revised CCCs incorporated UNICEF's commitment to working in partnership with international organizations, national authorities and civil society in order to strengthen risk reduction, disaster preparedness and response, and early recovery. During 2005 the UN's Inter-Agency Standing Committee (IASC), concerned with co-ordinating the international response to humanitarian disasters, developed a concept of organizing agency assistance to IDPs through the institutionalization of a 'Cluster Approach', comprising 11 core areas of activity. UNICEF is the lead agency for the clusters on Education (jointly with Save The Children); Nutrition; and Water, Sanitation and Hygiene. In addition, it leads the Gender-based Violence Area of Responsibility sub-cluster (jointly with UNFPA) and the Child Protection Area of Responsibility sub-cluster within the Protection Cluster.

Finance

UNICEF is funded by voluntary contributions from governments and non-governmental and private sector sources. UNICEF's income is divided into contributions for 'regular resources' (used for country programmes of co-operation approved by the Executive Board, programme support, and management and administration costs) and contributions for 'other resources' (for special purposes, including expanding the outreach of country programmes of co-operation, and ensuring capacity to deliver critical assistance to women and children, for example during humanitarian crises). UNICEF's total income in 2011 was US $3,711m., of which $2,260m. (60%) was from governments, $1,089m. (29%) from the private sector and non-governmental organizations, and $362m. (9%) from inter-organizational arrangements.

UNICEF's total expenditure in 2011 was $3,819m. Some 57% of the Fund's total programme expenditure in that year was allocated to activities in Africa south of the Sahara, 18% to activities in Asia, 7% to Latin America and the Caribbean, 4% to interregional projects, 3% to the Middle East and North Africa, and 2% to Central and Eastern Europe and the CIS.

UNICEF, UNDP and UNFPA are committed to integrating their budgets from 2014.

Publications

Progress for Children (in English, French and Spanish).

The State of the World's Children (annually, in Arabic, English, French, Russian and Spanish and about 30 other national languages).

UNICEF Annual Report (in English, French and Spanish).

UNICEF at a Glance (in English, French and Spanish).

UNICEF Humanitarian Action Report (annually).

Reports and studies; series on children and women; nutrition; education; children's rights; children in wars and disasters; working children; water, sanitation and the environment; analyses of the situation of children and women in individual developing countries.

Convention on the Rights of the Child

(Adopted by the General Assembly on 20 November 1989)

PREAMBLE

The States Parties to the present Convention,

Considering that, in accordance with the principles proclaimed in the Charter of the United Nations, recognition of the inherent dignity and of the equal and inalienable rights of all members of the human family is the foundation of freedom, justice and peace in the world,

Bearing in mind that the peoples of the United Nations have, in the Charter, reaffirmed their faith in fundamental human rights and in the dignity and worth of the human person, and have determined to promote social progress and better standards of life in larger freedom,

Recognizing that the United Nations has, in the Universal Declaration of Human Rights and in the International Covenants on Human Rights, proclaimed and agreed that everyone is entitled to all the rights and freedoms set forth therein, without distinction of any kind, such as race, colour, sex, language, religion, political or other opinion, national or social origin, property, birth or other status,

Recalling that, in the Universal Declaration of Human Rights, the United Nations has proclaimed that childhood is entitled to special care and assistance,

Convinced that the family, as the fundamental group of society and the natural environment for the growth and well-being of all its members and particularly children, should be afforded the necessary protection and assistance so that it can fully assume its responsibilities within the community,

Recognizing that the child, for the full and harmonious development of his or her personality, should grow up in a family environment, in an atmosphere of happiness, love and understanding,

Considering that the child should be fully prepared to live an individual life in society, and brought up in the spirit of the ideals proclaimed in the Charter of the United Nations, and in particular in the spirit of peace, dignity, tolerance, freedom, equality and solidarity,

Bearing in mind that the need to extend particular care to the child has been stated in the Geneva Declaration of the Rights of the Child of 1924 and in the Declaration of the Rights of the Child adopted by the General Assembly on 20 November 1959 and recognized in the Universal Declaration of Human Rights, in the International Covenant on Civil and Political Rights (in particular in articles 23 and 24), in the International Covenant on Economic, Social and Cultural Rights (in particular in article 10) and in the statutes and relevant instruments of specialized agencies and international organizations concerned with the welfare of children,

Bearing in mind that, as indicated in the Declaration of the Rights of the Child, 'the child, by reason of his physical and mental immaturity, needs special safeguards and care, including appropriate legal protection, before as well as after birth',

Recalling the provisions of the Declaration on Social and Legal Principles relating to the Protection and Welfare of Children, with Special Reference to Foster Placement and Adoption Nationally and Internationally; the United Nations Standard Minimum Rules for the Administration of Juvenile Justice (The Beijing Rules); and the Declaration on the Protection of Women and Children in Emergency and Armed Conflict,

Recognizing that, in all countries in the world, there are children living in exceptionally difficult conditions, and that such children need special consideration,

Taking due account of the importance of the traditions and cultural values of each people for the protection and harmonious development of the child,

Recognizing the importance of international co-operation for improving the living conditions of children in every country, in particular in the developing countries,

Have agreed as follows.

PART I

Article 1

For the purposes of the present Convention, a child means every human being below the age of eighteen years unless, under the law applicable to the child, majority is attained earlier.

Article 2

1. States Parties shall respect and ensure the rights set forth in the present Convention to each child within their jurisdiction without discrimination of any kind, irrespective of the child's or his or her parent's or legal guardian's race, colour, sex, language, religion, political or other opinion, national, ethnic or social origin, property, disability, birth or other status.

2. States Parties shall take all appropriate measures to ensure that the child is protected against all forms of discrimination or punishment on the basis of the status, activities, expressed opinions, or beliefs of the child's parents, legal guardians, or family members.

Article 3

1. In all actions concerning children, whether undertaken by public or private social welfare institutions, courts of law, administrative authorities or legislative bodies, the best interests of the child shall be a primary consideration.

2. States Parties undertake to ensure the child such protection and care as is necessary for his or her well-being, taking into account the rights and duties of his or her parents, legal guardians, or other individuals legally responsible for him or her, and, to this end, shall take all appropriate legislative and administrative measures.

3. States Parties shall ensure that the institutions, services and facilities responsible for the care or protection of children shall conform with the standards established by competent authorities, particularly in the areas of safety, health, in the number and suitability of their staff, as well as competent supervision.

Article 4

States Parties shall undertake all appropriate legislative, administrative, and other measures for the implementation of the rights recognized in the present Convention. With regard to economic, social and cultural rights, States Parties shall undertake such measures to the maximum extent of their available resources and, where needed, within the framework of international co-operation.

Article 5

States Parties shall respect the responsibilities, rights and duties of parents or, where applicable, the members of the extended family or community as provided for by local custom, legal guardians or other persons legally responsible for the child, to provide, in a manner consistent with the evolving capacities of the child, appropriate direction and guidance in the exercise by the child of the rights recognized in the present Convention.

Article 6

1. States Parties recognize that every child has the inherent right to life.

2. States Parties shall ensure to the maximum extent possible the survival and development of the child.

Article 7

1. The child shall be registered immediately after birth and shall have the right from birth to a name, the right to acquire a nationality and, as far as possible, the right to know and be cared for by his or her parents.

2. States Parties shall ensure the implementation of these rights in accordance with their national law and their obligations under the relevant international instruments in this field, in particular where the child would otherwise be stateless.

Article 8

1. States Parties undertake to respect the right of the child to preserve his or her identity, including nationality, name and family relations as recognized by law without unlawful interference.

2. Where a child is legally deprived of some or all of the elements of his or her identity, States Parties shall provide appropriate assistance and protection, with a view to re-establishing speedily his or her identity.

Article 9

1. States Parties shall ensure that a child shall not be separated from his or her parents against their will, except when competent authorities subject to judicial review determine, in accordance with applicable law and procedures, that such separation is necessary for the best interests of the child. Such determination

may be necessary in a particular case such as one involving abuse or neglect of the child by the parents, or one where the parents are living separately and a decision must be made as to the child's place of residence.

2. In any proceedings pursuant to paragraph 1 of the present article, all interested parties shall be given an opportunity to participate in the proceedings and make their views known.

3. States Parties shall respect the right of the child who is separated from one or both parents to maintain personal relations and direct contact with both parents on a regular basis, except if it is contrary to the child's best interests.

4. Where such separation results from any action initiated by a State Party, such as the detention, imprisonment, exile, deportation or death (including death arising from any cause while the person is in the custody of the State) of one or both parents or of the child, that State Party shall, upon request, provide the parents, the child or, if appropriate, another member of the family with the essential information concerning the whereabouts of the absent member(s) of the family unless the provision of the information would be detrimental to the well-being of the child. States Parties shall further ensure that the submission of such a request shall of itself entail no adverse consequences for the person(s) concerned.

Article 10

1. In accordance with the obligation of States Parties under article 9, paragraph 1, applications by a child or his or her parents to enter or leave a State Party for the purpose of family reunification shall be dealt with by States Parties in a positive, humane and expeditious manner. States Parties shall further ensure that the submission of such a request shall entail no adverse consequences for the applicants and for the members of their family.

2. A child whose parents reside in different States shall have the right to maintain on a regular basis, save in exceptional circumstances, personal relations and direct contacts with both parents. Towards that end and in accordance with the obligation of States Parties under article 9, paragraph 1, States Parties shall respect the right of the child and his or her parents to leave any country, including their own, and to enter their own country. The right to leave any country shall be subject only to such restrictions as are prescribed by law and which are necessary to protect the national security, public order (ordre public), public health or morals or the rights and freedoms of others and are consistent with the other rights recognized in the present Convention.

Article 11

1. States Parties shall take measures to combat the illicit transfer and non-return of children abroad.

2. To this end, States Parties shall promote the conclusion of bilateral or multilateral agreements or accession to existing agreements.

Article 12

1. States Parties shall assure to the child who is capable of forming his or her own views the right to express those views freely in all matters affecting the child, the views of the child being given due weight in accordance with the age and maturity of the child.

2. For this purpose, the child shall in particular be provided the opportunity to be heard in any judicial and administrative proceedings affecting the child, either directly, or through a representative or an appropriate body, in a manner consistent with the procedural rules of national law.

Article 13

1. The child shall have the right to freedom of expression; this right shall include freedom to seek, receive and impart information and ideas of all kinds, regardless of frontiers, either orally, in writing or in print, in the form of art, or through any other media of the child's choice.

2. The exercise of this right may be subject to certain restrictions, but these shall only be such as are provided by law and are necessary:

(a) For respect of the rights or reputations of others; or

(b) For the protection of national security or of public order (ordre public), or of public health or morals.

Article 14

1. States Parties shall respect the right of the child to freedom of thought, conscience and religion.

2. States Parties shall respect the rights and duties of the parents and, when applicable, legal guardians, to provide direction to the child in the exercise of his or her right in a manner consistent with the evolving capacities of the child.

3. Freedom to manifest one's religion or beliefs may be subject only to such limitations as are prescribed by law and are necessary to protect public safety, order, health or morals, or the fundamental rights and freedoms of others.

Article 15

1. States Parties recognize the rights of the child to freedom of association and to freedom of peaceful assembly.

2. No restrictions may be placed on the exercise of these rights other than those imposed in conformity with the law and which are necessary in a democratic society in the interests of national security or public safety, public order (ordre public), the protection of public health or morals or the protection of the rights and freedoms of others.

Article 16

1. No child shall be subjected to arbitrary or unlawful interference with his or her privacy, family, home or correspondence, nor to unlawful attacks on his or her honour and reputation.

2. The child has the right to the protection of the law against such interference or attacks.

Article 17

States Parties recognize the important function performed by the mass media and shall ensure that the child has access to information and material from a diversity of national and international sources, especially those aimed at the promotion of his or her social, spiritual and moral well-being and physical and mental health. To this end, States Parties shall:

(a) Encourage the mass media to disseminate information and material of social and cultural benefit to the child and in accordance with the spirit of article 29;

(b) Encourage international co-operation in the production, exchange and dissemination of such information and material from a diversity of cultural, national and international sources;

(c) Encourage the production and dissemination of children's books;

(d) Encourage the mass media to have particular regard to the linguistic needs of the child who belongs to a minority group or who is indigenous;

(e) Encourage the development of appropriate guidelines for the protection of the child from information and material injurious to his or her well-being, bearing in mind the provisions of articles 13 and 18.

Article 18

1. States Parties shall use their best efforts to ensure recognition of the principle that both parents have common responsibilities for the upbringing and development of the child. Parents or, as the case may be, legal guardians, have the primary responsibility for the upbringing and development of the child. The best interests of the child will be their basic concern.

2. For the purpose of guaranteeing and promoting the rights set forth in the present Convention, States Parties shall render appropriate assistance to parents and legal guardians in the performance of their child-rearing responsibilities and shall ensure the development of institutions, facilities and services for the care of children.

3. States Parties shall take all appropriate measures to ensure that children of working parents have the right to benefit from child-care services and facilities for which they are eligible.

Article 19

1. States Parties shall take all appropriate legislative, administrative, social and educational measures to protect the child from all

forms of physical or mental violence, injury or abuse, neglect or negligent treatment, maltreatment or exploitation, including sexual abuse, while in the care of parent(s), legal guardian(s) or any other person who has the care of the child.

2. Such protective measures should, as appropriate, include effective procedures for the establishment of social programmes to provide necessary support for the child and for those who have the care of the child, as well as for other forms of prevention and for identification, reporting, referral, investigation, treatment and follow-up of instances of child maltreatment described heretofore, and, as appropriate, for judicial involvement.

Article 20

1. A child temporarily or permanently deprived of his or her family environment, or in whose own best interests cannot be allowed to remain in that environment, shall be entitled to special protection and assistance provided by the State.

2. States Parties shall in accordance with their national laws ensure alternative care for such a child.

3. Such care could include, *inter alia*, foster placement, *kafalah* of Islamic law, adoption or if necessary placement in suitable institutions for the care of children. When considering solutions, due regard shall be paid to the desirability of continuity in a child's upbringing and to the child's ethnic, religious, cultural and linguistic background.

Article 21

States Parties that recognize and/or permit the system of adoption shall ensure that the best interests of the child shall be the paramount consideration and they shall:

(a) Ensure that the adoption of a child is authorized only by competent authorities who determine, in accordance with applicable law and procedures and on the basis of all pertinent and reliable information, that the adoption is permissible in view of the child's status concerning parents, relatives and legal guardians and that, if required, the persons concerned have given their informed consent to the adoption on the basis of such counselling as may be necessary;

(b) Recognize that inter-country adoption may be considered as an alternative means of a child's care, if the child cannot be placed in a foster or an adoptive family or cannot in any suitable manner be cared for in the child's country of origin;

(c) Ensure that the child concerned by inter-country adoption enjoys safeguards and standards equivalent to those existing in the case of national adoption;

(d) Take all appropriate measures to ensure that, in inter-country adoption, the placement does not result in improper financial gain for those involved in it;

(e) Promote, where appropriate, the objectives of the present article by concluding bilateral or multilateral arrangements or agreements, and endeavour, within this framework, to ensure that the placement of the child in another country is carried out by competent authorities or organs.

Article 22

1. States Parties shall take appropriate measures to ensure that a child who is seeking refugee status or who is considered a refugee in accordance with applicable international or domestic law and procedures shall, whether unaccompanied or accompanied by his or her parents or by any other person, receive appropriate protection and humanitarian assistance in the enjoyment of applicable rights set forth in the present Convention and in other international human rights or humanitarian instruments to which the said States are Parties.

2. For the purpose, States Parties shall provide, as they consider appropriate, co-operation in any efforts by the United Nations and other competent intergovernmental organizations or non-governmental organizations co-operating with the United Nations to protect and assist such a child and to trace the parents or other members of the family of any refugee child in order to obtain information necessary for reunification with his or her family. In cases where no parents or other members of the family can be found, the child shall be accorded the same protection as any other child permanently or temporarily deprived of his or her family environment for any reason, as set forth in the present Convention.

Article 23

1. States Parties recognize that a mentally or physically disabled child should enjoy a full and decent life, in conditions which ensure dignity, promote self-reliance and facilitate the child's active participation in the community.

2. States Parties recognize the right of the disabled child to special care and shall encourage and ensure the extension, subject to available resources, to the eligible child and those responsible for his or her care, of assistance for which application is made and which is appropriate to the child's condition and to the circumstances of the parents or others caring for the child.

3. Recognizing the special needs of a disabled child, assistance extended in accordance with paragraph 2 of the present article shall be provided free of charge, whenever possible, taking into account the financial resources of the parents or others caring for the child, and shall be designed to ensure that the disabled child has effective access to and receives education, training, health care services, rehabilitation services, preparation for employment and recreation opportunities in a manner conducive to the child's achieving the fullest possible social integration and individual development, including his or her cultural and spiritual development.

4. States Parties shall promote, in the spirit of international co-operation, the exchange of appropriate information in the field of preventive health care and of medical, psychological and functional treatment of disabled children, including dissemination of and access to information concerning methods of rehabilitation, education and vocational services, with the aim of enabling States Parties to improve their capabilities and skills to widen their experience in these areas. In this regard, particular account shall be taken of the needs of developing countries.

Article 24

1. States Parties recognize the right of the child to the enjoyment of the highest attainable standard of health and to facilities for the treatment of illness and rehabilitation of health. States Parties shall strive to ensure that no child is deprived of his or her right of access to such health care services.

2. States Parties shall pursue full implementation of this right and, in particular, shall take appropriate measures:

(a) To diminish infant and child mortality;

(b) To ensure the provision of necessary medical assistance and health care to all children with emphasis on the development of primary health care;

(c) To combat disease and malnutrition, including within the framework of primary health care, through, *inter alia*, the application of readily available technology and through the provision of adequate nutritious foods and clean drinking water, taking into consideration the dangers and risks of environmental pollution;

(d) To ensure appropriate pre-natal and post-natal health care for mothers;

(e) To ensure that all segments of society, in particular parents and children, are informed, have access to education and are supported in the use of basic knowledge of child health and nutrition, the advantages of breast-feeding, hygiene and environmental sanitation and the prevention of accidents;

(f) To develop preventive health care, guidance for parents and family planning education and services.

3. States Parties shall take all effective and appropriate measures with a view to abolishing traditional practices prejudicial to the health of children.

4. States Parties undertake to promote and encourage international co-operation with a view to achieving progressively the full realization of the right recognized in the present article. In this regard, particular account shall be taken of the needs of developing countries.

Article 25

States Parties recognize the right of a child who has been placed by the competent authorities for the purposes of care, protection or treatment of his or her physical or mental health, to a periodic review of the treatment provided to the child and all other circumstances relevant to his or her placement.

Article 26

1. States Parties shall recognize for every child the right to benefit from social security, including social insurance, and shall take the necessary measures to achieve the full realization of this right in accordance with their national law.

2. The benefits should, where appropriate, be granted, taking into account the resources and the circumstances of the child and persons having responsibility for the maintenance of the child, as well as any other consideration relevant to an application for benefits made by or on behalf of the child.

Article 27

1. States Parties recognize the right of every child to a standard of living adequate for the child's physical, mental, spiritual, moral and social development.

2. The parent(s) or others responsible for the child have the primary responsibility to secure, within their abilities and financial capacities, the conditions of living necessary for the child's development.

3. States Parties, in accordance with national conditions and within their means, shall take appropriate measures to assist parents and others responsible for the child to implement this right and shall in case of need provide material assistance and support programmes, particularly with regard to nutrition, clothing and housing.

4. States Parties shall take all appropriate measures to secure the recovery of maintenance for the child from the parents or other persons having financial responsibility for the child, both within the State Party and from abroad. In particular, where the person having financial responsibility for the child lives in a State different from that of the child, States Parties shall promote the accession to international agreements or the conclusion of such agreements, as well as the making of other appropriate arrangements.

Article 28

1. States Parties recognize the right of the child to education, and with a view to achieving this right progressively and on the basis of equal opportunity, they shall, in particular:

(a) Make primary education compulsory and available free to all;

(b) Encourage the development of different forms of secondary education, including general and vocational education, make them available and accessible to every child, and take appropriate measures such as the introduction of free education and offering financial assistance in case of need;

(c) Make higher education accessible to all on the basis of capacity by every appropriate means;

(d) Make educational and vocational information and guidance available and accessible to all children;

(e) Take measures to encourage regular attendance at schools and the reduction of drop-out rates.

2. States Parties shall take all appropriate measures to ensure that school discipline is administered in a manner consistent with the child's human dignity and in conformity with the present Convention.

3. States Parties shall promote and encourage international co-operation in matters relating to education, in particular with a view to contributing to the elimination of ignorance and illiteracy throughout the world and facilitating access to scientific and technical knowledge and modern teaching methods. In this regard, particular account shall be taken of the needs of developing countries.

Article 29

1. States Parties agree that the education of the child shall be directed to:

(a) The development of the child's personality, talents and mental and physical abilities to their fullest potential;

(b) The development of respect for human rights and fundamental freedoms, and for the principles enshrined in the Charter of the United Nations;

(c) The development of respect for the child's parents, his or her own cultural identity, language and values, for the national values of the country in which the child is living, the country from which he or she may originate, and for civilizations different from his or her own;

(d) The preparation of the child for responsible life in a free society, in the spirit of understanding, peace, tolerance, equality of sexes, and friendship among all peoples, ethnic, national and religious groups and persons of indigenous origin;

(e) The development of respect for the natural environment.

2. No part of the present article or article 28 shall be construed so as to interfere with the liberty of individuals and bodies to establish and direct educational institutions, subject always to the observance of the principle set forth in paragraph 1 of the present article and to the requirements that the education given in such institutions shall conform to such minimum standards as may be laid down by the State.

Article 30

In those States in which ethnic, religious or linguistic minorities or persons of indigenous origin exist, a child belonging to such a minority or who is indigenous shall not be denied the right, in community with other members of his or her group, to enjoy his or her own culture, to profess and practise his or her own religion, or to use his or her own language.

Article 31

1. States Parties recognize the right of the child to rest and leisure, to engage in play and recreational activities appropriate to the age of the child and to participate freely in cultural life and the arts.

2. States Parties shall respect and promote the right of the child to participate fully in cultural and artistic life and shall encourage the provision of appropriate and equal opportunities for cultural, artistic, recreational and leisure activity.

Article 32

1. States Parties recognize the right of the child to be protected from economic exploitation and from performing any work that is likely to be hazardous or to interfere with the child's education, or to be harmful to the child's health or physical, mental, spiritual, moral or social development.

2. States Parties shall take legislative, administrative, social and educational measures to ensure the implementation of the present article. To this end, and having regard to the relevant provisions of other international instruments, States Parties shall in particular:

(a) Provide for a minimum age or minimum ages for admission to employment;

(b) Provide for appropriate regulation of the hours and conditions of employment;

(c) Provide for appropriate penalties or other sanctions to ensure the effective enforcement of the present article.

Article 33

States Parties shall take all appropriate measures, including legislative, administrative, social and educational measures, to protect children from the illicit use of narcotic drugs and psychotropic substances as defined in the relevant international treaties, and to prevent the use of children in the illicit production and trafficking of such substances.

Article 34

States Parties undertake to protect the child from all forms of sexual exploitation and sexual abuse. For these purposes, States Parties shall in particular take all appropriate national, bilateral and multilateral measures to prevent:

(a) The inducement or coercion of a child to engage in any unlawful sexual activity;

(b) The exploitative use of children in prostitution or other unlawful sexual practices;

(c) The exploitative use of children in pornographic performances and materials.

Article 35

States Parties shall take all appropriate national, bilateral and multilateral measures to prevent the abduction of, the sale of or traffic in children for any purpose or in any form.

Article 36

States Parties shall protect the child against all other forms of exploitation prejudicial to any aspects of the child's welfare.

Article 37

States Parties shall ensure that:

(a) No child shall be subjected to torture or other cruel, inhuman or degrading treatment or punishment. Neither capital punishment nor life imprisonment without possibility of release shall be imposed for offences committed by persons below eighteen years of age;

(b) No child shall be deprived of his or her liberty unlawfully or arbitrarily. The arrest, detention or imprisonment of a child shall be in conformity with the law and shall be used only as a measure of last resort and for the shortest appropriate period of time;

(c) Every child deprived of liberty shall be treated with humanity and respect for the inherent dignity of the human person, and in a manner which takes into account the needs of persons of his or her age. In particular, every child deprived of liberty shall be separated from adults unless it is considered in the child's best interest not to do so and shall have the right to maintain contact with his or her family through correspondence and visits, save in exceptional circumstances;

(d) Every child deprived of his or her liberty shall have the right to prompt access to legal and other appropriate assistance, as well as the right to challenge the legality of the deprivation of his or her liberty before a court or other competent, independent and impartial authority, and to a prompt decision on any such action.

Article 38

1. States Parties undertake to respect and to ensure respect for rules of international humanitarian law applicable to them in armed conflicts which are relevant to the child.

2. States Parties shall take all feasible measures to ensure that persons who have not attained the age of fifteen years do not take a direct part in hostilities.

3. States Parties shall refrain from recruiting any person who has not attained the age of fifteen years into their armed forces. In recruiting among those persons who have attained the age of fifteen years but who have not attained the age of eighteen years, States Parties shall endeavour to give priority to those who are oldest.

4. In accordance with their obligations under international humanitarian law to protect the civilian population in armed conflicts, States Parties shall take all feasible measures to ensure protection and care of children who are affected by an armed conflict.

Article 39

States Parties shall take all appropriate measures to promote physical and psychological recovery and social reintegration of a child victim of: any form of neglect, exploitation, or abuse; torture or any other form of cruel, inhuman or degrading treatment or punishment; or armed conflicts. Such recovery and reintegration shall take place in an environment which fosters the health, self-respect and dignity of the child.

Article 40

1. States Parties recognize the right of every child alleged as, accused of, or recognized as having infringed the penal law to be treated in a manner consistent with the promotion of the child's sense of dignity and worth, which reinforces the child's respect for the human rights and fundamental freedoms of others and which takes into account the child's age and the desirability of promoting the child's reintegration and the child's assuming a constructive role in society.

2. To this end, and having regard to the relevant provisions of international instruments, States Parties shall, in particular, ensure that:

(a) No child shall be alleged as, be accused of, or recognized as having infringed the penal law by reason of acts or omissions that were not prohibited by national or international law at the time they were committed;

(b) Every child alleged as or accused of having infringed the penal law has at least the following guarantees:

(i) To be presumed innocent until proven guilty according to law;

(ii) To be informed promptly and directly of the charges against him or her, and, if appropriate, through his or her parents or legal guardians, and to have legal or other appropriate assistance in the preparation and presentation of his or her defence;

(iii) To have the matter determined without delay by a competent, independent and impartial authority or judicial body in a fair hearing according to law, in the presence of legal or other appropriate assistance and, unless it is considered not to be in the best interest of the child, in particular, taking into account his or her age or situation, his or her parents or legal guardians;

(iv) Not to be compelled to give testimony or to confess guilt; to examine or have examined adverse witnesses and to obtain the participation and examination of witnesses on his or her behalf under conditions of equality;

(v) If considered to have infringed the penal law, to have this decision and any measures imposed in consequence thereof reviewed by a higher competent, independent and impartial authority or judicial body according to law;

(vi) To have the free assistance of an interpreter if the child cannot understand or speak the language used;

(vii) To have his or her privacy fully respected at all stages of the proceedings.

3. States Parties shall seek to promote the establishment of laws, procedures, authorities and institutions specifically applicable to children alleged as, accused of, or recognized as having infringed the penal law, and, in particular:

(a) The establishment of a minimum age below which children shall be presumed not to have the capacity to infringe the penal law;

(b) Whenever appropriate and desirable, measures for dealing with such children without resorting to judicial proceedings, providing that human rights and legal safeguards are fully respected.

4. A variety of dispositions, such as care, guidance and supervision orders; counselling; probation; foster care; education and vocational training programmes and other alternatives to institutional care shall be available to ensure that children are dealt with in a manner appropriate to their well-being and proportionate both to their circumstances and the offence.

Article 41

Nothing in the present Convention shall affect any provisions which are more conductive to the realization of the rights of the child and which may be contained in:

(a) The law of a State party; or;

(b) International law in force for that State.

PART II

Article 42

States Parties undertake to make the principles and provisions of the Convention widely known, by appropriate and active means, to adults and children alike.

Article 43

1. For the purpose of examining the progress made by States Parties in achieving the realization of the obligations undertaken in the present Convention, there shall be established a Committee on the Rights of the Child, which shall carry out the functions hereinafter provided.

2. The Committee shall consist of 10 experts of high moral standing and recognized competence in the field covered by this Convention. The members of the Committee shall be elected by States Parties from among their nationals and shall serve in their personal capacity, consideration being given to equitable geographical distribution, as well as to the principal legal systems.

3. The members of the Committee shall be elected by secret ballot from a list of persons nominated by States Parties. Each State Party may nominate one person from among its own nationals.

4. The initial election to the Committee shall be held no later than six months after the date of the entry into force of the present Convention and thereafter every second year. At least four months before the date of each election, the Secretary-General of the United Nations shall address a letter to States Parties inviting them to submit their nominations within two months. The Secretary-General shall subsequently prepare a list in alphabetical order of all persons thus nominated, indicating States Parties which have nominated them, and shall submit it to the States Parties to the present Convention.

5. The elections shall be held at meetings of States Parties convened by the Secretary-General at United Nations Headquarters. At those meetings, for which two-thirds of States Parties shall constitute a quorum, the persons elected to the Committee shall be those who obtain the largest number of votes and an absolute majority of the votes of the representatives of States Parties present and voting.

6. The members of the Committee shall be elected for a term of four years. They shall be eligible for re-election if renominated. The term of five of the members elected at the first election shall expire at the end of two years; immediately after the first election, the names of these five members shall be chosen by lot by the Chairman of the meeting.

7. If a member of the Committee dies or resigns or declares that for any other cause he or she can no longer perform the duties of the Committee, the State Party which nominated the member shall appoint another expert from among its nationals to serve for the remainder of the term, subject to the approval of the Committee.

8. The Committee shall establish its own rules of procedure.

9. The Committee shall elect its officers for a period of two years.

10. The meetings of the Committee shall normally be held at United Nations Headquarters or at any other convenient place as determined by the Committee. The Committee shall normally meet annually. The duration of the meetings of the Committee shall be determined, and reviewed, if necessary, by a meeting of the States Parties to the present Convention, subject to the approval of the General Assembly.

11. The Secretary-General of the United Nations shall provide the necessary staff and facilities for the effective performance of the functions of the Committee under the present Convention.

12. With the approval of the General Assembly, the members of the Committee established under the present Convention shall receive emoluments from the United Nations resources on such terms and conditions as the Assembly may decide.

Article 44

1. States Parties undertake to submit to the Committee, through the Secretary-General of the United Nations, reports on the measures they have adopted which give effect to the rights recognized herein and on the progress made on the enjoyment of those rights:

(a) Within two years of the entry into force of the Convention for the State Party concerned;

(b) Thereafter every five years.

2. Reports made under the present article shall indicate factors and difficulties, if any, affecting the degree of fulfilment of the obligations under the present Convention. Reports shall also contain sufficient information to provide the Committee with a comprehensive understanding of the implementation of the Convention in the country concerned.

3. A State Party which has submitted a comprehensive initial report to the Committee need not in its subsequent reports submitted in accordance with paragraph 1(b) of the present article repeat basic information previously provided.

4. The Committee may request from States Parties further information relevant to the implementation of the Convention.

5. The Committee shall submit to the General Assembly, through the Economic and Social Council, every two years, reports on its activities.

6. States Parties shall make their reports widely available to the public in their own countries.

Article 45

In order to foster the effective implementation of the Convention and to encourage international co-operation in the field covered by the Convention:

(a) The specialized agencies, the United Nations Children's Fund and other United Nations organs shall be entitled to be represented at the consideration of the implementation of such provisions of the present Convention as fall within the scope of their mandate. The Committee may invite the specialized agencies, the United Nations Children's Fund and other competent bodies as it may consider appropriate to provide expert advice on the implementation of the Convention in areas falling within the scope of their respective mandates. The Committee may invite the specialized agencies, the United Nations Children's Fund and other United Nations organs to submit reports on the implementation of the Convention in areas falling within the scope of their activities;

(b) The Committee shall transmit, as it may consider appropriate, to the specialized agencies, the United Nations Children's Fund and other competent bodies, any reports from States Parties that contain a request, or indicate a need, for technical advice or assistance, along with the Committee's observations and suggestions, if any, on these requests or indications;

(c) The Committee may recommend to the General Assembly to request the Secretary-General to undertake on its behalf studies on specific issues relating to the rights of the child;

(d) The Committee may make suggestions and general recommendations based on information received pursuant to articles 44 and 45 of the present Convention. Such suggestions and general recommendations shall be transmitted to any State Party concerned and reported to the General Assembly, together with comments, if any, from States Parties.

PART III

Article 46

The present Convention shall be open for signature by all States.

Article 47

The present Convention is subject to ratification. Instruments of ratification shall be deposited with the Secretary-General of the United Nations.

Article 48

The present Convention shall remain open for accession by any State. The instruments of accession shall be deposited with the Secretary-General of the United Nations.

Article 49

1. The present Convention shall enter into force on the thirtieth day following the date of deposit with the Secretary-General of the United Nations of the twentieth instrument of ratification or accession.

2. For each State ratifying or acceding to the Convention after the deposit of the twentieth instrument of ratification or accession, the Convention shall enter into force on the thirtieth day after the deposit by such State of its instrument of ratification or accession.

Article 50

1. Any State Party may propose an amendment and file it with the Secretary-General of the United Nations. The Secretary-General shall thereupon communicate the proposed amendment to States Parties, with a request that they indicate whether they favour a conference of States Parties for the purpose of considering and voting upon the proposals. In the event that, within four months from the date of such communication, at least one-third of the States Parties favour such a conference, the Secretary-General shall convene the conference under the auspices of the United Nations. Any amendment adopted by a majority of States Parties present and voting at the conference shall be submitted to the General Assembly for approval.

2. An amendment adopted in accordance with paragraph 1 of the present article shall enter into force when it has been approved by the General Assembly of the United Nations and accepted by a two-thirds majority of States Parties.

3. When an amendment enters into force, it shall be binding on those States Parties which have accepted it, other States Parties still being bound by the provisions of the present Convention and any earlier amendments which they have accepted.

Article 51

1. The Secretary-General of the United Nations shall receive and circulate to all States the text of reservations made by States at the time of ratification or accession.

2. A reservation incompatible with the object and purpose of the present Convention shall not be permitted.

3. Reservations may be withdrawn at any time by notification to that effect addressed to the Secretary-General of the United Nations, who shall then inform all States. Such notification shall take effect on the date on which it is received by the Secretary-General.

Article 52

A State Party may denounce the present Convention by written notification to the Secretary-General of the United Nations. Denunciation becomes effective one year after the date of receipt of the notification by the Secretary-General.

Article 53

The Secretary-General of the United Nations is designated as the depositary of the present Convention.

Article 54

The original of the present Convention, of which the Arabic, Chinese, English, French, Russian and Spanish texts are equally authentic, shall be deposited with the Secretary-General of the United Nations.

In witness thereof the undersigned plenipotentiaries, being duly authorized thereto by their respective Governments, have signed the present Convention.

United Nations Conference on Trade and Development—UNCTAD

Address: Palais des Nations, 1211 Geneva 10, Switzerland.

Telephone: 229171234; **fax:** 229170057; **e-mail:** info@unctad.org; **internet:** www.unctad.org.

UNCTAD was established in December 1964. It is the principal instrument of the UN General Assembly concerned with trade and development, and is the focal point within the UN system for integrated treatment of trade and development and interrelated issues of finance, technology, investment, and sustainable development. It aims to help developing countries—particularly the Least Developed Countries, Small Island Developing States, Landlocked Developing Countries, economies in transition, and the so-called structurally weak, vulnerable and small economies—to maximize their trade and development opportunities, especially in view of the increasing globalization and liberalization of the world economy.

Organization

(June 2012)

CONFERENCE

The Conference is the organization's highest policy-making body and normally meets every four years at ministerial level to formulate major policy guidelines and to decide on UNCTAD's mandate and work priorities. The 13th session took place in Doha, Qatar, in April 2012. As well as its 194 members, many intergovernmental and non-governmental organizations (NGOs) participate in UNCTAD's work as observers.

TRADE AND DEVELOPMENT BOARD

The Trade and Development Board oversees the activities of UNCTAD in between the organization's quadrennial conferences. The Board comprises elected representatives from 153 UNCTAD member states and is responsible for ensuring the overall consistency of UNCTAD's activities, as well as those of its subsidiary bodies. The Board meets in a regular annual session lasting about 10 days, at which it examines global economic issues. It may also meet a further three times a year to deal with urgent policy issues and to address institutional matters.

COMMISSIONS

The Trade and Development Board has two Commissions: the Trade and Development Commission; and the Investment, Enterprise and Development Commission. The role of the commissions is to conduct policy dialogues, to consider the reports of expert meetings, to manage and recommend for approval the work programmes of expert meetings within their purview, and to promote and strengthen synergies among UNCTAD's three pillars of work: research and analysis; technical co-operation; and intergovernmental consensus-building. Each Commission holds one session per year. In addition to the Intergovernmental Group of Experts on Competition Law and Policy and the Intergovernmental Working Group of Experts on International Standards of Accounting and Reporting, the Commissions may convene up to eight expert meetings a year on specific issues. Of the eight, six have now been established as multi-year expert meetings and cover issues such as commodities, transport and trade facilitation, investment, enterprises and science, technology and innovation (STI), services, and South-South co-operation.

SECRETARIAT

The secretariat comprises the following divisions: Globalization and Development Strategies; Investment and Enterprise; International Trade in Goods and Services, and Commodities; Technology and Logistics; Africa, Least Developed Countries and Special Programmes; and Management.

The UNCTAD secretariat, comprising some 400 staff, undertakes policy analysis; monitoring, implementation and follow-up of decisions of intergovernmental bodies; technical co-operation in support of UNCTAD's policy objectives; and information exchanges and consultations of various types.

Secretary-General: Dr SUPACHAI PANITCHPAKDI (Thailand).

Deputy Secretary-General: PETKO DRAGANOV (Bulgaria).

Activities

UNCTAD's activities are underpinned by its three 'pillars': consensus-building; research, policy analysis and data collection; and technical assistance.

In April 2008 the 12th session of the Conference, convened in Accra, Ghana, on the theme 'Addressing the opportunities and challenges of globalization for development', adopted the Accra Accord, which built upon the São Paulo Consensus adopted by the 11th session, held in São Paulo, Brazil, in June 2004, while providing updated policy analysis, policy responses, and guidelines to strengthen UNCTAD and to enhance its development role, its impact, and its institutional effectiveness. The Accord served as a strategic framework for the work of the organization and established specific policy direction for the next four years. It requested UNCTAD to foster a better understanding of the feasible ways and means of ensuring that the positive impact of globalization and trade on development is maximized; to enhance its work on the special needs of the African continent and of Least Developed Countries; to enhance its work on the special needs and problems of Small Island Developing States, Landlocked Developing Countries, and other structurally weak, vulnerable and small economies; to assist transit developing countries with their special challenges in relation to infrastructure and transport; to make a contribution to the implementation and follow-up to the outcomes of relevant global conferences; and to continue to contribute to the achievement of internationally agreed development goals, including the UN Millennium Development Goals (MDGs).

UNCTAD has a clear mandate to assist with the implementation of: (i) the Programme of Action for LDCs, which resulted from the third UN Conference on the LDCs, held in May 2001; (ii) the Mauritius Strategy on the Programme of Action for the Sustainable Development of Small Island Developing States, adopted by the UN Conference on Small Islands held in Port Louis, Mauritius, in January 2005; and (iii) the Almatı Programme of Action, that was adopted in August 2003 by the International Ministerial Conference of Landlocked and Transit Developing Countries and Donor Countries and International Financial and Development Institutions on Transit Transport Co-operation. (See below.) As part of a concerted response to the ongoing global economic and food crises, G20 leaders agreed in November 2008 to help developing countries gain access to finance despite the challenging global financial conditions. UNCTAD continues to emphasise the importance of providing financial access to developing countries.

UNCTAD, with WTO, leads an initiative on promoting trade—through combating protectionism, including through the conclusion of the Doha round, and by strengthening aid-for-trade financing-for-trade initiatives—the third of nine activities that were launched in April 2009 by the UN System Chief Executives Board for Co-ordination (CEB), with the aim of alleviating the impact on poor and vulnerable populations of the developing global economic crisis.

In February 2012 the UNCTAD Secretary-General issued a report entitled *Development-led Globalization: Towards Sustainable and Inclusive Development Paths*, in which he urged a change of direction in the global economic system—a 'global new deal'—to enable more stable and inclusive economic progress. 'Development-centred globalization' was the theme of the 13th session of the UNCTAD conference held in Doha, Qatar, in April. During the 13th session the UNCTAD Secretary-General recommended the inclusion of two new initiatives in the follow up to the UN Conference on Sustainable Development (Rio+20), which was convened in June: the establishment of a Global Trade and Green Economy Forum, a new institutional space where evidence-based dialogue and solution sharing could be fostered with a view to addressing 'green protectionism'; and the creation of a scheme to support developing countries with identifying green export opportunities.

The March 2012 conference of heads of state or government of the so-called BRICS informal grouping of large emerging economies, comprising Brazil, Russia, India, People's Republic of China, and South Africa (together accounting for some 20% of global GDP), expressed commitment to advancing UNCTAD's work.

INTERNATIONAL TRADE IN GOODS AND SERVICES, AND COMMODITIES

In working to secure development gains from participation in international trade and globalization, the Division on International Trade in Goods and Services monitors and assesses trends in the international trading system from a development perspective. Among other activities, each year UNCTAD prepares an assessment of key developments in the international trading system for consideration and deliberation by the Trade and Development Board and the UN General Assembly. The Division quantifies the positive interaction between trade and development, and has developed the Trade and Development Index (TDI), covering 125 countries, as a diagnostic tool for policy-makers and researchers. It supports international trade and trade negotiations, and provides assistance to developing countries in clarifying and exploring the development dimension of the international trading system, particularly the WTO Doha Round negotiations, and in strengthening regional economic integration. It promotes South-South trade, including through trade finance and through the Global System of Trade Preferences among Developing Countries (GSTP); UNCTAD supports the second round of negotiations among GSTP participants, and services the 1989 GSTP Agreement. UNCTAD aims to increase the participation of developing countries in global services trade. Support is given to developing countries to enhance their knowledge of issues of particular concern to them relating to services, to assess the contribution of services to development, and to reform and formulate regulatory and institutional frameworks focused on building supply capacity. UNCTAD works to increase developing countries' participation in new and dynamic sectors of global trade, including creative products and industries, and serves as a global centre of excellence in managing trade data, statistics and related analytical software. It maintains a Trade Analysis and Information System (TRAINS) database, covering some 160 countries, and an Agricultural Trade Policy Simulation Model (ATPSM); and helps countries to set up competition policies and laws, and to develop voluntary norms to combat anti-competitive practices in national and global markets and to promote consumer welfare. UNCTAD is the focal point of work on competition policy and related consumer welfare within the UN system and hosts an annual meeting of an Intergovernmental Group of Experts on Competition Law and Policy. In 2005 UNCTAD established ad hoc voluntary peer reviews (VPR) on competition law and policy. Developing countries are also helped to design policies and strategies to strengthen their competitive productive capacities and trade-related infrastructures. The Conference aims to promote the achievement through trade of the UN MDGs, and to promote UN system-wide coherence on trade matters. It services a number of UN task forces and co-ordination mechanisms to facilitate greater synergy and co-operation in the UN's development work. A joint UNEP/UNCTAD Capacity Building Task Force on Trade, Environment and Development aims to strengthen the capacities of countries to address issues relating to trade, the environment and development. UNCTAD also supports research and technical assistance in a range of subjects linking trade and the environment, including organic agriculture, the use of renewable energy technologies and the protection of traditional knowledge. The 2009/10 edition of the triennial *Trade and Environment Review* focused on 'Promoting poles of clean growth to foster the transition to a more sustainable economy'.

UNCTAD and the WTO jointly manage the International Trade Centre (ITC), based in Geneva, which helps developing countries and countries with economies in transition to achieve sustainable human development through the export of goods and services.

INVESTMENT AND ENTERPRISE

As the focal point of the UN system on matters related to investment UNCTAD promotes the understanding of key issues, particularly matters related to foreign direct investment (FDI) and enterprise development. The Division on Investment and Enterprise (DIAE) also assists developing countries, in particular LDCs and countries with special needs, in formulating and implementing active policies aimed at boosting productive capacities and international competitiveness and in participating more fully in international investment agreements (IIAs). In order to accomplish this objective, the DIAE carries out research and policy analysis on the development impact of FDI in the areas of IIAs, national FDI policies, intellectual property, and enterprise development and business facilitation. An *IIA Monitor* is published four times a year. Technical assistance includes organizing seminars for policy-makers and the training of trade negotiators, some of it through a distance-learning programme. The annual *World Investment Report (WIR)* is a main point of reference for policy-makers and practitioners in this area, providing data on issues pertaining to FDI and transnational corporations (TNCs), as well as analysing trends and developments in FDI, examining the implications of activities by TNCs in relation to these trends, and assessing consequent international and national policy issues of relevance to developing countries. The 2011 edition of *WIR* had a special focus on the strategic use of non-equity modes by TNCs in their management of global value chains and international operations. The DIAE also assists developing countries in establishing an enabling policy framework for attracting and benefiting from FDI. In this respect, UNCTAD supports these nations in undertaking Investment Policy Reviews (IPRs), objective analyses of how national policy, regulatory and institutional systems attract or inhibit FDI; by 2012 some 32 IPRs had been implemented. UNCTAD also assists developing countries in implementing the recommendations of IPRs. Other capacity-building programmes include assistance to developing countries in collecting, improving, and harmonizing statistics on FDI; in negotiating international investment agreements; in investment promotion and facilitation; and in linking foreign affiliates and domestic enterprises. UNCTAD is also mandated to provide a platform for international dialogue on best practices in investment policies, and supports developing countries in promoting their enterprise development, through upgrading entrepreneurship, harmonizing international accounting and reporting standards, developing competitive insurance markets, and through an e-tourism initiative. UNCTAD's Empretec programme, initiated in 32 developing countries world-wide, trains and encourages entrepreneurs. The DIAE also services the Intergovernmental Group of Experts on International Standards on Accounting and Reporting (ISAR), which aims to assist developing countries and economies in transition with the implementation of best practices in corporate transparency and accounting. Since 2008 UNCTAD has organized a World Investment Forum, held every two years, to promote dialogue among government ministers, corporate executives, investors and heads of investment promotion agencies on investment-related issues and challenges. The third Forum was convened in Doha, Qatar, in April 2012.

GLOBALIZATION AND DEVELOPMENT STRATEGIES

UNCTAD works to promote policies and strategies at national and international levels, and analyses issues related to globalization, international trade and finance, in support of economic management for sustainable development. Every September UNCTAD publishes its flagship *Trade and Development Report (TDR)*. The 2012 *TDR* was to focus on income inequality. Through its Debt Management and Financial Analysis System (DMFAS), a joint programme with the World Bank, UNCTAD provides assistance to developing countries on debt management, helping debtor countries to analyse data, make projections, and plan strategies for debt repayment and reorganization with the help of modern information technology. By 2012 the programme had supported 69 countries. UNCTAD provides training for operators and senior officials to raise awareness of institutional reforms that might be necessary for effective debt management. UNCTAD also supports developing countries in their negotiations on debt owed to developed countries' governments, in the context of the Paris Club, and every year it provides a report on the external debt of developing countries to the UN General Assembly. Since 1995 UNCTAD has also provided technical assistance and economic analyses to support the Palestinian people and the development of the Palestinian economy. In 2008 the Accra Accord (see above) determined to intensify support to Palestine in order to alleviate economic and social hardships and to strengthen its state-building efforts.

TECHNOLOGY AND LOGISTICS

Within the UN system UNCTAD provides intellectual leadership and serves as a source of expertise in the areas of science, technology, innovation and information and communication technologies. Substantive and technical servicing is provided to the Commission on Science and Technology for Development (CSTD), and work is undertaken in the areas of science, technology and innovation policy, as well as technology transfer. In the area of information and communication technologies (ICTs), relevant mandates are implemented through policy research, and providing support to enable the participation of developing countries and transition economies in international discussions and policy debates. Furthermore, technical assistance projects are undertaken with a view to helping build the capacity of developing countries in the areas of science, technology, innovation and ICTs. UNCTAD's annual *Information Economy Report* tracks recent ICT trends and assesses strategies to enhance the development impact of these technologies in developing countries. The 2011 edition of the *Report* focused the use of ICTs to accelerate progress in private sector development. In 2004 UNCTAD established its Virtual Institute on Trade and Development, a special programme that aims to strengthen capacities at universities in developing and transition countries for the teaching and researching of trade issues. In June of that year UNCTAD launched an e-tourism initiative to help small economies and island developing countries reach their full tourism development potential using ICTs. In 2001 UNCTAD established its regular three-week flagship course on trade and development, 'Key Issues on the International Economic Agenda'. UNCTAD's work on trade logistics focuses on research and analysis, technical assistance and consensus building. Analytical studies and reports are prepared in the field of transport, and advice is provided to advance developing country policy makers' and traders' understanding of international trade mechanisms and frameworks. The ASYCUDA programme software, adopted by more than 90 countries world-wide, helps automate customs procedures and further facilitate trade transactions.

AFRICA AND SPECIAL PROGRAMMES

Development of Africa: UNCTAD undertakes analysis of African socio-economic issues and uses its findings to advance global understanding of that continent's development challenges, and to promote action at national, regional and international levels with a view to accelerating both regional development and greater participation by African countries in the global economy; UNCTAD co-operates closely with the New Partnership for Africa's development (NEPAD), with a particular focus on its agriculture, market access and diversification areas of activity; UNCTAD also participates in the annual regional consultations of UN agencies active in Africa. In July 2005, meeting in Gleneagles, Scotland, the annual summit of G8 leaders determined to double assistance to Africa by 2010, as first recommended by UNCTAD in 2000. Since 2000 UNCTAD has published an annual *Economic Development in Africa Report*, which analyses development issues specific to Africa and makes policy recommendations for African countries and the international community. The 2011 edition focused on 'Fostering industrial development in Africa in the new global environment'.

Landlocked Developing Countries (LLDCs): in 2012 there were 31 LLDCs, of which 15 were located in Africa, 12 were in Asia, two (Bolivia and Paraguay) were in Latin America, and two (Armenia and Moldova) were in Eastern Europe; LLDCs experience strong challenges to growth and development owing to factors including poor physical infrastructure, weak institutional and productive capacities, small domestic markets, remoteness from maritime ports and therefore world markets, and high vulnerability to external shocks; the need to transport goods through neighbouring territory tends to incur high transaction costs resulting in reduced competitiveness; UNCTAD's multidimensional approach to land-locked states includes developing adequate national transport networks and efficient transit systems, promoting regional or sub-regional economic integration, and encouraging FDI in economic activities that are not distance-sensitive. In 1995 the Global Framework for Transit Transport Co-operation between Land-locked and Transit Developing Countries and the Donor Community was endorsed by the UN General Assembly, with a view to enhancing transit systems and enabling LLDCs to reduce their marginalization from world markets. In 2003 the UN convened an international ministerial conference, in Almatı, Kazakhstan, which aimed to enhance transit transport co-operation between land-locked and transit developing countries. The resulting Almatı Declaration and Almatı Programme of Action addressed infrastructure development and maintenance, transit policy issues, and trade facilitation measures. UNCTAD participates in the implementation of the Almatı Programme of Action through analytical work on the transit transport and related development problems confronting LLDCs, and also through the provision of technical assistance to these countries in areas such as trade facilitation and electronic commerce. In 2005 the first meeting of LLDC Ministers responsible for trade, convened in Asunción, Paraguay, adopted the Asunción Platform for the Doha Development

Round, which aimed to harmonize the positions of LLDCs in multilateral trade negotiations.

Least Developed Countries (LDCs): UNCTAD aims to give particular attention to the needs of the world's 48 LDCs, the large majority of which (34) are in Africa; the UN has since 1971 (using established criteria based on gross national income per capita, weak human assets—as measured through a composite Human Assets Index, and economic vulnerability—as measured through a composite Economic Vulnerability Index) classified as LDCs states that are deemed highly disadvantaged in their development processes; in view of the UN's recognition of the particular challenges confronting LDCs, the development partners of these countries, including UN agencies and programmes, have adopted certain special support measures aimed at: reducing LDCs' competitive disadvantages in the global economy; supporting the development of LDCs' physical infrastructure and human resources; and enhancing their institutional capacities; LDC-specific treatment is focused on three main areas of international co-operation: the multilateral trading system (where special concessions, such as non-reciprocal market access preferences, are granted to LDCs); development financing (where donors are expected to give especially favourable consideration to LDCs when making decisions on concessionary financing); and technical assistance (with priority being given to LDCs under all UN development programming); UNCTAD's eighth session, held in February 1992, requested that detailed analyses of the socio-economic situations and domestic policies of the LDCs, of their resource needs, and of external factors affecting their economies, be undertaken as part of UNCTAD's work programme. The ninth session, held in April–May 1996, determined that particular attention be given to the problems of the LDCs in all areas of UNCTAD's work. The 10th session, convened in February 2000, focused on the impact of globalization on developing economies and on means of improving trade opportunities for LDCs. In June 2004 the 11th session noted the increasing marginalization of the LDCs in the global economy and urged UNCTAD to consider solutions to this marginalization. In April 2008 the 12th session emphasized the urgent need to take global action to protect the world's poor from the ongoing global financial and food crises and ensuing global recession. Three UN Conferences on the Least Developed Countries have been convened under UNCTAD auspices, in 1981, 1990, and 2001. LDC III, held in Brussels, in May 2001, adopted a Programme of Action for the Least Developed Countries for the Decade 2001–10, which was reviewed annually by UNCTAD. UNCTAD contributed to LDC IV, which took place in Istanbul, Turkey, in May 2011. LDC IV approved the Istanbul Programme of Action, which included a provision that national parliaments should be engaged in debating development strategies as well as in overseeing their implementation, and had the ultimate objective of enabling at least one-half of current LDCs to graduate from LDC status by 2020. UNCTAD publishes an annual *Least Developed Countries Report*, which in 2011 focused on the theme 'The Potential Role of South-South Co-operation for Inclusive and Sustainable Development'.

Small Island Developing States (SIDS): since 1974 the UN has recognized the particular problems of SIDS, which are deemed to be at greater risk of marginalization from the global economy than many other developing countries, owing to adverse consequences arising from their small size; remoteness from large markets (resulting in high transport costs); high economic vulnerability to economic and natural shocks beyond domestic control; fragile ecosystems and high exposure to globally induced phenomena such as rises in sea levels; and frequently unstable agricultural production, owing to increased exposure to natural disasters; there is no formal listing of SIDS, but, for analytical purposes, UNCTAD uses an unofficial list comprising 29 SIDS; the Global Conference on the Sustainable Development of SIDS (held in Barbados, in April–May 1994) adopted a Programme of Action for the Sustainable Development of SIDS; an International Meeting to Review the Implementation of the Programme of Action (convened in Mauritius, in January 2005) approved the Mauritius Strategy for the Further Implementation of the Programme of Action for the Sustainable Development of SIDS, which addressed the serious disadvantages suffered by many SIDS in the global economy; a High-level Review Meeting on the implementation of the Mauritius Strategy, convened in September 2010, adopted an Outcome Document reaffirming commitment to supporting SIDS' development efforts, noting with concern uneven progress made by SIDS towards achieving the MDGs, acknowledging the significant threat posed to SIDS by climate change and sea level rises, and recognizing the need to advance internationally a preventive approach towards alleviating the effects of natural disasters on SIDS, including reducing risks and properly integrating risk management into development policies.

SPECIAL UNIT ON COMMODITIES

UNCTAD, through its Special Unit on Commodities, provides analysis and technical co-operation and builds international consensus among member States on deepening understanding of the relationship between commodity production and trade and poverty reduction. Major areas of activity include focusing on making the commodity sector an instrument of poverty reduction by facilitating the access of small and poor commodity producers to markets; supporting diversification towards higher-value products and encouraging the stronger parts of the value chain to support the weaker parts; promoting the use of market-based instruments for generating finance, particularly for the disadvantaged parts of the value chain; focusing on the role of exchanges as facilitators for commodity-based development; publishing statistics; finding ways to enable producers to meet both official and private sector standards; developing ways of promoting broad-based economic development and diversification in mining-dependent areas; enhancing activities dealing with energy, particularly oil and gas, and organizing annual conferences on oil and gas trade and finance in Africa; and convening and servicing UN conferences relating to international commodity bodies. UNCTAD convenes annually a Global Commodities Forum, most recently in January 2012.

CHIEF EXECUTIVES BOARD (CEB) INTER-AGENCY CLUSTER ON TRADE AND PRODUCTIVE CAPACITY

UNCTAD leads the UN's CEB Inter-agency Cluster on Trade and Productive Capacity, which was established in April 2007 to co-ordinate trade and development operations at national and regional levels within the UN system. Other partner organizations in the Cluster are: UNIDO, UNDP, FAO, the International Trade Centre, WTO, the five UN Regional Commissions, UNEP, UNOPS, and (since December 2010) the UN Commission on International Trade Law. The Cluster has participated in pilot activities under the *Delivering as One* process.

Finance

The operational expenses of UNCTAD are borne by the regular budget of the UN, and amount to approximately US $50m. annually. Technical co-operation activities, financed from extra-budgetary resources, amount to some $25m. annually.

Publications

Development and Globalization: Facts and Figures.

Economic Development in Africa Report.

Information Economy Report.

Least Developed Countries Report (annually).

Review of Maritime Transport (annually).

Trade and Development Report (annually).

Trade and Environment Review.

UNCTAD Handbook of Statistics (annually, also available on DVD-Rom and online).

World Commodity Survey.

World Investment Report (annually).

Policy briefs, other abstracts, reviews and reports.

United Nations Development Programme—UNDP

Address: One United Nations Plaza, New York, NY 10017, USA.

Telephone: (212) 906-5300; **fax:** (212) 906-5364; **e-mail:** hq@undp.org; **internet:** www.undp.org.

The Programme was established in 1965 by the UN General Assembly. Its central mission is to help countries to eradicate poverty and achieve a sustainable level of human development, an approach to economic growth that encompasses individual well-being and choice, equitable distribution of the benefits of development, and conservation of the environment. UNDP advocates for a more inclusive global economy. UNDP co-ordinates global and national efforts to achieve the UN Millennium Development Goals.

Organization

(June 2012)

UNDP is responsible to the UN General Assembly, to which it reports through ECOSOC.

EXECUTIVE BOARD

The Executive Board is responsible for providing intergovernmental support to, and supervision of, the activities of UNDP and the UN Population Fund (UNFPA). It comprises 36 members: eight from Africa, seven from Asia and the Pacific, four from eastern Europe, five from Latin America and the Caribbean and 12 from western Europe and other countries. Members serve a three-year term.

SECRETARIAT

Offices and divisions at the Secretariat include: an Operations Support Group; Offices of the United Nations Development Group, the Human Development Report, Development Studies, Audit and Performance Review, Evaluation, and Communications; and Bureaux for Crisis Prevention and Recovery; Partnerships; Development Policy; and Management. Five regional bureaux, all headed by an assistant administrator, cover: Africa; Asia and the Pacific; the Arab states; Latin America and the Caribbean; and Europe and the Commonwealth of Independent States. UNDP's Administrator (the third most senior UN official, after the Secretary-General and the Deputy Secretary-General) is in charge of strategic policy and overall co-ordination of UN development activities (including the chairing of the UN Development Group), while the Associate Administrator supervises the operations and management of UNDP programmes.

Administrator: HELEN CLARK (New Zealand).

Associate Administrator: REBECA GRYNSPAN (Costa Rica).

Assistant Administrator and Director of the Bureau for Crisis Prevention and Recovery: JORDAN RYAN (USA).

Assistant Administrator and Director of the Bureau for Development Policy: OLAV KJØRVEN (Norway).

Assistant Administrator and Director of the Bureau of Management: JENS WANDEL (Denmark).

Assistant Administrator and Director of the Partnerships Bureau: SIGRID KAAG (Netherlands).

COUNTRY OFFICES

In almost every country receiving UNDP assistance there is an office, headed by the UNDP Resident Representative, who usually also serves as the UN Resident Co-ordinator, responsible for the co-ordination of all UN technical assistance and development activities in that country, so as to ensure the most effective use of UN and international aid resources.

Activities

UNDP describes itself as the UN's global development network, advocating for change and connecting countries to knowledge, experience and resources to help people build a better life. In 2012 UNDP was active in 177 countries. It provides advisory and support services to governments and UN teams with the aim of advancing sustainable human development and building national development capabilities. Assistance is mostly non-monetary, comprising the provision of experts' services, consultancies, equipment and training for local workers. Developing countries themselves contribute significantly to the total project costs in terms of personnel, facilities, equipment and supplies. UNDP also supports programme countries in attracting aid and utilizing it efficiently.

From the mid-1990s UNDP assumed a more active co-ordinating role within the UN system. In 1997 the UNDP Administrator was appointed to chair the UN Development Group (UNDG), which was established as part of a series of structural reform measures initiated by the UN Secretary-General, with the aim of preventing duplication and strengthening collaboration between all UN agencies, programmes and funds concerned with development. The UNDG promotes coherent policy at country level through the system of UN Resident Co-ordinators (see above), the Common Country Assessment mechanism (CCA, a process for evaluating national development needs), and the UN Development Assistance Framework (UNDAF, for planning and co-ordination development operations at country level, based on the CCA).

During the late 1990s UNDP undertook an extensive internal process of reform, which placed increased emphasis on its activities in the field and on performance and accountability. In 2001 UNDP established a series of Thematic Trust Funds to enable increased support of priority programme activities. In accordance with the more results-oriented approach developed under the reform process UNDP introduced a new Multi-Year Funding Framework (MYFF), which outlined the country-driven goals around which funding was to be mobilized, integrating programme objectives, resources, budget and outcomes. The MYFF was to provide the basis for the Administrator's Business Plans for the same duration and enables policy coherence in the implementation of programmes at country, regional and global levels. A Results-Oriented Annual Report (ROAR) was produced for the first time in 2000 from data compiled by country offices and regional programmes. New measures were introduced in 2006 to improve UNDP's management accountability, internal auditing, evaluation and procurement procedures.

The 2008–13 Strategic Plan emphasized UNDP's 'overarching' contribution to achieving sustainable human development through capacity development strategies, to be integrated into all areas of activity. (The UNDP Capacity Development Group, established in 2002 within the Bureau for Development Policy, organizes UNDP capacity development support at local and national level.) Other objectives identified by the 2008–13 Plan included strengthening national ownership of development projects and promoting and facilitating South-South co-operation.

In 2012 UNDP was working to advance the UN's development agenda through engagement with the MDGs Acceleration Framework (see below); through its participation in the UN Conference on Sustainable Development (UNCSD), which was held in Rio de Janeiro, Brazil, in June; and by contributing to the formulation of a post-2015 system-wide development framework. A new strategic plan was being developed for 2014–17, which aimed to strengthen UNDP's capacity to deliver results.

UNDP, jointly with the World Bank, leads an initiative on 'additional financing for the most vulnerable', the first of nine activities that were launched in April 2009 by the UN System Chief Executives Board for Co-ordination (CEB), with the aim of alleviating the impact on poor and vulnerable populations of the developing global economic crisis.

MILLENNIUM DEVELOPMENT GOALS

UNDP, through its leadership of the UNDG and management of the Resident Co-ordinator system, has a co-ordinating function as the focus of UN system-wide efforts to achieve the so-called Millennium Development Goals (MDGs), pledged by UN member governments attending a summit meeting of the UN

General Assembly in September 2000. The objectives were to establish a defined agenda to reduce poverty and improve the quality of lives of millions of people and to serve as a framework for measuring development. There are eight MDGs, as follows, for which one or more specific targets have been identified:

i) to eradicate extreme poverty and hunger, with the aim of reducing by 50% (compared with the 1990 figure) the number of people with an income of less than US $1 a day and those suffering from hunger by 2015, and to achieve full and productive employment and decent work for all, including women and young people;

ii) to achieve universal primary education by 2015;

iii) to promote gender equality and empower women, in particular to eliminate gender disparities in primary and secondary education by 2005 and at all levels by 2015;

iv) to reduce child mortality, with a target reduction of two-thirds in the mortality rate among children under five by 2015 (compared with the 1990 level);

v) to improve maternal health, specifically to reduce by 75% the numbers of women dying in childbirth and to achieve universal access to reproductive health by 2015 (compared with the 1990 level);

vi) to combat HIV/AIDS, malaria and other diseases, with targets to have halted and begun to reverse the incidence of HIV/AIDS, malaria and other major diseases by 2015 and to achieve universal access to treatment for HIV/AIDS for all those who need it by 2010;

vii) to ensure environmental sustainability, including targets to integrate the principles of sustainable development into country policies and programmes, to reduce by 50% (compared with the 1990 level) the number of people without access to safe drinking water by 2015, and to achieve significant improvement in the lives of at least 100m. slum dwellers by 2020;

viii) to develop a global partnership for development, including an open, rule-based, non-discriminatory trading and financial system, and efforts to deal with international debt, to address the needs of least developed countries and landlocked and small island developing states, to provide access to affordable, essential drugs in developing countries, and to make available the benefits of new technologies.

UNDP plays a leading role in efforts to integrate the MDGs into all aspects of UN activities at country level and to ensure that the MDGs are incorporated into national development strategies. The Programme supports efforts by countries, as well as regions and sub-regions, to report on progress towards achievement of the goals, and on specific social, economic and environmental indicators, through the formulation of MDG reports. These form the basis of a global report, issued annually by the UN Secretary-General since mid-2002. UNDP also works to raise awareness of the MDGs and to support advocacy efforts at all levels, for example through regional publicity campaigns, target-specific publications and the Millennium Campaign to generate support for the goals in developing and developed countries. UNDP provides administrative and technical support to the Millennium Project, an independent advisory body established by the UN Secretary-General in 2002 to develop a practical action plan to achieve the MDGs. Financial support of the Project is channelled through a Millennium Trust Fund, administered by UNDP. In January 2005 the Millennium Project presented its report, based on extensive research conducted by teams of experts, which included recommendations for the international system to support country level development efforts and identified a series of 'Quick Wins' to bring conclusive benefit to millions of people in the short-term. International commitment to achieve the MDGs by 2015 was reiterated at a World Summit, convened in September 2005. In December 2006 UNDP and the Spanish Government concluded an agreement on the establishment of the MDG Achievement Fund (MDG-F), which aims to support the acceleration of progress towards the achievement of the MDGs and to enhance co-operation at country level between UN development partners. UNDP and the UN Department of Economic and Social Affairs are lead agencies in co-ordinating the work of the Millennium Development Goals Gap Task Force, which was established by the UN Secretary-General in May 2007 to track, systematically and at both international and country level, existing international commitments in the areas of official development assistance, market access, debt relief, access to essential medicines and technology. In November the UN, in partnership with two major US companies, launched an online MDG Monitor (www.mdgmonitor.org) to track progress and to support organizations working to achieve the goals. In September 2010 UNDP launched the MDGs Acceleration Framework, which aimed to support countries in identifying and overcoming barriers to eradicating extreme poverty and achieving sustainable development.

DEMOCRATIC GOVERNANCE

UNDP supports national efforts to ensure efficient and accountable governance, to improve the quality of democratic processes, and to build effective relations between the state, the private sector and civil society, which are essential to achieving sustainable development. As in other practice areas, UNDP assistance includes policy advice and technical support, capacity-building of institutions and individuals, advocacy and public information and communication, the promotion and brokering of dialogue, and knowledge networking and sharing of good practices.

UNDP works to strengthen parliaments and other legislative bodies as institutions of democratic participation. It assists with constitutional reviews and reform, training of parliamentary staff, and capacity-building of political parties and civil organizations as part of this objective. UNDP undertakes missions to help prepare for and ensure the conduct of free and fair elections. It helps to build the long-term capacity of electoral institutions and practices within a country, for example by assisting with voter registration, the establishment of electoral commissions, providing observers to verify that elections are free and fair, projects to educate voters, and training journalists to provide impartial election coverage.

Within its justice sector programme UNDP undertakes a variety of projects to improve access to justice, in particular for the poor and disadvantaged, and to promote judicial independence, legal reform and understanding of the legal system. UNDP also works to promote access to information, the integration of human rights issues into activities concerned with sustainable human development, and support for the international human rights system.

UNDP is mandated to assist developing countries to fight corruption and improve accountability, transparency and integrity (ATI). It has worked to establish national and international partnerships in support of its anti-corruption efforts and used its role as a broker of knowledge and experience to uphold ATI principles at all levels of public financial management and governance. UNDP publishes case studies of its anti-corruption efforts and assists governments to conduct self-assessments of their public financial management systems.

In March 2002 a UNDP Governance Centre was inaugurated in Oslo, Norway, to enhance the role of UNDP in support of democratic governance and to assist countries to implement democratic reforms in order to achieve the MDGs. In 2012 the Centre's areas of focus were: access to information and e-governance; access to justice and rule of law; anti-corruption; civic engagement; electoral systems and processes; human rights; local governance; parliamentary development; public administration; and women's empowerment. The Democratic Governance Network (DGP-Net) allows discussion and the sharing of information. An iKnow Politics Network, supported by UNDP, aims to help women become involved in politics.

Within the democratic governance practice area UNDP supports more than 300 projects at international, country and city levels designed to improve conditions for the urban poor, in particular through improvement in urban governance. The Local Initiative Facility for Urban Environment (LIFE) undertakes small-scale projects in low-income communities, in collaboration with local authorities, the private sector and community-based groups, and promotes a participatory approach to local governance. UNDP also works closely with the UN Capital Development Fund to implement projects in support of decentralized governance, which it has recognized as a key element to achieving sustainable development goals.

UNDP aims to ensure that, rather than creating an ever-widening 'digital divide', ongoing rapid advancements in information and communications technology (ICT) are harnessed by poorer countries to accelerate progress in achieving sustainable human development. UNDP advises governments on ICT policy, promotes digital entrepreneurship in programme countries and works with private sector partners to provide reliable and affordable communications networks. The Bureau for Development Policy operates the Information and Communication Technologies for Development Programme, which aims to establish technology access centres in developing countries. A Sustainable Development Networking Programme focuses on expanding internet connectivity in poorer countries through building national capacities and supporting local internet sites. UNDP has used mobile internet units to train people even in isolated rural areas. In 1999 UNDP, in collaboration with an international communications company, Cisco Systems, and other partners, launched NetAid, an internet-based forum (accessible at www.netaid.org) for mobilizing and co-ordinating fundraising and other activities aimed at alleviating poverty and promoting sustainable human development in the developing world. With Cisco Systems and other partners, UNDP has worked to establish academies of information technology to support training and capacity-building in developing countries. UNDP and the World Bank jointly host the secretariat of the Digital Opportunity Task Force, a partnership between industrialized and developing countries, business and non-governmental organizations (NGOs) that was established in 2000. UNDP is a partner in the Global Digital Technology Initiative, launched in 2002 to strengthen the role of ICT in achieving the development goals of developing countries. In January 2004 UNDP and Microsoft Corporation announced an agreement to develop jointly ICT projects aimed at assisting developing countries to achieve the MDGs.

POVERTY REDUCTION

UNDP's activities to facilitate poverty eradication include support for capacity-building programmes and initiatives to generate sustainable livelihoods, for example by improving access to credit, land and technologies, and the promotion of strategies to improve education and health provision for the poorest elements of populations (especially women and girls). UNDP aims to help governments to reassess their development priorities and to design initiatives for sustainable human development. In 1996, following the World Summit for Social Development, which was held in Copenhagen, Denmark, in March 1995, UNDP launched the Poverty Strategies Initiative (PSI) to strengthen national capacities to assess and monitor the extent of poverty and to combat the problem. All PSI projects were to involve representatives of governments, the private sector, social organizations and research institutions in policy debate and formulation. Following the introduction, in 1999, by the World Bank and IMF of Poverty Reduction Strategy Papers (PRSPs), UNDP has helped governments to draft these documents, and, since 2001, has linked the papers to efforts to achieve and monitor progress towards the MDGs. In early 2004 UNDP inaugurated the International Poverty Centre, in Brasília, Brazil, which fosters the capacity of countries to formulate and implement poverty reduction strategies and encourages South-South co-operation in all relevant areas of research and decision-making. In particular, the Centre aims to assist countries to meet MDGs through research into and implementation of pro-poor policies that encourage social protection and human development, and through the monitoring of poverty and inequality. UNDP's Secretariat hosts the Special Unit for South-South Co-operation (SU/SSC), which was established by the United Nations General Assembly in 1978.

UNDP country offices support the formulation of national human development reports (NHDRs), which aim to facilitate activities such as policy-making, the allocation of resources, and monitoring progress towards poverty eradication and sustainable development. In addition, the preparation of Advisory Notes and Country Co-operation Frameworks by UNDP officials helps to highlight country-specific aspects of poverty eradication and national strategic priorities. In January 1998 the Executive Board adopted eight guiding principles relating to sustainable human development that were to be implemented by all country offices, in order to ensure a focus to UNDP activities. Since 1990 UNDP has published an annual *Human Development Report*, incorporating a Human Development Index, which ranks countries in terms of human development, using three key indicators: life expectancy, adult literacy and basic income required for a decent standard of living. UNDP's 2011 *Human Development Report*, published in November, focused on the need to address in tandem the urgent global challenges of achieving sustainability and equity, and identified policies at global and national level to advance progress. The Report includes a Human Poverty Index and a Gender-related Development Index, which assesses gender equality on the basis of life expectancy, education and income. Jointly with the International Labour Organization (ILO) UNDP operates a Programme on Employment for Poverty Reduction, which undertakes analysis and studies, and supports countries in improving their employment strategies. In late March 2012 the first Global Human Development Forum was convened, under UNDP auspices, in İstanbul, Turkey; delegates (comprising experts on development, and representatives of the UN, governments, the private sector and civil society) adopted the İstanbul Declaration, urging that the global development agenda should be redrawn, and calling for concerted global action against social inequities and environmental degradation.

UNDP is committed to ensuring that the process of economic and financial globalization, including national and global trade, debt and capital flow policies, incorporates human development concerns. It aimed to ensure that the Doha Development Round of World Trade Organization (WTO) negotiations should achieve an expansion of trade opportunities and economic growth to less developed countries. With the UN Conference on Trade and Development (UNCTAD), UNDP manages a Global Programme on Globalization, Liberalization and Sustainable Human Development, which aims to support greater integration of developing countries into the global economy. UNDP manages a Trust Fund for the Integrated Framework for Trade-related Technical Assistance to Least Developed Countries, which was inaugurated in 1997 by UNDP, the IMF, the International Trade Centre, UNCTAD, the World Bank and the WTO.

Jointly with the UN Economic Commission for Africa and other agencies, UNDP operates a project on Trade Capacity Development for Sub-Saharan Africa, to help African countries take a greater share of global markets, reinforce African negotiating capacities, and strengthen regional co-operation. In May 2008 UNDP launched a regional initiative to assist African countries in negotiating, managing and regulating large-scale investment contracts, particularly in the exploitation of natural resources, so as to ensure that the host country (and especially its poorest people) receives the maximum benefit.

In 1996 UNDP initiated a process of collaboration between city authorities world-wide to promote implementation of the commitments made at the 1995 Copenhagen summit for social development and to help to combat aspects of poverty and other urban problems, such as poor housing, transport, the management of waste disposal, water supply and sanitation. The World Alliance of Cities Against Poverty was formally launched in 1997, in the context of the International Decade for the Eradication of Poverty. The seventh global Forum of the Alliance took place in February 2010.

UNDP sponsors the International Day for the Eradication of Poverty, held annually on 17 October.

ENVIRONMENT AND ENERGY

UNDP plays a role in developing the agenda for international co-operation on environmental and energy issues, focusing on the relationship between energy policies, environmental protection, poverty and development. UNDP promotes development practices that are environmentally sustainable, for example through the formulation and implementation of Poverty Reduction Strategies and National Strategies for Sustainable Development. Together with the UN Environment Programme (UNEP) and the World Bank, UNDP is an implementing agency of the Global Environment Facility (GEF), which was established in 1991 to finance international co-operation in projects to benefit the environment.

UNDP recognizes that desertification and land degradation are major causes of rural poverty and promotes sustainable land management, drought preparedness and reform of land tenure as means of addressing the problem. It also aims to reduce poverty caused by land degradation through implementation of environmental conventions at a national and international level. In 2002 UNDP inaugurated an Integrated Drylands Development Programme which aimed to ensure that the needs of people living in arid regions are met and considered at a local and national level. The Drylands Development Centre implements the programme in 19 African, Arab and West Asian countries. UNDP is also concerned with sustainable management of forestries, fisheries and agriculture. Its Biodiversity Global Programme assists developing countries and communities to integrate issues relating to sustainable practices and biodiversity into national and global practices. Since 1992 UNDP has administered a Small Grants Programme, funded by the GEF, to support community-based initiatives concerned with biodiversity conservation, prevention of land degradation and the elimination of persistent organic pollutants. The Equator Initiative was inaugurated in 2002 as a partnership between UNDP, representatives of governments, civil society and businesses, with the aim of reducing poverty in communities along the equatorial belt by fostering local partnerships, harnessing local knowledge and promoting conservation and sustainable practices.

In 2006 UNDP inaugurated a new multi-partner initiative, Mangroves for the Future (MFF), to promote investment in coastal ecosystem conservation, in particular in those countries affected by the December 2004 tsunami, in order to support sustainable development. The project was to focus on mangrove swamps, which formerly provided a natural protection against flooding, but which have been cleared in order to provide land for rice-growing, fish-farming or shrimp-farming. In April 2008 a regional technical review forum of the initiative was convened, in Ahungalla, Sri Lanka, to assess programmes of work and national strategies. MFF was expanded to include Pakistan and Viet Nam, and to undertake regional coastal management projects.

In December 2005 UNDP (in collaboration with Fortis, a private sector provider of financial services) launched the MDG Carbon Facility, whereby developing countries that undertake projects to reduce emissions of carbon dioxide, methane and other gases responsible for global warming may sell their 'carbon credits' to finance further MDG projects. The first projects under the MDG Carbon Facility were inaugurated in February 2008, in Uzbekistan, the former Yugoslav republic of Macedonia, Yemen and Rwanda.

UNDP supports efforts to promote international co-operation in the management of chemicals. It was actively involved in the development of a Strategic Approach to International Chemicals Management which was adopted by representatives of 100 governments at an international conference convened in Dubai, UAE, in February 2006.

UNDP works to ensure the effective governance of freshwater and aquatic resources, and promotes co-operation in transboundary water management. It works closely with other agencies to promote safe sanitation, ocean and coastal management, and community water supplies. In 1996 UNDP, with the World Bank and the Swedish International Development Agency, established a Global Water Partnership to promote and implement water resources management. UNDP, with the GEF, supports a range of projects which incorporate development and ecological requirements in the sustainable management of international waters. including the Global Mercury Project, a project for improved municipal waste-water management in coastal cities of the African, Caribbean and Pacific states, a Global Ballast Water Management Programme and an International Waters Learning Exchange and Resources Network.

CRISIS PREVENTION AND RECOVERY

UNDP is not primarily a relief organization, but collaborates with other UN agencies in countries in crisis and with special circumstances to promote relief and development efforts, in order to secure the foundations for sustainable human development and thereby increase national capabilities to prevent or mitigate future crises. In particular, UNDP is concerned to achieve reconciliation, reintegration and reconstruction in affected countries, as well as to support emergency interventions and management and delivery of programme aid. It aims to facilitate the transition from relief to longer-term recovery and rehabilitation. Special development initiatives in post-conflict countries include the demobilization of former combatants and destruction of illicit small armaments, rehabilitation of communities for the sustainable reintegration of returning populations and the restoration and strengthening of democratic institutions. UNDP is seeking to incorporate conflict prevention into its development strategies. It has established a mine action unit within its Bureau for Crisis Prevention and Recovery in order to strengthen national and local de-mining capabilities including surveying, mapping and clearance of anti-personnel landmines. It also works to increase awareness of the harm done to civilians by cluster munitions, and participated in the negotiations that culminated in May 2008 with the adoption of an international Convention on Cluster Munitions, which in February 2010 received its 30th ratification, enabling its entry into force on 1 August. UNDP also works closely with UNICEF to raise awareness and implement risk reduction education programmes, and manages global partnership projects concerned with training, legislation and the socio-economic impact of anti-personnel devices. In 2005 UNDP adopted an '8-Point Agenda' aimed at improving the security of women and girls in conflict situations and promoting their participation in post-crisis recovery processes. In late 2006 UNDP began to administer the newly established Peacebuilding Fund, the purpose of which is to strengthen essential services to maintain peace in countries that have undergone conflict. During 2008 UNDP developed a new global programme aimed at strengthening the rule of law in conflict and post-conflict countries; the programme placed particular focus on women's access to justice, institution-building and transitional justice.

In 2006 UNDP launched an Immediate Crisis Response programme (known as 'SURGE') aimed at strengthening its capacity to respond quickly and effectively in the recovery phase following a conflict or natural disaster. Under the programme Immediate Crisis Response Advisors—UNDP staff with special expertise in at least one of 12 identified areas, including early recovery, operational support and resource mobilization—are swiftly deployed, in a 'SURGETeam', to UNDP country offices dealing with crises. In 2008 Immediate Crisis Response Advisors were deployed to northern Cameroon (in February) in response to a sudden influx of Chadian refugees; to Chad (also in February) to review the destruction of the local UNDP office in a period of violent unrest; to Myanmar (May) to assess the aftermath of Cyclone Nargis; and to Haiti (September) following a series of hurricanes there. In January 2009 a SURGETeam was deployed to assess the situation in Gaza, in view of the onset in December 2008 of an intense period of conflict. Following the earthquake that devastated Haiti in January 2010 a SURGETeam, comprising four experts on operations, recovery and security, was deployed immediately to assess the operational requirements of UNDP's office there; subsequently 24 SURGE advisers developed a SURGE work plan for the country.

UNDP is the focal point within the UN system for strengthening national capacities for natural disaster reduction (prevention, preparedness and mitigation relating to natural, environmental and technological hazards). UNDP's Bureau of Crisis Prevention and Recovery, in conjunction with the Office for the Co-ordination of Humanitarian Affairs and the secretariat of the International Strategy for Disaster Reduction, oversees the system-wide Capacity for Disaster Reduction Initiative (CADRI), which was inaugurated in 2007, superseding the former United Nations Disaster Management Training Programme. In February 2004 UNDP introduced a Disaster Risk Index that enabled vulnerability and risk to be measured and compared between countries and demonstrated the correspondence between human development and death rates following natural disasters. UNDP was actively involved in preparations for the second World Conference on Disaster Reduction, which was held in Kobe, Japan, in January 2005. Following the Kobe Conference UNDP initiated a new Global Risk Identification Programme. During 2005 the Inter-Agency Standing Committee, concerned with co-ordinating the international response to humanitarian disasters, developed a concept of providing assistance through a 'cluster' approach, comprising core areas of activity (see OCHA). UNDP was designated the lead agency for the Early Recovery cluster, linking the immediate needs following a disaster with medium- and long-term recovery efforts.

HIV/AIDS

UNDP regards the HIV/AIDS pandemic as a major challenge to development, and advocates making HIV/AIDS a focus of national planning and national poverty reduction strategies; supports decentralized action against HIV/AIDS at community level; helps to strengthen national capacities at all levels to combat the disease; and aims to link support for prevention activities, education and treatment with broader development planning and responses. UNDP places a particular focus on combating the spread of HIV/AIDS through the promotion of women's rights. UNDP is a co-sponsor, jointly with the World Health Organization (WHO) and other UN bodies, of the Joint UN Programme on HIV/AIDS (UNAIDS), which became operational on 1 January 1996. UNAIDS co-ordinates UNDP's HIV and Development Programme. UNDP works in partnership with the Global Fund to Fight HIV/AIDS, Tuberculosis and Malaria, in particular to support the local principal recipient of grant financing and to help to manage fund projects.

UNDP administers a global programme concerned with intellectual property and access to HIV/AIDS drugs, to promote wider and cheaper access to antiretroviral drugs, in accordance with the agreement on Trade-Related Aspects of Intellectual Property Rights (TRIPS), amended by the WTO in 2005 to allow countries without a pharmaceutical manufacturing capability to import generic copies of patented medicines.

Finance

UNDP and its various funds and programmes are financed by the voluntary contributions of members of the UN and the Programme's participating agencies, cost-sharing by recipient governments and third-party donors. In 2008 UNDP's gross regular (core) income was US $1,100m., and total non-core contributions amounted to $3,700m. Of total provisional programme expenditure of $4,096m. in 2008, some 34.9% was allocated to fostering democratic governance; 30.6% to achieving the MDGs and reducing human poverty; 16.0% to supporting crisis prevention and recovery; and 9.9% to managing energy and the environment for sustainable development. Some 28% of provisional total programme expenditure was allocated to Latin America and the Caribbean; 22% to Asia and the Pacific; 21% to Africa; 12% to the Arab states; and 8% to Europe and the CIS. For the period 2008–11 total voluntary contributions were projected at $20,600m., of which $5,300m. constituted regular (core) resources, $5,000m. bilateral donor contributions, $5,500m. contributions from multilateral partners, and $4,800m. cost-sharing by recipient governments.

UNDP, UNFPA and UNICEF are committed to integrating their budgets from 2014.

Publications

Annual Report of the Administrator.

Choices (quarterly).

Human Development Report (annually).

Poverty Report (annually).

Results-Oriented Annual Report.

Associated Funds and Programmes

UNDP is the central funding, planning and co-ordinating body for technical co-operation within the UN system. A number of associated funds and programmes, financed separately by means of voluntary contributions, provide specific services through the UNDP network. UNDP manages a trust fund to promote economic and technical co-operation among developing countries.

GLOBAL ENVIRONMENT FACILITY (GEF)

The GEF, which is managed jointly by UNDP, the World Bank (which hosts its secretariat) and UNEP, began operations in 1991 and was restructured in 1994. Its aim is to support projects in the six thematic areas of: climate change, the conservation of biological diversity, the protection of international waters, reducing the depletion of the ozone layer in the atmosphere, arresting land degradation and addressing the issue of persistent organic pollutants. Capacity-building to allow countries to meet their obligations under international environmental agreements, and adaptation to climate change, are priority cross-cutting components of these projects. The GEF acts as the financial mechanism for the Convention on Biological Diversity and the UN Framework Convention on Climate Change. UNDP is responsible for capacity-building, targeted research, pre-investment activities and technical assistance. UNDP also administers the Small Grants Programme of the GEF, which supports community-based activities by local NGOs, and the Country Dialogue Workshop Programme, which promotes dialogue on national priorities with regard to the GEF. In October 2010 donor countries pledged US $4,350m. for the fifth periodic replenishment of GEF funds (GEF-5), covering the period 2011–14.

Chair. and CEO: MONIQUE BARBUT (France).

Executive Co-ordinator of UNDP-GEF Unit: YANNICK GLEMAREC; 304 East 45th St, 9th Floor, New York, NY 10017, USA; fax (212) 906-6998; e-mail gefinfo@undp.org; internet www.undp.org/gef/.

MDG ACHIEVEMENT FUND (MDG-F)

The Fund, established in accordance with an agreement concluded in December 2006 between UNDP and the Spanish Government, aims to support the acceleration of progress towards the achievement of the MDGs and to advance country-level co-operation between UN development partners. The Fund operates through the UN development system and focuses mainly on financing collaborative UN activities addressing multi-dimensional development challenges. The Spanish Government provided initial financing to the Fund of nearly €528m., adding $98m. in September 2008. By 2012 some 128 programmes were under way in 49 countries, in the thematic areas of children and nutrition; climate change; conflict prevention; culture and development; economic governance; gender equality and women's empowerment; and youth employment.

Director of MDG-F Secretariat: SOPHIE DE CAEN (Canada); MDG-F Secretariat, c/o UNDP, One United Nations Plaza, New York, NY 10017, USA; tel. (212) 906-6180; fax (212) 906-5364; e-mail pb.mdgf.secretariat@undp.org; internet www.mdgfund.org.

MONTREAL PROTOCOL

Through its Montreal Protocol/Chemicals Unit UNDP collaborates with public and private partners in developing countries to assist them in eliminating the use of ozone-depleting substances (ODS), in accordance with the Montreal Protocol to the Vienna Convention for the Protection of the Ozone Layer, through the design, monitoring and evaluation of ODS phase-out projects and programmes. In particular, UNDP provides technical assistance and training, national capacity-building and demonstration projects and technology transfer investment projects.

PROGRAMME OF ASSISTANCE TO THE PALESTINIAN PEOPLE (PAPP)

PAPP, established in 1978, is committed to strengthening institutions in the Israeli-occupied Territories and emerging Palestinian autonomous areas, to creating employment opportunities and to stimulating private and public investment in the area to enhance trade and export potential. Examples of PAPP activities include the following: construction of sewage collection networks and systems in the northern Gaza Strip; provision of water to 500,000 people in rural and urban areas of the West Bank and Gaza; construction of schools, youth and health centres; support to vegetable and fish traders through the construction of cold storage and packing facilities; and provision of loans to strengthen industry and commerce. In January 2009, in response to the intensive bombardment of the Gaza Strip by

Israeli forces during December 2008–January 2009, with the stated aim of ending rocket attacks launched by Hamas and other militant groups on Israeli targets ('Operation Cast Lead'), PAPP distributed food packages to more than 30,000 Palestinians in the territory who were not served by UNRWA. In September 2011 PAPP launched a Consolidated Plan of Assistance, covering the period 2012–14, which aimed to support the Palestinian people in the following areas: energy resources; transport and management systems; affordable and adequate housing; education; public health services and systems; and heritage conservation.

UNDP Special Representative in the Occupied Palestinian Territories: Frode Mauring; POB 51359, Jerusalem; tel. (2) 6268200; fax (2) 6268222; e-mail registry.papp@undp.org; internet www.undp.ps.

SPECIAL UNIT FOR SOUTH-SOUTH CO-OPERATION (SU/SSC)

The SU/SSC, established in 1978 by the UN General Assembly and hosted by UNDP, aims to co-ordinate and support South-South co-operation in the political, economic, social, environmental and technical areas, and to support 'triangular' collaboration on a UN system-wide and global basis. The Special Unit organizes the annual UN Day for South-South Co-operation (December 19), and manages the UN Trust Fund for South-South Co-operation (UNFSC) and the Perez-Guerrero Trust Fund for Economic and Technical Co-operation among Developing Countries (PGTF), as well as undertaking programmes financed by UNDP.

Director: Yiping Zhou (People's Republic of China); 304 East 45th St, 12th Floor, New York, NY 11017, USA; tel. (212) 906-6944; fax (212) 906-6352; e-mail ssc.info@undp.org; internet ssc.undp.org.

UNDP DRYLANDS DEVELOPMENT CENTRE (DDC)

The Centre, based in Nairobi, Kenya, was established in February 2002, superseding the former UN Office to Combat Desertification and Drought (UNSO). (UNSO had been established following the conclusion, in October 1994, of the UN Convention to Combat Desertification in Those Countries Experiencing Serious Drought and/or Desertification, Particularly in Africa; in turn, UNSO had replaced the former UN Sudano-Sahelian Office.) The DDC was to focus on the following areas: ensuring that national development planning takes account of the needs of dryland communities, particularly in poverty reduction strategies; helping countries to cope with the effects of climate variability, especially drought, and to prepare for future climate change; and addressing local issues affecting the utilization of resources.

Officer-in-Charge: Elie Kodsie; UN Gigiri Compound, United Nations Ave, POB 30552, 00100 Nairobi, Kenya; tel. (20) 7624640; fax (20) 7624648; e-mail ddc@undp.org; internet www.undp.org/drylands.

UNDP-UNEP POVERTY-ENVIRONMENT INITIATIVE (UNPEI)

UNPEI, inaugurated in February 2007, supports countries in developing their capacity to launch and maintain programmes that mainstream poverty-environment linkages into national development planning processes, such as MDG achievement strategies and PRSPs. In May 2007 UNDP and UNEP launched the Poverty-Environment Facility (UNPEF) to co-ordinate, and raise funds in support of, UNPEI.

Officer-in-Charge: David Smith; UN Gigiri Compound, United Nations Avenue, POB 30552, 00100 Nairobi, Kenya; e-mail facility.unpei@unpei.org; internet www.unpei.org.

UNITED NATIONS CAPITAL DEVELOPMENT FUND (UNCDF)

The Fund was established in 1966 and became fully operational in 1974. It invests in poor communities in least developed countries (LDCs) through local governance projects and micro-finance operations, with the aim of increasing such communities' access to essential local infrastructure and services and thereby improving their productive capacities and self-reliance. UNCDF encourages participation by local people and local governments in the planning, implementation and monitoring of projects. The Fund aims to promote the interests of women in community projects and to enhance their earning capacities. A Special Unit for Microfinance (SUM), established in 1997 as a joint UNDP/UNCDF operation, was fully integrated into UNCDF in 1999. UNCDF/SUM helps to develop financial services for poor communities and supports UNDP's MicroStart initiative, which supports private sector and community-based initiatives in generating employment opportunities. UNCDF hosts the UN high-level Advisors Group on Inclusive Financial Sectors, established in respect of recommendations made during the 2005 International Year of Microcredit. In November 2008 UNCDF launched MicroLead, a US $26m. fund that was to provide loans to leading microfinance institutions and other financial service providers (MFIs/FSPs) in developing countries; MicroLead was also to focus on the provision of early support to countries in post-conflict situations. In 2010 UNCDF had a programme portfolio with a value of around $200m., in support of initiatives ongoing in 38 LDCs.

Executive Secretary: David Morrison (Canada); Two United Nations Plaza, 26th Floor, New York, NY 10017, USA; fax (212) 906-6479; e-mail info@uncdf.org; internet www.uncdf.org.

UNITED NATIONS VOLUNTEERS (UNV)

The United Nations Volunteers is an important source of middle-level skills for the UN development system supplied at modest cost, particularly in the least developed countries (LDCs). Volunteers expand the scope of UNDP project activities by supplementing the work of international and host-country experts and by extending the influence of projects to local community levels. UNV also supports technical co-operation within and among the developing countries by encouraging volunteers from the countries themselves and by forming regional exchange teams comprising such volunteers. UNV is involved in areas such as peace-building, elections, human rights, humanitarian relief and community-based environmental programmes, in addition to development activities.

The UN International Short-term Advisory Resources (UNISTAR) Programme, which is the private sector development arm of UNV, has increasingly focused its attention on countries in the process of economic transition. Since 1994 UNV has administered UNDP's Transfer of Knowledge Through Expatriate Nationals (TOKTEN) programme, which was initiated in 1977 to enable specialists and professionals from developing countries to contribute to development efforts in their countries of origin through short-term technical assignments. In March 2000 UNV established an Online Volunteering Service to connect development organizations and volunteers using the internet; in 2010, 127 online volunteers made their skills available through the Online Volunteering Service.

In December 2011 UNV issued the first *State of the World's Volunteerism Report*, on the theme 'Universal Values for Global Well-being'.

By 2012 the total number of people who had served as UNVs amounted to around 40,000, deployed to more than 140 countries. During 2010 some 7,765 national and international UNVs were deployed in 132 countries, on 7,960 assignments.

Executive Co-ordinator: Flavia Pansieri (Italy); POB 260111, 53153 Bonn, Germany; tel. (228) 8152000; fax (228) 8152001; e-mail information@unvolunteers.org; internet www.unv.org.

United Nations Environment Programme—UNEP

Address: POB 30552, Nairobi 00100, Kenya.

Telephone: (20) 621234; **fax:** (20) 623927; **e-mail:** unepinfo@unep.org; **internet:** www.unep.org.

The United Nations Environment Programme was established in 1972 by the UN General Assembly, following recommendations of the 1972 UN Conference on the Human Environment, in Stockholm, Sweden, to encourage international co-operation in matters relating to the human environment.

Organization

(June 2012)

GOVERNING COUNCIL

The main functions of the Governing Council (which meets every two years in ordinary sessions, with special sessions taking place in the alternate years) are to promote international co-operation in the field of the environment and to provide general policy guidance for the direction and co-ordination of environmental programmes within the UN system. It comprises representatives of 58 states, elected by the UN General Assembly, for four-year terms, on a regional basis. The Global Ministerial Environment Forum (first convened in 2000) meets annually as part of the Governing Council's regular and special sessions. The Governing Council is assisted in its work by a Committee of Permanent Representatives.

SECRETARIAT

Offices and divisions at UNEP headquarters include the Offices of the Executive Director and Deputy Executive Director; the Secretariat for Governing Bodies; Offices for Evaluation and Oversight, Programme Co-ordination and Management, Resource Mobilization, and Global Environment Facility Co-ordination; and Divisions of Communications and Public Information, Early Warning and Assessment, Environmental Policy Implementation, Technology, Industry and Economics, Regional Co-operation, and Environmental Law and Conventions.

Executive Director: ACHIM STEINER (Germany).

Deputy Executive Director: AMINA MOHAMED (Kenya).

REGIONAL OFFICES

UNEP maintains six regional offices. These work to initiate and promote UNEP objectives and to ensure that all programme formulation and delivery meets the specific needs of countries and regions. They also provide a focal point for building national, sub-regional and regional partnership and enhancing local participation in UNEP initiatives. A co-ordination office has been established at headquarters to promote regional policy integration, to co-ordinate programme planning, and to provide necessary services to the regional offices.

Africa: POB 30552, Nairobi, Kenya; tel. (20) 7624292; e-mail roainfo@unep.org; internet www.unep.org/roa.

Asia and the Pacific: United Nations Bldg, 2nd Floor, Rajadamnern Nok Ave, Bangkok 10200, Thailand; tel. (2) 288-1870; fax (2) 280-3829; e-mail uneproap@un.org; internet www.unep.org/roap.

Europe: 11–13 chemin des Anémones, 1219 Châtelaine, Geneva, Switzerland; tel. 229178279; fax 229178024; e-mail roe@unep.ch; internet www.unep.ch/roe.

Latin America and the Caribbean: Ciudad del Saber, Edif. 103, Avda Morse, Corregimiento de Ancón, Ciudad de Panamá, Panama; tel. 305-3100; fax 305-3105; e-mail enlace@pnuma.org; internet www.pnuma.org.

North America: 900 17th St NW, Suite 506, Washington, DC 20006, USA; tel. (202) 785-0465; fax (202) 785-2096; e-mail uneprona@un.org; internet www.rona.unep.org.

UNEP New York Office: DC-2 Bldg, Room 0803, Two United Nations Plaza, New York, NY 10017, USA; tel. (212) 963-8210; fax (212) 963-7341; e-mail unepnyo@un.org; internet www.unep.org/newyork.

West Asia: POB 10880, Manama, Bahrain; tel. 17812777; fax 17825110; e-mail uneprowa@unep.org.bh; internet www.unep.org.bh.

OTHER OFFICES

Convention on International Trade in Endangered Species of Wild Fauna and Flora (CITES): 15 chemin des Anémones, 1219 Châtelaine, Geneva, Switzerland; tel. 229178139; fax 227973417; e-mail info@cites.org; internet www.cites.org; Sec.-Gen. JOHN SCANLON (Australia).

Global Programme of Action for the Protection of the Marine Environment from Land-based Activities: GPA Co-ordination Unit, UNEP, POB 30552, 00100 Nairobi, Kenya; tel. (20) 7621206; fax (20) 7624249; internet www.gpa.unep.org.

Regional Co-ordinating Unit for East Asian Seas: UN Bldg, 2nd Floor, Rajadamnern Nok Ave, Bangkok 10200, Thailand; tel. (2) 288-1860; fax (2) 281-2428; e-mail kleesuwan.unescap@un.org; internet www.cobsea.org; Co-ordinator Dr ELLIK ADLER.

Regional Co-ordinating Unit for the Caribbean Environment Programme: 14–20 Port Royal St, Kingston, Jamaica; tel. 922-9267; fax 922-9292; e-mail rcu@cep.unep.org; internet www.cep.unep.org; Co-ordinator NELSON ANDRADE COLMENARES.

Secretariat of the Basel, Rotterdam and Stockholm Conventions: 11–13 chemin des Anémones, 1219 Châtelaine, Geneva, Switzerland; tel. 229178729; fax 229178098; e-mail brs@unep.org; internet www.basel.int; www.pic.int; www.pops.int; Exec. Sec. JIM WILLIS (USA).

Secretariat of the Mediterranean Action Plan on the Implementation of the Barcelona Convention: Leoforos Vassileos Konstantinou 48, POB 18019, 11610 Athens, Greece; tel. (210) 7273100; fax (210) 7253196; e-mail unepmedu@unepmap.gr; internet www.unepmap.org.

Secretariat of the Multilateral Fund for the Implementation of the Montreal Protocol: 1800 McGill College Ave, 27th Floor, Montréal, QC, Canada H3A 3J6; tel. (514) 282-1122; fax (514) 282-0068; e-mail secretariat@unmfs.org; internet www.multilateralfund.org; Chief Officer MARIA NOLAN.

UNEP/CMS (Convention on the Conservation of Migratory Species of Wild Animals) Secretariat: Hermann-Ehlers-Str. 10, 53113 Bonn, Germany; tel. (228) 8152402; fax (228) 8152449; e-mail secretariat@cms.int; internet www.cms.int; Exec. Sec. ELIZABETH MARUMA MREMA.

UNEP Division of Technology, Industry and Economics: 15 rue de Milan, 75441 Paris, Cedex 09, France; tel. 1-44-37-14-50; fax 1-44-37-14-74; e-mail unep.tie@unep.fr; internet www.unep.org/dtie; Dir SYLVIE LEMMET (France).

UNEP International Environmental Technology Centre (IETC): 2–110 Ryokuchi koen, Tsurumi-ku, Osaka 538-0036, Japan; tel. (6) 6915-4581; fax (6) 6915-0304; e-mail ietc@unep.or.jp; internet www.unep.or.jp; Dir PER BAKKEN.

UNEP Ozone Secretariat: POB 30552, Nairobi, Kenya; tel. (20) 762-3851; fax (20) 762-4691; e-mail ozoneinfo@unep.org; internet ozone.unep.org; Exec. Sec. MARCO GONZÁLEZ (Costa Rica).

UNEP Post-Conflict and Disaster Management Branch: 11–15 chemin des Anémones, 1219 Châtelaine, Geneva, Switzerland; tel. 229178530; fax 229178064; e-mail postconflict@unep.org; internet www.unep.org/disastersandconflicts; Chief Officer HENRIK SLOTTE.

UNEP Risoe Centre on Energy, Environment and Sustainable Development: Risoe Campus, Technical University of Denmark, Frederiksborgvej 399, Bldg 142, POB 49, 4000 Roskilde, Denmark; tel. 46-77-51-29; fax 46-32-19-99; e-mail unep@risoe.dtu.dk; internet uneprisoe.org; f. 1990 as the UNEP Collaborating Centre on Energy and Environment; supports UNEP in the planning and implementation of its energy-related policy and activities; provides technical support to governments towards the preparation of national Technology Needs Assessments on climate change adaptation; Head JOHN CHRISTENSEN.

UNEP-SCBD (Convention on Biological Diversity—Secretariat): 413 St Jacques St, Suite 800, Montréal, QC, Canada H2Y 1N9; tel. (514) 288-2220; fax (514) 288-6588; e-mail secretariat@cbd.int; internet www.cbd.int; Exec. Sec. BRAULIO FERREIRA DE SOUZA DIAS (Brazil).

UNEP Secretariat for the UN Scientific Committee on the Effects of Atomic Radiation: Vienna International Centre, Wagramerstr. 5, POB 500, 1400 Vienna, Austria; tel. (1) 26060-4330; fax (1) 26060-5902; e-mail malcolm.crick@unscear.org; internet www.unscear.org; Sec. Dr MALCOLM CRICK.

Activities

UNEP represents a voice for the environment within the UN system. It is an advocate, educator, catalyst and facilitator, promoting the wise use of the planet's natural assets for sustainable development. It aims to maintain a constant watch on the changing state of the environment; to analyse the trends; to assess the problems using a wide range of data and techniques; and to undertake or support projects leading to environmentally sound development. It plays a catalytic and co-ordinating role within and beyond the UN system. Many UNEP projects are implemented in co-operation with other UN agencies, particularly UNDP, the World Bank group, FAO, UNESCO and WHO. About 45 intergovernmental organizations outside the UN system and 60 international non-governmental organizations (NGOs) have official observer status on UNEP's Governing Council, and, through the Environment Liaison Centre in Nairobi, UNEP is linked to more than 6,000 non-governmental bodies concerned with the environment. UNEP also sponsors international conferences, programmes, plans and agreements regarding all aspects of the environment.

In February 1997 the Governing Council, at its 19th session, adopted a ministerial declaration (the Nairobi Declaration) on UNEP's future role and mandate, which recognized the organization as the principal UN body working in the field of the environment and as the leading global environmental authority, setting and overseeing the international environmental agenda. In June a special session of the UN General Assembly, referred to as 'Rio+5', was convened to review the state of the environment and progress achieved in implementing the objectives of the UN Conference on Environment and Development (UNCED—known as the Earth Summit), that had been held in Rio de Janeiro, Brazil, in June 1992. UNCED had adopted Agenda 21 (a programme of activities to promote sustainable development in the 21st century) and the 'Rio+5' meeting adopted a Programme for Further Implementation of Agenda 21 in order to intensify efforts in areas such as energy, freshwater resources and technology transfer. The meeting confirmed UNEP's essential role in advancing the Programme and as a global authority promoting a coherent legal and political approach to the environmental challenges of sustainable development. An extensive process of restructuring and realignment of functions was subsequently initiated by UNEP, and a new organizational structure reflecting the decisions of the Nairobi Declaration was implemented during 1999. UNEP played a leading role in preparing for the World Summit on Sustainable Development (WSSD), held in August–September 2002 in Johannesburg, South Africa, to assess strategies for strengthening the implementation of Agenda 21. Governments participating in the conference adopted the Johannesburg Declaration and WSSD Plan of Implementation, in which they strongly reaffirmed commitment to the principles underlying Agenda 21 and also pledged support to all internationally agreed development goals, including the UN Millennium Development Goals adopted by governments attending a summit meeting of the UN General Assembly in September 2000. Participating governments made concrete commitments to attaining several specific objectives in the areas of water, energy, health, agriculture and fisheries, and biodiversity. These included a reduction by one-half in the proportion of people world-wide lacking access to clean water or good sanitation by 2015, the restocking of depleted fisheries by 2015, a reduction in the ongoing loss in biodiversity by 2010, and the production and utilization of chemicals without causing harm to human beings and the environment by 2020. Participants determined to increase usage of renewable energy sources and to develop integrated water resources management and water efficiency plans. A large number of partnerships between governments, private sector interests and civil society groups were announced at the conference. The UN Conference on Sustainable Development (UNCSD) (also known as Earth Summit 2012 and as 'Rio+20'), convened in June 2012, again in Rio de Janeiro, determined that UNEP's role should be strengthened as the lead agency in setting the global environmental agenda and co-ordinating UN system-wide implementation of the environmental dimension of sustainable development. The Conference decided to ask the UN General Assembly, during its 67th session (commencing in September 2012), to adopt a resolution that would upgrade UNEP by establishing universal membership of the Governing Council; ensuring increased financial resources to enable the Programme to fulfil its mandate; strengthening UNEP's participation in the main UN co-ordinating bodies; and empowering UNEP to lead efforts to develop UN system-wide strategies on the environment.

In May 2000 UNEP's first annual Global Ministerial Environment Forum (GMEF), was held in Malmö, Sweden, attended by environment ministers and other government delegates from more than 130 countries. Participants reviewed policy issues in the field of the environment and addressed issues such as the impact on the environment of population growth, the depletion of earth's natural resources, climate change and the need for fresh water supplies. The Forum issued the Malmö Declaration, which identified the effective implementation of international agreements on environmental matters at national level as the most pressing challenge for policy-makers. The Declaration emphasized the importance of mobilizing domestic and international resources and urged increased co-operation from civil society and the private sector in achieving sustainable development. The GMEF was subsequently convened annually.

CLIMATE CHANGE

UNEP worked in collaboration with WMO to formulate the 1992 UN Framework Convention on Climate Change (UNFCCC), with the aim of reducing the emission of gases that have a warming effect on the atmosphere (known as greenhouse gases). (See Secretariat of the UN Framework Convention on Climate Change, below.) In 1998 UNEP and the World Meteorological Organization (WMO) established the Intergovernmental Panel on Climate Change (IPCC, see below), as an objective source of scientific information about the warming of the earth's atmosphere.

UNEP's climate change-related activities have a particular focus on strengthening the capabilities of countries (in particular developing countries) to integrate climate change responses into their national development processes, including improving preparedness for participating in UN Reduced Emissions from Deforestation and Forest Degradation (UN-REDD) initiatives; Ecosystem Based Adaptation; and Clean Tech Readiness.

UN-REDD, launched in September 2008 as a collaboration between UNEP, UNDP and FAO, aims to enable donors to pool resources (through a trust fund established for that purpose) to promote a transformation of forest resource use patterns. In August 2011 UN-REDD endorsed a Global Programme Framework covering 2011–15. Leaders from countries in the Amazon, Congo and Borneo-Mekong forest basins participated, in June 2011, in the Summit of Heads of State and Government on Tropical Forest Ecosystems, held in Brazzaville, Republic of the Congo; the meeting issued a declaration recognising the need to protect forests in order to combat climate change, and to conduct future mutual dialogue. In that month UNEP issued a report focusing on the economic benefits of expanding funding for forests.

UNEP's Technology Needs Assessment and Technology Action Plan aims to support some 35–45 countries with the implementation of improved national Technology Needs Assessments within the framework of the UNFCCC, involving, *inter alia*, detailed analysis of mitigation and adaptation technologies, and prioritization of these technologies. The UNEP Risoe Centre of Denmark supports governments in the preparation of these Assessments.

UNEP encourages the development of alternative and renewable sources of energy, as part of its efforts to mitigate climate change. To achieve this, UNEP has created the Global Network on Energy for Sustainable Development, linking 20 centres of excellence in industrialized and developing countries to conduct research and exchange information on environmentally sound energy technology resources. UNEP's Rural Energy Enterprise Development (REED) initiative helps the private sector to develop affordable 'clean' energy technologies, such as solar crop-drying and water-heating, wind-powered water pumps and efficient cooking stoves. UNEP is a member of the Global Bioenergy Partnership initiated by the G8 group of industrialized countries to support the sustainable use of biofuels. Through its Sustainable Transport Programme UNEP promotes the use of renewable fuels and the integration of environmental factors into transport planning, while the Sustainable Buildings and Construction Initiative promotes energy efficiency in the construction industry. In conjunction with UN-Habitat, UNDP, the World Bank and other organizations and institutions, UNEP promotes environmental concerns in urban planning and management through the Sustainable Cities Programme, and projects concerned with waste management, urban pollution and the impact of transportation systems.

During 2007 UNEP (with WMO and WTO) convened a second International Conference on Climate Change and Tourism, together with two meetings on sustainable tourism development and a conference on global eco-tourism.

In June 2009 UNEP and WTO jointly issued a report entitled *Trade and Climate Change*, reviewing the intersections between trade and climate change from the perspectives of: the science of climate change; economics; multilateral efforts to combat climate change; and the effects on trade of national climate change policies.

GREEN ECONOMY

In October 2008, in response to the global economic, fuel and food crises that escalated during that year, UNEP launched the *Green Economy Initiative (GEI)*, also known as the 'Global Green New Deal', which aimed to mobilize and refocus the global economy towards investments in clean technologies and the natural infrastructure (for example the infrastructures of forests and soils), with a view to, simultaneously, combating climate change and promoting employment. The UNEP Executive Director stated that the global crises were in part related to a broad market failure that promoted speculation while precipitating escalating losses of natural capital and nature-based assets, compounded by an over-reliance on finite, often subsidized fossil fuels. The three principal dimensions of the GEI were: the compilation of the *Green Economy* report, to provide an analysis of how public policy might support markets in accelerating the transition towards a low-carbon green economy; the Green Jobs Initiative, a partnership launched by UNEP, the ILO and the International Trade Union Confederation in 2007 (and joined in 2008 by the International Organisation of Employers); and the Economics of Ecosystems and Biodiversity (TEEB) partnership project, focusing on valuation issues. In April 2009 the UN System Chief Executives Board for Co-ordination (CEB) endorsed the GEI as the fourth of nine UN initiatives aimed at alleviating the impact of the global economic crisis on poor and vulnerable populations.

In June 2009 UNEP welcomed OECD's 'Green Growth' declaration, which urged the adoption of targeted policy instruments to promote green investment, and emphasized commitment to the realization of an ambitious and comprehensive post-2012 global climate agreement. In January 2012 UNEP, OECD, the World Bank, and the Global Green Growth Institute (established in June 2010 in Seoul, Republic of Korea) launched the Green Growth Knowledge Platform. The Platform, accessible at www.greengrowthknowledge.org, aims to advance efforts to identify and address major knowledge gaps in green growth theory and practice, and to support countries in formulating and implementing policies aimed at developing a green economy.

In January 2011 UNEP and the World Tourism Organization launched the Global Partnership for Sustainable Tourism, also comprising other UN agencies, OECD, 18 governments, and other partners, with the aim of guiding policy and developing projects in the area of sustainable tourism, providing a global platform for discussion, and facilitating progress towards a green economy.

UNEP Finance Initiatives (FI) is a programme encouraging banks, insurance companies and other financial institutions to invest in an environmentally responsible way: an annual FI Global Roundtable meeting is held, together with regional meetings. In April 2007 UNEP hosted the first annual Business for Environment (B4E) meeting, on corporate environmental responsibility, in Singapore; the 2012 meeting was to be held in April, in Berlin, Germany. During 2007 UNEP's Programme on Sustainable Consumption and Production established an International Panel for Sustainable Resource Management (comprising experts whose initial subjects of study were to be the environmental risks of biofuels and of metal recycling), and initiated forums for businesses and NGOs in this field. In May 2011 the International Panel issued a *Decoupling Report* that urged the separation of the global economic growth rate from the rate of natural resource consumption. The report warned that, by 2050, without a change of direction, humanity's consumption of minerals, ores, fossil fuels and biomass were on course to increase threefold. Later in May 2011 the Panel released a report focusing on the need to increase the recycling of metals world-wide.

In February 2009 UNEP issued a report, entitled *The Environmental Food Crisis: Environment's Role in Averting Future Food Crises*, that urged a transformation in the way that food is produced, handled and disposed of, in order to feed the world's growing population and protect the environment.

In 1994 UNEP inaugurated the International Environmental Technology Centre (IETC), based in Osaka, Japan. The Centre promotes and implements environmentally sound technologies for disaster prevention and post-disaster reconstruction; sustainable production and consumption; and water and sanitation (in particular waste-water management and more efficient use of rainwater).

EARLY WARNING AND ASSESSMENT

The Nairobi Declaration resolved that the strengthening of UNEP's information, monitoring and assessment capabilities was a crucial element of the organization's restructuring, in order to help establish priorities for international, national and regional action, and to ensure the efficient and accurate dissemination of information on emerging environmental trends and emergencies.

UNEP's Division of Early Warning and Assessment analyses the world environment, provides early warning information and assesses global and regional trends. It provides governments with data and helps them to use environmental information for decision-making and planning.

UNEP's Global Environment Outlook (GEO) process of environmental analysis and assessment, launched in 1995, is supported by an extensive network of collaborating centres. The fifth 'umbrella' report on the GEO process (*GEO-5*) was issued in June 2012, just in advance of the UN Conference on Sustainable Development. The fifth report assessed progress achieved towards the attainment of some 90 environmental challenges, and identified four objectives—the elimination of the production and use of ozone layer-depleting substances; the removal of lead from fuel; access to improved water supplies; and promoting research into reducing pollution of the marine environment—as the areas in which most progress had been made. Little or no progress, however, was found to have been attained in the pursuit of 24 objectives, including managing climate change, desertification and drought; and deterioration was found to have occurred in the state of the world's coral reefs. In recent years regional and national GEO reports have been issued focusing on Africa, the Andean region, the Atlantic and Indian oceans, Brazil, the Caucasus, Latin America and the Caribbean, North America, and the Pacific; and the following thematic GEO reports have been produced: *The Global Deserts Outlook* (2006) and *The Global Outlook for Ice and Snow* (2007). Various GEO technical reports have also been published.

UNEP's Global International Waters Assessment (GIWA) considers all aspects of the world's water-related issues, in particular problems of shared transboundary waters, and of future sustainable management of water resources. UNEP is also a sponsoring agency of the Joint Group of Experts on the Scientific Aspects of Marine Environmental Pollution and contributes to the preparation of reports on the state of the marine environment and on the impact of land-based activities on that environment. In November 1995 UNEP published a Global

Biodiversity Assessment, which was the first comprehensive study of biological resources throughout the world. The UNEP-World Conservation Monitoring Centre (UNEP-WCMC), established in June 2000 in Cambridge, United Kingdom, manages and interprets data concerning biodiversity and ecosystems, and makes the results available to governments and businesses. In October 2008 UNEP-WCMC, in partnership with the IUCN, launched a new online database of the world's national parks and protected areas; detailed images of more than 100,000 sites could be viewed on the site. In 2007 the Centre undertook the 2010 Biodiversity Indicators Programme, with the aim of supporting decision-making by governments so as to reduce the threat of extinction facing vulnerable species. UNEP is a partner in the International Coral Reef Action Network—ICRAN, which was established in 2000 to monitor, manage and protect coral reefs world-wide. In June 2001 UNEP launched the Millennium Ecosystem Assessment, which was completed in March 2005. Other major assessments undertaken include the International Assessment of Agricultural Science and Technology for Development; the Solar and Wind Energy Resource Assessment; the Regionally Based Assessment of Persistent Toxic Substances; the Land Degradation Assessment in Drylands; and the Global Methodology for Mapping Human Impacts on the Biosphere (GLOBIO) project.

In June 2010 delegates from 85 countries, meeting in Busan, Republic of Korea, at the third conference addressing the creation of a new Intergovernmental Science-Policy Platform on Biodiversity and Ecosystem Services (IPBES), adopted the Busan Outcome Document finalizing details of the establishment of the IPBES. The Platform, inaugurated in December 2010, following approval of the Outcome Document by the UN General Assembly, was to undertake, periodically, assessments, based on current scientific literature, of biodiversity and ecosystem outputs beneficial to humans, including timber, fresh water, fish and climatic stability. The first plenary session of IPBES was convened in October 2011.

UNEP's environmental information network includes the UNEP-INFOTERRA programme, which facilitates the exchange of environmental information through an extensive network of national 'focal points' (national environmental information centres, usually located in the relevant government ministry or agency). By 2012 177 countries were participating in the network, whereby UNEP promotes public access to environmental information, as well as participation in environmental concerns. UNEP's information, monitoring and assessment structures also serve to enhance early-warning capabilities and to provide accurate information during an environmental emergency.

DISASTERS AND CONFLICTS

UNEP aims to minimise environmental causes and consequences of disasters and conflicts, and supports member states in combating environmental degradation and natural resources mismanagement, deeming these to be underlying risk factors for conflicts and natural hazards. UNEP promotes the integration of environmental concerns into risk reduction policy and practices. In 2011 UNEP targeted activities aimed at reducing conflict and disaster risk at 16 countries, 12 of which had adopted national policies aimed at mitigating post-conflict and post-disaster environmental risks. During 2011 training on environment and disaster risk reduction was conducted in India, Sri Lanka and Thailand.

UNEP undertakes assessments to establish the risks posed by environmental impacts on human health, security and livelihoods, and provides field-based capacity building and technical support, in countries affected by natural disaster and conflict. Since 1999 UNEP has conducted post-crisis environmental assessments in Afghanistan, the Balkans, the Democratic Republic of the Congo, Lebanon, Nigeria (Ogoniland), the Palestinian territories, Rwanda, Sudan, and Ukraine, and in the countries affected by the 2004 Indian Ocean tsunami.

An independent report of the Senior Advisory Group to the UN Secretary General on Civilian Capacity in the Aftermath of Conflict, issued in February 2011, identified natural resources as a key area of focus and designated UNEP as the lead agency for identifying best practices in managing natural resources in support of peace building.

In May 2012 UNEP issued a report entitled *Greening the Blue Helmets: Environment, Natural Resources and UN Peacekeeping Operations*, which addressed the interaction between peacekeeping missions and natural resources and the broader environment, and emphasized the importance of minimizing the environmental impact of UN missions.

ENVIRONMENTAL GOVERNANCE

UNEP promotes international environmental legislation and the development of policy tools and guidelines in order to achieve the sustainable management of the world environment. It helps governments to implement multilateral environmental agreements, and to report on their results. At a national level it assists governments to develop and implement appropriate environmental instruments and aims to co-ordinate policy initiatives. Training in various aspects of environmental law and its applications is provided. The ninth Global Training Programme on Environmental Law and Policy was conducted by UNEP in November 2009; regional training programmes are also offered. UNEP supports the development of new legal, economic and other policy instruments to improve the effectiveness of existing environmental agreements. It updates a register of international environmental treaties, and publishes handbooks on negotiating and enforcing environmental law. It acts as the secretariat for a number of regional and global environmental conventions (see list above). In June 2011 UNEP launched the Multilateral Environmental Agreements Information and Knowledge Management Initiative, which aimed to expand the sharing of information on more than 12 international agreements relating to the protection of the environment.

In late June 2009 the first meeting was convened, in Belgrade, Serbia, of a new Consultative Group of Ministers and High-level Representatives on International Environment Governance; the meeting reviewed UNEP's role and stressed the linkages between sustainable environmental policies and development. From end-June–early July five successive UNEP Executive Directors and other prominent environmentalists met, in Glion, Switzerland, to discuss means of bringing about change in the functioning of the world economy to prioritize a sustainable approach to using and preserving the environment for the benefit of long-term human welfare.

UNEP is the principal UN agency for promoting environmentally sustainable water management. It regards the unsustainable use of water as one of the most urgent environmental issues, and estimates that two-thirds of the world's population will suffer chronic water shortages by 2025, owing to rising demand for drinking water as a result of growing populations, decreasing quality of water because of pollution, and increasing requirements of industries and agriculture. In 2000 UNEP adopted a new water policy and strategy, comprising assessment, management and co-ordination components. The Global International Waters Assessment (see above) is the primary framework for the assessment component. The management component includes the Global Programme of Action (GPA) for the Protection of the Marine Environment from Land-based Activities (adopted in November 1995), which focuses on the effects of pollution on freshwater resources, marine biodiversity and the coastal ecosystems of small island developing states. UNEP promotes international co-operation in the management of river basins and coastal areas and for the development of tools and guidelines to achieve the sustainable management of freshwater and coastal resources. In 2007 UNEP initiated a South-South Co-operation programme on technology and capacity-building for the management of water resources. UNEP provides scientific, technical and administrative support to facilitate the implementation and co-ordination of 14 regional seas conventions and 13 regional plans of action. UNEP's Regional Seas Programme aims to protect marine and coastal ecosystems, particularly by helping governments to put relevant legislation into practice.

UNEP was instrumental in the drafting of a Convention on Biological Diversity (CBD) to preserve the immense variety of plant and animal species, in particular those threatened with extinction. The Convention entered into force at the end of 1993; by June 2012 192 states and the European Union (EU) were parties to the CBD. The CBD's Cartagena Protocol on Biosafety (so called as it had been addressed at an extraordinary session of parties to the CBD convened in Cartagena, Colombia, in

February 1999) was adopted at a meeting of parties to the CBD in January 2000, and entered into force in September 2003; by June 2012 the Protocol had been ratified by 163 states parties. The Protocol regulates the transboundary movement and use of living modified organisms resulting from biotechnology, in order to reduce any potential adverse effects on biodiversity and human health. It establishes an Advanced Informed Agreement procedure to govern the import of such organisms. In January 2002 UNEP launched a major project aimed at supporting developing countries with assessing the potential health and environmental risks and benefits of genetically modified (GM) crops, in preparation for the Protocol's entry into force. In February the parties to the CBD and other partners convened a conference on ways in which the traditional knowledge and practices of local communities could be preserved and used to conserve highly threatened species and ecosystems. The sixth conference of parties to the CBD, held in April 2002, adopted detailed voluntary guidelines concerning access to genetic resources and sharing the benefits attained from such resources with the countries and local communities where they originate; a global work programme on forests; and a set of guiding principles for combating alien invasive species. In October 2010 the 10th conference of the parties to the CBD, meeting in Nagoya, Japan, approved the Nagoya-Kuala Lumpur Supplementary Protocol to the CBD, with a view to establishing an international regime on access and benefit sharing (ABS) of genetic resources, alongside a strategic 10-year Strategic Plan for Biodiversity, comprising targets and timetables to combat loss of the planet's nature-based resources. The Supplementary Protocol was opened for signature in March 2011, and by June 2012 had been signed by 92 states and ratified by five. The UN Decade on Biodiversity was being celebrated during 2011–20. UNEP supports co-operation for biodiversity assessment and management in selected developing regions and for the development of strategies for the conservation and sustainable exploitation of individual threatened species (e.g. the Global Tiger Action Plan). It also provides assistance for the preparation of individual country studies and strategies to strengthen national biodiversity management and research. UNEP administers the Convention on International Trade in Endangered Species of Wild Flora and Fauna (CITES), which entered into force in 1975 and comprised 175 states parties at June 2012. CITES has special programmes on the protection of elephants, falcons, great apes, hawksbill turtles, sturgeons, tropical timber (jointly with the International Tropical Timber Organization), and big leaf mahogany. Meeting in St Petersburg, Russia, in November 2010, at the International Tiger Forum, the heads of UNODC, the Convention on International Trade in Endangered Species of Wild Fauna and Flora (CITES), the World Customs Organization, INTERPOL and the World Bank jointly approved the establishment of a new International Consortium on Combating Wildlife Crime (ICCWC), with the aim of combating the poaching of wild animals and illegal trade in wild animals and wild animal products.

In December 1996 the Lusaka Agreement on Co-operative Enforcement Operations Directed at Illegal Trade in Wild Flora and Fauna entered into force, having been concluded under UNEP auspices in order to strengthen the implementation of the CBD and CITES in Eastern and Central Africa. UNEP and UNESCO jointly co-sponsor the Great Apes Survival Project (GRASP), which was launched in May 2001. GRASP supports, in 23 'great ape range states' (of which 21 are in Africa and two—Indonesia and Malaysia—in South-East Asia), the conservation of gorillas, chimpanzees, orang-utans and bonobos. GRASP's first intergovernmental meeting, held in Kinshasa, Democratic Republic of the Congo in September 2005, was attended by representatives of governments of great ape habitat states, donor and other interested states, international organizations, NGOs, and private-sector and academic interests. The meeting adopted a Global Strategy for the Survival of Great Apes, and the Kinshasa Declaration pledging commitment and action towards achieving this goal. GRASP, CITES and the World Association of Zoos and Aquariums jointly declared 2009 the Year of the Gorilla. In June 2009 160 government representatives participating in a conference to mark the Year of the Gorilla, convened in Frankfurt, Germany, issued the Frankfurt Declaration to Call for Better Protection of Gorillas.

The Convention on the Conservation of Migratory Species of Wild Animals (CMS, also referred to as the Bonn Convention), concluded under UNEP auspices in 1979, aims to conserve migratory avian, marine and terrestrial species throughout the range of their migration. The secretariat of the CMS is hosted by UNEP. At June 2012 there were 117 states parties to the Convention. A number of agreements and Memoranda of Understanding (MOU) concerning conservation have been concluded under the CMS. Agreements cover the conservation of African-Eurasian Migratory Waterbirds (1999), Populations of European Bats (1994), Small Cetaceans of the Baltic, North East Atlantic, Irish and North Seas (1994), Cetaceans of the Black Seas, Mediterranean and Contiguous Atlantic Area (2001), Seals in the Wadden Sea (1991), Albatrosses and Petrels (2004), and Gorillas and their Habitiats (2008). MOU cover the conservation of the Siberian Crane (1993), the Slender-billed Curlew (1994), Marine Turtles of the Atlantic Coast of Africa (1999), Marine Turtles of the Indian Ocean and South-east Asia (2001), the Great Bustard (2001), the Bukhara Deer (2002), the Aquatic Warbler (2003), the West African Elephant (2005), the Saiga Antelope (2005), Pacific Island Cetaceans (2006), the Ruddy-headed Goose (2006), Grassland Birds (2007), Atlantic Populations of the Mediterranean Monk Seal (2007), Dugongs (2007), the Manatee and Small Cetaceans of Western Africa and Macaronesia (2008), Migratory Birds of Prey in Africa and Eurasia (2008), High Andean Flamingos and their Habitats (2008), Migratory Sharks (2010), and the Southern Huemul (2010).

In October 1994 87 countries, meeting under UN auspices, signed a Convention to Combat Desertification (see UNDP Drylands Development Centre), which aimed to provide a legal framework to counter the degradation of arid regions. An estimated 75% of all drylands have suffered some land degradation, affecting approximately 1,000m. people in 110 countries. UNEP continues to support the implementation of the Convention, as part of its efforts to protect land resources. UNEP also aims to improve the assessment of dryland degradation and desertification in co-operation with governments and other international bodies, as well as identifying the causes of degradation and measures to overcome these.

ECOSYSTEM MANAGEMENT

The Millennium Ecosystem Assessment, a scientific study of the state of 24 ecosystems, that was commissioned by the UN Secretary-General and published in 2001, found that 15 of the ecosystems under assessment were being used unsustainably, thereby inhibiting, particularly in developing countries, the achievement of the UN MDGs of reducing poverty and hunger. UNEP's Ecosystem Management Programme aims to develop an adaptive approach that integrates the management of forests, land, freshwater, and coastal systems, focusing on sustaining ecosystems to meet future ecological needs, and to enhance human well-being. UNEP places particular emphasis on six ecosystem services deemed to be especially in decline: climate regulation; water regulation; natural hazard regulation; energy; freshwater; nutrient cycling; and recreation and ecotourism. Secondary importance is given to: water purification and waste treatment; disease regulation; fisheries; and primary production. UNEP supports governments in building capacity to promote the role of sustainably managed ecosystems in supporting social and economic development; assists national and regional governments in determining which ecosystem services to prioritize; and helps governments to incorporate an ecosystem management approach into their national and developmental planning and investment strategies.

UNEP's Billion Tree Campaign, initiated in February 2007, initially encouraged governments, community organizations and individuals to plant 1,000m. trees before the end of the year, and exceeded that target; by June 2012 some 12,599m. trees had been planted under the continuing campaign.

HARMFUL SUBSTANCES AND HAZARDOUS WASTE

UNEP administers the Basel Convention on the Control of Transboundary Movements of Hazardous Wastes and their Disposal, which entered into force in 1992 with the aim of preventing the uncontrolled movement and disposal of toxic and other hazardous wastes, particularly the illegal dumping of waste in developing countries by companies from industrialized countries. At June 2012 179 countries and the EU were parties to the Convention.

In 1996 UNEP, in collaboration with FAO, began to work towards promoting and formulating a legally binding international convention on prior informed consent (PIC) for hazardous chemicals and pesticides in international trade, extending a voluntary PIC procedure of information exchange undertaken by more than 100 governments since 1991. The Convention was adopted at a conference held in Rotterdam, Netherlands, in September 1998, and entered into force in February 2004. It aims to reduce risks to human health and the environment by restricting the production, export and use of hazardous substances and enhancing information exchange procedures. UNEP played a leading role in formulating a multilateral agreement to reduce and ultimately eliminate the manufacture and use of Persistent Organic Pollutants (POPs), which are considered to be a major global environmental hazard. The Stockholm Convention on POPs, targeting 12 particularly hazardous pollutants, was adopted by 127 countries in May 2001 and entered into force in May 2004. In May 2009 the fourth conference of parties to the Stockholm Convention agreed on a list of nine further POPs; these were incorporated into the Convention in an amendment that entered into force in August 2010.

In February 2009 140 governments agreed, under the auspices of UNEP, to launch negotiations on the development of an international treaty to combat toxic mercury emissions worldwide. The first session of the intergovernmental negotiating committee on preparing the proposed treaty was convened in June 2010, in Stockholm, Sweden. The second session was held January 2011, in Chiba, Japan, and a third took place in October–November, in Nairobi. Pending the adoption of the planned treaty (envisaged for 2013) it was agreed that a voluntary Global Mercury Partnership would address mercury pollution.

UNEP was the principal agency in formulating the 1987 Montreal Protocol to the Vienna Convention for the Protection of the Ozone Layer (1985), which provided for a 50% reduction in the production of chlorofluorocarbons (CFCs) by 2000. An amendment to the Protocol was adopted in 1990, which required complete cessation of the production of CFCs by 2000 in industrialized countries and by 2010 in developing countries. The Copenhagen Amendment, adopted in 1992, stipulated the phasing out of production of hydrochlorofluorocarbons (HCFCs) by 2030 in developed countries and by 2040 in developing nations. Subsequent amendments aimed to introduce a licensing system for all controlled substances, and imposed stricter controls on the import and export of HCFCs, and on the production and consumption of bromochloromethane (Halon-1011, an industrial solvent and fire extinguisher). In September 2007 the states parties to the Vienna Convention agreed to advance the deadline for the elimination of HCFCs: production and consumption were to be frozen by 2013, and were to be phased out in developed countries by 2020 and in developing countries by 2030. A Multilateral Fund for the Implementation of the Montreal Protocol was established in June 1990 to promote the use of suitable technologies and the transfer of technologies to developing countries, and support compliance by developing countries with relevant control measures. UNEP, UNDP, the World Bank and UNIDO are the sponsors of the Fund, which by February 2012 had approved financing for more than 6,875 projects and activities in 145 developing countries at a cost of more than US $2,800m. The eighth replenishment of the Fund, covering the period 2012–14, raised $400m. in new contributions from donors. In September 2009, following ratification by Timor-Leste, the Montreal Protocol, with 196 states parties, became the first agreement on the global environment to attain universal ratification. UNEP's OzonAction branch promotes information exchange, training and technological awareness, helping governments and industry in developing countries to undertake measures towards the cost-effective phasing-out of ozone-depleting substances.

UNEP encourages governments and the private sector to develop and adopt policies and practices that are cleaner and safer, make efficient use of natural resources, incorporate environmental costs, ensure the environmentally sound management of chemicals, and reduce pollution and risks to human health and the environment. In collaboration with other organizations UNEP works to formulate international guidelines and agreements to address these issues. UNEP also promotes the transfer of appropriate technologies and organizes conferences and training workshops to provide sustainable production practices. Relevant information is disseminated through the International Cleaner Production Information Clearing House. By 2012 UNEP, together with UNIDO, had established 47 National Cleaner Production Centres in developing and transition countries to promote a preventive approach to industrial pollution control. In October 1998 UNEP adopted an International Declaration on Cleaner Production, with a commitment to implement cleaner and more sustainable production methods and to monitor results. In 1997 UNEP and the Coalition for Environmentally Responsible Economies initiated the Global Reporting Initiative, which, with participation by corporations, business associations and other organizations, develops guidelines for voluntary reporting by companies on their economic, environmental and social performance. In April 2002 UNEP launched the 'Life Cycle Initiative', which evaluates the impact of products over their entire life cycle (from manufacture to disposal) and aims to assist governments, businesses and other consumers with adopting environmentally sound policies and practice, in view of the upward trend in global consumption patterns.

Through the International Register of Potentially Toxic Chemicals (IRPTC), used as a clearing house facility of relevant information, and by publishing further relevant information and technical reports, UNEP aims to facilitate access to data on chemicals and hazardous wastes, in order to assess and control health and environmental risks. UNEP provides technical support for implementing the Convention on Persistent Organic Pollutants (see above), encouraging the use of alternative pesticides, and monitoring the emission of pollutants through the burning of waste. UNEP administers the Strategic Approach to International Chemicals Management, adopted by the International Conference on Chemicals in 2006. With UNDP, UNEP helps governments to integrate sound management of chemicals into their development planning.

GLOBAL ENVIRONMENT FACILITY

UNEP, together with UNDP and the World Bank, is an implementing agency of the Global Environment Facility (GEF), established in 1991 to help developing countries, and those undergoing economic transition, to meet the costs of projects that benefit the environment in six specific areas: biological diversity, climate change, international waters, depletion of the ozone layer, land degradation and persistent organic pollutants. Important cross-cutting components of these projects include capacity-building to allow countries to meet their obligations under international environmental agreements (described above), and adaptation to climate change. During 1991–2011 some 522 projects were approved by the GEF to be implemented by UNEP, with a total value amounting to US $1,646m. UNEP services the Scientific and Technical Advisory Panel, which provides expert advice on GEF programmes and operational strategies.

COMMUNICATIONS AND PUBLIC INFORMATION

UNEP's public education campaigns and outreach programmes promote community involvement in environmental issues. Further communication of environmental concerns is undertaken through coverage in the press, broadcasting and electronic media, publications (see below), an information centre service and special promotional events, including World Environment Day (celebrated on 5 June; slogan in 2012: 'Green Economy: Does It Include You'), the Focus on Your World photography competition, and the awarding of the annual Sasakawa Prize (to recognize distinguished service to the environment by individuals and groups) and of the Champions of the Earth awards (for outstanding environmental leaders from each of UNEP's six regions). An annual Global Civil Society Forum (preceded by regional consultative meetings) is held in association with UNEP's Governing Council meetings. From April 2007 UNEP undertook a two-year programme on strengthening trade unions' participation in environmental processes. UNEP's Tunza programme for children and young people includes conferences, online discussions and publications. UNEP co-operates with the International Olympic Committee, the Commonwealth Games organizing body and international federations for football, athletics and other sports to encourage 'carbon neutral' sporting events and to use sport as a means of outreach.

Finance

Project budgetary resources approved by the Governing Council for UNEP's activities during 2012–13 totalled US $474m. UNEP is allocated a contribution from the regular budget of the United Nations, and derives most of its finances from voluntary contributions to the Environment Fund and to trust funds.

Publications

Annual Report.

CBTF (Capacity Building Task Force on Trade, Environment and Development) Newsletter.

DEWA/GRID Europe Quarterly Bulletin. E+ (Energy, Climate and Sustainable Development).

The Environment and Poverty Times.

Global 500.

Great Apes Survival Project Newsletter.

IETC (International Environmental Technology Centre) Insight.

Life Cycle Initiatives Newsletter.

Our Planet (quarterly).

Planet in Peril: Atlas of Current Threats to People and the Environment.

ROA (Regional Office for Africa) News (2 a year).

Tourism Focus (2 a year).

RRC.AP (Regional Resource Centre for Asia and the Pacific) Newsletter.

Sustainable Consumption Newsletter.

Tunza (quarterly magazine for children and young people).

UNEP Chemicals Newsletter.

UNEP Year Book.

World Atlas of Biodiversity.

World Atlas of Coral Reefs.

World Atlas of Desertification.

Studies, reports (including the *Global Environment Outlook* series), legal texts, technical guidelines, etc.

Associated Bodies

Secretariat of the UN Conference on Sustainable Development (UNCSD): Two UN Plaza, Rm DC2-2220 New York, NY 10017, USA; e-mail uncsd2012@un.org; internet www.uncsd2012.org/rio20/index.html; UNCSD (also known as Rio+20 and as the Earth Summit+20) was convened in Rio de Janeiro, Brazil, on 20–22 June 2012, with participation by more than 100 heads of state and government, and by an estimated 50,000 representatives of international and non-governmental organizations, civil society groups, and the private sector. Rio+20 commemorated the 20th anniversary of the 1992 UN Conference on Environment and Development (UNCED), also held in Rio de Janeiro, and the 10th anniversary of the World Summit on Sustainable Development (WSSD), staged in 2002, in Johannesburg, South Africa. In May 2010 the UN Secretary-General appointed the Under-Secretary-General for Economic and Social Affairs as the Secretary-General of Rio+20. A Conference Secretariat was established within the UN Department of Economic and Social Affairs. Rio+20 aims to assess progress towards, and secure renewed political commitment for sustainable development, with a focus on the following themes: (i) a green economy in the context of sustainable development and poverty eradication, and (ii) the Institutional Framework for Sustainable Development (IFSD). An inclusive preparatory process, involving stakeholders in the Conference, was implemented during 2010–June 2012. The UNCSD Secretariat, with other partners, prepared a series of briefs on Rio+20 issues—such as trade and the green economy; options for strengthening the IFSD; oceans; sustainable cities; green jobs and social inclusion; reducing disaster risk and building resilience; food security and sustainable agriculture; and water—to be made available to policy makers and other interested stakeholders as a basis for discussion. Heads of state and government, and high-level representatives, participating in Rio+20 endorsed an outcome document, entitled 'The Future We Want', which, *inter alia*, reaffirmed commitment to working towards an economically, socially and environmentally sustainable future, and to the eradication of poverty as an indispensable requirement for sustainable development; and deemed the implementation of green economy policy options, in the context of sustainable development and poverty eradication, to be an important tool for achieving sustainable development. The participants determined to strengthen the institutional framework and intergovernmental arrangements for sustainable development; and to establish a high-level intergovernmental forum to promote system-wide co-ordination and coherence of sustainable development policies and to follow up the implementation of sustainable development objectives. The forum was to build on the work of, and eventually replace, the UN Commission on Sustainable Development (see under ECOSOC), which was established in 1993 to oversee integration into the UN's work of UNCED's objectives; it was to meet for the first time in September 2013, at the start of the 68th UN General Assembly. The Conference invited all UN agencies and entities to mainstream sustainable development in their mandates, programmes, and strategies. The importance of enhancing the participation of developing countries in international economic decision-making was emphasized.

Secretary-General: SHA ZUKANG (People's Republic of China).

Executive Co-ordinators: H. ELIZABETH THOMPSON (Barbados), BRICE LALONDE (France).

Intergovernmental Panel on Climate Change (IPCC): established in 1988 by WMO and UNEP; comprises some 3,000 scientists as well as other experts and representatives of all UN member governments. Approximately every five years the IPCC assesses all available scientific, technical and socio-economic information on anthropogenic climate change. The IPCC provides, on request, scientific, technical and socio-economic advice to the Conference of the Parties to the UN Framework Convention on Climate Change (UNFCCC) and to its subsidiary bodies, and compiles reports on specialized topics, such as *Aviation and the Global Atmosphere*, *Regional Impacts of Climate Change*, and (issued in March 2012) *Managing the Risks of Extreme Events and Disasters to Advance Climate Change Adaptation*. The IPCC informs and guides, but does not prescribe, policy. In December 1995 the IPCC presented evidence to 120 governments, demonstrating 'a discernible human influence on global climate'. In 2001 the Panel issued its *Third Assessment Report,* in which it confirmed this finding and presented new and strengthened evidence attributing most global climate warming over the past 50 years to human activities. The IPCC's *Fourth Assessment Report*, the final instalment of which was issued in November 2007, concluded that increases in global average air and ocean temperatures, widespread melting of snow and ice, and the rising global average sea level, demonstrate that the warming of the climate system is unequivocal; that observational evidence from all continents and most oceans indicates that many natural systems are being affected by regional climate changes; that a global assessment of data since 1970 has shown that it is likely that anthropogenic warming has had a discernable influence on many physical and biological systems; and that other effects of regional climate changes are emerging. The *Fourth Assessment Report* was awarded a share of the Nobel Peace Prize for 2007. In January 2010 the IPCC accepted criticism that an assertion in the 2007 *Report*, concerning the rate at which Himalayan glaciers were melting, was exaggerated, and in February 2010 the Panel agreed that the *Report* had overstated the proportion of the Netherlands below sea level. In late February it was announced that an independent board of scientists would be appointed to review the work of the IPCC.

The *Fifth Assessment Report* of the IPCC was to be published in 2014. In May 2011 a meeting of delegates from IPCC member states determined that a 13-member executive committee, under the leadership of the IPCC Chairman, should be established to supervise the day-to-day operations of the Panel and to consider matters requiring urgent action.

Chair.: RAJENDRA K. PACHAURI (India).

Secretariat of the UN Framework Convention on Climate Change (UNFCCC): Haus Carstanjen, Martin-Luther-King-Str. 8, 53175 Bonn, Germany; tel. (228) 815-1000; fax (228) 815-1999; e-mail secretariat@unfccc.int; internet unfccc.int; WMO and UNEP worked together to formulate the Convention, in response to the first report of the IPCC, issued in August 1990, which predicted an increase in the concentration of 'greenhouse' gases (i.e. carbon dioxide and other gases that have a warming effect on the atmosphere) owing to human activity. The UNFCCC was signed in May 1992 and formally adopted at the UN Conference on Environment and Development, held in June. It entered into force in March 1994. It committed countries to submitting reports on measures being taken to reduce the emission of greenhouse gases and recommended stabilizing these emissions at 1990 levels by 2000; however, this was not legally binding. Following the second session of the Conference of the Parties (COP) of the Convention, held in July 1996, multilateral negotiations ensued to formulate legally binding objectives for emission limitations. At the third COP, held in Kyoto, Japan, in December 1997, 38 industrial nations endorsed mandatory reductions of combined emissions of the six major gases by an average of 5.2% during the five-year period 2008–12, to pre-1990 levels. The so-called Kyoto Protocol was to enter into force on being ratified by at least 55 countries party to the UNFCCC, including industrialized countries with combined emissions of carbon dioxide in 1990 accounting for at least 55% of the total global greenhouse gas emissions by developed nations. The fourth COP, convened in Buenos Aires, Argentina, in November 1998, adopted a plan of action to promote implementation of the UNFCCC and to finalize the operational details of the Kyoto Protocol. These included the Clean Development Mechanism, by which industrialized countries may obtain credits towards achieving their reduction targets by assisting developing countries to implement emission-reducing measures, and a system of trading emission quotas. The fifth COP, held in Bonn, Germany, in October–November 1999, and the first session of the sixth COP, convened in The Hague, Netherlands, in November 2000, failed to reach agreement on the implementation of the Buenos Aires plan of action, owing to a lack of consensus on several technical matters, including the formulation of an effective mechanism for ascertaining compliance under the Kyoto Protocol, and adequately defining a provision of the Protocol under which industrialized countries may obtain credits towards achieving their reduction targets in respect of the absorption of emissions resulting from activities in the so-called land-use, land-use change and forestry (LULUCF) sector. Further, informal, talks were held in Ottawa, Canada, in early December. Agreement on implementing the Buenos Aires action plan was finally achieved at the second session of the sixth COP, held in Bonn in July 2001. The seventh COP, convened in Marrakech, Morocco, in October–November, formally adopted the decisions reached in July, and elected 15 members to the Executive Board of the Clean Development Mechanism. In March 2002 the USA (the most prolific national producer of harmful gas emissions) announced that it would not ratify the Kyoto Protocol. The Kyoto Protocol eventually entered into force on 16 February 2005, 90 days after its ratification by Russia. Negotiations commenced in May 2007 on establishing a new international arrangement eventually to succeed the Kyoto Protocol. Participants in COP 13, convened in Bali, Indonesia, in December 2007, adopted the Bali Roadmap, detailing a two-year process leading to the planned conclusion of the schedule of negotiations in December 2009. Further rounds of talks were held during 2008 in Bangkok, Thailand (March–April); Bonn (June); and Accra, Ghana (August). The UN Climate Change Conference (COP 14), convened in Poznań, Poland, in December 2008, finalized the Kyoto Protocol's Adaptation Fund, which was to finance projects and programmes in developing signatory states that were particularly vulnerable to the adverse effects of climate change. Addressing the Conference, the UN Secretary-General urged the advancement of a 'Green New Deal', to address simultaneously the ongoing global climate and economic crises. COP 15 was held, concurrently with the fifth meeting of parties to the Kyoto Protocol, in Copenhagen, Denmark, in December 2009. Heads of state and government and other delegates attending the Conference approved the Copenhagen Accord, which determined that international co-operative action should be taken, in the context of sustainable development, to reduce global greenhouse gas emissions so as to hold the ongoing increase in global temperature below 2°C. It was agreed that enhanced efforts should be undertaken to reduce vulnerability to climate change in developing countries, with special reference to least developed countries, small island states and Africa. Developed countries agreed to pursue the achievement by 2020 of strengthened carbon emissions targets, while developing nations were to implement actions to slow down growth in emissions. A new Copenhagen Green Climate Fund was to be established to support climate change mitigation actions in developing countries, and a Technology Mechanism was also to be established, with the aim of accelerating technology development and transfer in support of climate change adaptation and mitigation activities. COP 16, convened, concurrently with the sixth meeting of parties to the Kyoto Protocol, in Cancun, Mexico, in November–December 2010, adopted several decisions (the 'Cancun Agreements'), which included mandating the establishment of a Cancun Adaptation Framework and associated Adaptation Committee, and approving a work programme which was to consider approaches to environmental damage linked to unavoidable impacts of climate change in vulnerable countries, as well as addressing forms of adaptation action, such as: strengthening the resilience of ecological systems; undertaking impact, vulnerability and adaptation assessments; engaging the participation of vulnerable communities in ongoing processes; and valuing traditional indigenous knowledge alongside the best available science. UN system-wide activities to address climate change are co-ordinated by an action framework established by the UN Chief Executives Board for Co-ordination under the UN *Delivering as One* commitment. By April 2012 the Kyoto Protocol had been ratified by 192 states and the European Community, including ratifications by industrialized nations with combined responsibility for 63.7% of greenhouse gas emissions by developed nations in 1990 (although excluding participation by the USA; in December Canada announced its intention to withdraw from the Protocol). COP 17, held in Durban, South Africa, in November–December 2011 concluded with an agreement on a 'Durban Platform for Enhanced Action'. The Platform incorporated agreements to extend the Kyoto provisions regarding emissions reductions by industrialized nations for a second phase (the commitment period, of either five or eight years, to be determined during 2012), to follow on from the expiry at end-2012 of the first commitment phase, and to initiate negotiations on a new, inclusive global emissions arrangement, to be concluded in 2015, that would come into effect in 2020 with 'legal force'. During the conference sufficient funds were committed to enable the Green Climate Fund to be inaugurated and a commitment was concluded to establish the Adaptation Committee.

Executive Secretary: CHRISTIANA FIGUERES (Costa Rica).

United Nations Framework Convention on Climate Change

(9 May 1992)

The Parties to this Convention,

Acknowledging that change in the Earth's climate and its adverse effect are a common concern of humankind,

Concerned that human activities have been substantially increasing the atmospheric concentrations of greenhouse gases, that these increases enhance the natural greenhouse effect, and that this will result on average in an additional warming of the Earth's surface and atmosphere and may adversely affect natural ecosystems and humankind,

Noting that the largest share of historical and current global emissions of greenhouse gases has originated in developed countries, that per capita emissions in developing countries are still relatively low and that the share of global emissions originating in developing countries will grow to meet their social and development needs,

Aware of the role and importance in terrestrial and marine ecosystems of sinks and reservoirs of greenhouse gases,

Noting that there are many uncertainties in predictions of climate change, particularly with regard to the timing, magnitude and regional patterns thereof,

Acknowledging that the global nature of climate change calls for the widest possible co-operation by all countries and their participation in an effective and appropriate international response, in accordance with their common but differentiated responsibilities and respective capabilities and their social and economic conditions,

Recalling the pertinent provisions of the Declaration of the United Nations Conference on the Human Environment, adopted at Stockholm on 16 June 1972,

Recalling also that States have, in accordance with the Charter of the United Nations and the principles of international law, the sovereign right to exploit their own resources pursuant to their own environmental and developmental policies, and the responsibility to ensure that activities within their jurisdiction or control do not cause damage to the environment of other States or of areas beyond the limits of national jurisdiction,

Reaffirming the principle of sovereignty of States in international co-operation to address climate change,

Recognizing that States should enact effective environmental legislation, that environmental standards, management objectives and priorities should reflect the environmental and developmental context to which they apply, and that standards applied by some countries may be inappropriate and of unwarranted economic and social cost to other countries, in particular developing countries, Recalling the provisions of the General Assembly ... on the United Nations Conference on Environment and Development, and ... on protection of global climate for present and future generations of mankind,

Recalling also the provisions of the General Assembly ... on the possible adverse effects of sea-level rise on islands and coastal areas, particularly low-lying coastal areas, and ... on the implementation of the Plan of Action to Combat Desertification,

Recalling further the Vienna Convention for the Protection of the Ozone Layer, 1985, and the Montreal Protocol on Substances that Deplete the Ozone Layer, 1987, as adjusted and amended on 29 June 1990,

Noting the Ministerial Declaration of the Second World Climate Conference adopted on 7 November 1990,

Conscious of the valuable analytical work being conducted by many States on climate change and of the important contributions of the World Meteorological Organization, the United Nations Environment Programme and other organs, organizations and bodies of the United Nations system, as well as other international and intergovernmental bodies, to the exchange of results of scientific research and the co-ordination of research,

Recognizing that steps required to understand and address climate change will be environmentally, socially and economically most effective if they are based on relevant scientific, technical and economic considerations and continually re-evaluated in the light of new findings in these areas,

Recognizing that various actions to address climate change can be justified economically in their own right and can also help in solving other environmental problems,

Recognizing also the need for developed countries to take immediate action in a flexible manner on the basis of clear priorities, as a first step towards comprehensive response strategies at the global, national and, where agreed, regional levels that take into account all greenhouse gases, with due consideration of their relative contributions to the enhancement of the greenhouse effect,

Recognizing further that low-lying and other small island countries, countries with low-lying coastal, arid and semi-arid areas or areas liable to floods, drought and desertification, and developing countries with fragile mountainous ecosystems are particularly vulnerable to the adverse effects of climate change,

Recognizing the special difficulties of those countries, especially developing countries, whose economies are particularly dependent on fossil fuel production, use and exportation, as a consequence of action taken on limiting greenhouse gas emissions,

Affirming that responses to climate change should be co-ordinated with social and economic development in an integrated manner with a view to avoiding adverse impacts on the latter, taking into full account the legitimate priority needs of developing countries for the achievement of sustained economic growth and the eradication of poverty,

Recognizing that all countries, especially developing countries, need access to resources required to achieve sustainable social and economic development and that, in order for developing countries to progress towards that goal, their energy consumption will need to grow, taking into account the possibilities for achieving greater energy efficiency and for controlling greenhouse gas emissions in general, including through the application of new technologies on terms which make such an application economically and socially beneficial,

Determined to protect the climate system for present and further generations,

Have agreed as follows.

Article 1

For the purposes of this Convention:

1. "Adverse effects of climate change" means changes in the physical environment or biota resulting from climate change which have significant deleterious effects on the composition, resilience or productivity of natural and managed ecosystems or on the operation of socio-economic systems or on human health and welfare.

2. "Climate change" means a change of climate which is attributed directly or indirectly to human activity that alters the composition of the global atmosphere and which is in addition to natural climate variability observed over comparable time periods.

3. "Climate system" means the totality of the atmosphere, hydrosphere, biosphere and geosphere and their interactions.

4. "Emissions" means the release of greenhouse gases and/or their precursors into the atmosphere over a specified area and period of time.

5. "Greenhouse gases" means those gaseous constituents of the atmosphere, both natural and anthropogenic, that absorb and re-emit infrared radiation.

6. "Regional economic integration organization" means an organization constituted by sovereign States of a given region which has competence in respect of matters governed by this Convention or its protocols and has been duly authorized, in accordance with its internal procedures, to sign, ratify, accept, approve or accede to the instruments concerned.

7. "Reservoir" means a component or components of the climate system where a greenhouse gas or a precursor of a greenhouse gas is stored.

8. "Sink" means any process, activity or mechanism which removes a greenhouse gas, an aerosol or a precursor of a greenhouse gas from the atmosphere.

9. "Source" means any process or activity which releases a greenhouse gas, an aerosol or a precursor of a greenhouse gas into the atmosphere.

Article 2

The ultimate objective of this Convention and any related legal instruments that the Conference of the Parties may adopt is to achieve, in accordance with the relevant provisions of the Convention, stabilization of greenhouse gas concentrations in the atmosphere at a level that would prevent dangerous anthropogenic interference with the climate system. Such a level should be achieved within a time-frame sufficient to allow ecosystems to adapt naturally to climate change, to ensure that food production is not threatened and to enable economic development to proceed in a sustainable manner.

Article 3

In their actions to achieve the objective of the Convention and to implement its provisions, the Parties shall be guided, *inter alia,* by the following:

1. The Parties should protect the climate system for the benefit of present and future generations of humankind, on the basis of equity and in accordance with their common but differentiated responsibilities and respective capabilities. Accordingly, the developed country Parties should take the lead in combating climate change and the adverse effects thereof.

2. The specific needs and special circumstances of developing country Parties, especially those that are particularly vulnerable to the adverse effects of climate change, and of those Parties, especially developing country Parties, that would have to bear a disproportionate or abnormal burden under the Convention, should be given full consideration.

3. The Parties should take precautionary measures to anticipate, prevent or minimize the causes of climate change and mitigate its adverse effects. Where there are threats of serious or irreversible damage, lack of full scientific certainty should not be used as a reason for postponing such measures, taking into account that policies and measures to deal with climate change should be cost-effective so as to ensure global benefits at the lowest possible cost. To achieve this, such policies and measures should take into account different socio-economic contexts, be comprehensive, cover all relevant sources, sinks and reservoirs of greenhouse gases and adaptation, and comprise all economic sectors. Efforts to address climate change may be carried out co-operatively by interested Parties.

4. The Parties have a right to, and should, promote sustainable development. Policies and measures to protect the climate system against human-induced change should be appropriate for the specific conditions of each Party and should be integrated with national development programmes, taking into account that economic development is essential for adopting measures to address climate change.

5. The Parties should co-operate to promote a supportive and open international economic system that would lead to sustainable economic growth and development in all Parties, particularly developing country Parties, thus enabling them better to address the problems of climate change. Measures taken to combat climate change, including unilateral ones, should not constitute a means of arbitrary or unjustifiable discrimination or a disguised restriction on international trade.

Article 4

1. All Parties, taking into account their common but differentiated responsibilities and their specific national and regional development priorities, objectives and circumstances, shall:

(a) Develop, periodically update, publish and make available to the Conference of the Parties, in accordance with Article 12, national inventories of anthropogenic emissions by sources and removals by sinks of all greenhouse gases not controlled by the Montreal Protocol, using comparable methodologies to be agreed upon by the Conference of the Parties;

(b) Formulate, implement, publish and regularly update national and, where appropriate, regional programmes containing measures to mitigate climate change by addressing anthropogenic emissions by sources and removals by sinks of all greenhouse gases not controlled by the Montreal Protocol, and measures to facilitate adequate adaptation to climate change;

(c) Promote and co-operate in the development, application and diffusion, including transfer, of technologies, practices and processes that control, reduce or prevent anthropogenic emissions of greenhouse gases not controlled by the Montreal Protocol in all relevant sectors, including the energy, transport, industry, agriculture, forestry and waste management sectors;

(d) Promote sustainable management, and promote and co-operate in the conservation and enhancement, as appropriate, of sinks and reservoirs of all greenhouses gases not controlled by the Montreal Protocol, including biomass, forests and oceans as well as other terrestrial, coastal and marine ecosystems;

(e) Co-operate in preparing for adaptation to the impacts of climate change; develop and elaborate appropriate and integrated plans for coastal zone management, water resources and agriculture, and for the protection and rehabilitation of areas, particularly in Africa, affected by drought and desertification, as well as floods;

(f) Take climate change considerations into account, to the extent feasible, in their relevant social, economic and environmental policies and actions, and employ appropriate methods, for example impact assessments, formulated and determined nationally, with a view to minimizing adverse effects on the economy, on public health and on the quality of the environment, of projects or measures undertaken by them to mitigate or adapt to climate change;

(g) Promote and co-operate in scientific, technological, technical, socio-economic and other research, systematic observation and development of data archives related to the climate system and intended to further the understanding and to reduce or eliminate the remaining uncertainties regarding the causes, effects, magnitude and timing of climate change and the economic and social consequences of various response strategies;

(h) Promote and co-operate in the full, open and prompt exchange of relevant scientific, technological, technical, socio-economic and legal information related to the climate system and climate change, and to the economic and social consequences of various response strategies;

(i) Promote and co-operate in education, training and public awareness related to climate change and encourage the widest participation in this process, including that of non-governmental organizations; and

(j) Communicate to the Conference of the Parties information related to implementation, in accordance with Article 12.

2. The developed country Parties and other Parties included in Annex I commit themselves specifically as provided for in the following:

(a) Each of these Parties shall adopt national policies and take corresponding measures on the mitigation of climate change, by limiting its anthropogenic emissions of greenhouse gases and protecting and enhancing its greenhouse gas sinks and reservoirs. These policies and measures will demonstrate that developed countries are taking the lead in modifying longer-term trends in anthropogenic emissions consistent with the objective of the Convention, recognizing that the return by the end of the present decade to earlier levels of anthropogenic emissions of carbon dioxide and other greenhouse gases not controlled by the Montreal Protocol would contribute to such modification, and taking into account the differences in these Parties' starting points and approaches, economic structures and resource bases, the need to maintain strong and sustainable economic growth, available technologies and other individual circumstances, as well as the need for equitable and appropriate contributions by each of these Parties to the global effort regarding that objective. These Parties may implement such policies and measures jointly with other Parties and may assist other Parties in contributing to the achievement of the objective of the Convention and, in particular, that of this sub-paragraph;

(b) In order to promote progress to this end, each of these Parties shall communicate, within six months of the entry into force of the Convention and periodically thereafter, and in accordance with Article 12, detailed information on its policies and measures referred to in sub-paragraph (a) above, as well as on its resulting projected anthropogenic emissions by sources and removals by sinks of greenhouse gases not controlled by the Montreal Protocol for the period referred to in sub-paragraph (a), with the aim of returning individually or jointly to their 1990 levels these anthropogenic emissions of carbon dioxide and other greenhouse gases not controlled by the Montreal Protocol. This information will be reviewed by the Conference of the Parties, at its first session and periodically thereafter, in accordance with Article 7;

(c) Calculations of emissions by sources and removals by sinks of greenhouse gases for the purposes of sub-paragraph (b) above should take into account the best available scientific knowledge, including of the effective capacity of sinks and the respective contributions of such gases to climate change. The Conference of the Parties shall consider and agree on methodologies for these calculations at its first session and review them regularly thereafter;

(d) The Conference of the Parties shall, at its first session, review the adequacy of sub-paragraphs (a) and (b) above. Such review shall be carried out in the light of the best available scientific information and assessment on climate change and its impacts, as well as relevant technical, social and economic information. Based on this review, the Conference of the Parties shall take appropriate action, which may include the adoption of amendments to the commitments in sub-paragraphs (a) and (b) above. The Conference of the Parties, at its first session, shall also take decisions regarding criteria for joint implementation as indicated in sub-paragraph (a) above. A second review of sub-paragraphs (a) and (b) shall take place not later than 31 December 1998, and thereafter at regular intervals determined by the Conference of the Parties, until the objective of the Convention is met;

(e) Each of these Parties shall;

(i) Co-ordinate as appropriate with other such Parties, relevant economic and administrative instruments developed to achieve the objective of the Convention; and

(ii) Identify and periodically review its own policies and practices which encourage activities that lead to greater levels of anthropogenic emissions of greenhouse gases not controlled by the Montreal Protocol than would otherwise occur.

(f) The Conference of the Parties shall review, not later than 31 December 1998, available information with a view to taking decisions regarding such amendments to the lists in Annexes I and II as may be appropriate, with the approval of the Party concerned;

(g) Any Party not included in Annex I may, in its instrument of ratification, acceptance, approval or accession, or at any time thereafter, notify the Depositary that it intends to be bound by sub-paragraphs (a) and (b) above. The Depositary shall inform the other signatories and Parties of any such notification.

3. The developed country Parties and other developed Parties included in Annex II shall provide new and additional financial resources to meet the agreed full costs incurred by developing country Parties in complying with their obligations under Article 12, paragraph 1. They shall also provide such financial resources, including for the transfer of technology, needed by the developing country Parties to meet the agreed full incremental costs of implementing measures that are covered by paragraph 1 of this Article and that are agreed between a developing country Party and the international entity or entities referred to in Article 11, in accordance with that Article. The implementation of these commitments shall take into account the need for adequacy and predictability in the flow of funds and the importance of appropriate burden-sharing among the developed country Parties.

4. The developed country Parties and other developed Parties included in Annex II shall also assist the developing country Parties that are particularly vulnerable to the adverse effects of climate change in meeting costs of adaptation to those adverse effects.

5. The developed country Parties and other developed Parties included in Annex II shall take all practicable steps to promote, facilitate and finance, as appropriate, the transfer of, or access to, environmentally sound technologies and know-how to other Parties, particularly developing country Parties, to enable them to implement the provisions of the Convention. In this process, the developed country Parties shall support the development and enhancement of endogenous capacities and technologies of developing country Parties. Other Parties and organizations in a position to do so may also assist in facilitating the transfer of such technologies.

6. In the implementation of their commitments under paragraph 2 above, a certain degree of flexibility shall be allowed by the Conference of the Parties to the Parties included in Annex I undergoing the process of transition to a market economy, in order to enhance the ability of these Parties to address climate change, including with regard to the historical level of anthropogenic emissions of greenhouse gases not controlled by the Montreal Protocol chosen as a reference.

7. The extent to which developing country Parties will effectively implement their commitments under the Convention will depend on the effective implementation by developed country Parties of their commitments under the Convention related to financial resources and transfer of technology and will take fully into account that economic and social development and poverty eradication are the first and overriding priorities of the developing country Parties.

8. In the implementation of the commitments in this Article, the Parties shall give full consideration to what actions are necessary under the Convention, including actions related to funding, insurance and the transfer of technology, to meet the specific needs and concerns of developing country Parties arising from the adverse effects of climate change and/or the impact of the implementation of response measures, especially on:

(a) Small island countries;

(b) Countries with low-lying coastal areas;

(c) Countries with arid and semi-arid areas, forested areas and areas liable to forest decay;

(d) Countries with areas prone to natural disasters;

(e) Countries with areas liable to drought and desertification;

(f) Countries with areas of high urban atmospheric pollution;

(g) Countries with areas with fragile ecosystems, including mountainous ecosystems;

(h) Countries whose economies are highly dependent on income generated from the production, processing and export, and/or on consumption of fossil fuels and associated energy-intensive products; and

(i) Land-locked and transit countries.

Further, the Conference of the Parties may take actions, as appropriate, with respect to this paragraph.

9. The Parties shall take full account of the specific needs and special situations of the least developed countries in their actions with regard to funding and transfer of technology.

10. The Parties shall, in accordance with Article 10, take into consideration in the implementation of the commitments of the Convention the situation of Parties, particularly developing country Parties, with economies that are vulnerable to the adverse effects of the implementation of measures to respond to climate change. This applies notably to Parties with economies that are highly dependent on income generated from the production, processing and export, and/or consumption of fossil fuels and associated energy-intensive products and/or the use of fossil fuels for which such Parties have serious difficulties in switching to alternatives.

Article 5

In carrying out their commitments under Article 4, paragraph 1 (g), the Parties shall:

(a) Support and further develop, as appropriate, international and intergovernmental programmes and networks or organizations aimed at defining, conducting, assessing and financing research, data collection and systematic observation, taking into account the need to minimize duplication of effort;

(b) Support international and intergovernmental efforts to strengthen systematic observation and national scientific and technical research capacities and capabilities, particularly in developing countries, and to promote access to, and the exchange of, data and analyses thereof obtained from areas beyond national jurisdiction; and

(c) Take into account the particular concerns and needs of developing countries and co-operate in improving their endogenous capacities and capabilities to participate in the efforts referred to in sub-paragraphs (a) and (b) above.

Article 6

In carrying out their commitments under Article 4, paragraph 1 (i), the Parties shall:

(a) Promote and facilitate at the national and, as appropriate, sub-regional and regional levels, and in accordance with national laws and regulations, and within their respective capacities:

(i) The development and implementation of educational and public awareness programmes on climate change and its effects;

(ii) Public access to information on climate change and its effects;

(iii) Public participation in addressing climate change and its effects and developing adequate responses; and

(iv) Training of scientific, technical and managerial personnel.

(b) Co-operate in and promote, at the international level, and, where appropriate, using existing bodies:

(i) The development and exchange of educational and public awareness material on climate change and its effects; and

(ii) The development and implementation of education and training programmes, including the strengthening of national institutions and the exchange or secondment of personnel to train experts in this field, in particular for developing countries.

Article 7

1. A Conference of the Parties is hereby established.

2. The Conference of the Parties, as the supreme body of this Convention, shall keep under regular review the implementation of the Convention and any related legal instruments that the Conference of the Parties may adopt, and shall make, within its mandate, the decisions necessary to promote the effective implementation of the Convention. To this end, it shall:

(a) Periodically examine the obligations of the Parties and the institutional arrangements under the Convention, in the light of the objective of the Convention, the experience gained in its implementation and the evolution of scientific and technological knowledge;

(b) Promote and facilitate the exchange of information on measures adopted by the Parties to address climate change and its effects, taking into account the differing circumstances, responsibilities and capabilities of the Parties and their respective commitments under the Convention;

(c) Facilitate, at the request of two or more Parties, the co-ordination of measures adopted by them to address climate change and its effects, taking into account the differing circumstances, responsibilities and capabilities of the Parties and their respective commitments under the Convention;

(d) Promote and guide, in accordance with the objective and provisions of the Convention, the development and periodic refinement of comparable methodologies, to be agreed on by the Conference of the Parties, *inter alia,* for preparing inventories of greenhouse gas emissions by sources and removals by sinks, and for evaluating the effectiveness of measures to limit the emissions and enhance the removals of these gases;

(e) Assess, on the basis of all information made available to it in accordance with the provisions of the Convention, the implementation of the Convention by the Parties, the overall effects of the measures taken pursuant to the Convention, in particular environmental, economic and social effects as well as their cumulative impacts and the extent to which progress towards the objective of the Convention is being achieved;

(f) Consider and adopt regular reports on the implementation of the Convention and ensure their publication;

(g) Make recommendations on any matters necessary for the implementation of the Convention;

(h) Seek to mobilize financial resources. . .

(i) Establish such subsidiary bodies as are deemed necessary for the implementation of the Convention;

(j) Review reports submitted by its subsidiary bodies and provide guidance to them;

(k) Agree upon and adopt, by consensus, rules of procedure and financial rules for itself and for any subsidiary bodies;

(l) Seek and utilize, where appropriate, the services and co-operation of, and information provided by, competent international organizations and intergovernmental and non-governmental bodies; and

(m) Exercise such other functions as are required for the achievement of the objective of the Convention as well as all other functions assigned to it under the Convention.

3. The Conference of the Parties shall, at its first session, adopt its own rules of procedure as well as those of the subsidiary bodies established by the Convention, which shall include decision-making procedures for matters not already covered by decision-making procedures stipulated in the Convention. Such procedures may include specified majorities required for the adoption of particular decisions.

4. The first session of the Conference of the Parties shall be convened by the interim secretariat referred to in Article 21 and shall take place not later than one year after the date of entry into force of the Convention. Thereafter, ordinary sessions of the Conference of the Parties shall be held every year unless otherwise decided by the Conference of the Parties.

5. Extraordinary sessions of the Conference of the Parties shall be held at such other times as may be deemed necessary by the Conference, or at the written request of any Party, provided that, within six months of the request being communicated to the Parties by the secretariat, it is supported by at least one-third of the Parties.

6. The United Nations, its specialized agencies and the International Atomic Energy Agency, as well as any State member thereof or observers thereto not Party to the Convention, may be represented at sessions of the Conference of the Parties as observers. Any body or agency, whether national or international, governmental or non-governmental, which is qualified in matters covered by the Convention, and which has informed the secretariat of its wish to be represented at a session of the Conference of the Parties as an observer, may be so admitted unless at least one-third of the Parties present object. The admission and participation of observers shall be subject to the rules of procedures adopted by the Conference of the Parties.

Article 8

1. A secretariat is hereby established.

2. The functions of the secretariat shall be:

(a) To make arrangements for sessions of the Conference of the Parties and its subsidiary bodies established under the Convention and to provide them with services as required;

(b) To compile and transmit reports submitted to it;

(c) To facilitate assistance to the Parties, particularly developing country Parties, on request, in the compilation and communication of information required in accordance with the provisions of the Convention;

(d) To prepare reports on its activities and present them to the Conference of the Parties;

(e) To ensure the necessary co-ordination with the secretariats of other relevant international bodies;

(f) To enter, under the overall guidance of the Conference of the Parties, into such administrative and contractual arrangements as may be required for the effective discharge of its functions; and

(g) To perform the other secretariat functions specified in the Convention and in any of its protocols and such other functions as may be determined by the Conference of the Parties.

3. The Conference of the Parties, at its first session, shall designate a permanent secretariat and make arrangements for its functioning.

Article 9

1. A subsidiary body for scientific and technological advice is hereby established to provide the Conference of the Parties and, as appropriate, its other subsidiary bodies with timely information and advice on scientific and technological matters relating to the Convention. This body shall be open to participation by all Parties and shall be multidisciplinary. It shall comprise government representatives competent in the relevant field of expertise. It shall report regularly to the Conference of the Parties on all aspects of its work.

2. Under the guidance of the Conference of the Parties, and drawing upon existing competent international bodies, this body shall:

(a) Provide assessments of the state of scientific knowledge relating to climate change and its effects;

(b) Prepare scientific assessments on the effects of measures taken in the implementation of the Convention;

(c) Identify innovative, efficient and state-of-the-art technologies and know-how and advise on the ways and means of promoting development and/or transferring such technologies;

(d) Provide advice on scientific programmes, international co-operation in research and development related to climate change, as well as on ways and means of supporting endogenous capacity-building in developing countries; and

(e) Respond to scientific, technological and methodological questions that the Conference of the Parties and its subsidiary bodies may put to the body.

3. The functions and terms of reference of this body may be further elaborated by the Conference of the Parties.

Article 10

1. A subsidiary body for implementation is hereby established to assist the Conference of the Parties in the assessment and review of the effective implementation of the Convention. This body shall be open to participation by all Parties and comprise government representatives who are experts on matters related to climate change. It shall report regularly to the Conference of the Parties on all aspects of its work.

2. Under the guidance of the Conference of the Parties, this body shall:

(a) Consider the information communicated in accordance with Article 12, paragraph 1, to assess the overall aggregated effect of the steps taken by the Parties in the light of the latest scientific assessments concerning climate change;

(b) Consider the information communicated in accordance with Article 12, paragraph 2, in order to assist the Conference of the Parties in carrying out the reviews required by Article 4, paragraph 2 (d); and

(c) Assist the Conference of the Parties, as appropriate, in the preparation and implementation of its decisions.

Article 11

1. A mechanism for the provision of financial resources on a grant or concessional basis, including for the transfer of technology, is hereby defined. It shall function under the guidance of and be accountable to the Conference of the Parties, which shall decide on its policies, programme priorities and eligibility criteria related to this Convention. Its operation shall be entrusted to one or more existing international entities.

2. The financial mechanism shall have an equitable and balanced representation of all Parties within a transparent system of governance.

3. The Conference of the Parties and the entity or entities entrusted with the operation of the financial mechanism shall agree upon arrangements to give effect to the above paragraphs, which shall include the following:

(a) Modalities to ensure that the funded projects to address climate change are in conformity with the policies, programme priorities and eligibility criteria established by the Conference of the Parties;

(b) Modalities by which a particular funding decision may be reconsidered in light of these policies, programme priorities and eligibility criteria;

(c) Provision by the entity or entities of regular reports to the Conference of the Parties on its funding operations, which is consistent with the requirement for accountability set out in paragraph 1 above; and

(d) Determination in a predictable and identifiable manner of the amount of funding necessary and available for the implementation of this Convention and the conditions under which that amount shall be periodically reviewed.

4. The Conference of the Parties shall make arrangements to implement the above-mentioned provisions at its first session, reviewing and taking into account the interim arrangements referred to in Article 21, paragraph 3, and shall decide whether these interim arrangements shall be maintained. Within four years thereafter, the Conference of the Parties shall review the financial mechanism and take appropriate measures.

5. The developed country Parties may also provide, and developing country Parties avail themselves of financial resources related to the implementation of the Convention through bilateral, regional and other multilateral channels.

Article 12

1. In accordance with Article 4, paragraph 1, each Party shall communicate to the Conference of the Parties, through the secretariat, the following elements of information:

(a) A national inventory of anthropogenic emissions by sources and removals by sinks of all greenhouse gases not controlled by the Montreal Protocol, to the extent its capacities permit, using comparable methodologies to be promoted and agreed upon by the Conference of the Parties;

(b) A general description of steps taken or envisaged by the Party to implement the Convention; and

(c) Any other information that the Party considers relevant to the achievement of the objective of the Convention and suitable for inclusion in its communication, including, if feasible, material relevant for calculations of global emission trends.

2. Each developed country Party and each other Party included in Annex I shall incorporate in its communication the following elements of information:

(a) A detailed description of the policies and measures that it has adopted to implement its commitment under Article 4, paragraphs 2(a) and 2(b); and

(b) A specific estimate of the effects that [those] policies and measures will have on anthropogenic emissions by its sources and removals by its sinks of greenhouse gases during the period referred to in Article 4, paragraph 2(a).

3. In addition, each developed country Party and each other developed Party included in Annex II shall incorporate details of measures taken in accordance with Article 4, paragraphs 3, 4 and 5.

4. Developing country Parties may, on a voluntary basis, propose projects for financing, including specific technologies, materials, equipment, techniques or practices that would be needed to implement such projects, along with, if possible, an estimate of all incremental costs, of the reductions of emissions and increments of removals of greenhouse gases, as well as an estimate of the consequent benefits.

5. Each developed country Party and each other Party included in Annex I shall make its initial communication within six months of the entry into force of the Convention for that Party. Each Party not so listed shall make its initial communication within three years of the entry into force of the Convention for that Party, or of the availability of financial resources in accordance with Article 4, paragraph 3. Parties that are least developed countries may make their initial communication at their discretion. The frequency of subsequent communications by all Parties shall be determined by the Conference of the Parties, taking into account the differentiated timetable set by this paragraph.

6. Information communicated by Parties under this Article shall be transmitted by the secretariat as soon as possible to the Conference of the Parties and to any subsidiary bodies concerned. If necessary, the procedures for the communication of information may be further considered by the Conference of the Parties.

7. From its first session, the Conference of the Parties shall arrange for the provision to developing country Parties of technical and financial support, on request, in compiling and communicating information under this Article, as well as in identifying the technical and financial needs associated with proposed projects and response measures under Article 4. Such support may be provided by other parties, by competent international organizations and by the secretariat, as appropriate.

8. Any group of Parties may, subject to guidelines adopted by the Conference of the Parties, and to prior notification to the Conference of the Parties, make a joint communication in

fulfilment of their obligations under this Article, provided that such a communication includes information on the fulfilment by each of these Parties of its individual obligations under the Convention.

9. Information received by the secretariat that is designated by a Party as confidential, in accordance with criteria to be established by the Conference of the Parties, shall be aggregated by the secretariat to protect its confidentiality before being made available to any of the bodies involved in the communication and review of information.

10. Subject to paragraph 9 above, and without prejudice to the ability of any Party to make public its communication at any time, the secretariat shall make communications by Parties under this Article publicly available at the time they are submitted to the Conference of the Parties.

Article 13

The Conference of the Parties shall, at its first session, consider the establishment of a multilateral consultative process, available to Parties on their request, for the resolution of questions regarding the implementation of the Convention.

Article 14

1. In the event of a dispute between any two or more Parties concerning the interpretation or application of the Convention, the Parties concerned shall seek a settlement of the dispute through negotiation or any other peaceful means of their own choice.

2. When ratifying, accepting, approving or acceding to the Convention, or at any time thereafter, a Party which is not a regional economic integration organization may declare in a written instrument submitted to the Depositary that, in respect of any dispute concerning the interpretation or application of the Convention, it recognizes as compulsory *ipso facto* and without special agreement, in relation to any Party accepting the same obligation:

(a) Submission of the dispute to the International Court of Justice, and/or

(b) Arbitration in accordance with procedures to be adopted by the Conference of the Parties as soon as practicable, in an annex on arbitration.

A Party which is a regional economic integration organization may make a declaration with like effect in relation to arbitration in accordance with the procedures referred to in sub-paragraph (b) above.

3. A declaration made under paragraph 2 above shall remain in force until it expires in accordance with its terms or until three months after written notice of its revocation has been deposited with the Depositary.

4. A new declaration, a notice of revocation or the expiry of a declaration shall not in any way affect proceedings pending before the International Court of Justice or the arbitral tribunal, unless the parties to the dispute otherwise agree.

5. Subject to the operation of paragraph 2 above, if after 12 months following notification by one Party to another that a dispute exists between them, the Parties concerned have not been able to settle their dispute through the means mentioned in paragraph 1 above, the dispute shall be submitted, at the request of any of the parties to the dispute, to conciliation.

6. A conciliation commission shall be created upon the request of one of the parties to the dispute. The commission shall be composed of an equal number of members appointed by each party concerned and a chairman chosen jointly by the members appointed by each party. The commission shall render a recommendatory award, which the parties shall consider in good faith ...

7. Additional procedures relating to conciliation shall be adopted by the Conference of the Parties, as soon as practicable, in an annex on conciliation.

Article 15

1. Any Party may propose amendments to the Convention.

2. Amendments to the Convention shall be adopted at an ordinary session of the Conference of the Parties. The text of any proposed amendment to the Convention shall be communicated to the Parties by the secretariat at least six months before the meeting at which it is proposed for adoption. The secretariat shall also communicate proposed amendments to the signatories to the Convention and, for information, to the Depositary [the Secretary-General of the UN].

3. The Parties shall make every effort to reach agreement on any proposed amendment to the Convention by consensus. If all efforts at consensus have been exhausted, and no agreement reached, the amendment shall as a last resort be adopted by a three-fourths majority vote of the Parties present and voting at the meeting. The adopted amendment shall be communicated by the secretariat to the Depositary, who shall circulate it to all Parties for their acceptance.

4. Instruments of acceptance in respect of an amendment shall be deposited with the Depositary. An amendment adopted in accordance with paragraph 3 above shall enter into force for those Parties having accepted it on the ninetieth day after the date of receipt by the Depositary of an instrument of acceptance by at least three-fourths of the Parties to the Convention.

5. The amendment shall enter into force for any other Party on the ninetieth day after the date on which that Party deposits with the Depositary its instrument of acceptance of the said amendment ...

Article 16

1. Annexes to the Convention shall form an integral part thereof and, unless otherwise expressly provided, a reference to the Convention constitutes at the same time a reference to any annexes thereto. Without prejudice to the provisions of Article 14, paragraphs 2(b) and 7, such annexes shall be restricted to lists, forms and any other material of a descriptive nature that is of a scientific, technical, procedural or administrative character.

2. Annexes to the Convention shall be proposed and adopted in accordance with the procedure set forth in Article 15, paragraphs 2, 3 and 4.

3. An annex that has been adopted in accordance with paragraph 2 above shall enter into force for all Parties to the Convention six months after the date of the communication by the Depositary to such Parties of the adoption of the annex, except for those Parties that have notified the Depositary, in writing, within that period of their non-acceptance of the annex. The annex shall enter into force for Parties which withdraw their notification of non-acceptance on the ninetieth day after the date on which withdrawal of such notification has been received by the Depositary.

4. The proposal, adoption and entry into force of amendments to annexes to the Convention shall be subject to the same procedure as that for the proposal, adoption and entry into force of annexes to the Convention in accordance with paragraphs 2 and 3 above.

5. If the adoption of an annex or an amendment to an annex involves an amendment to the Convention, that annex or amendment to an annex shall not enter into force until such time as the amendment to the Convention enters into force.

Article 17

1. The Conference of the Parties may, at any ordinary session, adopt protocols to the Convention.

2. The text of any proposed protocol shall be communicated to the Parties by the secretariat at least six months before such a session.

3. The requirements for the entry into force of any protocol shall be established by that instrument.

4. Only Parties to the Convention may be Parties to a protocol.

5. Decisions under any protocol shall be taken only by the Parties to the protocol concerned.

Articles 18–26

Voting, ratification, withdrawal and other general provisions.

ANNEX I

Australia	Japan
Austria	Latvia*
Belarus*	Lithuania*
Belgium	Luxembourg
Bulgaria*	Netherlands
Canada	New Zealand
Czechoslovakia†	Norway
Denmark	Poland*
European Economic Community	Portugal
	Romania*
Estonia*	Russian Federation*
Finland	Spain
France	Sweden
Germany	Switzerland
Greece	Turkey
Hungary*	Ukraine*
Iceland	United Kingdom
Ireland	United States of America
Italy	

* Countries that are undergoing the process of transition to a market economy.

† Czechoslovakia was succeeded by the Czech Republic and Slovakia from 31 December 1992.

ANNEX II

Australia	Italy
Austria	Japan
Belgium	Luxembourg
Canada	Netherlands
Denmark	New Zealand
European Economic Community	Norway
	Portugal
Finland	Spain
France	Sweden
Germany	Switzerland
Greece	Turkey
Iceland	United Kingdom
Ireland	United States of America

Kyoto Protocol to the United Nations Framework Convention on Climate Change

(11 December 1997)

The Parties to this Protocol,

Being Parties to the United Nations Framework Convention on Climate Change, hereinafter referred to as "the Convention",

In pursuit of the ultimate objective of the Convention as stated in its Article 2,

Recalling the provisions of the Convention,

Being guided by Article 3 of the Convention,

Pursuant to the Berlin Mandate adopted by decision 1/CP.1 of the Conference of the Parties to the Convention at its first session,

Have agreed as follows.

Article 1

Definitions

Article 2

1. Each Party included in Annex I, in achieving its quantified emission limitation and reduction commitments under Article 3, in order to promote sustainable development, shall:

(a) Implement and/or further elaborate policies and measures in accordance with its national circumstances, such as:

(i) Enhancement of energy efficiency in relevant sectors of the national economy;

(ii) Protection and enhancement of sinks and reservoirs of greenhouse gases not controlled by the Montreal Protocol, taking into account its commitments under relevant international environmental agreements; promotion of sustainable forest management practices, afforestation and reforestation;

(iii) Promotion of sustainable forms of agriculture in light of climate change considerations;

(iv) Research on, and promotion, development and increased use of, new and renewable forms of energy, of carbon dioxide sequestration technologies and of advanced and innovative environmentally sound technologies;

(v) Progressive reduction or phasing out of market imperfections, fiscal incentives, tax and duty exemptions and subsidies in all greenhouse gas emitting sectors that run counter to the objective of the Convention and application of market instruments;

(vi) Encouragement of appropriate reforms in relevant sectors aimed at promoting policies and measures which limit or reduce emissions of greenhouse gases not controlled by the Montreal Protocol;

(vii) Measures to limit and/or reduce emissions of greenhouse gases not controlled by the Montreal Protocol in the transport sector;

(viii) Limitation and/or reduction of methane emissions through recovery and use in waste management, as well as in the production, transport and distribution of energy;

(b) Co-operate with other such Parties to enhance the individual and combined effectiveness of their policies and measures adopted under this Article, pursuant to Article 4, paragraph 2(e)(i), of the Convention. To this end, these Parties shall take steps to share their experience and exchange information on such policies and measures, including developing ways of improving their comparability, transparency and effectiveness. The Conference of the Parties serving as the meeting of the Parties to this Protocol shall, at its first session or as soon as practicable thereafter, consider ways to facilitate such co-operation, taking into account all relevant information.

2. The Parties included in Annex I shall pursue limitation or reduction of emissions of greenhouse gases not controlled by the Montreal Protocol from aviation and marine bunker fuels, working through the International Civil Aviation Organization and the International Maritime Organization, respectively.

3. The Parties included in Annex I shall strive to implement policies and measures under this Article in such a way as to minimize adverse effects, including the adverse effects of climate change, effects on international trade, and social, environmental and economic impacts on other Parties, especially developing country Parties and in particular those identified in Article 4, paragraphs 8 and 9, of the Convention, taking into account Article 3 of the Convention. The Conference of the Parties serving as the meeting of the Parties to this Protocol may take further actions, as appropriate, to promote the implementation of the provisions of this paragraph.

4. The Conference of the Parties ..., if it decides that it would be beneficial to co-ordinate any of the policies and measures in paragraph 1(a) above, taking into account different national circumstances and potential effects, shall consider ways and means to elaborate the co-ordination of such policies and measures.

Article 3

1. The Parties included in Annex I shall, individually or jointly, ensure that their aggregate anthropogenic carbon dioxide equivalent emissions of the greenhouse gases listed in Annex A do not exceed their assigned amounts, calculated pursuant to their qualified emission limitation and reduction commitments inscribed in Annex B and in accordance with the provisions of this Article, with a view to reducing their overall emissions of such gases by at least 5 per cent below 1990 levels in the commitment period 2008 to 2012.

2. Each Party included in Annex I shall, by 2005, have made demonstrable progress in achieving its commitments under this Protocol.

3. The net changes in greenhouse gas emissions by sources and removals by sinks resulting from direct human-induced land-use change and forestry activities, limited to afforestation, reforestation and deforestation since 1990, measured as verifiable changes

in carbon stocks in each commitment period, shall be used to meet the commitments under this Article of each Party included in Annex I. The greenhouse gas emissions by sources and removals by sinks associated with those activities shall be reported in a transparent and verifiable manner and reviewed in accordance with Articles 7 and 8.

4. Prior to the first session of the Conference of the Parties serving as the meeting of the Parties to this Protocol, each Party included in Annex I shall provide, for consideration by the Subsidiary Body for Scientific and Technological Advice, data to establish its level of carbon stocks in 1990 and to enable an estimate to be made of its changes in carbon stocks in subsequent years. The Conference of the Parties ... shall, at its first session or as soon as practicable thereafter, decide upon modalities, rules and guidelines as to how, and which, additional human-induced activities related to changes in greenhouse gas emissions by sources and removals by sinks in the agricultural soils and the land-use change and forestry categories shall be added to, or subtracted from, the assigned amounts for Parties included in Annex I, taking into account uncertainties, transparency in reporting, verifiability, the methodological work of the Intergovernmental Panel on Climate Change (IPCC), the advice provided by the Subsidiary Body for Scientific and Technological Advice in accordance with Article 5 and the decisions of the Conference of the Parties. Such a decision shall apply in the second and subsequent commitment periods. A Party may choose to apply such a decision on these additional human-induced activities for its first commitment period, provided that these activities have taken place since 1990.

5. The Parties included in Annex I undergoing the process of transition to a market economy whose base year or period was established pursuant to decision 9/CP.2 of the Conference of the Parties at its second session shall use that base year or period for the implementation of their commitments under this Article. Any other Party included in Annex I undergoing the process of transition to a market economy which has not yet submitted its first national communication under Article 12 of the Convention may also notify the Conference of the Parties ... that it intends to use an historical base year or period other than 1990 for the implementation of its commitments under this Article. The Conference of the Parties ... shall decide on the acceptance of such notification.

6. Taking into account Article 4, paragraph 6, of the Convention, in the implementation of their commitments under this Protocol other than those under this Article, a certain degree of flexibility shall be allowed by the Conference of the Parties ... to the Parties included in Annex I undergoing the process of transition to a market economy.

7. In the first quantified emission limitation and reduction commitment period, from 2008 to 2012, the assigned amount for each Party included in Annex I shall be equal to the percentage inscribed for it in Annex B of its aggregate anthropogenic carbon dioxide equivalent emissions of the greenhouse gases listed in Annex A in 1990, or the base year or period determined in accordance with paragraph 5 above, multiplied by five. Those Parties included in Annex I for whom land-use change and forestry constituted a net source of greenhouse gas emissions in 1990 shall include in their 1990 emissions base year or period the aggregate anthropogenic carbon dioxide equivalent emissions by sources minus removals by sinks in 1990 from land-use change for the purposes of calculating their assigned amount.

8. Any Party included in Annex I may use 1995 as its base year for hydrofluorocarbons, perfluorocarbons and sulphur hexafluoride, for the purposes of the calculation referred to in paragraph 7 above.

9. Commitments for subsequent periods for Parties included in Annex I shall be established in amendments to Annex B to this Protocol, which shall be adopted in accordance with the provisions of Article 21, paragraph 7. The Conference of the Parties serving as the meeting of the Parties to this Protocol shall initiate the consideration of such commitments at least seven years before the end of the first commitment period referred to in paragraph 1 above.

10. Any emission reduction units, or any part of an assigned amount, which a Party acquires from another Party in accordance with the provisions of Article 6 or Article 17 shall be added to the assigned amount for the acquiring Party.

11. Any emission reduction units, or any part of an assigned amount, which a Party transfers to another Party in accordance with the provisions of Article 6 or of Article 17 shall be subtracted from the assigned amount for the transferring Party.

12. Any certified emission reductions which a Party acquires from another Party in accordance with the provisions of Article 12 shall be added to the assigned amount for the acquiring Party.

13. If the emissions of a Party included in Annex I in a commitment period are less than its assigned amount under this Article, this difference shall, on request of that Party, be added to the assigned amount for that Party for subsequent commitment periods.

14. Each Party included in Annex I shall strive to implement the commitments mentioned in paragraph 1 above in such a way as to minimize adverse social, environmental and economic impacts on developing country Parties, particularly those identified in Article 4, paragraphs 8 and 9, for the Convention. In line with relevant decisions ... on the implementation of those paragraphs, the Conference of the Parties ... shall, at its first session, consider what actions are necessary to minimize the adverse effects of climate change and/or the impacts of response measures on Parties referred to in those paragraphs. Among the issues to be considered shall be the establishment of funding, insurance and transfer of technology.

Article 4

1. Any Parties included in Annex I that have reached an agreement to fulfil their commitments under Article 3 jointly, shall be deemed to have met those commitments provided that their total combined aggregate anthropogenic carbon dioxide equivalent emissions of the greenhouse gases listed in Annex A do not exceed their assigned amounts calculated pursuant to their quantified emission limitation and reduction commitments inscribed in Annex B and in accordance with the provisions of Article 3. The respective emission level allocated to each of the Parties to the agreement shall be set out in that agreement.

2. The Parties to any such agreement shall notify the secretariat of the terms of the agreement on the date of deposit of their instruments of ratification, acceptance or approval of this Protocol, or accession thereto. The secretariat shall in turn inform the Parties and signatories to the Convention of the terms of the agreement.

3. Any such agreement shall remain in operation for the duration of the commitment period specified in Article 3, paragraph 7.

4. If Parties acting jointly do so in the framework of, and together with, a regional economic integration organization, any alteration in the composition of the organization after adoption of this Protocol shall not affect existing commitments under this Protocol. Any alteration in the composition of the organization shall only apply for the purposes of those commitments under Article 3 that are adopted subsequent to that alteration.

5. In the event of failure by the Parties to such an agreement to achieve their total combined level of emission reductions, each Party to that agreement shall be responsible for its own level of emissions set out in the agreement.

6. If Parties acting jointly do so in the framework of, and together with, a regional economic integration organization which is itself a Party to this Protocol, each member State of that regional economic integration organization individually, and together with the regional economic integration organization acting in accordance with Article 24, shall, in the event of failure to achieve the total combined level of emission reductions, be responsible for its level of emissions as notified in accordance with this Article.

Article 5

1. Each Party included in Annex I shall have in place, no later than one year prior to the start of the first commitment period, a national system for the estimation of anthropogenic emissions by sources and removals by sinks of all greenhouse gases not controlled by the Montreal Protocol. Guidelines for such national systems, which shall incorporate the methodologies specified in paragraph 2 below, shall be decided upon by the Conference of the Parties ...

2. Methodologies for estimating anthropogenic emissions by sources and removals by sinks of all greenhouse gases not controlled by the Montreal Protocol shall be those accepted by the IPCC and agreed upon by the Conference of the Parties at its third session. Where such methodologies are not used, appropriate adjustments shall be applied according to methodologies agreed upon by the Conference of the Parties. Based on the work of, *inter alia*, the IPCC and advice provided by the Subsidiary Body for Scientific and Technological Advice, the Conference of the Parties shall regularly review and, as appropriate, revise such methodologies and adjustments, taking fully into account any relevant decisions by the Conference of the Parties. Any revision to methodologies or adjustments shall be used only for the purposes of ascertaining compliance with commitments under Article 3 in respect of any commitment period adopted subsequent to that revision.

3. The global warming potentials used to calculate the carbon dioxide equivalence of anthropogenic emissions by sources and removals by sinks of greenhouse gases listed in Annex A shall be those accepted by the IPCC and agreed upon by the Conference of the Parties at its third session. Based on the work of, *inter alia*, the IPCC and advice provided by the Subsidiary Body for Scientific and Technological Advice, the Conference of the Parties ... shall regularly review and, as appropriate, revise the global warming potential of each such greenhouse gas ...

Article 6

1. For the purpose of meeting its commitments under Article 3, any Party included in Annex I may transfer to, or acquire from, any other such Party emission reduction units resulting from projects aimed at reducing anthropogenic emissions by sources or enhancing anthropogenic removals by sinks of greenhouse gases in any sector of the economy, provided that:

(a) Any such project has the approval of the Parties involved;

(b) Any such project provides a reduction in emissions by sources, or an enhancement of removals by sinks, that is additional to any that would otherwise occur;

(c) It does not acquire any emission reduction units if it is not in compliance with its obligations under Articles 5 and 7; and

(d) The acquisition of emission reduction units shall be supplemental to domestic actions for the purposes of meeting commitments under Article 3.

2. The Conference of the Parties serving as the meeting of the Parties to this Protocol may, at its first session or as soon as practicable thereafter, further elaborate guidelines for the implementation of this Article, including for verification and reporting.

3. A Party included in Annex I may authorize legal entities to participate, under its responsibility, in actions leading to the generation, transfer or acquisition under this Article of emission reduction units.

4. If a question of implementation by a Party included in Annex I of the requirements referred to in this Article is identified in accordance with the relevant provisions of Article 8, transfers and acquisitions of emission reduction units may continue to be made after the question has been identified, provided that any such units may not be used by a Party to meet its commitments under Article 3 until any issue of compliance is resolved.

Article 7

1. Each Party included in Annex I shall incorporate in its annual inventory of anthropogenic emissions by sources and removals by sinks of greenhouse gases not controlled by the Montreal Protocol, submitted in accordance with the relevant decisions of the Conference of the Parties, the necessary supplementary information for the purposes of ensuring compliance with Article 3, to be determined in accordance with paragraph 4 below.

2. Each Party included in Annex I shall incorporate in its national communication, submitted under Article 12 of the Convention, the supplementary information necessary to demonstrate compliance with its commitments under this Protocol, to be determined in accordance with paragraph 4 below.

3. Each Party included in Annex I shall submit the information required under paragraph 1 above annually, beginning with the first inventory due under the Convention for the first year of the commitment period after this Protocol has entered into force for that Party. Each such Party shall submit the information required under paragraph 2 above as part of the first national communication due under the Convention after this Protocol has entered into force and after the adoption of guidelines as provided for in paragraph 4 below. The frequency of subsequent submission of information required under this Article shall be determined by the Conference of the Parties serving as the meeting of the Parties to this Protocol, taking into account any timetable for the submission of national communications decided upon by the Conference of the Parties.

4. The Conference of the Parties serving as the meeting of the Parties to this Protocol shall adopt at its first session, and review periodically thereafter, guidelines of the preparation of the information required under this Article, taking into account guidelines for the preparation of national communications by Parties included in Annex I adopted by the Conference of the Parties. The Conference of the Parties serving as the meeting of the Parties to this Protocol shall also, prior to the first commitment period, decide upon modalities for the accounting of assigned amounts.

Article 8

1. The information submitted under Article 7 by each Party included in Annex I shall be reviewed by expert review teams ... as part of the annual compilation and accounting of emissions inventories and assigned amounts ... [and] as part of the review of communications.

2. Expert review teams shall be co-ordinated by the secretariat and shall be composed of experts selected from those nominated by Parties to the Convention and, as appropriate, by intergovernmental organizations, in accordance with guidance provided for this purpose by the Conference of the Parties.

3. The review process shall provide a thorough and comprehensive technical assessment of all aspects of the implementation by a Party of this Protocol. The export review teams shall prepare a report ... assessing the implementation of the commitments of the Party and identifying any potential problems in, and factors influencing, the fulfilment of commitments. Such reports shall be circulated by the secretariat to all Parties to the Convention. The secretariat shall list those questions of implementation indicated in such reports for further consideration by the Conference of the Parties ...

4. The Conference of the Parties ... shall adopt at its first session, and review periodically thereafter, guidelines for the review of implementation of this Protocol by expert review teams taking into account the relevant decisions of the Conference of the Parties.

Article 9

1. The Conference of the Parties ... shall periodically review this Protocol in the light of the best available scientific information and assessments on climate change and its impacts, as well as relevant technical, social and economic information ...

2. The first review shall take place at the second session of the Conference of the Parties serving as the meeting of the Parties to this Protocol. Further reviews shall take place at regular intervals and in a timely manner.

Article 10

All Parties, taking into account their common but differentiated responsibilities and their specific national and regional development priorities, objectives and circumstances, without introducing any new commitments for Parties not included in Annex I, but reaffirming existing commitments under Article 4, paragraph 1, of the Convention, and continuing to advance the implementation of these commitments in order to achieve sustainable development, taking into account Article 4, paragraphs 3, 5 and 7, of the Convention, shall:

(a) Formulate, where relevant and to the extent possible, cost-effective national and, where appropriate, regional programmes to improve the quality of local emission factors, activity data and/or models which reflect the socio-economic conditions of each Party for the preparation and periodic updating of national inventories of anthropogenic emissions by sources and removals by sinks of all greenhouse gases not controlled by the Montreal Protocol, using comparable methodologies to be agreed upon by the Conference of the Parties, and consistent with the guidelines for the preparation of national communications adopted by the Conference of the Parties;

(b) Formulate, implement, publish and regularly update national and, where appropriate, regional programmes containing measures to mitigate climate change and measures to facilitate adequate adaptation to climate change:

(i) Such programme would, *inter alia,* concern the energy, transport and industry sectors as well as agriculture, forestry and waste management. Furthermore, adaptation technologies and methods for improving spatial planning would improve adaptation to climate change; and

(ii) Parties included in Annex I shall submit information on action under this Protocol, including national programmes, in accordance with Article 7; and other Parties shall seek to include in their national communications, as appropriate, information on programmes which contain measures that the Party believes contribute to addressing climate change and its adverse impacts, including the abatement of increases in greenhouse gas emissions, and enhancement of and removals by sinks, capacity building and adaptation measures;

(c) Co-operate in the promotion of effective modalities for the development, application and diffusion of, and take all practicable steps to promote, facilitate and finance, as appropriate, the transfer of, or access to, environmentally sound technologies, know-how, practices and processes pertinent to climate change, in particular to developing countries, including the formulation of policies and programmes for the effective transfer of environmentally sound technologies that are publicly owned or in the public domain and the creation of an enabling environment for the private sector, to promote and enhance the transfer of, and access to, environmentally sound technologies;

(d) Co-operate in scientific and technical research and promote the maintenance and the development of systematic observation systems and development of data archives to reduce uncertainties related to the climate system, the adverse impacts of climate change and the economic and social consequences of various response strategies, and promote the development and strengthening of endogenous capacities and capabilities to participate in international and intergovernmental efforts, programmes and networks on research and systematic observation, taking into account Article 5 of the Convention;

(e) Co-operate in and promote at the international level, and, where appropriate, using existing bodies, the development and implementation of education and training programmes, including the strengthening of national capacity building, in particular human and institutional capacities and the exchange or secondment of personnel to train experts in this field, in particular for developing countries, and facilitate at the national level public awareness of, and public access to information on, climate change. Suitable modalities should be developed to implement these activities through the relevant bodies of the Convention, taking into account Article 6 of the Convention;

(f) Include in their national communications information on programmes and activities undertaken pursuant to this Article in accordance with relevant decisions of the Conference of the Parties; and

(g) Give full consideration, in implementing the commitments under this Article, to Article 4, paragraph 8, of the Convention.

Article 11

2. ... The developed country Parties and other developed Parties included in Annex II to the Convention shall:

(a) Provide new and additional financial resources to meet the agreed full costs incurred by developing country Parties in advancing the implementation of existing commitments under Article 4, paragraph 1(a) ...; and

(b) Also provide such financial resources, including for the transfer of technology, needed by the developing country Parties to meet the agreed full incremental costs of advancing the implementation of existing commitments under Article 4, paragraph 1, of the Convention that are covered by Article 10 and that are agreed between a developing country Party and the international entity or entities referred to in Article 11 of the Convention, in accordance with that Article. The implementation of these existing commitments shall take into account the need for adequacy and predictability in the flow of funds and the importance of appropriate burden-sharing among developed country Parties. The guidance to the entity or entities entrusted with the operation of the financial mechanism of the Convention in relevant decisions of the Conference of the Parties, including those agreed before the adoption of this Protocol, shall apply *mutatis mutandis* to the provisions of this paragraph.

3. The developed country Parties and other developed Parties in Annex II to the Convention may also provide, and developing country Parties avail themselves of, financial resources for the implementation of Article 10, through bilateral, regional and other multilateral channels.

Article 12

1. A clean development mechanism is hereby defined.

2. The purpose of the clean development mechanism shall be to assist Parties not included in Annex I in achieving sustainable development and in contributing to the ultimate objective of the Convention, and to assist Parties included in Annex I in achieving compliance with their quantified emission limitation and reduction commitments under Article 3.

3. Under the clean development mechanism:

(a) Parties not included in Annex I will benefit from project activities resulting in certified emission reductions; and

(b) Parties included in Annex I may use the certified emission reductions accruing from such project activities to contribute to compliance with part of their quantified emission limitation and reduction commitments under Article 3, as determined by the Conference of the Parties serving as the meeting of the Parties to this Protocol.

4. The clean development mechanism shall be subject to the authority and guidance of the Conference of the Parties serving as the meeting of the Parties to this Protocol and be supervised by an executive board of the clean development mechanism.

5. Emission reductions resulting from each project activity shall be certified by operational entities to be designated by the Conference of the Parties serving as the meeting of the Parties to this Protocol, on the basis of:

(a) Voluntary participation approved by each Party involved;

(b) Real, measurable, and long-term benefits related to the mitigation of climate change; and

(c) Reductions in emissions that are additional to any that would occur in the absence of the certified project activity.

6. The clean development mechanism shall assist in arranging funding of certified project activities as necessary.

7. The Conference of the Parties ... shall elaborate modalities and procedures with the objective of ensuring transparency, efficiency and accountability through independent auditing and verification of project activities.

8. The Conference of the Parties ... shall ensure that a share of the proceeds from certified project activities is used to cover administrative expenses as well as to assist developing country Parties that are particularly vulnerable to the adverse effects of climate change to meet the costs of adaptation.

9. Participation under the clean development mechanism, including in activities mentioned in paragraph 3(a) above and in the acquisition of certified emission reductions, may involve private and/or public entities, and is to be subject to whatever guidance may be provided by the executive board of the clean development mechanism.

10. Certified emission reductions obtained during the period from the year 2000 up to the beginning of the first commitment period can be used to assist in achieving compliance in the first commitment period.

Article 13

1. The Conference of the Parties, the supreme body of the Convention, shall serve as the meeting of the Parties to this Protocol.

2. Parties to the Convention that are not Parties to this Protocol may participate as observers in the proceedings of any session of the Conference of the Parties serving as the meeting of the Parties

to this Protocol ... Decisions under this Protocol shall be taken only by those that are Parties to this Protocol ...

Article 14

1. The secretariat established by Article 8 of the Convention shall serve as the secretariat of this Protocol.

2. Article 8, paragraph 2, of the Convention on the functions of the secretariat, and Article 8, paragraph 3, of the Convention on arrangements made for the functioning of the secretariat, shall apply *mutatis mutandis* to this Protocol. The secretariat shall, in addition, exercise the functions assigned to it under this Protocol.

Article 15

1. The Subsidiary Body for Scientific and Technological Advice and the Subsidiary Body for Implementation established by Articles 9 and 10 of the Convention shall serve as, respectively, the Subsidiary Body for Scientific and Technological Advice and the Subsidiary Body for Implementation of this Protocol. The provisions relating to the functioning of these two bodies under the Convention shall apply *mutatis mutandis* to this Protocol. Sessions of the meetings of the Subsidiary Body for Scientific and Technological Advice and the Subsidiary Body for Implementation of this Protocol shall be held in conjunction with the meetings of, respectively, the Subsidiary Body for Scientific and Technological Advice and the Subsidiary Body for Implementation of the Convention.

2. Parties to the Convention that are not Parties to this Protocol may participate as observers in the proceedings of any session of the subsidiary bodies. When the subsidiary bodies serve as the subsidiary bodies of this Protocol, decisions under this Protocol shall be taken only by those that are Parties to this Protocol ...

Article 16

The Conference of the Parties ... shall, as soon as praticable, consider the application to this Protocol of, and modify as appropriate, the multilateral consultative process referred to in Article 13 of the Convention, in the light of any relevant decisions that may be taken by the Conference of the Parties. Any multilateral consultative process that may be applied to this Protocol shall operate without prejudice to the procedures and mechanisms established in accordance with Article 18.

Article 17

The Conference of the Parties shall define the relevant principles, modalities, rules and guidelines, in particular for verification, reporting and accountability for emissions trading. The Parties included in Annex B may participate in emissions trading for the purposes of fulfilling their commitments under Article 3. Any such trading shall be supplemental to domestic actions for the purpose of meeting quantified emission limitation and reduction commitments under that Article.

Article 18

The Conference of the Parties serving as the meeting of the Parties to this Protocol shall, at its first session, approve appropriate and effective procedures and mechanisms to determine and to address cases of non-compliance with the provisions of this Protocol, including through the development of an indicative list of consequences, taking into account the cause, type, degree and frequency of non-compliance. Any procedures and mechanisms under this Article entailing binding consequences shall be adopted by means of an amendment to this Protocol.

Article 19

The provisions of Article 14 of the Convention on settlement of disputes shall apply *mutatis mutandis* to this Protocol.

Article 20

Amendments.

Article 21

Annexes.

Articles 22–28

Voting, ratification, reservations, etc.

United Nations High Commissioner for Refugees—UNHCR

Address: CP 2500, 1211 Geneva 2 dépôt, Switzerland.

Telephone: 227398111; **fax:** 227397312; **e-mail:** unhcr@unhcr.org; **internet:** www.unhcr.org.

The Office of the High Commissioner was established in 1951 to provide international protection for refugees and to seek durable solutions to their problems. In 1981 UNHCR was awarded the Nobel Peace Prize.

Organization

(June 2012)

HIGH COMMISSIONER

The High Commissioner is elected by the United Nations General Assembly on the nomination of the Secretary-General, and is responsible to the General Assembly and to the UN Economic and Social Council (ECOSOC).

High Commissioner: António Manuel de Oliveira Guterres (Portugal).

Deputy High Commissioner: Thomas Alexander Aleinikoff (USA).

EXECUTIVE COMMITTEE

The Executive Committee of the High Commissioner's Programme (ExCom), established by ECOSOC, gives the High Commissioner policy directives in respect of material assistance programmes and advice in the field of international protection. In addition, it oversees UNHCR's general policies and use of funds. ExCom, which comprises representatives of 66 states, both members and non-members of the UN, meets once a year.

ADMINISTRATION

Headquarters, based in Geneva, Switzerland, include the Executive Office, comprising the offices of the High Commissioner, the Deputy High Commissioner and the two Assistant High Commissioners (for Operations and Protection). The Inspector General, the Director of the UNHCR liaison office in New York, and the Director of the Ethics Office (established in 2008) report directly to the High Commissioner. The principal administrative Divisions cover: International Protection; Programme and Support Management; Emergency Security and Supply; Financial and Administrative Management; Human Resources Management; External Relations; and Information Systems and Telecommunications. A UNHCR Global Service Centre, based in Budapest, Hungary, was inaugurated in 2008 to provide administrative support to the Headquarters. There are five regional bureaux covering Africa, Asia and the Pacific, Europe, the Americas, and North Africa and the Middle East. In 2012 UNHCR employed around 7,190 regular staff, of whom about 85% were working in the field. At that time there were 396 UNHCR offices in 123 countries.

All UNHCR personnel are required to sign, and all interns, contracted staff and staff from partner organizations are required to acknowledge, a Code of Conduct, to which is appended the UN Secretary-General's bulletin on special measures for protection from sexual exploitation and sexual abuse. The post of

Senior Adviser to the High Commissioner on Gender Issues, within the Executive Office, was established in 2004.

Activities

The competence of the High Commissioner extends to any person who, owing to well-founded fear of being persecuted for reasons of race, religion, nationality or political opinion, is outside the country of his or her nationality and is unable or, owing to such fear or for reasons other than personal convenience, remains unwilling to accept the protection of that country; or who, not having a nationality and being outside the country of his or her former habitual residence, is unable or, owing to such fear or for reasons other than personal convenience, is unwilling to return to it. This competence may be extended, by resolutions of the UN General Assembly and decisions of ExCom, to cover certain other 'persons of concern', in addition to refugees meeting these criteria. Refugees who are assisted by other UN agencies, or who have the same rights or obligations as nationals of their country of residence, are outside the mandate of UNHCR.

In recent years there has been a significant shift in UNHCR's focus of activities. Increasingly UNHCR has been called upon to support people who have been displaced within their own country (i.e. with similar needs to those of refugees but who have not crossed an international border) or those threatened with displacement as a result of armed conflict. In addition, greater support has been given to refugees who have returned to their country of origin, to assist their reintegration, and UNHCR is working to enable local communities to support the returnees, frequently through the implementation of Quick Impact Projects (QIPs). In 2004 UNHCR led the formulation of a UN system-wide Strategic Plan for internally displaced persons (IDPs). During 2005 the UN's Inter-Agency Standing Committee (IASC), concerned with co-ordinating the international response to humanitarian disasters, developed a concept of organizing agency assistance to IDPs through the institutionalization of a 'Cluster Approach', currently comprising 11 core areas of activity (see OCHA). UNHCR is the lead agency for the clusters on Camp Co-ordination and Management (in conflict situations; the International Organization for Migration leads that cluster in natural disaster situations), Emergency Shelter, and (jointly with OHCHR and UNICEF) Protection.

From the mid-2000s the scope of UNHCR's mandate was widened from the protection of people fleeing persecution and violence to encompass, also, humanitarian needs arising from natural disasters.

In July 2006 UNHCR issued a '10 Point Plan of Action on Refugee Protection and Mixed Migration' (*10 Point Plan*), a framework document detailing 10 principal areas in which UNHCR might make an impact in supporting member states with the development of comprehensive migration strategies. The 10 areas covered by the Plan were as follows: co-operation among key players; data collection and analysis; protection-sensitive entry systems; reception arrangements; mechanisms for profiling and referral; differentiated processes and procedures; solutions for refugees; addressing secondary movements; return of non-refugees and alternative migration options; and information strategy. A revised version of the *10 Point Plan* was published in January 2007. Addressing the annual meeting of ExCom in October 2007 the High Commissioner, while emphasizing that UNHCR was not mandated to manage migration, urged a concerted international effort to raise awareness and comprehension of the broad patterns (including the scale, complexity, and causes—such as poverty and the pursuit of improved living standards) of global displacement and migration. In order to fulfil UNHCR's mandate to support refugees and others in need of protection within ongoing mass movements of people, he urged better recognition of the mixed nature of many 21st century population flows, often comprising both economic migrants and refugees, asylum seekers and victims of trafficking who required detection and support. It was also acknowledged that conflict and persecution—the traditional reasons for flight—were being increasingly compounded by factors such as environmental degradation and the detrimental effects of climate change. A Dialogue on Protection Challenges, convened by the High Commissioner in December 2007, agreed that the *10 Point Plan* should be elaborated further. Regional activities based on the Plan have been focused on Central America, Western Africa, Eastern Africa and Southern Asia; and on countries along the Eastern and South-Eastern borders of European Union member states.

In 2009 UNHCR launched the first annual Global Needs Assessment (GNA), with the aim of mapping comprehensively the situation and needs of populations of concern falling under the mandate of the Office. The GNA was to represent a blueprint for planning and decision-making for UNHCR, populations of concern, governments and other partners. In 2008 a pilot GNA, undertaken in eight countries, revealed significant unmet protection needs including in education, food security and nutrition, distribution of non-food items, health, access to clean water and sanitation, shelter, and prevention of sexual violence.

UNHCR's global strategic priorities for 2012–13 were: to promote a favourable protection environment; to promote fair protection processes and increase levels of documentation; to ensure security from violence and exploitation; to provide basic needs and services; and to pursue durable solutions.

At December 2010 the total global population of concern to UNHCR, based on provisional figures, amounted to 33.9m. At that time the refugee population world-wide totalled 10.5m., of whom 8.5m. were being hosted by developing countries. UNHCR was also concerned with some 197,626 recently returned refugees, 14.7m. IDPs, 2.9m. returned IDPs, 3.5m. stateless persons, and 837,478 asylum seekers. UNHCR maintains an online statistical population database.

UNHCR is one of the 10 co-sponsors of UNAIDS.

World Refugee Day, sponsored by UNHCR, is held annually on 20 June.

INTERNATIONAL PROTECTION

As laid down in the Statute of the Office, UNHCR's primary function is to extend international protection to refugees and its second function is to seek durable solutions to their problems. In the exercise of its mandate UNHCR seeks to ensure that refugees and asylum seekers are protected against *refoulement* (forcible return), that they receive asylum, and that they are treated according to internationally recognized standards. UNHCR pursues these objectives by a variety of means that include promoting the conclusion and ratification by states of international conventions for the protection of refugees. UNHCR promotes the adoption of liberal practices of asylum by states, so that refugees and asylum seekers are granted admission, at least on a temporary basis.

The most comprehensive instrument concerning refugees that has been elaborated at the international level is the 1951 United Nations Convention relating to the Status of Refugees. This Convention, the scope of which was extended by a Protocol adopted in 1967, defines the rights and duties of refugees and contains provisions dealing with a variety of matters which affect the day-to-day lives of refugees. The application of the Convention and its Protocol is supervised by UNHCR. The Office has actively encouraged states to accede to the Convention (which had 145 parties at June 2012) and the Protocol (146 parties at June 2012). Important provisions for the treatment of refugees are also contained in a number of instruments adopted at the regional level. These include the 1969 Convention Governing the Specific Aspects of Refugee Problems adopted by the Organization of African Unity (now the African Union—AU) member states in 1969, the European Agreement on the Abolition of Visas for Refugees, and the 1969 American Convention on Human Rights. In October 2009 AU member states adopted the AU Convention for the Protection and Assistance of IDPs in Africa, the first legally binding international treaty providing legal protection and support to internally displaced populations. An increasing number of states have also adopted domestic legislation and/or administrative measures to implement the international instruments, particularly in the field of procedures for the determination of refugee status. UNHCR has sought to address the specific needs of refugee women and children, and has also attempted to deal with the problem of military attacks on refugee camps, by adopting and encouraging the acceptance of a set of principles to ensure the safety of refugees. In recent years it has formulated a strategy designed to address the fundamental causes of refugee flows.

UNHCR has been increasingly concerned with the problem of statelessness, where people have no legal nationality, and promotes new accessions to the 1954 Convention Relating to the Status of Stateless Persons and the 1961 Convention on the Reduction of Statelessness. UNHCR maintains that a significant proportion of the global stateless population has not hitherto been systematically identified. In December 2011 UNHCR organized a ministerial meeting, in Geneva, to commemorate the 60th anniversary of the 1951 Refugee Convention and the 50th anniversary of the 1961 Convention on the Reduction of Statelessness, and to reaffirm commitment to the central role played by these instruments. A number of participants at the meeting made pledges to address statelessness, including improving procedures for identifying stateless people on their territories, enhancing civil registration systems, and raising awareness on the options available to stateless people.

ASSISTANCE ACTIVITIES

The first phase of an assistance operation uses UNHCR's capacity of emergency response. This enables UNHCR to address the immediate needs of refugees at short notice, for example, by employing specially trained emergency teams and maintaining stockpiles of basic equipment, medical aid and materials. A significant proportion of UNHCR expenditure is allocated to the next phase of an operation, providing 'care and maintenance' in stable refugee circumstances. This assistance can take various forms, including the provision of food, shelter, medical care and essential supplies. Also covered in many instances are basic services, including education and counselling.

As far as possible, assistance is geared towards the identification and implementation of durable solutions to refugee problems—this being the second statutory responsibility of UNHCR. Such solutions generally take one of three forms: voluntary repatriation, local integration or resettlement in another country. Where voluntary repatriation, increasingly the preferred solution, is feasible, the Office assists refugees to overcome obstacles preventing their return to their country of origin. This may be done through negotiations with governments involved, or by providing funds either for the physical movement of refugees or for the rehabilitation of returnees once back in their own country. Some 197,000 refugees repatriated voluntarily to their home countries in 2010. UNHCR supports the implementation of the Guidance Note on Durable Solutions for Displaced Persons, adopted in 2004 by the UN Development Group.

When voluntary repatriation is not an option, efforts are made to assist refugees to integrate locally and to become self-supporting in their countries of asylum. This may be done either by granting loans to refugees, or by assisting them, through vocational training or in other ways, to learn a skill and to establish themselves in gainful occupations. One major form of assistance to help refugees re-establish themselves outside camps is the provision of housing. In cases where resettlement through emigration is the only viable solution to a refugee problem, UNHCR negotiates with governments in an endeavour to obtain suitable resettlement opportunities, to encourage liberalization of admission criteria and to draw up special immigration schemes. During 2010 an estimated 73,000 refugees were resettled under UNHCR auspices.

UNHCR aims to integrate certain priorities into its programme planning and implementation, as a standard discipline in all phases of assistance. The considerations include awareness of specific problems confronting refugee women, the needs of refugee children, the environmental impact of refugee programmes and long-term development objectives. A Policy Development and Evaluation Service reviews systematically UNHCR's operational effectiveness.

EAST ASIA AND THE PACIFIC

In 1998 the Hong Kong authorities formally terminated the policy of granting a port of first asylum to Vietnamese 'boat people'. In February 2000 UNHCR welcomed a decision by the Hong Kong authorities to offer permanent residency status to the occupants of the last remaining Vietnamese detention camp (totalling 973 refugees and 435 'non-refugees'). By the end of May, when the camp was closed, more than 200 Vietnamese had failed to apply for residency. In 1995, in accordance with an agreement concluded with the People's Republic of China Government, UNHCR initiated a programme to redirect its local assistance to promote long-term self-sufficiency in the poorest settlements, including support for revolving-fund rural credit schemes. UNHCR favours the local integration of the majority of the Vietnamese refugee population in China as a durable solution to the situation. At 31 December 2010 there were an estimated 300,897 Vietnamese refugees in mainland China.

During 2012 UNHCR was advocating for the accession of the Hong Kong Special Administrative Region—which attracts mixed inflows of refugees, asylum seekers and economic migrants—to the 1951 United Nations Convention relating to the Status of Refugees (of which China is a signatory).

A large-scale process to resettle Myanma refugees from Thailand to third countries commenced in 2004. From 2009 UNHCR aimed to upgrade its activities in the Rakhine region of northern Myanmar, covering health, education, water and sanitation, agriculture and infrastructure improvement, in order to assist the reintegration of Muslim returnees to the area, as well as stateless residents (numbering around 750,000 in 2010). From late 2008 there were significant outflows of Muslims from Rakhine towards Malaysia, as well as to Indonesia and Thailand; UNHCR has worked with regional governments for the adoption of a collective approach to addressing the situation. UNHCR assisted 10,823 Myanma refugees with resettlement in 2010, reducing the numbers still sheltering in (nine) border camps to 95,718 at the end of that year. At 31 December 2010 there were some 76,120 Myanma refugees in Malaysia (all UNHCR-assisted), of whom 21,104 arrived during that year. In addition, an estimated 29,226 Myanma refugees (Rohingya Muslims) were receiving basic care from UNHCR in two camps in Bangladesh, having fled persecution in the 1990s. In 2012 UNHCR also aimed to improve the conditions of an estimated 200,000 unregistered Myanma refugees living outside its camps in Bangladesh.

UNHCR has sought access, so far unsuccessfully, to Laotian Hmong would-be asylum seekers sheltering since 2005 in temporary shelters in Thailand, whom the Thai authorities classify as illegal migrants. During 2005–10 some 7,500 Lao-Hmong were forcibly returned from Thailand to Laos, including some 4,000 who were returned en masse in December 2009.

In 2008 Thailand was the focus of a pilot project for UNHCR's Global Needs Assessment (formally inaugurated in 2009, see above). In view of the project's findings, UNHCR aimed to enhance its efforts to improve protection and to facilitate durable solutions for refugees in that country.

Renewed violent unrest in Timor-Leste that erupted in April 2006 resulted in significant new population displacement within the country, and, at the end of that year, more than 155,200 Timorese IDPs were of concern to UNHCR. During May–August 2006 the Office provided immediate relief to the newly uprooted IDPs, in the form of non-food items such as tents, and was subsequently involved in IDP protection and reconciliation activities. In January 2012 UNHCR formally ended its operations in Timor-Leste with the closure of its office in the capital, Dili.

UNHCR endeavours to facilitate safe passage to the Republic of Korea for people who have fled from the Democratic People's Republic of Korea to China and other countries in the region.

In February 2002 an Asia-Pacific regional ministerial conference on people smuggling, trafficking in persons and related transnational crime, held in Bali, Indonesia, launched the Bali Process, a series of regional capacity-building workshops, and other initiatives, with participation by UNHCR. The Process aimed, inter alia, to improve intelligence sharing; to enhance co-operation among law enforcement agencies, and between border agencies; to promote the enactment of national legislation relating to people smuggling; to encourage a focus on addressing the root causes of illegal migration; and to support states in adopting best practices in asylum management. Further regional ministerial conferences were convened to review the Bali Process in April 2003, April 2009, and March 2011. The March 2011 conference adopted a regional co-operation framework for combating people smuggling.

SOUTH ASIA

From the late 1970s civil strife in Afghanistan resulted in massive population displacements, including movements of refugees from that country into Pakistan and Iran which created a massive refugee population, reaching a peak of almost 6.3m. people in 1990. In September 2001, prompted by the threat of impending military action directed by a US-led global coalition against targets in the Taliban-administered areas of Afghanistan, UNHCR launched an emergency relief operation to cope with the potentially large further movement of Afghan refugees and IDPs. UNHCR urged the adoption of more liberal border policies by surrounding countries and began substantially to reinforce its presence in Iran and Pakistan. Emergency contingency plans were also formulated for a relief initiative to assist a projected increase in IDP numbers (in addition to the large numbers of people already displaced) inside Afghanistan. Large population movements out of cities were reported from the start of the international political crisis. An estimated 6m. Afghans (about one-quarter of the total population) were believed to be extremely vulnerable, requiring urgent food aid and other relief supplies. In mid-September all foreign UN field staff were withdrawn from Afghanistan for security reasons; meanwhile, in order to address the humanitarian situation, a Crisis Group was established by several UN agencies, including UNHCR, and a crisis management structure came into operation at UNHCR headquarters. In October (when air-strikes were initiated against Afghanistan) UNHCR opened a staging camp at a major crossing point on the Afghanistan-Pakistan border, and put in place a system for monitoring new refugee arrivals (implemented by local people rather than by UNHCR personnel). It was estimated that from October 2001–January 2002 about 50,000 Afghan refugees entered Pakistan officially, while about 150,000 crossed into the country at unofficial border points; many reportedly sought refuge with friends and relatives. Much smaller movements into Iran were reported. Spontaneous repatriations also occurred during that period (reportedly partly owing to the poor conditions at many camps in Pakistan), and UNHCR-assisted IDP returns were also undertaken. UNHCR resumed operations within Afghanistan in mid-November 2001, distributing supplies and implementing QIPs, for example the provision of warm winter clothing. From that month some 130,000 Afghan refugees in Pakistan were relocated from inadequate accommodation to new camps. In March 2002 tripartite accords on repatriation were concluded by UNHCR with the Afghan authorities and with Iran and Pakistan. During 2002–end-2010 more than 5m. refugees returned to Afghanistan from Pakistan and Iran; of these, 117,870 returned voluntarily, with UNHCR assistance, during 2010. The operational environment within Afghanistan, however, was highly challenging during the 2000s, with the security situation remaining extremely unstable in 2012. Where possible the Agency provides returning refugees with transport and an initial reintegration package, including a cash grant and food and basic household items, and monitors their situation. Particular focus is placed upon the situation of returnee women and prevention of gender-based violence, and on encouraging the return of professional workers, especially doctors and teachers. The Office also works to improve local infrastructure and water supply facilities, and has completed the construction of more than 200,000 shelter units. UNHCR aims to strengthen the capacity of the Afghan Government to manage the return and sustainable reintegration of refugees and IDPs. During 2012 UNHCR's access to IDPs in conflict zones in Afghanistan remained insecure and unreliable. At 31 December 2010 Pakistan was hosting some 1.9m. Afghan refugees. Meanwhile, some 1.0m. UNHCR-assisted Afghan refugees remained in Iran (in addition to about 1m. unregistered Afghan migrants), and 9,094 Afghan refugees remained in India (all UNHCR-assisted). In March 2009 UNHCR and the Pakistani authorities signed an accord extending the stay of Afghan refugees in Pakistan until the end of 2012.

In 1991–92 thousands of people of Nepalese ethnic origin living in Bhutan sought refuge from alleged persecution by fleeing to eastern Nepal. In December 2000 Bhutan and Nepal reached agreement on a joint verification mechanism for the repatriation of the refugees, which had been hitherto the principal issue precluding a resolution of the situation. The first verification of Bhutanese refugees was undertaken in March 2001. In March 2008 UNHCR launched an operation, in co-operation with the International Organization for Migration and the governments of Nepal and the resettlement countries, to resettle more than 10,000 Nepalese refugees from Bhutan, mainly to the USA. At end-December 2010 some 74,536 Bhutanese refugees remained in Nepal (compared with 107,000 at March 2008), of whom some 56,000 had expressed an interest in resettlement. In 2012 UNHCR was to facilitate the resettlement of up to 16,000 Bhutanese refugees from Nepal. During 2007 the Nepalese Government extended citizenship to some 2.6m. of the 3.5m. stateless people hitherto resident in Nepal.

During 1983–2001 hostilities between the Sri Lankan Government and Tamil separatists resulted in the displacement of more than 1m. Sri Lankan Tamil refugees (who sought shelter in India) and IDPs. Ongoing efforts by UNHCR to repatriate the Sri Lankan refugees were disrupted in late 1995 by an offensive by Sri Lankan government troops against the northern Jaffna peninsula, which caused a massive displacement of the local Tamil population. Increasing insecurity from late 1999 prompted further population movements. However, following the conclusion of a cease-fire agreement between the Sri Lankan Government and Tamil separatists in February 2002, the number of spontaneous returns accelerated. From April 2006 conflict between Tamil separatists and the Sri Lankan Government escalated once again, prompting a new wave of internal displacement and refugee movements to India during 2006–08, and in January 2008 the 2002 cease-fire agreement was abrogated, further intensifying the situation. Some 303,471 people were newly displaced during April 2006–October 2008, and a further 31,809 Sri Lankans were newly displaced during November 2008–February 2009. In May 2009 the Sri Lankan Government declared an end to military operations against the Tamil separatists. From 2006 UNHCR screened, registered and provided emergency accommodation for civilians displaced from the conflict zone, monitored the human rights situation, and advised the Sri Lankan authorities about the treatment of the displaced population. At 31 December 2010 there remained 273,772 Sri Lankan IDPs of concern to UNHCR and 161,128 recently returned IDPs, as well as an estimated 178,308 Sri Lankan refugees remaining in camps in southern India. By August 2011 some 395,000 IDPs had returned to their homes, with the IDP returns process expected to be completed in 2012. UNHCR's priorities for 2012 were to continue providing material assistance to, and monitoring the protection needs of, IDPs and returnees; to help build the capacity of national institutions and local agencies involved in reintegration activities; and to implement community-based QIPs. At end-December 2010 India's total refugee population of some 184,821 also included 100,003 refugees from China (mainly Tibetans).

CENTRAL ASIA

In the early 2000s UNHCR implemented an initiative to integrate locally up to 10,000 Tajik refugees of Kyrgyz ethnic origin in Kyrgyzstan and 12,500 Tajik refugees of Turkmen origin in Turkmenistan; this process was facilitated by the conclusion in mid-2003 of a Kyrgyz-Tajik agreement on a simplified procedure for citizenship acquisition. From 1 July 2006 UNHCR terminated refugee status for exiled Tajiks, although the Office continued to support their voluntary repatriation. By the end of that year most of the former Tajik refugees in Kyrgyzstan and Turkmenistan had become naturalized citizens of those countries, as planned; in 2008 all remaining Tajik refugees in Kyrgyzstan were granted Kyrgyz citizenship. UNHCR has helped the Kyrgyz authorities to integrate the former Tajiks. UNHCR ascertained that there were 21,157 stateless people residing in Kyrgyzstan at end-2010, either without documentation or holding expired USSR passports; the Office and the Kyrgyz authorities have aimed to work together to support applications by the stateless individuals for Kyrgyz citizenship.

During mid-2010 UNHCR distributed relief items (including tents, blankets and plastic sheeting) to some of an estimated 75,000 Kyrgyz refugees who had sought shelter in temporary camps and accommodation centres in Uzbekistan following the eruption of violent conflict in southern Kyrgyzstan in June. At that time UNHCR—which estimated that some 375,000 people had become displaced inside Kyrgyzstan, including some 40,000 with urgent shelter requirements—also established an emergency office in Jalal-Abad, southern Kyrgyzstan; worked to verify the number of displaced, to visit the areas where they were focused, and to assess their needs; and sent air deliveries of relief items to Osh, southern Kyrgyzstan. Furthermore some 75,000 Kyrgyz fled the violence to Uzbekistan. UNHCR co-ordinated the relief efforts in Uzbekistan, and also the protection and emergency shelter humanitarian clusters and non-food relief cluster within Kyrgyzstan.

From late 2001 about 9,000 Afghan refugees repatriated from Tajikistan under the auspices of UNHCR and the International Organization for Migration. UNHCR expressed concern following the adoption by the Tajikistan authorities in May 2002 of refugee legislation that reportedly contravened the 1951 Convention relating to the Status of Refugees and its 1967 Protocol. During 2006 nearly 1,500 Afghan refugees were resettled from Tajikistan to third countries, leaving a remaining Afghan refugee population in that country of about 1,000; UNHCR has pursued durable solutions for their local integration. Increasing numbers of Afghan asylum-seekers fled to Tajikistan in 2010.

In 2003 UNHCR agreed to participate in a European Union/UNDP Border Management Programme in Central Asia (BOMCA). At the request of the Uzbekistan Government UNHCR closed its Uzbekistan office in April 2006. A regional office for Central Asia was inaugurated in Almatı, Kazakhstan, in 2008. UNHCR assisted the Kazakh authorities with the preparation of draft national refugee legislation during that year.

UNHCR reported in 2010 that compliance with the Convention relating to the Status of Refugees was problematic in the Central Asia region. The Office's priorities in Central Asia in 2012 included registering and profiling people of concern using modern data collection tools; improving the regional capacity for refugee status determination; seeking to improve self-reliance among refugees and asylum seekers, with a particular focus on urban situations; and preventing and reducing statelessness.

NORTH AFRICA AND THE MIDDLE EAST

Given the lack of progress in achieving a settlement agreement for Western Sahara, UNHCR co-ordinates humanitarian assistance for the estimated 165,000 Sahrawis registered as refugees in five camps in the Tindouf area of Algeria. In September 2009 UNHCR resolved to expand its confidence-building programme, which was launched in 2004 mainly to facilitate family visits; by 2012 around 12,000 people had participated in family visits under the programme.

As a result of serious instability in Libya from mid-February 2011, nearly 100,000 people soon became displaced from the eastern coastal city of Benghazi and surrounding areas; furthermore large numbers (estimated at 656,000 by August) of Libyans and former foreign residents in Libya fled to nearby countries, including 57,221 Libyan nationals who were seeking shelter in Tunisia, and 63,747 Libyans in Egypt. UNHCR dispatched teams to Egypt and Libya to provide support. In response to the crisis within Libya, UNHCR—which maintained a small international staff in the Libyan capital, Tripoli, and organized presences in Benghazi and Tobruk in the east of the country—transported supplies into Libya and provided material assistance to refugees and other vulnerable groups there. During the initial months of the crisis UNHCR airlifted tents, and items such as blankets, sleeping mats, jerry cans, and kitchen sets, to several thousand people gathered in border areas. At the request of the Tunisian Government, UNHCR and other agencies established a number of camps at the Libya-Tunisia border. Furthermore, thousands of Libyans (mainly Berbers) fled Libya's Western Mountain region into Tunisia, the majority being accommodated there by local families. By late August UNHCR had registered nearly 60,000 Libyan refugees sheltering in southern Tunisia. UNHCR distributed ration cards to Libyan refugees in urban areas of Tunisia. UNHCR expressed reiterated concern in September 2011 for the safety of foreign nationals (mainly migrant workers) remaining in Libya. Sub-Saharan Africans were reported to be at particular risk of persecution. Meanwhile, in early 2011, UNHCR and IOM jointly conducted the humanitarian evacuation of more than 100,000 third country nationals from Egypt and Tunisia, which had also experienced serious civil unrest.

Yemen has historically hosted refugees from the Horn of Africa. Of an estimated 74,000 people who made the crossing in 2009, Ethiopians (numbering about 42,000) represented for the first time a larger group than Somalis; about 309 people were presumed to have drowned during the crossing in that year. UNHCR operates two reception centres to process incomers, and four other offices, in Yemen. At 31 December 2010 Yemen was hosting an estimated 190,092, mostly Somali (179,845), refugees; the majority of these were residing in urban areas, while some 11,000 were accommodated in the al-Kharaz camp. Ongoing violent conflict in northern Yemen has also generated internal displacement, and at the end of 2010 there were an estimated 220,994 IDPs in Yemen. In 2008 Yemen participated in a pilot project for UNHCR's Global Needs Assessment (formally inaugurated in 2009, see above). The Assessment recommended interventions to improve provision in the areas of food security and nutrition, non-food items, water and education. UNHCR's priorities in Yemen in 2011 included organizing joint screening teams with the Yemen Government to identify, protect and assist people of concern; improving the access of urban refugees to education, microcredit, vocational training, employment and business opportunities; and supporting the Government in identifying, registering and monitoring conflict-affected IDPs.

In view of an increase in irregular migrant and asylum seeker flows—mainly from Eritrea, Ethiopia, Iraq and Sudan—to and through Egypt (with many migrants and asylum seekers seeking to enter Israel illegally) in recent years, UNHCR has made efforts to identify asylum seekers and to assess their claims, as well as undertaking outreach activities focused on increased community participation in protection and assistance programmes and, through the provision of training, enhancing the capacity of the Egyptian authorities to provide refugee protection. The populations of concern to UNHCR, and also the poorest sectors of local communities, were made particularly vulnerable at that time by the high cost of living and the adverse global economic situation.

In March 2003, in view of the initiation of US-led military action against the Saddam Hussain regime in Iraq, UNHCR and the International Federation of Red Cross and Red Crescent Societies signed an agreement on co-operation in providing humanitarian relief in Iraq and neighbouring countries. From mid-2003, following the overthrow of the Saddam Hussain Government, UNHCR developed plans for the eventual phased repatriation of more than 500,000 of the large population of Iraqis exiled world-wide, and for the return to their homes of some 800,000 IDPs, contingent, however, upon the stabilization of the political and security situation in the country. The Office assumed responsibility for assisting about 50,000 refugees from other countries (including some 34,000 Palestinians—of whom an estimated 10,798 remained at end-2010) who had been supported by the previous Iraqi administration but were now suffering harassment; many had abandoned their homes in Iraq owing to insufficient security and inadequate supplies. Negotiations with Iran were initiated in mid-2003 to enable Iranian refugees to repatriate across the Iraq–Iran border. From March–May 2003, and following the bomb attack in August on the UN headquarters in Baghdad, all international UN humanitarian personnel were withdrawn from Iraq, leaving national staff to conduct operations on the ground. During 2003–05 some 315,000 spontaneous returns by Iraqi refugees and asylum seekers and 496,000 returns by IDPs were reported. However, owing to the ongoing unstable security situation, UNHCR and the Iraqi Interim Government (inaugurated in June 2004) discouraged Iraqi refugees from returning home, and UNHCR warned governments hosting Iraqi refugees against repatriation, as well as advising continued protection of Iraqi asylum seekers. During 2006–07, owing to escalating violent sectarian unrest, it was reported that more than 1.5m. Iraqis had become newly displaced and that many people—including skilled and professional workers—had left Iraq, further inhibiting the national recovery process. In April 2007 an International Conference on Addressing the Humanitarian Needs of Refugees and Internally Displaced Persons inside Iraq and in Neighbouring Countries was convened in Geneva by the UN High Commissioner for Refugees. UNHCR remains highly concerned for foreign refugees remaining in Iraq (totalling 34,655 at end-2010). UNHCR has a small international presence (re-established in March 2008) in Baghdad, Basrah, Erbil, Kirkuk and Mosul, and 15 Protection and Assistance Centres, as well as 40 mobile teams. Through its network of offices UNHCR monitors population movements and the well-being of refugees, IDPs and returnees throughout Iraq. At 31 December 2010, the total Iraqi IDP population amounted to 1.3m., around 200,000 IDPs having returned to their homes during that year. The Office provides returnees (who numbered 28,896 in 2010), in accordance with a case-by-case approach, with counselling, limited transportation and livelihood grants. UNHCR's priorities in Iraq in 2012 were to continue to provide for basic needs and essential services, including maintaining supplies of potable water, and building, maintaining and improving shelter structures; to promote security from violence and exploitation; to improve the quality of the Government's registration and profiling activities; to facilitate access to legal assistance for people of concern; and to pursue durable solutions for populations of concern.

At the end of 2010 it was estimated that there were 1m. Iraqis sheltering in Syria (135,200 UNHCR-assisted) and 450,000 (30,100 UNHCR-protected) in Jordan, as well as smaller groups of Iraqis in other neighbouring countries, placing considerable strain on local infrastructure and services. UNHCR significantly strengthened its outreach capacity in countries bordering Iraq from 2008, when the Iraqi refugee population became particularly vulnerable owing to sharp increases in food and commodity prices. In 2010 UNHCR and the Syrian Government concluded a Co-operation Agreement providing the legal basis for the Office's activities in that country. UNHCR registered some 23,000 newly arrived Iraqi refugees in Syria during 2010. In 2010 UNHCR's activities in support of Iraqi populations of concern included the provision of remedial classes; outreach to parents by education volunteers; distribution of education grants; and support with access to health care. UNHCR has particularly focused assistance on vulnerable refugees with specific needs, such as female-headed households, children and the elderly. During 2007–end-2010 114,300 Iraqi refugees were referred for resettlement, and more than 60,700 left for third countries. At end-2010 some 29,956 asylum applications by Iraqis (5,141 UNHCR-assisted) in other countries were pending, globally. UNHCR has pursued accelerated departures and additional resettlement opportunities for the most vulnerable Iraqi refugees. The violent unrest that emerged in Syria in 2011, and escalated in the first half of 2012, disrupted resettlement activities relating to Iraqi refugees there. During 2010 expenditure on the Iraq situation amounted to US $508m.

At the end of 2010 Kuwait was hosting 96,459 people of concern to UNHCR, mainly *bidoun* (stateless people, totalling 93,000), Iraqis and Palestinians.

In March 2012, in view of escalating unrest in Syria, which by then had displaced more than 200,000 people from their homes, humanitarian agencies appealed jointly for US $84m. to fund an inter-agency Syria Regional Response Plan. The Plan, led by UNHCR, aimed to assist more than 61,000 Syrians who had fled to neighbouring countries (which were continuing to keep their borders open to the influx). It was estimated at that time that around 13,750 Syrians had sought shelter in Jordan, 21,000 in Lebanon, 2,370 in Iraq, and 23,970 in Turkey. UNHCR's activities to alleviate the situation included implementing a cash assistance programme in Jordan, and outreach programmes to identify the most vulnerable refugees in Jordan and Lebanon; supplying food and household items to refugees, and rehabilitating homes and community centres, in those two countries; and airlifting tents and blankets to Turkey.

In March 2002 UNHCR signed a new agreement with the Iranian Government to grant access to the large Afghan refugee population in detention centres throughout that country and to undertake a screening programme for asylum seekers, in order to deal with the problem of undocumented refugees. During 2008 the Iranian authorities implemented an on-line refugee registration process, referred to as Amayesh III, under which the details of more than 900,000 people were registered; identity cards were issued to refugees registered under Amayesh III, and, subsequently, temporary work-permits began to be issued to Amayesh III card holders with a view to finding temporary solutions in Iran for the Afghan refugees. UNHCR envisaged utilizing the data collated under Amayesh III in its planning processes. During 2002–11 more than 5.7m. refugees returned to Afghanistan from Iran and Pakistan; of these, 117,870 returned voluntarily, with UNHCR assistance, during 2010. At 31 December 2010 some 1.0m. UNHCR-assisted Afghan refugees remained in Iran (in addition to about 1m. unregistered Afghan migrants).

SUB-SAHARAN AFRICA

UNHCR has provided assistance to refugees and internally displaced populations in many parts of the continent where civil conflict, violations of human rights, drought, famine or environmental degradation have forced people to flee their home regions. The majority of African refugees and returnees are located in countries that are themselves suffering major economic problems and are thus unable to provide the basic requirements of the uprooted people. In March 2004 a UNHCR-sponsored Dialogue on Voluntary Repatriation and Sustainable Reintegration in Africa endorsed the creation of an international working group—comprising African Governments, UN agencies, the AU and other partners—to support the return and sustainable reintegration of refugees in several African countries, including Angola, Burundi, the Democratic Republic of the Congo (DRC), Eritrea, Liberia, Rwanda, Sierra Leone, Somalia and Sudan. At 31 December 2010 there were an estimated 10.2m. people of concern to UNHCR in sub-Saharan Africa.

The Horn of Africa, afflicted by famine and long-term internal conflict, has suffered large-scale population movements in recent decades. During 1992–mid-2006 more than 1m. Somalis (of whom about 485,000 received UNHCR assistance) returned to their country, having sought sanctuary in neighbouring states following the January 1991 overthrow of the former Somali president Siad Barre. The humanitarian situation in Somalia has remained highly insecure, and deteriorated significantly during 2007–12. In 2010 more than 200,000 people were newly displaced within Somalia, and a further 70,000 fled as new refugees to neighbouring countries. At 31 December 2010 the Somalian IDP population totalled an estimated 1.5m. Severe food insecurity in southern areas of Somalia that escalated in 2011—with a state of famine officially declared in two areas from July 2011–early February 2012—exacerbated further the ongoing humanitarian crisis in that country. At September 2011 an estimated 3.7m. Somalis were estimated to be food-insecure, and many Somali rural households were reported to have migrated in search of food and support towards the conflict-affected Somali capital, Mogadishu, and into neighbouring countries. At that time most of Somalia was designated by the UN at security level 5 ('high'), with Mogadishu and other south-central areas at level 6 ('extreme insecurity'): therefore there was very limited access for humanitarian workers. Following the July 2011 famine declaration UNHCR distributed more than 27,000 emergency assistance packages to 174,000 IDPs in southern Somalia and Mogadishu, and supported nearly 270,000 IDPs throughout the country through the provision of emergency relief items such as blankets, mattresses, kitchen sets, and plastic sheeting. UNHCR maintains a presence in Puntland and in Somaliland, but directs its Somalia programme from Nairobi, Kenya. UNHCR is responsible for co-ordinating the UN's emergency shelter and protection clusters in Somalia, and, with OCHA, co-leads the Puntland IDP Task Force, established in late 2010 with the aim of devising a comprehensive strategy aimed at improving the situation of local IDPs. The Office's priorities within Somalia for 2012 were to protect people of concern within larger mixed migratory flows; to prioritize the most vulnerable asylum seekers in need of resettlement; to provide subsistence allowances to people of concern with urgent needs; to support initiatives aimed at promoting self-reliance and livelihood opportunities; to facilitate access to schools and health facilities; and to reduce xenophobia in host communities towards refugees and asylum seekers.

There was at 31 December 2010 an estimated total Somali refugee population of 770,148, of whom 351,773 were in Kenya (all assisted by UNHCR) and 179,845 in Yemen (98,855 UNHCR-assisted). During 2007 Kenya enacted a Refugee Act, in accordance with which it was to assume a more active role in managing the registration and status determination of refugees. In November 2010 UNHCR appealed to the Kenyan authorities to cease the ongoing forcible return to Somalia of up to 8,000 Somali refugees accommodated hitherto in the Mandera camp in northeast Kenya. By early 2012 some 443,500 Somali refugees were accommodated at Kenya's Dadaab complex of camps, comprising the Hagadera, Dagahaley, Ifo, Ifo East, Ifo West and Kambioos camps; Hagadera (with 134,590 Somali residents) was at that time the largest refugee camp in the world. UNHCR was to continue to protect and assist Somalian refugees during 2012, while considering possibilities for voluntary repatriation, local integration and resettlement. There were an estimated 300,000 Kenyan IDPs at 31 December 2010.

At 31 December 2010 an estimated 387,288 Sudanese were exiled as refugees, mainly in Chad, Uganda, Kenya, and Ethiopia, owing to a history of civil unrest in southern Sudan and the emergence in early 2003 of a new conflict zone in the western Sudanese province of Darfur (see below). The Ugandan Government, hosting an estimated 19,382 Sudanese refugees at end-2010 (all UNHCR-assisted), has provided new resettlement sites and, jointly with UNHCR and other partners, has developed a Self-Reliance Strategy, which envisages achieving self-sufficiency for the long-term refugee population through integrating services for refugees into existing local structures. In 2006 the Ugandan Government adopted a new Refugee Act that included gender-based persecution as grounds for granting refugee status. At end-2010 there were some 125,598 IDPs in Uganda, and some 302,991 returned Ugandan IDPs. In February 2006 UNHCR and Sudan signed tripartite agreements with Ethiopia, the DRC and the Central African Republic to provide a legal framework for the repatriation of Sudanese refugees remaining in those countries. From 2008 violent attacks committed by Ugandan Lord's Resistance Army rebels on communities in the southern Sudan-DRC-Central African Republic (CAR) border region displaced numerous southern Sudanese people, and forced thousands of displaced DRC villagers northwards into Sudan. At 31 December 2010 some 103,798 Eritreans were sheltering in Sudan, of whom 66,278 were receiving UNHCR assistance.

In August 2011, following the independence in July of South Sudan, the Sudanese Government amended legislation to deprive individuals who acquired South Sudan nationality of Sudanese citizenship. UNHCR expressed concern over the implications of this for significant numbers of people of mixed Sudanese/South Sudanese origin living in border areas. UNHCR's activities in South Sudan in 2012 were to focus on strengthening relevant institutional and legal frameworks; combating sexual and gender-based violence; protecting people at risk of statelessness; and supporting refugees, returnees, IDPs and host communities by targeting assistance at vulnerable families such as female-headed households, and implementing livelihoods programmes and QIPs. Mounting tensions in the first half of 2012 in disputed border areas between Sudan and South Sudan caused increasing numbers of Sudanese to flee to South Sudan and to Ethiopia. In late June 2012 UNHCR appealed urgently for extra resources to meet an estimated funding requirement of US $219m. to assist some 162,500 refugees in South Sudan and 36,500 in Ethiopia.

From April 2003 more than 200,000 refugees from Sudan's western Darfur region sought shelter across the Sudan-Chad border, having fled an alleged campaign of killing, rapes and destruction of property conducted by pro-government militias against the indigenous population. In addition, 2m.–3m. people became displaced within Darfur itself. The Office organized airlifts of basic household items to the camps, aimed to improve and expand refugees' access to sanitation, healthcare and education, to manage supplementary and therapeutic feeding facilities in order to combat widespread malnutrition, to provide psychosocial support to traumatized refugees, and to promote training and livelihood programmes. The Chad-Darfur operation has been hampered by severe water shortages resulting from the arid environment of the encampment areas, necessitating costly UNHCR deliveries of stored water, and by intense insecurity. A significant deterioration from 2006 in the security situation in the eastern areas of Chad bordering Darfur (where resources were already stretched to the limit), as well as in Darfur itself, led to further population displacement in the region, including the displacement of significant numbers of Chadians. At January 2012 some 39,500 Chadian refugees and Chadians in refugee-like situations were sheltering inside Darfur (of whom just under one-half were UNHCR-assisted), and there were also around 130,000 Chadian IDPs who had fled inwards from the Chad-Sudan border region. At end-December 2010 Chad was hosting 285,500 refugees from Darfur, accommodated in 12 UNHCR camps. UNHCR established a presence within western Darfur in June 2004, and in 2012 the Office was providing protection assistance to around 2.7m. displaced and returned Darfurians, as well as Chadian refugees, in the region. Following the establishment of the AU/UN Hybrid Operation in Darfur (UNAMID) in December 2007, UNHCR opened a liaison office near the UNAMID base in northern Darfur. UNHCR teams have undertaken efforts to train Sudanese managers of camps in Darfur in the areas of protection and human rights. The Office has also established in the area a number of women's centres providing support to survivors of sexual violence, and several centres for IDP youths, as well as rehabilitating conflict-damaged schools. In 2012 a gradual shift in programming from a primarily protection-oriented, camp-based approach to pursuing durable solutions was under way. A continuing volatile security situation in the CAR from 2003 resulted in significant population displacement into southern border areas of Chad; by 2012 more than 70,000 CAR refugees were accommodated by UNHCR in camps there, and at 31 December 2010 there were an estimated 192,529 IDPs inside the CAR.

UNHCR's activities in assisting refugees in West Africa have included a focus on the prevention of sexual and gender-based violence in refugee camps—a regional action plan to combat such violence was initiated in 2002—and collaboration with other agencies to ensure continuity between initial humanitarian assistance and long-term development support. UNHCR provided assistance to 120,000 people displaced by the extreme insecurity that developed in Côte d'Ivoire from September 2002. About 25,000 Côte d'Ivoire refugees fled to southern Liberia, and others sought shelter in Ghana, Guinea and Mali. In addition, between November and January 2003 an estimated 40,000 Liberian refugees in Côte d'Ivoire repatriated, in both spontaneous and partly UNHCR-assisted movements, having suffered harassment since the onset of the conflict. UNHCR initiated a number of QIPs aimed at rehabilitating the infrastructure of communities that were to receive returned Côte d'Ivoire refugees. At 31 December 2010 there were 514,515 IDPs in that country. As a consequence of unrest that erupted in Côte d'Ivoire following a disputed presidential election held in October–November 2010, an estimated 200,000 people became displaced from their homes in western Côte d'Ivoire, and some 150,000 Ivorian nationals fled to Liberia, during December 2010–April 2011. In response to the influx of Côte d'Ivoire refugees into Liberia, UNHCR facilitated the registration of the new refugees and mobilized the delivery of food aid and non-food relief items, as well as material for constructing a campsite. UNHCR planned to support some 55,000 Ivorian refugee returns, and 72,000 IDP returns in Côte d'Ivoire, during 2012.

Since 1993 the Great Lakes region of central Africa has experienced massive population displacement, causing immense operational challenges and demands on the resources of international humanitarian and relief agencies. During the late 1990s UNHCR resolved to work, in co-operation with UNDP and WFP, to rehabilitate areas previously inhabited by refugees in central African countries of asylum and undertook to repair roads, bridges and other essential transport infrastructure, improve water and sanitation facilities, and strengthen the education sector. However, the political stability of the Great Lakes region remained extremely uncertain, and, from August 1998, DRC government forces and rebels became involved in a civil war in which the militaries of several regional governments were also implicated. From late 1998 substantial numbers of DRC nationals fled to neighbouring countries (mainly Tanzania and Zambia) or were displaced within the DRC. Meanwhile, the DRC, in turn, was hosting a significant refugee population. In view of the conclusion, in December 2002, of a peace agreement providing for the staging of elections in the DRC after a transition period of 24 months, UNHCR planned for eventual mass refugee returns. The Office, in co-operation with other UN agencies, was to assist efforts to demobilize, disarm and repatriate former combatants. Owing to incessant rebel activity, insecurity continued to prevail, however, during 2003–12, in north-eastern areas of the DRC, resulting in further population displacements. In September 2005 UNHCR and the DRC and Tanzanian Governments signed a tripartite agreement on facilitating refugee returns of DRC refugees from Tanzania, and, during 2005–early

2012 UNHCR assisted 60,000 such returns. The status of Tanzania's Nyaragusu camp, sheltering mainly refugees from the DRC, was under review in 2012. A tripartite agreement on assistance was concluded by the Burundian and Tanzanian Governments and UNHCR in August 2003. In April 2010 the UN High Commissioner for Refugees expressed gratitude to the Tanzanian authorities for offering citizenship to 162,000 long-standing Burundian refugees. In February 2012 the Burundi-Tanzania-UNHCR tripartite commission confirmed that Tanzania's Mtabila camp, hosting 38,378 Burundian refugees, would close at the end of 2012, and that its residents would be repatriated to Burundi during April–November. UNHCR concluded similar tripartite accords in 2003 with the Rwandan Government and other states hosting Rwandan refugees, paving the way subsequently for significant voluntary refugee returns to Rwanda. In 2010 UNHCR assisted a total of 10,900 refugee returns to that country. The major populations of concern to UNHCR in the Great Lakes region at 31 December 2010 were, provisionally, as follows: 1.7m. IDPs, 460,740 returned IDPs and 166,366 refugees in the DRC; 157,167 IDPs in Burundi; 55,398 refugees in Rwanda; and a refugee population of 109,286 in Tanzania, very significantly reduced from 602,088 at end-2004. At the end of 2010 some 124,244 DRC refugees (all of whom were UNHCR-assisted) were sheltering in the Republic of the Congo. Long-standing DRC refugees in the Republic of the Congo are largely self-sufficient, with many refugees working as farmers and fishermen; the Office has aimed to promote the local integration of those unwilling to return to the DRC.

In September 2010 a regional conference on refugee protection and international migration, convened in Dar es Salaam, Tanzania, adopted an action plan to address mixed movements and irregular migration from eastern Africa, the Horn of Africa and the Great Lakes region to southern Africa; this was being implemented during 2011–12.

It was estimated that in all more than 4.3m. Angolans were displaced from their homes during the 1980s and 1990s, owing to long-term civil conflict. Following the signing of the Luanda Peace Agreement in April 2002 between the Angolan Government and rebels of the União National para a Independência Total de Angola, UNHCR made preparations for the voluntary repatriation of a projected 400,000 Angolan refugees sheltering elsewhere in southern Africa. By the end of 2004 the Office had rehabilitated the nine main repatriation corridors into Angola, and by the end of 2005 a total of nearly 4.4m. IDPs, refugees and demobilized fighters had reportedly returned home. UNHCR has assisted the Angolan Government with the development of a Sustainable Reintegration Initiative for returned refugees. From May 2009–early 2011 Angola forcibly returned home some 160,000 DRC refugees. In response to the initial forced repatriations, some 51,000 Angolan refugees were expelled from the DRC to Angola during 2009. An Angola-DRC agreement to suspend the mutual expulsions and enter into consultations, concluded in October 2009, was subsequently not adhered to by the Angolan authorities. At 31 December 2010 an estimated 134,858 Angolans were still sheltering in neighbouring countries, including 79,817 in the DRC and 25,265 in Zambia. HIV/AIDS- and mine-awareness training have been made available by UNHCR at refugee reception centres.

Zimbabwe was the country of origin of the largest number of asylum-seekers world-wide in 2010, with 149,400 new applications made by Zimbabwean nationals in that year.

THE AMERICAS AND THE CARIBBEAN

UNHCR's activities in Central and South America are currently guided by the Mexico Plan of Action (MPA), adopted in November 2004. The MPA aims to address ongoing population displacement problems in Latin America, with a particular focus on the humanitarian crisis in Colombia and the border areas of its neighbouring countries (see below), and the increasing numbers of refugees concentrated in urban centres in the region. The Cities of Solidarity pillar of the MPA assists UNHCR with facilitating the local integration and self-sufficiency of people in urban areas who require international protection; the Borders of Solidarity pillar addresses protection at international borders; and the Resettlement in Solidarity pillar promotes co-operation in resettling refugees. In November 2010 regional leaders adopted the Brasília Declaration on the Protection of Refugees and Stateless Persons in the Americas, in which they committed to revitalizing the MPA pillars.

UNHCR supports the Regional Conference on Migration (RCM, also know as the 'Puebla Process'), which was launched in March 1996 to promote regional co-operation on migration, and comprises the governments of Belize, Canada, Costa Rica, the Dominican Republic, El Salvador, Guatemala, Honduras, Mexico, Nicaragua, Panama and the USA. A Regional Conference on Refugee Protection and International Migration in the Americas, held in San José, Costa Rica, in November 2009, addressed key protection challenges in the context of an environment characterized by complex mixed migratory population movements.

In 1999 the Colombian Government approved an operational plan proposed by UNHCR to address a massive population displacement that had arisen in that country (escalating significantly from 1997), as a consequence of ongoing long-term internal conflict and alleged human rights abuses committed by paramilitary groups. In recent years the military capacity of the security forces has advanced, and demobilization of militants was undertaken during 2003–06. None the less, insecurity and population displacement have persisted within Colombia, exacerbated by a rise in organized crime and by the emergence of new illegal armed groups; some 100,000 Colombians were newly displaced in 2010. Indigenous and Afro-Colombian peoples in remote, rural districts, particularly along the Pacific Coast, in central areas, in Antioquia, and in border areas neighbouring Ecuador and Venezuela, have been particularly vulnerable. Intra-urban displacement among 1.7m. Colombian urban IDPs has also caused concern, with gang conflict contributing to an environment where sexual and gender-based violence, forced recruitment, and extortion have become commonplace. Measures, including the Government's Victims and Land Restitution Bill, signed in June 2011, have been introduced to enable the victims of forced displacement to claim reparations for and restitution of their holdings. Within Colombia UNHCR's protection activities have included ensuring an adequate, functioning legal framework for the protection of IDPs and enabling domestic institutions to supervise compliance with national legislation regarding the rights of IDPs; strengthening representation for IDPs and other vulnerable people; and developing local protection networks. UNHCR has also advised on public policy formulation in the areas of emergency response, IDP registration, health, education, housing, income-generation and protection of policy rights; and has endeavoured to promote durable solutions for IDPs, in particular local integration. The Office has also co-operated with UNICEF to improve the provision of education to displaced children. UNHCR works to provide legal protection and educational and medical support to around 500,000 Colombians who have fled to but not sought asylum in neighbouring countries. The Office's strategy for supporting countries receiving displaced Colombians (of whom the majority were not registered as refugees) has included border-monitoring activities, entailing the early warning of potential refugee movements, and provision of detailed country-of-origin data. UNHCR has offered technical assistance in relation to the Colombia-Ecuador Neighborhood Commission, established in 1989 and reactivated, following a period of inactivity, in November 2010. At the end of 2010 around 3.7m. IDPs within Colombia remained of concern to UNHCR. By that time an estimated 120,403 Colombians (52,059 UNHCR-assisted) were living as refugees in Ecuador, while 204,467 (21,067 UNHCR-assisted) Colombians were sheltering in Venezuela; the majority of these (in both countries) had not sought official protection but were living in 'refugee-like' situations. In 2012 UNHCR's presence in Colombia included 10 field offices and a branch office in Bogotá.

Following the devastating earthquake that struck Haiti in January 2010, UNHCR provided assistance to the international humanitarian response operation in the areas of camp registration and profiling matters; shelter co-ordination; and supporting OHCHR in its efforts to assist the displaced population outside Port-au-Prince and earthquake survivors living outside registered camps. UNHCR also implemented a number of QIPs, and provided material support to Haitian evacuees in the neighbouring Dominican Republic. In June 2010 UNHCR opened an office in Santo Domingo, Dominican Republic. In July 2011 UNHCR and OHCHR urged governments to suspend all involuntary returns to Haiti, owing to the ongoing fragile protection environment in that country and continuing displacement of some 680,000 people; the IDPs remained in more than 1,000 tented camps in earthquake-affected areas. During 2012 UNHCR was to support the authorities in reforming systems for recording civil documentation, including the registration of births, and in improving the legal framework relating to nationality. UNHCR's activities in the Dominican Republic in 2012 were to include assisting the authorities with addressing a backlog of asylum claims, helping to provide birth certificates and civil documentation to undocumented Haitian migrants and people of Haitian descent, to enable their access to legal protection and also to basic services. The Office was also to implement QIPs aimed at income generation and local infrastructure improvement in support of the most vulnerable undocumented Haitians in the Dominican Republic.

Canada and the USA are major countries of resettlement for refugees. UNHCR provides counselling and legal services for asylum seekers in these countries. At 31 December 2010 the estimated refugee populations totalled 165,549 in Canada and 264,574 in the USA, while asylum seekers numbered 51,025 and 6,285, respectively.

CENTRAL AND SOUTH-EASTERN EUROPE

The political changes in Central and Eastern Europe during the early 1990s resulted in a dramatic increase in the number of asylum seekers and displaced people in the region. UNHCR was the agency designated by the UN Secretary-General to lead the UN relief operation to assist those affected by the conflict in the former Yugoslavia. It was responsible for the supply of food and other humanitarian aid to the besieged capital of Bosnia and Herzegovina, Sarajevo, and to Muslim and Croatian enclaves in the country, under the armed escort of the UN Protection Force. Assistance was provided not only to Bosnian refugees in Croatia and displaced people within Bosnia and Herzegovina's borders, but also, in order to forestall further movements of people, to civilians whose survival was threatened. The operation was often seriously hampered by armed attacks (resulting, in some cases, in fatalities), distribution difficulties and underfunding from international donors. The Dayton peace agreement, which was signed in December 1995, bringing an end to the conflict, secured the right for all refugees and displaced persons freely to choose their place of residence within the new territorial arrangements of Bosnia and Herzegovina. Thus, the immediate effect of the peace accord was further population displacement, including a mass exodus of almost the entire Serb population of Sarajevo. Under the peace accord, UNHCR was responsible for planning and implementing the repatriation of all Bosnian refugees and displaced persons, then estimated at 2m.; however, there were still immense obstacles to freedom of movement, in particular for minorities wishing to return to an area dominated by a different politico-ethnic faction. Returns by refugees and IDPs (including significant numbers of refugees returning to areas where they represented minority ethnic communities) accelerated from 2000, owing to an improvement in security conditions. In July 2002 the heads of state of Bosnia and Herzogovina, Croatia and the Federal Republic of Yugoslavia (FRY, which was renamed Serbia and Montenegro in 2003, and was divided into separate sovereign states of Montenegro and Serbia in June 2006) met in Sarajevo with a view to resolving a number of outstanding issues, including the return of remaining refugees. In January 2005 the concerned parties adopted the Sarajevo Declaration, committing to resolve remaining population displacement issues through the 'Sarajevo Process' (also referred to as the '3x3 Initiative'). In March 2010 the foreign affairs ministers of Bosnia and Herzegovina, Croatia, Montenegro and Serbia convened in Belgrade, Serbia, at the International Conference: Durable Solutions for Refugees and IDPs: Co-operation Among Countries of the Region, to address continuing obstacles to durable solutions for those persons in the region who were continuing to live in a protracted refugee situation. The repossession by their rightful owners and reconstruction of illegally appropriated properties have been key issues for returned refugees to the region. In January 2011 the UN High Commissioner for Refugees appointed a personal envoy to assist the governments of Bosnia and Herzegovina, Croatia, Montenegro and Serbia in developing a binding common commitment and regional programme to address the protracted population displacement in the region. By December 2010 there was still an estimated total Bosnian refugee population of 63,004, of whom some 25,614 were receiving assistance from UNHCR. The majority of the Bosnian refugee population were in Germany and Serbia. At end-2010 there were also 113,365 IDPs of concern to UNHCR in Bosnia and Herzegovina. In 2012 the Office aimed to improve access to documentation (civil status documentation and late birth registration) for apparently stateless people in the region, with a particular focus on the Roma minority.

In the late 1990s attacks by Serbian forces against members of a separatist movement in the southern Serbian province of Kosovo and Metohija resulted in an estimated 1.3m. Kosovar Albanians being displaced. In June 1999, following a cease-fire accord and an agreement by the FRY to withdraw all forces and paramilitary units, UNHCR initiated a large-scale registration operation of Kosovar refugees and emergency operation to assist the displaced population within Kosovo. In mid-2000 UNHCR scaled down its emergency humanitarian activities in Kosovo and provided a UN Humanitarian Co-ordinator to oversee the transition to long-term reconstruction and development, in co-operation with the UN Interim Administration Mission in Kosovo (UNMIK). UNHCR and OSCE have periodically jointly assessed the situation of minority communities in Kosovo; minority returns (numbering during 2000–11 around 13,250 from Serbia to Kosovo, and 3,857 returning to places of origin within Kosovo) and integration have reportedly been impeded by discrimination against and intimidation of minorities in the province. Throughout the region UNHCR is concerned to reduce and prevent statelessness. The Office has undertaken a civil registration programme for undocumented IDPs in Kosovo and Serbia, particularly members of Roma, Ashkali and Egyptian communities in Kosovo, deemed to be at risk of statelessness. At the end of 2010 there were still 228,442 IDPs in Serbia. In addition, Serbia was hosting 73,608 refugees, of whom 21,047 were from Bosnia and Herzegovina and 52,483 from Croatia. UNHCR has expanded its durable solution programmes for IDPs in Serbia, by assisting with the construction of social housing, by providing cash grants to help people to move to the new accommodation, and by organizing self-reliance projects. At the end of 2010 more than 18,000 people remained displaced within Kosovo, of whom the majority were in the Mitrovica area. From 2010 forced returns from western European countries outnumbered voluntary returns to Kosovo, challenging Kosovo's capacity for absorption, reintegration, and its protection capabilities. Some 2,500 minority returns were envisaged in 2012.

EASTERN EUROPE

In June 2007, following the publication in June 2006 of its *10 Point Plan* for assisting member states with the management of refugee protection and mixed migration, UNHCR issued a '10 Point Plan of Action on Refugee Protection and Mixed Migration for Countries along the Eastern and South-Eastern Borders of European Union Member States', providing a framework for discussion between UNHCR and the governments of Belarus, Moldova and Ukraine, and also clarifying UNHCR's operational relationship in that subregion with the International Organization for Migration and non-governmental organizations. During 2007 UNHCR undertook a study on the local integration of refugees in Belarus, Moldova and Ukraine, at the request of those countries' governments.

In the early 1990s UNHCR co-ordinated international humanitarian efforts to assist some 500,000 people displaced by the conflict between Armenia and Azerbaijan. Of the 12 emergency camps established, the last were closed in December 2007. At 31 December 2010 Azerbaijan was still supporting an IDP population totalling 592,860. During 2011 UNHCR prioritized strengthening the national asylum system; promoting refugee self-sufficiency, particularly among those living in urban environments; giving advocacy for the rights of IDPs; and working for durable solutions fo IDPs, including local integration.

In Georgia, where almost 300,000 people left their homes as a result of civil conflict from 1991, UNHCR has attempted to encourage income-generating activities among the displaced population, to increase the Georgian Government's capacity to support those people and to assist the rehabilitation of people returning to their areas of origin. In July 2008 the Georgian authorities adopted a National IDP Action Plan, drafted with support from UNHCR, which was expected to provide a basis for future durable solutions. During August of that year UNHCR provided humanitarian assistance, including the distribution of blankets, jerry-cans and kitchen sets, to people affected by a period of violent insecurity that escalated in July between Georgian and South Ossetian separatist forces, further intensifying in early August when Georgia launched a military offensive on the South Ossetian capital Tskhinvali, a stronghold of the separatists, and Russian forces responded by supporting the South Ossetian counter-attack and by crossing into Georgian territory. The heightened insecurity resulted in the temporary displacement of some 134,000 people within Georgia and of nearly 35,000 from South to North Ossetia (Russian Federation). In the following month, once the conflict had abated, UNHCR teams began regular visits to assess the humanitarian situation in villages in the Georgia–South Ossetia buffer zone area north of the Georgian town of Gori. More than 32,000 of those who had fled from South to North Ossetia returned to their homes swiftly. There were 359,716 Georgian IDPs at 31 December 2010, including about 22,000 people who remained displaced by the August 2008 conflict. In 2008 Georgia was the focus of a pilot project for UNHCR's Global Needs Assessment (formally inaugurated in 2009, see above).

In late 1999 an estimated 7,000 refugees fleeing insecurity in Chechnya entered Georgia. UNHCR delivered food to the Chechen refugees and the host families with whom the majority were staying, and also assisted the refugees through shelter renovation, psychosocial support and the provision of childcare facilities and health and community development support, as well as monitoring refugee-host family relations. In 2009 UNHCR shifted its focus from materially assisting Chechen refugees remaining in Georgia (numbering about 1,000) to seeking a local integration solution for them. In 2007 Chechen refugees were granted temporary resident status in Georgia, and from April 2009 the Chechen refugees were permitted to apply through the Georgian authorities for the first time for Convention Travel Documents, issued in accordance with provisions of the 1951 Convention relating to the Status of Refugees.

In recent years UNHCR has conducted regular missions into the Russian separatist republic of Chechnya (the Chechen Republic of Ichkeriya) to monitor and support the reintegration of more than 200,000 IDPs who had fled civil unrest since the mid-1990s. UNHCR has also conducted interviews of returnees to Chechnya from neighbouring Ingushetiya in order to ensure that returns have been voluntary rather than enforced. It was estimated at end-2010 that around 6,500 Chechen refugees remained in Ingushetiya. At the end of 2010 there were reportedly still around 30,000 displaced people within Chechnya. There were also an estimated 3,500 Chechen IDPs in Dagestan. During 2003–10 some 255,000 IDPs were reported to have returned to Chechnya from elsewhere in the Russian Federation.

CO-OPERATION WITH OTHER ORGANIZATIONS

UNHCR works closely with other UN agencies, intergovernmental organizations and non-governmental organizations (NGOs) to increase the scope and effectiveness of its operations. Within the UN system UNHCR co-operates, principally, with the WFP in the distribution of food aid, UNICEF and WHO in the provision of family welfare and child immunization programmes, OCHA in the delivery of emergency humanitarian relief, UNDP in development-related activities and the preparation of guidelines for the continuum of emergency assistance to development programmes, and the Office of the UN High Commissioner for Human Rights. UNHCR also has close working relationships with the International Committee of the Red Cross and the International Organization for Migration. UNHCR planned to engage with nearly 700 NGOs in 2012–13. In recent years UNHCR has pursued a strategy to engage private sector businesses in supporting its activities through the provision of donations (cash contributions and 'in kind'), of loaned expertise, and of marketing related to designated causes.

TRAINING

UNHCR organizes training programmes and workshops to enhance the capabilities of field workers and non-UNHCR staff, in the following areas: the identification and registration of refugees; people-orientated planning; resettlement procedures and policies; emergency response and management; security awareness; stress management; and the dissemination of information through the electronic media.

Finance

The United Nations' regular budget finances a proportion of UNHCR's administrative expenditure. The majority of UNHCR's programme expenditure (about 98%) is funded by voluntary contributions, mainly from governments. The Private Sector and Public Affairs Service aims to increase funding from non-governmental donor sources, for example by developing partnerships with foundations and corporations. Following approval of the Unified Annual Programme Budget any subsequently identified requirements are managed in the form of Supplementary Programmes, financed by separate appeals. UNHCR's projected funding requirements for 2011 totalled US $3,320.0m.

Publications

Global Trends (annually).

Refugees (quarterly, in English, French, German, Italian, Japanese and Spanish).

Refugee Resettlement: An International Handbook to Guide Reception and Integration.

Refugee Survey Quarterly.

Refworld (annually).

Sexual and Gender-based Violence Against Refugees, Returnees and Displaced Persons: Guidelines for Prevention and Response.

The State of the World's Refugees (every 2 years).

Statistical Yearbook (annually).

UNHCR Handbook for Emergencies.

Press releases, reports.

Statistics

POPULATIONS OF CONCERN TO UNHCR BY REGION

('000 persons, at 31 December 2010, provisional figures)

	Refugees*	Asylum seekers	Returned refugees†	Others of concern‡
Africa	2,409	330	43	7,395
Asia	5,475	72	152	10,172
Europe	1,587	303	2	1,101
Latin America/ Caribbean	374	99	71	3,672
North America	430	57	—	—
Oceania	34	3	—	—
Total	10,550	837	198	22,340

* Includes persons recognized as refugees under international law, and also people receiving temporary protection and assistance outside their country but who have not been formally recognized as refugees.

† Refugees who returned to their place of origin during 2010.

‡ Mainly internally displaced persons (IDPs), former IDPs who returned to their place of origin during 2010, and stateless persons.

POPULATIONS OF CONCERN TO UNHCR BY COUNTRY*
('000 persons, at 31 December 2010, provisional figures)

	Refugees†	Asylum seekers	Returned refugees†	Others of concern†
Africa				
Burundi	29.4	12.1	4.8	158.2
Cameroon	104.3	2.4	—	—
CAR	21.6	1.2	0.0	192.5
Chad	347.9	0.1	0.0	181.0
DRC	161.3	0.9	16.6	2,182.1
Congo, Rep.	133.1	5.5	0.1	—
Côte d'Ivoire	26.2	0.3	0.0	537.1
Ethiopia	154.3	1.0	0.0	—
Kenya	402.9	28.0	0.3	320.0
Somalia	1.9	24.1	0.0	1,464.0
South Africa	57.9	171.7	—	—
Sudan	178.3	6.0	7.0	1,767.1
Tanzania	109.3	1.2	—	162.3
Uganda	135.8	20.8	0.1	428.6
Asia				
Afghanistan	6.4	0.0	118.0	1,193.5
Bangladesh	229.3	—	—	—
China, People's Republic‡	301.0	0.1	0.0	—
Egypt	95.1	25.1	14.3	0.1
India	184.8	3.7	—	—
Iran	1,073.4	1.8	0.0	—
Iraq	34.6	3.1	28.9	1,758.3
Jordan	450.9	2.2	—	—
Malaysia	81.5	11.3	—	120.0
Myanmar	—	—	—	859.4
Nepal	89.8	0.9	0.0	800.6
Pakistan	1,900.6	2.1	0.0	2,138.9
Sri Lanka	0.2	0.1	5.1	440.0
Syria	1,005.5	2.4	—	300.0
Thailand	96.7	10.3	—	542.5
Yemen	190.1	2.6	—	315.7
Europe				
Azerbaijan	1.9	0.0	—	594.9
Bosnia and Herzegovina	7.0	0.2	0.9	171.4
Estonia	0.0	0.0	—	101.0
France	200.7	48.6	—	1.1
Georgia	0.6	0.0	0.0	361.5
Germany	594.3	52.0	—	24.2
Latvia	0.1	0.1	—	326.9
Russian Federation	4.9	1.5	0.0	126.1
Serbia	73.6	0.2	0.4	238.7
Sweden	82.6	18.6	—	9.3
United Kingdom	238.2	14.9	—	0.2
Latin America/ Caribbean				
Colombia	0.2	0.2	0.0	3,672.1
Ecuador	121.2	49.9	—	—
Venezuela	201.5	15.9	—	—
North America				
Canada	165.5	51.0	—	—
USA	264.6	6.3	—	—

* The list includes only those countries having 100,000 or more persons of concern to UNHCR.
† See table above for definitions.
‡ Excluding Hong Kong Special Administrative Region.

ORIGIN OF MAJOR POPULATIONS OF CONCERN TO UNHCR*
('000 persons, 31 December 2010, provisional figures)

Origin	Population of concern to UNHCR
Afghanistan	4,404.5
Colombia	4,128.0
Iraq	3,387.5
DRC	2,718.6
Somalia	2,256.8
Pakistan	2,198.9
Sudan	2,185.2

* Data exclude (some 4,966,664 at 31 December 2010) Palestinian refugees who come under the mandate of UNRWA, although (at 31 December 2010) 96,545 Palestinians who are outside the UNRWA area of operation, for example those in Iraq and Libya, are considered to be of concern to UNHCR.

Convention relating to the Status of Refugees

(28 July 1951)

PREAMBLE

The High Contracting Parties

Considering that the Charter of the United Nations and the Universal Declaration of Human Rights approved on 10 December 1948 by the General Assembly have affirmed the principle that human beings shall enjoy fundamental rights and freedoms without discrimination,

Considering that the United Nations has, on various occasions, manifested its profound concern for refugees and endeavoured to assure refugees the widest possible exercise of these fundamental rights and freedoms,

Considering that it is desirable to revise and consolidate previous international agreements relating to the status of refugees and to extend the scope of and protection accorded by such instruments by means of a new agreement,

Considering that the grant of asylum may place unduly heavy burdens on certain countries, and that a satisfactory solution of a problem of which the United Nations has recognized the international scope and nature cannot therefore be achieved without international co-operation,

Expressing the wish that all States, recognizing the social and humanitarian nature of the problem of refugees will do everything within their power to prevent this problem from becoming a cause of tension between States,

Noting that the United Nations High Commissioner for Refugees is charged with the task of supervising international conventions providing for the protection of refugees, and recognizing that the effective co-ordination of measures taken to deal with this problem will depend upon the co-operation of States with the High Commissioner,

Have agreed as follows.

I. GENERAL PROVISIONS

Article 1

Definition of the term "Refugee".

A. For the purposes of the present Convention, the term "refugee" shall apply to any person who:

(1) Has been considered a refugee under the Arrangements of 12 May 1926 and 30 June 1928 or under the Conventions of 28 October 1933 and 10 February 1938, the Protocol of 14 September 1939 or the Constitution of the International Refugee Organization; Decisions of non-eligibility taken by the International Refugee Organization during the period of its activities shall not prevent the status of refugee being accorded

to persons who fulfil the conditions of paragraph 2 of this section;

(2) As a result of events occurring before 1 January 1951 and owing to well-founded fear of being persecuted for reasons of race, religion, nationality, membership of a particular social group or political opinion, is outside the country of his nationality and is unable or, owing to such fear, is unwilling to avail himself of the protection of that country; or who, not having a nationality and being outside the country of his former habitual residence as a result of such events, is unable or, owing to such fear, is unwilling to return to it.

In the case of a person who has more than one nationality, the term "the country of his nationality" shall mean each of the countries of which he is a national, and a person shall not be deemed to be lacking the protection of the country of his nationality if, without any valid reason based on well-founded fear, he has not availed himself of the protection of one of the countries of which he is a national.

B. (1) For the purposes of this Convention, the words "events occurring before 1 January 1951" in Article 1, Section A, shall be understood to mean either (a) 'events occurring in Europe before 1 January 1951'; or (b) 'events occurring in Europe or elsewhere before 1 January 1951'; and each Contracting State shall make a declaration at the time of signature, ratification or accession, specifying which of these meanings it applies for the purpose of its obligations under this Convention;

(2) Any Contracting State which has adopted alternative (a) may at any time extend its obligations by adopting alternative (b) by means of a notification addressed to the Secretary-General of the United Nations.

C. This Convention shall cease to apply to any person falling under the terms of Section A if:

(1) He has voluntarily re-availed himself of the protection of the country of his nationality; or

(2) Having lost his nationality, he has voluntarily re-acquired it; or

(3) He has acquired a new nationality, and enjoys the protection of the country of his new nationality; or

(4) He has voluntarily re-established himself in the country which he left or outside which he remained owing to fear of persecution; or

(5) He can no longer, because the circumstances in connection with which he has been recognized as a refugee have ceased to exist, continue to refuse to avail himself of the protection of the country of his nationality;

Provided that this paragraph shall not apply to a refugee falling under Section A(1) of this Article who is able to invoke compelling reasons arising out of previous persecution for refusing to avail himself of the protection of the country of nationality;

(6) Being a person who has no nationality he is, because the circumstances in connection with which he has been recognized as a refugee have ceased to exist, able to return to the country of his former habitual residence;

Provided that this paragraph shall not apply to a refugee falling under section A(1) of this Article who is able to invoke compelling reasons arising out of previous persecution for refusing to return to the country of his former habitual residence.

D. This Convention shall not apply to persons who are at present receiving from organs or agencies of the United Nations other than the United Nations High Commissioner for Refugees protection or assistance.

When such protection or assistance has ceased for any reason, without the position of such persons being definitively settled in accordance with the relevant resolutions adopted by the General Assembly of the United Nations, these persons shall ipso facto be entitled to the benefits of this Convention.

E. This Convention shall not apply to a person who is recognized by the competent authorities of the country in which he has taken residence as having the rights and obligations which are attached to the possession of the nationality of that country.

F. The provisions of this Convention shall not apply to any person with respect to whom there are serious reasons for considering that:

(a) He has committed a crime against peace, a war crime, or a crime against humanity, as defined in the international instruments drawn up to make provision in respect of such crimes;

(b) he has committed a serious non-political crime outside the country of refuge prior to his admission to that country as a refugee;

(c) he has been guilty of acts contrary to the purposes and principles of the United Nations.

Article 2

General obligations.

Every refugee has duties to the country in which he finds himself, which require in particular that he conform to its laws and regulations as well as to measures taken for the maintenance of public order.

Article 3

Non-discrimination.

The Contracting States shall apply the provisions of this Convention to refugees without discrimination as to race, religion or country of origin.

Article 4

Religion.

The Contracting States shall accord to refugees within their territories treatment at least as favourable as that accorded to their nationals with respect to freedom to practise their religion and freedom as regards the religious education of their children.

Article 5

Rights granted apart from this Convention.

Nothing in this Convention shall be deemed to impair any rights and benefits granted by a Contracting State to refugees apart from this Convention.

Article 6

The term "in the same circumstances".

For the purposes of this Convention, the term "in the same circumstances" implies that any requirements (including requirements as to length and conditions of sojourn or residence) which the particular individual would have to fulfil for the enjoyment of the right in question, if he were not a refugee, must be fulfilled by him, with the exception of requirements which by their nature a refugee is incapable of fulfilling.

Article 7

Exemption from reciprocity.

1. Except where this Convention contains more favourable provisions, a Contracting State shall accord to refugees the same treatment as is accorded to aliens generally.

2. After a period of three years' residence, all refugees shall enjoy exemption from legislative reciprocity in the territory of the Contracting States.

3. Each Contracting State shall continue to accord to refugees the rights and benefits to which they were already entitled, in the absence of reciprocity, at the date of entry into force of this Convention for that State.

4. The Contracting States shall consider favourably the possibility of according to refugees, in the absence of reciprocity, rights and benefits beyond those to which they are entitled according to paragraphs 2 and 3, and to extending exemption from reciprocity to refugees who do not fulfil the conditions provided for in paragraphs 2 and 3.

5. The provisions of paragraphs 2 and 3 apply both to the rights and benefits referred to in Articles 13, 18, 19, 21 and 22 of this Convention and to rights and benefits for which this Convention does not provide.

Article 8

Exemption from exceptional measures.

With regard to exceptional measures which may be taken against the person, property or interests of nationals of a foreign State, the Contracting States shall not apply such measures to a refugee who is formally a national of the said State solely on account of such nationality. Contracting States which, under their legislation, are prevented from applying the general principle expressed in this Article, shall, in appropriate cases, grant exemptions in favour of such refugees.

Article 9

Provisional measures.

Nothing in this Convention shall prevent a Contracting State, in time of war or other grave and exceptional circumstances, from taking provisionally measures which it considers to be essential to the national security in the case of a particular person, pending a determination by the Contracting State that that person is in fact a refugee and that the continuance of such measures is necessary in his case in the interests of national security.

Article 10

Continuity of residence.

1. Where a refugee has been forcibly displaced during the Second World War and removed to the territory of a Contracting State, and is resident there, the period of such enforced sojourn shall be considered to have been lawful residence within that territory.

2. Where a refugee has been forcibly displaced during the Second World War from the territory of a Contracting State and has, prior to the date of entry into force of this Convention, returned there for the purpose of taking up residence, the period of residence before and after such enforced displacement shall be regarded as one uninterrupted period for any purposes for which uninterrupted residence is required.

Article 11

Refugee seamen.

In the case of refugees regularly serving as crew members on board a ship flying the flag of a Contracting State, that State shall give sympathetic consideration to their establishment on its territory and the issue of travel documents to them or their temporary admission to its territory particularly with a view to facilitating their establishment in another country.

II. JURIDICAL STATUS

Article 12

Personal status.

1. The personal status of a refugee shall be governed by the law of the country of his domicile or, if he has no domicile, by the law of the country of his residence.

2. Rights previously acquired by a refugee and dependent on personal status, more particularly rights attaching to marriage, shall be respected by a Contracting State, subject to compliance, if this be necessary, with the formalities required by the law of that State, provided that the right in question is one which would have been recognized by the law of that State had he not become a refugee.

Article 13

Movable and immovable property.

The Contracting States shall accord to a refugee treatment as favourable as possible and, in any event, not less favourable than that accorded to aliens generally in the same circumstances, as regards the acquisition of movable and immovable property and other rights pertaining thereto, and to leases and other contracts relating to movable and immovable property.

Article 14

Artistic rights and industrial property.

In respect of the protection of industrial property, such as inventions, designs or models, trade marks, trade names, and of rights in literary, artistic, and scientific works, a refugee shall be accorded in the country in which he has his habitual residence the same protection as is accorded to nationals of that country. In the territory of any other Contracting State, he shall be accorded the same protection as is accorded in that territory to nationals of the country in which he has his habitual residence

Article 15

Right of association.

As regards non-political and non-profit-making associations and trade unions the Contracting States shall accord to refugees lawfully staying in their territory the most favourable treatment accorded to nationals of a foreign country, in the same circumstances.

Article 16

Access to courts.

1. A refugee shall have free access to the courts of law on the territory of all Contracting States.

2. A refugee shall enjoy in the Contracting State in which he has his habitual residence the same treatment as a national in matters pertaining to access to the Courts, including legal assistance and exemption from *cautio judicatem solvi.*

3. A refugee shall be accorded in the matters referred to in paragraph 2 in countries other than that in which he has his habitual residence the treatment granted to a national of the country of his habitual residence.

III. GAINFUL EMPLOYMENT

Article 17

Wage-earning employment.

1. The Contracting States shall accord to refugees lawfully staying in their territory the most favourable treatment accorded to nationals of a foreign country in the same circumstances, as regards the right to engage in wage-earning employment.

2. In any case, restrictive measures imposed on aliens or the employment of aliens for the protection of the national labour market shall not be applied to a refugee who was already exempt from them at the date of entry into force of this Convention for the Contracting State concerned, or who fulfils one of the following conditions:

(a) He has completed three years' residence in the country,

(b) He has a spouse possessing the nationality of the country of residence. A refugee may not invoke the benefits of this provision if he has abandoned his spouse,

(c) He has one or more children possessing the nationality of the country of residence.

3. The Contracting States shall give sympathetic consideration to assimilating the rights of all refugees with regard to wage-earning employment to those of nationals, and in particular of those refugees who have entered their territory pursuant to programmes of labour recruitment or under immigration schemes.

Article 18

Self-employment.

The Contracting States shall accord to a refugee lawfully in their territory treatment as favourable as possible and, in any event, not less favourable than that accorded to aliens generally in the same circumstances, as regards the right to engage on his own account in agriculture, industry, handicrafts and commerce and to establish commercial and industrial companies.

Article 19

Liberal professions.

1. Each Contracting State shall accord to refugees lawfully staying in their territory who hold diplomas recognized by the competent authorities of that State, and who are desirous of practising a liberal profession, treatment as favourable as possible and, in any event, not less favourable than that accorded to aliens generally in the same circumstances.

2. The Contracting States shall use their best endeavours consistently with their laws and constitutions to secure the settlement of such refugees in the territories, other than the metropolitan territory, for whose international relations they are responsible

IV. WELFARE

Article 20

Rationing.

Where a rationing system exists, which applies to the population at large and regulates the general distribution of products in short supply, refugees shall be accorded the same treatment as nationals.

Article 21

Housing.

As regards housing, the Contracting States, in so far as the matter is regulated by laws or regulations or is subject to the control of public authorities, shall accord to refugees lawfully staying in their territory treatment as favourable as possible and, in any event, not less favourable than that accorded to aliens generally in the same circumstances.

Article 22

Public education.

(1) The Contracting States shall accord to refugees the same treatment as is accorded to nationals with respect to elementary education.

(2) The Contracting States shall accord to refugees treatment as favourable as possible, and, in any event, not less favourable than that accorded to aliens generally in the same circumstances, with respect to education other than elementary education and, in particular, as regards access to studies, the recognition of foreign school certificates, diplomas and degrees, the remission of fees and charges and the award of scholarships.

Article 23

Public relief.

The Contracting States shall accord to refugees lawfully staying in their territory the same treatment with respect to public relief and assistance as is accorded to their nationals.

Article 24

Labour legislation and social security.

(1) The Contracting States shall accord to refugees lawfully staying in their territory the same treatment as is accorded to nationals in respect of the following matters:

(a) In so far as such matters are governed by laws or regulations or are subject to the control of administrative authorities: remuneration, including family allowances where these form part of remuneration, hours of work, overtime arrangements, holidays with pay, restrictions on home work, minimum age of employment, apprenticeship and training, women's work and the work of young persons, and the enjoyment of the benefits of collective bargaining;

(b) Social security (legal provisions in respect of employment injury, occupational diseases, maternity, sickness, disability, old age, death, unemployment, family responsibilities and any other contingency which, according to national laws or regulations, is covered by a social security scheme), subject to the following limitations: (i) There may be appropriate arrangements for the maintenance of acquired rights and rights in course of acquisition; (ii) National laws or regulations of the country of residence may prescribe special arrangements concerning benefits or portions of benefits which are payable wholly out of public funds, and concerning allowances paid to persons who do not fulfil the contribution conditions prescribed for the award of a normal pension.

(2) The right to compensation for the death of a refugee resulting from employment injury or from occupational disease shall not be affected by the fact that the residence of the beneficiary is outside the territory of the Contracting State.

(3) The Contracting States shall extend to refugees the benefits of agreements concluded between them, or which may be concluded between them in the future, concerning the maintenance of acquired rights and rights in the process of acquisition in regard to social security, subject only to the conditions which apply to nationals of the States signatory to the agreements in question.

(4) The Contracting States will give sympathetic consideration to extending to refugees so far as possible the benefits of similar agreements which may at any time be in force between such Contracting States and non-contracting States.

V. ADMINISTRATIVE MEASURES

Article 25

Administrative assistance.

(1) When the exercise of a right by a refugee would normally require the assistance of authorities of a foreign country to whom he cannot have recourse, the Contracting States in whose territory he is residing shall arrange that such assistance be afforded to him by their own authorities or by an international authority.

(2) The authority or authorities mentioned in paragraph 1 shall deliver or cause to be delivered under their supervision to refugees such documents or certifications as would normally be delivered to aliens by or through their national authorities.

(3) Documents or certifications so delivered shall stand in the stead of the official instruments delivered to aliens by or through their national authorities, and shall be given credence in the absence of proof to the contrary.

(4) Subject to such exceptional treatment as may be granted to indigent persons, fees may be charged for the services mentioned herein, but such fees shall be moderate and commensurate with those charged to nationals for similar services.

(5) The provisions of this Article shall be without prejudice to Articles 27 and 28.

Article 26

Freedom of movement.

Each Contracting State shall accord to refugees lawfully in its territory the right to choose their place of residence and to move freely within its territory, subject to any regulations applicable to aliens generally in the same circumstances.

Article 27

Identity papers.

The Contracting States shall issue identity papers to any refugee in their territory who does not possess a valid travel document.

Article 28

Travel documents.

(1) The Contracting States shall issue to refugees lawfully staying in their territory travel documents for the purpose of travel outside their territory unless compelling reasons of national security or public order otherwise require, and the provisions of the Schedule to this Convention shall apply with respect to such documents. The Contracting States may issue such a travel document to any other refugee in their territory; they shall in particular give sympathetic consideration to the issue of such a travel document to refugees in their territory who are unable to obtain a travel document from the country of their lawful residence.

(2) Travel documents issued to refugees under previous international agreements by parties thereto shall be recognized and treated by the Contracting States in the same way as if they had been issued pursuant to this article.

Article 29

Fiscal charges.

(1) The Contracting States shall not impose upon refugee duties, charges or taxes, of any description whatsoever, other or higher than those which are or may be levied on their nationals in similar situations.

(2) Nothing in the above paragraph shall prevent the application to refugees of the laws and regulations concerning charges in respect of the issue to aliens of administrative documents including identity papers.

Article 30

Transfer of assets.

(1) A Contracting State shall, in conformity with its laws and regulations, permit refugees to transfer assets which they have

brought into its territory, to another country where they have been admitted for the purposes of resettlement.

(2) A Contracting State shall give sympathetic consideration to the application of refugees for permission to transfer assets wherever they may be and which are necessary for their resettlement in another country to which they have been admitted.

Article 31

Refugees unlawfully in the country of refuge.

(1) The Contracting States shall not impose penalties, on account of their illegal entry or presence, on refugees who, coming directly from a territory where their life or freedom was threatened in the sense of Article 1, enter or are present in their territory without authorization, provided they present themselves without delay to the authorities and show good cause for their illegal entry or presence.

(2) The Contracting States shall not apply to the movements of such refugees restrictions other than those which are necessary and such restrictions shall only be applied until their status in the country is regularized or they obtain admission into another country. The Contracting States shall allow such refugees a reasonable period and all the necessary facilities to obtain admission into another country.

Article 32

Expulsion.

(1) The Contracting States shall not expel a refugee lawfully in their territory save on grounds of national security or public order.

(2) The expulsion of such a refugee shall be only in pursuance of a decision reached in accordance with due process of law. Except where compelling reasons of national security otherwise require, the refugee shall be allowed to submit evidence to clear himself, and to appeal to and be represented for the purpose before competent authority or a person or persons specially designated by the competent authority.

(3) The Contracting States shall allow such a refugee a reasonable period within which to seek legal admission into another country. The Contracting States reserve the right to apply during that period such internal measures as they may deem necessary.

Article 33

Prohibition of expulsion or return ('refoulement').

(1) No Contracting State shall expel or return ('refouler') a refugee in any manner whatsoever to the frontiers of territories where his life or freedom would be threatened on account of his race, religion, nationality, membership of a particular social group or political opinion.

(2) The benefit of the present provision may not, however, be claimed by a refugee whom there are reasonable grounds for regarding as a danger to the security of the country in which he is, or who, having been convicted by a final judgment of a particularly serious crime, constitutes a danger to the community of that country.

Article 34

Naturalization.

The Contracting States shall as far as possible facilitate the assimilation and naturalization of refugees. They shall in particular make every effort to expedite naturalization proceedings and to reduce as far as possible the charges and costs of such proceedings.

VI. EXECUTORY AND TRANSITORY PROVISIONS

Article 35

Co-operation of the national authorities with the United Nations.

(1) The Contracting States undertake to co-operate with the Office of the United Nations High Commissioner for Refugees, or any other agency of the United Nations which may succeed it, in the exercise of its functions, and shall in particular facilitate its duty of supervising the application of the provisions of this Convention.

(2) In order to enable the Office of the High Commissioner, or any other agency of the United Nations which may succeed it, to make reports to the competent organs of the United Nations, the Contracting States undertake to provide them in the appropriate form with information and statistical data requested concerning:

(a) the condition of refugees,

(b) the implementation of this Convention, and

(c) laws, regulations and decrees which are, or may hereafter be, in force relating to refugees.

Article 36

Information on national legislation.

The Contracting States shall communicate to the Secretary-General of the United Nations the laws and regulations which they may adopt to ensure the application of this Convention.

Article 37

Relation to previous Conventions.

Without prejudice to Article 28, paragraph 2, of this Convention, this Convention replaces, as between parties to it, the Arrangements of 5 July 1922, 31 May 1924, 12 May 1926, 30 June 1928 and 30 July 1935, the Conventions of 28 October 1933 and 10 February 1938, the Protocol of 14 September 1939 and the Agreement of 15 October 1946.

VII. FINAL CLAUSES

Article 38

Settlement of disputes.

Any dispute between parties to this Convention relating to its interpretation or application, which cannot be settled by other means, shall be referred to the International Court of Justice at the request of any one of the parties to the dispute.

Article 39

Signature, ratification and accession.

(1) This Convention shall be opened for signature at Geneva on 28 July 1951 and shall hereafter be deposited with the Secretary-General of the United Nations. It shall be open for signature at the European Office of the United Nations from 28 July to 31 August 1951 and shall be re-opened for signature at the Headquarters of the United Nations from 17 September 1951 to 31 December 1952.

(2) This Convention shall be open for signature on behalf of all States Members of the United Nations, and also on behalf of any other State invited to attend the Conference of Plenipotentiaries on the Status of Refugees and Stateless Persons or to which an invitation to sign will have been addressed by the General Assembly. It shall be ratified and the instruments of ratification shall be deposited with the Secretary-General of the United Nations.

(3) This Convention shall be open from 28 July 1951 for accession by the States referred to in paragraph 2 of this Article. Accession shall be effected by the deposit of an instrument of accession with the Secretary-General of the United Nations.

Article 40

Territorial application clause.

(1) Any state may, at the time of signature, ratification or accession, declare that this Convention shall extend to all or any of the territories for the international relations of which it is responsible. Such a declaration shall take effect when the Convention enters into force for the State concerned.

(2) At any time thereafter any such extension shall be made by notification addressed to the Secretary-General of the United Nations and shall take effect as from the ninetieth day after the day of receipt by the Secretary-General of the United Nations of this notification, or as from the date of entry into force of the Convention for the State concerned, whichever is the later.

(3) With respect to those territories to which this Convention is not extended at the time of signature, ratification or accession, each State concerned shall consider the possibility of taking the necessary steps in order to extend the application of this Convention to such territories, subject, where necessary for

constitutional reasons, to the consent of the governments of such territories.

Article 41

Federal clause.

In the case of a Federal or non-unitary State, the following provisions shall apply:

(a) With respect to those Articles of this Convention that come within the legislative jurisdiction of the federal legislative authority, the obligations of the Federal Government shall to this extent be the same as those of Parties which are not Federal States,

(b) With respect to those Articles of this Convention that come within the legislative jurisdiction of constituent States, provinces or cantons which are not, under the constitutional system of the federation, bound to take legislative action, the Federal Government shall bring such Articles with a favourable recommendation to the notice of the appropriate authorities of States, provinces or cantons at the earliest possible moment.

(c) A Federal State Party to this Convention shall, at the request of any other Contracting State transmitted through the Secretary-General of the United Nations, supply a statement of the law and practice of the Federation and its constituent units in regard to any particular provision of the Convention showing the extent to which effect has been given to that provision by legislative or other action.

Article 42

Reservations.

(1) At the time of signature, ratification or accession, any State may make reservations to articles of the Convention other than to Articles 1, 3, 4, 16(1), 33, 36–46 inclusive.

(2) Any State making a reservation in accordance with paragraph 1 of this article may at any time withdraw the reservation by a communication to that effect addressed to the Secretary-General of the United Nations.

Article 43

Entry into force.

(1) This Convention shall come into force on the ninetieth day following the day of deposit of the sixth instrument of ratification or accession.

(2) For each State ratifying or acceding to the Convention after the deposit of the sixth instrument of ratification or accession, the Convention shall enter into force on the ninetieth day following the date of deposit by such State of its instrument of ratification or accession.

Article 44

Denunciation.

(1) Any Contracting State may denounce this Convention at any time by a notification addressed to the Secretary-General of the United Nations.

(2) Such denunciation shall take effect for the Contracting State concerned one year from the date upon which it is received by the Secretary-General of the United Nations.

(3) Any State which has made a declaration or notification under Article 40 may, at any time thereafter, by a notification to the Secretary-General of the United Nations, declare that the Convention shall cease to extend to such territory one year after the date of receipt of the notification by the Secretary-General.

Article 45

Revision.

(1) Any Contracting State may request revision of this Convention at any time by a notification addressed to the Secretary-General of the United Nations.

(2) The General Assembly of the United Nations shall recommend the steps, if any, to be taken in respect of such request.

Article 46

Notifications by the Secretary-General of the United Nations. The Secretary-General of the United Nations shall inform all Members of the United Nations and non-member States referred to in Article 39:

(a) of declarations and notifications in accordance with Section B of Article 1;

(b) of signatures, ratifications and accessions in accordance with Article 39;

(c) of declarations and notifications in accordance with Article 40;

(d) of reservations and withdrawals in accordance with Article 42;

(e) of the date on which this Convention will come into force in accordance with Article 43;

(g) of requests for revision in accordance with Article 45.

IN FAITH WHEREOF the undersigned, duly authorized, have signed this Convention on behalf of their respective Governments, DONE at GENEVA, this twenty-eighth day of July, one thousand nine hundred and fifty-one, in a single copy, of which the English and French texts are equally authentic and which shall remain deposited in the archives of the United Nations, and certified true copies of which shall be delivered to all Members of the United Nations and to the non-member States referred to in Article 39

Protocol relating to the Status of Refugees

(signed 31 January 1967)

The States Parties to the present Protocol,

Considering that the Convention relating to the Status of Refugees done at Geneva on 28 July 1951 (hereinafter referred to as the Convention) covers only those persons who have become refugees as a result of events occurring before 1 January 1951,

Considering that new refugee situations have arisen since the Convention was adopted and that the refugees concerned may therefore not fall within the scope of the Convention,

Considering that it is desirable that equal status should be enjoyed by all refugees covered by the definition in the Convention irrespective of the dateline 1 January 1951,

Have agreed as follows.

Article 1

General provision.

1. The States Parties to the present Protocol undertake to apply Articles 2 to 34 inclusive of the Convention to refugees as hereinafter defined.

2. For the purpose of the present Protocol, the term 'refugee' shall, except as regards the application of paragraph 3 of this Article, mean any person within the definition of Article 1 of the Convention as if the words 'As a result of events occurring before 1 January 1951 and ... 'and the words' ... a result of such events', in Article 1 A (2) were omitted.

3. The present Protocol shall be applied by the States Parties hereto without any geographic limitation, save that existing declarations made by States already Parties to the Convention in accordance with Article 1 B (1) (a) of the Convention, shall, unless extended under Article 1 B (2) thereof, apply also under the present Protocol.

Article 2

Co-operation of the national authorities with the United Nations.

1. The States Parties to the present Protocol undertake to co-operate with the Office of the United Nations High Commissioner for Refugees, or any other agency of the United Nations which may succeed it, in the exercise of its functions, and shall in particular facilitate its duty of supervising the application of the provisions of the present Protocol.

2. In order to enable the Office of the High Commissioner, or any other agency of the United Nations which may succeed it, to

make reports to the competent organs of the United Nations, the States Parties to the present Protocol undertake to provide them with the information and statistical data requested, in the appropriate form, concerning: (a) The condition of refugees; (b) The implementation of the present Protocol; (c) Laws, regulations and decrees which are, or may hereafter be, in force relating to refugees.

Article 3

Information on national legislation.

The States Parties to the present Protocol shall communicate to the Secretary-General of the United Nations the laws and regulations which they may adopt to ensure the application of the present Protocol.

Article 4

Settlement of disputes.

Any dispute between States Parties to the present Protocol which relates to its interpretation or application and which cannot be settled by other means shall be referred to the International Court of Justice at the request of any one of the parties to the dispute.

Article 5

Accession.

The present Protocol shall be open for accession on behalf of all States Parties to the Convention and of any other State Member of the United Nations or member of any of the specialized agencies or to which an invitation to accede may have been addressed by the General Assembly of the United Nations. Accession shall be effected by the deposit of an instrument of accession with the Secretary-General of the United Nations.

Article 6

Federal clause.

In the case of a Federal or non-unitary State, the following provisions shall apply:

(a) With respect to those articles of the Convention to be applied in accordance with Article 1, paragraph 1, of the present Protocol that come within the legislative jurisdiction of the federal legislative authority, the obligations of the Federal Government shall to this extent be the same as those of States Parties which are not Federal States;

(b) With respect to those articles of the Convention to be applied in accordance with Article 1, paragraph 1, of the present Protocol that come within the legislative jurisdiction of constituent States, provinces or cantons which are not, under the constitutional system of the federation, bound to take legislative action, the Federal Government shall bring such articles with a favourable recommendation to the notice of the appropriate authorities of States, provinces or cantons at the earliest possible moment;

(c) A Federal State Party to the present Protocol shall, at the request of any other State Party hereto transmitted through the Secretary-General of the United Nations, supply a statement of the law and practice of the Federation and its constituent units in regard to any particular provision of the Convention to be applied in accordance with Article 1, paragraph 1, of the present Protocol, showing the extent to which effect has been given to that provision by legislative or other action.

Article 7

Reservations and declarations.

1. At the time of accession, any State may make reservations in respect of Article 4 of the present Protocol and in respect of the application in accordance with Article 1 of the present Protocol of any provisions of the Convention other than those contained in Articles 1, 3, 4, 16(1) and 33 thereof, provided that in the case of a State Party to the Convention reservations made under this Article shall not extend to refugees in respect of whom the Convention applies.

2. Reservations made by States Parties to the Convention in accordance with Article 42 thereof shall, unless withdrawn, be applicable in relation to their obligations under the present Protocol.

3. Any State making a reservation in accordance with paragraph 1 of this Article may at any time withdraw such reservation by a communication to that effect addressed to the Secretary-General of the United Nations.

4. Declarations made under Article 40, paragraphs 1 and 2, of the Convention by a State Party thereto which accedes to the present Protocol shall be deemed to apply in respect of the present Protocol, unless upon accession a notification to the contrary is addressed by the State Party concerned to the Secretary-General of the United Nations. The provisions of Article 40, paragraphs 2 and 3, and of Article 44, paragraph 3, of the Convention shall be deemed to apply *mutatis mutandis* to the present Protocol.

Articles 8–11

Entry into force, denunciation, notifications etc.

United Nations Human Settlements Programme—UN-Habitat

Address: POB 30030, 00100 Nairobi, Kenya.

Telephone: (20) 7623120; **fax:** (20) 7623477; **e-mail:** infohabitat@unhabitat.org; **internet:** www.unhabitat.org.

UN-Habitat was established as the United Nations Centre for Human Settlements, UNCHS-Habitat, in October 1978 to service the intergovernmental Commission on Human Settlements. It became a full UN programme in January 2002, serving as a focus for human settlements and sustainable urban development activities in the UN system. UN-Habitat was mandated by the Second UN Conference on Human Settlements, Habitat II, which was held in Istanbul, Turkey, in June 1996, to pursue the Habitat Agenda, focusing on the objectives of adequate shelter for all and sustainable human settlements in an urbanizing world; further mandates are derived from the September 2000 UN Millennium Forum Declaration and Agenda for Action, and from the June 2001 Habitat II review conference's Declaration on Cities and other Human Settlements in the New Millennium.

Organization

(June 2012)

GOVERNING COUNCIL

The Governing Council (formerly the Commission on Human Settlements) meets once every two years and has 58 members, serving for four years. Sixteen members are from Africa, 13 from Asia, 10 from Latin America and the Caribbean, six from eastern European countries, and 13 from western European and other countries. The Committee of Permanent Representatives to UN-Habitat, which meets at least four times a year, functions as an inter-sessional subsidiary body of the Governing Council. The Governing Council reports to the UN General Assembly through ECOSOC.

SECRETARIAT

The Secretariat services the Governing Council, implements its resolutions and ensures the integration and co-ordination of technical co-operation, research and policy advice. It comprises the Office of the Executive Director; the Regional and Technical Co-operation Division; the Monitoring and Research Division; the Shelter and Sustainable Human Settlements Development Division; and the Financing Human Settlements Division.

Executive Director: Dr JOAN CLOS (Spain).

REGIONAL OFFICES

Regional Office for Africa and the Arab States: POB 30030, Nairobi, Kenya 00100; tel. (20) 623221; fax (20) 623904; e-mail roaas@unhabitat.org; internet www.unhabitat.org/roaas.

Regional Office for Asia and the Pacific: ACROS Fukuoka Building, 8th Floor 1-1-1 Tenjin, Chuo-ku Fukuoka 810, Japan; tel. (92) 724-7121; fax (92) 724-7124; e-mail habitat.fukuoka@unhabitat.org; internet www.fukuoka.unhabitat.org.

Regional Office for Latin America and the Caribbean: Rua Rumânia 20, Cosme Velho 22240-140, Rio de Janeiro, Brazil; tel. (21) 3235-8550; fax (21) 3235-8566; e-mail rolac@habitat-lac.org; internet www.onuhabitat.org.

In addition, there are Liaison and Information Offices in Geneva, Switzerland; Brussels, Belgium; Budapest, Hungary; New York, USA; Beijing, the People's Republic of China; Moscow, Russia; and Chennai, India. A Best Practices Offices for City-to-City Co-operation is located in Barcelona, Spain. Habitat Programme Managers are located in almost 40 UNDP country offices.

Activities

Since 2008 at least one-half of the world's population has been resident in towns and cities (compared with about one-third in 1950; and forecast to rise to 70% by 2050). Africa is the most rapidly urbanizing continent: the proportion of Africans residing in urban areas is forecast to rise from nearly 40% in 2012 to 60% by 2050. Of the world's urban population, about one-third (about 1,000m. people) lives in slums without access to basic sanitation. Many local authorities do not have adequate mechanisms to monitor either formal or informal urban growth in a systematic manner. UN-Habitat supports and conducts capacity-building and operational research, provides technical co-operation and policy advice, and disseminates information with the aim of strengthening the development and management of human settlements. It is mandated to support the UN Millennium Development Goals (MDGs) of halving, by 2015, the proportion of people without sustainable access to safe drinking water and improving significantly the lives of at least 100m. slum dwellers by 2020.

In June 1996 representatives of 171 national governments and of more than 500 municipal authorities attending Habitat II adopted a Global Plan of Action (the 'Habitat Agenda'), which incorporated detailed programmes of action to realize economic and social development and environmental sustainability, and endorsed the conference's objectives of ensuring 'adequate shelter for all' and 'sustainable human settlements development in an urbanizing world'. UN-Habitat provides the leadership and serves as a focal point for the implementation of the Agenda. It collaborates with national governments, private sector and non-governmental institutions and UN bodies to achieve the objectives of Agenda 21 (see below). A special session of the UN General Assembly, entitled 'Istanbul + 5', was held in June 2001 to report on the implementation of the recommendations of the Habitat II conference. The special session adopted a Declaration on Cities and Other Human Settlements in the New Millennium that reaffirmed commitment to the objectives of the Habitat Agenda and urged an intensification of efforts towards eradicating widespread poverty, which was identified as the main impediment to achieving these, and towards promoting good governance. The special session also resolved to increase international co-operation in several other areas, including addressing HIV/AIDS, urban crime and violence, environmental issues, and the problems posed by conflicts and refugees; and recommended the enhancement of the status and role of UNCHS (Habitat). Consequently, in December 2001 the General Assembly authorized the elevation of the body to a full UN programme with a strengthened mandate to address and implement the Habitat Agenda and, in January 2002, UN-Habitat was inaugurated.

UN-Habitat's activities over the six-year period 2008–13 are governed by a medium-term strategic and institutional plan, adopted in April 2007, that aims by 2013 to help establish the necessary conditions for arresting the growth of slums and to set the stage for the subsequent reduction in and reversal of the number of slum dwellers world-wide. The plan focuses on: advocacy and monitoring; affordable land and housing; environmentally sound basic infrastructure and services; participatory urban planning, management and governance; and innovative human settlements finance, with each focus area accompanied by a set of strategic objectives and achievement indicators. In addition, a peer review mechanism comprising several Habitat Agenda partners was to be established during the period of the plan as a means of monitoring progress and achievement. UN-Habitat's work programme for 2012–13 was being implemented through the following four sub-programmes: Shelter and sustainable human development; Monitoring the Habitat Agenda; Regional and technical co-operation; and Human settlements financing.

In February 2009 UN-Habitat and the International Olympic Committee signed a Memorandum of Understanding aimed at encouraging the empowerment through sport of young people living in vulnerable and disadvantaged communities world-wide. It was envisaged that the agreement would support development through sport and would promote the MDGs to alleviate poverty and to improve the living conditions of slum dwellers everywhere. (More than one-half of slum dwellers are young people.) A follow-up committee was to meet annually to develop further a programme of international co-operation between the two organizations. In October 2010 UN-Habitat signed a partnership agreement with the University for Peace to support a Masters degree in Sustainable Urban Governance and Peace.

In June 2011 a UN-HABITAT Charter of Values was launched; this was to provide a framework underpinning joint activities with private sector partners.

UN-Habitat participated in the preparatory process for the UN Conference on Sustainable Development (Rio+20), which was convened in June 2012, in Rio de Janeiro, Brazil. In April 2011 the Governing Council adopted a resolution on 'Sustainable urban development through expanding equitable access to land, housing, basic services and infrastructure', underpinning UN-Habitat's contribution to Rio+20. 'Cities' were identified by the Conference Secretariat as one of the most critical sustainable development issues.

SHELTER AND SUSTAINABLE HUMAN SETTLEMENT DEVELOPMENT

The UN Housing Rights Programme (UNHRP), launched jointly by UN-Habitat and OHCHR in April 2002, supports states and other stakeholders with the implementation of their Habitat Agenda commitments to realizing the universal right to adequate housing. In 2004 UN-Habitat established an Advisory Group on Forced Evictions, with a mandate to monitor forced evictions of people with no or inadequate legal security of tenure, and to identify and promote alternatives including in situ upgrading of accommodation and negotiated resettlement. UN-Habitat's programme on Rapid Urban Sector Profiling for Sustainability (RUSPS) involves an accelerated action-oriented assessment of urban conditions in particular cities in seven thematic areas (governance; slums; gender and HIV/AIDS; urban environment; local economic development; basic urban services; and cultural heritage), with a view to developing and implementing tailor-made urban poverty reduction policies. Through its Strengthening Training Institutions programme UN-Habitat supports regional and national training institutions by organizing regional workshops to develop capacity-building strategies and to analyse training need assessments; by designing new training manuals and other tools; by developing, jointly with partners, generic training manuals and handbooks; by educating trainers; and by supporting institutions with the design and implementation of national training programmes. In addition, UN-Habitat supports training and other activities designed to strengthen management development (in particular in the provision and maintenance of services and facilities) at local and community level.

UN-Habitat implements a programme entitled 'Localizing Agenda 21' (LA21), to assist local authorities in developing countries to achieve more sustainable development and to address local environmental and infrastructure-related problems. The Programme targets secondary cities and supports city-to-city co-operation initiatives. A Sustainable Cities Programme, operated jointly with UNEP, is concerned with incorporating environmental issues into urban planning and management, in order to ensure sustainable and equitable development. The Programme is active in some 30 cities world-wide, although a prepared series of policy guidelines is used in many others. Some 95% of the Programme's resources are spent at city level to strengthen the capacities of municipal authorities and their public-, private- and community-sector partners in the field of environmental planning and management, with the objective that the concepts and approaches of the Programme are replicated throughout the region.

An Urban Management Programme aims to strengthen the contribution of cities and towns in developing countries towards human development, including economic growth, social advancements, the reduction of poverty and the improvement of the environment. The Programme (active in 140 cities in 58 countries) is an international technical co-operation project, of which UN-Habitat is the executing agency, the World Bank is an associated agency, while UNDP provides core funding and monitoring. The Programme is operated through regional offices, in collaboration with bilateral and multilateral support agencies, and brings together national and local authorities, community leaders and representatives of the private sector to consider specific issues and solutions to urban problems. The related Safer Cities Programme was initiated in 1996 to prevent and address urban violence through capacity-building at local government and city level. In November 2010 UN-Habitat, working with UNIFEM, now part of UN Women, inaugurated a Global Safe Cities for Women and Girls Programme. Pilot projects were to be implemented in the poorest areas of five cities: Quito (Ecuador), Cairo (Egypt), New Delhi (India), Port Moresby (Papua New Guinea) and Kigali (Rwanda). UN-Habitat's Global Campaign for Secure Tenure and Global Campaign on Urban Governance both emphasize urban poverty reduction.

UN-Habitat is supporting the development of a Sustainable Urban Development Network (SUD-Net) which aims to mobilize local, regional and global partners to achieve a multilateral and inter-disciplinary approach to sustainable urban development. SUD-Net envisaged strengthening capacity building at local level, involving the local community in decision-making, and promoting knowledge sharing and the exchange of good practices. A Cities in Climate Change Initiative was established in 2008 as a component of SUD-Net. It aimed to work with local governments and other bodies involved in the environmental planning and management process in order to address problems relating to climate change and to reduce greenhouse gas emissions. UN-Habitat was actively involved in the 15th Conference of the Parties (COP) of the UN Framework Convention on Climate Change (UNFCCC), which was held in Copenhagen, Denmark, in December 2009. In particular, it urged greater support to cities working to reduce the emission of harmful gases and to counter the impact of climate change. In September 2010 UN-Habitat, with UNEP and the World Bank, launched an International Standard for Determining Greenhouse Gas Emissions for Cities. In December, prior to the 16th COP of the UNFCCC, held in Cancun, Mexico, UN-Habitat joined with five other UN agencies in declaring their commitment to work to counter climate change.

UN-Habitat contributes to relief, rehabilitation and development activities undertaken by the UN in areas affected by regional and civil conflict. In December 2003 UN-Habitat signed a Memorandum of Understanding with UNHCR that covered several areas of co-operation including sheltering refugees and returnees, settlement and infrastructure planning, and property rights. Within the inter-agency emergency response system UN-Habitat provides shelter, water and sanitation under the Emergency Shelter and Early Recovery 'clusters'. UN-Habitat also provides assessment and technical support in the aftermath of natural disasters and is concerned with sustainable reconstruction, capacity-building, risk reduction and emergency preparedness activities and flood vulnerability reduction. Reconstruction and recovery activities are co-ordinated by the Risk and Disaster Management Unit. In November 2010 UN-Habitat concluded a technical assessment of the damage and housing needs resulting from extensive flooding in Pakistan in July–August.

In September 2011 the first annual 'Shelter Academy', a gathering of mayors and senior local government officials from Africa, Asia and Latin America, met in Rotterdam, Netherlands, to discuss the challenges that climate change presents to port cities.

FINANCING HUMAN SETTLEMENTS

UN-Habitat participates in implementing the human settlements component of Agenda 21, which was adopted at the UN Conference on Environment and Development in June 1992, and is also responsible for the chapter of Agenda 21 that refers to solid waste management and sewage-related issues. The Settlement Infrastructure and Environment Programme was initiated in 1992 to support developing countries in improving the environment of human settlements through policy advice and planning, infrastructure management and enhancing awareness of environmental and health concerns in areas such as water, sanitation, waste management and transport. In October 2002 UN-Habitat launched a Water and Sanitation Trust Fund, with the aim of supporting the goal of halving the proportion of the world's population lacking access to basic sanitation or clean water by 2015, that was set by the World Summit on Sustainable Development (WSSD), held in Johannesburg, South Africa, during August–September 2002 to assess strategies for strengthening the implementation of Agenda 21. The Water and Sanitation Programme promotes policy dialogue, information exchange, water education and awareness-raising; monitors progress towards achieving the MDG targets on improving access to safe water and sanitation; and designs replicable model-setting initiatives, i.e. the Lake Victoria Region Water and Sanitation Initiative and the Mekong Regional Water and Sanitation Initiative. The Water and Sanitation Programme incorporates two regional sub-programmes. The Managing Water for African Cities Programme, jointly co-ordinated by UN-Habitat and UNEP, promotes efficient water demand management, capacity-building to alleviate the environmental impact of urbanization on freshwater resources, information exchange on water management and conservation issues, and the exchange of best practices in urban water management. In March 2003 UN-Habitat and the Asian Development Bank (ADB) signed an agreement on the establishment of a parallel Water for Asian Cities Programme.

In 2009 UN-Habitat concluded preparations to establish a Global Water Operators' Partnership Alliance (GWOPA) secretariat, in accordance with decisions adopted at the fourth World Water Forum, held in Mexico, in March 2006. The first international conference of the GWOPA was convened in Zaragoza, Spain, in December 2009. The Alliance supports the establishment and development of regional Water Operators' Partnerships, and supports training and capacity building activities. The Alliance, in collaboration with Google and an international benchmarking network, has developed a Geo-Referenced Utility Benchmarking System (GRUBS) as a means of presenting utility performance (benchmarking) data in a searchable format online. The benchmarking of service providers was a key component of a separate h2.O Monitoring Services to Inform and Empower Initiative which aimed to improve methodologies for monitoring the urban environment and acquiring data and to enhance the effectiveness of investment planning. The project also envisaged the development and application of Urban Inequity Surveys and Citizen Report Cards.

UN-Habitat administers a Global Energy Network for Urban Settlements (GENUS) which aims to support and encourage partnerships between the public and private sector, governmental and non-governmental organizations, and other international, national and civil society agencies concerned with improving energy access for the urban poor, in order to advance best practices, technologies and capacity-building. The first GENUS workshop was convened in Yogyakara, Indonesia, in May 2009, with a focus on transport for the urban poor in Asia. A second was held in Nairobi, Kenya, in October, on slum electrification in Africa. In October 2010, at a meeting on 'Energy from Waste', held in San José, Costa Rica, GENUS in Latin America was inaugurated, with a focus on elaborating solutions for waste management.

In October 2003 UN-Habitat predicted that, owing to unprecedented urban growth, accompanied by poverty and social inequalities, the number of slum dwellers world-wide would double to about 2,000m. by 2030. The September 2005 World Summit of UN heads of state approved the development of a Slum Upgrading Facility (SUF) to improve access to credit and other resources for slum dwellers, in order to improve their homes and living conditions. Pilot projects were subsequently established in Ghana, Indonesia, Sri Lanka and Tanzania. Within each project Local Finance Facilities have been established, both at city and national level, to help communities access credit from local commercial banks.

In April 2007 the UN-Habitat Governing Council approved the establishment of a trust fund—the Experimental Reimbursable Seeding Operations and Other Innovative Mechanism (ERSO)—within the Habitat and Human Settlements Foundation, to support the financing of loans and credits for low-income housing, infrastructure and settlements upgrading. In November 2008 a new Opportunities Fund for Urban Youth-Led Development was inaugurated.

MONITORING AND RESEARCH

UN-Habitat maintains a Global Urban Observatory (GUO) to monitor implementation of the Habitat Agenda and to report on and support local and national plans of action and ongoing research and development. The Observatory operates through GUONet, a global network of regional, national and local urban observatories, and through partner institutions that provide training and other capacity-building expertise. The Observatory also maintains the GUO databases of urban indicators, statistics and city profiles. The Observatory works closely with the Best Practices and Local Leadership Programme, which was established in 1997 to support the implementation of the Habitat Agenda through the use of information and networking. In May 2008 the GUO helped to organize an expert meeting on slum identification, mapping and monitoring, held in Enschede, Netherlands; issues under discussion included methodologies for identifying slums, for example geo-information technologies such as Geographic Information Systems and Remote Sensing. In April 2011 UN-HABITAT launched www.urbangateway.org, a forum for knowledge-sharing among urban policy makers and managers globally.

In November 2004 UN-Habitat hosted the first meeting of the Global Research Network on Human Settlements (HS-Net). HS-Net was to act as a forum for human settlements researchers, research institutions and networks, and was to advise the UN-Habitat Secretariat on the preparation of its two 'flagship reports', the *Global Report on Human Settlements* and *State of the World's Cities*. For the two-year period 2010–11 UN-Habitat prepared, additionally, four editions of *State of the Region's Cities*, for Africa, Asia and the Pacific, Eastern Europe, and Latin America.

WORLD URBAN FORUM

UN-Habitat provides the secretariat of the World Urban Forum (WUF), the first of which was held in April–May 2002, in Nairobi, Kenya, with participation by national governments and Habitat Agenda partners. The Forum represented a merger of the former Urban Environment Forum and International Forum on Urban Poverty. It aims to promote international co-operation in shelter and urban development issues. The second WUF was held in Barcelona, Spain, in September 2004; the third in Vancouver, Canada, in June 2006; and the fourth in Nanjing, China, in November 2008. WUF 5 was held in Rio de Janeiro, Brazil, in March 2010. The sixth WUF was scheduled to be convened in Naples, Italy, in September 2012, on the theme 'The Urban Future'. Since 2006 a youth forum has been convened prior to the main Forum. In 2010 this was restructured as the World Urban Youth Assembly further to promote youth-led development.

ASSOCIATED BODY

Cities Alliance: 1818 H St, NW, Washington, DC, 20433 USA; tel. (202) 473-9233; fax (202) 522-3224; e-mail info@citiesalliance.org; internet www.citiesalliance.org; f. 1999, jointly by UNCHS (Habitat) and the World Bank, as a coalition of local authorities, governments and development organizations; aims to reduce urban poverty and improve the effectiveness of urban development co-operation and urban investment; in Sept. 2000 the UN Millennium Summit endorsed the Alliance's new Cities without Slums action plan as a target within its Millennium Development Goals i.e. 'by 2020, to have achieved a significant improvement in the lives of at least 100m. slum dwellers'; facilitates collaboration between govts and authorities to achieve best practices in slum upgrading initiatives; supports the formulation of city development strategies (CDS) in order to promote equitable and sustainable urban growth; in 2009 established a new CDS sub-group to develop a CDS conceptual framework; mems: UNEP, UN-Habitat, the World Bank, European Union, Shack/Slumdwellers International, United Cities and Local Government, World Association of the Major Metropolises (Metropolis), 16 national govts; assoc. mems: ILO, UNDP; Man. WILLIAM COBBETT.

Finance

UN-Habitat's work programme is financed from the UN regular budget, and from voluntary contributions to the UN Habitat and Human Settlements Foundation and to the Programme's technical co-operation activities. The approved budget for the two-year period 2012–13 amounted to US $393.2m. comprising a regular budget allocation of $22.4m., $180.7m. from the Habitat and Human Settlements Foundation (of which $110.5m. was for special purposes), and $190.0m. from the Technical Co-operation Fund.

Publications

Global Report on Human Settlements (annually).

State of the World's Cities (every 2 years).

State of the Region's Cities.

UMP e-Newsletter (quarterly).

Urban World (quarterly).

Technical reports and studies, occasional papers, bibliographies, directories.

United Nations Office on Drugs and Crime—UNODC

Address: Vienna International Centre, POB 500, 1400 Vienna, Austria.

Telephone: (1) 26060-0; **fax:** (1) 26060-5866; **e-mail:** unodc@unodc.org; **internet:** www.unodc.org.

The UN Office on Drugs and Crime (UNODC) was established in November 1997 (as the Office for Drug Control and Crime Prevention—ODCCP) to strengthen the UN's integrated approach to issues relating to drug control, crime prevention and international terrorism. A reform programme was launched in 2002 aimed at integrating further the Office's areas of activity. The Office was renamed in October of that year. It comprises two principal components: the United Nations Drug Programme and the United Nations Crime Programme.

Organization

(June 2012)

UNODC comprises the following four divisions: Operations; Treaty Affairs; Research and Public Affairs; and Management. There is a UNODC liaison office in New York and there are 54 field offices world-wide.

Executive Director: YURI FEDOTOV (Russia).

Activities

UNITED NATIONS DRUG PROGRAMME

The UN Drug Programme was established in 1991 as the UN International Drug Control Programme (UNDCP) and was renamed in 2002. It is responsible for co-ordinating the activities of all UN specialized agencies and programmes in matters of international drug control. The structures of the former Division of Narcotic Drugs, the UN Fund for Drug Abuse Control and the secretariat of the International Narcotics Control Board (see below) were integrated into the Programme. Accordingly, it became the focal point for promoting the UN Decade Against Drug Abuse (1991–2000) and for assisting member states to implement the Global Programme of Action that was adopted by the UN General Assembly in 1990 with the objective of achieving an international society free of illicit drugs and drug abuse. At a special session of the General Assembly, held in June 1998, heads of state and representatives of some 150 countries adopted a global strategy, formulated on the basis of UNDCP proposals, to reduce significantly the production of and demand for illicit substances over the next decade. UNDCP subsequently launched the Global Assessment Programme on Drug Abuse (GAP), which aimed to establish one global and nine regional drug abuse data systems to collect and evaluate data on the extent of and patterns of illegal substance abuse. In March 2009 UNODC reviewed progress since the 1998 General Assembly special session and adopted a Draft Political Declaration and Plan of Action on the future of drug control. The Declaration recognized that countries have a shared responsibility for solving the global drugs problem, and recommended a 'balanced and comprehensive approach', an emphasis on human rights, and a focus on health as a basis for international drugs policy. The Action Plan proposed some 30 solutions to problems in the following six areas of concern: reducing drug abuse and dependence; reducing the illicit supply of drugs; control of precursors and of amphetamine-type stimulants; international co-operation to eradicate the illicit cultivation of crops and to provide alternative development; countering money-laundering; and judicial co-operation. UNODC supports national monitoring systems that assess the extent and evolution of illicit crops in the world's principal drug-growing countries: Bolivia, Colombia and Peru (coca); Afghanistan, Laos and Myanmar (opium; Afghanistan accounted for around 90% of global opium supply in 2011); and Morocco (cannabis). Crop surveys are facilitated by a combination of satellite sensing (with the assistance of the European Space Agency), aerial surveillance and ground-level surveys, which provide a reliable collection and analysis mechanism for data on the production of illicit substances. UNODC's Alternative Development Programme supports projects to create alternative sources of income for farmers economically dependent on the production of illicit narcotic crops. In March 2012 UNODC and the UN Industrial Development Organization signed a Memorandum of Understanding on establishing a strategic partnership aimed at promoting grass-roots development and alternative livelihoods in poor rural communities hitherto dependent on the cultivation of illegal drugs crops. The UN Drug Programme aims to suppress trafficking in illegal substances and supports efforts to enhance regional and cross-border co-operation in implementing law enforcement initiatives. It serves as an international centre of expertise and information on drug abuse control, with the capacity to provide legal and technical assistance in relevant areas of concern. It supports governments in efforts to strengthen their institutional capacities for drug control (for example, drug identification and drug law enforcement training) and to prepare and implement national drug control 'action plans'.

The Programme's approach to reducing demand for illicit drugs combines strategies in the areas of prevention, treatment and rehabilitation. It sponsors activities to generate public awareness of the harmful effects of drug abuse, for example through its Global Youth Network project, which aims to involve young people in prevention activities, and through the system of goodwill ambassadors associated with its 'Sports Against Drugs' campaign. The Programme works with governments, as well as non-governmental and private organizations and local community partners, in the detection, treatment, rehabilitation and social reintegration of drug addicts. It also undertakes research to monitor the drugs problem: for example, assessing the characteristics of drug-takers and the substances being used in order to help identify people at risk of becoming drug-takers and to enhance the effectiveness of national programmes to address the issue (see also GAP, above).

Through the joint UNODC-World Customs Organization Container Control Programme, which has been operational since 2004 and consists of port control units that comprise both analysts and search teams of customs and police officers, maritime containers are systematically targeted and inspected with a view to ensuring that they have not been commandeered for criminal purposes; the Programme has intercepted containers that were in the process of carrying illicit drugs, as well as precursor chemicals, endangered species, hazardous materials and goods misleadingly labelled for fraudulent purposes. During 2010 UNODC launched the Airport Communication Project (AIRCOP), initially focusing on 10 international airports, located in West Africa, Brazil and Morocco. Under the Project, Joint Airport Interdiction Task Forces (JAITFs) were to be established with connections to international law enforcement databases and communication networks, to enable information sharing, including the instantaneous transmission between international airports of operational information on passengers and cargo, in order to facilitate the interception of illicit cargo.

The Programme promotes implementation of the following major treaties which govern the international drug control system: the Single Convention on Narcotic Drugs (1961) and a Protocol amending the Convention (1972); the Convention on Psychotropic Substances (1971); and the UN Convention against Illicit Traffic in Narcotic Drugs and Psychotropic Substances (1988). Among other important provisions, these treaties aim to restrict severely the production of narcotic drugs, while ensuring an adequate supply for medical and scientific purposes, to prevent profits obtained from the illegal sale of drugs being diverted into legal usage and to secure the extradition of drugs-traffickers and the transfer of proceedings for criminal prosecution. The Programme assists countries to adapt their national legislation and drug policies to facilitate their compliance with these conventions and to enhance co-ordinated inter-governmental efforts to control the movement of narcotic drugs. It services meetings of the International Narcotics Control Board (INCB), an independent body responsible for promoting and monitoring government compliance with the provisions of the drug control treaties, and of the Commission on Narcotic Drugs, which, as a functional committee of ECOSOC, is the main policy-making organ within the UN system on issues relating to international drug abuse control. The 52nd session of the Commission on Narcotic Drugs, held at UNODC headquarters in March 2009, adopted a Political Declaration and Plan of Action on International Co-operation towards an Integrated and Balanced Strategy to Counter the World Drug Problem. The INCB is promoting co-ordinated global action to prevent illicit internet sales of internationally controlled prescription drugs by so-called 'online pharmacies'. The increasing occurrence globally of abuse of prescription drugs was reported on by the INCB in February 2010.

UNODC co-operates closely with other international, regional and non-governmental organizations and maintains dialogue with agencies advocating drug abuse control. It is a co-sponsor of the Joint Programme on HIV/AIDS (UNAIDS), which was established on 1 January 1996. UNODC's participation is in recognition of the importance of international drug control efforts in preventing the spread of HIV/AIDS. In October 2004 UNODC and the World Customs Organization launched a joint Container Control Programme aimed at improving port control measures in developing countries.

Some 80% of opiates produced in Afghanistan are smuggled out of that country by transnational organized criminal groups via Iran and Pakistan, with the remainder being routed through central Asian countries; illegal trafficking threatens regional security and development and enriches criminal networks. In May 2003, at a Ministerial Conference on Drug Routes from Central Asia to Europe, convened in Paris, France, UNODC played a leading role in launching the Paris Pact, a partnership of more than 50 countries and international organizations aimed at combating the traffic in and consumption of Afghan opiates and related problems in affected countries along the Afghan opiates-trafficking routes. In June 2006 a further Ministerial Conference, on Drug Trafficking Routes from Afghanistan, held in Moscow, Russia, demonstrated support for the Paris Pact. In October 2007, within the frame of the Paris Pact, UNODC organized a meeting of senior international counter-narcotics officials, in Kabul, Afghanistan, aimed at strengthening efforts to restrict the supply of illicit drugs from Afghanistan. UNODC supports the Central Asia Regional Information and Co-ordination Centre (CARICC), which was established in Almatı, Kazakhstan, in February 2006, to combat illicit drugs-trafficking in that region. In April UNODC and the Collective Security Treaty Organization (then comprising Armenia, Belarus, Kazakhstan, Kyrgyzstan, Russia and Tajikistan; Uzbekistan joined in June) signed a protocol on developing joint projects and sharing information with the aim of addressing drugs-trafficking, terrorism and transborder crime in Central Asia. In December 2008 UNODC launched the Rainbow Strategy, a regional initiative comprising seven operational plans (covering areas such as precursor chemicals, border management, financial flows, and drug abuse prevention and treatment), aimed at facilitating the implementation of the Paris Pact. The Triangular Initiative, organized by UNODC and launched in June 2007, promotes drugs control co-operation between Afghanistan, Iran and Paksistan. In December 2011 UNODC launched a new regional programme for Afghanistan and neighbouring countries. Meeting in February 2012 partners in the Paris Pact adopted the Vienna Declaration on committing to act in a 'balanced and comprehensive manner' against the illicit Afghan opium trade.

In October 2008—during a High-level Conference on Drugs Trafficking as a Security Threat to West Africa, convened jointly by UNODC, ECOWAS and the Cape Verde Government, in Praia, Cape Verde—UNODC published a report identifying the expanding use in recent years of points in West Africa (particularly Guinea-Bissau and Ghana) as a transit route for narcotics being traded illegally between Latin America and Europe. The Executive Director of UNODC warned that West Africa was at risk of becoming an epicentre for drugs-trafficking, representing a serious threat to public health and security in the region. He proposed the establishment of a West African intelligence-sharing centre, and urged the promotion of development and the strengthening of the rule of law as a means of reducing regional vulnerability to drugs and crime. At the Conference ECOWAS adopted a Political Declaration on Drugs Trafficking and Organized Crime in West Africa, and approved an ECOWAS Regional Response Plan. In March 2009 UNODC and the African Union (AU) launched a joint project in support of a Plan of Action on Drug Control and Crime Prevention (2007–12) that had been adopted by the AU in December 2007. The UNODC-AU co-operation aimed to strengthen the policy-making, norm-setting and capacity-building capabilities of the AU Commission and sub-regional organizations (notably ECOWAS). In July 2009 UNODC released a report entitled *Transnational Trafficking and the Rule of Law in West Africa: A Threat Assessment*, which addressed the regional impact of trafficking in human beings, illicit drugs, petroleum, cigarettes, toxic waste and electronic waste ('e-waste'). The report also addressed the prevalence in West Africa of trafficking in counterfeit medications, including antibiotics, antiretroviral drugs and medicines to combat malaria and TB, many of which contained few active ingredients. In that month UNODC, other UN agencies, ECOWAS and INTERPOL launched the *West Africa Coast Initiative (WACI)*, which aimed to build national and regional capacities to combat drugs-trafficking and organized crime in, initially, four pilot post-conflict countries: Côte d'Ivoire, Guinea-Bissau, Liberia and Sierra Leone. In February 2010 the pilot countries signed the 'WACI- Freetown Commitment', endorsing the implementation of the initiative, and agreeing to establish specialized transnational crime units on their territories. WACI activities were to be expanded to Guinea during 2012.

UNITED NATIONS CRIME PROGRAMME

Through the United Nations Crime Programme, which is implemented by the Centre for International Crime Prevention (CICP), established in 1997, UNODC is responsible for crime prevention, criminal justice and criminal law reform. The Programme oversees the application of international standards and norms relating to these areas, for example the Minimum Rules for the Treatment of Prisoners, Conventions against Torture, and Other Cruel, Inhuman or Degrading Treatment or Punishment, and Safeguards Guaranteeing the Protection of the Rights of Those Facing the Death Penalty. The Programme provides member states with technical assistance to strengthen national capacities to establish appropriate legal and criminal justice systems and to combat transnational organized crime (see below). It supports the Commission on Crime Prevention and Criminal Justice, a functional committee of ECOSOC, which provides guidance in developing global anti-crime policies. The Programme manages the Global Programme against Corruption, a Global Programme on Organized Crime, which aims to analyse emerging transnational criminal organizations and assist countries to formulate strategies to combat the problem, and a Global Programme against Trafficking in Human Beings (trafficking in human beings for sexual exploitation or forced labour is regarded as the fastest-growing area of international organized crime). In March 2007 UNODC and partners initiated the UN Global Initiative to Fight Human Trafficking (UN.GIFT), with the aim of raising awareness world-wide of the phenomenon, promoting effective preventative measures, and improving law enforcement methods. In February 2008 UN.GIFT organized the Vienna Forum to Fight Human Trafficking, with participation by UN member states and agencies, other international organizations, academics, and representatives of the private sector and civil society. In February 2009 UNODC issued the *Global Report on Trafficking in Persons*, which used data drawn from 155 countries to compile an assessment of the world-wide scope of human trafficking and ongoing means of combating it. The Report included an overview of trafficking patterns, of legal steps taken in response, and also country-specific information on reported trafficking and prosecutions. The Report found sexual exploitation to be the most common purpose of human trafficking (representing 79% of incidences), followed by forced labour (18%), although it was stated that the prevalence of trafficking for forced labour may be under-represented. About one-fifth of known trafficking victims were reported to be children. Intra-regional and domestic trafficking were found to be more common than long-distance trafficking in persons. In March 2009 UNODC launched the Blue Heart Campaign against Human Trafficking, which aimed to use the media and the social networking arena to raise awareness of global trafficking. UNODC administers a UN Voluntary Trust Fund for Victims of Trafficking in Persons, which was established in November

2010 to support the objectives of a new UN Global Plan of Action to Combat Trafficking in Persons, adopted by the UN General Assembly in July of that year.

The CICP supported member states in the preparation of the UN Convention against Transnational Organized Crime (UNTOC, also known as the Palermo Convention), which was opened for signature in December 2000 at a UN conference on combating organized crime held in Sicily, Italy, and entered into force in September 2003. UNTOC has three additional Protocols: the Protocol to Prevent, Suppress and Punish Trafficking in Persons, especially Women and Children (entered into force December 2003, sometimes referred to as the 'Trafficking Protocol'); the Protocol against the Smuggling of Migrants by Land, Air and Sea (entered into force January 2004); and the Protocol against the Illicit Manufacturing and Trafficking in Firearms, Their Parts and Components and Ammunition (entered into force July 2005). The Programme assisted with the formulation of the UN Convention against Corruption (UNCAC), which was opened for signature in December 2003 in Mérida, Mexico, and entered into force in December 2005; the implementation of UNCAC in signatory states is monitored systematically under a mechanism established in November 2009. In April 2012 UNODC launched the Integrity Initial Public Offering (IPO) initiative, under which private companies and investors can finance efforts by developing countries to combat corruption, which is regarded as a major obstacle to sustainable development.

The UN Crime Programme promotes research and undertakes studies of new forms of crime prevention, in collaboration with the UN Interregional Crime and Justice Research Institute (UNICRI). It also maintains a UN Crime and Justice Information Network database (UNCJIN), which provides information on national crime statistics, publications and links to other relevant intergovernmental agencies and research and academic institutes. In October 2008 UNODC and INTERPOL signed a joint agreement establishing the first International Anti-Corruption Academy; the Academy, to be based in Laxenburg, Austria, was to provide training to police personnel, government officials, academics and representatives of NGOs and private sector entities. An online UNODC/INTERPOL training course, aimed at people engaged in international co-operation against terrorism, was launched in October 2009.

UNODC provides assistance to states in the area of penal reform, placing particular emphasis on training prison staff and responding to the needs of women and vulnerable prisoners. The 18th session of the Commission on Crime Prevention and Criminal Justice, hosted at UNODC headquarters in April 2009, promoted a shift from a punitive to a more rehabilitative approach to addressing crime, and urged a reduction in prison overcrowding and the advancement of the provision of legal aid in criminal justice systems. The meeting also discussed means of addressing the emergence of a 'global crime wave': the agenda covered issues including economic fraud (often conducted over the internet), identity-related crime, mafia penetration of the international financial system, and cyber-terrorism.

The UNODC's Terrorism Prevention Branch, established in 1999, researches trends in terrorist activity and assists countries to improve their capabilities to investigate and prevent acts of terrorism. The Branch promotes international co-operation in combating the problem, and has initiated a study into the connections between terrorist activity and other forms of crime. A comprehensive global database on global terrorism, including counter-terrorism conventions, national criminal laws and relevant case laws, was launched by UNODC in June 2009.

The UN Global Programme against Money Laundering (GPML), established in March 1999, assists governments with formulating legislation against money laundering and establishing and maintaining appropriate frameworks to counter the problem. GPML activities include the provision of technical assistance, training, and the collection, research and analysis of crime data. The Programme, in collaboration with other governmental organizations, law enforcement agencies and academic institutions, co-ordinates the International Money Laundering Information Network (IMoLIN), an internet-based information resource (accessible at www.imolin.org). IMoLIN incorporates the Anti-Money Laundering International Database (a comprehensive database on money-laundering legislation throughout the world that constituted a key element in the Office's activities in support of the elaboration of UNTOC—see above). At the first GPML Forum, held in the Cayman Islands in March 2000, the governments of 31 participating 'offshore' financial centres agreed in principle to adopt internationally accepted standards of financial regulation and measures against money laundering.

UNODC organized several regional preparatory meetings prior to the 11th UN Congress on Crime Prevention and Criminal Justice, which was held in Bangkok, Thailand, in April 2005.

In December 2008 the Executive Director of UNODC made a number of recommendations aimed at deterring, arresting and prosecuting individuals engaging in maritime piracy in waters off the Horn of Africa, including a proposal that so-called 'shipriders' should be deployed on warships operating in that area, with responsibility for arresting pirates and bringing them to justice in neighbouring countries. UNODC supports states in the region with the implementation of the UNTOC and other relevant international instruments. During 2009 UNODC launched a counter-piracy programme (CPP), with an initial focus on Kenya, where, by 2012, some 50 people had been convicted of piracy. The programme supports efforts to detain and prosecute piracy suspects, and supports financial intelligence units and law enforcement agencies in East Africa and the Horn of Africa. The CPP's mandate has been widened to cover six countries in the region. In February 2012 UNODC's Executive Director reported that, in 2011, pirates made US $170m. in ransom money from hijacking vessels, that the laundering of the proceeds of piracy was causing consumer prices to rise steeply in the Horn of Africa, and that illicit money flows linked to piracy were also being reinvested into other criminal activities, involving drugs, weaponry, alcohol smuggling, and human trafficking. In late 2012 UNODC, the World Bank and INTERPOL were jointly to issue a report on illicit financial flows linked to piracy. During November 2011 the UN Secretary-General sent an assessment mission—co-led by UNODC and the UN Department of Political Affairs—to several Gulf of Guinea states (Benin, Nigeria, Gabon and Angola) to determine the scope of the threat of piracy in the Gulf of Guinea region. Some 28 pirate attacks were reported in the Gulf of Guinea in 2011, a sharp increase over 11 attacks reported in 2010.

Meeting in St Petersburg, Russia, in November 2010, at the International Tiger Forum, the heads of UNODC, the Convention on International Trade in Endangered Species of Wild Fauna and Flora (CITES), the World Customs Organization, INTERPOL and the World Bank jointly approved the establishment of a new International Consortium on Combating Wildlife Crime (ICCWC), with the aim of combating the poaching of wild animals and illegal trade in wild animals and wild animal products.

In 2007 UNODC and the World Bank jointly launched the Stolen Asset Recovery (StAR) initiative, which aimed to address the theft of public assets from developing countries, and to promote direct government-to-government assistance. Activities to be implemented under StAR included developing and strengthening partnerships, and implementing pilot programmes aimed at recovering stolen assets through the provision of technical support, including the promotion of mutual legal assistance. In April 2009 the G20 recommended that StAR review and propose mechanisms to strengthen international co-operation relating to asset recovery.

A UNODC regional programme for Eastern Africa, covering 2009–12, was adopted in November 2009 by a regional ministerial conference on 'Promoting the Rule of Human Security in Eastern Africa', held in Nairobi, Kenya. The programme was based on the following three pillars: countering trafficking, organized crime and terrorism; combating corruption and promoting justice and integrity; and improving health and human development. In December 2010 UNODC and the League of Arab States jointly launched a five-year Regional Programme on Drug Control, Crime Prevention and Criminal Justice Reform for the Arab States, covering the period 2011–15, and based, similarly, on the following pillars: countering illicit trafficking, organized crime and terrorism; promoting justice and integrity; and drug prevention and improving health.

Finance

UNODC receives an allocation from the regular budget of the UN (US $40.9m. in 2012–13), although voluntary contributions from member states and private organizations represent the majority (about 90%) of its resources. UNODC's total projected resources for the two-year period 2012–13 amounted to some $417.8m.

Publications

Afghanistan Opium Survey (annual).

Bulletin on Narcotics.

Forum on Crime and Society.

eNews@UNODC (electronic newsletter).

Global Report on Crime and Justice.

Global Report on Trafficking in Persons.

Multilingual Dictionary of Narcotic Drugs and Psychotropic Substances Under International Control.

Technical Series.

The United Nations and Juvenile Justice: A Guide to International Standards and Best Practices.

UNODC Update (quarterly).

World Drug Report.

United Nations Peace-keeping

Address: Department of Peace-keeping Operations, Room S-3727-B, United Nations, New York, NY 10017, USA.

Telephone: (212) 963-8077; **fax:** (212) 963-9222; **internet:** www.un.org/Depts/dpko/.

United Nations peace-keeping operations have been conceived as instruments of conflict control. The UN has used these operations in various conflicts, with the consent of the parties involved, to maintain international peace and security, without prejudice to the positions or claims of parties, in order to facilitate the search for political settlements through peaceful means such as mediation and the good offices of the UN Secretary-General. Each operation is established with a specific mandate, which requires periodic review by the UN Security Council. In 1988 the United Nations Peace-keeping Forces were awarded the Nobel Peace Prize.

United Nations peace-keeping operations fall into two categories: peace-keeping forces and observer missions. Peace-keeping forces are composed of contingents of military and civilian personnel, made available by member states. These forces assist in preventing the recurrence of fighting, restoring and maintaining peace, and promoting a return to normal conditions. To this end, peace-keeping forces are authorized as necessary to undertake negotiations, persuasion, observation and fact-finding. They conduct patrols and interpose physically between the opposing parties. Peace-keeping forces are permitted to use their weapons only in self-defence.

Military observer missions are composed of officers (usually unarmed), who are made available, on the Secretary-General's request, by member states. A mission's function is to observe and report to the Secretary-General (who, in turn, informs the Security Council) on the maintenance of a cease-fire, to investigate violations and to do what it can to improve the situation. Peace-keeping forces and observer missions must at all times maintain complete impartiality and avoid any action that might affect the claims or positions of the parties.

A UN Stand-by Arrangements System (UNSAS) became operational in 1994; participating countries make available specialized civilian and military personnel as well as other services and equipment. In January 1995 the UN Secretary-General presented a report to the Security Council, reassessing the UN's role in peace-keeping. The document stipulated that UN forces in conflict areas should not be responsible for peace-enforcement duties, and included a proposal for the establishment of a 'rapid reaction' force, which would be ready for deployment within a month of being authorized by the Security Council. During 2000–08 the multinational UN Stand-by Forces High Readiness Brigade (SHIRBRIG), based in Denmark, was available to the UN, deploying troops to the UN Mission in Ethiopia and Eritrea (in 2000) and the UN Mission in Liberia (2003), and assisting (during 2004–05) with preparations for the deployment of the UN Mission in Sudan. In March 2003 a SHIRBRIG team supported ECOWAS in planning the deployment of a peace-keeping mission to Côte d'Ivoire. In 2007 it was asked to assist the African Union (AU) in planning its mission in Sudan (AMISOM), and, during 2008, it assisted the AU with the development of an African Standby Force. SHIRBRIG was fully disbanded in June 2009.

In August 2000 a report on UN peace-keeping activities prepared by a team of experts appointed by the Secretary-General assessed the aims and requirements of peace-keeping operations and recommended several measures to improve the performance of the Department of Peace-keeping Operations (DPKO), focusing on its planning and management capacity from the inception of an operation through to post-conflict peace-building activities, and on its rapid response capability. Proposed reforms included the establishment of a body to improve co-ordination of information and strategic analysis requirements; the promotion of partnership arrangements between member states (within the context of UNSAS) enabling the formation of several coherent multinational brigades, and improved monitoring of the preparedness of potential troop contributor nations, with a view to facilitating the effective deployment of most operations within 30 days of their authorization in a Security Council resolution; the adoption of 'on-call' reserve lists to ensure the prompt deployment of civilian police and specialists; the preparation of a global logistics support strategy; and a restructuring of the DPKO to improve administrative efficiency. The study also urged an increase in resources for funding peace-keeping operations and the adoption of a more flexible financing mechanism, and emphasized the importance of the UN's conflict prevention activities. In November the Security Council, having welcomed the report, adopted guidelines aimed at improving its management of peace-keeping operations, including providing missions with clear and achievable mandates. In June 2001 the Council adopted a resolution incorporating a Statement of principles on co-operation with troop-contributing countries, which aimed to strengthen the relationship between those countries and the UN and to enhance the effectiveness of peace-keeping operations. A new Rapid Deployment Level within UNSAS was inaugurated in July 2002. In 2004 the Department established a Special Investigation Team, at the request of the UN Secretary-General, which, in November, visited the Democratic Republic of the Congo to examine allegations of sexual exploitation and abuse committed by peace-keeping personnel. In July 2007 a new Department of Field Operations was established within the UN Secretariat to provide expert support and resources to enhance personnel, budget, information and communication technology, and other logistical aspects of UN peace-keeping operations in the field. At the same time a restructuring of the DPKO was initiated. A new Office for the Rule of Law and Security Institutions was established, and the Military Division was reconstituted as the Office of Military Affairs.

The UN's peace-keeping forces and observer missions are financed in most cases by assessed contributions from member states of the organization. In recent years a significant expansion in the UN's peace-keeping activities has been accompanied by a perpetual financial crisis within the organization, as a result of the increased financial burden and some member states' delaying payment. At 30 April 2012 outstanding assessed contributions to the peace-keeping budget amounted to some US $1,360m.

By June 2012 the UN had deployed a total of 67 peace-keeping operations, of which 13 were authorized in the period 1948–88 and 54 since 1988. At 31 May 2012 117 countries were contributing some 98,695 uniformed personnel to 16 ongoing operations, of whom 81,594 were peace-keeping troops, 14,492 police and 2,609 military observers.

In 2012 the DPKO was also directly supporting the UN Assistance Mission in Afghanistan, a political and peace-building mission that was established in March 2002.

African Union (AU)/UN Hybrid Operation in Darfur—UNAMID

Address: El Fasher, Sudan.

Joint AU-UN Special Representative: IBRAHIM GAMBARI (Nigeria).

Force Commander: Lt-Gen. PATRICK NYAMVUMBA (Rwanda).

Police Commissioner: JAMES OPPONG-BOANUH (Ghana).

Establishment and Mandate: UNAMID was established by a resolution of the UN Security Council in July 2007, authorized to take necessary action to support the implementation and verification of the Darfur Peace Agreement signed in May 2006 by the Sudanese Government and a rebel faction in Darfur, southern Sudan. UNAMID was also mandated to protect civilians, to provide security for humanitarian assistance, to support an inclusive political process, to contribute to the promotion of human rights and rule of law, and to monitor and report on the situation along the borders with Chad and the Central African Republic. An AU-UN Joint Mediation Support Team for Darfur (JMST) and a Tripartite Committee on UNAMID (including representatives of the UN, AU and Government of Sudan) meet periodically.

Activities: UNAMID assumed command of the AU Mission in Sudan (AMIS), comprising 10 battalions, in December 2007. In February 2008 UNAMID's Joint Special Representative signed a status of forces agreement with the minister of foreign affairs of Sudan, covering logistical aspects of the mission. In March UNAMID police units conducted their first confidence-building patrols in areas under rebel control in northern Darfur. In May UNAMID's Force Commander condemned aerial attacks against villages in northern Darfur, allegedly by Sudanese forces. Throughout 2008 an estimated 317,000 civilians were newly displaced from their homes in Darfur. A delegation of the UN Security Council visited the region in June and expressed concern at the mission's lack of adequate equipment and troop levels. In July 2008 the UN designated Darfur a 'security phase four' area (a designation that permits the UN to relocate staff temporarily pending an improvement in the security situation). At the end of June 2008 a new joint AU-UN Chief Mediator was appointed, based at UNAMID headquarters in El Fasher. A Joint Support Co-ordination Mechanism (JSCM) Office in Addis Ababa, Ethiopia, comprising liaison officers and communications equipment, was established in November to ensure effective consultation between the UN and AU headquarters. In October 2008 the UN Secretary-General reported that little progress had been achieved in the implementation of the 2006 Darfur Peace Agreement, that violent unrest continued to prevail, and that the conditions in Darfur were not conducive to undertaking a successful peace-keeping operation. From late 2008 activities were undertaken to bring the 10 former AMIS battalions up to full strength in terms of military personnel and equipment. Nevertheless, the Secretary-General reported in February 2009 (at which time the designated security level in Darfur remained at phase four) that UNAMID's operational capabilities continued to be limited by lack of critical and key military enabling equipment, logistical constraints, and the reluctance of many troop- and police-contributing countries to deploy to it well-trained personnel and efficient contingent-owned equipment. In addition, there was concern at restrictions on the movement of troops and on the issuing of visa and vehicle licence applications that were being imposed by the Sudanese authorities. In January 2009 UNAMID, jointly with OHCHR, issued a public report on a law enforcement operation by the Sudan Government in August 2008 against targets in Kalma camp for internally displaced persons (IDPs) in southern Darfur, that had resulted in 33 civilian fatalities and 108 civilian injuries; the report found that the use of force had been indiscriminate and disproportionate, in violation of international law. UNAMID has provided a security presence around Kalma camp. In early 2009 an escalation of violence in the Mahajeriya region of southern Darfur resulted in the displacement of some 46,000 people, the majority of whom moved to the Zam Zam refugee camp near El Fasher. UNAMID undertook to deliver daily water supplies, as well as to conduct protection patrols in and around the camp. The mission also began construction of a community policy centre in the camp. UNAMID provided security and other logistical support to help to ensure the continued distribution of humanitarian assistance following the expulsion from the country, in March, of 13 international non-governmental organizations (NGOs) and the dissolution of three national NGOs by the Sudanese authorities (who claimed that they had collaborated with investigations being conducted by the International Criminal Court). From late 2009 UNAMID provided logistical support to the Government's disarmament, demobilization and rehabilitation programme. In January 2010 the UN Secretary-General reported that the capability of UNAMID batallions in Darfur continued to be a cause of concern, with a number of units not having sufficient major equipment. At that time UNAMID undertook geophysical investigations to locate new water sources around mission camps. UNAMID assisted the former UN Mission in Sudan and the Sudanese authorities with transporting electoral materials to remote locations and with training more than 10,000 local police officers in preparation for the municipal, legislative and presidential elections that were held in April.

In March 2009 an AU High-Level Panel on Darfur (AUPD), led by the former President of South Africa, Thabo Mbeki, was established to address means of securing peace, justice, and reconciliation in Darfur. The panel conducted a series of hearings in Sudan over subsequent months, and, in October, issued a report of its findings and recommendations; a key recommendation was the creation of a hybrid court, comprising both AU and Sudanese judges, to prosecute crimes against humanity committed in Darfur. During October a new AU High-Level Implementation Panel (AUHIP) on Sudan was established, with a mandate to support the implementation of all AUPD recommendations, and to assist the relevant Sudanese parties with the implementation of a Comprehensive Peace Agreement (CPA) concluded in January 2005 (see under UNISFA). In November 2009 an inaugural conference of Darfurian civil society organizations was convened, in Doha, Qatar, in order to strengthen and to further political negotiations to achieve a peace settlement. A second conference was held in July 2010. In February and March 2010, respectively, two rebel groupings that had been operating in Darfur signed framework agreements with the Sudanese Government aimed at resolving the conflict; however, consequent negotiations with the largest rebel group, aimed at securing a cease-fire, stalled in May. During that month violent unrest in Darfur caused nearly 600 fatalities, the highest number since the deployment of the mission. UNAMID strengthened security measures and provided additional medical care in some of the larger IDP camps where inter-tribal conflict was becoming a major security concern. In late July 7,000 people in Kalma camp sought refuge at the UNAMID Community Policing Centre. In the following month UNAMID and the Sudanese Government agreed to establish a joint committee to resolve problems in Kalma, which hosted some 82,000 IDPs. In late August a consultative meeting of representatives of UNAMID, the AU, the USA and the Sudanese President agreed that UNAMID and the Sudanese Government would work closely together to improve the security situation in Darfur and to support stabilization and development of the region. The UN Secretary-General welcomed efforts by the Sudanese authorities to investigate, and restore order in the aftermath of, an attack launched in early September by armed assailants targeting local men attending the market in the Northern Darfur village of Tabarat, causing some 37 fatalities and precipitating the displacement of around 3,000 villagers.

In early April 2011 the Sudanese National Electoral Commission initiated preparations for a referendum to be held on the future status of Darfur, and requested material and technical assistance from UNAMID. Towards the end of April the JMST presented a draft peace agreement to the Sudan Government and rebel groupings. The draft agreement was considered by an All-Darfur Stakeholders' Conference, convened, with support from UNAMID, in Doha, Qatar, in late May; participants in the Conference endorsed a communiqué providing for the draft document (the Doha Document for Peace in Darfur—DDPD) to form the basis for achieving a permanent cease-fire and comprehensive Darfurian peace settlement. The DDPD addressed issues including power sharing, wealth sharing, human rights, justice and reconciliation, compensation, returns, and internal dialogue, and provided for the establishment of a Cease-fire Commission, a Darfur Regional Authority, and for a Darfuri to be appointed as the second Vice-President of Sudan. In June the UN Secretary-General welcomed the DDPD as the basis for resolving the Darfur conflict. In mid-July the Sudanese Government and the 'Liberation and Justice Movement', an alliance of rebel groupings, signed an accord on the adoption of the DDPD. Shortly afterwards the two sides also signed a Protocol on the Political Participation of the Liberation and Justice Movement and Integration of its Forces. Meanwhile, UNAMID, a participant in the DDPD Implementation Follow-on Commission, prepared, with civil society representatives, a plan for the dissemination throughout Darfur of information on the Document. In August UNAMID chaired the first meeting of the Cease-Fire Commission established under the provisions of the DDPD.

During late May–early June 2011 UNAMID intervened to assist 11 IDPs at Hassa Hissa camp who had been detained by a gang of youths also sheltering there; although the detainees were eventually released, it was reported in June that 11 IDPs in the area had been killed. At the beginning of May UNAMID and humanitarian agencies active in Darfur launched Operation Spring Basket, aimed at enhancing access to remote parts of Darfur and thereby providing humanitarian aid to around 400,000 beneficiaries. UNAMID continued to implement Quick Impact Projects in Darfur, in support of the education sector, infrastructure and local facilities. UNAMID, where requested, provides logistical and security support to humanitarian agencies assisting returnees to West Darfur. In response to reported cases of crop destruction by nomads in West Darfur, and complaints that returnees from Chad were also contributing to crop destruction, UNAMID liaised in the second half of 2011 with local crop protection committees. The formation in 2011 of a subcommittee comprising UNAMID and Sudanese government security entities led to a significant decrease in restrictions on the movements of UNAMID security patrols in the latter part of the year. There were continued reports of criminal attacks on UN personnel, including the theft of UNAMID vehicles, during 2008–12.

During January–March 2012 UNAMID undertook 14,172 ground patrols and 4,460 flights. In early March UNAMID completed the an operation to verify positions held by former rebels; information acquired during the verification operation was to be used by the Cease-fire Commission in disarmament, demobilization, and reintegration/integration planning. In April 2012 the UN Secretary-General stated that UNAMID personnel numbers would be adjusted downwards, and that troop numbers at various sites would be reconfigured, with the largest UNAMID presence being confined to areas with the highest risk of armed conflict. More frequent and longer patrols, with expanded use of temporary operating bases, were also recommended.

Operational Strength: UNAMID has an authorized strength of up to 19,555 military personnel and 6,432 police. The mission's operational strength at 31 May 2012 comprised 17,364 troops, 591 military observers and 5,511 police (in formed units, each comprising up to 140 personnel); the mission was supported by 475 UN Volunteers and (at 29 February 2012) by 1,097 international civilian personnel and 2,923 local civilian staff.

Finance: The budget for UNAMID amounted to US $1,689m. for the period 1 July 2011–30 June 2012, funded from a Special Account comprising assessed contributions from UN member states.

United Nations Disengagement Observer Force—UNDOF

Address: Camp Faouar, Syria.

Force Commander: Maj.-Gen. Natalio C. Ecarma (Philippines).

Establishment and Mandate: UNDOF was established for an initial period of six months by a UN Security Council resolution in May 1974, following the signature in Geneva, Switzerland, of a disengagement agreement between Syrian and Israeli forces. The mandate has since been extended by successive resolutions. The initial task of the mission was to take over territory evacuated in stages by the Israeli troops, in accordance with the disengagement agreement, to hand over territory to Syrian troops, and to establish an area of separation on the Golan Heights.

Activities: UNDOF continues to monitor the area of separation; it carries out inspections of the areas of limited armaments and forces; uses its best efforts to maintain the cease-fire; carries out demining activities; and undertakes activities of a humanitarian nature, such as arranging the transfer of prisoners and war-dead between Syria and Israel. The Force operates exclusively on Syrian territory.

During 2011 demonstrations by anti-Government protesters in Syria extended to the area of UNDOF's operations; the Force continued to supervise the area of separation using fixed positions and patrols, and undertook fortnightly inspections of equipment and force levels in the areas of limited armaments and forces. In mid-May and early June groups of Palestinian protesters gathered at a site known as the 'family shouting place', opposite the village of Majdal Chams in the area of limitation on the Israeli-occupied Golan side; on the second occasion the protesters attempted to breach the cease-fire line. UNDOF monitored the proceedings using armoured patrols, engaged with the Syrian and Israeli militaries, and attempted to diffuse tensions. Subsequently UNDOF strengthened its force protection measures, including the fortification of its positions. During the first half of 2012 UNDOF's area of operations continued to be affected by escalating instability in Syria. UNDOF continued to monitor the area of separation, through the use of fixed positions and patrols, to ensure the exclusion from it of military forces. In March officers of the Military Observer Group Golan reportedly came under gunfire.

Operational Strength: At 31 May 2012 the mission comprised 1,055 troops, and supported by 147 international and local civilian personnel (as at 29 February 2012). Military observers of UNTSO's Observer Group Golan help UNDOF in the performance of its tasks, as required.

Finance: The General Assembly appropriation for the operation over the period 1 July 2011–30 June 2012 amounted to US $50.5m.

United Nations Integrated Mission in Timor-Leste—UNMIT

Address: Dili, Timor-Leste.

Telephone: 3301400; **fax:** 3304410; **internet:** www.unmit.org.

Special Representative of the UN Secretary-General and Head of Office: Finn Reske-Nielsen (Denmark) (acting).

Police Commissioner: Luis Miguel Carrilho (Portugal).

Establishment and Mandate: In succession to the UN Mission in Support of East Timor (UNMISET), the UN Transitional Administration in East Timor (UNTAET) and the UN Office in Timor-Leste (UNOTIL), UNMIT was established by UN Security Council Resolution 1704 in August 2006 to support the Timor-Leste authorities with consolidating stability, promoting democratic governance and facilitating the process of national reconciliation. The mission was to co-operate with the Australian-led International Stabilization Force (ISF, also comprising troops from Malaysia, New Zealand and Portugal), which had been deployed to Timor-Leste in late May 2006 to secure key installations following an eruption of violent unrest in the previous month. The mission was authorized to assist with all aspects of the staging of the 2007 presidential and legislative elections, with restoring and maintaining public security, and with the promotion of human rights and justice.

Activities: In January 2007 UNMIT signed a trilateral agreement with the Timorese authorities and Australian Government to enhance co-ordination of all security-related activities. During the first half of 2007 the UNMIT police presence was expanded to provide full support to the Timorese national police and ISF in facilitating public security during the electoral process. In May

UNMIT reported that the presidential election, conducted in April–May, had been 'free and fair'. Parliamentary elections were conducted in late June, and in early August the Special Representative of the UN Secretary-General (SRSG) welcomed the establishment of a new coalition Government. The inauguration of the new Government, however, prompted renewed violent unrest in several districts of the country. Consequently, during August, UNMIT convened a meeting of representatives of national political groupings to address means of calming the unrest, and also offered practical assistance to the Timorese authorities towards restoring security and delivering humanitarian aid to those affected by the violence. In November a delegation of the UN Security Council visited the country. In February 2008 the UN condemned violent attacks against the Prime Minister and President in Timor-Leste. In that month, in extending UNMIT's mandate by one year, the Security Council requested that UNMIT continue to assist the Government to enhance the effectiveness of the judiciary, to review and reform the security sector, to co-ordinate donor co-operation for institutional capacity-building, and to assist in the formulation of poverty reduction and economic growth strategies. In June UNMIT confirmed that it was to assist the Timor-Leste authorities to undertake a comprehensive review of its security sector. In August the mission published a second report on the human rights situation in Timor-Leste, focusing on access to justice and the security sector. The mission's mandate was extended by a further 12-month period in February 2009. In March the Prime Minister and the SRSG announced that there was to be a gradual resumption of responsibilities for police operations by the national police force, the Policia Nacional de Timor-Leste (PNTL), contingent on the outcome of a joint assessment process. The first transfer of primary responsibility for policing from UNMIT to the PNTL was officially conducted in Lautém district in May 2009, and in September the PNTL assumed responsibility for the national police training centre, in Dili. In February 2010 the UN Security Council endorsed a recommendation of the Secretary-General to reconfigure the UNMIT police component, including its drawdown, in accordance with the phased transfer of policing responsibilities to the PNTL. In January a technical assessment mission was sent to Timor-Leste to make recommendations to the UN Secretary-General concerning UNMIT's role during 2010–12. By that time UNMIT had transferred responsibility to the PNTL for policing in 10 districts and six units, and an Immigration Department, Border Patrol Unit and INTERPOL office were operational. In February 2011 the UN Security Council, extending the mission's mandate by a further 12-month period, acknowledged the need for a continued UN police presence in the country in order to support further constitutional development, PNTL capacity building and preparations for presidential and parliamentary elections. (The former were conducted in March–April 2012, and the latter scheduled to be held in July). In late February 2011 a PNTL-UNMIT Police Joint Development Plan—with five priority areas for UNMIT police capacity-building support: legislation, training, administration, discipline and operations—was signed, and UNMIT police have subsequently focused on its implementation. By January 2012 UNMIT police had completed some 175 of the 576 activities provided for under the Plan. UNMIT supported the organization of local democratic governance forums during October–November 2011, and, in December, of a national forum on food security.

In September 2011 the SSRG and the Timor-Leste Government signed a Joint Transition Plan, to guide the transfer of UNMIT's responsibilities during the mission's withdrawal from the country, which was to be completed by December 2012.

Operational Strength: At 31 May 2012 UNMIT comprised 1,242 police officers and 33 military liaison officers; it was assisted by 268 UN Volunteers and (at 29 February 2012) by a team of 388 international and 874 local civilian staff.

Finance: The General Assembly apportioned US $196.1m. to finance the operation during the period 1 July 2011–30 June 2012.

United Nations Interim Administration Mission in Kosovo—UNMIK

Address: Priština, Kosovo.

Special Representative of the UN Secretary-General and Head of Office: FARID ZARIF (Afghanistan).

Establishment and Mandate: In June 1999 NATO suspended a 10-week aerial offensive against the then Federal Republic of Yugoslavia (which was renamed 'Serbia and Montenegro' in 2003 and divided into separate sovereign states of Montenegro and Serbia in June 2006), following an agreement by the Serbian authorities to withdraw all security and paramilitary forces from the southern province of Kosovo and Metohija, where Serbian repression of a separatist movement had prompted a humanitarian crisis and co-ordinated international action to resolve the conflict. The UN Security Council adopted Resolution 1244, which outlined the terms of a political settlement for Kosovo and provided for the deployment of international civilian and security personnel. The security presence, termed the Kosovo Peace Implementation Force (KFOR), was to be led by NATO, while the UN was to oversee all civilian operations. UNMIK was established under the terms of Resolution 1244 as the supreme legal and executive authority in Kosovo, with responsibility for all civil administration and for facilitating the reconstruction and rehabilitation of the province as an autonomous region. For the first time in a UN operation other organizations were mandated to co-ordinate aspects of the mission in Kosovo, under the UN's overall jurisdiction. The four key elements, or Pillars, of UNMIK were (I) humanitarian affairs (led by UNHCR); (II) civil administration; (III) democratization and institution-building (OSCE); and (IV) economic reconstruction (EU). At the end of the first year of UNMIK's presence the element of humanitarian assistance was phased out. A new Pillar (I), concerned with police and justice, was established in May 2001, under the direct leadership of the UN.

Activities, 1999–2002: On arriving in Kosovo at the end of June 1999, UNMIK and KFOR established a Joint Implementation Commission to co-ordinate and supervise the demilitarization of the Kosovo Liberation Army. UNMIK initiated a mass information campaign (and later administered new radio stations in Kosovo) to urge co-operation with the international personnel in the province and tolerance for all ethnic communities. A Mine Co-ordinating Centre supervised efforts to deactivate anti-personnel devices and to ensure the safety of the returning ethnic Albanian population. In July the UN Secretary-General's Special Representative (SRSG) took office, and chaired the first meeting of the Kosovo Transitional Council (KTC), which had been established by the UN as a multi-ethnic consultative organ, the highest political body under UNMIK, to help to restore law and order in the province and to reintegrate the local administrative infrastructure. In August a Joint Advisory Council on Legislative Matters was constituted, with representatives of UNMIK and the local judiciary, in order to consider measures to eliminate discrimination from the province's legal framework. At the end of July UNMIK personnel began to supervise customs controls at Kosovo's international borders. Other developments in the first few months of UNMIK's deployment included the inauguration of joint commissions on energy and public utilities, education, and health, a Technical Advisory Commission on establishing a judiciary and prosecution service, and, in October, the establishment of a Fuel Supervisory Board to administer the import, sale and distribution of petroleum. Central financial institutions for the province were inaugurated in November. In the same month UNMIK established a Housing and Property Directorate and a Claims Commission in order to resolve residential property disputes. In September the KTC agreed to establish a Joint Security Committee, in response to concerns at the escalation of violence in the province, in particular attacks on remaining Serbian civilians. In mid-December the leaders of the three main political groupings in Kosovo agreed on provisional power-sharing arrangements with UNMIK. The so-called Kosovo-UNMIK Joint Interim Administrative Structure established an eight-member executive Interim Administrative Council and a framework of administrative departments. In January 2000 UNMIK oversaw the inauguration of the Kosovo Protection Corps, a civilian agency comprising mainly former members of the newly demilitarized Kosovo Liberation Army, which was to provide an emergency response service and a humanitarian assistance capacity, to assist in de-mining operations and contribute to rebuilding local infrastructure. In August UNMIK, in view of its mandate to assist with the regeneration of the local economy, concluded an agreement with a multinational consortium to rehabilitate the Trepca non-ferrous mining complex. During mid-2000 UNMIK organized the voter registration process for municipal elections, which were held in late October. In mid-December the Supreme Court of Kosovo was inaugurated, comprising 16 judges appointed by the SRSG. During 2000 UNMIK police and KFOR co-operated in conducting joint security operations; the establishment of a special security task force to combat ethnically motivated political violence, comprising senior UNMIK police and KFOR members, was agreed in June. From January 2001 UNMIK international travel documents were distributed to Kosovars without Yugoslav passports. From June, in response to ongoing concern at violence between ethnic Albanians and security forces in the former Yugoslav republic of Macedonia (FYRM), UNMIK designated 19 authorized crossing points at Kosovo's international borders with Albania and the FYRM, and its boundaries with Montenegro and Serbia. In mid-May the SRSG signed the Constitutional Framework on Interim Self-Government, providing for the establishment of a Constitutional Assembly. UNMIK undertook efforts to register voters, in particular those from minority ethnic groups, and to continue to facilitate the return of displaced persons to their home communities. The last session of the KTC was held in October, and a general election was conducted, as scheduled, in mid-November. In December the SRSG inaugurated the new 120-member Assembly. However, disagreements ensued among the three main political parties represented in the Assembly concerning the appointment of the positions of President and Prime Minister. In February 2002 the SRSG negotiated an agreement with the leaders of the main political parties that resolved the deadlock in establishing the Interim Government. Accordingly, in March, the new President, Prime Minister and Interim Government were inaugurated, enabling the commencement of the process of developing self-governing institutions. In November the mission established the UNMIK Administration—Mitrovica, superseding parallel institutions that had operated hitherto in Serb-dominated northern Mitrovica, and thereby extending UNMIK's authority over all Kosovo. During that month a second series of municipal elections took place.

2003–05: In March 2003 a Transfer Council was established with responsibility for transferring competencies from UNMIK to the provisional institutions of self-government (PISG). In June UNMIK, with UNDP, launched a Rapid Response Returns Facility (RRRF) to assist returnees from inside and outside Kosovo through the provision of housing and socio-economic support. In October the SRSG invited Kosovan and Serb leaders, as well as representatives of the international Contact Group on the Balkans, to participate in direct talks. The outcome of the meeting, held in Vienna, Austria, was an agreement to pursue a process of direct dialogue. In March 2004 two working groups, concerned with energy and with missing persons, were established within the framework of direct dialogue; however, the process was suspended following serious ethnic violence that occurred during that month (see below). Also in October 2003 UNMIK established a task force to combat corruption, and concluded with Montenegro a Memorandum of Understanding (MOU) on Police Co-operation, with the aim of jointly targeting organized crime. In the following month a MOU was signed with the International Commission on Missing Persons, formalizing co-operation in using DNA technology to identify missing persons.

In December 2003 the SRSG and the Kosovan Prime Minister jointly launched *Standards for Kosovo*, drafted by the UN and partners and detailing eight fundamental democratic standards to be applied in the territory. Leaders of the Serb community declined to participate in the process. At the end of March 2004 the SRSG and Prime Minister Rexhapi launched the Kosovo Standards Implementation Plan, outlining 109 standards and goals, as a mechanism for reviewing the standards and assessing the progress of the PISG. In mid-March rioting erupted in Kosovska Mitrovica and violent clashes between Serb and Albanian communities occurred throughout the province. After two days of serious incidents 19 civilians were reported to have been killed, some 1,000 injured and an estimated 4,100 people from the Kosovan Serb, Roma and Ashkali communities had been displaced. In addition, 730 houses and 36 sites of cultural or religious importance had been damaged or destroyed. UNMIK undertook to restore the confidence of the affected communities, to assist with the reconstruction of damaged infrastructure, and to investigate the organizers and main perpetrators of the violence. It also initiated a review of its own operational procedures, as well as the conduct of local politicians. The priority areas for the mission were identified as providing a secure environment, including the protection of minorities, and ensuring the success of the Standards Implementation Plan. In August a newly appointed SRSG also re-emphasized the need to stimulate the local economy. In that month UNMIK, with UNDP and the local authorities, launched a youth employment creation project. In September UNMIK established a Financial Information Centre to help to deter money-laundering and other related offences. UNMIK assisted in preparations for legislative elections, to be held in October, and supported efforts to ensure a large and representative voter turn-out. In November the SRSG met the newly elected political leaders and agreed on the establishment of new ministries for energy and mining, local government, and returns and communities. The inaugural session of the new Assembly was convened in December. In that month the SRSG and the new Prime Minister, Ramush Haradinaj, concluded an agreement on making the Standards a priority for the Kosovan Government and on action for their implementation. In January 2005 a new UNMIK Senior Adviser on Minority Issues was appointed in order to assist the Government's efforts to integrate fully minorities into Kosovan society. In March Haradinaj resigned following notification of his indictment by the International Criminal Tribunal for the former Yugoslavia. UNMIK supported the establishment of a coalition administration, and announced the establishment of a new body to promote political consensus within the province. The first meeting of the so-called Kosovo Forum, to which all political leaders were invited, was convened in June. During March–May meetings of the working groups, convened within the framework of direct dialogue between Serbia and Kosovo, were held, concerned with missing persons, energy and return of displaced persons. In October the UN Secretary-General recommended that political negotiations on the future status of the province commence. A Special Envoy for the Future Status Process, Martii Ahtisaari, was appointed in the following month. In December new UNMIK regulations provided for the establishment of Ministries of Justice and of Internal Affairs.

2006–12: In March 2006 the Housing and Property Directorate was superseded by the Kosovo Property Agency. In August UNMIK and the Kosovan Ministry of Transport signed a memorandum governing the transfer of responsibility for the humanitarian transportation of minority communities in Kosovo from UNMIK to the Ministry. During that month the Interim Government approved the European Partnership Action Plan, which replaced the Kosovo Standards Implementation Plan during late 2006 as the basic reference document concerning standards. The 109 standards goals enshrined in the Standards Implementation Plan were incorporated into the Action Plan. Negotiations on the future status of Kosovo were organized by the Special Envoy for the Future Status Process during 2006, and in February 2007 he presented a Settlement Proposal to the relevant parties. The provisional Proposal, which provided for a Kosovan constitution, flag and national anthem and for Kosovo to apply for independent membership of international organizations, while remaining under close international supervision, was rejected by many Kosovan Serbs on the grounds that it appeared to advance the advent of a fully independent Kosovo, and also by extremist Kosovan Albanian elements since it did not guarantee immediate full independence. During violent protests against the proposals organized by radical Kosovo Albanians two protesters were killed by Kosovan and UNMIK police, leading to the resignations of the UNMIK Police Commissioner and the Kosovan Minister of Internal Affairs. The Special Envoy pursued further discussions with all parties; however, in March he declared an end to the negotiation process. A few days later he presented revisions to the Settlement Proposal. In April a delegation of the UN Security Council visited the region to consider the final settlement plans. In July the UN Secretary-General issued a technical assessment of the progress achieved in Kosovo towards implementing the Standards. He also noted ongoing ethnic tensions in the province that were threatening further progress and a low rate of minority returns. A troika of the Contact Group on Kosovo, comprising representatives of the EU, Russia and USA, was established to undertake intensive negotiations to determine a final status for the province. In December, however, the troika reported that no agreement had been reached.

UNMIK monitored the preparation for and conduct of a general election in Kosovo, held in November 2007. In February 2008 the mission appealed for restraint following a declaration of independence from Serbia, announced by the newly inaugurated Kosovan Assembly. In the following month the mission condemned a violent attack, by Serbian protesters, against a Court in northern Mitrovica, and subsequent clashes with UNMIK and KFOR personnel who regained control of the building. In early April the UN Secretary-General confirmed that UNMIK and the provisions of Security Council Resolution 1244 remained in effect and should be adhered to by the Kosovan and Serbian authorities. In mid-June a new Kosovan Constitution entered in force, providing for the transfer of executive powers from the UN to the elected authorities and for an EU police and justice mission to assume supervisory responsibilities from the UN. The UN Secretary-General confirmed that UNMIK was to be reconfigured; however, Serbian opposition to the Constitution and political divisions within the UN Security Council regarding the governance of the territory had prevented a new resolution being agreed. The EU 'Pillar' of the mission was terminated on 30 June. UNMIK worked closely with the EU to establish and deploy the EU Rule of Law Mission in Kosovo (EULEX), under the overall authority of the UN. In June the issuance of UNMIK travel documents was terminated as a result of a decision by the Kosovan authorities to produce national passports. UNMIK continued to monitor the implementation of the Standards for Kosovo programme and worked to strengthen co-operation between international agencies working in Kosovo. EULEX assumed responsibility for police and judicial functions in December, and reached full operational capacity in April 2009. Meanwhile, during 2009–10 UNMIK pursued practical co-operation with local authorities and reoriented its field presence to focus on areas occupied by ethnic non-Albanians. In July 2010 the International Court of Justice ruled that Kosovo had legitimately seceded from Serbia in February 2008. In mid-2010 UNMIK, jointly with the UN Kosovo Team, developed a new UN Strategic Framework for Kosovo, which was endorsed in September. During 2010–12 UNMIK continued its efforts to facilitate the participation of Kosovo in international and regional arrangements and conferences. By 31 December 2011 the UNMIK Human Rights Advisory Panel had completed 166 of a total of 525 cases under its consideration.

In 2012 UNMIK was continuing to facilitate dialogue among all communities in Kosovo. With a view to diffusing local tensions in northern areas, UNMIK has facilitated a new security co-ordination forum, comprising KFOR, EULEX, the OSCE and northern Kosovo Serb leaders. The mission monitors security arrangements provided to principal Serbian Orthodox religious sites, and facilitates UNESCO's cultural protection activities in Kosovo.

Operational Strength: At 31 May 2012 UNMIK comprised nine military officers and six civilian police officers, in addition to (at 29 February 2012) 148 international and 218 local civilian staff, and 24 UN Volunteers.

Finance: The General Assembly apportioned US $44.9m. to the Special Account for UNMIK to finance the operation during the period 1 July 2011–30 June 2012.

United Nations Interim Force in Lebanon—UNIFIL

Address: Naqoura, Lebanon.

Force Commander and Chief of Mission: Maj.-Gen. PAOLO SERRA (Italy).

Establishment and Mandate: UNIFIL was established by UN Security Council Resolution 425 in March 1978, following an invasion of Lebanon by Israeli forces. The force was mandated to confirm the withdrawal of Israeli forces, to restore international peace and security, and to assist the Government of Lebanon in ensuring the return of its effective authority in southern Lebanon. UNIFIL also extended humanitarian assistance, including the provision of food, water, and medical and dental services, to the population of the area, particularly following the second Israeli invasion of Lebanon in 1982. In April 1992, in accordance with its mandate, UNIFIL completed the transfer of part of its zone of operations to the control of the Lebanese army.

Activities, 1998–2005: In March 1998 the Israeli Government announced that it recognized Security Council Resolution 425, requiring the unconditional withdrawal of its forces from southern Lebanon. It stipulated, however, that any withdrawal of its troops must be conditional on receiving security guarantees from the Lebanese authorities. A formal decision to this effect, adopted on 1 April, was rejected by the Lebanese and Syrian Governments. In April 2000 the Israeli Government formally notified the UN Secretary-General of its intention to comply with Resolution 425. Later in that month the UN Secretary-General dispatched a team of experts to study the technical aspects of the impending implementation of the resolution, and sent a delegation, led by his then Special Co-ordinator for the Middle East Peace Process, Terje Roed-Larsen, and the Commander of UNIFIL, to consult with regional governments and groupings. The withdrawal of Israeli troops commenced in mid-May. Meanwhile, the Security Council endorsed an operational plan to enable UNIFIL to verify the withdrawal. All concerned parties were urged to co-operate with UNIFIL in order to ensure the full implementation of the resolution. In accordance with its mandate, UNIFIL was to be disbanded following the resumption by the Lebanese Government of effective authority and the normal responsibilities of a state throughout the area, including the re-establishment of law and order structures. In mid-June the UN Secretary-General confirmed that Israeli forces had fully evacuated from southern Lebanon. In spite of early reports of several Israeli violations of the line of withdrawal, in July the UN Secretary-General confirmed that no serious violations remained. UNIFIL, reinforced with additional troops, patrolled the area vacated by the Israeli forces, monitored the line of withdrawal, undertook de-mining activities, and continued to provide humanitarian assistance. From August the Lebanese Government deployed a Joint Security Force to the area and began re-establishing local administrative structures and reintegrating basic services into the rest of the country. However, the authorities declined to deploy military personnel along the border zone, on the grounds that a comprehensive peace agreement with Israel would first need to be achieved. In November, following two serious violations of the Blue Line in the previous month by both Israeli troops and Hezbollah militia, the Security Council urged the Lebanese Government to take effective control of the whole area vacated by Israel and to assume international responsibilities. In January 2001 the UN Secretary-General reported that UNIFIL no longer exercised control over the area of operation, which remained relatively stable. The Security Council endorsed his proposals to reconfigure the Force in order to focus on its remaining mandate of maintaining and observing the cease-fire along the line of withdrawal; this was completed by the end of 2002. In response to an increase from early 2002 in incidents generating tension in the area of UNIFIL's operation, reportedly perpetrated by Hezbollah and other militants, and continuous Israeli air violations of the Blue Line, Terje Roed-Larsen and the Secretary-General's Personal Representative for Southern Lebanon undertook diplomatic efforts aimed at restoring stability, and, despite restrictions on its movements, UNIFIL increased its patrols. In January 2003 the UN Secretary-General reported that the number of ground violations of the Blue Line had decreased significantly. From August, however, the number of reported violent incidents increased. Nonetheless, UNIFIL continued to work to clear areas of land of anti-personnel devices and to assist the integration of the formerly occupied zone into the rest of the country. In July 2004 UNIFIL representatives, with other UN officials, worked to defuse tensions following an alleged Hezbollah sniper attack against Israeli forces and subsequent Israeli violations of Lebanese airspace. At the end of that year the

UN expressed concern at further repeated violations of the Blue Line from both sides. A serious breach of the cease-fire occurred in May 2005. In June UNIFIL reported attacks on Israeli troop positions by Hezbollah militia and a forceful response by the Israeli Defence Force. In November UNIFIL brokered a cease-fire following further hostilities across the Blue Line, initiated by Hezbollah; however, there were reports of a missile attack on Israeli positions in the following month. The Security Council subsequently urged all parties to end violations of the Blue Line and called for the Lebanese Government to maintain order and exert greater authority throughout its territory.

2006–12: In mid-July 2006 a full-scale conflict erupted between the Israeli armed forces and Hezbollah, following the capture by Hezbollah of two Israeli soldiers, and the killing of three others. An estimated 1,000 Lebanese civilians were killed and 900,000 displaced from their homes during the unrest. A cease-fire between Hezbollah and Israel entered into effect in mid-August, following the adoption by the UN Security Council of Resolution 1701. The provisions of the resolution also demanded 'the immediate cessation by Hezbollah of all attacks and the immediate cessation by Israel of all offensive military operations' in Lebanon; welcomed a recent decision of the Lebanese Government to deploy 15,000 armed troops in southern Lebanon; increased the Force's authorized troop strength to a maximum of 15,000; and expanded its mandate to include monitoring the cease-fire, supporting the Lebanese troop deployment in southern Lebanon, facilitating humanitarian access to civilian communities, and assisting voluntary and safe returns of people displaced by the conflict.

In September 2006 a new Strategic Military Cell, reporting to the Under-Secretary-General for Peace-keeping Operations, was established to provide military guidance to UNIFIL. In the following month a Maritime Task Force was established, the first in a UN peace-keeping operation, to patrol the waters off the Lebanese coast in order to counter illegal trade in arms. A UN Mine Action Co-ordination Centre of South Lebanon was also established to co-ordinate efforts to locate and destroy unexploded munitions. In June 2007 six soldiers serving under UNIFIL were killed in a car bomb attack in south-eastern Lebanon. In January 2008 the Security Council condemned an attack on a UNIFIL patrol. In August the Security Council, while authorizing a 12-month extension to the mission's mandate, recognized UNIFIL's contribution to achieving a stable security environment since the 2006 conflict and welcomed an increase in co-ordinated activities between UNIFIL and Lebanese forces. In January 2009 UNIFIL initiated an investigation into evidence that rockets had been fired from Lebanon towards Israel, and others had been discovered ready to fire, and strengthened border patrols. A review of UNIFIL's operational effectiveness was conducted in late 2009; in February 2010 recommendations were issued, on the basis of the review, on means of making the Force in future more task-oriented and flexible. The review also emphasized the need to formalize a mechanism for regular strategic dialogue between UNIFIL and the Lebanese armed forces. In August the Force Commander convened an extraordinary tripartite meeting with senior representatives of the Lebanese Armed Forces and the Israeli Defense Forces, following a violent encounter along the Blue Line.

In February 2011 UNIFIL conducted a large-scale disaster preparedness exercise with the Lebanese Armed Forces in the Tyre area. The UN Security Council strongly condemned a terrorist attack perpetrated against a UNIFIL convoy near Saida in late July, injuring six peace-keepers. At the beginning of August Lebanese and Israeli forces briefly exchanged fire across the Blue Line in the Wazzani River area; UNIFIL subsequently investigated the incident, and made a number of recommendations aimed at preventing a recurrence. In 2011 UNIFIL undertook up to 10,000 patrols each month.

Worsening unrest in Syria in the first half of 2012 generated insecurity at the Lebanon–Syria border, and resulted in more than 10,000 Syrians seeking shelter on the Lebanese side. Illegal transfers of arms were also reportedly occurring across the boundary in both directions. At that time the UN Secretary-General was encouraging Lebanon and Syria to delineate fully their common border, in order to establish and finalize the formal demarcation of Lebanon's boundaries. The UN Secretary-General reported in April 2012, and deplored, that Israeli violations of Lebanese airspace—mainly by unmanned vehicles, but occasionally by fighter aircraft—were continuing to occur almost daily. He meanwhile called upon the leadership of Hezbollah (which, in early 2012, had made public acknowledgement of support received by the Iranian authorities) to cease making efforts to acquire weapons and build unilateral paramilitary capabilities.

Operational Strength: At 31 May 2012 the Force comprised 11,845 military personnel; it was supported (at 29 February 2012) by 348 international and 657 local civilian staff. UNIFIL is assisted in its tasks by military observers of the United Nations Truce Supervision Organization (see below).

Finance: The General Assembly appropriation for the operation for the period 1 July 2011–30 June 2012 amounted to US $545.5m.

United Nations Interim Security Force for Abyei—UNISFA

Address: Abyei Town, Sudan.

Head of Mission and Force Commander: Lt-Gen. TADESSE WEREDE TESFAY (Ethiopia).

Establishment and Mandate: Following the final conclusion in January 2005 of a Comprehensive Peace Agreement (CPA)—including a Protocol on the Resolution of the Conflict in Abyei Area (the 'Abyei Protocol'), signed in May 2004—between the Sudan Government and opposition Sudan People's Liberation Movement (SPLM), ongoing contention over the competing claims to land ownership in, and the future status of, Abyei presented an impediment to the implementation of the Agreement and to the advancement of stability in the region. From early January 2011, prior to the referendum held in that month on self-determination for South Sudan, heightened tensions and outbreaks of violence were reported in the disputed Abyei region (located at Sudan's border with South Sudan—which eventually gained independence on 9 July 2011). In mid-January and early March the parties to the Comprehensive Peace Agreement agreed on temporary security arrangements for the Abyei region; the ongoing insecurity, however, deteriorated further. Immediately prior to the establishment of UNISFA unrest in Abyei had escalated significantly, displacing around 113,000 people, including most of the civilian inhabitants of the town of Abyei. The 'Temporary Arrangements for the Administration and Security of the Abyei Area'—an accord adopted in mid-June 2011 by the Sudanese Government and rebels, governing the withdrawal of their respective forces from Abyei—facilitated the deployment of the peace-keeping operation. The Temporary Arrangements provided for the establishment of an Abyei Area Administration, to be administered jointly by an SPLM-nominated Chief Administrator and a Government-nominated Deputy, which was mainly to exercise powers determined in the Abyei Protocol to the CPA; responsibility for supervising security and stability, however, was transferred by the Temporary Arrangements to a newly-established Abyei Joint Oversight Committee, comprising members from each party to the conflict, as well as to an AU facilitator.

UNISFA was established by UN Security Resolution 1990 on 27 June 2011, with an initial mandated term of six months. The Force is mandated to protect civilians and humanitarian personnel in Abyei; to facilitate the free movement of humanitarian aid; to monitor and verify the redeployment of government and rebel forces from the Abyei Area; to participate in relevant Abyei Area bodies; to provide demining assistance and advice on technical matters; to strengthen the capacity of the Abyei Police Service; and, as necessary, to provide—in co-operation with the Abyei Police Service—security for the regional oil infrastructure. In December 2011 the UN Security Council expanded UNISFA's mandate to include assisting all parties in ensuring the observance of the Safe Demilitarized Border Zone, and advising, and supporting the operational activities of, the Joint Border Verification and Monitoring Mechanism (the creation of the Zone and Mechanism having been outlined in Agreements concluded in June 2011, see below); facilitating liaison between the parties; and supporting the parties, when requested, in developing effective bilateral management mechanisms along the border.

Later in December 2011 the mandate of the mission was extended for a period of five months.

Activities: Under the auspices of the 'Friends of Abyei', chaired by the Resident Co-ordinator in Sudan, a planning team, comprising representatives of UN agencies, donor and INGOs, developed during 2011 a humanitarian joint recovery programming strategy for Abyei; it was envisaged that people displaced by the violence in Abyei would only be returned there following the planned withdrawal of forces and the full deployment of UNISFA. At the end of June 2011 the parties to the conflict in Abyei signed an Agreement on Border Security, in which they reaffirmed commitment to a Joint Political and Security Mechanism, established under an agreement concluded in December 2010; and provided for the establishment of a Safe Demilitarized Border Zone, and Joint Border Verification and Monitoring Mechanism, pending the resolution of the status of disputed areas; UNISFA was mandated from December 2011 to provide force protection for Monitoring Mechanism. Since its inauguration UNISFA has conducted regular air and ground patrols, and has established permanent operating bases in Abyei Town, Agok, and Diffra. In February 2012 South Sudan and Sudan signed a Memorandum of Understanding on non-aggression and co-operation, committing each state to respecting the other's sovereignty and territorial integrity. In the following month the UN Secretary-General reported that the security situation in Abyei remained tense, owing to the continued presence—in violation of the June 2011 Agreement on Border Security—of unauthorized Sudanese armed forces, South Sudanese police, and rebels in the area; as well as owing to ongoing large-scale nomadic migration, and IDP returns. In April 2012, as tensions continued and violent clashes mounted, the UN Security Council demanded that Sudan and South Sudan redeploy their forces from Abyei; that the two sides withdraw forces from their joint border and cease escalating cross-border violence with immediate effect, with the support of UNISFA and through the establishment of a demilitarized border zone; that Sudanese rebels should vacate oilfields in Heglig (Sudan); that Sudan should cease aerial bombardments of South Sudan; and that a summit should be convened between the two states to resolve outstanding concerns. During April the African Union High-Level Implementation Panel (AUHIP) on Sudan (established in October 2009 and mandated to assist the relevant Sudanese parties with the implementation of the January 2005 CPA), presented to both parties a draft Joint Decision for Reduction of Tension, providing for the immediate cessation of hostilities between the two states, and the withdrawal of armed forces of each state from the territory of the other. At the end of April and early May 2012, respectively, South Sudan and Sudan agreed to abide by a seven-point Roadmap for Action by Sudan and South Sudan, approved in late April by the African Union (AU) Peace and Security Council. The AU Roadmap provided for: (i) the immediate cessation of all hostilities; (ii) the unconditional withdrawal of all armed forces to their respective sides of the border; (iii) the activation, within one week from the adoption of the Roadmap, of all necessary border security mechanisms; (iv) cessation of harbouring of, and support to, rebel groups active against the other state; (v) the activation of an ad hoc Committee to investigate complaints made by one party against the other; (vi) immediate cessation of hostile propaganda and inflammatory statements in the media, and against property, cultural and religious symbols belonging to the nationals of the other state; and (vii) implementation of pending aspects of the June 2011 Temporary Arrangements for the Administration and Security of the Abyei Area, most particularly the redeployment of all Sudanese and South Sudanese forces out of Abyei. In accordance with its commitment to the Roadmap, South Sudan withdrew its forces from Abyei in early May 2012, with logistical support from UNISFA; and, at the end of May, the mission confirmed that Sudan had also withdrawn its military from the area.

Operational Strength: At 31 May 2012 UNISFA comprised 3,813 troops and 120 military observers; it was supported by two UN Volunteers, and (as at 29 February 2012) by 35 international civilian staff members and by 12 local civilian personnel.

United Nations Military Observer Group in India and Pakistan—UNMOGIP

Address: Rawalpindi, Pakistan (November–April); Srinagar, India (May–October).

Head of Mission and Chief Military Observer: Maj.-Gen. YOUNG-BUM CHOI (Republic of Korea).

Establishment and Mandate: The Group was established in 1948 by UN Security Council resolutions aiming to restore peace in the region of Jammu and Kashmir, the status of which had become a matter of dispute between the Governments of India and Pakistan. Following a cease-fire that came into effect in January 1949 the military observers of UNMOGIP were deployed to assist in its observance. There is no periodic review of UNMOGIP's mandate.

Activities: In 1971, following the signature of a new cease-fire agreement, India claimed that UNMOGIP's mandate had lapsed, since it was originally intended to monitor the agreement reached in 1949. Pakistan, however, regarded UNMOGIP's mission as unchanged, and the Group's activities have continued, although they have been somewhat restricted on the Indian side of the 'line of control', which was agreed by India and Pakistan in 1972.

Operational Strength: At 31 May 2012 there were 42 military observers deployed on both sides of the 'line of control'; the mission was supported by 74 international and local civilian personnel (as at 29 February 2012).

Finance: The approved budget for the operation for the two-year period 2012–13 was US $21.1m.

United Nations Mission for the Referendum in Western Sahara—MINURSO

Address: el-Aaiún, Western Sahara.

Special Representative of the UN Secretary-General and Chief of Mission: WOLFGANG WEISBROD-WEBER (Germany).

Force Commander: Maj.-Gen. ABDUL HAFIZ (Bangladesh).

Establishment and Mandate: In April 1991 the UN Security Council endorsed the establishment of MINURSO to verify a cease-fire in the disputed territory of Western Sahara, which came into effect in September 1991, and to implement a settlement plan, involving the repatriation of Western Saharan refugees (in co-ordination with UNHCR), the release of all Sahrawi political prisoners, and the organization of a referendum on the future of the territory. Western Sahara is claimed by Morocco, the administering power since 1975, and by the Algerian-supported Frente Popular para la Liberación de Saguia el Hamra y Río de Oro—Frente Polisario. Although originally envisaged for January 1992, the referendum was postponed indefinitely. In 1992 and 1993 the UN Secretary-General's Special Representative (SRSG) organized negotiations between the Frente Polisario and the Moroccan Government, which were in serious disagreement regarding criteria for eligibility to vote in the plebiscite. In March 1993 the Security Council advocated that further efforts should be made to compile a satisfactory electoral list and to resolve the outstanding differences on procedural issues. The identification and registration operation was formally initiated in August 1994. In December 1995 the UN Secretary-General reported that the identification of voters had stalled, owing to persistent obstruction of the process on the part of the Moroccan and Frente Polisario authorities. In May 1996 the Security Council endorsed a recommendation of the Secretary-General to suspend the identification process until all sides demonstrate their willingness to co-operate with the mission. The Council decided that MINURSO's operational capacity should be reduced by 20%, with sufficient troops retained to monitor and verify the cease-fire.

Activities, 1997–2000: In early 1997 the Secretary-General of the UN attempted to revive the possibility of an imminent resolution of the dispute, amid increasing concerns that the opposing authorities were preparing for a resumption of hostilities in the event of a collapse of the existing cease-fire, and appointed James Baker, a former US Secretary of State, as his Personal Envoy to the region. In June Baker obtained the support of Morocco and the Frente Polisario, as well as Algeria and Mauritania (which border the disputed territory), to conduct further negotiations in order to advance the referendum process. Direct talks between senior representatives of the Moroccan Government and the Frente Polisario authorities were initiated later in that month, in Lisbon, Portugal, under the auspices of the UN, and attended by Algeria and Mauritania in an observer capacity. In September the two sides concluded an agreement that aimed to resolve the outstanding issues of contention and enable the referendum to be conducted in late 1998. The agreement included a commitment by both parties to identify eligible Sahrawi voters on an individual basis, in accordance with the results of the last official census in 1974, and a code of conduct to ensure the impartiality of the poll. In October 1997 the Security Council endorsed a recommendation of the Secretary-General to increase the strength of the mission, to enable it to supervise nine identification centres. The process of voter identification resumed in December.

In January 1998 the Security Council approved the deployment of an engineering unit to support MINURSO's de-mining activities. By early September of that year the initial identification process had been completed. However, the controversial issue of the eligibility of 65,000 members of three Saharan tribal groups remained unresolved. In October the Security Council endorsed a series of measures proposed by the UN Secretary-General to advance the referendum, including a strengthened Identification Commission to consider requests from any applicant from the three disputed tribal groups on an individual basis. The proposals also incorporated the need for an agreement by both sides with UNHCR with regard to arrangements for the repatriation of refugees. In November, following a visit to the region by the Secretary-General, the Frente Polisario accepted the proposals, and in March 1999 the Moroccan Government signed an agreement with the UN to secure the legal basis of the MINURSO operation. In May the Moroccan Government and the Frente Polisario agreed in principle to a draft plan of action for cross-border confidence measures. In July 1999 the UN published the first part of a provisional list of qualified voters. An appeals process then commenced, in accordance with the settlement plan. In late November almost 200 Moroccan prisoners of war were released by the Frente Polisario, following a series of negotiations led by the SRSG. The identification of applicants from the three disputed Saharan tribal groups was completed at the end of December. In January 2000 the second, final part of the provisional list of qualified voters was issued, and a six-week appeals process ensued. In December 1999 the Security Council acknowledged that persisting disagreements obstructing the implementation of the settlement plan (mainly concerning the processing and analysis of appeals, the release of remaining prisoners, and the repatriation of refugees) precluded any possibility of conducting the planned referendum before 2002.

2001–12: In June 2001 the Personal Envoy of the UN Secretary-General elaborated a draft Framework Agreement on the Status of Western Sahara as an alternative to the settlement plan. The draft Agreement envisaged the disputed area remaining part of Morocco, but with substantial devolution of authority. Any referendum would be postponed. The Security Council authorized Baker to discuss the proposals with all concerned parties. However, the Frente Polisario and Algeria rejected the draft Agreement. In November the Security Council, at the insistence of the Frente Polisario, requested the opinion of the UN Legal Counsel regarding the legality of two short-term reconnaissance licences granted by Morocco to international petroleum companies for operation in Western Sahara. In January 2002 the Secretary-General's Personal Envoy visited the region and met with leaders of both sides. He welcomed the release by the Frente Polisario of a further 115 Moroccan prisoners, but urged both sides to release all long-term detainees. In July the Frente Polisario released a further 101 Moroccan prisoners, leaving a total of 1,260 long-term detainees, of whom 816 had been held for more than 20 years. During February–November 2003 the Frente Polisario released 643 more prisoners. Morocco continued to detain 150 Sahrawi prisoners. In January the Secretary-General's Personal Envoy presented to both sides and to the Governments of neighbouring states a new arrangement for a political settlement, providing for self-determination, that had been requested by Resolution 1429 of the Security Council. In July the Frente Polisario accepted the so-called Peace Plan for Self-Determination of the People of Western Sahara. In April 2004, however, it was rejected by the Moroccan Government.

In March 2004 MINURSO co-operated with UNHCR to implement a family visits programme, providing for exchange of contacts of relatives divided by the dispute. MINURSO provided transport and other logistical support for the scheme, which was intended to be part of a series of humanitarian confidence-building measures. James Baker resigned as Personal Envoy of the Secretary-General in June. In September the SRSG, who had assumed responsibility for pursuing a political solution, held his first series of formal meetings with all parties to the dispute. In April 2005 the Secretary-General advised that MINURSO's force strength be maintained given the lack of progress in negotiating a political settlement. In July the Secretary-General appointed a new Personal Envoy for the Western Sahara, Peter van Walsum, who undertook his first visit to heads of state in the region in October in an attempt to review the 2003 Peace Plan. The Frente Polisario released all remaining Moroccan prisoners in August 2005.

In early 2006 Morocco established a Royal Advisory Council for Saharan Affairs that comprised Moroccan political parties and Sahrawi leaders, but not the Frente Polisario. In February a ministerial delegation of the Moroccan Government presented the member states of the Group of Friends of Western Sahara (France, Russia, Spain, the United Kingdom and the USA), as well as Germany and the UN Secretary-General, with the basics of a possible future plan for granting extended autonomy to Western Sahara. In April 2007 the UN Security Council reiterated a strong request that both parties enter into discussions without preconditions. In June direct talks between representatives of the Moroccan Government and the Frente Polisario, attended by representatives of Algeria and Mauritania, were held under the auspices of the Personal Envoy of the UN Secretary-General in Manhasset, NY, USA. Further negotiations were conducted in August. Both sides were reported to have agreed that the process should continue and that the current status quo in Western Sahara was unacceptable. The third and fourth rounds of discussions between the two sides, held in January and March 2008, respectively, secured further commitment by both sides to continue the process of negotiations. In February 2009 the newly appointed Personal Envoy, Christopher Ross, visited the region for the first time to meet with representatives of the Moroccan Government, Frente Polisario authorities and the Group of Friends. Ross visited the region for a second time in June to prepare for an informal meeting of the main parties. The talks, which were held in Dürnstein, Austria, in August, secured a commitment by the Moroccan Government and the Frente Polisario to continue negotiations as soon as possible. At a second informal meeting, held in Westchester County, NY, USA, in February 2010, both parties agreed once again to continue with negotiations; however, an *impasse* remained, concerning the issue of self-determination, with the Frente Polisario requesting a referendum for Western Sahara that would present multiple options, including independence, and the Moroccan Government favouring a negotiated autonomy for the area. At the third, fourth and fifth rounds of talks, held, respectively, in November and December 2010, and in January 2011, no significant progress was achieved. In early February 2011 the parties met with UNHCR to review the humanitarian confidence-building measures initiated during 2004. A sixth, seventh and eigth round of negotiations were convened in March. June and July 2011, and again ended in *impasse*, with each party continuing to reject the other's proposal as the sole basis of future negotiations. Negotiations were renewed in March 2012, at the Greentree Estate, in Manhasset, New York, USA, again without progression.

In the first half of 2012 MINURSO continued to monitor a temporary deployment line comprising 314 observation posts of the Royal Moroccan Army, positioned some 15 km to the west of the 'Berm' (the 2,700 km-long Moroccan-built wall separating the Moroccan- and Frente Polisario-controlled areas).

The mission has headquarters in the north and south of the disputed territory. There is a liaison office in Tindouf, Algeria, which was established in order to maintain contact with the Frente Polisario (which is based in Algeria) and the Algerian Government.

Operational Strength: At 31 May 2012 MINURSO comprised 216 military observers, 27 troops and six police officers; it was supported by 19 UN Volunteers, and (at 29 February 2012) by 162 international and 99 local civilian personnel.

Finance: The General Assembly appropriation to cover the cost of the mission for the period 1 July 2011–30 June 2012 amounted to US $63.2m.

United Nations Mission in Liberia—UNMIL

Address: Monrovia, Liberia.

Special Representative of the UN Secretary-General and Head of Mission: KARIN LANDGREN (Sweden).

Force Commander: Lt-Gen. MUHAMMAD KHALID (Pakistan).

Police Commissioner: JOHN NIELSEN (USA).

Establishment and Mandate: UNMIL was authorized by the UN Security Council in September 2003 to support the implementation of the cease-fire accord agreed in June and the Comprehensive Peace Agreement concluded in August by the parties to the conflict in Liberia. UNMIL was mandated to assist with the development of an action plan for the disarmament, demobilization, reintegration and, where appropriate, repatriation of all armed groups and to undertake a programme of voluntary disarmament; to protect civilians and UN personnel, equipment and facilities; to support humanitarian and human rights activities; to support the implementation of national security reforms; and, in co-operation with ECOWAS and other partners, to assist the National Transitional Government (inaugurated in mid-October) with the training of a national police force and the restructuring of the military. Troops were also to assist with the rehabilitation of damaged physical infrastructure, in particular the road network. On 1 October UNMIL assumed authority from an ECOWAS-led multinational force in Liberia (the ECOWAS Mission in Liberia—ECOMIL), which had been endorsed by the Security Council in August; ECOMIL's 3,600 troops were reassigned to UNMIL, which then had an authorized maximum strength of 15,000 military personnel.

Activities, 2003–05: In 2004 UNMIL's civil affairs component assessed the functional capacities of public administration structures, including government ministries, in order to assist the National Transitional Government in re-establishing authority throughout Liberia. UNMIL was to support the National Transitional Government in preparing the country for national elections, which were expected to be held in October 2005. In December 2003 the programme for disarmament, demobilization, rehabilitation and reintegration (DDRR) officially commenced when the first cantonment site was opened. However, the process was disrupted by an unexpectedly large influx of former combatants and a few days later the process was temporarily suspended. In mid-January 2004 an agreement was concluded by all parties on necessary prerequisites to proceeding with the programme, including the launch of an information campaign, which was to be co-ordinated and organized by UNMIL, and the construction of new reception centres and cantonment sites. The DDRR process resumed, under UNMIL command, in mid-April. A training programme for the country's new police service was inaugurated in July and the first UN-trained police officers were deployed at the end of the year. By July 2007 some 3,500 officers had graduated from the UN training programme. In August 2004 UNMIL launched a further vocational training scheme for some 640 former combatants to learn building skills. By the end of October, when the disarmament phase of the DDRR programme was officially terminated, more than 96,000 former combatants, including 10,000 child soldiers, had handed over their weapons. Some 7,200 commenced formal education. At the same time, however, UNMIL troops were deployed throughout the country to restore order, after an outbreak of sectarian hostilities prompted widespread looting and destruction of property and businesses. In early December the Special Representative of the UN Secretary-General (SRSG) hosted a meeting of the heads of all West African peace-keeping and political missions, in order to initiate a more integrated approach to achieving stability and peace throughout the region.

During 2005 UNMIL continued to work to integrate ex-combatants into society through vocational training schemes, and to support community rehabilitation efforts, in particular through the funding of Quick Impact Projects. By August an estimated 78,000 former combatants had participated in rehabilitation and reintegration schemes, funded bilaterally and by a Trust Fund administered by the UN Development Programme. A programme to enrol 20,000 disarmed combatants in formal education was initiated in November. UNMIL provided technical assistance to the National Elections Commission, which, in April, initiated a process of voter registration in preparation for presidential and legislative elections. UNMIL was also concerned with maintaining a peaceful and secure environment for the electoral campaigns and polling days and undertook a large-scale civic education campaign in support of the democratic election process. In October UNMIL, with the Transitional Government, established a Joint National Security Operations Centre. The elections were held, as scheduled, in October, with a second-round presidential poll in November.

2006–12: In 2006 UNMIL determined to strengthen its focus on the rule of law, economic recovery and good governance. It also pledged to support the new Government in efforts to remove UN sanctions against sales of rough diamonds and to become a member of the Kimberley Process Certification Scheme by providing air support for surveillance and mapping activities in mining areas. Throughout 2006 and 2007 UNMIL personnel undertook projects to rehabilitate and construct roads and bridges, police stations, courtrooms and educational facilities. The mission also initiated, with the support of other UN agencies, a scheme to create employment throughout the country. In March 2007 UNMIL initiated a Sports for Peace programme to promote national reconciliation. In late April the UN Security Council removed the embargo against sales of diamonds from Liberia, and in the following month UNMIL transferred control of the regional diamond certification office to the national authorities.

In September 2006 the UN Security Council endorsed a recommendation by the Secretary-General that a consolidation, drawdown and withdrawal plan for UNMIL should be developed and implemented; the consolidation phase was completed in December 2007. In August 2007 the UN Secretary-General recognized the efforts of the new Government in consolidating peace and promoting economic recovery in the country. In the following month the Security Council endorsed a plan to reduce UNMIL's military component by 2,450 troops between October and September 2008, and to reduce the number of police officers by 498 in the period April 2008–December 2010. In April 2008 the SRSG reported that greater progress was needed in the training and restructuring of Liberia's security forces to enable the proposed drawdown of UNMIL personnel and transfer of responsibility to proceed. In September 2008 the Security Council approved an increase of 240 in the authorized number of personnel deployed as part of UNMIL's police component, to provide strategic advice and expertise in specialized files and operational support to regular policing activities. UNMIL continued to monitor and control security incidents, local demonstrations, cross-border activities and drugs-trafficking. In June 2009 the UN Secretary-General issued a special report recommending a further reduction of UNMIL's military component, of some 2,029 troops, in the period October 2009–May 2010, and that UNMIL's mandate be revised to enable the mission to support the authorities in preparing for presidential and legislative elections to be held in late 2011. In accordance with a UN Security Council resolution adopted in September 2009, UNMIL, the UN country team in Liberia, the Liberian National Electoral Commission, and other stakeholders subsequently developed a multi-sector electoral assistance project, with a view to supporting the planned election. In July 2009 an UNMIL training programme for the new Armed Forces of Liberia was initiated. The Liberian Government officially assumed responsibilities for the development of the Armed Forces of Liberia in January 2010. In February UNMIL troops intervened to restore order in Lofa County, in north-western Liberia, following widespread inter-ethnic violence, during which four people died and several churches and mosques were set on fire. In September the SRSG reported that the security situation in the country was stable, but remained fragile. She observed that the country required greater national reconciliation and more progress towards resolving issues concerning access to land, strengthening public confidence in the justice system and developing an independent security sector. The third stage of UNMIL's drawdown was completed, as planned, in May. In February 2011 formal responsibility for guarding the Special Court for Sierra Leone was transferred from UNMIL to the Sierra Leone police force. In September 2010 the UN Security Council authorized UNMIL to assist the Liberian Government with staging the 2011 elections, through the provision of logistical support, co-ordination of international electoral assistance, and support for Liberian institutions and political parties in creating an atmosphere conducive to the conduct of peaceful elections.

Following the successful staging of legislative and presidential elections in October–November 2011, the UN Secretary-General sent a technical assessment mission to Liberia in February 2012 to assess progress made in achieving the mission's strategic objectives, and to evaluate the capacity of national security institutions and their ability to operate independently of UNMIL. The mission found that the security situation in Liberia remained fragile, and that there remained high levels of violent crime, and marked vulnerability of women and girls to sexual violence. Causes that were cited included an inadequate justice system and other weak state institutions; large numbers of unemployed, unskilled ex-combatants; ethnic divisions; and disputes over land ownership. In April 2012 the UN Secretary-General recommended a gradual reduction of UNMIL's strength, by around 4,200 troops, to be implemented in three phases during 2012–15. It was envisaged that thereafter a residual presence of about 3,750 troops would remain. Meanwhile, over that period, the mission was gradually to reconfigure, consolidating its presence in the capital, Monrovia, and in the Liberia–Côte d'Ivoire border area. The mission was also to develop a more mobile posture and a quick reaction capability. It was envisaged in early 2012 that the Liberian security forces would be fully operational by 2014.

The impact on Liberia of violent unrest in neighbouring Côte d'Ivoire during late 2010–early 2011, including an influx into Liberia of Ivorian combatants, represented a major security threat to Liberia in 2011, which the Liberian authorities and UNMIL worked to address. In July 2011 UNMIL destroyed a cache of weaponry and ammunition believed to have been hidden by Côte d'Ivoire combatants. From May that year the Liberian military, supported by UNMIL, increased its presence along the Liberia-Côte d'Ivoire border, and UNMIL and UNOCI intensified inter-mission co-operation, including undertaking joint border patrols under the so-called 'Operation Mayo'. In June UNMIL and UNOCI conducted a joint assessment mission in western Côte d'Ivoire. In 2011–12 UNMIL also conducted operations along Liberia's borders with Guinea and Sierra Leone, with the Liberian Government and the Guinean and Sierra Leone authorities. UNMIL strengthened its monitoring in 2011 of electoral, legal, political, public information, security and human rights matters prior to the elections conducted in October–November. Equal airtime was given by UNMIL Radio to all participating parties. The mission also co-ordinated international assistance to the electoral process through a Donor Co-ordination Group.

In June 2012 the heads of UNMIL and UNOCI, and government representatives from Liberia and Côte d'Ivoire, held a quadripartite meeting, in Abidjan, Côte d'Ivoire, on developing a strategy to enhance joint border security, following a fatal attack on UNOCI troops, and other fatal incidents, perpetrated in the border area during that month.

Operational Strength: At 31 May 2012 UNMIL comprised 7,750 troops, 119 military observers, and 1,313 police officers, supported by 224 UN Volunteers, and (as at 29 February 2012) by 480 international civilian personnel and 990 local civilian staff.

Finance: The General Assembly appropriation to the Special Account for UNMIL amounted to US $525.6m. for the period 1 July 2011–30 June 2012.

United Nations Mission in South Sudan—UNMISS

Address: Juba, Sudan.

Special Representative of the Secretary-General: Hilde Johnson (Norway).

Force Commander: Maj.-Gen. Moses Bisong Obi (Nigeria).

Establishment and Mandate: UNMISS was established in July 2011 upon the independence of South Sudan. The mission succeeded the former UN Mission in the Sudan (UNMIS). UNMISS is mandated to support the consolidation of peace, thereby fostering longer-term state-building and economic development; to support the South Sudan authorities with regard to conflict prevention, mitigation, and the protection of civilians; and to develop the new Government's capacity to provide security, to establish the rule of law, and to strengthen the security and justice sectors.

Activities: From July 2011 UNMISS liaised with the South Sudan Government and provided good offices to facilitate inclusive consultative processes involving all the stakeholders invested in nation-building. The mission responded to a request by the South Sudan authorities to support the development of a national security strategy; assisted, with UNDP, the South Sudan Disarmament, Demobilization and Reintegration Commission in preparing a disarmament, demobilization and reintegration policy; and cleared and opened (by November) some 121 km of road, through its Mine Action Service. During August–September the UNMISS Human Rights Unit undertook a fact-finding operation. UNMISS also supported the new Government's ratification of principal international human rights treaties, and monitored the harmonization of the national legislative framework with international human rights standards. In early August UNMISS and the Government of South Sudan signed a status-of-forces agreement guaranteeing the mission's freedom of movement throughout the new country; during the second half of 2011, however, UNMISS reported several restrictions on its movements. Planned deployments under UNMISS to Lord's Resistance Army (LRA)-affected areas were doubled, in comparison with deployments mandated under UNMIS. From the inception of UNMISS its forces were deployed mainly in response to violent unrest in Jonglei State, which persisted into 2012. Further UNMISS deployments in the second half of 2011 included deterrence operations in Western Equatoria, and a mission to support the integration of rebel forces in Pibor. UNMISS police activities focused on training and advising the new South Sudan Police Service.

From January 2012 relations between South Sudan and Sudan deteriorated significantly, owing to factors including the disputed delineation of the two countries' joint border, mutual accusations of support for anti-government rebel militia groups, control of the Sudanese territory of Abyei (Sudan, see under UNMISS), and the dependence at that time of landlocked South Sudan on the use of Sudanese infrastructure (a pipeline and Port Sudan) for the export of petroleum. In February South Sudan and Sudan signed a Memorandum of Understanding on non-aggression and co-operation, committing each state to respecting the other's sovereignty and territorial integrity. In early April an African Union High-Level Implementation Panel (AUHIP) on Sudan (established in October 2009), that was facilitating discussions between the two sides, presented to both parties a draft Joint Decision for Reduction of Tension, providing for the immediate cessation of hostilities between the two states, and the withdrawal of armed forces of each state from the territory of the other. Shortly afterwards the UN Security Council made several demands of both parties, including that they redeploy their forces from forward positions and end cross-border violence with immediate effect; that Sudan should cease aerial bombardments of South Sudan; that South Sudan and Sudan should redeploy forces from Abyei; and that a summit should be convened between the two states to resolve outstanding concerns. In mid-April an UNMISS support base was among buildings damaged by an aerial bombardment by Sudanese forces of Mayom, in Unity State, South Sudan, which resulted in several fatalities in that settlement. In early and late May, respectively, South Sudan and Sudan withdrew their forces from Abyei, in accordance with a seven-point Roadmap for Action by Sudan and South Sudan that was approved in late April by the African Union Peace and Security Council (see under the UN Interim Security Force for Abyei).

Operational Strength: UNMISS has an authorized strength comprising up to 7,000 military personnel and up to 900 civilian police personnel. At 31 May 2012 UNMISS comprised 5,157 troops, 139 military observers and 484 police officers; it was supported by 300 UN Volunteers and (as at 29 February 2012) by 779 international and 1,289 local civilian personnel.

United Nations Operation in Côte d'Ivoire—UNOCI

Address: Abidjan, Côte d'Ivoire.

Special Representative of the Secretary-General and Head of Mission: ALBERT (BERT) GERARD KOENDERS (Netherlands).

Force Commander: Maj.-Gen. MUHAMMAD IQBAL ASI (Pakistan).

Police Commissioner: Maj.-Gen. JEAN MARIE BOURRY (France).

Establishment and Mandate: UNOCI was authorized by the UN Security Council in February 2004 and began operations in early April. It was mandated to observe and monitor the implementation of the Linas-Marcoussis Accord, signed by the parties to the conflict in Côte d'Ivoire in January 2003, and hitherto supported by the UN Mission in Côte d'Ivoire (MINUCI), forces of the Economic Community of West African States—ECOWAS and French peace-keeping troops. UNOCI was authorized also to assist with the disarmament, demobilization and reintegration of rebel groups, to protect civilians and UN personnel, institutions and equipment, and to support ongoing humanitarian and human rights activities. With a contingent of the French *'Licorne'* peace-keeping force, UNOCI was to monitor a so-called Zone of Confidence separating the two areas of the country under government and rebel control.

Activities, 2003–04: In July 2003 all parties, attending a meeting of West African heads of state that had been convened by the UN Secretary-General and the President of Ghana, endorsed the Accra III Agreement identifying means of implementing the Linas-Marcoussis Accord. UNOCI was to participate in a tripartite monitoring group, together with ECOWAS and the African Union, to oversee progress in implementing the agreement. In mid-August UNOCI launched a radio station, in accordance with its mandate, to assist the process of national reunification, and in the following month established some secure transit routes between the areas under government and rebel control in order to facilitate travel and enable family reunions. None the less, by October UNOCI officials expressed concern at ongoing violations of human rights and a deterioration in security, as well as a lack of progress in implementing provisions of the peace accords.

In early November 2004 government troops violated the ceasefire and the Zone of Confidence by launching attacks against rebel Forces Nouvelles in the north of the country. An emergency session of the UN Security Council, convened following an escalation of the hostilities and a fatal air strike on a French peace-keeping unit, urged both sides to refrain from further violence. Security further deteriorated in the south of the country when French troops destroyed the government air force, prompting rioting in the capital, Abidjan, and violence directed towards foreign nationals. UNOCI assisted with the evacuation of foreign workers and their families and provided secure refuge for other personnel. In mid-November the Security Council imposed an immediate embargo on the sale or supply of armaments to Côte d'Ivoire and demanded a cessation of hostilities and of the use of media broadcasts to incite hatred and violence against foreigners. UNOCI was to monitor the terms of the resolution and to broadcast its own messages of support for the peace process. By the end of that month reports indicated that the security situation had improved and that some of the estimated 19,000 who fled the country to Liberia had started to return. In addition, conditions in the northern city of Bouaké were improving as water and electricity supplies were restored. In December UNOCI funded three Quick Impact Projects, in order to highlight the humanitarian aspect of the mission, and commenced joint patrols with government forces to uphold security in Abidjan.

2005–12: In February 2005 the UN Security Council demanded that all parties co-operate with UNOCI in compiling a comprehensive list of armaments under their control as preparation for implementing a programme of disarmament, demobilization and reintegration. In March UNOCI increased its presence in western regions of the country owing to an increase in reported violent incidents. In the following month UNOCI troops were deployed to the border regions with Liberia and Ghana in order to support implementation of the UN-imposed arms embargo. UNOCI troops also monitored the withdrawal of heavy weaponry by both government forces and the Forces Nouvelles. In June UN representatives condemned the massacre of almost 60 civilians in Duékoué, in the west of the country, and urged that an inquiry be held into the incident. UNOCI reinforcements were sent to restore stability in the area and undertook joint patrols with local forces. Later in that month the UN Security Council authorized an increase in UNOCI's military and civilian police components, as well as the redeployment of troops from other missions in the region in order to restore security in the country. In July UN troops, investigating reports of violent attacks by rebel groups, were prevented from entering two towns north of Abidjan. UNOCI later complained at further reported obstruction of human rights and civilian police teams. In spite of persisting concerns regarding the political and human rights situation in the country, UNOCI continued to provide logistical and technical assistance to the independent national electoral commission in preparing for elections, scheduled to be held in October; however, these were later postponed. A Transitional Government of National Unity was formed in December. In early 2006 UN property and personnel were subjected to hostile attacks during a period of unrest by groups protesting against a report of an International Working Group, co-chaired by the SRSG, that had recommended the dissolution of the national assembly (the mandate of which had already expired). Several hundred humanitarian personnel were evacuated from the country. At the end of February UNOCI initiated a large-scale operation to provide security for school examinations, to be held in the north of the country for the first time in three years. In June the Security Council authorized an increase in the mission's force strength by 1,025 military personnel and 475 police officers needed to strengthen security throughout the country and undertake disarmament operations. In October UNOCI conducted joint border patrols with UN forces in Liberia to monitor movements of combatants and weapons. In January 2007 the Security Council formally enlarged UNOCI's mandate to co-ordinate with UNMIL to monitor the arms embargo and to conduct a voluntary repatriation and resettlement programme for foreign ex-combatants. The Council's resolution also defined UNOCI's mandate as being to monitor the cessation of hostilities and movements of armed groups; to assist programmes for the disarmament, demobilization and reintegration of all combatants; to disarm and dismantle militias; to support population identification and voter registration programmes; to assist the reform of the security sector and other activities to uphold law and order; to support humanitarian assistance and the promotion of human rights; and to provide technical support for the conduct of free and fair elections no later than 31 October. A new political agreement to work towards national reconciliation was signed by leaders of the opposing parties in Ouagadougou, Burkina Faso, in March. According to the Ouagadougou Agreement the Zone of Confidence was to be dismantled and replaced by a UN-monitored 'green line'. UNOCI organized a series of meetings to ensure the support of traditional leaders for the peace process. In June UNOCI condemned a rocket attack on a plane carrying the country's Prime Minister. The process of disarmament was officially launched at the end of July; it was, however, hindered by underfunding of the arrangements for the reintegration of former militia members. In August 2008 UNOCI, in collaboration with UNDP, initiated a scheme of 'micro projects' to help to reduce poverty and youth unemployment and facilitate the reintegration of ex-combatants.

The redeployment of UNOCI troops from the former Zone of Confidence was completed by late July 2008, when the last observation post was officially closed. In April UNOCI announced that the presidential election was scheduled to be held later in that year on 30 November. UNOCI personnel were assisting in the rehabilitation of polling stations and in supporting the independent electoral commission. In July the SRSG met with the country's President to confirm UN support for the electoral process and plans to implement security arrangements. The process of voter identification and registration was formally inaugurated in mid-September, with UNOCI to provide transport and other logistical assistance in support of the electoral and registration processes. The electoral preparations, however, were disrupted by severe logistical problems, and in November the election was officially postponed. A new timetable, providing for the election to be held in November 2009 and for voter identification and registration processes to be concluded by 30 June, was announced in May; the election was, however, subsequently postponed once again, until 2010, owing to delays in preparing and publishing the provisional electoral list. The list was eventually issued in November 2009. In January 2010, however, a parallel list was found to be in existence, prompting the Côte d'Ivoire President in February to dissolve both the electoral commission and the national Government, in order to maintain the credibility of the process; a new electoral commission and Government were appointed at the end of that month. None the less, the consequent national tension and outbreak of violence caused the electoral process to remain stalled.

In view of a deterioration in the security situation in Guinea in late 2009 UNOCI forces intensified at that time air and ground patrols of the Côte d'Ivoire–Guinea border area.

During 2010 UNOCI developed, jointly with the Côte d'Ivoire military and French *'Licorne'* force, a co-ordinated plan for helping ensure the security of the planned election. In September an agreement on a final voters list was concluded by the leaders of the three main political parties, and this list was officially certified by the SRSG on 24 September. At the end of September the UN Security Council approved a temporary increase of UNOCI's authorized military and police personnel from 8,650 to 9,150, to be deployed with immediate effect. The first round of the long planned presidential election was held on 31 October, and, following certification of the results of the first round by the SRSG on 12 November, a second electoral round was contested by the two first round forerunners on 28 November. (The incumbent President, Laurent Gbagbo, had received the most votes at the first round, but by a margin that did not constitute an outright victory.) At the beginning of December the electoral commission, supported by the UN, confirmed that Gbagbo's opponent, Alassane Ouattara, had won the presidential election; on the following day, however, the national constitutional council rejected the final results, declaring Gbagbo to be the winner. International opinion, including the UN, African Union and ECOWAS, continued to endorse Ouattara as the rightfully elected new Ivorian President, and the UN Secretary-General and French Government rejected demands by Gbagbo, who refused to concede defeat to Ouattara, that UNOCI and *Licorne* troops should leave Côte d'Ivoire. From mid-December serious violent unrest erupted, with numerous fatalities, as well as obstructions to the movement and activities of UNOCI peacekeepers, and attacks on UN personnel and on the UNOCI headquarters, reported during late 2010–early 2011. In mid-January 2011 the Security Council authorized the deployment of an additional 2,000 military personnel to UNOCI, until end-June 2011; and extended, until end-June 2011, the temporary additional military and police capabilities authorized in September 2010.

On 30 March 2011 the UN Security Council adopted Resolution 1975, urging all Ivorian parties to respect the will of the electorate and therefore to acknowledge the election of Ouattara as Côte d'Ivoire President. Resolution 1975 emphasized that UNOCI might use 'all necessary measures' in executing its mandate to protect civilians under threat of attack. On the following day forces loyal to Ouattara advanced on Abidjan, while UNOCI peacekeepers took control of the capital's airport. In early April UNOCI and *Licorne* forces directed fire at pro-Gbagbo heavy artillery and armoured vehicles. On 9 April UNOCI troops fired on pro-Gbagbo forces, in response to a reported Gbagbo-sanctioned attack on Ouattara at an Abidjan hotel. UNOCI and *Licorne* air strikes were undertaken on the following day against pro-Gbagbo heavy weaponry, reportedly inflicting significant damage on the presidential palace. On 11 April forces loyal to Ouattara arrested Gbagbo, with assistance from *Licorne*; Gbagbo and his entourage were then placed under UNOCI guard. Ouattara was eventually inaugurated as President in May.

During the first half of May 2011 the UN Secretary-General dispatched an assessment mission to examine, and make a number of recommendations on, the situation in Côte d'Ivoire. The Secretary-General subsequently recommended that UNOCI play a greater role in helping the national authorities to stabilize the security situation, with a particular focus on Abidjan and western (including border) areas. Accordingly, UNOCI was to increase joint patrols with the Côte d'Ivoire military and police; and was to facilitate the resumption of law enforcement responsibilities by the police and gendarmerie; to deter the activities of militias; and to assist in the protection of civilians. UNOCI was also to continue to collect, secure and dispose of weaponry; and to assist in demining activities. It was recommended that UNOCI, in close co-operation with UNMIL, should enhance its support to the Côte d'Ivoire and Liberian authorities to monitor and address cross-border security challenges, and should increase patrols of the Côte d'Ivoire-Liberia border area (under the so-called 'Operation Mayo'); in June UNOCI and UNMIL conducted a joint assessment mission in western Côte d'Ivoire. It was recommended following the May assessment that UNOCI should provide assistance for the development of a UN justice support programme; support the capacity development for the police, gendarmerie and corrections officers; deploy an expert to work with the authorities on security sector reform; assist the Government in developing a new national programme for demobilization, disarmament and reintegration of combatants, and dismantling of militias, that would be tailored to the post April 2011 context; continue to support the registration and profiling of former combatants; support the organization and conduct of the legislative elections; and strengthen its human rights monitoring activities. UNOCI provided logistical and security support to facilitate the conduct of legislative elections that were held in Côte d'Ivoire in December 2011; in February 2012 the SSRG determined that the electoral process had been 'free, fair, just and transparent' in 193 of the 204 parliamentary constituencies that had been polled; results in the remaining constituencies had, however, been found by the Constitutional Court to be irregular, and had consequently been annulled. The elections in these constituencies were repeated at the end of February.

In late March 2012, having considered the findings of an assessment mission sent to Côte d'Ivoire in February, the UN Secretary-General recommended a reduction in UNOCI's authorized strength, and decided that the mission should adjust the scope of its deployment to cover more remote areas and to intensify its engagement with local communities. From April 2011–March 2012 UNOCI supported the Ivorian authorities in disarming 1,640 former combatants.

In June 2012 the heads of UNOCI and UNMIL, and government representatives from Côte d'Ivoire and Liberia, held a quadripartite meeting, in Abidjan, Côte d'Ivoire, on developing a strategy to enhance joint border security, following a fatal attack on UNOCI troops, and other fatal incidents, recently perpetrated in the border area.

Operational Strength: At 31 May 2012 UNOCI had an operational strength of 9,400 troops, 196 military observers and 1,337 police officers; it was supported by 293 UN Volunteers, and (at 29 February 2012) by 400 international and 758 local civilian personnel.

Finance: The General Assembly appropriated US $486.7m. to finance the mission during the period 1 July 2011–30 June 2012.

United Nations Organization Stabilization Mission in the Democratic Republic of the Congo—MONUSCO

Address: Kinshasa, Democratic Republic of the Congo.

Liaison offices are situated in Kigali (Rwanda) and Pretoria (South Africa). A logistics base is located in Entebbe, Uganda.

Special Representative of the UN Secretary-General and Chief of Mission: Roger Meece (USA).

Force Commander: Lt-Gen. Chander Prakash (India).

Police Commissioner: Abdallah Wafy (Niger).

Establishment and Mandate: On 1 July 2010 MONUSCO succeeded the former United Nations Mission in the Democratic Republic of the Congo (MONUC), which had been established by the UN Security Council in August 1999 and had been operational until the end of June 2010. MONUSCO was inaugurated—to reflect a new phase in the ongoing peace process in the Democratic Republic of the Congo (DRC)—as a consequence of the adoption, in late May 2010, of Security Council Resolution 1925. Resolution 1925 emphasized that the DRC regime (which had reportedly requested the full withdrawal of the UN peace-keeping presence) should bear primary responsibility for maintaining security and promoting peace-building and development in the country, and authorized MONUSCO's deployment until, initially, 30 June 2011 (the mandate was subsequently extended until 30 June 2012). MONUSCO was to comprise, initially, a maximum of 19,815 military personnel, 760 military observers, 391 police personnel and 1,050 members of formed police units, with future reconfigurations to be determined as the situation evolved on the ground. The mission was to use all necessary means to carry out its mandate, which focused on protecting civilians and humanitarian personnel, as well as protecting UN staff, facilities, installations and equipment; supporting the DRC regime in efforts towards stabilizing the country and consolidating peace, including helping with strengthening the capacity of the military and with police reforms, developing and implementing a multi-year joint UN justice support programme, consolidating state authority in areas freed from the control of armed militia, providing technical and logistics support for local and national elections at the request of the Government, and monitoring the arms embargo against rebel militia active in the DRC; providing human rights training to DRC government officials, security service personnel, journalists, and civil society organizations; and advancing child protection, combating sexual violence, and promoting the representation of women in decision-making roles. MONUSCO was to focus its military forces in eastern areas of the DRC, while maintaining a reserve force that could be deployed elsewhere at short notice. MONUSCO screens DRC battalion commanders for human rights violations prior to the provision of logistical and other support.

Activities: From mid-2010 MONUSCO implemented several Quick Impact Projects, including the establishment of new press and vocational training centres and the rehabilitation of play areas and schools. The mission continued to support the Government's disarmament, demobilization and rehabilitation initiative, and through its regional radio network the mission aimed to encourage defections from the Lord's Resistance Army (LRA) rebel group. In late July MONUSCO established a mobile base in Beni, North Kivu province, in order to enhance security for humanitarian personnel working to provide essential medical and food assistance to an estimated 90,000 people who had been temporarily displaced by an escalation of fighting in that area between the national armed forces and the Ugandan rebel group, the Allied Democratic Forces. In the following month three peace-keepers were killed in an attack on their base in Kirumba, North Kivu. In September MONUSCO initiated special patrols in North Kivu to enhance civilian protection following a series of violent attacks, including mass rapes, by illegal armed groups. During 2010–12 MONUSCO worked to launch community alert networks aimed at enhancing the protection of civilians; under the community alert system, settlements in isolated areas were enabled to request, through mission community liaison assistants, intervention to deter threatened attacks. MONUSCO also provided technical advice, logistical support, and police electoral security training, during the preparation for legislative and presidential elections that were held in November–December 2011, as well as providing security patrols before, during and after the electoral process. (The outcome of the presidential election was disputed.) During 2011 MONUSCO documented several hundred reported violations of human rights linked to the electoral process, affecting, in particular, political opposition supporters, journalists and human rights defenders.

During 2011 MONUSCO conducted 46 joint protection team missions with DRC armed forces, in North and South Kivu, Equateur, Ituri and Haut Uélé and Katanga. In late April MONUSCO implemented Operation Easter Shield, aimed an enhancing civilian protection and facilitating the delivery of humanitarian assistance in the northeastern Doruma area (bordering South Sudan), following reports of LRA attacks there. MONUSCO also undertook road rehabilitation activities in north-eastern DRC in 2011.

MONUSCO and the national armed forces launched the joint military operations 'Amani Kamilifu' and 'Radi Strike' in, respectively, February and March 2012, targeting militants in the Kivu provinces. MONUSCO undertook several military operations in the first half of 2012 to protect civilians in LRA-affected areas, and supported an initiative of the national armed forces to encourage LRA members to defect and to enter a disarmament, demobilization, repatriation, resettlement and reintegration process.

During late 2011 MONUSCO, with the UN DRC country team, finalized the 2011–13 UN Transitional Framework for the DRC, defining areas of collaboration between MONUSCO and other UN agencies.

Operational Strength: At 31 May 2012 MONUSCO comprised 17,042 troops, 730 military observers and 3,126 police officers (including formed police units), supported by 614 UN Volunteers and (at 29 February 2012) by 954 international and 2,864 local civilian personnel.

Finance: The budget for the mission amounted to US $1,419.9m. for the period 1 July 2011–30 June 2012, funded from a Special Account comprising assessed contributions from UN member states.

United Nations Peace-keeping Force in Cyprus—UNFICYP

Address: Nicosia, Cyprus.

Special Representative of the UN Secretary-General and Chief of Mission: LISA M. BUTTENHEIM (USA).

Force Commander: Maj.-Gen. CHAO LIU (People's Republic of China).

Establishment and Mandate: UNFICYP was established in March 1964 by a UN Security Council resolution (initially for a three-month duration) to prevent a recurrence of fighting between the Greek and Turkish Cypriot communities, and to contribute to the maintenance of law and order and a return to normal conditions. The Force controls a 180-km buffer zone, established (following the Turkish intervention in 1974) between the cease-fire lines of the Turkish forces and the Cyprus National Guard. It is mandated to investigate and act upon all violations of the cease-fire and buffer zone. The Force also performs humanitarian functions, such as facilitating the supply of electricity and water across the cease-fire lines, and offering emergency medical services.

In October 2004 the Security Council endorsed the recommendations of the Secretary-General's review team, which included a reduction in the mission's authorized strength from 1,230 to 860 military personnel, to include 40 military observers and liaison officers, and an increase in the deployment of civilian police officers from 44 to 69.

Activities, 1996–2005: In August 1996 serious hostilities between elements of the two communities in the UN-controlled buffer zone resulted in the deaths of two people and injuries to many others, including 12 UN personnel. Following further intercommunal violence, UNFICYP advocated the prohibition of all weapons and military posts along the length of the buffer zone. The Force also proposed additional humanitarian measures to improve the conditions of minority groups living in the two parts of the island. In July 1997 a series of direct negotiations between the leaders of the two communities was initiated, in the presence of the UN Secretary-General's Special Adviser; however, the talks were suspended at the end of that year. In November 1999 the Greek Cypriot and Turkish Cypriot leaders agreed to participate in proximity negotiations, to be mediated by the UN. Consequently, five rounds of these took place during the period December 1999–November 2000. In January 2002 a new series of direct talks between the leaders of the two communities commenced, under the auspices of the Secretary-General's Special Adviser. In May the Secretary-General visited Cyprus and met the two leaders. Further meetings between the Secretary-General and the two leaders took place in September (in Paris, France) and October (New York, USA). In November he submitted to them for consideration a document providing the basis for a comprehensive settlement agreement; a revised version of the document was released in the following month. A further revised version of the draft settlement plan document was presented to the leaders of the two communities during a visit by the Secretary-General to Cyprus in late February 2003. He urged that both sides put this to separate simultaneous referendums at the end of March, in the hope that, were the settlement plan approved, Cyprus would be able to accede to the European Union (EU) in a reunited state on 1 May 2004. Progress stalled, however, at a meeting between the two sides held in early March 2003 in The Hague, Netherlands. In April the Security Council adopted a resolution calling upon both parties to continue to work towards a settlement using the Secretary-General's plan as the unique basis for future negotiations. In reports to the Security Council the UN Secretary-General has consistently recognized UNFICYP as being indispensable to maintaining calm on the island and to creating the best conditions for his good offices. In November 2003 he noted that a number of restrictions placed on UNFICYP's activities during 2000 by the Turkish Cypriot authorities and Turkish forces remained in place. In February 2004 the Greek Cypriot and Turkish Cypriot leaders committed themselves to the Secretary-General's settlement plan. Negotiations on settling outstanding differences were chaired by the Secretary-General's Special Adviser for Cyprus throughout March. Despite a lack of agreement when the two sides met with the Secretary-General in late March, a finalized text was presented at the end of that month. The proposed Foundation Agreement was subsequently put to referendums in both sectors in April when it was approved by two-thirds of Turkish Cypriot voters, but rejected by some 75% of Greek Cypriot voters. In June the Secretary-General determined to undertake a comprehensive review of UNFICYP's mandate and force levels, in view of the political developments on the island, and announced his decision not to resume his good offices. In November 2004 UNFICYP troops initiated an EU-funded project to remove anti-personnel landmines from the buffer zone separating the two communities. A second phase of the project was launched in August 2005 (and completed in November 2006); it terminated in February 2011, by which time an estimated 27,000 landmines had been removed.

2006–12: In July 2006 the Turkish Cypriot leader and the Greek Cypriot President met, under the auspices of the UN Secretary-General. The leaders agreed on a set of principles and decisions aimed at reinstating the negotiating process. In September 2007 UNFICYP hosted a second meeting of the leaders of the two communities. They agreed on a need to initiate a settlement process and confirmed that they would continue a bi-communal dialogue under UN auspices. A new Greek Cypriot President was elected in February 2008. In the following month the Special Representative of the UN Secretary-General (SRSG) convened a meeting of the two leaders, who agreed to the establishment of technical committees and working groups in preparation for detailed political negotiations. The leaders also agreed to reopen a crossing between the two communities at Ledra Street, Nicosia. A ceremony to mark the event was held in early April. A second round of discussions was held, at the residence of the SRSG, in May. In July the two leaders agreed in principle on the issue of a single sovereignty and citizenship and initiated a review of the technical committees and working groups. Full negotiations on a political settlement for the island were inaugurated in early September, supported by the newly appointed Special Adviser of the UN Secretary-General, Alexander Downer. By August 2009 the two leaders had met 40 times in the preceding 12-month period, discussing issues concerning governance and power sharing, the EU, security and guarantees, territory, property, and economic matters. The second round of full negotiations commenced in September, and by September 2010 a further 44 meetings had been conducted. UNFICYP personnel during that year focused efforts on the maintenance of the military status quo, de-mining, and the facilitation of civilian activities in the buffer zone. In October the Limnitis/Yesilirmak crossing point was reopened. In November the UN Secretary-General met directly with the two leaders in order to reinvigorate the settlement discussions. A further meeting between the Secretary-General and the leaders of the two communities was convened in January 2011, at which both sides agreed to intensify efforts to reach substantive agreement. In June the UN Security Council strongly urged the leaders to advance the momentum of the negotiations. A meeting held in the following month between the Secretary-General and the Greek Cypriot and Turkish Cypriot leaders agreed on an intensified schedule of regular negotiations during late July–late October, with enhanced engagement by the UN. Two meetings covering contentious property ownership issues were convened in September between the two leaders, with the participation of UN property experts. In October 2011 and January 2012 further meetings were held between the UN Secretary-General and the two leaders, in Greentree, NY, USA, aimed at assessing progress made in the ongoing negotiations, and at addressing unresolved core issues, especially related to power-sharing, property, territory and citizenship. The series of meetings was continued, in Nicosia, in February–March 2012. In December 2011 the Security Council further extended UNFICYP's mandate, to 19 July 2012.

Operational Strength: At 31 May 2012 UNFICYP had an operational strength of 858 troops and 69 police officers; it was supported by 147 international and local civilian staff (as at 29 February 2012).

Finance: The General Assembly appropriated US $58.2m. to the Special Account for UNFICYP to finance the period 1 July 2011–30 June 2012.

United Nations Stabilization Mission in Haiti—MINUSTAH

Address: Port-au-Prince, Haiti.

Special Representative of the UN Secretary-General and Head of Mission: MARIANO FERNÁNDEZ (Chile).

Force Commander: Maj.-Gen. FERNANDO RODRIGUES GOULART (Brazil).

Police Commissioner: MARC TARDIF (Canada).

Establishment and Mandate: In early 2004 political tensions within Haiti escalated as opposition groups demanded political reforms and the resignation of President Jean-Bertrand Aristide. Increasingly violent public demonstrations took place throughout the country, in spite of diplomatic efforts by regional organizations to resolve the crisis, and in February armed opposition forces seized control of several northern cities. At the end of that month, with opposition troops poised to march on the capital and growing pressure from the international community, President Aristide tendered his resignation and fled the country. On that same day the UN Security Council, acting upon a request by the interim President, authorized the establishment of a Multinational Interim Force (MIF) to help to secure law and order in Haiti. The Council also declared its readiness to establish a follow-on UN mission. In April the Security Council agreed to establish MINUSTAH, which was to assume authority from the MIF with effect from 1 June. MINUSTAH was mandated to create a stable and secure environment, to support the transitional government in institutional development and organizing and monitoring elections, and to monitor the human rights situation. Among its declared objectives was the improvement of living conditions of the population through security measures, humanitarian actions and economic development.

Activities, 2004–09: In September 2004 MINUSTAH worked closely with other UN agencies and non-governmental organizations to distribute food and other essential services to thousands of people affected by a tropical storm, although at the end of that year MINUSTAH's priority continued to be the security situation in the country. By that time the following civil units had become fully operational: electoral assistance; child protection; gender; civil affairs; human rights; and HIV/AIDS. In January 2005 MINUSTAH, with the UN Development Programme, the Haitian Government and the Provisional Electoral Council, signed an agreement on the organization of local, parliamentary and presidential elections, to be held later in that year. In May the UN Secretary-General expressed concern at the security environment with respect to achieving political transition. In the following month the Security Council approved a temporary reinforcement of MINUSTAH to provide increased security in advance of the elections. The military component was to comprise up to 7,500 troops (an additional strength of 750 troops) and the civilian police force up to 1,897 officers. From mid-2005 MINUSTAH forces worked to improve security in the country, in particular to reduce the criminal activities of armed groups in poorer urban areas. In November MINUSTAH deployed experts to train electoral agents and supervisors; however, the electoral timetable was delayed. Presidential and legislative elections were conducted in early February 2006. MINUSTAH officers provided security during the voting and maintained order as the results were being clarified. The mission subsequently pledged to support a post-election process of national dialogue and reconciliation and measures to strengthen the country's police force in order to re-establish law and order in areas of the capital, Port-au-Prince. A second round of voting in the legislative election was conducted in April. In August the UN Security Council determined that the mission should strengthen its role in preventing crime and reducing community violence, in particular kidnappings and other activities by local armed groups. In February 2007 MINUSTAH launched a large-scale operation in the Cité Soleil quarter of Port-au-Prince in order to extend its security presence in the most vulnerable locations and to counter the activities of criminal gangs. At the same time UN personnel helped to rehabilitate education, youth and medical facilities in those areas. In April MINUSTAH provided security and logistical support during the conduct of local municipal and mayoral elections. By November an estimated 9,000 local police officers had graduated from MINUSTAH training institutes. Efforts to control gang violence and uphold security in the poorest urban areas were ongoing in 2007–09. In February 2008 MINUSTAH announced that it was to fund six local infrastructure improvement projects to generate temporary employment for 7,000 people in the Cité Soleil and Martissant districts of Port-au-Prince. In April there were violent local demonstrations concerning the rising cost of living, during which several MINUSTAH personnel were attacked and property was damaged. A contingent of the mission subsequently distributed food aid to some 3,000 families in the poorest quarters of the capital. In August–September MINUSTAH personnel undertook emergency relief and rehabilitation activities, including evacuation of local residents and the distribution of humanitarian aid, to assist some of the 800,000 people affected by tropical storms which struck the country consecutively during a period of three weeks. From mid-2008 MINUSTAH strengthened its presence along the country's border with the Dominican Republic to counter illegal drugs-trafficking and improve security in the region. In December the mission undertook its first joint operation with the local police authorities to seize illegal drugs. Later in that month it was announced that the first and second rounds of planned partial senatorial elections would be held, respectively, in April and June 2009; during December 2008–February 2009 MINUSTAH and the police authorities jointly conducted a security assessment of new voting centres. Also during December 2008 MINUSTAH, international donors and representatives of the Haitian Government participated in a workshop that resulted in the adoption of a legislative agenda for 2009. During 2009 MINUSTAH, as well as implementing projects aimed at reducing violence in the community, provided technical security capacity-building support to the national police.

2010–12: In January 2010 a major earthquake struck Haiti, and destroyed the MINUSTAH headquarters in Port-au-Prince. Subsequently it was confirmed that more than 60 mission staff had been killed, among them Hédi Annabi, the then Special Representative of the Secretary-General (SRSG), his deputy, and the acting police commissioner for the mission; almost 180 further UN personnel were unaccounted for. Later in January, following the natural disaster, the UN Security Council adopted a resolution increasing the strength of the mission, to enable it to support the immediate recovery, reconstruction and stability efforts in Haiti. The temporary deployment of an additional 680 police officers was authorized by the Security Council in June, in order to strengthen the capacity of the Haitian national police force. MINUSTAH extended technical, logistical and administrative assistance to the country's authorities in preparation for presidential and legislative elections, which were conducted in November. The Head of Mission maintained regular dialogue with all presidential candidates throughout the electoral process. MINUSTAH contributed to efforts to restore order and to maintain stability following violent reactions to preliminary election results in December. The mission developed a revised security strategy to ensure a stable environment for the second round of voting in the presidential election, held in March 2011. From October 2010 MINUSTAH provided logistical support to counter a severe outbreak of cholera, including the construction of temporary treatment centres, public education efforts, transportation of personnel, emergency medicines and supplies, and the distribution of potable water in affected areas. In January 2011 the UN Secretary-General appointed a panel of independent experts to assess the outbreak amid widespread speculation within the country that a contingent of MINUSTAH troops was the source. In May, following the publication of the report, the UN Secretary-General announced his intention to establish a task force to consider its findings and recommendations. During January 2011 MINUSTAH launched a major initiative, with the national police force, to seize known criminals, as well as to undertake youth training schemes in some of the poorest urban areas. In October the UN Security Council extended MINUSTAH's mandate until 15 October 2012, and authorized a reduction in the mission's authorized strength by 1,600 personnel, to be completed by mid-2012, in order to redress the mission's post-earthquake expansion. In January 2012 MINUSTAH reported that the post-earthquake population of IDPs in camps had reduced by two-thirds.

Operational Strength: At 31 May 2012 MINUSTAH comprised 7,283 troops and 3,126 police officers; there was also a support team of 559 international civilian staff and 1,358 local civilian staff (as at 29 February 2012), and 226 UN Volunteers.

Finance: The mission is financed by assessments in respect of a Special Account. The budget for the period 1 July 2011–30 June 2012 amounted to US $793.5m.

United Nations Supervision Mission in Syria—UNSMIS

Address: Damascus, Syria.

Head of Mission and Chief Military Observer: Maj.-Gen. Robert Mood (Norway).

Joint Special Envoy of the UN and the League of Arab States on the Syrian Crisis: Kofi Annan (Ghana).

Establishment and Mandate: UNSMIS was established by the UN Security Council in April 2012, for an initial period of 90 days, with a mandate to monitor a cease-fire between Syrian government forces and pro-democracy protesters, and to observe and support the full implementation of a six-point peace plan that had been proposed in March by the Joint Special Envoy of the UN and the League of Arab States on the Syrian Crisis, and accepted during that month by the Syrian authorities. UNSMIS was to be deployed 'expeditiously', subject to an assessment by the UN Secretary-General of relevant developments in Syria, including the consolidation of the—fragile—cease-fire. The UN Secretary-General demanded that the Syrian regime ensure UNSMIS's 'full, unimpeded, and immediate' freedom of movement and access, unobstructed communications, and safety.

The six-point Syrian peace plan, the implementation of which was to supported by UNSMIS, envisaged: (i) a commitment to working with the Joint Envoy in an inclusive Syrian-led political process aimed at addressing the legitimate aspirations and concerns of the Syrian people; (ii) a UN-monitored cease-fire by all parties, including a commitment by the Syrian regime to withdraw troops and heavy weaponry from population centres; (iii) a commitment to enabling the timely provision of humanitarian assistance to all areas affected by the fighting, and the immediate implementation of a daily two-hour humanitarian pause; (iv) the expedited release of arbitrarily arrested detainees; (v) free access and movement for journalists; and (vi) freedom of association and the right to demonstrate peacefully for all.

Activities: From late April 2012, following the deployment of UNSMIS, repeated violations of the terms of the six-point peace plan continued to be reported. In late May UNSMIS observers confirmed the indiscriminate massacre of an estimated 108 men, women and children, and the wounding of many more, resulting from the shelling of a residential neighbourhood—the rebel-controlled village of El-Houleh, near Homs—allegedly by forces loyal to the Syrian regime. The UN Security Council issued a statement unanimously condemning the atrocity, and demanded that the Syrian Government immediately cease the use of heavy weapons in population centres, as specified in the six-point plan.

In early June at least an estimated further 78 people, once again including women and children, were reported to have been killed in the western village of Qbeir, by pro-government militants, following the shelling of the area by government forces; UNSMIS observers en route to the site of the Qbeir massacre were reported to have been fired upon. A meeting of the Security Council, convened soon afterwards, reaffirmed commitment to the six-point plan while requesting that the UN Secretary-General put forward a range of options aimed at resolving the deepening crisis. On 16 June, in view of the escalating insecurity, UNSMIS suspended its patrols in Syria, while remaining committed to ending the violence. During March 2011–June 2012 around 10,000 people were reported to have been killed, and many more displaced, by the unrest.

Military Strength: At 14 June 2012 UNSMIS comprised 298 military observers, supported by 82 international and 30 local civilian staff.

Finance: The initial authorized budget for UNSMIS amounted to US $16.8m. for the period 21 April–20 July 2012, to be funded from a Special Account comprising assessed contributions from UN member states.

United Nations Truce Supervision Organization—UNTSO

Address: Government House, Jerusalem.

Head of Mission and Chief-of-Staff: Maj.-Gen. JUHA KILPIA (Finland).

Establishment and Mandate: UNTSO was established initially to supervise the truce called by the UN Security Council in Palestine in May 1948 and has assisted in the application of the 1949 Armistice Agreements. Its activities have evolved over the years, in response to developments in the Middle East and in accordance with the relevant resolutions of the Security Council. There is no periodic renewal procedure for UNTSO's mandate.

Activities: UNTSO observers assist UN peace-keeping forces in the Middle East, at present UNIFIL and UNDOF. The mission maintains offices in Beirut, Lebanon and Damascus, Syria. In addition, UNTSO operates a number of outposts in the Sinai region of Egypt to maintain a UN presence there. UNTSO observers have been available at short notice to form the nucleus of new peace-keeping operations.

In July 2006 the UN Secretary-General strongly condemned the killing by Israeli fire of four members of UNTSO who had been supporting UNIFIL during the full-scale conflict that erupted in that month between the Israeli armed forces and Hezbollah.

Military Strength: The operational strength of UNTSO at 31 May 2012 was 143 military observers. The mission is supported by 233 international and local civilian staff (as at 29 February 2012).

Finance: UNTSO expenditures are covered by the regular budget of the United Nations. The appropriation for the two-year period 2012–13 was US $70.3m.

United Nations Peace-keeping Operations and Observer Missions

A listing of all current and completed operations, in chronological order:

UNITED NATIONS TRUCE SUPERVISION ORGANIZATION (UNTSO)

Mandated to supervise the peace agreements in Palestine. Activities are ongoing (see above).

Duration: June 1948–.

Headquarters: Government House, Jerusalem.

UNITED NATIONS MILITARY OBSERVER GROUP IN INDIA AND PAKISTAN (UNMOGIP)

Established to help to restore peace in the disputed region of Jammu and Kashmir. Activities are ongoing (see above).

Duration: January 1949–.

Headquarters: Rawalpindi, Pakistan (November–April); Srinagar, India (May–October).

FIRST UNITED NATIONS EMERGENCY FORCE (UNEF I)

Aimed to secure and supervise the withdrawal of foreign troops from Egyptian territory and the cessation of hostilities between Egypt and Israel, and to maintain peaceful conditions in the area.

Duration: November 1956–June 1967.

Headquarters: Gaza.

UNITED NATIONS OBSERVATION GROUP IN LEBANON (UNOGIL)

Established to supervise the border between Lebanon and Syria, and, in particular, to ensure that there were no illegal crossings or supply of armaments.

Duration: June 1958–December 1958.

Headquarters: Beirut, Lebanon.

UNITED NATIONS OPERATION IN THE CONGO (ONUC)

Established, initially, to oversee the withdrawal of Belgian forces and the maintenance of law and order. Also aimed to maintain the territorial integrity of the Congo and prevent civil conflict or interference by foreign troops. After the withdrawal of the UN military contingent civilian operations continued, under the authority of the UN Technical Assistance Board.

Duration: July 1960–June 1964.

Headquarters: Léopoldville, Republic of the Congo (now Kinshasa, the Democratic Republic of the Congo).

UNITED NATIONS SECURITY FORCE IN WEST NEW GUINEA (NEW IRIAN) (UNSF)

Mandated to maintain peace and security during the transitional period pending transfer of the territory (previously under Dutch rule) to Indonesia.

Duration: October 1962–April 1963.

Headquarters: Hollandia, West New Guinea (now Jayapura, Irian Jaya).

UNITED NATIONS YEMEN OBSERVATION MISSION (UNYOM)

Established to observe the disengagement agreement and to secure the withdrawal of all foreign troops.

Duration: July 1963–September 1964.

Headquarters: San'a, Yemen.

UNITED NATIONS PEACE-KEEPING FORCE IN CYPRUS (UNFICYP)

Established to prevent further fighting between the Greek and Turkish Cypriot communities and to help to maintain law and order. Ongoing activities include supervision of a buffer-zone and other humanitarian tasks (see above).

Duration: March 1964–.

Headquarters: Nicosia, Cyprus.

MISSION OF THE REPRESENTATIVE OF THE SECRETARY-GENERAL IN THE DOMINICAN REPUBLIC (DOMREP)

Established to oversee a cease-fire between opposition movements.

Duration: May 1965–October 1966.

Headquarters: Santo Domingo, Dominican Republic.

UNITED NATIONS INDIA–PAKISTAN OBSERVATION MISSION (UNIPOM)

Established following the renewal of hostilities between India and Pakistan to supervise the cease-fire lines and the withdrawal of all armed personnel along the international border in areas outside of Kashmir.

Duration: September 1965–March 1966.

Headquarters: Amritsar, India; Lahore, Pakistan.

SECOND UNITED NATIONS EMERGENCY FORCE (UNEF II)

Established after the Arab–Israeli war to supervise a full cease-fire. Following peace agreements concluded in January 1994 and September 1995 UNEF supervised the redeployment of Egyptian and Israeli forces and established buffer zones in the region of the Suez Canal and in the Sinai Peninsula.

Duration: October 1973–July 1979.

Headquarters: Ismailia, Egypt.

UNITED NATIONS DISENGAGEMENT OBSERVER FORCE (UNDOF)

Established, initially, to supervise the disengagement of Syrian and Israeli forces, to monitor the withdrawal of Israeli troops and to establish an area of separation in the Golan Heights. Activities are ongoing (see above).

Duration: June 1974–.

Headquarters: Damascus, Syria.

UNITED NATIONS INTERIM FORCE IN LEBANON (UNIFIL)

Mandated to oversee the withdrawal of Israeli forces from southern Lebanon and to consolidate peace and security in the region. Activities are ongoing (see above).

Duration: March 1978–.

Headquarters: Naqoura, Lebanon.

UNITED NATIONS GOOD OFFICES MISSION IN AFGHANISTAN AND PAKISTAN (UNGOMAP)

Established to monitor the withdrawal of Soviet troops from Afghanistan, as well as the non-interference and non-intervention of troops between Afghanistan and Pakistan, in accordance with a peace accord signed in April 1988.

Duration: May 1988–March 1990.

Headquarters: Kabul, Afghanistan; Islamabad, Pakistan.

UNITED NATIONS IRAN–IRAQ MILITARY OBSERVER GROUP (UNIIMOG)

Its principal tasks were to monitor compliance with the cease-fire agreement, supervise the withdrawal of troops to internationally recognized boundaries, and facilitate confidence-building and other measures to reduce tensions between the two sides.

Duration: August 1988–February 1991.

Headquarters: Baghdad, Iraq.

UNITED NATIONS ANGOLA VERIFICATION MISSION I (UNAVEM I)

Mandated to verify the redeployment of Cuban troops, and their phased and eventual withdrawal from Angola.

Duration: January 1989–June 1991.

Headquarters: Luanda, Angola.

UNITED NATIONS TRANSITION GROUP (UNTAG)

Mandated to supervise democratic elections in Namibia and to ensure a peaceful transition to independence, in accordance with a UN Security Council resolution adopted in September 1978. The resolution was finally implemented in April 1989.

Duration: April 1989–March 1990.

Headquarters: Windhoek, Namibia.

UNITED NATIONS OBSERVER GROUP IN CENTRAL AMERICA (ONUCA)

Established to verify undertakings by five Central American Governments (those of Costa Rica, El Salvador, Guatemala, Honduras and Nicaragua) to cease aid to irregular forces, and to refrain from the use of the territory of one state for attacks on another.

Duration: November 1989–January 1992.

Headquarters: Tegucigalpa, Honduras.

UNITED NATIONS IRAQ–KUWAIT OBSERVATION MISSION (UNIKOM)

Mandated to monitor the demilitarized zone along the border between Iraq and Kuwait.

Duration: April 1991–October 2003.

Headquarters: Umm Qasr, Iraq. (In March 2003 relocated on a temporary basis to Kuwait City.)

UNITED NATIONS MISSION FOR THE REFERENDUM IN WESTERN SAHARA (MINURSO)

Responsible for the monitoring of a cease-fire, and for the organization and supervision of a referendum on the future of the disputed territory. Activities are ongoing (see above).

Duration: April 1991–.

Headquarters: el-Aaiún, Western Sahara.

UNITED NATIONS ANGOLA VERIFICATION MISSION II (UNAVEM II)

Established by the enlargement of the original UNAVEM mandate to enable the mission to perform new verification tasks arising from Peace Accords. The mission also observed general elections, held in September 1992, under an enlarged mandate.

Duration: June 1991–February 1995.

Headquarters: Luanda, Angola.

UNITED NATIONS OBSERVER MISSION IN EL SALVADOR (ONUSAL)

Mandated to monitor agreements concluded between the Government and opposition FMLN forces in El Salvador, and, in particular, the Agreement on Human Rights.

Duration: July 1991–April 1995.

Headquarters: San Salvador, El Salvador.

UNITED NATIONS ADVANCE MISSION IN CAMBODIA (UNAMIC)

Established to monitor the cease-fire, following the conclusion of a peace settlement between government and opposition factions. Absorbed into UNTAC (see below).

Duration: October 1991–March 1992.

Headquarters: Phnom Penh, Cambodia.

UNITED NATIONS PROTECTION FORCE (UNPROFOR)

Established to ensure the withdrawal of Yugoslav forces from Croatia and the demilitarization of three Serbian-held enclaves. Its mandate was subsequently enlarged to ensure the safe delivery of humanitarian assistance within Bosnia and Herzegovina, the withdrawal of Yugoslav troops from the Prevlaka peninsula in Croatia, and the removal of heavy weapons from neighbouring areas in Croatia and Montenegro. UNPROFOR also monitored compliance with the prohibition on military flights in Bosnian air-space.

Duration: March 1992–December 1995.

Headquarters: Zagreb, Croatia.

UNITED NATIONS TRANSITIONAL AUTHORITY IN CAMBODIA (UNTAC)

Mandated to organize and oversee democratic elections in Cambodia, and to supervise the administration of the country during the transitional period prior to the establishment of an elected government. Other duties included assisting the disarmament of Cambodian warring factions, the repatriation and resettlement of refugees, and the rehabilitation of the country's infrastructure.

Duration: March 1992–September 1993.

Headquarters: Phnom Penh, Cambodia.

UNITED NATIONS OPERATION IN SOMALIA I (UNOSOM I)

Responsible for monitoring a cease-fire between the principal warring factions in Somalia, promoting a political settlement, and the distribution of humanitarian aid. In December 1992 the UN Security Council endorsed the dispatch of a multinational force, under US command, to create a secure environment for the provision of humanitarian relief. UNOSOM remained responsible for humanitarian assistance and the political aspects of efforts to establish peace in Somalia.

Duration: April 1992–March 1993.

Headquarters: Mogadishu, Somalia.

UNITED NATIONS OPERATION IN MOZAMBIQUE (ONUMOZ)

Established to facilitate implementation of a peace agreement, signed in October 1992, between the Government and opposition RENAMO movement, including verification of the cessation of hostilities, supervision of the separation, demobilization and disarmament of forces, co-ordination of humanitarian operations, and organization of general elections.

Duration: December 1992–December 1994.

Headquarters: Maputo, Mozambique.

UNITED NATIONS OPERATION IN SOMALIA II (UNOSOM II)

Assumed control from the multinational force for the restoration and enforcement of peace, stability and law and order, as well as the rehabilitation of the country's political, economic and social structures and the enforcement of the disarmament of Somalia's principal conflicting factions.

Duration: March 1993–March 1995.

Headquarters: Mogadishu, Somalia.

UNITED NATIONS OBSERVER MISSION UGANDA–RWANDA (UNOMUR)

Established to monitor the border between Uganda and Rwanda, in order to prohibit the illegal supply of military assistance to Rwanda.

Duration: June 1993–September 1994.

Headquarters: Kabale, Uganda.

UNITED NATIONS OBSERVER MISSION IN GEORGIA (UNOMIG)

Established to monitor a cease-fire between Georgian and separatist Abkhazian forces. Under an enlarged mandate the mission was to monitor and verify implementation of a new agreement, signed in May 1994. It co-operated with troops from the Commonwealth of Independent States to facilitate the return of refugees and other displaced persons.

Duration: August 1993–June 2009.

Headquarters: Sukhumi, Georgia.

UNITED NATIONS OBSERVER MISSION IN LIBERIA (UNOMIL)

Established to verify implementation of a peace agreement signed by the conflicting parties in Liberia, including a lasting cease-fire and the disengagement of forces.

Duration: September 1993–September 1997.

Headquarters: Monrovia, Liberia.

UNITED NATIONS MISSION IN HAITI (UNMIH)

Established to maintain order during the transition of power from the military authorities to Haiti's exiled President Aristide. Under an enlarged mandate the mission provided technical assistance and monitored national elections.

Duration: September 1993–June 1996.

Headquarters: Port-au-Prince, Haiti.

UNITED NATIONS ASSISTANCE MISSION FOR RWANDA (UNAMIR)

Mandated to monitor a cease-fire agreement, signed in August 1993 and to help to maintain peace and security during the transitional peace process until the establishment of a new government. Its mandate was enlarged in May 1994, following the eruption of ethnic violence, to establish secure humanitarian areas and provide security for relief operations.

Duration: October 1993–March 1996.

Headquarters: Kigali, Rwanda.

UNITED NATIONS AOUZOU STRIP OBSERVER GROUP (UNASOG)

Established to verify the withdrawal of Libyan forces from the Aouzou Strip, in accordance with a decision of the International Court of Justice.

Duration: May 1994–June 1994.

Headquarters: Chad.

UNITED NATIONS MISSION OF OBSERVERS IN TAJIKISTAN (UNMOT)

Mandated to monitor a cease-fire agreement signed by the Tajik Government and opposition forces in September 1994, and subsequent peace accords, to facilitate the provision of humanitarian assistance, and to support the preparation of elections and the holding of a referendum.

Duration: December 1994–May 2000.

Headquarters: Dushanbe, Tajikistan.

UNITED NATIONS ANGOLA VERIFICATION MISSION III (UNAVEM III)

Mandated to supervise and monitor the terms of a new peace accord (the Lusaka Protocol) and to assist in the process of national reconciliation, reconstruction and mine-clearance.

Duration: February 1995–June 1997.

Headquarters: Luanda, Angola.

UNITED NATIONS CONFIDENCE RESTORATION OPERATION IN CROATIA (UNCRO)

Replaced UNPROFOR personnel in the disputed regions of Western Slavonia, Krajina, Eastern Slavonia and the Prevlaka peninsula, with the aim of enforcing a cease-fire, maintaining peace and freedom of movement, and monitoring the deployment of troops and weapons.

Duration: March 1995–January 1996.

Headquarters: Zagreb, Croatia.

UNITED NATIONS PREVENTIVE DEPLOYMENT FORCE (UNPREDEP)

Assumed the functions of the UNPROFOR contingent in the former Yugoslav republic of Macedonia, with the objective of upholding the stability of the territory.

Duration: March 1995–February 1999.

Headquarters: Skopje, the former Yugoslav republic of Macedonia.

UNITED NATIONS MISSION IN BOSNIA AND HERZEGOVINA (UNMIBH)

Incorporated the United Nations International Police Task Force and a United Nations civilian office.

Duration: December 1995–December 2002.

Headquarters: Sarajevo, Bosnia and Herzegovina.

UNITED NATIONS TRANSITIONAL ADMINISTRATION FOR EASTERN SLAVONIA, BARANJA AND WESTERN SIRMIUM (UNTAES)

Established to supervise the demilitarization of the region and its reintegration into Croatia, over a two-year period.

Duration: January 1996–January 1998.

Headquarters: Vukovar, Croatia.

UNITED NATIONS MISSION OF OBSERVERS IN PREVLAKA (UNMOP)

Assumed responsibility from UNCRO for monitoring the demilitarization of the Prevlaka peninsula.

Duration: January 1996–December 2002.

Headquarters: Dubrovnik, Croatia.

UNITED NATIONS SUPPORT MISSION IN HAITI (UNSMIH)

Continued the UN's presence in Haiti, after the expiry of UNMIH's mandate, in order to assist the Government to maintain a secure and stable environment and to strengthen the national police force.

Duration: July 1996–July 1997.

Headquarters: Port-au-Prince, Haiti.

UNITED NATIONS VERIFICATION MISSION IN GUATEMALA (MINUGUA)

Dispatched as a military attachment to the UN Mission for the Verification of Human Rights in Guatemala (authorized by the UN General Assembly) to verify a cease-fire agreement signed between the Government and opposition forces.

Duration: January 1997–May 1997.

Headquarters: Guatemala City, Guatemala.

UNITED NATIONS OBSERVER MISSION IN ANGOLA (MONUA)

Succeeded UNAVEM III with responsibility for overseeing the remaining tasks of the Lusaka peace accord, including the demobilization of the opposition UNITA forces and reinstatement of state administration throughout the country.

Duration: July 1997–February 1999.

Headquarters: Luanda, Angola.

UNITED NATIONS TRANSITION MISSION IN HAITI (UNTMIH)

Mandated to undertake specialist police training and to ensure the safety and freedom of movement of UN personnel working in the country.

Duration: August 1997–November 1997.

Headquarters: Port-au-Prince, Haiti.

UNITED NATIONS CIVILIAN POLICE MISSION IN HAITI (MIPONUH)

Established to complete UNTMIH's mandate of providing training and other technical assistance for law enforcement bodies and to support the process of national reconciliation.

Duration: December 1997–March 2000.

Headquarters: Port-au-Prince, Haiti.

UNITED NATIONS CIVILIAN POLICE SUPPORT GROUP

Established to monitor the activities of the Croatian police force and the welfare of populations returning to the Danube region following the withdrawal of UNTAES personnel.

Duration: January 1998–October 1998.

Headquarters: Vukovar and Zagreb, Croatia.

UNITED NATIONS MISSION IN THE CENTRAL AFRICAN REPUBLIC (MINURCA)

Assumed authority from a multinational force, with the aim of securing a peaceful environment, including the disarmament of rebel soldiers and other combatants, and of supporting preparations for legislative elections. Its mandate was enlarged in October 1998 to include support for the conduct of elections.

Duration: March 1998–February 2000.

Headquarters: Bangui, Central African Republic.

UNITED NATIONS OBSERVER MISSION IN SIERRA LEONE (UNOMSIL)

Aimed to promote stability and security in Sierra Leone following the restoration of a democratically elected government, including monitoring the disarmament and demobilization of opposition forces and respect for human rights.

Duration: July 1998–October 1999.

Headquarters: Freetown, Sierra Leone.

UNITED NATIONS INTERIM ADMINISTRATION MISSION IN KOSOVO (UNMIK)

Established as the supreme legal and executive authority in the province of Kosovo and Metohija, following the withdrawal of Serbian security and paramilitary forces from the province and the subsequent suspension by NATO of its aerial offensive against the Federal Republic of Yugoslavia. Activities are ongoing (see above).

Duration: June 1999–.

Headquarters: Priština, Kosovo, Yugoslavia.

UNITED NATIONS MISSION IN SIERRA LEONE (UNAMSIL)

Mandated to assist with the implementation of a peace accord signed by the Sierra Leone Government and rebel groups, to enforce a plan for the disarmament and demobilization of all former combatants and to facilitate the delivery of humanitarian assistance. Assisted the government to restore authority throughout the country, as necessary, to rebuild a national police force and to conduct democratic elections.

Duration: October 1999–December 2005.

Headquarters: Freetown, Sierra Leone.

UNITED NATIONS TRANSITIONAL ADMINISTRATION IN EAST TIMOR (UNTAET)

Established to exercise all judicial and executive authority in East Timor, following the organization by the UN of a popular referendum at which a majority of East Timorese voted in favour of independence for their territory.

Duration: October 1999–May 2002.

Headquarters: Dili, East Timor.

UNITED NATIONS MISSION IN THE DEMOCRATIC REPUBLIC OF THE CONGO (MONUC)

Mandated to assist with the implementation of a cease-fire agreement in the Democratic Republic of the Congo. Succeeded from 1 July 2010 by the United Nations Organization Stabilization Mission in the Democratic Republic of the Congo (MONUSCO), see below.

Duration: November 1999–June 2010.

Headquarters: Kinshasa, Democratic Republic of the Congo.

UNITED NATIONS MISSION IN ETHIOPIA AND ERITREA (UNMEE)

Mandated to assist with the implementation of a cease-fire agreement between Eritrea and Ethiopia.

Duration: July 2000–July 2008.

Headquarters: Asmara, Eritrea; Addis Ababa, Ethiopia.

UNITED NATIONS MISSION OF SUPPORT IN EAST TIMOR (UNMISET)

Mandated to support core administrative structures, provide interim law enforcement and security, and to assist the development of a national police force in newly independent Timor-Leste (East Timor).

Duration: May 2002–May 2005.

Headquarters: Dili, Timor-Leste.

UNITED NATIONS MISSION IN LIBERIA (UNMIL)

Mandated to support the implementation of the cease-fire accord agreed in June 2003 and Comprehensive Peace Agreement concluded in August by the parties to the conflict in Liberia, to assist with the development of an action plan for the disarmament, demobilization, reintegration and, where appropriate, repatriation of all armed groups and to undertake a programme of voluntary disarmament, to support the implementation of national security reforms, and to assist with the training of a national police force and the restructuring of the military. Activities are ongoing (see above).

Duration: September 2003–.

Headquarters: Monrovia, Liberia.

UNITED NATIONS OPERATION IN CÔTE D'IVOIRE (UNOCI)

Mandated to support the implementation of the Linas-Marcoussis cease-fire accord concluded in Côte d'Ivoire in January 2003 and to assist with the disarmament, demobilization and reintegration of rebel groups. Activities are ongoing (see above).

Duration: April 2004–.

Headquarters: Abidjan, Côte d'Ivoire.

UNITED NATIONS STABILIZATION MISSION IN HAITI (MINUSTAH)

Mandated to assume control from a multinational interim force in order to restore law and order, in co-operation with a transitional government, to investigate human rights abuses and to prepare for new elections. Activities are ongoing (see above).

Duration: June 2004–.

Headquarters: Port-au-Prince, Haiti

UNITED NATIONS OPERATION IN BURUNDI (ONUB)

Established to monitor and uphold the Arusha Agreement to restore peace in Burundi and bring about national reconciliation.

Duration: June 2004–Dec. 2006.

Headquarters: Bujumbura, Burundi.

UNITED NATIONS MISSION IN SUDAN (UNMIS)

Established to support implementation of a Comprehensive Peace Agreement, signed by parties to the conflict in Sudan in January 2005, and to contribute to international efforts to provide humanitarian assistance and to protect and promote human rights.

Duration: March 2005–July 2011.

Headquarters: Khartoum, Sudan.

UNITED NATIONS INTEGRATED MISSION IN TIMOR-LESTE (UNMIT)

Established to support the Timor-Leste authorities with consolidating stability, promoting democratic governance and facilitating the process of national reconciliation. Activities are ongoing (see above).

Duration: August 2006–.

Headquarters: Dili, Timor-Leste.

AFRICAN UNION (AU)/UN HYBRID OPERATION IN DARFUR (UNAMID)

Established to support implementation of the Darfur Peace Agreement and to assist the authorities with consolidating stability, promoting democratic governance and facilitating the process of national reconciliation. Activities are ongoing (see above).

Duration: July 2007–.

Headquarters: El Fasher, Sudan.

UNITED NATIONS MISSION IN THE CENTRAL AFRICAN REPUBLIC AND CHAD (MINURCAT)

Established as part of a multi-dimensional presence to create a secure environment in north-eastern CAR and eastern Chad. Activities are ongoing (see above).

Duration: September 2007–December 2010.

Headquarters: N'Djamena, Chad.

UNITED NATIONS ORGANIZATION STABILIZATION MISSION IN THE DEMOCRATIC REPUBLIC OF THE CONGO (MONUSCO)

Succeeded the United Nations Mission in the Democratic Republic of the Congo (MONUC), see above, in July 2010. Activities are ongoing (see above).

Duration: July 2010–.

Headquarters: Kinshasa, Democratic Republic of the Congo.

UNITED NATIONS INTERIM SECURITY FORCE FOR ABYEI (UNISFA)

Established in June 2011. Activities are ongoing.

Duration: June 2011–.

Headquarters: Abyei Town, Sudan.

UNITED NATIONS MISSION IN SOUTH SUDAN (UNMISS)

Succeeded the United Nations Mission in the Sudan (UNMIS), see above, in July 2011. Activities are ongoing (see above).

Duration: July 2011–.

Headquarters: Juba, South Sudan.

UNITED NATIONS SUPERVISION MISSION IN SYRIA (UNSMIS)

Established in April 2012. Activities are ongoing (see above).

Duration: April 2012–.

Headquarters: Damascus, Syria.

United Nations Peace-building

Address: Department of Political Affairs, United Nations, New York, NY 10017, USA.

Telephone: (212) 963-1234; **fax:** (212) 963-4879; **internet:** www.un.org/Depts/dpa/.

The Department of Political Affairs provides support and guidance to UN peace-building operations and political missions working in the field to prevent and resolve conflicts or to promote enduring peace in post-conflict societies.

The World Summit of UN heads of state held in September 2005 approved recommendations made by the UN Secretary-General in his March 2005 report entitled 'In Larger Freedom: Towards Development, Security and Human Rights for All' for the creation of an intergovernmental advisory Peace-building Commission. In December the UN Security Council and General Assembly authorized the establishment of the Commission; it was inaugurated, as a special subsidiary body of both the Council and Assembly, in June 2006. A multi-year standing peace-building fund, financed by voluntary contributions from member states and mandated to support post-conflict peace-building activities, was established in October 2006. A Peace-building Support Office was established within the UN Secretariat to administer the fund, as well as to support the Commission. In 2012 the Peace-building Commission was actively concerned with the situation in six African countries: Burundi, Central African Republic, Guinea, Guinea-Bissau, Liberia and Sierra Leone.

The UN Assistance Mission in Afghanistan is directed by the Department of Peace-keeping Operations.

Office of the Special Representative of the UN Secretary-General for West Africa—UNOWA

Address: BP 23851 Dakar-Ponty, 5 ave Carde, Immeuble Caisse de sécurité sociale, Dakar, Senegal.

Telephone: (221) 849-07-29; **fax:** (221) 842-50-95; **internet:** www.un.org/unowa.

Special Representative of the UN Secretary-General: SAID DJINNIT (Algeria).

Establishment and Mandate: UNOWA was established, with an initial three-year mandate, from January 2002, to elaborate an integrated approach by the United Nations to the prevention and management of conflict in West Africa; and to promote peace, security and development in the sub-region. (UNOWA's mandate has subsequently been renewed, most recently for a further three years until December 2013.) In pursuit of these objectives, the Special Representative of the Secretary-General (SRSG) meets regularly with the leaders of UN regional and political offices in West Africa.

Activities: UNOWA supports the development of a regional harmonized approach to disarmament, demobilization and reintegration in West Africa, and its projects have included an initiative to address cross-border challenges, such as mercenaries, child-soldiers and small arms proliferation. UNOWA also aims to support and facilitate a sub-regional approach to issues that impact stability in West Africa, in particular electoral processes and the transfer of power. UNOWA works with the Economic Community of West African States (ECOWAS), whose projects embrace security sector reform (identified as a key priority for the sub-region), small arms, transborder co-operation, etc. A trilateral partnership between UNOWA, the European Union and ECOWAS has also been established. In July 2009 UNOWA, with the UN Office on Drugs and Crime, the UN Department of Peace-keeping Operations and INTERPOL, inaugurated a West Africa Coast Initiative (WACI) to support the ECOWAS Regional Action Plan, which aimed to counter the problem of illicit drugs trafficking, organized crime, and drug abuse in West Africa. WACI provides advice, equipment, technical assistance and specialized training, and supports the establishment of Transnational Crime Units in each country. UNOWA, with the UN Office for the Co-ordination of Humanitarian Affairs (OCHA), has worked to address economic, political, security and humanitarian problems that confront the populations of certain border areas in West Africa through the development of integrated, multi-agency strategies in respect of four border clusters: Guinea/Côte d'Ivoire/Liberia/Sierra Leone (Guinea Forestière); Mali/Burkina Faso/Côte d'Ivoire/Ghana; Mauritania/Mali/Niger; and Senegal/The Gambia/Guinea-Bissau. UNOWA works closely with OCHA in strengthening the UN's regional humanitarian response. It is also concerned to promote respect for human rights and to support the full consideration of gender issues in conflict management and peace-building activities.

In May 2011 UNOWA organized a Regional Conference on Elections and Stability in West Africa, in Praia, Cape Verde; the Conference adopted the Praia Declaration on Elections and Stability in West Africa, identifying practical recommendations for improving electoral processes in the region. A round table meeting was convened in September, in New York, USA, by UNOWA and the International Peace Institute, further to discuss issues raised by the Conference. In the following month UNOWA supported the organization by the West African Human Rights Defenders Network of a panel discussion on the role of civil society organizations in elections; as a consequence of the panel discussion, civil society organizations in the subregion adopted a roadmap for the implementation of the Praia Declaration.

In early December 2011 UNOWA, jointly with OHCHR, ECOWAS, the African Union, the Mano River Union and the Organisation Internationale de la Francophonie, convened a Regional Conference on Impunity, Justice and Human Rights in West Africa, in Bamako, Mali; the Conference adopted the Bamako Declaration and a strategic framework, outlining recommendations aimed at strengthening good governance and the rule of law, in order to promote stability and development in West Africa.

In February 2012 the UN Security Council requested the UN Secretary-General to support, through UNOWA and UNOCA, states and sub-regional organizations in convening a joint Summit on combating maritime piracy in the Gulf of Guinea.

The SRSG serves as chairman of the Cameroon-Nigeria Mixed Commission, which has met regularly since December 2002, and hosts high level meetings of the heads of UN peace missions in West Africa. UNOWA conducts regional good offices missions.

Operational Strength: At 31 May 2012 UNOWA comprised three military advisers, and (as at 29 February 2012) 19 international civilian and 17 local civilian personnel.

Office of the United Nations Special Co-ordinator for Lebanon—UNSCOL

Address: UN House, Riad el-Solh Sq., POB 11, 8577 Beirut, Lebanon. **E-mail:** unscol-website@un.org; **internet:** unscol .unmissions.org.

Special Co-ordinator for Lebanon: DEREK PLUMBLY (United Kingdom).

Establishment and Mandate: The Office of the United Nations Special Co-ordinator for Lebanon was established in February 2007, replacing the Office of the Personal Representative of the UN Secretary-General for southern Lebanon (established in August 2000). The Office co-ordinates the UN presence in Lebanon and is the focal point for the core group of donor countries supporting Lebanon. The Office works closely with the expanded UN peace-keeping mission in Lebanon, UNIFIL. The Special Co-ordinator is responsible for supervising implementation of Security Council Resolution 1701, which was adopted in August 2006, and called for a cessation of hostilities in Lebanon.

Operational Strength: At 29 February 2012 UNSCOL comprised 21 international civilian and 61 local civilian personnel.

Office of the United Nations Special Co-ordinator for the Middle East Peace Process—UNSCO

Address: Gaza; Jerusalem; Ramallah.

Special Co-ordinator for the Middle East Peace Process: ROBERT R. SERRY (Netherlands).

Establishment and Mandate: The Office of the United Nations Special Co-ordinator for the Middle East (UNSCO) was established in June 1994 after the conclusion of the Declaration of Principles on Interim (Palestinian) Self-Government Arrangements—the 'Oslo Accord'. UNSCO was to seek, during the transition process envisaged by the Declaration, to ensure 'an adequate response to the needs of the Palestinian people and to mobilise financial, technical, economic and other assistance'. In 1995 UNSCO's mandate was reconfigured as the Office of the Special Co-ordinator for the Middle East Peace Process and Personal Representative of the Secretary-General to the Palestine Liberation Organization and the Palestine (National) Authority (PA).

Activities: The Office has been mandated to assist in all issues related to the humanitarian situation confronting the Palestinian people, and supports negotiations and the implementation of political agreements. The Regional Affairs Unit (RAU) of the Office assists in the fulfilment of that part of the Office's mandate that requires it to co-ordinate its work and to co-operate closely with all of the parties to the Middle East peace process, including the Governments of Israel, Lebanon, Syria, Jordan and Egypt, the PA, Palestinian civil society, the Arab League, and individual Arab states that have assumed a key role in facilitating the peace process. The Special Co-ordinator also collaborates closely with key international actors, in particular those that, together with the UN, constitute the Middle East Quartet, i.e. the European Union, Russia and the USA, and serves as the Envoy of the UN Secretary-General to the Quartet. In addition to the RAU, UNSCO maintains a Media Office and a Research Unit.

Operational Strength: At 29 February 2012 UNSCO comprised 31 international civilian and 29 local civilian personnel.

United Nations Assistance Mission in Afghanistan—UNAMA

Address: POB 5858, Grand Central Station, New York, NY 10163-5858, USA.

Telephone: (813) 246000; **fax:** (831) 246069; **e-mail:** spokesperson-unama@un.org; **internet:** www.unama-afg.org.

Special Representative of the UN Secretary-General: JÁN KUBIŠ (Slovakia).

Deputy Special Representative of the UN Secretary-General, Political Affairs: NICHOLAS HAYSOM (South Africa).

Deputy Special Representative of the UN Secretary-General, Relief, Recovery and Reconstruction: MICHAEL KEATING (United Kingdom).

Establishment and Mandate: The United Nations Assistance Mission in Afghanistan (UNAMA) was established by the UN Security Council in March 2002. UNAMA's mandate has subsequently been renewed annually, most recently to March 2013. The Mission was initially authorized to fulfil tasks assigned to the UN under the December 2001 Bonn Agreement on provisional arrangements for Afghanistan. The process determined by the Bonn Agreement terminated in September 2005. Subsequently UNAMA assumed responsibility for assisting the Afghan Government with the implementation of an Afghanistan Compact, which was adopted by the London Conference on Afghanistan, co-chaired by the UN and Afghanistan from 31 January–1 February 2006, as a framework for co-operation between the Afghan authorities, the UN and the international community. The Compact identifies three key and interdependent pillars of activity for its term: security; governance, rule of law and human rights; and economic and social development. In addition, the Compact aims to promote the elimination of Afghanistan's narcotics industry. UNAMA was mandated to provide political and strategic advice for the peace process; to provide good offices; to promote human rights; to provide technical assistance; and, in co-operation with the Afghan authorities, to manage all UN humanitarian relief, recovery, reconstruction and development activities. Peace-building tasks that fall under UNAMA's political mandate include the prevention and resolution of conflicts; building confidence and the promotion of national reconciliation; monitoring the political and human rights situation; and investigating human rights violations. As appropriate, UNAMA is charged with recommending corrective actions; maintaining dialogue with Afghan leaders, political parties, civil society groups, institutions and representatives of the central authorities; and undertaking good offices to foster the peace process.

Activities: UNAMA co-ordinates all of the activities of the UN system, whose programme of work is determined by Afghan needs and priorities. Nineteen UN agencies work together with their Afghan government counterparts and with national and international NGO partners. The Paris International Conference in Support of Afghanistan, convened in June 2008, agreed that UNAMA should expand its efforts to co-ordinate international activities in Afghanistan and endorsed a new Afghanistan National Development Strategy. In early 2009 UNAMA established a new political unit to co-ordinate efforts, in collaboration with local political parties, observers and civil society organizations, to promote a free and fair environment for the presidential and provincial council elections that were held in August. During that year UNAMA expanded its presence in the country to eight regional and 15 provincial offices. The London International Conference in Support of Afghanistan, convened in January 2010, renewed the commitment of the international community and Afghan authorities to the implementation of a reform-oriented nation-building agenda. In July an International Conference on Afghanistan, co-chaired by the UN, was convened for the first time in Kabul. The meeting endorsed a new Afghanistan National Development Strategy: Prioritization and Implementation Plan, for the period to mid-2013, which aimed to facilitate the transition to full Afghan governance. UNAMA was to support the so-called Kabul process by providing electoral assistance to the independent Afghan electoral commissions; fostering national political dialogue and regional engagement; promoting regional co-operation, though confidence-building measures and a Kabul Silk Road initiative (inaugurated in early 2010 by the SRSG to promote informal dialogue between the Government, the UN and Ambassadors of neighbouring countries); and co-ordinating UN and international aid in support of the Government's national development and governance priorities. In October the SRSG met members of a new High Peace Council, and concluded an agreement to provide technical and practical assistance to the Council in support of the process of national peace and reconciliation. In April 2011 three UNAMA international staff members were killed during violent protests near the UN compound in Mazar-e-Sharif. An international conference on Afghanistan held in Bonn, Germany, in December, confirmed long-term commitment to supporting Afghanistan through a newly designated Transformation Decade, to cover 2015–24, and noted the importance of the UN role, and that the mandate of UNAMA was under review as the Afghan authorities assumed increased leadership responsibilities. In late February 2012 a UNAMA compound in Kunduz, north-eastern Afghanistan, was attacked during violent protests that erupted following reports that US troops based in Afghanistan had unintentionally burned copies of the Koran.

During October 2010–August 2011 UNAMA conducted interviews with 379 inmates detained at 47 Afghan detention facilities operated either by the National Directorate of Security or by the national police, and, in October 2011, the mission released a report concluding that allegations by prisoners of mistreatment and torture at several of the facilities were credible. The report detailed a number of key recommendations aimed at preventing the recurrence of ill treatment of detainees.

UNAMA, jointly with OHCHR, issues an annual report on *Protection of Civilians in Armed Conflict*. The 2011 report, released in February 2012, found that civilian casualties arising from the Afghan conflict had, in 2011, risen for the fifth consecutive year, numbering 3,021, compared with 2,790 in 2010.

In November 2010 the UN signed an agreement with the Kuwaiti Government to establish a UNAMA Support Office in that country.

Operational Strength: At 31 May 2012 UNAMA comprised 17 military observers, four police personnel and 70 UN Volunteers; there were, in addition, 418 international civilian and 1,719 local civilian personnel (as at 29 February 2012).

United Nations Assistance Mission for Iraq—UNAMI

Address: Amman, Jordan.

Telephone: (6) 5504700; **fax:** (6) 5504705; **e-mail:** achouri@un.org; **internet:** www.uniraq.org.

Special Representative of the UN Secretary-General for Iraq: MARTIN KOBLER (Germany).

Deputy Special Representative of the UN Secretary-General for Political, Electoral and Constitutional Support: GYÖRGY BUSZTIN (Hungary).

Deputy Special Representative of the UN Secretary-General for Development and Humanitarian Support: JACQUELINE BADCOCK (United Kingdom).

Establishment and Mandate: The United Nations Assistance Mission for Iraq (UNAMI) was initially established by UN Security Council Resolution 1500 (14 August 2003) as a one-year mission to co-ordinate and support humanitarian efforts in post-conflict Iraq. Later in August, however, terrorist attacks on the UNAMI headquarters in Baghdad killed the newly appointed Special Representative of the UN Secretary-General for Iraq (and UN High Commissioner for Human Rights), Sergio Vieira de Mello, and 21 other UN personnel. UN international staff were subsequently withdrawn from Iraq, and, until the formation of the Iraqi Interim Government at the end of June 2004, UNAMI operated primarily from outside Iraq (from Cyprus, Jordan and Kuwait). Meanwhile, political and security concerns were urgently reviewed by the UN Secretary-General. UNAMI consists of two pillars—political and reconstruction and development—and a Human Rights Office (HRO), which maintains links with the Office of the Higher Commissioner for Human Rights. Generally, the work of the political pillar is carried out in support of the good offices and facilitation role of the Special Representative of the Secretary-General (SRSG). The political office also supports, as necessary, the HRO and the reconstruction and development pillar. In April–May 2004 the UN helped to establish an Independent Electoral Commission of Iraq (IECI). In accordance with the mandate afforded it under UN Security Council Resolution 1546 (June 2004), UNAMI assisted in the convening of an Iraqi national conference in August, including in the selection of a Consultative Council.

UNAMI is mandated, under Resolution 1546, 'to promote the protection of human rights, national reconciliation, and judicial and legal reform in order to strengthen the rule of law in Iraq'. Through two units, the HRO monitors and reports on the human rights situation and addresses the reconstruction of Iraqi national human rights institutions. HRO activities include providing technical support and training to the ministries of justice, defence and human rights; the establishment of a national centre for missing and disappeared persons in Iraq; and the establishment of a national human rights institution. UNAMI is also mandated to promote dialogue and effective procedures to resolve disputed international boundaries.

Activities: In January 2005 elections were held in Iraq to choose a Transitional National Assembly that would be charged with drafting a permanent constitution. These elections also formed the basis for the establishment of a Transitional Government and presidency. UNAMI's electoral unit assisted and advised the IECI, which was responsible for the organization and conduct of these elections. From May until October 2005, in response to requests for assistance from the Transitional Government, UNAMI provided support and advice to the constitution-making process. In early 2007 UNAMI facilitated and observed the process of reconfiguring the IECI as the Independent High Electoral Commission (IHEC). UNAMI continued to assist the IHEC in capacity- and institution-building and provided technical support during provincial and national legislative elections conducted in 2009–10. In December 2011 the Iraqi authorities requested that UNAMI serve in an impartial advisory capacity in the then ongoing process to select IHEC commissioners.

With regard to reconstruction and development, UNAMI aims are: to address the long-term challenge of achieving sustainable food security; to strengthen the overall quality of education and service delivery at all levels; to support policy development, and preserve and conserve the tangible and intangible Iraqi cultural heritage; to improve the human development situation in Iraq and promote good governance by strengthening institutional capacity, contributing to the creation of employment opportunities and providing policy advice; to support the national health strategy of the Iraqi Ministry of Health in meeting basic health needs; to formulate and implement programmes on institutional/policy reform, capacity building, and service provision necessary to rehabilitate and develop the infrastructure of human settlements; and to support the Iraqi authorities in providing adequate assistance and effective protection to uprooted populations in Iraq, and to assist them in preventing new displacement as well as in achieving durable solutions. UNAMI works closely with some 16 other UN agencies, funds and programmes to co-ordinate assistance activities through the UN Country Team for Iraq.

In April 2009 the Special Representative of the UN Secretary-General presented a report on the disputed internal boundaries of northern Iraq, concluding a year-long process of analysis and consultation. In June the Special Representative launched a Task Force on Dialogue, with senior representatives of the Iraqi Prime Minister and Kurdistan Regional Government. The Task Force convened, under UN auspices, regularly during late 2009 and the first half of 2010, to consider the UNAMI report and facilitate further political dialogue.

UNAMI endorsed the International Compact for Iraq, a five-year framework for co-operation between Iraq and the international community jointly chaired by the Iraqi Government and the UN Secretariat, that was launched in May 2007. In August the UN Security Council approved Resolution 1770, which expanded UNAMI's mandate to incorporate a responsibility to promote, support and facilitate the implementation of the International Compact, as well as the co-ordination and delivery of humanitarian assistance, and to support and advise on national reconciliation efforts. In August 2008 UNAMI and the Iraqi Government signed a UN Assistance Strategy for Iraq 2008–10, which focused on greater collaboration and co-financing of projects. In May 2010 a new UN Development Assistance Framework was signed by the UN and the Iraqi Government, covering the period 2011–14. It identified the priority areas for UN support being to contribute to: inclusive economic growth; environmental management; promoting good governance and protection of human rights; ensuring access to improved basic services for all; and investment in the capacities of women, youth and children to enable their full participation in all aspects of life in Iraq.

Operational Strength: At 31 May 2012 UNAMI personnel (based in Iraq, Jordan and Kuwait) comprised 392 troops, eight military advisers, and four police; they were assisted by 387 international civilian staff and 504 local civilian staff (as at 29 February 2012).

United Nations Office in Burundi—BNUB

Address: BP 6899, Gatumba Rd, Bujumbura, Burundi.

Telephone: 22205165; **internet:** binub.unmissions.org.

Special Representative of the UN Secretary-General and Head of Office: PARFAIT ONANGA-ANYANGA (Gabon).

Establishment and Mandate: The United Nations Office in Burundi (Bureau des Nations Unies au Burundi—BNUB) was established on 1 January 2011, as a successor to the UN Integrated Office in Burundi (BINUB), which had operated in the country since 2007. BNUB represented a commitment by the UN to maintaining a scaled-down presence in the country, for an initial 12-month period, in order to support the country's progress towards peace consolidation and long-term development. BNUB mandate was to support the efforts of the Burundi Government to strengthen the independence, capacities and legal frameworks of key national institutions, in accordance with international standards and principles; to facilitate political dialogue and broad-based participation in political life; to support efforts to fight impunity, in particular through the establishment of transitional justice mechanisms to strengthen national unity, and to promote justice and reconciliation within Burundi's society, and to provide operational support to the functioning of these bodies; to promote and protect human rights, and strengthen national capacities in that area; to ensure that all strategies and policies with respect to public finance and the economic sector, in particular the next Poverty Reduction Strategy Paper (PRSP), have a focus on peace-building, equitable growth, and addressing the needs of the most vulnerable population; and to provide support to Burundi's 2011 chairmanship of the East African Community, as well as providing advice, as requested, on regional integration issues. The Office was to work to ensure effective co-ordination among UN agencies in Burundi.

In December 2011 the UN Security Council extended the mandate of BNUB until 15 February 2013, emphasizing, in so doing, that significant challenges remained in areas including human rights, democratic governance, civilian protection, combating corruption, security sector reform, and promoting economic development.

Operational Strength: At 31 May 2012 BNUB comprised one military adviser, one police officer, and six UN Volunteers, as well as 52 international civilian staff and 65 local civilian staff (as at 29 February 2012).

United Nations Integrated Peace-building Office in Sierra Leone—UNIPSIL

Address: Cabenda Hotel, 14 Signal Hill Rd, POB 5, Freetown, Sierra Leone.

Telephone: (76) 692810; **internet:** unipsil.unmissions.org.

Executive Representative of the UN Secretary-General and Head of Mission: JENS ANDERS TOYBERG-FRANDZEN (Denmark).

Establishment and Mandate: The Office was established on 1 October 2008, in accordance with UN Security Council Resolution 1829 (4 August 2008), as a successor to the United Nations Integrated Office in Sierra Leone (UNIOSIL). UNIOSIL had been established in January 2006 following the expiry of the mandate of the large UN peace-keeping operation in Sierra Leone, UNAMSIL, and assisted the Government of Sierra Leone to consolidate peace and to build the capacity of national institutions to support democracy and economic and social development. The key elements of UNIPSIL's mandate were to support the Government of Sierra Leone: to identify and resolve tensions and areas of potential conflict; to monitor and promote human rights, democratic institutions and the rule of law, including efforts to counter transnational organized crime and drugs-trafficking; to consolidate good governance reforms, in particular anti-corruption bodies; to support decentralization; and to co-ordinate with and support the work of the Peace-building Commission, as well as the implementation of a Peace-building Co-operation Framework. UNIPSIL was to work closely with the Economic Community of West African States (ECOWAS), the Mano River Union, other international partners and other UN missions in the region. The head of UNIPSIL, the Executive Representative of the UN Secretary-General, also serves as the Resident Representative of the UN Development Programme and as the UN Resident and Humanitarian Co-ordinator. In December 2008 UNIPSIL, with all other UN agencies and programmes working in Sierra Leone, as well as the African Development Bank, adopted a Joint Vision to co-ordinate facilities and services in order to help to consolidate a sustainable peace in the country.

Operational Strength: At 31 May 2012 UNIPSIL comprised seven police personnel and eight UN Volunteers; it was supported by 37 international civilian and 31 local civilian personnel (as at 29 February 2012).

United Nations Integrated Peace-building Office in the Central African Republic—BINUCA

Address: BP 3338, PK 4 ave Boganda, Bangui, Central African Republic.

Telephone: 21-61-70-98; **internet:** binuca.unmissions.org.

Special Representative of the UN Secretary-General and Head of Office: MARGARET VOGT (Nigeria).

Establishment and Mandate: The United Nations Integrated Peace-building Office in the CAR (BINUCA) was inaugurated on 1 January 2010, replacing the UN Peace-building Office in the CAR (BONUCA), which was established in February 2000, following the withdrawal of the UN Peace-keeping Mission in the Central African Republic (MINURCA). BINUCA is mandated to support national and local efforts to develop governance reforms and electoral processes; to support the completion of disarmament, demobilization and reintegration programme activities; to help to restore state authority in the provinces; to promote respect for human rights and the rule of law; to support the UN Mission in the CAR and Chad (MINURCAT); and to ensure that child protection measures are observed. Successive extensions of BINUCA's mandate were approved by the Security Council in December 2010 and December 2011 (the former by one year, and the latter until 31 January 2013).

Operational Strength: At 31 May 2012 BINUCA comprised two military observers, two police and five UN Volunteers; in addition, it was supported by 67 international civilian and 75 local civilian personnel (as at 29 February 2012).

United Nations Integrated Peace-building Office in Guinea-Bissau—UNIOGBIS

Address: UN Bldg, CP 179, Rua Rui Djassi, Bissau, Guinea-Bissau.

Telephone: 20-36-18; **fax:** 20-36-13; **internet:** uniogbis .unmissions.org.

Special Representative of the UN Secretary-General and Head of Office: JOSEPH MUTABOBA (Rwanda).

Establishment and Mandate: Established to assist the Peace-building Commission in its multi-dimensional engagement with Guinea-Bissau, the United Nations Integrated Peace-building Office in Guinea-Bissau (UNIOGBIS) first became operational in January 2010, succeeding the UN Peace-building Office in Guinea-Bissau (UNOGBIS). Unlike other UN peace-building missions, UNOGBIS had not been preceded by a UN peace-keeping mission.

Activities: From 2003 the work of UNOGBIS, which preceded UNIOGBIS, focused on transition to civilian rule in the aftermath of a military coup that took place in that year. UNOGBIS was mandated by the UN Security Council to promote national reconciliation, respect for human rights and the rule of law; to support national capacity for conflict prevention; to encourage reform of the security sector and stable civil-military relations; to encourage government efforts to suppress trafficking in small arms; and to collaborate with a 'comprehensive peace-building strategy' to strengthen state institutions and mobilize international resources. In December 2007 the UN Security Council authorized a revised mandate for UNOGBIS to support efforts by the Guinea-Bissau authorities to counter illegal drugs-trafficking. UNOGBIS undertook training of electoral agents and journalists in preparation for legislative elections, conducted in November 2008, and co-ordinated the activities of international observers monitoring the voting. In June 2009 the UN Security Council endorsed the establishment of UNIOGBIS, which succeeded UNOGBIS from 1 January 2010. From mid-2010 UNIOGBIS facilitated the preparation of meetings of security and defence forces, as part of a National Reconciliation Conference process. It also worked to enhance the co-ordination and effectiveness of international assistance to further defence and security sector reform, co-operated with the UN Mine Action Service to assess the country's weapons and ammunition stockpiles, and supported the national authorities to combat human trafficking, drugs trafficking and other areas of organized crime. During 2011 UNIOGBIS, with UNDP, provided support to the organizing committee of the National Reconciliation Conference process. The Office also supported the ongoing constitutional review process, and provided technical and financial assistance to the National Technical Independent Mixed Commission, responsible for the selection of police officers. In September a model police station, established with support from UNIOGBIS, was inaugurated in Bissau; 12 further model police stations were planned.

Operational Strength: At 31 May 2012 UNIOGBIS comprised 16 police officers, two military advisers and six UN Volunteers; in addition, there were 53 international civilian and 52 local civilian personnel (as at 29 February 2012).

United Nations Political Office for Somalia—UNPOS

Address: UNPOS Public Information Office, POB 48246-00100, Nairobi, Kenya.

Telephone: (20) 7622131; **fax:** (20) 7622697; **e-mail:** unpos_pio@un.org; **internet:** unpos.unmissions.org.

Special Representative of the UN Secretary-General and Head of Office: AUGUSTINE P. MAHIGA (Tanzania).

Establishment and Mandate: The United Nations Political Office for Somalia (UNPOS) was established in 1995 with the objective of assisting the Secretary-General to advance peace and reconciliation in the country by utilizing its contacts with Somali leaders and civic organizations. Owing to the security situation in that country, UNPOS was administered from offices in Nairobi, Kenya. UNPOS provides good offices, co-ordinates international political support and financial assistance to peace and reconciliation initiatives, and monitors and reports on developments in the country. In 2002–04 UNPOS supported the Somali National Reconciliation Conference that was organized in Nairobi under the auspices of the Inter-governmental Authority on Development, and worked with international partners to facilitate agreement among Somali leaders on a transitional administration. By early 2005 the Conference had established a broad-based Transitional Federal Government, which was able to relocate to Somalia from its temporary base in Kenya. The UN Security Council consequently authorized UNPOS to promote reconciliation through dialogue between Somali parties; to assist efforts to address the 'Somaliland' issue; to co-ordinate the support of Somalia's neighbours and other international partners for the country's peace process; and to assume a leading political role in peace-building initiatives. In January 2012 the Special Representative of the Secretary-General (SRSG), with several core UNPOS staff members, relocated from Nairobi to the Somali capital, Mogadishu; the last SRSG to be based in Mogadishu had departed there in 1995. An UNPOS Public Information Office remained in Nairobi.

Activities: In spite of an outbreak of hostilities in May 2006, the Transitional Federal Institutions continued to function during that year and to co-operate with the UN's Special Representative to pursue peace negotiations. In May 2008 the Special Representative chaired inter-Somali peace negotiations, held in Djibouti. An agreement was reached in June, and formally signed in August, on the cessation of hostilities and the establishment of a Joint Security Committee and a High Level Committee on political issues. In March 2009 UNPOS organized a meeting, in Djibouti, with representatives of the Somali business community. A committee was established to develop and implement a strategy to support entrepreneurs. From mid-2009 UNPOS, with AMISOM and key members of the transitional Government and the international community acting in Somalia, met as a revised Joint Security Committee. In April 2010 UNPOS signed a Memorandum of Understanding with IGAD and AMISOM, in order to strengthen co-ordination of activities between the organizations in support of the peace process. In early 2011 UNPOS supported a consensus-building process to enable the transitional period of government to conclude, as determined under the Djibouti Peace Agreement, in August. In June the Special Representative facilitated the signing of the so-called Kampala Accord by the President and Speaker of the Transitional Federal Parliament providing for the establishment of a new interim administration to undertake the tasks necessary to end the transitional phase; a presidential election and election for a new Speaker were to take place no later than August 2012. In September 2011 the Special Representative helped to organize, in the Somali capital Mogadishu, a High Level Consultative Meeting on Ending Transition, attended by high level representatives of the Transitional Federal Institutions, the regional administrations serving Galmudug and Puntland, and other international partners. The meeting endorsed a roadmap for the forthcoming 12-month period. UNPOS was to establish a new dedicated unit to administer the implementation mechanisms identified in the roadmap.

Operational Strength: At 31 May 2012 UNPOS was composed of three military advisers and three police officers; there were, in addition, 54 international civilian and 31 local civilian personnel (as at 29 February 2012).

United Nations Regional Centre for Preventive Diplomacy for Central Asia—UNRCCA

Address: Aşgabat, Archabil Shaeli 43, Turkmenistan.

Special Representative of the UN Secretary-General and Head of Office: Miroslav Jenča (Slovakia).

Establishment and Mandate: The Centre was inaugurated in December 2007, with the objective of assisting and supporting the governments of Kazakhstan, Kyrgyzstan, Tajikistan, Turkmenistan and Uzbekistan to enhance their conflict prevention capacities through dialogue, confidence-building measures and partnerships, in order to respond to existing threats and emerging challenges in the Central Asian region. The Centre is administered by the UN Department of Political Affairs.

Activities: The Centre monitors and analyses the situation in Central Asia, including maintaining close contact with the UN Assistance Mission in Afghanistan, to attain early warning of potential conflict, co-ordinates the efforts of international agencies to promote sustainable development and conflict prevention, facilitates the implementation of regional and international agreements and frameworks of action, and organizes training, workshops and seminars. For the period 2012–14 the Centre identified the following as priority areas of activity: liaising with the governments of the region and, with their concurrence, with other parties concerned on issues relevant to preventive diplomacy; monitoring and analyzing the situation on the ground and providing the UN Secretary-General with current information related to conflict prevention efforts; maintaining contacts with relevant regional organizations, encouraging their peace-making efforts and initiatives, and facilitating co-ordination and information exchange with due regard to their specific mandates; providing a political framework and leadership for the preventive activities of the UN country teams in the region, and supporting the efforts of the Resident Co-ordinators; maintaining close contact with UNAMA to ensure a comprehensive and integrated analysis of the situation in the region. In December 2010 UNRCCA, with the UN Counter-Terrorism Implementation Task Force and the EU, convened the first of a series of expert meetings on measures to combat terrorism in Central Asia. In May 2011 the Centre hosted the third annual meeting of deputy ministers of foreign affairs of Central Asian countries, at which measures to enhance co-operation and strengthen stability in the region were discussed.

Operational Strength: At 29 February 2012 the Centre was served by eight international civilian and four local civilian personnel.

United Nations Regional Office for Central Africa—UNOCA

Address: BP 23773, Cité de la Démocratie, Villas 55–57, Libreville, Gabon.

Telephone: (241) 741-401; **fax:** (241) 741-402.

Special Representative of the UN Secretary-General: Abou Moussa (Chad).

Establishment and Mandate: UNOCA—covering the 10 member states of the Communauté économique des états de l'Afrique centrale (CEEAC): Angola, Burundi, Cameroon, Central African Republic, Chad, Democratic Republic of the Congo, Republic of the Congo, Equatorial Guinea, Gabon, and São Tomé and Príncipe—was inaugurated in March 2011, having been established through an exchange of letters, finalized in August 2010, between the UN Secretary-General and the UN Security Council. UNOCA is mandated, initially for a period of two years, to extend the UN's good offices and other assistance to regional states and organizations in support of preventive diplomacy and the consolidation of peace. The Office is also mandated to work closely with UN and other entities to address cross-border challenges, such as organized crime, trafficking in arms, and the activities of armed groups (including the Lord's Resistance Army).

Activities: UNOCA's priority areas of activity include: supporting conflict mediation, and, where requested, assisting with the peaceful conduct of elections in the region; facilitating cohesion in the general work of the UN in the region, including in partnership with other agencies, such as UNDP, UNODC, UN Women and OHCHR; promoting activities in partnership with the private sector and civil society networks; co-ordinating UN efforts in the region against armed groups; undertaking studies on regional challenges and threats; providing technical assistance aimed at advancing early warning and mediation capabilities; helping to build the capacity of CEEAC; promoting the formulation of a regional integrated approach to addressing cross-border insecurity; and combating maritime insecurity in the Gulf of Guinea.

In February 2012 the UN Security Council requested the UN Secretary-General to support, through UNOCA and UNOWA, states and sub-regional organizations in organizing a joint Summit to be held on combating maritime piracy in the Gulf of Guinea.

Operational Strength: At 31 May 2012 the Office comprised one military adviser, supported (as at 29 February 2012) by 17 international civilian and seven local civilian personnel.

United Nations Support Mission in Libya—UNSMIL

Address: Tripoli, Libya.

Special Representative of the UN Secretary-General: Ian Martin (United Kingdom).

Establishment and Mandate: Following the outbreak of conflict in Libya in February 2011, UNSMIL was established in September, for an initial period of three months, with a mandate to support Libya's transitional authorities in restoring public security and the rule of law; promoting inclusive political dialogue and national reconciliation; embarking upon the process of drafting a new constitution and preparing for democratic elections. UNSMIL is also mandated to support the Libyan authorities in extending state authority, through the strengthening of emerging accountable institutions; restoring public services; promoting and protecting human rights (particularly for vulnerable groups); supporting transitional justice; taking the immediate steps required to initiate economic recovery; and co-ordinating support that may be requested from other multilateral and bilateral actors. In December the UN Security Council extended the mission for a further three month period, and the mission's mandate was further extended, for 12 months, in March 2012: at that time the mandate was modified to include: assisting the Libyan authorities to define national needs and priorities; managing the process of democratic transition; promoting the rule of law and monitoring and protecting human rights, particularly those of women and vulnerable groups; restoring public security; countering the illicit proliferation of all arms and related materiel of all types, in particular man-portable surface-to-air missiles; co-ordinating international assistance; and building government capacity across all relevant sectors.

Operational Strength: At 29 February 2012 the Office was served by 56 international civilian personnel, two police, and three local civilian staff members.

United Nations Population Fund—UNFPA

Address: 605 Third Ave, New York, NY 10158, USA.

Telephone: (212) 297-5000; **fax:** (212) 370-0201; **e-mail:** hq@unfpa.org; **internet:** www.unfpa.org.

Created in 1967 as the Trust Fund for Population Activities, the UN Fund for Population Activities (UNFPA) was established as a Fund of the UN General Assembly in 1972 and was made a subsidiary organ of the UN General Assembly in 1979, with the UNDP Governing Council (now the Executive Board) designated as its governing body. In 1987 UNFPA's name was changed to the United Nations Population Fund (retaining the same acronym).

Organization

(June 2012)

EXECUTIVE DIRECTOR

The Executive Director, who has the rank of Under-Secretary-General of the UN, is responsible for the overall direction of the Fund, working closely with governments, other United Nations bodies and agencies, and non-governmental and international organizations to ensure the most effective programming and use of resources in population activities.

Executive Director: BABATUNDE OSOTIMEHIN (Nigeria).

Deputy Executive Director (Management): ANNE-BIRGITTE ALBRECTSEN (Denmark).

Deputy Executive Director (Programme): KATE GILMORE (Australia).

EXECUTING AGENCIES

UNFPA provides financial and technical assistance to developing countries and countries with economies in transition, at their request. In many projects assistance is extended through member organizations of the UN system (in particular, FAO, the ILO, UNESCO and WHO), although projects are executed increasingly by national governments themselves. The Fund may also call on the services of international, regional and national non-governmental and training organizations, as well as research institutions. In addition, UNFPA's nine country technical services teams, composed of experts from the UN, its specialized agencies and non-governmental organizations, assist countries at all stages of project/programme development and implementation.

FIELD ORGANIZATION

UNFPA operates field offices, each headed by an UNFPA Representative, in some 112 countries. In other countries UNFPA uses UNDP's field structure of Resident Representatives as the main mechanism for performing its work. The field offices assist governments in formulating requests for aid and co-ordinate the work of the executing agencies in any given country or area. UNFPA has nine regional technical services teams (see above). UNFPA has five regional offices, located in Bangkok, Thailand; Bratislava, Slovakia; Cairo, Egypt; Johannesburg, South Africa; and Panama City, Panama; five liaison offices, in Brussels, Belgium; Copenhagen, Denmark; Geneva, Switzerland; Tokyo, Japan; and Washington, DC, USA.

Activities

UNFPA aims to promote health, in particular reproductive health, and gender equality as essential elements of long-term sustainable development. It aims to assist countries, at their request, to formulate policies and strategies to reduce poverty and support development and to collect and analyse population data to support better understanding of their needs. UNFPA's activities are broadly defined by the Programme of Action adopted by the International Conference on Population and Development (ICPD), which was held in Cairo, Egypt, in September 1994; UNFPA was designated the lead agency in following up the objectives of Programme of Action, which envisaged universal access to reproductive health care services and family planning services, a reduction in infant, child and maternal mortality, a reduction in the rate of HIV infection, improving life expectancy at birth, and universal access to primary education for all children by 2015. The Programme also emphasized the necessity of empowering and educating women, in order to achieve successful sustainable human development. A special session of the UN General Assembly (entitled ICPD+5, and attended by delegates from 177 countries) was held in June–July 1999 to assess progress in achieving the objectives of the Cairo Conference and to identify priorities for future action. ICPD+5 adopted several key actions for further implementation of the Programme of Action. These included advancing understanding of the connections between poverty, gender inequalities, health, education, the environment, financial and human resources, and development; focusing on the economic and social implications of demographic change; greater incorporation of gender issues into social and development policies and greater involvement of women in decision-making processes; greater support for HIV/AIDS prevention activities; and strengthened political commitment to the reproductive health of adolescents. Several new objectives were adopted by the special session, including the achievement of 60% availability of contraceptives and reproductive health care services by 2005, 80% by 2010, with universal availability by 2015. The ICPD objectives were incorporated into the Millennium Development Goals (MDGs), agreed in September 2000 by a summit of UN heads of state or government, and have been included in national development frameworks and poverty reduction strategies. The 10th and 15th anniversaries of the ICPD were commemorated by meetings of the General Assembly convened in, respectively, October 2004 and October 2009. In February 2012 UNFPA launched a new website, icpdbeyond2014.org, providing formal updates on progress made under the IPCD Programme of Action. In May 2012 UNFPA helped to organize the fifth International Parliamentarians Conference on Population and Development, in Istanbul, Turkey, with participation by law-makers from 110 countries (the first such gathering having been held in November 2002 in Ottawa, Canada); the Conference adopted the Istanbul Declaration reaffirming commitment to the principles and goals of the 1994 Cairo Conference, and pledging to attempt to allocate at least 10% of national development and development assistance budgets towards population and reproductive health programmes. The overall objective for UNFPA's strategic plan for the period 2011–13, adopted by the Executive Board in October 2011, was to advance the right to sexual and reproductive health by accelerating progress towards the MDG of improving maternal health, with priority focus given to the goals of: reducing maternal deaths; and achieving universal access to reproductive health, including family planning (see below).

REPRODUCTIVE HEALTH AND RIGHTS

UNFPA recognizes that improving reproductive health is an essential requirement for improving the general welfare of the population and the basis for empowering women and achieving sustainable social and economic development. The ICPD succeeded in raising the political prominence of reproductive health issues and stimulating consideration by governments of measures to strengthen and restructure their health services and policies. In October 2007 the UN General Assembly officially incorporated the aim of achieving, by 2015, universal access to reproductive health into the target for Goal 5 of the MDGs. UNPFA supports the 'Every Woman Every Child' campaign and the Global Strategy for Women's and Children's Health, both launched in September 2010 at the commencement of the 65th session of the UN General Assembly. The campaign aims to mobilize global action to address major health challenges and thereby save the lives of 16m. women and children by 2015, and the Global Strategy represents a roadmap for identifying principal areas requiring enhanced funding, strengthened policy and improved service delivery. UNFPA encourages the integration of family planning into all maternal, child and other reproductive health care. Its efforts to improve the quality of these services include support for the training of healthcare personnel and promoting greater accessibility to education and services. Many reproductive health projects focus on the reduction of maternal mortality (i.e. deaths related to pregnancy), which was included as a central objective of the ICPD Programme, and recognized as a legitimate element of international human rights instruments concerning the right to life/survival. Projects to reduce maternal deaths, which amount to about 500,000 each year, have focused on improving accessibility to essential obstetric care and ensuring the provision of skilled attendance to women in labour. The ICPD reported that a major cause of maternal deaths was unsafe abortions, and urged governments to confront the issue as a major public health concern. UNFPA is concerned with reducing the use of abortion (i.e. its use as a means of family planning). UNFPA was an active member of a core planning group of international organizations and partnerships that organized the first Women Deliver conference, held in London, United Kingdom, in October 2007. Participants, including government ministers and representatives of organizations, private sector foundations and non-government bodies, endorsed a final commitment to increase investment in women's health and to make improving maternal health a development priority. In February 2008 UNFPA appealed for donations to its new Maternal Health Thematic Fund, which aimed to support efforts in 75 developing countries to improve maternal health care; by end-2010 some US $60 million in donations by the Thematic Fund. In addition to maternal deaths, an estimated 10m.–15m. women suffer serious or long-lasting illnesses or disabilities as a result of inadequate care in pregnancy and childbirth. In 2003 UNFPA launched a Global Campaign to End Fistula, which aims to improve the prevention and treatment of this obstetric condition in 30 countries in Africa and Asia and to achieve its elimination by 2015. UNFPA supports research into contraceptives and training in contraceptive technology. UNFPA organizes indepth studies on national contraceptive requirements and aims to ensure an adequate supply of contraceptives and reproductive health supplies to developing countries. In the early 2000s the Fund and other partners developed a Reproductive Health Commodity Strategy (RHCS), which aimed to improve developing countries' self-sufficiency in the management and provision of reproductive health commodities. In March 2012 UNFPA and UNICEF launched a Commission on Life-saving Commodities for Women and Children, which was to have participation by public, private and civil society stakeholders world-wide, and aimed to improve access to essential health supplies. UNFPA encourages partnerships between private sector interests and the governments of developing nations, with a view to making affordable commercial contraceptive products more easily available to consumers and thereby enabling governments to direct subsidies at the poorest sectors of society.

UNFPA is a co-sponsor of the Joint UN Programme on HIV/AIDS (UNAIDS), and is the UNAIDS convening agency with responsibility for young people and for condom programming, as well as taking a leading role in the UNAIDS inter-agency task team on gender and HIV/AIDS. The Fund, in co-operation with the other participants in UNAIDS, aims to strengthen the global response to the HIV/AIDS epidemic, and is also concerned to reduce levels of other sexually transmitted infections (STIs) and reproductive tract infections (RTIs), and of infertility. UNFPA gives special attention to the specific needs of adolescents, for example through education and counselling initiatives, and to women in emergency situations. The Fund maintains that meeting the reproductive health needs of adolescents is an urgent priority in combating poverty and HIV/AIDS. Through the joint Adolescent Girls Initiative, UNFPA, UNICEF and WHO promote policy dialogues in 10 countries. In May 2012 UNFPA welcomed a landmark resolution adopted by the UN Commission on Population and Development concerning the sexual and reproductive health, and reproductive rights, of adolescents and youth.

UNFPA takes a lead role in an emergency situation, following natural disaster or conflict, in providing basic supplies and services to protect reproductive health, in particular in the most vulnerable groups, i.e. young girls and pregnant women. It also helps to conduct rapid health assessments and censuses, supports counselling, education and training activities, and the construction of clinics and other health facilities, following humanitarian crises. UNFPA works with local authorities to prevent an escalation of sexual violence and to ensure that rapid and appropriate treatment and care is given to survivors of sexual violence.

POPULATION AND DEVELOPMENT

UNFPA promotes work on population as a central component of the goals of the international community to eradicate poverty and achieve sustainable development. UNFPA helps countries to formulate and implement comprehensive population policies as a part of any sustainable development strategies, and aims to ensure that the needs and concerns of women are incorporated into development and population policies. Research, educational and advocacy activities are undertaken to focus on specific aspects of development and population concern, for example migration, ageing and environmental sustainability. UNFPA provides assistance and training for national statistical offices in undertaking basic data collection, for example censuses and demographic surveys. UNFPA also provides assistance for analysis of demographic and socio-economic data, for research on population trends and for the formulation of government policies. A *State of World Population* report is published annually. The 2011 edition was issued in October of that year, the month when the global population was formally deemed to have reached 7,000m., and was subtitled 'People and possibilities in a world of 7 billion'; the 2011 report placed a strong emphasis on investment in young people. UNFPA supports a programme of fellowships in demographic analysis, data processing and cartography.

GENDER EQUALITY

A fundamental aspect of UNFPA's mission is to achieve gender equality, in order to promote the basic human rights of women and, through the empowerment of women, to support the elimination of poverty. Incorporated into all UNFPA activities are efforts to improve the welfare of women, in particular by providing reproductive choice, to eradicate gender discrimination, and to protect women from sexual and domestic violence and coercion. UNFPA's Strategic Framework on Gender Mainstreaming and Women's Empowerment for 2008–11 focused on the following six priority areas: setting policy for the ICPD Programme of Action and the MDGs; reproductive health; ending gender-based violence; adolescents and youth; emergency and post-emergency situations; and men and boys: partners for equality. The Fund aims to encourage the participation of women at all levels of decision- and policy-making and supports programmes that improve the access of all girls and women to education and grant women equal access to land, credit and employment opportunities. UNFPA aims to eradicate traditional practices that harm women, and works jointly with UNICEF to advance the eradication of female genital mutilation. UNFPA actively participates in efforts to raise awareness of and implement Resolution 1325 of the UN Security Council, adopted in October 2000, which addresses the impact of armed conflict on women and girls, the role of women in peace-building, and gender dimensions in peace processes and conflict resolution. Other activities are directed at particular issues concerning girls and adolescents and projects to involve men in reproductive health care initiatives.

Finance

UNFPA is supported entirely by voluntary contributions from governments and private donors. The Fund's total resources available for programme implementation in 2012–13 were forecast at US $1,459.6m. Institutional expenditure in that biennium was projected at $292.2m. Following the election of President Obama of the USA in January 2009, US funding, which had been suspended in 2002, was restored to UNFPA.

UNFPA, UNDP and UNICEF are committed to integrating their budgets from 2014.

Publications

Annual Report.

Campaign to End Fistula: The Year In Review (annually).

State of the World's Midwifery.

State of World Population (annually, in Arabic, English, French, Russian and Spanish).

Reports, technical publications, guidelines and manuals.

United Nations Relief and Works Agency for Palestine Refugees in the Near East—UNRWA

Address: Gamal Abd al-Nasser St, Gaza City.

Telephone: (8) 2887333; **fax:** (8) 2887555.

Address: Bayader Wadi Seer, POB 140157, Amman 11814, Jordan.

Telephone: (6) 5808100; **fax:** (6) 5808335; **e-mail:** unrwa-pio@unrwa.org; **internet:** www.unrwa.org.

UNRWA was established by the UN General Assembly to provide relief, health, education and welfare services for Palestine refugees in the Near East, initially on a short-term basis. UNRWA began operations in May 1950 and, in the absence of a solution to the refugee problem, its mandate has subsequently been extended by the General Assembly.

Organization

(June 2012)

UNRWA employs an international staff of about 120 and more than 24,200 local staff, mainly Palestine refugees. The Commissioner-General is the head of all UNRWA operations and reports directly to the UN General Assembly. UNRWA has no governing body, but its activities are reviewed annually by an Advisory Commission. In November 2005 the UN General Assembly approved an expansion of the Commission from 10 members to 21, reflecting the funding commitments in recent years of the governments concerned. It also authorized the Palestinian authorities, the European Community and the League of Arab States to attend as observers.

During 2007–10 UNRWA underwent a formal period of organizational development, aimed at strengthening its management capacity; thereafter the reform process continued, informally.

Commissioner-General: FILIPPO GRANDI (Italy).

Deputy Commissioner-General: MARGOT B. ELLIS (USA).

FIELD OFFICES

Each field office is headed by a director and has departments responsible for education, health and relief and social services programmes, finance, administration, supply and transport, legal affairs and public information. Operational support officers work in Gaza and the West Bank to monitor and report on the humanitarian situation and facilitate UNRWA field activities.

Gaza: POB 61; Al Azhar Rd, Rimal Quarter, Gaza City; tel. (8) 6777333; fax (8) 6777390.

Jordan: POB 143464, 11814 Amman; Al Zubeidi Bldg No. 16, Mustafa Bin Abdullah St, Barakeh, Tla'a Al-Ali, Amman; tel. (6) 5809100; fax (6) 5809134.

Lebanon: POB 11-0947, Beirut 1107 2060; Bir Hassan, Beirut; tel. (1) 840490; fax (1) 840466; e-mail lebanon@unrwa.org.

Syria: POB 4313; UN Compound, Mezzah Highway/Beirut Rd, Damascus; tel. (11) 6133035; fax (11) 6133047.

West Bank: POB 19149, Jerusalem; Sheik Jarrah Qtr, East Jerusalem; tel. (2) 5890400; fax (2) 5322714.

LIAISON OFFICES

Belgium: Centre d'Affaires ATEAC 11, rond point Schumann, 1040 Brussels; tel. (2) 256-75-85; fax (2) 256-75-03.

Egypt: 2 Dar-el-Shifa St, Garden City, POB 227, Cairo; tel. (2) 794-8502; fax (2) 794-8504.

Switzerland: Rms 92–94, Annex 1, Le Bocage, Palais des Nations, ave de la Paix, 1211 Geneva; tel. 229172057; fax 229170656.

USA: One United Nations Plaza, Room DC1-1265, New York, NY 10017; tel. (212) 963-2255; fax (212) 935-7899.

Activities

ASSISTANCE ACTIVITIES

Since 1950 UNRWA has been the main provider of relief, health, education and social services for Palestine refugees in Lebanon, Syria, Jordan, the West Bank and the Gaza Strip. For UNRWA's purposes, a Palestine refugee is one whose normal residence was in Palestine for a minimum of two years before the 1948 conflict and who, as a result of the Arab–Israeli hostilities, lost his or her home and means of livelihood. To be eligible for assistance, a refugee must reside in one of the five areas in which UNRWA operates and be in need. A refugee's descendants who fulfil certain criteria are also eligible for UNRWA assistance. After the renewal of Arab–Israeli hostilities in the Middle East in June 1967, hundreds of thousands of people fled from the fighting and from Israeli-occupied areas to east Jordan, Syria and Egypt. UNRWA provided emergency relief for displaced refugees and was additionally empowered by a UN General Assembly resolution to provide 'humanitarian assistance, as far as practicable, on an emergency basis and as a temporary measure' for those persons other than Palestine refugees who were newly displaced and in urgent need. In practice, UNRWA lacked the funds to aid the other displaced persons and the main burden of supporting them devolved on the Arab governments concerned. The Agency, as requested by the Government of Jordan in 1967 and on that Government's behalf, distributes rations to displaced persons in Jordan who are not registered refugees of 1948. UNRWA's emergency humanitarian support activities for Palestinian refugees include the provision of basic food and medical supplies; the implementation of a programme of emergency workdays, which aims to provide employment and income for labourers with dependants, while improving the local infrastructure; the provision of extra schooling days to make up for those missed because of the conflict, trauma counselling for children, and post-injury rehabilitation; and the reconstruction of shelters. UNRWA undertook a US $52m. emergency relief programme to support Palestinian refugees during 1982–85, following the Israeli invasion of southern Lebanon in June 1982. An expanded programme of assistance was implemented in the West Bank and Gaza during 1987–92 in response to the social and economic consequences of the so-called first Palestinian *intifada* (uprising) against Israel, and Israeli countermeasures. In June 2004 UNRWA and the Swiss Government hosted an international conference, convened in Geneva, with participation by representatives of 67 countries and 34 international organizations, aimed at addressing the humanitarian needs of Palestinian refugees; further to a decision of the conference a Department of Infrastructure and Camp Improvement was established at UNRWA headquarters, to address the deteriorating living conditions in many camps. In recent years diminishing funding has necessitated a retrenchment of the Agency's assistance activities, with the average annual spending per refugee falling by about one-half since 1975.

At 1 January 2012 UNRWA was providing essential services to 5m. registered refugees. Of these, an estimated 1.5m. (29%) were living in 58 camps serviced by the Agency (of which: 19 were in the West Bank; 12 were in Lebanon; 10 were in Jordan; nine were in Syria; and eight were in Gaza), while the remaining refugees had settled in local towns and villages of the host countries. UNRWA's three principal areas of activity are 'Acquired knowledge and skills', 'A long and healthy life', and 'A decent standard of living'. Some 85% of the Agency's 2012 regular budget was devoted to these three operational programmes.

'Acquired knowledge and skills' accounted for 53% of UNRWA's 2012 regular budget. In the 2011/12 school year there were 485,754 pupils enrolled in 699 UNRWA schools, and 19,217 educational staff. UNRWA also operated 10 vocational and teacher-training centres, which provided a total of 6,652 training places, and three other educational sciences faculties. Technical co-operation for the Agency's education programme is provided by UNESCO. During the 2010/11 school year UNRWA was prevented from enrolling some 40,000 eligible children in schools in Gaza as building materials required for the construction of necessary new schools had not been supplied to the territory since 2007. In March 2012 UNRWA convened an international conference in Brussels, Belgium, on the theme 'Engaging Youth: Palestine Refugees in a Changing Middle East', at which the Commissioner-General published a list of 10 'Youth Commitments' through which the Agency was to strengthen its support to young Palestinian refugees; these included expanding a pilot skills programme; providing enhanced vocational training and micro-finance opportunities; promoting fundraising towards scholarships; and increasing co-operation with global youth initiatives.

'Long and healthy lives' accounted for 19% of UNRWA's 2012 regular budget. At 1 January 2012 there were 138 primary health care units providing outpatient medical care, disease prevention and control, maternal and child health care and family planning services, of which 117 also offered dental care and a further 123 had laboratory services. At that time the number of health staff totalled 3,595. UNRWA also operates a hospital in the West Bank and offers assistance towards emergency and other secondary treatment, mainly through contractual agreements with non-governmental and private hospitals. Technical assistance for the health programme is provided by WHO. UNRWA offers mental health care to refugees, in particular children, experiencing psychological stress. The Agency aims to provide essential environmental health services. Nearly all camp shelters are connected to water networks, and by January 2012 87% were connected to sewerage networks.

'Decent standard of living' accounted for 13.5% of UNRWA's regular budget for 2012. These services comprise the distribution of food rations, the provision of emergency shelter and the organization of welfare programmes for the poorest refugees (at 1 January 2012 293,718 refugees, or nearly 6% of the total registered refugee population, were eligible to receive special hardship assistance). In 2012 UNRWA was providing technical and financial support to 49 women's programme centres and 35 community-based rehabilitation centres.

In order to encourage Palestinian self-reliance the Agency issues grants to ailing businesses and loans to families who qualify as special hardship cases. In 1991 UNRWA launched an income generation programme, which provides capital loans to small businesses and micro-enterprises with the objective of creating sustainable employment and eliminating poverty, particularly in the Occupied Territories. The programme was extended to Palestinian refugees in the West Bank in 1996 and in Jordan and Syria in 2003. By January 2012 265,571 loans, with a total estimated value of US $302m., had been awarded under the programme.

RECENT EMERGENCIES

From the commencement, in the second half of 2000, of the so-called second Palestinian al Aqsa *intifada* (uprising), and Israel's restriction from that time on the issuing of permits to enter or leave Gaza to only medical humanitarian cases, UNRWA became the lead agency with responsibility for the co-ordination and delivery of emergency assistance, as well as for monitoring the immediate needs of the local populations, and launched successive emergency appeals for assistance to Palestinian refugees in Gaza and the West Bank. The UNRWA Commissioner-General repeatedly expressed deep concern at the worsening humanitarian situation in the Palestinian territories, at the demolition of homes in Gaza and the West Bank by Israeli military forces, at the entry restrictions imposed by Israel against the Gaza Strip, which were causing extreme food shortages, and at restrictions on the movements of UN international staff within Gaza, which were severely impeding the Agency's activities. UNRWA repeatedly expressed concern at the construction by Israel, from 2002, of the West Bank 'security fence', or 'barrier', which was estimated to affect some 200,000 people through loss of land, water, agricultural resources and education, and hindered UNRWA's ability to provide and distribute humanitarian assistance. UNRWA has continued to monitor closely the construction and impact of the barrier.

Following the victory by the militant Islamic Resistance Movement (Hamas, opposed to any accommodation with Israel) at legislative elections held in the Palestinian Autonomous Territories in January 2006 and the installation of a Hamas-led administration there in March, the EU and USA announced that they would withhold direct aid to the Palestinian National Authority (PA), but would increase their contributions to humanitarian organizations engaged in the region. During 2006 UNRWA protested repeatedly that its activities in Gaza were being severely disrupted owing to the constant closure of the Karni crossing between Gaza and Israel. In late August the Agency reported that its operations in Gaza were nearly stalled and that the difficulties with access to the area had resulted in acute shortages of food, fuel and construction supplies. In July of that year UNRWA appealed for US $7.2m. to fund emergency humanitarian assistance for Palestinian refugees based in Lebanon and Syria who had been affected as a consequence of the conflict that erupted in that month between the Israeli armed forces and the militant Shi'a organization Hezbollah. The Agency was also assisting Lebanese civilians displaced by the conflict who had sought shelter in UNRWA schools. By the end of 2006 UNRWA reported its extreme concern at the socio-economic crisis affecting the Palestinian people, caused partly by the withholding of official donor assistance and ongoing restrictions on access and movement of people and goods. It launched an appeal for $246.2m. in emergency funding, mostly to meet basic humanitarian requirements, in 2007. In July 2007 UNRWA announced that it had suspended all public works rehabilitation and construction projects in Gaza owing to a lack of basic supplies resulting from a land, sea and air blockade imposed since June of that year on the Gaza Strip by Israel and Egypt (strengthening the existing border restrictions).

In May 2007 an outbreak of sectarian violence in northern Lebanon disrupted UNRWA's supply of humanitarian assistance and forced an estimated 27,000 people to leave their homes. In June UNRWA issued a flash appeal for US $12.7m. to meet the immediate needs of the displaced refugees and to improve the conditions at Beddawi camp, which was providing temporary shelter to the majority of those fleeing the fighting. In September UNRWA issued an emergency appeal for northern Lebanon, amounting to $54.8m. for the period 1 September 2007–

31 August 2008, to meet the needs of the affected population and to support the rehabilitation of the Nahr el-Bared camp, which had been extensively damaged by the fighting. In mid-2012 around 5,900 families remained displaced from Nahr el-Bared.

In December 2008 UNRWA issued an appeal for more than US $275m. in international donations for 2009 under the UN Consolidated Appeals Process (CAP), in view of the deepening vulnerability of Palestinian refugees affected by the continuing blockade imposed by Israel, entrenched poverty and unprecedented high levels of unemployment. The Agency stated that the dependency of Gaza and the West Bank on external aid had deepened during 2008. In late December, in response to the intensive bombardment of the Gaza Strip by Israeli forces that commenced at that time with the stated aim of ending rocket attacks launched by Hamas and other militant groups on Israeli targets, the UNRWA Commissioner-General expressed horror at the extensive destruction and loss of life caused by the Israeli action and, while recognizing Israel's legitimate security concerns, urged the Israeli military to cease the bombardment and to respect all international conventions regarding the protection of non-combatants in times of conflict to which Israel is a signatory. At the end of December UNRWA launched a flash appeal for $34m. to meet Gaza's urgent humanitarian requirements (including the provision of essential health supplies, food, cash assistance, materials for housing repairs, fuel, and shelter requirements for displaced Palestinian civilians) over a period of four months. Israeli air strikes were reported by UNRWA at that time to have inflicted significant damage to Gaza's fragile infrastructure and to have destroyed its public service capacity. The Agency, which had suspended its food assistance during the second half of December owing to insufficient supplies, demanded that border crossings should be reopened permanently. At the beginning of January 2009 Israeli forces initiated a ground invasion of Gaza.

In early January 2009 the UN Secretary-General urged an immediate cease-fire in Gaza and denounced as unacceptable recent Israeli attacks on three UNRWA-run schools that had resulted in a substantial number of civilian fatalities and injuries. At that time around 25 UNRWA schools were serving as temporary shelters to Palestinians who had been displaced by the ongoing violence. Soon afterwards UNRWA suspended its movements through Gaza (including, once again, food distribution) owing to Israeli air strikes on humanitarian convoys that had caused several fatalities. On 8 January the UN Security Council adopted Resolution 1860 demanding an immediate cease-fire in Gaza, culminating in the full withdrawal of Israeli forces; the unimpeded provision throughout Gaza of food, fuel and medical treatment; improved international arrangements to prevent arms and ammunition smuggling; intra-Palestinian reconciliation; and renewed efforts to achieve a comprehensive long-term peace between Israel and Palestine. In mid-January UNRWA's field headquarters in Gaza was struck and set alight by Israeli shells that reportedly contained incendiary white phosphorus; the UN Secretary-General protested strongly against the attack. On 18 January Israel, while maintaining its positions in Gaza, ceased hostilities; Hamas responded by announcing a week-long cessation of hostilities against Israeli targets, in order to permit Israel to withdraw its armed forces fully from the territory. The Israeli withdrawal was completed on 21 January. By the time of the cease-fire the Israeli offensive had reportedly killed 1,340 people in Gaza (including 460 children and 106 women), and had wounded some 5,320 people (including 1,855 children and 795 women). At the height of the crisis UNRWA provided refuge for 50,896 Palestinians in 50 shelters.

In late January 2009 the UN launched a flash appeal for US $615m. (in addition to its CAP appeal for 2009) to cover the emergency requirements of UNRWA and other aid agencies over a period of six–nine months in supporting civilians in Gaza through the provision of food, water, sanitation, health care and shelter, other basic services, education, psychological care, emergency repairs and rehabilitation, and clearing unexploded ordnance. At that time UNRWA was serving some 900,000 refugees in Gaza, while other civilians were being supported by the WFP. For several days in early February UNRWA suspended the importation of humanitarian supplies into Gaza following the confiscation by the Hamas authorities of deliveries of foodstuffs and blankets. At that time UNRWA's activities in Gaza were also being restricted by the refusal of the Israeli authorities to permit entry into the territory of nylon pellets for making plastic food distribution bags, and paper and exercise books for educational use. In early March the UN Secretary-General appealed to international donors participating in the International Conference on the Palestinian Economy and Gaza Reconstruction, convened in Sharm esh-Sheikh, Egypt, for contributions to support and rebuild Gaza. The Secretary-General emphasized at that meeting the importance of maintaining a durable cease-fire, open border crossings into Gaza, and Palestinian reconciliation. In August UNRWA issued a Gaza Ramadan Appeal, requesting an additional $181m. in donations to fund food assistance, shelter improvements, job creation and the rehabilitation of education and health facilities for the poorest and most vulnerable groups of refugees living in Gaza.

In January 2010 UNRWA launched its emergency appeal for that year, amounting to US $323.3m. At the end of May the UNRWA Commissioner-General and the UN Special Co-ordinator for the Middle East Peace Process issued a joint statement strongly condemning an attack perpetrated at that time by Israeli security forces against a flotilla of vessels that was travelling through international waters with the aim of carrying humanitarian aid to Gaza; the Israeli action resulted in the deaths of nine civilians and wounded more than 40 further passengers. The joint statement stressed that such fatalities would be avoidable if Israel were to terminate its blockade of Gaza. It was reported at the end of 2011 that UNRWA's funding appeal for that year (of US $379.7m.) was only 40% funded. In December 2011 UNRWA appealed for $318.2m. in support of its activities in 2012, of which $103.3m. was for Gaza and $214.9m. for the West Bank. Of the total amount nearly 80% was for the provision of emergency food and livelihood support for food-insecure families. A report issued by UNRWA in December 2011 found that, despite a recent expansion of economic activity in Gaza, the rate of unemployment amongst refugees there stood at 33.8% in the first half of 2011, one of the highest in the world. In January 2012 the UN General Assembly adopted a resolution that urged donor nations to increase contributions to the Agency, in order to address its funding shortfall.

Statistics

REFUGEES REGISTERED WITH UNRWA*
(1 January 2012)

Country	Number	% of total
Jordan	1,979,580	41
Gaza Strip	1,167,572	24
West Bank	727,471	15
Syria	486,946	10
Lebanon	436,154	9
Total	4,797,723	100

* Additionally, UNRWA was providing assistance in January 2012 to some 318,032 eligible other registered persons.

Finance

UNRWA is financed almost entirely by voluntary contributions from governments and the European Union, the remainder being provided by UN bodies, non-governmental organizations, business corporations and private sources, which also contribute to extra-budgetary activities. UNRWA's regular budget for 2012–13, covering recurrent expenditure on sectoral activities, totalled US $1,251m.

Publication

Annual Report of the Commissioner-General of UNRWA.

Reports on labour markets, microfinance, youth outreach, etc.

United Nations Training and Research Institutes

United Nations Institute for Disarmament Research—UNIDIR

Address: Palais des Nations, 1211 Geneva 10, Switzerland.

Telephone: 229173186; **fax:** 229170176; **e-mail:** unidir@unog.ch; **internet:** www.unidir.org.

UNIDIR is an autonomous institution within the United Nations. It was established by the General Assembly in 1980 for the purpose of undertaking independent research on disarmament and related problems, particularly international security issues. UNIDIR's statute became effective on 1 January 1985. The Director of UNIDIR reports annually to the General Assembly on the activities of the Institute. The UN Secretary-General's Advisory Board on Disarmament Studies functions as UNIDIR's Board of Trustees.

The work of the Institute is based on the following objectives: to provide the international community with more diversified and complete data on problems relating to international security, the armaments race and disarmament in all fields, so as to facilitate progress towards greater global security and towards economic and social development for all peoples; to promote informed participation by all states in disarmament efforts; to assist ongoing negotiations on disarmament, and continuing efforts to ensure greater international security at a progressively lower level of armaments, in particular nuclear weapons, by means of objective studies and analyses; and to conduct long-term research on disarmament in order to provide a general insight into the problems involved and to stimulate new initiatives for negotiations. UNIDIR's activities are grouped into the following five areas: weapons of mass destruction; weapons of societal disruption; security and society; emerging threats; and improving processes and creating synergies.

The work programme of UNIDIR is reviewed annually and is subject to approval by its Board of Trustees. During 2011 UNIDIR organized conferences, workshops and seminars on a range of issues, including: multilateral approaches to the nuclear fuel cycle; implementation of the 2010 NPT Review Conference Action Plan; global cybersecurity challenges, and 'international law and war in cyberspace'; developing an effective arms trade treaty; and space security. Examples of ongoing research projects in 2012 include: Supporting the Arms Trade Treaty Negotiations through Regional Discussions and Expertise Sharing (see below); Understanding Disarmament; Research and Development for an Evidence-based Reintegration Programming Tool; Emerging Security Threats; Weapons of Mass Destruction; International Co-operation Mechanisms on Nuclear Security; Norms on Explosive Weapons; Perspectives on Cyber War: Legal Frameworks and Transparency and Confidence Building; and Promoting Implementation of the NPT Action Plan 2012. Research projects are conducted within the Institute, or commissioned to individual experts or research organizations. For some major studies, multinational groups of experts are established. The Institute offers a research fellowship programme focusing on topics relating to regional security. UNIDIR maintains a database on research institutes (DATARIs) in the field of international security.

The Institute organizes (jointly with the Quaker United Nations Office and the Centre on Conflict, Development and Peacebuilding of the Graduate Institute of International and Development Studies) the Geneva Forum, which aims to serve as a focal point for discussion of disarmament and arms control issues, engaging government and non-governmental officials, UN personnel, media representatives and academics. The Geneva Forum publishes the *Media Guide to Disarmament and Arms Control.*

UNIDIR supported the preparatory process leading to the UN Conference on the Arms Trade Treaty, which was scheduled to be held in July 2012, in New York, with the aim of establishing a legally binding instrument to set the highest possible international standards of control and transparency to guide the import, export and transfer of conventional weapons.

The Institute is financed mainly by voluntary contributions from governments and public or private organizations. A contribution to the costs of the Director and staff may be provided from the UN regular budget.

Director: Theresa A. Hitchens (USA).

Publications: *Annual Report*, *Disarmament Forum* (quarterly), *UNIDIR Highlights*, research reports (6 a year), research papers (irregular).

United Nations Institute for Training and Research—UNITAR

Address: Palais des Nations, 1211 Geneva 10, Switzerland.

Telephone: 229178455; **fax:** 229178047; **e-mail:** info@unitar.org; **internet:** www.unitar.org.

UNITAR was established in 1963, as an autonomous body within the United Nations, in order to provide training for diplomats and other officials and to enhance the effectiveness of the UN. UNITAR's training activities, including seminars, workshops, distance and online training, and fellowships, are now open to any professional working in the relevant field. UNITAR established offices in New York, USA, (in 1996), in Hiroshima, Japan (in 2003), and in Brasília, Brazil (in 2010), to provide specialist or regional training activities.

UNITAR's Training Department is focused on three main areas of activity: peace, security and diplomacy; environment; and governance. The Peace, Security and Diplomacy Unit incorporates programmes on multilateral diplomacy, international law, peace-making and conflict prevention, and peacekeeping training. The Environment Unit manages programmes concerning environmental governance and law, chemicals and waste management, climate change, and biodiversity. Within the Governance Unit are programmes on public finance and trade, and on e-governance. The Unit also administers the Local Development and Decentralization Programme, which operates partly through a network of International Training Centres for Local Actors (CIFAL) to train local authorities in issues relating to sustainable development, the efficient management of local services, and urbanization.

UNITAR's Research Department is concerned with the application of new technologies to training and knowledge systems innovation. It administers the UNITAR Operational Satellite Applications Programme (UNOSAT) which aims to ensure that information from satellite earth observation is available and used effectively by relief and development organizations, as well as to help to monitor human rights and security and to support territorial planning. In 2003 UNOSAT developed a humanitarian rapid mapping service, providing rapid acquisition and processing of satellite imagery for use by agencies co-ordinating emergency relief, as well as recovery and rehabilitation efforts.

UNITAR is responsible for organizing annual retreats of the UN Secretary-General, and of the Departments of Peace-keeping Operations and of Political Affairs. The Institute also organizes an annual seminar of the Special Representatives of the UN Secretary-General. In April 2008 UNITAR inaugurated a Geneva Lecture Series which aimed to generate public awareness and engage leading personalities in a consideration of global challenges.

In November 2011, as part of a series of activities related to reform of the UN, UNITAR organized a workshop on 'System-wide Coherence in UN Development Activities', focusing on ongoing initiatives to improve co-ordination of the organization and its coherence mechanisms.

UNITAR is financed by voluntary contributions from UN member states, by donations from foundations and other non-governmental sources, and by income generated by its Reserve Fund.

Executive Director: Carlos Lopes (Guinea-Bissau) (outgoing).

United Nations Interregional Crime and Justice Research Institute—UNICRI

Address: Viale Maestri del Lavoro 10, 10127 Turin, Italy.

Telephone: (011) 6537111; **fax:** (011) 6313368; **e-mail:** information@unicri.it; **internet:** www.unicri.it.

The Institute was established in 1968 as the United Nations Social Defence Research Institute. Its present name was adopted by a resolution of ECOSOC in 1989. The Institute undertakes research, training and information activities in the fields of crime prevention and criminal justice, at international, regional and national levels.

In collaboration with national governments, UNICRI aims to establish a reliable base of knowledge and information on organized crime; to identify strategies for the prevention and control of crime, within the framework of contributing to socio-economic development and protecting human rights; and to design systems to support policy formulation, implementation and evaluation. UNICRI organizes workshops and conferences, and promotes the exchange of information through its international documentation centre on criminology. The Programme incorporates the following operational units: a department on Justice, Protection and Ethics, focusing on country projects, as well as victim surveys and biomedical research; a Security Governance/Counter Terrorism Laboratory, which provides support to the International Permanent Observatory (IPO) on Security during Major Events, as well as other regional security efforts (i.e. an IPO Americas network and the second phase of a European Union project on major events security, EU-SEC II), participates in the UN Counter-Terrorism Implementation Task Force, administers a 'programme of excellence' for policy-makers concerning security governance, and supports efforts to combat illicit trafficking in chemical, biological, radiological and nuclear weapons; an Emerging Crimes and Anti-Human Trafficking unit, incorporating projects concerned with trafficking in human beings, in particular women and children, and other emerging crimes, such as counterfeiting, environmental crime and 'cyber' crime; and a Training and Advanced Education Department, which administers educational courses, a summer school on migration, and a Masters of Law in International Organizations, International Criminal Law and Crime Prevention. During 2010–11 UNICRI, the ICTY and the OSCE Office for Democratic Institutions and Human Rights (ODIHR) implemented the EU-funded War Crimes Justice Project, aimed at strengthening the capacity of national judiciaries in the Balkans to address war crimes cases. In 2009 UNICRI inaugurated three regional offices of the Security Governance/Counter Terrorism Laboratory: in Lucca, Italy, to specialize in dialogue and innovation; in Lisbon, Portugal, to promote technical projects on public/private partnerships; and in Boston, USA, to focus on security in the urban environment. UNICRI maintains a Liaison Office in Rome, Italy, to strengthen collaboration with local institutions and civil bodies and with UN agencies. In June 2009 UNICRI opened a new office at the University of Pomezia, Italy, to conduct postgraduate, Masters and other specialized training courses.

UNICRI is funded by the United Nations Crime Prevention and Criminal Justice Fund, which is financed by voluntary contributions from UN member states, non-governmental organizations, academic institutions and other concerned bodies.

Director: Dr JONATHAN LUCAS (Seychelles).

Publications: *Brochure*, *F3–Freedom from Fear* (online journal, in collaboration with the Max Planck Institute for Foreign and International Criminal Law), training materials, reports, research studies.

United Nations Research Institute for Social Development—UNRISD

Address: Palais des Nations, 1211 Geneva 10, Switzerland.

Telephone: 229173020; **fax:** 229170650; **e-mail:** info@unrisd.org; **internet:** www.unrisd.org.

UNRISD was established in 1963 as an autonomous body within the United Nations, to conduct multi-disciplinary research into the social dimensions of contemporary problems affecting development.

The Institute aims to provide governments, development agencies, grass-roots organizations and scholars with a better understanding of how development policies and processes of economic, social and environmental change affect different social groups.

UNRISD research is undertaken in collaboration with a network of national research teams drawn from local universities and research institutions. UNRISD aims to promote and strengthen research capacities in developing countries. Its main focus areas are the eradication of poverty; the promotion of democracy and human rights; environmental sustainability; gender equality; and the effects of globalization. During 2010–14 UNRISD's research agenda 'Social Development in an Uncertain World' covered two main themes: social policies for inclusive and sustainable development' and 'political and institutional dynamics of social development'. In November 2009 UNRISD sponsored an international conference, convened in Geneva, Switzerland, addressing the Social and Political Dimensions of the Global Crisis: Implications for Developing Countries. In September 2010 UNRISD published a Flagship Report entitled *Combating Poverty and Inequality: Structural Change, Social Policy and Politics*, which resulted from major research initiatives, including on poverty reduction and poverty regimes, and on social policy in a development context.

The Institute is supported by voluntary grants from governments, and also receives financing from other UN organizations, and from various other national and international agencies.

Director: Dr SARAH COOK (United Kingdom).

Publications: *Conference News*, *e-Bulletin* (quarterly), *UNRISD News* (2 a year), discussion papers and monographs, special reports, programme and occasional papers.

United Nations System Staff College

Address: Viale Maestri del Lavoro 10, 10127 Turin, Italy.

Telephone: (011) 6535911; **fax:** (011) 6535902; **e-mail:** info@unssc.org; **internet:** www.unssc.org.

In July 2001 the UN General Assembly approved a statute for the UN System Staff College (UNSSC), which, it envisaged, would provide knowledge management, training and continuous learning opportunities for all UN personnel, with a view to developing UN system-wide co-operation and operational effectiveness. The inaugural meeting of the Board of Governors was held in November, and the College formally began operations on 1 January 2002. It aims to promote the exchange of knowledge and shared learning, to administer learning and training workshops, to provide support and expert advice, and to act as a clearing house for learning activities. It provides an online orientation course for new UN staff members and provides extensive learning support to the Resident Co-ordinators. A UN Leaders Programme, focusing on strategic leadership theory, practice and skills, was inaugurated in May 2009. In 2012 the College's activities were organized under the following programmes: the UN Leaders Programme; UN Coherence (including support of the *Delivering as One* agenda); Knowledge and Management; Peace and Security; and Development and Human Rights.

The UNSSC is financed by a combination of course fees, voluntary grants from governments and contributions in kind from various UN organizations in the form of staff secondments.

Director: CARLOS LOPES (Guinea-Bissau) (outgoing).

United Nations University—UNU

Address: 53–70, Jingumae 5-chome, Shibuya-ku, Tokyo 150-8925, Japan.

Telephone: (3) 5467-1212; **fax:** (3) 3499-2828; **e-mail:** mbox@unu.edu; **internet:** www.unu.edu.

The University is sponsored jointly by the UN and UNESCO. It is an autonomous institution within the UN, guaranteed academic freedom by a charter approved by the General Assembly in 1973. It is governed by a 28-member University Council of scholars and scientists, of whom 24 are appointed by the Secretary-General of the UN and the Director-General of UNESCO (who, together with the Executive Director of

UNITAR, are *ex officio* members of the Council; the Rector is also on the Council). The University works through networks of collaborating institutions and individuals. These include Associated Institutions (universities and research institutes linked with UNU under general agreements of co-operation). UNU undertakes multi-disciplinary research on problems that are the concern of the UN and its agencies, and works to strengthen research and training capabilities in developing countries. It administers joint graduate and international post-graduate courses and organizes an advanced seminar series and a global seminar series, which aims to generate awareness about contemporary global issues and the role of the UN in addressing them. In December 2008 the UNU Council endorsed the process of accreditation required for UNU to award its own degrees. In January 2009 UNU established a new Institute for Sustainability and Peace, which integrated the academic activities of two main programme areas: peace and governance, and environment and sustainable development. The Institute aimed to promote a transdisciplinary approach to issues affecting human security and sustainability.

The University oversees a network of research and training centres and programmes world-wide, comprising: the UNU Institute for Environment and Human Security (UNU-EHS), based in Bonn, Germany; the World Institute for Development Economics Research (UNU-WIDER) in Helsinki, Finland; the Economic and Social Research and Training Centre on Innovation and Technology (UNU-MERIT) in Maastricht, Netherlands; the International Institute for Software Technology (UNU-IIST) in Macao; the UNU Institute for Natural Resources in Africa (UNU-INRA) in Accra, Ghana (with a mineral resources unit in Lusaka, Zambia); the UNU Programme for Biotechnology in Latin America and the Caribbean (UNU-BIOLAC), based in Caracas, Venezuela; the International Leadership Institute (UNU-ILI) in Amman, Jordan; the Institute of Advanced Studies (UNU-IAS), based in Yokohama, Japan; the UNU International Network on Water, Environment and Health (UNU-INWEH) in Hamilton, Canada; the UNU Programme on Comparative Regional Integration Studies (UNU-CRIS), in Bruges, Belgium; the UNU Food and Nutrition Programme for Human and Social Development (UNU-FNP), based at Cornell University, USA; the UNU International Institute for Global Health (UNU-IIGH), based in Kuala Lumpur, Malaysia; the UNU Geothermal Training Programme (UNU-GTP) and UNU Fisheries Training Programme (UNU-FTP), both in Reykjavík, Iceland; and the UN-Water Decade Programme on Capacity Development, based in Bonn, Germany. In 1993 the UNU established a research centre focusing on international conflict (INCORE), as a joint project with the University of Ulster, United Kingdom.

The UNU Centre in Tokyo, Japan, co-ordinates much of the activities of the UNU and ensures close co-operation with the UN system. It is also supported by a Vice-Rectorate in Europe, based in Bonn, Germany, which is also responsible for promoting UNU's presence in Africa. In December 2008 the UNU Council approved an initiative to 'twin' institutes, in order to promote greater collaboration between centres in developed and less developed regions. The first twinning arrangement was to link the new Institute for Sustainability and Peace with UNU-INRA, in Ghana, and initiate a joint research project concerning education for sustainable development. A Memorandum of Understanding on the establishment of a new body, the UNU Institute for Integrated Management of Material Fluxes and Resources (UNU-FLORES) was signed in November 2010. The Institute was to be based in Dresden, Germany, with a twin institute in Maputo, Mozambique.

UNU is financed by voluntary contributions from UN member states.

Rector: Prof. Dr KONRAD OSTERWALDER (Switzerland).

Publications: *Our World 2.0* (online magazine), *UNU Update* (regular online newsletter), *UNU Press Newsletter* (quarterly), journals, abstracts, research papers.

University for Peace

Address: POB 138-6100, San José, Costa Rica.

Telephone: 2205-9000; **fax:** 2249-1929; **e-mail:** info@upeace.org; **internet:** www.upeace.org.

The University for Peace (UPEACE) was established in 1980 to conduct research on, *inter alia*, disarmament, mediation, the resolution of conflicts, the preservation of the environment, international relations, peace education and human rights. The Council of the University (the governing body, comprising 17 members) was reconstituted in March 1999, meeting for the first time since 1994, and initiated a programme of extensive reforms and expansion. A programme of short courses for advanced international training was reintroduced in 2001. In 2000 a Centre and Policy Institute was established in Geneva, Switzerland, and an Institute for Media, Peace and Security was inaugurated, with administrative headquarters in Paris, France. In 2001 the World Centre for Research and Training in Conflict Resolution was established in Bogotá, Colombia. In December 2006 UPEACE inaugurated a Human Rights Centre, which aimed to conduct research, education and training in theory and practice of human rights issues. A UPEACE Centre for Executive Education offers seminars and workshops to business executives and other professionals in fields concerning leadership, conflict resolution and peace education. In 2012 regular Masters degrees were available in Environmental Security and Peace (also with a specialization in Climate Change and Security); Gender and Peace-building; International Law and Human Rights; International Law and the Settlement of Disputes; International Peace Studies; Media, Peace and Conflict Studies; Natural Resources and Peace; Peace Education; Responsible Management and Sustainable Economic Development; and Sustainable Urban Governance and Peace.

UPEACE aims to develop a global network of partner institutions. A Central Asia Programme, concerned with education in peace-building and conflict prevention in the former Soviet Central Asia, was initiated in 2000. In January 2002 the University launched an Africa Programme, which aims to build African capacity for education, training and research on matters related to peace and security. A UPEACE Academic Advisory Council, mandated to improve the organization of the University's academic programme and build partnerships and networks with other academic institutions for collaboration in the areas of both teaching and research, was inaugurated in May 2003. Under an Asia Leaders Programme UPEACE offers a Master of Arts (MA) in International Peace Studies as a dual degree with the Ateneo de Manila University, the Philippines. A further dual MA for Asian students is offered in collaboration with the Hankuk University of Foreign Studies, Republic of Korea. An MA dual degree in Natural Resources and Sustainable Development is conducted with the American University in Washington, DC, USA. UPEACE aims to strengthen education capacities in developing countries. In September 2007 UPEACE, in collaboration with the Government of the Netherlands, initiated a programme to promote the teaching of peace and conflict studies in the Horn of Africa, the Middle East and South Asia. In November 2009 UPEACE signed a partnership agreement with the Peace and Sport international forum, based in Monaco, under which both organizations determined to establish a joint training programme.

Rector: JOHN J. MARESCA (USA).

Publications: *Peace and Conflict Review* (2 a year), *African Peace and Conflict Journal* (quarterly).

World Food Programme—WFP

Address: Via Cesare Giulio Viola 68, Parco dei Medici, 00148 Rome, Italy.

Telephone: (06) 65131; **fax:** (06) 6513-2840; **e-mail:** wfpinfo@wfp.org; **internet:** www.wfp.org.

WFP, the principal food assistance organization of the United Nations, became operational in 1963. It aims to alleviate acute hunger by providing emergency relief following natural or man-made humanitarian disasters, and supplies food assistance to people in developing countries to eradicate chronic undernourishment, to support social development and to promote self-reliant communities.

Organization

(June 2012)

EXECUTIVE BOARD

The governing body of WFP is the Executive Board, comprising 36 members, 18 of whom are elected by the UN Economic and Social Council (ECOSOC) and 18 by the Council of the Food and Agriculture Organization (FAO). The Board meets four times each year at WFP headquarters.

SECRETARIAT

WFP's Executive Director is appointed jointly by the UN Secretary-General and the Director-General of FAO and is responsible for the management and administration of the Programme. Around 90% of WFP staff members work in the field. WFP administers some 87 country offices, in order to provide operational, financial and management support at a more local level, and maintains six regional bureaux, located in Bangkok, Thailand (for Asia), Cairo, Egypt (for the Middle East, Central Asia and Eastern Europe), Panama City, Panama (for Latin America and the Caribbean), Johannesburg, South Africa (for Southern Africa), Kampala, Uganda (for Central and Eastern Africa), and Dakar, Senegal (for West Africa).

Executive Director: Ertharin Cousin (USA).

Activities

WFP is the only multilateral organization with a mandate to use food assistance as a resource. It is the second largest source of assistance in the UN, after the World Bank Group, in terms of actual transfers of resources, and the largest source of grant aid in the UN system. WFP handles more than one-third of the world's food assistance. WFP is also the largest contributor to South–South trade within the UN system, through the purchase of food and services from developing countries (at least three-quarters of the food purchased by the Programme originates in developing countries). WFP's mission is to provide food assistance to save lives in refugee and other emergency situations, to improve the nutrition and quality of life of vulnerable groups and to help to develop assets and promote the self-reliance of poor families and communities. WFP aims to focus its efforts on the world's poorest countries and to provide at least 90% of its total assistance to those designated as 'low-income food-deficit'. At the World Food Summit, held in November 1996, WFP endorsed the commitment to reduce by 50% the number of undernourished people, no later than 2015. During 2010 WFP food assistance, distributed through development projects, emergency operations (EMOPs) and protracted relief and recovery operations (PRROs), benefited some 109.2m. people, including 89m. women and children, and 15.4m. IDPs, in 75 countries. Total food deliveries in 2010 amounted to 4.6m. metric tons.

WFP rations comprise basic food items (staple foods such as wheat flour or rice; pulses such as lentils and chickpeas; vegetable oil fortified with vitamins A and D; sugar; and iodized salt). Where possible basic rations are complemented with special products designed to improve the nutritional intake of beneficiaries. These include fortified blended foods, principally 'Corn Soya Blend', containing important micronutrients; ready-to-use foods, principally peanut-based pastes enriched with vitamins and minerals trade-marked as 'Plumpy Doz' and 'Supplementary Plumpy', which are better suited to meeting the nutritional needs of young and moderately malnourished children; high energy biscuits, distributed in the first phases of emergencies when cooking facilities may be scarce; micronutrient powder ('sprinkles'), which can be used to fortify home cooking; and compressed food bars, given out during disaster relief operations when the distribution and preparation of local food is not possible. The Programme's food donations must meet internationally agreed standards applicable to trade in food products. In May 2003 WFP's Executive Board approved a policy on donations of genetically modified (GM) foods and other foods derived from biotechnology, determining that the Programme would continue to accept donations of GM/biotech food and that, when distributing it, relevant national standards would be respected. It is WFP policy to buy food as near to where it is needed as possible, with a view to saving on transport costs and helping to sustain local economies. From 2008 targeted cash and voucher schemes started to be implemented, as a possible alternative to food rations (see below). During 2011 WFP and several corporate partners started to implement pilot schemes in targeted areas in Bangladesh and Indonesia under a new Project Laser Beam (PLB) initiative, aimed at addressing child malnutrition. With other UN agencies, governments, research institutions, and representatives of civil society and of the private sector, WFP supports the Scaling up Nutrition (SUN) initiative, which was initiated in 2009, under the co-ordination of the UN Secretary-General's Special Representative for Food Security and Nutrition, with the aim of increasing the coverage of interventions that improve nutrition during the first 1,000 days of a child's life (such as exclusive breastfeeding, optimal complementary feeding practices, and provision of essential vitamins and minerals); and ensuring that nutrition plans are implemented at national level, and that government programmes take nutrition into account.

WFP aims to address the causes of chronic malnourishment, which it identifies as poverty and lack of opportunity. It emphasizes the role played by women (who are most likely to sow, reap, harvest and cook household food) in combating hunger, and endeavours to address the specific nutritional needs of women, to increase their access to food and development resources, and to promote girls' education. WFP estimates that females represent four-fifths of people engaged in farming in Africa and three-fifths of people engaged in farming in Asia, and that globally women are the sole breadwinners in one-third of households. Increasingly WFP distributes food assistance through women, believing that vulnerable children are more likely to be reached in this way. In September 2011 WFP and UN Women announced an agreement to provide income generating opportunities for women in rural areas. The Programme also focuses resources on supporting the nutrition and food security of households and communities affected by HIV/AIDS, and on promoting food security as a means of mitigating extreme poverty and vulnerability and thereby combating the spread and impact of HIV/AIDS. In February 2003 WFP and the Joint UN Programme on HIV/AIDS (UNAIDS) concluded an agreement to address jointly the relationship between HIV/AIDS, regional food shortages and chronic hunger, with a particular focus on Africa, Southeast Asia and the Caribbean. In October of that year WFP became a co-sponsor of UNAIDS. WFP also urges the development of new food assistance strategies as a means of redressing global inequalities and thereby combating the threat of conflict and international terrorism.

WFP is a participant in the High Level Task Force (HLTF) on the Global Food Security Crisis, which was established by the UN Secretary-General in April 2008 with the aim of addressing the global impact of soaring levels of food and commodity prices, and of formulating a comprehensive framework for action. WFP participated in the High-Level Conference on World Food Security and the Challenges of Climate Change and Bioenergy that was convened by FAO in June. At that time WFP determined to allocate some US $1,200m. in extra-budgetary funds to alleviate hunger in the worst-affected countries. In January 2009 the HLTF participated in a follow-up high-level meeting convened in Madrid, Spain, and attended also by 62 government ministers and representatives from 126 countries. The meeting agreed to initiate a consultation process with regard to the establishment of a Global Partnership for Agriculture, Food Security and Nutrition. WFP participated in a World Summit on Food Security, organized by FAO, in Rome, in November 2009, which aimed to secure greater coherence in the global governance of food security and set a 'new world food order'.

WFP, with FAO and IFAD, leads an initiative on ensuring food security by strengthening feeding programmes and expanding support to farmers in developing countries, the second of nine activities that were launched in April 2009 by the UN System Chief Executives Board for Co-ordination (CEB), with the aim of alleviating the impact on poor and vulnerable populations of the developing global economic crisis. WFP also solely leads an initiative on emergency activities to meet humanitarian needs and promote security, the seventh of the CEB activities launched in April 2009.

In June 2008 WFP's Executive Board approved a strategic plan, covering the period 2008–13, that shifted the focus of WFP's activities from the supply of food to the supply of food assistance, and provided a new institutional framework to support vulnerable populations affected by the ongoing global food crisis and by possible future effects of global climate change. The five principal objectives of the 2008–13 plan were: saving lives and protecting livelihoods in emergencies; preparing for emergencies; restoring and rebuilding lives after emergencies; reducing chronic hunger and undernutrition everywhere; and strengthening the capacity of countries to reduce hunger. The plan emphasized prevention of hunger through early warning systems and analysis; local purchase of food; the maintenance of efficient and effective emergency response systems; and the use of focused cash and voucher programmes (including electronic vouchers) to ensure the accessibility to vulnerable people in urban environments of food that was locally available but, owing to the high level of market prices and increasing unemployment, beyond their financial means. It was envisaged that the cash and voucher approach would reduce the cost to WFP of transporting and storing food supplies, and would also benefit local economies (both being long-term WFP policy objectives). Some 2.9m. people were assisted through cash and voucher programmes during 2010.

WFP has developed a range of mechanisms to enhance its preparedness for emergency situations (such as conflict, drought and other natural disasters) and to improve its capacity for responding effectively to crises as they arise. Through its Vulnerability Analysis and Mapping (VAM) project, WFP aims to identify potentially vulnerable groups by providing information on food security and the capacity of different groups for coping with shortages, and to enhance emergency contingency-planning and long-term assistance objectives. VAM produces food security analysis reports, guidelines, reference documents and maps. In 2009 VAM field units were operational in 43 countries worldwide. The key elements of WFP's emergency response capacity are its strategic stores of food and logistics equipment (drawn from 'stocks afloat': ships loaded with WFP food supplies that can be re-routed to assist in crisis situations; development project stocks redesignated as emergency project contingency reserves; and in-country borrowing from national food reserves enabled by bilateral agreements); stand-by arrangements to enable the rapid deployment of personnel, communications and other essential equipment; and the Augmented Logistics Intervention Team for Emergencies (ALITE), which undertakes capacity assessments and contingency-planning. When engaging in a crisis WFP dispatches an emergency preparedness team to quantify the amount and type of food assistance required, and to identify the beneficiaries of and the timescale and logistics (e.g. means of transportation; location of humanitarian corridors, if necessary; and designated food distribution sites, such as refugee camps, other emergency shelters and therapeutic feeding centres) underpinning the ensuing EMOP. Once the EMOP has been drafted, WFP launches an appeal to the international donor community for funds and assistance to enable its implementation. WFP special operations are short-term logistics and infrastructure projects that are undertaken to facilitate the movement of food aid, regardless of whether the food is provided by the Agency itself. Special operations typically complement EMOPs or longer rehabilitation projects.

During 2000 WFP led efforts, undertaken with other UN humanitarian agencies, for the design and application of local UN Joint Logistics Centre facilities, which aimed to co-ordinate resources in an emergency situation. In 2001 a UN Humanitarian Response Depot was opened in Brindisi, Italy, under the direction of WFP experts, for the storage of essential rapid response equipment. In that year the Programme published a set of guidelines on contingency planning. Since 2003 WFP has been mandated to provide aviation transport services to the wider humanitarian community. During 2005 the UN's Inter-Agency Standing Committee (IASC), concerned with co-ordinating the international response to humanitarian disasters, developed a concept of organizing agency assistance to IDPs through the institutionalization of a 'Cluster Approach', currently comprising 11 core areas of activity. WFP was designated the lead agency for the clusters on Emergency Telecommunications (jointly with OCHA and UNICEF) and Logistics. During January 2008–June 2009 WFP implemented a special operation to improve country-specific communications services in order to enhance country-level cluster capacities. A review of the humanitarian cluster approach, undertaken during 2010, concluded that a new cluster on Food Security should be established. The new cluster, established accordingly in 2011, is led jointly by WFP and FAO, and aims to combine expertise in food aid and agricultural assistance in order to boost food security and to improve the resilience of food-insecure disaster-affected communities.

WFP aims to link its relief and development activities to provide a continuum between short-term relief and longer-term rehabilitation and development. In order to achieve this objective, WFP aims to promote capacity-building elements within relief operations, e.g. training, income-generating activities and environmental protection measures; and to integrate elements that strengthen disaster mitigation into development projects, including soil conservation, reafforestation, irrigation infrastructure, and transport construction and rehabilitation. In all its projects WFP aims to assist the most vulnerable groups (such as nursing mothers and children) and to ensure that beneficiaries have an adequate and balanced diet. Through its development activities, WFP aims to alleviate poverty in developing countries by promoting self-reliant families and communities. No individual country is permitted to receive more than 10% of the Programme's available development resources. WFP's Food-for-Assets development operations pay workers living in poverty with food in return for participation in self-help schemes and labour-intensive projects, with the aim of enabling vulnerable households and communities to focus time and resources on investing in lasting assets with which to raise themselves out of poverty (rather than on day-to-day survival). Food-for-Assets projects provide training in new techniques for achieving improved food security (such as training in new agricultural skills or in the establishment of home gardening businesses); and include, for example, building new irrigation or terracing infrastructures; soil and water conservation activities; and allocating food rations to villagers to enable them to devote time to building schools and clinics. In areas undermined by conflict WFP offers food assistance as an incentive for former combatants to put down their weapons and learn new skills. WFP focuses on providing good nutrition for the first 1,000 days of life, from the womb to two years of age, in order to lay the foundations for a healthy childhood and adulthood. WFP's *1,000 days plus* approach supports children over the age of two through school feeding activities, which aim to expand educational opportunities for poor children (given that it is difficult for children to concentrate on studies without adequate food and nutrition, and that food-insecure households frequently have to choose between educating their children or making them work to help the family to survive), and to improve the quality of the teaching environment. During 2010 school feeding projects benefited 21.1m. children. As an incentive to promote the education of vulnerable children, including orphans and children with HIV/AIDS, and to encourage families to send their daughters to school, WFP also implements 'take-home ration' projects, under which it provides basic food items to certain households, usually including sacks of rice and cans of cooking oil. WFP's Purchase for Progress (P4P) programme, launched in September 2008, expands the Programme's long-term 'local procurement' policy, enabling smallholder and low-income farmers in developing countries to supply food to WFP's global assistance operations. Under P4P farmers are taught techniques and provided with tools to enable them to compete competitively in the market-place. P4P also aims to identify and test specific successful local practices that could be replicated to benefit small-scale farmers on a wider scale. During 2008–13 P4P initiatives were being piloted in 21 countries, in Africa, Latin America and Asia. By 2012 WFP had established links under P4P with more than 1,000 farmers' organizations representing more than 1.1m. farmers world-wide. In September 2009 WFP, the Global Alliance for Improved Nutrition and other partners launched Project Laser Beam (PLB), a five-year public-private partnership aimed at eradicating eradicating child malnutrition; PLB initially undertook pilot projects in Bangladesh and India.

Since 1999 WFP has been implementing PRROs, where the emphasis is on fostering stability, rehabilitation and long-term development for victims of natural disasters, displaced persons and refugees. PRROs are introduced no later than 18 months after the initial EMOP and last no more than three years. When undertaken in collaboration with UNHCR and other international agencies, WFP has responsibility for mobilizing basic food commodities and for related transport, handling and storage costs.

In 2009 WFP operational expenditure in Europe and the CIS amounted to US $50.4m. (1.3% of total operational expenditure in that year).

During July 2009–December 2011 WFP implemented a PRRO in Georgia—costing US $22.2m. and guided by an inter-agency needs assessment that was conducted in October 2008—to enable a smooth transition from emergency relief to livelihood creation and restoration for some 130,000 beneficiaries whose circumstances had been adversely affected by the military conflict over South Ossetia that erupted between Georgia and Russia in August 2008 (causing massive population displacement, loss of agricultural assets and disruption to livelihoods), as well as by the impact of the ongoing global financial crisis. WFP was also to continue to support highly vulnerable Georgians who had been displaced in 1992 through conflict, and to provide food assistance to Georgians affected by HIV/AIDS and TB. During August 2010–July 2015 WFP was undertaking a development programme aimed at improving access to education for some 370,000 vulnerable children in Tajikistan, and over the period 1 January 2011–31 December 2013 it was implementing a project aimed at assisting TB patients and their families in that country. In November 2008 WFP approved an EMOP to provide emergency winter assistance in early 2009 to food-insecure people in Kyrgyzstan; the EMOP was subsequently extended through the 2009–10 and 2010–11 winter seasons. A development programme to support sustainable school feeding was being undertaken in Armenia during mid-2010–mid-2013.

In 2009 WFP operational expenditure in Latin America and the Caribbean amounted to US $243.0m. Of the total regional expenditure $113.9m. was for emergency relief operations, $22.4m. for agricultural, rural and human resource development projects, and $4.2m. for special operations. During July 2011–June 2014 WFP was implementing a $13.6m. PRRO aimed at supporting 120,100 Colombian refugees sheltering in Ecuador. A PRRO implemented within Colombia over the period 2008–end-2011 provided food assistance to 530,000 IDPs and individuals in food-insecure communities affected by violent unrest. A country programme being undertaken in Nicaragua over the period 2008–12, at a cost of $18.6m. and with 225,000 planned beneficiaries, focused on improving mother-and-child health, and on the implementation of food for education and food for training projects. A country programme (costing $10m. and aimed at 125,000 beneficiaries) was being undertaken in Bolivia during 2008–12, with a focus on providing food-based interventions for children aged from two to five years; giving food assistance to primary school children and street children; and offering technical assistance in emergency preparedness and response to government institutions. During 2008–13 WFP's new P4P programme (see above) was being piloted in El Salvador, Honduras, Guatemala and Nicaragua.

WFP estimated in late 2009, immediately prior to the severe earthquake that struck Haiti in January 2010, that around one-third of the Haitian population was food-insecure. The agency has provided long-term support in the areas of nutrition and health, education, and disaster mitigation activities, to vulnerable people in that country who have been affected by political and civil unrest, successive natural disasters (including hurricanes), escalating food prices, and poor infrastructure. In January 2010 WFP appealed for US $475.3m. to fund a complex emergency humanitarian operation in response to the earthquake that caused devastation in Haiti in that month. WFP's relief activities aimed to target food assistance towards the most vulnerable survivors of the disaster, and were focused on the provision of school meals (aiming initially to reach 72,000 children in 148 schools in the Port-au-Prince area); a scheme to distribute nutritious food products (such as Supplementary Plumpy) to 53,000 children aged under five years, and to 16,000 pregnant and breast-feeding mothers; and the carefully targeted distribution to around 300,000 vulnerable families (comprising an estimated 1.5m. beneficiaries) of full food baskets including rice, beans, corn soya blend, oil and salt. In February WFP hosted a high-level meeting in Rome to launch a global partnership aimed at developing a future food security plan for Haiti.

In 2010 the five sub-regions of sub-Saharan Africa represented the main regional focus of WFP relief activities; during that year operational expenditure there amounted to US $2,340.8m. (59% of WFP's total annual operational expenditure), including $1,978.5m. for relief operations and $169.8m. for development projects. During 2008–13 WFP's new P4P programme (see above) was being piloted in Burkina Faso, the Democratic Republic of the Congo, Ethiopia, Ghana, Kenya, Liberia, Malawi, Mali, Mozambique, Rwanda, Sierra Leone, Sudan, Tanzania, Uganda and Zambia.

Drought-affected communities in the Horn of Africa are a particular focus of WFP's sub-Saharan Africa activities. By mid-2011, as a result of crop failure and livestock loss following two consecutive seasons of poor rainfall, a severe drought prevailed in the Horn of Africa, with southern Somalia, in particular, a focus of humanitarian emergency. The situation in Somalia was exacerbated by the long-term lack of effective government there, the inaccessibility of extensive rebel-controlled areas, and high food prices which had further limited access to adequate nutrition. An estimated 3.7m. southern Somalis were estimated to be suffering food insecurity at that time—with the rate of acute malnutrition reaching 30% in some areas—and, over the period July 2011–early February 2012, the UN declared a state of famine in two southern Somali regions. It was reported in July 2011 that many Somali rural households were migrating in search of food and support to the conflict-affected Somali capital, Mogadishu, as well as into neighbouring countries. During July 2011–December 2012 an EMOP was being undertaken which aimed to provide 239,820 metric tons of food assistance to 3.9m. beneficiaries in Somalia. Over the period January 2009–December 2011 some 130,271 Eritrean, Somali and Sudanese refugees sheltering in Ethiopia benefited from an $83.9m. PRRO. A $174.6m. PRRO to provide food assistance to 474,000 Somali and Sudanese refugees in Kenya, and 54,000 beneficiaries in the host population, was undertaken during the period 1 October 2009–30 September 2011. From 2009–13 WFP was implementing a country development programme, costing $106.3m., that was to support annually about 650,000 Kenyan primary school children in food-insecure areas and to assist annually around 78,000 food-insecure Kenyans affected by HIV/AIDS to graduate from food support. A one-year emergency operation in Sudan for 2010 aimed to provide 665,550 metric tons of food aid to 6.4m. beneficiaries at a cost of $873.7m. In April 2009 WFP approved a PRRO targeting an annual maximum of 881,000 beneficiaries in Uganda over April 2009–March 2012; the total cost of the PRRO amounted to $177.1m., including an allocation of $3m. to finance a pilot cash transfer scheme.

In 2010 and, again, from early 2012, the Sahel region of West Africa (including parts of Niger, Mali, Mauritania, Burkina Faso, Chad, Gambia, northern Nigeria and Senegal) was affected by severe drought, causing acute food insecurity. In early 2012, in response, WFP aimed to provide emergency food assistance to some 3.3m. beneficiaries in Niger, 750,000 in Mali, and 400,000 Mauritanians. The situation in northern areas of Mali was exacerbated from March by violent conflict, causing some 200,000 people to be displaced from their homes and a further

160,000 to seek shelter in neighbouring countries (Burkino Faso, Mauritania, Niger). A EMOP 'Assistance to Refugees and IDPs Affected by Insecurity in Mali' was under way during June–December 2012, and was to support some 550,000 people. A $46.4m. country development programme being implemented in Niger during 2009–13, and targeting 1.3m. beneficiaries, was to increase access to basic education, especially for girls; to strengthen the prevention and mitigation of food insecurity during lean periods; and to contribute to improving the health and nutritional status of patients living with HIV/AIDS and TB. In February 2009 WFP launched a cash transfer and voucher programme in urban areas of Ouagadougou, Burkina Faso (the first such programme to be implemented in Africa), targeting 120,000 people adversely affected by high food prices. Under the new programme family representatives were to be given over a six-month period up to six vouchers, valued at $3 each month, and exchangeable in participating shops for maize, cooking oil, sugar, salt and soap. Vulnerable families with young children were to receive rations of 'Plumpy Doz' (see above). In the following month a similar food voucher scheme was initiated in Bobo-Dioulasso, Burkina Faso, targeting 60,000 people. During September 2009–August 2011 WFP undertook a PRRO in Liberia, at a cost of US $39.8m., to assist the ongoing post-conflict recovery process there through livelihood asset rehabilitation; school feeding; nutrition interventions; and capacity-building, including the implementation of P4P schemes. At the beginning of January 2011 WFP commenced the distribution of high energy biscuits to the most vulnerable of more than 20,000 Côte d'Ivoire refugees who, owing to serious violent unrest, had fled to Liberia from late 2010. From February–July 2011 an EMOP to provide food aid to the Côte d'Ivoire refugees was undertaken; by April an estimated 150,000 Ivorian refugees had sought shelter in Liberia. During March–September 2011 WFP implemented an EMOP to provide food aid to 125,000 vulnerable Ivorian IDPs.

In 2009 WFP operational expenditure in the Middle East and North Africa amounted to US$175.2m. (4.4% of total operational expenditure in that year), including $161.7m. for emergency relief operations and $10.4m. for development operations. WFP has been engaged in preventing hunger in Iraq, undertaking activities including surveying food security, strengthening national capacity, assisting a newly established distribution system, and supporting a government-administered school feeding programme. From August 2010–July 2012 a PRRO was implemented in Iraq, benefiting nearly 1.8m. people through the provision of 189,504 metric tons of food assistance. According to a comprehensive food security and vulnerability analysis of Iraq published in November 2008, communities in 41 out of 115 districts of the country remained at that time vulnerable to food insecurity. An EMOP to assist 150,000 Iraqi refugees in Syria was undertaken during May 2010–March 2012. A mobile telephone-based system has been used to send food voucher codes to Iraqi beneficiaries of WFP assistance in Syria; the codes can be used to purchase items in local stores. In December 2007 WFP undertook a Rapid Food Security Needs Assessment of the situation in the Palestinian territories. In January 2009 WFP provided *meals-ready-to-eat* (MREs, which do not require conventional heating facilities) to people affected by the sustained Israeli military offensive against targets in Gaza that commenced in late December 2008, including to 16,000 Palestinians in UNRWA shelters and 7,000 Palestinians in hospitals. A global appeal, Operation Lifeline Gaza, was launched in January 2009 to fund the provision of WFP emergency assistance, initially for a 12-month period; Operation Lifeline Gaza was subsequently extended to 31 December 2011. In total some $4.8m. was allocated under the programme in the form of cash vouchers, and some $105.2m. in the form of food rations. From 1 January 2011–31 December 2012 WFP was implementing a project targeting food assistance in support of destitute and marginalized groups in the West Bank; the scheme was to help some 454,500 beneficiaries annually, focusing on meeting immediate food needs, enhancing food consumption, and improving dietery diversity, and aimed to promote long-term resilience by supporting the re-establishment of agricultural livelihoods in conflict-affected areas. An electronic food voucher system implemented by WFP in the Palestinian territories during 2010 assisted 32,000 people in the West Bank and more than 15,000 in Gaza; the vouchers could be spent in selected shops, thereby also benefiting local shop-owners and food producers. During 2009 a food safety net programme was introduced in Yemen to support vulnerable populations adversely affected by high food prices and conflict. A PRRO was being undertaken in Yemen during 1 January 2010–31 December 2012 aimed at alleviating acute food insecurity and very high incidence of malnutrition there. In mid-March 2012 a survey produced by WFP—in conjunction with UNICEF and the Yemen authorities—on the food situation in that country, reported that hunger had doubled since 2009, stating that nearly 5m. Yemenis were unable to produce or to buy sufficient food.

In response to the outbreak of conflict in Libya from mid-February 2011, WFP launched a US $4m. operation to augment and co-ordinate logistics and emergency telecommunications in that country. In mid-April WFP announced that it had opened a humanitarian corridor for the transportation of food and other assistance to communities in western areas of the country, which had hitherto been isolated by heavy fighting. A $121.6m. emergency operation aimed at supplying food aid to vulnerable populations affected by the conflict in Libya, and in Egypt and Tunisia (which had also been affected by violent unrest in early 2011), was implemented during March 2011–February 2012.

During October 2011–December 2012 WFP was undertaking an EMOP to assist some 500,000 people affected by violent unrest in Syria, through the distribution of supplementary food rations covering two-thirds of daily energy requirements.

In 2009 WFP operational expenditure in Asia amounted to US$763.4m. (19.2% of total operational expenditure in that year), including $650.8m. for emergency relief operations, $27.0m. for special operations, and $77.3m. for agricultural, rural and human resource development projects. During 2008–13 WFP's new P4P programme (see above) was being piloted in Afghanistan and Laos.

WFP has been active in Afghanistan, where violent conflict and natural disasters (mainly severe drought) have caused massive and protracted population displacement and food insecurity; the latter has been aggravated in recent years by volatile food prices. Restricted humanitarian access, limited institutional capacities, devastated infrastructure, and the country's landlocked geography have contributed to a crisis in which, by 2010, 31% of the population were estimated by WFP to be food-insecure, with a further 23% at risk of food insecurity. In April 2010 WFP launched a three-year PRRO throughout Afghanistan (to terminate in March 2013) which was to target a maximum of 7.6m. beneficiaries annually, at a total cost to the Programme of $1,204m. The PRRO aimed to provide food assistance to conflict- and disaster-affected people, IDPs and other vulnerable groups (such as malnourished children and pregnant and nursing women); to support—through the provision of basic education and basic skills training for women and girls—the re-establishment of the livelihoods of adversely-affected communities and families; and to advance the availability of TB treatment. A PRRO, costing $117.8m., was implemented during January–December 2011 to assist, through nutrition interventions and school-feeding, some 371,000 IDPs, returnees and host communities in northern Sri Lanka. An EMOP was undertaken from 1 August 2011–31 January 2012 with the aim of providing food assistance and early recovery support to an estimated 500,000 people displaced by flooding that occurred in eastern Sri Lanka during November 2010–January 2011. In 2009 a food safety net programme was introduced in Pakistan, to support vulnerable populations adversely affected by high food prices. In August 2010 WFP responded to severe flooding that devastated northern and central areas of Pakistan, seriously adversely affecting at least 15m. people and leaving an estimated 8m. survivors in need of urgent food assistance, by mobilizing its long-term local humanitarian presence to distribute food supplies throughout the affected areas. WFP appealed to the international community at that time for some $164m. to extend massively the scope of ongoing operations in Pakistan. A PRRO providing food assistance to 9.5m. beneficiaries in Pakistan, over the period 1 January 2011–31 December 2012, was targeted at flood-affected communities in Balochistan, Khyber Pakhtunkhwa, and the Federally Administered Tribal Areas of Pakistan.

The food situation in the Democratic People's Republic of Korea (North Korea) has required substantial levels of emergency food supplies in recent years, owing to natural disasters and consistently poor harvests. During 1995–99 an estimated 1.5m.–

3.5m. people died of starvation in North Korea. In August 2005 the North Korean Government requested WFP to shift its focus from emergency relief to development activities and consequently, in February 2006, WFP approved a US $102.2m. PRRO for North Korea, covering the period 1 April 2006–31 March 2008, which followed on from 10 successive emergency operations that had hitherto achieved some progress in reducing rates of malnutrition in that country. The two-year PRRO aimed to provide 150,000 metric tons of food aid to 1.9m. people, and to support the Government's strategy to achieve long-term food security. The operation provided for the distribution to young children and women of child-bearing age of vitamin- and mineral-enriched domestically produced foods, and for the allocation of cereal rations to underemployed communities with a view to enabling them to build and rehabilitate agricultural and other community assets. A short-term emergency operation to assist 215,000 people affected by floods that struck North Korea in August 2007 was implemented during August–November of that year. In June 2008 a WFP/FAO Rapid Food Security Assessment of that country found that access to food had deteriorated significantly since 2007, particularly for urban households in areas of low industrial activity, who had been severely affected by rising food and fuel prices, reductions in food rationing and decreasing rates of employment. WFP subsequently approved a $503.6m. EMOP covering the period 1 September 2008–30 November 2009 (later extended to June 2010), which aimed to target assistance at food-insecure populations through mother and child nutrition activities; food assistance to schools, elderly people and other vulnerable groups; and food for community development activities. WFP stated that comprehensive interventions were required to improve agricultural production in North Korea, and that, conditions permitting, humanitarian assistance would be reduced following the expiry of the emergency operation and the long-term development approach pursued under the 2006–08 PRRO would be resumed. Accordingly, in June 2010, a new PRRO was approved, initially covering the two-year period until June 2012, targeting 157,047 metric tons of nutrition support at women and children, at a total cost to WFP of $96m. In view of worsening food insecurity caused by high rainfall in 2010 and a harsh winter over 2010–11, the North Korean Government made a formal appeal to WFP in January 2011 requesting emergency food assistance. WFP, FAO and UNICEF conducted an inter-agency rapid food security assessment of the country during February–March. WFP initiated an EMOP covering 1 April 2011–30 June 2012, which aimed to support some 3.5m. vulnerable people (mainly women and children), incorporating and expanding activities launched under the PRRO initiated in June 2010. The PRRO was suspended, to be renewed following the completion of the EMOP.

A PRRO to improve the food security, nutrition status and livelihoods of vulnerable populations in Myanmar (targeting 2.0m. individuals), at a cost of US $121.8m., was being implemented during the three-year period 1 January 2010–31 December 2012. In late September 2007 WFP urged the Myanmar authorities to ease restrictions on the movement of food supplies that had been imposed owing to unrest in that country, as these were inhibiting WFP's implementation of its relief activities; assurances were reportedly received from the Myanmar regime at the end of that month that WFP would be permitted to undertake its scheduled food deliveries. In October WFP urged the Myanmar authorities to pursue critical social and economic reforms aimed at reducing poverty and hunger in that country, stating that international humanitarian assistance could not meet all the requirements of the Myanma population. An EMOP was undertaken during May–November 2008 to provide food assistance to 750,000 people in Myanmar, in response to the devastation caused by Cyclone Nargis in early May to domestic food stocks, livestock, crops, shrimp farms, fishing ponds, fish hatcheries, fishing boats and other food production assets.

An EMOP to provide food assistance to 1.6m. people whose livelihoods had been affected by long-term conflict in Mindanao, Philippines, was implemented over the period 1 June 2008–31 May 2009. From late September 2009 a series of typhoons resulted in extensive flooding in the Philippines, causing serious damage in the capital city, Manila, and in Luzon, the country's main rice-producing region. In response, WFP launched a US $57m. relief operation, which targeted assistance at more than 1m. people. Owing to further heavy rains, flooding and landslides in 2010–11 the operation was extended. In October 2011 WFP provided immediate food assistance (including High Energy Biscuits) to communities in northern Luzon whose lands were flooded by Typhoon Nesat. During 1 July 2010–31 December 2011 WFP implemented a development programme in Laos aimed at addressing malnutrition in mothers and children. In June 2011 WFP approved a country programme for Cambodia covering the period 2011–16, aimed at improving food security. In September 2008 a PRRO was approved to assist on average 255,600 vulnerable people in Timor-Leste per year over the two-year period 1 September 2008–31 August 2010; this was subsequently extended until August 2011.

Following a massive earthquake in the Indian Ocean in December 2004, which caused a series of tidal waves, or tsunamis, that devastated coastal regions in 14 countries in South and South-East Asia and East Africa, initial WFP emergency operations were funded from the Immediate Response Account (see below). In January 2005 WFP requested emergency funding of US $256m., of which $185m. was to support an initial six-month programme to provide food aid to 2m. people affected by the natural disaster, mainly in Sri Lanka, the Maldives and Indonesia, and $72m. was for three special operations, concerned with logistics augmentation, air support and the establishment of a UN Joint Logistics Centre for Inter-Agency Co-ordination, of which WFP was the lead agency. In Indonesia (close to the epicentre of the earthquake) WFP established new field offices and an emergency operations centre in the capital, Jakarta. From mid-2005 WFP focused its activities increasingly on recovery and rebuilding communities. A PRRO to provide nutritional and recovery support for vulnerable families in Indonesia (with 845,000 targeted individual beneficiaries) was undertaken during 1 January 2008–31 December 2010.

Finance

The Programme is funded by voluntary contributions from donor countries, intergovernmental bodies such as the European Commission, and the private sector. Contributions are made in the form of commodities, finance and services (particularly shipping). Commitments to the International Emergency Food Reserve (IEFR), from which WFP provides the majority of its food supplies, and to the Immediate Response Account of the IEFR (IRA), are also made on a voluntary basis by donors. WFP's projected budget for 2012 amounted to some US $5,484.4m. Contributions by donors were forecast at $3,750m.

Publications

Annual Report.

Food and Nutrition Handbook.

School Feeding Handbook.

World Hunger Series.

Statistics

OPERATIONAL EXPENDITURE IN 2009 BY REGION AND TYPE*
(US $ '000)

Region	Development	Relief	Special operations
Sub-Saharan Africa	187,950	2,171,822	28,958
Asia	77,256	650,793	27,036
Latin America and the Caribbean	22,353	113,970	4,232
North Africa and the Middle East	10,440	161,727	1,576
Europe and the CIS	—	499,992	413
Total†	275,906	3,239,887	176,364

* Excludes programme support and administrative costs.

† Includes operational expenditures such as trust fund expenditures that cannot be apportioned by project/operation.

SPECIALIZED AGENCIES WITHIN THE UN SYSTEM

Food and Agriculture Organization of the United Nations—FAO

Address: Viale delle Terme di Caracalla, 00100 Rome, Italy.

Telephone: (06) 5705-1; **fax:** (06) 5705-3152; **e-mail:** fao-hq@fao.org; **internet:** www.fao.org.

FAO, the first specialized agency of the UN to be founded after the Second World War, aims to alleviate malnutrition and hunger, and serves as a co-ordinating agency for development programmes in the whole range of food and agriculture, including forestry and fisheries. It helps developing countries to promote educational and training facilities and to create appropriate institutions.

MEMBERS

FAO has 191 member nations; the European Union is a member organization. The Faroe Islands and Tokelau are associate members.

Organization

(June 2012)

CONFERENCE

The governing body is the FAO Conference of member nations. It meets every two years, formulates policy, determines the organization's programme and budget on a biennial basis, and elects new members. It also elects the Director-General of the Secretariat and the Independent Chairman of the Council. Regional conferences are also held each year.

COUNCIL

The FAO Council is composed of representatives of 49 member nations, elected by the Conference for rotating three-year terms. It is the interim governing body of FAO between sessions of the Conference. There are eight main Governing Committees of the Council: the Finance and Programme Committees, and the Committees on Commodity Problems, Fisheries, Agriculture, Forestry, World Food Security, and Constitutional and Legal Matters.

SECRETARIAT

There are some 3,600 FAO staff, of whom about one-half are based at headquarters. FAO maintains five regional offices (see below), nine sub-regional offices, five liaison offices (in Yokohama, Japan; Washington, DC, USA, liaison with North America; Geneva, Switzerland and New York, USA, with the UN; and Brussels, Belgium, with the European Union), and some 74 country offices. Work is undertaken by the following departments: Agriculture and Consumer Protection; Economic and Social Development; Fisheries and Aquaculture; Forestry; Human, Financial and Physical Resources; Knowledge and Communication; Natural Resource Management and Environment; and Technical Co-operation.

Director-General: Dr José Graziano da Silva (Brazil).

REGIONAL OFFICES

Africa: POB 1628, Accra, Ghana; tel. (21) 675000; fax (21) 668427; e-mail fao-raf@fao.org; internet www.fao.org/world/regional/raf/index_en.asp; Regional Rep. Maria Helena de Morais Semedo; Sub-Regional Rep. for West Africa Musa Saihou Mbenga.

Asia and the Pacific: Maliwan Mansion, 39 Phra Atit Rd, Bangkok 10200, Thailand; tel. (2) 697-4000; fax (2) 697-4445; e-mail fao-rap@fao.org; internet www.fao.org/world/regional/rap; Regional Rep. Hiroyuki Konuma.

Europe and Central Asia: 1068 Budapest, Benczur u. 34, Hungary; tel. (1) 461-2000; fax (1) 351-7029; e-mail fao-seur@fao.org; internet www.fao.org/world/regional/reu; Regional Rep. Fernanda Guerrieri (Italy).

Latin America and the Caribbean: Avda Dag Hammarskjöld 3241, Casilla 10095, Vitacura, Santiago, Chile; tel. (2) 923-2100; fax (2) 923-2101; e-mail fao-rlc@field.fao.org; internet www.rlc.fao.org; Regional Rep. Raul Benitez.

Near East: 11 El-Eslah el-Zerai St, Dokki, POB 2223, Cairo, Egypt; tel. (2) 3316000; fax (2) 7495981; e-mail fao-rne@fao.org; internet www.fao.org/world/Regional/RNE/index_en.htm; Regional Rep. (vacant).

Activities

FAO aims to raise levels of nutrition and standards of living by improving the production and distribution of food and other commodities derived from farms, fisheries and forests. FAO's ultimate objective is the achievement of world food security, 'Food for All'. The organization provides technical information, advice and assistance by disseminating information; acting as a neutral forum for discussion of food and agricultural issues; advising governments on policy and planning; and developing capacity directly in the field.

In November 1996 FAO hosted the World Food Summit, which was held in Rome and was attended by heads of state and senior government representatives of 186 countries. Participants approved the Rome Declaration on World Food Security and the World Food Summit Plan of Action, with the aim of halving the number of people afflicted by undernutrition, then estimated to total 828m. world-wide, by no later than 2015. A review conference to assess progress in achieving the goals of the summit, entitled World Food Summit: Five Years Later, held in June 2002, reaffirmed commitment to this objective, which is also incorporated into the UN Millennium Development Goals (MDGs). During that month FAO announced the formulation of a global 'Anti-Hunger Programme', which aimed to promote investment in the agricultural sector and rural development, with a particular focus on small-scale farmers, and to enhance food access for those most in need, for example through the provision of school meals, schemes to feed pregnant and nursing mothers and food-for-work programmes. FAO hosts the UN System Network on Rural Development and Food Security, comprising some 20 UN bodies, which was established in 1997 as an inter-agency mechanism to follow-up the World Food Summits.

In November 1999 the FAO Conference approved a long-term Strategic Framework for the period 2000–15, which emphasized national and international co-operation in pursuing the goals of the 1996 World Food Summit. The Framework promoted interdisciplinarity and partnership, and defined three main global objectives: constant access by all people to sufficient, nutritionally adequate and safe food to ensure that levels of undernourishment were reduced by 50% by 2015 (see above); the continued contribution of sustainable agriculture and rural development to economic and social progress and well-being; and the conservation, improvement and sustainable use of natural resources. It identified five corporate strategies (each supported by several strategic objectives), covering the following areas: reducing food insecurity and rural poverty; ensuring enabling policy and regulatory frameworks for food, agriculture, fisheries and forestry; creating sustainable increases in the supply and availability of agricultural, fisheries and forestry products; conserving and enhancing sustainable use of the natural resource base; and generating knowledge. In October 2007 the report of an

Independent External Evaluation (IEE) into the role and functions of FAO recommended that the organization elaborate a plan for reform to ensure its continued efficiency and effectiveness. In November 2008 a Special Conference of member countries approved a three-year Immediate Plan of Action to reform the governance and management of the organization based on the recommendations of the IEE. In June 2012 the FAO Council endorsed a proposal of the Organization's Director-General to reallocate budgetary savings towards strengthening country offices, increasing strategic planning capacity, and funding more interdisciplinary activities.

In December 2007 FAO inaugurated an Initiative on Soaring Food Prices (ISFP) to help to boost food production in low-income developing countries and improve access to food and agricultural supplies in the short term, with a view to countering an escalation since 2006 in commodity prices. (During 2006–08 the Food Price Index maintained by FAO recorded that international prices for many basic food commodities had increased by around 60%, and the FAO Cereal Price Index, covering the prices of principal food staples such as wheat, rice and maize, recorded a doubling in the international price of grains over that period.) In April 2008 the UN Secretary-General appointed FAO's Director-General as Vice-Chairman of a High Level Task Force (HLTF) on the Global Food Security Crisis, which aimed to address the impact of the ongoing soaring levels of food and fuel prices and formulate a comprehensive framework for action. In June FAO hosted a High Level Conference on World Food Security and the Challenges of Climate Change and Bioenergy. The meeting adopted a Declaration on Food Security, urging the international donor community to increase its support to developing countries and countries with economies in transition. The Declaration also noted an urgent need to develop the agricultural sectors and expand food production in such countries and for increased investment in rural development, agriculture and agribusiness. In January 2009 a follow-up high level meeting was convened in Madrid, Spain, and attended by 62 government ministers and representatives from 126 countries. The meeting agreed to initiate a consultation process with regard to the establishment of a Global Partnership for Agriculture, Food Security and Nutrition to strengthen international co-ordination and governance for food security. FAO's long-standing Committee on World Food Security (CFS) underwent reform in 2009; henceforth the Committee was to be a central component of the new Global Partnership, and was to influence hunger elimination programmes at global, regional and national level, taking into account that food security relates not just to agriculture but also to economic access to food, adequate nutrition, social safety nets and human rights.

In May 2009 the EU donated €106m. to FAO, to support farmers and improve food security in 10 developing countries in Africa, Asia and the Caribbean that were particularly badly affected by the recently emerged global food crisis. Addressing the World Grain Forum, convened in St Petersburg, Russia, in June 2009, the FAO Director-General demanded a more effective and coherent global governance system to ensure future world food security, and urged that a larger proportion of development aid should be allocated to agriculture, to enable developing countries to invest in rural infrastructures. During June it was estimated that, in 2009, the number of people world-wide suffering chronic, daily hunger had risen to an unprecedented 1,020m., of whom an estimated 642m. were in Asia and the Pacific; 265m. in sub-Saharan Africa; 53m. in Latin America and the Caribbean; and 42m. in the Middle East and North Africa. Around 15m. people resident in developed countries were estimated at that time to be afflicted by chronic hunger. The *OECD-FAO Agricultural Outlook 2009–18*, issued in June 2009, found the global agriculture sector to be showing more resilience to the ongoing world-wide economic crisis than other sectors, owing to the status of food as a basic human necessity. However, the report warned that the state of the agriculture sector could become more fragile if the ongoing global downturn were to worsen. In July the FAO Director-General welcomed the L'Aquila Joint Statement on Global Food Security (promoting sustainable agricultural development), and the Food Security Initiative with commitments of US $20,000m., that were approved in that month by G8 leaders.

In mid-October 2009 a high-level forum of experts was convened by FAO to discuss policy on the theme 'How to Feed the World in 2050'. In November 2009 FAO organized a World Summit on Food Security, in Rome, with the aim of achieving greater coherence in the global governance of food security and setting a 'new world food order'. Leaders attending the Summit issued a declaration in which they adopted a number of strategic objectives, including: ensuring urgent action towards achieving World Food Summit objectives/the UN MDG relating to reducing undernutrition; promoting the new Global Partnership for Agriculture, Food Security and Nutrition and fully committing to reform of the CFS; reversing the decline in national and international funding for agriculture, food security and rural development in developing countries, and encouraging new investment to increase sustainable agricultural production; reducing poverty and working towards achieving food security and access to 'Food for All'; and confronting proactively the challenges posed by climate change to food security. The Summit determined to base its pursuit of these strategic objectives on the following *Five Rome Principles for Sustainable Global Food Security*: (i) investment in country-owned plans aimed at channelling resources to efficient results-based programmes and partnerships; (ii) fostering strategic co-ordination at national, regional and global level to improve governance, promote better allocation of resources, avoid duplication of efforts and identify response gaps; (iii) striving for a comprehensive twin-track approach to food security comprising direct action to combat hunger in the most vulnerable, and also medium- and long-term sustainable agricultural, food security, nutrition and rural development programmes to eliminate the root causes of hunger and poverty, including through the progressive realization of the right to adequate food; (iv) ensuring a strong role for the multilateral system by sustained improvements in efficiency, responsiveness, co-ordination and effectiveness of multilateral institutions; and (v) ensuring sustained and substantial commitment by all partners to investment in agriculture and food security and nutrition, with provision of necessary resources in a timely and reliable fashion, aimed at multi-year plans and programmes. The FAO Director-General welcomed a new 'Zero Hunger Challenge' initiative announced by the UN Secretary-General in June 2012, which aimed to eliminate malnutrition through measures including boosting the productivity of smallholders, creating sustainable food systems, and reducing food wastage.

FAO, with WFP and IFAD, leads an initiative to strengthen feeding programmes and expand support to farmers in developing countries, the second of nine activities that were launched in April 2009 by the UN System Chief Executives Board for Coordination (CEB), with the aim of alleviating the impact on poor and vulnerable populations of the developing global economic crisis.

With other UN agencies, FAO attended the Summit of the World's Regions on Food Insecurity, held in Dakar, Senegal, in January 2010. The summit urged that global governance of food security should integrate players on every level, and expressed support for the developing Global Partnership for Agriculture, Food Security and Nutrition.

In February 2011 the FAO Food Price Index, at 238 points, recorded the highest levels of global food prices since 1990, with prices having risen in each consecutive month during July 2010–February 2011 (and having, in December 2010, exceeded the previous peak reached during mid-2008). The Cereal Price Index also recorded in February 2011 the highest price levels since mid-2008. FAO maintains, additionally, a Dairy Price Index, an Oils/Fats Price Index, a Meat Price Index and a Sugar Price Index. In May 2012 the Food Price Index averaged 204 points.

In June 2011 agriculture ministers from G20 countries adopted an action plan aimed at stabilizing food price volatility and agriculture, with a focus on improving international policy co-ordination and agricultural production; promoting targeted emergency humanitarian food reserves; and developing, under FAO auspices, an Agricultural Market Information System (AMIS) to improve market transparency.

FAO's annual *State of Food Insecurity in the World* report (see below), compiled in 2011 with help from IFAD and WFP, maintained that volatile and high food prices were likely to continue, rendering poorer consumers, farmers and nations more vulnerable to poverty and hunger.

In May 2012 the CFS endorsed a set of landmark Voluntary Guidelines on the Responsible Governance of Tenure of Land, Fisheries and Forests in the Context of National Food Security, with the aim of supporting governments in safeguarding the rights of citizens to own or have access to natural resources. In June, in the context of the UN Conference on Sustainable Development, convened during that month in Rio de Janeiro, Brazil, FAO released a study that advocated for the promotion of energy-smart systems for food production and usage.

World Food Day, commemorating the foundation of FAO, is held annually on 16 October. In May 2010 FAO launched an online petition entitled the *1billionhungry project*, with the aim of raising awareness of the plight of people world-wide suffering from chronic hunger.

AGRICULTURE AND CONSUMER PROTECTION

FAO's overall objective is to lead international efforts to counter hunger and to improve levels of nutrition. Within this context FAO is concerned to improve crop and grassland productivity and to develop sustainable agricultural systems to provide for enhanced food security and economic development. It provides member countries with technical advice for plant improvement, the application of plant biotechnology, the development of integrated production systems and rational grassland management. There are groups concerned with the main field cereal crops, i.e. rice, maize and wheat, which *inter alia* identify means of enhancing production, collect and analyse relevant data and promote collaboration between research institutions, government bodies and other farm management organizations. In 1985 and 1990 FAO's International Rice Commission endorsed the use of hybrid rice, which had been developed in the People's Republic of China, as a means of meeting growing demand for the crop, in particular in the Far East, and has subsequently assisted member countries to acquire the necessary technology and training to develop hybrid rice production. In Africa FAO has collaborated with the West African Rice Development Association to promote and facilitate the use of new rice varieties and crop management practices. FAO actively promotes the concept of Conservation Agriculture, which aims to minimize the need for mechanical soil tillage or additional farming resources and to reduce soil degradation and erosion.

FAO is also concerned with the development and diversification of horticultural and industrial crops, for example oil seeds, fibres and medicinal plants. FAO collects and disseminates data regarding crop trials and new technologies. It has developed an information processing site, Ecocrop, to help farmers identify appropriate crops and environmental requirements. FAO works to protect and support the sustainable development of grasslands and pasture, which contribute to the livelihoods of an estimated 800m. people world-wide.

FAO's plant protection service incorporates a range of programmes concerned with the control of pests and the use of pesticides. In February 2001 FAO warned that some 30% of pesticides sold in developing countries did not meet internationally accepted quality standards. In November 2002 FAO adopted a revised International Code of Conduct on the Distribution and Use of Pesticides (first adopted in 1985) to reduce the inappropriate distribution and use of pesticides and other toxic compounds, particularly in developing countries. In September 1998 a new legally binding treaty on trade in hazardous chemicals and pesticides was adopted at an international conference held in Rotterdam, Netherlands. The so-called Rotterdam Convention required that hazardous chemicals and pesticides banned or severely restricted in at least two countries should not be exported unless explicitly agreed by the importing country. It also identified certain pesticide formulations as too dangerous to be used by farmers in developing countries, and incorporated an obligation that countries halt national production of those hazardous compounds. The treaty entered into force in February 2004. FAO co-operates with UNEP to provide secretariat services for the Convention. FAO has promoted the use of Integrated Pest Management (IPM) initiatives to encourage the use, at local level, of safer and more effective methods of pest control, such as biological control methods and natural predators.

FAO hosts the secretariat of the International Plant Protection Convention (first adopted in 1951, revised in 1997) which aims to prevent the spread of plant pests and to promote effective control measures. The secretariat helps to define phytosanitary standards, promote the exchange of information and extend technical assistance to contracting parties (177 at June 2012).

FAO is concerned with the conservation and sustainable use of plant and animal genetic resources. It works with regional and international associations to develop seed networks, to encourage the use of improved seed production systems, to elaborate quality control and certification mechanisms and to co-ordinate seed security activities, in particular in areas prone to natural or man-made disasters. FAO has developed a World Information and Early Warning System (WIEWS) to gather and disseminate information concerning plant genetic resources for food and agriculture and to undertake periodic assessments of the state of those resources. FAO is also developing, as part of the WIEWS, a Seed Information Service to extend information to member states on seeds, planting and new technologies. In June 1996 representatives of more than 150 governments convened in Leipzig, Germany, at an International Technical Conference organized by FAO to consider the use and conservation of plant genetic resources as an essential means of enhancing food security. The meeting adopted a Global Plan of Action, which included measures to strengthen the development of plant varieties and to promote the use and availability of local varieties and locally adapted crops to farmers, in particular following a natural disaster, war or civil conflict. In November 2001 the FAO Conference adopted the International Treaty on Plant Genetic Resources for Food and Agriculture (also referred to as the Seed Treaty), with the aim of providing a framework to ensure access to plant genetic resources and to related knowledge, technologies, and—through the Treaty's Benefit-sharing Fund (BSF)—funding. The Seed Treaty entered into force in June 2004, having received the required number of ratifications, and, by June 2012, had 127 states parties. The BSF assists poor farmers in developing countries with conserving, and also adapting to climate change, their most important food crops; in 2011 the Fund supported 11 high-impact projects for small-scale farmers in four regions. It was hoped that international donors would raise US $116m. for the BSF by 2014. By 2012 around 1,750 gene banks had been established world-wide, storing more than 7m. plant samples.

FAO's Animal Production and Health Division is concerned with the control and management of major animal diseases, and, in recent years, with safeguarding humans from livestock diseases. Other programmes are concerned with the contribution of livestock to poverty alleviation, the efficient use of natural resources in livestock production, the management of animal genetic resources, promoting the exchange of information and mapping the distribution of livestock around the world. In 2001 FAO established a Pro-Poor Livestock Policy Initiative to support the formulation and implementation of livestock-related policies to improve the livelihood and nutrition of the world's rural poor, with an initial focus on the Andean region, the Horn of Africa, West Africa, South Asia and the Mekong.

The Emergency Prevention System for Transboundary Animal and Plant Pests and Diseases (EMPRES) was established in 1994 to strengthen FAO's activities in the prevention, early warning, control and, where possible, eradication of pests and highly contagious livestock diseases (which the system categorizes as epidemic diseases of strategic importance, such as rinderpest or foot-and-mouth; diseases requiring tactical attention at international or regional level, e.g. Rift Valley fever; and emerging diseases, e.g. bovine spongiform encephalopathy—BSE). EMPRES has a desert locust component, and has published guidelines on all aspects of desert locust monitoring. FAO assumed responsibility for technical leadership and co-ordination of the Global Rinderpest Eradication Programme (GREP), which had the objective of eliminating that disease by 2011; in June 2011 the FAO Conference adopted a resolution declaring global freedom from rinderpest. In November 1997 FAO initiated a Programme Against African Trypanosomiasis, which aimed to counter the disease affecting cattle in almost one-third of Africa. In November 2004 FAO established a specialized Emergency Centre for Transboundary Animal Disease Operations (ECTAD) to enhance FAO's role in assisting member states to combat animal disease outbreaks and in co-ordinating international efforts to research, monitor and control transboundary disease crises. In May 2004 FAO and the World Organisation for Animal Health (OIE) signed an agreement to clarify their respective areas of competence and improve co-operation, in response to an increase in contagious transboundary animal diseases (such as foot-and-mouth disease and avian influenza, see below). The two bodies agreed to establish a global framework on the control of transboundary animal diseases, entailing improved international collaboration and circulation of information. In early 2006 FAO, OIE and the World Health Organization (WHO) agreed on the establishment of a Global Early Warning and Response System for Major Animal Diseases, including Zoonoses (GLEWS), in order to strengthen their joint capacity to detect, monitor and respond to animal disease threats. In October 2006 FAO inaugurated a new Crisis Management Centre (CMC) to co-ordinate (in close co-operation with OIE) the organization's response to outbreaks of H5N1 and other major emergencies related to animal or food health.

In September 2004 FAO and WHO declared an ongoing epidemic in certain east Asian countries of the H5N1 strain of highly pathogenic avian influenza (HPAI) to be a 'crisis of global importance': the disease was spreading rapidly through bird populations and was also transmitting to human populations through contact with diseased birds (mainly poultry). In that month FAO published *Recommendations for the Prevention, Control and Eradication of Highly Pathogenic Avian Influenza in Asia*. In April 2005 FAO and OIE established an international network of laboratories and scientists (OFFLU) to exchange data and provide expert technical advice on avian influenza. In the following month FAO, with WHO and OIE, launched a global strategy for the progressive control of the disease. In November a conference on Avian Influenza and Human Pandemic Influenza, jointly organized by FAO, WHO and OIE and the World Bank, issued a plan of action identifying a number of responses, including: supporting the development of integrated national plans for H5N1 containment and human pandemic influenza preparedness and response; assisting countries with the aggressive control of H5N1 and with establishing a more detailed understanding of the role of wild birds in virus transmission; nominating rapid response teams of experts to support epidemiological field investigations; expanding national and regional capacity in surveillance, diagnosis, and alert and response systems; expanding the network of influenza laboratories; establishing multi-country networks for the control or prevention of animal transboundary diseases; expanding the global antiviral stockpile; strengthening veterinary infrastructures; and mapping a global strategy and work plan for co-ordinating antiviral and influenza vaccine research and development. In June 2006 FAO and OIE convened a scientific conference on the spread and management of H5N1 that advocated early detection of the disease in wild birds, improved biosecurity and hygiene in the poultry trade, rapid response to disease outbreaks, and the establishment of a global tracking and monitoring facility involving participation by all relevant organizations, as well as by scientific centres, farmers' groupings, bird-watchers and hunters, and wildlife and wild bird habitat conservation bodies. The conference also urged investment in telemetry/satellite technology to improve tracking capabilities. International conference and pledging meetings on the disease were convened in Washington, DC, USA, in October 2005, Beijing, People's Republic of China, in January 2006, Bamako, Mali, in December and in New Delhi, India, in December 2007. In August 2008 a new strain of HPAI not previously recorded in sub-Saharan Africa was detected in Nigeria. In October the sixth international ministerial conference on avian influenza was convened in Sharm el-Sheikh, Egypt. FAO, with WHO, UNICEF, OIE, the World Bank and the UN System Influenza Co-ordinator, presented a new strategic framework, within the concept of 'One World, One Health', to improve understanding and co-operation with respect to emerging infectious diseases, to strengthen animal and public health surveillance and to enhance response mechanisms. During 2003–end-2011 outbreaks of H5N1 were recorded in 63 countries and territories, and some 250m. domestic and wild birds consequently died or were culled.

In December 2011 the conference of parties to the CMS officially ratified the establishment of a Scientific Task Force on Wildlife and Ecosystem Health, with FAO participation, reflecting a shift in focus from the isolated targeting avian influenza towards a 'One Health' policy of caring for the health of animals, humans, and the ecosystems that support them; a Task Force on Avian Influenza and Wild Birds, established under the CMS in August 2005, was to continue as a core focus area within the larger Scientific Task Force.

In April 2009, in response to a major outbreak in humans of the swine influenza variant pandemic (H1N1) 2009, the FAO Crisis Management Centre mobilized a team of experts to increase animal disease surveillance and maintain response readiness to protect the global pig sector from infection with the emerging virus. In early May FAO, OIE, WHO and WTO together issued a statement stressing that pork products handled in accordance with hygienic practices could not be deemed a source of infection.

In December 1992 FAO, with WHO, organized an International Conference on Nutrition, which approved a World Declaration on Nutrition and a Plan of Action, aimed at promoting efforts to combat malnutrition as a development priority. Since the conference, more than 100 countries have formulated national plans of action for nutrition, many of which were based on existing development plans such as comprehensive food security initiatives, national poverty alleviation programmes and action plans to attain the targets set by the World Summit for Children in September 1990. FAO promotes other efforts, at household and community level, to improve nutrition and food security, for example a programme to support home gardens. It aims to assist the identification of food-insecure and vulnerable populations, both through its *State of Food Insecurity in the World* reports and taking a lead role in the development of Food Insecurity and Vulnerability Information and Mapping Systems (FIVIMS), a recommendation of the World Food Summit. In 1999 FAO signed a Memorandum of Understanding with UNAIDS on strengthening co-operation to combat the threat posed by the HIV/AIDS epidemic to food security, nutrition and rural livelihoods. FAO is committed to incorporating HIV/AIDS into food security and livelihood projects, to strengthening community care and to highlighting the importance of nutrition in the care of those living with HIV/AIDS.

FAO is committed to promoting food quality and safety in all different stages of food production and processing. It supports the development of integrated food control systems by member states, which incorporate aspects of food control management, inspection, risk analysis and quality assurance. The joint FAO/WHO Codex Alimentarius Commission, established in 1962, aims to protect the health of consumers, ensure fair trade practices and promote the co-ordination of food standards activities at an international level. In January 2001 a joint team of FAO and WHO experts issued a report concerning the allergenicity of foods derived from biotechnology (i.e. genetically modified—GM—foods). In July the Codex Alimentarius Commission agreed the first global principles for assessing the safety of GM foods, and approved a series of maximum levels of environmental contaminants in food. In June 2004 FAO published guidelines for assessing possible risks posed to plants by living modified organisms. In July 2001 the Codex Alimentarius Commission adopted guidelines on organic livestock production, covering organic breeding methods, the elimination of growth hormones and certain chemicals in veterinary medicines, and the use of good quality organic feed with no meat or bone meal content. In January 2003 FAO organized a technical consultation on biological risk management in food and agriculture which recognized the need for a more integrated approach to so-called biosecurity, i.e. the prevention, control and management of risks to animal, human and plant life and health. FAO has subsequently developed a *Toolkit*, published in 2007, to help countries to develop and implement national biosecurity systems and to enhance biosecurity capacity.

FAO aims to assist member states to enhance the efficiency, competitiveness and profitability of their agricultural and food enterprises. FAO extends assistance in training, capacity-building and the formulation of agribusiness development strategies. It promotes the development of effective 'value chains', connecting primary producers with consumers, and supports other linkages within the agribusiness industry. Similarly, FAO aims to strengthen marketing systems, links between producers and retailers and training in agricultural marketing, and works to improve the regulatory framework for agricultural marketing.

FAO promotes the use of new technologies to increase agricultural production and extends a range of services to support mechanization, including training, maintenance, testing and the promotion of labour saving technologies. Other programmes are focused on farm management, post-harvest management, food and non-food processing, rural finance, and rural infrastructure. FAO helps reduce immediate post-harvest losses, with the introduction of improved processing methods and storage systems. FAO participates in PhAction, a forum of 12 agencies that was established in 1999 to promote post-harvest research and the development of effective post-harvest services and infrastructure.

FAO's Joint Division with the International Atomic Energy Agency (IAEA) is concerned with the use of nuclear techniques in food and agriculture. It co-ordinates research projects, provides scientific and technical support to technical co-operation projects and administers training courses. A joint laboratory in Seibersdorf, Austria, is concerned with testing biotechnologies and in developing non-toxic fertilizers (especially those that are locally available) and improved strains of food crops (especially from indigenous varieties). In the area of animal production and health, the Joint Division has developed progesterone-measuring and disease diagnostic kits. Other sub-programmes of the Joint Division are concerned with soil and water, plant breeding and nutrition, insect pest control and food and environmental protection.

In March 2011, in view of the severe damage suffered by the Fukushima Daiichi nuclear plant in Japan, following an earthquake and tsunami, FAO, the IAEA and WHO issued a joint statement on food safety issues in the aftermath of the emergency, emphasizing their commitment to mobilizing knowledge and expertise in support of the Japanese authorities.

NATURAL RESOURCES MANAGEMENT AND ENVIRONMENT

FAO is committed to promoting the responsible and sustainable management of natural resources and other activities to protect the environment. FAO assists member states to mitigate the impact of climate change on agriculture, to adapt and enhance the resilience of agricultural systems to climate change, and to promote practices to reduce the emission of greenhouse gases from the agricultural sector. In recent years FAO has strengthened its work in the area of using natural biomass resources as fuel, both at grassroots level and industrial processing of cash crops. In 2006 FAO established the International Bioenergy Platform to serve as a focal point for research, data collection, capacity-building and strategy formulation by local, regional and international bodies concerned with bioenergy. FAO also serves as the secretariat for the Global Bioenergy Partnership, which was inaugurated in May 2006 to facilitate the collaboration between governments, international agencies and representatives of the private sector and civil society in the sustainable development of bioenergy.

FAO aims to enhance the sustainability of land and water systems, and as a result to secure agricultural productivity, through the improved tenure, management, development and conservation of those natural resources. The organization promotes equitable access to land and water resources and supports integrated land and water management, including river basin management and improved irrigation systems. FAO has developed AQUASTAT as a global information system concerned with water and agricultural issues, comprising databases, country and regional profiles, surveys and maps. AquaCrop, CropWat and ClimWat are further productivity models and databases which have been developed to help to assess crop requirements and potential yields. Since 2003 FAO has participated in UN Water, an inter-agency initiative to co-ordinate existing approaches to water-related issues. In December 2008 FAO organized a Ministerial Conference on Water for Agriculture and Energy in Africa: 'the Challenges of Climate Change', in Sirte, Libya, which was attended by representatives of 48 African member countries and other representatives of international, regional and civil organizations.

Within the FAO's Natural Resources Management and Environment Department is a Research and Extension Division, which provides advisory and technical services to support national capacity-building, research, communication and education activities. It maintains several databases which support and facilitate the dissemination of information, for example relating to proven transferable technologies and biotechnologies in use in developing countries. The Division advises countries on communication strategies to strengthen agricultural and rural development, and has supported the use of rural radio. FAO is the UN lead agency of an initiative, 'Education for Rural People', which aims to improve the quality of and access to basic education for people living in rural areas and to raise awareness of the issue as an essential element of achieving the MDGs. The Research and Extension Division hosts the secretariat of the Global Forum on Agricultural Research, which was established in October 1996 as a collaboration of research centres, non-governmental and private sector organizations and development agencies. The Forum aims to strengthen research and promote knowledge partnerships concerned with the alleviation of poverty, the increase in food security and the sustainable use of natural resources. The Division also hosts the secretariat of the Science Council of the Consultative Group on International Agricultural Research (CGIAR), which, specifically, aims to enhance and promote the quality, relevance and impact of science within the network of CGIAR research centres and to mobilize global scientific expertise.

In September 2009 FAO published, jointly with the Centre for Indigenous People's Nutrition and Environment (CINE—based in McGill University, Montreal, Canada) a report entitled *Indigenous People's Food Systems: The Many Dimensions of Culture, Diversity and Environment for Nutrition and Health*, which aimed to demonstrate the wealth of knowledge on nutrition retained within indigenous communities world-wide.

FISHERIES AND AQUACULTURE

FAO aims to facilitate and secure the long-term sustainable development of fisheries and aquaculture, in both inland and marine waters, and to promote its contribution to world food security. In March 1995 a ministerial meeting of fisheries adopted the Rome Consensus on World Fisheries, which identified a need for immediate action to eliminate overfishing and to rebuild and enhance depleting fish stocks. In November the FAO Conference adopted a Code of Conduct for Responsible Fishing, which incorporated many global fisheries and aquaculture issues (including fisheries resource conservation and development, fish catches, seafood and fish processing, commercialization, trade and research) to promote the sustainable development of the sector. In February 1999 the FAO Committee on Fisheries adopted new international measures, within the framework of the Code of Conduct, in order to reduce over-exploitation of the world's fish resources, as well as plans of action for the conservation and management of sharks and the reduction in the incidental catch of seabirds in longline fisheries. The voluntary measures were endorsed at a ministerial meeting, held in March and attended by representatives of some 126 countries, which issued a declaration to promote the implementation of the Code of Conduct and to achieve sustainable management of fisheries and aquaculture. In March 2001 FAO adopted an international plan of action to address the continuing problem of so-called illegal, unreported and unregulated fishing (IUU). In that year FAO estimated that about one-half of major marine fish stocks were fully exploited, one-quarter under-exploited, at least 15% over-exploited, and 10% depleted or recovering from depletion. IUU was estimated to account for up to 30% of total catches in certain fisheries. In October FAO and the Icelandic Government jointly organized the Reykjavík Conference on Responsible Fisheries in the Marine Ecosystem, which adopted a declaration on pursuing responsible and sustainable fishing activities in the context of ecosystem-based fisheries management (EBFM). EBFM involves determining the boundaries of individual marine ecosystems, and maintaining or rebuilding the habitats and biodiversity of each of these so that all species will be supported at levels of maximum production. In March 2005 FAO's Committee of Fisheries adopted voluntary guidelines for the so-called eco-labelling and certification of fish and fish products, i.e. based on information regarding capture management and the sustainable use of resources. In March 2007 the Committee agreed to initiate a process of negotiating an internationally-binding agreement to deny port access to fishing vessels involved in IUU activities; the eventual 'Agreement on

Port State Measures to Prevent, Deter and Eliminate Illegal, Unreported and Unregulated Fishing' was endorsed by the Conference in November 2009.

FAO undertakes extensive monitoring, publishing every two years *The State of World Fisheries and Aquaculture*, and collates and maintains relevant databases. It formulates country and regional profiles and has developed a specific information network for the fisheries sector, GLOBEFISH, which gathers and disseminates information regarding market trends, tariffs and other industry issues. FAO aims to extend technical support to member states with regard to the management and conservation of aquatic resources, and other measures to improve the utilization and trade of products, including the reduction of post-harvest losses, preservation marketing and quality assurance. FAO promotes aquaculture (which contributes almost one-third of annual global fish landings) as a valuable source of animal protein and income-generating activity for rural communities. It has undertaken to develop an ecosystem approach to aquaculture (EAA) and works to integrate aquaculture with agricultural and irrigation systems. In February 2000 FAO and the Network of Aquaculture Centres in Asia and the Pacific (NACA) jointly convened a Conference on Aquaculture in the Third Millennium, which was held in Bangkok, Thailand, and attended by participants representing more than 200 governmental and non-governmental organizations. The Conference debated global trends in aquaculture and future policy measures to ensure the sustainable development of the sector. It adopted the Bangkok Declaration and Strategy for Aquaculture Beyond 2000.

FORESTRY

FAO is committed to the sustainable management of trees, forests and forestry resources. It aims to address the critical balance of ensuring the conservation of forests and forestry resources while maximising their potential to contribute to food security and social and economic development. In March 2009 the Committee on Forestry approved a new 10-year FAO Strategic Plan for Forestry, replacing a previous strategic plan initiated in 1999. The new plan, which was 'dynamic' and was to be updated regularly, covered the social, economic and environmental aspects of forestry. The first World Forest Week was held in March 2009 and the second in October 2010; 2011 was declared the International Year of Forests by the UN General Assembly.

FAO assists member countries to formulate, implement and monitor national forestry programmes, and encourages the participation of all stakeholders in developing plans for the sustainable management of tree and forest resources. FAO also helps to implement national assessments of those programmes and of other forestry activities. At a global level FAO undertakes surveillance of the state of the world's forests and publishes a report every two years. A separate *Forest Resources Assessment* is published every five years; the latest (for 2010) was initiated in March 2008. FAO is committed to collecting and disseminating accurate information and data on forests. It maintains the Forestry Information System (FORIS) to make relevant information and forest-related databases widely accessible.

FAO is a member of the Collaborative Partnership on Forests, which was established in April 2004 on the recommendation of the UN's Economic and Social Council. FAO organizes a World Forestry Congress, generally held every six years; the 13th Congress was convened in Buenos Aires, Argentina, in October 2009.

ECONOMIC AND SOCIAL DEVELOPMENT

FAO provides a focal point for economic research and policy analysis relating to food security and sustainable development. It produces studies and reports on agricultural development, the impact of development programmes and projects, and the world food situation, as well as on commodity prices, trade and medium-term projections. It supports the development of methodologies and guidelines to improve research into food and agriculture and the integration of wider concepts, such as social welfare, environmental factors and nutrition, into research projects. In November 2004 the FAO Council adopted a set of voluntary Right to Food Guidelines, and established a dedicated administrative unit, that aimed to 'support the progressive realization of the right to adequate food in the context of national food security' by providing practical guidance to countries in support of their efforts to achieve the 1996 World Food Summit commitment and UN MDG relating to hunger reduction. FAO's Statistical Division assembles, analyses and disseminates statistical data on world food and agriculture and aims to ensure the consistency, broad coverage and quality of available data. The Division advises member countries on enhancing their statistical capabilities. It maintains FAOSTAT as a core database of statistical information relating to nutrition, fisheries, forestry, food production, land use, population, etc. In 2004 FAO developed a new statistical framework, CountrySTAT, to provide for the organization and integration of statistical data and metadata from sources within a particular country. By 2012 CountrySTAT systems had been developed in 25 developing countries. FAO's internet-based interactive World Agricultural Information Centre (WAICENT) offers access to agricultural publications, technical documentation, codes of conduct, data, statistics and multimedia resources. FAO compiles and co-ordinates an extensive range of international databases on agriculture, fisheries, forestry, food and statistics, the most important of these being AGRIS (the International Information System for the Agricultural Sciences and Technology) and CARIS (the Current Agricultural Research Information System). In June 2000 FAO organized a high-level Consultation on Agricultural Information Management (COAIM), which aimed to increase access to and use of agricultural information by policy-makers and others. The second COAIM was held in September 2002 and the third meeting was convened in June 2007.

FAO's Global Information and Early Warning System (GIEWS), which become operational in 1975, maintains a database on and monitors the crop and food outlook at global, regional, national and sub-national levels in order to detect emerging food supply difficulties and disasters and to ensure rapid intervention in countries experiencing food supply shortages. It publishes regular reports on the weather conditions and crop prospects in sub-Saharan Africa and in the Sahel region, issues special alerts which describe the situation in countries or sub-regions experiencing food difficulties, and recommends an appropriate international response. FAO has also supported the development and implementation of Food Insecurity and Vulnerability Information and Mapping Systems (FIVIMS) and hosts the secretariat of the inter-agency working group on development of the FIVIMS. In October 2007 FAO inaugurated an online Global Forum on Food Security and Nutrition, to contribute to the compilation and dissemination of information relating to food security and nutrition throughout the world. In December 2008 a regular report issued by GIEWS identified 33 countries as being in crisis and requiring external assistance, of which 20 were in Africa, 10 in Asia and the Near East and three in Latin America and the Caribbean. All countries were identified as lacking the resources to deal with critical problems of food insecurity, including many severely affected by the high cost of food and fuel. The publication *Crop Prospects and Food Situation* reviews the global situation, and provides regional updates and a special focus on countries experiencing food crises and requiring external assistance, on a quarterly basis. *Food Outlook*, issued in June and November, analyses developments in global food and animal feed markets.

TECHNICAL CO-OPERATION

The Technical Co-operation Department has responsibility for FAO's operational activities, including policy development assistance to member countries; the mobilization of resources; investment support; field operations; emergency operations and rehabilitation; and the Technical Co-operation Programme.

FAO provides policy advice to support the formulation, implementation and evaluation of agriculture, rural development and food security strategies in member countries. It administers a project to assist developing countries to strengthen their technical negotiating skills, in respect to agricultural trade issues. FAO also aims to co-ordinate and facilitate the mobilization of extrabudgetary funds from donors and governments for particular projects. It administers a range of trust funds, including a Trust Fund for Food Security and Food Safety, established in 2002 to generate resources for projects to combat hunger, and the Government Co-operative Programme. FAO's Investment

Centre, established in 1964, aims to promote greater external investment in agriculture and rural development by assisting member countries to formulate effective and sustainable projects and programmes. The Centre collaborates with international financing institutions and bilateral donors in the preparation of projects, and administers cost-sharing arrangements, with, typically, FAO funding 40% of a project. The Centre is a co-chair (with the German Government) of the Global Donor Platform for Rural Development, which was established in 2004, comprising multilateral, donor and international agencies, development banks and research institutions, to improve the co-ordination and effectiveness of rural development assistance.

FAO's Technical Co-operation Programme, which was inaugurated in 1976, provides technical expertise and funding for small-scale projects to address specific issues within a country's agriculture, fisheries or forestry sectors. An Associate Professional Officers programme co-ordinates the sponsorship and placement of young professionals to gain experience working in an aspect of rural or agricultural development.

FAO's Special Programme for Food Security (SPFS), initiated in 1994, assists low-income countries with a food deficit to increase food production and productivity as rapidly as possible, primarily through the widespread adoption by farmers of improved production technologies, with emphasis on areas of high potential. Within the SPFS framework are national and regional food security initiatives, all of which aim towards the MDG objective of reducing the incidence of hunger by 50% by 2015. The SPFS is operational in more than 100 countries. The Programme promotes South-South co-operation to improve food security and the exchange of knowledge and experience. Some 40 bilateral co-operation agreements are in force, for example, between Gabon and the People's Republic of China, Egypt and Cameroon, and Viet Nam and Benin. In 2012 some 66 countries were categorized formally as 'low-income food-deficit'.

FAO organizes an annual series of fund-raising events, 'TeleFood', some of which are broadcast on television and the internet, in order to raise public awareness of the problems of hunger and malnutrition. Since its inception in 1997 public donations to TeleFood have exceeded some US $29m. (2012), financing more than 3,200 'grass-roots' projects in 130 countries. The projects have provided tools, seeds and other essential supplies directly to small-scale farmers, and have been especially aimed at helping women.

The Technical Co-operation Division co-ordinates FAO's emergency operations, concerned with all aspects of disaster and risk prevention, mitigation, reduction and emergency relief and rehabilitation, with a particular emphasis on food security and rural populations. FAO works with governments to develop and implement disaster prevention policies and practices. It aims to strengthen the capacity of local institutions to manage and mitigate risk and provides technical assistance to improve access to land for displaced populations in countries following conflict or a natural disaster. Other disaster prevention and reduction efforts include dissemination of information from the various early-warning systems and support for adaptation to climate variability and change, for example by the use of drought-resistant crops or the adoption of conservation agriculture techniques. Following an emergency FAO works with governments and other development and humanitarian partners to assess the immediate and longer-term agriculture and food security needs of the affected population. It has developed an Integrated Food Security and Humanitarian Phase Classification Scheme to determine the appropriate response to a disaster situation. Emergency co-ordination units may be established to manage the local response to an emergency and to facilitate and co-ordinate the delivery of inter-agency assistance. In order to rehabilitate agricultural production following a natural or man-made disaster FAO provides emergency seed, tools, other materials and technical and training assistance. During 2005 the UN's Inter-Agency Standing Committee, concerned with co-ordinating the international response to humanitarian disasters, developed a concept of providing assistance through a 'cluster' approach, comprising core areas of activity. FAO was designated the lead agency for the then Agriculture cluster. A review of the humanitarian cluster approach, undertaken during 2010, concluded that a new cluster on Food Security should be established, replacing the Agriculture cluster. The new cluster, established accordingly in 2011, is led jointly by FAO and WFP, and aims to combine expertise in agricultural assistance and food aid in order to boost food security and to improve the resilience of food-insecure disaster-affected communities. FAO also contributes the agricultural relief and rehabilitation component of the UN's Consolidated Appeals Process (CAP), which aims to co-ordinate and enhance the effectiveness of the international community's response to an emergency; by end-November 2011 FAO had received US $200m. in funding in response to its appeals under the 2011 CAP process. In April 2004 FAO established a Special Fund for Emergency and Rehabilitation Activities to enable it to respond promptly to a humanitarian crisis before making an emergency appeal for additional resources.

During 2008–early 2012 projects (providing fertilizers, seeds and other support necessary to ensure the success of harvests) were undertaken in more than 90 countries under the framework of the Initiative on Soaring Food Prices (see above); some US $314m. in project funding was provided by the EU Food Facility, while other projects (to the value of $37m.) were implemented through FAO's Technical Co-operation Programme.

FAO Statutory Bodies

(based at the Rome headquarters, unless otherwise indicated)

African Commission on Agricultural Statistics: c/o FAO Regional Office for Africa, POB 1628, Accra, Ghana; e-mail vincent.ngendakumana@fao.org; f. 1961 to advise member countries on the development and standardization of food and agricultural statistics; 37 member states.

African Forestry and Wildlife Commission: f. 1959 to advise on the formulation of forest policy and to review and co-ordinate its implementation on a regional level; to exchange information and advise on technical problems; 42 member states.

Agriculture, Land and Water Use Commission: c/o FAO Regional Office, POB 2223, Cairo, Egypt; f. 2000 by merger of the Near East Regional Commission on Agriculture and the Regional Commission on Land and Water Use in the Near East; 23 member states.

Animal Production and Health Commission for Asia and the Pacific: c/o FAO Regional Office, Maliwan Mansion, 39 Phra Atit Rd, Bangkok 10200, Thailand; f. 1975 to support national and regional livestock production and research; 17 member states.

Asia and Pacific Commission on Agricultural Statistics: c/o FAO Regional Office, Maliwan Mansion, 39 Phra Atit Rd, Bangkok 10200, Thailand; e-mail rap-statistics.fao.org; internet www.faorap-apcas.org; f. 1963; reviews recent developments in agricultural statistical systems, provides a platform for the exchange of ideas relating to the state of food and agricultural statistics in the region; senior officials responsible for the development of agricultural statistics from 25 member states.

Asia and Pacific Plant Protection Commission: c/o FAO Regional Office, Maliwan Mansion, Phra Atit Rd, Bangkok 10200, Thailand; f. 1956 (new title 1983) to strengthen international co-operation in plant protection to prevent the introduction and spread of destructive plant diseases and pests; 25 member states.

Asia-Pacific Fishery Commission: c/o FAO Regional Office, Maliwan Mansion, 39 Phra Atit Rd, Bangkok 10200, Thailand; f. 1948 to develop fisheries, encourage and co-ordinate research, disseminate information, recommend projects to governments, propose standards in technique and management measures; 20 member states.

Asia-Pacific Forestry Commission: internet www.apfcweb.org; f. 1949 to advise on the formulation of forest policy, and review and co-ordinate its implementation throughout the region; to exchange information and advise on technical problems; 29 member states.

Caribbean Plant Protection Commission: c/o FAO Sub-Regional Office for the Caribbean, POB 631-C, Bridgetown, Barbados; tel. 426-7110; fax 427-6075; e-mail fao-slac@fao.org; internet www.fao.org/world/subregional/slac; f. 1967 to preserve the existing plant resources of the area; 13 member states.

Codex Alimentarius Commission (Joint FAO/WHO Food Standards Programme): e-mail codex@fao.org; internet www.codexalimentarius.net; f. 1962 to make proposals for the co-ordination of all international food standards work and to publish a code of international food standards; Trust Fund to support participation by least-developed countries was inaugurated in 2003; there are numerous specialized Codex committees, e.g. for food labelling, hygiene, additives and contaminants, pesticide and veterinary residues, milk and milk products, and processed fruits and vegetables; and an intergovernmental task force on antimicrobial resistance; 184 member states and the European Union; 208 observers (at June 2012).

Commission for Controlling the Desert Locust in North-west Africa: f. 1971 to promote research on control of the desert locust in NW Africa.

Commission for Controlling the Desert Locust in South-west Asia: f. 1964 to carry out all possible measures to control plagues of the desert locust in Afghanistan, India, Iran and Pakistan.

Commission for Controlling the Desert Locust in the Central Region: c/o FAO Regional Office for the Near East, POB 2223, Cairo, Egypt; 16 member states.

Commission for Inland Fisheries of Latin America: Avda Dag Hammarskjöld 3241, Casilla 10095, Vitacura, Santiago, Chile; f. 1976 to promote, co-ordinate and assist national and regional fishery and limnological surveys and programmes of research and development leading to the rational utilization of inland fishery resources; 21 member states.

Commission on Genetic Resources for Food and Agriculture: internet www.fao.org/ag/cgrfa/default.htm; f. 1983 as the Commission on Plant Genetic Resources, renamed in 1995; provides a forum for negotiation on the conservation and sustainable utilization of genetic resources for food and agriculture, and the equitable sharing of benefits derived from their use; 164 member states.

Commission on Livestock Development for Latin America and the Caribbean: Avda Dag Hammarskjöld 3241, Casilla 10095, Vitacura, Santiago, Chile; f. 1986; 24 member states.

Commission on Phytosanitary Measures: f. 1997 as the governing body of the revised International Plant Protection Commission.

Committee for Inland Fisheries of Africa: f. 1971 to promote improvements in inland fisheries and aquaculture in Africa.

European Commission on Agriculture: f. 1949 to encourage and facilitate action and co-operation in technological agricultural problems among member states and between international organizations concerned with agricultural technology in Europe.

European Commission for the Control of Foot-and-Mouth Disease: internet www.fao.org/ag/againfo/commissions/en/eufmd/eufmd.html; f. 1953 to promote national and international action for the control of the disease in Europe and its final eradication.

European Forestry Commission: f. 1947 to advise on the formulation of forest policy and to review and co-ordinate its implementation on a regional level; to exchange information and to make recommendations; 27 member states.

European Inland Fisheries Advisory Commission: internet www.fao.org/fi/body/eifac/eifac.asp; f. 1957 to promote improvements in inland fisheries and to advise member governments and FAO on inland fishery matters; 34 member states.

Fishery Committee for the Eastern Central Atlantic: f. 1967.

General Fisheries Council for the Mediterranean—GFCM: internet www.fao.org/fi/body/rfb/index.htm; f. 1952 to develop aquatic resources, to encourage and co-ordinate research in the fishing and allied industries, to assemble and publish information, and to recommend the standardization of equipment, techniques and nomenclature.

Indian Ocean Fishery Commission: f. 1967 to promote national programmes, research and development activities, and to examine management problems; 41 member states.

International Poplar Commission: f. 1947 to study scientific, technical, social and economic aspects of poplar and willow cultivation; to promote the exchange of ideas and material between research workers, producers and users; to arrange joint research programmes, congresses, study tours; to make recommendations to the FAO Conference and to National Poplar Commissions.

International Rice Commission: internet www.fao.org/ag/AGP/AGPC/doc/field/commrice/welcome.htm; f. 1949 to promote national and international action on production, conservation, distribution and consumption of rice, except matters relating to international trade; supports the International Task Force on Hybrid Rice, the Working Group on Advanced Rice Breeding in Latin America and the Caribbean, the Inter-regional Collaborative Research Network on Rice in the Mediterranean Climate Areas, and the Technical Co-operation Network on Wetland Development and Management/Inland Valley Swamps; 60 member states.

Latin American and Caribbean Forestry Commission: f. 1948 to advise on formulation of forest policy and review and co-ordinate its implementation throughout the region; to exchange information and advise on technical problems; meets every two years; 31 member states.

Near East Forestry Commission: f. 1953 to advise on formulation of forest policy and review and co-ordinate its implementation throughout the region; to exchange information and advise on technical problems; 20 member states.

North American Forestry Commission: f. 1959 to advise on the formulation and co-ordination of national forest policies in Canada, Mexico and the USA; to exchange information and to advise on technical problems; three member states.

South West Indian Ocean Fisheries Commission: f. 2005 to promote the sustainable development and utilization of coastal fishery resources of East Africa and island states in that sub-region; 14 member states.

Western Central Atlantic Fishery Commission: f. 1973 to assist international co-operation for the conservation, development and utilization of the living resources, especially shrimps, of the Western Central Atlantic.

Finance

FAO's Regular Programme, which is financed by contributions from member governments, covers the cost of FAO's Secretariat, its Technical Co-operation Programme (TCP) and part of the cost of several special action programmes. The regular budget for the two-year period 2010–11 totalled US $1,000m. Much of FAO's technical assistance programme and emergency (including rehabilitation) support activities are funded from extra-budgetary sources, predominantly by trust funds that come mainly from donor countries and international financing institutions; voluntary donor contributions to FAO were projected at around $1,200m. in 2010–11.

Publications

Commodity Review and Outlook (annually).

Crop Prospects and Food Situation (5/6 a year).

Ethical Issues in Food and Agriculture.

FAO Statistical Yearbook (annually).

FAOSTAT Statistical Database (online).

Food Outlook (2 a year).

Food Safety and Quality Update (monthly; electronic bulletin).

Forest Resources Assessment.

The State of Agricultural Commodity Markets (every 2 years).

The State of Food and Agriculture (annually).

The State of Food Insecurity in the World (annually).

The State of World Fisheries and Aquaculture (every 2 years).

The State of the World's Forests (every 2 years).

Unasylva (quarterly).

Yearbook of Fishery Statistics.

Yearbook of Forest Products.

Commodity reviews, studies, manuals. A complete catalogue of publications is available at www.fao.org/icatalog/inter-e.htm.

International Atomic Energy Agency—IAEA

Address: POB 100, Wagramerstrasse 5, 1400 Vienna, Austria.

Telephone: (1) 26000; **fax:** (1) 26007; **e-mail:** official.mail@iaea.org; **internet:** www.iaea.org.

The International Atomic Energy Agency (IAEA) is an intergovernmental organization, established in 1957 in accordance with a decision of the General Assembly of the United Nations. Although it is autonomous, the IAEA is administratively a member of the United Nations, and reports on its activities once a year to the UN General Assembly. Its main objectives are to enlarge the contribution of atomic energy to peace, health and prosperity throughout the world and to ensure, so far as it is able, that assistance provided by it or at its request or under its supervision or control is not used in such a way as to further any military purpose. The 2005 Nobel Peace Prize was awarded, in two equal parts, to the IAEA and to the Agency's Director-General.

MEMBERS

The IAEA has 154 members. Some 72 intergovernmental and non-governmental organizations have formal agreements with the IAEA.

Organization

(June 2012)

GENERAL CONFERENCE

The Conference, comprising representatives of all member states, convenes each year for general debate on the Agency's policy, budget and programme. It elects members to the Board of Governors, and approves the appointment of the Director-General; it admits new member states.

BOARD OF GOVERNORS

The Board of Governors consists of 35 member states elected by the General Conference. It is the principal policy-making body of the Agency and is responsible to the General Conference. Under its own authority, the Board approves all safeguards agreements, important projects and safety standards.

SECRETARIAT

The Secretariat, comprising 2,338 staff at 31 December 2010, is headed by the Director-General, who is assisted by six Deputy Directors-General. The Secretariat is divided into six departments: Technical Co-operation; Nuclear Energy; Nuclear Safety and Security; Nuclear Sciences and Applications; Safeguards; and Management. A Standing Advisory Group on Safeguards Implementation advises the Director-General on technical aspects of safeguards.

Director-General: YUKIYA AMANO (Japan).

Activities

In recent years the IAEA has implemented several reforms of its management structure and operations. The three pillars supporting the Agency's activities are: technology (assisting research on and practical application of atomic energy for peaceful uses), safety, and verification (ensuring that special fissionable and other materials, services, equipment and information made available by the Agency or at its request or under its supervision are not used for any non-peaceful purpose).

IAEA organized several events on the sidelines of the June 2012 UN Conference on Sustainable Development (Rio+20), relating to sustainable energy, energy planning, food, oceans, and water. An IAEA International Ministerial Conference on Nuclear Energy in the 21st Century was scheduled to be convened in June 2013.

TECHNICAL CO-OPERATION AND TRAINING

The IAEA provides assistance in the form of experts, training and equipment to technical co-operation projects and applications world-wide, with an emphasis on radiation protection and safety-related activities. Training is provided to scientists, and experts and lecturers are assigned to provide specialized help on specific nuclear applications. The IAEA supported the foundation in September 2003 of the World Nuclear University, comprising a world-wide network of institutions that aim to strengthen international co-operation in promoting the safe use of nuclear power in energy production, and in the application of nuclear science and technology in areas including sustainable agriculture and nutrition, medicine, fresh water resources management and environmental protection.

FOOD AND AGRICULTURE

In co-operation with FAO, the Agency conducts programmes of applied research on the use of radiation and isotopes in fields including: efficiency in the use of water and fertilizers; improvement of food crops by induced mutations; eradication or control of destructive insects by the introduction of sterilized insects (radiation-based Sterile Insect Technique); improvement of livestock nutrition and health; studies on improving efficacy and reducing residues of pesticides, and increasing utilization of agricultural wastes; and food preservation by irradiation. The programmes are implemented by the Joint FAO/IAEA Division of Nuclear Techniques in Food and Agriculture and by the FAO/IAEA Agriculture and Biotechnology Laboratory, based at the IAEA's laboratory complex in Seibersdorf, Austria. A Training and Reference Centre for Food and Pesticide Control, based at Seibersdorf, supports the implementation of national legislation and trade agreements ensuring the quality and safety of food products in international trade. The Agency's Marine Environment Laboratory (IAEA-MEL), in Monaco, studies radionuclides and other ocean pollutants.

LIFE SCIENCES

In co-operation with the World Health Organization (WHO), the IAEA promotes the use of nuclear techniques in medicine, biology and health-related environmental research, provides training, and conducts research on techniques for improving the accuracy of radiation dosimetry.

The IAEA/WHO Network of Secondary Standard Dosimetry Laboratories (SSDLs) comprises 81 laboratories in 62 member states. The Agency's Dosimetry Laboratory in Seibersdorf performs dose inter-comparisons for both SSDLs and radiotherapy centres. The IAEA undertakes maintenance plans for nuclear laboratories; national programmes of quality control for nuclear medicine instruments; quality control of radioimmunoassay techniques; radiation sterilization of medical supplies; and improvement of cancer therapy through the IAEA Programme of Action for Cancer Therapy (PACT), inaugurated in 2004, and through which Agency works with WHO and other partners. In May 2009 the IAEA and WHO launched a new Joint Programme on Cancer Control, aimed at enhancing efforts to fight cancer in the developing world.

PHYSICAL AND CHEMICAL SCIENCES

The Agency's programme in physical sciences includes industrial applications of isotopes and radiation technology; application of nuclear techniques to mineral exploration and exploitation; radiopharmaceuticals; and hydrology, involving the use of isotope techniques for assessment of water resources. Nuclear data services are provided, and training is given for nuclear scientists from developing countries. The Physics, Chemistry and Instrumentation Laboratory at Seibersdorf supports the Agency's research in human health, industry, water resources and environment. The Abdus Salam International Centre for Theoretical Physics, based in Trieste, Italy, operates in accordance with a tripartite agreement in force between the IAEA, UNESCO and the Italian Government.

NUCLEAR POWER

In 2012 there were 435 nuclear power plants in operation and 63 reactors under construction world-wide. Nuclear power accounts for about 13% of total electrical energy generated globally. The IAEA helps developing member states to introduce nuclear-powered electricity-generating plants through assistance with planning, feasibility studies, surveys of manpower and infrastructure, and safety measures. The Agency also assesses life extension and decommissioning strategies for ageing nuclear power plants. It publishes books on numerous aspects of nuclear power, and provides training courses on safety in nuclear power plants and other topics. An energy data bank collects and disseminates information on nuclear technology, and a power-reactor information system monitors the technical performance of nuclear power plants. There is increasing interest in the use of nuclear reactors for seawater desalination and radiation hydrology techniques to provide potable water. In July 1992 the EC, Japan, Russia and the USA signed an agreement to co-operate in the engineering design of an International Thermonuclear Experimental Reactor (ITER); the People's Republic of China, Republic of Korea (South Korea) and India subsequently also joined the process. The project aims to demonstrate the scientific and technological feasibility of fusion energy, with the aim of providing a source of clean, abundant energy in the 21st century. In June 2005 the states participating in ITER agreed that the installation should be constructed in Cadarache, France, and in November 2006 an ITER Agreement was concluded, establishing, upon its entry into force in October 2007, a formal ITER organization, with responsibility for constructing, operating and decommissioning ITER. It was envisaged that ITER would enter fully into operation by 2026. In May 2001 the International Project on Innovative Nuclear Reactors and Fuel Cycles (INPRO) was inaugurated. INPRO, which has 28 members, aims to promote nuclear energy as a means of meeting future sustainable energy requirements and to facilitate the exchange of information by member states to advance innovations in nuclear technology. The IAEA is a permanent observer at the Generation IV International Forum (GIF), which was inaugurated in 2000 and aims to establish a number of international collaborative nuclear research and development agreements. In 2010 the IAEA established an Integrated Nuclear Infrastructure Group (ING), which aimed to integrate information from disparate databases to enable more effective planning; to offer training in the use of planning tools; to provide legislative assistance; to provide guidance on ensuring self-assessment capabilities among governmental and operating organizations; and to organize education and training materials. An advisory Technical Working Group on Nuclear Power Infrastructure was also initiated during 2010.

RADIOACTIVE WASTE MANAGEMENT

The Agency provides practical help to member states in the management of radioactive waste. The Waste Management Advisory Programme (WAMAP) was established in 1987, and undertakes advisory missions in member states. A code of practice to prevent the illegal dumping of radioactive waste was drafted in 1989, and another on the international transboundary movement of waste was drafted in 1990. A ban on the dumping of radioactive waste at sea came into effect in 1994, under the Convention on the Prevention of Marine Pollution by Dumping of Wastes and Other Matters. The IAEA was to determine radioactive levels, for purposes of the Convention, and provide assistance to countries for the safe disposal of radioactive wastes. A new category of radioactive waste—very low level waste (VLLW)—was introduced in the early 2000s. A VLLW repository, at Morvilliers, France, became fully operational in 2004. The Agency has issued modal regulations for the air, sea and land transportation of all radioactive materials.

In September 1997 the IAEA adopted a Joint Convention on the Safety of Spent Fuel Management and on the Safety of Radioactive Waste Management. The first internationally binding legal device to address such issues, the Convention was to ensure the safe storage and disposal of nuclear and radioactive waste, during both the construction and operation of a nuclear power plant, as well as following its closure. The Convention entered into force in June 2001, and had been ratified by 63 parties at June 2012.

NUCLEAR SAFETY

The IAEA's nuclear safety programme encourages international co-operation in the exchange of information, promoting implementation of its safety standards and providing advisory safety services. It includes the IAEA International Nuclear Event Scale (INES), which measures the severity of nuclear events, incidents and accidents; the Incident Reporting System; an emergency preparedness programme (which maintains an Emergency Response Centre, located in Vienna, Austria); operational safety review teams; the International Nuclear Safety Group (INSAG); the Radiation Protection Advisory Team; and a safety research co-ordination programme. The safety review teams provide member states with advice on achieving and maintaining a high level of safety in the operation of nuclear power plants, while research programmes establish risk criteria for the nuclear fuel cycle and identify cost-effective means to reduce risks in energy systems. A new version of the INES, issued in July 2008, incorporated revisions aimed at providing more detailed ratings of activities including human exposure to sources of radiation and the transportation of radioactive materials.

The nuclear safety programme promotes a global safety regime, which aims to ensure the protection of people and the environment from the effects of ionizing radiation and the minimization of the likelihood of potential nuclear accidents, etc. Through the Commission on Safety Standards (which has subcommittees on nuclear safety standards, radiation safety standards, transport safety standards and waste safety standards) the programme establishes IAEA safety standards and provides for their application. In September 2006 the IAEA published a new primary safety standard, the Fundamental Safety Principles, representing a unified philosophy of nuclear safety and protection that was to provide the conceptual basis for the Agency's entire safety standards agenda. The IAEA's *Safety Glossary Terminology Used in Nuclear Safety and Radiation Protection* is updated regularly. In 2010 IAEA established a Global Safety Assessment (G-SAN), facilitating collaboration between experts world-wide with the aim of harmonizing nuclear safety.

The Convention on the Physical Protection of Nuclear Material was signed in 1980, and committed contracting states to ensuring the protection of nuclear material during transportation within their territory or on board their ships or aircraft. In July 2005 delegates from 89 states party adopted a number of amendments aimed at strengthening the Convention.

Following a serious accident at the Chernobyl nuclear power plant in Ukraine (then part of the USSR) in April 1986, two conventions were formulated by the IAEA and entered into force in October. The first, the Convention on Early Notification of a Nuclear Accident, commits parties to provide information about nuclear accidents with possible transboundary effects at the earliest opportunity (it had 114 parties by June 2012); and the second, the Convention on Assistance in the Case of a Nuclear Accident or Radiological Emergency, commits parties to endeavour to provide assistance in the event of a nuclear accident or radiological emergency (this had 108 parties by June 2012). During 1990 the IAEA organized an assessment of the consequences of the Chernobyl accident, undertaken by an international team of experts, who reported to an international conference on the effects of the accident, convened at the IAEA headquarters in Vienna in May 1991. In February 1993 INSAG published an updated report on the Chernobyl incident, which emphasized the role of design factors in the accident, and the need to implement safety measures in the RBMK-type reactor. In March 1994 an IAEA expert mission visited Chernobyl and reported continuing serious deficiencies in safety at the defunct reactor and the units remaining in operation. An international conference reviewing the radiological consequences of the accident, 10 years after the event, was held in April 1996, co-sponsored by the IAEA, WHO and the European Commission. The last of the Chernobyl plant's three operating units was officially closed in December 2000. During the 2000s the IAEA was offering a wide range of assistance with the decommissioning of Chernobyl. In April 2009 the IAEA, UNDP, UNICEF and WHO launched the International Chernobyl Research and Information Network (ICRIN), a three-year initiative, costing US $2.5m., which aimed to provide up-to-date scientific information and sound practical advice to communities in areas of Ukraine, Belarus and Russia that remained affected by the

Chernobyl accident. In November 2008 the IAEA and other UN agencies approved a UN Action Plan on Chernobyl to 2016, which had been developed by UNDP, and was envisaged as a framework for the regeneration of these areas.

An International Convention on Nuclear Safety was adopted at an IAEA conference in June 1994. The Convention applies to land-based civil nuclear power plants: adherents commit themselves to fundamental principles of safety, and maintain legislative frameworks governing nuclear safety. The Convention entered into force in October 1996 and had been ratified by 75 states by June 2012.

In September 1997 more than 80 member states adopted a protocol to revise the 1963 Vienna Convention on Civil Liability for Nuclear Damage, fixing the minimum limit of liability for the operator of a nuclear reactor at 300m. Special Drawing Rights (SDRs, the accounting units of the IMF) in the event of an accident. The amended protocol also extended the length of time during which claims may be brought for loss of life or injury. It entered into force in October 2003. The International Expert Group on Nuclear Liability (INLEX) was established in the same year. A Convention on Supplementary Compensation for Nuclear Damage established a further compensatory fund to provide for the payment of damages following an accident; contributions to the Fund were to be calculated on the basis of the nuclear capacity of each member state. The Convention had four contracting states by June 2012.

In July 1996 the IAEA co-ordinated a study on the radiological situation at the Mururoa and Fangatauta atolls, following the French nuclear test programmes in the South Pacific. Results published in May 1998 concluded that there was no radiological health risk and that neither remedial action nor continued environmental monitoring was necessary.

The IAEA is developing a training course on measurement methods and risk analysis relating to the presence of depleted uranium (which can be used in ammunition) in post-conflict areas. In November 2000 IAEA specialists participated in a fact-finding mission organized by UNEP in Kosovo and Metohija, which aimed to assess the environmental and health consequences of the use of depleted uranium in ammunition by NATO during its 1999 aerial offensive against the then Federal Republic of Yugoslavia. (A report on the situation was published by UNEP in March 2001.) In June 2003 the Agency published the results of an assessment undertaken in 2002 of the possible long-term radiological impact of depleted uranium residues, derived from the 1991 Gulf War, at several locations in Kuwait; it determined that the residues did not pose a health threat to local populations.

In May 2001 the IAEA convened an international conference to address the protection of nuclear material and radioactive sources from illegal trafficking. In September, in view of the perpetration of major terrorist attacks against targets in the USA during that month, the IAEA General Conference addressed the potential for nuclear-related terrorism. It adopted a resolution that emphasized the importance of the physical protection of nuclear material in preventing its illicit use or the sabotage of nuclear facilities and nuclear materials. Three main potential threats were identified: the acquisition by a terrorist group of a nuclear weapon; acquisition of nuclear material to construct a nuclear weapon or cause a radiological hazard; and violent acts against nuclear facilities to cause a radiological hazard. In March 2002 the Board of Governors approved in principle an action plan to improve global protection against acts of terrorism involving nuclear and other radioactive materials. The plan addressed the physical protection of nuclear materials and facilities; the detection of malicious activities involving radioactive materials; strengthening national control systems; the security of radioactive sources; evaluation of security and safety at nuclear facilities; emergency response to malicious acts or threats involving radioactive materials; ensuring adherence to international guidelines and agreements; and improvement of programme co-ordination and information management. It was estimated that the Agency's upgraded nuclear security activities would require significant additional annual funding. In March 2003 the IAEA organized an International Conference on Security of Radioactive Sources, held in Vienna. In April 2005 the UN General Assembly adopted the International Convention for the Suppression of Acts of Nuclear Terrorism. The Convention, which opened for signature in September of that year and entered into force in July 2007, established a definition of acts of nuclear terrorism and urged signatory states to co-operate in the prevention of terrorist attacks by sharing information and providing mutual assistance with criminal investigations and extradition proceedings. Under the provisions of the Convention it was required that any seized nuclear or radiological material should be held in accordance with IAEA safeguards. By the end of 2010 a total of 1,980 incidents had been reported to the Illicit Trafficking Database (ITDB) since its creation in 1995; of the 147 incidents that were reported to have occurred during 2010, 13 involved illegal possession of and attempts to sell nuclear material or radioactive sources; 22 involved reported theft or loss; and 111 concerned discoveries of uncontrolled material, unauthorized disposals, and inadvertent unauthorized shipments and storage. The ITDB had 107 participant states in that year.

In June 2004 the Board of Governors approved an international action plan on the decommissioning of nuclear facilities; the plan was revised in 2007. In September 2007 the IAEA launched a Network of Centres of Excellence for Decommissioning. In 2012 the Agency was managing four ongoing international projects related to safe decommissioning.

In October 2008 the IAEA inaugurated the International Seismic Safety Centre (ISSC) within the Agency's Department of Safety and Security. The ISSC was to serve as a focal point for avoiding and mitigating the consequences of extreme seismic events on nuclear installations world-wide, and was to be supported by a committee of high-level experts in the following areas: geology and tectonics; seismology; seismic hazard; geotechnical engineering; structural engineering; equipment; and seismic risk. In August 2007, and January–February and December 2008, the IAEA sent missions to visit the Kashiwazaki-Kariwa nuclear power plant in Japan, in order to learn about the effects on that facility of an earthquake that struck it in July 2007, and to identify and recommend future precautions. In March 2011, in the aftermath of the severe earthquake and tsunami flooding that had struck and severely damaged Fukushima Daiichi nuclear power plant, the Japanese authorities requested IAEA support in monitoring the effects of the ensuing release of radiation on the environment and on human health. Accordingly, the IAEA dispatched radiation monitoring teams to Japan to provide assistance to local experts, with a particular focus on: worker radiation protection, food safety, marine and soil science, and Boiling Water Reactor (BWR) technology. In partnership with WMO, the IAEA also provided weather forecast updates as part of its immediate emergency response. In late March the IAEA, FAO and WHO issued a joint statement on food safety issues following the Fukushima nuclear emergency, emphasizing their commitment to mobilizing knowledge and expertise in support of the Japanese authorities. During late May–early June 2011 an IAEA team comprising 20 international experts visited Japan to assess the ongoing state of nuclear safety in that country. In 2011–12 the IAEA issued regular status reports on the situation at Fukushima Daiichi, covering environmental radiation monitoring; workers' exposure to radiation; and ongoing conditions at the plant.

In June 2011, in view of the Fukushima Daiichi accident, the IAEA Ministerial Conference on Nuclear Safety adopted a Ministerial Declaration which formed the basis of the first IAEA Action Plan for Nuclear Safety. The Plan, which was unanimously endorsed in September 2011 by the 55th General Conference, emphasized greater transparency in nuclear safety matters and the improvement of safety regimes, including the strengthening of peer reviews, emergency and response mechanisms, and national regulatory bodies. Safety standards were to be reviewed and an assessment of the vulnerabilities of nuclear power plants was to be undertaken. In March 2012 IAEA convened an International Experts' Meeting on Reactor and Spent Fuel Safety, and in June a meeting of experts was to be held on Enhancing Transparency and Communications Effectiveness in the Event of a Nuclear or Radiological Emergency.

DISSEMINATION OF INFORMATION

The International Nuclear Information System (INIS), which was established in 1970, provides a computerized indexing and abstracting service. Information on the peaceful uses of atomic energy is collected by member states and international organizations and sent to the IAEA for processing and dissemination (see list of publications below). The IAEA also co-operates with FAO in an information system for agriculture (AGRIS) and with the World Federation of Nuclear Medicine and Biology, and the non-profit Cochrane Collaboration, in maintaining an electronic database of best practice in nuclear medicine. The IAEA Nuclear Data Section provides cost-free data centre services and co-operates with other national and regional nuclear and atomic data centres in the systematic world-wide collection, compilation, dissemination and exchange of nuclear reaction data, nuclear structure and decay data, and atomic and molecular data for fusion.

SAFEGUARDS

The Treaty on the Non-Proliferation of Nuclear Weapons (known also as the Non-Proliferation Treaty or NPT), which entered into force in 1970, requires each 'non-nuclear-weapon state' (one which had not manufactured and exploded a nuclear weapon or other nuclear explosive device prior to 1 January 1967) which is a party to the Treaty to conclude a safeguards agreement with the IAEA. Under such an agreement, the state undertakes to accept IAEA safeguards on all nuclear material in all its peaceful nuclear activities for the purpose of verifying that such material is not diverted to nuclear weapons or other nuclear explosive devices. In May 1995 the Review and Extension Conference of parties to the NPT agreed to extend the NPT indefinitely, and reaffirmed support for the IAEA's role in verification and the transfer of peaceful nuclear technologies. At the next review conference, held in April–May 2000, the five 'nuclear-weapon states'—China, France, Russia, the United Kingdom and the USA—issued a joint statement pledging their commitment to the ultimate goal of complete nuclear disarmament under effective international controls. A further review conference was convened in May 2005. The 2010 review conference, held in May of that year, unanimously adopted an outcome document containing a 22-point action plan aimed at advancing nuclear disarmament, non-proliferation and the peaceful uses of nuclear energy over the following five years. The Conference also proposed that a regional conference should be convened to address means of eliminating nuclear and other weapons of mass destruction in the Middle East; resolved that the nuclear-weapon states should commit to further efforts to reduce and ultimately eliminate all types of nuclear weapons, including through unilateral, bilateral, regional and multilateral measures, with specific emphasis on the early entry into force and full implementation of the Treaty on Measures for the Further Reduction and Limitation of Strategic Offensive Arms (known as the New START Treaty), signed by the Presidents of Russia and the USA in April 2010; and determined that the Conference on Disarmament should immediately establish a subsidiary body to address nuclear disarmament within the context of an agreed and comprehensive programme of work. The Conference noted a five-point proposal of the UN Secretary-General for nuclear disarmament, including consideration of negotiations on a convention on nuclear weapons, and recognized the interests of non-nuclear-weapon states in constraining nuclear-weapon states' development of nuclear weapons. At June 2012 185 non-nuclear-weapon states and the five nuclear-weapon states were parties to the NPT. A number of non-nuclear-weapon states, however, had not complied, within the prescribed time-limit, with their obligations under the Treaty regarding the conclusion of the relevant safeguards agreement with the Agency.

The five nuclear-weapon states have concluded safeguards agreements with the Agency that permit the application of IAEA safeguards to all their nuclear activities, excluding those with 'direct national significance'. A Comprehensive Nuclear Test Ban Treaty (CTBT) was opened for signature in September 1996, having been adopted by the UN General Assembly. The Treaty was to enter into international law upon ratification by all 44 nations with known nuclear capabilities. A separate verification organization was to be established, based in Vienna. A Preparatory Commission for the treaty organization became operational in 1997. By June 2012 183 countries had signed the CTBT and 157 had ratified it, including 36 of the 44 states with known nuclear capabilities (known as the 'Annex II states', of which the remaining eight were: China, Egypt, Iran, Israel, and the USA, which were at that time signatories to the CTBT; and the Democratic People's Republic of Korea—North Korea, India, and Pakistan, which had not signed the Treaty). In October 1999 ratification of the CTBT was rejected by the US Senate. President Obama of the USA indicated in April 2009 that ratification of the Treaty would be pursued by his regime. The May 2010 NPT review conference determined that all nuclear-weapon states should undertake to ratify the CTBT, and emphasized that, pending the entry into force of the CTBT, all states should refrain from conducting test explosions of nuclear weapons.

Several regional nuclear weapons treaties require their member states to conclude comprehensive safeguards agreements with the IAEA, including the Treaty for the Prohibition of Nuclear Weapons in Latin America (Tlatelolco Treaty, with 33 states party at June 2012); the South Pacific Nuclear-Free Zone Treaty (Rarotonga Treaty, 13 states party at June 2012); the Treaty in the South-East Asia Nuclear-Weapon Free Zone (Treaty of Bangkok, adopted in 1995, 10 states party at June 2012); and the African Nuclear-Weapon Free Zone Treaty (Pelindaba Treaty, adopted in 1996, with 30 states party at June 2012). In September 2006 experts from Kazakhstan, Kyrgyzstan, Tajikistan, Turkmenistan and Uzbekistan adopted a treaty on establishing a Central Asian Nuclear Weapon Free Zone (CANWFZ); all five states subsequently ratified the treaty. At the end of 2010 IAEA safeguards agreements were in force with 175 states, covering 674 nuclear facilities. During that year the Agency conducted 1,983 inspections. Expenditure on the Safeguards Regular Budget for 2010 was €116.1m., and extra-budgetary programme expenditure amounted to €18.2m. The IAEA maintains an imagery database of nuclear sites, and is installing digital surveillance systems (including unattended and remote monitoring capabilities) to replace obsolete analogue systems.

In June 1995 the Board of Governors approved measures to strengthen the safeguards system, including allowing inspection teams greater access to suspected nuclear sites and to information on nuclear activities in member states, reducing the notice time for inspections by removing visa requirements for inspectors and using environmental monitoring (i.e. soil, water and air samples) to test for signs of radioactivity. In April 1996 the IAEA initiated a programme to prevent and combat illicit trafficking of nuclear weapons, and in May 1998 the IAEA and the World Customs Organization signed a Memorandum of Understanding to enhance co-operation in the prevention of illicit nuclear trafficking. In May 1997 the Board of Governors adopted a model additional protocol approving measures to strengthen safeguards further, in order to ensure the compliance of non-nuclear-weapon states with IAEA commitments. The new protocol compelled member states to provide inspection teams with improved access to information concerning existing and planned nuclear activities, and to allow access to locations other than known nuclear sites within that country's territory. By June 2012 116 states had ratified additional protocols to their safeguards agreements.

The IAEA's Safeguards Analytical Laboratory (at the Seibersdorf complex) analyses nuclear fuel-cycle samples collected by IAEA safeguards inspectors.

In April 1992 North Korea ratified a safeguards agreement with the IAEA. Subequently, however, that country refused to permit full access to all its facilities for IAEA inspectors to ascertain whether material capable of being used for the manufacture of nuclear weapons was being generated and stored. In March 1993 North Korea announced its intention to withdraw from the NPT, although, in June, it suspended this decision. In June 1994 the IAEA Board of Governors halted IAEA technical assistance to North Korea because of continuous violation of the NPT safeguards agreements. In the same month North Korea withdrew from the IAEA (though not from the NPT); however, it allowed IAEA inspectors to conduct safeguards activities at its Yongbyon nuclear site. In October the Governments of North Korea and the USA concluded an agreement whereby the former agreed to halt construction of two new nuclear reactors, on condition that it received international aid for the construction of two 'light water' reactors (which could not produce materials for the manufacture of nuclear weapons). North Korea also agreed to allow IAEA inspections of all its nuclear sites, but only after the installation of one of the light water reactors had been completed (entailing a significant time lapse). From 1995 the IAEA pursued technical discussions with the North Korean authorities as part of the Agency's efforts to achieve the full compliance with the IAEA safeguards agreement; however, little overall progress was achieved, owing to the obstruction of inspectors by the authorities in that country, including their refusal to provide samples for analysis. In accordance with a decision of the General Conference in September 2001, IAEA inspectors subsequently resumed a continuous presence in North Korea. The authorities in that country permitted low-level inspections of the Yongbyon site by an IAEA technical team in January and May 2002. However, in December, following repeated requests by the IAEA that North Korea verify the accuracy of reports that it was implementing an undeclared uranium enrichment programme, the authorities disabled IAEA safeguards surveillance equipment placed at three facilities in Yongbyon and took measures to restart reprocessing capabilities at the site, requesting the immediate withdrawal of the Agency's inspectors. In early January 2003 the IAEA Board of Governors adopted a resolution deploring North Korea's non-co-operation and urging its immediate and full compliance with the Agency. Shortly afterwards, however, North Korea announced its withdrawal from the NPT, while stating that it would limit its nuclear activities to peaceful purposes. In February the IAEA found North Korea to be in further non-compliance with its safeguards agreement, and condemned the reported successful reactivation of the Yongbyon reactor. In August a series of six-party talks on the situation was launched, involving North Korea, China, Japan, the Republic of Korea (South Korea), Russia and the USA, under the auspices of the Chinese Government. In September 2004 the General Conference adopted a resolution that urged North Korea to dismantle promptly and completely any nuclear weapons programme and to recognize the verification role of the Agency, while strongly encouraging the ongoing diplomatic efforts to achieve a peaceful outcome. In February 2005 North Korea suspended its participation in the six-party talks, and asserted that it had developed nuclear weapons as a measure of self-defence. The talks resumed during July–September, when the six parties signed a joint statement, in which North Korea determined to resume its adherence to the NPT and Agency safeguards, and consequently to halt its development of nuclear weapons; the USA and South Korea affirmed that no US nuclear weapons were deployed on the Korean Peninsula; the five other parties recognized North Korea's right to use nuclear energy for peaceful purposes, and agreed to consider at a later date the provision of a light water reactor to that country; and all parties undertook to promote co-operation in security and economic affairs. A timetable for future progress was to be established at the next phase of the six-party talks, the first session of which convened briefly in early November; North Korea, however, subsequently announced that it would only resume the talks pending the release by the USA of recently-frozen financial assets. In July 2006 the UN Security Council condemned a recent ballistic missile test by North Korea, noting the potential of such missiles to be used for delivering nuclear, chemical or biological payloads, and urged that country to return immediately to the six-party talks without precondition and work towards the implementation of the September 2005 joint statement. In early 2006 October the IAEA Director-General expressed serious concern in response to an announcement by North Korea that it had conducted a nuclear test. In mid-October the Security Council adopted Resolution 1718, demanding that North Korea suspend all activities related to its ballistic missile programme, abandon all nuclear weapons and existing nuclear programmes, abandon all other existing weapons of mass destruction and ballistic missile programmes in a complete, verifiable and irreversible manner, and return to the six-party talks. The Council also imposed sanctions against North Korea.

The six-party talks were resumed in February 2007, and resulted in an ad hoc agreement by all the participants that North Korea would shut down and seal—for the purpose of eventual abandonment—the Yongbyon facility, and would invite back IAEA personnel to conduct all necessary monitoring and verifications; that North Korea would discuss with the other parties a list of all its nuclear programmes; that it would would enter into negotiations with the USA aimed at resolving pending bilateral issues and moving toward full diplomatic relations; that the USA would initiate the process of removing the designation of North Korea as a state-sponsor of terrorism; that North Korea and Japan would start negotiations aimed at normalizing their relations; and that the parties would agree to co-operate in security and economic affairs (as detailed under the September 2005 joint statement). In the latter regard, the parties agreed to the provision of emergency energy assistance to North Korea. In July 2007 an IAEA team visited the country and verified the shutdown of the Yongbyon facility. Upon the resumption of the six-party talks in late September, the participants adopted an agreement wherein North Korea resolved to disable permanently its nuclear facilities.

In early June 2008 the IAEA Director-General asserted that, as long as the legal status of North Korea's accession to the NPT remained unclear, the safeguards responsibilities of the Agency towards North Korea were also uncertain. Later in June North Korea released documents outlining its capabilities in the areas of nuclear power and nuclear weapons. In the following month the participants in the next round of six-party talks agreed that a verification regime should be established, that the disablement of North Korea's Yongbyon nuclear facilities should be completed, and that assistance equivalent to 1m. tons of heavy fuel oil should be delivered to North Korea. In August the North Korean authorities announced their intention to reactivate the Yongbyon facility in reaction to the refusal, hitherto, of the USA to remove the country from its terrorism blacklist. In September the IAEA reported that all Agency seals and surveillance equipment had been removed from Yongbyon, and that North Korea would no longer sanction visits by IAEA inspectors to the reprocessing facility. In mid-October, shortly after the conclusion of an agreement between North Korea and USA on a series of measures aimed at verifying North Korea's denuclearization, and the US Government's subsequent removal of North Korea from its terrorism blacklist, the North Korean authorities permitted the return of IAEA inspectors to Yongbyon. A round of the six-party talks convened in December failed to reach agreement on the formulation of a verification protocol, which was to be based on the verification measures agreed in October.

In mid-April 2009 a long-range rocket test conducted by North Korea, in violation of UN Security Council Resolution 1718 (see above), was unanimously condemned by the Council. North Korea responded by announcing its withdrawal from the six-party talks; withdrawing from the ad hoc agreement concerning the Yongbyon facility reached in February 2007; stating its intention to restart the Yongbyon facility; and ceasing, with immediate effect, all co-operation with the IAEA. Accordingly, IAEA inspectors removed all seals and surveillance equipment from the Yongbyon complex and departed the country. A further nuclear test conducted by North Korea in late May 2009 was deplored by the Security Council, which strengthened the sanctions regime against that country, in June, and demanded that it rejoin the NPT. Reporting to the Board of Governors in June and September the IAEA Director-General urged all concerned parties to continue to work through diplomatic channels for a comprehensive solution that would bring North Korea back to the NPT and address that country's security concerns and humanitarian, economic and political requirements. In September 2011 the 55th IAEA Conference expressed concern at reports of the construction of a new uranium enrichment facility and light water reactor in North Korea. At the end of October discussions were held between North Korean and US government representatives concerning restarting the suspended six-party talks. It was announced at the end of February 2012 that North Korea, under new leadership since December 2011, had agreed to suspend uranium enrichment and nuclear testing, and to permit the return of IAEA inspectors, in return for significant provision of food aid from the USA. In March the North Korean authorities formally invited the IAEA to send a delegation to discuss technical issues relating to verifying activities at Yongbyon. In April the USA suspended the January agreement following a failed long-range missile launch, which North Korea declared to be an attempt to send a satellite into orbit. The UN Security Council condemned the launch as a violation of UN resolutions. Subsequently the IAEA carefully monitored the situation, and the Director-General announced in June that no delegation would be sent to North Korea in the immediate future.

In September 2003 the IAEA adopted a resolution demanding that the Iranian Government sign, ratify and fully implement an additional protocol to its safeguards agreement promptly and unconditionally. The Agency also urged Iran to suspend its uranium enrichment and reprocessing activities, pending satisfactory application of the provisions of the additional protocol. Iran issued a declaration of its nuclear activities in October, and, in December, signed an additional protocol and agreed to suspend uranium enrichment processing. The Agency dispatched inspectors to Iran from October to conduct an intensive verification process. In April 2004 the IAEA Director-General visited Iran and concluded an agreement on a joint action plan to address the outstanding issues of the verification process. Iran provided an initial declaration under the (as yet unratified) additional protocol in May. In June, however, the Director-General expressed his continued concern at the extent of Iranian co-operation with IAEA inspectors. In September the Board of Governors adopted a resolution in which it strongly regretted continuing enrichment-related and reprocessing activities by Iran and requested their immediate suspension. The Director-General announced in late November that the suspension had been verified. In August 2005 the Agency adopted a resolution condemning Iran for resuming uranium conversion. In the following month a further resolution was adopted by the Board of Governors, in support of a motion by the EU, citing Iran's non-compliance with the NPT and demanding that Iran accelerate its co-operation with the Agency regarding the outstanding issues. In February 2006 the Board of Governors adopted a resolution that recalled repeated failures by Iran to comply with its obligations under its NPT safeguards agreement, expressed serious concern at the nature of Iran's nuclear programme, and urged that, with a view to building confidence in the exclusively peaceful nature of the programme, Iran should suspend fully all activities related to uranium enrichment (reportedly resumed in January) and reprocessing; ratify and fully implement the additional protocol agreed in 2003; and implement transparency measures extending beyond its formal arrangements with the Agency. The resolution requested the IAEA Director-General to report the steps required of Iran to the UN Security Council and to inform the Security Council of all related IAEA documents and resolutions. In response, the Iranian authorities declared that they would suspend all legally non-binding measures imposed by the IAEA, including containment and surveillance measures provided for under the additional protocol, and that consequently all IAEA seals and cameras should be removed from Iranian sites by mid-February 2006. At the end of July the UN Security Council, having reviewed the relevant information provided by the IAEA Director-General, issued Resolution 1696, in which it demanded that Iran suspend all enrichment-related and reprocessing activities, including research and development, within a period of one month, and stipulated that non-compliance might result in the imposition on Iran of economic and diplomatic sanctions. The resolution requested that the IAEA Director-General submit to the Council at the end of August a report on Iran's response. The report, which was made public in mid-September, found that Iran had not suspended its enrichment-related activities and was still not in compliance with the provisions of the additional protocol. In December the Security Council imposed sanctions against Iran, and in March 2007 the Council imposed a ban on the export of arms from that country.

In June 2007 the IAEA Director-General and the Iranian authorities agreed to develop within 60 days a plan on the modalities for resolving outstanding safeguards implementation issues; accordingly, in August, a workplan on this area (also detailing procedures and timelines) was finalized. At that time the IAEA declared that previous Agency concerns about plutonium reprocessing activities in Iran were now resolved, as its findings had verified earlier statements made by the Iranian authorities. At the end of that month the IAEA Director-General reported that Iran had not yet suspended its uranium enrichment activities. The IAEA Director-General visited Iran in January 2008 to discuss with the Iranian administration means of accelerating the implementation of safeguards and confidence-building measures. It was agreed that remaining verification issues that had been specified in the August 2007 workplan should be resolved by mid-February 2008. In February 2008 the IAEA Board of Governors reported that Iran was still pursuing its uranium enrichment activities, and that the Iranian Government needed to continue to build confidence about the scope and purported peaceful nature of its nuclear programme. Consequently, in the following month, the UN Security Council adopted a new resolution on Iran in which it professed concern for the proliferation risk presented by the Iranian nuclear programme and authorized inspections of any cargo to and from Iran suspected of transporting prohibited equipment; strengthened the monitoring of Iranian financial institutions; and added names to the existing list of individuals and companies subject to asset and travel restrictions.

In May 2008 the IAEA Director-General, at the request of the UN Security Council, circulated a report to both the Security Council and the IAEA Board of Governors on the *Implementation of the NPT Safeguards Agreement and Relevant Provisions of Security Council Resolutions 1737 (2006), 1747 (2007), and 1803 (2008) in the Islamic Republic of Iran*, which concluded that there remained several areas of serious concern, including an ongoing 'green salt' project; high explosives testing; a missile re-entry vehicle project; some procurement activities of military-related institutions; outstanding substantive explanations regarding information with a possible military dimension; and Iran's continuing enrichment-related activities. In September the UN Security Council adopted a new resolution that reiterated demands that Iran cease enriching uranium. Reporting on the situation in February 2009, the IAEA Director-General stated that Iran continued to enrich uranium. Iran was urged once again to implement its additional protocol and other transparency measures.

In September 2009 the IAEA was informed by Iran that a second uranium enrichment facility was under construction in its territory; the Iranian authorities stated that the facility was to be used for peaceful purposes. The IAEA determined to send safeguards inspectors to examine the plant, located at an underground site near Qom, southwest of Tehran. In November the IAEA Board of Governors adopted a resolution urging Iran to suspend immediately construction at Qom; to engage with the IAEA on resolving all outstanding issues concerning its nuclear programme; to comply fully and without qualification with its safeguards obligations, specifically to provide requested clarifications regarding the purpose of the Qom enrichment plant and the chronology of its design and construction; and to confirm that no other undeclared facilities were planned or under construction. A report by the IAEA Secretary-General issued in February 2010 stated that, while the IAEA continued to verify the non-diversion of declared nuclear material in Iran, the Iranian authorities had not provided the necessary degree of co-operation to enable the Agency to confirm that all nuclear material in Iran was not being diverted for military purposes. In June the UN Security Council adopted Resolution 1929 strengthening the UN sanction regime against Iran. Resolution 1929 also established a panel of experts to assist with monitoring and enforcing the implementation of the Iran sanctions. In November 2011 the IAEA Board of Governors adopted a resolution expressing 'deep and increasing concern' over the unresolved issues regarding the Iranian nuclear programme and calling upon Iran to engage seriously and without preconditions in discussions aimed at restoring international confidence in the exclusively peaceful nature of its nuclear activities. With a view to intensifying dialogue, senior IAEA experts visited Iran in late January–early February 2012, and again in late February. On both occasions the IAEA team requested, but was denied, access to the military complex at Parchin, southeast of Tehran, which was suspected to be the site of an explosives containment vessel; clarification of unresolved issues relating to possible military dimensions of Iran's nuclear programme was not achieved. An IAEA report on the Iran situation, issued in late February, found that uranium enrichment had increased threefold since late 2011, in particular at the underground site near Qom; it was maintained by the Iranian authorities, however, that this material was required for a medical research reactor. The report also claimed that the installation of centrifuges at the Natanz uranium enrichment plant, in central Iran, had accelerated. Meeting in May 2012 the IAEA Director-General and senior Iranian officials determined to adopt a document on a 'Structured Approach' as a framework for discussions. Further negotiations aimed at finalizing the document took place in June.

The IAEA Conference adopted a resolution in September 2009 that expressed concern about Israel's nuclear capabilities and called upon Israel to accede to the NPT and to place all its nuclear facilities under comprehensive IAEA safeguards.

In June 2011 the IAEA Board of Governors adopted a resolution noting with serious concern the conclusion of the Agency that a building destroyed at Dair Alzour, Syria, in September 2007, was very likely an undeclared nuclear reactor; the resolution requested Syria to remedy urgently non-compliance with its Safeguards Agreement and called upon that country promptly to bring into force and implement an Additional Protocol to its Safeguards Agreement. IAEA officials visited Syria in October 2011 to pursue the matter, but were not granted sufficient access to locations believed to be functionally related to the Dair Alzour site. In November the IAEA Director-General demanded that Syria co-operate fully with the Agency in connection with unresolved issues relating to Dair Alzour and other locations.

In November 2011 the IAEA convened, in Vienna, a Forum on the Experience of Possible Relevance to the Creation of a Nuclear-Weapon-Free-Zone in the Middle East.

NUCLEAR FUEL CYCLE

The Agency promotes the exchange of information between member states on technical, safety, environmental, and economic aspects of nuclear fuel cycle technology, including uranium prospecting and the treatment and disposal of radioactive waste; it provides assistance to member states in the planning, implementation and operation of nuclear fuel cycle facilities and assists in the development of advanced nuclear fuel cycle technology. The Agency operates a number of databases and a simulation system related to the nuclear fuel cycle through its Integrated Nuclear Fuel Cycle Information System (iNFCIS). Every two years, in collaboration with OECD, the Agency prepares estimates of world uranium resources, demand and production.

Finance

The Agency is financed by regular and voluntary contributions from member states. Expenditure approved under the regular budget for 2012 amounted to some €333m., while the target for voluntary contributions to finance the IAEA technical co-operation programme in that year was €88m.

Publications

Annual Report.

Atoms for Peace.

Fundamental Safety Principles.

IAEA Bulletin (quarterly).

IAEA Newsbriefs (every 2 months).

IAEA Safety Glossary Terminology Used in Nuclear Safety and Radiation Protection.

IAEA Yearbook.

INIS Atomindex (bibliography, 2 a month).

INIS Reference Series.

INSAG Series.

Legal Series.

Meetings on Atomic Energy (quarterly).

The Nuclear Fuel Cycle Information System: A Directory of Nuclear Fuel Cycle Facilities.

Nuclear Fusion (monthly).

Nuclear Safety Review (annually).

Nuclear Technology Review (annually).

Panel Proceedings Series.

Publications Catalogue (annually).

Safety Series.

Technical Directories.

Technical Co-operation Report.

Treaty on the Non-Proliferation of Nuclear Weapons

(Signed 1 July 1968)

The States concluding this Treaty, hereinafter referred to as the 'Parties to the Treaty',

Considering the devastation that would be visited upon all mankind by a nuclear war and the consequent need to make every effort to avert the danger of such a war and to take measures to safeguard the security of peoples,

Believing that the proliferation of nuclear weapons would seriously enhance the danger of nuclear war,

In conformity with resolutions of the United Nations General Assembly calling for the conclusion of an agreement on the prevention of wider dissemination of nuclear weapons,

Undertaking to co-operate in facilitating the application of International Atomic Energy Agency safeguards on peaceful nuclear activities,

Expressing their support for research, development and other efforts to further the application, within the framework of the International Atomic Energy Agency safeguards system, of the principle of safeguarding effectively the flow of source and special fissionable materials by use of instruments and other techniques at certain strategic points,

Affirming the principle that the benefits of peaceful applications of nuclear technology, including any technological by-products which may be derived by nuclear-weapon States from the development of nuclear explosive devices, should be available for peaceful purposes to all Parties of the Treaty, whether nuclear-weapon or non-nuclear-weapon States,

Convinced that, in furtherance of this principle, all Parties to the Treaty are entitled to participate in the fullest possible exchange of scientific information for, and to contribute alone or in co-operation with other States to, the further development of the applications of atomic energy for peaceful purposes,

Declaring their intention to achieve at the earliest possible date the cessation of the nuclear arms race and to undertake effective measures in the direction of nuclear disarmament,

Urging the co-operation of all States in the attainment of this objective,

Recalling the determination expressed by the Parties to the 1963 Treaty banning nuclear weapon tests in the atmosphere, in outer space and under water in its Preamble to seek to achieve the discontinuance of all test explosions of nuclear weapons for all time and to continue negotiations to this end,

Desiring to further the easing of international tension and the strengthening of trust between States in order to facilitate the cessation of the manufacture of nuclear weapons, the liquidation of all their existing stockpiles, and the elimination from national arsenals of nuclear weapons and the means of their delivery pursuant to a Treaty on general and complete disarmament under strict and effective international control,

Recalling that, in accordance with the Charter of the United Nations, States must refrain in their international relations from the threat or use of force against the territorial integrity or political independence of any State, or in any other manner inconsistent with the Purposes of the United Nations, and that the establishment and maintenance of international peace and security are to be promoted with the least diversion for armaments of the world's human and economic resources,

Have agreed as follows.

Article I

Each nuclear-weapon State Party to the Treaty undertakes not to transfer to any recipient whatsoever nuclear weapons or other nuclear explosive devices or control over such weapons or explosive devices directly, or indirectly; and not in any way to assist, encourage, or induce any non-nuclear-weapon State to manufacture or otherwise acquire nuclear weapons or other nuclear explosive devices, or control over such weapons or explosive devices.

Article II

Each non-nuclear-weapon State Party to the Treaty undertakes not to receive the transfer from any transfer or whatsoever of nuclear weapons or other nuclear explosive devices or of control over such weapons or explosive devices directly, or indirectly; not to manufacture or otherwise acquire nuclear weapons or other nuclear explosive devices; and not to seek or receive any assistance in the manufacture of nuclear weapons or other nuclear explosive devices.

Article III

1. Each non-nuclear-weapon State Party to the Treaty undertakes to accept safeguards, as set forth in an agreement to be negotiated and concluded with the International Atomic Energy Agency in accordance with the Statute of the International Atomic Energy Agency and the Agency's safeguards system, for the exclusive purpose of verification of the fulfilment of its obligations assumed under this Treaty with a view to preventing diversion of nuclear energy from peaceful uses to nuclear weapons or other nuclear explosive devices. Procedures for the safeguards required by this article shall be followed with respect to source or special fissionable material whether it is being produced, processed or used in any principal nuclear facility or is outside any such facility. The safeguards required by this article shall be applied to all source or special fissionable material in all peaceful nuclear activities within the territory of such State, under its jurisdiction, or carried out under its control anywhere.

2. Each State Party to the Treaty undertakes not to provide: (a) source or special fissionable material, or (b) equipment or material especially designed or prepared for the processing, use or production of special fissionable material, to any non-nuclear-weapon State for peaceful purposes, unless the source or special fissionable material shall be subject to the safeguards required by this article.

3. The safeguards required by this article shall be implemented in a manner designed to comply with article IV of this Treaty, and to avoid hampering the economic or technological development of the Parties or international co-operation in the field of peaceful nuclear activities, including the international exchange of nuclear material and equipment for the processing, use or production of nuclear material for peaceful purposes in accordance with the provisions of this article and the principle of safeguarding set forth in the Preamble of the Treaty.

4. Non-nuclear-weapon States Party to the Treaty shall conclude agreements with the International Atomic Energy Agency to meet the requirements of this article either individually or together with other States in accordance with the Statute of the International Atomic Energy Agency. Negotiation of such agreements shall commence within 180 days from the original entry into force of this Treaty. For States depositing their instruments of ratification or accession after the 180-day period, negotiation of such agreements shall commence not later than the date of such deposit. Such agreements shall enter into force not later than eighteen months after the date of initiation of negotiations.

Article IV

1. Nothing in this Treaty shall be interpreted as affecting the inalienable right of all the Parties to the Treaty to develop research, production and use of nuclear energy for peaceful purposes without discrimination and in conformity with articles I and II of this Treaty.

2. All the Parties to the Treaty undertake to facilitate, and have the right to participate in, the fullest possible exchange of equipment, materials and scientific and technological information for the peaceful uses of nuclear energy. Parties to the Treaty in a position to do so shall also co-operate in contributing alone or together with other States or international organizations to the further development of the applications of nuclear energy for peaceful purposes, especially in the territories of non-nuclear-weapon States Party to the Treaty, with due consideration for the needs of the developing areas of the world.

Article V

Each party to the Treaty undertakes to take appropriate measures to ensure that, in accordance with this Treaty, under appropriate international observation and through appropriate international procedures, potential benefits from any peaceful applications of nuclear explosions will be made available to non-nuclear-weapon States Party to the Treaty on a nondiscriminatory basis and that the charge to such Parties for the explosive devices used will be as low as possible and exclude any charge for research and development. Non-nuclear-weapon States Party to the Treaty shall be able to obtain such benefits, pursuant to a special international agreement or agreements, through an appropriate international body with adequate representation of non-nuclear-weapon States. Negotiations on this subject shall commence as soon as possible after the Treaty enters into force. Non-nuclear-weapon States Party to the Treaty so desiring may also obtain such benefits pursuant to bilateral agreements.

Article VI

Each of the Parties to the Treaty undertakes to pursue negotiations in good faith on effective measures relating to cessation of the nuclear arms race at an early date and to nuclear disarmament, and on a Treaty on general and complete disarmament under strict and effective international control.

Article VII

Nothing in this Treaty affects the right of any group of States to conclude regional treaties in order to assure the total absence of nuclear weapons in their respective territories.

Article VIII

1. Any Party to the Treaty may propose amendments to this Treaty. The text of any proposed amendment shall be submitted to the Depositary Governments which shall circulate it to all Parties to the Treaty. Thereupon, if requested to do so by one-third or more of the Parties to the Treaty, the Depositary Governments shall convene a conference, to which they shall invite all the Parties to the Treaty, to consider such an amendment.

2. Any amendment to this Treaty must be approved by a majority of the votes of all the Parties to the Treaty, including the votes of all nuclear-weapon States Party to the Treaty and all other Parties which, on the date the amendment is circulated, are members of the Board of Governors of the International Atomic Energy Agency. The amendment shall enter into force for each Party that deposits its instrument of ratification of the amendment upon the deposit of such instruments of ratification by a majority of all the Parties, including the instruments of ratification of all nuclear-weapon States Party to the Treaty and all other Parties which, on the date the amendment is circulated, are members of the Board of Governors of the International Atomic Energy Agency. Thereafter, it shall enter into force for any other Party upon the deposit of its instrument of ratification of the amendment.

3. Five years after the entry into force of this Treaty, a conference of Parties to the Treaty shall be held in Geneva, Switzerland, in order to review the operation of this Treaty with a view to assuring that the purposes of the Preamble and the provisions of the Treaty are being realized. At intervals of five years thereafter, a majority of the Parties to the Treaty may obtain, by submitting a proposal to this effect to the Depositary Governments, the convening of further conferences with the same objective of reviewing the operation of the Treaty.

Article IX

1. This Treaty shall be open to all States for signature. Any State which does not sign the Treaty before its entry into force in accordance with paragraph 3 of this article may accede to it at any time.

2. This Treaty shall be subject to ratification by signatory States. Instruments of ratification and instruments of accession shall be deposited with the Governments of the United States of America, the United Kingdom of Great Britain and Northern Ireland and the Union of Soviet Socialist Republics, which are hereby designated the Depositary Governments.

3. This Treaty shall enter into force after its ratification by the States, the Governments of which are designated Depositaries of the Treaty, and forty other States signatory to this Treaty and the deposit of their instruments of ratification. For the purposes of this Treaty, a nuclear-weapon State is one which has manufactured and exploded a nuclear weapon or other nuclear explosive device prior to January 1 1967.

4. For States whose instruments of ratification or accession are deposited subsequent to the entry into force of this Treaty, it shall enter into force on the date of the deposit of their instruments of ratification or accession.

5. The Depositary Governments shall promptly inform all signatory and acceding States of the date of each signature, the date of deposit of each instrument of ratification or of accession, the date of the entry into force of this Treaty, and the date of receipt of any requests for convening a conference or other notices.

6. This Treaty shall be registered by the Depositary Governments pursuant to article 102 of the Charter of the United Nations.

Article X

1. Each Party shall in exercising its national sovereignty have the right to withdraw from the Treaty if it decides that extraordinary events, related to the subject matter of this Treaty, have jeopardized the supreme interests of its country. It shall give notice of such withdrawal to all other Parties to the Treaty and to the United Nations Security Council three months in advance. Such notice shall include a statement of the extraordinary events it regards as having jeopardized its supreme interests.

2. Twenty-five years after the entry into force of the Treaty, a conference shall be convened to decide whether the Treaty shall continue in force indefinitely, or shall be extended for an additional fixed period or periods. The decision shall be taken by a majority of the Parties to the Treaty.

Article XI

This Treaty, the English, Russian, French, Spanish and Chinese texts of which are equally authentic, shall be deposited in the archives of the Depositary Governments. Duly certified copies of this Treaty shall be transmitted by the Depositary Governments to the Governments of the signatory and acceding States.

In witness whereof the undersigned, duly authorized, have signed this Treaty.

Done in triplicate, at the cities of Washington, London and Moscow, this first day of July one thousand nine hundred sixty-eight.

International Bank for Reconstruction and Development—IBRD (World Bank)

Address: 1818 H St, NW, Washington, DC 20433, USA.

Telephone: (202) 473-1000; **fax:** (202) 477-6391; **e-mail:** pic@worldbank.org; **internet:** www.worldbank.org.

The IBRD was established in December 1945. Initially it was concerned with post-war reconstruction in Europe; since then its aim has been to assist the economic development of member nations by making loans where private capital is not available on reasonable terms to finance productive investments. Loans are made either directly to governments, or to private enterprises with the guarantee of their governments. The World Bank, as it is commonly known, comprises the IBRD and the International Development Association (IDA). The affiliated group of institutions, comprising the IBRD, IDA, the International Finance Corporation (IFC), the Multilateral Investment Guarantee Agency (MIGA) and the International Centre for Settlement of Investment Disputes (ICSID, see below), is referred to as the World Bank Group.

MEMBERS

There are 188 members. Only members of the International Monetary Fund (IMF) may be considered for membership in the World Bank. Subscriptions to the capital stock of the Bank are based on each member's quota in the IMF, which is designed to reflect the country's relative economic strength. Voting rights are related to shareholdings.

Organization

(June 2012)

Officers and staff of the IBRD serve concurrently as officers and staff in IDA. The World Bank has offices in New York, Brussels, Paris (for Europe), Frankfurt, London, Geneva and Tokyo, as well as in more than 100 countries of operation. Country Directors are located in some 30 country offices.

BOARD OF GOVERNORS

The Board of Governors consists of one Governor appointed by each member nation. Typically, a Governor is the country's finance minister, central bank governor, or a minister or an official of comparable rank. The Board normally meets once a year.

EXECUTIVE DIRECTORS

With the exception of certain powers specifically reserved to them by the Articles of Agreement, the Governors of the Bank have delegated their powers for the conduct of the general operations of the World Bank to a Board of Executive Directors which performs its duties on a full-time basis at the Bank's headquarters. There are 25 Executive Directors (see table below); each Director selects an Alternate. Five Directors are appointed by the five members having the largest number of shares of capital stock, and the rest are elected by the Governors representing the other members. The President of the Bank is Chairman of the Board.

The Executive Directors fulfil dual responsibilities. First, they represent the interests of their country or groups of countries. Second, they exercise their authority as delegated by the Governors in overseeing the policies of the Bank and evaluating completed projects. Since the Bank operates on the basis of consensus (formal votes are rare), this dual role involves frequent communication and consultations with governments so as to reflect accurately their views in Board discussions.

The Directors consider and decide on Bank policy and on all loan and credit proposals. They are also responsible for presentation to the Board of Governors at its Annual Meetings of an audit of accounts, an administrative budget, the *Annual Report* on the operations and policies of the World Bank, and any other matter that, in their judgement, requires submission to the Board of Governors. Matters may be submitted to the Governors at the Annual Meetings or at any time between Annual Meetings.

PRINCIPAL OFFICERS

The principal officers of the Bank are the President of the Bank, three Managing Directors, two Senior Vice-Presidents and 25 Vice-Presidents.

President and Chairman of Executive Directors: Dr Jim Yong Kim (USA) (from 1 July 2012).

Managing Directors: Sri Mulyani Indrawati (Indonesia), Mahmoud Mohieldin (Egypt), Caroline Anstey (United Kingdom).

Activities

The World Bank's primary objectives are the achievement of sustainable economic growth and the reduction of poverty in developing countries. In the context of stimulating economic growth the Bank promotes both private sector development and human resource development and has attempted to respond to the growing demands by developing countries for assistance in these areas. In September 2001 the Bank announced that it was to become a full partner in implementing the UN Millennium Development Goals (MDGs), and was to make them central to its development agenda. The objectives, which were approved by governments attending a special session of the UN General Assembly in September 2000, represented a new international consensus to achieve determined poverty reduction targets. The Bank was closely involved in preparations for the International Conference on Financing for Development, which was held in Monterrey, Mexico, in March 2002. The meeting adopted the Monterrey Consensus, which outlined measures to support national development efforts and to achieve the MDGs. During 2002/03 the Bank, with the IMF, undertook to develop a monitoring framework to review progress in the MDG agenda. The first *Global Monitoring Report* was issued by the Bank and the IMF in April 2004.

In October 2007 the Bank's President defined the following six strategic themes as priorities for Bank development activities: the poorest countries; fragile and post-conflict states; middle-income countries; global public goods; the Arab world; and knowledge and learning. In May 2008 the Bank established a Global Food Crisis Response Programme (GFRP, see below) to assist developing countries affected by the escalating cost of food production. In December the Bank resolved to establish a new facility to accelerate the provision of funds, through IDA, for developing countries affected by the global decline in economic and financial market conditions. The Bank participated in the meeting of heads of state and government of the Group of 20 (G20) leading economies, that was held in Washington, DC, USA, in November 2008 to address the global economic situation, and pursued close collaboration with other multinational organizations, in particular the IMF and OECD, to analyse the impact of the ongoing economic instability. In January 2009 the Bank's President proposed the establishment of a Vulnerability Fund to support essential investment projects in developing countries, to be financed by developed economies appropriating 0.7% of their economic stimulus measures to the Fund. During early 2009 the Bank elaborated its operational response to the global economic crisis. Three operational platforms were devised to address the areas identified as priority themes, i.e. protecting the most vulnerable against the effects of the crisis; maintaining long-term infrastructure investment programmes; and sustaining the potential for private sector-led economic growth and employment creation. Consequently, a new Vulnerability Financing Facility was established, incorporating the GFRP and a new Rapid Social Response Programme, to extend immediate assistance to the poorest groups in affected low- and middle-income countries. Infrastructure investment was to be supported through a new Infrastructure Recovery and Assets Platform, which was mandated to release funds to secure existing infrastructure projects and to finance new initiatives in support of longer-term economic development. Private sector support for infrastructure projects, bank recapitalization, microfinance, and trade financing was to be led by IFC.

In February 2009 the Bank, with the European Bank for Reconstruction and Development (EBRD) and the European Investment Bank, inaugurated a Joint International Financial Institutions (IFI) Action Plan to support the banking systems in central and eastern Europe and to finance lending to businesses in the region affected by the global economic crisis. Under the Plan the Banks initially committed €24,500m. over a two-year period. The Plan also identified the need to conduct joint assessments of the financing needs of the largest bank groups and to accelerate the delivery of co-ordinated assistance. The Action Plan concluded in March 2011, by which time more than €33,000m. had been provided under the initiative, including €9,600m. from the World Bank Group. A separate plan, the European Banking Co-ordination Initiative (the 'Vienna Initiative') was established in early 2009 in order to support banking operations in emerging European economies. The World Bank facilitated the establishment, in 2010, of two committees within the framework of the Initiative concerned with local currency finance development and with enhancing absorption of EU structural funds in emerging Europe. In 2011 two new committees were established (and co-chaired by the Bank) to consider non-performing loans in the region and the challenges of implementing the Basel III capital framework programme.

The Bank's efforts to reduce poverty include the compilation of country-specific assessments and the formulation of country assistance strategies (CASs) to review and guide the Bank's country programmes. In 1998/99 the Bank's Executive Directors endorsed a Comprehensive Development Framework (CDF) to effect a new approach to development assistance based on partnerships and country responsibility, with an emphasis on the interdependence of the social, structural, human, governmental, economic and environmental elements of development. The CDF, which aimed to enhance the overall effectiveness of development assistance, was formulated after a series of consultative meetings organized by the Bank and attended by representatives of governments, donor agencies, financial institutions, non-governmental organizations, the private sector and academics. In December 1999 the Bank introduced a new approach to implement the principles of the CDF, as part of its strategy to enhance the debt relief scheme for heavily indebted poor countries (HIPCs, see below). Applicant countries were requested to formulate, in consultation with external partners and other stakeholders, a results-oriented national strategy to reduce poverty, to be presented in the form of a Poverty Reduction Strategy Paper (PRSP). In cases where there might be some delay in issuing a full PRSP, it was permissible for a country to submit a less detailed 'interim' PRSP (I-PRSP) in order to secure the preliminary qualification for debt relief. The approach also requires the publication of annual progress reports. In 2001 the Bank introduced a new Poverty Reduction Support Credit to help low-income countries to implement the policy and institutional reforms outlined in their PRSP. Increasingly, PRSPs have been considered by the international community to be the appropriate country-level framework to assess progress towards achieving the MDGs.

FINANCIAL OPERATIONS

IBRD capital is derived from members' subscriptions to capital shares, the calculation of which is based on their quotas in the IMF. At 30 June 2011 the total subscribed capital of the IBRD was US $193,732m., of which the paid-in portion was $11,720m. (6.1%); the remainder is subject to call if required. Most of the IBRD's lendable funds come from its borrowing, on commercial terms, in world capital markets, and also from its retained earnings and the flow of repayments on its loans. IBRD loans carry a variable interest rate, rather than a rate fixed at the time of borrowing.

IBRD loans usually have a 'grace period' of five years and are repayable over 15 years or fewer. Loans are made to governments, or must be guaranteed by the government concerned, and are normally made for projects likely to offer a commercially viable rate of return. In 1980 the World Bank introduced structural adjustment lending, which (instead of financing specific projects) supports programmes and changes necessary to modify the structure of an economy so that it can restore or maintain its growth and viability in its balance of payments over the medium term.

The IBRD and IDA together made 362 new lending and investment commitments totalling US $43,005.6m. during the year ending 30 June 2011, compared with 354 (amounting to $58,747.1m.) in the previous year. During 2010/11 the IBRD alone approved commitments totalling $26,737.2m. (compared with $44,197.4m. in the previous year), of which $9,169.4m. (34%) was allocated to Latin America and the Caribbean, $6,369.6m. (24%) to projects in East Asia and the Pacific, and $5,470.0 (20%) to Europe and Central Asia. Disbursements by the IBRD in the year ending 30 June 2011 amounted to $21,879m. (For details of IDA operations, see separate chapter on IDA.)

IBRD operations are supported by medium- and long-term borrowings in international capital markets. During the year ending 30 June 2011 the IBRD's net income amounted to US $930m.

In September 1996 the World Bank/IMF Development Committee endorsed a joint initiative to assist HIPCs to reduce their debt burden to a sustainable level, in order to make more resources available for poverty reduction and economic growth. A new Trust Fund was established by the World Bank in November to finance the initiative. The Fund, consisting of an initial allocation of US $500m. from the IBRD surplus and other contributions from multilateral creditors, was to be administered by IDA. In early 1999 the World Bank and IMF initiated a comprehensive review of the HIPC initiative. By April meetings of the Group of Seven industrialized nations (G7) and of the governing bodies of the Bank and IMF indicated a consensus that the scheme needed to be amended and strengthened, in order to allow more countries to benefit from the initiative, to accelerate the process by which a country may qualify for assistance, and to enhance the effectiveness of debt relief. In June the G7 and Russia (known as the G8), meeting in Cologne, Germany, agreed to increase contributions to the HIPC Trust Fund and to cancel substantial amounts of outstanding debt, and proposed more flexible terms for eligibility. In September the Bank and IMF reached an agreement on an enhanced HIPC scheme. During the initial phase of the process to ensure suitability for debt relief, each applicant country should formulate a PRSP, and should demonstrate prudent financial management in the implementation of the strategy for at least one year, with support from the IMF and IDA. At the pivotal 'decision point' of the process, having thus developed and successfully applied the poverty reduction strategy, applicant countries still deemed to have an unsustainable level of debt were to qualify for interim debt relief from the IMF and IDA, as well as relief on highly concessional terms from other official bilateral creditors and multilateral institutions. During the ensuing 'interim period' countries were required successfully to implement further economic and social development reforms, as a final demonstration of suitability for securing full debt relief at the 'completion point' of the scheme. Data produced at the decision point was to form the base for calculating the final debt relief (in contrast to the original initiative, which based its calculations on projections of a country's debt stock at the completion point). In the majority of cases a sustainable level of debt was targeted at 150% of the net present value (NPV) of the debt in relation to total annual exports (compared with 200%–250% under the original initiative). Other countries with a lower debt-to-export ratio were to be eligible for assistance under the scheme, providing that their export earnings were at least 30% of GDP (lowered from 40% under the original initiative) and government revenue at least 15% of GDP (reduced from 20%). In March 2005 the Bank and the IMF implemented a new Debt Sustainability Framework in Low-income Countries to provide guidance on lending to low-income countries and to improve monitoring and prevention of the accumulation of unsustainable debt. In June finance ministers of the G8 proposed providing additional resources to achieve the full cancellation of debts owed by eligible HIPCs to assist those countries to meet their MDG targets. Countries that had reached their completion point were to qualify for immediate assistance. In July the heads of state and government of G8 countries requested that the Bank ensure the effective delivery of the additional funds and provide a framework for performance measurement. In September the Bank's Development Committee and the International Monetary and Financial Committee of the IMF endorsed the proposal, subsequently referred to as the Multilateral Debt Relief Initiative (MDRI). The Committees agreed to protect the financial capability of IDA, as one of the institutions (with the IMF and the African Development Bank) which was to meet the additional cancellation commitments, and to develop a monitoring programme. At July 2011 assistance committed under the HIPC initiative amounted to an estimated $76,000m. (in 2010 NPV terms), of which the World Bank Group had committed $14,900m. At that time the estimated costs of the MDRI amounted to $52,500m. in nominal value terms, of which the Bank's share amounted to an estimated $35,300m. By the end of 2011 32 countries (Afghanistan, Benin, Bolivia, Burkina Faso, Burundi, Cameroon, Central African Republic, Democratic Republic of the Congo, Republic of Congo, Ethiopia, The Gambia, Ghana, Guinea-Bissau, Guyana, Haiti, Honduras, Liberia, Madagascar, Malawi, Mali, Mauritania, Mozambique, Nicaragua, Niger, Rwanda, São Tomé and Príncipe, Senegal, Sierra Leone, Tanzania, Togo, Uganda and Zambia) had reached completion point under the enhanced HIPC initiative, while four countries had reached decision point. A further four countries were deemed eligible, or potentially eligible, for the initiative.

During 2000/01 the World Bank strengthened its efforts to counter the problem of HIV and AIDS in developing countries. In November 2001 the Bank appointed its first Global HIV/AIDS Adviser. In September 2000 a new Multi-Country HIV/AIDS Programme for Africa (MAP) was launched, initially with $500m., in collaboration with UNAIDS and other major donor agencies and non-governmental organizations. In February 2002 the Bank approved an additional $500m. for a second phase of MAP. A MAP initiative for the Caribbean, with a budget of $155m., was launched in 2001. The Bank has undertaken research into the long-term effects of HIV/AIDS, and hosts the Global HIV/AIDS Monitoring and Evaluation Support Team of UNAIDS. In November 2004 the Bank launched an AIDS Media Center to improve access to information regarding HIV/AIDS, in particular to journalists in developing countries. It has also established a resource library to strengthen HIV/AIDS monitoring and evaluation systems. In July 2009 the Bank published a report, with UNAIDS, concerned with the impact of the global economic crisis on HIV prevention and treatment programmes. A new regional report on HIV/AIDS in the Middle East and North Africa, entitled 'Time for Strategic Action', was published in June 2010.

In March 2007 the Board of Executive Directors approved an action plan to develop further its Clean Energy for Development Investment Framework, which had been formulated in response to a request by the G8 heads of state, meeting in Gleneagles, United Kingdom, in July 2005. The action plan focused on efforts to improve access to clean energy, in particular in sub-Saharan Africa; to accelerate the transition to low carbon-emission development; and to support adaptation to climate change. In October 2008 the Bank Group endorsed a new Strategic Framework on Development and Climate Change, which aimed to guide the Bank in supporting the efforts of developing countries to achieving growth and reducing poverty, while recognizing the operational challenges of climate change. In June 2010 the Bank appointed a Special Envoy to lead the Bank's representation in international discussions on climate change. In February 2012 the Bank supported the establishment of a Global Partnership for Oceans.

In February 2012 the Bank opened a new Global Centre on Conflict, Security and Development in Nairobi, Kenya, in order to enhance its support for the poorest people living in some 30 countries considered 'fragile' or affected by conflict. The Centre was to help co-ordinate development efforts in those countries, to improve the efficiency of financial support, and to serve as a focus for experts and practitioners to share knowledge and experience.

TECHNICAL ASSISTANCE AND ADVISORY SERVICES

In addition to providing financial services, the Bank also undertakes analytical and advisory services, and supports learning and capacity-building, in particular through the World Bank Institute, the Staff Exchange Programme and knowledge-sharing initiatives. The Bank has supported efforts, such as the Global Development Gateway, to disseminate information on development issues and programmes, and, since 1988, has organized the Annual Bank Conference on Development Economics (ABCDE) to provide a forum for the exchange and discussion of development-related ideas and research. In September 1995 the Bank initiated the Information for Development Programme (InfoDev) with the aim of fostering partnerships between governments, multilateral institutions and private-sector experts in order to promote reform and investment in developing countries through improved access to information technology.

The provision of technical assistance to member countries has become a major component of World Bank activities. The economic and sector work (ESW) undertaken by the Bank is the vehicle for considerable technical assistance and often forms the basis of CASs and other strategic or advisory reports. In addition, project loans and credits may include funds earmarked specifically for feasibility studies, resource surveys, management or planning advice, and training. The World Bank Institute has become one of the most important of the Bank's activities in technical assistance. It provides training in national economic management and project analysis for government officials at the middle and upper levels of responsibility. It also runs overseas courses aiming to build up local training capability, and administers a graduate scholarship programme. Technical assistance (usually reimbursable) is also extended to countries that do not need Bank financial support, e.g. for training and transfer of technology. The Bank encourages the use of local consultants to assist with projects and stimulate institutional capability.

The Project Preparation Facility (PPF) was established in 1975 to provide cash advances to prepare projects that may be financed by the Bank. In 1992 the Bank established an Institutional Development Fund (IDF), which became operational on 1 July; the purpose of the Fund was to provide rapid, small-scale financial assistance, to a maximum value of US $500,000, for capacity-building proposals. In 2002 the IDF was reoriented to focus on good governance, in particular financial accountability and system reforms.

ECONOMIC RESEARCH AND STUDIES

In the 1990s the World Bank's research, conducted by its own research staff, was increasingly concerned with providing information to reinforce the Bank's expanding advisory role to developing countries and to improve policy in the Bank's borrowing countries. The principal areas of current research focus on issues such as maintaining sustainable growth while protecting the environment and the poorest sectors of society, encouraging the development of the private sector, and reducing and decentralizing government activities.

Consultative Group on International Agricultural Research (CGIAR): founded in 1971 under the sponsorship of the World Bank (which provides its secretariat), FAO and UNDP. IFAD is also a co-sponsor. The Group was established to raise funds for international agricultural research work for improving crops and animal production in developing countries, and works in partnership with governments, international and regional organizations, private businesses and foundations to support 15 research centres; during 2010 CGIAR implemented a major reorganization: a CGIAR Fund, of which the Bank was nominated as trustee, was established as a multi-trust fund to administer donations to the various programmes, while a Consortium, governed by a 10-member board, was established to unite the strategic and funding supervision of the research centres; a new Independent Science Partnership Council was also established to promote the quality, relevance and impact of science in the CGIAR and to advise on strategic scientific issues; Chair. CGIAR Fund Council INGER ANDERSEN (Denmark); Chair. CGIAR Consortium Bd CARLOS PÉREZ DEL CASTILLO (Uruguay).

CO-OPERATION WITH OTHER ORGANIZATIONS

The World Bank co-operates with other international partners with the aim of improving the impact of development efforts. It collaborates with the IMF in implementing the HIPC scheme and the two agencies work closely to achieve a common approach to development initiatives. The Bank has established strong working relationships with many other UN bodies, in particular through a mutual commitment to poverty reduction objectives. In May 2000 the Bank signed a joint statement of co-operation with OECD. The Bank holds regular consultations with other multilateral development banks and with the European Union with respect to development issues. The Bank-NGO Committee provides an annual forum for discussion with non-governmental organizations (NGOs). Strengthening co-operation with external partners was a fundamental element of the Comprehensive Development Framework, which was adopted in 1998/99 (see above). In 2001/02 a Partnership Approval and Tracking System was implemented to provide information on the Bank's regional and global partnerships. In June 2007 the World Bank and the UN Office on Drugs and Crime launched a joint Stolen Asset Recovery (StAR) initiative, as part of the Bank's new Governance and Anti-Corruption (GAC) strategy. In April 2009 the G20 recommended that StAR review and propose mechanisms to strengthen international co-operation relating to asset recovery. The first global forum on stolen asset recovery and development was convened by StAR in June 2010.

In 1997 the Bank, in partnership with the IMF, UNCTAD, UNDP, the World Trade Organization (WTO) and the International Trade Commission, established an Integrated Framework for Trade-related Assistance to Least Developed Countries, at the request of the WTO, to assist those countries to integrate into the global trading system and improve basic trading capabilities. Also in 1997 a Partnerships Group was established to strengthen the Bank's work with development institutions, representatives of civil society and the private sector. The Group established a new Development Grant Facility, which became operational in October, to support partnership initiatives and to co-ordinate all of the Bank's grant-making activities. The Bank establishes and administers trust funds, open to contributions from member countries and multilateral organizations, NGOs, and private sector institutions, in order to support development partnerships. By 30 June 2011 the Bank had a portfolio of 1,038 active trust funds, with assets of some US $29,100m.

In June 1995 the World Bank joined other international donors (including regional development banks, other UN bodies, Canada, France, the Netherlands and the USA) in establishing a Consultative Group to Assist the Poorest (CGAP), which was to channel funds to the most needy through grass-roots agencies. An initial credit of approximately US $200m. was committed by the donors. The Bank manages the CGAP Secretariat, which is responsible for the administration of external funding and for the evaluation and approval of project financing. The CGAP provides technical assistance, training and strategic advice to microfinance institutions and other relevant bodies. As an implementing agency of the Global Environment Facility (GEF) the Bank assists countries to prepare and supervise GEF projects relating to biological diversity, climate change and other environmental protection measures. It is an example of a partnership in action which addresses a global agenda, complementing Bank country assistance activities. Other funds administered by the Bank include the Global Program to Eradicate Poliomyelitis, launched during the financial year 2002/03, the Least Developed Countries Fund for Climate Change, established in September 2002, an Education for All Fast-Track Initiative Catalytic Trust Fund, established in 2003/04, and a Carbon Finance Assistance Trust Fund, established in 2004/05. In 2006/07 the Bank established a Global Facility for Disaster Reduction and Recovery. In September 2007 the Bank's Executive Directors approved a Carbon Partnership Facility and a Forest Carbon Partnership Facility to support its climate change activities. In May 2008 the Bank inaugurated the Global Food Crisis Response Programme (GFRP) to provide financial support, with resources of some $1,200m., to help meet the immediate needs of countries affected by the escalating cost of food production and by food shortages. Grants and loans were to be allocated on the basis of rapid needs assessments, conducted by the Bank with FAO, WFP and IFAD. As part of the facility a Multi-Donor Trust Fund was established to facilitate co-ordination among donors and to leverage financial support for the rapid delivery of seeds and fertilizer to small-scale farmers. In April 2009 the Bank increased the resources available under the GFRP to $2,000m. By mid-2011 $1,500m. had been approved under the GFRP for initiatives in 40 countries, of which $1,155m. had been disbursed. In that month a new trust fund was established to support a Global Agriculture and Food Security Programme (GAFSP), with total donations amounting to $900m. from the Governments of Canada, Republic of Korea, Spain and the USA and the Bill and Melinda Gates Foundation. The first funds under the GAFSP were issued in June, amounting to $224m. to finance projects to improve agricultural productivity in Bangladesh, Haiti, Rwanda, Sierra Leone and Togo. In early November 2011 the Bank's President urged the forthcoming summit meeting of the G20 to address issues relating to food shortages and food price volatility.

The Bank is a lead organization in providing reconstruction assistance following natural disasters or conflicts, usually in collaboration with other UN agencies or international organizations, and through special trust funds. In May 2011 the Bank co-hosted, with the Global Facility for Disaster Reduction and Recovery and the UN International Strategy for Disaster Reduction, the first World Reconstruction Conference, which concluded an agreement to develop a framework for international co-operation in post disaster recovery and reconstruction. In November 2001 the Bank worked with UNDP and the Asian Development Bank to assess the needs of Afghanistan following the removal of the Taliban authorities in that country. At an International Conference on Reconstruction Assistance to

Afghanistan, held in Tokyo, Japan, in January 2002, the Bank's President proposed extending US $500m. in assistance over a 30-month period, and providing an immediate amount of $50m.–$70m. in grants. In May an Afghanistan Reconstruction Trust Fund was established to provide a co-ordinated financing mechanism to support the interim administration in that country. The Bank is the Administrator of the Trust, which is managed jointly by the Bank, the Asian Development Bank, the Islamic Development Bank and UNDP. By May 2010 contributions to the Trust Fund amounted to $4,361.2m., pledged by 30 countries, of which $3,715.4m. was paid-in. Disbursements under the Fund amounted to $3,112.0m. at that time. In May 2003 a Bank representative participated in an international advisory and monitoring board to assess reconstruction and development needs following international conflict in Iraq and removal of its governing regime. In October the Bank, with the UN Development Group, published a report identifying 14 priority areas for reconstruction, with funding requirements of $36,000m. over the period 2004–07, which was presented to an international donor conference held later in that month. The conference, held in Madrid, Spain, approved the establishment of an International Reconstruction Fund Facility for Iraq to channel international donations and to co-ordinate reconstruction activities. In January 2004 the Bank's Board of Executive Directors authorized the Bank to administer an integral part of the facility, the Iraq Trust Fund (ITF), to finance a programme of emergency projects and technical assistance. By January 2009 the ITF was financing 18 project grants, amounting to $481.6m. The Bank was a partner, with the Iraqi Government, the UN Secretariat, the IMF and other financial institutions, in the International Compact with Iraq, a five-year framework for co-operation that was launched in May 2007. At the end of 2004 the Bank responded immediately to assist countries affected by a massive earthquake and subsequent tsunami which devastated many coastal areas of some 14 countries in the Indian Ocean. Bank staff undertook assessments and other efforts to accelerate recovery planning, mobilize financial support and help to co-ordinate relief and recovery efforts. Some $672m. was allocated by the Bank, mainly in grants to be directed to Indonesia, Sri Lanka and the Maldives, for the first phase of reconstruction efforts. By June 2005 the Bank had committed more than $835m. to countries affected by the tsunami, in particular to repair damaged services, to assist the reconstruction of housing and to restore livelihoods. The Bank administers a Multi-Donor Trust Fund for Aceh and North Sumatra that was established by the Indonesian Government to manage some $500m. in pledged aid. By 30 September 2009 $685.2m. had been pledged for the Multi-Donor Trust Fund, of which some $399m. had been disbursed. In October 2005 the Bank, with the Asian Development Bank, undertook a preliminary damage and needs assessment following a massive earthquake in north-west Pakistan. The cost of the disaster was estimated at $5,200m., with initial reconstruction funding requirements of $3,500m. An international donors' conference was convened in November. In February 2007 the Bank approved a new framework policy to accelerate the response to a disaster or emergency situation in order to fund essential recovery and rehabilitation activities. In January 2010 the Bank issued $100m. in immediate emergency funding to support recovery efforts in Haiti following an earthquake which caused extensive damage and loss of life. By June the Bank had extended some $479m. in grants to support Haiti reconstruction and rehabilitation; at the end of May it cancelled the remaining $36m. outstanding debt owed by Haiti. The Bank acts as trustee of a multi-donor Haiti Reconstruction Fund, which was established in March at an international donors' conference.

The Bank has worked with FAO, WHO and the World Organisation of Animal Health (OIE) to develop strategies to monitor, contain and eradicate the spread of highly pathogenic avian influenza. In September 2005 the Bank organized a meeting of leading experts on the issue and in November it co-sponsored, with FAO, WHO and OIE, an international partners' conference, focusing on control of the disease and preparedness planning for any future related influenza pandemic in humans. In January 2006 the Bank's Board of Directors approved the establishment of a funding programme (the Global Program for Avian Influenza Control and Human Pandemic Preparedness and Response—GPAI), with resources of up to US $500m., to assist countries to combat the disease. Later in that month the Bank co-sponsored, with the European Commission and China, an International Ministerial Pledging Conference on Avian and Human Pandemic Influenza (AHI), convened in Beijing. Participants pledged some $1,900m. to fund disease control and pandemic preparedness activities at global, regional and country levels. Commitments to the AHI facility amounted to $126m. at January 2009. In June the Bank approved an additional $500m. to expand the GPAI in order to fund emergency operations required to prevent and control outbreaks of the new swine influenza variant pandemic (H1N1).

EVALUATION

The Independent Evaluation Group is an independent unit within the World Bank. It conducts Country Assistance Evaluations to assess the development effectiveness of a Bank country programme, and studies and publishes the results of projects after a loan has been fully disbursed, so as to identify problems and possible improvements in future activities. In addition, the department reviews the Bank's global programmes and produces the *Annual Review of Development Effectiveness*. In 1996 a Quality Assurance Group was established to monitor the effectiveness of the Bank's operations and performance. In March 2009 the Bank published an Action Plan on Aid Effectiveness, based on the Accra Agenda for Action that had been adopted in September 2008 during the Third High Level Forum on Aid Effectiveness, held in Ghana.

In September 1993 the Bank established an independent Inspection Panel, consistent with the Bank's objective of improving project implementation and accountability. The Panel, which became operational in September 1994, was to conduct independent investigations and report on complaints from local people concerning the design, appraisal and implementation of development projects supported by the Bank. By the end of 2011 the Panel had received 77 formal requests for inspection.

IBRD INSTITUTIONS

World Bank Institute (WBI): founded in March 1999 by merger of the Bank's Learning and Leadership Centre, previously responsible for internal staff training, and the Economic Development Institute (EDI), which had been established in 1955 to train government officials concerned with development programmes and policies. The new Institute aimed to emphasize the Bank's priority areas through the provision of training courses and seminars relating to poverty, crisis response, good governance and anti-corruption strategies. The Institute supports a Global Knowledge Partnership, which was established in 1997 to promote alliances between governments, companies, other agencies and organizations committed to applying information and communication technologies for development purposes. Under the EDI a World Links for Development programme was also initiated to connect schools in developing countries with partner establishments in industrialized nations via the internet. In 1999 the WBI expanded its programmes through distance learning, a Global Development Network, and use of new technologies. A new initiative, Global Development Learning Network (GDLN), aimed to expand access to information and learning opportunities through the internet, video conferences and organized exchanges. The WBI had also established 60 formal partnership arrangements with learning centres and public, private and non-governmental organizations to support joint capacity building programmes; many other informal partnerships were also in place. During 2009/10 new South-South Learning Middle-income country (MIC)–OECD Knowledge Exchange facilities were established. At 2012 the WBI was focusing its work on the following areas: fragile and conflict-affected states; governance; growth and competitiveness; climate change; health systems; public-private partnerships in infrastructure; and urban development; Vice-Pres. SANJAY PRADHAN (India); publs *Annual Report*, *Development Outreach* (quarterly), other books, working papers, case studies.

International Centre for Settlement of Investment Disputes (ICSID): founded in 1966 under the Convention of the Settlement of Investment Disputes between States and Nationals of Other States. The Convention was designed to encourage the growth of private foreign investment for economic development, by creating the possibility, always subject to the consent of both parties, for a Contracting State and a foreign investor who is a national of another Contracting State to settle any legal dispute that might arise out of such an investment by conciliation and/or arbitration before an impartial, international forum. The governing body of the Centre is its Administrative Council, composed of one representative of each Contracting State, all of whom have equal voting power. The President of the World Bank is (*ex officio*) the non-voting Chairman of the Administrative Council. At April 2012 381 cases had been registered with the Centre, of which 233 had been concluded and 148 were pending consideration. At that time 148 countries had signed and ratified the Convention to become ICSID Contracting States; Sec.-Gen. MEG KINNEAR (Canada).

Publications

Abstracts of Current Studies: The World Bank Research Program (annually).

African Development Indicators (annually).

Annual Report on Operations Evaluation.

Annual Report on Portfolio Performance.

Annual Review of Development Effectiveness.

Doing Business (annually).

Global Commodity Markets (quarterly).

Global Development Finance (annually).

Global Economic Prospects (annually).

ICSID Annual Report.

ICSID Review—Foreign Investment Law Journal (2 a year).

Joint BIS-IMF-OECD-World Bank Statistics on External Debt (quarterly).

News from ICSID (2 a year).

Poverty Reduction and the World Bank (annually).

Poverty Reduction Strategies Newsletter (quarterly).

Research News (quarterly).

Staff Working Papers.

The World Bank and the Environment (annually).

World Bank Annual Report.

World Bank Atlas (annually).

World Bank Economic Review (3 a year).

World Bank Research Observer.

World Development Indicators (annually).

World Development Report (annually).

Statistics

LENDING OPERATIONS, BY SECTOR
(projects approved, year ending 30 June; US $ million)

	2010	2011
Agriculture, fishing and forestry	2,618.2	2,128.8
Education	4,944.6	1,733.1
Energy and mining	9,925.1	5,807.4
Finance	9,136.5	897.5
Health and other social services	6,792.0	6,707.7
Industry and trade	1,251.3	2,167.9
Information and communication	146.3	640.3
Public administration, law and justice	10,828.1	9,673.5
Transportation	9,002.0	8,638.9
Water, sanitation and flood protection	4,102.8	4,617.7
Total	58,747.1	43,005.6

IBRD INCOME AND EXPENDITURE
(year ending 30 June; US $ million)

Revenue	2009	2010	2011
Income from loans	3,835	2,493	2,472
Income from investments and securities	603	367	367
Other income	599	1,248	1,431
Total income	5,037	4,108	4,270

Expenditure	2009	2010	2011
Borrowing expenses	2,739	1,750	1,687
Administrative expenses	1,244	1,421	1,457
Contributions to special programmes	197	168	147
Provision for loan losses	284	–32	–45
Other financial expenses	1	1	1
Total	4,465	3,308	3,247
Operating income	572	800	1,023
Effects of adjustment and accounting charge	2,542	–1,877	–93
Net income	3,114	–1,077	930

IBRD LOANS AND IDA CREDITS APPROVED, BY SECTOR AND REGION
(1 July 2010–30 June 2011; US $ million)

Sector	Africa	East Asia and Pacific	South Asia	Europe and Central Asia	Latin America and the Caribbean	Middle East and North Africa	Total
Agriculture, fishing and forestry	843.1	324.5	374.6	121.3	212.8	251.5	2,127.8
Education	497.6	163.7	463.8	220.4	347.6	40.0	1,733.1
Energy and mining	890.1	1,695.2	760.1	1,870.3	591.7	0.0	5,807.4
Finance	106.8	31.7	46.0	380.1	281.9	50.0	896.5
Health and other social services	591.4	289.8	1,298.6	1,203.7	3,088.9	234.3	6,706.7
Industry and trade	432.8	245.6	375.6	253.1	750.5	109.3	2,166.9
Information and communications	259.0	27.9	166.4	27.9	108.7	50.4	640.3
Public administration, law and justice	1,855.6	2,221.0	1,566.6	1,663.1	2,039.1	327.1	9,672.5
Transportation	937.9	1,941.9	3,913.5	242.5	1,119.6	482.5	8,637.9
Water, sanitation and flood protection	645.7	1,055.6	1,164.9	142.4	1,088.4	519.7	4,616.7
Total	7,060.0	7,997.0	10,130.0	6,124.7	9,629.2	2,064.7	43,005.6
of which: IBRD	55.9	6,369.6	3,730.4	5,470.0	9,169.4	1,941.9	26,737.2
IDA	7,004.1	1,627.4	6,399.6	654.7	459.8	122.8	16,268.4

IBRD OPERATIONS AND RESOURCES, 2006–11
(years ending 30 June; US $ million)

	2006/07	2007/08	2008/09	2009/10	2010/11
Loans approved	12,829	13,468	32,911	44,197	26,737
Gross disbursements	11,055	10,490	18,565	28,855	21,879
New medium- to long-term borrowings	10,209	15,526	39,092	31,696	29,722
Net income	–140	1,491	3,114	–1,077	930
Subscribed capital	189,801	189,801	189,918	189,943	193,732
Loans outstanding	97,805	99,050	105,698	120,103	132,459

Source: World Bank, *Annual Report 2011*.

EXECUTIVE DIRECTORS AND THEIR VOTING POWER

(May 2012)

Executive Director	Casting votes of	IBRD Total votes	IBRD % of total	IDA* Total votes	IDA* % of total
Appointed:					
IAN SOLOMON	USA	281,433	16.17	2,270,761	10.45
NOBUMITSU HIYASHI	Japan	165,694	9.52	1,882,463	8.66
INGRID G. HOVEN	Germany	82,700	4.75	1,219,662	5.61
AMBROISE FAYOLLE	France	73,945	4.25	833,247	3.83
SUSANNA MOOREHEAD	United Kingdom	73,945	4.25	1,215,716	5.60
Elected:					
KONSTANTIN HUBER (Austria)	Austria, Belarus†, Belgium, Czech Republic, Hungary, Kosovo, Luxembourg, Slovakia, Slovenia, Turkey	83,746	4.81	1,010,673	4.65
MARTA GARCIA (Spain)	Costa Rica, El Salvador, Guatemala, Honduras, Mexico, Nicaragua, Spain, Venezuela†	76,362	4.39	550,758	2.53
RUUD TREFFERS (Netherlands)	Armenia, Bosnia and Herzegovina, Bulgaria†, Croatia, Cyprus, Georgia, Israel, the former Yugoslav republic of Macedonia, Moldova, Montenegro, Netherlands, Romania†, Ukraine	73,269	4.21	934,771	4.30
MARIE-LUCIE MORIN (Canada)	Antigua and Barbuda†, The Bahamas, Barbados Belize, Canada, Dominica, Grenada, Guyana, Ireland, Jamaica†, Saint Christopher and Nevis, Saint Lucia, Saint Vincent and the Grenadines	70,131	4.03	967,022	4.45
MUKESH N. PRASAD (India)	Bangladesh, Bhutan, India, Sri Lanka	60,702	3.49	920,094	4.23
ROGERIO STUDART (Brazil)	Brazil, Colombia, Dominican Republic, Ecuador, Haiti, Panama, Philippines, Suriname†, Trinidad and Tobago	59,938	3.44	735,146	3.38
ANNA BRANDT (Sweden)	Denmark, Estonia, Finland, Iceland, Latvia, Lithuania, Norway, Sweden	59,697	3.43	1,152,024	5.30
SHAOLIN YANG	People's Republic of China	59,114	3.40	449,652	2.07
JOHN WHITEHEAD (New Zealand)	Australia, Cambodia, Kiribati, Republic of Korea, Marshall Islands, Federated States of Micronesia, Mongolia, New Zealand, Palau, Papua New Guinea, Samoa, Solomon Islands, Tuvalu, Vanuatu	58,060	3.34	860,664	3.96
PIERO CIPOLLONE (Italy)	Albania, Greece, Italy, Malta†, Portugal, San Marino†, Timor-Leste	56,705	3.26	689,313	3.17
JÖRG FRIEDEN (Switzerland)	Azerbaijan, Kazakhstan, Kyrgyzstan, Poland, Serbia, Switzerland, Tajikistan, Turkmenistan†, Uzbekistan	52,427	3.01	995,687	4.58
JAVED TALAT (Pakistan)	Afghanistan, Algeria, Ghana, Iran, Morocco, Pakistan, Tunisia	51,823	2.98	494,576	2.28
MERZA H. HASAN (Kuwait)	Bahrain†, Egypt, Iraq, Jordan, Kuwait, Lebanon, Libya, Maldives, Oman, Qatar†, Syria, United Arab Emirates, Yemen	47,335	2.72	516,226	2.38
VADIM GRISHIN	Russia	45,045	2.59	68,902	0.32
ABDULRAHMAN M. ALMOFADHI	Saudi Arabia	45,045	2.59	696,582	3.21
HEKINUS MANAO (Indonesia)	Brunei†, Fiji, Indonesia, Laos, Malaysia, Myanmar, Nepal, Singapore, Thailand, Tonga, Viet Nam	41,096	2.36	669,560	3.08
FELIX ALBERTO CAMARASA (Argentina)	Argentina, Bolivia, Chile, Paraguay, Peru, Uruguay†	37,499	2.15	331,177	1.52
RENOSI MOKATE (South Africa)	Angola, Nigeria, South Africa	30,322	1.74	224,365	1.03
AGAPITO MENDES DIAS (São Tomé and Príncipe)	Benin, Burkina Faso, Cameroon, Cape Verde, Central African Republic, Chad, Comoros, Democratic Republic of the Congo, Republic of the Congo, Côte d'Ivoire, Djibouti, Equatorial Guinea, Gabon, Guinea-Bissau, Mali, Mauritania, Mauritius, Niger, São Tomé and Príncipe, Senegal, Togo	27,742	1.59	1,024,528	4.72
HASSAN AHMED TAHA (Sudan)	Botswana, Burundi, Eritrea, Ethiopia, The Gambia, Kenya, Lesotho, Liberia, Malawi, Mozambique, Namibia†, Rwanda, Seychelles†, Sierra Leone, Sudan, Swaziland Tanzania, Uganda, Zambia, Zimbabwe	26,943	1.55	1,014,891	4.67

Note: Guinea (1,542 votes in IBRD and 33,987 in IDA), Madagascar (1,672 votes in IBRD and 54,982 in IDA), and Somalia (802 votes in IBRD and 10,506 in IDA) did not participate in the 2010 regular election of Executive Directors; South Sudan (1,687 votes in IBRD and 52,447 in IDA) became a member in April 2012.

* IDA as at 18 April 2012.

† Member of the IBRD only (not IDA).

International Development Association—IDA

Address: 1818 H Street, NW, Washington, DC 20433, USA.

Telephone: (202) 473-1000; **fax:** (202) 477-6391; **internet:** www.worldbank.org/ida.

The International Development Association began operations in November 1960. Affiliated to the IBRD, IDA advances capital to the poorer developing member countries on more flexible terms than those offered by the IBRD.

MEMBERS

IDA has 172 members.

Organization

(June 2012)

Officers and staff of the IBRD serve concurrently as officers and staff of IDA.

President and Chairman of Executive Directors: Dr Jim Yong Kim (USA) (from 1 July 2012).

Activities

IDA assistance is aimed at the poorer developing countries (i.e. those with an annual GNP per capita of less than US $1,175 were to qualify for assistance in 2011/12) in order to support their poverty reduction strategies. Under IDA lending conditions, credits can be extended to countries whose balance of payments could not sustain the burden of repayment required for IBRD loans. Terms are more favourable than those provided by the IBRD; credits are for a period of 35 or 40 years, with a 'grace period' of 10 years, and carry no, or very low, interest and service charges. From 1 July 2011 the maturity of credits was to be 25 or 40 years, with a grace period of five or 10 years. In 2012 81 countries were eligible for IDA assistance, including 10 small-island economies with a GNP per head greater than $1,175, but which would otherwise have little or no access to Bank funds, and 16 so-called 'blend borrowers' which are entitled to borrow from both IDA and the IBRD.

IDA's total development resources, consisting of members' subscriptions and supplementary resources (additional subscriptions and contributions), are replenished periodically by contributions from the more affluent member countries. In December 2007 an agreement was concluded to replenish IDA resources by some US $41,600m., for the period 1 July 2008–30 June 2011, of which $25,100m. was pledged by 45 donor countries. In March 2010 negotiations on the 16th replenishment of IDA funds (IDA16) commenced, in Paris, France. Participants determined that the overarching theme of IDA16 should be achieving development results, and the following areas of focus be 'special themes': gender; climate change; fragile and conflicted affected states; and crisis response. Replenishment meetings were subsequently held in Bamako, Mali, in June, and in Washington, DC, USA, in October. An agreement was concluded in December, at a meeting convened in Brussels, Belgium. The IDA16 replenishment amounted to $49,300m., to cover the period 1 July 2011–30 June 2014, of which $26,400m. was committed by 51 donor countries.

During the year ending 30 June 2011 new IDA commitments amounted to US $16,269m. for 230 projects, compared with $14,550m. for 190 projects in the previous year. Of total IDA assistance during 2010/11 $7,004m. (43%) was for Africa and $6,340m. (39%) for South Asia. In that financial year some 42% of lending was for infrastructure projects (including energy and mining, transportation, water sanitation and flood protection, and information and communications and technologies sectors), 23% for law, justice and public administration and 20% for social sector projects. In August 2010 the World Bank determined to reallocate some $900m. of IDA funding of planned and ongoing projects in order to support emergency relief and reconstruction activities in areas of Pakistan damaged by extensive flooding.

In December 2008 the Bank's Board of Executive Directors approved a new IDA facility, the Financial Crisis Response Fast Track Facility, to accelerate the provision of up to US $2,000m. of IDA15 resources to help the poorest countries to counter the impact of the global economic and financial crisis. The first operations approved under the Facility, in February 2009, were for Armenia (amounting to $35m.) and the Democratic Republic of Congo ($100m.) in support of employment creation and infrastructure development initiatives and meeting the costs of essential services. In December the Board of Executive Directors approved a pilot Crisis Response Window to deploy an additional $1,300m. of IDA funds to support the poorest countries affected by the economic crisis until the end of the IDA15 period (30 June 2011). The new facility was proposed during a mid-term review of IDA15, held in November, with the aim of assisting those countries to maintain spending on sectors critical to achieving the Millennium Development Goals. Permanent funding for the Crisis Response Window, which additionally was to assist low-income countries manage the impact of natural disasters, was agreed as part of the IDA16 replenishment accord in December 2010. In mid-2011 $250m. was allocated from the Crisis Response Window to provide relief and longer-term rehabilitation assistance to areas of the Horn of Africa affected by a severe drought. In September the World Bank announced that $30m. of those funds were to be disbursed through UNHCR in order to improve basic facilities in settlements occupied by persons displaced as a result of the drought. In December the World Bank's Board of Executive Directors approved the establishment of an Immediate Response Mechanism in order to accelerate the provision of assistance to IDA-eligible countries following a natural disaster or economic crisis.

IDA administers a Trust Fund, which was established in November 1996 as part of a World Bank/IMF initiative to assist heavily indebted poor countries (HIPCs). In September 2005 the World Bank's Development Committee and the International Monetary and Financial Committee of the IMF endorsed a proposal of the Group of Eight (G8) industrialized countries to cancel the remaining multilateral debt owed by HIPCs that had reached their completion point under the scheme (see IBRD). In December IDA convened a meeting of donor countries to discuss funding to uphold its financial capability upon its contribution to the so-called Multilateral Debt Relief Initiative (MDRI). IDA's participation in the scheme was approved by the Board of Executive Directors in March 2006 and entered into effect on 1 July. During IDA15 US $6,300m. was allocated to the provision of debt relief under the MDRI, $1,700m. under the HIPC initiative and a further $1,100m. to finance arrears clearance operations. At July 2011 the estimated cost of the HIPC initiative was $76,000m., of which IDA commitments totalled $14,900m.; IDA's contribution to the MDRI was estimated at $35,300m. in nominal value terms (or some 67% of the total cost of the MDRI). By the end of December 2011 32 countries had reached completion point to receive assistance under the initiative.

Publication

Annual Report.

Statistics

IDA OPERATIONS AND RESOURCES, 2007–11
(years ending 30 June; US $ million)

	2006/07	2007/08	2008/09	2009/10	2010/11
Commitments	11,867	11,235	14,041*	14,550	16,269
Disbursements	8,579	9,160	9,219	11,460	10,282
Number of projects	188	199	176	190	230

* Includes an HIPC grant of US $45.5m.
Source: World Bank, *Annual Report 2011*.

International Finance Corporation—IFC

Address: 2121 Pennsylvania Ave, NW, Washington, DC 20433, USA.

Telephone: (202) 473-3800; **fax:** (202) 974-4384; **e-mail:** information@ifc.org; **internet:** www.ifc.org.

IFC was founded in 1956 as a member of the World Bank Group to stimulate economic growth in developing countries by financing private sector investments, mobilizing capital in international financial markets, and providing technical assistance and advice to governments and businesses.

MEMBERS

IFC has 184 members.

Organization

(June 2012)

IFC is a separate legal entity in the World Bank Group. Executive Directors of the World Bank also serve as Directors of IFC. The President of the World Bank is *ex officio* Chairman of the IFC Board of Directors, which has appointed him President of IFC. Subject to his overall supervision, the day-to-day operations of IFC are conducted by its staff under the direction of the Executive Vice-President. The senior management team includes 10 Vice-Presidents responsible for regional and thematic groupings. At the end of June 2011 IFC had 3,354 staff members, of whom 54% were based in field offices in 86 countries.

PRINCIPAL OFFICERS

President: Dr Jim Yong Kim (USA) (from 1 July 2012).

Executive Vice-President: Lars Thunell (Sweden).

REGIONAL AND INDUSTRY DEPARTMENTS

IFC's regional departments cover: sub-Saharan Africa; East Asia and the Pacific; South Asia; Central and Eastern Europe; Southern Europe and Central Asia; Latin America and the Caribbean; and the Middle East and North Africa. They aim to develop strategies for member countries, promote businesses, and strengthen relations with governments and the private sector. The Industry Departments include Agribusiness; Environment and Social Development; Global Capital Markets Development; Global Financial Markets; Global Information and Communications Technologies (jointly managed with the World Bank); Global Manufacturing and Services; Health and Education; Infrastructure; Oil, Gas, Mining and Chemicals (jointly managed with the World Bank); Private Equity and Investment Funds; and Syndication and Resource Mobilization.

REGIONAL AND RESIDENT MISSIONS

There are Regional and Resident Missions in Australia, Bangladesh, Brazil, Cambodia, People's Republic of China, Dominican Republic, Egypt, Guyana, Haiti, India, Kazakhstan, Laos, Liberia, Mongolia, Russia, Serbia, South Africa, Sri Lanka, Trinidad and Tobago, Turkey, United Arab Emirates and Viet Nam. There are also Special Representatives in France, Germany and the United Kingdom (for Europe), an office in Tokyo, Japan, and other programme co-ordinators, managers and investment officers in more than 50 additional countries.

Activities

IFC aims to promote economic development in developing member countries by assisting the growth of private enterprise and effective capital markets. It finances private sector projects, through loans, the purchase of equity, quasi-equity products, and risk management services, and assists governments to create conditions that stimulate the flow of domestic and foreign private savings and investment. IFC may provide finance for a project that is partly state-owned, provided that there is participation by the private sector and that the project is operated on a commercial basis. IFC also mobilizes additional resources from other financial institutions, in particular through syndicated loans, thus providing access to international capital markets. IFC provides a range of advisory services to help to improve the investment climate in developing countries and offers technical assistance to private enterprises and governments. In 2008 IFC formulated a policy document to help to increase its impact in the three-year period 2009–11. The IFC Road Map identified five strategic 'pillars' as priority areas of activity: strengthening the focus on frontier markets (i.e. the lowest-income countries or regions of middle-income countries, those affected by conflict, or underdeveloped industrial sectors); building long-term partnerships with emerging 'players' in developing countries; addressing climate change and securing environmental and social sustainability; promoting private sector growth in infrastructure, health and education; and developing local financial markets. From late 2008 IFC's overriding concern was to respond effectively to the difficulties facing member countries affected by the global economic and financial crisis and to maintain a sustainable level of development. In particular it aimed to preserve and create employment opportunities, to support supply chains for local businesses, and to provide credit.

To be eligible for financing projects must be profitable for investors, as well as financially and economically viable; must benefit the economy of the country concerned; and must comply with IFC's environmental and social guidelines. IFC aims to promote best corporate governance and management methods and sustainable business practices, and encourages partnerships between governments, non-governmental organizations and community groups. In 2001/02 IFC developed a Sustainability Framework to help to assess the longer-term economic, environmental and social impact of projects. The first Sustainability Review was published in mid-2002. In 2002/03 IFC assisted 10 international banks to draft a voluntary set of guidelines (the Equator Principles), based on IFC's environmental, social and safeguard monitoring policies, to be applied to their global project finance activities. In September 2009 IFC initiated a Performance Standards Review Process to define new standards to be applied within the Equator Principles framework. At

January 2012 73 financial institutions had signed up to the Equator Principles.

In November 2004 IFC announced the establishment of a Global Trade Finance Programme (GTFP), with initial funding of some US $500m., which aimed to support small-scale importers and exporters in emerging markets, and to facilitate South–South trade in goods and services, by providing guarantees for trade transactions, as well as extending technical assistance and training to local financial institutions. Additional funding of $500m. was approved in January 2007, and in October 2008, by which time there were 147 confirming banks from 70 countries participating in the initiative and 126 issuing banks in 66 countries. In December, as part of a set of measures to support the global economy, the Board of Directors approved an expansion of the GTFP, doubling its funding to $3,000m. Other initiatives included the establishment of an Infrastructure Crisis Facility to provide investment for existing projects affected by a lack of private funding, and a new Bank Capitalization Fund (to be financed, up to $3,000m., with the Japan Bank for International Co-operation) to provide investment and advisory services to banks in emerging markets. In May 2009 IFC established an Asset Management Company, as a wholly owned subsidiary, to administer the Capitalization Fund. In February of that year IFC inaugurated a Microfinance Enhancement Facility, with a German development bank, to extend credit to microfinancing institutions and to support lending to low-income borrowers, with funds of up to $500m. IFC committed $1,000m. in funds to a new Global Trade Liquidity Program (GTLP), which was inaugurated by the World Bank Group in April, with the aim of mobilizing support of up to $50,000m. in trade transactions through financing extended by governments, other development banks and the private sector. In October IFC established a Debt and Asset Recovery Program to help to restore stability and growth by facilitating loan restructuring for businesses and by investing in funds targeting distressed assets and companies. IFC pledged to contribute $1,550m. to the Program over a three-year period, and aimed to mobilize resources through partnerships with other international financial institutions and private sector companies.

IFC's authorized capital is US $2,450m. At 30 June 2011 paid-in capital was $2,369m. The World Bank was originally the principal source of borrowed funds, but IFC also borrows from private capital markets. IFC's net income amounted to $1,579m. (after a $600m. grant transfer to IDA), compared with $1,746m. in 2009/10 (after a $600m. transfer to IDA). In December 2008 the Board of Directors approved a Sovereign Funds Initiative to enable IFC to raise and manage commercial capital from sovereign funds. In July 2010 the Board of Directors recommended a special capital increase of $130m., to raise authorized capital to $2,580m. The increase required the approval of the Board of Governors.

In the year ending 30 June 2011 project financing approved by IFC amounted to US $18,660m. for 518 projects in 102 countries (compared with $18,041 for 528 projects in the previous year). Of the total approved in 2010/11, $12,186m. was for IFC's own account, while $6,474m. was in the form of loan syndications and parallel loans, underwriting of securities issues and investment funds and funds mobilized by the IFC Asset Management Company. Generally, IFC limits its financing to less than 25% of the total cost of a project, but may take up to a 35% stake in a venture (although never as a majority shareholder). Disbursements for IFC's account amounted to $6,715m. in 2010/11.

In 2010/11 the largest proportion of investment commitments, for IFC's account, was allocated to Europe and Central Asia (26%); Latin America and the Caribbean received 24%, sub-Saharan Africa and East Asia and the Pacific each received 14%, the Middle East and North Africa received 11%, and South Asia 10%. In that year 33% of total financing committed was for global financial markets. Other commitments included infrastructure (17%) and manufacturing (12%).

IFC's Advisory Services are a major part of the organization's involvement with member countries to support the development of private enterprises and efforts to generate funding, as well as to enhance private sector participation in developing infrastructure. Advisory services cover the following five main areas of expertise: the business enabling environment (i.e improving the investment climate in a country); access to financing (including developing financing institutions, improving financial infrastructure and strengthening regulatory frameworks); infrastructure (mainly encouraging private sector participation); environment and social sustainability; and corporate advice (in particular in support of small and medium-sized enterprises—SMEs). In December 2008 the Board of Directors determined to provide additional funding to IFC advisory services in order to strengthen the capacity of financial institutions and governments to respond to the crisis in the global financial markets. At 30 June 2011 there were 642 active Advisory Service projects with a value of US $820m. Total expenditure on Advisory Services during that year amounted to $206.7m. IFC manages, jointly financed with the World Bank and MIGA, the Foreign Investment Advisory Service (FIAS), which provides technical assistance and advice on promoting foreign investment and strengthening the country's investment framework at the request of governments. Under the Technical Assistance Trust Funds Program (TATF), established in 1988, IFC manages resources contributed by various governments and agencies to provide finance for feasibility studies, project identification studies and other types of technical assistance relating to project preparation. In 2004 a Grassroots Business Initiative was established, with external donor funding, to support businesses that provide economic opportunities for disadvantaged communities in Africa, Latin America, and South and Southeast Asia. Since 2002 IFC has administered an online SME Toolkit to enhance the accessibility of business training and advice. By 2011 the service was available in 16 languages.

Since 2004 IFC has presented an annual Client Leadership Award to a chosen corporate client who most represents IFC values in innovation, operational excellence and corporate governance.

Publications

Annual Report.

Doing Business (annually).

Emerging Stock Markets Factbook (annually).

Lessons of Experience (series).

Outcomes (quarterly).

Results on the Ground (series).

Review of Small Businesses (annually).

Sustainability Report (annually).

Other handbooks, discussion papers, technical documents, policy toolkits, public policy journals.

Statistics

IFC OPERATIONS AND RESOURCES, 2009–11

(fiscal years ending 30 June; US $ million, unless otherwise stated)

	2009	2010	2011
Approved investments			
Number of new projects	447	528	518
Total investment programme*	14,509	18,042	18,660
Commitments for IFC's own account	10,547	12,664	12,186
Disbursements			
Total financing disbursed	7,598	9,648	8,744
For IFC's own account	5,640	6,793	6,715
Resources and income			
Borrowings	25,711	31,106	38,211
Paid-in capital	2,369	2,369	2,369
Retained earnings	13,042	14,788	16,367
Net income	–151	1,746	1,579

* Including parallel loans, structured finance, other mobilization and IFC initiatives, and IFC Asset Management Company.

Source: IFC, *Annual Report 2011*.

Multilateral Investment Guarantee Agency—MIGA

Address: 1818 H Street, NW, Washington, DC 20433, USA.

Telephone: (202) 473-6163; **fax:** (202) 522-2630; **internet:** www.miga.org.

MIGA was founded in 1988 as an affiliate of the World Bank. Its mandate is to encourage the flow of foreign direct investment to, and among, developing member countries, through the provision of political risk insurance and investment marketing services to foreign investors and host governments, respectively.

MEMBERS

MIGA has 177 member countries. Membership is open to all countries that are members of the World Bank.

Organization

(June 2012)

MIGA is legally and financially separate from the World Bank. It is supervised by a Council of Governors (comprising one Governor and one Alternate of each member country) and an elected Board of Directors (of no less than 12 members).

President: Dr Jim Yong Kim (USA) (from 1 July 2012).

Executive Vice-President: Izumi Kobayashi (Japan).

Activities

The convention establishing MIGA took effect in April 1988. Authorized capital was US $1,082m., although the convention provided for an increase of capital stock upon the admission of new members. In April 1998 the Board of Directors approved an increase in MIGA's capital base. A grant of $150m. was transferred from the IBRD as part of the package, while the capital increase (totalling $700m. callable capital and $150m. paid-in capital) was approved by MIGA's Council of Governors in April 1999. A three-year subscription period then commenced, covering the period April 1999–March 2002 (later extended to March 2003). At 30 June 2011 110 countries had subscribed $749.9m. of the general capital increase. At that time total subscriptions to the capital stock amounted to $1,912.8m., of which $364.9m. was paid-in.

MIGA guarantees eligible investments against losses resulting from non-commercial risks, under the following main categories:

(i) transfer risk resulting from host government restrictions on currency conversion and transfer;

(ii) risk of loss resulting from legislative or administrative actions of the host government;

(iii) repudiation by the host government of contracts with investors in cases in which the investor has no access to a competent forum;

(iv) the risk of armed conflict and civil unrest;

(v) risk of a sovereign not honouring a financial obligation or guarantee.

Before guaranteeing any investment, MIGA must ensure that it is commercially viable, contributes to the development process and is not harmful to the environment. During the fiscal year 1998/99 MIGA and IFC appointed the first Compliance Advisor and Ombudsman to consider the concerns of local communities directly affected by MIGA- or IFC-sponsored projects. In February 1999 the Board of Directors approved an increase in the amount of political risk insurance available for each project, from US $75m. to $200m. During 2003/04 MIGA established a new fund, the Invest-in-Development Facility, to enhance the role of foreign investment in attaining the Millennium Development Goals. In 2005/06 MIGA supported for the first time a project aimed at selling carbon credits gained by reducing greenhouse gas emissions; it provided US $2m. in guarantee coverage to the El Salvador-based initiative. In April 2009 the Board of Directors approved modifications to MIGA's policies and operational regulations in order to enhance operational flexibility and efficiency, in particular in the poorest countries and those affected by conflict. In November 2010 the Council of Governors approved amendments to MIGA's convention (the first since 1988) to broaden the eligibility for investment projects and to enhance the effectiveness of MIGA's development impact.

During the year ending 30 June 2011 MIGA issued 50 investment insurance contracts for 38 projects with a value of US $2,100m. (compared with 28 contracts amounting to $1,500m. in 2009/10). Since 1990 the total investment guarantees issued amounted to some $24,500m., through 1,030 contracts in support of 651 projects.

MIGA works with local insurers, export credit agencies, development finance institutions and other organizations to promote insurance in a country, to ensure a level of consistency among insurers and to support capacity-building within the insurance industry. MIGA also offers investment marketing services to help to promote foreign direct investment in developing countries and in transitional economies, and to disseminate information on investment opportunities. MIGA maintains an internet service (www.pri-center.com), providing access to political risk management and insurance resources, in order to support those objectives. In early 2007 MIGA's technical assistance services were amalgamated into the Foreign Advisory Investment Service (FIAS, see IFC), of which MIGA became a lead partner, along with IFC and the World Bank. During 2000/01 an office was established in Paris, France, to promote and co-ordinate European investment in developing countries, in particular in Africa and Eastern Europe. In March 2002 MIGA opened a regional office, based in Johannesburg, South Africa. In September a new regional office was inaugurated in Singapore, in order to facilitate foreign investment in Asia. A Regional Director for Asia and the Pacific was appointed, for the first time, in August 2010 to head a new Asian Hub, operating from offices in Singapore, Hong Kong SAR and the People's Republic of China.

In July 2004 an Afghanistan Investment Guarantee Facility, to be administered by MIGA, became operational to provide political risk guarantees for foreign investors in that country.

In November 2008 a West Bank and Gaza Investment Guarantee Trust Fund was inaugurated to encourage greater private sector investment in those territories. The new fund, co-sponsored by the European Investment Bank, the Japanese Government and the Palestinian (National) Authority, was to be administered by MIGA.

In April 2009 MIGA announced a new initiative to support financial institutions affected by the global economic crisis through broadened political risk guarantees for liquidity support or recapitalization of their banking subsidiaries. Some €3,000m. was allocated to finance investments in Europe and Central Asia.

Publications

Annual Report.

MIGA News (online newsletter; every 2 months).

World Investment and Political Risk (annually).

Other guides, brochures and regional briefs.

International Civil Aviation Organization—ICAO

Address: 999 University St, Montréal, QC H3C 5H7, Canada.
Telephone: (514) 954-8219; **fax:** (514) 954-6077; **e-mail:** icaohq@icao.int; **internet:** www.icao.int.

The Convention on International Civil Aviation was signed in Chicago in 1944. As a result, ICAO was founded in 1947 to develop the techniques of international air navigation and to help in the planning and improvement of international air transport.

MEMBERS

ICAO has 191 contracting states.

Organization

(June 2012)

ASSEMBLY

Composed of representatives of all member states, the Assembly is the organization's legislative body and meets at least once every three years. It reviews the work of the organization, sets out the work programme for the next three years, approves the budget and determines members' contributions. The 37th Assembly took place in September–October 2010.

COUNCIL

Composed of representatives of 36 member states, elected by the Assembly. It is the executive body, and establishes and supervises subsidiary technical committees and makes recommendations to member governments; meets in virtually continuous session; elects the President, appoints the Secretary-General, and administers the finances of the organization. The Council is assisted by the Air Navigation Commission, the Air Transport Committee, the Committee on Joint Support of Air Navigation Services, the Finance Committee, the Committee on Unlawful Interference and the Technical Co-operation Committee. The functions of the Council are:

(i) to adopt international standards and recommended practices and incorporate them as annexes to the Chicago Convention on International Civil Aviation;

(ii) to arbitrate between member states on matters concerning aviation and implementation of the Convention;

(iii) to investigate any situation which presents avoidable obstacles to development of international air navigation;

(iv) to take whatever steps are necessary to maintain safety and regularity of operation of international air transport;

(v) to provide technical assistance to the developing countries under the UN Development Programme and other assistance programmes.

President of the Council: Roberto Kobeh González (Mexico).

SECRETARIAT

The Secretariat, headed by a Secretary-General, is divided into five main divisions: the Air Navigation Bureau, the Air Transport Bureau, the Technical Co-operation Bureau, the Legal Bureau, and the Bureau of Administration and Services.

Secretary-General: Raymond Benjamin (France).

REGIONAL OFFICES

Asia and Pacific: 252/1 Vibhavadi-Rangsit Rd, Ladyao, Chatuchak, Bangkok 10900, Thailand; tel. (2) 537-8189; fax (2) 537-8199; e-mail apac@icao.int; internet www.bangkok.icao.int; Regional Dir Mokhtar Ahmed Awan.

Eastern and Southern Africa: Limuru Rd, Gigiri, POB 46294, Nairobi, Kenya; tel. (20) 7622395; fax (20) 7623028; e-mail icao@icao.unon.org; internet www.icao.int/esaf; Regional Dir Meshesha Belayneh.

European and North Atlantic: 3 bis Villa Émile-Bergerat, 92522 Neuilly-sur-Seine Cédex, France; tel. 1-46-41-85-85; fax 1-46-41-85-00; e-mail icaoeurnat@paris.icao.int; internet www.paris.icao.int; f. 1944; Regional Dir Luis Fonseca de Almeida.

Middle East: POB 85, Cairo Airport Post Office Terminal One, Cairo 11776, Egypt; tel. (2) 267-4840; fax (2) 267-4843; e-mail icaomid@cairo.icao.int; internet www.icao.int/mid; Regional Dir Mohamed R. M. Khonji.

North America, Central America and the Caribbean: Apdo Postal 5-377, CP 06500, México, DF, Mexico; tel. (55) 5250-3211; fax (55) 5203-2757; e-mail icao_nacc@mexico.icao.int; internet www.mexico.icao.int; Regional Dir L. J. Martin.

South America: ave Víctor Andrés Belaúnde 147, San Isidro, Lima, Peru; tel. (1) 611-8686; fax (1) 611-8689; e-mail mail@lima.icao.int; internet www.lima.icao.int; Regional Dir José Miguel Ceppi.

Western and Central Africa: 15 blvd de la République, BP 2356, Dakar, Senegal; tel. 839-9393; fax 823-6926; e-mail icaowacaf@dakar.icao.int; internet www.icao.int/wacaf; Regional Dir Mam Sait Jallow.

Activities

ICAO aims to ensure the safe and orderly growth of civil aviation; to encourage skills in aircraft design and operation; to improve airways, airports and air navigation; to prevent the waste of resources in unreasonable competition; to safeguard the rights of each contracting party to operate international air transport; and to prevent discriminatory practices. ICAO collects and publishes statistics relating to civil aviation. In October 2010 the Council adopted an ICAO Framework, detailing the following as strategic objectives for the period 2011–13: to enhance global civil aviation safety; to enhance global civil aviation security; and to foster the harmonized and economically viable development of international civil aviation in a manner that does not impact unduly on the environment. ICAO's first, second and third business plans, covering 2005–07, 2008–10, and 2011–13, respectively, placed a growing emphasis on performance planning and results-based management.

SAFETY

ICAO aims to ensure and enhance all aspects of air safety and security. A Global Aviation Safety Plan (GASP) was initiated in 1998 to promote safety measures. ICAO assists member countries to develop appropriate educational and training activities. It also supports programmes to assist the victims of aircraft accidents. A Universal Safety Oversight Audit Programme (USOAP) became operational on 1 January 1999, providing for mandatory, systematic and harmonized safety audits regularly to be undertaken in member states in fields including the airworthiness of aircraft, flight operations and personnel licensing, with results to be compiled in an Audit Findings and Differences Database. In October 2001 the Assembly approved the concept of an International Financial Facility for Aviation Safety (IFFAS) to provide funds to states to adhere to ICAO safety-related standards. The Facility became effective in 2003. In October 2004 the Assembly recognized the USOAP as having significantly contributed to raising the level of safety oversight world-wide and endorsed its expansion, from 1 January 2005, to incorporate, in a new comprehensive systems approach (CSA), all safety-related provisions of the annexes to the Chicago Convention; by the end of 2011 ICAO had completed 180 CSA audits, and four further audits were to be undertaken during 2012. The October 2004 Assembly also requested ICAO to accelerate the development of standards and guidance under its programme for the prevention of Controlled Flight Into Terrain accidents; urged contracting states strictly to control the movement and storage of man-portable defence systems; and resolved to review standards relating to the health of passengers and crews, as an integral element of safe air travel. In late 2005, following a series of aircraft accidents, ICAO determined to convene a meeting of Directors-General of Civil Aviation in order to assess the status of aviation safety, to identify ways to achieve improvements in safety standards, and to develop a new framework of safety measures. The conference, convened in March 2006, endorsed a Global Strategy for Aviation Safety. The declaration issued at the meeting stipulated that, *inter alia,* provisions should be implemented for safety-related information, including results of audits within the USOAP, to be shared among states, the public and other interested parties. Also at the March 2006 conference, the Directors-General endorsed Part I of a Global Aviation Safety Roadmap, delivered to ICAO in December of 2005 by the Industry Safety Strategy Group. The Roadmap identified mid- and long-term goals related to air-safety oversight and regulation matters. In December 2006 Part II of the Roadmap was finalized, outlining strategies for achieving these objectives. An updated GASP, based on the Roadmap, was published in June 2007, and in 2011 the GASP was enhanced further. In September 2007 the Assembly endorsed a new Comprehensive Regional Implementation Plan for Aviation Safety in Africa, which had been formulated by African governments, with representatives of the local civil aviation authorities and air industry. In September 2010 ICAO, the EU, the US Department of Transportation, and the International Air Transport Association, formally approved the establishment of a new Global Safety Information Exchange (GSIE), with the aim of improving the overall level of international aviation safety.

In December 2011 ICAO released the first *State of Global Aviation Safety* report, addressing global aviation safety performance. The report envisaged that the volume of scheduled aviation traffic world-wide, which had reached a record 30.5m. departures in 2010, would rise to 52m. annually by 2030.

ICAO maintains a Flight Safety Information Exchange (FSIX) website at www.icao.int/fsix/safety.cfm, to help to disseminate safety-related information, including safety and security audits, within the aviation community. The main subject areas cover safety oversight information, resolving safety deficiencies, regional regulations and safety management. It was announced in July 2008 that all states audited under the USOAP had given consent for ICAO to publish the audit findings on the FSIX website, in accordance with the outcome of the March 2006 conference of Directors-General of Civil Aviation.

In April 2010, in view of the eruption of the Eyjafjallajökull volcano, in Iceland, ICAO established the ICAO European and North Atlantic Volcanic Ash Task Force (EUR/NAT VATF), to establish a co-ordinated region-wide operational approach to volcanic ash emergencies. In the following month the Task Force agreed a common working agenda to improve contingency plans for preventing accidents in the wake of any future eruption, as well as minimizing disruptions of service and severe economic impact on the airline industry. In March 2012 ICAO issued a manual entitled *Flight Safety and Volcanic Ash*, which was based on the work of the Task Force, and aimed to provide air transport operators with a scientific basis for future post-volcanic eruption decision making.

SECURITY

In October 1998 a protocol to the Chicago Convention, prohibiting the use of weapons against civil aircraft in flight, entered into effect, having been adopted in 1984 following an attack on a Korean Airlines passenger flight. In 2000 ICAO developed model legislation to cover offences committed on board aircraft by unruly passengers (other than hijacking, sabotage etc., which are already governed by international legislation). Following the terrorist attacks perpetrated against targets in the USA in September 2001, involving the use of hijacked aircraft as weapons, the 33rd Assembly—held in September–October—adopted a Declaration on the Misuse of Civil Aircraft as Weapons of Destruction and Other Terrorist Acts involving Civil Aviation. The Declaration urged a review of ICAO's aviation security programme and consideration of the initiation of a programme to audit airport security arrangements and member states' civil aviation security programmes. In October the Council established a Special Group on Aviation War Risk Insurance to make recommendations on the development of a co-ordinated and long-term approach in this area. A proposal by the Special Group concerning the establishment of a Global Scheme on Aviation War Risk Insurance (Globaltime), to be provided by a non-profit entity with initial multilateral government support, was approved in principle by the Council in May 2002. A high-level ministerial conference, convened under ICAO auspices in February of that year to discuss preventing, combating and eradicating acts of terrorism involving civil aviation, and strengthening the organization's role in overseeing the adoption and national implementation of security-related standards and procedures, endorsed a global Aviation Security Plan of Action and reaffirmed the responsibility of states to ensure aviation security on their territories. The Plan provided for development of an effective global response to emerging threats; strengthened security-related provisions of the Convention on International Civil Aviation; and enhanced co-ordination of regional and sub-regional audit programmes. In June a Universal Security Audit Programme was launched, as part of the Aviation Security Plan of Action, to help to identify and correct deficiencies in the implementation of security-related standards. The first round of security audits of all contracting states was completed by the end of 2007, and a second cycle of audits was being implemented during 2008–13. A new Implementation Support and Development Branch was established in June 2007 to support member states with significant safety oversight or security deficiencies and to help to implement correction action plans. In September 2010 the Diplomatic Conference on Aviation Security, convened under ICAO auspices in Beijing, People's Republic of China, adopted two new international legal instruments: the Convention on the Suppression of Unlawful Acts Relating to International Civil Aviation, and the Protocol Supplementary to the Convention for the Suppression of Unlawful Seizure of Aircraft. In October 2010 the Assembly adopted the ICAO Declaration on Aviation Security, which included a roadmap aimed at further protecting global air transport from terrorist and other security threats, through the development of security screening procedures and increased capacity-building assistance. In the following month the Chicago Convention annex on security was amended to enhance air cargo security standards.

ICAO convened regional security conferences in New Delhi, India in September 2011; Dakar, Senegal, in October 2011; Moscow, Russia, in November 2011; Kuala Lumpur, Malaysia, in January 2012; Caracas, Venezuela, in February 2012; and Manama, Bahrain, in April 2012, under a process that was to culminate in a high-level global security conference, to be held in Montréal in September.

ICAO is developing a globally inter-operable system of Machine Readable Travel Documents (MRTDs), incorporating biometric identification data, in order to enhance airport and international security, and has provided technical assistance to support the efforts of contracting states to develop MRTDs. ICAO's objective that all states issue machine readable passports by 1 April 2010 was not universally met. The Organization has specified 24 November 2015 as the obligatory deadline for universal machine readable compliance, by which time non machine readable documents are to be phased out.

NAVIGATION

ICAO's Air Navigation Bureau develops technical studies for the Air Navigation Commission, as well as recommendations for standards and recommended practices relating to the safety, regularity and efficiency of international air navigation. Areas of activity include meteorology, automated data interchange systems, accident investigation and prevention, aviation medicine and air traffic management. In March 1998 the ICAO Council adopted a Global Air Navigation Plan for Communications, Navigation, Surveillance, and Air Traffic Management (CNS/ATM) Systems. In May an international conference was held in Rio de Janeiro, Brazil, to consider implementation of the CNS/ATM systems. The conference urged greater financing and co-operation between states to ensure that the CNS/ATM becomes the basis of a global ATM system. An Air Traffic Management Operational Concept Panel, which was to develop standards and recommend procedures for the development of an integrated ATM system, was convened for the first time in March–April 1999. In October 1998 the Assembly adopted a Charter on the Rights and Obligations of States relating to Global Navigation Satellite Systems (GNSS) to serve as an interim framework on the GNSS. A long-term legal framework on principles governing the GNSS, including a new international convention, remains under consideration. The 11th Air Navigation Conference, convened by ICAO in September–October 2003, in Montréal, endorsed an operational concept for a globally harmonized air navigation system that aimed to enhance safety and reduce airspace and airport congestion. In 2005 ICAO assisted countries and international organizations to develop preparedness strategies with regard to the threat of a pandemic of highly pathogenic avian influenza. In 2010 some 171 bilateral 'open skies' air services agreements, involving 103 states, were in force, as well as at least 15 liberalized agreements or arrangements at regional level. In April 2009 ICAO and major global aviation stakeholders adopted a declaration calling for the rapid implementation of Performance-based Navigation (PBN), a new air navigation concept setting clear performance targets for specific flight operations, and emphasizing the use of accurate satellite-based navigation aids, with the aim of contributing further to improving the safety, efficiency and sustainability of the global air transport system; all of the ICAO Regional Offices have established PBN task forces, which, with a global PBN Task Force, support countries' implementation of PBN.

ENVIRONMENTAL PROTECTION

ICAO activities with respect to the environment are primarily focused on areas that require a co-ordinated international approach, i.e. aircraft noise and engine emissions. International standards and guidelines for noise certification of aircraft and international provisions for the regulation of aircraft engine emissions have been adopted and published in Annex 16 to the Chicago Convention. ICAO provides briefings and written submissions to meetings of the parties to the United Nations Framework Convention on Climate Change (UNFCCC), having been recognized in the 1997 Kyoto Protocol to the UNFCCC as the global body through which industrialized nations were to pursue the limitation or reduction of so-called greenhouse gas emissions from international aviation. In 1998 ICAO's Committee on Aviation Environmental Protection (CAEP) recommended a reduction of 16% in the permissible levels of nitrogen oxides emitted by aircraft engines. The new limits, to be applicable to new engine designs from 2003, were adopted by the ICAO Council in early 1999. Further reduced limits were approved in 2004. In June 2001 the Council adopted a stricter noise standard (applicable from 1 January 2006) for jet and large propeller-driven aircraft, as well as new noise limits for helicopters and new provisions concerning re-certification. In October the Assembly approved a series of measures developed by the Committee concerning a balanced approach to aircraft noise and based on the following elements: quieter aircraft; land-use planning and management in the vicinity of airports; operational procedures for noise abatement; and operating restrictions. In 2008 the CAEP launched a series of Independent Expert (IE) reviews to establish technology and operational mid-term (i.e. 10-year) and long-term (20-year) objectives for progress in the reduction of noise, fuel burn and the emission of nitrogen oxides.

In September 2007 the ICAO Council determined to establish a new Group on International Aviation and Climate Change (GIACC), comprising senior government officials, in order to formulate an 'aggressive' programme of action on aviation and climate change, with a framework to help to achieve emissions reductions, for example through fuel efficiency targets and other voluntary measures. The GIACC held its inaugural meeting in February 2008. ICAO's first Environmental Report was published in September 2007, covering technical and policy aspects of aviation's impact on the environment. In October 2010 the 37th session of the ICAO Assembly adopted a resolution aimed at reducing the impact of aviation emissions on climate change, and providing a roadmap for action until 2050.

In June 2008 an online ICAO Carbon Emissions Calculator was launched, a methodology for estimating the carbon dioxide emissions from air travel for use in devising carbon footprint offset programmes.

ICAO SPECIFICATIONS

These are contained in annexes to the Chicago Convention, and in three sets of Procedures for Air Navigation Services (PANS Documents). The specifications are periodically revised in keeping with developments in technology and changing requirements. The 18 annexes to the Convention include personnel licensing, rules relating to the conduct of flights, meteorological services, aeronautical charts, air–ground communications, safety specifications, identification, air traffic control, rescue services, environmental protection, security and the transporting of dangerous goods. Technical Manuals and Circulars are issued to facilitate implementation.

TECHNICAL CO-OPERATION

ICAO's Technical Co-operation Bureau promotes the implementation of ICAO Standards and Recommended Practices, including the CNS/ATM (see above) and safety oversight measures, and assists developing countries in the execution of various projects, financed by UNDP and other sources. The TRAINAIR programme helps relevant institutions to develop a standard aviation training package, and promotes international co-operation in training and course development.

ICAO works in close co-operation with other UN bodies, such as the World Meteorological Organization, the UNFCCC, the International Telecommunication Union, the Universal Postal Union, the World Health Organization (WHO) and the International Maritime Organization. Non-governmental organizations which also participate in ICAO's work include the International Air Transport Association, the Airports Council International, the International Federation of Air Line Pilots' Associations, and the International Council of Aircraft Owner and Pilot Associations. In June 2003 ICAO published measures for preventing the spread by air travel of Severe Acute Respiratory Syndrome (SARS) and other contagious diseases, based on guidelines issued by WHO, and in 2009 ICAO supported member states in developing effective, globally harmonized national aviation contingency plans aimed at controlling the spread of pandemic (H1N1) 2009 (swine flu).

Finance

ICAO is financed mainly by contributions from member states. The authorized budget for the triennium 2011–13 totalled US 273.1m. (allocated as follows: $87.6m. in 2011, $90.2m. in 2012, and $95.3m. in 2013).

Publications

Annual Report of the Council.

Aviation Training Directory.

Directory of National Civil Aviation Administrations (online database).

ICAO Environmental Report.

ICAO Journal (6 a year, in English, French and Spanish).

State of Global Aviation Safety.

World of Civil Aviation.

Conventions, agreements, rules of procedures, regulations, technical publications and manuals.

International Fund for Agricultural Development—IFAD

Address: Via Paolo di Dono 44, 00142 Rome, Italy.

Telephone: (06) 54591; **fax:** (06) 5043463; **e-mail:** ifad@ifad.org; **internet:** www.ifad.org.

IFAD was established in 1977, following a decision by the 1974 UN World Food Conference, with a mandate to combat hunger and eradicate poverty on a sustainable basis in the low-income, food-deficit regions of the world. Funding operations began in January 1978.

MEMBERS

IFAD has 168 members.

Organization

(June 2012)

GOVERNING COUNCIL

Each member state is represented in the Governing Council (the Fund's highest authority) by a Governor and an Alternate. Sessions are held annually with special sessions as required. The Governing Council elects the President of the Fund (who also chairs the Executive Board) by a two-thirds majority for a four-year term. The President is eligible for re-election.

EXECUTIVE BOARD

Consists of 18 members and 18 alternates, elected by the Governing Council, who serve for three years. The Executive Board is responsible for the conduct and general operation of IFAD and approves loans and grants for projects; it holds three regular sessions each year. An independent Office of Evaluation reports directly to the Board.

The governance structure of the Fund is based on the classification of members. Membership of the Executive Board is distributed as follows: eight List A countries (i.e. industrialized donor countries), four List B (petroleum-exporting developing donor countries), and six List C (recipient developing countries), divided equally among the three Sub-List C categories (i.e. for Africa, Europe, Asia and the Pacific, and Latin America and the Caribbean).

President and Chairman of Executive Board: KANAYO F. NWANZE (Nigeria).

Vice-President: YUKIKO OMURA (Japan).

DEPARTMENTS

IFAD has three main administrative departments, each headed by an Assistant President: Finance and Administration; Programme Management (with five regional Divisions and a Technical Advisory Division); and External Affairs (including a Policy Division, Communication Division and a Resource Mobilization Unit). Offices of the General Counsel and of Internal Audit report to the Office of the President and Vice-President.

Activities

IFAD provides financing primarily for projects designed to improve food production systems in developing member states and to strengthen related policies, services and institutions. In allocating resources IFAD is guided by: the need to increase food production in the poorest food-deficit countries; the potential for increasing food production in other developing countries; and the importance of improving the nutrition, health and education of the poorest people in developing countries, i.e. small-scale farmers, artisanal fishermen, nomadic pastoralists, indigenous populations, rural women, and the rural landless. All projects emphasize the participation of beneficiaries in development initiatives, both at the local and national level. Issues relating to gender and household food security are incorporated into all aspects of its activities. IFAD is committed to achieving the Millennium Development Goals (MDGs), pledged by governments attending a special session of the UN General Assembly in September 2000, and, in particular, the objective to reduce by 50% the proportion of people living in extreme poverty by 2015. In 2001 the Fund introduced new measures to improve monitoring and impact evaluation, in particular to assess its contribution to achieving the MDGs.

In May 2011 the Executive Board adopted IFAD's Strategic Framework for 2011–15, in which it reiterated its commitment to improving rural food security and nutrition, and enabling the rural poor to overcome their poverty. The 2011–15 Strategic Framework was underpinned by five strategic objectives: developing a natural resource and economic asset base for poor rural communities, with improved resilience to climate change, environmental degradation and market transformation; facilitating access for the rural poor to services aimed at reducing poverty, improving nutrition, raising incomes and building resilience in a changing environment; supporting the rural poor in managing profitable, sustainable and resilient farm and non-farm enterprises and benefiting from decent employment opportunities; enabling the rural poor to influence policies and institutions that affect their livelihoods; and enabling institutional and policy environments that support agricultural production and the related non-farm activities.

From 2009 IFAD implemented a new business model, with the direct supervision of projects, and maintaining a stable presence in countries of operations, as its two main pillars. Consequently, by 2011 the Fund was directly supervising some 93% of the projects it was funding, compared with 18% in 2007.

IFAD is a participant in the High Level Task Force (HLTF) on the Global Food Security Crisis, which was established by the UN Secretary-General in April 2008 and aims to address the impact of soaring global levels of food and fuel prices and to formulate a comprehensive framework for action. In June IFAD participated in the High-Level Conference on World Food Security and the Challenges of Climate Change and Bioenergy, convened by FAO in Rome, Italy. The meeting adopted a Declaration on Food Security, which noted an urgent need to develop the agricultural sectors and expand food production in developing countries and countries with economies in transition, and for increased investment in rural development, agriculture and agribusiness. In January 2009 the HLTF participated in a follow-up high level meeting convened in Madrid, Spain, which agreed to initiate a consultation process with regard to the establishment of a Global Partnership for Agriculture, Food Security and Nutrition. IFAD was to contribute to a new Agricultural Market Information System (AMIS), aimed at increasing market transparency, which was agreed by a meeting of agriculture ministers from G20 countries, held in June 2011 to address the stabilization of food price volatility. In October 2011 IFAD and WFP helped FAO to compile its annual *State of Food Insecurity in the World* report, which maintained that volatile and high food prices were likely to continue, rendering poorer consumers, farmers and states more vulnerable to poverty and hunger. IFAD welcomed a commitment made, in May 2012, by G8 heads of state and government and leaders of African countries, to supporting a New Alliance for Food Security and Nutrition; the Alliance was to promote sustainable and inclusive agricultural growth over a 10-year period.

IFAD, with FAO and WFP, leads an initiative on ensuring food security by strengthening feeding programmes and expanding support to farmers in developing countries, the second of nine activities that were launched in April 2009 by the UN System Chief Executives Board for Co-ordination (CEB), with the aim of alleviating the impact on poor and vulnerable populations of the developing global economic crisis.

In March 2010 the Executive Board endorsed a new IFAD Climate Change Strategy, under which the Fund aimed to create a climate-smart portfolio, and to support smallholder farmers increase their resilience to climate change. During 2011 an Adaptation for Smallholder Agriculture Programme (ASAP) was developed; under ASAP finance for climate adaptation initiatives was to be integrated into IFAD-supported investments.

IFAD is a leading repository of knowledge, resources and expertise in the field of rural hunger and poverty alleviation. In 2001 it renewed its commitment to becoming a global knowledge institution for rural poverty-related issues. Through its technical assistance grants, IFAD aims to promote research and capacity-building in the agricultural sector, as well as the development of technologies to increase production and alleviate rural poverty. In recent years IFAD has been increasingly involved in promoting the use of communication technology to facilitate the exchange of information and experience among rural communities, specialized institutions and organizations, and IFAD-sponsored projects. Within the strategic context of knowledge management, IFAD has supported initiatives to establish regional electronic networks, such as Electronic Networking for Rural Asia/Pacific (ENRAP, conducted over three phases during the period 1998–2010), and FIDAMERICA in Latin America and the Caribbean (conducted over four phases during 1995–2009), as well as to develop other lines of communication between organizations, local agents and the rural poor.

IFAD is empowered to make both loans and grants. Loans are available on highly concessionary, hardened, intermediate and ordinary terms. Highly concessionary loans carry no interest but have an annual service charge of 0.75% and a repayment period of 40 years; loans approved on hardened terms carry no interest charge, have an annual service charge of 0.75%, and are repaid over 20 years; intermediate loans are subject to a variable interest charge, equivalent to 50% of the interest rate charged on World Bank loans, and are repaid over 20 years; and ordinary loans carry a variable interest charge equal to that levied by the World Bank, and are repaid over 15–18 years. New Debt Sustainability Framework (DSF) grant financing was introduced in 2007 in place of highly concessional loans for heavily indebted poor countries (HIPCs). In 2011 highly concessionary loans represented some 50.1% of total lending in that year, DSF grants 22.8%, intermediate loans 14.5%, ordinary loans 9.2%, and hardened loans 3.4%. Research and technical assistance grants are awarded to projects focusing on research and training, and for project preparation and development. In order to increase the impact of its lending resources on food production, the Fund seeks as much as possible to attract other external donors and beneficiary governments as cofinanciers of its projects. In 2011 external cofinancing accounted for some 18.8% of all project funding, while domestic contributions, i.e. from recipient governments and other local sources, accounted for 37.9%.

The IFAD Indigenous Peoples Assistance Facility was created in 2007 to fund microprojects that aim to build upon the knowledge and natural resources of indigenous communities and organizations. In September 2010, the Executive Board approved the establishment of a new Spanish Food Security Cofinancing Facility Trust Fund (the 'Spanish Trust Fund'), which is used to provide loans to IFAD borrower nations. On 31 December 2010 the Spanish Government provided, on a loan basis, €285.5m. to the Spanish Trust Fund.

In November 2006 IFAD was granted access to the core resources of the HIPC Trust Fund, administered by the World Bank, to assist in financing the outstanding debt relief on post-completion point countries participating in the HIPC debt relief initiative (see under IBRD). By December 2011 36 of 39 eligible countries had passed their decision points, thereby qualifying for HIPC debt relief assistance from IFAD, and 32 countries had reached completion point, thereby qualifying for full and irrevocable debt reduction.

At the end of 2011 total IFAD loans approved since 1978 amounted to US $12,865.8m. for 892 projects. During the same period the Fund approved 2,398 research and technical assistance grants, at a cost of $799.9m. In 2011 IFAD approved 32 loans and 19 DSF grants, amounting in total to $947.2m., for a total of 34 projects, as follows: $223.6m. for five projects in Eastern and Southern Africa (or 23.5% of the total committed in that year), $345.4m. for 10 operations in Asia and the Pacific (36.3%), $173.1m. for nine projects in Western and Central Africa (18.2%), $139.0m. for six projects in the Near East, North Africa and Europe (14.6%) and $70.6m. for four projects in Latin America and the Caribbean (7.4%). Research and technical assistance grants amounting to $51.2m. were awarded, bringing the total financial assistance approved in 2011 to $997.6m., compared with $845.4m. in the previous year.

IFAD's development projects usually include a number of components, such as infrastructure (e.g. improvement of water supplies, small-scale irrigation and road construction); input supply (e.g. improved seeds, fertilizers and pesticides); institutional support (e.g. research, training and extension services); and producer incentives (e.g. pricing and marketing improvements). IFAD also attempts to enable the landless to acquire income-generating assets: by increasing the provision of credit for the rural poor, it seeks to free them from dependence on the capital market and to generate productive activities.

In addition to its regular efforts to identify projects and programmes, IFAD organizes special programming missions to selected countries to undertake a comprehensive review of the constraints affecting the rural poor, and to help countries to design strategies for the removal of these constraints. In general, projects based on the recommendations of these missions tend to focus on institutional improvements at the national and local level to direct inputs and services to small farmers and the landless rural poor. Monitoring and evaluation missions are also sent to check the progress of projects and to assess the impact of poverty reduction efforts.

The Fund supports projects that are concerned with environmental conservation, in an effort to alleviate poverty that results from the deterioration of natural resources. In addition, it extends environmental assessment grants to review the environmental consequences of projects under preparation. IFAD administers the Global Mechanism of the 1996 Convention to Combat Desertification in those Countries Experiencing Drought and Desertification, particularly in Africa. The Mechanism mobilizes and channels resources for the implementation of the Convention, and IFAD is its largest financial contributor. IFAD is an executing agency of the Global Environmental Facility, specializing in the area of combating rural poverty and environmental degradation.

During 1998 the Executive Board endorsed a policy framework for the Fund's provision of assistance in post-conflict situations, with the aim of achieving a continuum from emergency relief to a secure basis from which to pursue sustainable development. In July 2001 IFAD and UNAIDS signed a Memorandum of Understanding on developing a co-operation agreement.

During the late 1990s IFAD established several partnerships within the agribusiness sector, with a view to improving performance at project level, broadening access to capital markets, and encouraging the advancement of new technologies. Since 1996 it has chaired the Support Group of the Global Forum on Agricultural Research (GFAR), which facilitates dialogue between research centres and institutions, farmers' organizations, non-governmental bodies, the private sector and donors. In October 2001 IFAD became a co-sponsor of the Consultative Group on International Agricultural Research (CGIAR). In 2006 IFAD reviewed the work of the International Alliance against Hunger, which was established in 2004 to enhance co-ordination among international agencies and non-governmental organizations concerned with agriculture and rural development, and national alliances against hunger. In November 2009 IFAD and the Islamic Development Bank concluded a US $1,500m. framework cofinancing agreement for jointly financing priority projects during 2010–12 in many of the 52 countries that had membership of both organizations.

Finance

In accordance with the Articles of Agreement establishing IFAD, the Governing Council periodically undertakes a review of the adequacy of resources available to the Fund and may request members to make additional contributions. A target of US $1,500m. was set for the ninth replenishment of IFAD funds, covering the period 2013–15. The provisional budget for administrative expenses for 2012 amounted to $144.1m., while some $12m. was budgeted in that year to the Fund's capital budget.

Publications

Annual Report.

IFAD Update (2 a year).

Rural Poverty Report.

Staff Working Papers (series).

International Labour Organization—ILO

Address: 4 route des Morillons, 1211 Geneva 22, Switzerland.

Telephone: 227996111; **fax:** 227988685; **e-mail:** ilo@ilo.org; **internet:** www.ilo.org.

The ILO was founded in 1919 to work for social justice as a basis for lasting peace. It carries out this mandate by promoting decent living standards, satisfactory conditions of work and pay and adequate employment opportunities. Methods of action include the creation of international labour standards; the provision of technical co-operation services; and research and publications on social and labour matters. In 1946 the ILO became a specialized agency associated with the UN. It was awarded the Nobel Peace Prize in 1969. The ILO's tripartite structure gives representation to employers' and workers' organizations alongside governments.

MEMBERS

The ILO has 185 members.

Organization

(June 2012)

INTERNATIONAL LABOUR CONFERENCE

The supreme deliberative body of the ILO, the Conference meets annually in Geneva, with a session devoted to maritime questions when necessary; it is attended by about 2,000 delegates, advisers and observers. National delegations are composed of two government delegates, one employers' delegate and one workers' delegate. Non-governmental delegates can speak and vote independently of the views of their national government. The Conference elects the Governing Body and adopts International Labour Conventions and Recommendations. Every two years the Conference adopts the ILO Budget. The 101st Conference was held in May–June 2012.

The President and Vice-Presidents hold office for the term of the Conference only.

GOVERNING BODY

The ILO's executive council meets three times a year in Geneva to decide policy and programmes. It is composed of 28 government members, 14 employers' members and 14 workers' members. Ten of the titular government seats are held permanently by 'states of chief industrial importance': Brazil, the People's Republic of China, France, Germany, India, Italy, Japan, Russia, the United Kingdom and the USA. The remaining 18 are elected from other countries every three years. Employers' and workers' members are elected as individuals, not as national candidates.

Among the Committees formed by the Governing Body are: the Programme, Financial and Administrative Committee; the Building Sub-Committee; the Committee on Freedom of Association; the Committee on Legal Issues and International Labour Standards; the Sub-Committee on Multinational Enterprises; the Committee on Employment and Social Policy; the Committee on Sectoral and Technical Meetings and Related Issues; the Committee on Technical Co-operation; the Working Party on the Social Dimension of Globalization; and the Working Party on the Functioning of the Governing Body and the International Labour Conference.

Chairperson: (2011–12) GREG VINES (Australia).

Employers' Vice-Chairperson: DANIEL FUNES DE RIOJA (Argentina).

Workers' Vice-Chairperson: LUC CORTEBEECK (Belgium).

INTERNATIONAL LABOUR OFFICE

The International Labour Office is the ILO's secretariat, operational headquarters and publishing house. It is staffed in Geneva and in the field by about 2,500 people of some 110 nationalities. Operations are decentralized to regional, area and branch offices in nearly 40 countries.

Director-General: JUAN O. SOMAVÍA (Chile) (until 30 September 2012), GUY RYDER (United Kingdom) (designate).

REGIONAL OFFICES

Africa: Africa Hall, 6th Floor, Menelik II Ave, Addis Ababa, Ethiopia; tel. (11) 544-4480; fax (11) 544-5573; e-mail addisababa@ilo.org.

Arab States: POB 11-4088, Beirut, Lebanon; tel. (1) 752400; fax (1) 752405; e-mail beirut@ilo.org.

Asia and the Pacific: POB 2-349, Bangkok 10200, Thailand; tel. (2) 881234; fax (2) 881735; e-mail bangkok@ilo.org.

Europe and Central Asia: 4 route des Morillons, 1211 Geneva 22, Switzerland; tel. 227996666; fax 227996061; e-mail europe@ilo.org.

Latin America and the Caribbean: Apdo Postal 14–124, Lima, Peru; tel. (1) 6150300; fax (1) 6150400; e-mail oit@oit.org.pe.

Activities

The ILO pursues the goal of 'Decent Work for All' and, in 1999, adopted a Decent Work Agenda, which has four basic pillars: employment, as the principal route out of poverty; rights, which empower men and women to escape from poverty; social protection, which safeguards against poverty; and tripartism and social dialogue, regarding the participation of employers' and workers' organizations as of key importance in shaping government policy for poverty reduction. Through the Decent Work Agenda the ILO supports the UN's Millennium Development Goals, adopted by UN heads of state participating in the Millennium Summit convened in September 2000.

STANDARDS AND FUNDAMENTAL PRINCIPLES AND RIGHTS AT WORK

One of the ILO's primary functions is the adoption by the International Labour Conference of conventions and recommendations setting minimum labour standards. Through ratification by member states, conventions create binding obligations to put their provisions into effect. Recommendations provide guidance as to policy and practice. By June 2012 a total of 189 conventions and 202 recommendations had been adopted, ranging over a wide field of social and labour matters. Together they form the International Labour Code. The Committee of Experts on the Application of Conventions and Recommendations and the Conference Committee on the Application of Standards monitor the adoption of international labour standards. In June 1998 the Conference adopted a Declaration on Fundamental Principles and Rights at Work, establishing four fundamental (core) labour standards: freedom of association, the abolition of forced labour, the abolition of child labour, and the elimination of discrimination in employment promotion, training and the protection of workers. All member states are obliged to observe these standards, whether or not they have ratified the corresponding international conventions. The following eight ILO core conventions have been identified by the Governing Body as fundamental to the rights of people at work, irrespective of the levels of development of individual member states: (relating to the core labour standard of freedom of association) Freedom of Association and Protection of the Right to Organise Convention (No. 87), Right to Organise and Collective Bargaining Convention (No. 98); (abolition of forced labour) Forced Labour Convention (No. 29), Abolition of Forced Labour Convention (No. 105); (equality) Equal Remuneration Convention (No. 100), Discrimination (Employment and Occupation) Convention (No. 111); (elimination of child labour) Minimum Age Convention (No. 138), Worst Forms of Child Labour Convention (No. 182). By June 2012 some 135 countries had ratified all of the core conventions; three member states: the Maldives, Marshall Islands, and Tuvalu, had ratified none of them. Since 2008 the following four conventions have been designated as priority 'governance conventions' (i.e. having particular significance from the perspective of governance): the Labour Inspection Convention (No. 81), Employment Policy Convention (No. 122), Labour Inspection (Agriculture) Convention (No. 129), and the Tripartite Consultation (International Labour Standards) Convention (No. 144).

In May 2003 the ILO issued the first global report on discrimination at work, *Time for Equality at Work*, compiled as a follow-up to the 1998 Declaration on Fundamental Principles and Rights at Work; *Equality for Work: The Continuing Challenge* was published in June 2011. In June 2012 the ILO released a *Global Estimate of Forced Labour*, which found that 20.9m. people globally (of whom 5.5m. were under 18 years of age) were trapped in forced labour, including through debt bondage and trafficking. Of an estimated 18.7m. people reported to be exploited in the private economy, some 14.2m. were believed to be trapped in activities such as domestic work, agriculture, construction and manufacturing (for example barely rewarded sweatshop work), and 4.5m. were believed to be victims of forced sexual exploitation. The ILO estimated that a further 2.2m. people were being exploited in organized forms of forced labour that failed to meet global standards, imposed, for example, by prisons or by the military.

From 1996 the ILO resolved to strengthen its efforts, working closely with UNICEF, to encourage member states to ratify and to implement relevant international standards on child labour. In June 1999 the International Labour Conference adopted the Worst Forms of Child Labour Convention (No. 182); the convention entered into force in November 2000. By June 2012 it had been ratified by 174 states. The Organization helped to organize an International Conference on Child Labour, convened in The Hague, Netherlands, in February 2002. A further Global Conference on Child Labour was held in The Hague, in May 2010, organized by the Government of the Netherlands in collaboration with the ILO; the meeting adopted a 'Roadmap' to strengthen the global effort to eliminate the worst forms of child labour. In November 2010 the Governing Body endorsed a new Global Plan of Action for achieving the elimination of the worst forms of child labour by 2016. By June 2012 the ILO's International Programme for the Elimination of Child Labour (IPEC, established in 1992) was operational in 88 countries. Under IPEC emphasis was placed on the elimination of the most severe forms of labour such as hazardous working conditions and occupations, child prostitution and trafficking of children. In addition, IPEC gives special attention to children who are particularly vulnerable, for example those under 12 years of age. IPEC launched a resource guide on child trafficking and sexual exploitation to coincide with the third World Congress against Sexual Exploitation of Children and Adolescents, convened in Rio de Janeiro, Brazil, in November 2008. The ILO-sponsored World Day against Child Labour is held annually on 12 June.

In June 2011 the International Labour Conference adopted the Convention on Decent Work for Domestic Workers, establishing global standards for up to 100m. domestic labourers world-wide.

EMPLOYMENT

The ILO aims to monitor, examine and report on the situation and trends in employment throughout the world, and considers the effects on employment and social justice of economic trade, investment and related phenomena. In October 2008 the ILO expressed concern that, without prompt and co-ordinated actions by governments, the numbers of unemployed and working poor world-wide were likely to rise severely as a result of the developing global financial crisis; it was predicted that the construction, automotive, tourism, finance, services and real estate sectors would be worst affected. ILO leads an initiative on promoting a 'Global Jobs Pact', the fifth of nine activities that were launched in April 2009 by the UN System Chief Executives Board for Co-ordination (CEB), with the aim of alleviating the impact on poor and vulnerable populations of the developing global economic crisis. The Global Jobs Pact is a co-ordinated labour recovery strategy, based on promoting sustainable enterprises. The International Labour Conference endorsed the new Pact in June 2009. In September, addressing a summit meeting of G20 leaders held in Pittsburgh, USA, which had welcomed the Pact, the ILO Director-General applauded the G20 leaders' stated commitment to implementing economic recovery plans that emphasized decent work and prioritized employment growth. In October the ILO reported that workers employed by and through temporary labour agencies were particularly badly affected by the continuing financial and economic crisis. The June 2010 session of the International Labour Conference urged governments to place employment and social protection at the centre of economic recovery policies. In June 2011 the ILO published a study entitled *The Global Crisis: Causes, responses and challenges*, focusing on the role that well-designed employment and social policies should play in promoting job creation and equitable economic growth. In December 2011 the ILO and the MasterCard Foundation launched Work4Youth, a partnership aimed at promoting decent work among young people. In January 2012 the ILO Director-General—addressing a panel on 'Averting a Lost Generation' at the 2012 annual meeting of the World Economic Forum, convened in Davos-Klosters, Switzerland—strongly urged the development of a new policy paradigm to promote inclusive employment opportunities for unemployed youth. In April the ILO and World Bank released a joint report entitled *Inventory of Policy Responses to the Financial and Economic Crisis*, and a companion web-based data tool that provided a detailed record of policies that had been implemented by governments during 2008–10 with a view to limiting the economic and social impacts of the global crisis and to boosting employment. It was envisaged that stocktaking and reviewing past crisis response measures would facilitate the design of efficient and effective policies to address future economic downturns.

In January 2012 the ILO estimated that 200m. workers world-wide (6% of the global labour force) were unemployed in 2011 (an increase of 27m. over 2007, prior to the impact of the continuing global economic and jobs crisis) and reported that around 1,520m. members of the global labour force were in vulnerable employment. In addition, it was estimated that around 456m. workers globally were living on or less than US $1.25 a day (categorized as 'working poor'). The ILO predicted at that time that some 400m. new jobs would need to be created over the next 10 years to avert a further increase in the level of unemployment, and estimated the rate of global youth unemployment in 2011 at 12.7%.

In February 2002 the ILO established a World Commission on the Social Dimension of Globalization to consider means of utilizing economic globalization to stimulate economic growth and reduce poverty. The Commission issued its final report, entitled *A Fair Globalization*, in February 2004; this was endorsed by the 92nd International Labour Conference, held in June. In March 2003 the ILO adopted the Global Employment Agenda, a comprehensive framework for managing changes to employment derived from the developing global economy, through investment in knowledge and skills, maintaining a healthy labour market and ensuring adequate social safety nets. In November 2007 the ILO convened a Forum on Decent Work for a Fair Globalization, in Lisbon, Portugal, comprising some 300 representatives of the ILO tripartite social partners, and other interested parties, to address the possibility of establishing a new Decent Work Movement to overcome growing global inequality. In June 2008, as the outcome of tripartite consultations based on the work of the World Commission on the Social Dimension of Globalization and its final report, the landmark *ILO Declaration on Social Justice for a Fair Globalization*, building on the Philadelphia Declaration (1944) and the Declaration on Fundamental Principles and Rights at Work (1998), was adopted by the International Labour Conference. The Declaration placed the Decent Work Agenda at the core of ILO activities.

The ILO's programme sector on skills, knowledge and employability supports governments in structuring policies for improved investment in learning and training for enhanced employability, productivity and social inclusion. The programme focuses on promoting access to training and decent work for specific groups, such as youths, the disabled, and workers in the informal economy, and on protecting the rights of the elderly. The Job Creation and Enterprise Development Programme aims to assist governments, employers, workers and other related groups with fostering a successful business environment, for example through the identification and implementation of appropriate policies, legal frameworks and management strategies, the promotion of access to business development and training services, and the promotion of local economic development programmes. It also incorporates a specific programme to promote the development of micro- and small enterprises, in co-operation with governments, communities and other social partners. The ILO's Gender Promotion Programme aims to promote effective gender mainstreaming and is responsible for a global programme for the creation of more and better jobs for women and men. The programme assists countries to develop and implement National Action Plans to achieve this objective. A programme on crisis response and reconstruction addresses the effect on employment of armed conflicts, natural disasters, social movements or political transitions, and financial and economic disruptions. The impact of current global financial and economic trends on employment creation, poverty alleviation and social exclusion are addressed by the ILO's Social Finance Programme. The programme works to reduce vulnerability, to create jobs through enterprise development, and to make financial policies more employment-sensitive, for example by providing information on microfinance and promoting microfinance institutions, and by conducting research on the impact of financial sector liberalization on the poor.

The Multinational Enterprise Programme is responsible for the promotion of and follow-up to the Tripartite Declaration of Principles concerning Multinational Enterprises and Social Policy, which was adopted in 1977 and amended in 2000. The Declaration provides international guidelines, agreed by governments and employers' and workers' organizations, on investment policy and practice. The programme is also responsible for co-ordinating work on corporate social responsibility, as well as for the ILO's participation in the Global Compact, an initiative of the UN Secretary-General, which was inaugurated in 2000, comprising leaders in the fields of business, labour and civil society who undertook to promote human rights, the fundamental principles of the ILO, and protection of the environment.

The ILO maintains technical relations with the IMF, the World Bank, OECD, the WTO and other international organizations on global economic issues, international and national strategies for employment, structural adjustment, and labour market and training policies. In May 2011 the ILO and OECD signed a Memorandum of Understanding on strengthening mutual co-operation. In September of that year the ILO and WTO jointly issued a publication entitled *Making Globalization Socially Sustainable*.

In 2007 the ILO, UNEP and the International Trade Union Confederation launched in partnership the Green Jobs Initiative (the International Organisation of Employers joined in 2008). The Initiative aims to promote the creation of decent jobs as a consequence of new environmental policies required to transform ongoing global environmental challenges. In September 2008 it released a report entitled *Green Jobs: Towards Decent Work in a Sustainable, Low-Carbon World*, the first comprehensive study on the impact of the emergent 'green economy' on the labour market.

SOCIAL PROTECTION

Access to an adequate level of social protection is recognized in the ILO's 1944 Declaration of Philadelphia, as well as in a number of international labour standards, as a basic right of all individuals. The ILO aims to enable countries to extend social protection to all groups in society and to improve working conditions and safety at work. The fundamental premise of the ILO's programme sector on socio-economic security is that basic security for all is essential for productive work and human dignity in the future global economy. The achievement of basic security is deemed to entail the attainment of basic humanitarian needs, including universal access to health services and a decent level of education. The programme aims to address the following concerns: what constitutes socio-economic security and insecurity in member countries; identifying the sources of such insecurity; and identifying economic, labour and social policies that could improve socio-economic security while promoting sustainable economic growth. The programme focuses on the following dimensions of work-based security: the labour market (the provision of adequate employment opportunities); employment (for example, protection against dismissal); occupational security (the opportunity to develop a career); work (protection against accidents, illness and stress at work); skills; income; and representation (the right to collective representation in the labour market, through independent trade unions and employers' associations, etc.). The ILO's Social Security Policy and Development Branch assists member states and constituents in the design, reform and implementation of social security policies based on the principles embodied in international labour standards, with a special focus on developing strategies to extend social security coverage. The Branch provides general research and analysis of social security issues; extends technical assistance to member states for designing, reforming and expanding social security schemes; provides services to enable community-based organizations to develop their own social security systems; promotes and oversees the implementation of ILO standards on social security; develops training programmes and materials; and disseminates information. The Financial, Actuarial and Statistical Services Branch aims to improve the financial planning, management and governance of national social security schemes and social protection systems. In June 2003 the ILO inaugurated a Global Campaign on Social Security and Coverage for All, with a particular focus on the informal economy. The ILO estimates that only one-fifth of the world's population has sufficient social security coverage. The key operational tool of the Campaign is the ILO's STEP (Strategies and Tools against Social Exclusion and Poverty) Programme which undertakes field work, research, training and the dissemination of knowledge to help to extend social protection and combat social exclusion. The International Social Security Association (ISSA), based at ILO headquarters, unites social security agencies and organizations, with the aim of supporting excellence in social security administration as a means of promoting the social dimension in the era of rapid economic globalization.

The ILO's Programme on Safety and Health at Work and the Environment aims to protect workers in hazardous occupations; to provide protection to vulnerable groups of workers outside the scope of normal protection measures; to improve the capacity of governments and employers' and workers' organizations to address workers' well-being, extend the scope of occupational health care etc.; and to ensure that policy-makers recognize and document the social and economic impact of implementing measures that enhance workers' protection. The ILO Guidelines on Occupational Safety and Health Management Systems (ILO-OSH 2001) provides a framework of action at an international, national and organizational level. The ILO's Conditions of Work Branch conducts research and provides advocacy, training and technical co-operation to governments and employers' and workers' organizations in areas such as wages, working time, maternity protection and life outside of work. The International Migration Branch focuses on protecting the rights, and promoting the integration, of migrant workers, forging international consensus on the management of migration, and furthering knowledge of international migration. In June 2004 the 92nd International Labour Conference adopted a plan of action providing for the development of a multilateral framework to extend labour protection standards to migrant workers. In December 2010 ILO and the OSCE jointly published a study entitled *Strengthening Migration Governance*. The ILO's Global Programme on HIV/AIDS and the World of Work, formally established in November 2000, issued a code of practice in May 2001, focusing on prevention, management and mitigation of the impact of HIV/AIDS on the world of work, support for HIV/AIDS-affected workers, and eliminating discrimination on the basis of perceived HIV status. The ILO is a co-sponsor of the Joint UN Programme on HIV/AIDS (UNAIDS), which was established on 1 January 1996 to co-ordinate and strengthen world-wide action against HIV/AIDS. In July 2004 an ILO report assessed the financial cost of HIV/AIDS in terms of loss of output and estimated the impact of the epidemic on the global labour force. The ILO adopted a Code of Practice on HIV/AIDS and the World of Work in October 2005. In June 2010 the International Labour Conference adopted a new international labour standard on HIV/AIDS and the world of work, representing the first international human rights instrument related to HIV/AIDS and employment. A new ILO list of occupational diseases was adopted by the Governing Body in March 2010; this aimed to assist member countries with the prevention, recording, notification and, where applicable, compensation of illnesses caused by work.

ILO, with WHO, leads the Social Protection Floor initiative, the sixth activity launched in April 2009 by CEB, to alleviate the effects of the global economic crisis. In October 2011 a Social

Protection Floor Advisory Group, launched in August 2010 under the initiative, issued a report entitled *Social Protection Floor for a Fair and Inclusive Globalization*, which urged that basic income and services should be guaranteed for all, stating that this would promote both stability and economic growth globally. A landmark Recommendation on a Social Protection Floor for All was adopted by the International Labour Conference in June 2012.

In December 2011 the ILO launched the ILO Global Business and Disability Network, a new global knowledge-sharing platform (accessible at www.businessanddisability.org), which was aimed at promoting the inclusion of people with disabilities in the workplace.

The ILO sponsors the World Day for Safety and Health at Work, held annually on 28 April.

SOCIAL DIALOGUE

This area was identified as one of the four strategic objectives in order to concentrate and reinforce the ILO's support for strengthening the process of tripartism, the role and activities of its tripartite constituents (i.e. governments, employers and workers' organizations), and, in particular, their capacity to engage in and to promote the use of social dialogue. The ILO recognizes that the enactment of labour laws, and ensuring their effective enforcement, collective bargaining and other forms of co-operation are important means of promoting social justice. It aims to assist governments and employers' and workers' organizations to establish sound labour relations, to adapt labour laws to meet changing economic and social needs, and to improve labour administration. In August 2006 ILO inaugurated a joint programme with the International Finance Corporation, 'Better Work', to improve labour standards within a competitive global market. In May 2009 both organizations signed a co-operation agreement to initiate a second phase of the programme in order to extend and expand its impact.

The Social Dialogue, Labour Law and Labour Administration Department maintains an International Observatory of Labour Law which provides information concerning national labour legislation and facilitates the dissemination of information regarding development in labour law throughout the world. The Department also supports the training and professional development of labour court judges and publishes the proceedings of meetings of European labour court judges.

A Committee on Freedom of Association examines allegations of abuses committed against trade union organizations and reports to the Governing Body. Reports of failure to implement the Freedom of Association and Protection of the Right to Organize Convention, 1948 (No. 87) are considered by the International Labour Conference.

From 1999 until June 2012 the ILO withheld technical co-operation from Myanmar, except to assist with combating forced labour, and that country was not invited to participate in ILO activities, owing to alleged use of forced labour there.

INSTITUTES

International Institute for Labour Studies (IILS): 4 route des Morillons, 1211 Geneva 22, Switzerland; tel. 227996128; fax 227998542; e-mail inst@ilo.org; established in 1960 and based at the ILO's Geneva headquarters, the Institute promotes the study and discussion of policy issues of concern to the ILO and its constituents, i.e. governments, employers and workers. The core theme of the Institute's activities is the interaction between labour institutions, development and civil society in a global economy. It identifies emerging social and labour issues by developing new areas for research and action, and encourages dialogue on social policy between the tripartite constituency of the ILO and the international academic community and other experts. The Institute maintains research networks, conducts courses, seminars and social policy forums, and supports internships and visiting scholar and internship programmes. The ILO Director-General is Chairman of the Board of the Institute.

International Training Centre of the ILO (ITC-ILO): Viale Maestri del Lavoro 10, 10127 Turin, Italy; tel. (011) 693-6111; fax (011) 663-8842; e-mail communications@itcilo.org; internet www.itcilo.org; f. 1964 by the ILO to offer advanced training facilities for managers, trainers and social partners, and technical specialists from ILO mem. states; became operational in 1965; the Centre has been increasingly used by its partners to provide training for improving the management of development and for building national capacities to sustain development programmes; through training and learning the ITC-ILO develops human resources and institutional capacity in pursuit of the ILO's goal of decent work for men and women; Exec. Dir PATRICIA O'DONOVAN.

Finance

The proposed regular budget for the two years 2012–13 was US $861.6m.

Publications

(in English, French and Spanish unless otherwise indicated)

Bulletin of Labour Statistics (quarterly).

Global Employment Trends.

Global Employment Trends for Youth.

Global Wage Report.

International Labour Review (quarterly).

International studies, surveys, works of practical guidance or reference (on questions of social policy, manpower, industrial relations, working conditions, social security, training, management development, etc).

Key Indicators of the Labour Market (2 a year).

Labour Law Documents (selected labour and social security laws and regulations; 3 a year).

Official Bulletin (3 a year).

Reports (for the annual sessions of the International Labour Conference, etc.; also in Arabic, Chinese and Russian).

World Employment Report (every 2–3 years).

World Labour Report (every 2 years).

World of Work (magazine issued in several languages; 5 a year).

Yearbook of Labour Statistics.

Also maintains a database on international labour standards, ILOLEX, and a database on national labour law, NATLEX, in electronic form.

Declaration concerning the aims and purpose of the International Labour Organization (Philadelphia Declaration)

(10 May 1944)

I. The Conference reaffirms the fundamental principles on which the Organization is based and, in particular, that:

(a) labour is not a commodity;

(b) freedom of expression and of association are essential to sustained progress;

(c) poverty anywhere constitutes a danger to prosperity everywhere;

(d) the war against want requires to be carried on with unrelenting vigour within each nation, and by continuous and concerted international effort in which the representatives of workers and employers, enjoying equal status with those of governments, join with them in free discussion and democratic decision with a view to the promotion of the common welfare.

II. Believing that experience has fully demonstrated the truth of the statement in the Constitution of the International Labour Organization that lasting peace can be established only if it is based on social justice, the Conference affirms that:

(a) all human beings, irrespective of race, creed or sex, have the right to pursue both their material well-being and their spiritual development in conditions of freedom and dignity, of economic security and equal opportunity;

(b) the attainment of the conditions in which this shall be possible must constitute the central aim of national and international policy;

(c) all national and international policies and measures, in particular those of an economic and financial character, should be judged in this light and accepted only in so far as they may be held to promote and not to hinder the achievement of this fundamental objective;

(d) it is a responsibility of the International Labour Organization to examine and consider all international economic and financial policies and measures in the light of this fundamental objective;

(e) in discharging the tasks entrusted to it the International Labour Organization, having considered all relevant economic and financial factors, may include in its decisions and recommendations any provisions which it considers appropriate.

III. The Conference recognizes the solemn obligation of the International Labour Organization to further among the nations of the world programmes which will achieve:

(a) full employment and the raising of standards of living;

(b) the employment of workers in the occupations in which they can have the satisfaction of giving the fullest measure of their skill and attainments and make their greatest contribution to the common well-being;

(c) the provision, as a means to the attainment of this end and under adequate guarantees for all concerned, of facilities for training and the transfer of labour, including migration for employment and settlement;

(d) policies in regard to wages and earnings, hours and other conditions of work calculated to ensure a just share of the fruits of progress to all, and a minimum living wage to all employed and in need of such protection;

(e) the effective recognition of the right of collective bargaining, the co-operation of management and labour in the continuous improvement of productive efficiency, and the collaboration of workers and employers in the preparation and application of social and economic measures;

(f) the extension of social security measures to provide a basic income to all in need of such protection and comprehensive medical care;

(g) adequate protection for the life and health of workers in all occupations;

(h) provision for child welfare and maternity protection;

(i) the provision of adequate nutrition, housing and facilities for recreation and culture;

(j) the assurance of equality of educational and vocational opportunity.

IV. Confident that the fuller and broader utilization of the world's productive resources necessary for the achievement of the objectives set forth in this Declaration can be secured by effective international and national action, including measures to expand production and consumption, to avoid severe economic fluctuations to promote the economic and social advancement of the less developed regions of the world, to assure greater stability in world prices of primary products, and to promote a high and steady volume of international trade, the Conference pledges the full co-operation of the International Labour Organization with such international bodies as may be entrusted with a share of the responsibility for this great task and for the promotion of the health, education and well-being of all peoples.

V. The conference affirms that the principles set forth in this Declaration are fully applicable to all peoples everywhere and that, while the manner of their application must be determined with due regard to the stage of social and economic development reached by each people, their progressive application to peoples who are still dependent, as well as to those who have already achieved self-government, is a matter of concern to the whole civilized world.

International Maritime Organization—IMO

Address: 4 Albert Embankment, London, SE1 7SR, United Kingdom.

Telephone: (20) 7735-7611; **fax:** (20) 7587-3210; **e-mail:** info@imo.org; **internet:** www.imo.org.

The Inter-Governmental Maritime Consultative Organization (IMCO) began operations in 1959, as a specialized agency of the UN to facilitate co-operation among governments on technical matters affecting international shipping. Its main functions are the achievement of safe, secure and efficient navigation, and the control of pollution caused by ships and craft operating in the marine environment. IMCO became IMO in 1982.

MEMBERS

IMO has 170 members and three associate members.

Organization

(June 2012)

ASSEMBLY

The Assembly consists of delegates from all member countries, who each have one vote. Associate members and observers from other governments and the international agencies are also present. Regular sessions are held every two years. The 27th session was convened in London, United Kingdom, in November 2011.

The Assembly is responsible for the election of members to the Council and approves the appointment of the Secretary-General of the Secretariat. It considers reports from all subsidiary bodies and decides the action to be taken on them; it votes the agency's budget and determines the work programme and financial policy. The Assembly also recommends to members measures to promote maritime safety and security, and to prevent and control maritime pollution from ships.

COUNCIL

The Council is the governing body of the Organization between the biennial sessions of the Assembly. Its members, representatives of 40 states, are elected by the Assembly for a term of two years. The Council appoints the Secretary-General; transmits reports by the subsidiary bodies, including the Maritime Safety Committee, to the Assembly, and reports on the work of the Organization generally; submits budget estimates and financial statements with comments and recommendations to the Assembly. The Council normally meets twice a year.

Facilitation Committee: The Facilitation Committee deals with measures to facilitate maritime travel and transport and matters arising from the 1965 Facilitation Convention. Membership is open to all IMO member states.

MARITIME SAFETY COMMITTEE

The Maritime Safety Committee is open to all IMO members. The Committee meets at least once a year and submits proposals to the Assembly on technical matters affecting the safety of shipping. In December 2002 a conference of contracting states to the 1974 International Convention for the Safety of Life at Sea (see below) adopted a series of security measures relating to the international maritime and port industries that had been formulated by the Safety Committee in view of the major terrorist attacks perpetrated against targets in the USA in September 2001. In January 2012 a Department for Member State Audit and Implementation Support was established within the Committee.

SUB-COMMITTEES:

Bulk Liquids and Gases*
Carriage of Dangerous Goods, Solid Cargoes, Containers
Fire Protection
Flag State Implementation*
Radiocommunications and Search and Rescue
Safety of Navigation
Ship Design and Equipment
Stability and Load Lines and Fishing Vessel Safety
Standards of Training and Watchkeeping

* Also sub-committees of the Marine Environment Protection Committee.

LEGAL COMMITTEE

Established by the Council in June 1967 to deal initially with legal issues connected with the loss of the tanker *Torrey Canyon,* and subsequently with any legal problems laid before IMO. Membership is open to all IMO member states.

MARINE ENVIRONMENT PROTECTION COMMITTEE

Established by the eighth Assembly (1973) to co-ordinate IMO's work on the prevention and control of marine pollution from ships, and to assist IMO in its consultations with other UN bodies, and with international organizations and expert bodies in the field of marine pollution. Membership is open to all IMO members.

TECHNICAL CO-OPERATION COMMITTEE

Evaluates the implementation of projects for which IMO is the executing agency, and generally reviews IMO's technical assistance programmes. Established in 1965 as a subsidiary body of the Council, and formally institutionalized by means of an amendment to the IMO constitution in 1984. Membership is open to all IMO member states.

SECRETARIAT

The Secretariat consists of the Secretary-General (who serves a four-year term of office), and a staff appointed by the Secretary-General and recruited on as wide a geographical basis as possible. The Secretariat comprises the following divisions: Administrative; Conference; Legal Affairs and External Relations; Marine Environment; Maritime Safety; and Technical Co-operation.

Secretary-General: Koji Sekimizu (Japan).

Activities

The 27th regular session of the Assembly, held in London in November 2011, adopted a high-level action plan for 2012–13, and approved a new Strategic Plan for the Organization. The Strategic Plan—covering the period 2012–17—focused on areas including the environmental impact of global shipping activities; the elimination of sub-standard shipping; piracy; and the implementation of effective measures to alleviate the humanitarian impact of piracy, and to address seaborne migration and stowaways. The Assembly also endorsed the appointment of a new Secretary-General, elected a new Council, approved the Organization's budget for 2012–13, and adopted a wide range of technical and other resolutions, including a resolution on combating piracy (see below).

From 2005 IMO brought to the attention of the UN Security Council serious concerns over acts of piracy and armed robbery being perpetrated against ships off the coast of Somalia and in the Gulf of Aden. In June, October and December 2008, November 2009, April and November 2010, and April and November 2011, the Security Council adopted successive resolutions on combating piracy. The issue was also one of the focal areas of a UN General Assembly resolution on 'Oceans and the law of the sea', adopted in February 2009. A high-level sub-regional meeting of states from the Western Indian Ocean, the Gulf of Aden and Red Sea areas, held under IMO auspices in Djibouti, in late January 2009, adopted the Djibouti Code of Conduct concerning the Repression of Piracy and Armed Robbery. The Code, which by June 2012 had been signed by 19 of the 21 countries eligible as signatories, promotes the implementation of those aspects of relevant UN Security Council resolutions, and of the February 2009 General Assembly resolution on Oceans and the law of the sea, which fall within IMO's area of competence. Signatories to the Code (which is supported by a dedicated trust fund) have agreed to co-operate lawfully in the apprehension, investigation and prosecution of people suspected of committing or facilitating acts of piracy; in the seizure of suspect vessels; in the rescue of ships, persons and property subject to acts of armed robbery; and to collaborate in the conduct of security operations. The Code also provides for sharing related information on matters related to maritime security. Meeting in May–June 2009 the Maritime Safety Committee approved revised guidance to governments, and also to shipowners, ship operators, ship masters and crews, on suppressing piracy. In December 2009 the IMO Assembly adopted a resolution supporting UN Security Council efforts to combat piracy, and also adopted a revised code of practice for investigating crimes of piracy and armed robbery against ships. The November 2011 IMO Assembly adopted a further resolution on 'combating piracy and armed robbery against ships in waters off the coast of Somalia', urging universal compliance with guidance promulgated by the Organization on preventive, evasive and defensive measures; encouraging governments to decide, as a matter of national policy, whether ships entitled to fly their flag should be authorized to carry privately contracted armed security personnel; strongly encouraging port and coastal states to promulgate their national policies on the embarkation, disembarkation and carriage of privately contracted armed security personnel and security-related equipment; and urging governments to ensure that owners and operators of ships entitled to fly their flag take fully into account the welfare of seafarers affected by piracy. In May 2012 the IMO hosted a Conference on Capacity Building to Counter Piracy off the Coast of Somalia, at which the Organization signed five strategic partnerships with UN agencies and the EU relating to building maritime infrastructure and law enforcement capacity, and to the implementation of the Djibouti Code of Conduct.

In December 2009 the 26th session of the Assembly determined that from 2015 the Organization's Member State Audit Scheme, aimed at comprehensively assessing national implementation of IMO instruments, should become mandatory.

In May 2010 the Maritime Safety Committee adopted a set of 'goal-based standards' (GBS)—structural standards conforming to functional requirements that had been developed by the Committee—with which, henceforth, newly constructed oil tankers and bulk carriers were to comply. The GBS were the first ever standards set by IMO for ship construction. At that time the Committee also adopted guidelines giving IMO a role in verifying compliance with the provisions of the International Convention for the Safety of Life at Sea (SOLAS) (see below). In July 2011 states parties to the MARPOL Convention adopted amendments to Annex VI (relating to prevention of air pollution from ships) to make mandatory the Energy Efficiency Design Index (EEDI), for new ships, of 400 gross tonnage and above, and the Ship Energy Efficiency Management Plan (SEEMP) for all ships. The revised regulations were expected to enter into force on 1 January 2013.

In June 2010 five new navigational areas (NAVAREAs) and meteorological areas (METAREAs), delineated by IMO and WMO respectively, were established in Arctic waters, expanding the World-Wide Navigational Warning System (WWNWS) into the region and thereby enabling ships operating there to receive necessary information about navigational and meteorological hazards. In 2012 the Sub-Committee on Ship Design and Equipment was developing a new mandatory Polar Code, which was to supplement relevant instruments, including MARPOL and SOLAS, to take into account risks specific to ships operating in remote and environmentally extreme polar waters.

In September 2010 IMO launched a new Seafarers' Rights International Centre, located at the London headquarters of the International Transport Workers' Federation.

In November 2011 IOM, jointly with the Intergovernmental Oceanographic Commission, UNDP, and FAO, released a *The Blueprint for Ocean and Coastal Sustainability*, aimed at improving the management of oceans and coastal areas.

IMO sponsors an annual Day of the Seafarer, held on 25 June. World Maritime Day is celebrated annually on 23 September; the theme for 2012 was to be 'IMO: One hundred years after the Titanic', and the role of the IMO in promoting safety at sea.

CONVENTIONS

(of which IMO is the depository)

Convention on Facilitation of International Maritime Traffic, 1965: came into force in March 1967.

International Convention on Load Lines, 1966: came into force in July 1968; Protocol, adopted in 1988, came into force in February 2000; numerous other amendments.

International Convention on Tonnage Measurement of Ships, 1969: Convention embodies a universal system for measuring ships' tonnage. Came into force in 1982.

International Convention relating to Intervention on the High Seas in Cases of Oil Pollution Casualties, 1969: came into force in May 1975; a Protocol adopted in 1973 came into force in 1983.

International Convention on Civil Liability for Oil Pollution Damage, 1969: came into force in June 1975; amended by Protocols of 1976, 1984 and 1992 (which was to replace the original Convention); further amendments to the 1992 Protocol, adopted in 2000, came into force in November 2003.

International Convention on the Establishment of an International Fund for Compensation for Oil Pollution Damage, 1971: came into force in October 1978; amended by Protocols of 1976, 1984 and 1992 (which replaced the original Convention); further amendments to the 1992 Protocol, adopted in 2000, came into force in November 2003; a Protocol to establish a Supplementary Fund was adopted in 2003 and came into force in March 2005.

Convention relating to Civil Liability in the Field of Maritime Carriage of Nuclear Material, 1971: came into force in 1975.

Special Trade Passenger Ships Agreement, 1971: came into force in 1974.

Convention on the International Regulations for Preventing Collisions at Sea, 1972: came into force in July 1977; numerous amendments.

Convention on the Prevention of Marine Pollution by Dumping of Wastes and Other Matter ('London Convention'), 1972: came into force in August 1975; numerous amendments, including, 1993, to incorporate a ban on low-level nuclear waste, which came into force in February 1994; Protocol, which was to replace the original Convention, adopted in 1996.

Hong Kong International Convention for the Safe and Environmentally Sound Recycling of Ships, 2009: adopted in May 2009, and opened for signature during September 2009–August 2010; was to enter into force 24 months after ratification by 15 states representing 40% of global merchant shipping by gross tonnage.

International Convention for Safe Containers, 1972: came into force in September 1977.

International Convention for the Prevention of Pollution from Ships, 1973: (as modified by the Protocol of 1978, known as MARPOL 73/78); came into force in October 1983; extended to include regulations to prevent air pollution in September 1997; came into force in May 2005; a revised MARPOL Annex VI: Prevention of Air Pollution from Ships was adopted in October 2008 and entered into force in July 2010; further amendments to Annex VI were adopted in July 2011 establishing a North American Emission Control Area; a revised MARPOL Annex III: Prevention of Pollution from Packaged Goods, and a revised MARPOL Annex V: Regulations for the Prevention of Pollution by Garbage from Ships, were approved in October 2010; in July 2011 a revision to Annex I, banning heavy fuel oil from the Antarctic region, was adopted.

International Convention for the Safety of Life at Sea (SOLAS), 1974: came into force in May 1980; a Protocol drawn up in 1978 came into force in May 1981; a second Protocol, of 1988, came into force in February 2000; amendments including special measures to enhance maritime safety came into force in July 2004, and further amendments strengthening international passenger ship safety regulations entered into force in July 2010.

Athens Convention relating to the Carriage of Passengers and their Luggage by Sea, 1974: came into force in April 1987.

Convention on the International Maritime Satellite Organization, 1976: came into force in July 1979.

Convention on Limitation of Liability for Maritime Claims, 1976: came into force in December 1986; a Protocol came into force in May 2004.

International Convention for the Safety of Fishing Vessels, Torremolinos, 1977: replaced by a Protocol adopted in 1993; to come into force 12 months after 15 countries with an aggregate fleet of at least 14,000 vessels of 24 metres in length and over have become parties thereto.

International Convention on Standards of Training, Certification and Watchkeeping (STCW) for Seafarers, 1978: came into force in April 1984; restructured by amendments that entered into force in February 1997, and further amendments adopted in June 2010; countries deemed to be implementing the Convention fully are recorded on a so-called 'white list'.

International Convention on Maritime Search and Rescue, 1979: came into force in June 1985.

Convention for the Suppression of Unlawful Acts against the Safety of Maritime Navigation, 1988: came into force in March 1992. Further Protocol adopted in October 2005.

Protocol for the Suppression of Unlawful Acts against the Safety of Fixed Platforms located on the Continental Shelf, 1988: came into force in March 1992; further Protocol adopted in October 2005.

International Convention on Salvage, 1989: came into force in July 1996.

International Convention on Oil Pollution, Preparedness, Response and Co-operation, 1990: came into force in May 1995.

International Convention on Maritime Liens and Mortgages, 1992: came into force in September 2004.

International Convention on Standards on Training, Certification and Watchkeeping for Fishing Vessel Personnel (STCW-F), 1995: will enter into force on 29 September 2012, 12 months after receiving the required 15 ratifications.

International Convention on Liability and Compensation for Damage in Connection with the Carriage of Hazardous and Noxious Substances by Sea, 1996: will come into force 18 months after 12 states of which four have not less than 2m. units of gross tonnage have become parties thereto.

International Convention on Civil Liability for Bunker Oil Pollution Damage, 2001: entered into force November 2008.

International Convention on the Control of Harmful Anti-fouling Systems on Ships, 2001: entered into force September 2008.

International Convention for the Control and Management of Ships' Ballast Water and Sediments, 2004: will come into force 12 months after 30 states representing not less than 35% of the world's merchant shipping tonnage have become parties thereto.

Nairobi International Convention on the Removal of Wrecks, 2007: will enter into force 12 months after 10 states have become parties thereto.

Port State Control Agreements: Paris Memorandum of Understanding (MOU) on Port State Control, 1982; Viña del Mar Agreement, 1992; Tokyo MOU, 1993; Caribbean MOU, 1996; Mediterranean MOU, 1997; Indian Ocean MOU, 1998; Abuja MOU, 1999; Black Sea, MOU, 2000. An International Ship and Port Facility Security Code was adopted under IMO auspices in December 2002 and entered into force in July 2004.

TRAINING INSTITUTES

IMO International Maritime Law Institute (IMLI): POB 31, Msida, MSD 1000, Malta; tel. 21319343; fax 21343092; e-mail info@imli.org; internet www.imli.org; f. 1988; provides degree courses, other training courses, study and research facilities for specialists in maritime law; promotes the development and dissemination of knowledge and expertise in the international legal regime of merchant shipping and related areas; Dir Prof. DAVID ATTARD; publs *IMLI News*, *IMLI e-News*, *IMLI Global Directory*.

World Maritime University (WMU): POB 500, Citadellsvägen 29, 201 24 Malmö, Sweden; tel. (40) 356300; fax (40) 128442; e-mail info@wmu.se; internet www.wmu.se; f. 1983; offers postgraduate courses in maritime disciplines, a master's and doctoral programme and professional development courses; undertakes various research projects; Pres. Prof. BJÖRN KJERFVE (USA/Sweden); publs *WMU News*, *WMU Handbook*, *WMU Journal of Maritime Affairs* (2 a year), several books on maritime issues.

OTHER AFFILIATED BODIES

Partnership in Environmental Management for the Seas of East Asia (PEMSEA): POB 2502, Quezon City, 1165 Philippines; tel. (2) 9292992; fax (2) 9269712; e-mail info@pemsea.org; internet www.pemsea.org; administered by UNOPS in conjunction with UNDP and the Global Environment Facility; aims to build interagency, intersectoral and intergovernmental partnerships for the implementation of the Sustainable Development Strategy for the Seas of East Asia (SDS-SEA).

Regional Marine Pollution Emergency Response Centre for the Mediterranean Sea (REMPEC): Maritime House, Lascaris Wharf, Valletta VLT 1921, Malta; tel. 21337296; fax 21339951; e-mail rempec@rempec.org; internet www.rempec.org; f. 1976 as the Regional Oil Combating Centre for the Mediterranean Sea; administered by IMO in conjunction with the Regional Seas Programme of the UN Environment Programme; aims to develop measures to prevent and combat pollution from ships in the Mediterranean; responsible for implementing a new EU-funded regional project, initiated in November 2005, for Euro-Mediterranean co-operation on maritime safety and prevention of pollution from ships; Dir FRÉDÉRIC HÉBERT (France).

Regional Marine Pollution Emergency, Information and Training Center for the Wider Caribbean Region: Fokkerweg 26, Willemstad Curaçao, Netherlands Antilles; tel. 461-4012; fax 461-1996; e-mail rempeitc@cep.unep.org; internet cep.unep.org/racrempeitc; f. 1995; aims to help prevent and respond to major pollution incidents in the region's marine environment; administered by IMO in conjunction with UNEP's Regional Seas Programme.

Finance

Contributions are received from the member states, with the amount paid calculated according to the tonnage of a member state's merchant fleet. The 10 top contributors in 2010 were: Panama, Liberia, Bahamas, Marshall Islands, the United Kingdom, Greece, Singapore, Malta, Japan and the People's Republic of China. The budget appropriation for the two years 2012–13, approved by the Assembly in November 2011, amounted to £62.2m., comprising £30.5m. for 2012 and £31.7m. for 2013.

Publications

IMO News (quarterly).

Ships' Routeing.

Numerous specialized publications, including international conventions of which IMO is the depository.

International Monetary Fund—IMF

Address: 700 19th St, NW, Washington, DC 20431, USA.

Telephone: (202) 623-7000; **fax:** (202) 623-4661; **e-mail:** publicaffairs@imf.org; **internet:** www.imf.org.

The IMF was established at the same time as the World Bank in December 1945, to promote international monetary co-operation, to facilitate the expansion and balanced growth of international trade and to promote stability in foreign exchange.

MEMBERS

The IMF has 188 members.

Organization

(June 2012)

Managing Director: CHRISTINE LAGARDE (France).

First Deputy Managing Director: DAVID LIPTON (USA).

Deputy Managing Directors: NAOYUKI SHINOHARA (Japan), NEMAT SHAFIK (Egypt/United Kingdom/USA), MIN ZHU (People's Republic of China).

BOARD OF GOVERNORS

The highest authority of the Fund is exercised by the Board of Governors, on which each member country is represented by a Governor and an Alternate Governor. The Board normally meets once a year. The Board of Governors has delegated many of its powers to the Executive Directors. However, the conditions governing the admission of new members, adjustment of quotas and the election of Executive Directors, as well as certain other important powers, remain the sole responsibility of the Board of Governors. The voting power of each member on the Board of Governors is related to its quota in the Fund (see table below).

In September 1999 the Board of Governors adopted a resolution to transform the Interim Committee of the Board of Governors (established in 1974) into the International Monetary and Financial Committee (IMFC). The IMFC, which held its inaugural meeting in April 2000, comprises 24 members, representing the same countries or groups of countries as those on the Board of Executive Directors (see below). It advises and reports to the Board on matters relating to the management and adaptation of the international monetary and financial system, sudden disturbances that might threaten the system and proposals to amend the Articles of Agreement, but has no decision-making authority.

The Development Committee (the Joint Ministerial Committee of the Boards of Governors of the World Bank and the IMF on the Transfer of Real Resources to Developing Countries, created in 1974, with a structure similar to that of the IMFC) reviews development policy issues and financing requirements.

BOARD OF EXECUTIVE DIRECTORS

The 24-member Board of Executive Directors, responsible for the day-to-day operations of the Fund, is in continuous session in Washington, under the chairmanship of the Fund's Managing Director or Deputy Managing Directors. The USA, United Kingdom, Germany, France and Japan each appoint one Executive Director. There is also one Executive Director each from the People's Republic of China, Russia and Saudi Arabia, while the remainder are elected by groups of all other member countries. As in the Board of Governors, the voting power of each member is related to its quota in the Fund, but in practice the Executive Directors normally operate by consensus. In December 2010 the Board of Governors endorsed a proposal to amend the composition of the Board of Executive Directors in order to increase the representation of emerging dynamic economies and developing countries. The proposal, which required ratification of an Amendment to the Articles of Agreement by members holding 85% of the total voting power, also provided for Board to be fully elected.

The Managing Director of the Fund serves as head of its staff, which is organized into departments by function and area. In 2012 the Fund employed some 2,400 staff members from 144 countries.

REGIONAL REPRESENTATION

There is a network of regional offices and Resident Representatives in more than 90 member countries. In addition, special information and liaison offices are located in Tokyo, Japan (for Asia and the Pacific), in New York, USA (for the United Nations), and in Europe (Paris, France; Geneva, Switzerland; Belgium, Brussels; and Warsaw, Poland, for Central Europe and the Baltic states).

Paris Office: 64–66 ave d'Iéna, 75116 Paris, France; tel. 1-40-69-30-70; fax 1-47-23-40-89; Dir of the IMF Offices in Europe EMMANUEL VAN DER MENSBRUGGHE (Belgium).

Regional Office for Asia and the Pacific: 21F Fukoku Seimei Bldg, 2-2-2, Uchisaiwai-cho, Chiyodu-ku, Tokyo 100, Japan; tel. (3) 3597-6700; fax (3) 3597-6705; f. 1997; Dir SHOGO ISHII (Japan).

Regional Office for Central Europe and the Baltics: 00-108 Warsaw, 37C Zielna, Poland; tel. (22) 3386700; fax (22) 3386500; e-mail cee-office@imf.org; f. 2005; Senior Regional Rep. MARK ALLEN.

Activities

The purposes of the IMF, as defined in the Articles of Agreement, are:

(i) To promote international monetary co-operation through a permanent institution which provides the machinery for consultation and collaboration on monetary problems;

(ii) To facilitate the expansion and balanced growth of international trade, and to contribute thereby to the promotion and maintenance of high levels of employment and real income and to the development of members' productive resources;

(iii) To promote exchange stability, to maintain orderly exchange arrangements among members, and to avoid competitive exchange depreciation;

(iv) To assist in the establishment of a multilateral system of payments in respect of current transactions between members and in the elimination of foreign exchange restrictions which hamper the growth of trade;

(v) To give confidence to members by making the general resources of the Fund temporarily available to them, under adequate safeguards, thus providing them with the opportunity to correct maladjustments in their balance of payments, without resorting to measures destructive of national or international prosperity;

(vi) In accordance with the above, to shorten the duration of and lessen the degree of disequilibrium in the international balances of payments of members.

In joining the Fund, each country agrees to co-operate with the above objectives. In accordance with its objective of facilitating the expansion of international trade, the IMF encourages its members to accept the obligations of Article VIII, Sections two, three and four, of the Articles of Agreement. Members that accept Article VIII undertake to refrain from imposing restrictions on the making of payments and transfers for current international transactions and from engaging in discriminatory currency arrangements or multiple currency practices without IMF approval. At the end of 2011 some 90% of members had accepted Article VIII status.

In 2000/01 the Fund established an International Capital Markets Department to improve its understanding of financial markets and a separate Consultative Group on capital markets to serve as a forum for regular dialogue between the Fund and representatives of the private sector. In mid-2006 the International Capital Markets Department was merged with the Monetary and Financial Systems Department to create the Monetary and Capital Markets Department, with the intention of strengthening surveillance of global financial transactions and monetary arrangements. In June 2008 the Managing Director presented a new Work Programme, comprising the following four immediate priorities for the Fund: to enable member countries to deal with the current crises of reduced economic growth and escalating food and fuel prices, including efforts by the Fund to strengthen surveillance activities; to review the Fund's lending instruments; to implement new organizational tools and working practices; and to advance further the Fund's governance agenda.

The deceleration of economic growth in the world's major economies in 2007 and 2008 and the sharp decline in global financial market conditions, in particular in the second half of 2008, focused international attention on the adequacy of the governance of the international financial system and of regulatory and supervisory frameworks. The IMF aimed to provide appropriate and rapid financial and technical assistance to low-income and emerging economies most affected by the crisis and to support a co-ordinated, multinational recovery effort. The Fund worked closely with the Group of 20 (G20) leading economies to produce an Action Plan, in November 2008, concerned with strengthening regulation, transparency and integrity in financial markets and reform of the international financial system. In March 2009 the IMF released a study on the 'Impact of the Financial Crisis on Low-income Countries', and in that month convened, with the Government of Tanzania, a high-level conference, held in Dar es Salaam, to consider the effects of the global financial situation on African countries, as well as areas for future partnership and growth. Later in that month the Executive Board approved a series of reforms to enhance the effectiveness of the Fund's lending framework, including new conditionality criteria, a new flexible credit facility and increased access limits (see below).

In April 2009 a meeting of G20 heads of state and government, convened in London, United Kingdom, determined to make available substantial additional resources through the IMF and other multinational development institutions in order to strengthen global financial liquidity and support economic recovery. There was a commitment to extend US $250,000m. to the IMF in immediate bilateral financial contributions (which would be incorporated into an expanded New Arrangements to Borrow facility) and to support a general allocation of special drawing rights (SDRs), amounting to a further $250,000m. It was agreed that additional resources from sales of IMF gold were to be used to provide $6,000m. in concessional financing for the poorest countries over the next two to three years. The G20 meeting also resolved to implement several major reforms to strengthen the regulation and supervision of the international financial system, which envisaged the IMF collaborating closely with a new Financial Stability Board. In September G20 heads of state and government endorsed a Mutual Assessment Programme, which aimed to achieve sustainable and balanced growth, with the IMF providing analysis and technical assistance. In January 2010 the IMF initiated a process to review its mandate and role in the 'post-crisis' global economy. Short-term priorities included advising countries on moving beyond the policies they implemented during the crisis; reviewing the Fund's mandate in surveillance and lending, and investigating ways of improving the stability of the international monetary system; strengthening macro-financial and cross-country analyses, including early warning exercises; and studying ways to make policy frameworks more resilient to crises. In November 2011 G20 heads of state and government, meeting in Cannes, France, agreed to initiate an immediate review of the Fund's resources, with a view to securing global financial stability which had been undermined by high levels of debt in several euro area countries. In December European Union heads of state and government agreed to allocate to the IMF additional resources of up to $270,000m. in the form of bilateral loans.

A joint meeting of the IMFC, G20 finance ministers and governors of central banks, convened in April 2012, in Washington, DC, USA, welcomed a decision in March by euro area member states to strengthen European firewalls through broader reform efforts and the availability of central bank swap lines, and determined to enhance IMF resources for crisis prevention and resolution, announcing commitments from G20 member states to increasing, by more than US $430,000m., resources to be made available to the IMF as part of a protective firewall to serve the entire IMF membership. Additional resources pledged by emerging economies (notably by the

People's Republic of China, Brazil, India, Mexico and Russia) at a meeting of G20 heads of state and government held in June, in Los Cabos, Baja California Sur, Mexico, raised the universal firewall to $456,000m.

The IMF's annual evaluation of the euro area, undertaken by a dedicated IMF mission in May–June 2012, in accordance with Article IV of the Articles of Agreement, found the euro area financial crisis to have reached a critical stage, with markets remaining under acute stress; the mission recommended the forceful pursuit of stronger European Monetary Union, accompanied by wide-ranging structural reforms aimed at advancing economic growth.

In September 2011 the IMF joined other international financial institutions active in the Middle East and North Africa region to endorse the so-called Deauville Partnership, established by the G8 in May to support political and economic reforms being undertaken by several countries, notably Egypt, Jordan, Morocco and Tunisia. The Fund was committed to supporting those countries to maintain economic and financial stability, and to promote inclusive growth.

SPECIAL DRAWING RIGHTS

The SDR was introduced in 1970 as a substitute for gold in international payments, and was intended eventually to become the principal reserve asset in the international monetary system. SDRs are allocated to members in proportion to their quotas. In October 1996 the Executive Board agreed to a new allocation of SDRs in order to achieve their equitable distribution among member states (i.e. all members would have an equal number of SDRs relative to the size of their quotas). In particular, this was deemed necessary since 38 countries that had joined the Fund since the last allocation of SDRs in 1981 had not yet received any of the units of account. In September 1997, at the annual meeting of the Executive Board, a resolution approving a special allocation of SDR 21,400m. was passed, in order to ensure an SDR to quota ratio of 29.32%, for all member countries. The proposed Fourth Amendment to the Articles of Agreement was to come into effect following its acceptance by 60% of member countries, having 85% of the total voting power. The final communiqué of the G20 summit meeting, held in April, endorsed the urgent ratification of the Fourth Amendment. In August the Amendment entered into force, having received approval by the USA. The special allocation, equivalent to some US $33,000m., was implemented on 9 September.

In August 2009 the Board of Governors approved a third general allocation of SDRs, amounting to SDR 161,200m., which become available to all members, in proportion to their existing quotas, effective from 28 August.

From 1974 to 1980 the SDR was valued on the basis of the market exchange rate for a basket of 16 currencies, belonging to the members with the largest exports of goods and services; since 1981 it has been based on the currencies of the five largest exporters (France, Germany, Japan, the United Kingdom and the USA), although the list of currencies and the weight of each in the SDR valuation basket is revised every five years. In January 1999 the IMF incorporated the new currency of the European Economic and Monetary Union, the euro, into the valuation basket; it replaced the French and German currencies, on the basis of their conversion rates with the euro as agreed by the EU. From 1 January 2006 the relative weights assigned to the currencies in the valuation basket were redistributed. The value of the SDR averaged US $1.57868 in 2011, and at 21 June 2012 stood at $1.521750.

The Second Amendment to the Articles of Agreement (1978) altered and expanded the possible uses of the SDR in transactions with other participants. These 'prescribed holders' of the SDRs have the same degree of freedom as Fund members to buy and sell SDRs and to receive or use them in loans, pledges, swaps, donations or settlement of financial obligations.

QUOTAS

Each member is assigned a quota related to its national income, monetary reserves, trade balance and other economic indicators. A member's subscription is equal to its quota and is payable partly in SDRs and partly in its own currency. The quota determines a member's voting power, which is based on one vote for each SDR 100,000 of its quota *plus* the 250 votes to which each member is entitled. A member's quota also determines its access to the financial resources of the IMF, and its allocation of SDRs.

Quotas are reviewed at intervals of not more than five years, to take into account the state of the world economy and members' different rates of development. Special increases, separate from the general review, may be made in exceptional circumstances. In June 1990 the Board of Governors authorized proposals for a Ninth General Review of quotas. At the same time the Board stipulated that the quota increase, of almost 50%, could occur only after the Third Amendment of the IMF's Articles of Agreement had come into effect. The amendment provides for the suspension of voting and other related rights of members that do not fulfil their obligations under the Articles. By September 1992 the necessary proportion of IMF members had accepted the amendment, and it entered into force in November. The 10th General Review of quotas was concluded in December 1994, with the Board recommending no further increase in quotas. In October 1996 the Fund's Managing Director advocated an increase in quotas under the latest review of at least two-thirds in the light of the IMF's reduced liquidity position. (The IMF had extended unprecedentedly large amounts in stand-by arrangements during the period 1995–96, notably to Mexico and Russia.) In January 1998 the Board of Governors adopted a resolution in support of an increase in quotas of 45%. The required consent of member states constituting 85% of total quotas had been granted by January 1999 to enable the 11th General Review of Quotas to enter into effect. The 12th General Review was initiated in December 2001, and was concluded at the end of January 2003 without an increase in quotas. The 13th General Review was concluded, without an increase in quotas, in January 2008. In September 2006 the Board of Governors adopted a resolution on Quota and Voice Reform in the IMF, representing a two-year reform package aimed at improving the alignment of the quota shares of member states to represent more accurately their relative positions in the global economy and also to enhance the participation and influence of emerging market and low-income countries. An immediate ad hoc quota increase was approved for China, the Republic of Korea, Mexico and Turkey. In March 2008 the Executive Board approved a second round of ad hoc quota increases as part of the proposed extensive reform of the governance and quota structure, which also committed the Fund to regular, five-yearly realignments of quotas. The proposals were to come into effect upon being accepted by member states representing 85% of total votes. In April 2009 G20 heads of state and government further endorsed the quota and voice reform measures and urged the IMF to complete a general review of quotas by January 2011. The 2008 Quota and Voice Reform agreement entered into effect in March 2011, providing for quota increases for 54 member countries with emerging or dynamic economies and an increase in basic votes for low-income countries, in order to strengthen their participation mechanism. In November 2010 the Executive Board responded to a request by the G20 for a further realignment of quotas, and in December the Board of Governors endorsed an agreement concluding the 14th General Review of Quotas to provide for a 100% increase in quotas, to some SDR 476,800m. and adjustment of quota shares to ensure appropriate representation for emerging economies and developing countries. The agreement included a commitment to undertake a comprehensive review of the quota formula by January 2013 and to conclude a 15th General Review by January 2014. The reforms required acceptance of three-fifths of members representing 85% of voting power in order to enter into effect. At 21 June 2012 total quotas in the Fund amounted to SDR 238,116.4m.

RESOURCES

Members' subscriptions form the basic resource of the IMF. They are supplemented by borrowing. Under the General Arrangements to Borrow (GAB), established in 1962, the Group of Ten industrialized nations (G10—Belgium, Canada, France, Germany, Italy, Japan, the Netherlands, Sweden, the United Kingdom and the USA) and Switzerland (which became a member of the IMF in May 1992 but which had been a full participant in the GAB from April 1984) undertake to lend the Fund as much as SDR 17,000m. in their own currencies to assist in fulfilling the balance of payments requirements of any member of the group, or in response to requests to the Fund from countries with balance of payments problems that could threaten the stability of the international monetary system. In 1983 the Fund entered into an agreement with Saudi Arabia, in association with the GAB, making available SDR 1,500m., and other borrowing arrangements were completed in 1984 with the Bank for International Settlements, the Saudi Arabian Monetary Agency, Belgium and Japan, making available a further SDR 6,000m. In 1986 another borrowing arrangement with Japan made available SDR 3,000m. In May 1996 GAB participants concluded an agreement in principle to expand the resources available for borrowing to SDR 34,000m., by securing the support of 25 countries with the financial capacity to support the international monetary system. The so-called New Arrangements to Borrow (NAB) was approved by the Executive Board in January 1997. It was to enter into force, for an initial five-year period, as soon as the five largest potential creditors participating in NAB had approved the initiative and the total credit arrangement of participants endorsing the scheme had reached at least SDR 28,900m. While the GAB credit arrangement was to remain in effect, the NAB was expected to be the first facility to be activated in the event of the Fund's requiring supplementary resources. In July 1998 the GAB was activated for the first time in more than 20 years in order to provide funds of up to US $6,300m. in support of an IMF emergency assistance package for Russia (the first time the GAB had been used for a non-participant). The NAB became effective in November, and was used for the first time as part of an extensive programme of support for Brazil, which was adopted by the IMF in early December. (In March 1999, however, the activation was cancelled.) In November 2008 the Executive Board initiated an assessment of IMF resource requirements and options for supplementing resources in view of an exceptional increase in demand for IMF assistance. In February 2009 the Board approved the terms of a borrowing agreement with the Government of Japan to extend some SDR 67,000m. (some $100,000m.) in supplemental funding, for an initial one-year period. In April G20 heads of state and government resolved to expand the NAB facility, to incorporate all G20 economies, in order to increase its resources by up to SDR 367,500m. ($500,000m.). The G20 summit meeting held in September confirmed that it had contributed the additional resources to the NAB. In April 2010 the IMF's Executive Board approved the expansion and enlargement of NAB borrowing arrangements; these came into effect in March 2011, having completed the ratification process. By December 37 members or state institutions were participating in the NAB, and had committed SDR 366,116m. in supplementary resources.

FINANCIAL ASSISTANCE

The Fund makes resources available to eligible members on an essentially short-term and revolving basis to provide members with temporary assistance to contribute to the solution of their payments problems. Before making a purchase, a member must show that its balance of payments or reserve position makes the purchase necessary. Apart from this requirement, reserve tranche purchases (i.e. purchases that do not bring the Fund's holdings of the member's currency to a level above its quota) are permitted unconditionally. Exchange transactions within the Fund take the form of members' purchases (i.e. drawings) from the Fund of the currencies of other members for the equivalent amounts of their own currencies.

With further purchases, however, the Fund's policy of conditionality means that a recipient country must agree to adjust its economic policies, as stipulated by the IMF. All requests other than for use of the reserve tranche are examined by the Executive Board to determine whether the proposed use would be consistent with the Fund's policies, and a member must discuss its proposed adjustment programme (including fiscal, monetary, exchange and trade policies) with IMF staff. New guidelines on conditionality, which, *inter alia*, aimed to promote national ownership of policy reforms and to introduce specific criteria for the implementation of conditions given different states' circumstances, were approved by the Executive Board in September 2002. In March 2009 the Executive Board approved reforms to modernize the Fund's conditionality policy, including greater use of pre-set qualification criteria and monitoring structural policy implementation by programme review (rather than by structural performance criteria).

Purchases outside the reserve tranche are made in four credit tranches, each equivalent to 25% of the member's quota; a member must reverse the transaction by repurchasing its own currency (with SDRs or currencies specified by the Fund) within a specified time. A credit tranche purchase is usually made under a 'Stand-by Arrangement' with the Fund, or under the Extended Fund Facility. A Stand-by Arrangement is normally of one or two years' duration, and the amount is made available in instalments, subject to the member's observance of 'performance criteria'; repurchases must be made within three-and-a-quarter to five years. An Extended Arrangement is normally of three years' duration, and the member must submit detailed economic programmes and progress reports for each year; repurchases must be made within four-and-a-half to 10 years. In October 1994 the Executive Board approved an increase in members' access to IMF resources, on the basis of a recommendation by the then Interim Committee. The annual access limit under IMF regular tranche drawings, Stand-by Arrangements and Extended Fund Facility credits was increased from 68% to 100% of a member's quota, with the cumulative access limit set at 300%. In March 2009 the Executive Board agreed to double access limits for non-concessional loans to 200% and 600% of a member's quota for annual and cumulative access respectively. In 2009/10 regular funding arrangements approved (and augmented) amounted to SDR 74,175m. (compared with SDR 66,736m. in the previous financial year and SDR 1,333m. in 2007/08).

In October 1995 the Interim Committee of the Board of Governors endorsed recent decisions of the Executive Board to strengthen IMF financial support to members requiring exceptional assistance. An Emergency Financing Mechanism was established to enable the IMF to respond swiftly to potential or actual financial crises, while additional funds were made available for short-term currency stabilization. The Mechanism was activated for the first time in July 1997, in response to a request by the Philippines Government to reinforce the country's international reserves, and was subsequently used during that year to assist Thailand, Indonesia and the Republic of Korea. It was used in 2001 to accelerate lending to Turkey. In September 2008 the Mechanism was activated to facilitate approval of a Stand-by Arrangement amounting to SDR 477.1m. for Georgia, which urgently needed to contain its fiscal deficit and undertake rehabilitation measures following a conflict with Russia in the previous month. In November the Board approved a Stand-by Arrangement of SDR 5,169m., under the Emergency Financing Mechanism procedures, to support an economic stabilization programme in Pakistan, one for Ukraine, amounting to SDR 11,000m., and another of SDR 10,538m. for Hungary, which constituted 1,015% of its quota, to counter exceptional pressures on that country's banking sector and the Government's economic programme. An arrangement for Latvia, amounting to SDR 1,522m., was approved in the following month. In May 2010 the Board endorsed a three-year Stand-by Arrangement for Greece amounting to SDR 26,400m., accounting for some 2,400% of that country's new quota (under the 2008 quota reform). The Arrangement was approved under the Emergency Financing Mechanism, as part of a joint financial assistance package with the euro area countries, which aimed to alleviate Greece's sovereign debt crisis and to support an economic recovery and reform programme. In July 2011 the Fund completed a fourth review of the country's economic performance under the Stand-by Arrangement, enabling a further disbursement of SDR 2,900m. In March 2012, following the cancellation of the Stand-by Arrangement, the Executive Board approved an allocation of SDR 23,800m. to be distributed over four years under the Extended Fund Facility—representing access to IMF resources amounting to 2,159% of Greece's quota—in support of the country's ongoing economic adjustment programme; some SDR 1,400m, was to be disbursed immediately.

In October 2008 the Executive Board approved a new Short-Term Liquidity Facility (SLF) to extend exceptional funds (up to 500% of quotas) to emerging economies affected by the turmoil in international financial markets and economic deceleration in advanced economies. Eligibility for lending under the new Facility was to be based on a country's record of strong macroeconomic policies and having a sustainable level of debt. In March 2009 the Executive Board decided to replace the SLF with a Flexible Credit Line (FCL) facility, which, similarly, was to provide credit to countries with strong economic foundations, but was also to be primarily considered as precautionary. In addition, it was to have a longer repayment period (of up to five years) and have no access 'cap'. The first arrangement under the FCL was approved in April for Mexico, making available funds of up to SDR 31,528m. for a one-year period. Three FCL arrangements, amounting to SDR 52,184m., were approved in 2009/10, accounting for more than 70% of Fund lending commitments in that year.

In January 2006 a new Exogenous Shocks Facility (ESF) was established to provide concessional assistance to economies adversely affected by events deemed to be beyond government control, for example commodity price changes, natural disasters, or conflicts in neighbouring countries that disrupt trade. Loans under the ESF were to be offered on the same terms as those of the Poverty Reduction and Growth Facility (PRGF) for low-income countries without a PRGF in place. In September 2008 modifications to the ESF were approved, including a new rapid-access component (to provide up to 25% of a country's quota) and a high-access component (to provide up to 75% of quota). These came into effect in late November.

In January 2010 the Fund introduced new concessional facilities for low-income countries as part of broader reforms to enhance flexibility of lending and to focus support closer to specific national requirements. The three new facilities aimed to support country-owned programmes to achieve macroeconomic positions consistent with sustainable poverty reduction and economic growth. They carried zero interest rate, although this was to be reviewed every two years. An Extended Credit Facility (ECF) succeeded the existing PRGF to provide medium-term balance of payments assistance to low-income members. ECF loans were to be repayable over 10 years, with a five-and-a-half-year grace period. A Standby Credit Facility (SCF) replaced the high-access component of the Exogenous Shocks Facility (see above) in order to provide short-term balance of payments financial assistance, including on a precautionary basis. SCF loans were to be repayable over eight years, with a grace period of four years. A new Rapid Credit Facility was to provide rapid financial assistance to members requiring urgent balance of payments assistance, under a range of circumstances. Loans were repayable over 10 years, with a five-and-a-half-year grace period.

In May 2001 the Executive Board decided to provide a subsidized loan rate for emergency post-conflict assistance for PRGF-eligible countries, in order to facilitate the rehabilitation of their economies and to improve their eligibility for further IMF concessionary arrangements. In January 2005 the Executive Board decided to extend the subsidized rate for natural disasters.

During 2010/11 members' purchases from the general resources account amounted to SDR 26,616m., compared with SDR 21,087m. in the previous year. Outstanding IMF credit at 30 April 2011 totalled SDR 70,421m., compared with SDR 46,350m. in the previous year.

IMF participates in the initiative to provide exceptional assistance to heavily indebted poor countries (HIPCs), in order to help them to achieve a sustainable level of debt management. The initiative was formally approved at the September 1996 meeting of the Interim Committee, having received the support of the 'Paris Club' of official creditors, which agreed to increase the relief on official debt from 67% to 80%. In all 41 HIPCs were identified, of which 33 were in sub-Saharan Africa. Resources for the HIPC initiative were channelled through the PRGF Trust. In early 1999 the IMF and the World Bank initiated a comprehensive review of the HIPC scheme, in order to consider modifications of the initiative and to strengthen the link between debt relief and poverty reduction. A consensus emerged among the financial institutions and leading industrialized nations to enhance the scheme, in order to make it available to more countries, and to accelerate the process of providing debt relief. In September the IMF Board of Governors expressed its commitment to undertaking an off-market transaction of a percentage of the Fund's gold reserves (i.e. a sale, at market prices, to central banks of member countries with repayment obligations to the Fund, which were then to be made in gold), as part of the funding arrangements of the enhanced HIPC scheme; this was undertaken during the period December 1999–April 2000. Under the enhanced initiative it was agreed that countries seeking debt relief should first formulate, and successfully implement for at least one year, a national poverty reduction strategy (see above). In May 2000 Uganda became the first country to qualify for full debt relief under the enhanced scheme. In September 2005 the IMF and the World Bank endorsed a proposal of the Group of Eight (G8) nations to achieve the cancellation by the IMF, IDA and the African Development Bank of 100% of debt claims on countries that had reached completion point under the HIPC initiative, in order to help them to achieve their Millennium Development Goals. The debt cancellation was to be undertaken within the framework of a Multilateral Debt Relief Initiative (MDRI). The IMF's Executive Board determined, additionally, to extend MDRI debt relief to all countries with an annual per caput GDP of US $380, to be financed by IMF's own resources. Other financing was to be made from existing bilateral contributions to the PRGF Trust Subsidy Account. In December the Executive Board gave final approval to the first group of countries assessed as eligible for 100% debt relief under the MDRI, including 17 countries that had reached completion point at that time, as well as Cambodia and Tajikistan. The initiative became effective in January 2006 once the final consent of the 43 contributors to the PRGF Trust Subsidy Account had been received. By the end of 2011 a further 15 countries had qualified for MDRI relief. As at July the IMF had committed some $6,500m. in debt relief under the HIPC initiative, of a total of $76,000m. pledged for the initiative (in 2010 net present value terms); at that time the cost to the IMF of the MDRI amounted to some $3,900m. (in nominal value terms). In June 2010 the Executive Board approved the establishment of a Post-Catastrophe Debt Relief Trust (PCDR Trust) to provide balance of payments assistance to low-income members following an exceptional natural disaster.

SURVEILLANCE

Under its Articles of Agreement, the Fund is mandated to oversee the effective functioning of the international monetary system. Accordingly, the Fund aims to exercise firm surveillance over the exchange rate policies of member states and to assess whether a country's economic situation and policies are consistent with the objectives of sustainable development and domestic and external stability. The Fund's main tools of surveillance are regular, bilateral consultations with member countries conducted in accordance with Article IV of the Articles of Agreement, which cover fiscal and monetary policies, balance of payments and external debt developments, as well as policies that affect the economic performance of a country, such as the labour market, social and environmental issues and good governance, and aspects of the country's capital accounts, and finance and banking sectors. In April 1997 the Executive Board agreed to the voluntary issue of Press Information Notices (PINs) following each member's Article IV consultation, to those member countries wishing to make public the Fund's views. Other background papers providing information on and analysis of economic developments in individual countries continued to be made available. The Executive Board monitors global economic developments and discusses policy implications from a multilateral perspective, based partly on World Economic Outlook reports and Global Financial Stability Reports. In addition, the IMF studies the regional implications of global developments and policies pursued under regional fiscal arrangements. The Fund's medium-term strategy, initiated in 2006, determined to strengthen its surveillance policies to reflect new challenges of globalization for international financial and macroeconomic stability. In June 2007 the Executive Board approved a Decision on Bilateral Surveillance to update and clarify principles for a member's exchange rate policies and to define best practice for the Fund's bilateral surveillance activities. In October 2008 the Board adopted a Statement of Surveillance Priorities, based on a series of economic and operational policy objectives, for the period 2008–11. The need to enhance surveillance and economic transparency was a priority throughout 2009 as the Fund assessed the global economic and financial crisis and its own role in future crisis prevention. The IMF, with the UN Department for Economic and Social Affairs, leads an initiative to strengthen monitoring and analysis surveillance, and to implement an effective warning system, one of nine initiatives that were endorsed in April 2009 by the UN System Chief Executives Board for Co-ordination (CEB), with the aim of alleviating the impact of the global crisis on poor and vulnerable populations. In September 2010 the Executive Board decided that regular financial stability assessments, within the Financial Sector Assessment Programme framework (see below), were to be a mandatory exercise for 25 jurisdictions considered to have systemically important financial sectors.

In April 1996 the IMF established the Special Data Dissemination Standard (SDDS), which was intended to improve access to reliable economic statistical information for member countries that have, or are seeking, access to international capital markets. In March 1999 the IMF undertook to strengthen the Standard by the introduction of a new reserves data template. By December 2011 69 countries had subscribed to the Standard. The financial crisis in Asia, which became apparent in mid-1997, focused attention on the importance of IMF surveillance of the economies and financial policies of member states and prompted the Fund further to enhance the effectiveness of its surveillance through the development of international standards in order to maintain fiscal transparency. In December 1997 the Executive Board approved a new General Data Dissemination System (GDDS), to encourage all member countries to improve the production and dissemination of core economic data. The operational phase of the GDDS commenced in May 2000. By December 2011 102 countries were participating in the GDDS. The Fund maintains a Dissemination Standards Bulletin Board, which aims to ensure that information on SDDS subscribing countries is widely available.

In April 1998 the then Interim Committee adopted a voluntary Code of Good Practices on Fiscal Transparency: Declaration of Principles, which aimed to increase the quality and promptness of official reports on economic indicators, and in September 1999 it adopted a Code of Good Practices on Transparency in Monetary and Financial Policies: Declaration of Principles. The IMF and World Bank jointly established a Financial Sector Assessment Programme (FSAP) in May 1999, initially as a pilot project, which aimed to promote greater global financial security through the preparation of confidential detailed evaluations of the financial sectors of individual countries. In September 2009 the IMF and World Bank determined to enhance the FSAP's surveillance effectiveness with new features, for example introducing a risk assessment matrix, targeting it more closely to country needs, and improving its cross-country analysis and perspective. As part of the FSAP Fund staff may conclude a Financial System Stability Assessment (FSSA), addressing issues relating to macroeconomic stability and the strength of a country's financial system. A separate component of the FSAP are Reports on the Observance of Standards and Codes (ROSCs), which are compiled after an assessment of a country's implementation and observance of internationally recognized financial standards.

In March 2000 the IMF Executive Board adopted a strengthened framework to safeguard the use of IMF resources. All member countries making use of Fund resources were to be required to publish annual central bank statements audited in accordance with internationally accepted standards. It was also agreed that any instance of intentional misreporting of information by a member country should be made public. In the following month the Executive Board approved the establishment of an Independent Evaluation Office (IEO) to conduct objective evaluations of IMF policy and operations. The Office commenced activities in July 2001. In 2008/09 the Office concluded an evaluation report on IMF Involvement in International Trade Policy Issues for consideration by the Board. In January 2010 the Office published a report on IMF Interactions with Member Countries. At that time two further projects were under development: the IMF's Research Agenda, and the IMF's Role in the Run-up to the Current Financial and Economic Crisis.

In April 2001 the Executive Board agreed on measures to enhance international efforts to counter money-laundering, in particular through the Fund's ongoing financial supervision activities and its programme of assessment of offshore financial centres (OFCs). In November the IMFC, in response to the terrorist attacks against targets in the USA, which had occurred in September, resolved, *inter alia*, to strengthen the Fund's focus on surveillance, and, in particular, to extend measures to counter money-laundering to include the funds of terrorist organizations. It determined to accelerate efforts to assess offshore centres and to provide technical support to enable poorer countries to meet international financial standards. In March 2004 the Board of Directors resolved that an anti-money laundering and countering the financing of terrorism (AML/CFT) component be introduced into regular OFC and FSAP assessments conducted by the Fund and the World Bank, following a pilot programme undertaken from November 2002 with the World Bank, the Financial Action Task Force and other regional supervisory bodies. The first phase of the OFC assessment programme was concluded in February 2005, at which time 41 of 44 contacted jurisdictions had been assessed and the reports published. In May 2008 the IMF's Executive Board agreed to integrate the OFC programme into the FSAP.

TECHNICAL ASSISTANCE

Technical assistance is provided by special missions or resident representatives who advise members on every aspect of economic management, while more specialized assistance is provided by the IMF's various departments. In 2000/01 the IMFC determined that technical assistance should be central to the IMF's work in crisis prevention and management, in capacity-building for low-income countries, and in restoring macroeconomic stability in countries following a financial crisis. Technical assistance activities subsequently underwent a process of review and reorganization to align them more closely with IMF policy priorities and other initiatives.

Since 1993 the IMF has delivered some technical assistance, aimed at strengthening local capacity in economic and financial management, through regional centres. The first, established in that year, was a Pacific Financial Technical Assistance Center, located in Fiji. A Caribbean Regional Technical Assistance Centre (CARTAC), located in Barbados, began operations in November 2001. In October 2002 an East African Regional Technical Assistance Centre (East AFRITAC), based in Dar es Salaam, Tanzania, was inaugurated and a second AFRITAC was opened in Bamako, Mali, in May 2003, to cover the West African region. In October 2004 a new technical assistance centre for the Middle East (METAC) was inaugurated, based in Beirut, Lebanon. A regional technical assistance centre for Central Africa, located in Libreville, Gabon, was inaugurated in 2006/07. The fourth AFRITAC, located in Port Louis, Mauritius, serving Southern Africa and the Indian Ocean, was inaugurated in October 2011. A Regional Technical Assistance Centre for Central America, Panama and the Dominican Republic (CAPTAC-DR), was inaugurated in June 2009, in Guatemala City, Guatemala. In September 2002 the IMF signed a Memorandum of Understanding with the African Capacity Building Foundation to strengthen collaboration, in particular within the context of a new IMF Africa Capacity-Building Initiative.

The IMF Institute, which was established in 1964, trains officials from member countries in macroeconomic management, financial analysis and policy, balance of payments methodology and public finance. The IMF Institute also co-operates with other established regional training centres and institutes in order to refine its delivery of technical assistance and training services. The IMF is a co-sponsor, with the Austrian authorities, the EBRD, OECD and WTO, of the Joint Vienna Institute, which was opened in the Austrian capital in October 1992 and which trains officials from former centrally-planned economies in various aspects of economic management and public administration. In May 1998 an IMF-Singapore Regional Training Institute (an affiliate of the IMF Institute) was inaugurated, in collaboration with the Singaporean Government, in order to provide training for officials from the Asia-Pacific region. In 1999 a Joint Regional Training Programme, administered with the Arab Monetary Fund, was established in the United Arab Emirates. During 2000/01 the Institute established a new joint training programme for government officials of the People's Republic of China, based in Dalian, Liaoning Province. A Joint Regional Training Centre for Latin America became operational in Brasília, Brazil, in 2001. In July 2006 a Joint India-IMF Training Programme was inaugurated in Pune, India.

Publications

Annual Report.

Balance of Payments Statistics Yearbook.

Civil Society Newsletter (quarterly).

Direction of Trade Statistics (quarterly and annually).

Emerging Markets Financing (quarterly).

F & D—Finance and Development (quarterly).

Financial Statements of the IMF (quarterly).

Global Financial Stability Report (2 a year).

Global Monitoring Report (annually, with the World Bank).

Government Finance Statistics Yearbook.

Handbook on Securities Statistics (published jointly by IMF, BIS and the European Central Bank).

IMF Commodity Prices (monthly).

IMF Financial Activities (weekly, online).

IMF in Focus (annually).

IMF Research Bulletin (quarterly).

IMF Survey (monthly, and online).

International Financial Statistics (monthly and annually).

Joint BIS-IMF-OECD-World Bank Statistics on External Debt (quarterly).

Quarterly Report on the Assessments of Standards and Codes.

Staff Papers (quarterly).

World Economic Outlook (2 a year).

Other country reports, regional outlooks, economic and financial surveys, occasional papers, pamphlets, books.

Statistics

QUOTAS
(SDR million)

	June 2012
Afghanistan	161.9
Albania	60.0
Algeria	1,254.7
Angola	286.3
Antigua and Barbuda	13.5
Argentina	2,117.1
Armenia	92.0
Australia	3,236.4
Austria	2,113.9
Azerbaijan	160.9
Bahamas	130.3
Bahrain	135.0
Bangladesh	533.3
Barbados	67.5
Belarus	386.4
Belgium	4,605.2
Belize	18.8
Benin	61.9
Bhutan	6.3
Bolivia	171.5
Bosnia and Herzegovina	169.1
Botswana	87.8
Brazil	4,250.5
Brunei	215.2
Bulgaria	640.2
Burkina Faso	60.2
Burundi	77.0
Cambodia	87.5
Cameroon	185.7
Canada	6,369.2
Cape Verde	9.6
Central African Republic	55.7
Chad	66.6
Chile	856.1
China, People's Republic	9,525.9
Colombia	774.0
Comoros	8.9
Congo, Democratic Republic	533.0
Congo, Republic	84.6
Costa Rica	164.1
Côte d'Ivoire	325.2
Croatia	365.1
Cyprus	158.2
Czech Republic	1,002.2
Denmark	1,891.4
Djibouti	15.9
Dominica	8.2
Dominican Republic	218.9
Ecuador	347.8
Egypt	943.7
El Salvador	171.3
Equatorial Guinea	52.3
Eritrea	15.9
Estonia	93.9
Ethiopia	133.7
Fiji	70.3
Finland	1,263.8
France	10,738.5
Gabon	154.3
The Gambia	31.1
Georgia	150.3
Germany	14,565.5
Ghana	369.0
Greece	1,101.8
Grenada	11.7
Guatemala	210.2
Guinea	107.1
Guinea-Bissau	14.2
Guyana	90.9
Haiti	81.9
Honduras	129.5
Hungary	1,038.4
Iceland	117.6
India	5,821.5
Indonesia	2,079.3
Iran	1,497.2
Iraq	1,188.4
Ireland	1,257.6
Israel	1,061.1
Italy	7,882.3
Jamaica	273.5
Japan	15,628.5
Jordan	170.5
Kazakhstan	365.7
Kenya	271.4
Kiribati	5.6
Korea, Republic	3,366.4
Kosovo	59.0
Kuwait	1,381.1
Kyrgyzstan	88.8
Laos	52.9
Latvia	142.1
Lebanon	266.4
Lesotho	34.9
Liberia	129.2
Libya	1,123.7
Lithuania	183.9
Luxembourg	418.7
Macedonia, former Yugoslav republic	68.9
Madagascar	122.2
Malawi	69.4
Malaysia	1,773.9
Maldives	10.0
Mali	93.3
Malta	102.0
Marshall Islands	3.5
Mauritania	64.4
Mauritius	101.6
Mexico	3,625.7
Micronesia, Federated States	5.1

—continued	June 2012
Moldova	123.2
Mongolia	51.1
Montenegro	27.5
Morocco	588.2
Mozambique	113.6
Myanmar	258.4
Namibia	136.5
Nepal	71.3
Netherlands	5,162.4
New Zealand	894.6
Nicaragua	130.0
Niger	65.8
Nigeria	1,753.2
Norway	1,883.7
Oman	237.0
Pakistan	1,033.7
Palau	3.1
Panama	206.6
Papua New Guinea	131.6
Paraguay	99.9
Peru	638.4
Philippines	1,019.3
Poland	1,688.4
Portugal	1,029.7
Qatar	302.6
Romania	1,030.2
Russia	5,945.4
Rwanda	80.1
Saint Christopher and Nevis	8.9
Saint Lucia	15.3
Saint Vincent and the Grenadines	8.3
Samoa	11.6
San Marino	22.4
São Tomé and Príncipe	7.4
Saudi Arabia	6,985.5
Senegal	161.8
Serbia	467.7
Seychelles	10.9
Sierra Leone	103.7

—continued	June 2012
Singapore	1,408.0
Slovakia	427.5
Slovenia	275.0
Solomon Islands	10.4
Somalia	44.2
South Africa	1,868.5
South Sudan	123.0
Spain	4,023.4
Sri Lanka	413.4
Sudan	169.7
Suriname	92.1
Swaziland	50.7
Sweden	2,395.5
Switzerland	3,458.5
Syria	293.6
Tajikistan	87.0
Tanzania	198.9
Thailand	1,440.5
Timor-Leste	8.2
Togo	73.4
Tonga	6.9
Trinidad and Tobago	335.6
Tunisia	286.5
Turkey	1,455.8
Turkmenistan	75.2
Tuvalu	1.8
Uganda	180.5
Ukraine	1,372.0
United Arab Emirates	752.5
United Kingdom	10,738.5
USA	42,122.4
Uruguay	306.5
Uzbekistan	275.6
Vanuatu	17.0
Venezuela	2,659.1
Viet Nam	460.7
Yemen	243.5
Zambia	489.1
Zimbabwe	353.4

FINANCIAL ACTIVITIES
(SDR million, year ending 30 April)

Type of Transaction	2006	2007	2008	2009	2010	2011
Total disbursements	2,559	2,806	1,952	17,082	22,488	27,527
Purchases by facility (General Resources Account)*	2,156	2,329	1,468	16,363	21,087	26,616
Loans under PRGF/ECF/ESF arrangements	403	477	484	719	1,402	914
Repurchases and repayments	35,991	14,678	3,324	2,301	764	3,412
Repurchases	32,783	14,166	2,905	1,833	275	2,268
SAF/PRGF/ECF/ESF loan repayments	3,208	512	419	468	489	1,144
Total outstanding credit provided by Fund (end of year)	23,144	11,216	9,844	24,625	46,350	70,421
Of which:						
General Resources Account	19,227	7,334	5,896	20,426	41,238	65,539
SAF Arrangements	9	9	9	9	9	9
PRGF/ ECF/ESF Arrangements†	3,819	3,785	3,873	4,124	5,037	4,807
Trust Fund	89	89	66	66	66	66

* Including reserve tranche purchases.
† Including Saudi Fund for Development associated loans.

Source: IMF, *Annual Report 2011*.

BOARD OF EXECUTIVE DIRECTORS
(June 2012)

Director	Casting Votes of	Total Votes	%
Appointed:			
MEG LUNDSAGER	USA	421,961	16.75
MITSUHIRO FURUSAWA	Japan	157,022	6.23
HUBERT TEMMEYER	Germany	146,392	5.81
AMBROISE FAYOLLE	France	108,122	4.29
ALEXANDER GIBBS	United Kingdom	108,122	4.29
Elected:			
WILLY KIEKENS (Belgium)	Austria, Belarus, Belgium, Czech Republic, Hungary, Kosovo, Luxembourg, Slovakia, Slovenia, Turkey	125,191	4.97
CARLOS PÉREZ-VERDÍA (Mexico)	Costa Rica, El Salvador, Guatemala, Honduras, Mexico, Nicaragua, Spain, Venezuela	117,029	4.64
MENNO SNEL (Netherlands)	Armenia, Bosnia and Herzegovina, Bulgaria, Croatia, Cyprus, Georgia, Israel, the former Yugoslav republic of Macedonia, Moldova, Montenegro, Netherlands, Romania, Ukraine	113,835	4.52
ARRIGO SADUN (Italy)	Albania, Greece, Italy, Malta, Portugal, San Marino, Timor-Leste	107,223	4.26
DER JIUN CHIA (Singapore)	Brunei, Cambodia, Fiji, Indonesia, Laos, Malaysia, Myanmar, Nepal, Philippines, Singapore, Thailand, Tonga, Viet Nam	99,023	3.81
TAO ZHANG	People's Republic of China	95,996	3.81
CHRISTOPHER LEGG (Australia)	Australia, Kiribati, Republic of Korea, Marshall Islands, Federated States of Micronesia, Mongolia, New Zealand, Palau, Papua New Guinea, Samoa, Seychelles, Solomon Islands, Tuvalu, Uzbekistan, Vanuatu	91,302	3.62
THOMAS HOCKIN (Canada)	Antigua and Barbuda, The Bahamas, Barbados, Belize, Canada, Dominica, Grenada, Ireland, Jamaica, Saint Christopher and Nevis, Saint Lucia, Saint Vincent and the Grenadines	90,672	3.60
BENNY ANDERSEN (Denmark)	Denmark, Estonia, Finland, Iceland, Latvia, Lithuania, Norway, Sweden	85,615	3.40
MOAKETSI MAJORO (Lesotho)	Angola, Botswana, Burundi, Eritrea, Ethiopia, The Gambia, Kenya, Lesotho, Liberia, Malawi, Mozambique, Namibia, Nigeria, Sierra Leone, South Africa, Sudan, Swaziland, Tanzania, Uganda, Zambia, Zimbabwe	81,022	3.22
A. SHAKOUR SHAALAN (Egypt)	Bahrain, Egypt, Iraq, Jordan, Kuwait, Lebanon, Libya, Maldives, Oman, Qatar, Syria, United Arab Emirates, Yemen	81,061	3.18
ARVIND VIRMANI (India)	Bangladesh, Bhutan, India, Sri Lanka	70,693	2.81
PAULO NOGUEIRA BATISTA, Jr (Brazil)	Brazil, Colombia, Dominican Republic, Ecuador, Guyana, Haiti, Panama, Suriname, Trinidad and Tobago	70,616	2.80
AHMED ABDULKARIM ALKHOLIFEY	Saudi Arabia	70,592	2.80
RÉNE WEBER (Switzerland)	Azerbaijan, Kazakhstan, Kyrgyzstan, Poland, Serbia, Switzerland, Tajikistan, Turkmenistan	69,818	2.77
ALEKSEI V. MOZHIN	Russia	60,191	2.39
JAFAR MOJARRAD (Iran)	Afghanistan, Algeria, Ghana, Iran, Morocco, Pakistan, Tunisia	57,071	2.26
ALFREDO MACLAUGHLIN (Argentina)	Argentina, Bolivia, Chile, Paraguay, Peru, Uruguay	46,317	1.84
KOSSI ASSIMAIDOU (Togo)	Benin, Burkina Faso, Cameroon, Cape Verde, Central African Republic, Chad, Comoros, Democratic Republic of the Congo, Republic of the Congo, Côte d'Ivoire, Djibouti, Equatorial Guinea, Gabon, Guinea-Bissau, Mali, Mauritius, Niger, Rwanda, São Tomé and Príncipe, Senegal, Togo	38,973	1.55

Note: The total number of votes does not include the votes of Guinea, Madagascar, Somalia and South Sudan (amounting to 0.27% of the total of votes in the General Department and the Special Drawing Rights Department), as these countries did not participate in the 2010 election of Executive Directors.

International Telecommunication Union—ITU

Address: Place des Nations, 1211 Geneva 20, Switzerland.

Telephone: 227305111; **fax:** 227337256; **e-mail:** itumail@itu.int; **internet:** www.itu.int.

Founded in 1865, ITU became a specialized agency of the UN in 1947. It acts *inter alia* to encourage world co-operation for the improvement and national use of telecommunications to promote technical development, to harmonize national policies in the field, and to promote the extension of telecommunications throughout the world.

MEMBERS

ITU has 193 member states. More than 700 scientific and technical companies, public and private operators, broadcasters and other organizations are also ITU members.

Organization

(June 2012)

PLENIPOTENTIARY CONFERENCE

The supreme organ of ITU; normally meets every four years. The main tasks of the Conference are to elect ITU's leadership, establish policies, revise the Constitution and Convention (see below) and approve limits on budgetary spending. The 2010 Conference was held in Guadalajara, Mexico, in October; the 2014 Conference was scheduled to be convened in Busan, Republic of Korea.

WORLD CONFERENCES ON INTERNATIONAL TELECOMMUNICATIONS

The World Conferences on International Telecommunications are held at the request of members and after approval by the Plenipotentiary Conference. The World Conferences are authorized to review and revise the regulations applying to the provision and operation of international telecommunications services. Separate Conferences are held by the Union's three sectors (see below): Radiocommunication Conferences (every two or three years); Telecommunication Standardization Assemblies (every four years or at the request of one-quarter of ITU members); and Telecommunication Development Conferences (every four years).

ITU COUNCIL

The Council meets annually in Geneva and is composed of 48 members elected by the Plenipotentiary Conference.

The Council ensures the efficient co-ordination and implementation of the work of the Union in all matters of policy, administration and finance, in the interval between Plenipotentiary Conferences, and approves the annual budget.

GENERAL SECRETARIAT

The Secretary-General is elected by the Plenipotentiary Conference and is assisted by a Co-ordination Committee that also comprises the Deputy Secretary-General and the Directors of the three sector Bureaux. The General Secretariat comprises departments for Administration and Finance; Conferences and Publications; Information Services; Internal Audit; ITU Telecom (conference organization); Legal Affairs; and Strategic Planning and Membership. The Secretariat's staff totals some 800, representing more than 80 nationalities; the official and working languages are Arabic, Chinese, English, French, Russian and Spanish.

Secretary-General: HAMADOUN I. TOURÉ (Mali).

Deputy Secretary-General: HOULIN ZHAO (People's Republic of China).

Constitution and Convention

Between 1865 and 1992 each Plenipotentiary Conference adopted a new Convention of ITU. At the Additional Plenipotentiary Conference held in December 1992, in Geneva, Switzerland, a new Constitution and Convention were signed. They were partially amended by the following two Plenipotentiary Conferences held in Kyoto, Japan, in 1994, and Minneapolis, USA, in 1998. The Constitution contains the fundamental provisions of ITU, whereas the Convention contains other provisions which complement those of the Constitution and which, by their nature, require periodic revision.

The Constitution establishes the purposes and structure of the Union, contains the general provisions relating to telecommunications and special provisions for radio, and deals with relations with the UN and other organizations. The Convention establishes the functioning of the Union and the three sectors, and contains the general provisions regarding conferences and assemblies. Both instruments are further complemented by the *Radio Regulations* and the *International Telecommunications Regulations* (see below).

Activities

In December 1992 an Additional Plenipotentiary Conference, convened in Geneva, Switzerland, determined that the ITU should be restructured into three sectors corresponding to its main functions: standardization; radiocommunication; and development. In October 1994 the ordinary Plenipotentiary Conference, held in Kyoto, Japan, adopted ITU's first strategic plan. In November 1998 the Conference, convened in Minneapolis, USA, adopted a second strategic plan, for the period 1999–2003, which recognized new trends and developments in the world telecommunication environment, such as globalization, liberalization, and greater competition, assessed their implications for ITU, and proposed new strategies and priorities to enable the Union to function effectively. The meeting approved the active involvement of ITU in governance issues relating to the internet, and recommended that a World Summit on the Information Society (WSIS, see below) be convened, given the rapid developments in that field. In October 2002 the Plenipotentiary Conference, convened in Marrakesh, Morocco, adopted a third strategic plan, for the period 2004–07 which emphasized ITU's role in facilitating universal access to the global information economy and society. ITU was to take a lead role in UN initiatives concerning information and communication technologies and support all efforts to overcome the digital divide. The 2006 Conference, held in November, in Antalya, Turkey, adopted a fourth strategic plan covering the period 2008–11, which outlined the future course of the Union, and endorsed ITU's essential role in 'Bridging the Digital Divide' and in leading the multi-stakeholder process for the follow-up and implementation of relevant WSIS objectives. Main thematic areas of focus include: the implementation of the ITU's Global Cybersecurity Agenda; pursuing the objective of 'connecting the unconnected' by 2015; developing emergency telecommunications as a critical pillar of disaster management; and implementing the Next Generation Network (NGN) Global Standards Initiative. In October 2010 the Plenipotentiary Conference, held in Guadalajara, Mexico, adopted new strategic and financial plans for the period 2012–15, as well as a series of resolutions concerning, *inter alia*, enhanced collaboration with relevant international organizations and regional registries in the development of Internet Protocol-based networks and internet governance, the implementation of a programme of work on confirmity and interoperability, bridging the standardization gap between developed and developing countries, supporting further NGN development and its deployment in developing countries, promoting collation of information relating to human exposure to electromagnetic fields, and the establishment of a new Council Working Group on internet-related public policy issues.

ITU's Telecom division organizes major global and regional conferences which bring together governments, non-governmental bodies and representatives of the telecommunications industry. The next major conference, ITU World Telecoms, was scheduled to be held in Dubai, in October 2012.

The Global Cybersecurity Agenda (GCA) was formulated as part of ITU's commitments to implement the WSIS 'Action Line' on building confidence and security in the use of information and communication technologies, and was inaugurated in May 2007. It aimed to provide a framework for international co-operation to enhance confidence in and the security of the information society, structured on the following five work areas: legal measures; technical and procedural measures; organizational structures; capacity building; and international co-operation. In September 2008 ITU signed a Memorandum of Understanding (MOU) with the International Multilateral Partnership against Cyber Threats (IMPACT) to collaborate in efforts to strengthen cybersecurity and to transfer the operations and administration of the GCA to IMPACT. In November ITU inaugurated a Child Online Protection (COP) initiative, to be incorporated into the GCA framework, in order to address the specific cybersecurity issues relating to young people. A new COP Global Initiative was launched in November 2010 to promote the implementation, through national action plans, industry codes of conduct, awareness training etc, of previously developed strategies and guidelines. In May 2011 ITU signed an MOU with the UN Office on Drugs and Crime to promote co-operation at a global level to counter cyber crime. At the same time a separate MOU was signed with Symantec, a private provider of security intelligence and systems management.

ITU, with UNIDO and WIPO, leads an initiative on promoting technology and innovation, the eighth of nine activities that were launched in April 2009 by the UN System Chief Executives Board for Co-ordination (CEB), with the aim of alleviating the impact on poor and vulnerable populations of the developing global economic crisis.

In May 2010 ITU, with UNESCO, established a Broadband Commission for Digital Development, to comprise high level representatives of governments, industry and international agencies concerned with the effective deployment of broadband networks as an essential element of economic and social development objectives. The Commission released its first report, with a series of recommendations for the rapid development of broadband world-wide, in September, prior to the UN Millennium Development Goal Review Summit. A second report, focusing on bringing high-speed connectivity to the poorest communities, was issued in June 2011.

The ITU publishes an annual report entitled *Measuring the Information Society*, which includes an ICT Development Index (IDI), measuring the state of ICT development world-wide (covering 152 countries in the 2011 edition, released in September of that year). The report also features an ICT Price Basket, reflecting the combined cost of mobile-cellular, fixed-telephone and fixed-broadband tariffs.

WORLD SUMMIT ON THE INFORMATION SOCIETY

ITU took a lead role in organizing the WSIS, which was held, under the auspices of the UN Secretary-General, in two phases: the first took place in Geneva in December 2003, and the second in Tunis, Tunisia in November 2005. The Geneva meeting, attended by representatives of 175 countries, recognized the central role of ITU in building an information society and approved a Declaration of Principles and Plan of Action, which urged co-operation by public and private sector stakeholders, civil society interests and UN agencies in encouraging new projects and partnerships aimed at bridging the so-called international digital divide. It entrusted ITU with addressing issues relating to cybersecurity. The second meeting adopted the Tunis Agenda for the Information Society, which called upon the UN Secretary-General to establish an Internet Governance Forum (IGF), with a view to establishing a more inclusive dialogue on global internet policy. In March 2006 the UN Secretary-General announced that a small secretariat would be formed to assist with convening the planned Forum, the first session of which was held in Athens, Greece, in October–November. IGFs have subsequently been held annually (September 2011: Nairobi, Kenya; September 2012: Baku, Azerbaijan). ITU hosts an annual WSIS Forum, in May, to address issues relating to follow-up and implementation by all stakeholders in the process. A UN Group on the Information Society was established in April 2006 to address UN implementation of the WSIS Plan of Action.

RADIOCOMMUNICATION SECTOR

The role of the sector (ITU-R) is globally to manage, and to ensure the equitable and efficient use of, the radio-frequency spectrum by all radiocommunication services, including those that use satellite orbits (the latter being in increasing demand from fixed, mobile, amateur, broadcasting, emergency telecommunications, environmental monitoring and communications services, global positioning systems, meteorology and space research services). The sector also conducts studies, and adopts recommendations on sector issues. The *Radio Regulations*, which first appeared in 1906, include general rules for the assignment and use of frequencies and the associated orbital positions for space stations. They include a Table of Frequency Allocations (governing the use of radio frequency bands between 9 kHz and 400 GHz) for the various radio services (*inter alia* radio broadcasting, television, radio astronomy, navigation aids, point-to-point service, maritime mobile, amateur). They are reviewed and revised by the World Radiocommunication Conferences: the most recent revision was issued in 2008. The technical work on issues to be considered by the conferences is conducted by Radiocommunication Assemblies, on the basis of recommendations made by Study Groups. These groups of experts study technical questions relating to radiocommunications, according to a study programme formulated by the Assemblies. The Assemblies may approve, modify or reject any recommendations of the Study Groups, and are authorized to establish new groups and to abolish others. The procedural rules used in the application of the Radio Regulations may be considered by a Radio Regulations Board, which may also perform duties relating to the allocation and use of frequencies and consider cases of interference. ITU-R is responsible for defining and recommending standards and frequency arrangements for international mobile telecommunications (IMT), in collaboration with governments, industry and the private sector. In October 2007 the Radiocommunication Assembly agreed to define as 'IMT-Advanced' new systems and capabilities that extend beyond the existing 'IMT 2000' systems. In January 2012 the Radiocommunication Assembly specified standards for IMT-Advanced technologies and agreed that 'LTE-Advanced' and WirelessMAN-Advanced' met the criteria for classification as IMT-Advanced.

The January 2012 Radiocommunication Assembly determined to conduct further studies on the development of a continuous time standard, aimed at replacing the current system of 'Coordinated Universal Time' (UTC), and repressing the use of 'leap seconds' that is standardized within UTC.

The administrative work of the sector is the responsibility of the Radiocommunication Bureau, which is headed by an elected Director, who is assisted by an Advisory Group. The Bureau co-ordinates the work of Study Groups, provides administrative support for the Radio Regulations Board, and works alongside the General Secretariat to prepare conferences and to provide relevant assistance to developing countries. The Bureau maintains the Maritime Mobile Access and Retrieval System (MARS), which provides access to operational information registered in the ITU maritime database.

Director: François Rancy (France).

TELECOMMUNICATION STANDARDIZATION SECTOR

The Telecommunication Standardization sector (ITU-T) studies technical, operational and tariff issues in order to standardize telecommunications throughout the world. The sector's conferences adopt the *International Telecommunications Regulations*, which establish ITU guidelines to guarantee the effective provision of telecommunication services. Recommendations may be approved outside of the four-year interval between conferences if a sectoral Study Group (comprising private and public sector experts) concludes such action to be urgent. Study Groups are engaged in the following areas of interest: operational aspects of service provision, networks and performance; tariff and accounting principles; telecommunication management; protection against electromagnetic environmental effects; outside plant and related indoor installations; integrated broadband cable networks and television and sound transmission; signalling requirements and protocols; performance and quality of service; NGN; optical and other transport network infrastructures; multimedia terminals, systems and applications; security, languages and telecommunications softwares; and mobile telecommunications networks. The Telecommunication Standardization Advisory Group (TSAG) reviews sectoral priorities, programmes, operations and administrative matters, and establishes, organizes and provides guidelines to the Study Groups. The 2004 World Telecommunication Standardization Assembly (WTSA), convened in October, in Florianópolis, Brazil, adopted an action plan for addressing the global standardization gap. Consequently a Group on Bridging the Standardization Gap was established within the TSAG. The 2008 WTSA was held in Johannesburg, South Africa, in October; it was preceded for the first time by a Global Standards Symposium that addressed means of enabling increased participation by developing countries in the standards making process, as well as considering challenges to the standards agenda, such as accessibility and climate change. ITU Global Standards Initiatives cover: Identity Management; Internet Protocol; Television; and NGN. The 2008 WTSA *inter alia* resolved to reduce greenhouse gas emissions arising from the use of ICTs. The 2012 WTSA was scheduled to be convened in November, in Dubai, UAE.

Preparations for conferences and other meetings of the sector are made by the Telecommunication Standardization Bureau. It administers the application of conference decisions, as well as relevant provisions of the International Telecommunications Regulations. The Bureau is headed by an elected Director, who is assisted by an Advisory Group. The Director reports to conferences and to the ITU Council on the activities of the sector.

Director: MALCOLM JOHNSON (United Kingdom).

TELECOMMUNICATION DEVELOPMENT SECTOR

The sector's objectives are to facilitate and enhance telecommunications development by offering, organizing and co-ordinating technical co-operation and assistance activities, to promote the development of telecommunication infrastructure, networks and services in developing countries, to facilitate the transfer of appropriate technologies and the use of resources, and to provide advice on issues specific to telecommunications. The sector implements projects under the UN development system or other funding arrangements. In January 2005 ITU launched an initiative to establish a network of some 100 Multipurpose Community Telecentres in 20 African countries, with the aim of providing broader access to ICTs. A global development initiative entitled 'Connect the World' was introduced by ITU in June, with the aim of providing access to ICTs to 1,000m. people without connectivity. The initiative, involving 22 stakeholders, was developed within the context of the WSIS agenda to encourage new projects and partnerships to bridge the digital divide. The first in a series of regional summits was held in October 2007 in Kigali, Rwanda, with the aim of mobilizing the human, financial and technical resources required to close ICT gaps throughout Africa. The summit generated investment commitments in excess of US $5,500m., and agreed to accelerate ICT connectivity goals in the region to 2012 (from 2015). The second summit, 'Connect CIS', was convened in Minsk, Belarus, in November 2009. Since 2001 ITU has supported the establishment of Internet Training Centres, by working in partnership with multinational and local private companies and training institutes. By December 2010 80 Centres had been established under the initiative.

The sector holds conferences regularly to encourage international co-operation in the development of telecommunications, and to determine strategies for development. Conferences consider the result of work undertaken by Study Groups on issues of benefit to developing countries, including development policy, finance, network planning and operation of services. The fourth World Telecommunication Development Conference (WTDC), convened in March 2006, in Doha, Qatar, addressed development priorities in the context of the Digital Divide, and the promotion of international co-operation to strengthen telecommunication infrastructure and institutions in developing countries. The fifth WTDC, held in Hyderabad, India, in May–June 2010, adopted the Hyderabad Action Plan, detailing strategies for fostering future global ICT and telecommunications development. Availability of NGN and extensive access to broadband services, wireless technologies and the internet were deemed to be catalysts for advancing a global information society and worldwide economic, social and cultural development.

ITU aims to support international humanitarian efforts in the event of an emergency by deploying temporary telecommunications and assessing the damage to the information infrastructure and its rehabilitation needs. ITU played a key role in drafting and promoting the Tampere Convention on the Provision of Telecommunication Resources for Disaster Mitigation and Relief Operations that was signed in 1998 and entered into force in January 2005. The Convention aimed to facilitate the deployment and use of telecommunications equipment in an emergency situation, in particular by removing regulatory barriers.

The administrative work of the sector is conducted by the Telecommunication Development Bureau, which may also study specific problems presented by a member state. The Director of the Bureau reports to conferences and the ITU Council, and is assisted by an Advisory Board.

Director: BRAHIMA SANOU (Burkina Faso).

Finance

The budget for the two-year period 2012–13 amounted to 319.1m. Swiss francs.

Publications

ITU Global Directory.

ITU News (10 a year, in English, French and Spanish).

ITU Yearbook of Statistics (annually).

Measuring the Information Society.

Operational Bulletin.

WSIS Stocktaking Report (annually).

Conventions, databases, statistics, regulations, technical documents and manuals, conference documents.

United Nations Educational, Scientific and Cultural Organization—UNESCO

Address: 7 place de Fontenoy, 75352 Paris 07 SP, France.

Telephone: 1-45-68-10-00; **fax:** 1-45-67-16-90; **e-mail:** bpi@unesco.org; **internet:** www.unesco.org.

UNESCO was established in 1946 'for the purpose of advancing, through the educational, scientific and cultural relations of the peoples of the world, the objectives of international peace and the common welfare of mankind'.

MEMBERS

UNESCO has 195 members (including Palestine, given full membership in October 2011) and six associate members.

Organization

(June 2012)

GENERAL CONFERENCE

The supreme governing body of the Organization, the Conference meets in ordinary session once in two years and is composed of representatives of the member states. It determines policies, approves work programmes and budgets and elects members of the Executive Board.

EXECUTIVE BOARD

The Board, comprising 58 members, prepares the programme to be submitted to the Conference and supervises its execution; it meets twice a year.

SECRETARIAT

The organization is headed by a Director-General, appointed for a four-year term. There are Assistant Directors-General for the main thematic sectors, i.e education, natural sciences, social and human sciences, culture, and communication and information, as well as for the support sectors of external relations and co-operation and of administration.

Director-General: Irina Bokova (Bulgaria).

CO-OPERATING BODIES

In accordance with UNESCO's constitution, national Commissions have been set up in most member states. These help to integrate work within the member states and the work of UNESCO. Most member states also have their own permanent delegations to UNESCO. UNESCO aims to develop partnerships with cities and local authorities.

FIELD CO-ORDINATION

UNESCO maintains a network of offices to support a more decentralized approach to its activities and enhance their implementation at field level. Cluster offices provide the main structure of the field co-ordination network. These cover a group of countries and help to co-ordinate between member states and with other UN and partner agencies operating in the area. In 2012 there were 27 cluster offices covering 148 states. In addition 21 national offices serve a single country, including those in post-conflict situations or economic transition and the nine most highly populated countries. The regional bureaux (see below) provide specialized support at a national level.

REGIONAL BUREAUX

Regional Bureau for Education in Africa (BREDA): 12 ave L. S. Senghor, BP 3318, Dakar, Senegal; tel. 849-23-23; fax 823-86-23; e-mail dakar@unesco.org; internet www.dakar.unesco.org; Dir Ann Therese Ndong-Jatta.

Regional Bureau for Science and Technology in Africa: POB 30592, Nairobi, Kenya; tel. (20) 7621-234; fax (20) 7622-750; e-mail nairobi@unesco.org; internet www.unesco-nairobi.org; f. 1965 to execute UNESCO's regional science programme, and to assist in the planning and execution of national programmes; Dir Joseph M. G. Massaquoi.

Regional Bureau for Education in the Arab States: POB 5244, Cité Sportive, Beirut, Lebanon; tel. (1) 850013; fax (1) 834854; e-mail beirut@unesco.org; internet www.unesco.org/en/beirut; Dir Hamed al-Hammami.

Regional Bureau for Sciences in the Arab States: 8 Abdel Rahman Fahmy St, Garden City, Cairo 11511, Egypt; tel. (2) 7945599; fax (2) 7945296; e-mail cairo@unesco.org; internet www.unesco.org/new/en/cairo/natural-sciences; also covers informatics; Dir Dr Tarek Shawki.

Regional Bureau for Science and Culture in Europe and North America: Palazzo Zorzi, 4930 Castello, 30122 Venice, Italy; tel. (041) 260-1511; fax (041) 528-9995; e-mail veniceoffice@unesco.org; internet www.unesco.org/venice; Dir Yolande Valle-Neff.

Regional Bureau for Culture in Latin America and the Caribbean (ORCALC): Calzada 551, esq. d, Vedado, Havana 4, Cuba; tel. (7) 833-3438; fax (7) 833-3144; e-mail habana@unesco.org.cu; internet www.unesco.org.cu; f. 1950; activities include research and programmes of cultural development and cultural tourism; maintains a documentation centre and a library of 14,500 vols; Dir Herman van Hooff; publs *Oralidad* (annually), *Boletín Electrónico* (quarterly).

Regional Bureau for Education in Latin America and the Caribbean (OREALC): Calle Enrique Delpiano 2058, Providencia, Santiago, Chile; Casilla 127, Correo 29, Providencia, Santiago, Chile; tel. (2) 472-4600; fax (2) 655-1046; e-mail santiago@unesco.org; internet www.unesco.org/santiago; f. 1963; Dir Jorge Sequeira.

Regional Bureau for Science for Latin America and the Caribbean: Calle Dr Luis Piera 1992, 2°, Casilla 859, 11000 Montevideo, Uruguay; tel. 2413 2075; fax 2413 2094; e-mail orcyt@unesco.org.uy; internet www.unesco.org.uy; also cluster office for Argentina, Brazil, Chile, Paraguay, Uruguay; Dir Jorge Grandi.

Regional Bureau for Education in Asia and the Pacific: POB 967, Bangkok 10110, Thailand; tel. (2) 391-0577; fax (2) 391-0866; e-mail bangkok@unescobkk.org; internet www.unescobkk.org; Dir Gwang-Jo Kim.

Regional Science Bureau for Asia and the Pacific: UNESCO Office, Jalan Galuh II 5, Kebayoran Baru, Jakarta 12110, Indonesia; tel. (21) 7399818; fax (21) 72796489; e-mail jakarta@unesco.org; internet www.unesco.or.id; Dir Hubert J. Gijzen.

Activities

In the implementation of all its activities UNESCO aims to contribute to achieving the UN Internationally Agreed Development Goals, and the UN Millennium Development Goal (MDG) of halving levels of extreme poverty by 2015, as well as other MDGs concerned with education and sustainable development. UNESCO was the lead agency for the International Decade for a Culture of Peace and Non-violence for the Children of the World (2001–10). In November 2007 the General Conference approved a medium-term strategy to guide UNESCO during the period 2008–13. UNESCO's central mission as defined under the strategy was to contribute to building peace, the alleviation of poverty, sustainable development and intercultural dialogue through its core programme sectors (Education; Natural Sciences; Social and Human Sciences; Culture; and Communication and Information). The strategy identified five 'overarching objectives' for UNESCO in 2008–13, within this programme framework: Attaining quality education for all; Mobilizing scientific knowledge and science policy for sustainable development; Addressing emerging ethical challenges; Promoting cultural diversity and intercultural dialogue; and Building inclusive knowledge societies through information and communication.

The 2008–13 medium-term strategy reaffirmed the organization's commitment to prioritizing Africa and its development efforts. In particular, it was to extend support to countries in post-conflict and disaster situations and strengthen efforts to achieve international targets and those identified through the New Partnership for Africa's Development (NEPAD, see under African Union). A further priority for UNESCO, to be implemented through all its areas of work, was gender equality. Specific activities were to be pursued in support of the welfare of youth, least developed countries and small island developing states.

EDUCATION

UNESCO recognizes education as an essential human right, and an overarching objective for 2008–13 was to attain quality education for all. Through its work programme UNESCO is committed to achieving the MDGs of eliminating gender disparity at all levels of education and attaining universal primary education in all countries by 2015. The focus of many of UNESCO's education initiatives are the nine most highly-populated developing countries (Bangladesh, Brazil, the People's Republic of China, Egypt, India, Indonesia, Mexico, Nigeria and Pakistan), known collectively as the E-9 ('Education-9') countries.

UNESCO leads and co-ordinates global efforts in support of 'Education for All' (EFA), which was adopted as a guiding principle of UNESCO's contribution to development following a world conference, convened in March 1990. In April 2000 several UN agencies, including UNESCO and UNICEF, and other partners sponsored the World Education Forum, held in Dakar, Senegal, to assess international progress in achieving the goal of Education for All and to adopt a strategy for further action (the 'Dakar Framework'), with the aim of ensuring universal basic education by 2015. The Dakar Framework, incorporating six specific goals, emphasized the role of improved access to education in the reduction of poverty and in diminishing inequalities within and between societies. UNESCO was appointed as the lead agency in the implementation of the Framework, focusing on co-ordination, advocacy, mobilization of resources, and information-sharing at international, regional and national levels. It was to oversee national policy reforms, with a particular focus on the integration of EFA objectives into national education plans. An EFA Global Action Plan was formulated in 2006 to reinvigorate efforts to achieve EFA objectives and, in particular, to provide a framework for international co-operation and better definition of the roles of international partners and of UNESCO in leading the initiative. UNESCO's medium-term strategy for 2008–13 committed the organization to strengthening its role in co-ordinating EFA efforts at global and national levels, promoting monitoring and capacity-building activities to support implementation of EFA objectives, and facilitating mobilization of increased resources for EFA programmes and strategies (for example through the EFA-Fast Track Initiative, launched in 2002 to accelerate technical and financial support to low-income countries).

UNESCO advocates 'Literacy for All' as a key component of Education for All, regarding literacy as essential to basic education and to social and human development. UNESCO is the lead agency of the UN Literacy Decade (2003–12), which aims to formulate an international plan of action to raise literacy standards throughout the world and to assist policy-makers to integrate literacy standards and goals into national education programmes. The Literacy Initiative for Empowerment (LIFE) was developed as an element of the Literacy Decade to accelerate efforts in some 35 countries where illiteracy is a critical challenge to development. UNESCO is also the co-ordinating agency for the UN Decade of Education for Sustainable Development (2005–14), through which it aims to establish a global framework for action and strengthen the capacity of education systems to incorporate the concepts of sustainable development into education programmes. The April 2000 World Education Forum recognized the global HIV/AIDS pandemic to be a significant challenge to the attainment of Education for All. UNESCO, as a co-sponsor of UNAIDS, takes an active role in promoting formal and non-formal preventive health education. Through a Global Initiative on HIV/AIDS and Education (EDUCAIDS) UNESCO aims to develop comprehensive responses to HIV/AIDS rooted in the education sector, with a particular focus on vulnerable children and young people. An initiative covering the 10-year period 2006–15, the Teacher Training Initiative in sub-Saharan Africa, aims to address the shortage of teachers in that region (owing to HIV/AIDS, armed conflict and other causes) and to improve the quality of teaching.

A key priority area of UNESCO's education programme is to foster quality education for all, through formal and non-formal educational opportunities. It assists members to improve the quality of education provision through curricula content, school management and teacher training. UNESCO aims to expand access to education at all levels and to work to achieve gender equality. In particular, UNESCO aims to strengthen capacity-building and education in natural, social and human sciences and promote the use of new technologies in teaching and learning processes. In May 2010 UNESCO, jointly with ITU, established a Broadband Commission for Digital Development, to comprise high level representatives of governments, industry and international agencies concerned with the effective deployment of broadband networks as an essential element of economic and social development objectives.

The Associated Schools Project (ASPnet—comprising more than 9,000 institutions in 180 countries in 2012) has, since 1953, promoted the principles of peace, human rights, democracy and international co-operation through education. It provides a forum for dialogue and for promoting best practices. At tertiary level UNESCO chairs a University Twinning and Networking (UNITWIN) initiative, which was established in 1992 to establish links between higher education institutions and to foster research, training and programme development. A complementary initiative, Academics Across Borders, was inaugurated in November 2005 to strengthen communication and the sharing of knowledge and expertise among higher education professionals. In October 2002 UNESCO organized the first Global Forum on International Quality Assurance, Accreditation and the Recognition of Qualifications to establish international standards and promote capacity-building for the sustainable development of higher education systems.

Within the UN system UNESCO is responsible for providing technical assistance and educational services in the context of emergency situations. This includes establishing temporary schools, providing education for refugees and displaced persons, as well as assistance for the rehabilitation of national education systems. In Palestine, UNESCO collaborates with UNRWA to assist with the training of teachers, educational planning and rehabilitation of schools. In February 2010 UNESCO agreed to form an International Co-ordination Committee in support of Haitian culture, in view of the devastation caused by an earthquake that had struck that country in January, causing 230,000 fatalities and the destruction of local infrastructure and architecture.

In February 2010 a high-level meeting on Education for All, comprising ministers of education and international co-operation, and representatives from international and regional organizations, civil society and the private sector, was held to assess the impact on education of the ongoing global economic crisis, and to consider related challenges connected to social marginalization.

NATURAL SCIENCES

The World Summit on Sustainable Development, held in August–September 2002, recognised the essential role of science (including mathematics, engineering and technology) as a foundation for achieving the MDGs of eradicating extreme poverty and ensuring environmental sustainability. UNESCO aims to promote this function within the UN system and to assist member states to utilize and foster the benefits of scientific and technical knowledge. A key objective for the medium-term strategy (2008–13) was to mobilize science knowledge and policy for sustainable development. Throughout the natural science programme priority was to be placed on Africa, least developed countries and small island developing states. The Local and Indigenous Knowledge System (LINKS) initiative aims to strengthen dialogue among traditional knowledge holders, natural and social scientists and decision-makers to enhance the conservation of biodiversity, in all disciplines, and to secure an active and equitable role for local communities in the governance of resources. In June 2012, in advance of the UN Conference on Sustainable Development (Rio+20), which was convened later in that month, UNESCO, with the International Council of Scientific Unions and other partners, participated in a Forum on Science, Technology and Innovation for Sustainable Development, addressing the role to be played by science and innovation in promoting sustainable development, poverty eradication, and the transition to a green economy.

In November 1999 the General Conference endorsed a Declaration on Science and the Use of Scientific Knowledge and an agenda for action, which had been adopted at the World Conference on Science, held in June–July 1999, in Budapest, Hungary. By leveraging scientific knowledge, and global, regional and country level science networks, UNESCO aims to support sustainable development and the sound management of natural resources. It also advises governments on approaches to natural resource management, in particular the collection of scientific data, documenting and disseminating good practices and integrating social and cultural aspects into management structures and policies. UNESCO's Man and the Biosphere Programme supports a world-wide network of biosphere reserves (comprising 580 biosphere reserves in 114 countries in 2012), which aim to promote environmental conservation and research, education and training in biodiversity and problems of land use (including the fertility of tropical soils and the cultivation of sacred sites). The third World Congress of Biosphere Reserves, held in Madrid, Spain, in February 2008, adopted the Madrid Action Plan, which aimed to promote biosphere reserves as the main internationally-designated areas dedicated to sustainable development. UNESCO also supports a Global Network of National Geoparks (89 in 27 countries in 2012) which was inaugurated in 2004 to promote collaboration among managed areas of geological significance to exchange knowledge and expertise and raise awareness of the benefits of protecting those environments. UNESCO organizes regular International Geoparks Conferences; the fifth was held in May 2012, in Unzen Volcanic Area Global Geopark, Japan.

UNESCO promotes and supports international scientific partnerships to monitor, assess and report on the state of Earth systems. With the World Meteorological Organization and the International Council of Science, UNESCO sponsors the World Climate Research Programme, which was established in 1980 to determine the predictability of climate and the effect of human activity on climate. UNESCO hosts the secretariat of the World Water Assessment Programme (WWAP), which prepares the periodic *World Water Development Report*. UNESCO is actively involved in the 10-year project, agreed by more than 60 governments in February 2005, to develop a Global Earth Observation System of Systems (GEOSS). The project aims to link existing and planned observation systems in order to provide for greater understanding of the earth's processes and dissemination of detailed data, for example predicting health epidemics or weather phenomena or concerning the management of ecosystems and natural resources. UNESCO's Intergovernmental Oceanographic Commission serves as the Secretariat of the Global Ocean Observing System. The International Geoscience Programme, undertaken jointly with the International Union of Geological Sciences (IUGS), facilitates the exchange of knowledge and methodology among scientists concerned with geological processes and aims to raise awareness of the links between geoscience and sustainable socio-economic development. The IUGS and UNESCO jointly initiated the International Year of Planet Earth (2008).

UNESCO is committed to contributing to international efforts to enhance disaster preparedness and mitigation. Through education UNESCO aims to reduce the vulnerability of poorer communities to disasters and improve disaster management at local and national levels. It also co-ordinates efforts at an international level to establish monitoring networks and early-warning systems to mitigate natural disasters, in particular in developing tsunami early-warning systems in Africa, the Caribbean, the South Pacific, the Mediterranean Sea and the North East Atlantic similar to those already established for the Indian and Pacific oceans. Other regional partnerships and knowledge networks were to be developed to strengthen capacity-building and the dissemination of information and good practices relating to risk awareness and mitigation and disaster management. Disaster education and awareness were to be incorporated as key elements in the UN Decade of Education for Sustainable Development (see above). UNESCO is also the lead agency for the International Flood Initiative, which was inaugurated in January 2005 at the World Conference on Disaster Reduction, held in Kobe, Japan. The Initiative aims to promote an integrated approach to flood management in order to minimize the damage and loss of life caused by floods, mainly with a focus on research, training, promoting good governance and providing technical assistance. The fifth International Conference on Flood Management was convened in Tsukuba, Japan, in September 2011.

A priority of the natural science programme has been to promote policies and strengthen human and institutional capacities in science, technology and innovation. At all levels of education UNESCO aims to enhance teaching quality and content in areas of science and technology and, at regional and sub-regional level, to strengthen co-operation mechanisms and policy networks in training and research. With the International Council of Scientific Unions and the Third World Academy of Sciences, UNESCO operates a short-term fellowship programme in the basic sciences and an exchange programme of visiting lecturers.

UNESCO is the lead agency of the New Partnership for Africa's Development (NEPAD) Science and Technology Cluster and the NEPAD Action Plan for the Environment.

SOCIAL AND HUMAN SCIENCES

UNESCO is mandated to contribute to the world-wide development of the social and human sciences and philosophy, which it regards as of great importance in policy-making and maintaining ethical vigilance. The structure of UNESCO's Social and Human Sciences programme takes into account both an ethical and standard-setting dimension, and research, policy-making, action in the field and future-oriented activities. One of UNESCO's so-called overarching objectives in the period 2008–13 was to address emerging ethical challenges.

A priority area of UNESCO's work programme on Social and Human Sciences has been to promote principles, practices and ethical norms relevant for scientific and technological development. The programme fosters international co-operation and dialogue on emerging issues, as well as raising awareness and promoting the sharing of knowledge at regional and national levels. UNESCO supports the activities of the International Bioethics Committee (IBC—a group of 36 specialists who meet under UNESCO auspices) and the Intergovernmental Bioethics Committee, and hosts the secretariat of the 18-member World Commission on the Ethics of Scientific Knowledge and Technology (COMEST), established in 1999, which aims to serve as a forum for the exchange of information and ideas and to promote dialogue between scientific communities, decision-makers and the public.

The priority Ethics of science and technology element aims to promote intergovernmental discussion and co-operation; to conduct explorative studies on possible UNESCO action on environmental ethics and developing a code of conduct for scientists; to enhance public awareness; to make available teaching expertise and create regional networks of experts; to promote the development of international and national databases on ethical issues; to identify ethical issues related to emerging technologies; to follow up relevant declarations, including the Universal Declaration on the Human Genome and Human Rights (see below); and to support the Global Ethics Observatory, an online world-wide database of information on applied bioethics and other applied science- and technology-related areas (including environmental ethics) that was launched in December 2005 by the IBC.

UNESCO itself provides an interdisciplinary, multicultural and pluralistic forum for reflection on issues relating to the ethical dimension of scientific advances, and promotes the application of international guidelines. In May 1997 the IBC approved a draft version of a Universal Declaration on the Human Genome and Human Rights, in an attempt to provide ethical guidelines for developments in human genetics. The Declaration, which identified some 100,000 hereditary genes as 'common heritage', was adopted by the UNESCO General Conference in November and committed states to promoting the dissemination of relevant scientific knowledge and co-operating in genome research. In October 2003 the General Conference adopted an International Declaration on Human Genetic Data, establishing standards for scientists working in that field, and in October 2005 the General Conference adopted the Universal Declaration on Bioethics and Human Rights. At all levels UNESCO aims to raise awareness and foster debate about the ethical implications of scientific and technological developments and promote exchange of experiences and knowledge between governments and research bodies.

UNESCO recognizes that globalization has a broad and significant impact on societies. It is committed to countering negative trends of social transformation by strengthening the links between research and policy formulation by national and local authorities, in particular concerning poverty eradication. In that respect, UNESCO promotes the concept that freedom from poverty is a fundamental human right. In 1994 UNESCO initiated an international social science research programme, the Management of Social Transformations (MOST), to promote capacity-building in social planning at all levels of decision-making. In 2003 the Executive Board approved a continuation of the programme but with a revised strategic objective of strengthening links between research, policy and practice. In 2008–13 UNESCO aimed to promote new collaborative social science research programmes and to support capacity-building in developing countries.

UNESCO aims to monitor emerging social or ethical issues and, through its associated offices and institutes, formulate preventative action to ensure they have minimal impact on the attainment of UNESCO's objectives. As a specific challenge UNESCO is committed to promoting the International Convention against Doping in Sport, which entered into force in 2007. UNESCO also focuses on the educational and cultural dimensions of physical education and sport and their capacity to preserve and improve health.

Fundamental to UNESCO's mission is the rejection of all forms of discrimination. It disseminates information aimed at combating racial prejudice, works to improve the status of women and their access to education, promotes equality between men and women, and raises awareness of discrimination against people affected by HIV/AIDS, in particular among young people. In 2004 UNESCO inaug-urated an initiative to enable city authorities to share experiences and collaborate in efforts to counter racism, discrimination, xenophobia and exclusion. As well as the International Coalition of Cities against Racism, regional coalitions were to be formed with more defined programmes of action. An International Youth Clearing House and Information Service (INFOYOUTH) aims to increase and consolidate the information available on the situation of young people in society, and to heighten awareness of their needs, aspirations and potential among public and private decision-makers. Supporting efforts to facilitate dialogue among different cultures and societies and promoting opportunities for reflection and consideration of philosophy and human rights, for example the celebration of World Philosophy Day, are also among UNESCO's fundamental aims.

CULTURE

In undertaking efforts to preserve the world's cultural and natural heritage UNESCO has attempted to emphasize the link between culture and development. In December 1992 UNESCO established the World Commission on Culture and Development, to strengthen links between culture and development and to prepare a report on the issue. The first World Conference on Culture and Development was held in June 1999, in Havana, Cuba. In November 2001 the General Conference adopted the UNESCO Universal Declaration on Cultural Diversity, which affirmed the importance of intercultural dialogue in establishing a climate of peace. UNESCO's medium-term strategy for 2008–13 recognized the need for a more integrated approach to cultural heritage as an area requiring conservation and development and one offering prospects for dialogue, social cohesion and shared knowledge.

UNESCO aims to promote cultural diversity through the safeguarding of heritage and enhancement of cultural expressions. In January 2002 UNESCO inaugurated the Global Alliance on Cultural Diversity, to promote partnerships between governments, non-governmental bodies and the private sector with a view to supporting cultural diversity through the strengthening of cultural industries and the prevention of cultural piracy. In October 2005 the General Conference approved an International Convention on the Protection of the Diversity of Cultural Expressions. It entered into force in March 2007 and the first session of the intergovernmental committee servicing the Convention was convened in Ottawa, Canada, in December.

UNESCO's World Heritage Programme, inaugurated in 1978, aims to protect historic sites and natural landmarks of outstanding universal significance, in accordance with the 1972 UNESCO Convention Concerning the Protection of the World Cultural and Natural Heritage, by providing financial aid for restoration, technical assistance, training and management planning. The medium-term strategy for 2008–13 acknowledged that new global threats may affect natural and cultural heritage. It also reinforced the concept that conservation of sites contributes to social cohesion. During mid-2011–mid-2012 the 'World Heritage List' comprised 936 sites globally, of which 725 had cultural significance, 183 were natural landmarks, and 28 were of 'mixed' importance. Examples include: the Great Barrier Reef (in Australia), the Galapagos Islands (Ecuador), Chartres Cathedral (France), the Taj Mahal at Agra (India), Auschwitz concentration camp (Poland), the historic sanctuary of Machu Picchu (Peru), Robben Island (South Africa), the Serengeti National Park (Tanzania), and the archaeological site of Troy (Turkey). Some 36 new sites were being considered in June 2012 for inscription onto the List for 2012–13. UNESCO also maintains a 'List of World Heritage in Danger', comprising 35 sites during mid-2011–mid-2012, in order to attract international attention to sites particularly at risk from the environment or human activities.

UNESCO supports the safeguarding of humanity's non-material 'intangible' heritage, including oral traditions, music, dance and medicine. An Endangered Languages Programme was initiated in 1993. By 2012 the Programme estimated that, of some 6,700 languages spoken world-wide, about one-half were endangered. It works to raise awareness of the issue, for example through publication of the *Atlas of the World's Languages in Danger of Disappearing*, to strengthen local and national capacities to safeguard and document languages, and administers a Register of Good Practices in Language Preservation. In October 2003 the UNESCO General Conference adopted a Convention for the Safeguarding of Intangible Cultural Heritage, which provided for the establishment of an intergovernmental committee and for participating states to formulate national inventories of intangible heritage. The Convention entered into force in April 2006 and the intergovernmental committee convened its inaugural session in November. The second session was held in Tokyo, Japan, in September 2007. A Representative List of the Intangible Cultural Heritage of Humanity, inaugurated in November 2008, comprised, at June 2012, 232 elements ('masterpieces of the oral and intangible heritage of humanity') deemed to be of outstanding value; these included: Chinese calligraphy; falconry; several dances, such as the tango, which originated in Argentina and Uruguay, and the dances of the Ainu in Japan; the chant of the Sybil on Majorca, Spain; and the Ifa Divination System (Nigeria). The related List of Intangible Cultural Heritage in Need of Urgent Safeguarding comprised 27 elements in June 2012, such as the Naqqāli form of story-telling in Iran, the Saman dance in Sumatra, Indonesia, and the Qiang New Year Festival in Sichuan Province, China. UNESCO's culture programme also aims to safeguard movable cultural heritage and to support and develop museums as a means of preserving heritage and making it accessible to society as a whole.

In November 2001 the General Conference authorized the formulation of a Declaration against the Intentional Destruction of Cultural Heritage. In addition, the Conference adopted the Convention on the Protection of the Underwater Cultural Heritage, covering the protection from commercial exploitation of shipwrecks, submerged historical sites, etc., situated in the territorial waters of signatory states. UNESCO also administers the 1954 Hague Convention on the Protection of Cultural Property in the Event of Armed Conflict and the 1970 Convention on the Means of Prohibiting and Preventing the Illicit Import, Export and Transfer of Ownership of Cultural Property. In 1992 a World Heritage Centre was established to enable rapid mobilization of international technical assistance for the preservation of cultural sites. Through the World Heritage Information Network (WHIN), a world-wide network of more than 800 information providers, UNESCO promotes global awareness and information exchange.

UNESCO aims to support the development of creative industries and or creative expression. Through a variety of projects UNESCO promotes art education, supports the rights of artists, and encourages crafts, design, digital art and performance arts. In October 2004 UNESCO launched a Creative Cities Network to facilitate public and private sector partnerships, international links, and recognition of a city's unique expertise. In 2012 the following cities were participating in the Network: Aswan (Egypt), Icheon (Republic of Korea), Kanazawa (Japan) and Santa Fe (Mexico) (UNESCO Cities of Craft and Folk Art); Berlin (Germany), Buenos Aires (Argentina), Graz (Austria), Montreal (Canada), Nagoya and Kobe (Japan), Seoul (Republic of Korea), Shanghai and Shenzhen (China), Saint-Etienne (France) (UNESCO Cities of Design); Chengdu (China), Östersund (Sweden), Popayan (Colombia) (UNESCO Cities of Gastronomy); Dublin (Republic of Ireland), Edinburgh (United Kingdom), Iowa City (USA), Melbourne (Australia), Reykjavik (Iceland) (UNESCO Cities of Literature); Bologna (Italy), Ghent (Belgium), Glasgow (United Kingdom), Seville (Spain) (UNESCO Cities of Music); Bradford (United Kingdom), Sydney (Australia) (UNESCO Cities of Film); and Lyon (France) (UNESCO City of Media Arts). UNESCO is active in preparing and encouraging the enforcement of international legislation on copyright, raising awareness on the need for copyright protection to uphold cultural diversity, and is contributing to the international debate on digital copyright issues and piracy.

Within its ambition of ensuring cultural diversity, UNESCO recognizes the role of culture as a means of promoting peace and dialogue. Several projects have been formulated within a broader concept of Roads of Dialogue. In Central Asia a project on intercultural dialogue follows on from an earlier multi-disciplinary study of the ancient Silk Roads trading routes linking Asia and Europe, which illustrated many examples of common heritage. Other projects include a study of the movement of peoples and cultures during the slave trade, a Mediterranean Programme, the Caucasus Project and the Arabia Plan, which aims to promote world-wide knowledge and understanding of Arab culture. UNESCO has overseen an extensive programme of work to formulate histories of humanity and regions, focused on ideas, civilizations and the evolution of societies and cultures. These have included the *General History of Africa, History of Civilizations of Central Asia,* and *History of Humanity*. UNESCO endeavoured to consider and implement the findings of the Alliance of Civilizations, a high-level group convened by the UN Secretary-General that published a report in November 2006. UNESCO signed a Memorandum of Understanding with the Alliance during its first forum, convened in Madrid, Spain, in January 2008.

UNESCO was designated as the lead UN agency for organizing the International Year for the Rapprochement of Cultures (2010). In February 2010, at the time of the launch of the International Year, the UNESCO Director-General established a High Panel on Peace and Dialogue among Cultures, which was to provide guidance on means of advancing tolerance, reconciliation and balance within societies world-wide.

COMMUNICATION AND INFORMATION

UNESCO regards information, communication and knowledge as being at the core of human progress and well-being. The Organization advocates the concept of knowledge societies, based on the principles of freedom of expression, universal access to information and knowledge, promotion of cultural diversity, and equal access to quality education. In 2008–13 it determined to consolidate and implement this concept, in accordance with the Declaration of Principles and Plan of Action adopted by the World Summit on the Information Society (WSIS) in November 2005.

A key strategic objective of building inclusive knowledge societies was to be through enhancing universal access to communication and information. At national and global levels UNESCO promotes the rights of freedom of expression and of access to information. It promotes the free flow and broad diffusion of information, knowledge, data and best practices, through the development of communications infrastructures, the elimination of impediments to freedom of expression, and the development of independent and pluralistic media, including through the provision of advisory services on media legislation, particularly in post-conflict countries and in countries in transition. UNESCO recognizes that the so-called global 'digital divide', in addition to other developmental differences between countries, generates exclusion and marginalization, and that increased participation in the democratic process can be attained through strengthening national communication and information capacities. UNESCO promotes policies and mechanisms that enhance provision for marginalized and disadvantaged groups to benefit from information and community opportunities. Activities at local and national level include developing effective 'infostructures', such as libraries and archives and strengthening low-cost community media and information access points, for example through the establishment of Community Multimedia Centres (CMCs). Many of UNESCO's principles and objectives in this area are pursued through the Information for All Programme, which entered into force in 2001. It is administered by an intergovernmental council, the secretariat of which is provided by UNESCO. UNESCO also established, in 1982, the International Programme for the Development of Communication (IPDC), which aims to promote and develop independent and pluralistic media in developing countries, for example by the establishment or modernization of news agencies and newspapers and training media professionals, the promotion of the right to information, and through efforts to harness informatics for development purposes and strengthen member states' capacities in this field. In March 2011 the IPDC approved funding for 93 new media development projects in developing and emerging countries world-wide.

UNESCO supports cultural and linguistic diversity in information sources to reinforce the principle of universal access. It aims to raise awareness of the issue of equitable access and diversity, encourage good practices and develop policies to strengthen cultural diversity in all media. In 2002 UNESCO established Initiative B@bel as a multidisciplinary programme to promote linguistic diversity, with the aim of enhancing access of under-represented groups to information sources as well as protecting underused minority languages. In December 2009 UNESCO and the Internet Corporation for Assigned Names and Numbers (ICANN) signed a joint agreement which aimed to promote the use of multilingual domain names using non-Latin script, with a view to promoting linguistic diversity. UNESCO's Programme for Creative Content supports the development of and access to diverse content in both the electronic and audiovisual media. The Memory of the World project, established in 1992, aims to preserve in digital form, and thereby to promote wide access to, the world's documentary heritage. Documentary material includes stone tablets, celluloid, parchment and audio recordings. By 2012 245 inscriptions had been included on the project's register; three inscriptions originated from international organizations: the Archives of the ICRC's former International Prisoners of War Agency, 1914–23, submitted by the ICRC, and inscribed in 2007; the League of Nations Archives, 1919–46, submitted by the UN Geneva Office, and inscribed in 2009; and the UNRWA Photo and Film Archives of Palestinian Refugees' Documentary Heritage, submitted by UNRWA, and also inscribed in 2009. In September 2012 UNESCO was to organize an International Conference on the 'Memory of the World in the Digital Age: Digitization and Preservation', in Vancouver, Canada. UNESCO also supports other efforts to preserve and disseminate digital archives and, in 2003, adopted a Charter for the Preservation of Digital Heritage. In April 2009 UNESCO launched the internet based World Digital Library, accessible at www.wdl.org, which aims to display primary documents (including texts, charts and illustrations), and authoritative explanations, relating to the accumulated knowledge of a broad spectrum of human cultures.

UNESCO promotes freedom of expression, of the press and independence of the media as fundamental human rights and the basis of democracy. It aims to assist member states to formulate policies and legal frameworks to uphold independent and pluralistic media and infostructures and to enhance the capacities of public service broadcasting institutions. In regions affected by conflict UNESCO supports efforts to establish and maintain an independent media service and to use it as a means of consolidating peace. UNESCO also aims to develop media and information systems to respond to and mitigate the impact of disaster situations, and to integrate these objectives into wider UN peace-building or reconstruction initiatives. UNESCO is the co-ordinating agency for 'World Press Freedom Day', which is held annually on 3 May; it also awards an annual World Press Freedom Prize. A conference convened in Tunis, Tunisia, in celebration of the May 2012 World Press Freedom Day—held on the theme 'New Voices: Media Freedom Helping to Transform Societies', with a focus on the transition towards democracy in several countries of North Africa and the Middle East—adopted the Carthage Declaration, urging the creation of free and safe environments for media workers and the promotion of journalistic ethics. The Declaration also requested UNESCO to pursue implementation of the UN Plan of Action on the Safety of Journalists and the Issue of Impunity, which had been drafted with guidance from UNESCO, and endorsed in April by the UN System Chief Executives Board for Co-ordination. UNESCO maintains an Observatory on the Information Society, which provides up-to-date information on the development of new ICTs, analyses major trends, and aims to raise awareness of related ethical, legal and societal issues. UNESCO promotes the upholding of human rights in the use of cyberspace. In 1997 it organized the first International Congress on Ethical, Legal and Societal Aspects of Digital Information ('INFOethics').

UNESCO promotes the application of information and communication technology for sustainable development. In particular it supports efforts to improve teaching and learning processes through electronic media and to develop innovative literacy and education initiatives, such as the ICT-Enhanced Learning (ICTEL) project. UNESCO also aims to enhance understanding and use of new technologies and support training and ongoing learning opportunities for librarians, archivists and other information providers.

Finance

UNESCO's activities are funded through a regular budget provided by contributions from member states and extrabudgetary funds from other sources, particularly UNDP, the World Bank, regional banks and other bilateral Funds-in-Trust arrangements. UNESCO co-operates with many other UN agencies and international non-governmental organizations.

UNESCO's Regular Programme budget for the two years 2012–13 was US $685.7m.

In response to a decision, in late October 2011, by a majority of member states participating in the UNESCO General Conference to admit Palestine as a new member state, the USA decided to withhold from UNESCO significant annual funding. In 2012 a formal application (submitted in October 2011 by the Executive President of the Palestinian Authority) for full UN membership for Palestine—and thereby formal recognition as an independent state—remained under consideration by the UN Security Council.

Publications

(mostly in English, French and Spanish editions; Arabic, Chinese and Russian versions are also available in many cases)

Atlas of the World's Languages in Danger of Disappearing (online).

Copyright Bulletin (quarterly).

Encyclopedia of Life Support Systems (online).

Education for All Global Monitoring Report.

International Review of Education (quarterly).

International Social Science Journal (quarterly).

Museum International (quarterly).

Nature and Resources (quarterly).

The New Courier (quarterly).

Prospects (quarterly review on education).

UNESCO Sources (monthly).

UNESCO Statistical Yearbook.

UNESCO World Atlas of Gender Equality in Education.

World Communication Report.

World Educational Report (every 2 years).

World Heritage Review (quarterly).

World Information Report.

World Science Report (every 2 years).

Books, databases, video and radio documentaries, statistics, scientific maps and atlases.

Specialized Institutes and Centres

Abdus Salam International Centre for Theoretical Physics: Strada Costiera 11, 34151 Trieste, Italy; tel. (040) 2240111; fax (040) 224163; e-mail sci_info@ictp.it; internet www.ictp.it; f. 1964; promotes and enables advanced study and research in physics and mathematical sciences; organizes and sponsors training opportunities, in particular for scientists from developing countries; aims to provide an international forum for the exchange of information and ideas; operates under a tripartite agreement between UNESCO, IAEA and the Italian Government; Dir Fernando Quevedo (Guatemala).

International Bureau of Education (IBE): POB 199, 1211 Geneva 20, Switzerland; tel. 229177800; fax 229177801; e-mail doc.centre@ibe.unesco.org; internet www.ibe.unesco.org; f. 1925, became an intergovernmental organization in 1929 and was incorporated into UNESCO in 1969; the Council of the IBE is composed of representatives of 28 member states of UNESCO, designated by the General Conference; the Bureau's fundamental mission is to deal with matters concerning educational content, methods, and teaching/learning strategies; an International Conference on Education is held periodically; Dir Clementina Acedo (Venezuela); publs *Prospects* (quarterly review), *Educational Innovation* (newsletter), educational practices series, monographs, other reference works.

UNESCO European Centre for Higher Education (CEPES): Str. Stirbei Vodà 39, 010102 Bucharest, Romania; tel. (1) 313-0839; fax (1) 312-3567; e-mail info@cepes.ro; f. 1972; Head of Office a. i. Peter J. Wells.

UNESCO Institute for Information Technologies in Education: 117292 Moscow, ul. Kedrova 8, Russia; tel. (495) 129-29-90; fax (495) 129-12-25; e-mail info@iite.ru; internet www.iite.ru; the Institute aims to formulate policies regarding the development of, and to support and monitor the use of, information and communication technologies in education; it conducts research and organizes training programmes; Chair Badarch Dendev (acting).

UNESCO Institute for Life-long Learning: Feldbrunnenstr. 58, 20148 Hamburg, Germany; tel. (40) 448-0410; fax (40) 410-7723; e-mail uil@unesco.org; internet www.unesco.org/uil/index.htm; f. 1951, as the Institute for Education; a research, training, information, documentation and publishing centre, with a particular focus on adult basic and further education and adult literacy; Dir Arne Carlsen.

UNESCO Institute for Statistics: CP 6128, Succursale Centre-Ville, Montréal, QC, H3C 3J7, Canada; tel. (514) 343-6880; fax (514) 343-6882; e-mail uis@unesco.org; internet www.uis.unesco.org; f. 2001; collects and analyses national statistics on education, science, technology, culture and communications; Dir Hendrik van der Pol (Netherlands).

UNESCO Institute for Water Education: Westvest 7, 2611 AX Delft, Netherlands; tel. (15) 2151-715; fax (15) 2122-921; e-mail info@unesco-ihe.org; internet www.unesco-ihe.org; f. 2003; activities include education, training and research; and co-ordination of a global network of water sector organizations; advisory and policy-making functions; setting international standards for postgraduate education programmes; and professional training in the water sector; Rector András Szöllösi-Nagy.

UNESCO International Centre for Technical and Vocational Education and Training: UN Campus, Hermann-Ehlers-Str. 10, 53113 Bonn, Germany; tel. (228) 8150-100; fax (228) 8150-199; e-mail info@unevoc.unesco.org; internet www.unevoc.unesco.org; f. 2002; promotes high-quality lifelong technical and vocational education in UNESCO's member states, with a particular focus on young people, girls and women, and the disadvantaged; Head SHYAMAL MAJUMDAR (India).

UNESCO International Institute for Capacity Building in Africa (UNESCO–IICBA): ECA Compound, Africa Ave, POB 2305, Addis Ababa, Ethiopia; tel. (11) 5445284; fax (11) 514936; e-mail info@unesco-iicba.org; internet www.unesco-iicba.org; f. 1999 to promote capacity building in the following areas: teacher education; curriculum development; educational policy, planning and management; and distance education; Dir ARNALDO NHAVOTO.

UNESCO International Institute for Educational Planning (IIEP): 7–9 rue Eugène Delacroix, 75116 Paris, France; tel. 1-45-03-77-00; fax 1-40-72-83-66; e-mail info@iiep.unesco.org; internet www.unesco.org/iiep; f. 1963; serves as a world centre for advanced training and research in educational planning; aims to help all member states of UNESCO in their social and economic development efforts, by enlarging the fund of knowledge about educational planning and the supply of competent experts in this field; legally and administratively a part of UNESCO, the Institute is autonomous, and its policies and programme are controlled by its own Governing Board, under special statutes voted by the General Conference of UNESCO; a satellite office of the IIEP is based in Buenos Aires, Argentina; Dir KHALIL MAHSHI (Jordan).

UNESCO International Institute for Higher Education in Latin America and the Caribbean: Avda Los Chorros con Calle Acueducto, Edif. Asovincar, Altos de Sebucán, Apdo 68394, Caracas 1062-A, Venezuela; tel. (212) 286-0555; fax (212) 286-0527; e-mail prensa@unesco.org.ve; internet www.iesalc.unesco.org.ve; Dir PEDRO HENRÍQUEZ GUAJARDO (acting).

United Nations Industrial Development Organization—UNIDO

Address: Vienna International Centre, Wagramerstr. 5, POB 300, 1400 Vienna, Austria.

Telephone: (1) 260260; **fax:** (1) 2692669; **e-mail:** unido@unido.org; **internet:** www.unido.org.

UNIDO began operations in 1967, as an autonomous organization within the UN Secretariat, and became a specialized agency of the UN in 1985. UNIDO's objective is to promote sustainable industrial development in developing nations and states with economies in transition. It aims to assist such countries to integrate fully into the global economic system by mobilizing knowledge, skills, information and technology to promote productive employment, competitive economies and sound environment.

MEMBERS

UNIDO has 174 members.

Organization

(June 2012)

GENERAL CONFERENCE

The General Conference, which consists of representatives of all member states, meets once every two years. It is the chief policy-making organ of the Organization, and reviews UNIDO's policy concepts, strategies on industrial development and budget. The 14th General Conference was convened, in Vienna, Austria, in November–December 2011, on the theme 'The new industrial revolution: making it sustainable'.

INDUSTRIAL DEVELOPMENT BOARD

The Board consists of 53 members elected by the General Conference for a four-year period. It reviews the implementation of the approved work programme, the regular and operational budgets and other General Conference decisions, and, every four years, recommends a candidate for the post of Director-General to the General Conference for appointment.

PROGRAMME AND BUDGET COMMITTEE

The Committee, consisting of 27 members elected by the General Conference for a two-year term, assists the Industrial Development Board in preparing work programmes and budgets.

SECRETARIAT

The Secretariat comprises the office of the Director-General and three divisions, each headed by a Managing Director: Programme Development and Technical Co-operation; Programme Co-ordination and Field Operations; and Administration. In 2012 UNIDO employed around 700 regular staff members at its headquarters and other established offices.

Director-General: KANDEH YUMKELLA (Sierra Leone).

FIELD REPRESENTATION

UNIDO has 17 country offices and 12 regional offices. UNIDO's field activities throughout the world are assisted annually by around 2,800 experts.

Activities

UNIDO bases its assistance on two core functions: serving as a global forum for generating and disseminating industry-related knowledge; and designing and implementing technical co-operation programmes in support of its clients' industrial development efforts. The two core functions are complementary and mutually supportive: policy-makers benefit from experience gained in technical co-operation projects, while, by helping to define priorities, the Organization's analytical work identifies where technical co-operation will have greatest impact. Its assistance is also underpinned by the following three thematic priorities: poverty reduction through productive activities; trade capacity-building; and environment and energy. The comprehensive services provided by UNIDO cover:

(i) Industrial governance and statistics;

(ii) Promotion of investment and technology;

(iii) Industrial competitiveness and trade;

(iv) Private sector development;

(v) Agro-industries;

(vi) Sustainable energy and climate change;

(vii) The Montreal Protocol;

(viii) Environment management.

UNIDO promotes the achievement by 2015 of all the Millennium Development Goals (MDGs) adopted by the September 2000 UN Millennium Summit, with a particular focus on using industrial development in support of: eradicating extreme poverty and hunger; promoting gender equality and empowering women; ensuring environmental protection; and developing a global partnership for development. In December 2005 the 11th session of the General Conference adopted a *Strategic Long-term Vision Statement* covering the period 2005–15, focused on promoting the Organization's three thematic priorities.

UNIDO participates in the UN System Chief Executives' Board for Co-ordination—CEB's Inter-Agency Cluster on Trade and Productive Capacity, chaired by UNCTAD and also comprising UNDP, FAO, the International Trade Centre (ITC), WTO and the UN regional commissions; the Cluster, in line with the UN's *Delivering as One* agenda, aims to co-ordinate trade and development operations at the national and regional levels within the UN system. In March 2008 UNIDO organized a high-level dialogue entitled UN System-wide Coherence: The Next Steps, with a view to mapping future UN inter-agency co-operation.

UNIDO, with ITU and WIPO, leads an initiative on promoting technology and innovation, the eighth of nine activities that were launched in April 2009 by the CEB, with the aim of alleviating the impact on poor and vulnerable populations of the developing global economic crisis.

UNIDO also supports collaborative efforts between countries with complementary experience or resources in specific sectors. The investment and technology promotion network publicizes investment opportunities, provides information to investors and promotes business contacts between industrialized and developing countries and economies in transition. UNIDO is increasingly working to achieve investment promotion and transfer of technology and knowledge among developing countries. The Organization has developed several databases, including the Biosafety Information Network Advisory Service (BINAS), the Business Environment Strategic Toolkit (BEST), Industrial Development Abstracts (IDA, providing information on technical co-operation), and the International Referral System on Sources of Information (IRS).

In November 2011 UNIDO published a new *Connectedness Index*, measuring and ranking national 'knowledge networks' to assist private sector policy makers; the report was subtitled 'Networks for prosperity: achieving development goals through knowledge sharing'.

UNIDO has helped to establish and operate the following International Technology Centres: the International Centre for Science and High Technology (based in Trieste, Italy); the International Centre for Advancement of Manufacturing Technology (Bangalore, India); the UNIDO Regional Centre for Small Hydro Power (Trivandum, India); the Centre for the Application of Solar Energy (Perth, Australia); the International Centre of Medicine Biotechnology (Obolensk, Russia); the International Materials Assessment and Application Centre (Rio de Janeiro, Brazil); the International Centre for Materials Technology Promotion (Beijing, People's Republic of China); and the Shenzhen International Technology Promotion Centre (also in China).

The Organization promotes South-South industrial co-operation. A UNIDO Centre for South-South Industrial Co-operation (UCSSIC) was established in India, and, in July 2008, a further UCSSIC was inaugurated in Beijing.

POVERTY REDUCTION THROUGH PRODUCTIVE ACTIVITIES

UNIDO provides support to policy-making bodies in developing countries to promote competitive industries and private sector development, with a particular focus on: the creation of competitiveness intelligence units in major public and private sector institutions; and the establishment of industrial observatories, with the role of monitoring global trade and industry trends, and benchmarking national and company performance. During 2007 UNIDO introduced an online private sector development toolkit, to provide support to policy-makers.

Encouraging foreign direct investment, and promoting technology transfer and technology diffusion projects aimed at strengthening developing countries' national innovation systems, are key elements of the Organization's poverty reduction strategy.

UNIDO implements a programme for small and medium-sized enterprise (SME) cluster development, which aims to enhance linkages between small businesses and support institutions, in order to assist them with realizing their full growth potential. A Rural and Women's Entrepreneurship Development Programme promotes businesses in developing countries with a particular focus on women and youth. UNIDO recognizes that agro-based industries play a major role in the transition from traditional rural to competitive manufacturing-based economies, and therefore supports the development of the skills and technologies required to advance those industries in developing countries. In the area of food-processing programmes have been initiated to upgrade agro-based value chains, and to open market channels for agro-products. Through its efforts to strengthen developing countries' food supplies and facilitate access to markets, technology and investment, UNIDO also contributes to UN system-wide efforts to address the ongoing global food security crisis. In April 2008 UNIDO, jointly with FAO, IFAD and the Indian Government, organized the Global Agro-Industries Forum: Improving Competitiveness and Development Impact, convened in New Delhi, India; and in November UNIDO helped to organize an International Conference on Sharing Innovative Agribusiness Solutions, held in Cairo, Egypt. The Organization also implements projects aimed at restoring agro-industries that have been adversely affected by violent conflict and natural disasters, and has undertaken studies and projects aimed at strengthening the textile and garment industries.

In March 2012 UNIDO and the UN Office on Drugs and Crime signed a Memorandum of Understanding on establishing a strategic partnership aimed at promoting grass-roots development and alternative livelihoods in poor rural communities hitherto dependent on the cultivation of illegal drugs crops.

UNIDO provides advice to governmental agencies and industrial institutions to improve the management of human resources. The Organization also undertakes training projects to develop human resources in specific industries, and aims to encourage the full participation of women in economic progress through gender awareness programmes and practical training to improve women's access to employment and business opportunities.

UNIDO participated in the Third United Nations Conference on the Least Developed Countries (LDC-III), held in Brussels, Belgium, in May 2001. The Organization launched a package of 'deliverables' (special initiatives) in support of the Programme of Action adopted by the Conference, which emphasized the importance of productive capacity in the international development agenda. These related to energy, market access (the enablement of LDCs to participate in international trade), and SME networking and cluster development (with a particular focus on agro-processing and metal-working). LDC-IV was convened in May–June 2011 in Istanbul, Turkey.

UNIDO places a major focus on industrialization in Africa, the advancement of which is regarded as essential to that continent's full integration into the global economy; challenges include the prevalence there of LDCs, limited industrial skills and technological capabilities, weak support from institutions, inadequate financing and underdeveloped domestic and regional markets. UNIDO welcomed the African Union Action Plan for the Accelerated Industrial Development of Africa, which was launched in January 2008, and promotes African regional integration as beneficial for the industrialization of the continent. UNIDO plays a leading role in co-ordinating Africa Industrialization Day, held annually on 20 November. UNIDO has developed national programmes for 24 African countries; these have emphasized capacity-building for the enhancement of industrial competitiveness and private sector development, which is regarded as a major priority for the transformation of African economies. The basic philosophy has been to identify, jointly with key stakeholders in major industrial sub-sectors, the basic tools required to determine their national industrial development needs and priorities. This process has facilitated the definition and establishment of comprehensive national medium- and long-term industrial development agendas. In March 2010 UNIDO convened a high-level conference, in Abuja, Nigeria, on means of developing agribusiness and agro-industries in Africa; the conference endorsed a new African Agribusiness and Agro-industries Development Initiative (known as '3ADI'), a programme framework and funding mechanism enabling public and private sector interests to mobilize resources for investment in development of the African agri-food sector.

TRADE CAPACITY-BUILDING

UNIDO implements programmes that build industrial capacities, in both public and private institutions, to formulate policies and strategies for developing trade competitiveness. The Organization has developed a comprehensive programme to improve deficiencies in standards, metrology, accreditation and conformity infrastructure, to help developing countries overcome technical barriers while improving product quality, to meet the standards required in the global trading arena. UNIDO also helps countries to comply with global sanitary and phyto-sanitary standards. Efforts in the area of post-conflict rebuilding of quality infrastructures have been undertaken. UNIDO's industrial business development services—such as business incubators, rural entrepreneurship development and SME cluster development—for SME support institutions are aimed at enabling SMEs to play a key role in economic growth. Aid-for-trade activities are undertaken, including programmes that link debt swaps to trade-related technical co-operation. The Organization assists with the establishment of export consortia, through which SMEs can pool knowledge, financial resources and contacts to improve their export potential while also reducing costs. Promotion of business partnership has been strengthened through the Organization's world-wide network of investment and technology promotion offices, investment promotion units, and subcontracting and partnership exchanges. UNIDO contributes to the UN Global Compact aimed at promoting corporate social responsibility (CSR). In 2008 the Organization prepared a paper entitled *CSR, SMEs and Public Policy in Middle and Low Income Countries: Issues and Options for UNIDO*, which explored the links between public policy interventions, SMEs and CSR.

UNIDO has pursued efforts to overcome the so-called 'digital divide' between and within countries. The Organization has helped to develop electronic and mobile business for SMEs in developing countries and economies in transition. It has also launched an internet-based electronic platform, UNIDO Exchange (accessible at exchange.unido.org) for sharing intelligence and fostering business partnerships. UNIDO's Technology Foresight initiative, launched in 1999, involves the systematic visualization of long-term developments in the areas of science, technology, industry, economy and society, with the aim of identifying technologies capable of providing future economic and social benefits. The initiative is being implemented in Asia, Latin America and the Caribbean, and in Central and Eastern Europe and the CIS.

In March 2002, while participating in the International Conference on Financing and Development, held in Monterrey, Mexico, UNIDO launched an initiative designed to facilitate access to international markets for developing countries and countries with transitional economies by assisting them in overcoming barriers to trade.

ENVIRONMENT AND ENERGY

UNIDO's Energy and Climate Change Branch supports patterns of energy use by industry that are environmentally sustainable and likely to mitigate climate change. UNIDO encourages energy efficiency and implements a programme to promote access to renewable sources of energy, essential for conducting modern productive activities. UNIDO has organized a number of conferences relating to renewable energy. In April 2009 a report was issued entitled *UNIDO and Renewable Energy: Greening the Industrial Agenda*, outlining the Organization's renewable energy promotion efforts. In August–September 2002 the Organization participated in the World Summit on Sustainable Development (WSSD), held in Johannesburg, South Africa, at which it launched an initiative seeking to promote rural energy for productive use. UNIDO's Lighting up Rural Africa programme develops small hydropower projects for rural electrification and industrial usage. The Global Mercury Project focuses on reducing mercury pollution caused by artisanal gold mining, and a Participatory Control of Desertification and Poverty Reduction in the Arid and Semi-Arid High Plateau Ecosystems of Eastern Morocco scheme, jointly developed with IFAD, promotes natural regeneration and efficient land use. UNIDO is engaged in capacity building activities for developing biotechnology projects. In October 2010 UNIDO participated in the fourth global ministerial conference on renewable energy, which took place in New Delhi, India, on the theme 'Upscaling and Mainstreaming Renewables for Energy Security, Climate Change and Economic Development'; the first, second and third conferences had been held in Bonn, Germany, in June 2004; in Beijing, China, in November 2005; and Washington, USA, in March 2008. In June 2012 UNIDO organized several events on the sidelines of the UN Conference on Sustainable Development (Rio+20), and, with UNEP and the UN Global Compact, launched a new Green Industry Platform, which aimed to mainstream climate, environmental and social dimensions into business operations.

In September 2009 UNIDO, with UNEP, ILO, ESCAP and the Philippines Government organized the International Conference on Green Industry in Asia, in Manila; the conference adopted the Manila Declaration and Framework for Action, detailing measures aimed at reducing the resource-intensity and carbon emissions of Asian industries. UNIDO subsequently focused on developing a series of activities aimed at assisting the implementation of the Framework in those Asian countries wishing to implement it, including the preparation of green industry policy guidelines and of country status reports on eco-efficiency. Green-industry pilot programmes were to be undertaken in Asia and elsewhere.

As one of the implementing agencies of the Multilateral Fund for the Implementation of the Montreal Protocol, UNIDO implements projects that help developing countries to reduce the use of ozone-depleting substances. From 2007 the Organization contributed to the formulation of national plans in support of the freezing by 2013 of the production of hydrochlorofluorocarbons (HCFCs). It is also involved in implementing the Kyoto Protocol of the Framework Convention on Climate Change (relating to greenhouse gas emissions) in old factories world-wide. UNIDO has helped to develop 10 national ozone units responsible for designing, monitoring and implementing programmes to phase out ozone-depleting substances. By December 2008 33 National Cleaner Production Centres (NCPCs), five National Cleaner Production Programmes, and, in Latin America, a regional network of cleaner production centres, had been established, under a joint UNIDO/UNEP programme that was launched in 1994 to promote the use and development of environmentally sustainable technologies and to build national capacities in cleaner production. In February 2010 UNIDO, in partnership with the Norwegian Government and the Global Carbon Capture and Storage Institute, launched a project aimed at developing a global technology roadmap for carbon capture and storage for industrial processes.

The Director-General of UNIDO serves as the chairperson of UN-Energy, the inter-agency mechanism that aims to promote system-wide co-operation in the UN's response to energy-related issues. UNIDO, on behalf on UN-Energy, identifies areas for collaboration between the UN and private sector in addressing challenges posed by climate change and the achievement of sustainable development.

In December 2007 the General Conference endorsed a Strategic Approach to International Chemicals Management. A programme promoting chemical leasing encourages improved co-operation between chemicals producers and users, and helps companies to comply with environmental regulations. UNIDO has supported countries with the preparation of national implementation plans for the effective removal of persistent organic pollutants. The Organization has undertaken a number of technical assistance projects and schemes aimed at helping countries to adopt energy management standards, and has also co-operated with the International Organization for Standardization on the development of an international energy management standard.

UNIDO and UN-Energy supported the UN Global Compact in organizing the annual Private Sector Forum, held in September 2011, in New York, USA, at which the UN Secretary-General launched a new initiative, Sustainable Energy for All by 2030, and a high-level group responsible for its implementation.

The 2011 edition of UNIDO's annual *Industrial Development Report*, issued in January 2012, highlighted the importance of prioritizing industrial energy efficiency in the pursuit of sustainable industrial development, with a particular focus on developing countries.

Finance

The provisional regular budget for the two years 2012–13 amounted to €153.2m., financed mainly by assessed contributions payable by member states. There was an operational budget of some €27.9m. for the same period, financed mainly by voluntary contributions. The Industrial Development Fund is used by UNIDO to finance development projects that fall outside the usual systems of multilateral funding.

Publications

Annual Report.

Connectedness Index.

Development of Clusters and Networks of SMEs.

Gearing up for a New Development Agenda.

Industrial Development Report.

Industry for Growth into the New Millennium.

International Yearbook of Industrial Statistics (annually).

Making It: Industry for Development (quarterly).

Manual for the Evaluation of Industrial Projects.

Manual for Small Industrial Businesses.

Reforming the UN System—UNIDO's Need-Driven Model.

UNIDOScope (monthly, electronic newsletter).

Using Statistics for Process Control and Improvement: An Introduction to Basic Concepts and Techniques.

World Information Directory of Industrial Technology and Investment Support Services.

Several other manuals, guidelines, numerous working papers and reports.

Universal Postal Union—UPU

Address: Case Postale 13, 3000 Bern 15, Switzerland.

Telephone: 313503111; **fax:** 313503110; **e-mail:** info@upu.int; **internet:** www.upu.int.

The General Postal Union was founded by the Treaty of Berne (1874), beginning operations in July 1875. Three years later its name was changed to the Universal Postal Union. In 1948 the UPU became a specialized agency of the UN. The UPU promotes the sustainable development of high-quality, universal, efficient and accessible postal services.

MEMBERS

The UPU has 192 members.

Organization

(June 2012)

CONGRESS

The supreme body of the Union is the Universal Postal Congress, which meets, in principle, every four years. Congress focuses on general principles and broad policy issues. It is responsible for the Constitution (the basic act of the Union), the General Regulations (which contain provisions relating to the application of the Constitution and the operation of the Union), changes in the provision of the Universal Postal Convention, approval of the strategic plan and budget parameters, formulation of overall policy on technical co-operation, and for elections and appointments. Amendments to the Constitution are recorded in Additional Protocols, of which there are currently seven. The 24th Congress was convened in Geneva, Switzerland, in July–August 2008, under the chairmanship of Kenya. The 25th Universal Postal Congress was scheduled to be held in Doha, Qatar, during September–October 2012.

COUNCIL OF ADMINISTRATION

The Council meets annually at Bern. It is composed of a Chairman and representatives of 41 member countries of the Union elected by the Universal Postal Congress on the basis of an equitable geographical distribution. It is responsible for supervising the affairs of the Union between Congresses. The Council also considers policies that may affect other sectors, such as standardization and quality of service, provides a forum for considering the implications of governmental policies with respect to competition, deregulation and trade-in-service issues for international postal services, and considers intergovernmental aspects of technical co-operation. The Council approves the Union's budget, supervises the activities of the International Bureau and takes decisions regarding UPU contacts with other international agencies and bodies. It is also responsible for promoting and co-ordinating all aspects of technical assistance among member countries. The Council has a subsidiary WTO Issues Project Group.

POSTAL OPERATIONS COUNCIL (POC)

As the technical organ of the UPU, the POC, which holds annual sessions and comprises 40 elected member countries, is responsible for the operational, economic and commercial aspects of international postal services. The POC has the authority to amend and enact the Detailed Regulations of the Universal Postal Convention, on the basis of decisions made at Congress. It promotes the studies undertaken by some postal services and the introduction of new postal products. It also prepares and issues recommendations for member countries concerning uniform standards of practice. On the recommendation of the 1999 Beijing Congress the POC established a Standards Board with responsibility for approving standards relating to telematics, postal technology and Electronic Data Interchange (EDI). The POC aims to assist national postal services to modernize postal products, including letter and parcel post, financial services and expedited mail services.

CONSULTATIVE COMMITTEE

The Consultative Committee, established in September 2004 by the 23rd (Bucharest) Congress, provides a platform for dialogue between postal industry stakeholders and represents the interests of the wider international postal sector. It has 27 members, comprising non-governmental organizations representing customers, delivery service providers, workers' organizations, suppliers of goods and services to the postal sector and other organizations. Membership of the Committee is open to non-government organizations with an interest in international postal services, representing customers, delivery service providers, suppliers of goods and services to the postal sector, and workers' organizations; and also to private companies with an interest in international postal services, such as private operators, direct marketers, international mailers, and printers. All members are extended full observer status in all organs of the Union. The Committee convenes twice a year, in Bern, to coincide with meetings of the Council of Administration and the Postal Operations Council.

INTERNATIONAL BUREAU

The day-to-day administrative work of the UPU is executed through the International Bureau, which provides secretariat and support facilities for the UPU's bodies. It serves as an instrument of liaison, information and consultation for the postal administration of the member countries and promotes technical co-operation among Union members. It also acts as a clearing house for the settlement of accounts between national postal administrations for inter-administration charges related to the exchange of postal items and international reply coupons. The Bureau supports the technical assistance programmes of the UPU, organizes regular conferences and workshops, and serves as an intermediary between the UPU, the UN, its agencies and other international organizations, customer organizations and private delivery services. Increasingly the Bureau has assumed a greater role in postal administration, through two co-operatives: the Telematics Co-operative and the Express Mail Service (EMS) Co-operative. The Telematics Co-operative, with voluntary participation by public, semi-public, and private postal operators, supports the use of new technologies in the improvement and expansion of postal services. Its operational arm is the Postal Technology Centre (PTC, supported by five Regional Support Centres world-wide), which manages three core activities: Post*Net, a global postal communication network, using EDI to provide monitoring services, a track-and-trace system, and postal remuneration and billing; the International Postal System (IPS), an integrated international mail management system, providing automated processing of dispatches and end-to-end tracking of items; and the International Financial System (IFS), a software application facilitating international money order services. The EMS Co-operative, comprising (at June 2012) 172 EMS designated operators covering 90% of global EMS traffic, regulates the provision of a high-quality, competitive global EMS service, and operates through an EMS Unit. Seven UPU Regional Project Co-ordinators support the implementation of postal development projects world-wide.

Director-General of the International Bureau: EDOUARD DAYAN (France).

Deputy Director-General: GUOZHONG HUANG (People's Republic of China).

Activities

The essential principles of the Union are the following:

(i) to develop social, cultural and commercial communication between people through the efficient operation of the postal services;

(ii) to guarantee freedom of transit and free circulation of postal items;

(iii) to ensure the organization, development and modernization of the postal services;

(iv) to promote and participate in postal technical assistance between member countries;

(v) to ensure the interoperability of postal networks by implementing a suitable policy of standardization;

(vi) to meet the changing needs of customers;

(vii) to improve the quality of service.

In addition to the Constitution and the General Regulations, the Universal Postal Convention is also a compulsory Act of the UPU (binding on all member countries), in view of its importance in the postal field and historical value. The Convention and its Detailed Regulations contain the common rules applicable to the international postal service and provisions concerning letter- and parcel-post. The Detailed Regulations are agreements concluded by the national postal administrations elected by Congress to the POC. The POC is empowered to revise and enact these, taking into account decisions made at Congress.

The 24th Congress, convened in Geneva, Switzerland (under the chairmanship of Kenya), in July–August 2008, adopted a new Postal Payment Services Agreement and its Regulations (the original version of which was adopted by the 1999 Beijing Congress to replace the former Money Orders, Giro and Cash-on-Delivery Agreements). The Agreement (adherence to which is optional for UPU member states) aims to enable postal operators to operate faster, more secure and more accessible electronic money transfer services to communities without access to banks in developing regions that have poor access to formal money transfer networks.

In recent years the UPU has reviewed its activities and has focused on the following factors underlying the modern postal environment: the growing role played by technology; the expanding reach of the effects of globalization; and the need to make the customer the focus of new competitive strategies. In October 2002 the UPU organized a Strategy Conference entitled 'Future Post', at which delegates representing governments and postal services addressed challenges confronting the postal industry. The 23rd Congress, held in September–October 2004, adopted the Bucharest World Postal Strategy, detailing a number of objectives to be pursued in the postal sector over the next four years; a new package of proposals for so-called terminal dues; a new quality of standards and targets for international mail services; a resolution relating to security, the combating of terrorism and prevention of money-laundering through use of the mail network; and a proposal to amend the UPU Convention to recognize legally the Electronic Postmark as an optional postal service. In July–August 2008 the 24th Congress adopted the Nairobi Postal Strategy to guide the Union's activities during 2009–12. The Strategy focused on modernizing global postal services at all levels, in terms of institutional reform, improvement in the quality of service, security of postal services, and promoting a universal postal service (UPS); and also in terms of raising awareness of the impact of postal services on the environment and climate change. The UPU Secretary-General stated during the 24th Congress that UPU's future agenda would focus on e-commerce, technological development, intelligent mail, facilitation of international trade and exchanges, electronic money transfers, sustainable development, international co-operation, postal infrastructure at the service of development policies, and improvements to the UPS. The 24th Congress determined to establish minimum security standards and processes for postal operators, and to invite postal administrations to co-operate more closely with customs authorities to identify counterfeit or pirated articles dispatched through the mail. In December 2009 UPU released the results of its first world-wide survey of greenhouse gas emissions generated by postal operations. At the UN Climate Change Conference, held in Copenhagen, Denmark, later in that month, UPU pledged to promote more environmentally-friendly methods of processing and delivering mail. In September 2010 UPU organized a Strategy Conference, in Nairobi, to initiate the process of defining a new global postal strategy prior to the 25th Congress. The meeting concluded that the adoption of new technologies and the diversification of postal services were critical elements of a future strategy. In January 2012 UPU released a study monitoring the development of postal e-services, which were divided into: e-post services (such as internet-access points in post offices, postal electronic mailboxes and online direct mail); e-finance services (electronic invoicing, electronic remittances, electronic bill payments); e-commerce services (online subscriptions to periodicals, secure web certificates); and e-government services (including electronic payment of retirement pensions, online passport applications, electronic customs documents).

In April 2011 a new UPU inter-committee security group, with participation by postal operators and international organizations, met for the first time to pursue the development and application of global postal security standards.

In January 2010 UPU established a task force of postal experts to co-ordinate efforts to support and rehabilitate postal services in Haiti, following a devastating earthquake in that country. In November 2011 a new UPU Emergency and Solidarity Fund (ESF) became operational; the ESF was to facilitate the recovery of basic postal services in countries affected by natural disaster and armed conflict, and was to be financed by voluntary contributions from governments and postal sector partners.

POSTAL ENVIRONMENT

The 2004 Bucharest Congress approved a UPU policy on extraterritorial offices of exchange (ETOEs), defined as offices of facilities operated by or in connection with a postal operator on the territory of another country for the commercial purpose of drawing business in markets outside its national territory. The Council of Administration's WTO Issues Project Group monitors developments on trade in services, keeps member states informed on trade developments, and promotes awareness of WTO issues of interest to the UPU. In recent years the UPU has been concerned with developing the role of the postal sector in the modern information society and in reducing the digital divide between industrialized and developing nations. The UPU pursues the following objectives in line with the Geneva Plan of Action adopted during the first phase of the World Summit on the Information Society convened in December 2003: facilitating, through the global postal infrastructure, unprecedented access to knowledge and ICTs; advancing the physical, electronic and financial dimensions of the global postal network; transferring postal administrations' expertise in physical communications management to the internet (particularly in the areas of identity management and SPAM control); and helping to build confidence and security in the use of ICTs. At the World

Telecommunication Development Conference, convened in Hyderabad, India, in May–June 2010, the UPU, jointly with the International Telecommunication Union, launched a publication on innovation in the postal sector, entitled *ICTs, New Services and Transformation of the Post*. The UPU conducts market analysis to assist postal administrations in adapting to globalization and technological advances in world markets. A Postal Economics Programme implemented by the UPU conducts economic research aimed at analysing the uneven postal sector development of developing countries and providing growth models for the postal sectors of developing countries. In recent years the UPU has focused on the role of postal administrations in supporting the use of e-commerce activities by micro- and small enterprises in least developed and developing countries.

On 1 October 2003 a new UPU clearing system (UPU*Clearing) became operational to enable postal operators to exchange bills electronically. During 2004 the UPU sponsored an application to the Internet Corporation for Assigned Names and Numbers (ICANN) to obtain a top-level internet domain, .post, for use, *inter alia*, by national and other postal operators, postal-related organizations, regional associations, UPU-regulated services, and trademarks and brand names. Negotiations between ICANN and the UPU on contract terms for the .post domain were concluded in October 2009 and an agreement was signed in December.

In March 2007 the UPU and the International Air Transport Association signed a Memorandum of Understanding on developing and harmonizing standards and increasing the use of technologies (such as bar coding, radio frequency identification, and the processing of electronic data) to improve air mail flows.

UPU helps to organize a regular World Postal Business Forum, which addresses postal sector challenges and trends; the 2011 Forum was convened in September, in Stuttgart, Germany, concurrently with the 15th annual POST-EXPO, an exhibition displaying recent post-related technological innovations and systems. The 16th POST-EXPO was scheduled to be held in September 2012, in Brussels, Belgium.

POSTAL DEVELOPMENT

The UPU's International Bureau undertakes quality tests on postal products and services world-wide, monitoring some 900 international links through the use of test letters and parcels; the Bureau also publishes end-to-end delivery standards. The UPU sends consultants to selected countries to promote the implementation of improvements in quality of service. The first phase of testing a new performance-measuring facility, the Global Monitoring System (GMS), was initiated in August 2009 by postal operators in 21 countries. The GMS commenced operations in January 2010.

The UPU has conducted research into the effects of postal sector regulatory reforms. The UPU's Integrated Postal Reform and Development Plan (IPDP) aims to enhance co-operation in promoting postal sector reform; under IPDP guidelines the principal aim of the postal sector reform process is to ensure that the state obligation to provide the UPS is met, and that the conditions required to modernize the postal sector are established, with a view to benefiting both individual citizens and business. Through its programme on development co-operation the UPU provides postal technical assistance to developing member countries. The 2008 Congress and the Nairobi Postal Strategy promoted the regional implementation of global development strategies; UPU implements a Regional Development Plan (RDP) aimed at providing a coherent framework for regional development activities.

The UPU has undertaken projects to develop human resources in the postal sector. It has developed guides, training materials and training models through its Trainpost programme, and organizes capacity-building training workshops in developing countries and on a regional basis. The UPU promotes environmental sustainability in the postal sector, encouraging recycling programmes and the use of environment-friendly products and resources. The UPU has produced guidelines on cost accounting to be used as a management tool by postal administrations.

The 1999 Congress approved the establishment of a Quality of Service Fund, which was to be financed by industrialized member countries (by a 7.5% increase in dues) in order to support service improvement projects in developing member states. The Fund became operative in 2001 and had by the end of 2010 approved 570 projects, benefiting some 150 national postal services. The 2008 Congress determined to extend the Fund's period of operation (originally to have expired in that year) to 2016.

Finance

All of the UPU's regular budget expenses are financed by member countries, based on a contribution class system. The UPU's annual budget amounts to some 37m. Swiss francs.

Publications

Postal Statistics.

*POST*Info* (online newsletter of postal technology centre).

Union Postale (quarterly, in French, German, English, Arabic, Chinese, Spanish and Russian).

UPU EDI Messaging Standards.

UPU Technical Standards.

Other guides and industry reports.

World Health Organization—WHO

Address: 20 ave Appia, 1211 Geneva 27, Switzerland.

Telephone: 227912111; **fax:** 227913111; **e-mail:** info@who.int; **internet:** www.who.int.

WHO, established in 1948, is the lead agency within the UN system concerned with the protection and improvement of public health.

MEMBERS

WHO has 194 members.

Organization

(June 2012)

WORLD HEALTH ASSEMBLY

The Assembly meets in Geneva, once a year. It is responsible for policy-making and the biennial programme and budget; appoints the Director-General; admits new members; and reviews budget contributions. The 65th Assembly was convened in May 2012.

EXECUTIVE BOARD

The Board is composed of 34 health experts designated by a member state that has been elected by the World Health Assembly to serve on the Board; each expert serves for three years. The Board meets at least twice a year to review the Director-General's programme, which it forwards to the Assembly with any recommendations that seem necessary. It advises on questions referred to it by the Assembly and is responsible for putting into effect the decisions and policies of the Assembly. It is also empowered to take emergency measures in case of epidemics or disasters. Meeting in November 2011 the Board agreed several proposals on reforms to the Organization aimed at improving health outcomes, achieving greater coherence in global health matters, and promoting organizational efficiency and transparency.

Chairman: Dr Mihaly Kökény (Hungary).

SECRETARIAT

Director-General: Dr Margaret Chan (People's Republic of China).

Deputy Director-General: Dr Anarfi Asamoa-Baah (Ghana).

Assistant Directors-General: Dr Bruce Aylward (Canada) (Polio, Emergencies and Country Collaboration), Flavia Bustreo (Italy) (Family, Women's and Children's Health), Oleg Chestnov (Italy) (Non-communicable Diseases and Mental Health), Dr Carissa F. Etienne (Dominica) (Health Systems and Services), Keiji Fukuda (USA) (Health Security and Environment), Mohamed Abdi Jama (Somalia) (General Management), Marie-Paule Kieny (France) (Innovation, Information, Evidence and Research), Hiroki Nakatani (Japan) (HIV/ AIDS, TB, Malaria and Neglected Tropical Diseases).

PRINCIPAL OFFICES

Each of WHO's six geographical regions has its own organization, consisting of a regional committee representing relevant member states and associate members, and a regional office staffed by experts in various fields of health.

Africa Office: Cité du Djoue BP 06, Brazzaville, Republic of the Congo; tel. 83-91-00; fax 83-95-01; e-mail regafro@whoafro.org; internet www.afro.who.int; Dir Dr Luís Gomes Sambo (Angola).

Americas Office: Pan-American Health Organization, 525 23rd St, NW, Washington, DC 20037, USA; tel. (202) 974-3000; fax (202) 974-3663; e-mail director@paho.org; internet www.paho .org; also administers The Caribbean Epidemiology Centre (CAREC); Dir Dr Mirta Roses Periago (Argentina).

Eastern Mediterranean Office: POB 7608, Abdul Razzak al Sanhouri St, Cairo (Nasr City) 11371, Egypt; tel. (2) 2765000; fax (2) 6702492; e-mail postmaster@emro.who.int; internet www.emro.who.int; Dir Dr Ala Alwan (Iraq).

Europe Office: 8 Scherfigsvej, 2100 Copenhagen Ø, Denmark; tel. 39-17-17-17; fax 39-17-18-18; e-mail postmaster@euro.who .int; internet www.euro.who.int; Dir Zsuzsanna Jakab (Hungary).

International Health Regulations Coordination—WHO Lyon Office: 58 ave Debourg, 69007 Lyon, France; tel. 4-72-71-64-70; fax 4-72-71-64-71; e-mail ihrinfo@who.int; internet www.who.int/ihr/lyon/en/index.html; supports (with regional offices) countries in strengthening their national surveillance and response systems, with the aim of improving the detection, assessment and notification of events, and responding to public health risks and emergencies of international concern under the International Health Regulations.

South-East Asia Office: World Health House, Indraprastha Estate, Mahatma Gandhi Rd, New Delhi 110002, India; tel. (11) 23370804; fax (11) 23379507; e-mail registry@searo.who.int; internet www.searo.who.int; Dir Dr Samlee Plianbangchang.

Western Pacific Office: POB 2932, Manila 1000, Philippines; tel. (2) 5288001; fax (2) 5211036; e-mail pio@wpro.who.int; internet www.wpro.who.int; Dir Dr Shin Young Soo (Republic of Korea).

WHO Centre for Health Development: I. H. D. Centre Bldg, 9th Floor, 5–1, 1-chome, Wakinohama-Kaigandori, Chuo-ku, Kobe, Japan; tel. (78) 230-3100; fax (78) 230-3178; e-mail wkc@wkc.who.int; internet www.who.or.jp; f. 1995 to address health development issues; Dir Alex Ross (USA).

WHO European Office for Investment for Health and Development: Palazzo Franchetti, S. Marco 2847, 30124 Venice, Italy; tel. (041) 279-3865; fax (041) 279-3869; e-mail info@ihd.euro.who.int; f. 2003 to develop a systematic approach to the integration of social and economic factors into European countries' development strategies.

WHO Mediterranean Centre for Health Risk Reduction (WMC): rue du Lac Windermere, BP 40, 1053 Les Berges du Lac, Tunisia; tel. (71) 964-681; fax (71) 764-4558; e-mail info@ wmc.who.int; f. 1997; advocates globally for appropriate health policies; trains health professionals; supports capacity-building for community action at grassroots level; works closely with WHO's regional offices.

Activities

WHO is the UN system's co-ordinating authority for health (defined as 'a state of complete physical, mental and social well-being and not merely the absence of disease and infirmity'). WHO's objective is stated in its constitution as 'the attainment by all peoples of the highest possible level of health'. The Organization's core functions, outlined in its 11th programme of work covering 2006–15, are to provide leadership on global public health matters, in partnership, where necessary, with other agencies; to help shape the global health research agenda; to articulate ethical and evidence-based policy options; to set, and monitor the implementation of, norms and standards; to monitor and assess health trends; and to provide technical and policy support to member countries. Aid is provided in emergencies and natural disasters.

In its work WHO adheres to a six-point agenda covering: promoting development; fostering health security; strengthening health systems; harnessing research, information and evidence; enhancing partnerships; and improving performance.

WHO has developed a series of international classifications, including the *International Statistical Classification of Disease and Related Health Problems (ICD)*, providing an etiological framework of health conditions, and currently in its 10th edition; and the complementary *International Classification of Functioning, Disability and Health (ICF)*, which describes how people live with their conditions.

WHO keeps diseases and other health problems under constant surveillance, promotes the exchange of prompt and accurate information and of notification of outbreaks of diseases, and administers the International Health Regulations (the most recently revised version of which entered into force in June 2007). It sets standards for the quality control of drugs, vaccines and other substances affecting health. It formulates health regulations for international travel.

It collects and disseminates health data and carries out statistical analyses and comparative studies in such diseases as cancer, heart disease and mental illness.

It receives reports on drugs observed to have shown adverse reactions in any country, and transmits the information to other member states.

It promotes improved environmental conditions, including housing, sanitation and working conditions. All available information on effects on human health of the pollutants in the environment is critically reviewed and published.

A global programme of collaborative research and exchange of scientific information is carried out in co-operation with about 1,200 national institutions. Particular stress is laid on the widespread communicable diseases of the tropics, and the countries directly concerned are assisted in developing their research capabilities. Co-operation among scientists and professional groups is encouraged. The organization negotiates and sustains national and global partnerships. It may propose international conventions and agreements. The organization promotes the development and testing of new technologies, tools and guidelines. It assists in developing an informed public opinion on matters of health.

WHO's first global strategy for pursuing 'Health for all' was adopted in May 1981 by the 34th World Health Assembly. The objective of 'Health for all' was identified as the attainment by all citizens of the world of a level of health that would permit them to lead a socially and economically productive life, requiring fair distribution of available resources, universal access to essential health care, and the promotion of preventive health care. In May 1998 the 51st World Health Assembly renewed the initiative, adopting a global strategy in support of 'Health for all in the 21st century', to be effected through regional and national health policies. The new framework was to build on the primary health care approach of the initial strategy, but aimed to strengthen the emphasis on quality of life, equity in health and access to health services.

In the implementation of all its activities WHO aims to contribute to achieving by 2015 the UN Millennium Development Goals (MDGs) that were agreed by the September 2000 UN Millennium Summit. WHO has particular responsibility for the MDGs of: reducing child mortality, with a target reduction of two-thirds in the mortality rate among children under five; improving maternal health, with a specific goal of reducing by 75% the numbers of women dying in childbirth; and combating HIV/AIDS, malaria and other diseases. In addition, it directly supports the following Millennium 'targets': halving the proportion of people suffering from malnutrition; halving the proportion of people without sustainable access to safe drinking water and basic sanitation; and providing access, in co-operation with pharmaceutical companies, to affordable, essential drugs in developing countries. Furthermore, WHO reports on 17 health-related MDG indicators; co-ordinates, jointly with the World Bank, the High-Level Forum on the Health MDGs, comprising government ministers, senior officials from developing countries, and representatives of bilateral and multilateral agencies, foundations, regional organizations and global partnerships; and undertakes technical and normative work in support of national and regional efforts to reach the MDGs.

The 2006–15 11th General Programme of Work defined a policy framework for pursuing the principal objectives of building healthy populations and combating ill health. The Programme took into account: increasing understanding of the social, economic, political and cultural factors involved in achieving better health and the role played by better health in poverty reduction; the increasing complexity of health systems; the importance of safeguarding health as a component of humanitarian action; and the need for greater co-ordination among development organizations. It incorporated four interrelated strategic directions: lessening excess mortality, morbidity and disability, especially in poor and marginalized populations; promoting healthy lifestyles and reducing risk factors to human health arising from environmental, economic, social and behavioural causes; developing equitable and financially fair health systems; and establishing an enabling policy and an institutional environment for the health sector and promoting an effective health dimension to social, economic, environmental and development policy. WHO is the sponsoring agency for the Health Workforce Decade (2006–15).

During 2005 the UN's Inter-Agency Standing Committee (IASC), concerned with co-ordinating the international response to humanitarian disasters, developed a concept of organizing agency assistance to IDPs through the institutionalization of a 'Cluster Approach', comprising 11 core areas of activity. WHO was designated the lead agency for the Health Cluster. The 65th World Health Assembly, convened in May 2012, adopted a resolution endorsing WHO's role as Health Cluster lead and urging international donors to allocate sufficient resources towards health sector activities during humanitarian emergencies.

WHO, with ILO, leads the Social Protection Floor initiative, the sixth of nine activities that were launched in April 2009 by the UN System Chief Executives Board for Co-ordination (CEB), with the aim of alleviating the impact on poor and vulnerable populations of the global economic downturn. In October 2011 a Social Protection Floor Advisory Group, launched in August 2010 under the initiative, issued a report entitled *Social Protection Floor for a Fair and Inclusive Globalization*, which urged that basic income and services should be guaranteed for all, stating that this would promote both stability and economic growth globally.

COMMUNICABLE DISEASES

WHO identifies infectious and parasitic communicable diseases as a major obstacle to social and economic progress, particularly in developing countries, where, in addition to disabilities and loss of productivity and household earnings, they cause nearly one-half of all deaths. Emerging and re-emerging diseases, those likely to cause epidemics, increasing incidence of zoonoses (diseases or infections passed from vertebrate animals to humans by means of parasites, viruses, bacteria or unconventional agents), attributable to factors such as environmental changes and changes in farming practices, outbreaks of unknown etiology, and the undermining of some drug therapies by the spread of antimicrobial resistance, are main areas of concern. In recent years WHO has noted the global spread of communicable diseases through international travel, voluntary human migration and involuntary population displacement.

WHO's Communicable Diseases group works to reduce the impact of infectious diseases world-wide through surveillance and response; prevention, control and eradication strategies; and research and product development. The group seeks to identify new technologies and tools, and to foster national development through strengthening health services and the better use of existing tools. It aims to strengthen global monitoring of important communicable disease problems, and to create consensus and consolidate partnerships around targeted diseases and collaborates with other groups at all stages to provide an integrated response. In 2000 WHO and several partner institutions in epidemic surveillance established the Global Outbreak Alert and Response Network (GOARN). Through the Network WHO aims to maintain constant vigilance regarding outbreaks of disease and to link world-wide expertise to provide an immediate response capability. From March 2003 WHO, through the Network, was co-ordinating the international investigation into the global spread of Severe Acute Respiratory Syndrome (SARS), a previously unknown atypical pneumonia. From the end of that year WHO was monitoring the spread through several Asian countries of the virus H5N1 (a rapidly mutating strain of zoonotic highly pathogenic avian influenza—HPAI) that was transmitting to human populations through contact with diseased birds, mainly poultry. It was feared that H5N1 would mutate into a form transmissable from human to human. In March 2005 WHO issued a *Global Influenza Preparedness Plan*, and urged all countries to develop national influenza pandemic preparedness plans and to stockpile antiviral drugs. In May, in co-operation with FAO and the World Organisation for Animal Health (OIE), WHO launched a Global Strategy for the Progressive Control of Highly Pathogenic Avian Influenza. A conference on Avian Influenza and Human Pandemic Influenza that was jointly organized by WHO, FAO, OIE and the World Bank in November 2005 issued a plan of action identifying a number of responses, including: supporting the development of integrated national plans for H5N1 containment and human pandemic influenza preparedness and response; assisting countries with the aggressive control of H5N1 and with establishing a more detailed understanding of the role of wild birds in virus transmission; nominating rapid response teams of experts to support epidemiological field investigations; expanding national and regional capacity in surveillance, diagnosis, and alert and response systems; expanding the network of influenza laboratories; establishing multi-country networks for the control or prevention of animal transboundary diseases; expanding the global antiviral stockpile; strengthening veterinary infrastructures; and mapping a global strategy and work plan for co-ordinating antiviral and influenza vaccine research and development. An International Pledging Conference on Avian and Human Influenza, convened in January 2006 in Beijing, People's Republic of China, and co-sponsored by the World Bank, European Commission and Chinese Government, in co-operation with WHO, FAO and OIE, requested a minimum of US $1,200m. in funding towards combating the spread of the virus. By 5 June 2012 a total of 605 human cases of H5N1 had been laboratory confirmed, in Azerbaijan, Bangladesh, Cambodia, China, Djibouti, Egypt, Indonesia, Iraq, Laos, Myanmar, Nigeria, Pakistan, Thailand, Turkey and Viet Nam, resulting in 357 deaths. Cases in poultry had become endemic in parts of Asia and Africa, and outbreaks in poultry had also occurred in some European and Middle Eastern countries.

In April 2009 GOARN sent experts to Mexico to work with health authorities there in response to an outbreak of confirmed human cases of a new variant of swine influenza A(H1N1) that had not previously been detected in animals or humans. In late April, by which time cases of the virus had been reported in the USA and Canada, the Director-General of WHO declared a 'public health emergency of international concern'. All countries were instructed to activate their national influenza pandemic preparedness plans (see above). At the end of April the level of pandemic alert was declared to be at phase five of a six-phase

(phase six being the most severe) warning system that had been newly revised earlier in the year. Phase five is characterized by human-to-human transmission of a new virus into at least two countries in one WHO region. On 11 June WHO declared a global pandemic (phase six on the warning scale, characterized by human-to-human transmission in two or more WHO regions). The status and development of pandemic influenza vaccines was the focus of an advisory meeting of immunization experts held at the WHO headquarters in late October. In June 2010 the WHO Director-General refuted allegations, levelled by a British medical journal and by the Parliamentary Assembly of the Council of Europe, regarding the severity of pandemic (H1N1) 2009 and the possibility that the Organization had, in declaring the pandemic, used advisers with a vested commercial interest in promoting pharmaceutical industry profitability. In August 2010 the WHO Director-General declared that transmission of the new H1N1 virus had entered a post-pandemic phase.

A severe outbreak of infection with Enterohemorrhagic Escherichia Coli (EHEC), and the related Haemolytic Uraemic Syndrome (HUS), believed to have originated in raw bean and seed sprouts, occurred in Germany from late May–July 2011. By 21 July some 857 cases of HUS (including 32 fatalities), and 3,078 cases of infection with EHEC (16 fatalities), had been reported in that country. In addition, some 51 HUS cases (two fatalities) and 89 EHEC cases (no fatalities) had been reported in a further 15 countries, almost all in recent visitors to Germany. In early June WHO confirmed that the cases involved a rare strain of EHEC that had never before been reported in a mass outbreak.

One of WHO's major achievements was the eradication of smallpox. Following a massive international campaign of vaccination and surveillance (begun in 1958 and intensified in 1967), the last case was detected in 1977 and the eradication of the disease was declared in 1980. In May 1996 the World Health Assembly resolved that, pending a final endorsement, all remaining stocks of the variola virus (which causes smallpox) were to be destroyed on 30 June 1999, although 500,000 doses of smallpox vaccine were to remain, along with a supply of the smallpox vaccine seed virus, in order to ensure that a further supply of the vaccine could be made available if required. In May 1999, however, the Assembly authorized a temporary retention of stocks of the virus until 2002. In late 2001, in response to fears that illegally held virus stocks could be used in acts of biological terrorism (see below), WHO reassembled a team of technical experts on smallpox. In January 2002 the Executive Board determined that stocks of the virus should continue to be retained, to enable research into more effective treatments and vaccines. World Health Assemblies (most recently in May 2011) have affirmed that the remaining stock of variola virus should be destroyed following the completion of the ongoing research. The state of variola virus research was to be reviewed in 2014, by the 67th World Health Assembly, which was to discuss nominating a deadline for the destruction of the remaining virus stocks.

In 1988 the World Health Assembly launched the Global Polio Eradication Initiative (GPEI), which aimed, initially, to eradicate poliomyelitis by the end of 2000; this target was subsequently extended to 2013 (see below). Co-ordinated periods of Supplementary Immunization Activity (SIA, facilitated in conflict zones by the negotiation of so-called 'days of tranquility'), including National Immunization Days (NIDs), Sub-National Immunization Days (SNIDs), mop-up campaigns, VitA campaigns (Vitamin A is administered in order to reduce nutritional deficiencies in children and thereby boost their immunity), and Follow up/ Catch up campaigns, have been employed in combating the disease, alongside the strengthening of routine immunization services. Since the inauguration of the GPEI WHO has declared the following regions 'polio-free': the Americas (1994); Western Pacific (2000); and Europe (2002). Furthermore, type 2 wild poliovirus has been eradicated globally (since 1999), although a type 2 circulating vaccine-derived poliovirus (cVDPV) was reported to be active in northern Nigeria during 2006–early 2010. In January 2004 ministers of health of affected countries, and global partners, meeting under the auspices of WHO and UNICEF, adopted the Geneva Declaration on the Eradication of Poliomyelitis, in which they made a commitment to accelerate the drive towards eradication of the disease, by improving the scope of vaccination programmes. Significant progress in eradication of the virus was reported in Asia during that year. In sub-Saharan Africa, however, an outbreak originating in northern Nigeria in mid-2003—caused by a temporary cessation of vaccination activities in response to local opposition to the vaccination programme—had spread, by mid-2004, to 10 previously polio-free countries. These included Côte d'Ivoire and Sudan, where ongoing civil unrest and population displacements impeded control efforts. During 2004–05 some 23 African governments, including those of the affected West and Central African countries, organized, with support from the African Union, a number of co-ordinated mass vaccination drives, which resulted in the vaccination of about 100m. children. By mid-2005 the sub-regional epidemic was declared over; it was estimated that since mid-2003 it had resulted in the paralysis of nearly 200 children. In Nigeria itself, however, the number of confirmed wild poliovirus cases had by 2006 escalated to 1,122 from 202 in 2002. In February 2007 the GPEI launched an intensified eradication effort aimed at identifying and addressing the outstanding operational, technical and financial barriers to eradication. The May 2008 World Health Assembly adopted a resolution urging all remaining polio-affected member states to ensure the vaccination of every child during each SIA. By the end of 2008, having received independent advice that the intensified eradication effort initiated in 2007 had demonstrated that the remaining challenges to eradication were surmountable, the GPEI endorsed a strategic plan covering the period 2009–13 (replacing a previous plan for 2004–08), with the aim of achieving the interruption of type 1 wild poliovirus transmission in India, and the cessation of all prolonged outbreaks in Africa by the end of 2009; the interruption of all poliovirus transmission in Afghanistan, India and Pakistan, of type 1 wild poliovirus transmission in Nigeria, and of all wild poliovirus transmission elsewhere in Africa, by end-2010; the interruption of type 3 wild poliovirus transmission in Nigeria by end-2011; and the eradication of new cVDPVs within six months of detection by end-2013. During 2009, however, polio outbreaks, which were subsequently eradicated, occurred in 10 of 15 previously polio-free countries in Africa. In June 2010 a new strategic plan, covering 2010–12, was launched, incorporating the following targets: cessation in mid-2010 of all polio outbreaks with onset in 2009; cessation by end-2010 of all re-established wild poliovirus transmission; cessation by end-2011 of all transmission in at least two of the four countries designated at that time as polio-endemic (i.e. Afghanistan, India, Nigeria, and Pakistan); and the cessation by end-2012 of all transmission. Some 650 polio cases were confirmed world-wide in 2011, of which 340 were in the then four polio-endemic countries (Pakistan, 198 cases; Afghanistan, 80 cases; Nigeria, 61 cases; and India one case), and 310 cases were recorded in non-endemic countries (including 132 cases in Chad and 93 cases in Democratic Republic of the Congo). (In 1988, in comparison, 35,000 cases had been confirmed in 125 countries, with the actual number of cases estimated at around 350,000.) India was declared to be no longer polio-endemic in February 2012.

WHO's Onchocerciasis Control Programme in West Africa (OCP), active during 1974–2002, succeeded in eliminating transmission in 10 countries in the region, excepting Sierra Leone, of onchocerciasis ('river blindness', spread by blackflies, and previously a major public health problem and impediment to socio-economic development in West Africa). It was estimated that under the OCP some 18m. people were protected from the disease, 600,000 cases of blindness prevented, and 25m. ha of land were rendered safe for cultivation and settlement. The former headquarters of the OCP, based in Ouagadougou, Burkina Faso, was transformed into a Multi-disease Surveillance Centre. In January 1996 another initiative, the African Programme for Onchocerciasis Control (APOC), covering 19 countries outside West Africa, became operational, with funding co-ordinated by the World Bank and with WHO as the executing agency.

The Onchocerciasis Elimination Programme in the Americas (OEPA), launched in 1992, co-ordinates work to control the disease in six Latin American countries where it is endemic. In January 1998 a new 20-year programme to eliminate lymphatic filariasis was initiated, with substantial funding and support from two major pharmaceutical companies, and in collaboration with the World Bank, the Arab Fund for Economic and Social Development and the governments of Japan, the United Kingdom and the USA. South American trypanosomiasis ('Chagas disease') is endemic in Central and South America, causing the deaths of some 45,000 people each year and infecting a further 16m.–18m. A regional intergovernmental commission is implementing a programme to eliminate Chagas from the Southern Cone region of Latin America. The countries of the Andean region of Latin America initiated a plan for the elimination of transmission of Chagas disease in February 1997, and a similar plan was launched by Central American governments in October. In July 2007, to combat the expansion of Chagas disease into some European countries, the Western Pacific, and the USA, as well as the re-emergence of the disease in areas such as the Chaco, in Argentina and Bolivia, where it was thought to have been eradicated, WHO established a Global Network for Chagas Disease Elimination.

WHO is committed to the elimination of leprosy (the reduction of the prevalence of leprosy to less than one case per 10,000 population). The use of a highly effective combination of three drugs (known as multi-drug therapy—MDT) resulted in a reduction in the number of leprosy cases world-wide from 10m.–12m. in 1988 to 213,036 registered cases in January 2010. In 2008 some 249,007 cases were detected in 121 countries. The number of countries having more than one case of leprosy per 10,000 had declined to four by January 2007 (Brazil, Democratic Republic of the Congo, Mozambique and Nepal), compared with 122 in 1985. The country with the highest prevalence of leprosy cases in 2007 was Brazil (3.21 per 10,000 population) and the country with the highest number of cases was India (139,252). The Global Alliance for the Elimination of Leprosy was launched in November 1999 by WHO, in collaboration with governments of affected countries and several private partners, including a major pharmaceutical company, to support the eradication of the disease through the provision of free MDT treatment; WHO has supplied free MDT treatment to leprosy patients in endemic countries since 1995. In June 2005 WHO adopted a Strategic Plan for Further Reducing the Leprosy Burden and Sustaining Leprosy Control Activities, covering the period 2006–10 and following on from a previous strategic plan for 2000–05. In 1998 WHO launched the Global Buruli Ulcer Initiative, which aimed to co-ordinate control of and research into Buruli ulcer, another mycobacterial disease. In July of that year the Director-General of WHO and representatives of more than 20 countries, meeting in Yamoussoukro, Côte d'Ivoire, signed a declaration on the control of Buruli ulcer. In May 2004 the World Health Assembly adopted a resolution urging improved research into, and detection and treatment of, Buruli ulcer.

The Special Programme for Research and Training in Tropical Diseases, established in 1975 and sponsored jointly by WHO, UNDP and the World Bank, as well as by contributions from donor countries, involves a world-wide network of some 5,000 scientists working on the development and application of vaccines, new drugs, diagnostic kits and preventive measures, and applied field research on practical community issues affecting the target diseases.

The objective of providing immunization for all children by 1990 was adopted by the World Health Assembly in 1977. Six diseases (measles, whooping cough, tetanus, poliomyelitis, tuberculosis and diphtheria) became the target of the Expanded Programme on Immunization (EPI), in which WHO, UNICEF and many other organizations collaborated. As a result of massive international and national efforts, the global immunization coverage increased from 20% in the early 1980s to the targeted rate of 80% by the end of 1990. In 2006 WHO, UNICEF and other partners launched the Global Immunization Vision and Strategy (GIVS), a global 10-year framework, covering 2006–15, aimed at reducing deaths due to vaccine-preventable diseases by at least two-thirds compared to 2000 levels, by 2015; and increasing national vaccination coverage levels to at least 90%. In 2009 the global child vaccination coverage rate was estimated at 82%.

In June 2000 WHO released a report entitled 'Overcoming Antimicrobial Resistance', in which it warned that the misuse of antibiotics could render some common infectious illnesses unresponsive to treatment. At that time WHO issued guidelines which aimed to mitigate the risks associated with the use of antimicrobials in livestock reared for human consumption.

HIV/AIDS, TB, MALARIA AND NEGLECTED DISEASES

Combating the human immunodeficiency virus/acquired immunodeficiency syndrome (HIV/AIDS), tuberculosis (TB) and malaria are organization-wide priorities and, as such, are supported not only by their own areas of work but also by activities undertaken in other areas. TB is the principal cause of death for people infected with the HIV virus and an estimated one-third of people living with HIV/AIDS globally are co-infected with TB. In July 2000 a meeting of the Group of Seven industrialized nations and Russia, convened in Genoa, Italy, announced the formation of a new Global Fund to Fight AIDS, TB and Malaria (as previously proposed by the UN Secretary-General and recommended by the World Health Assembly).

The HIV/AIDS epidemic represents a major threat to human well-being and socio-economic progress. Some 95% of those known to be infected with HIV/AIDS live in developing countries, and AIDS-related illnesses are the leading cause of death in sub-Saharan Africa. It is estimated that more than 25m. people world-wide died of AIDS during 1981–2008. WHO supports governments in developing effective health sector responses to the HIV/AIDS epidemic through enhancing their planning and managerial capabilities, implementation capacity, and health systems resources. The Joint UN Programme on HIV/AIDS (UNAIDS) became operational on 1 January 1996, sponsored by WHO and other UN agencies; the UNAIDS secretariat is based at WHO headquarters. Sufferers of HIV/AIDS in developing countries have often failed to receive advanced antiretroviral (ARV) treatments that are widely available in industrialized countries, owing to their high cost. In May 2000 the World Health Assembly adopted a resolution urging WHO member states to improve access to the prevention and treatment of HIV-related illnesses and to increase the availability and affordability of drugs. A WHO-UNAIDS HIV Vaccine Initiative was launched in that year. In June 2001 governments participating in a special session of the UN General Assembly on HIV/AIDS adopted a Declaration of Commitment on HIV/AIDS. WHO, with UNAIDS, UNICEF, UNFPA, the World Bank, and major pharmaceutical companies, participates in the 'Accelerating Access' initiative, which aims to expand access to care, support and ARVs for people with HIV/AIDS. In March 2002, under its 'Access to Quality HIV/AIDS Drugs and Diagnostics' programme, WHO published a comprehensive list of HIV-related medicines deemed to meet standards recommended by the Organization. In April WHO issued the first treatment guidelines for HIV/AIDS cases in poor communities, and endorsed the inclusion of HIV/AIDS drugs in its *Model List of Essential Medicines* (see below) in order to encourage their wider availability. The secretariat of the International HIV Treatment Access Coalition, founded in December of that year by governments, non-governmental organizations, donors and others to facilitate access to ARVs for people in low- and middle-income countries, is based at WHO headquarters. In September 2006, Brazil, Chile, France, Norway and the United Kingdom launched UNITAID, an international drug purchase facility aiming to provide sustained, strategic market intervention, with a view to reducing the cost of medicines for priority diseases and increasing the supply of drugs and diagnostics. In July 2008, UNITAID created the Medicines Patent Pool; the Pool, a separate entity, was to focus on increasing access to HIV medicines in developing countries. The Pool is funded by UNITAID, under a five-year arrangement. By the end of 2010 an estimated 6.6m. people in developing and middle-income countries were receiving appropriate HIV treatment, compared with 4m. at end-2008. In May 2011 the 64th World Health Assembly adopted a new Global Health Sector Strategy on HIV/AIDS, covering 2011–15, which aimed to promote greater innovation in HIV prevention, diagnosis, treatment, and the improvement of care services to facilitate universal access to care for HIV patients. WHO supports the following *Three Ones* principles, endorsed in April 2004 by a high-level meeting organized by UNAIDS, the United Kingdom and the USA, with the aim of strengthening national responses to the HIV/AIDS pandemic: for every country there should be one agreed national HIV/AIDS action framework; one national AIDS co-ordinating authority; and one agreed monitoring and evaluation system.

In December 2011 the UN General Assembly adopted a Political Declaration on HIV/AIDS, outlining 10 targets to be attained by 2015: reducing by 50% sexual transmission of HIV; reducing by 50% HIV transmission among people who inject drugs; eliminating new HIV infections among children, and reducing AIDS-related maternal deaths; ensuring that at least 15m. people living with HIV are receiving ARVs; reducing by 50% TB deaths in people living with HIV; reaching annual global investment of at least US $22,000m. in combating AIDS in low- and medium-resource countries; eliminating gender inequalities and increasing the capacity of women and girls to self-protect from HIV; promoting the adoption of legislation and policies aimed at eliminating stigma and discrimination against people living with HIV; eliminating HIV-related restrictions on travel; strengthening the integration of the AIDS response in global health and development efforts.

The total number of people world-wide living with HIV/AIDS at December 2010 was estimated at 34.0m., including some 2.7m. children under 15 years of age. It was reported that 2.6m. people were newly infected during that year. At December 2010 an estimated 22.9m. people in sub-Saharan Africa were estimated to have HIV/AIDS, of whom 1.9m. were newly affected during that year. More people were living with HIV/AIDS in South Africa than in any other country world-wide (an estimated 5.6m., with an estimated national adult prevalence rate of 17.8%, at end-2009), while the national adult prevalence rates at that time were 25.9% in Swaziland, 24.8% in Botswana, and 23.6% in Lesotho, and exceeded 10% in Malawi, Mozambique, Namibia, Zambia and Zimbabwe.

In 1995 WHO established a Global Tuberculosis Programme to address the challenges of the TB epidemic, which had been declared a global emergency by the Organization in 1993. According to WHO estimates, one-third of the world's population carries the TB bacillus. In 2009 this generated 9.4m. new active cases (1.1m. in people co-infected with HIV), and killed 1.7m. people (0.4m. of whom were also HIV-positive). Some 22 high-burden countries account for four-fifths of global TB cases. The largest concentration of TB cases is in South-East Asia. WHO provides technical support to all member countries, with special attention given to those with high TB prevalence, to establish effective national tuberculosis control programmes. WHO's strategy for TB control includes the use of the expanded DOTS (direct observation treatment, short-course) regime, involving the following five tenets: sustained political commitment to increase human and financial resources and to make TB control in endemic countries a nation-wide activity and an integral part of the national health system; access to quality-assured TB sputum microscopy; standardized short-course chemotherapy for all cases of TB under proper case-management conditions; uninterrupted supply of quality-assured drugs; and maintaining a recording and reporting system to enable outcome assessment. Simultaneously, WHO is encouraging research with the aim of further advancing DOTS, developing new tools for prevention, diagnosis and treatment, and containing new threats (such as the HIV/TB co-epidemic). Inadequate control of DOTS in some areas, leading to partial and inconsistent treatments, has resulted in the development of drug-resistant and, often, incurable strains of TB. The incidence of so-called Multidrug Resistant TB (MDR-TB) strains, that are unresponsive to at least two of the four most commonly used anti-TB drugs, has risen in recent years, and WHO estimates that about four-fifths are 'super strains', resistant to at least three of the main anti-TB drugs; an estimated 3.3% of new TB cases were reported to be MDR in 2009. MDR-TB cases occur most frequently in Eastern Europe, Central Asia, the People's Republic of China, and India; it was reported in 2010 that in certain areas of the former Soviet Union up to 28% of all new TB cases were MDR. WHO has developed DOTS-Plus, a specialized strategy for controlling the spread of MDR-TB in areas of high prevalence. By August 2010 59 countries had reported at least one case of Extensive Drug Resistant TB (XDR-TB), defined as MDR-TB plus resistance to additional drugs. XDR-TB is believed to be most prevalent in Eastern Europe and Asia. In 2007 WHO launched the Global MDR/XDR Response Plan, which aimed to expand diagnosis and treatment to cover, by 2015, some 85% of TB patients with MDR-TB.

The 'Stop TB' partnership, launched by WHO in 1999, in partnership with the World Bank, the US Government and a coalition of non-governmental organizations, co-ordinates the Global Plan to Stop TB, which represents a roadmap for TB control covering the period 2006–15. The Global Plan aims to facilitate the achievement of the MDG of halting and beginning to reverse by 2015 the incidence of TB by means of access to quality diagnosis and treatment for all; to supply ARVs to 3m. TB patients co-infected with HIV; to treat nearly 1m. people for MDR-TB (this target was subsequently altered by the 2007 Global MDR/XDR Response Plan, see above); to develop a new anti-TB drug and a new vaccine; and to develop rapid and inexpensive diagnostic tests at the point of care. A second phase of the Global Plan, launched in late 2010 and covering 2011–15, updated the Plan to take account of actual progress achieved since its instigation in 2006. The Global TB Drug Facility, launched by 'Stop TB' in 2001, aims to increase access to high-quality anti-TB drugs for sufferers in developing countries. In 2007 'Stop TB' endorsed the establishment of a new Global Laboratory Initiative with the aim of expanding laboratory capacity.

In December 2010 WHO endorsed a new rapid nucleic acid amplification test (NAAT) that provided an accurate diagnosis of TB in around 100 minutes; it was envisaged that NAAT, by eliminating the current wait of up to three months for a TB diagnosis, would greatly enhance management of the disease and patient care.

In October 1998 WHO, jointly with UNICEF, the World Bank and UNDP, formally launched the Roll Back Malaria (RBM) programme. The disease acutely affects at least 350m.–500m. people, and kills an estimated 1m. people, every year. Some 85% of all malaria cases occur in sub-Saharan Africa. It is estimated that the disease directly causes 18% of all child deaths in that region. The global RBM Partnership, linking governments, development agencies, and other parties, aims to mobilize resources and support for controlling malaria. The RBM Partnership Global Strategic Plan for the period 2005–15, adopted in November 2005, lists steps required to intensify malaria control interventions with a view to attaining targets set by the Partnership for 2010 and 2015 (the former targets include: ensuring the protection of 80% of people at risk from malaria and the diagnosis and treatment within one day of 80% of malaria patients, and reducing the global malaria burden by one-half compared with 2000 levels; and the latter: achieving a 75% reduction in malaria morbidity and mortality over levels at 2005). WHO recommends a number of guidelines for malaria control, focusing on the need for prompt, effective antimalarial treatment, and the issue of drug resistance; vector control, including the use of insecticide-treated bednets; malaria in pregnancy; malaria epidemics; and monitoring and evaluation activities. WHO, with several private and public sector partners, supports the development of more effective anti-malaria drugs and vaccines through the 'Medicines for Malaria' venture.

Joint UN Programme on HIV/AIDS (UNAIDS): 20 ave Appia, 1211 Geneva 27, Switzerland; tel. 227913666; fax 227914187; e-mail communications@unaids.org; internet www.unaids.org; established in 1996 to lead, strengthen and support an expanded response to the global HIV/AIDS pandemic; activities focus on prevention, care and support, reducing vulnerability to infection, and alleviating the socio-economic and human effects of HIV/AIDS; launched the Global Coalition on Women and AIDS in Feb. 2004; guided by UN Security Council Resolution 1308, focusing on the possible impact of AIDS on social instability and emergency situations, and the potential impact of HIV on the health of international peace-keeping personnel; by the UN Millennium Development Goals adopted in Sept. 2000; by the Declaration of Commitment on HIV/AIDS agreed in June 2001 by the first-ever Special Session of the UN General Assembly on HIV/AIDS, which acknowledged the AIDS epidemic as a 'global emergency'; and the Political Declaration on HIV/AIDS, adopted by the June 2006 UN General Assembly High Level Meeting on AIDS; launched the Global Coalition on Women and AIDS in Feb. 2004; co-sponsors: WHO, UN Women, UNICEF, UNDP, UNFPA, UNODC, the ILO, UNESCO, the World Bank, WFP, UNHCR; Exec. Dir MICHEL SIDIBÉ (Mali).

NON-COMMUNICABLE DISEASES AND MENTAL HEALTH

The Non-communicable Diseases (NCDs) and Mental Health group comprises departments for the surveillance, prevention and management of uninfectious diseases, and departments for health promotion, disability, injury prevention and rehabilitation, substance abuse and mental health. Surveillance, prevention and management of NCDs, tobacco, and mental health are organization-wide priorities.

Addressing the social and environmental determinants of health is a main priority of WHO. Tobacco use, unhealthy diet and physical inactivity are regarded as common, preventable risk factors for the four most prominent NCDs: cardiovascular diseases, cancer, chronic respiratory disease and diabetes. It is estimated that the four main NCDs are collectively responsible for an estimated 35m. deaths—60% of all deaths—globally each year, and that up to 80% of cases of heart disease, stroke and type 2 diabetes, and more than one-third of cancers, could be prevented by eliminating shared risk factors, the main ones being: tobacco use, unhealthy diet, physical inactivity and harmful use of alcohol. WHO envisages that the disease burden and mortality from these diseases will continue to increase, most rapidly in Africa and the Eastern Mediterranean, and that the highest number of deaths will occur in the Western Pacific region and in South-East Asia. WHO aims to monitor the global epidemiological situation of NCDs, to co-ordinate multinational research activities concerned with prevention and care, and to analyse determining factors such as gender and poverty. The 53rd World Health Assembly, convened in May 2000, endorsed a Global Strategy for the Prevention and Control of NCDs. In May 2008 the 61st World Health Assembly endorsed a new Action Plan for 2008–13 for the Global Strategy for the Prevention and Control of NCDs, based on the vision of the 2000 Global Strategy. The Action Plan aimed to provide a roadmap establishing and strengthening initiatives on the surveillance, prevention and management of NCDs, and emphasized the need to invest in NCD prevention as part of sustainable socioeconomic development planning.

The sixth Global Conference on Health Promotion, convened jointly by WHO and the Thai Government, in Bangkok, Thailand, in August 2005, adopted the Bangkok Charter for Health Promotion in a Globalized World, which identified ongoing key challenges, actions and commitments.

In May 2004 the World Health Assembly endorsed a Global Strategy on Diet, Physical Activity and Health; it is estimated that more than 1,000m. adults world-wide are overweight, and that, of these, some 300m. are clinically obese. WHO has studied obesity-related issues in co-operation with the International Association for the Study of Obesity (IASO). The International Task Force on Obesity, affiliated to the IASO, aims to encourage the development of new policies for managing obesity. WHO and FAO jointly commissioned an expert report on the relationship of diet, nutrition and physical activity to chronic diseases, which was published in March 2003.

WHO's programmes for diabetes mellitus, chronic rheumatic diseases and asthma assist with the development of national initiatives, based upon goals and targets for the improvement of early detection, care and reduction of long-term complications. WHO's cardiovascular diseases programme aims to prevent and control the major cardiovascular diseases, which are responsible for more than 14m. deaths each year. It is estimated that one-third of these deaths could have been prevented with existing scientific knowledge. The programme on cancer control is concerned with the prevention of cancer, improving its detection and cure, and ensuring care of all cancer patients in need. In May 2004 the World Health Assembly adopted a resolution on cancer prevention and control, recognizing an increase in global cancer cases, particularly in developing countries, and stressing that many cases and related deaths could be prevented. The resolution included a number of recommendations for the improvement of national cancer control programmes. In May 2009 WHO and the IAEA launched a Joint Programme on Cancer Control, aimed at enhancing efforts to fight cancer in the developing world. WHO is a co-sponsor of the Global Day Against Pain, which is held annually on 11 October. The Global Day highlights the need for improved pain management and palliative care for sufferers of diseases such as cancer and AIDS, with a particular focus on patients living in low-income countries with minimal access to opioid analgesics, and urges recognition of access to pain relief as a basic human right.

The WHO Human Genetics Programme manages genetic approaches for the prevention and control of common hereditary diseases and of those with a genetic predisposition representing a major health factor. The Programme also concentrates on the further development of genetic approaches suitable for incorporation into health care systems, as well as developing a network of international collaborating programmes.

WHO works to assess the impact of injuries, violence and sensory impairments on health, and formulates guidelines and protocols for the prevention and management of mental problems. The health promotion division promotes decentralized and community-based health programmes and is concerned with developing new approaches to population ageing and encouraging healthy lifestyles and self-care. It also seeks to relieve the negative impact of social changes such as urbanization, migration and changes in family structure upon health. WHO advocates a multi-sectoral approach—involving public health, legal and educational systems—to the prevention of injuries, which represent 16% of the global burden of disease. It aims to support governments in developing suitable strategies to prevent and mitigate the consequences of violence, unintentional injury and disability. Several health promotion projects have been undertaken, in collaboration between WHO regional and country offices and other relevant organizations, including: the Global School Health Initiative, to bridge the sectors of health and education and to promote the health of school-age children; the Global Strategy for Occupational Health, to promote the health of the working population and the control of occupational health risks; Community-based Rehabilitation, aimed at providing a more enabling environment for people with disabilities; and a communication strategy to provide training and support for health communications personnel and initiatives. In 2000 WHO, UNESCO, the World Bank and UNICEF adopted the joint Focusing Resources for Effective School Health (FRESH Start) approach to promoting life skills among adolescents.

WHO supports the UN Convention, and its Optional Protocol, on the Rights of Persons with Disabilities, which came into force in May 2008, and seeks to address challenges that prevent the full participation of people with disabilities in the social, economic and cultural lives of their communities and societies; at that time the WHO Director-General appointed a Taskforce on Disability to ensure that WHO was reflecting the provisions of the Convention overall as an organization and in its programme of work.

In February 1999 WHO initiated a new programme, 'Vision 2020: the Right to Sight', which aimed to eliminate avoidable blindness (estimated to be as much as 80% of all cases) by 2020. Blindness was otherwise predicted to increase by as much as twofold, owing to the increased longevity of the global population.

The Tobacco or Health Programme aims to reduce the use of tobacco, by educating tobacco-users and preventing young people from adopting the habit. In 1996 WHO published its first report on the tobacco situation world-wide. According to WHO, about one-third of the world's population aged over 15 years smoke tobacco, which causes nearly 6m. deaths each year (through lung cancer, heart disease, chronic bronchitis and other effects); in 2012 WHO estimated that tobacco would lead to more than 8m. deaths annually by 2030. In 1998 the 'Tobacco Free Initiative', a major global anti-smoking campaign, was established. In May 1999 the World Health Assembly endorsed the formulation of a Framework Convention on Tobacco Control (FCTC) to help to combat the increase in tobacco use (although a number of tobacco growers expressed concerns about the effect of the convention on their livelihoods). The FCTC entered into force in February 2005. The greatest increase in tobacco use is forecast to occur in developing countries. In 2008 WHO published a comprehensive analysis of global tobacco use and control, the *WHO Report on the Global Tobacco Epidemic*, which designated abuse of tobacco as one of the principal global threats to health, and predicted that during the latter part of the 21st century the vast majority of tobacco-related deaths would occur in developing countries. The Report identified and condemned a global tobacco industry strategy to target young people and adults in the developing world, and it detailed six key proven strategies, collectively known as the 'MPOWER package', that were aimed at combating global tobacco use: monitoring tobacco use and implementing prevention policies; protecting people from tobacco smoke; offering support to people to enable them to give up tobacco use; warning about the dangers of tobacco; enforcing bans on tobacco advertising, promotion and sponsorship; and raising taxes on tobacco. The MPOWER package provided a roadmap to support countries in building on their obligations under the FCTC. The FCTC obligates its states parties to require 'health warnings describing the harmful effects of tobacco use' to appear on packs of tobacco and their outside packaging, and recommends the use of warnings that contain pictures. WHO provides technical and other assistance to countries to support them in meeting this obligation through the Tobacco Free Initiative. WHO encourages governments to adopt tobacco health warnings meeting the agreed criteria for maximum effectiveness in convincing consumers not to smoke: these appear on both the front and back of a cigarette pack, should cover more than half of the pack, and should contain pictures.

WHO's Mental Health and Substance Abuse department was established in 2000 from the merger of formerly separate departments to reflect the many common approaches in managing mental health and substance use disorders.

WHO defines mental health as a 'state of well-being in which every individual realizes his or her own potential, can cope with the normal stresses of life, can work productively and fruitfully, and is able to make a contribution to her or his community'. WHO's Mental Health programme is concerned with mental health problems that include unipolar and bipolar affective disorders, psychosis, epilepsy, dementia, Parkinson's disease, multiple sclerosis, drug and alcohol dependency, and neuropsychiatric disorders such as post-traumatic stress disorder, obsessive compulsive disorder and panic disorder. Although, overall, physical health has improved, mental, behavioural and social health problems are increasing, owing to extended life expectancy and improved child mortality rates, and factors such as war and poverty. WHO aims to address mental problems by increasing awareness of mental health issues and promoting improved mental health services and primary care. In October 2008 WHO launched the so-called mental health Gap Action Programme (mhGAP), which aimed to improve services addressing mental, neurological and substance use disorders, with a special focus on low and middle income countries. It was envisaged that, with proper care, psychosocial assistance and medication, many millions of patients in developing countries could be treated for depression, schizophrenia, and epilepsy; prevented from attempting suicide; and encouraged to begin to lead normal lives. A main focus of mhGAP concerns forging strategic partnerships to enhance countries' capacity to combat stigma commonly associated with mental illness, reduce the burden of mental disorders, and promote mental health. WHO is a joint partner in the Global Campaign against Epilepsy: Out of the Shadows, which aims to advance understanding, treatment, services and prevention of epilepsy world-wide.

The Substance Abuse programme addresses the misuse of all psychoactive substances, irrespective of legal status and including alcohol. WHO provides technical support to assist countries in formulating policies with regard to the prevention and reduction of the health and social effects of psychoactive substance abuse, and undertakes epidemiological surveillance and risk assessment, advocacy and the dissemination of information, strengthening national and regional prevention and health promotion techniques and strategies, the development of cost-effective treatment and rehabilitation approaches, and also encompasses regulatory activities as required under the international drugs-control treaties in force. In May 2010 WHO endorsed a new global strategy to reduce the harmful use of alcohol; this promoted measures including taxation on alcohol, minimizing outlets selling alcohol, raising age limits for those buying alcohol, and the employment of effective measures to deter people from driving while under the influence of alcohol.

In June 2010 WHO launched the Global Network of Age-Friendly Cities, as part of a broader response to the ageing of populations world-wide. The Network aims to support cities in creating urban environments that would enable older people to remain active and healthy.

FAMILY AND COMMUNITY HEALTH

WHO's Family and Community Health group addresses the following areas of work: child and adolescent health, research and programme development in reproductive health, making pregnancy safer and men's and women's health. Making pregnancy safer is an organization-wide priority. The group's aim is to improve access to sustainable health care for all by strengthening health systems and fostering individual, family and community development. Activities include newborn care; child health, including promoting and protecting the health and development of the child through such approaches as promotion of breast-feeding and use of the mother-baby package, as well as care of the sick child, including diarrhoeal and acute respiratory disease control, and support to women and children in difficult circumstances; the promotion of safe motherhood and maternal health; adolescent health, including the promotion and development of young people and the prevention of specific health problems; women, health and development, including addressing issues of gender, sexual violence, and harmful traditional practices; and human reproduction, including research related to contraceptive technologies and effective methods. In addition, WHO aims to provide technical leadership and co-ordination on reproductive health and to support countries in their efforts to ensure that people: experience healthy sexual development and maturation; have the capacity for healthy, equitable and responsible relationships; can achieve their reproductive intentions safely and healthily; avoid illnesses, diseases and injury related to sexuality and reproduction; and receive appropriate counselling, care and rehabilitation for diseases and conditions related to sexuality and reproduction.

WHO supports the 'Global Strategy for Women's and Children's Health', launched by heads of state and government participating in the September 2010 UN Summit on the MDGs; some US $40,000m. has been pledged towards women's and child's health and achieving goals (iv) Reducing Child Mortality and (v) Improving Maternal Health. In May 2012 the World Health Assembly adopted a resolution on raising awareness of early marriage (entered into by more than 30% of women in developing countries) and adolescent pregnancy, and the consequences thereof for young women and infants.

In September 1997 WHO, in collaboration with UNICEF, formally launched a programme advocating the Integrated Management of Childhood Illness (IMCI). IMCI recognizes that pneumonia, diarrhoea, measles, malaria and malnutrition cause some 70% of the approximately 11m. childhood deaths each year, and recommends screening sick children for all five conditions, to obtain a more accurate diagnosis than may be achieved from the results of a single assessment. WHO encourages national programmes aimed at reducing childhood deaths as a result of diarrhoea, particularly through the use of oral rehydration therapy and preventive measures. In November 2009 WHO and UNICEF launched a Global Action Plan for the Prevention and Control of Pneumonia (GAPP), which aimed to accelerate pneumonia control through a combination of interventions of proven benefit. Accelerated efforts by WHO to promote vaccination against measles through its Measles Initiative (subsequently renamed the Measles and Rubella Initiative), established in 2001, contributed to a three-quarters reduction in global mortality from that disease over the period 2000–10. In April 2012 WHO and other partners launched a global strategy that aimed to eliminate measles deaths and congenital rubella syndrome.

In March 1996 WHO's Centre for Health Development opened at Kobe, Japan. The Centre researches health developments and other determinants to strengthen policy decision-making within the health sector.

SUSTAINABLE DEVELOPMENT AND HEALTHY ENVIRONMENTS

The Sustainable Development and Healthy Environments group focuses on the following areas of work: health in sustainable development; nutrition; health and environment; food safety; and emergency preparedness and response. Food safety is an organization-wide priority.

WHO promotes recognition of good health status as one of the most important assets of the poor. The Sustainable Development and Healthy Environment group seeks to monitor the advantages and disadvantages for health, nutrition, environment and development arising from the process of globalization (i.e. increased global flows of capital, goods and services, people, and knowledge); to integrate the issue of health into poverty reduction programmes; and to promote human rights and equality. Adequate and safe food and nutrition is a priority programme area. WHO collaborates with FAO, WFP, UNICEF and other UN agencies in pursuing its objectives relating to nutrition and food safety. It has been estimated that 780m. people world-wide cannot meet basic needs for energy and protein, more than 2,000m. people lack essential vitamins and minerals, and that 170m. children are malnourished. In December 1992 WHO and FAO hosted an international conference on nutrition, at which a World Declaration and Plan of Action on Nutrition was adopted to make the fight against malnutrition a development priority. Following the conference, WHO promoted the elaboration and implementation of national plans of action on nutrition. WHO aims to support the enhancement of member states' capabilities in dealing with their nutrition situations, and addressing scientific issues related to preventing, managing and monitoring protein-energy malnutrition; micronutrient malnutrition, including iodine deficiency disorders, vitamin A deficiency, and nutritional anaemia; and diet-related conditions and NCDs such as obesity (increasingly affecting children, adolescents and adults, mainly in industrialized countries), cancer and heart disease. In 1990 the World Health Assembly resolved to eliminate iodine deficiency (believed to cause mental retardation); a strategy of universal salt iodization was launched in 1993. In collaboration with other international agencies, WHO is implementing a comprehensive strategy for promoting appropriate infant, young child and maternal nutrition, and for dealing effectively with nutritional emergencies in large populations. Areas of emphasis include promoting healthcare practices that enhance successful breast-feeding; appropriate complementary feeding; refining the use and interpretation of body measurements for assessing nutritional status; relevant information, education and training; and action to give effect to the International Code of Marketing of Breast-milk Substitutes. The food safety programme aims to protect human health against risks associated with biological and chemical contaminants and additives in food. With FAO, WHO establishes food standards (through the work of the Codex Alimentarius Commission and its subsidiary committees) and evaluates food additives, pesticide residues and other contaminants and their implications for health. The programme provides expert advice on such issues as food-borne pathogens (e.g. listeria), production methods (e.g. aquaculture) and food biotechnology (e.g. genetic modification). In July 2001 the Codex Alimentarius Commission adopted the first global principles for assessing the safety of genetically modified (GM) foods. In March 2002 an intergovernmental task force established by the Commission finalized 'principles for the risk analysis of foods derived from biotechnology', which were to provide a framework for assessing the safety of GM foods and plants. In the following month WHO and FAO announced a joint review of their food standards operations. In February 2003 the FAO/WHO Project and Fund for Enhanced Participation in Codex was launched to support the participation of poorer countries in the Commission's activities. WHO supports, with other UN agencies, governments, research institutions, and representatives of civil society and of the private sector, the initiative on Scaling up Nutrition (SUN), which was initiated in 2009, under the co-ordination of the UN Secretary-General's Special Representative for Food Security and Nutrition, with the aim of increasing the coverage of interventions that improve nutrition during the first 1,000 days of a child's life (such as exclusive breastfeeding, optimal complementary feeding practices, and provision of essential vitamins and minerals); and ensuring that nutrition plans are implemented at national level, and that government programmes take nutrition into account. The activities of SUN are guided by the Framework for Scaling up Nutrition, which was published in April 2010; and by the SUN Roadmap, finalized in September 2010.

WHO's programme area on environmental health undertakes a wide range of initiatives to tackle the increasing threats to health and well-being from a changing environment, especially in relation to air pollution, water quality, sanitation, protection against radiation, management of hazardous waste, chemical safety and housing hygiene. In 2008 it was estimated that some 1,200m. people world-wide had no access to clean drinking water, while a further 2,600m. people are denied suitable sanitation systems. WHO helped launch the Water Supply and Sanitation Council in 1990 and regularly updates its *Guidelines for Drinking Water Quality*. In rural areas the emphasis continues to be on the provision and maintenance of safe and sufficient water supplies and adequate sanitation, the health aspects of rural housing, vector control in water resource management, and the safe use of agrochemicals. In urban areas assistance is provided to identify local environmental health priorities and to improve municipal governments' ability to deal with environmental conditions and health problems in an integrated manner; promotion of the 'Healthy City' approach is a major component of the programme. Other programme activities include environmental health information development and management, human resources development, environmental health planning methods, research and work on problems relating to global environment change, such as UV-radiation. The WHO Global Strategy for Health and Environment, developed in response to the WHO Commission on Health and Environment which reported to the UN Conference on Environment and Development in June 1992, provides the framework for programme activities. In May 2008 the 61st World Health Assembly adopted a resolution urging member states to take action to address the impact of climate change on human health.

Through its International EMF Project WHO is compiling a comprehensive assessment of the potential adverse effects on human health deriving from exposure to electromagnetic fields (EMF). In May 2011 the International Agency for Research on Cancer, an agency of WHO, classified radiofrequency EMF as possibly carcinogenic to humans, on the basis of an increased risk for glioma (malignant brain cancer) associated with the use of wireless phones.

WHO's work in the promotion of chemical safety is undertaken in collaboration with the ILO and UNEP through the International Programme on Chemical Safety (IPCS), the Central Unit for which is located in WHO. The Programme provides internationally evaluated scientific information on chemicals, promotes the use of such information in national programmes, assists member states in establishment of their own chemical safety measures and programmes, and helps them strengthen their capabilities in chemical emergency preparedness and response and in chemical risk reduction. In 1995 an Inter-organization Programme for the Social Management of Chemicals was established by UNEP, the ILO, FAO, WHO, UNIDO and OECD, in order to strengthen international co-operation in the field of chemical safety. In 1998 WHO led an international assessment of the health risk from bendocine disruptors (chemicals which disrupt hormonal activities).

In September 2005 a forum comprising representatives of WHO, IAEA, UNDP, UNEP, FAO, OCHA, the World Bank and the UN Scientific Committee on the effects of Atomic Radiation, and the governments of Belarus, Russia and Ukraine, issued an assessment of the long-term health, environmental and socio-economic effects of the 1986 Chornobyl (Chernobyl) nuclear reactor accident.

Since the major terrorist attacks perpetrated against targets in the USA in September 2001, WHO has focused renewed attention on the potential malevolent use of bacteria (such as bacillus anthracis, which causes anthrax), viruses (for example, the variola virus, causing smallpox) or toxins, or of chemical agents, in acts of biological or chemical terrorism. In September 2001 WHO issued draft guidelines entitled 'Health Aspects of Biological and Chemical Weapons'.

Within the UN system, WHO's Department of Emergency and Humanitarian Action co-ordinates the international response to emergencies and natural disasters in the health field, in close co-operation with other agencies and within the framework set out by the UN's Office for the Co-ordination of Humanitarian Affairs. In this context, WHO provides expert advice on epidemiological surveillance, control of communicable diseases, public health information and health emergency training. Its emergency preparedness activities include co-ordination, policy-making and planning, awareness-building, technical advice, training, publication of standards and guidelines, and research. Its emergency relief activities include organizational support, the provision of emergency drugs and supplies and conducting technical emergency assessment missions. The Division's objective is to strengthen the national capacity of member states to reduce the adverse health consequences of disasters. In responding to emergency situations, WHO always tries to develop projects and activities that will assist the national authorities concerned in rebuilding or strengthening their own capacity to handle the impact of such situations. WHO appeals through the UN's inter-agency Consolidated Appeals Process (CAP) for funding for its emergency humanitarian operations.

WHO's emergency response to a severe earthquake in the Pacific Ocean, measuring 9.0 on the international Richter scale, and a tsunami, that in mid-March 2011 devastated northeastern coastal areas of Japan and destroyed part of the Fukushima Daiichi nuclear plant, included collating available technical guidelines on nuclear issues; developing plans to address potential nuclear-related human health needs that might arise from the incident; making available funds for initiating training and planning to address related psycho-social issues; and issuing information on food safety. In late March 2011 WHO, FAO and the IAEA issued a joint statement on food safety issues in the aftermath of the Fukushima nuclear emergency, emphasizing their commitment to mobilizing knowledge and expertise in support of the Japanese authorities.

HEALTH TECHNOLOGY AND PHARMACEUTICALS

WHO's Health Technology and Pharmaceuticals group, made up of the departments of essential drugs and other medicines, vaccines and other biologicals, and blood safety and clinical technology, covers the following areas of work: essential medicines—access, quality and rational use; immunization and vaccine development; and world-wide co-operation on blood safety and clinical technology. Blood safety and clinical technology are an organization-wide priority.

The Department of Essential Drugs and Other Medicines promotes public health through the development of national drugs policies and global guidelines and through collaboration with member countries to promote access to essential drugs, the rational use of medicines and compliance with international drug-control requirements. The department comprises four teams: Policy Access and Rational Use; the Drug Action Programme; Quality, Safety and the Regulation of Medicines; and Traditional Medicine.

The Department of Vaccines and Other Biologicals undertakes activities related to quality assurance and safety of biologicals; vaccine development; vaccine assessment and monitoring; access to technologies; and the development of policies and strategies aimed at maximizing the use of vaccines.

The Policy Access and Rational Use team and the Drug Action Programme assist in the development and implementation by member states of pharmaceutical policies, in ensuring a supply of essential drugs of good quality at low cost, and in the rational use of drugs. Other activities include global and national operational research in the pharmaceutical sector, and the development of technical tools for problem solving, management and evaluation. The Policy Access and Rational Use team also has a strong advocacy and information role, promulgated through a periodical, the *Essential Drugs Monitor*, an extensive range of technical publications, and an information dissemination programme targeting developing countries.

The Quality, Safety and Regulation of Medicines team supports national drug-regulatory authorities and drug-procurement agencies and facilitates international pharmaceutical trade through the exchange of technical information and the harmonization of internationally respected norms and standards. In particular, it publishes the *International Pharmacopoeia (Ph. Int.)*, the *Consultative List of International Nonproprietary Names for Pharmaceutical Substances*, and annual and biennial reports of Expert Committees responsible for determining relevant international standards for the manufacture and specification of pharmaceutical and biological products in international commerce. It provides information on the safety and efficacy of drugs, with particular regard to counterfeit and substandard projects, to health agencies and providers of health care, and it maintains the pharmaceuticals section of the UN *Consolidated List of Products whose Consumption and/or Sale have been Banned, Withdrawn, Severely Restricted or Not Approved by Governments*. The *WHO Model List of Essential Medicines* is updated about every two years and is complemented by corresponding model prescribing information; the 17th *Model List* was published in March 2011. The first *Model List of Medicines for Children* was produced in October 2007. The *WHO Model Formulary* (current edition: 2008) gives detailed information on the safe and effective use of all essential drugs. The first *WHO Model Formulary for Children*, listing more than 240 essential medicines, as well as recommended usage, dosage, adverse effects and contraindications, for treating children between the ages 0–12, was issued in June 2010.

The Traditional Medicine team encourages and supports member states in the integration of traditional medicine into national healthcare systems and in the appropriate use of traditional medicine, through the provision of technical guidelines, standards and methodologies. In May 2002 WHO adopted a strategy on the regulation of traditional medicine and complementary or alternative medicines (TM/CAM). A WHO Congress on Traditional Medicine was held in November 2008, in Beijing, People's Republic of China.

In January 1999 the Executive Board adopted a resolution on WHO's Revised Drug Strategy which placed emphasis on the inequalities of access to pharmaceuticals, and also covered specific aspects of drugs policy, quality assurance, drug promotion, drug donation, independent drug information and rational drug use. Plans of action involving co-operation with member states and other international organizations were to be developed to monitor and analyse the pharmaceutical and public health implications of international agreements, including trade agreements. In April 2001 experts from WHO and the World Trade Organization participated in a workshop to address ways of lowering the cost of medicines in less developed countries. In the following month the World Health Assembly adopted a resolution urging member states to promote equitable access to essential drugs, noting that this was denied to about one-third of the world's population. WHO participates with other partners in the 'Accelerating Access' initiative, which aims to expand access to antiretroviral drugs for people with HIV/AIDS.

WHO reports that 2m. children die each year of diseases for which common vaccines exist. In September 1991 the Children's Vaccine Initiative (CVI) was launched, jointly sponsored by the Rockefeller Foundation, UNDP, UNICEF, the World Bank and WHO, to facilitate the development and provision of children's vaccines. The CVI has as its ultimate goal the development of a single oral immunization shortly after birth that will protect against all major childhood diseases. An International Vaccine Institute was established in Seoul, Republic of Korea, as part of the CVI, to provide scientific and technical services for the production of vaccines for developing countries. A comprehensive survey, *State of the World's Vaccines and Immunization*, was published by WHO, jointly with UNICEF, in 1996; revised editions of the survey were issued in 2003 and 2010. In 1999 WHO, UNICEF, the World Bank and a number of public and private sector partners formed the Global Alliance for Vaccines and Immunization (GAVI), which aimed to expand the provision of existing vaccines and to accelerate the development and introduction of new vaccines and technologies, with the ultimate goal of protecting children of all nations and from all socio-economic backgrounds against vaccine-preventable diseases.

WHO supports states in ensuring access to safe blood, blood products, transfusions, injections, and healthcare technologies.

INFORMATION, EVIDENCE AND RESEARCH

The Information, Evidence and Research group addresses the following areas of work: evidence for health policy; health information management and dissemination; and research policy and promotion and organization of health systems. Through the generation and dissemination of evidence the Information, Evidence and Research group aims to assist policy-makers assess health needs, choose intervention strategies, design policy and monitor performance, and thereby improve the performance of national health systems. The group also supports international and national dialogue on health policy.

WHO co-ordinates the Health InterNetwork Access to Research Initiative (HINARI), which was launched in July 2001 to enable relevant authorities in developing countries to access biomedical journals through the internet at no or greatly reduced cost, in order to improve the world-wide circulation of scientific information; by 2012 more than 8,500 journals and 7,000 e-books were being made available to health institutions in more than 100 countries.

In 2004 WHO developed the World Alliance on Patient Safety, further to a World Health Assembly resolution in 2002. Since renamed WHO Patient Safety, the programme was launched to facilitate the development of patient safety policy and practice across all WHO member states.

HEALTH DAYS

World Health Day is observed on 7 April every year, and is used to promote awareness of a particular health topic ('Aging and health: good health adds life to years', in 2012). World Leprosy Day is held every year on 30 January, World TB Day on 24 March, World No Tobacco Day on 31 May, World Heart Day on 24 September, World Mental Health Day on 10 October, World Diabetes Day, in association with the International Diabetes Federation, on 14 November, World AIDS Day on 1 December, and World Asthma Day on 11 December.

ASSOCIATED AGENCY

International Agency for Research on Cancer: 150 Cours Albert Thomas, 69372 Lyon Cedex 08, France; tel. 4-72-73-84-85; fax 4-72-73-85-75; e-mail www@iarc.fr; internet www.iarc.fr; established in 1965 as a self-governing body within the framework of WHO, the Agency organizes international research on cancer. It has its own laboratories and runs a programme of research on the environmental factors causing cancer. Mems: Australia, Belgium, Canada, Denmark, Finland, France, Germany, Italy, Japan, Netherlands, Norway, Spain, Sweden, Switzerland, United Kingdom, USA; Dir Dr CHRISTOPHER WILD (United Kingdom).

Finance

WHO's regular budget is provided by assessment of member states and associate members. An additional fund for specific projects is provided by voluntary contributions from members and other sources, including UNDP and UNFPA.

A total programme budget of US $4,804m. was proposed for the two years 2012–13; of the total some $3,419m. (71.2%) was allocated to WHO programmes; $922m. (19.2%) to special programmes and collaborative arrangements; and $462m. (9.6%) to outbreak and crisis response (governed by acute emergency events).

WHO PROPOSED BUDGET APPROPRIATIONS BY REGION, 2012–13

Region	Amount (US $ million)	% of total budget
Africa	1,409	29.3
Americas	257	5.3
South-East Asia	505	10.5
Europe	266	5.5
Eastern Mediterranean	725	15.1
Western Pacific	316	6.6
Headquarters	1,325	27.6
Total	4,804	100.0

Publications

Bulletin of WHO (monthly).

Eastern Mediterranean Health Journal (annually).

International Classification of Functioning, Disability and Health—ICF.

International Pharmacopoeia.

International Statistical Classification of Disease and Related Health Problems.

International Travel and Health.

Model List of Essential Medicines (every two years).

Pan-American Journal of Public Health (annually).

3 By 5 Progress Report.

Toxicological Evaluation of Certain Veterinary Drug Residues in Food (annually).

Weekly Epidemiological Record (in English and French, paper and electronic versions available).

WHO Drug Information (quarterly).

WHO Global Atlas of Traditional, Complementary and Alternative Medicine.

WHO Model Formulary.

WHO Report on the Global Tobacco Epidemic.

World Health Report (annually, in English, French and Spanish).

World Cancer Report.

World Malaria Report (with UNICEF).

Zoonoses and Communicable Diseases Common to Man and Animals.

Technical report series; catalogues of specific scientific, technical and medical fields available.

World Intellectual Property Organization—WIPO

Address: 34 chemin des Colombettes, BP 18, 1211 Geneva 20, Switzerland.

Telephone: 223389111; **fax:** 227335428; **e-mail:** wipo.mail@wipo.int; **internet:** www.wipo.int.

WIPO was established by a Convention signed in Stockholm in 1967, which came into force in 1970. It became a specialized agency of the UN in December 1974.

MEMBERS

WIPO has 185 members.

Organization

(June 2012)

GENERAL ASSEMBLY

The General Assembly is one of the three WIPO governing bodies, and is composed of all states that are party to the WIPO Convention and that are also members of any of the WIPO-administered Unions (see below). The Assembly meets in ordinary session once a year to agree on programmes and budgets. It elects the Director-General, who is the executive head of WIPO. Prior to the adoption of a new Treaty, the General Assembly may convene a Diplomatic Conference (a high-level meeting of member states) to finalize negotiations.

CONFERENCE

All member states are represented in the Conference, which meets in ordinary session once every two years.

CO-ORDINATION COMMITTEE

Countries belonging to the Committee are elected from among the member states of WIPO, the Executive Committee of the International Union for the Protection of Industrial Property (Paris Union, relating to the Paris Convention, see below), the Executive Committee of the International Union for the Protection of Literary and Artistic Works (Berne Union, relating to the Berne Convention, also see below), and, *ex officio*, Switzerland. It meets in ordinary session once a year.

ASSEMBLIES OF THE UNIONS

The Assemblies of member states of the Paris Union, the Berne Union, the other Unions of WIPO-administered international agreements (the Budapest Union, Hague Union, Lisbon Union, Locarno Union, Madrid Union—Marks, Nice Union, PCT (Patent Co-operation Treaty) Union, Strasbourg Agreement Concerning the International Patent Classification—IPC—Union, and Vienna Union), and the Assemblies of member states of the Rome Convention Intergovernmental Committee, the Patent Law Treaty, WIPO Copyright Treaty, and of the WIPO Performances and Phonograms Treaty) also contribute to the WIPO decision-making process. In September 2009 meetings of the WIPO Assemblies were, for the first time, preceded by a two-day high-level ministerial gathering ('ministerial segment').

INTERNATIONAL BUREAU

The International Bureau, as WIPO's secretariat, prepares the meetings of the various bodies of WIPO and the Unions, mainly through the provision of reports and working documents. It organizes the meetings, and sees that the decisions are communicated to all concerned, and, as far as possible, that they are carried out.

The International Bureau implements projects and initiates new ones to promote international co-operation in the field of intellectual property. It acts as an information service and publishes reviews. It is also the depository of most of the treaties administered by WIPO.

Separate regional bureaux, under the co-ordination of the International Bureau, channel technical assistance to member states in the Middle East, Africa, the Far East and Australasia, and Latin America and the Caribbean.

Director-General: FRANCIS GURRY (Australia).

There are four ad hoc Standing Committees, comprising experts, on: Law of Patents; Law of Trademarks, Industrial Designs and Geographical Indications; Copyright and Related Rights; and Information Technologies. A Standing Committee may establish a working group to examine specific issues in detail. There is also a Committee on Development and Intellectual Property, and an Advisory Committee on Enforcement. Some 250 non-governmental organizations have observer status at WIPO. WIPO has co-ordination offices in Brussels, Belgium; Toyko, Japan; Singapore; and New York, USA.

Activities

WIPO works to ensure that the rights of creators and owners of intellectual property (IP), 'creations of the mind', are protected throughout the world, with a view to facilitating the advancement of science, technology and the arts and promoting international trade. IP comprises two principal branches: industrial property (patents and other rights in technological inventions, rights in trademarks, industrial designs, geographical indications—including appellations of origin, etc.) and copyright and related rights (covering literary, musical, artistic and photographic works; and also the rights of performing artists in their performances, of producers of phonograms in their recordings, and of broadcasters in their audiovisual media broadcasts). IP rights enable the owner of a copyright, patent or trademark (the 'creator') to benefit from their work. In December 2008 member states adopted a revised strategic framework for WIPO comprising the following nine strategic goals: promoting the balanced evolution of the international normative framework for IP; providing premier global IP services; facilitating the use of IP for development; co-ordinating and developing a global IP infrastructure; developing as a world reference source for IP information and analysis; promoting international co-operation on building respect for IP; addressing IP in relation to global policy issues; developing a responsive communications interface between WIPO, its member states and all stakeholders; and developing an efficient administrative and financial support structure to enable the Organization better to deliver its programmes.

In October 2008 a WIPO strategic realignment programme (SRP) was launched, which was to introduce a corporate culture and to review the Organization's strategic objectives, structures, programmes and resources, to enable it to fulfill its mandate more effectively. In September 2010 member states endorsed proposed reforms to the Organization and adopted a new medium-term strategic plan for 2011–15, based on the Organization's nine strategic goals.

WIPO administers and encourages member states to sign and enforce international treaties relating to the protection of IP, of which the most fundamental are the Paris Convention for the Protection of Industrial Property (1883), the Berne Convention for the Protection of Literary and Artistic Works (1886), and the Patent Co-operation Treaty (PCT).

WIPO's Advisory Committee on Enforcement (ACE, established in October 2002) co-ordinates with other organizations and the private sector to enforce IP rights by combating piracy and counterfeiting; promoting public education; implementing national and regional training programmes for relevant stakeholders; and facilitating, through its IPEIS Electronic Forum, the exchange of information on enforcement issues. WIPO helps to organize the periodic Global Congress on Combating Counterfeiting and Piracy, which was established in 2004 as an international forum of senior public sector representatives and business leaders who gather to develop strategies against counterfeiting and piracy.

WIPO organizes an annual World Intellectual Property Day, held on 26 April; the theme for 2012 was 'Visionary Innovators'.

GLOBAL IP INFRASTRUCTURE

The co-ordination and development of a global IP infrastructure, to enhance the world-wide promotion of science, new technologies and innovation, was one of the new strategic goals approved by WIPO member states in December 2008. In September 2009 a WIPO global symposium of IP authorities met to discuss means of establishing a more accessible, digital and borderless global IP infrastructure. In 2012 the global IP infrastructure comprised the following pillars: IP institutions and authorities; capacity-building and networking; electronic data interchange among IP offices; international classifications in the fields of trademarks and industrial design; standards and technical agreements; databases; services; and an information-sharing forum (the Global Symposium of IP Authorities, of which the third was convened in September 2011).

DEVELOPING LAWS AND STANDARDS

One of WIPO's major activities is the progressive development and harmonization of IP laws, standards, and practices among its member states, in the areas of industrial property law and copyright law. The organization prepares new treaties and undertakes the revision of the existing treaties that it administers. WIPO administers international classifications established by treaties and relating to inventions, marks and industrial designs: periodically it reviews these to ensure their improvement in terms of coverage and precision. WIPO also carries out studies on issues in the field of IP that could be the subject of model laws or guidelines for implementation at national or international levels. The organization seeks to simplify and harmonize national IP legislation and procedures (for example through implementation of the Trademark Law Treaty, 1994, and development of the Patent Law Treaty, 2000) in order to make the registration of IP more easily accessible.

WIPO implements two programmes that provide legal and technical assistance on the formulation of strong IP laws and systems specifically to, respectively, developing countries and countries with economies in transition.

WIPO DIGITAL AGENDA

WIPO promotes the development of the use of Information and Communication Technology (ICT) for storing, accessing and using valuable IP data, and to provide a forum for informed debate and for the exchange of expertise on IP. The rapid advancement of digital communications networks has posed challenges regarding the protection and enforcement of IP rights. WIPO has undertaken a range of initiatives to address the implications for copyright and industrial property law, and for electronic commerce transcending national jurisdictions. WIPO's Electronic Commerce Section co-ordinates programmes and activities relating to the IP aspects of electronic commerce. In September 1999 WIPO organized the first International Conference on Electronic Commerce and IP; the 'WIPO Digital Agenda', which establishes a series of guidelines and objectives, was launched by the Organization at the Conference. The second International Conference on Electronic Commerce and IP was held in September 2001. In January 2001, under its Digital Agenda, WIPO launched WIPOnet, a global digital network of IP information sources capable of transmitting confidential data. The Organization also manages WIPO Gold, launched in June 2010 as an online repository of searchable IP data, and maintains WIPO Lex, an online search facility for IP national laws and treaties.

IP FOR DEVELOPMENT

WIPO aims to support governments and organizations in establishing policies and structures to harness the potential of IP for development. In 2005 WIPO founded an Office for Strategic Use of IP for Development (OSUIPD), which comprises the following four divisions: the Creative Industries Division (CID); the IP and Economic Development Division (IPEDD); the IP and New Technologies Division (IPNT Division); and the Small and Medium-Sized Enterprises Division (SMEs Division). The OSUIPD supports member states—with a particular focus on developing countries and those with economies in transition—in successfully utilizing the IP system for cultural, economic and social development; assists SMEs; and aims to enhance capacity in the area of managing IP assets.

In May 2005 WIPO, jointly with UNCTAD, UNIDO, WHO and the WTO, organized an international seminar focusing on IP and Development and IP and Public Policy. Areas covered included biodiversity; competition policy; copyright and related rights in the digital environment; creating value from intellectual property (IP) assets; national best practices; public health; traditional knowledge; and technology transfer. WIPO has subsequently organized a number of international and national seminars on the strategic use of IP for economic and social development. In April 2012 WIPO and UNIDO agreed to strengthen co-operation relating to IP in the areas of science and technology, promoting innovation, private sector development, and building trade capacity.

In September 2007 WIPO member states adopted the WIPO Development Agenda. The Agenda comprises a series of recommendations that incorporate 45 agreed proposals covering the following six clusters of activities: Technical Assistance and Capacity Building; Norm-setting, Flexibilities, Public Policy and Public Knowledge; Technology Transfer, ICT and Access to Knowledge; Assessments, Evaluation and Impact Studies; Institutional Matters including Mandate and Governance; and Other Issues (for example, ensuring that IP enforcement is viewed within the context of broader societal interests). A Committee on Development and IP (CDIP) was established in October 2007 to formulate a work programme for the implementation of these recommendations, and to monitor their implementation. The OSUIPD co-operates closely with all departments of WIPO involved in the implementation of the Development Agenda.

WIPO aims to modernize national IP systems. It offers technical assistance to increase the capabilities of developing countries to benefit from the international IP framework, with a view to promoting the optimal use of human and other resources and thereby contributing to national prosperity. WIPO supports governments with IP-related institution-building, human resources development, and preparation and implementation of legislation. The OSUIPD helps countries to formulate national IP strategies. The WIPO Worldwide Academy, established in March 1998, undertakes training, teaching and research on IP matters, focusing particularly on developing countries. The Academy maintains a Distance Learning Centre using online facilities, digital multimedia technology and video conferencing. WIPO's Information and Documentation Centre holds extensive reference materials. Under its Digital Agenda WIPO aims to assist the integration of developing countries into the internet environment, particularly through the use of WIPOnet (see above). In March 2007 WIPO helped to organize the first annual symposium for IP academies, in Rio de Janeiro, Brazil, which established the Global Network of IP Academies (GNIPA) as a framework for co-operation. The fifth GNIPA symposium was convened in August 2011, in Washington, DC, USA.

WIPO advises countries on obligations under the WTO's agreement on Trade-Related Aspects of IP Rights (TRIPS). The two organizations have jointly implemented a technical co-operation initiative to assist least developed countries with harmonizing their national legislative and administrative structures in compliance with the TRIPS accord; the original deadline for completion of the initiative, 1 January 2006, was extended in November 2005 to 1 July 2013.

WIPO presented a programme of action to the Third UN Conference on the Least Developed Countries (LDCs-III, held in Brussels, Belgium in May 2001), which was aimed at strengthening LDCs' IP systems. In May 2009 WIPO launched a Japan-funded programme aimed at promoting the use of IP in Africa and LDCs as a catalyst for economic and commercial development. Representatives of LDCs attending a WIPO high-level forum on the strategic use of intellectual property for prosperity and development, held in July 2009, reaffirmed commitment to integrating IP and innovation strategies into their national development planning. WIPO participated in the preparation of LDC-IV, which was held in May 2011, in Istanbul, Turkey.

WIPO, with ITU and UNIDO, leads an initiative on promoting technology and innovation, the eighth of nine activities that were launched in April 2009 by the UN System Chief Executives Board for Co-ordination (CEB), with the aim of alleviating the impact on poor and vulnerable populations of the developing global economic crisis.

In June 2011 WIPO launched a new project to establish a common digital platform across 11 countries in West Africa, with the aim of simplifying the identification of protected musical works in that region.

COPYRIGHT AND RELATED RIGHTS

Through its Copyright and Related Rights sector WIPO works on the development of international norms and standards in the area of copyright and related rights (these being legal concepts and instruments that both protect the rights of creators of works and aim to contribute to national development); and also actively promotes, through the organization of meetings and seminars, the so-called 'WIPO Internet Treaties' (the WIPO Copyright Treaty—WCT and WIPO Performances and Phonograms Treaty—WPPT), which were enacted as part of the WIPO Digital Agenda with the aim of updating copyright law in the light of new digital technologies. In July 2008 WIPO convened an international workshop on digital preservation and copyright.

In July 2007 the Organization published the *WIPO Guide on Managing Intellectual Property for Museums*, which acknowledged that institutions of the cultural heritage community in industrialized countries were increasingly regarded as owners of shared IP resources (for example, their own contextualized or interpretative authoritative content), rather than as merely users of IP, and aimed to assist museums and the broader cultural heritage community to use the international IP system to enhance the future management of their collections in the digital environment. In May 2011 WIPO and the International Council of Museums (ICOM) signed a Memorandum of Understanding on collaboration in the management of IP options, and in the mediation of disputes, in the area of cultural heritage and museums, with a particular focus on copyright issues, traditional knowledge and traditional cultural expressions, and the digitization of cultural artifacts.

SMALL AND MEDIUM-SIZED ENTERPRISES

A programme focusing on the IP concerns of small and medium-sized enterprises was approved by the WIPO General Assembly in September 2000. An International Forum on IP and SMEs, organized jointly by WIPO and the Italian Government in Milan, Italy in February 2001, adopted the Milan Plan of Action for helping SMEs to benefit fully from the IP system. WIPO publishes a number of guides and manuals aimed specifically at SMEs.

TRADITIONAL KNOWLEDGE, EXPRESSIONS OF FOLKLORE, GENETIC RESOURCES

In view of the advances in technology and economic globalization in recent years WIPO has focused increasingly on the relationship between IP and issues such as traditional knowledge (TK), biological diversity, environmental protection and human rights. In 1998–99 WIPO made fact-finding visits to 3,000 TK stakeholders in 60 locations world-wide, and in 2001, following an open review of the 1998–99 consultations, the Organization published the first ever report on the IP concerns of holders of TK. In April 2000 the organization convened its first Meeting on IP and Genetic Resources (GR). A WIPO Intergovernmental Committee on IP and GR, TK and Folklore (IGC) was established in September of that year. In January 2002 an international forum organized by WIPO adopted the Muscat Declaration on IP and TK, recognizing the contribution of TK to international co-operation. In October 2005 the WIPO Voluntary Fund for Accredited Indigenous and Local Communities was inaugurated with a view to supporting the participation of accredited indigenous and local communities in the work of the IGC. In December 2006 the 10th session of the IGC identified 10 key questions relating to the protection of traditional cultural expressions (TCE) and expressions of folklore (EoF), and to the protection of TK. A commentary process on the issues raised was subsequently undertaken. In December 2007 WIPO convened a roundtable on building the capacity of indigenous communities in the area of IP, TK, GR and TCE. The 12th session of the IGC, convened in February 2008, determined to prepare a working document that was to describe, and to illustrate any gaps in, the existing provisions at international level providing protection for TCE/EoF; and that was to consider means of addressing any gaps identified. The resulting 'gap analyses' were reviewed by the 13th IGC session, convened in October of that year. In July 2009 the 14th session of the IGC agreed on the future negotiation and adoption of an internationally legally binding instrument aimed at ensuring the effective protection of biodiversity, TK, GR and TCEs. Text-based negotiations on the proposed legal framework were initiated in May 2010, and, in February 2012, the 20th session of the IGC consolidated proposals arising from the negotiations into a single text, which was to be considered by the WIPO General Assembly in October 2012.

WIPO's Creative Heritage Project supports indigenous communities with the employment of new digital technologies to record and archive expressions of their cultural heritage. The Project manages the WIPO Creative Heritage Digital Gateway, an internet portal to collections of indigenous cultural heritage. A pilot project was launched in September 2008 under the auspices of the Creative Heritage Project to provide training to specific indigenous communities in documenting their cultural traditions, in archiving the documentation relating to their heritage, and in protecting their rights regarding the authorization of third party use of this material; the first focus of the initiative was the Kenyan Maasai.

In September 2007 WIPO launched a series of open-policy symposia to address issues related to the use and impact of IP in the life sciences; the fourth round of symposia, convened in April 2008, addressed using life sciences patent landscaping for public policy purposes. WIPO has commissioned expert analyses of the patent landscapes relating to priority areas of concern for public health policy-makers, including avian influenza and neglected diseases.

In November 2009 WIPO supported the Indian Government in convening an International Conference on TK, in New Delhi, India, with participation by international experts in TK, GR and TCEs.

ENFORCEMENT OF IP RIGHTS

WIPO's Advisory Committee on Enforcement (ACE) provides technical assistance and co-ordinates with other organizations and with the private sector to combat counterfeiting and piracy activities; provides public education; supports the implementation of national and regional training programmes; and promotes the exchange of information on enforcement issues.

ARBITRATION AND MEDIATION CENTRE

WIPO maintains the WIPO Arbitration and Mediation Centre, which became operational in October 1994, to facilitate the settlement of IP disputes between private parties. Since its inception the Centre has deliberated on more than 210 requests for arbitration (relating to, *inter alia*, patent infringements, patent licenses, software licenses, distribution agreements for pharmaceutical products, research and development agreements, trademark co-existence agreements, consultancy agreements, and joint venture agreements); and more than 70 requests for mediation (relating to, *inter alia*, patent disputes, software/ICT, copyright, trademark co-existence, employment issues in an IP context, and engineering disputes). The Centre organizes arbitrator and mediator workshops and assists in the development of WIPO model contract clauses and industry-specific resolution schemes. The Centre offers parties to disputes the option of using the WIPO Electronic Case Facility (WIPO ECAF), which provides for secure web-based filing, storing and retrieval of case-related submissions.

The Arbitration and Mediation Centre also offers a Domain Name Dispute Resolution service, which plays a leading role in reviewing cases of conflict between trademarks and internet domain names (such as com, .net, .org, and .info), and some 65 country code top-level domains (ccTLDs), in accordance with the Uniform Domain Name Dispute Resolution Policy (UDRP) that was, on WIPO's recommendation, adopted by the Internet Corporation for Assigned Names and Numbers—ICANN in October 1999. WIPO's first Internet Domain Name Process, a series of international consultations, undertaken in 1999, issued several recommendations for controlling the abuse of trademarks on the internet. A second Internet Domain Name Process, completed in 2001, addressed the improper registration of other identifiers ('cybersquatting'), including standard non-proprietary names for pharmaceutical substances, names and acronyms of intergovernmental organizations, geographical indications and terms, and trade names. By 2012 more than 20,000 cases, relating to some 35,000 separate domain names, and involving parties from 153 countries, had been administered by WIPO under UDRP procedures; the principal areas of complainant activity were information technology and pharmaceuticals. From December 2009 the Centre offered a paperless UDRP process, which became mandatory in March 2010. In addition to UDRP cases, the Centre deals with cases relating to registrations in the start-up phase of new domains, in accordance with so-called 'Sunrise' policies. WIPO publishes an online Legal Index of WIPO UDRP Panel Decisions and also maintains an online database of cybersquatting cases: a record 2,764 complaints regarding alleged cybersquatting were filed with the Centre in 2011.

INTERNATIONAL REGISTRATION SERVICES

WIPO maintains the following international registration services:

International registration of trademarks: operating since 1893; during 2011 there were 42,270 registrations and 21,754 renewals of trademarks; publ. *WIPO Gazette of International Marks* (every two weeks).

International deposit of industrial designs: operating since 1928; during 2011 2,363 applications were made for deposits, renewals and prolongations of 12,033 industrial designs; publ. *International Designs Bulletin* (monthly).

International applications for patents: operating since 1978; provisionally, 181,900 record copies of international applications for patents under the PCT were received in 2011, with the fastest area of growth in the area of digital communications; publ. *World Intellectual Property Indicators* (annually), *PCT Review* (annually), *Weekly Published PCT Data* (monthly, on dvd, from www.wipo.int/patentscope/en/data/data_download.html). A series of Patent Colloquia were convened during October 2006–November 2007, aimed at enhancing the international patent system.

WIPO-ADMINISTERED TREATIES

INTELLECTUAL PROPERTY TREATIES

(status at June 2012)

The IP Treaties administered by WIPO define internationally agreed basic standards of IP protection in each member state.

Paris Convention for the Protection of Industrial Property: signed 20 March 1883, last revised in 1967; 174 states party.

Berne Convention for the Protection of Literary and Artistic Works: signed 9 Sept. 1886, last revised in 1971; 165 states party.

Madrid Agreement for the Repression of False or Deceptive Indications of Source on Goods: signed 14 April 1891; 35 states party.

Rome Convention for the Protection of Performers, Producers of Phonograms and Broadcasting Organizations: signed 26 October 1961; 91 states party.

Phonograms Convention for the Protection of Producers of Phonograms against Unauthorized Duplication of their Phonograms: signed 29 October 1971; 77 states party.

Brussels Convention Relating to the Distribution of Programme-carrying Signals Transmitted by Satellite: signed 21 May 1974; 35 states party.

Nairobi Treaty on the Protection of the Olympic Symbol: signed 26 September 1981; 50 states party.

Treaty on the International Registration of Audiovisual Works (Film Register Treaty): signed 20 April 1989; 13 states party.

Trademark Law Treaty: signed 27 October 1994; 52 states party.

WIPO Copyright Treaty (WCT): signed 20 December 1996; 89 states party.

WIPO Performances and Phonograms Treaty (WPPT): signed 20 December 1996; 89 states party.

Patent Law Treaty, 2000: entered into force 28 April 2005; 32 states party.

Singapore Treaty on the Law of Trademarks: entered into force 16 March 2009; 26 states party.

Washington Treaty on Intellectual Property in Respect of Integrated Circuits: signed 26 May 1989; three ratifications.

GLOBAL PROTECTION SYSTEM TREATIES

(status at June 2012)

WIPO administers a small number of treaties, listed below, that cover inventions (patents), trademarks and industrial designs, under which one international registration or filing has effect in any of the relevant signatory states. The services provided by WIPO under its so-called Global Protection System treaties simplify the registration process and reduce the cost of making individual applications or filings in each country in which protection for a given IP right is sought. The most widely used of these treaties is the PCT, under which a single international patent application is valid in all signatory countries selected by the applicant. The PCT system has expanded rapidly in recent years. The PCT-SAFE (Secure Applications Filed Electronically) system became operational in February 2004, safeguarding the electronic filing of patent applications. Patent applications can be accessed through WIPO's PatentScope search facility. The corresponding treaties concerning the international registration of trademarks and industrial designs are, respectively, the Madrid Agreement (and its Protocol), and the Hague Agreement. From 1 January 2010 the earliest of the three Acts of the Hague Agreement (the 1934 London Act, deemed to be obsolete) was suspended to streamline the administration of the Agreement.

Madrid Agreement Concerning the International Registration of Marks: signed 14 April 1891; 56 states party.

The Hague Agreement Concerning the International Registration of Industrial Designs: signed 16 November 1925; 60 states party.

Lisbon Agreement for the Protection of Appellations of Origin and their International Registration: signed 31 October 1958; 27 states party.

Patent Co-operation Treaty (PCT): signed 19 June 1970; 144 states party.

Budapest Treaty on the International Recognition of the Deposit of Micro-organisms for the Purposes of Patent Procedure: signed 28 April 1977; 76 states party.

Protocol Relating to the Madrid Agreement Concerning the International Registration of Marks: signed 28 June 1989; 87 contracting states.

INTERNATIONAL CLASSIFICATION TREATIES

(status at June 2012)

The International Classification Treaties administered by WIPO create classification systems that organize information concerning inventions, trademarks and industrial designs. The International Classification treaties have established permanent committees of experts mandated periodically to revise and update the classification systems.

Locarno Agreement Establishing an International Classification for Industrial Designs: signed 8 October 1968; 52 states party.

Nice Agreement Concerning the International Classification of Goods and Services for the Purposes of the Registration of Marks: signed 15 June 1957; 83 states party.

Strasbourg Agreement Concerning the International Patent Classification (IPC): signed 24 March 1971; 62 states party.

Vienna Agreement Establishing an International Classification of the Figurative Elements of Marks: signed 12 June 1973; 31 states party.

Finance

The approved budget for the two years 2012–13 amounted to 647.4m. Swiss francs. Around 85% of WIPO's revenue derives from the international registration systems maintained by the organization; the remainder derives mainly from contributions by member states.

Publications

Les appellations d'origine (annually, in French).

Hague Yearly Review.

Intellectual Property Statistics.

International Designs Bulletin (weekly, in English and French).

Madrid System Annual Report.

PCT Newsletter (monthly).

PCT Yearly Review.

WIPO Gazette of International Marks (weekly, in English and French).

WIPO Handbook.

World Intellectual Property Indicators (annually).

WIPO Magazine (every 2 months, in English, French and Spanish).

WIPO Overview.

A collection of industrial property and copyright laws and treaties; a selection of publications related to intellectual property.

World Meteorological Organization—WMO

Address: 7 bis, ave de la Paix, CP 2300, 1211 Geneva 2, Switzerland.

Telephone: 227308111; **fax:** 227308181; **e-mail:** wmo@wmo.int; **internet:** www.wmo.int.

WMO was established in 1950 and was recognized as a Specialized Agency of the UN in 1951, operating in the fields of meteorology, climatology, operational hydrology and related fields, as well as their applications.

MEMBERS

WMO has 189 members.

Organization

(June 2012)

WORLD METEOROLOGICAL CONGRESS

The supreme body of the Organization, the Congress, is convened every four years and represents all members; it adopts regulations, and determines policy, programme and budget. The 16th Congress was held in May–June 2011. An extraordinary session of the Congress was to be convened in October 2012.

EXECUTIVE COUNCIL

The Council has 37 members and meets at least once a year to prepare studies and recommendations for the Congress; it supervises the implementation of Congress resolutions and regulations, informs members on technical matters and offers advice.

SECRETARIAT

The Secretariat acts as an administrative, documentary and information centre; undertakes special technical studies; produces publications; organizes meetings of WMO constituent bodies; acts as a link between the meteorological and hydrometeorological services of the world, and provides information for the general public. The WMO Secretariat hosts the secretariat of the intergovernmental Group on Earth Observations (GEO), which was founded by participants at the Earth Observation Summit convened in Washington, DC, USA, in July 2003.

Secretary-General: MICHEL JARRAUD (France).

Deputy Secretary-General: JEREMIAH LENGOASA (South Africa).

REGIONAL ASSOCIATIONS

Members are grouped in six Regional Associations (Africa, Asia, Europe, North America, Central America and the Caribbean, South America and the South-West Pacific), whose task is to co-ordinate meteorological activity within their regions and to examine questions referred to them by the Executive Council. Sessions are held at least once every four years.

TECHNICAL COMMISSIONS

The Technical Commissions are composed of experts nominated by the members of the Organization. Sessions are held at least once every four years. The Commissions cover the following areas: Basic Systems; Climatology; Instruments and Methods of Observation; Atmospheric Sciences; Aeronautical Meteorology; Agricultural Meteorology; Hydrology; Oceanography and Marine Meteorology.

WORLD CLIMATE CONFERENCE

The First World Climate Conference was convened in 1979 and the Second World Climate Conference took place in 1990. WMO co-operated with other UN agencies to prepare for the third World Climate Conference, which was convened, in Geneva, in August–September 2009.

Activities

In June 2011 the 16th World Meteorological Congress determined that WMO's five priority areas of activity during 2011–15 would be: developing the newly-endorsed Global Framework for Climate Services; enhancing the agency's contribution to disaster risk reduction; improving observation and information systems; strengthening developing countries' capacity to share in scientific advances and their applications; and advancing the efficiency of meteorological services in the aviation sector. The 16th Congress also recommended that WMO should prepare a cross-cutting Capacity Development Strategy to co-ordinate and enhance existing capacity building activities.

GLOBAL FRAMEWORK FOR CLIMATE SERVICES

The third World Climate Conference, convened in August–September 2009, resolved to establish the Global Framework for Climate Services, to act as a platform for dialogue on climate change between providers of climate services (for example national meteorological and hydrometeorological services) and service users, such as policy-makers and farmers. The new Framework, developed by a High-level Task Force during 2010–early 2011, was endorsed by the 16th World Meteorological Congress in June 2011. An extraordinary session of the World Meteorological Congress was to be convened in October 2012 to review and adopt a draft implementation plan of the new Global Framework.

WORLD WEATHER WATCH (WWW) PROGRAMME

Combining facilities and services provided by the members, the Programme's primary purpose is to make available meteorological and related geophysical and environmental information enabling them to maintain efficient meteorological services. Facilities in regions outside any national territory (outer space, ocean areas and Antarctica) are maintained by members on a voluntary basis. In May 2007 the 15th WMO Congress made a number of decisions aimed at improving the WWW Programme, including instruments and observation methods and assisting developing countries to strengthen their operational capacities. WMO's World Weather Information Services website (worldweather.wmo.int) provides weather observations in nine languages.

Antarctic Activities: co-ordinates WMO activities related to the Antarctic, in particular the surface and upper-air observing programme, plans the regular exchange of observational data and products needed for operational and research purposes, studies problems related to instruments and methods of observation peculiar to the Antarctic, and develops appropriate regional coding practices. Contacts are maintained with scientific bodies dealing with Antarctic research and with other international organizations on aspects of Antarctic meteorology.

Data Management: monitors the integration of the different components of the WWW Programme, with the intention of increasing the efficiency of, in particular, the Global Observing System, the Global Data Processing System and the Global Telecommunication System. The Data Management component of the WWW Programme develops data handling procedures and standards for enhanced forms of data representation, in order to aid member countries to process large volumes of meteorological data.

Emergency Response Activities: assists national meteorological services to respond effectively to man-made environmental emergencies, particularly nuclear accidents, through the development, co-ordination and implementation of WMO/IAEA established procedures and response mechanisms for the provision and exchange of observational data and specialized transport model products. In the immediate aftermath of the devastating earthquake and tsunami flooding that struck Japan in March 2011, disabling the Fukushima Daiichi nuclear power plant, WMO, in partnership with the IAEA, undertook weather forecast monitoring.

Global Data Processing and Forecasting System: consists of World Meteorological Centres (WMCs) in Melbourne (Australia), Moscow (Russia) and Washington, DC (USA); 40 Regional/Specialized Meteorological Centres (RSMCs); and 188 National Meteorological Centres. The WMCs and RSMCs provide analyses, forecasts and warnings for exchange on the Global Telecommunications System. Some centres concentrate on the monitoring and forecasting of environmental quality and special weather phenomena, such as tropical cyclones, monsoons, droughts, etc., which have a major impact on human safety and national economies. These analyses and forecasts are designed to assist the members in making local and specialized forecasts.

Global Observing System: makes simultaneous observations at around 11,000 land stations. Meteorological information is also received from 3,000 aircraft, 7,000 ships, 600 drifting buoys, and nine polar orbiting and six geostationary meteorological satellites. About 160 members operate some 1,300 ground stations equipped to receive picture transmissions from geostationary and polar-orbiting satellites.

WMO Integrated Global Observing Systems (WIGOS): approved by the 15th World Meteorological Congress (2007). The 16th World Meteorological Congress (2011) decided that priority should be given to developing WIGOS to enable it to become operational by 2016.

WMO Information System (WIS): became operational in January 2012 as a single co-ordinated global infrastructure responsible for telecommunications and data management, aimed at expanding the global exchange of weather, climate and water data. It was conceived of as a pillar of WMO's activities for managing and moving weather, climate and water information in the 21st century. The core infrastructure of the WIS consists of: Global Information System Centres (GISCs), Data Collection or Production Centres (DCPCs), and National Centres (NCs).

Global Telecommunication System: provides telecommunication services for the rapid collection and exchange of meteorological information and related data; consists of: the Main Telecommunication Network (MTN), six Regional Meteorological Telecommunication networks, and the national telecommunication networks. The system operates through 183 National Meteorological Centres, 29 Regional Telecommunications Hubs and the three WMCs.

Instruments and Methods of Observation Programme: promotes the world-wide standardization of meteorological and geophysical instruments and methods of observation and measurement to meet agreed accuracy requirements. It provides related guidance material and training assistance in the use and maintenance of the instruments.

System Support Activity: provides guidance and support to members in the planning, establishment and operation of the WWW Programme. It includes training, technical co-operation support, system and methodology support, operational WWW evaluations, advanced technology support, an operations information service, and the WWW Programme referral catalogue.

Tropical Cyclone Programme: established in response to UN General Assembly Resolution 2733 (XXV), aims to develop national and regionally co-ordinated systems to ensure that the loss of life and damage caused by tropical cyclones and associated floods, landslides and storm surges are reduced to a minimum. The Programme supports the transfer of technology, and includes five regional tropical cyclone bodies covering more than 60 countries, to improve warning systems and collaboration with other international organizations in activities related to disaster mitigation. The 16th World Meteorological Congress determined that the Programme should be strengthened to provide capacity-building support to Least Developed Countries and Small Island Developing States.

WORLD CLIMATE PROGRAMME

Adopted by the Eighth World Meteorological Congress (1979), the World Climate Programme (WCP) comprises the following components: World Climate Data and Monitoring Programme (WCDMP), World Climate Applications and Climate Information Services (CLIPS) Programme (WCASP), World Climate Impact Assessment and Response Strategies Programme (WCIRP), World Climate Research Programme (WCRP). The 16th World Meteorological Congress (2011) adopted a restructured and strengthened World Climate Programme and decided that it would be a key programme in the delivery of the newly-endorsed Global Framework for Climate Services. The WCP is supported by the Global Climate Observing System (GCOS), which provides comprehensive observation of the global climate system, involving a multi-disciplinary range of atmospheric, oceanic, hydrologic, cryospheric and biotic properties and processes. The objectives of the WCP are: to use existing climate information to improve economic and social planning; to improve the understanding of climate processes through research, so as to determine the predictability of climate and the extent of man's influence on it; and to detect and warn governments of impending climate variations or changes, either natural or man-made, which may significantly affect critical human activities.

Co-ordination of the overall Programme is the responsibility of WMO, together with direct management of the WCDMP and WCASP. The UN Environment Programme (UNEP) has accepted responsibility for the WCIRP, while the WCRP is jointly administered by WMO, the International Council for Science (ICSU) and UNESCO's Intergovernmental Oceanographic Commission. Other organizations involved in the Programme include FAO, WHO, and the Consultative Group on International Agricultural Research (CGIAR). In addition, the WCP supports the WMO/UNEP Intergovernmental Panel on Climate Change and the implementation of international agreements, such as the UN Framework Convention on Climate Change; and co-ordinates climate activities within WMO.

World Climate Applications and Climate Information and Services Programme (WCASP): promotes applications of climate knowledge in the areas of food production, water, energy (especially solar and wind energy), urban planning and building, human health, transport, tourism and recreation.

World Climate Data and Monitoring Programme (WCDMP): aims to make available reliable climate data for detecting and monitoring climate change for both practical applications and research purposes. The major projects are: the Climate Change Detection Project (CCDP); development of climate databases; computer systems for climate data management (CLICOM); the World Data and Information Referral Service (INFOCLIMA); the Climate Monitoring System; and the Data Rescue (DARE) project.

World Climate Impact Assessment and Response Strategies Programme (WCIRP): aims to make reliable estimates of the socio-economic impact of climate changes, and to assist in forming national policies accordingly. It concentrates on: study of the impact of climate variations on national food systems; assessment of the impact of man's activities on the climate, especially through increasing the amount of carbon dioxide and other radiatively active gases in the atmosphere; and developing the methodology of climate impact assessments.

World Climate Research Programme (WCRP): organized jointly with the Intergovernmental Oceanographic Commission of UNESCO and the ICSU, to determine to what extent climate can be predicted, and the extent of man's influence on climate. Its three specific objectives are: establishing the physical basis for weather predictions over time ranges of one to two months; understanding and predicting the variability of the global climate over periods of several years; and studying the long-term variations and the response of climate to natural or man-made influence over periods of several decades. Studies include: changes in the atmosphere caused by emissions of carbon dioxide, aerosols and other gases; the effect of cloudiness on the radiation balance; the effect of ground water storage and vegetation on evaporation; the Arctic and Antarctic climate process; and the effects of oceanic circulation changes on the global atmosphere.

Global Climate Observing System (GCOS): aims to ensure that data on climate are obtained and made available for: climate system monitoring and climate change detection and attribution; assessing impacts of, and vulnerability to, climate variability and change, e.g. extreme events, terrestrial ecosystems, etc., and analysing options for adaptation; research to improve understanding, modelling and prediction of the climate system; and application to sustainable economic development. The strategy of the GCOS has been to work with its international and regional partners and to engage countries both directly and through international fora such as WMO, other GCOS sponsors and the UN Framework Convention on Climate Change.

ATMOSPHERIC RESEARCH AND ENVIRONMENT PROGRAMME

This major Programme aims to help members to implement research projects; to disseminate relevant scientific information; to draw the attention of members to outstanding research problems of major importance, such as atmospheric composition and environment changes; and to encourage and help members to incorporate the results of research into operational forecasting or other appropriate techniques, particularly when such changes of procedure require international co-ordination and agreement.

Global Atmosphere Watch (GAW): a world-wide system that integrates most monitoring and research activities involving the long-term measurement of atmospheric composition, and is intended to serve as an early warning system to detect further changes in atmospheric concentrations of 'greenhouse' gases, changes in the ozone layer and associated ultraviolet radiation, and in long-range transport of pollutants, including acidity and toxicity of rain, as well as the atmospheric burden of aerosols. The instruments of these globally standardized observations and related research are a set of 22 global stations in remote areas and, in order to address regional effects, some 200 regional stations measuring specific atmospheric chemistry parameters, such as ozone and acid deposition. GAW is the main contributor of data on chemical composition and surface ultraviolet radiation to the GCOS. Through GAW, WMO has collaborated with the UN Economic Commission for Europe (ECE) and has been responsible for the meteorological part of the Monitoring and Evaluation of the Long-range Transmission of Air Pollutants in Europe. In this respect, WMO has arranged for the establishment of two Meteorological Synthesizing Centres (Oslo, Norway, and Moscow, Russia) which provide daily analysis of the transport of pollution over Europe. GAW also gives attention to atmospheric chemistry studies, prepares scientific assessments and encourages integrated environmental monitoring. Quality Assurance/Science Activity Centres have been established to ensure an overall level of quality in GAW. Atmospheric composition information is maintained by and available through a series of six GAW World Data Centres. GAW operates the GAW Urban Environment Meteorological Research Programme (GURME), which assists National Meteorological and Hydrological Services (NMHSs) in dealing with regional and urban pollution monitoring and forecasting, through the provision of guide-lines and information on the requisite measuring and modelling infrastructures, and by bringing together NMHSs, regional and city administrations and health authorities. GURME is being developed in co-operation with the World Health Organization.

WMO and other agencies support UNESCO's International Oceanographic Commission with implementing tsunami warning systems for the Caribbean region, the north-eastern Atlantic, the Mediterranean and connected seas, and the Pacific. An Indian Ocean Tsunami Warning and Mitigation System became operational in June 2006. In May 2007 the 15th WMO Congress stressed the importance of developing and maintaining tsunami warning systems and ocean forecast/warning systems.

Physics of Clouds and Weather Modification Research Programme: encourages scientific research on cloud physics and chemistry, with special emphasis on interaction between clouds and atmospheric chemistry, as well as weather modification such as precipitation enhancement ('rain-making') and hail suppression. It provides information on world-wide weather modification projects, and guidance in the design and evaluation of experiments. It also studies the chemistry of clouds and their role in the transport, transformation and dispersion of pollution.

Tropical Meteorology Research Programme: aims to promote and co-ordinate members' research efforts into such important problems as monsoons, tropical cyclones, meteorological aspects of droughts in the arid zones of the tropics, rain-producing tropical weather systems, and the interaction between tropical and mid-latitude weather systems. This should lead to a better understanding of tropical systems and forecasting, and thus be of economic benefit to tropical countries.

World Weather Research Programme (WWRP): promotes the development and application of improved weather forecasting techniques. The Programme is primarily concerned with forecasting weather events that have the potential to cause considerable socio-economic dislocation. Advances in forecasting capability are pursued through a combination of improved scientific understanding (gained through field experiments and research), forecast technique development, the demonstration of new forecasting capabilities, and the transfer of these advances to all NMHSs in conjunction with related training through various Research Development Projects (RDPs) and Forecast Demonstration Projects (FDPs). In particular, THORPEX: a Global Atmospheric Research Programme, is being developed and implemented as part of the WWRP to accelerate improvements in the accuracy of 1–14-day weather forecasts in order to achieve social and economic benefits. The Programme builds upon ongoing advances within the basic research and operational forecasting communities. It aims to make progress by enhancing international collaboration between these communities and with users of forecast products.

APPLICATIONS OF METEOROLOGY PROGRAMME

Public Weather Services Programme: assists members in providing reliable and effective weather and related services for the benefit of the public. The main objectives of the Programme are: to strengthen members' capabilities to meet the needs of the community through the provision of comprehensive weather and related services, with particular emphasis on public safety and welfare; and to foster a better understanding by the public of the capabilities of national meteorological services and how best to use their services.

Agricultural Meteorology Programme: the study of weather and climate as they affect agriculture and forestry, the selection of crops and their protection from disease and deterioration in storage, soil conservation, phenology and physiology of crops and productivity and health of farm animals; the Commission for Agricultural Meteorology supervises the applications projects and also advises the Secretary-General in his efforts to co-ordinate activities in support of food production. There are also special activities in agrometeorology to monitor and combat drought and desertification, to apply climate and real-time weather information in agricultural planning and operations, and to help improve the efficiency of the use of human labour, land, water and energy in agriculture; close co-operation is maintained with FAO, centres of CGIAR and UNEP. The 16th World Meteorological Congress (2011) approved the use of a standardized meteorological drought index to enhance drought monitoring and early warning systems.

Aeronautical Meteorology Programme: provides operational meteorological information required for safe, regular and efficient air navigation, as well as meteorological assistance to non-real-time activities of the aviation industry. The objective is to ensure the world-wide provision of cost-effective and responsive aviation operations. The Programme is implemented at global, regional and national levels, the Commission for Aeronautical Meteorology (CAeM) playing a major role, taking into account relevant meteorological developments in science and technology, studying aeronautical requirements for meteorological services, promoting international standardization of methods, procedures and techniques, and considering requirements for basic and climatological data as well as aeronautical requirements for meteorological observations and specialized instruments and enhanced understanding and awareness of the impact of aviation on the environment. Activities under this Programme are carried out, where relevant, with the International Civil Aviation Organization (ICAO) and in collaboration with users of services provided to aviation.

Marine Meteorology and Oceanography Programme: undertakes operational monitoring of the oceans and the maritime atmosphere; collection, exchange, archival recording and management of marine data; processing of marine data, and the provision of marine meteorological and oceanographic services in support of the safety of life and property at sea and of the efficient and economic operation of all sea-based activities. The joint WMO/Intergovernmental Oceanographic Commission (IOC) Technical Commission for Oceanography and Marine Meteorology (JCOMM) has broad responsibilities in the overall management of the Programme. Many programme elements are undertaken jointly with the IOC, within the context of JCOMM, and also of the Global Ocean Observing System (GOOS). Close co-operation also occurs with the International Maritime Organization (IMO), as well as with other bodies both within and outside the UN system.

HYDROLOGY AND WATER RESOURCES PROGRAMME

The overall objective of this major Programme is to apply hydrology to meet the needs of sustainable development and use of water and related resources; for the mitigation of water-related disasters; and to ensure effective environment management at national and international levels. The 16th World Meteorological Congress (2011) determined that the Programme should be strengthened to meet a growing need for sustainable water resources management. The Programme consists of the following mutually supporting component programmes:

Programme on Basic Systems in Hydrology (BSH): provides the basis and framework for the majority of the scientific and technical aspects of WMO activities in hydrology and water resources. The BSH covers the collection, transmission and storage of data, the transfer of operationally proven technology through the Hydrological Operational Multipurpose System (HOMS), and the development of the World Hydrological Cycle Observing System (WHYCOS), with the aim of improving countries' capacity to supply reliable water-related data, and manage and exchange accurate and timely water resources information.

Programme on Forecasting and Applications in Hydrology (FAH): covers aspects of the Hydrology and Water Resources Programme relating to hydrological modelling and forecasting, and to the application of hydrology in studies of global change. The FAH organizes activities in support of water resources development and management, and hazard mitigation, and promotes interdisciplinary co-operation to enhance flood forecasting at the national, regional and global level. The Programme is linked to the World Climate and Tropical Cyclone programmes.

Programme on Sustainable Development of Water Resources (SDW): encourages the full participation of hydrological services in national planning and in the implementation of actions consequent to the relevant recommendations of the United Nations Conference on Environment and Development (UNCED, held in Rio de Janeiro, Brazil, in 1992), and the World Summit on Sustainable Development (WSSD, held in Johannesburg, South Africa, in 2002).

Programme on Capacity Building in Hydrology and Water Resources (CBH): provides a framework under which National Hydrological Services (NHSs) are supported in their institutional development, through education and training activities, development of guidance material, assistance in the preparation of water legislation, reorganization of services and changes in administrative and legal frameworks.

Programme on Water-related Issues (WRI): maintains WMO's important role in international activities relating to water resource assessment and hydrological forecasting. A major aspect of this component programme is the organization's collaboration with other UN agencies.

Other WMO programmes contain hydrological elements, which are closely co-ordinated with the Hydrology and Water Resources Programme. These include the Tropical Cyclone Programme, the World Climate Programme, and the Global Energy and Water Budget Experiment of the World Climate Research Programme.

EDUCATION AND TRAINING PROGRAMME

The overall objective of this Programme is to assist members in developing adequately trained staff to meet their responsibilities for providing meteorological and hydrological information services.

Activities include surveys of the training requirements of member states, the development of appropriate training programmes, the monitoring and improvement of the network of 23 Regional Meteorological Training Centres, the organization of training courses, seminars and conferences and the preparation of training materials. The Programme also arranges individual training programmes and the provision of fellowships. The Panel of Experts on Education and Training was established by the Executive Council to serve as an advisory body on all aspects of technical and scientific education and of training in meteorology and operational hydrology.

TECHNICAL CO-OPERATION PROGRAMME

The objective of the WMO Technical Co-operation Programme is to assist developing countries in improving their meteorological and hydrological services so that they can serve the needs of their people more effectively. This is achieved through improving, *inter alia,* their early warning systems for severe weather; their agricultural-meteorological services, to facilitate more reliable and fruitful food production; and the assessment of climatological factors for economic planning. At a regional level the Programme concentrates on disaster prevention and mitigation. In 2006 a Severe Weather Forecasting Demonstration Project was launched in southeastern Africa; the 15th WMO Congress (2007) determined that this should be expanded and implemented throughout Africa and in the southwest Pacific region, and the 16th Congress decided that it should be expanded further.

Programme for the Least Developed Countries: has as its long-term objective enhancement of the capacities of the NMHSs of LDCs so that they can contribute efficiently and in a timely manner to socio-economic development efforts. Priority areas are poverty alleviation and natural disaster preparedness and mitigation. Specific projects will be developed for individual countries and at a sub-regional level for countries in Africa, Asia and the Pacific.

Voluntary Co-operation Programme (VCP): WMO assists members in implementing the WWW Programme to develop an integrated observing and forecasting system. Member governments contribute equipment, services and fellowships for training, in addition to cash donations.

WMO also carries out assistance projects under Trust Fund arrangements, financed by national authorities, either for activities in their own country or in a beneficiary country and managed by UNDP, the World Bank, regional development banks, the European Union and others. WMO provides assistance to UNDP in the development of national meteorological and hydrological services, in the application of meteorological and hydrological data to national economic development, and in the training of personnel.

REGIONAL PROGRAMME

WMO's Regional Programme cuts across the other major WMO programmes of relevance to the regions and addresses meteorological, hydrological and other geophysical issues which are unique to and of common concern to a region or group of regions. It provides a framework for the formulation of most of the global WMO Programmes and serves as a mechanism for their implementation at the national, subregional and regional levels. The Programme provides support to the WMO regional associations and contributes to the development of NMHSs through capacity-building and other priority activities identified by members or relevant economic groups and organizations within the respective regions.

NATURAL DISASTER PREVENTION AND MITIGATION PROGRAMME

The purpose of this cross-cutting Programme is to ensure the integration of relevant activities being carried out by the various WMO programmes in the area of disaster prevention and mitigation, and to provide for the effective co-ordination of pertinent WMO activities with the related activities of international, regional and national organizations, including civil defence organizations. The Programme should also provide scientific and technical support to WMO actions made in response to disaster situations, and its activities should emphasize pre-disaster preparedness and be based on activities within a number of WMO programmes, including the Public Weather Services and other components of the Applications of Meteorology Programme. The Programme will serve as a vehicle for enabling the delivery of increasingly accurate and reliable warnings of severe events, especially through co-ordinating WMO actions aimed at improving mechanisms and communications for the delivery, use and evaluation of warnings, provision of prompt advice and assistance to members; and at enhancing effective international co-operation and collaboration.

SPACE PROGRAMME

The 14th WMO Congress, held in 2003, initiated this new, cross-cutting programme to increase the effectiveness of, and contributions from, satellite systems for WMO programmes. Congress recognized the critical importance of data, products and services provided by the expanded space-based component of the GCOS. In recent years the use by WMO members of satellite data, products and services has grown tremendously, to the benefit of almost all WMO programmes and WMO-supported programmes. The 53rd session of the Executive Council adopted a landmark decision to expand the space-based component of the GCOS to include appropriate research and development ('R&D') and environmental satellite missions. The Congress agreed that the Commission for Basic Systems should continue to play a leading role, in full consultation with the other technical commissions for the Space Programme. Anticipated benefits from the Programme include an increasing contribution to the development of the GCOS, as well as to that of other WMO-supported programmes and associated observing systems, through the provision of continuously improved data, products and services, from both operational and R&D satellites. The Programme also aims to facilitate and promote the wider availability and meaningful utilization world-wide of such improved data. The 16th Congress agreed to pursue the development of an architecture for climate monitoring from space.

INTERNATIONAL POLAR DECADE AND GLOBAL CRYOSPHERE WATCH

WMO considers the polar regions (including the 'Third Pole'—the Himalayan and Tibetan Plateau) as extremely important in terms of their impact on global weather, water and climate. WMO, jointly with the International Council for Science, sponsored the International Polar Year (IPY), which was observed during March 2007–March 2008, although the full scientific programme associated with the IPY covered two annual cycles over the period March 2007–March 2009. The IPY focused on the Arctic and Antarctic polar regions and involved more than 200 projects addressing a wide range of physical, biological and social areas of research. The 16th World Meteorological Congress (2011) agreed to work with other international organizations to organize a future International Polar Decade. The 16th Congress also supported the need to establish an observational framework for polar regions, including an Antarctic Observing Network; determined to support a Global Integrated Polar Prediction System; and decided to develop, with international partners, the Global Cryosphere Watch. The Congress emphasized the significance, in terms of climate change prediction, of the cryosphere—i.e. water in its frozen state, including snow cover, sea, lake and river ice, glaciers, ice caps, ice sheets and permafrost, spanning all latitudes, in approximately 100 countries.

CO-OPERATION WITH OTHER BODIES

As a Specialized Agency of the UN, WMO actively participates in the UN system. Within the UN *Delivering as One* process WMO and UNESCO were assigned the lead role in developing a Climate Knowledge Base. WMO, in addition, has concluded a number of formal agreements and working arrangements with international organizations both within and outside the UN system, at the intergovernmental and non-governmental level. As a result, WMO participates in major international conferences convened under the auspices of the UN or other organizations. In 1988 WMO, jointly with UNEP, established the Intergovernmental Panel on Climate Change as an advisory scientific body concerned with assessing and reporting the scientific, technical and socio-economic information relating to climate change. In response to the first report of the Panel, published in 1990, WMO and UNEP worked together to formulate the UN Framework Convention on Climate Change, which was signed in May 1992 and entered into force in March 1994. Other co-sponsored programmes are the World Climate Research Programme, the Global Climate Observing System, and the Global Ocean Observing System.

INTERNATIONAL DAY

World Meteorological Day is observed every year on 23 March. The theme in 2012 was 'Powering our future with weather, climate and water'.

Finance

WMO is financed by contributions from members on a proportional scale of assessment. For the 16th financial period, the four years 2012–15, a regular budget of 276m. Swiss francs was approved, and voluntary resources were projected at 175m. Swiss francs. Outside this budget, WMO implements a number of projects as executing agency for UNDP or else under trust fund.

Publications

Annual Report.

MeteoWorld.

WMO Bulletin (quarterly in English, French, Russian and Spanish).

World Climate News.

Reports, technical regulations, manuals and notes and training publications.

World Tourism Organization—UNWTO

Address: Capitán Haya 42, 28020 Madrid, Spain.

Telephone: (91) 5678100; **fax:** (91) 5713733; **e-mail:** omt@unwto.org; **internet:** www.world-tourism.org.

The World Tourism Organization (UNWTO) was formally established in 1975 following transformation of the International Union of Official Travel Organisations into an intergovernmental body, in accordance with a resolution of the UN General Assembly approved in 1969. The organization became a specialized agency of the UN in December 2003. It aims to promote and develop sustainable tourism, in particular in support of socio-economic growth in developing countries.

MEMBERS

155 member states, seven territories as associate members, 418 affiliate members.

Organization

(June 2012)

GENERAL ASSEMBLY

The General Assembly meets every two years to approve the budget and programme of work of the organization and to consider issues of concern for the tourism sector. It consists of representatives of all full and associate members; affiliate members and representatives of other international organizations participate as observers. The 19th General Assembly was convened in Gyeongju, Republic of Korea, in October 2011.

EXECUTIVE COUNCIL

The Council, comprising 29 members elected by the General Assembly, is the governing body responsible for supervising the activities of the organization. It meets twice a year. The following specialized committees are subsidiary organs of the Council and advise on management and programme content: Programme; Budget and Finance; Statistics and Macroeconomic Analysis of Tourism; Market Intelligence and Promotion; Sustainable Development of Tourism; and Quality Support and Trade. In addition, there is a World Committee on Tourism Ethics and a Subcommittee for the Review of Applications for Affiliate Membership.

REGIONAL COMMISSIONS

There are six regional commissions, comprising all members and associate members from that region, which meet at least once a year to determine the organization's priorities and future activities in the region. The commissions cover Africa, the Americas, East Asia and the Pacific, Europe, the Middle East, and South Asia.

SECRETARIAT

The Secretariat is responsible for implementing the organization's work programme. The Secretary-General is supported by three Executive Directors, all based at headquarters. A regional support office for Asia and the Pacific is based in Osaka, Japan. Six regional representatives, based at the Secretariat, support national tourism authorities, act as a liaison between those authorities and international sources of finance, and represent the body at national and regional events.

Secretary-General: TALEB RIFAI (Jordan).

AFFILIATE MEMBERS

UNWTO is unique as an intergovernmental body in extending membership to operational representatives of the industry and other related sectors, for example transport companies, educational institutions, insurance companies, publishing groups. A UNWTO Education Council aims to support UNWTO's education and human resource development activities. It undertakes research projects, grants awards for innovation and the application of knowledge in tourism, and co-ordinates a tourism labour market observatory project. The UNWTO Business Council groups together the affiliate members from the private sector and aims to promote and facilitate partnerships between the industry and governments. A third group of the affiliate membership is the UNWTO Destinations Council, which acts as an operational body supporting the UNWTO Destination Management programme with particular concern for issues relevant to tourist destinations, for example local tourism marketing, economic measurements and management of congestion.

Chair. of Board of UNWTO Affiliate Members (2012–13): GEORGE DRAKOPOULOS (Greece).

Activities

The World Tourism Organization promotes the development of responsible, sustainable and universally accessible tourism within the broad context of contributing to economic development, international prosperity and peace and respect for human rights. As a UN specialized agency UNWTO aims to emphasize the role of tourism as a means of supporting socio-economic development and achieving the UN Millennium Development Goals (MDGs). Through its network of affiliated members UNWTO extends its activities and objectives to the private sector, tourism authorities and educational institutions. In October 2008 the Executive Council approved the establishment of a Tourism Resilience Committee, which was to consider the response of the tourist industry to the deterioration of the global economy and the role of tourism in economic stimulus programmes. The Committee convened for the first time in January 2009. In September WMO published a 'Roadmap for Recovery' which highlighted the role of tourism and travel in job creation and economic recovery, including its contribution to creating a 'green economy'. The Roadmap was endorsed by the General Assembly, meeting in October. At that time ministers of tourism of several industrialized and developing economies determined to form a grouping to promote the Roadmap at high-level international discussions. Meetings of the so-called T.20 were subsequently convened, with the full support of UNWTO, in Johannesburg, South Africa, in February 2010; in Buyeo, Republic of Korea, in October of that year; in Paris, France, in October 2011; and in Mérida, Mexico, in May 2012. UNWTO welcomed a declaration issued by the 2012 Mérida meeting urging that priority be given to advancing visa facilitation as a means of stimulating economic growth and creating employment through travel. The fifth T20 meeting was to be held during 2013, in Russia. In March 2011 UNWTO, with the Government of Andorra, organized an inaugural Global Tourism Forum, which brought together representatives of international agencies, private sector companies, and other partners, to promote the role of tourism in a sustainable global economic recovery and to harness collective support for the competitive and responsible development of the tourism sector.

DEVELOPMENT ASSISTANCE

UNWTO aims to support member states to develop and promote their tourist industry in order to contribute to socio-economic growth and poverty alleviation. Activities to transfer technical skills and knowledge to developing countries are fundamental tasks for the organization. It aims to assist member countries to develop tourism plans and strategies and helps to secure and manage specific development projects, for example the formulation of tourism legislation in Syria, hotel classification in Bolivia and statistics development in Botswana. Other aspects of developing tourism concern the involvement of local communities, fostering public-private partnerships and the preservation of cultural and natural heritage. UNWTO maintains a register of specialized consultants and firms to undertake appropriate missions.

In September 2002 at the World Summit on Sustainable Development, held in Johannesburg, South Africa, UNWTO, in collaboration with the UN Conference on Trade and Development (UNCTAD), launched the Sustainable Tourism-Eliminating Poverty (ST-EP) initiative. It aimed to encourage social, economic and ecologically sustainable tourism with the aim of alleviating poverty in the world's poorest countries. In September 2004 UNWTO signed an agreement with the Republic of Korea providing for the establishment of a ST-EP Foundation in the capital, Seoul. UNWTO has conducted a series of capacity-building seminars and other training activities concerning tourism and poverty alleviation, within the framework of the ST-EP initiative. It convenes an annual ST-EP forum, in Berlin, Germany, to involve a range of tourism agencies and companies in the scheme. Project identification missions have been conducted in some 30 developing countries with a focus on local level tourism development and small-scale entrepreneurial schemes. The first Pan-African Conference on Sustainable Tourism Management in African National Parks and Protected Areas was scheduled to be convened by UNWTO in Arusha, Tanzania, in October 2012.

MARKET, COMPETITIVENESS AND STATISTICS

UNWTO aims to ensure that quality standards and safety and security aspects are incorporated into all tourism products and services. It is also concerned with the social impact of tourism and the regulatory trading framework. UNWTO has formulated international standards for tourism measurement and reporting. It compiles comprehensive tourism statistics and forecasts. A Tourism Satellite Account (TSA) was developed to analyse the economic impact of tourism. It was endorsed by the UN Statistical Commission in 2000 and is recognized as a framework for providing internationally comparable data. (An updated Recommended Methodological Framework was introduced in 2008.) The TSA is also considered by UNWTO to be a strategic project within the broader objective of developing a system of tourism statistics. In October 2005 a world conference on TSAs, held in the Iguazu region of Argentina, Brazil and Paraguay, agreed on 10 defined objectives to extend and develop the use of TSAs. Further international conferences on tourism statistics have been held in Malaga, Spain, in October 2008, and in Bali, Indonesia, in March–April 2009.

UNWTO assists governments and tourist professionals to identify, analyse and forecast tourism trends and to assess the relative performance of each country's tourist industry. The organization also assists member states with tourism promotion through marketing tools and the formulation of tourism development strategies. A Market Intelligence and Promotion Committee was formally established in October 2002. Following the terrorism attacks against targets in the USA in September 2001 a Tourism Recovery Committee was established to monitor events affecting tourism, to help to restore confidence in the industry and to strengthen UNWTO activities concerned with safety and security.

In 1991 UNWTO's General Assembly approved a series of Recommended Measures for Tourism Safety which member states were encouraged to apply. UNWTO has established a Safety and Security in Tourism Network to consider aspects of the recommended measures and to facilitate collaboration between institutions and experts concerned with safety and security issues. The Network publishes national factsheets on safety and security in countries and tourist destinations, compiled by a designated national tourism administration focal point, for use by tourism professionals and the general public. Other essential quality standards promoted by the organization are hygiene and food safety, accessibility, product and pricing transparency and authenticity. UNWTO is also concerned with ensuring that tourist activities are in keeping with the surrounding environment. UNWTO was a co-organizer of official events on Tourism for a Sustainable Future and Green Innovation in Tourism, held on the sidelines of the UN Conference on Sustainable Development, which was convened in Rio de Janeiro, Brazil, in June 2012.

In January 2005 the Executive Council convened its first ever emergency session in response to the devastation of many coastal areas in the Indian Ocean caused by a series of earthquakes and tsunamis at the end of 2004. The Council, meeting in Phuket, Thailand, along with other regional organizations, private sector representatives and tourism experts, adopted an action plan to support the recovery of the tourism sector in many of the affected areas, to help to restore tourist confidence in the region and to rehabilitate tourism infrastructure, in particular in Thailand, the Maldives, Indonesia and Sri Lanka. A co-ordinating unit to oversee the longer-term projects was established in February 2005 and its functions were integrated into UNWTO's broader emergency response framework in mid-2006. In 2005 UNWTO pledged its commitment to working with governments and the private sector to incorporate tourism concerns into preparedness programmes relating to the threat of highly pathogenic avian influenza. A Tourism Emergency Response Network (TERN) was established in April 2006 as a grouping of travel organizations committed to supporting UN efforts to respond to avian influenza and the threat of a potential human pandemic. UNWTO maintains a tourism emergency tracking system, which identifies recent outbreaks of the disease. In 2008 UNWTO developed a new online service, SOS.travel, to support crisis preparedness and management within the tourist industry and to enable individual travellers to enhance their own personal safety and security.

UNWTO participates as an observer at the World Trade Organization on issues relating to trade in tourism services, with particular concern to negotiations under the General Agreement on Trade in Services (GATS) for a separate annex on tourism. UNWTO hosts a voluntary working group on liberalization.

In order to generate awareness of tourism among the international community UNWTO sponsors a World Tourism Day, held each year on 27 September. In 2011 the official events were hosted by Egypt, focusing on 'Linking Cultures'. The theme of the 2012 events was to be 'Tourism and Sustainable Energy: Powering Sustainable Development'.

SUSTAINABLE TOURISM DEVELOPMENT

UNWTO aims to encourage and facilitate the application of sustainable practices within the tourism industry. It publishes guides on sustainable development and compilations for good practices for use by local authorities. UNWTO has also published manuals for tourism planning at regional, national and local level and has organized seminars on planning issues in developing countries. UNWTO actively promotes voluntary initiatives for sustainability including labelling schemes, certification systems and awards.

In 1999 UNWTO was mandated, together with the UN Environment Programme (UNEP), to assume responsibility for the International Year of Ecotourism which was held in 2002, as well as all preparatory and follow-up activities. A World Ecotourism Summit, which was convened in Québec, Canada in May, was attended by delegates from 132 countries. It resulted in the Québec Declaration, containing guidelines for sustainable ecotourism development and management. UNWTO publishes a series of compilations of good practices for small and medium-sized businesses involved with ecotourism. UNWTO sponsored the first International Conference on Climate Change and Tourism, which was held in Djerba, Tunisia, in April 2003. A final declaration of the conference urged that UNWTO take the lead in focusing international attention on the issue and called upon all parties to continue research efforts, to encourage sustainability in tourism, to generate awareness and to implement defined actions. The second International Conference on Climate Change and Tourism, organized by UNWTO, UNEP and WMO, was convened in Davos, Switzerland, in October 2007. The meeting concluded the Davos Declaration, which urged greater action by the tourism sector to respond to the challenges of climate change, for example by employing new energy efficiency technologies, in order to support the objectives of the UN Millennium Development Goals. UNWTO supported the development of a new initiative to promote responsible and sustainable tourism, which was inaugurated as the 'Live the Deal' global campaign during the 15th Conference of the Parties to the UN Framework Convention on Climate Change, held in Copenhagen, Denmark, in December 2009.

In January 2011 UNWTO and UNEP launched the Global Partnership for Sustainable Tourism, also comprising other UN agencies, the OECD, 18 governments, and other partners, with the aim of guiding policy and developing projects in the area of sustainable tourism, providing a global platform for discussion, and facilitating progress towards a green economy.

In May 2011 UNWTO participated in a special event on Tourism for Sustainable Development and Poverty Reduction, which was organized at the fourth UN Conference on Least Developed Countries (LDC-IV), held in Istanbul, Turkey. Tourism is a major source of export earnings in more than one-half of LDCs.

In early 2012 UNWTO and the Ramsar Convention on Wetlands jointly supported the annual celebration, on 2 February, of World Wetlands Day, on the theme 'Wetlands and Tourism'; the two bodies collaborated at that time in producing information material on the topic of sustainable tourism and Wetland sites (such as the Great Barrier Reef, Australia, and the Okavango Delta in Botswana).

In 1997 a Task Force for the Protection of Children from Sexual Exploitation in Tourism was established by UNWTO as a forum for governments, industry associations and other organizations to work together with the aim of identifying, preventing and eradicating the sexual exploitation of children. In March 2007 the mandate of the Task Force was expanded to include protection of children and young people against all forms of exploitation in tourism, including child labour and trafficking. In November 2008 the Task Force, meeting during the World Travel Market in London, United Kingdom, inaugurated a new 'Protect Children Campaign' to generate awareness of the abuse of children and to harness global support for its protection efforts. In 1999 the General Assembly adopted a Global Code of Ethics for Tourism. The Code, which was endorsed by a special resolution of the UN General Assembly in 2001, aims to protect resources upon which tourism depends and to ensure that the economic benefits of tourism are distributed equitably. A World Committee on Tourism Ethics, established in 2003 to support the implementation of the Code, held its first meeting in Rome, Italy, in February 2004 and has subsequently been convened on an annual basis. A permanent secretariat for the Committee was inaugurated in November 2008. In March 2000 UNWTO, with

UNESCO and UNEP, established a Tour Operators Initiative to encourage socially responsible tourism development within the industry.

In November 2007 the General Assembly resolved to appoint the organization's first Special Adviser on Women and Tourism.

In 1994 UNWTO, in co-operation with UNESCO, initiated a project to promote tourism, in support of economic development, along the traditional Silk Road trading routes linking Asia and Europe. In October 2004 a Silk Road Tourism Office was opened in Samarkand, Uzbekistan. In December 2008 UNWTO, in collaboration with UNDP, initiated a UN Silk Road City award scheme further to promote tourism and development along the trading route. In October 2009 the General Assembly adopted the Astana Declaration in support of a Silk Road Initiative, which aimed to promote the tourism potential of the countries along the Silk Road. The fifth international meeting of participants in the Silk Road project was convened in Samarkand, in October 2010. Representatives of 26 countries endorsed UNWTO's development of a Silk Road Action Plan. An updated Silk Road Action Plan was approved at a ministerial meeting held in March 2012, in Berlin, Germany. In 1995 UNWTO and UNESCO launched the Slave Route project to stimulate tourism and raise cultural awareness in several West African countries. In October 2007 UNWTO hosted an International Conference on Tourism, Religion and the Dialogue of Cultures, in Córdoba, Spain, to contribute to the discussion and promotion of the UN initiative for an Alliance of Civilizations.

EDUCATION AND KNOWLEDGE MANAGEMENT

UNWTO is committed to supporting education and training within the tourism industry and to developing a network of specialized research and training institutes. Most activities are undertaken by the UNWTO Education Council and the Themis Foundation. A specialized office concerned with human resource development was opened in September 2003, in Andorra. In September 2010 UNWTO inaugurated a Knowledge Network (UNWTO.Know) of institutes, universities, and public and private organizations, with the aim of facilitating a broad approach to the development of tourism policy, governance and practices. The inaugural meeting of UNWTO.Know took place in Madrid, Spain, in January 2011. In June of that year the Network, which by that time comprised more than 120 institutions from 40 countries, organized the UNWTO Algarve Forum, held in Vilamoura, Portugal, with participation by more than 300 representatives from the tourism sector, as well as academics. The Forum, conceived as a means of bridging theory and practice in tourism, adopted the Algarve Consensus, detailing guidelines and policy programmes aimed at directing the future development and good governance of the sector.

UNWTO Themis Foundation: Avinguda Dr Vilanova 9, Edif. Thaïs 4c, Andorra la Vella, Andorra; tel. 802600; fax 829955; e-mail wto.themis@andorra.ad; internet themis.unwto.org; aims to promote quality and efficiency in tourism education and training. Works closely with the human resource development programme of UNWTO and promotes UNWTO's specialized training products and services, in particular the TedQual certification and the Practicum programme for tourism officials; Exec. Dir OMAR VALDEZ.

INFORMATION AND COMMUNICATIONS

In January 2004 UNWTO hosted the first World Conference on Tourism Communications. Regular regional conferences have since been organized, within the framework of a Special Programme for Capacity Sharing in International Tourism Communications (TOURCOM), to enhance the capacity of regional and national tourism authorities to apply international standards and best practices to the promotion and communication of tourism.

UNWTO aims to act as a clearing house of information for the tourist industry. A UNWTO Documentation Centre collates extensive information on tourism activities and promotes access to and exchange of information among member states and affiliated partners. The Centre offers access to tourism legislation and other regulatory procedures through its LEXTOUR database on the internet. The Centre also administers a tourism information database (INFODOCTOUR). A Thesaurus on Tourism and Leisure Activities was published in 2001.

Finance

The budget for the two-year period 2012–13 amounted to €25.2m.

Publications

Compendium of Tourism Statistics.

Tourism Market Trends (annually).

Yearbook of Tourism Statistics.

UNWTOBC Interactive (monthly).

UNWTO News (3 a year, in English, French and Spanish).

UNWTO World Tourism Barometer (3 a year).

Other research or statistical reports, studies, guidelines and factsheets.

PART THREE

Major Non-UN Organizations

AFRICAN DEVELOPMENT BANK—AfDB

Address: Statutory Headquarters: rue Joseph Anoma, 01 BP 1387, Abidjan 01, Côte d'Ivoire.

Telephone: 20-20-44-44; **fax:** 20-20-49-59; **e-mail:** afdb@afdb.org; **internet:** www.afdb.org.

Address: Temporary Relocation Agency: 15 ave du Ghana, angle des rues Pierre de Coubertin et Hedi Nouira, BP 323, 1002 Tunis Belvédère, Tunisia.

Telephone: (71) 103-900; **fax:** (71) 351-933.

Established in 1964, the Bank began operations in July 1966, with the aim of financing economic and social development in African countries. The Bank's headquarters are officially based in Abidjan, Côte d'Ivoire. Since February 2003, however, in view of ongoing insecurity in Côte d'Ivoire, the Bank's operations have been conducted, on a long-term temporary basis, from Tunis, Tunisia.

AFRICAN MEMBERS*

Algeria	Equatorial Guinea	Namibia
Angola	Eritrea	Niger
Benin	Ethiopia	Nigeria
Botswana	Gabon	Rwanda
Burkina Faso	The Gambia	São Tomé and Príncipe
Burundi	Ghana	Senegal
Cameroon	Guinea	Seychelles
Cape Verde	Guinea-Bissau	Sierra Leone
Central African Republic	Kenya	Somalia
Chad	Lesotho	South Africa
Comoros	Liberia	Sudan
Congo, Democratic Republic	Libya	Swaziland
Congo, Republic	Madagascar	Tanzania
Côte d'Ivoire	Malawi	Togo
Djibouti	Mali	Tunisia
Egypt	Mauritania	Uganda
	Mauritius	Zambia
	Morocco	Zimbabwe
	Mozambique	

* An application for full membership of the Bank was submitted in May 2011 by the authorities of South Sudan (which, in July, became an independent state); this remained under review at June 2012. In September 2011 the Bank and the South Sudan Government signed an agreement on general co-operation, enabling the extension of financial and technical support to South Sudan pending that country's accession to full Bank membership.

There are also 24 non-African members.

Organization

(June 2012)

BOARD OF GOVERNORS

The highest policy-making body of the Bank, which also elects the Board of Directors and the President. Each member country nominates one Governor, usually its Minister of Finance and Economic Affairs, and an alternate Governor or the Governor of its Central Bank. The Board meets once a year. The 2012 meeting was convened in Arusha, Tanzania, in May–June.

BOARD OF DIRECTORS

The Board, elected by the Board of Governors for a term of three years, is responsible for the general operations of the Bank and meets on a weekly basis. The Board has 20 members.

OFFICERS

The President is responsible for the organization and the day-to-day operations of the Bank under guidance of the Board of Directors. The President is elected for a five-year term and serves as the Chairperson of the Board of Directors. The President oversees the following senior management: Chief Economist; Vice-Presidents of Finance, Corporate Services, Country and Regional Programmes and Policy, Sector Operations, and Infrastructure, Private Sector and Regional Integration; Auditor General; General Counsel; Secretary-General; and Ombudsman. Bank field offices are located in some 30 member countries under a strategy of decentralization. The Bank plans to establish three external representation offices: for the Americas, to be based in Washington, DC, USA (from 2012); for Asia, to be based in Tokyo, Japan (also from 2012); and for Europe, to be based in Brussels, Belgium (from 2013).

Executive President and Chairperson of Board of Directors: DONALD KABERUKA (Rwanda).

FINANCIAL STRUCTURE

The African Development Bank (AfDB) Group of development financing institutions comprises the African Development Fund (ADF) and the Nigeria Trust Fund (NTF), which provide concessionary loans, and the AfDB itself. The Group uses a unit of account (UA), which, at December 2011, was valued at US $1.53257.

The capital stock of the Bank was at first exclusively open for subscription by African countries, with each member's subscription consisting of an equal number of paid-up and callable shares. In 1978, however, the Governors agreed to open the capital stock of the Bank to subscription by non-regional states on the basis of nine principles aimed at maintaining the African character of the institution. The decision was finally ratified in May 1982, and the participation of non-regional countries became effective on 30 December. It was agreed that African members should still hold two-thirds of the share capital, that all loan operations should be restricted to African members, and that the Bank's President should always be a national of an African state. In May 1998 the Board of Governors approved an increase in capital of 35%, and resolved that the non-African members' share of the capital be increased from 33.3% to 40%. In May 2010 the Board of Governors approved a general capital increase of 200%. At 31 December 2011 the Bank's authorized capital was UA 66,054.5m. (compared with UA 67,687.5m. at the end of 2010); subscribed capital at the end of 2011 was UA 37,322.0m. (of which the paid-up portion was UA 3,289.1m.)

Activities

At the end of 2011 the Bank Group had approved total lending of UA 67,949m. since the beginning of its operations in 1967. In 2011 the Group approved 184 lending operations amounting to UA 5,720.3m., compared with UA 4,099.8m. in the previous year. Of the total amount approved in 2011 UA 4,128.0m. was for loans and grants, UA 1,350.9m. for heavily indebted poor countries (HIPC) debt relief, UA 53.4m. for equity participation and UA 188.1m. for special funds. Of the total loans and grants approved in 2011, UA 1,572.3m. (38%) was for infrastructure projects (of which UA 1,005.4m. was for transportation); UA 853.2m. (21%) was for multisector projects; and UA 802.3m. (19%) for projects in the finance sector. Some 24% of Bank Group loan and grant approvals in 2011 were allocated to countries in West Africa, 21.9% to North Africa, 14.8% to East Africa, 11% to Central Africa, and 9.8% to Southern Africa.

In 2006 the Bank established a High Level Panel of eminent personalities to advise on the Bank's future strategic vision. The Panel issued its report, 'Investing in Africa's future—The AfDB in the 21st Century', in February 2008. In May the Bank's President announced that the new medium-term strategy for 2008–12 was to focus on the achievement of the Millennium Development Goals (MDGs) and on shared and sustainable economic growth. It envisaged a significant increase in Bank operations and in its institutional capacity. A Roadmap on Development Effectiveness was approved by the Board in March 2011, focusing on areas deemed most likely to bring about transformational change, including strengthening transparency and accountability; and accelerating decentralization. In mid-

2008 the Bank established an African Food Crisis Response initiative to extend accelerated support to members affected by the sharp increase in the cost of food and food production. The initiative aimed to reduce short-term food poverty and malnutrition, with funds of some UA 472.0m., and to support long-term sustainable food security, with funding of UA 1,400m. In February 2009 the Bank hosted a meeting of the heads of multilateral development banks and of the IMF to discuss recent economic developments, the responses of each institution and future courses of action. In March the Bank's Board of Directors endorsed four new initiatives to help to counter the effects of the crisis: the establishment of an Emergency Liquidity Facility, with funds of some US $1,500m., to assist members with short-term financing difficulties; a new Trade Finance Initiative, with funds of up to $1,000m., to provide credit for trade financing operations; a Framework for the Accelerated Resource Transfer of ADF Resources; and enhanced policy advisory support. The Bank also agreed to contribute $500m. to a multinational Global Trade Liquidity Program, which commenced operations in mid-2009. In September the Bank initiated a consultative process for a sixth general capital increase. An increase of 200% was endorsed by a committee of the governing body representing the Bank's shareholders, meeting in April 2010, in order to enable the Bank to sustain its increased level of lending. The capital increase was formally approved by the Board of Governors in May.

In November 2008 the Bank hosted a special conference of African ministers of finance and central bank governors to consider the impact on the region of the contraction of the world's major economies and the recent volatility of global financial markets. The meeting determined to establish a Committee of African Finance Ministers and Central Bank Governors, comprising 10 representatives from each Bank region, with a mandate to examine further the impact of the global financial crisis on Africa, to review the responses by member governments, and to develop policy options. The so-called Committee of Ten (C10) convened for its inaugural meeting in Cape Town, South Africa, in January 2009. In March the C10 adopted a paper outlining the major concerns of African countries in preparation for the meeting of heads of state of the Group of 20 (G20) leading economies, held in London, United Kingdom, in early April. The third meeting of the Committee, held in Abuja, Nigeria, in July, reviewed economic indicators and developments since the G20 meeting and appealed for all commitments to low-income countries pledged at the summit to be met. The Committee also issued a series of messages for the next G20 summit meeting, held in Pittsburgh, USA, in September, including a request for greater African participation in the G20 process and in international economic governance. The fourth meeting of the C10, convened in February 2010, determined that it should meet formally two times a year, with other informal meetings and meetings of deputies to be held in between; the Secretariat of the Committee was to be provided by the AfDB.

In May 2011 the Group of Eight (G8) industrialized nations, in collaboration with regional and international financial institutions and the governments of Egypt and Tunisia, established a Deauville Partnership to support political and economic reforms being undertaken by several countries in North Africa and the Middle East, notably Egypt, Jordan, Morocco and Tunisia. The AfDB supported the establishment of the Partnership and was to chair a Co-ordination Platform. In September Kuwait, Qatar, Saudi Arabia, Turkey and the UAE joined the Partnership.

Since 1996 the Bank has collaborated closely with international partners, in particular the World Bank, in efforts to address the problems of HIPCs (see IBRD). Of the 41 countries identified as potentially eligible for assistance under the scheme, 33 were in sub-Saharan Africa. Following the introduction of an enhanced framework for the initiative, the Bank has been actively involved in the preparation of Poverty Reduction Strategy Papers, that provide national frameworks for poverty reduction programmes. In April 2006 the Board of Directors endorsed a new Multilateral Debt Relief Initiative (MDRI), which provided for 100% cancellation of eligible debts from the ADF, the IMF and the International Development Association to secure additional resources for countries to help them attain their MDGs. ADF's participation in the MDRI, which became effective in September, was anticipated to provide some UA 5,570m. (US $8,540m.) in debt relief.

The Bank contributed funds for the establishment, in 1986, of the Africa Project Development Facility, which assists the private sector in Africa by providing advisory services and finance for entrepreneurs: it was managed by the International Finance Corporation (IFC), until replaced by the Private Enterprise Partnership for Africa in April 2005. In 1989 the Bank, in co-ordination with IFC and the UN Development Programme (UNDP), created the African Management Services Company (AMSCo), which provides management support and training to private companies in Africa. The Bank is one of three multilateral donors, with the World Bank and UNDP, supporting the African Capacity Building Foundation, which was established in 1991 to strengthen and develop institutional and human capacity in support of sustainable development activities. The Bank hosts the secretariat of an Africa Investment Consortium, which was inaugurated in October 2005 by several major African institutions and donor countries to accelerate efforts to develop the region's infrastructure. An Enhanced Private Sector Assistance Initiative was established, with support from the Japanese Government, in 2005 to support the Bank's strategy for the development of the private sector. The Initiative incorporated an Accelerated Cofinancing Facility for Africa and a Fund for African Private Sector Assistance. In October 2010 the Board of Directors agreed to convert the Fund into a multi-donor trust fund.

In November 2006 the Bank Group, with the UN Economic Commission for Africa (ECA), organized an African Economic Conference (AEC), which has since become an annual event. The sixth AEC was held in Addis Ababa, Ethiopia, in October 2011, on the theme 'Green Economy and Structural Transformation in Africa'. In September 2011 the Bank organized a regional meeting on peace-building and state-building in Africa, in preparation for the Fourth High Level Forum on Aid Effectiveness, which was held in Busan, Republic of Korea, in November–December.

In March 2000 African ministers of water resources endorsed an African Water Vision and a Framework for Action to pursue the equitable and sustainable use and management of water resources in Africa in order to facilitate socio-economic development, poverty alleviation and environmental protection. An African Ministers' Council on Water (AMCOW) was established in April 2002 to provide the political leadership and focus for implementation of the Vision and the Framework for Action. AMCOW requested the Bank to establish and administer an African Water Facility Special Fund, in order to provide the financial requirements for achieving their objectives; this became operational in December. In March the Bank approved a Rural Water Supply and Sanitation Initiative to accelerate access in member countries to sustainable safe water and basic sanitation, in order to meet the requirements of several MDGs. In March 2008 the Bank hosted the first African Water Week, organized jointly with AMCOW, on the theme of 'Accelerating Water Security for the Socio-economic Development of Africa'. The Bank co-ordinated and led Africa's regional participation in the Sixth World Water Forum, which was held in Marseilles, France, in March 2012. The Bank was actively involved in preparing for the fourth Africa Carbon Forum, which was convened in Addis Ababa, Ethiopia, in April 2012 (previous fora having been held in September 2008, March 2010 and July 2011).

The Bank hosts the secretariat of the Congo Basin Forest Fund, which was established in June 2008, as a multi-donor facility, with initial funding from Norway and the United Kingdom, to protect and manage the forests in that region.

Through the Migration and Development Trust Fund, launched in 2009, the Bank supports the development of financial services for migrant workers, and facilitates channelling remittances towards productive uses in workers' countries of origin.

The Bank provides technical assistance to regional member countries in the form of experts' services, pre-investment feasibility studies, and staff training. Much of this assistance is financed through bilateral trust funds contributed by non-African member states. The Bank's African Development Institute provides training for officials of regional member countries in order to enhance the management of Bank-financed projects and, more broadly, to strengthen national capacities for promoting sustainable development. The Institute also manages an AfDB/Japan Fellowship programme that provides scholarships to African students to pursue further education. A Joint Africa Institute, established jointly by the Bank, the World Bank and the IMF, was operational from November 1999–end-2009, offering training opportunities and strengthening capacity building. In 1990 the Bank established the African Business Round Table (ABR), which is composed of the chief executives of Africa's leading corporations. The ABR aims to strengthen Africa's private sector, promote intra-African trade and investment, and attract foreign investment to Africa. The ABR is chaired by the Bank's Executive President. In 2008 the Bank endorsed a Governance Strategic Directions and Action Plan as a framework for countering corruption and enhancing democratic governance in Africa in the period 2008–12.

In 1990 a Memorandum of Understanding (MOU) for the Reinforcement of Co-operation between the Organization of African Unity, now African Union (AU), the UN Economic Commission for Africa and the AfDB was signed by the three organizations. A joint secretariat supports co-operation activities between the organizations. In March 2009 a new Coalition for Dialogue on Africa (CoDA) was inaugurated by the Bank, the ECA and the AU. In 1999 a Co-operation Agreement was formally concluded between the Bank and the Common Market for Eastern and Southern Africa (COMESA). In March 2000 the Bank signed an MOU on its strategic partnership with the World Bank. Other MOUs were signed during that year with the United Nations Industrial Development Organization, the World Food Programme, and the Arab Maghreb Union. In September 2008 the Bank supported the establishment of an African Financing Partnership, which aimed to mobilize private sector resources through partnerships with regional development finance institutions. The Bank hosts the secretariat of the Partnership. It also hosts the secretariat of the Making Finance Work for Africa Partnership, which was established, by the G8, in October 2007, in order to support the development of the financial sector in the sub-Saharan region. In December 2010 the Bank signed an MOU with the Islamic Development Bank to promote economic development in common member countries through co-financing and co-ordinating projects in priority areas. It signed an MOU with the European Bank for Reconstruction and Development (EBRD) in September 2011. The Bank is actively involved in the New Partnership for Africa's Development (NEPAD), established in 2001 to promote sustainable development and eradicate poverty throughout the region. Since 2004 it has been a strategic partner in NEPAD's African Peer Review Mechanism. In 2011 the Bank supported the development of a Program for Infrastructure Development in Africa (PIDA), as a joint initiative with NEPAD and the AU.

AFRICAN DEVELOPMENT BANK

The Bank makes loans at a variable rate of interest, which is adjusted twice a year, plus a commitment fee of 0.75%. Lending approved amounted to UA 3,689.4m. for 59 operations in 2011, including resources allocated under the HIPC debt relief initiative, the Post-conflict Country Facility (see below), and equity participations, compared with UA 2,581.1m., again for 59 operations, in the previous year. Lending for private sector projects amounted to UA 868.9m. in 2011. Since October 1997 new fixed and floating rate loans have been made available.

AFRICAN DEVELOPMENT FUND

The ADF commenced operations in 1974. It grants interest-free loans to low-income African countries for projects with repayment over 50 years (including a 10-year grace period) and with a service charge of 0.75% per annum. Grants for project feasibility studies are made to the poorest countries.

In May 1994 donor countries withheld any new funds owing to dissatisfaction with the Bank's governance. In May 1996, following the implementation of various institutional reforms to strengthen the Bank's financial management and decision-making capabilities and to reduce its administrative costs, an agreement was concluded on the seventh replenishment of ADF resources. In December 2004 donor countries pledged some US $5,400m. for the 10th replenishment of the ADF covering the three-year period 2005–07; it was agreed that poverty reduction and the promotion of sustainable growth would remain the principal objectives of the Fund under ADF-10. In December 2007 donor countries committed $8,900m. to replenish the Fund for the period 2008–10 (ADF-11), during which there was to be a focus on infrastructure, governance and regional integration. The funding arrangements for ADF-11 allocated UA 408m. to a new Fragile States Facility to support the poorer regional member countries, in particular those in a post-conflict or transitional state. The Facility was to incorporate the Post-Conflict Country Facility, which was established in 2003 to help certain countries to clear their arrears and accelerate their progress within the HIPC process. An agreement was concluded by donors in October 2010 to increase contributions to the Fund by 10.6%, to some $9,350m., under ADF-12, covering the period 2011–13. ADF-12 was to support ongoing institutional reform and capacity building, as well as efforts to stimulate economic growth in Africa's lowest income countries. Operational priorities included climate change adaptation and mitigation measures, regional economic integration, and private sector development.

In 2011 lending under the ADF amounted to UA 1,831.9m. for 87 projects, compared with UA 1,456.7m. for 65 projects in the previous year.

NIGERIA TRUST FUND

The Agreement establishing the NTF was signed in February 1976 by the Bank and the Government of Nigeria. The Fund is administered by the Bank and its loans are granted for up to 25 years, including grace periods of up to five years, and carry 0.75% commission charges and 4% interest charges. The loans are intended to provide financing for projects in co-operation with other lending institutions. The Fund also aims to promote the private sector and trade between African countries by providing information on African and international financial institutions able to finance African trade.

Operations under the NTF were suspended in 2006, pending a detailed assessment and consideration of the Fund's activities which commenced in November. The evaluation exercise was concluded in July 2007 and an agreement was reached in November to authorize the Fund to continue activities for a further 10-year period. Three operations, amounting to UA 10.9m., were approved in 2011.

Publications

Annual Report.

Annual Development Effectiveness Review.

AfDB Business Bulletin (10 a year).

AfDB Statistics Pocketbook.

AfDB Today (every 2 months).

African Competitiveness Report.

African Development Report (annually).

African Development Review (3 a year).

African Economic Outlook (annually, with OECD).

African Statistical Journal (2 a year).

Annual Procurement Report.

Economic Research Papers.

Gender, Poverty and Environmental Indicators on African Countries (annually).

OPEV Sharing (quarterly newsletter).

Quarterly Operational Summary.

Selected Statistics on African Countries (annually).

Summaries of operations and projects, background documents, Board documents.

Statistics

SUMMARY OF BANK GROUP OPERATIONS
(millions of UA)

	2010	2011	Cumulative total*
AfDB approvals†			
Number	59	59	1,318
Amount	2,581.13	3,689.43	36,008.07
Disbursements	1,339.85	1868.79	20,541.59
ADF approvals†			
Number	65	87	2,474
Amount	1,456.72	1,831.86	25,540.06
Disbursements	1,165.84	1,296.65	16,098.51
NTF approvals			
Number	2	3	85
Amount	29.53	10.88	382.21
Disbursements	5.02	8.67	235.74
Special Funds‡			
Number	13	35	108
Amount approved	32.38	188.12	329.23
Group total†			
Number	139	184	3,985
Amount approved	4,099.75	5,720.29	67,949.00
Disbursements	2,510.70	3,174.11	38,744.62

* Since the initial operations of the three institutions (1967 for AfDB, 1974 for ADF and 1976 for NTF).

† Approvals include loans and grant operations, private and public equity investments, emergency operations, HIPC debt relief, loan reallocations and guarantees, the Post-Conflict Country Facility and the Fragile States Facility.

‡ Includes the African Water Fund, the Rural Water Supply and Sanitation Initiative, the Global Environment Facility, the Congo Basin Forest Fund, the Fund for African Private Sector Assistance, and the Migration and Development Trust Fund.

Source: African Development Bank, *Annual Report 2011*.

BANK GROUP APPROVALS BY SECTOR, 2011

Sector	Number of projects	Amount (millions of UA)
Agriculture and rural development	11	145.6
Social	27	451.3
Education	6	39.0
Health	2	56.0
Other	19	356.3
Infrastructure	36	1,572.3
Water supply and sanitation	5	139.1
Energy supply	12	420.1
Communication	1	7.6
Transportation	18	1,005.4
Finance	11	802.3
Multisector	47	853.2
Industry, mining and quarrying	2	293.7
Environment	1	9.6
Total (loans and grants)	135	4,128.0
HIPC debt relief	7	1,350.9
Equity participations	7	53.4
Special funds	35	188.1
Other approvals	49	1,592.6
Total approvals	184	5,720.3

Source: African Development Bank, *Annual Report 2011*.

AFRICAN UNION—AU

Address: Roosvelt St, Old Airport Area, POB 3243, Addis Ababa, Ethiopia.

Telephone: (11) 5517700; **fax:** (11) 5517844; **e-mail:** webmaster@africa-union.org; **internet:** au.int.

In May 2001 the Constitutive Act of the African Union entered into force. In July 2002 the African Union (AU) became fully operational, replacing the Organization of African Unity (OAU), which had been founded in 1963. The AU aims to support unity, solidarity and peace among African states; to promote and defend African common positions on issues of shared interest; to encourage human rights, democratic principles and good governance; to advance the development of member states by encouraging research and by working to eradicate preventable diseases; and to promote sustainable development and political and socio-economic integration, including co-ordinating and harmonizing policy between the continent's various 'regional economic communities' (see below).

MEMBERS*

Algeria	Eritrea	Nigeria
Angola	Ethiopia	Rwanda
Benin	Gabon	São Tomé and Príncipe
Botswana	The Gambia	Senegal
Burkina Faso	Ghana	Seychelles
Burundi	Guinea	Sierra Leone
Cameroon	Guinea-Bissau†	Somalia
Cape Verde	Kenya	South Africa
Central African Republic	Lesotho	South Sudan‡
Chad	Liberia	Sudan
Comoros	Libya	Swaziland
Congo, Democratic Republic	Madagascar†	Tanazania
Congo, Republic	Malawi	Togo
Côte d'Ivoire	Mali†	Tunisia
Dijbouti	Mauritania†	Uganda
Egypt	Mauritius	Zambia
Equatorial Guinea	Mozambique	Zimbabwe
	Namibia	
	Niger	

* The Sahrawi Arab Democratic Republic (SADR–Western Sahara) was admitted to the OAU in February 1982, following recognition by more than one-half of the member states, but its membership was disputed by Morocco and other states which claimed that a two-thirds' majority was needed to admit a state whose existence was in question. Morocco withdrew from the OAU with effect from November 1985, and has not applied to join the AU. The SADR ratified the Constitutive Act in December 2000 and is a full member of the AU.

† Mauritania's participation in the activities of the AU was suspended in August 2008, following the overthrow of its constitutional Government in a military coup d'état. In March 2009 Madagascar's participation in the activities of the AU was suspended, following the forced resignation of its elected President and transfer of power to the military. Mali was suspended from AU participation after the overthrow of that country's Government by a military coup in March 2012, and, in April, Guinea-Bissau was also suspended following a military coup, pending the restoration of constitutional order.

‡ South Sudan (which became independent on 9 July 2011) was admitted as a member of the AU in August 2011.

Note: The Constitutive Act stipulates that member states in which Governments accede to power by unconstitutional means are liable to suspension from participating in the Union's activities and to the imposition of sanctions by the Union.

Organization

(June 2012)

ASSEMBLY

The Assembly, comprising member countries' heads of state and government, is the supreme organ of the Union and meets at least once a year (with alternate sessions held in Addis Ababa, Ethiopia) to determine and monitor the Union's priorities and common policies and to adopt its annual work programme. Resolutions are passed by a two-thirds' majority, procedural matters by a simple majority. Extraordinary sessions may be convened at the request of a member state and on approval by a two-thirds' majority. A chairperson is elected at each meeting from among the members, to hold office for one year. The Assembly ensures compliance by member states with decisions of the Union, adopts the biennial budget, appoints judges of the African Court of Human and Peoples' Rights, and hears and settles disputes between member states. The first regular Assembly meeting was held in Durban, South Africa, in July 2002, and a first extraordinary summit meeting of the Assembly was convened in Addis Ababa in February 2003. The 18th ordinary session of the Assembly took place in Addis Ababa, in January 2012. The 19th ordinary session was to convene in July 2012, also in Addis Ababa. The theme of both 2012 summits was 'Boosting Intra-African Trade'. The location of the 19th session was moved from Lilongwe, Malawi, owing to the Malawi Government's refusal to host President al-Bashir of Sudan, who had been indicted by the International Criminal Court on genocide charges.

Chairperson: (2012/13) YAYI BONI (Pres. of Benin).

EXECUTIVE COUNCIL

Consists of ministers of foreign affairs and others and meets at least twice a year (in February and July), with provision for extraordinary sessions. The Council's Chairperson is the minister of foreign affairs (or another competent authority) of the country that has provided the Chairperson of the Assembly. Prepares meetings of, and is responsible to, the Assembly. Determines the issues to be submitted to the Assembly for decision, co-ordinates and harmonizes the policies, activities and initiatives of the Union in areas of common interest to member states, and monitors the implementation of policies and decisions of the Assembly.

PERMANENT REPRESENTATIVES COMMITTEE

The Committee, which comprises Ambassadors accredited to the AU and meets at least once a month. It is responsible to the Executive Council, which it advises, and whose meetings, including matters for the agenda and draft decisions, it prepares.

COMMISSION

The Commission is the permanent secretariat of the organization. It comprises a Chairperson (elected for a four-year term of office by the Assembly), Deputy Chairperson and eight Commissioners (responsible for: peace and security; political affairs; infrastructure and energy; social affairs; human resources, science and technology; trade and industry; rural economy and agriculture; and economic affairs) who are elected on the basis of equal geographical distribution. Members of the Commission serve a term of four years and may stand for re-election for one further term of office. Further support staff assist the smooth functioning of the Commission. The Commission represents the Union under the guidance of, and as mandated by, the Assembly and the Executive Council, and reports to the Executive Council. It deals with administrative issues, implements the decisions of the Union, and acts as the custodian of the Constitutive Act and Protocols, and other agreements. Its work covers the following domains: control of pandemics; disaster management; international crime and terrorism; environmental management; negotiations relating to external trade; negotiations relating to external debt; population, migration, refugees and displaced persons; food security; socio-economic integration; and all other areas where a common position has been established by Union member states. It has responsibility for the co-ordination of AU activities and meetings.

In 2012 plans were under way to transform the Commission into a new African Union Authority. The 18th ordinary session of the Assembly, held in January 2012, was to have elected a new Chairperson of the Commission, to replace Jean Ping, but failed to reach agreement on Ping's successor. A dedicated meeting on the election of a successor Chairperson that was convened by AU heads of state in May, in Cotonou, Benin, also ended in *impasse*.

It was hoped that the next Chairperson would be elected in July, by the 19th Assembly session.

Chairperson: JEAN PING (Gabon).

SPECIALIZED TECHNICAL COMMITTEES

There are specialized committees for monetary and financial affairs; rural economy and agricultural matters; trade, customs and immigration matters; industry, science and technology, energy, natural resources and environment; infrastructure; transport, communications and tourism; health, labour and social affairs; and education, culture and human resources. These have responsibility for implementing the Union's programmes and projects.

PAN-AFRICAN PARLIAMENT

The Pan-African Parliament comprises five deputies (including at least one woman) from each AU member state, presided over by an elected President assisted by four Vice-Presidents. The President and Vice-Presidents must equitably represent the central, northern, eastern, southern and western African states. The Parliament convenes at least twice a year; an extraordinary session may be called by a two-thirds' majority of the members. The Parliament currently has only advisory and consultative powers. Its eventual evolution into an institution with full legislative authority is planned. The Parliament is headquartered at Midrand, South Africa.

President: Dr MOUSSA IDRISS NDÉLÉ (Chad).

AFRICAN COURT OF JUSTICE AND HUMAN RIGHTS

An African Court of Human and Peoples' Rights (ACHPR) was created following the entry into force in January 2004 of the Protocol to the African Charter on Human and Peoples' Rights Establishing the ACHPR (adopted in June 1998). In February 2009 a protocol (adopted in July 2003) establishing an African Court of Justice entered into force. The Protocol on the Statute of the African Court of Justice and Human Rights, aimed at merging the ACHPR and the African Court of Justice, was opened for signature in July 2008, and had, by June 2012, been ratified by three states.

PEACE AND SECURITY COUNCIL

The Protocol to the Constitutive Act of the African Union Relating to the Peace and Security Council of the African Union entered into force on 26 December 2003; the 15-member elected Council was formally inaugurated in May 2004. It acts as a decision-making body for the prevention, management and resolution of conflicts.

ECONOMIC, SOCIAL AND CULTURAL COUNCIL

The Economic, Social and Cultural Council (ECOSOCC), inaugurated in March 2005, was to have an advisory function and to comprise representatives of civic, professional and cultural bodies at national, regional and diaspora levels. Its main organs were to be: an elected General Assembly; Standing Committee; Credential Committee; and Sectoral Cluster Communities. It is envisaged that the Council will strengthen the partnership between member governments and African civil society. The General Assembly. was inaugurated in September 2008. The Sectoral Cluster Communities were to be established to formulate opinions and influence AU decision-making in the following 10 areas: peace and security; political affairs; infrastructure and energy; social affairs and health; human resources, science and technology; trade and industry; rural economy and agriculture; economic affairs; women and gender; and cross-cutting programmes.

NEW PARTNERSHIP FOR AFRICA'S DEVELOPMENT (NEPAD)

NEPAD Planning and Co-ordination Agency (NPCA): POB 1234, Halfway House, Midrand, 1685 South Africa; tel. (11) 313-3716; fax (11) 313-3684; e-mail africam@nepad.org; internet www.nepad.org; f. Feb. 2010, as a technical body of the AU, to replace the former NEPAD Secretariat, with the aim of improving the country-level implementation of projects; NEPAD was launched in 2001 as a long-term strategy to promote socio-economic development in Africa; adopted Declaration on Democracy, Political, Economic and Corporate Governance and the African Peer Review Mechanism in June 2002; the July 2003 AU Maputo summit decided that NEPAD should be integrated into AU structures and processes; a special 'Brainstorming on NEPAD' summit, held in Algiers, Algeria in March 2007, issued a 13-point communiqué on the means of reforming the Partnership; a further Review Summit on NEPAD, convened in Dakar, Senegal, in April 2008, reaffirmed the centrality of NEPAD as the overarching developmental programme for Africa; the UN allocated US $12.6m. in support of NEPAD under its 2012–13 budget; CEO Dr IBRAHIM ASSANE MAYAKI.

PROPOSED INSTITUTIONS

In 2012 three financial institutions, for managing the financing of programmes and projects, remained to be established: an African Central Bank; an African Monetary Fund; and an African Investment Bank.

Activities

In May 1963 30 African heads of state adopted the Charter of the Organization of African Unity. In May 1994 the Abuja Treaty Establishing the African Economic Community (AEC, signed in June 1991) entered into force.

An extraordinary summit meeting, convened in September 1999, in Sirte, Libya, at the request of the then Libyan leader Col al-Qaddafi, determined to establish an African Union, based on the principles and objectives of the OAU and AEC, but furthering African co-operation, development and integration. Heads of state declared their commitment to accelerating the establishment of regional institutions, including a pan-African parliament, a court of human and peoples' rights and a central bank, as well as the implementation of economic and monetary union, as provided for by the Abuja Treaty Establishing the AEC. In July 2000 at the annual OAU summit meeting, held at Lomé, Togo, 27 heads of state and government signed the draft Constitutive Act of the African Union, which was to enter into force one month after ratification by two-thirds of member states' legislatures; this was achieved on 26 May 2001. The Union was inaugurated, replacing the OAU, on 9 July 2002, at a summit meeting of heads of state and government held in Durban, South Africa, after a transitional period of one year had elapsed since the endorsement of the Act in July 2001. During the transitional year, pending the transfer of all assets and liabilities to the Union, the OAU Charter remained in effect. A review of all OAU treaties was implemented, and those deemed relevant were retained by the AU. The four key organs of the AU were launched in July 2002. Morocco is the only African country that is not a member of the AU. The AU aims to strengthen and advance the process of African political and socio-economic integration initiated by the OAU. The Union operates on the basis of both the Constitutive Act and the Abuja Treaty.

The AU has the following areas of interest: peace and security; political affairs; infrastructure and energy; social affairs; human resources, science and technology; trade and industry; rural economy and agriculture; and economic affairs. In July 2001 the OAU adopted a New African Initiative, which was subsequently renamed the New Partnership for Africa's Development (NEPAD). NEPAD, which was officially launched in October, represents a long-term strategy for socio-economic recovery in Africa and aims to promote the strengthening of democracy and economic management in the region. The heads of state of Algeria, Egypt, Nigeria, Senegal and South Africa played leading roles in its preparation and management. In June 2002 NEPAD heads of state and government adopted a Declaration on Democracy, Political, Economic and Corporate Governance and announced the development of an African Peer Review Mechanism (APRM—whose secretariat was to be hosted by the UN Economic Commission for Africa). Meeting during that month the Group of Seven industrialized nations and Russia (the G8) welcomed the formation of NEPAD and adopted an Africa Action Plan in support of the initiative. The inaugural summit of the AU Assembly, held in Durban, South Africa, in July 2002, issued a Declaration on the Implementation of NEPAD, which urged all member states to adopt the Declaration on Democracy, Political, Economic and Corporate Governance and to participate in the peer review process. By June 2012 some 11 nations had completed the APRM process. NEPAD focuses on the following sectoral priorities: infrastructure (covering information and communication technologies, energy, transport, water and sanitation); human resources development; agriculture; culture; science and technology; mobilizing resources; market access; and the environment. It implements action plans concerned with capacity building, the environment, and infrastructure. The summit meeting of the AU Assembly convened in Maputo, Mozambique, in July 2003 determined that NEPAD should be integrated into AU structures and processes. In March 2007 a special NEPAD summit held in Algiers, Algeria, issued a 13-point communiqué on the best means of achieving this objective without delay. The centrality of NEPAD as the overarching developmental programme for Africa was reaffirmed by a further summit meeting, convened in Dakar, Senegal, in April 2008, which also published a number of further key decisions aimed at guiding the future orientation of the Partnership. In February 2010 African leaders approved the establishment of the NEPAD Planning and Co-ordination Agency (NPCA), a technical body of the AU, to replace the former NEPAD Secretariat, with the aim of improving the implementation of projects at country level. The Chairperson of the African Union Commission (AUC) exercises supervisory authority over the NPCA. NEPAD's Programme for Infrastructure Development in Africa (PIDA), of which the African Development Bank is executing agency, aims to develop the continental energy, ICT, transport and transboundary water resources infrastructures. Some 80 programmes and projects aimed at regional integration, with a particular focus on developing the continental infrastructure, were being undertaken in the context of an AU/NEPAD African Action Plan (AAP) covering the period 2010–15.

The eighth AU Assembly, held in January 2007 in Cairo, Egypt, adopted a decision on the need for a 'Grand Debate on the Union Government', concerned with the possibility of establishing an AU Government as a precursor to the eventual creation of a United States of Africa. The ninth Assembly, convened in July 2007 in Accra, Ghana, adopted the Accra Declaration, in which AU heads of state and government expressed commitment to the formation of a Union Government of Africa and ultimate aim of creating a United States of Africa, and pledged, as a means to this end, to accelerate the economic and political integration of the African continent; to rationalize, strengthen and harmonize the activities of the regional economic communities; to conduct an immediate audit of the organs of the AU ('Audit of the Union'); and to establish a ministerial committee to examine the concept of the Union Government. A panel of eminent persons was subsequently established to conduct the proposed institutional Audit of the Union; the panel became operational at the beginning of September, and presented its review to the 10th Assembly, which was held in January–February 2008 in Addis Ababa. A committee comprising 10 heads of state was appointed to consider the findings detailed in the review.

In March 2005 the UN Secretary-General issued a report on the functioning of the United Nations which included a clause urging donor nations to focus particularly on the need for a 10-year plan for capacity-building within the AU. The UN System-wide Support to the AU and NEPAD was launched in 2006, following on from the UN System-wide Special Initiative on Africa, which had been undertaken over the decade 1996–2005.

In May 2012, with a view to increasing the involvement in the African development agenda of people of African origin living beyond the continent, the AU hosted the first Global African Diaspora Summit, in Midrand, South Africa.

PEACE AND SECURITY

The Protocol to the Constitutive Act of the African Union Relating to the Establishment of the Peace and Security Council, adopted by the inaugural AU summit of heads of state and government in July 2002, entered into force in December 2003, superseding the 1993 Cairo Declaration on the OAU Mechanism for Conflict Prevention, Management and Resolution. The Protocol provides for the development of a collective peace and security framework (known as the African Peace and Security Architecture—APSA). This includes a 15-country Peace and Security Council, operational at the levels of heads of state and government, ministers of foreign affairs, and permanent representatives, to be supported by a five-member advisory Panel of the Wise, a Continental Early Warning System, an African Standby Force (ASF) and a Peace Fund (superseding the OAU Peace Fund, which was established in June 1993). In March 2004 the Executive Council elected 15 member states to serve on the inaugural Peace and Security Council. The activities of the Peace and Security Council include the promotion of peace, security and stability; early warning and preventive diplomacy; peace-making mediation; peace support operations and intervention; peace-building activities and post-conflict reconstruction; and humanitarian action and disaster management. The Council was to implement the common defence policy of the Union, and to ensure the implementation of the 1999 OAU Convention on the Prevention and Combating of Terrorism (which provided for the exchange of information to help counter terrorism and for signatory states to refrain from granting asylum to terrorists). Member states were to set aside standby troop contingents for the planned ASF, which was to be mandated to undertake observation, monitoring and other peace-support missions; to deploy in member states as required to prevent the resurgence or escalation of violence; to intervene in member states as required to restore stability; to conduct post-conflict disarmament and demobilization and other peace-building activities; and to provide emergency humanitarian assistance. The Council was to harmonize and co-ordinate the activities of other regional security mechanisms. An extraordinary AU summit meeting, convened in Sirte, Libya, in February 2004, adopted a declaration approving the establishment of the multinational ASF, comprising five regional brigades—the Central African Multinational Force (FOMAC), the Eastern Africa Standby Force (EASF), the ECOWAS Standby Force (ESF), the North African Regional Capability (NARC), and the SADC Standby Brigade (SADCBRIG)—to be deployed in African-led peace support operations. A Policy Framework Document on the establishment of the ASF and the Military Staff Committee was approved by the third regular summit of AU heads of state, held in July 2004. It is envisaged that the ASF, which is composed of rapidly deployable multidimensional military, police and civilian capabilities, will become fully operational by 2015. In October 2010 the ASF conducted an exercise known as 'AMANI AFRICA', with pan-continental participation, in Addis Ababa, Ethiopia. A roadmap on achieving the full operationalization of the ASF was under development in 2012.

The extraordinary OAU summit meeting convened in Sirte, Libya, in September 1999 determined to hold a regular ministerial Conference on Security, Stability, Development and Co-operation in Africa (CSSDCA): the first CSSDCA took place in Abuja, Nigeria, in May 2000. The CSSDCA process provides a forum for the development of policies aimed at advancing the common values of the AU and AEC in the areas of peace, security and co-operation. In December 2000 OAU heads of state and government adopted the Bamako Declaration, concerned with arresting the circulation of small arms and light weapons (SALW) on the continent. It was envisaged that the Central African Convention for the Control of SALW, their Ammunition, Parts and Components that can be used for their Manufacture, Repair or Assembly (Kinshasa Convention), adopted by central African states in April 2010, would contribute to the AU's SALW control capacity. In September 2011 AU member states, met in Lomé, Togo, to debate a draft strategy on SALW control and to elaborate an African Common Position on an Arms Trade Treaty (ATT) in advance of the UN Conference on an ATT, which was to take place in July 2012. In May 2012 an African Regional Consultation on the ATT was organized at AU headquarters by the Regional Centre for Peace and Disarmament in Africa (UNREC, a subsidiary of the UN Office for Disarmament Affairs).

In May 2003 the AU, UNDP and UN Office for Project Services agreed a US $6.4m. project entitled 'Support for the Implementation of the Peace and Security Agenda of the African Union'. In June of that year a meeting of the G8 and NEPAD adopted a Joint Africa/G8 Plan to enhance African capabilities to undertake Peace Support Operations. Within the framework of the Plan, a consultation between the AU, the NEPAD Secretariat, the G8, the African regional economic communities, as well as the European Union (EU) and UN and other partners, was convened in Addis Ababa in April 2005. In September 2002 and October 2004 the AU organized high-level intergovernmental meetings on preventing and combating terrorism in Africa. An AU Special Representative on Protection of Civilians in Armed Conflict Situations in Africa was appointed in September 2004.

In January 2005 the AU Non-Aggression and Common Defence Pact was adopted to promote co-operation in developing a common defence policy and to encourage member states to foster an attitude of non-aggression. The Pact, which entered into force in December 2009, establishes measures aimed at preventing inter- and intra-state conflicts and arriving at peaceful resolutions to conflicts. It also sets out a framework defining, *inter alia,* the terms 'aggression' and 'intervention' and determining those situations in which intervention may be considered an acceptable course of action. As such, the Pact stipulates that an act, or threat, of aggression against an individual member state is to be considered an act, or threat, of aggression against all members states.

In recent years the AU has been involved in peace-making and peace-building activities in several African countries and regions.

In April 2003 the AU authorized the establishment of a 3,500-member African Mission in Burundi (AMIB) to oversee the implementation of cease-fire accords in that country, support the disarmament and demobilization of former combatants, and ensure favourable conditions for the deployment of a future UN peace-keeping presence. In June 2004 AMIB was terminated and its troops 'rehatted' as participants in the then newly authorized UN Operation in Burundi (ONUB, which was terminated in 2006).

The July 2003 Maputo Assembly determined to establish a post-conflict reconstruction ministerial committee on Sudan. The first meeting of the committee, convened in March 2004, resolved to dispatch an AU team of experts to southern Sudan to compile a preliminary assessment of that region's post-conflict requirements; this was undertaken in late June. In early April, meeting in N'Djamena, Chad, the Sudan Government and other Sudanese parties signed, under AU auspices, a Humanitarian Cease-fire Agreement providing for the establishment of an AU-led Cease-fire Commission and for the deployment of an AU military observer mission (the AU Mission in the Sudan—AMIS) to the western Sudanese region of Darfur, where widespread violent unrest (including reportedly systematic attacks on the indigenous civilian population by pro-government militias), resulting in a grave humanitarian crisis, had prevailed since early 2003. Following the adoption in late May 2004 of an accord on the modalities for the implementation of the Humanitarian Cease-fire Agreement (also providing for the future deployment of an armed protection force as an additional component of AMIS, as requested by a recent meeting of the Peace and Security Council), the Cease-fire Commission was inaugurated at the end of that month and, at the beginning of June, the Commission's headquarters were opened in El Fasher, Sudan; some 60 AMIS military observers were dispatched to the headquarters during that month. In early July the AU Assembly agreed to increase the strength of AMIS to 80 observers. From mid-2004 the AU mediated contact between the parties to the conflict in Darfur on the achievement of a negotiated peace agreement. AMIS's military component, agreed in May 2004, initially comprising 310 troops from Nigeria and Rwanda and mandated to monitor the cease-fire and protect the Mission, began to be deployed in August. In October the Peace and Security Council decided to expand AMIS into a full peace-keeping operation, eventually to comprise 3,300 troops, police and civilian support staff. The mission's mandate was enhanced to include promoting increased compliance by all parties with the cease-fire agreement and helping with the process of confidence-building; responsibility for monitoring compliance with any subsequent agreements; assisting IDP and refugee returns; and contributing to the improvement of the security situation throughout Darfur. In April 2005 the Peace and Security Council authorized the further enhancement of AMIS to comprise, by the end of September, some 6,171 military personnel, including up to 1,560 civilian police personnel. A pledging conference for the mission, convened in April, resulted in commitments from AU partners and some member states totalling US $291.6m.; the promised funding included $77.4m. from the EU and $50m. from the USA. In January 2005 a Comprehensive Peace Agreement (CPA)—including a Protocol on the Resolution of the Conflict in Abyei Area (the 'Abyei Protocol'), signed in May 2004—was finalized between the Sudan Government and opposition Sudan People's Liberation Movement (SPLM); continuing contention, however, over competing claims to land ownership in, and the future status of, the Abyei region (located at Sudan's border with South Sudan) hindered the Agreement's implementation. In March 2006 the Peace and Security Council agreed, in principle, to support the transformation of AMIS into a UN operation. In late April, following talks in Abuja, Nigeria, AU mediators submitted a proposed peace agreement to representatives of the Sudanese Government and rebel groups; the so-called Darfur Peace Agreement (DPA) was signed on 5 May by the Sudanese Government and the main rebel grouping (the Sudan Liberation Movement).

In August 2006 the UN Security Council expanded the mandate of UNMIS to provide for its deployment to Darfur, in order to enforce a cease-fire and support the implementation of DPA. The Council also requested the UN Secretary-General to devise jointly with the AU, in consultation with the parties to the DPA, a plan and schedule for a transition from AMIS to a sole UN operation in Darfur. The Sudanese Government, however, initially rejected the concept of an expanded UN peace-keeping mission, on the grounds that it would compromise national sovereignty. Eventually, in late December, the UN, AU and Sudanese Government established a tripartite mechanism which was to facilitate the implementation of a UN-formulated three-phase approach, endorsed by the AU Peace and Security Council in November, that would culminate in a hybrid AU/UN mission in Darfur. In January 2007 UNMIS provided AMIS with supplies and extra personnel under the first ('light') phase of the approach; the second ('heavy') phase, finalized in that month, was to involve the delivery of force enablers, police units, civilian personnel and mission support items. UNMIS continued to make efforts to engage the non-signatories of the DPA in the political process in Darfur. In June the AU and UN special representatives for Darfur defined a political roadmap to lead eventually to full negotiations in support of a peaceful settlement to the sub-regional conflict. In August the first AU/UN-chaired 'pre-negotiation' discussions with those rebel groups in Darfur that were not party to the DPA approved an agreement on co-operation in attempting to secure a settlement.

In June 2007 the Sudanese Government agreed to support unconditionally the deployment of the Hybrid UN/AU Operation in Darfur (UNAMID); UNAMID was authorized by the UN Security Council in the following month, with a mandated force ceiling of up to 26,000 troops and police officers, supported by 5,000 international and local civilian staff, and a mandate to take necessary action to support the implementation and verification of the May 2006 Darfur Peace Agreement. UNAMID was also mandated to protect civilians, to provide security for humanitarian assistance, to support an inclusive political process, to contribute to the promotion of human rights and rule of law, and to monitor and report on the situation along the borders with Chad and the Central African Republic (CAR). An AU-UN Joint Mediation Support Team for Darfur (JMST) and a Tripartite Committee on UNAMID (including representatives of AU, the UN and Government of Sudan), meet periodically. UNAMID assumed command of AMIS (then comprising 10 battalions) in December 2007. In February 2008 UNAMID's Joint Special Representative signed a status of forces agreement with the minister of foreign affairs of Sudan, covering logistical aspects of the mission. In March UNAMID police units conducted their first confidence-building patrols in areas under rebel control in northern Darfur. In May UNAMID's Force Commander condemned aerial attacks against villages in northern Darfur, allegedly by Sudanese forces.

At the end of June 2008 a new joint AU-UN Chief Mediator was appointed, based at UNAMID headquarters in El Fasher. A Joint Support Co-ordination Mechanism (JSCM) Office in Addis Ababa, comprising liaison officers and communications equipment, was established in November to ensure effective consultation between AU headquarters and the UN. In October 2008 the UN Secretary-General reported that little progress had been achieved in the implementation of the 2006 Darfur Peace Agreement and that violent unrest continued to prevail, and that the conditions in Darfur were not conducive to undertaking a successful peace-keeping operation. From 2008 activities were under way to bring the 10 former AMIS battalions up to full strength in terms of military personnel and equipment. Nevertheless, the UN Secretary-General reported in February 2009 that UNAMID's operational capabilities continued to be limited by lack of critical and key military enabling equipment, logistical constraints, and the reluctance of many troop- and police-contributing countries to deploy to it well-trained personnel and efficient contingent-owned equipment. In January 2010 the UN Secretary-General reported that the capability of UNAMID batallions in Darfur continued to be a cause of concern, with a number of units not having sufficient major equipment.

In March 2009 an AU High-Level Panel on Darfur (AUPD), led by the former President of South Africa, Thabo Mbeki, was established to address means of securing peace, justice, and reconciliation in Darfur. The panel conducted a series of hearings in Sudan over subsequent months, and, in October, issued a report of its findings and recommendations; a key recommendation was the creation of a hybrid court, comprising both AU and Sudanese judges, to prosecute crimes against humanity committed in Darfur. During October a new AU High-Level Implementation Panel (AUHIP) on Sudan was established, with a mandate to support the implementation of all AUPD recommendations, and to assist the relevant Sudanese parties with the implementation of the January 2005 CPA. In November 2009 an inaugural conference of Darfurian civil society organizations was convened, in Doha, Qatar, in order to strengthen and to further political negotiations to achieve a peace settlement. A second conference was held in July 2010. In February and March 2010, respectively, two rebel groupings that had been operating in Darfur signed framework agreements with the Sudanese Government aimed at resolving the conflict; however, consequent negotiations with the largest rebel group, aimed at securing a cease-fire, stalled in May. During that month violent unrest in Darfur caused nearly 600 fatalities, the highest number since the deployment of the mission. UNAMID strengthened security measures and provided additional medical care in some of the larger IDP camps. In late August a consultative meeting of representatives of UNAMID, the AU, the USA and the Sudanese President agreed that UNAMID and the Sudanese Government would work closely together to improve the security situation in Darfur and to support stabilization and development of the region.

In April 2011 the Sudanese National Electoral Commission initiated preparations for a referendum to be held on the future status of Darfur, and requested material and technical assistance from UNAMID. Towards the end of April the JMST presented a draft peace agreement to the Sudan Government and rebel groupings. The agreement was considered by an All-Darfur Stakeholders' Conference, convened, with support from UNAMID, in Doha, Qatar, in late May; participants in the Conference endorsed a communiqué providing for the draft document (the Doha Document for Peace in Darfur—DDPD) to form the basis for achieving a permanent cease-fire and comprehensive Darfurian peace settlement. The DDPD addressed issues including power sharing, wealth sharing, human rights, justice and reconciliation, compensation, returns, and internal dialogue, and provided for the establishment of a Cease-fire Commission, a Darfur Regional Authority, and for a Darfuri to be appointed as the second Vice-President of Sudan. In June the UN Secretary-General welcomed the DDPD as the basis for resolving the Darfur conflict. In mid-July the Sudanese Government and the 'Liberation and Justice Movement', an alliance of rebel groupings, signed an accord on the adoption of the DDPD. Shortly afterwards the two sides also signed a Protocol on the Political Participation of the Liberation and Justice Movement and Integration of its Forces. Meanwhile, UNAMID, a participant in the DDPD Implementation Follow-on Commission, prepared, with civil society representatives, a plan for the dissemination throughout Darfur of information on the Document. In August UNAMID chaired the first meeting of the Cease-Fire Commission established under the provisions of the DDPD. The formation in 2011 of a subcommittee comprising UNAMID and Sudanese government security entities led to a significant decrease in restrictions on the movements of UNAMID security patrols in the latter part of the year. There were continued reports of criminal attacks on UN personnel, including the theft of UNAMID vehicles, during 2008–12. In early March 2012 UNAMID completed an operation to verify positions held by former rebels; information acquired during the verification operation was to be used by the Cease-fire Commission in disarmament, demobilization, and reintegration/integration planning. In the following month the UN Secretary-General stated that UNAMID personnel numbers would be adjusted downwards, and that troop numbers at various sites would reconfigured, with the largest UNAMID presence being confined to areas with the highest risk of armed conflict. More frequent and longer patrols, with expanded use of temporary operating bases, was also recommended.

UNAMID's operational strength in May 2012 comprised 17,364 troops, 591 military observers and 5,511 police officers. At June 2012 UNAMID was being led by the Joint AU-UN Special Representative, Ibrahim Gambari.

From January 2011, when a referendum was held on future self-determination for South Sudan, violent tensions escalated significantly in Abyei, and had, by July, when South Sudan's independence was achieved, displaced around 113,000 people. In July UNSMIS was succeeded by a new UN mission, the UN Mission in South Sudan (UNMISS). A further UN mission, the UN Interim Security Force for Abyei (UNISFA) was established in June. The 'Temporary Arrangements for the Administration and Security of the Abyei Area'—an accord adopted in mid-June by the Sudanese Government and rebels, governing the withdrawal of their respective forces from Abyei—vested responsibility for supervising security and stability in the region in an Abyei Joint Oversight Committee, comprising members from each party to the conflict, and also in an AU Facilitator. From January 2012 relations between South Sudan and Sudan deteriorated significantly, owing to factors including the disputed delineation of the two countries' joint border, mutual accusations of support for anti-government rebel militia groups, South Sudan's dependency on the use of Sudanese infrastructure (a pipeline and Port Sudan) for the export of petroleum, and sovereignty over Abyei. In February the two countries signed a Memorandum of Understanding on non-aggression and co-operation, committing each state to respecting the other's sovereignty and territorial integrity. In early April AUHIP, facilitating discussions between the two sides, presented to both parties a draft Joint Decision for Reduction of Tension, providing for the immediate cessation of hostilities between the two states, and the withdrawal of armed forces of each state from the territory of the other. In late April the AU Peace and Security Council approved a seven-point Roadmap for Action by Sudan and South Sudan, aimed at normalizing relations between the two states. The Roadmap provided for: (i) the immediate cessation of all hostilities; (ii) the unconditional withdrawal of all armed forces to their respective sides of the border; (iii) the activation, within one week from the adoption of the Roadmap, of all necessary border security mechanisms; (iv) cessation of harbouring of, and support to, rebel groups active against the other state; (v) the activation of an ad hoc Committee to investigate complaints made by one party against the other; (vi) immediate cessation of hostile propaganda and inflammatory statements in the media, and against property, cultural and religious symbols belonging to the nationals of the other state; and (vii) implementation of pending aspects of the June 2011 Temporary Arrangements for the Administration and Security of the Abyei Area, most particularly the redeployment, within two weeks, of all Sudanese and South Sudanese forces out of Abyei. In late April 2012 the AU Commission welcomed South Sudan's acceptance of the Roadmap, and in early May the Sudan Government approved the document. In accordance with its commitment to the Roadmap, South Sudan withdrew its forces from Abyei in early May 2012, with logistical support from UNISFA; and, at the end of May, UNISFA confirmed that Sudan had also withdrawn its military from the area.

Meeting in January 2006 the Peace and Security Council accepted in principle the future deployment of an AU Peace Support Mission in Somalia, with a mandate to support that member country's transitional federal institutions; meanwhile, it was envisaged that an IGAD peace support mission (IGASOM, approved by IGAD in January 2005 and endorsed by that month's AU summit) would be stationed in Somalia. In mid-March 2006 the IGAD Assembly reiterated its support for the deployment of IGASOM, and urged the UN Security Council to grant an exemption to the UN arms embargo applied to Somalia in order to facilitate the regional peace support initiative. At a consultative meeting on the removal of the arms embargo, convened in mid-April, in Nairobi, Kenya, representatives of the Somali transitional federal authorities presented for consideration by the AU and IGAD a draft national security and stabilization plan. It was agreed that a detailed mission plan should be formulated to underpin the proposed AU/IGAD peace missions. In January 2007 the Peace and Security Council authorized the deployment of the AU Mission in Somalia (AMISOM), in place of the proposed IGASOM. AMISOM was to be deployed for an initial period of six months, with a mandate to contribute to the political stabilization of Somalia. It was envisaged that AMISOM would evolve into a UN operation focusing on the post-conflict restoration of Somalia. In the following month the UN Security Council endorsed AMISOM and proposed that it should eventually be superseded by such a UN operation. AMISOM became operational in May 2007. In mid-September 2009 the AU strongly condemned terrorist attacks that were perpetrated against the AMISOM headquarters in Mogadishu, Somalia, killing more than 20 people, including the Deputy Force Commander of the Mission, and injuring a further 40. In October 2010 Flt Lt Jerry Rawlings, the former President of Ghana, was appointed as the AU High Representative on Somalia. AMISOM reached its then mandated strength of 8,000 troops in November 2010. In the following month the UN Security Council, concerned at continuing unrest and terrorist attacks, extended AMISOM's mandate until 30 September 2011 and requested the AU to increase the mission's numbers to 12,000. AMISOM's mandate was extended further, in September 2011, until 31 October 2012. In so doing, the UN Security Council requested the AU urgently to increase the mission's strength to the then mandated level of 12,000. In late February 2012 the Security Council voted unanimously to enhance the mission further, to comprise 17,700 troops, and to expand its areas of operation. At that time the Council also banned trade in charcoal with Somalia, having identified that commodity as a significant source of revenue for militants. In January 2012 the Peace and Security Council adopted a Strategic Concept for future AMISOM Operations

In February 2008 the AU welcomed the efforts of African leaders, including the outgoing Chairman of the AU Assembly, President Kufuor of Ghana, and the former UN Secretary-General, Kofi Annan, to secure a peaceful outcome to the political crisis and violent unrest that had erupted in Kenya following the disputed outcome of a presidential election staged in December 2007. In March 2008 the Pan-African Parliament sent an observer mission to monitor the legislative and presidential elections that were held concurrently in Zimbabwe. In February 2009 the Assembly welcomed ongoing political progress in Zimbabwe and demanded the immediate suspension of international sanctions against that country.

In November 2008 the AU and International Conference on the Great Lakes Region jointly convened, in Nairobi, Kenya, with participation by the UN Secretary-General, a regional summit on ongoing heightened insecurity in eastern regions of the Democratic Republic of the Congo.

In August 2008, following the overthrow of its constitutional Government in a military *coup d'état*, Mauritania was suspended from participating in the activities of the AU. Guinea was suspended from the AU during December 2008–December 2010, also following a *coup d'état*; Guinea's membership suspension was lifted in view of presidential elections held in 2010. In March 2009 the AU suspended Madagascar from participation in its activities, following the forced resignation of the elected President, Mark Ravalomanana, and transfer of power to the military. In February 2010 Niger was suspended from participation in AU activities, following a *coup d'état*; Niger's membership suspension was lifted in March 2011, following the successful organization, in October 2010, of a referendum on a new constitution, and of legislative and presidential elections in early 2011.

In March 2011 a High-Level Ad Hoc Committee on Libya, comprising the leaders of Republic of the Congo, Mali, Mauritania, South Africa and Uganda, was formed to facilitate dialogue among the parties to the conflict that had emerged in Libya in early 2011. In mid-March the Committee urged an immediate halt to the military intervention in Libya that followed the adoption by the UN Security Council of Resolution 1973, which, *inter alia*, imposed a no-fly zone in Libya's airspace and authorized UN member states to take 'all necessary measures to protect civilians and civilian populated areas under threat of attack' by forces loyal to Col al-Qaddafi, 'while excluding a foreign occupation force of any form on any part of Libyan territory'. During March the Committee developed a Roadmap for the Peaceful Resolution of the Crisis in Libya, which urged an immediate cessation of hostilities; the facilitation by the Libyan authorities of the delivery of humanitarian assistance to vulnerable populations; the protection of all foreign nationals, including African migrant workers; the adoption and implementation of political reforms to eliminate the causes of the conflict; and better co-ordination of the international community's crisis resolution efforts. In early April it was reported that the Libyan regime had accepted the provisions of the AU Roadmap; the opposition forces active in Libya, however, refused to approve it, demanding that al-Qaddafi relinquish power. The 17th regular summit of AU heads of state and government, convened in late June–early July 2011, endorsed a set of Proposals on a Framework Agreement for a Political Solution to the Crisis in Libya, which had been developed by the High-Level Ad Hoc Committee in the context of the AU Roadmap. The summit also determined to disregard the arrest warrant for al-Qaddafi and members of his regime that had been issued in late June by the International Criminal Court. In early July the High-Level Ad Hoc Committee formally presented the Proposals for a Framework Agreement to the parties to the Libyan conflict; these were rejected by the rebel forces.

In mid-August 2011, following several months of civil conflict in Libya, and of Security Council Resolution 1973-mandated NATO action there, anti-government forces began to make significant advances against the al-Qaddafi regime, and, by 23 August, the rebels had taken control of the Libyan capital, Tripoli, and had conquered al-Qaddafi's fortified compound in the city. Meeting shortly afterwards, at the level of heads of state and government, the AU Peace and Security Council noted with deep appreciation the efforts undertaken by the High-Level Ad Hoc Committee on Libya in pursuit of a political solution to the ongoing conflict, within the context of the AU Roadmap and the Proposals on a Framework Agreement. The Council urged Libyan stakeholders to accelerate the process leading to the formation of an all-inclusive transitional government for that country, and emphasized the commitment of the AU to work with the UN, the Arab League, the Organization of Islamic Cooperation, NATO, and the EU, in support of the Libyan people. In late September the AU reiterated its concerns for the security of African migrant workers based in Libya. In September 2011 the AU recognized the National Transitional Council as the de facto government of Libya.

In early 2011 the Peace and Security Council held a series of meetings to consider ongoing unrest in Côte d'Ivoire, where the security situation had deteriorated following the refusal of the outgoing President Laurent Gbagbo to acknowledge the outcome of presidential elections held in 2010, and consequently to cede power. In late January 2011 the Council, meeting at the level of heads of state and government, determined to establish a High-level Panel on Côte d'Ivoire. The Panel, which was inaugurated at the end of that month, included five African leaders, the AU Chairperson, and the President of the ECOWAS Commission. Meeting in mid-March 2011 the Peace and Security Council decided that an AU High Representative should be appointed to pursue a peaceful resolution of the Côte d'Ivoire political crisis, through the implementation of peace proposals developed by the High-level Panel. The legitimately elected President, Alassane Ouattara, was eventually inaugurated in May 2011.

Following the overthrow of the legitimate Government of Mali by the military in March 2012 that country was suspended from participation in AU activities. The AU Commission, recalling the 'fundamental principle of the intangibility of borders inherited by the African countries at their accession to independence' expressed its 'total rejection' of a unilateral declaration, made in early April by separatist militants of the National Movement for the Liberation of Azawad (MNLA), who, supported by Islamist forces, had just seized land in the Kidal, Gao and Tombouctou regions of northern Mali, that this was, henceforth, to be known as the independent entity of Azawad. The Commission affirmed the AU's full support for efforts being undertaken by ECOWAS to protect Mali's unity and territorial integrity, both through mediation and through the envisaged deployment there of the ECOWAS Standby Force. It was reported in mid-June that the AU had requested the UN Security Council to draft a resolution endorsing military intervention against the militants in northern Mali. In April 2012 Guinea-Bissau was also suspended from the AU, following a military coup, pending the restoration of constitutional order.

The EU assists the AU financially in the areas of: peace and security; institutional development; governance; and regional economic integration and trade. In June 2004 the European Commission activated for the first time its newly-established Africa Peace Facility (APF), which aims to contribute to the African peace and security agenda, including, since 2007, conflict prevention, post-conflict stabilization, and accelerating decision making and co-ordination processes. During 2007–12 APF funds were chanelled as follows: €607m. to peace support operations (the Fund's core area of activity); €100m. towards the operationalization of the African Peace and Security Architecture and Africa-EU dialogue; €20m. for unforeseen contingencies; and €15m. towards early response. A €300m. replenishment of the APF, to cover 2011–13, was agreed in August 2011. It was announced in March 2012 that €11.4m. would be allocated through the APF over the period 1 February 2012–31 January 2014 towards the training of the ASF, and towards the establishment of an African e-library comprising documentation of relevance to the Force.

Since October 2007 APF and UN funding have jointly financed the deployment of UNAMID (with the APF financing of UNAMID and AUHIP totalling €305m). AMISOM was allocated €208m. in APF funding during 2007–12. The APF has, furthermore, channelled more than €90m. towards peace support operations in the CAR, including support for the deployment, since July 2008, of the Mission for the Consolidation of Peace in the CAR—MICOPAX, which, under the auspices of the Communauté économique des états de l'Afrique centrale, superseded the Multinational Force in the Central African Republic (established in 2002). MICOPAX has a military strength of around 520 troops, and a civilian component that includes a police unit of 150 officers.

INFRASTRUCTURE, ENERGY AND THE ENVIRONMENT

Meeting in Lomé, Togo, in July 2001, OAU heads of state and government authorized the establishment of an African Energy Commission (AFREC), with the aim of increasing co-operation in energy matters between Africa and other regions. AFREC was launched in February 2008. It was envisaged at that time that an African Electrotechnical Standardization Commission (AFSEC) would also become operational, as a subsidiary body of AFREC.

In 1964 the OAU adopted a Declaration on the Denuclearization of Africa, and in April 1996 it adopted the African Nuclear Weapons Free Zone Treaty (also known as the 'Pelindaba Treaty'), which identifies Africa as a nuclear weapons-free zone and promotes co-operation in the peaceful uses of nuclear energy.

In 1968 OAU member states adopted the African Convention on the Conservation of Nature and Natural Resources. The Bamako Convention on the Ban of the Import into Africa and the Control of Transboundary Movement and Management of Hazardous Wastes within Africa was adopted by OAU member states in 1991 and entered into force in April 1998.

In June 2010 a consultative meeting was convened between the AU, COMESA, IGAD, and other regional partners, aimed at advancing co-ordination and harmonization of their activities governing the environment. It was envisaged that the AU should facilitate the development of a comprehensive African Environmental Framework, to guide pan-continental and REC environmental activities. At that time the AU was in the process of integrating two regional fora—the African Ministerial Conference on Water and the African Ministerial Conference on the Environment—into its structures, as specialized institutes.

The 17th regular summit of AU heads of state and government, held in late June–early July 2011, adopted a decision inviting member states to work on a common African position for the landmark United Nations Conference on Sustainable Development—UNCSD (also referred to as Rio+20), which was to be held in Rio de Janeiro, Brazil, in June 2012. Consequently an Africa Regional Preparatory Conference for UNCSD was convened, under the auspices of ECA, in October 2011. The Conference noted emerging challenges to continental sustainable development, including low adaptive capacity to the effects of consequences of climate change; increasing severe biodiversity loss, desertification and land degradation, aggravated by the effects of climate change; and rapid urbanization. The conference urged the international community to meet its commitments to the continent in terms of transfer of financial and technological resources, and committed African states to enhancing efforts to improve national governance and development effectiveness, and to developing national strategies for sustainable development.

In February 2007 the first Conference of African Ministers responsible for Maritime Transport was convened to discuss maritime transport policy in the region. A draft declaration was submitted at the Conference, held in Abuja, Nigeria, outlining the AU's vision for a common maritime transport policy aimed at 'linking Africa' and detailing programmes for co-operation on maritime safety and security and the development of an integrated transport infrastructure. The subsequently adopted Abuja Maritime Transport Declaration formally provided for an annual meeting of maritime transport ministers, to be hosted by each region in turn in a rotational basis. In July 2009 the AU Assembly decided to establish an African Agency for the Protection of Territorial and Economic Waters of African Countries. In June 2011 a task force was inaugurated to lead the development and implementation of a new '2050 Africa's Integrated Maritime Strategy' (2050 Aim-Strategy); the Strategy was to address maritime challenges affecting the continent, including the development of aquaculture and offshore renewable energy resources; unlawful activities, such as illegal fishing, acts of maritime piracy (particularly in the Gulfs of Aden and Guinea), and trafficking in arms and drugs; and environmental pressures, such as loss of biodiversity, degradation of the marine environment, and climate change. The first Conference of African Ministers responsible for Maritime-related Affairs was held in April 2012, alongside a workshop on developing the 2050 AIM-Strategy.

In January 2012 the Executive Council endorsed a new African Civil Aviation Policy (AFCAP); and also endorsed the African Action Plan for the UN 2011–20 Decade of Action on Road Safety.

POLITICAL AND SOCIAL AFFAIRS

The African Charter on Human and People's Rights, which was adopted by the OAU in 1981 and entered into force in October 1986, provided for the establishment of an 11-member African Commission on Human and People's Rights, based in Banjul, The Gambia. A Protocol to the Charter, establishing an African Court of People's and Human Rights, was adopted by the OAU Assembly of Heads of State in June 1998 and entered into force in January 2004. In February 2009 a protocol (adopted in July 2003) establishing an African Court of Justice entered into force. The Protocol on the Statute of the African Court of Justice and Human Rights, aimed at merging the African Court of Human and Peoples' Rights and the African Court of Justice, was opened for signature in July 2008. A further Protocol, relating to the Rights of Women, was adopted by the July 2003 Maputo Assembly. The African Charter on the Rights and Welfare of the Child was opened for signature in July 1990 and entered into force in November 1999. A Protocol to the Abuja Treaty Establishing the AEC relating to the Pan-African Parliament, adopted by the OAU in March 2001, entered into force in December 2003. The Parliament was inaugurated in March 2004 and was, initially, to exercise advisory and consultative powers only, although its eventual evolution into an institution with full legislative powers is envisaged. In March 2005 the advisory Economic, Social and Cultural Council was inaugurated.

The July 2002 inaugural summit meeting of AU heads of state and government adopted a Declaration Governing Democratic Elections in Africa, providing guidelines for the conduct of national elections in member states and outlining the AU's electoral observation and monitoring role. In April 2003 the AU Commission and the South African Independent Electoral Commission jointly convened an African Conference on Elections, Democracy and Governance. In February 2012 a new African Charter on Democracy, Elections and Governance entered into force, having been ratified at that time by 15 AU member states.

In recent years several large population displacements have occurred in Africa, mainly as a result of violent conflict. In 1969 OAU member states adopted the Convention Governing the Specific Aspects of Refugee Problems in Africa, which entered into force in June 1974 and had been ratified by 45 states at June 2012. The Convention promotes close co-operation with UNHCR. The AU maintains a Special Refugee Contingency Fund to provide relief assistance and to support repatriation activities, education projects, etc., for displaced people in Africa. In October 2009 AU member states participating in a regional Special Summit on Refugees, Returnees and IDPs in Africa, convened in Kampala, Uganda, adopted the AU Convention for the Protection and Assistance of IDPs in Africa, the first legally binding international treaty providing legal protection and support to people displaced within their own countries by violent conflict and natural disasters; the Convention had received four ratifications by June 2012. The AU aims to address pressing health issues affecting member states, including the eradication of endemic parasitic and infectious diseases and improving access to medicines. An African Summit on HIV/AIDS, TB and other related Infectious Diseases was convened, under OAU auspices, in Abuja in March 2001 and, in May 2006, an AU Special Summit on HIV/AIDS, TB and Malaria was convened, also in Abuja, to review the outcomes of the previous Summit. The 2006 Special Summit adopted the Abuja Call for Accelerated Action on HIV/AIDS, TB and Malaria, and, in September of that year AU ministers of health adopted the Maputo Plan of Action for the operationalisation of the Continental Policy Framework for Sexual and Reproductive Health, covering 2007–10, aimed at advancing the goal of achieving universal access to comprehensive sexual and reproductive health services in Africa; in July 2010 the Plan was extended over the period 2010–15. In January 2012 the 18th AU Assembly meeting decided to revitalize AIDS Watch Africa (AWA), an advocacy platform established in April 2001, and hitherto comprising several regional heads of states, to be henceforth an AU Heads of State and Government Advocacy and Accountability Platform with continent-wide representation. AWA's mandate was to be extended to cover, also, TB and malaria. In March 2012 NEPAD and UNAIDS signed an agreement on advancing sustainable responses to HIV/AIDS, health and development across Africa. An AU Scientific, Technical and Research Commission is based in Lagos, Nigeria.

In July 2004 the Assembly adopted the Solemn Declaration on Gender Equality in Africa (SDGEA), incorporating a commitment to reporting annually on progress made towards attaining gender equality. The first conference of ministers responsible for women's affairs and gender, convened in Dakar, Senegal, in October 2005, adopted the Implementation Framework for the SDGEA, and Guidelines for Monitoring and Reporting on the SDGEA, in support of member states' reporting responsibilities.

The seventh AU summit, convened in Banjul, The Gambia, in July 2006, adopted the African Youth Charter, providing for the implementation of youth policies and strategies across Africa, with the aim of encouraging young African people to participate in the development of the region and to take advantage of increasing opportunities in education and employment. The Charter outlined the basic rights and responsibilities of youths, which were divided into four main categories: youth participation; education and skills development; sustainable livelihoods; and health and well-being. The Charter, which entered into force in August 2010, also details the obligations of member states towards young people.

In December 2007 the AU adopted a Plan of Action on Drug Control and Crime Prevention covering the period 2007–12, and determined to establish a follow-up mechanism to monitor and evaluate its implementation. In March 2009 the AU and UNODC (which in October 2008 had published a report identifying the expanding use in recent years of West Africa as a transit route for narcotics being illegally traded between Latin America and Europe) launched a joint initiative to support the Plan. The AU-UNODC co-operation aimed to strengthen the policy-making, norm-setting and capacity-building capabilities of the AU Commission and sub-regional organizations (notably ECOWAS).

AU efforts to combat human trafficking are guided by the 2006 Ouagadougou Action Plan to Combat Trafficking in Human Beings. In June 2009 the AU launched AU COMMIT, a campaign aimed at raising the profile of human trafficking on the regional development agenda. It was estimated at that time that nearly 130,000 people in sub-Saharan Africa and 230,000 in North Africa and the Middle East had been recruited into forced labour, including sexual exploitation, as a result of trafficking; many had also been transported to Western Europe and other parts of the world.

TRADE, INDUSTRY AND ECONOMIC CO-OPERATION

In October 1999 a conference on Industrial Partnerships and Investment in Africa was held in Dakar, Senegal, jointly organized by the OAU with UNIDO, the ECA, the African Development Bank and the Alliance for Africa's Industrialization. In June 1997 the first meeting between ministers of the OAU and the EU was convened in New York, USA. In April 2000 the first EU-Africa summit of heads of state and government was held in Cairo, under the auspices of the EU and OAU. The summit adopted the Cairo Plan of Action, which addressed areas including economic integration, trade and investment, private-sector development in Africa, human rights and good governance, peace and security, and development issues such as education, health and food security. The second EU-Africa summit meeting was initially to have been held in April 2003 but was postponed, owing to disagreements concerning the participation of President Mugabe of Zimbabwe, against whom the EU had imposed sanctions. In February 2007 the EU and the AU began a period of consultation on a joint EU-Africa Strategy, aimed at outlining a long-term vision of the future partnership between the two parties. The Strategy was adopted by the second EU-Africa Summit, which was convened, finally, in December 2007, in Lisbon, Portugal (with participation by President Mugabe). The third EU-Africa Summit, held in November 2010, in Tripoli, Libya, confirmed commitment to the Strategy and adopted an action plan on co-operation, covering 2011–13. A fourth EU-Africa Business Forum was convened alongside the November 2010 summit. A Joint Africa-EU Task Force meets regularly, most recently in March 2012, to consider areas of co-operation.

Co-operation between African states and the People's Republic of China is undertaken within the framework of the Forum on China-Africa Co-operation (FOCAC). The first FOCAC ministerial conference was held in October 2000; the second in December 2003; the third (organized alongside a China-Africa leaders' summit) in November 2006; and the fourth in November 2009. The fifth FOCAC ministerial conference was scheduled to be held in July 2012. Africa–USA trade is underpinned by the US African Growth and Opportunity Act (AGOA), adopted in May 2000 to promote the development of free market economies in Africa. Regular Africa-EU and Africa-South America ('ASA') summits are convened. The second ASA summit, convened by the AU and Union of South American Nations—UNASUR in Porlamar, Margarita Island, Venezuela, in September 2009, adopted the Margarita Declaration and Action Plan, covering issues of common concern, including combating climate change, and developing an alternative financial mechanism to address the global economic crisis. The third ASA summit took place in May 2012, in Malabo, Equatorial Guinea.

The AU aims to reduce obstacles to intra-African trade and to reverse the continuing disproportionate level of trade conducted by many African countries with their former colonial powers. In June 2005 an AU conference of Ministers of Trade was convened, in Cairo, to discuss issues relating to the development of Trade in Africa, particularly in the context of the World Trade Organization's (WTO) Doha Work Programme. The outcome of the meeting was the adoption of the Cairo Road Map on the Doha Work Programme, which addressed several important issues including the import, export and market access of agricultural and non-agricultural commodities, development issues and trade facilitation.

The 1991 Abuja Treaty Establishing the AEC initially envisaged that the Economic Community would be established by 2028, following a gradual six-phase process involving the co-ordination, harmonization and progressive integration of the activities of all existing and future sub-regional economic unions. (There are 14 so-called 'regional economic communities', or RECs, in Africa, including the following major RECs that are regarded as the five pillars, or building blocks, of the AEC: the Common Market for Eastern and Southern Africa—COMESA, the Communauté économique des états de l'Afrique centrale—CEEAC, the Economic Community of West African States—ECOWAS, the Southern African Development Community—SADC, and the Union of the Arab Maghreb. The subsidiary RECs are: the Communauté économique et monétaire de l'Afrique centrale—CEMAC, the Community of Sahel-Saharan States—CEN-SAD, the East African Community—EAC, the Economic Community of the Great Lakes Countries, the Intergovernmental Authority on Development—IGAD, the Indian Ocean Commission—IOC, the Mano River Union, the Southern African Customs Union, and the Union économique et monétaire ouest-africaine—UEMOA.) The inaugural meeting of the AEC took place in June 1997. In July 2007 the ninth AU Assembly adopted a Protocol on Relations between the African Union and the RECs, aimed at facilitating the harmonization of policies and ensuring compliance with the schedule of the Abuja Treaty.

In January 2012 the 18th summit of AU leaders endorsed a new Framework, Roadmap and Architecture for Fast Tracking the Establishment of a Continental Free Trade Area (CFTA), and an Action Plan for Boosting Intra-African Trade. The summit determined that the implementation of the CFTA process should follow these milestones: the finalization by 2014 of the EAC-COMESA-SADC Tripartite FTA initiative; the completion during 2012–14 of other REC FTAs; the consolidation of the Tripartite and other regional FTAs into the CFTA initiative during 2015–16; and the establishment of an operational CFTA by 2017. The January 2012 summit invited ECOWAS, CEEAC, CEN-SAD and the Union of the Arab Maghreb to draw inspiration from the EAC-COMESA-SADC Tripartite initiative and to establish promptly a second pole of regional integration, thereby accelerating continental economic integration. The summit welcomed the UN Conference on Sustainable Development (UNCSD), scheduled to be held in June of that year, and recognized the need to strengthen the AU's institutional framework for sustainable development, deeming that promoting the transition to 'green' and 'blue' economies would accelerate continental progress towards sustainable development.

In February 2008 the AU Assembly endorsed the AU Action Plan for the Accelerated Industrial Development of Africa (AIDA), which had been adopted in September 2007 by the first extraordinary session of the Conference of African Ministers of Industry. The Action Plan details a set of programme and activities aimed at stimulating a competitive and sustainable industrial development process.

A roadmap and plan of action for promoting microfinance in Africa was finalized in 2009, and is under consideration.

The AU leadership participated in the summit meeting of G8 heads of state and government that was convened in Huntsville, Canada, in June 2010; the summit also included an African Outreach meeting with the leaders of Algeria, Ethiopia, Malawi, Nigeria, Senegal and South Africa.

In October 2010 the AU, ECA and African Development Bank established a Joint Secretariat to enhance coherence and collaboration in support of Africa's development agenda.

RURAL ECONOMY AND AGRICULTURE

In July 2003 the second Assembly of heads of state and government adopted the Maputo Declaration on Agriculture and Food Security in Africa, focusing on the need to revitalize the agricultural sector and to combat hunger on the continent by developing food reserves based on African production. The leaders determined to deploy policies and budgetary resources to remove current constraints on agricultural production, trade and rural development; and to implement the Comprehensive Africa Agriculture Programme (CAADP). The CAADP, which is implemented through NEPAD, focuses on the four pillars of sustainable land and water management; market access; food supply and hunger; and agricultural research. CAADP heads of state have agreed the objective of allocating at least 10% of national budgets to investment in agricultural productivity. The CAADP aims by 2015 to achieve dynamic agricultural markets between African countries and regions; good participation in and access to markets by farmers; a more equitable distribution of wealth for rural populations; more equitable access to land, practical and financial resources, knowledge, information, and technology for sustainable development; development of Africa's role as a strategic player in the area of agricultural science and technology; and environmentally sound agricultural production and a culture of sustainable management of natural resources.

In December 2006 AU leaders convened at a Food Security Summit in Abuja adopted a declaration of commitment to increasing intra-African trade by promoting and protecting as strategic commodities at the continental level cotton, legumes, maize, oil palm, rice and beef, dairy, fisheries and poultry products; and promoting and protecting as strategic commodities at the sub-regional level cassava, sorghum and millet. The AU leaders also declared a commitment to initiating the implementation of the NEPAD Home-grown School Feeding Project, the African Regional Nutrition Strategy, the NEPAD African Nutrition Initiative, and the NEPAD 10-Year Strategy for Combating Vitamin and Mineral Deficiency.

In December 2006 the AU adopted the Great Green Wall of the Sahara and Sahel Initiative (GGWSSI), comprising a set of cross-sectoral actions and interventions (including tree planting) that were aimed at conserving and protecting natural resources, halting soil degradation, reducing poverty, and increasing land productivity in some 20 countries in the Sahara and Sahel areas.

The AU's Programme for the Control of Epizootics (PACE) has co-operated with FAO to combat the further spread of the Highly Pathogenic Avian Influenza (H5N1) virus, outbreaks of which were reported in poultry in several West African countries in the 2000s; joint activities have included establishing a regional network of laboratories and surveillance teams and organizing regional workshops on H5N1 control.

In April 2009 AU ministers responsible for agriculture met to address the challenges to the continent posed by high food prices, climate change and the ongoing global financial and economic crisis. In July 2009 the 13th regular session of the Assembly issued a Declaration on Land Issues and Challenges in Africa, and the Sirte Declaration on Investing in Agriculture for Economic Growth and Food Security. The Sirte Declaration urged member states to review their land sector policies, and determined to undertake studies on the establishment of an appropriate institutional framework, and to launch an African Fund for Land Policy, in support of these efforts. The meeting also urged the establishment of a 'South to South Forum for Agricultural Development in Africa', recommitted to the Maputo Declaration, and urged member states to expand efforts to accelerate the implementation of the CAADP.

In January 2011 the Executive Council endorsed the Accelerated African Agribusiness and Agro-Industries Development Initiative (3ADI), which had been launched at a high-level conference on the development of agribusiness and agro-industries in Africa, convened in Abuja, Nigeria, in March 2010. The framework for the implementation of the 3ADI is the Strategy for the Implementation of the AU Plan of Action for the Accelerated Industrial Development of Africa (AIDA), adopted by African ministers responsible for industry, in October 2008; the Ministerial Action Plan for the Least Developed Countries (LDCs), adopted in December 2009 by LDC ministers responsible for industry and trade; and the Abuja Declaration on Development of Agribusiness and Agro-industries in Africa, adopted by the March 2010 Abuja high-level conference. The initiative aims to mobilize private sector investment, from domestic, regional and international sources, in African agribusiness and agro-industrial development, with the long-term objective of achieving, by 2020, highly productive and profitable agricultural value chains.

The First Conference of African Ministers of Fisheries and Aquaculture (CAMFA) was convened in September 2010, in Banjul, The Gambia. In January 2011 the Executive Council urged member states to adopt and integrate ecosystem approaches in their national and regional fisheries management plans; to strengthen measures to address Illegal, Unreported and Unregulated (IUU) fishing; and to eliminate barriers to intra-regional trade in fish and fishery products.

HUMANITARIAN RESPONSE

In December 2005 a ministerial conference on disaster reduction in Africa, organized by the AU Commission, adopted a programme of action for the implementation of the Africa Regional Strategy for Disaster Risk Reduction (2006–15), formulated in the context of the Hyogo Framework of Action that had been agreed at the World Conference on Disaster Reduction held in Kobe, Japan, in January 2005. A second ministerial conference on disaster reduction, convened in April 2010, urged all member states, and the RECs, to take necessary measures to implement the programme of action. In August 2010 the AU and OCHA signed an agreement detailing key areas of future co-operation on humanitarian issues, with the aim of strengthening the AU's capacity in the areas of disaster preparedness and response, early warning, co-ordination, and protection of civilians affected by conflict or natural disaster.

In late August 2011 AU leaders convened at the first AU Pledging Conference promised to donate some US $350m. towards relief efforts to alleviate the impact of severe drought and famine in the Horn of Africa, which was reported at that time to be affecting up to 12.5m. people.

Finance

The 2012 budget, adopted by the Executive Council in December 2011, totalled US $274.9m., comprising an operational budget of $114.8m. and a programme budget $159.3m. Some 75% of the operational budget is financed by contributions from Algeria, Egypt, Libya, Nigeria and South Africa. Around 90% of programme budgetary funding derives from the AU's development partners.

Specialized Agencies

African Academy of Languages (ACALAN): BP 10, Koulouba-Bamako, Mali; tel. 2023-84-47; fax 2023-84-47; e-mail acalan@acalan.org; internet www.acalan.org; f. 2006 to foster continental integration and development through the promotion of the use—in all domains—of African languages; aims to restore the role and vitality of indigenous languages (estimated to number more than 2,000), and to reverse the negative impact of colonialism on their perceived value; implements a Training of African Languages Teachers and Media Practitioners Project; a core programme is the promotion of the Pan-African Masters and PhD Program in African Languages and Applied Linguistics (PANMAPAL), inaugurated in 2006 at the University of Yaoundé 1 (Cameroon), Addis Ababa University (Ethiopia), and at the University of Cape Town (South Africa); identified in 2009 some 41 'Vehicular Cross-Border Languages'; Vehicular Cross-Border Language Commissions were to be established for 12 of these: Beti-fang and Lingala (Central Africa); Kiswahili, Somali and Malagasy (East Africa); Standard modern Arab and Berber (North Africa); Chichewa/Chinyanja and Setswana (Southern Africa); and Hausa, Mandenkan and Fulfulde (West Africa); in Dec. 2011 organized a workshop on African languages in cyberspace; ACALAN is developing a linguistic Atlas for Africa; Exec. Dir Dr SOZINHO FRANCISCO MATSINHE.

African Civil Aviation Commission (AFCAC): 1 route de l'Aéroport International LSS, BP 2356, Dakar, Senegal; tel. 859-88-00; fax 820-70-18; e-mail secretariat@afcac.org; internet www.afcac.org; f. 1969 to co-ordinate civil aviation matters in Africa and to co-operate with ICAO and other relevant civil aviation bodies; promotes the development of the civil aviation industry in Africa in accordance with provisions of the 1991 Abuja Treaty; fosters the application of ICAO Standards and Recommended Practices; examines specific problems that might hinder the development and operation of the African civil aviation industry; 53 mem states; promotes co-ordination and better utilization and development of African air transport systems and the standardization of aircraft, flight equipment and training programmes for pilots and mechanics; organizes working groups and seminars, and compiles statistics; Sec.-Gen. IYABO SOSINA.

African Telecommunications Union (ATU): ATU Secretariat, POB 35282 Nairobi, 00200 Kenya; tel. (20) 4453308; fax (20) 4453359; e-mail sg@atu-uat.org; internet www.atu-uat.org; f. 1999 as successor to Pan-African Telecommunications Union (f. 1977); promotes the rapid development of information communications in Africa, with the aim of making Africa an equal participant in the global information society; works towards universal service and access and full inter-country connectivity; promotes development and adoption of appropriate policies and regulatory frameworks; promotes financing of development; encourages co-operation between members and the exchange of information; advocates the harmonization of telecommunications policies; 46 national mems, 18 associate mems comprising fixed and mobile telecoms operators; Sec.-Gen. ABDOULKARIM SOUMAILA.

Pan-African Institute of Education for Development (IPED): 49 ave de la Justice, BP 1764, Kinshasa I, Democratic Republic of the Congo; tel. (81) 2686091; fax (81) 2616091; internet iped-auobs.org; f. 1973, became specialized agency in 1986, present name adopted 2001; undertakes educational research and training, focuses on co-operation and problem-solving, acts as an observatory for education; responsible for Education Management Information Systems (EMIS) under the Second Decade for Education for Africa (2006–15); publs *Bulletin d'Information* (quarterly), *Revue africaine des sciences de l'éducation* (2 a year), *Répertoire africain des institutions de recherche* (annually).

Pan-African News Agency (PANAPRESS): BP 4056, ave Bourguiba, Dakar, Senegal; tel. 869-12-34; fax 824-13-90; e-mail panapress@panapress.com; internet www.panapress.com; f. 1979 as PanAfrican News Agency, restructured under current name in 1997; regional headquarters in Khartoum, Sudan; Lusaka, Zambia; Kinshasa, Democratic Republic of the Congo; Lagos, Nigeria; Tripoli, Libya; began operations in May 1983; receives information from national news agencies and circulates news in Arabic, English, French and Portuguese; publs *Press Review*, *In-Focus*.

Pan-African Postal Union (PAPU): POB 6026, Arusha, Tanzania; tel. (27) 2543263; fax (27) 2543265; e-mail sg@papu.co.tz; internet www.upap-papu.org; f. 1980 to extend members' co-operation in the improvement of postal services; 43 mem. countries; Sec.-Gen. RODAH MASAVIRU; publ. *PAPU News*.

Supreme Council for Sport in Africa (SCSA): POB 1363, Yaoundé, Cameroon; tel. 223-95-80; fax 223-45-12; e-mail scsa_yaounde@yahoo.com; f. 1966; co-ordinating authority and forum for the development and promotion of sports in Africa; hosts All Africa Games, held every four years; mems: sports ministers from 53 countries; Sec.-Gen. MVUZO MBEBE (South Africa); publ. *Newsletter* (monthly).

Summary of Constitutive Act of the African Union

(adopted at Lomé, Togo, on 11 July 2000; entered into force on 26 May 2001)

Article 1

Definition of terms and abbreviations used in the Constitutive Act.

Article 2

Establishment of the African Union in accordance with the provisions of the Act.

Objectives of the Union:

(a) To achieve greater unity and solidarity between the African countries and their peoples.

(b) To defend the sovereignty, territorial integrity and independence of its Member States.

(c) To accelerate the political and socio-economic integration of the continent.

(d) To promote and defend African common positions on issues of interest to the continent and its peoples.

(e) To encourage international co-operation, taking due account of the Charter of the United Nations and the Universal Declaration of Human Rights.

(f) To promote peace, security, and stability on the continent.

(g) To promote democratic principles and institutions, popular participation and good governance.

(h) To promote and protect human and peoples' rights in accordance with the African Charter on Human and Peoples' Rights and other relevant human rights instruments.

(i) To establish the necessary conditions which enable the continent to play its rightful role in the global economy and in international negotiations.

(j) To promote sustainable development at the economic, social and cultural levels as well as the integration of African economies.

(k) To promote co-operation in all fields of human activity to raise the living standards of African peoples.

(l) To co-ordinate and harmonize policies between existing and future Regional Economic Communities for the gradual attainment of the objectives of the Union.

(m) To advance the development of the continent by promoting research in all fields, in particular in science and technology.

(n) To work with relevant international partners in the eradication of preventable diseases and the promotion of good health on the continent.

Article 4

The Union shall function in accordance with the following principles:

(a) Sovereign equality and interdependence among Member States of the Union.

(b) Respect of borders existing on achievement of independence.

(c) Participation of the African peoples in the activities of the Union.

(d) Establishment of a common defence policy for the African Continent.

(e) Peaceful resolution of conflicts among Member States of the Union through such appropriate means as may be decided upon by the Assembly.

(f) Prohibition of the use of force or threat to use force among Member States of the Union.

(g) Non-interference by any Member State in the internal affairs of another.

(h) The right of the Union to intervene in a Member State pursuant to a decision of the Assembly in respect of grave circumstances, namely war crimes, genocide and crimes against humanity.

(i) Peaceful co-existence of Member States and their right to live in peace and security.

(j) The right of Member States to request intervention from the Union in order to restore peace and security.

(k) Promotion of self-reliance within the framework of the Union.

(l) Promotion of gender equality.

(m) Respect for democratic principles, human rights, the rule of law and good governance.

(n) Promotion of social justice to ensure balanced economic development.

(o) Respect for the sanctity of human life, condemnation and rejection of impunity and political assassination, acts of terrorism and subversive activities.

(p) Condemnation and rejection of unconstitutional changes of governments.

Article 5

Establishment of the organs of the Union: the Assembly of the Union; the Executive Council; the Pan-African Parliament; the Court of Justice; the Commission; the Permanent Representatives Committee; the Specialized Technical Committees; the Economic, Social, and Cultural Council; and the Financial Institutions.

Articles 6–9

The Assembly of Heads of State and Government is the supreme organ of the Union. The Assembly meets at least once a year in ordinary session and, at the request of any Member State and on approval by a two-thirds majority of the Member States, may meet in extraordinary session. The Assembly determines the common policies of the Union; takes decisions on reports and recommendations from the other organs of the Union; may establish other organs of the Union; monitors the implementation of policies and decisions of the Union and ensures compliance by all Member States; adopts the budget of the Union; gives directives to the Executive Council on the management of conflicts, war and other emergency situations and the restoration of peace; makes and terminates the appointment of judges of the Court of Human and Peoples' Rights; appoints the Chairman of the Commission and his or her deputy or deputies and the Commissioners of the Commission and determines their functions and terms of office. The Assembly may delegate any of its powers and functions to any organ of the Union.

Articles 10–13

The Executive Council, composed of the ministers of foreign affairs or other ministers or authorities designated by the member states, and responsible to the Assembly, co-ordinates and takes decisions on policies in areas of common interest to the Member States, including: foreign trade; energy, industry and mineral resources; food, agricultural and animal resources, livestock production and forestry; water resources and irrigation; environmental protection, humanitarian action and disaster response and relief; transport and communications; insurance; education, culture, health and human resources development; science and technology; nationality, residency and immigration matters; social security; establishment of a system of African rewards, medals and prizes.

Article 14–16

Establishment of the Specialized Technical Committees on: Rural Economy and Agricultural Matters; Monetary and Financial Affairs; Trade, Customs, and Immigration Matters; Industry, Science and Technology, Energy, Natural Resources and Environment; Transport Communications and Tourism; Health Labour and Social Affairs; and Education Culture and Human. Each Committee prepares, co-ordinates and reviews projects and programmes of the Union.

Article 17

Concerns the establishment of a Pan-African Parliament to ensure the full participation of African peoples in the development and economic integration of the continent. (The composition, powers, functions and organization of the Parliament shall be defined in a protocol relating thereto.)

Article 18

Establishment of a Court of Justice. (The composition, functions and organization of the Court shall be defined in a protocol relating thereto.)

Article 19

Establishment of the financial institutions of the Union (whose rules and regulations shall be defined in protocols relating thereto): the African Central Bank; the African Monetary Fund; and the African Investment Bank.

Article 20

Establishment of a Commission of the Union to act as the Union's Secretariat.

Article 21

Establishment of a Permanent Representatives Committee responsible for preparing the work of the Executive Council and acting on the instructions of the Council.

Article 22

Establishment of the Economic, Social and Cultural Council, composed of different social and professional groups from Union Member States, as an advisory organ.

Article 23

The Assembly shall determine the appropriate sanctions to be imposed on any Member State that defaults on payment of its contributions to the budget of the Union in the following manner: denial of the right to speak at meetings, to vote, to present candidates for any position or post within the Union, or to benefit from any activity or commitments therefrom. Furthermore, any Member State that fails to comply with the decisions and policies of the Union may be subject to sanctions, such as the denial of transport and communications links with other Member States or other measures of a political or economic nature.

Article 24

Establishment of the Headquarters of the Union in Addis Ababa, Ethiopia.

Article 25

The working languages of the Union and all its institutions shall be African languages, Arabic, English, French and Portuguese.

Article 26

The Court shall be seized with matters of interpretation arising from the application or implementation of the Act. (Pending its establishment such matters shall be submitted to the Assembly of the Union, which shall decide by a two-thirds majority.)

Article 29

Any African State may notify the Chairman of the Commission of its intention to accede to this Act and to be admitted as a member of the Union. Admission shall be decided by a simple majority of the Member States.

Article 30

Governments that come to power through unconstitutional means shall not be allowed to participate in the activities of the Union.

Article 31

Any State wishing to withdraw from the Union must give one year's written notification to the Chairman of the Commission.

Article 32

Amendments or revisions of this Act may be submitted to the Chairman of the Commission by any Member State and shall be adopted by the Assembly by consensus or by a two-thirds majority.

Article 33

This Act replaces the Charter of the Organization of African Unity. It takes precedence over and supersedes any inconsistent or contrary provisions of the Treaty establishing the African Economic Community.

ANDEAN COMMUNITY OF NATIONS

(COMUNIDAD ANDINA DE NACIONES—CAN)

Address: Paseo de la República 3895, San Isidro, Lima 27; Apdo 18-1177, Lima 18, Peru.

Telephone: (1) 4111400; **fax:** (1) 2213329; **e-mail:** contacto@comunidadandina.org; **internet:** www.comunidadandina.org.

The organization was established in 1969 as the Acuerdo de Cartagena (the Cartagena Agreement), also referred to as the Grupo Andino (Andean Group) or the Pacto Andino (Andean Pact). In March 1996 member countries signed a Reform Protocol of the Cartagena Agreement, in accordance with which the Andean Group was superseded in August 1997 by the Andean Community of Nations (CAN). The Community was to promote greater economic, commercial and political integration within a new Andean Integration System (Sistema Andino de Integración), comprising the organization's bodies and institutions.

MEMBERS

Bolivia Colombia Ecuador Peru

Note: Argentina, Brazil, Chile, Paraguay and Uruguay are associate members. Mexico, Panama and Spain have observer status. Venezuela withdrew from the Community in April 2006.

Organization

(June 2012)

ANDEAN PRESIDENTIAL COUNCIL

The presidential summits, which had been held annually since 1989, were formalized under the 1996 Reform Protocol of the Cartagena Agreement as the Andean Presidential Council. The Council is the highest-level body of the Andean Integration System, and provides the political leadership of the Community.

COMMISSION

The Commission consists of a plenipotentiary representative from each member country, with each country holding the presidency in turn. The Commission is the main policy-making organ of the Andean Community, and is responsible for co-ordinating Andean trade policy.

COUNCIL OF FOREIGN MINISTERS

The Council of Foreign Ministers meets annually or whenever it is considered necessary, to formulate common external policy and to co-ordinate the process of integration.

GENERAL SECRETARIAT

In August 1997 the General Secretariat assumed the functions of the Board of the Cartagena Agreement. The General Secretariat is the body charged with implementation of all guidelines and decisions issued by the bodies listed above. It submits proposals to the Commission for facilitating the fulfilment of the Community's objectives. Members are appointed for a three-year term. Under the reforms agreed in March 1996 the Secretary-General is elected by the Council of Foreign Ministers for a five-year term, and has enhanced powers to adjudicate in disputes arising between member states, as well as to manage the sub-regional integration process. There are three Directors-General.

Secretary-General a.i.: Dr Adalid Contreras Baspineiro (Bolivia).

PARLIAMENT

Parlamento Andino: Avda 13, No. 70-61, Bogotá, Colombia; tel. (1) 217-3357; fax (1) 348-2805; e-mail correo@parlamentoandino.org; internet www.parlamentoandino.org; f. 1979; comprises five members from each country, and meets in each capital city in turn; makes recommendations on regional policy; in April 1997 a new protocol was adopted that provided for the election of members by direct and universal voting; Pres. Rebeca Delgado Burgoa (Bolivia).

COURT OF JUSTICE

Tribunal de Justicia de la Comunidad Andina: Juan de Dios Martínez Mera 34-380 y Portugal, Sector Iglesia de Fátima, Quito, Ecuador; tel. (2) 3331417; e-mail tjca@tribunalandino.org.ec; internet www.tribunalandino.org.ec; f. 1979, began operating in 1984; a protocol approved in May 1996 (which came into force in August 1999) modified the Court's functions; its main responsibilities are to resolve disputes among member countries and interpret community legislation; comprises one judge from each member country, appointed for a six-year renewable period; the Presidency is assumed annually by each judge in turn; Pres. (2012) José Vicente Troya Jaramillo (Ecuador).

Activities

In May 1979, at Cartagena, Colombia, the Presidents of the then five member countries signed the 'Mandate of Cartagena', which envisaged greater economic and political co-operation, including the establishment of more sub-regional development programmes (especially in industry). In May 1989 the Group undertook to revitalize the process of Andean integration, by withdrawing measures that obstructed the programme of trade liberalization, and by complying with tariff reductions that had already been agreed upon. In May 1991, in Caracas, Venezuela, a summit meeting of the Andean Group agreed the framework for the establishment of a free trade area on 1 January 1992 (achieved in February 1993) and for an eventual Andean common market.

In March 1996 heads of state, meeting in Trujillo, Peru, agreed to a substantial restructuring of the Andean Group. They signed the Reform Protocol of the Cartagena Agreement, providing for the establishment of the Andean Community of Nations, which was to have greater ambitious economic and political objectives. Consequently, in August 1997 the Andean Community was inaugurated, and the Group's Junta was replaced by a new General Secretariat, headed by a Secretary-General with enhanced executive and decision-making powers. The initiation of these reforms was designed to accelerate harmonization in economic matters.

In April 2006 the President of Venezuela announced his intention to withdraw that country from the Andean Community, with immediate effect, expressing opposition to the bilateral free trade agreements signed by Colombia and Peru with the USA, on the grounds that they would undermine efforts to achieve regional economic integration. The Community countered that Venezuela's commitment to Andean integration had been placed in doubt by its declared allegiance to other regional groupings, in particular the Mercado Común del Sur (Mercosur).

In June 2012 Colombia and Peru, together with Chile and Mexico, inaugurated the Pacific Alliance, aimed at furthering eonomic integration.

POLITICAL CO-OPERATION

In June 2002 Community ministers of defence and of foreign affairs approved an Andean Charter for Peace and Security, establishing principles and commitments for the formulation of a policy on sub-regional security, the establishment of a zone of peace, joint action in efforts to counter terrorism, and the limitation of external defence spending. Other provisions included commitments to eradicate illegal trafficking in firearms, ammunition and explosives, to expand and reinforce confidence-building measures, and to establish verification mechanisms to strengthen dialogue and efforts in those areas. In January 2003 the Community concluded a co-operation agreement with Interpol providing for collaboration in combating national and transnational crime, and in June the presidential summit adopted an Andean Plan for the Prevention, Combating and Eradication of Small, Light Weapons. The heads of state, convened in Quirama, Colombia, also endorsed a new strategic direction for the Andean integration process based on developing the Andean common market, common foreign policy and social agenda, the physical integration of South America, and sustainable development.

A sub-regional workshop to formulate an Andean Plan to Fight Corruption was held in April 2005, organized by the General Secretariat and the European Commission. Heads of state expressed their commitment to the Plan in mid-2007, and in September 2008 Offices of the Controller General and other supervisory bodies in Andean countries agreed to implement the Plan. In November a meeting was convened, at the request of heads of state, of a Community Council of treasury or finance ministers, heads of central banks and ministers responsible for economic planning, in order to analyse the effects on the region of the severe global economic and financial downturn. The Council met again in February 2009 to consider various technical studies that had been undertaken.

At the 13th presidential summit, held in Valencia, Venezuela, in June 2001, heads of state adopted an Andean Co-operation Plan for the Control of Illegal Drugs and Related Offences, designed to promote a united approach to combating these problems. In July 2005 the Council of Foreign Ministers approved an Andean Alternative Development Strategy, which aimed to support sustainable local development initiatives, including alternatives to the production of illegal drug crops. In August 2009 the Council approved a financing agreement with the European Union (EU) to implement an anti-illegal drug programme in the Andean Community.

In June 2003 ministers of foreign affairs and foreign trade adopted 16 legal provisions aimed at giving maximum priority to the social dimension of integration within the Community, including a measure providing for mobility of workers between member countries. A new Andean passport system, which had been approved in 2001, entered into effect in December 2005.

TRADE

A council for customs affairs met for the first time in January 1982, aiming to harmonize national legislation within the group. In December 1984 the member states launched a common currency, the Andean peso, aiming to reduce dependence on the US dollar and to increase regional trade. The new currency was to be supported by special contributions to the Fondo Andino de Reservas (now the Fondo Latinoamericano de Reservas) amounting to US $80m., and was to be 'pegged' to the US dollar, taking the form of financial drafts rather than notes and coins.

The 'Caracas Declaration' of May 1991 provided for the establishment of an Andean free trade area (AFTA), which entered into effect (excluding Peru—see below) in February 1993. Heads of state also agreed in May 1991 to create a common external tariff (CET), to standardize member countries' trade barriers in their dealings with the rest of the world, and envisaged the eventual creation of an Andean common market. In December heads of state defined four main levels of external tariffs (between 5% and 20%). In August 1992 the Group approved a request by Peru for the suspension of its rights and obligations under the Pact, thereby enabling the other members to proceed with hitherto stalled negotiations on the CET. Peru was readmitted as a full member of the Group in 1994, but participated only as an observer in the ongoing negotiations.

In November 1994 ministers of trade and integration, meeting in Quito, Ecuador, concluded a final agreement on a four-tier structure of external tariffs (although Bolivia was to retain a two-level system). The CET agreement came into effect on 1 February 1995, covering 90% of the region's imports which were to be subject to the following tariff bands: 5% for raw materials; 10%–15% for semi-manufactured goods; and 20% for finished products. In order to reach an agreement, special treatment and exemptions were granted, while Peru, initially, was to remain a 'non-active' member of the accord. In June 1997 an agreement was concluded to ensure Peru's continued membership of the Community, which provided for that country's integration into AFTA. The Peruvian Government determined to eliminate customs duties on some 2,500 products with immediate effect. The process of incorporating Peru into AFTA was completed by January 2006.

In May 1999 the 11th presidential summit agreed to establish the Andean Common Market by 2005; the Community adopted a policy on border integration and development to prepare the border regions of member countries for the envisaged free circulation of people, goods, capital and services, while consolidating sub-regional security. In June 2001 the Community agreed to recognize national identification documents issued by member states as sufficient for tourist travel in the sub-region. Community heads of state, meeting in January 2002 at a special Andean presidential summit, agreed to consolidate and improve the free trade zone by mid-2002 and apply a new CET (with four levels, i.e. 0%, 5%, 10% and 20%). To facilitate this process a common agricultural policy was to be adopted and macroeconomic policies were to be harmonized. In October member governments determined the new tariff levels applicable to 62% of products and agreed the criteria for negotiating levels for the remainder. Although the new CET was to become effective on 1 January 2004, this date was subsequently postponed. In January 2006 ministers of trade approved a working programme to define the Community's common tariff policy, which was to incorporate a flexible CET. The value of intra-Community trade totalled some US $5,774m. in 2009, and increased to $7,810m. in 2010.

In May 2011 the Commission approved the establishment of an Andean Committee on Micro, Small and Medium-sized Enterprises (MSMEs), mandated to advise and support the Commission and General Secretariat in efforts to support MSMEs. At the same time the Commission endorsed the establishment of an Andean Observatory on MSMEs as a mechanism for monitoring the development and needs of MSMEs in the sub-region, as well as the impact of corporate policy instruments on their competitiveness.

EXTERNAL RELATIONS

In September 1995 heads of state of member countries identified the formulation of common positions on foreign relations as an important part of the process of relaunching the integration initiative. A Protocol Amending the Cartagena Agreement was signed in June 1997 to confirm the formulation of a common foreign policy. During 1998 the General Secretariat held consultations with government experts, academics, representatives of the private sector and other interested parties to help formulate a document on guidelines for a common foreign policy. The guidelines, establishing the principles, objectives and mechanisms of a common foreign policy, were approved by the Council of Foreign Ministers in 1999. In July 2004 Andean ministers of foreign affairs approved new guidelines for an Andean common policy on external security. The ministers, meeting in Quito, Ecuador, also adopted a Declaration on the Establishment of an Andean Peace Zone, free from nuclear, chemical or biological weapons. In April 2005 the Community Secretariat signed a Memorandum of Understanding with the Organization for the Prohibition of Chemical Weapons, which aimed to consolidate the Andean Peace Zone, assist countries to implement the Chemical Arms Convention and promote further collaboration between the two groupings.

A co-operation agreement with the EU was signed in April 1993, establishing a Mixed Commission to further deliberation and co-operation between the two organizations. A Euro-Andean Forum is held periodically to promote mutual co-operation, trade and investment. In February 1998 the Community signed a co-operation and technical assistance agreement with the EU in order to combat drugs trafficking. At the first summit meeting of Latin American and Caribbean (LAC) and EU leaders held in Rio de Janeiro, Brazil, in June 1999, Community-EU discussions were held on strengthening economic, trade and political co-operation and on the possibility of concluding an Association Agreement. In May 2002 the EU adopted a Regional Strategy for the Andean Community covering the period 2002–06. Following the second LAC and EU summit meeting, held in May 2002 in Madrid, Spain, a Political Dialogue and Co-operation Agreement was signed in December 2003. In May 2004 a meeting of the two sides held during the third LAC-EU summit, in Guadalajara, Mexico, confirmed that an EU-CAN Association Agreement was a common strategic objective. In January 2005 an ad hoc working group was established in order to undertake a joint appraisal exercise on regional economic integration. The fourth LAC and EU summit meeting, held in Vienna, Austria, in May 2006, approved the establishment of an EU-LAC Parliamentary Assembly; this was inaugurated in November. Negotiations on an Association Agreement were formally inaugurated at the meeting of Andean heads of state held in Tarifa, Bolivia, in June 2007, and the first round of negotiations was held in September. In May 2008 heads of state of the Andean Community confirmed that they would continue to negotiate the agreement as a single group; however, in December the EU announced that it was to commence negotiations for separate free trade agreements with Colombia and Peru. Bolivia criticized the decision as undermining the Andean integration process. In March 2010 the EU-CAN Mixed Commission agreed on a programme of co-operation in 2011–13, with funding commitments of €17.5m. for projects concerned with economic integration, countering illicit drugs production and trafficking, and environmental protection. An EU-CAN summit meeting was held in Madrid in May 2010.

Since December 1991 exports from Andean Community countries have benefited from preferential access to US markets under the Andean Trade Preference Act. In August 2002 the legislation was renewed and amended under a new Andean Trade Preference and Drug Eradication Act, which provided duty free access for more than 6,000 products with the objective of supporting legal trade transactions in order to help to counter the production and trafficking of illegal narcotic drugs. The Act was initially scheduled to expire in December 2006, but has been periodically extended by the US Congress. In December 2008 the US President suspended Bolivia's eligibility under the Act owing to its failure to meet its counternarcotics requirements.

In August 1999 the Secretary-General of the Community visited Guyana in order to promote bilateral trading opportunities and to strengthen relations with the Caribbean Community. The Community held a meeting on trade relations with the Caribbean Community during 2000.

In March 2000 the Andean Community concluded an agreement to establish a political consultation and co-operation mechanism with the People's Republic of China. At the first ministerial meeting within this framework, which took place in October 2002, it was agreed that consultations would be held thereafter on a biennial basis. The first meeting of the Council of Foreign Ministers with the Chinese Vice-President took place in January 2005. A high-level meeting between senior officials from Community member states and Japan was organized in December 2002; further consultations were to be convened, aimed at cultivating closer relations.

In April 1998, at the 10th Andean presidential summit, an agreement was signed with Panama establishing a framework for negotiations providing for the conclusion of a free trade accord by the end of 1998 and for Panama's eventual associate membership of the Community. A political dialogue and co-operation agreement, a requirement for Panama's associate membership status, was signed by both sides in September 2007. Mexico was invited to assume observer status in September 2004. In November 2006 Mexico and the Andean Community signed an agreement to establish a mechanism for political dialogue and co-operation in areas of mutual interest. The first meeting of the mechanism was held in New York, USA, in September 2007. In November 2004 the Community signed a framework agreement with the Central American Integration System (SICA) to strengthen dialogue and co-operation between the two blocs of countries. In January 2011 the Secretaries-General of the two organizations, meeting in San Salvador, El Salvador, determined to reactivate the agreement and pursue greater collaboration.

The Community signed a framework agreement with Mercosur on the establishment of a free trade accord in April 1998. Although negotiations between the Community and Mercosur were subsequently delayed, bilateral agreements between the countries of the two groupings were extended. Preferential tariff agreements were concluded with Brazil and Argentina, entering into effect in July 1999 and August 1999 and August 2000, respectively. The Community commenced negotiations on drafting a preferential tariff agreement with (jointly) El Salvador, Guatemala and Honduras in March 2000. In September leaders of the Community and Mercosur, meeting at a summit of Latin American heads of state, determined to relaunch negotiations, with a view to establishing a free trade area. In July 2001 ministers of foreign affairs of the two groupings approved the establishment of a formal mechanism for political dialogue and co-ordination in order to facilitate negotiations and to enhance economic and social integration. In December 2003 Mercosur and the Andean Community signed an Economic Complementary Agreement providing for free trade provisions, according to which tariffs on 80% of trade between the two groupings were to be phased out by 2014 and tariffs to be removed from the remaining 20% of, initially protected, products by 2019. The accord did not enter into force in July 2004, as planned, owing to delays in drafting the tariff reduction schedule. Members of the Latin American Integration Association (Aladi) remaining outside Mercosur and the Andean Community—Cuba, Chile and Mexico—were to be permitted to apply to join the envisaged larger free trade zone. In July 2005 the Community granted Argentina, Brazil, Paraguay and Uruguay associate membership of the grouping, as part of efforts to achieve a reciprocal association agreement. Chile was granted observer status in December 2004, and in September 2006 was formally invited to join the Community as an associate member. In December the first meeting of the CAN-Chile Joint Commission was convened in Cochabamba, Bolivia. An agreement on Chile's full participation in all Community bodies and mechanisms was approved in July 2007. In February 2010 ministers of foreign affairs of the Community and Mercosur agreed to establish a CAN–Mercosur Mixed Commission to facilitate enhanced co-operation between the countries of the two organizations.

In December 2004 leaders from 12 Latin American countries attending a pan-South American summit, convened in Cusco, Peru, approved in principle the creation of a new South American Community of Nations (SACN). It was envisaged that negotiations on the formation of the new Community, which was to entail the merger of the Andean Community, Mercosur and Aladi (with the participation of Chile, Guyana and Suriname), would be completed within 15 years. A region-wide meeting of ministers of foreign affairs was held in April 2005, within the framework of establishing the SACN. The first South American Community meeting of heads of state convened in September, in Brasília, Brazil. The meeting issued mandates to the heads of sub-regional organizations to consider integration processes, the convergence of economic agreements and common plans of action.

In April 2007, at the first South American Energy Summit, held in Margarita Island, Venezuela, heads of state endorsed the establishment of a Union of South American Nations (UNASUR), to replace the SACN as the lead organization for regional integration. It was envisaged that UNASUR would have political decision-making functions, supported by a small permanent secretariat, to be located in Quito, and would co-ordinate on economic and trade matters with the Andean Community, Mercosur and Aladi. At a summit meeting convened in May 2008, in Brasília, a constitutional document formally establishing UNASUR was signed. In December Brazil hosted a Latin American and Caribbean Summit on Integration and Development, which aimed to strengthen the commitment by all countries in the region to work together in support of sustainable development. The meeting issued the Salvador Declaration, which pledged support to strengthen co-operation among the regional and sub-regional groupings, to pursue further consultation and joint efforts to counter regional effects of the global financial crisis, and to promote closer collaboration on issues including energy, food security, social development, physical infrastructure and natural disaster management. The first informal meeting of the General Secretariat of the Andean Community and UNASUR was held in January 2010, in Lima, Peru.

At a special meeting of the Andean Council of Presidents, held in Bogotá, Colombia, in November 2011, heads of state agreed to strengthen the CAN, and requested that the acting Secretary-General of the Community identify jointly, with the General Secretariats of both Mercosur and UNASUR, common and complementary elements and differences prior to the future convergence of the three processes.

Spain was awarded observer status in August 2011.

INDUSTRY AND ENERGY

In May 1987 member countries signed the Quito Protocol, modifying the Cartagena Agreement, to amend the strict rules that had formerly been imposed on foreign investors in the region. In March 1991 the Protocol was amended, with the aim of further liberalizing foreign investment and stimulating an inflow of foreign capital and technology. External and regional investors were to be permitted to repatriate their profits (in accordance with the laws of the country concerned) and there was no stipulation that a majority share-holding must eventually be transferred to local investors. A further directive, adopted in March, covered the formation of multinational enterprises to ensure that at least two member countries have a shareholding of 15% or more of the capital, including the country where the enterprise was to be based. These enterprises were entitled to participate in sectors otherwise reserved for national enterprises, subject to the same conditions as national enterprises in terms of taxation and export regulations, and to gain access to the markets of all member countries. In September 1999 Colombia, Ecuador and Venezuela signed an accord to facilitate the production and sale of vehicles within the region; the agreement became effective in January 2000.

In November 1988 member states established a bank, the Banco Intermunicipal Andino, which was to finance public works. In October 2004 a sub-regional committee on small and medium-sized enterprises (SMEs) endorsed efforts by the Community Secretariat to establish an Andean System of SME Guarantees to facilitate their access to credit.

In May 1995 the Group initiated a programme to promote the use of cheap and efficient energy sources and greater co-operation in the energy sector. The programme planned to develop a regional electricity grid. During 2003 efforts were undertaken to establish an Andean Energy Alliance, with the aim of fostering the development of integrated electricity and gas markets, as well as developing renewable energy sources, promoting 'energy clusters' and ensuring regional energy security. The first meeting of ministers of energy, electricity, hydrocarbons and mines, convened in Quito, Ecuador, in January 2004, endorsed the Alliance. In August 2011 representatives of Andean electricity regulatory bodies, including that of Chile, agreed upon transitional arrangements to provide for trade in surplus electricity and greater interconnectivity. Andean Community heads of state, meeting in Bogotá, Colombia, in November, pledged to boost the integration of regional energy. In February 2012 the Community held the first meeting of representatives of mining and environment authorities to discuss issues relating to illegal mining activities, in order to promote co-ordinated efforts against those activities, and to initiate the development of a legal directive to counter illegal mining.

TRANSPORT AND COMMUNICATIONS

The Andean Community has pursued efforts to improve infrastructure throughout the region. In 1983 the Commission formulated a plan to assist land locked Bolivia, particularly through improving roads connecting it with neighbouring countries and the Pacific Ocean. An 'open skies' agreement, giving airlines of member states equal rights to airspace and airport facilities within the grouping, was signed in May 1991. In June 1998 the Commission approved the establishment of an Andean Commission of Land Transportation Authorities, to oversee the operation and development of land transportation services. Similarly, an Andean Committee of Water Transportation Authorities was established to ensure compliance with Community regulations regarding ocean transportation activities. The Community aims to facilitate the movement of goods throughout the region by the use of different modes of transport ('multimodal transport') and to guarantee operational standards. It also intends to harmonize Community transport regulations and standards with those of Mercosur countries. In September 2005 the first summit meeting of the proposed SACN issued a declaration to support and accelerate infrastructure, transport and communications integration throughout the region.

In August 1996 a regulatory framework was approved for the development of a commercial Andean satellite system. In December 1997 the General Secretariat approved regulations for granting authorization for the use of the system; the Commission subsequently granted the first Community authorization to an Andean multinational enterprise (Andesat), comprising 48 companies from all five member states. In 1994 the Community initiated efforts to establish digital technology infrastructure throughout the Community: the resulting Andean Digital Corridor comprises ground, underwater and satellite routes providing a series of cross-border interconnections between the member countries. In 2000 an Andean Internet System was operational in Colombia, Ecuador and Venezuela. In May 1999 the Andean Committee of Telecommunications Authorities agreed to remove all restrictions to free trade in telecommunications services (excluding sound broadcasting and television) by 1 January 2002. The Committee also determined to formulate provisions on interconnection and the safeguarding of free competition and principles of transparency within the sector. In November 2006 the Andean Community approved a new regulatory framework for the commercial exploitation of the Andean satellite system belonging to member states.

Asociación de Empresas de Telecomunicaciones de la Comunidad Andina (ASETA): Calle La Pradera E7–41 y San Salvador, Casilla 17-1106042, Quito, Ecuador; tel. (2) 256-3812; fax (2) 256-2499; e-mail aseta@aseta.org; internet www.aseta.org; f. 1974; co-ordinates improvements in national telecommunications services, in order to contribute to the further integration of the countries of the Andean Community; Sec.-Gen. MARCELO LÓPEZ ARJONA.

RURAL DEVELOPMENT AND FOOD SECURITY

In 1984 the Andean Food Security System was created to develop the agrarian sector, replace imports progressively with local produce, and improve rural living conditions. In April 1998 the Presidential Council instructed the Commission, together with ministers of agriculture, to formulate an Andean Common Agricultural Policy, including measures to harmonize trade policy instruments and legislation on animal and plant health. The 12th Andean presidential summit, held in June 2000, authorized the adoption of the concluded Policy and the enforcement of a plan of action for its implementation. In January 2002, at the special Andean presidential summit, it was agreed that all countries in the bloc would adopt price stabilization mechanisms for agricultural products.

In July 2004 Andean ministers of agriculture approved a series of objectives and priority actions to form the framework of a Regional Food Security Policy. Also in July Andean heads of state endorsed the Andean Rural Development and Agricultural Competitiveness Programme to promote sub-regional efforts in areas such as rural development, food security, production competitiveness, animal health and technological innovation. In October 2005 ministers of trade and of agriculture approved the establishment of a special fund to finance the programme, the Fund for Rural Development and Agricultural Productivity. In late 2010 it was reported that the Fund was part-financing 14 production projects in rural and border areas where poverty was prevalent.

ENVIRONMENT

In March–April 2005 the first meeting of an Andean Community Council of Ministers of the Environment and Sustainable Development was convened, in Paracas, Peru. An Andean Environmental Agenda, covering the period 2006–10, aimed to strengthen the capacities of member countries with regard to environmental and sustainable development issues, in particular biodiversity, climate change and water resources. In accordance with the Agenda the Community was working to establish an Andean Institute for Biodiversity, and to establish and implement regional strategies on integrated water resource management and on climate change. In June 2007 the Secretariat signed an agreement with Finland to develop a regional biodiversity programme in the Amazon region of Andean member countries (BioCAN). The Council of Foreign Ministers, meeting in February 2010, approved implementation of BioCAN. In October 2007 the Secretariat organized Clima Latino, hosted by two city authorities in Ecuador, comprising conferences, workshops and cultural events at which climate change was addressed. The Community represented member countries at the conference of parties to the UN Framework Convention on Climate Change, held in Bali, Indonesia, in December, and demanded greater international political commitment and funding to combat the effects of climate change, in particular to monitor and protect the Amazon rainforest. In November 2011, at a special meeting of the Andean Council of Presidents in Bogotá, Colombia, heads of state asserted their intention to work together to reach a common position for the UN Conference on Sustainable Development ('Rio+20'), which was held in June 2012.

In July 2002 an Andean Committee for Disaster Prevention and Relief (CAPRADE) was established to help mitigate the risk and impact of natural disasters in the sub-region. CAPRADE was to be responsible for implementing the Andean Strategy for Disaster Prevention and Relief, which was approved by the Council of Foreign Ministers in July 2004. A new Strategy for Natural Disaster Prevention and Relief was approved in August 2009, which aimed to link activities for disaster prevention and relief to those related to the environmental agenda, climate change and integrated water management. An Andean University Network in Risk Management and Climate Change promotes information exchange between some 32 institutions.

SOCIAL INTEGRATION

Several formal agreements and institutions have been established within the framework of the Andean Integration System to enhance social development and welfare. In May 1999 the 11th Andean presidential summit adopted a 'multidimensional social agenda' focusing on job creation and on improvements in the fields of education, health and housing throughout the Community. In June 2000 the 12th presidential summit instructed the Andean institutions to prepare individual programmes aimed at consolidating implementation of the Community's integration programme and advancing the development of the social agenda, in order to promote greater involvement of representatives of civil society. In July 2004 Community heads of state declared support for a new Andean Council of Social Development Ministers. Other bodies established in 2003/04 included Councils of Ministers of Education and of Ministers responsible for Cultural Policies, and a Consultative Council of Municipal Authorities. During 2009 work was undertaken to develop and implement an Integral Plan for Social Development, first approved by the Council of Foreign Ministers in September 2004. In August 2009 the Council of Foreign Ministers endorsed the establishment of an Andean Council of Authorities of Women's Affairs as a forum for regional consideration of equal opportunities and gender issues. In March 2010 representatives of Andean cultural authorities determined to initiate an Andean Development Plan for Cultural Industries. In the previous month a Permanent Working Network on Andean Cinema was established. In December Andean ministers of foreign affairs endorsed 2011 as the Andean Year of Social Integration, which aimed to promote Community policies and initiatives regarding equality, cohesion and social and territorial integration. In July 2011 Andean ministers responsible for social development approved 11 Andean Social Development Objectives, which they pledged to achieve by 2019, and a new Andean Economic and Social Cohesion Strategy to support the accomplishment of those targets.

In June 2007 Community heads of state approved the establishment of a Working Committee on Indigenous People's Rights. In July the Community convened the first forum of intellectuals and researchers to strengthen the debate on indigenous issues and their incorporation into the integration process. A Consultative Council of Indigenous Peoples of the Andean Community was founded in September to promote the participation of representatives of indigenous communities in the Andean integration process.

INSTITUTIONS

Consejo Consultivo de Pueblos Indígenos de la Comunidad Andina (Consultative Council of Indigenous Peoples of the Andean Community): Paseo de la República 3895, Lima, Peru; tel. (1) 4111400; fax (1) 2213329; f. 2007; first meeting held in September 2008; aims to strengthen the participation of indigenous peoples in the sub-regional integration process.

Consejo Consultivo Empresarial Andino (Andean Business Advisory Council): Asociación Nacional de Industriales, Calle 73, No. 8–13, Bogotá, Colombia; tel. (1) 3268500; fax (1) 3473198; e-mail jnarino@andi.com.co; first meeting held in Nov. 1998; an advisory institution within the framework of the Sistema Andino de Integración; comprises elected representatives of business organizations; advises Community ministers and officials on integration activities affecting the business sector; Chair. JUAN CAMILO NARIÑO ALCOCER (Colombia).

Consejo Consultivo Laboral Andino (Andean Labour Advisory Council): Paseo de la República 3832, Of. 502, San Isidro, Lima 27, Peru; tel. (1) 6181701; fax (1) 6100139; e-mail cutperujcb@gmail.com; internet www.ccla.org.pe; f. 1998; an advisory institution within the framework of the Sistema Andino de Integración; comprises elected representatives of labour organizations; advises Community ministers and officers on related labour issues; Chair. VÍCTOR JOSÉ PARDO RODRÍGUEZ (Colombia).

Convenio Andrés Bello (Andrés Bello Agreement): Avda Carrera 20 85-60, Bogotá, Colombia; tel. (1) 644-9292; fax (1) 610-0139; e-mail ecobello@col1.telecom.com.co; internet www.convenioandresbello.org; f. 1970, modified in 1990; aims to promote integration in the educational, technical and cultural sectors; a new Inter-institutional Co-operation Agreement was signed with the Secretariat of the CAN in Aug. 2003; mems: Bolivia, Chile, Colombia, Cuba, Dominican Republic, Ecuador, Mexico, Panama, Paraguay, Peru, Spain, Venezuela; Exec. Sec. Dr FRANCISCO HUERTA MONTALVO (Ecuador).

Convenio Hipólito Unanue (Hipólito Unanue Agreement): Edif. Cartagena, Paseo de la República 3832, 3°, San Isidro, Lima, Peru; tel. (1) 2210074; fax (1) 2222663; e-mail postmaster@conhu.org.pe; internet www.orasconhu.org; f. 1971 on the occasion of the first meeting of Andean ministers of health; became part of the institutional structure of the Community in 1998; aims to enhance the development of health services, and to promote regional co-ordination in areas such as environmental health, disaster preparedness and the prevention and control of drug abuse; Exec. Sec. Dr CAROLINE CHANG CAMPOS (Ecuador).

Convenio Simón Rodríguez (Simón Rodríguez Agreement): Paseo de la República 3895, esq. Aramburú, San Isidro, Lima 27, Peru; tel. (1) 4111400; fax (1) 2213329; promotes a convergence of social and labour conditions throughout the Community, for example, working hours and conditions, employment and social security policies, and to promote the participation of workers and employers in the sub-regional integration process; Protocol of Modification signed in June 2001; ratification process ongoing.

Corporación Andina de Fomento (CAF) (Andean Development Corporation): Torre CAF, Avda Luis Roche, Altamira, Apdo 5086, Caracas, Venezuela; tel. (212) 2092111; fax (212) 2092444; e-mail infocaf@caf.com; internet www.caf.com; f. 1968, began operations in 1970; aims to encourage the integration of the Andean countries by specialization and an equitable distribution of investments; conducts research to identify investment opportunities, and prepares the resulting investment projects; gives technical and financial assistance; and attracts internal and external credit; auth. cap. US $10,000m.; subscribed or underwritten by the governments of member countries, or by public, semi-public and private sector institutions authorized by those governments; the Board of Directors comprises representatives of each country at ministerial level; mems: the Andean Community, Argentina, Brazil, Chile, Costa Rica, Jamaica, Mexico, Panama, Paraguay, Spain, Trinidad and Tobago, Uruguay, Venezuela, and 15 private banks in the Andean region; Exec. Pres. ENRIQUE GARCÍA RODRÍGUEZ (Bolivia).

Fondo Latinoamericano de Reservas (FLAR) (Latin American Reserve Fund): Avda 82 12–18, 7°, POB 241523, Bogotá, Colombia; tel. (1) 634-4360; fax (1) 634-4384; e-mail flar@flar.net; internet www.flar.net; f. 1978 as the Fondo Andino de Reservas to support the balance of payments of member countries, provide credit, guarantee loans, and contribute to the harmonization of monetary and financial policies; adopted present name in 1991, in order to allow the admission of other Latin American countries; in 1992 the Fund began extending credit lines to commercial cos for export financing; it is administered by an Assembly of the ministers of finance and economy of the member countries, and a Board of Directors comprising the Presidents of the central banks of the member states; mems: Bolivia, Colombia, Costa Rica, Ecuador, Peru,

Uruguay, Venezuela; subscribed cap. US $2,343.8m. cap. p.u. $1,864.5m. (31 Aug. 2010); Exec. Pres. ANA MARÍA CARRASQUILLA.

Universidad Andina Simón Bolívar (Simón Bolívar Andean University): Real Audiencia 73, Casilla 545, Sucre, Bolivia; tel. (4) 6460265; fax (4) 6460833; e-mail uasb@uasb.edu.bo; internet www.uasb.edu.bo; f. 1985; institution for postgraduate study and research; promotes co-operation between other universities in the Andean region; branches in Quito (Ecuador), La Paz (Bolivia), Caracas (Venezuela) and Cali (Colombia); Pres. (Sucre Office) JOSÉ LUIS GUITIÉRREZ SARDÁN.

Publications

Reports, working papers, sector documents, council proceedings.

ARAB FUND FOR ECONOMIC AND SOCIAL DEVELOPMENT—AFESD

Address: POB 21923, Safat, 13080 Kuwait.

Telephone: 24959000; **fax:** 24815760; **e-mail:** hq@arabfund.org; **internet:** www.arabfund.org.

Established in 1968 by the Economic Council of the Arab League, the Fund began its operations in 1974. It participates in the financing of economic and social development projects in the Arab states.

MEMBERS

All member countries of the League of Arab States.

Organization

(June 2012)

BOARD OF GOVERNORS

The Board of Governors consists of a Governor and an Alternate Governor appointed by each member of the Fund. The Board of Governors is considered as the General Assembly of the Fund, and has all powers.

BOARD OF DIRECTORS

The Board of Directors is composed of eight Directors elected by the Board of Governors from among Arab citizens of recognized experience and competence. They are elected for a renewable term of two years.

The Board of Directors is charged with all the activities of the Fund and exercises the powers delegated to it by the Board of Governors.

Director-General and Chairman of the Board of Directors: ABDLATIF YOUSUF AL-HAMAD (Kuwait).

FINANCIAL STRUCTURE

The Fund's authorized capital is 800m. Kuwaiti dinars (KD) divided into 80,000 shares having a value of KD 10,000 each. In April 2008 the Board of Governors approved a transfer of KD 1,337m. from the Fund's additional capital reserves to paid-up capital, increasing subscribed capital from KD 663m. to KD 2,000m. At 31 December 2011 shareholders' equity amounted to KD 2,717.2m. (including KD 717m. in reserves).

Activities

Pursuant to the Agreement Establishing the Fund (as amended in 1997 by the Board of Governors), the purpose of the Fund is to contribute to the financing of economic and social development projects in the Arab states and countries by:

1. Financing economic development projects of an investment character by means of loans granted on concessionary terms to governments and public enterprises and corporations, giving preference to projects which are vital to the Arab entity, as well as to joint Arab projects;
2. Financing private sector projects in member states by providing all forms of loans and guarantees to corporations and enterprises (possessing juridical personality), participating in their equity capital, and providing other forms of financing and the requisite financial, technical and advisory services, in accordance with such regulations and subject to such conditions as may be prescribed by the Board of Directors;
3. Forming or participating in the equity capital of corporations possessing juridical personality, for the implementation and financing of private sector projects in member states, including the provision and financing of technical, advisory and financial services;
4. Establishing and administering special funds with aims compatible with those of the Fund and with resources provided by the Fund or other sources;
5. Encouraging, directly or indirectly, the investment of public and private capital in a manner conducive to the development and growth of the Arab economy;
6. Providing expertise and technical assistance in the various fields of economic development.

The Fund co-operates with other Arab organizations such as the Arab Monetary Fund, the League of Arab States and the Organization of Arab Petroleum Exporting Countries in preparing regional studies and conferences, for example in the areas of human resource development, demographic research and private sector financing of infrastructure projects. It also acts as the secretariat of the Co-ordination Group of Arab National and Regional Development Financing Institutions. These organizations work together to produce a *Joint Arab Economic Report*, which considers economic and social developments in the Arab states. In March 2011 the Fund hosted the first in a series of annual Arab Development Symposiums, to be organized jointly with the World Bank. The inaugural Symposium concerned 'Water and Food Security in the Arab World'. In September the Fund endorsed the so-called Deauville Partnership, which had been established by the Group of Eight industrialized countries in May in order to assist countries in the Middle East and North Africa undergoing social and economic transformations. The Fund joined some nine other international financial institutions active in the region to establish a Co-ordination Platform to facilitate and promote collaboration among the institutions extending assistance under the Partnership.

During 2011 the Fund approved 12 loans, totalling KD 340m., to help finance public sector projects in six member countries. One private sector project was appraised in 2011: a storage services initiative in Abu Rawash, Egypt. At the end of that year total lending since 1974 amounted to KD 7,219.1m., which had helped to finance 580 projects in 17 Arab countries. In 2011 42% of financing was for energy and electricity projects, while 32% was for projects in the transport and telecommunications sector. During the period 1974–2011 33.4% of project financing was for energy and electric power projects, 25.9% for projects in the area of transport and telecom, 14.9% for agriculture and rural development, 10.0% for water and sewerage, 7.4% in the area of social services, and 6.1% for industry and mining.

During 2011 the Fund extended 37 inter-Arab and national grants, totalling KD 13.4m., providing for technical assistance, training, research activities and other emergency assistance programmes. The cumulative total number of grants provided by the end of 2011 was 983, with a value of KD 175.9m.

In December 1997 AFESD initiated an Arab Fund Fellowships Programme, which aimed to provide grants to Arab academics to conduct university teaching or advanced research. During 2010 the Fund contributed US $100m. to a new Special Account to finance small and medium-sized private sector projects in Arab countries, which had first been proposed in January 2009. The Fund administers the Account, and hosted its inaugural meeting in October 2010.

Publications

Annual Report.

Joint Arab Economic Report (annually).

Statistics

LOANS BY SECTOR

Sector	2011 Amount (US $ million)	2011 %	1974–2011 %
Infrastructure sectors	260.0	76.5	69.3
Transport and telecommunications	110.0	32.3	25.9
Energy and electricity	142.0	41.8	33.4
Water and sewerage	8.0	2.4	10.0
Productive sectors	50.0	14.7	21.0
Industry and mining	0.0	0.0	6.1
Agriculture and rural development	50.0	14.7	14.9
Social services	30.0	8.8	7.4
Other	0.0	0.0	2.3
Total	340.0	100.0	100.0

Source: AFESD, *Annual Report 2011*.

ARAB MONETARY FUND

Address: Arab Monetary Fund Bldg, Corniche Rd, POB 2818, Abu Dhabi, United Arab Emirates.

Telephone: (2) 6171400; **fax:** (2) 6326454; **e-mail:** centralmail@amfad.org.ae; **internet:** www.amf.org.ae.

The Agreement establishing the Arab Monetary Fund was approved by the Economic Council of Arab States in Rabat, Morocco, in April 1976 and entered into force on 2 February 1977.

MEMBERS

Algeria	Morocco
Bahrain	Oman
Comoros	Palestine
Djibouti	Qatar
Egypt	Saudi Arabia
Iraq*	Somalia*
Jordan	Sudan*
Kuwait	Syria
Lebanon	Tunisia
Libya	United Arab Emirates
Mauritania	Yemen

* From July 1993 loans to Iraq, Somalia and Sudan were suspended as a result of non-repayment of debts to the Fund. Sudan was readmitted in April 2000, following a settlement of its arrears; a Memorandum of Understanding, to incorporate new loan repayments was concluded in September 2001. An agreement to reschedule Iraq's outstanding arrears was concluded in 2008.

Organization

(June 2012)

BOARD OF GOVERNORS

The Board of Governors is the highest authority of the Arab Monetary Fund. It formulates policies on Arab economic integration and the liberalization of trade among member states. With certain exceptions, it may delegate to the Board of Executive Directors some of its powers. The Board of Governors is composed of a governor and a deputy governor appointed by each member state for a term of five years. It meets at least once a year; meetings may also be convened at the request of half the members, or of members holding half of the total voting power.

BOARD OF EXECUTIVE DIRECTORS

The Board of Executive Directors exercises all powers vested in it by the Board of Governors and may delegate to the Director-General such powers as it deems fit. It is composed of the Director-General and eight non-resident directors elected by the Board of Governors. Each director holds office for three years and may be re-elected.

DIRECTOR-GENERAL

The Director-General of the Fund is appointed by the Board of Governors for a renewable five-year term, and serves as Chairman of the Board of Executive Directors.

The Director-General supervises Committees on Loans, Investments, and Administration. Other offices include the Economic and Technical Department, the Economic Policy Institute, the Investment Department, the Legal Department, an Internal Audit Office, and the Finance and Computer Department.

Director-General and Chairman of the Board of Executive Directors: Dr Jassim Abdullah al-Mannai.

FINANCE

The Arab Accounting Dinar (AAD) is a unit of account equivalent to three IMF Special Drawing Rights (SDRs). (The average value of the SDR in 2011 was US $1.57868.)

In April 1983 the authorized capital of the Fund was increased from AAD 288m. to AAD 600m. The new capital stock comprised 12,000 shares, each having the value of AAD 50,000. At the end of 2010 total paid-up capital was AAD 596.04m.

CAPITAL SUBSCRIPTIONS

(million Arab Accounting Dinars, 31 December 2010)

Member	Paid-up capital
Algeria	77.90
Bahrain	9.20
Comoros	0.45
Djibouti	0.45
Egypt	58.80
Iraq	77.90
Jordan	9.90
Kuwait	58.80
Lebanon	9.20
Libya	24.69
Mauritania	9.20
Morocco	27.55
Oman	9.20
Palestine	3.96
Qatar	18.40
Saudi Arabia	88.95
Somalia	7.35
Sudan	18.40
Syria	13.25
Tunisia	12.85
United Arab Emirates	35.30
Yemen	28.30
Total*	596.04

* Excluding Palestine's share (AAD 3.96m.), which was deferred by a Board of Governors' resolution in 1978.

Activities

The creation of the Arab Monetary Fund was seen as a step towards the goal of Arab economic integration. It assists member states in balance of payments difficulties, and also has a broad range of aims.

The Articles of Agreement define the Fund's aims as follows:

(*a*) to correct disequilibria in the balance of payments of member states;

(*b*) to promote the stability of exchange rates among Arab currencies, to render them mutually convertible, and to eliminate restrictions on current payments between member states;

(*c*) to establish policies and modes of monetary co-operation to accelerate Arab economic integration and economic development in the member states;

(*d*) to tender advice on the investment of member states' financial resources in foreign markets, whenever called upon to do so;

(*e*) to promote the development of Arab financial markets;

(*f*) to promote the use of the Arab dinar as a unit of account and to pave the way for the creation of a unified Arab currency;

(*g*) to co-ordinate the positions of member states in dealing with international monetary and economic problems; and

(*h*) to provide a mechanism for the settlement of current payments between member states in order to promote trade among them.

The Arab Monetary Fund functions both as a fund and a bank. It is empowered:

(*a*) to provide short- and medium-term loans to finance balance of payments deficits of member states;

(*b*) to issue guarantees to member states to strengthen their borrowing capabilities;

(*c*) to act as intermediary in the issuance of loans in Arab and international markets for the account of member states and under their guarantees;

(*d*) to co-ordinate the monetary policies of member states;

(*e*) to manage any funds placed under its charge by member states;

(*f*) to hold periodic consultations with member states on their economic conditions; and

(*g*) to provide technical assistance to banking and monetary institutions in member states.

Loans are intended to finance an overall balance of payments deficit and a member may draw up to 75% of its paid-up subscription, in convertible currencies, for this purpose unconditionally (automatic loans). A member may, however, obtain loans in excess of this limit, subject to agreement with the Fund on a programme aimed at reducing its balance of payments deficit (ordinary and extended loans, equivalent to 175% and 250% of its quota respectively). From 1981 a country receiving no extended loans was entitled to a loan under the Inter-Arab Trade Facility (discontinued in 1989) of up to 100% of its quota. In addition, a member has the right to borrow under a compensatory loan in order to finance an unexpected deficit in its balance of payments resulting from a decrease in its exports of goods and services or a large increase in its imports of agricultural products following a poor harvest. In 2009 the access limit was doubled to 100% of paid-up capital.

Automatic and compensatory loans are repayable within three years, while ordinary and extended loans are repayable within five and seven years, respectively. Loans are granted at concessionary and uniform rates of interest that increase with the length of the period of the loan. In 1996 the Fund established the Structural Adjustment Facility, initially providing up to 75% of a member's paid-up subscription and later increased to 175%. This may include a technical assistance component comprising a grant of up to 2% of the total loan. In 2009, in order to enhance the flexibility and effectiveness of its lending to meet the needs of member countries affected by the global financial crisis, the Fund determined to extend an access limit of 175% for lending for both the public finance sector and for the financial and banking sector under the Structural Adjustment Facility. In 2007 the Fund established an Oil Facility to assist petroleum-importing member countries to counter the effects of the escalation in global fuel prices. Eligible countries were entitled to borrow up to 200% of their paid-up subscription under the new Facility. A new Short Term Liquidity Facility was approved in 2009 to provide resources to countries with previously strong track records undergoing financial shortages owing to the sharp contraction in international trade and credit.

Over the period 1978–2010 the Fund extended 150 loans amounting to AAD 1,317m. During 2010 the Fund approved lending of AAD 118m. (compared with AAD 99m. in 2009), including two Structural Adjustment Loans, amounting to AAD 65m., for public finance reforms in Jordan and Morocco, an Extended Loan, amounting to AAD 43m., for Yemen, and a Compensatory Loan, amounting to AAD 10m., to Jordan.

The Fund's technical assistance activities are extended through either the provision of experts to the country concerned or in the form of specialized training of officials of member countries. In view of the increased importance of this type of assistance, the Fund established, in 1988, the Economic Policy Institute (EPI), which offers regular training courses and specialized seminars for middle-level and senior staff, respectively, of financial and monetary institutions of the Arab countries. During 2010 the EPI organized 17 training events, attended by 532 people. In April 1999 the Fund signed a Memorandum of Understanding with the International Monetary Fund (IMF) to establish a joint regional training programme. The Fund also co-operates with the IMF in conducting workshops and technical advice missions under the Arab Credit Reporting Initiative and the Arab Debt Markets Development Initiative.

AMF collaborates with Arab Fund for Economic and Social Development (AFESD), the Arab League and the Organization of Arab Petroleum Exporting Countries in writing and publishing a *Joint Arab Economic Report*. The Fund also co-operates with AFESD, with the technical assistance of the IMF and the World Bank, in organizing an annual seminar. The Fund provides the secretariat for the Council of Arab Central Banks, comprising the governors of central banks and the heads of the monetary agencies in Arab countries. In 1991 the Council established the Arab Committee on Banking Supervision. In 2005 the Council inaugurated a second technical grouping, the Arab Committee on Payments and Settlements Systems. In September 2011 the Fund endorsed the so-called Deauville Partnership, which had been established by the Group of Eight industrialized countries in May in order to assist countries in the Middle East and North Africa undergoing social and economic transformations. The Fund joined some nine other international financial institutions active in the region to establish a Co-ordination Platform to facilitate and promote collaboration among the institutions extending assistance under the Partnership.

TRADE PROMOTION

Arab Trade Financing Program (ATFP): POB 26799, Arab Monetary Fund Bldg, 7th Floor, Corniche Rd, Abu Dhabi, United Arab Emirates; tel. (2) 6316999; fax (2) 6316793; e-mail finadmin@atfp.ae; internet www.atfp.org.ae; f. 1989 to develop and promote trade between Arab countries and to enhance the competitive ability of Arab exporters; operates by extending lines of credit to Arab exporters and importers through national agencies (some 200 agencies designated by the monetary authorities of 19 Arab and five other countries); the Arab Monetary Fund provided 50% of ATFP's authorized capital of US $500m; participation was also invited from private and official Arab financial institutions and joint Arab/foreign institutions; administers the Inter-Arab Trade Information Network (IATIN), and organizes Buyers-Sellers meetings to promote Arab goods; by the end of 2010 the Program had extended lines of credit with a total value of $8,580m; Chair. and Chief Exec. Dr Jassim Abdullah al-Mannai; publ. *Annual Report* (Arabic and English).

Publications

Annual Report.

Arab Countries: Economic Indicators (annually).

Foreign Trade of the Arab Countries (annually).

Joint Arab Economic Report (annually).

Money and Credit in the Arab Countries.

National Accounts of the Arab Countries (annually).

Quarterly Bulletin.

Reports on commodity structure (by value and quantity) of member countries' imports from and exports to other Arab countries; other studies on economic, social, management and fiscal issues.

Statistics

LOANS APPROVED, 1978–2010

Type of loan	Number of loans	Amount (AAD '000)
Automatic	59	301,474
Ordinary	12	104,751
Compensatory	16	130,785
Extended	24	340,344
Structural Adjustment Facility	26	355,927
Oil Facility	2	18,814
Inter-Arab Trade Facility (cancelled in 1989)	11	64,730
Total	150	1,316,825

LOANS APPROVED, 2010

Borrower	Type of loan	Amount (AAD '000)
Jordan	Structural Adjustment Facility	17,185
	Automatic loan	9,820
Morocco	Structural Adjustment Facility	47,863
Yemen	Extended loan	43,000

Source: *Annual Report 2010.*

ASIA-PACIFIC ECONOMIC COOPERATION—APEC

Address: 35 Heng Mui Keng Terrace, Singapore 119616.

Telephone: 68919600; **fax:** 68919690; **e-mail:** info@apec.org; **internet:** www.apec.org.

The Asia-Pacific Economic Cooperation (APEC) was initiated in November 1989, in Canberra, Australia, as an informal consultative forum. Its aim is to promote multilateral economic co-operation on issues of trade and investment.

MEMBERS

Australia	Japan	Philippines
Brunei	Korea, Republic	Russia
Canada	Malaysia	Singapore
Chile	Mexico	Taiwan*
China, People's Republic	New Zealand	Thailand
Hong Kong	Papua New Guinea	USA
Indonesia	Peru	Viet Nam

* Admitted as Chinese Taipei.

Note: APEC has three official observers: the Association of Southeast Asian Nations (ASEAN) Secretariat; the Pacific Economic Cooperation Council; and the Pacific Islands Forum Secretariat. Observers may participate in APEC meetings and have full access to all related documents and information.

Organization

(June 2012)

ECONOMIC LEADERS' MEETINGS

The first meeting of APEC heads of government was convened in November 1993, in Seattle, Washington, USA. Subsequently, each annual meeting of APEC ministers of foreign affairs and of economic affairs has been followed by an informal gathering of the leaders of the APEC economies, at which the policy objectives of the grouping are discussed and defined. The 18th Economic Leaders' Meeting was convened in November 2011 in Honolulu, Hawaii.

MINISTERIAL MEETINGS

APEC ministers of foreign affairs and ministers of economic affairs meet annually. These meetings are hosted by the APEC Chair, which rotates each year, although it was agreed, in 1989, that alternate Ministerial Meetings were to be convened in an ASEAN member country. A Senior Officials' Meeting (SOM) convenes regularly between Ministerial Meetings to co-ordinate and administer the budgets and work programmes of APEC's committees and working groups. Other meetings of ministers are held on a regular basis to enhance co-operation in specific areas.

SECRETARIAT

In 1992 the Ministerial Meeting, held in Bangkok, Thailand, agreed to establish a permanent secretariat to support APEC activities. The Secretariat became operational in February 1993. In accordance with a decision of the 2007 Leaders' Meeting, from 1 January 2010 an Executive Director with a three-year fixed term of office was appointed (hitherto the Executive Director had served a one-year term). A Policy Support Unit was established within the Secretariat in 2008.

Executive Director: MUHAMAD NOOR YACOB (Malaysia).

COMMITTEES

Budget and Management Committee (BMC): f. 1993 as Budget and Administrative Committee, present name adopted 1998; advises APEC senior officials on budgetary, administrative and managerial issues. The Committee reviews the operational budgets of APEC committees and groups, evaluates their effectiveness and conducts assessments of group projects. In 2005 the APEC Support Fund (ASF) was established under the auspices of the BMC, with the aim of supporting capacity-building programmes for developing economies; subsidiary funds of the ASF have been established relating to human security and avian influenza.

Committee on Trade and Investment (CTI): f. 1993 on the basis of a Declaration signed by ministers meeting in Seattle, Washington, USA, in order to facilitate the expansion of trade and the development of a liberalized environment for investment among member countries; undertakes initiatives to improve the flow of goods, services and technology in the region. Supports Industry Dialogues to promote collaboration between public and private sector representatives in the following areas of activity: Automotive; Chemical; Non-ferrous Metal; and Life Sciences Innovation. An Investment Experts' Group was established in 1994, initially to develop non-binding investment principles. In May 1997 an APEC Tariff Database was inaugurated, with sponsorship from the private sector. A Market Access Group was established in 1998 to administer CTI activities concerned with non-tariff measures. In 2001 the CTI finalized a set of nine non-binding Principles on Trade Facilitation, which aimed to help eliminate procedural and administrative impediments to trade and to increase trading opportunities. A Trade Facilitation Action Plan (TFAP) was approved in 2002. By 2005 a strategy was adopted to systematize transparency standards. TFAP II, which aimed to reduce trade transaction costs by 5% during 2007–10, was endorsed by the APEC ministers responsible for trade in July 2007 and by APEC leaders in September; an assessment of achievements made under TFAP II was under way in 2011. In 2007 the Electronic Commerce Steering Group, established in 1999, became aligned to the CTI. An Investment Facilitation Action Plan (IFAP) was undertaken during 2008–10, with the aim of assisting investment flows into the region. The most recent (seventh) edition of the official *Guide to the Investment Regimes of the APEC Member Economies* was published in January 2011.

Economic Committee (EC): f. 1994 following an agreement, in November, to transform the existing ad hoc group on economic trends and issues into a formal committee; aims to enhance APEC's capacity to analyse economic trends and to research and report on issues affecting economic and technical co-operation in the region. In addition, the Committee is considering the environmental and development implications of expanding population and economic growth. During 2007–10 the EC implemented a work plan on the implementation of the Leaders' Agenda to Implement Structural Reform (LAISR, agreed in November 2004 by the 12th Economic Leaders' Meeting, see below).

SOM Steering Committee on ECOTECH (SCE): f. 1998 to assist the SOM with the co-ordination of APEC's economic and technical co-operation programme (ECOTECH); reconstituted in 2006, with an enhanced mandate to undertake greater co-ordination and oversee project proposals of the working groups; monitors and evaluates project implementation and also identifies initiatives designed to strengthen economic and technical co-operation in infrastructure.

ADVISORY COUNCIL

APEC Business Advisory Council (ABAC): Philamlife Tower, 43rd Floor, 8767 Paseo de Roxas, Makati City, 1226 Metro Manila, Philippines; tel. (2) 8454564; fax (2) 8454832; e-mail abacsec@pfgc.ph; internet www.abaconline.org; an agreement to establish ABAC, comprising up to three senior representatives of the private sector from each APEC member economy, was concluded at the Ministerial Meeting held in Nov. 1995. ABAC is mandated to advise member states on the implementation of APEC's Action Agenda and on other business matters, and to provide business-related information to APEC fora. ABAC meets three or four times each year and holds an annual CEO Summit alongside the annual APEC Economic Leaders' Meeting; Exec. Dir ZIYAVUDIN MAGOMEDOV (USA) (2012).

Activities

APEC is focused on furthering objectives in three key areas, or 'pillars': trade and investment liberalization; business facilitation; and economic and technical co-operation. It was initiated in 1989 as a forum for informal discussion between the then six ASEAN members and their six dialogue partners in the Pacific, and, in particular, to promote trade liberalization in the Uruguay Round of negotiations, which were being conducted under the General Agreement on Tariffs and Trade (GATT). The Seoul Declaration, adopted by ministers meeting in the Republic of Korea (South Korea) in November 1991, defined the objectives of APEC.

ASEAN countries were initially reluctant to support any more formal structure of the forum, or to admit new members, owing to concerns that it would undermine ASEAN's standing as a regional grouping and be dominated by powerful non-ASEAN economies. In August 1991 it was agreed to extend membership to the People's Republic of China, Hong Kong and Taiwan (subject to conditions imposed by China, including that a Taiwanese official of no higher than vice-ministerial level should attend the annual meeting of ministers of foreign affairs). Mexico and Papua New Guinea acceded to the organization in November 1993, and Chile joined in November 1994. The summit meeting held in November 1997 agreed that Peru, Russia and Viet Nam should be admitted to APEC at the 1998 meeting, but imposed a 10-year moratorium on further expansion of the grouping.

In September 1992 APEC ministers agreed to establish a permanent secretariat. In addition, the meeting created an 11-member non-governmental Eminent Persons Group (EPG), which was to assess trade patterns within the region and propose measures to promote co-operation. At the Ministerial Meeting in Seattle, Washington, USA, in November 1993, members agreed on a framework for expanding trade and investment among member countries, and to establish a permanent committee (the CTI, see above) to pursue these objectives.

In August 1994 the EPG proposed the following timetable for the liberalization of all trade across the Asia-Pacific region: negotiations for the elimination of trade barriers were to commence in 2000 and be completed within 10 years in developed countries, 15 years in newly industrialized economies and by 2020 in developing countries. Trade concessions could then be extended on a reciprocal basis to non-members in order to encourage world-wide trade liberalization, rather than isolate APEC as a unique trading bloc. In November 1994 the meeting of APEC heads of government adopted the Bogor Declaration of Common Resolve, which endorsed the EPG's timetable for free and open trade and investment in the region by the year 2020. Other issues incorporated into the Declaration included the implementation of GATT commitments in full and strengthening the multilateral trading system through the forthcoming establishment of the World Trade Organization (WTO), intensifying development co-operation in the Asia-Pacific region and expanding and accelerating trade and investment programmes. In November 1995 the Ministerial Meeting decided to dismantle the EPG, and to establish the APEC Business Advisory Council (ABAC), consisting of private sector representatives.

Meeting in Osaka, Japan, in November 1995, APEC heads of government adopted the Osaka Action Agenda as a framework to achieve the commitments of the Bogor Declaration. Part One of the Agenda identified action areas for the liberalization of trade and investment and the facilitation of business, for example, customs procedures, rules of origin and non-tariff barriers. It incorporated agreements that the process was to be comprehensive, consistent with WTO commitments, comparable among all APEC economies and non-discriminatory. Each member economy was to ensure the transparency of its laws, regulations and procedures affecting the flow of goods, services and capital among APEC economies and to refrain from implementing any trade protection measures. A second part of the Agenda was to provide a framework for further economic and technical co-operation between APEC members in areas such as energy, transport, infrastructure, small and medium-sized enterprises (SMEs) and agricultural technology. In order to resolve a disagreement concerning the inclusion of agricultural products in the trade liberalization process, a provision for flexibility was incorporated into the Agenda, taking into account diverse circumstances and different levels of development in APEC member economies. Liberalization measures were to be implemented from January 1997 (i.e. three years earlier than previously agreed). A Trade and Investment Liberalization and Facilitation Special Account was established to finance projects in support of the implementation of the Osaka Action Agenda. Each member economy was to prepare an Individual Action Plan (IAP) on efforts to achieve the trade liberalization measures, that were to be reviewed annually.

In November 1996 the Economic Leaders' Meeting, held in Subic Bay, Philippines, approved the Manila Action Plan for APEC (MAPA), which incorporated the IAPs and other collective measures aimed at achieving the trade liberalization and co-operation objectives of the Bogor Declaration, as well as the joint activities specified in the second part of the Osaka Agenda. Heads of government also endorsed a US proposal to eliminate tariffs and other barriers to trade in information technology products by 2000 and determined to support efforts to conclude an agreement to this effect at the forthcoming WTO conference; however, they insisted on the provision of an element of flexibility in achieving trade liberalization in this sector.

The 1997 Economic Leaders' Meeting, held in Vancouver, Canada, in November, was dominated by concern at the financial instability that had affected several Asian economies during that year. The final declaration of the summit meeting endorsed a framework of measures that had been agreed by APEC deputy ministers of finance and central bank governors at an emergency meeting convened in the previous week in Manila, Philippines (the so-called Manila Framework for Enhanced Asian Regional Cooperation to Promote Financial Stability). The meeting, attended by representatives of the IMF, the World Bank and the Asian Development Bank, committed all member economies receiving IMF assistance to undertake specified economic and financial reforms, and supported the establishment of a separate Asian funding facility to supplement international financial assistance (although this was later rejected by the IMF). APEC ministers of finance and governors of central banks were urged to accelerate efforts for the development of the region's financial and capital markets and to liberalize capital flows in the region. Measures were to include strengthening financial market supervision and clearing and settlement infrastructure, the reform of pension systems, and promoting co-operation among export credit agencies and financing institutions. The principal item on the Vancouver summit agenda was an initiative to enhance trade liberalization, which, the grouping insisted, should not be undermined by the financial instability in Asia. The following 15 economic sectors were identified for 'early voluntary sectoral liberalization' ('EVSL'): environmental goods and services; fish and fish products; forest products; medical equipment and instruments; toys; energy; chemicals; gems and jewellery; telecommunications; oilseeds and oilseed products; food; natural and synthetic rubber; fertilizers; automobiles; and civil aircraft. The implementation of EVSL was to encompass market opening, trade facilitation, and economic and technical co-operation activities.

In May 1998 APEC finance ministers met in Canada to consider the ongoing financial and economic crisis in Asia and to review progress in implementing efforts to alleviate the difficulties experienced by several member economies. The ministers agreed to pursue activities in the following three priority areas: capital market development; capital account liberalization; and strengthening financial systems (including corporate governance). The region's economic difficulties remained the principal topic of discussion at the Economic Leaders' Meeting held in Kuala Lumpur, Malaysia, in November. A final declaration reiterated their commitment to co-operation in pursuit of sustainable economic recovery and growth, in particular through the restructuring of financial and corporate sectors, promoting and facilitating private sector capital flows, and efforts to strengthen the global financial system. The meeting endorsed a proposal by ABAC to establish a partnership for equitable growth, with the aim of enhancing business involvement in APEC's programme of economic and technical co-operation. Other initiatives approved included an Agenda of APEC Science and Technology Industry Cooperation into the 21st Century (for which China announced it was to establish a special fund), and an Action Programme on Skills and Development in APEC. Japan's persisting opposition to a reduction of tariffs in the fish and forestry sectors prevented the conclusion of tariff negotiations under the EVSL scheme, and it was therefore agreed that responsibility for managing the tariff reduction element of the initiative should be transferred to the WTO.

In September 1999 political dialogue regarding civil conflict in East Timor (now Timor-Leste) dominated the start of the annual meetings of the grouping, held in Auckland, New Zealand, although the issue remained separate from the official agenda. The Economic Leaders' Meeting considered measures to sustain the economic recovery in Asia and endorsed the APEC Principles to Enhance Competition and Regulatory Reform (for example, transparency, accountability, non-discrimination) as a framework to strengthen APEC markets and to enable further integration and implementation of the IAPs. Also under discussion was the forthcoming round of multilateral trade negotiations, to be initiated by the WTO. The heads of government proposed the objective of completing a single package of trade agreements within three years and endorsed the abolition of export subsidies for agricultural products. The meeting determined to support the efforts of China, Russia, Taiwan and Viet Nam to accede to WTO membership. An APEC Business Travel Card scheme, to facilitate business travel within the region, was inaugurated in 1999, having been launched on a trial basis in 1997; card holders receive fast-track passage through designated APEC immigration processing lanes at major airports, and multiple short term-entry entitlements to participating economies. By 2012 more than 80,000 individuals were registered under the scheme, in which 18 economies were participating fully. The November 2011 Leaders' Meeting determined to launch an APEC Travel Facilitation Initiative, which was to address means of facilitating faster, easier and more secure travel through the region.

The Economic Leaders' Meeting for 2000, held in Brunei in November, urged that an agenda for the now-stalled round of multilateral trade negotiations should be formulated without further delay. The meeting endorsed a plan of action to promote the utilization of advances in information and communications technologies in member economies, for the benefit of all citizens. It adopted the aim of tripling the number of people in the region with access to the internet by 2005, and determined to co-operate with business and education sector interests to attract investment and expertise in the pursuit of this goal. A proposal that the Democratic People's Republic of Korea (North Korea) be permitted to participate in APEC working groups was approved at the meeting.

The 2001 Economic Leaders' Meeting, held in October, in Shanghai, China, condemned the terrorist attacks against targets in the USA of the previous month and resolved to take action to combat the threat of international terrorism. The heads of government declared terrorism to be a direct challenge to APEC's vision of free, open and prosperous economies, and concluded that the threat made the continuing move to free trade, with its aim of bolstering economies, increasing prosperity and encouraging integration, even more of a priority. Leaders emphasized the importance of sharing the benefits of globalization, and adopted the Shanghai Accord, which identified development goals for APEC during its second decade and clarified measures for achieving the Bogor goals within the agreed timetable. A process of IAP Peer Reviews was initiated. (By late 2005 the process had been concluded for each member economy.) The meeting also outlined the e-APEC Strategy developed by the e-APEC Task Force established after the Brunei Economic Leaders' meeting. Considering issues of entrepreneurship, structural and regulatory reform, competition, intellectual property rights and information security, the strategy aimed to facilitate technological development in the region. Finally, the meeting adopted a strategy document relating to infectious diseases in the Asia Pacific region, which aimed to promote a co-ordinated response to combating HIV/AIDS and other contagious diseases.

In September 2002 a meeting of APEC ministers of finance was held in Los Cabos, Mexico. Ministers discussed the importance of efforts to combat money-laundering and the financing of terrorism. The meeting also focused on ways to strengthen global and regional economic growth, to advance fiscal and financial reforms and to improve the allocation of domestic savings for economic development. The theme of the 2002 Economic Leaders' Meeting, held in the following month in Los Cabos, was 'Expanding the Benefits of Cooperation for Economic Growth and Development—Implementing the Vision'. The meeting issued a statement on the implementation of APEC standards of transparency in trade and investment liberalization and facilitation. Leaders also issued a statement on fighting terrorism and promoting growth. In February the first conference to promote the Secure Trade in the APEC Region (STAR) initiative was convened in Bangkok, Thailand, and attended by representatives of all APEC member economies as well as senior officers of private sector companies and relevant international organizations. The second STAR conference was held in Viña del Mar, Chile, in March 2004; the third in Incheon, South Korea, in February 2005; the fourth in Hanoi, Viet Nam, in February 2006; the fifth in Sydney, Australia, in June 2007; the sixth in Lima, Peru, in August 2008; the seventh in Singapore, in July 2009; and the eighth in Washington, DC, USA, in September 2011.

The 2003 Economic Leaders' Meeting, convened in October, in Bangkok, Thailand, considered means of advancing the WTO's stalled Doha round of trade negotiations, emphasizing the central importance of its development dimension, and noted progress made hitherto in facilitating intra-APEC trade. The meeting also addressed regional security issues, reiterating the Community's commitment to ensuring the resilience of APEC economies against the threat of terrorism. The Leaders adopted the Bangkok Declaration on Partnership for the Future, which identified the following areas as priority concerns for the group: the promotion of trade and investment liberalization; enhancing human security; and helping people and societies to benefit from globalization. The Bangkok meeting also issued a statement on health security, which expressed APEC's determination to strengthen infrastructure for the detection and prevention of infectious diseases, as well as the surveillance of other threats to public health, and to ensure a co-ordinated response to public health emergencies, with particular concern to the outbreak, earlier in the year, of Severe Acute Respiratory Syndrome (SARS).

The 12th Economic Leaders' Meeting was held in Santiago, Chile, in November 2004, on the theme 'One Community, Our Future'. The meeting reaffirmed the grouping's commitment to the Doha Development Agenda, and endorsed the package of agreements concluded by the WTO in July. The meeting approved a Santiago Initiative for Expanded Trade in APEC, to promote further trade and investment liberalization in the region and advance trade facilitation measures. Other areas discussed were human security, HIV/AIDS and other emerging infectious diseases, and energy security. Efforts to combat corruption and promote good governance included a Santiago Commitment to Fight Corruption and Ensure Transparency, the APEC Course of Action on Fighting Corruption and Ensuring Transparency, and a Leaders' Agenda to Implement Structural Reform (LAISR). LAISR covers the following five policy areas: regulatory reform; competition policy; public sector governance; corporate governance; and strengthening economic and legal infrastructure.

In September 2005 APEC finance ministers, meeting in Jeju, South Korea, discussed two main issues: the increased importance of capital flows among member economies, particularly those from worker remittances; and the challenge presented by the region's ageing population. The meeting resolved to promote capital account liberalization and to develop resilient and efficient capital markets. It also adopted the 'Jeju Declaration on Enhancing Regional Cooperation against the Challenges of Population Ageing', in which it acknowledged the urgency of such domestic reforms such as creating sustainable pension systems, providing an increased range of savings products and improving financial literacy. In November 2005 the 13th Economic Leaders' Meeting endorsed a Busan Roadmap to the Bogor Goals, based on an assessment of action plans, which outlined key priorities and frameworks. Particular focus was drawn to support for the multilateral trading system, efforts to promote high quality regional trade agreements and free trade agreements, and strengthened collective and individual action plans. It also incorporated a Busan Business Agenda and commitments to a strategic approach to capacity building and to a pathfinder approach to promoting trade and investment in the region, through work on areas such as intellectual property rights, anti-corruption, secure trade and trade facilitation.

The 14th Economic Leaders' Meeting, held in Hanoi, Viet Nam, in November 2006 on the theme 'Towards One Dynamic Community for Sustainable Development and Prosperity', reaffirmed support for the stalled negotiations on the WTO's Doha Development Agenda; adopted the Hanoi Action Plan on the implementation of the Busan Roadmap (endorsed by the 2005 Leaders' Meeting); endorsed the APEC Action Plan on Prevention and Response to Avian and Influenza Pandemics; and expressed strong concern at the nuclear test conducted by North Korea in October.

The participants at the 15th Economic Leaders' Meeting, convened in Sydney, Australia, in September 2007, on the theme 'Strengthening our Community, Building a Sustainable Future', adopted a Declaration on Climate Change, Energy Security and Clean Development, wherein they acknowledged the need to ensure energy supplies to support regional economic growth while also preserving the quality of the environment. The Declaration incorporated an Action Agenda and agreements to establish an Asia-Pacific Network for Energy Technology and an Asia-Pacific Network for Sustainable Forest Management and Rehabilitation. The Economic Leaders also issued a statement once again affirming the need successfully to resolve the stalled WTO Doha Development Round; endorsed a report on means of further promoting Asia-Pacific economic integration; agreed to examine the options and prospects for the development of a Free Trade Area of the Asia-Pacific (FTAAP); welcomed efforts by the Economic Committee to enhance the implementation of the LAISR; endorsed the second Trade Facilitation Action Plan, which aimed to achieve a 5% reduction in business and trade transaction costs by 2010; determined to strengthen the protection and enforcement of intellectual property rights in the region; and approved the Anti-corruption Principles for the Public and Private Sectors, and related codes of conduct, that had been adopted in June 2007 by the Anti-corruption and Transparency Experts' Task Force and endorsed by the September 2007 Ministerial Meeting.

The 16th Economic Leaders' Meeting, held in November 2008, in Lima, Peru, under the theme 'A New Commitment to Asia-Pacific Development', addressed the implications for the region of the then deteriorating global economic situation. The APEC Leaders urged the promotion of good Corporate Social Responsibility (CSR) practices in the region; commended the progress made hitherto in examining the prospects for establishing the proposed FTAAP; and urged ministers of finance to examine more fully means of optimizing linkages between private infrastructure finance and economic growth and development. Expressing deep concern at the impact on the region of volatile global food prices, and at food shortages in some developing economies, the meeting determined to support the regional implementation of the Comprehensive Framework for Action of the UN Task Force on the Global Food Security Crisis, and to increase technical co-operation and capacity-building measures aimed at fostering the growth of the agricultural sector.

Convened in November 2009, in Singapore, the 17th Economic Leaders' Meeting expressed support for the goals of the G20 'Framework for Strong, Sustainable and Balanced Growth' (adopted in September), and adopted a Declaration on a New Growth Paradigm for a Connected Asia-Pacific in the 21st Century, aimed at navigating a future post-global economic crisis landscape; reaffirming commitment to addressing issues related to the threat of climate change; and welcoming the implementation of a peer review of energy efficiency in APEC economies.

The first APEC Ministerial Meeting on Food Security, held in October 2010, in Niigata, Japan, endorsed a new APEC Action Plan on Food Security. In November the 18th Economic Leaders' Meeting, held in Yokohama, Japan, adopted the APEC Leaders' Growth Strategy, representing a comprehensive long-term framework for promoting high-quality growth in the region. The Growth Strategy included an action plan, which was to outline work towards progress in the areas of structural reform; human resource and entrepreneurship development; human security; green growth; and the development of a knowledge-based economy. Progress in the implementation of the Growth Strategy was to be reviewed in 2015. The November 2010 Leaders' Meeting also endorsed a report and issued an assessment on the state of progress towards achieving the Bogor Goals. Leaders reaffirmed strong commitment to pursuing the proposed FTAAP and towards achieving a successful conclusion to the Doha Development Agenda, while determining to refrain from adopting protectionist measures until 2014. In May 2011 APEC and the World Bank concluded a Memorandum of Understanding on strengthening collaboration on food safety in the Asia-Pacific region. In September a session of APEC ministers and senior government officials, and leaders from the private sector, meeting in San Francisco, USA, adopted the San Francisco Declaration on Women and the Economy, outlining means of realizing the as yet untapped full potential of women to contribute to the regional economy, and welcoming the establishment of an APEC Policy Partnership on Women and the Economy (PPWE), which had been endorsed by senior officials in May.

The 19th Leaders' Meeting, convened in Honolulu, Hawaii, in November 2011, adopted the Honolulu Declaration 'Toward a Seamless Regional Economy', which, *inter alia*, instructed regional officials to consider new approaches to the then stalled negotiations on concluding the Doha Development Round; reaffirmed commitment to anti-protectionism; determined to advance a set of policies to promote market-driven innovation policy; committed to implementing plans towards the establishment of an APEC New Strategy for Structural Reform and an APEC Cross Border Privacy Rules System; committed, further, to promoting green growth, including through encouraging member economies, in 2012, to develop an APEC list of environmental goods contributing directly to the Community's sustainable development objectives, to which applied tariff rates were to be reduced to 5% or less by end-2015; aspired to reduce regional energy intensity by 45% by 2035, to take specific steps to promote energy-smart low-carbon communities, and to incorporate low-emissions development strategies into national economic growth plans; welcomed the San Francisco Declaration on Women and the Economy and pledged to monitor its implementation; and determined to enhance the role of the private sector in APEC, through greater contribution to its working groups and the establishment of new public-private policy partnerships. The second APEC Ministerial Meeting on Food Security, convened in May 2012, in Kazan, Russia, issued the Kazan Declaration on APEC Food Security, representing a comprehensive assessment of member states' food security issues, and an updated framework for addressing them.

SPECIAL TASK GROUPS

These may be established by the Senior Officials' Meeting to identify issues and make recommendations on areas for consideration by the grouping.

Counter Terrorism Task Force (CTTF): established in February 2003 to co-ordinate implementation of the Leaders' Statement on Fighting Terrorism and Promoting Growth, which had been adopted in October 2002. It was subsequently mandated to implement all other APEC initiatives to enhance human security. The CTTF assists member economies to identify and assess counter-terrorism needs and co-ordinates individual Counter Terrorism Action Plans, which identify measures required and the level of implementation achieved to secure trade.

Mining Task Force (MTF): the first meeting of the MTF was convened in May 2008, in Arequipa, Peru. The Task Force was to provide a unified, cohesive mining, minerals and metals forum for APEC member economies. Its ongoing work programme includes undertaking a study on means of attracting investment to the regional mining sector, with a particular focus on investment; the regulatory framework; and the availability of skilled workforces. A Conference on Sustainable Development of the Mining Sector in the APEC Region was held in July 2009, in Singapore.

WORKING GROUPS

APEC's structure of working groups aims to promote practical and technical co-operation in specific areas, and to help implement individual and collective action plans in response to the directives of the Economic Leaders and meetings of relevant ministers.

Agricultural Technical Co-operation (ATCWG): formally established as an APEC expert's group in 1996, and incorporated into the system of working groups in 2000. The ATCWG aims to enhance the role of agriculture in the economic growth of the region and to promote co-operation in the following areas: conservation and utilization of plant and animal genetic resources; research, development and extension of agricultural biotechnology; processing, marketing, distribution and consumption of agricultural products; plant and animal quarantine and pest management; development of an agricultural finance system; sustainable agriculture; and agricultural technology transfer and training. The ATCWG has primary responsibility for undertaking recommendations connected with the implementation of the APEC Food System, which aims to improve the efficiency of food production, supply and trade within member economies. The ATCWG has conducted projects on human resource development in post-harvest technology and on capacity building, safety assessment and communication in biotechnology. A high-level policy dialogue on agricultural biotechnology was initiated in 2002. Following the outbreak of so-called avian flu and its impact on the region's poultry industry, in 2004 it was agreed that the ATCWG would develop the enhanced biosecurity planning and surveillance capacity considered by APEC's member economies as being essential to protect the region's agricultural sector from the effects of future outbreaks of disease. A quarantine regulators' seminar on Implementing Harmonised Arrangements for Ensuring Effective Quarantine Treatments, and an APEC Workshop on Avian Influenza Risks in the Live Bird Market System, were organized in 2008; and in August 2009 a symposium on the Approach of Organic Agriculture: New Markets, Food Security and a Clean Environment was held. In April 2010 a *Report on Developing and Applying a Traceability System in Agriculture Production and Trade* was issued. The ATCWG contributed to the development of the APEC Action Plan on Food Security, which was endorsed by the October 2010 APEC Ministerial Meeting on Food Security. The 15th ATCWG meeting, held in Washington, DC, USA, in February 2011, agreed to promote agricultural technical transfer and co-operation within the APEC region; consequently, in November 2011, an APEC Agricultural Technology Transfer Forum was held, in Beijing, China, on the theme 'Strengthening Agricultural Technology Transfer for Food Security in the APEC Region'. A workshop on developing a regional food security information platform, comprising general information and statistical data, was convened in February 2011; the platform was expected to be finalized in 2012. In 2011 an APEC Experts Group on Illegal Logging and Associated Trade was established to enhance co-operation in addressing concerns surrounding illegal logging, and to promote sustainable forest management.

Anti-corruption and Transparency (ACT): the ACT was upgraded to a working group in March 2011, having been established as a task force in 2004. The Ministerial Meeting, held in Santiago, Chile, in November 2004, endorsed the establishment of the ACT to implement an APEC Course of Action on Fighting Corruption and Ensuring Transparency. Following its establishment the ACT worked to promote ratification and implementation of the UN Convention against Corruption, to strengthen measures to prevent and combat corruption and to sanction public officials found guilty of corruption, to promote public-private partnerships, and to enhance co-operation within the region to combat problems of corruption. An APEC Anti-Counterfeiting and Piracy Initiative was launched in mid-2005. In June 2007 the ACT approved a Code of Conduct for Business, in collaboration with ABAC, a set of Conduct Principles for Public Officials, and Anti-corruption Principles for the Public and Private Sectors. In February 2010 the ACT endorsed the final result of a project entitled 'Stocktaking of Bilateral and Regional Arrangements on Anti-corruption Matters Between/Among APEC Member Economies'. An ACT Workshop on Successful Training Techniques for Implementing the Principles of Conduct for Public Officials was held in September 2010, in Sendai, Japan. The work plan for 2012 included promoting the implementation of existing APEC anti-corruption commitments; convening a workshop in July, in Phuket, Thailand, on Effectively Combating Corruption and Illicit Trade through Tracking Cross-Border Financial Flows, International Asset Recovery and Anti-Money-Laundering Efforts; and implementing a three-year project on enhancing anti-corruption and money-laundering efforts using financial flow tracking techniques.

Emergency Preparedness (EPWG): established in March 2005, as a special task force, in response to the devastating natural disaster that had occurred in the Indian Ocean in late December 2004; upgraded to a working group in 2010. The EPWG is mandated to co-ordinate efforts throughout APEC to enhance disaster management capacity building, to strengthen public awareness regarding natural disaster preparedness, prevention and survival, and to compile best practices. An APEC Senior Disaster Management Co-ordinator Seminar, convened in Cairns, Australia, in August 2007, and comprising representatives of APEC member economies and of international humanitarian organizations, determined to support the development of a three- to five-year emergency preparedness strategic plan. The fourth APEC Emergency Management CEOs' Forum was held in January 2010, in Kobe, Japan. In October 2011 the EPWG organized a workshop on 'school earthquake and tsunami safety in APEC economies'.

Energy (EWG): APEC ministers responsible for energy convened for the first time in August 1996 to discuss major energy challenges confronting the region. The main objectives of the EWG, established in 1990, are: the enhancement of regional energy security and improvement of the fuel supply market for the power sector; the development and implementation of programmes of work promoting the adoption of environmentally sound energy technologies and promoting private sector investment in regional power infrastructure; the development of energy efficiency guidelines; and the standardization of testing facilities and results. The EWG is supported by five expert groups, on clean fossil energy, efficiency and conservation, energy data and analysis, new and renewable energy technologies, and minerals and energy exploration and development; and by two task forces, on renewable energy and energy efficiency financing, and biofuels. In March 1999 the EWG resolved to establish a business network to improve relations and communications with the private sector. The first meeting of the network took place in April. In May 2000 APEC energy ministers meeting in San Diego, California, USA, launched the APEC 21st Century Renewable Energy Initiative, which aimed to encourage co-operation in and advance the utilization of renewable energy technologies, envisaging the establishment of a Private Sector Renewable Energy Forum. In June 2003 APEC energy ministers agreed on a framework to implement APEC's Energy Security Initiative. The first meeting of ministers responsible for mining was convened in Santiago, Chile, in June 2004. In 2004, amid challenges to energy security and unusually high oil prices, the EWG was instructed by APEC Economic Leaders to accelerate the implementation of the Energy Security Initiative, a strategy aimed at responding to temporary supply disruptions and at addressing the broader challenges facing the region's energy supply by means of longer-term policy. In October 2005 APEC ministers responsible for energy convened in Gyeongju, South Korea, to address the theme 'Securing APEC's Energy Future: Responding to Today's Challenges for Energy Supply and Demand'. Meeting in May 2007 in Darwin, Australia, under the theme 'Achieving Energy Security and Sustainable Development through Efficiency, Conservation and Diversity', energy ministers directed the EWG to formulate a voluntary Energy Peer Review Mechanism. The ministers welcomed the work of the Asia-Pacific Partnership on Clean Development and Climate, launched in January 2006 by Australia, China, India, Japan, South Korea and the USA. In June 2010 energy ministers gathered, in Fukui, Japan, under the theme 'Low Carbon Path to Energy Security'. Pursuant to the Osaka Action Agenda adopted by APEC Economic Leaders in 1995, the Asia Pacific Energy Research Centre (APERC) was established in July 1996 in Tokyo, Japan; APERC's mandate and programmes focus on energy sector development in APEC member states. APERC maintains a comprehensive regional Energy Database. Meeting in Kaohsiung, Taiwan, in October 2011, the EWG set a target to reduce APEC regional energy intensity by 45% by 2035; this was endorsed by the November 2011 Leaders' Meeting. In March 2012 the EWG, convened in Kuala Lumpur, Malaysia, discussed an 'Action Agenda to move APEC toward an Energy Efficient, Sustainable, Low-Carbon Transport Future', which had been adopted by the first APEC Joint Transportation and Energy Ministerial Conference, convened in September 2011, in San Francisco, USA.

Health: in October 2003 a Health Task Force (HTF) was established, on an ad hoc basis, to implement health-related activities as directed by APEC leaders, ministers and senior officials, including a Health Safety Initiative, and to address health issues perceived as potential threats to the region's economy, trade and security, in particular emerging infectious diseases. The HTF convened for the first time in Taiwan, in April 2004. It was responsible for enhancing APEC's work on preventing, preparing for and mitigating the effects of highly pathogenic avian influenza (avian flu) and any future related human influenza pandemic. APEC organized an intergovernmental meeting on Avian and Pandemic Influenza Preparedness and Response, convened in Brisbane, Australia, in October 2005. In May 2006 a Ministerial Meeting on Avian and Influenza Pandemics, held in Da Nang, Viet Nam, endorsed an APEC Action Plan on the Prevention of and Response to Avian and Influenza Pandemics. In June 2007 APEC ministers of health, meeting in Sydney, Australia, determined to reconstitute the HTF as the Health Working Group. The Group convened for its first official meeting in February 2008. Meeting in June 2010, the HWG identified the following priority areas: enhancing preparedness for combating vector-borne diseases, including avian and human pandemic influenza, and HIV/AIDS; capacity-building in the areas of health promotion and prevention of lifestyle-related diseases; improving health outcomes through advances in health information technologies; and strengthening health systems in each member economy. In September 2011 the HWG considered the development of an APEC Action Plan to Reduce the Economic Burden of Non-Communicable Disease.

Human Resources Development (HRD): established in 1990; comprises three networks: the Capacity Building Network, with a focus on human capacity building, including management and technical skills development and corporate governance; the Education Network, promoting effective learning systems and supporting the role of education in advancing individual, social and economic development; and the Labour and Social Protection Network, concerned with promoting social integration through the strengthening of labour markets, the development of labour market information and policy, and improvements in working conditions and social safety net frameworks. The HRD undertakes activities through these networks to implement ministerial and leaders' directives. A voluntary network of APEC study centres links higher education and research institutions in member economies. Private sector participation in the HRD has been strengthened by the establishment of a network of APEC senior executives responsible for human resources management. Recent initiatives have included a cyber-education co-operation project, a workshop on advanced risk management, training on the prevention and resolution of employment and labour disputes, and an educators' exchange programme on the use of information technology in education. In 2012 the HRD was to undertake a project on 'Advancing Inclusive Growth through Social Protection'. A seminar on strengthening the social protection system was to be convened in July 2012, in the Philippines. Meeting in February 2012, in Moscow, Russia, the HRD adopted the Moscow Initiative on fostering public-private partnership in the working group's activities.

Industrial Science and Technology (ISTWG): aims to contribute to sustainable development in the region, improve the availability of information, enhance human resources development in the sector, improve the business climate, promote policy dialogue and review and facilitate networks and partnerships. Accordingly, the ISTWG has helped to establish an APEC Virtual Centre for Environmental Technology Exchange in Japan; a Science and Technology Industrial Parks Network; an International Molecular Biology Network for the APEC Region; an APEC Centre for Technology Foresight, based in Thailand; and the APEC Science and Technology Web, an online database. During 1997 and 1998 the ISTWG formulated an APEC Action Framework on Emerging Infectious Diseases and developed an Emerging Infections Network (EINet), based at the University of Washington, Seattle, USA. In March 2004 the fourth meeting of science ministers was held in Christchurch, New Zealand, the first since 1998. ISTWG's work plan for 2010–15 outlined the following goals: enhanced economic growth, trade and investment opportunities, and sustainable development; improved quality of life and a cleaner environment; a safe and secure society; human resource capacity building; enhanced international science and technology networks; improved interconnection between research and innovation; and strengthened technological co-operation.

Oceans and Fisheries (OFWG): formed in 2011 by the merger of the former Fisheries Working Group (FWG) and Marine Resource Conservation Working Group (MRCWG); promotes initiatives within APEC to protect the marine environment and its resources, and to maximize the economic benefits and sustainability of fisheries resources for all APEC members; previously the FWG and MRCWG had held a number of joint sessions focusing on areas of common interest, such as: management strategies for regional marine protected areas, fishery resources and aquaculture; exotic marine species introduction; capacity building in the fields of marine and fishery resources and coral reef conservation; combating destructive fishing practices; aquaculture; and information sharing. The OFWG was to implement the October 2010 Paracas Declaration on Healthy Oceans and Fisheries Management Towards Food Security, focusing on sustainable development and protection of the marine environment, which built upon the previous Seoul Oceans Declaration (2002) and Bali Plan of Action (2005).

Policy Partnership on Women and the Economy (PPWE): established in May 2011 as a public-private mechanism to integrate gender considerations into APEC activities, replacing the former Gender Focal Point Network (GFPN, established in 2002); provides policy advice on gender issues and promotes gender equality; aims to provide linkages between the APEC secretariat, working groups, and economies, to advance the economic integration of women in the APEC region for the benefit of all members; at the inaugural meeting of the PPWE, convened in San Francisco, USA, in September 2011, member states address four policies areas regarded as key in increasing economic participation by women: access to capital; access to markets; capacity and skills building; and women's leadership; the meeting also adopted terms of reference and endorsed the San Francisco Declaration on Women and the Economy, urging APEC member states to take concrete actions to realize the full potential of women and integrate them more fully into APEC economies; an APEC Women's Entrepreneurship Summit was held in September–October 2010, in Gifu, Japan; in 2005, the GFPN recommended that women's participation in the APEC Business Advisory Council (ABAC) should be increased, following which several member economies have nominated at least one female delegate to ABAC; a *Gender Experts List* and a *Register of Best Practices on Gender Integration* are maintained.

Small and Medium Enterprises (SMEWG): established in 1995, as the Ad Hoc Policy Level Group on Small and Medium Enterprises (SMEs), with a temporary mandate to oversee all APEC activities relating to SMEs. It supported the establishment of an APEC Centre for Technical Exchange and Training for Small and Medium Enterprises, which was inaugurated at Los Baños, near Manila, Philippines, in September 1996. A five-year action plan for SMEs was endorsed in 1998. The group was redesignated as a working group, with permanent status, in 2000. In August 2002 the SMEWG's action plan was revised to include an evaluation framework to assist APEC and member economies in identifying and analysing policy issues. In the same month a sub-group specializing in micro-enterprises was established. The first APEC Incubator Forum was held in July–August 2003, in Taiwan, to promote new businesses and support their early development. During 2003 the SMEWG undertook efforts to develop a special e-APEC Strategy for SMEs. In 2004 the APEC SME Coordination Framework was finalized. The 12th APEC SME ministerial meeting, held in Daegu, South Korea, in September 2005, adopted the 'Daegu Initiative on SME Innovation Action Plan', which provided a framework for member economies to create economic and policy environments more suitable to SME innovation. In 2006 the APEC Private Sector Development Agenda was launched. The sixth APEC SME Technology Conference and Fair was convened in June–July 2010, in Fuzhou, China. In December 2011 the 33rd APEC SME meeting considered drafting a SME Strategic Plan to cover the period 2013–16; this was to have three main priority areas: improving the business environment; market access and internationalization; and capacity-building management.

Telecommunications and Information (TEL): incorporates three steering groups concerned with different aspects of the development and liberalization of the sector—Liberalization; ICT development; and Security and prosperity. Activities are guided by directives of ministers responsible for telecommunications, who first met in 1995, in South Korea, and adopted a Seoul Declaration on Asia Pacific Information Infrastructure (APII). The second ministerial meeting, held in Gold Coast, Australia, in September 1996, adopted more detailed proposals for liberalization of the sector in member economies. In June 1998 ministers, meeting in Singapore, agreed to remove technical barriers to trade in telecommunications equipment (although Chile and New Zealand declined to sign up to the arrangement). At their fourth meeting, convened in May 2000 in Cancún, Mexico, telecommunications ministers approved a programme of action that included measures to bridge the 'digital divide' between developed and developing member economies, and adopted the APEC Principles on International Charging Arrangements for Internet Services and the APEC Principles of Interconnection. The fifth ministerial meeting, held in May 2002, issued a Statement on the Security of Information and Communications Infrastructures; a compendium of IT security standards has been disseminated in support of the Statement. A Mutual Recognition Arrangement Task Force (MRATF) (under the Liberalization steering group) implements a mutual recognition arrangement for conformity assessment of telecommunications equipment. An APEC Digital Prosperity Checklist is under development, with the aim of promoting ICT as a means of fuelling economic growth; the first and second seminars on the implementation of the Checklist were conducted, respectively, in July 2009 and March 2010. An Asia-Pacific Information Infrastructure (APII) Testbed Network Project, which aimed to facilitate researchers' and engineers' work and to promote the use of new generation internet, and a Stock-Take on Regulatory Convergence are also ongoing. TEL is implementing a Strategic Action Plan over 2010–15, with a focus on universal broadband access.

Tourism (TWG): established in 1991, with the aim of promoting the long-term sustainability of the tourism industry, in both environmental and social terms. The TWG administers a Tourism Information Network and an APEC International Centre for Sustainable Tourism. The first meeting of APEC ministers of tourism, held in South Korea in July 2000, adopted the Seoul Declaration on the APEC Tourism Charter. The TWG's work plan is based on four policy goals inherent in the Seoul Declaration, namely: the removal of impediments to tourism business and investment; increased mobility of visitors and increased demand for tourism goods and services; sustainable management of tourism; and enhanced recognition of tourism as a vehicle for economic and social development. At a meeting of the TWG in April 2001, APEC and the Pacific Asia Travel Association (PATA) adopted a Code for Sustainable Tourism. The Code is designed for adoption and implementation by a variety of tourism companies and government agencies. It urges members to conserve the natural environment, ecosystems and biodiversity; respect local traditions and cultures; conserve energy; reduce pollution and waste; and ensure that regular environmental audits are carried out. In 2004 the TWG published a report on Best Practices in Safety and Security to Safeguard Tourism against Terrorism. In October 2004 the 'Patagonia Declaration on Tourism in the APEC region' was endorsed at the third tourism ministers' meeting in Punta Arenas, Chile. The Declaration set out a strategic plan to ensure the viability of the regional tourism industry by measuring sustainability, safety and security and developing niche projects such as sports and health tourism. The fourth meeting of tourism ministers, held in Hoi An, Viet Nam, in October 2006, adopted the 'Hoi An Declaration on Tourism', which aimed to promote co-operation in developing sustainable tourism and investment in the region, with a focus on the following areas: encouragement of private sector participation in a new APEC Tourism and Investment Forum, and the promotion of the APEC Tourism Fair, both of which were to be held on the sidelines of tourism sector ministerial meetings; and liberalization of the air routes between the cultural heritage sites of APEC member states. In April 2008 tourism ministers, meeting in Lima, Peru, adopted the 'Pachacamac Declaration on Responsible Tourism'. The TWG recognizes tourism as a vehicle of social development, as well as an economic force. The sixth meeting of APEC tourism ministers, convened in Nara, Japan, in September 2010 considered tourism as an engine for economic growth. Meeting in May 2011 the TWG agreed to increase private sector involvement in future meetings.

Transportation (TPTWG): undertakes initiatives to enhance the efficiency and safety of the regional transportation system, in order to facilitate the development of trade. The TPTWG focuses on three main areas: improving the competitiveness of the transportation industry; promoting a safe and environmentally sound regional transportation system; and human resources development, including training, research and education. The TPTWG has published surveys, directories and manuals on all types of transportation systems, and has compiled an inventory on regional co-operation on oil spills preparedness and response arrangements. A Road Transportation Harmonization Project aims to provide the basis for common standards in the automotive industry in the Asia-Pacific region. The TPTWG has established an internet database on ports and the internet-based Virtual Centre for Transportation Research, Development and Education. It plans to develop a regional action plan on the implementation of Global Navigation Satellite Systems, in consultation with the relevant international bodies. A Special Task Force was established by the TPTWG in 2003 to assist member economies to implement a new International Ship and Port Facility Security Code, sponsored by the International Maritime Organization, which entered into force on 1 July 2004. In April 2004 an Aviation Safety Experts' Group met for the first time since 2000. In July 2004 the fourth meeting of APEC ministers of transport directed the TPTWG to prepare a strategy document to strengthen its activities in transport liberalization and facilitation. A Seminar on Post Tsunami Reconstruction and Functions of Ports Safety was held in 2005. The fifth APEC Transportation ministerial meeting was held in Adelaide, Australia, in March 2007; the sixth, convened in Manila, Philippines, in April 2009, issued a joint ministerial statement detailing the following future focus areas for the TPTWG: liberalization and facilitation of transport services; seamless transportation services; aviation safety and security; land transport and mass transit safety and security; maritime safety and security; sustainable transport; industry involvement; and information sharing. The seventh meeting of APEC transport ministers, convened in September 2011, in San Francisco, USA, pledged to increase co-operation on greener, more energy-efficient co-operation. The first APEC Joint Transportation and Energy Ministerial Conference, also convened in September, in San Francisco, adopted an 'Action Agenda to move APEC toward an Energy Efficient, Sustainable, Low-Carbon Transport Future'.

Publications

ABAC Report to APEC Leaders (annually).

APEC at a Glance (annually).

APEC Business Travel Handbook.

APEC Economic Outlook (annually).

APEC Economic Policy Report.

APEC Energy Handbook (annually).

APEC Energy Statistics (annually).

APEC Outcomes and Outlook.

Guide to the Investment Regimes of the APEC Member Economies (every three years).

Key APEC Documents (annually).

Towards Knowledge-based Economies in APEC.

Trade and Investment Liberalization in APEC.

Working group reports, regional directories, other irregular surveys.

Seoul Declaration

(14 November 1991)

OBJECTIVES

Representatives of Australia, Brunei, Canada, the People's Republic of China, Hong Kong, Indonesia, Japan, the Republic of Korea, Malaysia, New Zealand, the Philippines, Singapore, Taiwan, Thailand and the USA, meeting in Seoul, the Republic of Korea, from 12 to 14 November 1991 at ministerial level,

Recognizing that the dynamic growth of economies in the Asia-Pacific region has brought with it growing economic interdependence and strong common interests in maintaining the region's economic dynamism;

Conscious of the vital interests shared by the Asia-Pacific economies in the expansion of free trade and investment, both at the regional and global level, and of the dangers inherent in protectionism;

Recognizing that the healthy and balanced development of economic interdependence within the Asia-Pacific region based upon openness and a spirit of partnership is essential for the prosperity, stability and progress of the entire region;

Convinced that closer co-operation is needed to utilize more effectively human and natural resources of the Asia-Pacific region so as to attain sustainable growth of its economies, while reducing economic disparities among them, and improve the economic and social well-being of its peoples;

Recalling the productive outcome of their two previous meetings held in Canberra, Australia, during 5–7 November 1989 and in Singapore, during 29–31 July 1990, the basic principles for Asia-Pacific Economic Cooperation which emerged therefrom, and the process of consultations and co-operation evolving among the participating Asia-Pacific economies;

Acknowledging the important contribution made by the Association of Southeast Asian Nations (ASEAN) and the pioneering role played by the Pacific Economic Cooperation Conference (PECC) in fostering closer regional links and dialogue;

Recognizing the important role played by the GATT in fostering a healthy and open multilateral trading system, in reducing barriers to trade and in eliminating discriminatory treatment in international commerce;

Believing that Asia-Pacific Economic Cooperation should serve as an exemplary model of open regional co-operation;

Do hereby declare as follows.

1. The objectives of Asia-Pacific Economic Cooperation (hereinafter referred to as APEC) will be:

(a) to sustain the growth and development of the region for the common good of its peoples and, in this way, to contribute to the growth and development of the world economy;

(b) to enhance the positive gains, both for the region and the world economy, resulting from increasing economic interdependence, including by encouraging the flow of goods, services, capital and technology;

(c) to develop and strengthen the open multilateral trading system in the interest of Asia-Pacific and all other economies;

(d) to reduce barriers to trade in goods and services and investment among participants in a manner consistent with GATT principles, where applicable, and without detriment to other economies.

SCOPE OF ACTIVITY

2. APEC will focus on those economic areas where there is scope to advance common interests and achieve mutual benefits, including through:

(a) exchange of information and consultation on policies and developments relevant to the common efforts of APEC economies to sustain growth, promote adjustment and reduce economic disparities;

(b) development of strategies to reduce impediments to the flow of goods and services and investment world-wide and within the region;

(c) promotion of regional trade, investment, financial resource flows, human resources development, technology transfer, industrial co-operation and infrastructure development;

(d) co-operation in specific sectors such as energy, environment, fisheries, tourism, transportation and telecommunications.

3. In each of these fields, APEC will seek:

(a) to improve the identification and definition of the region's common interests and where appropriate, to project these interests in multilateral forums such as the GATT;

(b) to improve the understanding of the policy concerns, interests and experiences of economic partners, particularly of their international implications, and to help promote consistency in policy-making in appropriate areas;

(c) to develop practical programmes of economic co-operation to contribute to economic dynamism and improved living standards throughout the region;

(d) to enhance and promote the role of the private sector and the application of free market principles in maximizing the benefits of regional co-operation.

MODE OF OPERATION

4. Co-operation will be based on:

(a) the principle of mutual benefit, taking into account differences in the stages of economic development and in the socio-political systems, and giving due consideration to the needs of developing economies; and

(b) a commitment to open dialogue and consensus-building, with equal respect for the views of all participants.

5. APEC will operate through a process of consultation and exchange of views among high-level representatives of APEC economies, drawing upon research, analysis and policy ideas contributed by participating economies and other relevant organizations including the ASEAN and the South Pacific Forum (SPF) Secretariats and the PECC.

6. Recognizing the important contribution of the private sector to the dynamism of APEC economies, APEC welcomes and encourages active private sector participation in appropriate APEC activities.

PARTICIPATION

7. Participation in APEC will be open, in principle, to those economies in the Asia-Pacific region which:

(a) have strong economic linkages in the Asia-Pacific region; and

(b) accept the objectives and principles of APEC as embodied in this Declaration.

8. Decisions regarding future participation in APEC will be made on the basis of a consensus of all existing participants.

9. Non-participant economies or organizations may be invited to the meetings of APEC upon such terms and conditions as may be determined by all existing participants.

ORGANIZATION

10. A ministerial meeting of APEC participants will be held annually to determine the direction and nature of APEC activities within the framework of this Declaration and decide on arrangements for implementation. Participants who wish to host ministerial meetings will have the opportunity to do so, with the host in each case providing the chairman of the meeting.

11. Additional ministerial meetings may be convened as necessary to deal with specific issues of common interest.

12. Responsibility for developing the APEC process in accord with the decisions of the ministerial meetings and the work programme determined at those meetings will lie with a senior officials' meeting of representatives from each participant. The senior officials' meeting will be chaired by a representative of the host of the subsequent annual ministerial meeting, and will make necessary preparations for that meeting.

13. Each project on the work programme will be pursued by a working group composed of representatives from participants, co-ordinated by one or more participants. The working groups will identify specific areas of co-operation and policy options relating to each project.

THE FUTURE OF APEC

14. Recognizing the ongoing and dynamic nature of the APEC process, APEC will retain the flexibility to evolve in line with the changes in regional economic circumstances and the global economic environment, and in response to the economic policy challenges facing the Asia-Pacific region.

ASIAN DEVELOPMENT BANK—ADB

Address: 6 ADB Ave, Mandaluyong City, 0401 Metro Manila, Philippines; POB 789, 0980 Manila, Philippines.

Telephone: (2) 6324444; **fax:** (2) 6362444; **e-mail:** information@adb.org; **internet:** www.adb.org.

The ADB commenced operations in December 1966. The Bank's principal functions are to provide loans and equity investments for the economic and social advancement of its developing member countries, to give technical assistance for the preparation and implementation of development projects and programmes and advisory services, to promote investment of public and private capital for development purposes, and to respond to requests from developing member countries for assistance in the co-ordination of their development policies and plans.

MEMBERS

There are 48 member countries and territories within the ESCAP region and 19 others (see list of subscriptions below).

Organization

(June 2012)

BOARD OF GOVERNORS

All powers of the Bank are vested in the Board, which may delegate its powers to the Board of Directors except in such matters as admission of new members, changes in the Bank's authorized capital stock, election of Directors and President, and amendment of the Charter. One Governor and one Alternate Governor are appointed by each member country. The Board meets at least once a year. The 45th meeting was held in Manila, Philippines, in May 2012.

BOARD OF DIRECTORS

The Board of Directors is responsible for general direction of operations and exercises all powers delegated by the Board of Governors, which elects it. Of the 12 Directors, eight represent constituency groups of member countries within the ESCAP region (with about 65% of the voting power) and four represent the rest of the member countries. Each Director serves for two years and may be re-elected.

Three specialized committees (the Audit Committee, the Budget Review Committee and the Inspection Committee), each comprising six members, assist the Board of Directors in exercising its authority with regard to supervising the Bank's financial statements, approving the administrative budget, and reviewing and approving policy documents and assistance operations.

The President of the Bank, though not a Director, is Chairman of the Board.

Chairman of Board of Directors and President: HARUHIKO KURODA (Japan).

Vice-Presidents: ZHAO XIAOYU (People's Republic of China), STEPHEN P. GROFF (USA), BINDU LOHANI (Nepal), LAKSHMI VENKATACHALAM (India), THIERRY DE LONGUEMAR (France).

ADMINISTRATION

The Bank had 2,958 staff, from 59 countries, at 31 December 2011.

Five regional departments cover Central and West Asia, East Asia, the Pacific, South Asia, and South-East Asia. Other departments and offices include Anti-corruption and Integrity, Central Operations Services, Co-financing Operations, Economics and Research, Private Sector Operations, Regional and Sustainable Development, Risk Management, Strategy and Policy, as well as other administrative units.

There are Bank Resident Missions in Afghanistan, Armenia, Azerbaijan, Bangladesh, Cambodia, the People's Republic of China, Georgia, India, Indonesia, Kazakhstan, Kyrgyzstan, Laos, Mongolia, Nepal, Pakistan, Papua New Guinea, Sri Lanka, Tajikistan, Thailand, Turkey, Uzbekistan and Viet Nam, all of which report to the head of the regional department. In addition, the Bank maintains a Country Office in the Philippines, a Special Liaison Office in Timor-Leste, a Pacific Liaison and Co-ordination Office in Sydney, Australia, and a South Pacific Sub-Regional Mission, based in Fiji. Representative Offices are located in Tokyo, Japan, Frankfurt am Main, Germany (for Europe), and Washington, DC, USA (for North America).

INSTITUTE

ADB Institute (ADBI): Kasumigaseki Bldg, 8th Floor, 2–5 Kasumigaseki 3-chome, Chiyoda-ku, Tokyo 100-6008, Japan; tel. (3) 3593-5500; fax (3) 3593-5571; e-mail info@adbi.org; internet www.adbi.org; f. 1997 as a subsidiary body of the ADB to research and analyse long-term development issues and to disseminate development practices through training and other capacity-building activities; Dean Dr MASAHIRO KAWAI (Japan).

FINANCIAL STRUCTURE

The Bank's ordinary capital resources (which are used for loans to the more advanced developing member countries) are held and used entirely separately from its Special Funds resources (see below). In May 2009 the Board of Governors approved a fifth General Capital Increase (GCI V), increasing the Bank's resources by some 200% to US $165,000m. By 31 December 2011 the Bank had received subscriptions equivalent to 99.2% of the shares authorized under GCI V.

At 31 December 2011 the position of subscriptions to the capital stock was as follows: authorized US $163,336m.; subscribed $162,487m.

The Bank also borrows funds from the world capital markets. Total borrowings during 2011 amounted to US $14,008.8m. (compared with $14,940.1m. in 2010). At 31 December 2011 total outstanding debt amounted to $58,257.3m.

In July 1986 the Bank abolished the system of fixed lending rates, under which ordinary operations loans had carried interest rates fixed at the time of loan commitment for the entire life of the loan. Under the present system the lending rate is adjusted every six months, to take into account changing conditions in international financial markets.

Activities

Loans by the ADB are usually aimed at specific projects. In responding to requests from member governments for loans, the Bank's staff assesses the financial and economic viability of projects and the way in which they fit into the economic framework and priorities of development of the country concerned. In 1985 the Bank decided to expand its assistance to the private sector, hitherto comprising loans to development finance institutions, under government guarantee, for lending to small and medium-sized enterprises; a programme was formulated for direct financial assistance, in the form of equity and loans without government guarantee, to private enterprises. During the early 1990s the Bank aimed to expand its role as project financier by providing assistance for policy formulation and review and promoting regional co-operation, while placing greater emphasis on individual country requirements. During that period the Bank also introduced a commitment to assess development projects for their impact on the local population and to avoid all involuntary resettlement where possible and established a formal procedure for grievances, under which the Board may authorize an inspection of a project by an independent panel of experts, at the request of the affected community or group. The currency instability and ensuing financial crises affecting many Asian economies in 1997/98 prompted the Bank to reflect on its role in the region. The Bank resolved to strengthen its activities as a broad-based development institution, rather than solely as a project financier, through lending policies, dialogue, co-financing and technical assistance.

In November 1999 the Board of Directors approved a new overall strategy objective of poverty reduction, which was to be the principal consideration for all future Bank activities. The strategy incorporated key aims of supporting sustainable, grass-roots based economic growth, social development and good governance. From 2000 the Bank refocused its country strategies, projects and lending targets to complement the poverty reduction strategy. In addition, it initiated a process of consultation to formulate a long-term strategic framework, based on the target of reducing by 50% the incidence of extreme poverty by 2015, one of the so-called Millennium Development Goals (MDGs) identified by the UN General Assembly. The framework, establishing the operational priorities and principles for reducing poverty, was approved in March 2001. A review of the strategy, initiated at the end of 2003, concluded that more comprehensive, results-oriented monitoring and evaluation be put in place. It also recommended a closer alignment of Bank operations with national poverty reduction strategies and determined to include capacity development as a new overall thematic priority for the Bank, in addition to environmental sustainability, gender and development, private sector development and regional co-operation. In mid-2004 the Bank initiated a separate reform agenda to incorporate the strategy approach 'Managing for development results' throughout the organization. In April 2005 a Regional Monitoring Unit was replaced by an Office of Regional Economic Integration, which aimed to promote economic co-operation and integration among developing member countries and to contribute to economic growth throughout the whole region. In July 2006 the Bank adopted a strategy to promote regional co-operation and integration in order to combat poverty through collective regional and cross-border activities.

In June 2006 the Bank convened a panel of eminent persons to assess the Bank's future role within the region. The report of the panel, submitted in March 2007, prompted further wide-ranging consultations. In May 2008 the Board of Governors, convened in Madrid, Spain, endorsed a new long-term strategic framework to cover the period 2008–20 ('Strategy 2020'), replacing the previous 2001–15 strategic framework, in recognition of the unprecedented economic growth of recent years and its associated challenges, including the effect on natural resources, inadequate infrastructure to support economic advances, and widening disparities both within and between developing member countries. Under the strategy the Bank determined to refocus its activities onto three critical agendas: inclusive economic growth; environmentally sustainable growth; and regional integration. It determined also to initiate a process of restructuring its operations into five core areas of specialization, to which some 80% of lending was to be allocated by 2012: infrastructure; environment, including climate change; regional co-operation and integration; financial sector development; and education. The Bank resolved to act as an agent of change, stimulating economic growth and widening development assistance, for example by supporting the private sector with more risk guarantees, investment and other financial instruments, placing greater emphasis on good governance, promoting gender equality and improving accessibility to and distribution of its knowledge services. It also committed to expanding its partnerships with other organizations, including with the private sector and other private institutions.

In September 2008 the Bank organized a high level conference, attended by representatives of multilateral institutions, credit rating agencies, regulatory and supervisory bodies and banks to discuss and exchange ideas on measures to strengthen the region's financial markets and contain the global financial instability evident at that time. In March 2009 the Bank hosted a South Asia Forum on the Impact of the Global Economic and Financial Crisis, as the first of a proposed series of sub-regional conferences. At the end of that month the Bank expanded its Trade Finance Facilitation Program (TFFP, inaugurated in 2004) to support the private sector by increasing its exposure limit to guarantee trade transactions from US $150m. to $1,000m. In May 2009 the Board of Governors approved a general capital increase of some 200% to enable the Bank to extend the lending required to assist countries affected by the global economic downturn, as well as to support the longer-term development objectives of Strategy 2020. In June 2009 the Board of Directors approved a new Countercyclical Support Facility, with resources of $3,000m., to extend short-term, fast-disbursing loans to help developing member countries to counter the effects of the global financial crisis. Countries eligible for the funds were required to formulate a countercyclical development programme, to include plans for investment in public infrastructure or social safety net initiatives. The Board approved an additional $400m, to be made available through the Asian Development Fund (ADF), for countries with no access to the Bank's ordinary capital resources.

In 2011 the Bank's total financing operations amounted to US $21,718m, compared with $17,514m. in the previous year. Of the total amount approved in 2011, $12,605m. was for 114 loans, of which loans from ordinary capital resources totalled $9,250m., while loans from the ADF amounted to $2,213m. In 2011 the Bank approved 23 grants amounting to $614m. financed mainly by the ADF, as well as by other Special Funds (see below) and bilateral and multilateral sources. It also approved funding of $148m. for 212 technical assistance projects, $239m. for six equity investments, and $417m. in guarantees for four projects. During 2011 $7,695m. of the total financing approved came from co-financing partners, for 180 investment and technical assistance projects, compared with $5,431m. in 2010.

An Operations Evaluation Office prepares reports on completed projects, in order to assess achievements and problems. In April 2000 the Bank announced that some new loans would be denominated in local currencies, in order to ease the repayment burden on recipient economies.

The Bank co-operates with other international organizations active in the region, particularly the World Bank, the IMF, UNDP and APEC, and participates in meetings of aid donors for developing member countries. In May 2001 the Bank and UNDP signed a Memorandum of Understanding (MOU) on strategic partnership, in order to strengthen co-operation in the reduction of poverty, for example the preparation of common country assessments and a common database on poverty and other social indicators. Also in 2001 the Bank signed an MOU with the World Bank on administrative arrangements for co-operation, providing a framework for closer co-operation and more efficient use of resources. In May 2004 the Bank signed a revised MOU with ESCAP to enhance co-operation activities to achieve the MDGs. In November 2011 the Bank signed an MOU with the EBRD to strengthen mutual co-operation in their mutual countries of operation. In early 2002 the Bank worked with the World Bank and UNDP to assess the preliminary needs of the interim administration in Afghanistan, in preparation for an International Conference on Reconstruction Assistance to Afghanistan, held in January, in Tokyo, Japan. The Bank pledged to work with its member governments to provide highly concessional grants and loans of some US $500m. over two-and-a-half years, with a particular focus on road reconstruction, basic education, and agricultural irrigation rehabilitation. In June 2008, at an international donors' conference held in Paris, France, the Bank pledged up to $1,300m. to finance infrastructure projects in Afghanistan in the coming five years. A new policy concerning co-operation with non-governmental organizations (NGOs) was approved by the Bank in 1998. The Bank administers an NGO Centre to provide advice and support to NGOs on involvement in country strategies and development programmes.

In June 2004 the Bank approved a new policy to provide rehabilitation and reconstruction assistance following disasters or other emergencies. The policy also aimed to assist developing member countries with prevention, preparation and mitigation of the impact of future disasters. At the end of December the Bank announced assistance amounting to US $325m. to finance immediate reconstruction and rehabilitation efforts in Indonesia, the Maldives and Sri Lanka, which had been severely damaged by the tsunami that had spread throughout the Indian Ocean as a result of a massive earthquake that had occurred close to the west coast of Sumatra, Indonesia. Of the total amount $150m. was to be drawn as new lending commitments from the ADF. Teams of Bank experts undertook to identify priority operations and initiated efforts, in co-operation with governments and other partner organizations, to prepare for more comprehensive reconstruction activities. In accordance with the 2004 policy initiative, an interdepartmental task force was established to co-ordinate the Bank's response to the disaster. In January 2005, at a Special ASEAN Leaders' Meeting, held in Jakarta, Indonesia, the Bank pledged assistance amounting to $500m.; later in that month the Bank announced its intention to establish a $600m. Multi-donor Asian Tsunami Fund to accelerate the provision of reconstruction and technical assistance to countries most affected by the disaster. In March 2006 the Bank hosted a high-level co-ordination meeting on rehabilitation and reconstruction assistance to tsunami-affected countries. In October the Bank, with representatives of the World Bank, undertook an immediate preliminary damage and needs assessment following a massive earthquake in north-western Pakistan, which also affected remote parts of Afghanistan and India. The report identified relief and reconstruction requirements totalling some $5,200m. The Bank made an initial contribution of $80m. to a Special Fund (see below) and also pledged concessional support of up to $1,000m. for rehabilitation and reconstruction efforts in the affected areas. In August 2010 the Bank announced that it was to extend up to $2,000m. in emergency rehabilitation and reconstruction assistance to Pakistan, large areas of which had been severely damaged by flooding. The Bank agreed to undertake, jointly with the World Bank, a damage and needs assessment to determine priority areas of action.

The Bank has actively supported regional, sub-regional and national initiatives to enhance economic development and promote economic co-operation within the region. The Bank is the main co-ordinator and financier of a Greater Mekong Sub-region (GMS) programme, initiated in 1992 to strengthen co-operation between Cambodia, China, Laos, Myanmar, Thailand and Viet Nam. Projects undertaken have included transport and other infrastructure links, energy projects and communicable disease control. The first meeting of GMS heads of state was convened in Phnom-Penh, Cambodia, in November 2002. A second summit was held in Kunming, China, in July 2005, and a third summit in Vientiane, Laos, in March 2008, on the theme 'Enhancing Competitiveness through Greater Connectivity'. In June a GMS Economic Corridors Forum was held, in Kunming, to accelerate development of economic corridors in the sub-region. A second Forum was convened in Phnom-Penh, in September 2009, and a third in Vientiane, in June 2011. Other sub-regional initiatives supported by the Bank include the Central Asian Regional Economic Co-operation (CAREC) initiative, the South Asia Sub-regional Economic Cooperation (SASEC) initiative, the Indonesia, Malaysia, Thailand Growth Triangle (IMT-GT), and the Brunei, Indonesia, Malaysia, Philippines East ASEAN Growth Area (BIMP-EAGA).

SPECIAL FUNDS

The Bank is authorized to establish and administer Special Funds. The Asian Development Fund (ADF) was established in 1974 in order to provide a systematic mechanism for mobilizing and administering resources for the Bank to lend on concessionary terms to the least-developed member countries. In 1998 the Bank revised the terms of ADF. Since 1 January 1999 all new project loans are repayable within 32 years, including an eight-year grace period, while quick-disbursing programme loans have a 24-year maturity, also including an eight-year grace period. The previous annual service charge was redesignated as an interest charge, including a portion to cover administrative expenses. The new interest charges on all loans are 1%–1.5% per annum. In May 2008 30 donor countries pledged US $4,200m. towards the ninth replenishment of ADF resources (ADF X), which totalled $11,300m. to provide resources for the four-year period 2009–12. The total amount included replenishment of the Technical Assistance Special Fund (TASF—see below). Meetings were held in September and December 2011 on the 10th replenishment of ADF resources (ADF XI), to cover 2013–16. During 2011 ADF loans approved amounted to $1,955m.

The Bank provides technical assistance grants from its TASF. The fourth replenishment of its resources was approved in August 2008 for the period 2009–12. By the end of 2011 the Fund's total resources amounted to US $1,845m. During 2011 $140m. was approved under the TASF project preparation, advisory and capacity development activities. A fifth TASF replenishment was to cover 2013–16. The Japan Special Fund (JSF) was established in 1988 to provide finance for technical assistance by means of grants, in both the public and private sectors. The JSF aims to help developing member countries to restructure their economies, enhance the opportunities for attracting new investment, and recycle funds. The Japanese Government had committed a total of 112,900m. yen (equivalent to some $973.7m.) to the JSF by the end of 2011. The Bank administers the ADB Institute Special Fund, which was established to finance the ADB Institute's operations. By 31 December 2011 cumulative commitments to the Special Fund amounted to 20,000m. yen and A$1m. (or $183.7m.).

During the period February 2005–December 2010 the ADB operated an Asian Tsunami Fund, initiated with funds of US $600m. (of which $50m. were not utilized) to accelerate the provision of reconstruction and technical assistance to countries most affected by the natural disaster that had affected the Indian Ocean region in December 2004. During November 2005–June 2011 the Bank managed a Pakistan Earthquake Fund, launched with a commitment from the Bank of $80m., to help to deliver emergency grant financing and technical assistance required for rehabilitation and reconstruction efforts following the massive earthquake that had occurred in October 2005. In February 2007 the Bank established, with an initial $40.0m., the Regional Co-operation and Integration Fund to fund co-operation and integration activities. By the end of 2011 the Fund's total resources amounted to $53.1m., of which $4.1m. was uncommitted. In April 2008 the Bank established a Climate Change Fund, with an initial contribution of $40.0m. By 31 December 2011 total resources amounted to $51.1m., of which $14.2m. was uncommitted. In April 2009 the Bank's Board of Directors approved the establishment of an Asia Pacific Disaster Response Fund (APDRF) to extend rapid assistance to developing countries following a natural disaster. Some $40.0m. from the Asian Tsunami Fund was transferred to inaugurate the APDRF, which was mandated to provide grants of up to $3.0m. to fund immediate humanitarian relief operations. The APDRF was used in late September to provide assistance for more than 300,000 families in the Philippines affected by extensive flooding and damage to infrastructure caused by a tropical storm. In the following month the Bank approved $1.0m. from the Fund to support emergency efforts in Samoa, following an earthquake and tsunami. In August 2010 $3.0m. was approved under the APDRF to extend immediate emergency assistance following devastating flooding in Pakistan. At that time the Bank established a special flood reconstruction fund to administer donor contributions for relief and rehabilitation efforts in Pakistan. At 31 December 2011 the APDRF's total resources amounted to $40.2m., of which $12.4m. remained uncommitted.

TRUST FUNDS

The Bank also manages and administers several trust funds and other bilateral donor arrangements. The Japanese Government funds the Japan Scholarship Program, under which 2,823 scholarships had been awarded to recipients from 35 member countries between 1988 and 2011. In May 2000 the Japan Fund for Poverty Reduction was established, with an initial contribution of 10,000m. yen (approximately US $92.6m.) by the Japanese Government, to support ADB-financed poverty reduction and social development activities. During 2011 the Fund expanded its scope of activity to provide technical assistance grants. By the end of 2011 cumulative resources available to the Fund totalled $504.3m. In March 2004 a Japan Fund for Public Policy Training was established, with an initial contribution by the Japanese Government, to enhance capacity building for public policy management in developing member countries.

The majority of grant funds in support of the Bank's technical assistance activities are provided by bilateral donors under channel financing arrangements (CFAs), the first of which was negotiated in 1980. CFAs may also be processed as a thematic financing tool, for example concerned with renewable energy, water or poverty reduction, enabling more than one donor to contribute. A Co-operation Fund for Regional Trade and Financial Security Initiative was established in July 2004, with contributions by Australia, Japan and the USA, to support efforts to combat money laundering and the financing of terrorism. Other financing partnerships facilities may also be established to mobilize additional financing and investment by development partners. In November 2006 the Bank approved the establishment of an Asia Pacific Carbon Fund (within the framework of a Carbon Market Initiative) to finance clean energy projects in developing member countries. To complement this Fund a new Future Carbon Fund was established, in July 2008, to provide resources for projects beyond 2012 (when the Kyoto Protocol regulating trade in carbon credits was to expire). In December 2006 the Bank established a Water Financing Partnership Facility to help to achieve the objectives of its Water Financing Program. In April 2007 a Clean Energy Financing Partnership Facility (CEFPF) was established, further to provide investment in clean energy projects for developing member countries. An Asian Clean Energy Fund and an Investment Climate Facilitation Fund were established in 2008 within the framework of the CEFPF. A separate Carbon Capture and Storage Fund was established, under the CEFPF, with funding from the Australian Government, in July 2009. In November the Bank, with funding from the United Kingdom, initiated a five-year strategic partnership to combat poverty in India. In the following month the Bank established a multi-donor Urban Financing Partnership Facility. In November 2010 the Board of Directors approved the establishment of an Afghanistan Infrastructure Trust Fund, to be administered by the Bank, to finance and co-ordinate donor funding for infrastructure projects in that country.

In April 2010 the Board of Directors agreed to allocate US $130m. to a new Credit Guarantee and Investment Facility, established by ASEAN + 3 governments, with a further capital contribution of some $570m., in order to secure longer-term financing for local businesses and to support the development of Asian bond markets.

Finance

Internal administrative expenses were budgeted at US $544.8m. for 2012.

Publications

ADB Business Opportunities (monthly).

ADB Institute Newsletter.

ADB Review (monthly).

Annual Report.

Asia Bond Monitor (quarterly).

Asia Capital Markets Monitor (annually).

Asia Economic Monitor (2 a year).

Asian Development Outlook (annually; an *Update* published annually).

Asian Development Review (2 a year).

Basic Statistics (annually).

Development Asia (2 a year).

Key Indicators for Asia and the Pacific (annually).

Law and Policy Reform Bulletin (annually).

Sustainability Report.

Studies and technical assistance reports, information brochures, guidelines, sample bidding documents, staff papers.

Statistics

SUBSCRIPTIONS AND VOTING POWER
(31 December 2011)

Country	Voting power (% of total)	Subscribed capital (% of total)
Regional:		
Afghanistan	0.33	0.03
Armenia	0.54	0.30
Australia	4.94	5.80
Azerbaijan	0.66	0.45
Bangladesh	1.12	1.02
Bhutan	0.30	0.01
Brunei	0.58	0.35
Cambodia	0.34	0.05
China, People's Republic	5.47	6.46
Cook Islands	0.30	0.00
Fiji	0.35	0.07
Georgia	0.57	0.34
Hong Kong	0.74	0.55
India	5.38	6.35
Indonesia	4.44	5.17
Japan	12.82	15.65
Kazakhstan	0.95	0.81
Kiribati	0.30	0.00
Korea, Republic	4.34	5.05
Kyrgyzstan	0.54	0.30
Laos	0.31	0.01
Malaysia	2.48	2.73
The Maldives	0.30	0.00
Marshall Islands	0.30	0.00
Micronesia, Federated States	0.30	0.00
Mongolia	0.31	0.02
Myanmar	0.74	0.55
Nauru	0.30	0.00
Nepal	0.42	0.15
New Zealand	1.53	1.54
Pakistan	2.05	2.19
Palau	0.30	0.00
Papua New Guinea	0.37	0.09
Philippines	2.21	2.39
Samoa	0.30	0.00
Singapore	0.57	0.34
Solomon Islands	0.30	0.01
Sri Lanka	0.76	0.58
Taiwan	1.17	1.09
Tajikistan	0.53	0.29
Thailand	1.39	1.37
Timor-Leste	0.31	0.01
Tonga	0.30	0.00
Turkmenistan	0.50	0.25
Tuvalu	0.30	0.00
Uzbekistan	0.84	0.68
Vanuatu	0.30	0.01
Viet Nam	0.57	0.34
Sub-total	65.07	63.43
Non-regional:		
Austria	0.57	0.34
Belgium	0.57	0.34
Canada	4.50	5.25
Denmark	0.57	0.34
Finland	0.57	0.34
France	2.17	2.33
Germany	3.77	4.34
Ireland	0.57	0.34
Italy	1.75	1.81
Luxembourg	0.57	0.34
Netherlands	1.12	1.03
Norway	0.57	0.34
Portugal	0.39	0.11
Spain	0.57	0.34
Sweden	0.57	0.34
Switzerland	0.77	0.59
Turkey	0.57	0.34
United Kingdom	1.94	2.05
USA	12.82	15.65
Sub-total	34.93	36.57
Total	100.000	100.000

LOAN APPROVALS BY SECTOR

Sector	2011 Amount (US $ million)	2011 %	1968–2011 Amount
Agriculture and natural resources	844.2	7.0	20,468.4
Education	540.0	4.3	6,718.8
Energy	3,941.7	31.3	36,899.1
Finance	180.0	1.4	20,517.7
Health and social protection	20.0	0.2	3,852.9
Industry and trade	—	—	4,588.0
Public sector management	529.8	4.2	14,510.1
Transport and information and communication technology (ICT)	3,602.1	28.6	44,725.3
Water supply and other municipal infrastructure and services	1,176.0	9.3	15,236.8
Multi-sector	1,771.7	14.1	12,186.5
Total	12,605.5	100.0	179,709.7

APPROVALS BY COUNTRY, 2011
(US $ million)

Country	Ordinary Capital loans	ADF loans	Total approvals*
Afghanistan	—	—	300.4
Armenia	65.0	48.6	114.3
Azerbaijan	500.0	—	643.6
Bangladesh	480.0	450.0	2,292.5
Bhutan	—	19.9	27.6
Cambodia	—	67.0	102.4
China, People's Republic	1,439.8	25.0	1,947.9
Cook Islands	4.7	—	6.0
Georgia	140.0	120.0	1,688.5
India	2,872.9	20.0	3,126.7
Indonesia	580.0	—	809.3
Kazakhstan	207.0	—	207.6
Kiribati	—	7.6	23.9
Kyrgyzstan	—	55.0	55.5
Laos	448.2	41.9	537.7
Maldives	—	—	1.1
Marshall Islands	—	—	0.3
Mongolia	—	65.0	95.6
Nepal	—	154.0	62.9
Pakistan	940.2	320.0	2,886.1
Papua New Guinea	165.0	74.1	300.5
Philippines	362.0	—	441.3
Samoa	—	10.8	10.3
Solomon Islands	—	—	10.3
Sri Lanka	199.3	82.3	391.7
Tajikistan	—	—	167.3
Thailand	170.0	—	1,090.8
Timor-Leste	—	—	24.4
Tonga	—	—	39.9
Turkmenistan	125.0	—	125.0
Uzbekistan	940.2	320.0	2,886.1
Vanuatu	—	15.8	61.4
Viet Nam	1,031.4	364.8	3,604.6
Total	10,650.4	1,954.9	21,717.6

* Includes guarantees, equity investments, grants, technical assistance financing and co-financing.

Source: Asian Development Bank, *Annual Report 2011*.

ASSOCIATION OF SOUTHEAST ASIAN NATIONS—ASEAN

Address: 70A Jalan Sisingamangaraja, POB 2072, Jakarta 12110, Indonesia.

Telephone: (21) 7262991; **fax:** (21) 7398234; **e-mail:** public@aseansec.org; **internet:** www.aseansec.org.

ASEAN was established in August 1967 in Bangkok, Thailand, to accelerate economic progress and to increase the stability of the South-East Asian region. In November 2007 its 10 members signed an ASEAN Charter, which, after ratification by all member states, was formally to accord the grouping the legal status of an intergovernmental organization. The Charter entered into force on 15 December 2008.

MEMBERS

Brunei	Malaysia	Singapore
Cambodia	Myanmar	Thailand
Indonesia	Philippines	Viet Nam
Laos		

Organization

(June 2012)

SUMMIT MEETING

The summit meeting is the highest authority of ASEAN, bringing together the heads of state or government of member countries. The first meeting was held in Bali, Indonesia, in February 1976. The new ASEAN Charter specified that summit meetings were to be convened at least twice a year, hosted by the member state holding the Chairmanship of the organization (a position that rotates on an annual basis). The 20th summit meeting was held in Phnom Penh, Cambodia, in April 2012.

ASEAN CO-ORDINATING COUNCIL

The inaugural meeting of the Council was convened in December 2008, upon the entering into force of the new ASEAN Charter. Comprising the ministers of foreign affairs of member states, the Council was to meet at least twice a year to assist in the preparation of summit meetings, to monitor the implementation of agreements and summit meeting decisions and to co-ordinate ASEAN policies and activities.

ASEAN COMMUNITY COUNCILS

Three new Community Councils were established within the framework of the ASEAN Charter in order to pursue the objectives of the different pillars of the grouping and to enhance regional integration and co-operation. The ASEAN Political-Security Community Council, the ASEAN Economic Community Council and the ASEAN Socio-Cultural Community Council each meet at least twice a year, chaired by the appropriate government minister of the country holding ASEAN Chairmanship. Each Council oversees a structure of Sectoral Ministerial Bodies, many of which had established mandates as ministerial meetings, councils or specialized bodies.

COMMITTEE OF PERMANENT REPRESENTATIVES

The Committee, according to the new Charter, was to comprise a Permanent Representative appointed, at ambassadorial level, by each member state. Its functions were to include supporting the work of ASEAN bodies, liaising with the Secretary-General, and facilitating ASEAN co-operation with external partners.

SECRETARIATS

A permanent secretariat was established in Jakarta, Indonesia, in 1976 to form a central co-ordinating body. The Secretariat comprises the Office of the Secretary-General and Bureaux relating to Economic Integration and Finance, External Relations and Co-ordination, and Resources Development. The Secretary-General holds office for a five-year term and is assisted by four Deputy Secretaries-General, increased from two in accordance with the new ASEAN Charter. Two were to remain as nominated positions, rotating among member countries for a non-renewable term of three years; the two new positions of Deputy Secretary-General were to be openly recruited on a renewable three-year term. Each member country is required to maintain an ASEAN National Secretariat to co-ordinate implementation of ASEAN decisions at the national level and to raise awareness of the organization and its activities within that country. In July 2009 the first ASEAN Secretariat Policy Forum was convened with the aim of promoting public debate on the activities of the Secretariat.

ASEAN Committees in Third Countries (composed of heads of diplomatic missions) may be established to promote ASEAN's interests and to support the conduct of relations with other countries and international organizations.

Secretary-General: Dr SURIN PITSUWAN (Thailand) (until 31 Dec. 2012), LE LUONG MINH (Viet Nam) (designate).

Deputy Secretary-General, for the ASEAN Political Security Community: NYAN LYNN (Myanmar).

Deputy Secretary-General, for the ASEAN Economic Community: Dr LIM HONG HIN (Brunei).

Deputy Secretary-General, for the ASEAN Socio-Cultural Community: MISRAN KARMAIN (Malaysia).

Deputy Secretary-General, for Community and Corporate Affairs: BAGAS HAPSORO (Indonesia).

Activities

ASEAN was established in 1967 with the signing of the ASEAN Declaration, otherwise known as the Bangkok Declaration, by the ministers of foreign affairs of Indonesia, Malaysia, the Philippines, Singapore and Thailand. In February 1976 the first ASEAN summit meeting adopted the Treaty of Amity and Co-operation in South-East Asia and the Declaration of ASEAN Concord. Brunei joined the organization in January 1984, shortly after attaining independence. Viet Nam was admitted as the seventh member of ASEAN in July 1995. Laos and Myanmar joined in July 1997 and Cambodia was formally admitted in April 1999, fulfilling the organization's ambition to incorporate all 10 countries in the sub-region.

In December 1997 ASEAN heads of government agreed upon a series of commitments to determine the development of the grouping into the 21st century. The so-called Vision 2020 envisaged ASEAN as 'a concert of Southeast Asian nations, outward looking, living in peace, stability and prosperity, bonded together in partnership in dynamic development and in a community of caring societies'. In October 2003 ASEAN leaders adopted a declaration known as 'Bali Concord II', which committed signatory states to the creation of an ASEAN Economic Community, an ASEAN Security Community and an ASEAN Socio-Cultural Community. In December 2005 heads of state determined to establish a High Level Task Force to formulate a new ASEAN Charter. The finalized document, codifying the principles and purposes of the grouping and according it the legal status of an intergovernmental organization, was signed in November 2007 by ASEAN heads of government attending the 13th summit meeting, convened in Singapore. In July 2008 the ASEAN Ministerial Meeting of ministers of foreign affairs reaffirmed their commitment to ratifying the Charter by the 14th summit meeting, scheduled to be held in Bangkok, Thailand, in December. Early in that month, however, the summit meeting was postponed, owing to political instability in Thailand. None the less, the Charter entered into force on 15 December, having been ratified by each member state. The occasion was commemorated at a Special ASEAN Foreign Ministers' Meeting, convened at the Secretariat, which consequently became the inaugural meeting of the new ASEAN Co-ordinating Council.

In March 2009, at the end of the reconvened 14th summit meeting, held in Cha-am and Hua Hin, Thailand, ASEAN heads of state and government signed the Cha-am Hua Hin Declaration on the Roadmap for an ASEAN Community (2009–15), comprising Blueprints on the ASEAN Political Security, Economic, and Socio-cultural Communities as well as a second Initiative for ASEAN Integration Work Plan. The meeting also issued a Statement on the Global Economic and Financial Crisis, which emphasised the need for co-ordinated policies and joint actions to restore financial stability and to safeguard economic growth in the region.

In October 2010 ASEAN heads of state, meeting in Hanoi, Viet Nam, adopted a Master Plan on ASEAN Connectivity, which identified priority projects to enhance communications and community-building in three dimensions: physical, institutional and people-to-people. The November 2011 summit meeting of ASEAN heads of state, held in Bali, agreed to consider the possibility of developing a 'Connectivity Master Plan Plus' in future, with the aim of expanding the Connectivity initiative beyond the immediate ASEAN region. The November 2011 meeting also adopted a declaration on 'Bali Concord III', promoting a common ASEAN platform on global issues of common interest and concern, based on a shared ASEAN global view.

TRADE AND ECONOMIC CO-OPERATION

In January 1992 heads of government, meeting in Singapore, signed an agreement to create an ASEAN Free Trade Area (AFTA) by 2008. In accordance with the agreement, a common effective preferential tariff (CEPT) scheme came into effect in January 1993. The CEPT covered all manufactured products, including capital goods, and processed agricultural products (which together accounted for two-thirds of intra-ASEAN trade), but was to exclude unprocessed agricultural products. Tariffs were to be reduced to a maximum of 20% within a period of five to eight years and to 0%–5% during the subsequent seven to 10 years. Fifteen categories were designated for accelerated tariff reduction. In October 1993 ASEAN trade ministers agreed to modify the CEPT, with only Malaysia and Singapore having adhered to the original tariff reduction schedule. The new AFTA programme, under which all member countries except Brunei were scheduled to begin tariff reductions from 1 January 1994, substantially enlarged the number of products to be included in the tariff reduction process (i.e. on the so-called 'inclusion list') and reduced the list of products eligible for protection. In September 1994 ASEAN ministers of economic affairs agreed to accelerate the implementation of AFTA, advancing the deadline for its entry into operation from 2008 to 1 January 2003. Tariffs were to be reduced to 0%–5% within seven to 10 years, or within five to eight years for products designated for accelerated tariff cuts. In July 1995, Viet Nam was admitted as a member of ASEAN and was granted until 2006 to implement the AFTA trade agreements. In December 1995 heads of government, at a meeting convened in Bangkok, Thailand, agreed to extend liberalization to certain service industries, including banking, telecommunications and tourism. In July 1997 Laos and Myanmar became members of ASEAN and were granted a 10-year period, from 1 January 1998, to comply with the AFTA schedule.

In December 1998, meeting in Hanoi, Viet Nam, heads of government approved a Statement on Bold Measures, detailing ASEAN's strategies to deal with the economic crisis that had prevailed in the region since late 1997. These included incentives to attract investors, for example a three-year exemption on corporate taxation, accelerated implementation of the ASEAN Investment Area (AIA, see below), and advancing the AFTA deadline, for the original six members, to 2002, with some 85% of products to be covered by the arrangements by 2000, and 90% by 2001. It was envisaged that the elimination of tariffs would be achieved by 2015, by the original six members, or by 2018, by the new members. The Hanoi Plan of Action, which was also adopted at the meeting as a framework for the development of the organization over the period 1999–2004, incorporated a series of measures aimed at strengthening macroeconomic and financial co-operation and enhancing economic integration. In April 1999 Cambodia, on being admitted as a full member of ASEAN, signed an agreement to implement the tariff reduction programme over a 10-year period, commencing 1 January 2000. Cambodia also signed a declaration endorsing the commitments of the 1998 Statement on Bold Measures. In May 2000 Malaysia was granted a special exemption to postpone implementing tariff reductions on motor vehicles for two years from 1 January 2003. In November 2000 a protocol was approved permitting further temporary exclusion of products from the CEPT scheme for countries experiencing economic difficulties. On 1 January 2002 AFTA was formally realized among the original six signatories (Brunei, Indonesia, Malaysia, the Philippines, Singapore and Thailand), which had achieved the objective of reducing to less than 5% trade restrictions on 96.24% of products on the inclusion list. By 1 January 2005 tariffs on just under 99% of products on the 2005 CEPT inclusion list had been reduced to the 0%–5% range among the original six signatory countries, with the average tariff standing at 1.93%. With regard to Cambodia, Laos, Myanmar and Viet Nam, some 81% of products fell within the 0%–5% range. On 1 August 2008 comprehensive revised CEPT rules of origin came into effect.

To complement AFTA in facilitating intra-ASEAN trade, member countries committed to the removal of non-tariff barriers (such as quotas), the harmonization of standards and conformance measures, and the simplification and harmonization of customs procedures. In June 1996 the Working Group on Customs Procedures completed a draft legal framework for regional co-operation, designed to simplify and harmonize customs procedures, legislation and product classification. The agreement was signed in March 1997 at the inaugural meeting of ASEAN finance ministers. (Laos and Myanmar signed the customs agreement in July and Cambodia assented to it in April 1999.) In 2001 ASEAN finalized its system of harmonized tariff nomenclature, implementation of which commenced in the following year. In November the summit meeting determined to extend ASEAN tariff preferences to ASEAN's newer members from January 2002, under the ASEAN Integration System of Preferences (AISP), thus allowing Cambodia, Laos, Myanmar and Viet Nam tariff-free access to the more developed ASEAN markets earlier than the previously agreed target date of 2010. In April 2002 ASEAN ministers of economic affairs signed an agreement to facilitate intra-regional trade in electrical and electronic equipment by providing for the mutual recognition of standards (for example, testing and certification). The agreement was also intended to lower the costs of trade in those goods, thereby helping to maintain competitiveness.

In November 2000 heads of government endorsed an Initiative for ASEAN Integration (IAI), which aimed to reduce economic disparities within the region through effective co-operation, with a particular focus on assisting the newer signatory states, i.e. Cambodia, Laos, Myanmar and Viet Nam. In July 2002 the AMM endorsed an IAI Work Plan, covering 2002–08, which had the following priority areas: human resources development; infrastructure; information and communications technology (ICT); and regional economic integration. Much of the funding for the Initiative came from ASEAN's external partners, including Australia, India, Japan, Norway and the Republic of Korea (South Korea). A second IAI Work Plan, covering the period 2009–15, was adopted by ASEAN heads of state and government in March 2009.

The Bali Concord II, adopted in October 2003, affirmed commitment to existing ASEAN economic co-operation frameworks, including the Hanoi Plan of Action (and any subsequently agreed regional plans of action) and the IAI, and outlined plans for the creation, by 2020, of an integrated ASEAN Economic Community (AEC), entailing: the harmonization of customs procedures and technical regulations by the end of 2004; the removal of non-tariff trade barriers and the establishment of a network of free trade zones by 2005; and the progressive withdrawal of capital controls and strengthening of intellectual property rights. An ASEAN legal unit was to be established to strengthen and enhance existing dispute settlement systems. (A Protocol on Enhanced Dispute Settlement Mechanism was signed in November 2004.) The free movement of professional and skilled workers would be facilitated by standardizing professional requirements and simplifying visa procedures, with the adoption of a single ASEAN visa requirement envisaged by 2005. In 2004 ASEAN economic and trade ministers worked closely, in co-operation with the private sector, to produce a roadmap for the integration of 11 sectors identified as priority areas in the AEC plan of action. In July the ASEAN Ministerial Meeting reviewed progress in preparing the Vientiane Action Programme (VAP), the proposed successor to the Hanoi Plan of Action. In November the 10th meeting of ASEAN heads of state, held in Vientiane, Laos, endorsed the VAP with commitments to deepen regional integration and narrow the development gap within the grouping. An ASEAN Development Fund was to be established to support the implementation of the VAP and other action programmes. The leaders adopted two plans of action (concerning security and sociocultural affairs) to further the implementation of the Bali Concord II regarding the establishment of a three-pillared ASEAN Community, which included the AEC. An ASEAN Framework Agreement for Integration of the Priority Sectors and its Protocols was also signed. Import duties (on 85% of products) were to be eliminated by 2007 for the original members (including Brunei) and by 2012 for newer member states in 11 sectors, accounting for more than 50% of intra-ASEAN trade in 2003. A Blueprint and Strategic Schedule for realizing the AEC by 2015 was approved by ASEAN ministers of economic affairs in August 2007 and was signed by ASEAN heads of state, meeting in November. During 2008 ASEAN developed a 'scorecard' mechanism to track the implementation of the Blueprint by member countries. The first AEC Scorecard was published in April 2010, which demonstrated that 73% of the targets set by the Blueprint had been achieved. In March 2009 heads of state agreed that the new Roadmap for an ASEAN Community should replace the VAP. In May 2010 an ASEAN Trade in Goods Agreement entered into force, which aimed to consolidate all trade commitments and tariff liberalization schedules.

In November 1999 an informal meeting of leaders of ASEAN countries, the People's Republic of China, Japan and South Korea (designating themselves 'ASEAN + 3') issued a Joint Statement on East Asian Co-operation, in which they agreed to strengthen regional unity, and addressed the long-term possibility of establishing an East Asian common market and currency. In July 2000 ASEAN + 3 ministers of foreign affairs convened an inaugural formal summit in Bangkok, Thailand, and in October ASEAN + 3 economic affairs ministers agreed to hold their hitherto twice-yearly informal meetings on an institutionalized basis. In November an informal meeting of ASEAN + 3 leaders approved further co-operation in various sectors and initiated a feasibility study into a proposal to establish a regional free trade area. In May 2001 ASEAN + 3 ministers of economic affairs endorsed a series of projects for co-operation in ICT, environment, small and medium-sized enterprises, Mekong Basin development, and harmonization of standards. In July 2002 ASEAN + 3 ministers of foreign affairs declared their support for other regional initiatives, namely an Asia Co-operation Dialogue, which was initiated by the Thai Government in June, and an Initiative for Development in East Asia (IDEA), which had been announced by the Japanese Government in January. An IDEA ministerial meeting was convened in Tokyo, in August. ASEAN + 3 ministers of labour convened in May 2003. In September the sixth consultation between ASEAN + 3 ministers of economic affairs was held, at which several new projects were endorsed, including two on e-commerce. During 2004 an ASEAN + 3 Unit was established in the ASEAN Secretariat. In November the ASEAN summit meeting agreed to convene a meeting of an East Asia grouping, to be developed in parallel with the ASEAN + 3 framework.

In October 2008 ASEAN heads of state held a special meeting, in Beijing, China, to consider the impact on the region of the deceleration of growth in the world's most developed economies and the ongoing instability of global financial markets. The meeting was followed by a specially convened ASEAN + 3 summit to discuss further regional co-operation to counter the impact of the crisis. In April 2010 ASEAN heads of state, convened in Hanoi, Viet Nam, adopted an ASEAN Strategy for Economic Recovery and Development to ensure sustainable recovery from the global financial and economic crisis. Leaders determined to strengthen efforts to enhance financial monitoring and surveillance, to foster infrastructure and sustainable development and to achieve regional economic integration. The Strategy determined to pursue the ASEAN Connectivity Initiative, which had been approved at the 15th summit in October 2009, as well as efforts to develop a Master Plan on ASEAN Connectivity.

In August 2010 an inaugural meeting of ministers of economic affairs of Cambodia, Laos, Myanmar and Viet Nam (the so-called 'CLMV' countries) was convened, in Da Nang, Viet Nam, further to strengthen intra-economic and trade relations. In particular, the meeting considered measures to enhance trade promotion and to narrow the development gap between the CLMV countries and other countries in the region.

FINANCE AND INVESTMENT

In 1987 heads of government agreed to accelerate regional financial co-operation in order to support intra-ASEAN trade and investment. They adopted measures to increase the role of ASEAN currencies in regional trade, to assist negotiations on the avoidance of double taxation, and to improve the efficiency of tax and customs administrators. An ASEAN Reinsurance Corporation was established in 1988, with initial authorized capital of US $10m. Other measures to attract greater financial resource flows in the region, including an ASEAN Plan of Action for the Promotion of Foreign Direct Investment and Intra-ASEAN Investment, were implemented during 1996.

In February 1997 ASEAN central bank governors agreed to strengthen efforts to combat currency speculation through the established network of foreign exchange repurchase agreements. However, from mid-1997 several Asian currencies were undermined by speculative activities. Subsequent unsuccessful attempts to support the foreign exchange rates contributed to a collapse in the value of financial markets in some countries and to a reversal of the region's economic growth, at least in the short term, while governments undertook macroeconomic structural reforms. In December ASEAN ministers of finance, meeting in Malaysia, agreed to liberalize markets for financial services and to strengthen surveillance of member country economies, to help prevent further deterioration of the regional economy. The ministers also endorsed a proposal for the establishment of an Asian funding facility to provide emergency assistance in support of international credit and structural reform programmes.

In October 1998 ministers of economic affairs, meeting in Manila, Philippines, signed a Framework Agreement on an ASEAN Investment Area (AIA), which was to provide for equal treatment of domestic and other ASEAN direct investment proposals within the grouping by 2010, and of all foreign investors by 2020. The meeting also confirmed that the proposed ASEAN Surveillance Process (ASP), to monitor the economic stability and financial systems of member states, would be implemented with immediate effect, and would require the voluntary submission of economic information by all members to a monitoring committee, to be based in Jakarta, Indonesia. The ASP and the Framework Agreement on the AIA were incorporated into the Hanoi Plan of Action, adopted by heads of state in December 1998. The summit meeting also resolved to accelerate reforms, particularly in the banking and financial sectors, in order to strengthen the region's economies, and to promote the liberalization of the financial services sector. In March 1999 ASEAN ministers of trade and industry, meeting in Phuket, Thailand, as the AIA Council, agreed to open their manufacturing, agriculture, fisheries, forestry and mining industries to foreign investment. Investment restrictions affecting those industries were to be eliminated by 2003 in most cases, although Laos and Viet Nam were granted until 2010. In addition, ministers adopted a number of measures to encourage investment in the region, including access to three-year corporate income tax exemptions, and tax allowances of 30% for investors. The AIA agreement formally entered into force in June 1999, having been ratified by all member countries. In September 2001 ministers agreed to accelerate the full realization of the AIA for non-ASEAN investors in manufacturing, agriculture, forestry, fishing and mining sectors. The date for full implementation was advanced to 2010 for the original six ASEAN members and to 2015 for the newer members. In August 2007 the AIA Council determined to revise the Framework Agreement on the AIA in order to implement a more comprehensive investment arrangement in support of the establishment of the AEC; consequently a new ASEAN Comprehensive Investment Agreement (ACIA) entered into force in April 2012.

In May 2000, ASEAN + 3 ministers of economic affairs, meeting in Chiang Mai, Thailand, proposed the establishment of an enhanced currency swap mechanism, enabling countries to draw on liquidity support to defend their economies during balance of payments difficulties or speculative currency attacks and to prevent future financial crises. The so-called Chiang Mai Initiative Multilateralization (CMIM) on currency swap arrangements was formally approved by ASEAN + 3 finance ministers in May 2001. In August 2003 ASEAN + 3 finance ministers agreed to establish a Finance Co-operation Fund, to be administered by the ASEAN Secretariat; the Fund was to support ongoing economic reviews relating to projects such as the CMIM. An Asian Bond Markets Initiative (ABMI) was launched by ASEAN + 3 countries in 2003 to develop local currency denominated bond markets. In February 2009 ministers of finance of ASEAN + 3 countries convened a special meeting, in Phuket, Thailand, to consider the impact on the region of the global economic and financial crisis, and issued an Action Plan to Restore Economic and Financial Stability of the Asian Region. Ministers agreed to expand the CMIM (from US $80,000m. to $120,000m.) and to establish an independent regional surveillance unit to strengthen economic monitoring. The CMIM entered into force in March 2010. In May ASEAN + 3 finance ministers, convened in Tashkent, Uzbekistan, announced the launch, within the ABMI framework, of a Credit Guarantee and Investment Facility, with an initial capital of $700m., as a trust fund of the Asian Development Bank. Ministers also acknowledged that agreement had been reached on the establishment, in Singapore, of an ASEAN + 3 Macroeconomic Research Office, to monitor and analyse regional economies and to support the effectiveness of the CMIM. The Office was inaugurated in April 2011. In May 2012 ASEAN + 3 ministers of finance and governors of central banks, meeting in Manila, the Philippines, agreed further to expand the CMIM (from $120,000m. to $240,000m.), and to initiate a crisis prevention mechanism: the 'CMIM Precautionary Line (CMIM-PL)'; they also adopted an 'ABMI New Roadmap+', aimed at enhancing the Bond Markets Initiative.

POLITICS AND SECURITY

In 1971 ASEAN members endorsed a declaration envisaging the establishment of a Zone of Peace, Freedom and Neutrality (ZOPFAN) in the South-East Asian region. This objective was incorporated in the Declaration of ASEAN Concord, which was adopted at the first summit meeting of the organization, held in Bali, Indonesia, in February 1976. Heads of state also signed a Treaty of Amity and Co-operation, establishing principles of mutual respect for the independence and sovereignty of all nations, non-interference in the internal affairs of one another and settlement of disputes by peaceful means. The Treaty was amended in December 1987 by a protocol providing for the accession of Papua New Guinea and other non-member countries in the region. In January 1992 ASEAN leaders agreed that there should be greater co-operation on security matters within the grouping, and that ASEAN's post-ministerial conferences (PMCs) should be used as a forum for discussion of questions relating to security with dialogue partners and other countries. In July 1992 Viet Nam and Laos signed ASEAN's Treaty of Amity and Co-operation. Cambodia acceded to the Treaty in January 1995 and Myanmar signed it in July.

In December 1995 ASEAN heads of government, meeting in Bangkok, Thailand, signed a treaty establishing a South-East Asia Nuclear-Weapon Free Zone (SEANWFZ). The treaty was also signed by Cambodia, Myanmar and Laos. It was extended to cover the offshore economic exclusion zones of each country. On ratification by all parties, the treaty was to prohibit the manufacture or storage of nuclear weapons within the region. Individual signatories were to decide whether to allow port visits or transportation of nuclear weapons by foreign powers through territorial waters. The treaty entered into force in March 1997. ASEAN senior officials were mandated to oversee implementation of the treaty, pending the establishment of a permanent monitoring committee. In July 1999 China and India agreed to observe the terms of the SEANWFZ.

In July 1992 the ASEAN Ministerial Meeting issued a statement calling for a peaceful resolution of the dispute concerning the strategically significant Spratly Islands in the South China Sea, which are claimed, wholly or partly, by China, Viet Nam, Taiwan, Brunei, Malaysia and the Philippines. In 1999 ASEAN established a special committee to formulate a code of conduct for the South China Sea to be observed by all claimants to the Spratly Islands. In November 2002 ASEAN and China's ministers of foreign affairs adopted a Declaration on the Conduct (DOC) of Parties in the South China Sea, agreeing to promote a peaceful environment and durable solutions for the area, to resolve territorial disputes by peaceful means, to refrain from undertaking activities that would aggravate existing tensions (such as settling unpopulated islands and reefs), and to initiate a regular dialogue of defence officials. In December 2004 in Kuala Lumpur, Malaysia, at the first senior officials' meeting between ASEAN and China on the implementation of the DOC, it was agreed to adopt the Terms of Reference of the newly established joint working group as a step towards enhancing security and stability in the South China Sea.

In July 1997 ASEAN ministers of foreign affairs reiterated their commitment to the principle of non-interference in the internal affairs of other countries. However, the group's efforts in negotiating a political settlement to the internal conflict in Cambodia marked a significant shift in diplomatic policy towards one of 'constructive intervention', which had been proposed by Malaysia's Deputy Prime Minister in recognition of the increasing interdependence of the region. At the Ministerial Meeting in July 1998 Thailand's Minister of Foreign Affairs, supported by his Philippine counterpart, proposed that the grouping formally adopt a policy of 'flexible engagement'. The proposal, based partly on concerns that the continued restrictions imposed by the Myanmar authorities on dissident political activists was damaging ASEAN relations with its dialogue partners, was to provide for the discussion of the affairs of other member states when they have an impact on neighbouring countries. While rejecting the proposal, other ASEAN ministers agreed to pursue a more limited version, referred to as 'enhanced interaction', and to maintain open dialogue within the grouping. In September 1999 the unrest prompted by the popular referendum on the future of East Timor (now Timor-Leste) and the resulting humanitarian crisis highlighted the unwillingness of some ASEAN member states to intervene in other member countries and undermined the political unity of the grouping. A compromise agreement, enabling countries to act on an individual basis rather than as representatives of ASEAN, was formulated prior to an emergency meeting of ministers of foreign affairs, held during the APEC meetings in Auckland, New Zealand. Malaysia, the Philippines, Singapore and Thailand declared their support for the establishment of a multinational force to restore peace in East Timor and committed troops to participate in the Australian-led operation. At their informal summit in November 1999 heads of state approved the establishment of an ASEAN Troika, which was to be constituted as an ad hoc body comprising the foreign ministers of the Association's current, previous and future chairmanship with a view to providing a rapid response mechanism in the event of a regional crisis.

On 12 September 2001 ASEAN issued a ministerial statement on international terrorism, condemning the attacks of the previous day in the USA and urging greater international co-operation to counter terrorism. The seventh summit meeting in November issued a Declaration on a Joint Action to Combat Terrorism. This condemned the September attacks, stated that terrorism was a direct challenge to ASEAN's aims, and affirmed the grouping's commitment to strong measures to counter terrorism. The summit encouraged member countries to sign (or ratify) the International Convention for the Suppression of the Financing of Terrorism, to strengthen national mechanisms against terrorism, and to work to deepen co-operation, particularly in the area of intelligence exchange; international conventions to combat terrorism would be studied to see if they could be integrated into the ASEAN structure, while the possibility of developing a regional anti-terrorism convention was discussed. The summit noted the need to strengthen security co-operation to restore investor confidence. In its Declaration and other notes, the summit explicitly rejected any attempt to link terrorism with religion or race, and expressed concern for the suffering of innocent Afghanis during the US military action against the Taliban authorities in Afghanistan. The summit's final Declaration was worded so as to avoid any mention of the US action, to which Muslim ASEAN states such as Malaysia and Indonesia were strongly opposed. In November 2002 the eighth summit meeting adopted a Declaration on Terrorism, reiterating and strengthening the measures announced in the previous year. (See, also, Transnational Crime, below.)

The ASEAN Charter that entered into force in December 2008 envisaged the establishment of a new ASEAN human rights body. It was to extend, for the first time within the grouping, a formal structure for the promotion and protection of human rights and fundamental freedoms. In July 2009 the ASEAN Ministerial Meeting of ministers of foreign affairs adopted the terms of reference of the body, which had been drafted by a High Level Panel. It was to be established as the ASEAN Intergovernmental Commission on Human Rights (AICHR) and composed of a national expert representative from each member state. At the same meeting, ASEAN ministers urged the authorities in Myanmar to release all political detainees, including the main opposition leader Aung San Suu Kyi, in order to enable them to participate freely in elections scheduled to be conducted in 2010. In August 2009 Thailand, acting in its capacity as the ASEAN Chair, expressed deep disappointment at the sentencing of Aung San Suu Kyi for allegedly breaching the terms of her house arrest. (Aung San Suu Kyi was eventually released in November 2010.) The inaugural meeting of the AICHR was held at the ASEAN Secretariat in March–April 2010. The Commission considered the formulation of rules of procedure, the development of a five-year work plan and priority activities for 2010/11.

In May 2011 ASEAN heads of state, meeting in Jakarta, Indonesia, urged ministers of foreign affairs to elaborate plans to establish an ASEAN Institute for Peace and Reconciliation.

ASEAN Regional Forum (ARF): In July 1993 the meeting of ASEAN ministers of foreign affairs sanctioned the establishment of a forum to discuss and promote co-operation on security issues within the region, and, in particular, to ensure the involvement of China in regional dialogue. The ARF was informally initiated during that year's PMC, comprising the ASEAN countries, its dialogue partners (at that time Australia, Canada, the European Community, Japan, South Korea, New Zealand and the USA), and China, Laos, Papua New Guinea, Russia and Viet Nam. The first formal meeting of the ARF was conducted in July 1994, following the Ministerial Meeting held in Bangkok, Thailand, and it was agreed that the ARF would be convened on an annual basis. The 1995 meeting, held in Brunei, in August, attempted to define a framework for the future of the Forum. It was perceived as evolving through three stages: the promotion of confidence-building (including disaster relief and peace-keeping activities); the development of preventive diplomacy; and the elaboration of approaches to conflict. The third ARF, convened in July 1996, which was attended for the first time by India and Myanmar, agreed a set of criteria and guiding principles for the future expansion of the grouping. In particular, it was decided that the ARF would only admit as participants countries that had a direct influence on the peace and security of the East Asia and Pacific region. The ARF held in July 1997 reviewed progress made in developing the first two 'tracks' of the ARF process, through the structure of inter-sessional working groups and meetings. The Forum's consideration of security issues in the region was dominated by concern at the political situation in Cambodia; support was expressed for ASEAN mediation to restore stability within that country. Mongolia was admitted into the ARF at its meeting in July 1998. India rejected a proposal that Pakistan attend the meeting to discuss issues relating to both countries' testing of nuclear weapons. The meeting ultimately condemned the testing of nuclear weapons in the region, but declined to criticize specifically India and Pakistan. In July 1999 the ARF warned the Democratic People's Republic of Korea (North Korea) not to conduct any further testing of missiles over the Pacific. At the seventh meeting of the ARF, convened in Bangkok, in July 2000, North Korea was admitted to the Forum. The meeting considered the positive effects and challenges of globalization, including the possibilities for greater economic interdependence and for a growth in transnational crime. The eighth ARF meeting in July 2001 in Hanoi, Viet Nam, pursued these themes, and also discussed the widening development gap between nations. The meeting agreed to enhance the role of the ARF Chairman, enabling him to issue statements on behalf of ARF participants and to organize events during the year. The ninth ARF meeting, held in Bandar Seri Begawan, Brunei, in July 2002, assessed regional and international security developments, and issued a statement of individual and collective intent to prevent any financing of terrorism. The statement included commitments by participants to freeze the assets of suspected individuals or groups, to implement international financial standards and to enhance co-operation and the exchange of information. In October the Chairman, on behalf of all ARF participants, condemned the terrorist bomb attacks committed against tourist targets in Bali, Indonesia. Pakistan joined the ARF in July 2004. In November the first ARF Security Policy Conference was held in Beijing, China. The Conference recommended developing various aspects of bilateral and multilateral co-operation, including with regard to non-traditional security threats. Timor-Leste and Bangladesh became participants in the ARF in July 2005. In July 2006 the ARF issued statements on 'co-operation in fighting cyber attacks and terrorist misuse of cyber space' and on disaster management and emergency responses, which determined to formulate guidelines for enhanced co-operation in humanitarian operations. In January 2007 an ARF maritime security shore exercise was conducted, in Singapore. In March the first ARF Defense Ministers Retreat was convened, in Bali. The 14th ARF, held in Manila, Philippines, in July, approved the establishment of a 'Friends of the Chair' mechanism, comprising three ministers, to promote preventive diplomacy and respond rapidly to political crises. In July 2008 the 15th ARF determined further to strengthen co-operation in natural disaster preparedness and relief operations and resolved to organize training in those areas and a disaster relief exercise. At that time North Korea acceded to ASEAN's Treaty of Amity and Co-operation. The USA acceded to the Treaty in July 2009; Canada and Turkey acceded to the Treaty in July 2010. In July 2009, the ARF marked its 15th anniversary by adopting a Vision Statement for the period up to 2020. It reaffirmed its commitment to 'building a region of peace, friendship and prosperity' and proposed measures to strengthen the ARF and to develop security-based partnerships. In the following 12-month period inter-sessional meetings of the ARF were held on disaster relief, maritime security, confidence-building measures and preventive diplomacy, counter-terrorism and transnational crime, and non-proliferation and disarmament. The 17th meeting of the ARF, convened in Hanoi, in July 2010, adopted a Plan of Action to implement the Vision Statement 2020. The meeting also discussed security in the South China Sea, preparations for a general election in Myanmar and efforts to achieve the denuclearization of the Korean Peninsula.

Since 2000 the ARF has published the *Annual Security Outlook*, to which participating countries submit assessments of the security prospects in the region.

In October 2010 the first so-called ASEAN Defence Ministers' Meeting (ADMM) Plus was held, in Hanoi, incorporating ASEAN ministers and their counterparts from eight dialogue partner countries, i.e. Australia, China, Japan, South Korea, New Zealand, Russia and the USA. The new body was intended to complement the work of the ARF.

TRANSNATIONAL CRIME

In June 1999 the first ASEAN Ministerial Meeting on Transnational Crime (AMMTC) was convened. Regular meetings of senior officials and ministers were subsequently held. The third AMMTC, in October 2001, considered initiatives to combat transnational crime, which was defined as including terrorism, trafficking in drugs, arms and people, money-laundering, cyber-crime, piracy and economic crime. In May 2002 ministers responsible for transnational crime issues convened a Special Ministerial Meeting on Terrorism, in Kuala Lumpur, Malaysia. The meeting approved a work programme to implement a plan of action to combat transnational crime, including information exchange, the development of legal arrangements for extradition, prosecution and seizure, the enhancement of co-operation in law enforcement, and the development of regional security training programmes. In a separate initiative Indonesia, Malaysia and the Philippines signed an agreement on information exchange and the establishment of communication procedures. Cambodia acceded to the agreement in July. In November 2004 ASEAN leaders adopted an ASEAN Declaration against Trafficking in Persons, Particularly Women and Children, which aimed to strengthen co-operation to prevent and combat trafficking, through, *inter alia*, the establishment of a new regional focal network, information-sharing procedures and standardized immigration controls. In May 2011 ASEAN leaders issued a joint statement on enhancing co-operation against trafficking in persons in South East Asia. The Plan of Action of the ASEAN Security Community (envisaged by the Bali Concord II—see above) had as its five key areas: political development; shaping and sharing of norms; conflict prevention; conflict resolution; and post-conflict peace building. In November 2004 eight member countries, namely Brunei, Cambodia, Indonesia, Malaysia, Laos, the Philippines, Singapore and Viet Nam, signed a Treaty on Mutual Legal Assistance in Criminal Matters in Kuala Lumpur, Malaysia.

In January 2007 ASEAN leaders, meeting in Cebu, Philippines, signed an ASEAN Convention on Counter Terrorism. The Convention entered into force in May 2011, having received the required ratification by six member states: Brunei, Cambodia, the Philippines, Singapore, Thailand and Viet Nam.

INDUSTRY

The ASEAN-Chambers of Commerce and Industry (CCI) aims to enhance ASEAN economic and industrial co-operation and the participation in these activities of the private sector. In March 1996 a permanent ASEAN-CCI secretariat became operational at the ASEAN Secretariat. The first AIA Council-Business Sector Forum was convened in September 2001, with the aim of developing alliances between the public and private sectors. An ASEAN Business Advisory Council held its inaugural meeting in April 2003.

The ASEAN Industrial Co-operation (AICO) scheme, initiated in 1996, encourages companies in the ASEAN region to undertake joint manufacturing activities. Products derived from an AICO arrangement benefit immediately from a preferential tariff rate of 0%–5%. The AICO scheme superseded the ASEAN industrial joint venture scheme, established in 1983. The attractiveness of the scheme was expected slowly to diminish as ASEAN moves towards the full implementation of the CEPT scheme. ASEAN has initiated studies of new methods of industrial co-operation within the grouping, with the aim of achieving further integration. In April 2004 ASEAN economic ministers signed a Protocol to Amend the Basic Agreement on the AICO Scheme, which aimed to maintain its relevance. As from 1 January 2005 the tariff rate for Brunei, Cambodia, Indonesia, Laos, Malaysia and Singapore was 0%; for the Philippines 0%–1%, for Thailand 0%–3% and for Myanmar and Viet Nam 0%–5%.

The ASEAN Consultative Committee on Standards and Quality (ACCSQ) aims to promote the understanding and implementation of quality concepts, considered to be important in strengthening the economic development of a member state and in helping to eliminate trade barriers. ACCSQ comprises three working groups: standards and information; conformance and assessment; and testing and calibration. A Standards and Quality Bulletin is published regularly to disseminate information and promote transparency on standards, technical regulations and conformity assessment procedures. In September 1994 an ad hoc Working Group on Intellectual Property (IP) Co-operation was established, with a mandate to formulate a framework agreement on intellectual property co-operation and to strengthen ASEAN activities in intellectual property protection. An ASEAN Intellectual Property Right (IPR) Action Plan covering the period 2011–15 aims, *inter alia,* to promote a balanced IP system taking into account the varying levels of development of member states, to develop national or regional legal and policy infrastructures to address the evolving demands of the IP landscape, and to ensure that IP is utilized as a tool for innovation and development.

In 1988 the ASEAN Fund was established, with capital of US $150m., to provide finance for portfolio investments in ASEAN countries, in particular for small and medium-sized enterprises (SMEs). The Hanoi Plan of Action, which was adopted by ASEAN heads of state in December 1998, incorporated a series of initiatives to enhance the development of SMEs, including training and technical assistance, co-operation activities and greater access to information. In September 2004 ASEAN economic ministers approved an ASEAN Policy Blueprint for SME Development 2004–14, first proposed by a working group in 2001, which comprised strategic work programmes and policy measures for the development of SMEs in the region. The first meeting of a new ASEAN SME Advisory Board was held in Singapore, in June 2011.

In January 2007 senior officials concluded a five-year ASEAN plan of action to support the development and implementation of national occupational safety and health frameworks. In May 2010 ASEAN ministers responsible for labour adopted a Work Programme for the period 2010–15, which aimed to support the realization of the ASEAN Community and to further the objectives of achieving adequate social protection for all workers in the region and fostering productive employment.

FOOD, AGRICULTURE AND FORESTRY

In October 1983 a ministerial agreement on fisheries co-operation was concluded, providing for the joint management of fish resources, the sharing of technology, and co-operation in marketing. In July 1994 a Conference on Fisheries Management and Development Strategies in the ASEAN region resolved to enhance fish production through the introduction of new technologies, aquaculture development, improvements of product quality and greater involvement by the private sector. In June 2011 the ministerial session of the ASEAN-Southeast Asian Fisheries Development Center Conference on Sustainable Fisheries for Sustainable Development adopted a resolution on Sustainable Fisheries for Food Security for the ASEAN Region Towards 2020, to be implemented through individual and collective efforts among member states.

Co-operation in forestry is focused on joint projects, funded by ASEAN's dialogue partners, which include a Forest Tree Seed Centre, an Institute of Forest Management and the ASEAN Timber Technology Centre. In 2005 an Ad Hoc Experts Working Group on International Forest Policy Processes was created, to support the development of ASEAN joint positions and approaches on regional and international forest issues. An ASEAN Social Forestry Network was also established in that year. In November 2007 ASEAN ministers responsible for forestry issued a statement on strengthening forest law enforcement and governance.

There is an established ASEAN programme of training and study exchanges for farm workers, agricultural experts and members of agricultural co-operatives. Other areas of co-operation aim to enhance food security and the international competitiveness of ASEAN food, agriculture and forestry products, to promote the sustainable use and conservation of natural resources, to encourage greater involvement by the private sector in the food and agricultural industry, and to strengthen joint approaches on international and regional issues. An ASEAN Task Force has been formed to harmonize regulations on agricultural products derived from biotechnology. In December 1998 heads of state determined to establish an ASEAN Food Security Information Service to enhance the capacity of member states to forecast and manage food supplies. In 1999 agriculture ministers endorsed guidelines on assessing risk from genetically modified organisms (GMOs) in agriculture, to ensure a common approach. In 2001 work was undertaken to increase public and professional awareness of GMO issues, through workshops and studies. In October ASEAN + 3 ministers of agriculture and forestry met for the first time, and discussed issues of poverty alleviation, food security, agricultural research and human resource development. An East Asia Emergency Rice Reserve (enhancing the original emergency rice reserve scheme, established in 1979) was initiated by ASEAN + 3 ministers in 2003 as a pilot project. In October 2004 ministers of agriculture and forestry, meeting in Yangon, Myanmar, endorsed a Strategic Plan of Action on ASEAN Co-operation in Food, Agriculture and Forestry 2005–10. The ministers also approved certain regional food standards, endorsed the establishment of an ASEAN Animal Health Trust Fund, and resolved to establish a Task Force to co-ordinate regional co-operation for the control and eradication of highly pathogenic avian influenza (HPAI). A Regional Strategy for the Progressive Control and Eradication of HPAI, covering the period 2008–10, was endorsed at a meeting of ASEAN ministers of agriculture and forestry held in November 2007. The meeting also determined to establish an ASEAN Network on Aquatic Animal Health Centres to strengthen diagnostic and certification measures of live aquatic animals within the region. In October 2010 ASEAN ministers of agriculture and forestry endorsed a 'Roadmap Towards an HPAI-Free ASEAN Community by 2020', as a strategic framework to address avian influenza and other transboundary and zoonotic diseases of significant priority to the region.

In February–March 2009 ASEAN heads of state, meeting in Cha-am and Hua Hin, Thailand, adopted an Integrated Food Security Framework and a Strategic Plan of Action on Food Security in the ASEAN Region. An ASEAN-FAO Regional Conference on Food Security was held in Bangkok, Thailand, in May. In October 2010 ministers endorsed the transformation of the ASEAN + 3 Emergency Rice Reserve into a permanent scheme for meeting emergency food requirements and improving food security.

MINERALS AND ENERGY

The ASEAN Centre for Energy (ACE), based in Jakarta, Indonesia, provides an energy information network, promotes the establishment of interconnecting energy structures among ASEAN member countries, supports the development of renewable energy resources and encourages co-operation in energy efficiency and conservation. An ASEAN energy business forum is held annually and attended by representatives of the energy industry in the private and public sectors. In November 1999 a Trans-ASEAN Gas Pipeline Task Force was established and in April 2000 an ASEAN Interconnection Masterplan Study Working Group was established to formulate a study on the power grid. In July 2002 ASEAN ministers of energy signed a Memorandum of Understanding (MOU) to implement the pipeline project, involving seven interconnections. In early 2005 the Trans-Thai-Malaysia Gas Pipeline became operational. In June 2004 the first meeting of ASEAN + 3 energy ministers was also convened in June 2004. Later in that year a permanent Secretariat of the heads of ASEAN Power Utilities/Authorities was established on a three-year rotation basis. An MOU on the regional power grid initiative was signed by ministers of energy, meeting in August 2007. In July 2009 ministers of energy adopted an ASEAN Plan of Action for Energy Cooperation (APAEC) 2010–15.

A Framework of Co-operation in Minerals was adopted by an ASEAN working group of experts in August 1993. The group has also developed a programme of action for ASEAN co-operation in the development and utilization of industrial minerals, to promote the exploration and development of mineral resources, the transfer of mining technology and expertise, and the participation of the private sector in industrial mineral production. The programme of action is implemented by an ASEAN Regional Development Centre for Mineral Resources, which also conducts workshops and training programmes relating to the sector. In August 2005 ASEAN ministers responsible for minerals held an inaugural meeting, in Kuching, Malaysia. A second meeting was convened, in October 2008, in Manila, Philippines; and a third in December 2011, in Hanoi, Viet Nam. An ASEAN Minerals Co-operation Action Plan for 2011–15 aimed to promote information sharing on minerals; to facilitate and enhance trade and investment in the sector; and to promote environmentally and socially sustainable practices.

TRANSPORT

ASEAN objectives for the transport sector include developing multi-modal transport, harmonizing road transport laws and regulations, improving air space management and developing ASEAN legislation for the carriage of dangerous goods and waste by land and sea. In September 1999 ASEAN ministers of transport and communications adopted a programme of action for development of the sector in 1999–2004. By September 2001, under the action programme, a harmonized road route numbering system had been completed, a road safety implementation work plan agreed, and two pilot courses, on port management and traffic engineering and safety, had been adopted. A Framework Agreement on Facilitation of Goods in Transit entered into force in October 2000. In September 2002 ASEAN transport ministers signed Protocol 9 on Dangerous Goods, one of the implementing protocols under the framework agreement, which provided for the simplification of procedures for the transportation of dangerous goods within the region using internationally accepted rules and guidelines. In November 2004 the ASEAN Transport Action Plan 2005–10 was adopted. A roadmap to support the development of an integrated and competitive maritime transport sector in the ASEAN region was signed by ministers of transport in November 2007. At the same time an agreement to strengthen co-operation in maritime cargo and passenger transport was signed with China. The November 2008 meeting of ministers of transport concluded an ASEAN Framework Agreement on the Facilitation of Inter-State Transport. In November 2010 ASEAN ministers of transport adopted a successor Transport Action Plan, for the period 2011–15, which incorporated measures to support the realization of the AEC by 2015 and the regional transport priorities of the Master Plan on ASEAN Connectivity.

In October 2001 ministers approved the third package of commitments for the air and transport sectors under the ASEAN framework agreement on services (according to which member countries were to liberalize the selling and marketing of air and maritime transport services). A protocol to implement the fourth package of commitments was signed by ministers in November 2004. In September 2002 ASEAN senior transport officials signed the MOU on air freight services, which represented the first stage in full liberalization of air freight services in the region. As one of the priority sectors within the ASEAN Framework Agreement for Integration of the Priority Sectors and its Protocols, air travel in the region was to be fully integrated by 2010. The Action Plan for ASEAN Air Transport Integration and Liberalization 2005–15 was adopted in November 2004. The Master Plan for ASEAN Connectivity, adopted by heads of state in October 2010, incorporated objectives for the development and implementation of an ASEAN Single Aviation Market, as well as an ASEAN Single Shipping Market, by 2015.

TELECOMMUNICATIONS

ASEAN aims to achieve interoperability and interconnectivity in the telecommunications sector. In November 2000 ASEAN heads of government approved an e-ASEAN Framework Agreement to promote and co-ordinate e-commerce and internet utilization. The Agreement incorporated commitments to develop and strengthen ASEAN's information infrastructure, in order to provide for universal and affordable access to communications services. Tariff reduction on information and communication technology (ICT) products was to be accelerated, with the aim of eliminating all tariffs in the sector by 2010. In July 2001 the first meeting of ASEAN ministers responsible for telecommunications (TELMIN) was held, in Kuala Lumpur, Malaysia, during which a Ministerial Understanding on ASEAN co-operation in telecommunications and ICT was signed. In September ASEAN ministers of economic affairs approved a list of ICT products eligible for the elimination of duties under the e-ASEAN Framework Agreement. This was to take place in three annual tranches, commencing in 2003 for the six original members of ASEAN and in 2008 for the newer member countries. During 2001 ASEAN continued to develop a reference framework for e-commerce legislation. In September 2003 the third ASEAN telecommunications ministerial meeting adopted a declaration incorporating commitments to harness ASEAN technological advances, create digital opportunities and enhance ASEAN's competitiveness in the field of ICT. The ministers also endorsed initiatives to enhance cybersecurity, including the establishment of computer emergency response teams in each member state. In August 2004 an ASEAN ICT Fund was established to accelerate implementation of the grouping's ICT objectives. At the fifth meeting of telecommunications ministers, held in Hanoi, Viet Nam, in September 2005, the Hanoi Agenda on Promoting Online Services and Applications was adopted. 'ASEANconnect', a web portal collating all essential information and data regarding ICT activities and initiatives within ASEAN, was also launched. In August 2007 ASEAN telecommunications ministers, convened in Siem Reap, Cambodia, endorsed a commitment to enhance universal access of ICT services within ASEAN, in particular to extend the benefits of ICT to rural communities and remote areas. At the same time ministers met their counterparts from China, Japan and South Korea to strengthen co-operation in ICT issues. An ASEAN Connectivity Initiative, approved by ASEAN heads of state in October 2009, envisaged greater investment and targets for co-operation in ICT, as well as transport, energy and cross-border movement of goods and people. A Master Plan on ASEAN Connectivity (MPAC) was adopted by heads of state meeting in Hanoi, in October 2010. In September 2011 ASEAN and the ADB signed an agreement to establish the ASEAN Infrastructure Fund (AIF), which was to channel funding to support regional infrastructure development and MPAC. In January 2011 ASEAN telecommunications ministers adopted an ASEAN ICT Masterplan 2015 ('AIM2015').

SCIENCE AND TECHNOLOGY

ASEAN's Committee on Science and Technology (COST) supports co-operation in food science and technology, meteorology and geophysics, microelectronics and ICT, biotechnology, non-conventional energy research, materials science and technology, space technology applications, science and technology infrastructure and resources development, and marine science. There is an ASEAN Science Fund, used to finance policy studies in science and technology and to support information exchange and dissemination.

The Hanoi Plan of Action, adopted in December 1998, envisaged a series of measures aimed at promoting development in the fields of science and technology, including the establishment of networks of science and technology centres of excellence and academic institutions, the creation of a technology scan mechanism, the promotion of public and private sector co-operation in scientific and technological (particularly ICT) activities, and an increase in research on strategic technologies. In September 2001 the ASEAN Ministerial Meeting on Science and Technology, convened for its first meeting since 1998, approved a new framework for the implementation of ASEAN's Plan of Action on Science and Technology during the period 2001–04. The Plan aimed to help less developed member countries become competitive in the sector and integrate into regional co-operation activities. In September 2003 ASEAN and China inaugurated a Network of East Asian Think-tanks to promote scientific and technological exchange. In November 2004 a Ministerial Meeting on Science and Technology decided to establish an ASEAN Virtual Institute of Science and Technology with the aim of developing science and technology human resources in the region. In August 2006 an informal Ministerial Meeting on Science and Technology endorsed in principle a Plan of Action on Science and Technology for 2007–11, focusing on the following areas of activity: environment and disaster management; new and renewable energy; open source software system; and food safety and security. An ASEAN Plan of Action on Science and Technology for 2012–17 covered: food security; an early warning system for natural disasters; biofuels; development and application of open source software; and climate change.

ENVIRONMENT

An ASEAN Agreement on the Conservation of Nature and Natural Resources was signed in July 1985. In April 1994 a ministerial meeting on the environment approved long-term objectives on environmental quality and standards for the ASEAN region, aiming to enhance joint action in addressing environmental concerns. At the same time, ministers adopted standards for air quality and river water to be achieved by all ASEAN member countries by 2010. In June 1995 ministers agreed to co-operate to counter the problems of transboundary pollution. An ASEAN Regional Centre for Biodiversity Conservation (ARCBC) was established in February 1999.

In December 1997 ASEAN heads of state endorsed a Regional Haze Action Plan to address the environmental problems resulting from forest fires, which had afflicted several countries in the region throughout that year. A Haze Technical Task Force undertook to implement the plan, with assistance from the UN Environment Programme. Sub-regional fire-fighting arrangement working groups for Sumatra and Borneo were established in April 1998 and in May the Task Force organized a regional workshop to strengthen ASEAN capacity to prevent and alleviate the haze caused by the extensive fires. A pilot project of aerial surveillance of the areas in the region most at risk of forest fires was initiated in July. In December heads of government resolved to establish an ASEAN Regional Research and Training Centre for Land and Forest Fire Management. In March 2002 members of the working groups on sub-regional fire-fighting arrangements for Sumatra and Borneo agreed to intensify early warning efforts and surveillance activities in order to reduce the risks of forest fires. In June ASEAN ministers of the environment signed an Agreement on Transboundary Haze Pollution, which was intended to provide a legal basis for the Regional Haze Action Plan. The Agreement, which entered into force in November 2003, required member countries to co-operate in the prevention and mitigation of haze pollution, for example, by responding to requests for information by other states and facilitating the transit of personnel and equipment in case of disaster. The Agreement also provided for the establishment of an ASEAN Co-ordination Centre for Transboundary Haze Pollution Control. The first conference of parties to the Agreement was held in November 2004. An ASEAN Specialized Meteorological Centre (ASMC) based in Singapore, plays a primary role in long-range climatological forecasting, early detection and monitoring of fires and haze. In August 2005, guided by the ASEAN Agreement on Transboundary Haze Pollution, member countries activated bilateral and regional mechanisms to exchange information and mobilize resources to deal with severe fires in Sumatra (Indonesia), peninsular Malaysia and southern Thailand. In September 2007 ASEAN ministers agreed to establish a sub-regional Technical Working Group to focus on addressing land and forest fires in the northern part of the region.

In May 2001 environment ministers launched the ASEAN Environment Education Action Plan (AEEAP), with the aim of promoting public awareness of environmental and sustainable development issues. In November 2003 ASEAN + 3 ministers responsible for the environment agreed to prioritize environmental activities in the following areas: environmentally sustainable cities; global environmental issues; land and forest fires and transboundary haze pollution; coastal and marine environment; sustainable forest management; freshwater resources; public awareness and environmental education; promotion of green technologies and cleaner production; and sustainable development monitoring and reporting. The Vientiane Action Plan (see above) incorporated objectives for environmental and natural resource management for the period 2004–10. In September 2005 the ASEAN Centre for Biodiversity, funded jointly by ASEAN and the European Union (EU), was inaugurated in La Union, near Manila, the Philippines. In that month ministers of the environment approved an ASEAN Strategic Plan of Action on Water Resources Management. The ASEAN summit meeting convened in November 2007 was held on the theme of 'energy, environment, climate change, and sustainable development'. A final Declaration on Environmental Sustainability incorporated specific commitments to strengthen environmental protection management, to respond to climate change and to work towards the conservation and sustainable management of natural resources. A Special Ministerial Meeting on the environment was held in Hua Hin, Thailand, in September 2009. The meeting reviewed ongoing programmes and approved the establishment of an ASEAN Working Group on Climate Change. In the following month ASEAN environment ministers endorsed the terms of reference of an ASEAN Climate Change Initiative and adopted a Singapore Resolution on Environmental Sustainability and Climate Change, recognising the need for closer co-operation in responding to climate change. In April 2010 ASEAN heads of state, meeting in Hanoi, Viet Nam, adopted a Leaders' Statement on Joint Response to Climate Change, which reaffirmed ASEAN's commitment to securing a new legally binding agreement on carbon emissions and to strengthening ASEAN efforts to counter and respond to climate change.

SOCIAL WELFARE AND DEVELOPMENT

ASEAN is concerned with a range of social issues including youth development, the role of women, health and nutrition, education and labour affairs. In December 1993 ASEAN ministers responsible for social affairs adopted a Plan of Action for Children, which provided a framework for regional co-operation for the survival, protection and development of children in member countries. ASEAN supports efforts to combat drug abuse and illegal drugs-trafficking. It aims to promote education and drug-awareness campaigns throughout the region, and administers a project to strengthen the training of personnel involved in combating drug abuse. In July 1998 ASEAN ministers of foreign affairs signed a Joint Declaration for a Drug-Free ASEAN, which envisaged greater co-operation among member states, in particular in information exchange, educational resources and legal procedures, in order to eliminate the illicit production, processing and trafficking of narcotic substances by 2020. (This deadline was subsequently advanced to 2015.)

In December 1998 ASEAN leaders approved a series of measures aimed at mitigating the social impact of the financial and economic crises that had affected many countries in the region. Plans of Action were formulated on issues of rural development and poverty eradication, while Social Safety Nets, which aimed to protect the most vulnerable members of society, were approved. The summit meeting emphasized the need to promote job generation as a key element of strategies for economic recovery and growth. The IAI, launched in November 2000 (see above) aimed to close the widening development gap between ASEAN members. The Plan of Action for the ASEAN Socio-Cultural Community (envisaged in the Bali Concord II—see above) was adopted by ASEAN leaders in November 2004. The first ASEAN + 3 Ministerial Meeting for social welfare and development was convened in Bangkok, Thailand, in December, at which it was agreed that the three key areas of co-operation were to be: the promotion of a community of caring societies in the region; developing policies and programmes to address the issue of ageing; and addressing human resource development in the social sector. In July 2005 it was agreed to establish an ASEAN Development Fund, to which each member country would make an initial contribution of US $1m. An ASEAN Commission on the Promotion and Protection of the Rights of Women and Children was inaugurated in April 2010. A Strategic Framework and Plan of Action for Social Welfare, Family and Children for the period 2011–15 had the following objectives: promoting the welfare of children by safeguarding their rights, ensuring their survival and their full development; protecting children from abuse, discrimination and exploitation; protecting the elderly by supporting community-based support systems to supplement the role of the family as primary caregiver; strengthening regional co-operation to promote self-reliance of older persons and persons with disabilities; strengthening national social welfare and social protection national capacities; and developing family support and family life education programmes.

The seventh ASEAN summit meeting, held in November 2001, declared work on combating HIV and AIDS to be a priority. The second phase of a work programme to combat AIDS and provide help for sufferers was endorsed at the meeting. Heads of government expressed their readiness to commit the necessary resources for prevention and care, and to attempt to obtain access to cheaper drugs. An ASEAN task force on AIDS has been operational since March 1993. An ASEAN Co-operation Forum on HIV/AIDS was held in February 2003, in Bangkok. An East Asia and Pacific Consultation on Children and AIDS was convened in March 2006 and identified nine urgent actions to respond to children affected by HIV/AIDS. In April 2003 a Special ASEAN Leaders' Meeting on Severe Acute Respiratory Syndrome (SARS) endorsed the recommendations of ministers of health, who convened in special session a few days previously, and agreed to establish an ad hoc ministerial-level Joint Task Force to follow-up and monitor implementation of those decisions. Co-operation measures approved included public information and education campaigns, health and immigration control procedures, and the establishment of an early-warning system on emerging infectious diseases. In June 2006 ASEAN ministers responsible for health adopted a declaration entitled 'ASEAN Unity in Health Emergencies'. In June 2008 ASEAN inaugurated an internet-based information centre on emerging infectious diseases in the ASEAN + 3 countries to exchange data relating to infection outbreaks and surveillance. In May 2009 ASEAN + 3 ministers of health convened a Special Meeting on Influenza A(H1N1), a new strain of swine flu that had recently emerged as a serious threat to humans. The meeting agreed to strengthen surveillance and effective responses; to implement national pandemic preparedness plans; and to ensure effective public communication. It urged regional co-operation to promote surveillance and the transfer of technology, in relation to the production of vaccines. An International Ministerial Conference on Animal and Pandemic Influenza was convened in Hanoi, Viet Nam, in April 2010. The meeting commended the efforts to counter infectious diseases, but noted the continued threat of highly pathogenic avian influenza (HPAI—see above).

In November 2011 ASEAN ministers approved a new framework action plan on rural development and poverty eradication, covering the period 2011–15, to address the following priorities: sustainable rural development and rural economic growth; food security and food sovereignty amid climate change; social protection and safety nets; development of infrastructure and human resources in rural areas; constituency building for rural development and poverty eradication; and monitoring and evaluation of the poverty reduction in the region.

In January 1992 the ASEAN summit meeting resolved to establish an ASEAN University Network (AUN) to hasten the development of a regional identity. A draft AUN Charter and Agreement were adopted in 1995. The Network aims to strengthen co-operation within the grouping, develop academic and professional human resources and transmit information and knowledge. The 17 universities linked by the Network carry out collaborative studies and research programmes. Three more universities became members of the AUN in November 2006. At the seventh ASEAN summit in November 2001 heads of government agreed to establish the first ASEAN University, in Malaysia. In August 2005 it was agreed to convene a regular ASEAN Ministerial Meeting on education; the first meeting was held in March 2006. In March 2007 education ministers determined to restart an ASEAN Student Exchange Programme.

In January 2007 ASEAN heads of government signed a Declaration on the Protection and Promotion of the Rights of Migrant Workers, which mandated countries to promote fair and appropriate employment protection, payment of wages, and adequate access to decent working and living conditions for migrant workers. A Committee on the Implementation of the ASEAN Declaration held its inaugural meeting in September 2008.

DISASTER MANAGEMENT

An ASEAN Committee on Disaster Management was established in early 2003 and worked to formulate a framework for co-operation in disaster management and emergency response. In January 2005 a Special ASEAN Leaders' Meeting was convened in Jakarta, Indonesia, to consider the needs of countries affected by an earthquake and devastating tsunami that had occurred in the Indian Ocean in late December 2004. The meeting, which was also attended by the UN Secretary-General, the President of the World Bank and other senior envoys of donor countries and international organizations, adopted a Declaration on Action to Strengthen Emergency Relief, Rehabilitation, Reconstruction and Prevention on the Aftermath of Earthquake and Tsunami Disaster. In July 2005 an ASEAN Agreement on Disaster Management and Emergency Response was signed in Vientiane, Laos. The Agreement stated as its objective the provision of mechanisms that would effectively reduce the loss of life and damage to the social, economic and environmental assets of the region and the response to disaster emergencies through concerted national efforts and increased regional and international co-operation. By October 2009 the Agreement had been ratified by each member state and it entered into force in December. In May 2009 ASEAN, with the World Bank and UN International Strategy for Disaster Reduction, announced a new co-operation programme to strengthen disaster reduction, including reducing vulnerability to natural hazards, and disaster management in South-East Asia.

TOURISM

National tourist organizations from ASEAN countries meet regularly to assist in co-ordinating the region's tourist industry, and a Tourism Forum is held annually to promote the sector. (In January 2012 the Forum was held in Manado, North Sulawesi, Indonesia.) The first formal meeting of ASEAN ministers of tourism was held in January 1998, in Cebu, Philippines. The meeting adopted a Plan of Action on ASEAN Co-operation in Tourism, which aimed to promote intra-ASEAN travel, greater investment in the sector, joint marketing of the region as a single tourist destination and environmentally sustainable tourism. In January 1999 the second meeting of ASEAN ministers of tourism agreed to appoint country co-ordinators to implement various initiatives, including research to promote the region as a tourist destination in the 21st century, and to develop a cruise ship industry; and the establishment of a network of ASEAN Tourism Training Centres to develop new skills and technologies in the tourist industry. The third meeting of tourism ministers, held in Bangkok, Thailand, in January 2000, agreed to reformulate the Visit ASEAN Millennium Year initiative as a long-term Visit ASEAN programme. This was formally launched in January 2001. The first phase of the programme promoted brand awareness through an intense marketing effort; the second phase, initiated at the fifth meeting of tourism ministers, held in Yogyakarta, Indonesia, in January 2002, was to direct campaigns towards end-consumers. Ministers urged member states to abolish all fiscal and non-fiscal travel barriers to encourage tourism, including intra-ASEAN travel. Tourism ministers from the ASEAN + 3 countries attended the meeting for the first time. In November the eighth summit of heads of state adopted a framework agreement on ASEAN co-operation in tourism, aimed at facilitating domestic and intra-regional travel. ASEAN national tourism organizations signed an implementation plan for the agreement in May 2003, when they also announced a Declaration on Tourism Safety and Security. In January 2011 ASEAN ministers of tourism approved a new ASEAN Tourism Strategic Plan for the period 2011–15. The Plan envisaged promoting the region as a single tourist destination, developing a set of ASEAN tourism standards with a certification process, and enabling visitors to travel throughout the region with a single visa.

CULTURE AND INFORMATION

Regular workshops and festivals are held in visual and performing arts, youth music, radio, television and films, and print and interpersonal media. In addition, ASEAN administers a News Exchange and provides support for the training of editors, journalists and information officers. In 2000 ASEAN adopted new cultural strategies, with the aim of raising awareness of the grouping's objectives and achievements, both regionally and internationally. The strategies included: producing ASEAN cultural and historical educational materials; promoting cultural exchanges; and achieving greater exposure of ASEAN cultural activities and issues in the mass media. An ASEAN Youth Camp was held for the first time in that year, and subsequently has been organized on an annual basis. An ASEAN Youth Forum is convened on the sidelines of the ASEAN summit meeting (most recently in Phnom Penh, Cambodia, in April 2012). ASEAN ministers responsible for culture and arts (AMCA) met for the first time in October 2003. The fourth ministerial meeting was convened, with their ministerial counterparts from the ASEAN + 3 countries, in Clark, Angelus City (Pampanga province), Philippines, in March 2010. The fourth ASEAN Festival of Arts was held concurrently, on the theme 'The Best of ASEAN', while Clark was named as the first ASEAN City of Culture.

In July 1997 ASEAN ministers of foreign affairs endorsed the establishment of an ASEAN Foundation to promote awareness of the organization and greater participation in its activities; this was inaugurated in July 1998 and is based at the ASEAN secretariat building (www.aseanfoundation.org).

EXTERNAL RELATIONS

ASEAN's external relations have been pursued through a dialogue system, initially with the objective of promoting co-operation in economic areas with key trading partners. The system has been expanded in recent years to encompass regional security concerns and co-operation in other areas, such as the environment. The ARF (see above) emerged from the dialogue system, and more recently the formalized discussions of ASEAN with China, Japan and South Korea (ASEAN + 3) has evolved as a separate process with its own strategic agenda. In February 2000 a meeting of ASEAN heads of state and the Secretary-General of the United Nations (UN) took place in Bangkok, Thailand. (A second ASEAN-UN summit was held in September 2005, in New York, USA, and a third was convened in October 2010, in Hanoi, Viet Nam.) In December 2006 the UN General Assembly granted ASEAN permanent observer status at its meetings.

In December 2005 the first East Asia Summit (EAS) meeting was convened, following the ASEAN leaders' meeting in Kuala Lumpur, Malaysia. It was attended by ASEAN member countries, China, Japan, South Korea (the '+ 3' countries), India, Australia and New Zealand; Russia participated as an observer. The meeting agreed to pursue co-operation in areas of common interest and determined to meet annually. It concluded a Declaration on Avian Influenza Prevention, Control and Response. At the second EAS meeting, held in Cebu, Philippines, in January 2007, a Declaration on East Asian Energy Security was adopted. An inaugural meeting of East Asian ministers of energy was convened in August. The third summit meeting was convened in Singapore, in November; it issued the Singapore Declaration on Climate Change, Energy and the Environment and held discussions on issues of mutual concern. The fourth EAS, scheduled to be held in Bangkok, in December 2008, was postponed owing to civil unrest, and was again deferred, in April 2009, owing to violent anti-government demonstrations at a new venue in Pattaya, Thailand. A statement by EAS heads of state, issued in June, declared their support for efforts to counter the global economic and financial crisis, including measures agreed by the G20, completion of the World Trade Organization's Doha Round, and a Comprehensive Economic Partnership in East Asia Initiative. Russia and the USA participated fully in the EAS for the first time at the sixth summit meeting, held in Bali, Indonesia, in November 2011.

European Union: In March 1980 a co-operation agreement was signed between ASEAN and the European Community (EC, as the EU was known prior to its restructuring on 1 November 1993), which provided for the strengthening of existing trade links and increased co-operation in the scientific and agricultural spheres. A Joint Co-operation Committee met in November (and annually thereafter). An ASEAN-EC Business Council was launched in December 1983 to promote private sector co-operation. The first meeting of ministers of economic affairs from ASEAN and EC member countries took place in October 1985. In December 1990 the Community adopted new guidelines on development co-operation, with an increase in assistance to Asia, and a change in the type of aid given to ASEAN members, emphasizing training, science and technology and venture capital, rather than assistance for rural development. In October 1992 the EC and ASEAN agreed to promote further trade between the regions, as well as bilateral investment, and made a joint declaration in support of human rights. An EU-ASEAN Junior Managers Exchange Programme was initiated in November 1996, as part of efforts to promote co-operation and understanding between the industrial and business sectors in both regions. In December 2000 an ASEAN-EU Ministerial Meeting was held in Vientiane, Laos. Both sides agreed to pursue dialogue and co-operation and issued a joint declaration that accorded support for the efforts of the UN Secretary-General's special envoy towards restoring political dialogue in Myanmar. Myanmar agreed to permit an EU delegation to visit the country and political opposition leaders in early 2001. In September the Joint Co-operation Committee, meeting for the first time since 1999, resolved to strengthen policy dialogue, in particular in areas fostering regional integration. An ASEAN-EU Business Network was established in Brussels, Belgium, in 2001, to develop political and commercial contacts between the two sides. An ASEAN-EU Business Summit meeting was convened for the first time in May 2011, in Jakarta, Indonesia.

In May 1995 ASEAN and EU senior officials endorsed an initiative to strengthen relations between the two economic regions within the framework of an Asia-Europe Meeting of heads of government (ASEM). The first ASEM was convened in Bangkok, Thailand, in March 1996, at which leaders approved a new Asia-Europe Partnership for Greater Growth. The second ASEM summit meeting, held in April 1998, focused heavily on economic concerns. In February 1997 ministers of foreign affairs of countries participating in ASEM met in Singapore. Despite ongoing differences regarding human rights issues, in particular concerning ASEAN's granting of full membership status to Myanmar and the situation in East Timor (which precluded the conclusion of a new co-operation agreement), the Ministerial Meeting issued a final joint declaration, committing both sides to strengthening co-operation and dialogue on economic, international and bilateral trade, security and social issues. The third ASEM summit meeting was convened in Seoul, South Korea in October 2000. At the 14th ASEAN-EU Ministerial Meeting, held in Brussels, in January 2003, delegates adopted an ASEAN-EU Joint Declaration on Co-operation to Combat Terrorism. An

ASEM seminar on combating terrorism was held in Beijing, China, in October. In February 2003 the EU awarded €4.5m. under the ASEAN-EU Programme on Regional Integration Support (APRIS) to enhance progress towards establishing AFTA. (The first phase of the APRIS programme was concluded in September 2006, and a second three-year phase, APRIS II, was initiated in November with a commitment by the EU of €7.2m.) In April 2003 the EU proposed the creation of a regional framework, the Trans-Regional EU-ASEAN Trade Initiative (TREATI), to address mutual trade facilitation, investment and regulatory issues. It was suggested that the framework might eventually result in a preferential trade agreement. In January 2004 a joint statement was issued announcing a roadmap for implementing the TREATI and an EU-ASEAN work plan for that year. The fifth ASEM meeting of heads of state and government was held in Hanoi, Viet Nam, in October, attended for the first time by the 10 new members of the EU and by Cambodia, Laos, and Myanmar. At the session of the Joint Co-operation Committee held in February 2005, in Jakarta, Indonesia, it was announced that the European Commission's communication entitled 'A New Partnership with Southeast Asia', issued in July 2003, would form the basis for the development of the EU's relations with ASEAN, along with Bali Concord II and the VAP. Under the new partnership, the TREATI would represent the framework for dialogue on trade and economic issues, whereas the READI (Regional EC ASEAN Dialogue Instrument) would be the focus for non-trade issues. The sixth ASEM, convened in Helsinki, Finland, in September 2006, on the theme '10 Years of ASEM: Global Challenges and Joint Responses', was attended for the first time by the ASEAN Secretariat, Bulgaria, India, Mongolia, Pakistan and Romania. The participants adopted a Declaration on Climate Change, aimed at promoting efforts to reach consensus in international climate negotiations, and the Helsinki Declaration on the Future of ASEM, detailing guidelines and practical recommendations for developing future ASEM co-operation. A Declaration on an Enhanced Partnership was endorsed in March 2007 and a plan of action to pursue strengthened co-operation was adopted at an ASEAN-EU summit meeting held in November. The seventh ASEM summit, convened in Beijing, China, in October 2008, issued a Declaration on Sustainable Development, focusing on the MDGs, climate change and energy security, and social cohesion. In May 2009 ASEAN and EU ministers of foreign affairs signed a declaration committing both sides to completing EU accession to the Treaty of Amity and Co-operation as a priority. The 18th ASEAN-EU Ministerial Meeting was held in Madrid, Spain, in May 2010, on the theme of 'Partners in Regional Integration'. The eighth ASEM summit took place in October, in Brussels. During the meeting Australia, New Zealand and Russia acceded to the grouping. The ninth ASEM summit was to be convened in Japan, in November 2012.

People's Republic of China: Efforts to develop consultative relations between ASEAN and China were initiated in 1993. Joint Committees on economic and trade co-operation and on scientific and technological co-operation were subsequently established. The first formal consultations between senior officials of the two sides were held in April 1995. In July 1996, in spite of ASEAN's continued concern at China's territorial claims to the Spratly Islands in the South China Sea, China was admitted to the PMC as a full dialogue partner. In February 1997 a Joint Co-operation Committee was established to co-ordinate the China-ASEAN dialogue and all aspects of relations between the two sides. Relations were further strengthened by the decision to form a joint business council to promote bilateral trade and investment. China participated in the informal summit meeting held in December, at the end of which both sides issued a joint statement affirming their commitment to resolving regional disputes through peaceful means. China was a participant in the first official ASEAN + 3 meeting of foreign ministers, which was convened in July 2000. An ASEAN-China Experts Group was established in November, to consider future economic co-operation and free trade opportunities. The Group held its first meeting in April 2001 and proposed a framework agreement on economic co-operation and the establishment of an ASEAN-China free trade area within 10 years (with differential treatment and flexibility for newer ASEAN members). Both proposals were endorsed at the seventh ASEAN summit meeting in November 2001. In November 2002 an agreement on economic co-operation was concluded by the ASEAN member states and China. The Framework Agreement on Comprehensive Economic Co-operation between ASEAN and China entered into force in July 2003, and envisaged the establishment of an ASEAN-China Free Trade Area (ACFTA) by 2010 (with the target for the newer member countries being 2015). The Agreement provided for strengthened co-operation in key areas including agriculture, information and telecommunications, and human resources development. It was also agreed to implement the consensus of the Special ASEAN-China Leaders' Meeting on SARS, held in April 2003, and to set up an ASEAN + 1 special fund for health co-operation. In October China acceded to the Treaty on Amity and Co-operation and signed a joint declaration with ASEAN on Strategic Partnership for Peace and Prosperity on strengthening co-operation in politics, economy, social affairs, security and regional and international issues. It was also agreed to continue consultations on China's accession to the SEANWFZ and to expedite the implementation of the Joint Statement on Co-operation in the Field of Non-Traditional Security Issues and the Declaration on the Conduct of Parties in the South China Sea. In November 2004 ASEAN and China signed the Agreement on Trade in Goods and the Agreement on Dispute Settlement Mechanism of the Framework Agreement on Comprehensive Economic Co-operation, to be implemented from 1 July 2005. A Plan of Action to Implement ASEAN-China Joint Declaration on Strengthening Strategic Partnership for Peace and Prosperity was also adopted by both parties at that time. In August 2005 ASEAN signed an MOU with China on cultural co-operation. An ASEAN-China Agreement on Trade in Services was signed in January 2007, within the Framework Agreement on Comprehensive Economic Co-operation, and entered into force on 1 July. The final component of the Framework Agreement, an ASEAN-China Investment Agreement, was signed in August 2009. Accordingly, ACFTA entered fully into effect on 1 January 2010. In November 2007 the ASEAN-China summit resolved that the environment should be included as a priority area for future co-operation and endorsed agreements concluded earlier in that month to strengthen co-operation in aviation and maritime transport. An ASEAN-China Environmental Co-operation Centre was formally inaugurated in Beijing, in May 2011. It was announced in October 2011 that China was to establish a mission to ASEAN during 2012.

Japan: The first meeting between the two sides at ministerial level was held in October 1992. At this meeting, and subsequently, ASEAN requested Japan to increase its investment in member countries and to make Japanese markets more accessible to ASEAN products, in order to reduce the trade deficit with Japan. Since 1993 ASEAN-Japanese development and cultural co-operation has expanded under schemes including the Inter-ASEAN Technical Exchange Programme, the Japan-ASEAN Co-operation Promotion Programme and the ASEAN-Japan Friendship Programme. In December 1997 Japan, attending the informal summit meeting in Malaysia, agreed to improve market access for ASEAN products and to provide training opportunities for more than 20,000 young people in order to help develop local economies. In December 1998 ASEAN heads of government welcomed a Japanese initiative to allocate US $30,000m. to promote economic recovery in the region. In mid-2000 a new Japan-ASEAN General Exchange Fund (JAGEF) was established to promote and facilitate the transfer of technology, investment and personnel. In November 1999 Japan, with China and South Korea, attending an informal summit meeting of ASEAN, agreed to strengthen economic and political co-operation with the ASEAN countries, to enhance political and security dialogue, and to implement joint infrastructure and social projects. Japan participated in the first official ASEAN + 3 meeting of foreign ministers, which was convened in July 2000. In recent years Japan has provided ICT support to ASEAN countries, and has offered assistance in environmental and health matters and for educational training and human resource development (particularly in engineering). In October 2003 ASEAN and Japan signed a Framework for Comprehensive Partnership. In December Japan concluded a joint action plan with ASEAN with provisions on reinforcing economic integration within ASEAN and enhancing competitiveness, and on addressing terrorism, piracy and other transnational issues. A joint declaration was also issued on starting discussions on the possibility of establishing an ASEAN-Japan FTA by 2012 (with the newer ASEAN countries participating from 2017). Negotiations on a Comprehensive Economic Partnership Agreement were initiated in April 2005 and concluded in November 2007. The accord was signed in April 2008 and entered into force on 1 December. In July 2004 Japan acceded to the Treaty on Amity and Co-operation. In November the ASEAN-Japan summit meeting adopted the ASEAN-Japan Joint Declaration for Co-operation in the Fight Against International Terrorism. In July 2008 ASEAN concluded a formal partnership agreement with the new Japan International Co-operation Agency, with the aim of working together to strengthen ASEAN integration and development. In April 2011 a Special ASEAN-Japan Ministerial Meeting was convened, in Jakarta, Indonesia, to reaffirm mutual support, in particular in respect to Japan's recovery from a massive earthquake in the previous month.

Australia and New Zealand: In 1999 ASEAN and Australia undertook to establish the ASEAN-Australia Development Co-operation Programme (AADCP), to replace an economic co-operation programme that had begun in 1974. In August 2002 the two sides signed a formal MOU on the AADCP. It was to comprise three core elements, with assistance amounting to $A45m.: a Program Stream, to address medium-term issues of economic integration and competitiveness; a Regional Partnerships Scheme for smaller collaborative activities; and the establishment of a Regional Economic Policy Support Facility within the ASEAN Secretariat. In July 2009 ASEAN and Australia signed an MOU on the implementation of a second phase of the AADCP.

In September 2001 ASEAN ministers of economic affairs signed a Framework for Closer Economic Partnership (CEP) with their counterparts from Australia and New Zealand (the Closer Economic Relations—CER—countries), and agreed to establish a Business Council to involve the business communities of all countries in the CEP. In November 2004 a Commemorative Summit, marking 30 years of dialogue between the nations, took place between ASEAN leaders and those of Australia and New Zealand at which it was agreed to launch negotiations on a free trade agreement. In July 2005 New Zealand signed ASEAN's Treaty of Amity and Co-operation; Australia acceded to the Treaty in December. In August 2007 the Australian and ASEAN ministers of foreign affairs signed a Joint Declaration on a Comprehensive Partnership, and in November they agreed upon a plan of action to implement the accord. An agreement establishing an ASEAN–Australia–New Zealand free trade area was negotiated during 2008 and signed in Cha-am/Hua Hin, Thailand, in February 2009. An ASEAN-New Zealand Joint Declaration on Comprehensive Partnership for the period 2010-2015 was signed by ministers of foreign affairs of both sides in July 2010.

South Asia: In July 1993 both India and Pakistan were accepted as sectoral partners, providing for their participation in ASEAN meetings in sectors such as trade, transport and communications and tourism. An ASEAN-India Business Council was established, and met for the first time, in New Delhi, in February 1995. In December 1995 the ASEAN summit meeting agreed to enhance India's status to that of a full dialogue partner; India was formally admitted to the PMC in July 1996. At a meeting of the ASEAN-India Working Group in March 2001 the two sides agreed to pursue co-operation in new areas, such as health and pharmaceuticals, social security and rural development. The fourth meeting of the ASEAN-India Joint Co-operation Committee in January 2002 agreed to strengthen co-operation in these areas and others, including technology. The first ASEAN-India consultation between ministers of economic affairs, which took place in September, resulted in the adoption as a long-term objective, of the ASEAN-India Regional Trade and Investment Area. The first ASEAN-India summit at the level of heads of state was held in Phnom-Penh, Cambodia, in November. In October 2003 India acceded to the Treaty of Amity and Co-operation and signed a joint Framework Agreement on Comprehensive Economic Co-operation, which was to enter into effect in July 2004. The objectives of the Agreement included: strengthening and enhancing economic, trade and investment co-operation; liberalizing and promoting trade in goods and services; and facilitating economic integration within ASEAN. It was also agreed that negotiations would begin on establishing an ASEAN-India Regional Trade and Investment Area (RTIA), including a free trade area, for Brunei, Indonesia, Malaysia, Singapore and Thailand. A Partnership for Peace, Progress and Shared Prosperity was signed at the third ASEAN-India summit, held in November 2004. At the sixth summit meeting, held in November 2007, it was noted that annual bilateral ASEAN-India trade had reached US $20,000m. ASEAN-India agreements on trade in goods and on a dispute settlement mechanism were concluded in August 2008. The agreement on trade in goods was signed by both sides in August 2009, enabling the RTIA to enter into force on 1 January 2010.

An ASEAN-Pakistan Joint Business Council met for the first time in February 2000. In early 2001 both sides agreed to co-operate in projects relating to new and renewable energy resources, ICT, agricultural research and transport and communications. Pakistan acceded to the Treaty on Amity and Co-operation in July 2004. In January 2007 Timor-Leste acceded to the Treaty; Sri Lanka and Bangladesh acceded in August.

Republic of Korea: In July 1991 the Republic of Korea (South Korea) was accepted as a 'dialogue partner' in ASEAN, and in December a joint ASEAN-Korea Chamber of Commerce was established. South Korea participated in ASEAN's informal summit meetings in December 1997 and November 1999 (see above), and took part in the first official ASEAN + 3 meeting of ministers of foreign affairs, convened in July 2000. South Korea's assistance in the field of ICT has become particularly valuable in recent years. In March 2001, in a sign of developing co-operation, ASEAN and South Korea exchanged views on political and security issues in the region for the first time. South Korea acceded to the Treaty on Amity and Co-operation in November 2004. In that month an ASEAN-Korea summit meeting agreed to initiate negotiations on the establishment of a free trade area between the two sides. The Framework Agreement on Comprehensive Economic Co-operation, providing for the establishment of an ASEAN-Korea Free Trade Area, was signed in December 2005, eliminating tariffs on some 80% of products, with effect from 1 January 2010. In May 2006 governments of both sides (excluding Thailand, owing to a dispute concerning trade in rice) signed an Agreement on Trade in Goods. An ASEAN–Korea agreement on trade in services entered into force in May 2009. An ASEAN-Korea Investment Agreement was signed in June.

Russia: In March 2000 the first ASEAN-Russia business forum opened in Kuala Lumpur, Malaysia. In July 2004 ASEAN and Russia signed a Joint Declaration to Combat International Terrorism, while in November Russia acceded to the Treaty of Amity and Co-operation. The first ASEAN-Russia summit meeting was held in December 2005. The leaders agreed on a comprehensive programme of action to promote co-operation between both sides in the period 2005–15. This included commitments to co-operate in areas including counter-terrorism, human resources development, finance and economic activities and science and technology. In July 2008 both sides adopted a roadmap to further implementation of the comprehensive programme of action.

USA and Canada: In 1990 ASEAN and the USA established an ASEAN-US Joint Working Group, the purpose of which was to review ASEAN's economic relations with the USA and to identify measures by which economic links could be strengthened. In recent years, dialogue has increasingly focused on political and security issues. In August 2002 ASEAN ministers of foreign affairs met with their US counterpart, and signed a Joint Declaration for Co-operation to Combat International Terrorism. At the same time, the USA announced the ASEAN Co-operation Plan, which was to include activities in the fields of ICT, agricultural biotechnology, health, disaster response and training for the ASEAN Secretariat. In July 2009 the USA signed ASEAN's Treaty of Amity and Co-operation. The first official ASEAN meeting with the US President took place in November, in Singapore. Both sides resolved to enhance collaboration and to establish an ASEAN-US Eminent Persons Group. A second ASEAN-US leaders' meeting was held in September 2010, and a third in November 2011.

ASEAN-Canadian co-operation projects include fisheries technology, the telecommunications industry, use of solar energy, and a forest seed centre. A Working Group on the Revitalization of

ASEAN-Canada relations met in February 1999. At a meeting in Bangkok, Thailand, in July 2000, the two sides agreed to explore less formal avenues for project implementation. A Work Plan for ASEAN-Canada Co-operation 2007–10 was adopted in August 2007.

Indo-China: In June 1996 ministers of ASEAN countries, and of Cambodia, China, Laos and Myanmar adopted a framework for ASEAN-Mekong Basin Development Co-operation. The initiative aimed to strengthen the region's cohesiveness, with greater co-operation on issues such as drugs-trafficking, labour migration and terrorism, and to facilitate the process of future expansion of ASEAN. Groups of experts and senior officials were to be convened to consider funding issues and proposals to link the two regions, including a gas pipeline network, rail links and the establishment of a common time zone. In December 1996 the working group on rail links appointed a team of consultants to conduct a feasibility study of the proposals. The completed study was presented at the second ministerial conference on ASEAN-Mekong Basin Development Co-operation, convened in Hanoi, Viet Nam, in July 2000. At the November 2001 summit China pledged US $5m. to assist with navigation along the upper stretches of the Mekong River, while other means by which China could increase its investment in the Mekong Basin area were considered. At the meeting South Korea was invited to become a core member of the grouping. Other growth regions sponsored by ASEAN include the Brunei, Indonesia, Malaysia, Philippines, East ASEAN Growth Area (BIMP-EAGA), the Indonesia, Malaysia, Singapore Growth Triangle (IMS-GT), and the West-East Corridor within the Mekong Basin Development initiative.

Gulf States: In June 2009 ASEAN ministers of foreign affairs held an inaugural meeting with their counterpart from the Co-operation Council for the Arab States of the Gulf (GCC). The meeting, convened in Manama, Bahrain, adopted a GCC-ASEAN Joint Vision as a framework for future co-operation between the two groupings. A second meeting, held in Singapore, in May–June 2010, approved an ASEAN–GCC Action Plan, which identified specific measures for closer co-operation to be undertaken in the two-year period 2010–12.

Publications

Annual Report.

Annual Security Report.

ASEAN Investment Report (annually).

ASEAN State of the Environment Report (1st report: 1997; 2nd report: 2000; 3rd report: 2006; 4th report: 2009).

Business ASEAN (quarterly).

ASEAN Updates.

Public Information Series, briefing papers, documents series, educational materials.

The ASEAN Declaration (Bangkok Declaration)

(8 August 1967)

The Presidium Minister for Political Affairs/Minister for Foreign Affairs of Indonesia, the Deputy Prime Minister of Malaysia, the Secretary of Foreign Affairs of the Philippines, the Minister for Foreign Affairs of Singapore and the Minister of Foreign Affairs of Thailand;

Mindful of the existence of mutual interests and common problems among countries of South-East Asia and convinced of the need to strengthen further the existing bonds of regional solidarity and co-operation;

Desiring to establish a firm foundation for common action to promote regional co-operation in South-East Asia in the spirit of equality and partnership and thereby contribute towards peace, progress and prosperity in the region;

Conscious that in an increasingly interdependent world, the cherished ideals of peace, freedom, social justice and economic well-being are best attained by fostering good understanding, good neighbourliness and meaningful co-operation among the countries of the region already bound together by ties of history and culture;

Considering that the countries of South-East Asia share a primary responsibility for strengthening the economic and social stability of the region and ensuring their peaceful and progressive national development, and that they are determined to ensure their stability and security from external interference in any form or manifestation in order to preserve their national identities in accordance with the ideals and aspirations of their peoples;

Affirming that all foreign bases are temporary and remain only with the expressed concurrence of the countries concerned and are not intended to be used directly or indirectly to subvert the national independence and freedom of States in the area or prejudice the orderly processes of their national development;

Do hereby declare:

First, the establishment of an Association for Regional Co-operation among the countries of South-East Asia to be known as the Association of South-East Asian Nations (ASEAN).

Second, that the aims and purposes of the Association shall be:

1. To accelerate the economic growth, social progress and cultural development in the region through joint endeavours in the spirit of equality and partnership in order to strengthen the foundation for a prosperous and peaceful community of South-East Asian Nations;
2. To promote regional peace and stability through abiding respect for justice and the rule of law in the relationship among countries of the region and adherence to the principles of the United Nations Charter;
3. To promote active collaboration and mutual assistance on matters of common interest in the economic, social, cultural, technical, scientific and administrative fields;
4. To provide assistance to each other in the form of training and research facilities in the educational, professional, technical and administrative spheres;
5. To collaborate more effectively for the greater utilization of their agriculture and industries, the expansion of their trade, including the study of the problems of international commodity trade, the improvement of their transportation and communications facilities and the raising of the living standards of their peoples;
6. To promote South-East Asian studies;
7. To maintain close and beneficial co-operation with existing international and regional organizations with similar aims and purposes, and explore all avenues for even closer co-operation among themselves.

Third, that to carry out these aims and purposes, the following machinery shall be established:

(a) Annual Meeting of Foreign Ministers, which shall be by rotation and referred to as ASEAN Ministerial Meeting. Special Meetings of Foreign Ministers may be convened as required;

(b) A Standing committee, under the chairmanship of the Foreign Minister of the host country or his representative and having as its members the accredited Ambassadors of the other member countries, to carry on the work of the Association in between Meetings of Foreign Ministers;

(c) Ad hoc Committees and Permanent Committees of specialists and officials on specific subjects;

(d) A National Secretariat in each member country to carry out the work of the Association on behalf of that country and to service the Annual or Special Meetings of Foreign Ministers, the Standing Committee and such other committees as may hereafter be established.

Fourth, that the Association is open for participation to all States in the South-East Asian Region subscribing to the aforementioned aims, principles and purposes.

Fifth, that the Association represents the collective will of the nations of South-East Asia to bind themselves together in friendship and co-operation and, through joint efforts and sacrifices, secure for their peoples and for posterity the blessings of peace, freedom and prosperity.

Treaty of Amity and Co-operation in South-East Asia

(24 February 1976)

The High Contracting Parties:

Conscious of the existing ties of history, geography and culture, which have bound their peoples together

Anxious to promote regional peace and stability through abiding respect for justice and the rule of law and enhancing regional resilience in their relations

Desiring to enhance peace, friendship and mutual co-operation on matters affecting South-East Asia consistent with the spirit and principles of the Charter of the United Nations, the Ten Principles adopted by the Asian-African Conference in Bandung on 25 April 1955, the Declaration of the Association of South-East Asian Nations signed in Bangkok on 8 August 1967, and the Declaration signed in Kuala Lumpur on 27 November 1971

Convinced that the settlement of differences or disputes between their countries should be regulated by rational, effective and sufficiently flexible procedures, avoiding negative attitudes which might endanger or hinder co-operation

Believing in the need for co-operation with all peace-loving nations, both within and outside South-East Asia, in the furtherance of world peace, stability and harmony

Solemnly agree to enter into a Treaty of Amity and Co-operation as follows.

I. PURPOSE AND PRINCIPLES

Article 1.

The purpose of this Treaty is to promote perpetual peace, everlasting amity and co-operation among their peoples which would contribute to their strength, solidarity and closer relationship.

Article 2.

In their relations with one another, the High Contracting Parties shall be guided by the following fundamental principles:

(a) Mutual respect for the independence, sovereignty, equality, territorial integrity and national identity of all nations;

(b) The right of every State to lead its national existence free from external interference, subversion or coercion;

(c) Non-interference in the internal affairs of one another;

(d) Settlement of differences or disputes by peaceful means;

(e) Renunciation of the threat or use of force;

(f) Effective co-operation among themselves.

II. AMITY

Article 3.

In pursuance of the purpose of this Treaty the High Contracting Parties shall endeavour to develop and strengthen the traditional, cultural and historical ties of friendship, good neighbourliness and co-operation which bind them together and shall fulfil in good faith the obligations assumed under this Treaty. In order to promote closer understanding among them, the High Contracting Parties shall encourage and facilitate contract and intercourse among their peoples.

III. CO-OPERATION

Article 4.

The High Contracting Parties shall promote active co-operation in the economic, social, technical, scientific and administrative fields as well as in matters of common ideals and aspirations of international peace and stability in the region and all other matters of common interest.

Article 5.

Pursuant to Article 4 the High Contracting Parties shall exert their maximum efforts multilaterally as well as bilaterally on the basis of equality, non-discrimination and mutual benefit.

Article 6.

The High Contracting Parties shall collaborate for the acceleration of the economic growth in the region in order to strengthen the foundation for a prosperous and peaceful community of nations in South-East Asia. To this end, they shall promote the greater utilization of their agricultural and industries, the expansion of their trade and the improvement of their economic infrastructure for the mutual benefit of their peoples. In this regard, they shall continue to explore all avenues for close and beneficial co-operation with other States as well as international and regional organizations outside the region.

Article 7.

The High Contracting Parties, in order to achieve social justice and to raise the standards of living of the peoples of the region, shall intensify economic co-operation. For this purpose, they shall adopt appropriate regional strategies for economic development and mutual assistance.

Article 8.

The High Contracting Parties shall strive to achieve the closest co-operation on the widest scale and shall seek to provide assistance to one another in the form of training and research facilities in the social, cultural, technical, scientific and administrative fields.

Article 9.

The High Contracting Parties shall endeavour to foster co-operation in the furtherance of the cause of peace, harmony, and stability in the region. To this end, the High Contracting Parties shall maintain regular contacts and consultations with one another on international and regional matters with a view to co-ordinating their views and policies.

Article 10.

Each High Contracting Party shall not in any manner or form participate in any activity which shall constitute a threat to the political and economic stability, sovereignty, or territorial integrity of another High Contracting Party.

Article 11.

The High Contracting Parties shall endeavour to strengthen their respective national resilience in their political, economic, socio-cultural as well as security fields in conformity with their respective ideals and aspirations, free from external interference as well as internal subversive activities in order to preserve their respective national identities.

Article 12.

The High Contracting Parties in their efforts to achieve regional prosperity and security, shall endeavour to co-operate in all fields for the promotion of regional resilience, based on the principles of self-confidence, self-reliance, mutual respect, co-operation of solidarity which will constitute the foundation for a strong and viable community of nations in South-East Asia.

IV. PACIFIC SETTLEMENT OF DISPUTES

Article 13.

The High Contracting Parties shall have the determination and good faith to prevent disputes from arising. In the case of disputes on matters directly affecting them, the High Contracting Parties shall refrain from the threat or use of force and shall at all times settle such disputes among themselves through friendly negotiations.

Article 14.

To settle disputes through regional processes, the High Contracting Parties shall constitute, as a continuing body, a High Council comprising a Representative at ministerial level from each of the High Contracting Parties to take cognizance of the existence of disputes or situations likely to disturb regional peace and harmony.

Article 15.

In the event no solution is reached through direct negotiations, the High Council shall take cognizance of the dispute or the situation and shall recommend to the parties in dispute appropriate means of settlement such as good offices, mediation, inquiry or conciliation. The High Council may, however, offer its good offices, or upon agreement of the parties in dispute, constitute itself into a committee of mediation, inquiry or conciliation. When deemed necessary, the High Council shall recommend appropriate measures for the prevention of a deterioration of the dispute of the situation.

Article 16.

The foregoing provision of this Chapter shall not apply to a dispute unless all the parties to the dispute agree to their application to that dispute. However, this shall not preclude the other High Contracting Parties not party to the dispute from offering all possible assistance to settle the said dispute. Parties to the dispute should be well disposed towards such offers of assistance.

Article 17.

Nothing in this Treaty shall preclude recourse to the modes of peaceful settlement contained in Article 33 (1) of the Charter of the United Nations. The High Contracting Parties which are parties to a dispute should be encouraged to take initiatives to solve it by friendly negotiations before resorting to the other procedures provided for in the Charter of the United Nations.

V. GENERAL PROVISIONS

(Articles 18–20).

Charter of the Association of Southeast Asian Nations

(signed 20 November 2007)

PREAMBLE

We the peoples of the Member States of the Association of Southeast Asian Nations (ASEAN), as represented by the Heads of State or Government of Brunei Darussalam, the Kingdom of Cambodia, the Republic of Indonesia, the Lao People's Democratic Republic, Malaysia, the Union of Myanmar, the Republic of the Philippines, the Republic of Singapore, the Kingdom of Thailand and the Socialist Republic of Viet Nam:

Noting with satisfaction the significant achievements and expansion of ASEAN since its establishment in Bangkok through the promulgation of The ASEAN Declaration;

Recalling the decisions to establish an ASEAN Charter in the Vientiane Action Programme, the Kuala Lumpur Declaration on the Establishment of the ASEAN Charter and the Cebu Declaration on the Blueprint of the ASEAN Charter;

Mindful of the existence of mutual interests and interdependence among the peoples and Member States of ASEAN which are bound by geography, common objectives and shared destiny;

Inspired by and united under One Vision, One Identity and One Caring and Sharing Community;

United by a common desire and collective will to live in a region of lasting peace, security and stability, sustained economic growth, shared prosperity and social progress, and to promote our vital interests, ideals and aspirations;

Respecting the fundamental importance of amity and cooperation, and the principles of sovereignty, equality, territorial integrity, non-interference, consensus and unity in diversity;

Adhering to the principles of democracy, and good governance, respect for rights and fundamental freedoms;

Resolved to ensure sustainable development for the benefit of present and future generations and to place the well-being, livelihood and welfare of the peoples at the centre of the ASEAN community building process;

Convinced of the need to strengthen existing bonds of regional solidarity to realise an ASEAN Community that is politically cohesive, economically integrated and socially responsible in order to effectively respond to current and future challenges and opportunities;

Committed to intensifying community building through enhanced regional cooperation and integration, in particular by establishing an ASEAN Community comprising the ASEAN Security Community, the ASEAN Economic Community and the ASEAN Socio-Cultural Community, as provided for in the Bali Declaration of ASEAN Concord II;

Hereby decide to establish, through this Charter, the legal and institutional framework for ASEAN;

And to this end, the Heads of State or Government of the Member States of ASEAN, assembled in Singapore on the historic occasion of the 40th anniversary of the founding of ASEAN, have agreed to this Charter.

CHAPTER I. PURPOSES AND PRINCIPLES

Article 1

The Purposes of ASEAN are:

1. To maintain and enhance peace, security and stability and further strengthen peace-oriented values in the region;

2. To enhance regional resilience by promoting greater political, security, economic and socio-cultural co-operation;

3. To preserve Southeast Asia as a Nuclear Weapon-Free Zone and free of all other weapons of mass destruction;

4. To ensure that the peoples and Member States of ASEAN live in peace with the world at large in a just, democratic and harmonious environment;

5. To create a single market and production base which is stable, prosperous, highly competitive and economically integrated with effective facilitation for trade and investment in which there is free flow of goods, services and investment; facilitated movement of business persons, professionals, talents and labour; and freer flow of capital;

6. To alleviate poverty and narrow the development gap within ASEAN through mutual assistance and cooperation;

7. To strengthen democracy, enhance good governance and the rule of law, and to promote and protect human rights and fundamental freedoms, with due regard to the rights and responsibilities of the Member States of ASEAN;

8. To respond effectively, in accordance with the principle of comprehensive security, to all forms of threats, transnational crimes and transboundary challenges;

9. To promote sustainable development so as to ensure the protection of the region's environment, the sustainability of its natural resources, the preservation of its cultural heritage and the high quality of life of its peoples;

10. To develop human resources through closer cooperation in education and life-long learning, and in science and technology, for the empowerment of the peoples of ASEAN and for the strengthening of the ASEAN Community;

11. To enhance the well-being and livelihood of the peoples of ASEAN by providing them with equitable access to opportunities for human development, social welfare and justice;

12. To strengthen co-operation in building a safe, secure and drug-free environment for the peoples of ASEAN;

13. To promote a people-oriented ASEAN in which all sectors of society are encouraged to participate in, and benefit from, the process of ASEAN integration and community building;

14. To promote an ASEAN identity through the fostering of greater awareness of the diverse culture and heritage of the region; and

15. To maintain the centrality and proactive role of ASEAN as the primary driving force in its relations and cooperation with its external partners in a regional architecture that is open, transparent and inclusive.

Article 2

1. In pursuit of the Purposes stated in Article 1, ASEAN and its Member States reaffirm and adhere to the fundamental principles contained in the declarations, agreements, conventions, concords, treaties and other instruments of ASEAN.

2. ASEAN and its Member States shall act in accordance with the following Principles:

(a) respect for the independence, sovereignty, equality, territorial integrity and national identity of all ASEAN Member States;

(b) shared commitment and collective responsibility in enhancing regional peace, security and prosperity;

(c) renunciation of aggression and of the threat or use of force or other actions in any manner inconsistent with international law;

(d) reliance on peaceful settlement of disputes;

(e) non-interference in the internal affairs of ASEAN Member States;

(f) respect for the right of every Member State to lead its national existence free from external interference, subversion and coercion;

(g) enhanced consultations on matters seriously affecting the common interest of ASEAN;

(h) adherence to the rule of law, good governance, the principles of democracy and constitutional government;

(i) respect for fundamental freedoms, the promotion and protection of human rights, and the promotion of social justice;

(j) upholding the United Nations Charter and international law, including international humanitarian law, subscribed to by ASEAN Member States;

(k) abstention from participation in any policy or activity, including the use of its territory, pursued by any ASEAN Member State or non-ASEAN State or any non-State actor, which threatens the sovereignty, territorial integrity or political and economic stability of ASEAN Member States;

(l) respect for the different cultures, languages and religions of the peoples of ASEAN, while emphasising their common values in the spirit of unity in diversity;

(m) the centrality of ASEAN in external political, economic, social and cultural relations while remaining actively engaged, outward-looking, inclusive and non-discriminatory; and

(n) adherence to multilateral trade rules and ASEAN's rules-based regimes for effective implementation of economic commitments and progressive reduction towards elimination of all barriers to regional economic integration, in a market-driven economy.

CHAPTER II. LEGAL PERSONALITY

Article 3

ASEAN, as an inter-governmental organisation, is hereby conferred legal personality.

CHAPTER III. MEMBERSHIP

Article 4

The Member States of ASEAN are Brunei Darussalam, the Kingdom of Cambodia, the Republic of Indonesia, the Lao People's Democratic Republic, Malaysia, the Union of Myanmar, the Republic of the Philippines, the Republic of Singapore, the Kingdom of Thailand and the Socialist Republic of Viet Nam.

Article 5

1. Member States shall have equal rights and obligations under this Charter.

2. Member States shall take all necessary measures, including the enactment of appropriate domestic legislation, to effectively implement the provisions of this Charter and to comply with all obligations of membership.

3. In the case of a serious breach of the Charter or noncompliance, the matter shall be referred to Article 20.

Article 6

1. The procedure for application and admission to ASEAN shall be prescribed by the ASEAN Coordinating Council.

2. Admission shall be based on the following criteria:

(a) location in the recognised geographical region of Southeast Asia;

(b) recognition by all ASEAN Member States;

(c) agreement to be bound and to abide by the Charter; and

(d) ability and willingness to carry out the obligations of Membership.

3. Admission shall be decided by consensus by the ASEAN Summit, upon the recommendation of the ASEAN Coordinating Council.

4. An applicant State shall be admitted to ASEAN upon signing an Instrument of Accession to the Charter.

CHAPTER IV. ORGANS

Article 7

1. The ASEAN Summit shall comprise the Heads of State or Government of the Member States.

2. The ASEAN Summit shall:

(a) be the supreme policy-making body of ASEAN;

(b) deliberate, provide policy guidance and take decisions on key issues pertaining to the realisation of the objectives of ASEAN, important matters of interest to Member States and all issues referred to it by the ASEAN Co-ordinating Council, the ASEAN Community Councils and ASEAN Sectoral Ministerial Bodies;

(c) instruct the relevant Ministers in each of the Councils concerned to hold ad hoc inter-Ministerial meetings, and address important issues concerning ASEAN that cut across the Community Councils. Rules of procedure for such meetings shall be adopted by the ASEAN Coordinating Council;

(d) address emergency situations affecting ASEAN by taking appropriate actions;

(e) decide on matters referred to it under Chapters VII and VIII;

(f) authorise the establishment and the dissolution of Sectoral Ministerial Bodies and other ASEAN institutions; and

(g) appoint the Secretary-General of ASEAN, with the rank and status of Minister, who will serve with the confidence and at the pleasure of the Heads of State or Government upon the recommendation of the ASEAN Foreign Ministers Meeting.

3. ASEAN Summit Meetings shall be:

(a) held twice annually, and be hosted by the Member State holding the ASEAN Chairmanship; and

(b) convened, whenever necessary, as special or ad hoc meetings to be chaired by the Member State holding the ASEAN Chairmanship, at venues to be agreed upon by ASEAN Member States.

Article 8

1. The ASEAN Co-ordinating Council shall comprise the ASEAN Foreign Ministers and meet at least twice a year.

2. The ASEAN Co-ordinating Council shall:

(a) prepare the meetings of the ASEAN Summit;

(b) co-ordinate the implementation of agreements and decisions of the ASEAN Summit;

(c) co-ordinate with the ASEAN Community Councils to enhance policy coherence, efficiency and cooperation among them;

(d) co-ordinate the reports of the ASEAN Community Councils to the ASEAN Summit;

(e) consider the annual report of the Secretary-General on the work of ASEAN;

(f) consider the report of the Secretary-General on the functions and operations of the ASEAN Secretariat and other relevant bodies;

(g) approve the appointment and termination of the Deputy Secretaries-General upon the recommendation of the Secretary-General; and

(h) undertake other tasks provided for in this Charter or such other functions as may be assigned by the ASEAN Summit.

3. ASEAN Summit Meetings shall be:

(a) held twice annually, and be hosted by the Member State holding the ASEAN Chairmanship; and

(b) convened, whenever necessary, as special or ad hoc meetings to be chaired by the Member State holding the ASEAN Chairmanship, at venues to be agreed upon by ASEAN Member States.

4. The ASEAN Co-ordinating Council shall be supported by the relevant senior officials.

Article 9

1. The ASEAN Community Councils shall comprise the ASEAN Political-Security Community Council, ASEAN Economic Com-

munity Council, and ASEAN Socio-Cultural Community Council.

2. Each ASEAN Community Council shall have under its purview the relevant ASEAN Sectoral Ministerial Bodies.

3. Each Member State shall designate its national representation for each ASEAN Community Council meeting.

4. In order to realise the objectives of each of the three pillars of the ASEAN Community, each ASEAN Community Council shall:

(a) ensure the implementation of the relevant decisions of the ASEAN Summit;

(b) co-ordinate the work of the different sectors under its purview, and on issues which cut across the other Community Councils; and

(c) submit reports and recommendations to the ASEAN Summit on matters under its purview.

5. Each ASEAN Community Council shall meet at least twice a year and shall be chaired by the appropriate Minister from the Member State holding the ASEAN Chairmanship.

6. Each ASEAN Community Council shall be supported by the relevant senior officials.

Article 10

1. ASEAN Sectoral Ministerial Bodies shall:

(a) function in accordance with their respective established mandates;

(b) implement the agreements and decisions of the ASEAN Summit under their respective purview;

(c) strengthen cooperation in their respective fields in support of ASEAN integration and community building; and

(d) submit reports and recommendations to their respective Community Councils.

2. Each ASEAN Sectoral Ministerial Body may have under its purview the relevant senior officials and subsidiary bodies to undertake its functions as contained in Annex 1. The Annex may be updated by the Secretary-General of ASEAN upon the recommendation of the Committee of Permanent Representatives without recourse to the provision on Amendments under this Charter.

Article 11

1. The Secretary-General of ASEAN shall be appointed by the ASEAN Summit for a non-renewable term of office of five years, selected from among nationals of the ASEAN Member States based on alphabetical rotation, with due consideration to integrity, capability and professional experience, and gender equality.

2. The Secretary-General shall:

(a) carry out the duties and responsibilities of this high office in accordance with the provisions of this Charter and relevant ASEAN instruments, protocols and established practices;

(b) facilitate and monitor progress in the implementation of ASEAN agreements and decisions, and submit an annual report on the work of ASEAN to the ASEAN Summit;

(c) participate in meetings of the ASEAN Summit, the ASEAN Community Councils, the ASEAN Co-ordinating Council, and ASEAN Sectoral Ministerial Bodies and other relevant ASEAN meetings;

(d) present the views of ASEAN and participate in meetings with external parties in accordance with approved policy guidelines and mandate given to the Secretary-General; and

(e) recommend the appointment and termination of the Deputy Secretaries-General to the ASEAN Coordinating Council for approval.

3. The Secretary-General shall also be the Chief Administrative Officer of ASEAN.

4. The Secretary-General shall be assisted by four Deputy Secretaries-General with the rank and status of Deputy Ministers. The Deputy Secretaries-General shall be accountable to the Secretary-General in carrying out their functions.

5. The four Deputy Secretaries-General shall be of different nationalities from the Secretary-General and shall come from four different ASEAN Member States.

6. The four Deputy Secretaries-General shall comprise:

(a) two Deputy Secretaries-General who will serve a non-renewable term of three years, selected from among nationals of the ASEAN Member States based on alphabetical rotation, with due consideration to integrity, qualifications, competence, experience and gender equality; and

(b) two Deputy Secretaries-General who will serve a term of three years, which may be renewed for another three years. These two Deputy Secretaries-General shall be openly recruited based on merit.

7. The ASEAN Secretariat shall comprise the Secretary-General and such staff as may be required.

8. The Secretary-General and the staff shall:

(a) uphold the highest standards of integrity, efficiency, and competence in the performance of their duties;

(b) not seek or receive instructions from any government or external party outside of ASEAN; and

(c) refrain from any action which might reflect on their position as ASEAN Secretariat officials responsible only to ASEAN.

9. Each ASEAN Member State undertakes to respect the exclusively ASEAN character of the responsibilities of the Secretary-General and the staff, and not to seek to influence them in the discharge of their responsibilities.

Article 12

1. Each ASEAN Member State shall appoint a Permanent Representative to ASEAN with the rank of Ambassador based in Jakarta.

2. The Permanent Representatives collectively constitute a Committee of Permanent Representatives, which shall:

(a) support the work of the ASEAN Community Councils and ASEAN Sectoral Ministerial Bodies;

(b) co-ordinate with ASEAN National Secretariats and other ASEAN Sectoral Ministerial Bodies;

(c) liaise with the Secretary-General of ASEAN and the ASEAN Secretariat on all subjects relevant to its work;

(d) facilitate ASEAN co-operation with external partners; and

(e) perform such other functions as may be determined by the ASEAN Co-ordinating Council.

Article 13

Each ASEAN Member State shall establish an ASEAN National Secretariat which shall:

(a) serve as the national focal point;

(b) be the repository of information on all ASEAN matters at the national level;

(c) co-ordinate the implementation of ASEAN decisions at the national level;

(d) co-ordinate and support the national preparations of ASEAN meetings;

(e) promote ASEAN identity and awareness at the national level; and

(f) contribute to ASEAN community building.

Article 14

1. In conformity with the purposes and principles of the ASEAN Charter relating to the promotion and protection of human rights and fundamental freedoms, ASEAN shall establish an ASEAN human rights body.

2. This ASEAN human rights body shall operate in accordance with the terms of reference to be determined by the ASEAN Foreign Ministers Meeting.

Article 15

1. The ASEAN Foundation shall support the Secretary- General of ASEAN and collaborate with the relevant ASEAN bodies to support ASEAN community building by promoting greater awareness of the ASEAN identity, people-to-people interaction, and close collaboration among the business sector, civil society, academia and other stakeholders in ASEAN.

2. The ASEAN Foundation shall be accountable to the Secretary-General of ASEAN, who shall submit its report to the ASEAN Summit through the ASEAN Co-ordinating Council.

CHAPTER V. ENTITIES ASSOCIATED WITH ASEAN

CHAPTER VI. IMMUNITIES AND PRIVILEGES

CHAPTER VII. DECISION-MAKING

Article 20

1. As a basic principle, decision-making in ASEAN shall be based on consultation and consensus.

2. Where consensus cannot be achieved, the ASEAN Summit may decide how a specific decision can be made.

3. Nothing in paragraphs 1 and 2 of this Article shall affect the modes of decision-making as contained in the relevant ASEAN legal instruments.

4. In the case of a serious breach of the Charter or noncompliance, the matter shall be referred to the ASEAN Summit for decision.

Article 21

1. Each ASEAN Community Council shall prescribe its own rules of procedure.

2. In the implementation of economic commitments, a formula for flexible participation, including the ASEAN Minus X formula, may be applied where there is a consensus to do so.

CHAPTER VIII. SETTLEMENT OF DISPUTES

Article 22

1. Member States shall endeavour to resolve peacefully all disputes in a timely manner through dialogue, consultation and negotiation.

2. ASEAN shall maintain and establish dispute settlement mechanisms in all fields of ASEAN co-operation.

Article 23

1. Member States which are parties to a dispute may at any time agree to resort to good offices, conciliation or mediation in order to resolve the dispute within an agreed time limit.

2. Parties to the dispute may request the Chairman of ASEAN or the Secretary-General of ASEAN, acting in an ex officio capacity, to provide good offices, conciliation or mediation.

Article 24

1. Disputes relating to specific ASEAN instruments shall be settled through the mechanisms and procedures provided for in such instruments.

2. Disputes which do not concern the interpretation or application of any ASEAN instrument shall be resolved peacefully in accordance with the Treaty of Amity and Co-operation in Southeast Asia and its rules of procedure.

3. Where not otherwise specifically provided, disputes which concern the interpretation or application of ASEAN economic agreements shall be settled in accordance with the ASEAN Protocol on Enhanced Dispute Settlement Mechanism.

Article 25

Where not otherwise specifically provided, appropriate dispute settlement mechanisms, including arbitration, shall be established for disputes which concern the interpretation or application of this Charter and other ASEAN instruments.

Article 26

When a dispute remains unresolved, after the application of the preceding provisions of this Chapter, this dispute shall be referred to the ASEAN Summit, for its decision.

Article 27

1. The Secretary-General of ASEAN, assisted by the ASEAN Secretariat or any other designated ASEAN body, shall monitor the compliance with the findings, recommendations or decisions resulting from an ASEAN dispute settlement mechanism, and submit a report to the ASEAN Summit.

2. Any Member State affected by non-compliance with the findings, recommendations or decisions resulting from an ASEAN dispute settlement mechanism, may refer the matter to the ASEAN Summit for a decision.

Article 28

Unless otherwise provided for in this Charter, Member States have the right of recourse to the modes of peaceful settlement contained in Article 33(1) of the Charter of the United Nations or any other international legal instruments to which the disputing Member States are parties.

CHAPTER IX. BUDGET AND FINANCE

CHAPTER X. ADMINISTRATION AND PROCEDURE

Article 31

1. The Chairmanship of ASEAN shall rotate annually, based on the alphabetical order of the English names of Member States.

2. ASEAN shall have, in a calendar year, a single Chairmanship by which the Member State assuming the Chairmanship shall chair:

(a) the ASEAN Summit and related summits;

(b) the ASEAN Co-ordinating Council;

(c) the three ASEAN Community Councils;

(d) where appropriate, the relevant ASEAN Sectoral Ministerial Bodies and senior officials; and

(e) the Committee of Permanent Representatives.

Article 32

The Member State holding the Chairmanship of ASEAN shall:

(a) actively promote and enhance the interests and wellbeing of ASEAN, including efforts to build an ASEAN Community through policy initiatives, coordination, consensus and cooperation;

(b) ensure the centrality of ASEAN;

(c) ensure an effective and timely response to urgent issues or crisis situations affecting ASEAN, including providing its good offices and such other arrangements to immediately address these concerns;

(d) represent ASEAN in strengthening and promoting closer relations with external partners; and

(e) carry out such other tasks and functions as may be mandated.

Article 33

ASEAN and its Member States shall adhere to existing diplomatic protocol and practices in the conduct of all activities relating to ASEAN. Any changes shall be approved by the ASEAN Co-ordinating Council upon the recommendation of the Committee of Permanent Representatives.

Article 34

The working language of ASEAN shall be English.

CHAPTER XI. IDENTITY AND SYMBOLS

CHAPTER XII. EXTERNAL RELATIONS

Article 41

1. ASEAN shall develop friendly relations and mutually beneficial dialogue, cooperation and partnerships with countries and sub-regional, regional and international organisations and institutions.

2. The external relations of ASEAN shall adhere to the purposes and principles set forth in this Charter.

3. ASEAN shall be the primary driving force in regional arrangements that it initiates and maintain its centrality in regional co-operation and community building.

4. In the conduct of external relations of ASEAN, Member States shall, on the basis of unity and solidarity, co-ordinate and endeavour to develop common positions and pursue joint actions.

5. The strategic policy directions of ASEAN's external relations shall be set by the ASEAN Summit upon the recommendation of the ASEAN Foreign Ministers Meeting.

6. The ASEAN Foreign Ministers Meeting shall ensure consistency and coherence in the conduct of ASEAN's external relations.

7. ASEAN may conclude agreements with countries or sub-regional, regional and international organisations and institutions. The procedures for concluding such agreements shall be prescribed by the ASEAN Co-ordinating Council in consultation with the ASEAN Community Councils.

Article 42

1. Member States, acting as Country Coordinators, shall take turns to take overall responsibility in co-ordinating and promoting the interests of ASEAN in its relations with the relevant Dialogue Partners, regional and international organisations and institutions.

2. In relations with the external partners, the Country Co-ordinators shall, inter alia:

(a) represent ASEAN and enhance relations on the basis of mutual respect and equality, in conformity with ASEAN's principles;

(b) co-chair relevant meetings between ASEAN and external partners; and

(c) be supported by the relevant ASEAN Committees in Third Countries and International Organisations.

Article 43

1. ASEAN Committees in Third Countries may be established in non-ASEAN countries comprising heads of diplomatic missions of ASEAN Member States. Similar Committees may be established relating to international organisations. Such Committees shall promote ASEAN's interests and identity in the host countries and international organisations.

2. The ASEAN Foreign Ministers Meeting shall determine the rules of procedure of such Committees.

Article 44

1. In conducting ASEAN's external relations, the ASEAN Foreign Ministers Meeting may confer on an external party the formal status of Dialogue Partner, Sectoral Dialogue Partner, Development Partner, Special Observer, Guest, or other status that may be established henceforth.

2. External parties may be invited to ASEAN meetings or cooperative activities without being conferred any formal status, in accordance with the rules of procedure.

Article 45

1. ASEAN may seek an appropriate status with the United Nations system as well as with other sub-regional, regional, international organisations and institutions.

2. The ASEAN Coordinating Council shall decide on the participation of ASEAN in other sub-regional, regional, international organisations and institutions.

Article 46

Non-ASEAN Member States and relevant inter-governmental organisations may appoint and accredit Ambassadors to ASEAN. The ASEAN Foreign Ministers Meeting shall decide on such accreditation.

CHAPTER XIII.

General and Final Provisions.

BANK FOR INTERNATIONAL SETTLEMENTS—BIS

Address: Centralbahnplatz 2, 4002 Basel, Switzerland.

Telephone: 612808080; **fax:** 612809100; **e-mail:** email@bis.org; **internet:** www.bis.org.

The Bank for International Settlements was founded pursuant to the Hague Agreements of 1930 to promote co-operation among national central banks and to provide additional facilities for international financial operations.

Organization

(June 2012)

GENERAL MEETING

The General Meeting is held annually in June and is attended by representatives of the central banks of countries in which shares have been subscribed. The central banks of the following 56 authorities are entitled to attend and vote at General Meetings of the BIS: Algeria, Argentina, Australia, Austria, Belgium, Bosnia and Herzegovina, Brazil, Bulgaria, Canada, Chile, the People's Republic of China, Croatia, the Czech Republic, Denmark, Estonia, Finland, France, Germany, Greece, Hong Kong SAR, Hungary, Iceland, India, Indonesia, Ireland, Israel, Italy, Japan, the Republic of Korea, Latvia, Lithuania, the former Yugoslav republic of Macedonia, Malaysia, Mexico, the Netherlands, New Zealand, Norway, the Philippines, Poland, Portugal, Romania, Russia, Saudi Arabia, Serbia, Singapore, Slovakia, Slovenia, South Africa, Spain, Sweden, Switzerland, Thailand, Turkey, the United Kingdom and the USA. The European Central Bank became a BIS shareholder in December 1999.

BOARD OF DIRECTORS

The Board of Directors is responsible for the conduct of the Bank's operations at the highest level. It comprises the Governors in office of the central banks of Belgium, France, Germany, Italy, and the United Kingdom, as well as the Chairman of the Board of Governors of the US Federal Reserve System. Each of those six *ex officio* members may appoint another director of the same nationality. The Bank's statutes provide for the election to the Board of not more than nine Governors of other member central banks. As at June 2012 those of Canada, People's Republic of China, Japan, Mexico, the Netherlands, Sweden and Switzerland and the President of the European Central Bank were elected members of the Board. In June 2005 an extraordinary general meeting amended the statutes to abolish the position of President of the Bank, which had been jointly vested with chairmanship of the Board since 1948.

Chairman of the Board: CHRISTIAN NOYER (France).

MANAGEMENT

At March 2012 the Bank employed some 616 staff members, from 54 countries. The main departments are the General Secretariat, the Monetary and Economic Department and the Banking Department. In July 1998 the BIS inaugurated its first overseas administrative unit, the Representative Office for Asia and the Pacific, which is based in Hong Kong. A Regional Treasury dealing room became operational at the Hong Kong office in October 2000, with the aim of improving access for Asian central banks to BIS financial services during their trading hours. In November 2002 a Representative Office for the Americas was inaugurated in Mexico City, Mexico.

General Manager: JAIME CARUANA (Spain).

Representative Office for Asia and the Pacific: Two International Finance Centre, 78th Floor, 8 Finance St, Central, Hong Kong, Special Administrative Region, People's Republic of China; tel. 28787100; fax 28787123.

Representative Office for the Americas: Torre Chapultepec, Rubén Darío 281, 17th Floor, Col. Bosque de Chapultepec, Del. Miguel Hidalgo, 11580 Mexico, D.F., Mexico; tel. (55) 91380290; fax (55) 91380299; e-mail americas@bis.org.

Activities

The BIS is an international financial institution whose role is to promote international monetary and financial co-operation, and to fulfil the function of a 'central banks' bank'. Although it has the legal form of a company limited by shares, it is an international organization governed by international law, and enjoys special privileges and immunities in keeping with its role (a Headquarters Agreement was concluded with Switzerland in 1987). The participating central banks were originally given the option of subscribing the shares themselves or arranging for their subscription in their own countries. In January 2001, however, an extraordinary general meeting amended the Bank's statutes to restrict ownership to central banks. Accordingly, all shares then held by private shareholders (representing 14% of the total share capital) were repurchased at a compensation rate of 16,000 Swiss francs per share. An additional compensation payment was required following a decision by the Hague Arbitral Tribunal (provided for in the 1930 Hague Agreements) in September 2003.

FINANCE

Until the end of the 2002/03 financial year the Bank's unit of account was the gold franc. An extraordinary general meeting in March 2003 amended the Bank's statutes to redenominate the Bank's share capital in Special Drawing Rights (SDRs), the unit of account of the IMF, with effect from 1 April 2003, in order to enhance the efficiency and transparency of the Bank's operations. The meeting decided that the nominal value of shares would be rounded down from SDR 5,696 at 31 March 2003 to SDR 5,000, entailing a reduction of 12.2% in the total share capital. The excess of SDR 92.1m. was transferred to the Bank's reserve funds. The authorized capital of the Bank at 31 March 2012 was SDR 3,000m., divided into 600,000 shares of equal value.

BANKING OPERATIONS

The BIS assists central banks in managing and investing their foreign exchange and gold reserves: in 2012 some 140 international financial institutions and central banks from all over the world had deposits with the BIS, representing around 3% of world foreign exchange reserves.

The BIS uses the funds deposited with it partly for lending to central banks. Its credit transactions may take the form of swaps against gold; covered credits secured by means of a pledge of gold or marketable short-term securities; credits against gold or currency deposits of the same amount and for the same duration held with the BIS; unsecured credits in the form of advances or deposits; or standby credits, which in individual instances are backed by guarantees given by member central banks.

The BIS also engages in traditional types of investment: funds not required for lending to central banks are placed in the market as deposits with commercial banks and purchases of short-term negotiable paper, including Treasury bills. Such operations constitute a major part of the Bank's business. Increasingly, the Bank has developed its own investment services for central banks, including short-term products and longer-term financial instruments.

Central banks' monetary reserves often need to be available at short notice, and need to be placed with the BIS at short term, for fixed periods and with clearly defined repayment terms. The BIS has to match its assets to the maturity structure and nature of its commitments, and must therefore conduct its business with special regard to maintaining a high degree of liquidity.

The Bank's operations must be in conformity with the monetary policy of the central banks of the countries concerned. It is not permitted to make advances to governments or to open current accounts in their name. Real estate transactions are also excluded.

INTERNATIONAL MONETARY CO-OPERATION

Governors of central banks meet for regular discussions at the BIS to co-ordinate international monetary policy and to promote stability in the international financial markets. There is close co-operation with the IMF and the World Bank. The BIS participates in meetings of the so-called Group of 10 (G10) industrialized nations (see IMF), which has been a major forum for discussion of international monetary issues since its establishment in 1962. Governors of central banks of the G10 countries convene for regular Basel Monthly Meetings. In 1971 a Standing Committee of the G10 central banks was established at the BIS to consider aspects of the development of Euro-currency markets. In February 1999 the G10 renamed the body the Committee on the Global Financial System, and approved a revised mandate to undertake systematic short-term monitoring of global financial system conditions; longer-term analysis of the functioning of financial markets; and the articulation of policy recommendations aimed at improving market functioning and promoting stability. A Markets Committee (formerly known as the Committee on Gold and Foreign Exchange, established in 1962) comprises senior officials responsible for market operations in the G10 central banks. It meets regularly to consider developments in foreign exchange and related financial markets, possible future trends and short-run implications of events on market functioning. In 1990 a Committee on Payment and Settlement Systems was established to monitor and analyse developments in domestic payment, settlement and clearing systems, and cross-border and multi-currency systems. It meets three times a year. The Irving Fisher Committee on Central Bank Statistics, a forum of central bank users and compilers of statistics, has operated under the auspices of the BIS since January 2006.

In 1974 the Governors of central banks of the G10 set up the Basel Committee on Banking Supervision (whose secretariat is provided by the BIS) to co-ordinate banking supervision at the international level. The Committee pools information on banking supervisory regulations and surveillance systems, including the supervision of banks' foreign currency business, identifies possible danger areas and proposes measures to safeguard the banks' solvency and liquidity. An International Conference of Banking Supervisors is held every two years. In 1997 the Committee published new guidelines, entitled Core Principles for Effective Banking Supervision, that were intended to provide a comprehensive set of standards to ensure sound banking. In 1998 the Committee was concerned with the development and implementation of the Core Principles, particularly given the ongoing financial and economic crisis affecting several Asian countries and instability of other major economies. A Financial Stability Institute was established in 1999, jointly by the BIS and Basel Committee, to enhance the capacity of central banks and supervisory bodies to implement aspects of the Core Principles, through the provision of training programmes and other policy workshops. In January 2001 the Committee issued preliminary proposals on capital adequacy rules. In June 2004 the Committee approved a revised framework of the International Convergence of Capital Measurement and Capital Standards (also known as Basel II), which aimed to promote improvements in risk management and strengthen the stability of the financial system. An updated version of the revised framework, as well as a new version of the Amendment to the Capital Accord to incorporate market risks, was issued in November 2005. The updated versions also incorporated a paper concerned with trading activities and the treatment of double default effects prepared by a joint working group of the Committee and the International Organization of Securities Commissions. In October 2006 the International Conference of Banking Supervisors endorsed an enhanced version of the Core Principles (and its associated assessment methodology), incorporating stricter guidelines to counter money-laundering and to strengthen transparency. The Basel II capital framework began to be implemented by countries and banks from 1 January 2007. The Committee's Accord Implementation Group undertook to promote full implementation of the accord, to provide supervisory guidance and review procedures. In January 2009 the Committee proposed a package of enhanced measures to strengthen the Basel II capital framework. In June the Committee agreed to broaden its membership to include representatives from the Group of 20 (G20) countries not currently in the Committee, i.e. Argentina, Indonesia, Saudi Arabia, South Africa and Turkey. In addition, Hong Kong, Special Administrative Region, and Singapore were invited to become members. The first meeting of the expanded Committee, convened in July, approved the enhancements to the Basel II capital framework. In July 2010 a reformed capital framework programme, Basel III, was agreed by Committee's Group of Central Bank Governors and Heads of Supervision. In accordance with an agreement concluded by G20 ministers of finance in the previous month, Basel III regulations were to be phased in gradually, with some elements, for example those concerning liquidity, not becoming mandatory until 2018. In September 2010 the Group announced further agreements substantially to strengthen global capital requirements, including raising common equity levels in relation to risk-weighted assets, and introducing capital conservation buffers from 2016. The regulatory framework was endorsed by a meeting of the G20 heads of state and government held in Seoul, Republic of Korea, in November 2010.

The BIS hosts the secretariat of the Financial Stability Board, which was established (as the Financial Stability Forum) following a meeting in February 1999 of ministers of finance and governors of the central banks of the Group of Seven (G7) industrialized nations. Its aim was to strengthen co-operation among the world's largest economies and economic bodies in order to improve the monitoring of international finance, to reduce the tendency for financial shocks to spread from one economy to another, and thus to prevent a recurrence of economic crises such as those that occurred in 1997 and 1998. Working groups have studied aspects of highly leveraged, or unregulated, institutions, offshore financial centres, short-term capital flows, deposit insurance schemes and measures to promote implementation of international standards. In March 2009 membership was expanded to include all G20 economies, as well as Spain and the European Commission. In the following month G20 heads of state and government, meeting in London, United Kingdom, determined to re-establish the Financial Stability Forum as the Financial Stability Board, with an expanded mandate to develop and implement strengthened financial regulation and supervision. The inaugural meeting of the Board was convened in June.

Since January 1998 the BIS has hosted the secretariat of the International Association of Insurance Supervisors, which aims to promote co-operation within the insurance industry with regard to effective supervision and the development of domestic insurance markets. It also hosts the secretariat of the International Association of Deposit Insurers, founded in May 2002.

RESEARCH

The Bank's Monetary and Economic Department conducts research, particularly into monetary and financial questions; collects and publishes data on securities markets and international banking developments; and administers a Data Bank for central banks. Examples of recent research and policy analysis include inflation targeting procedures, structural changes in foreign exchange markets, financial risks and the business cycle, international capital flows, and transmission mechanism of monetary policy. In 2004 the BIS established a Central Bank Research Hub to promote and facilitate the dissemination of economic research published by central banks. Statistics on aspects of the global financial system are published regularly, including details on international banking activities, international and domestic securities markets, derivatives, global foreign exchange markets, external debt, and payment and settlement systems. In September 2006 a three-year Asian research programme was initiated, concerned with monetary policy and exchange rates and analysing financial markets and institutions. Following the conclusion of the programme in August 2009, a more permanent research presence in the region was under consideration. The Bank is a co-sponsor, with the UN, Euro Banking Association, Eurostat, OECD, the IMF and the World Bank, of the Statistical Data and Metadata Exchange initiative, established in June 2002.

AGENCY AND TRUSTEE FUNCTIONS

Throughout its history the BIS has undertaken various duties as Trustee Fiscal Agent or Depository with regard to international loan agreements. In October 2005 the BIS served in an escrow agent role in a loan with the Central Bank of Nigeria; the arrangement was terminated upon the final release of funds in February 2007.

In April 1994 the BIS assumed new functions in connection with the rescheduling of Brazil's external debt, which had been agreed by the Brazilian Government in November 1993. In accordance with two collateral pledge agreements, the BIS acts in the capacity of Collateral Agent to hold and invest collateral for the benefit of the holders of certain US dollar-denominated bonds, maturing in 15 or 30 years, which have been issued by Brazil under the rescheduling arrangements. The Bank acts in a similar capacity for Peru, in accordance with external debt agreements concluded in November 1996 and a collateral agreement signed with the BIS in March 1997, and for Côte d'Ivoire, under a restructuring agreement signed in May 1997 and collateral agreement signed in March 1998.

Publications

Annual Report (in English, French, German, Italian and Spanish).

BIS Consolidated Banking Statistics (every 6 months).

BIS Papers (series).

Central Bank Survey of Foreign Exchange and Derivatives Market Activity (every 3 years).

International Journal of Central Banking (quarterly).

Joint BIS-IMF-OECD-World Bank Statistics on External Debt (quarterly).

Quarterly Review.

Regular OTC Derivatives Market Statistics (every 6 months).

Statistics

STATEMENT OF ACCOUNT

(In SDR millions; 31 March 2012)

Assets		%
Gold and gold deposits . . .	35,912.7	14.0
Cash and on sight a/c with banks	4,077.8	1.6
Treasury bills	53,492.3	20.9
Loans and advances	22,757.1	8.9
Securities	124,088.5	48.5
Miscellaneous	15,342.4	6.0
Total	255,670.8	100.0

Liabilities		%
Deposits (gold)	19,624.0	7.7
Deposits (currencies) . . .	195,778.5	76.6
Accounts payable	16,745.5	6.6
Other liabilities	5,143.5	2.0
Shareholders' equity	18,379.3	7.2
Total	255,670.8	100.0

Source: BIS, *Annual Report*.

CARIBBEAN COMMUNITY AND COMMON MARKET—CARICOM

Address: POB 10827, Georgetown, Guyana.

Telephone: (2) 222-0001; **fax:** (2) 222-0171; **e-mail:** info@caricom.org; **internet:** www.caricom.org.

CARICOM was formed in 1973 by the Treaty of Chaguaramas, signed in Trinidad, as a movement towards unity in the Caribbean; it replaced the Caribbean Free Trade Association (CARIFTA), founded in 1965. A revision of the Treaty of Chaguaramas (by means of nine separate Protocols), in order to institute greater regional integration and to establish a CARICOM Single Market and Economy (CSME), was instigated in the 1990s and completed in July 2001. The single market component of the CSME was formally inaugurated on 1 January 2006.

MEMBERS

Antigua and Barbuda	Jamaica
Bahamas*	Montserrat
Barbados	Saint Christopher and Nevis
Belize	Saint Lucia
Dominica	Saint Vincent and the Grenadines
Grenada	Suriname
Guyana	Trinidad and Tobago
Haiti	

*The Bahamas is a member of the Community but not the Common Market.

ASSOCIATE MEMBERS

Anguilla	Cayman Islands
Bermuda	Turks and Caicos Islands
British Virgin Islands	

Note: Aruba, Colombia, Dominican Republic, Mexico, Puerto Rico, and Venezuela have observer status with the Community.

Organization

(June 2012)

HEADS OF GOVERNMENT CONFERENCE AND BUREAU

The Conference is the final authority of the Community and determines policy. It is responsible for the conclusion of treaties on behalf of the Community and for entering into relationships between the Community and international organizations and states. Decisions of the Conference are generally taken unanimously. Heads of government meet annually, although intersessional meetings may be convened.

At a special meeting of the Conference, held in Trinidad and Tobago in October 1992, participants decided to establish a Heads of Government Bureau, with the capacity to initiate proposals, to update consensus and to secure the implementation of CARICOM decisions. The Bureau became operational in December, comprising the Chairman of the Conference, as Chairman, as well as the incoming and outgoing Chairmen of the Conference, and the Secretary-General of the Conference, in the capacity of Chief Executive Officer.

COMMUNITY COUNCIL OF MINISTERS

In October 1992 CARICOM heads of government agreed that a Caribbean Community Council of Ministers should be established to replace the existing Common Market Council of Ministers as the second highest organ of the Community. Protocol I amending the Treaty of Chaguaramas, to restructure the organs and institutions of the Community, was formally adopted at a meeting of CARICOM heads of government in February 1997 and was signed by all member states in July. The inaugural meeting of the Community Council of Ministers was held in Nassau, Bahamas, in February 1998. The Council consists of ministers responsible for community affairs, as well as other government ministers designated by member states, and is responsible for the development of the Community's strategic planning and co-ordination in the areas of economic integration, functional co-operation and external relations.

COURT OF JUSTICE

Caribbean Court of Justice (CCJ): 134 Henry St, POB 1768, Port of Spain, Trinidad and Tobago; tel. 623-2225; e-mail info@caribbeancourtofjustice.org; internet www.caribbeancourtofjustice.org; inaugurated in April 2005; an agreement establishing the Court was formally signed by 10 member countries in February 2001, and by two further states in February 2003; in January 2004 a revised agreement on the establishment of the CCJ, which incorporated provision for a Trust Fund, entered into force; serves as a tribunal to enforce rights and to consider disputes relating to the CARICOM Single Market and Economy; intended to replace the Judicial Committee of the Privy Council as the Court of Final Appeal (effective for Barbados, Belize and Guyana in 2010); Pres. Sir DENNIS BYRON (Saint Christopher and Nevis).

MINISTERIAL COUNCILS

The principal organs of the Community are assisted in their functions by the following bodies, established under Protocol I amending the Treaty of Chaguaramas: the Council for Trade and Economic Development (COTED); the Council for Foreign and Community Relations (COFCOR); the Council for Human and Social Development (COHSOD); and the Council for Finance and Planning (COFAP). The Councils are responsible for formulating policies, promoting their implementation and supervising co-operation in the relevant areas.

SECRETARIAT

The Secretariat is the main administrative body of the Caribbean Community. The functions of the Secretariat are to service meetings of the Community and of its Committees; to take appropriate follow-up action on decisions made at such meetings; to carry out studies on questions of economic and functional co-operation relating to the region as a whole; to provide services to member states at their request in respect of matters relating to the achievement of the objectives of the Community. The Secretariat incorporates Directorates, each headed by an Assistant Secretary-General, for Trade and Economic Integration; Foreign and Community Relations; Human and Social Development; and CARIFORUM.

Secretary-General: IRWIN LAROCQUE (Dominica).

Activities

The Heads of Government meeting, convened in Montego Bay, Jamaica, in July 2010, agreed to establish a seven-member high-level committee to draft proposals on a new governance structure for CARICOM, in order to address concerns regarding the implementation of community decisions. The report, entitled *Turning around CARICOM: Proposals to restructure the Secretariat*, was presented to heads of government, convened for an intersessional meeting in Paramaribo, Suriname, in March 2012.

ECONOMIC CO-OPERATION

The Caribbean Community's main field of activity is economic integration, by means of a Caribbean Common Market. The Secretariat and the Caribbean Development Bank undertake research on the best means of tackling economic difficulties, and meetings of the chief executives of commercial banks and of central bank officials are also held with the aim of strengthening regional co-operation. In March 2009 heads of government, meeting in Belize City, Belize, resolved to pursue a regional strategy to counter the effects on the region of the severe global economic and financial downturn. A new Heads of Government Task Force on the Regional Financial and Economic Crisis held its inaugural meeting in August, in Jamaica.

In July 1984 heads of government agreed to establish a common external tariff (CET) on certain products, in order to protect domestic industries. They urged structural adjustment in the economies of the region, including measures to expand production and reduce imports. In 1989 the Conference of Heads of Government agreed to implement, by July 1993, a series of measures to encourage the creation of a single Caribbean market. These included the establishment of a CARICOM Industrial Programming Scheme; the inauguration of the CARICOM Enterprise Regime; facilitation of travel for CARICOM nationals within the region; full implementation of the rules of origin and the revised scheme for the harmonization of fiscal incentives; free movement of skilled workers; removal of all remaining regional barriers to trade; establishment of a regional system of air and sea transport; and the introduction of a scheme for regional capital movement. A CARICOM Export Development Council, established in November 1989, undertook a three-year export development project to stimulate trade within CARICOM and to promote exports outside the region. In August 1990 CARICOM heads of government mandated the governors of CARICOM members' central banks to begin a study of the means to achieve monetary union within CARICOM; they also institutionalized biannual meetings of CARICOM ministers of finance and senior finance officials.

The initial deadline of 1991 for the establishment of a CET was not achieved. At a special meeting, held in October 1992, CARICOM heads of government agreed to reduce the maximum level of tariffs from 45% to between 30% and 35%, to be in effect by 30 June 1993 (the level was to be further lowered, to 25%–30% by 1995). The Bahamas, however, was not party to these trading arrangements (since it is a member of the Community but not of the Common Market), and Belize was granted an extension for the implementation of the new tariff levels. At the Heads of Government Conference, held in July 1995 in Guyana, Suriname was admitted as a full member of CARICOM and acceded to the treaty establishing the Common Market. It was granted until 1 January 1996 for implementation of the tariff reductions.

The 1995 Heads of Government Conference approved additional measures to promote the single market. The free movement of skilled workers (mainly graduates from recognized regional institutions) was to be permitted from 1 January 1996. At the same time an agreement on the mutual protection and provision of social security benefits was to enter into force. In July 1996 the heads of government agreed to extend the provisions of free movement to sports men and women, musicians and others working in the arts and media.

In July 1997 the Conference, meeting in Montego Bay, Jamaica, determined to accelerate economic integration, with the aim of completing a single market by 1999. At the meeting 11 member states signed Protocol II amending the Treaty of Chaguaramas, which constituted a central element of a CARICOM Single Market and Economy (CSME), providing for the right to establish enterprises, the provision of services and the free movement of capital and labour throughout participating countries. A regional collaborative network was established to promote the CSME. In July 1998, at the meeting of heads of government, held in Saint Lucia, an agreement was signed with the Insurance Company of the West Indies to accelerate the establishment of a Caribbean Investment Fund, which was to mobilize foreign currency from extra-regional capital markets for investment in new or existing enterprises in the region. Some 60% of all funds generated were to be used by CARICOM countries and the remainder by non-CARICOM members of the Association of Caribbean States.

In November 2000 a special consultation on the single market and economy was held in Barbados, involving CARICOM and government officials, academics, and representatives of the private sector, labour organizations, the media, and other regional groupings. In February 2001 heads of government agreed to establish a new high-level sub-committee to accelerate the establishment of the CSME and to promote its objectives. The sub-committee was to be supported by a Technical Advisory Council, comprising representatives of the public and private sectors. By June all member states had signed and declared the provisional application of Protocol II. By May 2007 12 countries had completed the fourth phase of the CET.

In October 2001 CARICOM heads of government, convened for a special emergency meeting, considered the impact on the region's economy of the terrorist attacks perpetrated against targets in the USA in the previous month. The meeting resolved to enhance aviation security, implement promotion and marketing campaigns in support of the tourist industry, and approach international institutions to assist with emergency financing. The economic situation, which had been further adversely affected by the reduced access to the European Union (EU) banana market, the economic downturn in the USA, and the effects on the investment climate of the OECD Harmful Taxation Initiative, was considered at the Heads of Government Conference, held in Guyana, in July 2002.

On 1 January 2006 the single market component of the CSME was formally inaugurated, with Barbados, Belize, Guyana, Jamaica, Suriname and Trinidad and Tobago as active participants. Six more countries (Antigua and Barbuda, Dominica, Grenada, Saint Christopher and Nevis, Saint Lucia, Saint Vincent and the Grenadines) formally joined the single market in July. At the same time CARICOM heads of government approved a contribution formula allowing for the establishment of a regional development fund. In February 2007 an inter-sessional meeting of the Conference of Heads of Government, held in Saint Vincent and the Grenadines, approved a timetable for the full implementation of the CSME: phase I (mid-2005–08) for the consolidation of the single market and the initiation of a single economy; phase II (2009–15) for the consolidation and completion of the single economy process, including the harmonization and co-ordination of economic policies in the region and the establishment of new institutions to implement those policies. In July 2007 CARICOM heads of government endorsed the report, *Towards a Single Development Vision and the Role of the Single Economy*, on which the elaboration of the CSME was based. In January 2008 a Caribbean Competition Commission was inaugurated, in Paramaribo, Suriname, to enforce the rules of competition within the CSME. In February Haiti signed the revised Treaty of Chaguaramas. The Caribbean Development Fund (CDF), launched in mid-2008, with initial finances of US $60m. commenced full operations in August 2009. A Convocation on the CSME was convened in Bridgetown, Barbados, in October, as part of a wider appraisal of the CSME. In February 2011 heads of government signed an agreement to enable the CDF to grant funds on preferential terms to low-income member countries.

In December 2007 a special meeting of the Conference of Heads of Government, convened in Georgetown, Guyana, considered issues relating to regional poverty and the rising cost of living in member states. The meeting resolved to establish a technical team to review the CET on essential commodities to determine whether it should be removed or reduced to deter inflationary pressures. The meeting also agreed to review the supply and distribution of food throughout the region, including transportation issues affecting the price of goods and services, and determined to expand agricultural production and agro-processing. Efforts to harness renewable energy sources were to be strengthened to counter rising fuel prices.

REGIONAL INTEGRATION

In 1989 CARICOM heads of government established the 15-member West Indian Commission to study regional political and economic integration. The Commission's final report, submitted in July 1992, recommended that CARICOM should remain a community of sovereign states (rather than a federation), but should strengthen the integration process and expand to include the wider Caribbean region. It recommended the formation of an Association of Caribbean States (ACS), to include all the countries within and surrounding the Caribbean Basin. In November 1997 the Secretaries-General of CARICOM and the ACS signed a Co-operation Agreement to formalize the reciprocal procedures through which the organizations work to enhance and facilitate regional integration. Suriname was admitted to CARICOM in July 1995. In July 1997 the Heads of Government Conference agreed to admit Haiti as a member, although the terms and conditions of its accession to the organization were not finalized until July 1999. In July 2001 the CARICOM Secretary-General formally inaugurated a CARICOM Office in Haiti, which aimed to provide technical assistance in preparation of Haiti's accession to the Community. In January 2002 a CARICOM special mission visited Haiti, following an escalation of the political violence that had started in the previous month. Ministers of foreign affairs emphasized the need for international aid for Haiti when they met their US counterpart in February. Haiti was admitted as the 15th member of CARICOM at the Heads of Government Conference, held in July.

During 1998 CARICOM was concerned by the movement within Nevis to secede from its federation with Saint Christopher. In July heads of government agreed to dispatch a mediation team to the country (postponed until September). The Heads of Government Conference held in March 1999 welcomed the establishment of a Constitutional Task Force by the local authorities to prepare a draft constitution, on the basis of recommendations of a previous constitutional commission and the outcome of a series of public meetings. In July 1998 heads of government expressed concern at the hostility between the Government and opposition groupings in Guyana. The two sides signed an agreement, under CARICOM auspices, and in September a CARICOM mediation mission visited Guyana to promote further dialogue. CARICOM has declared its support for Guyana in its territorial disputes with Venezuela and Suriname. A CARICOM electoral observer mission monitored the conduct of a general election in Guyana in November 2011.

In February 1997 Community heads of government signed a new Charter of Civil Society for the Community, which set out principles in the areas of democracy, government, parliament, freedom of the press and human rights. In July 2002 a conference was held, in Liliendaal, Guyana, attended by representatives of civil society and CARICOM heads of government. The meeting issued a statement of principles on 'Forward Together', recognizing the role of civil society in meeting the challenges to the region. It was agreed to hold regular meetings and to establish a task force to develop a regional strategic framework for pursuing the main recommendations of the conference. In February 2007 an inter-sessional meeting of CARICOM heads of government determined to add security (including crime) as a fourth pillar of regional integration, in addition to those identified: economic integration; co-ordination of foreign policy; and functional co-operation.

CO-ORDINATION OF FOREIGN POLICY

The co-ordination of foreign policies of member states is listed as one of the main objectives of the Community in its founding treaty. Activities include strengthening member states' position in international organizations; joint diplomatic action on issues of particular interest to the Caribbean; joint co-operation arrangements with third countries and organizations; and the negotiation of free trade agreements with third countries and other regional groupings. In April 1997 CARICOM inaugurated a Caribbean Regional Negotiating Machinery (CRNM) body, based in Kingston, Jamaica, to co-ordinate and strengthen the region's presence at external economic negotiations. The main areas of activity were negotiations to establish a Free Trade Area of the Americas (FTAA—now stalled), ACP relations with the EU, and multilateral trade negotiations under the World Trade Organization (WTO). In July 2009 the CRNM was renamed the Office of Trade Negotiations, reporting directly to the Council for Trade and Economic Development; its mandate was expanded to include responsibility for all external trade negotiations on behalf of the Community, with immediate priority to be placed on negotiations with Canada. Since 2001 CARICOM has conducted regular meetings with representatives of the United Nations. The sixth meeting, convened in July 2011, agreed to revise the existing Regional Strategic Framework for co-operation and to initiate negotiations towards a more effective mechanism for UN activities in the region.

In July 1991 Venezuela applied for membership of CARICOM, and offered a non-reciprocal free trade agreement for CARICOM exports to Venezuela, over an initial five-year period. In October 1993 the newly established Group of Three (Colombia, Mexico and Venezuela) signed joint agreements with CARICOM and Suriname on combating drugs-trafficking and on environmental protection. In June 1994 CARICOM and Colombia concluded an agreement on trade, economic and technical co-operation, which, *inter alia*, gives special treatment to the least-developed CARICOM countries. CARICOM has observer status in the Latin American Rio Group.

In 1992 Cuba applied for observer status within CARICOM, and in July 1993 a joint commission was inaugurated to establish closer ties between CARICOM and Cuba and provide a mechanism for regular dialogue. In July 1997 the heads of government agreed to pursue consideration of a free trade accord between the Community and Cuba. A Trade and Economic Agreement was signed by the two sides in July 2000, and in February 2001 a CARICOM office was established in Cuba. At the first meeting of heads of state and government in December 2002, convened in Havana, Cuba, it was agreed to commemorate the start of diplomatic relations between the two sides, some 30 years previously, on 8 December each year as Cuba/CARICOM Day. The second summit meeting, held in December 2005 in Bridgetown, Barbados, agreed to strengthen co-operation in education, culture and the environment, access to health care and efforts to counter international terrorism. A second meeting of CARICOM-Cuba ministers of foreign affairs was convened in May 2007 (the first having taken place in July 2004). The third meeting at the level of heads of state and government was held in December 2008 in Santiago de Cuba, Cuba. CARICOM leaders urged the new US administration to reconsider its restrictions on trade with Cuba. A similar appeal was made at the fourth summit meeting, convened in December 2011, in Port-of-Spain, Trinidad and Tobago. The meeting also focused on collaboration with regard to the illegal trafficking of drugs and small arms.

In February 1992 ministers of foreign affairs from CARICOM and Central American states met to discuss future co-operation, in view of the imminent conclusion of the North American Free Trade Agreement (NAFTA) between the USA, Canada and Mexico. It was agreed that a consultative forum would be established to discuss the possible formation of a Caribbean and Central American free trade zone. In October 1993 CARICOM declared its support for NAFTA, but requested a 'grace period', during which the region's exports would have parity with Mexican products, and in March 1994 requested that it should be considered for early entry into NAFTA.

In May 1997 a meeting of CARICOM heads of government and the US President established a partnership for prosperity and security, and arrangements were instituted for annual consultations between the ministers of foreign affairs of CARICOM countries and the US Secretary of State. However, the Community failed to secure a commitment by the USA to grant the region's exports 'NAFTA-parity' status, or to guarantee concessions to the region's banana industry. The USA's opposition to a new EU banana policy (which was to terminate the import licensing system, extending import quotas to 'dollar' producers, while maintaining a limited duty-free quota for Caribbean producers) was strongly criticized by CARICOM leaders, meeting in July 1998. In March 1999 the Inter-Sessional meeting of the Conference of Heads of Government issued a statement condemning the imposition by the USA of sanctions against a number of EU imports, in protest at the revised EU banana regime, and the consequences of this action on Caribbean economies, and agreed to review its co-operation with the USA under the partnership for prosperity and security.

In August 1998 CARICOM and the Dominican Republic signed a free trade accord, covering trade in goods and services, technical barriers to trade, government procurement, and sanitary and phytosanitary measures and standards. A protocol to the agreement was signed in April 2000, following the resolution of differences concerning exempted items. The accord was ratified by the Dominican Republic in February 2001 and entered partially into force on 1 December. A Task Force to strengthen bilateral relations was established in 2007 and held its first meeting in November 2008. In November 2001 the CARICOM Secretary-General formally inaugurated a Caribbean Regional Technical Assistance Centre (CARTAC), in Barbados, to provide technical advice and training to officials from member countries and the Dominican Republic in support of the region's development. The Centre's operations are managed by the IMF.

In March 2000 heads of government issued a statement supporting the territorial integrity and security of Belize in that country's ongoing border dispute with Guatemala. CARICOM subsequently urged both countries to implement the provisions of an agreement signed in November and has continued to monitor the situation regularly.

In February 2002 the first meeting of heads of state and of government of CARICOM and the Central American Integration System (SICA) was convened in Belize City, Belize. The meeting aimed to strengthen co-operation between the groupings, in particular in international negotiations, efforts to counter transnational organized crime, and support for the regions' economies. In late 2002 a joint CARICOM-Spain commission was inaugurated to foster greater co-operation between the two parties. In March 2004 CARICOM signed a free trade agreement with Costa Rica.

In January 2004 CARICOM heads of government resolved to address the escalating political crisis in Haiti. Following a visit by a high-level delegation to that country early in the month discussions were held with representatives of opposition political parties and civil society groups. At the end of January several CARICOM leaders met with Haiti's President Aristide and members of his Government and announced a Prior Action Plan, incorporating opposition demands for political reform. The Plan, however, was rejected by opposition parties since it permitted Aristide to complete his term-in-office. CARICOM, together with the OAS, continued to pursue diplomatic efforts to secure a peaceful solution to the crisis. On 29 February Aristide resigned and left the country and a provisional president was appointed. In March CARICOM heads of government determined not to allow representatives of the new interim administration to participate in the councils of the Community until constitutional rule had been reinstated. In July heads of government resolved to send a five-member ministerial team to Haiti to discuss developments in that country with the interim authorities. In July 2005 CARICOM heads of government expressed concern at the deterioration of the situation in Haiti, but reiterated their readiness to provide technical assistance for the electoral process, under the auspices of the UN mission. In March 2006 the CARICOM Chairman endorsed the results of the presidential election, conducted in February, and pledged to support Haiti's return to democratic rule. In August 2010 CARICOM sent a joint election observation mission (JEOM), with the OAS, to monitor presidential and legislative elections in Haiti, scheduled for November. Although the JEOM reported several procedural irregularities in the voting process, and expressed concern at allegations by some candidates and their supporters of fraudulence or intimidation at polling stations, it confirmed that the elections were valid. The mission remained in Haiti in early 2011 in order to monitor the second round of voting in the presidential election, held in March.

In March 2006 a CARICOM-Mexico Joint Commission signed an agreement to promote future co-operation, in particular in seven priority areas. The first summit level meeting between heads of state and government of Mexico and CARICOM was held in February 2010, in Riviera Maya, Mexico. In February 2007 the Secretaries-General of CARICOM and SICA signed a plan of action on future co-operation between the two groupings. A second CARICOM-SICA meeting of heads of state and of government was convened in May, in Belize. The meeting endorsed the plan of action and, in addition, instructed their ministers of foreign affairs and of trade to pursue efforts to negotiate a free trade agreement, to be based on that signed by CARICOM with Costa Rica (see above). Trade negotiations were formally inaugurated in August. The third CARICOM-SICA summit meeting was convened in El Salvador, in August 2011. A joint declaration recognized the need to develop transport and cultural links, and detailed measures to strengthen co-operation in international environmental negotiations, combating transnational crime, disaster management, the prevention of non-communicable diseases, and the management of migratory fish stocks in the Caribbean Sea.

In March 2006 CARICOM ministers of foreign affairs met with the US Secretary of State and agreed to strengthen co-operation and enhance bilateral relations. In June 2007 a major meeting, the 'Conference on the Caribbean: a 20/20 Vision', was held in Washington, DC, USA. A series of meetings was held to consider issues and challenges relating to CARICOM's development and integration efforts and to the strengthening of relations with other countries in the region and with the USA. An Experts' Forum was hosted by the World Bank, a Private Sector Dialogue was held at the headquarters of the Inter-American Development Bank, and a Diaspora Forum was convened at the OAS. A summit meeting of CARICOM heads of government and US President George W. Bush was held in the context of the Conference, at which issues concerning trade, economic growth and development, security and social investment were discussed. A second Conference on the Caribbean was held in New York, USA, in June 2008. A meeting of CARICOM foreign ministers with the US Secretary of State was held in June 2010, in Barbados, at which a series of commitments was concluded to enhance co-operation on a range of issues including energy security, climate change, health and trade relations.

CRIME AND SECURITY

In December 1996 CARICOM heads of government determined to strengthen comprehensive co-operation and technical assistance to combat illegal drugs-trafficking. The Conference decided to establish a Caribbean Security Task Force to help to formulate a single regional agreement on maritime interdiction, incorporating agreements already concluded by individual members. A Regional Drugs Control Programme at the CARICOM Secretariat aims to co-ordinate regional initiatives with the overall objective of reducing the demand and supply of illegal substances.

In July 2000 the Heads of Government meeting issued a statement strongly opposing the OECD Harmful Tax Initiative, under which punitive measures had been threatened against 35 countries, including CARICOM member states, if they failed to tighten taxation legislation. The meeting also condemned a separate list, issued by OECD's Financial Action Task Force on Money Laundering (FATF), which identified 15 countries, including five Caribbean states, of failing to counter effectively international money-laundering. The statement reaffirmed CARICOM's commitment to fighting financial crimes and support for any necessary reform of supervisory practices or legislation, but insisted that national taxation jurisdictions, and specifically competitive regimes designed to attract offshore business, was not a matter for OECD concern. CARICOM remained actively involved in efforts to counter the scheme, and in April 2001 presented its case to the US President. In September the FATF issued a revised list of 19 'unco-operative jurisdictions', including Dominica, Grenada, Saint Christopher and Nevis and Saint Vincent and the Grenadines. In early 2002 most Caribbean states concluded a provisional agreement with OECD to work to improve the transparency and supervision of offshore sectors.

In July 2001 heads of government resolved to establish a task force to be responsible for producing recommendations for a forthcoming meeting of national security advisers. In October heads of government convened an emergency meeting in Nassau, the Bahamas, to consider the impact of the terrorist attacks against the USA that had occurred in September. The meeting determined to convene immediately the so-called Task Force on Crime and Security in order to implement new policy directives. It was agreed to enhance co-ordination and collaboration of security services throughout the region, in particular in intelligence gathering, analysis and sharing in relation to crime, illicit drugs and terrorism, and to strengthen security at airports, seaports and borders. In July 2002 heads of government agreed on a series of initiatives recommended by the Task Force to counter the escalation in crime and violence. These included strengthening border controls, preparing national anti-crime master plans, establishing broad-based National Commissions on law and order and furthering the exchange of information and intelligence.

In July 2005 CARICOM heads of government endorsed a new Management Framework for Crime and Security, which provided for regular meetings of a Council of Ministers responsible for national security and law enforcement, a Security Policy Advisory Committee, and the establishment of an Implementation Agency for Crime and Security. Several co-ordinated security measures were implemented during the cricket world cup, which was held across the region in early 2007. In July CARICOM heads of government agreed in principle to extend these security efforts, including the introduction of a voluntary CARICOM Travel Card, CARIPASS, to facilitate the establishment of a single domestic space. An agreement to implement CARIPASS was signed by heads of state and government meeting in Dominica, in March 2010; the installation of the CARIPASS system was ongoing in 2012.

In April 2010 US President Barack Obama announced a Caribbean Basin Security Initiative (CBSI), which was to structure its regional security policy around a bilateral partnership with CARICOM, in particular to advance public safety and security, substantially to reduce trafficking of illicit substances and to promote social justice. In the following month an inaugural Caribbean-US Security Co-operation Dialogue was held, in Washington, DC, to pursue discussion of the CBSI. The first meeting of a CBSI Commission was convened in Kingston, Jamaica, in November. Also in November, at the second meeting of the CARICOM-US Security Co-operation Dialogue, held in the Bahamas, officials agreed to facilitate region-wide information sharing, and to develop a regional juvenile justice policy.

In September 2011 a delegation from the UN Office on Drugs and Crime met with officials from CARICOM's Implementation Agency for Crime and Security in Trinidad and Tobago. Discussions centred on strengthening regional forensics capacity, the proliferation of illegal guns, human trafficking, smuggling of migrants, and money-laundering.

INDUSTRY, ENERGY AND THE ENVIRONMENT

A protocol relating to the CARICOM Industrial Programming Scheme (CIPS), approved in 1988, is the Community's instrument for promoting the co-operative development of industry in the region. Protocol III amending the Treaty of Chaguaramas, with respect to industrial policy, was opened for signature in July 1998. The Secretariat has established a national standards bureau in each member country to harmonize technical standards. In 1999 members agreed to establish a new CARICOM Regional Organisation for Standards and Quality (CROSQ), as a successor to the Caribbean Common Market Standards Council. The agreement to establish CROSQ, to be located in Barbados, was signed in February 2002.

The CARICOM Alternative Energy Systems Project provides training, assesses energy needs and conducts energy audits. Efforts in regional energy development are directed at the collection and analysis of data for national energy policy documents. Implementation of a Caribbean Renewable Energy Development Programme, a project initiated in 1998, commenced in 2004. The Programme aimed to remove barriers to renewable energy development, establish a foundation for a sustainable renewable energy industry, and to create a framework for co-operation among regional and national renewable energy projects. A Caribbean Renewable Energy Fund was established to provide equity and development financing for renewable energy projects.

In January 2001 the Council for Trade and Economic Development approved the development of a specialized CARICOM agency to co-ordinate the gathering of information and other activities relating to climate change. The Caribbean Community Climate Change Centre became operational in early 2004 and was formally inaugurated, in Belmopan, Belize, in August 2005. It serves as an official clearing house and repository of data relating to climate change in the Caribbean region, provides advice to governments and other expertise for the development of projects to manage and adapt to climate change, and undertakes training. The results of the Centre's Mainstreaming Adaptation to Climate Change (MACC) Project were presented to governments at a Caribbean Climate Change Conference, held in Saint Lucia, in March 2009. In June 2012, during the UN Conference on Sustainable Development, held in Rio de Janeiro, Brazil, the Centre, the Indian Ocean Commission and the Secretariat of the Pacific Regional Environment Programme signed two agreements on co-operation in addressing climate change and promoting sustainable development. In July 2008 CARICOM heads of government established a Task Force on Climate Change and Development to consider future action in relation to developments in energy and climate change, and in particular food insecurity caused by global rising food and fuel prices. The inaugural meeting of the Task Force was held in November, in Saint Lucia. In March 2012 CARICOM heads of government endorsed an 'Implementation Plan for the Regional Framework for Achieving Development Resilient to Climate Change', to cover the period 2011–21.

TRANSPORT, COMMUNICATIONS AND TOURISM

In 1997 CARICOM heads of government considered a number of proposals relating to air transportation, tourism, human resource development and capital investment, which had been identified by Community ministers of tourism as critical issues in the sustainable development of the tourist industry. The heads of government requested ministers to meet regularly to develop tourism policies, and in particular to undertake an in-depth study of human resource development issues in 1998. A regional summit on tourism was held in the Bahamas in December 2001. A new Caribbean passport was introduced in January 2005; all 12 member countries participating in the CSME were issuing the document by 2009.

A Caribbean Confederation of Shippers' Councils represents the interests of regional exporters and importers. A Multilateral Agreement Concerning the Operations of Air Services within the Caribbean Community entered into force in November 1998, providing a formal framework for the regulation of the air transport industry and enabling CARICOM-owned and -controlled airlines to operate freely within the region. In July 1999 heads of government signed Protocol VI amending the Treaty of Chaguaramas providing for a common transportation policy, with harmonized standards and practices, which was to be an integral component of the development of a single market and economy. In November 2001 representatives of national civil aviation authorities signed a Memorandum of Understanding, providing for the establishment of a regional body, the Regional Aviation Safety Oversight System. This was succeeded, in July 2008, by a Caribbean Aviation Safety and Security Oversight System upon the signing of an agreement by Barbados, Guyana, Saint Lucia and Trinidad and Tobago.

In 1989 the Caribbean Telecommunications Union was established to oversee developments in regional telecommunications. In July 2006 the Conference of Heads of Government, convened in Saint Christopher and Nevis, mandated the development of C@ribNET, a project to extend the availability of high speed internet access throughout the region. In May 2007 the inaugural meeting of a Regional Information Communications and Technology Steering Committee was held, in Georgetown, Guyana, to determine areas of activity for future co-operation in support of the establishment of a Caribbean Information Society.

AGRICULTURE AND FISHERIES

In July 1996 the CARICOM summit meeting agreed to undertake wide-ranging measures in order to modernize the agricultural sector and to increase the international competitiveness of Caribbean agricultural produce. The CARICOM Secretariat was to support national programmes with assistance in policy formulation, human resource development and the promotion of research and technology development in the areas of productivity, marketing, agri-business and water resources management. Protocol V amending the Treaty of Chaguaramas, which was concerned with agricultural policy, was opened for signature by heads of government in July 1998. In July 2002 heads of government approved an initiative to develop a CARIFORUM Special Programme for Food Security. CARICOM Governments have continually aimed to generate awareness of the economic and social importance of the banana industry to the region, in particular within the framework of the WTO multilateral trade negotiations.

In July 2005 CARICOM heads of government issued a statement protesting against proposals by the European Commission, issued in the previous month, to reform the EU sugar regime. Particular concern was expressed at a proposed price reduction in the cost of refined sugar of 39% over a four-year period. The heads of government insisted that, in accordance with the ACP-EU Cotonou Agreement, any review of the Sugar Protocol was required to be undertaken with the agreement of both parties and with regard to safeguarding benefits. In December CARICOM heads of government held a special meeting to discuss the EU sugar and banana regimes, in advance of a ministerial meeting of the WTO, held in Hong Kong that month. The Conference reiterated the potentially devastating effects on regional economies of the sugar price reduction and proposed new banana tariffs, and expressed the need for greater compensation and for the WTO multilateral negotiations to address fairly issues of preferential access. Negotiations between the ACP Caribbean signatory countries (the so-called CARIFORUM) and the EU on an Economic Partnership Agreement to succeed the Cotonou Agreement, which had commenced in April 2004, were concluded in December 2007. In January 2008 CARICOM's Council for Trade and Economic Development resolved to conduct an independent review of the new agreement. The agreement was signed (initially, with the exception of Guyana and Haiti) in October.

A Caribbean Regional Fisheries Mechanism was established in 2002 to promote the sustainable use of fisheries and aquaculture resources in the region. It incorporates a Caribbean Fisheries Forum, which serves as the main technical and scientific decision-making body of the Mechanism. In March 2010 a Caribbean Agricultural Health and Food Safety Agency (CAHFSA) was inaugurated in Paramaribo, Suriname.

HEALTH AND SOCIAL POLICY

In 1984 CARICOM and the Pan-American Health Organization launched 'Caribbean Co-operation in Health' with projects to be undertaken in six main areas: environmental protection, including the control of disease-bearing pests; development of human resources; chronic non-communicable diseases and accidents; strengthening health systems; food and nutrition; maternal and child health care; and population activities. A second phase of the initiative commenced in 1992. In 2001 CARICOM established the Pan-Caribbean Partnership against HIV/AIDS (PANCAP), with the aim of reducing the spread and impact of HIV and AIDS in member countries. In February 2002 PANCAP initiated regional negotiations with pharmaceutical companies to secure reductions in the cost of anti-retroviral drugs.

A Caribbean Environmental Health Institute (see below) aims to promote collaboration among member states in all areas of environmental management and human health. In July 2001 heads of government, meeting in the Bahamas, issued the Nassau Declaration on Health, advocating greater regional strategic co-ordination and planning in the health sector and institutional reform, as well as increased resources. In February 2006 PANCAP and UNAIDS organized a regional consultation on the outcomes of country-based assessments of the HIV/AIDS crisis that had been undertaken in the region, and formulated a Regional Roadmap for Universal Access to HIV and AIDS Prevention, Care, Treatment and Support over the period 2006–10. A special meeting of COHSOD, convened in June 2006, in Trinidad and Tobago, issued the Port of Spain Declaration on the Education Sector Response to HIV and AIDS, which committed member states to supporting the Roadmap through education policy. In September 2007 a special regional summit meeting on chronic non-communicable diseases was held in Port of Spain, Trinidad and Tobago. In July 2008 CARICOM heads of government endorsed a new Caribbean Regional Strategy Framework on HIV and AIDS for the period 2008–12. In March 2010 Caribbean heads of government approved the establishment of a Caribbean Public Health Agency (CARPHA), which was intended to promote a co-ordinated approach to public health issues, in accordance with the Nassau Declaration. CARPHA became a legally established entity in July 2011. The operational development of CARPHA, including the full integration of the core functions of the existing five regional health institutions, was scheduled to be completed by 2014.

CARICOM education programmes have included the improvement of reading in schools through assistance for teacher training and ensuring the availability of low-cost educational material throughout the region. In July 1997 CARICOM heads of government adopted the recommendations of a ministerial committee, which identified priority measures for implementation in the education sector. These included the objective of achieving universal, quality secondary education and the enrolment of 15% of post-secondary students in tertiary education by 2005, as well as improved training in foreign languages and science and technology. In March 2004 CARICOM ministers of education endorsed the establishment of a Caribbean Knowledge and Learning Network (CKLN) to strengthen tertiary education institutions throughout the region and to enhance knowledge sharing. The CKLN, which also co-ordinates and manages the development of C@ribNET, was formally inaugurated in July, in co-operation with the OECS, in Grenada. A Caribbean Vocational Qualification was introduced in 2007.

From the late 1990s youth activities have been increasingly emphasized by the Community. These have included new programmes for disadvantaged youths, a mechanism for youth exchange and the convening of a Caribbean Youth Parliament. CARICOM organizes a biennial Caribbean Festival of Arts (CARIFESTA). CARIFESTA X was staged in Georgetown, Guyana, in August 2008. As a result of the poor economic climate, the Bahamas withdrew its offer to hold the festival in 2010. In July 2011 Suriname announced that it was to host CARIFESTA XI, in 2013. A CARICOM Regional Sports Academy was inaugurated, in Paramaribo, Suriname, in March 2012.

EMERGENCY ASSISTANCE

A Caribbean Disaster Emergency Response Agency (CDERA) was established in 1991 to co-ordinate immediate disaster relief, primarily in the event of hurricanes. In January 2005, meeting on the sidelines of the fifth Summit of the Alliance of Small Island States, in Port Louis, Mauritius, the Secretaries-General of CARICOM, the Commonwealth, the Pacific Islands Forum and the Indian Ocean Commission determined to take collective action to strengthen the disaster preparedness and response capabilities of their member countries in the Caribbean, Pacific and Indian Ocean areas. In September 2006 CARICOM, the EU and the Caribbean ACP states signed a Financing Agreement for Institutional Support and Capacity Building for Disaster Management in the Caribbean, which aimed to support CDERA by providing €3.4m. to facilitate the implementation of revised legislation, improved co-ordination between countries in the region and the increased use of information and communications technology in emergency planning. A new Caribbean Catastrophe Risk Insurance Facility (CCRIF), a multi-country initiative enabling participating states to draw funds for responding immediately to adverse natural events, such as earthquakes and hurricanes, became operational in June 2007, with support from international donors, including the Caribbean Development Bank and the World Bank. In September 2009 a new Caribbean Disaster Emergency Management Agency (CDEMA) formally replaced the CDERA, which had 18 participating states.

In January 2010 CARICOM provided immediate assistance to Haiti, after a massive earthquake caused extensive damage and loss of life in the country. A Tactical Mission was deployed to assess relief requirements and logistics, in particular in providing health services. A Special Co-ordinator, to be based in Haiti, was appointed to ensure the effectiveness of the Community's assistance, working closely with CDEMA and other international relief efforts. At the International Donors' Conference Towards a New Future for Haiti, held in New York, USA, in March, UN member countries and other international partners pledged US $5,300m. in support of an Action Plan for the National Recovery and Development of the country. CARICOM pledged to support the Haitian Government in working with the international community and to provide all necessary institutional and technical assistance during the rehabilitation process. CARICOM was represented on the Board of the Interim Commission for the Reconstruction of Haiti, inaugurated in June, following a World Summit on the Future of Haiti, held to discuss the effective implementation of the Action Plan. In April 2011 CARICOM heads of government expressed serious concern at the slow disbursement of international pledges towards the reconstruction effort.

INSTITUTIONS

The following are among the institutions formally established within the framework of CARICOM:

Assembly of Caribbean Community Parliamentarians: c/o CARICOM Secretariat; an intergovernmental agreement on the establishment of a regional parliament entered into force in August 1994; inaugural meeting held in Barbados in May 1996. Comprises up to four representatives of the parliaments of each member country, and up to two of each associate member. It aims to provide a forum for wider community involvement in the process of integration and for enhanced deliberation on CARICOM affairs; authorized to issue recommendations for the Conference of Heads of Government and to adopt resolutions on any matter arising under the Treaty of Chaguaramas.

Caribbean Agricultural Research and Development Institute (CARDI): UWI Campus, St Augustine, Trinidad and Tobago; tel. 645-1205; fax 645-1208; e-mail infocentre@cardi.org; internet www.cardi.org; f. 1975; aims to contribute to the competitiveness and sustainability of Caribbean agriculture by generating and transferring new and appropriate technologies and by developing effective partnerships with regional and international entities; Exec. Dir Dr ARLINGTON CHESNEY; publs *CARDI Weekly*, *CARDI Review*, technical bulletin series.

Caribbean Centre for Development Administration (CARICAD): Weymouth Corporate Centre, 1st Floor, Roebuck St, St Michael, Barbados; tel. 427-8535; fax 436-1709; e-mail info@caricad.net; internet www.caricad.net; f. 1980; aims to assist governments in the reform of the public sector and to strengthen their managerial capacities for public administration; promotes the involvement of the private sector, non-governmental organizations and other bodies in all decision-making processes; Exec. Dir JENNIFER ASTAPHAN.

Caribbean Community Climate Change Centre (5Cs): Lawrence Nicholas Bldg, 2nd Floor, Ring Rd, POB 563, Belmopan, Belize; tel. 822-1094; fax 822-1365; e-mail kleslie1@caribbeanclimate.bz; internet www.caribbeanclimate.bz; f. 2005 to co-ordinate the region's response to climate change; Exec. Dir Dr KENRICK LESLIE.

Caribbean Competition Commission: Hendrikstraat 69, Paramaribo, Suriname; tel. 491480; f. 2008; to enforce the rules of competition of the CARICOM Single Market and Economy; Chair. Dr KUSHA HARAKSINGH (Trinidad and Tobago); Exec. Dir BERTHA ISIDORE.

Caribbean Disaster Emergency Management Agency (CDEMA): Bldg 1, Manor Lodge, Lodge Hill, St Michael, Barbados; tel. 425-0386; fax 425-8854; e-mail cdera@caribsurf.com; internet www.cdera.org; f. 1991; aims to respond with immediate assistance following a request by a participating state in the event of a natural or man-made disaster; co-ordinates other relief efforts; assists states to establish disaster preparedness and response capabilities; incorporates national disaster organizations, headed by a co-ordinator, in each participating state; Exec. Dir JEREMY COLLYMORE.

Caribbean Environmental Health Institute (CEHI): POB 1111, The Morne, Castries, St Lucia; tel. 4522501; fax 4532721; e-mail cehi@candw.lc; internet www.cehi.org.lc; f. 1980 (began operations in 1982); provides technical and advisory services to member states in formulating environmental health policy legislation and in all areas of environmental management (for example, solid waste management, water supplies, beach and air pollution, and pesticides control); promotes, collates and disseminates relevant research; conducts courses, seminars and workshops throughout the region; Exec. Dir PATRICIA AQUING (Trinidad and Tobago).

Caribbean Examinations Council: The Garrison, St Michael 20, Barbados; tel. 436-6261; fax 429-5421; e-mail cxcezo@cxc.org; internet www.cxc.org; f. 1972; develops syllabuses and conducts examinations for the Caribbean Advanced Proficiency Examination (CAPE), the Caribbean Secondary Education Certificate (CSEC) and the Caribbean Certificate of Secondary Level Competence (CCSLC); mems: govts of 16 English-speaking countries and territories; Registrar and CEO Dr DIDACUS JULES.

Caribbean Food and Nutrition Institute (CFNI): UWI Campus, POB 140, St Augustine, Trinidad and Tobago; tel. 645-2917; fax 663-1544; e-mail cfni@cablenett.net; internet www.paho.org/cfni; f. 1967 to serve the governments and people of the region and to act as a catalyst among persons and organizations concerned with food and nutrition through research and field investigations, training in nutrition, dissemination of information, advisory services and production of educational material; a specialized centre of the Pan American Health Organization; mems: all English-speaking Caribbean territories, including the mainland countries of Belize and Guyana; Dir Dr FITZROY HENRY; publs *CAJANUS* (quarterly), *Nyam News* (monthly), *Nutrient-Cost Tables* (quarterly), educational material.

Caribbean Meteorological Organization (CMO): POB 461, Port of Spain, Trinidad and Tobago; tel. 622-4711; fax 622-0277; e-mail cmohq@cmo.org.tt; internet www.cmo.org.tt; f. 1973 as successor to Caribbean Meteorological Service (founded 1951) to co-ordinate regional activities in meteorology, operational hydrology and allied sciences; became a specialized institution of CARICOM in 1973; comprises a Council of Government Ministers, a Headquarters Unit, the Caribbean Meteorological Foundation and the Caribbean Institute for Meteorology and Hydrology, located in Barbados; mems: govts of 16 countries and territories represented by the National Meteorological and Hydro-meteorological Services; Co-ordinating Dir TYRONE W. SUTHERLAND.

Caribbean Telecommunications Union (CTU): Victoria Park Suites, 3rd Floor, 14–17 Victoria Sq., Port of Spain, Trinidad and Tobago; tel. 627-0281; fax 623-1523; internet www.ctu.int; f. 1989; aims to co-ordinate the planning and development of telecommunications in the region; encourages the development of regional telecommunications standards, the transfer of technology and the exchange of information among national telecommunications administrations; membership includes mems of CARICOM and other countries in the region, private sector orgs and non-governmental orgs; Sec.-Gen. BERNADETTE LEWIS (Trinidad and Tobago).

CARICOM Implementation Agency for Crime and Security (IMPACS): Sagicor Bldg, Ground Floor, 16 Queen's Park West, Port of Spain, Trinidad and Tobago; tel. 622-0245; fax 628-9795; e-mail enquiries@caricomimpacs.org; internet www.caricomimpacs.org; f. 2006 as a permanent institution to co-ordinate activities in the region relating to crime and security; incorporates two sub-agencies: a Joint Regional Communications Centre and a Regional Intelligence Fusion Centre; Exec. Sec. a.i. FRANCIS FORBES (Jamaica).

CARICOM Regional Organisation for Standards and Quality: Baobab Towers, Warrens, St Michael, Barbados; tel. 622-7677; fax 622-7678; e-mail crosq.caricom@crosq.org; internet www.crosq.org; f. 2002; aims to enhance and promote the implementation of standards, infrastructure and quality verification throughout the region and liaise with international standards orgs; CEO WINSTON BENNETT.

Council of Legal Education: c/o Gordon St, St Augustine, Trinidad and Tobago; tel. 662-5860; fax 662-0927; internet www.clecaribbean.com; f. 1971; responsible for the training of members of the legal profession; administers law schools in Jamaica, Trinidad and Tobago, and the Bahamas; mems: govts of 12 countries and territories; Chair. E. ANN HENRY (Antigua and Barbuda).

ASSOCIATE INSTITUTIONS

Caribbean Development Bank: POB 408, Wildey, St Michael, Barbados; tel. 431-1600; fax 426-7269; e-mail info@caribank.org; internet www.caribank.org; f. 1969 to stimulate regional economic growth through support for agriculture, industry, transport and other infrastructure, tourism, housing and education; in May 2010 the Board of Governors approved an ordinary capital increase of some US $1,000m., including a paid-up component of $216m.; in 2011 new loans, grants and equity investments approved totalled US $166.5m., bringing the cumulative total to $3,914.8m.; total assets $875.2m. (31 Dec. 2011); mems: CARICOM states, and Canada, the People's Republic of China, Colombia, Germany, Italy, Mexico, United Kingdom, Venezuela; Pres. Dr. WARREN SMITH (Jamaica).

Caribbean Law Institute: Florida State University College of Law, Tallahassee, Florida,32306-1601 USA; tel. (850) 644-7731; fax (850) 644-7729; internet www.law.fsu.edu/centers/cli/index.html; f. 1988 to harmonize and modernize commercial laws in the region; a Caribbean Law Institute Centre is based at the University of the West Indies, in Bridgetown, Barbados; Dir PROF.ELWIN GRIFFITHS.

Other Associate Institutions of CARICOM, in accordance with its constitution, are the University of Guyana, the University of the West Indies and the Secretariat of the Organisation of Eastern Caribbean States.

Publications

CARICOM Perspective (annually).

CARICOM View (6 a year).

CENTRAL AMERICAN INTEGRATION SYSTEM

(SISTEMA DE LA INTEGRACIÓN CENTROAMERICANA—SICA)

Address: Final Blv. Cancillería, Ciudad Merliot, Antiguo Cuscatlán, La Libertad, San Salvador, El Salvador.

Telephone: 2248-8800; **fax:** 2248-8899; **e-mail:** info.sgsica@sica.int; **internet:** www.sica.int.

Founded in December 1991, when the heads of state of six Central American countries signed the Protocol of Tegucigalpa to the agreement establishing the Organization of Central American States (f. 1951), creating a new framework for regional integration. A General Secretariat of the Sistema de la Integración Centroamericana (SICA) was inaugurated in February 1993 to co-ordinate the process of political, economic, social cultural and environmental integration and to promote democracy and respect for human rights throughout the region.

MEMBERS

Belize	Guatemala	Nicaragua
Costa Rica	Honduras	Panama
El Salvador		

ASSOCIATE MEMBER

Dominican Republic

Note: Argentina, Australia, Brazil, Chile, France, Germany, Italy, Japan, Republic of Korea, Mexico, Peru, Spain, Taiwan and the USA have observer status with SICA.

Organization

(June 2012)

SUMMIT MEETINGS

The meetings of heads of state of member countries serve as the supreme decision-making organ of SICA.

COUNCIL OF MINISTERS

Ministers of foreign affairs of member states meet regularly to provide policy direction for the process of integration.

EXECUTIVE COMMITTEE

Comprises a government representative of each member state tasked with ensuring the implementation of decisions adopted by heads of state or the Council of Ministers, and with overseeing the activities of the General Secretariat.

CONSULTATIVE COMMITTEE

The Committee comprises representatives of business organizations, trade unions, academic institutions and other federations concerned with the process of integration in the region. It is a fundamental element of the integration system and assists the Secretary-General in determining the organization's policies.

GENERAL SECRETARIAT

The General Secretariat of SICA was established in February 1993 to co-ordinate the process of enhanced regional integration. It comprises Directorates-General of Social Integration, Economic Integration, and of Environmental Affairs.

In September 1997 Central American Common Market (CACM) heads of state, meeting in the Nicaraguan capital, signed the Managua Declaration in support of further regional integration and the establishment of a political union. In February 1998 heads of state resolved to establish a Unified General Secretariat to integrate the institutional aspects of the grouping in a single office, to be located in San Salvador, El Salvador. A new headquarters for the organization was inaugurated in July 2011.

Secretary-General: Juan Daniel Alemán Gurdián.

CORE INSTITUTIONS

Central American Parliament (PARLACEN)

12 Avda 33-04, Zona 5, 01005 Guatemala City, Guatemala; tel. 2424-4600; fax 2424-4610; e-mail comunica@parlacen.int; internet www.parlacen.org.gt; officially inaugurated in 1991; comprises 20 elected representatives of Domincan Republic, El Salvador, Guatemala, Honduras, Nicaragua and Panama, as well as former Presidents and Vice-Presidents of mem. countries; Haiti awarded observer status in Feb. 2012; Pres. Manolo Pichardo (Dominican Republic); publ. *Foro Parlamentario.*

Central American Court of Justice

Apdo Postal 907, Managua, Nicaragua; tel. 266-6273; fax 266-4604; e-mail cortecen@ccj.org.ni; internet portal.ccj.org.ni; officially inaugurated in 1994; tribunal authorized to consider disputes relating to treaties agreed within the regional integration system; in February 1998 Central American heads of state agreed to limit the number of magistrates in the Court to one per country.

SPECIALIZED SECRETARIATS

In addition to those listed below, various technical or executive secretariat units support meetings of ministerial Councils, concerned *inter alia*with women, housing, health and finance.

Secretaría General de la Coordinación Educativa y Cultural Centroamericana (SG-CECC): 400m este y 25m norte de la Iglesia Santa Teresita en Barrio Escalante, 262-1007 San José, Costa Rica; tel. 2283-7719; e-mail sgcecc@racsa.co.cr; internet www.sica.int/cecc; f. 1982; promotes development of regional programmes in the fields of education and culture; Sec.-Gen. María Eugenia Paniagua Padilla.

Secretaría de Integración Económica Centroamericana (SIECA): 4a Avda 10–25, Zona 14, Apdo 1237, 01901 Guatemala City, Guatemala; tel. 2368-2151; fax 2368-1071; e-mail info@sieca.int; internet www.sieca.int; f. 1960 to assist the process of economic integration and the creation of a Central American Common Market (CACM—established by the organization of Central American States under the General Treaty of Central American Economic Integration, signed in December 1960 and ratified by Costa Rica, Guatemala, El Salvador, Honduras and Nicaragua in September 1963); supervises the correct implementation of the legal instruments of economic integration, conducts relevant studies at the request of the CACM, and arranges meetings; comprises departments covering the working of the CACM: negotiations and external trade policy; external co-operation; systems and statistics; finance and administration; also includes a unit for co-operation with the private sector and finance institutions, and a legal consultative committee; Sec.-Gen. Ernesto Torres Chico (El Salvador); publs *Anuario Estadístico Centroamericano de Comercio Exterior*, *Carta Informativa* (monthly), *Cuadernos de la SIECA* (2 a year), *Estadísticas Macroeconómicas de Centroamérica* (annually), *Series Estadísticas Seleccionadas de Centroamérica* (annually), *Boletín Informativo* (fortnightly).

Secretaría Ejecutiva del Consejo Monetario Centroamericano (SECMCA) (Central American Monetary Council): 400m suroeste de la Rotonda La Bandera, Barrio Dent, Contiguo al BANHVI, San José, Costa Rica; tel. 2280-9522; fax 2524-1062; e-mail secma@secmca.org; internet www.secmca.org; f. 1964 by the presidents of Central American central banks, to co-ordinate monetary policies; Exec. Sec. William Calvo Villegas; publs *Boletín Estadístico* (annually), *Informe Económico* (annually).

Secretaría de la Integración Social Centroamericana (SISCA): Final Boulevard Cancillería, Distrito El Espino Ciudad Merliot, Antiguo Cuscatlán, La Libertad, El Salvador; tel. 2248-8857; fax 2248-8896; e-mail info.sisca@sica.int; internet www.sica.int/sisca; f. 1995; co-ordinates various intergovernmental secretariats, including regional councils concerned with social security, sport and recreation, and housing and human settlements; Sec. ANA HAZEL ESCRICH.

Secretaría Ejecutiva de la Comisión Centroamericana de Ambiente y Desarrollo (SE-CCAD): Final Boulevard Cancillería, Distrito El Espino Ciudad Merliot, Antiguo Cuscatlán, La Libertad, El Salvador; tel. 2248-8800; fax 2248-8894; e-mail info.ccad@sica.int; internet www.sica.int/ccad; f. 1989 to enhance collaboration in the promotion of sustainable development and environmental protection; Exec. Sec. NELSON ORLANDO TREJO AGUILAR (Honduras).

Secretaría de Integración Turística Centroamericana (SITCA): Blv. Orden de Malta 470, Santa Elena, Antiguo Cuscatlán, San Salvador, El Salvador; tel. 2248-8837; fax 2248-8897; e-mail info.stcct@sica.int; internet www.sica.int/cct; f. 1965 to develop regional tourism activities; provides administrative support to the Central American Tourism Council, comprising national ministers and directors of tourism; Dir MERCEDES MELÉNDEZ DE MENA.

Secretaría del Consejo Agropecuario Centroamericano (SCAC): 600m noreste del Cruce de Ipis-Coronado, San Isidro de Coronado, Apdo Postal 55-2200, San José, Costa Rica; tel. 2216-0303; fax 2216-0285; e-mail coreca@iica.ac.cr; internet www.sica.int/cac; f. 1991 to determine and co-ordinate regional policies and programmes relating to agriculture and agroindustry; Exec. Sec. JULIO O. CALDERÓN ARTIEDA.

OTHER SPECIALIZED INSTITUTIONS

Agriculture and Fisheries

Organismo Internacional Regional de Sanidad Agropecuaria (OIRSA) (International Regional Organization of Plant Protection and Animal Health): Calle Ramón Belloso, Final Pasaje Isolde, Colonia Escalón, Apdo (01) 61, San Salvador, El Salvador; tel. 2209-9200; fax 2263-1128; e-mail oirsa@oirsa.org; internet www.oirsa.org; f. 1953 for the prevention of the introduction of animal and plant pests and diseases unknown in the region; research, control and eradication programmes of the principal pests present in agriculture; technical assistance and advice to the ministries of agriculture and livestock of member countries; education and qualification of personnel; mems: Belize, Costa Rica, Dominican Republic, El Salvador, Guatemala, Honduras, Mexico, Nicaragua, Panama; Exec. Dir GUILLERMO ENRIQUE ALVARADO DOWNING.

Unidad Coordinadora de la Organización del Sector Pesquero y Acuícola del Istmo Centroamericano (OSPESCA) (Organization of Fishing and Aquaculture in Central America): Blv. Orden de Malta 470, Santa Elena, Antiguo Cuscatlán, San Salvador, El Salvador; tel. 2248-8841; fax 2248-8899; e-mail info.ospesca@sica.int; internet www.sica.int/ospesca; f. 1995, incorporated into SICA in 1999; Regional Co-ordinator MARIO GONZÁLEZ RECINOS.

Education, Health and Sport

Consejo Superior Universitario Centroamericano (CSUCA) (Central American University Council): Avda Las Américas 1–03, Zona 14, International Club Los Arcos, 01014 Guatemala City, Guatemala; tel. 2367-1833; fax 2367-4517; e-mail sg@csuca.org; internet www.csuca.org; f. 1948 to guarantee academic, administrative and economic autonomy for universities and to encourage regional integration of higher education; maintains libraries and documentation centres; Council of 32 mems; mems: 18 universities, in Belize, Costa Rica (four), Dominican Republic, El Salvador, Guatemala, Honduras (two), Nicaragua (four) and Panama (four); Sec.-Gen. JUAN ALFONSO FUENTES SORIA; publs *Estudios Sociales Centroamericanos* (quarterly), *Cuadernos de Investigación* (monthly), *Carta Informativa de la Secretaría General* (monthly).

Instituto de Nutrición de Centro América y Panamá (INCAP) (Institute of Nutrition of Central America and Panama): Calzada Roosevelt 6–25, Zona 11, Apdo Postal 1188-01901, Guatemala City, Guatemala; tel. 2472-3762; fax 2473-6529; e-mail info.incap@sica.int; internet www.sica.int/incap; f. 1949 to promote the development of nutritional sciences and their application and to strengthen the technical capacity of member countries to reach food and nutrition security; provides training and technical assistance for nutrition education and planning; conducts applied research; disseminates information; maintains library (including about 600 periodicals); administered by the Pan American Health Organization and the World Health Organization; mems: CACM mems, Belize and Panama; Dir CAROLINA SIÚ; publ. *Annual Report*.

Consejo del Istmo Centroamericano de Deportes y Recreación (CODICADER) (Committee of the Central American Isthmus for Sport and Recreation): Blv. Orden de Malta 470, Santa Elena, Antiguo Cuscatlán, San Salvador, El Salvador; tel. 2248-8857; fax 2248-8899; internet www.sica.int/sisca/codicader; f. 1992.

Energy and the Environment

Secretaría Ejecutiva de la Comisión Regional de Recursos Hidráulicos (SE-CRRH): 500 mts norte, 200 oeste y 25 norte de Super Blvd Pavas, San José, Costa Rica; tel. 2231-5791; fax 2296-0047; e-mail secretaria@recursoshidricos.org; internet www.recursoshidricos.org; f. 1966; mems: Belize, Costa Rica, El Salvador, Guatemala, Honduras, Nicaragua, Panama.

Secretaría Ejecutiva del Consejo de Electrificación de América Central (CEAC) (Central American Electrification Council): Apdo 0816, 01552 Panamá, Panama; tel. 501-3942; fax 501-3990; e-mail jmontesi@cel.gob.sv; internet www.ceaconline.org; f. 1985; Exec. Sec. JULIO ROBERTO ALVAREZ VILLATORO.

Finance

Banco Centroamericano de Integración Económica (BCIE) (Central American Bank for Economic Integration): Blv. Suyapa, Contigua a Banco de Honduras, Apdo 772, Tegucigalpa, Honduras; tel. 2240-2231; fax 2240-2183; e-mail MNunez@bcie.org; internet www.bcie.org; f. 1961 to promote the economic integration and balanced economic development of member countries; finances public and private development projects, particularly those related to industrialization and infrastructure; auth. cap. US $2,000m; regional mems: Costa Rica, El Salvador, Guatemala, Honduras, Nicaragua; non-regional mems: Argentina, Colombia, Dominican Republic, Mexico, Panama, Spain, Taiwan; Exec. Pres. NICK RISCHBIETH; publs *Annual Report*, *Revista de la Integración y el Desarrollo de Centroamérica*.

Organización Centroamericana y del Caribe de Entidades Fiscalizadores Superiores (OCCEFS) (Organization of Central American and Caribbean Supreme Audit Institutions): Tribunal Superior de Cuentas de la República de Honduras, Centro Cívico Gubernamental, Col. Las Brisas Comayagüela, Honduras; tel. and fax 234-5210; internet www.sica.int/occefs; f. 1995 as the Organización Centroamericana de Entidades Fiscalizadores Superiores, within the framework of the Organización Latinoamericana y del Caribe de Entidades Fiscalizadoras Superiores; assumed present name in 1998; aims to promote co-operation among members, facilitate exchange of information, and provide technical assistance; Exec. Sec. JORGE BOGRÁN RIVERA (Honduras).

Public Administration

Centro de Coordinación para la Prevención de Desastres Naturales en América Central (CEPREDENAC): Avda Hincapié 21–72, Zona 13 Guatemala City, Guatemala; tel. and fax 2390-0200; e-mail info.cepredenac@sica.int; internet www.sica.int/cepredenac; f. 1988, integrated into SICA in 1995; aims to strengthen the capacity of the region to reduce its vulnerability to natural disasters; Exec. Sec. IVAN MORALES.

Instituto Centroamericano de Administración Pública (ICAP) (Central American Institute of Public Administration): Apdo Postal 10025-1000, San José, Costa Rica; tel. 2234-1011; fax 2225-2049; e-mail info@icap.ac.cr; internet www.icap.ac.cr; f. 1954 by the five Central American Republics and the UN, with later participation by Panama; the Institute aims to train the region's public servants, provide technical assistance and carry out research leading to reforms in public administration.

Science and Technology

Comisión para el Desarrollo Científico y Tecnológico de Centroamérica y Panamá (CTCAP) (Committee for the Scientific and Technological Development of Central America and Panama): 3A Avda 13–28, Zona 1, Guatemala City, Guatemala; tel. and fax 2228-6019; internet www.sica.int/ctcap; f. 1976; Pres. ROSA MARÍA AMAYA FABIÁN DE LÓPEZ.

Transport and Communications

Comisión Centroamericana de Transporte Marítimo (COCATRAM): Frente al costado oeste del Hotel Mansión Teodolinda, Barrio Bolonia, Apdo Postal 2423, Managua, Nicaragua; tel. 2222-3667; fax 222-2759; e-mail drojas@cocatram.org.ni; internet www.cocatram.org.ni; f. 1981; Exec. Dir OTTO NOACK SIERRA; publ. *Boletín Informativo*.

Comisión de Telecomunicaciones de Centroamérica (COMTELCA) (Commission for Telecommunications in Central America): Col. Palmira, Edif. Alpha 608, Avda Brasil, Apdo 1793, Tegucigalpa, Honduras; tel. 2220-1011; fax 2220-1197; e-mail sec@comtelca.org; internet www.comtelca.org; f. 1966 to co-ordinate and improve the regional telecommunications network; Dir-Gen. RAFAEL A. MARADIAGA.

Corporación Centroamericana de Servicios de Navegación Aérea (COCESNA) (Central American Air Navigation Services Corporation): Apdo 660, 150 sur de Aeropuerto de Toncontín, Tegucigalpa, Honduras; tel. 2234-3360; fax 2234-2550; e-mail notam@cocesna.org; internet www.cocesna.org; f. 1960; offers radar air traffic control services, aeronautical telecommunications services, flight inspections and radio assistance services for air navigation; provides support in the areas of safety, aeronautical training and aeronautical software; Exec. Pres. BAYARDO PAGOADA FIGUEROA.

Activities

In June 1990 the presidents of the CACM countries (Costa Rica, El Salvador, Guatemala, Honduras and Nicaragua) signed a declaration welcoming peace initiatives in El Salvador, Guatemala and Nicaragua, and appealing for a revitalization of CACM, as a means of promoting lasting peace in the region. In December the presidents committed themselves to the creation of an effective common market, proposing the opening of negotiations on a comprehensive regional customs and tariffs policy by March 1991, and the introduction of a regional 'anti-dumping' code by December 1991. They requested the support of multilateral lending institutions through investment in regional development, and the cancellation or rescheduling of member countries' debts. In December 1991 the heads of state of the five CACM countries and Panama signed the Protocol of Tegucigalpa; in February 1993 the General Secretariat of SICA was inaugurated to co-ordinate the integration process in the region.

In June 2009 SICA ministers of foreign affairs, meeting in Managua, Nicaragua, issued a special declaration condemning the removal, by military force, of the Honduran President Manuel Zelaya and the illegal detention of members of his Government. SICA heads of state subsequently met in an extraordinary session and agreed a series of immediate measures, including the suspension of all meetings with the new Honduran authorities, the suspension—through the Central American Bank for Economic Integration—of all loans and disbursements to Honduras, and support for an Organization of American States (OAS) resolution demanding a reinstatement of the democratically elected government. Costa Rica and Panama recognized the results of a general election, held in November. In July 2010 SICA heads of state (excluding the Nicaraguan President) signed a Special Declaration on Honduras, permitting that country's full participation in the grouping and supporting its readmission into the OAS.

EXTERNAL RELATIONS

In February 1993 the European Community (now European Union—EU) signed a new framework co-operation agreement with the CACM member states extending the programme of economic assistance and political dialogue initiated in 1984; a further co-operation agreement with the EU was signed in early 1996. In May 2002 ministers of foreign affairs of Central America and the EU agreed a new agenda for a formalized dialogue and priority areas of action, including environmental protection, democracy and governance, and poverty reduction. The meeting determined to work towards the eventual conclusion of an Association Agreement, including an agreement on free trade, although the latter was to be conditional upon the completion of the Doha Round of multilateral negotiations on trade liberalization and upon the attainment of a sufficient level of economic integration in Central America. It was agreed that meetings between the two sides, at ministerial level, were to be held each year. In December 2003 an EU-Central America Political Dialogue and Co-operation Agreement was signed to replace an existing (1993) framework accord. A new Regional Strategy, for 2007–13, was concluded in March 2007, with an allocation of €75.0m.

A framework agreement with the Andean Community was signed with the SICA in November 2004 to strengthen dialogue and co-operation between the two blocs of countries. In January 2011 the Secretaries-General of the two organizations, meeting in San Salvador, El Salvador, determined to reactivate the agreement and pursue greater collaboration.

In May 2008 Brazil was invited to become an observer of SICA. In June 2009 the Council of Ministers agreed to admit Japan as an extra-regional observer of the grouping. The agreement was formalized with the Japanese Government in January 2010. The Republic of Korea was approved as an observer at the meeting of heads of state held in July 2011. In June, meanwhile, at the International Conference in Support of the Regional Strategy for Central America and Mexico, the US Secretary of State announced that the USA was to apply for regional observer status with SICA. This was approved at the SICA summit meeting held in December, and granted by the signing of a Memorandum of Understanding in May 2012. At the December 2011 meeting Australia and France became extra-regional observers; Peru was admitted with regional observer status in February 2012.

A meeting of SICA heads of state and the Secretary-General of the United Nations, Ban Ki-Moon, took place in Guatemala, in March 2011.

TRADE AGREEMENTS AND ECONOMIC INTEGRATION

In October 1993 the presidents of the CACM countries and Panama signed a protocol to the 1960 General Treaty, committing themselves to full economic integration in the region (with a common external tariff of 20% for finished products and 5% for raw materials and capital goods) and creating conditions for increased free trade. The countries agreed to accelerate the removal of internal non-tariff barriers, but no deadline was set. Full implementation of the protocol was to be 'voluntary and gradual', owing to objections on the part of Costa Rica and Panama. In May 1994, however, Costa Rica committed itself to full participation in the protocol. In March 1995 a meeting of the Central American Monetary Council discussed and endorsed a reduction in the tariff levels from 20% to 15% and from 5% to 1%. Efforts to adopt this as a common policy were hindered by the implementation of these tariff levels by El Salvador on a unilateral basis, from 1 April, and the subsequent modifications by Guatemala and Costa Rica of their external tariffs. In March 2002 Central American leaders adopted the San Salvador Plan of Action for Central American Economic Integration, establishing several objectives as the basis for the future creation of a regional customs union, with a single tariff. CACM heads of state, meeting in December in Costa Rica, adopted the 'Declaration of San José', supporting the planned establishment of the Central American customs union.

In May 1997 the heads of state of CACM member countries, together with the Prime Minister of Belize, conferred with the then US President, Bill Clinton, in Costa Rica. The leaders resolved to establish a Trade and Investment Council to promote trade relations; however, Clinton failed to endorse a request from CACM members that their products receive preferential access to US markets, on similar terms to those from Mexico agreed under the North American Free Trade Agreement (NAFTA). During the 1990s the Central American Governments pursued negotiations to conclude free trade agreements with Mexico, Panama and the members of the Caribbean Community and Common Market (CARICOM). Nicaragua signed a bilateral accord with Mexico in December (Costa Rica already having done so in 1994). El Salvador, Guatemala and Honduras jointly concluded a free trade arrangement with Mexico in May 2000. In November 1997, at a special summit meeting of CACM heads of state, an agreement was reached with the President of the Dominican Republic to initiate a gradual process of incorporating that country into the process of Central American integration, with the aim of promoting sustainable development throughout the region. A free trade accord with the Dominican Republic was concluded in April 1998, and formally signed in November.

In April 2001 Costa Rica concluded a free trade accord with Canada; the other four CACM countries commenced negotiations with Canada in November with the aim of reaching a similar agreement. In February 2002 Central American heads of state convened an extraordinary summit meeting in Managua, Nicaragua, at which they resolved to implement measures to further the political and economic integration of the region. The leaders determined to pursue initial proposals for a free trade accord with the USA, a Central American Free Trade Area (CAFTA), during the visit to the region of the then US President George W. Bush in the following month, and, more generally, to strengthen trading relations with the EU. They also pledged to resolve all regional conflicts by peaceful means. Earlier in February the first meeting of heads of state or government of Central American and CARICOM countries took place in Belize, with the aim of strengthening political and economic relations between the two groupings. The meeting agreed to work towards concluding common negotiating positions, for example in respect of the World Trade Organization.

Negotiations on CAFTA between the CACM countries and the USA were initiated in January 2003. An agreement was concluded between the USA and El Salvador, Guatemala, Honduras and Nicaragua in December, and with Costa Rica in January 2004. Under the resulting US-Central America Free Trade Agreement some 80% of US exports of consumer and industrial goods and more than 50% of US agricultural exports to CAFTA countries were to become duty-free immediately upon its entry into force, with remaining tariffs to be eliminated over a 10-year period for consumer and industrial goods and over a 15-year period for agricultural exports. Almost all CAFTA exports of consumer and industrial products to the USA were to be duty-free on the Agreement's entry into force. The Agreement was signed by the US Trade Representative and CACM ministers of trade and economy, convened in Washington, DC, USA, in May 2004. It required ratification by all national legislatures before entering into effect. Negotiations on a US-Dominican Republic free trade agreement, to integrate the Dominican Republic into CAFTA, were concluded in March and the agreement was signed in August. The so-called DR-CAFTA accord was formally ratified by the USA in August 2005. Subsequently the agreement has entered into force with El Salvador on 1 March 2006, Honduras and Nicaragua on 1 April, Guatemala on 1 July, the Dominican Republic on 1 March 2007, and Costa Rica on 1 January 2009.

In May 2006 a meeting of EU and Central American heads of state resolved to initiate negotiations to conclude an Association Agreement. The first round of negotiations was concluded in San José, Costa Rica, in October 2007; subsequent rounds were held in Brussels, Belgium, in February 2008, in San Salvador, in April, in Brussels in July, in Guatemala City, Guatemala, in October, and in Brussels, in January 2009. In April the seventh round of negotiations, being held in Tegucigalpa, Honduras, was suspended when the delegation from Nicaragua withdrew from the talks. The process was suspended in July owing to the political crisis in Honduras. Negotiations to conclude the accord resumed in February 2010; Panama participated in the negotiations as a full member for the first time in March. The Association Agreement was formally signed by both sides in May. It provided for immediate duty-free access into the EU for some 92% of Central American products into the EU (48% for EU goods entering Central America), with the remainder of tariffs (on all but 4% of products) being phased out over a 15-year period. The accord also incorporated new import quotas for meat, dairy products and rice, and market access agreements for car manufacturers and the service industry.

In February 2007 the Secretaries-General of SICA and CARICOM signed a plan of action to foster greater co-operation in areas including foreign policy, international trade relations, security and combating crime, and the environment. Meetings of ministers of foreign affairs and of the economy and foreign trade were convened in the same month at which preparations were initiated for trade negotiations between the two groupings. In May the second Central American-CARICOM summit meeting was convened, in Belize City, Belize. Heads of state and of government endorsed the efforts to enhance co-operation between the organizations and approved the elaboration of a free trade agreement, based on the existing bilateral accord signed between CARICOM and Costa Rica. Formal negotiations were inaugurated at a meeting of ministers of trade in August. In December 2010 SICA heads of state, meeting in Belize, resolved to strengthen co-operation with CARICOM and the Association of Caribbean States. The third meeting of SICA and CARICOM heads of state or government was held in August 2011, in San Salvador. Also in August, the OAS convened a high-level meeting of CEOs and business executives from the two blocs to discuss measures to expand trade and investment in the region following the global economic downturn.

In May 2008 SICA heads of state and government met their Brazilian counterparts in San Salvador. The summit meeting reaffirmed the willingness of both sides to enhance political and economic co-operation with the grouping of Southern Common Market (Mercosur) countries and determined to establish mechanisms, in particular, to promote trade and political dialogue.

FINANCIAL CO-OPERATION

In January 2007 the Treaty on Payment Systems and the Liquidation of Assets in Central America and the Dominican Republic was presented to the Secretary-General of SICA. The treaty aimed to increase greater financial co-operation and further develop the financial markets in the region.

In December 2008 a summit meeting, convened in San Pedro Sula, Honduras, adopted a plan of urgent measures to address the effects of the global economic and financial downturn, including a commitment of greater investment in infrastructure projects and the establishment of a common credit fund. Heads of state ratified an agreement to establish a Central American Statistical Commission (Centroestad) to develop a regional statistics service, provide technical statistical assistance to member countries and harmonize national and regional statistics.

INTEGRATED DISASTER RISK MANAGEMENT, ENERGY AND CLIMATE CHANGE

In December 1994 SICA member states and the USA signed a joint declaration (CONCAUSA), covering co-operation in the following areas: conservation of biodiversity; sound management of energy; environmental legislation; and sustainable economic development. In June 2001 both sides signed a renewed and expanded CONCAUSA, now also covering co-operation in addressing climate change, and in disaster preparedness.

In October 1999 SICA heads of state adopted a strategic framework for the period 2000–04 to strengthen the capacity for the physical, social, economic and environmental infrastructure of Central American countries to withstand the impact of natural disasters. In particular, programmes for the integrated management and conservation of water resources, and for the prevention of forest fires were to be implemented.

In June 2001 the heads of state and representatives of Belize, Costa, Rica, El Salvador, Guatemala, Honduras, Mexico, Nicaragua and Panama agreed to activate a Puebla-Panamá Plan (PPP) to promote sustainable social and economic development in the region and to reinforce integration efforts among Central America and the southern states of Mexico (referred to as Mesoamerica). The heads of state identified the principal areas for PPP initiatives, including tourism, road integration, telecommunications, energy interconnection, and the prevention and mitigation of disasters. In June 2002 the heads of state of seven countries, and the Vice-President of Panama, convened in Mérida, Mexico, during an investment fair to promote the Plan and reiterated their support for the regional initiatives. The meeting was also held within the framework of the 'Tuxtla dialogue mechanism', so-called after an agreement signed in 1991 between Mexico and Central American countries, to discuss co-ordination between the parties, in particular in social matters, health, education and the environment. Regular 'Tuxtla' summit meetings convened subsequently.

Representatives of SICA and of Colombia, the Dominican Republic and Mexico adopted the Declaration of Romana in June 2006, wherein they agreed to implement the Mesoamerican Energy Integration Program, aimed at developing regional oil, electricity and natural gas markets, promoting the use of renewable energy, and increasing electricity generation and interconnection capacity across the region. In the following month, at the eighth Tuxtla summit, convened in Panama, SICA member states approved the legal framework for the Central American Electrical Connection System (known as SIEPAC), which was to be co-funded by the Central American Bank for Economic Integration and the Inter-American Development Bank. In June 2008 the 10th Tuxtla summit meeting, convened in Villahermosa, Mexico, agreed to establish the Mesoamerican Integration and Development Project to supersede the PPP. The new Project was to incorporate ongoing initiatives on highways and infrastructure and implement energy, electricity and information networks.

In November 2007 SICA heads of state endorsed a Sustainable Energy Strategy for Central America 2020. Its main areas of concern were: access to energy by the least advantaged populations; the rational and efficient use of energy; renewable sources of energy; biofuels for the transport sector; and climate change. A joint summit on the environment and climate change in Central America and the Caribbean was held with CARICOM representatives in San Pedro Sula, Honduras, in May 2008.

SICA heads of state ratified an agreement, in July 2010, to accelerate efforts to reduce the region's vulnerability to natural disasters and the effects of climate change. They determined to establish a special regional fund to finance the initiative. At the third SICA-CARICOM meeting, held in San Salvador, El Salvador, in August 2011, heads of state welcomed an initiative by Panama to establish a Regional Humanitarian Logistic Assistance Centre to respond to emergency situations in the region within 24 to 48 hours. The meeting recognized the need to strengthen transport and cultural links and detailed measures to bolster co-operation in international environmental negotiations and disaster management. In December, at the summit meeting of SICA heads of state, environmental preservation and tackling natural disasters were central to the agenda, and members agreed to adopt the constitution of a Central American Fund for the Promotion of Integrated Risk Management to provide technical assistance and resources as needed.

HEALTH AND TOURISM

At the meeting of CACM heads of state in December 2002, the establishment of a new Central American Tourism Agency was announced. In July 2011 SICA heads of state declared 2012 to be the Central American Year of Sustainable Tourism.

In June 2008 the SICA summit meeting, convened in San Salvador, El Salvador, reiterated concerns regarding escalating petroleum and food prices, and welcomed several initiatives concerned with strengthening the region's food security (see above). During the SICA-CARICOM heads of state meeting in El Salvador, in August 2011, it was agreed that the two organizations would collaborate on the early detection (and prevention) of non-communicable diseases.

REGIONAL SECURITY

In March 2005 SICA ministers responsible for security, defence and the interior resolved to establish a special regional force to combat crime, drugs and arms trafficking and terrorism. In June 2008 SICA heads of state and government, convened in San Salvador, agreed to establish a peace-keeping operations unit within the secretariat in order to co-ordinate participation in international peace-keeping missions.

In June 2008 the US Congress approved US $65m. to fund a Central American initiative to counter drugs-trafficking and organized crime, as part of a larger agreement arranged with the Mexican Government (the so-called Mérida Initiative). The scheme was subsequently relaunched as the Central American Regional Security Initiative, with additional approved funds of some $100m. to provide equipment, training, and technical assistance to build the capacity of Central American institutions to counter crime. In February 2010, at a meeting of the Inter-American Development Bank (IDB), several countries and other multilateral organizations determined to establish a Group of Friends for Central American Security, in order to support the region to counter organized crime. In March 2011 US President Obama announced the establishment of a Central American Citizen Security Partnership to strengthen law enforcement and to provide young people with alternatives to organized crime.

In early 2011 an Ad Hoc Regional Expert Task Force was established to help to elaborate a regional security strategy, in advance of an international conference, convened in Guatemala City, Guatemala, in June. At the International Conference in Support of the Regional Security Strategy for Central America and Mexico, the US Secretary of State committed US $300m. in support of security initiatives, including more specialized police units and a new SICA Regional Crime Observatory. Negotiations to formulate a Central American Security Strategy (Estrategia de Seguridad de Centroamérica—ESCA), based on 22 priority projects identified at the International Conference, recommenced in September. ESCA's main activities were to incorporate combating crime and preventing violence, rehabilitation of offenders, prison management, and institutional strengthening. In February 2012 the IDB hosted a meeting of the SICA Security Commission and the so-called Group of Friends of the Central America Security Strategy to inaugurate an initial eight ESCA projects.

COMMON MARKET FOR EASTERN AND SOUTHERN AFRICA—COMESA

Address: COMESA Secretariat, Ben Bella Rd, POB 30051, 101101 Lusaka, Zambia.

Telephone: (1) 229725; **fax:** (1) 225107; **e-mail:** comesa@comesa.int; **internet:** www.comesa.int.

The COMESA treaty was signed by member states of the Preferential Trade Area for Eastern and Southern Africa (PTA) in November 1993. COMESA formally succeeded the PTA in December 1994. COMESA aims to strengthen the process of regional economic and social development that was initiated under the PTA, with the ultimate aim of merging with the other regional economic communities of the African Union.

MEMBERS

Burundi	Malawi
Comoros	Mauritius
Congo, Democratic Republic	Rwanda
Djibouti	Seychelles
Egypt	South Sudan*
Eritrea	Sudan
Ethiopia	Swaziland
Kenya	Uganda
Libya	Zambia
Madagascar	Zimbabwe

* South Sudan, which achieved independence on 9 July 2011, was admitted to COMESA in October of that year.

Organization

(June 2012)

AUTHORITY

The Authority of the Common Market is the supreme policy organ of COMESA, comprising heads of state or government of member countries. The inaugural meeting of the Authority took place in Lilongwe, Malawi, in December 1994. The 15th summit meeting was held in October 2011, in Lilongwe, Malawi, on the theme 'Harnessing Science and Technology for Development'.

COUNCIL OF MINISTERS

Each member government appoints a minister to participate in the Council. The Council monitors COMESA activities, including supervision of the Secretariat, recommends policy direction and development, and reports to the Authority.

A Committee of Governors of Central Banks advises the Authority and the Council of Ministers on monetary and financial matters.

COURT OF JUSTICE

The sub-regional Court is vested with the authority to settle disputes between member states and to adjudicate on matters concerning the interpretation of the COMESA treaty. The Court is composed of seven judges, who serve terms of five years' duration. The Court was restructured in 2005 to comprise a First Instance division and an Appellate division.

President: NZAMBA KITONGA (Kenya).

SECRETARIAT

COMESA's Secretariat comprises the following divisions: Administration; Budget and finance; Gender and social affairs; Infrastructure development; Investment Promotion; Private Sector Development; and Trade customs and monetary affairs. There are also units at the Secretariat dealing with legal and institutional affairs, and climate change.

Secretary-General: SINDISO NWENGYA (Zimbabwe).

Activities

COMESA aims to promote economic and social progress, co-operation and integration in member states. A strategic plan, endorsed by the COMESA Authority at its 14th summit meeting convened in August 2010, governs COMESA's medium-term goals and activities during the period 2011–15, prioritizing integration; enhancing productive capacity for global competitiveness; infrastructure development; cross-cutting issues such as gender and social development, climate change, statistics, peace and security, knowledge-based capacity and human capital; co-operation and partnership; and institutional development. COMESA supports capacity-building activities and the establishment of other specialized institutions (see below).

In May 1999 COMESA established a Free Trade Area (FTA) Committee to facilitate and co-ordinate preparations for the creation of the common market envisaged under the COMESA treaty. An extraordinary summit of COMESA heads of state or government, held in October 2000, inaugurated the FTA, with nine initial members: Djibouti, Egypt, Kenya, Madagascar, Malawi, Mauritius, Sudan, Zambia and Zimbabwe. Burundi and Rwanda became members of the FTA in January 2004, and Swaziland undertook in April to seek the concurrence of the Southern African Customs Union, of which it is also a member, to allow it to participate in the FTA. Trading practices within the FTA have been fully liberalized, including the elimination of non-tariff barriers, thereby enabling the free internal movement of goods, services and capital. The COMESA Customs Union (CU), with a common external tariff (CET) set at 0% for capital goods and raw materials, 10% for intermediate goods and 25% for finished products, was launched at the 13th annual summit meeting of the Authority, in June 2009. It was envisaged that the Customs Union would be fully operational in 2012. A Protocol establishing the COMESA Fund, which assists member states in addressing structural imbalances in their economies, came into effect in November 2006. COMESA plans to form an economic community (entailing monetary union and the free movement of people between member states) by 2014. The COMESA Regional Investment Agency (RIA), based in Cairo, Egypt, was inaugurated in June 2006, its founding charter having been adopted in June 2005 by the 10th summit meeting of the Authority. An Agreement on the establishment of a COMESA Common Investment Area (CCIA) was adopted by the Authority at its May 2007 summit meeting. The May 2007 meeting also endorsed the establishment of an 'Aid for Trade' unit in the COMESA Secretariat, which was to assist countries with the identification and implementation of projects aimed at removing trade-related supply constraints. A COMESA Competition Commission, based in Blantyre, Malawi, was inaugurated in December 2008. In June 2009 a regional payments and settlement system (REPSS), headquartered in Lusaka, Zambia, was launched.

In February 2000 a COMESA economic forum was convened in Cairo, Egypt. The seventh COMESA Business Forum was organized in October 2011, in Lilongwe, Malawi, on the sidelines of the 15th summit of the Authority. The COMESA RIA sponsors annual investment fora: the fourth forum was convened in Dubai, United Arab Emirates, in March 2011.

Co-operation programmes have been implemented by COMESA in the financial, agricultural, transport and communications, industrial, and energy sectors. A regional food security programme aims to ensure continuous adequate food supplies. COMESA works with private sector interests through the African Union (AU) Comprehensive African Agricultural Development Programme (CAADP) to improve agricultural performance. The CAADP undertook efforts in 2008 to strengthen regional capacity to address food insecurity, promoting robust markets and long-term competitiveness. COMESA maintains a Food and Agricultural Marketing Information System (FAMIS), providing up-to-date data on the sub-regional food security situation. In 1997 COMESA heads of state advocated that the food sector be supported by the implementation of an irrigation action plan for the region. The organization supports the establishment of common agricultural standards and phytosanitary regulations throughout the region in order to stimulate trade in food crops. In March 2005 more than 100 standards on quality assurance, covering mainly agricultural products, were adopted. Meeting for the first time in November 2002, COMESA ministers of agriculture determined to formulate a regional policy on genetically modified organisms. At their second meeting, held in October 2004, ministers of agriculture agreed to prioritize agriculture in their development efforts, and—in accordance with a Declaration of the AU—the objective of allocating at least 10% of national budgets to agriculture and rural development. In September 2008 COMESA ministers of agriculture launched the Alliance for Commodity Trade in Eastern and Southern Africa (ACTESA), with the aim of integrating small farmers into national, regional and international markets. ACTESA became a specialized agency of COMESA in June 2009. In March 2010 COMESA and ACTESA signed an agreement aimed at accelerating the implementation of regional initiatives in agriculture, trade and investment. Other organization-wide initiatives include a road customs declaration document, a scheme for third-party motor vehicle insurance, a system of regional travellers cheques, and a regional customs bond guarantee scheme. A COMESA Telecommunications Company (COMTEL) was registered in May 2000. In January 2003 the Association of Regulators of Information and Communication for Eastern and Southern Africa was launched, under the auspices of COMESA. An Eastern Africa Power Pool (EAPP) has been established by COMESA, comprising Burundi, Democratic Republic of the Congo, Djibouti, Ethiopia, Kenya, Sudan, Tanzania and Uganda. COMESA and the Southern African Development Community (SADC) have the joint objective of eventually linking the EAPP and the Southern Africa Power Pool. COMESA maintains a priority list of regional infrastructure projects, and, in 2008, launched an interactive database recording the status of the projects.

In May 1999 the COMESA Authority resolved to establish a Committee on Peace and Security comprising ministers of foreign affairs from member states. It was envisaged that the Committee would convene at least once a year to address matters concerning regional stability. (Instability in certain member states was regarded as a potential threat to the successful implementation of the FTA.) The Committee met for the first time in 2000. It was announced in September 2002 that the COMESA Treaty was to be amended to provide for the establishment of a formal conflict prevention and resolution structure to be governed by member countries' heads of state. COMESA participates, with other regional economic communities (RECs) in the AU's Continental Early Warning System, and has, since 2008, taken part in joint technical meetings and training sessions in this respect. In June 2009 COMESA inaugurated the regional COMWARN early warning system, which was to monitor indicators of vulnerability to conflict in member states. The seventh meeting of the Committee, held in November 2006, recommended the establishment of a COMESA Committee of Elders, which was to undertake preventive peace-building assignments; the Committee of Elders held its inaugural meeting in December 2011. The seventh meeting of COMESA ministers of foreign affairs also decided that COMESA's peace and security activities should focus in particular on the economic dimensions of conflicts.

Following a recommendation by the AU, in January 2007, that climate change adaptation strategies should be integrated into African national and sub-regional development planning and activities, COMESA launched a Climate Change Initiative, which aims to improve economic and social resilience to the impacts of climate change. In July 2010 COMESA, the EAC and SADC adopted a five-year Tripartite Programme on Climate Change Adaptation and Mitigation in the COMESA-EAC-SADC region.

A joint COMESA-EAC-IGAD observer mission was dispatched to monitor presidential and legislative elections that took place in Uganda in February 2011. COMESA also sent an observer mission to monitor the conduct of the presidential, legislative and local government elections that were held in late September in Zambia.

From COMESA's establishment there were concerns on the part of member states, as well as other regional non-member countries, in particular South Africa, of adverse rivalry between COMESA and the SADC and of a duplication of roles. In 1997 Lesotho and Mozambique terminated their membership of COMESA owing to concerns that their continued participation in the organization was incompatible with their SADC membership. Tanzania withdrew from COMESA in September 2000, reportedly also in view of its dual commitment to that organization and to SADC. In June 2003 Namibia announced its withdrawal from COMESA. The summit meeting of COMESA heads of state or government held in May 2000 expressed support for an ongoing programme of co-operation by the Secretariats of COMESA and SADC aimed at reducing the duplication of roles between the two organizations, and urged further mutual collaboration. A co-ordinating task force was established in 2001, and was joined by the EAC (becoming the COMESA-EAC-SADC Task Force) in 2005, as the EAC became involved in the REC co-operation programme. The Regional Trade Facilitation Programme covering southern and eastern Africa, and based in Pretoria, South Africa, provides secretariat services to the Task Force.

In October 2008 the first tripartite COMESA-EAC-SADC summit was convened, in Kampala, Uganda, to discuss the harmonization of policy and programme work by the three RECs. Leaders of the 26 countries attending the Kampala summit approved a roadmap towards the formation of a common FTA and the eventual establishment of a single African Economic Community (a long-term objective of AU co-operation). A COMESA-EAC-SADC Joint Competition Authority was established at the tripartite summit. At the second tripartite summit, held in June 2011, in Johannesburg, South Africa, negotiations were initiated on the establishment of the proposed COMESA-EAC-SADC Tripartite FTA. In January 2012 AU leaders endorsed a new Framework, Roadmap and Architecture for Fast Tracking the Establishment of a Continental FTA (referred to as CFTA), and an Action Plan for Boosting Intra-African Trade, which planned for the consolidation of the COMESA-EAC-SADC Tripartite FTA with other regional FTAs into the CFTA initiative during 2015–16; and the establishment of an operational CFTA by 2017. COMESA has co-operated with other sub-regional organizations to finalize a common position on co-operation between African ACP countries and the European Union (EU) under the Cotonou Agreement (concluded in June 2000, see chapter on the EU).

In February 2010 COMESA and ECOWAS concluded a Memorandum of Understanding aimed at enhancing private sector development in their regions, and at advancing pan-African economic integration.

In June 2010 a consultative meeting was convened between COMESA, the AU, IGAD, and other regional partners, aimed at advancing co-ordination and harmonization of their activities related to the environment.

In September 2006 the COMESA Regional Economic and Trade Integration Program (CRETIP) was adopted by COMESA and the USA; under CRETIP, COMESA receives US assistance towards the implementation of programmes promoting COMESA–USA trade, regional trade, and the institutional strengthening of the COMESA Secretariat. In August 2007 COMESA appointed a Special Representative to the Middle East to establish partnerships with that region and to promote trade opportunities.

COMESA INSTITUTIONS

African Trade Insurance Agency (ATI): POB 10620, 00100-GPO, Nairobi, Kenya; tel. (20) 27269999; fax (20) 2719701; e-mail info@ati-aca.org; internet www.ati-aca.org; f. 2001 to promote trade and investment activities throughout the region; mems: 13 African countries; CEO George O. Otieno.

Alliance for Commodity Trade in Eastern and Southern Africa (ACTESA): Corporate Park, Alick Nkhata Rd, Lusaka, 10101 Zambia; tel. 211-253572; e-mail info@actesacomesa.org; internet www.actesacomesa.org; f. 2008, became a specialized agency of COMESA in June 2009; aims to integrate small farmers into national, regional and international markets; CEO Dr Chungu Mwila.

COMESA Bankers Association: Private Bag 271, Kapeni House, 1st Floor, Blantyre, Malawi; tel. and fax (1) 674236; e-mail info@comesabankers.org; internet www.comesabankers.org; f. 1987 as the PTA Association of Commercial Banks; name changed as above in 1994; aims to strengthen co-operation between banks in the region; organizes training activities; conducts studies to harmonize banking laws and operations; implements a bank fraud prevention programme; mems: 55 commercial banking orgs in Burundi, Egypt, Eritrea, Ethiopia, Kenya, Malawi, Rwanda, Sudan, Swaziland; Exec. Sec. ERIC C. CHINKANDA (acting).

COMESA Leather and Leather Products Institute (LLPI): POB 2358, 1110 Addis Ababa, Ethiopia; tel. (11) 4390928; fax (11) 4390900; e-mail comesa.llpi@ethionet.et; internet www.comesa-llpi.org/index.php; f. 1990 as the PTA Leather Institute; mems: 17 COMESA mem. states; Chair. WILSON MAZIMBA.

COMESA Regional Investment Authority (COMESA-RIA): 3 Salah Salem Rd, Nasr City, Cairo, Egypt; tel. (2) 405-5428; fax (2) 405-5421; e-mail info@comesaria.org; internet www.comesaria.org; Man. HEBA SALAMA.

Compagnie de réassurance de la Zone d'échanges préférentiels (ZEP-RE) (PTA Reinsurance Co): ZEP-RE Place, Longonot Rd, Upper Hill, POB 42769, 00100 Nairobi, Kenya; tel. (20) 2738221; fax (20) 2738444; e-mail mail@zep-re.com; internet www.zep-re.com; f. 1992 (began operations on 1 Jan. 1993); provides local reinsurance services and training to personnel in the insurance industry; total assets US $103.1m. (2010); Chair. Dr MICHAEL GONDWE; Man. Dir RAJNI VARIA.

East African Power Pool (EAPP): Bole Sub City, Gulz Aziz Bldg, Addis Ababa Ethiopia; tel. (11) 6183694; fax (11) 6183694; e-mail eapp@eappool.org; internet www.eappool.org/eng/about.html; in Feb. 2005 energy ministers from Burundi, DRC, Egypt, Ethiopia, Kenya, Rwanda and Sudan signed the Inter-Governmental Memorandum of Understanding on the establishment of the Eastern Africa Power Pool (EAPP); EAPP was adopted by COMESA as a specialized institution in 2006; Tanzania and Libya joined in 2010 and 2011, respectively; Exec. Sec. JASPER ODUOR.

Eastern and Southern African Trade and Development Bank: NSSF Bldg, 22nd/23rd Floor, Bishop's Rd, POB 48596, 00100 Nairobi, Kenya; tel. (20) 2712250; fax (20) 2711510; e-mail official@ptabank.org; internet www.ptabank.org; f. 1983 as PTA Development Bank; aims to mobilize resources and finance COMESA activities to foster regional integration; promotes investment and co-financing within the region; in Jan. 2003 the US dollar replaced the UAPTA (PTA unit of account) as the Bank's reporting currency; shareholders: 15 COMESA mem. states, the People's Republic of China, Somalia, Tanzania and the African Development Bank; total assets US $1,055.9m. (Dec. 2010); Pres. and CEO ADMASSU Y. TADESSE (Ethiopia).

Federation of National Associations of Women in Business in Eastern and Southern Africa (FEMCOM): Off Queens Drive, Area 6, Plot No. 170, POB 1499, Lilongwe, Malawi; tel. (1) 205-908; e-mail info@femcomcomesa.org; internet www.femcomcomesa.org; f. 1993; self-standing secretariat launched in 2009; aims to promote programmes that integrate women into regional trade and development activities, with a particular focus on the areas of agriculture, fishing, energy, communications, industry, mining, natural resources, trade, services, and transport; has chapters in all COMESA mem. states; Exec. Dir KATHERINE ICHOYA.

Finance

COMESA is financed by member states.

Publications

Annual Report of the Council of Ministers.

Asycuda Newsletter.

COMESA Journal.

COMESA Trade Directory (annually).

COMESA Trade Information Newsletter (monthly).

e-comesa (monthly newsletter).

Demand/supply surveys, catalogues and reports.

COMMONWEALTH

Address: Commonwealth Secretariat, Marlborough House, Pall Mall, London, SW1Y 5HX, United Kingdom.

Telephone: (20) 7747-6500; **fax:** (20) 7930-0827; **e-mail:** info@commonwealth.int; **internet:** www.thecommonwealth.org.

The Commonwealth is a voluntary association of 53 independent states, comprising about one-quarter of the world's population. It includes the United Kingdom and most of its former dependencies, and former dependencies of Australia and New Zealand (themselves Commonwealth countries).

The evolution of the Commonwealth began with the introduction of self-government in Canada in the 1840s; Australia, New Zealand and South Africa became independent before the First World War. At the Imperial Conference of 1926 the United Kingdom and the Dominions, as they were then called, were described as 'autonomous communities within the British Empire, equal in status', and this change was enacted into law by the Statute of Westminster, in 1931.

The modern Commonwealth began with the entry of India and Pakistan in 1947, and of Sri Lanka (then Ceylon) in 1948. In 1949, when India decided to become a republic, the Commonwealth Heads of Government agreed to replace allegiance to the British Crown with recognition of the British monarch as Head of the Commonwealth, as a condition of membership. This was a precedent for a number of other members (see Heads of State and Heads of Government, below).

MEMBERS*

Antigua and Barbuda	Kenya	Saint Vincent and the Grenadines
Australia	Kiribati	Samoa
Bahamas	Lesotho	Seychelles
Bangladesh	Malawi	Sierra Leone
Barbados	Malaysia	Singapore
Belize	The Maldives	Solomon Islands
Botswana	Malta	South Africa
Brunei	Mauritius	Sri Lanka
Cameroon	Mozambique	Swaziland
Canada	Namibia	Tanzania
Cyprus	Nauru	Tonga
Dominica	New Zealand	Trinidad and Tobago
The Gambia	Nigeria	Tuvalu
Ghana	Pakistan	Uganda
Grenada	Papua New Guinea	United Kingdom
Guyana	Rwanda	Vanuatu
India	Saint Christopher and Nevis	Zambia
Jamaica	Saint Lucia	

* Ireland, South Africa and Pakistan withdrew from the Commonwealth in 1949, 1961 and 1972, respectively. In October 1987 Fiji's membership was declared to have lapsed (following the proclamation of a republic there). It was readmitted in October 1997, but was suspended from participation in meetings of the Commonwealth in June 2000. Fiji was formally readmitted to Commonwealth meetings in December 2001 following the staging of free and fair legislative elections in August–September. However, following a further military coup in December 2006, Fiji was once again suspended from participation in meetings of the Commonwealth, and, in September 2009, Fiji's Commonwealth membership was fully suspended. Pakistan rejoined the Commonwealth in October 1989. However, it was suspended from participation in meetings during the period October 1999–May 2004 and, once again, during November 2007–May 2008. South Africa rejoined in June 1994. Nigeria's membership was suspended in November 1995; it formally resumed membership in May 1999, when a new civilian government was inaugurated. In 1995 Mozambique became a member, the first to have no historical or administrative connection with another Commonwealth country. Tuvalu, previously a special member of the Commonwealth with the right to participate in all activities except full Meetings of Heads of Government, became a full member in September 2000. In March 2002 Zimbabwe was suspended from participation in meetings of the Commonwealth. Zimbabwe announced its withdrawal from the Commonwealth in December 2003. Rwanda was admitted to membership of the Commonwealth in November 2009. In June 2011 Nauru was reinstated as a full member of the Commonwealth, having been classed as a 'member in arrears' from 2003. In 2012 the Commonwealth was considering possible future membership for South Sudan, which attained independence in July 2011.

AUSTRALIAN EXTERNAL TERRITORIES

Ashmore and Cartier Islands	Coral Sea Islands Territory
Australian Antarctic Territory	Heard Island and the McDonald Islands
Christmas Island	Norfolk Island
Cocos (Keeling) Islands	

NEW ZEALAND DEPENDENT AND ASSOCIATED TERRITORIES

Cook Islands	Ross Dependency
Niue	Tokelau

UNITED KINGDOM OVERSEAS TERRITORIES

Anguilla	Gibraltar
Bermuda	Isle of Man
British Antarctic Territory	Montserrat
British Indian Ocean Territory	Pitcairn Islands
British Virgin Islands	St Helena, Ascension, Tristan da Cunha
Cayman Islands	South Sandwich Islands
Channel Islands	Turks and Caicos Islands
Falkland Islands	

HEADS OF STATE AND HEADS OF GOVERNMENT

At June 2012 21 member countries were monarchies and 33 were republics. All Commonwealth countries accept Queen Elizabeth II as the symbol of the free association of the independent member nations and as such the Head of the Commonwealth. Of the 33 republics, the offices of Head of State and Head of Government were combined in 22: Botswana, Cameroon, Cyprus, The Gambia, Ghana, Guyana, Kenya, Kiribati, Malawi, the Maldives, Mozambique, Namibia, Nauru, Nigeria, Rwanda, Seychelles, Sierra Leone, South Africa, Sri Lanka, Tanzania, Uganda and Zambia. The two offices were separated in the remaining 11: Bangladesh, Dominica, Fiji, India, Malta, Mauritius, Pakistan, Samoa, Singapore, Trinidad and Tobago and Vanuatu.

Of the monarchies, the Queen is Head of State of the United Kingdom and of 15 others, in each of which she is represented by a Governor-General: Antigua and Barbuda, Australia, the Bahamas, Barbados, Belize, Canada, Grenada, Jamaica, New Zealand, Papua New Guinea, Saint Christopher and Nevis, Saint Lucia, Saint Vincent and the Grenadines, Solomon Islands and Tuvalu. Brunei, Lesotho, Malaysia, Swaziland and Tonga are also monarchies, where the traditional monarch is Head of State.

The Governors-General are appointed by the Queen on the advice of the Prime Ministers of the country concerned. They are wholly independent of the Government of the United Kingdom.

HIGH COMMISSIONERS

Governments of member countries are represented in other Commonwealth countries by High Commissioners, who have a status equivalent to that of Ambassadors.

Organization

(June 2012)

The Commonwealth is not a federation: there is no central government nor are there any rigid contractual obligations such as bind members of the United Nations.

Commonwealth members subscribe to the ideals of the Declaration of Commonwealth Principles unanimously approved by a meeting of heads of government in Singapore in 1971.

Members also approved the Gleneagles Agreement concerning apartheid in sport (1977); the Lusaka Declaration on Racism and Racial Prejudice (1979); the Melbourne Declaration on relations between developed and developing countries (1981); the New Delhi Statement on Economic Action (1983); the Goa Declaration on International Security (1983); the Nassau Declaration on World Order (1985); the Commonwealth Accord on Southern Africa (1985); the Vancouver Declaration on World Trade (1987); the Okanagan Statement and Programme of Action on Southern Africa (1987); the Langkawi Declaration on the Environment (1989); the Kuala Lumpur Statement on Southern Africa (1989); the Harare Commonwealth Declaration (1991); the Ottawa Declaration on Women and Structural Adjustment (1991); the Limassol Statement on the Uruguay Round of multilateral trade negotiations (1993); the Millbrook Commonwealth Action Programme on the Harare Declaration (1995); the Edinburgh Commonwealth Economic Declaration (1997); the Fancourt Commonwealth Declaration on Globalization and People-centred Development (1999); the Coolum Declaration on the Commonwealth in the 21st Century: Continuity and Renewal (2002); the Aso Rock Commonwealth Declaration and Statement on Multilateral Trade (2003); the Malta Commonwealth Declaration on Networking for Development (2005); the Munyonyo Statement on Respect and Understanding (2007); the Marlborough House Statement on Reform of International Institutions (2008); the Commonwealth Climate Change Declaration (2009); and the Perth Declaration on Food Security Principles (2011). In October 2011 Commonwealth heads of government agreed that a non-binding Charter of the Commonwealth, embodying the principles contained in previous declarations, should be drafted.

MEETINGS OF HEADS OF GOVERNMENT

Commonwealth Heads of Government Meetings (CHOGMs) are private and informal and operate not by voting but by consensus. The emphasis is on consultation and exchange of views for co-operation. A communiqué is issued at the end of every meeting. Meetings are normally held every two years in different capitals in the Commonwealth. The 2011 meeting was convened in Perth, Australia, at the end of October. The 2013 and 2015 meetings were to be held, respectively, in Sri Lanka and in Mauritius.

OTHER CONSULTATIONS

The Commonwealth Ministerial Action Group on the Harare was formed in 1995 to support democracy in member countries (see Activities, below). It comprises a group of nine ministers of foreign affairs, with rotating membership.

Since 1959 Commonwealth finance ministers have met in the week prior to the annual meetings of the IMF and the World Bank. Ministers responsible for civil society, education, the environment, foreign affairs, gender issues, health, law, tourism and youth also hold regular meetings.

Senior officials—cabinet secretaries, permanent secretaries to heads of government and others—meet regularly in the year between meetings of heads of government to provide continuity and to exchange views on various developments.

COMMONWEALTH SECRETARIAT

The Secretariat, established by Commonwealth heads of government in 1965, operates as an intergovernmental organization at the service of all Commonwealth countries. It organizes consultations between governments and runs programmes of co-operation. Meetings of heads of government, ministers and senior officials decide these programmes and provide overall direction. A Board of Governors, on which all eligible member governments are represented, meets annually to review the Secretariat's work and approve its budget. The Board is supported by an Executive Committee which convenes four times a year to monitor implementation of the Secretariat's work programme. The Secretariat is headed by a secretary-general, elected by heads of government.

In 2002 the Secretariat was restructured, with a view to strengthening the effectiveness of the organization to meet the priorities determined by the meeting of heads of government held in Coolum, Australia, in March 2002. Under the reorganization the number of deputy secretaries-general was reduced from three to two. Certain work divisions were amalgamated, while new units or sections, concerned with youth affairs, human rights and good offices, were created to strengthen further activities in those fields. Accordingly, the Secretariat's divisional structure is as follows: Legal and constitutional affairs; Political affairs; Corporate services; Communications and public affairs; Strategic planning and evaluation; Economic affairs; Governance and institutional development; Social transformation programmes; Youth affairs (from 2004); and Special advisory services. (Details of some of the divisions are given under Activities, below.) In addition there are units responsible for human rights and project management and referrals, and an Office of the Secretary-General.

The Secretariat's strategic plan for 2008/09–2011/12, approved by the Board of Governors in May 2008, set out two main, long-term objectives for the Commonwealth. The first, 'Peace and Democracy', was to support member countries in preventing or resolving conflicts, to strengthen democracy and the rule of law, and to achieve greater respect for human rights. The second, 'Pro-Poor Growth and Sustainable Development', was to support policies for economic growth and sustainable development, particularly for the benefit of the poorest people, in member countries. Four programmes were to facilitate the pursuit of the first objective: Good Offices for Peace; Democracy and Consensus Building; Rule of Law; and Human Rights. The second objective was to be pursued through the following four programmes: Public Sector Development; Economic Development; Environmentally Sustainable Development; and Human Development.

Secretary-General: KAMALESH SHARMA (India).

Deputy Secretaries-General: MMASEKGOA MASIRE-MWAMBA (Botswana), RANSFORD SMITH (Jamaica).

Assistant Secretary-General for Corporate Affairs: STEPHEN CUTTS (United Kingdom).

Activities

PROMOTING DEMOCRACY, HUMAN RIGHTS AND DEVELOPMENT

In October 1991 heads of government, meeting in Harare, Zimbabwe, issued the Harare Commonwealth Declaration, in which they reaffirmed their commitment to the Commonwealth Principles declared in 1971, and stressed the need to promote sustainable development and the alleviation of poverty. The Declaration placed emphasis on the promotion of democracy and respect for human rights and resolved to strengthen the Commonwealth's capacity to assist countries in entrenching democratic practices. In November 1995 Commonwealth heads of government, convened in New Zealand, formulated and adopted the Millbrook Commonwealth Action Programme on the Harare Declaration, to promote adherence by member countries to the fundamental principles of democracy and human rights (as proclaimed in the 1991 Declaration). The Programme incorporated a framework of measures to be pursued in support of democratic processes and institutions, and actions to be taken in response to violations of the Harare Declaration principles, in particular the unlawful removal of a democratically elected government. A Commonwealth Ministerial Action Group on the Harare Declaration (CMAG) was established in December 1995 to implement this process and to assist the member country involved to comply with the Harare principles. In March 2002 Commonwealth leaders expanded CMAG's mandate to enable the Group to consider action against serious violations of the Commonwealth's core values perpetrated by elected administrations as well as by military regimes. In October 2011 the Perth summit of Commonwealth leaders agreed a series of reforms aimed at strengthening the role of CMAG in addressing serious violations of Commonwealth political values; these included clearer guidelines and time frames for engagement when the situation in a country causes concern, with a view to shifting from a reactive to a more proactive role.

The October 2011 heads of government reconstituted CMAG's membership to comprise over the next biennium the ministers responsible for foreign affairs of Australia, Bangladesh, Canada, Jamaica, the Maldives (suspended from the Group in February 2012), Sierra Leone, Tanzania, Trinidad and Tobago, and Vanuatu.

In February 2012 CMAG placed the Maldives on its formal agenda, having considered a report from a Commonwealth ministerial mission that reviewed an allegedly forced transfer of presidential power, in early February, between former President Mohamed Nasheed and the incumbent President Mohammed Waheed. CMAG urged the initiation of immediate dialogue between the two sides, with a view to setting a date for early elections, and welcomed the appointment of a Special Envoy of the Commonwealth Secretary-General to address the situation in the Maldives. (Sir Donald McKinnon, who had been Secretary-General of the Commonwealth during 2000–08, assumed the role of Special Envoy on 1 March.) CMAG also placed in abeyance the Maldives' ongoing Group membership, owing to its inclusion on the Group's formal agenda. In June the Group welcomed a commitment made in May by the Maldives authorities to strengthening a national Commission of National Inquiry mandated to investigate the February events; the reformed Commission was relaunched in mid-June.

In December 2006, following the overthrow of the Fijian Government by the military, an extraordinary meeting of CMAG determined that Fiji should be suspended from meetings of the Commonwealth, pending the reinstatement of democratic governance. In September 2007 the Group urged the Fijian authorities to hold a democratic general election by March 2009 and determined to keep the situation in that country under review; the March 2009 election deadline was not, however, met by the Fijian authorities. CMAG expressed support at the March meeting for ongoing political dialogue in Fiji, jointly mediated by the Commonwealth and the UN. In April the Commonwealth Secretary-General condemned the unconstitutional conduct of the Fijian authorities in abrogating the Constitution, dismissing the judiciary and announcing that democratic elections were to be postponed to 2014, following a judgment by Fiji's Court of Appeal declaring the appointment of the current interim government to be unlawful and urging the prompt restoration of democracy. Meeting at the end of July, CMAG demanded that the Fijian regime reactivate by 1 September 2009 the Commonwealth- and UN-mediated political dialogue process, leading to the staging of elections no later than October 2010. At the beginning of September 2009 the Commonwealth Secretary-General announced that the Fijian regime had not acted to meet CMAG's demands and that Fiji's Commonwealth membership was consequently fully suspended with immediate effect. Meeting in September 2010 and April 2011 CMAG reiterated its concern at the situation in Fiji and maintained the suspension of Fiji's Commonwealth membership.

In March 2002, meeting in Coolum, near Brisbane, Australia, Commonwealth heads of government adopted the Coolum Declaration on the Commonwealth in the 21st Century: Continuity and Renewal, which reiterated commitment to the organization's principles and values. Leaders at the meeting condemned all forms of terrorism and endorsed a Plan of Action for combating international terrorism, establishing a Commonwealth Committee on Terrorism, convened at ministerial level, to oversee the implementation of the Plan. The leaders welcomed the Millennium Development Goals (MDGs) adopted by the UN General Assembly; requested the Secretary-General to constitute an expert group on implementing the objectives of the Fancourt Commonwealth Declaration on Globalization and People-Centred Development (see Economic Co-operation, below); pledged continued support for small states; and urged renewed efforts to combat the spread of HIV/AIDS. They also endorsed a Commonwealth Local Government Good Practice Scheme, to be managed by the Commonwealth Local Government Forum (established in 1995). The heads of government adopted a report on the future of the Commonwealth drafted by the High Level Review Group. The document recommended strengthening the Commonwealth's role in conflict prevention and resolution and support of democratic practices; enhancing the 'good offices' role of the Secretary-General; better promoting member states' economic and development needs; strengthening the organization's role in facilitating member states' access to international assistance; and promoting increased access to modern information and communications technologies.

In concluding the 2003 meeting heads of government issued the Aso Rock Commonwealth Declaration, which emphasized their commitment to strengthening development and democracy, and incorporated clear objectives in support of these goals. Priority areas identified included efforts to eradicate poverty and attain the MDGs, to strengthen democratic institutions, empower women, promote the involvement of civil society, combat corruption and recover assets (for which a working group was to be established), facilitate finance for development, address the spread of HIV/AIDS and other diseases, combat illicit trafficking in human beings, and promote education. The leaders also adopted a separate statement on multilateral trade, in particular in support of the stalled Doha Round of World Trade Organization (WTO) negotiations.

The 2007 meeting of Commonwealth heads of government, convened in Kampala, Uganda, in November, issued the Munyonyo Statement on Respect and Understanding, which commended the work of the Commonwealth Commission on Respect and Understanding (established in 2005) and endorsed its recently published report entitled *Civil Paths to Peace* aimed at building tolerance and understanding of diversity.

In November 2009 Commonwealth heads of government, meeting in Trinidad and Tobago, welcomed recent progress in the discussion of border disputes between Belize and Guatemala, and between Guyana and Venezuela. They expressed support for negotiations on the reunification of Cyprus, initiated in 2008, and welcomed the recent agreement on power-sharing in Zimbabwe. They urged the renewal of commitment to the non-proliferation of nuclear weapons at the next Non-Proliferation Treaty review conference (convened in May 2010), and the negotiation of a comprehensive Arms Trade Treaty (on conventional weapons) at a conference to be held in July 2012. Heads of government also urged the conclusion of a UN treaty on international terrorism and discussed combating piracy and human trafficking. In July 2010, in view of a decision of the 2009 heads of government meeting, a new Commonwealth Eminent Persons Group (EPG) was inaugurated, with a mandate to make recommendations on means of strengthening the organization. During June 2010 the Commonwealth Secretariat hosted the first Small States Biennial Conference.

The summit of heads of government held in Perth, Australia, in October 2011, issued the Perth Declaration on Food Security Principles, reaffirming the universal right to safe, sufficient and nutritious food. The summit agreed that a Charter of the Commonwealth, proposed by the EPG, should be drafted, embodying the principles contained in previous declarations; and that the appointment of a Commonwealth Commissioner for Democracy, Rule of Law and Human Rights, also recommended by the EPG, should be considered.

Political Affairs Division: assists consultation among member governments on international and Commonwealth matters of common interest. In association with host governments, it organizes the meetings of heads of government and senior officials. The Division services committees and special groups set up by heads of government dealing with political matters. The Secretariat has observer status at the United Nations, and the Division manages a joint office in New York to enable small states, which would otherwise be unable to afford facilities there, to maintain a presence at the United Nations. The Division monitors political developments in the Commonwealth and international progress in such matters as disarmament and the Law of the Sea. It also undertakes research on matters of common interest to member governments, and reports back to them. The Division is involved in diplomatic training and consular co-operation.

In 1990 Commonwealth heads of government mandated the Division to support the promotion of democracy by monitoring the preparations for and conduct of parliamentary, presidential or other elections in member countries at the request of national governments. In May 2010 a new Commonwealth Network of National Election Management Bodies was inaugurated; the Network aims to enhance collaboration among institutions, thereby boosting standards. Commonwealth observer groups were dispatched to observe legislative elections held in Lesotho in May 2012; and in Papua New Guinea, in June.

Under the reorganization of the Secretariat in 2002 a Good Offices Section was established within the Division to strengthen and support the activities of the Secretary-General in addressing political conflict in member states and in assisting countries to adhere to the principles of the Harare Declaration. The Secretary-General's good offices may involve discreet 'behind the scenes' diplomacy to prevent or resolve conflict and assist other international efforts to promote political stability.

Human Rights Unit: undertakes activities in support of the Commonwealth's commitment to the promotion and protection of fundamental human rights. It develops programmes, publishes human rights materials, co-operates with other organizations working in the field of human rights, in particular within the UN system, advises the Secretary-General, and organizes seminars and meetings of experts. It also provides training for police forces, magistrates and government officials in awareness of human rights. The Unit aims to integrate human rights standards within all divisions of the Secretariat.

Legal and Constitutional Affairs Division: promotes and facilitates co-operation and the exchange of information among member governments on legal matters and assists in combating financial and organized crime, in particular transborder criminal activities. It administers, jointly with the Commonwealth of Learning (see below), a distance training programme for legislative draftsmen and assists governments to reform national laws to meet the obligations of international conventions. The Division organizes the triennial meeting of ministers, Attorneys General and senior ministry officials concerned with the legal systems in Commonwealth countries. It has also initiated four Commonwealth schemes for co-operation on extradition, the protection of material cultural heritage, mutual assistance in criminal matters and the transfer of convicted offenders within the Commonwealth. It liaises with the Commonwealth Magistrates' and Judges' Association, the Commonwealth Legal Education Association, the Commonwealth Lawyers' Association (with which it helps to prepare the triennial Commonwealth Law Conference for the practising profession), the Commonwealth Association of Legislative Counsel, and with other international non-governmental organizations. The Division provides in-house legal advice for the Secretariat. The Commonwealth Law Bulletin, published four times a year, reports on legal developments in and beyond the Commonwealth. The Commonwealth Human Rights Law Digest (three a year) contains details of decisions relating to human rights cases from across the Commonwealth.

ECONOMIC AND ENVIRONMENTAL CO-OPERATION

In May 1998 the Commonwealth Secretary-General appealed to the Group of Eight industrialized nations (G8) to accelerate and expand the initiative to ease the debt burden of the most heavily indebted poor countries (HIPCs—see World Bank and the IMF). In October Commonwealth finance ministers reiterated their appeal to international financial institutions to accelerate the HIPC initiative. The meeting also issued a Commonwealth Statement on the global economic crisis and endorsed proposals to help to counter the difficulties experienced by several countries. These measures included a mechanism to enable countries to suspend payments on all short-term financial obligations at a time of emergency without defaulting, assistance to governments to attract private capital and to manage capital market volatility, and the development of international codes of conduct regarding financial and monetary policies and corporate governance. In March 1999 the Commonwealth Secretariat hosted a joint IMF-World Bank conference to review the HIPC scheme and initiate a process of reform. In November Commonwealth heads of government, meeting in South Africa, declared their support for measures undertaken by the World Bank and IMF to enhance the HIPC initiative. At the end of an informal retreat the leaders adopted the Fancourt Commonwealth Declaration on Globalization and People-Centred Development, which emphasized the need for a more equitable spread of wealth generated by the process of globalization, and expressed a renewed commitment to the elimination of all forms of discrimination, the promotion of people-centred development and capacity building, and efforts to ensure that developing countries benefit from future multilateral trade liberalization measures. In June 2002 the Commonwealth Secretary-General urged more generous funding of the HIPC initiative. Meetings of ministers of finance from Commonwealth member countries participating in the HIPC initiative are convened twice a year, as the Commonwealth Ministerial Debt Sustainability Forum. The Secretariat aims to assist HIPCs and other small economies through its Debt Recording and Management System (DRMS), which was first used in 1985 and updated in 2002; in July 2010 Liberia became the 60th country to join the System. In July 2005 the Commonwealth Secretary-General welcomed an initiative of the G8 to eliminate the debt of those HIPCs that had reached their completion point in the process, in addition to a commitment substantially to increase aid to Africa.

In February 1998 the Commonwealth Secretariat hosted a meeting of intergovernmental organizations to promote co-operation between small island states and the formulation of a unified policy approach to international fora. A second meeting was convened in March 2001, where discussions focused on the forthcoming WTO ministerial meeting and OECD's Harmful Tax Competition Initiative. In September 2000 Commonwealth ministers of finance, meeting in Malta, reviewed the OECD initiative and agreed that the measures, affecting many member countries with offshore financial centres, should not be imposed on governments. The ministers mandated the involvement of the Commonwealth Secretariat in efforts to resolve the dispute; a joint working group was subsequently established by the Secretariat with the OECD. In April 2002 a meeting on international co-operation in the financial services sector, attended by representatives of international and regional organizations, donors and senior officials from Commonwealth countries, was held under Commonwealth auspices in Saint Lucia. In September 2005 Commonwealth finance ministers, meeting in Barbados, considered new guidelines for Public Financial Management Reform.

In November 2005 Commonwealth heads of government issued the Malta Declaration on Networking the Commonwealth for Development, expressing their commitment to making available to all the benefits of new technologies and to using information technology networks to enhance the effectiveness of the Commonwealth in supporting development. The meeting endorsed a new Commonwealth Action Programme for the Digital Divide and approved the establishment of a special fund to enable implementation of the programme's objectives. Accordingly a Commonwealth Connects programme was established in August 2006 to develop partnerships and help to strengthen the use of and access to information technology in all Commonwealth countries; a Commonwealth Connects web portal—www.commonwealthconnects.org—was launched at the October 2011 heads of government summit. The 2005 Heads of Government Meeting also issued the Valletta Statement on Multilateral Trade, emphasizing their concerns that the Doha Round of WTO negotiations proceed steadily, on a development-oriented agenda, to a successful conclusion and reiterating their objectives of achieving a rules-based and equitable international trading system. A separate statement drew attention to the specific needs and challenges of small states and urged continued financial and technical support, in particular for those affected by natural disasters.

The Commonwealth Climate Change Action Plan, adopted by heads of government in November 2007, acknowledged that climate change posed a serious threat to the very existence of some small island states within the Commonwealth, and to the low-lying coastal areas of others. It offered unqualified support for the UN Framework Convention on Climate Change, and recognized the need to overcome technical, economic and policy-making barriers to reducing carbon emissions, to using renewable energy, and to increasing energy efficiency. The Plan undertook to assist developing member states in international negotiations on climate change; to support improved land use management, including the use of forest resources; to investigate the carbon footprint of agricultural exports from member countries; to increase support for the management of natural disasters in member countries; and to provide technical assistance to help least developed members and small states to assess the implications of climate change and adapt accordingly. A high-level meeting on climate finance, convened in London, in January 2011, determined to establish a working group to advance climate-related Commonwealth initiatives; and to integrate work on climate-related finance mechanisms into the next (2012–16) strategic plan.

In June 2008 the Commonwealth issued the Marlborough House Statement on Reform of International Institutions, declaring that ongoing global financial turbulence and soaring food and fuel prices highlighted the poor responsiveness of some international organizations mandated to promote economic stability, and determining to identify underlying principles and actions required to reform the international system. In November 2009 heads of government reiterated the need for reform in the UN system, demanding greater representation for developing countries in international economic decision-making, with particular reference to the IMF and the World Bank. They expressed concern that many Commonwealth countries were falling behind the MDG targets, and resolved to strengthen existing networks of co-operation: in particular, they undertook to take measures to improve the quality of data used in policy-making, and to strengthen the links between research and policy-making. A new Commonwealth Partnership Platform Portal was to provide practical support for sharing ideas and best practices. Heads of government also undertook to promote investment in science, technology and innovation.

Economic Affairs Division: organizes and services the annual meetings of Commonwealth ministers of finance and the ministerial group on small states and assists in servicing the biennial meetings of heads of government and periodic meetings of environment ministers. It engages in research and analysis on economic issues of interest to member governments and organizes seminars and conferences of government officials and experts. The Division actively supports developing Commonwealth countries to participate in the Doha Round of multilateral trade negotiations and is assisting the ACP group of countries to negotiate economic partnership agreements with the European Union. It continues to help developing countries to strengthen their links with international capital markets and foreign investors. The Division also services groups of experts on economic affairs that have been commissioned by governments to report on, among other things, protectionism; obstacles to the North-South negotiating process; reform of the international financial and trading system; the debt crisis; management of technological change; the impact of change on the development process; environmental issues; women and structural adjustment; and youth unemployment. A separate section within the Division addresses the specific needs of small states and provides technical assistance. The work of the section covers a range of issues including trade, vulnerability, environment, politics and economics. In 2000 a Commonwealth Secretariat/World Bank Joint Task Force on Small States finalized a report entitled *Small States: Meeting Challenges in the Global Economy*. A review of the report was issued in 2005. In June 2010 the first Commonwealth Biennial Small States Conference was convened, in London, comprising representatives of small states from the Africa, Asia-Pacific and Caribbean regions. In January 2011 a new Commonwealth Small States Office was inaugurated in Geneva, Switzerland; the Office was to provide subsidized office space for the Geneva-based diplomatic missions of Commonwealth small states, and business facilities for both diplomatic personnel and visiting delegations from small member states. The Economic Affairs Division also co-ordinates the Secretariat's environmental work and manages the Iwokrama International Centre for Rainforest Conservation and Development.

The Division supported the establishment of a Commonwealth Private Investment Initiative (CPII) to mobilize capital, on a regional basis, for investment in newly privatized companies and in small and medium-sized businesses in the private sector. The first regional fund under the CPII, the Commonwealth Africa Investment Fund (Comafin), was operational during the period July 1996–end-December 2006, and made 19 investments (of which three were subsequently written off) to assist businesses across nine sectors in seven countries in sub-Saharan Africa. A Pan-Commonwealth Africa Partners Fund was launched in 2002, which aimed to help existing businesses expand to become regional or pan-African in scope. In 1997 an investment fund for the Pacific Islands (known as the Kula Fund) was launched; a successor fund (Kula Fund II), with financing of some $20m., was launched in October 2005, with the aim of injecting capital into the smaller Pacific Island countries. A $200m. South Asia Regional Fund (SARF) was established in October 1997. In 1998 the Tiona Fund for the Commonwealth Caribbean was inaugurated, at a meeting of Commonwealth finance ministers; this was subsequently absorbed into the Caribbean Investment Fund (established in 1993 by member states of the Caribbean Community and Common Market—CARICOM).

SOCIAL WELFARE

Social Transformation Programmes Division: consists of three sections concerned with education, gender and health.

The **Education Section** arranges specialist seminars, workshops and co-operative projects, and commissions studies in areas identified by ministers of education, whose meetings it also services. Its areas of work include improving the quality of and access to basic education; strengthening science, technology and mathematics education in formal and non-formal areas of education; improving the quality of management in institutions of higher learning and basic education; improving the performance of teachers; strengthening examination assessment systems; and promoting the movement of students between Commonwealth countries. The Section also promotes the elimination of gender disparities in education, support for education in difficult circumstances, such as areas affected by conflict or natural disasters, and mitigating the impact of HIV and AIDS on education. It attempts to address the problems of scale particular to smaller member countries, and encourages collaboration between governments, the private sector and other non-governmental organizations.

The **Gender Affairs Section** is responsible for the implementation of the Commonwealth Plan of Action for Gender Equality, covering the period 2005–15, which succeeded the Commonwealth Plan of Action on Gender and Development (adopted in 1995 and updated in 2000). The Plan of Action supports efforts towards achieving the MDGs, and the objectives of gender equality adopted by the 1995 Beijing Declaration and Platform for Action and the follow-up Beijing + 5 review conference, held in 2000, and Beijing + 10 in 2005. Gender equality, poverty eradication, promotion of human rights, and strengthening democracy are recognized as intrinsically interrelated, and the Plan has a particular focus on the advancement of gender mainstreaming in the following areas: democracy, peace and conflict; human rights and law; poverty eradication and economic empowerment; and HIV/AIDS.

The **Health Section** organizes ministerial, technical and expert group meetings and workshops, to promote co-operation on health matters, and the exchange of health information and expertise. The Section commissions relevant studies and provides professional and technical advice to member countries and to the Secretariat. It also supports the work of regional health organizations and promotes health for all people in Commonwealth countries.

The **Youth Affairs Division**, reporting directly to a Deputy Secretary-General, was established within the Secretariat in 2002, acquiring divisional status in 2004.

The Division administers the Commonwealth Youth Programme (CYP), which was initiated in 1973 to promote the involvement of young people in the economic and social development of their countries. The CYP, funded through separate voluntary contributions from governments, was awarded a budget of £2.8m. for 2009/10. The Programme's activities are in three areas: Youth Enterprise and Sustainable Livelihoods; Governance, Development and Youth Networks; and Youth Work Education and Training. Regional centres are located in Zambia (for Africa), India (for Asia), Guyana (for the Caribbean), and Solomon Islands (for the Pacific). The Programme administers a Youth Study Fellowship scheme, a Youth Project Fund, a Youth Exchange Programme (in the Caribbean), and a Youth Development Awards Scheme. It also holds conferences and seminars, carries out research and disseminates information. The CYP Diploma in Youth Development Work is offered by partner institutions in 45 countries, primarily through distance education. The Commonwealth Youth Credit Initiative, initiated in 1995, provides funds and advice for young entrepreneurs setting up small businesses. A Plan of Action for Youth Empowerment, covering the period 2007–15, was approved by the sixth meeting of Commonwealth ministers responsible for youth affairs, held in Nassau, Bahamas, in May 2006. The first Commonwealth Youth Games was held in Edinburgh, United Kingdom in 2000, and has been convened every four years since. The eighth Commonwealth Youth Forum was convened in Freemantle, Australia, in October 2011.

TECHNICAL ASSISTANCE

Commonwealth Fund for Technical Co-operation (CFTC): f. 1971 to facilitate the exchange of skills between member countries and to promote economic and social development; it is administered by the Commonwealth Secretariat and financed by voluntary subscriptions from member governments. The CFTC responds to requests from member governments for technical assistance, such as the provision of experts for short- or medium-term projects, advice on economic or legal matters, and training programmes. Public sector development, allowing member states to build on their capacities, is the principal element in CFTC activities. This includes assistance for improvement of supervision and combating corruption; improving economic management, for example by advising on exports and investment promotion; strengthening democratic institutions, such as electoral commissions; and improvement of education and health policies. The CFTC also administers the Langkawi awards for the study of environmental issues, which is funded by the Canadian Government; the CFTC budget for 2009/10 amounted to £29.2m, supplemented by external resources through partnerships.

CFTC activities are mainly implemented by the following divisions:

Governance and Institutional Development Division: strengthens good governance in member countries, through advice, training and other expertise in order to build capacity in national public institutions. The Division administers the Commonwealth Service Abroad Programme (CSAP), which is funded by the CFTC. The Programme extends short-term technical assistance through highly qualified volunteers. The main objectives of the scheme are to provide expertise, training and exposure to new technologies and practices, to promote technology transfers and sharing of experiences and knowledge, and to support community workshops and other local activities.

Special Advisory Services Division: provides advice and technical assistance in four principal areas: debt management; economic and legal services; enterprise and agriculture; and trade.

Finance

The Secretariat's budget for 2009/10 amounted to £15.0m. Member governments meet the cost of the Secretariat through subscriptions on a scale related to income and population.

Publications

Advisory (annual newsletter of the Special Advisory Services Division).

Global (electronic magazine).

Commonwealth News (weekly e-mail newsletter).

Report of the Commonwealth Secretary-General (every 2 years).

Small States Digest (periodic newsletter).

Numerous reports, studies and papers (catalogue available).

Commonwealth Organizations

(in the United Kingdom, unless otherwise stated)

The two principal intergovernmental organizations established by Commonwealth member states, apart from the Commonwealth Secretariat itself, are the Commonwealth Foundation and the Commonwealth of Learning. In 2012 there were nearly 90 other professional or advocacy organizations bearing the Commonwealth's name and associated with or accredited to the Commonwealth, a selection of which are listed below.

PRINCIPAL INTERGOVERNMENTAL ORGANIZATIONS

Commonwealth Foundation: Marlborough House, Pall Mall, London, SW1Y 5HY; tel. (20) 7930-3783; fax (20) 7839-8157; e-mail geninfo@commonwealth.int; internet www.commonwealthfoundation.com; f. 1966; intergovernmental body promoting people-to-people interaction, and collaboration within the non-governmental sector of the Commonwealth; supports non-governmental organizations, professional associations and Commonwealth arts and culture; awards an annual Commonwealth Writers' Prize; funds are provided by Commonwealth govts; Chair. Simone de Comarmond (Seychelles); Dir Vijay Krishnarayan (Trinidad and Tobago); publ. *Commonwealth People* (quarterly).

Commonwealth of Learning (COL): 1055 West Hastings St, Suite 1200, Vancouver, BC V6E 2E9, Canada; tel. (604) 775-8200; fax (604) 775-8210; e-mail info@col.org; internet www.col.org; f. 1987 by Commonwealth Heads of Government to promote the devt and sharing of distance education and open learning resources, including materials, expertise and technologies, throughout the Commonwealth and in other countries; implements and assists with national and regional educational programmes; acts as consultant to international agencies and national governments; conducts seminars and studies on specific educational needs; core financing for COL is provided by Commonwealth governments on a voluntary basis; COL has an annual budget of approx. C $12m; Pres. and CEO Prof. Asha Kanwar (India); publ. *Connections*.

The following represents a selection of other Commonwealth organizations:

ADMINISTRATION AND PLANNING

Commonwealth Association for Public Administration and Management (CAPAM): L'Esplanade Laurier, 300 Laurier Ave West, West Tower, Room A1245, Ottawa, ON K1A 0M7, Canada; tel. (416) 996-5026; fax (416) 947-9223; e-mail capam@capam.org; internet www.capam.org; f. 1994; aims to promote sound management of the public sector in Commonwealth countries and to assist those countries undergoing political or financial reforms; an international awards programme to reward innovation within the public sector was introduced in 1997, and is awarded every 2 years; more than 1,200 individual mems and 80 institutional memberships in some 80 countries; Pres. Paul Zahra (Malta); Exec. Dir and CEO David Waung.

Commonwealth Association of Planners: c/o Royal Town Planning Institute in Scotland, 18 Atholl Crescent, Edinburgh, EH3 8HQ; tel. (131) 229-9628; fax (131) 229-9332; e-mail annette.odonnell@rtpi.org.uk; internet www.commonwealth-planners.org; aims to develop urban and regional planning in Commonwealth countries, to meet the challenges of urbanization and the sustainable development of human settlements; Pres. Christine Platt (South Africa); Sec.-Gen. Clive Harridge (United Kingdom).

Commonwealth Local Government Forum: 16a Northumberland Ave, London, WC2N 5AP; tel. (20) 7389-1490; fax (20) 7389-1499; e-mail info@clgf.org.uk; internet www.clgf.org.uk; works to promote democratic local government in Commonwealth countries, and to encourage good practice through conferences, programmes, research and the provision of information; regional offices in Fiji, India and South Africa.

AGRICULTURE AND FORESTRY

Commonwealth Forestry Association: Crib, Dinchope, Craven Arms, Shropshire, SY7 9JJ; tel. (1588) 672868; fax (870) 0116645; e-mail cfa@cfa-international.org; internet www.cfa-international.org; f. 1921; produces, collects and circulates information relating to world forestry and promotes good management, use and conservation of forests and forest lands throughout the world; mems: 1,200; Chair. John Innes (Canada); Pres. Jim Ball (United Kingdom); publs *International*

Forestry Review (quarterly), *Commonwealth Forestry News* (quarterly), *Commonwealth Forestry Handbook* (irregular).

Royal Agricultural Society of the Commonwealth: Royal Highland Centre, Ingleston, Edinburgh, EH28 8NF; tel. (131) 335-6200; fax (131) 335-6229; e-mail rasc@commagshow.org; internet www.commagshow.org; f. 1957 to promote development of agricultural shows and good farming practice, in order to improve incomes and food production in Commonwealth countries.

Standing Committee on Commonwealth Forestry: Forestry Commission, 231 Corstorphine Rd, Edinburgh, EH12 7AT; tel. (131) 314-6405; fax (131) 316-4344; e-mail jonathan.taylor@forestry.gsi.gov.uk; internet www.cfc2010.org; f. 1923 to provide continuity between Confs, and to provide a forum for discussion on any forestry matters of common interest to mem. govts which may be brought to the Cttee's notice by any mem. country or organization; 54 mems; June 2010 Conference: Edinburgh, United Kingdom; Sec. JONATHAN TAYLOR.

BUSINESS

Commonwealth Business Council: 18 Pall Mall, London, SW1Y 5LU; tel. (20) 7024-8200; fax (20) 7024-8201; e-mail info@cbcglobal.org; internet www.cbcglobal.org; f. 1997 by the Commonwealth Heads of Government Meeting to promote co-operation between governments and the private sector in support of trade, investment and development; the Council aims to identify and promote investment opportunities, in particular in Commonwealth developing countries, to support countries and local businesses to work within the context of globalization, to promote capacity building and the exchange of skills and knowledge (in particular through its Information Communication Technologies for Development programme), and to encourage co-operation among Commonwealth members; promotes good governance; supports the process of multilateral trade negotiations and other liberalization of trade and services; represents the private sector at government level; Dir-Gen. and CEO Sir ALAN COLLINS.

EDUCATION AND CULTURE

Association of Commonwealth Universities (ACU): Woburn House, 20-24 Tavistock Sq., London, WC1H 9HF; tel. (20) 7380-6700; fax (20) 7387-2655; e-mail info@acu.ac.uk; internet www.acu.ac.uk; f. 1913; promotes international co-operation and understanding; provides assistance with staff and student mobility and development programmes; researches and disseminates information about universities and relevant policy issues; organizes major meetings of Commonwealth universities and their representatives; acts as a liaison office and information centre; administers scholarship and fellowship schemes; operates a policy research unit; mems: c. 500 universities in 36 Commonwealth countries or regions; Sec.-Gen. Prof. JOHN WOOD; publs include *Yearly Review*, *Commonwealth Universities Yearbook*, *ACU Bulletin* (quarterly), *Who's Who of Executive Heads: Vice-Chancellors, Presidents, Principals and Rectors*, *International Awards*, student information papers (study abroad series).

Commonwealth Association of Museums: R.R.1, De Winton, Alberta, T0L 0X0, Canada; tel. and fax (403) 938-3190; e-mail irvinel@fclc.com; internet www.maltwood.uvic.ca/cam; f. 1985; professional asscn working for the improvement of museums throughout the Commonwealth; encourages links between museums and assists professional development and training through distance learning, workshops and seminars; general assembly held every three or four years; mems in 38 Commonwealth countries; Pres. Prof. LOIS IRVINE.

Commonwealth Association of Science, Technology and Mathematics Educators (CASTME): 7 Lion Yard, Tremadoc Rd, London, SW4 7NQ; tel. (20) 7819-3936; e-mail castme@lect.org; internet www.castme.org; f. 1974; special emphasis is given to the social significance of education in these subjects; organizes an Awards Scheme to promote effective teaching and learning in these subjects, and biennial regional seminars; Chair. COLIN MATHESON; publ. *CASTME Journal* (3 a year).

Commonwealth Council for Educational Administration and Management: POB 1891, Penrith, NSW 2751, Australia; tel. (2) 4732-1211; fax (2) 4732-1711; e-mail admin@cceam.org; internet www.cceam.org; f. 1970; aims to foster quality in professional development and links among educational administrators; holds national and regional conferences, as well as visits and seminars; mems: 24 affiliated groups representing 3,000 persons; Pres. Prof. FRANK CROWTHER; publ. *International Studies in Educational Administration* (2 a year).

Commonwealth Education Trust: New Zealand House, 6th Floor, 80 Haymarket, London, SW1Y 4TE; tel. (20) 7024-9822; fax (20) 7024-9833; e-mail info@commonwealth-institute.org; internet www.commonwealtheducationtrust.org; f. 2007 as the successor trust to the Commonwealth Institute; funds the Centre of Commonwealth Education, established in 2004 as part of Cambridge University; supports the Lifestyle of Our Kids (LOOK) project initiated in 2005 by the Commonwealth Institute (Australia); Chief Exec. JUDY CURRY.

Institute of Commonwealth Studies: South Block, 2nd Floor, Senate House, Malet Street, London, WC1E 7HU; tel. (20) 7862-8844; fax (20) 7862-8813; e-mail ics@sas.ac.uk; internet commonwealth.sas.ac.uk; f. 1949 to promote advanced study of the Commonwealth; provides a library and meeting place for postgraduate students and academic staff engaged in research in this field; offers postgraduate teaching; Dir Prof. PHILIP MURPHY; publs *Annual Report*, *Collected Seminar Papers*, *Newsletter*, *Theses in Progress in Commonwealth Studies*.

HEALTH AND WELFARE

Commonwealth Medical Trust (COMMAT): BMA House, Tavistock Sq., London, WC1H 9JP; tel. (20) 7272-8492; fax (1689) 890609; e-mail office@commat.org; internet www.commat.org; f. 1962 (as the Commonwealth Medical Association) for the exchange of information; provision of techical co-operation and advice; formulation and maintenance of a code of ethics; promotes the Right to Health; liaison with WHO and other UN agencies on health issues; meetings of its Council are held every three years; mems: medical asscns in Commonwealth countries; Dir MARIANNE HASLEGRAVE.

Commonwealth Nurses' Federation: c/o Royal College of Nursing, 20 Cavendish Sq., London, W1G 0RN; tel. (20) 7647-3593; fax (20) 7647-3413; e-mail jill@commonwealthnurses.org; internet www.commonwealthnurses.org; f. 1973 to link national nursing and midwifery asscns in Commonwealth countries; aims to influence health policy, develop nursing networks, improve nursing education and standards, and strengthen leadership; inaugural Conference held in March 2012 (in London); Exec. Sec. JILL ILIFFE.

Commonwealth Organization for Social Work: Halifax, Canada; tel. (902) 455-5515; e-mail moniqueauffrey@eastlink.ca; internet www.commonwealthsw.org; promotes communication and collaboration between social workers in Commonwealth countries; provides network for information and sharing of expertise; Sec.-Gen. MONIQUE AUFFREY (Canada).

Commonwealth Pharmacists Association: 1 Lambeth High St, London, SE1 7JN; tel. (20) 7572-2216; fax (20) 7572-2504; e-mail admin@commonwealthpharmacy.org; internet www.commonwealthpharmacy.org; f. 1970 (as the Commonwealth Pharmaceutical Association) to promote the interests of pharmaceutical sciences and the profession of pharmacy in the Commonwealth; to maintain high professional standards, encourage links between members and the creation of nat. asscns; and to facilitate the dissemination of information; holds conferences (every four years) and regional meetings; mems: pharmaceutical asscns from over 40 Commonwealth countries; Pres. RAYMOND ANDERSON (United Kingdom); publ. *Quarterly Newsletter*.

Commonwealth Society for the Deaf (Sound Seekers): 34 Buckingham Palace Rd, London, SW1W 0RE; tel. (20) 7233-5700; fax (20) 7233-5800; e-mail sound.seekers@btinternet.com; internet www.sound-seekers.org.uk; f. 1959; undertakes initiatives to establish audiology services in developing Commonwealth countries, including mobile clinics to provide outreach services; aims to educate local communities in aural hygiene and the prevention of ear infection and deafness; provides audiological equipment and organizes the training of audiological maintenance technicians; conducts research into the causes and prevention of deafness; Chief Exec. GARY WILLIAMS; publ. *Annual Report*.

Royal Commonwealth Ex-Services League: Haig House, 199 Borough High St, London, SE1 1AA; tel. (20) 3207-2413; fax (20) 3207-2115; e-mail mgordon-roe@commonwealthveterans.org.uk; internet www.commonwealthveterans.org.uk; links the ex-service orgs in the Commonwealth, assists ex-servicemen of the Crown who are resident abroad; holds conferences every four years; 56 mem. orgs in 48 countries; Grand Pres. HRH The Duke of EDINBURGH; publ. *Annual Report*.

Sightsavers (Royal Commonwealth Society for the Blind): Grosvenor Hall, Bolnore Rd, Haywards Heath, West Sussex, RH16 4BX; tel. (1444) 446600; fax (1444) 446688; e-mail info@sightsavers.org; internet www.sightsavers.org; f. 1950 to prevent blindness and restore sight in developing countries, and to provide education and community-based training for incurably blind people; operates in collaboration with local partners in some 30 developing countries, with high priority given to training local staff; Chair. Lord NIGEL CRISP; Chief Exec. Dr CAROLINE HARPER; publ. *Sight Savers News*.

INFORMATION AND THE MEDIA

Commonwealth Broadcasting Association: 17 Fleet St, London, EC4Y 1AA; tel. (20) 7583-5550; fax (20) 7583-5549; e-mail cba@cba.org.uk; internet www.cba.org.uk; f. 1945; general conferences are held every two years (2012: Brisbane, Australia, in April); mems: c. 100 in more than 50 countries; Pres. MONEEZA HASHMI; Sec.-Gen. SALLY-ANN WILSON; publs *Commonwealth Broadcaster* (quarterly), *Commonwealth Broadcaster Directory* (annually).

Commonwealth Journalists Association: c/o Canadian Newspaper Association, 890 Yonge St, Suite 200, Toronto, ON M4W 3P4, Canada; tel. (416) 575-5377; fax (416) 923-7206; e-mail cantleyb@commonwealthjournalists.com; internet www.commonwealthjournalists.com; f. 1978 to promote co-operation between journalists in Commonwealth countries, organize training facilities and conferences, and foster understanding among Commonwealth peoples; Pres. RITA PAYNE (United Kingdom); publ. *Newsletter* (3 a year).

CPU Media Trust (Association of Commonwealth Newspapers, News Agencies and Periodicals): e-mail webform@cpu.org.uk; internet www.cpu.org.uk; f. 2008 as a 'virtual' organization charged with carrying on the aims of the Commonwealth the Commonwealth Press Union (CPU, f. 1950, terminated 2008); promotes the welfare of the Commonwealth press; Chair. GUY BLACK.

LAW

Commonwealth Lawyers' Association: c/o Institute of Advanced Legal Studies, 17 Russell Sq., London, WC1B 5DR; tel. (20) 7862-8824; fax (20) 7862-8816; e-mail cla@sas.ac.uk; internet www.commonwealthlawyers.com; f. 1983 (fmrly the Commonwealth Legal Bureau); seeks to maintain and promote the rule of law throughout the Commonwealth, by ensuring that the people of the Commonwealth are served by an independent and efficient legal profession; upholds professional standards and promotes the availability of legal services; organizes the biannual Commonwealth Law Conference; Chair. LAURENCE WATT; publs *The Commonwealth Lawyer*, *Clarion*.

Commonwealth Legal Advisory Service: c/o British Institute of International and Comparative Law, Charles Clore House, 17 Russell Sq., London, WC1B 5DR; tel. (20) 7862-5151; fax (20) 7862-5152; e-mail contact@biicl.org; internet www.biicl.org; f. 1962; financed by the British Institute and by contributions from Commonwealth govts; provides research facilities for Commonwealth govts and law reform commissions; publ. *New Memoranda* series.

Commonwealth Legal Education Association: c/o Legal and Constitutional Affairs Division, Commonwealth Secretariat, Marlborough House, Pall Mall, London, SW1Y 5HX; tel. (20) 7747-6415; fax (20) 7004-3649; e-mail clea@commonwealth.int; internet www.clea-web.com; f. 1971 to promote contacts and exchanges and to provide information regarding legal education; Pres. DAVID MACQUOID-MASON; Gen. Sec. SELINA GOULBOURNE; publ. *Commonwealth Legal Education Association Newsletter* (3 a year).

Commonwealth Magistrates' and Judges' Association: Uganda House, 58–59 Trafalgar Sq., London, WC2N 5DX; tel. (20) 7976-1007; fax (20) 7976-2394; e-mail info@cmja.org; internet www.cmja.org; f. 1970 to advance the administration of the law by promoting the independence of the judiciary, to further education in law and crime prevention and to disseminate information; confs and study tours; corporate membership for asscns of the judiciary or courts of limited jurisdiction; assoc. membership for individuals; Pres. Hon. Mrs Justice NORMA WADE-MILLER; Sec.-Gen. Dr KAREN BREWER; publs *Commonwealth Judicial Journal* (2 a year), *CMJA News*.

PARLIAMENTARY AFFAIRS

Commonwealth Parliamentary Association: Westminster House, Suite 700, 7 Millbank, London, SW1P 3JA; tel. (20) 7799-1460; fax (20) 7222-6073; e-mail hq.sec@cpahq.org; internet www.cpahq.org; f. 1911 to promote understanding and co-operation between Commonwealth parliamentarians; organization: Exec. Cttee of 35 MPs responsible to annual Gen. Assembly; 176 brs in national, state, provincial and territorial parliaments and legislatures throughout the Commonwealth; holds annual Commonwealth Parliamentary Confs and seminars; also regional confs and seminars; Chair. Sir ALAN HASELHURST; Sec.-Gen. Dr WILLIAM F. SHIJA; publ. *The Parliamentarian* (quarterly).

SCIENCE AND TECHNOLOGY

Commonwealth Association of Architects: POB 1166, Stamford, PE2 2HL; tel. and fax (1780) 238091; e-mail info@comarchitect.org; internet www.comarchitect.org; f. 1964; aims to facilitate the reciprocal recognition of professional qualifications; to provide a clearing house for information on architectural practice; and to encourage collaboration. Plenary conferences every three years; regional conferences are also held; 38 societies of architects in various Commonwealth countries; Pres. MUBASSHAR HUSSAIN; Exec. Dir TONY GODWIN; publs *Handbook*, *Objectives and Procedures: CAA Schools Visiting Boards*, *Architectural Education in the Commonwealth* (annotated bibliography of research), *CAA Newsnet* (2 a year), a survey and list of schools of architecture.

Commonwealth Engineers' Council: c/o Institution of Civil Engineers, One Great George St, London, SW1P 3AA; tel. (20) 7222-7722; e-mail secretariat@ice.org.uk; internet www.cec.ice.org.uk; f. 1946; links and represents engineering institutions across the Commonwealth, providing them with an opportunity to exchange views on collaboration and mutual support; holds international and regional conferences and workshops; mems: 45 institutions in 44 countries; Sec.-Gen. NEIL BAILEY.

Commonwealth Telecommunications Organization: 64-66 Glenthorne Rd, London, W6 0LR; tel. (20) 8600-3800; fax (20) 8600-3819; e-mail info@cto.int; internet www.cto.int; f. 1967 as an international development partnership between Commonwealth and non-Commonwealth governments, business and civil society organizations; aims to help to bridge the digital divide and to achieve social and economic development by delivering to developing countries knowledge-sharing programmes in the use of information and communication technologies in the specific areas of telecommunications, IT, broadcasting and the internet; CEO Prof. TIM UNWIN; publs *CTO Update* (quarterly), *Annual Report*, *Research Reports*.

Conference of Commonwealth Meteorologists: c/o International Branch, Meteorological Office, FitzRoy Rd, Exeter, EX1 3PB; tel. (1392) 885680; fax (1392) 885681; e-mail commonwealth@metoffice.gov.uk; internet www.commonwealthmet.org; links national meteorological and hydrological services in Commonwealth countries; conferences held every four years.

SPORT AND YOUTH

Commonwealth Games Federation: 2nd Floor, 138 Piccadilly, London, W1J 7NR; tel. (20) 7491-8801; fax (20) 7409-7803; e-mail info@thecgf.com; internet www.thecgf.com; the Games were first held in 1930 and are now held every four years; participation is limited to competitors representing the mem. countries of the Commonwealth; 2014 games: Glasgow, United

Kingdom; mems: 72 affiliated bodies; Pres. HRH Prince IMRAN (Malaysia); CEO MICHAEL HOOPER.

Commonwealth Youth Exchange Council: 7 Lion Yard, Tremadoc Rd, London, SW4 7NQ; tel. (20) 7498-6151; fax (20) 7622-4365; e-mail ival@cyec.org.uk; internet www.cyec.org.uk; f. 1970; promotes contact between groups of young people of the United Kingdom and other Commonwealth countries by means of educational exchange visits, provides information for organizers and allocates grants; provides host governments with technical assistance for delivery of the Commonwealth Youth Forum, held every two years; since July 2011 administers the Commonwealth Teacher Exchange Programme; mems: 222 orgs, 134 local authorities, 88 voluntary bodies; Chief Exec. V. S. G. CRAGGS; publs *Contact* (handbook), *Exchange* (newsletter), *Final Communiqués* (of the Commonwealth Youth Forums), *Safety and Welfare* (guidelines for Commonwealth Youth Exchange groups).

RELATIONS WITHIN THE COMMONWEALTH

Commonwealth Countries League: 37 Priory Ave, Sudbury, HA0 2SB; tel. (20) 8248-3275; e-mail info@ccl-int.org; internet www.ccl-int.org; f. 1925; aims to secure equality of liberties, status and opportunities between women and men and to promote friendship and mutual understanding throughout the Commonwealth; promotes women's political and social education and links together women's organizations in most countries of the Commonwealth; an education sponsorship scheme was established in 1967 to finance the secondary education of bright girls from lower income backgrounds in their own Commonwealth countries; the CCL Education Fund was sponsoring more than 300 girls throughout the Commonwealth (2012); Exec. Chair. MARJORIE RENNIE; publs *News Update* (3 a year), *Annual Report*.

Commonwealth War Graves Commission: 2 Marlow Rd, Maidenhead, SL6 7DX; tel. (1628) 634221; fax (1628) 771208; internet www.cwgc.org; casualty and cemetery enquiries; e-mail casualty.enq@cwgc.org; f. 1917 (as Imperial War Graves Commission); responsible for the commemoration in perpetuity of the 1.7m. members of the Commonwealth Forces who died during the wars of 1914–18 and 1939–45; provides for the marking and maintenance of war graves and memorials at some 23,000 locations in 150 countries; mems: Australia, Canada, India, New Zealand, South Africa, United Kingdom; Pres. HRH The Duke of KENT; Dir-Gen. ALAN PATEMAN-JONES.

Council of Commonwealth Societies: c/o Royal Commonwealth Society, 25 Northumberland Ave, London, WC2N 5AP; tel. (20) 7766-9206; fax (20) 7930-9705; e-mail ccs@rcsint.org; internet www.rcsint.org/day; f. 1947; provides a forum for the exchange of information regarding activities of member orgs which promote understanding among countries of the Commonwealth; co-ordinates the distribution of the Commonwealth Day message by Queen Elizabeth II, organizes the observance of and promotes Commonwealth Day, and produces educational materials relating to the occasion; seeks to raise the profile of the Commonwealth; mems: 30 official and unofficial Commonwealth orgs; Chair. Lord ALAN WATSON.

Royal Commonwealth Society: 25 Northumberland Ave, London, WC2N 5AP; tel. (20) 7766-9200; fax (20) 7930-9705; e-mail info@thercs.org; internet www.thercs.org; f. 1868; to promote international understanding of the Commonwealth and its people; organizes meetings and seminars on topical issues, projects for young people, a youth leadership programme, and cultural and social events; Pres. Baroness PRASHAR; Dir Dr DANNY SRISKANDARAJAH; publs *RCS Exchange* (3 a year), conference reports.

Royal Over-Seas League: Over-Seas House, Park Place, St James's St, London, SW1A 1LR; tel. (20) 7408-0214; fax (20) 7499-6738; e-mail info@rosl.org.uk; internet www.rosl.org.uk; f. 1910 to promote friendship and understanding in the Commonwealth; club houses in London and Edinburgh; membership is open to all British subjects and Commonwealth citizens; Dir-Gen. Maj.-Gen. RODDY PORTER; publ. *Overseas* (quarterly).

Victoria League for Commonwealth Friendship: 55 Leinster Sq., London, W2 4PW; tel. (20) 7243-2633; fax (20) 7229-2994; e-mail enquiries@victorialeague.co.uk; internet www.victorialeague.co.uk; f. 1901; aims to further personal friendship among Commonwealth peoples and to provide hospitality for visitors; maintains Student House, providing accommodation for students from Commonwealth countries; has branches elsewhere in the UK and abroad; Chair. LYN D. HOPKINS; Gen. Man. DOREEN HENRY; publ. *Annual Report*.

Declaration of Commonwealth Principles

(agreed by the Commonwealth Heads of Government Meeting at Singapore, 22 January 1971)

The Commonwealth of Nations is a voluntary association of independent sovereign states, each responsible for its own policies, consulting and co-operating in the common interests of their peoples and in the promotion of international understanding and world peace.

Members of the Commonwealth come from territories in the six continents and five oceans, include peoples of different races, languages and religions, and display every stage of economic development from poor developing nations to wealthy industrialized nations. They encompass a rich variety of cultures, traditions and institutions.

Membership of the Commonwealth is compatible with the freedom of member-governments to be non-aligned or to belong to any other grouping, association or alliance. Within this diversity all members of the Commonwealth hold certain principles in common. It is by pursuing these principles that the Commonwealth can continue to influence international society for the benefit of mankind.

We believe that international peace and order are essential to the security and prosperity of mankind; we therefore support the United Nations and seek to strengthen its influence for peace in the world, and its efforts to remove the causes of tension between nations.

We believe in the liberty of the individual, in equal rights for all citizens regardless of race, colour, creed or political belief, and in their inalienable right to participate by means of free and democratic political processes in framing the society in which they live. We therefore strive to promote in each of our countries those representative institutions and guarantees for personal freedom under the law that are our common heritage.

We recognize racial prejudice as a dangerous sickness threatening the healthy development of the human race and racial discrimination as an unmitigated evil of society. Each of us will vigorously combat this evil within our own nation.

No country will afford to regimes which practise racial discrimination assistance which in its own judgment directly contributes to the pursuit or consolidation of this evil policy. We oppose all forms of colonial domination and racial oppression and are committed to the principles of human dignity and equality.

We will therefore use all our efforts to foster human equality and dignity everywhere, and to further the principles of self-determination and non-racialism.

We believe that the wide disparities in wealth now existing between different sections of mankind are too great to be tolerated. They also create world tensions. Our aim is their progressive removal. We therefore seek to use our efforts to overcome poverty, ignorance and disease, in raising standards of life and achieving a more equitable international society.

To this end our aim is to achieve the freest possible flow of international trade on terms fair and equitable to all, taking into account the special requirements of the developing countries, and to encourage the flow of adequate resources, including governmental and private resources, to the developing countries, bearing in mind the importance of doing this in a true spirit of partnership and of establishing for this purpose in the developing countries conditions which are conducive to sustained investment and growth.

We believe that international co-operation is essential to remove the causes of war, promote tolerance, combat injustice, and secure development among the peoples of the world. We are convinced that the Commonwealth is one of the most fruitful associations for these purposes.

In pursuing these principles the members of the Commonwealth believe that they can provide a constructive example of the multi-national approach which is vital to peace and progress in the modern world. The association is based on consultation, discussion and co-operation.

In rejecting coercion as an instrument of policy they recognize that the security of each member state from external aggression is a matter of concern to all members. It provides many channels for continuing exchanges of knowledge and views on professional, cultural, economic, legal and political issues among member states.

These relationships we intend to foster and extend, for we believe that our multi-national association can expand human understanding and understanding among nations, assist in the elimination of discrimination based on differences of race, colour or creed, maintain and strengthen personal liberty, contribute to the enrichment of life for all, and provide a powerful influence for peace among nations.

The Lusaka Declaration on Racism and Racial Prejudice

The Declaration, adopted by heads of government in 1979, includes the following statements:

(i) the peoples of the Commonwealth have the right to live freely in dignity and equality, without any distinction or exclusion based on race, colour, sex, descent, or national or ethnic origin;

(ii) while everyone is free to retain diversity in his or her culture and lifestyle this diversity does not justify the perpetuation of racial prejudice or racially discriminatory practices;

(iii) everyone has the right to equality before the law and equal justice under the law; and

(iv) everyone has the right to effective remedies and protection against any form of discrimination based on the grounds of race, colour, sex, descent, or national or ethnic origin.

We reject as inhuman and intolerable all policies designed to perpetuate apartheid, racial segregation or other policies based on theories that racial groups are or may be inherently superior or inferior.

We reaffirm that it is the duty of all the peoples of the Commonwealth to work together for the total eradication of the infamous policy of apartheid which is internationally recognized as a crime against the conscience and dignity of mankind and the very existence of which is an affront to humanity.

We agree that everyone has the right to protection against acts of incitement to racial hatred and discrimination, whether committed by individuals, groups or other organizations.

Inspired by the principles of freedom and equality which characterise our association, we accept the solemn duty of working together to eliminate racism and racial prejudice. This duty involves the acceptance of the principle that positive measures may be required to advance the elimination of racism, including assistance to those struggling to rid themselves and their environment of the practice.

Being aware that legislation alone cannot eliminate racism and racial prejudice, we endorse the need to initiate public information and education policies designed to promote understanding, tolerance, respect and friendship among peoples and racial groups.

We note that racism and racial prejudice, wherever they occur, are significant factors contributing to tension between nations and thus inhibit peaceful progress and development. We believe that the goal of the eradication of racism stands as a critical priority for governments of the Commonwealth committed as they are to the promotion of the ideals of peaceful and happy lives for their people.

Harare Commonwealth Declaration

The following are the major points of the Declaration adopted by heads of government at the meeting held in Harare, Zimbabwe, in 1991:

Having reaffirmed the principles to which the Commonwealth is committed, and reviewed the problems and challenges which the world, and the Commonwealth as part of it, face, we pledge the Commonwealth and our countries to work with renewed vigour, concentrating especially in the following areas: the protection and promotion of the fundamental political values of the Commonwealth; equality for women, so that they may exercise their full and equal rights; provision of universal access to education for the population of our countries; continuing action to bring about the end of apartheid and the establishment of a free, democratic, non-racial and prosperous South Africa; the promotion of sustainable development and the alleviation of poverty in the countries of the Commonwealth; extending the benefits of development within a framework of respect for human rights; the protection of the environment through respect for the principles of sustainable development which we enunciated at Langkawi; action to combat drugs trafficking and abuse and communicable diseases; help for small Commonwealth states in tackling their particular economic and security problems; and support of the United Nations and other international institutions in the world's search for peace, disarmament and effective arms control; and in the promotion of international consensus on major global political, economic and social issues.

To give weight and effectiveness to our commitments we intend to focus and improve Commonwealth co-operation in these areas. This would include strengthening the capacity of the Commonwealth to respond to requests from members for assistance in entrenching the practices of democracy, accountable administration and the rule of law.

In reaffirming the principles of the Commonwealth and in committing ourselves to pursue them in policy and action in response to the challenges of the 1990s, in areas where we believe that the Commonwealth has a distinctive contribution to offer, we the Heads of Government express our determination to renew and enhance the value and importance of the Commonwealth as an institution which can and should strengthen and enrich the lives not only of its own members and their peoples but also of the wider community of peoples of which they are a part.

COMMONWEALTH OF INDEPENDENT STATES—CIS

Address: 220000 Minsk, Kirava 17, Belarus.

Telephone: (17) 222-35-17; **fax:** (17) 227-23-39; **e-mail:** postmaster@www.cis.minsk.by; **internet:** www.cis.minsk.by.

The Commonwealth of Independent States (CIS) is a voluntary association of 11 states, established at the time of the collapse of the USSR in December 1991.

MEMBERS

Armenia	Moldova
Azerbaijan	Russia
Belarus	Tajikistan
Kazakhstan	Ukraine
Kyrgyzstan	Uzbekistan

Note: Azerbaijan formally became a member of the CIS in September 1993. Georgia was admitted to the CIS in December 1993. In August 2009 Georgia's membership was terminated. Ukraine ratified the foundation documents that established the CIS in 1991 but has not yet ratified the CIS Charter. Turkmenistan has associate membership, reduced from full membership in August 2005.

Organization

(June 2012)

COUNCIL OF HEADS OF STATE

This is the supreme body of the CIS, on which all the member states of the Commonwealth are represented at the level of head of state, for discussion of issues relating to the co-ordination of Commonwealth activities and the development of the Minsk Agreement. Decisions of the Council are taken by common consent, with each state having equal voting rights. The Council meets at least once a year. An extraordinary meeting may be convened on the initiative of the majority of Commonwealth heads of state. The chairmanship of the Council is normally rotated among member states.

COUNCIL OF HEADS OF GOVERNMENT

This Council convenes for meetings at least once every three months; an extraordinary sitting may be convened on the initiative of a majority of Commonwealth heads of government. The two Councils may discuss and take necessary decisions on important domestic and external issues, and may hold joint sittings.

Working and auxiliary bodies, composed of authorized representatives of the participating states, may be set up on a permanent or interim basis on the decision of the Council of Heads of State and the Council of Heads of Government.

EXECUTIVE COMMITTEE

The Executive Committee was established by the Council of Heads of State in April 1999 to supersede the previous Secretariat, the Inter-state Economic Committee and other working bodies and committees, in order to improve the efficient functioning of the organization. The Executive Committee co-operates closely with other CIS bodies including the councils of foreign ministers and defence ministers; the Economic Council; Council of Border Troops Commanders; the Collective Security Council; the Secretariat of the Council of the Inter-parliamentary Assembly; and the Inter-state Committee for Statistics.

Executive Secretary and Chairman of the Executive Committee: SERGEI N. LEBEDEV (Russia).

Activities

On 8 December 1991 the heads of state of Belarus, Russia and Ukraine signed the Minsk Agreement, providing for the establishment of a Commonwealth of Independent States. Formal recognition of the dissolution of the USSR was incorporated in a second treaty (the Alma-Ata Declaration), signed by 11 heads of state in the then Kazakh capital, Alma-Ata (Almatı), later in that month.

In March 1992 a meeting of the CIS Council of Heads of Government decided to establish a commission to examine the resolution that 'all CIS member states are the legal successors of the rights and obligations of the former Soviet Union'. Documents relating to the legal succession of the Soviet Union were signed at a meeting of heads of state in July. In April an agreement establishing an Inter-parliamentary Assembly (IPA), signed by Armenia, Belarus, Kazakhstan, Kyrgyzstan, Russia, Tajikistan and Uzbekistan, was published. The first Assembly was held in Bishkek, Kyrgyzstan, in September, attended by delegates from all these countries, with the exception of Uzbekistan.

A CIS Charter was adopted at the meeting of the heads of state in Minsk, Belarus, in January 1993. The Charter, providing for a defence alliance, an inter-state court and an economic co-ordination committee, was to serve as a framework for closer co-operation and was signed by all of the members except for Turkmenistan and Ukraine; by 2012 Ukraine had still not signed the Charter.

In May 1994 the CIS and UNCTAD signed a co-operation accord. A similar agreement was concluded with the UN Economic Commission for Europe in June 1996. Working contacts have also been established with the ILO, UNHCR, WHO and the European Union (EU). In June 1998 the IPA approved a decision to sign the European Social Charter (see Council of Europe); a declaration of co-operation between the Assembly and the OSCE Parliamentary Assembly was also signed.

In April 1996 the Council of Heads of Government approved a long-term plan for the integrated development of the CIS, incorporating measures for further socio-economic, military and political co-operation. Meeting in April 1999 the Council of Heads of Government adopted guidelines for restructuring the CIS and for the future development of the organization. Economic co-operation was to be a priority area of activity, and in particular, the establishment of a free trade zone. In June 2000 the Councils of Heads of State and Government issued a declaration concerning the maintenance of strategic stability, approved a plan and schedule for pursuing economic integration, and adopted a short-term programme for combating international terrorism (perceived to be a significant threat in central Asia). An informal CIS 10-year 'jubilee' summit, convened in November 2001, adopted a statement identifying the collective pursuit of stable socio-economic development and integration on a global level as the organization's principal objectives. A summit of heads of state convened in January 2003 agreed that the position of Chairman of the Council of Heads of State (hitherto held by consecutive Russian presidents) should be rotated henceforth among member states. Leonid Kuchma, then President of Ukraine, was elected as the new Chairman. (In September 2004, however, Russia's then President Vladimir Putin was reappointed temporarily as the Chairman of the Council, owing to a perceived deterioration in the international security situation and a declared need for experienced leadership.) A summit meeting convened in September 2003, in Yalta, Ukraine, focused on measures to combat crime and terrorism, and endorsed an economic plan for 2003–10.

In September 2004 the CIS Council of Heads of State, meeting in Astana, Kazakhstan, was dominated by consideration of measures to combat terrorism and extremist violence, following a month in which Russia, including North Ossetia, had experienced several atrocities committed against civilian targets. As part of a wider consideration of a reorganization of the CIS, the Council resolved to establish a Security Council.

Member states of the CIS have formed alliances of various kinds among themselves, thereby potentially undermining the unity of the Commonwealth. In March 1996 Belarus, Kazakhstan, Kyrgyzstan and Russia signed the Quadripartite Treaty for greater integration. This envisaged the establishment of a 'New Union', based, initially, on a common market and customs union, and was to be open to all CIS members and the Baltic states. Consequently, these countries (with Tajikistan) became founding members of the Eurasian Economic Community (EurAsEC), inaugurated in October 2001. In April 1996 Belarus and Russia signed the Treaty on the Formation of a Community of Sovereign Republics (CSR), which provided for extensive economic, political and military co-operation. In April 1997 the two countries signed a further Treaty of Union and, in addition, initialled the Charter of the Union, which detailed the procedures and institutions designed to develop a common infrastructure, a single currency and a joint defence policy within the CSR, with the eventual aim of 'voluntary unification of the member states'. The Charter was signed in May and ratified by the respective legislatures the following month. The Union's Parliamentary Assembly, comprising 36 members from the legislature of each country, convened in official session for the first time shortly afterwards. Progress within the framework of the CSR stalled, however, in the early 2000s. Azerbaijan, Georgia, Moldova and Ukraine co-operated increasingly from the late 1990s as the so-called GUAM group, which envisaged implementing joint economic and transportation initiatives (such developing a Eurasian Trans-Caucasus transportation corridor) and establishing the GUAM Free Trade Zone. Uzbekistan was a member of the group during the period April 1999–May 2005, during which time it was known as 'GUUAM'. The group agreed in September 2000 to convene regular annual summits of member countries' heads of state and to organize meetings of ministers of foreign affairs at least twice a year. Meeting in Kyiv, Ukraine, in May 2006 the heads of state of Azerbaijan, Georgia, Moldova and Ukraine adopted a charter formally inaugurating GUAM as a full international organization and renaming it Organization for Democracy and Economic Development—GUAM. The heads of state suggested at that time that the GUAM countries might withdraw from the CIS. In April 2003 Armenia, Belarus, Kazakhstan, Kyrgyzstan, Tajikistan and Russia established the Collective Security Treaty Organization (see below). In 1994 Kazakhstan, Kyrgyzstan, Tajikistan and Uzbekistan formed the Central Asian Economic Community. In February 2002 those countries relaunched the grouping as the Central Asian Co-operation Organization (CACO), to indicate that co-operation between member states had extended to political and security matters. Russia joined the organization in 2004. In October 2005, at a summit of CACO leaders in St Petersburg, Russia, it was announced that the organization would be merged with EurAsEC. This was achieved in January 2006 with the accession to EurAsEC of Uzbekistan, which had hitherto been the only member of CACO that did not also belong to the Community. In November 2008 Uzbekistan announced a temporary withdrawal from EurAsEC.

The CIS regularly sends observer teams to monitor legislative and presidential elections in member states. In March 2005 Ukraine announced that it was to suspend its participation in the CIS Election Monitoring Organization (CIS-EMO, registered as a non-governmental organization in December 2003), owing to discrepancies in the findings of the observers of that body with those of the OSCE during the Ukrainian presidential election that was held in October and December 2004. The CIS Convention on Democratic Elections Standards, Electoral Rights and Freedoms in Member States, adopted in October 2002, has been ratified by Armenia, Kyrgyzstan, Moldova, Russia and Tajikistan.

In August 2005 a number of recommendations aimed at restructuring the organs of the CIS, with a view to increasing the overall efficiency of the organization, were presented to the summit of the Council of Heads of State, which was held in Kazan, Russia. Several declarations were signed at the Kazan summit, including a document on co-operation in humanitarian projects and combating illegal migration; however, a consensus on far-reaching reform of the organization failed to be reached by CIS leaders at that time. The heads of state of Armenia, Georgia, Turkmenistan (which had downgraded its full membership of the CIS to associate membership in 2005) and Ukraine did not attend an informal summit of CIS leaders convened in Moscow, Russia, in July 2006.

At the 2007 CIS summit meeting, held in Dushanbe, Tajikistan, in October, CIS heads of state (excluding those of Georgia and Turkmenistan) adopted the 'Concept for Further Development of the CIS' and an action plan for its implementation. Azerbaijan endorsed the document, but reserved the right to abstain from implementing certain clauses. The Concept cited the 'long-term formation of an integrated economic and political association' as a major objective of the Commonwealth, and determined that the multi-sector nature of the organization should be retained and that the harmonized development of its interacting spheres should continue to be promoted. Further goals detailed in the Concept included: supporting regional socio-economic stability and international security; improving the economic competitiveness of member states; supporting the accession of member states to the World Trade Organization (WTO); improving regional living standards and conditions; promoting inter-parliamentary co-operation; increasing co-operation between national migration agencies; harmonizing national legislation; and standardizing CIS structures and bodies. The state chairing the Council of Heads of State was to have responsibility for co-ordinating the implementation of the Concept. Leaders attending the Dushanbe summit also determined to establish a special body to oversee migration in the region and adopted an agreement aimed at promoting the civil rights of migrants.

In mid-August 2008, following a period of conflict between Georgian and Russian forces earlier in that month, Georgia announced its intention to withdraw from the CIS; this came into effect in August 2009. The 2008 regular CIS summit meeting was convened in Bishkek, Kyrgyzstan, in October, without the participation of Azerbaijan, (outgoing) Georgia, or Ukraine. Leaders attending the summit meeting considered—and determined to send for revision—a draft 'CIS Economic Development Strategy until 2020' and also discussed means of alleviating the regional impact of the ongoing global financial crisis. The 2009 CIS summit meeting was hosted by the Moldovan Government in Chişinău, in October, without participation by the heads of state of Tajikistan, Turkmenistan or Uzbekistan. The meeting endorsed the 'CIS Economic Development Strategy until 2020', discussed strengthening member states' co-operation in combating the impact of the global financial crisis, and adopted a joint action plan of related measures. It also addressed advancing co-operation in the humanitarian and collective security spheres. The heads of state adopted a Declaration on the forthcoming 65th anniversary commemorating the end of the Second World War, and declared 2010 as CIS Year of Veterans. Leaders participating in the 2010 summit meeting, convened in December, in Moscow, signed an agreement on advancing military co-operation until 2015, as well as concluding agreements addressing CIS common border policy; trafficking in humans and drugs; terrorism; and combating extremist terrorist activity. The 2011 summit meeting was held in September, in Dushanbe; participation by Azerbaijan, Belarus and Uzbekistan was at only prime ministerial level. The summit gave consideration to a report analysing progress during the first 20 years of the CIS, and to a draft programme on co-operation in combating illegal migration during 2012–14. Food security was a priority area of focus for CIS member states at that time. The 2012 summit meeting was to be held in November, in Aşgabat, Turkmenistan.

In May 2009 the heads of state or government of Armenia, Azerbaijan, Belarus, Georgia, Moldova and Ukraine, and representatives of the EU and the heads of state or government, and other representatives, of its member states, convened in Prague, Czech Republic, issued a Joint Declaration on establishing an Eastern Partnership. The main goal of the Eastern Partnership (to be facilitated through a specific Eastern dimension of the EU's European Neighbourhood Policy) was, through EU support for political and socio-economic reforms in interested partner countries, to create the necessary conditions to accelerate political association and further economic integration with the EU.

ECONOMIC AFFAIRS

At a meeting of the Council of Heads of Government in March 1992 agreement was reached on repayment of the foreign debt of the former USSR. Agreements were also signed on pensions, joint tax policy and the servicing of internal debt. In May an accord on repayment of inter-state debt and the issue of balance of payments statements was adopted by the heads of government, meeting in Tashkent, Uzbekistan. In July it was decided to establish an economic court in Minsk, Belarus.

The CIS Charter, adopted in January 1993, provided for the establishment of an economic co-ordination committee. In February, at a meeting of the heads of foreign economic departments, a foreign economic council was formed. In May all member states, with the exception of Turkmenistan, adopted a declaration of support for increased economic union and, in September, agreement was reached by all states except Ukraine and Turkmenistan on a framework for economic union, including the gradual removal of tariffs and creation of a currency union. Turkmenistan was subsequently admitted as a full member of the economic union in December 1993 and Ukraine as an associate member in April 1994.

At the Council of Heads of Government meeting in September 1994 all member states, except Turkmenistan, agreed to establish an Inter-state Economic Committee to implement economic treaties adopted within the context of an economic union. The establishment of a payments union to improve the settlement of accounts was also agreed. In April 1998 CIS heads of state resolved to incorporate the functions of the Inter-state Economic Committee, along with those of other working bodies and sectional committees, into a new CIS Executive Committee.

Guidelines adopted by the Council of Heads of State in April 1999 concerning the future development of the CIS identified economic co-operation and the establishment of a free trade zone (see Trade) as priority areas for action. Improving the economic competitiveness of member states was a primary focus of the 'Concept for the Integrated Economic Development of the CIS' that was adopted by the organization's October 2007 summit meeting. A 'CIS Economic Development Strategy until 2020' was adopted by the October 2009 Chişinău summit.

TRADE

Agreement was reached on the free movement of goods between republics at a meeting of the Council of Heads of State in February 1992, and in April 1994 an agreement on the creation of a CIS free trade zone (envisaged as the first stage of economic union) was concluded. In July a council of the heads of customs committees, meeting in Moscow, approved a draft framework for customs legislation in CIS countries, to facilitate the establishment of a free trade zone. The framework was approved by all the participants, with the exception of Turkmenistan. Draft customs union legislation was approved by the first session of the Inter-state Economic Committee, held in November 1994. In April 1999 CIS heads of state signed a protocol to the 1994 free trade area accord, which aimed to accelerate co-operation. In June 2000 the Council of Heads of State adopted a plan and schedule for the implementation of priority measures related to the creation of the free trade zone, and at the September 2003 summit meeting Russia, Belarus, Kazakhstan and Ukraine signed the Union of Four agreement establishing the framework for a Common Economic Space (CES, see below).

The development of a customs union and the strengthening of intra-CIS trade were objectives endorsed by all participants, with the exception of Georgia, at the Council of Heads of Government meeting held in March 1997. In March 1998 Russia, Belarus, Kazakhstan and Kyrgyzstan signed an agreement establishing a customs union, which was to be implemented in two stages: firstly, the removal of trade restrictions and the unification of trade and customs regulations; followed by the integration of economic, monetary and trade policies. In February 1999 Tajikistan signed the 1998 agreement to become the fifth member of the customs union. In October 1999 the heads of state of the five member states of the customs union reiterated their political determination to implement the customs union and approved a programme to harmonize national legislation to create a single economic space. In May 2000 the heads of state announced their intention to raise the status of the customs union to that of an inter-state economic organization, and, in October, the leaders signed the founding treaty of EurAsEC. Under the new structure member states aimed to formulate a unified foreign economic policy, and, taking into account existing customs agreements, collectively to pursue the creation of the planned single economic space. In the following month the five member governments signed an agreement enabling visa-free travel within the new Community. (Earlier in 2000 Russia had withdrawn from a CIS-wide visa-free travel arrangement agreed in 1992. Kazakhstan, Turkmenistan and Uzbekistan subsequently withdrew from the agreement, and Belarus announced its intention to do so in late 2005.) In December 2000 member states of the Community adopted several documents aimed at facilitating economic co-operation. EurAsEC, governed by an inter-state council based in Astana, Kazakhstan, was formally inaugurated in October 2001. In October 2003 the Community was granted observer status at the UN. The Union of Four agreement on establishing the framework for a CES, adopted in September 2003 by the leaders of Belarus, Kazakhstan, Russia and Ukraine, envisaged the creation of a free trade zone and the gradual harmonization of tariffs, customs and transport legislation. While participation at each stage would remain optional, decisions would be obligatory and certain areas of sovereignty would eventually be ceded to a council of heads of state and a commission. The Union of Four accord entered into force in April 2004. Meeting on the sidelines of the CIS summit held in October 2007, EurAsEC leaders determined to establish a fully operational customs union over the next three years, with Belarus, Kazakhstan and Russia as the founding members, and Kyrgyzstan, Tajikistan and Uzbekistan to join at a later date, once they had achieved the requisite accession conditions. Ukraine, which was also committed to participation in the GUAM Free Trade Zone, was not at that time participating actively in the negotiating process on the CES. It was envisaged that the CES, open to accession by other CIS member states, would form the basis of the planned wider EurAsEC economic integration. Despite significant growth in the gross domestic product of the poorer states of the CIS at that time (Armenia, Azerbaijan, Georgia, Kyrgyzstan, Moldova, Tajikistan and Uzbekistan, then known as the 'CIS-7'), in April 2005 the IMF called for greater harmonization of trade rules within the CIS, as well as liberalization of transit policies and the removal of non-tariff barriers. The customs union between Russia, Belarus and Kazakhstan entered into formal existence on 1 January 2010, when a common external tariff was adopted; on 1 July 2010 a harmonized customs code came into force. In December of that year the heads of state of Russia, Belarus and Kazakhstan signed several agreements aimed at finalizing the establishment of the planned CES, and in November 2011 they signed a declaration on Eurasian economic integration and adopted a roadmap outlining integration processes aimed at creating a Eurasian Economic Union, to be established, provisionally, by 1 Jan. 2015, and to be based on the customs union and proposed CES. In October 2011, in St Petersburg, the leaders of Russia, Armenia, Belarus, Kazakhstan, Kyrgyzstan, Moldova, Tajikistan, and Ukraine (therefore all CIS states except for Azerbaijan, Uzbekistan and Turkmenistan) signed an agreement establishing the CIS Free Trade Area—CISFTA; this aimed to simplify trade and economic relations, and to regulate a free trade regime, replacing several previous multilateral agreements and around 100 bilateral agreements. The CIS leaders also adopted an accord on basic principles of currency regulation and currency controls within the CIS.

The CIS maintains a 'loose co-ordination' on issues related to applications by member states to join the WTO. Supporting the accession of member states to the WTO was a primary focus of the Concept for Further Development of the CIS that was adopted by the October 2007 summit meeting of the Commonwealth. Russia, Belarus and Kazakhstan, whose customs union entered into formal existence in 2010, see above, aim to synchronize their positions on WTO accession.

BANKING AND FINANCE

In February 1992 CIS heads of state agreed to retain the rouble as the common currency for trade between the republics. However, in July 1993, in an attempt to control inflation, notes printed before 1993 were withdrawn from circulation and no new ones were issued until January 1994. Despite various agreements to recreate the 'rouble zone', including a protocol agreement signed in September 1993 by six states, it effectively remained confined to Tajikistan, which joined in January 1994, and Belarus, which joined in April. Both those countries proceeded to introduce national currencies in May 1995. In January 1993, at the signing of the CIS Charter, the member countries endorsed the establishment of an inter-state bank to facilitate payments between the republics and to co-ordinate monetary credit policy. Russia was to hold 50% of shares in the bank, but decisions were to be made only with a two-thirds' majority approval. In December 2000, in accordance with the CSR and Treaty of Union (see above), the Presidents of Belarus and Russia signed an agreement providing for the adoption by Belarus of the Russian currency from 1 January 2005, and for the introduction of a new joint Union currency by 1 January 2008; the adoption by Belarus of the Russian currency was, however, subsequently postponed. Following the entry into formal existence on 1 January 2010 of the customs union between Belarus, Russia and Kazakhstan (see above), the introduction of a new common currency unit for the members of the union was under consideration.

In October 2004 Russia and Kazakhstan announced a proposal to establish a CIS Development Bank, with capital of €1m.

REGIONAL SECURITY

At a meeting of heads of government in March 1992 agreements on settling inter-state conflicts were signed by all participating states (except Turkmenistan). At the same meeting an agreement on the status of border troops was signed by five states. In May a five-year Collective Security Treaty was signed. In July further documents were signed on collective security and it was agreed to establish joint peace-making forces to intervene in CIS disputes. (CIS peace-keeping forces were sent into Tajikistan, and Abkhazia, Georgia during 1993–2000, and 1994–2009, respectively.) In December 1993 the Council of Defence Ministers agreed to establish a secretariat to co-ordinate military co-operation. In November 1995 the Council of Defence Ministers authorized the establishment of a Joint Air Defence System, to be co-ordinated largely by Russia. In the context of the CSR (see above) Russia and Belarus also agreed to develop a joint air defence unit, although implementation of this was postponed. (In February 2009 the two states announced plans to proceed with the establishment of a joint integrated air defence system.) In April 1999 Armenia, Belarus, Kazakhstan, Kyrgyzstan, Russia and Tajikistan signed a protocol to extend the Collective Security Treaty (while Azerbaijan, Georgia and Uzbekistan withdrew from the agreement). In April 1998 the Council proposed drawing up a draft programme for military and technical co-operation between member countries and also discussed procedures advising on the use and maintenance of armaments and military hardware. The programme was approved by CIS heads of state in October 2002.

In October 2000 the six signatory states to the Collective Security Treaty signed an agreement on the Status of Forces and Means of Collective Security Systems, establishing a joint rapid deployment function. The so-called CIS Collective Rapid Reaction Force was to be assembled to combat insurgencies, with particular reference to transborder terrorism from Afghanistan, and also to deter transborder illegal drugs-trafficking. In June 2001 a CIS Anti-terrorism Centre was established in Moscow. A Central Asian subdivision of the CIS Anti-Terrorism Centre was established in Bishkek, Kyrgyzstan, in October 2002. In October 2001, in response to the major terrorist attacks perpetrated in September against targets in the USA—allegedly co-ordinated by militant fundamentalist Islamist leader Osama bin Laden—the parties to the Collective Security Treaty adopted a new anti-terrorism plan. In December 2002 the committee of the Collective Security Treaty member countries adopted a protocol on the exchange of expertise and information on terrorist organizations and their activities. In April 2003 the signatory states determined to establish the Collective Security Treaty Organization (CSTO); ratification of its founding documents was completed by September, when it applied for UN observer status (granted in December 2004). The CIS summit in September 2003 approved draft decisions to control the sale of portable anti-aircraft missiles and to set up a joint co-ordination structure to address illegal immigration. During September 2004 the CIS Council of Heads of State determined to establish a Security Council, comprising the ministers responsible for foreign affairs and for defence, and heads of security and border control.

The signatory countries to the Collective Security Treaty participate in regular so-called CIS Southern Shield joint military exercises. A summit meeting of CSTO leaders held in October 2007 endorsed documents enabling the future establishment of CSTO joint peace-keeping forces and the creation of a co-ordination council for the heads of member states' emergency response agencies. In July 2008 the Council of Defence Ministers, convened in Bishkek, discussed strengthening air defence co-operation until 2015. In February 2009 the participating states in the CSTO determined to develop a rapid reaction military force, which would be deployed to combat terrorists and in response to regional emergencies. A meeting of the Council of Defence Ministers held in June 2009, in Moscow, addressed conceptual approaches to the development of military co-operation among CIS countries until 2015.

An Agreement on the Co-operation of the CIS Member States in Combating Trafficking in Persons, Human Organs and Tissues was adopted in November 2005 and has been ratified by Azerbaijan, Armenia, Belarus, Kyrgyzstan and Russia. In August 2005 CIS member states adopted a blueprint on joint co-operation in combating terrorism and extremism; the blueprint provided for the exchange of relevant information between member states and for the extradition of individuals suspected of financing or committing terrorist acts. In October 2009 CIS heads of states approved a number of additional measures for strengthening border control.

OTHER ACTIVITIES

An agreement on legislative co-operation was signed at an Inter-Parliamentary Conference in January 1992; joint commissions were established to co-ordinate action on economy, law, pensions, housing, energy and ecology. The CIS Charter, formulated in January 1993, provided for the establishment of an inter-state court. In October 1994 a Convention on the rights of minorities was adopted at the meeting of the heads of state; this has been ratified by Azerbaijan, Armenia, Belarus, Kyrgyzstan and Tajikistan. In May 1995, at the sixth plenary session of the IPA, several acts to improve co-ordination of legislation were approved, relating to migration of labour, consumer rights, and the rights of prisoners of war; revised legislation on labour migration and the social protection of migrant workers was adopted in November 2005. A CIS Convention on Human Rights and Fundamental Freedoms, adopted at that time, and incorporating the Statute of a proposed CIS Commission on Human Rights, has been ratified by Belarus, Kyrgyzstan, Russia and Tajikistan. In November 2006 an agreement on the protection of participants in the criminal justice system was signed by eight member states. In November 2008 the CIS Convention on the Legal Status of Working Migrants and their Families was signed by the heads of member states.

The creation of a Council of Ministers of Internal Affairs was approved at the heads of state meeting in January 1996; the Council was to promote co-operation between the law enforcement bodies of member states. The IPA has approved a number of model laws, relating to areas including banking and financial services; charity; defence; ecology, the economy; education; the regulation of refugee problems; combating terrorism; and social issues, including obligatory social insurance against production accidents and occupational diseases.

The CIS has held a number of discussions relating to the environment. In July 1992 agreements were concluded to establish an Inter-state Ecological Council. It was also agreed in that month to establish *Mir*, an inter-state television and radio company. In October 2002 a decision was made by CIS heads of government to enhance mutual understanding and co-operation between members countries through *Mir* radio and television broadcasts. In February 1995 the IPA established a Council of Heads of News Agencies, in order to promote the concept of a single information area. CIS leaders meeting in Moscow in May 2005 agreed to sign a declaration aimed at enhancing co-operation between CIS members in the humanitarian, cultural and scientific spheres.

A Connect CIS Summit was convened by the International Telecommunications Union and partners in Minsk, Belarus, in November 2009, with participation by CIS leaders and representatives from businesses and financial institutions, with the aim of mobilizing the financial and technical resources required to facilitate a swift regional transition towards a digital infrastructure and services. The Summit urged greater investment in regional ICT broadband access.

The Minsk Agreement

(8 December 1991)

PREAMBLE

We, the Republic of Belarus, the Russian Federation and the Republic of Ukraine, as founder states of the Union of Soviet Socialist Republics (USSR), which signed the 1922 Union Treaty, further described as the high contracting parties, conclude that the USSR has ceased to exist as a subject of international law and a geopolitical reality.

Taking as our basis the historic community of our peoples and the ties which have been established between them, taking into account the bilateral treaties concluded between the high contracting parties;

striving to build democratic law-governed states; intending to develop our relations on the basis of mutual recognition and respect for state sovereignty, the inalienable right to self-determination, the principles of equality and non-interference in internal affairs, repudiation of the use of force and of economic or any other methods of coercion, settlement of contentious problems by means of mediation and other generally recognized principles and norms of international law;

considering that further development and strengthening of relations of friendship, good-neighbourliness and mutually beneficial co-operation between our states correspond to the vital national interests of their peoples and serve the cause of peace and security;

confirming our adherence to the goals and principles of the United Nations Charter, the Helsinki Final Act and other documents of the Conference on Security and Co-operation in Europe;

and committing ourselves to observe the generally recognized internal norms on human rights and the rights of peoples, we have agreed the following:

Article 1.

The high contracting parties form the Commonwealth of Independent States.

Article 2.

The high contracting parties guarantee their citizens equal rights and freedoms regardless of nationality or other distinctions. Each of the high contracting parties guarantees the citizens of the other parties, and also persons without citizenship that live on its territory, civil, political, social, economic and cultural rights and freedoms in accordance with generally recognized international norms of human rights, regardless of national allegiance or other distinctions.

Article 3.

The high contracting parties, desiring to promote the expression, preservation and development of the ethnic, cultural, linguistic and religious individuality of the national minorities resident on their territories, and that of the unique ethno-cultural regions that have come into being, take them under their protection.

Article 4.

The high contracting parties will develop the equal and mutually beneficial co-operation of their peoples and states in the spheres of politics, the economy, culture, education, public health, protection of the environment, science and trade and in the humanitarian and other spheres, will promote the broad exchange of information and will conscientiously and unconditionally observe reciprocal obligations.

The parties consider it a necessity to conclude agreements on co-operation in the above spheres.

Article 5.

The high contracting parties recognize and respect one another's territorial integrity and the inviolability of existing borders within the Commonwealth.

They guarantee openness of borders, freedom of movement for citizens and of transmission of information within the Commonwealth.

Article 6.

The member states of the Commonwealth will co-operate in safeguarding international peace and security and in implementing effective measures for reducing weapons and military spending. They seek the elimination of all nuclear weapons and universal total disarmament under strict international control.

The parties will respect one another's aspiration to attain the status of a non-nuclear zone and a neutral state.

The member states of the Commonwealth will preserve and maintain under united command a common military-strategic space, including unified control over nuclear weapons, the procedure for implementing which is regulated by a special agreement.

They also jointly guarantee the necessary conditions for the stationing and functioning of and for material and social provision for the strategic armed forces. The parties contract to pursue a harmonized policy on questions of social protection and pension provision for members of the services and their families.

Article 7.

The high contracting parties recognize that within the sphere of their activities, implemented on the equal basis through the common co-ordinating institutions of the Commonwealth, will be the following:

co-operation in the sphere of foreign policy;

co-operation in forming and developing the united economic area, the common European and Eurasian markets, in the area of customs policy;

co-operation in developing transport and communication systems;

co-operation in preservation of the environment, and participation in creating a comprehensive international system of ecological safety;

migration policy issues;

and fighting organized crime.

Article 8.

The parties realize the planetary character of the Chernobyl catastrophe and pledge themselves to unite and co-ordinate their efforts in minimizing and overcoming its consequences.

To these ends they have decided to conclude a special agreement which will take consideration of the gravity of the consequences of this catastrophe.

Article 9.

The disputes regarding interpretation and application of the norms of this agreement are to be solved by way of negotiations between the appropriate bodies, and, when necessary, at the level of heads of the governments and states.

Article 10.

Each of the high contracting parties reserves the right to suspend the validity of the present agreement or individual articles thereof, after informing the parties to the agreement of this a year in advance.

The clauses of the present agreement may be addended to or amended with the common consent of the high contracting parties.

Article 11.

From the moment that the present agreement is signed, the norms of third states, including the former USSR, are not permitted to be implemented on the territories of the signatory states.

Article 12.

The high contracting parties guarantee the fulfilment of the international obligations binding upon them from the treaties and agreements of the former USSR.

Article 13.

The present agreement does not affect the obligations of the high contracting parties in regard to third states.

The present agreement is open for all member states of the former USSR to join, and also for other states which share the goals and principles of the present agreement.

Article 14.

The city of Minsk is the official location of the co-ordinating bodies of the Commonwealth.

The activities of bodies of the former USSR are discontinued on the territories of the member states of the Commonwealth.

The Alma-Ata Declaration

(21 December 1991)

PREAMBLE

The independent states:

The Republic of Armenia, the Republic of Azerbaijan, the Republic of Belarus, the Republic of Kazakhstan, the Republic of Kyrgyzstan, the Republic of Moldova, the Russian Federation, the Republic of Tajikistan, the Republic of Turkmenistan, the Republic of Ukraine and the Republic of Uzbekistan;

seeking to build democratic law-governed states, the relations between which will develop on the basis of mutual recognition and respect for state sovereignty and sovereign equality, the inalienable right to self-determination, principles of equality and non-interference in the internal affairs, the rejection of the use of force, the threat of force and economic and any other methods of pressure, a peaceful settlement of disputes, respect for human rights and freedoms, including the rights of national minorities, a conscientious fulfilment of commitments and other generally recognized principles and standards of international law;

recognizing and respecting each other's territorial integrity and the inviolability of the existing borders;

believing that the strengthening of the relations of friendship, good neighbourliness and mutually advantageous co-operation, which has deep historic roots, meets the basic interests of nations and promotes the cause of peace and security;

being aware of their responsibility for the preservation of civilian peace and inter-ethnic accord;

being loyal to the objectives and principles of the agreement on the creation of the Commonwealth of Independent States;

are making the following statement.

THE DECLARATION

Co-operation between members of the Commonwealth will be carried out in accordance with the principle of equality through co-ordinating institutions formed on a parity basis and operating in the way established by the agreements between members of the Commonwealth, which is neither a state, nor a super-state structure.

In order to ensure international strategic stability and security, allied command of the military-strategic forces and a single control over nuclear weapons will be preserved, the sides will respect each other's desire to attain the status of a non-nuclear and (or) neutral state.

The Commonwealth of Independent States is open, with the agreement of all its participants, to the states—members of the former USSR, as well as other states—sharing the goals and principles of the Commonwealth.

The allegiance to co-operation in the formation and development of the common economic space, and all-European and Eurasian markets, is being confirmed.

With the formation of the Commonwealth of Independent States, the USSR ceases to exist. Member states of the Commonwealth guarantee, in accordance with their constitutional procedures, the fulfilment of international obligations, stemming from the treaties and agreements of the former USSR.

Member states of the Commonwealth pledge to observe strictly the principles of this declaration.

Agreement on Strategic Forces

(30 December 1991)

Guided by the necessity for a co-ordinated and organized solution to issues in the sphere of the control of the strategic forces and the single control over nuclear weapons, the Republic of Armenia, the Republic of Azerbaijan, the Republic of Belarus, the Republic of Kazakhstan, the Republic of Kyrgyzstan, the Republic of Moldova, the Russian Federation, the Republic of Tajikistan, the Republic of Turkmenistan, the Republic of Ukraine and the Republic of Uzbekistan, subsequently referred to as 'the member states of the Commonwealth', have agreed on the following:

Article 1.

The term 'strategic forces' means: groupings, formations, units, institutions, the military training institutes for the strategic missile troops, for the air force, for the navy and for the air defences; the directorates of the Space Command and of the airborne troops, and of strategic and operational intelligence, and the nuclear technical units and also the forces, equipment and other military facilities designed for the control and maintenance of the strategic forces of the former USSR (the schedule is to be determined for each state participating in the Commonwealth in a separate protocol).

Article 2.

The member states of the Commonwealth undertake to observe the international treaties of the former USSR, to pursue a co-ordinated policy in the area of international security, disarmament and arms control, and to participate in the preparation and implementation of programmes for reductions in arms and armed forces. The member states of the Commonwealth are immediately entering into negotiations with one another and also with other states which were formerly part of the USSR, but which have not joined the Commonwealth, with the aim of ensuring guarantees and developing mechanisms for implementing the aforementioned treaties.

Article 3.

The member states of the Commonwealth recognize the need for joint command of strategic forces and for maintaining unified control of nuclear weapons, and other types of weapons of mass destruction, of the armed forces of the former USSR.

Article 4.

Until the complete elimination of nuclear weapons, the decision on the need for their use is taken by the President of the Russian Federation in agreement with the heads of the Republic of Belarus, the Republic of Kazakhstan and the Republic of Ukraine, and in consultation with the heads of the other member states of the Commonwealth.

Until their destruction in full, nuclear weapons located on the territory of the Republic of Ukraine shall be under the control of the Combined Strategic Forces Command, with the aim that they not be used and be dismantled by the end of 1994, including tactical nuclear weapons by 1 July 1992.

The process of destruction of nuclear weapons located on the territory of the Republic of Belarus and the Republic of Ukraine shall take place with the participation of the Republic of Belarus, the Russian Federation and the Republic of Ukraine under the joint control of the Commonwealth states.

Article 5.

The status of strategic forces and the procedure for service in them shall be defined in a special agreement.

Article 6.

This agreement shall enter into force from the moment of its signing and shall be terminated by decision of the signatory states or the Council of Heads of State of the Commonwealth.

This agreement shall cease to apply to a signatory state from whose territory strategic forces or nuclear weapons are withdrawn.

Note: The last nuclear warheads were removed from Kazakhstan in April 1995, from Belarus in March 1996 and from Ukraine in May–June 1996. All strategic offensive arms in Belarus and Kazakhstan have been destroyed, and those in Ukraine are being eliminated.

COOPERATION COUNCIL FOR THE ARAB STATES OF THE GULF

Address: POB 7153, Riyadh 11462, Saudi Arabia.

Telephone: (1) 482-7777; **fax:** (1) 482-9089; **internet:** www.gcc-sg.org.

More generally known as the Gulf Cooperation Council (GCC), the organization was established on 25 May 1981 by six Arab states.

MEMBERS*

Bahrain	Oman	Saudi Arabia
Kuwait	Qatar	United Arab Emirates

* In December 2001 the Supreme Council admitted Yemen (which applied to join the organization as a full member in 1996) as a member of the GCC's Arab Bureau of Education for the Gulf States, as a participant in meetings of GCC ministers of health and of labour and social affairs, and, alongside the GCC member states, as a participant in the biennial Gulf Cup football tournament. In September 2008 Yemen's inclusion in future GCC development planning was approved and Yemen was admitted to GCC control and auditing apparatuses. Negotiations are ongoing on the full accession of Yemen to the GCC by 2016. In May 2011 the GCC invited Jordan and Morocco to submit membership applications.

Organization

(June 2012)

SUPREME COUNCIL

The Supreme Council is the highest authority of the GCC. It comprises the heads of member states and holds one regular session annually, and in emergency session if demanded by two or more members. The Council also convenes an annual consultative meeting. The Presidency of the Council is undertaken by each state in turn, in alphabetical order. The Supreme Council draws up the overall policy of the organization; it discusses recommendations and laws presented to it by the Ministerial Council and the Secretariat General in preparation for endorsement. The GCC's charter provided for the creation of a commission for the settlement of disputes between member states, to be attached to and appointed by the Supreme Council. The Supreme Council convenes the commission for the settlement of disputes on an ad hoc basis to address altercations between member states as they arise. The 32nd annual meeting of the Supreme Council was convened in December 2011 in Riyadh, Saudi Arabia.

CONSULTATIVE COMMISSION

The Consultative Commission, comprising 30 members (five from each member state) nominated for a three-year period, acts as an advisory body, considering matters referred to it by the Supreme Council.

COMMISSION FOR THE SETTLEMENT OF DISPUTES

The Commission for the Settlement of Disputes is formed by the Supreme Council for each case, on an ad hoc basis in accordance with the nature of each specific dispute.

MINISTERIAL COUNCIL

The Ministerial Council consists of the ministers of foreign affairs of member states (or other ministers acting on their behalf), meeting every three months, and in emergency session if demanded by two or more members. It prepares for the meetings of the Supreme Council, and draws up policies, recommendations, studies and projects aimed at developing co-operation and co-ordination among member states in various spheres. GCC ministerial committees have been established in a number of areas of co-operation; sectoral ministerial meetings are held periodically.

SECRETARIAT GENERAL

The Secretariat assists member states in implementing recommendations by the Supreme and Ministerial Councils, and prepares reports and studies, budgets and accounts. The Secretary-General is appointed by the Supreme Council for a three-year term renewable once. The position is rotated among member states in order to ensure equal representation. The Secretariat comprises the following divisions and departments: Political Affairs; Economic Affairs; Human and Environmental Affairs; Military Affairs; Security; Legal Affairs; the Office of the Secretary-General; Finance and Administrative Affairs; a Patent Bureau; an Administrative Development Unit; an Internal Auditing Unit; an Information Centre; and a Telecommunications Bureau (based in Bahrain). Assistant Secretaries-General, in charge of Political Affairs; Economic Affairs; Human and Environmental Affairs; Military Affairs; Security, are appointed by the Ministerial Council upon the recommendation of the Secretary-General. All member states contribute in equal proportions towards the budget of the Secretariat. There is a GCC delegation office in Brussels, Belgium, of which the head is appointed by the Ministerial Council for a three-year term of office.

Secretary-General: ABDUL LATIF BIN RASHID AL-ZAYANI (Bahrain).

Activities

The GCC was established following a series of meetings of foreign ministers of the states concerned, culminating in an agreement on the basic details of its charter on 10 March 1981. The Charter was signed by the six heads of state on 25 May. It describes the organization as providing 'the means for realizing co-ordination, integration and co-operation' in all economic, social and cultural affairs. In December 2011 the 32nd summit of the Supreme Council welcomed a proposal by King Abdullah of Saudi Arabia specifying that the basis of GCC collaboration should progress from the stage of co-operation to full union (as an 'Arab Gulf Union Council'). The summit directed the Ministerial Council to form in 2012 a specialized commission, to comprise three members from each member state, to study the proposal.

COMPREHENSIVE DEVELOPMENT STRATEGY FOR 2010–25

In December 1998 the Supreme Council approved a long-term strategy for regional development, covering the period 2000–25, and aimed at achieving integrated, sustainable development in all member states and the co-ordination of national development plans. Meeting in December 2010 the 31st summit of GCC heads of state adopted a revised comprehensive development strategy for member states, covering 2010–25. The updated strategy identified several ongoing challenges including: promoting integration over competition, and collective over national development efforts, within the grouping; scarcity of water resources in the region, the high salinity content in local water, and the high cost of alternative water resources; limitations on cultivating farming lands; the disproportionate engagement of national citizens in state employment and dependence on foreign workers in the non-governmental labour market; incompatibility between educational and training goals and the needs of the labour market (the region has a large non-resident population); investment decline in certain sectors, and migration of national capital abroad owing to limited local investment opportunities; the existence of budgetary deficits; the potential impacts of climate change on the environment; and global development, security and economic challenges. The following strategic goals were outlined: pursuing a framework enabling sustainable development; ensuring adequate water for development needs; achieving self-sufficiency in meeting the security and defence needs of the GCC development process; achieving integrated economic partnership; eliminating sources of vulnerability from the GCC economic environment; deriving maximum benefit from infrastructure facilities; technical and scientific capacity building; enhancing social development in the areas of education and training, health, and intellectual and cultural development; and enhancing the productivity of the GCC labour force.

ECONOMIC CO-OPERATION

In November 1981 GCC ministers drew up a Unified Economic Agreement covering freedom of movement of people and capital, the abolition of customs duties, technical co-operation, harmonization of banking regulations and financial and monetary co-ordination. At the same time GCC heads of state approved the formation of a Gulf Investment Corporation, to be based in Kuwait (see below). In March 1983 customs duties on domestic products of the Gulf states were abolished, and new regulations allowing free movement of workers and vehicles between member states were also introduced. A common minimum customs levy (of between 4% and 20%) on foreign imports was imposed in 1986. In February 1987 the governors of the member states' central banks agreed in principle to co-ordinate their rates of exchange, and this was approved by the Supreme Council in November. It was subsequently agreed to link the Gulf currencies to a 'basket' of other currencies. In April 1993 the Gulf central bank governors decided to allow Kuwait's currency to become part of the GCC monetary system that was established following Iraq's invasion of Kuwait in order to defend the Gulf currencies. In May 1992 GCC trade ministers announced the objective of establishing a GCC common market. Meeting in September GCC ministers reached agreement on the application of a unified system of tariffs by March 1993. A meeting of the Supreme Council, held in December 1992, however, decided to mandate GCC officials to formulate a plan for the introduction of common external tariffs, to be presented to the Council in December 1993. Only the tax on tobacco products was to be standardized from March 1993, at a rate of 50% (later increased to 70%). In April 1994 ministers of finance agreed to pursue a gradual approach to the unification of tariffs. A technical committee, which had been constituted to consider aspects of establishing a customs union, met for the first time in June 1998. In November 1999 the Supreme Council concluded an agreement to establish the customs union by 1 March 2005. However, in December 2001 the Supreme Council, meeting in Muscat, Oman, adopted a new agreement on regional economic union ('Economic Agreement Between the Arab GCC States'), which superseded the 1981 Unified Economic Agreement. The new accord brought forward the deadline for the establishment of the proposed customs union to 1 January 2003 and provided for a standard tariff level of 5% for foreign imports (with the exception of 53 essential commodities previously exempted by the Supreme Council). The agreement also provided for the introduction, by January 2010, of a GCC single currency, linked to the US dollar (this deadline, however, was not met—see below). The Supreme Council also authorized the creation of a new independent authority for overseeing the unification of specifications and standards throughout member states.

The GCC customs union was launched, as planned, on 1 January 2003. In July the GCC entered into negotiations with Yemen on harmonizing economic legislation. In December 2005 the Supreme Council approved standards for the introduction of the planned single currency. The GCC Common Market was inaugurated on 1 January 2008. Oman and the United Arab Emirates (UAE) withdrew from the process to introduce a single currency in 2007 and 2009, respectively. An accord on Gulf Monetary Union was signed in June 2009 by Bahrain, Kuwait, Qatar and Saudi Arabia, and was approved by the 30th meeting of the Supreme Council, held in Kuwait in December. In May 2010 the GCC Secretary-General stated that the introduction of the single currency was unlikely to occur for at least five years.

In April 1993 GCC central bank governors agreed to establish a joint banking supervisory committee, in order to devise rules for GCC banks to operate in other member states. In December 1997 GCC heads of state authorized guidelines to this effect. These were to apply only to banks established at least 10 years previously with a share capital of more than US $100m.

The 29th summit meeting of heads of state, held in Muscat, Oman, in December 2008, discussed the ongoing global financial crisis, and directed relevant ministerial committees to intensify co-ordination among member states to mitigate the negative impact of the global situation on the region's economies.

The sixth GCC Economic Forum was held in Dubai, United Arab Emirates, in February 2010.

TRADE AND INDUSTRY

In 1982 a ministerial committee was formed to co-ordinate trade policies and development in the region. Technical subcommittees were established to oversee a strategic food reserve for the member states, and joint trade exhibitions (which were generally held every year until responsibility was transferred to the private sector in 1996). In 1986 the Supreme Council approved a measure whereby citizens of GCC member states were enabled to undertake certain retail trade activities in any other member state, with effect from 1 March 1987. In September 2000 GCC ministers of commerce agreed to establish a technical committee to promote the development of electronic commerce and trade among member states.

In 1976 the GCC member states formed the Gulf Organization for Industrial Consulting, based in Doha, Qatar, which promotes regional industrial development. In 1985 the Supreme Council endorsed a common industrial strategy for the Gulf states. It approved regulations stipulating that priority should be given to imports of GCC industrial products, and permitting GCC investors to obtain loans from GCC industrial development banks. In November 1986 resolutions were adopted on the protection of industrial products, and on the co-ordination of industrial projects, in order to avoid duplication. In 1989 the Ministerial Council approved the Unified GCC Foreign Capital Investment Regulations, which aimed to attract foreign investment and to co-ordinate investments amongst GCC countries. Further guidelines to promote foreign investment in the region were formulated during 1997. In December 1999 the Supreme Council amended the conditions determining rules of origin on industrial products in order to promote direct investment and intra-Community trade. In December 1992 the Supreme Council endorsed Patent Regulations for GCC member states to facilitate regional scientific and technological research. A GCC Patent Office for the protection of intellectual property in the region was established in 1998. In December 2006 the Supreme Council endorsed a system to unify trademarks in GCC states.

In December 2001 the Supreme council adopted unified procedures and measures for facilitating the intra-regional movement of people and commercial traffic, as well as unified standards in the areas of education and health care. In August 2003 the GCC adopted new measures permitting nationals of its member states to work in, and to seek loans from financial institutions in, any other member state. In December 2005 the Supreme Council approved a plan to unify member states' trade policies. The Council adopted further measures aimed at facilitating the movement of people, goods and services between member countries, with consideration given to environmental issues and consumer protection, and agreed to permit GCC citizens to undertake commercial activities in all member states.

AGRICULTURE

The GCC states aim to achieve food security through the best utilization of regional natural resources. A unified agricultural policy for GCC countries was endorsed by the Supreme Council in November 1985, and revised in December 1996. Efforts were also made to harmonize legislation relating to water conservation, veterinary vaccines, insecticides, fertilizers, fisheries and seeds. Unified agricultural quarantine laws were adopted by the Supreme Council in December 2001. In 2006 an agreement was entered into with the FAO on the regional implementation of a technical programme on agricultural quarantine development, aimed at protecting the agricultural sector from plant disease epidemics. A permanent committee on fisheries aims to co-ordinate national fisheries policies, to establish designated fishing periods and to undertake surveys of the fishing potential in the Arabian (Persian) Gulf. In December 2010 the summit meeting of GCC leaders called for a comprehensive review of agricultural sector development, with a focus on policies aimed at preserving water resources; the regional scarcity of water, and its high saline content, have been an area of concern.

COMMUNICATIONS, INFORMATION AND TRANSPORT

GCC ministers responsible for telecoms, posts and information technology, and ministers of information, convene regularly. The 2001 Economic Agreement provided for member states to take all necessary means to ensure the integration of their telecommunication policies, including telephone, post and data network services. A simplified passport system was approved in 1997 to facilitate travel between member countries. In December 2006 the Supreme Council requested that all GCC members conclude studies on the implementation of a GCC rail network, which was to interconnect all member states, with a view to enhancing economic development. It was announced in 2010 that the GCC states would invest nearly US $119,600m. in infrastructure projects during 2010–20, with developing the regional rail infrastructure accounting for some 90% of the investment. A report, issued in April 2011, on the status of GCC infrastructure development schemes, stated that some $452m. of infrastructure projects were under way in the region. It was envisaged that increased expenditure on infrastructure projects, representing a diversification from petroleum-based growth, might strengthen the regional economy during the ongoing global economic slowdown.

ENERGY AND ENVIRONMENT

The 1981 Unified Economic Agreement stated that member states should harmonize their policies in hydrocarbons industry, with regard to extraction, refining, marketing, processing, pricing, exploitation and development of energy resources; and that member states should develop common oil policies and take common positions at the international level. The 2001 Economic Agreement expanded upon this.

In 1982 a ministerial committee was established to co-ordinate hydrocarbons policies and prices. Ministers adopted a petroleum security plan to safeguard individual members against a halt in their production, to form a stockpile of petroleum products, and to organize a boycott of any non-member country when appropriate. In December 1987 the Supreme Council adopted a plan whereby a member state whose petroleum production was disrupted could 'borrow' petroleum from other members, in order to fulfil its export obligations. GCC petroleum ministers hold occasional co-ordination meetings to discuss the agenda and policies of OPEC, to which all six member states belong. In December 1988 the Supreme Council authorized the development of a long-term petroleum policy, and adopted a regional emergency policy for oil products. In November 2003 ministers of petroleum determined to develop a GCC Common Mining Law.

The Unified Economic Agreement provided for the establishment and co-ordination of an infrastructure of power-generating stations and desalination plans. The 2001 Economic Agreement also stressed that member states should adopt integrated economic policies with regard to developing the basic utilities infrastructure. During the early 1990s proposals were formulated to integrate the electricity networks of the six member countries. In December 1997 GCC heads of state declared that work should commence on the first stage of the plan, under the management of an independent authority. The estimated cost of the project was more than US $6,000m. However, it was agreed not to invite private developers to participate in construction of the grid, but that the first phase of the project should be financed by member states (to contribute 35% of the estimated $2,000m. required), and by loans from commercial banking and international monetary institutions. The Gulf Council Interconnection Authority was established in 1999, with its headquarters in Dammam, Saudi Arabia. In 2001 a GCC Electric Interconnection Commission was established, which was to support the project. The first phase of the project was completed, and in trial operation, by 2009.

In February 2001 GCC ministers responsible for water and electricity determined to formulate a common water policy for the region. Ministers responsibility for electricity and water approved an Electric Interconnection Agreement in November 2009, setting out the relations between the contracting parties. A GCC conference on Power and Water Desalination was convened in Qatar in October 2011. A Common Water Emergency Plan is under development.

In December 2006 the Supreme Council declared its intention to pursue the use of nuclear energy technology in the GCC region. The Council commissioned a study to develop a joint nuclear energy programme, but emphasized that any development of this technology would be for peaceful purposes only and fully disclosed to the international community. In February 2009 representatives of GCC member states attended a workshop organized by the IAEA.

In December 2001 GCC member states adopted the Convention on the Conservation of Wildlife and their Natural Habitats in the Countries of the GCC; the Convention entered into force in April 2003. In December 2007 the Supreme Council adopted a green environment initiative, aimed at improving the efficiency and performance of environmental institutions in member states.

CULTURAL CO-OPERATION

The GCC Folklore Centre, based in Doha, Qatar, was established in 1983 to collect, document and classify the regional cultural heritage, publish research, sponsor and protect regional folklore, provide a database on Gulf folklore, and to promote traditional culture through education. The December 2005 summit of heads of state adopted the 'Abu Dhabi Declaration', which stressed that member states should place a strong focus on education and on the development of human resources in order better to confront global challenges. Periodically cultural fora are held, including on: folklore (most recently in 2001); poetry (2004); drama (2009); and intellectual matters (2006). An occasional Exhibition of Creative Arts and Arabic Calligraphy is convened, most recently in 2006.

REGIONAL SECURITY

Although no mention of defence or security was made in the original charter, the summit meeting which ratified the charter also issued a statement rejecting any foreign military presence in the region. The Supreme Council meeting in November 1981 agreed to include defence co-operation in the activities of the organization: as a result, defence ministers met in January 1982 to discuss a common security policy, including a joint air defence system and standardization of weapons. In November 1984 member states agreed to form the Peninsula ('Al Jazeera') Shield Force for rapid deployment against external aggression, comprising units from the armed forces of each country under a central command to be based in north-eastern Saudi Arabia.

In December 1987 the Supreme Council approved a joint pact on regional co-operation in matters of security. In August 1990 the Ministerial Council condemned Iraq's invasion of Kuwait as a violation of sovereignty, and demanded the withdrawal of all Iraqi troops from Kuwait. The Peninsula Shield Force was not sufficiently developed to be deployed in defence of Kuwait. During the crisis and the ensuing war between Iraq and a multinational force which took place in January and February 1991, the GCC developed closer links with Egypt and Syria, which, together with Saudi Arabia, played the most active role among the Arab countries in the anti-Iraqi alliance. In March the six GCC nations, Egypt and Syria formulated the 'Declaration of Damascus', which announced plans to establish a regional peace-keeping force. The Declaration also urged the abolition of all weapons of mass destruction in the area, and recommended the resolution of the Palestinian question by an international conference. In June Egypt and Syria, whose troops were to have formed the largest proportion of the proposed peace-keeping force, announced their withdrawal from the project, reportedly as a result of disagreements with the GCC concerning the composition of the force and the remuneration involved. In December 1997 the Supreme Council approved plans for linking the region's military telecommunications networks and establishing a common early warning system. In December 2000 GCC leaders adopted a joint defence pact aimed at enhancing the grouping's defence capability. The pact formally committed member states to defending any other member state from external attack, envisaging the expansion of the Peninsula Shield Force from 5,000 to 22,000 troops and the creation of a new rapid deployment function within the Force. In March 2001 the

GCC member states inaugurated the first phase of the long-envisaged joint air defence system. In December GCC heads of state authorized the establishment of a supreme defence council, comprising member states' ministers of defence, to address security-related matters and supervise the implementation of the joint defence pact. The council was to convene on an annual basis. Meeting in emergency session in early February 2003 GCC ministers of defence and foreign affairs agreed to deploy the Peninsula Field Force in Kuwait, in view of the then impending US military action against neighbouring Iraq. The full deployment of 3,000 Peninsula Shield troops to Kuwait was completed in early March; the force was withdrawn two months later. In December 2005 the Supreme Council, meeting in Abu Dhabi, UAE, agreed that the Peninsula Shield Force should be reconstituted. Proposals to develop the Force were endorsed by the 2006 heads of state summit, held in December, in Riyadh. In December 2009 the 30th Supreme Council meeting ratified a new defence strategy that included upgrading the capabilities of the Peninsula Shield, undertaking joint military projects, and pursuing co-operation in combating the illegal trade of armaments to GCC member states.

In November 1994 a security agreement, to counter regional crime and terrorism, was concluded by GCC states. The pact, however, was not signed by Kuwait, which claimed that a clause concerning the extradition of offenders was in contravention of its constitution. The GCC welcomed a judgement made in March 2001 by the International Court of Justice awarding Bahrain sovereignty of the Hawar islands, while supporting Qatar's sovereignty over certain other territories; this settled a territorial dispute that had been a long-term cause of tension between the two GCC member countries.

In December 1997 the Council expressed concern at the escalation of tensions owing to Iraq's failure to co-operate with the UN Special Commission (UNSCOM). In February 1998 the US Secretary of Defense visited each of the GCC countries in order to generate regional support for any punitive military action against Iraq, given that country's obstruction of UN weapons inspectors. Kuwait was the only country to declare its support for the use of force (and to permit the use of its bases in military operations against Iraq), while other member states urged a diplomatic solution to the crisis. The GCC supported an agreement concluded between the UN Secretary-General and the Iraqi authorities at the end of February 1998, and urged Iraq to co-operate with UNSCOM in order to secure an end to the problem and a removal of the international embargo against the country. This position was subsequently reiterated by the Supreme Council. In September 2002 the US Secretary of State met representatives of the GCC to discuss ongoing US pressure on the UN Security Council to draft a new resolution insisting that Iraq comply with previous UN demands, setting a time frame for such compliance and authorizing the use of force against Iraq in response to non-compliance. In March 2003, in response to the initiation of US-led military action against Iraq for perceived non-compliance with the resulting Security Council resolution (1441, adopted in November 2002), the GCC Secretary-General urged the resumption of negotiations in place of military conflict. The GCC summit meeting held in Kuwait, in December 2003, issued a statement accepting the USA's policies towards Iraq at that time, emphasizing the importance of UN participation there, condemning ongoing operations by terrorist forces, and denoting the latter as anti-Islamic. In December 2009 the 30th Supreme Council meeting emphasized the GCC's support for Iraq's sovereignty, independence and territorial integrity, on non-interference in Iraq's internal affairs, and on the preservation of its Arab and Islamic identity; and urged inclusive national reconciliation.

In 1992 Iran extended its authority over the island of Abu Musa, which it had administered under a joint arrangement with the UAE since 1971. In September 1992 the GCC Ministerial Council condemned Iran's continued occupation of the island and efforts to consolidate its presence, and reiterated support of UAE sovereignty over Abu Musa, as well as the largely uninhabited Greater and Lesser Tunb islands (also claimed by Iran). All three islands are situated in the approach to the Strait of Hormuz, through which petroleum exports are transported. The GCC has condemned repeated military exercises conducted by Iran in the waters around the disputed islands as a threat to regional security and a violation of the UAE's sovereignty. Successive GCC summit meetings have restated support for the UAE's right to regain sovereignty over the three islands (and over their territorial waters, airspace, continental shelf and economic zone). In December 2010 the 31st summit meeting stated disappointment at the failure of repeated contacts with Iran over the matter. The meeting welcomed international efforts to engage with Iran over its controversial nuclear programme, particularly by the 5+1 Group (comprising the People's Republic of China, France, Germany, Russia and the United Kingdom).

In March 2011, in response to a request from the Bahrain Government following a series of violent clashes between opposition protesters and security forces in that country, the GCC dispatched a contingent of Peninsula Shield Force troops (numbering some 1,000 from Saudi Arabia and 500 from the UAE, with more than 100 armoured vehicles), to Bahrain to protect strategic facilities and help maintain order.

The December 2005 summit of GCC heads of state issued a statement declaring that the Gulf region should be a zone free of weapons of mass destruction.

The December 2009 meeting of the Supreme Council stated concern over acts of marine piracy in the Gulf of Aden, the Red Sea and other regional waterways, and emphasized the need to intensify co-operation in challenging the perpetrators. The December 2010 summit meeting expressed appreciation at efforts made by the GCC naval forces in combating maritime piracy and protecting shipping corridors.

In July 2007 the Ministerial Council determined to establish a GCC Disaster Control Center; a team of experts in disaster management was to be established there. In December 2010 the GCC summit approved a regional plan of action to prepare for and respond to radiation risks.

EXTERNAL RELATIONS

In June 1988 an agreement was signed by GCC and European Community (EC) ministers on economic co-operation; this took effect from January 1990. Under the accord a joint ministerial council (meeting on an annual basis) was established, and working groups were subsequently created to promote co-operation in several specific areas, including business, energy, the environment and industry. In October 1990 GCC and EC ministers of foreign affairs commenced negotiations on formulating a free trade agreement. GCC heads of state, meeting in December 1997, condemned statements issued by the European Parliament, as well as by other organizations, regarding human rights issues in member states and insisted they amounted to interference in GCC judicial systems. In January 2003 the GCC established a customs union (see above), which was a precondition of the proposed GCC-European Union (EU, as the restructured EC was now known) free trade agreement. Negotiations on the agreement, initiated in 2003, had, by 2012, still not been concluded. In June 2010 the GCC and EU adopted a Joint Action Programme for 2010–13, aimed at strengthening economic, financial and monetary co-operation, as well as co-operation in other key strategic areas of investment, including trade, energy and the environment, transport, industry, telecommunications and information technology, education and scientific research. In April 2008 the GCC and the European Free Trade Association (EFTA) finalized negotiations on the conclusion of a bilateral free trade agreement; the agreement was signed in July 2009, in Norway.

In September 1994 GCC ministers of foreign affairs decided to end the secondary and tertiary embargo on trade with Israel. In December 1996 the foreign ministers of the Damascus Declaration states, convened in Cairo, Egypt, requested the USA to exert financial pressure on Israel to halt the construction of settlements on occupied Arab territory. In December 2001 GCC heads of state issued a statement holding Israeli government policy responsible for the escalating crisis in the Palestinian territories. The consultative meeting of heads of state held in May 2002 declared its support for a Saudi-proposed initiative aimed at achieving a peaceful resolution of the crisis. GCC heads of state summits have repeatedly urged the international community to encourage Israel to sign the Nuclear Non-Proliferation Treaty.

In June 1997 ministers of foreign affairs of the Damascus Declaration states agreed to pursue efforts to establish a free trade zone throughout the region, which they envisaged as the nucleus of a future Arab common market. Meanwhile, the Greater Arab Free Trade Area, an initiative of the League of Arab States, entered into effect on 1 January 2005.

The GCC-USA Economic Dialogue, which commenced in 1985, convenes periodically as a government forum to promote co-operation between the GCC economies and the USA. Since the late 1990s private sector interests have been increasingly represented at sessions of the Dialogue. It was announced in March 2001 that a business forum was to be established under the auspices of the Dialogue, to act as a permanent means of facilitating trade and investment between the GCC countries and the USA.

In January 2008 the last of four rounds of negotiations between the GCC member states and Singapore on the creation of a GCC-Singapore Free Trade Area (GSFTA) was concluded; the agreement establishing the GSFTA was signed, in Doha, Qatar, in December 2008. An inaugural meeting of ministers of foreign affairs of the GCC and the Association of Southeast Asian Nations (ASEAN) was held in June 2009, in Manama, Bahrain. The meeting adopted a GCC-ASEAN Joint Vision as a framework for future co-operation between the two groupings. A second meeting, held in Singapore, in May–June 2010, approved an ASEAN-GCC Action Plan, which identified specific measures for closer co-operation to be undertaken in the two-year period 2010–12.

The GCC Secretary-General denounced the major terrorist attacks that were perpetrated in September 2001 against targets in the USA. Meeting in an emergency session in mid-September, in Riyadh, Saudi Arabia, GCC ministers of foreign affairs agreed to support the aims of the developing international coalition against terrorism. Meanwhile, however, member states urged parallel international resolve to halt action by the Israeli security forces against Palestinians. In December the Supreme Council declared the organization's full co-operation with the anti-terrorism coalition. In December 2006 the Supreme Council determined to establish a specialized security committee to counter terrorism.

In March 2011 GCC leaders issued a statement urging the League of Arab States to take measures to protect citizens in Libya from the effects of violent measures against opposition elements being taken at that time by the regime of the then Libyan leader Col Muammar al-Qaddafi. In October 2011 the Council met in emergency session to discuss ongoing violent unrest in Syria, where suppression by the regime of anti-government protests during that year had resulted in more than 3,000 civilian fatalities. In early 2012 all GCC member states withdrew their diplomatic presence from Syria in protest at the Syrian regime's violent suppression of mass anti-government protests.

In April 2011, in response to mounting political unrest in Yemen, the GCC proposed a mediation plan whereby President Saleh of Yemen would resign and receive immunity from prosecution, anti-Government activists would desist from protesting, and a new government of national unity would be appointed, pending the staging of a presidential election within two months of Saleh's proposed withdrawal. Saleh, however, refused to sign the plan at that time, and, in late May, the GCC mediation attempt was suspended. In September Saleh indicated that he might be willing to approve the plan although opposition elements expressed scepticism that Saleh would fully adhere to the peace initiative. In October the UN Security Council unanimously approved a resolution that expressed serious concern over the worsening security situation in Yemen; demanded that all sides immediately reject the use of violence to achieve their political goals; and called on all parties to sign the GCC peace initiative. In late November President Saleh finally signed the GCC-mediated agreement. Accordingly Saleh relinquished his constitutional powers and, in February 2012, presidential elections were held.

INVESTMENT CORPORATION

Gulf Investment Corporation (GIC): POB 3402, Safat 13035, Kuwait; tel. 2225000; fax 2225010; e-mail gic@gic.com.kw; internet www.gic.com.kw; f. 1983 by the six member states of the GCC, each contributing 16.6% of the total capital; total assets US $5,776m. (Dec. 2010); investment chiefly in the Gulf region, financing industrial projects (including pharmaceuticals, chemicals, steel wire, aircraft engineering, aluminium, dairy produce and chicken-breeding); provides merchant banking and financial advisory services, and in 1992 was appointed to advise the Kuwaiti Government on a programme of privatization; CEO and Chief Investment Officer HISHAM ABDULRAZZAQ AL-RAZZUQI; publ. *The GIC Gazetteer* (annually).

Gulf International Bank: POB 1017, ad-Dowali Bldg, 3 Palace Ave, Manama 317, Bahrain; tel. 17534000; fax 17522633; e-mail info@gibbah.com; internet www.gibonline.com; f. 1976 by the six GCC states and Iraq; became a wholly owned subsidiary of the GIC (without Iraqi shareholdings) in 1991; in April 1999 a merger with Saudi Investment Bank was concluded; total assets US $16,800m. (Dec. 2011); CEO Dr YAHYA ALYAHYA.

Publications

GCC News (monthly, available online in Arabic).

GCC: A Statistical Glance.

Statistical Bulletin on Water.

At-Ta'awun (periodical).

COUNCIL OF ARAB ECONOMIC UNITY

Address: 1113 Corniche el-Nil, 4th Floor, POB 1 Mohammed Fareed, 11518 Cairo, Egypt.

Telephone: (2) 5755321; **fax:** (2) 5754090.

Established in 1957 by the Economic Council of the League of Arab States. The first meeting of the Council of Arab Economic Unity was held in 1964.

MEMBERS

Egypt	Palestine
Iraq	Somalia
Jordan	Sudan
Libya	Syria
Mauritania	Yemen

Organization

(June 2012)

COUNCIL

The Council consists of representatives of member states, usually ministers of economy, finance and trade. It meets twice a year; meetings are chaired by the representative of each country for one year.

GENERAL SECRETARIAT

Entrusted with the implementation of the Council's decisions and with proposing work plans, including efforts to encourage participation by member states in the Arab Economic Unity Agreement. The Secretariat also compiles statistics, conducts research and publishes studies on Arab economic problems and on the effects of major world economic trends.

Secretary-General: MOHAMMED AL-RABEE (Yemen).

COMMITTEES

The following permanent committees have been established: customs issues; monetary and finance; economic; permanent representatives; and follow-up.

Activities

The Council undertakes to co-ordinate measures leading to a customs union subject to a unified administration; conduct market and commodity studies; assist with the unification of statistical terminology and methods of data collection; conduct studies for the formation of new joint Arab companies and federations; and to formulate specific programmes for agricultural and industrial co-ordination and for improving road and railway networks.

ARAB ECONOMIC INTEGRATION

Based on a resolution passed by the Council in August 1964, an Arab Common Market was to be established, with its implementation to be supervised by the Council. Customs duties and other taxes on trade between the member countries were to be eliminated in stages prior to the adoption of a full customs union, and ultimately all restrictions on trade between the member countries, including quotas, and restrictions on residence, employment and transport, were to be abolished. In practice, however, little progress was achieved in the development of an Arab common market during 1964–2000. In 2001 the Council's efforts towards liberalizing intra-Arab trade were intensified. A meeting of Council ministers of economy and trade convened in Baghdad, Iraq, in June, approved an executive programme for developing the proposed common market, determined to establish a compensation fund to support the integration of the least developed Arab states into the regional economy, and agreed to provide technical assistance for Arab states aiming to join the World Trade Organization. In May 2001 Egypt, Jordan, Morocco and Tunisia (all then participants in the Euro-Mediterranean Partnership, re-launched in 2008 as the Union for the Mediterranean—see European Union), while convened in Agadir, Morocco, had issued the 'Agadir Declaration' in which they determined to establish an Arab Mediterranean Free Trade Zone. The so-called Agadir Agreement on the establishment of a Free Trade Zone between the Arabic Mediterranean Nations was signed in February 2004, came into force in July 2006, and entered its implementation phase in March 2007. Tariff-free trade between the 17 participants in the Greater Arab Free Trade Area (GAFTA, implemented by the Arab League, also known as the 'Pan-Arab Free Trade Area') entered into force on 1 January 2005. The signatories to the Agadir Agreement are also members of GAFTA. Progress towards achieving Arab economic integration was considered at the first ever Economic, Development and Social summit meeting of Arab leaders, convened in January 2009 in Kuwait, under the auspices of the Arab League; a second summit was held in January 2011, in Sharm el-Sheikh, Egypt.

Council agreements aimed at encouraging Arab investment include an accord on Non-Double Taxation, Tax Evasion, and Establishing Common Rules on Income and Capital (adopted in December 1997); an accord on Non-Double Taxation and Income Tax Evasion (December 1998); an accord on Investment Promotion and Protection (June 2000); and an accord on Investment Dispute Settlement in Arab Countries (December 2000).

JOINT VENTURES

A number of multilateral organizations in industry and agriculture have been formed on the principle that faster development and economies of scale may be achieved by combining the efforts of member states. In industries that are new to the member countries Arab Joint Companies are formed, while existing industries are co-ordinated by the setting up of Arab Specialized Unions. The unions are for closer co-operation on problems of production and marketing, and to help companies deal as a group in international markets. The companies are intended to be self-supporting on a purely commercial basis; they may issue shares to citizens of the participating countries.

Arab Joint Companies:

Arab Company for Drug Industries and Medical Appliances (ACDIMA): POB 925161, Amman 11190, Jordan; tel. (6) 5821618; fax (6) 5821649; e-mail acdima@go.com.jo; internet www.acdima.com; f. 1976.

Arab Company for Livestock Development (ACOLID): POB 5305, Damascus, Syria; tel. (11) 666037; internet www.acolid.com.

Arab Mining Company: POB 20198, Amman, Jordan; tel. (6) 5663148; fax (6) 5684114; e-mail armico@armico.com; internet www.armico.com; f. 1974.

Specialized Arab Unions and Federations:

Arab Co-operative Union: POB 452, Duki, Giza, Egypt; tel. (2) 3442348; fax (2) 3038481; e-mail co_opunion@yahoo.com; f. 1985.

Arab Federation for Paper, Printing and Packaging Industries: POB 5456, Baghdad, Iraq; tel. (1) 887-2384; fax (1) 886-9639; e-mail info@afpppi.com; internet www.afpppi.com; f. 1977; 250 mems.

Arab Federation for Oil and Gas Technologies: POB 954183, Amman 11954, Jordan; tel. (6) 5511170; fax (6) 5541986; e-mail info@afogt.com; internet www.afogt.com; f. 2011.

Arab Federation of Engineering Industries: POB 14429, Damascus, Syria; e-mail ahyafi@scs-net.org; internet www.arab-fei.com; f. 1975.

Arab Federation of Food Industries: POB 13025, Baghdad, Iraq; e-mail g-secretary@arabffi.org; internet www.arabffi.org; f. 1976.

Arab Federation of Leather Industries: POB 2188, Damascus, Syria; f. 1978.

Arab Federation of Shipping: POB 1161, Baghdad, Iraq; tel. (1) 717-4540; fax (1) 717-7243; e-mail secretariat@afos-shipping.org; f. 1979; 22 mems.

Arab Federation of Textile Industries: POB 16062, Aleppo, Syria; f. 1976.

Arab Iron and Steel Union: BP 4, Chéraga, Algiers, Algeria; tel. (21) 36-27-04; fax (21) 37-19-75; e-mail relex@solbarab.com; internet www.arabsteel.info; f. 1972; Gen. Sec. MUHAMMAD LAID LACHGAR.

Arab Seaports Federation: POB 21514 el-Shalat Gdns, Egypt; tel. and fax 4818791; e-mail arabport@yahoo.com; internet www.aspf.org.eg; f. 1977; Sec.-Gen. Rear Adm. ESSAM EDDIN BADAWY.

Arab Sugar Federation: POB 195, Khartoum, Sudan; f. 1977.

Arab Union for Cement and Building Materials: POB 9015, Damascus, Syria; tel. (11) 6118598; fax (11) 6111318; e-mail aucbm@scs-net.org; internet www.aucbm.org; f. 1977; 22 mem. countries, 103 mem. cos; Sec.-Gen. AHMAD AL-ROUSAN; publ. *Cement and Building Materials Review* (quarterly).

Arab Union of Fish Producers: POB 15064, Baghdad, Iraq; tel. (1) 425-2588; f. 1976.

Arab Union of Land Transport: POB 926324, Amman 11190, Jordan; tel. (6) 5663153; fax (6) 5664232; e-mail ault@go.com.jo; internet auolt.org; f. 1977.

Arab Union of the Manufacturers of Pharmaceuticals and Medical Appliances: POB 81150, Amman 11181, Jordan; tel. (6) 4654306; fax (6) 4648141; internet www.aupam.com; f. 1986.

Arab Union of the Manufacturers of Tyres and Rubber Products: POB 6599, Alexandria, Egypt; f. 1993.

Arab Union of Railways (UACF): POB 6599, Aleppo, Syria; tel. (21) 2667270; fax (21) 2686000; e-mail uacf@scs-net.org; f. 1979.

Federation of Arab Travel Agents Associations (FATAA): POB 7090, Amman, Jordan.

General Arab Insurance Federation: 8 Kaser en-Nil St, POB 611, 11511 Cairo, Egypt; tel. (2) 5743177; fax (2) 5762310; e-mail info@gaif.org; internet www.gaif.org; f. 1964.

Inter-Arab Union of Hotels and Tourism (IAUHT): rue Maysaloun, Damascus, Syria; tel. (11) 2232323; fax (11) 2245762; f. 1994.

Union of Arab Contractors: Cairo, Egypt; f. 1995.

Union of Arab Investors: Cairo, Egypt; f. 1995.

JOINT VENTURES

A number of multilateral organizations in industry and agriculture have been formed on the principle that faster development and economies of scale may be achieved by combining the efforts of member states. In industries that are new to the member countries Arab Joint Companies are formed, while existing industries are co-ordinated by the setting up of Arab Specialized Unions. The unions are for closer co-operation on problems of production and marketing, and to help companies deal as a group in international markets. The companies are intended to be self-supporting on a purely commercial basis; they may issue shares to citizens of the participating countries.

Publications

Annual Bulletin for Arab Countries' Foreign Trade Statistics.

Annual Bulletin for Official Exchange Rates of Arab Currencies.

Arab Economic Unity Bulletin (2 a year).

Demographic Yearbook for Arab Countries.

Economic Report (2 a year).

Guide to Studies prepared by Secretariat.

Progress Report (2 a year).

Statistical Yearbook for Arab Countries.

Yearbook for Intra-Arab Trade Statistics.

Yearbook of National Accounts for Arab Countries.

COUNCIL OF THE BALTIC SEA STATES—CBSS

Address: Slussplan 9, POB 2010, 103 11 Stockholm, Sweden.
Telephone: (8) 440-19-20; **fax:** (8) 440-19-44; **e-mail:** cbss@cbss.org; **internet:** www.cbss.org.

The Council of the Baltic Sea States (CBSS) was established in 1992 to develop co-operation between member states.

MEMBERS

Denmark	Iceland	Poland
Estonia	Latvia	Russia
Finland	Lithuania	Sweden
Germany	Norway	

The European Commission also has full membership status. Observers: Belarus, France, Italy, the Netherlands, Romania, Slovakia, Spain, Ukraine, United Kingdom, USA.

Organization

(June 2012)

PRESIDENCY

The presidency is occupied by member states for one year, on a rotating basis (1 July 2011–30 June 2012: Germany; 1 July 2012–30 June 2013: Russia). Summit meetings of heads of government are convened every two years. The ninth summit meeting was convened in Stralsund, Germany, in May 2012.

MINISTERIAL COUNCIL

The Council comprises the ministers of foreign affairs of each member state and a representative of the European Commission. The Council meets every two years and aims to serve as a forum for guidance, direction of work and overall co-ordination among participating states. The 17th, extraordinary, session of the Council was convened in Plön, Germany, in February 2012. Chairmanship of the Council rotates annually among member states and is responsible for co-ordinating the Council's activities between ministerial sessions, with assistance from the Committee of Senior Officials. (Other ministers also convene periodically, on an ad hoc basis by their own decision.)

COMMITTEE OF SENIOR OFFICIALS—CSO

The Committee consists of senior officials of the ministries of foreign affairs of the member states and of the European Commission. It serves as the main discussion forum and decision-making body for matters relating to the work of the Council, and monitors, facilitates and aims to co-ordinate the activities of all structures for CBSS co-operation. The Chairman of the Committee, from the same country serving as President of the CBSS, meets regularly with the previous and future Chairmen. The so-called Troika aims to maintain information co-operation, promote better exchange of information, and ensure more effective decision-making. The CSO monitors the work of the Expert Group on Nuclear and Radiation Safety, the Task Force against Trafficking in Human Beings, the Expert Group on Co-operation on Children at Risk, the Expert Group on Youth Affairs, the Lead Country Function of the EuroFaculty Project in Pskov (in Russia, see below), the Expert Group on Maritime Policy, and the Expert Group on Sustainable Development—Baltic 21.

SECRETARIAT

The tasks of the Secretariat include providing technical and organizational support to the chairmanship, structures and working bodies of the Ministerial Council; co-ordinating CBSS activities; managing the CBSS archives and information databases; and maintaining contacts with governments and other organizations operational in the region. The Secretariat includes a Children's Unit, and it hosts the Secretariat of Northern Dimension Partnership in Public Health and Social Well-being. In May 2012 the ninth summit meeting endorsed a decision of the Committee of Senior Officials to establish a Project Support Facility to be administered by the Secretariat.

Director: JAN LUNDIN (Sweden).

Activities

The CBSS was established in March 1992 as a forum to enhance and strengthen co-operation between countries in the Baltic Sea region. At a meeting of the Council in Kalmar, Sweden, in July 1996, ministers adopted an Action Programme as a guideline for CBSS activities. The main programme areas covered stable and participatory political development; economic integration and prosperity; and protection of the environment. The third summit meeting of CBSS heads of government, held at Kolding, Denmark, in April 2000, recommended a restructuring of the organization to consolidate regional intergovernmental, multilateral co-operation in all sectors. In June the ninth meeting of the CBSS Council approved the summit's recommendations. The 10th ministerial session, held in Hamburg, Germany, in June 2001, adopted a set of guidelines regarding the strengthening of the CBSS. Heads of government attending the seventh summit of Baltic Sea States, held in Riga, Latvia, in June 2008, endorsed a Declaration on the Reform of the CBSS, listing the following five future priority areas of co-operation for member states: environment (which may include climate change); economic development; energy; education and culture; and civil security and the human dimension. The 15th ministerial session, held in Helsingør, Denmark, in June 2009, endorsed new terms of reference of the CBSS and of its Secretariat, updated in view of the 2008 Declaration on the Reform of the CBSS. Meeting in Vilnius, Lithuania, in June 2010, the eighth summit of heads of government adopted the Vilnius Declaration on 'A Vision for the Baltic Region by 2020'.

The ministerial session held in May 1994 determined to appoint an independent Commissioner on Democratic Development, concerned with democratic institutions and human rights, to serve a three-year term of office, from October of that year. The Commissioner's mandate was subsequently twice extended for three years, in July 1997 and June 2000, and was terminated in December 2003.

At the first Baltic Sea States summit, held in Visby, Sweden, in May 1996, heads of government agreed to establish a Task Force on Organized Crime to counter drugs-trafficking, strengthen judicial co-operation, increase the dissemination of information, impose regional crime-prevention measures, improve border controls and provide training. The Task Force's mandate has been successively renewed, most recently, by the 10th Baltic Sea States summit, until 31 December 2016. In January 1998 the second summit meeting, convened in Riga, Latvia, agreed to enhance co-operation in the areas of civic security and border control. The third Baltic Sea summit, held in April 2000, authorized the establishment of a Task Force on Communicable Disease Control, which was mandated to formulate a joint plan aimed at improving disease control throughout the region, and also to strengthen regional co-operation in combating the threat to public health posed by a significant increase in communicable diseases, in particular HIV/AIDS. The Task Force presented its final report to the CBSS summit meeting held in June 2004. It was recognized that some of the structures of the Task Force could be pursued through the Northern Dimension Partnership in Public Health and Social Well-Being (NDPHS, see below). A Task Force against Trafficking in Human Beings was established in November 2006.

The Council has founded a number of groups, comprising experts in specific fields, which aim to report on and recommend action on issues of concern to the Council (see under the Committee of Senior Officials). In January 2009 the Council inaugurated the CBSS EuroFaculty Pskov programme, aimed at upgrading business/economics education at two higher education institutions in the western Russian Pskov region (bordering Estonia and Latvia); a second phase of the EuroFaculty Pskov programme was to commence in October 2012. A CBSS

EuroFaculty programme was implemented during 2000–07 at the Immanuel Kant State University in Kaliningrad, Russia.

A Baltic Business Advisory Council was established in 1996 with the aim of facilitating the privatization process in the member states in transition and promoting small and medium-sized enterprises. A Roadmap on Investment Promotion, drafted by the Working Group on Economic Co-operation, was approved by the sixth summit meeting of CBSS heads of government, held in Reykjavik, Iceland, in June 2006. A Ministerial Conference on Trade and Economy was held in Stockholm, Sweden, in May 2007.

The environmental state of the Baltic Sea, which is one of the world's busiest shipping routes, and associated issues such as eutrophication, overfishing, unsustainable production, and marine littering, are of great concern to the Council. In January 2001 the CBSS Council agreed to establish a unit in the CBSS secretariat to implement Baltic 21, the regional variant (adopted by the CBSS in 1998) of Agenda 21, the programme of action agreed by the UN Conference on Environment and Development, held in Rio de Janeiro, Brazil, in June 1992. From January 2010 Baltic 21 was integrated into the structure of the CBSS as the Expert Group on Sustainable Development—Baltic 21. The Expert Group and BASREC (see below) co-hosted an event on the sidelines of the June 2012 UN Conference on Sustainable Development (Rio+20). The 16th session of the Ministerial Council, held in June 2011, in Oslo, Norway, endorsed a new CBSS Strategy on Sustainable Development for 2010–15, with a focus on the following four strategic areas of co-operation: climate change; sustainable urban and rural development; sustainable consumption and production; and innovation and education for sustainable development. In June 2010 funding was approved by the Baltic Sea Region Programme of the European Union (EU) for a new Baltic Sea Region Climate Change Adaptation Strategy (BALTADAPT), to be implemented, with participation by 11 partners from seven countries, under the auspices of Baltic 21. The CBSS was to convene a high-level Policy Forum on Climate Change Adaptation in Berlin, Germany, in April 2012. The Baltic Sea Region Energy Co-operation (BASREC) has its own secretariat function and council of senior energy officials, administered by the CBSS Secretariat. BASREC also has ad hoc groups on electricity markets, gas markets, energy efficiency and climate change. The 17th, extraordinary, ministerial session, held in February 2012, adopted a Declaration on Energy Security, highlighting future areas of policy focus. These included: diversification; reciprocity; security of supplies; environmental aspects and sustainability; and nuclear safety standards. The promotion of the sustainable and balanced spatial development of the region is addressed within the framework of the Visions and Strategies around the Baltic Sea (VASAB) co-operation.

The CBSS organizes annual co-ordination meetings to provide a forum and framework of co-operation for its strategic partners in the Baltic Sea area, including the B7 Baltic Island Network (comprising the seven largest Baltic Sea islands), the Baltic Development Forum, the Baltic Sea Forum, the Helsinki Commission and the Union of the Baltic Cities. The CBSS seeks synergies with the Arctic Council, the Barents Euro-Arctic Council, the Nordic Council of Ministers, and the EU's Northern Dimension co-operation framework. The Council contributed to the implementation of Northern Dimension Action Plans (NDAPs) for 2000–03 and 2004–06. In 2006 the CBSS prepared and presented to the European Commission a survey on the future of Northern Dimension co-operation. This contributed to the development of a long-term Northern Dimension Policy Framework Document that was adopted, alongside a Political Declaration on the Northern Dimension, in November 2006, in place of the previous NDAPs, with a view to renewing the co-operation. The first ministerial meeting of the renewed Northern Dimension co-operation was convened in St Petersburg, Russia, in October 2008. Ongoing Northern Dimension initiatives that are supported by CBSS member states include the Northern Dimension Environment Partnership (NDEP), established in 2001; the NDPHS, which was established in 2003; and the development of a Northern Dimension Partnership on Transport and Logistics, approved in October 2008. An EU Strategy for the Baltic Sea Region (EUSBSR) was adopted by the European Council in October 2009. In January 2012 the CBSS Secretariat became lead partner of a EUSBSR flagship project on macro-regional risk scenarios and gaps identification.

Finance

The Secretariat is financed by contributions of the governments of the Council's 11 member states. Ongoing activities and co-operation projects are funded through voluntary contributions from member states on the basis of special contribution schemes. Some €1.7m. was budgeted in 2012 for core Secretariat expenditure, the Expert Group on Sustainable Development—Baltic 21, and the Task Force against Trafficking in Human Beings, and a budget of €2.7m. was forecast for 2013 (including a €1m. contribution to a new Project Support Facility).

Publication

Balticness Light (quarterly).

COUNCIL OF EUROPE

Address: Ave de l'Europe, 67075 Strasbourg Cedex, France.

Telephone: 3-88-41-20-33; **fax:** 3-88-41-27-45; **e-mail:** infopoint@coe.int; **internet:** www.coe.int.

The Council was founded in May 1949 to achieve a greater unity between its members, to facilitate their social progress and to uphold the principles of parliamentary democracy, respect for human rights and the rule of law. Membership has risen from the original 10 to 47.

MEMBERS*

Albania	Lithuania
Andorra	Luxembourg
Armenia	Macedonia, former Yugoslav republic
Austria	Malta
Azerbaijan	Moldova
Belgium	Montenegro
Bosnia and Herzegovina	Monaco
Bulgaria	Netherlands
Croatia	Norway
Cyprus	Poland
Czech Republic	Portugal
Denmark	Romania
Estonia	Russia
Finland	San Marino
France	Serbia
Georgia	Slovakia
Germany	Slovenia
Greece	Spain
Hungary	Sweden
Iceland	Switzerland
Ireland	Turkey
Italy	Ukraine
Latvia	United Kingdom
Liechtenstein	

* Belarus is a state candidate for membership of the Council of Europe. Canada, the Holy See, Japan, Mexico and the USA have observer status with the Committee of Ministers. The parliaments of Canada, Israel and Mexico have observer status with the Parliamentary Assembly.

Organization

(June 2012)

COMMITTEE OF MINISTERS

The Committee consists of the ministers of foreign affairs of all member states (or their deputies, who are usually ministers' permanent diplomatic representatives in Strasbourg); it decides all matters of internal organization, makes recommendations to governments and draws up conventions and agreements with binding effect; it also discusses matters of political concern, such as European co-operation, compliance with member states' commitments, in particular concerning the protection of human rights, and considers possible co-ordination with other institutions, such as the European Union (EU) and the Organization for Security and Co-operation in Europe (OSCE). The Committee meets weekly at deputy ministerial level and once a year (in May or November) at ministerial level. Six two-day meetings are convened each year to supervise the execution of judgments of the European Court of Human Rights (see below).

CONFERENCES OF SPECIALIZED MINISTERS

There are 20 Conferences of specialized ministers, meeting regularly for intergovernmental co-operation in various fields.

PARLIAMENTARY ASSEMBLY

President: JEAN-CLAUDE MIGNON (France).

Secretary-General of the Parliamentary Assembly: WOJCIECH SAWICKI (Poland).

Chairman of the Socialist Group: ANDREAS GROSS (Switzerland).

Chairman of the Group of the European People's Party: LUCA VOLONTÈ (Italy).

Chairman of the Alliance of Liberals and Democrats for Europe: ANNE BRASSEUR (Luxembourg).

Chairman of the European Democrat Group: ROBERT WALTER (United Kingdom).

Chairman of the Unified European Left Group: TINY KOX (Netherlands).

Members are elected or appointed by their national parliaments from among the members thereof; political parties in each delegation follow the proportion of their strength in the national parliament. Members do not represent their governments, speaking on their own behalf. At June 2012 the Assembly had 318 members (and 318 substitutes): 18 each for France, Germany, Italy, Russia and the United Kingdom; 12 each for Poland, Spain, Turkey and Ukraine; 10 for Romania; seven each for Belgium, the Czech Republic, Greece, Hungary, the Netherlands, Portugal and Serbia; six each for Austria, Azerbaijan, Bulgaria, Sweden and Switzerland; five each for Bosnia and Herzegovina, Croatia, Denmark, Finland, Georgia, Moldova, Norway and Slovakia; four each for Albania, Armenia, Ireland and Lithuania; three each for Cyprus, Estonia, Iceland, Latvia, Luxembourg, the former Yugoslav republic of Macedonia, Malta, Montenegro and Slovenia; and two each for Andorra, Liechtenstein, Monaco and San Marino. The parliaments of Canada, Israel and Mexico have permanent observer status. (Belarus's special 'guest status' was suspended in January 1997.)

The Assembly meets in ordinary session once a year. The session is divided into four parts, generally held in the last full week of January, April, June and September. The Assembly submits Recommendations to the Committee of Ministers, passes Resolutions, and discusses reports on any matters of common European interest. It is also a consultative body to the Committee of Ministers, and elects the Secretary-General, the Deputy Secretary-General, the Secretary-General of the Assembly, the Council's Commissioner for Human Rights, and the members of the European Court of Human Rights.

The parliament of Morocco (since June 2011) and the Palestine National Council (since October 2011) hold 'Partner for Democracy' status at the Parliamentary Assembly, which aims to provide democracy-building support to national legislatures in regions neighbouring the Council of Europe area.

Standing Committee: represents the Assembly when it is not in session, and may adopt Recommendations to the Committee of Ministers and Resolutions on behalf of the Assembly. Consists of the President, Vice-Presidents, Chairmen of the Political Groups, Chairmen of the Ordinary Committees and Chairmen of national delegations. Meetings are usually held at least twice a year.

Ordinary Committees: political affairs; legal and human rights; economic affairs and development; social, health and family affairs; culture, science and education; environment, agriculture, and local and regional affairs; migration, refugees and population; rules of procedure and immunities; equal opportunities for women and men; honouring of obligations and commitments by member states of the Council of Europe.

SECRETARIAT

The Secretariat incorporates the Secretariats and Registry of the institutions of the Council. There are Directorates of Communication and Research, Strategic Planning, Protocol and Internal Audit, and the following Directorates-General: Political Affairs; Legal Affairs; Human Rights; Social Cohesion; Education, Culture and Heritage, Youth and Sport; and Administration and Logistics.

Secretary-General: THORBJØRN JAGLAND (Norway).

Deputy Secretary-General: MAUD DE BOER-BUQUICCHIO (Netherlands).

EUROPEAN COURT OF HUMAN RIGHTS

The Court was established in 1959 under the European Convention on Human Rights. It has compulsory jurisdiction and is competent to consider complaints lodged by states party to the European Convention and by individuals, groups of individuals or non-governmental organizations (NGOs) claiming to be victims of breaches of the Convention's guarantees. The Court comprises one judge for each contracting state. The Court sits in three-member Committees, empowered to declare applications inadmissible in the event of unanimity and where no further examination is necessary, seven-member Chambers, and a 17-member Grand Chamber. Chamber judgments become final three months after delivery, during which period parties may request a rehearing before the Grand Chamber, subject to acceptance by a panel of five judges. Grand Chamber judgments are final. The Court's final judgments are binding on respondent states and their execution is supervised by the Committee of Ministers. Execution of judgments includes payment of any pecuniary just satisfaction awarded by the Court, adoption of specific individual measures to erase the consequences of the violations found (such as striking out of impugned convictions from criminal records, reopening of judicial proceedings, etc.), and general measures to prevent new similar violations (e.g. constitutional and legislative reforms, changes of domestic case-law and administrative practice, etc.). When the Committee of Ministers considers that the measures taken comply with the respondent state's obligation to give effect to the judgment, a final resolution is adopted that terminates the supervision of the case. In June 2009 the Court adopted a new policy establishing seven categories of case, and aiming to focus resources on the cases ('priority applications') deemed to be most important. The EU Treaty of Lisbon, which entered into force in December 2009, committed the EU to pursuing accession to the Court. During 2011 the Court delivered 1,511 judgments, and some 149,450 cases were pending at 31 March 2012.

President: Sir NICHOLAS BRATZA (United Kingdom).

Registrar: ERIK FRIBERGH (Sweden).

CONGRESS OF LOCAL AND REGIONAL AUTHORITIES OF THE COUNCIL OF EUROPE (CLRAE)

The Congress was established in 1994, incorporating the former Standing Conference of Local and Regional Authorities, in order to protect and promote the political, administrative and financial autonomy of local and regional European authorities by encouraging central governments to develop effective local democracy. The Congress comprises two chambers—a Chamber of Local Authorities and a Chamber of Regions—with a total membership of 318 elected representatives (and 318 elected substitutes). Annual sessions are mainly concerned with local government matters, regional planning, protection of the environment, town and country planning, and social and cultural affairs. A Standing Committee, drawn from all national delegations, meets between plenary sessions of the Congress. Four Statutory Committees (Institutional; Sustainable Development; Social Cohesion; Culture and Education) meet twice a year in order to prepare texts for adoption by the Congress.

The Congress advises the Council's Committee of Ministers and the Parliamentary Assembly on all aspects of local and regional policy and co-operates with other national and international organizations representing local government. The Congress monitors implementation of the European Charter of Local Self-Government, which was opened for signature in 1985 and provides common standards for effective local democracy. Other legislative guidelines for the activities of local authorities and the promotion of democracy at local level include the 1980 European Outline Convention on Transfrontier Co-operation, and its Additional Protocol which was opened for signature in 1995; a Convention on the Participation of Foreigners in Public Life at Local Level (entered into force in 1997); and the European Charter for Regional or Minority Languages (entered into force 1998). In addition, the European Urban Charter (adopted 1992) defines citizens' rights in European towns and cities, for example in the areas of transport, urban architecture, pollution and security; the European Landscape Convention (entered into force in March 2004) details an obligation for public authorities to adopt policies and measures at local, regional, national and international level for the protection, management and planning of landscapes; and the Charter on the Participation of Young People in Municipal and Regional Life (adopted in 1992 and revised in 2003), sets out guidelines for encouraging the active involvement of young people in the promotion of social change in their municipality or region. In May 2005 the Congress concluded an agreement with the EU Committee of the Regions on co-operation in ensuring local and regional democracy and self-government.

The Congress produces 'monitoring reports' on the state of local democracy in member countries, and is responsible for the monitoring of local and regional elections and for setting standards in electoral matters. It was envisaged that during 2011–12 the Congress would enhance its monitoring activities, broaden the scope of election observation, develop the provision of targeted post-monitoring and post-observation assistance, streamline its thematic activities, and introduce as a new priority area of focus the local dimension of human rights.

In September 2011 the Congress convened a Summit of Mayors on Roma, in Strasbourg, with participation by representatives of European municipalities, regions, institutions and networks, and Roma and traveller organizations. The Summit issued a final Declaration which supported the establishment of a new European Alliance of Cities and Regions for Roma Inclusion, with a view to enhancing future co-operation.

President: KEITH WHITMORE (United Kingdom).

Activities

In an effort to harmonize national laws, to put the citizens of member countries on an equal footing and to pool certain resources and facilities, the Council of Europe has concluded a number of conventions and agreements covering particular aspects of European co-operation. Since 1989 the Council has undertaken to increase co-operation with all countries of the former Eastern bloc and to facilitate their accession to the organization. In October 1997 heads of state or government of member countries convened for only the second time (the first meeting took place in Vienna, in October 1993) with the aim of formulating a new social model to consolidate democracy throughout Europe. The meeting endorsed a Final Declaration and an Action Plan, which established priority areas for future Council activities, including fostering social cohesion; protecting civilian security; promoting human rights; enhancing joint measures to counter cross-border illegal trafficking; and strengthening democracy through education and other cultural activities. In addition, the meeting generated renewed political commitment to the Programme of Action against Corruption, which has become a key element of Council activities. A third meeting of heads of state or government was held in Warsaw, Poland, in May 2005. In a Final Declaration and an Action Plan the meeting defined the principal tasks of the Council in the coming years, i.e. promoting human rights and the rule of law, strengthening the security of European citizens and fostering co-operation with other international and European organizations. The Council's activities have three cross-cutting themes: children; democracy; and combating violence. In January 2011 the Parliamentary Assembly adopted a resolution recommending that a Council of Europe summit should be convened with the aim of redefining the role of the Council and giving it a new political impetus.

HUMAN RIGHTS

The protection of human rights is one of the Council of Europe's basic goals, to be achieved in four main areas: the effective supervision and protection of fundamental rights and freedoms; identification of new threats to human rights and human dignity; development of public awareness of the importance of human rights; and promotion of human rights education and professional training. The most significant treaties in this area include: the European Convention for the Protection of Human Rights and Fundamental Freedoms (European Convention on Human Rights) (which was adopted in 1950 and entered into force in 1953); the European Social Charter; the European Convention for the Prevention of Torture and Inhuman or Degrading Treatment or Punishment; the Framework Convention for the Protection of National Minorities; the European Charter for Regional or Minority Languages; and the Convention on Action against Trafficking in Human Beings.

The Steering Committee for Human Rights is responsible for inter-governmental co-operation in the field of human rights and fundamental freedoms; it works to strengthen the effectiveness of systems for protecting human rights and to identify potential threats and challenges to human rights. The Committee has been responsible for the elaboration of several conventions and other legal instruments including the following protocols to the European Convention on Human Rights: Protocol No. 11, which entered into force in November 1998, resulting in the replacement of the then existing institutions—the European Commission of Human Rights and the European Court of Human Rights—by a single Court, working on a full-time basis; Protocol No. 12, which entered into force in April 2005, enforcing a general prohibition of discrimination; No. 13, which entered into force in July 2003, guaranteeing the abolition of the death penalty in all circumstances (including in time of war); and No. 14, which entered into force on 1 June 2010, aiming to enhance the effectiveness of the Court by improving implementation of the European Convention on Human Rights at national level and the processing of applications, and accelerating the execution of the Court's decisions.

The EU Treaty of Lisbon, which entered into force in December 2009, provided for accession by the EU to the European Convention on Human Rights. Formal negotiations on EU accession commenced in July 2010. During 2011–12 a Joint Informal Body, comprising members of the Parliamentary Assembly and members of the European Parliament, met several times to discuss the accession process.

The Steering Committee for Human Rights was responsible for the preparation of the European Ministerial Conference on Human Rights, held in Rome in November 2000, to commemorate the 50th anniversary of the adoption of the European Convention on Human Rights. The Conference highlighted, in particular, 'the need to reinforce the effective protection of human rights in domestic legal systems as well as at the European level'.

The Council of Europe Commissioner for Human Rights (whose office was established by a resolution of the Council's Committee of Ministers in May 1999) promotes respect for human rights in member states.

In May 2012 the Commissioner emphasized the importance of effective national human rights structures (NHRSs)—including independent commissions, equality bodies, ombudsmen, and police complaints mechanisms—in protecting vulnerable sectors of society during the period of economic and social austerity that was ongoing in many European countries.

Commissioner for Human Rights: NILS MUIŽNIEKS (Latvia).

EUROPEAN COMMITTEE FOR THE PREVENTION OF TORTURE AND INHUMAN OR DEGRADING TREATMENT OR PUNISHMENT (CPT)

The Committee was established under the 1987 Convention for the Prevention of Torture as an integral part of the Council of Europe's system for the protection of human rights. The Committee, comprising independent experts, aims to examine the treatment of persons deprived of their liberty with a view to strengthening, if necessary, the protection of such persons from torture and from inhuman or degrading treatment or punishment. It conducts periodic visits to police stations, prisons, detention centres, and all other sites where persons are deprived of their liberty by a public authority, in all states parties to the Convention, and may also undertake ad hoc visits when the Committee considers them necessary. After each visit the Committee drafts a report of its findings and any further advice or recommendations, based on dialogue and co-operation. By June 2012 the Committee had published 267 reports and had undertaken 321 visits (195 periodic and 126 ad hoc).

President: LATIF HÜSEYNOV (Azerbaijan).

EUROPEAN SOCIAL CHARTER

The European Social Charter, in force since 1965, is the counterpart of the European Convention on Human Rights, in the field of protection of economic and social rights. A revised Charter, which amended existing guarantees and incorporated new rights, was opened for signature in May 1996, and entered into force on 1 July 1999. By June 2012 27 member states had ratified the Charter and 32 had ratified the revised Charter. Rights guaranteed by the Charter concern all individuals in their daily lives in matters of housing, health, education, employment, social protection, movement of persons and non-discrimination. The European Committee of Social Rights considers reports submitted to it annually by member states. It also considers collective complaints submitted in the framework of an Additional Protocol (1995), providing for a system which entered into force in July 1998, permitting trade unions, employers' organizations and NGOs to lodge complaints on alleged violations of the Charter. The Committee, composed of 15 members, decides on the conformity of national situations with the Charter. When a country does not bring a situation into conformity, the Committee of Ministers may, on the basis of decisions prepared by a Governmental Committee (composed of representatives of each Contracting Party), issue recommendations to the state concerned, inviting it to change its legislation or practice in accordance with the Charter's requirements.

President of the European Committee of Social Rights: LUIS JIMENA QUESADA (Spain).

FRAMEWORK CONVENTION FOR THE PROTECTION OF NATIONAL MINORITIES

In 1993 the first summit meeting of Council of Europe heads of state and government, held in Vienna, mandated the Committee of Ministers to draft 'a framework convention specifying the principle that States commit themselves to respect in order to assure the protection of national minorities'. A special committee was established to draft the so-called Framework Convention for the Protection of National Minorities, which was then adopted by the Committee in November 1994. The Convention was opened for signature in February 1995, entering into force in February 1998. Contracting parties (39 states at June 2012) are required to submit reports on the implementation of the treaty at regular intervals to an Advisory Committee composed of 18 independent experts. The Advisory Committee adopts an opinion on the implementation of the Framework Convention by the contracting party, on the basis of which the Committee of Ministers adopts a resolution. A Conference entitled 10 Years of Protecting National Minorities and Regional or Minority Languages was convened in March 2008 to review the impacts of, and the role of regional institutions in implementing, both the Framework Convention and the Convention on Minority Languages. In October 2010 a high-level meeting of the Council of Europe adopted the Strasbourg Declaration on Roma, detailing guiding principles and priorities to encourage the empowerment and inclusion of Roma/Gypsy people in Europe (who were estimated to number 10m.–12m. at that time); the Declaration outlined the establishment of a new European Training Programme for Roma Mediators, which was to enable the provision of legal and administrative advice to Roma communities.

Head, Secretariat: MICHÈLE AKIP.

RACISM AND INTOLERANCE

In October 1993 heads of state and of government, meeting in Vienna, resolved to reinforce a policy to combat all forms of intolerance, in response to the increasing incidence of racial hostility and intolerance towards minorities in European societies. A European Commission against Racism and Intolerance (ECRI) was established by the summit meeting to analyse and assess the effectiveness of legal, policy and other measures taken by member states to combat these problems. It became operational in March 1994. The European conference against racism, held in October 2000, requested that ECRI should be reinforced and, in June 2002, the Committee of Ministers of the Council of Europe adopted a new Statute for ECRI that consolidated its role as an independent human rights monitoring body focusing on issues related to racism and racial discrimination. Members of ECRI are appointed on the basis of their recognized expertise in the field; they are independent and impartial in fulfilling their mandate. ECRI undertakes activities in three programme areas: country-by-country approach; work on general themes; and relations with civil society. In the first area of activity, ECRI analyses the situation regarding racism and intolerance in each of the member states, in order to advise governments on measures to combat these problems. In December 1998 ECRI completed a first round of reports for all Council members. A second series of country reports was completed in December 2002 and a third monitoring cycle, focusing on implementation and 'specific issues', was undertaken during 2003–07. The fourth series of country reports was being compiled during 2008–12. ECRI's work on general themes includes the preparation of policy recommendations and guidelines on issues of importance to combating racism and intolerance. ECRI also collects and disseminates examples of good practices relating to these issues. Under the third programme area ECRI aims to disseminate information and raise awareness of the problems of racism and intolerance among the general public.

EQUALITY BETWEEN WOMEN AND MEN

The Steering Committee for Equality between Women and Men (CDEG—an intergovernmental committee of experts) is responsible for encouraging action at both national and Council of Europe level to promote equality of rights and opportunities between the two sexes. Assisted by various specialist groups and committees, the CDEG is mandated to establish analyses, studies and evaluations, to examine national policies and experiences, to devise concerted policy strategies and measures for implementing equality and, as necessary, to prepare appropriate legal and other instruments. It is also responsible for preparing the European Ministerial Conferences on Equality between Women and Men. The main areas of CDEG activities are the comprehensive inclusion of the rights of women (for example, combating violence against women and trafficking in human beings) within the context of human rights; the issue of equality and democracy, including the promotion of the participation of women in political and public life; projects aimed at studying the specific equality problems related to cultural diversity, migration and minorities; positive action in the field of equality between men and women and the mainstreaming of equality into all policies and programmes at all levels of society. In October 1998 the Committee of Ministers adopted a Recommendation to member states on gender mainstreaming; in May 2000 it approved a Recommendation on action against trafficking in human beings for the purpose of sexual exploitation; and in May 2002 it adopted a Recommendation on the protection of women from violence. Following a decision of the meeting of heads of state or government convened in Warsaw in May 2005, a Council of Europe Task Force to Combat Violence against Women, including Domestic Violence was established. In June 2006 the Committee of Ministers adopted the Blueprint of the Council of Europe Campaign to Combat Violence against Women, including Domestic Violence, which had been drafted by the Task Force. In May 2009 the Council of Europe published a *Handbook on the Implementation of Gender Budgeting*.

MEDIA AND COMMUNICATIONS

Article 10 of the European Convention on Human Rights (freedom of expression and information) forms the basis for the Council of Europe's activities in the area of mass media. Implementation of the Council of Europe's work programme concerning the media is undertaken by the Steering Committee on the Media and New Communication Services (CDMC), which comprises senior government officials and representatives of professional organizations, meeting in plenary session twice a year. The CDMC is mandated to devise concerted European policy measures and appropriate legal instruments. Its underlying aims are to further freedom of expression and information in a pluralistic democracy, and to promote the free flow of information and ideas. The CDMC is assisted by various specialist groups and committees. Policy and legal instruments have been developed on subjects including: exclusivity rights; media concentrations and transparency of media ownership; protection of journalists in situations of conflict and tension; independence of public-service broadcasting, protection of rights holders; legal protection of encrypted television services; media and elections; protection of journalists' sources of information; the independence and functions of broadcasting regulatory authorities; and coverage of legal proceedings by the media. These policy and legal instruments (mainly in the form of non-binding recommendations addressed to member governments) are complemented by the publication of studies, analyses and seminar proceedings on topics of media law and policy. The CDMC has also prepared a number of international binding legal instruments, including the European Convention on Transfrontier Television (adopted in 1989 and ratified by 34 countries by June 2012), the European Convention on the Legal Protection of Services Based on or Consisting of Conditional Access (ratified by nine countries at June 2012), and the European Convention Relating to Questions on Copyright Law and Neighbouring Rights in the Context of Transfrontier Broadcasting by Satellite (ratified by two countries at June 2012).

In March 2005 the Council's Committee of Ministers adopted a declaration on freedom of expression and information in the media in the context of the fight against terrorism. A declaration on the independence and functions of regulatory authorities for the broadcasting sector was adopted by the Committee of Ministers in March 2008. In that month the Committee also adopted a Recommendation on the Use of Internet Filters aimed at promoting a balance between freedom of expression and the protection of children against harmful material published on the internet.

SOCIAL COHESION

In June 1998 the Committee of Ministers established the European Committee for Social Cohesion (CDCS). The CDCS has the following responsibilities: to co-ordinate, guide and stimulate co-operation between member states with a view to promoting social cohesion in Europe; to develop and promote integrated, multidisciplinary responses to social issues; and to promote the social standards embodied in the European Social Charter and other Council of Europe instruments, including the European Code of Social Security. In 2002 the CDCS published the *Report on Access to Social Rights in Europe*, concerning access to employment, housing and social protection. The Committee supervises an extensive programme of work on children, families and the elderly. In March 2004 the Committee of Ministers approved a revised version of the Council's Strategy for Social Cohesion (adopted in July 2000).

The European Code of Social Security and its Protocol entered into force in 1968; by June 2012 the Code had been ratified by 21 states and the Protocol by seven states. These instruments set minimum standards for medical care and the following benefits: sickness; old age; unemployment; employment injury; family; maternity; invalidity; and survivor's benefit. A revision of these instruments, aiming to provide higher standards and greater flexibility, was completed for signature in 1990 and had been ratified by one member state (the Netherlands) at June 2012.

The European Convention on Social Security, in force since 1977, currently applies in Austria, Belgium, Italy, Luxembourg, the Netherlands, Portugal, Spain and Turkey; most of the provisions apply automatically, while others are subject to the conclusion of additional multilateral or bilateral agreements. The Convention is concerned with establishing the following four fundamental principles of international law on social security: equality of treatment; unity of applicable legislation; conservation of rights accrued or in course of acquisition; and payment of benefits abroad. In 1994 a Protocol to the Convention, providing for the enlargement of the personal scope of the Convention, was opened for signature; by June 2012 it had been ratified only by Portugal.

In May 2011 a Group of Eminent Persons, appointed by the Secretary-General, released a report entitled 'Living Together: Combining Freedom and Diversity in 21st Century Europe', which identified threats to the values of the Council of Europe deriving from rising intolerance and increasing diversity in European populations, and outlined proposed responses.

HEALTH

Through a series of expert committees, the Council aims to ensure constant co-operation in Europe in a variety of health-related fields, with particular emphasis on health services and patients' rights, for example: equity in access to health care; quality assurance; health services for institutionalized populations (prisoners, elderly in homes); discrimination resulting from health status; and education for health. These efforts are supplemented by the training of health personnel. Recommendations adopted by the Committee of Ministers in the area of health cover blood, cancer control, disabilities, health policy development and promotion, health services, the protection of human rights and dignity of persons with mental disorder, the organization of palliative care, the role of patients, transplantation, access to health care by vulnerable groups, and the impact of new information technologies on health care.

A Partial Agreement in the Social and Public Health Field aims to protect the consumer from potential health risks connected with commonplace or domestic products, including asbestos, cosmetics, flavouring substances, pesticides, pharmaceuticals and products that have a direct or indirect impact on the human food chain, and also has provisions on the integration of people with disabilities. Two European treaties have been concluded within the framework of this Partial Agreement: the European Agreement on the Restriction of the use of Certain Detergents in Washing and Cleaning Products, and the Convention on the Elaboration of a European Pharmacopoeia (establishing legally binding standards for medicinal substances, auxiliary substances, pharmaceutical preparations, vaccines for human and veterinary use and other articles). The latter Convention entered into force in eight signatory states in May 1974 and, by June 2012 had been ratified by 37 states and the EU. WHO, and seven European and 13 non-European states, participate (as at June 2012) as observers in the sessions of the European Pharmacopoeia Commission. In 1994 a procedure on certification of suitability to the European Pharmacopoeia monographs for manufacturers of substances for pharmaceutical use was established. A network of official control laboratories for human and veterinary medicines was established in 1995, open to all signatory countries to the Convention and observers at the Pharmacopoeia Commission. The seventh edition of the European Pharmacopoeia, in force since 1 January 2011, is updated regularly in its electronic version, and includes more than 2,000 harmonized European standards, or 'monographs', 268 general methods of analysis and 2,210 reagents.

The 1992 Recommendation on A Coherent Policy for People with Disabilities contains the policy principles for the rehabilitation and integration of people with disabilities. This model programme recommends that governments of all member states develop comprehensive and co-ordinated national disability policies taking account of prevention, diagnosis, treatment education, vocational guidance and training, employment, social integration, social protection, information and research. It has set benchmarks, both nationally and internationally. The 1995 Charter on the Vocational Assessment of People with Disabilities states that a person's vocational abilities and not disabilities should be assessed and related to specific job requirements. The 2001 Resolution on Universal Design aims to improve accessibility, recommending the inclusion of Universal Design principles in the training for vocations working on the built environment. The 2001 Resolution on New Technologies recommends formulating national strategies to ensure that people with disabilities benefit from new technologies. In April 2006 the Council of Europe Committee of Ministers adopted a Recommendation endorsing a recently drafted Council of Europe action plan for 2006–15, with the aim of promoting the rights and full participation of people with disabilities in society and of improving the quality of life of people with disabilities in Europe.

In the co-operation group to combat drug abuse and illicit drugs trafficking (Pompidou Group), 35 states work together, through meetings of ministers, officials and experts, to counteract drug abuse. The Group follows a multidisciplinary approach embracing, in particular, legislation, law enforcement, prevention, treatment, rehabilitation and data collection. In January 2007 the Group initiated an online register of ongoing drug research projects; a revised version of the register was launched in April 2008.

A new Council of Europe Convention on the Counterfeiting of Medical Products and Similar Crimes Involving Threats to Public Health ('Medicrime Convention') was opened for signature in October 2011 and had 15 signatories at June 2012.

Improvement of blood transfusion safety and availability of blood and blood derivatives has been ensured through European Agreements and guidelines. Advances in this field and in organ transplantation are continuously assessed by expert committees.

In April 1997 the first international convention on biomedicine was opened for signature at a meeting of health ministers of member states, in Oviedo, Spain. The so-called Convention for the Protection of Human Rights and the Dignity of Human Beings with Respect to the Applications of Biology and Medicine incorporated provisions on scientific research, the principle of informed patient consent, organ and tissue transplants and the prohibition of financial gain and disposal of a part of the human body. It entered into force on 1 November 1999 (see below).

POPULATION AND MIGRATION

The European Convention on the Legal Status of Migrant Workers, in force since 1983, has been ratified by Albania, France, Italy, Moldova, the Netherlands, Norway, Portugal, Spain, Sweden, Turkey and the Ukraine. The Convention is based on the principle of equality of treatment for migrant workers and the nationals of the host country as to housing, working conditions, and social security. It also upholds the principle of the right to family reunion. An international consultative committee, representing the parties to the Convention, monitors the application of the Convention.

In 1996 the European Committee on Migration concluded work on a project entitled 'The Integration of Immigrants: Towards Equal Opportunities' and the results were presented at the sixth conference of European ministers responsible for migration affairs, held in Warsaw. At the conference a new project, entitled 'Tensions and Tolerance: Building better integrated communities across Europe' was initiated; it was concluded in 1999. During the period 1977–2005 an ad hoc committee of experts on the Legal Aspects of Territorial Asylum Refugees and Stateless Persons (CAHAR) assisted the Committee on Migration with examining migration issues at the pan-European level. In 2002 CAHAR prepared a Recommendation relating to the detention of asylum seekers. In May 2005 the Committee of Ministers adopted *Twenty Guidelines on Forced Return of Illegal Residents*, which had been drafted by CAHAR. The European Committee on Migration was responsible for activities concerning Roma/Gypsies in Europe, in co-ordination with other relevant Council of Europe bodies. In December 2004 a European Roma and Travellers Forum, established in partnership with the Council of Europe, was inaugurated. The eighth Council of Europe conference of ministers responsible for migration affairs, convened in Kyiv, Ukraine, in September 2008, adopted a final declaration on pursuing an integrated approach to addressing economic migration, social cohesion and development. In May 2011 a consultation meeting on Council of Europe activities in the area of migration, addressing the human rights dimension of migration; procedures for asylum and return; and questions relating to the social integration of migrants, was convened in Athens, Greece, with participation by experts and representatives of UNHCR and the EU Fundamental Rights Agency.

In May 2006 the Council of Europe adopted a Convention on the avoidance of statelessness in relation to state succession. It was reported in August 2011 by the Council's Commissioner for Human Rights that there were at that time up to 589,000 stateless people in Europe.

The European Population Committee, an intergovernmental committee of scientists and government officials responsible for population matters, monitors and analyses population trends throughout Europe and informs governments, research centres and the public of demographic developments and their impact on policy decisions. It compiles an annual statistical review of regional demographic developments and publishes the results of studies on population issues.

LEGAL AFFAIRS

The European Committee on Legal Co-operation develops co-operation between member states in the field of law, with the objective of harmonizing and modernizing public and private law, including administrative law and the law relating to the judiciary. The Committee is responsible for expert groups which consider issues relating to administrative law, efficiency of justice, family law, nationality, information technology and data protection.

Numerous conventions and Recommendations have been adopted, and followed up by appropriate committees or groups of experts, on matters which include: efficiency of justice; nationality; legal aid; rights of children; data protection; information technology; children born out of wedlock; animal protection; adoption; information on foreign law; and the legal status of NGOs.

In December 1999 the Convention for the Protection of Human Rights and the Dignity of Human Beings with Respect to the Applications of Biology and Medicine: Convention on Human Rights and Biomedicine entered into force, as the first internationally binding legal text to protect people against the misuse of biological and medical advances. It aims to preserve human dignity and identity, rights and freedoms, through a series of principles and rules. Additional protocols develop the Convention's general provisions by means of specialized texts. A Protocol prohibiting the medical cloning of human beings was approved by Council heads of state and government in 1998 and entered into force on 1 March 2001. A Protocol on the transplantation of human organs and tissue was opened for signature in January 2002 and entered into force in May 2006, and a Protocol concerning biomedical research opened for signature in January 2005 and entered into force in September 2007. Work on draft protocols relating to protection of the human embryo and foetus, and genetics is ongoing. A Recommendation on xenotransplantation was adopted by the Committee of Ministers in 2003.

In 2001 an Additional Protocol to the Convention for the protection of individuals with regard to automatic processing of personal data was adopted. The Protocol, which opened for signature in November, concerned supervisory authorities and transborder data flows. It entered into force in July 2004.

In 2001 the European Committee for Social Cohesion (CDCS) approved three new conventions on contact concerning children, legal aid, and 'Information Society Services'. In 2002 the CDCS approved a Recommendation on mediation on civil matters and a resolution establishing the European Commission for the Efficiency of Justice (CEPEJ). The aims of the CEPEJ are: to improve the efficiency and functioning of the justice system of member states, with a view to ensuring that everyone within their jurisdiction can enforce their legal rights effectively, increasing citizen confidence in the system; and to enable better implementation of the international legal instruments of the Council of Europe concerning efficiency and fairness of justice.

A Convention on Contact concerning Children was adopted in May 2003. It entered into force in September 2005 and by June 2012 had been ratified by seven states. A new convention on the Protection of Children against Sexual Exploitation and Sexual Abuse was adopted in July 2007 and entered into force in July 2010; by June 2012 it had received 19 ratifications.

A Convention on Preventing and Combating Violence against Women and Domestic Violence was adopted in May 2011, and was to enter into force following its 10th ratification (it had 20 signatories and one ratification at June 2012).

The Consultative Council of European Judges has prepared a framework global action plan for judges in Europe. In addition, it has contributed to the implementation of this programme by the adoption of opinions on standards concerning the independence of the judiciary and the irremovability of judges, and on the funding and management of courts.

A Committee of Legal Advisers on Public and International Law (CAHDI), comprising the legal advisers of ministers of foreign affairs of member states and of several observer states, is authorized by the Committee of Ministers to examine questions of public international law, and to exchange and, if appropriate, to co-ordinate the views of member states. The CAHDI functions as a European observatory of reservations to international treaties. Recent activities of the CAHDI include the preparation of a Recommendation on reactions to inadmissible reservations to international treaties, the publication of a report on state practice with regard to state succession and recognition, and another on expression of consent of states to be bound by a treaty.

With regard to crime, expert committees and groups operating under the authority of the European Committee on Crime Problems have prepared conventions on such matters as extradition, mutual assistance, recognition and enforcement of foreign judgments, transfer of proceedings, suppression of terrorism, transfer of prisoners, compensation payable to victims of violent crime, money-laundering, confiscation of proceeds from crime and corruption.

A Convention on Cybercrime, adopted in 2001, entered into force in July 2004 and by June 2012 had received 35 ratifications. In 2003 member states concluded an additional Protocol to the Convention relating to the criminalization of acts of a racist and xenophobic nature committed through computer systems; this entered into force in March 2006 and had been ratified by 20 countries at June 2012. The Council of Europe organizes an annual conference on cybercrime (in 2011 held in November, in Strasbourg). The 2008 conference, convened in April, adopted guidelines aimed at improving co-operation between crime investigators and internet service providers.

A Multidisciplinary Group on International Action against Terrorism, established in 2001, elaborated a protocol that updated the 1977 European Convention on the Suppression of Terrorism. In 2002 the Council's Committee of Ministers adopted a set of 'guidelines on Human Rights and the Fight against Terrorism'. In 2003 a Committee of Experts on Terrorism (CODEXTER) was inaugurated, with a mandate to oversee and co-ordinate the Council's counter-terrorism activities in the legal field. CODEXTER formulated the Council of Europe Convention for the Prevention of Terrorism, which was opened for signature in May 2005 and entered into force in June 2007. By June 2012 the Convention for the Prevention of Terrorism had been ratified by 29 member states. In 2006 the Council of Europe launched a campaign to combat trafficking, which seeks to raise awareness of the extent of trafficking in present-day Europe and to emphasize the measures that can be taken to prevent it. The campaign also promotes participation in the Convention on Action against Trafficking in Human Beings; the Convention entered into force in February 2008 and, by June 2012, had been ratified by 36 countries.

The Group of States Against Corruption (GRECO) became operational in 1999 and became a permanent body of the Council in 2002. At June 2012 it had 49 members (including the USA). A monitoring mechanism, based on mutual evaluation and peer pressure, GRECO assesses members' compliance with Council instruments for combating corruption, including the Criminal Law Convention on Corruption, which entered into force in July 2002 (and by June 2012 had been ratified by 43 states), and its Additional Protocol (which entered into force in February 2005). The evaluation procedure of GRECO is confidential but it has become practice to make reports public after their adoption. GRECO's First Evaluation Round was completed during 2001–02, and the Second Evaluation Round was conducted during 2003–06. The Third Evaluation Round, which was undertaken during 2007–11, covered member states' compliance with, *inter alia*, requirements of the Criminal Law Convention on Corruption and its Additional Protocol, and the area of transparency of political party funding. GRECO's Fourth Evaluation Round commenced in January 2012. In May 2012 GRECO urged member states to establish transparent systems for regulating the funding of political parties and election campaigns. During 2012 GRECO was, for the first time, considering the prevention of corruption among members of parliament and of judiciaries in member states; the first countries to be evaluated in this respect were Estonia, Finland, Latvia, Poland, Slovenia and the United Kingdom.

The Select Committee of Experts on the Evaluation of Anti-Money Laundering Measures (MONEYVAL) became operational in 1998. It is responsible for mutual evaluation of the anti-money-laundering measures in place in 20 Council of Europe states that are not members of the Financial Action Task Force (FATF). The MONEYVAL mechanism is based on FATF practices and procedures. States are evaluated against the relevant international standards in the legal, financial and law enforcement sectors. In the legal sector this includes evaluation of states' obligations under the Council of Europe Convention on Laundering, Search, Seizure and Confiscation of the Proceeds from Crime and on the Financing of Terrorism, which entered into force in May 2008. With effect from 1 January 2011 MONEYVAL was elevated to the status of an independent monitoring mechanism, reporting directly to the Committee of Ministers. After the terrorist attacks against targets in the USA on 11 September 2001, the Committee of Ministers adopted revised terms of reference, which specifically include the evaluation of measures to combat the financing of terrorism. MONEYVAL undertook its first round of on-site visits during 1998–2000. Its second round, focusing even more closely on the effectiveness of national systems, began in 2001 and was completed in 2004. MONEYVAL's third evaluation round, covering the period

2005–10, was being conducted in accordance with a comprehensive global methodology agreed with the FATF, FATF-style regional bodies, the IMF and the World Bank, and was evaluating the effectiveness of enforcement measures in place to combat the financing of terrorism as well as money laundering. The evaluations of MONEYVAL are confidential, but summaries of adopted reports are made public.

A Criminological Scientific Council, composed of specialists in law, psychology, sociology and related sciences, advises the Committee and organizes criminological research conferences and colloquia. A Council for Penological Co-operation organizes regular high-level conferences of directors of prison administrations and is responsible for collating statistical information on detention and community sanctions in Europe. The Council prepared the European Prison Rules in 1987 and the European Rules on Community Sanctions (alternatives to imprisonment) in 1992. A council for police matters was established in 2002.

In May 1990 the Committee of Ministers adopted a Partial Agreement to establish the European Commission for Democracy through Law, to be based in Venice, Italy. The so-called Venice Commission was enlarged in February 2002 and in June 2012 comprised all Council of Europe member states in addition to Kyrgyzstan (which joined in 2004), Chile (2005), the Republic of Korea (2006), Algeria and Morocco (2007), Israel and Tunisia (2008), Peru and Brazil (2009), and Mexico (2010). The Commission is composed of independent legal and political experts, mainly senior academics, supreme or constitutional court judges, members of national parliaments, and senior public officers. Its main activity is constitutional assistance and it may supply opinions upon request, made through the Committee of Ministers, by the Parliamentary Assembly, the Secretary-General or any member states of the Commission. Other states and international organizations may request opinions with the consent of the Committee of Ministers. The Commission is active throughout the constitutional domain, and has worked on issues including legislation on constitutional courts and national minorities, electoral law and other legislation with implications for national democratic institutions. The creation of the Council for Democratic Elections institutionalized co-operation in the area of elections between the Venice Commission, the Parliamentary Assembly of the Council of Europe, and the Congress of Regional and Local Authorities of the Council of Europe. The Commission disseminates its work through the UniDem (University for Democracy) programme of seminars, the CODICES database, and the *Bulletin of Constitutional Case-Law*. In May 2005 Council heads of state decided to establish a new Forum for the Future of Democracy, with the aim of strengthening democracy and citizens' participation.

The promotion of local and regional democracy and of transfrontier co-operation constitutes a major aim of the Council's intergovernmental programme of activities. The Steering Committee on Local and Regional Democracy (CDLR) serves as a forum for representatives of member states to exchange information and pursue co-operation in order to promote the decentralization of powers, in accordance with the European Charter on Local Self-Government. The CDLR's principal objectives are to improve the legal, institutional and financial framework of local democracy and to encourage citizen participation in local and regional communities. In December 2001 the Committee of Ministers adopted a Recommendation on citizens' participation in public life at local level, drafted on the basis of the work conducted by the CDLR. The CDLR publishes comparative studies and national reports, and aims to identify guidelines for the effective implementation of the principles of subsidiarity and solidarity. Its work also constitutes a basis for the provision of aid to Central and Eastern European countries in the field of local democracy. The CDLR is responsible for the preparation and follow-up of Conferences of Ministers responsible for local and regional government.

Intergovernmental co-operation with the CDLR is supplemented by specific activities aimed at providing legislative advice, supporting reform and enhancing management capabilities and democratic participation in European member and non-member countries. These activities are specifically focused on the democratic stability of Central and Eastern European countries. The programmes for democratic stability in the field of local democracy draw inspiration from the European Charter of Local Self-Government, operating at three levels of government: at intergovernmental level, providing assistance in implementing reforms to reinforce local or regional government, in compliance with the Charter; at local or regional level, co-operating with local and regional authorities to build local government capacity; and at community level, co-operating directly with individual authorities to promote pilot initiatives. Working methods include: awareness-raising conferences; legislative opinion involving written opinions, expert round-tables and working groups; and seminars, workshops and training at home and abroad.

In February 2005 the 14th session of the conference of European ministers responsible for local and regional government adopted the Budapest Agenda for Delivering Good Local and Regional Governance in 2005–10, which identified challenges confronting local and regional democracy in Europe and actions to be taken in response to them. In October 2007 the 15th session of the conference adopted the Valencia Declaration, recommitting to the implementation of the Budapest Agenda and endorsing a new Council of Europe Strategy on Innovation and Good Governance at Local Level. The 15th session also determined to draft an additional protocol to the European Charter on Local Self-Government consolidating at European level the right to democratic participation, citizens' right to information, and the duties of authorities relating to these rights; this was opened for signature in November 2009. The 16th session, held in Utrecht, Netherlands, in October 2009, adopted the 'Utrecht Declaration on Good Local and Regional Governance in Turbulent Times: The Challenge of Change'.

The policy of the Council of Europe on transfrontier co-operation between territorial communities or authorities is implemented through two committees. The Committee of Experts on Transfrontier Co-operation, working under the supervision of the CDLR, aims to monitor the implementation of the European Outline Convention on Transfrontier Co-operation between Territorial Communities or Authorities; to make proposals for the elimination of obstacles, in particular of a legal nature, to transfrontier and interterritorial co-operation; and to compile 'best practice' examples of transfrontier co-operation in various fields of activity. In 2002 the Committee of Ministers adopted a Recommendation on the mutual aid and assistance between central and local authorities in the event of disasters affecting frontier areas. A Committee of Advisers for the development of transfrontier co-operation in Central and Eastern Europe is composed of six members appointed or elected by the Secretary-General, the Committee of Ministers and the Congress of Local and Regional Authorities of Europe. Its task is to guide the promotion of transfrontier co-operation in Central and Eastern European countries, with a view to fostering good neighbourly relations between the frontier populations, especially in particularly sensitive regions. Its programme comprises: conferences and colloquies designed to raise awareness on the Outline Convention; meetings in border regions between representatives of local communities with a view to strengthening mutual trust; and legal assistance to, and restricted meetings with, national and local representatives responsible for preparing the legal texts for ratification and/or implementation of the Outline Convention. The priority areas outlined by the Committee of Advisers include South-East Europe, northern Europe around the Baltic Sea, the external frontiers of an enlarged EU, and the Caucasus.

EDUCATION, CULTURE AND HERITAGE

The European Cultural Convention covers education, culture, heritage, sport and youth. Programmes on education, higher education, culture and cultural heritage are managed by four steering committees. A new Council of Europe cultural governance observatory, CultureWatchEurope is under development, with a mandate to monitor the follow-up to all relevant Council of Europe Conventions; to act as a forum for the exchange of information on culture, and on cultural and natural heritage; to observe ongoing relevant policies, practices, trends and emerging issues; to highlight good practice; and to analyse and advise on policy.

The education programme consists of projects on education for democratic citizenship and human rights, history teaching, intercultural dialogue, instruments and policies for plurilingualism, the education of European Roma/Gypsy children, teaching remembrance—education for the prevention of crimes against humanity, and the 'Pestalozzi' training programme for education professionals. The Council of Europe's main focus in the field of higher education is, in co-operation with the EU, on the Bologna Process, which was launched in 1999 with the aim of establishing a European Higher Education Area, including education networks and student exchanges at all levels. In May 2007 the Council of Europe and the EU signed a Memorandum of Understanding confirming mutual co-operation in the promotion of democratic citizenship and human rights education and reaffirming commitment to the Bologna Process. In April 2009 ministers responsible for higher education in the member countries of the Bologna Process adopted the priorities for the European Higher Education Area until 2020, with an emphasis on the importance of life long learning, expanding access to higher education, and mobility. In March 2010 the Bologna Process ministers for higher education adopted the Budapest-Vienna Declaration officially launching the European Higher Education Area. Other Council of Europe activities in the area of education include the partial agreement for the European Centre for Modern Languages located in Graz, Austria, the Network for School Links and Exchanges, and the European Schools Day competition, organized in co-operation with the EU.

In December 2000 the Committee of Ministers adopted a Declaration on Cultural Diversity, formulated in consultation with other organizations (including the EU and UNESCO), which created a framework for developing a European approach to valuing cultural diversity. A European Charter for Regional or Minority Languages entered into force in 1998, with the aim of protecting regional or minority languages, which are considered to be a threatened aspect of Europe's cultural heritage. It was intended to promote the use in private and public life of languages traditionally used within a state's territory. The Charter provides for a monitoring system enabling states, the Council of Europe and individuals to observe and follow up its implementation. The meeting of heads of state or government convened in Warsaw, Poland, in May 2005 identified intercultural dialogue as a means of promoting tolerance and social cohesion; this was supported by the Faro Declaration on the Council of Europe's Strategy for Developing Intercultural Dialogue adopted by ministers of culture convened in Faro, Portugal, in October of that year. In May 2008 the Council of Europe organized, in Liverpool, United Kingdom, a conference on intercultural cities, which addressed replacing a multicultural approach to cultural diversity with an intercultural outlook, encouraging interaction between and hybridization of cultures, with a view to generating a richer common cultural environment. A new Council of Europe Intercultural Cities Programme was launched at the conference. In that month the Committee of Ministers adopted a *White Paper on Intercultural Dialogue* which stated that clear reference to the universal values of democracy, human rights, and the rule of law must underpin the use of intercultural dialogue as a means of addressing the complex issues raised by increasingly culturally diverse societies.

The Framework Convention on the Value of Cultural Heritage for Society (known as the Faro Framework Convention), which entered into force in June 2011, establishes principles underpinning the use and development of heritage in Europe in the globalization era.

The European Audiovisual Observatory, established in 1992, collates and circulates information on legal, production, marketing and statistical issues relating to the audiovisual industry in Europe, in the four sectors of film, television, video and DVD, and new media. The European Convention for the Protection of Audiovisual Heritage and its Protocol were opened for signature in November 2001; the first document entered into force in January 2008, and had been ratified by eight countries at June 2012. The Eurimages support fund, in which 36 member states participate, helps to finance co-production of films. The Convention for the Protection of the Architectural Heritage and the Protection of the Archaeological Heritage provide a legal framework for European co-operation in these areas. The European Heritage Network is being developed to facilitate the work of professionals and state institutions and the dissemination of good practices in more than 30 countries of the states party to the European Cultural Convention.

YOUTH

In 1972 the Council of Europe established the European Youth Centre (EYC) in Strasbourg. A second residential centre was created in Budapest in 1995. The centres, run with and by international non-governmental youth organizations representing a wide range of interests, provide about 50 residential courses a year (study sessions, training courses, symposia). A notable feature of the EYC is its decision-making structure, by which decisions on its programme and general policy matters are taken by a Programming Committee composed of an equal number of youth organizations and government representatives. The ninth Council of Europe Conference of Ministers responsible for Youth was scheduled to take place in St Petersburg, Russia, in September 2012.

The European Youth Foundation (EYF) aims to provide financial assistance to European activities of non-governmental youth organizations and began operations in 1973. Since that time more than 300,000 young people have benefited directly from EYF-supported activities. The Steering Committee for Youth conducts research in youth-related matters and prepares for ministerial conferences.

In 1997 the Council of Europe and the European Youth Information and Counselling Agency (EYRICA) concluded a partnership agreement on developing the training of youth information workers. EYRICA maintains SHEYRICA, an online platform supporting youth information workers. In November 2004 the EYRICA General Assembly adopted the European Youth Information Charter; in 2012 some 13,000 EYRICA youth workers were providing young people with general information in accordance with the principles of the Charter. In 2012 EYRICA comprised 24 member organizations, as well as seven affiliated and three co-operating organizations, which were active in more than 7,500 youth information centres in 28 countries.

SPORT

The Committee for the Development of Sport, founded in 1977, oversees sports co-operation and development on a pan-European basis, bringing together all the 50 (as at June 2012) states party to the European Cultural Convention. Its activities focus on the implementation of the European Sport Charter and Code of Sports Ethics (adopted in 1992 and revised in 2001), the role of sport in society, the provision of assistance in sports reform to new member states in Central and Eastern Europe, and the practice of both recreational and high-level sport. A Charter on Sport for Disabled Persons was adopted in 1986. The Committee also prepares the Conferences of European Ministers responsible for Sport (usually held every four years) and has been responsible for drafting two important conventions to combat negative influences on sport. The European Convention on Spectator Violence and Misbehaviour at Sport Events (1985) provides governments with practical measures to ensure crowd security and safety, particularly at football matches. The Anti-Doping Convention (1989) has been ratified by 51 countries (as at June 2012); it is also open to non-European states. In October 2004 the ministerial conference, convened in Budapest, Hungary, adopted principles of good governance in sport. In May 2007 the Committee of Ministers adopted the Enlarged Partial Agreement on Sport (EPAS), which aimed to develop a framework for a pan-European platform of intergovernmental sports co-operation and to set international standards.

ENVIRONMENT AND SUSTAINABLE DEVELOPMENT

In 1995 the Pan-European Biological and Landscape Diversity Strategy (PEBLDS), formulated by the Committee of Ministers, was endorsed at a ministerial conference of the UN Economic Commission for Europe, which was held in Sofia, Bulgaria. The Strategy is implemented jointly by the Council of Europe and UNEP, in close co-operation with the European Community. In particular, it provides for implementation of the Convention on Biological Diversity. It promotes the development of the Pan-European Ecological Network (PEEN), supporting the conservation of a full range of European ecosystems, habitats, species and landscapes, and physically linking core areas through the preservation (or restoration) of ecological corridors.

The Convention on the Conservation of European Wildlife and Natural Habitats (Bern Convention), which was signed in 1979 and entered into force in June 1982, gives total protection to 693 species of plants, 89 mammals, 294 birds, 43 reptiles, 21 amphibians, 115 freshwater fishes, 113 invertebrates and their habitats. The Convention established a network of protected areas known as the 'Emerald Network'. The Council awards the European Diploma for protection of sites of European significance, supervises a network of biogenetic reserves, and co-ordinates conservation action for threatened animals and plants. A European Convention on Landscape, to provide for the management and protection of the natural and cultural landscape in Europe, was adopted by the Committee of Ministers in 2000 and entered into force in July 2004.

Regional disparities constitute a major obstacle to the process of European integration. Conferences of ministers responsible for regional/spatial planning (CEMAT) are held to discuss these issues. In 2000 they adopted guiding principles for sustainable development of the European continent and, in 2001, a resolution detailing a 10-point programme for greater cohesion among the regions of Europe. In September 2003 the 13th CEMAT, convened in Ljubljana, Slovenia, agreed on strategies to promote the sustainable spatial development of the continent, including greater public participation in decision-making, an initiative to revitalize the countryside and efforts to prevent flooding. The 14th meeting was held in Portugal, in October 2006, and the 15th was convened in July 2010, in Moscow, Russia, on the theme 'Challenge of the Future: Sustainable Spatial Development of the European Continent in a Changing World'.

EXTERNAL RELATIONS

Agreements providing for co-operation and exchange of documents and observers have been concluded with the UN and its agencies, and with most of the European intergovernmental organizations and the Organization of American States. Relations with non-member states, other organizations and NGOs are co-ordinated by the Directorate-General of Political Affairs. In 2001 the Council and European Commission signed a joint declaration on co-operation and partnership, which provided for the organization and funding of joint programmes.

Israel, Canada and Mexico are represented in the Parliamentary Assembly by observer delegations, and certain European and other non-member countries participate in or send observers to certain meetings of technical committees and specialized conferences at intergovernmental level. Full observer status with the Council was granted to the USA in 1995, to Canada and Japan in 1996 and to Mexico in 1999. The Holy See has had a similar status since 1970.

The European Centre for Global Interdependence and Solidarity (the 'North-South Centre') was established in Lisbon, Portugal, in 1990, in order to provide a framework for European co-operation in this area and to promote pluralist democracy and respect for human rights. The Centre is co-managed by parliamentarians, governments, NGOs and local and regional authorities. Its activities are divided into three programmes: public information and media relations; education and training for global interdependence; and dialogue for global partnership. The Centre organizes workshops, seminars and training courses on global interdependence and convenes international colloquies on human rights.

The partial European and Mediterranean Major Hazards Agreement (EUR-OPA), adopted in 1987, facilitates co-operation between European and non-European southern Mediterranean countries in the field of major natural and technological disasters, covering knowledge of hazards, risk prevention, risk management, post-crisis analysis and rehabilitation.

Since 1993 the Council of Europe and EU have jointly established a co-operative structure of programmes to assist the process of democratic reform in Central and Eastern European countries that were formerly under communist rule. The majority of ongoing joint programmes are country-specific (for example, programmes focused on Albania (inaugurated in 1993), on Armenia, Azerbaijan and Georgia (1999), on Bosnia and Herzegovina (2003), Moldova (1997), Russia (1996), Serbia (2001), and Ukraine (1995). Sub-regional multilateral thematic programmes have also been implemented, for example on combating organized crime and corruption, and on the protection of national minorities. A scheme of Democratic Leadership Programmes for the training of political leaders has been implemented. Within the framework of the co-operation programme 21 information and documentation offices have been established in Central and Eastern European countries.

Finance

The budget is financed by contributions from members on a proportional scale of assessment (using population and gross domestic product as common indicators). The budgets for both 2012 and 2013 totalled €240m.

Publications

Activities Report (in English and French).

The Bulletin (newsletter of the CLRAE, quarterly).

Bulletin On Constitutional Case-Law (3–4 times a year, in English and French).

The Council of Europe: 800 million Europeans (introductory booklet).

Education Newsletter (3 a year).

The Europeans (electronic bulletin of the Parliamentary Assembly).

The Fight Against Terrorism, Council of Europe Standards (in English and French).

Human Rights and the Environment (in English, French and Italian).

Human Rights Information Bulletin (3 a year, in English and French).

The Independent (newsletter of the North-South Centre, 3 a year).

Iris (legal observations of the European audiovisual observatory, monthly).

Naturopa (2 a year, in 15 languages).

Penological Information Bulletin (annually, in English and French).

The Pompidou Group Newsletter (3 a year).

Recent Demographic Developments in Europe (annually, in English and French).

Social Cohesion Developments (3 a year).

Yearbook of Film, Television and Multimedia in Europe (in English and French).

Associated Body

Council of Europe Development Bank (CEB): 55 ave Kléber, 75116 Paris, France; tel. 1-47-55-55-00; fax 1-47-55-37-82; e-mail info@coebank.org; internet www.coebank.org; f. April 1956 as the Council of Europe Resettlement Fund, subsequently renamed as the Council of Europe Social Development Fund, with the present name adopted in Nov. 1999; a multilateral development bank with a social development mandate; grants loans for investment projects with a social purpose: priority projects seek to solve social problems related to the presence of refugees, displaced persons or forced migrants; additionally, the Bank finances projects in other fields contributing directly to strengthening social cohesion in Europe, including: job creation and preservation in small and medium-sized enterprises; social housing; improving urban living conditions; health and education infrastructure; managing the environment; and supporting public infrastructure; established in 2008 a Human Rights Trust Account to finance technical projects in the field of human rights protection; at 31 Dec. 2011 this had received total contributions of €6.1m. and had disbursed €3.6m; total assets: €26,083m. (2011); in 2011 the Bank approved new projects with a value of €2,110m; Governor ROLF WENZEL.

European Social Charter

(4 November 1950; text as revised 3 May 1996)

PREAMBLE

The governments signatory hereto, being members of the Council of Europe

Considering that the aim of the Council of Europe is the achievement of greater unity between its members for the purpose of safeguarding and realising the ideals and principles which are their common heritage and of facilitating their economic and social progress, in particular by the maintenance and further realisation of human rights and fundamental freedoms;

Considering that in the European Convention for the Protection of Human Rights and Fundamental Freedoms signed at Rome on 4 November 1950, and the Protocols thereto, the member States of the Council of Europe agreed to secure to their populations the civil and political rights and freedoms therein specified;

Considering that in the European Social Charter opened for signature in Turin on 18 October 1961 and the Protocols thereto, the member States of the Council of Europe agreed to secure to their populations the social rights specified therein in order to improve their standard of living and their social well-being;

Recalling that the Ministerial Conference on Human Rights held in Rome on 5 November 1990 stressed the need, on the one hand, to preserve the indivisible nature of all human rights, be they civil, political, economic, social or cultural and, on the other hand, to give the European Social Charter fresh impetus;

Resolved, as was decided during the Ministerial Conference held in Turin on 21 and 22 October 1991, to update and adapt the substantive contents of the Charter in order to take account in particular of the fundamental social changes which have occurred since the text was adopted;

Recognising the advantage of embodying in a Revised Charter, designed progressively to take the place of the European Social Charter, the rights guaranteed by the Charter as amended, the rights guaranteed by the Additional Protocol of 1988 and to add new rights

Have agreed as follows:

PART I

The Parties accept as the aim of their policy, to be pursued by all appropriate means both national and international in character, the attainment of conditions in which the following rights and principles may be effectively realised:

1. Everyone shall have the opportunity to earn his living in an occupation freely entered upon.
2. All workers have the right to just conditions of work.
3. All workers have the right to safe and healthy working conditions.
4. All workers have the right to a fair remuneration sufficient for a decent standard of living for themselves and their families.
5. All workers and employers have the right to freedom of association in national or international organizations for the protection of their economic and social interests.
6. All workers and employers have the right to bargain collectively.
7. Children and young persons have the right to a special protection against the physical and moral hazards to which they are exposed.
8. Employed women, in case of maternity, have the right to a special protection.
9. Everyone has the right to appropriate facilities for vocational guidance with a view to helping him choose an occupation suited to his personal aptitude and interests.
10. Everyone has the right to appropriate facilities for vocational training.
11. Everyone has the right to benefit from any measures enabling him to enjoy the highest possible standard of health attainable.
12. All workers and their dependents have the right to social security.
13. Anyone without adequate resources has the right to social and medical assistance.
14. Everyone has the right to benefit from social welfare services.
15. Disabled persons have the right to independence, social integration and participation in the life of the community.
16. The family as a fundamental unit of society has the right to appropriate social, legal and economic protection to ensure its full development.
17. Children and young persons have the right to appropriate social, legal and economic protection.
18. The nationals of any one of the Parties have the right to engage in any gainful occupation in the territory of any one of the others on a footing of equality with the nationals of the latter, subject to restrictions based on cogent economic or social reasons.
19. Migrant workers who are nationals of a Party and their families have the right to protection and assistance in the territory of any other Party.
20. All workers have the right to equal opportunities and equal treatment in matters of employment and occupation without discrimination on the grounds of sex.
21. Workers have the right to be informed and to be consulted within the undertaking.
22. Workers have the right to take part in the determination and improvement of the working conditions and working environment in the undertaking.
23. Every elderly person has the right to social protection.
24. All workers have the right to protection in cases of termination of employment.
25. All workers have the right to protection of their claims in the event of the insolvency of their employer.
26. All workers have the right to dignity at work.
27. All persons with family responsibilities and who are engaged or wish to engage in employment have a right to do so without being subject to discrimination and as far as possible without conflict between their employment and family responsibilities.
28. Workers' representatives in undertakings have the right to protection against acts prejudicial to them and should be afforded appropriate facilities to carry out their functions.
29. All workers have the right to be informed and consulted in collective redundancy procedures.
30. Everyone has the right to protection against poverty and social exclusion.
31. Everyone has the right to housing.

PART II

The Parties undertake, as provided for in Part III, to consider themselves bound by the obligations laid down in the following articles and paragraphs.

Article 1. The right to work.

With a view to ensuring the effective exercise of the right to work, the Parties undertake:

1. to accept as one of their primary aims and responsibilities the achievement and maintenance of as high and stable a level of employment as possible, with a view to the attainment of full employment;
2. to protect effectively the right of the worker to earn his living in an occupation freely entered upon;
3. to establish or maintain free employment services for all workers;
4. to provide or promote appropriate vocational guidance, training and rehabilitation.

Article 2. The right to just conditions of work.

With a view to ensuring the effective exercise of the right to just conditions of work, the Parties undertake:

1. to provide for reasonable daily and weekly working hours, the working week to be progressively reduced to the extent that the increase of productivity and other relevant factors permit;

2. to provide for public holidays with pay;

3. to provide for a minimum of four weeks' annual holiday with pay;

4. to eliminate risks in inherently dangerous or unhealthy occupations, and where it has not yet been possible to eliminate or reduce sufficiently these risks, to provide for either a reduction of working hours or additional paid holidays for workers engaged in such occupations;

5. to ensure a weekly rest period which shall, as far as possible, coincide with the day recognised by tradition or custom in the country or region concerned as a day of rest;

6. to ensure that workers are informed in written form, as soon as possible, and in any event not later than two months after the date of commencing their employment, of the essential aspects of the contract or employment relationship;

7. to ensure that workers performing night work benefit from measures which take account of the special nature of the work.

Article 3. The right to safe and healthy working conditions.

With a view to ensuring the effective exercise of the right to safe and healthy working conditions, the Parties undertake, in consultation with employers' and workers' organizations:

1. to formulate, implement and periodically review a coherent national policy on occupational safety, occupational health and the working environment. The primary aim of this policy shall be to improve occupational safety and health and to prevent accidents and injury to health arising out of, linked with or occurring in the course of work, particularly by minimising the causes of hazards inherent in the working environment;

2. to issue safety and health regulations;

3. to provide for the enforcement of such regulations by measures of supervision;

4. to promote the progressive development of occupational health services for all workers with essentially preventive and advisory functions.

Article 4. The right to a fair remuneration.

With a view to ensuring the effective exercise of the right to a fair remuneration, the Parties undertake:

1. to recognize the right of workers to a remuneration such as will give them and their families a decent standard of living;

2. to recognize the right of workers to an increased rate of remuneration for overtime work, subject to exceptions in particular cases;

3. to recognize the right of men and women workers to equal pay for work of equal value;

4. to recognize the right of all workers to a reasonable period of notice for termination of employment;

5. to permit deductions from wages only under conditions and to the extent prescribed by national laws or regulations or fixed by collective agreements or arbitration awards.

The exercise of these rights shall be achieved by freely concluded collective agreements, by statutory wage-fixing machinery, or by other means appropriate to national conditions.

Article 5. The right to organize.

With a review to ensuring or promoting the freedom of workers and employers to form local, national or international organizations for the protection of their economic and social interests and to join those organizations, the Parties undertake that national law shall not be such as to impair, nor shall it be so applied as to impair, this freedom. The extent to which the guarantees provided for in this article shall apply to the police shall be determined by national laws or regulations. The principle governing the application to the members of the armed forces of these guarantees and the extent to which they shall apply to persons in this category shall equally be determined by national laws or regulations.

Article 6. The right to bargain collectively.

With a view to ensuring the effective exercise of the right to bargain collectively, the Parties undertake:

1. to promote joint consultation between workers and employers;

2. to promote, where necessary and appropriate, machinery for voluntary negotiations between employers or employers' organizations and workers' organizations, with a view to the regulation of terms and conditions of employment by means of collective agreements;

3. to promote the establishment and use of appropriate machinery for conciliation and voluntary arbitration for the settlement of labour disputes;

and recognize:

4. the right of workers and employers to collective action in cases of conflicts of interest, including the right to strike, subject to obligations that might arise out of collective agreements previously entered into.

Article 7. The right of children and young persons to protection.

With a view to ensuring the effective exercise of the right of children and young persons to protection, the Parties undertake:

1. to provide that the minimum age of admission to employment shall be 15 years, subject to exceptions for children employed in prescribed light work without harm to their health, morals or education;

2. to provide that the minimum age of admission to employment shall be 18 years with respect to prescribed occupations regarded as dangerous or unhealthy;

3. to provide that persons who are still subject to compulsory education shall not be employed in such work as would deprive them of the full benefit of their education;

4. to provide that the working hours of persons under 18 years of age shall be limited in accordance with the needs of their development, and particularly with their need for vocational training;

5. to recognize the right of young workers and apprentices to a fair wage or other appropriate allowances;

6. to provide that the time spent by young persons in vocational training during the normal working hours with the consent of the employer shall be treated as forming part of the working day;

7. to provide that employed persons of under 18 years of age shall be entitled to a minimum of four weeks' annual holiday with pay;

8. to provide that persons under 18 years of age shall not be employed in night work with the exception of certain occupations provided for by national laws or regulations;

9. to provide that persons under 18 years of age employed in occupations prescribed by national laws or regulations shall be subject to regular medical control;

10. to ensure special protection against physical and moral dangers to which children and young persons are exposed, and particularly against those resulting directly or indirectly from their work.

Article 8. The right of employed women to protection of maternity.

With a view to ensuring the effective exercise of the right of employed women to the protection of maternity, the Parties undertake:

1. to provide either by paid leave, by adequate social security benefits or by benefits from public funds for employed women to take leave before and after childbirth up to a total of at least fourteen weeks;

2. to consider it as unlawful for an employer to give a women notice of dismissal during the period from the time she notifies her employer that she is pregnant until the end of her maternity leave, or to give her notice of dismissal at such a time that the notice would expire during such a period;

3. to provide that mothers who are nursing their infants shall be entitled to sufficient time off for this purpose;

4. to regulate the employment in night work of pregnant women, women who have recently given birth and women nursing their infants;

5. to prohibit the employment of pregnant women, women who have recently given birth or who are nursing their infants in underground mining and all other work which is unsuitable

by reason of its dangerous, unhealthy or arduous nature and to take appropriate measures to protect the employment rights of these women.

Article 9. The right to vocational guidance.

With a view to ensuring the effective exercise of the right to vocational guidance, the Parties undertake to provide or promote, as necessary, a service which will assist all persons, including the handicapped, to solve problems related to occupational choice and progress, with due regard to the individual's characteristics and their relation to occupational opportunity: this assistance should be available free of charge, both to young persons, including schoolchildren, and to adults.

Article 10. The right to vocational training.

With a view to ensuring the effective exercise of the right to vocational training, the Parties undertake:

1. to provide or promote, as necessary, the technical and vocational training of all persons, including the handicapped, in consultation with employers' and workers' organizations, and to grant facilities for access to higher technical and university education, based solely on individual aptitude;

2. to provide or promote a system of apprenticeship and other systematic arrangements for training young boys and girls in their various employments;

3. to provide or promote, as necessary:

(a) adequate and readily available training facilities for adult workers;

(b) special facilities for the retraining of adult workers needed as a result of technological development or new trends in employment;

4. to provide or promote, as necessary, special measures for the retraining and reintegration of the long-term unemployed;

5. to encourage the full utilisation of the facilities provided by appropriate measures such as:

(a) reducing or abolishing any fees or charges;

(b) granting financial assistance in appropriate cases;

(c) including in the normal working hours time spent on supplementary training taken by the worker, at the request of his employer, during employment;

(d) ensuring, through adequate supervision, in consultation with the employers' and workers' organizations, the efficiency of apprenticeship and other training arrangements for young workers, and the adequate protection of young workers generally.

Article 11. The right to protection of health.

With a view to ensuring the effective exercise of the right to protection of health, the Parties undertake, either directly or in co-operation with public or private organizations, to take appropriate measures designed *inter alia*:

1. to remove as far as possible the causes of ill-health;

2. to provide advisory and educational facilities for the promotion of health and the encouragement of individual responsibility in matters of health;

3. to prevent as far as possible epidemic, endemic and other diseases, as well as accidents.

Article 12. The right to social security.

With a view to ensuring the effective exercise of the right to social security, the Parties undertake:

1. to establish or maintain a system of social security;

2. to maintain the social security system at a satisfactory level at least equal to that necessary for the ratification of the European Code of Social Security;

3. to endeavour to raise progressively the system of social security to a higher level;

4. to take steps, by the conclusion of appropriate bilateral and multilateral agreements or by other means, and subject to the conditions laid down in such agreements, in order to ensure:

(a) equal treatment with their own nationals of the nationals of other Parties in respect of social security rights, including the retention of benefits arising out of social security legislation, whatever movements the persons protected may undertake between the territories of the Parties;

(b) the granting, maintenance and resumption of social security rights by such means as the accumulation of insurance or employment periods completed under the legislation of each of the Parties.

Article 13. The right to social and medical assistance.

With a view to ensuring the effective exercise of the right to social and medical assistance, the Parties undertake:

1. to ensure that any person who is without adequate resources and who is unable to secure such resources either by his own efforts or from other sources, in particular by benefits under a social security scheme, be granted adequate assistance, and, in case of sickness, the care necessitated by his condition;

2. to ensure that persons receiving such assistance shall not, for that reason, suffer from a diminution of their political or social rights;

3. to provide that everyone may receive by appropriate public or private services such advice and personal help as may be required to prevent, to remove, or to alleviate personal or family want;

4. to apply the provisions referred to in paragraphs 1, 2 and 3 of this article on an equal footing with their nationals to nationals of other Parties lawfully within their territories, in accordance with their obligations under the European Convention on Social and Medical Assistance, signed at Paris on 11 December 1953.

Article 14. The right to benefit from social welfare services.

With a view to ensuring the effective exercise of the right to benefit from social welfare services, the Parties undertake:

1. to promote or provide services which, by using methods of social work, would contribute to the welfare and development of both individuals and groups in the community, and to their adjustment to the social environment;

2. to encourage the participation of individuals and voluntary or other organizations in the establishment and maintenance of such services.

Article 15. The right of persons with disabilities to independence, social integration and participation in the life of the community.

With a view to ensuring to persons with disabilities, irrespective of age and the nature and origin of their disabilities, the effective exercise of the right to independence, social integration and participation in the life of the community, the Parties undertake, in particular:

1. to take the necessary measures to provide persons with disabilities with guidance, education and vocational training in the framework of general schemes wherever possible or, where this is not possible, through specialized bodies, public or private;

2. to promote their access to employment through all measures tending to encourage employers to hire and keep in employment persons with disabilities in the ordinary working environment and to adjust the working conditions to the needs of the disabled or, where this is not possible by reason of the disability, by arranging for or creating sheltered employment according to the level of disability. In certain cases, such measures may require recourse to specialized placement and support services;

3. to promote their full social integration and participation in the life of the community in particular through measures, including technical aids, aiming to overcome barriers to communication and mobility and enabling access to transport, housing, cultural activities and leisure.

Article 16. The right of the family to social, legal and economic protection.

With a view to ensuring the necessary conditions for the full development of the family, which is a fundamental unit of society, the Parties undertake to promote the economic, legal and social protection of family life by such means as social and family benefits, fiscal arrangements, provision of family housing, benefits for the newly married and other appropriate means.

Article 17. The right of children and young persons to social, legal and economic protection.

With a view to ensuring the effective exercise of the right of children and young persons to grow up in an environment which encourages the full development of their personality and of their physical and mental capacities, the Parties undertake, either directly or in co-operation with public and private organizations, to take all appropriate and necessary measures designed:

1. (a) to ensure that children and young persons, taking account of the rights and duties of their parents, have the care, the assistance, the education and the training they need, in particular by providing for the establishment or maintenance of institutions and services sufficient and adequate for this purpose;

(b) to protect children and young persons against negligence, violence or exploitation;

(c) to provide protection and special aid from the state for children and young persons temporarily or definitively deprived of their family's support;

2. to provide to children and young persons a free primary and secondary education as well as to encourage regular attendance at schools.

Article 18. The right to engage in a gainful occupation in the territory of other Parties.

With a view to ensuring the effective exercise of the right to engage in a gainful occupation in the territory of any other Party, the Parties undertake:

1. to apply existing regulations in a spirit of liberality;

2. to simplify existing formalities and to reduce or abolish chancery dues and other charges payable by foreign workers or their employers;

3. to liberalize, individually or collectively, regulations governing the employment of foreign workers;

and recognize:

4. the right of their nationals to leave the country to engage in a gainful occupation in the territories of the other Parties.

Article 19. The right of migrant workers and their families to protection and assistance.

With a view to ensuring the effective exercise of the right of migrant workers and their families to protection and assistance in the territory of any other Party, the Parties undertake:

1. to maintain or to satisfy themselves that there are maintained adequate and free services to assist such workers, particularly in obtaining accurate information, and to take all appropriate steps, so far as national laws and regulations permit, against misleading propaganda relating to emigration and immigration;

2. to adopt appropriate measures within their own jurisdiction to facilitate the departure, journey and reception of such workers and their families, and to provide, within their own jurisdiction, appropriate services for health, medical attention and good hygienic conditions during the journey;

3. to promote co-operation, as appropriate, between social services, public and private, in emigration and immigration countries;

4. to secure for such workers lawfully within their territories, insofar as such matters are regulated by law or regulations or are subject to the control of administrative authorities, treatment not less favourable than that of their own nationals in respect of the following matters:

(a) remuneration and other employment and working conditions;

(b) membership of trade unions and enjoyment of the benefits of collective bargaining;

(c) accommodation.

5. to secure for such workers lawfully within their territories treatment not less favourable than that of their own nationals with regard to employment taxes, dues or contributions payable in respect of employed persons;

6. to facilitate as far as possible the reunion of the family of a foreign worker permitted to establish himself in the territory;

7. to secure for such workers lawfully within their territories treatment not less favourable than that of their own nationals in respect of legal proceedings relating to matters referred to in this article;

8. to secure that such workers lawfully residing within their territories are not expelled unless they endanger national security or offend against public interest or morality;

9. to permit, within legal limits, the transfer of such parts of the earnings and savings of such workers as they may desire;

10. to extend the protection and assistance provided for in this article to self-employed migrants insofar as such measures apply;

11. to promote and facilitate the teaching of the national language of the receiving state or, if there are several, one of these languages, to migrant workers and members of their families.

12. to promote and facilitate, as far as practicable, the teaching of the migrant worker's mother tongue to the children of the migrant worker.

Article 20. The right to equal opportunities and equal treatment in matters of employment and occupation without discrimination on the grounds of sex.

With a view to ensuring the effective exercise of the right to equal opportunities and equal treatment in matters of employment and occupation without discrimination on the grounds of sex, the Parties undertake to recognize that right and to take appropriate measures to ensure or promote its application in the following fields:

(a) access to employment, protection against dismissal and occupational reintegration;

(b) vocational guidance, training, retraining and rehabilitation;

(c) terms of employment and working conditions, including remuneration;

(d) career development, including promotion.

Article 21. The right to information and consultation.

With a view to ensuring the effective exercise of the right of workers to be informed and consulted within the undertaking, the Parties undertake to adopt or encourage measures enabling workers or their representatives, in accordance with national legislation and practice:

(a) to be informed regularly or at the appropriate time and in a comprehensible way about the economic and financial situation of the undertaking employing them, on the understanding that the disclosure of certain information which could be prejudicial to the undertaking may be refused or subject to confidentiality; and

(b) to be consulted in good time on proposed decisions which could substantially affect the interests of workers, particularly on those decisions which could have an important impact on the employment situation in the undertaking.

Article 22. The right to take part in the determination and improvement of the working conditions and working environment.

With a view to ensuring the effective exercise of the right of workers to take part in the determination and improvement of the working conditions and working environment in the undertaking, the Parties undertake to adopt or encourage measures enabling workers or their representatives, in accordance with national legislation and practice, to contribute:

(a) to the determination and the improvement of the working conditions, work organization and working environment;

(b) to the protection of health and safety within the undertaking;

(c) to the organisation of social and socio-cultural services and facilities within the undertaking;

(d) to the supervision of the observance of regulations on these matters.

Article 23. The right of elderly persons to social protection.

With a view to ensuring the effective exercise of the right of elderly persons to social protection, the Parties undertake to adopt or encourage, either directly or in co-operation with public or private organizations, appropriate measures designed in particular:

1. to enable elderly persons to remain full members of society for as long as possible, by means of:

(a) adequate resources enabling them to lead a decent life and play an active part in public, social and cultural life;

(b) provision of information about services and facilities available for elderly persons and their opportunities to make use of them.

2. to enable elderly persons to choose their life-style freely and to lead independent lives in their familiar surroundings for as long as they wish and are able, by means of:

(a) provision of housing suited to their needs and their state of health or of adequate support for adapting their housing;

(b) the health care and the services necessitated by their state.

3. to guarantee elderly persons living in institutions appropriate support, while respecting their privacy, and participation in decisions concerning living conditions in the institution.

Article 24. The right to protection in cases of termination of employment.

With a view to ensuring the effective exercise of the right of workers to protection in cases of termination of employment, the Parties undertake to recognize:

(a) the right of all workers not to have their employment terminated without valid reasons for such termination connected with their capacity or conduct or based on the operational requirements of the undertaking, establishment or service;

(b) the right of workers whose employment is terminated without a valid reason to adequate compensation or other appropriate relief.

To this end the Parties undertake to ensure that a worker who considers that his employment has been terminated without a valid reason shall have the right to appeal to an impartial body.

Article 25. The right of workers to the protection of their claims in the event of the insolvency of their employer.

With a view to ensuring the effective exercise of the right of workers to the protection of their claims in the event of the insolvency of their employer, the Parties undertake to provide that workers' claims arising from contracts of employment or employment relationships be guaranteed by a guarantee institution or by any other effective form of protection.

Article 26. The right to dignity at work.

With a view to ensuring the effective exercise of the right of all workers to protection of their dignity at work, the Parties undertake, in consultation with employers' and workers' organizations:

1. to promote awareness, information and prevention of sexual harassment in the workplace or in relation to work and to take all appropriate measures to protect workers from such conduct;

2. to promote awareness, information and prevention of recurrent reprehensible or distinctly negative and offensive actions directed against individual workers in the workplace or in relation to work and to take all appropriate measures to protect workers from such conduct.

Article 27. The right of workers with family responsibilities to equal opportunities and equal treatment.

With a view to ensuring the exercise of the right to equality of opportunity and treatment for men and women workers with family responsibilities and between such workers and other workers, the Parties undertake:

1. to take appropriate measures:

(a) to enable workers with family responsibilities to enter and remain in employment, as well as to re-enter employment after an absence due to those responsibilities, including measures in the field of vocational guidance and training;

(b) to take account of their needs in terms of conditions of employment and social security;

(c) to develop or promote services, public or private, in particular child daycare services and other childcare arrangements.

2. to provide a possibility for either parent to obtain, during a period after maternity leave, parental leave to take care of a child, the duration and conditions of which should be determined by national legislation, collective agreements or practice;

3. to ensure that family responsibilities shall not, as such, constitute a valid reason for termination of employment.

Article 28. The right of workers' representatives to protection in the undertaking and facilities to be accorded to them.

With a view to ensuring the effective exercise of the right of workers' representatives to carry out their functions, the Parties undertake to ensure that in the undertaking:

(a) they enjoy effective protection against acts prejudicial to them, including dismissal, based on their status or activities as workers' representatives within the undertaking;

(b) they are afforded such facilities as may be appropriate in order to enable them to carry out their functions promptly and efficiently, account being taken of the industrial relations system of the country and the needs, size and capabilities of the undertaking concerned.

Article 29. The right to information and consultation in collective redundancy procedures.

With a view to ensuring the effective exercise of the right of workers to be informed and consulted in situations of collective redundancies, the Parties undertake to ensure that employers shall inform and consult workers' representatives, in good time prior to such collective redundancies, on ways and means of avoiding collective redundancies or limiting their occurrence and mitigating their consequences, for example by recourse to accompanying social measures aimed, in particular, at aid for the redeployment or retraining of the workers concerned.

Article 30. The right to protection against poverty and social exclusion.

With a view to ensuring the effective exercise of the right to protection against poverty and social exclusion, the Parties undertake:

(a) to take measures within the framework of an overall and co-ordinated approach to promote the effective access of persons who live or risk living in a situation of social exclusion or poverty, as well as their families, to, in particular, employment, housing, training, education, culture and social and medical assistance;

(b) to review these measures with a view to their adaptation if necessary.

Article 31. The right to housing.

With a view to ensuring the effective exercise of the right to housing, the Parties undertake to take measures designed:

1. to promote access to housing of an adequate standard;

2. to prevent and reduce homelessness with a view to its gradual elimination;

3. to make the price of housing accessible to those without adequate resources.

PART III

Article A. Undertakings.

1. Subject to the provisions of Article B below, each of the Parties undertakes:

(a) to consider Part I of this Charter as a declaration of the aims which it will pursue by all appropriate means, as stated in the introductory paragraph of that part;

(b) to consider itself bound by at least six of the following nine articles of Part II of this Charter: Articles 1, 5, 6, 7, 12 13, 16, 19 and 20;

(c) to consider itself bound by an additional number of articles or numbered paragraphs of Part II of the Charter which it may select, provided that the total number of articles or numbered paragraphs by which it is bound is not less than sixteen articles or sixty-three numbered paragraphs.

2. The articles or paragraphs selected in accordance with sub-paragraphs b and c of paragraph 1 of this article shall be notified to the Secretary-General of the Council of Europe at the time when the instrument of ratification, acceptance or approval is deposited.

3. Any Party may, at a later date, declare by notification addressed to the Secretary-General that it considers itself bound by any articles or any numbered paragraphs of Part II of the Charter which it has not already accepted under the terms of paragraph 1 of this article. Such undertakings subsequently

given shall be deemed to be an integral part of the ratification, acceptance or approval and shall have the same effect as from the first day of the month following the expiration of a period of one month after the date of the notification.

4. Each Party shall maintain a system of labour inspection appropriate to national conditions.

Article B. Links with the European Social Charter and the 1988 Additional Protocol.

No Contracting Party to the European Social Charter or Party to the Additional Protocol of 5 May 1988 may ratify, accept or approve this Charter without considering itself bound by at least the provisions corresponding to the provisions of the European Social Charter and, where appropriate, of the Additional Protocol, to which it was bound.

Acceptance of the obligations of any provision of this Charter shall, from the date of entry into force of those obligations for the Party concerned, result in the corresponding provision of the European Social Charter and, where appropriate, of its Additional Protocol of 1988 ceasing to apply to the Party concerned in the event of that Party being bound by the first of those instruments or by both instruments.

PART IV

Article C. Supervision of the implementation of the undertakings contained in this Charter.

The implementation of the legal obligations contained in this Charter shall be submitted to the same supervision as the European Social Charter.

Article D. Collective complaints.

1. The provisions of the Additional Protocol to the European Social Charter providing for a system of collective complaints shall apply to the undertakings given in this Charter for the States which have ratified the said Protocol.

2. Any State which is not bound by the Additional Protocol to the European Social Charter providing for a system of collective complaints may when depositing its instrument of ratification, acceptance or approval of this Charter or at any time thereafter, declare by notification addressed to the Secretary-General of the Council of Europe, that it accepts the supervision of its obligations under this Charter following the procedure provided for in the said Protocol.

PART V

Article E. Non-discrimination.

The enjoyment of the rights set forth in this Charter shall be secured without discrimination on any ground such as race, colour, sex, language, religion, political or other opinion, national extraction or social origin, health, association with a national minority, birth or other status.

Article F. Derogations in time of war or public emergency.

1. In time of war or other public emergency threatening the life of the nation any Party may take measures derogating from its obligations under this Charter to the extent strictly required by the exigencies of the situation, provided that such measures are not inconsistent with its other obligations under international law.

2. Any Party which has availed itself of this right of derogation shall, within a reasonable lapse of time, keep the Secretary-General of the Council of Europe fully informed of the measures taken and of the reasons therefor. It shall likewise inform the Secretary-General when such measures have ceased to operate and the provisions of the Charter which it has accepted are again being fully executed.

Article G. Restrictions.

1. The rights and principles set forth in Part I when effectively realised, and their effective exercise as provided for in Part II, shall not be subject to any restrictions or limitations not specified in those parts, except such as are prescribed by law and are necessary in a democratic society for the protection of the rights and freedoms of others or for the protection of public interest, national security, public health, or morals.

2. The restrictions permitted under this Charter to the rights and obligations set forth herein shall not be applied for any purpose other than that for which they have been prescribed.

Article H. Relations between the Charter and domestic law or international agreements.

The provisions of this Charter shall not prejudice the provisions of domestic law or of any bilateral or multilateral treaties, conventions or agreements which are already in force, or may come into force, under which more favourable treatment would be accorded to the persons protected.

Article I. Implementation of the undertakings given.

1. Without prejudice to the methods of implementation foreseen in these articles the relevant provisions of Articles 1 to 31 of Part II of this Charter shall be implemented by:

(a) laws or regulations;

(b) agreements between employers or employers' organizations and workers' organizations;

(c) combination of those two methods;

(d) other appropriate means.

2. Compliance with the undertakings deriving from the provisions of paragraphs 1, 2, 3, 4, 5 and 7 of Article 2, paragraphs 4, 6 and 7 of Article 7, paragraphs 1, 2, 3 and 5 of Article 10 and Articles 21 and 22 of Part II of this Charter shall be regarded as effective if the provisions are applied, in accordance with paragraph 1 of this article, to the great majority of the workers concerned.

Article J. Amendments.

PART VI

Articles K–O. General provisions.

APPENDIX

Note: In accordance with Article N of the Charter, the Appendix forms an integral part of the revised document.

Scope of the Revised European Social Charter in terms of persons protected

1. Without prejudice to Article 12, paragraph 4, and Article 13, paragraph 4, the persons covered by Articles 1 to 17 and 20 to 31 include foreigners only in so far as they are nationals of other Parties lawfully resident or working regularly within the territory of the Party concerned, subject to the understanding that these articles are to be interpreted in the light of the provisions of Articles 18 and 19. This interpretation would not prejudice the extension of similar facilities to other persons by any of the Parties.

2. Each Party will grant to refugees as defined in the Convention relating to the Status of Refugees, signed in Geneva on 28 July 1951 and in the Protocol of 31 January 1967, and lawfully staying in its territory, treatment as favourable as possible, and in any case not less favourable than under the obligations accepted by the Party under the said convention and under any other existing international instruments applicable to those refugees.

3. Each Party will grant to stateless persons as defined in the Convention on the Status of Stateless Persons done in New York on 28 September 1954 and lawfully staying in its territory, treatment as favourable as possible and in any case not less favourable than under the obligations accepted by the Party under the said instrument and under any other existing international instruments applicable to those stateless persons.

Part II

Article 1, paragraph 2.

This provision shall not be interpreted as prohibiting or authorizing any union security clause or practice.

Article 2, paragraph 6.

Parties may provide that this provision shall not apply:

(a) to workers having a contract or employment relationship with a total duration not exceeding one month and/or with a working week not exceeding eight hours;

(b) where the contract or employment relationship is of a casual and/or specific nature, provided, in these cases, that its non-application is justified by objective considerations.

Article 3, paragraph 4.

It is understood that for the purposes of this provision the functions, organization and conditions of operation of these services shall be determined by national laws or regulations, collective agreements or other means appropriate to national conditions.

Article 4, paragraph 4.

This provision shall be so understood as not to prohibit immediate dismissal for any serious offence.

Article 4, paragraph 5.

It is understood that a Party may give the undertaking required in this paragraph if the great majority of workers are not permitted to suffer deductions from wages either by law or through collective agreements or arbitration awards, the exceptions being those persons not so covered.

Article 6, paragraph 4.

It is understood that each Party may, insofar as it is concerned, regulate the exercise of the right to strike by law, provided that any further restriction that this might place on the right can be justified under the terms of Article G.

Article 7, paragraph 2.

This provision does not prevent Parties from providing in their legislation that young persons not having reached the minimum age laid down may perform work insofar as it is absolutely necessary for their vocational training where such work is carried out in accordance with conditions prescribed by the competent authority and measures are taken to protect the health and safety of these young persons.

Article 7, paragraph 8.

It is understood that a Party may give the undertaking required in this paragraph if it fulfils the spirit of the undertaking by providing by law that the great majority of persons under eighteen years of age shall not be employed in night work.

Article 8, paragraph 2.

This provision shall not be interpreted as laying down an absolute prohibition. Exceptions could be made, for instance, in the following cases:

(a) if an employed woman has been guilty of misconduct which justifies breaking off the employment relationship;

(b) if the undertaking concerned ceases to operate;

(c) if the period prescribed in the employment contract has expired.

Article 12, paragraph 4.

The words 'and subject to the conditions laid down in such agreements' in the introduction to this paragraph are taken to imply *inter alia* that with regard to benefits which are available independently of any insurance contribution, a Party may require the completion of a prescribed period of residence before granting such benefits to nationals of other Parties.

Article 13, paragraph 4.

Governments not Parties to the European Convention on Social and Medical Assistance may ratify the Charter in respect of this paragraph provided that they grant to nationals of other Parties a treatment which is in conformity with the provisions of the said convention.

Article 16.

It is understood that the protection afforded in this provision covers single-parent families.

Article 17.

It is understood that this provision covers all persons below the age of 18 years, unless under the law applicable to the child majority is attained earlier, without prejudice to the other specific provisions provided by the Charter, particularly Article 7.

This does not imply an obligation to provide compulsory education up to the above-mentioned age.

Article 19, paragraph 6.

For the purpose of applying this provision, the term 'family of a foreign worker' is understood to mean at least the worker's spouse and unmarried children, as long as the latter are considered to be minors by the receiving State and are dependent on the migrant worker.

Article 20.

1. It is understood that social security matters, as well as other provisions relating to unemployment benefit, old age benefit and survivor's benefit, may be excluded from the scope of this article.

2. Provisions concerning the protection of women, particularly as regards pregnancy, confinement and the post-natal period, shall not be deemed to be discrimination as referred to in this article.

3. This article shall not prevent the adoption of specific measures aimed at removing *de facto* inequalities.

4. Occupational activities which, by reason of their nature or the context in which they are carried out, can be entrusted only to persons of a particular sex may be excluded from the scope of this article or some of its provisions. This provision is not to be interpreted as requiring the Parties to embody in laws or regulations a list of occupations which, by reason of their nature or the context in which they are carried out, may be reserved to persons of a particular sex.

Article 21 and 22.

1. For the purpose of the application of these articles, the term 'workers' representatives' means persons who are recognized as such under national legislation or practice.

2. The terms 'national legislation and practice' embrace as the case may be, in addition to laws and regulations, collective agreements, other agreements between employers and workers' representatives, customs as well as relevant case law.

3. For the purpose of the application of these articles, the term 'undertaking' is understood as referring to a set of tangible and intangible components, with or without legal personality, formed to produce goods or provide services for financial gain and with power to determine its own market policy.

4. It is understood that religious communities and their institutions may be excluded from the application of these articles, even if these institutions are 'undertakings' within the meaning of paragraph 3. Establishments pursuing activities which are inspired by certain ideals or guided by certain moral concepts, ideals and concepts which are protected by national legislation, may be excluded from the application of these articles to such an extent as is necessary to protect the orientation of the undertaking.

5. It is understood that where in a state the rights set out in these articles are exercised in the various establishments of the undertaking, the Party concerned is to be considered as fulfilling the obligations deriving from these provisions.

6. The Parties may exclude from the field of application of these articles, those undertakings employing less than a certain number of workers, to be determined by national legislation or practice.

Article 22.

1. This provision affects neither the powers and obligations of states as regards the adoption of health and safety regulations for workplaces, nor the powers and responsibilities of the bodies in charge of monitoring their application.

2. The terms 'social and socio-cultural services and facilities' are understood as referring to the social and/or cultural facilities for workers provided by some undertakings such as welfare assistance, sports fields, rooms for nursing mothers, libraries, children's holiday camps, etc.

Article 23, paragraph 1.

For the purpose of the application of this paragraph, the term 'for as long as possible' refers to the elderly person's physical, psychological and intellectual capacities.

Article 24.

1. It is understood that for the purposes of this article the terms 'termination of employment' and 'terminated' mean termination of employment at the initiative of the employer.

2. It is understood that this article covers all workers but that a Party may exclude from some or all of its protection the following categories of employed persons:

(a) workers engaged under a contract of employment for a specified period of time or a specified task;

(b) workers undergoing a period of probation or a qualifying period of employment, provided that this is determined in advance and is of a reasonable duration;

(c) workers engaged on a casual basis for a short period.

3. For the purpose of this article the following, in particular, shall not constitute valid reasons for termination of employment:

(a) trade union membership or participation in union activities outside working hours, or, with the consent of the employer, within working hours;

(b) seeking office as, acting or having acted in the capacity of a workers' representative;

(c) the filing of a complaint or the participation in proceedings against an employer involving alleged violation of laws or regulations or recourse to competent administrative authorities;

(d) race, colour, sex, marital status, family responsibilities, pregnancy, religion, political opinion, national extraction or social origin;

(e) maternity or parental leave;

(f) temporary absence from work due to illness or injury.

4. It is understood that compensation or other appropriate relief in case of termination of employment without valid reasons shall be determined by national laws or regulations, collective agreements or other means appropriate to national conditions.

Article 25.

1. It is understood that the competent national authority may, by way of exemption and after consulting organizations of employers and workers, exclude certain categories of workers from the protection provided in this provision by reason of the special nature of their employment relationship.

2. it is understood that the definition of the term 'insolvency' must be determined by national law and practice.

3. The workers' claims covered by this provision shall include at least:

(a) the workers' claims for wages relating to a prescribed period, which shall not be less than three months under a privilege system and eight weeks under a guarantee system, prior to the insolvency or to the termination of employment;

(b) the workers' claims for holiday pay due as a result of work performed during the year in which the insolvency or the termination of employment occurred;

(c) the workers' claims for amounts due in respect of other types of paid absence relating to a prescribed period, which shall not be less than three months under a privilege system and eight weeks under a guarantee system, prior to the insolvency or the termination of the employment.

4. National laws or regulations may limit the protection of workers' claims to a prescribed amount, which shall be of a socially acceptable level.

Article 26.

It is understood that this article does not require that legislation be enacted by the Parties.

It is understood that paragraph 2 does not cover sexual harassment.

Article 27.

It is understood that this article applies to men and women workers with family responsibilities in relation to their dependent children as well as in relation to other members of their immediate family who clearly need their care or support where such responsibilities restrict their possibilities of preparing for, entering, participating in or advancing in economic activity. The terms 'dependent children' and 'other members of their immediate family who clearly need their care and support' mean persons defined as such by the national legislation of the Party concerned.

Article 28 and 29.

For the purpose of the application of this article, the term 'workers' representatives' means persons who are recognized as such under national legislation or practice.

Part III

It is understood that the Charter contains legal obligations of an international character, the application of which is submitted solely to the supervision provided for in Part IV thereof.

Part V

Article E.

A differential treatment based on an objective and reasonable justification shall not be deemed discriminatory.

Article F.

The terms 'in time of war or other public emergency' shall be so understood as to cover also the threat of war.

Article I.

It is understood that workers excluded in accordance with the appendix to Articles 21 and 22 are not taken into account in establishing the number of workers concerned.

Article J.

The term 'amendment' shall be extended so as to cover also the addition of new articles to the Charter.

Convention for Protection of Human Rights and Fundamental Freedoms (European Convention on Human Rights)

(4 November 1950)

Note: The text of the Convention has been amended according to the provisions of Protocol II, which entered into force on 1 November 1998 and replaced all previous protocols.

The governments signatory hereto, being members of the Council of Europe;

Considering the Universal Declaration of Human Rights proclaimed by the General Assembly of the United Nations on 10 December 1948;

Considering that this Declaration aims at securing the universal and effective recognition and observance of the Rights therein declared;

Considering that the aim of the Council of Europe is the achievement of greater unity between its members and that one of the methods by which that aim is to be pursued is the maintenance and further realisation of human rights and fundamental freedoms;

Reaffirming their profound belief in those fundamental freedoms which are the foundation of justice and peace in the world and are best maintained on the one hand by an effective political democracy and on the other by a common understanding and observance of the human rights upon which they depend;

Being resolved, as the governments of European countries which are like-minded and have a common heritage of political traditions, ideals, freedom and the rule of law, to take the first steps for the collective enforcement of certain of the rights stated in the Universal Declaration

Have agreed as follows:

Article 1. Obligation to respect human rights.

The High Contracting Parties shall secure to everyone within their jurisdiction the rights and freedoms defined in Section I of this Convention.

I. RIGHTS AND FREEDOMS

Article 2. Right to life.

1. Everyone's right to life shall be protected by law. No one shall be deprived of his life intentionally save in the execution of a sentence of a court following his conviction of a crime for which this penalty is provided by law.

2. Deprivation of life shall not be regarded as inflicted in contravention of this article when it results from the use of force which is no more than absolutely necessary:

(a) in defence of any person from unlawful violence;

(b) in order to effect a lawful arrest or to prevent the escape of a person lawfully detained;

(c) in action lawfully taken for the purpose of quelling a riot or insurrection.

Article 3. Prohibition of torture.

No one shall be subjected to torture or to inhuman or degrading treatment or punishment.

Article 4. Prohibition of slavery and forced labour.

1. No one shall be held in slavery or servitude.

2. No one shall be required to perform forced or compulsory labour.

3. For the purpose of this article the term 'forced or compulsory labour' shall not include:

(a) any work required to be done in the ordinary course of detention imposed according to the provisions of Article 5 of this Convention or during conditional release from such detention;

(b) any service of a military character or, in case of conscientious objectors in countries where they are recognized, service exacted instead of compulsory military service;

(c) any service exacted in case of an emergency or calamity threatening the life or well-being of the community;

(d) any work or service which forms part of normal civic obligations.

Article 5. Right to liberty and security.

1. Everyone has the right to liberty and security of person. No one shall be deprived of his liberty save in the following cases and in accordance with a procedure prescribed by law:

(a) the lawful detention of a person after conviction by a competent court;

(b) the lawful arrest or detention of a person for non-compliance with the lawful order of a court or in order to secure the fulfilment of any obligation prescribed by law;

(c) the lawful arrest or detention of a person effected for the purpose of bringing him before the competent legal authority on reasonable suspicion of having committed an offence or when it is reasonably considered necessary to prevent his committing an offence or fleeing after having done so;

(d) the detention of a minor by lawful order for the purpose of educational supervision or his lawful detention for the purpose of bringing him before the competent legal authority;

(e) the lawful detention of persons for the prevention of the spreading of infectious diseases, of persons of unsound mind, alcoholics or drug addicts or vagrants;

(f) the lawful arrest or detention of a person to prevent his effecting an unauthorized entry into the country or of a person against whom action is being taken with a view to deportation or extradition.

2. Everyone who is arrested shall be informed promptly, in a language which he understands, of the reasons for his arrest and of any charge against him.

3. Everyone arrested or detained in accordance with the provisions of paragraph 1.c of this article shall be brought promptly before a judge or other officer authorized by law to exercise judicial power and shall be entitled to trial within a reasonable time or to release pending trial. Release may be conditioned by guarantees to appear for trial.

4. Everyone who is deprived of his liberty by arrest or detention shall be entitled to take proceedings by which the lawfulness of his detention shall be decided speedily by a court and his release ordered if the detention is not lawful.

5. Everyone who has been the victim of arrest or detention in contravention of the provisions of this article shall have an enforceable right to compensation.

Article 6. Right to a fair trial.

1. In the determination of his civil rights and obligations or of any criminal charge against him, everyone is entitled to a fair and public hearing within a reasonable time by an independent and impartial tribunal established by law. Judgment shall be pronounced publicly but the press and public may be excluded from all or part of the trial in the interests of morals, public order or national security in a democratic society, where the interests of juveniles or the protection of the private life of the parties so require, or to the extent strictly necessary in the opinion of the court in special circumstances where publicity would prejudice the interests of justice.

2. Everyone charged with a criminal offence shall be presumed innocent until proved guilty according to law.

3. Everyone charged with a criminal offence has the following minimum rights:

(a) to be informed promptly, in a language which he understands and in detail, of the nature and cause of the accusation against him;

(b) to have adequate time and facilities for the preparation of his defence;

(c) to defend himself in person or through legal assistance of his own choosing or, if he has not sufficient means to pay for legal assistance, to be given it free when the interests of justice so require;

(d) to examine or have examined witnesses against him and to obtain the attendance and examination of witnesses on his behalf under the same conditions as witnesses against him;

(e) to have the free assistance of an interpreter if he cannot understand or speak the language used in court.

Article 7. No punishment without law.

1. No one shall be held guilty of any criminal offence on account of any act or omission which did not constitute a criminal offence under national or international law at the time when it was committed. Nor shall a heavier penalty be imposed than the one that was applicable at the time the criminal offence was committed.

2. This article shall not prejudice the trial and punishment of any person for any act or omission which, at the time when it was committed, was criminal according to the general principles of law recognized by civilized nations.

Article 8. Right to respect for private and family life.

1. Everyone has the right to respect for his private and family life, his home and his correspondence.

2. There shall be no interference by a public authority with the exercise of this right except such as is in accordance with the law and is necessary in a democratic society in the interests of national security, public safety or the economic well-being of the country, for the prevention of disorder or crime, for the protection of health or morals, or for the protection of the rights and freedoms of others.

Article 9. Freedom of thought, conscience and religion.

1. Everyone has the right to freedom of thought, conscience and religion; this right includes freedom to change his religion or belief and freedom, either alone or in community with others and in public or private, to manifest his religion or belief, in worship, teaching, practice and observance.

2. Freedom to manifest one's religion or beliefs shall be subject only to such limitations as are prescribed by law and are necessary in a democratic society in the interests of public safety, for the protection of public order, health or morals, or for the protection of the rights and freedoms of others.

Article 10. Freedom of expression.

1. Everyone has the right to freedom of expression. This right shall include freedom to hold opinions and to receive and impart information and ideas without interference by public authority and regardless of frontiers. This article shall not prevent States from requiring the licensing of broadcasting, television or cinema enterprises.

2. The exercise of these freedoms, since it carries with it duties and responsibilities, may be subject to such formalities, conditions, restrictions or penalties as are prescribed by law and are necessary in a democratic society, in the interests of national security, territorial integrity or public safety, for the prevention of disorder or crime, for the protection of health or morals, for the protection of the reputation or rights of others, for preventing the disclosure of information received in confidence, or for maintaining the authority and impartiality of the judiciary.

Article 11. Freedom of assembly and association.

1. Everyone has the right to freedom of peaceful assembly and to freedom of association with others, including the right to form and to join trade unions for the protection of his interests.

2. No restrictions shall be placed on the exercise of these rights other than such as are prescribed by law and are necessary in a democratic society in the interests of national security or public safety, for the prevention of disorder or crime, for the protection of health or morals or for the protection of the rights and freedoms of others. This article shall not prevent the imposition of lawful restrictions on the exercise of these rights by members of the armed forces, of the police or of the administration of the State.

Article 12. Right to marry.

Men and women of marriageable age have the right to marry and to found a family, according to the national laws governing the exercise of this right.

Article 13. Right to an effective remedy.

Everyone whose rights and freedoms as set forth in this Convention are violated shall have an effective remedy before a national authority notwithstanding that the violation has been committed by persons acting in an official capacity.

Article 14. Prohibition of discrimination.

The enjoyment of the rights and freedoms set forth in this Convention shall be secured without discrimination on any ground such as sex, race, colour, language, religion, political or other opinion, national or social origin, association with a national minority, property, birth or other status.

Article 15. Derogation in time of emergency.

1. In time of war or other public emergency threatening the life of the nation any High Contracting Party may take measures derogating from its obligations under this Convention to the extent strictly required by the exigencies of the situation, provided that such measures are not inconsistent with its other obligations under international law.

2. No derogation from Article 2, except in respect of deaths resulting from lawful acts of war, or from Articles 3, 4 (paragraph 1) and 7 shall be made under this provision.

3. Any High Contracting Party availing itself of this right of derogation shall keep the Secretary-General of the Council of Europe fully informed of the measures which it has taken and the reasons therefor. It shall also inform the Secretary-General of the Council of Europe when such measures have ceased to operate and the provisions of the Convention are again being fully executed.

Article 16. Restrictions on political activity of aliens.

Nothing in Articles 10, 11 and 14 shall be regarded as preventing the High Contracting Parties from imposing restrictions on the political activity of aliens.

Article 17. Prohibition of abuse of rights.

Nothing in this Convention may be interpreted as implying for any State, group or person any right to engage in any activity or perform any act aimed at the destruction of any of the rights and freedoms set forth herein or at their limitation to a greater extent than is provided for in the Convention.

Article 18. Limitation on use of restrictions on rights.

The restrictions permitted under this Convention to the said rights and freedoms shall not be applied for any purpose other than those for which they have been prescribed.

II. EUROPEAN COURT OF HUMAN RIGHTS

Article 19. Establishment of the Court.

To ensure the observance of the engagements undertaken by the High Contracting Parties in the Convention and the Protocols thereto, there shall be set up a European Court of Human Rights, hereinafter referred to as 'the Court'. It shall function on a permanent basis.

Article 20. Number of judges.

The Court shall consist of a number of judges equal to that of the High Contracting Parties.

Article 21. Criteria for office.

1. The judges shall be of high moral character and must either possess the qualifications required for appointment to high judicial officer or be jurisconsults of recognized competence.

2. The judges shall sit on the Court in their individual capacity.

3. During their term of office the judges shall not engage in any activity which is incompatible with their independence, impartiality or with the demands of a full-time office; all questions arising from the application of this paragraph shall be decided by the Court.

Article 22. Election of judges.

1. The judges shall be elected by the Parliamentary Assembly with respect to each High Contracting Party by a majority of votes cast from a list of three candidates nominated by the High Contracting Party.

2. The same procedure shall be followed to complete the Court in the event of the accession of new High Contracting Parties and in filling casual vacancies.

Article 23. Terms of office.

1. The judges shall be elected for a period of six years. They may be re-elected. However, the terms of office of one-half of the judges elected at the first election shall expire at the end of three years.

2. The judges whose terms of office are to expire at the end of the initial period of three years shall be chosen by lot by the Secretary-General of the Council of Europe immediately after their election.

3. In order to ensure that, as far as possible, the terms of office of one-half of the judges are renewed every three years, the Parliamentary Assembly may decide, before proceeding to any subsequent election, that the term or terms of office of one or more judges to be elected shall be for a period other than six years but not more than nine and not less than three years.

4. In cases where more than one term of office is involved and where the Parliamentary Assembly applies the preceding paragraph, the allocation of the terms of office shall be effected by a drawing of lots by the Secretary-General of the Council of Europe immediately after the election.

5. A judge elected to replace a judge whose term of office has not expired shall hold office for the remainder of his predecessor's term.

6. The terms of office of judges shall expire when they reach the age of 70.

7. The judges shall hold office until replaced. They shall, however, continue to deal with such cases as they already have under consideration.

Article 24. Dismissal.

No judge may be dismissed from his office unless the other judges decide by a majority of two-thirds that he has ceased to fulfil the required conditions.

Article 25. Registry and legal secretaries.

The Court shall have a registry, the functions and organization of which shall be laid down in the rules of the Court. The Court shall be assisted by legal secretaries.

Article 26. Plenary Court.

The plenary Court shall:

(a) elect its President and one or two Vice-Presidents for a period of three years; they may be re-elected;

(b) set up Chambers, constituted for a fixed period of time;

(c) elect the Presidents of the Chambers of the Court; they may be re-elected;

(d) adopt the rules of the Court, and

(e) elect the Registrar and one or more Deputy Registrars.

Article 27. Committees, Chambers and Grand Chamber.

1. To consider cases brought before it, the Court shall sit in committees of three judges, in Chambers of seven judges and in a Grand Chamber of seventeen judges. The Court's Chambers shall set up committees for a fixed period of time.

2. There shall sit as an *ex officio* member of the Chamber and the Grand Chamber the judge elected in respect of the State Party

concerned or, if there is none or if he is unable to sit, a person of its choice who shall sit in the capacity of judge.

3. The Grand Chamber shall also include the President of the Court, the Vice-Presidents, the Presidents of the Chambers and other judges chosen in accordance with the rules of the Court. When a case is referred to the Grand Chamber under Article 43, no judge from the Chamber which rendered the judgment shall sit in the Grand Chamber, with the exception of the President of the Chamber and the judge who sat in respect of the State Party concerned.

Article 28. Declarations of inadmissibility by committees.

A committee may, by a unanimous vote, declare inadmissible or strike out of its list of cases an application submitted under Article 34 where such a decision can be taken without further examination. The decision shall be final.

Article 29. Decisions by Chambers on admissibility and merits.

1. If no decision is taken under Article 28, a Chamber shall decide on the admissibility and merits of individual applications submitted under Article 34.

2. A Chamber shall decide on the admissibility and merits of inter-State applications submitted under Article 33.

3. The decision on admissibility shall be taken separately unless the Court, in exceptional cases, decides otherwise.

Article 30. Relinquishment of jurisdiction to the Grand Chamber.

Where a case pending before a Chamber raises a serious question affecting the interpretation of the Convention or the protocols thereto, or where the resolution of a question before the Chamber might have a result inconsistent with a judgment previously delivered by the Court, the Chamber may, at any time before it has rendered its judgment, relinquish jurisdiction in favour of the Grand Chamber, unless one of the parties to the case objects.

Article 31. Powers of the Grand Chamber.

The Grand Chamber shall.

(a) determine applications submitted either under Article 33 or Article 34 when a Chamber has relinquished jurisdiction under Article 30 or when the case has been referred to it under Article 43; and

(b) consider requests for advisory opinions submitted under Article 47.

Article 32. Jurisdiction of the Court.

1. The jurisdiction of the Court shall extend to all matters concerning the interpretation and application of the Convention and the protocols thereto which are referred to it as provided in Articles 33, 34 and 47.

2. In the event of dispute as to whether the Court has jurisdiction, the Court shall decide.

Article 33. Inter-State cases.

Any High Contracting Party may refer to the Court any alleged breach of the provisions of the Convention and the protocols thereto by another High Contracting Party.

Article 34. Individual applications.

The Court may receive applications from any person, non-governmental organization or group of individuals claiming to be the victim of a violation by one of the High Contracting Parties of the rights set forth in the Convention or the protocols thereto. The High Contracting Parties undertake not to hinder in any way the effective exercise of this right.

Article 35. Admissibility criteria.

1. The Court may only deal with the matter after all domestic remedies have been exhausted, according to the generally recognized rules of international law, and within a period of six months from the date on which the final decision was taken.

2. The Court shall not deal with any application submitted under Article 34 that

(a) is anonymous; or

(b) is substantially the same as a matter that has already been examined by the Court or has already been submitted to another procedure of international investigation or settlement and contains no relevant new information.

3. The Court shall declare inadmissible any individual application submitted under Article 34 which it considers incompatible with the provisions of the Convention or the protocols thereto, manifestly ill-founded, or an abuse of the right of application.

4. The Court shall reject any application which it considers inadmissible under this Article. It may do so at any stage of the proceedings.

Article 36. Third party intervention.

1. In all cases before a Chamber of the Grand Chamber, a High Contracting Party one of whose nationals is an applicant shall have the right to submit written comments and to take part in hearings.

2. The President of the Court may, in the interest of the proper administration of justice, invite any High Contracting Party which is not a party to the proceedings or any person concerned who is not the applicant to submit written comments or take part in hearings

Article 37. Striking out applications.

1. The Court may at any stage of the proceedings decide to strike an application out of its list of cases where the circumstances lead to the conclusion that

(a) the applicant does not intend to pursue his application; or

(b) the matter has been resolved; or

(c) for any other reason established by the Court, it is no longer justified to continue the examination of the application.

However, the Court shall continue the examination of the application if respect for human rights as defined in the Convention and the protocols thereto so requires.

2. The Court may decide to restore an application to its list of cases if it considers that the circumstances justify such a course

Article 38. Examination of the case and friendly settlement proceedings.

1. If the Court declares the application admissible, it shall

(a) pursue the examination of the case, together with the representatives of the parties, and if need be, undertake an investigation, for the effective conduct of which the States concerned shall furnish all necessary facilities;

(b) place itself at the disposal of the parties concerned with a view to securing a friendly settlement of the matter on the basis of respect for human rights as defined in the Convention and the protocols thereto.

2. Proceedings conducted under paragraph 1(b) shall be confidential.

Article 39. Finding of a friendly settlement.

If a friendly settlement is effected, the Court shall strike the case out of its list by means of a decision which shall be confined to a brief statement of the facts and of the solution reached.

Article 40. Public hearings and access to documents.

1. Hearings shall be in public unless the Court in exceptional circumstances decides otherwise.

2. Documents deposited with the Registrar shall be accessible to the public unless the President of the Court decides otherwise.

Article 41. Just satisfaction.

If the Court finds that there has been a violation of the Convention or the protocols thereto, and if the internal law of the High Contracting Party concerned allows only partial reparation to be made, the Court shall, if necessary, afford just satisfaction to the injured party.

Article 42. Judgments of Chambers.

Judgments of Chambers shall become final in accordance with the provisions of Article 44, paragraph 2.

Article 43. Referral to the Grand Chamber.

1. Within a period of three months from the date of the judgment of the Chamber, any party to the case may, in exceptional cases, request that the case be referred to the Grand Chamber.

2. A panel of five judges of the Grand Chamber shall accept the request if the case raises a serious question affecting the interpretation or application of the Convention or the protocols thereto, or a serious issue of general importance.

3. If the panel accepts the request, the Grand Chamber shall decide the case by means of a judgment.

Article 44. Final judgments.

1. The judgment of the Grand Chamber shall be final.

2. The judgment of a Chamber shall become final

(a) when the parties declare that they will not request that the case be referred to the Grand Chamber; or

(b) three months after the date of the judgment, if reference of the case to the Grand Chamber has not been requested; or

(c) when the panel of the Grand Chamber rejects the request to refer under Article 43.

3. The final judgment shall be published.

Article 45. Reasons for judgments and decisions.

1. Reasons shall be given for judgments as well as for decisions declaring applications admissible or inadmissible.

2. If a judgment does not represent, in whole or in part, the unanimous opinion of the judges, any judge shall be entitled to deliver a separate opinion

Article 46. Binding force and execution of judgments.

1. The High Contracting Parties undertake to abide by the final judgment of the Court in any case to which they are parties.

2. The final judgment of the Court shall be transmitted to the Committee of Ministers, which shall supervise its execution

Article 47. Advisory opinions.

1. The Court may, at the request of the Committee of Ministers, give advisory opinions on legal questions concerning the interpretation of the Convention and the protocols thereto.

2. Such opinions shall not deal with any question relating to the content or scope of the rights or freedoms defined in Section I of the Convention and the protocols thereto, or with any other question which the Court or the Committee of Ministers might have to consider in consequence of any such proceedings as could be instituted in accordance with the Convention.

3. Decision of the Committee of Ministers to request an advisory opinion of the Court shall require a majority vote of the representatives entitled to sit on the Committee.

Article 48. Advisory jurisdiction of the Court.

The Court shall decide whether a request for an advisory opinion submitted by the Committee of Ministers is within its competence as defined in Article 47.

Article 49. Reasons for advisory opinions.

1. Reasons shall be given for advisory opinions of the Court.

2. . If the advisory opinion does not represent, in whole or in part, the unanimous opinion of the judges, any judge shall be entitled to deliver a separate opinion.

3. Advisory opinions of the Court shall be communicated to the Committee of Ministers.

Article 50. Expenditure on the Court.

The expenditure on the Court shall be borne by the Council of Europe.

Article 51. Privileges and immunities of judges.

The judges shall be entitled, during the exercise of their functions, to the privileges and immunities provided for in Article 40 of the Statute of the Council of Europe and in the agreements made thereunder.

III. MISCELLANEOUS PROVISIONS

Article 52. Inquiries by the Secretary-General.

On receipt of a request from the Secretary-General of the Council of Europe any High Contracting Party shall furnish an explanation of the manner in which its internal law ensures the effective implementation of any of the provisions of the Convention.

Article 53. Safeguard for existing human rights.

Nothing in this Convention shall be construed as limiting or derogating from any of the human rights and fundamental freedoms which may be ensured under the laws of any High Contracting Party or under any other agreement to which it is a Party.

Article 54. Powers of the Committee of Ministers.

Nothing in this Convention shall prejudice the powers conferred on the Committee of Ministers by the Statute of the Council of Europe.

Article 55. Exclusion of other means of dispute settlement.

The High Contracting Parties agree that, except by special agreement, they will not avail themselves of treaties, conventions or declarations in force between them for the purpose of submitting, by way of petition, a dispute arising out of the interpretation or application of this Convention to a means of settlement other than those provided for in this Convention.

Article 56. Territorial application.

1. Any State may at the time of its ratification or at any time thereafter declare by notification addressed to the Secretary-General of the Council of Europe that the present Convention shall, subject to paragraph 4 of this Article, extend to all or any of the territories for whose international relations it is responsible.

2. The Convention shall extend to the territory or territories named in the notification as from the thirtieth day after the receipt of this notification by the Secretary-General of the Council of Europe.

3. The provisions of this Convention shall be applied in such territories with due regard, however, to local requirements.

4. Any State which has made a declaration in accordance with paragraph 1 of this article may at any time thereafter declare on behalf of one or more of the territories to which the declaration relates that it accepts the competence of the Court to receive applications from individuals, non-governmental organizations or groups of individuals as provided by Article 34 of the Convention.

Article 57. Reservations.

Article 58. Denunciation.

Article 59. Signature and ratification.

ECONOMIC COMMUNITY OF WEST AFRICAN STATES—ECOWAS

Address: ECOWAS Executive Secretariat, 101 Yakubu Gowon Crescent, PMB 401, Asokoro, Abuja, Nigeria.

Telephone: (9) 3147647; **fax:** (9) 3147646; **e-mail:** info@ecowas.int; **internet:** www.ecowas.int.

The Treaty of Lagos, establishing ECOWAS, was signed in May 1975 by 15 states, with the object of promoting trade, co-operation and self-reliance in West Africa. Outstanding protocols bringing certain key features of the Treaty into effect were ratified in November 1976. Cape Verde joined in 1977. A revised ECOWAS treaty, designed to accelerate economic integration and to increase political co-operation, was signed in July 1993.

MEMBERS

Benin	Ghana	Niger
Burkina Faso	Guinea	Nigeria
Cape Verde	Guinea-Bissau*	Senegal
Côte d'Ivoire	Liberia	Sierra Leone
The Gambia	Mali	Togo

* Guinea-Bissau was suspended from participation in meetings of the Community from the end of April 2012, pending the restoration of constitutional order, following the overthrow of the legitimate Government earlier in that month.

Organization

(June 2012)

AUTHORITY OF HEADS OF STATE AND GOVERNMENT

The Authority is the supreme decision-making organ of the Community, with responsibility for its general development and realization of its objectives. The Chairman is elected annually by the Authority from among the member states. The Authority meets at least once a year in ordinary session. The 41st ordinary session was to be convened at the end of June 2012, in Yammasoukro, Côte d'Ivoire.

COUNCIL OF MINISTERS

The Council consists of two representatives from each member country; the chairmanship is held by a minister from the same member state as the Chairman of the Authority. The Council meets at least twice a year, and is responsible for the running of the Community.

ECOWAS COMMISSION

The ECOWAS Commission, formerly the Executive Secretariat, was inaugurated in January 2007, following a decision to implement a process of structural reform taken at the January 2006 summit meeting of the Authority. Comprising a President, a Vice-President and seven Commissioners, the Commission is elected for a four-year term, which may be renewed once only.

President: KADRÉ DÉSIRÉ OUÉDRAOGO (Burkina Faso).

TECHNICAL COMMITTEES

There are nine technical committees, formerly specialized technical commissions, which prepare Community projects and programmes in the following areas:

(i) Administration and Finance;

(ii) Agriculture, Environment and Water Resources;

(iii) Communication and Information Technology;

(iv) Human Development and Gender;

(v) Infrastructure;

(vi) Legal and Judicial Affairs;

(vii) Macro-economic Policy;

(viii) Political Affairs, Peace and Security; and

(ix) Trade, Customs and Free Movement of Persons.

ECOWAS PARLIAMENT

The inaugural session of the 120-member ECOWAS Parliament, based in Abuja, Nigeria, was held in November 2000. The January 2006 summit meeting of the Authority determined to restructure the Parliament, in line with a process of wider institutional reform. The number of seats was reduced from 120 to 115 and each member of the Parliament was to be elected for a four-year term (reduced from five years). The second legislature was inaugurated in November 2006. There is a co-ordinating administrative bureau, comprising a speaker and four deputy speakers, and there are also eight standing committees (reduced in number from 13) covering each of the Parliament's areas of activity.

Speaker: IKE EKWEREMADU (Nigeria).

ECOWAS COURT OF JUSTICE

The Court of Justice, established in January 2001, is based in Abuja, and comprises seven judges who serve a five-year renewable term of office. At the January 2006 summit meeting the Authority approved the creation of a Judicial Council, comprising qualified and experienced persons, to contribute to the establishment of community laws. The Authority also approved the inauguration of an appellate division within the Court. The judges will hold (non-renewable) tenure for four years.

President: NANA AWA DABOYA (Togo).

Activities

ECOWAS aims to promote co-operation and development in economic, social and cultural activities, to raise the standard of living of the people of the member countries, to increase and maintain economic stability, to improve relations among member countries and to contribute to the progress and development of Africa. ECOWAS is committed to abolishing all obstacles to the free movement of people, services and capital, and to promoting: harmonization of agricultural policies; common projects in marketing, research and the agriculturally based industries; joint development of economic and industrial policies and elimination of disparities in levels of development; and common monetary policies.

Initial slow progress in achieving many of ECOWAS's aims was attributed *inter alia* to the reluctance of some governments to implement policies at the national level and their failure to provide the agreed financial resources; to the high cost of compensating loss of customs revenue; and to the existence of numerous other intergovernmental organizations in the region (in particular the Union économique et monétaire ouest-africaine—UEMOA, which replaced the francophone Communauté économique de l'Afrique de l'ouest in 1994). In respect of the latter obstacle to progress, however, ECOWAS and UEMOA resolved in February 2000 to create a single monetary zone (see below). In October ECOWAS and the European Union (EU) held their first joint high-level meeting, at which the EU pledged financial support for ECOWAS's economic integration programme, and in April 2001 it was announced that the IMF had agreed to provide technical assistance for the programme.

A revised treaty for the Community was drawn up by an ECOWAS Committee of Eminent Persons in 1991–92, and was signed at the ECOWAS summit conference that took place in Cotonou, Benin, in July 1993. The treaty designated the achievement of a common market and a single currency as economic objectives, while in the political sphere it envisaged the establishment of an ECOWAS parliament, an economic and social council, and an ECOWAS court of justice to enforce Community decisions (see above). The treaty also formally assigned the Community with the responsibility of preventing and settling regional conflicts. At a summit meeting held in Abuja, in August 1994, ECOWAS heads of state and government signed a protocol agreement for the establishment of a regional parliament. The meeting also adopted a Convention on Extradition of non-political offenders. The new ECOWAS treaty entered into effect in August 1995, having received the required number of ratifications. A draft protocol providing for the creation of a mechanism for the prevention, management and settlement of conflicts, and for the maintenance of peace in the region, was approved by ECOWAS heads of state and government in December 1999. In December 2000 Mauritania, a founding member, withdrew from the Community.

In May 2002 the ECOWAS Authority met in Yamoussoukro, Côte d'Ivoire, to develop a regional plan of action for the implementation of the New Partnership for Africa's Development (NEPAD). In January 2006 the Authority, meeting in Niamey, Niger, commended the recent establishment of an ECOWAS Project Development and Implementation Unit, aimed at accelerating the implementation of regional infrastructural projects in sectors such as energy, telecommunications and transport. Also at that meeting the Authority approved further amendments to the revised ECOWAS treaty to provide for institutional reform.

Meeting in Abuja, in June 2007, the Authority adopted a long-term ECOWAS Strategic Vision, detailing the proposed establishment by 2020 of a West African region-wide borderless, stateless space and single economic community. In January 2008 the Authority adopted a comprehensive strategy document proposing a number of initiatives and programmes aimed at reducing poverty in West Africa. The Authority also approved the establishment of a statistics development support fund, and the ECOWAS Common Approach on Migration.

TRADE AND MONETARY UNION

In 1990 ECOWAS heads of state and government agreed to adopt measures that would create a single monetary zone and remove barriers to trade in goods that originated in the Community. ECOWAS regards monetary union as necessary to encourage investment in the region, since it would greatly facilitate capital transactions with foreign countries. In September 1992 it was announced that, as part of efforts to enhance monetary co-operation and financial harmonization in the region, the West African Clearing House was to be restructured as the West African Monetary Agency (WAMA). As a specialized agency of ECOWAS, WAMA was to be responsible for administering an ECOWAS exchange rate system (EERS) and for establishing the single monetary zone. In July 1996 the Authority agreed to impose a common value-added tax (VAT) on consumer goods, in order to rationalize indirect taxation and to stimulate greater intra-Community trade. In August 1997 ECOWAS heads of state and government authorized the introduction of a regional travellers' cheque scheme. (The scheme was formally inaugurated in October 1998, and the cheques, issued by WAMA in denominations of a West African Unit of Account and convertible into each local currency at the rate of one Special Drawing Right—SDR—see IMF—entered into circulation on 1 July 1999.) In December 1999 the ECOWAS Authority determined to pursue a 'Fast Track Approach' to economic integration, involving a two-track implementation of related measures. In April 2000 seven, predominantly anglophone, ECOWAS member states—Cape Verde, The Gambia, Ghana, Guinea, Liberia, Nigeria and Sierra Leone—issued the 'Accra Declaration', in which they agreed to establish a second West African monetary union (the West African Monetary Zone—WAMZ) to co-exist initially alongside UEMOA, which unites eight, mainly francophone, ECOWAS member states. As preconditions for adopting a single currency and common monetary and exchange rate policy, the member states of the second West African monetary union were (under the supervision of a newly established ECOWAS Convergence Council, comprising member states' ministers of finance and central bank governors) to attain a number of convergence criteria, including: a satisfactory level of price stability; sustainable budget deficits; a reduction in inflation; and the maintenance of an adequate level of foreign exchange reserves. The two complementary monetary unions were expected to harmonize their economic programmes, with a view to effecting an eventual merger, as outlined in an action plan adopted by ECOWAS and UEMOA in February 2000. The ECOWAS Authority summit held in December 2000, in Bamako, Mali, adopted an Agreement Establishing the WAMZ, approved the establishment of a West African Monetary Institute to prepare for the formation of a West African Central Bank (WACB), and determined that the harmonization of member countries' tariff structures should be accelerated to facilitate the implementation of the planned customs union. In December 2001 the Authority determined that the currency of the WAMZ (and eventually the ECOWAS-wide currency) would be known as the 'eco' and authorized the establishment during 2002 of an exchange rate mechanism. This was achieved in April. Meeting in November 2002 the heads of state and government determined that a forum of WAMZ ministers of finance should be convened on a regular basis to ensure the effective implementation of fiscal policies. In May 2004 ECOWAS and UEMOA signed an agreement that provided for the establishment of a Joint Technical Secretariat to enhance the co-ordination of their programmes.

Owing to slower-than-anticipated progress in achieving the convergence criteria required for monetary union, past deadlines for the inauguration of the WAMZ and launch of the 'eco' were not met. In May 2009 the Convergence Council adopted a new roadmap towards realizing the single currency for West Africa by 2020. Under the roadmap (of which an updated version was released in March 2010), the harmonization of the regulatory and supervisory framework for banking and other financial institutions, the establishment of the payment system infrastructure for cross-border transactions and of the payment system infrastructure in Guinea, The Gambia and Sierra Leone, and also the ongoing integration of regional financial markets, were all to be finalized during 2009–early 2013. The roadmap envisaged that, by 2014, ratification of the legal instruments for the creation of the WAMZ would have been achieved, and that during 2014 the WACB, WAMZ Secretariat and West African Financial Supervisory Agency would be established. The WAMZ monetary union was finally to enter into effect before or at the start of 2015, with the 'eco' scheduled to enter into circulation in January 2015. In October 2011 the Convergence Council adopted supplementary acts to facilitate the process of establishing the single currency. The documents included: the Guideline on the Formation of a Multi-year Programme on Convergence with ECOWAS; and the Draft Supplementary Act on Convergence and Macroeconomic Stability Pact among Member States, the latter constituting a formal commitment by signatories to ensure economic policy co-ordination, to strengthen economic convergence and to increase macroeconomic stability.

In January 2006 the Authority approved the implementation of a four-band common external tariff (CET) that was to align the WAMZ tariff structure with that of UEMOA, as follows: a 0% tariff would be applied to social goods (for example, educational and medical equipment); 5% would be levied on raw materials and most agricultural inputs; 10% on intermediate goods and rice; and 20% on finished consumer products. At the inaugural meeting of the Joint ECOWAS–UEMOA Management Committee of the ECOWAS CET, convened in July 2006, members agreed on a roadmap for implementing the uniform tariff system. The roadmap also outlined the legal framework for the introduction of the CET. In December 2011 a meeting of the Joint Committee agreed on a timetable for concluding the draft CET, in order to be able to present it for adoption by the ECOWAS Council of Ministers during 2012.

In December 1992 ECOWAS ministers agreed on the institutionalization of an ECOWAS trade fair, in order to promote trade liberalization and intra-Community trade. The first trade fair was held in Dakar, Senegal, in 1995; the sixth was held in Lomé, Togo, in November–December 2011, on the theme 'Strengthening intra-Community trade through public private partnership'. In September an ECOWAS Investment Forum was held in Lagos, Nigeria (following an inaugural event held in Brussels, Belgium, in the previous year), during which member states were called upon to implement measures to reduce risk and improve investor confidence and the business climate. ECOWAS business fora are organized periodically (the fourth, with a focus on ICT, was scheduled to be held in The Gambia in September 2012). A feasibility study for the establishment of an ECOWAS Investment Guarantee/Reinsurance Agency was under consideration in 2012.

An extraordinary meeting of ministers of trade and industry was convened in May 2008 to discuss the impact on the region of the rapidly rising cost at that time of basic food items. In December the ECOWAS Authority warned that the ongoing global financial crisis might undermine the region's economic development, and called for a regional strategy to minimize the risk.

TRANSPORT AND COMMUNICATIONS

In July 1992 the ECOWAS Authority formulated a Minimum Agenda for Action for the implementation of Community agreements regarding the free movement of goods and people, for example the removal of non-tariff barriers, the simplification of customs and transit procedures and a reduction in the number of control posts on international roads. However, implementation of the Minimum Agenda was slow. In April 1997 Gambian and Senegalese finance and trade officials concluded an agreement on measures to facilitate the export of goods via Senegal to neighbouring countries, in accordance with ECOWAS protocols relating to inter-state road transit arrangements. An Inter-state Road Transit Authority has been established. A Brown Card scheme provides recognized third-party liability insurance throughout the region. In January 2003 Community heads of state and government approved the ECOWAS passport; by 2011 the passport was being issued by Benin, Guinea, Liberia, Niger, Nigeria and Senegal.

In February 1996 ECOWAS and several private sector partners established ECOAir Ltd, based in Abuja, Nigeria, which was to develop a regional airline. In December 2007, following a recommendation by the Authority, a new regional airline, ASKY (Africa Sky) was established, which initiated operations in January 2010. A regional shipping company, ECOMARINE, commenced operations in February 2003. In October 2011 West African ministers of transported concluded a series of measures to establish a common regulatory regime for the airline industry in order to improve the viability of regional airlines and to support regional integration.

An ECOWAS programme for the development of an integrated regional road network comprises: the Trans-West African Coastal Highway, linking Lagos, Nigeria, with Nouackchott, Mauritania (4,767 km), and envisaged as the western part of an eventual Pan-African Highway; and the Trans-Sahelian Highway, linking Dakar, Senegal, with N'Djamena, Chad (4,633 km). By 2006 about 83% of the coastal route was reportedly complete, and by 2001 about 87% of the trans-Sahelian route had reportedly been built. It was reported in January 2009 that construction companies were tendering to complete the Nigerian section of the Coastal Highway. In 2003 the African Development Bank agreed to finance a study on interconnection of the region's railways.

In August 1996 the initial phase of a programme to improve regional telecommunications was reported to have been completed. A second phase of the programme (INTELCOM II), which aimed to modernize and expand the region's telecommunications services, was initiated by ECOWAS heads of state in August 1997. A West African Telecommunications Regulators' Association was established, under the auspices of ECOWAS, in September 2000. The January 2006 summit meeting of the Authority approved a new Special Fund for Telecommunications to facilitate improvements to cross-border telecommunications connectivity. In May ECOWAS ministers of information and telecommunications agreed guidelines for harmonizing the telecommunications sector. In January 2007 ECOWAS leaders adopted a regional telecommunications policy and a regulatory framework that covered areas including interconnection to ICT and services networks, license regimes, and radio frequency spectrum management. A common, liberalized ECOWAS telecommunications market is envisaged. In October 2008 ECOWAS ministers responsible for telecommunications and ICT adopted regional legislation on combating cybercrime. In October 2011 ECOWAS ministers of ICT and telecommunications, meeting in Yamoussoukro, Côte d'Ivoire, adopted a series of priority projects to be undertaken in the next five years, including the elaboration of a regulation on access to submarine cable landing stations and national rights of way. The meeting recommended the establishment of a Directorate of Telecoms-ICT and Post sectors by late 2012, in order to improve ECOWAS's operational capacity and to enhance the planning and monitoring of these sectors at the Community level.

ECONOMIC AND INDUSTRIAL DEVELOPMENT

In June 2010 the Council of Ministers adopted the West African Common Industrial Policy (WACIP), and a related action plan and supplementary acts. WACIP aimed to diversify and expand the regional industrial production base by supporting the creation of new industrial production capacities as well as developing existing capacities. WACIP envisaged the expansion of intra-ECOWAS trade from 13% to 40% by 2030, through enhancing skills, industrial competitiveness and quality infrastructure, with a particular focus on the areas of information, communications and transport.

TIn September 2008 the inaugural meeting was convened of an ECOWAS–People's Republic of China economic and trade forum, which aimed to strengthen bilateral relations and discuss investment possibilities in the development of infrastructure, financial services, agriculture and the exploitation of natural resources. A second forum was convened in March 2012, in Accra, Ghana.

In November 1984 ECOWAS heads of state and government approved the establishment of a private regional investment bank, Ecobank Transnational Inc. ECOWAS has a 10% share in the bank, which is headquartered in Lomé, Togo.

In September 1995 Nigeria, Ghana, Togo and Benin resolved to develop a gas pipeline to connect Nigerian gas supplies to the other countries. In August 1999 the participating countries, together with two petroleum companies operating in Nigeria, signed an agreement on the financing and construction of the 600-km West African Gas Pipeline, which was to extend from the Nigerian capital, Lagos, to Takoradi, Ghana. It became operational in late 2007. The implementation of a planned energy exchange scheme, known as the West African Power Pool Project (WAPP), is envisaged as a means of efficiently utilizing the region's hydro-electricity and thermal power capabilities by transferring power from surplus producers to countries unable to meet their energy requirements. An ECOWAS Energy Protocol, establishing a legal framework for the promotion of long-term co-operation in the energy sector, was adopted in 2003. In May of that year the Community decided to initiate the first phase of WAPP, to be implemented in Benin, Côte d'Ivoire, Ghana, Niger, Nigeria and Togo, at an estimated cost of US $335m. In January 2005 the Authority endorsed a revised masterplan for the implementation of WAPP, which was scheduled to be completed by 2020. In July 2005 the World Bank approved a $350m. facility to support the implementation of WAPP, which became fully operational in January 2006.

In November 2008 the Authority approved the establishment of a Regional Centre for Renewable Energy and Energy Efficiency (ECREEE), to be based in Praia, Cape Verde, and also endorsed the establishment of an ECOWAS Regional Electricity Regulatory Authority, to be based in Accra. The Authority also adopted a joint ECOWAS/UEMOA action plan on priority regional infrastructure projects. ECREEE was inaugurated in 2009, and a Secretariat was established in July 2010. In September 2011 the ECOWAS Commission signed a €2.3m. grant contract with the EU for an ECREEE project on energy efficiency in West Africa.

In April 2009 ministers responsible for the development of mineral resources endorsed an ECOWAS Directive on the Harmonization of Guiding Principles and Policies in the Mining Sector. An ad hoc committee to monitor the implementation of the Directive convened in May 2011.

REGIONAL SECURITY

The revised ECOWAS treaty, signed in July 1993, incorporates a separate provision for regional security, requiring member states to work towards the maintenance of peace, stability and security. In December 1997 an extraordinary meeting of ECOWAS heads of state and government was convened in Lomé, Togo, to consider the future stability and security of the region. It was agreed that a permanent mechanism should be established for conflict prevention and the maintenance of peace. ECOWAS leaders also reaffirmed their commitment to pursuing dialogue to prevent conflicts, co-operating in the early deployment of peacekeeping forces and implementing measures to counter trans-border crime and the illegal trafficking of armaments and drugs. At the meeting ECOWAS leaders acknowledged the role of the ECOWAS Cease-fire Monitoring Group (ECOMOG) in restoring constitutional order in Liberia and expressed their appreciation of the force's current efforts in Sierra Leone (see below). In March 1998 ECOWAS ministers of foreign affairs, meeting in Yamoussoukro, Côte d'Ivoire, resolved that ECOMOG should become the region's permanent peace-keeping force, and agreed to undertake a redefinition of the command structure within the organization in order to strengthen decision-making and the legal status of the ECOMOG force.

In December 1999 ECOWAS heads of state and government, meeting in Lomé, Togo, approved a draft protocol to the organization's treaty, providing for the establishment of a Permanent Mechanism for the Prevention, Management and Settlement of Conflicts and the Maintenance of Peace in the Region, and for the creation of a Mediation and Security Council, to comprise representatives of 10 member states, elected for two-year terms. The Council was to be supported by an advisory Council of Elders (also known as the Council of the Wise), comprising 32 eminent statesmen from the region; this was inaugurated in July 2001. ECOMOG was to be transformed from an ad hoc cease-fire monitoring group into a permanent standby force available for immediate deployment to avert emerging conflicts in the region. In January 2003 the Council of Elders was recomposed as a 15-member body with a representative from each member state. In December 2006 a Technical Committee of Experts on Political Affairs, Peace and Security was established as a subsidiary body of the Mediation and Security Council.

In October 1998 the ECOWAS Authority determined to implement a renewable three-year moratorium on the import, export or manufacture of small armaments in order to enhance the security of the sub-region. In March 1999 the Programme of Co-ordination and Assistance for Security and Development (PCASED) was launched to complement the moratorium. The moratorium was renewed for a further three years in July 2001. (In 2004 ECOWAS announced its intention to transform the moratorium into a convention and PCASED was decommissioned.) In June 2006 the Authority adopted the ECOWAS Convention on Small Arms and Light Weapons, their Ammunitions and other Materials, with the aim of regulating the importation and manufacture of such weapons. The ECOWAS Small Arms Control Programme (ECOSAP) was inaugurated in that month, based in Bamako, Mali, aimed at improving the capacity of national and regional institutions to reduce the proliferation of small weapons across the region. During 1999 ECOWAS member states established the Intergovernmental Action Group Against Money Laundering in Africa (GIABA), which was mandated to combat drug-trafficking and money laundering throughout the region; a revised regulation for GIABA adopted by the Authority in January 2006 expanded the Group's mandate to cover regional responsibility for combating terrorism. Representatives from ECOWAS member states met in Ouagadougou, Burkina Faso, in September 2007 to draft a new West African strategy for enhanced drug control. In October 2008—during a High-level Conference on Drugs Trafficking as a Security Threat to West Africa, convened by ECOWAS jointly with the UN Office on Drugs and Crime (UNODC) and the Cape Verde Government, in Praia, Cape Verde—the Executive Director of UNODC warned that West Africa was at risk of becoming an epicentre for drugs trafficking, representing a serious threat to public health and security in the region. He proposed the establishment of a West African intelligence-sharing centre, and urged the promotion of development and the strengthening of the rule of law as a means of reducing regional vulnerability to drugs and crime. At the Conference ECOWAS adopted a Political Declaration on Drugs Trafficking and Organized Crime in West Africa, and approved an ECOWAS Regional Response Plan. In April 2009 ECOWAS ministers with responsibility for issues relating to trafficking in persons adopted a policy aimed at establishing a legal mechanism for protecting and assisting victims of trafficking. In July 2009 ECOWAS, UNODC, other UN agencies, and INTERPOL launched the West Africa Coast Initiative (WACI), which aimed to build national and regional capacities to combat drugs trafficking and organized crime in, initially, four pilot post-conflict countries: Côte d'Ivoire, Guinea-Bissau, Liberia and Sierra Leone. In February 2010 the pilot countries signed the 'WACI-Freetown Commitment', endorsing the implementation of the initiative, and agreeing to establish specialized transnational crime units on their territories. WACI activities were to be expanded to Guinea during 2012. In March 2010 ECOWAS, the African Union, the International Organization for Migration and UNODC launched an initiative to develop a roadmap for implementing in West Africa the Ouagadougou Action Plan to Combat Trafficking in Human Beings (adopted by the AU in 2006).

An ECOWAS Warning and Response Network (ECOWARN) asseses threats to regional security. In June 2004 the Community approved the establishment of the ECOWAS Standby Force (ESF), comprising 6,500 troops, including a core rapid reaction component, the ECOWAS Task Force, numbering around 2,770 soldiers (deployable within 30 days). The ECOWAS Defence and Security Commission approved the operational framework for the ESF in April 2005. A training exercise for the logistics component of the ESF was conducted, in Ouagadougou, Burkina Faso, in June 2009.

In January 2005 the Authority authorized the establishment of humanitarian depot, to be based in Bamako, Mali, and a logistics depot, to be based in Freetown, Sierra Leone, with a view to expanding regional humanitarian response capacity. In December 2009 the Sierra Leone Government allocated land for the construction on the planned Freetown depot, and, in February 2011, ECOWAS signed Memoranda of Understanding with WFP and with the Government of Mali relating to the planned creation of the Bamako ECOWAS Humanitarian Depot, which, once established, was to provide storage for food and non-food items, and for emergency equipment. An ECOWAS Emergency Response Team (EERT) was established in 2007.

In October 2006 it was reported that ECOWAS planned to introduce a series of initiatives in each of the member states under a Peace and Development Project (PADEP). The Project intended to foster a 'culture of peace' among the member states of ECOWAS, strengthening social cohesion and promoting economic integration, democracy and good governance.

In March 2008 an ECOWAS Network of Electoral Commissions, comprising heads of member states' institutions responsible for managing elections, was established with the aim of ensuring the transparency and integrity of regional elections and helping to entrench a culture of democracy.

Guinea's membership of ECOWAS was suspended in January 2009, following a *coup d'état* in December 2008. The inaugural meeting of an International Contact Group on Guinea (ICG-G), co-chaired by ECOWAS and the AU Commission, and also comprising representatives of other regional and international organizations, was held in February 2009. Meeting in October, in its eighth session, the ICG-G strongly condemned brutal acts perpetrated by armed troops in Guinea against women and other unarmed civilians in late September. The ICG-G also invited ECOWAS, with support from partners, to establish an international observer and protection mission to contribute to the establishment of an atmosphere of security in Guinea. An extraordinary summit of the ECOWAS Authority, held in mid-October, urged the establishment of a transitional regime in Guinea. Also in October 2009, Niger's ECOWAS membership was suspended, following the refusal of that country's authorities to respond to a request by ECOWAS to postpone a controversial presidential election. ECOWAS condemned a *coup d'état* which took place in Niger in February 2010. In June 2010 the Mediation and Security Council expressed satisfaction with progress being made towards the restoration of democracy in both Guinea (where a presidential election was held, in two rounds, in June and November 2010) and Niger (where a 12-month timetable outlining the return to democratic rule had been adopted, in April, by the military regime). A meeting of the Authority in March 2011 ended the membership suspensions of both Guinea and Niger.

The President of the ECOWAS Commission participated in an AU High-level Panel appointed in January 2011 to address ongoing unrest in Côte d'Ivoire, where the security situation had deteriorated following the refusal of the outgoing President Laurent Gbagbo to acknowledge the outcome of presidential elections held in 2010, and consequently to cede power. The legitimately elected President, Alassane Ouattara, was eventually inaugurated in May 2011. In September the President of the Commission led an ECOWAS delegation to Côte d'Ivoire to assess that country's post-conflict humanitarian and economic needs. The President appointed Oluwole Coker as his Special Representative to Côte d'Ivoire in order to facilitate the provision and distribution of ECOWAS assistance. In the same month five ECOWAS heads of state met to consider the deteriorating security situation along the borders between Côte d'Ivoire and Liberia.

In April 2011 ECOWAS initiated a series of regional measures to combat the increased incidence of piracy, in co-operation with the Communauté économique des états de l'Afrique centrale (CEEAC—Economic Community of Central African States). In October the UN Security Council adopted Resolution 2018 which urged ECOWAS, the CEEAC and the Gulf of Guinea Commission to develop a comprehensive regional action plan against piracy and armed robbery at sea.

In October 2011 ECOWAS dispatched a 150-member observer mission to monitor the presidential and legislative elections in Liberia. An enlarged mission, comprising 200 observers, returned to the country in November in order to monitor the second round of voting in the presidential poll. In February 2012 ECOWAS heads of state and government authorized a Joint AU–ECOWAS high-level mission to Senegal, in order to promote political dialogue and to ensure peaceful, fair and transparent forthcoming elections. An observer mission was dispatched to Senegal in late February to monitor the presidential poll.

In March 2009 ECOWAS Chiefs of Defence agreed to deploy a multidisciplinary group to monitor and co-ordinate security sector reforms in Guinea-Bissau, following the assassinations of the military Chief of Staff and President of that country at the beginning of the month. The ECOWAS Chiefs of Defence also demanded a review of ECOWAS legislation on conflict prevention and peace-keeping. In November 2010 ECOWAS and the Comunidade dos Países de Língua Portuguesa (CPLP) adopted an ECOWAS-CPLP road map on reform of the defence and security sector in Guinea-Bissau. In March 2012 an 80-member ECOWAS observation mission monitored the first round of a presidential election held in Guinea-Bissau following the death in office, in January, of the President. In mid-April, before the planned second round of the Guinea-Bissau presidential election, scheduled for later in that month, a military junta usurped power by force and established a Transitional National Council (TNC), comprising military officers and representatives of political parties that had been in opposition to the legitimate government. The ECOWAS Commission strongly condemned the military coup and denounced the establishment of the TNC. An ECOWAS high-level delegation visited Guinea-Bissau in mid-April to hold discussions with the military leadership.

In mid-March 2012 the President of the ECOWAS Commission led a fact-finding mission to Mali, in view of escalating unrest in northern areas of that country arising from attacks by separatist militants of the National Movement for the Liberation of Azawad (MNLA). The Commission condemned all acts of violence committed by the MNLA. In late March ECOWAS heads of state and government convened an extraordinary summit to discuss the recent illegal overthrow, by the Comité National de Redressement pour la Démocratie et la Restauration de l'Etat (CNRDRE), of the legitimate government of Mali's elected President Amadou Touré, and also to address the separatist violence ongoing in the north of the country. The regional leaders suspended Mali from participating in all decision-making bodies of ECOWAS pending the restoration of constitutional order, and imposed sanctions (including a ban on travel and an assets freeze) on members of the CNRDRE and their associates. The summit appointed President Blaise Compaoré of Burkina Faso as ECOWAS mediator, with a mandate to facilitate dialogue between the legitimate Mali Government and the CNRDRE regime on achieving a return to civilian rule, and also on means of terminating the northern rebellion. Meanwhile, in early April, MNLA rebels, assisted by Islamist forces, seized land in the Kidal, Gao and Tombouctou regions of northern Mali, unilaterally declaring this to be the independent entity of Azawad. At that time the Commission denounced a 'Declaration of Independence by the MNLA for the North of Mali', reminding all militants that Mali is an 'indivisible entity', and stating that ECOWAS would be prepared to use all necessary measures, including force, to ensure Mali's territorial integrity. An emergency meeting of ECOWAS Joint Chiefs of Defence Staff, held in early April, adopted preparatory measures for the rapid deployment of the ESF to Mali if necessary. On 6 April representatives of the CNRDRE and the ECOWAS mediation team, under the chairmanship of Compaoré, signed an accord that was intended to lead to a return to full constitutional rule; the accord entailed the appointment of a new interim president, who was to lead a transitional administration pending the staging of democratic elections. Accordingly, an interim president, Dioncounda Traoré, was sworn in on 12 April, and ECOWAS sanctions against Mali were withdrawn. The CNRDRE, however, subsequently appeared to influence the political process: in late April Traoré announced a new government, which included three posts held by military officers and no ministers from the former Touré government.

An extraordinary summit meeting of ECOWAS heads of state and government convened in late April 2012 decided to deploy troops from the ESF to both Guinea-Bissau and Mali to support in both countries a swift restoration of constitutional order. Sanctions, including economic measures and targeted individual penalties, were to be imposed if the military in either country continued to obstruct the democratic process. The summit meeting urged military leaders in both countries to release civilians who had been detained during the coups and to ensure the safety of officials from the former legitimate administrations. The meeting stipulated that democratic elections should be held in both Guinea-Bissau and Mali within 12 months. It was reported that the ESF contingent in Guinea-Bissau (which arrived in that country in mid-May) would comprise around 620 troops, and that the ESF presence in Mali would number at least 3,000. A seven-nation Contact Group on Guinea-Bissau (comprising Benin, Cape Verde, The Gambia, Guinea, Senegal and Togo, and chaired by Nigeria) was established by the extraordinary summit, with a mandate to follow up its decisions. At the end of April diplomatic, economic and financial sanctions were imposed on military leaders and their associates in Guinea-Bissau, in view of the failure of talks between the Contact Group and Guinea-Bissau stakeholders to secure an arrangement for restoring constitutional rule within a 12-month period. Meeting in early May an extraordinary summit of the Authority condemned violent clashes that had erupted in Bamako, the Malian capital, from the end of April, and welcomed the availability of the President of Nigeria, Goodluck Jonathan, to assist, as 'Associate Mediator', Compaoré in pursuing a negotiated resolution to the conflict in northern Mali. Later in May the President of the Commission condemned a violent assault on Traoré, the interim Malian President, by opponents protesting against the length of his term of office. At the end of that month the President of the Commission reaffirmed support to the transitional authorities and warned that sanctions would be imposed on those deemed to be disrupting the transitional process. ECOWAS heads of state and government attending a consultative meeting on the situation in Mali that was organized in early June, in Lomé, Togo, on the sidelines of the 16th UEMOA summit, strongly condemned acts of rape, robbery, and killing, and the desecration of cultural sites, allegedly being perpetrated by armed groups in northern Mali. The meeting instructed the ECOWAS Commission to continue with preparations for the deployment of the ESF in Mali, and urged the Community and the AU to seek UN Security Council approval for the operation.

PAST PEACE-KEEPING OPERATIONS

The ECOWAS cease-fire monitoring group, ECOMOG, was established in 1990, when it was dispatched to Liberia in an attempt to enforce a cease-fire between conflicting factions there and to help restore public order. It remained in that country until October 1999, undertaking roles including disarmament of rebel soldiers, maintaining security during presidential and legislative elections, and restructuring the national security forces. A second military force, the ECOWAS Mission in Liberia, ECOMIL, was authorized in July 2003 to protect civilians following political disturbances in the Liberian capital, Monrovia. The 3,500 ECOMIL troops transferred to a UN-mandated mission in October.

In August 1997 ECOMOG was mandated by ECOWAS heads of state and government to monitor a cease-fire in Sierra Leone negotiated with the dissident Armed Forces Revolutionary Council (ARFC), which had removed the president, Ahmed

Tejan Kabbah, from office earlier in that year. ECOMOG was also mandated to upholding international sanctions against the new authorities. In February 1999 ECOMOG troops assumed control of Freetown from ARFC and the rebel Revolutionary United Front (RUF) control. Following the return of Kabbah in March, it was agreed that ECOMOG forces, then numbering some 10,000, were to remain in the country in order to ensure the full restoration of peace and security, to assist in the restructuring of the armed forces and to help to resolve the problems of the substantial numbers of refugees and internally displaced persons. ECOMOG's mandate in Sierra Leone was further adapted, following the signing of a political agreement in July, to support the consolidation of peace in that country and national reconstruction. In October a new UN mission, UNAMSIL, assumed many of the functions then being performed by ECOMOG, including the provision of security at Lungi international airport and at other key installations, buildings and government institutions in the Freetown area. In consequence the ECOMOG contingent was withdrawn in April 2000.

In February 1999 a 600-strong ECOMOG Interposition Force was dispatched to Guinea-Bissau to help uphold a cease-fire agreement between government and rebel factions in that country, to supervise the border region with Senegal and to facilitate the delivery of humanitarian assistance. The Force was withdrawn, however, in June following the removal from office of President João Vieira.

In September 2002 an extraordinary summit meeting of ECOWAS heads of state and government was convened in Accra, Ghana, to address the violent unrest that had erupted in Côte d'Ivoire during that month. The meeting condemned the attempt to overthrow democratic rule and constitutional order and established a high-level contact group, comprising the heads of state of Ghana, Guinea-Bissau, Mali, Niger, Nigeria and Togo, to prevail upon the rebel factions to end hostilities, and to negotiate a general framework for the resolution of the crisis. The contact group helped to mediate a cease-fire in the following month; this was to be monitored by an ECOWAS military mission in Côte d'Ivoire (ECOMICI), which was also to be responsible for ensuring safe passage for deliveries of humanitarian assistance. In March 2003, following the conclusion in January by the parties to the conflict of a peace agreement, signed at Marcoussis, France, ECOWAS chiefs of staff endorsed the expansion of ECOMICI from 1,264 to a maximum of 3,411 troops, to monitor the implementation of the peace agreement in co-operation with the UN Mission in Côte d'Ivoire (MINUCI), and French forces. In April 2004 authority was transferred from ECOMICI and MINUCI to the newly established UN Operation in Côte d'Ivoire (UNOCI). In mid-June ECOWAS heads of state and government convened at a summit to address means of reviving the implementation of the stalled Marcoussis peace accord. A high-level meeting of ECOWAS heads of state and government, other African leaders, the Chairperson of the AU, and the parties to the Côte d'Ivoire conflict, held in Accra in late July, affirmed that a monitoring mechanism, comprising representatives of ECOWAS, the AU, Côte d'Ivoire and the UN, should produce regular reports on progress towards peace in Côte d'Ivoire.

AGRICULTURE AND THE ENVIRONMENT

The Community enforces a certification scheme for facilitating the monitoring of animal movement and animal health surveillance and protection in the sub-region. In February 2001 ECOWAS ministers of agriculture adopted an action plan for the formulation of a common agricultural policy, as envisaged under the ECOWAS treaty. An ECOWAS Regional Agricultural Policy (ECOWAP) was endorsed by the January 2005 Authority summit. In January 2006 the Authority approved an action plan for the implementation of ECOWAP. The Policy was aimed at enhancing regional agricultural productivity with a view to guaranteeing food sufficiency and standards. In October 2011 a high-level consultative meeting of ECOWAS and FAO officials determined that ECOWAP was the most effective means of countering the effects of food price increases and volatility.

ECOWAS promotes implementation of the UN Convention on Desertification Control and supports programmes initiated at national and sub-regional level within the framework of the treaty. Together with the Permanent Inter-State Committee on Drought Control in the Sahel—CILSS, ECOWAS has been designated as a project leader for implementing the Convention in West Africa. Other environmental initiatives include a regional meteorological project to enhance meteorological activities and applications, and in particular to contribute to food security and natural resource management in the sub-region. ECOWAS pilot schemes have formed the basis of integrated control projects for the control of floating (or invasive aquatic) weeds in five water basins in West Africa, which had hindered the development of the local fishery sectors. A rural water supply programme aims to ensure adequate water for rural dwellers in order to improve their living standards. The first phase of the project focused on schemes to develop village and pastoral water points in Burkina Faso, Guinea, Mali, Niger and Senegal, with funds from various multilateral donors.

In September 2009 a regional conference, convened in Lomé, Togo, to address the potential effects of rapid climate change on regional stability, issued the Lomé Declaration on Climate Change and Protection of Civilians in West Africa, and recommended the establishment of a fund to support communities suffering the negative impact of climate change. In March 2010 ECOWAS ministers responsible for agriculture, environment and water resources adopted a Framework of Strategic Guidelines on the Reduction of Vulnerability and Adaptability to Climate Change in West Africa, outlining the development of regional capacities to build up resilience and adaptation to climate change and severe climatic conditions. ECOWAS supports the development and implementation by member states of Nationally Appropriate Mitigation Actions (NAMAs).

SOCIAL PROGRAMME

The following organizations have been established within ECOWAS: the Organization of Trade Unions of West Africa, which held its first meeting in 1984; the West African Universities' Association, the ECOWAS Youth and Sports Development Centre (EYSDC), the ECOWAS Gender Development Centre (EGDC), and the West African Health Organization (WAHO), which was established in 2000 by merger of the West African Health Community and the Organization for Co-ordination and Co-operation in the Struggle against Endemic Diseases. ECOWAS and the European Commission jointly implement the West African Regional Health Programme, which aims to improve the co-ordination and harmonization of regional health policies, with a view to strengthening West African integration. In December 2001 the ECOWAS summit of heads of state and government adopted a plan of action aimed at combating trafficking in human beings and authorized the establishment of an ECOWAS Criminal Intelligence Bureau. In March 2009 ECOWAS ministers of education, meeting in Abuja, Nigeria, identified priority activities for advancing the regional implementation of regional activities relating to the AU-sponsored Second Decade of Education in Africa (2006–15). In the following month ECOWAS ministers responsible for labour and employment adopted a regional labour policy. In February 2012 the ECOWAS Commission and the International Labour Organization determined to collaborate in order to address the challenges of child labour in West Africa. The Commission resolved to harmonize national action plans relating to child labour and to formulate a regional strategy. Since 2010 the EYSDC has organized the biennial 'ECOWAS Games' (September 2010: Abuja, Nigeria; June 2012: Accra, Ghana; 2014: to be held in Côte d'Ivoire).

SPECIALIZED AGENCIES

ECOWAS Bank for Investment and Development (EBID): BP 2704, 128 blvd du 13 janvier, Lomé, Togo; tel. 22-21-68-64; fax 22-21-86-84; e-mail bidc@bidc-ebid.org; internet www.bidc-ebid.org; f. 2001, replacing the former ECOWAS Fund for Co-operation, Compensation and Development; comprises two divisions, a Regional Investment Bank and a Regional Development Fund; Pres. Bashir M. Ifo.

West African Monetary Agency (WAMA): 11–13 ECOWAS St, PMB 218, Freetown, Sierra Leone; tel. 224485; fax 223943; e-mail wamao@amao-wama.org; internet www.wama-amao.org; f. 1975 as West African Clearing House; agreement founding WAMA signed by governors of ECOWAS central banks in

March 1996; administers transactions between its eight member central banks in order to promote sub-regional trade and monetary co-operation; administers ECOWAS travellers' cheques scheme. Mems: Banque Centrale des Etats de l'Afrique de l'Ouest (serving Benin, Burkina Faso, Côte d'Ivoire, Guinea-Bissau, Mali, Niger, Senegal, Togo) and the central banks of Cape Verde, The Gambia, Ghana, Guinea, Liberia, Nigeria and Sierra Leone; Dir-Gen. Prof. MOHAMED BEN OMAR NDIAYE; publ. *Annual Report*.

West African Monetary Institute (WAMI): Gulf House, Tetteh Quarshie Interchange, Cantonments 75, Accra, Ghana; tel. (30) 2743801; fax (30) 2743807; e-mail info@wami-imao.org; internet www.wami-imao.org; f. by the ECOWAS Authority summit in December 2000 to prepare for the establishment of a West African Central Bank, currently scheduled for 2014; Dir-Gen. TEI KITCHER (acting).

West African Health Organization (WAHO): 01 BP 153 Bobo-Dioulasso 01, Burkina Faso; tel. and fax (226) 975772; e-mail wahooas@wahooas.org; internet www.wahooas.org; f. 2000 by merger of the West African Health Community (f. 1978) and the Organization for Co-ordination and Co-operation in the Struggle against Endemic Diseases (f. 1960); aims to harmonize member states' health policies and to promote research, training, the sharing of resources and diffusion of information; Dir-Gen. Dr PLACIDO MONTEIRO CARDOSO (Guinea-Bissau); publ. *Bulletin Bibliographique* (quarterly).

West African Power Pool (WAPP): 06 BP 2907, Zone des Ambassade, PK 6 Cotonou, Benin; tel. 21-37-41-95; fax 21-37-41-96; e-mail info@ecowapp.org; internet www.ecowapp.org; f. 1999; new organization approved as a Specialized Agency in Jan. 2006; inaugural meeting held in July 2006; aims to facilitate the integration of the power systems of member nations into a unified regional electricity market; Gen. Sec. AMADOU DIALLO; publ. *WAPP Newsletter* (intermittent).

Finance

Under the revised treaty, signed in July 1993, ECOWAS was to receive revenue from a community tax, based on the total value of imports from member countries. In July 1996 the summit meeting approved a protocol on a community levy, providing for the imposition of a 0.5% tax on the value of imports from a third country. In August 1997 the Authority of Heads of State and Government determined that the community levy should replace budgetary contributions from member states as the organization's principal source of finance. The protocol came into force in January 2000, having been ratified by nine member states, with the substantive regime entering into effect on 1 January 2003. The January 2006 meeting of the Authority approved a budget of US $121m. for the operations of the Community in that year.

Publications

Annual Report.

Contact.

ECOWAS National Accounts.

ECOWAS News.

ECOWAS Newsletter.

West African Bulletin.

ECONOMIC COOPERATION ORGANIZATION—ECO

Address: 1 Golbou Alley, Kamranieh St, POB 14155-6176, Tehran, Iran.

Telephone: (21) 22831733; **fax:** (21) 22831732; **e-mail:** registry@ecosecretariat.org; **internet:** www.ecosecretariat.org.

The Economic Cooperation Organization (ECO) was established in 1985 as the successor to the Regional Cooperation for Development, founded in 1964.

MEMBERS

Afghanistan	Kyrgyzstan	Turkey
Azerbaijan	Pakistan	Turkmenistan
Iran	Tajikistan	Uzbekistan
Kazakhstan		

The 'Turkish Republic of Northern Cyprus' has been granted special guest status.

Organization

(June 2012)

SUMMIT MEETING

The first summit meeting of heads of state and of government of member countries was held in Tehran, Iran, in February 1992. Summit meetings are generally held at least once every two years. The 11th summit meeting was held in Istanbul, Turkey, in December 2010.

COUNCIL OF MINISTERS

The Council of Ministers, comprising ministers of foreign affairs of member states, is the principal policy- and decision-making body of ECO. It meets at least once a year.

REGIONAL PLANNING COUNCIL

The Council, comprising senior planning officials or other representatives of member states, meets at least once a year. It is responsible for reviewing programmes of activity and evaluating results achieved, and for proposing future plans of action to the Council of Ministers.

COUNCIL OF PERMANENT REPRESENTATIVES

Permanent representatives or Ambassadors of member countries accredited to Iran meet regularly to formulate policy for consideration by the Council of Ministers and to promote implementation of decisions reached at ministerial or summit level.

SECRETARIAT

The Secretariat is headed by a Secretary-General, who is supported by two Deputy Secretaries-General. The following Directorates administer and co-ordinate the main areas of ECO activities: Trade and investment; Transport and communications; Energy, minerals and environment; Agriculture, industry and tourism; Project and economic research and statistics; Human resources and sustainable development; and International relations. The Secretariat services regular ministerial meetings held by regional ministers of agriculture; energy and minerals; finance and economy; industry; trade and investment; and transport and communications.

Secretary-General: YAHYA P. MAROOFI (Afghanistan).

Activities

The Regional Cooperation for Development (RCD) was established in 1964 as a tripartite arrangement between Iran, Pakistan and Turkey, which aimed to promote economic co-operation between member states. ECO replaced the RCD in 1985, and seven additional members were admitted to the Organization in November 1992. The main areas of co-operation are transport (including the building of road and rail links, of particular importance as seven member states are landlocked), telecommunications and post, trade and investment, energy (including the interconnection of power grids in the region), minerals, environmental issues, industry, and agriculture. ECO priorities and objectives for each sector are defined in the Quetta Plan of Action and the Istanbul Declaration; an 'Almaty Outline Plan', which was adopted in 1993, is specifically concerned with the development of regional transport and communication infrastructure. Meeting in October 2005, in Astana, Kazakhstan, the ECO Council of Ministers adopted a document entitled *ECO Vision 2015*, detailing basic policy guidelines for the organization's activities during 2006–15, and setting a number of targets to be achieved in the various areas of regional co-operation. The 10th ECO summit meeting, convened in Tehran, Iran, in March 2009, reaffirmed commitment to ongoing co-operation, and observed that the global financial crisis had originated in factors such as world-wide systemic weaknesses, unsound practices, and excessive use of resources, necessitating closer future co-operation among member states. At the 11th summit meeting, held in Istanbul, Turkey, in December 2010, it was reported that Iraq had applied to join the Organization.

In 1990 an ECO College of Insurance was inaugurated. A joint Chamber of Commerce and Industry was established in 1993. The third ECO summit meeting, held in Islamabad, Pakistan, in March 1995, concluded formal agreements on the establishment of several other regional institutes and agencies: an ECO Trade and Development Bank, headquartered in Istanbul (with main branches in Tehran and Islamabad) (the Bank's headquarters was inaugurated in late 2006, and commenced operations in 2008); a joint shipping company (now operational), airline (project abandoned, see below), and an ECO Cultural Institute (inaugurated in 2000), all based in Iran; and an ECO Reinsurance Company (draft articles of agreement relating to its creation were finalized in May 2007) and an ECO Science Foundation, with headquarters in Pakistan. In addition, heads of state and of government endorsed the creation of an ECO eminent persons group and signed the following two agreements in order to enhance and facilitate trade throughout the region: the Transit Trade Agreement (which entered into force in December 1997) and the Agreement on the Simplification of Visa Procedures for Businessmen of ECO Countries (which came into effect in March 1998). In May 2001 the Council of Ministers agreed to terminate the ECO airline project, owing to its unsustainable cost, and to replace it with a framework agreement on co-operation in the field of air transport.

In September 1996, at an extraordinary meeting of the ECO Council of Ministers, held in Izmir, Turkey, member countries signed a revised Treaty of Izmir, the Organization's founding charter. An extraordinary summit meeting, held in Aşgabat, Turkmenistan, in May 1997, adopted the Aşgabat Declaration, emphasizing the importance of the development of the transport and communications infrastructure and the network of trans-national petroleum and gas pipelines through bilateral and regional arrangements in the ECO area. In May 1998, at the fifth summit meeting, held in Almatı, Kazakhstan, ECO heads of state and of government signed a Transit Transport Framework Agreement (TTFA) and a Memorandum of Understanding (MOU) to help combat the cross-border trafficking of illegal goods. (The TTFA entered into force in May 2006.) The meeting also agreed to establish an ECO Educational Institute in Ankara, Turkey; in April 2012 the Institute was formally inaugurated. In June 2000 the sixth ECO summit encouraged member states to participate in the development of information and communication technologies through the establishment of a database of regional educational and training institutions specializing in that field. The seventh ECO summit, held in Istanbul, in October 2002, adopted the Istanbul Declaration, which outlined a strengthened and more proactive economic orientation for the Organization.

Convening in conference for the first time in March 2000, ECO ministers of trade signed a Framework Agreement on ECO Trade Cooperation (ECOFAT), which established a basis for the expansion of intra-regional trade. The Framework Agreement envisaged the eventual adoption of an accord providing for the gradual elimination of regional tariff and non-tariff barriers between member states. The so-called ECO Trade Agreement (ECOTA) was endorsed at the eighth ECO summit meeting, held in Dushanbe, Tajikistan, in September 2004. Heads of state and government urged member states to ratify ECOTA at the earliest opportunity, in order to achieve their vision of an ECO free trade area by 2015. The meeting also requested members to ratify and implement the Transit Transport Framework Agreement (see above), to support economic co-operation throughout the region. In May 2011 the Permanent Steering Committee on Economic Research, meeting for the first time, adopted the ECO Plan of Action for Economic Research.

ECO ministers of agriculture, convened in July 2002, in Islamabad, adopted a declaration on co-operation in the agricultural sector, which specified that member states would contribute to agricultural rehabilitation in Afghanistan, and considered instigating a mechanism for the regional exchange of agricultural and cattle products. In December 2004, meeting in Antalya, Turkey, agriculture ministers approved the Antalya Declaration on ECO Cooperation in Agriculture and adopted an ECO plan of action on drought management and mitigation. In March 2007, meeting in Tehran, ECO ministers of agriculture approved the concept of an ECO Permanent Commission for Prevention and Control of Animal Diseases and Control of Animal Origin Food-Borne Diseases (ECO-PCPCAD). ECO implements a Regional Programme for Food Security (RPFS), supported by FAO, which comprises nine regional components, as well as a country programme for community-based food production in Afghanistan. In April 2007 an ECO experts' group convened to develop a work plan on biodiversity in the ECO region with the aim of promoting co-operation towards achieving a set of agreed biodiversity targets over the period 2007–15. The ECO member states agreed, in July 2008, to establish the ECO Seed Association (ECOSA); ECOSA hosted its first international seed trade conference in December 2009, and a second in October 2010; a third was held in November 2011. In December 2008 the first ECO expert meeting on tourism adopted a plan of action on ECO co-operation in the field of ecotourism, covering 2009–13. In September 2007 the ECO Regional Center for Risk Management of Natural Disasters was inaugurated in Mashhad, Iran; the Center was to promote co-operation in drought monitoring and early warning. The sixth ECO International Conference on Disaster Risk Management was convened in February 2012, in Kabul, Afghanistan. In February 2006 a high-level group of experts on health was formed; its first meeting, held in the following month, focused on the spread of avian influenza in the region. The first ECO ministerial meeting on health, convened in February 2010, considered means of enhancing co-operation on health issues with regard to attaining relevant UN Millennium Development Goals, and addressed strengthening co-operation in the areas of blood transfusion and pharmaceuticals. The meeting adopted the Baku Declaration, identifying key priority areas for future ECO area health co-operation. In June 2011 ECO environment ministers adopted a Framework Plan of Action on Environmental Cooperation and Global Warming, covering the period 2011–15.

A meeting of ministers of industry, convened in November 2005, approved an ECO plan of action on privatization, envisaging enhanced technical co-operation between member states, and a number of measures for increasing cross-country investments; and adopted a declaration on industrial co-operation. The first meeting of the heads of ECO member states' national statistics offices, convened in January 2008 in Tehran, adopted the ECO Framework of Cooperation in Statistics and a related plan of action. An ECO Trade Fair was staged in Pakistan, in July 2008. The Organization maintains ECO TradeNet, an internet-based repository of regional trade information.

ECO has co-operation agreements with several UN agencies and other international organizations in development-related activities. In December 2007 the ECO Secretary-General welcomed, as a means of promoting regional peace and security, the inauguration of the UN Regional Centre for Preventive Diplomacy in Central Asia (UNRCCA), based in Aşgabat. In that month ECO and the Shanghai Cooperation Organization signed an MOU on mutual co-operation in areas including trade and transportation, energy and environment, and tourism. An ECO-International Organization on Migration MOU on co-operation was concluded in January 2009. In March 2011 ECO, the UN Economic Commission for Europe and the Islamic Development Bank signed a trilateral MOU on co-operation. ECO has been granted observer status at the UN, OIC and WTO.

ECO prioritizes activities aimed at combating the cultivation of and trade in illicit drugs in the region (which is the source of more than one-half of global seizures of opium, with more than 90% of global opium production occuring in Afghanistan, and many ECO member states are used in transit for its distribution). An ECO-UNODC Drug Control and Co-ordination Unit was inaugurated, in Tehran, in July 1999. In 2011 the ECO Secretariat and European Commission were jointly implementing a project entitled 'Fight against Illicit Drug Trafficking from/to Afghanistan'. The inaugural meeting of heads of INTERPOL of ECO member states was held in June 2010, in Tehran, and, in August, the first conference of ECO police chiefs with responsibility for anti-narcotics was convened, also in Tehran.

In November 2001 the UN Secretary-General requested ECO to take an active role in efforts to restore stability in Afghanistan and to co-operate closely with his special representative in that country. In June 2002 the ECO Secretary-General participated in a tripartite ministerial conference on co-operation for development in Afghanistan that was convened under the auspices of the UN Development Programme and attended by representatives from Afghanistan, Iran and Pakistan. ECO operates a Special Fund for the Reconstruction of Afghanistan, which was established in April 2004; at December 2011 US $11.2m. had been pledged to the Fund. By that time the Fund had approved four ECO projects targeted towards the education and health sectors. ECO envisages connecting Afghanistan to the regional rail road system. In January 2010 the ECO Secretary-General participated in a Regional Summit Meeting of Afghanistan and Neighbours, hosted by the Turkish Government in Istanbul, with participation by representatives of regional governments and organizations; and, in July 2010, he attended the first International Conference on Afghanistan to be convened on that country's territory, in the Afghan capital, Kabul.

Finance

Member states contribute to a centralized administrative budget.

Publications

ECO Annual Economic Report.

ECO Bulletin (quarterly).

ECO Economic Journal.

ECO Environment Bulletin.

EUROPEAN BANK FOR RECONSTRUCTION AND DEVELOPMENT—EBRD

Address: One Exchange Square, London, EC2A 2JN, United Kingdom.

Telephone: (20) 7338-6000; **fax:** (20) 7338-6100; **e-mail:** generalenquiries@ebrd.com; **internet:** www.ebrd.com.

The EBRD was founded in May 1990 and inaugurated in April 1991. Its object is to contribute to the progress and the economic reconstruction of the countries of Central and Eastern Europe, and, from 2011–12, transitional economies in the Southern and Eastern Mediterranean, that undertake to respect and put into practice the principles of multi-party democracy, pluralism, the rule of law, respect for human rights and a market economy.

MEMBERS

Countries of Operations:

Albania	Moldova
Armenia	Mongolia
Azerbaijan	Montenegro
Belarus	Poland
Bosnia and Herzegovina	Romania
Bulgaria	Russia
Croatia	Serbia
Estonia	Slovakia
Georgia	Slovenia
Hungary	Tajikistan
Kazakhstan	Turkey
Kyrgyzstan	Turkmenistan
Latvia	Ukraine
Lithuania	Uzbekistan
Macedonia, former Yugoslav republic	

Other EU members*:

Austria	Ireland
Belgium	Italy
Cyprus	Luxembourg
Czech Republic	Malta
Denmark	Netherlands
Finland	Portugal
France	Spain
Germany	Sweden
Greece	United Kingdom

EFTA† members:

Iceland	Norway
Liechtenstein	Switzerland

Other countries:

Australia	Republic of Korea
Canada	Mexico
Egypt‡	Morocco‡
Israel	New Zealand
Japan	Tunisia‡
Jordan‡	USA

* The European Union (EU) and the European Investment Bank (EIB) are also shareholder members in their own right.

† European Free Trade Association.

‡ Jordan and Tunisia were admitted as members of the EBRD in January 2012; during 2012 a process was under way to enable those two countries, as well as Egypt and Morocco (both founding members of the Bank), to become countries of operations.

Organization

(June 2012)

BOARD OF GOVERNORS

The Board of Governors, to which each member appoints a Governor (normally the minister of finance of that country) and an alternate, is the highest authority of the EBRD. It elects the President of the Bank. The Board meets each year. The 2012 meeting was held in London, United Kingdom, in May.

BOARD OF DIRECTORS

The Board, comprising 23 directors, elected by the Board of Governors for a three-year term, is responsible for the organization and operations of the EBRD.

ADMINISTRATION

The EBRD's operations are conducted by its Banking Department, headed by the First Vice-President. Three other Vice-Presidents oversee departments of Finance; Risk Management, Human Resources and Nuclear Safety; and Environment, Procurement and Administration. Other offices include Internal Audit; Communications; the Evaluation Department; and Offices of the President, the Secretary-General, the General Counsel, the Chief Economist and the Chief Compliance Officer. A structure of country teams, industry teams and operations support units oversee the implementation of projects. The EBRD has 34 local offices in 26 countries. At December 2011 there were 1,203 staff at the Bank's headquarters (75%) and 403 staff in the Resident Offices.

President: Sir SUMA CHAKRABARTI (United Kingdom) (from 3 July 2012).

First Vice-President: VAREL FREEMAN (USA).

FINANCIAL STRUCTURE

In May 2010 EBRD shareholders agreed to increase the Bank's capital from €20,000m. to €30,000m., through use of a temporary increase in callable capital of €9,000m. and a €1,000m. transfer from reserves to paid-in capital. At 31 December 2011 paid-in capital amounted to €6,197m.

Activities

The Bank was founded to assist the transition of the economies of Central Europe, Southern and Eastern Europe and the Caucasus, and Central Asia and Russia towards a market economy system, and to encourage private enterprise. The Agreement establishing the EBRD specifies that 60% of its lending should be for the private sector, and that its operations do not displace commercial sources of finance. The Bank helps the beneficiaries to undertake structural and sectoral reforms, including the dismantling of monopolies, decentralization, and privatization of state enterprises, to enable these countries to become fully integrated in the international economy. To this end, the Bank promotes the establishment and improvement of activities of a productive, competitive and private nature, particularly small and medium-sized enterprises (SMEs), and works to strengthen financial institutions. It mobilizes national and foreign capital, together with experienced management teams, and helps to develop an appropriate legal framework to support a market-orientated economy. The Bank provides extensive financial services, including loans, equity and guarantees, and aims to develop new forms of financing and investment in accordance with the requirements of the transition process. In 2006 the Bank formally began to implement a strategy to withdraw, by 2010, from countries where the transition to a market economy was nearing completion, i.e. those now members of the European Union (EU, see below), and strengthen its focus on and resources to Russia, the Caucasus and Central Asia. New operations in the Czech Republic were terminated at the end of 2007. Mongolia and Montenegro became new countries of operations in 2006. In November 2008 Turkey, which had been a founding member of the Bank, became the 30th country of operations. In May 2011 the Group of Eight major industrialized nations (G8) declared their support for an expansion of the Bank's geographical mandate to support transitional economies in the Southern and Eastern Mediterranean (SEMED) region. In March the Bank signed a new

Memorandum of Understanding (MOU) with the European Investment Bank (EIB) and European Commission to enhance co-operation in activities outside of the EU region. MOUs with the African Development Bank and the Islamic Development Bank were signed in September. At that time the EBRD joined other international financial institutions active in the Middle East and North Africa region to endorse the so-called Deauville Partnership, established by G8 in May to support political and economic reforms being undertaken by several countries, notably Egypt, Jordan, Morocco and Tunisia. Jordan and Tunisia were admitted as members of the EBRD in January 2012; during that year a process was under way to enable those two countries, as well as Egypt and Morocco (both founding members of the Bank), to become countries of operations. It was envisaged that the EBRD would be able to invest up to €2,500m. annually across the four countries, with a focus on the development of SMEs, in order to stimulate job creation, entrepreneurship and growth. Initial flows of grant-funded technical assistance to the planned four new countries of operations commenced in late 2011; a dedicated fund to enable investments in the four countries was to be established in 2012.

During 2011 the Bank continued to support its countries of operations affected by the global financial and economic crisis by approving its largest ever amount of investment commitments. During the crisis the Bank aimed, in particular, to maintain the flow of credit to SMEs, to uphold investor confidence in local economies, to ensure the continuation of projects providing essential jobs and economic stimulus, and to initiate the restructuring of private and public institutions.

In the year ending 31 December 2011 the EBRD approved 380 operations, involving funds of €9,051m., compared with €9,009m. for 386 operations in the previous year. During 2011 some 32% of all project financing committed was allocated to the financial sector, including loans to SMEs through financial intermediaries, while 30% was for the corporate sector, including agribusiness, manufacturing, property, tourism, telecommunications and new media, 20% for energy projects, comprising natural resources and the power sector, and 18% was infrastructure projects. Some 36% of the Bank's commitments in 2011 was for projects in Russia, 19% for Eastern Europe and the Caucasus, 16% for Turkey, 14% for countries in South-Eastern Europe, 10% for Central Europe and the Baltic states, and 3% for Central Asia. By the end of 2011 the Bank had approved 3,374 projects since it commenced operations, for which financing of €71,146m. had been approved. In addition, the Bank had mobilized resources amounting to an estimated €138,605m., bringing the total project value to €210,665m.

In 1999 the Bank established a Trade Facilitation Programme to extend bank guarantees in order to promote trading capabilities, in particular for SMEs. An increasing number of transactions are intra-regional arrangements. In December 2008 the Bank's Board of Directors agreed to expand the Programme's budget for 2009, from €800m. to €1,500m., in order to provide exceptional assistance to countries affected by the global deceleration of economic growth and contraction in credit markets. During 2009, however, the Programme was less widely used than anticipated, owing to a sharp decline in foreign trade transactions and a reluctance on the part of local banks to expose themselves to more risk. In 2011 the Bank financed 1,616 trade transactions under the Programme, amounting to more than €1,000m. (compared with 1,274 transactions amounting to €774m. in the previous year). In February 2009 the Bank established a Corporate Support Facility, with funds of €250m., to assist medium-sized businesses to counter the economic downturn. In the same month the EBRD, with the World Bank and the EIB, inaugurated a Joint International Financial Institutions (IFI) Action Plan to support the banking systems in Central and Eastern Europe and to finance lending to businesses in the region affected by the global economic crisis. Under the Plan the Banks initially committed €24,500m. over a two-year period. The IFI Action Plan was concluded in March 2011, at which time €33,200m. had been provided under the joint initiative, of which €8,100m. was provided by the EBRD. A parallel plan, the European Banking Co-ordination Initiative (the 'Vienna Initiative'), was implemented during 2008–09 to promote dialogue between authorities in emerging European economies, official multilateral donors and private banks. In early 2010 the Bank initiated a Local Currency and Capital Market Initiative ('Vienna Plus') aimed at addressing the regional impact of new global regulatory standards on bank capital adequacy and liquidity, as well as the challenges confronting emerging economies in managing non?performing loans. The EBRD chaired a committee, established under the Initiative framework, concerning local currency finance development, and in 2011 co-chaired, with the World Bank, a new committee on the challenges of implementing the Basel III capital framework programme. During the second half of 2011, at which time financial crisis in several euro area countries raised the risk of contagion in the financial sectors of many of the EBRD's countries of operations, the Bank took a leading role in developing 'Vienna 2.0', which aimed to support nation-based regulatory responses, and to limit systemic risks from parent bank deleveraging in the region.

From 2002 the EBRD, together with the World Bank, the IMF and the Asian Development Bank, sponsored the CIS-7 initiative, which aimed to generate awareness of the difficulties of transition for seven low-income countries of the Commonwealth of Independent States (Armenia, Azerbaijan, Georgia, Kyrgyzstan, Moldova, Tajikistan, Uzbekistan), strengthen international and regional co-operation, and promote reforms to achieve economic growth. A review of the scheme was published in April 2004. In that month a new initiative was launched to increase activities in those CIS states, designated 'Early Transition Countries' (ETCs), in particular to stimulate private sector business development, market activity and financing of small-scale projects. In November the Bank established a multi-donor ETC Fund to administer donor pledges and grant financing in support of EBRD projects in those countries. In 2006 Mongolia was incorporated into the ETC grouping. In 2007 the Bank's resident office in Tbilisi, Georgia, was transformed into a regional focal point for specialized activities in the Caucasus and Moldova. Belarus and Turkmenistan joined the ETC programme in 2009 and 2010 respectively. During 2011 Bank commitments for the ETCs increased substantially to more than €1,000m. for 120 projects Financing from the ETC Fund amounted to €75m. during 2004–11. In May 2011 an ETC Local Currency Lending Programme was initiated, with donor support from the ETC Fund, Switzerland, the USA, and the EBRD Shareholders Special Fund (see below). By May 2012 the Programme had been introduced in Armenia, Georgia, Kyrgyzstan, Moldova and Tajikistan.

High priority is given to attracting external finance for Bank-sponsored projects, in particular in countries at advanced stages of transition, from government agencies, international financial institutions, commercial banks and export credit agencies. The EBRD's Technical Co-operation Funds Programme (TCFP) aims to facilitate access to the Bank's capital resources for countries of operations by providing support for project preparation, project implementation and institutional development. Resources for technical co-operation originate from regular TCFP contributions, specific agreements and contributions to Special Funds. The Baltic Investment Programme, which is administered by Nordic countries, consists of two special funds to co-finance investment and technical assistance projects in the private sectors of Baltic states. The Funds are open to contributions from all EBRD member states. The Russia Small Business Fund (RSBF) was established in 1994 to support local SMEs through similar investment and technical co-operation activities. In November 2006 a new Western Balkans Fund was established as a multi-donor facility to support economic growth and the business environment in Albania, Bosnia and Herzegovina, the former Yugoslav republic of Macedonia, Montenegro and Serbia (including Kosovo). A Western Balkans Local Enterprise Facility was also established in 2006. In November 2009 a Western Balkans Investment Framework was inaugurated by the EBRD, the European Commission, the European Investment Bank and the Council of Europe Development Bank, to co-ordinate the leverage and use of donor funds in support of priority projects in the region. In mid-2008 the Bank established a Neighbourhood Investment Facility to provide technical assistance and grants mainly for infrastructure projects. An Investment Facility for Central Asia was launched in June 2010 to provide additional grant funding for energy and environmental sustainability projects in Kazakhstan, Kyrgyzstan, Tajikistan, Turkmenistan and Uzbekistan. Other financing mechanisms that the EBRD uses to address the needs of the region include Regional Venture Funds, which invest equity in privatized companies, in particular in Russia, and provide relevant management assistance, and the Central European Agency Lines, which disburse lines of credit to small-scale projects through local intermediaries.

An Enterprise Growth Programme—EGP (formerly the Turn-Around Management initiative, and renamed in 2011) provides practical assistance to senior managers of industrial enterprises to facilitate the expansion of businesses in a market economy. A Small Business Support Team—SBS (known until 2011 as the Business Advisory Services scheme) complements the Enterprise Growth Programme by undertaking projects to improve competitiveness, strategic planning, marketing and financial management in SMEs. In 2011 the SBS raised €23.9m. from donors for several new initiatives and ongoing programmes in all regions. During the second half of that year the EGP and SBS conducted feasibility studies in Egypt, Morocco and Tunisia, which were in the process of becoming countries of operation, and in late 2011 two EGP projects were initiated in Egypt. In May 2008 the Bank agreed to establish a Shareholders Special Fund (SSF), with resources of €115m., in order to support technical co-operation and grant operations. Further allocations of resources, including of €150m. in May 2010, brought the total committed by the Bank to €295m. by the end of that year.

In 2001 the EBRD collaborated with other donor institutions and partners to initiate a Northern Dimension Environmental Partnership (NDEP) to strengthen and co-ordinate environmental projects in northern Europe. The Partnership, which became operational in November 2002, includes a 'nuclear window' to address the nuclear legacy of the Russian Northern Fleet. The Bank administers the NDEP Support Fund, as well as a number of other funds specifically to support the promotion of nuclear safety: the Nuclear Safety Account (NSA), a multilateral programme of action established in 1993; the Chornobyl (Chernobyl) Shelter Fund (CSF), established in 1997; and International Decommissioning Support Funds (IDSFs), which have enabled the closure of nuclear plants for safety reasons where this would otherwise have been prohibitively costly, in Bulgaria, Lithuania and Slovakia. In 1997 a CSF-financed Chornobyl Unit 4 Shelter Implementation Plan (SIP) was initiated to assist Ukraine in stabilizing the protective sarcophagus covering the damaged Chornobyl reactor. The first-stage Unit 4 shelter was completed in December 2006. A contract for construction of a New Safe Confinement (NSC) of the destroyed Unit 4 was signed in 2007; the NSC was scheduled to be completed by October 2015.

The EBRD's founding Agreement specifies that all operations are to be undertaken in the context of promoting environmentally sound and sustainable development. It undertakes environmental audits and impact assessments in areas of particular concern, which enable the Bank to incorporate environmental action plans into any project approved for funding. An Environment Advisory Council assists with the development of policy and strategy in this area. In May 2006 the Bank launched the first, three-year, phase of a Sustainable Energy Initiative (SEI), committing to invest in energy efficiency and renewable energy projects in the region. A second phase of the SEI (SEI-2) was initiated in 2009, with enhanced activities in areas including transport energy efficiency, climate change adaptation and the stationary use of biomass. SEI-3, with a financing target of €4,500m.–€6,500m., was launched in May 2012, focusing on projects in areas including large industry energy efficiency; cleaner energy supply; municipal infrastructure energy efficiency; support to carbon market development in the region; energy efficiency of buildings; biomass energy; gas flaring reduction; transport energy efficiency, and climate change adaptation. Over the period 2006–end-2011 the Bank invested €8,800m. in SEI projects. A separate Multilateral Carbon Credit Fund was established, in December 2006, in co-operation with the EIB, providing a means by which countries may obtain carbon credits from emission-related projects. By early 2012 the Fund was fully subscribed with resources totalling €208.5m. In December 2009 the Bank contributed €25m. to a new joint Southeast Europe Energy Efficiency Fund (SE4F), which aimed to expand the availability of and access to sustainable energy finance in the western Balkans and Turkey. A new multi-donor EBRD Water Fund, with a particular focus on water projects in Central Asia, was established in July 2010.

Publications

Annual Report.
Donor Report (annually).
Economics of Transition (quarterly).
Law in Transition (2 a year).
People and Projects (annually).
Sustainability Report (annually).
Transition Report (annually).
Working papers, fact sheets.

Statistics

BANK COMMITMENTS BY SUB-REGION AND COUNTRY
(in € million)

	2011	Cumulative to 31 Dec. 2011
Central Europe and the Baltic States		
Croatia	158	2,619
Czech Republic	0	1,136
Estonia	20	539
Hungary	124	2,599
Latvia	19	581
Lithuania	2	600
Poland	892	5,445
Slovakia	68	1,654
Slovenia	103	739
Sub-total	1,385	15,871
South-Eastern Europe		
Albania	96	665
Bosnia and Herzegovina	94	1,389
Bulgaria	92	2,450
Macedonia, former Yugoslav republic	220	950
Montenegro	43	283
Romania	449	5,585
Serbia	533	2,939
Sub-total	1,527	14,234
Eastern Europe and the Caucasus		
Armenia	93	516
Azerbaijan	289	1,503
Belarus	194	839
Georgia	187	349
Moldova	69	97
Ukraine	1,019	7,512
Sub-total	1,851	12,616
Central Asia		
Kazakhstan	289	4,377
Kyrgyzstan	66	405
Mongolia	62	364
Tajikistan	28	247
Turkmenistan	23	162
Uzbekistan	3	755
Sub-total	470	6,309
Russia	2,928	20,581
Turkey	890	1,535
Total	9,051	71,146

Note: Financing for regional projects is allocated to the relevant countries.

Source: EBRD, *Annual Report 2011*.

EUROPEAN SPACE AGENCY—ESA

Address: 8–10 rue Mario Nikis, 75738 Paris Cedex 15, France.

Telephone: 1-53-69-76-54; **fax:** 1-53-69-75-60; **e-mail:** contactesa@esa.int; **internet:** www.esa.int.

ESA was established in 1975 to provide for, and to promote, European co-operation in space research and technology, and their applications, for exclusively peaceful purposes. It replaced the European Space Research Organisation (ESRO) and the European Launcher Development Organisation (both founded in 1962).

ESA has liaison offices in Brussels, Belgium, Moscow, Russia and Washington, DC, USA, as well as offices in Houston, Texas, USA, to support International Space Station activities, and at the Guyana Space Centre, located in Kourou, French Guyana. ESA owns the launch and launcher production facilities at Kourou. The Agency also operates ground/tracking stations around the world.

MEMBERS*

Austria	Luxembourg
Belgium	Netherlands
Czech Republic	Norway
Denmark	Portugal
Finland	Romania
France	Spain
Germany	Sweden
Greece	Switzerland
Ireland	United Kingdom
Italy	

* Estonia, Hungary, Poland, and Slovenia have 'European Co-operating State' status. Canada has signed an agreement for close co-operation with ESA, including representation on the ESA Council. Cyprus, Israel, Latvia, and Slovakia have also signed Co-operation Agreements.

Organization

(June 2012)

COUNCIL

The Council is composed of representatives of all member states. It is responsible for formulating policy and meets at ministerial or delegate level.

ADMINISTRATION

ESA's activities are divided into the following 10 Directorates, each headed by a Director who reports directly to the Director-General: Earth Observation Programmes; Technical and Quality Management; Launchers; Human Spaceflight; Resources Management; Legal Affairs and External Relations; Science and Robotic Exploration; Telecommunications and Integrated Applications; Galileo Programme and Navigation-related Activites; Operations; and Infrastructure.

Director-General: JEAN-JACQUES DORDAIN (France).

ESA CENTRES

European Astronaut Centre (EAC): Cologne, Germany. As a subsidiary of the Directorate of Human Spaceflight, manages all European astronaut activities and trains European and international partner astronauts on the European elements of the International Space Station. The Centre employs 16 European astronauts.

European Space Astronomy Centre (ESAC): Villafranca del Castillo, Spain. A centre of excellence for space science and a base for ESA astrophysics and solar system missions. Hosts a virtual observatory.

European Space Operations Centre (ESOC): Darmstadt, Germany. Responsible for all satellite operations and the corresponding ground facilities and communications networks.

European Space Research and Technology Centre (ESTEC): Noordwijk, Netherlands. ESA's principal technical establishment, at which the majority of project teams are based, together with the space science department and the technological research and support engineers; provides the appropriate testing and laboratory facilities.

European Space Research Institute (ESRIN): Frascati, Italy. Responsible for the corporate exploitation of Earth observation data from space.

Activities

ESA's tasks are to define and put into effect a long-term European space policy of scientific research and technological development and to encourage all members to co-ordinate their national programmes with those of ESA to ensure that Europe maintains a competitive position in the field of space technology. ESA's basic activities cover studies on future projects; technological research; and shared technical investments, information systems and training programmes. These, and the science programme, are mandatory activities to which all members must contribute; other programmes are optional and members may determine their own level of participation. In November 2000 the ESA Council and the Council of the European Union (EU) adopted parallel resolutions endorsing a European strategy for space. The strategy, which had been jointly prepared in 1999 and was entitled *Europe and Space: A New Chapter*, aimed to strengthen the foundation for European space activities; advance scientific knowledge; and to use the technical capabilities developed in connection with space activities to secure wider economic and social benefits. ESA collaborated with the European Commission in the preparation of a Green Paper on EU Space Policy, which assessed Europe's strengths and weaknesses in the sector. In May 2004 a framework agreement entered into force providing the legal basis for structured co-operation between ESA and the European Commission. The framework agreement provides for a co-ordinating ESA-European Commission secretariat, and for joint consultations between the ESA Council and the EU Council (known as the Space Council). The European Space Policy (based on an EU White Paper, drafted with ESA support, and adopted in 2004) was adopted in May 2007, providing a common political framework for space activities in Europe. In June 2011 ESA and the European Defence Agency concluded an administrative arrangement on co-operation.

ESA is committed to pursuing international co-operation to achieve its objective of developing the peaceful applications of space technology. ESA works closely with both the US National Aeronautics and Space Administration (NASA) and the Russian Federal Space Agency ('Roscosmos'). In 2003 ESA and the Russian Government signed an Agreement on Co-operation and Partnership in the Exploration and Use of Outer Space for Peaceful Purposes, succeeding a similar agreement concluded with the USSR in 1990. Also, 'European Co-operating State Agreements' (a legal instrument designed to replace existing co-operation agreements between ESA and European states seeking closer relations with the Agency) are in force with Estonia, Hungary, Poland and Slovenia, providing for technical training and joint projects in the fields of space science, Earth observation and telecommunications. ESA assists other transitional and developing countries to expand their space activities. It works closely with other international organizations, in particular the EU and EUMETSAT. ESA has observer status with the UN Committee on the Peaceful Uses of Outer Space and co-operates closely with the UN's Office of Outer Space Affairs, in particular through the organization of a training and fellowship programme. ESA has also developed a co-operative relationship with Japan, with a special focus on data relay satellites and the exchange of materials for the International Space Station.

In March–April 2009 ESA convened the fifth European Conference on Space Debris.

SCIENCE AND ROBOTIC EXPLORATION

The first European scientific space programmes were undertaken under the aegis of ESRO, which launched seven satellites during 1968–72. The Science Programme is a mandatory activity of the Agency and forms the basis of co-operation between member states. Among the most successful scientific satellites and probes subsequently launched by ESA are the Giotto probe, launched in 1985 to study the composition of Halley's comet and reactivated in 1990 to observe the Grigg-Skjellerup comet in July 1992; and Hipparcos, which, between 1989 and 1993, determined the precise astronomic positions and distances of more than 1m. stars. In November 1995 ESA launched the Infrared Space Observatory (the operational phase of which lasted until April 1998, and was followed by a post-operational period ending in 2006), which successfully conducted pre-planned scientific studies providing data on galaxy and star formation and on interstellar matter. ESA collaborated with NASA in the Ulysses space project (a solar polar mission that was launched in October 1990 and terminated in June 2009, as the spacecraft's orbital path became too far removed from the Earth to allow sufficient transmission of data); the Solar and Helispheric Observatory (SOHO, launched in December 1995 to study the internal structure of the sun); and the Hubble Space Telescope. The Agency is committed to co-operation with NASA on the JWST (James Webb Space Telescope), the successor of the Hubble Space telescope, scheduled to be launched in 2014. In May 2012 ESA received delivery of the Mid InfraRed Instrument (MIRI), the first instrument that it had commissioned for the JWST. In October 1997 the Huygens space probe was launched under the framework of a joint NASA–ESA project (the Cassini/Huygens mission) to study the planet Saturn and its largest moon, Titan, where it landed in January 2005. In August 2009 ESA and NASA agreed in principle to establish a Mars Exploration Joint Initiative (MEJI), which was to launch (in 2016, 2018 and 2020) landers and orbiters to conduct astrobiological, geological, geophysical and other investigations; samples were to be returned to Earth from Mars during the 2020s. The LISA Pathfinder mission (see below) is to be conducted with NASA.

In December 1999 the X-Ray Multimirror Mission (XMM–Newton) was launched from Kourou, French Guyana. It was envisaged that XMM–Newton, the most powerful X-ray telescope ever placed in orbit, would investigate the origin of galaxies, the formation of black holes, etc. Four cluster satellites, launched from Baikonur, Russia, in July–August 2000, were, in association with SOHO (see above), to explore the interaction between the Earth's magnetic field and electrically charged particles transported on the solar wind. In October 2002 INTEGRAL (International Gamma-Ray Astrophysical Laboratory) was successfully launched by a Russian Proton vehicle, to study the most violent events perceptible in the Universe.

ESA's space missions are an integral part of its long-term science programme, Horizon 2000, which was initiated in 1984. In 1994 a new set of missions was defined, to enable the inclusion of projects using new technologies and participation in future international space activities, which formed the Horizon 2000 Plus extension covering the period 2005–16. Together they were called Horizons 2000.

In November 2003 the Science Programme Committee initiated a new long-term space science programme, Cosmic Vision, initially to cover the period 2004–14. Under the programme three main projects—Astrophysics, Solar System Science, and Fundamental Physics—were to be developed in production groups, missions within each to be built synergistically, where possible using common technologies and engineering teams. Projects included: Herschel, exploring the infrared and microwave Universe (the Herschel Space Observatory, designed to investigate the formation of stars and galaxies, was launched in mid-May 2009); Planck, studying the cosmic microwave background (launched in May 2009); GAIA, the ultimate galaxy mapper (to be launched in 2013); Rosetta, launched in March 2004, to rendez vous with and land on a comet; Mars Express, a Mars orbiter carrying the Beagle 2 lander (launched in 2003; contact with Beagle 2 was, however, lost in January 2004); Venus Express, a Venus orbiter (launched 2005, entered into orbit around Venus in April 2006); SMART-1, which was to demonstrate solar propulsion technology while on course to the Moon (launched 2003); BepiColombo, a mission to Mercury (to be launched in 2014); and SMART-2, a technology demonstration mission.

In accordance with a new phase of Cosmic Vision, focusing on 2015–25, further missions are to be undertaken, including LISA Pathfinder, a joint mission with NASA, searching for gravitational waves (to be launched in 2013); and Solar Orbiter, which aims to take a closer look at the Sun (to be launched in 2017). Other missions under consideration include: Cross-Scale (Investigating Multi-scale Coupling in Space Plasmas); Euclid (mapping the geometry of the dark universe; to be launched in 2019); Plato (next generation planet finder); Spica (an infrared space telescope for cosmology and astrophyics), Laplace/EJSM (mission to Europa and Jupiter system); and Xeus/Ixo (X-ray observatory for the extreme and evolving universe).

EARTH OBSERVATION

ESA has contributed to the understanding and monitoring of the Earth's environment through its satellite projects. From 1977–2002 ESA launched seven Meteosat spacecraft (financed and owned by EUMETSAT, but ESA-operated until December 1995) into geosynchronous orbit, to provide continuous meteorological data, mainly for the purposes of weather forecasting. The first and second Meteosat Second Generation—MSG satellates, MSG-1 and MSG-2, were launched in August 2002 and December 2005, respectively. The launch of MSG-3 was scheduled for July 2012. In 2012 ESA and EUMETSAT were developing a more advanced Meteosat Third Generation (MTG) operational geostationary meteorological satellite system, which was to be inaugurated in 2015. ESA and EUMETSAT have also collaborated on the METOP/EPS (EUMETSAT Polar System) programme, to provide observations from polar orbit. The first METOP satellite was launched in October 2006.

In 1991 ESA launched the ERS-1 satellite, which carried sophisticated instruments to measure the Earth's surface and its atmosphere. A second ERS satellite was launched in April 1995 with the specific purpose of measuring the stratospheric and tropospheric ozone. ENVISAT, the largest and most advanced European-built observation satellite, was launched in February 2002 from Kourou, French Guyana, with the aim of monitoring exceptional natural events, such as volcanic eruptions; and of providing detailed assessments of: the impact of human activities on the Earth's atmosphere, as well as of land and coastal processes. In April 2012 contact with ENVISAT was lost and in the following month that mission was terminated.

ESA Earth Explorer missions aim to enhance understanding of the Earth's system with a view to supporting efforts to address the challenges posed by ongoing global change, i.e. climate change and also the large-scale impact on Earth of the growing human population and continued economic expansion. The Agency has selected six such missions, of which three are 'Core' (responding to specific areas of public concern) and three are 'Opportunity' (quick implementation missions aimed at addressing areas of immediate environmental concern). The Core missions are as follows: GOCE (see below); the Atmospheric Dynamics Mission (ADM)-Aeolus, which, when launched in 2013, will aim to demonstrate measurements of vertical wind profiles from space; and the Earth Clouds Aerosols and Radiation Explorer (Earth-CARE), which, once launched in 2013, will aim to improve the representation and understanding of the Earth's radiative balance in climate and numerical forecast models. The Opportunity missions are: the Soil Moisture and Ocean Salinity (SMOS) mission, launched in November 2009, which aims to further understanding of the Earth's water cycle; CryoSat-2 (see below); and Swarm, scheduled to be launched in 2012, which was to produce the best survey to date of the geomagnetic field and its temporal evolution.

In June 1998 the ESA Council approved the initiation of activities related to the Living Planet Programme, designed to increase understanding of environmental issues. In May 1999 the Council committed funds for a research mission, CryoSat, to be undertaken, in order to study the impact of global warming on polar ice caps. However, the launch of CryoSat was aborted in October 2005. A CryoSat recovery plan, completed in February 2006, provided for the development of a CryoSat-2 mission, with the same objectives; CryoSat-2 was eventually launched in April 2010. The Gravity Field and Steady-State Ocean Circulation Explorer (GOCE) mission, launched in March 2009, was to use a unique measurement technique to recover geodetic precision data on the Earth's gravity field. ESA is responsible for the space component of the European Commission's Global Monitoring for Environment and Security (GMES) programme and aimed to launch an earth observation satellite, Sentinel-2, specifically to monitor the land environment, in 2012. In November 2008 the Council approved a Space Situational Awareness (SSA) preparatory programme, for an initial three-year period, to develop a capability to monitor potentially hazardous objects and natural phenomena.

As part of the Treaty Enforcement Services using Earth Observation (TESEO) initiative, agreed in 2001, ESA satellites provide data for a wide range of environmental activities including monitoring wetlands, ensuring compliance with Kyoto Protocol emission targets and combating desertification. Similarly, ESA has agreements with UNESCO to protect wildlife and sites of historic interest, in support of the Convention Concerning the Protection of the World Cultural and Natural Heritage.

TELECOMMUNICATIONS AND INTEGRATED APPLICATIONS

ESA commenced the development of communications satellites in 1968. These have since become the largest markets for space use and have transformed global communications, with more than 100 satellites circling the Earth for the purposes of telecommunications. The main series of operational satellites developed by ESA are the European Communications Satellites (ECS), based on the original orbital test satellite and used by EUTELSAT, and the Maritime Communications Satellites (MARECS), which have been leased for operations to Inmarsat (see International Mobile Satellite Organization).

An Advanced Relay and Technology Mission Satellite (ARTEMIS) has been developed by ESA to test and operate new telecommunications techniques, and in particular to enable the relay of information directly between satellites. ARTEMIS was launched in July 2001. In 1998 ESA, together with the EU and EUROCONTROL continued to implement a satellite-based navigation system to be used for civilian aircraft and maritime services, similar to the two existing systems operational for military use. ESA was also working with the EU and representatives of the private sector to enhance the region's role in the development of electronic media infrastructure to meet the expanding global demand. In May 1999 the Council approved funding for a satellite multimedia programme, Advanced Research in Telecommunications Systems (Artes), which aimed to support the development of satellite systems and services for delivering information through high-speed internet access. Ongoing in 2012 were: Artes-1 (focused on strategic analysis); Artes-3–4 (seeking to improve the near-term competitiveness of the satcom industry through the development of equipment including terminals, processors and antennas for ground or space); Artes-5 (seeking to develop a more sustained long-term technological basis for European industrial effectiveness, and divided into Artes-5.1, involving projects initiated by and also fully funded by the Agency, and Artes-5.2, comprising projects initiated by industry and 75% ESA-funded); Artes-7, dedicated to the implementation of an European Data Relay Satellite (EDRS) system; Artes-8, focused on the development of the Alphasatis satellite that, with Inmarsat, was to incorporate the first stage of the Alphabus multi-purpose geostationary communications platform; Artes-10, a satellite-based communication system that was to complement a new EU air traffic management system; Artes-11, aimed at developing the Small GEO System, a satellite incorporating advanced payload technology; Artes-20, dedicated to the development, implementation and pilot operations of Integrated Applications (combined satellite operations); Artes-21, developing the Automatic Identification System, a short-range coastal tracking system.

GALILEO PROGRAMME AND NAVIGATION-RELATED ACTIVITIES

ESA and the European Commission are collaborating to design and develop a European global satellite and navigation system, *Galileo*. The project, scheduled to be fully deployed during 2013, will provide a highly accurate global positioning service by means of 30 satellites (of which 27 will be operational and three active spares), a global network of 20 Galileo Sensor Stations (GSSs), and two Galileo Control Centres (GCCs), based in Europe. ESA, in co-operation with the European Commission and Eurocontrol, is implementing the EGNOS System. EGNOS is the European contribution to the Global Navigation Satellite System phase 1 (GNSS-1) and will provide an improved navigation and positioning service for all users of the (American) GPS and (Russian) GLONASS systems. It is envisaged that EGNOS will serve as a major regional component of a seamless, world-wide augmentation system for navigation, aimed at meeting the demanding requirements for aircraft navigation, and comprising (in addition to EGNOS in Europe): WAAS in the USA; MSAS in Japan; and GAGAN in India. The GNSS aims to use the *Galileo*, GPS and GLONASS systems to provide an integrated satellite navigation service of unprecedented accuracy and global coverage under civilian control.

LAUNCHERS

The European requirement for independent access to space first manifested itself in the early 1970s against the background of strategic and commercial interests in telecommunications and Earth observation. As a consequence, and based on knowledge gained through national programmes, ESA began development of a space launcher. The resulting Ariane rocket was first launched in December 1979. The project, which incorporated four different launchers; Ariane-1 to Ariane-4, subsequently became an essential element of ESA's programme activities and, furthermore, developed a successful commercial role in placing satellites into orbit. The last flight of Ariane-4 took place in February 2003. From 1985 ESA worked to develop the more powerful Ariane-5 launcher, which has been in commercial operation since 1999, launched from the ESA facility at the Guyana Space Centre. In December 2000 the ESA Council approved the Vega Small Launcher Development and the P80 Advanced Solid Propulsion Stage programmes. The first Vega launch took place in February 2012. A Future Launcher Preparatory Programme is being defined.

HUMAN SPACEFLIGHT

In the 1980s and 1990s Europe gained access to human space technology and operations through Spacelab, which ESA developed as the European contribution to the US Space Shuttle Programme, and through two joint Euromir missions on the Russian space station, Mir. Since the mid-1980s ESA has supported space research in the life and physical sciences through its microgravity programmes. A considerable scientific output has been achieved in key areas such as crystal growth, solidification physics, fluid sciences, thermophysical properties, molecular and cell biology, developmental biology, exobiology and human physiology. The latest microgravity programme, approved in November 2001, is the ESA Programme in Life and Physical Sciences and Applications (ELIPS). ESA is a partner in the International Space Station (ISS), which was initiated by the US Government in 1984, and subsequently developed as a joint project between five partners—Canada, Europe, Japan, Russia and the USA. ESA's main contributions to the ISS are the Columbus Laboratory (launched in February 2008); and the 'Jules Verne', 'Johannes Kepler' and 'Edoardo Amaldi' unmanned Automated Transfer Vehicles (ATVs), launched in March 2008, February 2011 and March 2012, respectively; these provide logistical support to the ISS. The Columbus laboratory accommodates European multi-user research facilities: Biolab; Fluid Science Laboratory, European Physiology Modules, Material Science Laboratory (all developed within the Microgravity Facilities for the Columbus Programme); and European Drawer Rack and European Stowage Rack (both within the ISS Utilization Programme). In the framework of the ISS agreements with the USA, ESA is allocated 51% usage of Columbus, the remainder being allocated to NASA. In addition to the experiment accommodation capabilities on Columbus, the European Zero-G Airbus, operated under ESA contract by Novespace, provides European researchers short-duration access to microgravity conditions for a wide variety of experiments, ranging from precursor experiments for the ISS to student experiments. Droptowers and sounding rockets provide additional short-duration opportunities. The ESA Directorate of Human Spaceflight also provides European researchers with flight opportunities on unmanned Russian Foton and Bion capsules.

Finance

All member states contribute to ESA's mandatory programme activities (studies on future projects; technological research; shared technical investments, information systems and training programmes; and the science programme) on a scale based on their national income, and are free to decide on their level of commitment in optional programmes. The total budget for 2012 amounted to about €4,020m., with €861.4m. (21.4%) allocated to earth observation (an optional programme), €720.7m. (17.9%) to navigation (optional), €570.0m. (14.4%) to launchers (optional), €479.7m. (11.9%) to space science (mandatory), and €413.3m. (10.3%) to human spaceflight (optional).

Publications

CONNECT.
ECSL News.
ESA Annual Report.
ESA Bulletin (quarterly).
Eurocomp (newsletter).
PFF—Preparing for the Future.
Monographs and conference proceedings.

EUROPEAN UNION—EU

The European Coal and Steel Community (ECSC) was created by a treaty signed in Paris on 18 April 1951 (effective from 25 July 1952) to pool the coal and steel production of the six original members. It was seen as a first step towards a united Europe. The European Economic Community (EEC) and European Atomic Energy Community (Euratom) were established by separate treaties signed in Rome, Italy, on 25 March 1957 (effective from 1 January 1958), the former to create a common market and to approximate economic policies, the latter to promote growth in nuclear industries. The common institutions of the three Communities were established by a treaty signed in Brussels, Belgium, on 8 April 1965 (effective from 1 July 1967).

The EEC was formally changed to the European Community (EC) under the Treaty on European Union (effective from 1 November 1993, and renamed from December 2009, see below), although in practice the term EC had been used for several years to describe the three Communities together. The new Treaty established a European Union (EU), which introduced citizenship thereof and aimed to increase intergovernmental co-operation in economic and monetary affairs; to establish a common foreign and security policy; and to introduce co-operation in justice and home affairs. The EU was placed under the supervision of the European Council (comprising heads of state or of government of member countries), while the EC continued to exist, having competence in matters relating to the Treaty of Rome and its amendments.

The Treaty of Paris establishing the ECSC expired on 23 July 2002, resulting in the termination of the ECSC legal regime and procedures and the dissolution of the ECSC Consultative Committee. The ECSC's assets and liabilities were transferred to the overall EU budget, while rights and obligations arising from international agreements drawn up between the ECSC and third countries were devolved to the EC.

With the entry into force, on 1 December 2009, of the Treaty of Lisbon amending the Treaty on European Union and the Treaty establishing the European Community, the Treaty on European Union was renamed the Treaty on the Functioning of the European Union, with all references to the European 'Community' changed to the 'Union'. Euratom continued to exist, alongside the EU.

Meetings of the principal organs take place in Brussels, Luxembourg and Strasbourg, France. The Treaty of Lisbon provided for the posts of President of the European Council and High Representative of the Union for Foreign Affairs and Security Policy; and for an 18-month troika comprising groups of three successive governments holding the rotating six-month presidency of the Council of the European Union.

Presidency of the Council of the European Union: Cyprus (July–December 2012); Ireland (January–June 2013); Lithuania (July 2013–December 2013).

President of the European Council: Herman Van Rompuy (Belgium).

High Representative of the Union for Foreign Affairs and Security Policy: Catherine Ashton (United Kingdom).

Secretary-General of the Council of the European Union: Uwe Corsepius (Germany).

President of the European Commission: José Manuel Durão Barroso (Portugal).

President of the European Parliament: Martin Schulz (Germany).

MEMBERS

Austria	Germany*	Netherlands*
Belgium*	Greece	Poland
Bulgaria	Hungary	Portugal
Cyprus	Ireland	Romania
Czech Republic	Italy*	Slovakia
Denmark	Latvia	Slovenia
Estonia	Lithuania	Spain
Finland	Luxembourg*	Sweden
France*	Malta	United Kingdom

* Original members.

ENLARGEMENT

The six original members (Belgium, France, Germany, Italy, Luxembourg and the Netherlands) were joined in the European Communities (later the European Union—EU) on 1 January 1973 by Denmark, Ireland and the United Kingdom, and on 1 January 1981 by Greece. In a referendum held in February 1982, the inhabitants of Greenland voted to end their membership of the Community, entered into when under full Danish rule. Greenland's withdrawal took effect from 1 February 1985. Portugal and Spain became members on 1 January 1986. Following the reunification of Germany in October 1990, the former German Democratic Republic immediately became part of the Community, although a transitional period was allowed before certain Community legislation took effect there. Austria, Finland and Sweden became members on 1 January 1995.

At the Copenhagen summit on 13 December 2002, an historic agreement was reached when the European Council agreed that 10 candidate countries, comprising eight in Central and Eastern Europe (the Czech Republic, Estonia, Hungary, Latvia, Lithuania, Poland, Slovakia and Slovenia), and Malta and Cyprus, should join the EU on 1 May 2004. The leaders of the 10 new member states signed the accession treaty in Athens, Greece, on 16 April 2003. The Treaty of Athens had to be ratified by all 25 states prior to accession on 1 May 2004. The 15 existing member states opted to ratify the Treaty in parliament whereas the future member states, except Cyprus (the Cypriot Parliament unanimously approved accession to the EU on 14 July 2003), adopted the Treaty by referendum. A referendum took place in Malta on 8 March 2003, Slovenia on 23 March, Hungary on 12 April, Lithuania on 10 and 11 May, Slovakia on 16 and 17 May, Poland on 7 and 8 June, the Czech Republic on 15 and 16 June, Estonia on 14 September and Latvia on 20 September; each poll recorded a majority in favour of accession. Under the terms of the Treaty, only the Greek Cypriot sector of Cyprus was to be admitted to the EU in the absence of a settlement on the divided status of the island, although the EU made clear its preference for the accession of a united Cyprus. In April 2004, however, in a referendum on a UN-proposed reunification settlement held only a few days before Cyprus was scheduled to join the EU, some 76% of Greek Cypriot voters rejected the proposal. At the same time, some 65% of Turkish Cypriot voters endorsed the settlement. Both communities would have had to approve the proposed reunification in order for Cyprus to commence its membership of the EU undivided. Consequently, only the Greek sector of the island assumed EU membership from 1 May.

Romania submitted its formal application for EU membership on 22 June 1995, while Bulgaria applied for membership on 14 December. Following the Helsinki European Council's decision in December 1999, accession negotiations started with Romania and Bulgaria in February 2000. The Commission concluded in November 2003 that Bulgaria had a functioning market economy and would be able to perform within the EU in the near future provided it continued to implement its reform programme. In October 2004 a report by the European Commission described Romania as a functioning market economy, although it confirmed that endemic corruption, ethnic minority rights and human trafficking remained, *inter alia*, areas of concern in both countries. In the same strategy document, the Commission proposed a new clause in accession treaties under which membership negotiations could be suspended if candidate countries failed to fulfil the economic and political criteria established in Copenhagen, Denmark, in December 2002, according to which a prospective member must: be a stable democracy, respecting human rights, the rule of law, and the protection of minorities; have a functioning market economy; and adopt the common rules, standards and policies that make up the body of EU law. Bulgaria and Romania provisionally completed formal negotiations in June and December 2004, respectively, and this was confirmed at the Brussels European Council meeting of 17 December. The Commission formally approved the accession applications of Romania and Bulgaria on 22 February 2005. Bulgaria and Romania signed a joint accession treaty on 25 April. In September 2006 the Commission recommended that Romania and Bulgaria should accede to the EU as planned;

both countries formally became members of the Union on 1 January 2007, with the entry into force of their joint accession treaty.

Croatia submitted its application for membership of the EU in February 2003, and membership negotiations finally commenced in October 1995. Negotiations were completed in June 2011, and Croatia signed an accession treaty on 9 December. Croatia was expected to accede to full membership of the EU in July 2013, following approval of EU membership by a referendum held in that country in January 2012.

Turkey, which had signed an association agreement with the EC in 1963 (although this was suspended between 1980 and 1986, following a military coup), applied for membership of the EU on 14 April 1987. As a populous, predominantly Muslim nation, with a poor record on human rights and low average income levels, Turkey encountered objections to its prospective membership, which opponents claimed would disturb the balance of power within the EU and place an intolerable strain on the organization's finances. The Helsinki European Council of 1999, however, granted Turkey applicant status and encouraged it to undertake the requisite political and economic reforms for eventual membership. By accelerating the pace of reforms, Turkey had made significant progress towards achieving compliance with the Copenhagen criteria by 2004, including far-reaching reforms of the Constitution and the penal code. Turkish ambitions for EU membership were adversely affected in April 2004 by the failure of the UN plan for the reunification of Cyprus, which was rejected in a referendum by the Greek Cypriots in the south of the island (see above). Cyprus has been divided since 1974 when Turkey invaded the northern third of the country in response to a Greek-sponsored coup aiming to unite the island with Greece. Turkey refuses to recognize the Greek Cypriot Government and is the only country to recognize the Government of the northern section of the country, known as the 'Turkish Republic of Northern Cyprus', where it has 30,000 troops deployed. The requirement for the successful resolution of all territorial disputes with members of the EU meant that failure to reach a settlement in Cyprus remained a significant impediment to Turkey's accession to the EU, although the Turkish authorities had expressed strong support for the peace plan. In December 2004, however, the EU agreed to begin accession talks with Turkey in early October 2005, although it specified a number of conditions, including the right to impose 'permanent safeguard' clauses in any accession accord. The safeguard clauses related to the freedom of movement of Turkish citizens within the EU (seeking to allay fears about large numbers of low-paid Turkish workers entering other EU member states) and restrictions on the level of subsidy available to Turkey for its infrastructure development or agriculture. The EU warned that negotiations could last between 10 and 15 years and that eventual membership was not guaranteed. Turkey was also obliged to sign a protocol to update its association agreement with the EU prior to accession negotiations in October, to cover the 10 new members that had joined the organization in May 2004, including Cyprus. The Turkish Government had previously refused to grant effective recognition to the Greek Cypriot Government and, although it signed the protocol at the end of July 2005, it still insisted that the extension of the association agreement did not constitute formal recognition. In a report issued in November 2006, the Commission demanded that Turkey open its ports to Cypriot ships by mid-December, in compliance with its agreement to extend its customs union to the 10 new member states in 2005. Turkey announced that there could be no progress on this issue until the EU implemented a regulation drafted in 2004 to end the economic isolation of the 'Turkish Republic of Northern Cyprus', the adoption of which had been blocked by Cyprus. In December 2006, therefore, the EU Council stipulated that talks would not commence in eight policy areas affected by the restrictions placed on Cypriot traffic by Turkey. In its 2011 annual report on enlargement strategy and progress, the Commission expressed regret that negotiations had not opened in any new policy areas for over a year. By March 2012 negotiations had opened in 13 of the total of 33 policy areas, with talks provisionally closed in one area; 18 areas remained blocked.

At a summit of EU leaders in Brussels in December 2005, the former Yugoslav Republic of Macedonia (FYRM) was granted candidate status, joining Croatia and Turkey. However, no date was established for the initiation of accession negotiations. A summit of the Council convened in June 2008 determined that, as a precondition of the FYRM's accession, an ongoing dispute with Greece concerning its name (Macedonia also being the name of a region of Greece) must be satisfactorily resolved. Montenegro applied for EU membership in December 2008, and the European Council confirmed Montenegro's status as a candidate country in December 2010. In October 2011 the European Commission declared that Montenegro had fulfilled the political and economic criteria needed to begin EU membership negotiations. Upon the Commission's recommendation, the European Council agreed in December to initiate the accession process, and negotiations were expected to commence in 2012, dependent on further progress in combating corruption and organized crime in that country. In July 2009 Iceland's legislature voted to apply for EU membership, and membership negotiations commenced in July 2010. By December 2011 talks had opened in 11 policy areas.

Serbia applied for EU membership in December 2009, and in October 2011 the European Commission recommended to the Council that Serbia should be granted candidate status. On 1 March 2012 the European Council agreed officially to give Serbia the status of a candidate country for EU membership. Albania submitted a membership application in April 2009. In November 2010 the European Commission adopted an Opinion on Albanian membership of the EU, which recommended that Albania should be considered as a candidate for membership once it had fulfilled the necessary political and economic criteria.

INSTITUTIONAL REFORM

In February 2002 a Convention on the Future of Europe was opened in Brussels, Belgium, chaired by former French President Valéry Giscard d'Estaing. The Convention, which had been agreed upon at the Laeken summit in December 2001, when the European Council adopted the Declaration on the Future of the European Union, included in its remit 60 or more topics aimed at reforming EU institutions to ensure the smooth functioning of the Union after enlargement. The full text of the draft constitutional treaty was submitted to the Council of the European Union in July 2003. The draft was discussed at the Intergovernmental Conference (IGC), which was composed of the representatives of the member states and the accession countries, from October to December.

Heads of state and of government attending an EU summit held in Brussels, in December 2003, failed to agree the final text of the proposed constitution, owing to conflicting views over the issue of voting rights. At a summit meeting held in Brussels, in June 2004, the heads of state and of government of the then 25 EU member states approved a draft constitutional treaty, having reached a compromise over voting rights. The draft constitutional treaty was formally signed in Rome, Italy, in October by the heads of state or of government of the 25 member states and the three candidate countries of Bulgaria, Romania and Turkey, although it remained subject to ratification by each member nation (either by a vote in the national legislature or by a popular referendum). The future of the constitutional treaty became uncertain following its rejection in national referendums held in France and the Netherlands, in May and June 2005, respectively, and seven countries (the Czech Republic, Denmark, Finland, Ireland, Portugal, Sweden and the United Kingdom) announced plans to postpone a national referendum.

In June 2007, at a summit in Brussels, the European Council agreed to convene an IGC to draft a new treaty. At an informal summit of the European Council held in Lisbon, Portugal, in mid-October, agreement was reached on the final text of a new reform treaty. The resulting Treaty of Lisbon amending the Treaty on European Union and the Treaty establishing the European Community was signed in Lisbon, on 13 December, by the heads of state or of government of the now 27 member states. The Treaty of Lisbon revised existing treaties, and retained much of the content of the abandoned constitutional treaty, including its scheme for Council of the European Union voting rights (whereby measures would require the support of at least 55% of EU states, representing at least 65% of the total population, see below; this aimed to ensure that smaller member states—particularly the new Eastern European members—could not be overruled by a small but powerful group of senior members). During 2008 the parliaments of most member states voted to ratify the Treaty. However, in June 2008 voters in Ireland, which was constitutionally bound to conduct a popular referendum on the issue, rejected ratification. In December the European Council agreed to a number of concessions, including the removal of a provision in the Treaty for a reduction in the number of European Commissioners (see below), and relating to taxation, the family, and state neutrality, with the aim of securing its ratification by all EU member states by the end of 2009. A new referendum, held in Ireland in early October 2009, approved the Treaty. In early November, following a ruling by the Constitutional Court of the Czech Republic that its provisions were compatible with the country's Constitution, the Czech Republic became the final EU country to ratify the Treaty of Lisbon. The Treaty entered into force on 1 December 2009.

PRINCIPAL ELEMENTS OF THE TREATY OF LISBON

The Treaty of Lisbon (formally known as the Treaty of Lisbon amending the Treaty on European Union and the Treaty establishing the European Community) sought to redefine the functions and procedures of the institutions of the EU. It created a High Representative of the Union for Foreign Affairs and Security Policy (appointed by the European Council by qualified majority with the agreement of the President of the Commission) to represent the EU internationally, combining the former roles of EU Commissioner responsible for external relations and EU High Representative for the Common Foreign and Security Policy (although foreign policy remains subject to a national veto). The High Representative of the Union for Foreign Affairs and Security Policy is mandated by the Council, but is also one of the Vice-Presidents of the Commission and chairs the External Relations Council. The Lisbon Treaty also provides for the creation of a new permanent president of the European Council, elected by the European Council for a period of two and one-half years, renewable once; the creation of this role aims to promote coherence and continuity in policy-making. The system of a six-month rotating presidency has been retained for the different Council formations (except for the External Relations Council, chaired by the new High Representative of the Union for Foreign Affairs and Security Policy). A new system of fixed 18-month troikas (groups of three presidencies) has been introduced, sharing the presidencies of most configurations of the Council, to facilitate overall co-ordination and continuity of work. The Lisbon Treaty provides for a revised system of qualified majority voting in the Council (see Council of the European Union). The European Parliament's legislative powers are consolidated under the Treaty, which grants the Parliament the right of co-decision with the Council of the European Union in an increased number of policy areas, giving it a more prominent role in framing legislation. The maximum number of seats in the European Parliament is raised to 751 (to be fully effective from 2014, see European Parliament). The European Commission retains its composition of one commissioner for each member state. The Treaty establishing the European Community (also known as the Treaty of Rome) is renamed as the Treaty on the Functioning of the European Union, with references to the 'Community' replaced by 'Union'. The Lisbon Treaty attempts to improve democracy and transparency within the Union, introducing the right for EU citizens to petition the Commission to introduce new legislation and enshrining the principles of subsidiarity (that the EU should only act when an objective can be better achieved at the supranational level, implying that national powers are the norm) and proportionality (that the action should be proportional to the desired objective). National parliaments are given the opportunity to examine EU legislation to ensure that it rests within the EU's remit, and legislation may be returned to the Commission for reconsideration if one-third of member states find that a proposed law breaches these principles. The Treaty of Lisbon enables enhanced co-operation for groups numbering at least one-third (i.e. currently nine) of the member states. The Treaty provides a legal basis for the EU defence force, with a mutual defence clause, and includes the stipulation that the EU has the power to sign treaties and sit on international bodies as a legal entity in its own right. The new framework also provides for the establishment of a European public prosecutor's office to combat EU fraud and cross-border crime and the right to dual citizenship (i.e. of the EU as well as of a member state), and includes arrangements for the formal withdrawal of a member state from the EU.

Union Institutions

The EU provides an information service, Europe Direct, online at europa.eu/europedirect/index_en.htm.

EUROPEAN COMMISSION

Address: 200 rue de la Loi, 1049 Brussels, Belgium.

Telephone: (2) 299-11-11; **fax:** (2) 295-01-38; **e-mail:** forename.surname@ec.europa.eu; **internet:** ec.europa.eu.

Please note: in an e-mail address, when the forename and/or the surname are composed of more than one word, the different words are linked by a hyphen. If help is needed, you may send a message to address-information@ec.europa.eu requesting the correct e-mail address of the correspondent.

MEMBERS OF THE COMMISSION
(2010–14)

President: JOSÉ MANUEL DURÃO BARROSO (Portugal).

Vice-President and High Representative of the Union for Foreign Affairs and Security Policy: CATHERINE ASHTON (United Kingdom).

Vice-President, responsible for Justice, Fundamental Rights and Citizenship: VIVIANE REDING (Luxembourg).

Vice-President, responsible for Competition: JOAQUÍN ALMUNIA (Spain).

Vice-President, responsible for Transport: SIIM KALLAS (Estonia).

Vice-President, responsible for the Digital Agenda: NEELIE KROES (Netherlands).

Commissioner, responsible for Industry and Entrepreneurship: ANTONIO TAJANI (Italy).

Commissioner, responsible for Inter-Institutional Relations and Administration: MAROŠ ŠEFČOVIČ (Slovakia).

Commissioner, responsible for the Environment: JANEZ POTOČNIK (Slovenia).

Commissioner, responsible for Economic and Monetary Affairs and the Euro: OLLI REHN (Finland).

Commissioner, responsible for Development: ANDRIS PIEBALGS (Latvia).

Commissioner, responsible for Internal Market and Services: MICHEL BARNIER (France).

Commissioner, responsible for Education, Culture, Multilingualism and Youth: ANDROULLA VASSILIOU (Cyprus).

Commissioner, responsible for Taxation and Customs Union, Audit and Anti-Fraud: ALGIRDAS ŠEMETA (Lithuania).

Commissioner, responsible for Trade: KAREL DE GUCHT (Belgium).

Commissioner, responsible for Health and Consumer Policy: JOHN DALLI (Malta).

Commissioner, responsible for Research, Innovation and Science: MÁIRE GEOGHEGAN-QUINN (Ireland).

Commissioner, responsible for Financial Programming and Budget: JANUSZ LEWANDOWSKI (Poland).

Commissioner, responsible for Maritime Affairs and Fisheries: MARIA DAMANAKI (Greece).

Commissioner, responsible for International Co-operation, Humanitarian Aid and Crisis Response: KRISTALINA GEORGIEVA (Bulgaria).

Commissioner, responsible for Energy: GÜNTHER H. OETTINGER (Austria).

Commissioner, responsible for Regional Policy: JOHANNES HAHN (Austria).

Commissioner, responsible for Climate Action: CONNIE HEDEGAARD (Denmark).

Commissioner, responsible for Enlargement and European Neighbourhood Policy: ŠTEFAN FÜLE (Czech Republic).

Commissioner, responsible for Employment, Social Affairs and Inclusion: LÁSZLÓ ANDOR (Hungary).

Commissioner, responsible for Home Affairs: CECILIA MALMSTRÖM (Sweden).

Commissioner, responsible for Agriculture and Rural Development: DACIAN CIOLOŞ (Romania).

The European Commission, like the European Parliament and Council of the European Union, was established in the 1950s under the EU's founding Treaties. The functions of the Commission are four-fold: to propose legislation to the European Parliament and the Council of the European Union; to implement EU policies and programmes adopted by the European Parliament and to manage and implement the budget; to enforce European law, in conjunction with the Court of Justice, in all the member states; and to represent the EU in international affairs and to negotiate agreements between the EU and other organizations or countries.

A new Commission is appointed for a five-year term, normally within six months of the elections to the European Parliament. The Governments of the member states agree on an individual to designate as the new Commission President. The President-designate then selects the other members of the Commission, following discussions with the member state Governments. In the performance of their duties, the members of the Commission are forbidden to seek or accept instructions from any government or other body, or to engage in any other paid or unpaid professional activity. The nominated President and other members of the Commission must be approved as a body by the European Parliament before they can take office. Once approved, the Commission may nominate a number of its members as Vice-President. Any member of the Commission, if he or she no longer fulfils the conditions required for the performance of his or her duties, or commits a serious offence, may be declared removed from office by the Court of Justice. The Court may, furthermore, on the petition of the Council of the European Union or of the Commission itself, provisionally suspend any member of the Commission from his or her duties. The European Parliament has the authority to dismiss the entire Commission by adopting a motion of censure. The number of members of the Commission may be amended by a unanimous vote of the Council of the European Union.

The members of the Commission, also known as the College, meet once a week and a collective decision is made on policy following a presentation by the relevant Commissioner. The Commission's staff is organized into Directorates-General and Services. The Directorates-General are each responsible for a particular policy area and they devise and draft the Commission's legislative proposals, which become official when adopted by the Commission.

In January 1999 Commissioners accused of mismanagement and corruption retained their positions following a vote of censure by Parliament. However, Parliament appointed a five-member Committee of Independent Experts to investigate allegations of fraud, mismanagement and nepotism within the Commission. In March two new codes of conduct for Commissioners were announced, and the Committee published a report that criticized the Commission's failure to control the administration of the budget and other measures implemented by each department. As a consequence of the report the Commission agreed, collectively, to resign, although Commissioners retained their positions, and exercised limited duties, until their successors were appointed. In late March EU heads of state and of government nominated Romano Prodi, the former Italian Prime Minister, as the next President of the Commission. His appointment, and that of his interim team of Commissioners, were duly ratified by Parliament in September, subject to conditions that formed the foundation of a future inter-institutional agreement between Parliament and the Commission. The Commission retained its powers, but undertook to be more open in its dealings with the Parliament.

In January 2004 the Commission launched legal proceedings against the Economic and Financial Council of Ministers (ECOFIN—which comprises the national ministers responsible for finance). The Commission sought a ruling from the European Court of Justice on the legality of ECOFIN's decision to suspend disciplinary procedures against France and Germany, both of which intended to exceed the budget deficit limit of 3% of gross domestic product (GDP), imposed under the Stability and Growth Pact, for the third consecutive year. In July the European Court of Justice ruled that ECOFIN's intervention was not compatible with EU legislation but that ministers retained ultimate control over the implementation of the pact. In November 2005, in response to diminishing public confidence in EU institutions, the Commission launched the European Transparency Initiative, with the aim of strengthening ethical rules for EU policy-makers, increasing the transparency of lobbying and ensuring the openness of the institutions.

Meanwhile, on 1 May 2004, following the accession of 10 new member states, the 20 existing members of the Commission were joined by 10 new members (one from each new member state). For the first six months of their term of office, although considered full members, they worked alongside existing Commissioners and were not allocated their own departments. From 1 November, when a new Commission was to begin its mandate, there were to be 25 members of the Commission, one from each member state as stipulated by the Treaty of Nice (prior to 1 May, large countries had been permitted two Commissioners, while smaller countries had one). In late October, however, the incoming President of the European Commission, José Manuel Durão Barroso, withdrew his proposed team of commissioners, in order to avoid defeat in the investiture vote in the European Parliament. The reconstituted Commission (two members were replaced and one was allocated a new portfolio) was approved by the European Parliament and took office on 22 November. In January 2007, following the accession of Bulgaria and Romania, the number of Commissioners increased to 27. As it was feared that too large an increase in the number of Commissioners would be prejudicial to collective responsibility, it was initially determined that from 2014 the number would be reduced to a level determined by the Council. However, in December 2008, in response to Ireland's rejection of the Lisbon Treaty in a national referendum in June, the European Council agreed a number of legal guarantees intended to address voters' objections, including a commitment that every member state would have one Commissioner. (The Irish electorate approved the Treaty in October 2009, and it entered into force in December of that year.)

The second Barroso Commission, for 2010–14, was approved by the European Parliament in January 2010 and inaugurated in the following month. The mandate of the previous commission (that should have expired in October 2009) had been lengthened temporarily to accommodate delays in the appointment of the new Commission that were caused by the later than anticipated entry into force of the Lisbon Treaty.

DIRECTORATES-GENERAL AND SERVICES

POLICIES

Directorate-General for Agriculture and Rural Development: 130 rue de la Loi, 1049 Brussels; tel. (2) 295-32-40; fax (2) 295-01-30; e-mail agri-library@ec.europa.eu; internet ec.europa.eu/dgs/agriculture; Dir-Gen. JOSÉ MANUEL SILVA RODRIGUEZ.

Directorate-General for Budget: 45 ave d'Auderghem, 1049 Brussels; tel. (2) 299-11-11; fax (2) 295-95-85; e-mail budget@ec.europa.eu; internet ec.europa.eu/dgs/budget; Dir-Gen. HERVÉ JOUANJEAN.

Directorate-General for Climate Action: 1049 Brussels; e-mail ec.europa.eu/dgs/clima/contact_en.htm (contact form); internet ec.europa.eu/dgs/climateaction/index_en.htm; f. Feb. 2010; Dir-Gen. JOS DELBEKE.

Directorate-General for Competition: 70 rue Joseph II, 1049 Brussels; tel. (2) 299-11-11; fax (2) 295-01-28; e-mail infocomp@ec.europa.eu; internet ec.europa.eu/competition; f. 1958; Dir-Gen. ALEXANDER ITALIANER.

Directorate-General for Economic and Financial Affairs: 1049 Brussels; tel. (2) 299-11-11; fax (2) 298-08-23; e-mail staffdir@ec.europa.eu; internet ec.europa.eu/economy_finance; Dir-Gen. MARCO BUTI.

Directorate-General for Education and Culture: 200 rue de la Loi, 1049 Brussels; tel. (2) 299-11-11; fax (2) 295-60-85; e-mail eac-info@ec.europa.eu; internet ec.europa.eu/dgs/education_culture; Dir-Gen. JAN TRUSZCZYŃSKI.

Directorate-General for Employment, Social Affairs and Inclusion: 200 rue de la Loi, 1049 Brussels; tel. (2) 299-11-11; e-mail ec.europa.eu/social/contact (contact form); internet ec.europa.eu/social; Dir-Gen. JACOBUS RICHELLE.

Directorate-General for Energy: 200 rue de la Loi, 1049 Brussels; tel. (2) 299-11-11; fax (2) 295-01-50; e-mail ec.europa.eu/energy/contact/index_en.htm (contact form); internet ec.europa.eu/energy/index_en.htm; Dir-Gen. PHILIP LOWE.

Directorate-General for Health and Consumers: 4 rue Breydel, 1049 Brussels; tel. (2) 299-11-11; fax (2) 296-62-98; e-mail sanco-mailbox@ec.europa.eu; internet ec.europa.eu/dgs/health_consumer/index_en.htm; Dir-Gen. PAULA TESTORI COGGI.

Directorate-General for Home Affairs: 46 rue du Luxembourg, 1050 Brussels; tel. (2) 299-11-11; fax (2) 296-74-81; e-mail forename.surname@ec.europa.eu; internet ec.europa.eu/dgs/home-affairs/index_en.htm; Dir-Gen. STEFANO MANSERVISI.

Directorate-General for Internal Market and Services: rue de Spa, 1000 Brussels; e-mail markt-info@ec.europa.eu; internet ec.europa.eu/dgs/internal_market; Dir-Gen. JONATHAN FAULL.

Directorate-General for Justice: 200 rue de la Loi, 10549 Brussels; tel. (2) 299-11-11; fax (2) 296-74-81; e-mail forename.surname@ec.europa.eu; internet ec.europa.eu/justice/index_en.htm; Dir-Gen. FRANÇOISE LE BAIL.

Directorate-General for Maritime Affairs and Fisheries: 99 rue de Joseph II, 1000 Brussels; tel. (2) 299-11-11; fax (2) 299-30-40; e-mail fisheries-info@ec.europa.eu; internet ec.europa.eu/fisheries; Dir-Gen. LOWRI EVANS.

Directorate-General for Mobility and Transport (DG Move): 24–28 rue Demot, 1040 Brussels; tel. (2) 299-11-11; fax (2) 295-01-50; e-mail ec.europa.eu/transport/contact/index_en.htm (contact form); internet ec.europa.eu/transport/index_en.htm; Dir-Gen. MATTHIAS RUETE.

Directorate-General for Regional Policy: 23 rue Père de Deken, 1040 Brussels; tel. (2) 296-06-34; fax (2) 296-60-03; e-mail regio-info@ec.europa.eu; internet ec.europa.eu/dgs/regional_policy; Dir-Gen. WALTER DEFFAA.

Directorate-General for Research: 21 rue de Champ de Mars, 1050 Brussels; tel. (2) 299-11-11; fax (2) 295-82-20; e-mail research@cec.eu.int; internet ec.europa.eu/dgs/research; Dir-Gen. ROBERT-JAN SMITS.

Enterprise and Industry Directorate-General: 45 ave d'Auderghem, 1049 Brussels; tel. (2) 299-11-11; fax (2) 296-99-30; e-mail info-enterprises@ec.europa.eu; internet ec.europa.eu/enterprise; Dir-Gen. DANIEL CALLEJA CRESPO.

Environment Directorate-General: 5 ave de Beaulieu, 1160 Brussels; tel. (2) 299-11-11; fax (2) 299-11-05; e-mail envinfo@ec.europa.eu; internet ec.europa.eu/environment; Dir-Gen. KARL FALKENBERG.

Information Society and Media Directorate-General: 24 ave de Beaulieu, 1049 Brussels; tel. (2) 299-93-99; fax (2) 299-94-99; e-mail infso-desk@ec.europa.eu; internet ec.europa.eu/dgs/information_society; Dir-Gen. ROBERT MADELIN.

Taxation and the Customs Union Directorate-General: 59 rue Montoyer, 1000 Brussels; tel. (2) 299-11-11; fax (2) 295-07-56; e-mail librarian-information@ec.europa.eu; internet ec.europa.eu/taxation_customs/index_en.htm; Dir-Gen. HEINZ ZOUREK.

EXTERNAL RELATIONS

Directorate-General for Enlargement: 200 rue de la Loi, 1049 Brussels; tel. (2) 299-96-96; fax (2) 296-84-90; e-mail elarg-info@ec.europa.eu; internet ec.europa.eu/dgs/enlargement; Dir-Gen. STEFANO SAFFINO.

Directorate-General for Trade (DG Trade): 200 rue de la Loi, 1049 Brussels; tel. (2) 299-11-11; fax (2) 299-10-29; e-mail trade-unit3@ec.europa.eu; internet ec.europa.eu/dgs/trade; Dir-Gen. JEAN-LUC DEMARTY.

Directorate-General for Development and Co-operation (EuropeAid): 15 rue de la Science, 1049 Brussels; tel. (2) 299-21-43; fax (2) 296-49-26; e-mail development@ec.europa.eu; internet ec.europa.eu/development/AboutGen_en.cfm; Dir-Gen. FOKIAN FOTIADIS.

Humanitarian Aid Office (ECHO): 88 rue d'Arlon, 1040 Brussels; tel. (2) 299-11-11; fax (2) 295-45-78; e-mail echo-info@ec.europa.eu; internet ec.europa.eu/echo; Dir CLAUS SØRENSEN.

GENERAL SERVICES

Directorate-General for Communication: 45 ave d'Auderghem, SDME 2/2, 1049 Brussels; tel. (2) 299-11-11; fax (2) 295-01-43; e-mail comm-web@ec.europa.eu; internet ec.europa.eu/dgs/communication; Dir-Gen. GREGORY PAULGER.

European Anti-Fraud Office: 30 rue Joseph II, 1000 Brussels; tel. (2) 296-29-76; fax (2) 296-08-53; e-mail olaf-courrier@ec.europa.eu; internet ec.europa.eu/anti_fraud/index_en.htm; Dir-Gen. GIOVANNI KESSLER.

Eurostat (Statistical Office of the European Communities): Bâtiment Joseph Bech, 5 Rue Alphonse Weicker, 2721 Luxembourg; tel. 43-01-33-444; fax 43-01-35-349; e-mail eurostat-pressoffice@ec.europa.eu; internet epp.eurostat.ec.europa.eu; Dir-Gen. WALTER RADERMACHER.

Joint Research Centre (JRC): 200 rue de la Loi, 1049 Brussels; tel. (2) 297-41-81; fax (2) 299-63-22; e-mail jrc-info@ec.europa.eu; internet ec.europa.eu/dgs/jrc; Dir-Gen. DOMINIQUE RISTORI.

Office for Official Publications of the European Communities (Publications Office): 2 rue Mercier, 2985 Luxembourg; tel. 29-291; fax 29-29-44-619; e-mail info@publications.europa.eu; internet www.publications.europa.eu; Dir-Gen. MARTINE REICHERTS.

Secretariat-General: 45 ave d'Auderghem, 1049 Brussels; tel. (2) 299-11-11; fax (2) 296-05-54; e-mail sg-info@ec.europa.eu; internet ec.europa.eu/dgs/secretariat_general; Sec.-Gen. CATHERINE DAY.

INTERNAL SERVICES

Bureau of European Policy Advisers (BEPA): 200 rue de la Loi, 1049 Brussels; tel. (2) 299-11-11; fax (2) 295-23-05; e-mail bepa-info@ec.europa.eu; internet ec.europa.eu/dgs/policy_advisers; Head JEAN-CLAUDE THÉBAULT.

Data Protection Officer of the European Commission: 1049 Brussels; tel. (2) 226-87-50; fax (2) 296-38-91; e-mail data-protection-officer@ec.europa.eu; internet ec.europa.eu/dataprotectionofficer; Data Protection Officer PHILIPPE RENAUDIÈRE.

Directorate-General for Human Resources and Security: 200 rue de la Loi, 1040 Brussels; tel. (2) 299-11-11; fax (2) 299-62-76; e-mail forename.surname@ec.europa.eu; internet ec.europa.eu/dgs/human-resources/index_en.htm; Dir-Gen. IRÈNE SOUKA.

Directorate-General for Informatics (DIGIT): rue Alcide de Gasperi, 2920 Luxembourg; e-mail digit-europa@ec.europa.eu; internet ec.europa.eu/dgs/informatics; Dir-Gen. FRANCISCO GARCÍA MORÁN.

Directorate-General for Interpretation: 200 rue de la Loi, 1040 Brussels; tel. (2) 299-11-11; e-mail scic-euroscic@ec.europa.eu; internet scic.ec.europa.eu/europa/jcms/j_8/home; Head of Service MARCO BENEDETTI.

Directorate-General for Translation (DGT): 200 rue de la Loi, 1040 Brussels; rue de Genève, 1140 Brussels; tel. (2) 299-11-11; fax (2) 296-97-69; e-mail dgt-webmaster@ec.europa.eu; internet ec.europa.eu/dgs/translation; Dir-Gen. RYTIS MARTIKONIS (acting).

Internal Audit Service (IAS): 200 rue de la Loi, 1049 Brussels; tel. (2) 299-11-11; fax (2) 295-41-40; e-mail ias-europa@ec.europa.eu; internet ec.europa.eu/dgs/internal_audit/index_en.htm; Internal Auditor of the European Commission BRIAN GRAY.

Legal Service: 85 ave des Nerviens, 1049 Brussels; tel. (2) 299-11-11; fax (2) 296-30-86; e-mail oib-info@ec.europa.eu; internet ec.europa.eu/dgs/legal_service; Dir-Gen. LUIS ROMERO REQUENA.

Office for Infrastructure and Logistics in Brussels (OIB): Garderie Wilson, 16 rue Wilson, 1040 Brussels; fax (2) 295-76-41; e-mail oib-info@ec.europa.eu; internet ec.europa.eu/oib; Dir GÁBOR ZUPKÓ.

Office for Infrastructure and Logistics in Luxembourg (OIL): Luxembourg; e-mail oil-cad@ec.europa.eu; internet ec.europa.eu/oil; Dir MARIAN O'LEARY.

EUROPEAN COUNCIL

Address: Justus Lipsius Bldg, 175 rue de la Loi, 1048 Brussels, Belgium.

Telephone: (2) 281-61-11; **fax:** (2) 281-69-34; **internet:** www.european-council.europa.eu.

The European Council was the name used to describe summit meetings of the heads of state or of government of the EU member states, their ministers of foreign affairs, and senior officials of the European Commission. The Council met at least twice a year, in the member state that exercised the Presidency of the Council of the European Union, or in Brussels. Until 1975 summit meetings were held less frequently, on an ad hoc basis, usually to adopt major policy decisions regarding the future development of the Community. In answer to the evident need for more frequent consultation at the highest level, it was decided at the summit meeting held in Paris in December 1974 to convene the meetings on a regular basis, under the rubric of the European Council. There was no provision made for the existence of the European Council in the Treaty of Rome, but its position was acknowledged and regularized in the Single European Act (1987). Its role was further strengthened in the Treaty on European Union, which entered into force on 1 November 1993. As a result of the Treaty, the European Council became directly responsible for common policies within the fields of common foreign and security policy and justice and home affairs.

Under the Treaty of Lisbon, which came into force at the beginning of December 2009, the European Council became an institution shaping the EU's development and defining its political priorities. In November 2009, prior to the entry into force of the Treaty, an informal meeting of EU heads of state and of government elected Herman Van Rompuy of Belgium to the new position of President of the European Council, for a period of two years and six months, renewable once. He took office upon the entry into force of the Treaty. The European Council comprises the heads of state or of government of the member states, together with its President and the President of the Commission; the High Representative is also involved in the activities of the European Council, which performs no legislative function, and meets twice every six months, as convened by its President. If required, the President may convene special meetings of the European Council.

COUNCIL OF THE EUROPEAN UNION

Address: Justus Lipsius Bldg, 175 rue de la Loi, 1048 Brussels, Belgium.

Telephone: (2) 281-61-11; **fax:** (2) 281-69-34; **e-mail:** press.office@consilium.europa.eu; **internet:** www.consilium.europa.eu.

The Council of the European Union (until November 1993 known formally as the Council of Ministers of the European Communities and still sometimes referred to as the Council of Ministers) is the only institution that directly represents the member states. It is the Community's principal decision-making body, acting, as a rule, only on proposals made by the Commission, and has six main responsibilities: to approve EC legislation (in many fields it legislates jointly with the European Parliament); to co-ordinate the broad economic policies of the member states; to conclude international agreements between the EU and one or more states or international organizations; to approve the EU budget (in conjunction with the European Parliament); to develop the EU's Common Foreign and Security Policy (CFSP), on the basis of guidelines drawn up by the European Council; and to co-ordinate co-operation between the national courts and police forces in criminal matters. The Council is composed of representatives of the member states, each Government delegating to it one of its members, according to the subject to be discussed (the Council has nine different configurations). These meetings are generally referred to as the Agriculture and Fisheries Council, the Transport, Telecommunications and Energy Council, etc. The General Affairs and External Relations Council, the Economic and Financial Affairs Council (ECOFIN) and the Agriculture and Fisheries Council each normally meet once a month. The Presidency is exercised for a term of six months by each member of the Council in rotation. A new, fixed 18-month troika system (groups of three presidencies) was introduced under the Treaty of Lisbon, which entered into force on 1 December 2009. The current group of presidencies is as follows: Denmark, January–June 2012; Cyprus, July–December 2012; Ireland, January–June 2013). The troika shares the presidencies of most configurations of the Council, with the aim of facilitating overall co-ordination and continuity of work.

The Treaty of Rome prescribed three types of voting (depending on the issue under discussion): simple majority, qualified majority and unanimity. Amendments to the Treaty of Rome (the Single European Act), effective from July 1987, restricted the right of veto, and were expected to accelerate the development of a genuine common market: they allowed proposals relating to the dismantling of barriers to the free movement of goods, persons, services and capital to be approved by a majority vote in the Council, rather than by a unanimous vote. Unanimity was still required, however, for certain areas, including harmonization of indirect taxes, legislation on health and safety, veterinary controls, and environmental protection; individual states retained control over immigration rules and the prevention of terrorism and of drugs-trafficking. The Treaty of Amsterdam, which came into force on 1 May 1999, extended the use of qualified majority voting (QMV) to a number of areas previously subject to unanimous decision. Under the terms of the Treaty of Nice, which came into force on 1 February 2003, a further range of areas (mostly minor in nature and relating to appointments to various EU institutions) that had previously been subject to national vetoes became subject to QMV. With the expansion of the EU to 25 members in 2004, and subsequently to 27 members in 2007, and the consequent reduced likelihood of unanimity in Council decisions, the use of QMV in an even broader range of decisions was intended to minimize so-called policy drag. The 2009 Lisbon Treaty provided for the further extension of QMV, which was newly defined, to areas that had previously been subject to national vetoes (from 2014, see below).

The Single European Act introduced a 'co-operation procedure' whereby a proposal adopted by a qualified majority in the Council must be submitted to the European Parliament for approval: if the Parliament rejects the Council's common position, unanimity shall be required for the Council to act on a second reading, and, if the Parliament suggests amendments, the Commission must re-examine the proposal and forward it to the Council again. A 'co-decision procedure' was introduced in 1993 by the Treaty on European Union. The procedure allowed a proposal to be submitted for a third reading by a so-called Conciliation Committee, composed equally of Council representatives and members of the European Parliament. The Treaty of Amsterdam simplified the co-decision procedure, and extended it to matters previously resolved under the co-operation procedure, although the latter remained in place for matters concerning economic and monetary union.

Under the Treaty of Amsterdam, the Secretary-General of the Council also took the role of High Representative, responsible for the co-ordination of the common foreign and security policy. The Council Secretary-General is supported by a policy planning and early warning unit.

The Treaty of Nice, which came into force in February 2003, addressed institutional issues that remained outstanding under the Treaty of Amsterdam and that had to be settled before the enlargement of the EU in 2004, and various other issues not directly connected with enlargement. The main focus of the Treaty was the establishment of principles governing the new distribution of seats in the European Parliament, the new composition of the Commission and a new definition of QMV within the Council of the European Union. From 1 May 2004 (when the 10 accession states joined the EU) until 31 October, there were transitional arrangements for changing the weighting of votes in the Council. In accordance with the provisions incorporated in the Treaty of Nice, from 1 November the new weighting system was as follows: France, Germany, Italy and the United Kingdom 29 votes each; Poland and Spain 27 votes each; the Netherlands 13 votes; Belgium, the Czech Republic, Greece, Hungary and Portugal 12 votes each; Austria and Sweden 10 votes each; Denmark, Finland, Ireland, Lithuania and Slovakia seven votes each; Cyprus, Estonia, Latvia, Luxembourg and Slovenia four votes each; and Malta three votes. A qualified majority was reached if a majority of member states (in some cases a two-thirds' majority) approved and if a minimum of 232 votes out of a total of 321 was cast in favour (which was 72.3% of the total—approximately the same share as under the previous system). In addition, a member state could request confirmation that the votes in favour represented at least 62% of the total population of the EU. Should this not be the case, the decision would not be adopted by the Council. The number of weighted votes required for the adoption of a decision (referred to as the 'qualified majority threshold') was to be reassessed on the accession of any additional new member state. Accordingly, in January 2007, with the accession of Romania and Bulgaria, which were allocated, respectively, 14 and 10 votes, the 'qualified majority threshold' was increased to 255 votes, which represented 73.9% of the new total of 345 votes. It was widely held that the voting system according to the Treaty of Nice was overly complicated and that it gave undue power to certain less populous countries, notably Spain and Poland (which both held 27 votes each, compared with Germany, which, with a population of at least twice the size of those in Spain and Poland, controlled 29 votes).

Reforms approved under the 2009 Treaty of Lisbon made provision for the extension and redefinition of QMV in the Council of the European Union and the ending of the system of national vetoes in a number of further policy areas (including combating climate change, energy, emergency aid, and security). Under a system to be gradually introduced during 2014–17, a qualified majority was to be defined as representing at least 55% of the members of the Council, composed of at least 15 of them and representing member states comprising at least 65% of the EU's population (although a blocking minority would have to include at least four member states). The Lisbon Treaty includes a provision allowing the European Council to agree, by unanimity and subject to prior unanimous approval by national legislatures, to introduce QMV in an area currently requiring unanimity (except in a small number of areas including defence, foreign policy and taxation), thus obviating the need for treaty change.

GENERAL SECRETARIAT

Secretary-General of the Council of the European Union: Uwe Corsepius (Germany).

Secretary-General's Private Office: Head of Cabinet Marek Mora.

Legal Service: Dir-Gen./Legal Adviser Hubert Legal.

Directorates-General:

A (Administration): Dir-Gen. William Shapcott.

B (Agriculture, Fisheries, Social Affairs and Health): Dir-Gen. Ángel Boixareu Carrera.

C (Foreign Affairs, Enlargement and Civil Protection): Dir-Gen. Leonardo Schiavo.

D (Justice and Home Affairs): Dir-Gen. Rafael Fernández-Pita y González (acting).

E (Environment, Education, Transport and Energy): Dir-Gen. Jarosław Pietras.

F (Communication and Transparency): Dir-Gen. Reijo Kempinnen.

G (Economic and Social Affairs): Dir-Gen. Carsten Pillath.

PERMANENT REPRESENTATIVES OF MEMBER STATES

(June 2012)

Austria: Walter Grahammer; 30 ave de Cortenberg, 1040 Brussels; tel. (2) 234-51-00; fax (2) 235-63-00; e-mail bruessel-ov@bmeia.gv.at.

Belgium: Dirk Wouters; 61–63 rue de la Loi, 1040 Brussels; tel. (2) 233-21-11; fax (2) 231-10-75; e-mail dispatch.belgoeurop@diplobel.fed.be.

Bulgaria: Dimiter Tzantchev; 49 sq. Marie-Louise, 1000 Brussels; tel. (2) 235-83-00; fax (2) 374-91-88; e-mail info@bg-permrep.eu; internet www.bg-permrep.eu.

Cyprus: Kornelios S. Korneliou; 61 ave de Cortenberg, 1000 Brussels; tel. (2) 739-51-11; fax (2) 735-45-52; e-mail cy.perm.rep@mfa.gov.cy.

Czech Republic: Milena Vicenová; 15 rue Caroly, 1050 Brussels; tel. (2) 213-91-11; fax (2) 213-91-86; e-mail eu.brussels@embassy.mzv.cz; internet www.czechrep.be.

Denmark: Jeppe Tranholm-Mikkelsen; 73 rue d'Arlon, 1040 Brussels; tel. (2) 233-08-11; fax (2) 230-93-84; e-mail brurep@um.dk.

Estonia: Matti Maasikas; 11–13 rue Guimard, 1040 Brussels; tel. (2) 227-39-10; fax (2) 227-39-25; e-mail permrep.eu@mfa.ee; internet www.eu.estemb.be.

Finland: Jan Store; 100 rue de Trèves, 1040 Brussels; tel. (2) 287-84-11; fax (2) 287-84-05; e-mail forename.surname@formin.fi; internet www.finland.eu.

France: Philippe Etienne; 14 place de Louvain, 1000 Brussels; tel. (2) 229-82-11; fax (2) 230-99-50; e-mail courrier.bruxelles-dfra@diplomatie.gouv.fr; internet www.rpfrance.org.

Germany: Peter Tempel; 8–14 rue Jacques de Lalaing, 1040 Brussels; tel. (2) 787-10-00; fax (2) 787-20-00; e-mail info@eu-vertretung.de; internet www.eu-vertretung.de.

Greece: Theodoros N. Sotiropoulos; 19–21 rue Jacques de Lalaing, 1040 Brussels; tel. (2) 551-56-11; fax (2) 551-56-51; e-mail mea.bruxelles@rp-grece.be; internet www.greekembassy-press.be.

Hungary: Péter Györkös; 92–98 rue de Trèves, 1040 Brussels; tel. (2) 234-12-00; fax (2) 372-07-84; e-mail sec.beu@kum.hu; internet www.hunrep.be.

Ireland: Rory Montgomery; 50 rue Froissart, 1040 Brussels; tel. (2) 230-85-80; fax (2) 230-32-03; e-mail irlprb@dfa.ie; internet www.irelandrepbrussels.be.

Italy: Ferdinando Nelli Feroci; 5–11 rue du Marteau, 1000 Brussels; tel. (2) 220-04-11; fax (2) 219-34-49; e-mail rpue@rpue.esteri.it; internet www.italiaue.esteri.it.

Latvia: Ilze Juhansone; 23 ave des Arts, 1000 Brussels; tel. (2) 238-31-00; fax (2) 238-32-50; e-mail permrep.eu@mfa.gov.lv; internet www.mfa.gov.lv/brussels.

Lithuania: Raimundas Karoblis; 41–43 rue Belliard, 1040 Brussels; tel. (2) 771-01-40; fax (2) 401-98-77; e-mail office@eurep.mfa.lt; internet www.eurep.mfa.lt.

Luxembourg: Christian Braun; 75 ave de Cortenberg, 1000 Brussels; tel. (2) 737-56-00; fax (2) 737-56-10; e-mail forename.surname@rpue.etat.lu.

Malta: Richard Cachia Caruana; 25 rue d'Archimède, 1000 Brussels; tel. (2) 343-01-95; fax (2) 343-01-06; e-mail maltarep@gov.mt.

Netherlands: Pieter de Gooijer; 4–10 ave de Cortenberg, 1040 Brussels; tel. (2) 679-15-11; fax (2) 679-17-75; e-mail BRE@minbusa.nl; internet eu.nlvertegenwoordiging.org.

Poland: Jan Tombiński; 139 rue Stevin, 1000 Brussels; tel. (2) 780-42-00; fax (2) 780-42-97; e-mail bebrustpe@msz.gov.pl; internet www.brukselaeu.polemb.net.

Portugal: Domingos Fezas Vital; 12 ave de Cortenberg, 1040 Brussels; tel. (2) 286-42-11; fax (2) 231-00-26; e-mail reper@reper-portugal.be; internet www.reper-portugal.be.

Romania: Mihnea Ioan Motoc; 12 rue Montoyer, 1000 Brussels; tel. (2) 700-06-40; fax (2) 700-06-41; e-mail bru@rpro.eu; internet www.ue.mae.ro.

Slovakia: IVAN KORČOK; 79 ave de Cortenberg, 1000 Brussels; tel. (2) 743-68-11; fax (2) 743-68-88; e-mail eu.brussels@mzv.sk; internet www.mzv.sk/szbrusel.

Slovenia: RADO GENORIO; 44 rue du Commerce, 1000 Brussels; tel. (2) 213-63-00; fax (2) 213-63-01; e-mail pr.spbr@gov.si; internet www.mzz.gov.si.

Spain: ALFONSO DASTIS QUECEDO; 52 blvd du Régent, 1000 Brussels; tel. (2) 509-86-11; fax (2) 511-19-40; e-mail reperue@reper.maec.es; internet www.es-ue.org.

Sweden: DAG HARTELIUS; 30 place de Meeûs, 1000 Brussels; tel. (2) 289-56-11; fax (2) 289-56-00; e-mail representationen.bryssel@foreign.ministry.se; internet www.sweden.gov.se/sb/d/2250.

United Kingdom: JON CUNLIFFE; 10 ave d'Auderghem, 1040 Brussels; tel. (2) 287-82-11; fax (2) 282-89-00; e-mail ukrep@fco.gov.uk; internet ukeu.fco.gov.uk/en.

Preparation and co-ordination of the Council's work (with the exception of agricultural issues, which are handled by the Special Committee on Agriculture) is entrusted to a Committee of Permanent Representatives (COREPER), which meets in Brussels on a weekly basis and which consists of the permanent representatives of the member countries to the Union (who have senior ambassadorial status). A staff of national civil servants assists each ambassador.

EUROPEAN EXTERNAL ACTION SERVICE—EEAS

Address: 1 ave de Cortenberg, Brussels, 1046 Belgium.

Telephone: (2) 584-11-11; **internet:** www.eeas.europa.eu.

The Treaty of Lisbon, which entered into force at the beginning of December 2009, created the new position of High Representative of the Union for Foreign Affairs and Security, to which Catherine Ashton was appointed for a five-year term. In July 2010 the European Parliament approved the creation of the European External Action Service (EEAS), which was formally established at the beginning of December, as the EU's foreign policy and diplomatic service. The High Representative of the Union for Foreign Affairs and Security Policy, who is also a Vice-President of the Commission, is responsible for the co-ordination of the EEAS, and chairs monthly meetings of the Foreign Affairs Council, which comprises EU ministers of foreign affairs, of defence and of development. The EEAS, an independent body, combines the functions of the Commission and the Council hitherto responsible for foreign affairs.

High Representative of the Union for Foreign Affairs and Security Policy: CATHERINE ASHTON (United Kingdom).

Executive Secretary-General: PIERRE VIMONT (France).

Chief Operating Officer: DAVID O'SULLIVAN (Ireland).

EUROPEAN PARLIAMENT

Address: Centre Européen, Plateau du Kirchberg, BP 1601, 2929 Luxembourg.

Telephone: 4300-1; **fax:** 4300-29494; **internet:** www.europarl.europa.eu.

PRESIDENT AND MEMBERS

President: MARTIN SCHULZ (Germany).

Members: Members of the Parliament are elected for a five-year term by direct universal suffrage and proportional representation by the citizens of the member states. Members sit in the Chamber in transnational political, not national, groups. The Parliament elected in June 2009 was initially composed of 736 members; the Treaty of Lisbon, which entered into force on 1 December 2009, however, makes provision for a total of 751 seats.

The European Parliament has three main roles: sharing with the Council of the European Union the power to legislate; holding authority over the annual Union budget (again, jointly with the Council), including the power to adopt or reject it in its entirety; and exercising a measure of democratic control over the executive organs of the European Communities, the Commission and the Council. Notably, it has the power to dismiss the European Commission as a whole by a vote of censure (requiring a two-thirds' majority of the votes cast, which must also be a majority of the total parliamentary membership). The Parliament does not exercise the authority, however, to dismiss individual Commissioners. Increases in parliamentary powers were brought about through amendments to the Treaty of Rome. The Single European Act, which entered into force on 1 July 1987, introduced, in certain circumstances where the Council normally adopts legislation through majority voting, a co-operation procedure involving a second parliamentary reading, enabling the Parliament to amend legislation. Community agreements with third countries require parliamentary approval. The Treaty on European Union, which came into force in November 1993, introduced the co-decision procedure, permitting a third parliamentary reading (see the Council of the European Union). The Treaty also gives the Parliament the right potentially to veto legislation, and allows it to approve or reject the nomination of Commissioners (including the President of the Commission). The Parliament appoints the European Ombudsman from among its members, who investigates reports of maladministration in Community institutions. The Treaty of Amsterdam, which entered into force in May 1999, expanded and simplified the Parliament's legislative role. The co-decision procedure between the Parliament and the Council was extended into a wider range of policy areas. The Treaty also stipulated that the President of the Commission must be formally approved by the Parliament. In addition, international agreements, treaty decisions and the accession of new member states all require the assent of the Parliament. The Treaty of Nice, which came into force in February 2003, further extended the use of co-decision and introduced a new distribution of seats in the Parliament. The Treaty of Lisbon again extended the Parliament's right of co-decision with the Council, and made provision for a maximum number of seats of 751 (750 voting members and the President), with each member state being entitled to a minimum of six and a maximum of 96 seats, on a proportional basis (see below). Under the Treaty 18 additional seats were allocated to 12 member states, while Germany was to lose three of its former seats.

The Parliament elected in June 2009, prior to the entry into force of the Lisbon Treaty in December, initially comprised the 736 members provided for by the Nice Treaty. However, in December 2008 EU heads of state and of government had agreed a compromise composition for the 2009–14 Parliament, which was to comprise the 736 members elected in June 2009 (including the three extra German representatives elected legitimately under the terms of the Nice Treaty), plus the 18 additional members provided for by the Lisbon Treaty (see below for distribution), thereby temporarily raising the total number of members to 754, until the election of the next, 751-member Parliament in 2014. In order to enable the 18 additional members (who would technically hold observer status, to enable their participation in the 2009–14 Parliament) to assume their responsibilities, a transitional change to the Lisbon Treaty was required. On 17 June 2010 the European Council agreed to launch an Intergovernmental Conference to negotiate the required amendment. The amendment was adopted six days later, subject to ratification by the national legislatures of member states. Ratification was completed in November 2011, and the amendment entered into force on 1 December 2011. Moreover, from April 2012 Croatia sent a further 12 members, with observer status, to the Parliament; they would become full members in July 2013, upon Croatia's admission to the EU.

The distribution of seats among the 27 members provided for by the Lisbon Treaty is as follows: Germany 96 members (with, exceptionally, 99, in accordance with the provisions of the Nice Treaty, to hold seats during 2009–14); France 74 (compared with 72 provided for under the Nice Treaty); the United Kingdom 73 (including one additional member); Italy 73 (one additional member); Spain 54 (four); Poland 51 (one); Romania 33; the Netherlands 26 (one); Portugal (with one additional member), Belgium, the Czech Republic, Greece and Hungary 22 each; Sweden 20 (two additional members); Austria 19 (two); Bulgaria 18 (one additional member); Denmark, Finland and Slovakia 13 each; Ireland and Lithuania 12 each; Latvia nine (one); Slovenia eight (one); and Malta (with one additional member), Cyprus, Estonia and Luxembourg six each.

Political Groups

	Distribution of seats (March 2012)
Group of the European People's Party (Christian Democrats) (EPP)	271
Group of the Progressive Alliance of Socialists and Democrats (S/D)	190
Group of the Alliance of Liberals and Democrats for Europe (ALDE)	85
Group of the Greens/European Free Alliance (Verts/EFA)	58
European Conservatives and Reformists Group (ECR)	53
Confederal Group of the European United Left/ Nordic Green Left (GUE/NGL)	34
Europe of Freedom and Democracy Group (EFD)	33
Non-affiliated (NA)	30
Total	754

With effect from June 2009 the minimum number of members required to form a political group under the Parliament's rules of procedure has been fixed at 25, from a minimum of seven member states (previously 20 members were required from a minimum of six member states).

The Parliament has an annual session, divided into around 12 one-week meetings, attended by all members and normally held in Strasbourg, France. The session opens with the March meeting. Committee meetings, political group meetings and additional plenary sittings of the Parliament are held in Brussels, while the parliamentary administrative offices are based in Luxembourg.

The budgetary powers of the Parliament (which, together with the Council of the European Union, forms the Budgetary Authority of the Communities) were increased to their present status by a treaty of 22 July 1975. Under this treaty the Parliament can amend non-agricultural spending and reject the draft budget, acting by a majority of its members and two-thirds of the votes cast. The Parliament debates the draft budget in two successive readings, and it does not come into force until it has been signed by the President of the Parliament. The Parliament's Committee on Budgetary Control (COCOBU) monitors how the budget is spent, and each year the Parliament decides whether to approve the Commission's handling of the budget for the previous financial year (a process technically known as 'granting a discharge').

The Parliament is run by a Bureau comprising the President, 14 Vice-Presidents elected from its members by secret ballot to serve for two-and-a-half years, and the five members of the College of Quaestors. The Conference of Presidents is the political governing body of the Parliament, with responsibility for formulating the agenda for plenary sessions and the timetable for the work of parliamentary bodies, and for establishing the terms of reference and the size of committees and delegations. It comprises the President of the Parliament and the Chairmen of the political groups.

The majority of the Parliament's work is conducted by 22 Standing Parliamentary Committees, which correspond to different policy areas and various European Commission agencies: Foreign Affairs; Development; International Trade; Budgets; Budgetary Control; Economic and Monetary Affairs; Employment and Social Affairs; Environment, Public Health and Food Safety; Industry, Research and Energy; Internal Market and Consumer Protection; Transport and Tourism; Regional Development; Agriculture and Rural Development; Fisheries; Culture and Education; Legal Affairs; Civil Liberties, Justice and Home Affairs; Constitutional Affairs; Women's Rights and Gender Equality; Petitions; Human Rights; and Security Defence.

The first direct elections to the European Parliament took place in June 1979, and Parliament met for the first time in July. The second elections were held in June 1984 (with separate elections held in Portugal and Spain in 1987, following the accession of these two countries to the Community), the third in June 1989, and the fourth in June 1994. Direct elections to the European Parliament were held in Sweden in September 1995, and in Austria and Finland in October 1996. The fifth European Parliament was elected in June 1999, and the sixth in June 2004, following the mass accession of 10 new member states in May of that year. Elections to the seventh European Parliament were held on 4–7 June 2009; the rate of participation by the electorate was 43.1%.

EUROPEAN OMBUDSMAN

Address: 1 ave du Président Robert Schuman, BP 30403, 67001 Strasbourg Cedex, France.

Telephone: 3-88-17-23-13; **fax:** 3-88-17-90-62; **e-mail:** euro-ombudsman@europarl.eu.int; **internet:** www.ombudsman.europa.eu/home/en/default.htm.

The position was created by the Treaty on European Union (the Maastricht Treaty), and the first Ombudsman took office in July 1995. The Ombudsman is appointed by the European Parliament (from among its own members) for a renewable five-year term (to run concurrently with that of the European Parliament). He is authorized to receive complaints (from EU citizens, businesses and institutions, and from anyone residing or having their legal domicile in an EU member state) regarding maladministration in Community institutions and bodies (except in the Court of Justice and Court of First Instance), to make recommendations, and to refer any matters to the Parliament. The Ombudsman submits an annual report on his activities to the European Parliament.

European Ombudsman: Prof. NIKIFOROS DIAMANDOUROS (Greece).

COURT OF JUSTICE OF THE EUROPEAN UNION

Address: Cour de justice de l'Union européenne, 2925 Luxembourg.

Telephone: 4303-1; **fax:** 4303-2600; **e-mail:** info@curia.europa.eu; **internet:** curia.europa.eu/jcms/jcms/Jo2_7024.

As the EU's judicial institution, the Court of Justice acts as a safeguard of EU legislation and has jurisdiction over cases concerning member states, EU institutions, undertakings or individuals. EU legislation has been technically known as European Union law since the entry into force in December 2009 of the Treaty of Lisbon, which invested the EU with legal personality; prior to that it was known as Community law. The Court ensures uniform interpretation and application of European Union law throughout the EU. The 27 Judges and the eight Advocates-General are each appointed for a term of six years, after which they may be reappointed for one or two further periods of three years. The role of the Advocates-General is—publicly and impartially—to deliver reasoned opinions on the cases brought before the Court. There is normally one Judge per member state, whose name is put forward by the Government of that member state. These proposed appointments are then subject to a vote in the Council of the European Union. For the sake of efficiency, when the Court holds a plenary session only 13 Judges—sitting as a 'Grand Chamber'—have to attend. The President of the Court, who has overall charge of the Court's work and presides at hearings and deliberations, is elected by the Judges from among their number for a renewable term of three years. The majority of cases are dealt with by one of the eight chambers, each of which consists of a President of Chamber and three or five Judges. The Court may sit in plenary session in cases of particular importance or when a member state or Union institution that is a party to the proceedings so requests. Judgments are reached by a majority vote and are signed by all Judges involved in the case, irrespective of how they voted. The Court has jurisdiction to award damages. It may review the legality of acts (other than recommendations or opinions) of the Council, the Commission or the European Central Bank, of acts adopted jointly by the European Parliament and the Council, and of Acts adopted by the Parliament and intended to produce legal effects vis-à-vis third parties. It is also competent to give judgment on actions by a member state, the Council or the Commission on grounds of lack of competence, of infringement of an essential procedural requirement, of infringement of a Treaty or of any legal rule relating to its application, or of misuse of power. The Court of Justice may hear appeals, on a point of law only, from the Court of First Instance.

The Court is empowered to hear certain other cases concerning the contractual and non-contractual liability of the Communities and disputes between member states in connection with the objects of the Treaties. It also gives preliminary rulings at the request of national courts on the interpretation of the Treaties, of Union legislation, and of the Brussels Convention on Jurisdiction and the Enforcement of Judgments in Civil and Commercial Matters.

President of the Court of Justice: VASSILIOS SKOURIS (Greece).

Registrar: ALFREDO CALOT ESCOBAR (Spain).

GENERAL COURT

Address: Cour de justice de l'Union européenne, 2925 Luxembourg.

Telephone: 4303-1; **fax:** 4303-2600; **internet:** curia.europa.eu/jcms/jcms/Jo2_7033.

The General Court was established, as the Court of First Instance of the European Communities, by the European Council by a decision of October 1988, and began operations in 1989. Its current name was adopted following the entry into force of the Treaty of Lisbon on 1 December 2009. In order to help the Court of Justice deal with the thousands of cases brought before it and to offer citizens better legal protection, the General Court (which, although independent, is attached to the Court of Justice) deals with cases brought by individuals, legal entities and member states against the actions of EU institutions. The decisions of the General Court may be subject to appeal to the Court of Justice, on issues of law, within two months. As with the Court of Justice, the composition of the General Court is based on 27 Judges (one from each member state, appointed for a renewable term of six years), one President (elected from among the 27 Judges for a renewable period of three years) and eight chambers. The General Court has no permanent Advocates-General.

Within the framework of the Treaty of Nice, which provided for the creation of additional judicial panels in specific areas, in November 2004 the Council decided to establish the Civil Service Tribunal in order to reduce the number of cases brought before the Tribunal of First Instance. The specialized tribunal, which had been fully constituted by December 2005, exercises jurisdiction in the first instance in disputes between the EU and its staff. Its decisions are subject to appeal on questions of law only to the General Court and, in exceptional cases, to review by the European Court of Justice. The Council appoints the tribunal's seven Judges for a period of six years, and the President is elected by the Judges from among their number for a period of three years. The Council is charged with ensuring that as many member states as possible are represented in the tribunal.

President of the General Court: MARC JAEGER (Luxembourg).

Registrar: EMMANUEL COULON (France).

President of the Civil Service Tribunal: SEAN VAN RAEPENBUSCH (Belgium).

EUROPEAN COURT OF AUDITORS

Address: 12 rue Alcide de Gasperi, 1615 Luxembourg.

Telephone: 4398-1; **fax:** 4393-42; **e-mail:** eca-info@eca.europa.eu; **internet:** www.eca.europa.eu.

The European Court of Auditors (ECA) was created by the Treaty of Brussels, which was signed on 22 July 1975, and commenced its duties in late 1977. It was given the status of an institution on a par with the Commission, the Council, the Court of Justice and the Parliament by the Treaty on European Union. It is the institution responsible for the external audit of the resources managed by the EU. It consists of 27 members (one from each member state) who are appointed for renewable six-year terms (under a qualified majority voting system) by the Council of the European Union, after consultation with the European Parliament (in practice, however, the Council simply endorses the candidates put forward by the member states). The members elect the President of the Court from among their number for a renewable term of three years.

The Court is organized and acts as a collegiate body. It adopts its decisions by a majority of its members. Each member, however, has a direct responsibility for the audit of certain sectors of Union activities.

The Court examines the accounts of all expenditure and revenue of the EU and of any body created by them in so far as the relevant constituent instrument does not preclude such examination. It examines whether all revenue has been received and all expenditure incurred in a lawful and regular manner and whether the financial management has been sound. The audit is based on records, and if necessary is performed directly in the institutions of the Union, in the member states and in other countries. In the member states the audit is carried out in co-operation with the national audit bodies. The Court of Auditors draws up an annual report after the close of each financial year. The Court provides the Parliament and the Council with a statement of assurance as to the reliability of the accounts, and the legality and regularity of the underlying transactions. It may also, at any time, submit observations on specific questions (usually in the form of special reports) and deliver opinions at the request of one of the institutions of the Union. It assists the European Parliament and the Council in exercising their powers of control over the implementation of the budget, in particular within the framework of the annual discharge procedure, and gives its prior opinion on financial regulations, on the methods and procedure whereby budgetary revenue is made available to the Commission, and on the formulation of rules concerning the responsibility of authorizing officers and accounting officers and concerning appropriate arrangements for inspection.

President: VÍTOR MANUEL SILVA CALDEIRA (Portugal).

Secretary-General: EDUARDO RUIZ GARCÍA (Spain).

EUROPEAN CENTRAL BANK

Address: Kaiserstr. 29, 60311 Frankfurt am Main, Germany; Postfach 160319, 60066 Frankfurt am Main, Germany.

Telephone: (69) 13440; **fax:** (69) 13446000; **e-mail:** info@ecb.europa.eu; **internet:** www.ecb.int/home/html/index.en.html.

The European Central Bank (ECB) was formally established on 1 June 1998, replacing the European Monetary Institute, which had been operational since January 1994. The Bank has the authority to issue the single currency, the euro, which replaced the European Currency Unit (ECU) on 1 January 1999, at the beginning of Stage III of Economic and Monetary Union (EMU), in accordance with the provisions of the Treaty on European Union (the Maastricht Treaty). One of the ECB's main tasks is to maintain price stability in the euro area (i.e. in those member states that have adopted the euro as their national currency). This is achieved primarily by controlling the money supply and by monitoring price trends. The Bank's leadership is provided by a six-member Executive Board, appointed by common agreement of the presidents or prime ministers of the 17 euro area countries for a non-renewable term of eight years (it should be noted that the Statute of the European System of Central Banks—ESCB—provides for a system of staggered appointments to the first Executive Board for members other than the President in order to ensure continuity). The Executive Board is responsible for the preparation of meetings of the Governing Council, the implementation of monetary policy in accordance with the guidelines and decisions laid down by the Governing Council and for the current business of the ECB. The ECB and the national central banks of all EU member states together comprise the ESCB. The Governing Council, which is the ECB's highest decision-making body and which consists of the six members of the Executive Board and the governors of the central banks of countries participating in EMU, meets twice a month. The prime mission of the Governing Council is to define the monetary policy of the euro area, and, in particular, to fix the interest rates at which the commercial banks can obtain money from the ECB. The General Council is the ECB's third decision-making body; it comprises the ECB's President, the Vice-President and the governors of the central banks of all EU member states.

President: MARIO DRAGHI (Italy).

Vice-President: VITOR MANUEL RIBEIRO CONSTÂNCIO (Portugal).

EUROPEAN INVESTMENT BANK

Address: 100 blvd Konrad Adenauer, 2950 Luxembourg.

Telephone: 4379-1; **fax:** 4377-04; **e-mail:** info@eib.org; **internet:** www.eib.org.

The European Investment Bank (EIB) is the EU's international financing institution, and was created in 1958 by the six founder member states of the European Economic Community. The shareholders are the member states of the EU, which have all subscribed to the bank's capital. The bulk of the EIB's resources comes from borrowings, principally public bond issues or private placements on capital markets inside and outside the Union.

The EIB's principal task, defined by the Treaty of Rome, is to work on a non-profit basis, making or guaranteeing loans for investment projects that contribute to the balanced and steady development of EU member states. Throughout the Bank's history, priority has been given to financing investment projects that further regional development within the Union. The EIB also finances projects that improve communications, protect and improve the environment, promote urban development, strengthen the competitive position of industry and encourage industrial integration within the Union, support the activities of small and medium-sized enterprises (SMEs), and help ensure the security of energy supplies. Following a recommendation of the Lisbon European Council in March 2000 for greater support for SMEs, the Board of Governors set up the EIB Group, consisting of the EIB and the European Investment Fund. The EIB also provides finance for developing countries in Africa, the Caribbean and the Pacific, under the terms of the Cotonou Agreement (see p. 527), the successor agreement to the Lomé Convention; for countries in the Mediterranean region, under a new Euro-Mediterranean investment facility established in 2002; and for accession countries in Central and Eastern Europe. Lending outside the EU is usually based on Union agreements, but exceptions have been made for specific projects in certain countries, such as Russia.

The Board of Governors of the EIB, which usually meets once a year, lays down general directives on credit policy, approves the annual report and accounts and decides on capital increases. The Board of Directors meets once a month, and has sole power to take decisions in respect of loans, guarantees and borrowings. The Bank's President presides over meetings of the Board of Directors. The day-to-day management of operations is the responsibility of the Management Committee, which is the EIB's collegiate executive body and recommends decisions to the Board of Directors. The Audit Committee, which reports to the Board of Governors regarding the management of operations and the maintenance of the Bank's accounts, is an independent body comprising three members who are appointed by the Board of Governors for a renewable three-year term.

Board of Governors: The Board of Governors comprises one minister (usually the minister with responsibility for finance or economic affairs) from each member state.

Chair.: JEAN-CLAUDE JUNCKER (Luxembourg).

Board of Directors: The Board of Directors consists of 28 directors, appointed for a renewable five-year term, with one director appointed by each member state and one by the European Commission. There are 16 alternates, also appointed for a renewable five-year term, meaning that some of these positions will be shared by groupings of countries. Since 1 May 2004 decisions have been taken by a majority consisting of at least one-third of members entitled to vote and representing at least 50% of the subscribed capital.

Management Committee: Comprises the President and seven Vice-Presidents, nominated for a renewable six-year term by the Board of Directors and approved by the Board of Governors. The President presides over the meetings of the Management Committee but does not vote.

President: WERNER HOYER (Germany).

Audit Committee: The Audit Committee is composed of three members and three observers, appointed by the Governors for a term of office of three years.

Chair.: ERIC MATHAY (Belgium).

EUROPEAN INVESTMENT FUND

Address: 96 blvd Konrad Adenauer, 2968 Luxembourg.

Telephone: 2485-1; **fax:** 2485-81301; **e-mail:** info@eif.org; **internet:** www.eif.org.

The European Investment Fund was founded in 1994 as a specialized financial institution to support the growth of small and medium-sized enterprises (SMEs). Its operations are focused on the provision of venture capital, through investment in funds that support SMEs, and on guarantee activities to facilitate access to finance for SMEs. In all its activities the Fund aims to maintain a commercial approach to investment, and to apply risk-sharing principles. The Fund manages the SME Guarantee Facility. The Joint European Resources for Micro to Medium Enterprises (JEREMIE) initiative, which was launched in May 2006, enables EU member countries and regions to use part of their allocation of structural funds to obtain financing that is specifically targeted to support SMEs. The European Investment Fund is operational in the member states of the EU and in accession countries.

Chief Executive: RICHARD PELLY (United Kingdom).

EUROPEAN ECONOMIC AND SOCIAL COMMITTEE

Address: 99 rue Belliard, 1040 Brussels.

Telephone: (2) 546-90-11; **fax:** (2) 513-48-93; **e-mail:** info@eesc.europa.eu; **internet:** www.eesc.europa.eu.

The Committee was set up by the 1957 Rome Treaties. It is advisory and is consulted by the Council of the European Union or by the European Commission, particularly with regard to agriculture, free movement of workers, harmonization of laws and transport, as well as legislation adopted under the Euratom Treaty. In certain cases consultation of the Committee by the Commission or the Council is mandatory. In addition, the Committee has the power to deliver opinions on its own initiative.

The Committee has a tripartite structure with members belonging to one of three groupings: the Employers' Group; the Workers' Group; and the Various Interests' Group, which includes representatives of social, occupational, economic and cultural organizations. The Committee is appointed for a renewable term of four years by the unanimous vote of the Council of the European Union. The 344 members are nominated by national governments, but are appointed in their personal capacity and are not bound by any mandatory instructions. Germany, France, Italy and the United Kingdom have 24 members each, Spain and Poland have 21, Romania 15, Belgium, Bulgaria, Greece, the Netherlands, Portugal, Austria, Sweden, the Czech Republic and Hungary 12, Denmark, Ireland, Finland, Lithuania and Slovakia nine, Estonia, Latvia and Slovenia seven, Luxembourg and Cyprus six, and Malta five. The Committee is served by a permanent and independent General Secretariat, headed by the Secretary-General.

President: STAFFAN NILSSON (Italy) (Various Interests' Group).

Secretary-General: MARTIN WESTLAKE (United Kingdom).

COMMITTEE OF THE REGIONS—COR

Address: 99–101 rue Belliard, 1040 Brussels.

Telephone: (2) 282-22-11; **fax:** (2) 282-23-25; **e-mail:** info@cor.europa.eu; **internet:** www.cor.europa.eu.

The Treaty on European Union provided for a committee to be established, with advisory status, comprising representatives of regional and local bodies throughout the EU. The first meeting of the CoR was held in March 1994. It may be consulted on EU proposals concerning economic and social cohesion, trans-European networks, public health, education and culture, and may issue an opinion on any issue with regional implications. The CoR meets in plenary session five times a year.

The entry into force of the Lisbon Treaty, in December 2009, empowered the CoR, on the basis of a simple majority vote, to challenge at the European Court of Justice any new EU legislation—relating to the policy areas where the Committee may be consulted—that is deemed to infringe the principle of 'subsidiarity', i.e. that decisions should be taken as closely as possible to the citizens.

The number of members of the CoR is equal to that of the European Economic and Social Committee. Members are appointed for a renewable term of four years by the Council, acting unanimously on the proposals from the respective member states. The Committee elects its principal officers from among its members for a two-year term.

President: MERCEDES BRESSO (Italy).

First Vice-President: RAMÓN LUIS VALCÁRCEL SISO (Spain).

AGENCIES

Agency for the Co-operation of Energy Regulators—ACER
1000 Ljubljana, Trg republike 3, Slovenia; tel. 082-053400; e-mail info@acer.europa.eu; internet www.acer.europa.eu; f. 2011; ACER aims to facilitate cross-border energy trade, to co-ordinate the activities of national energy regulators and to help to prevent conflict between them, in order to encourage competition and to ensure fair prices for both consumers and businesses. The agency's opening coincided with the entry into force of the EU's third energy package on the internal market.

President: ALBERTO POTOTSCHNIG (Italy).

Body of European Regulators for Electronic Communications—BEREC

2nd Floor, Z. A. Meierovica Bulv. 14, Riga 1050, Latvia; tel. 6611-7590; e-mail berec@berec.europa.eu; internet erg.eu.int/Default.htm.

Established by a regulation of the European Parliament in Nov. 2009, replacing the European Regulators Group (ERG).

Administrative Manager: ANDO REHEMAA (Estonia).

Community Plant Variety Office—CPVO

POB 10121, 49101 Angers Cédex 2, France; 3 blvd Maréchal Foch, 49000 Angers, France; tel. 2-41-25-64-00; fax 2-41-25-64-10; e-mail cpvo@cpvo.europa.eu; internet www.cpvo.europa.eu.

Began operations in April 1995, with responsibility for granting intellectual property rights for plant varieties. Supervised by an Administrative Council, and managed by a President, appointed by the Council of the European Union. A Board of Appeal has been established to consider appeals against certain technical decisions taken by the Office. Publishes an annual report listing valid Community plant variety rights, their owners and their expiry dates.

President: BART P. KIEWIET (Netherlands).

Euratom Supply Agency

Euroforum Bldg, 10 rue Robert Stumper, 2920 Luxembourg; tel. 4301-36738; fax 4301-38139; internet ec.europa.eu/euratom/index.html.

The Euratom Supply Agency commenced operations in 1960, having been established by the Euuratom Treaty to ensure the regular and equitable supply of nuclear energy throughout EU member states.

Director: STAMATIOS TSALAS (Belgium).

European Agency for the Management of Operational Co-operation at the External Borders—FRONTEX

Rondo ONZ 1, 00-124 Warsaw, Poland; tel. (22) 5449500; fax (22) 5449501; e-mail frontex@frontex.europa.eu; internet www.frontex.europa.eu.

Established by a regulation of the European Parliament in October 2004, the Agency's primary responsibility is the creation of an integrated border management system, in order to ensure a high and uniform level of control and surveillance. The Agency began operations on 1 May 2005.

Executive Director: Col ILKKA PERTTI JUHANI LAITINEN (Finland).

European Agency for Safety and Health at Work—EU-OSHA

Gran Vía 33, 48009 Bilbao, Spain; tel. (94) 4794360; fax (94) 4794383; e-mail information@osha.europa.eu; internet osha.europa.eu.

Began operations in 1996. Aims to encourage improvements in the working environment, and to make available all necessary technical, scientific and economic information for use in the field of health and safety at work. The Agency supports a network of Focal Points in the member states of the EU, in the member states of the European Free Trade Association (EFTA) and in the candidate states of the EU.

Director: Dr CHRISTA SEDLATSCHEK (Austria).

European Aviation Safety Agency—EASA

Postfach 101253, 50452 Köln, Germany; Ottoplatz 1, 50679 Köln, Germany; tel. (221) 89990000; fax (221) 89990999; e-mail info@easa.europa.eu; internet easa.europa.eu/home.php.

Established by a regulation of the European Parliament in July 2002; the mission of the agency is to establish and maintain a high, uniform level of civil aviation safety and environmental protection in Europe. The Agency commenced full operations in September 2003, and moved to its permanent seat, in Köln, Germany, in November 2004.

Executive Director: PATRICK GOUDOU (France).

European Centre for the Development of Vocational Training—Cedefop

POB 22427, 551 02 Thessaloníki, Greece; Evropis 123, 570 01 Thessaloníki, Greece; tel. (30) 2310490111; fax (30) 2310490049; e-mail info@cedefop.europa.eu; internet www.cedefop.europa.eu.

Established in 1975, Cedefop assists policy-makers and other officials in member states and partner organizations in issues relating to vocational training policies, and assists the European Commission in the development of these policies. Manages a European Training Village internet site (www.trainingvillage.gr/etv/default.asp).

Director: CHRISTIAN F. LETTMAYR (Austria) (acting).

European Centre for Disease Prevention and Control—ECDC

17183 Stockholm, Sweden; Tomtebodavägen 11A, Solna, Sweden; tel. (8) 586-01000; fax (8) 586-01001; e-mail info@ecdc.europa.eu; internet www.ecdc.europa.eu.

Founded in 2005 to strengthen European defences against infectious diseases. It works with national health protection bodies to develop disease surveillance and early warning systems across Europe.

Director: Dr MARC SPRENGER (Netherlands).

European Chemicals Agency—ECHA

Annankatu 18, Helsinki, Finland; POB 400, 00121 Helsinki, Finland; tel. (9) 686180; e-mail press@echa.europa.eu; internet echa.europa.eu.

The European Chemicals Agency (ECHA) was established by regulations of the European Parliament and the European Council in 2006, and became fully operational in June 2008. The objective of the ECHA is to supervise and undertake the technical, scientific and administrative aspects of the Registration, Evaluation, Authorization and Restriction of Chemicals (REACH) throughout the EU and in Iceland, Liechtenstein and Norway. It also supports and runs a national helpdesk, and disseminates information on chemicals to the public.

Executive Director: GEERT DANCET (Finland).

European Defence Agency—EDA

17–23 rue des Drapiers, 1050 Brussels, Belgium; tel. (2) 504-28-00; fax (2) 504-28-15; e-mail info@eda.europa.eu; internet www.eda.europa.eu.

Founded in July 2004 and became operational in 2005; aims to help member states to improve their defence capabilities for crisis management under the European Security and Defence Policy. The Steering Board is composed of the ministers responsible for defence of 26 member states (all states except Denmark).

Head of the Agency and Chairman of the Steering Board: Catherine Ashton (United Kingdom).

Chief Executive: Claude-France Arnould (France).

European Environment Agency—EEA

6 Kongens Nytorv, 1050 Copenhagen K, Denmark; tel. 33-36-71-00; fax 33-36-71-99; e-mail eea@eea.europa.eu; internet www.eea.europa.eu.

Became operational in 1994, having been approved in 1990, to gather and supply information to assist the drafting and implementation of EU policy on environmental protection and improvement. Iceland, Liechtenstein, Norway, Switzerland and Turkey are also members of the Agency. The Agency publishes frequent reports on the state of the environment and on environmental trends.

Executive Director: Prof. Jacqueline McGlade (United Kingdom).

European Fisheries Control Agency—CFCA

Edificio Odriozola, Avda García Barbón, 36201 Vigo, Spain; tel. (98) 6120610; e-mail efca@efca.europa.eu; internet cfca.europa.eu/pages/home/home.htm.

Established in April 2005 to improve compliance with regulations under the 2002 reform of the Common Fisheries Policy. The EFCA aims to ensure the effectiveness of enforcement by sharing EU and national methods of fisheries' control, monitoring resources and co-ordinating activities.

Executive Director: Pascal Savouret (France).

European Food Safety Authority—EFSA

Via Carlo Magno 1a, 43126 Parma, Italy; tel. (39-0521) 036111; fax (39-0521) 036110; e-mail info@efsa.europa.eu; internet www.efsa.europa.eu.

Established by a regulation of the European Parliament in February 2002 and began operations in May 2003; the primary responsibility of the Authority is to provide independent scientific advice on all matters with a direct or indirect impact on food safety. The Authority will carry out assessments of risks to the food chain and scientific assessment on any matter that may have a direct or indirect effect on the safety of the food supply, including matters relating to animal health, animal welfare and plant health. The Authority will also give scientific advice on genetically modified organisms (GMOs), and on nutrition in relation to European Union law.

Executive Director: Catherine Geslain-Lanéelle (France).

European Foundation for the Improvement of Living and Working Conditions—CCP

Wyattville Rd, Loughlinstown, Dublin 18, Ireland; tel. (1) 2043100; fax (1) 2826456; e-mail postmaster@eurofound.europa.eu; internet www.eurofound.europa.eu.

Established in 1975, the Foundation aims to provide information and advice on European living and working conditions, industrial relations, and the management of change to employers, policy-makers, governments and trade unions, by means of comparative data, research and analysis. In 2001 the Foundation established the European Monitoring Centre on Change (EMCC) to help disseminate information and ideas on the management and anticipation of change in industry and enterprise.

Director: Jorma Karppinen (Finland).

European GNSS Supervisory Authority—GSA

56 Rue de la Loi, 1049 Brussels, Belgium; tel. (2) 297-16-16; fax (2) 296-72-38; e-mail news@gsa.europa.eu; internet www.gsa.europa.eu.

The European GNSS Supervisory Authority (GSA) was established in July 2004, to oversee all public interests relating to European Global Navigation Satellite System (GNSS) programmes. On 1 January 2007 the GSA officially took over the tasks previously assigned to the Galileo Joint Undertaking (GJU), which had been established in May 2002 by the EU and the European Space Agency to manage the development phase of the Galileo programme. The strategic objectives of the GSA include the achievement of a fully operational Galileo system, capable of becoming the world's leading civilian satellite navigation system, and Europe's only GNSS.

Executive Director: Carlo des Dorides (Italy).

European Institute for Gender Equality

Švitrigailos g. 11m, Vilnius, Lithuania; tel. (5) 239-4140; internet eige.europa.eu.

The European Institute for Gender Equality was established in May 2007, initially in Brussels, Belgium, to help EU member states and institutions to promote gender equality, combat gender discrimination and disseminate information on gender issues. The institute collects and interprets relevant data, to develop methodologies and tools to help integrate gender across all policy areas, to facilitate discussion and the adoption of best practices, and to raise awareness of gender issues. The institute comprises a management board, which is the decision-making body, together with a consultative experts' forum. The budget for 2007–13 is €52.5m.

Director: Virginija Langbakk (Sweden).

European Institute of Innovation and Technology

Infopark 1/E, 1117 Budapest, Neumann Janos ut., Hungary; tel. (1) 481-93-00.

The Agency was established in 2008 with the aim of increasing sustainable growth and competitiveness in Europe by reinforcing the EU's innovation capacity.

Director: José Manuel Leceta (Spain).

European Joint Undertaking for ITER and the Development of Fusion Energy—Fusion for Energy

2 Josep Pla, Torres Diagonal Litoral, Edificio B3, 08019 Barcelona, Spain; tel. (93) 320-18-00; fax (93) 489-75-37; e-mail info@f4e.europa.eu; internet fusionforenergy.europa.eu.

The Agency was established in 2007, as a Joint Undertaking under the European Atomic Energy Community (Euratom) Treaty, by a decision of the Council of the European Union (see Energy). Its members comprise the EU member states, Euratom and Switzerland.

Director: Frank Briscoe (United Kingdom).

European Judicial Co-operation Unit—EUROJUST

Maanweg 174, 2516 The Hague, the Netherlands; tel. (70) 4125000; fax (70) 4125005; e-mail info@eurojust.europa.eu; internet www.eurojust.europa.eu.

Established in 2002 to improve co-operation and co-ordination between member states in the investigation and prosecution of serious cross-border and organized crime. The EUROJUST College is composed of one member (a senior prosecutor or judge) nominated by each member state.

President of the College: Aled Williams (United Kingdom).

Administrative Director: Klaus Rackwitz (Germany).

European Maritime Safety Agency—EMSA

Cais do Sodré, 1249-206 Lisbon, Portugal; tel. (21) 1209200; fax (21) 1209210; e-mail information@emsa.europa.eu; internet www.emsa.europa.eu.

Established by a regulation of the European Parliament in June 2002; the primary responsibility of the Agency is to provide technical and scientific advice to the Commission in the field of maritime safety and prevention of pollution by ships, and, from April 2012, oil and gas rigs. The Agency held its inaugural meeting in December 2002, and in December 2003 it was decided that the permanent seat of the Agency would be Lisbon, Portugal. Norway and Iceland are also members of EMSA.

Executive Director: Markku Mylly (Finland).

European Medicines Agency—EMA

7 Westferry Circus, Canary Wharf, London, E14 4HB, United Kingdom; tel. (20) 7418-8400; fax (20) 7418-8416; e-mail infol@ema.europa.eu; internet www.ema.europa.eu.

Established in 1995 for the evaluation, authorization and supervision of medicinal products for human and veterinary use.

Executive Director: Guido Rasi (Sweden).

European Monitoring Centre for Drugs and Drug Addiction—EMCDDA

Cais do Sodré, 1249-289 Lisbon, Portugal; tel. (21) 1210200; fax (21) 8131711; e-mail info@emcdda.europa.eu; internet www.emcdda.europa.eu.

Founded in 1993 and became fully operational at the end of 1995, with the aim of providing member states with objective, reliable and comparable information on drugs and drug addiction in order to assist in combating the problem. The Centre co-operates with other European and international organizations and non-EU countries. The Centre publishes an *Annual Report on the State of the Drugs Problem in Europe*. A newsletter, *Drugnet Europe*, is published quarterly.

Executive Director: WOLFGANG GÖTZ (Germany).

European Network and Information Security Agency—ENISA

POB 1309, 710 01 Heraklion, Crete, Greece; Science and Technology Park of Crete, Vassilika Vouton, 700 13 Heraklion, Crete, Greece; tel. (2810) 391280; fax (2810) 391410; e-mail info@enisa.europa.eu; internet www.enisa.europa.eu.

Established by a regulation of the European Parliament in March 2004; commenced operations in 2005. The primary responsibilities of the Agency are to promote closer European co-ordination on the security of communications networks and information systems and to provide assistance in the application of EU measures in this field. The agency publishes a quarterly magazine.

Executive Director: Dr UDO HELMBRECHT (Germany).

European Police College—CEPOL

CEPOL House, Bramshill, Hook, Hampshire, RG27 0JW, United Kingdom; tel. (1256) 60-26-68; fax (1256) 60-29-96; e-mail secretariat@cepol.europa.eu; internet www.cepol.europa.eu.

Founded in 2005 to help create a network of senior police officers throughout Europe, to encourage cross-border co-operation in combating crime, and to improve public security and law and order through the organization of training activities and research.

Director: Dr FERENC BÁNFI (Hungary).

European Police Office—EUROPOL

POB 90850, 2509 The Hague, the Netherlands; Raamweg 47, The Hague, the Netherlands; tel. (70) 3025000; fax (70) 3025896; e-mail info@europol.europa.eu; internet www.europol.europa.eu.

Established in 1992, EUROPOL is a law enforcement organization that aims to aid EU member states to combat organized crime, by handling criminal intelligence throughout Europe and promoting co-operation between the law enforcement bodies of member countries; became a full EU agency, with an enhanced mandate for combating international crime, in Jan. 2010.

Director: ROB WAINWRIGHT (United Kingdom).

European Railway Agency—ERA

120 rue Marc Lefrancq, 59300 Valenciennes, France; tel. 3-27-09-65-00; fax 3-27-33-40-65; e-mail press-info@era.europa.eu; internet www.era.europa.eu.

Established by a regulation of the European Parliament in April 2004; the primary responsibility of the Agency is to reinforce the safety and interoperability of railways in the EU.

Executive Director: MARCEL VERSLYPE (Belgium).

European Training Foundation—ETF

Villa Gualino, Viale Settimio Severo 65, 10133 Turin, Italy; tel. (011) 630-22-22; fax (011) 630-22-00; e-mail info@etf.europa.eu; internet www.etf.europa.eu.

The Foundation, which was established in 1990 and became operational in 1994, provides policy advice to the European Commission and to the EU's partner countries, to support vocational education and training reform. The ETF works in the countries surrounding the EU, which are involved either in the European Neighbourhood Partnership Instrument, or in the enlargement process under the Instrument for Pre-accession Assistance. The ETF also works in a number of other countries from Central Asia. The ETF also gives technical assistance to the European Commission for the implementation of the Trans-European Mobility Programme for University Studies (TEMPUS), which focuses on the reform of higher education systems in partner countries.

Director: MADLEN SERBAN (Romania).

European Union Agency for Fundamental Rights—FRA

Schwarzenbergplatz 11, 1040 Vienna, Austria; tel. (1) 580300; fax (1) 58030699; e-mail information@fra.europa.eu; internet fra.europa.eu.

Founded in March 2007, replacing the European Monitoring Centre on Racism and Xenophobia (EUMC). The Agency aims to provide assistance to EU member states on fundamental rights matters during the application of EU law. The FRA continues the work of the EUMC on racism, xenophobia, anti-Semitism and related intolerance, and utilizes its experience of data collection methods and co-operation with governments and international organizations. In addition, the FRA gives significant emphasis to increasing public awareness of rights issues and to co-operation with civil society.

Director: MORTEN KJAERUM (Denmark).

European Union Institute for Security Studies—EUISS

100 ave de Suffren, 75015 Paris, France; tel. 1-56-89-19-30; fax 1-56-89-19-31; e-mail institute@iss.europa.eu; internet www.iss.europa.eu.

Established by a Council Joint Action in July 2001, and inaugurated in January 2002. The Institute aims to help implement and develop the EU's Common Foreign and Security Policy (CFSP), and carries out political analysis and forecasting. The Institute produces several publications: the Chaillot Papers, Occasional Papers and a quarterly Newsletter, as well as books containing in-depth studies of specialized topics.

Director: ÁLVARO DE VASCONCELOS (Portugal).

European Union Satellite Centre—EUSC

Apdo de Correos 511, Torréjon de Ardoz, 28850 Madrid, Spain; tel. (91) 6786000; fax (91) 6786006; e-mail info@eusc.europa.eu; internet www.eusc.europa.eu.

Established by a Council Joint Action in July 2001 and operational from 1 January 2002. The Centre is dedicated to providing material derived from the analysis of satellite imagery in support of the Common Foreign and Security Policy.

Director: TOMAŽ LOVRENČIČ (Slovenia).

Office for Harmonization in the Internal Market (Trade Marks and Designs)—OHIM

Apdo. de Correos 77, 03080 Alicante, Spain; Avda de Europa 4, 03008 Alicante, Spain; tel. (96) 5139100; fax (96) 5131344; e-mail information@oami.europa.eu; internet www.oami.europa.eu.

Established in 1993 to promote and control trade marks and designs throughout the EU.

President: ANTÓNIO CAMPINOS (Portugal).

Translation Centre for the Bodies of the European Union—CdT

Bâtiment Nouvel Hémicycle, 1 rue du Fort Thüngen, 1499 Luxembourg; tel. 4217-11-1; fax 4217-11-220; e-mail cdt@cdt.europa.eu; internet www.cdt.europa.eu.

Established in 1994 to meet the translation needs of other decentralized Union agencies.

Director: GAILĖ DAGILIENĖ (Lithuania).

Activities of the Community

STRATEGIC FRAMEWORK

Meeting in March 2000, the European Council launched the Lisbon Strategy, which was elaborated at subsequent meetings of the Council and rested on three pillars: an economic pillar preparing for a transition to a competitive, knowledge-based economy, with a focus on research and development; a social pillar that covered investment in human resources and combating social exclusion, with a focus on education, training and employment policy; and an environmental pillar, focused on disconnecting economic growth from the depletion of natural resources.

On 17 June 2010 the Council adopted the Europe 2020 strategic policy framework, the successor to the Lisbon Strategy, which seeks to consolidate the Lisbon Strategy's achievements with respect to economic growth and the creation of jobs. EU-wide targets were agreed in five policy areas. By 2020 at least 75% of those aged between 20 and 64 years are to be in employment; 3% of the EU's total gross domestic product (GDP) is to be invested in research and innovation; greenhouse gas emissions are to be reduced by at least 20%, compared with levels in 1990, with 20% of energy produced to be renewable, and with energy efficiency to be increased by 20%; at least 40% of those aged 30–34 years are to have completed higher education, and 10% more children are to complete their schooling; and there are to be at least 20m. fewer people living in, or threatened by, poverty and social exclusion.

AGRICULTURE

Agriculture (including rural development) is by far the largest single item on the EU budget, accounting for 42% of annual expenditure in 2010, although this represented a significant reduction compared with 1984, when agriculture accounted for 70% of expenditure.

Co-operation in the EU has traditionally been at its most highly organized in the area of agriculture. The Common Agricultural Policy (CAP), which took effect from 1962, was originally devised to ensure food self-sufficiency for Europe following the food shortages of the post-war period and to ensure a fair standard of living for the agricultural community. Its objectives are described in the Treaty of Rome. The markets for agricultural products have been progressively organized following three basic principles: unity of the market (products must be able to circulate freely within the Union and markets must be organized according to common rules); EU preference (products must be protected from low-cost imports and from fluctuations on the world market); and common financial responsibility: the European Agricultural Guarantee Fund (which replaced the European Agricultural Guidance and Guarantee Fund in 2007) finances the export of agricultural products to third countries, intervention measures to regulate agricultural markets, and direct payments to farmers.

Agricultural prices are, in theory, fixed each year at a common level for the EU as a whole, taking into account the rate of inflation and the need to discourage surplus production of certain commodities. Export subsidies are paid to enable farmers to sell produce at the lower world market prices without loss. When market prices of certain cereals, sugar, some fruits and vegetables, dairy produce and meat fall below a designated level, the Community intervenes, and buys a quantity, which is then stored until prices recover.

Serious reform of the CAP began in 1992, following strong criticism of the EC's agricultural and export subsidies during the Uruguay Round of negotiations on the General Agreement on Tariffs and Trade (GATT, see World Trade Organization—WTO) in 1990. In May 1992 ministers adopted a number of reforms, which aimed to transfer the Community's agricultural support from upholding prices to maintaining farmers' incomes, thereby removing the incentive to over-produce. Intervention prices were reduced, and farmers were compensated by receiving additional grants, which, in the case of crops, took the form of a subsidy per hectare of land planted. To qualify for these subsidies, arable farmers (except for those with the smallest farms) were obliged to remove 15% of their land from cultivation (the 'set-aside' scheme). Incentives were given for alternative uses of the withdrawn land (e.g. forestry).

In March 1999, at the Berlin European Council, the EU Heads of Government concluded an agreement on a programme, Agenda 2000, which aimed to reinforce Community policies and to restructure the financial framework of the EU with a view to enlargement. In terms of agriculture, it was decided to continue the process of agricultural reform begun in 1992 with particular emphasis on environmental concerns, safeguarding a fair income for farmers, streamlining legislation and decentralizing its application. A further element of reform was the increased emphasis on rural development, which was described as the 'second pillar' of the CAP in Agenda 2000. The objective was to restore and increase the competitiveness of rural areas, through supporting employment, diversification and population growth. In addition, producers were to be rewarded for the preservation of rural heritage. Forestry was recognized as an integral part of rural development (previous treaties of the EU had made no provision for a comprehensive common forestry policy).

The accession of 10 new states to the EU in May 2004 had major implications for the CAP, in that the enlargement doubled the EU's arable land area and its farming population. In October 2002 it was agreed that the enlargement process would be part-funded by a deal to maintain farm subsidies at 2006 levels until 2013, with a 1% annual correction for inflation, and that the new members would be offered direct farm payments at 25% of the level paid to existing member states, rising in stages to 100% over 10 years.

In July 2002 the Commissioner responsible for Agriculture, Rural Development and Fisheries proposed directing more funds towards the rural development policy and severing the link between direct payments to farmers and production (a policy styled 'decoupling'). The reforms suggested were, however, vigorously opposed by the main beneficiaries of the existing system, notably France. A revised plan was submitted, which restored the link between subsidies and production for certain products while still adhering to the principle of decoupling.

The compromise deal for CAP reform was agreed in June 2003, and the agreement was ratified by the Council of the European Union and the accession states in September. Production-linked subsidies were to be replaced by a Single Farm Payment, subsidies previously received, rather than tied to current production levels, and was also to be linked to environmental, food safety and animal welfare standards. Obligatory decoupling was only partial for beef, cereal and mutton, with production still accounting for as much as 25% of payments for cereals and as much as 40% for beef. Overall, however, 90% of payments would no longer be linked to production. The agreement contained a commitment to reduce all payments above €5,000 a year by 3% in 2005, by 4% in 2006 and by 5% in 2007. Increased resources were to be directed towards rural development projects, protecting the environment and improvements to food quality; organic farmers and those offering high-quality produce with special guarantees were to receive grants of up to €3,000 a year for five years. Under the principle of 'modulation', an increasing percentage of direct farm subsidies was to be retained by individual member states to finance rural development measures. The equivalent of at least 80% of the funds gathered in each member state (90% in Germany) was to be spent in that country. Implementation of the CAP reforms agreed in June 2003 commenced on 1 January 2005.

Meanwhile, in April 2004 the EU Council of Ministers of Agriculture reached agreement for CAP reform of the olive oil, cotton, hops and tobacco sectors. The principle of decoupling aid from production was to be extended to these commodities. A significant share of the existing production-linked payments was to be transferred to the Single Farm Payment (which was provided independently of production), although production-linked subsidies were permitted of up to 60% for tobacco, 40% for olive oil, 35% for cotton and 25% for hops. Moreover, full decoupling in the tobacco sector was to be introduced progressively over the four years to 2010 and rural development aid was to finance conversion to other crops in tobacco-producing areas. The remaining production aid for olive oil was to be directed at maintaining olive groves with environmental or social value. In September 2006 the European Court of Justice annulled the CAP provisions on cotton, proposing a slightly revised reform of the support scheme in November 2007. The new proposal maintained the support arrangements agreed in 2004 (i.e. production-linked subsidies of up to 35%), but provided for additional funding for support measures in cotton-producing regions and the creation of a 'label of origin' to enhance the promotion of EU cotton.

The EU finally agreed on reforms to the sugar industry in November 2005, following a WTO ruling earlier in the year (after an action brought by Brazil, Australia and Thailand) that the current level of subsidy breached legal limits. In 2005 the EU sugar sector was still characterized by large subsidies, high internal prices, and imports by African, Caribbean and Pacific (ACP) countries on favourable terms under quotas. The EU produced large surpluses of sugar, which were disposed of on the world market to the detriment of more competitive producers, notably developing countries. The reforms, which were implemented from July 2006, included the gradual reduction of the internal EU market price (which was three times the international price for the commodity in 2005) by 36% by 2009, and direct aid payments of €6,300m. over the four years of the phased introduction of the reforms to EU sugar producers as compensation. A fundamental element in the reform of the EU sugar sector was the establishment of a restructuring fund, financed by sugar producers, to ease the transition to greater competitiveness. The objective was to remove a total of some 6m. metric tons of sugar quota during the four-year reform period. Amendments to the sugar-restructuring scheme were adopted in October 2007 in an attempt to encourage greater participation, and, by the conclusion of the reform period, in early 2009, some 5.8m. metric tons of sugar quota had been renounced.

At the Doha Round of the WTO in Hong Kong in December 2005, agreement was reached on the elimination of export subsidies on farm goods by the end of 2013. This represented a concession by the EU but was three years later than the date sought by the USA and developing countries.

A new regulation laying down specific rules concerning the fruit and vegetables sector was adopted in September 2007 and entered into force in January 2008. Notable reforms included: the integration of the sector into the Single Farm Payment scheme; the requirement that producer organizations allocate at least 10% of their annual expenditure to environmental concerns; an increase in EU funding for the promotion of fruit and vegetable consumption and for organic production; and the abolition of export subsidies for fruit and vegetables. In April ministers of agriculture adopted a new regulation on the reform of the wine sector. The regulation provided, *inter alia*, for the inclusion of the sector in the Single Farm Payment scheme, while distillation subsidies were to be gradually withdrawn by 2012, releasing funds for measures such as wine promotion in third countries and the modernization of vineyards and cellars. In addition, the regulation provided for the introduction of a voluntary, three-year scheme, under which wine producers were to receive subsidies over a three-year period, with the aim of removing surplus and uncompetitive wine from the market.

In May 2008 the European Commission proposed a number of regulations to reform and simplify the CAP further in 2009–13, including additional reductions in production-linked payments and increased funding for rural development. In November 2008 the European Council reached agreement on the proposed reforms, which: raised the rate of decoupling in those countries that maintained the link between subsidy and production; provided for reform of the dairy sector; abolished the set-aside scheme from 2009; and provided for payments to farms qualifying for subsidies of at least €5,000 a year to be reduced gradually, so that by 2012 10% of funds (compared with the existing 5%) would be transferred to the rural development budget (large-scale farms would be required to transfer a greater proportion of funds). Milk quotas were to be increased by 1% per year in 2009–13, before their eventual expiry in 2015.

As a result of severe decline in dairy prices from 2008, in June 2009 the Commissioner for Agriculture and Rural Development established a High Level Experts' Group on Milk (HLG), comprising representatives of the 27 EU member states, and chaired by the Director-General for Agriculture and Rural Development. The HLG sought to identify medium- and long-term measures for stabilizing the market and incomes, and increasing transparency, given the expiry of milk quotas from 1 April 2015. The HLG held 10 meetings between October 2009 and June 2010, and identified significant problems in the supply chain. In late September 2010 its proposals for addressing the problems were endorsed by the Council's Presidency. These required endorsement by the Council of Agriculture Ministers and the European Parliament, and were expected to enter into effect in 2012.

In mid-November 2010 the European Commission launched the consultation process on further reform of the CAP with the adoption of a communication entitled 'The CAP towards 2020: meeting the food, natural resources and territorial challenges of the future', based on the results of public debate on the issue of CAP reform, which were summarized at a conference held in Brussels, Belgium, in July 2010. In mid-October 2011 the Commission announced a set of legislative proposals aimed at simplifying the CAP from 2014, while ensuring greater transparency, and the long-term sustainability, competitiveness and diversity of the agricultural sector. Income support was to be available only to economically active farmers, and was to be subject to a fixed maximum rate, and distributed more evenly. Improved tools for managing economic crises were to be introduced, to reduce the impact of volatility in the prices of raw agricultural materials; the Commission proposed the introduction of 'safety nets' (specifically intervention and storage arrangements), and the establishment of insurance and mutual funds. There were also plans to introduce a 'green' component to reward environmental competitiveness by directing up to 30% of the value of direct payments towards encouraging better use of natural resources. The budget for agricultural research and innovation was to be increased two-fold, supported by the creation of a new European Innovation Partnership. The Commission proposed increasing support for producer organizations, developing inter-professional organizations, and encouraging direct sales by producers to customers. Sugar quotas were to be removed by the end of 2015. Two targeted Rural Development policy objectives were to seek to develop, maintain and improve ecosystems; and help maximize the efficiency of resources and combat climate change. Farmers under 40 years of age were to receive inducements to enter the sector (some 65% of farmers were aged at least 55 years). The administration of the CAP was also to be simplified.

Food safety is a significant issue in the EU, especially since the first case of bovine spongiform encephalopathy (BSE), a transmissible disease that causes the brain tissue to degenerate, was diagnosed in cattle in the United Kingdom in 1986. The use of meat and bone meal (MBM) in animal feed was identified as possibly responsible for the emergence of the disease, and was banned for use in cattle feed in the United Kingdom in 1988. MBM was banned throughout the EU from 1994 for ruminants and in December 2000 for all animals. The possible link between BSE and new variant Creutzfeldt-Jakob disease (vCJD), a degenerative brain disease that affects humans, led to a collapse in consumer confidence in the European beef market in 1996. By January 2011 176 people were believed to have contracted vCJD in the United Kingdom, the location of the vast majority of cases.

In July 1997 ministers of agriculture voted to introduce a complete ban on the use for any purpose of 'specified risk materials' (SRMs—i.e. those parts and organs most likely to carry the BSE prion disease agent) from cattle, sheep and goats. The ban was implemented in January 1999. The scope of legislation on undesirable substances in animal feed was extended in May 2002, to cover additives. In May 2001 new legislation was adopted by the European Parliament and the Agriculture Council that consolidated much of the existing legislation on BSE and other transmissible spongiform encephalopathies (TSEs) in bovine, ovine and caprine animals. The new TSE Regulation, which replaced previous emergency legislation and clarified the rules for the prevention, control and eradication of TSEs, came into force on 1 July 2001. Every year the Commission approves programmes aimed at monitoring, controlling and eradicating animal diseases, with a special focus on zoonoses, which are transmissible from animal carriers to humans.

The EU's Food and Veterinary Office was established in April 1997 to ensure that the laws on food safety, animal health and welfare, and plant health are applied in all member states. The office carries out audits and checks on food safety in member states and in third countries exporting agricultural produce to the EU. Legislation establishing the European Food Safety Authority (EFSA) was signed in January 2002; the new body was to provide independent scientific advice and support on matters with a direct or indirect impact on food safety. It was to have no regulatory or judicial power, but would co-operate closely with similar bodies in the member states. The first meeting of the EFSA management board took place in September, and its Advisory Forum was convened for the first time in March 2003. In September 2007 the European Commission adopted a communication setting out the EU's animal health strategy for 2007–13. The aims of the new strategy were: to ensure a high level of public health and food safety by reducing the risks posed to humans by problems with animal health; to promote animal health by preventing or reducing the incidence of animal diseases, thus also protecting farming and the rural economy; to improve economic growth, cohesion and competitiveness in animal-related sectors; and to promote farming and animal welfare practices that prevent threats to animal health and minimize the environmental impact of raising animals. In January 2012 the European Commission adopted a new animal health strategy for 2012–15, the objective of which is to improve animal welfare throughout the EU, by adopting new, comprehensive legislation on animal welfare, while strengthening existing actions.

In June 1995 the Agriculture Council agreed to new rules on the welfare of livestock during transport. The agreement, which came into effect in 1996, limited transport of livestock to a maximum of eight hours in any 24-hour period, and stipulated higher standards for their accommodation and care while in transit. In January 1996 the Commission proposed a ban on veal crates, which came into effect from January 1998. In April 2001 the Commission adopted new rules for long-distance animal transport, setting out the required standards of ventilation, temperature and humidity control. A new regulation aimed at further enhancing the welfare of animals during transport was adopted in December 2004. To ensure improved enforcement of the rules, a satellite navigation system was to be introduced from January 2007 to track vehicles carrying livestock. In June 1999 EU agriculture ministers agreed to end battery egg production within the EU by 2012; in December 2000 a regulation was adopted requiring EU producers to indicate the rearing method on eggs and egg-packaging. A new directive laying out minimum standards for the protection of pigs, including provisions banning the use of individual stalls for pregnant sows and gilts, increasing their living space, and allowing them to have permanent access to materials for rooting, was applicable from January 2003 to holdings newly built or rebuilt and from January 2013 to all holdings. A similar directive was adopted in June 2007 for the protection of chickens kept for meat production, laying out minimum standards in areas such as stocking density, lighting, litter and ventilation; it was to be implemented by member states within three years. Following 13 years of negotiations, in November 2002 agreement was finally reached between the European Parliament and the member states to ban the sale, import and export of virtually all cosmetic products tested after 11 March 2009 on animals in the EU, and to halt from 11 March 2013 all animal testing for cosmetics. Accordingly, on 11 March 2009 testing on animals was outlawed in seven mandatory tests of toxicity following a single application (namely tests for absorption through the skin, skin irritancy, sensitivity to light, eye irritancy, corrosivity, genetic toxicity and acute toxicity), with eight further tests, designed to establish longer-term toxicity following multiple applications (e.g. tendency to cause cancer or birth defects), to be banned by the 2013 deadline. In October 2009 the European Commission adopted a report (compiled with a view to facilitating political debate with other institutions) that outlined options for labelling products with the objective of enabling consumers to identify good animal welfare practices and to provide an economic incentive to producers to make advances in the area of animal welfare. The report considered the possible future establishment of an animal welfare-orientated European Network of Reference Centres to provide technical support for the development and implementation of animal welfare policies, including in the areas of certification and labelling.

The EU has adopted a number of protective measures to prevent the introduction of organisms harmful to plants and plant products. Regulations governing the deliberate release of genetically modified organisms (GMOs) into the environment have been in force since October 1991, with an approval process based on a case-by-case analysis of the risks to human health and the environment. A total of 18 GMOs were authorized for use in the EU under this directive. An updated directive took effect in October 2002, which introduced principles for risk assessment, long-term monitoring requirements and full labelling and traceability obligations for food and feed containing more than 0.9% GM ingredients. A further regulation adopted by the Commission in January 2004 specified a system to identify and trace each GMO product used in the production of all food and animal feeds, completing the EU's regulatory framework on the authorization, labelling and traceability of GMOs. All of the accession states had adopted EU regulations on GM products by 2004, despite fears raised by environmental groups that inadequate testing facilities would prevent the implementation of effective labelling procedures. By June 2009 15 EU member states had adopted specific legislation on the co-existence of GMOs with conventional and organic crops. In March 2010 the European Commission announced that Amflora, a genetically modified potato, had been authorized for cultivation in the EU for industrial use.

In 2004 the Commission, with support from the Council, presented a European action plan for organic food and farming, comprising 21 measures, aimed at promoting the development of organic farming in the EU. The Council also adopted a regulation improving legal protection for organic farming methods and established a programme on the conservation, collection and utilization of genetic resources in agriculture. In 2005 the Commission adopted a proposal for new regulations defining objectives and principles for organic production, clarifying labelling rules and regulating imports. The new regulation on production and labelling was adopted in June 2007 and came into force on 1 January 2009. The new rules concerning imports of organic foods were approved in December 2006. From July 2010 all pre-packaged EU organic products were required to carry an EU organic food logo.

FISHERIES

The Common Fisheries Policy (CFP) came into effect in January 1983 after seven years of negotiations, particularly concerning the problem of access to fishing grounds. The CFP confirmed a 200-mile (370-km) zone around the regional coastline (excluding the Mediterranean) within which all members had access to fishing, and allowed exclusive national zones of six miles with access between six and 12 miles from the shore for other countries according to specified historic rights. Rules furthering conservation (e.g. standards for fishing tackle) were imposed under the policy, with checks by a Community fisheries inspectorate. A body of inspectors answerable to the Commission monitored compliance with the quotas and with technical measures in Community and some international waters.

In December 1992 EC ministers agreed to extend the CFP for a further 10-year period. Two years later ministers concluded a final agreement on the revised CFP, allowing Spain and Portugal to be integrated into the policy by 1 January 1996. A compromise accord was reached regarding access to waters around Ireland and off south-west Great Britain (referred to as the 'Irish box'), by means of which up to 40 Spanish vessels were granted access to 80,000 sq miles of the 90,000 sq mile area. However, the accord was strongly opposed by Irish and British fishermen. In October 1995 fisheries ministers agreed a regime to control fishing in the 'Irish box', introducing stricter controls and instituting new surveillance measures.

The organization of fish marketing involves common rules on size, weight, quality and packing and a system of guide prices established annually by the Council of the European Union. Fish are withdrawn from the market if prices fall too far below the guide price, and compensation may then be paid to the fishermen. Export subsidies are paid to enable the export of fish onto the lower-priced world market, and import levies are imposed to prevent competition from low-priced imports. A new import regime took effect from May 1993. This enabled regional fishermen's associations to increase prices to a maximum of 10% over the Community's reference price, although this applied to both EU and imported fish.

In June 1998 the Council of the European Union overcame long-standing objections from a number of member states and adopted a ban on the use of drift nets in the Atlantic Ocean and the Mediterranean Sea, in an attempt to prevent the unnecessary deaths of marine life such as dolphins and sharks. The ban, which was introduced in January 2002, partially implemented a 1992 UN resolution demanding a complete cessation of drift-net fishing. A series of compensatory measures aimed to rectify any short-term detrimental impact on EU fishing fleets. In March 2004 the Council approved a ban on the use of drift nets in the Baltic Sea, and, in April, it adopted a regulation stipulating the use of active acoustic deterrent devices on fishing nets throughout most EU waters to prevent dolphins and porpoises from becoming fatally entangled in the nets.

With concern over stocks continuing to mount (it was calculated in the early 2000s that cod stocks in the North Sea had fallen to one-10th of their level at 1970), in June 2002 the

Commission proposed to establish a procedure for setting total allowable catches (TACs) so as to achieve a significant increase in mature fish stocks, with limits on the fishing effort fixed in accordance with the TACs. The Commission also proposed the temporary closure of areas where endangered species had congregated, and more generous EU aid for the decommissioning of vessels (aid for the modernization of vessels, which tends to increase the fishing catch, was to be reduced). By 2002 the Commission had also been alerted to the critical depletion of deep-sea species, the commercialization of which had become increasingly attractive in the 1990s as other species became less abundant. For the first time, in December 2002, the Commission introduced catch limits for deep-water fish species, complemented by a system of deep-sea fishing permits. In 2004 the Commission extended the scope of the use of TACs to more fish stocks and introduced a number of closed areas for heavily depleted species.

Initially structural assistance actions for fisheries were financed by the European Agricultural Guidance and Guarantee Fund (which was replaced by the European Agricultural Guarantee Fund in 2007). Following the reform of funding programmes in 1993, a separate fund, the Financial Instrument for Fisheries Guidance (FIFG), was set up. The instrument's principal responsibilities included the decommissioning of vessels and the creation, with foreign investors, of joint ventures designed to reduce the fishing effort in EU waters. The fund also supported the building and modernizing of vessels, developments in the aquaculture sector, and the creation of protected coastal areas. From January 2007 the FIFG was replaced by the simplified European Fisheries Fund, covering the period 2007–13, which grants financial support to facilitate the implementation of the CFP (see below).

Radical reform of the CFP, aimed at ensuring the sustainable development of the industry, was announced during 2002. The Commission proposed a new multi-annual framework—which was to replace the existing Multi-Annual Guidance Programme—MAGP—for the efficient conservation of resources and the management of fisheries, incorporating environmental concerns. The new measures were introduced on 1 January 2003, replacing the basic rules that had governed the CFP since 1993, and substantially amending structural assistance in the fisheries sector under the FIFG. The new framework provided for a long-term approach to attaining and maintaining fish stocks, designed to encourage member states to achieve a better balance between the fishing capacity of their fleets and available resources. Under the terms of the new framework quotas for catches of cod, whiting and haddock were substantially reduced, fishermen were guaranteed only nine days a month at sea (with provision to extend this to 15 days in some circumstances), and public funding for the renewal or modernization of fishing boats was abolished after 2004 (with the exception of funding for the provision of aid to improve security and working conditions on board). In addition, measures were announced to develop co-operation among the various fisheries authorities and to strengthen the uniformity of control and sanctions throughout the EU. The Commission inspectors had their powers extended to ensure the equity and efficacy of the enforcement of EU regulations. In an attempt to compensate for the ongoing decline of the EU fishing fleet, a number of socio-economic measures were introduced, including the provision of aid from member states to fishermen and vessel owners who had temporarily to halt their fishing activities and the granting of aid to fishermen to help them retrain to convert to professional activities outside the fisheries sector, while permitting them to continue fishing on a part-time basis. A new regulation setting up an emergency fund to encourage the decommissioning of vessels (known as the 'Scrapping Fund') was also adopted.

In July 2004 the Council adopted a common framework on the establishment of regional advisory councils (RACs), as part of the 2002 reform, to enable scientists, fishermen and other interested parties to work together to identify ways of maintaining sustainable fisheries. In November 2004 the first RAC, for the North Sea, was instituted in Edinburgh, Scotland. The Pelagic RAC and the North Western Waters RAC, based, respectively, in Amsterdam, Netherlands, and Dublin, Ireland, were created in August and September 2005. A Baltic Sea RAC, based in Copenhagen, Denmark, was set up in March 2006. The RAC for Long Distance Waters and the RAC for the South Western Waters were established in March and April 2007, while the last RAC (for the Mediterranean Waters) was established in September 2008. During 2006, for the first time, TACs and quotas for the Baltic Sea were discussed separately from those covering other Community waters. Meanwhile, in March 2005 the European Commission announced its decision to initiate a consultation process on a new integrated EU maritime policy aimed at developing the potential of the maritime economy in an environmentally sustainable manner. In October 2007 the Commission presented a communication on integrated maritime policy, which was endorsed by the Council in December. An accompanying action plan included fisheries-related initiatives such as a scheme to strengthen international co-operation against destructive deep-sea fishing practices and measures to halt imports of illegal fisheries products.

In April 2005, in order to improve further compliance with the CFP as reformed in 2002, the Council of Ministers agreed to establish a Community Fisheries Control Agency (CFCA). The Agency, through the implementation of joint deployment plans, aims to strengthen the uniformity and effectiveness of enforcement of fisheries regulations by pooling EU and individual countries' means of control and monitoring and by co-ordinating enforcement activities. The CFCA (now the European Fisheries Control Agency—EFCA) adopted five joint deployment plans for 2009, three of which covered the regulated fisheries in the North Atlantic, and cod fisheries in the Baltic, North Sea and adjacent areas; and two of which covered the cod fisheries in Western Waters, and the regulated fisheries in waters beyond the national fisheries jurisdiction in the North Eastern Atlantic.

In July 2006, in order to facilitate, within the framework of the CFP, a sustainable European fishing and aquaculture industry, the Agriculture and Fisheries Council adopted a regulation on the establishment of a European Fisheries Fund (EFF), which replaced the FIFG on 1 January 2007. The Fund was to support the industry as it adapted its fleet in order to make it more competitive, and to promote measures to protect the environment. It was also to assist the communities that were most affected by the resulting changes to diversify their economic base. The EFF was to remain in place for seven years, with a total budget of some €3,800m. The regulation also set forth detailed rules and arrangements regarding structural assistance, including an obligation on all member states to draw up a national strategic plan for their fisheries sectors. Assistance was henceforth to be channelled through a single national EFF programme.

In January 2009 the European Commission adopted the first EU Plan of Action for the Conservation and Management of Sharks, which also aimed to protect related species, such as skates and rays, and was to apply wherever the EU fleet operates, both within and outside European waters. At the beginning of January 2010 a framework of new rules to strengthen the CFP control system entered into force, in accordance with which no country was to be given preferential treatment over another, thereby promoting, it was envisaged, a culture of compliance throughout the sector. The framework comprised three separate, yet inter-related, regulations on: combating illegal, unreported and unregulated (IUU) fishing; authorizations for the EU fleet operating outside EU waters; and establishing a control system for ensuring compliance with CFP rules. Under the new IUU regulation, all marine fishery products traded with the EU were to be certified and their origin traceable under a comprehensive catch certification scheme.

Legally bound to review some areas of the CFP by 2012, and concerned to address depleted stock levels and fleet overcapacity, the European Commission launched a consultation process on CFP reform in April 2009; following the termination of the consultations in December, the Commission published a report in April 2010. Five structural failings of the CFP were identified: the issue of fleet overcapacity; the need to refocus the CFP on the ecological sustainability of fish stocks and the minimization of 'discards' (dead fish or other marine organisms caught in excess of quotas that are dumped overboard, having been caught unintentionally); the desire to adapt fisheries governance away from centralized control, towards regionalized implementation of principles; involving the sector in resource management and implementation of the CFP; and developing a culture of compliance with rule. The Commission published its draft proposals for reform in July 2011. The proposals provided for returning fish stocks to sustainable levels by 2015, using a multi-annual, ecosystem approach. The discard system was to be gradually abandoned. The proposals provided for the establishment of clear targets and timetables to prevent overfishing, and to benefit small-scale fisheries, while providing transferrable fishing concessions. The Commission intended the new framework for fisheries policy to enter into force in 2013, following its approval by the European Parliament and the Council. In December 2011 the European Commission proposed the establishment of a new European Maritime and Fisheries Fund (EMFF) to co-ordinate the EU's maritime and fisheries policies in 2014–20. The EMFF, which was expected to have a budget of some €6,500m., was to be responsible for implementing the objectives of the revised CFP, assisting fishermen to adapt to more sustainable methods of fishing and helping coastal areas to diversify their economies.

Bilateral fisheries agreements have been signed with other countries (Norway, Iceland and the Faroe Islands) allowing limited reciprocal fishing rights and other advantages ('reciprocity agreements'), and with some African and Indian Ocean countries and Pacific Islands that receive technical and financial assistance in strengthening their fishing industries in return for allowing EU boats to fish in their waters ('fisheries partnership agreements'). Following the withdrawal of Greenland from the Community in February 1985, Community vessels retained fishing rights in Greenland waters, in exchange for financial compensation. In recent years, however, owing to growing competition for scarce fish resources, it has become increasingly difficult for the EU to conclude bilateral fisheries agreements giving its fleets access to surplus fish stocks in the waters of third countries.

Of the 10 new states that joined the EU in 2004, only four had sizeable fishing industries (Poland, Estonia, Latvia and Lithuania); the combined total annual catch of these four states in the early 2000s was equivalent to less than 7% of the EU total. Prior to their membership, the accession states were obliged to establish the necessary administrative capacity for applying the obligations arising from the CFP, including the modernization and renewal of old fishing vessels, the joint conservation of resources, the training of fisheries inspectors, the implementation and monitoring of common marketing standards, the introduction of EU health and hygiene standards, the management of structural policy in fisheries and aquaculture, and the compilation of a register of fishing vessels. In December 2005 the International Baltic Sea Fishery Commission (IBSFC) ceased its activities. Following the accession of Estonia, Latvia, Lithuania and Poland to the EU in 2004, membership of the IBSFC had been reduced to only two parties, the EU and Russia, and the negotiations that had formerly been conducted within its framework could now be undertaken bilaterally.

RESEARCH AND INNOVATION

In the amendments to the Treaty of Rome, effective from July 1987, a section on research and technology (subsequently restyled 'research and innovation') was included for the first time, defining the extent of Community co-operation in this area. Most of the funds allocated to research and innovation are granted to companies or institutions that apply to participate in EU research programmes.

A new Competitiveness and Innovation Framework Programme (CIP) was formally approved by the Council of the European Union in October 2006. The CIP for 2007–13 has an overall budget of €3,621m., and is divided into three operational programmes: the Entrepreneurship and Innovation Programme (EIP); the Information Communication Technologies Policy Support Programme (ICT-PSP); and the Intelligent Energy Europe Programme (IEE). In December 2006 the Council adopted a decision establishing the Seventh Framework Programme for research and technological development (FP7), and also established the Seventh Framework Programme of Euratom, for nuclear research and training activities in 2007–11, with a budget of €2,702m. A budget of €48,770m. was approved for the four specific programmes into which FP7 had been structured: co-operation (€32,413m.); ideas (to be implemented by the European Research Council—ERC—€7,510m.); people (€4,750m.); and capacities (€4,097m.). Joint technology initiatives (JTIs), in which industry, research organizations and public authorities would form public-private partnerships to pursue common research objectives, were a major new element of FP7. In December 2007 the Council adopted resolutions establishing ARTEMIS, a JTI involving research into embedded computer systems (specialized computer components dedicated to a specific task that are part of a larger system); the Clean Sky JTI, which aimed to develop environmentally sound and reasonably priced aircraft; the Innovative Medicines Initiative (IMI), which aimed to attract pharmaceutical research and development to Europe, in order to improve access to the newest and most effective medicines; and Nanoelectronics Technologies 2020 (ENIAC), a JTI which aimed to develop European nanoelectronic capabilities. In May 2008 the Council approved the establishment of the Fuel Cells and Hydrogen JTI, which aims to develop new hydrogen energy and fuel cell technologies for use in transport, and stationary and portable applications.

In February 2006 the Commission recommended the establishment of a European Institute of Technology (EIT), to promote excellence in higher education, research and innovation, and based on a Europe-wide network of 'knowledge and innovation communities' (KIC—partnerships comprising higher education institutions, research organizations, companies and other interested parties). The EU's contribution to the EIT was forecast at €308.7m. during 2008–13. A directive on the establishment of the EIT (now known as the European Institute of Innovation and Technology) came into force in April 2008, and the inaugural meeting of the EIT's 18-member governing board took place in September. The first KICs were chosen in December 2009, focusing on: climate change mitigation and adaptation; sustainable energy; and the information and communication society. In April 2010 the EIT's headquarters moved to Budapest, Hungary.

In October 2010 the Commission adopted a communication on the new Innovation Union, part of the 10-year Europe 2020 Strategy, designed to help steer the EU economy out of the economic crisis, by encouraging global competitiveness and innovation. From 2014 FP7 was to be superseded by Horizon 2020, a financial instrument to aid implementation of the Innovation Union. Horizon 2020, which was to have a budget of €80,000m., was to combine all the research and innovation funding now provided through the FP7, the CIP and the EIT. The CIP was to be replaced by a new Programme for the Competitiveness of Enterprises and Small and Medium-sized Enterprises (COSME), which was to have an individual budget of €2,500m. for 2014–20.

In January 2000 the Commission launched an initiative to establish a European Research Area (ERA). The aim was to promote the more effective use of scientific resources within a single area, in order to enhance the EU's competitiveness and create jobs. Detailed plans for the creation of the ERC, as an independent funding body for science, were incorporated in the FP7 agenda. The 22 founding members of a Scientific Council, responsible for determining the scientific funding strategy of the ERC and defining methods of peer review and proposal evaluation, held their inaugural meeting in October 2005. The ERC commenced operations in February 2007, with a budget of €7,500m. The ERC's Dedicated Implementation Structure, the Council's executive agency responsible for applying the strategies and methodologies defined by the Scientific Council, became operational in July 2009. The mandate of a new European Research Area Committee (ERAC) was approved by the Council in May 2010; the Committee, which replaced the Scientific and Technical Research Committee (CREST) established in 1995, provides strategic policy advice to the Council, the Commission and the EU member states on research and innovation issues of relevance to the ERA.

In July 1997 the European Parliament approved the Life Patent Directive, a proposal aiming to harmonize European rules on gene patenting in order to promote research into genetic diseases, despite objections over the ethical implications. In December 2004, at a meeting of the Council of the European Union, Germany, Austria and Italy reiterated their strong opposition to proposed EU funding of embryo research; consequently, the proposal was blocked and a moratorium on central funding was extended indefinitely, although the Commission remained free to approve stem cell research projects on a case-by-case basis and in accordance with strict ethical guidelines.

The EU is making efforts to integrate space science into its research activities, and has increasingly been collaborating with the European Space Agency (ESA). In September 2000 the EU and ESA adopted a joint European strategy for space, and in the following year the two bodies established a joint task force. In November 2003 negotiations on a framework agreement for structured co-operation between the EU and ESA were concluded. The European Space Policy, providing a common political framework for space activities in Europe, was adopted in May 2007. The European Commission, ESA and Eurocontrol developed the European Geostationary Navigation Overlay Service (EGNOS), the first pan-European satellite navigation system, which extends the US GPS system, and is suitable for use in challenging navigational situations in which safety is critical (for example, guiding boats through narrow channels). In April 2009 ownership of EGNOS was transferred to the European Commission. In October the European Commission announced the launch of the free EGNOS Open Service. The European Commission and ESA are also collaborating to design and develop a European satellite and navigation system, Galileo, to consist of about 30 satellites, a global network of tracking stations, and central control facilities in Europe. The European Global Navigation Satellite System (GNSS) Supervisory Authority (GSA) aims to use the Galileo, GPS and Global Navigation Satellite (GLONASS) systems to provide a global, integrated satellite navigation service under civilian control.

The Joint Research Centre (JRC) was established under the European Atomic Energy Community. Directed by the European Commission, but relying for much of its funding on individual contracts, the JRC is a collection of seven institutes, based at five different sites around Europe—Ispra, Italy; Geel, Belgium; Karlsruhe, Germany; Seville, Spain; and Petten, Netherlands. While nuclear research and development remain major concerns of the institutes, their research efforts have diversified substantially over the years. The JRC identified seven priority areas to be addressed under FP7: food safety; biotechnology, chemicals and health; the environment (including climate change and natural disasters); energy and transport; nuclear energy, safety and security; the Lisbon Strategy, information society and rural development; and internal and external security, anti-fraud measures and development aid. Nuclear work accounts for about one-quarter of all JRC activities, with the share accounted for by non-nuclear work increasing. The JRC also provides technical assistance to applicant countries. The JRC's budget for the FP7 period was €1,751m. for non-nuclear activities and €517m. for nuclear activities.

In 2005 the Enterprise and Industry Directorate-General launched the PRO INNO ('Promoting innovation in Europe') initiative, which aimed to foster trans-European co-operation between national and sub-national innovation programmes and activities. The INNO-Policy TrendChart provides detailed information about innovation trends in 39 countries in Europe, the Mediterranean region, North America and Asia. In order to analyse the EU's performance, the Commission used a set of performance indicators to draw up a so-called European Innovation Scoreboard (EIS). After the adoption by the Commission of the Innovation Union in October 2010, the EIS was re-established as the Innovation Union Scoreboard (IUS), in order to monitor implementation of the Innovation Union. The IUS for 2011, published in February 2012, uses 25 research and innovation-related indicators, and covers the 27 EU member states, as well as Croatia, Iceland, the former Yugoslav republic of Macedonia, Norway, Serbia, Switzerland and Turkey. Denmark, Finland, Germany and Sweden were designated 'European innovation leaders', outperforming the rest of Europe. However, when compared with major global competitor nations, a significant gap remained between the EU and the superior performance in innovation of Japan, the Republic of Korea and the USA.

The EU also co-operates with non-member countries in bilateral research projects. The Commission and 38 (mainly European) countries—including EU members as individuals—participate, as full members, in the EUREKA programme of research and development in market-orientated industrial technology, which was launched in 1985; in addition to the full members, the Republic of Korea is designated a EUREKA associated country, and Albania and Bosnia and Herzegovina participate in EUREKA projects through a network of National Information Points (NIPs). EUREKA (the acronym of the European Research Co-ordination Agency), sponsors projects focusing on robotics, engineering, information technology and environmental science, allows resources to be pooled and promotes collaboration. Most of EUREKA's funding is provided by private sources. The Community research and development information service (CORDIS) disseminates findings in the field of advanced technology.

ENERGY

The treaty establishing the European Atomic Energy Community (Euratom) came into force on 1 January 1958. This was designed to encourage the growth of the nuclear energy industry in the Community by conducting research, providing access to information, supplying nuclear fuels, building reactors and establishing common laws and procedures. A common market for nuclear materials was introduced in 1959 and there is a common insurance scheme against nuclear risks. In 1977 the Commission began granting loans on behalf of Euratom to finance investment in nuclear power stations and the enrichment of fissile materials. An agreement with the International Atomic Energy Agency (IAEA) entered into force in the same year, to facilitate co-operation in research on nuclear safeguards and controls. The EU's Joint Research Centre (JRC, see Research and Innovation) conducts research on nuclear safety and the management of radioactive waste.

The Joint European Torus (JET) is an experimental thermonuclear machine designed to pioneer new processes of nuclear fusion, using the 'Tokamak' system of magnetic confinement to heat gases to very high temperatures and bring about the fusion of tritium and deuterium nuclei. Fusion powers stars and is viewed as a 'cleaner' approach to energy production than nuclear fission and fossil fuels. Switzerland is also a member of the JET project (formally inaugurated in 1984), which is based at Culham in the United Kingdom and which is funded by the European Commission. In 1991 JET became the first fusion facility in the world to achieve significant production of controlled fusion power. The European Fusion Development Agreement (EFDA), which entered into force in March 1999, and a new JET implementing agreement, which came into force in January 2000, provide the framework for the collective use of the JET facilities. In 1988 work began with representatives of Japan, the former USSR and the USA on the joint design of an International Thermonuclear Experimental Reactor (ITER), based on JET but with twice its capacity. In mid-2005 the six participant teams in the ITER project (the People's Republic of China, the EU—represented by Euratom, Japan, the Republic of Korea, Russia and the USA), organized under the auspices of the IAEA, agreed that the vast trial reactor would be located in Cadarache, in southern France. In late 2005 India also became a full partner in the project. The main aim of ITER is to demonstrate the potential for fusion to generate electrical power (ITER would be the first fusion experiment with a net output of power) as well as to collect the data required to design and operate the first electricity-producing plant. In March 2007 the Council established the European Joint Undertaking for ITER and the Development of Fusion Energy (Fusion for Energy) to manage the EU's contribution to ITER. Overall responsibility for ITER was formally assumed by the newly established ITER International Fusion Energy Organization in November, following the ratification of a joint implementation agreement by all seven participants in the project. The construction of the project was expected to be accomplished during 2011–16, after which the reactor would remain operational for 20 years, at a total estimated cost of €10,000m., of which the EU was to contribute about 50%.

Legislation on the completion of the 'internal energy market', adopted in 1990, aimed to encourage the sale of electricity and gas across national borders in the Community by opening national networks to foreign supplies, obliging suppliers to publish their prices and co-ordinating investment in energy. Energy ministers reached agreement in June 1996 on rules for the progressive liberalization of the electricity market. In December 1997 the Council agreed rules to allow the gas market to be opened up in three stages, over a 10-year period.

In 2000 European electricity and gas energy regulators established the Council of European Energy Regulators (CEER), a not-for-profit association that promotes voluntary co-operation. In 2001 the Commission amended the timetable for liberalizing the electricity and gas markets: by 2003 all non-domestic consumers were to have the freedom to choose their electricity supplier; by 2004 non-domestic consumers were to have the freedom to choose their gas supplier; and by 2005 all consumers, domestic and non-domestic, would be able to choose both suppliers. In June 2002 the European Council confirmed amended target dates for the complete two-stage liberalization of the markets: opening up by July 2004 for non-domestic users and by July 2007 for domestic users. The European Regulators Group for electricity and gas (ERGEG) was established in November 2003 to act as an advisory group of independent national regulatory authorities to assist the European Commission in consolidating the internal market for electricity and gas. In early 2006 the ERGEG launched a regional initiative which created three gas and seven electricity zones within the EU. The initiative focused on removing barriers to market integration at a regional level, in order to facilitate the creation of a single competitive market. In October 2009 the CEER helped to organize the fourth World Forum on Energy Regulation, convened in Athens, Greece.

In October 2005 the EU signed a treaty establishing an Energy Community, which entered into force in July 2006. The contracting parties to the treaty comprise Albania, Bosnia and Herzegovina, Croatia, the former Yugoslav Republic of Macedonia, Montenegro, Serbia and the UN Interim Administration Mission in Kosovo. Moldova subsequently became a member in May 2010, and Ukraine joined in February 2011. Georgia, Norway and Turkey have been admitted as observers. The treaty, which aimed to facilitate the creation of an integrated pan-European market for electricity and gas, required the signatories to adopt EU energy regulations. The treaty provided for the liberalization of electricity and gas markets within participating countries by 2008 for non-domestic users, and by 2015 for domestic users. The World Bank estimated that this planned extension of the single European market for electricity and gas would lead to investment of €21,000m. in energy infrastructure in South-Eastern Europe over 15 years. In March 2006 the Commission adopted a Green Paper on developing a common European energy policy, which included recommendations on the appointment of a single energy regulator, the creation of an integrated European power grid and the negotiation of a new long-term pact with Russia on energy supplies. In December the Commission issued a final warning ('reasoned opinion') to 16 member states, including Germany, the United Kingdom, Spain, France and Italy, for having failed to open up sufficiently their energy markets. The final report of a competition inquiry, published in January 2007, identified high levels of market concentration, vertical integration of supply, production and infrastructure and collusion between operators to share markets as the main obstacles to the effective integration of the energy market. The Commission recommended the more stringent enforcement of regulations within an improved regulatory framework for energy liberalization.

The Commission has consistently urged the formation of an effective overall energy policy. The five-year programmes, SAVE and SAVE II, introduced respectively in 1991 and 1995, aimed to establish energy efficiency (e.g. reduction in the energy consumption of vehicles and the use of renewable energy) as a criterion for all EU projects. SAVE was integrated into Energy, Environment and Sustainable Development (EESD), initiated under the Fifth Framework Programme (FP5) for 1998–2002 and subsequently incorporated into a new, overarching plan, Intelligent Energy for Europe (IEE), which was adopted by the Commission for 2003–06 as part of the Sixth Framework Programme (FP6). IEE aimed to strengthen the security of supply and to promote energy efficiency and renewable energy sources (RES) such as wind, solar, biomass and small-scale hydropower. IEE has continued and expanded under a new Competitiveness and Innovation Framework Programme (CIP), in conjunction with the Seventh Framework Programme (FP7) for research during 2007–13. Under CIP, the so-called IEE 2 incorporated three separate elements: energy efficiency (SAVE); RES for the production of electricity and heat (ALTENER); and the energy aspects of transport (STEER); IEE 2 was allocated a budget of €730m. The EU Sustainable Energy Europe Campaign, covering 2005–11, and including an annual European Sustainable Energy Week, aims to accelerate private investment in sustainable energy technologies, to spread best practices, and to encourage alliances among sustainable energy stakeholders. A European Council Directive issued in April 2006 required each member state to submit a National Energy Efficiency Action Plan (NEEAP) to the European Commission by the end of June 2007, demonstrating means of achieving an energy savings target of 9% by 2016.

In order to help the EU to meet its joint commitment under the Kyoto Protocol to reduce greenhouse gas emissions by 8% from 1990 levels by 2012, and to encourage the use of more efficient energy technologies, in July 2003 the Council established the Emissions Trading Scheme, now Emissions Trading System (ETS). Under the scheme, which came into force in January 2005, individual companies were allocated a free greenhouse gas emission allowance by national governments. If they reduced emissions beyond their allocated quota, they would be allowed to sell their credits on the open market. During the first phase, covering 2005–07, ETS was only applied to large industrial and energy undertakings in certain sectors and only covered carbon dioxide emissions. Several member states opted to extend the scope of ETS for the second trading period (2008–12), and it incorporated revised rules for monitoring and reporting, more stringent restrictions on emissions, and an increased number of combustion sources. The third trading period (2013–20) will introduce significant changes, including harmonized allocation methodologies and additional emissions and installations.

In January 2007 the Commission attempted to initiate a more coherent integration of the EU energy and climate policies by incorporating in its proposals a comprehensive series of measures addressing the issue of climate change, while emphasizing the interdependency between security of supply and the promotion of sustainable energy sources. The measures included the establishment of a biennial Strategic Energy Review (SEER) to monitor progress in all aspects of energy policy, which was to constitute the basis for future action plans to be adopted by the Council and the Parliament. The Council endorsed the proposals in March; it also stated that its strategic objective was to limit the increase in the average global temperature to no more than 2°C above pre-industrial levels. The EU was to commit itself to reducing its greenhouse gas emissions by 20% (compared with their 1990 levels) by 2020. At the same time, the renewable energy sector was to supply 20% of EU energy by 2020, compared with 6.6% in 1990, and the share of biofuels in overall consumption of energy by the transport sector was to increase by 10%, also by 2020. New legislation was to facilitate the market penetration of renewable energy sources, while individual member states were to decide whether to develop their nuclear electricity sectors. The development of a European strategic energy technology plan was agreed. It was to be instrumental in increasing research into sustainable technologies (including low-carbon technology) by 50% by 2014. In November 2007 the Commission duly launched the European Strategic Energy Technology Plan (SET-Plan), in which it outlined plans to introduce six new industrial initiatives, focusing on wind power; solar power; biofuels; carbon dioxide capture, transport and storage; the electricity grid (including the creation of a centre to implement a research programme on the European transmission network); and sustainable nuclear fission.

Energy ministers from the EU member states and 12 Mediterranean countries agreed at a meeting held in June 1996 in Trieste, Italy, to develop a Euro-Mediterranean gas and electricity network. The first Euro-Med Energy Forum was held in May 1997, and an action plan for 1998–2002 was adopted in May 1998. In May 2003 the energy ministers of the Euro-Med partnership (including the ministers from the 10 accession states) adopted a declaration launching the Second Regional Energy Plan (2003–06). The Energy Forum that took place in September 2006, to agree on priorities for 2007–10, advocated the continued integration of Euro-Med energy markets, the development of energy projects of common interest, and of sustainable energy. The fifth Euro-Med ministerial conference on energy, held in Cyprus in December 2007, endorsed an action plan for further energy co-operation, covering 2008–13, which was to receive funding of €12,400m. from the European Investment Bank. Priorities included: the harmonization of regional energy markets and legislation; the promotion of sustainable development in the energy sector; and the development of initiatives of common interest in areas such as infrastructure, investment financing and research and development.

In 1997 the Community agreed to help a number of newly independent Eastern European countries to overcome energy problems by means of the Interstate Oil and Gas Transport to Europe programme (INOGATE). The overall aim of this programme was to improve the security of Europe's energy supply by promoting the regional integration of the oil and gas pipeline systems both within Eastern Europe itself and towards the export markets of Europe and the West in general, while acting as a catalyst for attracting private investors and international financial institutions to these pipeline projects. INOGATE originally formed part of the TACIS (Technical Assistance to the Commonwealth of Independent States) programme (see External Relations). However, under the Umbrella Agreement of INOGATE, which officially came into force as an international treaty in February 2001, the programme is open to all interested countries. In November 2006, as a continuation of the Baku initiative inaugurated in November 2004 under the umbrella of INOGATE, the EU and the governments of countries in the Caspian and Black Sea regions adopted a new Energy Road Map, which established a long-term plan of action. The Road Map provided for enhanced energy co-operation between all of the partners involved in such areas as the integration of energy markets on the basis of the EU internal energy market; the improvement of energy security by addressing issues of energy exports/imports; supply diversification; energy transit; sustainable energy development; and the securing of investment for projects of common interest.

At the sixth EU-Russia summit, held in Paris in October 2000, the two sides agreed to institute an energy dialogue on a regular basis with a view to establishing a strategic EU-Russia energy partnership. The dialogue was subsequently structured around joint thematic research groups to analyse issues of common interest, notably in the areas of energy strategies and balances, investment, technology transfers, energy infrastructures and energy efficiency and the environment. From 2001 annual progress reports were presented to EU-Russia summit meetings. However, following the disruption in January 2006 of Russian gas supplies to the EU via Ukraine, which demonstrated the extent of the EU's dependency on Russian gas (about one-quarter of gas supplied to the EU is from Russia), a European Parliament resolution emphasized that there was an urgent need to secure a more stable, reciprocal and transparent EU-Russia energy framework. Reductions in crude oil supplies from Russia to the EU in early 2007, resulting from a dispute between Russia and the transit country, Belarus, led to further demands for measures to enhance the security of the Union's energy supply. In April a restructuring of the thematic groups of the EU-Russia energy dialogue was agreed, to cover energy strategies, forecasts and scenarios; market developments; and energy efficiency. At an EU-Russia summit meeting held in Mafra, Portugal, in October it was agreed to establish a system to provide early warnings of threats to the supply of natural gas and petroleum to the EU.

In addition, the EU promotes trans-European networks (TENs, see also Transport), with the aim of developing European energy, telecommunications and transport through the interconnection and opening-up of national networks. In 2003 a revision of the guidelines for the TEN-Energy (TEN-E) programme was undertaken to take into account the priorities of the enlarged EU. The revised guidelines, adopted by the Council in July 2006, sought: to enhance the security of energy supplies in Europe; to strengthen the internal energy market of the enlarged EU; to support the modernization of energy systems in partner countries; to increase the share of renewable energies, in particular in electricity generation; and to facilitate the realization of major new energy infrastructure projects. The TEN-E networks policy, in particular, aimed to secure and diversify additional gas import capacity from sources in Russia, the Caspian Basin, northern Africa and the Middle East. The budget agreed for the TEN-E programme for 2007–13 totalled €155m. In October 2011 the European Commission published a proposal for a regulation on guidelines for trans-European energy infrastructure, which aimed to ensure the completion of energy networks (12 priority corridors were identified) and storage facilities by 2020.

In November 1999 the Commission indicated the need to strengthen the EU's Northern Dimension energy policy (covering Scandinavia, the Baltic states and north-west Russia) through the reinforcement of international co-operation, the opening-up of markets, the promotion of competition and the improvement of nuclear safety. In a communication in September 2000, the Commission set out a new EU strategy on nuclear safety in Central and Eastern Europe and the former Soviet states. The strategy entailed supporting those countries in their efforts to improve operating safety, strengthening their regulatory frameworks, and closing reactors that could not be upgraded to an acceptable standard. The fifth enlargement of the EU, completed in January 2007 with the accession of Bulgaria and Romania, had implications for nuclear safety, since seven of the 12 new member states had nuclear reactors, mostly of the old Soviet design. The closure of two ageing reactors was one of the preconditions for Bulgaria's accession to the EU. In June 2009 the European Council issued a Directive that established a common binding legal framework for the safety of nuclear installations.

EU member states are required to maintain minimum stocks of crude oil and/or petroleum products. In accordance with a European Council Directive issued in September 2009 member states were to ensure, by 31 December 2012, that these correspond to, at the very least, 90 days of average daily net imports or to 61 days of average daily internal consumption. A Green Paper of March 2006, entitled 'Towards a European strategy for the security of energy supply', re-emphasized the links between security of supply, the creation of a liberalized, integrated EU energy market and the development of sustainable energy. To protect energy supplies against the risk of natural catastrophes, terrorist threats, political risks and rising oil and gas prices, it recommended the following measures: the development of smart electricity networks; the establishment of a European Energy Supply observatory to monitor supply and demand patterns in EU energy markets; improved network security through increased collaboration and exchange of information between transmission system operators under an overarching European centre of energy networks; a solidarity mechanism to ensure rapid assistance to any member state confronted by damage to its essential infrastructure; and common standards to protect infrastructure and the development of a common European voice to promote partnerships with third countries. In May 2007 an EU Network of Energy Security Correspondents (NESCO) was launched to provide early warnings, and so enhance the Community's ability to react to pressure on external energy security.

In October 2008 the first meeting of a new Citizens' Energy Forum, organized by the Commission, took place in London, United Kingdom, bringing together consumer associations, industry representatives, national regulators, and government authorities to discuss issues affecting energy consumers, including billing, smart metering and the protection of vulnerable consumers, in order to serve as a platform to ensure consumer rights in the EU energy market; the Forum met annually thereafter.

In mid-June 2009 the Council formally adopted a new liberalization agreement for the EU's gas and electricity markets, known as the Third Energy Package (the Second Energy Package had been agreed in 2003), which was to enter into effect in 2011–13, and which established common rules for the internal markets in gas and electricity; included regulations on conditions for access to natural gas transmission networks and the network for cross-border exchanges in electricity; and provided for the establishment of an Agency for the Co-operation of Energy Regulators. The Third Energy Package aimed to: separate energy supply and production from network operations; ensure fair competition both within the EU, and with respect to third countries; strengthen the national energy regulators; and create a new Agency for the Co-operation of Energy Regulators (ACER), together with European Networks of Transmission Operators for electricity (ENTSO-E) and for gas (ENTSO-G). In July the new ENTSO-E took over all the operational tasks of the six existing European Transmission System Operators associations. The new ENTSO-G was established at the beginning of December, and comprises 33 Transmission System Operators from 22 European countries in an effort to facilitate progress towards the creation of a single energy market.

In November 2010 the European Commission adopted a communication entitled 'Energy 2020: a strategy for competitive, sustainable and secure energy', which defined the Commission's energy priorities for the next 10 years, focusing on the need to save energy; to ensure a competitive market with secure energy supplies; to promote technological advances; and to encourage effective international negotiation. In early February 2011 the first EU energy summit was held, in Brussels, Belgium, at which an agreement was adopted on a number of strategic energy-related areas. In particular, the summit concluded that work should be undertaken to develop a transparent, rule-governed relationship with Russia. The summit also made clear its intention to promote investment in renewable energy, and sustainable low-carbon technologies; to accelerate the liberalization of energy markets, in order to bring them into accordance with EU law (about one-half of the EU member states had liberalized their energy markets, but only Denmark had fully implemented the latest legislation; some 60 infringement proceedings had been brought against member states for failing to open up their markets); to improve adherence to the 2020 20% energy-efficiency target (which aimed to reduce the use of greenhouse gases by 20%, to increase the proportion of renewable energy used to 20%, and to improve overall energy efficiency by 20% by 2020); and to investigate the potential extraction and use of unconventional fossil fuel sources, such as shale gas and oil shale, favoured, in particular, by Poland.

Since June 2005 annual formal ministerial meetings of the EU-Organization of the Petroleum Exporting Countries (OPEC) Energy Dialogue have been convened; the eighth ministerial Dialogue, convened in Vienna, Austria, in June 2011, agreed to conduct a workshop to review the findings of a study on technological development in the road transport sector; to finalize preparations for a proposed EU-OPEC Energy Technology Centre; and to address the major challenges affecting oil and gas exploration and production activities, such as the safety of offshore operations and the shortage of human resources.

ENTERPRISE AND INDUSTRY

Industrial co-operation was the earliest activity of the Community. The treaty establishing the European Coal and Steel Community (ECSC) came into force in July 1952, and by the end of 1954 nearly all barriers to trade in coal, coke, steel, pig iron and scrap iron had been removed. The ECSC treaty expired in July 2002, and the provisions of the ECSC treaty were incorporated in the EEC treaty, on the grounds that it was no longer appropriate to treat the coal and steel sectors separately.

In the late 1970s and 1980s measures were adopted radically to restructure the steel industry in response to a dramatic reduction in world demand for steel. During the 1990s, however, new technologies and modern production processes were introduced, and the European steel sector showed signs of substantial recovery. Privatization and cross-border mergers also improved the industry's competitive performance, and by the 2000s Europe was a competitive global exporter. In March 2004 the European Commission and major stakeholders in the European steel industry launched the European Steel Technology Platform, the long-term aim of which was to help the sector meet the challenges of the global marketplace, changing supply and demand patterns, environmental objectives, and the simplification of EU and national legislation and regulation in this field. In addition, the May 2004 enlargement of the EU increased the need for extensive restructuring of the steel industries. The steel industry played a relatively larger role in the 10 new member states, compared with the existing 15 members. In 2008 the European steel industry produced 198m. metric tons of steel, compared with some 160m. tons in the early 2000s. The industry directly employed around 420,000 EU citizens (with several times this number employed in the steel-processing, -usage and -recycling industries) in 2008. A decrease in production resulting from the global economic downturn, however, caused up to 170,000 steel sector employees to be laid off, either temporarily or permanently, or to adopt short-time working patterns in 2009.

The European textiles and clothing industry has been seriously affected by overseas competition over an extended period. From 1974 the Community participated in the Multi-Fibre Arrangement (MFA, see World Trade Organization), to limit imports from low-cost suppliers overseas. However, as a result of the Uruguay Round of GATT (General Agreement on Tariffs and Trade) trade negotiations, the quotas that existed under the MFA were progressively eliminated during 1994–2004 in accordance with an Agreement on Textiles and Clothing. An action plan for the European textiles and clothing industry was drawn up in 1997. A report published by the Commission in 2000 established future priorities for the sector, focusing on preparations for the enlargement of the EU and systems for co-operation in the 'new economy'. Particular importance was attached to ensuring a smooth transition to the quota-free world environment (from 1 January 2005), to enable third countries currently exporting to the EU to maintain their competitive position, and to secure for EU textiles and clothing industries in third countries market access conditions similar to those offered by the EU. A high-level group on textiles and clothing, established by the Commission in order to encourage debate on initiatives to facilitate the sectors' adjustment to major challenges, and to improve their competitiveness, published its first report in 2004.

In May 2005, in response to a dramatic increase in clothing exports from the People's Republic of China since 1 January, the EU imposed limits on textiles imports from that country. In June the EU and the Chinese Government agreed import quotas on 10 clothing and textiles categories until 2008, but by August several of the quotas for 2005 had already been breached. In September the dispute was resolved when it was agreed that one-half of the estimated 80m. Chinese garments that had been impounded at European ports would be released and the remainder counted against the quotas for 2006. In September 2006 the high-level group on textiles and clothing published its second report, which sought, *inter alia*, to chart the likely development of the sector up to 2020. In October 2007 the European Commission and China agreed that, following the expiry in 2008 of the agreement on import quotas, a monitoring system would be introduced to track, but not limit, the issuing of export licences in China and the import of goods into the EU for eight clothing and textiles categories. Trade in textiles and clothing was fully liberalized from January 2009, following which China continued to increase its market share in Europe.

Production in EU member states' shipyards fell drastically from the 1970s, mainly as a result of competition from shipbuilders in the Far East. In the first half of the 1980s a Council directive allowed for subsidies to help reorganize the shipbuilding industry and to increase efficiency, but subsequently rigorous curbs on state aid to the industry were introduced. State aid was eventually withdrawn in early 2001. From 2000 construction activity increased somewhat. However, the number of new orders declined sharply from the latter half of 2008 as a result of the global economic downturn.

In April 2002 the Commission adopted its fifth report on the state of global shipbuilding. It confirmed previous observations that, in the absence of an international agreement, the market was in crisis, owing to the extremely low prices offered by shipyards in the Republic of Korea (South Korea). In May the EU agreed to launch WTO procedures against South Korea, and to establish a 'temporary defensive mechanism' (TDM) of state subsidies to protect European shipbuilding against unfair South Korean practices.

Harmonization of national company law to form a common legal structure within the Community has led to the adoption of directives on disclosure of information, company capital, internal mergers, the accounts of companies and of financial institutions, the division of companies, the qualification of auditors, single-member private limited companies, mergers, take-over bids, and the formation of joint ventures.

The European Patent Convention (EPC) was signed in 1973 and entered into force in 1977. Revisions to the Convention were agreed in November 2000, and a revised EPC entered into force on 13 December 2007. In June 1997 the Commission published proposals to simplify the European patent system through the introduction of a unitary Community patent, to remove the need to file patent applications with individual member states. Upon the entry into force in December 2009 of the Lisbon Treaty, which provided a new legal basis for the establishment of unitary intellectual property titles within the EU, the proposed Community patent was renamed the EU patent. During that month the European Council agreed a draft regulation on the EU patent, in accordance with which it was envisaged that the EU would accede to the EPC (which would require further revision to the Convention), and the European Patent Office (EPO, based in Munich, Germany) would grant EU patents with unitary effect throughout the territory of the EU. Infringement and validity issues relating to the planned EU patent were to be addressed by a proposed European and EU Patents Court. In June 2011 the EU Council agreed to draw up two EU regulations on the unitary patent, concerning increased co-operation on unitary patent protection, and the associated translation arrangements.

An Office for Harmonization in the Internal Market (OHIM), based in Alicante, Spain, was established in December 1993, and is responsible for the registration of Community trademarks and for ensuring that these receive uniform protection throughout the EU.

The liberalization of Community public procurement has played an important role in the establishment of the internal market. From January 1993 the liberalization of procurement was extended to include public utilities in the previously excluded sectors of energy, transport, drinking water and telecommunications. In 1996 the Commission launched the Système d'information pour les marchés publics (SIMAP) programme, to give information on rules, procedures and opportunities in the public procurement market, and to encourage the optimum use of information technology in public procurement. In 2002 the European Parliament adopted a regulation aimed at simplifying the rules on procurement of contract notices, by introducing a single system for classifying public procurement, to be used by all public authorities; a regulation updating the classification system was adopted in November 2007. The European Public Procurement Network was established in January 2003. The objective of this network, which comprises all EU member states, EU candidate countries, European Economic Area (EEA) members, Switzerland and other European countries, was to strengthen the application of public procurement rules through a mutual exchange of experience. Reforms to the EU's public procurement directives were adopted in 2004 in an attempt to make the often complex rules more transparent, efficient and comprehensible. In November 2007 a directive was adopted with the aim of improving the effectiveness of review procedures concerning the award of public contracts.

In 1990 the European Council adopted two directives with the aim of removing the tax obstacles encountered by companies operating across borders: the Merger Directive was designed to reduce tax measures that could hamper business reorganization and the Parent-Subsidiary Directive abolished double taxation of profit distributed between parent companies in one member state and their subsidiaries in others. In October 2001 the European Council adopted two legislative instruments enabling companies to form a European Company (known as a Societas Europaea—SE). A vital element of the internal market, the legislation gave companies operating in more than one member state the option of establishing themselves as single companies, thereby able to function throughout the EU under one set of rules and through a unified management system; companies might be merged to establish an SE. The legislation was aimed at making cross-border enterprise management more flexible and less bureaucratic, and at helping to improve competitiveness. In July 2003 the Council adopted similar legislation enabling co-operatives to form a European Co-operative Society (Societas Cooperativa Europaea—SCE). In September 2004 the Commission established a working group to advance the development of a common consolidated corporate tax base (CCCTB). In February 2005 the Council approved an amendment to the Merger Directive of 1990, extending its provisions to cover a wider range of companies, including SEs and SCEs. A directive aimed at facilitating cross-border mergers of limited liability companies was adopted by the European Parliament and the Council in October 2005. The establishment of SPEs from mid-2008 (see below) aimed to facilitate the operation of small and medium-sized enterprises (SMEs) across borders.

In September 1995 a Commission report outlined proposals to improve the business environment for SMEs. In March 1996 the Commission agreed new guidelines for state aid to SMEs. Aid for the acquisition of patent rights, licences, expertise, etc., was to be allowed at the same level as that for tangible investment. A Charter for Small Enterprises, approved in June 2000, aimed to support SMEs in areas such as education and training, the development of regulations, and taxation and financial matters, and to increase representation of the interests of small businesses at national and EU level. In November 2005 the Commission launched a new policy framework for SMEs, proposing specific actions in five areas: promoting entrepreneurship and skills; improving SMEs' access to markets; simplifying regulations; improving SMEs' growth potential; and strengthening dialogue and consultation with SME stakeholders. In January 2007 the Commission launched an action programme aimed at reducing unnecessary administrative burdens on companies, primarily SMEs, by one-quarter by 2012, focusing on 13 priority areas, including company law, employment relations, taxation, agriculture and transport. In addition, 10 'fast-track' measures were identified, which, it was estimated, would reduce the burden on businesses by €1,300m. per year. A high-level group of experts was appointed in November 2007 to advise the Commission on the implementation of the action programme, which had been endorsed by the Council in March. In June 2008 the Commission adopted the Small Business Act for Europe (SBA), which was endorsed by the EU Council of Ministers in December. The SBA aimed further to streamline bureaucratic procedures for SMEs, and to enable businesses to establish a European Private Company (Societas Privata Europaea—SPE), which would operate according to uniform principles in all member states, thereby simplifying procedures for SMEs operating across borders. By 2010 there were more than 20m. SMEs in the EU, accounting for 99% of all EU enterprises. In February 2011 the results of a review of the SBA's work in 2008–10 was published. The review concluded that some 100,000 SMEs had benefited from the Competitiveness and Innovation Framework Programme 2007–13; a new late payment directive required public authorities to pay suppliers within 30 days, improving cash flow; the resources (both financial and in terms of time taken) required to establish a new SME had been reduced; simplified online procedures and opportunities for joint bidding had facilitated the participation of SMEs in public procurement; and the establishment of a new EU SME Centre in China had helped SMEs to access Chinese markets. The review also identified a number of priority areas for further action: the need to assist SMEs in accessing finance, for investment and growth, for example by improving access to loan guarantees and venture capital markets, as well as targeted measures aimed at making investors more aware of the benefits of SMEs; improving regulation; enhancing the ability of SMEs fully to utilize the common market, with proposals for a Common Consolidated Corporate Tax Base, measures to facilitate cross-border debt recovery, and a revision of the European standardization system to make it more accessible to SMEs; and assisting SMEs in dealing with the issues of globalization and climate change.

The European Investment Bank provides finance for small businesses by means of 'global loans' to financial intermediaries. A mechanism providing small businesses with subsidized loans was approved by ministers in April 1992.

The Enterprise Europe Network, launched in February 2008, comprises contact points providing information and advice to businesses, in particular SMEs, on EU matters, in 51 countries, including the EU member states, EU candidate countries, members of the EEA, and other participating third countries. The EU's other information services for business include the Community Research and Development Information Service (CORDIS, see Research and Innovation) and the internet-based Your Europe: Business, which brings together advice and data from various sources. In addition, around 147 accredited Business and Innovation Centres (BICs) were operating in the 27 EU countries by 2008, with a mission to promote entrepreneurship and the creation of innovative businesses, and to assist existing companies to enhance their prospects through innovation.

In January 2000 the EU's Directorates-General for Industry and SMEs and for Innovation were transformed into one Directorate-General for Enterprise Policy (subsequently restyled the Enterprise and Industry Directorate-General). The Commission subsequently adopted a Multiannual Programme for Enterprise and Entrepreneurship (MAP) covering 2001–05, aimed particularly at SMEs. Stronger measures were proposed for the protection of intellectual property rights (IPRs), and the harmonization of legislation on IPRs was advocated (differences between national laws in this respect could constitute protectionist barriers to the EU's principle of free movement of goods and services). In April 2004 a directive was adopted on the enforcement of IPRs, to make it easier to enforce copyrights, patents and trademarks in the EU and to punish those who tampered with technical mechanisms designed to prevent copying or counterfeiting. In July 2005 the Commission proposed a second directive on the enforcement of IPRs, which would impose criminal penalties for infringements, to supplement the civil and administrative measures contained in the 2004 directive; the draft directive remained under consideration. Meanwhile, in November 2004 the Commission announced plans to commence monitoring certain countries (particularly China, Ukraine and Russia) to check that they were making genuine efforts to halt the production of counterfeit goods. In October 2005 the Commission launched a new industrial policy, proposing eight new initiatives or actions targeted at specific sectors, including pharmaceuticals, defence, and information and communication technologies, as well as cross-sectoral initiatives on: competitiveness; energy and the environment; IPRs; improved regulation; research and innovation; market access; skills; and managing structural change. In January 2007 the MAP, which had been extended until the end of 2006, was succeeded by an Entrepreneurship and Innovation Programme under a wider Competitiveness and Innovation Framework Programme for 2007–13, with a budget of some €3,600m. In January 2009 the EU and China agreed an action plan on advancing closer customs co-operation relating to IPR protection, and signed an agreement aimed at enhancing co-operation in monitoring trade and preventing trafficking in chemicals used in the illicit manufacture of narcotic drugs.

The European Business Angels Network (EBAN) provides a means of introduction between SMEs and investors and encourages the exchange of expertise. The Commission also promotes inter-industry co-operation between enterprises in the EU and in third countries through the TransAtlantic Business Dialogue (TABD), the Canada-Europe Round Table, the EU-Japan Business Round Table, the Mercosur-Europe Business Forum (MEBF), the EU-Russia Industrialists' Round Table, the EU-India Business Dialogue, the EU-Indonesia Business Dialogue and the European-Israeli Business Dialogue.

COMPETITION

The Treaty of Rome establishing the European Economic Community provided for the creation of a common market based on the free movement of goods, persons, services and capital. The EU's competition policy aims to guarantee the unity of this internal market, by providing access to a range of high-quality goods and services, at competitive prices. It seeks to prevent anti-competitive practices by companies or national authorities, and to outlaw monopolization, protective agreements and abuses of dominant positions. Overall, it aims to create a climate favourable to innovation, while protecting the interests of consumers.

The Commission has wide investigative powers in the area of competition policy. It may act on its own initiative, or after a complaint from a member state, firm or individual, or after being notified of agreements or planned state aid. Before taking a decision, the Commission organizes hearings; its decisions can be challenged before the Court of First Instance and the Court of Justice, or in national courts.

The Treaty of Rome prohibits any state aid that distorts or threatens to distort competition in the common market (e.g. by discriminating in favour of certain firms or the production of certain goods); however, some exceptions are permitted where the proposed aid may have a beneficial impact in overall Union terms. As an integral part of competition policy, control of state aid, including balancing the negative effects of aid on competition with its positive effects on the common interest, helps to maintain competitive markets. The procedural rules on state aid were consolidated and clarified in a regulation in 1999, and provided for several exemptions, notably regarding the provision of aid to small and medium-sized enterprises (SMEs) and for training. The EU has drawn up 'regional aid maps' designed to concentrate aid in those regions with the most severe development problems. A State Aid Action Plan (SAAP), covering the five-year period 2005–09, was adopted by the Commission in June 2005 as a roadmap for the reform of state aid policy. The SAAP streamlined procedures (which had become increasingly complex, and challenged by EU enlargement) to provide member states with a clear and predictable state aid framework. It promoted targeting state aid towards improving the competitiveness of European industry and towards the creation of sustainable jobs, thereby advancing the Lisbon Strategy. It provided for aid to be utilized as a means of achieving objectives of common interest, such as services of general economic interest, social and regional cohesion, employment, research and development, sustainable development, and promotion of cultural diversity, and for redressing inefficiencies in the functioning of markets ('market failures') with a view to promoting growth. Amid widespread recession, in December 2008 the European Commission adopted a Temporary Framework for State Aid, which aimed to assist member states in co-ordinating the provision of credit facilities to businesses until 2010, in order to protect and restore their viability in the long term. The Temporary Framework was subsequently extended until the end of 2011. In February 2012 the Commission published a guidance paper on state aid-compliant financing, and restructuring and privatization of state-owned enterprises. Since 2001 the Commission has analysed state aid granted by member states in its State Aid Scoreboard. According to the Scoreboard published in December 2011, and excluding targeted crisis measures, the total amount of state aid granted by EU member states in 2010 was some €73,700m., equivalent to 0.6% of EU gross domestic product (GDP). In the same year, crisis-support measures, such as the recapitalization of the financial sector, totalled €121,300m. (equivalent to some 1% of EU GDP); some €11,700m. of aid (equivalent to some 0.9% of EU GDP) was granted under the Temporary Framework. By the beginning of October 2011, the Commission had approved financial crisis measures for 22 member states, and aid measures for 26 member states had been approved under the temporary framework. The Commission acts to recover any illegal or incompatible state aid: recovery of such aid disbursed since 1 January 2000 exceeded €11,500m. by the end of June 2011.

The Treaty of Rome prohibits agreements and concerted practices between firms resulting in the prevention, restriction or distortion of competition within the common market. This ban applies both to horizontal agreements (between firms at the same stage of the production process) and vertical agreements (between firms at different stages). The type of agreements and practices that are prohibited include: price-fixing; imposing conditions on sale; seeking to isolate market segments; imposing production or delivery quotas; agreements on investments; establishing joint sales offices; market-sharing agreements; creating exclusive collective markets; agreements leading to discrimination against other trading parties; collective boycotting; and voluntary restraints on competitive behaviour. Certain types of co-operation considered to be positive, such as agreements promoting technical and economic progress, may be exempt.

In addition, mergers that would significantly impede competition in the common market are banned. The Commission examines prospective mergers in order to decide whether they are compatible with competition principles. In July 2001 the EU blocked a merger between two US companies for the first time, on the grounds that EU companies would be adversely affected. In December the Commission launched a review of its handling of mergers and acquisitions, focusing on the speed of decisions and on bringing European competition standards in line with those in the USA and elsewhere. A new merger regulation was adopted in January 2004 and came into force in May, introducing some flexibility into the time frame for investigations into proposed mergers.

The Commission is attempting to abolish monopolies in the networks supplying basic services to member states. In June 2002 the Council adopted a directive on the opening up of postal services. Liberalization has also been pursued in the gas and electricity, telecommunications and transport sectors. In July 2002 the Commission approved a plan to open the car industry to greater competition, by applying new EU-wide rules for car sales, giving car dealers the freedom to operate anywhere in the EU. The reforms, which were strongly opposed by car manufacturers and by the French and German Governments, came into effect in October 2005. In June the Commission launched inquiries into competition in the electricity and gas markets and in the retail banking and business insurance sectors. In January 2007 the Commission adopted the final report of the inquiry into the gas and electricity markets, concluding that consumers and businesses were disadvantaged by inefficiency and expense. Particular problems that were identified by the final report were high levels of market concentration; vertical integration of supply, generation and infrastructure, leading to a lack of equal access to and insufficient investment in infrastructure; and possible collusion between incumbent operators to share markets. The Commission announced its intention to pursue action in individual cases, within the framework of anti-trust, merger control and state aid regulations, and to act to improve the regulatory framework for energy liberalization. The adoption of the final report was accompanied by the adoption of a comprehensive package of measures to establish a New Energy Policy for Europe, with the aim of combating climate change and prompting energy security and competitiveness within the EU. The final report of the inquiry into the retail banking sector, published in January 2007, indicated a number of concerns in the markets for payment cards, payments systems and retail banking products. In particular, the report noted that there were large variations in merchant and interchange fees for payment cards, barriers to entry into the markets for payment systems and credit registers, impediments to customer mobility and product tying. In response to these findings, the Commission announced that it would use its powers, within the framework of competition regulations and in close collaboration with national authorities, to combat serious abuses. The final report of the inquiry into the business insurance sector, published in September, raised concerns about the widespread practice of premium alignment in the reinsurance and coinsurance markets when more than one insurer is involved in covering a single risk and about lack of transparency in the remuneration of insurance brokers, as well as the risk of conflicts of interest jeopardizing the objectivity of brokers' advice to clients.

In February 2006, in a first reading, the European Parliament adopted a draft directive aimed at opening up the services sector to cross-border competition. The directive had proved controversial, with opponents fearing it would lead to lower wages, lower standards of social and environmental protection and an influx of foreign workers. The Parliament notably amended the directive so that a company offering services in another country would be governed by the rules and regulations of the country in which the service was being provided (rather than those of the company's home country, as the Commission had favoured). The Parliament excluded a number of areas from the future directive's scope, including broadcasting, audiovisual services, legal services, social services, gambling and public health, and also agreed a list of legitimate reasons that a country could cite for restricting the activities of foreign service providers, such as national security, public health and environmental protection. Those in favour of the directive claimed that it had been severely weakened by the Parliament. In December, having been approved by the Parliament at its second reading earlier in that month, the directive was adopted by the Parliament and the Council of the European Union and entered into force.

In 2003 the Commission worked to establish detailed provisions for a modernized framework for anti-trust and merger control in advance of the enlargement of the EU in May 2004. In that month major changes to EU competition law and policy (including substantive and procedural reform of the European Community Merger Regulation) entered into force. As part of the reforms, national competition authorities, acting as a network, and national courts were to become much more involved in the enforcement of competition rules, and companies were to be required to conduct more self-assessment of their commercial activities. In March the US Department of Justice had criticized the EU's anti-trust action against the US computer software company Microsoft. The European Commission imposed a fine of €497m. and instructed the company to disclose elements of its programming (within 120 days) to facilitate the development of competitive products. Microsoft appealed against the decision in the Court of First Instance in Luxembourg in June and the EU penalties were temporarily suspended. In December, however, the Court rejected Microsoft's appeal to delay the implementation of the EU sanctions pending the final outcome of the company's main appeal against the Commission's anti-trust decision. In July 2006 the Commission imposed a fine of €280.5m. on Microsoft, and threatened to impose heavier penalties on the company in future, for its failure to comply with the EU's demand that it should provide complete and accurate information to permit interoperability between its Windows operating system and rivals' work-group servers. The Commission was also legally entitled to impose a further daily fine of €0.5m., backdated to December 2005, on the company if the royalty fees it charged for the use of its technical information were found to be excessive. In March 2007 the Commission communicated a statement of objection to Microsoft, stating its preliminary view that there was no significant innovation in submissions made by the company from December 2005 in respect of compliance with the Commission's anti-trust action of March 2004, and that the royalty fees proposed were therefore unreasonable. In September 2007 the Court of First Instance rejected Microsoft's appeal against the 2004 anti-trust decision. Microsoft announced in October 2007 that it would accept the Court's ruling and comply with the Commission's demands. In December 2009 the Commission made legally binding, for five years from March 2010, a commitment offered by Microsoft in October 2009 to give consumers of its Windows operating system a choice of web browser beyond Microsoft's own Internet Explorer, and, thereby, to remove a long-term obstacle to competition and innovation. Meanwhile, in May 2009 the Commission imposed a fine of €1,060m. on the Intel Corporation, after concluding that it had abused its strong position in the central processing unit (CPU) market by making reimbursements to computer manufacturers, provided that they bought CPUs from Intel, and by making direct payments to Europe's largest computer retailer, Media Saturn Holding, on condition that its stock solely comprised computers containing Intel CPUs. In addition, Intel made direct payments to computer manufacturers to postpone or halt the launch of specific products containing competitors' CPUs and to restrict the sales avenues available to such products.

In October 2004 the USA initiated dispute procedures at the World Trade Organization (WTO) in protest at alleged massive state subsidies to the civil aircraft manufacturer Airbus. However, the EU took retaliatory action regarding state subsidies to the US aircraft manufacturer Boeing. An attempt, from January 2005, to settle the dispute through bilateral talks failed, and both sides renewed their cases at the WTO in May. In July the WTO agreed to establish two panels to examine the complaints of the USA and the EU; members of the panels were appointed in October. In November 2006 the US case against Airbus was formally presented; a preliminary report on the situation, issued by the WTO in September 2009, determined that Airbus had received illegal subsidies totalling US $13,000m., but did not find the EU systematically to have abused global trade rules. The case of the EU against Boeing was presented in March 2007, and in March 2011 the WTO ruled that Boeing had received illegal US subsidies worth more than $5,000m.

In mid-January 2008 the Commission initiated an inquiry into the pharmaceuticals sector, in response to indications that fewer new medicines were entering the market, and that the launch of generic medicines appeared to be subject to unnecessary delays. In July 2009 the Commission adopted the final report of the sector inquiry into pharmaceuticals, which confirmed that originator companies use a variety of methods to extend the commercial life of their products prior to generic entry, and which confirmed a decline in the number of new medicines reaching the market and indicated that pharmaceutical companies might have created obstacles to market entry. The Commission planned to increase monitoring of pharmaceuticals companies in order to identify breaches of anti-trust legislation in the sector, and to identify defensive patenting strategies. To reduce the risk that settlements between originator and generic companies are concluded at the expense of consumers, the Commission undertakes to carry out further focused monitoring of settlements that limit or delay the market entry of generic drugs.

The international affairs unit of the Directorate-General for Competition co-operates with foreign competition authorities and promotes competition instruments in applicant countries, where it also provides technical assistance. The unit works within the framework of international organizations such as the WTO, the Organisation for Economic Co-operation and Development (OECD) and the United Nations Conference on Trade and Development (UNCTAD). Dedicated co-operation agreements on competition policy have been signed with the USA, Canada and Japan, while other forms of bilateral co-operation on competition issues exist with a number of other countries and regions. In addition, in 2001 the European Commission was a founding member of the International Competition Network, an informal forum for competition authorities from around the world.

TELECOMMUNICATIONS, INFORMATION TECHNOLOGY AND BROADCASTING

In 1991 the Council adopted a directive requiring member states to liberalize their rules on the supply of telecommunications terminal equipment, thus ending the monopolies of national telecommunications authorities. In the same year, the Council adopted a plan for the gradual introduction of a competitive market in satellite communications; a directive relating to the liberalization of satellite telecommunications equipment and services came into force in late 1994, but allowed for deferment until 1 January 1996. In October 1995 the European Commission adopted a directive liberalizing the use of cable telecommunications, requiring member states to permit a wide range of services, in addition to television broadcasts, on such networks. The EU market for mobile telephone networks was opened to full competition as a result of a directive adopted by the Commission in January 1996, which obliged member states to abolish all exclusive and special rights in this area, and establish open and fair licensing procedures for digital services. All the major EU telecommunications markets were, in principle, open to competition from 1998.

In February 2000 the Commission requested that national competition authorities, telecommunications regulators, mobile network operators and service providers give information on conditions and price structures for national and international mobile services. In response to concerns regarding the increased cost for EU citizens of using a mobile telephone when travelling in another EU country, a new regulation fixing a maximum rate for so-called roaming charges entered into force in June 2007. In order to enhance the transparency of retail prices, mobile telephony providers were also required to inform their customers of the charges applicable to them when making and receiving calls in another member state. In July 2011 the Commission published a proposal to further amend the application of roaming charges for EU mobile telephone users, by imposing new maximum rates, increasing competition, and allowing consumers to sign a separate, additional contract for data roaming with a company other than their contracted domestic mobile service provider.

In July 2000 a comprehensive reform of the regulatory framework for telecommunications—the 'telecoms package'—was launched. The reform aimed to update EU regulations to take account of changes in the telecommunications, media and information technology (IT) sectors. Noting the continuing convergence of these sectors, the Commission aimed to develop a single regulatory framework for all transmission networks and associated services, in order to exploit the full potential for growth, competition and job creation. The Commission recommended, as a priority, the introduction of a regulation on unbundled access to the local loop (the final connection of telephone wires into the home). The lack of competition in this part of the network was considered a significant obstacle to the widespread provision of low-cost internet access. The regulation obliged incumbent operators to permit shared and full access to the local loop by the end of 2000. In December 2001 the European Parliament voted to adopt a compromise telecoms package. This gave the Commission powers to oversee national regulatory regimes and, in some cases, to overrule national regulatory authorities. The package included a framework directive and three specific directives (covering issues of authorization, access and interconnection, universal service and users' rights) and measures to ensure harmonized conditions in radio spectrum policy. By the end of 2003 the EU regulatory framework for electronic communications had been completely implemented; during subsequent years, however, the Commission initiated legal proceedings against a number of member states for either their failure fully to transpose the new rules of competition in their national laws or for incorrect implementation of the framework. In November 2009 the European Parliament and the Council of Ministers agreed a reform of the EU's telecommunications rules; the new rules, which were to be fully incorporated into national legislation by June 2011, aimed to provide consumers with more choice by reinforcing competition between operators; to promote investment in new communication infrastructures, notably by freeing radio spectrum for wireless broadband services; and to make communication networks more reliable and more secure, for example by introducing new measures to combat unsolicited e-mail, viruses, etc. To improve regulation and competition, and reinforce co-operation between national telecommunications regulators in an attempt to facilitate the creation of pan-European services, a new Body of European Regulators for Electronic Communications (BEREC) was inaugurated in January 2010.

The '.eu' top-level domain name, aimed at giving individuals, organizations and companies the option of having a pan-European identity for their internet presence, was launched in December 2005, when registration commenced for applicants with prior rights, such as trademark holders and public bodies; registration was open to all from April 2006. The European Registry of Internet Domain Names (ERID) reported in February 2010 that the number of registered '.eu' domain names had exceeded 3.2m.

Information and communication technologies (ICT) was one of the main themes of the co-operation programme of the Seventh Framework Programme for research, technological development and demonstration activities (FP7, covering 2007–13)—see Research and Innovation. The development of ICT was allocated €9,050m. in the budget for 2007–13. Aims included strengthening Europe's scientific and technology base in ICTs; stimulating innovation through ICT use; and ensuring that progress in ICTs is rapidly transformed into benefits for citizens, businesses, industry and governments. The Interchange of Data between Administrations (IDA) initiative supported the rapid electronic exchange of information between EU administrations—in January 2005 the IDA was renamed the Interoperable Delivery of pan-European eGovernment Services to Public Administrations, Businesses and Citizens (IDAbc) programme. An action plan promoting safer use of the internet, extended in March 2002 until December 2004, aimed to combat illegal and harmful content on global networks. In December 2004 the EU approved a new programme, called Safer Internet Plus (2005–08), to promote safer use of the internet and new online technologies and to combat illegal and harmful content (particularly child pornography and violent and racist material). The renewed Safer Internet programme for 2009–13 was awarded a budget of €55m., and aimed to combat both illegal content and harmful conduct such as the 'grooming' of children by paedophiles (where an adult establishes contact with a child via the internet, under false pretences, with the intention of arranging a meeting with that child for the purposes of committing a sexual offence) and bullying.

In 1992 a White Paper proposed the establishment of trans-European networks (TENs) in telecommunications, energy and transport, in order to improve infrastructure and assist in the development of the common market. Following the liberalization of the telecommunications market in 1998, efforts in this area were concentrated on support (through the eTEN programme) for the development of broadband networks and multimedia applications. The eTEN programme, which expired in 2006, focused strongly on public services and its objectives were based on the EU's stated aim of 'an information society for all'. The ICT Policy Support Programme (ICT PSP), part of the wider Competitiveness and Innovation Framework Programme (CIP, covering 2007–13), was designed to build on the former eTEN programme by stimulating innovation and competitiveness through the wider uptake and best use of ICT by citizens, governments and businesses. A budget of €728m. was allocated to the ICT PSP for 2007–13.

In October 2003 new digital privacy legislation aimed at combating unwanted commercial e-mails (known collectively as 'spam') came into force across the EU. The new rules required companies to gain consent before sending e-mails and introduced a ban on the use of 'spam' throughout the EU. It was widely recognized, however, that concerted international action was required, since most of the 'spam' entering Europe originated from abroad (particularly from the USA). In February 2005 13 European countries agreed to share information and pursue complaints across borders in an effort to combat unsolicited e-mails. A European Network and Information Security Agency (ENISA) became fully operational in October 2004. The main aims of the Agency, which is based in Heraklion, Greece, are to promote closer European co-ordination on information security and to provide assistance in the application of EU measures in this field. ENISA periodically monitors anti-spam activities. A 2009 ENISA survey of measures taken by European e-mail service providers to combat spam in their networks found that less than 5% of EU e-mail traffic at that time was delivered to inboxes. In February 2010 ENISA, which reported that 211m. internet users in Europe were regularly accessing online social networking sites (SNSs), released a list of 17 'golden rules' to enable consumers to protect themselves from online risk.

In 1991 a directive ('Television without Frontiers') came into force, establishing minimum standards for television programmes to be broadcast freely throughout the Community: limits were placed on the amount of time devoted to advertisements, a majority of programmes broadcast were to be from the Community, where practicable, and governments were allowed to forbid the transmission of programmes considered morally harmful. In November 2002 the Commission adopted a communication on the promotion and distribution of television programmes. In July 2003 the Commission reiterated proposals (originally presented at the Lisbon summit in March 2000) to help film and audiovisual production companies to have access to external funding from banks and other financial institutions by covering some of the costs of the guarantees demanded by these institutions and/or part of the cost of a loan ('discount contract loan') for financing the production of their works. In May 2005 the Commission urged EU member states to accelerate the changeover from analogue to digital broadcasting, setting a target of 2012 for shutting down analogue services. In December 2005 the Commission proposed a modernization of the Television without Frontiers directive in view of rapid technological and market developments in the audiovisual sector. A reduction in the regulatory burden on providers of television and similar services was envisaged, as well as the introduction of more flexible rules on advertising. National rules on the protection of minors, against incitement to hatred and against surreptitious advertising would be replaced with an EU-wide minimum standard of protection. The proposals distinguished between so-called 'linear' services (e.g. scheduled broadcasting via traditional television, the internet or mobile cellular telephones) and 'non-linear' services, such as on-demand films or news, which would be subject only to a basic set of minimum principles. The modernized Television without Frontiers directive, renamed the Audiovisual Media Services without Frontiers directive, was adopted by the European Parliament in November 2007. The deadline for implementation of the legislation by member states was December 2009, although this was not universally met. In July 2007 the Commission adopted a strategy urging member states and industry to facilitate and accelerate the introduction of mobile television (the transmission of traditional and on-demand audiovisual content to a mobile device), encouraging the use of DVB-H (Digital Video Broadcasting for Handhelds) technology as the single European standard. This strategy was endorsed by the Council in November.

The MEDIA programme was introduced in 1991 to provide financial support to the television and film industry. MEDIA 2007, covering the period 2007–13, was formally adopted by the European Parliament and the Council in November 2007, with a budget of €755m. MEDIA 2007's principal objectives are: to preserve and enhance European cultural diversity and its cinematographic and audiovisual heritage, and to guarantee Europeans' access to it and foster intercultural dialogue; to increase the circulation of European audiovisual works both within and outside the EU; and to reinforce the competitiveness of the European audiovisual sector within the framework of an open and competitive market. In January 2011 the Commission launched a loan guarantee mechanism, the MEDIA Production Guarantee Fund, within the framework of MEDIA 2007; the Fund was to facilitate access to bank credits for European audiovisual companies during 2011–13.

In October 2009 the European Commission published a report on cross-border consumer e-commerce that detailed concerns with ongoing barriers to completing online purchases across EU borders and so to achieving progress towards the creation of a digital single market. Difficulties were, in particular, caused by traders not shipping their products to certain countries or not offering suitable means for cross-border payment; the countries where consumers were least able to buy cross-border products online were Belgium, Bulgaria, Latvia and Romania. The number of broadband subscribers in the EU had reached 120m. by July 2009, equivalent to 24% of the population, compared with 48.4m. subscribers (10.6%) at July 2005.

In March 2010 the European Commission launched the Europe 2020 strategy, which established the Digital Agenda for Europe as one of seven principal initiatives. The Digital Agenda for Europe, which replaced the i2010 initiative, aimed to exploit the full economic and social potential of ICT resources, in particular the internet, in order to promote innovation and economic growth, through the creation of a digital single market. The Commission identified seven principal objectives: the creation of a new single, online market; improved standards and interoperability for ICT; enhanced trust and security for those using the internet; improved access to very fast internet speeds; improved research and innovation; improved digital literacy; and using ICT to address issues of importance to society throughout Europe, such as mitigating rising health costs and digitising the EU's cultural heritage.

TRANSPORT

The establishment of a common transport policy is stipulated in the Treaty of Rome, with the aim of gradually standardizing the national regulations that hinder the free movement of traffic within the Community, such as the varying safety and licensing rules, diverse restrictions on the size of lorries, and frontier-crossing formalities. A White Paper in 1992 set out a common transport policy for the EU. The paper proposed the establishment of trans-European networks (TENs) to improve transport, telecommunications and energy infrastructure throughout the Community, as well as the integration of transport systems and measures to protect the environment and improve safety.

The overall aim of the EU's trans-European transport network (TEN-T) policy, which included so-called intelligent transport systems and services, was to unite the various national networks into a single European network, by eliminating bottlenecks and adding missing links. As a result of the accession of 10 new member states in 2004, a further 16 TEN-T projects, in addition to 14 ongoing projects, were identified as being priorities for the enlarged Union. The Commission estimated that all 30 TEN-T projects would require investment of €225,000m. for completion by 2020, of which around €140,000m. would be required in 2007–13. The total cost of completing the TEN-T was estimated at €600,000m. In July 2005 the Commission nominated six co-ordinators with a four-year mandate to facilitate dialogue between member states on transnational TEN-T projects in an attempt to accelerate their completion; two further co-ordinators were appointed in 2007, and in July 2009 the co-ordinators' mandate was extended for a further four-year term. A Trans-European Transport Network Executive Agency was established in November 2006 to manage priority projects. The first annual ministerial conference on the future of TEN-T, held in October 2009, with participation by delegates from the EU member states, the Balkans, the Western Mediterranean and Africa, and from Norway, Switzerland, Russia and Turkey, determined to strengthen co-operation to facilitate the creation of a sustainable infrastructure network, and outlined common priorities until 2020. In October 2010 the Commission published the first mid-term review of the TEN-T programme. Of the 92 large-scale infrastructure projects under way, 48 were deemed to be making sufficient progress to reach completion in December 2013, as planned; a further 39 projects were given a revised deadline, of 2015, while the remaining five were to be cancelled. It has been estimated that the completion of TEN-T could reduce transport-generated carbon dioxide emissions by 6.3m. metric tons per year by 2020.

The EU has increasingly focused on integrating environmental issues and questions of sustainable development into transport policy. In September 2001 the Commission adopted a White Paper on Transport Policy for 2010, setting out a framework designed to accommodate the forecast strong growth in demand for transport on a sustainable basis. The policy aimed to shift the balance between modes of transport by 2010, by revitalizing railways, promoting maritime and inland waterway transport systems, and by linking up different kinds of transport. The paper proposed an action plan and a strategy designed gradually to break the link between economic and transport growth, with the aim of reducing pressure on the environment and relieving congestion. A communication on an action plan for the deployment of intelligent transport systems in Europe, issued by the Commission in December 2008, promoted the use of information and communications technologies to enable the development of cleaner, more efficient (including energy efficient) and safer transport systems.

In March 2011 the Commission published a new White Paper on Transport Policy for a Single European Transport Area, which aimed to create a competitive and environmentally efficient transport system by 2050. The Commission detailed 40 separate initiatives for the next decade with the objective of building a competitive transport system to increase mobility; removing barriers; and aiding economic growth and employment. The proposals sought to reduce substantially Europe's dependence on imported petroleum and to reduce carbon emissions in the transport sector by 60% by 2050. Principal goals for fulfilment by 2050 included: removing conventionally fuelled cars from cities; ensuring that 40% of aviation fuels used were sustainable, low-carbon fuels; and reducing shipping emissions by at least 40%.

In 1991 directives were adopted by the Council on the compulsory use of safety belts in vehicles weighing less than 3.5 metric tons. Further regulations applying to minibuses and coaches were introduced in 1996. In June 2000 the Commission issued a communication setting out measures to improve the safety and efficiency of road transport and to ensure fair competition. These included road traffic monitoring, the regulation of employed drivers' working time, and regularity of employment conditions. In November 2002 the European Parliament adopted a directive on speed limitation devices for certain categories of motor vehicles, including haulage vehicles and passenger vehicles carrying more than eight passengers. In March 2006 the European Parliament and Council adopted a regulation reducing maximum driving times and increasing obligatory rest periods for professional drivers and a directive increasing the number of checks on lorries; the new legislation entered into force in April 2007.

In 1992 ministers of transport approved an 'open skies' arrangement that would allow any EC airline to operate domestic flights within another member state (with effect from 1 April 1997). In November 2002 the European Court of Justice ruled that bilateral open skies treaties, or Air Services Agreements (ASAs), between countries were illegal if they discriminated against airlines from other member states; the ruling was in response to a case brought by the Commission against eight member states that had concluded such agreements with the USA. In response to the ruling, in June 2003 the Commission and member states identified two ways of resolving the issues: either bilateral negotiations between each member state concerned and its partners, amending each bilateral ASA separately, or single 'horizontal' agreements negotiated by the Commission on behalf of the member states. Each horizontal agreement aims to amend the relevant provisions of all existing bilateral ASAs in the context of a single negotiation with one third country. By May 2006 separate bilateral negotiations had led to changes with 39 partner states, representing the correction of 69 bilateral agreements, while by December 2007 horizontal negotiations had led to changes with 32 partner states. In 2004–05 the Commission initiated infringement proceedings against a number of member states that were persisting in maintaining discriminatory bilateral air agreements with the USA. At the same time the Commission was conducting negotiations with the USA in an attempt to conclude an overall open skies agreement, under which a common aviation area would be created. In November 2005 a preliminary agreement was concluded with the USA, and in early March 2007 EU and US negotiators concluded a draft accord. The EU-US aviation agreement, encompassing some 60% of global air traffic, was approved by EU ministers of transport later in March and formally signed in April.

In June 2006 the European Commission signed a political agreement with the eight new EU member states from Central and South-Eastern Europe, Bulgaria, Romania, Norway, Iceland and the countries of the Western Balkans on the creation of a European Common Aviation Area (ECAA). The establishment of the ECAA involved the harmonization of standards and regulations on safety, security, competition policy, social policy and consumer rights, as well as the establishment of a single market for aviation.

In July 1994, despite EU recommendations for tighter controls on subsidies awarded to airlines, as part of efforts to increase competitiveness within the industry, the Commission approved substantial subsidies that had been granted by the French and Greek governments to their respective national airlines. Subsequently the Commission specified that state assistance could be granted to airlines 'in exceptional, unforeseen circumstances, outside the control of the company'. Following the terrorist attacks perpetrated against targets in the USA in September 2001, and the consequent difficulties suffered by the air transport sector, the EU ruled that a degree of aid or compensation was permissible, but stressed that this must not lead to distortion of competition. In October the Commission proposed to establish common rules in the field of civil aviation security, to strengthen public confidence in air transport following the terrorist attacks on the USA. Issues addressed included securing cockpits, improving air-ground communications and using video cameras in aircraft. Member states also agreed to incorporate into Community law co-operation arrangements on security measures. These measures covered control of access to sensitive areas of airports and aircraft, control of passengers and hand luggage, control and monitoring of hold luggage, and training of ground staff. In October 2006 the Commission adopted a regulation restricting the liquids that air passengers were allowed to carry beyond certain screening points at airports and onto aircraft. The new regulation, introduced in response to the threat posed to civil aviation security by home-made liquid explosives, was to be applied to all flights departing from member states' airports.

In July 2002 the European Parliament adopted a regulation creating a European Aviation Safety Agency (EASA). The EASA (which officially opened its permanent seat in Köln, Germany, in December 2004) was to cover all aircraft registered in member states, unless agreed otherwise. The Commission has also formulated ground rules for inquiries into civil air incidents and has issued proposals for assessing the safety of aircraft registered outside the EU. In April 2008 a regulation entered into force that extended the responsibilities of the EASA, particularly regarding control over pilots' licences and the regulation of airlines based in third countries operating in the EU. In December 2005 EU ministers of transport approved a regulation introducing a Europe-wide 'blacklist' of unsafe airlines and granting passengers the right to advance information about the identity of the air carrier operating their flight.

In December 1999 the Commission presented a communication on streamlining air traffic management (ATM) to create a Single European Sky (SES), of which the overall aim was to restructure the EU's airspace on the basis of traffic, rather than national frontiers. In December 2002 EU ministers of transport agreed on a package of measures under which the separate European ATM providers would be regulated as a single entity, and EU airspace over 28,500 ft (approximately 8,690 m) would be under unified control. A first package of SES legislation (SES I), bringing ATM under the common transport policy, was adopted by the European Parliament and Council in April 2004. In November 2005 the European Commission launched SESAR, a Single European Sky industrial and technological programme to develop a new ATM system. The project consisted of three phases: the definition phase (2005–07), costing €60m. (co-funded by the Commission and the European Organisation for the Safety of Air Navigation—EUROCONTROL); the development phase (2008–13), estimated to cost around €300m. per year (co-funded by the Commission, EUROCONTROL and the industry); and the deployment phase (2014–20), to be financed by the industry. A regulation creating the SESAR Joint Undertaking, a public-private entity managing the development stage of the project, was formally approved by the Council and Parliament in February 2007. Meanwhile, in April 2006 a directive was adopted on the introduction of a Community air traffic controller licence, with the aim of raising safety standards and improving the operation of the ATM system. In March 2009 the Council adopted a decision endorsing a new SESAR ATM Master Plan as the initial version of a planned European ATM Master Plan. Also during that month the European Parliament approved a second package of SES legislation (SES II), incorporating improvements aimed at addressing environmental challenges and fuel cost efficiency.

In 1986 progress was made towards the establishment of a common maritime transport policy, with the adoption of regulations on unfair pricing practices, safeguard of access to cargoes, application of competition rules and the eventual elimination of unilateral cargo reservation and discriminatory cargo-sharing arrangements. In December 1990 the Council approved, in principle, the freedom for shipping companies to provide maritime transport anywhere within the Community. Cabotage by sea began to be introduced from January 1993 and was virtually complete by January 1999. Cabotage was also introduced in the inland waterways transport sector in 1993. By January 2000 the inland waterways market had been liberalized, although obstacles to the functioning of the single market subsequently persisted, including differing technical regulations among member states. The 2001 White Paper on European Transport Policy proposed the development of Motorways of the Sea, which aimed to shift a proportion of freight traffic from the road system to short sea shipping, or to a combination of short sea shipping and other modes of transport in which road journeys were minimized. In March 2005 the European Commission launched a consultation process on a new integrated EU maritime policy aimed at developing the potential of the maritime economy in an environmentally sustainable manner. The commissioners responsible for sea-related policies were charged with preparing a consultation paper addressing all economic and recreational maritime activities, such as shipping, fishing, oil and gas extraction, use of wind and tidal power, shipbuilding, tourism and marine research. The resultant Green Paper was adopted by the Commission in June 2006. Following the conclusion of a consultation process based on the document, in October 2007 the Commission presented a communication on its vision for the integrated maritime policy, which was endorsed by the Council in December. An accompanying action plan included initiatives such as a European strategy for marine research; national integrated maritime policies; an integrated network for maritime surveillance; a European marine observation and data network; and a strategy to mitigate the effects of climate change on coastal regions.

In March 2000 the Commission adopted a communication on the safety of the seaborne oil trade. It proposed the introduction of a first package of short-term measures to strengthen controls, including the right to refuse access to substandard ships, more stringent inspections and a generalization of the ban on single-hull oil tankers. In May the Commission adopted a proposal to harmonize procedures between bulk carriers and terminals, in order to reduce the risk of accidents caused by incorrect loading and unloading. In the same month the Commission signed a memorandum of understanding (MOU) with several countries on the establishment of the Equasis database, intended to provide information on the safety and quality of ships. In December the Commission set out a second package of safety measures, broad agreement was reached on the first package, and the EU agreed to accelerate the gradual introduction of double-hull tankers (single-hull tankers were being phased out from the end of 2010). In June 2002 the European Parliament established by regulation the European Maritime Safety Agency (the permanent seat of which was to be located in Lisbon, Portugal); its tasks were to include preparing legislation in the field of maritime safety, co-ordination of investigations following accidents at sea, assisting member states in implementing maritime safety measures, and providing assistance to candidate countries. In March 2004 the Agency was given additional responsibility for combating pollution caused by ships. In November 2005 the Commission proposed a third package of maritime safety measures, including a requirement that member states ensure that ships flying their flags comply with international standards; an improvement in the quality and effectiveness of ship inspections, with increased targeting of vessels deemed to pose the greatest risk and less frequent inspections of high-quality ships; and an obligation that member states designate an independent authority responsible for the prior identification of places of refuge for ships in distress. The Commission noted that the EU had become a major maritime power, accounting for some 25% of the world's fleet.

In April 1998 the Commission published a report on railway policy, with the aim of achieving greater harmonization, the regulation of state subsidies and the progressive liberalization of the rail-freight market. In October 1999 EU ministers of transport concluded an agreement that was regarded as a precursor to the full liberalization and revitalization of the rail-freight market. Rail transport's share of the total freight market had declined substantially since the 1970s, but it was widely recognized that, in terms of environmental protection and safety, transport of freight by rail was greatly preferable to road haulage. The agreement provided for the extension of access to a planned core Trans-European Rail Freight Network (TERFN, covering some 50,000 km), with a charging system designed to ensure optimum competitiveness. During 2000–04 the EU adopted three 'railway packages', which dealt with the progressive deregulation of the rail market. However, a number of EU member states vehemently opposed granting full access to their national railway networks. Other measures incorporated in the packages included developing a common approach to rail safety; upholding principles of interoperability; and setting up a European Railway Agency (ERA). The ERA was established by a regulation of the European Parliament in April 2004. The main aim of the Agency, the permanent seat of which was inaugurated in Lille/Valenciennes, France, in June 2005, was to reinforce the safety and interoperability of railways in the EU. In March 2005 the European Commission and representatives of the rail industry signed an MOU on the deployment of a European Rail Traffic Management System (ERTMS) on a major part of the European network. The ERTMS, a single European rail signalling system, was intended to enhance safety and reduce infrastructure costs in the longer term; existing national systems were to be gradually withdrawn within 10–12 years. In December 2006 the Commission presented a communication proposing measures to remove technical and operational barriers to international rail activities, with the aim of making the rail industry more competitive, particularly in relation to road and air transport; the simplification of procedures for the approval of locomotives for operational service across the EU; and the extension of the powers of the ERA.

The Marco Polo II programme, which was being implemented during 2007–13 (having succeeded the original Marco Polo programme, covering 2003–06, which, in turn, had replaced an earlier PACT—pilot action for combined transport—scheme), was allocated a budget of €400m. Marco Polo II, the scope of which extended to countries bordering the EU, aimed to reduce road congestion by increasing the utilization of sea, rail and inland waterways routes for freight traffic, and to improve the environmental performance of the intermodal network within the EU, thereby contributing to an efficient and sustainable transport system.

A directive adopted in April 2004 aimed to establish an electronic toll collection system across the EU that would apply to roads, tunnels, bridges, ferries and urban congestion-charging schemes. Notably, all new electronic toll systems brought into service from 1 January 2007 were required to use at least one of three prescribed existing technologies.

JUSTICE AND HOME AFFAIRS

Under the Treaty on European Union, EU member states undertook to co-operate in the areas of justice and home affairs, particularly in relation to the free movement of people between member states. Issues of common interest were defined as asylum policy; border controls; immigration; drug addiction; fraud; judicial co-operation in civil and criminal matters; customs co-operation; and police co-operation for the purposes of combating terrorism, drugs-trafficking and other serious forms of international crime. In view of the sensitivity of many of the issues involved in this sphere, the EU affords great weight to the positions and opinions of individual states. There tends to be a greater degree of flexibility than in other areas, and requirements are frequently less stringent.

The EU's draft Charter of Fundamental Rights, which was signed in December 2000, outlines the rights and freedoms recognized by the EU. It includes civil, political, economic and social rights, with each based on a previous charter, convention, treaty or jurisprudence. The charter may be used to challenge decisions taken by the Community institutions and by member states when implementing EU law. A reference to the charter, making it legally binding, was included in the Treaty of Lisbon amending the Treaty on European Union and the Treaty establishing the European Community (previously known as the Reform Treaty), which was signed in December 2007 and entered into force in December 2009. A protocol to the Treaty of Lisbon limited the application of the charter in the United Kingdom and Poland to rights recognized by national legislation in those countries. In June 2005 the European Commission adopted a proposal for a regulation establishing an EU Agency for Fundamental Rights. The regulation was adopted in its final form in February 2007, allowing the establishment of the Agency, as the successor to the European Monitoring Centre on Racism and Xenophobia, on 1 March. In April the specific programme 'Fundamental Rights and Citizenship' was established under the framework programme 'Fundamental Rights and Justice'. With a budget of €94m. for 2007–13, the Programme aimed to promote the development of a European society based on respect for fundamental rights; to strengthen civil society organizations and to encourage a dialogue with them regarding fundamental rights; to combat racism, xenophobia and anti-Semitism; and to improve contacts between legal, judicial and administrative authorities and the legal professions.

In July 2010 the Directorate-General for Justice, Freedom and Security was divided into the Directorate-General for Justice and the Directorate-General for Home Affairs. The new Directorate-General for Justice comprises three directorates: Civil Justice; Criminal Justice; and Fundamental Rights and Citizenship.

In December 2009 the European Council adopted the Stockholm Programme, which aimed to provide a framework in 2010–14 for the creation of an 'open and secure Europe serving and protecting its citizens'. The Programme's objectives were to promote European citizenship and fundamental rights; to achieve a Europe of law and justice; to develop an internal EU security strategy; to promote, through integrated border management and visa policies, access to Europe; to develop a forward-looking and comprehensive European migration and asylum policy; and to develop the external dimension of EU freedom, security and justice policy. Cyber-security (developing a single system for the protection of personal data), combating terrorism and organized crime, and border control were all to be addressed by the new agenda. Ensuring equal rights for migrants, finer monitoring of migration patterns and labour trends, and closer co-operation with non-EU countries on managing migration flows were areas of focus.

A European Police Office (Europol), facilitating the exchange of information between police forces, operates from The Hague, Netherlands. A special Europol unit dealing with the trafficking of illicit drugs and nuclear and radioactive materials began work in 1994. Europol's mandate has been extended to cover illegal immigrants, stolen vehicles, paedophilia and terrorist activities, money-laundering and counterfeiting of the euro and other means of payment. From 1 January 2010 Europol became a full EU agency, with a stronger mandate and enhanced capability for combating serious international crime and terrorism.

The EU convention on extradition, signed by ministers of justice in September 1996 prior to ratification by national governments, simplified and accelerated procedures in this area, reduced the number of cases where extradition could be refused, and made it easier to extradite members of criminal organizations. In November 1997 the Commission proposed an extension to European law to allow civil and commercial judgments made in the courts of member states to be enforced throughout the whole of the EU. A regulation on the mutual recognition and enforcement of such judgments came into force in March 2001 across the EU, with the exception of Denmark. In 2000 a convention on mutual assistance in criminal matters (such as criminal hearings by video and telephone conference and cross-border investigations) was adopted.

The Grotius-Civil programme of incentives and exchanges for legal practitioners was established in 1996. It was designed to aid judicial co-operation between member states by improving reciprocal knowledge of legal and judicial systems. The successor programme, Grotius II, focused on general and criminal law. In February 2002 the EU established a 'Eurojust' unit, composed of prosecutors, magistrates and police officers from member states, to help co-ordinate prosecutions and support investigations into incidences of serious organized crime. A European Police College (CEPOL) has also been created, initially consisting of a network of existing national training institutes; in December 2003, however, the European Council decided that a permanent CEPOL institution would be established at Bramshill in the United Kingdom. CEPOL was formally established as an EU agency in 2005.

In March 2000 an action programme to develop a European strategy for the prevention and control of organized crime was adopted. A European crime prevention network was formally established in May 2001. There are also agreements within the EU on co-operation between financial intelligence units and between police forces for the purposes of combating child pornography. In addition, the EU has a common strategy designed to help Russia combat organized crime. The EU ran the FALCONE programme—a series of incentives, training opportunities and exchanges for those responsible for the fight against organized crime in individual member states. The STOP (sexual treatment of persons) programme operated a similar system for those responsible for combating trade in humans and the sexual exploitation of children. Several programmes, including Grotius II, STOP and FALCONE, were merged into a single framework programme, called AGIS, in January 2003. In 2006 AGIS, which covered police and judicial co-operation in criminal matters, was terminated and succeeded by new programmes, adopted by the Council in February 2007 and covering the period 2007–13, with a focus on internal security (with an overall budget of €745m.) and criminal justice (with an overall budget of some €196m.).

In September 2001 member states harmonized their definitions of human trafficking and set common minimum prison sentences. In January 2005 the European Commission adopted a proposal for a framework decision on the fight against organized crime, in which it sought to harmonize the definition of what constitutes a criminal organization. A White Paper on exchanges of information on criminal convictions in the EU was also adopted, proposing, notably, that a computerized mechanism be established to allow the criminal record offices of the member states to share information. In June, in a communication on developing a 'strategic concept' on tackling organized crime, the Commission recommended the development of common methodologies among national and EU bodies involved in combating organized crime, as well as an EU crime statistics system.

The European Monitoring Centre for Drugs and Drug Addiction (EMCDDA) is based in Lisbon, Portugal. In 2000 Norway became the first non-EU state to be admitted to EMCDDA. The EU is working with other third countries to tackle issues of drugs demand and supply. In December 2004 the European Council endorsed an EU strategy on drugs (2005–12), which set out the framework, objectives and priorities for two consecutive four-year action plans. A drug prevention and information programme was adopted in September 2007. With a budget of €21m. for 2007–13, the programme's general objectives were to prevent and reduce drugs use and dependence; to enhance information on the effects of drugs use; and to support the implementation of the EU drugs strategy and action plans.

Measures related to the abolition of customs formalities at intra-community frontiers were completed by mid-1991, and entered into force in January 1993. In June 1990 Belgium, France, Germany, Luxembourg and the Netherlands, meeting in Schengen, Luxembourg, signed a convention to implement an earlier agreement (concluded in 1985 at the same location), abolishing frontier controls on the free movement of persons from 1993. Delay in the establishment of the Schengen Information System (SIS), providing a computer network on suspect persons or cargo for use by the police forces of signatory states, resulted in the postponement of the implementation of the new agreement. Seven countries (Belgium, France, Germany, Luxembourg, the Netherlands, Portugal and Spain) agreed to implement the agreement with effect from March 1995. Frontier controls at airports on those travelling between the seven countries were dismantled during a three-month transition period, which ended on 1 July 1995 (although France retained all of its land-border controls until March 1996, when border controls with Spain and Germany were lifted, although controls on borders with the Benelux countries were retained owing to fear over the transportation of illicit drugs). Italy joined the 'Schengen Group' in October 1997, and Austria in December. Border controls for both countries were removed in 1998. Denmark, Finland and Sweden (and non-EU members Norway and Iceland) were admitted as observers of the accord from 1 May 1996, and all five countries joined the Schengen Group in March 2001. Meanwhile, in March 1999 signatories of the Schengen accords on visa-free border crossings began to waive visa requirements with Estonia, Latvia and Lithuania. The Treaty of Amsterdam, which came into effect on 1 May, incorporated the so-called Schengen *acquis* (comprising the 1985 agreement, 1990 convention and additional accession protocols and executive decisions), in order to integrate it into the framework of the EU. The Treaty permitted the United Kingdom and Ireland to maintain permanent jurisdiction over their borders and rules of asylum and immigration. Countries acceding to the EU after 2000 were automatically to adhere to the Schengen arrangements. In February 2002 the Council approved Ireland's participation in some of the provisions of the Schengen *acquis*.

Following the enlargement of the EU in May 2004, border controls between the 15 existing members and the 10 new members remained in force until 2007. Although the 10 new states technically belonged to the Schengen agreement, the Commission decided that the SIS computer network was not large enough to incorporate data from 10 more countries. Work on a new computerized information system, SIS II, began in 2002 but suffered delays and is not expected to be completed until 2013. Pending deployment of SIS II, a modified version of SIS, named SISone4ALL, was introduced to allow the extension of the Schengen area to proceed. In December 2007 the provisions of the Schengen agreement were applied to the land and sea borders of nine of the 10 countries that joined the EU in 2004, with controls at airports removed, accordingly, in March 2008. The inclusion of Cyprus in the Schengen area was postponed. The admission of Bulgaria and Romania (which were both subject to ongoing concerns regarding their progress in combating corruption and organized crime) to the Schengen area was vetoed in both December 2010 and September 2011. Switzerland, a non-EU member, joined the Schengen area in December 2008, and Liechtenstein was expected to join in the future.

In November 2000 the Commission adopted a communication outlining a common asylum procedure and providing for a uniform status, valid throughout the EU, for persons granted asylum. In March 2001 a common list of countries whose citizens required visas to enter the EU was adopted. The EU has also developed the so-called Eurodac database for co-ordinating information on the movements of asylum seekers; Eurodac allows for the comparison of fingerprints of refugees. In April 2004 the Council adopted a directive establishing a common European definition of a refugee, aimed at curtailing movement from state to state until one is reached that is prepared to give protection. In February 2002 the European Council adopted a comprehensive plan to combat illegal immigration. Priority areas included visa policy, readmission and repatriation policies, the monitoring of borders, the role of Europol and penalties. A European Agency for the Management of Operational Co-operation at the External Borders of the European Union (FRONTEX) was established by a regulation of the European Parliament in October 2004, the primary responsibility of which was the creation of an integrated border management system. The Agency commenced operations on 1 May 2005, with its seat at Warsaw, Poland. The role of FRONTEX was to be enhanced during 2010–14, under the Stockholm Programme. In June 2004 the Council adopted a decision concerning the development of a system for the exchange of visa data between member states, the Visa Information System (VIS). The VIS was intended to enhance the internal security of member states and contribute to the fight against illegal immigration. In September 2005 the Commission presented a package of measures on asylum and immigration. The proposals included the application of common standards to the return of illegal immigrants, the adoption of a more coherent approach to the integration of migrants, the encouragement of migrants to contribute to the development of their home countries, and the introduction of Regional Protection Programmes to assist refugees remaining in their regions of origin and their host countries. In December, in a move towards the creation of a common European asylum system, the Justice and Home Affairs Council adopted a directive on asylum procedures, setting minimum standards for granting and withdrawing refugee status, as well as an action plan on preventing human trafficking. A new framework programme entitled 'Solidarity and Management of Migration Flows' was adopted in December 2006 with the aim of improving management of migratory flows at EU level. Allocated an overall budget of €4,020m. for 2007–13, the programme was divided into four specific policy areas, each with its own financial instrument: the control and surveillance of external borders (External Borders Fund, €1,820m.); the return of third country nationals residing illegally in the EU (European Return Fund, €676m.); the integration of legally resident third country nationals (European Integration Fund, €825m.); and asylum (European Refugee Fund—first established in 2000—€699m.). In June 2008 the Commission adopted a communication on principles, actions and tools relating to a common immigration policy for Europe, and a policy plan on asylum. The latter provided the framework for the second phase of the creation of the common European asylum system. In December the European Parliament and Council of the EU adopted a directive on determining common standards and procedures for returning illegally staying third country nationals from member states, and, in May 2009, the Council adopted a directive on the enforcement of sanctions and measures against employers engaging illegal immigrants. It was estimated at that time that up to 8m. illegal immigrants were residing in the EU. A new European Migration Network, fully established following a directive of the Council adopted in May 2008, having been launched in 2003 as a pilot project, aims to provide current and comparable information on migration and asylum. In November 2011 the EU Immigration Portal was launched, to provide practical information for foreign nationals interested in moving to the EU, or seeking to move between EU countries. In December the Single Permit Directive was adopted, establishing rights for non-EU workers residing lawfully in an EU member state.

EDUCATION, TRAINING AND CULTURE

The Treaty of Rome, although not covering education directly, gave the Community the role of establishing general principles for implementing a common vocational training policy. The Treaty on European Union urged greater co-operation on education policy, including encouraging exchanges and mobility for students and teachers, distance learning and the development of European studies. The Bologna Process was launched in 1999 with the aim of establishing a European Higher Education Area, including education networks and student exchanges. In May 2007 the EU and the Council of Europe signed a memorandum of understanding confirming mutual co-operation in the promotion of democratic citizenship and human rights education and their joint commitment to the Bologna Process. In November 2007 the Council adopted a resolution on modernising universities to aid Europe's competitiveness in the global knowledge economy. In April 2009 ministers responsible for higher education in the member countries of the Bologna Process adopted the priorities for the European Higher Education Area until 2020, with an emphasis on the importance of lifelong learning, expanding access to higher education, and mobility. In March 2010 the Bologna Process ministers for higher education adopted the Budapest-Vienna Declaration officially launching the European Higher Education Area. Meanwhile, in May 2009 the Council had adopted Education and Training 2020 (ET 2020), a strategic framework for European co-operation in education and training, which identified four principal objectives: to facilitate lifelong learning and mobility; to improve the quality of education and training; to promote equality, social cohesion and citizenship; and to help develop creativity and innovation in education and training. ET 2020 also provided for support for the Bologna intergovernmental process, which focuses on higher education.

The postgraduate European University Institute (EUI) was founded in Florence, Italy, in 1972, with departments of history and civilization, economics, law, and political and social sciences. The EUI is also the depository for the historical archives of the EC institutions. Approximately 140 new research students enrol at the Institute each year. An Academy of European Law was founded within the EUI in 1990, and in 1992 the Robert Schuman Centre for Advanced Studies was established to develop inter-disciplinary and comparative postdoctoral research. The Jean Monnet programme, which supports institutions and activities in the field of European integration, finances the establishment of Jean Monnet chairs at universities throughout the world; the programme targets disciplines in which EU developments are an increasingly important part of the subject studied—e.g. European law, European economic and political integration, and the history of the European construction process. The establishment of a network of Jean Monnet Centres of Excellence was approved in 1998; the network was extended beyond Europe in 2001, and by 2012 it was active in 72 countries world-wide.

The EU's Lifelong Learning Programme, an integrated action programme covering 2007–13, and with an overall budget of €6,970m., incorporated as sub-programmes four existing educational and training initiatives—Comenius (for schools), Erasmus (for higher education), Grundtvig (for adult education) and the Leonardo da Vinci programme (see below)—as well as the Jean Monnet programme, and introduced a new Transversal programme to facilitate activities involving more than one area of education, such as language learning and innovation in information and communication technologies. An educational information network, Eurydice, which began operations in 1980, provides data on and analyses of European national education systems and policies. Eurydice is co-ordinated by an Education, Audiovisual and Culture Executive Agency in Brussels, Belgium, and comprises national units based in the 33 Lifelong Learning programme countries.

The Erasmus educational exchange programme, which was launched in 1987, enables students throughout Europe to travel to other EU countries to study and work as part of their degree programme. The first Erasmus Mundus programme ran from 2004–08 as a global mobility programme, promoting intercultural co-operation, and the EU as a centre of academic excellence, by enabling highly qualified students and academics living outside the EU to pursue Masters or doctorate programmes at EU universities. In October 2008 the European Parliament approved a second Erasmus Mundus programme for 2009–13, with an estimated budget of €950m.

The EU's Youth in Action programme, with a total budget of €885m., covers the period 2007–13, replacing the previous Youth programme for 2000–06. Objectives of Youth in Action include: fostering a sense of citizenship, solidarity and mutual understanding in young people; enhancing the quality of support systems for youth activities; and promoting European co-operation in youth policy. In March 2005 the Council adopted a European Pact for Youth, which focused on improving the education, training, mobility, vocational integration and social inclusion of young Europeans, while facilitating the reconciliation of family life and working life.

In November 2011 the European Commission proposed a new EU programme for education, training, youth and sport, Erasmus for All, which was intended to replace both the Lifelong Learning and the Youth in Action programmes. The Commission intended to introduce the new programme in 2014, with a budget of €19,000m. The proposal required approval by the European Council and the European Parliament.

Covering 2007–13, the fourth phase of the Trans-European Mobility Scheme for University Studies (TEMPUS, the first phase of which was launched in 1990) aims to support the modernization of higher education, and to create an area of co-operation between institutions in EU member countries and partner countries surrounding the EU. TEMPUS IV covers 27 partner countries in Central and Eastern Europe, Central Asia, North Africa and the Middle East. The European Training Foundation (ETF), which was established in Turin, Italy, in 1995, and the mandate of which was revised in December 2008, aims to support developing and transition countries in the promotion of human capital development, i.e. advancing skills and competences through the improvement of vocational education and training systems.

The European Centre for the Development of Vocational Training (Centre Européen pour le Développement de la Formation Professionnelle—CEDEFOP) was established in Berlin, Germany, in 1975. The centre relocated to Thessaloníki, Greece, in 1995. Much of CEDEFOP's recent work has focused on the employment problems encountered by women, especially those who wish to return to work after a long absence, on encouraging the participation of older workers in vocational training, and on addressing the needs of low-skilled people. The Leonardo da Vinci programme was introduced in 1994 to help European citizens to enhance their skills and to improve the quality and accessibility of vocational training. The programme supports lifelong learning policies and promotes transnational projects in an effort to increase mobility and foster innovation in European vocational education and training. The EUROPASS programme, which was officially launched in February 2005 and which brought into a single framework several existing tools for the transparency of diplomas, certificates and competences, was aimed at promoting both occupational mobility, between countries as well as across sectors, and mobility for learning purposes. In September 2006 the Commission proposed the establishment of a European qualifications framework (EQF), based on eight reference levels of qualifications, with the aim of further promoting mobility and lifelong learning. Member states were required to relate their own qualifications systems to the EQF by 2010, and by 2012 every new qualification issued in the EU was to have a reference to the appropriate EQF level. The EQF was formally adopted in April 2008.

The EU's Culture 2007 programme, covering the period 2007–13, and with a total budget of some €400m., replaced a previous Culture 2000 agenda, and focused on three priorities: the mobility of those working in the cultural sector; the transnational circulation of works of art; and intercultural dialogue. In November 2007 the Council endorsed the first European strategy for culture policy, which had three main objectives: the promotion of cultural diversity and intercultural dialogue; the promotion of culture as a catalyst for creativity; and the promotion of culture as a vital element in the EU's international relations. The EU's Culture programme supports several prizes, which are awarded in recognition of excellence in architecture, cultural heritage, literature and music. In November 2008 the Europeana project was launched, funded by the European Commission, with the aim of creating an online digital library to make Europe's cultural heritage accessible to the public (www.europeana.net). By July 2010 the collection comprised some 10m. items.

The European City of Culture initiative was launched in 1985 (and renamed the European Capital of Culture initiative in 1999). Member states nominate one or more cities in turn, according to an agreed chronological order. The capitals of culture are then formally selected by the Council on the recommendation of the Commission, taking into account the view of a selection panel. Since 2009 there have been two annual capitals of culture from member states, including one from the new, post-May 2004, membership, plus a maximum of one city from European non-member countries. Guimarães (Portugal) and Maribor (Slovenia) were selected as capitals for culture for 2012; Marseille (France) and Košice (Slovakia) for 2013; and Umeå (Sweden) and Rīga (Latvia) for 2014.

EMPLOYMENT, SOCIAL AFFAIRS AND INCLUSION

The Single European Act, which entered into force in 1987, added to the original Treaty of Rome articles that emphasized the need for 'economic and social cohesion' in the Community, i.e. the reduction of disparities between the various regions. This was to be achieved principally through the existing 'structural funds'—the European Regional Development Fund, the European Social Fund, and the Guidance Section of the European Agricultural Guidance and Guarantee Fund, which was replaced by the European Fund for Agricultural Development in 2007. In 1988 the Council declared that Community operations through the structural funds, the European Investment Bank and other financial instruments should have five priority objectives: (i) promoting the development and structural adjustment of the less-developed regions (where gross domestic product per head was less than 75% of the Community average); (ii) converting the regions, frontier regions or parts of regions seriously affected by industrial decline; (iii) combating long-term unemployment among people above the age of 25; (iv) providing employment for young people (under the age of 25); and (v) with a view to the reform of the common agricultural policy (CAP), speeding up the adjustment of agricultural structures and promoting the development of rural areas.

In 1989 the Commission proposed a Charter of Fundamental Social Rights of Workers (later known as the Social Charter), covering freedom of movement, fair remuneration, improvement of working conditions, the right to social security, freedom of association and collective wage agreements, the development of participation by workers in management, and sexual equality. The Charter was approved (with some modifications) by the heads of government of all Community member states, except the United Kingdom, in December. On the insistence of the United Kingdom, the chapter on social affairs of the Treaty on European Union, negotiated in December 1991, was omitted from the Treaty to form a separate protocol (the Community Charter of Fundamental Social Rights for Workers, or so-called Social Charter, complete with an opt-out arrangement for the United Kingdom). In September 1994 ministers adopted the first directive to be approved under the Social Charter, concerning the establishment of mandatory works councils in multinational companies; this came into force in September 1996. In April 1996 the Commission proposed that part-time, fixed-term and temporary employees should receive comparable treatment to permanent, full-time employees. A directive ensuring equal treatment for part-time employees was adopted by the Council in December 1997. A directive on parental leave, the second directive to be adopted under the Social Charter, provided for a statutory minimum of three months' unpaid leave to allow parents to care for young children, and was adopted in June 1996. In May 1997 the new Government of the United Kingdom approved the Social Charter, which was to be incorporated into the Treaty of Amsterdam. The Treaty, which entered into force in May 1999, consequently removed the opt-out clause and incorporated the Social Chapter in the revised Treaty of Rome. In December the Council adopted amendments extending the two directives adopted under the Charter to include the United Kingdom.

The Treaty of Amsterdam authorized the European Council to take action against all types of discrimination. Several directives and programmes on gender equality and equal opportunities have been approved and the Commission has initiated legal proceedings against a number of member states before the European Court of Justice for infringements. In December 2006 the Council and Parliament approved the establishment of a European Institute for Gender Equality, which was founded in 2007; initially temporarily located in Brussels, Belgium, it is now based in Vilnius, Lithuania. In June 2000 the Council adopted a directive implementing the principle of equal treatment regardless of racial or ethnic origin in employment, education, social security, health care and access to goods and services. This was followed in November by a directive establishing a framework for equal treatment regardless of religion or belief, disability, age or sexual orientation. A joint seminar was held in February 2004, in Brussels, by the Commission and the European Jewish Congress, to discuss Jewish community concerns that anti-Semitism was increasing in Europe. In June 2005 the Commission presented a framework strategy on non-discrimination and equal opportunities, aimed at ensuring the full implementation and enforcement by member states of anti-discrimination legislation. In March 2007 the EU Agency for Fundamental Rights (FRA), based in Vienna, replaced the former European Monitoring Centre on Racism and Xenophobia (EUMC). The FRA, which immediately assumed the mandate of the EUMC regarding racism and xenophobia, was gradually to develop knowledge, expertise and work programmes in respect of other fundamental rights. The Agency maintains an information network (the European Information Network on Racism and Xenophobia—RAXEN) and a database.

Numerous directives on health and safety in the workplace have been adopted by the Community. The Major Accident Hazards Bureau (MAHB), which was established in 1996 and is based at the Joint Research Centre in Ispra, Italy, helps to prevent and to mitigate industrial accidents in the EU. To this end, MAHB maintains a Major Accident Reporting System database and a Community Documentation Centre on Industrial Risk. There is also a European Agency for Health and Safety at Work, which was established in 1995 in Bilbao, Spain. The Agency has a health and safety information network composed of 'focal points' in each member state, in the candidate countries and in the four European Free Trade Association (EFTA) states. In February 2007 the Commission adopted a new five-year strategy for health and safety at work, which aimed to reduce work-related illness and accidents by 25% by 2012.

In June 1993 the Working Time Directive (WTD) was approved, restricting the working week to a maximum duration of 48 hours, except where overtime arrangements are agreed with trade unions. The WTD also prescribed minimum rest periods and a minimum of four weeks' paid holiday a year. However, certain categories of employee were exempt from the maximum 48-hour week rule, including those in the transport sector, those employed in offshore oil extraction, fishermen and junior hospital doctors. In April 2000 agreement was reached on gradually extending some or all of the rights of the WTD to cover most excluded workers. A Road Transport Directive, which applies to mobile workers who participate in road transport activities covered by EU drivers' hours rules, was adopted in March 2002 and took effect in March 2005. In January 2004 the Commission launched a review of the WTD following an increase in the use of its opt-out clause by a number of member states. In May 2005, however, in a first reading, the European Parliament voted in favour of proposals to phase out the opt-out clause (except for the police, army and emergency services, and chief executive officers and senior managers) and to count all on-call time as working time, although members agreed with the Commission regarding the use of a one-year reference period for calculating the average working week. In December 2008 the European Parliament voted to phase out the WTD opt-out clause within three years of the entry into force of a revised directive; however, negotiations on WTD reform subsequently broke down. A European Commission report published in December 2010 indicated that five member states (Bulgaria, Cyprus, Estonia, Malta and the United Kingdom) permitted the opt-out to be used, without restriction on sector, while 11 further member states allowed, or were introducing, limited use of the opt-out clause. In contrast, four member states made use of the opt-out clause in 2003.

The European Foundation for the Improvement of Living and Working Conditions (Eurofound), which was established in Dublin, Ireland, in 1975, undertakes four-year research and development programmes in the fields of employment, sustainable development, equal opportunities, social cohesion, health and well-being, and participation. Prior to the EU's enlargement in May 2004, Eurofound made available wide-ranging new data and analysis on living and working conditions in the existing member states and in the accession and candidate states. The Foundation utilizes monitoring tools including the European Industrial Relations Observatory (EIRO), the European Working Conditions Observatory (EWCO), and the European Monitoring Centre on Change (EMCC). Every four years Eurofound conducts surveys on Quality of Life in Europe; and surveys are also carried out on European Working Conditions; and on European companies.

An employment body, European Employment Services (EURES), launched in 1994, maintains a web portal and operates as a network of more than 750 specialist advisers across Europe, who (with the co-operation of national public employment services, trade unions, employers' organizations, local authorities, etc., and with access to a detailed database) provide the three basic EURES services of information, guidance and placement to both job seekers and employers interested in the European job market. EURES has a particularly effective role to play in cross-border regions where there are significant degrees of cross-border commuting by employees. EURES, which covers the countries of the European Economic Area (EEA) and Switzerland, also provides a public database of employment vacancies and a database through which job seekers can make their curricula vitae available to a wide range of employers.

Under the European employment strategy, initiated in 1997 and incorporated in the Treaty of Amsterdam, an Employment Committee was established in 2000 to oversee the co-ordination of the employment strategies of the member states and an employment package was to be presented (as a joint effort by the Council of the European Union and the Commission) each year. The package contains reports on member states' performances, individual recommendations and policy guidelines for the future. In December 2007 EU ministers responsible for employment and social affairs adopted a set of common principles of 'flexicurity' (a combination of flexibility and security) that member states should follow when developing labour market policies. This new approach was based on four components: effective labour market policies; flexible and reliable contractual arrangements; comprehensive lifelong learning strategies; and modern and adequate social protection systems. At an EU summit in Brussels at the end of January 2012 the European Council pledged to increase efforts to provide jobs for young people, in particular by identifying EU member states with the highest rates of unemployment among young people, and diverting funds to facilitate the provision of training or access to employment, and establish apprenticeship schemes. The Council also sought the completion of the single market, and the promotion of cross-border labour mobility; and the provision of assistance to small and medium-sized enterprises (SMEs). The overall EU unemployment rate was 9.9% in December 2011, while the rate of employment in the euro area was 10.4%.

All 15 of the longer-standing members of the EU (EU-15), except the United Kingdom, Ireland and Sweden, had planned to impose at least a two-year period of restriction on immigrants from the eight formerly communist new member states (EU-8—the Czech Republic, Estonia, Hungary, Latvia, Lithuania, Poland, Slovenia and Slovakia) after their accession to the EU in May 2004, to prevent their labour markets being saturated with inexpensive labour. Workers from the new member states Malta and Cyprus were allowed into existing EU countries without any restrictions. All EU-15 states were required to apply EU legislation on free movement and open their labour markets to the EU-8 in 2011, and to Bulgaria and Romania by 2014. By early 2012 work restrictions on citizens of Bulgaria and Romania remained in place in Austria, France, Germany, Ireland, Holland, Luxembourg, Malta and the United Kingdom. A European Commission report published in 2009 estimated that the number of EU-8 nationals residing in EU-15 countries had risen from around 900,000 before enlargement to some 1.9m. in 2007, with Ireland and the United Kingdom as the main destination for new workers; meanwhile, over the same period, the number of Bulgarian and Romanian workers resident in EU-15 states was estimated to have increased from about 700,000 to nearly 1.9m., with Italy and Spain as the principal destination countries.

A European Social Protection Committee was established in June 2000. In addition, the EU administers MISSOC—the Mutual Information System on Social Protection in the EU member states and the EEA. Switzerland is also included in MISSOC. In February 2005 the European Commission launched its Social Agenda (2005–10) for modernizing the EU's social model. The Agenda focused on providing jobs and equal opportunities for all and ensuring that the benefits of the EU's growth and employment creation schemes reached all levels of society. A renewed Agenda was adopted by the European Commission in July 2008, focusing on seven priority areas: children and youth; investment in people; mobility; longer, healthier lives; combating poverty and social exclusion; fighting discrimination and promoting equality; and global opportunities, access and solidarity. Meanwhile, a new programme for employment and social solidarity (PROGRESS) had been established to provide financial support for the implementation of the objectives set out in the Social Agenda. With an overall budget of €743m. for 2007–13, PROGRESS replaced four previous programmes that had expired in 2006 and was to cover the policy areas of social protection and inclusion, employment, non-discrimination, gender equality and working conditions.

The Charter of Fundamental Rights (CFR) was proclaimed at the Nice Summit of the European Council in December 2000. The text of the CFR consists of seven chapters, covering dignity, freedoms, equality, solidarity, citizens' rights, justice and general provisions. No new rights were actually created as part of the CFR; rather, it presents in a single document the existing rights and freedoms enjoyed by EU citizens through the European Convention on Human Rights, the Charter of Fundamental Social Rights of Workers and various other EU treaties. The CFR became legally binding following the entry into force in December 2009 of the Treaty of Lisbon. (A protocol limited the application of the CFR in the Czech Republic, Poland and the United Kingdom.) In February 2010 the EU, a single legal entity under the terms of the Lisbon Treaty, acceded to the European Convention on Human Rights (ECHR), thereby enabling the European Court of Human Rights to verify future EU compliance with the provisions of the ECHR.

The EU disability strategy has three main focuses: co-operation between the Commission and the member states; the full participation of people with disabilities; and ensuring disability issues are fully recognized in policy formulation (particularly with regard to employment). Ongoing EU activities relating to disability include dialogue with the European Disability Forum and a European Day of Disabled People, which takes place in December each year. A disability action plan for 2004–10 aimed to enhance the economic and social integration of people with disabilities. In November 2010 the Commission launched the EU Disability Strategy 2010–20, which established plans for the forthcoming decade. In the Strategy's first five years the Commission aimed to: improve accessibility to goods and services for people with disabilities, and to consider proposing a European Accessibility Act; help disabled people to exercise their right to vote; use the European Platform Against Poverty to reduce the risk of poverty; ensure that the European Social Fund offered ongoing support to disability-related projects; carry out data collection with the aim of improving opportunities for the employment of disabled people; develop policies to ensure inclusive education; facilitate the mutual recognition of disability cards and related entitlements throughout Europe; and promote the rights of people with disabilities through the EU's external action.

CONSUMER PROTECTION AND HEALTH

Consumer protection is one of the stated priorities of EU policy, and has been implemented via a series of action programmes covering areas such as safety of products and services (e.g. food additives, safety of toys and childcare articles, packaging and labelling of goods), protecting consumers' economic and legal interests, and promoting consumer representation. A number of measures have been taken to strengthen consumer power, by promoting consumer associations and drawing up a requirement for fair commercial practices. The EU consumer policy strategy for 2007–13 was adopted in March 2007, subtitled 'Empowering consumers, enhancing their welfare, effectively protecting them'.

In December 2009 the European Commission adopted a new set of Rapid Alert System for Non-Food Consumer Products (known as RAPEX) guidelines. The RAPEX system (inaugurated in 2004) facilitates the rapid exchange of information between member states of measures taken to restrict or prevent the marketing or use of products deemed to pose a serious risk to the health and safety of consumers. The Commission publishes a weekly report of recent RAPEX notifications. In July 2009 a new Toy Safety Directive entered into force, which aimed to ensure that toys produced in and/or sold to consumers in the EU meet the highest safety requirements, and included limiting the amounts of certain chemicals that may be contained in materials used in the production of toys.

The Dolceta—Online Consumer Education initiative of the European Commission (launched in June 2005; managed by the European Association for University Lifelong Learning in co-operation with the European Association for Adult Education, and national teams; and accessible at www.dolceta.eu) aims to educate European consumers in areas including consumer rights; financial services; product safety; sustainable consumption; and services (utilities, telecommunications, transport and postal services).

In February 1997 the Commission extended the function of its directorate-general on consumer policy to incorporate consumer health protection. This decision (which followed widespread consumer concerns regarding the bovine spongiform encephalopathy (BSE) crisis—see Agriculture) was designed to ensure that sufficient importance was given to food safety. The European

Food Safety Authority was established to assume responsibility for providing the Commission with scientific advice on food safety. With a wide brief to cover all stages of food production and supply right through to consumers, the Authority has been based in Parma, Italy, since June 2005. In March 2004 the Commission adopted a decision to establish three new scientific steering committees in the fields of consumer products, health and environmental risks, and emerging and newly identified health risks. In July 1998 an Institute for Health and Consumer Protection (IHCP), attached to the Commission's Joint Research Centre, was established (see ihcp.jrc.ec.europa.eu).

In July 2001 the Commission developed its rules on the labelling and tracing of genetically modified organisms (GMOs, see Agriculture). During 2004 a framework was developed for the creation of international guidelines on the measurement of chemical and biological elements in food and other products. The system would facilitate the detection of GMOs and the measurement of sulphur content in motor fuels. New legislation on the safety of food and animal feed came into force in January 2005. Business operators were required to ensure the safety of their products and apply appropriate systems and procedures to establish the traceability of food, feed, food-producing animals and all substances incorporated into foodstuffs at all stages of production, processing and distribution. An Advisory Group on the Food Chain and Animal and Plant Health was established by the Commission in March and held its inaugural meeting in July. A Community Register of Feed Additives was first published in November, in accordance with a regulation on additives for use in animal nutrition. A regulation requiring that all health claims on food, drinks or food supplements be substantiated by independent experts was adopted in December 2006. In January of that year new regulations on food and animal feed hygiene, applying to every stage of the food chain, entered into force. At the same time, an EU-wide ban on the use of antibiotics in animal feed to stimulate growth took effect, as part of efforts to reduce the non-essential use of antibiotics in order to address the problem of micro-organisms becoming resistant to traditional medical treatments. In November 2009 the European Commission published, as a basis for future discussion, a working paper on means of addressing so-called anti-microbial resistance (AMR) which, it was reported, was causing annually around 25,000 human fatalities in the EU region.

In January 2005 a European Consumer Centres Network (ECC-Net) was established to provide a single point of contact in each member state for consumers to obtain information about their rights and assistance in pursuing complaints, particularly in cases concerning cross-border purchases. The ECC-NET handled 71,292 cases in 2010, of which 12,622 related to the rights of air travellers. Legislation increasing the compensation rights of air travellers took effect in February 2005. New rights to compensation and assistance in the event of cancellations or long delays were introduced, compensation was increased for passengers unable to board a flight owing to overbooking by the airline and cover was extended to passengers travelling on charter or domestic flights. In November 2009 the European Commission launched a public consultation on revising EU legislation relating to package travel, to take account of advances made in recent years in internet and low-cost airline usage. Also in that month the Commission published a report on airline charges which found that frequently it had been airline practice to incorporate some basic operational costs (including handling charges, fuel charges and booking fees) into the 'taxes and charges' category, rendering it difficult for consumers to make comparisons between offers or to identify the value of national taxes and airport charges that might be refunded against unused tickets.

The Consumer Protection Co-operation Network (CPC), comprising public authorities responsible for enforcing legislation to protect the interests of consumers in the event of cross-border disputes, was officially launched in February 2007. The first of a series of EU 'sweeps'—joint investigations and enforcement actions aimed at evaluating compliance with consumer laws in particular markets—was conducted in September 2007, into misleading advertising and unfair practices on airline ticket-selling websites, and in November it was revealed that irregularities had been discovered on more than 50% of the sites checked. Following such investigations, national enforcement authorities act to ensure that companies found to have been compromising consumer rights improve their practices. The results of a 'sweep' focusing on the provision of online mobile cellular telephone services, initiated in June 2008, were published in November 2009. In September 2010 the results of the second phase of a 'sweep' investigating online distributors of electronic goods (such as mobile cellular telephones, digital cameras and personal music players) were published; 84% of the websites checked for breach of EU consumer legislation in 26 member states, plus Iceland and Norway, were found to comply with EU laws, compared with 44% in 2009. The breaches identified involved misleading information on consumer rights, incorrect tariffs, and failures to provide traders' contact details; such sites were compelled to make adjustments, and, if necessary, penalties were imposed. In July 2009 the European Commission published a blueprint for a proposed standardized EU-wide method for classifying and reporting consumer complaints. In November 2011 the Commission adopted a directive on Alternative Dispute Resolution (ADR), which sought to ensure that all contractual disputes between consumers and providers could be resolved without recourse to the courts. A new Regulation on Online Dispute Resolution sought to create an online presence ('ODR platform') throughout the EU, which could be consulted by both consumers and businesses in order to enable them to settle disputes concerning the online purchase of goods from other EU member countries.

In February 2005 the European Parliament approved a new directive to harmonize the framework across the EU for banning unfair commercial practices. The new legislation, which clarified consumers' rights, banned pressure selling and misleading marketing and facilitated cross-border trade, took effect in December 2007, although only 14 member states had implemented the directive by that time. In February 2003 the Commission adopted an action plan for a more coherent and standardized European contract law. Substantive work towards the long-term aim of developing a Common Frame of Reference, which would contain clear definitions of legal terms, fundamental principles and coherent model rules of contract law, was ongoing.

A programme of action in the field of health, for the period 2008–13, entitled 'Together for Health', was adopted in October 2007, with a budget of €321.5m. Its three general objectives were: to improve citizens' health security; to promote health, including the reduction of health inequalities; and to generate and disseminate health information and knowledge. Meanwhile, the Commission adopted a new health strategy for the same period with the aims of fostering good health in an ageing Europe, protecting citizens from health threats, and supporting dynamic health systems and new technologies.

In December 2008—in view of estimates that annually 8%–12% of patients admitted to EU hospitals suffered largely preventable harm from the health care they received, including contracting health care-associated infections, such as those caused by the bacterium MRSA (methicillin-resistant staphylococcus aureus)—the Commission adopted a Communication and proposal for a Council Recommendation on specific actions that member states could take, either individually, collectively or with the Commission, to improve the safety of patients.

In September 2009 the European Commission determined to limit health risks to consumers derived from exposure to noise from personal music players; it was decided that default settings on personal music players should be set at safe exposure levels, and that clear warnings should be provided alerting consumers to the possible adverse effects of excessive exposure to high sound levels.

Various epidemiological surveillance systems are in operation, covering major communicable diseases. An early warning and response system (EWRS) to help member states deal with outbreaks of diseases was in place by the end of 2000. In April 2004 the European Parliament and the Council adopted a regulation establishing a European Centre for Disease Prevention and Control (ECDC), to enable the EU to share its disease control expertise more effectively and to allow multinational investigation teams to be drawn up quickly and efficiently. The Centre, based in Sweden, became operational in May 2005. The ECDC's European Programme for Intervention Epidemiology Training (EPIET) provides training and practical experience in intervention epidemiology at national centres for surveillance and communicable diseases control within the EU. In late April 2009 an extraordinary meeting of EU health ministers was convened, in Luxembourg, to address the emergence of a new variant of swine influenza (A/H1N1), referred to from June as pandemic (H1N1) 2009. The directorate-general with responsibility for Health took control of the co-ordinated response to pandemic (H1N1) 2009 within the framework of the EWRS. In September 2009 the European Commission adopted the EU Strategy on Pandemic (H1N1) 2009, aimed at supporting member states in their efforts to respond efficiently to it, and focusing on the importance of co-ordination across sectors and between states.

In September 2009 the European Commission launched a new European Partnership for Action against Cancer, which was to bring together relevant organizations to pool expertise with the aim of lowering the number of new cancer cases arising in the EU by some 15%, by 2020. During 2006–08 the EU member states, and Iceland and Norway, implemented the Vaccine European New Integrated Collaboration Effort (VENICE) project, which aimed to broaden knowledge and best practices on vaccination; a follow-up project, VENICE II, was launched in December 2008. The first European conference on vaccination and immunization—Eurovaccine 2009, organized and funded by the ECDC, and convened in Stockholm, Sweden, in December 2009—addressed topics including vaccinating against pandemic (H1N1) 2009 and the formulation of strategies for eliminating measles throughout Europe.

Under the Treaty on European Union, the EU assumed responsibility for the problem of drug addiction; a European Monitoring Centre for Drugs and Drug Addiction (EMCDDA, see Justice and Home Affairs) was established in Lisbon, Portugal, in 1995. In March 2005 an EU Platform for Action on Diet, Physical Activity and Health was launched, as part of an overall strategy on nutrition and physical activity being developed by the Commission to address rising levels of obesity. The Commission initiated a public consultation in December on how to reduce obesity levels and the prevalence of associated chronic diseases in the EU. In May 2007 the Commission adopted a White Paper on nutrition- and obesity-related health issues, in which it urged food manufacturers to reduce levels of salt, fat and sugar in their products and emphasized the need to encourage Europeans to undertake more physical activity. A European Alcohol and Health Forum, comprising more than 40 businesses and non-governmental organizations, was formed in June 2007 to focus on initiatives to protect European citizens from the harmful use of alcohol. In October 2006 the Commission had adopted a communication setting out an EU strategy to support member states in reducing alcohol-related harm.

The European Commission states that tobacco use is the largest single cause of premature death and disease in the EU. In July 2005 an EU directive came into effect that prohibited tobacco advertising in the print media, on radio and over the internet, as well as the sponsorship by tobacco companies of cross-border cultural and sporting events. The directive applied only to advertising and sponsorship with a cross-border dimension. Tobacco advertising on television had already been banned in the EU in the early 1990s. In June 2009, after extensive consultation, the Commission adopted a proposal for a Council recommendation on the introduction by 2012 of national legislation to protect citizens from exposure to tobacco smoke. At February 2011 comprehensive legislation on providing a smoke-free environment had been enacted in 10 EU countries, with complete bans on smoking in enclosed public places, on public transport and in workplaces in force in Ireland and the United Kingdom.

The Food Supplements Directive, which was approved in 2002 and was designed to strengthen controls on the sale of natural remedies, vitamin supplements and mineral plant extracts, came into effect in August 2005. Under the legislation, only vitamins and minerals on an approved list could be used in supplements and restrictions were to be placed on the upper limits of vitamin doses. In July 2005 the European Court of Justice had confirmed the validity of the directive, which had been challenged by a group of consumers' and retail associations in the United Kingdom.

In June 2008 an EU high-level conference entitled 'Together for Mental Health and Well-being' launched the European Pact for Mental Health and Well-being, to be implemented through thematic conferences during 2009–10 focusing on five priority areas: prevention of suicide and depression; mental health in youth and education; mental health in workplace settings; mental health in older people; and combating stigma and social exclusion.

In October 2009 the European Commission adopted a strategy and action plan for combating HIV/AIDS in the EU and neighbouring countries in 2009–13, with a focus on the following principal areas: HIV prevention and testing; targeting priority groups most at risk of HIV; and targeting regions with a higher proportion of people at risk. The strategy had the following overall objectives: to reduce new HIV infections across all European countries by 2013; to improve patients' access to prevention, treatment and support; and to ameliorate the quality of life of those living with, affected by or most vulnerable to HIV/AIDS in Europe and neighbouring countries.

It was envisaged that the enlargement of the EU in May 2004, and again in January 2007, providing for the incorporation of 12 new member states, would cause a number of problems for the Union with regard to public health policy given that, in general, the health status indicators of the majority of the accession states compared poorly with the EU average. Some of the new member states, which (with only one or two exceptions) had few resources to spend on health, had serious problems with communicable diseases (particularly HIV/AIDS), and the health systems of most were in need of improvement. In October 2009 the European Commission announced a series of actions aimed at helping member states and other actors to address inequalities in health provision and life expectancy within and between individual EU member states. Member states and stakeholders were to be helped to identify best practices; and the Commission was to publish regular relevant statistics, and also to issue reports on inequalities and their impact and on successful strategies for addressing them. It was to support countries by using EU funds towards improving primary care facilities, water provision, sanitation and housing renewal. An initial report on progress towards combating health inequalities was to be released in 2012.

Since 1 January 2006 EU member states have issued European Health Insurance Cards (EHICs), which entitle residents to receive state-provided medical treatment in the event of suffering either an accident or illness while visiting temporarily states within the European Economic Area (EEA) and Switzerland.

ENVIRONMENT

Environmental action by the EU was initiated in 1972. The Maastricht Treaty on European Union, which entered into force in November 1993, gave environmental action policy status, and the Treaty of Amsterdam identified sustainable development as one of the Community's overall aims. In June 1998 European heads of state and government launched the Cardiff Process, requiring the integration of environmental considerations into all EU policies.

The EU's sixth environmental action programme (2002–12), Environment 2010: Our Future, Our Choice, emphasized the continuing importance of the integration of environmental considerations into other EU policies, focusing on four priority areas: climate change, nature and biodiversity; environment; health and quality of life; and the management of natural resources and waste. The programme also identified explicitly the measures required to implement successfully the EU's sustainable development strategy. In addition, it sought to encourage greater public participation in environmental debates.

The environment was one of the 10 themes of the 'co-operation' specific programme of the Seventh Framework Programme (FP7) for research, technological development and demonstration activities covering 2007–13 (see Research and Innovation). With a budget of €1,900m., a wide range of environmental research activities were allocated funding under FP7, grouped into four areas: climate change, pollution and risks; sustainable management of resources; environmental technologies; and earth observation and assessment tools for sustainable development. The Institute for Environment and Sustainability, located in Ispra, Italy, was created in 2001 as part of the Joint Research Centre to provide research-based support to the development and implementation of European environmental policies.

In 1990 the EC established the European Environment Agency (EEA, see p. 478) to monitor environmental issues and provide advice. The agency, which is located in Copenhagen, Denmark, and which became operational in November 1994, also provides targeted information to policy-makers and the public and disseminates comparable environmental data. The agency is open to non-EU countries and it was the first EU body to have members from the accession states.

From November 2009 the online European Pollutant Release and Transfer Register (E-PRTR) replaced the former European Pollutant Emission Register (EPER). The E-PRTR provides data (updated annually, with records commencing in 2007) for EU member states on 91 substances released to air, water and land and 65 sectors of industrial activity, including data on transfers of waste and waste-water from industrial facilities to other locations, and data on emissions caused by accidents at industrial facilities. The European Parliament approved legislation in April 2004 aimed at making firms causing pollution liable for the costs of repairing the damage caused to natural habitats, water resources and wildlife. In December 2007 the Commission adopted a new directive on reducing industrial emissions, which was to replace seven existing directives. The directive was intended, *inter alia*, to tighten emission limits in certain industrial sectors, to introduce minimum standards for environmental inspections of industrial installations and to extend the scope of legislation to cover other polluting activities, such as medium-sized combustion plants.

In May 2007 the Council and Parliament adopted a new funding programme, LIFE+, following on from a LIFE programme established in 1992; LIFE+ was to be the EU's single financial instrument targeting only the environment. With a budget of €2,143m. for the period 2007–13, LIFE+ consists of three thematic components: nature and biodiversity; environment policy and governance; and information and communication. LIFE+ supports projects throughout the EU, as well as in some candidate, acceding and neighbouring countries. Between 1992 and 2009 some 3,316 projects were co-financed by LIFE/LIFE+.

The EU has approved numerous international instruments relating to the environment, including the Vienna Convention for the Protection of the Ozone Layer, and its protocol, controlling the production of chlorofluorocarbons (CFCs); the Stockholm Convention on Persistent Organic Pollutants; and the Kyoto Protocol. In June 2000 the Commission launched the European Climate Change Programme (ECCP), which aimed to identify and develop a strategy needed to meet commitments under the Kyoto Protocol, and to incorporate climate change concerns into various EU policies. A second phase of the ECCP (under which more than 30 measures had been implemented since its establishment in 2000), ECCP II, was launched in October 2005, with the aim of reviewing the progress of individual member states towards achieving their individual targets on reducing emissions, and developing a framework for EU climate change policy beyond the expiry of the Kyoto Protocol in 2012. In January 2007, in a communication ('Limiting Global Climate Change to 2° Celsius: The Way Ahead for 2020 and Beyond'), the Commission set out proposals for climate change management, which were aimed at limiting the increase in the average global temperature to no more than 2°C above pre-industrial levels. In March 2007, at a summit meeting, EU leaders set a number of joint targets as part of the continued effort to combat the effects of global warming, which, together, it was claimed, constituted the Union's first ever comprehensive agreement on climate and energy policy. Consequently, in April 2009, the Council adopted new climate change legislation, committing EU member states to reducing carbon dioxide emissions by 20% in 2013–20, compared with emissions levels in 1990. The Council also agreed to increase the use of renewable energy sources to 20% (10% for transport energy consumption) by 2020, and to increase energy efficiency by 20% by the same date. Meeting in January 2010, the European Council and the European Commission published a joint letter in which they formally stated the willingness of the EU to adhere to emission reduction targets detailed in the non-binding Copenhagen Accord, which had been agreed in December 2009 by heads of state and government and other delegates attending the UN Climate Change Conference that had been convened in Copenhagen, originally with the objective of finalizing negotiations on a successor instrument to the Kyoto Protocol. The Copenhagen Accord determined that international co-operative action should be taken, in the context of sustainable development, to reduce global greenhouse gas emissions so as to hold the ongoing increase in global temperature below 2°C; in accordance with its April 2009 commitments, the EU had pledged a unilateral commitment to reduce the overall emissions by 20% of 1990 levels by 2020, and made a conditional offer to increase this reduction in emissions to 30%, provided that other major emitters agreed to assume their fair share of global emissions reduction efforts.

In February 2010 a Directorate-General for Climate Action was established, to help mitigate the consequences of climate change, to ensure targets on climate change are met, and to oversee the EU Emissions Trading System (ETS). The ETS, which was launched in January 2005, obliges companies that exceed their allocation of carbon dioxide emissions to buy extra allowances from more efficient companies or incur considerable fines. In November 2006 the Commission initiated a review of the EU ETS, proposing an expansion of its coverage to new sectors and emissions and the further harmonization of its application between member states. Legislation on a revised ETS was adopted by the Commission in April 2009. The revised ETS was to be effective from 2013–20, capping the overall level of permissible emissions, while allowing allowances to be traded as required. The total annual allowance was to decline each year, in order to reduce gradually the overall emissions level; 12% of ETS revenues were to be invested in a fund designed to encourage poorer member states to modernize their industry. Exemptions were to apply to industrial sectors considered to be at risk of 'carbon leakage', through the relocation of factories to countries located outside the EU, or the acquisition of EU industries by non-EU competitors. A directive incorporating the aviation sector into the EU ETS, with a view to capping aviation sector emissions, entered into force in February 2009. In October 2007 the European Commission announced that it had reached an agreement with the three countries of the EEA on linking their respective emissions trading systems. In the same month the Commission became a founding member of the International Carbon Action Partnership (ICAP), which convenes a Global Carbon Market Forum for countries and regions with mandatory emissions capping and trading systems.

Europe 2020 is the EU's strategy for growth until 2020, as part of which the Commission's flagship initiative for a resource-efficient Europe focuses on sustainable growth and a move towards a resource-efficient, low-carbon economy. In March 2011 the Commission adopted detailed proposals concerned with bringing about the transition to a competitive, low-carbon EU economy, by reducing domestic carbon emissions by between 80% and 95% by 2050. A so-called roadmap for a resource-efficient Europe was adopted by the Commission in September.

In June 1996 the Commission agreed a strategy, drawn up in collaboration with the European petroleum and car industries and known as the Auto-Oil Programme, for reducing harmful emissions from road vehicles by between 60% and 70% by 2010 in an effort to reduce air pollution. The programme committed member states to the progressive elimination of leaded petrol by 2000 (with limited exemptions until 2005). From 2000 petrol-powered road vehicles were to be fitted with 'on-board diagnostic' (OBD) systems to monitor emissions. Diesel vehicles were to be installed with OBD systems by 2005. Under Auto-Oil II, the directive was revised in 2003, establishing specifications to come into force on 1 January 2005, with new limits on sulphur content of both petrol and diesel. Moreover, lower limits would come into force for all fuel marketed from December 2009, although there would be limited availability from 2005. In July 1998 the Commission announced plans to reduce pollution from nuclear power stations by reducing emissions of sulphur dioxides, nitrogen oxides and dust by one-half. A new directive limiting the sulphur content of marine fuel came into force in August 2005. In April 2009 the Council and the European Parliament adopted a regulation on setting carbon dioxide emissions performance standards for new passenger cars, as part of an integrated approach to reducing carbon dioxide emissions from light-duty vehicles to no more than 120g per km by 2012.

In September 2005 the European Commission presented a thematic strategy on air pollution, prepared under the auspices of Clean Air for Europe (CAFE), a programme of technical analysis and policy development launched in March 2001. While covering all major pollutants, the new air quality policy focused on particulates and ground-level ozone pollution, which were known to pose the greatest risk to human health. The strategy aimed to cut the annual number of premature deaths from pollution-related diseases by almost 40% by 2020, compared with the 2000 level, and also to reduce the area of forests and other ecosystems suffering damage from airborne pollutants. In April 2008 a new air quality directive was approved by the Council, which merged five existing pieces of legislation into a single directive, and imposed limits on fine particle emissions (PM2.5) from vehicles, agriculture and small-scale industry for the first time. Emissions of PM2.5 in urban areas were to be reduced by 20% by 2020, compared with 2010 levels. The European Commission estimated that some 370,000 EU citizens died each year from conditions linked to air pollution.

In October 2005 the Commission proposed a strategy to protect the marine environment, which aimed to ensure that all EU marine waters were environmentally healthy by 2021. This was the second of seven thematic strategies to be adopted under the sixth environmental action programme (2002–12). The Commission proposed strategies on the prevention and recycling of waste and the sustainable use of natural resources in December 2005, and on the urban environment in January 2006. In July the Commission proposed a directive aimed at establishing a framework for achieving a more sustainable use of pesticides by reducing the risks posed by pesticides to human health and the environment (its sixth thematic strategy). In September the Commission adopted a comprehensive strategy dedicated to soil protection, including a proposal for a directive setting forth common principles for soil protection across the EU. A directive on the assessment and management of flood risks entered into force in November 2007, requiring member states to conduct preliminary assessments by 2011 to identify river basins and associated coastal areas at risk of flooding, to develop flood-risk maps by 2013 for areas deemed to be at risk, and to establish flood-risk management plans for these areas by 2015. In March 2009 the European Commission finalized an EU-wide review of the safety—to consumers, farmers, local residents, passers-by and animals—of existing pesticides used in plant protection products that were on the market before 1993; the review had resulted in the removal from sale of more than two-thirds of the substances assessed.

In September 2000 the EU adopted a directive on end-of-life vehicles (ELVs), containing measures for the collection, treatment, recovery and disposal of such waste. The ruling forced manufacturers to pay for the disposal of new cars from July 2002 and of old cars from January 2007. The directive set recycling and recovery targets, restricted the use of heavy metals in new cars from 2003, and specified that ELVs might only be dismantled by authorized agencies. EU directives on waste electronic and electrical equipment and the restriction of the use of certain hazardous substances in electronic and electrical equipment came into force in February 2003. The directives were based on the premise of producer responsibility and aimed to persuade producers to improve product design in order to facilitate recycling and disposal. Increased recycling of electrical and electronic equipment would limit the total quantity of waste going to final disposal. Under the legislation consumers would be able to return equipment free of charge from August 2005. In order to prevent the generation of hazardous waste, the second directive required the substitution of various heavy metals (lead, mercury, cadmium, and hexavalent chromium) and brominated flame retardants in new electrical and electronic equipment marketed from July 2006. In January 2005 the Commission adopted a new strategy on reducing mercury pollution, which was endorsed by EU ministers of the environment in June. A regulation banning mercury exports from the EU by 2011 was proposed by the Commission in October 2006. In September 2007 a directive was adopted on phasing out, by April 2009, the use of toxic mercury in measuring devices in cases where it could be substituted by safer alternatives; this was expected to lead to an annual reduction of 33 metric tons in mercury emissions in the EU.

A regulation revising EU laws on trade in wild animals and plants was adopted by ministers of the environment in December 1996. A series of directives adopted in 2002 formulated new EU policy on the conservation of wild birds, fishing and protection for certain species of whales. Every three years the Commission publishes an official report on the conservation of wild birds. In January 2010 the Commission issued a communication detailing possible future options for biodiversity policy after 2010, to succeed a previous agenda of halting biodiversity loss in the Union by 2010. The communication envisaged a long-term vision, towards 2050, for preserving and, as far as possible, restoring biodiversity, to be preceded by medium-term objectives to be achieved by 2020.

As part of the EU's efforts to promote awareness of environmental issues and to encourage companies to do likewise, the voluntary Eco-Management and Audit Scheme (EMAS) was launched in April 1995. Under the scheme, participating industrial companies undergo an independent audit of their environmental performance. In addition, the EU awards 'eco-labels' for products that limit harmful effects on the environment (including foodstuffs, beverages and pharmaceutical products, among others). The criteria to be met are set by the EU Eco-Labelling Board (EUEB).

In October 2003 the Commission presented a new environmental policy—the Registration, Evaluation and Authorisation of Chemicals system (REACH)—which was originally intended to collate crucial safety information on tens of thousands of potentially dangerous chemicals used in consumer goods industries. However, following intensive lobbying by the chemical industry sector, the scope of REACH was reduced (for example, the number of chemicals to be tested was cut and the number of chemicals that would require licences was also substantially curtailed). The European Parliament approved the proposed legislation in a first reading in November 2005, and in December the Council reached a political agreement on REACH. Environmentalists criticized ministers for weakening the legislation by relaxing the conditions set by the Parliament for authorization of the most dangerous chemicals. The REACH regulation was formally adopted in December 2006. The European Chemicals Agency, which is responsible for managing REACH, commenced operations in Helsinki, Finland, in June 2007. In December 2008 the Commission adopted a regulation aligning the EU system of classification, labelling and packaging of chemical substances and mixtures to the UN Globally Harmonized System of Classification and Labelling of Chemicals.

SECURITY AND DEFENCE

Under the Single European Act, which came into force on 1 July 1987 (amending the Treaty of Rome), it was formally stipulated for the first time that member states should inform and consult each other on foreign policy matters (as was already, in practice, often the case). In June 1992 the Petersberg Declaration of Western European Union (WEU) defined the role of WEU as the defence component of the EU and outlined the 'Petersberg tasks' relating to crisis management, including humanitarian, peace-keeping and peace-making operations, which could be carried out under WEU authority (now EU authority). In 1992 France and Germany established a joint force called Eurocorps, based in Strasbourg, France, which was later joined by Belgium, Spain and Luxembourg. An agreement was signed in January 1993 that specified that Eurocorps troops could serve under the command of the North Atlantic Treaty Organization (NATO), thus relieving concern, particularly from the United Kingdom and the USA, that the Eurocorps would undermine NATO's role in Europe. In May member states of the Eurocorps agreed to make the Eurocorps available to WEU. WEU also ratified in May 1995 the decision by Spain, France, Italy and Portugal to establish land and sea forces, the European Operational Rapid Force (EUROFOR) and the European Maritime Force (EUROMARFOR) respectively, which were also to undertake the Petersberg tasks under the auspices of WEU. Several other multinational forces also belonged to Forces Answerable to the WEU (FAWEU). At the EU summit in Köln, Germany, in June 1999, EU member states accepted a proposal for the Eurocorps to be placed at the disposal of the EU for crisis response operations. At the end of that year Eurocorps member states agreed to transform the Eurocorps into a rapid reaction corps headquarters available both to the EU and NATO. In 2002 NATO certified the Eurocorps as a NATO high readiness force, which required the headquarters (Eurocorps HQ) to be open to all NATO members as well as those from the EU; thus representatives from Austria, Canada, Finland, Greece, Italy, the Netherlands, Poland, Turkey and the United Kingdom are integrated into Eurocorps HQ. During early 2004–early 2005 an HQ Eurocorps European staff took the lead of the NATO International Security Assistance Force in Afghanistan (ISAF) for the duration of its sixth mandate.

The Maastricht Treaty on European Union, which came into force on 1 November 1993, provided for joint action by member governments in matters of common foreign and security policy (CFSP), and envisaged the formation of a European security and defence policy (ESDP), with the possibility of a common defence force, although existing commitments to NATO were to be honoured. The Treaty raised WEU to the rank of an 'integral part of the development of the Union', while preserving its institutional autonomy, and gave it the task of elaborating and implementing decisions and actions with defence implications.

The Treaty of Amsterdam, which entered into force in May 1999, aimed to strengthen the concept of a CFSP within the Union and incorporated a process of common strategies to coordinate external relations with a third party. Under the Amsterdam Treaty, WEU was to provide the EU with access to operational capability for undertaking the so-called Petersberg tasks. In March 1999 representatives of the Commission and NATO held a joint meeting, for the first time, to discuss the conflict in the southern Serbian province of Kosovo. The Treaty introduced the role of High Representative for the CFSP. In April a meeting of NATO Heads of State and of Government determined that NATO's equipment, personnel and infrastructure would be available to any future EU military operation. In June the European Council, meeting in Köln, determined to strengthen the ESDP, stating that the EU needed a capacity for autonomous action, without prejudice to actions by NATO and acknowledging the supreme prerogatives of the UN Security Council. The European Council initiated a process of assuming direct responsibility for the Petersberg tasks, which were placed at the core of the ESDP process. In December, following consultation with NATO, the European Council, meeting in Helsinki, Finland, adopted the European Defence Initiative, comprising the following goal: by 2003 the EU should be able to deploy within 60 days and for a period of up to one year a rapid reaction force, comprising up to 60,000 national troops from member states, capable of implementing the full range of Petersberg tasks. At the Helsinki meeting, the establishment of three permanent military institutions was proposed: a Political and Security Committee (PSC); a Military Committee; and a Military Staff. The PSC, which was fully established by 2001, monitors the international situation, helps to define policies and assess their implementation, encourages dialogue and, under the auspices of the Council, takes responsibility for the political direction of capability development. In the event of a crisis situation, it oversees the strategic direction of any military response, proposes political objectives and supervises their enactment. The Military Committee gives military advice to the PSC, and comprises the chiefs of defence of member states, represented by military delegates. It serves as a forum for military consultation and co-operation and deals with risk assessment, the development of crisis management and military relations with non-EU European NATO members, accession countries, and NATO itself. Meanwhile, the Military Staff, comprising experts seconded by the member states, provides the EU with an early-warning capability, takes responsibility for strategic planning for the Petersberg tasks and implements the Military Committee's policies. Permanent arrangements have been agreed for EU-NATO consultation and co-operation in this area. The process of transferring the crisis management responsibilities of WEU to the EU was finalized by July 2001. From January 2007 a new EU Operations Centre (OpsCentre), located in Brussels, Belgium, was available as a third option for commanding EU crisis management missions. Hitherto autonomous EU operations were commanded either with recourse to NATO's command structure or from the national operational headquarters of one of five member states (France, Germany, Greece, Italy and the United Kingdom). Although the EU OpsCentre was to have a permanent staff of only eight core officers, it was envisaged that a total of 89 officers and civilians would be able to begin planning an operation within five days of the Council deciding to activate the centre, achieving full capability to command the operation within 20 days.

In December 2001 the EU announced that the rapid reaction force was ready to undertake small-scale crisis management tasks. A deal was agreed at the Copenhagen summit in December 2002 on sharing planning resources with NATO. In January 2003 EU forces were deployed for the first time in an international peace-keeping role (when 500 police officers were dispatched to Bosnia and Herzegovina to take over policing duties from the existing UN force). In March the European Parliament voted to approve the EU's first military mission, allowing 450 lightly armed EU troops to take over from NATO peace-keepers in the former Yugoslav republic of Macedonia.

In June 2004 the European Council approved the creation of a European Defence Agency, which commenced operations later that year. The European Defence Agency was to be responsible for improving the EU's defence capabilities in relation to crisis management and for promoting co-operation on research and procurement, strengthening the European defence industrial and technological base and developing a competitive European defence equipment market. In November 2007 EU ministers responsible for defence adopted a framework for a joint strategy on defence research and technology.

In June 2000 the EU established a civilian crisis management committee. In the same month the European Council defined four priority areas for civilian crisis management: developing the role of the police; strengthening the rule of law; strengthening civilian administrations; and improving civil protection. In February 2001 the Council adopted a regulation creating a rapid reaction mechanism (RRM) to improve the EU's civilian capacity to respond to crises. The mechanism bypassed cumbersome decision-making processes, to enable civilian experts in fields such as mine clearance, customs, police training, election-monitoring, institution-building, media support, rehabilitation and mediation to be mobilized speedily. In November 2006 the Council and Parliament adopted a regulation establishing an Instrument for Stability for 2007–13, replacing the RRM.

The common security and defence policy (CSDP), as the ESDP was renamed, remained an integral part of the CFSP under the Treaty of Lisbon, which entered into force, becoming the new legal basis for the CFSP, in December 2009. According to the Lisbon Treaty, the progressive framing of a common defence policy was intended to lead to a common defence, following a unanimous decision of the European Council. A mutual defence clause and a solidarity clause (in the event of a member state becoming the victim of a terrorist attack or natural or man-made disaster) were included, and joint disarmament operations, military advice and assistance, conflict prevention and post-conflict stabilization were added to the Petersberg tasks. The Lisbon Treaty introduced the office of High Representative of the Union for Foreign Affairs and Security Policy (uniting the previous roles of High Representative for the CFSP and External Affairs Commissioner), and provided for the establishment of the European External Action Service (with a diplomatic function, and supporting the work of and reporting to the High Representative). The High Representative leads the External Relations Council, is also a Vice-President of the European Commission, and heads political dialogue with international partners. Most decisions on the CFSP are to continue to be adopted at intergovernmental level and by consensus of all member states.

In November 2004 EU ministers responsible for defence agreed to create several Battlegroups (BGs) for eventual deployment to crisis areas. BGs were to comprise up to 1,500 troops and were to be capable of being deployed within 10 days of a unanimous decision from EU member states and the creation of a battle plan and would be equipped to stay in an area for up to four months. Each group was to be commanded by a 'lead nation' and associated with a force headquarters. The BGs reached initial operational capacity in January 2005, meaning that at least one was on standby every six months. France, Italy, Spain and the United Kingdom set up their own BGs. The creation of the BGs was partly to compensate for the inadequacies of the rapid reaction force of 60,000 troops, which, while theoretically declared ready for action in May 2003, in practice was adversely affected by shortfalls in equipment, owing to a lack of investment in procurement and research and a failure to co-ordinate purchases among member states. In November 2005 it was announced that 15 BGs would be created, and additional groups were subsequently proposed. In January 2007 the BGs reached full operational capacity, meaning that two BG operations could be undertaken concurrently; no BG deployments had, however, taken place by mid-2012.

The Justice and Home Affairs Council held an emergency meeting in September 2001 following the terrorist attacks on the USA. It determined a number of measures to be taken to improve security in the Community. First, the Council sought to reach a common definition of acts of terrorism, and to establish higher penalties for such acts. The new definition included 'cyber' and environmental attacks. The Council decided that, for the perpetrators of terrorist attacks, as well as those involved in other serious crimes (including trafficking in arms, people and drugs and money-laundering), the process of extradition would ultimately be replaced by a procedure for handover based on a European arrest warrant. In the mean time, member states were urged to implement the necessary measures to allow the existing conventions on extradition to enter into force. The member states reached agreement on the arrest warrant in December; under the agreement, covering 32 serious offences, EU countries may no longer refuse to extradite their own nationals. The warrant entered into force in eight of the then 15 EU member states on 1 January 2004 (the seven other member states having failed to meet the implementation deadline of 31 December 2003). The European arrest warrant had been implemented in all member states by mid-2005. The Council also determined to accelerate the implementation of the convention on mutual assistance in criminal matters and to establish a joint investigation team. Member states were encouraged to ratify the convention on combating the financing of terrorism and to exercise greater rigour in the issuing of travel documents. The heads of the security and intelligence services of member states met in October 2001, in the first EU-wide meeting of this kind, to discuss the co-ordinated action to be taken to curb terrorism. They were to meet in regular sessions thereafter. A team of counter-terrorist specialists, established within Europol, was to produce an assessment of terrorist threats to EU states, indicating the likely nature and location of any such attacks. Rapid links were forged with US counterparts—in December Europol signed a co-operation agreement on the exchange of strategic information (excluding personal data) with the USA; in December 2002 the agreement was extended to include the exchange of personal data. The heads of the EU's anti-terrorist units also held a meeting following the September 2001 attacks, to discuss issues such as joint training exercises, equipment sharing, the joint procurement of equipment and possible joint operations. Prior to these emergency meetings, intelligence and security information had been shared bilaterally and on a small scale. Terrorist bombings in Madrid, Spain, in March 2004 gave added impetus to EU initiatives aimed at improving travel-document security and impeding the cross-border movements of terrorists. Following the attacks, the EU created the new position of Counter-terrorist Co-ordinator, the principal responsibilities of whom included enhancing intelligence-sharing among EU members and promoting the implementation of agreed EU anti-terrorism measures, some of which had been impeded by the legislative processes of individual member states. The Justice and Home Affairs Council held an extraordinary meeting following the terrorist attacks in London, United Kingdom, in July 2005, at which ministers pledged to accelerate the adoption and implementation of enhanced counter-terrorism measures, focusing on issues such as the financing of terrorism, information-sharing by law enforcement authorities, police co-operation and the retention of telecommunications data by service providers. In December the Council adopted a new EU counter-terrorism strategy focused on preventing people embracing terrorism, protecting citizens and infrastructure, pursuing and investigating suspects, and responding to the consequences of an attack. A specific strategy for combating radicalization and the recruitment of terrorists was approved at the same time. Despite concerns over privacy rights, the Council also reached agreement on a draft directive on the retention of telecommunications data for a period of between six months and two years for use in anti-terrorism investigations. Police would have access to information about telephone calls, text messages and internet data, but not to the exact content. The directive was approved by the European Parliament later that month. In November 2007 the Commission adopted a series of proposals on the criminalization of terrorist training, recruitment and public provocation to commit terrorist offences, on the prevention of the use of explosives by terrorists and on the use of airline passenger information in law enforcement investigations.

Under the European code of conduct on arms exports, the EU publishes an annual report on defence exports based on confidential information provided by each member state. EU member states must withhold export licences to countries where it is deemed that arms sales might lead to political repression or external aggression. The Community funds projects aimed at the collection and destruction of weapons in countries emerging from conflict. The EU is strongly committed to nuclear non-proliferation. Under its programme of co-operation with Russia, the Union works to dismantle or destroy nuclear, chemical and biological weapons and weapons of mass destruction.

In September 2004 five European ministers responsible for defence signed an agreement in Noordwijk, Netherlands, to establish a police force, which could be deployed internationally for post-conflict peace-keeping duties and maintaining public order. The European Gendarmerie Force (EGF), which was officially inaugurated at its headquarters (EGF HQ) in Vicenza, Italy, in January 2006, was to be capable of deploying a mission of up to 800 gendarmes within 30 days, which could be reinforced. EGF HQ has developed a comprehensive operational system for crisis management, to be at the prompt disposal of EU and other international organizations, including the UN, NATO and the Organization for Security and Co-operation in Europe (OSCE). In 2007 the EGF became involved with EUFOR-Althea (in Bosnia and Herzegovina), and in February 2010 the EGF commenced an operational commitment within the NATO Training Mission in Afghanistan, to contribute to the development of the Afghan National Police. From December 2008 the EGF comprised members from France, Italy, the Netherlands, Portugal, Romania and Spain; Poland's military gendarmerie is also a partner.

For details of military operations that the EU has undertaken in third countries, see the specific regional information.

FINANCIAL SERVICES AND CAPITAL MOVEMENTS

Freedom of capital movement and the creation of a uniform financial area were regarded as vital for the completion of the EU's internal market by 1992. In 1987, as part of the liberalization of the flow of capital, a Council directive came into force whereby member states were obliged to remove restrictions on three categories of transactions: long-term credits related to commercial transactions; acquisition of securities; and the admission of securities to capital markets. In June 1988 the Council of Ministers approved a directive whereby all restrictions on capital movements (financial loans and credits, current and deposit account operations, transactions in securities and other instruments normally dealt in on the money market) were to be removed by 1 July 1990. A number of countries were permitted to exercise certain restrictions until the end of 1992, and further extensions were then granted to Portugal and Greece. With the entry into force of the Maastricht Treaty in November 1993, the principle of full freedom of capital movements was incorporated into the structure of the EU.

The EU worked to develop a single market in financial services throughout the 1990s. In October 1998 the Commission drew up a framework for action in the financial services sector. This communication was followed by a Financial Services Action Plan (FSAP) in May 1999, with three strategic objectives: to establish a single market in wholesale financial services; to make retail markets open and secure; and to strengthen the rules on prudential supervision in order to keep pace with new sources of financial risk. The prudential supervision of financial conglomerates (entities offering a range of financial services in areas such as banking, insurance and securities), which were developing rapidly, was identified as an area of particular importance. During 2002 a directive was drawn up on the supplementary supervision of such businesses, in recognition of the increasing consolidation in the financial sector and the emergence of cross-sector financial groups. Individual targets specified in the 1999 FSAP included removing the outstanding barriers to raising capital within the EU; creating a coherent legal framework for supplementary pension funds; and providing greater legal certainty in cross-border securities trading.

In November 2003 the Commission adopted a package of seven measures aiming to establish a new organizational architecture in all financial services sectors. The Commission stressed that this initiative was required urgently if the FSAP was to be implemented and enforced effectively. The deadline of 2005 for the adoption of the FSAP measures was largely met, with 98% of the measures having been completed, and their implementation by member states was being closely monitored by the Commission. In December 2005 the Commission presented its financial services policy for 2005–10, identifying five priorities: to consolidate progress and ensure effective implementation and enforcement of existing rules; to extend the 'better regulation principles' (i.e. transparency, wide consultation and thorough evaluation) to all policy-making; to enhance supervisory co-operation and convergence; to create greater competition between service providers, especially those active in retail markets; and to expand the EU's external influence in globalizing capital markets.

In July 2001 progress towards the creation of a single financial market was impeded by the European Parliament's rejection of a proposed takeover directive that had been under negotiation for 12 years. The directive had aimed to ensure that shareholders were treated in the same way throughout the EU after takeover bids, and had sought to create a single Community framework governing takeovers. The proposed directive was eventually approved by the European Parliament (with a number of strategic amendments) in December 2003. The Council gave its final approval to the directive in March 2004, and it came into force in May. The takeover directive was due to be incorporated into member states' national laws by 20 May 2006. In February 2007 a report by the Commission on the implementation of the takeover directive indicated that the continued use by a large number of member states of exemptions from the directive's main provisions (which were not mandatory) might bring about new barriers in the EU takeover market, rather than eliminate existing ones. A directive enhancing the rights of shareholders of listed companies was adopted in June; member states were to implement the directive within two years.

A directive on Community banking, adopted in 1977, laid down common prudential criteria for the establishment and operation of banks in member states. A second banking directive, adopted in 1989, aimed to create a single community licence for banking, thereby permitting a bank established in one member country to open branches in any other. The directive entered into force on 1 January 1993. Related measures were subsequently adopted, with the aim of ensuring the capital adequacy of credit institutions and the prevention of money-laundering by criminals. In September 1993 ministers approved a directive on a bank deposit scheme to protect account holders. These directives were consolidated into one overall banking directive in March 2000. Non-bank institutions may be granted a 'European passport' once they have complied with the principles laid down in the EU's first banking directive on the mutual recognition of licences, prudential supervision and supervision by the home member state. Non-bank institutions must also comply with the directive on money-laundering. In May 2001 a directive on the reorganization and closure of failed credit institutions with branches in more than one member state was agreed; it entered into force in May 2004. The capital requirements directive, which was adopted in June 2006, provided for the introduction of a supervisory framework on capital measurement and capital standards in accordance with the Basel II rules agreed by the Basel Committee on Banking Supervision (see Bank for International Settlements). The new framework aimed to enhance consumer protection and strengthen the stability of the financial system by fostering improved risk management among financial institutions. In October 2008, in response to the ongoing crisis in global financial markets, the European Commission proposed amendments to the existing capital requirement directive, revising the rules on bank capital requirements with the aim of reinforcing the stability of the financial system; under the revised directive, banks were to be restricted in lending beyond a specified limit to any one party, while national supervisory authorities were to have a better overview of cross-border banking group activities.

In September 2000 a directive was issued governing the actions of non-bank institutions with regard to the issuance of 'electronic money' (money stored on an electronic device, for example a chip card or in a computer memory). The directive authorized non-bank institutions to issue electronic money on a non-professional basis, with the aim of promoting a 'level playing field' with other credit institutions. Other regulations oblige the institutions to redeem electronic money at par value in coins and bank notes, or by transfer without charge. A review of this directive, prompted by various market developments since its introduction, such as the use of pre-paid telephone cards, which some member states considered as electronic money and others did not, was proposed by the Commission in July 2006 and was to follow the approval of the directive on payment services. The directive on payment services, which was adopted in November 2007, provided the legal framework for the creation of the Single Euro Payments Area (SEPA), an initiative designed to make all electronic payments across the euro area, for example by credit card, debit card, bank transfer or direct debit, as straightforward, efficient and secure as domestic payments within a single member state. From November 2009 non-bank institutions were also permitted to provide payment services under the new directive, thus opening the market to competition.

In July 1994 the third insurance co-ordination directives, relating to life assurance and non-life insurance, came into effect, creating a framework for an integrated Community insurance market. The directive on the reorganization and winding-up of insurance undertakings was adopted by the EU in February 2001 and came into force in April 2003. The main aim of the directive was to provide greater consumer protection and it formed part of a wider drive to achieve a consistent approach to insolvency proceedings across the EU. A new directive on life assurance was adopted in November 2002, superseding all previous directives in this field. In May 2005 the EU adopted a fifth motor insurance directive, which considerably increased the minimum amounts payable for personal injuries and damage to property and designated pedestrians and cyclists as specific categories of victims who are entitled to compensation. A directive on reinsurance was adopted in November; companies specializing in this area had not previously been specifically regulated by EU legislation. In July 2007 the Commission proposed a thorough reform of EU insurance legislation, which was designed to improve consumer protection, modernize supervision, deepen market integration and increase the international competitiveness of European insurers. The new system, known as Solvency II, would introduce more extensive solvency requirements for insurers, in order to guarantee that they have sufficient capital to withstand adverse events, covering not only traditional insurance risks, but also economic risks, including market risk (such as a fall in the value of an insurer's investments), credit risk (for example when debt obligations are not met) and operational risk (such as malpractice or system failure). In addition, insurers would be compelled to devote significant resources to the identification, measurement and proactive management of risks. The directive on Solvency II (replacing 14 existing directives), was adopted in May 2009 and it was envisaged that the new system would be operational by 1 January 2013. The European Insurance and Occupational Pensions Committee works to improve co-operation with national supervisory authorities.

In September 2007 the Council and Parliament adopted a directive designed to harmonize procedural rules and assessment criteria throughout the Community with regard to acquisitions and increases of shareholdings in the banking, insurance and securities sectors. A directive aimed at modernizing and simplifying rules on value-added tax (VAT) for financial and insurance services was proposed by the Commission in November. It was noted that although these services were generally exempt from VAT, the exemption was not being applied uniformly by member states and that a clear definition of exempt services was therefore required.

In May 1993 ministers adopted a directive on investment services, which (with effect from 1 January 1996) allowed credit institutions to offer investment services in any member state, on the basis of a licence held in one state. The 1999 FSAP aimed to achieve the further convergence of national approaches to investment, in order to increase the effectiveness of the 1993 directive. The directive on the market in financial services, which was adopted in April 2004 to replace the 1993 directive, aimed to allow investment firms to operate throughout the EU on the basis of authorization in their home member state and to ensure that investors enjoyed a high level of protection when employing investment firms, regardless of their location in the EU. The directive entered into force in November 2007.

In late 1999 the Commission put forward proposals to remove tax barriers and investment restrictions affecting cross-border pension schemes, as variations among member states in the tax liability of contributions to supplementary pension schemes were obstructing the transfer of pension rights from one state to another, contradicting the Treaty of Rome's principles of free movement. In October 2000 a specific legal framework for institutions for occupational retirement provision (IORPs) was proposed. This seeks to abolish barriers to investment by pension funds and would permit the cross-border management of IORP pension schemes, with mutual recognition of the supervisory methods in force. In September 2003 the occupational pensions directive (IORP directive), which was designed to allow workers of multinational companies to have access to cross-border employer pension schemes, became EU law. Implementation, which had been due within two years, was subject to delays.

In November 1997 the Commission adopted proposals to co-ordinate tax policy among member states. The measures aimed to simplify the transfer of royalty and interest payments between member states and to prevent the withholding of taxes. In February 1999 the European Parliament endorsed a proposal by the Commission to harmonize taxation further, through the co-ordination of savings taxes. In November 2000 ministers of finance agreed on a proposed savings tax directive, the details of which were endorsed in July 2001. This directive set out rules on the exchange of information on savings accounts of individuals resident in one EU country and receiving interest in another. However, in December Austria, Luxembourg and Belgium abandoned the agreement, insisting that they would only comply if other tax havens in Europe, such as Monaco, Liechtenstein and Switzerland, were compelled to amend their banking secrecy laws.

Two proposed directives were issued in November 2000, the first relating to interest and royalties and the second concerning the code of conduct for business taxation. Together with the savings tax directive, these were known as the EU tax package. The EU ministers of finance finally reached agreement on the terms of the package in June 2003. The package consisted of a political code of conduct to eliminate harmful business tax regimes; a legislative measure to ensure an effective minimum level of taxation of savings income; and a legislative measure to eliminate source taxes on cross-border payments of interest and royalties between associated companies. The Council of the EU reached agreement on the controversial savings tax directive (after 15 years of negotiation) in June 2004; the directive entered into force on 1 July 2005. The aim of the directive was to prevent EU citizens from avoiding taxes on savings by keeping their money in foreign bank accounts. Under the directive, each member state would ultimately be expected to provide information to other member states on interest paid from that member state to individual savers resident in those other member states. For a transitional period, Belgium, Luxembourg and Austria were to be allowed to apply a withholding tax instead, at a rate of 15% for the first three years (2005–07), 20% for the subsequent three years (2008–10) and 35% from 1 July 2011. Negotiations had been concluded with Switzerland, Liechtenstein, Monaco, Andorra and San Marino to ensure the adoption of equivalent measures in those countries to allow effective taxation of savings income paid to EU residents.

The May 2000 convention on mutual assistance in criminal matters (see Justice and Home Affairs) committed member states to co-operation in combating economic and financial crime. In May 2001 the Council adopted a framework decision on preventing fraud and counterfeiting in non-cash means of payment, recognizing this as a criminal offence. An EU conference in Paris, France, in February 2002 (which was also attended by representatives of seven candidate countries and Russia) agreed to tackle money-laundering by setting minimum secrecy levels and compelling internet service providers to identify operators of suspect financial deals. Following the terrorist attacks on the USA in September 2001, the EU attempted to accelerate the adoption of the convention combating the financing of terrorism, and began work on a new directive on 'freezing' assets or evidence related to terrorist crimes. In October 2005 a regulation on the compulsory declaration at EU borders of large amounts (i.e. more than €10,000) of cash (including banknotes and cheques) entered into force. The aim of this measure, which applied only to the external borders of the Union, was to prevent the entry into the EU of untraceable money, which could then be used to fund criminal or terrorist activities. A third money-laundering directive (which was extended to cover terrorist financing as well as money-laundering) was also adopted in that month. In November 2006 the Council and Parliament adopted a regulation aimed at ensuring that law enforcement authorities have access to basic information on the payer of transfers of funds in the context of investigating terrorists and tracing their assets.

In February 2001 the Commission launched a complaints network for out-of-court settlements in the financial sector (FIN-NET), to help consumers find amicable solutions in cases where the supplier is in another member state. A directive establishing harmonized rules on the cross-border distance-selling of financial services was adopted in June 2002. The first meeting took place in June 2006 of the Financial Services Consumer Group, a permanent committee, comprising representatives of consumer organizations from each of the member states as well as those active at EU level, established by the Commission to discuss financial services policies and proposals of particular relevance to consumers. In December 2007 the Commission published a White Paper proposing measures to improve the competitiveness and efficiency of European residential mortgage markets by facilitating the cross-border supply and funding of mortgage credit and by increasing the diversity of products available.

The European Commission convened regularly from late 2008 to address the crisis. In October 2008 the President of the European Commission established a high-level group on financial supervision in the EU to decide means of building more effective European and global supervision for financial institutions. Shortly afterwards the heads of state or government of the euro area countries issued a Declaration on a Concerted European Action Plan of the Euro Area Countries, outlining measures to ensure liquidity for financial institutions and co-operation among European states. In mid-October the European Commission proposed a revision to the deposit guarantee schemes directive, which would increase the minimum protection for bank deposits to €100,000. A summit of the Council held in mid-October urged further concerted and global action to protect the financial market system and the best interests of tax-payers. It emphasized the need for further action to strengthen European and international financial market rules and supervision. In mid-December the European Council approved a European Economic Recovery Plan (EERP), outlining a co-ordinated European response to the crisis, involving a three-part approach, based on a new European financial market architecture; a framework plan for the recovery of the real economy, to stimulate jobs and economic growth; and a global response to the financial crisis (see Economic Co-operation). In January 2009 the European Commission adopted decisions aimed at strengthening the supervisory framework for the EU financial markets. The high-level group on financial supervision in the EU, established in October 2008, published a report in February 2009 that analysed the complexity and principal causes of the financial crisis; identified priority areas requiring regulatory change; detailed proposals for far-reaching reforms within the EU aimed at stabilizing the financial markets; and proposals for changes at international level to prevent the recurrence of such a crisis. In mid-March the European Council adopted a common European position, based on constructing a rules- and values-based form of globalization, for a summit of the Group of Twenty (G20), which was held in early April. The Commission participated in the Financial Stability Forum which the April G20 meeting determined to establish, with a mandate to strengthen world-wide financial regulation and supervision; the Forum's inaugural meeting was held in June.

In September 2009, with a view to strengthening EU financial supervision, the Commission adopted proposals for the creation of a European Systemic Risk Board (ESRB), which was to monitor and assess risks to the stability of the financial system as a whole; and a European System of Financial Supervisors (ESFS), which would have the capacity to address recommendations and warnings issued to member states and to the European supervisory authorities. The ESFS was to comprise three European Supervisory Authorities (ESAs): a European

Banking Authority; a European Securities and Markets Authority; and a European Insurance and Occupational Pensions Authority. These authorities were to be responsible for helping to rebuild confidence, develop a single set of financial rules, seek solutions to problems involving cross-border firms, and prevent the accumulation of risks that could undermine the stability of the financial system. In September 2010 the European Parliament endorsed the new supervisory framework, which was confirmed by ministers of the economy and of finance (the ECOFIN Council) in mid-November. The three ESAs and the ESRB were established in January 2011 to replace the supervisory committees hitherto in place.

ECONOMIC CO-OPERATION

A review of the economic situation is presented annually by the Commission, analysing recent developments and short- and medium-term prospects. Economic policy guidelines for the following year are adopted annually by the Council.

The following objectives for the end of 1973 were agreed by the Council in 1971, as the first of three stages towards European economic and monetary union: the narrowing of exchange rate margins to 2.25%; creation of a medium-term pool of reserves; co-ordination of short- and medium-term economic and budgetary policies; a joint position on international monetary issues; harmonization of taxes; creation of the European Monetary Co-operation Fund (EMCF); and creation of the European Regional Development Fund.

The narrowing of exchange margins (the 'snake') came into effect in 1972; however, Denmark, France, Ireland, Italy and the United Kingdom later floated their currencies, with only Denmark permanently returning to the arrangement. Sweden and Norway also linked their currencies to the 'snake', but Sweden withdrew from the arrangement in August 1977, and Norway withdrew in December 1978.

The European Monetary System (EMS) came into force in March 1979, with the aim of creating closer monetary co-operation, leading to a zone of monetary stability in Europe, principally through an Exchange Rate Mechanism (ERM), supervised by the ministries of finance and the central banks of member states. Not all Community members participated in the ERM: Greece did not join, Spain joined only in June 1989, the United Kingdom in October 1990 and Portugal in April 1992. To prevent wide fluctuations in the value of members' currencies against each other, the ERM fixed for each currency a central rate in European Currency Units (ECUs, see below), based on a 'basket' of national currencies; a reference rate in relation to other currencies was fixed for each currency, with established fluctuation margins. Central banks of the participating states intervened by buying or selling currencies when the agreed margin was likely to be exceeded. Each member placed 20% of its gold reserves and dollar reserves, respectively, into the EMCF, and received a supply of ECUs to regulate central bank interventions. Short- and medium-term credit facilities were given to support the balance of payments of member countries. The EMS was initially put under strain by the wide fluctuations in the exchange rates of non-Community currencies and by the differences in economic development among members, which led to nine realignments of currencies in 1979–83. Subsequently greater stability was achieved, with only two realignments of currencies between 1984 and 1988. In 1992–93, however, there was great pressure on currency markets, necessitating further realignments; in September 1992 Italian and British membership of the ERM was suspended. In July 1993, as a result of intensive currency speculation on European financial markets (forcing the weaker currencies to the very edge of their permitted margins), the ERM almost collapsed. In response to the crisis, EC ministers of finance decided to widen the fluctuation margins allowed for each currency, except in the cases of Germany and the Netherlands, which agreed to maintain their currencies within the original limits. The new margins were regarded as allowing for so much fluctuation in exchange rates as to represent a virtual suspension of the ERM, although some countries, notably France and Belgium, expressed their determination to adhere as far as possible to the original 'bands' in order to fulfil the conditions for eventual monetary union. In practice, most currencies remained within the former narrower bands during 1994. Austria became a member of the EMS in January 1995, and its currency was subject to ERM conditions. While Sweden decided to remain outside the EMS, Finland joined in October 1996. In November of that year the Italian lira was readmitted to the ERM.

The Intergovernmental Conference on Economic and Monetary Union, initiated in December 1990, was responsible for the drafting of the economic and monetary provisions of the Treaty on European Union, which came into force on 1 November 1993. The principal feature of the Treaty's provisions on Economic and Monetary Union (EMU), which was to be implemented in three stages, was the gradual introduction of a single currency, to be administered by a single central bank.

In December 1995 the European Council confirmed that Stage III of EMU was to begin on 1 January 1999 and confirmed the economic conditions for member states wishing to participate in it. The meeting decided that the proposed single currency would be officially known as the euro. Member countries remaining outside the monetary system, whether or not by choice, would still be part of the single market. Technical preparations for the euro were confirmed during a meeting of the European Council in Dublin, Ireland, in December 1996. The heads of government endorsed the new ERM and the legal framework for the euro, and approved the Stability and Growth Pact (SGP), intended to ensure that member countries maintained strict budgetary discipline. In March 1998 Greece was admitted to the ERM, causing a 14% devaluation of its national currency. In May of that year it was confirmed by a meeting of heads of state and of government that Greece failed to fulfil the conditions required for the adoption of a single currency from 1999. The meeting agreed that existing ERM central rates were to be used to determine the final rates of exchange between national currencies and the euro. A European Central Bank (ECB) was established in June 1998, which was to be accountable to a European Forum, comprising members of the European Parliament (MEPs) and chairmen of the finance committees of the national parliaments of EU member countries.

Although all of the then 15 members of the EU endorsed the principle of monetary union, with France and Germany the most ardent supporters, some countries had political doubts about joining. In October 1997 both the United Kingdom and Sweden confirmed that they would not participate in EMU from 1999. Denmark was also to remain outside the single currency. In May 1998 heads of state and government confirmed that 11 countries would take part in Stage III of EMU. It was agreed that existing ERM central rates were to be used to determine the final rates of exchange between national currencies and the euro. A European Central Bank (ECB) was established in June 1998.

On 31 December 1998 the ECOFIN Council adopted the conversion rates for the national currencies of the countries participating in the single currency. The euro was formally launched on 1 January 1999. ERM-II, the successor to the ERM, was launched on the same day. Both Greece and Denmark joined ERM-II, but in September 2000 some 53% of Danish voters participating in a national referendum rejected the adoption of the euro. On 1 January 2001 Greece became the 12th EU member state to adopt the euro. In September 2003 the majority of Swedish voters—some 56%—participating in a national referendum chose to reject Sweden's adoption of the euro.

The SGP, endorsed by the European Council in 1996, was instituted with the intention of ensuring that member countries maintain strict budgetary discipline during Stage III of monetary union, of which it was regarded as the cornerstone. Under its original terms, member states were obliged to keep budget deficits within 3% of gross domestic product (GDP), or face fines, and to bring their budgets close to balance by 2004. However, during 2002 the Pact was strongly criticized for being inflexible, when a number of countries could not meet its requirements. In September 2002 the 2004 deadline for reaching a balanced budget was extended by two years, although the 3% limit for budgetary deficit remained, while some concessionary provision was introduced to allow countries with low levels of long-term debt to increase investment spending by running larger short-term budget deficits.

In November 2003 France and Germany, which were both likely to breach the budget deficit of 3% for a third consecutive year, persuaded the EU ministers responsible for finance to suspend the disciplinary procedure (triggered by their failure to meet the 3% limit in 2002) under which they could have faced punitive fines. The refusal of France and Germany to restrict their expenditure provoked anger among some smaller EU countries that had implemented strict austerity programmes in order to comply with the Pact. In January 2004 the European Commission launched a legal action against the Council of Finance Ministers in the European Court of Justice, seeking clarification of whether the Council had acted illegally in temporarily suspending the budget rules. The SGP faced additional pressure with the pending enlargement of the EU, as its framework would have to apply to the 10 candidate countries, even though their economies were very diverse.

All 10 countries that joined the EU on 1 May 2004 (Cyprus, the Czech Republic, Estonia, Hungary, Latvia, Lithuania, Malta, Poland, Slovakia and Slovenia) were obliged to participate in EMU; however, adoption of the euro was dependent on the fulfilment of the same Maastricht convergence criteria as the initial entrants, which comprised conditions regarding inflation, debt, budget deficit, long-term interest rates and exchange rate stability. The exchange rate criteria included the requirement to spend at least two years in ERM-II. Although the currency was permitted to fluctuate 15% either side of a central rate or, by common agreement, within a narrower band, the ECB specified that the limit of 2.25% would be applied when judging whether countries had achieved sufficient stability to join the euro area. The entry into the euro area of the new member states was not expected to affect the ECB's monetary policy, as the new member states only accounted for about 5% of the GDP of the enlarged EU. Although many of the new member countries were keen to adopt the euro as soon as possible, the ECB warned of the risks associated with early membership of ERM-II, sharing widespread concerns that the required fiscal austerity and loss of flexibility over exchange rate policy would stifle economic growth in the accession countries. Moreover, currencies would also become vulnerable to speculative attacks once they entered ERM-II. Owing to differences in the economies of the new member states, progress towards adoption of the euro varied significantly. In June 2004 Estonia, Lithuania and Slovenia joined ERM-II. In May 2006, in a specific convergence report drawn up at the request of Slovenia and Lithuania to assess their readiness to adopt the euro, the Commission concluded that Slovenia met all of the conditions for admission to the euro area, while Lithuania should retain its current status as a member state with a derogation. Slovenia duly adopted the euro on 1 January 2007. Cyprus, Latvia and Malta joined ERM-II on 2 May 2005, followed by Slovakia on 28 November. Cyprus and Malta were admitted to the euro area on 1 January 2008, and Slovakia adopted the euro on 1 January 2009. Estonia adopted the euro on 1 January 2011, increasing the number of countries in the euro area to 17.

In September 2004 revised figures released by Greece revealed previous gross under-reporting of the country's national budgetary deficit and debt figures. It was subsequently established that Greece had not complied with membership rules for the single currency in 2000, the year in which it qualified to join. Greece received a formal warning from the Commission in December 2004 for publishing inaccurate data concerning its public finances for 1997–2003. In April 2009 the Council placed Greece under excessive deficit procedures, setting a deadline of 2010 for correction of the deficit to below 3%, on the basis of a Commission proposal which, in turn, had been based on an estimated Greek budgetary deficit equivalent to 3.7% of GDP in 2008. In December 2009—by which time Greece's 2008 budgetary deficit had been revised up to 7.7% and the 2009 deficit was being estimated at 12.7%, attributable to factors such as the effects of the ongoing economic crisis, absence of corrective measures and fiscal slippage—the Council determined that the Greek authorities had not taken sufficient effective action to correct the deficit. The estimated 12.7% Greek budgetary deficit for 2009 was deemed potentially destabilizing to markets and to the entire euro area, and the unreliable reporting of public finance statistics was a significant cause of concern: in this respect it was reported in early 2010 that the Commission was considering reforms that would in future enable Eurostat to audit national statistical agencies.

In January 2010 the ECOFIN Council advised the Greek Government to embrace a far-reaching economic reform plan aimed at gradually reducing Greece's budget deficit (by 4% by the end of 2010, initially); the plan was endorsed by the Commission in early February 2010. In early February the European Commission also, using new powers given under the Treaty of Lisbon, imposed a new 'quasi-permanent' surveillance system on the management of Greece's public finances. Furthermore, the Commission issued a formal warning to the Greek authorities regarding the need to pursue policies consistent with the broad economic guidelines adopted by the Council, and launched infringement proceedings against Greece relating to the submission of erroneous statistical data. Soon afterwards EU heads of state and government issued a statement emphasizing that all euro area members were required to conduct sound national policies in line with agreed rules, while committing the euro area member states to taking determined and co-ordinated action, if need be, to safeguard financial stability in the euro area as a whole. In mid-February 2010 the Council gave notice to Greece to correct its excessive deficit (to below 3% of GDP) by 2012, setting out a timetable for corrective measures, and issued a formal recommendation to Greece to bring its economic policies into line with broad EU economic policy guidelines and thereby remove the risk of jeopardizing the overall proper functioning of economic and monetary union. In May 2010 the European Commission, the European Central Bank (ECB) and the IMF reached agreement with Greece on a programme intended to stabilize the Greek economy, in accordance with which funding of €110,000m. would be provided over a period of three years, of which €80,000m. was to originate from the countries of the euro area. In accordance with the terms of the programme, Greece was required to implement further budget cuts, increase taxation, and carry out substantial reforms of the pensions and social security systems.

In early July 2011 EU ministers of finance approved the disbursement of further lending to Greece, temporarily alleviating the threat of default. In late October 2011 EU leaders agreed further emergency measures designed to help resolve the euro area debt crisis. The agreement provided for the recapitalization of private banks; provided for losses of one-half of the banks' holdings of Greek debt; and sought to increase the financial strength of the European Financial Stability Facility (EFSF—see below). In February 2012 the EU, the ECB and the IMF approved further lending to Greece, worth some €130,000m. However, its disbursement remained dependent on the rapid adoption of further reductions in expenditure and guarantees of their implementation, despite the approval of a series of austerity measures by Greece. Following inconclusive legislative elections on 6 May, new elections were held on 17 June. The election of a coalition Government led by the centre-right New Democracy party was widely interpreted as indicating popular support for continued Greek membership of the euro area. Meanwhile, in early June euro area ministers of finance agreed to providing lending of up to €100,000m. to recapitalize the Spanish banking sector. The funding was expected to be provided by two EU rescue funds, the temporary EFSF and the new, permanent crisis mechanism, the European Stability Mechanism (ESM, see below). After Greece, Ireland, Portugal and Spain, in late June Cyprus became the fifth member of the euro area to seek emergency EU funding.

Meanwhile, in 2008 a sharp contraction in global credit markets had prompted EU Governments to offer widespread financial assistance to support failing banks amid the onset of recession throughout the EU. In mid-November a Group of Twenty (G20) summit meeting was held in Washington, DC, USA, at the EU's instigation, in order to discuss measures to help stimulate economic recovery world-wide, improve the regulation of financial markets, aid international governance, and reject protectionism. In December the European Council adopted a European Economic Recovery Plan (EERP), worth around €200,000m., equivalent to some 1.5% of the EU's total GDP, and representing a co-ordinated response to the situation. The plan aimed to restore consumer and business confidence, to restart lending, and to stimulate investment in EU economies and create jobs, by increasing investments in infrastructure and important sectors of the economy—including the automotive industry, construction and green technologies—while making full use of the flexibility offered in the SGP. The EERP proposed that member states should co-ordinate national budgetary stimulus packages in order to optimize their impact and avoid secondary consequences, as negative effects spread from one country to another. A Commission report on the EU economy issued in September 2009 found the ongoing recession to be the deepest since the 1930s, and stated that a comprehensive, co-ordinated recession 'exit strategy' (emphasizing investment in renewable energy sources and green infrastructure) should be developed, for implementation as soon as economic recovery was apparent.

In early May 2010 euro area member states agreed to the establishment of a new, temporary institution, the EFSF, with a lending capacity of €4,400m., which aimed to maintain financial stability in the euro area through the provision of rapid financial assistance to member countries. In late June heads of state and of government agreed to expand the EFSF's remit and increase its guarantee commitments from €4,400m. to €7,800m., equivalent to a lending capacity of €4,400m. The EFSF's scope was further expanded in late July, and all amendments to the EFSF Framework entered into force in mid-October 2011. The EFSF is based in Luxembourg, and is backed by guarantees from 14 of the euro area's 17 members (Greece, Ireland and Portugal were exempted). Meanwhile, in October 2010 the European Council had agreed to establish a permanent crisis mechanism, the ESM, to safeguard the financial stability of the euro area. Combined with strengthened economic governance and monitoring, the ESM, which was to have an overall lending capacity of €500,000m., aimed to prevent the development of future crises. In late July 2011 EU heads of state and of government taking part in an emergency Euro Area Summit in Brussels, Belgium, agreed to reduce EFSF interest rates and extend the maturities of future loans issued to Greece, Ireland and Portugal, in an effort to strengthen their financial programmes.

On 9 December 2011 the majority of EU member states reached agreement in principal on new fiscal arrangements, designed to increase fiscal discipline and convergence in the euro area. The Treaty on Stability, Coordination and Governance (TSCG) in the Economic and Monetary Union (or fiscal compact), *inter alia*, required member states to maintain a balanced budget (or a deficit of no more than 0.5% of nominal GDP). Agreement was reached on increased co-operation on economic policy, and an acceleration of arrangements for the introduction of the ESM. In March 2012 25 heads of state and of government signed the TSCG, which required ratification by 12 euro area member states; the United Kingdom and the Czech Republic refused to sign the agreement. In Ireland, the TSCG was approved by a referendum, which took place at the end of May.

In mid-December 2011 new rules, comprising five regulations and one directive (the 'six-pack'), came into effect, applying to both the procedures within the SGP that are designed to prevent excessive deficits, and the excessive deficit procedure (EDP), which is the corrective branch of the pact. New measures, specifically financial disincentives and fines, were to be applied to non-compliant euro area members in an effort to strengthen the efficacy of the SGP. At January 2012 23 of the 27 EU member states were subject to an EDP (with the exception of Estonia, Finland, Luxemburg and Sweden).

THE EURO

With the creation of the European Monetary System (EMS) in 1979, a new monetary unit, the European Currency Unit (ECU), was adopted. Its value and composition were identical to those of the European Unit of Account (EUA) already used in the administrative fields of the Community. The ECU was a composite monetary unit, in which the relative value of each currency was determined by the gross national product and the volume of trade of each country. Assigned the function of the unit of account used by the European Monetary Co-operation Fund, the ECU was also used as the denominator for the Exchange Rate Mechanism (ERM); as the denominator for operations in both the intervention and the credit mechanisms; and as a means of settlement between monetary authorities of the European Community. From April 1979 the ECU was also used as the unit of account for the purposes of the Common Agricultural Policy (CAP). From 1981 it replaced the EUA in the general budget of the Community; the activities of the European Development Fund (EDF) under the Lomé Convention; the balance sheets and loan operations of the European Investment Bank (EIB); and the activities of the European Coal and Steel Community (ECSC). In June 1985 measures were adopted by the governors of the Community's central banks, aiming to strengthen the EMS by expanding the use of the ECU, for example, by allowing international monetary institutions and the central banks of non-member countries to become 'other holders' of ECUs. From September 1989 the Portuguese and Spanish currencies were included in the composition of the ECU. The composition of the ECU 'basket' of national currencies was 'frozen' with the entry into force of the Treaty on European Union on 1 November 1993, and remained unchanged until the termination of the ECU on 31 December 1998. (Consequently the currencies of Austria, Finland and Sweden, on those countries' accession to the EU, were not represented in the ECU 'basket'.)

As part of Stage III of the process of Economic and Monetary Union (EMU), the ECU was replaced by a single currency, the euro (€), on 1 January 1999, at a conversion rate of 1:1. Initially the euro was used for cashless payments and accounting purposes, while the traditional national currencies, then considered as 'sub-units' of the euro, continued to be used for cash payments. On 1 January 2002 euro coins and banknotes entered into circulation in the then 12 participating countries, and, by the end of February, the former national currencies of all of the participating countries had been withdrawn. The euro's value in national currencies is calculated and published daily, and stood at €1 = US $1.322 on 26 April 2012, at which time there were 17 participating countries.

A payments settlement system, known as TARGET (Trans-European Automated Real-time Gross Settlement Express Transfer), was introduced for countries participating in EMU on 4 January 1999. An upgraded version of the system, TARGET2, was launched in November 2007. The Single Euro Payments Area (SEPA), which was introduced gradually from 2008, was designed to enable all electronic payments across the euro area to be made as efficiently and securely as domestic payments within a single member state.

Three interest rates are set for the euro area: the rate on the main refinancing operations, providing most of the banking system's liquidity; the rate on the deposit facility, which may be used by banks making overnight deposits with the euro system; and the rate on the marginal lending facility, which offers overnight credit to banks from the euro system. From October 2008 refinancing operations were conducted through a fixed-rate tender procedure, having been conducted as variable rate tenders since June 2000. During the second half of 2008 and early 2009 the ECB considerably reduced interest rates with the aim of stimulating non-inflationary growth and contributing to financial stability. The ECB reduced the fixed refinancing rate progressively from 3.75% in October 2008 to 1.0% at 13 May 2009 (that rate remaining in force until 13 April 2011). The rates set in 2009 represented the lowest euro area rates (whether variable or fixed) set in the decade since January 1999. On 13 April 2011 the fixed refinancing rate was increased to 1.25%. From 14 December 2011 the fixed refinancing rate was 1.0%.

External Relations

CENTRAL AND SOUTH-EASTERN EUROPE

During the late 1980s the extensive political changes and reforms in Eastern European countries led to a strengthening of links with the EC. Agreements on trade and economic co-operation were concluded with several countries. Community heads of government agreed in December 1989 to establish a European Bank for Reconstruction and Development—EBRD, with participation by member states of the Organisation for Economic Co-operation and Development—OECD and the Council for Mutual Economic Assistance, to promote investment in Eastern Europe; the EBRD began operations in April 1991. In the 1990s 'Europe Agreements' were signed with Czechoslovakia, Hungary and Poland (1991), Bulgaria and Romania (1993), Estonia, Latvia and Lithuania (1995), and Slovenia (1996), which led to formal applications for membership of the EU. On 1 May 2004 the Czech Republic, Estonia, Hungary, Latvia, Lithuania, Poland, Slovakia and Slovenia acceded to the EU. Bulgaria and Romania formally joined the EU on 1 January 2007.

In July 2006 an Instrument for Pre-Accession Assistance (IPA) was adopted by the Council, which replaced the former PHARE (Poland/Hungary Aid for Restructuring of Economies) and other such programmes (Instrument for Structural Policies for Pre-Accession—ISPA; Special Accession Programme for Agriculture and Rural Development—SAPARD; Community Assistance for Reconstruction, Development and Stabilisation, with reference to the Western Balkans—CARDS; and the Turkey instrument) from January 2007. The IPA aims to provide targeted assistance to candidate countries for membership of the EU (Croatia, Iceland, the former Yugoslav republic of Macedonia—FYRM, Montenegro, Serbia and Turkey by April 2012) or those that are potential candidate countries (e.g. Albania and Bosnia and Herzegovina). In March 2008 the Commission launched the Civil Society Facility, a new financing arrangement under the IPA, which aims to support the development of civil society in South-Eastern Europe, by strengthening the political role of civil society organizations; developing cross-border projects; and familiarizing representatives of civil society with EU affairs. In November the Commission adopted the IPA Multi-Annual Financial Framework for 2010–12, comprising five components: transition and institution building; cross-border co-operation; regional development; human resources development; and rural development. Candidate countries Croatia and the FYRM were allocated €471.8m. and €296.8m. for 2010–12, respectively; Albania was to receive €285.1m.; Bosnia and Herzegovina €324.3m.; Kosovo €4,631.4m.; Montenegro €104.1m.; and Serbia €608.2m. (Turkey was also eligible for funding under the IPA.)

In June 1999 the EU, in conjunction with the Group of Seven industrialized nations and Russia (the Group of Eight—G8), regional governments and other organizations concerned with the stability of the region, launched the Stability Pact for South Eastern Europe, a comprehensive conflict-prevention strategy, which was placed under the auspices of the Organization for Security and Co-operation in Europe (OSCE). The Stability Pact aimed to strengthen the efforts of the countries of South-Eastern Europe in fostering peace, democracy, respect for human rights and economic prosperity. In April 2008 the Stability Pact was replaced by a Regional Co-operation Council, based in Sarajevo, Bosnia and Herzegovina.

In March 1997 the EU sent two advisory delegations to Albania to help to restore order after violent unrest and political instability erupted in that country. It was announced in early April that the EU was to provide humanitarian aid of some ECU 2m., to be used for emergency relief. In September 2002 the European Parliament voted in support of opening negotiations for a Stabilization and Association Agreement (SAA) with Albania, following satisfactory progress in that country, with regard to presidential voting and electoral reform. In November 2005 the Commission urged Albania to increase its efforts to combat organized crime and corruption, to enhance media freedom and to conduct further electoral reform. Negotiations on the signature of an SAA with Albania, which officially commenced at the end of January 2003, were completed in February 2006. The SAA was formally signed in June and entered into force in April 2009. In April 2009 Albania applied for the status of a candidate country for EU membership. In November 2010 the European Commission agreed to introduce visa liberalization for Albania, with effect from mid-December. The Commission considered that Albania had made substantial efforts to meet the EU's political, economic and legislative criteria during the preceding year, but that further reform was required before it could be considered suitable for candidate status, owing, in particular, to the inefficacy of the public administration and the political impasse that had followed the legislative elections of June 2009. In January 2011 more than 20,000 people took part in an anti-Government demonstration in the Albanian capital, Tirana, which led to violent clashes between police and protesters. EU officials condemned the excessive use of force, and urged political dialogue. Following local elections in May, the EU's Commissioner responsible for Enlargement and European Neighbourhood Policy criticized the conduct of the elections (which were marred by controversy and disputes between the two main political parties), declaring that they demonstrated the urgent need for electoral reform. In October the European Commission again failed to recommend candidate status for Albania, citing insufficient progress in meeting the EU's political criteria.

A co-operation agreement was signed with Yugoslavia in 1980 (but was not ratified until April 1983), allowing tariff-free imports and Community loans. New financial protocols were signed in 1987 and 1991. However, EC aid was suspended in July 1991, following the declarations of independence by the Yugoslav republics of Croatia and Slovenia, and the subsequent outbreak of civil conflict. Efforts were made in the ensuing months by EC ministers of foreign affairs to negotiate a peaceful settlement, and a team of EC observers was maintained in Yugoslavia from July, to monitor successive cease-fire agreements. In October the EC proposed a plan for an association of independent states, to replace the Yugoslav federation: this was accepted by all of the Yugoslav republics except Serbia, which demanded a redefinition of boundaries to accommodate within Serbia all predominantly Serbian areas. In November the application of the Community's co-operation agreements with Yugoslavia was suspended (with exemptions for the republics which co-operated in the peace negotiations). In January 1992 the Community granted diplomatic recognition to the former Yugoslav republics of Croatia and Slovenia, and in April it recognized Bosnia and Herzegovina, while withholding recognition from Macedonia (owing to pressure from the Greek Government, which feared that the existence of an independent Macedonia would imply a claim on the Greek province of the same name). In May EC ambassadors were withdrawn from the Yugoslav capital, Belgrade, in protest at Serbia's support for aggression by Bosnian Serbs against other ethnic groups in Bosnia and Herzegovina, and in the same month the Community imposed a trade embargo on Serbia and Montenegro.

In April 1994, following a request from EU ministers of foreign affairs, a Contact Group, consisting of France, Germany, the United Kingdom, the USA and Russia, was initiated to undertake peace negotiations. In the following month ministers of foreign affairs of the USA, Russia and the EU (represented by five member states) jointly endorsed a proposal to divide Bosnia and Herzegovina in proportions of 49% to the Bosnian Serbs and 51% to the newly established Federation of Muslims and Croats. The proposal was rejected by the Bosnian Serb assembly in July and had to be abandoned after the Muslim-Croat Federation also withdrew its support. In July the EU formally assumed political control of Mostar, in southern Bosnia and Herzegovina, in order to restore the city's administrative infrastructure.

In September 1995 the EU supported US-led negotiations in Geneva, Switzerland, to devise a plan to end the conflict in Bosnia and Herzegovina. The plan closely resembled the previous proposals of the Contact Group: two self-governing entities were to be created within Bosnia and Herzegovina, with 51% of territory being allocated to the Muslim-Croat Federation and 49% to Bosnian Serbs. The proposals were finally agreed after negotiations in Dayton, OH, USA, in November 1995, and an accord was signed in Paris, France, in December.

In January 1996 the EU announced its intention to recognize Yugoslavia (Serbia and Montenegro). During 1996–99 the EU allocated ECU 1,000m. for the repatriation of refugees, restructuring the economy and technical assistance, in addition to ECU 1,000m. in humanitarian aid provided since the beginning of the conflict in the former Yugoslavia.

In 2000 the EU published a roadmap for Bosnia and Herzegovina, outlining measures that must be undertaken by the Government prior to the initiation of a feasibility study on the formulation of an SAA. In September 2002 the Commission reported that Bosnia and Herzegovina had essentially adhered to the terms of the roadmap. In January 2003 a new EU Police Mission (EUPM) took over from the UN peace-keeping force in Bosnia and Herzegovina. This was the first operation under the common European Security and Defence Policy. The EUPM was re-established in 2006, and aimed to support the police-reform process and continue to help to combat organized crime. Meanwhile, on 28 January 2004 the Bosnian Government issued a decree providing for the reunification of Mostar (divided between Croat- and Bosnian-controlled municipalities since 1993) into a single administration, thereby fulfilling one of the major preconditions for the signature of an SAA with the EU. In December 2004 7,000 troops (EUFOR) were deployed under EU command in Bosnia and Herzegovina, taking over from

NATO, with a mission (Operation Althea) to ensure stability in the country. From the end of March 2007 EUFOR-Althea was downsized to comprise the Multinational Maneuver Battalion, of around 2,000 troops. Negotiations on an SAA officially commenced in November 2005, and an SAA with the EU was initialled in December 2007, and signed in mid-June 2008. In November 2010 the European Commission agreed to introduce visa liberalization for Bosnia and Herzegovina, with effect from mid-December. Following state and entity elections in October, the failure to establish a state-level government was cited by the European Commission in October 2011 as a major obstacle to progress in reforms. In November the Commission announced that it was to grant pre-accession funds of some €200m. during 2012–13 to support government reform efforts. (A new state Council of Ministers was finally formed in February 2012.)

An SAA was signed with Croatia in October 2001. In February 2003 Croatia submitted a formal application for membership of the EU. In December 2004 the European Council announced that negotiations on membership would commence in mid-March 2005, provided that Croatia co-operated fully with the International Criminal Tribunal for the former Yugoslavia (ICTY). The SAA entered into force in February 2005. In early 2005 the only outstanding issue between Croatia and the ICTY was the need for the arrest and transfer to The Hague of the retired Gen. Ante Gotovina, who went into hiding in 2001 when the ICTY charged him with war crimes against ethnic Serbs during a military operation in 1995. The planned accession talks with Croatia were postponed in March 2005, following an official report by the Chief Prosecutor at the ICTY, Carla Del Ponte, which stated that the Croatian authorities had failed to demonstrate full co-operation with the ICTY. However, in early October Del Ponte issued an assessment stating that Croatia's co-operation with the ICTY had improved, and negotiations were initiated. In December Gotovina was apprehended in the Canary Islands, Spain, thereby removing the main perceived obstacle to EU membership. A border dispute with Slovenia threatened progress towards membership from late 2008; however, a referendum held in Slovenia in early June 2010 secured support for the resolution of the dispute by international arbitration. In November the Commission praised Croatia's progress towards meeting the criteria for EU membership, but urged that further efforts be made to combat corruption and organized crime, to undertake administrative reform, protect ethnic minorities and to aid the repatriation of refugees. Croatia completed membership negotiations on 30 June 2011, and signed the Treaty of Accession on 9 December. Accession was due to take place in 2013, following popular approval of Croatian membership of the EU in a referendum held in late January 2012.

In December 1993 six member states of the EU formally recognized the FYRM as an independent state, but in February 1994 Greece imposed a commercial embargo against the FYRM, on the grounds that the use of the name and symbols (e.g. on the state flag) of 'Macedonia' was a threat to Greek national security. In March, however, ministers of foreign affairs of the EU decided that the embargo was in contravention of EU law, and in April the Commission commenced legal proceedings in the European Court of Justice against Greece. In September 1995 Greece and the FYRM began a process of normalizing relations, after the FYRM agreed to change the design of its state flag. In October Greece ended its economic blockade of the FYRM. A trade and co-operation agreement with the FYRM entered into force in January 1998. In April 2001 an SAA was signed with the FYRM. At the same time, an interim agreement was adopted, allowing for trade-related matters of the SAA to enter into effect in June, without the need for formal ratification by the national parliaments of the EU member states. (The SAA provided for the EU to open its markets to 95% of exports from the FYRM.) However, the Macedonian Government was informed that it would be required to deliver concessions to the ethnic Albanian minority population prior to entering into the agreement. In 2002 the remit of the European Agency for Reconstruction, which had been originally established to implement aid programmes in Kosovo, was extended to include the FYRM. On 31 March 2003 a NATO contingent in the FYRM was replaced by an EU-led mission, Operation Concordia, comprising 350 military personnel. It was replaced in December by a 200-member EU police mission, Operation Proxima, which, in addition to maintaining security and combating organized crime, was to advise the Macedonian police forces. Operation Proxima's mandate expired at the end of 2005. The SAA entered into force in April 2004. A formal application for membership of the EU was submitted in March of that year, and the FYRM was granted candidate status in December 2005. In October 2009 the European Commission recommended that accession negotiations with the FYRM commence; however, Greece objected to the initiation of membership negotiations while the dispute over the country's name remained unresolved. In mid-December visa liberalization entered into force for travel within the Schengen area. In progress reports in November 2010 and October 2011, the European Commission confirmed that the FYRM's unresolved dispute with Greece remained the only main obstacle to the commencement of accession negotiations. Despite the continued impasse, in March 2012 the FYRM began a preliminary dialogue with the EU, which was designed to reduce the length of any future official membership negotiations.

In 1998 the escalation of violence in the Serbian province of Kosovo (Federal Republic of Yugoslavia—FRY), between Serbs and the ethnic Albanian majority, prompted the imposition of sanctions by EU ministers of foreign affairs. In March ministers agreed to impose an arms embargo, to halt export credit guarantees to Yugoslavia and to restrict visas for Serbian officials. A ban on new investment in the region was imposed in June. In the same month, military observers from the EU, Russia and the USA were deployed to Kosovo. During October the Yugoslav Government allowed a team of international experts to investigate atrocities in the region, under an EU mandate. Several EU countries participated in the NATO military offensive against Yugoslavia, which was initiated in March 1999 owing to the continued repression of ethnic Albanians in Kosovo by Serbian forces. Ministers approved a new series of punitive measures in April, including an embargo on the sale or supply of petroleum to the Yugoslav authorities and an extension of a travel ban on Serbian officials and business executives. Humanitarian assistance was extended to provide relief for the substantial numbers of refugees who fled Kosovo amid the escalating violence, in particular to assist the Governments of Albania and the FYRM.

In September 1999 EU ministers responsible for foreign affairs agreed to ease sanctions against Kosovo and Montenegro. In October the EU began to implement an Energy for Democracy initiative, with the objective of supplying some €5m.-worth of heating oil to Serbian towns controlled by groups in opposition to the Yugoslav President, Slobodan Milošević. In February 2000 the EU suspended its ban on the Yugoslav national airline. However, the restrictions on visas for Serbian officials were reinforced. Kosovo received a total of €474.7m. under EU programmes in 2000 and the EU was the largest financial contributor to the province in 2001.

In May 2000 the EU agreed an emergency aid package to support Montenegro against destabilization by Serbia. Following the election of a new administration in the FRY in late 2000, the EU immediately withdrew all remaining sanctions, with the exception of those directed against Milošević and his associates, and pledged financial support of €200m. The FRY was welcomed as a full participant in the stabilization and association process (see below). The EU insisted that the FRY must co-operate fully with the ICTY. Following the arrest of Milošević by the FRY authorities in April 2001, the first part of the EU's aid package for that year (amounting to €240m.) was released. During 2002 EU humanitarian aid to Serbia totalled €37.5m., to assist the large numbers of refugees and displaced persons. Negotiations on an SAA between the State Union of Serbia and Montenegro (as the FRY became known in February 2003) and the EU commenced in November 2005, but were terminated in May 2006, owing to the country's failure fully to co-operate with the ICTY. Following Montenegro's declaration of independence on 3 June 2006, the Narodna skupština Republike Srbije (National Assembly of the Republic of Serbia) confirmed that Serbia was the official successor state of the State Union of Serbia and Montenegro. On 12 June the EU recognized Montenegrin independence, and the Serbian Government officially recognized Montenegro as an independent state three days later. At the end of September the Narodna skupština adopted a new Constitution, which was confirmed by referendum in late October. In early June 2007 the President of the European Commission invited Serbia to resume negotiations on an SAA, following the arrest, within Serbia, of Zdravko Tolimir, a former Bosnian Serb army officer. A visa facilitation and readmission agreement between Serbia and the EU came into force at the beginning of 2008. In late February the EU suspended negotiations with Serbia on an SAA, after violence broke out in Belgrade following the declaration of independence by Kosovo (see below). However, on 29 April EU ministers of foreign affairs signed the SAA, in what was widely perceived as an effort to strengthen popular support for reformist parties contesting the forthcoming elections. The SAA with Serbia was accompanied by a provisional document granting Serbia access to benefits based on the SAA before all EU members had ratified the Agreement; however, its implementation was to be suspended until EU member states agreed unanimously on Serbia's full co-operation with the ICTY. In late July Radovan Karadžić, a former President of Republika Srpska, Bosnia and Herzegovina, whose arrest on charges of war crimes, including genocide, had long been sought by the ICTY, was apprehended in Belgrade. In mid-December 2009 visa liberalization was implemented for Serbian citizens travelling within the Schengen area. In late December Serbia formally applied for membership of the EU. At the end of March 2010 the Narodna skupština passed a resolution condemning the massacre of up to 8,000 Muslim male civilians by Serb forces in July 1995, in Srebrenica, Bosnia and Herzegovina. In June 2010 the EU agreed to begin the ratification process for the SAA with Serbia, following a positive assessment of Serbia's co-operation with the ICTY. In late July the International Court of Justice (ICJ) issued a non-binding, advisory opinion that Kosovo's declaration of independence on 17 February 2008 had not breached international law, Security Council Resolution 1244 or the constitutional framework. Serbia reaffirmed its intention to continue to withhold recognition of independence for Kosovo. In early September 2010, however, the UN General Assembly adopted a joint, non-binding, EU-Serbia resolution, according to which Serbia agreed to participate in direct talks with Kosovo, under the aegis of the EU. Subsequently, in late October EU ministers of foreign affairs agreed to request that the Commission assess Serbia's application for candidacy. In late May 2011 the Serbian authorities arrested the Bosnian Serb former military leader Ratko Mladić in northern Serbia. The arrest of the final major war crimes suspect to be indicted by the ICTY, the Croatian Serb Goran Hadžić, was announced in late July. In October the European Commission issued a report stating that Serbia had made sufficient progress towards meeting EU criteria for a formal recommendation to be made that it become a candidate country. In December, nevertheless, Serbia failed to secure membership status at an EU summit meeting in Brussels owing to the insistence of a number of EU leaders that the issue of Serbia's refusal to recognize Kosovo first be resolved. At the end of February 2012, the Romanian Government unexpectedly presented objections to Serbia's candidacy relating to the treatment of the Vlach ethnic minority in Serbia, which were withdrawn following an agreement between Serbian and Romanian officials. EU heads of state and government officially approved Serbia's candidate status on 1 March (following significant progress in dialogue between Serbian and Kosovo representatives in Brussels), although no date for the beginning of accession negotiations was announced.

Following the declaration of independence by Montenegro in June 2006, the EU Council pledged to develop the relationship of the EU with Montenegro as a sovereign state. The first Enhanced Permanent Dialogue meeting between Montenegro and the EU was held in the Montenegrin capital, Podgorica, in late July. On the same day the Council adopted a mandate for the negotiation of an SAA with Montenegro (based on the previous mandate for negotiations with the State Union of Serbia and Montenegro). Negotiations were initiated in September, and in October 2007 Montenegro signed an SAA with the EU, which entered into force on 1 May 2010. Meanwhile, Montenegro had applied for membership of the EU in December 2008. A visa facilitation and readmission agreement between Montenegro and the EU came into force at the beginning of 2008, and from 19 December 2009 Montenegrin citizens were no longer required to hold a visa to travel within the Schengen area. Following a recommendation by the European Commission in the previous month, in mid-December 2010, at a meeting of the EU Council, held in Brussels, Montenegro was formally granted the status of a candidate country for EU membership. In March 2011 the European Parliament adopted a resolution commending Montenegro's progress towards EU integration. In October the Commission recommended that accession negotiations be opened with Montenegro, stating that the Government had made satisfactory progress towards meeting the criteria for EU membership, although stipulating that sustained efforts were necessary in the area of the rule of law, particularly in combating corruption and organized crime.

On 17 February 2008 the Assembly of Kosovo endorsed a declaration establishing the province as a sovereign state, independent from Serbia. Serbia immediately protested that the declaration of independence contravened international law and demanded that it be annulled. The USA extended recognition to Kosovo on the following day, and a large number of EU member nations announced their intention to do so. A supervisory EU mission in Kosovo (the EU Rule of Law Mission in Kosovo—EULEX), to comprise some 1,900 foreign personnel, became operational after a 120-day transition period (although full deployment was delayed). Following the deployment of EULEX, UNMIK had been scheduled to transfer authority to government institutions in Kosovo. However, after both Serbia and Russia challenged the legality of EULEX, it was agreed that the two missions would co-exist under joint command. It was also anticipated that a NATO presence would remain in Kosovo for a period of five years, in order to oversee Kosovo's security. On 15 June a new Constitution came into force in Kosovo (Serbia refused to accept its introduction in Serb-dominated northern Kosovo). In late October an agreement was signed with the USA, providing for its participation in EULEX. EULEX assumed responsibility from UNMIK for police and judicial functions in December. In December 2008 EULEX Kosovo became operational, and by April 2009 the mission was being deployed to full operational capacity. In July 2010 the European Parliament adopted a resolution that reiterated its desire for all EU member states to recognize Kosovo's independence, the legality of which was upheld by the advisory opinion of the ICJ later that month. At June 2012 91 UN member nations, including 22 EU member states, had formally recognized Kosovo, and many diplomatic missions in Prishtina had become embassies. However, several EU member states (Cyprus, Greece, Romania, Slovakia and Spain) had announced their intention to withhold recognition of Kosovo as an independent state. In February 2012 the European Commission proposed the undertaking of a feasibility study for an SAA with Kosovo. In June the mandate of EULEX was extended until mid-2014.

EASTERN EUROPE, RUSSIA AND THE CIS

In the late 1980s the extensive political changes and reforms in Eastern Europe led to a strengthening of links with the EC. In December 1989 EC heads of government agreed to establish the European Bank for Reconstruction and Development (EBRD) to promote investment in Eastern Europe, with participation by member states of the Organisation for Economic Co-operation and Development (OECD) and the Council for Mutual Economic Assistance (CMEA), which provided economic co-operation and co-ordination in the communist bloc between 1949 and 1991. The EBRD began operations in April 1991. In the same year the EC established the Technical Assistance to the Commonwealth of Independent States (TACIS) programme, to promote the development of successful market economies and to foster democracy in the countries of the former USSR through the provision of expertise and training. (TACIS initially extended assistance to the Baltic states; in 1992, however, these became eligible for assistance under PHARE and withdrew from TACIS. Mongolia was eligible for TACIS assistance in 1991–2003, but was subsequently covered by the Asia Latin America—ALA programme.)

In March 2003 the European Commission launched a European Neighbourhood Policy (ENP) with the aim of enhancing co-operation with countries adjacent to the enlarged Union. A new European Neighbourhood and Partnership Instrument (ENPI) replaced TACIS and MEDA (which was concerned with EU co-operation with Mediterranean countries) from 2007. All countries covered by the ENP (Armenia, Azerbaijan, Belarus, Georgia, Moldova, Ukraine and several Mediterranean countries) were to be eligible for support under the ENPI. Russia was not covered by the ENP, and the relationship between Russia and the EU was described as a Strategic Partnership, which was also to be funded by the ENPI. In accordance with the ENP, in December 2004 the EU agreed Action Plans with Moldova and Ukraine, establishing targets for political and economic co-operation. These Plans were adopted by EU ministers of foreign affairs and the two countries concerned in February 2005. ENP Action Plans for Armenia, Azerbaijan and Georgia were developed in 2005 and published in late 2006. A visa facilitation and readmission agreement with Georgia was concluded in January 2011. The EU did not enter into discussions on a Plan with Belarus, stating that it first required the country to hold free and fair elections in order to establish a democratic form of government (see below). The eventual conclusion of more ambitious relationships with partner countries achieving sufficient progress in meeting the priorities set out in the Action Plans (through the negotiation of European Neighbourhood Agreements) was envisaged.

In June 2007 the European Council adopted The EU and Central Asia: Strategy for a New Partnership, which aimed to develop bilateral and regional co-operation in a wide number of areas. An initial progress report was published in June 2008. In May 2009 the heads of state or government of Armenia, Azerbaijan, Belarus, Georgia, Moldova and Ukraine, and representatives of the EU and the heads of state or government, and other representatives, of its member states, convened in Prague, Czech Republic, issued a joint declaration on establishing an Eastern Partnership. The Eastern Partnership (facilitated through a specific Eastern dimension of the ENP) aimed, through support for political and socio-economic reforms in interested partner countries, to create the necessary conditions to accelerate political association and further economic integration with the EU.

In 1992 EU heads of government decided to replace the agreement on trade and economic co-operation that had been concluded with the USSR in 1989 with new Partnership and Co-operation Agreements (PCAs), providing a framework for closer political, cultural and economic relations between the EU and the former republics of the USSR. An Interim Agreement with Russia on trade concessions came into effect in February 1996, giving EU exporters improved access to the Russian market for specific products, and at the same time abolishing quantitative restrictions on some Russian exports to the EU; a PCA with Russia came into effect in December 1997. In January 1998 the first meeting of the Co-operation Council for the EU-Russia PCA was held, and in July an EU-Russia Space Dialogue was established. In June 1999 the EU adopted a Common Strategy on Russia. This aimed to promote the consolidation of democracy and rule of law in the country; the integration of Russia into the common European economic and social space; and regional stability and security. At the sixth EU-Russia summit, held in October 2000, both parties agreed to initiate a regular energy dialogue, with the aim of establishing an EU-Russia Energy Partnership. However, the status of Kaliningrad, a Russian enclave situated between Poland and Lithuania, became an increasing source of contention as the EU prepared to admit those two countries. Despite opposition from Russia, the EU insisted that residents of Kaliningrad would need a visa to cross EU territory. In November 2002, at an EU-Russia summit meeting held in Brussels, Belgium, a compromise agreement was reached, according to which residents of the enclave were to be issued with multiple-transit travel documentation; the new regulations took effect in July 2003. Also in November 2002, the EU granted Russian exporters market economy status, in recognition of the progress made by Russia to liberalize its economy. At a summit held in St Petersburg, Russia, in May 2003, the EU and Russia agreed to improve their co-operation by creating four 'common spaces' within the framework of the PCA. The two sides agreed to establish a common economic space; a common space for freedom, security and justice; a space for co-operation on external security; and for research, education and culture. However, relations between the EU and Russia remained strained by Russia's opposition to EU enlargement, partly owing to fears of a detrimental effect on the Russian economy, as some of its neighbouring countries (significant markets for Russian goods) were obliged to introduce EU quotas and tariffs. In February 2004 the European Commission made proposals to improve the efficacy of EU-Russia relations, given their increased dependence, the enlargement due to take place in May, and unresolved territorial conflicts in a number of countries close to the Russian and EU borders (Azerbaijan, Georgia and Moldova). In May, at a bilateral summit held in the Russian capital, Moscow, the EU agreed to support Russia's membership of the World Trade Organization (WTO), following Russia's extension in April of its PCA with the EU to 10 accession states. The Russian President, Vladimir Putin, signed legislation ratifying the Kyoto Protocol of the UN Convention on Climate Change in November, following EU criticism of the country's failure to do so. The Kyoto Protocol entered into force in February 2005. Consultations on human rights took place between the EU and Russia for the first time in March of that year, in Luxembourg. At a summit held in Moscow in May the two sides adopted a single package of 'roadmaps', to facilitate the creation of the four common spaces in the medium term. As part of the common space on freedom, security and justice, agreements on visa facilitation (simplifying the procedures for issuing short-stay visas) and on readmission (setting out procedures for the return of people found to be illegally resident in the territory of the other party) were reached in October, and were signed at the EU-Russia summit held in Sochi, Russia, in May 2006. In July the Commission approved draft negotiating directives for a new EU-Russia Agreement to replace the PCA, which was to come to the end of its initial 10-year period in December 2007. The PCA remained in force pending the conclusion of a new agreement. In March 2007 the Commission published a Country Strategy Paper for EU-Russia relations in 2007–13. Associated with the paper was a National Indicative Programme for Russia for 2007–10, which envisaged that financial allocations from the EU to Russia during that period would amount to €30m. annually. Financial co-operation was intended to focus on the common spaces and the package of road maps for their creation. At an EU-Russia summit meeting held in Mafra, Portugal, in October 2007, it was agreed to establish a system to provide early warning of threats to the supply of natural gas and petroleum to the EU, following the serious disruption of supplies to EU countries from Russia, via Belarus, in previous years. In November 2008 the European Commission, the USA and 15 other countries attending an energy summit in Baku, Azerbaijan, signed a declaration urging increased co-operation in projects aimed at improving co-operation in energy projects in the Caspian Sea region, in order to diversify supply routes. In January 2009 the European Commission proposed to contribute €250m. towards funding the planned Nabucco gas pipeline, which was to channel about 5%–10% of Europe's gas requirements (originating in the Caspian region and the Middle East, including Azerbaijan, Egypt, Iraq and Turkmenistan) from Erzurum, Turkey, to Baumgarten an der March, Austria, possibly also with an extension pipeline to Poland. Construction of the Nabucco pipeline was scheduled to commence in 2013, and gas was scheduled to start flowing through it in 2017.

On 8 August 2008 Georgia launched a military offensive in the separatist republic of South Ossetia, prompting retaliatory intervention by Russia. A cease-fire agreement was brokered four days later, with the assistance of French President Nicolas Sarkozy, whose country held the rotating Presidency of the Council of the European Union. However, Russia's failure to withdraw its troops from Georgian territory by the end of August, and its decision to recognize the independence of the republics of South Ossetia and Abkhazia, resulted, at the beginning of September, in an agreement by EU leaders to postpone talks with Russia on the new EU-Russia agreement, which had been scheduled to commence later that month. Following further negotiations with Sarkozy, Russia subsequently agreed to withdraw its troops from Georgia by 10 October. Meanwhile, in early September EU ministers responsible for foreign affairs reached agreement on the deployment of an EU Monitoring Mission (EUMM) to Georgia from 1 October. EUMM comprised some 350 personnel from 22 countries, and was mandated to monitor adherence to peace agreements signed in Georgia in August and September 2008, and to contribute to stability throughout Georgia and the surrounding region. EUMM's field office structure was strengthened in September 2009. An EU-Russia summit meeting took place in Nice, France, in November. The

EU noted that Russia had fulfilled most of its obligations in Georgia, but that further progress was needed with regard to the withdrawal of troops from two locations in South Ossetia. In November 2008 EU ministers of foreign affairs agreed to resume talks with Russia on the new EU-Russia agreement, which remained ongoing.

In February 1994 the EU Council of Ministers agreed to pursue closer economic and political relations with Ukraine, following an agreement by that country to renounce control of nuclear weapons on its territory. A PCA was signed by the two sides in June. In December EU ministers of finance approved a loan totalling ECU 85m., conditional on Ukraine's implementation of a strategy to close the Chernobyl (Chornobyl) nuclear power plant. An Interim Trade Agreement with Ukraine came into force in February 1996; this was replaced by a PCA in March 1998. In December 1999 the EU adopted a Common Strategy on Ukraine, aimed at developing a strategic partnership on the basis of the PCA. The Chernobyl plant closed in December 2000. The EU has provided funding to cover the interim period prior to the completion of two new reactors (supported by the EBRD and the European Atomic Energy Community—Euratom) to replace the plant's generating capacity. The EU Action Plan for Ukraine adopted in February 2005 envisaged enhanced co-operation in many areas. At a summit held in the Ukrainian capital, Kyiv, in December, the EU and Ukraine signed agreements on aviation and on Ukraine's participation in the EU's Galileo civil satellite navigation and positioning system and a memorandum of understanding (MOU) on increased co-operation in the energy sector. Ukraine reiterated its strategic goal to be integrated fully into the EU, and the EU pledged support for Ukraine's bid to join the WTO (Ukraine became a member of the WTO in May 2008). Meanwhile, in November 2005 an EU Border Assistance Mission to monitor Ukraine's border with Moldova (EUBAM) was launched at the request of both countries' Governments (deployed for an initial period of two years, subsequently extended, and ongoing at 2012). In February 2008 EU ministers of foreign affairs attended a conference on the EU's Black Sea Synergy programme, held in Kyiv, Ukraine. Following the accession to the EU of the littoral states Bulgaria and Romania, the programme aims to improve co-operation between countries bordering the Black Sea, as well as between members of the Black Sea region and the EU. In September, at an EU-Ukraine summit, held in Paris, France, the EU announced plans to commence negotiations towards an Association Agreement with Ukraine, which would supersede the PCA. In November 2009 an EU-Ukraine Association Agenda was adopted, replacing the EU Action Plan. In March 2011 an MOU on the National Indicative Programme for Ukraine for 2011–13 was signed, allocating some €470m. to Ukraine, focusing on three principal areas: good governance and the rule of law; progress pertaining to the EU-Ukraine Association Agreement (including plans for the creation of a deep and comprehensive free trade area—DCFTA); and sustainable development. An EU-Ukraine free trade agreement was finalized in late October 2011, but the signature of the agreement, which was to form part of the EU-Ukraine Association Agreement, risked delay, owing to EU concerns over the prosecution of opposition politicians in that country. In mid-October Yuliya Tymoshenko, a former Prime Minister and the principal political opponent of the President of Ukraine, Viktor Yanukovych, had been sentenced to seven years' imprisonment for abuse of office, after a trial that she claimed was politically motivated. In December the European Parliament urged the EU-Ukraine association agreement to be initialled rapidly, asserting that the agreement could help to bring about political change. The Agreement was initialled at the end of March 2012.

Prior to 2009 Russia and Ukraine held annual negotiations on the renewal of gas supply contracts. A dispute between Russia and Ukraine over gas prices in January 2006 was of considerable concern to the EU, which relied on Russia for some 25% of its gas (with some member states entirely dependent on imports from Russia), most of which passed through Ukraine. In January 2009, owing to the failure of negotiations to agree the 2009 prices for Ukraine's consumption and Russia's gas transit through Ukraine, Russia suspended gas supplies to Ukraine, stating that it would pump only sufficient gas for customers further down the pipeline. Later in January a 10-year deal on prices was concluded between Russia and Ukraine and supplies to Ukraine were resumed. In March 2009 the EU, Ukraine, international financial institutions, gas industry representatives and other partners participated in a Joint EU-Ukraine International Investment Conference on the Rehabilitation of Ukraine's Gas Transit System, to discuss the future modernization of the system, with a view to improving the sustainability, reliability and efficiency of the infrastructure and helping to secure long-term supplies of gas to the rest of Europe.

In April 2008, following a visit to Turkmenistan by the Commissioner for External Relations and European Neighbourhood Policy, the Turkmenistani authorities pledged to supply some 10,000m. cu m of natural gas per year to the EU from 2009 (thereby enabling EU member states to reduce their reliance on Russian gas supplies). A memorandum of mutual understanding and co-operation on energy issues was signed between the EU and Turkmenistan in May.

In January 2011 the Commission signed a joint declaration on gas delivery for Europe, in Baku. According to the agreement, Azerbaijan guaranteed substantial, long-term gas supplies to EU markets, while the EU provided access to its markets for Azerbaijani gas, via a planned Southern Gas Corridor.

An Interim Agreement with Belarus was signed in March 1996. However, in February 1997 the EU suspended negotiations for the conclusion of the Interim Agreement and for a PCA in view of serious reverses to the development of democracy in that country. EU technical assistance programmes were suspended, with the exception of aid programmes and those considered directly beneficial to the democratic process. In 1999 the EU announced that the punitive measures would be withdrawn gradually upon the attainment of certain benchmarks. In 2000 the EU criticized the Belarusian Government for failing to accept its recommendations on the conduct of the legislative elections held in October. In November 2002 EU member states imposed a travel ban on President Alyaksandr Lukashenka and other senior Belarusian officials, in protest against the lack of democracy and the declining human rights situation in the country; the ban was lifted in April 2003. In September 2004 the European Parliament condemned Lukashenka's attempt to secure a third term of office by scheduling a referendum to change the country's Constitution, which permitted a maximum of two terms. The EU subsequently imposed a travel ban on officials responsible for the allegedly fraudulent legislative elections and the referendum held in Belarus in October, which abolished limits on the number of terms that the President was permitted to serve. The Council, nevertheless, reiterated the EU's willingness to develop closer relations with Belarus if Lukashenka were to introduce fundamental democratic and economic reforms. As part of efforts to support civil society and democratization, in September the European Commission initiated a €2m. project to increase access in Belarus to independent sources of news and information. In April 2006, following Lukashenka's re-election in the previous month, the EU extended the travel ban imposed in 2004 to include Lukashenka and 30 government ministers and other officials. In November 2006, in a communication to the Belarusian authorities, the EU detailed the benefits that Belarus could expect to gain, within the framework of the European Neighbourhood Policy, were the country to embark on a process of democratization and to show due respect for human rights and the rule of law. In October 2008 EU ministers of foreign affairs agreed to soften sanctions against Belarus, which released three high-profile political prisoners from detention in August, by suspending the travel ban on Lukashenka and other officials. In November 2009 the Council noted positive developments in EU-Belarus relations, with the development of an EU-Belarus Human Rights Dialogue, increased technical co-operation and the country's active participation in the Eastern Partnership. However, owing to a lack of progress with regard to human rights and democracy, the Council agreed to retain restrictive measures in place against a number of Belarusian officials. At the end of September 2011 Belarusian officials failed to attend a summit meeting of the Eastern Partnership, held in Warsaw, Poland. The meeting was attended by representatives of Armenia, Azerbaijan, Georgia, Moldova and Ukraine, but the EU was unable to secure support for a statement demanding the safeguarding of human rights and democracy in Belarus. In October 2011 the EU agreed to retain restrictive measures against Belarusian officials for a further 12-month period. In January 2012 the EU noted a worsening in the human rights situation in Belarus, and announced that it was to expand its list of banned officials (then numbering 210) to some 336; in response, in February Belarus expelled EU diplomats and the Polish ambassador from the country, and recalled its own ambassadors.

In May 1997 an Interim Agreement with Moldova entered into force; this was replaced by a PCA in July 1998. The first EU-Moldova Co-operation Council meeting was held in the same month in Brussels. Interim Agreements entered into force during 1997 with Kazakhstan (April), Georgia (September) and Armenia (December). An Interim Agreement with Azerbaijan entered into force in March 1999. A PCA with Turkmenistan was signed in May 1998 and an Interim Agreement with Uzbekistan entered into force in June. By the end of that year PCAs had been signed with all the countries of the CIS, except Tajikistan, owing to political instability in that country. All remaining Agreements had entered into force by 1 July 1999, with the exception of those negotiated with Belarus and Turkmenistan. A PCA with Tajikistan was eventually signed in October 2004, and entered into force in January 2010.

OTHER EUROPEAN COUNTRIES

The members of the European Free Trade Association (EFTA) concluded bilateral free trade agreements with the EEC and the ECSC during the 1970s. On 1 January 1984 the last tariff barriers were eliminated, thus establishing full free trade for industrial products between the Community and EFTA members. Some EFTA members subsequently applied for membership of the EC: Austria in 1989, Sweden in 1991, and Finland, Switzerland and Norway in 1992. Formal negotiations on the creation of a European Economic Area (EEA), a single market for goods, services, capital and labour among EC and EFTA members, began in June 1990, and were concluded in October 1991. The agreement was signed in May 1992 (after a delay caused by a ruling of the Court of Justice of the EC that a proposed joint EC-EFTA court, for adjudication in disputes, was incompatible with the Treaty of Rome; EFTA members then agreed to concede jurisdiction to the Court of Justice on cases of competition involving both EC and EFTA members, and to establish a special joint committee for other disputes). In a referendum in December, Swiss voters rejected ratification of the agreement, and the remaining 18 countries signed an adjustment protocol in March 1993, allowing the EEA to be established without Switzerland (which was to have observer status). The EEA entered into force on 1 January 1994. Despite the rejection of the EEA by the Swiss electorate, the Swiss Government declared its intention to continue to pursue its application for membership of the EU. Formal negotiations on the accession to the EU of Austria, Finland and Sweden began on 1 February, and those on Norway's membership started on 1 April. Negotiations were concluded in March 1994. Heads of government of the four countries signed treaties of accession to the EU in June, which were to come into effect from 1995, subject to approval by a national referendum in each country. Accession to the EU was endorsed by the electorates of Austria, Finland and Sweden in June, October and November 1994, respectively. Norway's accession, however, was rejected in a national referendum (by 52.4% of voters) conducted at the end of November. The success of the campaign opposing Norway's entry to the EU was attributed to several factors: in particular, fears that an influx of cheaper agricultural goods from the EU would lead to bankruptcies and unemploymen, and that stocks of fish would be severely depleted if EU boats were granted increased access to Norwegian waters. There was also widespread concern that national sovereignty would be compromised by the transfer to the EU of certain executive responsibilities. From 1994 Norway's relations with the EU were based on full participation in the EEA as well as involvement (at non-signatory level) in the EU's Schengen Agreement. Austria, Finland and Sweden became members of the EU on 1 January 1995. Liechtenstein, which became a full member of EFTA in September 1991, joined the EEA on 1 May 1995.

In 1999 Switzerland signed seven bilateral free trade agreements with the EU, mainly relating to trade liberalization (known together as Bilateral I). A referendum was held in March 2001 on whether to begin 'fast-track' accession negotiations with the EU. Participation in the ballot was high and the motion was rejected by 77% of voters; however, the Swiss application remains open. The first EU-Switzerland summit meeting took place in Brussels, Belgium, in May 2004, after which nine sectoral agreements (together known as Bilateral II, and covering areas such as savings tax, fraud, the Schengen Agreement on border controls and the environment) were signed by the two parties. The participation of Switzerland in the Schengen area and the extension of the agreement on the free movement of persons to the 10 states that joined the EU in May 2004 were approved by Swiss voters in public referendums in June and September 2005. A protocol on these measures and on Bilateral II was signed in October 2004 and entered into force in April 2006.

Despite the fact that Iceland joined EFTA in 1970 and ratified the EEA in 1993 (although the extension of the single market legislation excluded agriculture and fisheries management, as in Norway and Liechtenstein), it did not thereafter apply for EU membership. Although opposition to Iceland's joining the EU persisted at government level in the first half of the 2000s, relations between the EU and Iceland had generally developed smoothly since 1993—notably, Iceland negotiated participation in the Schengen Agreement (although, as a signatory, it was not involved in decision-making within the agreement). Following a serious economic crisis in Iceland in 2008, in July 2009 the Icelandic Parliament voted in favour of making an application for membership of the EU. Accession negotiations with Iceland opened in July 2010, and by December 2011 talks had opened in 11 of the total of 33 policy areas.

In November 2008 the European Commission adopted a communication on the EU and the Arctic Region, which emphasized the adverse effects of climate change and technological activities in that region. The Commission identified three principal goals: to preserve the region, in co-operation with its indigenous population; to encourage the sustainable use of natural resources; and to aid improved multilateral governance. In January 2011 the European Parliament adopted a resolution on EU policy in the High North, which emphasized the need for a co-ordinated approach to EU activity in the Arctic Region.

The EU's Northern Dimension programme covers the Baltic Sea, Arctic Sea and north-west Russia regions. It aims to address the specific challenges of these areas and to encourage co-operation with external states. The Northern Dimension programme operates within the framework of the EU-Russia PCA and the TACIS programme, as well as other agreements and financial instruments. An Action Plan for the Northern Dimension in the External and Cross-border Policies of the EU, covering 2000–03, was adopted in June 2000. The Plan detailed objectives in the following areas of co-operation: environmental protection; nuclear safety and nuclear waste management; energy; transport and border-crossing infrastructure; justice and internal affairs; business and investment; public health and social administration; telecommunications; and human resources development. The first conference of Northern Dimension foreign ministers was held in Helsinki, Finland, in November 1999. At a ministerial conference on the Northern Dimension held in October 2002, guidelines were adopted for a second Action Plan for the Northern Dimension in the External and Cross-border Policies of the EU, covering 2004–06. The second Action Plan, which was formally adopted in October 2003, set out strategic priorities and objectives in five priority areas: economy and infrastructure; social issues (including education, training and public health); environment, nuclear safety and natural resources; justice and home affairs; and cross-border co-operation. Under the Northern Dimension programme, priority was given to efforts to integrate Russia into a common European economic and social area through projects dealing with environmental pollution, nuclear risks and cross-border organized crime. At a Northern Dimension summit meeting held in Helsinki, Finland, in November 2006, the leaders of the EU, Iceland, Norway and Russia endorsed a new Policy Framework Document and Northern Dimension Political Declaration, replacing the three-year action plans hitherto in place with a new common regional policy. In October 2009 a memorandum of understanding was signed in Naples, Italy, by the European Commission and 11 northern European countries, establishing the Northern Dimension Partnership on Transport and Logistics, which sought to develop important transport links in northern Europe.

A trade agreement with Andorra entered into force on 1 January 1991, establishing a customs union for industrial products, and allowing duty-free access to the EC for certain Andorran agricultural products. A wide-ranging co-operation agreement with Andorra and an agreement on the taxation of savings income were signed in November 2004 and entered into force in July 2005. Similar agreements on the taxation of savings income also took effect in Liechtenstein, Monaco and San Marino in July 2005. Negotiations on a co-operation and customs union agreement between the EC and San Marino were concluded in December 1991; the agreement entered into force in May 2002. The euro became the sole currency in circulation in Andorra, Monaco, San Marino and the Vatican City at the beginning of 2002.

THE MIDDLE EAST AND THE MEDITERRANEAN

A scheme to negotiate a series of parallel trade and co-operation agreements encompassing almost all of the non-member states on the coast of the Mediterranean was formulated by the European Community (EC) in 1972. Association Agreements, intended to lead to customs union or the eventual full accession of the country concerned, had been signed with Greece (which eventually became a member of the Community in 1981) in 1962, Turkey in 1964 and Malta in 1971; a fourth agreement was signed with Cyprus in 1972. (In May 2004 Malta and Cyprus became members of the European Union—EU, as the EC became known in May 2003.) These established free access to the Community market for most industrial products and tariff reductions for most agricultural products. Annexed were financial protocols under which the Community was to provide concessional finance. During the 1970s a series of agreements covering trade and economic co-operation were concluded with the Arab Mediterranean countries and Israel, all establishing free access to EC markets for most industrial products. Access for agricultural products was facilitated, although some tariffs remained. In 1982 the Commission formulated an integrated plan for the development of its own Mediterranean regions and recommended the adoption of a new policy towards the non-Community countries of the Mediterranean. This was to include greater efforts towards diversifying agriculture, in order to avoid surpluses of items such as citrus fruits, olive oil and wine (which the Mediterranean countries all wished to export to the Community) and to reduce these countries' dependence on imported food. From 1 January 1993 the majority of agricultural exports from Mediterranean non-Community countries were granted exemption from customs duties.

In June 1995 the European Council endorsed a proposal by the Commission to reform and strengthen the Mediterranean policy of the EU. In November a conference of ministers of foreign affairs of the EU member states, 11 Mediterranean non-member countries (excluding Libya) and the Palestinian authorities was convened in Barcelona, Spain. The conference issued the Barcelona Declaration, outlining the main objective of the partnership, which was to create a region of peace, security and prosperity. The Declaration set the objective of establishing a Euro-Mediterranean free trade area. The process of co-operation and dialogue under this agreement became known as the Euro-Mediterranean Partnership (or Barcelona Process, until 2008, when this was renamed as the Union for the Mediterranean, see below).

In March 2008 the European Council approved a proposal formally to transform the Barcelona Process into a Union for the Mediterranean. In mid-July heads of state and of government from the 27 EU member states and from the member states and observers of the Barcelona Process attended the Paris Summit for the Mediterranean, at which the new Union for the Mediterranean was officially launched. Bosnia and Herzegovina, Croatia, Monaco and Montenegro were also admitted to the Union for the Mediterranean. Six co-operation projects were approved at the summit, which were to focus on: improving pollution levels in the Mediterranean; constructing maritime and land highways; civil protection; the creation of a Mediterranean Solar Plan; the establishment of a Euro-Mediterranean University (which was established in Slovenia in June 2008); and the launch of a Mediterranean Business Development Initiative. Various institutions were to be established to support the Union for the Mediterranean, including a joint Secretariat and a Joint Permanent Committee, to be based in Brussels. A meeting of Euro-Mediterranean ministers of foreign affairs, convened in Marseilles, in November, endorsed the new Union. A Euro-Mediterranean Regional and Local Assembly (ARLEM) held its inaugural meeting in Barcelona in January 2010, and a Secretariat was established in Barcelona in March.

The European Neighbourhood Policy (ENP) was established by the European Commission in 2004, to enhance co-operation with 16 countries neighboured the EU following its enlargement. Algeria, Egypt, Israel, Jordan, Lebanon, Libya, Morocco, the Palestinian Autonomous Areas, Syria and Tunisia were covered by the ENP (which became known as the Southern Neighbourhood), which was intended to complement the Barcelona Process, in addition to several countries to the east of the Union (the Eastern Neighbourhood). Under the ENP, the EU has negotiated bilateral Action Plans with 12 neighbouring countries, establishing targets for further political and economic co-operation over a three- to five-year period. The Action Plans aimed to build on existing contractual relationships between the partner country and the EU (e.g. an Association Agreement or a Partnership and Co-operation Agreement). The eventual conclusion of more ambitious relationships with partner countries achieving sufficient progress in meeting the priorities set out in the Action Plans (through the negotiation of European Neighbourhood Agreements) was envisaged.

The EU's primary financial instrument for the implementation of the Euro-Mediterranean Partnership was the MEDA programme, providing support for the reform of economic and social structures within partnership countries. It was followed by MEDA II, which was granted a budget of €5,350m. for 2000–06. In 2007 a new European Neighbourhood and Partnership Instrument (ENPI) replaced MEDA and the Technical Assistance to the Commonwealth of Independent States (TACIS) programme (which was concerned with EU co-operation with the countries of the former USSR). ENPI was conceived as a flexible, policy-orientated instrument to target sustainable development and conformity with EU policies and standards. In 2007–13 some €12,000m. was to be made available, within its framework, to support ENP Action Plans and the Strategic Partnership with Russia. An ENPI cross-border co-operation programme was to cover activities across the external borders of the EU in the south and the east, supported by funds totalling €1,180m. in 2007–13.

Turkey, which had signed an Association Agreement with the EC in 1963 (although this was suspended between 1980 and 1986 following a military coup), applied for membership of the EU in April 1987. Accession talks began in October 2005 (see Enlargement).

Co-operation agreements concluded in the 1970s with the Maghreb countries (Algeria, Morocco and Tunisia), the Mashreq countries (Egypt, Jordan, Lebanon and Syria) and Israel covered free access to the Community market for industrial products, customs preferences for certain agricultural products, and financial aid in the form of grants and loans from the EIB. A co-operation agreement negotiated with the Republic of Yemen was non-preferential. In June 1992 the EC approved a proposal to conclude new bilateral agreements with the Maghreb countries, incorporating the following components: political dialogue; financial, economic, technical and cultural co-operation; and the eventual establishment of a free trade area. A Euro-Mediterranean Association Agreement with Tunisia was signed in July 1995 and entered into force in March 1998. A similar agreement with Morocco (concluded in 1996) entered into force in March 2000. (In July 1987 Morocco applied to join the Community, but its application was rejected on the grounds that it is not a European country.) In March 1997 negotiations were initiated between the European Commission and representatives of the Algerian Government on a Euro-Mediterranean Association Agreement that would incorporate political commitments relating to democracy and human rights; this was signed in December 2001 and entered into force in September 2005. An Association Agreement with Jordan was signed in November 1997 and entered into force in May 2002. A Euro-Mediterranean Association Agreement with Egypt (which has been a major beneficiary of EU financial co-operation since the 1970s) was signed in June 2001 and was fully ratified in June 2004. In May 2001 Egypt, together with Jordan, Tunisia and Morocco, issued the Agadir Declaration, in which they determined to establish an Arab

Mediterranean Free Trade Zone. The so-called Agadir Agreement on the establishment of a Free Trade Zone between the Arabic Mediterranean Nations was signed in February 2004, entered into force in July 2006, and entered its implementation phase in March 2007. An interim EU Association Agreement with Lebanon was signed in June 2002, and entered into force in April 2006. Protracted negotiations on an Association Agreement with Syria were concluded in October 2004 and a revised version of the Agreement was initialled in December 2008.

In January 1989 the EC and Israel eliminated the last tariff barriers to full free trade for industrial products. A Euro-Mediterranean Association Agreement with Israel was signed in 1995, providing further trade concessions and establishing an institutional political dialogue between the two parties. The agreement entered into force in June 2000. In late 2004 an ENP Action Plan on further co-operation was agreed by the EU and Israel; it was adopted by the EU in February 2005 and by the Israeli authorities in April of that year.

Following the signing of the September 1993 Israeli-Palestine Liberation Organization (PLO) peace agreement, the EC committed substantial funds in humanitarian assistance for the Palestinians. A Euro-Mediterranean Interim Association Agreement on Trade and Co-operation was signed with the PLO in February 1997 and entered into force in July. In April 1998 the EU and the Palestinian (National) Authority (PA) signed a security co-operation agreement. The escalation of violence between Israel and the Palestinians from September 2000 resulted in a deterioration in EU-Israel relations. The EU formed part of the Quartet (alongside the UN, the USA and Russia), which was established in July 2002 to monitor and aid the implementation of Palestinian civil reforms, and to guide the international donor community in its support of the Palestinian reform agenda. In September the Quartet put forward a peace plan aiming at a final settlement, which was published in April 2003. In late 2004 the EU agreed an Action Plan with the PA; it was adopted by the EU in February 2005 and by the PA in May. In November, on the basis of an agreement reached by Israel and the PA following Israel's withdrawal from Gaza and the northern West Bank, the EU established an EU Border Assistance Mission (EU BAM Rafah), which monitored operations at the Rafah border crossing between Egypt and the Gaza Strip until June 2007. An EU Police Mission for the Palestinian Territories (EUPOL COPPS) commenced operations in January 2006, with an initial three-year mandate, subsequently extended to 2012, to support the PA in establishing sustainable and effective policing arrangements. At March 2012 the mission comprised 41 international staff and 70 local personnel. EU observation missions monitored Palestinian presidential and legislative elections in January 2005 and January 2006, respectively. In June 2006 EU member states and the European Commission established the Temporary International Mechanism (TIM), an emergency assistance mechanism to provide support directly to the Palestinian people. After the formation of a new, interim Government under Dr Salam Fayyad, the EU renewed co-operation with, and assistance to, the PA. The militant Islamist group Hamas refused to recognize the legitimacy of the interim administration. On 1 February 2008 the European Commission launched a new mechanism, known as PEGASE, to support the PRDP, with a wider remit than the TIM. PEGASE aimed to support activities in four principal areas: governance (including fiscal reform, security and the rule of law); social development (including social protection, health and education); economic and private-sector development; and development of public infrastructure (in areas such as water, the environment and energy). In February 2009 the European Commission's Humanitarian Aid Office (ECHO) agreed to allocate €58m. towards a global plan to assist the most vulnerable population groups affected by the Israeli–Palestinian conflict. Meeting in Trieste, Italy, in June 2009, the Quartet issued a statement welcoming commitments made by the new Israeli Prime Minister, Binyamin Netanyahu, and President Mahmud Abbas to seek a two-state solution, and stressed the need for the conclusion of peace agreements between Israel and Syria and between Israel and Lebanon. In December 2010 some 26 prominent political figures, including the former High Representative of the Common Foreign and Security Policy and Secretary-General of the Council of the European Union and of the Western European Union Javier Solana and 10 former heads of state, wrote to the EU Council President Herman Van Rompuy, the High Representative of the Union for Foreign Affairs and Security Policy Catherine Ashton, and all EU heads of state and of government, urging the EU to strengthen its response to Israel's continued construction of settlements in the Palestinian Autonomous Areas.

Talks were held with Iran in April 1992 on the establishment of a co-operation accord. In December the Council of Ministers recommended that a 'critical dialogue' be undertaken with Iran, owing to the country's significance to regional security. In April 1997 the 'critical dialogue' was suspended and ambassadors were recalled from Iran, after a German court found the Iranian authorities responsible for having ordered the murder of four Kurdish dissidents in Berlin in 1992. Later that month ministers of foreign affairs resolved to restore diplomatic relations with Iran, in order to protect the strong trading partnership. In November 2000 an EU-Iran Working Group on Trade and Investment met for the first time to discuss the possibility of increasing and diversifying trade and investment. During 2002 attempts were made to improve relations with Iran, as negotiations began in preparation for a Trade and Co-operation Agreement. An eventual trade deal was to be linked to progress in political issues, including human rights, weapons proliferation and counter-terrorism. In mid-2003 the EU (in conformity with US policy) warned Iran to accept stringent new nuclear inspections, and threatened the country with economic repercussions (including the abandonment of the proposed trade agreement) unless it restored international trust in its nuclear programme. A 'comprehensive dialogue' between the EU and Iran (which replaced the 'critical dialogue' in 1998) was suspended by Iran in December 2003. In January 2005 the EU resumed trade talks with Iran after the Iranian authorities agreed to suspend uranium enrichment. However, these talks were halted by the Commission in August, following Iran's resumption of uranium conversion to gas (the stage before enrichment). Following Iran's removal of international seals from a nuclear research facility in January 2006, the EU supported moves to refer Iran to the UN Security Council. In mid-2006, during a visit to Tehran, Javier Solana presented to the Iranian authorities new proposals by the international community on how negotiations on Iran's nuclear programme could be initiated. In December, in a declaration on Iran, the Council criticized the country's failure to implement measures required by both the International Atomic Energy Agency (IAEA) and the UN Security Council in respect of its nuclear programme, and warned that this failure would be to the detriment of EU-Iran relations. EU trade sanctions against Iran were strengthened in August 2008, after Iran failed to halt its uranium-enrichment programme. In July 2010 EU ministers of foreign affairs adopted a new set of sanctions, prohibiting investment, technical assistance and technology transfers to Iran's energy sector, and also targeting the country's financial services, insurance and transport sectors. Sanctions were strengthened in May 2011. In October an IAEA report expressed strong concern that Iran's nuclear programme related to military technology. EU sanctions were strengthened in January 2012, when a ban on imports of Iranian crude oil was imposed and the assets of the Iranian central bank within the EU were frozen. The EU also has strong concerns over the human rights situation in Iran, particularly following the increased repression that followed the presidential election of 2009. As a consequence, the EU has imposed sanctions on 61 people believed to be responsible for significant human rights abuses; in March 2012 EU ministers of foreign affairs expanded these sanctions to cover a further 17 individuals.

A co-operation agreement between the EC and the countries of the Gulf Cooperation Council (GCC), which entered into force in January 1990, provided for co-operation in industry, energy, technology and other fields. Negotiations on a full free trade pact began in October, but it was expected that any agreement would involve transition periods of some 12 years for the reduction of European tariffs on 'sensitive products' (i.e. petrochemicals). In November 1999 the GCC Supreme Council agreed to establish a customs union (a precondition of the proposed EU-GCC free trade agreement); the union was established in January 2003. At the 20th EU-GCC Joint Council and Ministerial Meeting, held in Luxembourg in June 2010, an EU-GCC Joint Action Programme for 2010–13 was adopted, with the aim of strengthening co-operation in a number of areas, principally economic and financial co-operation; trade and industry; energy and the environment; transport, telecommunications and information technology; education and research; and culture.

The increased tension in the Middle East prior to the US-led military action in Iraq in March 2003 placed considerable strain on relations between member states of the EU, and exposed the lack of a common EU policy on Iraq. In February 2003 the European Council held an extraordinary meeting to discuss the crisis in Iraq, and issued a statement reiterating its commitment to the UN. In April, however, the EU leaders reluctantly accepted a dominant role for the USA and the United Kingdom in post-war Iraq, and Denmark, Spain and the Netherlands announced plans to send peace-keeping troops to Iraq. At the Madrid Donors' Conference in October the EU and its accession states pledged more than €1,250m. (mainly in grants) for Iraq's reconstruction. In March 2004 the Commission adopted a programme setting three priorities for reconstruction assistance to Iraq in that year: restoring the delivery of principal public services; increasing employment and reducing poverty; and strengthening governance, civil society and human rights. The EU welcomed the handover of power by the Coalition Provisional Authority to the Iraqi Interim Government in June 2004 and supported the holding of elections to the Transitional National Assembly in Iraq in January 2005. An EU integrated rule-of-law mission for Iraq, to provide training in management and criminal investigation to staff and senior officials from the judiciary, the police and the penitentiary, commenced operations in July, with an initial mandate of 12 months. In December 2006 an agreement was signed on the establishment of a European Commission delegation office in the Iraqi capital, Baghdad. In June of that year, in response to the formation of a new Iraqi Government, the Commission set forth its proposals for an EU-wide strategy to govern EU relations with Iraq. The strategy comprised five objectives: overcoming divisions within Iraq and building democracy; promoting the rule of law and human rights; supporting the Iraqi authorities in the delivery of basic services; supporting the reform of public administration; and promoting economic reform. In November negotiations commenced on a trade and co-operation agreement with Iraq; at a round of negotiations on the agreement held in February 2009, participants agreed to upgrade the draft accord to a more comprehensive draft partnership agreement, which would provide for annual ministerial meetings and the establishment of a joint co-operation council. In November the EU and Iraq completed negotiations on the partnership and co-operation agreement, which had still to be signed. A memorandum of understanding on a strategic energy partnership between the EU and the Iraqi Government was signed in January 2010. Between 2003 and the end of 2008 the EU provided €933m. in reconstruction and humanitarian assistance to Iraq. The EU allocated €66m. towards development co-operation with Iraq during 2009–10 (€42m. for 2009 and €24m. for 2010). In November 2010 the EU adopted a Joint Strategy Paper for Iraq for 2011–13, which aimed to assist Iraq in making optimum use of its resources through: capacity-building activities relating to good governance; promoting education in order to aid socio-economic recovery; building institutional capacity; water management and agriculture.

A series of large-scale demonstrations in Tunisia, prompted by the self-immolation of a young Tunisian man in protest at state restrictions in mid-December 2010, led President Zine al-Abidine Ben Ali to flee the country in mid-January 2011. An EU-Tunisia Task Force was established to ensure the improved co-ordination of support for Tunisia's political and economic transition, the first meeting of which took place in late September in the capital, Tunis. Negotiations towards the agreement of a Deep and Comprehensive Free Trade Area (DCFTA) were due to be initiated in 2012.

Mass protests also took place in Egypt in early 2011, which resulted in the resignation of the Egyptian President Lt-Gen. Muhammad Hosni Mubarak on 11 February. In mid-February a series of violent clashes broke out between anti-Government protesters in Libya and armed forces loyal to the Libyan leader, Col Muammar al-Qaddafi. By 22 February it was reported that protesters had taken control of Benghazi and large parts of eastern Libya. At the end of February the Council of the EU adopted a UN Security Council Resolution on Libya, prohibiting the sale to that country of arms and ammunition, and agreed to impose additional sanctions against those responsible for the violent repression of the civilian protests, halting trade in any equipment that could be utilized for such purposes. The Council also imposed a visa ban on several people, including al-Qaddafi and other members of his family, and froze the assets of al-Qaddafi and 25 other people. On 1 April 2011 the Council agreed to establish EUFOR Libya to help support the provision of humanitarian assistance, and to facilitate the movement of displaced people, in response to the crisis situation in Libya, if its deployment were requested by the UN Office for the Coordination of Humanitarian Affairs. After al-Qaddafi went into hiding in late August, and forces in support of the opposition National Transitional Council (NTC) took control of the capital, Tripoli, the European Council agreed measures to support the Libyan economy and to assist the UN mission in Libya. Some €30m. was to be provided to aid the NTC in its efforts to stabilize the country. A number of hitherto frozen assets were released in support of humanitarian and civilian needs, and a ban on the use of European air space by Libyan aircraft was removed. At the end of August the EU opened an office in Tripoli. At an international conference held in Paris, France, in early September, the EU agreed to initiate assessments of the needs of the NTC in the fields of security, communication, civil society, border management and procurement, and a further €50m. was to be made available for longer-term support programmes. On 20 October it was confirmed that Qaddafi had been captured and killed during fighting in his home city of Sirte; three days later the NTC formally declared 'national liberation'. In mid-November the EU's Tripoli office was formally upgraded, becoming the headquarters of the new EU delegation to Libya.

Meanwhile, from mid-March 2011 anti-Government protests in Syria were violently suppressed by the authorities. In response, the EU imposed a number of restrictive measures, including an arms embargo and targeted sanctions, comprising a travel ban and the freezing of assets, against those deemed to be responsible for, or involved with, the repression. In May bilateral EU-Syria co-operation programmes were suspended, as were preparations for new areas of co-operation. The Syrian authorities continued to implement harsh measures in an attempt to quell demonstrations against the rule of President Bashar al-Assad; by mid-October the Office of the UN High Commissioner for Human Rights estimated that more than 3,000 people had been killed in Syria since protests began. In March 2012 the EU imposed its 13th set of sanctions on the Syrian authorities since the protests began.

Unrest also developed in Yemen in early 2011, with escalating conflict between forces loyal to Saleh and tribal groups, and ongoing protests against Field Marshal Ali Abdullah Saleh's rule in several cities. In late November the EU expressed satisfaction at the signature in Riyadh of the agreement for political transition signed by President Saleh and senior Yemeni officials, under the auspices of the GCC. The EU provided some €20m. in additional humanitarian aid to Yemen in 2011, and welcomed the presidential election that took place in late February 2012, and the subsequent inauguration of President Field Marshal Abd al-Rabbuh Mansur al-Hadi, prior to legislative elections in 2014.

After demonstrations commenced in the capital of Bahrain, Manama, in early 2011, the EU urged restraint, and exhorted all parties to take part in negotiations. None the less, protests were violently repressed, and the EU's High Representative dispatched a senior EU envoy to Bahrain for talks. The EU welcomed the establishment, in June, of the Bahrain Independent Commission of Inquiry (BICI)—an independent, international commission of judicial and human rights experts—to investigate both the causes of the unrest and allegations of human rights violations.

In late February 2011, at a Senior Officials' meeting to discuss the instability in the Middle East (which became widely known as the 'Arab Spring'), EU High Representative Catherine Ashton identified the need to respond in three ways: by helping to develop 'deep democracy', through a process of political reform, democratic elections, institution-building, measures to combat corruption, and support for the independent judiciary and civil society; through economic development; and by facilitating the movement of people and of communications, while avoiding mass migration. In late September the European Commission agreed to new economic support for the Middle East. The

Support for Partnership Reform and Inclusive Growth (SPRING) programme was to be allocated a budget of €350m. in additional funds for 2011–12, and was to provide support on a so-called more-for-more basis to those countries that demonstrated progress in implementing democratic reforms. The Civil Society Facility was to be established, with a budget of €26.4m., with the objective of strengthening the capacity of civil society to promote reform and increase public accountability. By December 2011 the European Commission had provided funds amounting to some €80.5m. to help the refugee crisis in North Africa, while EU member states had provided a further €73.0m.

SUB-SAHARAN AFRICA

The first Africa-EU summit, representing the institutionalization of Africa-EU dialogue, was convened in April 2000, in Cairo, Egypt. The second summit was held in December 2007, in Lisbon, Portugal (having been postponed from 2003 owing to concerns over the participation of President Mugabe of Zimbabwe, see below). The 2007 Lisbon summit adopted a Joint Africa-EU Strategy as a vision and road map, providing an overarching long-term framework for future political co-operation, to be implemented through successive short-term action plans. The First Action Plan of the Joint Strategy identified eight areas for strategic partnership during 2008–10: peace and security; democratic governance and human rights; trade, regional integration and infrastructure; achievement of the UN Millennium Development Goals; energy; climate change; migration, mobility and employment; and science, information society and space. The third Africa-EU summit, with the theme of 'investment, economic growth and job creation' was held in Tripoli, Libya, in November 2010. An action plan for 2011–13 was adopted, focusing on the following principal areas of co-operation: peace and security; democratic governance and human rights; regional integration, trade and infrastructure; the UN's eight Millennium Development Goals; energy; climate change and the environment; migration, mobility and employment; and science, the information society and space.

In June 2004 the European Commission activated for the first time its newly established Africa Peace Facility (APF), which provided €12m. in support of African Union (AU) humanitarian and peace-monitoring activities in Darfur (Sudan). In 2007 the EU and the AU agreed to expand the APF to cover the prevention of conflict and post-conflict stabilization, and to facilitate decision-making and co-ordination. APF funds were allocated accordingly: €600m. for Peace Support Operations, the principal focus of the APF; €100m. to aid capacity-building efforts, specifically in the context of the African Peace and Security Architecture (APSA) and Africa-EU dialogue; €15m. to support the Early Response Mechanism; and €40m. for contingencies.

During 2002 the European Council condemned the worsening human rights situation in Zimbabwe, and imposed a range of targeted sanctions, including a travel ban on and freezing of the assets of certain members of the leadership, an arms embargo, and the suspension of development aid. Sanctions relating to Zimbabwe have been extended repeatedly on an annual basis. In September 2009 an EU delegation visited Zimbabwe for the first time since the imposition of sanctions, and indicated that further progress was needed to end human rights violations there. The majority of the sanctions were extended in February 2010 and February 2011. In February 2012 the EU welcomed developments towards the formation of a Government of National Unity, and agreed to remove sanctions from 51 people and 20 entities with immediate effect.

The EU, together with, *inter alia*, the UN Secretary-General, US President Barack Obama, the IMF and the Economic Community of West African States (ECOWAS), recognized Alassane Ouattara as the legitimate victor of a run-off election to decide the presidency of Côte d'Ivoire in November 2010; however, in early December the country's constitutional council released results indicating that incumbent President Laurent Gbagbo had won the election. Widespread disruption and violence followed the disputed elections. In mid-January 2011 the EU imposed sanctions against Côte d'Ivoire, which were subsequently strengthened at the end of that month. Ouattara was officially sworn in as President in May. In July the EU adopted five programmes, which allocated some €125m. to Côte d'Ivoire to support vocational training, road maintenance, health and the management of public finances, and to strengthen civil society organizations.

The EU maintains several missions in Africa. During June–September 2003 an EU military operation, codenamed Artemis, was conducted in the Democratic Republic of the Congo (DRC). In June 2005 1,400 EUSEC RD Congo peace-keepers were dispatched to attempt to curb ongoing ethnic violence in the DRC; the mandate of EUSEC RD Congo was scheduled to terminate at the end of September 2012. In October 2007 the Council approved a EUFOR operation (EUFOR Chad/CAR), comprising 3,300 troops, to support a UN mission in eastern Chad and north-eastern Central African Republic (MINURCAT) in efforts to improve security in those regions, where more than 200,000 people from the Darfur region of western Sudan had sought refuge from violence in their own country. The force began deployment in early 2008. In March 2009 EUFOR Chad/CAR's mandate expired and MINURCAT assumed the EU force's military and security responsibilities. In December 2008 Operation EU NAVFOR Somalia—Operation Atalanta, the EU's first maritime military operation, reached its initial operational capacity; Operation EU NAVFOR Somalia was established in support of UN Security Council resolutions aimed at deterring and repressing acts of piracy and armed robbery in waters off the coast of Somalia, and protecting vulnerable vessels in that area (including vessels delivering humanitarian aid to displaced persons in Somalia). The mandate of EU NAVFOR Somalia was due to expire in December 2012, subsequently extended to December 2014. In February 2010 the Council of the European Union established the EU Training Mission for Somalia (EUTM Somalia), to help strengthen the Somali transitional federal Government, in particular through providing military training to 2,000 security force recruits; EUTM Somalia became operational in April. An EU mission in support of security sector reform in Guinea-Bissau was established in February 2008, and its mandate expired in September 2010.

There are EU Special Representatives to the African Union and for the Great Lakes Region.

LATIN AMERICA

A non-preferential trade agreement was signed with Uruguay in 1974, and economic and commercial co-operation agreements with Mexico in 1975 and with Brazil in 1980. A five-year co-operation agreement with the members of the Central American Common Market and with Panama entered into force in 1987, as did a similar agreement with the member countries (see below) of the Andean Group (now the Andean Community). Co-operation agreements were signed with Argentina and Chile in 1990, and in that year tariff preferences were approved for Bolivia, Colombia, Ecuador and Peru, in support of those countries' efforts to combat drugs-trafficking. In May 1992 an inter-institutional co-operation agreement was signed with the Southern Common Market (Mercado Común del Sur—Mercosur); in the following month the European Community (EC) and the member states of the Andean Group (Bolivia, Colombia, Ecuador, Peru and Venezuela) initialled a new co-operation agreement, which was to broaden the scope of economic and development co-operation and enhance trade relations, and a new co-operation agreement was signed with Brazil. In July 1993 the EC introduced a tariff regime to limit the import of bananas from Latin America, in order to protect the banana-producing countries of the African, Caribbean and Pacific (ACP) group, then linked to the EC by the Lomé Convention. (In December 2009, in resolution to a long dispute over the tariff regime, the EU and Latin American states initialled the EU-Latin America Bananas Agreement, which provided for a gradual reduction in the tariff rate.)

From 1996 the European Union (EU, as the EC became in 1993) forged closer links with Latin America, by means of strengthened political ties, an increase in economic integration and free trade, and co-operation in other areas. In April 1997 the EU extended further trade benefits to the countries of the Andean Community. In September 2009 the Commission adopted 'The European Union and Latin America: Global Players in Partnership', updating an earlier communication, published in 2005, on 'A Stronger Partnership between the European Union and Latin America'.

In July 1997 the EU and Mexico concluded an Economic Partnership, Political Co-ordination and Co-operation Agreement (the Global Agreement) and an interim agreement on trade. The accords were signed in December, and entered into effect in 2000. In November 1999 the EU and Mexico concluded a free trade agreement, which provided for the removal of all tariffs on bilateral trade in industrial products by 2007. The first meeting of the Joint Council established by the Economic Partnership, Political Co-ordination and Co-operation Agreement between the EU and Mexico was held in February 2001; further meetings have since been held on a regular basis. In July 2008, in acknowledgement of the gradual strengthening of EU-Mexico relations, the European Commission proposed the establishment of a Strategic Partnership with Mexico. An EU-Mexico summit meeting was held in Comillas, Spain, in May 2010.

In June 1996 the EU and Chile signed a framework agreement on political and economic co-operation, which provided for a process of bilateral trade liberalization, as well as co-operation in other industrial and financial areas. An EU-Chile Joint Council was established. In November 1999 the EU and Chile commenced practical negotiations on developing closer political and economic co-operation, within the framework of a proposed Association Agreement. In November 2002 the EU and Chile signed an association and free trade agreement, which entered into force in March 2005; it provided for the liberalization of trade within seven years for industrial products and 10 years for agricultural products. The first meeting of the Association Council set up by the agreement took place in Athens, Greece, in March 2003, and the second was held in Luxembourg in May 2005. Representatives of civil society met within the framework of the Association Agreement for the first time in late 2006. In May 2008 the EU and Chile determined to establish a joint Association for Development and Innovation. The fourth EU-Chile summit meeting was held in Madrid, Spain, in May 2010.

In May 2007 the European Commission proposed to launch a Strategic Partnership with Brazil, in recognition of its increasing international prominence and strong bilateral ties with Europe. The first EU-Brazil summit was duly held in Lisbon, Portugal, in July; the fifth EU-Brazil summit took place in Brussels, Belgium, in October 2011.

In late December 1994 the EU and Mercosur signed a joint declaration that aimed to promote trade liberalization and greater political co-operation. In September 1995, at a meeting in Montevideo, Uruguay, a framework agreement on the establishment of a free trade regime between the two organizations was initialled. The agreement was formally signed in December. In July 1998 the European Commission voted to commence negotiations towards an interregional Association Agreement with Mercosur, which would strengthen existing co-operation agreements. Negotiations were initiated in April 2000 (focusing on the three pillars of political dialogue, co-operation, and establishing a free trade area), and were extended in May 2008 to cover the additional pillars of science and technology, infrastructure, and renewable energy.

The first ministerial conference between the EC and the Rio Group of Latin American and Caribbean states took place in April 1991; since then high-level joint ministerial meetings have been held every two years. The first summit meeting of all EU and Latin American and Caribbean heads of state or government was held in Rio de Janeiro, Brazil, in June 1999, when a strategic partnership was launched. A second EU-Latin America/Caribbean (EU-LAC) summit took place in Madrid, in May 2002, and covered co-operation in political, economic, social and cultural fields. A political dialogue and co-operation agreement with the Andean Community and its member states was signed in December 2003. At the third EU-LAC summit meeting, held in Guadalajara, Mexico, in May 2004 it was agreed by the two parties that an Association Agreement, including a free trade area, was a common objective. In December 2005 the European Commission proposed a renewed strategy for strengthening the strategic partnership with Latin America, ahead of the fourth EU-LAC summit, held in Vienna, Austria, in May 2006. Its proposals included increasing political dialogue between the two regions, stimulating economic and commercial exchanges, encouraging regional integration, addressing inequality and adapting the EU's development and aid policy to correspond more closely to conditions in Latin America. At the fourth EU-LAC summit it was decided that negotiations for Association Agreements with Central America and with the Andean Community should be initiated. The summit also endorsed a proposal to establish an EU-Latin America parliamentary assembly. The assembly met for the first time in November 2006. In May 2010 the sixth EU-LAC summit was convened, in Madrid, on the theme 'Innovation and Technology for Sustainable Development and Social Inclusion'. In June 2007 the EU and the Andean Community initiated negotiations on the planned Association Agreement in Tarija, Bolivia. However, negotiations were suspended in June 2008, reportedly owing to divergent views of the aims and scope of the trade provisions. In January 2009 negotiations recommenced between three of the Andean Community countries, Colombia, Ecuador and Peru, with the goal of concluding a multi-party trade agreement; Ecuador provisionally suspended its participation in the negotiations in July. Negotiations were concluded on 1 March 2010, with an agreement on trade between the EU and Colombia and Peru, providing for the liberalization of trade in 65% of industrial products with Colombia, and 80% with Peru. Talks on an Association Agreement between the EU and the countries of Central America (Costa Rica, El Salvador, Guatemala, Honduras, Nicaragua and Panama) commenced in Costa Rica in October 2007, but negotiations were suspended temporarily during 2009 owing to the unstable political situation in Honduras. In May 2010 the EU concluded negotiations on an Association Agreement with Central America, covering three areas: trade; political dialogue; and co-operation. The European Commission was expected to provide total funding of some €3,000m. to Latin America, some €840m. to the countries of Central America, and some €50m. to the Andean Community in 2007–13. In 2007 the EU also concluded negotiations for an Economic Partnership Agreement with the Caribbean Forum (CARIFORUM) grouping of 16 Caribbean states.

Cuba remained the only Latin American country that did not have a formal economic co-operation agreement with the EU. In June 1995 a Commission communication advocated greater economic co-operation with Cuba; this policy was criticized by the US Government, which maintained an economic embargo against Cuba. Later that year the EU agreed to make the extent of economic co-operation with Cuba (a one-party state) contingent on progress towards democracy. An EU legation office opened in the Cuban capital, Havana, in March 2003, and the EU supported a renewed application by Cuba to join the successor to the Lomé Convention, the Cotonou Agreement. However, human rights abuses perpetrated by the Cuban regime in April (the imprisonment of a large number of dissidents) led to the downgrading of diplomatic relations with Cuba by the EU, the instigation of an EU policy of inviting dissidents to embassy receptions in Havana (the so-called cocktail wars) and the indefinite postponement of Cuba's application to join the Cotonou Agreement. In May Cuba withdrew its application for membership, and in July the Cuban President, Fidel Castro, announced that the Government would not accept aid from the EU and would terminate all political contact with the organization. In December 2004 the EU proposed a compromise—namely not to invite any Cubans, whether government ministers or dissidents, to future embassy receptions—but reiterated its demand that Cuba unconditionally release all political prisoners who remained in detention (several dissidents had already been released). Cuba announced in January 2005 that it was restoring diplomatic ties with all EU states. At the end of that month the EU temporarily suspended the diplomatic sanctions imposed on Cuba in mid-2003 and announced its intention to resume a 'constructive dialogue' with the Cuban authorities. In March 2005 the European Commissioner responsible for Development and Humanitarian Aid visited Cuba, and held meetings with the Cuban President, as well as several dissidents. The EU extended the temporary suspension of diplomatic sanctions against Cuba for one year in June, and again in mid-2006 and mid-2007, in the hope that constructive dialogue would bring about reform in the areas of human rights and democratization and the release of further political prisoners. Sanctions were lifted in June 2008, although the decision was to be subject to an annual review. In May 2010 the European Commission adopted a country strategy paper on Cuba, which identified three priority areas for intervention: food security; the environment, and adaptation to climate change; and exchanges of expertise, training and studies. Some €20m. was allocated to Cuba for the period 2011–13.

The EU's natural disaster prevention and preparedness programme (Dipecho) has targeted earthquake, flood, hurricane, and volcanic eruption preparedness throughout Latin America and the Caribbean. By March 2010 EU humanitarian assistance for Haiti (including planned pledges), in the aftermath of the earthquake that devastated the country's infrastructure, totalled more than €320m. (from member states and the European Commission). Emergency relief from the European Commission was worth over €120m., including €3m. in emergency funding allocated within 24 hours of the earthquake taking place. Following an outbreak of cholera in October 2010, an alert system was put in place, and the Commission approved new funding of some €10m. at the end of December to help fund the efforts of the European Commission's Humanitarian Aid Office (ECHO) to provide support for health staff; to implement preventive strategies, such as the promotion of chlorination and a hygiene-awareness campaign; and to improve the collection and analysis of health-related data.

FAR EAST AND AUSTRALASIA

Relations between the EU and the Association of Southeast Asian Nations (ASEAN) were based on a Co-operation Agreement of 1980. In March 2007, at an EU-ASEAN ministerial meeting held in Nuremberg, Germany, ASEAN and the EU made the Nuremberg Declaration on an EU-ASEAN Enhanced Partnership, and a Plan of Action was approved to strengthen co-operation during 2007–12. In September an EU-ASEAN commemorative summit took place in Singapore, to mark 30 years of co-operation between the two organizations.

In May 1995 ASEAN and EU senior officials endorsed an initiative to convene an Asia-Europe Meeting of heads of government (ASEM), which takes places every two years. The first ASEM summit was held in March 1996 in Bangkok, Thailand. The second ASEM summit, convened in the United Kingdom in April 1998, established an ASEM Trust Fund, under the auspices of the World Bank, to alleviate the social impact of financial crisis. Other initiatives adopted by ASEM were an Asia-Europe Co-operation Framework (AECF) to co-ordinate political, economic and financial co-operation, a Trade Facilitation Action Plan, and an Investment Promotion Action Plan, which incorporated a new Investment Experts Group. ASEM VI, convened in Helsinki, Finland, in September 2006, addressed the theme '10 Years of ASEM: Global Challenges and Joint Responses'. The participants adopted a Declaration on Climate Change, aimed at promoting efforts to reach consensus in international climate negotiations, and the Helsinki Declaration on the Future of ASEM, detailing practical recommendations for developing future ASEM co-operation. ASEM VII was held in Beijing, People's Republic of China, in October 2008. The meeting had the theme 'Vision and Action: Towards a Win-Win Solution', focusing on advancing dialogue regarding mutually beneficial co-operation on economic and social and cultural issues, and on sustainable development. The meeting resulted in the Beijing Declaration on Sustainable Development, which recognized the challenges posed to sustainable development by increasing global population, environmental degradation, depletion of resources, and deteriorating ecological 'carrying' capacity. The eighth ASEM summit meeting took place in Brussels, Belgium, in October 2010.

A trade agreement was signed with China in 1978 and renewed in May 1985. In June 1989, following the violent repression of the Chinese pro-democracy movement by Chinese Government, the EC imposed economic sanctions and an embargo on arms sales to that country. In October 1990 it was decided that relations with China should be 'progressively normalized'. The EU has supported China's increased involvement in the international community and, in particular, supported its application for membership of the WTO. The first EU-China meeting of heads of government was convened in April 1998. In November the President of the Commission made an official visit to China and urged that country to remove trade restrictions imposed on European products. In the same month the EU and Hong Kong signed a co-operation agreement to combat drugs-trafficking and copyright piracy. A bilateral trade agreement between the EU and China was concluded in May 2000, removing a major barrier to China's accession to the World Trade Organization; this was approved in November 2001. A third EU-China summit meeting was held in Beijing in October 2000. At the fourth summit, convened in September 2001, the two sides agreed to strengthen and widen political dialogue and to continue discussions on human rights issues. In March 2002 the European Commission approved a strategy document setting out a framework for co-operation between the EU and China in 2002–06, and in September the fifth EU-China summit discussed trade relations and future co-operation on illegal immigrants and tourism. At the sixth EU-China summit, held in Beijing in October 2003, two agreements were signed establishing a new dialogue on industrial policy and confirming China's participation in the 'Galileo' project; in addition, a memorandum of understanding (MOU) was initialled, paving the way for Chinese tourist groups to travel to the EU more easily. At the seventh EU-China summit, which took place in The Hague, Netherlands, in December 2004, the two sides further strengthened their maturing strategic partnership. A joint declaration was signed on nuclear non-proliferation and arms control, and agreements were also concluded on customs co-operation, and science and technology. The eighth summit, held in Beijing in September 2005, marked the 30th anniversary of the establishment of EU-China diplomatic relations. During the meeting, the establishment of an EU-China partnership on climate change was confirmed. The two sides also agreed to move towards early negotiations on a new framework agreement, and two MOUs were signed on labour, employment and social affairs and on the initiation of a dialogue on energy and transport strategies. The ninth EU-China summit, convened in September 2006, agreed that negotiations should be initiated on concluding a comprehensive Partnership and Co-operation Agreement (PCA) and on updating the 1985 trade and economic co-operation agreement. In October 2006, in a strategy communication, the Commission set forth details of a new agenda for EU-China relations, the priorities of which included support for China's transition towards greater openness and political pluralism and co-operation on climate change. In a separate policy paper, the Commission detailed a new strategy for expanding EU-China relations in the areas of trade and investment. Negotiations for a comprehensive PCA were launched in January 2007. The 10th EU-China summit took place in Beijing in November 2007. At the meeting, heads of state and of government witnessed the signature of a €500m. framework loan from the European Investment Bank to support efforts to tackle climate change. In January 2009 China and EU adopted nine agreements aimed at strengthening joint co-operation. Convened in Prague, Czech Republic, in May, the 11th EU-China summit addressed issues including the ongoing global financial and economic crisis and climate change. At the 12th EU-China summit, held in Nanjing in November, the two sides agreed to make efforts to facilitate the further implementation of the EU-China Joint Declaration on Climate Change, and agreed to strengthen the existing Partnership on Climate Change. The 13th EU-China summit took place in Brussels in October 2010, at which it was decided to designate 2011 as the EU-China Year of Youth.

A framework agreement on trade and co-operation between the EU and the Republic of Korea was signed in 1996 and entered into force in April 2001. In September 1997 the EU joined the Korean Peninsula Energy Development Organization, an initiative founded in 1995 to increase nuclear safety and reduce the risk of nuclear proliferation from the energy programme of the Democratic People's Republic of Korea (DPRK). Meanwhile, in May 2007 the EU and the Republic of Korea had commenced negotiations towards the adoption of a free trade agreement, and an agreement was initialled in October 2009. The deal, which provided for the elimination of almost all duties in the agricultural and industrial sectors, was signed formally at an EU-Republic of Korea summit meeting, held in Brussels in October 2010. The agreement was approved by the European Parliament in February 2011, with the addition of a clause ensuring that new Korean legislation on carbon dioxide limits from cars would not damage the interests of European car-makers. The free trade agreement entered into force in July of that year. Meanwhile, in June 2008 negotiations had commenced, aimed at updating the mutual framework agreement. In May 2010 the EU and the Republic of Korea signed a new framework agreement on bilateral relations. At the EU-Korea summit meeting of October 2010 the EU and the Republic of Korea also agreed further to strengthen their relationship, by forming a Strategic Partnership, which provided for increased commitment to co-operation by both parties.

In September 1999, for the first time, ministerial-level discussions took place between the EU and the DPRK at the UN General Assembly. In May 2001 the EU announced that it was to establish diplomatic relations with the DPRK to facilitate the Union's efforts in support of reconciliation in the Korean Peninsula and, in particular, in support of economic reform and the easing of the acute food and health problems in the DPRK. However, the implementation of a Country Strategy Paper, adopted in March 2002, was suspended, and there no plan for its renewal. In October 2002 the EU expressed its deep concern after the DPRK admitted that it had conducted a clandestine nuclear weapons programme, in serious breach of the country's international non-proliferation commitments. In the following month the EU stated that failure to resolve the nuclear issue would jeopardize the future development of EU-DPRK relations. In response to the DPRK's announcement in October 2006 that it had conducted a nuclear test, the EU strongly condemned the 'provocative' action and urged the DPRK to abandon its nuclear programme. In April 2009 the EU strongly condemned the DPRK for launching a rocket in contravention of relevant UN Security Council resolutions. In December 2010 the Council reinforced sanctions in place against a number of individuals and entities in the DPRK.

In June 1992 the EC signed trade and co-operation agreements with Mongolia and Macao, with respect for democracy and human rights forming the basis of envisaged co-operation. The 10th EU-Mongolia joint committee, held in Brussels in September 2007, focused on political and economic issues, and concluded that negotiations would be initiated on a PCA. An agreement on aviation was also reached, as a result of which legal certainty was to be restored to 11 air service agreements between Mongolia and individual EU member states. The 13th EU-Macao joint committee met in Brussels in December. A co-operation accord was formally signed with Viet Nam in July 1995, under which the EU agreed to increase quotas for Vietnamese textiles products, to support the country's efforts to join the WTO and to provide aid for environmental and public management projects. The agreement entered into force in June 1996. A permanent EU mission to Viet Nam was established in February 1996. In October 2004 the EU and Viet Nam concluded a bilateral agreement on market access in preparation for Viet Nam's accession to the WTO, which took place in January 2007. In addition, an agreement signed in December 2004 lifted all EU quantitative restrictions for Vietnamese textiles with effect from 1 January 2005. In May 2007 the EU and Viet Nam commenced negotiations on a new PCA, to replace that of 1995. Non-preferential co-operation agreements were signed with Laos and Cambodia in April 1997. The agreement with Laos (which emphasized development assistance and economic co-operation) entered into force on 1 December; the agreement with Cambodia was postponed owing to adverse political developments in that country. The EU concluded a textiles agreement with Laos, which provisionally entered into force in December 1998; as a result of the agreement, exports of textiles to the EU from Laos increased significantly. In 1998 the EU provided financial assistance to support preparations for a general election in Cambodia, and dispatched observers to monitor the election, which was held in July. The EU co-operation agreement with Cambodia entered into force in November 1999. EU-Cambodia relations were further enhanced with the opening of an EU delegation in Phnom-Penh in early 2002 and a Cambodian embassy in Brussels in late 2004. In September 1999 the EU briefly imposed an arms embargo against Indonesia, which was at that time refusing to permit the deployment of an international peace-keeping force in East Timor (now Timor-Leste). In April 2005 the EU extended preferential trade conditions to Indonesia, which meant that the country would benefit from lower customs duties in certain sectors. From September of that year the EU, together with contributing countries from ASEAN, as well as Norway and Switzerland, deployed a monitoring mission in the Indonesian province of Aceh to supervise the implementation of a peace agreement between the Government of Indonesia and the separatist Gerakan Aceh Merdeka (Free Aceh Movement). Having achieved its aims, the mission was concluded in December 2006. In November 2009 an EU-Indonesia PCA was signed.

In October 1996 the EU imposed strict limits on entry visas for Myanma officials, because of Myanmar's refusal to allow the Commission to send a mission to the country to investigate allegations of forced labour. In March 1997 EU ministers of foreign affairs agreed to revoke Myanmar's special trade privileges under the Generalized System of Preferences (GSP). The EU successively extended its ban on arms exports to Myanmar and its prohibition on the issuing of visas. In April 2003 a new 'Common Position' was adopted by the EU, which consolidated and extended the scope of existing sanctions against Myanmar and strengthened the arms embargo; EU sanctions were further extended in April 2004 in view of the military regime's failure to make any significant progress in normalizing the administration of the country and addressing the EU's concerns with regard to human rights. EU ministers of foreign affairs agreed to Myanmar's participation in ASEM V in October at a level below head of government. Following the summit, however, the EU revised the Common Position, further broadening sanctions against Myanmar, as the military regime had failed to comply with certain demands, including the release from house arrest of the opposition leader Aung San Suu Kyi. The Common Position was renewed in April 2006, November 2007, and April 2009. In August 2009 an amended Common Position was adopted, extending sanctions to the Myanmar judiciary, following proceedings against Aung San Suu Kyi related to alleged violation of the terms of her house arrest. Restrictive measures against Myanmar were renewed in April 2010. Legislative elections in Myanmar in November of that year (which were followed by the release of Suu Kyi) were criticized by the EU and other international observers. However, a civilian Government took power, and a degree of reform was being undertaken. In April 2012 the EU agreed to suspend most of the sanctions in place against Myanmar, in recognition of the significant political changes in that country; an arms embargo remained in place.

The EU's long-term assistance strategy for Timor-Leste has focused on stabilization and dialogue, combating poverty, and humanitarian support. Under the EU country strategy for Timor-Leste during 2008–13, rural development was to be strengthened, with a view to achieving sustained poverty reduction and food security, and the health sector and capacity building were to be supported.

Textiles exports by Asian countries have caused concern in the EU, owing to the depressed state of its textiles industry. In 1982 bilateral negotiations were held under the former Multi-Fibre Arrangement (MFA, see WTO) with Asian producers, notably Hong Kong, the Republic of Korea and Macao. Agreements were eventually reached involving reductions in clothing quotas and 'anti-surge' clauses to prevent flooding of European markets. In 1986 new bilateral negotiations were held and agreements were reached with the principal Asian textiles exporters, for the period 1987–91 (later extended to December 1993, when the Uruguay Round of GATT negotiations was finally concluded): in most cases a slight increase in quotas was permitted. Under the conclusions of the Uruguay Round, the MFA was replaced by an Agreement on Textiles and Clothing (ATC), which provided for the progressive elimination of the quotas that existed under the MFA during 1994–2004. In January 1995 bilateral textiles agreements, signed by the EU with India, Pakistan and China, specified certain trade liberalization measures to be undertaken, including an increase of China's silk export quota. In May 2005 the EU imposed limits on textiles imports from China, in response to a dramatic increase in Chinese clothing exports since the expiry of the ATC on 1 January. In June the EU and the Chinese Government agreed import quotas on 10 clothing and textiles categories until 2008, but by August several of the quotas for 2005 had already been breached. In September the dispute was resolved when it was agreed that one-half of the estimated 80m. Chinese garments that had been impounded at European ports would be released and the remainder counted against the quotas for 2006. Also in September 2005 a report published by the high-level group on textiles and clothing—established by the Commission in 2003—sought, *inter alia*, to chart the likely development of the sectors up to 2020. With regard to the quota-free environment for textiles and clothing that had been introduced at the beginning of 2005, the report noted that a Commission statement released in mid-2006 had indicated that the disruptive impact of liberalization of Chinese textiles exports to the EU had been confined to a fairly restricted range of product categories. None the less, China's share of exports to the EU of products in the liberalized categories had risen markedly, to the detriment of traditional EU suppliers. Overall, however, only a modest increase in EU imports of textiles and clothing (in both the liberalized categories and in total) had occurred. The statement noted, too, that China was becoming a key growth market for exports of textiles and clothing from the EU. In October 2007 the European Commission agreed not to renew quotas on textiles from China, but instead to introduce a system of monitoring imports.

Numerous discussions have been held since 1981 on the EU's increasing trade deficit with Japan, and on the failure of the Japanese market to accept more European exports. In July 1991 the heads of government of Japan and of the EC signed a joint declaration on closer co-operation in both economic and political matters. The European office of the EU-Japan Industrial Co-operation Centre was opened in Brussels in June 1996; the Centre, which was established in 1987 as a joint venture between the Japanese Government and the European Commission, sought to increase industrial co-operation between the EU and Japan. In October 1996 the WTO upheld a long-standing complaint brought by the EU that Japanese taxes on alcoholic spirits discriminated against certain European products. In January 1998 an EU-Japan summit meeting was held, followed by a meeting at ministerial level in October. Subsequent summits (the 19th was held in Brussels in April 2011) have aimed to strengthen dialogue.

Regular consultations are held with Australia at ministerial and senior official level. In January 1996 the Commission proposed a framework agreement to formalize the EU's trade and political relationship with that country. In September, however, after the Australian Government had objected to the human rights clause contained in all EU international agreements, negotiations were suspended. In June 1997 a joint declaration was signed, committing both sides to greater political, cultural and economic co-operation. In 2001 a National Europe Centre, based at the Australian National University in Canberra, was established jointly by the EU and the University to consolidate EU-Australia relations. The EU-Australia ministerial consultations convened in Melbourne, Australia, in April 2003, adopted a five-year Agenda for Co-operation. In October 2008 ministers of foreign affairs from the EU and Australia, meeting in Paris, France, adopted a Partnership Framework, outlining future co-operation in the areas of: foreign policy and security issues; trade; relations with Asia and the Pacific; environment; and science, technology and education. The Partnership Framework was updated at a meeting of ministers of foreign affairs held in Stockholm, Sweden, in October 2009. In March 1997 New Zealand took a case relating to import duties to the WTO, which later ruled against the EU. A joint declaration detailing areas of co-operation and establishing a consultative framework to facilitate the development of these was signed in May 1999. Mutual recognition agreements were also signed with Australia and New Zealand in 1999, with the aim of facilitating bilateral trade in industrial products. In March 2004 a European Commission Delegation was inaugurated in Wellington, New Zealand. In September 2007 a new joint declaration on relations and co-operation was adopted by the EU and New Zealand, replacing the 1999 joint declaration and 2004 action plan.

SOUTH ASIA

Bilateral non-preferential co-operation agreements were signed with Bangladesh, India, Pakistan and Sri Lanka between 1973 and 1976. A further agreement with India, extended to include co-operation in trade, industry, energy, science and finance, came into force in December 1981. A third agreement, which entered into effect in August 1994, included commitments to develop co-operation between the two sides and improve market access, as well as on the observance of human rights and democratic principles. The first EU-India summit meeting was held in Lisbon, Portugal, in June 2000. In November 2004 the EU and India signed a 'strategic partnership' agreement, which was expected significantly to improve their relationship; the agreement—described as a reflection of 'India's growing stature and influence'—meant that India became a special EU partner alongside the USA, Canada, the People's Republic of China and Russia. The sixth EU-India summit meeting, held in New Delhi, India, in September 2005, adopted a joint action plan to implement the strategic partnership. It was agreed to establish a dialogue on security issues, disarmament and non-proliferation, to increase co-operation in efforts to combat terrorism, and to create a high-level trade group to examine ways of strengthening economic relations. An agreement on India's participation in the EU's Galileo civil satellite navigation and positioning system was also signed. The country strategy paper for 2007–13 allocated funds totalling some €470m. to India, focusing on the implementation of the joint action plan and the country's pursuit of the Millennium Development Goals agreed by UN member Governments in 2000, concentrating on health and education. The 10th EU-India summit was held in Brussels, Belgium, in December 2010, and a joint declaration on international terrorism was adopted. The first India-EU Joint Working Group on Counter-Terrorism met in New Delhi in January 2012. The most recent EU-India summit was held in New Delhi in February, at which participants welcomed the progress that had been made in ongoing negotiations towards the finalization of an India-EU Broad-based Trade and Investment Agreement (BTIA).

A new accord with Sri Lanka, designed to promote co-operation in areas such as trade, investment and protection of the environment, entered into force in April 1995. In mid-August 2010 the EU temporarily withheld certain trade preferences for Sri Lanka, after an investigation confirmed that three UN conventions relating to human rights had failed to be fully implemented.

The EU has provided support for democracy and peace in Nepal, which formally abolished the monarchy in May 2008, following multi-party legislative elections. In January 2011 an EU-Nepal memorandum of understanding on the Multi-Annual Indicative Programme for 2011–13 was signed. Bilateral co-operation focuses on three principal areas: education; stability and peace-building; and trade and strengthening of economic capacity building.

A new agreement with Pakistan on commercial and economic co-operation entered into force in May 1986; in May 1992 an agreement was signed on measures to stimulate private investment in Pakistan. A draft co-operation agreement was initialled with Pakistan in April 1998. However, following a military coup in Pakistan in October 1999, the agreement was suspended. Political dialogue with Pakistan recommenced on an ad hoc basis in November 2000, and the co-operation agreement was signed in November 2001; a joint statement was issued on the occasion, in which Pakistan reiterated its firm commitment to return to democratic government. The co-operation agreement with Pakistan entered into force in April 2004. The EU pledged assistance for Pakistan amounting to €398m. in 2007–13, compared with €125m. in development co-operation funding granted in 2002–06. In February 2008 the EU deployed an Election Observation Mission to Pakistan, to monitor the conduct of the general election. The first EU-Pakistan summit was held in June 2009, and a second EU-Pakistan summit was held in Brussels, Belgium, in June 2010. In February 2012 the Council adopted a five-year EU-Pakistan engagement plan, which aimed to promote peace and stability in the region.

Meanwhile, the new co-operation accord with Bangladesh (which replaced the 1976 commercial co-operation agreement) was signed in May 2000 and came into force in March 2001. In 2007–13, within the framework of a country strategy paper, assistance pledged to Bangladesh totalled €403m.

The EU pledged assistance for the reconstruction of Afghanistan following the removal of the Taliban regime in late 2001, and in 2002 announced development aid of €1,000m. for 2002–06, in addition to humanitarian aid. (By the end of 2006 the total of €1,000m. had been exceeded.) In March 2003 the European Commission hosted, along with the World Bank, the Afghanistan High Level Strategic Forum. The Government of Afghanistan convened the meeting to discuss with its principal partners, donors and multilateral organizations the progress and future vision for state-building in Afghanistan, as well as the long-term funding requirements for reconstruction. In 2004–05 the EU provided substantial support for the election process in Afghanistan, dispatching a Democracy and Election Support Mission to assess the presidential election, which was held in October 2004, and a full Election Observation Mission to monitor legislative and provincial elections, which took place in September 2005. In November the EU and Afghanistan adopted a joint declaration on a new partnership aimed at promoting Afghanistan's political and economic development and strengthening EU-Afghan relations. Increased co-operation was envisaged in areas such as political and economic governance, judicial reform, counter-narcotics measures, and human rights, while the declaration also provided for a regular political dialogue, in the form of annual meetings at ministerial level. The EU welcomed the launch by the UN-sponsored London Conference on Afghanistan, held on 31 January–1 February 2006, of the Afghanistan Compact, representing a framework for co-operation between the Government of Afghanistan, the UN and the international community for a five-year period. The EU pledged €1,030m. in development assistance to Afghanistan over 2007–13. In May 2007 the Council adopted a Joint Action on an EU police mission to Afghanistan; EUPOL, comprising some 160 police officers, was officially launched on 15 June, and aimed to help develop a police force in Afghanistan that would work to respect human rights and operate within the framework of the rule of law, and to address the issue of police reform at central, regional and provincial levels. In May 2010 the Council extended EUPOL's mandate for a three-year period, terminating at the end of May 2013. Assistance provided by the EU focused on the principal areas of concern identified in the National Development Strategy for Afghanistan, which was adopted by the Paris Declaration at a donors' conference held in France on 12 June 2008, and which included strengthening the judicial system; rural development, to combat narcotics production by promoting alternatives to poppy cultivation; and supporting the health sector. The EU agreed to provide food and other humanitarian assistance amounting to €35m. in 2009 to vulnerable civilians in Afghanistan and to Afghan refugees sheltering in Pakistan and Iran. An EU Election Observation Mission was dispatched to monitor the presidential and provincial elections held in Afghanistan in August. In October a Plan for Enhanced EU Engagement in Afghanistan and Pakistan was approved by EU ministers of foreign affairs. The Plan emphasized the need to strengthen sub-national governance, the police and the judiciary in Afghanistan; the importance of co-ordinated EU support for national programmes and the process of reintegration; and support for the electoral structure and the development of democratic institutions.

THE USA AND CANADA

A framework agreement for commercial and economic co-operation between the Community and Canada was signed in Ottawa in 1976. It was superseded in 1990 by a Declaration on EC-Canada Relations. In February 1996 the Commission proposed closer ties with Canada and an action plan including early warning to avoid trade disputes, elimination of trade barriers, and promotion of business contacts. An action plan and joint political declaration were signed in December.

Canadian and EU leaders meet regularly at bilateral summits. At the Ottawa summit meeting held in December 1996, a political declaration on EU-Canada relations was adopted, specifying areas for co-operation. At a summit held in Ottawa in March 2004, Canada and the EU adopted a Partnership Agenda to promote political and economic co-operation. In November 2005 Canada and the EU signed an agreement creating a framework for Canada's participation in the EU's crisis management operations.

A number of specific agreements were concluded between the Community and the USA: a co-operation agreement on the peaceful use of atomic energy entered into force in 1959, and agreements on environmental matters and on fisheries came into force in 1974 and 1984, respectively. Additional agreements provide for co-operation in other fields of scientific research and development, while bilateral contacts take place in many areas not covered by a formal agreement. A Transatlantic Declaration on EC-US relations was concluded in November 1990: the two parties agreed to consult each other on important matters of common interest, and to increase formal contacts. A new Transatlantic Agenda for EU-US relations was signed by the US President and the Presidents of the European Commission and the European Council at a meeting in Madrid, Spain, in December 1995. In May 1998, at an EU-US summit held in London, the United Kingdom, a new Transatlantic Economic Partnership (TEP) was launched, to remove technical trade barriers, eliminate industrial tariffs, establish a free trade area in services, and further liberalize measures relating to government procurement, intellectual property and investment. (The agricultural and audiovisual sectors were excluded from the TEP.) In June 2005 an EU-US economic summit reached agreement on an initiative to enhance transatlantic economic integration and growth; the first informal EU-US economic ministerial meeting took place in Brussels in November. In January 2006 the Commission hosted the first high-level EU-US Regulatory Co-operation Forum, which aimed to minimize barriers to bilateral trade. At an EU-US summit held in April 2007, in Washington, DC, USA, a new Framework for Advancing Transatlantic Economic Integration between the USA and the EU was adopted. A new Transatlantic Economic Council, a political body established to monitor and facilitate bilateral co-operation in order to promote economic integration, met for the first time in November. In November 2009, at an EU-US summit held in Washington, DC, the EU and the US agreed to re-launch their High Level Consultative Group on Development and to hold annual ministerial meetings to increase co-operation on development policy, initially focused on three areas: food security and agricultural development; climate change; and the Millennium Development Goals. On the margins of the summit, the first meeting of a ministerial-level EU-US Energy Council, which had been launched in September, and aimed to strengthen transatlantic dialogue on energy matters, took place. An EU-US summit was held in Lisbon, Portugal, in November 2010. The summit focused on three principal issues: economic growth and the creation of employment, including in new and emerging business areas; addressing global challenges, such as climate change and international development; and strengthening security for citizens. At the summit meeting held in Washington, DC, in November 2011 the EU and the USA agreed to expand the work of the Transatlantic Economic Council, and to maintain and increase work on energy security and research in the EU-US Energy Council.

The USA has frequently criticized the Common Agricultural Policy, which it regards as creating unfair competition for US exports by its system of export refunds and preferential agreements. In 1998 the World Trade Organization (WTO) upheld a US complaint about the EU ban on imports of hormone-treated beef, which had led to a retaliatory US ban on meat imports from the EU. Following the EU's refusal to repeal the ban by May 1999, the WTO authorized the imposition by the USA and Canada of retaliatory sanctions for each year that the ban was in place. In March 2008 a WTO panel ruled that scientific evidence did not support the imposition of the import ban by the EU; Canada and the USA were also criticized for their failure to repeal their retaliatory measures against the EU. Meanwhile, in June 2003, at a US-EU summit in Washington, DC, it was acknowledged that agriculture remained a major obstacle to agreement in the Doha Round of the WTO. In May the USA had further strained relations by filing a WTO complaint, supported by Argentina and Canada, to end the EU's de facto moratorium on genetically modified food, which began in 1998 and was based on European safety concerns, on the grounds that it was an unfair trade barrier. Another issue of contention between the USA and the EU was the EU's banana import regime (see African, Caribbean and Pacific countries). At a WTO Ministerial Conference held in Hong Kong in December 2005 to advance the Doha Round of negotiations, agreement was reached on the elimination of export subsidies on agricultural goods by the end of 2013.

In October 1996 EU ministers of foreign affairs agreed to pursue in the WTO a complaint regarding the effects on European businesses of the USA's trade embargo against Cuba, formulated in the Helms-Burton Act. In April 1997 the EU and the USA approved a temporary resolution of the Helms-Burton dispute, whereby the US Administration was to limit the application of sanctions in return for a formal suspension of the WTO case. In mid-1996 the US Congress had adopted legislation imposing an additional trade embargo (threatening sanctions against any foreign company investing more than US $40m. in energy projects in a number of prescribed states, including Iran and Libya), the presence of which further complicated the EU-US debate in September 1997, when a French petroleum company, Total, provoked US anger, owing to its proposed investment in an Iranian natural gas project. In May 1998 an EU-US summit meeting reached agreement on the Transatlantic Economic Partnership (see above). The USA agreed to exempt European companies from the trade embargo on Iran and Libya, and to seek congressional approval for an indefinite waiver for the Helms-Burton Act, thereby removing the threat of sanctions from Total. The EU had allowed the WTO case to lapse in April, but it warned that a new WTO panel would be established if the USA took action against European companies trading with Cuba. In return, the EU agreed to increase co-operation in combating terrorism and the proliferation of weapons of mass destruction and to discourage investment in expropriated property.

In July 1997 the EU became involved in intensive negotiations with the US aircraft company Boeing over fears that its planned merger with McDonnell Douglas would harm European interests. In late July the EU approved the merger, after Boeing accepted concessions including an agreement to dispense with exclusivity clauses for 20-year supply contracts and to maintain McDonnell Douglas as a separate company for a period of 10 years. In June the EU and the USA agreed to introduce a mutual recognition agreement, which was to enable goods (including medicines, pharmaceutical products, telecommunications equipment and electrical apparatus) undergoing tests in Europe to be marketed in the USA or Canada without the need for further testing. In August 2004 a fresh trade dispute erupted between the USA and the EU over the subsidies that the two sides paid to their respective aircraft industries. The USA claimed that the financial support European governments provided to aircraft manufacturer Airbus was in breach of world trade rules, while the EU stated that the same was true of the US Administration's subsidies for Boeing. The USA made a formal complaint to the WTO over the EU's support for Airbus in October; the EU immediately responded in kind by filing a complaint regarding the US financial assistance to Boeing. Following the failure of bilateral talks to resolve the dispute, in July 2005 the WTO agreed to establish two panels to examine the complaints of the USA and the EU; members of the panels were appointed in October. In November 2006 the US case against Airbus was formally presented. In May 2011 a WTO appeals panel ruled that some EU subsidies to Airbus had been illegal. The case of the EU against Boeing was presented in March 2007. In March 2012 a WTO panel of appeal ruled that subsidies granted to Boeing by the US Government were incompatible with international trade rules.

In July 2002 the Commission submitted a complaint to the WTO regarding tax exemptions granted to US companies exporting goods via subsidiaries established in tax-free countries (foreign sales corporations). The WTO found in favour of the Commission and authorized the EU to levy punitive tariffs of up to US $4,000m. in compensation for the US tax exemptions, which benefited large companies, including Boeing and Microsoft, and which the WTO ruled were discriminatory and should be abolished. In February 2003 the EU released a final list of about 50,000 goods that would be subjected to tariffs of 100%, but postponed implementation of the sanctions, pending the progress of a bill to amend the tax law in the US Congress. In March 2004, however, the legislation remained in place and the EU began the phased imposition of duties (initially at 5%, but increasing by 1% every month) on a range of US exports. This represented the first time that the EU had taken retaliatory action against the USA in a trade dispute. In October the US President, George W. Bush, signed legislation that repealed the tax exemptions from 1 January 2005 but contained transitional provisions allowing for exemptions to be maintained for some exporters until the end of 2006 and for an indefinite period on certain binding contracts. The EU appealed to the WTO regarding the transitional provisions, suspending sanctions from January 2005 pending a ruling. In September a WTO panel concluded that, despite the changes to its legislation, the USA had not fully abided by previous rulings and that the tax exemptions maintained under transitional provisions violated WTO rules. In February 2006 the WTO upheld this ruling, rejecting an appeal from the USA. The USA amended its legislation in May and EU sanctions were terminated in the same month.

From 1 May 2005 the EU imposed an additional 15% duty on a range of US goods (including paper, farm goods, textiles and machinery) as punishment for the failure of the USA to revoke a clause in its anti-dumping legislation, known as the Byrd Amendment. The Byrd Amendment, which was promulgated in October 2000, made provision for funds accruing from the payment of anti-dumping and anti-subsidy duties to be paid to the US companies that filed the complaint. The WTO ruled the Amendment illegal in 2002, but the USA failed to repeal the legislation by the deadline of December 2003. In February 2006 the European Commission welcomed the enactment in the USA of legislation repealing the Byrd Amendment (however, under a transition clause, duties imposed on goods imported into the USA until 30 September 2007 were to be distributed after their collection, which, under US practice, could take place several years after the import).

Some member states criticized the USA's objections to the establishment of the International Criminal Court (which came into effect in The Hague, Netherlands, in 2003), while there was also criticism of the USA's strategy towards Iraq in early 2003 (see the Middle East and the Mediterranean), as the EU emphasized that only the UN Security Council could determine whether military action in Iraq was justified. The EU-US annual summit held in June, however, emphasized the need for transatlantic co-operation following the overthrow by a US-led coalition force of Saddam Hussain's regime in Iraq, stressing the need to unite against global terrorism and the proliferation of weapons of mass destruction.

A visit to several European countries by the US Secretary of State, Condoleezza Rice, in December 2005 was largely overshadowed by allegations, published in November, that the USA's Central Intelligence Agency (CIA) had used European airports to transport suspected Islamist militants to secret detention centres in Eastern Europe for interrogation in an illegal programme of so-called extraordinary rendition. Rice acknowledged the practice of rendition, but denied that prisoners were tortured and refused to comment on the alleged existence of CIA prisons in Eastern Europe. In late November the EU requested clarification from the USA about the alleged secret prisons and transfer flights, while the Council of Europe established an inquiry into the matter. Meanwhile, the European Parliament formed its own 46-member committee to investigate the allegations. The final report of the Parliament's inquiry, published in February 2007, rejected extraordinary rendition as an illegal instrument used by the USA in the fight against terrorism. The report noted that secret detention facilities may have been located at US military bases in Europe, and deplored the acquiescence of some member states in illegal CIA operations and the failure of the EU Council of Ministers to co-operate with the inquiry.

AFRICAN, CARIBBEAN AND PACIFIC (ACP) COUNTRIES

In June 2000, meeting in Cotonou, Benin, heads of state and of government of the EU and African, Caribbean and Pacific (ACP) countries concluded a new 20-year partnership accord between the EU and ACP states. The EU-ACP Partnership Agreement, known as the Cotonou Agreement, entered into force on 1 April 2003 (although many of its provisions had been applicable for a transitional period since August 2000), following ratification by the then 15 EU member states and more than the requisite two-thirds of the ACP countries. Previously, the principal means of co-operation between the Community and developing countries were the Lomé Conventions. The First Lomé Convention (Lomé I), which was concluded at Lomé, Togo, in February 1975 and came into force on 1 April 1976, replaced the Yaoundé Conventions and the Arusha Agreement. Lomé I was designed to provide a new framework of co-operation, taking into account the varying needs of developing ACP countries. The Second Lomé Convention entered into force on 1 January 1981 and the Third Lomé Convention on 1 March 1985 (trade provisions) and 1 May 1986 (aid). The Fourth Lomé Convention, which had a 10-year commitment period, was signed in December 1989: its trade provisions entered into force on 1 March 1990, and the remainder entered into force in September 1991.

The Cotonou Agreement was to cover a 20-year period from 2000 and was subject to revision every five years. A financial protocol was attached to the Agreement, which indicated the funds available to the ACP through the European Development Fund (EDF), the main instrument for Community aid for development co-operation in ACP countries. The ninth EDF, covering the initial five-year period from March 2000, provided a total budget of €13,500m., of which €1,300m. was allocated to regional co-operation and €2,200m. was for the new investment facility for the development of the private sector. In addition, uncommitted balances from previous EDFs amounted to a further €2,500m. The new Agreement envisaged a more participatory approach with more effective political co-operation to encourage good governance and democracy, increased flexibility in the provision of aid to reward performance, and a new framework for economic and trade co-operation. Its objectives were to alleviate poverty, contribute to sustainable development and integrate the ACP economies into the global economy. Negotiations to revise the Cotonou Agreement were initiated in May 2004 and concluded in February 2005. The political dimension of the Agreement was broadly strengthened and a reference to co-operation in counter-terrorism and the prevention of the proliferation of weapons of mass destruction was included. The revised Cotonou Agreement was signed on 24 June 2005.

Under the provisions of the new accord, the EU was to finalize free trade arrangements (replacing the previous non-reciprocal trade preferences) with the most-developed ACP countries during 2000–08; these would be structured around a system of six regional free trade zones, and would be designed to ensure full compatibility with World Trade Organization (WTO) provisions. Once in force, the agreements would be subject to revision every five years. The first general stage of negotiations for the Economic Partnership Agreements (EPAs), involving discussions with all ACP countries regarding common procedures, began in September 2002. The regional phase of EPA negotiations to establish a new framework for trade and investment commenced in October 2003. Negotiations had been scheduled for completion in mid-2007 to allow for ratification by 2008, when the WTO exception for existing arrangements expired. However, the negotiation period was subsequently extended. Some 36 ACP states have signed full or interim EPAs, covering the liberalization of goods and agricultural products. The EPAs have attracted some criticism for their focus on trade liberalization and their perceived failure to recognize the widespread poverty of ACP countries.

In March 2010 negotiations were concluded on the second revision of the Cotonou Agreement, which sought to take into account various factors, including the increasing importance of enhanced regional co-operation and a more inclusive partnership in ACP countries; the need for security; efforts to meet the Millennium Development Goals; the new trade relationship developed following the expiry of trade preferences at the end of 2007; and the need to ensure the effectiveness and coherence of international aid efforts. The second revised Cotonou Agreement was formally signed in Ouagadougou, Burkina Faso, in June 2010, and entered into effect, on a provisional basis, at the beginning of November.

Meanwhile, the EU had launched an initiative to allow free access to the products of the least-developed ACP nations by 2005. Stabex and Sysmin, instruments under the Lomé Conventions designed to stabilize export prices for agricultural and mining commodities, respectively, were replaced by a system called FLEX, introduced in 2000, to compensate ACP countries for short-term fluctuations in export earnings. In February 2001 the EU agreed to phase out trade barriers on imports of everything but military weapons from the world's 48 least-developed countries, 39 of which were in the ACP group. Duties on sugar, rice, bananas and some other products were to remain until 2009 (these were withdrawn from October of that year). In May 2001 the EU announced that it would cancel all outstanding debts arising from its trade accords with former colonies of member states.

One major new programme set up on behalf of the ACP countries and financed by the EDF was Pro€Invest, which was launched in 2002, with funding of €110m. over a seven-year period. In October 2003 the Commission proposed to incorporate the EDF into the EU budget (it had previously been a fund outside the EU budget, to which the EU member states made direct voluntary contributions). The cost-sharing formula for the 25 member states would automatically apply, obviating the need for negotiations about contributions for the 10th EDF. The Commission proposal was endorsed by the European Parliament in April 2004. Despite the fears of ACP countries that the enlargement of the EU could jeopardize funding, the 10th EDF was agreed in December 2005 by the European Council and provided funds of €22,682m. for 2008–13.

On 1 July 1993 the EC introduced a regime to allow the preferential import into the Community of bananas from former French and British colonies in the Caribbean. This was designed to protect the banana industries of ACP countries from the availability of cheaper bananas, produced by countries in Latin America. Latin American and later US producers brought a series of complaints before the WTO, claiming that the EU banana import regime was in contravention of free trade principles. The WTO upheld their complaints on each occasion leading to adjustments of the complex quota and tariffs systems in place. Following the WTO authorization of punitive US trade sanctions, in April 2001 the EU reached agreement with the USA and Ecuador on a new banana regime. Under the new accord, the EU was granted the so-called Cotonou waiver, which allowed it to maintain preferential access for ACP banana exports, in return for the adoption of a new tariff-only system for bananas from Latin American countries from 1 January 2006. The Latin American producers were guaranteed total market access under the agreement and were permitted to seek arbitration if dissatisfied with the EU's proposed tariff levels. Following the WTO rejection of EU proposals for tariff levels of €230 and €187 per metric ton (in comparison with existing rates of €75 for a quota of 2.2m. tons and €680 thereafter), in November 2005 the EU announced that a tariff of €176, with a duty-free quota of 775,000 metric tons for ACP producers, would be implemented on 1 January 2006. In late 2006 Ecuador initiated a challenge to the EU's proposals at the WTO. Twelve other countries subsequently initiated third-party challenges to the proposals at the WTO, in support of the challenge by Ecuador. In April 2008 the WTO upheld the challenge by Ecuador, and ordered the EU to align its tariffs with WTO regulations. In December 2009 representatives from the EU and Latin American countries initialled the Geneva Agreement on Trade in Bananas (GATB), which aimed to end the dispute. Under the Agreement, which made no provision for import quotas, the EU was gradually to reduce its import tariff on bananas from Latin American countries, from €176 per metric ton to €114 per ton by 2017. In March 2010 The EU also approved the implementation of Banana Accompanying Measures, which aimed to mobilize €190m. to support the 10 main ACP banana-exporting countries in adjusting to the anticipated increase in market competition from Latin America during 2010–13. (ACP countries would continue to benefit from duty- and quota-free access to EU markets.) For their part, Latin American banana-producing countries undertook not to demand further tariff reductions; and to withdraw several related cases against the EU that were pending at the WTO. In response to the Agreement, the US authorities determined to settle ongoing parallel complaints lodged with the WTO against the EU relating to bananas.

Following a WTO ruling at the request of Brazil, Australia and Thailand in 2005 that the EU's subsidized exports of sugar breached legal limits, reform of the EU's sugar regime was required by May 2006. Previously, the EU purchased fixed quotas of sugar from ACP producers at two or three times the world price, the same price that it paid to sugar growers in the EU. In November 2005 the EU agreed to reform the sugar industry through a phased reduction of its prices for white sugar of 36% by 2009 (which was still twice the market price in 2005). Compensation to EU producers amounted to €6,300m. over the four years beginning in January 2006, but compensation to ACP producers was worth just €40m. in 2006. Development campaigners and impoverished ACP countries, notably Jamaica and Guyana, condemned the plans.

In June 1995 negotiations opened with a view to concluding a wide-ranging trade and co-operation agreement with South Africa, including the eventual creation of a free trade area (FTA). The accord was approved by heads of state and of government in March 1999, after agreement was reached to eliminate progressively, over a 12-year period, the use of the terms 'port' and 'sherry' to describe South African fortified wines. The accord provided for the removal of duties from about 99% of South Africa's industrial exports and some 75% of its agricultural products within 10 years, while South Africa was to liberalize its market for some 86% of EU industrial goods (with protection for the motor vehicle and textiles industries), within a 12-year period. The accord also introduced increased development assistance for South Africa after 1999. The long-delayed agreement was finally signed in January 2002, allowing South African wines freer access to the EU market. Under the terms of the agreement, South Africa was allowed to export 42m. litres of wine a year duty-free to the EU, in exchange for abandoning the use of names such as 'sherry', 'port', 'ouzo' or 'grappa'. In March 1997 the Commission approved a Special Protocol for South Africa's accession to the Lomé Convention, and in April South Africa attained partial membership. Full membership was withheld, as South Africa was not regarded as, in all respects, a developing country, and was therefore not entitled to aid provisions. The EU and South Africa launched a strategic partnership in November 2006. In May 2007 the two sides agreed an Action Plan, which aimed to develop political dialogue and increase co-operation on a range of economic, social and other issues. The first EU-South Africa summit meeting was held in Bordeaux, France, in July 2008.

In May 2003 Timor-Leste joined the ACP and the ACP-EC Council of Ministers approved its accession to the ACP-EC Partnership Agreement. Cuba, which had been admitted to the ACP in December 2000, was granted observer status. Cuba withdrew its application to join the Cotonou Agreement in July 2003.

Article 96 of the Cotonou Agreement, which provides for suspension of the Agreement in specific countries in the event of violation of one of its essential elements (respect for human rights, democratic principles and the rule of law), was invoked against Haiti in 2001, and this was extended annually to December 2004. However, relations with Haiti were in the process of normalization from September of that year.

ACP-EU INSTITUTIONS

The three institutions of the Cotonou Agreement are the Council of Ministers, the Committee of Ambassadors and the Joint Parliamentary Assembly.

Council of Ministers: comprises the members of the Council of the European Union and members of the EU Commission and a member of the Government of each ACP signatory to the Cotonou Agreement; meets annually.

Committee of Ambassadors: comprises the Permanent Representative of each member state to the European Union and a representative of the EU Commission and the Head of Mission (ambassador) of each ACP state accredited to the EU; assists the Council of Ministers and meets regularly, in particular to prepare the session of the Council of Ministers.

Joint Parliamentary Assembly: EU and ACP countries are equally represented; attended by parliamentary delegates from each of the ACP countries and an equal number of members of the European Parliament; two co-presidents are elected by the Assembly from each of the two groups; meets twice a year; 24 vice-presidents (12 EU and 12 ACP) are also elected by the Assembly and with the co-presidents constitute the Bureau of the Joint Parliamentary Assembly, which meets several times a year; Co-Pres LOUIS MICHEL, MUSIKARI KOMBO.

Secretariat of the ACP-EC Council of Ministers: 175 rue de la Loi, 1048 Brussels, Belgium; tel. (2) 281-61-11; fax (2) 281-69-34; Co-Secretaries ALDA SILVEIRA REIS, Dr MOHAMED IBN CHAMBAS.

Centre for the Development of Enterprise (CDE): 52 ave Herrmann Debroux, 1160 Brussels, Belgium; tel. (2) 679-18-11; fax (2) 679-26-03; e-mail info@cde.int; internet www.cde.int/index.aspx; f. 1977 to encourage and support the creation, expansion and restructuring of industrial companies (mainly in the fields of manufacturing and agro-industry) in the ACP states by promoting co-operation between ACP and European companies, in the form of financial, technical or commercial partnership, management contracts, licensing or franchise agreements, sub-contracts, etc.; manages the Pro€Invest programme; Dir JEAN-ERICK ROMAGNE.

Technical Centre for Agricultural and Rural Co-operation (CTA): Postbus 380, 6700 AJ Wageningen, Netherlands; tel. (317) 467100; fax (317) 460067; e-mail cta@cta.int; internet www.cta.int/index.htm; f. 1984 to improve the flow of information among agricultural and rural development stakeholders in ACP countries; Dir MICHAEL HAILU.

ACP INSTITUTIONS

ACP Council of Ministers: composed of a member of Government for each ACP state or a government-designated representative; the principal decision-making body for the ACP group; meets twice annually; ministerial sectoral meetings are held regularly.

ACP Committee of Ambassadors: the second decision-making body of the ACP Group; it acts on behalf of the Council of Ministers between ministerial sessions and is composed of the ambassadors or one representative from every ACP State.

ACP Secretariat: ACP House, 451 ave Georges Henri, Brussels, Belgium; tel. (2) 743-06-00; fax (2) 735-55-73; e-mail info@acpsec.org; internet www.acpsec.org; Sec.-Gen. Dr MOHAMED IBN CHAMBAS (Ghana).

On 15 April 2005 27 ACP countries signed a charter creating the ACP Consultative Assembly, which formalized the existing inter-parliamentary co-operation between the ACP member states.

THE ACP STATES

Angola
Antigua and Barbuda
Bahamas
Barbados
Belize
Benin
Botswana
Burkina Faso
Burundi
Cameroon
Cape Verde
Central African Republic
Chad
Comoros
Congo, Democratic Republic
Congo, Republic
Cook Islands
Côte d'Ivoire
Cuba
Djibouti
Dominica
Dominican Republic
Equatorial Guinea
Eritrea
Ethiopia
Fiji
Gabon
The Gambia
Ghana
Grenada
Guinea
Guinea-Bissau
Guyana
Haiti
Jamaica
Kenya
Kiribati
Lesotho
Liberia
Madagascar
Malawi
Mali
Marshall Islands
Mauritania
Mauritius
Federated States of Micronesia
Mozambique
Namibia
Nauru
Niger
Nigeria
Niue
Palau
Papua New Guinea
Rwanda
Saint Christopher and Nevis
Saint Lucia
Saint Vincent and the Grenadines
Samoa
São Tomé and Príncipe
Senegal
Seychelles
Sierra Leone
Solomon Islands
Somalia
South Africa
Sudan
Suriname
Swaziland
Tanzania
Timor-Leste
Togo
Tonga
Trinidad and Tobago
Tuvalu
Uganda
Vanuatu
Zambia
Zimbabwe

GENERALIZED PREFERENCES

In July 1971 the Community introduced a generalized system of preferences (GSP) for tariffs in favour of developing countries, ensuring duty-free entry to the EC of all manufactured and semi-manufactured industrial products, including textiles, but subject in certain circumstances to preferential limits. Preferences, usually in the form of a tariff reduction, are also offered on some agricultural products. In 1980 the Council agreed to the extension of the scheme for a second decade (1981–90): at the same time it adopted an operational framework for industrial products, giving individual preferential limits based on the degree of competitiveness of the developing country concerned. From the end of 1990 an interim scheme was in operation, pending the introduction of a revised scheme based on the outcome of the Uruguay Round of GATT negotiations on international trade (which were finally concluded in December 1993). Since 1977 the Community has progressively liberalized GSP access for the least-developed countries by according them duty-free entry on all products and by exempting them from virtually all preferential limits. In 1992–93 the GSP was extended to Albania, the Baltic states, the CIS and Georgia; in September 1994 it was extended to South Africa.

In December 1994 the European Council adopted a revised GSP to operate during 1995–98. It provided additional trade benefits to encourage the introduction by governments of environmentally sound policies and of internationally recognized labour standards. Conversely, a country's preferential entitlement could be withdrawn, for example, if it permitted forced labour. Under the new scheme, preferential tariffs amounted to 85% of the common customs duty for very sensitive products (for example, most textiles products), and 70% or 35% for products classified as sensitive (for example, chemicals and electrical goods). The common customs duty was suspended for non-sensitive products (for example, paper, books and cosmetics). In accordance with the EU's foreign policy objective of focusing on the development of the world's poorest countries, duties were eliminated in their entirety (with the exception of arms and ammunition) for 49 least-developed countries (LDCs). Duties were also suspended for a further five Latin American countries, conditional on the implementation of campaigns against the production and trade of illegal drugs. The GSP for 1999–2001 largely extended the existing scheme unchanged. The next GSP regulation, for 2002–04 (subsequently extended until the end of 2005), was revised to expand product coverage and improve preferential margins. In May 2003 new regulations were adopted enabling certain countries to be exempted from the abolition of tariff preferences on export of their products to the EU if that sector was judged to be in crisis.

Under the GSP for 2006–08, the coverage of the general arrangement was extended to a further 300 products, mostly in the agriculture and fishery sectors, bringing the total number of products covered to some 7,200. The focus of the new regime was on developing countries most in need. Additional preferences were granted under a new GSP+ incentive scheme to particularly vulnerable countries pursuing good governance and sustainable development policies (judged by their ratification and implementation of relevant international conventions). Bolivia, Colombia, Costa Rica, Ecuador, El Salvador, Georgia, Guatemala, Honduras, Moldova, Mongolia, Nicaragua, Panama, Peru, Sri Lanka and Venezuela were declared eligible for GSP+, which took effect, exceptionally, on 1 July 2005, replacing the special arrangements to combat drugs production and trafficking in force under the previous GSP. Under the GSP for 2009–11, the GSP+ scheme was also retained, as was an initiative in support of LDCs, Everything but Arms (introduced in 2001), which granted those countries duty- and quota-free access to EU markets.

In May 2011 the Commission agreed that the existing GSP should remain in place ('roll over') until the end of 2013, in order to avoid the system lapsing and to enable applications for GSP+ to continue to be submitted, while a new, revised GSP was agreed. The objectives of the new system, which was to come into effect by January 2014, were to target fewer countries, focusing on the most needy; to strengthen GSP+ and to bolster the effectiveness of trade concessions for LDCs through the Everything but Arms scheme; and to increase the system's transparency and stability, while removing the need for its renewal every three years.

AID TO DEVELOPING AND NON-EU COUNTRIES

The main channels for EU aid to developing countries are the Cotonou Agreement and the Mediterranean Financial Protocols, but technical and financial aid and assistance for refugees, training, trade promotion and co-operation in industry, energy, science and technology are also provided to about 30 countries in Asia and Latin America. The European Commission's Humanitarian Aid Office (ECHO) was established in 1991, with a mandate to co-ordinate the provision of emergency humanitarian assistance and food aid. ECHO, which became fully operational in 1993 and is based in Brussels, finances operations conducted by non-governmental organizations and international agencies, with which it works in partnership. Relations between ECHO and its partners are governed by Framework Partnership Agreements (FPAs), which define roles and responsibilities in the implementation of humanitarian operations financed by the EU. In December 2003 ECHO signed an FPA with the International Committee of the Red Cross, the International Federation of Red Cross and Red Crescent Societies, and the national Red Cross societies of the EU member states and Norway. A new FPA with non-governmental organizations entered into force on 1 January 2004; this agreement expired on 30 December 2007, and a revised FPA came into force on 1 January 2008. ECHO's relations with UN agencies are covered by a Financial and Administrative Framework Agreement signed in April 2003. ECHO aims to meet the immediate needs of victims of natural and man-made disasters world-wide, in such areas as assisting displaced persons, health, and mine-clearing programmes. In 2010 ECHO committed funds totalling €1,115m. to humanitarian assistance.

In December 2008 the European Council and European Parliament endorsed a new €1,000m. EU Food Facility, aimed at alleviating the global crisis in food security in 2009–11, by supporting agricultural sector programmes and projects in 23 developing countries. In March 2009 the European Commission made its first EU Food Facility financing decision, adopting a €314m. package of projects.

Allocations by ECHO towards sub-Saharan Africa in 2010 included €131m. to distribute food and aid the implementation of other life-saving activities (for example, in the areas of sanitation, hygiene and shelter) in Sudan, €47m. to help refugees in the Democratic Republic of the Congo, €38m. to support vulnerable refugee populations, to combat a cholera epidemic and to aid drought in the Sahel region in Chad, and €96m. to provide support to populations affected by drought in the Horn of Africa (Djibouti, Ethiopia, Kenya, Somalia and Uganda). In January–September 2011 the EU also contributed some €160m. in emergency funding to help those affected by the continuing severe drought throughout the Horn of Africa region.

In 2010 ECHO provided €51m. in humanitarian and food aid to support populations in the Occupied Palestinian Territories; €18m. to respond to humanitarian needs in and around Iraq; €10m. to Western Sahara; €10m. to Yemen; and €7m. to aid Palestinian refugees in Lebanon.

Finance

BUDGET

The EU budget, which funds EU policies and finances all the EU institutions, is limited by agreement of all the member states. The Commission puts forward spending proposals, which have to be approved by the European Parliament and the Council of the European Union. The Parliament signs the agreed budget into law. Revenue for the budget comes from customs duties, sugar levies, payments based on value-added tax (VAT) and contributions from the member states based on their gross national income (GNI). The Commission is accountable each year to the European Parliament for its use of EU funds. External audits are carried out by the European Court of Auditors. To combat fraud, the European Anti-Fraud Office (OLAF) was established in June 1999.

The general budget contains the expenditure of the six main EU institutions—the Commission, the Council, Parliament, the Court of Justice, the Court of Auditors, and the Economic and Social Committee and the Committee of the Regions—of which Commission expenditure (covering administrative costs and expenditure on operations) forms the largest proportion. Expenditure is divided into two categories: that necessarily resulting from the Treaties (compulsory expenditure) and other (non-compulsory) expenditure. The budgetary process is aided by the establishment of Financial Perspectives, which are spending plans covering a number of years, thus guaranteeing the security of long-term EU projects and activities. Although the Financial Perspective limits expenditure in each policy area for each of the years covered, a more detailed annual budget still has to be agreed each year. The Commission presents the preliminary draft annual budget in late April or early May of the preceding year and the adopted budget is published in February of the relevant year. If the budget has not been adopted by the beginning of the financial year, monthly expenditure may amount to one-12th of the appropriations adopted for the previous year's budget. The Commission may (even late in the year during which the budget is being executed) revise estimates of revenue and expenditure, by presenting supplementary and/or amending budgets. Expenditure under the general budget is financed by 'own resources', comprising agricultural duties (on imports of agricultural produce from non-member states), customs duties, application of VAT on goods and services, and (since 1988) a levy based on the GNI of member states. Member states are obliged to collect 'own resources' on the Community's behalf.

In January 2006 the European Commission proposed an action plan to simplify the audit system, following the Court of Auditors' failure to approve the EU's accounts for the 11th consecutive year. The Commission criticized member states, which supervise about 80% of EU spending, and suggested the harmonization of audit systems across the member states.

In May 2006 a new financial framework for the enlarged EU was formally adopted, when the European Parliament, the Council and the Commission signed an inter-institutional agreement on budgetary discipline and sound financial management, which entered into force at the beginning of January 2007. According to the framework, the EU was to focus on three main priority areas in 2007–13: integrating the single market to achieve sustainable growth by promoting competitiveness, cohesion and the preservation and management of natural resources; promoting the concept of European citizenship by prioritizing freedom, justice and security, and ensuring access to basic public goods and services; and establishing a strong global influence for Europe through its regional responsibilities, through emphasizing sustainable development, and by contributing to security. According to the agreement, which was amended in December 2007, the average annual upper limit on payment appropriations for 2007–13 amounted to 1.03% of the GNI of the 27 member states. Meanwhile, in mid-December 2006 the Council adopted new financial regulations, which aimed to improve the management of EU expenditure; the regulations demanded the publication of a list of all those receiving EU funds. All provisions of the Financial Regulation and its Implementing Rules had entered into force by 1 May 2007.

On 1 December 2011 the European Parliament endorsed the 2012 EU budget, which provided for payment appropriations of €129,100m., (representing 0.98% of the member states' GNI) and commitment appropriations of €147,200m. (1.12% of GNI). The largest proportion of spending, 45.9%, was to be allocated towards the promotion of increased economic competitiveness and greater cohesion between the 27 member states in the pursuit of growth and employment, with the aim of reactivating economic activity and overcoming the adverse economic and financial climate.

In late June 2011 the European Commission, in the course of preparations for the 2014–20 Multi-annual Financial Framework, proposed to increase the transparency and fairness of the system for financing the EU budget by introducing a new financial transaction tax (FTT). In late September the Commission presented a directive on the proposed FTT, which would be levied on all transactions between financial institutions, provided that at least one of those institutions was located in the EU; it was proposed that the exchange of shares and bonds be taxed at a rate of 0.1%, and derivatives at a rate of 0.01%, with effect from 1 January 2014. Two-thirds of revenue from the FTT was to be directed to the EU budget, thereby reducing the GNI-based contributions of member states, while the remaining one-third would be retained by individual member states.

FUNDING PROGRAMMES

In July 2006 the Council and the European Parliament adopted five new regulations that were to constitute the legal basis for the pursuit of cohesion objectives in 2007–13. A general regulation indicated common principles and standards for the implementation of three 'structural funds' (principal instruments for financing EU-wide economic and social restructuring, addressing regional disparities and supporting regional development): the European Regional Development Fund (ERDF), the European Social Fund (ESF) and the Cohesion Fund. The regulation on the ERDF defined the scope of its interventions, among them the promotion of private and public investments assisting in the reduction of regional disparities across the EU. Funding priorities were identified as research, innovation, environmental protection and risk prevention. The regulation concerning the ESF determined that it should be implemented in accordance with European employment strategy in 2007–13, and that it should focus on increasing the flexibility of workers and enterprises, enhancing access to and participation in the labour market, reinforcing social inclusion—by such means as combating discrimination—and promoting partnership for reform in the areas of employment and inclusion. In view of its application to member states with a GNI of less than 90% of the Community average, the new regulation concerning the Cohesion Fund extended eligibility for its support to the new member states, in addition to Greece and Portugal. Spain was also to qualify for the Cohesion Fund, but on a transitional basis. A fifth regulation established a European Grouping of Territorial Co-operation, whose aim was to facilitate cross-border and transnational/interregional co-operation between regional and local authorities.

In 2007–13 the ERDF, the ESF and the Cohesion Fund were to contribute to three objectives: convergence (ERDF, ESF and the Cohesion Fund); regional competitiveness and employment (ERDF and ESF); and European territorial co-operation (ERDF). The convergence objective was to concern 84 regions in 17 of the 27 member states and, on a 'phasing-out' basis, a further 16 regions where per head gross domestic product was only slightly more than the threshold of 75% of the EU average. Indicative allocations for the convergence objective in 2007–13 (expressed in 2004 prices) were to total €251,100m. The regional competitiveness and employment objective was to apply to 168 regions in the 27 member states, 13 of which were so-called 'phasing-in' regions, eligible for special financial allocations. Indicative allocations for the regional competitiveness and employment objective were to total €49,100m., including €10,400m. for the phasing-in regions. A total of €7,750m. was to be made available for the European territorial co-operation objective in 2007–13.

In addition to the funds listed below, four financial instruments were created in 2007. Jasper and Jasmine were developed to provide technical assistance, Jeremie to improve access to finance for small and medium-sized businesses, and Jessica to provide support for urban development.

COHESION FUND

The Treaty on European Union and its protocol on economic and social cohesion provided for the establishment of a Cohesion Fund, which began operating on 1 April 1993, with a mandate to subsidize projects in the fields of the environment and trans-European energy and communications networks in member states with a per-head gross national income of less than 90% of the Community average. The Fund's total budget 2007–13 was €61,590m.

EUROPEAN AGRICULTURAL FUND FOR RURAL DEVELOPMENT—EAFRD

The EAFRD was created in September 2005 and came into operation at the beginning of 2007. It replaced the Guidance Section of the European Agricultural Guidance and Guarantee Fund (which previously financed the Common Agricultural Policy–CAP) and the rural development measures previously financed under the Guarantee section. It is responsible for the single financial contribution under the CAP to rural development programmes.

EUROPEAN AGRICULTURAL GUARANTEE FUND—EAGF

The EAGF was created in September 2005 to replace the Guarantee Section of the European Agricultural Guidance and Guarantee Fund. It came into operation at the beginning of 2007 and, *inter alia*, provides direct payments to farmers under the CAP, finance for the export of agricultural products to third countries, and intervention measures to regulate agricultural markets.

EUROPEAN FISHERIES FUND—EFF

The EFF, covering the period 2007–13, came into operation on 1 January 2007, replacing, with a simplified programming process, the former Financial Instrument for Fisheries Guidance (established in 1993). The EFF grants financial support to facilitate the implementation of the Common Fisheries Policy.

EUROPEAN REGIONAL DEVELOPMENT FUND—ERDF

Payments began in 1975. The Fund is intended to compensate for the unequal rate of development in different EU regions. It finances investment leading to the creation or maintenance of jobs, improvements in infrastructure, local development initiatives and the business activities of small and medium-sized enterprises in 'least favoured regions'.

EUROPEAN SOCIAL FUND—ESF

The Fund (established in 1960) provides resources with the aim of combating long-term unemployment and facilitating the integration into the labour market of young people and the socially disadvantaged. It also supports schemes to help workers to adapt to industrial changes.

EUROPEAN UNION SOLIDARITY FUND—EUSF

The EUSF was established in 2002 to support disaster response activities in member states.

BUDGET EXPENDITURE: COMMITMENT APPROPRIATIONS

(€ million)

	2011	2012
Sustainable growth	53,629.0	55,336.7
Preservation and growth of natural resources	55,945.9	57,034.2
Citizenship, freedom, security and justice	1,738.1	1,484.3
EU as a global player	7,242.5	6,955.1
Administration	8,171.5	8,277.7
Total	126,727.1	129,088.0

Source: Official Journal of the European Union, *Definitive Adoption of the European Union's General Budget for the Financial Year 2012.*

REVENUE

(€ million)

Source of revenue	2011	2012
Customs duties and sugar levies	16,667.0	19,294.6
VAT-based resource	14,126.0	14,498.9
GNI-based resource	87,496.5	93,718.8
Other revenue	8,437.6	1,575.7
Total	126,727.1	129,088.0

Source: Official Journal of the European Union, *Definitive Adoption of the European Union's General Budget for the Financial Year 2012.*

NATIONAL CONTRIBUTION TO THE EU BUDGET

Country	Contribution for 2011 (€ million)	% of total
Austria	2,505.3	2.3
Belgium	3,342.9	3.1
Bulgaria	328.7	0.3
Cyprus	165.3	0.2
Czech Republic	1,318.1	1.2
Denmark	2,247.6	2.1
Estonia	130.4	0.1
Finland	1,707.2	1.6
France	19,075.6	17.6
Germany	21,189.9	19.6
Greece	2,183.1	2.0
Hungary	922.9	0.9
Ireland	1,264.0	1.2
Italy	14,517.6	13.4
Latvia	157.2	0.1
Lithuania	259.0	0.2
Luxembourg	277.6	0.3
Malta	54.9	0.1
Netherlands	4,263.7	3.9
Poland	3,501.5	3.2
Portugal	1,552.8	1.4
Romania	1,170.3	1.1
Slovakia	630.7	0.6
Slovenia	338.5	0.3
Spain	9,625.7	8.9
Sweden	2,679.8	2.5
United Kingdom	12,918.3	11.9
Total	108,328.7	100.0

Source: European Commission.

Publications*

The Courier ACP-EU (every 2 months, in English, French, Portuguese and Spanish on ACP-EU affairs).

EUR-Lex (treaties, legislation and judgments; internet europa.eu .int/eur-lex/lex).

European Economy Research Letter (3 a year).

General Report on the Activities of the European Union (annually; internet europa.eu/generalreport/en/welcome.htm).

Official Journal of the European Union (website on which all contracts from the public sector that are valued above a certain threshold must be published; internet www.ojec.com).

Publications of the European Communities (quarterly).

Information sheets, background reports and statistical documents.

* Most publications are available in all of the official languages of the Union and are available free of charge online. They can be obtained from the Office for Official Publications of the European Communities (Publications Office), 2 rue Mercier, 2985 Luxembourg; tel. 29291; fax 495719; e-mail info@publications.europa.eu; internet publications.europa.eu/index_-en.htm.

European Union Fundamental and other Treaties

The following treaties have formed the basis of EU legislation:

Treaty establishing the European Coal and Steel Community (Treaty of Paris), effective from 25 July 1952—23 July 2002. Leaders signing the Treaty of Paris at the same time signed the Europe Declaration, stating that the creation of the new Community gave 'proof of their determination to create the first supranational institution and that thus they are laying the true foundation of an organized Europe'.

Treaty establishing the European Atomic Energy Community (Treaty of Rome/Euratom Treaty), effective from 1 January 1958. Amended by subsequent treaties, including the Merger Treaty, the Treaty on European Union, the Treaty of Amsterdam and the Treaty of Nice.

Treaty on the Functioning of the European Union (Treaty of Rome), known until the entry into force of the Treaty of Lisbon (which replaced all references to 'Community' with 'Union') as the Treaty establishing the European Economic Community, effective from 1 January 1958. Amended by subsequent treaties, including the Merger Treaty, the Single European Act, the Treaty on European Union, the Treaty of Amsterdam, the Treaty of Rome, the Treaty of Nice, and the Treaty of Lisbon.

The Single European Act (SEA). On 1 July 1987 amendments to the Treaties of Paris and Rome, in the form of the SEA, came into effect, following ratification by all the Member States. The Act contained provisions aiming to complete by 31 December 1992 the creation of a single Community market—'an area without internal frontiers in which the free movement of goods, persons, services and capital is ensured'. Other provisions increased Community co-operation in research and technology, social policy (particularly the improvement of working conditions), economic and social cohesion (reduction of disparities between regions), environmental protection, creation of economic and monetary union, and foreign policy. It allowed the Council of Ministers to take decisions by a qualified majority vote on matters which previously, under the Treaty of Rome, had required unanimity; this applied principally to matters relating to the establishment of the internal market. The Act increased the powers of the European Parliament to delay and amend legislation, by introducing a new co-operation procedure for major decisions concerned with the completion of the internal market, although the Council retained final decision-making powers. The Act provided for the establishment of the Court of First Instance. The Act also provided for the establishment of a secretariat for European political co-operation on matters of foreign policy.

Treaty on European Union (Maastricht Treaty). Effective from 1 November 1993. Amended by the Treaty of Amsterdam, the Treaty of Nice, and the Treaty of Lisbon. Established the European Union, with a 'pillar' structure, comprising: the European Community (EC), Common Foreign and Security Policy (CFSP), and Justice and Home Affairs pillars. (The pillar structure was subsequently disbanded by provisions of the Treaty of Lisbon.) Enabled the development of the euro (currency). At the meeting of the European Council in December 1992, it was agreed that Denmark was to be exempted from certain central provisions of the Maastricht Treaty, including those regarding monetary union, European citizenship and defence (subject to approval by a second Danish referendum, which ratified the Treaty in May 1993). A protocol to the Treaty was approved and a separate agreement signed by all Member States except the United Kingdom on social policy, based on the Charter of Fundamental Social Rights (the Social Charter) of 1989. Following the decision of the Government of the United Kingdom to subscribe to the Social Charter with effect from May 1997, the Treaty of Amsterdam (below) incorporated the protocol based on the Charter (by amending the Treaty of Rome establishing the European Economic Community).

Treaty of Amsterdam. Effective from 1 May 1999. Subsequently amended by the Treaty of Nice. Introduced process of reform to EU institutions, prior to the ensuing membership enlargement process, and increased the powers of the European Parliament. A Protocol to the Treaty incorporated the Schengen *acquis* on the freedom of movement of persons across internal European Union boundaries in order to integrate it into the framework of the European Union. The *acquis* includes the Schengen Agreement, signed on 14 June 1985 between the Governments of the States of the Benelux Economic Union, the Federal Republic of Germany and France; the Implementation Convention, signed in Schengen on 19 June 1990 between Belgium, the Federal Republic of Germany, France, Luxembourg and the Netherlands; and subsequent Accession Protocols and Agreements to the 1985 Agreement and the 1990 Implementation Convention; and decisions and declarations adopted by the Executive Committee established by the Implementation Convention, as well as acts adopted for the implementation of the Convention by the organs upon which the Executive Committee has conferred decision-making powers.

Treaty of Nice. Effective from 1 February 2003. Amended the Treaty on European Union, the Treaties establishing the European Communities and Certain Related Acts. Reformed EU voting procedures, enabling the enlargement of the Union in 2004. Provided for the establishment of subsidiary courts. Enabled punitive sanctions to be imposed against member states.

Treaty of Lisbon amending the Treaty on European Union and the Treaty establishing the European Community; entered into force 1 December 2009. Aimed to redefine the functions and procedures of the EU and to enhance its efficiency and democratic transparency, finalizing a process started with the Treaty of Amsterdam and Treaty of Nice. Amended the former Treaty establishing the European Community (Treaty of Rome), renaming it the Treaty on the Functioning of the European Union, and replacing references to the 'Community' with 'Union'. Incorporated into the Treaty on the Functioning of the European Union a reference to the EU Charter of Fundamental Rights (drafted and proclaimed in 2000, but with uncertain legal status hitherto), rendering that document legally binding. Gave equal legal base to the Treaty on the Functioning of the European Union, the Treaty on European Union, and the Charter of Fundamental Rights, which thereafter constituted the legal basis of the EU. Provided for the posts of President of the European Council and High Representative of the Union for Foreign Affairs and Security Policy (appointed by the European Council by qualified majority with the agreement of the President of the Commission), to represent the EU internationally; and for an 18-month troika comprising groups of three successive governments holding the rotating six-month presidency of the Council of the European Union. Provided for a revised system of qualified majority voting in the Council. Granted the European Parliament the right of co-decision with the Council of the European Union in an increased number of policy areas, giving it a more prominent role in framing legislation. Raised the number of seats in the European Parliament to 751 (to be fully effective from 2014). Enshrined the principles of subsidiarity (that the EU should only act when an objective can be better achieved at the supranational level, implying that national powers are the norm) and proportionality (that the action should be proportional to the desired objective). Provided a legal basis for the EU defence force, with a mutual defence clause, and included the stipulation that the EU has the power to sign treaties and sit on international bodies as a legal entity in its own right. Provided for the establishment of a European public prosecutor's office. Included arrangements for the formal withdrawal of a member state from the EU.

The following additional treaties have been signed by Member States of the European Union:

Treaty Instituting a Single Council and a Single Commission of the European Communities (Merger Treaty): signed in Brussels on 8 April 1965 by the six original members. This Treaty was repealed by the Treaty of Amsterdam.

Treaty Modifying Certain Budgetary Arrangements of the European Communities and of the Treaty Instituting a Single Council and a Single Commission of the European Communities: signed in Luxembourg on 22 April 1970 by the six original members.

Treaty Concerning the Accession of the Kingdom of Denmark, Ireland, the Kingdom of Norway and the United Kingdom of Great Britain and Northern Ireland to the European Economic Community and the European Atomic Energy Community: signed in Brussels on 22 January 1972 (amended on 1 January 1973, owing to the non-accession of Norway).

Treaty of Accession of the Hellenic Republic to the European Economic Community and to the European Atomic Energy Community: signed in Athens on 28 May 1979.

Treaty of Accession of the Portuguese Republic and the Kingdom of Spain to the European Economic Community and to the European Atomic Energy Community: signed in Lisbon and Madrid on 12 June 1985.

Note: Accession of new members to the European Coal and Steel Community was enacted separately, by a Decision of the European Council.

Treaty Concerning the Accession of the Kingdom of Norway, the Republic of Austria, the Republic of Finland and the Kingdom of Sweden to the European Union: signed in Corfu on 24 June 1994 (amended on 1 January 1995, owing to the non-accession of Norway).

Treaty of Accession of the Czech Republic, Estonia, Cyprus, Latvia, Lithuania, Hungary, Malta, Poland, Slovenia and Slovakia; signed in Athens on 16 April 2003.

Treaty of Accession of Bulgaria and Romania; signed in Neumünster Abbey, Luxembourg, on 25 April 2005.

Treaty on Stability, Coordination and Governance in the Economic and Monetary Union: signed in Brussels, in March 2012 by all member states, with the exception of the Czech Republic and the United Kingdom.

FRANC ZONE

Address: c/o Direction de la Communication (Service de Presse), Banque de France, 48 rue Croix-des-Petits-Champs, 75049, Paris Cedex 01, France.

Telephone: 1-42-92-39-08; **fax:** 1-42-92-39-40; **e-mail:** infos@banque-france.fr; **internet:** www.banque-france.fr/en/eurosystem-international/franc-zone-and-development-financing.html.

MEMBERS*

Benin	French Overseas Territories
Burkina Faso	Gabon
Cameroon	Guinea-Bissau
Central African Republic	Mali
Chad	Niger
Comoros	Senegal
Republic of the Congo	Togo
Côte d'Ivoire	
Equatorial Guinea	

* Prior to 1 January 2002, when the transition to a single European currency (euro) was finalized (see below), the Franc Zone also included Metropolitan France, the French Overseas Departments (French Guiana, Guadeloupe, Martinique and Réunion), the French Overseas Collectivité Départementale (Mayotte) and the French Overseas Collectivité Territoriale (St Pierre and Miquelon). The French Overseas Territory (French Polynesia) and the French Overseas Countries (New Caledonia and the Wallis and Futuna Islands) have continued to use the franc CFP (franc des Comptoirs français du Pacifique, 'French Pacific franc').

Apart from Guinea and Mauritania (see below), all of the countries that formerly comprised French West and Equatorial Africa are members of the Franc Zone. The former West and Equatorial African territories are still grouped within the two currency areas that existed before independence, each group having its own variant on the CFA, issued by a central bank: the franc de la Communauté Financière d'Afrique ('franc CFA de l'Ouest'), issued by the Banque centrale des états de l'Afrique de l'ouest—BCEAO, and the franc Coopération financière en Afrique centrale ('franc CFA central'), issued by the Banque des états de l'Afrique centrale—BEAC.

The following states withdrew from the Franc Zone during the period 1958–73: Guinea, Tunisia, Morocco, Algeria, Mauritania and Madagascar. Equatorial Guinea, formerly a Spanish territory, joined the Franc Zone in January 1985, and Guinea-Bissau, a former Portuguese territory, joined in May 1997.

The Comoros, formerly a French Overseas Territory, did not join the Franc Zone following its unilateral declaration of independence in 1975. However, the franc CFA was used as the currency of the new state and the Institut d'émission des Comores continued to function as a Franc Zone organization. In 1976 the Comoros formally assumed membership. In July 1981 the Banque centrale des Comores replaced the Institut d'émission des Comores, establishing its own currency, the Comoros franc.

The Franc Zone operates on the basis of agreements concluded between France and each group of member countries, and the Comoros. The currencies in the Franc Zone were formerly linked with the French franc at a fixed rate of exchange. However, following the introduction of the euro (European single currency) in January 1999, within the framework of European economic and monetary union, in which France was a participant, the Franc Zone currencies were effectively linked at fixed parity to the euro (i.e. parity was based on the fixed conversion rate for the French franc and the euro). From 1 January 2002, when European economic and monetary union was finalized and the French franc withdrawn from circulation, the franc CFA, Comoros franc and franc CFP became officially pegged to the euro, at a fixed rate of exchange. (In accordance with Protocol 13 on France, appended to the 1993 Maastricht Treaty on European Union, France was permitted to continue issuing currencies in its Overseas Territories—i.e. the franc CFP—following the completion of European economic and monetary union.) All the convertability arrangements previously concluded between France and the Franc Zone remained in force. Therefore, Franc Zone currencies are freely convertible into euros, at the fixed exchange rate, guaranteed by the French Treasury. Each group of member countries, and the Comoros, has its own central issuing bank, with overdraft facilities provided by the French Treasury. (The issuing authority for the French Overseas Territories is the Institut d'émission d'outre-mer, based in Paris, France.) Monetary reserves are held mainly in the form of euros. The BCEAO and the BEAC are authorized to hold up to 35% of their foreign exchange holdings in currencies other than the euro. Franc Zone ministers of finance normally meet twice a year to review economic and monetary co-operation. The meeting is normally attended by the French Minister of Co-operation and Francophony.

During the late 1980s and early 1990s the economies of the African Franc Zone countries were adversely affected by increasing foreign debt and by a decline in the prices paid for their principal export commodities. The French Government, however, refused to devalue the franc CFA, as recommended by the IMF. In 1990 the Franc Zone governments agreed to develop economic union, with integrated public finances and common commercial legislation. In April 1992, at a meeting of Franc Zone ministers, a treaty on the insurance industry was adopted, providing for the establishment of a regulatory body for the industry, the Conférence Intrafricaine des Marchés d'Assurances (CIMA), and for the creation of a council of Franc Zone ministers responsible for the insurance industry, with its secretariat in Libreville, Gabon. (A code of conduct for members of CIMA entered into force in February 1995.) At the meeting held in April 1992 ministers also agreed that a further council of ministers was to be created with the task of monitoring the social security systems in Franc Zone countries. A programme drawn up by Franc Zone finance ministers concerning the harmonization of commercial legislation in member states through the establishment of l'Organisation pour l'Harmonisation en Afrique du Droit des Affaires (OHADA) was approved by the Franco-African summit in October. A treaty to align corporate and investment regulations was signed by 11 member countries in October 1993.

In August 1993, in view of financial turmoil related to the continuing weakness of the French franc and the abandonment of the European exchange rate mechanism, the BCEAO and the BEAC determined to suspend repurchasing of francs CFA outside the Franc Zone. Effectively this signified the temporary withdrawal of guaranteed convertibility of the franc CFA with the French franc. Devaluations of the franc CFA and the Comoros franc (by 50% and 33.3%, respectively) were implemented in January 1994. Following the devaluation the CFA countries embarked on programmes of economic adjustment, designed to stimulate growth and to ensure eligibility for development assistance from international financial institutions. France established a special development fund of FFr 300m. to alleviate the immediate social consequences of the devaluation, and announced substantial debt cancellations. The IMF, which had strongly advocated a devaluation of the franc CFA, and the World Bank approved immediate soft-credit loans, technical assistance and cancellations or rescheduling of debts. In January 1996 Afristat, a research and training institution based in Bamako, Mali, commenced activities to support national statistical organizations in participating states in order to strengthen their economic management capabilities. The IMF and the World Bank have continued to support economic development efforts in the Franc Zone. France provides debt relief to Franc Zone member states eligible under the World Bank's initiative for heavily indebted poor countries (HIPCs). In April 2001 the African Franc Zone member states determined jointly to develop anti-money-laundering legislation.

In February 2000 the Union économique et monétaire ouest-africaine (UEMOA) and the Economic Community of West African States (ECOWAS) adopted an action plan for the creation of a single West African Monetary Zone and consequent replacement of the franc Communauté financière africaine by a single West African currency (see below).

In accordance with an agreement concluded between the Banque de France and the French Government in March 1994, and subsequently revised in June 2011, the Banque's Franc Zone and Development Financing Studies Division acts as the secretariat for six-monthly meetings of Franc Zone ministers of finance; conducts studies on Franc Zone economies; and produces, in conjunction with the BCEAO, the BEAC and the Banque centrale des Comoros, the *Rapport Annuel de la Zone Franc*. The 2010 report found that, in the aftermath of the global economic downturn that commenced in 2008, economic growth of 4.3% was recorded in the UEMOA area in 2010, compared with 3.0% in 2009 (attributable in particular to good agricultural sector performance, and public investment in infrastructure); and economic growth of 4.3% was also recorded in the CEMAC region in that year, recovering from 1.8% in 2009. Owing to the impact of a rise in foreign direct investment flows, and of debt cancellation under the Multilateral Debt Relief Initiative endorsed in September 2005 by the World Bank and IMF, the balance of payments positions of UEMOA, CEMAC and the Comoros were reported to show substantial surpluses in 2010.

CURRENCIES OF THE FRANC ZONE

1 franc CFA = €0.00152. CFA stands for Communauté financière africaine in the West African area and for Coopération financière en Afrique centrale in the Central African area. Used in the monetary areas of West and Central Africa, respectively.

1 Comoros franc = €0.00201. Used in the Comoros, where it replaced the franc CFA in 1981.

1 franc CFP = €0.00839. CFP stands for Comptoirs français du Pacifique. Used in New Caledonia, French Polynesia and the Wallis and Futuna Islands.

WEST AFRICA

Union économique et monétaire ouest-africaine (UEMOA): BP 543, Ouagadougou 01, Burkina Faso; tel. 31-88-73; fax 31-88-72; e-mail commission@uemoa.int; internet www.uemoa.int; f. 1994; promotes regional monetary and economic convergence, and envisages the eventual creation of a sub-regional common market. A preferential tariff scheme, eliminating duties on most local products and reducing by 30% import duties on many Union-produced industrial goods, became operational on 1 July 1996; in addition, from 1 July, a community solidarity tax of 0.5% was imposed on all goods from third countries sold within the Union, in order to strengthen UEMOA's capacity to promote economic integration. (This was increased to 1% in December 1999.) In June 1997 UEMOA heads of state and government agreed to reduce import duties on industrial products originating in the Union by a further 30%. An inter-parliamentary committee, recognized as the predecessor of a UEMOA legislature, was inaugurated in Mali in March 1998. In September Côte d'Ivoire's stock exchange was transformed into the Bourse regionale des valeurs mobilières, a regional stock exchange serving the Union, in order to further economic integration. On 1 January 2000 internal tariffs were eliminated on all local products (including industrial goods) and a joint external tariff system, in five bands of between 0% and 20%, was imposed on goods deriving from outside the new customs union. Guinea-Bissau was excluded from the arrangement owing to its unstable political situation. The UEMOA member countries also belong to ECOWAS and, in accordance with a decision taken in April 2000, aim to harmonize UEMOA's economic programme with that of a planned second West African monetary union (the West African Monetary Zone—WAMZ), to be established by the remaining—mainly anglophone—ECOWAS member states by January 2015 (as currently scheduled). A merger of the two complementary monetary unions, and the replacement of the franc Communauté financière africaine by a new single West African currency (the 'eco', initially to to be adopted by the WAMZ), is eventually envisaged. In January 2003 member states adopted a treaty on the establishment of a UEMOA parliament. During 2006–10 UEMOA implemented a regional economic programme aimed at developing regional infrastructures. UEMOA adopted in March 2009 a Regional Initiative for Sustainable Energy, aiming to meet all regional electricity needs by 2030. A subsidiary mortgage refinancing institution (Caisse Régionale de Refinancement Hypothécaire de l'UEMOA—CRRH-UEMOA) was established in July 2010. The 16th summit of UEMOA heads of state and government was held in Lomé, Togo, in June 2012. Mems: Benin, Burkina Faso, Côte d'Ivoire, Guinea-Bissau, Mali, Niger, Senegal and Togo; Pres. CHEIKH HADJIBOU SOUMARÉ (Senegal).

Banque centrale des états de l'Afrique de l'ouest (BCEAO): ave Abdoulaye Fadiga, BP 3108, Dakar, Senegal; tel. 839-05-00; fax 823-93-35; e-mail webmaster@bceao.int; internet www.bceao.int; f. 1962; central bank of issue for the mems of UEMOA; total assets 8,370.1m. francs CFA (31 Dec. 2009); mems: Benin, Burkina Faso, Côte d'Ivoire, Guinea-Bissau, Mali, Niger, Senegal and Togo; Gov. TIEMOKO MEYLIET KONE (Côte d'Ivoire); publs *Annual Report, Notes d'Information et Statistiques* (monthly), *Annuaire des banques, Bilan des banques et établissements financiers* (annually).

Banque ouest-africaine de développement (BOAD): 68 ave de la Libération, BP 1172, Lomé, Togo; tel. 221-42-44; fax 221-52-67; e-mail boadsiege@boad.org; internet www.boad.org; f. 1973 to promote the balanced development of mem. states and the economic integration of West Africa; a Guarantee Fund for Private Investment in West Africa, established jtly by BOAD and the European Investment Bank in Dec. 1994, aims to guarantee medium- and long-term credits to private sector businesses in the region; in April 2012, jointly with CDC Climat and Proparco (see Agence française de développement), BOAD launched the Fonds carbone pour l'Afrique (FCA), aimed at financing a green economy in West Africa; auth. cap. 1,050,000m. francs CFA (30 June 2010); mems: Benin, Burkina Faso, Côte d'Ivoire, Guinea-Bissau, Mali, Niger, Senegal, Togo; Pres. CHRISTIAN ADOVELANDE (Benin); publs *Rapport Annuel, BOAD en Bref* (quarterly).

Bourse Régionale des Valeurs Mobilières (BRVM): 18 rue Joseph Anoma, BP 3802, Abidjan 01, Côte d'Ivoire; tel. 20-32-66-85; fax 20-32-66-84; e-mail brvm@brvm.org; internet www.brvm.org; f. 1998; regional electronic stock exchange; Dir-Gen. JEAN-PAUL GILLET.

CENTRAL AFRICA

Communauté économique et monétaire de l'Afrique centrale (CEMAC): BP 969, Bangui, Central African Republic; tel. and fax 21-61-47-81; fax 21-61-21-35; e-mail secemac@cemac.int; internet www.cemac.int; f. 1998; formally inaugurated as the successor to the Union douanière et économique de l'Afrique centrale (UDEAC, f. 1966) at a meeting of heads of state held in Malabo, Equatorial Guinea, in June 1999; aims to promote the process of sub-regional integration within the framework of an economic union and a monetary union; CEMAC was also to comprise a parliament and sub-regional tribunal; UDEAC established a common external tariff for imports from other countries and administered a common code for investment policy and a Solidarity Fund to counteract regional disparities of wealth and economic development; mems: Cameroon, Central African Republic, Chad, Republic of the Congo, Equatorial Guinea, Gabon; Pres. ANTOINE NTSIMI (Cameroon).

At a summit meeting in December 1981, UDEAC leaders agreed in principle to form an economic community of Central African states (Communauté économique des états de l'Afrique centrale—CEEAC), to include UDEAC members and Burundi, Rwanda, São Tomé and Príncipe and Zaire (now Democratic Republic of the Congo). CEEAC began operations in 1985.

Banque de développement des états de l'Afrique centrale (BDEAC): place du Gouvernement, BP 1177, Brazzaville, Republic of the Congo; tel. 281-18-85; fax 281-18-80; e-mail bdeac@bdeac.org; internet www.bdeac.org; f. 1975; auth. cap. 250,000m. francs CFA (30 Sept. 2011) (BDEAC's auth. cap. was increased by 100% in 2010); shareholders: Cameroon, Central African Republic, Chad, Republic of the Congo, Gabon, Equatorial Guinea, AfDB, BEAC, France, Germany and Kuwait; Pres. MICHAËL ADANDÉ.

Banque des états de l'Afrique centrale (BEAC): 736 ave Mgr François Xavier Vogt, BP 1917, Yaoundé, Cameroon; tel. 223-40-30; fax 223-33-29; e-mail beac@beac.int; internet www.beac.int; f. 1973 as the central bank of issue of Cameroon, the Central African Republic, Chad, Republic of the Congo, Equatorial Guinea and Gabon; a monetary market, incorporating all national financial institutions of the BEAC countries, came into effect on 1 July 1994; cap. 88,000m. francs CFA (Dec. 2009); Gov. LUCAS ABAGA NCHAMA (Equatorial Guinea); publs *Rapport Annuel*, *Etudes et statistiques* (monthly).

CENTRAL ISSUING BANKS

Banque centrale des Comores: place de France, BP 405, Moroni, Comoros; tel. (773) 1814; fax (773) 0349; e-mail bancecom@snpt.km; internet www.bancecom.com; f. 1981; Gov. ABOUDOU MOHAMED CHAFIOUN.

Banque centrale des états de l'Afrique de l'ouest: see above.

Banque des états de l'Afrique centrale: see above.

Institut d'émission d'outre-mer (IEOM): 5 rue Roland Barthes, 75012 Paris Cedex 12, France; tel. 1-53-44-41-41; fax 1-43-47-51-34; e-mail direction@iedom-ieom.fr; internet www.ieom.fr; f. 1966; issuing authority for the French Overseas Territories; Dir-Gen. NICOLAS DE SEZE.

FRENCH ECONOMIC AID

France's connection with the African Franc Zone countries involves not only monetary arrangements, but also includes comprehensive French assistance in the forms of budget support, foreign aid, technical assistance and subsidies on commodity exports.

Official French financial aid and technical assistance to developing countries is administered by the following agencies:

Agence française de développement (AFD): 5 rue Roland Barthes, 75598 Paris Cedex 12, France; tel. 1-53-44-31-31; fax 1-44-87-99-39; e-mail com@afd.fr; internet www.afd.fr; f. 1941; fmrly the Caisse française de développement—CFD; French development bank that lends money to member states and former member states of the Franc Zone and several other states, and executes the financial operations of the FSP (see below). Following the devaluation of the franc CFA in January 1994, the French Government cancelled some FFr 25,000m. in debt arrears owed by member states to the CFD. The CFD established a Special Fund for Development and the Exceptional Facility for Short-term Financing to help to alleviate the immediate difficulties resulting from the devaluation. Serves as the secretariat for the Fonds français pour l'environnement mondial (f. 1994). Has, together with private shareholders, an interest in the development investment company PROPARCO (f. 1977). Since 2000 the AFD has been implementing France's support of the World Bank's HIPC initiative; Pres. PIERRE-ANDRÉ PERISSOL; CEO DOV ZERAH.

Fonds de Solidarité Prioritaire (FSP): c/o Ministry of Foreign and European Affairs, 37 quai d'Orsay, 75351 Paris, France; tel. 1-43-17-53-53; fax 1-43-17-52-03; internet www.diplomatie.gouv.fr; f. 2000, taking over from the Fonds d'aide et de coopération (f. 1959) the administration of subsidies from the French Government to 54 countries of the Zone de solidarité prioritaire; FSP is administered by the French Ministry of Foreign and European Affairs, which allocates budgetary funds to it.

INTER-AMERICAN DEVELOPMENT BANK—IDB

Address: 1300 New York Ave, NW, Washington, DC 20577, USA.

Telephone: (202) 623-1000; **fax:** (202) 623-3096; **e-mail:** pic@iadb.org; **internet:** www.iadb.org.

The Bank was founded in 1959 to promote the individual and collective development of Latin American and Caribbean countries through the financing of economic and social development projects and the provision of technical assistance. From 1976 membership was extended to include countries outside the region.

MEMBERS

Argentina	Ecuador	Nicaragua
Austria	El Salvador	Norway
Bahamas	Finland	Panama
Barbados	France	Paraguay
Belgium	Germany	Peru
Belize	Guatemala	Portugal
Bolivia	Guyana	Slovenia
Brazil	Haiti	Spain
Canada	Honduras	Suriname
Chile	Israel	Sweden
China, People's Rep.	Italy	Switzerland
Colombia	Jamaica	Trinidad and Tobago
Costa Rica	Japan	United Kingdom
Croatia	Republic of Korea	USA
Denmark	Mexico	Uruguay
Dominican Republic	Netherlands	Venezuela

Organization

(June 2012)

BOARD OF GOVERNORS

All the powers of the Bank are vested in a Board of Governors, consisting of one Governor and one alternate appointed by each member country (usually ministers of finance or presidents of central banks). The Board meets annually, with special meetings when necessary. The 53nd annual meeting was held in Montevideo, Uruguay, in March 2012.

BOARD OF EXECUTIVE DIRECTORS

The Board of Executive Directors is responsible for the operations of the Bank. It establishes the Bank's policies, approves loan and technical co-operation proposals that are submitted by the President of the Bank, and authorizes the Bank's borrowings on capital markets.

There are 14 executive directors and 14 alternates. Each Director is elected by a group of two or more countries, except the Directors representing Canada and the USA. The USA holds 30% of votes on the Board, in respect of its contribution to the Bank's capital. The Board has five permanent committees, relating to: Policy and evaluation; Organization, human resources and board matters; Budget, financial policies and audit; Programming; and a Steering Committee.

ADMINISTRATION

In December 2006 the Board of Executive Directors approved a new structure which aimed to strengthen the Bank's country focus and improve its operational efficiency. Three new positions of Vice-Presidents were created. Accordingly the executive structure comprised the President, Executive Vice-President and Vice-Presidents for Countries (with responsibility for four regional departments); Sectors and Knowledge; Private Sector and Non-sovereign Guaranteed Operations; and Finance and Administration. The principal Offices were of the Auditor-General, Outreach and Partnerships, External Relations, Risk Management, and Strategic Planning and Development Effectiveness. An Independent Consultation and Investigation Mechanism to monitor compliance with the Bank's environmental and social policies, was established in February 2010. The Bank has country offices in each of its borrowing member states, and special offices in Paris, France and in Tokyo, Japan. There are some 1,800 Bank staff (excluding the Board of Executive Directors and the Evaluation Office), of whom almost 30% are based in country offices. The total Bank group administrative expenses for 2011 amounted to US $618m.

President: LUIS ALBERTO MORENO (Colombia).

Executive Vice-President: JULIE T. KATZMAN (USA).

Activities

Loans are made to governments and to public and private entities for specific economic and social development projects and for sectoral reforms. These loans are repayable in the currencies lent and their terms range from 12 to 40 years. Total lending authorized by the Bank amounted to US $207,122m. by the end of 2011. During 2011 the Bank approved loans and guarantees amounting to $10,671m., of which Ordinary Capital loans totalled $10,400m. (compared with a total of $12,136m. in 2010). Disbursements on Ordinary Capital loans amounted to $7,902m. in 2011, compared with $10,341m. in the previous year. Some 167 projects were approved in 2011, of which 142 were investment projects. In October 2008 the Bank announced measures to help to counter the effects on the region of the downturn in the world's major economies and the restrictions on the availability of credit. It resolved to accelerate lending and establish an emergency liquidity facility, with funds of up to $6,000m., in order to sustain regional economic growth and to support social welfare programmes.

In March 2009 the Board of Governors agreed to initiate a capital review, in recognition of unprecedented demand for Bank resources owing to the sharp contraction of international capital markets. An agreement to increase the Bank's authorized capital by US $70,000m. was concluded in March 2010 and endorsed, as the Ninth General Capital Increase (IDB-9), by the Board of Governors in July. Of the total increase, $1,700m. was expected to be paid in by member countries over a five-year period. At the end of 2011 the subscribed Ordinary Capital stock, including inter-regional capital, which was merged into it in 1987, totalled $104,980m., of which $4,339m. was paid-in and $100,641m. was callable. The callable capital constitutes, in effect, a guarantee of the securities that the Bank issues in the capital markets in order to increase its resources available for lending.

In 2011 operating income amounted to US $836m. At the end of 2011 total borrowings outstanding amounted to $58,015m., compared with $57,874m. at the end of the previous year.

The Fund for Special Operations (FSO) enables the Bank to make concessional loans for economic and social projects where circumstances call for special treatment, such as lower interest rates and longer repayment terms than those applied to loans from the ordinary resources. Assistance may be provided to countries adversely affected by economic crises or natural disasters through an Emergency Lending Program. In March 2007 the Board of Governors approved a reform of the Bank's concessional lending (at the same time as endorsing arrangements for participation in the Multilateral Debt Relief Initiative, see below), and resolved that FSO lending may be 'blended' with Ordinary Capital loans by means of a parallel lending mechanism. At 31 December 2011 cumulative FSO lending amounted to $19,204m., and in 2011 FSO lending totalled $181m. The terms and conditions of IDB-9, approved by the Board of Governors in July 2010, incorporated a commitment to replenish FSO resources by $479m.

On 1 January 2012 a new Flexible Financing Facility (FFF) entered into effect, which was, thereafter, to be the only financial product platform for approval of all new Ordinary Capital sovereign guaranteed loans.

In June 2007 a new IDB Grant Facility (GRF) was established, funded by transfers from the FSO, to make available resources for specific projects or countries in specific circumstances. By the end of 2011 resources had only been granted to support reconstruction and development in Haiti. In accordance with IDB-9 the Board of Governors may approve transfers of Ordinary Capital to the GRF. Accordingly, in March 2011 the Board approved the transfer of US $200m. from Ordinary Capital. During 2011 the Bank approved grants to Haiti from the GRF totalling $241m. In May 2011 the Board of Governors approved a new Small and Medium-sized Enterprises (SME) Financing Facility, with funds of up to $100m. in order to improve access to finance for SMEs, to promote job creation and stimulate economic growth.

In 1998 the Bank agreed to participate in an initiative of the IMF and the World Bank to assist heavily indebted poor countries (HIPCs) to maintain a sustainable level of debt. Also in 1998, following projections of reduced resources for the FSO, borrowing member countries agreed to convert about US $2,400m. in local currencies held by the Bank, in order to maintain a convertible concessional Fund for poorer countries, and to help to reduce the debt-servicing payments under the HIPC initiative. In mid-2000 a committee of the Board of Governors endorsed a financial framework for the Bank's participation in an enhanced HIPC initiative, which aimed to broaden the eligibility criteria and accelerate the process of debt reduction. The Bank was to provide $896m. (in net present value), in addition to $204m. committed under the original scheme, of which $307m. was for Bolivia, $65m. for Guyana, $391m. for Nicaragua and $133m. for Honduras. The Bank assisted the preparation of national Poverty Reduction Strategy Papers, a condition of reaching the 'completion point' of the process. In January 2007 the Bank concluded an agreement to participate in the Multilateral Debt Relief Initiative (MDRI), which had been approved by the World Bank and IMF in 2005 as a means of achieving 100% cancellation of debts for eligible HIPCs. The agreement to support the MDRI was endorsed by the Bank's Board of Governors in March 2007. Under the initiative the eligible completion point countries, along with Haiti (which had reached 'decision point' in November 2006), were to receive additional debt relief amounting to some $3,370m. in principal payments and $1,000m. in future interest payments, cancelling loan balances with the FSO (outstanding as of 31 December 2004). Haiti reached 'completion point' under the HIPC initiative in June 2009. Accordingly, FSO delivered debt relief under the enhanced HIPC initiative and the MDRI amounting to some $419m. The general capital increase, approved in 2010, intended to provide for cancellation of all Haiti's outstanding debts to the Bank. In September 2010 the US Government made available an advance contribution of $204m. to the FSO, enabling the Bank to announce the cancellation of Haiti's outstanding debts, amounting to $484m.

In June 2006 the Bank inaugurated a new initiative, Opportunities for the Majority, to improve conditions for low-income communities throughout the region. Under the scheme the Bank was to support the development of partnerships between communities, private sector bodies and non-governmental organizations to generate employment, deliver services and integrate poorer members of society into the productive economy. During 2011 a total of 11 projects were approved under the initiative with a value of US $48.4m. By the end of that year the initiative was supporting 32 projects in low-income communities in the region, with a total commitment of $190.2m.

In March 2007 the Bank's Board of Governors endorsed the Sustainable Energy and Climate Change Initiative (SECCI), which aimed to expand the development and use of biofuels and other sources of renewable energy, to enhance energy efficiency and to facilitate adaptation to climate change. A Bank fund, with an initial US $20m. in resources, was established to finance feasibility studies and technical co-operation projects. In November 2009 the Bank signed a Memorandum of Understanding with the Asian Development Bank to support projects and programmes that promote sustainable, low-carbon transport in both regions. In accordance with the priorities of the lending agreement approved along with IDB-9 in July 2010, support for climate change adaptation initiatives and other projects concerned with renewable energy and environmental sustainability was expected to reach 25% of total lending by the end of 2015.

The Bank supports a range of consultative groups in order to strengthen donor co-operation with countries in the Latin America and Caribbean region, in particular to co-ordinate emergency relief and reconstruction following a natural disaster or to support peace efforts within a country. In November 2001 the Bank hosted the first meeting of a Network for the Prevention and Mitigation of Natural Disasters in Latin America and the Caribbean, which was part of a regional policy dialogue, sponsored by the Bank to promote broad debate on strategic issues. In April 2006 the Bank established the Disaster Prevention Fund, financed through Ordinary Capital funds, to help countries to improve their disaster preparedness and reduce their vulnerability to natural hazards. A separate Multidonor Disaster Prevention Trust Fund was established at the end of 2006 to finance technical assistance and investment in preparedness projects.

In July 2004 the Bank co-hosted an international donor conference, together with the World Bank, the EU and the UN, to consider the immediate and medium-term needs for Haiti following a period of political unrest. Some US $1,080m. was pledged at the conference, of which the Bank's contribution was $260m. In April 2009 international donors, meeting under the Bank's auspices, pledged further contributions of $324m. to Haiti's economic and social development. In January 2010 the Bank determined to redirect undisbursed funds of up to $90m. to finance priority emergency assistance and reconstruction efforts in Haiti following a devastating earthquake. In March the Board of Governors agreed to cancel Haiti's outstanding debt and to convert undisbursed loans in order to provide grant assistance amounting to $2,000m. over the coming 10 years. In mid-March the Bank organized a conference of representatives of the private sector in Haiti, in preparation for the International Donors' Conference, which was then held at the end of that month in New York, USA. The Bank also supported the Haitian Government in preparing, jointly with the UN, World Bank and European Commission, a Preliminary Damage and Needs Assessment report for presentation at the Conference. During 2011 the Bank committed some $241m. in grants to Haiti, in particular to fund the provision of basic services, education reform, and to support small farmers; of this, some $175m. was disbursed.

An increasing number of donor countries have placed funds under the Bank's administration for assistance to Latin America, outside the framework of the Ordinary Resources and the Bank's Special Operations. These include the Social Progress Trust Fund (set up by the USA in 1961); the Venezuelan Trust Fund (set up in 1975); the Japan Special Fund (1988); and other funds administered on behalf of Austria, Belgium, Canada, Chile, Denmark, Finland, France, Israel, Italy, Japan, the Netherlands, Norway, Portugal, Spain, Sweden, Switzerland, the United Kingdom and the EU. A Program for the Development of Technical Co-operation was established in 1991, which is financed by European countries and the EU. During 2011 co-financing by bilateral and multilateral sources amounted to some US $2,010.48m.

The Bank provides technical co-operation to help member countries to identify and prepare new projects, to improve loan execution, to strengthen the institutional capacity of public and private agencies, to address extreme conditions of poverty and to promote small- and micro-enterprise development. The Bank has established a special co-operation programme to facilitate the transfer of experience and technology among regional programmes. Technical co-operation operations are mainly financed by income from the FSO and donor trust funds. The Bank supports the efforts of the countries of the region to achieve economic integration and has provided extensive technical support for the formulation of integration strategies in the Andean, Central American and Southern Cone regions. In June 2010 the Bank agreed to collaborate with the Spanish Government, the Bill and Melinda Gates Foundation and the Carlos Slim Health Institute in administering a new 'Salud Mesoamérica 2015' initiative, which aimed to support efforts to achieve the millennium development health objectives in the region over a five-year period. The Bank is a member of the technical co-ordinating committee of the Integration of Regional Infrastructure in South America initiative, which aimed to promote multinational development projects, capacity-building and integration in that region. In September 2006 the Bank established a new fund to support the preparation of infrastructure projects, InfraFund, with an initial US $20m. in resources. In 2005 the

Bank inaugurated a Trade Finance Facilitation Program (TFFP) to support economic growth in the region by expanding the financing available for international trade activities. The programme was given permanent status in November 2006. In May 2008 the Bank launched a training initiative within the framework of the TFFP. In January 2009 the Bank determined to expand the TFFP to include loans, as well as guarantees, and to increase the programme limit from $400m. to $1,000m. By June 2012 there were 77 issuing banks from 20 Latin American and Caribbean countries participating in the programme, and 265 confirming banks from 53 countries world-wide. In September 2009 the Bank supported the establishment, jointly with the MIF, IIC, Andean Development Corporation, the US private investment corporation and a Swiss investment management company, of a Microenterprise Growth Facility (MIGROF), which aimed to provide up to $250m. to microfinance institutions in Latin America and the Caribbean.

AFFILIATES

Inter-American Investment Corporation (IIC): 1350 New York Ave, NW, Washington, DC 20577, USA; tel. (202) 623-3900; fax (202) 623-2360; e-mail iicmail@iadb.org; internet www.iic.int; f. 1986 as a legally autonomous affiliate of the Inter-American Development Bank, to promote the economic development of the region; commenced operations in 1989; initial capital stock was US $200m., of which 55% was contributed by developing member nations, 25.3% by the USA, and the remainder by non-regional members; in 2001 the Board of Governors of the Bank agreed to increase the IIC's capital to $500m; places emphasis on investment in small and medium-sized enterprises without access to other suitable sources of equity or long-term loans; developed FINPYME as an online service to support SMEs and to improve their access to potential sources of financing; in 2011 the IIC approved 71 operations with commitments amounting to $465m., with an additional $463m. mobilized from other sources; mems: 44 countries as shareholders; Gen. Man. Jacques Rogozinski; publ. *Annual Report* (in English, French, Portuguese and Spanish).

Multilateral Investment Fund (MIF) (Fondo Multilateral de Inversiones (FOMIN): 1300 New York Ave, NW, Washington, DC 20577, USA; tel. (202) 942-8211; fax (202) 942-8100; e-mail mifcontact@iadb.org; internet www.iadb.org/mif; f. 1993 as an autonomous fund administered by the Bank, to promote private sector development in the region; the 21 Bank members who signed the initial draft agreement in 1992 to establish the Fund pledged to contribute US $1,200m.; the Fund's activities are undertaken through three separate facilities concerned with technical co-operation, human resources development and small enterprise development; in 2000 a specialist working group, established to consider MIF operations, recommended that it target its resources on the following core areas of activity: small business development; market functioning; and financial and capital markets; the Bank's Social Entrepreneurship Program makes available credit to individuals or groups without access to commercial or development loans; some $10m. is awarded under the programme to fund projects in 26 countries; a Microenterprise Forum, 'Foromic', is held annually (Oct. 2012: Barbados); in April 2005 38 donor countries agreed to establish MIF II, and replenish the Fund's resources with commitments totalling $502m.; MIF II came into effect in March 2007; in mid-2010 MIF supported the establishment of an Emergency Liquidity Program for Haiti; during 2011 MIF approved $108m. to finance 74 operations; Gen. Man. Nancy Lee; publ. *MicAméricas*.

INSTITUTIONS

Instituto para la Integración de América Latina y el Caribe (INTAL) (Institute for the Integration of Latin America and the Caribbean): Esmeralda 130, 17°, 1035 Buenos Aires, Argentina; tel. (11) 4320-1850; fax (11) 4320-1865; e-mail intal@iadb.org; internet www.iadb.org/intal; f. 1965 under the auspices of the Inter-American Development Bank; undertakes research on all aspects of regional integration and co-operation and issues related to international trade, hemispheric integration and relations with other regions and countries of the world; activities come under four main headings: regional and national technical co-operation projects on integration; policy fora; integration fora; and journals and information; hosts the secretariat of the Integration of Regional Infrastructure in South America (IIRSA) initiative; maintains an extensive Documentation Center and various statistical databases; Dir Ricardo Carciofi; publs *Integración y Comercio/Integration and Trade* (2 a year), *INTAL Monthly Newsletter, Informe Andino/Andean Report, CARICOM Report, Informe Centroamericano/Central American Report, Informe Mercosur/Mercosur Report* (2 a year).

Inter-American Institute for Social Development (INDES): 1350 New York Ave, NW, Washington, DC 20057, USA; fax (202) 623-2008; e-mail indes@iadb.org; internet indes.iadb.org; commenced operations in 1995; aims to support the training of senior officials from public sector institutions and organizations involved with social policies and social services; organizes specialized sub-regional courses and seminars and national training programmes; produces teaching materials and also serves as a forum for the exchange of ideas on social reform; Head Juan Cristobal Bonnefoy (Chile).

Publications

Annual Report (in English, French, Portuguese and Spanish).

Development in the Americas (series).

Development Effectiveness Overview (annually).

IDB Edu (quarterly).

Puentes (periodic civil society newsletter).

Revelation of Expectations in Latin America (periodic analysis of market expectations of inflation and growth).

Brochure series, occasional papers, working papers, reports.

Statistics

APPROVALS BY SECTOR, 2011*

Sector	Amount (US $ million)	% of total	Number of projects
Infrastructure and Environment	6,711	62	71
Agriculture and rural development	565	5	11
Energy	1,585	15	22
Environmental protection and natural disasters	410	4	8
Tourism	115	1	3
Transportation	2,249	21	11
Water and sanitation	1,788	16	16
Institutional capacity and finance	3,163	29	62
Capital markets	707	6	22
Industry	252	2	2
Microenterprises	52	0	2
Multisector credit and preinvestment	55	1	2
Private sector development	31	0	2
Reform/modernization of the state	1,226	11	24
Urban development and housing	841	8	8
Integration and trade	94	1	13
Social sector	943	21	9
Education	465	7	12
Health	128	2	5
Science and technology	—	—	—
Social investment	350	3	11
Total	10,911	100.0	167

* Includes loans, guarantees, and operations financed by the IDB Grant Facility.

YEARLY AND CUMULATIVE LOANS AND GUARANTEES, 1961–2011
(US $ million; after cancellations and exchange adjustments)

Country	Total Amount* 2011	Total Amount* 1961–2011	Ordinary Capital 1961–2011	Fund for Special Operations 1961–2011	Funds in Administration 1961–2011
Argentina	1,312.7	31,434.1	30,740.0	644.9	49.2
Bahamas	131.0	633.4	620.4	—	2.0
Barbados	70.0	696.4	635.4	41.7	19.0
Belize	10.0	183.7	183.7	—	—
Bolivia	259.1	4,646.1	1,961.9	2,612.0	72.2
Brazil	2,188.0	42,004.6	40,314.4	1,555.9	134.3
Chile	91.8	6,472.2	6,221.1	206.3	44.8
Colombia	785.2	18,184.7	17,330.6	767.6	86.5
Costa Rica	132.4	3,642.1	3,133.7	371.1	137.2
Dominican Republic	464.8	4,668.9	3,826.5	753.4	89.0
Ecuador	568.8	6,837.3	5,744.5	998.1	97.7
El Salvador	263.1	4,562.9	3,609.9	806.2	146.8
Guatemala	50.3	4,450.5	3,651.3	729.5	69.7
Guyana	17.0	1,232.9	209.2	1,016.8	6.9
Haiti	241.0	2,018.3	—	1,154.3	864.0
Honduras	172.0	3,728.3	1,200.5	2,462.7	65.1
Jamaica	328.0	3,244.9	2,871.8	174.6	198.9
Mexico	1,638.3	30,093.4	29,376.9	559.0	157.5
Nicaragua	107.0	4,696.7	651.8	2,447.2	68.0
Panama	228.2	4,054.3	3,716.6	296.6	41.4
Paraguay	170.0	3,000.4	2,298.1	690.0	12.3
Peru	450.0	10,241.9	9,580.0	440.8	221.1
Suriname	80.0	292.5	286.1	6.4	—
Trinidad and Tobago	290.0	1,657.1	1,601.3	30.6	25.2
Uruguay	317.6	5,537.4	5,391.4	104.2	41.8
Venezuela	120.0	7,229.0	7,054.7	101.4	72.9
Regional	425.0	4,076.5	3,828.9	233.6	14.0
Total	12,464.2	197,025.4	176,179.9	19,054.1	1,791.4

* Includes non-sovereign guaranteed loans, net of participations, and guarantees, as applicable. Excludes the IDB Grant Facility or lines of credit approved and guarantees issued under the Trade Finance Facilitation Program.
Source: Inter-American Development Bank, *Annual Report 2011*.

INTERGOVERNMENTAL AUTHORITY ON DEVELOPMENT—IGAD

Address: Ave Georges Clemenceau, BP 2653, Djibouti.

Telephone: 354050; **fax:** 356994; **internet:** igad.int.

The Intergovernmental Authority on Development (IGAD), established in 1996 to supersede the Intergovernmental Authority on Drought and Development (IGADD, founded in 1986), aims to co-ordinate the sustainable socio-economic development of member countries, to combat the effects of drought and desertification, and to promote regional food security.

MEMBERS*

Djibouti	Kenya	South Sudan	Uganda
Ethiopia	Somalia	Sudan	

* In April 2007 Eritrea suspended its IGAD membership; the IGAD Council of Ministers has subsequently engaged with Eritrea to promote its return to the organization. South Sudan was admitted as the seventh member of the organization in November 2011.

Organization

(June 2012)

ASSEMBLY

The Assembly, consisting of heads of state and of government of member states, is the supreme policy-making organ of the Authority. It holds a summit meeting at least once a year. The chairmanship of the Assembly rotates among the member countries on an annual basis.

Chairman: MELES ZENAWI (Ethiopia).

COUNCIL OF MINISTERS

The Council of Ministers is composed of the minister of foreign affairs and one other minister from each member state. It meets at least twice a year and approves the work programme and the annual budget of the Secretariat.

COMMITTEE OF AMBASSADORS

The Committee of Ambassadors comprises the ambassadors or plenipotentiaries of member states to Djibouti. It convenes as regularly as required to advise and assist the Executive Secretary concerning the interpretation of policies and guidelines and the realization of the annual work programme.

SECRETARIAT

The Secretariat, the executive body of IGAD, is headed by the Executive Secretary, who is appointed by the Assembly for a term of four years, renewable once. In addition to the Office of the Executive Secretary, the Secretariat comprises the following three divisions: Agriculture and Environment; Economic Co-operation; and Political and Humanitarian Affairs, each headed by a director. A workshop was convened in September 2011 to discuss the future organizational restructuring of IGAD.

Executive Secretary: MAHBOUB MAALIM (Kenya).

Activities

IGADD was established in 1986 by Djibouti, Ethiopia, Kenya, Somalia, Sudan and Uganda, to combat the effects of aridity and desertification arising from the severe drought and famine that has periodically affected the Horn of Africa. Eritrea became a member of IGADD in September 1993, following its proclamation as an independent state. In April 1995, at an extraordinary summit meeting held in Addis Ababa, Ethiopia, heads of state and of government resolved to reorganize and expand the Authority. In March 1996 IGAD was endorsed to supersede IGADD, at a second extraordinary summit meeting of heads of state and of government, held in Nairobi, Kenya. The meeting led to the adoption of an agreement for a new organizational structure and the approval of an extended mandate to co-ordinate and harmonize policy in the areas of economic co-operation and political and humanitarian affairs, in addition to its existing responsibilities for food security and environmental protection.

IGAD aims to achieve regional co-operation and economic integration. To facilitate this, IGAD assists the governments of member states to maximize resources and co-ordinates efforts to initiate and implement regional development programmes and projects. In this context, IGAD promotes the harmonization of policies relating to agriculture and natural resources, communications, customs, trade and transport; the implementation of programmes in the fields of social sciences, research, science and technology; and effective participation in the global economy. Meetings between IGAD ministers of foreign affairs and the IGAD Partners' Forum (IPF), comprising the grouping's donors, are convened periodically to discuss issues such as food security and humanitarian affairs. In October 2001 delegates from IGAD and representatives of government and civil society in member states initiated a process to establish an IGAD-Civil Society Forum; the founding assembly of the Forum was convened in Nairobi, in July 2003. In August 2008 a meeting was held with the UN Development Programme (UNDP) on mobilizing resources and capacity building for the regional organization. Negotiations were conducted during 2008 on formulating a regional Integration Plan to cover all sectors of IGAD's activity. In February 2009 the IGAD Executive Secretary chaired a technical meeting, in Djibouti, which aimed to chart a road map for future integration.

In October 2003 the 10th IGAD summit meeting ratified a decision of the eighth summit, held in November 2000, to absorb the Harare, Zimbabwe- and Nairobi-based Drought Monitoring Centre (an initiative of 24 eastern and southern African states inaugurated in 1989 under the auspices of UNDP and the World Meteorological Organization) as a specialized institution of IGAD; the Centre was renamed the IGAD Climate Prediction and Applications Centre (ICPAC). In April 2007 ICPAC was fully integrated into IGAD.

A Protocol establishing the Inter-parliamentary Union of IGAD (IPU-IGAD), signed in February 2004 by the participants in the first meeting of regional speakers of parliament, entered into force in November 2007; IPU-IGAD was to be based in Addis Ababa.

In January 2008 the IGAD Regional AIDS Partnership Program (IRAPP) was launched, with a particular focus on protecting mobile communities (for example pastoralists, internally displaced persons, and refugees) at risk of HIV/AIDS. IRAPP was implementing a common regional strategic plan for combating HIV/AIDS, targeting cross-border and mobile populations, over the period 2011–16. Jointly with the World Bank the IGAD Secretariat is developing a mechanism for monitoring the occurrence of HIV/AIDS in member states.

In June 2006 IGAD launched the IGAD Capacity Building Program Against Terrorism (ICPAT), a four-year programme based in Addis Ababa, which aimed to combat the reach of international terrorism through the enhancement of judicial measures and interdepartmental co-operation, improving border control activities, supporting training and information-sharing, and promoting strategic co-operation. In April 2009 a meeting of IGAD justice ministers, organized by ICPAT, approved a draft IGAD Convention on Extradition, and also a draft Convention on Mutual Legal Assistance. In October 2011 a new IGAD Security Sector Program (ISSP) was launched, focusing on initiatives in the areas of counter-terrorism; organized crime; maritime security; and capacity building of security institutions.

A draft framework for an IGAD Gender Peer Review Mechanism is under consideration; it is envisaged that the Mechanism would be a means of addressing the issue of violence against women in the region as well as other matters relating to women's progress. In December 2009 the first IGAD Women's Parliamentary Conference, convened in Addis Ababa, adopted a declaration on the Enhancement of Women's Participation and Representation in Decision-Making Positions. In April 2011 IGAD convened a conference on women and peace, considering the engagement of women in peace-building and security initiatives in the region.

In October 2011 IGAD was granted observer status at the UN General Assembly.

FOOD SECURITY AND ENVIRONMENTAL PROTECTION

IGAD seeks to achieve regional food security, the sustainable development of natural resources and environmental protection, and to encourage and assist member states in their efforts to combat the consequences of drought and other natural and man-made disasters. The region suffers from recurrent droughts, which severely impede crop and livestock production. Natural and man-made disasters increase the strain on resources, resulting in annual food deficits. About 80% of the IGAD sub-region is classified as arid or semi-arid, and some 40% of the region is unproductive, owing to severe environmental degradation. Activities to improve food security and preserve natural resources have included: the introduction of remote-sensing services; the development of a Marketing Information System and of a Regional Integrated Information System (RIIS); the establishment of training and credit schemes for fishermen; research into the sustainable production of drought-resistant, high-yielding crop varieties; transboundary livestock disease control and vaccine production; the control of environmental pollution; the promotion of alternative sources of energy in the home; the management of integrated water resources; the promotion of community-based land husbandry; training programmes in grain marketing; and the implementation of the International Convention to Combat Desertification. IGAD's Livestock Marketing Information System (LMIS) aims to improve food security in the sub-region.

In June 2008 the IGAD Assembly, meeting in a climate of escalating global food prices and shortfalls in regional imports of foodstuffs, issued a Declaration on the Current High Food Price Crisis, in which it resolved to pursue policies aimed at improving sustainable food production; urged IGAD's partners to support regional agricultural development programmes; determined to enhance the regional drought, climate change monitoring, and early warning mechanisms; and announced that a regional emergency reserve fund would be established. In addition the Authority decided to establish a ministerial task force to assess regional emergency food aid requirements with a view to launching an international appeal for assistance. In July an IGAD meeting on regional food security and risk management, held in Nairobi, Kenya, addressed means of improving social protection and disaster risk management strategies and policies. In December 2009 IGAD and the World Food Programme (WFP) concluded a Memorandum of Understanding (MOU) aimed at enhancing mutual co-operation with a view to improving food and nutrition security in the IGAD region. An executive body, technical committee and co-ordination office were to be established to facilitate the implementation of the MOU.

In November 2011 IGAD and partner countries held a consultative meeting entitled 'Ending Drought Emergencies in the Horn of Africa', in response to ongoing severe drought and an ensuing food security crisis, that had resulted in some 13m. people in the region requiring food assistance. The meeting determined the institutional arrangements for implementing a Horn of Africa Disaster Resilience and Sustainability Initiative: Ending Drought Emergencies, which had been launched by regional heads of state in September. The meeting also agreed to establish an IGAD Platform, intended as an enhanced partnership with donors facilitating long-term investment—particularly in regional arid and semi-arid lands—to end the recurrence of drought emergencies.

IGAD adopted an Environment and Natural Resources Strategy in April 2007, identifying a number key strategic objectives that were to guide future sub-regional environmental programmes. In June 2010 a consultative meeting was convened between IGAD, the African Union (AU), the Common Market for Eastern and Southern African (COMESA), and other regional partners, aimed at advancing the co-ordination and harmonization of their activities governing the environment.

ECONOMIC CO-OPERATION

The Economic Co-operation division concentrates on the development of a co-ordinated infrastructure for the region, in particular in the areas of transport and communications, to promote foreign, cross-border and domestic trade and investment opportunities. IGAD seeks to harmonize national transport and trade policy and thereby to facilitate the free movement of people, goods and services. The improvements to infrastructure also aim to facilitate more timely interventions in conflicts, disasters and emergencies in the sub-region. Projects under way include: the construction of missing segments of the Trans-African Highway and the Pan African Telecommunications Network; the removal of barriers to trade and communications; improvements to ports and inland container terminals; and the modernization of railway and telecommunications services. In November 2000 the IGAD Assembly determined to establish an integrated rail network connecting all member countries. In addition, the heads of state and government considered the possibility of drafting legislation to facilitate the expansion of intra-IGAD trade. The development of economic co-operation has been impeded by persisting conflicts in the sub-region (see below). In August 2010 an IGAD Business Forum was held, in Kampala, Uganda.

POLITICAL AND HUMANITARIAN AFFAIRS

The field of political and humanitarian affairs focuses on conflict prevention, management and resolution through dialogue. The division's primary aim is to restore peace and stability to member countries affected by conflict, in order that resources may be diverted for development purposes. Efforts have been pursued to strengthen capacity for conflict prevention and to relieve humanitarian crises. The ninth IGAD summit meeting, held in Khartoum, Sudan, in January 2002, adopted a protocol to IGAD's founding agreement establishing a conflict early warning and response mechanism (CEWARN). CEWARN, which is based in Addis Ababa, Ethiopia, collects and analyses information for the preparation of periodic early warning reports concerning the potential outbreak of violent conflicts in the region. In February 2006 IGAD convened a ministerial conference on refugees, returnees and internally displaced persons, to consider means of addressing the burden posed by population displacement in member states; at that time it was estimated that 11m. people had been forcibly displaced from their homes in the region. In May 2008 IGAD, the AU and the International Organization for Migration (IOM) jointly organized a workshop, held in Addis Ababa, on inter-state and intra-regional co-operation on migration; an IGAD Regional Consultative Process (IGAD-RCP) on migration was launched, with the aim of building member countries' management capacities. In February 2012 a meeting of the IGAD-RCP considered the possibility of developing a regional action plan for Diaspora engagement in development. IGAD contributes to efforts to raise awareness of the AU's 2006 Ouagadougou Action Plan to Combat Trafficking in Human Beings, and supports the AU COMMIT campaign, launched in June 2009 to combat human trafficking.

The Executive Secretary of IGAD participated in the first summit meeting of all East African heads of state and government, convened in April 2005 in Addis Ababa; the meeting agreed to establish an Eastern African Standby Brigade (EASBRIG). EASBRIG, the development of which is co-ordinated by IGAD, will form the regional component of the AU African Standby Force. In November 2009 EASBRIG undertook a field training exercise ('Exercise Amani Carana') in Djibouti.

In 2008 a new IGAD Peace and Security Strategy was devised. In August IGAD chaired the first meeting of the steering committee on Conflict Prevention Management and Resolution (CPMR), comprising IGAD, COMESA and the East African Community (EAC), which aimed to promote a co-ordinated approach to peace and security in the region.

In September 1995 negotiations between the Sudanese Government and opposition leaders were initiated, under the auspices of IGAD, with the aim of resolving the conflict in southern Sudan; these were subsequently reconvened periodically. In March 2001 IGAD's mediation committee on southern Sudan, chaired by (then) President Daniel arap Moi of Kenya, publicized a seven-point plan for a peaceful settlement of the conflict. In June, at a regional summit on the situation in Sudan convened by IGAD, it was agreed that a permanent negotiating forum comprising representatives of the parties to the conflict would be established at the Authority's secretariat. In July 2002 the Sudanese Government and the main rebel grouping in that country signed, under IGAD auspices, in Machakos, Kenya, a protocol providing for a six-year period of autonomy for southern Sudan to be followed by a referendum on self-determination, and establishing that northern Sudan would be governed in accordance with *Shari'a* law and southern Sudan by a secular judicial system. Peace negotiations subsequently continued under IGAD auspices. A cease-fire agreement was concluded by the parties to the conflict in October, to which an addendum was adopted in February 2003, recommending the deployment of an IGAD verification and monitoring team to oversee compliance with the agreement. In September of that year the parties to the conflict signed an accord on interim security arrangements. During 2003–04 IGAD mediated several further accords that paved the way for the conclusion, in January 2005, of a final Comprehensive Peace Agreement (CPA). An extraordinary session of the IGAD Council of Ministers, convened in January 2010, in Addis Ababa, expressed concern regarding the ongoing status of the implementation of the CPA and directed the IGAD Secretariat to develop programmes and seminars aimed at promoting a culture of peace in Sudan. An extraordinary summit meeting of the IGAD Assembly, held in March, *inter alia* emphasized the centrality of IGAD's role in the full implementation of the CPA; directed the IGAD Secretariat to open immediately a liaison office in Juba, Sudan, to follow up the implementation of the CPA; directed the IGAD Secretariat to accept an invitation to observe the April 2010 Sudanese elections; and directed the IGAD Secretariat to convene, in collaboration with the IPF and the parties to the CPA, an international Donors' Conference for Sudan. The IGAD monitoring team dispatched to observe the presidential and legislative elections in Sudan, in April, found them to be 'credible', while noting that technical problems had occurred and that the electoral authorities had been overwhelmed by the magnitude of their task. Following the referendum on self-determination for South Sudan, held in January 2011, and South Sudan's consequent attainment of independence in July, the new nation was admitted to IGAD in November 2011. The 20th extraordinary session of the Authority, held in January 2012, noted with concern deteriorating relations between Sudan and South Sudan, and strongly urged both states to refrain from actions that might undermine the resolution of outstanding issues under the CPA. In February 2012 the IGAD Executive Secretary reiterated the position of the AU that a warrant issued in November 2011 by the Kenyan High Court for the arrest of Sudanese President Omar al-Bashir—indicted by the International Criminal Court on charges of including crimes against humanity and genocide—contravened the interests of peace, stability and economic development in the region, and risked undermining the peace process being undertaken by IGAD in Sudan. In April 2012 the IGAD Executive Secretariat issued a statement expressing deep concern at escalating conflict between Sudan and South Sudan, urging the two sides to adhere to a Memorandum of Understanding signed in February on non-aggression and co-operation, and fully supporting the ongoing mediation efforts of an AU High Level and Implementation Panel.

In May–August 2000 a conference aimed at securing peace in Somalia was convened in Arta, Djibouti, under the auspices of IGAD. The conference appointed a transitional Somali legislature, which then elected a transitional national president. The eighth summit of IGAD heads of state and government, held in Khartoum, in November, welcomed the conclusion in September of an agreement on reconciliation between the new Somali transitional administration and a prominent opposition alliance, and determined that those member countries that neighboured Somalia (the 'frontline states' of Djibouti, Ethiopia and Kenya) should co-operate in assisting the process of reconstruction and reconciliation in that country. The summit appointed a special envoy to implement IGAD's directives concerning the Somali situation. In January 2002 the ninth IGAD summit meeting determined that a new conference for promoting reconciliation in Somalia (where insecurity continued to prevail) should be convened, under IGAD's auspices. The leaders also issued a statement condemning international terrorism and urged Somalia, in particular, to make a firm commitment to eradicating terrorism. The second Somalia reconciliation conference, initiated in October, in Eldoret, Kenya, under IGAD auspices, issued a Declaration on Cessation of Hostilities, Structures and Principles of the Somalia National Reconciliation Process, as a basis for the pursuit of a peace settlement. In February 2003 the conference was relocated to Nairobi, Kenya. In January 2004 the Nairobi conference determined to establish a new parliament; this was inaugurated in August. In January 2005 IGAD heads of state and government authorized the deployment of a Peace Support Mission to Somalia (IGASOM) to assist the transitional federal authorities there, pending the subsequent deployment of an AU peace force; this arrangement was endorsed in the same month by the AU. In mid-March 2006 the IGAD Assembly reiterated its support for the planned deployment of IGASOM, and urged the UN Security Council to grant an exemption to the UN arms embargo applied to Somalia in order to facilitate the regional peace support initiative. At a consultative meeting on the removal of the arms embargo, convened in mid-April, in Nairobi, representatives of the Somali transitional federal authorities presented for consideration by IGAD and the AU a draft national security and stabilization plan. It was agreed that a detailed mission plan should be formulated to underpin the proposed IGAD/AU peace missions. In January 2007 the AU Peace and Security Council authorized the deployment of the AU Mission in Somalia (AMISOM) in place of the proposed IGASOM.

An extraordinary meeting of the IGAD Council of Ministers, held in New York, USA, in September 2008, noted with serious concern the ongoing escalation in acts of piracy in waters off the Somalian coast, and urged the international community to take co-ordinated action to safeguard maritime safety in the region. In December a new IGAD Facilitator for the Somali peace process was appointed. Meeting in May 2009 an extraordinary session of the IGAD Council of Ministers urged the UN Security Council to impose (except for humanitarian personnel) a no-fly zone over Somalia and blockades on identified Somali seaports, and also to impose targeted sanctions against all those providing assistance to extremists—including foreign forces—who were continuing to attack AMISOM and otherwise to destabilize that country. A further extraordinary meeting of IGAD leaders, convened in June 2009, on the sidelines of the AU summit, in Sirte, Libya, noted with deep concern the continuing poor security situation in Somalia; urged the UN Security Council to consider enabling front-line states to deploy troops to Somalia if necessary; committed IGAD member states individually and collectively to establishing an internal mechanism to effect the sanctions called for in May and to enact legislation aimed at combating piracy; and directed the IGAD Secretariat to accord full support to the grouping's Facilitator for the Somali peace process. In mid-September IGAD, the UN, the European Union (EU), the League of Arab States and the respective Governments of Norway and the USA issued a joint statement strongly condemning suicide car bomb attacks that were perpetrated by Islamic extremists against the AMISOM headquarters in Mogadishu, Somalia, killing more than 20 people, including the Deputy Force Commander of the Mission, and injuring a further 40. The January 2010 IGAD extraordinary summit gathering determined to send a ministerial delegation to selected partner countries and organizations to solicit their support for the Somali transitional federal authorities; and welcomed the imposition by the UN Security Council in December 2009 of punitive sanctions against the Eritrean political and military leadership, who were found to have provided political, financial and logistical support to armed groups engaged in undermining the reconciliation process in Somalia, and to have acted aggressively towards Djibouti. The Kampala Accord, signed in June 2011 by the President of the Somali transitional federal authorities and the Speaker of the transitional legislature, and related Roadmap on its implementation, outlined a schedule for national elections, and determined that the IGAD and EAC heads of state, with UN and AU co-operation, should establish a political bureau to oversee and advance the Somali peace process. The January 2012 extraordinary session of the Authority endorsed a new IGAD

Somalia Inland Strategy and Action Plan to Prevent and Counter Piracy.

At the beginning of February 2008 IGAD heads of state and government convened in Addis Ababa, on the sidelines of the 10th Assembly of the AU, to discuss the violent unrest that had erupted in Kenya in the aftermath of that country's December 2007 disputed general election; following the meeting an IGAD ministerial delegation was dispatched to Kenya as a gesture of regional solidarity with the Kenyan people and with a peace initiative led by the former UN Secretary-General, Kofi Annan. IGAD sent an observer mission to monitor the national referendum on a new draft constitution held in Kenya in August 2010.

Publications

Annual Report.

IGAD News (2 a year).

Proceedings of the Summit of Heads of State and Government; Reports of the Council of Ministers' Meetings.

INTERNATIONAL CHAMBER OF COMMERCE—ICC

Address: 38 cours Albert 1er, 75008 Paris, France.

Telephone: 1-49-53-28-28; **fax:** 1-49-53-28-59; **e-mail:** webmaster@iccwbo.org; **internet:** www.iccwbo.org.

The ICC, founded in 1919, is the primary world business organization, representing enterprises world-wide from all business sectors. The ICC aims to promote cross-border trade and investment and to support enterprises in meeting the challenges and opportunities presented by globalization. The ICC regards trade as a force for peace and prosperity. In the 2000s the ICC underwent an extensive process of reform.

MEMBERS

ICC membership comprises corporations, national professional and sectoral associations, business and employer federations, chambers of commerce, and individuals involved in international business from more than 130 countries. National Committees or Groups have been formed in some 85 countries and territories to co-ordinate ICC objectives and functions at the national level.

Organization

(June 2012)

ICC WORLD COUNCIL

The ICC World Council is the governing body of the organization. It meets twice a year and is composed of members nominated by the National Committees. Ten direct members, from countries where no National Committee exists, may also be invited to participate. The Council elects the Chairman and Vice-Chairman for terms of two years. Ten 'direct' members originating in countries that do not have a national committee may also be invited to participate in the meetings of the World Council.

Chairman: GÉRARD WORMS (France).

EXECUTIVE BOARD

The Executive Board consists of up to 30 business leaders and ex officio members appointed by the ICC World Council upon recommendation of the Chairman. Members serve for a three-year term, one-third of the members retiring at the end of each year. It ensures the strategic direction of ICC activities and the implementation of its policies, and meets at least three times each year.

INTERNATIONAL SECRETARIAT

The ICC International Secretariat, based in Paris, is the operational arm of the ICC. It implements the work programme approved by the ICC World Council, providing intergovernmental organizations with commercial views on issues that directly affect business operations. The International Secretariat is led by the Secretary-General, who is appointed by the World Council on the recommendation of the Executive Board. A regional office for Asia, based in Singapore, was inaugurated in January 2010.

Secretary-General: JEAN-GUY CARRIER (Canada).

NATIONAL COMMITTEES AND GROUPS

Each affiliate is composed of leading business organizations and individual companies. It has its own secretariat, monitors issues of concern to its national constituents, and draws public and government attention to ICC policies.

WORLD CHAMBERS CONGRESS

The ICC's World Chambers Federation (WCF) organizes the ICC's supreme World Chambers Congress every two years; the seventh was convened in Mexico City, Mexico, in June 2011.

CONFERENCES

Regular ICC topical conferences and seminars, organized by ICC Events, disseminate ICC expertise in various fields including international arbitration, trade, banking and commercial practice.

COMMISSIONS

Policy Commissions:

Commission on Arbitration;

Commission on Banking Technique and Practice;

Commission on Commercial Practice;

Corporate Responsibility and Anti-corruption;

Commission on Competition;

Commission on Customs and Trade Regulations;

Commission on E-business, IT and Telecoms;

Commission on Environment and Energy;

Commission on Financial Services and Insurance;

Commission on Intellectual Property;

Commission on Marketing and Advertising;

Commission on Taxation;

Commission on Trade and Investment Policy;

Commission on Transport and Logistics.

ADVISORY GROUPS

Corporate Economist Advisory Group;

G20 Advisory Group.

OTHER BODIES

ICC Commercial Crime Services;

ICC Services (incorporates ICC Events and ICC Publications);

ICC World Chambers Federation.

ICC Commercial Crime Services Divisions:

International Maritime Bureau (IMB): a Piracy Reporting Centre provides the most accurate and up-to-date information to shippers regarding pirate activity on the world's oceans.

Financial Investigation Bureau (FIB): works to detect financial fraud before it occurs by allowing banks and other financial institutions access to a database of shared information.

Counterfeiting Intelligence Bureau (CIB): runs a number of initiatives to protect against counterfeiting including Counterforce, Countertech and Countersearch international networks, the Counterfeit Pharmaceutical Initiative, the IHMA's Hologram Image Register and the Universal Hologram Scanner.

Activities

The ICC's main activities are setting voluntary rules guiding the conduct of international trade, arbitrating trade disputes, and establishing policy.

The various Commissions of the ICC (listed above) are composed of more than 500 practising business executives and experts from all sectors of economic life, nominated by National Committees. ICC recommendations must be adopted by a Commission following consultation with National Committees, and then approved by the ICC World Council or Executive Board, before they can be regarded as official ICC policies. Meetings of Commissions are generally held twice a year. Task Forces are frequently constituted by Commissions to undertake specific projects and report back to their parent body. The Commissions produce a wide array of specific codes and guidelines of direct use to the world business community; formulate statements and initiatives for presentation to governments and international bodies; and comment constructively and in detail on proposed actions by intergovernmental organizations and governments that are likely to affect business.

The ICC works closely with other international organizations. It has undertaken a broad range of activities with the UN, the World Trade Organization (WTO), the European Union (EU) and many other intergovernmental bodies. The ICC presidency meets annually with the leader of the country hosting the Group of Eight (G8) summit to discuss business aspects of the meeting. A G20 Advisory Group, comprising chief executives from major global corporations and other business leaders, aims to support the effective targeting of G20 policy development. In June 2012 the ICC initiated a G20 Business Scorecard, with the aim of evaluating the G20's performance in response to business recommendations in the areas of financing for growth and development; green growth; trade and investment; and transparency and anti-corruption.

The ICC plays a part in combating international crime connected with commerce through its Commercial Crime Services (CCS). Based in London, United Kingdom, the CCS operates according to two basic principles: to prevent and investigate commercial crime and to facilitate the prosecution of criminals involved in such crimes. In July 2008 the ICC issued guidelines on establishing and implementing internal whistle-blowing programmes within businesses, aimed at exposing fraud. In March 2009 the ICC, in partnership with Transparency International, the UN Global Compact and the World Economic Forum, launched RESIST (Resisting Extortions and Solicitations in International Transactions), a tool providing recommendations to assist businesses with responding to attempted solicitation and extortion from clients.

Following the launch of the ICC's Business Action to Stop Counterfeiting and Piracy (BASCAP) initiative in November 2004, more than 150 companies and trade associations have become actively engaged in a set of projects designed to combat counterfeiting and piracy and increase awareness of the economic and social harm such activities cause. In March 2008 chief executive officers and senior corporate executives participating in BASCAP convened in New York, USA, with representatives of the World Customs Organization, World Intellectual Property Organization and US Government to discuss means of co-operation in addressing counterfeiting and piracy. The BASCAP delegates urged the prompt negotiation of an Anti-Counterfeiting Trade Agreement (ACTA). In October BASCAP published a set of intellectual property (IP) guidelines aimed at supporting businesses in managing copyright and branded materials, and deterring trade in counterfeit goods. In March 2010 BASCAP noted that jobs in creative industries were under threat from piracy, increasingly caused by illicit use of the internet (so-called digital piracy). In June 2010 BASCAP released an Arabic version of its IP guidelines for businesses. In February 2011 the ICC warned that the global economic and social impacts of counterfeiting and piracy would reach US $1,700,000m. by 2015, putting at risk 2.5m. legitimate jobs annually. The ICC issues an annual *Intellectual Property Roadmap*.

The International Maritime Bureau of the ICC compiles an annual *Global Piracy Report*, detailing incidents of maritime piracy. The 2012 Report, issued in April, reported an increase in the first quarter of that year in cases (totalling 10) of armed robbery at sea off the coast of West Africa, attributing this to the activities of Nigerian pirates, who were reported to be widening their range. Some 43 attacks by armed pirates were reported off the coast of Somalia over that period.

The ICC provides a framework for settling international commercial disputes. The Commission on Arbitration acts as a forum for experts and also reviews the ICC's dispute settlement services, for example regarding the deployment of new technologies. In 2011 the ICC International Court of Arbitration, which was established in 1923, received 796 requests for arbitration, concerning 2,293 parties from 139 countries. Other ICC services for dispute resolution include its Rules of Arbitration (updated Rules entered into force from 1 January 2012, the Rules having previously been revised in 1998), its Alternative Dispute Resolution, and the International Centre for Expertise. The latter administers ICC Rules of Expertise and Rules for Documentary Credit and Dispute Resolution Expertise (DOCDEX). The International Centre for Expertise was to administer the seven-month objection period that commenced in June 2012 in relation to applications received by the Internet Corporation for Assigned Names and Numbers (ICANN)'s expanded generic TLDs (gTLDs) programme. In June 2008 the ICC's Dispute Resolution Library was migrated to the internet, providing online access to ICC documentation on international dispute resolution.

The ICC's World Chambers Federation (WCF), a global network of chambers of commerce, acts as a platform for interaction and exchange of best practice. It is responsible for the ATA Carnet temporary export document system. The WCF also organizes the biennial World Chambers Federation Congresses. At the sixth Congress, convened in Kuala Lumpur, Malaysia, in June 2009, the WCF signed a co-operation agreement with the UN. The seventh WCF Congress was held in June 2011, in Mexico City, Mexico, on the theme 'Enterprise—Network—Prosperity; and the eighth was scheduled to be held in Doha, Qatar, in April 2013, themed as 'Opportunities for All'. In June 2008, in Stockholm, Sweden, the ICC launched the first ICC World Business Summit, as a forum for business decision makers in government and in the private sector. The Summit was convened on the theme 'World Economy at a Crossroads', and addressed the risks to the global economy posed by rising protectionism and increasing threats to IP rights. The second World Business Summit was held in June 2010, on the theme 'New Global Economic Realities: Asia-Pacific Perspectives'.

The ICC has developed rules and guidelines relating to electronic transactions, including guidelines for ethical advertising on the internet and for data protection. The ICC has devised a system of standard trade definitions most commonly used in international sales contracts ('Incoterms') and the Uniform Customs and Practice (UCP) for Documentary Credits, used by banks to finance international trade. An updated set of Incoterms ('Incoterms 2010') entered into force in January 2011. The UCP for Documentary Credits were most recently updated in 2007 (the 'UCP 600' edition). There are also ICC voluntary codes for eliminating extortion and bribery, and for promoting sound environmental management practices. The first ICC Trade Finance Summit was held in Beijing, People's Republic of China, in October 2011. A new Consolidated ICC Code of Advertising and Marketing Communications was launched in September 2011, detailing standards for marketers selling over the internet, and aimed also at strengthening protection for online consumers.

In mid-2006 the ICC launched the Business Action to Support the Information Society (BASIS) initiative, which aims to project, at international fora, the global business outlook on issues relating to the information society, such as internet governance, and the use of information and communications technologies in promoting development. BASIS contributes to the annual policy-setting Internet Governance Forum, established in 2005 by the World Summit on the Information Society.

In January 2010 the ICC launched a new global framework for responsible environmental marketing communications. The ICC led the engagement of the global business sector in preparations for the UN Conference on Sustainable Development (Rio+20), convened in Rio de Janeiro, Brazil, in June 2012.

In co-operation with the Ifo Institute for Economic Research, the ICC has since 1981 compiled a quarterly *World Economic Survey*. The *Survey* edition that was issued in February 2009 reported the lowest ever recorded global economic index, confirming the prevalence of global recession; the *Survey* index rose, however, in subsequent quarters; by the May 2012 edition, which was based on the input of more than 1,101 economic experts in 121 countries, it stood at only marginally below its long-term average and a positive outlook was given.

Finance

The ICC is a private, non-profit-making organization financed partly by contributions from National Committees and other members, according to the economic importance of the country that each represents, and partly by revenue from fees for various services and from sales of publications.

Publications

Annual Report.

Documentary Credits Insight (quarterly).

Global Piracy Report (annually).

ICC Banking Commission Opinions.

ICC International Court of Arbitration Bulletin.

Intellectual Property Roadmap (annually).

World Economic Survey (jointly with the Ifo Institute for Economic Research, quarterly).

Publications on general and technical business and trade-related subjects are also available online.

INTERNATIONAL CRIMINAL COURT

Address: Maanweg 174, 2516 AB The Hague, Netherlands.

Telephone: (70) 5158515; **fax:** (70) 5158555; **e-mail:** otp.informationdesk@icc-cpi.int; **internet:** www.icc-cpi.int.

The International Criminal Court (ICC) was established by the Rome Statute of the International Criminal Court, adopted by 120 states participating in a UN Diplomatic Conference in July 1998. The Rome Statute (and therefore the temporal jurisdiction of the ICC) entered into force on 1 July 2002, 60 days after ratification by the requisite 60th signatory state in April. The ICC is a permanent, independent body, in relationship with the UN, that aims to promote the rule of law and punish the most serious international crimes. The Rome Statute reaffirmed the principles of the UN Charter and stated that the relationship between the Court and the UN system should be determined by a framework relationship agreement between the states parties to the Rome Statute and the UN General Assembly: under the so-called negotiated relationship agreement, which entered into force in October 2004, upon signature by the Court's President and the Secretary-General of the UN, there was to be mutual exchange of information and documentation to the fullest extent and co-operation and consultation on practical matters, and it was stipulated that the Court might, if deemed appropriate, submit reports on its activities to the UN Secretary-General and propose to the Secretary-General items for consideration by the UN.

The Court comprises the Presidency (consisting of a President and first and second Vice-Presidents), Chambers (including a Pre-Trial Chamber, Trial Chamber and Appeals Chamber) with 18 permanent judges, Office of the Prosecutor (comprising the Chief Prosecutor and up to two Deputy Prosecutors), and Registry. The judges must each have a different nationality and equitably represent the major legal systems of the world, a fair geographical distribution, and a fair proportion of men and women. They are elected by the Assembly of States Parties to the Rome Statute from two lists, the first comprising candidates with established competence in criminal law and procedures and the second comprising candidates with established competence in relevant areas of international law, to terms of office of three, six or nine years. The President and Vice-Presidents are elected by an absolute majority of the judges for renewable three-year terms of office. The Chief Prosecutor is elected by an absolute majority of states parties to the Rome Statute to an unrenewable nine-year term of office. The first judges were elected to the Court in February 2003, the first Presidency in March, and the first Chief Prosecutor in April.

The Court has established a Victims Trust Fund to finance compensation, restitution or rehabilitation for victims of crimes (individuals or groups of individuals). The Fund is administered by the Registry and supervised by an independent board of directors. By mid-2012 the Trust Fund had supported more than 80,000 victims from the Democratic Republic of the Congo and northern Uganda.

By June 2012 15 cases in seven situations had been brought before the Court. Three situations were being addressed by the Court that had been referred to it by states party to the Rome Statute relating to occurrences on their territories; two situations were being pursued that had been referred by the UN Security Council; and investigations *proprio motu* were being conducted into situations in Kenya and Côte d'Ivoire (see below).

Situation in Uganda: referred to the Court in January 2004 by the Ugandan Government; the Chief Prosecutor agreed to open an investigation into the situation in July 2004; relates to the long-term unrest in the north of the country; in October 2005 the Court unsealed warrants of arrest (issued under seal in July) against five commanders of the Ugandan Lord's Resistance Army (LRA), including the LRA leader, Joseph Kony; in July 2007 the Court's proceedings against one of the named commanders were terminated on the grounds that he had been killed during LRA rebel activities in August 2006; the other four suspects remained at large at June 2012.

Situation in the DRC: referred in April 2004 by the DRC Government; the Chief Prosecutor agreed to open an investigation into the situation in June 2004; relates to alleged war crimes; in March 2006 Thomas Lubanga Dyilo, a DRC militia leader, was arrested by the Congolese authorities and transferred to the Court, thereby becoming the first ICC indictee to be captured; Lubanga was charged with conscripting child soldiers, a sealed warrant for his arrest having been issued in February; in July 2007 warrants of arrest were issued for the DRC rebel commanders Germain Katanga and Mathieu Ngudjolo Chui; Katanga was transferred into the custody of the Court in October 2007 and Ngudjolo Chui in February 2008; in April 2008 the Court unsealed a warrant of arrest for the rebel leader Bosco Ntaganda; Lubanga's trial—the first conducted by the Court—commenced in January 2009; the Prosecution concluded its presentation of its case in the trial of Lubanga in July 2009; Lubanga was found guilty in mid-March 2012, in the first verdict given by the Court; the trial in the case of Katanga and Ngudjolo Chui (the Court's second trial) commenced in November 2009; in December 2011 charges relating to crimes against humanity and other war crimes were withdrawn against Callixte Mbarushimana, an alleged rebel leader who had been arrested by the French authorities in October 2010 and transferred to the custody of the Court in January 2011; Ntaganda remained at large at June 2012.

Situation in the Central African Republic (CAR): referred in January 2005 by the CAR Government; the Chief Prosecutor agreed to open an investigation into the situation in May 2005; relates to war crimes and crimes against humanity allegedly committed during the period October 2002–March 2003; in May 2008 the Court issued a warrant of arrest for Jean-Pierre Bemba Gombo, the leader of the Mouvement du Libération du Congo (the 'Banyamulenge'); Bemba Gombo was transferred into the custody of the Court in July 2008, and his trial commenced in November 2010.

Situation in Darfur, Sudan: referred to the Court in March 2005 by the UN Security Council on the basis of the recently issued report of an International Commission of Inquiry on Darfur; the Chief Prosecutor agreed to open an investigation into the situation in June 2005; relates to the situation prevailing in Darfur since 1 July 2002; the UN Secretary-General handed the Chief Prosecutor a sealed list of 51 names of people identified in the report as having committed crimes under international law; in April 2007 the Court issued warrants for the arrests of Ahmad Harun, a former Sudanese government minister, and Ali Kushayb, a leader of the Sudanese Janjaweed militia, who were both accused of perpetrating war crimes and crimes against humanity; both remained at large at June 2012; in July 2008 the Chief Prosecutor presented evidence that Sudan's President Omar al-Bashir had been responsible for committing alleged war crimes, including crimes against humanity and genocide, in Darfur; an arrest warrant for President al-Bashir was issued by the Court in March 2009; a second arrest warrant for President al-Bashir was issued in July 2010, charging him with genocide against three ethnic groups in Darfur; al-Bashir had not surrendered to the Court at June 2012; in May 2009 a summons was issued against the militia leader Bahr Idriss Abu Garda, who appeared voluntarily before the Court later in that month; the Pre-Trial Chamber examining the Garda case declined, in February 2010, to confirm the charges against him; in June 2010 Abdallah Banda Abakaer Nourain and Saleh Mohammed Jerbo Jamus surrendered voluntarily to the Court, having been accused, with Abu Garda, of attacking the Haskanita African Union (AU) camp in September–October 2007 and causing the deaths of 12 peace-keeping troops deployed to the former AU Mission in Sudan; on 1 March 2012 the Court issued an arrest warrant for the Sudanese Minister of Defence, Abdelrahim Mohamed Hussein, for crimes against humanity and war crimes committed during August 2003–March 2004, when he was the country's Minister for the Interior, as detailed in the case of Harun and Kushayb (see above).

Situation in Kenya: in November 2009 the Presidency of the Court decided to assign the situation in Kenya (relating to violent unrest following the December 2007 presidential elections there) to a Pre-Trial Chamber; in July 2009 the International Commission of Inquiry on Post-Election Violence (known also as the Waki Commission), which had been established by the Kenyan

Government in February 2008, presented the Court Prosecutor with documentation, supporting materials, and a list of people suspected of being implicated in the violent unrest; on 31 March 2010 Pre-Trial Chamber II granted the Prosecution authorization to open an investigation *proprio motu* into the situation of Kenya; in March 2011 the ICC issued summonses for six Kenyans alleged to be criminally responsible for crimes against humanity; charges against five of the six: William Samoei Ruto, Joshua Arap Sang, Henry Kiprono Kosgey, Francis Kirimi Muthaura, and Uhuru Muigai Kenyatta were confirmed in January 2012.

Situation in Libya: referred to the Court in February 2011 by the UN Security Council; in the following month the Prosecutor agreed to open an investigation into the situation in Libya since February 2011; in late June 2011 the Court issued arrest warrants against the Libyan leader Col Muammar al-Qaddafi, Saif al-Islam (his son), and Abdullah Al-Senussi (his former Head of Military Intelligence), regarding crimes against humanity (murder and persecution) committed in Libya—through the state apparatus and security forces—from 15 February until at least 28 February; in September 2011 the ICC Prosecutor requested INTERPOL to issue a Red Notice for the arrest of the three Libyan indictees; Col Qaddafi was killed during fighting with opposition forces on 20 October; in late November Saif al-Islam was detained in southern Libya; it was subsequently reported that, despite the ICC indictment, the Libyan authorities intended to bring al-Islam to trial within Libya on charges of relating to murder and rape; Abdullah Al-Senussi was also detained by Libyan security forces in mid-March 2012.

Situation in Côte d'Ivoire: in early October 2011 an ICC Pre-Trial Chamber agreed, at the request of the Prosecutor, to commence an investigation into alleged crimes committed in Côte d'Ivoire between 28 November 2010 and 12 April 2011, during a period of civil unrest resulting from disputed presidential election results, and to consider also any crimes that may be committed in the future in the context of this situation; in late November 2011 the former president, Laurent Gbagbo, who had been in Ivorian custody since April, was transferred to the Court to face charges of crimes against humanity; in February 2012 the Court expanded the scope of the Côte d'Ivoire investigation also to include crimes within the jurisdiction of the Court allegedly committed during the period 19 September 2002–28 November 2010.

The Office of the Prosecutor also receives communications from civilian individuals and organizations relating to alleged crimes that come under the Court's jurisdiction; by 31 May 2011 9,214 such communications had been received since July 2002.

The Court also conducts an Outreach Programme, which pursues activities (through community, legal, academic, and media divisions) aimed at raising awareness and understanding of the Court's mandate in the communities most affected by the situations and cases being addressed (i.e. currently in the CAR, Darfur—Sudan, the DRC, and Uganda). During 1 October 2009–1 October 2010 more than 46,499 individuals participated in 422 Outreach Programme activities.

By June 2012 121 states had ratified the Rome Statute.

THE JUDGES
(June 2012)

	Term ends*
President: SANG-HYUN SONG (Republic of Korea)	2015
First Vice-President: SANJI MMASENONO MONAGENG (Botswana)	2018
Second Vice President: CUNO JAKOB TARFUSSER (Italy)	2018
HANS-PETER KAUL (Germany)	2015
AKUA KUENYEHIA (Ghana)	2015
ERKKI KOURULA (Finland)	2015
ANITA UŠACKA (Latvia)	2015
EKATERINA TRENDAFILOVA (Bulgaria)	2015
JOYCE ALUOCH (Kenya)	2018
CHRISTINE VAN DEN WYNGAERT (Belgium)	2018
SILVIA ALEJANDRA FERNÁNDEZ DE GURMENDI (Argentina)	2018
KUNIKO OZAKI (Japan)	2018
MIRIAM-DEFENSOR SANTIAGO (Philippines)	2021
HOWARD MORRISON (United Kingdom)	2021
ANTHONY T. CARMONA (Trinidad and Tobago)	2021
OLGA HERRERA CARBUCCIA (Dominican Republic)	2021
ROBERT FREMR (Czech Republic)	2021
CHILE EBOE-OSUJI (Nigeria)	2021

* Each term ends on 10 March of the year indicated.

Chief Prosecutor: FATOU B. BENSOUDA (The Gambia).

Registrar: SILVANA ARBIA (Italy).

Finance

The proposed budget for the International Criminal Court for 2012 amounted to €111m.

Publication

ICC Weekly Update (electronic publication).

Other International Criminal Tribunals

EXTRAORDINARY CHAMBERS IN THE COURTS OF CAMBODIA—ECCC

Address: National Rd 4, Chaom Chau Commune, Dangkao District, POB 71, Phnom-Penh, Cambodia.

Telephone: (23) 219824; **fax:** (23) 219841; **e-mail:** info@eccc.gov.kh; **internet:** www.eccc.gov.kh.

Formally established as the Extraordinary Chambers in the Courts of Cambodia for the Prosecution of Crimes Committed during the Period of Democratic Kampuchea, the ECCC was inaugurated in July 2006 on the basis of an agreement concluded in June 2003 between the Cambodian Government and the UN. The ECCC is mandated to prosecute senior leaders of the former Khmer Rouge regime for serious contraventions of Cambodian and international law—including crimes against humanity, genocide and war crimes—committed during the period 17 April 1975–6 January 1979. The ECCC is a hybrid Cambodian tribunal with international participation, combining Cambodian and international judges and personnel. It applies international standards and acts independently of the Cambodian Government and the UN. The ECCC comprises a Pre-Trial Chamber, Trial Chamber and Supreme Court Chamber; an Office of the Co-Prosecutors; an Office of the Co-Investigating Judges; a Defence Support section; a Victims' Unit; and an Office of Administration. The UN Assistance to the Khmer Rouge Trials (UNAKRT) provides technical assistance to the ECCC. Victims may file complaints before the ECCC, and may apply to become Civil Parties to the proceedings. By 2012 some 3,866 people had been admitted as Civil Parties in Case 002 (ongoing, see below). In February 2009 the ECCC initiated proceedings ('Case 001') against its first defendent, Kaing Guek Eav (also known as 'Duch'), who had been charged under international law with crimes against humanity and grave breaches of the Geneva Conventions, and under Cambodian national law with homicide and torture offences, in relation to his former role under the Khmer Rouge regime as director of Tuol Sleng prison, where at least 15,000 prisoners had been tortured and executed. The presentation of evidence in the Kaing Guek Eav case was concluded in September 2009, and closing statements were made in November. In July 2010 Kaing Guek Eav was found guilty and sentenced to 35 years of imprisonment; in February 2012, following an appeal in that case, lodged in March 2011, Kaing Guek Eav's sentence was increased to life imprisonment. In September 2010 four other senior figures in the Khmer Rouge regime (Nuon Chea, formerly the Deputy Secretary of the Party of Democratic Kampuchea; Ieng Sary, formerly Minister of Foreign Affairs; Khieu Samphan, formerly President of the State Presidium; and Ieng Thirith, formerly Minister of Social Affairs and Action) were indicted on charges of crimes against humanity, grave breaches of the Geneva Conventions, genocide, and offences under the Cambodian criminal code ('Case 002'). In January 2011 the Pre-Trial Chamber ordered the case to be sent for trial. In September the Trial Chamber ordered the division of Case 002 into a series of smaller trials, which were to be tried and adjudicated separately. The first trial was to focus on the forced movement of population and related charges of crimes against humanity. In November the Trial Chamber ordered the unconditional release from detention of Ieng Thirith on the grounds that she was unfit to stand trial; trial proceedings against the remaining three defendants commenced on 21 November. In September 2009 the International Prosecutor, submitting to investigating judges a confidential list of the names of five additional suspects, requested a formal judicial investigation into two further cases ('Case 003' and 'Case 004', the subject matter of which also remained confidential). In October 2011 the Court's then International Co-Investigating Judge resigned, citing attempted interference by government officials in the investigation into Cases 003 and 004. His successor submitted his resignation on similar grounds in March 2012.

National Co-Prosecutor: CHEA LEANG (Cambodia).

International Co-Prosecutor: ANDREW T. CAYLEY (United Kingdom).

National Co-Investigating Judge: YOU BUNLENG (Cambodia).

International Co-Investigating Judge: (vacant).

SPECIAL TRIBUNAL FOR LEBANON

Address: POB 115, 2260 AC Leidschendam, Netherlands.

Telephone: (70) 800-3400; **e-mail:** stl-pressoffice@un.org; **internet:** www.stl-tsl.org.

In March 2006 the UN Security Council adopted a resolution requesting the UN Secretary-General to negotiate an agreement with the Lebanese Government on the establishment of an international tribunal to try those suspected of involvement in a terrorist attack that, in February 2005, had killed 23 people, including the former Prime Minister of Lebanon, Rafik Hariri. The resulting agreement on the Special Tribunal for Lebanon was endorsed by the Security Council in May 2007. The Tribunal, which became operational on 1 March 2009, comprises both international and Lebanese judges and applies Lebanese (not international) law. On its establishment the Tribunal took over the mandate of a terminated UN International Independent Investigation Commission (UNIIIC), which had been created by a resolution of the Security Council in April 2005 in order to gather evidence and assist the Lebanese authorities in their investigation into the February 2005 attacks, and whose mandate had later been expanded to investigate other assassinations that had occurred before and after the February 2005 attack. A Defence Office has been established within the Tribunal to protect the rights of the suspects, accused and their counsel, providing legal assistance and support where necessary. In June 2011 the Tribunal passed to the Lebanese authorities arrest warrants for four Lebanese suspects, Salim Jamil Ayyash, Mustafa Amine Badreddine, Hussein Hassan Oneissi and Assad Hassan Sabra, who were indicted on charges of conspiracy to commit a terrorist act; in February 2012 the Tribunal announced that it would try the four suspects *in absentia*, as it appeared that they had absconded. Also in February 2012, the UN Secretary-General extended the mandate of the Special Tribunal for a further three years, with effect from 1 March. The Tribunal maintains an office in Beirut, Lebanon.

President of the Court: Sir DAVID BARAGWANATH (New Zealand).

Chief Prosecutor: NORMAN FARELL (Canada).

Registrar: HERMAN VON HEBEL (Netherlands).

Head of Defence Office: FRANÇOIS ROUX (France).

SPECIAL COURT FOR SIERRA LEONE

Address: Jomo Kenyatta Rd, New England, Freetown, Sierra Leone.

Telephone: (22) 297000; **fax:** (22) 297001; **e-mail:** scsl-mail@un.org; **internet:** www.sc-sl.org.

The Court was established in January 2002 by agreement of the UN and the government of Sierra Leone, pursuant to a UN Security Council resolution of August 2000 to establish an independent Special Court to prosecute those 'bearing the greatest responsibility for committing violations against humanitarian law' committed in the territory of Sierra Leone since 20 November 1996. The Court is funded entirely by voluntary contributions. The Court indicted in total some 13 people, although two indictments were withdrawn in December 2003 following the deaths of two of the accused, and, following the death of another of the accused, a further indictment was terminated in May 2007. Trial proceedings commenced in June 2004. Three cases involving eight defendants have been completed. In April 2006 the Special Court for Sierra Leone and the ICC concluded a Memorandum of Understanding in accordance with which the Special Court was to use the courtroom and detention facilities of the ICC for the planned trial of Charles Taylor, the former President of Liberia, who had been indicted in March 2003 on 17 counts (subsequently reduced to 11) of crimes against humanity and violations of international law, relating to his 'acts or omissions' in relation to the activities of the rebel forces of the Sierra Leone Revolutionary United Front. Taylor, who had been arrested in Nigeria and transferred to the Special Court in March 2006, was taken to the ICC's detention centre in The Hague, Netherlands, in June of that year. Taylor's trial commenced in June 2007. It was adjourned shortly afterwards and reconvened in January 2008. In February 2009 the Prosecution formally closed its case. The Defence case was conducted during July 2009–March 2011. In late April 2012 Taylor was found guilty of aiding and abetting the crimes on which he had been indicted, while acquitted of bearing criminal responsibility and 'joint enterprise' in the commission of the crimes; he was sentenced, in May, to 50 years' imprisonment. Taylor was the first former head of state to be found guilty of charges relating to war crimes by an international court.

President of the Court: JON KAMANDA (Sierra Leone).

Chief Prosecutor: BRENDA HOLLIS (USA).

Registrar: BINTA MANSARAY (Sierra Leone).

INTERNATIONAL OLYMPIC COMMITTEE

Address: Château de Vidy, 1001 Lausanne, Switzerland.

Telephone: 216216111; **fax:** 216216216; **internet:** www.olympic.org.

The International Olympic Committee was founded in 1894 to ensure the regular celebration of the Olympic Games.

Organization

(June 2012)

INTERNATIONAL OLYMPIC COMMITTEE

The International Olympic Committee (IOC) is a non-governmental international organization comprising 115 members—who are representatives of the IOC in their countries and not their countries' delegates to the IOC, and include 15 active Olympic athletes, 15 National Olympic Committee presidents, 15 International Sports Federation presidents, and 70 other individuals—as well as 24 Honorary members and three Honor members. The members meet in session at least once a year. A Nomination Commission examines and reports to the Executive Board on each candidate for membership of the IOC.

The IOC is the final authority on all questions concerning the Olympic Games and the Olympic Movement. There are 205 recognized National Olympic Committees, which are the sole authorities responsible for the representation of their respective countries at the Olympic Games. The IOC may give recognition to International Federations which undertake to adhere to the Olympic Charter, and which govern sports that comply with the IOC's criteria.

An International Council of Arbitration for Sport (ICAS) has been established. ICAS administers the Court of Arbitration for Sport which hears cases brought by competitors.

EXECUTIVE BOARD

The session of the IOC delegates to the Executive Board the authority to manage the IOC's affairs. The President of the Board is elected for an eight-year term, and is eligible for re-election once for an additional term of four years. The Vice-Presidents are elected for four-year terms, and may be re-elected after a minimum interval of four years. Members of the Board are elected to hold office for four years. The Executive Board generally meets four to five times per year.

President: Dr JACQUES ROGGE (Belgium).

Vice-Presidents: THOMAS BACH (Germany), ZAIQING YU (People's Republic of China), MARIO PESCANTE (Italy), SER MIANG NG (Singapore).

Members of the Board: DENIS OSWALD (Switzerland), RENÉ FASEL (Switzerland), FRANK FREDERICKS (Namibia), NAWAL EL MOUTAWAKEL (Morocco), RICHARD L. CARRIÓN (Puerto Rico), CRAIG REEDIE (United Kingdom), JOHN D. COATES (Australia), SAM RAMSAMY (South Africa), GUNILLA LINSBERG (Sweden).

IOC COMMISSIONS

Athletes' Commission: f. 1981; comprising active and retired athletes, represents their interests; convenes an Athletes' Forum every two years; may issue recommendations to the Executive Board.

Commission for Culture and Olympic Education: f. 2000 by merger of the Culture Commission (f. 1968) and the IOC Commission for the International Olympic Academy and Olympic Education (f. 1961).

Entourage Commission: f. 2010 to address issues relating to members of Olympic athletes' entourages, such as sports coaches and trainers.

Ethics Commission: f. 1999 to develop and monitor rules and principles to guide the selection of hosts for the Olympic Games, and the organization and execution of the Games; the activities of the Ethics Commission are funded by the Foundation for Universal Olympic Ethics, inaugurated in 2001.

Evaluation Commission: prepares a technical assessment of candidate cities' bids to host the Olympic Games, analysing their suitability.

Finance Commission: aims to ensure the efficient management of the IOC's financial resources.

International Relations Commission: f. 2002 to promote a positive relationship between the Olympic Movement and national governments and public authorities.

Juridical Commission: f. 1974 to provide legal opinions and perform other tasks of a legal nature.

Marketing Commission: helps to perpetuate the work of the Olympic Movement through the provision of financial resources and programmes aimed at protecting and enhancing the Olympic image and Olympic values.

Medical Commission: f. 1967; concerned with the protection of the health of athletes, respect for medical and sport ethics, and equality for all competing athletes; a new Olympic Movement Medical Code entered into force in October 2009.

Nominations Commission: f. 1999 to institute a procedure for electing and re-electing IOC members.

Olympic Philately, Numismatic and Memorabilia Commission: f. 1993; aims to increase awareness of the Olympic ideal through the promotion of Olympic commemorative paraphenalia.

Olympic Programme Commission: reviews, and analyses the Olympic programme of sports, disciplines and events; develops recommendations on the principles and structure of the programme.

Olympic Solidarity Commission: f. 1971; assists National Olympic Committees (NOCs); responsible for managing and administering the share of television rights allocated to NOCs.

Press Commission: advises Olympic Games organizing committees on the provision of optimum working conditions for the written and photographic media.

Radio and Television Commission: advises Olympic Games organizing committees and national broadcasting organizations on the provision of the optimum working conditions for the broadcast media.

Sport and Environment Commission: f. 1995 to promote environmental protection and sustainable development.

Sport and Law Commission: f. 1996 to act as a forum for discussion of legal issues concerning the Olympic Movement.

Sport for All Commission: f. 1983 to encourage and support the principles of Sport for All.

TV Rights and New Media Commission: prepares and implements overall IOC strategy for future broadcast rights negotiations.

Women and Sport Commission: f. 2004 (by transformation of a working group, f. 1995 to advise the Executive Board on policies to promote women in sport).

In addition, co-ordination commissions for specific Olympic Games are founded after the election of a host city to oversee and assist the organizing committee in the planning and management of the Games: in June 2012 co-ordination commissions were in force for London Summer Olympic Games 2012; Sochi Winter Olympic Games 2014; Nanjing Youth Olympic Games 2014; Rio de Janeiro Summer Olympic Games 2016; and PyeongChang Winter Olympic Games 2018.

OLYMPIC CONGRESS

Olympic Congresses are held periodically, on particular themes, to gather together the different components of the Olympic Movement with the aim of analysing the Movement's strengths and weaknesses and evaluating ongoing opportunities and challenges. The first Congress (Paris, France, 1894) addressed the theme 'Re-establishment of the Olympic Games'; the most recent, the 13th Congress (Copenhagen, Denmark, October 2009) was convened on the theme 'The Role of the Olympic Movement in Society and in all Regions of the World'.

ADMINISTRATION

The administration of the IOC is under the authority of the Director-General, who is appointed by the Executive Board, on the proposal of the President, and is assisted by Directors responsible for the following administrative sectors: international co-operation; Olympic Games co-ordination; finance, marketing and legal affairs; technology; control and co-ordination of operations; communications; and medical.

Director-General: CHRISTOPHE DE KEPPER.

Activities

The fundamental principles of the Olympic movement are:

Olympism is a philosophy of life, exalting and combining, in a balanced whole, the qualities of body, will and mind. Blending sport with culture, education and respect for the environment, Olympism seeks to create a way of life based on the joy found in effort, the educational value of good example and respect for universal fundamental ethical principles.

Under the supreme authority of the IOC, the Olympic movement encompasses organizations, athletes and other persons who agree to be guided by the Olympic Charter. The criterion for belonging to the Olympic movement is recognition by the IOC.

The goal of the Olympic movement is to contribute to building a peaceful and better world by educating youth through sport practised without discrimination of any kind and in the Olympic spirit, which requires mutual understanding with a spirit of friendship, solidarity and fair play.

The activity of the Olympic movement is permanent and universal. It reaches its peak with the bringing together of the athletes of the world at the great sport festival, the Olympic Games.

The Olympic Charter is the codification of the fundamental principles, rules and bye-laws adopted by the IOC. It governs the organization and operation of the Olympic movement and stipulates the conditions for the celebration of the Olympic Games. In March 1999, following the publication in January of the results of an investigation into allegations of corruption and bribery, an extraordinary session of the IOC was convened, at which the six Committee members were expelled for violating rules relating to Salt Lake City's bid to host the Olympic Winter Games in 2002; four other members had already resigned, while an Executive Board member had received disciplinary action. The President of the IOC retained his position after receiving a vote of confidence. The session approved a number of reform measures, including the establishment of a new independent Ethics Commission to oversee cities' bids to host the Olympic Games, and the establishment of a commission mandated to recommend far-reaching reforms to the internal structure of the organization and to the bidding process. In December 1999, having considered the recommendations of the Commission, the IOC adopted 50 reforms aimed at creating a more open, responsive and accountable organization. These included a new permanent procedure for the elimination of member visits to bid cities, the application of terms of office, limiting the expansion of the Summer Games, and the election of 15 active athletes to the IOC membership.

In response to ongoing concern at drugs abuse in sport an independent World Anti-Doping Agency (WADA) was established by the IOC in November 1999 and, on 1 January 2000, an Anti-Doping Code entered into effect. Participants attending the World Conference on Doping in Sport, held in Copenhagen, Denmark, in March 2003, adopted the Copenhagen Declaration on Doping in Sport and promoted the World Anti-Doping Code, formulated by WADA, as the basis for combating such abuses.

In July 2000 the IOC established a subsidiary International Olympic Truce Foundation, and an International Olympic Truce Centre, based in Athens, Greece, with the aim of promoting a culture of peace through the pursuit of sport and the Olympic ideals. In early 2002 the Olympic Games Study Commission was established to address means of reducing the cost and complexity of the Games. The Commission presented a full report of its findings, incorporating several recommendations for the future organization of the Games, to the 115th Session of the IOC, held in Prague, Czech Republic, in July 2003. The Commission was subsequently dissolved. In November 2002 the Olympic Programme Commission made a full review of the sports programme for the first time since 1936. It decided to cap the number of sports at 28, the number of events at 300, and the number of participating athletes at 10,500.

In July 2007 the IOC determined to establish Summer and Winter Youth Olympic Games (YOG); the first Summer YOG were held in August 2010, in Singapore, and the first Winter YOG were staged in January 2012, in Innsbrück, Austria. In October 2009 the IOC was granted observer status at the UN. The 13th Olympic Congress, convened in that month, in Copenhagen, approved a set of 66 recommendations with a particular emphasis on youth and athletes, including proposals to promote greater engagement by young people in sport; to improve the protection of athletes medically, psychologically, and in retirement; to make full use of new digital technology, and to establish a digital task force in this respect; and to utilize the YOG as a model for youth competition.

ASSOCIATED BODIES

International Committee for Fair Play: Istvánmezei út 1-3, 1146 Budapest, Hungary; tel. (1) 460-6057; fax (1) 460-6956; e-mail cifp@fairplayinternational.org; internet www.fairplayinternational.org; f. 1963 to defend and promote good sportsmanship; organizes annual World Fair Play Awards; Pres. Dr JENŐ KAMUTI; Sec.-Gen. JEAN DURRY (France).

World Anti-Doping Agency (WADA): Stock Exchange Tower, Suite 1700, 800 Place Victoria, POB 120 Montréal, QC H4Z 1B7, Canada; tel. (514) 904-9232; fax (514) 904-8650; e-mail info@wada-ama.org; internet www.wada-ama.org; f. 1999; aims to promote and co-ordinate efforts to achieve drug-free sport; the World Anti-Doping Program focuses on three pillars: the 2000 World Anti-Doping Code, International Standards, and Models of Best Practice and Guidelines; principal areas of activity are: monitoring compliance with the Code; co-operation with law enforcement; science and medicine; anti-doping co-ordination; anti-doping development; education; and athlete outreach; initiated, in 2000, an Independent Observer (IO) programme for the random testing of athletes, and observing and reporting on doping control and results management processes, at major events; and, in 2005, launched the internet-based Anti-Doping Administration and Management System (ADAMS), a clearing house for anti-doping data, such as laboratory results, 'therapeutic use exemptions', and information relating to Anti-Doping Rule Violations (ADRVs); Pres. JOHN FAHEY; Dir-Gen. DAVID HOWMAN.

The World Olympics Association, uniting competitors from past Olympic Games, and the International Paralympic Committee are affiliates of the IOC.

THE GAMES OF THE OLYMPIAD

The Olympic Summer Games take place during the first year of the Olympiad (period of four years) that they are to celebrate. They are the exclusive property of the IOC, which entrusts their organization to a host city seven years in advance.

1896 Athens	1964 Tokyo
1900 Paris	1968 Mexico City
1904 St Louis	1972 Munich
1908 London	1976 Montreal
1912 Stockholm	1980 Moscow
1920 Antwerp	1984 Los Angeles
1924 Paris	1988 Seoul
1928 Amsterdam	1992 Barcelona
1932 Los Angeles	1996 Atlanta
1936 Berlin	2000 Sydney
1948 London	2004 Athens
1952 Helsinki	2008 Beijing
1956 Melbourne	2012 London
1960 Rome	2016 Rio de Janeiro

The programme of the Games must include at least 15 of the total number of Olympic sports (sports governed by recognized International Federations and admitted to the Olympic programme by decision of the IOC at least seven years before the Games). The Olympic summer sports are: aquatics (including swimming, diving and water polo); archery; athletics; badminton; baseball; basketball; boxing; canoeing; cycling; equestrian sports; fencing, football; gymnastics; handball; field hockey; judo; modern pentathlon; rowing; sailing; shooting; softball; table tennis; tae kwondo; tennis; triathlon; volleyball; weight-lifting; wrestling.

OLYMPIC WINTER GAMES

The Olympic Winter Games comprise competitions in sports practised on snow and ice. Since 1994 they have been held in the second calendar year following that in which the Games of the Olympiad take place.

1924 Chamonix
1928 St Moritz
1932 Lake Placid
1936 Garmisch-Partenkirchen
1948 St Moritz
1952 Oslo
1956 Cortina d'Ampezzo
1960 Squaw Valley
1964 Innsbrück
1968 Grenoble
1972 Sapporo
1976 Innsbrück
1980 Lake Placid
1984 Sarajevo
1988 Calgary
1992 Albertville
1994 Lillehammer
1998 Nagano
2002 Salt Lake City
2006 Turin
2010 Vancouver
2014 Sochi
2018 Pyeongchang

The Winter Games may include biathlon, bobsleigh, curling, ice hockey, luge, skating, skiing, ski jumping, and snowboarding.

YOUTH OLYMPIC GAMES

Athletes aged between 14 and 18 years may compete in the Youth Olympic Games.

2010 Singapore (Summer)
2012 Innsbrück (Winter)
2014 Nanjing (Summer)
2016 Lillehammer (Winter)

Finance

The IOC derives marketing revenue from the sale of broadcast rights, the Olympic Partners sponsorship Programme, local sponsorship, ticketing, and licensing. Some 8% of this is retained for the Committee's operational budget, with the remainder allocated to Olympic organizing committees, National Olympic Committees and teams, and international sports federations.

Publications

IOC Newsletter (weekly).

Olympic Review (quarterly).

INTERNATIONAL ORGANIZATION FOR MIGRATION—IOM

Address: 17 route des Morillons, CP 71, 1211 Geneva 19, Switzerland.

Telephone: 227179111; **fax:** 227986150; **e-mail:** info@iom .int; **internet:** www.iom.int.

The Intergovernmental Committee for Migration (ICM) was founded in 1951 as a non-political and humanitarian organization with a predominantly operational mandate, including the handling of humane, orderly and planned migration to meet specific needs of emigration and immigration countries; and the processing and movement of refugees, displaced persons and other individuals in need of international migration services to countries offering them resettlement opportunities. In 1989 ICM's name was changed to the International Organization for Migration (IOM). IOM was admitted as an observer to the UN General Assembly in 1992.

MEMBERS

Afghanistan
Albania
Algeria
Angola
Antigua and Barbuda
Argentina
Armenia
Australia
Austria
Azerbaijan
Bahamas
Bangladesh
Belarus
Belgium
Belize
Benin
Bolivia
Bosnia and Herzegovina
Botswana
Brazil
Bulgaria
Burkina Faso
Burundi
Cambodia
Cameroon
Canada
Cape Verde
Central African Republic
Chad
Chile
Colombia
Comoros
Congo, Democratic Republic
Congo, Republic
Costa Rica
Côte d'Ivoire
Croatia
Cyprus
Czech Republic
Denmark
Djibouti
Dominican Republic
Ecuador
Egypt
El Salvador
Estonia
Ethiopia
Finland
France
Gabon
The Gambia
Georgia
Germany
Ghana
Greece
Guatemala
Guinea
Guinea-Bissau
Guyana
Haiti
Holy See
Honduras
Hungary
India
Iran
Ireland
Israel
Italy
Jamaica
Japan
Jordan
Kazakhstan
Kenya
Korea, Republic
Kyrgyzstan
Latvia
Lesotho
Liberia
Libya
Lithuania
Luxembourg
Madagascar
Mali
Maldives
Malta
Mauritania
Mauritius
Mexico
Micronesia, Federated States
Moldova
Mongolia
Montenegro
Morocco
Mozambique
Namibia
Nauru
Nepal
Netherlands
New Zealand
Nicaragua
Niger
Nigeria
Norway
Pakistan
Panama
Paraguay
Peru
Philippines
Poland
Portugal
Romania
Rwanda
Senegal
Serbia
Seychelles
Sierra Leone
Slovakia
Slovenia
Somalia
South Africa
South Sudan
Spain
Sri Lanka
Sudan
Swaziland
Sweden
Switzerland
Tajikistan
Tanzania
Thailand
Timor-Leste
Togo
Trinidad and Tobago
Tunisia
Turkey
Uganda
Ukraine
United Kingdom
USA
Uruguay
Vanuatu
Venezuela
Viet Nam
Yemen
Zambia
Zimbabwe

Observers: Bahrain, Bhutan, People's Republic of China, Cuba, Indonesia, former Yugoslav republic of Macedonia, Papua New Guinea, Qatar, Russia, San Marino, São Tomé and Príncipe, Saudi Arabia and Turkmenistan. In addition, 85 international, governmental and non-governmental organizations hold observer status with IOM.

Organization

(June 2012)

IOM is governed by a Council that is composed of representatives of all member governments, and has the responsibility for making final decisions on policy, programmes and financing. An Executive Committee of nine member governments elected by the Council examines and reviews the organization's work; considers and reports on any matter specifically referred to it by the Council; advises the Director-General on any matters that he may refer to it; makes, between sessions of the Council, any urgent decisions on matters falling within the competence of the Council, which are then submitted for approval by the Council; and presents advice or proposals to the Council or the Director-General on its own initiative. The Director-General is responsible to the Council and the Executive Committee. Alongside the Director-General's Office there are offices of International Migration Law and Legal Affairs; Management Co-ordination; Information Technology and Communications; and Gender Co-ordination. In recent years IOM has transferred some administrative functions from its headquarters to two administrative centres, located in Manila, Philippines, and Ciudad del Saber, Panama. Plans are under way to establish a Capacity-Building Office in Africa. In July 2010 a Field Implementation Team was established, mandated to oversee a reorganization of IOM's field activities, including the establishment of eight new regional offices.

Director-General: William Lacy Swing (USA).

Deputy Director-General: Laura Thompson Chacón (Costa Rica).

Activities

IOM aims to provide assistance to member governments in meeting the operational challenges of migration, to advance understanding of migration issues, to encourage social and economic development through migration and to work towards effective respect of the human dignity and well-being of migrants. It provides a full range of migration assistance to, and sometimes de facto protection of, migrants, refugees, displaced persons and other individuals in need of international migration services. This includes recruitment, selection, processing, medical examinations, and language and cultural orientation courses, placement, activities to facilitate reception and integration and other advisory services. IOM co-ordinates its refugee activities with the UN High Commissioner for Refugees (UNHCR) and with governmental and non-governmental partners. In May 1997 IOM and UNHCR signed a Memorandum of Understanding that aimed to facilitate co-operation between the two organizations. Since it commenced operations in February 1952 IOM is estimated to have provided assistance to more than 12m. migrants. IOM estimates that migrants comprise some 3% of the global population, and that some 15%–20% of migrant movements are unregulated. In 2010 IOM provided movement assistance to 269,931 individuals, including the resettlement of 101,685 refugees, and repatriation of a further 13,196. During 2010 IOM undertook 2,302 active projects, of which 690 were initiated in that year; some 33% of the total number of projects were implemented in Europe, 21% in Africa, and 19% in Asia and Oceania. In 2010 38% of ongoing projects related to regulating migration (38%), 28% to movement, emergency and post-crisis migration management, and 10% to facilitating migration.

IOM's International Migration Law (IML) and Legal Affairs Department promotes awareness and knowledge of the legal instruments that govern migration at national, regional and international level; provides training and capacity-building services connected with IML; and researches IML. IOM maintains an international database of IML.

IOM provides information and advice to support the efforts of governments and other stakeholders to formulate effective national, regional and global migration management policies and strategies; and conducts research, aimed at guiding migration policy and practice, in areas including migration trends and data, IML, migration and development, health and migration, counter-trafficking, labour migration, trade, remittances, irregular migration, integration and return migration.

IOM was a founder member with other international organizations of the inter-agency Global Migration Group (GMG, established as the Geneva Migration Group in April 2003 and renamed in 2006). The GMG provides a framework for discussion among the heads of member organizations on the application of decisions and norms relating to migration, and for stronger leadership in addressing related issues. Since 2007 the GMG has organized an annual Global Forum for Migration and Development (GFMD). The 2010 GFMD, convened in Puerto Vallarta, Mexico, in November, addressed the theme 'Partnerships for Migration and Human Development—Shared Prosperity, Shared Responsibility'. The 2011 GFMD took the form of a series of decentralized small-scale action-oriented meetings world-wide, focused on the theme 'Action on Migration and Development—Coherence, Capacity and Co-operation', and culminated in a final conference of Friends of the GFMD, held in Geneva, in December. GFMD 2012 was to be hosted by Mauritius, in accordance with the traditional centralized format, with a main meeting to be convened towards the end of the year.

In October 2005 IOM's Director-General inaugurated a new Business Advisory Board, comprising 13 business leaders representing a cross section of global concerns. It was envisaged that the initiative would promote an effective partnership between IOM and the private sector aimed at supporting the planning, development and implementation of improved mobility policies and practices.

IOM acknowledges a direct link between migration and both climate change and environmental degradation; so-called 'environmental migration' (both cross-border and internal) is particularly prevalent in the world's poorest countries. In March 2011 IOM organized a workshop aimed at assisting the international community in preparing for environmental migration.

In June 2007 the IOM Council adopted a comprehensive 12-point strategy, which was to be incorporated into all of the activities of the organization.

IOM operates within the framework of the main service areas outlined below.

MIGRATION AND DEVELOPMENT

IOM places a strategic focus on advancing a positive relationship between migration and development; on fostering a deeper understanding of the linkages between migration and development; and on enhancing the benefits that well-managed migration can have for the development, growth and prosperity of migrants' countries of origin and of destination, as well as for the migrants personally. IOM's activities in this area include strengthening the capacity of governments and other stakeholders to engage expatriate migrant communities in development processes in their countries of origin; promoting economic and community development in places from which there is a high level of emigration; enhancing the development impact of remittances; and facilitating the return and reintegration of qualified nationals. There are two main branches of Migration and Development programming: Migration and Economic/Community Development; and Capacity Building Through Qualified Human Resources and Experts.

IOM's Migration and Economic/Community Development programme area covers three principal fields of activity. First, IOM seeks to maximize the positive potential from migration for the development of countries of origin and destination, promoting an increase in more development-oriented migration policies, and implementing initiatives aimed at building the capacity of governments and other stakeholders in countries of origin to involve their migrant populations in home country development projects. Second, IOM aims to address the root causes of economically motivated migration by assisting governments and other actors with the strategic focusing of development activities to expand economic opportunities and improve social services and infrastructures in regions experiencing outward or returning migration. Third, IOM promotes data collection, policy dialogue and dissemination of good practices, and pilot project implementation, in the area of remittances (funds sent home by migrant workers, mainly in the form of private money transfers), with the aim of improving the development impact of remittances. IOM helped to organize the Global Consultation on Migration, Remittances and Development: Responding to the Global Economic Crisis from a Gender Perspective, which was convened in June–July 2009, in Switzerland; the meeting adopted a communiqué detailing policy recommendations.

IOM's Capacity Building Through Qualified Human Resources and Experts programme area focuses on the return from abroad and socio-economic reintegration of skilled and qualified nationals. Return and Reintegration of Qualified Nationals (RQN) and similar projects include recruitment, job placement, transport and limited employment support services, and aim to influence the economic and social environment in countries of origin in a manner conducive to further returns. IOM also focuses on the recruitment and selection of highly trained workers and professionals to fill positions in priority sectors of the economy in developing countries for which qualified persons are not available locally, taking into account national development priorities as well as the needs and concerns of receiving communities.

A programme to encourage the Return and Reintegration of Qualified Afghan Nationals (RQAFN), co-funded by the European Commission, and a Return and Reintegration of Qualified Nationals to Sudan programme, were ongoing in 2012. In 2005 IOM, the United Nations Volunteers (UNV) and the Iraqi Government established an ongoing RQN–Transfer of Knowledge Through Expatriate Nationals (TOKTEN) programme for Iraq, known as 'Iraqis Rebuilding Iraq', with funding from the International Reconstruction Fund Facility for Iraq. In addition, IOM operates the Migration for Development in Africa (MIDA) institutional capacity-building programme, which provides a framework for transferring skills and resources from African migrants to their countries of origin. For example, in 2012 a MIDA project was encouraging expatriate Ghanaian health professionals to provide training to health workers in Ghana. IOM and the UN Development Programme (UNDP) jointly implement the Qualified Expatriate Somali Technical Support (QUESTS)-MIDA scheme, which aims to engage technical expertise in the areas of policy and legislation, human resources management, and public financial management, among the Somali diaspora, to support the rebuilding of key governance foundations in parts of Somalia. IOM and the European Union jointly fund a scheme to support Rwandan students abroad and encourage their return to Rwanda.

In 2010 migrants were estimated to have remitted some US $325,000m. to developing countries of origin. In March 2009 IOM and FAO agreed to collaborate on supporting agricultural projects in home countries funded by remittances from migrants in OECD member states.

From April 2006–June 2008 IOM and the Netherlands Government undertook the Temporary Return of Qualified Nationals (TRQN) project, with the aim of supporting reconstruction and development efforts in Afghanistan, Bosnia and Herzegovina, Kosovo, Montenegro, Serbia, Sierra Leone and Sudan. Under the TRQN, IOM provided logistical and financial assistance to experts originating in any of the target countries who were also nationals of or had residence in the Netherlands, to help them participate in projects aimed at enriching the target countries. TRQN II was undertaken during July 2009–July 2011, in support of development efforts in Afghanistan, Bosnia and Herzegovina, Ethiopia, Georgia, Sierra Leone and Sudan.

IOM offers Assisted Voluntary Return (AVR) services to migrants and governments, with the aim of facilitating the efficient and humane return and reintegration of migrants who wish to repatriate voluntarily to their countries of origin. Pre-departure, transportation and post-arrival assistance is provided to unsuccessful asylum seekers, migrants in irregular situations, migrants stranded in transit, stranded students, etc. AVR services can be tailored to the particular needs of specific groups, such as vulnerable migrants. IOM established a Stranded Migrant Facility in 2005.

During October 2006–October 2007 IOM implemented the pilot Return and Reintegration in Countries of Origin (IRRiCO) project, which aimed to establish an internet-based database of relevant information in support of voluntary returns and reintegration, for use both by service providers and by migrants considering returning home. IRRiCO II, with the participation of 20 countries of origin and nine European countries, was launched in September 2008.

The IOM Development Fund (founded in 2001 as the '1035 Facility', and renamed in January 2012) supports developing member states and member states with economies in transition with the implementation of migration management capacity-building projects. By June 2012 some 370 projects in 112 member states had been supported by the Fund, at a cost of US $32m.

FACILITATING MIGRATION

Integrated world markets, transnational business networks and the rapid growth of ICTs have contributed to large-scale movements of workers, students, family members, and other migrants. IOM implements programmes that assist governments and migrants with recruitment, language training, pre-departure cultural orientation, pre-consular support services, arrival reception, and integration, and has introduced initiatives in areas including document verification, migrant information, interviews, applicant testing and logistical support. There are three main branches of Facilitating Migration programming: Labour Migration; Migrant Processing and Assistance; and Migrant Integration.

Through its Labour Migration activities, IOM aims to promote regulated orderly labour migration while combating illegal, often clandestine, migration; and and to foster the economic and social development of countries of origin, transit and destination. Jointly with governments and other agencies, IOM has developed specific labour migration programmes that include elements such as capacity building; pre-departure training; return and reintegration support; and regional dialogue and planning.

Through its Migrant Processing and Assistance activities IOM provides assistance to facilitate migration under organized and regular migration schemes that are tailored to meet specific programme needs and cover the different stages of the migration process: information and application, interview and approval, and post-approval (including pre-departure counselling and cultural orientation). Similar assistance is also provided to experts participating in international technical co-operation activities, to students studying abroad and, in some cases, to their dependents.

IOM's Migration Integration activities promote strategies aimed at enabling migrants to adjust easily to new environments abroad and focus on the dissemination of information on the rights and obligations of migrants and refugees in home and in host countries, the provision of advisory and counselling services, and the reinforcement of their skills. In addition IOM promotes awareness-raising activities in host societies that highlight the positive contributions that migrants can make, with a view to reducing the risks of discrimination and xenophobia.

REGULATING MIGRATION

IOM aims to counter the growing problem of smuggling and trafficking in migrants, which has resulted in several million people being exploited by criminal agents and employers. IOM aims to provide shelter and assistance for victims of trafficking; to provide legal and medical assistance to migrants uncovered in transit or in the receiving country; and to offer voluntary return and reintegration assistance. The organization maintains the IOM Global Human Trafficking Information Management System (also known as the IOM Global Database), which aims to facilitate the management of assistance for victims of trafficking. IOM organizes mass information campaigns in countries of origin, in order to highlight the risks of smuggling and trafficking, and aims to raise general awareness of the problem. The most common countries of origin covered in the database are Belarus, Bulgaria, the Dominican Republic, Moldova, Romania and Ukraine. IOM also provides training to increase the capacity of governments and other organizations to counter irregular migration. Since 1996 IOM has worked in Cambodia and Thailand to help victims of trafficking to return home. A transit centre has been established on the border between the two countries, where assessments are carried out, advice is given, and the process of tracing families is undertaken. IOM has campaigned for the prevention of trafficking in women from the Baltic states. IOM launched a series of new training modules in November 2006, designed to enhance the knowledge and understanding of the issues of human trafficking.

Through its Technical Co-operation on Migration Division, IOM offers advisory services to governments on the optimum administrative structures, policy, legislation, operational systems and human resource systems required to regulate migration. IOM technical co-operation also focuses on capacity-building projects such as training courses for government migration officials, and analysis of and suggestions for solving emerging migration problems. Throughout these activities, IOM aims to maintain an emphasis on the rights and well-being of migrants, and in particular to ensure that the specific needs of migrant women are incorporated into programmes and policies.

In October 2009 IOM launched a campaign entitled 'What Lies Behind the Things We Buy?', which aimed to draw attention to the use of trafficked and exploited labour in the manufacture of cheap goods.

MOVEMENT, EMERGENCY AND POST-CRISIS RESPONSE

IOM provides services to assist with the resettlement of individuals accepted under regular national immigration programmes; these include: supporting the processing of relevant documentation; medical screening; arranging safe transportation; and, in some cases, the provision of language training and cultural orientation. IOM also assists with the voluntary repatriation of refugees, mainly in support of UNHCR's voluntary repatriation activities.

In emergency situations IOM provides transportation and humanitarian assistance to individuals requiring evacuation, as well as providing support to countries of temporary protection. IOM supports internally displaced populations through the provision of emergency shelter and relief materials. Post-emergency movement assistance for returning displaced populations is also provided (mainly internally displaced perons—IDPs, demobilized soldiers and persons affected by natural disasters). In post-crisis situations it actively supports governments in the reconstruction and rehabilitation of affected communities and offers short-term community and micro-enterprise development programmes. In such situations IOM's activities may include health sector assistance and counter-trafficking awareness activities, psycho-social support, capacity building for disaster transportation and logistics; and registration and information management of affected populations.

During 2005 the UN developed a concept of organizing humanitarian agency assistance to IDPs through the institutionalization of a 'Cluster Approach', currently comprising 11 core areas of activity. IOM was designated the lead humanitarian agency for the cluster on Camp Co-ordination and Management in natural disaster situations (UNHCR was to lead that cluster in conflict situations).

Since April 2003, following the launching in March of US-led military action against the Saddam Hussain regime in Iraq, IOM has been lead organization for emergency distributions of food and non-food items (NFIs) for the displaced population inside Iraq, and has co-ordinated the assessment and monitoring of Iraqi IDPs, including providing data on their numbers, locations and needs. IOM works to restore essential services, including the provision of drinking water, good sanitation, health, and education, in central and southern Iraq. By 2012 IOM had established community management teams and technical consultative boards in Iraq, with a view to empowering local communities to identify and implement sustainable long-term development structures. In April 2009 IOM was appointed the partner with responsibility for transportation of NFIs in the UN-managed 'common pipeline' operation for Darfur and northern Sudan; by December IOM had delivered about 2.3m. NFIs in Darfur. IOM was responsible for organizing the out-of-country registration and voting process for the referendum on independence for southern Sudan that took place in January 2011; following its attainment of independence in July 2011, South Sudan became a member of IOM.

CLAIMS PROGRAMMES

IOM was designated as one of the implementing organizations of the settlement agreement concluded between survivors of the Nazi Holocaust and Swiss banks. IOM established the Holocaust Victim Assets Programme (HVAP) to process claims made by certain target groups. A German Forced Labour Compensation Programme (GFLCP) was founded to process applications for claims of forced labour and personal injury and for property loss. By September 2005 IOM had recommended payment in respect of 18,431 of a total of 49,371 claims received under the HVAP, while claims received under the GFLCP included 332,307 for slave and forced labour, 41,837 for personal injury and 34,997 for property loss. Under the terms of the settlement agreement, with regard to 'looted assets', IOM was mandated to distribute US $20.5m. to humanitarian programmes, specifically to assist elderly Roma and Sinti, Jehovah's Witnesses, disabled and homosexual victims and targets of Nazi persecution. The HVAP and GFLCP were terminated in December 2006.

IOM provides assistance and advice to the Commission for Resolution of Real Property Disputes (CRRPD), an independent agency of the Government of Iraq that was established in March 2006 to resolve claims on property in Iraq relating to the period 17 July 1968–9 April 2003.

In 2012 IOM was implementing a 'Technical Assistance to the Administrative Reparation Programme in Colombia' initiative, launched in January 2008, with the aim of supporting the Colombian authorities in compensating—as an act of solidarity—the victims of violence inflicted by illegal armed militia in that country.

MIGRATION HEALTH

IOM's Migration Health Department aims to ensure that migrants are fit to travel, do not pose a danger to those travelling with them, and that they receive medical attention and care when necessary. IOM also undertakes research and other technical support and policy development activities in the field of health care. Medical screening of prospective migrants is routinely conducted, along with immunizations and specific counselling, e.g. for HIV/AIDS. IOM administers programmes for disabled refugees and undertakes medical evacuation of people affected by conflict. Under its programmes for health assistance and advice, IOM conducts health education programmes, training for health professionals in post-conflict regions, and assessments of availability and access to health care for migrant populations. IOM provides assistance for post-emergency returning populations, through the rehabilitation of health infrastructures; provision of medical supplies; mental health programmes, including psychosocial support; and training of personnel.

IOM collaborates with government health authorities and relevant intergovernmental and non-governmental organizations. In September 1999 IOM and UNAIDS signed a co-operation framework to promote awareness on HIV/AIDS issues relating to displaced populations, and to ensure that the needs of migrants are incorporated into national and regional AIDS strategies. In October IOM and the World Health Organization (WHO) signed an agreement to strengthen collaborative efforts to improve the health care of migrants. IOM maintains a database of its tuberculosis diagnostic and treatment programmes, which facilitates the management of the disease. An information system on immigration medical screening data was being developed to help to analyse disease trends among migrants.

International Centre for Migration and Health

11 route du Nant-d'Avril, 1214 Geneva, Vernier, Switzerland; tel. 227831080; fax 227831087; e-mail secretariat@icmhd.ch; internet www.icmhd.ch.

Established in March 1995, by IOM and the University of Geneva, with the support of WHO, to respond to the growing needs for information, documentation, research, training and policy development in migration health; designated as a WHO collaborating centre for health-related issues among people displaced by disasters.

Executive Director: Dr MANUEL CARBALLO.

Finance

IOM's proposed operational budget for 2012 totalled US $615.4m.

Publications

Global Eye on Human Trafficking (quarterly).

International Migration (quarterly).

IOM Harare Newsletter.

IOM News (quarterly, in English, French and Spanish).

Migration (2 a year).

Migration and Climate Change.

Migration Health Annual Report.

Report by the Director-General (in English, French and Spanish).

Trafficking in Migrants (quarterly).

World Migration Report (annually).

Research reports, *IOM Info Sheets* surveys and studies.

INTERNATIONAL RED CROSS AND RED CRESCENT MOVEMENT

The International Red Cross and Red Crescent Movement (known as 'Red Cross Red Crescent') is a world-wide independent humanitarian organization, comprising three main components: the International Committee of the Red Cross (ICRC), founded in 1863; the International Federation of Red Cross and Red Crescent Societies (the Federation), founded in 1919; and National Red Cross and Red Crescent Societies in 185 countries; as well as Magen David Adom, an Israeli society equivalent to the Red Cross and Red Crescent Societies. In 1997 all constituent parts of the Movement adopted the Seville Agreement on co-operation in the undertaking of international relief activities. The Agreement excludes activities that are entrusted to individual components by the statutes of the Movement or the Geneva Conventions.

Organization

INTERNATIONAL CONFERENCE

The supreme deliberative body of the Movement, the Conference comprises delegations from the ICRC, the Federation and the National Societies, and of representatives of States Parties to the Geneva Conventions (see below). The Conference's function is to determine the general policy of the Movement and to ensure unity in the work of the various bodies. It usually meets every four to five years, and is hosted by the National Society of the country in which it is held. The 30th International Conference was held in Geneva, Switzerland, in November 2007.

The 29th International Conference, held in Geneva in June 2006, approved membership of the Palestinian Red Crescent Society and the Israeli society Magen David Adom. A Third Additional Protocol (Protocol III—see below) to the Geneva Conventions was adopted in December 2005 and entered into force in January 2007. Protocol III recognizes as third emblem of the Movement a red crystal, which is deemed to be a neutral symbol devoid of political or religious connotations.

STANDING COMMISSION

The Commission meets at least twice a year in ordinary session. It promotes harmony in the work of the Movement, and examines matters which concern the Movement as a whole. It is formed of two representatives of the ICRC, two of the Federation, and five members of National Societies elected by the Conference.

COUNCIL OF DELEGATES

The Council comprises delegations from the National Societies, from the ICRC and from the Federation. The Council is the body where the representatives of all the components of the Movement meet to discuss matters that concern the Movement as a whole.

In November 1997 the Council adopted an Agreement on the organization of the activities of the Movement's components. The Agreement aimed to promote increased co-operation and partnership between the Movement's bodies, clearly defining the distribution of tasks between agencies. In particular, the Agreement aimed to ensure continuity between international operations carried out in a crisis situation and those developed in its aftermath.

Fundamental Principles of the Movement

Humanity: The International Red Cross and Red Crescent Movement, born of a desire to bring assistance without discrimination to the wounded on the battlefield, endeavours, in its international and national capacity, to prevent and alleviate human suffering wherever it may be found. Its purpose is to protect life and health and to ensure respect for the human being. It promotes mutual understanding, friendship, co-operation and lasting peace among all peoples.

Impartiality: It makes no discrimination as to nationality, race, religious beliefs, class or political opinions. It endeavours to relieve the suffering of individuals, being guided solely by their needs, and to give priority to the most urgent cases of distress.

Neutrality: In order to continue to enjoy the confidence of all, the Movement may not take sides in hostilities or engage in controversies of a political, racial, religious or ideological nature.

Independence: The Movement is independent. The National Societies, while auxiliaries in the humanitarian services of their governments and subject to national laws, must retain their autonomy so that they may always be able to act in accordance with the principles of the Movement.

Voluntary Service: It is a voluntary relief movement not prompted by desire for gain.

Unity: There can be only one Red Cross or Red Crescent Society in any one country. It must be open to all. It must carry on its humanitarian work throughout the territory.

Universality: The International Red Cross and Red Crescent Movement, in which all National Societies have equal status and share equal responsibilities and duties in helping each other, is world-wide.

International Committee of the Red Cross—ICRC

Address: 19 ave de la Paix, 1202 Geneva, Switzerland.

Telephone: 227346001; **fax:** 227332057; **e-mail:** press.gva@icrc.org; **internet:** www.icrc.org.

Founded in 1863, the ICRC is at the origin of the Red Cross and Red Crescent Movement, and co-ordinates all international humanitarian activities conducted by the Movement in situations of conflict. New statutes of the ICRC, incorporating a revised institutional structure, entered into force in July 1998.

The ICRC is an independent institution of a private character composed exclusively of Swiss nationals. Members are co-opted, and their total number may not exceed 25. The international character of the ICRC is based on its mission and not on its composition.

Organization

(June 2012)

ASSEMBLY

The Assembly is the supreme governing body of the ICRC. It formulates policy, defines the Committee's general objectives and strategies, oversees its activities, and approves its budget and accounts. The Assembly is composed of the members of the ICRC, and is collegial in character. The President and Vice-Presidents of the ICRC hold the same offices in the Assembly.

President: PETER MAURER (from 1 July 2012).

Vice-Presidents: CHRISTINE BEERLI, OLIVIER VODOZ.

ASSEMBLY COUNCIL

The Council (formerly the Executive Board) is a subsidiary body of the Assembly, to which the latter delegates certain of its responsibilities. It prepares the Assembly's activities and takes decisions on matters within its competence. The Council is composed of five members elected by the Assembly and is chaired by the President of the ICRC.

Members: PETER MAURER, CHRISTINE BEERLI, CLAUDE LE COULTRE, ROLF SOIRON, BRUNO STAFFELBACH.

DIRECTORATE

The Directorate is the executive body of the ICRC, overseeing the efficient running of the organization and responsible for the application of the general objectives and institutional strategies decided by the Assembly. Members are appointed by the Assembly to serve a four-year term.

Director-General: YVES DACCORD.

Members: PIERRE KRÄHENBÜHL (Director of Operations), HELEN ALDERSON (Director of Financial Resources and Logistics), CHARLOTTE LINDSEY-CURTET (Director of Communication and Information Management), PHILIP SPOERRI (Director for International Law and Co-operation within the Movement), CAROLINE WELCH-BALLENTINE (Director of Human Resources).

Activities

The International Committee of the Red Cross was founded in 1863 in Geneva, by Henry Dunant and four of his friends. The original purpose of the Committee was to promote the foundation, in every country, of a voluntary relief society to assist wounded soldiers on the battlefield (the origin of the National Societies of the Red Cross or Red Crescent), as well as the adoption of a treaty protecting wounded soldiers and all those who come to their rescue. The mission of the ICRC was progressively extended through the Geneva Conventions (see below). The present activities of the ICRC consist in giving legal protection and material assistance to military and civilian victims of wars (international wars, internal strife and disturbances), in promoting and monitoring the application of international humanitarian law (IHL), and, in recent years, in providing humanitarian assistance in situations of violence other than armed conflicts: in 2011 the ICRC provided emergency assistance to civilians affected by violent disturbances in Egypt, Tunisia, Yemen and Syria. (The situation in Syria escalated into armed conflict in 2012.) The ICRC takes into account the legal standards and the specific cultural, ethical and religious features of the environment in which it operates. It aims to influence the conduct of all actual and potential perpetrators of violence by seeking direct dialogue with combatants. In 1990 the ICRC was granted observer status at the UN General Assembly. The ICRC overall programme of activities covers the following areas:

The protection of vulnerable individuals and groups under IHL, including activities related to ensuring respect for detainees (monitoring prison conditions), respect for civilians, reuniting relatives separated in conflict situations and restoring family links, and tracing missing persons;

The implementation of assistance activities, aimed at restoring a sufficient standard of living to victims of armed conflict, including the provision of medical aid and emergency food supplies, initiatives to improve water supply, basic infrastructure and access to health care, and physical rehabilitation assistance (for example to assist civilians injured by landmines);

Preventive action, including the development and implementation of IHL and dissemination of humanitarian principles, with a view to protecting non-combatants from violence;

The use of humanitarian diplomacy to raise awareness of humanitarian issues among states and within international organizations;

Building private sector relations;

Co-operation with National Societies.

The ICRC Advisory Service, established in 1996, offers legal and technical assistance to national authorities with incorporating IHL into their national legislation, assists them in their implementation of IHL, maintains a database on IHL, and publishes specialist documents. A Documentation Centre has also been established for exchanging information on national measures and activities aimed at promoting humanitarian law in countries. The Centre is open to all states and National Societies, as well as to interested institutions and the general public. In 2010 the ICRC maintained contact with the military in some 160 countries, with nearly 80 armed militia, and with a number of private military and security companies with the intention of ensuring that they are knowledgable about and comply with IHL. A Senior Workshop on International Rules Governing Military Operations is organized annually by the ICRC to provide guidance to combatants.

In April 1998 the Assembly endorsed a plan of action, based on the following four priorities identified by the 'Avenir' project to define the organization's future role, that had been launched in 1996: improving the status of international humanitarian action and knowledge of and respect for IHL; carrying out humanitarian action in closer proximity to victims, with long-term plans and identified priorities; strengthening dialogue with all parties (including launching joint appeals with other organizations if necessary); and increasing the ICRC's efficiency. In December 2003 the 28th International Conference of the Red Cross and Red Crescent adopted an Agenda for Humanitarian Action. The main components of the Agenda, which had the overall theme 'protecting human dignity', were: respecting and restoring the dignity of persons and families missing as a result of conflict situations; strengthening controls on weapons development, proliferation and use; lessening the impact of disasters through the implementation of disaster risk reduction measures and improving preparedness and response mechanisms; and reducing vulnerability to the effects of disease associated with lack of access to comprehensive prevention, care and treatment.

The ICRC's Institutional Strategy covering the period 2011–14 focused on the following four priority areas: reinforcing the ICRC's scope of action; strengthening the Committee's contextualized, multidisciplinary response; shaping the debate on legal and policy issues related to the Committee's mission; and optimizing the Committee's performance. The ICRC has noted in recent years that, while some conflicts remain underpinned by territorial or ideological disputes, increasing numbers of conflicts and so-called situations of violence are being fuelled by pressure to secure control over natural resources, and that there is evidence of increasing activity by economically predatory armed elements. Fragile humanitarian situations are complicated by other factors, including weapons proliferation; environmental degradation; mass migration to cities and increased urban violence; and acts of terrorism and anti-terrorism operations. The ICRC has identified two principal challenges to the neutral and independent implementation of its humanitarian activities: developing a refined understanding of the diversity and specificity of armed conflicts and other situations of violence; and addressing meaningfully the many needs of affected civilian populations. During 2011–15 the ICRC was undertaking a Health Care in Danger project, which aimed to enhance protection of the sick and wounded, and address other negative impacts, in cases where illegal and violent acts obstruct the delivery of health provision or endanger health care staff, during armed conflict and other situations of violence.

The ICRC consistently reviews the 1980 UN Convention on prohibitions or restrictions on the use of certain conventional weapons which may be deemed to be excessively injurious or to have indiscriminate effects and its protocols. In September 1997 the ICRC participated in an international conference, held in Oslo, Norway, which adopted the Convention on the Prohibition of the Use, Stockpiling, Production and Transfer of Anti-personnel Mines and on their Destruction. The Convention entered into force on 1 March 1999. In April 1998 the Swiss Government established a Geneva International Centre for Humanitarian Demining, in co-operation with the UN and the ICRC, to co-ordinate the destruction of landmines world-wide. The ICRC was a principal advocate for the formulation of the Convention on Cluster Munitions, which was opened for signature in December 2008, and entered into force on 1 August 2010.

In 1995 the ICRC adopted a Plan of Action concerning Children in Armed Conflicts, to promote the principle of non-recruitment and non-participation in armed conflict of children under the age of 18 years. A co-ordinating group was established, with representatives of the individual National Societies and the International Federation of Red Cross and Red Crescent Societies. The ICRC participated in drafting the Optional Protocol to the Convention on the Rights of the Child, which was adopted by the UN General Assembly in May 2000 and entered into force in February 2002, raising from 15 to 18 years the minimum age for recruitment in armed conflict.

The ICRC's presence in the field is organized under the following three categories: responsive action, aimed at addressing the immediate effects of crises; remedial action, with an emphasis on rehabilitation; and environment-building activities, aimed at creating political, institutional, humanitarian and economic situations that are suitable for generating respect for human rights. ICRC operational delegations focus on responsive action and remedial action, while environment-building is undertaken by ICRC regional delegations. The regional delegations undertake humanitarian diplomacy efforts (e.g. networking, promoting IHL and distributing information), logistical support to operational delegations, and their own operations; they also have an early warning function, alerting the ICRC to developing conflict situations. The ICRC targets its activities at the following groups: 'victims', comprising civilians affected by violent crises, people deprived of their freedom, and the wounded and sick (whether civilians or weapon-bearers); and institutions and individuals with influence, i.e. national and local authorities, security forces, representatives of civil society, and ICRC National Societies. Children, women, internally displaced people and missing persons are of particular concern to the ICRC.

The ICRC's 'Family Links' internet pages (accessible at www.familylinks.icrc.org) aim to reunite family members separated by conflict or disaster situations. In February 2003 the ICRC launched 'The Missing', a major initiative that aimed to raise awareness of the issue of persons unaccounted for owing to armed conflict or internal violence. The ICRC assisted with the preparation of the International Convention for the Protection of all Persons from Enforced Disappearance, adopted by the UN General Assembly in December 2006, and representing the first international treaty to prohibit practices facilitating enforced disappearance. Meeting in November 2007 prior to the 30th International Conference, the Council of Delegates adopted the Restoring Family Links Strategy for the International Red Cross and Red Crescent Movement, covering the period 2008–18.

In 2007 the ICRC adopted a rapid deployment and response approach. During 2010 this was used to meet large-scale humanitarian requirements following the devastating earthquake that struck Haiti in January, and following the eruption in June of violent inter-ethnic unrest in Kyrgyzstan. In 2011 rapid deployment and response were deployed in Côte d'Ivoire, affected by serious unrest early in the year following a disputed presidential election result in November 2010, and also in Libya, where unrest and conflict also prevailed from early 2011, and where the ICRC had no previous operational framework.

During 2010 ICRC representatives visited some 500,928 prisoners (30,674 individually) held in 1,783 places of detention in 71 countries world-wide. A total of 160,338 messages were collected from and 145,114 distributed to family members separated by conflict; and 12,795 phone calls were facilitated between family members. Some 3,822 individuals who were the subject of other tracing requests were located; 1,983 unaccompanied minors and separated children were reunited with their families; and some 614 demobilized child soldiers were reunited with their families. Regular substantial assistance was provided to 294 hospitals, 351 health care facilities, and to 81 physical rehabilitation centres world-wide. Food was distributed by the ICRC in that year to more than 4.9m. beneficiaries and essential household and hygiene items to more than 4.7m. ICRC activities in the areas of water, sanitation and construction benefited some 10m. people and ICRC sustainable food production programmes and micro-economic initiatives supported more than 3.2m. people.

In 2012 the ICRC was actively concerned with around 80 conflicts and was undertaking major operations in (in order of budgetary priority): Afghanistan (provisionally allocated 88.9m. Swiss francs), Somalia (70.2m.), Iraq (67.3m.), Pakistan (66.2m.), the Democratic Republic of the Congo (54.1m.), Sudan (54.6m.), Israel and the Palestinian territories (52.6m.), Yemen (37.6m.), Colombia (33.1m.), and South Sudan (which attained independence in July 2011) (25.0m.).

In 2011 around 1,780 ICRC personnel were deployed in Afghanistan. Activities included protecting detainees and enabling them to maintain contact with their families; monitoring the conduct of hostilities and supporting the implementation of IHL; assisting the disabled and wounded; supporting the provision of hospital care; improving water and sanitation services; and building the capacity of the Afghan Red Crescent Society. From October 2010 Somalia was affected by severe drought, prompting the ICRC, working with the Somali Red Crescent Society (SCRS), to provide food assistance to more than 800,000 people. During June–October 2011 the ICRC and SCRS launched 11 new outpatient therapeutic feeding programmes and nine mobile health teams; the ICRC also delivered water to 11 drought-affected areas of Somalia, benefiting up to 700,000 persons and their livestock, as well as renovating 46 water supply infrastructures, with a view to improving groundwater sources and surface water storage facilities. During 2011 the ICRC also distributed essential household items to more than 260,000 new Somali IDPs, displaced by conflict, and provided seeds and tools to nearly 100,000 farmers, with the aim of boosting food production.

In April 2009 the ICRC and IFRC launched a joint website, www.ourworld-yourmove.org, which aimed to highlight ongoing humanitarian crises.

THE GENEVA CONVENTIONS

Since its inception the ICRC has been a leader in the process of improving and complementing IHL. In 1864, one year after its foundation, the ICRC submitted to the states called to a Diplomatic Conference in Geneva a draft international treaty for 'the Amelioration of the Condition of the Wounded in Armies in the Field'. This treaty was adopted and signed by 12 states, which thereby bound themselves to respect as neutral wounded soldiers and those assisting them. This was the first Geneva Convention.

With the development of technology and weapons, the introduction of new means of waging war, and the manifestation of certain phenomena (the great number of prisoners of war during World War I; the enormous number of displaced persons and refugees during World War II; the internationalization of internal conflicts in recent years), it was considered necessary to develop other international treaties to protect new categories of war victims.

There are now four Geneva Conventions, adopted on 12 August 1949: I—to protect wounded and sick in armed forces on land, as well as medical personnel; II—to protect the same categories of people at sea, as well as the shipwrecked; III—concerning the treatment of prisoners of war; IV—for the protection of civilians in time of war. Two Additional Protocols were adopted on 8 June 1977, for the protection of victims in international armed conflicts (Protocol I) and in non-international armed conflicts (Protocol II). A Third Additional Protocol (Protocol III), endorsing the red crystal as an additional emblem of the Movement, was adopted on 8 December 2005 and entered into force on 14 January 2007.

By June 2012 194 states were parties to the Geneva Conventions; 171 were parties to Protocol I, 166 to Protocol II and 59 to Protocol III.

Finance

The ICRC's work is financed by a voluntary annual grant from governments parties to the Geneva Conventions, the European Commission, voluntary contributions from National Red Cross and Red Crescent Societies and by gifts and legacies from private donors. The ICRC's provisional budget for 2012 allocated

180.8m. Swiss francs to headquarters, and 969.5m. Swiss francs to field operations.

In October 2005, as part of a long-term strategy to diversify funding sources, the ICRC launched a Corporate Support Group in partnership with seven Swiss-based companies, which had been selected in accordance with ethical guidelines based on ICRC's mandate and on the principles and statutes of the International Red Cross and Red Crescent Movement. Contributions from Corporate Support Group Partners is used to fund both staff training and operational activities.

Publications

Annual Report (editions in English, French and Spanish).

FORUM series.

The Geneva Conventions (texts and commentaries).

ICRC News (weekly, English, French, German and Spanish editions).

International Review of the Red Cross (quarterly in English and French; annually in Arabic, Russian and Spanish).

The Additional Protocols (texts and commentaries).

The Missing.

Various publications on subjects of Red Cross Red Crescent interest (medical studies, IHL, etc.), some in electronic form.

International Federation of Red Cross and Red Crescent Societies

Address: 17 chemin des Crêts, Petit-Saconnex, CP 372, 1211 Geneva 19, Switzerland.

Telephone: 227304222; **fax:** 227330395; **e-mail:** secretariat@ifrc.org; **internet:** www.ifrc.org.

The Federation was founded in 1919 (as the League of Red Cross Societies). It works on the basis of the Principles of the Red Cross and Red Crescent Movement to inspire, facilitate and promote all forms of humanitarian activities by the National Societies, with a view to the prevention and alleviation of human suffering, and thereby contribute to the maintenance and promotion of peace in the world. The Federation acts as the official representative of its member societies in the field. The Federation maintains close relations with many inter-governmental organizations, the UN and its Specialized Agencies, and with non-governmental organizations. It has permanent observer status with the UN.

MEMBERS

National Red Cross and Red Crescent Societies in 187 countries, and Magen David Adom, Israel's equivalent of the Red Cross Society (at June 2012).

Organization

(June 2012)

GENERAL ASSEMBLY

The General Assembly is the highest authority of the Federation and meets every two years in commission sessions (for development, disaster relief, health and community services, and youth) and plenary sessions. It is composed of representatives from all National Societies that are members of the Federation.

GOVERNING BOARD

The Board (formerly the Executive Council) meets every six months and is composed of the President of the Federation, nine Vice-Presidents, representatives of 16 National Societies elected by the Assembly, and the Chairman of the Finance Commission. Its functions include the implementation of decisions of the General Assembly; it also has powers to act between meetings of the Assembly.

President: TADATERU KONOÉ (Japan).

ZONES

International Federation Africa Zone Office: 44 Wierda Rd, West Wierda Valley, 2196 Sandton, Johannesburg, South Africa; tel. (11) 303-9700; fax (11) 884-0230; Dir ALASAN SENGHORE (Gambia).

International Federation Americas Zone Office: Gaillard Ave, Bldg 806, Ciudad del Saber, Clayton, Panama City, Panama; Dir XAVIER CASTELLANOS (Ecuador).

International Federation Asia-Pacific Zone Office: The AmpWalk Suite, 9.06 (North Block), 218 Jalan Ampang, 50450 Kuala Lumpur, Malaysia; tel. (39) 207–5700; fax (32) 161-0670; Dir JAGAN CHAPAGAIN (Nepal).

International Federation Middle East and North Africa Zone Office: c/o Al Shmeisani, Maroof Al Rasafi St, Bldg 19, Amman, Jordan; tel. (6) 5681060; fax (6) 5694556; Dir ABDEL KARIM BENSIALI (Algeria).

International Federation Europe Zone Office: Berkenye u. 13–15, 1025 Budapest, Hungary; tel. (1) 888-4500; fax (1) 336-1516; Dir ANITTA UNDERLIN (Denmark).

GLOBAL SENIOR MANAGEMENT TEAM

Under the Federation's guiding Strategy 2020, adopted in 2009, responsibility for operational and routine decision-making was transferred in 2010 to the Directors of the Zone offices (established in that year). The Zone Directors were appointed to the newly-established Global Senior Management Team, which also comprises the Secretary-General and Under-Secretaries-General for: Governance and Management Services; Humanitarian Values and Diplomacy; and Programme Services.

COMMISSIONS

Development Commission;

Disaster Relief Commission;

Finance Commission;

Health and Community Services Commission;

Youth Commission.

The Commissions meet, in principle, twice a year, before the Governing Board meeting. Members are elected by the Assembly under a system that ensures each Society a seat on one Commission.

SECRETARIAT

The Secretariat assumes the statutory responsibilities of the Federation in the field of relief to victims of natural disasters, refugees and civilian populations who may be displaced or exposed to abnormal hardship. In addition, the Secretariat promotes and co-ordinates assistance to National Societies in developing their basic structure and their services to the community. Under the Federation's Strategy 2020 a new business model was adopted for the Secretariat, with the following five business lines: raising humanitarian standards; improving services for vulnerable people; advancing sustainable development; enhancing the Federation's influence and support for its activities; and deepening the tradition of 'togetherness'.

Four Business Groups were established, on: Programme Services, National Society and Knowledge Development, Governance and Management; Humanitarian Values and Diplomacy; Programme Services; and National Society and Knowledge Development. The Secretary-General nominates honorary and special envoys for specific situations.

Secretary-General: BEKELE GELETA (Canada and Ethiopia).

Activities

In November 2005 the Assembly adopted a Global Agenda, comprising the following objectives which aimed to contribute to the attainment of the UN Millennium Development Goals: to reduce the deaths, injuries and impact of disasters on peoples' lives; to improve methods of dealing with public health crises; to combat intolerance and discrimination; and to build Red Cross and Red Crescent capacity at the community level to prepare for and cope with threats to lives and livelihoods.

In April 2008, in response to rapidly increasing food prices world-wide, the Federation launched a new five-year community-based food security initiative in 15 countries in Africa, with the aim of fostering resilience to fluctuating food prices by supporting local agriculture projects in the areas of microfinance, sustainable farming, small-scale irrigation and the development of food security early alert systems. Addressing the Group of Eight summit of industrialized nations in July, the Federation's Secretary-General urged participating states to support such long-term community-based food insecurity prevention programmes, stating that the ongoing food crisis represented a long-term phenomenon.

In November 2009, following extensive consultation within the Movement, the Assembly adopted Strategy 2020, outlining the Federation's objectives and strategies for the next 10 years, and replacing the previous Strategy 2010 (adopted in 1999). Strategy 2020 focused on a common vision (inspiring, encouraging, facilitating and promoting at all times all forms of humanitarian activities by national societies, with a view to preventing and alleviating suffering and thereby promoting dignity and world peace), and detailed three strategic aims for the Federation and its member national societies: saving lives, protecting livelihoods, and strengthening recovery from disasters and crises; enabling healthy and safe living; and promoting social inclusion and a culture of non-violence and peace. These were to be delivered through three enabling actions: building strong national Red Cross and Red Crescent societies; pursuing humanitarian diplomacy to prevent and reduce vulnerability in a globalized world; and functioning effectively as the International Federation (entailing the decentralization of authority to offices representing five geographical 'Zones').

DISASTER RESPONSE

The Federation supports the establishment of emergency response units, which aim to act effectively and independently to meet the needs of victims of natural or man-made disasters. The units cover basic health care provision, referral hospitals, water sanitation, logistics, telecommunications and information units. The Federation advises National Societies in relief health. A Disaster Relief Emergency Fund (DREF) was established in 1985 to ensure the availability of immediate financial support for emergency response actions. In 2012 DREF's budget totalled 18m. Swiss francs. In the event of a disaster the following areas are covered: communicable disease alleviation and vaccination; psychological support and stress management; health education; the provision of medicines; and the organization of mobile clinics and nursing care. The Societies also distribute food and clothing to those in need and assist in the provision of shelter and adequate sanitation facilities and in the management of refugee camps. The 2005 Global Agenda provided for a significant increase in Federation activities, in particular in the provision of emergency shelter, following natural disasters.

During 2005 the UN's Inter-Agency Standing Committee (IASC), concerned with co-ordinating the international response to humanitarian disasters, developed a concept of organizing agency assistance to IDPs through the institutionalization of a 'Cluster Approach', comprising nine core areas of activity. The Federation was designated the lead agency for the Emergency Protection (in natural disasters) cluster.

DEVELOPMENT

The Federation undertakes capacity-building activities with the National Societies to train and develop staff and volunteers and to improve management structures and processes, in particular in the area of disaster-preparedness. Blood donor programmes are often undertaken by National Societies, sometimes in conjunction with the World Health Organization. The Federation supports the promotion of these programmes and the implementation of quality standards. Other activities in the health sector aim to strengthen existing health services and promote community-based health care and first aid; the prevention of HIV/AIDS and substance abuse; and health education and family planning initiatives. The Federation also promotes the establishment and development of education and service programmes for children and for other more vulnerable members of society, including the elderly and disabled. Education projects support the promotion of humanitarian values.

Finance

The permanent Secretariat of the Federation is financed by the contributions of member Societies on a pro-rata basis. Each relief action is financed by separate, voluntary contributions, and development programme projects are also financed on a voluntary basis.

Publications

Annual Report.

Handbook of the International Red Cross and Red Crescent Movement (with the ICRC).

Red Cross Red Crescent Magazine (quarterly, in English, French and Spanish).

Weekly News.

World Disasters Report (annually).

Newsletters on several topics; various guides and manuals for Red Cross and Red Crescent activities.

Summary of the Four Geneva Conventions

The four Geneva Conventions summarized below were adopted on 12 August 1949 by the Diplomatic Conference for the Establishment of International Conventions for the Protection of Victims of War, convened in Geneva, Switzerland, from 21 April–12 August 1949. The Conventions entered into force on 21 October 1950. Some of the text is common to all four Conventions, notably that dealing with the following: the circumstances in which the Conventions are to be applied (Articles 1–3 of the First Convention); scrutiny of how the Conventions are applied (Articles 8–11 of the First Convention); making the Conventions widely known and enforcing penal sanctions for any breach (Articles 47–53 of the First Convention).

First Geneva Convention

(The Geneva Convention for the Amelioration of the Condition of the Wounded and Sick in Armed Forces in the Field)

CHAPTER I: GENERAL PROVISIONS

Articles 1–3

1. Persons taking no active part in the hostilities, including members of armed forces who have laid down their arms and those placed hors de combat by sickness, wounds, detention or

any other cause, shall in all circumstances be treated humanely, without any adverse distinction founded on race, colour, religion or faith, sex, birth or wealth. The following acts are prohibited at any time and in any place whatsoever with respect to the above mentioned persons: violence to life and person, in particular murder, mutilation, cruel treatment and torture; taking of hostages; outrages upon personal dignity, in particular humiliating and degrading treatment; the passing of sentences and the carrying out of executions without previous judgment pronounced by a regularly constituted court, affording all the judicial guarantees which are recognized as indispensable by civilized peoples.

2. The wounded and sick shall be collected and cared for.

Articles 4–7

Neutral Powers shall apply the provisions of the Convention to the wounded and sick, medical personnel and chaplains of the armed forces of the Parties to the conflict, received or interned in their territory, as well as to dead persons found. For the protected persons who have fallen into the hands of the enemy, the present Convention shall apply until their final repatriation.

Articles 8–11

The present Convention shall be applied with the cooperation and under the scrutiny of the Protecting Powers whose duty it is to safeguard the interests of the Parties to the conflict. For this purpose the Protecting Powers may appoint, apart from their diplomatic or consular staff, delegates from among their own nationals or the nationals of other neutral Powers. The provisions of the Convention constitute no obstacle to the humanitarian activities of the International Committee of the Red Cross (ICRC) or any other impartial humanitarian organization. The Detaining Power may request that a neutral state or a humanitarian organization, such as the ICRC, undertake the functions of a Protecting Power. Where there is disagreement between the Parties to the conflict as to the application of the Convention, the Protecting Powers shall assist in settling the disagreement.

CHAPTER II: WOUNDED AND SICK

Articles 12–13

Members of the armed forces and other persons mentioned below, who are wounded or sick, shall be respected and protected in all circumstances. They shall be treated humanely and cared for by the Party to the conflict in whose power they may be, without any adverse distinction founded on sex, race, nationality, religion, political opinions, or any other similar criteria. Any attempts upon their lives, or violence to their persons, shall be strictly prohibited: they shall not be murdered or exterminated, subjected to torture or to biological experiments; they shall not wilfully be left without medical assistance and care, nor shall conditions exposing them to contagion or infection be created. Only urgent medical reasons will authorize priority in the order of treatment to be administered. Women shall be treated with all consideration due to their sex. The Convention applies to the wounded and sick of members of the armed forces of a Party to the conflict, including militias and volunteer corps; members of other militias and volunteer corps, including organized resistance movements; members of regular armed forces who profess allegiance to a government not recognized by the Detaining Power; authorized persons who accompany the armed forces (e.g. civil members of military air crews, war correspondents, supply contractors, and members of labour units and welfare services); members of the merchant marine and crews of civil aircraft; and inhabitants of a non-occupied territory who take arms to resist invading forces.

Articles 14–18

The wounded and sick of a belligerent who fall into enemy hands shall be prisoners of war and the provisions of international law concerning prisoners of war shall apply to them. Parties to the conflict shall take all possible measures to search for and collect the wounded and sick, to protect them against pillage and ill-treatment, to ensure their adequate care, and to search for the dead and prevent their being despoiled. When possible a suspension of fire shall be arranged to permit the removal, exchange and transport of the wounded left on the battlefield, or from a besieged or encircled area. Parties to the conflict shall record the particulars of each wounded, sick or dead person of the adverse Party falling into their hands and forward the information to the Information Bureau for prisoners of war (established under the Third Convention: see below); this information is to include certificates of death or authenticated lists of the dead. Documents or articles of importance to the next of kin shall be collected and forwarded through the same Bureau. The dead are to be identified and honourably interred, and their graves marked and registered. The military authorities may appeal to the charity of the inhabitants voluntarily to collect and care for the wounded and sick. No-one may ever be molested or convicted for having nursed the wounded or sick.

CHAPTER III: MEDICAL UNITS AND ESTABLISHMENTS

Articles 19–21

Hospitals and mobile medical units may in no circumstances be attacked, but are to be respected and protected by the Parties to the conflict. If they fall into the hands of the adverse Party their personnel shall be free to pursue their duties. This protection shall not cease unless the hospitals or medical units are used to commit acts harmful to the enemy, and then only if due warning is given. Hospital zones may be established to protect the wounded and sick from the effects of war, and the Parties concerned may conclude agreements on mutual recognition of such zones. The Protecting Powers and the ICRC are invited to lend their good offices to facilitate the institution and recognition of hospital zones.

CHAPTER IV: PERSONNEL

Articles 24–32

Medical personnel exclusively engaged in the search for, or the collection, transport or treatment of the wounded or sick, or in the prevention of disease, administrative staff of medical units, and chaplains attached to the armed forces, shall be respected and protected in all circumstances; likewise the staff of National Red Cross Societies and of other authorized voluntary aid societies. If these personnel fall into the hands of the adverse Party they shall be retained only in so far as the health and spiritual needs of prisoners of war require: they shall not be deemed prisoners of war, and if not indispensable they shall be returned to the Party to the conflict to whom they belong, as soon as possible. Members of the armed forces specially trained as hospital orderlies, nurses or stretcher-bearers shall likewise be respected and protected if they are carrying out these duties when they come into contact with the enemy; if captured they shall be prisoners of war, but shall be employed on their medical duties as the need arises. Medical personnel from a neutral country may not be detained.

CHAPTER V: BUILDINGS AND MATERIAL

Articles 33–34

The material of mobile medical units of the armed forces which fall into the hands of the enemy shall be reserved for the care of the wounded and sick. The buildings, material and stores of fixed medical establishments of the armed forces may not be diverted from that purpose as long as they are required for the care of the wounded and sick, except in cases of urgent military necessity, when other arrangements must first be made for the welfare of the patients. The material and stores defined above shall not be intentionally destroyed. The right of requisition recognized for belligerents by the laws and customs of war shall not be exercised except in case of urgent necessity, and only after the welfare of the wounded and sick has been ensured.

CHAPTER VI: MEDICAL TRANSPORTS

Articles 35–37

Transports of wounded and sick or of medical equipment shall be respected and protected. If captured, the care of the wounded and sick that they contain must be ensured. Medical aircraft (bearing agreed identifying marks and flying at agreed heights, times and routes) shall not be attacked, but respected by the belligerents. Unless agreed otherwise, flights over enemy or enemy-occupied territory are prohibited. Such aircraft may fly over or land on the territory of neutral Powers, by agreement with the latter. Unless agreed otherwise between the neutral Power and the Parties to the conflict, the wounded and sick who are disembarked on neutral territory shall be detained by the neutral Power, where so required by international law, in such a manner that they cannot again take part in operations of war.

CHAPTER VII: THE DISTINCTIVE EMBLEM

Articles 38–44

As a compliment to Switzerland, the heraldic emblem of the red cross on a white ground (formed by reversing the Federal colours of Switzerland) is retained as the emblem and distinctive sign of the Medical Service of armed forces. The red crescent or the red lion and sun on a white ground are also recognized by the Convention. The emblem is to be used on flags, armlets and identity cards. The distinctive flag shall be hoisted only over such medical units as are entitled to be respected under the convention, and only with the consent of the military authorities.

CHAPTER VIII: EXECUTION OF THE CONVENTION

Articles 45–48

Each Party to the conflict, acting through its commander-in-chief, shall ensure the detailed execution of the preceding Articles. The High Contracting Parties undertake, in time of peace as in war, to disseminate the text of the Convention as widely as possible and to encourage the study of the text in programmes of military and civil instruction, so that the principles thereof may become known to the entire population, in particular to the armed fighting forces, the medical personnel and the chaplains.

CHAPTER IX: REPRESSION OF ABUSES AND INFRACTIONS

Articles 49–54

The High Contracting Parties undertake to enact any legislation necessary to provide effective penal sanctions for persons committing, or ordering to be committed, grave breaches of the Convention. Each High Contracting Party shall be under the obligation to search for these persons and shall bring them, regardless of their nationality, before its own courts, or hand them over to another High Contracting Party for trial. In all circumstances, the accused persons shall benefit by safeguards of proper trial and defence. Grave breaches comprise any of the following acts, if committed against persons or property protected by the Convention: wilful killing, torture or inhuman treatment, including biological experiments, wilfully causing great suffering or serious injury to body or health, and extensive destruction and appropriation of property, not justified by military necessity and carried out unlawfully and wantonly. At the request of a Party to the conflict, an enquiry shall be instituted, in a manner to be decided between the interested Parties, concerning any alleged violation of the Convention: once the violation has been established, the Parties to the conflict shall repress it with the least possible delay. The unauthorized use of the emblem or designation 'Red Cross' or 'Geneva Cross' or any imitation thereof, shall be prohibited.

FINAL PROVISIONS

Articles 55–64

These Articles concern details of the translation, signature and ratification of the Convention. Article 63 states that each of the High Contracting Parties shall be at liberty to denounce the present Convention: the denunciation shall be notified in writing to the Swiss Federal Council, which shall then transmit it to the Governments of all the High Contracting Parties, and it shall take effect one year after the notification. If the denouncing Power is involved in a conflict, the denunciation shall not take effect until peace has been concluded, and until after operations connected with the release and repatriation of persons protected by the Convention have been terminated.

ANNEXES

Annex I is a draft agreement relating to the establishment of hospital zones (as mentioned in Article 23, above). Annex II concerns the suggested wording of an identity card for medical and religious personnel attached to the armed forces.

Second Geneva Convention

(The Geneva Convention for the Amelioration of the Condition of Wounded, Sick and Shipwrecked Members of Armed Forces at Sea)

The text of this Convention is largely identical to that of the First Geneva Convention, except where it specifically refers to those involved in war at sea.

Article 4

In case of hostilities between land and naval forces of Parties to the conflict, the provisions of the present Convention shall apply only on board ship. Forces put ashore shall immediately become subject to the provisions of the First Geneva Convention.

Article 12

Members of the armed forces and other persons in the categories specified in Article 13 of the First Geneva convention (above), who are at sea and who are wounded, sick or shipwrecked, shall be respected and protected in all circumstances, it being understood that the term 'shipwreck' means shipwreck from any cause and includes forced landings at sea by or from aircraft.

Articles 14–16

All warships of a belligerent Party shall have the right to demand that the wounded, sick or shipwrecked on board military and other hospital ships shall be surrendered, provided that the wounded and sick are in a fit state to be moved, and that the warship can provide adequate facilities. If wounded, sick or shipwrecked persons are taken on board a neutral warship or neutral military aircraft, it shall be ensured, where so required by international law, that they can take no further part in operations of war. The wounded, sick and shipwrecked of a belligerent who fall into enemy hands shall be prisoners of war. The captor may decide whether it is expedient to hold them or to convey them to a port in the captor's own country, to a neutral port or even to a port in enemy territory. In the last case prisoners of war thus returned to their home country may not serve for the duration of the war.

Articles 22–35

Military hospital ships, that is ships built or equipped solely with a view to assisting the wounded, sick or shipwrecked, may not be attacked or captured, but shall be respected and protected, on condition that their names and descriptions have been notified to the Parties to the conflict ten days before the ships are employed. This also applies to hospital ships used by National Red Cross Societies and by authorized relief organizations belonging to a Party to the conflict or to a neutral country. Small craft used for coastal rescue operations shall also be respected and protected. The vessels described above shall afford relief and assistance to the wounded, sick and shipwrecked, without distinction of nationality. The High Contracting Parties undertake not to use these vessels for any military purpose. The Parties to the conflict shall have the right to control and search these vessels. The protection to which hospital ships are entitled shall not cease unless they are used to commit acts harmful to the enemy, and then only after due warning has been given. Hospital ships may not use a secret code for their wireless or other means of communication.

Article 36

The religious, medical and hospital personnel of hospital ships and their crews shall be respected and protected; they may not be captured during the time they are in the service of the ship, whether or not there are wounded and sick on board.

Article 38

Ships chartered for the purpose shall be authorized to transport equipment exclusively intended for the treatment of wounded and sick members of armed forces or for the prevention of disease, provided that the particulars of their voyage have been notified to and approved by the adverse Power.

Article 43

Hospital ships shall be distinctively marked: all exterior surfaces shall be white, and dark red crosses, as large as possible, shall be painted on each side of the hull and on the horizontal surfaces, so as to afford the greatest possible visibility from the sea and the air. A white flag with a red cross shall be flown from the mainmast. Coastal lifeboats and all small craft used by the Medical Service shall be similarly marked. These signs may only be used for indicating or protecting the vessels mentioned above, and the High Contracting Parties shall take the necessary measures to prevent abuse of the distinctive signs.

Third Geneva Convention

(The Geneva Convention relative to the Treatment of Prisoners of War)

PART I: GENERAL PROVISIONS

Articles 1–11

The text of the first three Articles is the same as that in Articles 1–3 of the First Geneva Convention. Article 4 defines prisoners of war (PoWs) by the same criteria as those defining persons covered by the First Geneva Convention (Article 13 of the First Convention). It adds that the following shall likewise be treated as PoWs: persons belonging, or having belonged, to the armed forces of the occupied country if the occupying Power considers it necessary to intern them; and persons belonging to one of the above categories who have been received by neutral or non-belligerent Powers on their territory and whom these Powers are required to intern under international law. Articles 8–11 provide for the scrutiny of the application of the Convention, as in Articles 8–11 of the First Geneva Convention.

PART II: GENERAL PROTECTION OF PRISONERS OF WAR

Articles 12–16

Prisoners of war are in the hands of the enemy Power, but not of the individuals or military units who have captured them. The detaining Power is responsible for the treatment given them. PoWs must at all times be humanely treated. No PoW may be subjected to physical mutilation, or to medical or scientific experiments of any kind. PoWs must at all times be protected, particularly against acts of violence or intimidation, and against insults and public curiosity. Measures of reprisal against PoWs are prohibited. PoWs are entitled to respect for their persons and their honour. Women shall be treated with all the regard due to their sex, and shall benefit by treatment as favourable as that granted to men. PoWs shall retain the full civil capacity which they enjoyed at the time of their capture. The Power detaining PoWs shall be bound to provide free of charge for their maintenance and for medical attention. All PoWs shall be treated alike, without any adverse distinction based on race, nationality, religious belief or political opinions.

PART III: CAPTIVITY

Section I: Beginning of Captivity

Articles 17–20

When questioned, a PoW is bound to give only his surname, first name, rank, date of birth, and army, regimental, personal or serial number, or equivalent information. No physical or mental torture, nor any other form of coercion, may be inflicted on PoWs to secure information from them. PoWs who refuse to answer may not be threatened, insulted or exposed to disadvantageous treatment. PoWs may keep their personal possessions, except for weapons, military equipment and military documents. PoWs shall be evacuated, as soon as possible after their capture, to camps in an area far enough from the combat zone for them to be out of danger. Evacuation of PoWs shall be effected humanely and in conditions similar to those for the forces of the Detaining Power in their changes of station: the PoWs must be supplied with the necessary food, water, clothing and medical attention, and any stay in transit camps shall be as brief as possible.

Section II: Internment of Prisoners of War

Chapter I: General Observations

Articles 21–24

The Detaining Power may subject PoWs to internment. It may impose on them the obligation of not leaving, beyond certain limits, the camp where they are interned, or if the camp is fenced in, of not going outside its perimeter. PoWs may not be held in close confinement, except under penal and disciplinary sanctions or where necessary to safeguard their health. PoWs may be partially or wholly released on parole or promise. They may be interned only in premises located on land and affording every guarantee of hygiene and healthfulness, and shall be assembled according to their nationality, language and customs. No PoW may be detained in areas where he may be exposed to the fire of the combat zone, nor may his presence be used to render certain areas immune from military operations. PoWs shall have shelters against air bombardment and other hazards of war, to the same extent as the local civilian population. PoW camps shall be indicated in the daytime by the letters PW or PG, or other agreed markings, clearly visible from the air.

Chapter II: Quarters, Food and Clothing

Articles 25–28

PoWs shall be quartered under conditions as favourable as those for the forces of the Detaining Power who are billeted in the same area, particularly as regards dormitory space and installations. Premises shall be adequately heated and lighted, and protected against damp and the danger of fire. Separate dormitories shall be provided for women PoWs. Daily food rations must be sufficient to ensure good health, and sufficient drinking water, clothing and footwear must be provided. Canteens shall be installed in all camps, where PoWs may procure food, soap, tobacco and ordinary articles in daily use, at a tariff not in excess of local market prices.

Chapter III: Hygiene and Medical Attention

Articles 29–32

The Detaining Power shall be bound to take all sanitary measures necessary to ensure the cleanliness and healthfulness of camps and to prevent epidemics. Hygienic conveniences and washing facilities shall be provided and kept clean, with separate facilities for women PoWs. Every camp shall have an adequate infirmary where PoWs may have the attention they require. Medical inspections of PoWs shall be held at least once a month.

Chapter IV: Medical Personnel and Chaplains retained to assist Prisoners of War

Article 33

Medical personnel and chaplains retained by the Detaining Power to assist PoWs shall not be considered as PoWs. They shall receive as a minimum all the benefits and protection of the present Convention, and be granted all facilities necessary for medical care of and religious ministration to PoWs. The senior medical officer in each camp shall be responsible to the camp military authorities for everything connected with the activities of retained medical personnel. Although they shall be subject to the internal discipline of the camp in which they are retained, such personnel may not be compelled to carry out any work other than that concerned with their medical or religious duties.

Chapter V: Religious, Intellectual and Physical Activities

Articles 34–38

PoWs shall enjoy complete latitude in the exercise of their religious duties. Chaplains who fall into the hands of the enemy Power and who remain or are retained with a view to assisting PoWs, shall be allowed to minister to them. PoWs who are ministers of religion shall be at liberty to minister freely to the members of their community. The Detaining Power shall encourage the practice of intellectual, educational and recreational pursuits, sports and games among prisoners, and shall provide adequate premises and equipment. Prisoners shall have opportunities for taking physical exercise. Sufficient open spaces shall be provided for this purpose.

Chapter VI: Discipline

Articles 43–45

Every PoW camp shall be put under the immediate authority of a responsible commissioned officer of the regular armed forces of the Detaining Power, who shall possess a copy of the Convention and ensure that its provisions are known to the camp staff and the guard, and shall be responsible, under the direction of his government, for its application. In every camp the text of the Convention shall be available to prisoners in their own language. Regulations, orders, notices and publications relating to the conduct of PoWs shall be issued in a language that they can understand. The use of weapons against PoWs, especially against those who are attempting to escape, shall constitute an extreme measure, which shall always be preceded by appropriate warnings.

Chapter VII: Rank of Prisoners of War

Articles 43–45

The Parties to the conflict shall communicate to one another the titles and ranks of all the persons qualifying as PoWs, in order to ensure equality of treatment between prisoners of equivalent rank. Officers and prisoners of equivalent status shall be treated with the regard due to their rank and age. In order to ensure service in officers' camps, other ranks of the same armed forces shall be assigned as orderlies. Supervision of the mess by the officers themselves shall be facilitated in every way. PoWs other than officers and prisoners of equivalent status shall be treated with the regard due to their rank and age. Supervision of the mess by the prisoners themselves shall be facilitated in every way.

Chapter VIII: Transfer of Prisoners of War after their Arrival in Camp

Articles 46–48

The Detaining Power, when deciding upon the transfer of PoWs, shall take into account the interests of the prisoners themselves, more especially so as not to increase the difficulty of their repatriation. The transfer of PoWs shall always be effected humanely and in conditions not less favourable than those under which the forces of the Detaining Power are transferred. Sick or wounded PoWs shall not be transferred as long as their recovery may be endangered by the journey, unless their safety imperatively demands it. Prisoners may take their personal effects with them, and inform their next of kin of their new postal address.

Section III: Labour of Prisoners of War

Articles 49–57

The Detaining Power may utilize the labour of PoWs who are physically fit, taking into account their age, sex, rank and physical aptitude, and with a view to maintaining them in good health. Non-commissioned officers shall only be required to do supervisory work. If officers or persons of equivalent status ask for suitable work, it shall be found for them, so far as possible, but they may not be compelled to work. Apart from camp administration and maintenance, PoWs may be compelled to do only such work as is included in the following classes: agriculture; industries connected with the production or extraction of raw materials, and manufacturing, with the exception of metallurgical, machinery and chemical industries; public works and building operations which have no military character or purpose; transport and handling of non-military stores; commercial business; arts and crafts; domestic service; non-military public utility services. PoWs must be granted suitable working conditions, regulations, training and protection similar to those of the nationals of the Detaining Power. No PoW may be employed, except as a volunteer, in labour which is unhealthy, dangerous (including the removal of mines) or humiliating. Working hours and rest periods are to be similar to those permitted for local civilian nationals of the Detaining Power, who are employed in the same work. The fitness of PoWs for work shall be periodically verified by medical examinations. The organization of labour detachments shall be similar to that of PoW camps, and every labour detachment shall remain administratively part of a PoW camp, whose commander is responsible for them.

Section IV: Financial Resources of Prisoners of War

Articles 58–68

The Detaining Power may determine the maximum amount of money that prisoners may have in their possession. Any amount in excess shall be placed to their separate accounts. The Detaining Power shall grant all PoWs a monthly advance of pay, according to rank. They shall be paid a fair working rate of pay by the detaining authorities direct. PoWs shall be permitted to receive remittances of money addressed to them individually or collectively. The Detaining Power shall hold an account for each PoW, and on the termination of captivity he shall be given a statement showing the credit balance due to him. Advances of pay are considered as made on behalf of the Power on which the PoW depends, and shall form the subject of arrangements between the Powers concerned, at the close of hostilities.

Section V: Relations of Prisoners of War with the Exterior

Articles 69–77

Immediately upon capture, or not more than one week after arrival at a camp, every PoW shall be enabled to write directly to his family and to the Central Prisoners of War Information Agency (see Article 123, below), informing them of his capture, address and state of health. PoWs shall be allowed to send and receive letters, subject to censorship. They may receive parcels and relief shipments. If military operations prevent the transport of mail, the ICRC or any other approved organization may undertake the conveyance of it.

Section VI: Relations between Prisoners of War and the Authorities

Chapter I: Complaints of Prisoners respecting the Conditions of Captivity

Article 78

PoWs shall have the right to make requests to the military authorities in whose power they are, regarding their conditions of captivity, and have the unrestricted right to apply to the representatives of the Protecting Powers, either directly or through their prisoners' representative, to make a complaint regarding their conditions of captivity. Even if the requests or complaints are recognized to be unfounded, they may not give rise to any punishment.

Chapter II: Prisoners' Representatives

Articles 79–81

In all places where there are PoWs, except in those where there are officers, the prisoners shall freely elect by secret ballot, every six months, prisoners' representatives entrusted with representing them before the military authorities, the Protecting Powers, the ICRC and any other organization which may assist them, and with furthering the well-being of the PoWs. In camps for officers or mixed camps, the senior officer present acts as the prisoners' representative. The prisoners' representative must have the same nationality, language and customs as those he represents.

Chapter III: Penal and Disciplinary Sanctions

Articles 82–98

A PoW shall be subject to the laws, regulations and orders in force in the armed forces of the Detaining Power, and the Detaining Power may take judicial or disciplinary measures in respect of any offence. A PoW shall be tried only by a military court, unless a member of the armed forces of the Detaining Power would be tried in a civil court for the same offence. The court must guarantee independence and impartiality. PoWs may not be sentenced to any penalties except those provided for in respect of members of the armed forces of the Detaining Power who have committed the same acts. Collective punishment for individual acts, corporal punishment, imprisonment in premises without daylight, and any form of torture or cruelty, are forbidden. No PoW may be deprived of his rank by the Detaining Power. Disciplinary punishments comprise: a fine; discontinuance of privileges; fatigue duties (not for officers); or confinement; they may not be inhuman, brutal or dangerous to the prisoner's health. The duration of any single punishment shall not exceed 30 days. PoWs who have successfully escaped and are recaptured shall not be liable to any punishment. PoWs who are caught attempting to escape shall be liable only to a disciplinary punishment, even if it is a repeated offence, but may be subjected to special surveillance.

Articles 99–108

With regard to judicial proceedings, no PoW may be tried or sentenced for an act which is not forbidden by the law of the Detaining Power or by international law, in force at the time when the act was committed. No coercion may be exerted on a PoW to induce him to admit guilt, and no PoW may be convicted without an opportunity to present his defence and the assistance of a qualified advocate. If the Detaining Power has decided to institute judicial proceedings against a PoW, it shall notify the Protecting Power as soon as possible, and at least three weeks before the opening of the trial. Any judgment and sentence pronounced upon a PoW shall be immediately reported to the Protecting Power. If the death penalty is pronounced, the sentence shall not be executed until at least six months after the Protecting Power has received notification. Sentences shall be served in the same establishments and under the same conditions as in the case of the armed forces of the Detaining Power; these conditions shall conform to the requirements of health and humanity. A woman PoW on whom such a sentence has been pronounced shall be confined separately and under the supervision of women.

PART IV: TERMINATION OF CAPTIVITY

Section I: Direct Repatriation and Accommodation in Neutral Countries

Articles 109–117

Parties to the conflict are bound to send back to their own country PoWs who are seriously wounded or seriously ill, if fit for travel. The wounded and sick may be accommodated in a neutral country if this is likely to increase their prospects of recovery. Mixed Medical Commissions (see Annex II, below) shall be appointed to make decisions concerning sick and wounded PoWs. No repatriated person may be employed on active military service.

Section II: Release and Repatriation at the Close of Hostilities

Articles 118–119

PoWs shall be released and repatriated without delay after the cessation of active hostilities. The costs of repatriation shall be equitably shared between the Detaining Power and the Power on which the prisoners depend. Repatriation shall be effected in conditions similar to those laid down for the transfer of PoWs (Articles 46–48, above). Articles of value and foreign currency shall be restored to them, and they may take their personal effects with them, or these may be forwarded by the Detaining Power.

PoWs against whom criminal proceedings are pending may be detained until the end of the proceedings and the completion of the punishment; the same shall apply to prisoners already convicted of an indictable offence.

Section III: Death of Prisoners of War

Articles 120–121

Wills of PoWs shall be drawn up in accordance with the legislation of their countries of origin, and after death the will shall be transmitted to the Protecting Power. Death certificates and details of the place of burial of all persons who die as PoWs shall be forwarded to the PoW Information Bureau. The burial or cremation of a PoW shall be preceded by a medical examination and report. The detaining authorities shall ensure that PoWs are honourably buried, if possible according to the rites of their own religion, and their graves respected, maintained and marked, and the particulars recorded with a Graves Registration Service established by the Detaining Power.

PART V: INFORMATION BUREAUX AND RELIEF SOCIETIES FOR PRISONERS OF WAR

Articles 122–125

Upon the outbreak of a conflict and in all cases of occupation, each of the Parties to the conflict shall institute an official Information Bureau to receive information on PoWs and transmit it to their next of kin, to make enquiries concerning PoWs, and to collect and pass on the personal possessions of PoWs who have been repatriated, escaped or died. A Central Prisoner of War Information Agency shall be created in a neutral country, to collect and transmit information on PoWs. Subject to the measures which the Detaining Powers may consider essential to ensure their security, the representatives of religious organizations, relief societies or other organizations assisting PoWs shall receive facilities for visiting prisoners and distributing relief supplies. The special position of the ICRC in this field shall be recognized and respected at all times.

PART VI: EXECUTION OF THE CONVENTION

Articles 126–132

Representatives of the Protecting Powers shall have permission to go to all places where PoWs may be and interview the prisoners without witnesses. They shall have full liberty to select the places they wish to visit, and the duration and frequency of visits shall not be restricted. The delegates of the ICRC shall enjoy the same prerogatives. The text covering the widespread dissemination of the Convention and the undertaking by the High Contracting Parties to enact legislation that will provide effective penal sanctions for persons committing grave breaches of the Convention is largely identical with that of Articles 47–52 of the First Geneva Convention (see above): to the list of grave breaches included there, this section adds compelling a PoW to serve in the forces of the hostile Power and wilfully depriving a PoW of the rights of fair and regular trial.

Articles 133–143

This section concerns details of the translation, signature and ratification of the Convention, with provision for denunciation of the Convention by a High Contracting Party (as in Article 63 of the First Geneva Convention).

ANNEXES

Annex I is a model agreement concerning repatriation of wounded and sick PoWs, giving extensive medical criteria. Annex II gives regulations concerning the Mixed Medical Commissions provided for in Article 112: they are to comprise three members, two of whom, appointed by the ICRC, shall belong to a neutral country, while the third shall be appointed by the Detaining Power. Annex III comprises regulations concerning collective relief. Annex IV gives the wording of identity cards and other documents.

Fourth Geneva Convention

(The Geneva Convention relative to the Protection of Civilian Persons in Time of War)

PART I: GENERAL PROVISIONS

The text of the first three Articles is the same as that of Articles 1–3 in the First Geneva Convention (see above).

Articles 4–12

Persons protected by the Convention are those who find themselves, in case of a conflict or occupation, in the hands of a Party to the conflict or Occupying Power of which they are not nationals. Nationals of a state which is not bound by the Convention are not protected by it. Persons protected by the first three Conventions shall not be considered as protected persons within the meaning of the present Convention. In the territory of a Party to the conflict, an individual who is suspected of or engaged in activities hostile to the security of the State is not entitled to claim rights and privileges under the Convention that would be prejudicial to the security of the State. Where in occupied territory an individual protected person is detained as a spy or saboteur, he shall, where military security so requires, forfeit rights of communication under the Convention. Such persons shall be treated with humanity and not be deprived of the rights of fair and regular trial. In the territory of Parties to the conflict, the application of the Convention shall cease on the close of military operations, and in the case of occupied territory, one year afterwards. The text on provision for scrutiny of how the Convention is applied is similar to that in Articles 8–11 of the First Geneva Convention.

PART II: GENERAL PROTECTION OF POPULATIONS AGAINST CERTAIN CONSEQUENCES OF WAR

Articles 13–26

The provisions of Part II cover the whole of the populations of the countries in conflict, without any adverse distinction based on race, nationality, religion or political opinion, and are intended to alleviate the sufferings caused by war. Parties to a conflict may establish hospital and safety zones to protect from the effects of war wounded, sick and aged persons, children under 15, expectant mothers and mothers of children under seven. In the regions where fighting is taking place, the Parties may establish neutralized zones to shelter wounded and sick combatants and non-combatants, and civilians who take no part in hostilities and perform no work of a military character while residing in the zones. They shall endeavour to conclude local agreements for the removal of wounded, sick, infirm and aged persons, children and maternity cases, from besieged or encircled areas, and for the passage of ministers of religion and medical personnel and equipment to such areas. Civilian hospitals may not be the object of attack, unless they are used to commit acts harmful to the enemy, and then only after due warning has been given. Protection is given to medical personnel, convoys of vehicles, hospital trains, vessels and aircraft carrying wounded and sick civilians, and consignments of medical stores. Parties to the conflict shall ensure that children under 15 who are orphaned or separated from their families as a result of war are not left to their own resources, and that their maintenance, the exercise of their religion and their education are facilitated; the Parties shall facilitate the reception of such children in a neutral country for the duration of the conflict. All persons in the territory of a Party to the conflict, or in an occupied territory, shall be enabled to give personal news to members of their families, and to receive news from them, without undue delay. Each Party shall facilitate enquiries made by members of families dispersed owing to the war.

PART III: STATUS AND TREATMENT OF PROTECTED PERSONS

Section I: Provisions common to the Territories of the Parties to the Conflict and to Occupied Territories

Articles 27–34

Protected persons are entitled, in all circumstances, to respect for their persons, their honour, their family rights, their religious convictions and practices, and their manners and customs. They shall at all times be humanely treated, and protected against all acts of violence or threats thereof and against insults and public curiosity. Women shall especially be protected against any attack on their honour, in particular against rape, enforced prostitution, or any form of indecent assault. All protected persons shall be treated with the same consideration, regardless of race, religion or political opinion. The presence of a protected person may not be used to render certain points or areas immune from military operations. No physical or moral coercion shall be exercised against protected persons to obtain information from them or from third parties. No measure may be taken to cause the physical suffering or extermination of protected persons, through murder, torture, corporal punishment, mutilation and medical or scientific experiments not necessitated by medical treatment, or any other measures of brutality by civilian or military agents. No protected person may be punished for an offence he has not personally committed. Collective penalties and all measures of intimidation or of terrorism are prohibited, likewise pillage, reprisals and the taking of hostages.

Section II: Aliens in the Territory of a Party to the Conflict

Articles 35–46

All protected persons who desire to leave the territory at the outset of or during a conflict shall be entitled to do so, unless their departure is contrary to the national interest: their application to leave shall be decided in accordance with regularly established procedures, as rapidly as possible. They may take necessary funds and possessions. Departures shall be carried out in satisfactory conditions as regards safety, hygiene, sanitation and food. The situation of protected persons who are aliens shall continue to be regulated, in principle, by the provisions concerning aliens in time of peace. They are entitled to the same treatment as the nationals of the State concerned in receiving medical attention, being allowed to move away from dangerous areas, and receiving preferential treatment for children under 15 years, pregnant women and mothers of children under seven. Protected persons who, as a result of the war, have lost their gainful employment, shall be granted the opportunity to find paid employment, on an equal basis with the nationals of the Party to the conflict in whose territory they are. Where a Party to the conflict applies methods of control which prevent a protected person from supporting himself, the Party shall ensure his support and that of his dependants. Protected persons may be compelled to work only to the same extent as nationals of the Party to the conflict in whose territory they are, and shall have the benefit of the same working conditions and safeguards. The internment or placing in assigned residence of protected persons may be ordered only if the security of the Detaining Power makes it absolutely necessary. Any protected person who has been interned or placed in assigned residence shall be entitled to have this action reconsidered by an appropriate court or administrative board designated by the Detaining Power for that purpose. The Detaining Power shall as soon as possible give the Protecting Power the names of internees. The Detaining Power shall not treat refugees as enemy aliens exclusively on the basis of their being nationals de jure of an enemy state when, in fact, they do not enjoy the protection of any government. Protected persons may be transferred by the Detaining Power only to a Power which is a party to the Convention, and after the Detaining Power has satisfied itself of the willingness and ability of the transferee Power to apply the Convention. In no circumstances shall a protected person be transferred to a country where he may have reason to fear persecution for political opinions or religious beliefs. These provisions do not constitute an obstacle to the extradition of protected persons accused of offences against ordinary criminal law. Restrictive measures regarding protected persons and their property shall be cancelled as soon as possible after the close of hostilities.

Section III: Occupied Territories

Articles 47–50

Protected persons who are in occupied territory shall not be deprived of the benefits of the Convention by any change introduced, as a result of the occupation, into the institutions or government of the territory. Protected persons who are not nationals of the Power whose territory is occupied may leave the territory (subject to the provisions of Article 35: see above). Individual or mass forcible transfers and deportations are prohibited, although the Occupying Power may evacuate an area if the security of the population or imperative military reasons demand it: such evacuees shall be transferred back to their homes as soon as hostilities in the area have ceased. The Occupying Power shall ensure that proper accommodation is provided for the evacuees, and the Protecting Power shall be informed at once of any transfers and evacuations. The Occupying Power shall not deport or transfer parts of its own civilian population into the territory it occupies. It shall facilitate the proper working of all institutions devoted to the care and education of children, and arrange for the maintenance of children who are orphaned or separated from their families as a result of the war

Articles 51–52

The Occupying Power may not compel protected persons to serve in its armed or auxiliary forces. No pressure or propaganda which aims at securing voluntary enlistment is permitted. The Occupying Power may not compel protected persons to work unless they are over 18, and then only on work which is necessary either for the needs of the army of occupation, or for the public utility services, or for the feeding, sheltering, clothing, transportation or health of the population of the occupied country. They may not be compelled to undertake any work which would involve them in military operations. Workers shall be paid a fair wage and the legislation in force in the occupied country concerning working conditions and safeguards shall be applicable.

Articles 53–58

Destruction of private or state property by the Occupying Power is prohibited, except where it is rendered absolutely necessary by military operations. The Occupying Power may not alter the status of public officials or judges in the occupied territories, or apply sanctions to them should they abstain from fulfilling their functions for reasons of conscience: this prohibition does not affect the right of the Occupying Power to remove public officials from their posts. The Occupying Power has the duty of ensuring the food and medical supplies of the population. It may not requisition supplies except for use by the occupation forces and administration personnel, and then only if the requirements of the civilian population have been met. It has the duty of maintaining medical and hospital establishments and services, public health and hygiene in the occupied territory; it may requisition civilian hospitals only temporarily for the care of military wounded and sick, on condition that the needs of the civilian population are met. It shall permit ministers of religion to give spiritual assistance to the members of their religious communities.

Articles 59–63

If the whole or part of the occupied territory is inadequately supplied, the Occupying Power shall facilitate relief schemes by states or by impartial humanitarian organizations such as the ICRC. Relief consignments shall in no way relieve the Occupying Power of any of its responsibilities. Recognized National Red Cross Societies and similar relief societies shall be permitted to pursue their activities.

Articles 64–69

The penal laws of the occupied territory shall remain in force unless they constitute a threat to the security of the Occupying Power or an obstacle to the application of the Convention. The Occupying Power may, however, subject the population of the occupied territory to provisions which are essential to enable the Occupying Power to fulfil its obligations under the Convention, to maintain the orderly government of the territory, and to ensure the security of the Occupying Power. The penal provisions enacted by the Occupying Power shall not come into force before they have been published and brought to the knowledge of the inhabitants in their own language, and their effect shall not be retroactive. In the case of a breach of these penal provisions, the Occupying Power may hand over the accused to its properly constituted, non-political military courts, on condition that these courts sit in the occupied country. Protected persons who commit an offence which is solely intended to harm the Occupying Power, but which does not constitute an attempt on the life or limb of members of the occupying forces or administration, nor a grave collective danger, nor seriously damage the property of the occupying forces, shall be liable to internment or simple imprisonment proportionate to the offence committed. The death penalty may only be imposed where the protected person is guilty of espionage, serious acts of sabotage or offences which have caused the death of one or more persons, provided that such offences were punishable by death under the law of the occupied territory in force before the occupation began. The death penalty may not be pronounced against a person who was under 18 years of age at the time of the offence.

Articles 70–78

Protected persons shall not be arrested or convicted by the Occupying Power for acts committed or for opinions expressed before the occupation, except for breaches of the laws and customs of war. No sentence shall be pronounced by the competent courts of the Occupying Power except after a regular trial. The Protecting Power shall be informed of all proceedings instituted by the Occupying Power against protected persons in respect of charges involving the death penalty or imprisonment for two years or more. Accused persons have the right to be assisted by a qualified advocate and an interpreter, and shall have the right of appeal. No death sentence shall be carried out until six months after the Protecting Power has been notified. If convicted, protected persons shall serve their sentences in the occupied country, under conditions sufficient to keep them in good health. If the Occupying Power considers it necessary, for reasons of security, to take safety measures concerning protected persons, it may, at the most, subject them to assigned residence or to internment.

Section IV: Regulations for the Treatment of Internees

Chapter I: General Provisions

Articles 79–82

The Parties to the conflict shall not intern protected persons, except in accordance with the provisions of the Articles summarized in the previous paragraphs. Internees shall retain their full civil capacity. Parties to the conflict who intern protected persons shall be bound to provide free of charge for their maintenance and medical care, and for the support of their dependants if necessary. The Detaining Power shall, as far as possible, accommodate internees according to their nationality, language and customs. Members of the same family, especially parents and children, shall be interned together, with facilities for leading a proper family life.

Chapters II–XI: Places and Conditions of Internment

Articles 83–131

The Detaining Power shall not set up places of internment in areas particularly exposed to the dangers of war. Internment camps shall be indicated by the letters IC, or other agreed marking, so as to be clearly visible from the air. Internees shall be accommodated and administered separately from prisoners of war and from persons deprived of liberty for any other reason. Every place of internment shall be put under the authority of a responsible officer chosen from the regular military forces or the regular civil administration of the Detaining Power: the officer in charge must possess a copy of the Convention and is responsible for its application, and must instruct the staff in charge of internees accordingly. The text of the Convention shall be posted inside the place of internment, in a language which the internees understand. Provisions for hygienic living conditions, adequate food and clothing, medical attention, facilities for intellectual and physical activities and correspondence, retention of possessions, internees' representatives, disciplinary punishments, the transfer of internees, and the procedures to be followed after the death of an internee, are similar to those stipulated for prisoners of war under the Third Geneva Convention (see above). Children shall be allowed to attend school, either within the place of internment or outside. The Detaining Power shall not employ internees as workers unless they so desire: working conditions and payment shall not be inferior to those obtaining for work of the same nature in the same district.

Chapter XII: Release and Repatriation

Articles 132–135

Each interned person shall be released by the Detaining Power as soon as the reasons which necessitated his internment no longer exist, and as soon as possible after the close of hostilities. Internees against whom penal proceedings are pending, for offences not exclusively subject to disciplinary penalties, may be detained until the close of the proceedings and the completion of the penalty. The High Contracting Parties shall endeavour, upon the close of hostilities or occupation, to ensure the return of all internees to their last place of residence, or to facilitate their repatriation.

Section V: Information Bureaux and Central Agency

Articles 136–141

Upon the outbreak of a conflict and in all cases of occupation, each of the Parties to the conflict shall establish an official Information Bureau, responsible for receiving and transmitting information in respect of the protected persons who are in its power: each of the Parties to the conflict shall give its Bureau information on any protected persons who are kept in custody for more than two weeks, subjected to assigned residence, or interned. Each national Bureau shall also be responsible for collecting and forwarding the personal possessions left by protected persons who have been released or repatriated, escaped or died. A Central Information Agency for protected persons, in particular for internees, shall be created in a neutral country: it may be the same as that created for prisoners of war under the Third Geneva Convention (Article 123).

PART IV: EXECUTION OF THE CONVENTION

Articles 142–143

This section makes provision for the assistance of protected persons by representatives of the Protecting Powers and of religious organizations and relief societies (in particular the ICRC), similar to that given to prisoners of war under the Third Geneva Convention (Articles 125–126).

Articles 144–149

These Articles, largely common to all four Conventions, provide for the widespread dissemination of the Convention and the undertaking by the High Contracting Parties to enact legislation that will provide effective penal sanctions for persons committing grave breaches of the Convention (see under the First Geneva Convention, Articles 47–54).

Articles 150–159

This section concerns details of the translation, signature and ratification of the Convention, with provision for denunciation of the Convention by a High Contracting Party (as in Article 63 of the First Geneva Convention).

ANNEXES

Annex I is a draft agreement relating to hospital and safety zones. Annex II comprises draft regulations concerning collective relief.

Convention on the Prohibition of the Use, Stockpiling, Production and Transfer of Anti-personnel Mines and on their Destruction

(entered into force 1 March 1999)

The State Parties:

Determined to put an end to the suffering and casualties caused by anti-personnel mines, that kill or maim hundreds of people every week, mostly innocent and defenceless civilians and especially children, obstruct economic development and reconstruction, inhibit the repatriation of refugees and internally displaced persons, and have other severe consequences for years after emplacement;

Believing it necessary to do their utmost to contribute in an efficient and co-ordinated manner to face the challenge of removing anti-personnel mines placed throughout the world, and to assure their destruction;

Wishing to do their utmost in providing assistance for the care and rehabilitation, including the social and economic reintegration of mine victims;

Recognizing that a total ban of anti-personnel mines would also be an important confidence-building measure;

Welcoming the adoption of the Protocol on Prohibitions or Restrictions on the Use of Mines, Booby-Traps and Other Devices, as amended on 3 May 1996, annexed to the Convention on Prohibitions or Restrictions on the Use of Certain Conventional Weapons Which May Be Deemed to Be Excessively Injurious or to Have Indiscriminate Effects, and calling for the early ratification of this Protocol by all States which have not yet done so;

Welcoming also United Nations General Assembly Resolution 51/45 S of 10 December 1996 urging all States to pursue vigorously an effective, legally-binding international agreement to ban the use, stockpiling, production and transfer of anti-personnel landmines;

Welcoming furthermore the measures taken over the past years, both unilaterally and multilaterally, aiming at prohibiting, restricting or suspending the use, stockpiling, production and transfer of anti-personnel mines;

Stressing the role of public conscience in furthering the principles of humanity as evidenced by the call for a total ban of anti-personnel mines and recognizing the efforts to that end undertaken by the International Red Cross and Red Crescent Movement, the International Campaign to Ban Landmines and numerous other non-governmental organizations around the world;

Recalling the Ottawa Declaration of 5 October 1996 and the Brussels Declaration of 27 June 1997 urging the international community to negotiate an international and legally binding agreement prohibiting the use, stockpiling, production and transfer of anti-personnel mines;

Emphasizing the desirability of attracting the adherence of all States to this Convention, and determined to work strenuously towards the promotion of its universalization in all relevant fora including, *inter alia*, the United Nations, the Conference on Disarmament, regional organizations, and groupings, and review conferences of the Convention on Prohibitions or Restrictions on the Use of Certain Conventional Weapons Which May Be Deemed to Be Excessively Injurious or to Have Indiscriminate Effects;

Basing themselves on the principle of international humanitarian law that the right of the parties to an armed conflict to choose methods or means of warfare is not unlimited, on the principle that prohibits the employment in armed conflicts of weapons, projectiles and materials and methods of warfare of a nature to cause superfluous injury or unnecessary suffering and on the principle that a distinction must be made between civilians and combatants;

Have agreed as follows:

Article 1.

General obligations

1. Each State Party undertakes never under any circumstances:

(a) To use anti-personnel mines;

(b) To develop, produce, otherwise acquire, stockpile, retain or transfer to anyone, directly or indirectly, anti-personnel mines;

(c) To assist, encourage or induce, in any way, anyone to engage in any activity prohibited to a State Party under this Convention.

2. Each State Party undertakes to destroy or ensure the destruction of all anti-personnel mines in accordance with the provisions of this Convention.

Article 2.

Definitions

1. "Anti-personnel mine" means a mine designed to be exploded by the presence, proximity or contact of a person and that will incapacitate, injure or kill one or more persons. Mines designed to be detonated by the presence, proximity or contact of a vehicle as opposed to a person, that are equipped with anti-handling devices, are not considered anti-personnel mines as a result of being so equipped.

2. "Mine" means a munition designed to be placed under, on or near the ground or other surface area and to be exploded by the presence, proximity or contact of a person or a vehicle.

3. "Anti-handling device" means a device intended to protect a mine and which is part of, linked to, attached to or placed under the mine and which activates when an attempt is made to tamper with or otherwise intentionally disturb the mine.

4. "Transfer" involves, in addition to the physical movement of anti-personnel mines into or from national territory, the transfer of title to and control over the mines, but does not involve the transfer of territory containing emplaced anti-personnel mines.

5. "Mined area" means an area which is dangerous due to the presence or suspected presence of mines.

Article 3.

Exceptions

1. Notwithstanding the general obligations under Article 1, the retention or transfer of a number of anti-personnel mines for the development of and training in mine detection, mine clearance, or mine destruction techniques is permitted. The amount of such mines shall not exceed the minimum number absolutely necessary for the above-mentioned purposes.

2. The transfer of anti-personnel mines for the purpose of destruction is permitted

Article 4.

Destruction of stockpiled anti-personnel mines.

Except as provided for in Article 3, each State Party undertakes to destroy or ensure the destruction of all stockpiled anti-personnel mines it owns or possesses, or that are under its jurisdiction or control, as soon as possible but not later than four years after the entry into force of this Convention for that State Party.

Article 5.

Destruction of anti-personnel mines in mined areas

1. Each State Party undertakes to destroy or ensure the destruction of all anti-personnel mines in mined areas under its jurisdiction or control, as soon as possible but not later than ten years after the entry into force of this Convention for that State Party.

2. Each State Party shall make every effort to identify all areas under its jurisdiction or control in which anti-personnel mines are known or suspected to be emplaced and shall ensure as soon as possible that all anti-personnel mines in mined areas under its jurisdiction or control are perimeter-marked, monitored and protected by fencing or other means, to ensure the effective exclusion of civilians, until all anti-personnel mines contained therein have been destroyed. The marking shall at least be to the standards set out in the Protocol on Prohibitions or Restrictions on the Use of Mines, Booby-Traps and Other Devices, as amended on 3 May 1996, annexed to the Convention on Prohibitions or Restrictions on the Use of Certain Conventional Weapons Which May Be Deemed to Be Excessively Injurious or to Have Indiscriminate Effects.

3. If a State Party believes that it will be unable to destroy or ensure the destruction of all anti-personnel mines referred to in paragraph 1 within that time period, it may submit a request to a Meeting of the States Parties or a Review Conference for an extension of the deadline for completing the destruction of such anti-personnel mines, for a period of up to ten years.

4. Each request shall contain:

(a) The duration of the proposed extension.

(b) A detailed explanation of the reasons for the proposed extension, including:

(i) The preparation and status of work conducted under national demining programmes;

(ii) The financial and technical means available to the State Party for the destruction of all the anti-personnel mines; and

(iii) Circumstances which impede the ability of the State Party to destroy all the anti-personnel mines in mined areas.

(c) The humanitarian, social, economic, and environmental implications of the extension; and

(d) Any other information relevant to the request for the proposed extension.

5. The Meeting of the States Parties or the Review Conference shall, taking into consideration the factors contained in paragraph 4, assess the request and decide by a majority of votes of States Parties present and voting whether to grant the request for an extension period.

6. Such an extension may be renewed upon the submission of a new request in accordance with paragraphs 3, 4 and 5 of this Article. In requesting a further extension period a State Party shall submit relevant additional information on what has been undertaken in the previous extension period pursuant to this Article.

Article 6.

International co-operation and assistance

1. In fulfilling its obligations under this Convention each State Party has the right to seek and receive assistance, where feasible, from other States Parties to the extent possible.

2. Each State Party undertakes to facilitate and shall have the right to participate in the fullest possible exchange of equipment, material and scientific and technological information concerning the implementation of this Convention. The States Parties shall not impose undue restrictions on the provision of mine clearance equipment and related technological information for humanitarian purposes.

3. Each State Party in a position to do so shall provide assistance for the care and rehabilitation, and social and economic reintegration, of mine victims and for mine awareness programmes. Such assistance may be provided, *inter alia*, through the United Nations system, international, regional or national organizations or institutions, the International Committee of the Red Cross, national Red Cross and Red Crescent societies and their International Federation, non-governmental organizations, or on a bilateral basis.

4. Each State Party in a position to do so shall provide assistance for mine clearance and related activities. Such assistance may be provided, *inter alia*, through the United Nations system, international or regional organizations or institutions, non-governmental organizations or institutions, or on a bilateral basis, or by contributing to the United Nations Voluntary Trust Fund for Assistance in Mine Clearance, or other regional funds that deal with demining.

5. Each State Party in a position to do so shall provide assistance for the destruction of stockpiled anti-personnel mines.

6. Each State Party undertakes to provide information to the database on mine clearance established within the United Nations system, especially information concerning various means and technologies of mine clearance, and lists of experts, expert agencies or national points of contact on mine clearance.

7. States Parties may request the United Nations, regional organizations, other States Parties or other competent intergovernmental or non-governmental fora to assist its authorities in the elaboration of a national demining programme to determine, *inter alia*:

(a) The extent and scope of the anti-personnel mine problem

(b) The financial, technological and human resources that are required for the implementation of the programme

(c) The estimated number of years necessary to destroy all anti-personnel mines in mined areas under the jurisdiction or control of the concerned State Party

(d) Mine awareness activities to reduce the incidence of mine-related injuries or deaths

(e) Assistance to mine victims

(f) The relationship between the Government of the concerned State Party and the relevant governmental, intergovernmental or non-governmental entities that will work in the implementation of the programme.

8. Each State Party giving and receiving assistance under the provisions of this Article shall co-operate with a view to ensuring the full and prompt implementation of agreed assistance programmes.

Article 7.

Transparency measures

1. Each State Party shall report to the Secretary-General of the United Nations as soon as practicable, and in any event not later than 180 days after the entry into force of this Convention for that State Party on:

(a) The national implementation measures referred to in Article 9;

(b) The total of all stockpiled anti-personnel mines owned or possessed by it, or under its jurisdiction or control, to include a breakdown of the type, quantity and, if possible, lot numbers of each type of anti-personnel mine stockpiled;

(c) To the extent possible, the location of all mined areas that contain, or are suspected to contain, anti-personnel mines under its jurisdiction or control, to include as much detail as possible regarding the type and quantity of each type of anti-personnel mine in each mined area and when they were emplaced;

(d) The types, quantities and, if possible, lot numbers of all anti-personnel mines retained or transferred for the development of and training in mine detection, mine clearance or mine destruction techniques, or transferred for the purpose of destruction, as well as the institutions authorized by a State Party to retain or transfer anti-personnel mines, in accordance with Article 3;

(e) The status of programmes for the conversion or decommissioning of anti-personnel mine production facilities;

(f) The status of programmes for the destruction of anti-personnel mines in accordance with Articles 4 and 5, including details of the methods which will be used in destruction, the location of all destruction sites and the applicable safety and environmental standards to be observed;

(g) The types and quantities of all anti-personnel mines destroyed after the entry into force of this Convention for that State Party, to include a breakdown of the quantity of each type of anti-personnel mine destroyed, in accordance with Articles 4 and 5, respectively, along with, if possible, the lot numbers of each type of anti-personnel mine in the case of destruction in accordance with Article 4;

(h) The technical characteristics of each type of anti-personnel mine produced, to the extent known, and those currently owned or possessed by a State Party, giving, where reasonably possible, such categories of information as may facilitate identification and clearance of anti-personnel mines; at a minimum, this information shall include the dimensions, fusing, explosive content, metallic content, colour photographs and other information which may facilitate mine clearance; and

(i) The measures taken to provide an immediate and effective warning to the population in relation to all areas identified under paragraph 2 of Article 5.

2. The information provided in accordance with this Article shall be updated by the States Parties annually, covering the last calendar year, and reported to the Secretary-General of the United Nations not later than 30 April of each year.

3. The Secretary-General of the United Nations shall transmit all such reports received to the States Parties.

Article 8.

Facilitation and clarification of compliance

1. The States Parties agree to consult and co-operate with each other regarding the implementation of the provisions of this Convention, and to work together in a spirit of co-operation to facilitate compliance by States Parties with their obligations under this Convention.

2. If one or more States Parties wish to clarify and seek to resolve questions relating to compliance with the provisions of this Convention by another State Party, it may submit, through the Secretary-General of the United Nations, a Request for Clarification of that matter to that State Party. Such a request shall be accompanied by all appropriate information. Each State Party shall refrain from unfounded Requests for Clarification, care being taken to avoid abuse. A State Party that receives a Request for Clarification shall provide, through the Secretary-General of the United Nations, within 28 days to the requesting State Party all information which would assist in clarifying this matter.

3. If the requesting State Party does not receive a response through the Secretary-General of the United Nations within that time period, or deems the response to the Request for Clarification to be unsatisfactory, it may submit the matter through the Secretary-General of the United Nations to the next Meeting of the States Parties. The Secretary-General of the United Nations shall transmit the submission, accompanied by all appropriate information pertaining to the Request for Clarification, to all States Parties. All such information shall be presented to the requested State Party which shall have the right to respond.

4. Pending the convening of any meeting of the States Parties, any of the States Parties concerned may request the Secretary-General of the United Nations to exercise his or her good offices to facilitate the clarification requested.

5. The requesting State Party may propose through the Secretary-General of the United Nations the convening of a Special Meeting of the States Parties to consider the matter. The Secretary-General of the United Nations shall thereupon communicate this proposal and all information submitted by the States Parties concerned, to all States Parties with a request that they indicate whether they favour a Special Meeting of the States Parties, for the purpose of considering the matter. In the event that within 14 days from the date of such communication, at least one-third of the States Parties favours such a Special Meeting, the Secretary-General of the United Nations shall convene this Special Meeting of the States Parties within a further 14 days. A quorum for this Meeting shall consist of a majority of States Parties.

6. The Meeting of the States Parties or the Special Meeting of the States Parties, as the case may be, shall first determine whether to consider the matter further, taking into account all information submitted by the States Parties concerned. The Meeting of the States Parties or the Special Meeting of the States Parties shall make every effort to reach a decision by consensus. If despite all efforts to that end no agreement has been reached, it shall take this decision by a majority of States Parties present and voting.

7. All States Parties shall co-operate fully with the Meeting of the States Parties or the Special Meeting of the States Parties in the fulfilment of its review of the matter, including any fact-finding missions that are authorized in accordance with paragraph 8.

8. If further clarification is required, the Meeting of the States Parties or the Special Meeting of the States Parties shall authorize a fact-finding mission and decide on its mandate by a majority of States Parties present and voting. At any time the requested State Party may invite a fact-finding mission to its territory. Such a mission shall take place without a decision by a Meeting of the States Parties or a Special Meeting of the States Parties to authorize such a mission. The mission, consisting of up to 9 experts, designated and approved in accordance with paragraphs 9 and 10, may collect additional information on the spot or in other places directly related to the alleged compliance issue under the jurisdiction or control of the requested State Party.

9. The Secretary-General of the United Nations shall prepare and update a list of the names, nationalities and other relevant data of qualified experts provided by States Parties and communicate it to all States Parties. Any expert included on this list shall be regarded as designated for all fact-finding missions unless a State Party declares its non-acceptance in writing. In the event of non-acceptance, the expert shall not participate in fact-finding missions on the territory or any other place under the jurisdiction or control of the objecting State Party, if the non-acceptance was declared prior to the appointment of the expert to such missions.

10. Upon receiving a request from the Meeting of the States Parties or a Special Meeting of the States Parties, the Secretary-General of the United Nations shall, after consultations with the requested State Party, appoint the members of the mission, including its leader. Nationals of States Parties requesting the fact-finding mission or directly affected by it shall not be appointed to the mission. The members of the fact-finding mission shall enjoy privileges and immunities under Article VI of the Convention on the Privileges and Immunities of the United Nations, adopted on 13 February 1946.

11. Upon at least 72 hours notice, the members of the fact-finding mission shall arrive in the territory of the requested State Party at the earliest opportunity. The requested State Party shall take the necessary administrative measures to receive, transport and accommodate the mission, and shall be responsible for ensuring the security of the mission to the maximum extent possible while they are on territory under its control.

12. Without prejudice to the sovereignty of the requested State Party, the fact-finding mission may bring into the territory of the requested State Party the necessary equipment which shall be used exclusively for gathering information on the alleged compliance issue. Prior to its arrival, the mission will advise the requested State Party of the equipment that it intends to utilize in the course of its fact-finding mission.

13. The requested State Party shall make all efforts to ensure that the fact-finding mission is given the opportunity to speak with all relevant persons who may be able to provide information related to the alleged compliance issue.

14. The requested State Party shall grant access for the fact-finding mission to all areas and installations under its control where facts relevant to the compliance issue could be expected to be collected. This shall be subject to any arrangements that the requested State Party considers necessary for:

(a) The protection of sensitive equipment, information and areas;

(b) The protection of any constitutional obligations the requested State Party may have with regard to proprietary rights, searches and seizures, or other constitutional rights; or

(c) The physical protection and safety of the members of the fact-finding mission.

In the event that the requested State Party makes such arrangements, it shall make every reasonable effort to demonstrate through alternative means its compliance with this Convention.

15. The fact-finding mission may remain in the territory of the State Party concerned for no more than 14 days, and at any particular site no more than 7 days, unless otherwise agreed.

16. All information provided in confidence and not related to the subject matter of the fact-finding mission shall be treated on a confidential basis.

17. The fact-finding mission shall report, through the Secretary-General of the United Nations, to the Meetings of the States Parties or the Special Meeting of the States Parties the results of its findings.

18. The Meeting of the States Parties or the Special Meeting of the States Parties shall consider all relevant information, including the report submitted by the fact-finding mission, and may request the requested State Party to take measures to address the compliance issue within a specified period of time. The requested State Party shall report on all measures taken in response to this request.

19. The Meeting of the States Parties or the Special Meeting of the States Parties may suggest to the States Parties concerned ways and means to further clarify or resolve the matter under consideration, including the initiation of appropriate procedures in conformity with international law. In circumstances where the issue at hand is determined to be due to circumstances beyond the control of the requested State Party, the Meeting of the States Parties or the Special Meeting of the States Parties may recommend appropriate measures, including the use of co-operative measures referred to in Article 6.

20. The Meeting of the States Parties or the Special Meeting of the States Parties shall make every effort to reach its decisions referred to in paragraphs 18 and 19 by consensus, otherwise by a two-thirds majority of States Parties present and voting.

Article 9.

National implementation measures.

Each State Party shall take all appropriate legal, administrative and other measures, including the imposition of penal sanctions, to prevent and suppress any activity prohibited to a State Party under this Convention undertaken by persons or on territory under its jurisdiction or control.

Article 10.

Settlement of disputes

1. The States Parties shall consult and co-operate with each other to settle any dispute that may arise with regard to the application or the interpretation of this Convention. Each State Party may bring any such dispute before the Meeting of the States Parties.

2. The Meeting of the States Parties may contribute to the settlement of the dispute by whatever means it deems appropriate, including offering its good offices, calling upon the States Parties to a dispute to start the settlement procedure of their choice and recommending a time-limit for any agreed procedure.

3. This Article is without prejudice to the provisions of this Convention on facilitation and clarification of compliance.

Article 11.

Meetings of the States Parties

1. The States Parties shall meet regularly in order to consider any matter with regard to the application or implementation of this Convention, including:

(a) The operation and status of this Convention;

(b) Matters arising from the reports submitted under the provisions of this Convention;

(c) International co-operation and assistance in accordance with Article 6;

(d) The development of technologies to clear anti-personnel mines;

(e) Submissions of States Parties under Article 8; and

(f) Decisions relating to submissions of States Parties as provided for in Article 5.

2. The First Meeting of the States Parties shall be convened by the Secretary-General of the United Nations within one year after the entry into force of this Convention. The subsequent meetings

shall be convened by the Secretary-General of the United Nations annually until the first Review Conference.

3. Under the conditions set out in Article 8, the Secretary-General of the United Nations shall convene a Special Meeting of the States Parties.

4. States not parties to this Convention, as well as the United Nations, other relevant international organizations or institutions, regional organizations, the International Committee of the Red Cross and relevant non-governmental organizations may be invited to attend these meetings as observers in accordance with the agreed Rules of Procedure.

Article 12.
Review Conferences

1. A Review Conference shall be convened by the Secretary-General of the United Nations five years after the entry into force of this Convention. Further Review Conferences shall be convened by the Secretary-General of the United Nations if so requested by one or more States Parties, provided that the interval between Review Conferences shall in no case be less than five years. All States Parties to this Convention shall be invited to each Review Conference.

2. The purpose of the Review Conference shall be:

(a) To review the operation and status of this Convention;

(b) To consider the need for and the interval between further Meetings of the States Parties referred to in paragraph 2 of Article 11;

(c) To take decisions on submissions of States Parties as provided for in Article 5; and

(d) To adopt, if necessary, in its final report conclusions related to the implementation of this Convention.

3. States not parties to this Convention, as well as the United Nations, other relevant international organizations or institutions, regional organizations, the International Committee of the Red Cross and relevant non-governmental organizations may be invited to attend each Review Conference as observers in accordance with the agreed Rules of Procedure.

Article 13.
Amendments

1. At any time after the entry into force of this Convention any State Party may propose amendments to this Convention. Any proposal for an amendment shall be communicated to the Depositary, who shall circulate it to all States Parties and shall seek their views on whether an Amendment Conference should be convened to consider the proposal. If a majority of the States Parties notify the Depositary no later than 30 days after its circulation that they support further consideration of the proposal, the Depositary shall convene an Amendment Conference to which all States Parties shall be invited.

2. States not parties to this Convention, as well as the United Nations, other relevant international organizations or institutions, regional organizations, the International Committee of the Red Cross and relevant non-governmental organizations may be invited to attend each Amendment Conference as observers in accordance with the agreed Rules of Procedure.

3. The Amendment Conference shall be held immediately following a Meeting of the States Parties or a Review Conference unless a majority of the States Parties request that it be held earlier.

4. Any amendment to this Convention shall be adopted by a majority of two-thirds of the States Parties present and voting at the Amendment Conference. The Depositary shall communicate any amendment so adopted to the States Parties.

5. An amendment to this Convention shall enter into force for all States Parties to this Convention which have accepted it, upon the deposit with the Depositary of instruments of acceptance by a majority of States Parties. Thereafter it shall enter into force for any remaining State Party on the date of deposit of its instrument of acceptance.

Article 14.
Costs

1. The costs of the Meetings of the States Parties, the Special Meetings of the States Parties, the Review Conferences and the Amendment Conferences shall be borne by the States Parties and States not parties to this Convention participating therein, in accordance with the United Nations scale of assessment adjusted appropriately.

2. The costs incurred by the Secretary-General of the United Nations under Articles 7 and 8 and the costs of any fact-finding mission shall be borne by the States Parties in accordance with the United Nations scale of assessment adjusted appropriately.

Article 15.
Signature

This Convention, done at Oslo, Norway, on 18 September 1997, shall be open for signature at Ottawa, Canada, by all States from 3 December 1997 until 4 December 1997, and at the United Nations Headquarters in New York from 5 December 1997 until its entry into force.

Article 16.
(Ratification, acceptance, approval or accession)

Article 17.
(Entry into force)

Article 18.
(Provisional application)

Article 19.
Reservations

The Articles of this Convention shall not be subject to reservations.

Article 20.
Duration and withdrawal

1. This Convention shall be of unlimited duration.

2. Each State Party shall, in exercising its national sovereignty, have the right to withdraw from this Convention. It shall give notice of such withdrawal to all other States Parties, to the Depositary and to the United Nations Security Council. Such instrument of withdrawal shall include a full explanation of the reasons motivating this withdrawal.

3. Such withdrawal shall only take effect six months after the receipt of the instrument of withdrawal by the Depositary. If, however, on the expiry of that six-month period, the withdrawing State Party is engaged in an armed conflict, the withdrawal shall not take effect before the end of the armed conflict.

4. The withdrawal of a State Party from this Convention shall not in any way affect the duty of States to continue fulfilling the obligations assumed under any relevant rules of international law.

INTERNATIONAL SEABED AUTHORITY

Address: 14–20 Port Royal St, Kingston, Jamaica.

Telephone: 922-9105; **fax:** 922-0195; **e-mail:** webmaster@isa.org.jm; **internet:** www.isa.org.jm.

The Authority is an autonomous international organization established in accordance with the United Nations Convention on the Law of the Sea—UNCLOS (which was adopted in April 1982 and entered into force in November 1994) and the Agreement Relating to the Implementation of Part XI of the Convention (which was adopted in 1994 and entered into force in July 1996). The Authority was founded in November 1994 and became fully operational in June 1996.

Organization

(June 2012)

ASSEMBLY

The Assembly is the supreme organ of the Authority, consisting of representatives of all member states. In conjunction with the Council, it formulates the Authority's general policies. It elects Council members and members of the Finance Committee. It also approves the budget, submitted by the Council on the recommendation of the Finance Committee. The 17th session of the Assembly was convened in July 2011. The 18th session was to be convened in July 2012.

COUNCIL

The Council, elected by the Assembly for four-year terms, acts as the executive organ of the Authority. It consists of 36 members, comprising the four states that are the largest importers or consumers of seabed minerals, the four largest investors in seabed minerals, the four major exporters of seabed minerals, six developing countries representing special interests, and 18 members covering all the geographical regions.

LEGAL AND TECHNICAL COMMISSION

The Legal and Technical Commission, comprising 25 experts elected for five-year terms, assists the Council by making recommendations concerning seabed activities, assessing the environmental implications of activities in the area, proposing measures to protect the marine environment, and reviewing the execution of exploration contracts.

FINANCE COMMITTEE

The Committee, comprising 15 experts, was established to make recommendations to the Assembly and the Council on all financial and budgetary issues.

SECRETARIAT

The Secretariat provides administrative services to all the bodies of the Authority and implements the relevant work programmes. It comprises the Office of the Secretary-General, Offices of Resources and Environmental Monitoring, Legal Affairs, and Administration and Management. Under the terms of the 1994 Agreement Relating to the Implementation of Part XI of the Convention, the Secretariat is performing the functions of the Enterprise, the organ through which the Authority carries out deep-seabed mining operations (directly or through joint ventures). It is envisaged that the Enterprise will eventually operate independently of the Secretariat.

Secretary-General: Nii Allotey Odunton (Ghana).

Activities

The Authority, functioning as an autonomous international organization in relationship with the UN, implements UNCLOS. All states party to the Convention (161 and the European Union as at June 2012) are members. The Convention covers the uses of ocean space: navigation and overflight, resource exploration and exploitation, conservation and pollution, and fishing and shipping; as well as governing conduct on the oceans; defining maritime zones; establishing rules for delineating sea boundaries; assigning legal rights, duties and responsibilities to states; and providing machinery for the settlement of disputes. Its main provisions are as follows:

Coastal states are allowed sovereignty over their territorial waters of up to 12 nautical miles in breadth; foreign vessels are to be allowed 'innocent passage' through these waters;

Ships and aircraft of all states, including landlocked states, are allowed 'transit passage' through straits used for international navigation; states bordering these straits can regulate navigational and other aspects of passage;

Archipelagic states (composed of islands and interconnecting waters) have sovereignty over a sea area enclosed by straight lines drawn between the outermost points of the islands;

Coastal states and inhabited islands are entitled to proclaim a 200-mile exclusive economic zone (EEZ) with respect to natural resources and jurisdiction over certain activities (such as protection and preservation of the environment), and rights over the adjacent continental shelf, up to 350 miles from the shore under specified circumstances;

All states have freedom of navigation, overflight, scientific research and fishing within the EEZ, in addition to the right to lay submarine cables and pipelines, but must co-operate in measures to conserve living resources;

A 'parallel system' is to be established for exploiting the international seabed, where all activities are to be supervised by the International Seabed Authority (ISA); landlocked and geographically disadvantaged states have the right to participate, on an equitable basis, in the exploitation of an appropriate part of the surplus of living resources of the EEZs of coastal states of the same region or sub-region;

Coastal states have sovereign rights over the continental shelf (the national area of the seabed, which can extend up to 200 nautical miles from the shore) for exploring and exploiting its natural resources; the UN Commission on the Limits of the Continental Shelf shall make recommendations to states on the shelf's outer boundaries when it extends beyond 200 miles;

All states party to the Convention share, through the Authority, the revenue generated from exploiting non-living resources from any part of the continental shelf extending beyond 200 miles; the distribution of revenue is determined according to equitable sharing criteria, taking into account the interests and needs of developing and landlocked states;

States are bound to control pollution and co-operate in forming preventive rules, and incur penalties for failing to combat pollution; states bordering enclosed, or semi-enclosed, waters are bound to co-operate in managing living resources, environmental policies and research activities;

Marine scientific research in the zones under national jurisdiction is subject to the prior consent of the coastal state, but consent may be denied only under specific circumstances;

States are bound to co-operate in the development and transfer of marine technology 'on fair and reasonable terms and conditions' and with proper regard for all legitimate interests;

States are obliged to settle by peaceful means disputes on the application and interpretation of the Convention; disputes must be submitted to a compulsory procedure entailing decisions binding on all parties.

The Convention provides for the establishment of an International Tribunal for the Law of the Sea (see below), which has exclusive jurisdiction over disputes relating to the international seabed area. In July 1994 the UN General Assembly adopted the Agreement Relating to the Implementation of Part XI of the Convention. At June 2012 there were 141 states party to the Agreement. The original Part XI, concerning the exploitation of the international ocean bed, and particularly the minerals to be found there (chiefly manganese, cobalt, copper and nickel), envisaged as the 'common heritage of mankind', had not been supported by the USA and other industrialized nations on the grounds that countries possessing adequate technology for deep sea mining would be insufficiently represented in the ISA; that the operations of private mining consortia would be unacceptably limited by the stipulations that their technology should be shared with the Authority's 'Enterprise'; and that production should be limited in order to protect land-based mineral producers. Under the 1994 Agreement there was to be no mandatory transfer of technology, the Enterprise was to operate according to commercial principles; and there were to be no production limits, although a compensation fund was to assist land-based producers adversely affected by seabed mining. By June 2012 the USA had not yet ratified either the Convention or the Agreement. An agreement on the implementation of the provisions of the Convention relating to the conservation and management of straddling and highly migratory fish stocks was opened for signature in December 1995 and entered into force in December 2001; by June 2012 it had been ratified by 78 states.

The comprehensive set of rules, regulations and procedures being developed by the ISA to govern prospecting, exploration and exploitation of marine minerals in the international seabed 'Area' (defined as the seabed and subsoil beyond the limits of national jurisdictions) are known as the 'Mining Code'. So far the Mining Code comprises the Regulations for Prospecting and Exploration for Polymetallic Nodules in the Area, adopted by the Authority in July 2000; and the Regulations for Prospecting and Exploration for Polymetallic Sulphides, adopted in May 2010 by the 16th session of the Authority. A third set of regulations, on prospecting and exploration for cobalt-rich crusts, were drafted in 2011, and were to be endorsed in July 2012 by the 18th session of the Assembly. The Authority maintains a database on polymetallic nodules (POLYDAT) and a central data repository (CDR) for all marine minerals in the seabed. In November 2008 the ISA organized a seminar, jointly with the Government of Brazil, to address challenges relating to marine mineral resources in the South and Equatorial Atlantic Oceans. The Legal and Technical Commission has issued recommendations for the guidance of contractors on regarding the assessment of the environmental impacts of exploration for polymetallic nodules. In November 2011 the ISA organized a workshop on 'environmental management needs for exploration and exploitation of deep seabed minerals'.

In 2005 the ISA launched a project to make a geological model (comprising a set of digital and hard copy maps and tables describing predicted metal content and abundance of deposits, as well as related error estimates) of the Clarion-Clipperton Fracture Zone (CCZ) exploration area, which is located south-east of Hawaii in the Equatorial North Pacific Ocean and has the largest known deposits world-wide of seabed polymetallic nodules. In December 2009 the Authority organized a workshop aimed at finalizing the CCZ geological model as well as a Prospector's Guide for the Zone. An international workshop was held in November 2010 to advise on the formulation of a CCZ environmental management plan and strategic environmental assessment. A geological model project is under development for the ISA's second designated exploration area, the Central Indian Basin of the Indian Ocean.

Pursuant to the Regulations for Prospecting and Exploration for Polymetallic Nodules in the Area, 11 deep sea exploration contracts have been signed by the ISA and registered pioneer investors. In July 2011 and January 2012, respectively, companies from Nauru and Tonga became the first investors to sign exploration contracts with the ISA relating to polymetallic nodules in areas of the CCZ that have been reserved—in accordance with a provision of UNCLOS—for entities from developing countries.

In February 2008 the ISA launched a new Endowment Fund aimed at promoting and supporting collaborative marine scientific research in the international seabed area. The Fund awards fellowships to scientists and technical personnel from developing countries through its Technical Assistance Programme-Marine Scientific Research (TAP-MAR). By end-2011 the Fund was financing training and research activities for 16 scientists and technicians from 14 developing countries. Following the conclusion in June 2009 of a Memorandum of Understanding between the Authority and the People's Republic of China, in November China agreed to fund postgraduate studies in marine science at a Chinese university for up to five candidates from ISA developing member states.

Finance

The Authority's budget is adopted by the Assembly on the recommendations of both the Council and the Finance Committee. The budget for the Authority for the biennium 2011–12 was US $13.0m. The administrative expenses of the Authority are met by assessed contributions from its members.

Publications

Basic Texts of the ISA (in English, French and Spanish).

Handbook (annually).

The Law of the Sea: Compendium of Basic Documents.

Selected decisions of sessions of the Authority, consultations, documents, rules of procedure, technical reports and studies, etc.

Associated Institutions

The following were also established under the terms of the Convention:

Commission on the Limits of the Continental Shelf: Division for Ocean Affairs and the Law of the Sea, Rm DC2-0450, United Nations, New York, NY 10017, USA; tel. (212) 963-3966; fax (212) 963-5847; e-mail doalos@un.org; internet www.un.org/Depts/los/clcs_new/clcs_home.htm; 21 members, serving a five-year term (currently June 2012–June 2017); responsible for making recommendations regarding the establishment of the outer limits of the continental shelf of a coastal state, where the limit extends beyond 200 nautical miles (370 km); Chair. GALO CARRERA HURTADO (Mexico).

International Tribunal for the Law of the Sea: Am Internationalen Seegerichtshof 1, 22609 Hamburg, Germany; tel. (40) 35607-0; fax (40) 35607-245; e-mail itlos@itlos.org; internet www.itlos.org; inaugurated in 1996; 21 judges; responsible for interpreting the Convention and ruling on disputes brought by states parties to the Convention on matters within its jurisdiction; Registrar PHILIPPE GAUTIER (Belgium).

INTERNATIONAL TRADE UNION CONFEDERATION—ITUC

Address: 5 blvd du Roi Albert II, bte 1, 1210 Brussels, Belgium.

Telephone: (2) 224-02-10; **fax:** (2) 201-58-15; **e-mail:** info@ituc-csi.org; **internet:** www.ituc-csi.org.

ITUC was established in November 2006 by the merger of the International Confederation of Free Trade Unions (ICFTU, founded in 1949 by trade union federations that had withdrawn from the World Federation of Trade Unions), the World Confederation of Labour (WCL, founded in 1920 as the International Federation of Christian Trade Unions and reconstituted and renamed in 1968), and eight national trade union organizations. ITUC aims to defend and promote the rights of working people by encouraging co-operation between trade unions, and through global campaigning and advocacy. The principal areas of activity are: trade union and human rights; the economy, society and the workplace; equality and non-discrimination; and international solidarity. The principles of trade union democracy and independence are enshrined in ITUC's Constitution. In November 2006, following its establishment, ITUC ratified an agreement with the so-called Global Unions (global trade union federations, see list below) and the Trade Union Advisory Committee to the OECD (TUAC) to form a Council of Global Unions, with the aims of promoting trade union membership and advancing common trade union interests world-wide. In 2007 ITUC, UNEP and the ILO launched the Green Jobs Initiative (the International Organisation of Employers joined the partnership in 2008). The Initiative aims to promote the creation of decent jobs as a consequence of new environmental policies required to transform ongoing global environmental challenges.

MEMBERS

There were 308 member organizations in 153 countries and territories with 175m. members (at June 2012).

Organization

(June 2012)

WORLD CONGRESS

The Congress, the highest authority of ITUC, meets in ordinary session at least once every four years. The first Congress was held in Vienna, Austria, in November 2006; and the second was convened in Vancouver, Canada, in June 2010.

Delegations from national federations vary in size on the basis of their paying membership. The Congress examines past activities and financial reports of the Confederation; reports on the activities of ITUC's regional organizations and on the Council of Global Unions (the structured partnership with the global union federations and TUAC); addresses general policy questions; maps out future plans; considers proposals for amendments to the Constitution and any other proposals submitted by member organizations; and elects the General Council, the General Secretary and the Confederation's three auditors. The General Secretary leads the Secretariat and is an ex officio member of the General Council and of the Executive Bureau.

GENERAL COUNCIL

Elected by the Congress, the General Council comprises 78 members, of whom 70 represent regions (Europe: 24; the Americas: 18; Asia-Pacific: 15; Africa: 11; 'open' regional membership: two); six members are nominated by the Women's Committee; and two members are nominated by the Youth Committee. The Council meets at least once a year and acts as the supreme authority of the Confederation between World Congresses, with responsibility for directing the activities of the Confederation and effecting decisions and recommendations of the Congress. The Council's agenda is prepared by the General Secretary.

The Council has appointed the following Committees:

Human and Trade Union Rights Committee;

Women's Committee;

Youth Committee.

EXECUTIVE BUREAU

At its first meeting after the regular World Congress the General Council elects an Executive Bureau, comprising the President, the General Secretary and up to 25 members of the General Council. The Executive Bureau is authorized to address questions of urgency that arise between meetings of the General Council, or which are entrusted to it by the General Council. The Bureau meets at least twice a year.

President: MICHAEL SOMMER (Germany).

SECRETARIAT

General Secretary: SHARAN BURROW (Australia).

The General Secretary is supported by two Deputy General Secretaries.

BRANCH OFFICES

ITUC Amman Office: POB 925875, Amman 11190, Jordan; tel. (6) 5603181; fax (6) 5603185; e-mail itu-jor@orange.jo; Co-ordinator NEZAM QAHOUSH; ITUC Co-ordinator of the Iraqi Workers Project RALF ERBEL.

ITUC CIS Office: Leninskiy Prospect 42, 119119 Moscow, Russia; tel. (495) 938-7356; fax (495) 930-7671; e-mail ituc.mos@gmail.com.

ITUC Geneva Office: 46 ave Blanc, 1202 Geneva, Switzerland; tel. 227384202; fax 227381082; e-mail genevaoffice@ituc-csi.org; Dir RAQUEL GONZALEZ.

ITUC/Global Unions Washington Office: 888 16th St, Washington, DC 20006, USA; tel. (202) 974-8120; fax (202) 974-8122; e-mail washingtonoffice@ituc-csi.org; Rep. PETER BAKVIS.

ITUC South-East European Office: 71000 Sarajevo, Topal Osman paše 26/iv, Bosnia and Herzegovina; tel. (33) 715305; fax (33) 664676; e-mail seeoffice@ituc-csi.ba; Co-ordinator ENISA SALIMOVIC.

There are also Permanent Representatives accredited to FAO (Rome), IMO (London), UNIDO and IAEA (Vienna), and to UNEP and UN-Habitat (Nairobi).

REGIONAL ORGANIZATIONS

African Regional Organisation of ITUC (ITUC-Africa): route Internationale d'Atakpamé, POB 4101, Lomé, Togo; tel. and fax 225-07-10; e-mail info@ituc-africa.org; internet www.ituc-africa.org; f. 2007; Gen. Sec. KWASI ADU-AMANKWAH.

ITUC Regional Organisation for Asia-Pacific (ITUC-AP): 9th Floor, NTUC Centre, One Marina Blvd, Singapore 018989; tel. 63273590; fax 63273576; e-mail gs@ituc-ap.org; internet www.ituc-ap.org; f. 2007; Gen. Sec. NORIYUKI SUZUKI.

Pan-European Regional Council (PERC): 5 blvd du Roi Albert II, bte 1, 1210, Brussels, Belgium; tel. (2) 224-03-19; fax (2) 201-58-15; e-mail perc@ituc-csi.org; internet perc.ituc-csi.org; Gen. Sec. BERNADETTE SEGOL.

Trade Union Confederation of the Americas (TUCA): Rua Formosa 367, Centro CEP 01049-000, São Paulo, Brazil; tel. (11) 21040750; fax (11) 21040751; e-mail sede@csa-csi.org; internet www.csa-csi.org; f. 2008; Gen. Sec. VICTOR BÁEZ MOSQUEIRA.

Finance

Affiliated organizations pay an affiliation fee per 1,000 members per annum, which finances ITUC's activities. The Confederation's budget amounts to some €11m. annually.

A Solidarity Fund, financed by contributions from affiliated organizations, supports the development and practice of democratic trade unionism world-wide and assists workers and trade unionists victimized by repressive political measures.

Global Union Federations

Building and Wood Workers International (BWI): 54 route des Acacias, 1227 Carouge, Switzerland; tel. 228273777; fax 228273770; e-mail info@bwint.org; internet www.bwint.org; f. 2005 by merger of International Federation of Building and Woodworkers (f. 1934) and World Federation of Building and Wood Workers (f. 1936); mems: 328 national unions with a membership of around 12m. workers in 130 countries; organization: Congress, World Council, World Board; Pres. KLAUS WIESEHÜGEL (Germany); Gen. Sec. AMBET YUSON (Philippines); publ. *BWI Online on the web* (daily).

Education International (EI): 5 blvd du Roi Albert II, 1210 Brussels, Belgium; tel. (2) 224-06-11; fax (2) 224-06-06; e-mail info@ei-ie.org; internet www.ei-ie.org; f. 1993; the fmr World Confederation of Teachers (f. 1962) merged with EI in 2006; aims to represent the causes of teachers and education employees and to promote the development of education; advocates for free quality public education for all, deeming education to be a 'human right and a public good'; regards literacy as the cornerstone of all sustainable societies, and the key to breaking the poverty cycle and halting the spread of HIV/AIDS; mems: 401 organizations representing 30m. teachers and education workers in 172 countries; Pres. SUSAN HOPGOOD (Australia); Gen. Sec. FRED VAN LEEUWEN (Netherlands).

International Federation of Chemical, Energy, Mine and General Workers' Unions (ICEM): 20 rue Adrien Lachenal, 1207 Geneva, Switzerland; tel. 223041840; fax 223041841; e-mail info@icem.org; internet www.icem.org; f. 1995 by merger of the International Federation of Chemical, Energy and General Workers' Unions (f. 1907) and the Miners' International Federation (f. 1890); mems: 355 trade unions covering more than 20m. workers in 115 countries; main sectors cover energy industries; chemicals; pharmaceuticals and biotechnology; mining and extraction; pulp and paper; rubber; ceramics; glass; building materials; and environmental services; Pres. SENZENI ZOKWANA; Gen. Sec. MANFRED WARDA (Germany); publs *ICEM Info* (quarterly), *ICEM Focus on Health, Safety and Environment* (2 a year), *ICEM Update* (irregular).

International Federation of Journalists (IFJ): International Press Centre, 155 rue de la Loi, 1040 Brussels, Belgium; tel. (2) 235-22-00; fax (2) 235-22-19; e-mail ifj@ifj.org; internet www.ifj.org; f. 1952 to link national unions of professional journalists dedicated to the freedom of the press, to defend the rights of journalists, and to raise professional standards; it conducts surveys, assists in trade union training programmes, organizes seminars and provides information; it arranges fact-finding missions in countries where press freedom is under pressure, and issues protests against the persecution and detention of journalists and the censorship of the mass media; holds Congress every three years (May 2010: Cadiz, Spain); mems: 156 unions in more than 100 countries, comprising 600,000 individuals; Pres. JIM BOUMELHA (United Kingdom); Gen. Sec. ELIZABETH (BETH) COSTA (Brazil); publ. *IFJ Direct Line* (every 2 months).

International Metalworkers' Federation (IMF): 54 bis route des Acacias, CP 1516, 1227 Geneva, Switzerland; tel. 223085050; fax 223085055; e-mail info@imfmetal.org; internet www.imfmetal.org; f. 1893; mems: represents the collective interests of 25m. metalworkers from more than 200 unions in 100 countries; holds Congress every four years (May 2009: Göteborg, Sweden); has five regional offices; six industrial departments; World Company Councils for unions in multinational corporations; Pres. BERTHOLD HUBER (Germany); Gen. Sec. JYRKI RAINA (Finland); publs *IMF News Briefs* (weekly), *Metal World* (quarterly).

International Textile, Garment and Leather Workers' Federation (ITGLWF): 8 rue Joseph Stevens (bte 4), 1000 Brussels, Belgium; tel. (2) 512-26-06; fax (2) 511-09-04; e-mail office@itglwf.org; internet www.itglwf.org; f. 1970; mems: 217 unions covering 10m. workers in 110 countries; normally holds Congress every five years (Dec. 2009: Frankfurt, Germany); Gen. Sec. KLAUS PRIEGNITZ (Germany).

International Transport Workers' Federation (ITF): 49–60 Borough Rd, London, SE1 1DR, United Kingdom; tel. (20) 7403-2733; fax (20) 7357-7871; e-mail mail@itf.org.uk; internet www.itfglobal.org; f. 1896; hosts the Seafarers' Rights International Centre (f. 2010); scheduled to convene in Sept. 2012, in Casablanca, Morocco, the first of a series of Maritime Roundtables, focusing on building links between dockers' and seafarers unions; organizes and negotiates on behalf of crews working on ships flying Flags of Convenience (FOCs); mems: national trade unions covering 4.5m. workers in 690 unions in 153 countries; holds Congress every four years; has eight Industrial Sections; Pres. PADDY CRUMLIN (Australia); Gen. Sec. DAVID COCKROFT (United Kingdom); publ. *Transport International* (quarterly).

International Union of Food, Agricultural, Hotel, Restaurant, Catering, Tobacco and Allied Workers' Associations (IUF): 8 rampe du Pont-Rouge, 1213 Petit-Lancy, Switzerland; tel. 227932233; fax 227932238; e-mail iuf@iuf.org; internet www.iuf.org; f. 1920; mems: 384 affiliated organizations covering about 12m. workers in 120 countries; holds Congress every five years (May 2012: Geneva, Switzerland); Gen. Sec. RON OSWALD; publ. bi-monthly bulletins.

Public Services International (PSI): 45 ave Voltaire, BP9, 01211 Ferney-Voltaire Cédex, France; tel. 4-50-40-64-64; fax 4-50-40-73-20; e-mail psi@world-psi.org; internet www.world-psi.org; f. 1907; represents 20m. people working in the public services around the world; PSI is an officially recognized non-governmental organization for the public sector within the ILO; mems: 690 unions and professional associations covering 20m. workers in 161 countries; holds Congress every five years (Nov. 2012: Durban, South Africa); Pres. DAVE PRENTIS (United Kingdom); Gen. Sec. PETER WALDORFF (Denmark); publ. *Focus* (quarterly).

Union Network International (UNI): 8–10 ave Reverdil, 1260 Nyon, Switzerland; tel. 223652100; fax 223652121; e-mail contact@uniglobalunion.org; internet www.uniglobalunion.org; f. 2000 by merger of Communications International (CI), the International Federation of Commercial, Clerical, Professional and Technical Employees (FIET), the International Graphical Federation (IGF), and Media and Entertainment International (MEI); mems: 900 unions in more than 150 countries, representing 20m. people; activities cover the following sectors: cleaning and security, commerce, finance, gaming, graphical and packaging, hair and beauty, IT and services, media, entertainment and arts, post and logistics, social insurance, telecommunications, tourism, temporary and agency work; third World Congress was held in Nagasaki, Japan, in Nov. 2010, and the fourth was scheduled to be held in Cape Town, South Africa, in 2014; Pres. JOSEPH DE BRUYN (Australia); Gen. Sec. PHILIP J. JENNINGS (United Kingdom); publs *UNIinfo* (quarterly), *UNInet News* (monthly).

INTER-PARLIAMENTARY UNION—IPU

Address: 5 chemin du Pommier, CP 330, 1218 Le Grand Saconnex/Geneva, Switzerland.

Telephone: 229194150; **fax:** 229194160; **e-mail:** postbox@mail.ipu.org; **internet:** www.ipu.org.

Founded in 1889, the IPU aims to promote peace, co-operation and representative democracy by providing a forum for multilateral political debate between representatives of national parliaments.

MEMBERS

National parliaments of 162 sovereign states; 10 international parliamentary associations (associate members): the Andean Parliament; Central American Parliament; CEEAC Parliament; East African Legislative Assembly; ECOWAS Parliament; European Parliament; Latin American Parliament; Parliamentary Assembly of the Council of Europe; Transitional Arab Parliament; and UEMOA Inter-Parliamentary Committee. Most member states are affiliated to one of six geopolitical groupings, known as the African, Arab, Asia-Pacific, Eurasia, Latin American and '12-Plus' (European) groups.

Organization

(June 2012)

ASSEMBLY

The Assembly (formerly known as the Inter-Parliamentary Conference and renamed in April 2003) is the main statutory body of the IPU, comprising eight to 10 representatives from each member parliament. It meets twice a year to discuss current issues in world affairs and to make political recommendations. Other specialized meetings of parliamentarians may also be held, on a global or regional basis. The Assembly is assisted by the following three plenary Standing Committees: on Peace and International Security; Sustainable Development, Finance and Trade; and Democracy and Human Rights. The 126th Assembly was convened in Kampala, Uganda, in March–April 2012.

GOVERNING COUNCIL

The Governing Council (formerly the Inter-Parliamentary Council, renamed in April 2003) comprises two representatives of each member parliament, usually from different political groups. It is responsible for approving membership and the annual programme and budget of the IPU, and for electing the Secretary-General. The Council may consider substantive issues and adopt resolutions and policy statements, in particular on the basis of recommendations from its subsidiary bodies.

President: ABDELWAHAD RADI (Morocco).

MEETING OF WOMEN PARLIAMENTARIANS

The Meeting is a mechanism for co-ordination between women parliamentarians. Convened twice a year, on the occasion of IPU statutory meetings, the Meeting aims to address subjects of common interest, to formulate strategies to develop the IPU's women's programme, to strengthen their influence within the organization and to ensure that women are elected to key positions. The Meeting is assisted by a Co-ordinating Committee.

SUBSIDIARY BODIES

In addition to the thematic Standing Committees of the IPU Assembly, various other committees and groups undertake and co-ordinate IPU activities in specific areas. The following bodies are subsidiary to the IPU Council:

Standing Committee on Peace and International Security;

Standing Committee on Sustainable Development, Finance and Trade;

Standing Committee on Democracy and Human Rights;

Committee on the Human Rights of Parliamentarians;

Committee on Middle East Questions;

Committee on UN Affairs;

Group of Facilitators for Cyprus;

Ad Hoc Committee to Promote Respect for International Humanitarian Law;

Co-ordinating Committee of the Meeting of Women MPs;

Gender Partnership Group.

The Association of Secretaries-General of Parliaments (ASGP), an autonomous, self-managing body that meets during the IPU Assembly, has consultative status at the IPU.

EXECUTIVE COMMITTEE

The Committee, comprising 17 members and presided over by the President of the Council, oversees the administration of the IPU and advises the Council on membership, policy and programme, and any other matters referred to it.

SECRETARIAT

Secretary-General: ANDERS B. JOHNSSON (Sweden).

Activities

PROMOTION OF REPRESENTATIVE DEMOCRACY

This is one of the IPU's core areas of activity, and covers a wide range of concerns, such as democracy, gender issues, human rights and ethnic diversity, parliamentary action to combat corruption, and links between democracy and economic growth. The IPU sets standards and guidelines, provides technical assistance for strengthening national representative institutions, promotes human rights and the protection of members of parliament, supports partnership between men and women in politics, and promotes knowledge of the functioning of national parliaments. In September 1997 the Council adopted a Universal Declaration on Democracy. The IPU subsequently published a study entitled *Democracy: Its Principles and Achievements*.

The IPU aims to improve knowledge of the functioning of national parliaments by gathering and disseminating information on their constitutional powers and responsibilities, structure, and membership, and on the electoral systems used. The IPU also organizes international seminars and gatherings for parliamentarians, officials, academics and other experts to study the functioning of parliamentary institutions. A Technical Co-operation Programme aims to mobilize international support in order to improve the capabilities, infrastructure and technical facilities of national parliaments and enhance their effectiveness. Under the Programme, the IPU may provide expert advice on the structure of legislative bodies, staff training, and parliamentary working procedures, and provide technical equipment and other resources. There is a Parliamentary Resource Centre at IPU headquarters.

In 1993 the Council resolved that the IPU be present at all national elections organized, supervised or verified by the UN. The IPU has reported on the rights and responsibilities of election observers and issued guidelines on the holding of free and fair elections. These include the 1994 *Declaration on Criteria for Free and Fair Elections*, a study entitled *Free and Fair Elections* (initially published in 1994, and re-issued in a new, expanded version in 2006), *Codes of Conduct for Elections*, and *Tools for Parliamentary Oversight* (issued in 2008).

The IPU maintains a special database (PARLINE) on parliaments of the world, giving access to information on the structure and functioning of all existing parliaments, and on national elections. It conducts regular world studies on matters regarding the structure and functioning of parliaments. It also maintains a separate database (PARLIT) comprising literature from around the world on constitutional, electoral and parliamentary matters.

In August–September 2000 the IPU organized the first international conference of presiding officers of national parliaments. The second speakers' conference took place in September 2005, and the third in July 2010. The sixth annual meeting of women speakers of parliament, organized by the IPU jointly with the Swiss Government, also took place in July 2010.

INTERNATIONAL PEACE AND SECURITY

The IPU aims to promote conflict resolution and international security through political discussion. Certain areas of conflict are monitored by the Union on an ongoing basis (for example, Cyprus and the Middle East), while others are considered as they arise. In February 2011 the IPU President strongly condemned the use of military force by the Libyan authorities against political demonstrators in that country, and, in the following month, he similarly condemned the use by the Côte d'Ivoire authorities of force against political protesters. In early April 2012 the 126th IPU Assembly issued a statement expressing profound concern at the overthrow, in late March, of Mali's legitimate authorities by the military; and adopted a resolution demanding the immediate cessation of violence and human rights violations in Syria, and requesting the IPU to dispatch an international parliamentary fact-finding mission to that country to assess the situation there. The 126th Assembly also adopted a resolution inviting all states and parliaments to consider the lessons to be drawn from the Middle East, North Africa, Europe, the USA, and elsewhere, on the need for democratic reform, and on the need for governments to provide their citizens with basic employment and economic opportunities, and to guarantee equal opportunities for all; and urged that an international parliamentary conference should be convened, under IPU auspices, on the role of youth in politics and current technological developments.

The objectives outlined at the first Conference on Security and Co-operation in the Mediterranean (CSCM), held in June 1992, were integrated as a structured process of the IPU. A second CSCM was held in Valletta, Malta, in November 1995, and a third was convened in Marseilles, France, in March–April 2000. In February 2005 participants attending the fourth CSCM, held in Nafplion, Greece, agreed to terminate the process and establish in its place a Parliamentary Assembly of the Mediterranean (PAM); the inaugural session of the PAM was convened in Amman, Jordan, in September 2006.

The IPU has worked constantly to promote international and regional efforts towards disarmament, as part of the process of enhancing peace and security. Issues that have been discussed by the Assembly include nuclear non-proliferation, a ban on testing of nuclear weapons, and a global register of arms transfers.

SUSTAINABLE DEVELOPMENT

The Standing Committee for Sustainable Development, Finance and Trade guides the IPU's work in this area, with a broad approach of linking economic growth with social, democratic, human welfare and environmental considerations. Issues of world economic and social development on which the IPU has approved recommendations include employment in a globalizing world, the globalization of economy and liberalization of trade, Third World debt and its impact on the integration of those countries affected into the process of globalization, international mass migration and other demographic problems, and the right to food. The IPU co-operates with programmes and agencies of the UN, in particular in the preparation and follow-up of major socio-economic conferences, including the World Summit for Social Development, which was held in Copenhagen, Denmark, in March 1995; the Fourth World Conference on Women, held in Beijing, People's Republic of China, in September 1995; and the World Food Summit, held in Rome, Italy, in November 1996. In September 1996 a tripartite meeting of parliamentary, governmental and inter-governmental representatives, convened at the UN headquarters in New York, USA, considered legislative measures to pursue the objectives of the World Summit for Social Development. Since 2000 the IPU has aimed to bring to the attention of national parliaments the Millennium Development Goals (MDGs) that were adopted by UN leaders in September of that year, and were to be achieved by 2015. In May 2012 the UN General Assembly adopted a resolution calling for enhanced engagement between the UN, IPU and national parliaments, on major issues such as democracy, peace, development and human rights, and urging the IPU to continue mobilizing efforts aimed at attaining the MDGs, and to encourage parliaments to contribute to formulating post-2015 development objectives. At the end of May 2012 the IPU sponsored an Africa Parliamentary Conference on the MDGs, with a focus on the role of African parliamentarians in accelerating efforts to meet the MDGs and on their participation in discussions on the post-2015 development agenda. The IPU and the European Parliament jointly organize an annual parliamentary conference on the World Trade Organization (WTO), which addresses issues including access to markets, the development dimension of the multilateral trading system, agriculture and subsidies. The conference aims to add a parliamentary dimension to multilateral co-operation on trade matters and thereby to enhance the transparency of the WTO's activities and to strengthen democracy at international level.

Activities to protect the environment are undertaken within the framework of sustainable development. In 1984 the first Inter-Parliamentary Conference on the Environment, convened in Nairobi, Kenya, advocated the inclusion of environmental considerations into the development process. The IPU was actively involved in the preparation of the UN Conference on Environment and Development (UNCED), which was held in Rio de Janeiro, Brazil, in June 1992. Subsequently the IPU's environment programme focused on implementing the recommendations of UNCED, and identifying measures to be taken at parliamentary level to facilitate that process. The IPU monitors the actual measures taken by national parliaments to pursue the objective of sustainable development, as well as emerging environmental problems. In 1997 the IPU published the *World Directory of Parliamentary Bodies for Environment*. In April 2005 the Assembly held an emergency debate on the role of parliaments in the prevention of natural disasters and the protection of vulnerable groups. In October 2011 the 125th Assembly debated sustainable development. The IPU participated in the preparations for the June 2012 UN Conference on Sustainable Development (Rio+20), seeking input from member parliaments, and lobbying for the clear presentation in the draft Rio+20 outcome document of the role of parliaments in advancing sustainable development policies. During the Conference the IPU organized a Parliamentary Briefing.

In November 2007 the IPU, in co-operation with the UN Development Programme (UNDP), UNAIDS and the Philippines legislature, convened the first Global Parliamentary Meeting on HIV/AIDS, at which participating parliamentary representatives addressed the role of national legislatures in responding to the HIV/AIDS pandemic.

The IPU and UNDP concluded a comprehensive Memorandum of Understanding in November 2007 aimed at expanding mutual co-operation in support of world-wide democratic governance; future areas of co-operation were to cover national budgetary processes; and parliamentary activities aimed at advancing the achievement of the UN Millennium Development Goals (MDGs) and at implementing UN treaties and conventions, and strategies aimed at poverty reduction and the empowerment of women. The IPU welcomed a resolution adopted in December 2010 by the UN General Assembly on co-operation between the UN, national parliaments and the IPU.

In May 2009, in Geneva, the IPU convened a parliamentary conference on the ongoing global financial and economic crisis. The role of parliaments in developing South-South and 'triangular' (where two countries form a partnership to assist a third country) co-operation, with a view to accelerating achievement of the MDGs, and parliamentary action to ensure global food security, were addressed by the IPU Assembly in October.

IPU co-ordinated a two-year consultation process aimed at incorporating the concerns of national parliaments into the outcome of the Fourth UN Conference for the Least Developed Countries (LDV IV), convened in Istanbul, Turkey, in May 2011. LDC IV approved the Istanbul Programme of Action, which included a provision that national parliaments should be engaged in debating development strategies as well as in overseeing their implementation.

HUMAN RIGHTS AND HUMANITARIAN LAW

The IPU aims to incorporate human rights concerns, including employment, the rights of minorities, and gender issues, in all areas of activity. The Assembly and specialized meetings of parliamentarians frequently consider and make relevant recommendations on human rights issues. A five-member Committee on the Human Rights of Parliamentarians is responsible for the consideration of complaints relating to alleged violations of the human rights of members of parliament, for example state harassment, arbitrary arrest and detention, unfair trail and violation of parliamentary immunity, based on a procedure adopted by the IPU in 1976, when the Committee was established. The Committee conducts hearings and site missions to investigate a complaint and communicates with the authorities of the country concerned. If no settlement is reached at that stage, the Committee may then publish a report for the Governing Council and submit recommendations on specific measures to be adopted. During 2010 the Committee addressed cases of allegations of human rights violations against 306 current or former members of parliament in 35 countries.

The IPU works closely with the International Committee of the Red Cross to uphold respect for international humanitarian law (IHL). It supports the implementation of the Geneva Conventions and their Additional Protocols, and the adoption of appropriate national legislation. In 1995 the Council adopted a special resolution to establish a reporting mechanism at the parliamentary level to ensure respect for IHL. Consequently IPU initiated a world survey on legislative action regarding the application of IHL, as well as efforts to ban anti-personnel landmines. In April and September 1998 the Council adopted special resolutions on parliamentary action to secure the entry into force (achieved in March 1999) and implementation of the Convention on the Prohibition of the Use, Stockpiling, Production and Transfer of Anti-personnel Mines and on their Destruction, which had been signed by representatives of some 120 countries meeting in Ottawa, Canada, in December 1997.

In February 2008 the IPU and the UN Office on Drugs and Crime (UNODC) jointly organized a Parliamentary Forum on Human Trafficking, convened in Vienna, Austria, in the context of the global Vienna Forum to Fight Human Trafficking; in April 2009 the IPU and UNODC jointly issued *Combating Trafficking in Persons: a Handbook for Parliamentarians*. In April 2010 the Assembly issued a declaration on 'Co-operation and shared responsibility in the global fight against organized crime, in particular drug trafficking, illegal arms trafficking, trafficking in persons, and cross-border terrorism'.

In November 2010 participants in the international parliamentary conference on 'Parliaments, minorities and indigenous peoples', convened in Chiapas, Mexico, adopted the 'Chiapas Declaration' aimed at improving the situation of minorities and indigenous peoples.

WOMEN IN POLITICS

In conjunction with UN Women, IPU publishes an annual survey on progress made towards increasing female representation in parliament since the 1995 Fourth World Conference on Women (see above). The March 2012 *Women in Politics* survey reported that, at 1 January of that year, only 27 countries world-wide had achieved female parliamentary representation of 30% or more, and that there were at that time only 17 female elected heads of state or government. In September 2008 the IPU noted that Rwanda had become the first country with more than 50% female parliamentary representation, and, by 2012 Andorra also had also reached that benchmark.

The IPU aims to promote the participation of women in the political and parliamentary decision-making processes, and, more generally, in all aspects of society. It organizes debates and events on these issues and maintains an online statistical database on women in politics, compiled by regular world surveys, as well as a women in politics bibliographic database. The IPU also actively addresses wider issues of concern to women, such as literacy and education, women in armed conflicts, women's contribution to development, and women in the electoral process. The eradication of violence against women was the subject of a special resolution adopted by the Conference in 1991. The Meeting of Women MPs has monitored efforts by national authorities to implement the recommendations outlined in the resolution. In 1996 the IPU promoted the Framework for Model Legislation on Domestic Violence, formulated by the UN Special Rapporteur on the issue, which aimed to assist national parliaments in preparing legislation to safeguard women. At the Fourth World Conference on Women, held in Beijing, People's Republic of China, in September 1995, the IPU organized several events to bring together parliamentarians and other leading experts, diplomats and officials to promote the rights of women and of children. In February 1997 the IPU organized a Specialized Inter-Parliamentary Conference, in New Delhi, India, entitled 'Towards partnership between men and women in politics'. Following the Conference the IPU established a Gender Partnership Group, comprising two men and two women, within the Executive Committee, to ensure that IPU activities and decisions serve the interests and needs of all members of the population. The Group was authorized to report to the IPU Council.

The IPU aims to promote the importance of women's role in economic and social development and their participation in politics as a democratic necessity, and recognizes the crucial role of the media in presenting the image of women. Within the context of the 1997 New Delhi Conference, the IPU organized a second Round Table on the Image of Women Politicians in the Media (the first having been convened in November 1989). The debate urged fair and equal representation of women politicians by the media and for governments to revise their communications policies to advance the image of female parliamentarians.

In March 2007 IPU, jointly with UNDP, UNIFEM (from 2011 part of UN Women) and other partners, launched the International Knowledge Network of Women in Politics (iKNOW Politics), an online workspace aimed at supporting government officials, researchers, etc., in achieving the objective of advancing female participation in politics.

In 2008 the IPU launched a three-year programme to support parliaments to make ending violence against women a priority at the national level.

In April 2009 the IPU Assembly discussed means of accelerating progress towards securing the rights of adolescent girls to survival, education, health care, and protection, while emphasizing that the empowerment of adolescent girls belongs at the core of the development agenda and efforts towards achieving the UN Millennium Development Goals. In April 2012 the Assembly adopted a resolution on Access to Health as a Basic Right: the Role of Parliaments in Addressing Challenges to Securing the Health of Women and Children.

EDUCATION, SCIENCE AND CULTURE

Activities in these sectors are often subject to consideration by statutory meetings of the Assembly. Assembly resolutions have focused on the implementation of educational and cultural policies designed to foster greater respect for demographic values, adopted in April 1993; on bioethics and its implications world-wide for human rights protection, adopted in April 1995; and on the importance of education and culture as prerequisites for securing sustainable development (with particular emphasis on the education of women and the application of new information technologies), necessitating their high priority status in national budgets, adopted in April 2001. Specialized meetings organized by the IPU have included the Asia and Pacific Inter-Parliamentary Conference on 'Science and technology for regional sustainable development', held in Tokyo, Japan, in June 1994, and the Inter-Parliamentary Conference on 'Education, science, culture and communication on the threshold of the 21st century', organized jointly with UNESCO, and held in Paris, France, in June 1996. In October 2003 the IPU and UNESCO launched a network of national focal points linking the IPU's member parliaments and UNESCO, with the aim of circulating information and improving co-operation in the area of education, science, culture and communications.

In November 2006, the IPU and the UN Department of Economic and Social Affairs inaugurated the Rome, Italy-based Global Centre for Information and Communication Technologies in Parliament. The Centre, whose establishment was endorsed at the World Summit of the Information Society held in November 2005 in Tunis, Tunisia, is mandated to act as a clearing house for information, research, innovation, technology and technical assistance, and to promote a structured dialogue among parliaments, centres of excellence, international organizations, civil society, private sector interests, and international donors.

In October 2007 IPU, in conjunction with the UN Department for Economic and Social Affairs and the Association of Secretaries-General of Parliament, with support from the Global Centre for ICT in Parliament, convened the first World e-Parliament Conference, with participation by members of parliament, parliamentary officials, academics, and representatives of international organizations and of civil society. The e-Conference aimed to identify best practices in the use of new technologies to modernize parliamentary processes and communications. The IPU has, since 2008, issued an annual *World e-Parliament Report*.

Finance

The IPU is financed by its members, mainly from assessed contributions from member states. In addition, external financial support, primarily from voluntary donor contributions and UNDP, is received for some special activities. The 2012 annual budget amounted to 13.7m. Swiss francs.

Publications

Activities of the Inter-Parliamentary Union (annually).

Chronicle of Parliamentary Elections (annually).

Free and Fair Elections.

Global Parliamentary Report.

IPU Information Brochure (annually).

World Directory of Parliamentary Human Rights Bodies.

World Directory of Parliaments (annually).

World e-Parliament Report (annually).

The World of Parliaments (quarterly).

Other handbooks, reports and surveys, documents, proceedings of the Assembly.

ISLAMIC DEVELOPMENT BANK

Address: POB 5925, Jeddah 21432, Saudi Arabia.

Telephone: (2) 6361400; **fax:** (2) 6366871; **e-mail:** idbarchives@isdb.org; **internet:** www.isdb.org.

The Bank was established following a conference of Ministers of Finance of member countries of the then Organization of the Islamic Conference (now Organization of Islamic Cooperation—OIC), held in Jeddah in December 1973. Its aim is to encourage the economic development and social progress of member countries and of Muslim communities in non-member countries, in accordance with the principles of the Islamic *Shari'a* (sacred law). The Bank formally opened in October 1975. The Bank and its associated entities—the Islamic Research and Training Institute, the Islamic Corporation for the Development of the Private Sector, the Islamic Corporation for the Insurance of Investment and Export Credit, and the International Islamic Trade Finance Corporation—constitute the Islamic Development Bank Group.

MEMBERS

There are 56 members.

Organization

(June 2012)

BOARD OF GOVERNORS

Each member country is represented by a governor, usually its Minister of Finance, and an alternate. The Board of Governors is the supreme authority of the Bank, and meets annually. The 37th meeting was held in Khartoum, Sudan, in March–April 2012. The 38th meeting was scheduled to be convened in Dushanbe, Tajikistan, in May 2013.

BOARD OF EXECUTIVE DIRECTORS

The Board consists of 18 members, half of whom are appointed by the eight largest subscribers to the capital stock of the Bank; the remaining eight are elected by Governors representing the other subscribers. Members of the Board of Executive Directors are elected for three-year terms. The Board is responsible for the direction of the general operations of the Bank.

ADMINISTRATION

President of the Bank and Chairman of the Board of Executive Directors: Dr AHMAD MOHAMED ALI AL-MADANI (Saudi Arabia).

Vice-President Corporate Services: Dr AHMET TIKTIK (Turkey).

Vice-President Finance: Dr ABDULAZIZ BIN MOHAMED BIN ZAHIR AL HINAI (Oman).

Vice-President Operations: BIRAMA BOUBACAR SIDIBE (Mali).

REGIONAL OFFICES

Kazakhstan: 050000 Almatı, Aiteki bi 67; tel. (727) 272-70-00; fax (727) 250-13-02; e-mail idbroa@isdb.org; Dir HISHAM TALEB MAAROUF.

Malaysia: Menara Bank Pembangunan Bandar Wawasan, Level 13, Jalan Sultan Ismail, 508250 Kuala Lumpur; tel. (3) 26946627; fax (3) 26946626; e-mail ROKL@isdb.org.

Morocco: Km 6.4, Ave Imam Malik Route des Zaers, POB 5003, Rabat; tel. (3) 7757191; fax (3) 7775726.

Senegal: 18 blvd de la République, Dakar; tel. (33) 889-1144; fax (33) 823-3621; e-mail RODK@isdb.org; Dir SIDI MOHAMED OULD TALEB.

FINANCIAL STRUCTURE

The Bank's unit of account is the Islamic Dinar (ID), which is equivalent to the value of one Special Drawing Right (SDR) of the IMF (average value of the SDR in 2011 was US $1.57868). In May 2006 the Bank's Board of Governors approved an increase in the authorized capital from ID 15,000m. to ID 30,000m. An increase in subscribed capital, from ID 15,000m. to ID 16,000m. was approved by the Board of Governors in June 2008. In June 2010 the Board of Governors approved a further increase in subscribed capital to ID 18,000m. At 25 November 2011 total committed subscriptions amounted to ID 17,782.6m.

SUBSCRIPTIONS
(million Islamic Dinars, as at 25 November 2011)

Afghanistan	9.93	Maldives	9.23
Albania	9.23	Mali	18.19
Algeria	459.22	Mauritania	9.77
Azerbaijan	18.19	Morocco	91.69
Bahrain	25.88	Mozambique	9.23
Bangladesh	182.16	Niger	24.63
Benin	20.80	Nigeria	1,384.00
Brunei	45.85	Oman	50.92
Burkina Faso	24.63	Pakistan	459.22
Cameroon	45.85	Palestine	19.55
Chad	9.77	Qatar	1,297.50
Comoros	4.65	Saudi Arabia	4,249.60
Côte d'Ivoire	4.65	Senegal	52.80
Djibouti	4.96	Sierra Leone	4.96
Egypt	1,278.67	Somalia	4.96
Gabon	54.58	Sudan	83.21
The Gambia	9.23	Suriname	9.23
Guinea	45.85	Syria	18.49
Guinea-Bissau	4.96	Tajikistan	4.96
Indonesia	406.48	Togo	4.96
Iran	1,491.20	Tunisia	19.55
Iraq	48.24	Turkey	1,165.86
Jordan	78.50	Turkmenistan	4.96
Kazakhstan	19.29	Uganda	24.63
Kuwait	985.88	United Arab Emirates	1,357.20
Kyrgyzstan	9.23	Uzbekistan	4.80
Lebanon	9.77	Yemen	92.38
Libya	1,704.46		
Malaysia	294.01		

Activities

The Bank adheres to the Islamic principle forbidding usury, and does not grant loans or credits for interest. Instead, its methods of project financing are: provision of interest-free loans, mainly for infrastructural projects which are expected to have a marked impact on long-term socio-economic development; provision of technical assistance (e.g. for feasibility studies); equity participation in industrial and agricultural projects; leasing operations, involving the leasing of equipment such as ships, and instalment sale financing; and profit-sharing operations. Funds not immediately needed for projects are used for foreign trade financing. Under the Bank's trade financing operations funds are used for importing commodities for development purposes (i.e. raw materials and intermediate industrial goods, rather than consumer goods), with priority given to the import of goods from other member countries. In 2005 the Bank initiated a consultation process, led by a commission of eminent persons, to develop a new long-term strategy for the Bank. A document on the AH 1440 (2020) Vision was published in March 2006. It recommended that the Bank redefine its mandate and incorporate a broad focus on comprehensive human development, with priority concerns to be the alleviation of poverty and improvements to health, education and governance. The new strategy also envisaged greater community involvement in Bank operations and more support given to local initiatives. In October 2008 the Bank organized a forum to consider the impact of the international economic and financial crisis on the Islamic financial system. The meeting resolved to establish a Task Force for Islamic Finance and Global Financial Stability, which met for the first time in January 2009, in Kuala Lumpur, Malaysia. In May the Board of Executive Directors agreed to double ordinary capital resources operations over a three-year period in order to support economic recovery in member countries. In the following month the Board of Governors approved the measure, along with others in support of mitigating the effects of the global financial crisis. During that year the Bank resolved to accelerate implementation of a major reform programme to enhance its relevance and impact in member countries, in accordance with the AH 1440 (2020) Vision. The Bank also adopted a Thematic Strategy for Poverty Reduction and Comprehensive Human Development to focus efforts to achieve the Vision's objectives.

By 25 November 2011 the Bank had approved a total of ID 25,526.7m. (equivalent to some US $37,350.5m.) for project financing since operations began in 1976, including ID 264.1m. ($371.7m.) for technical assistance, in addition to ID 28,491.6m. ($39,951.7m.) for foreign trade financing, and ID 556.0m. ($723.4m.) for special assistance operations, excluding amounts for cancelled operations. Total net approved operations amounted to ID 54,574.3m. ($79,025.5m.) at that time.

During the Islamic year 1432 (7 December 2010–25 November 2011) the Bank approved a net total of ID 6,973.0m., for 398 operations, compared with ID 4,550.3m. for 367 operations in the previous year. Of the total approved in AH 1432 ID 239.6m. was approved for 40 loans, supporting projects concerned with the education and health sectors, infrastructural improvements, and agricultural developments. The Bank approved 98 technical assistance operations during that year in the form of grants and loans, amounting to ID 22.5m. Trade financing approved amounted to ID 2,056.2m. for 77 operations. During AH 1432 the Bank's total disbursements totalled ID 3,347.8m., bringing the total cumulative disbursements since the Bank began operations to ID 36,626.2m.

During AH 1427 the Bank's export financing scheme was formally dissolved, although it continued to fund projects pending the commencement of operations of the International Islamic Trade Finance Corporation (ITFC). The Bank also finances other trade financing operations, including the Islamic Corporation for the Development of the Private Sector (ICD, see below), the Awqaf Properties Investment Fund and the Treasury Department. In addition, a Trade Co-operation and Promotion Programme supports efforts to enhance trade among OIC member countries. In June 2005 the Board of Governors approved the establishment of the ITFC as an autonomous trade promotion and financing institution within the Bank Group. The inaugural meeting of the ITFC was held in February 2007. In May 2006 the Board of Governors approved a new fund to reduce poverty and support efforts to achieve the UN Millennium Development Goals, in accordance with a proposal of the OIC. It was inaugurated, as the Islamic Solidarity Fund for Development, in May 2007, and became operational in early 2008. By the end of the Islamic year 1432 capital contributions to the Fund amounted to US $1,633m., of a total of $2,639m. that had been pledged by 43 countries.

In AH 1407 (1986/87) the Bank established an Islamic Bank's Portfolio for Investment and Development (IBP) in order to promote the development and diversification of Islamic financial markets and to mobilize the liquidity available to banks and financial institutions. During AH 1428 resources and activities of the IBP were transferred to the newly established ITFC. The Bank's Unit Investment Fund (UIF) became operational in 1990, with the aim of mobilizing additional resources and providing a profitable channel for investments conforming to *Shari'a*. The initial issue of the UIF was US $100m., which was subsequently increased to $325m. The Fund finances mainly private sector industrial projects in middle-income countries and also finances short-term trade operations. The Bank also mobilizes resources from the international financial markets through the issuance of the International Islamic Sukuk bond. In October 1998 the Bank announced the establishment of a new fund to invest in infrastructure projects in member states. The Bank committed $250m. to the fund, which was to comprise $1,000m. equity capital and a $500m. Islamic financing facility. In January 2009 the Bank launched a second phase of the infrastructure fund. In November 2001 the Bank signed an agreement with Malaysia, Bahrain, Indonesia and Sudan for the establishment of an Islamic financial market. In April 2002 the Bank, jointly with governors of central banks and the Accounting and Auditing Organization for Islamic Financial Institutions, concluded an agreement, under the auspices of the IMF, for the establishment of an Islamic Financial Services Board. The Board, to be located in Kuala Lumpur, Malaysia, was intended to elaborate and harmonize standards for best practices in the regulation and supervision of the Islamic financial services industry.

The Bank's Special Assistance Programme was initiated in AH 1400 to support the economic and social development of Muslim communities in non-member countries, in particular in the education and health sectors. It also aimed to provide emergency aid in times of natural disasters, and to assist Muslim refugees throughout the world. Operations undertaken by the Bank are financed by the Waqf Fund (formerly the Special Assistance Account). By the end of the Islamic year 1432 some ID 556.0m. (US $723.4m.) had been approved under the Waqf Fund Special Assistance Programme for 1,415 operations. Other assistance activities include scholarship programmes, technical co-operation projects and the sacrificial meat utilization project (see below). In addition the Bank supports recovery, rehabilitation and reconstruction efforts in member countries affected by natural disasters or conflict.

In October 2002 the Bank's Board of Governors, meeting in Burkina Faso, adopted the Ouagadougou Declaration on the co-operation between the Bank group and Africa, which identified priority areas for Bank activities, for example education and the private sector. The Bank pledged US $2,000m. to finance implementation of the Declaration over the five year period 2004–08. A successor initiative, the IDB Special Programme for the Development of Africa, was endorsed at a summit meeting of the OIC held in March 2008. The Bank committed $4,000m. to the Programme for the next five-year period, 2008–12. By the end of the Islamic year 1432 $3,980m. had been approved under the Programme, of which $1,400m. had been disbursed. During the Islamic year 1431 the Bank initiated a Membership Country Partnership (MCP) Strategy to strengthen dialogue with individual member countries and to contribute more effectively to their medium- and long-term development plans. By the end of AH 1432 five MCPs were being implemented, in Indonesia, Mali, Mauritania, Turkey and Uganda, and one had been completed for Pakistan.

In June 2008 the Board of Governors inaugurated the Jeddah Declaration Initiative, with an allocation of $1,500m. in funds over a five-year period, to assist member countries to meet the escalating costs of food and to attain greater food security. In November 2009 the Bank concluded a co-financing agreement with IFAD, with funds of up to $1,500m., to support priority projects concerned with food security and rural development in the poorest member countries in Africa and Asia. The agreement was signed by the presidents of the two organizations in February 2010. During 2011 the Bank contributed to the preparation of an Action Plan on Food Price Volatility and Agriculture, which was adopted by heads of state and government of the Group of 20 industrialized and emerging economies (G20) in November. The Bank also contributed, through participation in a working group and high-level panel, to the elaboration of a G20 Multilateral Development Bank Infrastructure Action Plan. In April the Bank collaborated with the World Bank Group to inaugurate an Arab Financing Facility for Infrastructure in roder to support national and cros-border infrastructure development, in particular through use of public–private partnerships. In September the Bank participated in a meeting of ministers of finance of the Group of Eight industrialized nations (G8) and high-level representatives of international financial institutions active in the Middle East and North Africa region to further support of the so-called Deauville Partnership, which had been established in May in order to assist countries in the region undergoing social and economic transformations. The Bank was a founding member of the new Co-ordination Platform to facilitate and promote collaboration among the institutions extending assistance under the Partnership.

In AH 1404 (1983/84) the Bank established a scholarship programme for Muslim communities in non-member countries to provide opportunities for students to pursue further education or other professional training. The programme also assists 12 member countries on an exceptional basis. By the end of the Islamic year 1432 6,794 people had graduated and 4,977 were undertaking studies under the scheme. The Merit Scholarship Programme, initiated in AH 1412 (1991/92), aims to develop scientific, technological and research capacities in member countries through advanced studies and/or research. A total of 760 scholarships had been awarded by the end of AH 1432. In AH 1419 (1998/99) a Scholarship Programme in Science and Technology for IDB Least Developed Member Countries became operational for students in 20 eligible countries. By the end of the Islamic year 1432 404 students had received scholarships under the programme. The Bank awards annual prizes for science and technology to promote excellence in research and development and in scientific education.

The Bank's Programme for Technical Co-operation aims to mobilize technical capabilities among member countries and to promote the exchange of expertise, experience and skills through expert missions, training, seminars and workshops. In December 1999 the Board of Executive Directors approved two technical assistance grants to support a programme for the eradication of illiteracy in the Islamic world, and one for self-sufficiency in human vaccine production. The Bank also undertakes the distribution of meat sacrificed by Muslim pilgrims. The Bank was the principal source of funding of the International Centre for Biosaline Agriculture, which was established in Dubai, UAE, in September 1999.

BANK GROUP ENTITIES

International Islamic Trade Finance Corporation: Jeddah, Saudia Arabia; tel. (2) 6361400; fax (2) 6371064; e-mail info@itfc-idb.org; internet www.itfc-idb.org; f. 2007; commenced operations Jan. 2008; aims to promote trade and trade financing in Bank member countries, to facilitate access to public and private capital, and to promote investment opportunities; during the Islamic year 1432 the ITFC approved US $3,033m. for 66 trade financing operations; auth. cap. US $3,000m.; subs. cap. $750m. (Nov. 2011); CEO Dr WALID AL-WOHAIB.

Islamic Corporation for the Development of the Private Sector (ICD): POB 54069, Jeddah 21514, Saudi Arabia; tel. (2) 6441644; fax (2) 6444427; e-mail icd@isdb.org; internet www.icd-idb.org; f. 1999; to identify opportunities in the private sector, provide financial products and services compatible with Islamic law, mobilize additional resources for the private sector in member countries, and encourage the development of Islamic financing and capital markets; approved 22 projects amounting to US $364.8 in the Islamic year 1432; the Bank's share of the capital is 50%, member countries 30% and public financial institutions of member countries 20%; auth. cap. US $2,000m., subs. cap. $875m. (Nov. 2011); mems: 47 countries, the Bank, and 5 public financial institutions; CEO and Gen. Man. KHALID M. AL-ABOODI.

Islamic Corporation for the Insurance of Investment and Export Credit (ICIEC): POB 15722, Jeddah 21454, Saudi Arabia; tel. (2) 6445666; fax (2) 6379504; e-mail idb.iciec@isdb.org.sa; internet www.iciec.com; f. 1994; aims to promote trade and the flow of investments among member countries of the OIC through the provision of export credit and investment insurance services; a representative office was opened in Dubai, UAE, in May 2010; auth. cap. increased from ID 150m. to ID 400m. in July 2011; mems: 40 member states and the Islamic Development Bank (which contributes two-thirds of its capital); Gen. Man. Dr ABDEL RAHMAN A. TAHA.

Islamic Research and Training Institute: POB 9201, Jeddah 21413, Saudi Arabia; tel. (2) 6361400; fax (2) 6378927; e-mail irti@isdb.org; internet www.irti.org; f. 1982 to undertake research enabling economic, financial and banking activities to conform to Islamic law, and to provide training for staff involved in development activities in the Bank's member countries; the Institute also organizes seminars and workshops, and holds training courses aimed at furthering the expertise of government and financial officials in Islamic developing countries; Dir-Gen. Dr AZMI OMAR (Malaysia); publs *Annual Report, Islamic Economic Studies* (2 a year), various research studies, monographs, reports.

Publication

Annual Report.

Statistics

OPERATIONS APPROVED, ISLAMIC YEAR 1432
(7 December 2010–25 November 2011)

Type of operation	Number of operations	Amount (million Islamic Dinars)
Total project financing	272	3,255.5
Project financing	174	3,233.0
Technical assistance	98	22.5
Trade financing operations*	77	2,056.2
Special assistance operations	49	9.6
Total†	398	5,321.3

* Including operations by the ITFC, the ICD, the UIF, Treasury operations, and the Awqaf Properties Investment Fund.
† Excluding cancelled operations.

DISTRIBUTION OF PROJECT FINANCING AND TECHNICAL ASSISTANCE BY SECTOR, ISLAMIC YEAR 1432
(7 December 10–25 November 2011)

Sector	Number of operations	Amount (million Islamic Dinars)	%
Agriculture	29	422.1	15.5
Education	38	219.2	8.0
Energy	15	782.5	28.7
Finance	50	147.4	5.4
Health	21	202.2	7.4
Industry and mining	5	15.5	0.6
Information and communications	4	35.1	1.3
Public administration	1	0.2	0.0
Transportation	13	505.1	18.5
Water, sanitation and urban services	22	397.6	14.6
Total*	198	2,727.1	100.0

* Excluding cancelled operations.

Source: Islamic Development Bank, *Annual Report 1432 H.*

LATIN AMERICAN INTEGRATION ASSOCIATION—LAIA

(ASOCIACIÓN LATINOAMERICANA DE INTEGRACIÓN—ALADI)

Address: Cebollatí 1461, Casilla 20.005, 11200 Montevideo, Uruguay.

Telephone: 2410 1121; **fax:** 2419 0649; **e-mail:** sgaladi@aladi.org; **internet:** www.aladi.org.

The Latin American Integration Association was established in August 1980 to replace the Latin American Free Trade Association, founded in February 1960.

MEMBERS

Argentina	Cuba	Paraguay
Bolivia	Ecuador	Peru
Brazil	Mexico	Uruguay
Chile	Panama	Venezuela
Colombia		

Observers: People's Republic of China, Costa Rica, Dominican Republic, El Salvador, Guatemala, Honduras, Italy, Japan, Republic of Korea, Nicaragua, Pakistan, Portugal, Romania, Russia, San Marino, Spain, Switzerland and Ukraine; also the UN Economic Commission for Latin America and the Caribbean, the UN Development Programme, the Andean Development Corporation, the European Union, the Ibero-American General Secretariat (SEGIB), the Inter-American Development Bank, the Inter-American Institute for Co-operation on Agriculture, the Latin American Economic System, the Organization of American States, and the Pan American Health Organization/World Health Organization.

Organization

(June 2012)

COUNCIL OF MINISTERS

The Council of Ministers of Foreign Affairs is responsible for the adoption of the Association's policies. It meets when convened by the Committee of Representatives.

CONFERENCE OF EVALUATION AND CONVERGENCE

The Conference, comprising plenipotentiaries of the member governments, assesses the integration process and encourages negotiations between members. It also promotes the convergence of agreements and other actions on economic integration. The Conference meets when convened by the Committee of Representatives.

COMMITTEE OF REPRESENTATIVES

The Committee, the permanent political body of the Association, comprises a permanent and a deputy representative from each member country. The Committee is the main forum for the negotiation of ALADI's initiatives and is responsible for the correct implementation of the Treaty and its supplementary regulations. There are the following auxiliary bodies:

Advisory Commission for Financial and Monetary Affairs.

Advisory Commission on Customs Valuation.

Advisory Council for Enterprises.

Advisory Council for Export Financing.

Advisory Council for Customs Matters.

Budget Commission.

Commission for Technical Support and Co-operation.

Council for Financial and Monetary Affairs: comprises the Presidents of member states' central banks, who examine all aspects of financial, monetary and exchange co-operation.

Council of National Customs Directors.

Council on Transport for Trade Facilitation.

Labour Advisory Council.

Nomenclature Advisory Commission.

Sectoral Councils.

Tourism Council.

GENERAL SECRETARIAT

The General Secretariat is the technical body of the Association; it submits proposals for action, carries out research and evaluates activities. The Secretary-General is elected for a three-year term, which is renewable. There are two Assistant Secretaries-General.

Secretary-General: CARLOS ÁLVAREZ (Argentina).

Activities

The Latin American Free Trade Association (LAFTA) was an intergovernmental organization, created by the Treaty of Montevideo in February 1960 with the object of increasing trade between the Contracting Parties and of promoting regional integration, thus contributing to the economic and social development of the member countries. The Treaty provided for the gradual establishment of a free trade area, which would form the basis for a Latin American Common Market. Reduction of tariff and other trade barriers was to be carried out gradually until 1980. In June 1980, however, it was decided that LAFTA should be replaced by a less ambitious and more flexible organization, the Latin American Integration Association (Asociación Latinoamericana de Integración—ALADI), established by the 1980 Montevideo Treaty, which came into force in March 1981, and was fully ratified in March 1982. The Treaty envisaged an area of economic preferences, comprising a regional tariff preference for goods originating in member states (in effect from 1 July 1984) and regional and partial scope agreements (on economic complementation, trade promotion, trade in agricultural goods, scientific and technical co-operation, the environment, tourism, and other matters), taking into account the different stages of development of the members, and with no definite timetable for the establishment of a full common market. By 2010 intra-ALADI exports were estimated to total US $133,151m., an increase of almost 25% from the previous year, when trade declined owing to adverse global economic conditions. The estimated total of intra-ALADI trade in 2011 amounted to $160,000m.

Certain LAFTA institutions were retained and adapted by ALADI, e.g. the Reciprocal Payments and Credits Agreement (1965, modified in 1982) and the Multilateral Credit Agreement to Alleviate Temporary Shortages of Liquidity, known as the Santo Domingo Agreement (1969, extended in 1981 to include mechanisms for counteracting global balance of payments difficulties and for assisting in times of natural disaster).

Agreements concluded under ALADI auspices include a regional tariff preference agreement, whereby members allow imports from other member states to enter with tariffs 20% lower than those imposed on imports from other countries, and a Market Opening Lists agreement in favour of the three least developed member states, which provides for the total elimination of duties and other restrictions on imports of certain products. Other 'partial scope agreements' (in which two or more member states participate), include: renegotiation agreements (pertaining to tariff cuts under LAFTA); trade agreements covering particular industrial sectors; the agreements establishing the Southern Common Market (Mercosur) and the Group of Three (G-3); and agreements covering agriculture, gas supply, tourism, environmental protection, books, transport, sanitation and trade facilitation. A new system of tariff nomenclature, based on the 'harmonized system', was adopted from 1 January 1990 as a basis for common trade negotiations and statistics. General regimes on safeguards and rules of origin entered into force in

1987. The Secretariat convenes meetings of entrepreneurs in various private industrial sectors, to encourage regional trade and co-operation.

ALADI has worked to establish multilateral links or agreements with Latin American non-member countries or integration organizations, and with other developing countries or economic groups outside the continent. In February 1994 the Council of Ministers of Foreign Affairs urged that ALADI should become the co-ordinating body for the various bilateral, multilateral and regional accords (with the Andean Community, Mercosur and G-3, etc.), with the aim of eventually forming a region-wide common market. The General Secretariat initiated studies in preparation for a programme to undertake this co-ordinating work. At the same meeting in February there was a serious disagreement regarding the proposed adoption of a protocol to the Montevideo Treaty to enable Mexico to participate in the North American Free Trade Agreement (NAFTA), while remaining a member of ALADI. However, in June the first Interpretative Protocol to the Montevideo Treaty was signed by the Ministers of Foreign Affairs: the Protocol allows member states to establish preferential trade agreements with developed nations, with a temporary waiver of the most favoured nation clause, subject to the negotiation of unilateral compensation. In December 2011 the Secretary-General of ALADI welcomed the establishment of the Community of Latin American and Caribbean States as further means of strengthening regional integration and of formulating a unified regional position in global fora. In March 2012 ALADI hosted a ministerial meeting, attended by high-level representatives of other regional organizations, which discussed current approaches to development in Latin America.

Mercosur (comprising Argentina, Brazil, Paraguay and Uruguay) aims to conclude free trade agreements with the other members of ALADI. In March 2001 ALADI signed a co-operation agreement with the Andean Community to facilitate the exchange of information and consolidate regional and sub-regional integration. In December 2003 Mercosur and the Andean Community signed an Economic Complementary Agreement, and in April 2004 they concluded a free trade agreement, to come into effect on 1 July 2004 (although later postponed). Those ALADI member states remaining outside Mercosur and the Andean Community would be permitted to apply to join the envisaged larger free trade zone.

In May 2012 ALADI member states met to exchange information and views on sustainability and the Green Economy in advance of the UN Conference on Sustainable Development (Rio+20), which was convened in the following month.

Publications

Noticias ALADI (monthly, in Spanish).

Estadísticas y Comercio (quarterly, in Spanish).

Reports, studies, brochures, texts of agreements.

LEAGUE OF ARAB STATES

Address: POB 11642, Arab League Bldg, Tahrir Sq., Cairo, Egypt.

Telephone: (2) 575-0511; **fax:** (2) 574-0331; **internet:** www.arableagueonline.org.

The League of Arab States (more generally known as the Arab League) is a voluntary association of sovereign Arab states, designed to strengthen the close ties linking them and to co-ordinate their policies and activities and direct them towards the common good of all the Arab countries. It was founded in March 1945.

MEMBERS

Algeria	Lebanon	Somalia
Bahrain	Libya*	Sudan
Comoros	Mauritania	Syria*
Djibouti	Morocco	Tunisia
Egypt	Oman	United Arab Emirates
Iraq	Palestine†	Yemen
Jordan	Qatar	
Kuwait	Saudi Arabia	

* Libya was suspended from participation in meetings of the League in February 2011. It was readmitted in August following an agreement that the new Libyan Transitional Council would represent the country at the League. In mid-November Syria was suspended from meetings of the League.

† Palestine is considered to be an independent state, and therefore a full member of the League.

Organization

(June 2012)

COUNCIL

The supreme organ of the Arab League, the Council consists of representatives of the member states, each of which has one vote, and a representative for Palestine. The Council meets ordinarily every March, normally at the League headquarters, at the level of heads of state ('kings, heads of state and emirs'), and in March and September at the level of ministers of foreign affairs. The summit level meeting reviews all issues related to Arab national security strategies, co-ordinates supreme policies of the Arab states towards regional and international issues, reviews recommendations and reports submitted to it by meetings at foreign minister level, appoints the Secretary-General of the League, and is mandated to amend the League's Charter. Decisions of the Council at the level of heads of state are passed on a consensus basis. Meetings of ministers of foreign affairs assess the implementation of summit resolutions, prepare relevant reports, and make arrangements for subsequent summits. Committees comprising a smaller group of foreign ministers may be appointed to follow up closely summit resolutions. Extraordinary summit meetings may be held at the request of one member state or the Secretary-General, if approved by a two-thirds' majority of member states. Extraordinary sessions of ministers of foreign affairs may be held at the request of two member states or of the Secretary-General. The presidency of ordinary meetings is rotated in accordance with the alphabetical order of the League's member states. Unanimous decisions of the Council are binding upon all member states of the League; majority decisions are binding only on those states that have accepted them.

The Council is supported by technical and specialized committees advising on financial and administrative affairs, information affairs and legal affairs. In addition, specialized ministerial councils have been established to formulate common policies for the regulation and the advancement of co-operation in the following sectors: communications; electricity; environment; health; housing and construction; information; interior; justice; social affairs; tourism; transportation; and youth and sports.

GENERAL SECRETARIAT

The administrative and financial offices of the League. The Secretariat carries out the decisions of the Council, and provides financial and administrative services for the personnel of the League. General departments comprise: the Bureau of the Secretary-General, Arab Affairs, Economic Affairs, Information Affairs, Legal Affairs, Palestine Affairs, Political International Affairs, Military Affairs, Social Affairs, Administrative and Financial Affairs, and Internal Audit. In addition, there is a Documentation and Information Centre, an Arab League Centre in Tunis, Tunisia, an Arab Fund for Technical Assistance in African States, a Higher Arab Institute for Translation in Algiers, Algeria, a Music Academy in Baghdad, Iraq, and a Central Boycott Office, based in Damascus, Syria (see below). The following bodies have also been established: an administrative court; an investment arbitration board; and a higher auditing board.

The Secretary-General is appointed at summit meetings of the Council by a two-thirds' majority of the member states, for a five-year, renewable term. He appoints the Assistant Secretaries-General and principal officials, with the approval of the Council. He has the rank of ambassador, and the Assistant Secretaries-General have the rank of ministers plenipotentiary.

Secretary-General: NABIL AL-ARABI (Egypt).

DEFENCE AND ECONOMIC CO-OPERATION

Groups established under the Treaty of Joint Defence and Economic Co-operation, concluded in 1950 to complement the Charter of the League.

Arab Unified Military Command: f. 1964 to co-ordinate military policies for the liberation of Palestine.

Economic and Social Council: compares and co-ordinates the economic policies of the member states; supervises the activities of the Arab League's specialized agencies. The Council is composed of ministers of economic affairs or their deputies; decisions are taken by majority vote. The first meeting was held in 1953. In February 1997 the Economic and Social Council adopted the Executive Programme of the League's (1981) Agreement to Facilitate and Develop Trade Among Arab Countries, with a view to establishing a Greater Arab Free Trade Area (see below).

Joint Defence Council: supervises implementation of those aspects of the treaty concerned with common defence. Composed of ministers of foreign affairs and of defence; decisions by a two-thirds' majority vote of members are binding on all.

Permanent Military Commission: f. 1950; composed of representatives of army general staffs; main purpose: to draw up plans of joint defence for submission to the Joint Defence Council.

ARAB TRANSITIONAL PARLIAMENT

Inaugurated in December 2005, the Arab Transitional Parliament, based in Damascus, Syria, comprises 88 members (four delegates from each Arab state, including some representing non-elected bodies). The Transitional Parliament is eventually to be replaced by a Permanent Arab Parliament, a Statute for which remains under discussion. The interim body (which has no legislative function) aims to encourage dialogue between member states and to provide a focal point for joint Arab action.

OTHER INSTITUTIONS OF THE LEAGUE

Other bodies established by resolutions adopted by the Council of the League:

Administrative Tribunal of the Arab League: f. 1964; began operations 1966.

Arab Fund for Technical Assistance to African Countries: f. 1975 to provide technical assistance for development projects by providing African and Arab experts, grants for scholarships and training, and finance for technical studies.

Central Boycott Office: POB 437, Damascus, Syria; f. 1951 to prevent trade between Arab countries and Israel, and to enforce a boycott by Arab countries of companies outside the region that conduct trade with Israel.

Higher Auditing Board: comprises representatives of seven member states, elected every three years; undertakes financial and administrative auditing duties.

Investment Arbitration Board: examines disputes between member states relating to capital investments.

SPECIALIZED AGENCIES

All member states of the Arab League are also members of the Specialized Agencies, which constitute an integral part of the Arab League. (See also the Arab Fund for Economic and Social Development, the Arab Monetary Fund, Council of Arab Economic Unity and the Organization of Arab Petroleum Exporting Countries.)

Arab Academy for Science, Technology and Maritime Transport (AASTMT): POB 1029, Alexandria, Egypt; tel. (3) 5622388; fax (3) 5622525; internet www.aast.edu; f. 1975 as Arab Maritime Transport Academy; provides specialized training in marine transport, engineering, technology and management; Pres. Prof. Dr ISMAIL ABDEL GHAFAR ISMAIL; publs *Maritime Research Bulletin* (monthly), *Journal of the Arab Academy for Science, Technology and Maritime Transport* (2 a year).

Arab Administrative Development Organization (ARADO): 2 El-Hegaz St, POB 2692 al-Horreia, Heliopolis, Cairo, Egypt; tel. (2) 22580006; fax (2) 22580077; e-mail arado@arado.org.eg; internet www.arado.org.eg; f. 1961 (as Arab Organization of Administrative Sciences), became operational in 1969; administration development, training, consultancy, research and studies, information, documentation; promotes Arab and international co-operation in administrative sciences; includes Arab Network of Administrative Information; maintains an extensive digital library; 20 Arab state members; Dir-Gen. Prof. REFAT ABDELHALIM ALFAOURI; publs *Arab Journal of Administration* (biannual), *Management Newsletter* (quarterly), research series, training manuals.

Arab Atomic Energy Agency (AAEA): POB 402, El-Manzah 1004, 1004 Tunis, Tunisia; tel. (71) 808400; fax (71) 808450; e-mail aaea@aaea.org.tn; internet www.aaea.org.tn; f. 1988; Dir-Gen. Prof. Dr ABDELMAJID MAHJOUB (Tunisia); publs *The Atom and Development* (quarterly), other publs in the field of nuclear sciences and their applications in industry, biology, medicine, agriculture, food irradiation and seawater desalination.

Arab Bank for Economic Development in Africa (Banque arabe pour le développement économique en Afrique—BADEA): Sayed Abd ar-Rahman el-Mahdi St, POB 2640, Khartoum 11111, Sudan; tel. (1) 83773646; fax (1) 83770600; e-mail badea@badea.org; internet www.badea.org; f. 1973 by Arab League; provides loans and grants to African countries to finance development projects; paid-up cap. US $2,800m. (Dec. 2010); in 2010 the Bank approved loans and grants totalling $192.0m. and technical assistance for feasibility studies and institutional support amounting to $30m.; by the end of 2010, total net loan and grant commitments approved since funding activities began in 1975 amounted to $2,223.6m; during 2010 the Bank contributed $13.91m. to the heavily indebted poor countries initiative, bringing the cumulative total to $186.3. since the scheme commenced in 1997; subscribing countries: all countries of the Arab League, except the Comoros, Djibouti, Somalia and Yemen; recipient countries: all countries of the African Union, except those belonging to the Arab League; Chair. YOUSEF IBRAHEM AL-BASSAM (Saudi Arabia); Dir-Gen. ABDELAZIZ KHELEF (Algeria); publs *Annual Report Co-operation for Development* (quarterly), studies on Afro-Arab co-operation, periodic brochures.

Arab Center for the Studies of Arid Zones and Dry Lands (ACSAD): POB 2440, Damascus, Syria; tel. (11) 5743039; fax (11) 5743063; e-mail email@acsad.org; internet www.acsad.org; f. 1968 to conduct regional research and development programmes related to water and soil resources, plant and animal production, agro-meteorology, and socio-economic studies of arid zones; holds conferences and training courses and encourages the exchange of information by Arab scientists; Dir-Gen. RAFIK ALI SALEH.

Arab Industrial Development and Mining Organization: rue France, Zanagat al-Khatawat, POB 8019, Rabat, Morocco; tel. (37) 772600; fax (37) 772188; e-mail id@aidmo.org; internet www.aidmo.org; f. 1990 by merger of Arab Industrial Development Organization, Arab Organization for Mineral Resources and Arab Organization for Standardization and Metrology; comprises a 13-member Executive Council, a High Consultative Committee of Standardization, a High Committee of Mineral Resources and a Co-ordination Committee for Arab Industrial Research Centres; a Council of ministers of member states responsible for industry meets every two years; in Sept. 2011 organized, jointly with ESCWA, a conference on 'The Role of Green Industries in Promoting Socio-Economic Development in the Arab Countries'; Dir-Gen. MOHAMED BIN YOUSEF; publs *Arab Industrial Development* (monthly and quarterly newsletters).

Arab Investment & Export Credit Guarantee Corporation: POB 23568, Safat 13096, Kuwait; tel. 4959000; fax 4959596; e-mail operations@dhaman.org; internet www.dhaman.org; f. 1974; insures Arab investors for non-commercial risks, and export credits for commercial and non-commercial risks; undertakes research and other activities to promote inter-Arab trade and investment; total assets US $354.5m. (Dec. 2010); mems: 21 Arab countries and four multilateral Arab financial institutions; Dir-Gen. FAHAD RASHID AL-IBRAHIM; publs *News Bulletin* (quarterly), *Arab Investment Climate Report* (annually).

Arab Labour Organization: POB 814, Cairo, Egypt; tel. (2) 3362721; fax (2) 3484902; internet www.alolabor.org; f. 1965 for co-operation between member states in labour problems; unification of labour legislation and general conditions of work wherever possible; research; technical assistance; social insurance; training, etc; the organization has a tripartite structure: governments, employers and workers; Dir-Gen. AHMAD MUHAMMAD LUQMAN; publs *ALO Bulletin* (monthly), *Arab Labour Review* (quarterly), *Legislative Bulletin* (annually), series of research reports and studies concerned with economic and social development issues in the Arab world.

Arab League Educational, Cultural and Scientific Organization (ALECSO): ave Mohamed V, POB 1120, Tunis, Tunisia; tel. (71) 784-466; fax (71) 784-496; e-mail alecso@email.ati.tn; internet www.alecso.org.tn; f. 1970 to promote and co-ordinate educational, cultural and scientific activities in the Arab region; 21 mem. states; regional units: Arab Centre for Arabization, Translation, Authorship, and Publication—Damascus, Syria; Institute of Arab Manuscripts—Cairo, Egypt; Institute of Arab Research and Studies—Cairo, Egypt; Khartoum International Institute for Arabic Language—Khartoum, Sudan; and the Arabization Co-ordination Bureau—Rabat, Morocco; Dir-Gen. MOHAMED-EL AZIZ BEN ACHOUR; publs *Arab Journal of Culture* (2 a year), *Arab Journal of Education* (2 a year), *Arab Journal of Science and Information* (2 a year), *Arab Bulletin of Publications* (annually), *ALECSO Newsletter* (monthly).

Arab Organization for Agricultural Development (AOAD): 7 al-Amarat St, POB 474, Khartoum 11111, Sudan; tel. (1) 83472176; fax (1) 83471402; e-mail info@aoad.org; internet www.aoad.org; f. 1970; began operations in 1972 to contribute to co-operation in agricultural activities, and in the development of natural and human resources for agriculture; compiles data, conducts studies, training and food security programmes; includes Information and Documentation Centre, Arab Centre for Studies and Projects, and Arab Institute of Forestry and Biodiversity; Dir-Gen. Dr TARIQ MOOSA AL-ZADJALI; publs *Agricultural Statistics Yearbook*, *Annual Report on Agricultural Development, the State of Arab Food Security* (annually), *Agriculture and Development in the Arab World* (quarterly), *Accession Bulletin* (every 2 months), *AOAD Newsletter* (monthly), *Arab Agricultural Research Journal, Arab Journal for Irrigation Water Management* (2 a year).

Arab Satellite Communications Organization (ARABSAT): POB 1038, Diplomatic Quarter, Riyadh 11431, Saudi Arabia; tel. (1) 4820000; fax (1) 4887999; e-mail info@arabsat.com; internet www.arabsat.com; f. 1976; regional satellite telecommunications organization providing television, telephone and data exchange services to members and private users; operates five satellites, which cover all Arab and Western European countries; suspended satellite broadcasts to Syria in June 2012, at the request of the League Council; Pres. and CEO KHALID AHMED BALKHEYOUR.

Arab States Broadcasting Union (ASBU): POB 250, 1080 Tunis Cedex; rue 8840, Centre Urbain Nord, Tunisia; tel. (71)

843505; fax (71) 843054; e-mail asbu@asbu.intl.tn; internet www.asbu.net; f. 1969 to promote and study broadcasting subjects, to exchange expertise and technical co-operation in broadcasting; conducts training and audience research; 28 active mems, seven participating mems, 19 assoc. mems; Pres. of Exec. Council MOHAMED HATEM SULEIMAN (Sudan); publ. *Arab Broadcasters* (quarterly).

Activities

The League was founded in 1945 with the signing of the Pact of the Arab League. A Cultural Treaty was signed in the following year. In 1952, agreements were concluded on extradition, writs, letters of request and the nationality of Arabs outside their country of origin, and in the following year a Convention was adopted on the privileges and immunities of the League. At an emergency summit meeting held in 1985, two commissions were established to mediate in disagreements between Arab states (between Jordan and Syria, Iraq and Syria, Iraq and Libya, and Libya and the Palestine Liberation Organization (PLO). The League's headquarters, which had been transferred from Cairo, Egypt, to Tunis, Tunisia, in 1979, were relocated back to Cairo in 1990. At a meeting of the Council held in September 2000, ministers of foreign affairs of member states adopted an Appendix to the League's Charter that provided for the Council to meet ordinarily every March at the level of a summit conference of heads of state ('kings, heads of state and emirs'). The Council was to continue to meet at foreign ministerial level every March and September. In October 2002 Libya announced plans to withdraw from the League, although these were subsequently suspended. In July the Egyptian Government unveiled a series of measures aimed at strengthening the League, including the adoption of majority voting and the establishment of a body to resolve conflicts in the region (previously agreed at the 1996 summit and sanctioned by member states' foreign ministers in 2000). The 2004 summit meeting of Arab League heads of state, scheduled to be held in Tunis in late March, was postponed by the Tunisian Government two days in advance following disagreements among member states over a number of issues on the summit's agenda, including democratic reforms in Arab states and the proposed reforms to the League. The meeting, which was eventually held in May, approved a *Pledge of Accord and Solidarity* that committed the League heads of state to implementing in full decisions of the League. The Arab leaders also stated their commitment to conducting political, economic and social reforms, respect for human rights, and to strengthening the role of women, despite continuing opposition from several member states. In March 2007 the summit meeting of heads of state, held in Riyadh, Saudi Arabia, determined that in future Arab consultative summits should be convoked when deemed necessary to address specific issues. The 22nd Arab League summit meeting, held in Sirte, Libya, in March 2010, approved the formation of a committee comprising the Egyptian, Iraqi, Libyan, Qatari and Yemeni heads of state, and the League Secretary-General, with a mandate to oversee the development of a new structure for joint Arab action. The committee prepared documentation on proposed reforms for consideration by an extraordinary summit of the League that was held in early October, also in Sirte.

From February–August 2011 the League suspended Libya from participation in its meetings owing to the use of military force against opposition movements in that country (see below). In mid-November Syria was suspended from meetings of the League, on similar grounds. The emerging civil unrest in countries in the region, notably, in addition, in Egypt, Tunisia and Yemen, led to the 23rd summit meeting, initially scheduled to be held in March 2011, being postponed until March 2012.

In mid-May 2011 a meeting of League ministers of foreign affairs unanimously elected Nabil al-Arabi, hitherto the Egyptian minister of foreign affairs, as the new Secretary-General of the League.

The 23rd summit meeting of Arab League heads of state, convened in Baghdad, Iraq, in late March 2012, endorsed, and called for the immediate implementation of, a six-point plan on resolving the Syrian crisis that had been recently proposed by the Arab League-UN Joint Special Envoy on the Syrian Crisis. The UN Secretary-General attended the summit, owing to the inclusion of the Syrian crisis on its agenda. Saudi Arabia, seeking the imposition of stronger measures against the Syrian regime, and having reportedly failed to secure the agreement of the Iraqi Government to invite Syrian opposition representatives to the summit meeting, was represented at the gathering at the level of Ambassador. Egypt and Qatar also sent delegates lower than the level of head of state. The Amir of Kuwait participated in the meeting, representing the first visit by a Kuwaiti leader to Baghdad since prior to the 1990 invasion Kuwait by Iraq. Regional water shortages and means of coping with natural disasters were also discussed by the summit.

In early 2012 the League submitted the prospective domain name .arab for registration under the Internet Corporation for Assigned Names and Numbers (ICANN)'s expanded generic top-level domains (gTLD) programme; it was envisaged that approval would be granted in 2013.

SECURITY

In 1950 Arab League member states concluded a Joint Defence and Economic Co-operation Treaty. An Arab Deterrent Force was established by the Arab League Council in June 1976 to supervise attempts at that time to cease hostilities in Lebanon; the Force's mandate was terminated in 1983. In April 1998 Arab League ministers of the interior and of justice adopted the Arab Convention for the Suppression of Terrorism, which incorporated security and judicial measures, such as extradition arrangements and the exchange of evidence. The agreement entered into effect in May 2000, 30 days after being ratified by at least seven member countries. In August 1998 the League denounced terrorist bomb attacks against the US embassies in Kenya and Tanzania. Nevertheless, it condemned US retaliatory military action, a few days later, against suspected terrorist targets in Afghanistan and Sudan, and endorsed a request by the Sudanese Government that the Security Council investigate the incident. An emergency meeting of the League's Council, convened in mid-September 2001 in response to major terrorist attacks on the USA, perpetrated by militant Islamist fundamentalists, condemned the atrocities, while urging respect for the rights of Arab and Muslim US citizens. The Secretary-General subsequently emphasized the need for co-ordinated global anti-terrorist action to have clearly defined goals and to be based on sufficient consultations and secure evidence. He also deplored anti-Islamic prejudice, and stated that US-led action against any Arab state would not be supported and that Israeli participation in an international anti-terrorism alliance would be unacceptable. A meeting of League ministers of foreign affairs in Doha, Qatar, in early October condemned international terrorism but did not express support for retaliatory military action by the USA and its allies. In December a further emergency meeting of League foreign affairs ministers was held to discuss the deepening Middle East crisis. In January 2002 the League appointed a commissioner responsible for promoting dialogue between civilizations. The commissioner was mandated to encourage understanding in Western countries of Arab and Muslim civilization and viewpoints, with the aim of redressing perceived negative stereotypes (especially in view of the Islamist fundamentalist connection to the September 2001 terrorist atrocities). In April 2003 the Secretary-General expressed his regret that the Arab states had failed to prevent the ongoing war in Iraq, and urged the development of a new regional security order. In November the UN Secretary-General appointed the Secretary-General of the League to serve as the Arab region's representative on the UN High-Level Panel on Threats, Challenges and Change. In March 2007 the League's summit meeting resolved to establish an expert-level task force to consider national security issues.

In December 2010 the Arab League and the UN Office on Drugs and Crime jointly launched a five-year Regional Programme on Drug Control, Crime Prevention and Criminal Justice Reform for the Arab States, covering the period 2011–15, and based on the following pillars: countering illicit trafficking, organized crime and terrorism; promoting justice and integrity; and drug prevention and improving health.

LIBYA

In December 1991 the League expressed solidarity with Libya, which was under international pressure to extradite two government agents who were suspected of involvement in the explosion which destroyed a US passenger aircraft over Lockerbie, United Kingdom, in December 1988. In March 1992 the League appointed a committee to seek to resolve the disputes between Libya and the USA, the United Kingdom and France over the Lockerbie bomb and the explosion which destroyed a French passenger aircraft over Niger in September 1989. The League condemned the UN's decision, at the end of March, to impose sanctions against Libya, and appealed for a negotiated solution. In September 1997 Arab League ministers of foreign affairs advocated a gradual removal of international sanctions against Libya, and agreed that member countries should permit international flights to leave Libya for specific humanitarian and religious purposes and when used for the purpose of transporting foreign nationals. In August 1998 the USA and United Kingdom accepted a proposal of the Libyan Government, supported by the Arab League, that the suspects in the Lockerbie case be tried in The Hague, Netherlands, under Scottish law. In March 1999 the League's Council determined that member states would suspend sanctions imposed against Libya, once arrangements for the trial of the suspects in the Lockerbie case had been finalized. (The suspects were transferred to a detention centre in the Netherlands in early April, whereupon the UN Security Council suspended its sanctions against Libya.) At the end of January 2001, following the completion of the trial in The Hague of the two Libyans accused of complicity in the Lockerbie case (one of whom was found guilty and one of whom was acquitted), the Secretary-General of the League urged the UN Security Council fully to terminate the sanctions against Libya that had been suspended in 1999. Meeting in mid-March, the League's Council pledged that member states would not consider themselves bound by the (inactive) UN sanctions. In early September 2002 the Council deplored the USA's continuing active imposition of sanctions against Libya and endorsed Libya's right to claim compensation in respect of these.

In mid-February 2011, in protest against violent measures taken by the regime of the Libyan leader Col Muammar al-Qaddafi against opposition groupings, the Libyan delegate to the League resigned his representative position. An emergency session of the League convened soon afterwards suspended Libya from participation in meetings of the League. The League supported the adoption by the UN Security Council, in March, of Resolution 1973, which imposed a no-fly zone in Libya's airspace, strengthened sanctions against the Qaddafi regime, demanded an immediate cease-fire, and authorized member states to take 'all necessary measures to protect civilians and civilian populated areas under threat of attack' by forces loyal to Qaddafi, 'while excluding a foreign occupation force of any form on any part of Libyan territory'. Following the instigation of the UN-mandated military action in Libya, the League Secretary-General reportedly emphasized that the focus of the military intervention ought to be on the protection of civilians and ought not to exceed the mandate to impose a no-fly zone. In August, as opposition forces captured the Libyan capital, Tripoli, the League Secretary-General offered full solidarity to the new Libyan National Transitional Council, as the legitimate representative of the Libyan people. Libya was readmitted to full League membership at the end of that month. The League at that time urged the international community to release all assets and property of the Libyan state, previously blocked by economic sanctions. Following the death of al-Qaddafi in October the Secretary-General urged unity and extended the League's full support for the country's transition.

SYRIA

By August 2011 it was estimated that around 2,200 anti-government street protesters had been killed by security forces—deploying tanks and snipers—during several months of unrest in Syria. A meeting of Arab League foreign ministers convened in that month issued a statement urging the Syrian regime to act reasonably, stop the ongoing bloodshed, and respect the 'legitimate demands' of the Syrian people. The meeting also determined that the League Secretary-General, Nabil al-Arabi, would visit the Syrian authorities with a peace initiative aimed at resolving the situation through dialogue. Accordingly, talks were held between the Secretary-General and President Bashar al-Assad in the Syrian capital, Damascus, in early September. It was reported that al-Arabi and al-Assad discussed measures aimed at accelerating political reforms in Syria, and that the League Secretary-General stated his rejection of foreign intervention in the Syrian situation. The League's peace initiative was, however, reportedly rejected by both the Syrian authorities and protesters. In October al-Arabi led a further delegation to the country, amid an escalation of attacks by the security forces. In mid-November the League, meeting in emergency session, voted to suspend Syria from participation in meetings of the League, and to impose economic and diplomatic sanctions in protest at the violent repression of political opponents and civilian demonstrators by the government, and its failure to implement a peace initiative. The resolution was endorsed by 18 members; Syria, Lebanon and Yemen voted against the suspension (Iraq abstained). The measures came into effect four days later, when no concessions had been made by the Syrian authorities. On 19 December the Syrian authorities reportedly agreed to the League's peace plan to withdraw security forces and heavy weapons from civilian areas, to initiate negotiations with the opposition movement and to release political prisoners. The Arab League was to send an observer mission to the country, with an initial mandate of one month, in order to monitor compliance with the measures. However, within days of the arrival of the first 50 observers, on 26 December, the mission was strongly criticized for its ineffectiveness in preventing further government attacks and its inability to act independently of the authorities to assess accurately the level of violence. On 9 January 2012 Arab League ministers of foreign affairs met to consider the mission's initial findings and to discuss demands for its withdrawal. The meeting agreed to maintain and to reinforce the mission and demanded that the Syrian authorities co-operate fully. On 22 January Arab League ministers agreed on a plan of action to end the conflict, requiring President Assad to transfer his authority to an interim government within two months, and democratic parliamentary and presidential elections to be conducted within six months. The proposals were to be submitted for approval by the UN Security Council. They were rejected, the following day, by the Syrian authorities. The ministerial meeting agreed to extend the monitoring mission. Saudi Arabia, however, decided to withdraw from the operation. On 24 January members of the Gulf Cooperation Council also resolved to withdraw their monitors. A few days later the League announced that it was suspending the mission owing to a sharp deterioration in the security situation in Syria. In early February Russia and the People's Republic of China vetoed a draft resolution at the UN Security Council to endorse the League's peace plan for Syria. In mid-February League ministers adopted a resolution providing for the termination of the suspended monitoring mission; ending diplomatic co-operation with the Syrian regime; and proposing the creation of a joint Arab-UN peace-keeping mission to Syria. Later in that month the Secretaries-General of the League and of the UN appointed Kofi Annan—formerly the UN Secretary-General (until 2006)—as their Joint Special Envoy on the Syrian Crisis; in March Nasser al-Kidwa, a former minister of foreign affairs in the Palestine National Authority, and Jean-Marie Guéhenno, a former UN Under-Secretary-General for Peace-keeping Operations, were appointed as Deputy Joint Special Envoys. Towards the end of February an international conference on the situation in Syria, which had escalated significantly, was convened in Tunis, Tunisia, by the 'Friends of Syria', a coalition initiated by France and the USA, with League support (specifically, with endorsement from Qatar and Saudi Arabia), following China and Russia's veto of the Security Council's draft resolution on Syria. The conference urged the UN to consider establishing a peace-keeping mission for Syria. In late March the Syrian Government announced its acceptance of a six-point peace plan proposed earlier in that month by Annan. The plan envisaged: (i) a commitment to working with the Joint Envoy in an inclusive Syrian-led political process aimed at addressing the legitimate aspirations and concerns of the Syrian people; (ii) a UN-monitored cease-fire by all parties, including a commitment by the Syrian regime to withdraw troops and heavy weaponry from population centres; (iii) a commitment to enabling the timely provision of humanitarian assistance to all areas affected by the fighting, and the immediate implementation of a daily two-hour humanitarian pause; (iv) the expedited release of arbitrarily arrested detainees; (v) free access and movement for journalists;

and (vi) freedom of association and the right to demonstrate peacefully for all. The plan did not demand explicitly the resignation of Syrian President Assad. Shortly afterwards Arab League heads of state, gathered at a summit meeting in Baghdad, Iraq, endorsed the plan, and called for its immediate and full implementation. In mid-April the UN Security Council—taking note of an assessment by the League-UN Joint Special Envoy that the parties to the Syrian violence appeared to be observing a cessation of fire, and that the Syrian Government had begun to implement its commitments under the plan—authorized an advance team of up to 30 unarmed military observers to monitor the cease-fire, pending the deployment of a full cease-fire supervision mission. Soon afterwards, as violence had escalated since the attempt to impose a cease-fire, and Syrian forces had not withdrawn from urban areas, the UN Secretary-General requested that a full team of 300 unarmed observers should be promptly deployed. Consequently, on 21 April, the UN Security Council unanimously authorized the establishment of the UN Supervision Mission in Syria (UNSMIS), initially for a period of 90 days, with a mandate to monitor the cessation of violence and to observe and support the full implementation of the six-point peace plan. Repeated violations of the terms of the peace plan continued, however, to be reported. In late May the UN Security Council issued a statement unanimously condemning—as an 'outrageous use of force against the civilian population' constituting a violation of applicable international law—the indiscriminate massacre (confirmed by UNSMIS observers), of an estimated 108 men, women and children, and the wounding of many more, resulting from the shelling of a residential neighbourhood—the rebel-controlled village of El-Houleh, near Homs—allegedly by Syrian government forces. The Council also condemned the killing of civilians in El-Houleh by shooting at close range and by severe physical abuse. Reiterating its full support to the efforts of the Arab League-UN Joint Special Envoy for the implementation of his six-point plan, the Council demanded that the Syrian Government immediately cease the use of heavy weapons in population centres, and immediately return its troops to their barracks. In early June the 'Free Syrian Army' group of anti-government militants announce that it was no longer committed to the six-point peace plan. Shortly afterwards at least an estimated further 78 people, again including women and children, were reported to have been killed in the western village of Qbeir, by pro-government militants, following the shelling of the area by government forces. A meeting of the Security Council held soon afterwards, with participation by the Arab League and UN Secretaries-General and the Joint Special Envoy, requested the UN Secretary-General to put forward a range of options for resolving the Syrian crisis. On 16 June, in view of the escalating insecurity, UNSMIS suspended its patrols in Syria, while remaining committed to ending the violence. By mid-2012 the number of civilians killed in the conflict since March 2011 was estimated at around 10,000; many more people were estimated to have been displaced from their homes. In June 2012 an extraordinary ministerial-level meeting of the League Council requested the Arab Satellite Communications Organization and the Egyptian company Nilesat to suspend broadcasts via Arab Satellites of official and private Syrian television channels.

Joint Special Envoy of the League of Arab States and the UN on the Syrian Crisis: KOFI ANNAN (Ghana).

TRADE AND ECONOMIC CO-OPERATION

In 1953 Arab League member states formed an Economic and Social Council. In 1956 an agreement was concluded on the adoption of a Common Tariff Nomenclature. In 1962 an Arab Economic Unity Agreement was concluded. The first meeting of the Council of Arab Economic Unity took place in June 1964. An Arab Common Market Agreement was endorsed by the Council in August. In February 1997 the Economic and Social Council adopted the Executive Programme of the (1981) Agreement to Facilitate and Develop Trade Among Arab Countries, with a view to creating a Greater Arab Free Trade Area (GAFTA), which aimed to facilitate and develop trade among participating countries through the reduction and eventual elimination of customs duties over a 10-year period (at a rate of 10% per year), with effect from January 1998. In February 2002 the Economic and Social Council agreed to bring forward the inauguration of GAFTA to 1 January 2005. Consequently customs duties, which, according to schedule, had been reduced by 50% from January 1998–January 2002, were further reduced by 10% by January 2003, 20% by January 2004, and a final 20% by January 2005. GAFTA entered into force, as planned, with 17 participating countries (accounting for about 94% of the total volume of intra-Arab trade). The Council agreed to supervise the implementation of the free trade agenda and formally to review its progress twice a year.

The first ever Economic, Development and Social summit meeting of Arab leaders was held in January 2009, in Kuwait, under the auspices of the Arab League. The second Economic, Development and Social summit meeting was convened in January 2011, in Sharm el-Sheikh, Egypt.

WATER RESOURCES

In April 1993 the Council approved the creation of a committee to consider the political and security aspects of water supply in Arab countries. In March 1996, following protests by Syria and Iraq that extensive construction work in southern Turkey was restricting water supply in the region, the Council determined that the waters of the Euphrates and Tigris rivers be shared equitably between the three countries. In April an emergency meeting of the Council issued a further endorsement of Syria's position in the dispute with Turkey.

The inaugural session of a new Arab Ministerial Water Council was convened in June 2009. The Council gave consideration to the development of an Arab Water Strategy; this was launched in March 2011.

ARAB–ISRAELI AFFAIRS

The League regards Palestine as an independent state and therefore as a full League member. In 1951 a Central Boycott Office was established, in Damascus, Syria, to oversee the prevention of trade between Arab countries and Israel, and to enforce a boycott by Arab countries of companies outside the region that conduct trade with Israel. The second summit conference of Arab heads of state, convened in 1964, welcomed the establishment of the PLO.

In April 1993 the League pledged its commitment to the ongoing US-sponsored Middle East Peace Process. Following the signing of the Israeli-PLO Oslo peace accords in September the Council convened in emergency session, at which it approved the agreement. In 1994 the League condemned a decision of the Gulf Cooperation Council (GCC), announced in late September, to end the secondary and tertiary trade embargo against Israel, by which member states refuse to trade with international companies that have investments in Israel. A statement issued by the League insisted that the embargo could be removed only on the decision of the Council.

In March 1995 Arab ministers of foreign affairs approved a resolution urging Israel to renew the Nuclear Non-Proliferation Treaty. The resolution stipulated that failure by Israel to do so would cause Arab states to seek to protect legitimate Arab interests by alternative means. In May an extraordinary session of the Council condemned a decision by Israel to confiscate Arab-owned land in East Jerusalem for resettlement. The Israeli Government announced the suspension of its expropriation plans. The 2009 Arab League summit stated that the International Atomic Energy Agency (IAEA) should provide guarantees on Israel's nuclear facilities and activities.

In June 1996 an extraordinary summit conference of Arab League heads of state was convened, the first since 1990, in order to formulate a united Arab response to the election, in May 1996, of a new government in Israel. The conference (from which Iraq was excluded from the meeting in order to ensure the attendance of the Gulf member states) urged Israel to honour its undertaking to withdraw from the Occupied Territories, including Jerusalem, and to respect the establishment of an independent Palestinian state, in order to ensure the success of the peace process. A final communiqué of the meeting warned that Israeli co-operation was essential to prevent Arab states from reconsidering their participation in the peace process and the re-emergence of regional tensions. In September the League met in emergency session following an escalation of civil unrest in Jerusalem and the Occupied Territories. The League urged the UN Security Council to prevent further alleged Israeli aggression against the

Palestinians. In November the League criticized Israel's settlement policy, and at the beginning of December it convened in emergency session to consider measures to end any expansion of the Jewish population in the West Bank and Gaza. In March 1997 the Council met in emergency session in response to the Israeli Government's decision to proceed with construction of a new settlement at Har Homa (Jabal Abu-Ghunaim) in East Jerusalem. At the end of March ministers of foreign affairs of Arab League states agreed to end all efforts to secure normal diplomatic relations with Israel (although binding agreements already in force with Egypt, Jordan and Palestine were exempt) and to close diplomatic offices and missions while construction work continued in East Jerusalem.

In March 1999 a meeting of the League's Council expressed support for a UN resolution convening an international conference to facilitate the implementation of agreements applying to Israel and the Occupied Territories, condemned Israel's refusal to withdraw from the Occupied Territories without a majority vote in favour from its legislature, as well as its refusal to resume peace negotiations with Lebanon and Syria that had ended in 1996, and advocated the publication of evidence of Israeli violence against Palestinians. The Council considered other issues, including the need to prevent further Israeli expansion in Jerusalem and the problem of Palestinian refugees, and reiterated demands for international support to secure Israel's withdrawal from the Golan Heights. In June the League condemned an Israeli aerial attack on Beirut and southern Lebanon. In November the League demanded that Israel compensate Palestinians for alleged losses incurred by their enforced use of the Israeli currency. In late December, prior to a short-lived resumption of Israeli-Syrian peace negotiations, the League reaffirmed its full support for Syria's position.

In February 2000 the League strongly condemned an Israeli aerial attack on southern Lebanon; the League's Council changed the venue of its next meeting, in March, from the League's Cairo headquarters to Beirut as a gesture of solidarity with Lebanon. The League welcomed the withdrawal of Israeli forces from southern Lebanon in May, although it subsequently condemned continuing territorial violations by the Israeli military. At a meeting of the Council in early September resolutions were passed urging international bodies to avoid participating in conferences in Jerusalem, reiterating a threatened boycott of a US chain of restaurants that was accused of operating a franchise in an Israeli settlement in the West Bank, and opposing an Israeli initiative for a Jewish emblem to be included as a symbol of the International Red Cross and Red Crescent Movement. At an emergency summit meeting convened in late October in response to mounting insecurity in Jerusalem and the Occupied Territories, 15 Arab heads of state, senior officials from six countries and Yasser Arafat, the then Palestinian National Authority (PA) leader, strongly rebuked Israel, which was accused of inciting the ongoing violent disturbances by stalling the progress of the peace process. The summit determined to 'freeze' co-operation with Israel, requested the formation of an international committee to conduct an impartial assessment of the situation, urged the UN Security Council to establish a mechanism to bring alleged Israeli 'war criminals' to trial, and requested the UN to approve the creation of an international force to protect Palestinians residing in the Occupied Territories. The summit also endorsed the establishment of an 'al-Aqsa Fund', with a value of US $800m., which was to finance initiatives aimed at promoting the Arab and Islamic identity of Jerusalem, and a smaller 'Jerusalem Intifada Fund' to support the families of Palestinians killed in the unrest. A follow-up committee was subsequently established to implement the resolutions adopted by the emergency summit.

In January 2001 a meeting of Arab League ministers of foreign affairs reviewed a proposed framework agreement, presented by outgoing US President Clinton, which aimed to resolve the continuing extreme tension between the Israeli and Palestinian authorities. The meeting agreed that the issues dominating the stalled Middle East peace process should not be redefined, strongly objecting to a proposal that, in exchange for Palestinian assumption of control over Muslim holy sites in Jerusalem, Palestinians exiled at the time of the foundation of the Israeli state in 1948 should forgo their claimed right to return to their former homes. In March 2001 the League's first ordinary annual summit-level Council was convened, in Amman, Jordan. The summit issued the Amman Declaration, which emphasized the promotion of Arab unity, and demanded the reversal of Israel's 1967 occupation of Arab territories. Heads of state attending the summit requested that the League consider means of reactivating the now relaxed Arab economic boycott of Israel. In May 2001 League ministers of foreign affairs determined that all political contacts with Israel should be suspended in protest at aerial attacks by Israel on Palestinian targets in the West Bank. In July representatives of 13 member countries met in Damascus, Syria, under the auspices of the Central Boycott Office. The meeting declared unanimous support for reactivated trade measures against Israeli companies and foreign businesses dealing with Israel. In August an emergency meeting of ministers of foreign affairs of the member states was convened at the request of the Palestinian authorities to address the recent escalation of hostilities and Israel's seizure of institutions in East Jerusalem. The meeting, which was attended by the League's Secretary-General and the leader of the PA, Yasser Arafat, aimed to formulate a unified Arab response to the situation.

In early March 2002 a meeting of League foreign ministers agreed to support an initiative proposed by Crown Prince Abdullah of Saudi Arabia aimed at brokering a peaceful settlement to the, by then, critical Palestinian–Israeli crisis. The Saudi-backed plan—entailing the restoration of 'normal' Arab relations with Israel and acceptance of its right to exist in peace and security, in exchange for a full Israeli withdrawal from the Occupied Territories, the establishment of an independent Palestinian state with East Jerusalem at its capital, and the return of refugees—was unanimously endorsed, as the first-ever pan-Arab Palestinian-Israeli peace initiative, by the summit-level Council held in Beirut in late March. The plan urged compliance with UN Security Council Resolution 194 concerning the return of Palestinian refugees to Israel, or appropriate compensation for their property; however, precise details of eligibility criteria for the proposed return, a contentious issue owing to the potentially huge numbers of refugees and descendants of refugees involved, were not elaborated. Conditions imposed by Israel on Yasser Arafat's freedom of movement deterred him from attending the summit. At the end of March the League's Secretary-General condemned the Israeli military's siege of Arafat's presidential compound in Ramallah (initiated in retaliation against a succession of Palestinian bomb attacks on Israeli civilians). In April an extraordinary Council meeting, held at the request of Palestine to consider the 'unprecedented deterioration' of the situation in the Palestinian territories, accused certain states (notably the USA) of implementing a pro-Israeli bias that enabled Israel to act outside the scope of international law and to ignore relevant UN resolutions, and accused Israel of undermining international co-operation in combating terrorism by attempting to equate its actions towards the Palestinian people with recent anti-terrorism activities conducted by the USA. A meeting organized by the Central Boycott Office at the end of April agreed to expand boycott measures and assessed the status of 17 companies believed to have interests in Israel. Israel's termination of its siege of Arafat's Ramallah compound in early May was welcomed by the Secretary-General. Following an aerial raid by the Israeli military on targets in Gaza in late July, the League urged a halt to the export of weaponry, particularly F-16 military aircraft, to Israel. A Council meeting held in early September agreed to intensify Arab efforts to expose Israeli atrocities against the Palestinians and urged the international community to provide protection and reparations for Palestinians. The Council authorized the establishment of a committee to address the welfare of imprisoned Palestinians and urged the USA and the United Kingdom to reconsider their policies on exporting weaponry to Israel, while issuing a resolution concerning the danger posed by Israel's possession of weapons of mass destruction. In early October the Secretary-General expressed concern at new US legislation aimed at securing the relocation of the USA's embassy in Israel from Tel-Aviv to Jerusalem, stating that this represented a symbolic acceptance of Jerusalem as the Israeli capital, in contravention of relevant UN resolutions.

In November 2003 the League welcomed the adoption by the UN Security Council of a resolution endorsing the adoption in April by the so-called 'Quartet', comprising envoys from the UN, the European Union (EU), Russia and the USA, of a 'performance-based roadmap to a permanent two-state solution to the

Israeli–Palestinian conflict'. In January 2004 the International Court of Justice (ICJ) authorized the participation of the League in proceedings relating to a request for an advisory opinion on the *Legal Consequences of the Construction of a Wall in the Occupied Palestinian Territory*, referred to the ICJ by the UN General Assembly in late 2003; the League welcomed the ICJ's conclusions on the case, published in July 2004. The 2004 summit meeting of Arab League heads of state, held in Tunis, Tunisia, in May, condemned contraventions of international law by the Israeli Government, in particular continuing settlement activities and the use of unjudicial killings and other violence, and focused on the humanitarian situation of Palestinians recently displaced by large-scale house demolitions in Rafah, Gaza. In January 2005 the League welcomed the election of Mahmud Abbas as the new Executive President of the PA, following the death in November 2004 of Yasser Arafat.

In March 2007 the annual summit meeting of the League reaffirmed the League's support for the 2002 peace initiative proposed by Crown Prince Abdullah of Saudi Arabia, and urged the Israeli authorities to resume direct negotiations based on the principles of the initiative. In July 2007 the ministers of foreign affairs of Egypt and Jordan, representing the League, visited Israel to promote the 2002 initiative. The March 2009 League summit meeting condemned the intensive military assault on Gaza perpetrated by Israeli forces (with the stated aim of ending rocket attacks launched by Hamas and other militant groups on Israeli targets) during late December 2008–mid-January 2009. The summit urged Israel to establish a time frame for committing to the peace process. In October an emergency meeting of the League condemned attacks by the Israeli armed forces on the al-Aqsa Mosque in Jerusalem.

The March 2010 summit meeting, held in Sirte, Libya, agreed, in its final declaration, all Israeli measures seeking to alter the features and demographic, humanitarian and historic situation of occupied Jerusalem to be invalid and unacceptable, while appealing to the international community (particularly the UN Security Council, the EU and UNESCO) to act to save East Jerusalem and maintain the al-Aqsa Mosque. The meeting's declaration urged that a special session of the UN General Assembly should be held with a view to halting Israeli measures that contravened international law, and mandated the formation of a League legal committee to follow up the issue of the 'judaization' of East Jerusalem and the confiscation of Arab property, and to take these issues before national and international courts with appropriate jurisdiction.

In June 2010, in response to an Israeli raid at the end of May on a flotilla of vessels carrying humanitarian aid through international waters towards the Gaza Strip, resulting in nine civilian fatalities and wounding at least 40 further people, the League Secretary-General visited Gaza in a gesture of solidarity towards the Palestinian people. During the visit he demanded the termination of the blockade imposed since 2006 by Israel against Gaza. The League was critical of a UN-commissioned report on the flotilla incident, released in September 2011, which, while concluding that the Israeli army had used 'excessive and unreasonable' force, also found the Israeli naval blockade of Gaza to have been imposed as a 'legitimate security measure' to prevent weapons from reaching Gaza by sea, and found that the flotilla had acted recklessly in attempting to breach the naval blockade.

In July 2011 the recently appointed League Secretary-General, Nabil al-Arabi, announced that the League would request the UN to grant full membership—and consequently recognition as an independent state—to Palestine; in September the Executive President of the Palestinian Authority submitted a formal application to the UN Secretary-General for Palestine's admission to that organization.

CONFLICT IN SUB-SAHARAN AFRICA

In 1992 the League attempted to mediate between the warring factions in Somalia. In early June 2002 the League appointed a special representative to Somalia to assist with the ongoing reconciliation efforts in that country.

In early September 2002 the Council established a committee to encourage peace efforts in Sudan. In May 2004 representatives of the League participated in an African Union (AU) fact-finding mission to assess the ongoing humanitarian crisis in Darfur, Sudan. In August an emergency meeting of League ministers of foreign affairs, convened to address the situation in Darfur, declared support for the Sudanese Government's measures to disarm Arab militias and punish human rights violations there. In November the League was asked to join a panel appointed to monitor the cease-fire agreement that had been adopted in April by the parties to the Darfur conflict. In March 2006 the meeting of heads of state agreed to offer financial support to the AU Mission in Sudan, deployed to the Darfur region of that country. The summit meeting in March 2007 expressed continued support for all peace accords signed between conflicting parties in Sudan. In March 2009 the summit of heads of state expressed full support and solidarity with Sudan in rejecting the legitimacy of the arrest warrant that had been issued earlier in that month by the International Criminal Court against President Omar al-Bashir of Sudan.

In October 2010 the League and the AU jointly organized an Afro-Arab summit, held in Sirte, Libya; leaders attending the summit endorsed a new Strategic Plan of the Afro-Arab Co-operation, covering the period 2011–15. The next Afro-Arab summit was scheduled to be held in Kuwait, during 2013.

Finance

The League's budget for 2010 totalled US $61.2m., including $58.8m. for the League Secretariat and $5m. allocated to the Arab Fund for Technical Assistance in African States.

Publications

Arab Perspectives—Sh'oun Arabiyya (monthly).

Journal of Arab Affairs (monthly).

Bulletins of treaties and agreements concluded among the member states, essays, regular publications circulated by regional offices.

The Pact of the League of Arab States

(22 March 1945)

Article 1. The League of Arab States shall be composed of the: independent Arab States that have signed this Pact.

Every independent Arab state shall have the right to adhere to the League. If it desires to do so, it shall submit a request which will be deposited with the Permanent Secretariat-General and submitted to the Council at the first meeting held after submission of the request.

Article 2. The League has as its purpose the strengthening of the relations between the member states; the co-ordination of their policies in order to achieve co-operation between them and to safeguard their independence and sovereignty; and a general concern with the affairs and interests of the Arab countries. It has also as its purpose the close co-operation of the member states, with due regard to the organization and circumstances of each state, on the following matters:

(*a*) Economic and financial affairs, including trade, customs, currency, and questions of agriculture and industry

(*b*) Communications, including railways, roads, aviation, navigation, telegraphs and posts

(*c*) Cultural affairs

(*d*) Nationality, passports, visas, execution of judgments, and extradition of criminals

(*e*) Social affairs

(*f*) Health problems.

Article 3. The League shall possess a Council composed of the representatives of the member states of the League; each state shall have a single vote, irrespective of the number of its representatives.

It shall be the task of the Council to achieve the realization of the objectives of the League and to supervise the execution of agreements which the member states have concluded on the questions enumerated in the preceding article, or on any other questions.

It likewise shall be the Council's task to decide upon the means by which the League is to co-operate with the international bodies to be created in the future in order to guarantee security and peace and regulate economic and social relations.

Article 4. For each of the questions listed in Article 2 there shall be set up a special committee in which the member states of the League shall be represented. These committees shall be charged with the task of laying down the principles and extent of co-operation. Such principles shall be formulated as draft agreements, to be presented to the Council for examination preparatory to their submission to the aforesaid states.

Representatives of the other Arab countries may take part in the work of the aforesaid committees. The Council shall determine the conditions under which these representatives may be permitted to participate and the rules governing such representation.

Article 5. Any resort to force in order to resolve disputes arising between two or more member states of the League is prohibited. If there should rise among them a difference which does not concern a state's independence, sovereignty, or territorial integrity, and if the parties to the dispute have recourse to the Council for the settlement of this difference, the decision of the Council shall then be enforceable and obligatory.

In such a case, the states between whom the difference has arisen shall not participate in the deliberations and decisions of the Council.

The Council shall mediate in all differences which threaten to lead to war between two member states, or a member state and a third state, with a view to bringing about their reconciliation.

Decisions of arbitration and mediation shall be taken by majority vote.

Article 6. In case of aggression or threat of aggression by one state against a member state, the state which has been attacked or threatened with aggression may demand the immediate convocation of the Council.

The Council shall by unanimous decision determine the measures necessary to repulse the aggression. If the aggressor is a member state, its vote shall not be counted in determining unanimity.

If, as a result of the attack, the government of the state attacked finds itself unable to communicate with the Council, that state's representative in the Council shall have the right to request the convocation of the Council for the purpose indicated in the foregoing paragraph. In the event that this representative is unable to communicate with the Council, any member state of the League shall have the right to request the convocation of the Council.

Article 7. Unanimous decisions of the Council shall be binding upon all member states of the League; majority decisions shall be binding only upon those states that have accepted them.

In either case the decisions of the Council shall be enforced in each member state according to its respective basic laws.

Article 8. Each member state shall respect the systems of government established in the other member states and regard them as exclusive concerns of those states. Each shall pledge to abstain from any action calculated to change established systems of government.

Article 9. States of the League which desire to establish closer co-operation and stronger bonds than are provided by this Pact may conclude agreements to that end.

Treaties and agreements already concluded or to be concluded in the future between a member state and another state shall not be binding or restrictive upon other members.

Article 10. The permanent seat of the League of Arab States is established in Cairo. The Council may, however, assemble at any other place it may designate.

Article 11. The Council of the League shall convene in ordinary session twice a year, in March and in September. It shall convene in extraordinary session upon the request of two member states of the League whenever the need arises.

Article 12. The League shall have a permanent Secretariat-General which shall consist of a Secretary-General, Assistant Secretaries, and an appropriate number of officials.

The Council of the League shall appoint the Secretary-General by a majority of two-thirds of the states of the League. The Secretary-General, with the approval of the Council, shall appoint the Assistant Secretaries and the principal officials of the League.

The Council of the League shall establish an administrative regulation for the functions of the Secretariat-General and matters relating to the Staff.

The Secretary-General shall have the rank of Ambassador and the Assistant Secretaries that of Ministers Plenipotentiary.

Article 13. The Secretary-General shall prepare the draft of the budget of the League and shall submit it to the Council for approval before the beginning of each fiscal year.

The Council shall fix the share of the expenses to be borne by each state of the League. This share may be reconsidered if necessary.

Article 14. (confers diplomatic immunity on officials).

Article 15. The first meeting of the Council shall be convened at the invitation of the head of the Egyptian Government. Thereafter it shall be convened at the invitation of the Secretary-General.

The representatives of the member states of the League shall alternately assume the presidency of the Council at each of its ordinary sessions.

Article 16. Except in cases specifically indicated in this Pact, a majority vote of the Council shall be sufficient to make enforceable decisions on the following matters:

(*a*) Matters relating to personnel

(*b*) Adoption of the budget of the League

(*c*) Establishment of the administrative regulations for the Council, the Committees, and the Secretariat-General

(*d*) Decisions to adjourn the sessions.

Article 17. Each member state of the League shall deposit with the Secretariat-General one copy of every treaty or agreement concluded or to be concluded in the future between itself and another member state of the League or a third state.

Article 18. (deals with withdrawal).

Article 19. (deals with amendment).

Article 20. (deals with ratification).

ANNEX REGARDING PALESTINE

Since the termination of the last great war, the rule of the Ottoman Empire over the Arab countries, among them Palestine, which has become detached from that Empire, has come to an end. She has come to be autonomous, not subordinate to any other state.

The Treaty of Lausanne proclaimed that her future was to be settled by the parties concerned.

However, even though she was as yet unable to control her own affairs, the Covenant of the League (of Nations) in 1919 made provision for a regime based upon recognition of her independence.

Her international existence and independence in the legal sense cannot, therefore, be questioned, any more than could the independence of the Arab countries.

Although the outward manifestations of this independence have remained obscured for reasons beyond her control, this should not be allowed to interfere with her participation in the work of the Council of the League.

The states signatory to the Pact of the Arab League are therefore of the opinion that, considering the special circumstances of Palestine and until that country can effectively exercise its independence, the Council of the League should take charge of the selection of an Arab representative from Palestine to take part in its work.

ANNEX REGARDING CO-OPERATION WITH COUNTRIES WHICH ARE NOT MEMBERS OF THE COUNCIL

Whereas the member states of the League will have to deal in the Council as well as in the committees with matters which will benefit and affect the Arab world at large;

And whereas the Council has to take into account the aspirations of the Arab countries which are not members of the Council and has to work toward their realization;

Now therefore, it particularly behoves the states signatory to the Pact of the Arab League to enjoin the Council of the League, when considering the admission of those countries to participation in the committees referred to in the Pact, that it should do its utmost to co-operate with them, and furthermore, that it should spare no effort to learn their needs and understand their aspirations and hopes; and that it should work thenceforth for their best interests and the safeguarding of the future with all the political means at its disposal.

NORTH AMERICAN FREE TRADE AGREEMENT—NAFTA

Address: *(Canadian section)* 111 Sussex Drive 5th Floor Ottawa, ON K1N 1J1.

Telephone: (613) 992-9388; **fax:** (613) 992-9392; **e-mail:** canada@nafta-sec-alena.org; **internet:** www.nafta-sec-alena.org/canada.

Address: *(Mexican section)* Blvd Adolfo López Mateos 3025, 2°, Col Héroes de Padierna, 10700 México, DF.

Telephone: (55) 5629-9630; **fax:** (55) 5629-9637; **e-mail:** mexico@nafta-sec-alena.org.

Address: *(US section)* 14th St and Constitution Ave, NW, Room 2061, Washington, DC 20230.

Telephone: (202) 482-5438; **fax:** (202) 482-0148; **e-mail:** usa@nafta-sec-alena.org; **internet:** www.nafta-sec-alena.org.

The North American Free Trade Agreement (NAFTA) grew out of the free trade agreement between the USA and Canada that was signed in January 1988 and came into effect on 1 January 1989. Negotiations on the terms of NAFTA, which includes Mexico in the free trade area, were concluded in October 1992 and the Agreement was signed in December. The accord was ratified in November 1993 and entered into force on 1 January 1994; the full implementation of the provisions of the accord was achieved in January 2008. The NAFTA Secretariat is composed of national sections in each member country.

MEMBERS

Canada Mexico USA

MAIN PROVISIONS OF THE AGREEMENT

Under NAFTA almost all restrictions on trade and investment between Canada, Mexico and the USA were removed during the period 1 January 1994–1 January 2008. Tariffs on trade between the USA and Mexico in 94% of agricultural products were eliminated immediately, with trade restrictions on further agricultural products initially protected by tariff-rate quotas (TRQs) and eliminated more gradually; tariffs on the most import-sensitive staple agricultural commodities, including Mexican exports to the USA of sugar and selected horticultural products and US exports to Mexico of corn, high fructose corn syrup, dry edible beans and non-fat dry milk, were abolished on 1 January 2008.

NAFTA also provided for the phasing out by 2004 of tariffs on automobiles and textiles between all three countries; and for Mexico to open its financial sector to US and Canadian investment, with all restrictions to be removed by 2008. Mexico was to liberalize government procurement, removing preferential treatment for domestic companies over a 10-year period. Barriers to investment were removed in most sectors, with exemptions for petroleum in Mexico, culture in Canada and airlines and radio communications in the USA. In April 1998 the fifth meeting of the three-member ministerial Free Trade Commission (see below), held in Paris, France, agreed to remove tariffs on some 600 goods, including certain chemicals, pharmaceuticals, steel and wire products, textiles, toys, and watches, from 1 August. As a result of that agreement, a number of tariffs were eliminated as much as 10 years earlier than had been originally planned.

In transport, it was initially planned that heavy goods vehicles would have complete freedom of movement between the three countries by 2000. However, owing to concerns on the part of the US Government relating to the implementation of adequate safety standards by Mexican truck drivers, the 2000 deadline for the free circulation of heavy goods vehicles was not met. In February 2001 a five-member NAFTA panel of experts appointed to adjudicate on the dispute ruled that the USA was violating the Agreement. In December the US Senate approved legislation entitling Mexican long-haul trucks to operate anywhere in the USA following compliance with rigorous safety checks to be enforced by US inspectors.

In the case of a sudden influx of goods from one country to another that adversely affects a domestic industry, the Agreement makes provision for the imposition of short-term 'snap-back' tariffs.

Disputes are to be settled in the first instance by intergovernmental consultation. If a dispute is not resolved within 30 to 40 days, a government may call a meeting of the Free Trade Commission. The Commission's Advisory Committee on Private Commercial Disputes and its Advisory Committee on Private Commercial Disputes Regarding Agricultural Goods recommend procedures for the resolution of such complex disputes. If the Commission is unable to settle an issue a panel of experts in the relevant field is appointed to adjudicate. In June 1996 Canada and Mexico announced their decision to refer the newly enacted US 'Helms-Burton' legislation on trade with Cuba to the Commission. They claimed that the legislation, which provides for punitive measures against foreign companies that engage in trade with Cuba, imposed undue restrictions on Canadian and Mexican companies and was, therefore, in contravention of NAFTA. However, at the beginning of 1997 certain controversial provisions of the Helms-Burton legislation were suspended for a period of six months by the US Administration. The relevant provisions have continued subsequently to be suspended at six-monthly intervals.

In December 1994 NAFTA members issued a formal invitation to Chile to seek membership of the Agreement. Formal discussions on Chile's entry began in June 1995, but were stalled in December when the US Congress failed to approve 'fast-track' negotiating authority for the US Government, which was to have allowed the latter to negotiate a trade agreement with Chile, without risk of incurring a line-by-line veto from the US Congress. In February 1996 Chile began high-level negotiations with Canada on a wide-ranging bilateral free trade agreement. Chile, which already had extensive bilateral trade agreements with Mexico, was regarded as advancing its position with regard to NAFTA membership by means of the proposed accord with Canada. The bilateral agreement, which provided for the extensive elimination of customs duties by 2002, was signed in November 1996 and ratified by Chile in July 1997. However, in November 1997 the US Government was obliged to request the removal of the 'fast-track' proposal from the legislative agenda, owing to insufficient support within Congress.

In April 1998 heads of state of 34 countries, meeting in Santiago, Chile, agreed formally to initiate the negotiating process to establish a Free Trade Area of the Americas (FTAA). The US Government had originally proposed creating the FTAA through the gradual extension of NAFTA trading privileges on a bilateral basis. However, the framework agreed upon by ministers of trade of the 34 countries, meeting in March, provided for countries to negotiate and accept FTAA provisions on an individual basis and as part of a sub-regional economic bloc. It was envisaged that the FTAA would exist alongside the sub-regional associations, including NAFTA. At a special summit of the Americas, held in January 2004 in Monterrey, Mexico, the leaders adopted a declaration committing themselves to the eventual establishment of the FTAA; however, they did not specify a completion date for the negotiations. In March the negotiations were suspended, and in 2012 they remained so.

ADDITIONAL AGREEMENTS

During 1993, as a result of domestic pressure, the new US Government negotiated two 'side agreements' with its NAFTA partners, which were to provide safeguards for workers' rights and the environment. A Commission for Labor Cooperation was established under the North American Agreement on Labor Cooperation (NAALC) to monitor implementation of labour accords and to foster co-operation in that area. Panels of experts, with representatives from each country, were established to adjudicate in cases of alleged infringement of workers' rights or environmental damage. The panels were given the power to impose fines and trade sanctions, but only with regard to the USA and Mexico; Canada, which was opposed to such measures, was to enforce compliance with NAFTA by means of its own legal system. The Commission for Environmental Cooperation (CEC), initiated in 1994 under the provisions of the 1993 North American Agreement on Environmental Cooperation (which complements the relevant environmental provisions of NAFTA), addresses regional environmental concerns, assists in the prevention of potential trade and environmental conflicts, advises on the environmental impact of trade issues, encourages private sector investment in environmental trade issues, and promotes the effective enforcement of environmental law. In co-operation with mapping agency partners CEC produces the *North American Environmental Atlas*. During 1994–early 2012 the CEC adopted numerous resolutions, including on the sound management of chemicals, the environmentally sound management and tracking of hazardous wastes and hazardous recyclable materials, the conservation of butterflies and birds, the availability of pollutant release and transfer data, and on co-operation in the conservation of biodiversity. The CEC-financed North American Fund for Environmental Cooperation (NAFEC), established in 1995, supports community environmental projects.

With regard to the NAALC, National Administration Offices have been established in each of the three NAFTA countries in order to monitor labour issues and to address complaints about non-compliance with domestic labour legislation. However, punitive measures in the form of trade sanctions or fines (up to US $20m.) may only be imposed in the specific instances of contravention of national legislation regarding child labour, a minimum wage or health and safety standards.

Border Environmental Cooperation Commission (BECC): POB 221648 El Paso, TX 79913 USA; tel. (877) 277-1703; e-mail becc@cocef.org; internet www.cocef.org/eng; f. 1993; supports the co-ordination of projects for the improvement of infrastructure and monitors the environmental impact of NAFTA on the US–Mexican border area; by June 2012 the BECC had certified 194 projects, at a cost of US $4,317.5m.; Gen. Man. MARIA ELENA GINER (USA).

Commission for Environmental Cooperation (CEC): 393 rue St Jacques Ouest, Bureau 200, Montréal, QC H2Y IN9, Canada; tel. (514) 350-4300; fax (514) 350-4314; e-mail info@cec.org; internet www.cec.org; f. 1994; Exec. Dir EVAN LLOYD; publs *Annual Report*, *Taking Stock* (annually), industry reports, policy studies.

Commission for Labor Cooperation: 1211 Connecticut Ave, NW Suite 400, Washington, DC 20036, USA; tel. (202) 464-1100; fax (202) 464-9490; e-mail info@naalc.org; internet www.naalc.org; f. 1994; Exec. Dir (vacant); publ. *Annual Report*.

North American Development Bank (NADB/NADBank): 203 South St Mary's, Suite 300, San Antonio, TX 78205, USA; tel. (210) 231-8000; fax (210) 231-6232; internet www.nadbank.org; f. 1993; mandated to finance environmental and infrastructure projects along the US–Mexican border; at June 2012 the NADB had authorized capital of US $3,000m., subscribed equally by Mexico and the USA, of which $450m. was paid-up; Man. Dir GERÓNIMO GUTIÉRREZ FERNÁNDEZ (Mexico); publs *Annual Report*, *NADBank News*.

NORTH ATLANTIC TREATY ORGANIZATION—NATO

Address: blvd Léopold III, 1110 Brussels, Belgium.

Telephone: (2) 707-41-11; **fax:** (2) 707-45-79; **e-mail:** natodoc@hq.nato.int; **internet:** www.nato.int.

The Atlantic Alliance was established on the basis of the 1949 North Atlantic Treaty as a defensive political and military alliance of a group of European states (then numbering 10) and the USA and Canada. The Alliance aims to provide common security for its members through co-operation and consultation in political, military and economic fields, as well as scientific, environmental, and other non-military aspects. The objectives of the Alliance are implemented by NATO. Since the collapse of the communist governments in Central and Eastern Europe, from 1989 onwards, and the dissolution, in 1991, of the Warsaw Treaty of Friendship, Co-operation and Mutual Assistance (the Warsaw Pact), which had hitherto been regarded as the Alliance's principal adversary, NATO has undertaken a fundamental transformation of its structures and policies to meet the new security challenges in Europe.

MEMBERS*

Albania	Greece	Poland
Belgium	Hungary	Portugal
Bulgaria	Iceland	Romania
Canada	Italy	Slovakia
Croatia	Latvia	Slovenia
Czech Republic	Lithuania	Spain
Denmark	Luxembourg	Turkey
Estonia	Netherlands	United Kingdom
France	Norway	USA
Germany		

* Greece and Turkey acceded to the Treaty in 1952, and the Federal Republic of Germany in 1955. France withdrew from the integrated military structure of NATO in 1966, although remaining a member of the Atlantic Alliance; in 1996 France resumed participation in some, but not all, of the military organs of NATO. Spain acceded to the Treaty in 1982, but remained outside the Alliance's integrated military structure until 1999. The Czech Republic, Hungary and Poland were formally admitted as members of NATO in March 1999. In March 2003 protocols of accession, amending the North Atlantic Treaty, were adopted by the 19 NATO member states with a view to admitting Bulgaria, Estonia, Latvia, Lithuania, Romania, Slovakia and Slovenia to the Alliance. In March 2004, the protocols of accession having been ratified by all of the member states, those seven countries were formally invited to join NATO and, on 29 March, they acceded to the Treaty. On 1 April 2009 Albania and Croatia acceded to the Treaty.

Organization

(June 2012)

NORTH ATLANTIC COUNCIL

The Council, the highest authority of the Alliance, is composed of representatives of the 28 member states. It meets at the level of Permanent Representatives, ministers of foreign affairs, or heads of state and government, and, at all levels, has effective political and decision-making authority. Ministerial meetings are held at least twice a year. Occasional meetings of defence ministers are also held. At the level of Permanent Representatives the Council meets at least once a week. A meeting of heads of state and government was convened in Lisbon, Portugal, in November 2010.

The Secretary-General of NATO is Chairman of the Council, and each year a minister of foreign affairs of a member state is nominated honorary President, following the English alphabetical order of countries.

Decisions are taken by common consent and not by majority vote. The Council is a forum for wide consultation between member governments on major issues, including political, military, economic and other subjects, and is supported by the Senior or regular Political Committee, the Military Committee and other subordinate bodies.

PERMANENT REPRESENTATIVES

Albania: Artur Kuko.

Belgium: Rudolf Huygelen.

Bulgaria: Todor Churov.

Canada: Yves Brodeur.

Croatia: Igor Pokaz.

Czech Republic: Martin Povejšil.

Denmark: Carsten Søndergaard.

Estonia: Jüri Luik.

France: Philippe Errera.

Germany: Martin Erdmann.

Greece: Tryphon Paraskevopoulos.

Hungary: István Kovács.

Iceland: Thorstein Ingolfsson.

Italy: Riccardo Sessa.

Latvia: Māris Riekstiņš.

Lithuania: Kęstutis Jankauskas.

Luxembourg: Jean-Jacques Welfring.

Netherlands: Frank Majoor.

Norway: Vegard Ellefsen.

Poland: Jacek Najder.

Portugal: João Mira Gomes.

Romania: Sorin Dumitru Ducaru.

Slovakia: František Kašický.

Slovenia: Andrej Benedejčič.

Spain: José de Carvajal.

Turkey: Haydar Berk.

United Kingdom: Mariot Leslie.

USA: Ivo H. Daalder.

Note: NATO partner countries are represented by heads of diplomatic missions or liaison officers located at NATO headquarters.

DEFENCE PLANNING COMMITTEE

Most defence matters are dealt with in the Defence Planning Committee, composed of representatives of all member countries except France. The Committee provides guidance to NATO's military authorities and, within the field of its responsibilities, has the same functions and authority as the Council. Like the Council, it meets regularly at ambassadorial level and assembles twice a year in ministerial sessions, when member countries are represented by their ministers of defence.

NUCLEAR PLANNING GROUP

Defence ministers of countries participating in the Defence Planning Committee meet regularly in the Nuclear Planning Group (NPG) to discuss specific policy issues relating to nuclear forces, such as safety, deployment issues, nuclear arms control and proliferation. The NPG is supported by a Staff Group, composed of representatives of all members participating in the NPG, which meets at least once a week. The NPG High Level Group, chaired by the USA and comprising national policy-makers and experts, exists as a senior advisory body to the NPG in respect of nuclear policy and planning issues.

OTHER COMMITTEES

There are also committees for political affairs, economics, military medical services, armaments, defence review, science, infrastructure, logistics, communications, civil emergency planning, information and cultural relations, and civil and military budgets. In addition, other committees consider specialized subjects such as NATO pipelines, air traffic management, etc. Since 1992 most of these committees have consulted on a regular basis with representatives from central and eastern European countries.

INTERNATIONAL SECRETARIAT

The Secretary-General is Chairman of the North Atlantic Council, the Defence Planning Committee and the Nuclear Planning Group. He is the head of the International Secretariat, with staff drawn from the member countries. He proposes items for NATO consultation and is generally responsible for promoting consultation and co-operation in accordance with the provisions of the North Atlantic Treaty. He is empowered to offer his help informally in cases of disputes between member countries, to facilitate procedures for settlement.

Secretary-General: ANDERS FOGH RASMUSSEN (Denmark).

Deputy Secretary-General: ALEXANDER VERSHBOW (USA).

There is an Assistant Secretary-General for each of the operational divisions listed below.

PRINCIPAL DIVISIONS

Division of Defence Investment: responsible for enhancing NATO's defence capacity (including armaments planning, air defence and security investment) by developing and investing in the Alliance's assets and capabilities; Asst Sec.-Gen. PATRICK AUROY (France).

Division of Defence Policy and Planning: responsible for defence planning, nuclear policy and defence against weapons of mass destruction; Asst Sec.-Gen. HÜSEYIN DIRIÖZ (Turkey).

Division of Emerging Security Challenges: co-ordinates the Alliance approach to security issues, including terrorism, the proliferation of weapons of mass destruction, cyber threats, and energy security challenges; Asst Sec.-Gen. GÁBOR IKLÓDY (Hungary).

Division of Political Affairs and Security Policy: is concerned with regional, economic and security affairs and relations with other international organizations and partner countries; Asst Sec.-Gen. DIRK BRENGELMANN (Germany).

Division of Public Diplomacy: responsible for dissemination of information on NATO's activities and policies through the media, the official website and print publications as well as seminars and conferences; manages the Science for Peace and Security programme and the information offices in Russia and Ukraine; Asst Sec.-Gen. KOLINDA GRABAR KITAROVIĆ (Croatia).

Executive Management Division: ensures the efficient running of the International Secretariat and provides support to elements such as conference services, information management and human and financial resources; Asst Sec.-Gen. WILLIAM A. EATON (USA).

Operations Division: responsible for the Alliance's crisis management and peace-keeping activities and civil emergency planning and exercises; incorporates the Euro-Atlantic Disaster Response Coordination Centre (EADRCC) and the NATO Situation Centre; Asst Sec.-Gen. STEPHEN EVANS (United Kingdom).

Military Organization

MILITARY COMMITTEE

Composed of the allied Chiefs-of-Staff, or their representatives, of all member countries: the highest military body in NATO under the authority of the Council. Meets at least twice a year at Chiefs-of-Staff level and remains in permanent session with Permanent Military Representatives. It is responsible for making recommendations to the Council and Defence Planning Committee and Nuclear Planning Group on military matters and for supplying guidance on military questions to Supreme Allied Commanders and subordinate military authorities. The Committee is supported by an International Military Staff.

Chairman: Gen. KNUD BARTELS (Denmark).

COMMANDS

In June 2011 NATO ministers of defence approved a reform of the existing command structure, in order to enhance its effectiveness and affordability, with the number of command headquarters and personnel to be significantly reduced. In addition to the two strategic commands, of Operations and Transformation, there were to be two main Joint Force Headquarters, each able to deploy a major joint operation into theatre, comprising a Combined Air Operations Centre and static air, land and maritime commands. The Command Structure was to be supported by a Communication and Information Systems Group. Implementation of the reforms was to be completed by 2015.

Allied Command Operations: Casteau, Belgium—Supreme Headquarters Allied Powers Europe—SHAPE; Supreme Allied Commander Europe—SACEUR Adm. JAMES G. STAVRIDIS (USA).

Allied Command Transformation: Norfolk, Virginia, USA; Supreme Allied Commander Transformation—SACT Lt-Gen. STÉPHANE ABRIAL (France).

Activities

The common security policy of the members of the North Atlantic Alliance is to safeguard peace through the maintenance of political solidarity and adequate defence at the lowest level of military forces needed to deter all possible forms of aggression. Each year, member countries take part in a Defence Review, designed to assess their contribution to the common defence in relation to their respective capabilities and constraints. Allied defence policy is reviewed periodically by ministers of defence.

Political consultations within the Alliance take place on a permanent basis, under the auspices of the North Atlantic Council (NAC), on all matters affecting the common security interests of the member countries, as well as events outside the North Atlantic Treaty area.

Co-operation in environmental, scientific and technological fields takes place in the NATO Science Committee and in its Committee on the Challenges of Modern Society. Both these bodies operate an expanding international programme of science fellowships, advance study institutes and research grants. NATO has also pursued co-operation in relation to civil emergency planning. These activities represent NATO's 'Third Dimension'.

Since the 1980s the Alliance has been actively involved in co-ordinating policies with regard to arms control and disarmament issues designed to bring about negotiated reductions in conventional forces, intermediate and short-range nuclear forces and strategic nuclear forces. A Verification Co-ordinating Committee was established in 1990. In April 1999 the summit meeting determined to improve co-ordination on issues relating to weapons of mass destruction through the establishment of a separate centre at NATO headquarters. At a summit meeting of the Conference on Security and Co-operation in Europe (CSCE), later renamed the Organization for Security and Co-operation in Europe (OSCE), in November 1990 the member countries of NATO and the Warsaw Pact signed an agreement limiting Conventional Armed Forces in Europe (CFE), whereby conventional arms would be reduced to within a common upper limit in each zone. The two groups also issued a Joint Declaration, stating that they were no longer adversaries and that none of their weapons would ever be used 'except in self-defence'. In March 1992, under the auspices of the CSCE, the ministers of foreign affairs of the NATO and of the former Warsaw Pact countries (with Russia, Belarus, Ukraine and Georgia taking the place of the USSR) signed the 'Open Skies' treaty. Under this treaty, aerial reconnaissance missions by one country over another were to be permitted, subject to regulation. The eight former Soviet republics with territory in the area of application of the CFE Treaty committed themselves to honouring its obligations in June. At the summit meeting of the OSCE in December 1996 the signatories of the CFE Treaty agreed to begin negotiations on a revised treaty governing conventional weapons in Europe. In July 1997 the CFE signatories concluded an agreement on Certain Basic Elements for Treaty Adaptation, which provided for substantial reductions in the maximum levels of conventional military equipment at national and territorial level, replacing the previous bloc-to-bloc structure of the Treaty. The Adapted CFE Treaty was concluded and signed in November 1999, at an OSCE meeting held in Istanbul, Turkey. At the same time, a series of agreements or Commitments, was approved which required Russia to withdraw forces from and reduce levels of military equipment in Georgia and Moldova, a process to be monitored by NATO. In April 2007 NATO ministers of foreign affairs held immediate discussions following an announcement by Russia's President that it intended to suspend unilaterally its implementation of CFE obligations. An extraordinary conference of parties to the CFE was convened in June to consider Russia's security concerns; in the following month, however, the Russian Government announced that it was to suspend obligations under the Treaty, with effect from mid-December. In April 2008 NATO heads of state and government urged Russia to resume its implementation of the Treaty. The Lisbon Summit Declaration, issued by NATO heads of state and government in November 2010, reaffirmed political commitment to the CFE process, but insisted that the existing *impasse* could not continue indefinitely.

In January 1994 NATO heads of state and government welcomed the entry into force of the Maastricht Treaty, establishing the European Union (EU, superseding the EC). The Treaty included an agreement on the development of a common foreign and security policy, which was intended to be a mechanism to strengthen the European pillar of the Alliance. NATO subsequently co-operated with Western European Union (WEU, now defunct) in support of the development of a European Security and Defence Identity. In June 1996 NATO ministers of foreign affairs reached agreement on the implementation of a 'Combined Joint Task Force (CJTF) concept'. Measures were to be taken to establish the 'nuclei' of these task forces at certain NATO headquarters, which would provide the basis for missions that could be activated at short notice for specific purposes such as crisis management and peace-keeping. The summit meeting held in April 1999 confirmed NATO's willingness to establish a direct NATO-EU relationship. The first formal meeting of the Military Committees of the EU and NATO took place in June 2001 to exchange information relating to the development of EU-NATO security co-operation. In November 2003 NATO and the EU conducted a joint crisis management exercise for the first time. In order to support an integrated security structure in Europe, NATO also co-operates with the OSCE and has provided assistance for the development of the latter's conflict prevention and crisis management activities. In September 2008 a Joint Declaration on UN/NATO Secretariat Co-operation was signed by the Secretaries-General of the two organizations to strengthen practical co-operation, in particular in crisis management. In November 2010 NATO heads of state and government endorsed an Action Plan to incorporate into all aspects of Alliance planning, training and operations the provisions of the UN Security Council Resolution 1325 on Women, Peace and Security.

In January 2001 NATO established an ad hoc working committee in response to concerns expressed by several member governments regarding the health implications of the use of depleted uranium munitions during the Alliance's military intervention in the Balkans. The committee was to co-ordinate the compilation of information regarding the use of depleted uranium and to co-operate with the Yugoslav authorities in the rehabilitation of the local environment. An extraordinary meeting of chiefs of military medical services, including surgeons-general and medical experts, was also convened to consider the issue.

On 12 September 2001 the NAC agreed to invoke, for the first time, Article 5 of the North Atlantic Treaty, providing for collective self-defence, in response to terrorist attacks against targets in the USA that had taken place on the previous day. The measure was formally implemented in early October after the US authorities presented evidence substantiating claims that the attacks had been directed from abroad. The NAC endorsed eight specific US requests for logistical and military support in its efforts to counter terrorism, including enhanced sharing of intelligence and full access to airfields and ports in member states. It also agreed to dispatch five surveillance aircraft to help to patrol US airspace and directed the standing naval force to the Eastern Mediterranean (see 'Operation Active Endeavour', below). In December NATO ministers of defence initiated a review of military capabilities and defences with a view to strengthening its ability to counter international terrorism.

In November 2002 NATO heads of state and government, convened in Prague, Czech Republic, approved a comprehensive reform of the Alliance's capabilities in order to reflect a new operational outlook and enable the transition to smaller, more flexible forces. The command structure was to be reduced and redefined, under operational and functional strategic commands, while a NATO Response Force (NRF), comprising a flexible and interoperable force of readily deployable land, sea and air elements, was to be established. The meeting agreed on further measures to strengthen NATO's capabilities to defend against terrorism and approved a broader commitment to improve and develop modern warfare capabilities. The Prague Summit initiatives were endorsed by a meeting of NATO defence ministers in June 2003. In March 2005 the NAC approved a charter formally to establish an organization to manage an Active Layered Theatre Ballistic Missile Defence programme, which aimed to establish a new collective defence capability. The NRF was inaugurated in October 2003, with a force strength of 9,500 troops. It was intended to enable NATO to react swiftly and efficiently in new areas of operation, such as evacuations, disaster management and counter-terrorism. By October 2004 the NRF had reached its initial operating capacity, comprising some 17,000 troops. It reached its full capacity, of 25,000 troops, in November 2006.

In April 2003 an agreement was signed by six member states—the Czech Republic, Denmark, Germany, the Netherlands, Norway and Poland—formally establishing the Civil-Military Co-operation Group North. The group was to be based at Budel, Netherlands, and was intended to provide NATO commanders with a co-ordinated approach to civil-military co-operation during crises and in post-conflict areas.

Periodic reviews of NATO's structures have been undertaken in response to changes in the security environment. In November 1991 NATO heads of government, convened in Rome, Italy, recommended a radical restructuring of the organization in view of the fundamental changes then taking place in Central and Eastern Europe; the restructuring entailed further reductions in military forces in Europe, active involvement in international peace-keeping operations, increased co-operation with other international institutions and close co-operation with its former adversaries, the USSR and the countries of Eastern Europe. The basis for NATO's revised force structure was incorporated into a Strategic Concept, which was adopted in the Rome Declaration issuing from the summit meeting. The concept provided for the maintenance of a collective defence capability, with a reduced dependence on nuclear weapons. Substantial reductions in the size and levels of readiness of NATO forces were undertaken, in order to reflect the Alliance's strictly defensive nature, and forces were reorganized within a streamlined integrated command structure. Forces were categorized into immediate and rapid reaction forces (including the ACE Rapid Reaction Corps—ARRC, which was inaugurated in October 1992), main defence forces and augmentation forces, which may be used to reinforce any NATO region or maritime areas for deterrence, crisis management or defence. During 1998 work was undertaken on the formulation of an updated Strategic Concept, reflecting the changing security environment and defining NATO's future role and objectives, which recognized a broader sphere of influence and confirmed NATO to be the principal generator of security in the Euro-Atlantic area. It emphasized NATO's role in crisis management and a renewed commitment to partnership and dialogue. The document was approved at a special summit meeting, convened in Washington, DC, USA, in April 1999, to commemorate the 50th anniversary of the Alliance. A separate initiative was approved to assist member states to adapt their defence capabilities to meet changing security requirements, for example improving the means of troop deployment and equipping and protecting forces. A summit meeting convened in Istanbul, Turkey in June 2004, evaluated progress made in transforming the Alliance's capabilities. In November 2006 NATO heads of state and government, meeting in Riga, Latvia, endorsed and made public a Comprehensive Political Guidance document which aimed to provide a framework and direction for the Alliance in the next 10–15 years. In particular, it identified the likely capability requirements of future operations, the need to respond to new threats and challenges, such as terrorism and the spread of weapons of mass destruction, and the development of relations with non-NATO countries. In June 2007 NATO ministers of defence, meeting to review the transformation of the Alliance's operational capabilities, agreed to assess the political and military implications of a possible redeployment of US missile defences in Europe. In April 2008 a NATO summit meeting, convened in Bucharest, Romania, reviewed progress in transforming the Alliance. It endorsed an Action Plan of proposals to develop and implement a NATO strategy for a comprehensive approach to existing and future security challenges. The meeting recognized the importance of working in partnership with the UN and EU and of strengthening co-operation with other countries and regional alliances. The meeting highlighted issues of arms control, nuclear non-proliferation and disarmament as being of particular concern. NATO's 60th anniversary summit meeting, convened in early April 2009, in Strasbourg, France and Kehl, Germany, adopted a Declaration on Alliance Security, reaffirming the basic values, principles and purposes of the Alliance, and determined to develop a new Strategic Concept that was to define NATO's longer-term role in the 21st century. The process of defining a new Strategic Concept was launched in July at a security conference attended by representatives of allied and partner governments, international organizations, the private sector, and civil society, including non-governmental organizations, academia and the media. In May 2010 a Group of Experts, appointed by the Secretary-General, presented a report to the NAC incorporating an analysis and recommendations for the new Strategic Concept. Further detailed deliberations were pursued over the next few months. The Strategic Concept, entitled *Active Engagement, Modern Defence*, was adopted by NATO heads of state and government, meeting in Lisbon, Portugal, in November. The document identified the challenges posed by the contemporary security environment and sought to enhance NATO's defence and deterrence capacities accordingly, while reaffirming its core tasks of collective defence, crisis management and co-operative security. NATO leaders approved the development of a new European missile defence capability, as well as measures to enhance cyber defence capabilities. They also endorsed an extensive reform of NATO's civil and military command structures, in order to enhance the organization's efficiency and flexibility.

In January 2012 the Secretary-General's first Annual Report (covering 2011) was published. In March 2012 the Secretary-General presented 'NATO 2020', a vision for the Alliance's medium-term future; this focused on the vigorous pursuit of so-called 'smart defence': acquiring, and maintaining, capabilities by means of greater collaboration, coherence and focus of effort, rather than through greater resources. In May 2012 a summit meeting of NATO heads of state and government, convened in Chicago, USA, announced readiness to work towards establishing, at the request of the Afghanistan Government, a mission to provide training and assistance to the Afghan Security Forces, including the Afghan Special Operations Forces, following on from the planned departure of ISAF at the end of 2014. The summit tasked the Council to commence, immediately, work on the military planning process for the proposed new mission. The summit also endorsed new NATO Policy Guidelines on Counter-Terrorism, mandated the Council to prepare an action plan aimed at improving NATO's terrorist threat awareness capabilities, and endorsed a Chicago Defence Declaration and Defence Package, outlining a vision of, and guidelines towards achieving, a new capabilities objective: 'NATO Forces 2020'—modern, closely connected forces equipped, trained, exercised and commanded in a manner that would enable them to operate jointly, and with partners, in any environment. The summit declared an interim NATO Ballistic Missile Defence (BMD) capacity, and tasked the Council to review on a regular basis the implementation of BMD capabilities.

In late June 2012 Turkey announced that it would pursue consultations within the Council, under Article 4 of the North Atlantic Treaty, invoked when the territorial integrity, political independence or security of any of the parties is threatened, following the shooting down by Syrian forces of a Turkish military jet; allegedly the attack was not forewarned and the jet was unarmed and in international airspace.

PARTNERSHIPS

In May 1997 a Euro-Atlantic Partnership Council (EAPC) was inaugurated as a successor to the North Atlantic Co-operation Council (NACC), that had been established in December 1991 to provide a forum for consultation on political and security matters with the countries of central and eastern Europe, including the former Soviet republics. An EAPC Council was to meet monthly at ambassadorial level and twice a year at ministerial level. It was to be supported in its work by a steering committee and a political committee. The EAPC was to pursue the NACC Work Plan for Dialogue, Partnership and Co-operation and incorporate it into a new Work Plan, which was to include an expanded political dimension of consultation and co-operation among participating states. The Partnership for Peace (PfP) programme, which was established in January 1994 within the framework of the NACC, was to remain an integral element of the new co-operative mechanism. The PfP incorporated practical military and defence-related co-operation activities that had originally been part of the NACC Work Plan. Participation in the PfP requires an initial signature of a framework agreement, establishing the common principles and objectives of the partnership, the submission of a presentation document, indicating the political and military aspects of the partnership and the nature of future co-operation activities and the development of individual partnership programmes establishing country-specific objectives. In June 1994 Russia, which had previously opposed the strategy as being the basis for future enlargement of NATO, signed the PfP framework document, which included a declaration envisaging an 'enhanced dialogue' between the two sides. Despite its continuing opposition to any enlargement of NATO, in May 1995 Russia agreed to sign a PfP Individual Partnership Programme, as well as a framework document for NATO-Russian dialogue and co-operation beyond the PfP. During 1994 a Partnership Co-ordination Cell (PCC), incorporating representatives of all partnership countries, became operational in Mons, Belgium. The PCC, under the authority of the NAC, aims to co-ordinate joint military activities and planning in order to implement PfP programmes. The first joint military exercises with countries of the former Warsaw Pact were conducted in September. NATO began formulating a PfP Status of Forces Agreement (SOFA) to define the legal status of Allies' and partners' forces when they are present on each other's territory; the PfP SOFA was opened for signature in June 1995. The new EAPC was to provide a framework for the development of an enhanced PfP programme, which NATO envisaged would become an essential element of the overall European security structure. Accordingly, the military activities of the PfP were to be expanded to include all Alliance missions and incorporate all NATO committees into the PfP process, thus providing for greater co-operation in crisis management, civil emergency planning and training activities. In addition, all PfP member countries were to participate in the CJTF concept through a structure of Partners Staff Elements, working at all levels of the Alliance military structure. Defence ministers of NATO and the 27 partner countries were to meet regularly to provide the political guidance for the enhanced Planning and Review Process of the PfP. In December 1997 NATO ministers of foreign affairs approved the establishment of a Euro-Atlantic Disaster Response Co-ordination Centre (EADRCC), and a non-permanent Euro-Atlantic Disaster Response Unit. The EADRCC was inaugurated in June 1998 and immediately commenced operations to provide relief to ethnic Albanian refugees fleeing the conflict in the Serbian province of Kosovo. In November the NAC approved the establishment of a network of PfP training centres, the first of which was inaugurated in Ankara, Turkey. The centres were a key element of a Training and Education Programme, which was endorsed at the summit meeting in April 1999. A policy of establishing individual PfP Trust Funds was approved in September 2000. These aimed to provide support for military reform and demilitarization activities in partners countries, in particular the destruction of anti-personnel landmines. In November 2002 heads of state and government, meeting in Prague, Czech Republic, endorsed a new initiative to formulate Individual Partnership Action Plans (IPAPs) designed to strengthen bilateral relations with a partner country, improve the effectiveness of NATO assistance in that country, and provide for intensified political dialogue. The Istanbul summit meeting in

June 2004 agreed to strengthen co-operation with partner countries in the Caucasus and Central Asia. A Special Representative of the Secretary-General to the two regions was appointed in September. In October the first IPAP was signed with Georgia, with the aim of defining national security and defence objectives, reforms and country-specific NATO assistance. IPAPs were concluded with Azerbaijan in May 2005, Armenia in December, Kazakhstan in January 2006 and with Moldova in May. Bosnia and Herzegovina and Montenegro joined the PfP process in December 2006. (Serbia also joined at that time.) In April 2008 both countries were invited to begin an Intensified Dialogue with NATO. Montenegro concluded an IPAP in June and held its first consultation under the Intensified Dialogue in that month. The IPAP with Bosnia and Herzegovina was concluded in September. In December 2009 NATO ministers of foreign affairs agreed to invite Montenegro to join the Membership Action Plan (MAP—see below), and determined that Bosnia and Herzegovina join MAP once further institutional reforms had been implemented.

The enlargement of NATO, through the admission of new members from the former USSR and Central and Eastern European countries, was considered to be a progressive means of contributing to the enhanced stability and security of the Euro-Atlantic area. In December 1996 NATO ministers of foreign affairs announced that invitations to join the Alliance would be issued to some former eastern bloc countries during 1997. The NATO Secretary-General and member governments subsequently began intensive diplomatic efforts to secure Russia's tolerance of these developments. It was agreed that no nuclear weapons or large numbers of troops would be deployed on the territory of any new member country in the former Eastern bloc. In May 1997 NATO and Russia signed the Founding Act on Mutual Relations, Co-operation and Security, which provided for enhanced Russian participation in all NATO decision-making activities, equal status in peace-keeping operations and representation at the Alliance headquarters at ambassadorial level, as part of a recognized shared political commitment to maintaining stability and security throughout the Euro-Atlantic region. A NATO-Russian Permanent Joint Council (PJC) was established under the Founding Act, and met for the first time in July; the Council provided each side with the opportunity for consultation and participation in the other's security decisions, but without a right of veto. In March 1999 Russia condemned NATO's military action against the Federal Republic of Yugoslavia and announced the suspension of all relations within the framework of the Founding Act, as well as negotiations on the establishment of a NATO mission in Moscow. The PJC convened once more in May 2000, and subsequent meetings were held in June and December. In February 2001 the NATO Secretary-General agreed with the then acting Russian President a joint statement of commitment to pursuing dialogue and co-operation. A NATO information office was opened in Moscow in that month. In December an agreement was concluded by NATO ministers of foreign affairs and their Russian counterpart to establish an eventual successor body to the PJC. The new NATO-Russia Council (NRC), in which NATO member states and Russia were to have equal status in decision-making, was inaugurated in May 2002. The Council aimed to strengthen co-operation in issues including counter-terrorism, crisis management, nuclear non-proliferation, and arms control. The third NATO-Russia conference on the role of the military in combating terrorism was convened in April 2004. In September the Council issued a joint statement condemning atrocities committed against civilians in North Ossetia and other parts of the Russian Federation. In April 2005, at an informal meeting of the ministers of foreign affairs of the NATO-Russia Council, Russia signed the PfP Status of Forces Agreement that provides a legal framework for the movement to and from Allied countries, partner countries and Russia of military personnel and support staff. In June a meeting of the Council endorsed Political-Military Guidance towards Enhanced Interoperability between Russian and NATO forces, thereby facilitating the preparation of those forces for possible joint operations. In April 2006 an informal meeting of the Council's ministers of foreign affairs reviewed NATO-Russia co-operation to date and adopted recommendations identifying interoperability, a pilot Afghanistan counter-narcotics project, a co-operative airspace initiative (CAI) and intensified political dialogue as the priority areas for future co-operation. In April 2008 the NRC, meeting at the level of heads of state, determined to extend on a permanent basis the joint project on counter-narcotics training of Afghan and Central Asian personnel and to accelerate the CAI project to ensure it reaches full operational capability by the end of 2009. In June 2008 NATO's Secretary-General urged Russia to withdraw some 400 troops from the Abkhazian region of Georgia and to respect that country's territorial integrity. In August meetings of the NRC were suspended owing to Russia's military action in Georgia, which the Alliance deemed to be 'disproportionate'. In December NATO ministers of foreign affairs agreed to initiate a gradual resumption of contacts with Russia. In April 2009 the meeting of NATO heads of state and government determined to resume normal relations with Russia. A meeting of the NRC at ministerial level was convened in June, in Corfu, Greece, at which all sides agreed to resume full political and military co-operation within the framework of the NRC. In September NATO's new Secretary-General, Anders Fogh Rasmussen, spoke on the importance of renewing and revitalizing NATO's strategic partnership with Russia. Later in that month he met with the Russian Minister of Foreign Affairs, in New York, USA, to discuss areas in which practical co-operation could be strengthened. In December the NRC, meeting at the level of foreign ministers, agreed on an extensive 2010 work programme, including renewed military co-operation, and initiated a Joint Review of 21st Century Common Security Challenges. At a meeting of the NRC, held in September 2010, discussions focused on strengthening practical co-operation and enhancing security in Europe. In November the NRC met at the level of heads of state. Both sides agreed on the need for a new strategic partnership, based on the presumption that they no longer posed a mutual threat. The declaration issued by NATO heads of state and government, meeting at that time in Lisbon, Portugal, incorporated an invitation to Russia to co-operate with the development of a new European missile defence capability. In June 2011 the first joint exercise was conducted under the CAI. In early July the NRC met in Sochi, Russia. The meeting reaffirmed the commitment of both sides to pursuing co-operation in missile defence, as well as other areas of mutual concern.

In May 1997 NATO ministers of foreign affairs, meeting in Sintra, Portugal, concluded an agreement with Ukraine providing for enhanced co-operation between the two sides; the so-called Charter on a Distinctive Relationship was signed at the NATO summit meeting held in Madrid, Spain, in July. In May 1998 NATO agreed to appoint a permanent liaison officer in Ukraine to enhance co-operation between the two sides and assist Ukraine to formulate a programme of joint military exercises. The first NATO-Ukraine meeting at the level of heads of state took place in April 1999. A NATO-Ukraine Commission (NUC) met for the first time in March 2000. In February 2005, at a NATO-Ukraine summit meeting, NATO leaders expressed support for Ukraine's reform agenda and agreed to strengthen co-operation with the country. In view of its commitment to strengthened co-operation, NATO announced that it would launch a project, the largest of its kind ever undertaken, to assist Ukraine in the decommissioning of old ammunitions, small arms and light weapons stockpiles. In April NATO invited Ukraine to begin an 'Intensified Dialogue' on its aspirations to NATO membership and on the necessary relevant reforms that it would be required to undertake. In the same month NATO and Ukraine effected an exchange of letters preparing the way for Ukraine to support 'Operation Active Endeavour' (see below). In June talks held between NATO ministers of defence and their Ukrainian counterpart focused on NATO's assistance to Ukraine in the reform of its defence and security sectors. In October the NATO-Ukraine Commission held its first meeting within the framework of the Intensified Dialogue initiated in April. A meeting of the ministers of defence of the NATO-Ukraine Commission held in June 2006 discussed Ukraine's defence policy and the ongoing transformation of the Ukrainian armed forces. In this context, ministers confirmed that the NATO-Ukraine Joint Working Group on Defence Reform should remain a key mechanism. In April 2008 NATO heads of state and government approved, in principle, Ukraine's future membership of the Alliance. The NAC, headed by the Secretary-General, visited Ukraine for a series of meetings in June. In August 2009 a Declaration to Complement the Charter on a Distinctive Partnership between NATO and Ukraine was signed, which emphasized the NUC's role in strengthening political dialogue and co-operation between the two sides and in securing reforms necessary for Ukraine to join the Alliance.

In August 2008 an extraordinary meeting of the NAC was convened to discuss an escalation of conflict in Georgia. The meeting expressed solidarity with Georgia's actions to counter attacks by separatist forces in Abkhazia and South Ossetia and deplored as disproportionate the use of force by Russia. Several days later the NAC held a special ministerial meeting to demand a peaceful, lasting solution to the conflict based on respect for Georgia's independence, sovereignty and territorial integrity. The meeting agreed that NATO would support Georgia in assessing damage to civil infrastructure, as well as in re-establishing an air traffic system and advising on cyber defence issues. Ministers also determined to establish a NATO-Georgia Commission, to strengthen co-operation and political dialogue between the two sides and to oversee Georgia's future application for NATO membership. A Framework Document to establish the Commission was signed by NATO's Secretary-General and Georgia's Prime Minister in the Georgian capital, Tbilisi, in September; the inaugural session of the Commission was convened immediately. The first meeting of the Commission at ministerial level was convened in December. In that month NATO ministers of foreign affairs agreed to establish a NATO Liaison Office in Tbilisi. The Office was inaugurated in October 2010 during a visit by the Secretary-General to Georgia. In December 2008 NATO foreign ministers also determined that Georgia should develop an Annual National Programme, replacing its existing IPAP, as a framework for co-operation with the Alliance and the implementation of reforms needed to fulfil membership criteria.

The Madrid summit meeting in July 1997 endorsed the establishment of a Mediterranean Co-operation Group to enhance NATO relations with Egypt, Israel, Jordan, Mauritania, Morocco and Tunisia. The Group was to provide a forum for regular political dialogue between the two groupings and to promote co-operation in training, scientific research and information exchange. In April 1999 NATO heads of state endorsed measures to strengthen the so-called Mediterranean Dialogue. Algeria joined the Mediterranean Dialogue in February 2000. The June 2004 summit meeting determined to enhance the Mediterranean Dialogue and launched a new 'Istanbul Co-operation Initiative' (ICI) aimed at promoting broader co-operation with the Middle East; Bahrain, Kuwait, Qatar and the UAE have joined the ICI. In February 2012 an ICI seminar was convened to consider means of deepening the partnership, and to discuss ongoing security challenges in the Middle East and North Africa. In February 2006 NATO and Mediterranean Dialogue partner countries convened their first meeting at the level of ministers of defence. In April, under the chairmanship of NATO's Deputy Secretary-General, the NAC and representatives of the seven Mediterranean Dialogue countries met in Rabat, Morocco, in order to review their co-operation to date and to discuss its future prospects. All countries were encouraged to formulate Individual Co-operation Programmes (ICPs) as a framework for future co-operation. In November NATO heads of state and government, meeting in Riga, Latvia, inaugurated a NATO Training Co-operation Initiative to extend defence and specialist training and expertise with Mediterranean Dialogue and ICI partner countries. The Initiative aimed to help those countries to strengthen their defence structures and enhance the interoperability of their armed forces with those of the Alliance. Egypt signed an ICP with NATO in October 2007, and Jordan concluded its ICP in April 2009. In April 2011, convened in Berlin, NATO ministers of foreign affairs approved a More Efficient and Flexible Partnership Policy, providing for '28+' meetings between NATO and partner countries in more flexible formats, beyond and within existing partnership frameworks. Consequently a meeting on Indian Ocean counter-piracy activities was held in September, with participation by representatives of 47 interested states and organizations. In May 2012 Mongolia and NATO agreed an ICP. The NATO summit convened in that month recognized that new standards of consultation and practical co-operation with partner countries had been achieved during the implementation, in 2011, of Operation Unified Protector in Libya, and, agreed to pursue more regular consultations on security issues through the Mediterranean Dialogue and ICI frameworks, as well as through bilateral consultations and the new flexible formats. The summit agreed to consider providing support to partners, where requested, in areas including security institution building, defence modernization, and civil-military relations. An offer by Kuwait to host an ICI Regional Centre was welcomed.

In July 1997 heads of state and government formally invited the Czech Republic, Hungary and Poland to begin accession negotiations. Accession Protocols for the admission of those countries were signed in December and required ratification by all member states. The three countries formally became members of NATO in March 1999. In April the NATO summit meeting, held in Washington, DC, USA, initiated a new Membership Action Plan (MAP) to extend practical support to aspirant member countries and to formalize a process of reviewing applications. In March 2003 protocols of accession, amending the North Atlantic Treaty, were adopted by the then 19 NATO member states with a view to admitting Bulgaria, Estonia, Latvia, Lithuania, Romania, Slovakia and Slovenia to the Alliance. In March 2004, the protocols of accession having been ratified by all of the member states, those seven countries were formally invited to join NATO and, on 29 March, they acceded to the Treaty. In April 2008 NATO heads of state and government, meeting in Bucharest, Romania, invited Albania and Croatia to commence accession negotiations and declared support for Georgia and Ukraine to apply for MAP status. It was also agreed that accession negotiations with the former Yugoslav republic of Macedonia, which joined the MAP programme in 1999, would be initiated as soon as a mutually acceptable solution to the issue over the country's name has been reached with Greece. The Accession Protocols for Albania and Croatia were signed by NATO ministers of foreign affairs in July, and those countries formally acceded to the Treaty on 1 April 2009. Montenegro was invited to join MAP in December; at that time NATO ministers confirmed that Bosnia and Herzegovina would participate in MAP as soon as further institutional reforms had been implemented. In April 2010 NATO ministers of foreign affairs invited Bosnia and Herzegovina to join MAP, conditional on full registration of its defence properties.

In November 2010 the Lisbon summit meeting determined to reform NATO's structure of partnership mechanisms, in order to enhance the flexibility and efficiency of co-operation arrangements.

OPERATIONS

During the 1990s NATO increasingly developed its role as a mechanism for peace-keeping and crisis management. In June 1992 NATO ministers of foreign affairs, meeting in Oslo, Norway, announced the Alliance's readiness to support peace-keeping operations under the aegis of the CSCE on a case-by-case basis: NATO would make both military resources and expertise available to such operations. In July NATO, in co-operation with WEU, undertook a maritime operation in the Adriatic Sea to monitor compliance with the UN Security Council's resolutions imposing sanctions against the Yugoslav republics of Serbia and Montenegro. In December NATO ministers of foreign affairs expressed the Alliance's readiness to support peace-keeping operations under the authority of the UN Security Council. From April 1993 NATO fighter and reconnaissance aircraft began patrolling airspace over Bosnia and Herzegovina in order to enforce the UN prohibition of military aerial activity over the country. In addition, from July NATO aircraft provided protective cover for troops from the UN Protection Force in Yugoslavia (UNPROFOR) operating in the 'safe areas' established by the UN Security Council. In February 1994 NATO conducted the first of several aerial strikes against artillery positions that were violating heavy weapons exclusion zones imposed around 'safe areas' and threatening the civilian populations. Throughout the conflict the Alliance also provided transport, communications and logistics to support UN humanitarian assistance in the region.

The peace accord for the former Yugoslavia, which was initialled in Dayton, USA, in November 1995, and signed in Paris, France, in December, provided for the establishment of a NATO-led Implementation Force (IFOR) to ensure compliance with the treaty, in accordance with a strictly defined timetable and under the authority of a UN Security Council mandate. In December a joint meeting of allied foreign and defence ministers endorsed the military structure for the peace mission, entitled 'Operation Joint Endeavour', which was to involve approximately 60,000 troops from 31 NATO and non-NATO countries. IFOR, which constituted NATO's largest military operation ever, formally assumed responsibility for peace-keeping in Bosnia and Herzegovina from the UN on 20 December.

By mid-1996 the military aspects of the Dayton peace agreement had largely been implemented under IFOR supervision. Substantial progress was achieved in the demobilization of soldiers and militia and in the cantonment of heavy weaponry. During 1996 IFOR personnel undertook many activities relating to the civilian reconstruction of Bosnia and Herzegovina, including the repair of roads, railways and bridges, reconstruction of schools and hospitals, delivery of emergency food and water supplies, and emergency medical transportation. IFOR also co-operated with, and provided logistical support for, the Office of the High Representative of the International Community in Bosnia and Herzegovina, which was charged with overseeing implementation of the civilian aspects of the Bosnian peace accord. IFOR assisted the OSCE in preparing for and overseeing the all-Bosnia legislative elections that were held in September, and provided security for displaced Bosnians who crossed the inter-entity boundary in order to vote in their towns of origin. In December NATO ministers of foreign affairs approved a follow-on operation, with an 18-month mandate, to be known as the Stabilization Force (SFOR). SFOR was to be about one-half the size of IFOR, but was to retain 'the same unity of command and robust rules of engagement' as the previous force. Its principal objective was to maintain a safe environment at a military level to ensure that the civil aspects of the Dayton peace accord could be fully implemented, including the completion of the de-mining process, the repatriation of refugees, rehabilitation of local infrastructure and preparations for municipal elections. In December 1997 NATO ministers of defence confirmed that SFOR would be maintained at its current strength of some 31,000 troops, subject to the periodic six-monthly reviews. In February 1998 NATO resolved to establish within SFOR a specialized unit to respond to civil unrest and uphold public security. At the same time the NAC initiated a series of security co-operation activities to promote the development of democratic practices and defence mechanisms in Bosnia and Herzegovina. In October 1999 the NAC agreed to implement a reduction in SFOR's strength to some 20,000 troops, as well as a revision of its command structure, in response to the improved security situation in Bosnia and Herzegovina. In May 2002 NATO determined to reduce SFOR to 12,000 troops by the end of that year, and in December 2003 NATO defence ministers undertook to reduce NATO's presence to some 7,000 troops by mid-2004. The June 2004 summit meeting determined to terminate SFOR's mandate at the end of 2004, and endorsed a new European Union (EU) mission, EUFOR, in Bosnia and Herzegovina. NATO maintains a military headquarters in Sarajevo, in order to continue to assist the authorities in Bosnia and Herzegovina in matters of defence reform.

In March 1998 an emergency session of the NAC was convened at the request of the Albanian Government, which was concerned at the deteriorating security of its border region with the Serbian province of Kosovo and Metohija. In June NATO defence ministers authorized the formulation of plans for air-strikes against Serbian targets, which were finalized in early October. However, the Russian Government remained strongly opposed to the use of force and there was concern among some member states over whether there was sufficient legal basis for NATO action without further UN authorization. Nevertheless, in mid-October, following Security Council condemnation of the humanitarian situation in Kosovo, the NAC agreed on limited air-strikes against Serbian targets, with a 96-hour delay on the 'activation order'. At the same time the US envoy to the region, Richard Holbrooke, concluded an agreement with President Milošević to implement the conditions of a UN resolution (No. 1199). A 2,000-member international observer force, under the auspices of the OSCE, was to be established to monitor compliance with the agreement, supported by a NATO Co-ordination Unit, based in the former Yugoslav republic of Macedonia (FYRM), to assist with aerial surveillance. In mid-November NATO ambassadors approved the establishment of a 1,200–1,800-strong multinational force, under French command, to assist in any necessary evacuation of OSCE monitors. A NATO Kosovo Verification Command Centre was established in Kumanovo, north-east FYRM, later in that month.

On 24 March 1999 an aerial offensive against the Federal Republic of Yugoslavia (which was renamed 'Serbia and Montenegro' in 2003 and divided into separate states of Montenegro and Serbia in 2006) was initiated by NATO, with the declared aim of reducing that country's capacity to commit attacks on the Albanian population. The first phase of the allied operation was directed against defence facilities, followed, a few days later, by the second phase which permitted direct attacks on artillery positions, command centres and other military targets in a declared exclusion zone south of the 44th parallel. The escalation of the conflict prompted thousands of Albanians to flee Kosovo, while others were reportedly forced from their homes by Serbian security personnel, creating massive refugee populations in neighbouring countries. In early April 1999 NATO ambassadors agreed to dispatch some 8,000 troops, as an ACE Mobile Force Land operation (entitled 'Operation Allied Harbour'), to provide humanitarian assistance to the estimated 300,000 refugees in Albania at that time and to provide transportation to relieve overcrowded camps, in particular in border areas. Refugees in the FYRM were to be assisted by the existing NATO contingent (numbering some 12,000 troops by early April), which was permitted by the authorities in that country to construct new camps for some 100,000 displaced Kosovans. An additional 1,000 troops were transferred from the FYRM to Albania in mid-May in order to construct a camp to provide for a further 65,000 refugees. NATO's 50th anniversary summit meeting, held in Washington, DC, USA, in late April, was dominated by consideration of the conflict and of the future stability of the region. A joint statement declared the determination of all Alliance members to increase economic and military pressure on President Milošević to withdraw forces from Kosovo. In particular, the meeting agreed to prevent shipments of petroleum reaching Serbia through Montenegro, to complement the embargo imposed by the EU and a new focus of the bombing campaign which aimed to destroy the fuel supply within Serbia. However, there was concern on the part of several NATO governments with regard to the legal and political aspects of implementing the embargo. The meeting failed to adopt a unified position on the use of ground forces. Following further intensive diplomatic efforts to secure a cease-fire in Kosovo, on 9 June a Military Technical Agreement was signed between NATO and the Federal Republic of Yugoslavia, incorporating a timetable for the withdrawal of all Serbian security personnel. On the following day the UN Security Council adopted Resolution 1244, which authorized an international security presence in Kosovo, the Kosovo Peace Implementation Force (KFOR), under NATO command, and an international civilian presence, the UN Interim Administration Mission in Kosovo (UNMIK). The NAC subsequently suspended the air-strike campaign, which, by that time, had involved some 38,000 sorties. An initial 20,000 KFOR troops entered Kosovo on 12 June. A few days later an agreement was concluded with Russia, providing for the joint responsibility of Pristina airport with a NATO contingent and for the participation of some 3,600 Russian troops in KFOR, reporting to the country command in each sector. On 20 June the withdrawal of Yugoslav troops from Kosovo was completed, providing for the formal ending of NATO's air campaign. KFOR's immediate responsibility was to create a secure environment to facilitate the safe return of refugees, and, pending the full deployment of UNMIK, to assist the reconstruction of infrastructure and civil and political institutions. In addition, NATO troops were to assist personnel of the international tribunal to investigate sites of alleged violations of human rights and mass graves. In January 2000 NATO agreed that the Eurocorps defence force would assume command of KFOR headquarters in April. In February an emergency meeting of the NAC was convened to review the situation in the divided town of Mitrovicë (Kosovska Mitrovica), northern Kosovo, where violent clashes had occurred between the ethnic populations and five people had died during attempts by KFOR to impose order. The NAC expressed its determination to reinforce KFOR's troop levels. In October KFOR worked with OSCE and UN personnel to maintain a secure environment and provide logistical assistance for the holding of municipal elections in Kosovo. During the year KFOR attempted to prevent the movement and stockpiling of illegal armaments in the region. A Weapons Destruction Programme was successfully conducted by KFOR between April 2000–December 2001; a second programme was initiated in March 2002, while an Ammunition Destruction Programme commenced in January. In May the NAC approved a modification of KFOR's mission that was designed to facilitate the introduction of a more regional approach to operations and permit a reduction in KFOR's strength from 38,000 troops to some 33,200 by the end of the year. In July 2003, in view of progress made in the security situation, the withdrawal of the Russian contingent from KFOR was effected. In March 2004, in response to renewed inter-ethnic violence in Kosovo, NATO deployed additional troops from previously designated operational and strategic reserve forces in order to support operations undertaken by KFOR to protect Kosovar Serbs and other ethnic minorities in addition to ethnic Albanians. In February 2006 direct UN-led talks between Serbian and Kosovo Albanian officials on the future status of Kosovo commenced in Vienna, Austria. By the end of 2007, however, the two sides had failed to reach agreement. NATO's ministers of foreign affairs, meeting in December 2007, agreed that KFOR would remain in the province, at current troop levels, unless the UN Security Council decided otherwise. In February 2008 Kosovo's newly elected government issued a unilateral declaration of independence from Serbia, supported by many EU countries. NATO's Secretary-General and NAC reaffirmed the commitment to maintain a force in Kosovo and to support any future arrangements. In June 2009 NATO defence ministers announced a gradual reduction in KFOR troop numbers, given improvements in the security environment, and envisaged the force becoming a 'deterrent presence'. In February 2010 NATO ministers of defence reviewed the situation in Kosovo and welcomed the conclusion of the first phase adjusting KFOR to a deterrent force. At that time there were some 10,700 troops under NATO command in Kosovo (compared with some 15,500 in January 2009).

In March 2001 Albanian separatists in the FYRM escalated their campaign in the north of that country prompting thousands of Albanians to flee into Kosovo. KFOR troops attempted to prevent Kosovo Albanians from supporting the rebels, fighting as the National Liberation Army (NLA), in order to avert further violence and instability. NATO dispatched military and political missions to meet with the Macedonian authorities, and agreed that Serbian troops were to be permitted to enter the ground safety zone in the Presevo valley (bordering on Kosovo and the FYRM) to strengthen security and prevent it becoming a safe haven for the rebel fighters. In June NATO troops supervised the withdrawal of some 300 armed Albanian rebels who had been besieged in a town neighbouring Skopje, the Macedonian capital. A cease-fire agreement, mediated by NATO, was concluded by the Macedonian authorities and Albanian militants in early July. An agreement regarding disarmament and conditions for ethnic minorities, as well as for the immediate withdrawal of troops, was concluded in August. Some 3,800 NATO troops were deployed at the end of that month, under so-called 'Operation Essential Harvest'. At the end of the operation's 30-day mandate almost 4,300 guns had been surrendered, together with 400,000 mines, grenades and ammunition rounds. The NLA formally disbanded, in accordance with the peace agreement. The NAC approved a successor mission, 'Task Force Fox', comprising 700 troops, to protect the civilian observers of the accord (to be deployed by the EU and OSCE). In June 2002 a team from NATO headquarters met with the Macedonian authorities to discuss measures to enhance the country's co-operation with the Alliance. In November, as the expiry of the extended mandate of Task Force Fox approached, NATO agreed, at the request of the FYRM authorities, to deploy a new peace-keeping mission, 'Operation Allied Harmony', from December in order to afford continued protection to the civilian observers of the cease-fire accord and to assist the Macedonian authorities to assume responsibility for security. On 31 March 2003 NATO's mission in the FYRM was succeeded by an EU-led operation.

In September 2001, following the terrorist attacks against targets in the USA and the decision to invoke Article 5 of the North Atlantic Treaty, NATO redirected the standing naval force to provide an immediate Alliance presence in the Eastern Mediterranean. In the following month 'Operation Active Endeavour' was formally launched, to undertake surveillance and monitoring of maritime trade in the region and to detect and deter terrorist activity, including illegal trafficking. In February 2003 the NAC agreed to extend the operation to escort non-military vessels through the Strait of Gibraltar; this aspect of the mission was suspended in May 2004. In March 2004 the NAC determined to expand the operation to the whole of the Mediterranean and to seek the support of this extension, through their active participation in the operation, by participants in the EAPC and the PfP programme. An Exchange of Letters between NATO and Russia, concluded in December 2004, facilitated the implementation from February 2006 of joint training activities. In September 2006 NATO authorized the participation of a Russian naval ship in the operation. The NAC approved the active involvement of a Ukrainian ship in the operation in May 2007. By 2012 more than 100,000 vessels had been monitored under the operation, and some 155 compliant boardings had taken place.

In August 2003 NATO undertook its first mission outside of the Euro-Atlantic area when it assumed command of the UN-mandated International Security Assistance Force (ISAF) in Afghanistan. In October the office of a Senior Civilian Representative was established to liaise with the national government and representatives of the international community and advance NATO's politico-military objectives in the country. In December NATO ministers of defence agreed progressively to extend ISAF's mission in Afghanistan beyond the capital, Kabul. The transfer of command of the Kunduz Provincial Reconstruction Team (PRT) to NATO in January 2004 represented the first step of that expansion. In June the summit meeting, held in Istanbul, Turkey, determined to expand the ISAF in order to assist the Afghan authorities to extend and exercise authority across the country. A first phase of the mission's expansion, involving the establishment of PRTs in Baghlan, Feyzabad, Mazar-e-Sharif and Meymana, had been completed by October of that year. In December the NAC authorized a second expansionary phase, which envisaged the establishment of four PRTs in western provinces of Afghanistan. This was undertaken in 2005. In September an additional 2,000 NATO troops were temporarily deployed to Afghanistan to provide security during provincial and parliamentary elections, held in that month. In December NATO ministers of foreign affairs endorsed a revised operational plan to incorporate a Stage 3 and Stage 4 Expansion of ISAF. The Stage 3 and Stage 4 Expansions, achieved, respectively, in July and October 2006, entailed extending operations to cover the entire country and establishing 15 additional PRTs, five regional commands and two forward support bases (in Kandahar and Khost). Additional ISAF officers were dispatched to mentor and liaise with national army units, support government programmes to disarm rebel groups and support government and international programmes to counter illicit narcotic production. NATO continued to emphasize immediate reconstruction and development activities, through its civil military co-operation units, working closely with government and local and community leaders, and co-operated with the Pakistani military and Afghan National Army through a Tripartite Commission and a Joint Intelligence and Operations Centre. In September 2006 NATO's Secretary-General signed a declaration with the Afghan President establishing a Framework for Enduring Co-operation in Partnership, committing NATO to long-term support for the country's efforts to secure democratic government and territorial integrity. In April 2008 NATO heads of state and government, meeting in Bucharest, Romania, confirmed that ISAF remained a priority for the Alliance and expressed a long-term commitment to achieving peace and security in Afghanistan. In June the Secretary-General participated in an International Conference in Support of Afghanistan, hosted by the French Government in Paris. In April 2009 heads of state and government, and leaders of partner countries contributing to ISAF, attending the NATO summit, issued a Declaration on Afghanistan, in which they stated their long-term commitment to that country, pledged the deployment there of additional military forces for electoral support and for training and mentoring the Afghan National Army, and announced the establishment of a NATO Training

Mission in Afghanistan (NTM-A). Further initiatives to enhance the training for Afghan National Security Forces, to improve the command and control structure of ISAF and to deploy NATO airborne warning and control aircraft to Afghanistan, were approved by NATO defence ministers meeting in June. In October NATO defence ministers and ministers from non-NATO contributing countries agreed a set of key priorities for the coming year: placing the Afghan population at the core of Alliance activities in that country; building further the capacity of the national security forces; promoting better governance; and engaging with Afghanistan's neighbours, in particular with Pakistan. NTM-A was formally established in that month. In February 2010 ISAF initiated a joint military offensive with Afghan national security forces, entitled Operation Moshtarak, in order to reassert government authority and to protect the civilian population in southern Helmand province. In April an informal meeting of NATO and ISAF ministers of foreign affairs agreed on a roadmap to structure a transition process of handing over full sovereignty to the Afghan authorities. At the same time ministers adopted an Afghan First Policy to strengthen the local Afghan economy. A joint framework for transition to full Afghan ownership of its national security by the end of 2014 was endorsed at an international conference on Afghanistan, convened in Kabul, in July 2010. The transition process, was endorsed at the NATO summit meeting in November 2010. At that time ISAF 's troop strength totalled 130,930 from 40 contributing nations. NATO heads of state and government also reaffirmed their long-term commitment to ensuring the stability of Afghanistan. In March 2011 the Afghan President confirmed that from July troops would be withdrawn and power transferred to local authorities in a first tranche of areas. Accordingly, responsibility for security of Bamiyan province, central Lashkar Gah, and Mehter Lam in eastern Afghanistan was transferred to Afghan forces in July. The transition process started in a second tranche of Afghan areas in December 2011. At an International Conference on Afghanistan, held in that month in Bonn, Germany, NATO committed to supporting Afghanistan through its 'Transformation Decade' beyond 2014. In early February 2012 a meeting of NATO and ISAF defence ministers determined that the process of transition to Afghan security ownership was on course, and reaffirmed the objective that the Afghan security forces should have full responsibility for security across the country by end-2014. Later in February 2012 ISAF personnel were temporarily withdrawn from government ministries in and around Kabul following the killing of two ISAF officers inside the Afghan Ministry of Interior; violent protests had erupted at that time over reports that US troops based in Afghanistan had unintentionally burned copies of the Koran. The 2012 NATO summit, held in May (shortly after the commencement of the third tranche of the transition process), determined to initiate the planning process for a new mission to continue training and advising the Afghan security forces, within the context of the Framework for Enduring Co-operation in Partnership and at the behest of the Afghan Government, following the 2014 transfer of power.

In June 2004 NATO heads of state and government, meeting in Istanbul, Turkey, agreed to offer assistance to the newly inaugurated Iraqi Interim Government with the training of its security forces. The meeting also endorsed a new NATO Policy on Combating Trafficking in Human Beings, with the aim of supporting the efforts of countries and international organizations to counter the problem. In July a NATO Training Implementation Mission was initiated to undertake the training commitments in Iraq. In December the NAC authorized an expansion of the Mission, of up to 300 personnel, and the establishment of an Iraq Training, Education and Doctrine Centre. The expanded operation was to be called the NATO Training Mission–Iraq (NTM-I). In September 2005 an Iraqi Joint Staff College was inaugurated. In July 2009 NATO and the Iraqi Government signed a long-term agreement regarding the training of Iraqi Security Forces. NTM-I expanded its remit in 2010 to include training of border personnel. NTM-1 was terminated in December 2011. In April 2011 Iraq was granted NATO partner status. It was announced in May 2012 that a NATO Transition Cell had been established in Iraq to support the development of the partnership.

In April 2005 the African Union (AU) requested NATO assistance to support its peace-keeping mission in Darfur, western Sudan, where civil conflict had caused a severe humanitarian crisis. In May the NAC provisionally agreed to provide logistical support for the mission. Further consultations were held with the AU, UN and EU. In June the NAC confirmed that it would assist in the expansion of the AU mission (AMIS) by airlifting supplementary AU peace-keepers into the region. No NATO combat troops were to be deployed to Darfur. The first airlifts were undertaken in July and in August NATO agreed to transport civilian police officers. NATO established a Senior Military Liaison Officer team, in Addis Ababa, Ethiopia, to liaise with the AU. In June 2006 the AU requested enhanced NATO assistance for its peace-keeping mission in Darfur, including the certification of troops allocated to the peace-keeping force, assistance with lessons learned and support in the establishment of a joint operations centre. NATO undertook staff training to further the mission's capacity-building activities. In November NATO ministers extended its support for proposals by the AU and UN to undertake a hybrid peace-keeping mission in Darfur. NATO support to AMIS was concluded on 31 December 2007 when the mission was transferred to the UN/AU operation. In June 2007 NATO agreed to support an AU mission in Somalia by providing strategic airlifts for deployment of personnel and equipment. The 2012 NATO summit agreed to extend strategic airlift support, and also maritime life support, to AMISOM, and to support the development of the AU's long-term peace-keeping capabilities, including the African Standby Force. In October 2008 NATO ministers of defence, meeting in Budapest, Hungary, agreed to initiate a temporary assignment, Operation Allied Provider, in support of a request by the UN Secretary-General, to protect ships chartered by the World Food Programme to deliver humanitarian aid to Somalia. The mission was also mandated to conduct patrols to deter piracy and other criminal acts against merchant shipping in the high risk areas in the Gulf of Aden. The Operation was concluded in mid-December. NATO resumed its counter-piracy operations in that region in March 2009, under Operation Allied Protector. A successor mission, Operation Ocean Shield, was approved in August and incorporated a new training element to enable countries in the region to strengthen their counter-piracy capabilities. In March 2012 the mandate of Operation Ocean Shield was extended to the end of 2014.

From October 2005 until 1 February 2006 NATO undertook a mission to provide relief to areas of north-west Pakistan severely damaged and isolated by a massive earthquake. NATO airlifted relief supplies into the region, transported civilians and official personnel, and deployed some 1,200 engineers and troops to assist with road clearance and the construction of shelters and other local infrastructure. In August 2010 the NAC agreed to a request from the Pakistani Government to provide assistance in the delivery of humanitarian supplies, donated by international organizations following extensive flooding in large parts of the country.

In March 2011 NATO initiated Operation Unified Protector, using ships and aircraft operating in the Central Mediterranean, in order to monitor and enforce an arms embargo against the Libyan authorities, which had been imposed by the UN Security Council (Resolution 1973, adopted on 17 March) in response to the violent oppression of an opposition movement in that country. Later in that month NATO members determined to enforce the UN-sanctioned no-fly zone over Libya, alongside a military operation to prevent further attacks on civilians and civilian-populated areas, undertaken by a multinational coalition under British, France and US command. A few days later, on 27 March, NATO member states agreed to assume full command of the operation to protect civilians in Libya (formal transfer of command took place on 31 March). On 28 March NATO's Secretary-General attended an international conference on Libya, held in London, United Kingdom, at which it was agreed to establish a Contact Group to give political guidance to the international community's response to the situation. The first meeting of the Contact Group was held in Doha, Qatar, in April. (The Contact Group was replaced in September by a Group of Friends of the New Libya.) In early June NATO ministers extended Operation Unified Protector for a further 90 days (from 27 June); in September the Operation was extended once again for 90 days. In late October, following the capture by opposition forces of the last remaining government-controlled city, Sirte, and the arrest (and subsequent death) of the Libyan leader, Col Muammar al-Qaddafi, the North Atlantic Council resolved to conclude the Operation with effect from the end of that month. By the time of its conclusion NATO and its partners had conducted more than 26,500 air sorties over Libya, including 9,700 strike missions. Nineteen vessels were deployed during the Operation to monitor and enforce the arms embargo, supported by patrol aircraft. Over 3,100 ships were hailed, 300 boarded and 11 denied transit to port under the Operation.

NATO Agencies

In November 2010 NATO heads of state and government agreed to realign the Agency structure and consolidate the functions and programmes of the then 14 entities along three major programmatic themes: Support; Communications and information systems; and Procurement. The Agency Reform plan was approved in June 2011. Accordingly, a NATO Support Agency (headquartered in Capellen, Luxembourg); a NATO Communications and Information Agency (headquartered in Brussels, Belgium); and a NATO Procurement Agency (also based in Brussels) were to become operational in 2012. A new Science and Technology Organization was also to be established. The future of the existing, Brussels-based, NATO Standardization Agency was to be reviewed in 2014; otherwise, all the functions hitherto performed by the outgoing entities were to be transferred to the new Agencies, in some cases as programme offices of the new Agencies.

Finance

As NATO is an international, not a supra-national, organization, its member countries themselves decide the amount to be devoted to their defence effort and the form which the latter will assume. Thus, the aim of NATO's defence planning is to develop realistic military plans for the defence of the Alliance at reasonable cost. Under the annual defence planning process, political, military and economic factors are considered in relation to strategy, force requirements and available resources. The procedure for the co-ordination of military plans and defence expenditures rests on the detailed and comparative analysis of the capabilities of member countries. All installations for the use of international forces are financed under a common-funded infrastructure programme. In accordance with the terms of the Partnership for Peace strategy, partner countries undertake to make available the necessary personnel, assets, facilities and capabilities to participate in the programme. The countries also share the financial cost of military exercises in which they participate.

Publications

NATO publications (in English and French, with some editions in other languages) include:

NATO Basic Texts.

NATO Handbook.

NATO Ministerial Communiqués.

NATO Review (quarterly, in 24 languages).

NATO Update (monthly, electronic version only).

Secretary-General's Annual Report.

Economic and scientific publications.

North Atlantic Treaty

(signed 4 April 1949, as amended by protocols signed on the accession of Greece, Turkey, Germany and Spain)

The Parties to this Treaty reaffirm their faith in the purposes and principles of the Charter of the United Nations and their desire to live in peace with all peoples and all governments.

They are determined to safeguard the freedom, common heritage and civilization of their peoples, founded on the principles of democracy, individual liberty and the rule of law.

They seek to promote stability and well-being in the North Atlantic area. They are resolved to unite their efforts for collective defence and for the preservation of peace and security.

They therefore agree to this North Atlantic Treaty:

Article 1

The Parties undertake, as set forth in the Charter of the United Nations, to settle any international dispute in which they may be involved by peaceful means in such a manner that international peace and security and justice are not endangered, and to refrain in their international relations from the threat or use of force in any manner inconsistent with the purposes of the United Nations.

Article 2

The Parties will contribute toward the further development of peaceful and friendly international relations by strengthening their free institutions, by bringing about a better understanding of the principles upon which these institutions are founded, and by promoting conditions of stability and well-being. They will seek to eliminate conflict in their international economic policies and will encourage economic collaboration between any or all of them.

Article 3

In order more effecitvely to achieve the objectives of this Treaty, the Parties, separately and jointly, by means of continuous and effective self-help and mutual aid, will maintain and develop their individual and collective capacity to resist armed attack.

Article 4

The Parties will consult together whenever, in the opinion of any of them, the territorial integrity, political independence or security of any of the Parties is threatened.

Article 5

The Parties agree that an armed attack against one or more of them in Europe or North America shall be considered an attack against them all and consequently they agree that, if such an armed attack occurs, each of them, in exercise of the right of individual or collective self-defence recognised by Article 51 of the Charter of the United Nations, will assist the Party or Parties so attacked by taking forthwith, individually and in concert with the other Parties, such action as it deems necessary, including the use of armed force, to restore and maintain the security of the North Atlantic area.

Any such armed attack and all measures taken as a result thereof shall immediately be reported to the (UN) Security Council. Such measures shall be terminated when the Security Council has taken the measures necessary to restore and maintain international peace and security.

Article 6

For the purpose of Article 5, an armed attack on one or more of the Parties is deemed to include an armed attack:

—on the territory of any of the Parties in Europe or North America, on the Algerian Departments of France*, on the territory of Turkey or on the Islands under the jurisdiction of any of the Parties in the North Atlantic area north of the Tropic of Cancer;

—on the forces, vessels, or aircraft of any of the Parties, when in or over these territories or any other area in Europe in which occupation forces of any of the Parties were stationed on the date when the Treaty entered into force or the Mediterranean Sea or the North Atlantic area north of the Tropic of Cancer.

Article 7

This treaty does not affect, and shall not be interpreted as affecting in any way the rights and obligations under the Charter of the Parties which are members of the United Nations, or the primary responsibility of the Security Council for the maintenance of international peace and security.

Article 8

Each Party declares that none of the international engagements now in force beween it and any other of the Parties or any third State is in conflict with the provisions of this Treaty, and undertakes not to enter into any international engagement in conflict with this Treaty.

Article 9

The Parties hereby establish a Council, on which each of them shall be represented, to consider matters concerning the implementation of this Treaty. The Council shall be so organised as to be able to meet promptly at any time. The Council shall set up such subsidiary bodies as may be necessary; in particular it shall establish immediately a defence committee which shall recommend measures for the implementation of Articles 3 and 5.

Article 10

The Parties may, by unanimous agreement, invite any other European State in a position to further the principles of this Treaty and to contribute to the security of the North Atlantic area to accede to this Treaty. Any State so invited may become a Party to the Treaty by depositing its instrument of accession with the Government of the United States of America. The Government of the United States of America will inform each of the Parties of the deposit of each such instrument of accession.

Article 11

This Treaty shall be ratified and its provisions carried out by the Parties in accordance with their respective constitutional processes. The instruments of ratification shall be deposited as soon as possible with the Government of the United States of America, which will notify all the other signatories of each deposit. The Treaty shall enter into force between the States which have ratified it as soon as the ratifications of the majority of the signatories, including the ratifications of Belgium, Canada, France, Luxembourg, the Netherlands, the United Kingdom and the United States, have been deposited and shall come into effect with respect to other States on the date of the deposit of their ratifications.

Article 12

After the Treaty has been in force for ten years, or at any time thereafter, the Parties shall, if any of them so requests, consult together for the purpose of reviewing the Treaty, having regard for the factors then affecting peace and security in the North Atlantic area, including the development of universal as well as regional arrangements under the Charter of the United Nations for the maintenance of international peace and security.

Article 13

After the Treaty has been in force for twenty years, any Party may cease to be a Party one year after its notice of denunciation has been given to the Government of the United States of America, which will inform the Governments of the other Parties of the deposit of each notice of denunciation.

Article 14

This Treaty, of which the English and French texts are equally authentic, shall be deposited in the archives of the Government of the United States of America. Duly certified copies will be transmitted by that Government to the Governments of other signatories.

* In January 1963, the North Atlantic Council noted that insofar as the former Algerian Departments of France were concerned, the relevant clauses of this Treaty had become inapplicable as from July 1962.

ORGANISATION FOR ECONOMIC CO-OPERATION AND DEVELOPMENT—OECD

Address: 2 rue André-Pascal, 75775 Paris Cedex 16, France.
Telephone: 1-45-24-82-00; **fax:** 1-45-24-85-00; **e-mail:** webmaster@oecd.org; **internet:** www.oecd.org.

OECD was founded in 1961, replacing the Organisation for European Economic Co-operation (OEEC) which had been established in 1948 in connection with the Marshall Plan. It constitutes a forum for governments to discuss, develop and attempt to co-ordinate their economic and social policies. The organization aims to promote policies designed to achieve the highest level of sustainable economic growth, employment and increase in the standard of living, while maintaining financial stability and democratic government, and to contribute to economic expansion in member and non-member states and to the expansion of world trade.

MEMBERS

Australia	Hungary	Norway
Austria	Iceland	Poland
Belgium	Ireland	Portugal
Canada	Israel	Slovakia
Chile	Italy	Slovenia
Czech Republic	Japan	Spain
Denmark	Republic of Korea	Sweden
Estonia	Luxembourg	Switzerland
Finland	Mexico	Turkey
France	Netherlands	United Kingdom
Germany	New Zealand	USA
Greece		

Note: Accession talks were ongoing with Russia in 2012.
The European Commission also takes part in OECD's work. Brazil, the People's Republic of China, India, Indonesia and South Africa are regarded as 'key partner' countries.

Organization

(June 2012)

COUNCIL

The governing body of OECD is the Council, at which each member country is represented. The Council meets from time to time (usually once a year) at the level of government ministers, with the chairmanship rotated among member states. It also meets regularly at official level, when it comprises the Secretary-General and the Permanent Representatives of member states to OECD. It is responsible for all questions of general policy and may establish subsidiary bodies as required, to achieve the aims of the organization. Decisions and recommendations of the Council are adopted by mutual agreement of all its members.

HEADS OF PERMANENT DELEGATIONS

(with ambassadorial rank)

Australia: Christopher Barrett.
Austria: Wolfgang Petritsch.
Belgium: Yves Haesendonck.
Canada: Judith LaRocque.
Chile: Raúl Sáez.
Czech Republic: Karel Dyba.
Denmark: Poul Eric Dam Kristensen.
Estonia: Marten Kokk.
Finland: Antti Kuosmanen.
France: Pascale Andréani.
Germany: Johannes Westerhoff.
Greece: Konstantina (Tina) Birmpili.
Hungary: Istvan Mikola.
Iceland: Berglind Asgeirstdottir.
Ireland: Michael Forbes.
Israel: Nimrod Barkan.
Italy: Carlo Maria Oliva.
Japan: Motohide Yoshikawa.
Republic of Korea: Kyung-wook Hur.
Luxembourg: Georges Santer.
Mexico: Agustín García-López Loaeza.
Netherlands: Edmond H. Wellenstein.
New Zealand: Rosemary Banks.
Norway: Tore Eriksen.
Poland: Pawel Wojciechowski.
Portugal: (vacant).
Slovakia: Ingrid Brocková.
Slovenia: Andrej Rant.
Spain: Ricardo Díez-Hochleitner.
Sweden: Anders Ahnlid.
Switzerland: Stefan Flückiger.
Turkey: Kadri Ecvet Tezcan.
United Kingdom: Nicholas (Nick) Bridge.
USA: Karen F. Kornbluh.
European Union: Maria-Francesca Spatolisano.

EXECUTIVE COMMITTEE

The Executive Committee prepares the work of the Council. It is also called upon to carry out specific tasks where necessary. In addition to its regular meetings, the Committee meets occasionally in special sessions attended by senior government officials.

SECRETARIAT

The Council, the committees and other bodies in OECD are assisted by an independent international secretariat headed by the Secretary-General. An Executive Director is responsible for the management of administrative support services. There are OECD Centres in Berlin, Germany; Mexico City, Mexico; Tokyo, Japan; and Washington, DC, USA.

Secretary-General: José Ángel Gurría Treviño (Mexico).

Deputy Secretaries-General: Pier Carlo Padoan (Italy) (OECD Chief Economist), Rintaro Tamaki (Japan), Richard A. Boucher (USA), Yves Leterme (Belgium).

Chief of Staff and 'Sherpa to the G20': Gabriela Ramos (Mexico).

SPECIAL BODIES

African Partnership Forum.
Centre for Educational Research and Innovation (CERI).
Development Centre.
Financial Action Task Force.
Global Project 'Measuring the Progress of Societies'.
International Energy Agency.
International Transport Forum.
Nuclear Energy Agency.
Partnership for Democratic Governance Advisory Unit.
Sahel and West Africa Club.

Activities

In 2011 OECD resolved to strengthen its multilateral policy approach in order to fulfil its founding ambitions, and adopted a new directive entitled 'Better Policies for Better Lives'. In its 50th Anniversary Vision Statement, published in May, OECD also resolved to adopt a New Paradigm for Development, with greater collaboration within the organization and strengthened partnerships with non-member countries, and to work Towards a Global Policy Network.

ECONOMIC POLICY

OECD aims to promote stable macroeconomic environments in member and non-member countries. The Economics Department works to identify priority concerns for governments and to assess the economic implications of a broad range of structural issues, such as ageing, labour market policies, migration, public expenditure and financial market developments. *Economic Outlook*, analysing the major trends in short-term economic prospects and key policy issues, is published twice a year. The main organ for the consideration and direction of economic policy is the Economic Policy Committee, which comprises governments' chief economic advisers and central bankers, and meets two or three times a year.

The Economic and Development Review Committee, comprising all member countries, is responsible for surveys of the economic situation and macroeconomic and structural policies of each member country. A report, including specific policy recommendations, is issued every 12 to 18 months on each country, after an examination carried out by the Committee.

In December 2008 OECD published a *Strategic Response to the Global Financial and Economic Crisis* (developed collectively by the OECD Council, Committees and Secretariat), which aimed to address regulatory and policy failures in a comprehensive manner, and focused on strengthening and implementing principles and guidelines, and on identifying regulatory gaps in, the areas of finance, competition and governance; and monitoring developments and identifying policy options to promote the restoration of sustainable long-term growth. From early 2009 OECD co-ordinated an initiative, also comprising the ILO, the IMF, the World Bank and the World Trade Organization (WTO), to compile *A 'Global Charter'/'Legal Standard', Inventory of Possible Policy Instruments*; this audit of the existing range of economic and social policy instruments, a preliminary version of which was issued in March, was to be a single, coherent repository of policy recommendations, guidelines and principles of best practice, and was regarded as a work in progress aimed at strengthening the regulatory framework. The five organizations contributing to the *Inventory* had been invited by the G8 summit held in Hokkaido, Japan, in June 2008, to enhance their co-operation. The meeting of G20 heads of state and government held, for the first time with OECD participation, in April 2009, determined to re-launch the Financial Stability Board, which comprises senior representatives of national financial authorities, international financial institutions, international regulatory and supervisory groupings, and committees of central bank experts, and aims to stabilize and strengthen the functioning of the financial markets. The meeting issued as its final communiqué a global plan for recovery and reform, outlining commitments that included strengthening financial supervision and regulation and reforming global financial institutions, and supporting consideration of a new charter for promoting sustainable economic development. In June G8 ministers responsible for finance, meeting in Lecce, Italy, endorsed a 'Global Standard for the 21st Century' through the adoption of the Lecce Framework of Common Principles and Standards for Propriety, Integrity and Transparency; the Lecce Framework, as the Global Standard was known thereafter, was supported by OECD and was approved by G8 heads of state and government held in L'Aquila, Italy, in July. It was envisaged that OECD would continue to play a leading role in its development. In April 2011 OECD reported that global economic recovery was advancing and was reaching self-sustaining levels throughout the OECD area. Owing to the devastating earthquake and tsunami that struck Japan in mid-March, projections for economic growth in that country were excluded at that time. In November, in the context of a serious debt crisis within several euro area countries, OECD's *Economic Outlook* urged member countries to implement decisive policies, including a substantial increase in the capacity of the European Financial Stability Fund, in order to prevent sovereign defaults, credit contraction and bank failures. OECD economic surveys of the euro area and EU issued in March 2012 urged far-reaching reforms to taxation systems, education systems, and to product and labour markets, in order to rebalance euro area economies and restore economic growth and competitiveness. In May 2012 OECD launched a new Skills Strategy, which aimed to support governments in boosting employment and building economic resilience through the promotion of skills education and training.

STATISTICS

Statistical data and related methodological information are collected from member governments and, where possible, consolidated, or converted into an internationally comparable form. The Statistics Directorate maintains and makes available data required for macroeconomic forecasting, i.e. national accounts, the labour force, foreign trade, prices, output, and monetary, financial, industrial and other short-term statistics. Work is also undertaken to develop new statistics and new statistical standards and systems in areas of emerging policy interest (such as sustainable development). In addition, the Directorate shares with non-member countries member states' experience in compiling statistics. In the early 2000s a new Statistical Information System, incorporating new technical infrastructure, was developed which aimed to improve the efficiency of data collection, processing, storage etc., to improve the quality of OECD statistics, and to enhance accessibility to the data. The first World Forum on Statistics, Knowledge and Policy was held in November 2004, in Palermo, Italy. At the second Forum, held in Istanbul, Turkey, in June 2007, on the theme 'Measuring and Fostering the Progress of Societies', OECD, the European Commission, the OIC, the UN, UNDP and the World Bank issued the Istanbul Declaration, in which they made a commitment to measuring and fostering the progress of societies with a view to improving policy-making and advancing democracy and the well-being of citizens. The Declaration was subsequently opened to wider signature. A Global Project on Measuring the Progress of Societies, with OECD participation, was launched in 2008. The third World Forum on Statistics, Knowledge and Policy was convened in Busan, Republic of Korea (South Korea), in October 2009, on the theme 'Charting Progress, Building Visions, Improving Life'; the fourth Forum was to be convened in October 2012, in New Delhi, India.

In September 2010 OECD launched the iLibrary, a new platform providing comprehensive access to statistical data, working papers, books and journals.

DEVELOPMENT CO-OPERATION

The Development Assistance Committee (DAC) is the principal body through which OECD deals with issues relating to co-operation with developing countries and is one of the key forums in which the major bilateral donors work together to increase their effectiveness in support of sustainable development. The DAC is supported by the Development Co-operation Directorate, which monitors aid programmes and resource flows, compiles statistics and seeks to establish codes of practice in aid. There are also working parties on statistics, aid evaluation, gender equality and development co-operation and environment; and networks on poverty reduction, good governance and capacity development, and conflict, peace and development co-operation. The DAC holds an annual high-level meeting of ministers responsible for international aid, and heads of aid agencies from member governments, with senior officials from the World Bank, the IMF and UNDP.

The DAC's mission is to foster co-ordinated, integrated, effective and adequately financed international efforts in support of sustainable economic and social development. Recognizing that developing countries themselves are ultimately responsible for their own development, the DAC concentrates on how international co-operation can contribute to the population's ability to overcome poverty and participate fully in society. Principal activities include: adopting authoritative policy guidelines; conducting periodic critical reviews of members' programmes of development co-operation; providing a forum for dialogue, exchange of experience and the building of international consensus on policy and management issues; and publishing statistics and reports on aid and other resource flows to developing countries and countries in transition. A working set of indicators of development progress has been established by the DAC, in collaboration with experts from UN agencies (including the World Bank) and from developing countries.

In February 2003 OECD/DAC co-sponsored a High-Level Forum on Aid Effectiveness, held in Rome, Italy. The second

High-Level Forum, convened in February–March 2005, in Paris, France, endorsed the Paris Declaration on Aid Effectiveness, and agreed a number of country-based action plans, for donor and recipient countries, aimed at improving aid effectiveness. In addition, the meeting reviewed OECD's contribution to achieving the UN Millennium Development Goals, issues relating to development, peace and security, and a report on development effectiveness in the context of the New Partnership for Africa's Development (NEPAD). The Accra Agenda for Action, adopted in September 2008 by the third High-Level Forum convened in Accra, Ghana, included further country-based action plans tailored to advance progress in aid effectiveness. In November–December 2011 the fourth High-Level Forum, convened in Busan, South Korea, reviewed progress in implementing the principles of the Paris Declaration. A Busan Partnership for Effective Development Co-operation was signed to foster a framework for co-operation by developed and developing countries, emerging economies, civil society and private funders.

In 2010 official development assistance (ODA) from DAC donor countries totalled US $129,000m. The five largest ODA donors in 2010 were France, Germany, Japan, the United Kingdom and the USA.

Development Centre: f. 1962; acts as a forum for dialogue and undertakes research and policy analysis in order to assist the development of policy to stimulate economic and social growth in developing and emerging economies; membership open to both OECD and non-OECD countries.

Sahel and West Africa Club: f. 1976, initially to support countries affected by drought in the Sahel region of Africa; expanded to include other countries in West Africa in 2001; acts as an informal discussion grouping between some 17 African countries and OECD members.

African Partnership Forum: f. 2003, following a meeting of heads of state of the G8, in Evian, France; comprises representatives of G8 countries, NEPAD and major bilateral and multilateral development partners; meets twice a year; aims to strengthen efforts in support of Africa's development.

PUBLIC GOVERNANCE AND TERRITORIAL DEVELOPMENT

The Public Governance and Territorial Development Directorate is concerned with identifying changing needs in society and in markets, and with helping countries to adapt their governmental systems and territorial policies. One of the Directorate's primary functions is to provide a forum for exchanging ideas on how to meet the challenges countries face in the area of governance. It is concerned with improving public sector governance through comparative data and analysis, the setting and promotion of standards, and the facilitation of transparency and peer review, as well as to encourage the participation of civil society in public governance. The Public Management Committee (PUMA) serves as a forum for senior officials responsible for the central management systems of government, providing information, analysis and recommendations on public management and governing capacity. A Working Party of Senior Budget Officials is the principal international forum for issues concerning international budgeting. In 1992 a joint initiative of OECD and the European Union (EU), operating within OECD, was established to support good governance in the countries of Central and Eastern Europe that were to accede to, or were candidates for either accession to or association with, the EU. The so-called Support for Improvement in Governance and Management (SIGMA) programme assists in the reform and modernization of public institutions in those countries and assesses their progress in those areas. OECD undertakes Reviews of Public Sector Integrity in member and non-member states to assist policy makers to improve policies, adopt good practices and implement established principles and standards. In March 2012 OECD hosted, in Mexico City, Mexico, a high-level meeting on e-government, which reviewed new digital public sector management tools.

In October 2007 OECD, with UNDP, the Organization of American States and the Inter-American Development Bank, inaugurated the Partnership for Democratic Governance (PDG), to assist developing countries to improve governance and strengthen their accountability and effectiveness. OECD hosts an advisory unit of the initiative. The OECD Secretary-General acts as chairperson of the PDG.

The Territorial Development Policy Committee assists central governments with the design and implementation of more effective, area-based strategies, encourages the emergence of locally driven initiatives for economic development, and promotes better integration of local and national approaches. Generally, the Committee's work programme emphasizes the need for innovative policy initiatives and exchange of knowledge in a wide range of policies, such as entrepreneurship and technology diffusion and issues of social exclusion and urban deprivation. National and regional territorial reviews are undertaken to analyse economic and social trends and highlight governance issues.

TRADE AND AGRICULTURE

Through the Trade and Agriculture Directorate OECD works to support a rules-based multilateral trading system with the objective of promoting further trade liberalization; and to assess government support to the agricultural sector in OECD and principal emerging economies, while assessing the medium-term outlook for agricultural markets and advising on policies for the sustainable use of farm and fisheries resources.

The OECD Trade Committee supports the continued liberalization and efficient operation of the multilateral trading system, with the aim of contributing to the expansion of world trade on a non-discriminatory basis, and thereby advancing standards of living and sustainable development. Its activities include examination of issues concerning trade relations among member countries as well as relations with non-member countries, and consideration and discussion of trade measures taken by a member country which adversely affect another's interests. The Committee holds regular consultations with civil society organizations.

A Working Party on Export Credits and Credit Guarantees serves as a forum for the discussion and co-ordination of export credit policies. OECD maintains an Export Credit Arrangement, which provides a framework for the use of officially supported export credits, stipulating the most generous financial terms and conditions available. Governments participating in the Arrangement meet regularly. In 2000 the Working Party agreed an Action Statement on Bribery and Officially Supported Export Credits; this was strengthened and converted into an OECD Recommendation in December 2006. In June 2007 the OECD Council adopted a Revised Recommendation on Common Approaches to the Environment and Officially Supported Export Credits (updated from 2003).

The Trade Committee considers the challenges that are presented to the existing international trading system by financial or economic instability, the process of globalization of production and markets and the ensuing deeper integration of national economies. OECD is committed to the Doha Development Agenda, the framework for the multilateral trade negotiations currently being pursued by the WTO. OECD and the WTO have established a joint database that provides information about trade-related technical assistance and capacity building in respect of trade policy and regulation; trade development; and infrastructure. In accordance with the Doha Agenda OECD is undertaking analysis of the implications on business of the growing number of regional trade agreements and the relationship between those agreements and the multilateral system. OECD hosts an annual Global Forum on Trade. The 2011 event was convened in November, in Paris, to highlight the initial work of an International Collaborative Initiative on Trade and Employment.

OECD undertakes analysis of relevant issues and advises governments, in particular in relation to policy reform, trade liberalization and sustainable agriculture and fisheries. OECD is also a focal point for global efforts in the certification and standardization of products, packaging and testing procedures, though its agricultural codes and schemes. A Committee for Agriculture reviews major developments in agricultural policies, deals with the adaptation of agriculture to changing economic conditions, elaborates forecasts of production and market prospects for the major commodities, identifies best practices for limiting the impact of agricultural production on the environment, promotes the use of sustainable practices in the sector and considers questions of agricultural development in emerging and transition economies. A separate Fisheries Committee carries out similar tasks in its sector, and, in particular, analyses the consequences of policy measures with a view to promoting responsible and sustainable fisheries. The Directorate administers a Biological Resources in Agriculture programme, which sponsors research fellowships as well as workshops and conferences, to enhance international co-operation in priority areas of agro-food research.

In February 2010 ministers of agriculture from OECD states met, for the first time since 1998, to discuss global food security in relation to issues such as population growth, food demand in affluent industrialized societies, pressure on land and water, and climate change; agriculture ministers from non-member countries with significant agricultural sectors or food markets also participated in the meeting. In January 2011 the OECD Secretary-General stated that volatility in food and commodity prices was undermining efforts to address global poverty and hunger, and was threatening economic growth, and urged governments to co-operate in mitigating extreme swings in market prices. The *OECD-FAO Agricultural Outlook 2011–20*, published in June 2011, found that while a good harvest in the near future might lead to a reduction in commodity prices compared with extremely high levels reached earlier in 2011, nevertheless cereal prices might average up to 20% higher and meat prices up to 30% higher during 2011–20, compared with 2001–10 price levels. It was noted that higher commodity prices were leading to rising consumer price inflation in many countries, raising concern for food security and economic stability in some developing countries. Boosting investment in agriculture and reinforcing rural development in developing countries were urged.

ENTREPRENEURSHIP AND LOCAL DEVELOPMENT

In June 2000 OECD convened a Ministerial Conference on Small and Medium-sized Enterprises (SMEs), in Bologna, Italy, and initiated a process to promote SMEs and entrepreneurship policies. Within the context of the so-called Bologna Process, an OECD Global Conference on SME and Entrepreneurship Funding was held in March 2006, in Brasilia, Brazil. In July 2004 OECD established a Centre for Entrepreneurship, SMEs and Local Development, responsible for promoting OECD work on entrepreneurship and for bringing together experts in the field. In addition, it disseminates best practices on the design, implementation and evaluation of initiatives to promote entrepreneurship, SMEs and local economic and employment development. The Centre administers OECD's Local Economic and Employment Development (LEED) programme, which aims to promote the creation of employment through innovative strategies and recommendations to local governments and communities.

A Tourism Committee promotes sustainable growth in the tourism sector and encourages the integration of tourism issues into other policy areas. A Global Forum on Tourism Statistics is convened every two years.

FINANCIAL AND ENTERPRISE AFFAIRS

Promoting the efficient functioning of markets and enterprises and strengthening the multilateral framework for trade and investment is the responsibility of the main OECD committees and working groups supported by the Directorate for Financial and Enterprise Affairs. The Directorate analyses emerging trends, provides policy guidelines and recommendations, gives examples of best practice and maintains benchmarks to measure progress.

The Committee on Capital Movements and Invisible Transactions monitors the implementation of the Codes of Liberalization of Invisible Transactions and of Current Invisible Operations as legally binding norms for all member countries. The Committee on International Investment and Multinational Enterprises monitors the OECD Guidelines for Multinational Enterprises, a corporate Code of Conduct recommended by OECD member governments, business and labour units. A Declaration on International Investment and Multinational Enterprises, while non-binding, contains commitments on the conduct and treatment of foreign-owned enterprises established in member countries. It is subject to periodic reviews, the most recent of which was concluded in May 2011. By the end of that year 43 countries had subscribed to the Declaration. Negotiations on a Multilateral Agreement on Investment (MAI), initiated by OECD ministers in 1995 to provide a legal framework for international investment, broke down in October 1998, although 'informal consultation' on the issue was subsequently pursued. In June 2008 the OECD Council, meeting at ministerial level, adopted a declaration on sovereign wealth funds (SWFs) and policies for recipient countries, to ensure a fair and transparent investment environment. The declaration was also endorsed by the governments of Chile, Estonia and Slovenia. The development of a non-binding 'Model Investment Treaty', to facilitate negotiations and foster more consistency in investment procedures, is under consideration by OECD.

The Committee on Competition Law and Policy promotes the harmonization of national competition policies, co-operation in competition law enforcement, common merger reporting rules and pro-competitive regulatory reform, the development of competition laws and institutions, and efforts to change policies that restrain competition. The Committee on Financial Markets exercises surveillance over recent developments, reform measures and structural and regulatory conditions in financial markets. It aims to promote international trade in financial services, to encourage the integration of non-member countries into the global financial system, and to improve financial statistics. The Insurance Committee monitors structural changes and reform measures in insurance markets, for example the liberalization of insurance markets, financial insolvency, co-operation on insurance and reinsurance policy, the monitoring and analysis of regulatory and structural developments, and private pensions and health insurance. A working party on private pensions meets twice a year. In 2002 OECD member governments approved guidelines for the administration of private pension funds, the first initiative they had taken to set international standards for the governance and supervision of collective pension funds. Specialized work on public debt is undertaken by the Working Party on Government Debt Management. An OECD Global Forum on Public Debt Management and Emerging Government Securities Markets is convened each year.

In May 1997 the OECD Council endorsed plans to introduce a global ban on the corporate bribery of public officials. The OECD Convention on Bribery of Foreign Public Officials in International Business Transactions entered into force in February 1999 and, by June 2012, had been ratified by all OECD member states and five non-member countries (Argentina, Brazil, Bulgaria, Russia and South Africa). All signatory states were required to undergo a 'phase I' review of legislation conformity with anti-bribery standards and help to compile a 'phase II' country report assessing the structures in place to enforce these laws and their effectiveness. In May 2009 the OECD Council adopted a Recommendation on the Non-Tax Deductibility of Bribes and in December adopted a Recommendation for Further Combating Bribery of Foreign Public Officials in order to strengthen the existing legal framework for combating bribery and corruption. All signatory states were required to implement the new measures. In 2010, OECD member states, and key partner countries, adopted a Declaration on Propriety, Integrity and Transparency in the Conduct of International Business and Finance.

In March 2011 it was announced that OECD was developing a new initiative, entitled 'clean.gov.biz', to improve the co-ordination of anti-corruption and transparency initiatives, firstly within member countries, and then, in an expanded version, to incorporate all other relevant players, including governments, international organizations, and the private sector.

In May 1999 ministers endorsed a set of OECD Principles for Corporate Governance, covering ownership and control of corporate entities, the rights of shareholders, the role of stakeholders, transparency, disclosure and the responsibilities of boards. In 2000 these became one of the 12 core standards of global financial stability, and they are used as a benchmark by other international financial institutions. A revised set of Principles was published in 2004. OECD collaborates with the World Bank and other organizations to promote good governance world-wide, for example through regional round tables and the Global Corporate Governance Forum. OECD provides the secretariat for the Financial Action Task Force on Money

Laundering (FATF), which develops and promotes policies to combat money-laundering. In February 2011 the G20 ministers of finance and central bank governors tasked OECD and the Financial Stability Board with developing a new set of principles on consumer protection in financial services. The resulting draft guidelines were agreed at a meeting of G20 ministers in October, and were to be incorporated into a broader regulatory framework.

TAXATION

OECD promotes internationally accepted standards and practices of taxation, and provides a forum for the exchange of information and experience of tax policy and administration. The Committee on Fiscal Affairs is concerned with promoting the removal of tax barriers, monitoring the implementation and impact of major tax reforms, developing a neutral tax framework for electronic commerce, and studying the tax implications of the globalization of national economies. A Centre for Tax Policy and Administration supports the work of the Committee. Other activities include the publication of comparable statistics on taxation and guidelines on transfer pricing, and the study of tax evasion and tax and electronic commerce. OECD is a sponsor, with the IMF and the World Bank, of an International Tax Dialogue. OECD administers a network of Multilateral Tax Centres that provide workshops and a venue for exchanges between national officials and OECD experts.

Since 1998 OECD has promoted co-ordinated action for the elimination of so-called 'harmful' tax practices, designed to reduce the incidence of international money-laundering, and the level of potential tax revenue lost by OECD members. In mid-2000 OECD launched an initiative to abolish 'harmful tax systems', identifying a number of offshore jurisdictions as tax havens lacking financial transparency, and inviting these to co-operate by amending national financial legislation. Several of the countries and territories named agreed to follow a timetable for reform, with the aim of eliminating such practices by the end of 2005. Others, however, were reluctant to participate. (The USA also strongly opposed the initiative.) In April 2002 OECD announced that co-ordinated defensive measures would be implemented against non-complying jurisdictions ('un-co-operative tax havens') from early 2003. OECD has also highlighted examples of preferential tax regimes in member countries. In May 2009 the Committee removed the remaining three jurisdictions, Andorra, Liechtenstein and Monaco, from the list of un-co-operative tax havens, following commitments made by those authorities to implement recommended standards of transparency and effective exchange of information.

OECD convenes a Global Forum on Transparency and Exchange of Information for Tax Purposes to promote co-operation and dialogue with non-member countries. In September 2009 the Global Forum determined to implement a strengthened global monitoring and peer review process to ensure full implementation by members of their commitments. The Forum agreed to expand its membership, emphasizing that all members shared an equal footing; agreed to accelerate negotiations processes; and decided to establish a co-ordinated technical assistance programme aimed at supporting smaller jurisdictions rapidly to implement standards. In March 2010 the Global Forum initiated a peer review process for its member jurisdictions (which numbered 109 in June 2012). In October 2011 the Forum agreed guidelines on the co-ordination of technical assistance and adopted a progress report on international compliance with standards of exchange of tax information. Reviews of 59 tax jurisidictions were presented to the G20 meeting of heads of state in November. At the meeting G20 countries signed together a Protocol amending the Convention on Mutual Administrative Assistance in Tax Matters (first developed by OECD and the Council of Europe in 1988), which aimed to promote exchange of information on tax examinations, evasion and collection between member and non-member states. By June 2012 the Protocol had been ratified by 15 states. In April 2012 the Global Forum announced the completion of peer reviews of a further 11 jurisdictions. Also at that time the Forum released three supplementary reports, for Barbados, Bermuda and Qatar. which assessed their compliance with previous Forum recommendations. A further nine reviews (bringing to 79 the number of reviews completed since March 2010), and a further three supplementary reports (on Antigua and Barbuda, Estonia, and the Seychelles) were completed in June 2012. At that time 17 more reviews were under way. From the second half of 2012 the Forum's focus was to move towards exchange of information in practice and advancing co-operation between 'competent authorities'. In January 2010 the Global Forum established an Informal Task Force on Tax and Development, comprising business and civil society interests, and NGOs, from OECD and developing countries. In May 2012 the Informal Task Force launched a 'Tax Inspectors Without Borders' initiative, which aimed to support developing countries in strengthening their tax systems.

ENVIRONMENT

The OECD Environment Directorate works in support of the Environment Policy Committee (EPOC) on environmental issues. EPOC assesses performance; encourages co-operation on environmental policy; promotes the integration of environmental and economic policies; works to develop principles, guidelines and strategies for effective environmental management; provides a forum for member states to address common problems and share data and experience; and promotes the sharing of information with non-member states. The Directorate conducts peer reviews of environmental conditions and progress. A first cycle of 32 Environmental Performance Reviews of member and selected non-member countries was completed in 2000, and a second cycle was undertaken during 2001–09. A third cycle, initiated in 2009, was ongoing in 2012. The Directorate aims to improve understanding of past and future trends through the collection and dissemination of environmental data.

OECD programmes and working parties on the environment consider a range of issues, including the harmonization of biotechnology regulation, the environmental impact of production and consumption, natural resource management, trade and investment and the environment, and chemical safety. In some cases working parties collaborate with other Directorates (for example, the working parties on Trade and Environment and on Agriculture and Environment). An Experts Group on Climate Change, based in the Environment Directorate, undertakes studies related to international agreements on climate change.

In May 2001 OECD ministers of the environment, convened in Paris, France, adopted the OECD Environmental Strategy for the 21st Century, containing recommendations for future work, with a focus on fostering sustainable development, and strengthening co-operation with non-member countries and partnerships with the private sector and civil society. The strategy identified several issues requiring urgent action, such as the generation of municipal waste, increased car and air travel, greenhouse gas emissions, groundwater pollution, and the exploitation of marine fisheries. The meeting endorsed guidelines for the provision of environmentally sustainable transport, as well as the use of a set of key environmental indicators. A review of the key indicators was presented to a meeting of environment ministers, convened in April 2004. The *Global Environment Outlook to 2030*, issued in March 2008, indicated that wide-ranging climate change might be achieved without negatively impacting economic growth, if efficient policy instruments were employed. In June 2009 OECD member countries, candidate countries, and key partner countries issued a declaration on 'Green Growth', urging the adoption of targeted policy instruments to promote green investment, and emphasizing their commitment to the realization of an ambitious and comprehensive post-2012 global climate agreement. In March 2012 OECD published *Global Environment Outlook to 2050: Consequences of Inaction*. OECD ministers of the environment meeting in that month considered the following main concerns identified by the report: energy demands, air pollution, natural resources and biodiversity, and global water demand. The meeting was convened on the theme 'Making Green Growth Deliver', which aimed to secure sustainable socio-economic development, in accordance with OECD's Green Growth Strategy, launched in May 2011. In January 2012 OECD, jointly with UNEP, the World Bank and the Global Green Growth Institute, established a Green Growth Knowledge Platform to compile and disseminate research and policy experience concerning green growth.

OECD organized events on 'Tailoring Green Growth Strategies to Country Circumstances' and 'Green Growth and Developing Countries' on the sidelines of the UN Conference on Sustainable Development (Rio+20), convened in Rio de Janeiro, Brazil, in June 2012.

SCIENCE, TECHNOLOGY AND INDUSTRY

The Directorate for Science, Technology and Industry aims to assist member countries in formulating, adapting and implementing policies that optimize the contribution of science, technology, industrial development and structural change to economic growth, employment and social development. It provides indicators and analysis on emerging trends in these fields, identifies and promotes best practices, and offers a forum for dialogue. In February 2008 OECD, as part of its then International Futures Programme (which was merged into the Directorate in April 2011) inaugurated a Global Forum on Space Economics to provide a focus for international debate and co-operation on economic issues affecting the development of space infrastructure and other space-related activities.

Areas considered by the Committee for Scientific and Technological Policy include the management of public research, technology and innovation, and intellectual property rights. A Working Party on Biotechnology was established in 1993 to pursue study of biotechnology and its applications, including issues such as scientific and technological infrastructure, and the relation of biotechnology to sustainable industrial development. Statistical work on biotechnology is undertaken by a Working Party of National Experts on Science and Technology Indicators. In 1992 a megascience forum was established to bring together senior science policy officials to identify and pursue opportunities for international co-operation in scientific research. It was succeeded, in 1999, by the Global Science Forum which meets two times a year. A Global Biodiversity Information Facility (GBIF) began operations in 2001 to connect global biodiversity databases in order to make available a wide range of data online. In September 2011 OECD hosted a Global Forum on the Knowledge Economy, which focused on improving national science and innovation policies, and science and innovation for inclusive development.

The Committee for Information, Computer and Communications Policy monitors developments in telecommunications and information technology and their impact on competitiveness and productivity, with an emphasis on technological and regulatory convergence. It also promotes the development of new guidelines and analyses trade and liberalization issues. The Committee maintains a database of communications indicators and telecommunications tariffs. A Working Party on Information Security and Privacy promotes a co-ordinated approach to efforts to enhance trust in the use of electronic commerce. In August 2004 an OECD Task Force was established to co-ordinate efforts to counter unsolicited e-mail ('spam'). OECD supports the Digital Opportunities Task Force (Dot.force) which was established in June 2000 by the G8 to recommend action with a view to eliminating the so-called 'digital divide' between developed and less developed countries and between different population sectors within nations. OECD's Global Conference on Telecommunications Policy for the Digital Environment, held in January 2002, emphasized the importance of competition in the sector and the need for regulatory reform. A ministerial meeting on the Future of the Internet Economy was held in Seoul, South Korea, in June 2008. A follow-up High-Level Meeting on the Internet Economy: Generating Innovation and Growth, was convened in June 2011, in Paris.

The Committee on Industry and the Business Environment focuses on industrial production, business performance, innovation and competitiveness in industrial and services sectors, and policies for private sector development in member and selected non-member economies. In recent years the Committee has addressed issues connected with globalization, regulatory reform, SMEs, and the role of industry in sustainable development. Business and industry policy fora explore a variety of issues with the private sector, for example new technologies or environmental strategies for industry, and develop recommendations. The Working Party on SMEs and Entrepreneurship conducts an ongoing review of the contribution of SMEs to growth and employment and carries out a comparative assessment of best practice policies. (See also the Bologna Process.)

The Transport Division of the Directorate for Science, Technology and Industry considers aviation, maritime, shipbuilding, road and intermodal transport issues. Maritime Transport and Steel Committees aim to promote multilateral solutions to sectoral friction and instability based on the definition and monitoring of rules. The Working Party on Shipbuilding seeks to establish normal competitive conditions in that sector, especially through dialogue with non-OECD countries. In January 2004 a new Transport Research Centre was established by merger of OECD's road transport and intermodal linkages research programme and the economic research activities of the European Conference of Ministers of Transport. A new report, entitled *Strategic Transport Infrastructure Needs to 2030* was published in March 2012.

International Transport Forum (ITF): in May 2006 the European Conference of Ministers of Transport agreed to establish and become integrated into a new International Transport Forum; the inaugural meeting of the Forum was held in May 2008, in Leipzig, Poland.

EMPLOYMENT, LABOUR AND SOCIAL AFFAIRS

The Employment, Labour and Social Affairs Committee is concerned with the development of the labour market and selective employment policies to ensure the utilization of human capital at the highest possible level and to improve the quality and flexibility of working life, as well as the effectiveness of social policies; it plays a central role in addressing OECD's concern to reduce high and persistent unemployment through the creation of high-quality jobs. The Committee's work covers such issues as the role of women in the economy, industrial relations, measurements of unemployment, and the development of an extensive social database. The Committee also carries out single-country and thematic reviews of labour market policies and social assistance systems. It has assigned a high priority to work on the policy implications of an ageing population and on indicators of human capital investment. In May 2011 OECD and the ILO signed an MOU on strengthening mutual co-operation. Both organizations provided analysis and support to the G20 meeting of ministers of labour and employment, held in September 2011, in Cannes, France. The heads of both organizations expressed concern that world unemployment was almost 200m. and urged G20 members to prioritize employment and social protection in the policy debate.

OECD undertakes analysis of health care and health expenditure issues, and reviews the organization and performance of health systems. In May 2004 OECD ministers responsible for health reviewed a three-year project to evaluate and analyse the performance of health care systems in member countries. Upon their recommendation a new Group on Health was established in January 2005 to direct a further programme of work, to be supported by a new Health Division within the Directorate of Employment, Labour and Social Affairs. Social policy areas of concern include benefits and wages, family-friendly policies, and the social effects of population ageing. In 2011 OECD launched a Better Life Index to enhance understanding of the impact of policy options on quality of life.

A Non-Member Economies and International Migration Division works on social policy issues in emerging economies and economies in transition, especially relating to education and labour market reforms and to the economic and social aspects of migration. The Directorate undertakes regular analysis of trends in international migration, including consideration of its economic and social impact, the integration of immigrants, and international co-operation in the control of migrant flows.

In January 2011 OECD issued a study entitled *Housing and the Economy: Policies for Renovation*, which offered governments a roadmap for developing sounder housing policy through the promotion of reforms in areas such as financial sector regulation, taxation, the regulation of rental markets, and the provision of social housing. The study also found that national policies favouring home ownership over renting had reduced residential and labour mobility, which in turn undermined recovery in employment levels.

EDUCATION

The Directorate for Education was created in 2002 in order to raise the profile of OECD's work, which is conducted in the context of its view of education as a lifelong activity. The

Directorate comprises Divisions on Education and Training, Indicators and Analysis, Education Management, and Infrastructure. Programmes undertaken by the Directorate include a Programme for Co-operation with non-member Economies, the Programme of International Student Assessments (PISA), the Programme on Institutional Management in Higher Education and the Programme on Education Building, as well as regular peer reviews of education systems. A Programme for the International Assessment of Adult Competencies (PIAAC) was launched in 2011 to measure skills and comptencies of individuals to contribute to society. The results were expected to be published in 2013. In February 2012 OECD published a report which encouraged governments to increase investment in disadvantaged schools in order to reduce school failure, increase economic growth and help to contribute to a fairer society.

Centre for Educational Research and Innovation (CERI): f. 1968; an independently funded programme within the Directorate for Education; promotes the development of research activities in education, together with experiments of an advanced nature, designed to test innovations in educational systems and to stimulate research and development.

CO-OPERATION WITH NON-MEMBER ECONOMIES

The Centre for Co-operation with Non-Members (CCNM) was established in January 1998, by merger of the Centre for Co-operation with Economies in Transition (founded in 1990) and the Liaison and Co-ordination Unit. It serves as the focal point for the development of policy dialogue with non-member economies, managing multi-country, thematic, regional and country programmes. These include a Baltic Regional Programme, Programmes for Russia and for Brazil, an Emerging Asian Economies Programme and the OECD Programme of Dialogue and Co-operation with China. The Centre also manages OECD's various Global Forums, which discuss a wide range of specific issues that defy resolution in a single country or region, for example international investment, sustainable development, biotechnology, and trade. The Centre co-ordinates and maintains OECD's relations with other international organizations. An integral part of the CCNM is the joint venture with the EU, the Support for Improvement in Governance and Management (SIGMA) programme, which is directed towards the transition economies of Central and Eastern Europe.

Non-member economies are invited by the CCNM, on a selective basis, to participate in or observe the work of certain OECD committees and working parties. The Centre also provides a limited range of training activities in support of policy implementation and institution building. In 1994 the OECD Centre for Private Sector Development, based in Istanbul, Turkey, commenced operations as a joint project between the OECD and the Turkish Government to provide policy advice and training to administrators from transitional economies in Eastern Europe, Central Asia and Transcaucasus. Subsequently, the Centre has evolved into a regional forum for policy dialogue and co-operation with regard to issues of interest to transitional economies. The CCNM is also a sponsor of the Joint Vienna Institute, which offers a variety of administrative, economic and financial management courses to participants from transition economies. In May 2007 OECD invited Chile, Estonia, Israel, Russia and Slovenia to initiate discussions with a view to future membership of the organization. So-called 'roadmaps' for negotiations were agreed with those five 'accession countries' in December. Chile, Slovenia, Israel and Estonia formally acceded to the Organization in May, July, September and December 2010, respectively.

In 2007 OECD launched an Enhanced Engagement Initiative. Participating ('key partner') countries—Brazil, China, India, Indonesia and South Africa—are encouraged to participate directly in the work of the Organisation and are important partners in dialogue. The 50th Anniversary Vision Statement adopted in May 2011 by the Ministerial Council placed priority on developing new forms of partnership with each of the key partner countries.

In November 2006 OECD's Trade Union Advisory Committee (TUAC) ratified an agreement with the International Trade Union Confederation and the so-called Global Unions (global trade union federations) to form a Council of Global Unions, with the aims of promoting trade union membership and advancing common trade union interests world-wide.

OECD administered a support unit to the Heiligendamm L'Aquila Process, which was launched, with a two-year mandate, in July 2009, to follow on from the Heiligendamm Process (inaugurated in June 2007 with the aim of strengthening relations between the G8 and principal emerging economies). The Heiligendamm L'Aquila Process aimed to broaden the thematic framework addressed by the Heiligendamm Process: cross-border investment; innovation and intellectual property; energy and climate change; and development, in particular in Africa.

Finance

OECD's total budget for 2011 amounted to €342m.

Publications

OECD Annual Report.

African Economic Outlook (annually).

Agricultural Policies in Emerging Economies (annually).

Agricultural Policies in OECD Countries.

Development Co-operation Report (annually).

Economic Policy Reforms (annually).

Education at a Glance (annually).

Energy Balances of Non-OECD Countries (annually).

Energy Balances of OECD Countries (annually).

Geographical Distribution of Financial Flows to Developing countries (annually).

Going for Growth (annually).

Health at a Glance.

Information Technology Outlook (every two years).

International Migration Outlook (annually).

Labour Force Statistics.

Latin American Economic Outlook (annually).

Measuring Globalisation.

Measuring Innovation.

National Accounts at a Glance.

OECD Economic Surveys (every 12 to 18 months for each country).

OECD Employment Outlook (annually).

OECD Environmental Outlook to 2030.

OECD Factbook (annually).

OECD Information Technology Outlook.

OECD Observer (every 2 months).

OECD Transfer Pricing Guidelines for Multinational Enterprises and Tax Administrations.

OECD Yearbook.

Pensions at a Glance.

Perspectives on Global Development (annually).

Regions at a Glance.

Southeast Asian Economic Outlook (annually).

Society at a Glance.

Tax Co-operation.

Numerous specialized reports, working papers, books and statistics on economic and social subjects are also published.

International Energy Agency—IEA

Address: 9 rue de la Fédération, 75739 Paris Cedex 15, France.

Telephone: 1-40-57-65-00; **fax:** 1-40-57-65-09; **e-mail:** info@iea.org; **internet:** www.iea.org.

The Agency was established by the OECD Council Decision Establishing an International Energy Agency to develop co-operation on energy questions among participating countries.

MEMBERS

Australia	Hungary	Portugal
Austria	Ireland	Slovakia
Belgium	Italy	Spain
Canada	Japan	Sweden
Czech Republic	Republic of Korea	Switzerland
Denmark	Luxembourg	Turkey
Finland	Netherlands	United Kingdom
France	New Zealand	USA
Germany	Norway*	
Greece	Poland	

* Norway participates in the IEA under a special Agreement.

In October 2010 the Governing Board determined that negotiations should commence on the future admission of Chile to the IEA. The European Commission also takes part in the IEA's work as an observer.

Organization

(June 2012)

GOVERNING BOARD

Composed of ministers or senior officials of the member governments. Meetings are held every two years at ministerial level and five times a year at senior official level. Decisions may be taken by a special weighted majority on a number of specified subjects, particularly concerning emergency measures and emergency reserve commitments; a simple weighted majority is required for procedural decisions and decisions implementing specific obligations in the agreement. Unanimity is required only if new obligations, not already specified in the agreement, are to be undertaken.

SECRETARIAT

The Secretariat comprises the following Directorates: Energy Markets and Security (with three divisions: Oil Industry and Markets; Emergency Policy; and Energy Diversification); Global Energy Dialogue (four divisions: an office on co-operation with dialogue countries in the Asia-Pacific region, Latin America, and sub-Saharan Africa; an office on co-operation with dialogue countries in Europe, the Middle East and North Africa; Country Studies; and Energy Technology Collaboration); Sustainable Energy Policy and Technology (two divisions: Energy Efficiency and Environment; and Energy Technology Policy); and Employment at the IEA. There are also the following Standing Groups and Committees: Standing Group on Long-Term Co-operation; Standing Group on the Oil Market; Standing Group on Emergency Questions; Committee on Energy Research and Technology (with working parties); and the Standing Group on Global Energy Dialogue.

Executive Director: Maria van der Hoeven (Netherlands).

Activities

The Agreement on an International Energy Programme was signed in November 1974 and formally entered into force in January 1976. The Agreement commits the participating countries of the IEA to share petroleum in certain emergencies, to strengthen co-operation in order to reduce dependence on petroleum imports, to increase the availability of information on the petroleum market, to co-operate in the development and co-ordination of energy policies, and to develop relations with the petroleum-producing and other petroleum-consuming countries. In mid-2011 IEA countries possessed total reserves of petroleum totalling more than 4,100m. barrels, of which 1,600m. barrels were in public stocks kept exclusively for emergency purposes.

The IEA collects, processes and disseminates statistical data and information on all aspects of the energy sector, including production, trade, consumption, prices and greenhouse gas emissions. The IEA promotes co-operation among policy-makers and energy experts to discuss common energy issues, to enhance energy technology and research and development, in particular projects concerned with energy efficiency, conservation and protection of the environment, and to engage major energy producing and consuming non-member countries.

The IEA has developed a system of emergency measures to be used in the event of a reduction in petroleum supplies. Under the International Energy Programme, member states are required to stock crude oil equivalent to 90 days of the previous year's net imports. These measures, which also include demand restraint, were to take effect in disruptions exceeding 7% of the IEA or individual country average daily rate of consumption. A more flexible system of response to oil supply disruption has also been developed under the Co-ordinated Energy Response Measures in 1984. By mid-2012 IEA member states had collectively made available to the market additional supplies of petroleum three times. Firstly in the lead-up to the 1991 Gulf War. Secondly in September 2005, in response to concerns at interruptions to the supply of petroleum from the Gulf of Mexico, following extensive hurricane damage to oil rigs, pipeline and refineries (that action was terminated in December). In June 2011 IEA member states agreed for the third time collectively to release emergency oil stocks (60m. barrels over an initial period of 30 days), in response to ongoing disruption of oil supplies from Libya; it was feared that continuing pressure on petroleum markets at that time might undermine the fragile global economic recovery. Meeting in Camp David, Maryland, USA, in May 2012, the leaders of the G8 industrialized nations indicated their readiness to request the IEA to stand by to release emergency oil stocks should international sanctions on Iran (imposed in reaction to international concern at that country's nuclear programme) result in disruption to the global supply.

The IEA undertakes emergency response reviews and workshops, and publishes an Emergency Management Manual to facilitate a co-ordinated response to a severe disruption in petroleum supplies. The Oil Markets and Emergency Preparedness Office monitors and reports on short-term developments in the petroleum market. It also considers other related issues, including international crude petroleum pricing, petroleum trade and stock developments and investments by major petroleum-producing countries.

Through its Energy Technology Office the IEA promotes international collaboration in this field and the participation of energy industries to facilitate the application of new technologies, through effective transfer of knowledge, technology innovation and training. Member states have initiated over 40 Multilateral Technology Initiatives (also referred to as Implementing Agreements), which provide a framework for international collaboration and information exchange in specific areas, including renewable energy, fossil fuels, end-use technologies and fusion power. OECD member states, non-member states, the energy producers and suppliers are encouraged to participate in these Agreements. The Committee on Energy Research and Technology, which supports international collaboration, is serviced by four expert bodies: Working Parties on Fossil Fuels, Renewable Energy Technologies and Energy End-Use Technologies and a Fusion Power Co-ordinating Committee. In May 2011 the IEA issued two roadmaps on solar electricity: the Solar Photovoltaic Roadmap and the Concentrating Solar Power Roadmap; the Agency predicted at that time that by 2050 solar energy could represent up to 25% of global electricity production. In April 2011 the IEA produced its first *Clean Energy Progress Report*, providing an overview of key policy developments in the field of clean energy technologies. Later in April the IEA issued a roadmap on *Biofuels for Transport*, assessing that by 2050 biofuels could provide up to 27% of world transportation fuel. In October 2011 OECD and the IEA released a joint statement in support of reform of fossil fuel subsidies, in order to promote investment in renewable energy and encourage greater energy efficiency.

The IEA Long-Term Co-operation Programme is designed to strengthen the security of energy supplies and promote stability in world energy markets. It provides for co-operative efforts to conserve energy, to accelerate the development of alternative energy sources by means of both specific and general measures, to strengthen research and development of new energy technologies and to remove legislative and administrative obstacles to increased energy supplies. Regular reviews of member countries' efforts in the fields of energy conservation and accelerated development of alternative energy sources assess the effectiveness of national programmes in relation to the objectives of the Agency.

The IEA actively promotes co-operation and dialogue with non-members and international organizations in order to promote global energy security, environmental protection and economic development. The IEA holds bilateral and regional technical meetings and conducts surveys and reviews of the energy situation in non-member countries. Co-operation agreements with key energy-consuming countries, including India and China, are a priority. The Agency also has co-operation agreements with Russia and the Ukraine and works closely with the petroleum-producing countries of the Middle East. In the latter states the IEA has provided technical assistance for the development of national energy legislation, regulatory reform and energy efficiency projects. The IEA is represented on the Executive Committee of the International Energy Forum (formerly the Oil Producer-Consumer Dialogue) to promote greater co-operation and understanding between petroleum producing and consuming countries. It is also active in the Joint Oil Data Initiative (JODI), a collaborative initiative of seven international organizations to improve oil data transparency.

Recognizing that ongoing energy trends are not sustainable and that an improved balance should be sought between energy security, economic development, and protection of the environment, the IEA supports analysis of actions to mitigate climate change; studies of the implications of the Kyoto Protocol to the UN Framework Convention on Climate Change (UNFCCC), and the development of new international commitments on climate change alleviation following the end of the Kyoto Protocol's first commitment period in 2012; and analysis of policies designed to reduce greenhouse gas emissions, including emissions trading. It is a partner in the Global Bioenergy Partnership and is active in the Renewable Energy and Efficiency Partnership (REEEP). Since 2001 the IEA has organized, with the International Emissions Trading Association and the Electric Power Research Institute, an annual workshop of greenhouse gas emissions trading. The Agency also analyses the regulation and reform of energy markets, especially for electricity and gas. The IEA Regulatory Forum held in February 2002 considered the implications for security of supply and public service of competition in energy markets. In July 2005 heads of state of the Group of Eight industrialized nations (G8) approved a plan of action mandating a clean, competitive and sustainable energy future. The IEA was requested to make recommendations towards achieving the plan of action and has submitted reports to each subsequent annual summit meeting. In July 2008 the G8 heads of state, convened in Hokkaido, Japan, endorsed an IEA initiative to develop roadmaps for new energy technologies, in particular carbon capture and storage projects. The IEA participated in the 2009 G8 summit, held in L'Aquila, Italy, in July. In December 2009 the IEA presented to the UN Climate Change Conference (the 15th conference of parties of the UNFCCC), held in Copenhagen, Denmark, a blueprint for delivering in future on ambitious climate change goals; the Agency also urged participating governments to promote new investment in clean energy. At the 2010 Climate Change Conference, held in December, in Cancún, Mexico, the IEA urged the increased adoption worldwide of clean energy solutions.

In March 2009 the IEA inaugurated a new Energy Business Council, which was mandated to meet twice a year to assess the impact of the global financial crisis on energy markets, and to address climate change and other energy issues.

Publications

CO^2 Emissions from Fuel Combustion (annually).

Coal Information (annually).

Electricity Information (annually).

Energy Balances and Energy Statistics of OECD and non-OECD Countries (annually).

Energy Policies of IEA Countries (annually).

Key World Energy Statistics.

Natural Gas Information (annually).

Natural Gas Market Review (annually).

Oil Information (annually).

Oil Market Report (monthly).

Renewables Information (annually).

World Energy Outlook (annually).

Other reports, studies, statistics, country reviews.

OECD Nuclear Energy Agency—NEA

Address: Le Seine Saint-Germain, 12 blvd des Îles, 92130 Issy-les-Moulineaux, France.

Telephone: 1-45-24-82-00; **fax:** 1-45-24-11-10; **e-mail:** nea@oecd-nea.org; **internet:** www.oecd-nea.org.

The NEA was established in 1958 to further the peaceful uses of nuclear energy. Originally a European agency, it has since admitted OECD members outside Europe.

MEMBERS

The NEA has 30 member states. Russia's accession to the NEA from 1 January 2013, as its 31st member, was formally approved in May 2012.

Organization

(June 2012)

STEERING COMMITTEE FOR NUCLEAR ENERGY

Meets twice a year. Comprises senior representatives of member governments, presided over by a chairman. Reports directly to the OECD Council.

SECRETARIAT

Director-General: Luis Enrique Echávarri (Spain).

MAIN COMMITTEES

Committee on Nuclear Regulatory Activities.

Committee on Radiation Protection.

Committee on the Safety of Nuclear Installations.

Committee for Technical and Economic Studies on Nuclear Development and the Fuel Cycle (Nuclear Development Committee).

Nuclear Law Committee.

Nuclear Science Committee.

Radioactive Waste Management Committee.

NEA DATA BANK

The Data Bank was established in 1978, as a successor to the Computer Programme Library and the Neutron Data Compilation Centre. The Data Bank develops and supplies data and computer programmes for nuclear technology applications to users in laboratories, industry, universities and other areas of interest. Under the supervision of the Nuclear Science Committee, the Data Bank collates integral experimental data, and functions as part of a network of data centres to provide direct data services. It was responsible for co-ordinating the development of the Joint Evaluation Fission and Fusion (JEFF) data reference library, and works with the Radioactive Waste Management Division of the NEA on the Thermonuclear Database project (see below).

Activities

The NEA's mission is to assist its member countries in maintaining and further developing, through international co-operation, the scientific, technological and legal bases required for the safe, environmentally friendly and economical use of nuclear energy for peaceful purposes. It maintains a continual survey with the co-operation of other organizations, notably the International Atomic Energy Agency (IAEA), of world uranium resources, production and demand, and of economic and technical aspects of the nuclear fuel cycle.

A major part of the Agency's work is devoted to the safety and regulation of nuclear power, including co-operative studies and projects related to the prevention of nuclear accidents and the long-term safety of radioactive waste disposal systems. The Committee on Nuclear Regulatory Activities contributes to developing a consistent and effective regulatory response to current and future challenges. These challenges include operational experience feedback, increased public expectations concerning safety in the use of nuclear energy, industry initiatives to improve economics and inspection practices, the necessity to ensure safety over a plant's entire life cycle, and new reactors and technology. The Committee on the Safety of Nuclear Installations contributes to maintaining a high level of safety performance and safety competence by identifying emerging safety issues through the analysis of operating experience and research results, contributing to their resolution and, when needed, establishing international research projects. The Radioactive Waste Management Committee assists member countries in the management of radioactive waste and materials, focusing on the development of strategies for the safe, sustainable and broadly acceptable management of all types of radioactive waste, in particular long-lived waste and spent fuel. The Committee on Radiation Protection and Public Health, comprising regulators and protection experts, aims to identify new and emerging issues, analyse their impact and recommend action to address issues and to enhance protection regulation and implementation. It is served by various expert groups and a working party on nuclear emergency matters. The Nuclear Development Committee supports member countries in formulating nuclear energy policy, addressing issues of relevance for governments and the industry at a time of nuclear technology renaissance and sustained government interest in ensuring long-term security of energy supply, reducing the risk of global climate change and pursuing sustainable development. The aim of the NEA nuclear science programme is to help member countries identify, share, develop and disseminate basic scientific and technical knowledge used to ensure safe and reliable operation of current nuclear systems, as well as to develop next-generation technologies. The main areas covered are reactor physics, fuel behaviour, fuel cycle physics and chemistry, critical safety and radiation shielding. The Nuclear Law Committee (NLC) promotes the harmonization of legislation governing the peaceful uses of nuclear energy in member countries and in selected non-member countries. It supports the modernization and strengthening of national and international nuclear liability regimes. Under the supervision of the NLC, the NEA also compiles, analyses and disseminates information on nuclear law through a regular publications programme and organizes the International School of Nuclear Law educational programme. The NEA co-operates with non-member countries of Central and Eastern Europe and the CIS in areas such as nuclear safety, radiation protection and nuclear law.

In January 2005 a policy group of the Generation IV International Forum (GIF) confirmed arrangements under which the NEA would provide technical secretariat support to the GIF, including the funding of this activity by GIF members through voluntary contributions. The GIF is a major international initiative aimed at developing the next generation of nuclear energy systems. In September 2006 the NEA was selected to perform the technical secretariat functions for the Multinational Design Evaluation Programme (MDEP), which had been established to share the resources and knowledge accumulated by national nuclear regulatory authorities during their assessment of new reactor designs, with the aim of improving both the efficiency and the effectiveness of the process.

The NEA offered its support to the Government of Japan in mid-March 2011, following the destabilization of the Fukushima nuclear power plant by an earthquake and tsunami in that month. In response to the Fukushima incident the Agency activated its Flashnews system, facilitating the swift exchange of information among nuclear regulators, and also established a senior-level task group to exchange information, co-ordinate activities and examine the implications for future nuclear plant management. In June the NEA and the French G8 presidency jointly organized a *Forum on the Fukushima Daiichi Accident: Insights and Approaches*. In January 2012 an NEA panel of experts met with members of the Japanese Advisory Committee for the Prevention of Nuclear Accidents and the special Japanese Task Force for the Reform of Nuclear Safety Regulations and Organizations to discuss improving approaches to the regulation and oversight of nuclear facilities.

JOINT PROJECTS

Joint projects and information exchange programmes enable interested countries to share the costs of pursuing research or the sharing of data, relating to particular areas or problems, with the support of the NEA.

NUCLEAR SAFETY

OECD Halden Reactor Project: launched in Jan. 2009, with an initial mandate until Dec. 2011, extended until 2014; based in Halden, Norway; experimental boiling heavy water reactor, which became an OECD project in 1958; from 1964, under successive agreements with participating countries, the reactor has been used for long-term testing of water reactor fuels and for research into automatic computer-based control of nuclear power stations; the main focus is on nuclear fuel safety and man-machine interface; some 130 nuclear energy research institutions and authorities in 19 countries participate in the project.

OECD/NEA Behaviour of Iodine Project Phase 2: initiated in April 2011, with a mandate until March 2014; aims to examine iodine behaviour in a nuclear reactor containment building following a severe accident.

OECD/NEA Cabri Water Loop Project: initiated in 2000, with a mandate until 2015; conducted at the Institute for Protection and Nuclear Safety (IPNS), based in France; investigates the capacity of high burn-up fuel to withstand sharp power peaks that may occur in power reactors owing to rapid reactivity insertion in the reactor core (i.e. reactivity-initiated accidents); 19 participating orgs.

OECD/NEA Fire Propagation in Elementary, Multi-rooms Scenarios (PRISME) Project-2: initiated in Jan. 2006, with a mandate until Dec. 2010; PRISME-2 was mandated to operate from July 2011–June 2016; aims to support the qualification of fire codes and the development of fire protection strategies; eight participating countries.

OECD/NEA Loss of Forced Coolant (LOFC) Project: initiated in March 2011, with a mandate until March 2013; conducting an integrated large-scale test of LOFC in the Japan Atomic Energy Agency high temperature test reactor.

OECD/NEA PKL-2 Project: initiated in April 2008 with a mandate until Sept. 2011; investigated safety issues relating to current pressurised water reactor (PWR) plants and new PWR design concepts; a concluding workshop was scheduled for Oct. 2012, and a three-and-a-half year follow-up project was expected to commence during that year.

OECD/NEA Rig of Safety Assessment (ROSA-2) Project: initiated in April 2009, with a mandate until 30 Sept. 2012; aims to resolve key safety issues relating to light water reactor (LWR) thermal hydraulics.

OECD/NEA Sandia Fuel Project (SFP): launched in July 2009, with a mandate until Feb. 2013; aims to provide experimental data relevant to the hydraulic and ignition phenomena of prototypic water reactor fuel assemblies.

OECD/NEA Source Term Evaluation and Mitigation (STEM) Project: initiated in July 2011, with a mandate until June 2015; aims to improve the general evaluation of the source term, to provide better information for diagnosis and prognosis of the progression of an accident, to allow for better evaluation of the potential release of radioactive materials; seven participating countries.

OECD/NEA Steam Explosion Resolution for Nuclear Applications (SERENA) Project: launched in October 2007, with a mandate until March 2012; established to assess the capabilities of fuel-coolant interaction computer codes to predict steam explosion-induced loads in reactor situations; 11 participating countries.

OECD/NEA Studsvik Cladding Integrity Project: phase 2 covers July 2009–June 2014 (phase 1 covered July 2004–June 2009); aims to generate high quality experimental data to improve understanding of the dominant failure mechanisms for water reactor fuels, and to devise means for reducing fuel failures

OECD/NEA Thermal-hydraulics, Hydrogen, Aerosols, Iodine (ThAI) Project-2: launched in January 2007, with a mandate until December 2009; ThAI-2 was launched in July 2011, and mandated until June 2014; the initial project was designed to provide data for the evaluation and simulation of hydrogen and fission product interactions, supporting accident simulation models; phase 2 was aimed at addressing remaining questions and providing experimental data for relevant HTGR graphite dust transport issues, specific Water Cooled Reactors aerosol and iodine issues and hydrogen mitigation under accidental circumstances; 11 participating countries.

RADIOACTIVE WASTE MANAGEMENT

International Co-operative Programme on Decommissioning: initiated in 1985; promotes exchange of technical information and experience for ensuring that safe, economic and optimum environmental options for decommissioning are used; 12 participating countries.

Thermochemical Database (TDB) Project: aims to develop a quality-assured, comprehensive thermodynamic database of selected chemical elements for use in the safety assessment of radioactive waste repositories; data are selected by review teams; phase II commenced in 1998 and phase III commenced in Feb. 2003; phase IV, studying inorganic species and compounds of iron, was ongoing during 2008–12; 12 participating countries and 17 participating organizations.

RADIATION PROTECTION

Information System on Occupational Exposure (ISOE): initiated in 1992 and co-sponsored by the IAEA; maintains largest database world-wide on occupational exposure to ionizing radiation at nuclear power plants; participants: 323 reactors (some of which are either defunct or actively decommissioning) in 29 countries.

Finance

The Agency's annual budget amounts to some €10.4m., while funding of €3.0m. is made available for the Data Bank. These sums may be supplemented by members' voluntary contributions.

Publications

Annual Report.

NEA News (2 a year).

Nuclear Energy Data (annually).

Nuclear Law Bulletin (2 a year).

Publications on a range of issues relating to nuclear energy, reports and proceedings.

ORGANIZATION FOR SECURITY AND CO-OPERATION IN EUROPE—OSCE

Address: Wallnerstrasse 6, 1010 Vienna, Austria.

Telephone: (1) 514-36-0; **fax:** (1) 514-36-96; **e-mail:** info@osce.org; **internet:** www.osce.org.

The OSCE was established in 1972 as the Conference on Security and Co-operation in Europe (CSCE), providing a multilateral forum for dialogue and negotiation. It produced the Helsinki Final Act of 1975 on East–West relations (see below). The areas of competence of the CSCE were expanded by the Charter of Paris for a New Europe (1990), which transformed the CSCE from an ad hoc forum into an organization with permanent institutions, and the Helsinki Document 1992. In December 1994 the summit conference adopted the new name of OSCE, in order to reflect the organization's changing political role and strengthened secretariat.

PARTICIPATING STATES

Albania	Greece	Portugal
Andorra	Hungary	Romania
Armenia	Iceland	Russia
Austria	Ireland	San Marino
Azerbaijan	Italy	Serbia
Belarus	Kazakhstan	Slovakia
Belgium	Kyrgyzstan	Slovenia
Bosnia and Herzegovina	Latvia	Spain
Bulgaria	Liechtenstein	Sweden
Canada	Lithuania	Switzerland
Croatia	Luxembourg	Tajikistan
Cyprus	Macedonia, former Yugoslav republic	Turkey
Czech Republic	Malta	Turkmenistan
Denmark	Moldova	Ukraine
Estonia	Monaco	United Kingdom
Finland	Montenegro	USA
France	Netherlands	Uzbekistan
Georgia	Norway	Vatican City (Holy See)
Germany	Poland	

Organization

(June 2012)

SUMMIT CONFERENCES

Heads of state or government of OSCE participating states convene periodically to set priorities and the political orientation of the organization. The sixth conference was held in Istanbul, Turkey, in November 1999. A seventh summit meeting was convened, in Astana, Kazakhstan, in December 2010.

MINISTERIAL COUNCIL

The Ministerial Council (formerly the Council of Foreign Ministers) comprises ministers of foreign affairs of member states. It is the central decision-making and governing body of the OSCE and meets every year in which no summit conference is held. The 18th Ministerial Council was held in Vilnius, Lithuania, in December 2011, and the 19th was to be held in Dublin, Ireland, in December 2012. The first informal meeting of ministers was held in Corfu, Greece, in June 2009. A second informal ministerial meeting was convened in Almatı, Kazakhstan, in July 2010.

PERMANENT COUNCIL

The Council, which is based in Vienna, Austria, is responsible for day-to-day operational tasks. Members of the Council, comprising the permanent representatives of member states to the OSCE, convene weekly. The Council is the regular body for political consultation and decision-making, and may be convened for emergency purposes.

FORUM FOR SECURITY CO-OPERATION

The Forum for Security Co-operation (FSC), comprising representatives of delegations of member states, meets weekly in Vienna to negotiate and consult on measures aimed at strengthening security and stability throughout Europe. Its main objectives are negotiations on arms control, disarmament, and confidence- and security-building measures (CSBMs); regular consultations and intensive co-operation on matters related to security; and the further reduction of the risks of conflict. The FSC is also responsible for the implementation of CSBMs; the preparation of seminars on military doctrine; the holding of annual implementation assessment meetings; and the provision of a forum for the discussion and clarification of information exchanged under agreed CSBMs.

CHAIRPERSON-IN-OFFICE

The Chairperson-in-Office (CiO) is vested with overall responsibility for executive action. The position is held by a minister of foreign affairs of a member state for a one-year term. The CiO is assisted by a Troika, consisting of the preceding, current and incoming chairpersons; ad hoc steering groups; and special or personal representatives, who are appointed by the CiO with a clear and precise mandate to assist in dealing with specific issues, crises or conflicts.

Chairperson-in-Office: EAMON GILMORE (Ireland) (2012).

SECRETARIAT

The Secretariat comprises the following principal units: the Conflict Prevention Centre; the Action against Terrorism Unit; the Anti-trafficking Assistance Unit; the Office of the Co-ordinator of OSCE Economic and Environmental Activities; External Co-operation, the Strategic Police Matters Unit; the Training Section; a Department of Human Resources; and the Department of Management and Finance, responsible for technical and administrative support activities. The OSCE maintains an office in Prague, Czech Republic, which assists with documentation and information activities.

The position of Secretary-General was established in December 1992 and the first appointment to the position was made in June 1993. The Secretary-General is appointed by the Ministerial Council for a three-year term of office. The Secretary-General is the representative of the CiO and is responsible for the management of OSCE structures and operations.

Secretary-General: LAMBERTO ZANNIER (Italy).

Co-ordinator of OSCE Economic and Environmental Activities: GORAN SVILANOVIĆ (Serbia).

Director of Conflict Prevention Centre: ADAM KOBIERACKI (Poland).

Senior Police Advisor: KNUT DREYER (Sweden).

Special Representative and Co-ordinator for Combating Trafficking in Human Beings: MARIA GRAZIA GIAMMARINARO (Italy)..

OSCE Specialized Bodies

High Commissioner on National Minorities

POB 20062, 2500 EB The Hague, Netherlands; tel. (70) 3125500; fax (70) 3635910; e-mail hcnm@hcnm.org; internet www.osce.org/hcnm.

The office of High Commissioner on National Minorities was established in December 1992. The High Commissioner is an instrument for conflict prevention, tasked with identifying ethnic tensions that have the potential to develop into conflict, thereby endangering peace, stability or relations between OSCE participating states, and to promote their early resolution. The High Commissioner works in confidence and provides strictly confidential reports to the OSCE CiO. The High Commissioner is appointed by the Ministerial Council, on the recommendation of the Senior Council, for a three-year term.

High Commissioner: KNUT VOLLEBAEK (Norway).

Office for Democratic Institutions and Human Rights (ODIHR)

Aleje Ujazdowskie 19, 00-557 Warsaw, Poland; tel. (22) 520-06-00; fax (22) 520-06-05; e-mail office@odihr.pl; internet www.osce.org/odihr.

Established in July 1999, the ODIHR has responsibility for promoting human rights, democracy and the rule of law. The Office provides a framework for the exchange of information on and the promotion of democracy-building, respect for human rights and elections within OSCE states. In addition, it co-ordinates the monitoring of elections and provides expertise and training on constitutional and legal matters.

Director: JANEZ LENARČIČ (Slovenia).

Office of the Representative on Freedom of the Media

Wallnerstrasse 6, 1010 Vienna, Austria; tel. (1) 512-21-450; fax (1) 512-21-459; e-mail pm-fom@osce.org; internet www.osce.org/fom.

The office was established by a decision of the Permanent Council in November 1997 to strengthen the implementation of OSCE commitments regarding free, independent and pluralistic media.

Representative: DUNJA MIJATOVIĆ (Bosnia and Herzegovina).

Parliamentary Assembly

Radhusstraede 1, 1466 Copenhagen K, Denmark; tel. 33-37-80-40; fax 33-37-80-30; e-mail osce@oscepa.dk; internet www.oscepa.org.

In April 1991 parliamentarians from the CSCE countries agreed on the creation of a pan-European parliamentary assembly. Its inaugural session was held in Budapest, Hungary, in July 1992. The Parliamentary Assembly, which is composed of 320 members from 55 parliaments, meets annually. It comprises a Standing Committee, a Bureau and three General Committees and is supported by a Secretariat in Copenhagen, Denmark.

President: PETROS EFTHYMIOU (Greece).

Secretary-General: R. SPENCER OLIVER (USA).

OSCE Related Bodies

COURT OF CONCILIATION AND ARBITRATION

Villa Rive-Belle, 266 route de Lausanne, 1292 Chambésy, Geneva, Switzerland; tel. 227580025; fax 227582510; e-mail cca.osce@bluewin.ch; internet www.osce.org/cca.

An OSCE Convention on Conciliation and Arbitration, providing for the establishment of the Court, was concluded in 1992 and entered into effect in December 1994. The first meeting of the Court was convened in May 1995. OSCE states that have ratified the Convention may submit a dispute to the Court for settlement by the Arbitral Tribunal or the Conciliation Commission.

President: ROBERT BADINTER (France).

JOINT CONSULTATIVE GROUP (JCG)

The states that are party to the Treaty on Conventional Armed Forces in Europe (CFE), which was concluded within the CSCE framework in 1990, established the Joint Consultative Group (JCG). The JCG, which meets in Vienna, addresses questions relating to compliance with the Treaty; enhancement of the effectiveness of the Treaty; technical aspects of the Treaty's implementation; and disputes arising out of its implementation. There are currently 30 states participating in the JCG.

OPEN SKIES CONSULTATIVE COMMISSION

The Commission promotes implementation of the Treaty on Open Skies, which was signed by members of NATO and the former members of the Warsaw Pact (with Russia, Belarus, Ukraine and Georgia taking the place of the USSR) in March 1992. Under the accord, aerial reconnaissance missions by one country over another were permitted, subject to regulation. Regular meetings of the Commission are serviced by the OSCE secretariat.

Activities

In July 1990 heads of government of the member countries of the North Atlantic Treaty Organization (NATO) proposed to increase the role of the CSCE 'to provide a forum for wider political dialogue in a more united Europe'. The Charter of Paris for a New Europe, which undertook to strengthen pluralist democracy and observance of human rights, and to settle disputes between participating states by peaceful means, was signed in November. At the summit meeting the Treaty on Conventional Armed Forces in Europe (CFE), which had been negotiated within the framework of the CSCE, was signed by the member states of NATO and of the Warsaw Pact. The Treaty limits non-nuclear air and ground armaments in the signatory countries. The summit conference that was held in Lisbon, Portugal, in December 1996 agreed to adapt the CFE Treaty, in order to further arms reduction negotiations on a national and territorial basis. In November 1999 a revised CFE Treaty was signed, providing for a stricter system of limitations and increased transparency, which was to be open to other OSCE states not currently signatories. The US and European Union (EU) governments determined to delay ratification of the Agreement of the Adaptation of the Treaty until Russian troop levels in the Caucasus had been reduced.

The Council of Foreign Ministers met for the first time in Berlin, Germany, in June 1991. The meeting adopted a mechanism for consultation and co-operation in the case of emergency situations, to be implemented by the Council of Senior Officials (CSO; subsequently renamed the Senior Council, which was dissolved in 2006, with all functions transferred to the Permanent Council). A separate mechanism regarding the prevention of the outbreak of conflict was also adopted, whereby a country can demand an explanation of 'unusual military activity' in a neighbouring country. These mechanisms were utilized in July in relation to the armed conflict in Yugoslavia between the Republic of Croatia and the Yugoslav Government. In August a meeting of the CSO resolved to reinforce the CSCE's mission in Yugoslavia and in September the CSO agreed to impose an embargo on the export of armaments to Yugoslavia. In October the CSO determined to establish an observer mission to monitor the observance of human rights in Yugoslavia.

In January 1992 the Council of Foreign Ministers agreed to alter the Conference's rule of decision-making by consensus in order to allow the CSO to take appropriate action against a participating state 'in cases of clear and gross violation of CSCE commitments'. This development was precipitated by the conflict in Yugoslavia, where the Yugoslav Government was held responsible by the majority of CSCE states for the continuation of hostilities and was suspended from the grouping. The meeting also agreed that the CSCE should undertake fact-finding and conciliation missions to areas of tension, with the first such mission to be sent to Nagornyi Karabakh, the largely Armenian-populated enclave in Azerbaijan.

The meeting of heads of state and government, held in Helsinki, Finland, in July 1992, adopted the Helsinki Document, in which participating states defined the terms of future CSCE peace-keeping activities. Conforming broadly to UN practice, operations would be undertaken only with the full consent of the parties involved in any conflict and only if an effective cease-fire were in place. The CSCE may request the use of the military resources of NATO, the Commonwealth of Independent States (CIS), the EU or other international bodies. The Helsinki Document declared the CSCE a 'regional arrangement' in the sense of Chapter VIII of the UN's Charter, which states that such a regional grouping should attempt to resolve a conflict in the region before referring it to the Security Council.

In 1993 the First Implementation Meeting on Human Dimension Issues (the CSCE term used with regard to issues concerning human rights and welfare) took place. The Meeting, for which the ODIHR serves as a secretariat, provides a now annual forum for the exchange of news regarding OSCE commitments in the fields of human rights and democracy.

Also in 1993 the first annual Economic Forum was convened to focus on the transition to and development of free market economies as an essential aspect of democracy-building. It was renamed the Economic and Environment Forum in 2007 to incorporate consideration of environmental security matters. The first Preparatory Meeting of the 20th Forum was convened in February 2012 (in Vienna Austria), and the second was held in April (in Dublin, Ireland). The theme of the 20th Forum was 'Promoting Security and Stability through Good Governance'.

In December 1993 a Permanent Committee (later renamed the Permanent Council) was established in Vienna, providing for greater political consultation and dialogue through its weekly meetings. In December 1994 the summit conference redesignated the CSCE as the Organization for Security and Co-operation in Europe (OSCE) and endorsed the role of the organization as the primary instrument for early warning, conflict prevention and crisis management in the region. The conference adopted a 'Code of Conduct on Politico-Military Aspects of Security', which set out principles to guide the role of the armed forces in democratic societies. In December 1996 the summit conference convened in Lisbon, Portugal, adopted the 'Lisbon Declaration on a Common and Comprehensive Security Model for Europe for the 21st Century', committing all parties to pursuing measures to ensure regional security. A Security Model Committee was established and began to meet regularly during 1997 to consider aspects of the Declaration. In November the Office of the Representative on Freedom of the Media was established in Vienna, to support the OSCE's activities in this field. In the same month a new position of Co-ordinator of OSCE Economic and Environmental Activities was created.

In November 1999 OSCE heads of state and of government, convened in Istanbul, Turkey, signed a new Charter for European Security, which aimed to formalize existing norms regarding the observance of human rights and to strengthen co-operation with other organizations and institutions concerned with international security. The Charter focused on measures to improve the operational capabilities of the OSCE in early warning, conflict prevention, crisis management and post-conflict rehabilitation. Accordingly, Rapid Expert Assistance and Co-operation (REACT) teams were to be established to enable the organization to respond rapidly to requests from participating states for assistance in crisis situations. The REACT programme became operational in April 2001. The 1999 summit meeting also adopted a revised Vienna Document on confidence- and security-building measures and a Platform for Co-operative Security as a framework for co-operation with other organizations and institutions concerned with maintaining security in the OSCE area.

In April 2000 the OSCE High Commissioner on National Minorities issued a report reviewing the problems confronting Roma and Sinti populations in OSCE member states. In April 2001 the ODIHR launched a programme of assistance for the Roma communities of south-eastern Europe. In November 2000 an OSCE Document on Small Arms and Light Weapons was adopted, aimed at curtailing the spread of armaments in member states. A workshop on implementation of the Document was held in February 2002. In mid-November 2000 the Office of the Representative on Freedom of the Media organized a conference, staged in Dushanbe, Tajikistan, of journalists from Kazakhstan, Kyrgyzstan, Tajikistan and Uzbekistan. In February 2001 the ODIHR established an Anti-Trafficking Project Fund to help to finance its efforts to combat trafficking in human beings.

In September 2001 the Secretary-General condemned terrorist attacks perpetrated against targets in the USA, by militant Islamist fundamentalists. In early October OSCE member states unanimously adopted a statement in support of the developing US-led global coalition against international terrorism. In December the Ministerial Council, meeting in Romania, approved the 'Bucharest Plan of Action' outlining the organization's contribution to countering terrorism. An Action against Terrorism Unit was established within the Secretariat to co-ordinate and help to implement the counter-terrorism initiatives. A Personal Representative for Terrorism was appointed by the CiO in January 2002. Also in December 2001 the OSCE sponsored, with the then UN Office for Drug Control and Crime Prevention (ODCCP), an International Conference on Security and Stability in Central Asia, held in Bishkek, Kyrgyzstan. The meeting, which was attended by representatives of more than 60 countries and organizations, was concerned with strengthening efforts to counter terrorism and providing effective support to the Central Asian states. At a Ministerial Council meeting held in Porto, Portugal, in December 2002, the OSCE issued a Charter on Preventing Terrorism, which condemned terrorism 'in all its forms and manifestations' and called upon member states to work together to counter, investigate and prosecute terrorist acts. The charter also acknowledged the links between terrorism, organized crime and trafficking in human beings. At the same time, a political declaration entitled 'Responding to Change' was adopted, in which member states pledged their commitment to mutual co-operation in combating threats to security. The OSCE's first Annual Security Review Conference was held in Vienna, in July 2003. The meeting elaborated a range of practical options for addressing the new threats and challenges, including the introduction of common security features on travel documentation, stricter controls on manual portable air defence systems and the improvement of border security and policing methods. Security issues were also the subject of the Rotterdam Declaration, adopted by some 300 members of the Parliamentary Assembly in July, which stated that it was imperative for the OSCE to maintain a strong field presence and for field missions to be provided with sufficient funding and highly trained staff. It also recommended that the OSCE assume a role in unarmed peace-keeping operations.

In July 2003 the Permanent Council adopted a new Action Plan to Combat Trafficking in Human Beings. The Plan was endorsed by the Ministerial Council, held in Maastricht, Netherlands, in December. The Council approved the appointment of a Special Representative on Combating Trafficking in Human Beings, mandated to raise awareness of the issues and to ensure member governments comply with international procedures and conventions, and the establishment of a special unit within the Secretariat. In July 2004 the Special Representative organized an international conference to consider issues relating to human trafficking, including human rights, labour, migration, organized crime, and minors. Participants agreed to establish an Alliance against Trafficking in Persons, which aimed to consolidate co-operation among international and non-governmental organizations.

During July 2003 the first OSCE conference on the effects of globalization was convened in Vienna, attended by some 200 representatives from international organizations. Participants called for the advancement of good governance in the public and private sectors, the development of democratic institutions and the creation of conditions that would enable populations to benefit from the global economy. At a meeting of the Ministerial Council, convened in Maastricht, in December, member states endorsed a document that aimed to address risks to regional security and stability arising from stockpiles of conventional ammunition through, *inter alia*, detailing practical steps for their destruction. In December 2004 the Ministerial Council, meeting in Sofia, Bulgaria, condemned terrorist attacks that had been committed during the year, including in Madrid, Spain, in March, and in Beslan, Russia, in September. The meeting issued a statement expressing determination to pursue all measures to prevent and combat international terrorism, while continuing to protect and uphold human rights. In order to consider OSCE's capacity to address new security challenges, and to provide a new strategic vision for the organization, the Council resolved to establish a Panel of Eminent Persons on Strengthening the Effectiveness of the OSCE. The Panel presented its report, comprising some 70 recommendations, to the Permanent Council in June 2005. In December 2008 the Ministerial Council, convened in Helsinki, determined to pursue a high-level dialogue on strengthening the legal framework of OSCE. In June 2009 OSCE ministers of foreign affairs, meeting in an informal session in Greece, inaugurated the Corfu Process to structure further dialogue on future European security. A Ministerial Declaration on the Corfu Process was adopted by the Ministerial Council in December, which determined to use it to strengthen a free, democratic and integrated Europe. The Declaration was to serve as a roadmap for dialogue focusing on: OSCE norms, principles and commitments; conflict resolution; arms control and confidence- and security-building regimes; transnational and multidimensional threats and challenges; common economic and environmental challenges; human rights and fundamental freedoms, as well as democracy and the rule of law; and enhancing the OSCE's effectiveness and interaction with other organizations and institutions. In July 2010 a second informal ministerial meeting, convened in Almatı, Kazakhstan, reviewed progress in implementing the Corfu Process, as well as the Organization's response to insecurity in Kyrgyzstan. Later in that month the Permanent Council endorsed a decision to deploy a 52-member Police Advisory Group to Kyrgyzstan in order to facilitate law enforcement efforts in areas of ethnic unrest. In December OSCE and the ILO jointly published a study entitled *Strengthening Migration Governance*.

In December 2010 OSCE heads of state and government, meeting in Astana, Kazakhstan, adopted the 'Astana Commemorative Declaration: Towards a Security Community', which reaffirmed the core principles and commitments of the organization. The Declaration asserted that commitments in the three security dimensions, i.e. human, politico-military, and economic and environmental, are matters of direct and legitimate concern to all participating states. In spite of a lack of full consensus to adopt a framework for future action, the Declaration urged greater efforts to resolve conflicts and to undertake conflict prevention, to update the Vienna Document 1999 (concerning confidence- and security-building measures), and to enhance energy security dialogue.

In December 2011 the Ministerial Council, convened in Vilnius, Lithuania, adopted a decision on 'enhancing OSCE capabilities in early warning, early action, dialogue facilitation, mediation support and post-conflict rehabilitation on an operational level', tasking the Secretary-General with ensuring that the Secretariat's Conflict Prevention Centre assumes the role of focal point for the systematic collection, collation, analysis and assessment of relevant early warning signals, and calling for increased exchange of information and co-ordination between the OSCE executive structures. Other decisions made by the Council included: enhancing engagement with Afghanistan and Partners for Co-operation; promoting equal opportunities for women in the economic sphere; addressing transnational threats; strengthening dialogue on transport; and addressing small arms, light weapons and stockpiles of conventional ammunition. A declaration on combating all forms of human trafficking was adopted.

The OSCE maintains regular formal dialogue and co-operation with certain nominated countries. Afghanistan, Australia, Japan, the Republic of Korea, Mongolia and Thailand have the status of 'Asian Partners for Co-operation' with the OSCE, while Algeria, Egypt, Israel, Jordan, Morocco and Tunisia are 'Mediterranean Partners for Co-operation'. Regular consultations are held with these countries in order to discuss security issues of common concern. In October 2004 OSCE deployed a team of observers to monitor the presidential election in Afghanistan, representing the organization's first election mission in a partner country. In October 2008 OSCE participating states and Mediterranean partner countries convened, in Amman, Jordan, at conference level, to discuss regional security. In the following month a conference was held in the Afghan capital, Kabul, to strengthen co-operation between the OSCE and its Asian partner countries. An OSCE-Japan conference, convened in Tokyo, Japan, in June 2009, considered how the OSCE and Asian partner states should best address global security challenges. In December 2010 OSCE heads of state and government resolved to enhance interaction with its Partners for Co-operation. The annual conference of all OSCE Asian Partners for Co-operation was convened in 2011 in Ulan Bator, Mongolia, in May. The December 2011 Ministerial Conference adopted a decision on Partners for Co-operation, which commended the voluntary reform processes ongoing in some Mediterranean partner countries; reaffirmed the OSCE's readiness, through its executive structures, when requested, to assist the Partners for Co-operation in their voluntary implementation of OSCE norms, principles and commitments; decided to enhance the Partnership for Co-operation by broadening dialogue, intensifying political consultations, strengthening practical co-operation and further sharing best practices, according to the needs and priorities identified by the Partners; and determined to strengthen regular high-level dialogue with the Partners for Co-operation.

OSCE provides technical assistance to the Southeast European Co-operative Initiative.

FIELD OPERATIONS IN CENTRAL AND SOUTH-EASTERN EUROPE

OSCE Mission in Kosovo: 38000 Priština, Beogradska 32; tel. (38) 500162; fax (38) 240711; e-mail press.omik@osce.org; internet www.osce.org/kosovo; f. July 1999 as an integral component of an international operation, led by the UN, with specific responsibility for democracy- and institution-building; in 2012 the Mission was operating five regional centres: in Mitrovica/Mitrovice, Pejë/Peć, Prizren, Gjilan/Gnjilane, and Prishtinë/Priština, as well as more than 30 municipal teams throughout Kosovo; succeeded a 2,000-member OSCE Kosovo Verification Mission (KVM), established to monitor compliance with the terms of a cease-fire between Serbian authorities and ethnic Albanian separatists in the formerly autonomous province of Kosovo and Metohija; helped to establish and/or administer a police training school and inspectorate, an Institute for Civil Administration, the Department for Democratic Governance and Civil Society, the Office of the Ombudsperson, a Kosovo Centre for Public Safety Education and Development and a Press Council; in early 2002 the Mission initiated training sessions for members of the new Kosovo Assembly; in mid-2004 the Mission initiated an Out-of-Kosovo voting scheme to update the voter registration for forthcoming Assembly elections and, following the election in Oct., the Mission, with other partner organizations co-ordinated under an Assembly Support Initiative, again undertook an induction programme for newly elected members; the Mission provided technical assistance for the preparation of national and municipal assembly elections, held in Nov. 2007, and, following the new government's unilateral declaration of independence, issued in Feb. 2008, determined to support the country's new institutions, and monitor their work for compliance with human rights standards; following the reconfiguration of the UN operation in Kosovo, and reduction of its field presence, the OSCE Mission has assumed greater responsibility for monitoring and reporting on the security situation and compliance with human rights standards; a Mission report on the functioning of the Kosovo justice system, released in Jan. 2012, found that improvements were still required to establish a fully independent judiciary; in Feb. the Head of the Misson expressed concern over recent security incidents affecting the Kosovo Serb community in the eastern Gjilan/Gnjilane region; in early May the Mission undertook a ballot facilitation operation to enable eligible voters to participate in the Serbian presidential and parliamentary elections; Head of Mission WERNER ALMHOFER (Austria).

OSCE Mission to Bosnia and Herzegovina: 71000 Sarajevo, Fra Andjela Zvizdovica 1; tel. (33) 752100; fax (33) 442479; e-mail info.ba@osce.org; internet www.oscebih.org; f. Dec. 1995 to achieve the objectives of the peace accords for the former Yugoslavia, in particular to oversee the process of democratization; in 2012 had 13 field offices, and an additional office in Brcko (the so-called 'Brcko Team'); helped to organize and monitor national elections, held in Sept. 1996, municipal elections, held in Sept. 1997, elections to the National Assembly of the Serb Republic and to the Bosnian Serb presidency in Nov., a general election, conducted in Sept. 1998, and legislative elections held in Nov. 2000; the Mission's responsibility for elections in the country ended in Nov. 2001 when a new permanent Election Commission was inaugurated, to which the Mission was to provide support; other key areas of Mission activity are the promotion of democratic values, monitoring and promoting respect for human rights, strengthening the legal system, assisting with the creation of a modernized, non-discriminatory education system and establishing democratic control over the armed forces; in Sept. 2004 the agreement on confidence- and security-building measures, mandated under the Dayton peace accords, was suspended in acknowledgement of the country's extensive political reforms and in Dec. the Mission transferred its co-chairmanship of the country's Defence Reform Commission (DRC) to the new NATO headquarters in Sarajevo, although representatives of the Mission continued to be involved in work of the DRC; in June 2008 the Mission concluded a long-term legislative strengthening programme, which included the development of an intranet system for the country's Parliamentary Assembly; responsibility for a project to promote greater legislative transparency and accessibility, Open Parliament, was transferred to the national Parliament in July 2009; the Mission supports implementation of the sub-regional arms control agreement, although responsibility for inspection missions was assumed by the national armed forces from Jan. 2010; during 2011–12 the Mission was implementing a Citizens' Academy project, aimed at encouraging citizens to engage with local government; Head of Mission FLETCHER M. BURTON (USA).

OSCE Mission to Montenegro: 81000 Podgorica, Bul. Svetog Petra Cetinjskog bb; tel. (81) 401401; fax (81) 406431; internet www.osce.org/montenegro; f. June 2006 following the country's declaration of independence from Serbia; supports the reform processes required to achieve European and Euro-Atlantic integration, i.e. democratization processes, legislative reform and institution-building, police and media reform, and activities to promote environmental protection and economic development; in March 2011 the Mission organized a regional conference of ministers responsible for justice and interior affairs in order to strengthen co-operation in judicial and policing matters; the Head of Mission and the Montenegro Ministry of Justice concluded a Memorandum of Understanding on judicial reform in Dec. 2011; Head of Mission ŠARŪNAS ADOMAVIČIUS (Lithuania).

OSCE Mission to Serbia: 11000 Belgrade, Čakorska 1; tel. (11) 3606100; fax (11) 3606119; e-mail ppiu-serbia@osce.org; internet www.osce.org/serbia; f. Jan. 2001 as the OSCE Mission to the Federal Republic of Yugoslavia (FRY, renamed the OSCE Mission to Serbia and Montenegro in 2003 and divided into two separate Missions in June 2006); the initial mandate of the Mission was to assist in the areas of democracy and protection of human rights and in the restructuring and training of law enforcement agencies and the judiciary, to provide advice to government authorities with regard to reform of the media, and, in close co-operation with the United Nations High Commissioner for Refugees, to facilitate the return of refugees to and from neighbouring countries as well as within the FRY; until Dec. 2011 the Mission provided on-site field support to the Basic Police Training Centre in Sremska Kamenica; in March 2002 the Mission facilitated the census process in southern Serbia; in June 2003 the Mission initiated an Outreach Campaign, to ensure regular visits by Mission representatives to more remote municipalities, and undertook a border-policing project in an effort to reduce human trafficking and organized crime in Serbia and Montenegro; the Mission supported the formulation and implementation of new procedures to counter organized crime; a seminar on effective and transparent methods for managing temporarily-seized assets was organized by the Mission in April 2011; in 2012 the Mission aimed to support Serbia's efforts to build accountable and effective democratic institutions, to uphold human rights, to establish a stable and inclusive civil society, and to enhance environmental protection measures; supports the activities of the Citizen's Protector/Ombudsman, the Commissioner for the Protection of Equality and the Judicial Training Academy; in 2012 the Mission had an office in Bujanovac, southern Serbia, a training facility in Novi Pazar, and an advanced police training centre in Zemun; Head of Mission DIMITRIOS KYPREOS (Greece).

OSCE Presence in Albania: Sheraton Tirana Hotel & Towers, 1st Floor, Sheshi 'Italia', Tirana; tel. (4) 2235993; fax (4) 2235994; e-mail post.albania@osce.org; internet www.osce.org/albania; f. in March 1997 to help to restore political and civil stability, which had been undermined by the collapse of national pyramid saving schemes at the start of the year; in 2012 the Presence had four field stations, in Gjirokaster, Kukes, Shkoder and Vlora; from March 1998 to the conclusion of a political settlement for Kosovo and Metohija in mid-1999 the Presence was mandated to monitor the country's borders with the Kosovan region of southern Serbia and to prevent any spillover effects from the escalating crisis; from Sept. 1998 the Presence became the Co-Chair, with the EU, of the Friends of Albania group, which brought together countries and international bodies concerned with the situation in Albania; in accordance with an updated mandate, approved in Dec. 2003, the Presence provides advice and support to the Albanian Government regarding democratization, the rule of law, the media, human rights, anti-trafficking, weapons collection, election preparation and monitoring, and the development of civil society; it supports an Economics and Environment Unit and an Elections Unit, which, since the parliamentary elections of 2001, has facilitated the process of electoral reform, including modernization of the civil registration system; in 2010 the Presence assisted the Albanian Government with drafting legislation concerning parliamentary oversight of the intelligence and security services and in 2011 extended technical assistance to the Central Elections Commission in preparing for local government elections, that were conducted in May; Head of Presence EUGEN WOLLFARTH (Germany).

OSCE Spillover Monitor Mission to Skopje: MK-1000 Skopje, 11 Oktomvri str. 25, QBE Building; tel. (2) 3234000; fax (2) 3234234; e-mail info-MK@osce.org; f. Sept. 1992 to help to prevent the conflict in the former Yugoslavia from destabilizing the former Yugoslav republic of Macedonia (FYRM), with an initial mandate of overseeing the border region, monitoring human rights and promoting the development of democratic institutions, including an independent media; supports implementation of the Ohrid framework political agreement, signed in August 2001, initially through the deployment of international confidence-building monitors and police advisers, the recruitment and training of police cadets, and measures to strengthen local self-government; since 2002 the Mission has supported the Office of the Ombudsman, and in June 2007 initiated a second phase of the support project, including a new public awareness campaign; in early 2009 the Mission worked to strengthen the integrity of the electoral process for presidential and municipal elections that were conducted in March; in April 2010 Skopje missions of the OSCE, EU, NATO and USA reiterated the need for full commitment to the Ohrid Framework Agreement and for reinforced political dialogue; a short-term OSCE observer mission monitored parliamentary elections held in June 2011; in July the Mission organized a regional conference on the introduction of legal aid and the improvement of practices to promote access to justice throughout south-eastern Europe; in Jan. 2012 the Mission organized a workshop aimed at strengthening regional co-operation and dialogue to promote an effective response to human- and child-trafficking; in March 2012 the Head of Mission condemned recent violent incidents in Skopje; Head of Mission RALF BRETH (Germany).

In January 2012 the OSCE closed its Office in Zagreb, which had been established in January 2008, replacing a former OSCE Mission to Croatia.

FIELD OPERATIONS IN EASTERN EUROPE AND CENTRAL ASIA

An OSCE Mission to Georgia was established in 1992 to work towards a political settlement between disputing factions within the country. Since 1994 the Mission has contributed to efforts to define the political status of South Ossetia and has supported UN peace-keeping and human rights activities in Abkhazia. In 1997 the Mission established a field office in Tskhinvali (South Ossetia). In December 1999 the Permanent Council, at the request of the Government of Georgia expanded the mandate of the existing OSCE Mission to Georgia to include monitoring that country's border with the Chechen Republic of Ichkeriya (Chechnya). The first permanent observation post opened in February 2000 and the monitoring team was fully deployed by July. In December 2001 the Permanent Council approved an expansion in the border monitoring mission to cover the border between Georgia and Ingushetia. A further expansion, to include monitoring Georgia's border with Dagestan, was effected from January 2003. A special envoy of the OSCE Chairperson visited Georgia in July 2004 following a deterioration in the security situation. In November the Mission assisted the Georgian Government to develop an Action Plan to combat trafficking in human beings. In the same month the Mission helped to organize a national workshop on combating money-laundering and suppressing the financing of terrorism. In April 2005 the OSCE Permanent Council established a Training Assistance Programme for some 800 Georgian border guards. In June 2006 OSCE participating states pledged more than €10m. in support of projects for social and economic rehabilitation in the zone of the Georgian–Ossetian conflict. The donors' conference was the first of its kind to be organized by the OSCE. During 2007 the Mission continued to support activities concerned with police reform, human rights monitoring and education, munitions disposal, border control and management, counter-trafficking, and strengthening local democracy. OSCE observers participated in an international mission to monitor parliamentary elections held in May 2008. In July the Mission signed a Memorandum of Understanding with the Georgian Ministry of Defence to implement a three-year plan to strengthen local capacity for the dismantling and disposal of munitions. In the same month the Mission organized a training course for officials on the protection of human rights and fundamental freedoms. At that time the OSCE expressed concern at escalating tensions between the Georgian and Ossetian authorities. In August intensive fighting broke out when Georgian forces entered the territory and attempted to seize control of Tskhinvali. The resulting counter-attack by Ossetian troops, supported by additional Russian land and air forces, contributed to extensive civilian casualties, population displacement and damage to the region's infrastructure. The OSCE participated in diplomatic efforts to secure a cease-fire and convened a special meeting of the Permanent Council to discuss the organization's contribution to stabilizing the post-conflict situation. Members agreed to expand the Mission to Georgia by 100 military monitoring officers, of whom 20 were to be deployed immediately to the areas adjacent to South Ossetia. In late August the CiO and the Head of the Mission to Georgia visited the worst affected areas. In the following month the Head of Mission met the Russian Minister of Foreign Affairs to discuss issues relating to the freedom of movement of the Mission's unarmed monitors and the need for the effective delivery of humanitarian aid. In October the OSCE met with senior representatives of the UN and EU, in Geneva, Switzerland, to consider the stability and security of the region and the situation of displaced persons. The Mission to Georgia was terminated upon the expiry of its mandate on 31 December 2008, as agreement had not been reached by that time on continuing it into 2009, owing to Russia's insistence on a new mandate for the mission that excluded any arrangement sustaining Georgia's territorial claims on South Ossetia and Abkhazia, and Georgia's opposition to this. In February 2009 the OSCE Permanent Council agreed to extend, until 30 June, the mandate of the OSCE unarmed monitors in Georgia. During the first six months of 2009 intensive diplomatic efforts were undertaken to conclude an agreement on a continued OSCE presence in Georgia; there was failure, however, to achieve consensus by the end of June when, as planned, the unarmed monitors were withdrawn.

On 31 March 2011 the OSCE Office in Minsk closed, following a decision by the authorities in Belarus not to extend its mandate. The Office had opened in January 2003, as a successor to an OSCE Advisory and Monitoring Group, with a mandate to promote institution-building, to consolidate the rule of law, to strengthen relations with civil society and to assist the Government of Belarus in developing economic and environmental activities.

OSCE Centre in Aşgabat: 744005 Aşgabat, Türkmenbasi Shayoly 15, Turkmenistan; tel. (12) 35-30-92; fax (12) 35-30-41; e-mail info_tm@osce.org; internet www.osce.org/ashgabat/; f. Jan. 1999 (following a decision of the Permanent Council, in July 1998, to establish a permanent presence in the country); works to support greater collaboration between the authorities and the OSCE and the implementation of OSCE principles, to facilitate contacts with other local and international institutions and organizations working in the region and to assist in arranging regional seminars, events and visits by OSCE personnel; courses and workshops organized by the Centre in 2011 included best practices in police training, travel document security, anti-corruption measures, protecting human rights while countering terrorism, and contemporary global journalism; Head of Centre Sergei Belyaev (Russia).

OSCE Centre in Astana: 010000 Astana, Beibitshilik 10, Kazakhstan; tel. (7172) 32-68-04; fax (7172) 32-83-04; internet www.osce.org/astana; f. June 2007, as successor to an OSCE Centre in Almatı (f. Jan. 1999); mandated to support greater co-operation between the authorities and the OSCE, as well as the implementation of OSCE principles, to facilitate contacts with other local and international institutions and organizations working in the region, to assist in arranging regional seminars, events and visits by OSCE personnel, and to support the Government of Kazakhstan, for example by training officials and raising awareness of OSCE activities; matters addressed by seminars and courses organized by the Centre in 2010/11 included freedom of peaceful assembly, corporate social accountability, environmental protection, criminal justice reform, including the development of a probation system, the establishment of a national preventive mechanism to monitor the use of torture in detention centres, and gender equality; in June 2011 hosted a regional forum on internet development in Central Asia; Head of Centre Natalia Zarudna (Ukraine).

OSCE Centre in Bishkek: 720001 Bishkek, Toktogula 139, Kyrgyzstan; tel. (312) 66-50-15; fax (312) 66-31-69; e-mail pm-kg@osce.org; internet www.osce.org/bishkek/; f. Jan. 1999 (following a decision of the Permanent Council, in July 1998, to establish a permanent presence in the country); works to support greater collaboration between the authorities and the OSCE and the implementation of OSCE principles, to facilitate contacts with other local and international institutions and organizations working in the region and to assist in arranging regional seminars, events and visits by OSCE personnel; established a field office in Osh, in 2000, to oversee operations in Kyrgyzstan's southern provinces; supports the OSCE Academy in Bishkek, which was inaugurated in Dec. 2002 as a regional centre for training, research and dialogue, in particular in security-related issues; following an escalation of civil and political tensions after legislative elections in Feb.–March 2005, the Centre offered to provide a forum for dialogue between the authorities and opposition groups; following political upheaval and civil and ethnic violence in April and June 2010 the Centre worked closely with the interim authorities to alleviate political tension and to promote dialogue and reconciliation; in Sept. the Centre facilitated contacts between political and non-governmental groups and the Head of an OSCE Police Advisory Group, which was deployed from Jan. 2011 in a primarily consultative role; prior to parliamentary elections, held in Oct. 2010, the Centre worked to ensure compliance with an electoral Code of Conduct signed by representatives of 26 political parties, to advise on the role of prosecutors, to promote impartial media reporting and to ensure the safety of journalists; organized a training course on multi-ethnic policing in July 2011; also in July, supported a meeting on the development of a new national action plan to combat human trafficking; in March 2012 co-hosted, jointly with the World Bank, UNODC and the Kyrgyz Government, a workshop on assessing the risk of money laundering; in 2012 the Centre aimed to focus its activities on six strategic priority areas: border security and management, including customs training; rule of law; good governance; legislation; environmental protection; and regional co-operation; Head of Centre Andrew Tesoriere (United Kingdom).

OSCE Mission to Moldova: 2012 Chişinău, str. Mitropolit Dosoftei 108; tel. (22) 22-34-95; fax (22) 22-34-96; e-mail moldova@osce.org; internet www.osce.org/moldova/; f. Feb. 1993, in order to assist conflicting parties in that country to pursue negotiations on a political settlement for the Transniestrian region, as well as to observe the military situation in the region and to provide advice on issues of human and minority rights, democratization and the repatriation of refugees; the Mission's mandate was expanded in Dec. 1999 to ensure the full removal and destruction of Russian ammunition and armaments and to co-ordinate financial and technical assistance for the withdrawal of foreign troops and the destruction of weapons; in June 2001 the Mission established a tripartite working group, with representatives of the Russian Ministry of Defence and the local authorities in Transnistria, to assist and support the process of disposal of munitions; destruction of heavy weapons began in mid-2002, under the supervision of the Mission; in Sept. 2004 the OSCE Mission financed a workshop as part of a two-year project concerned with 'strengthening protection and assistance to victims of trafficking, adults and minors'; during 2005 the OSCE Mission hosted negotiations which resulted in the Transnistrian authorities extending permanent registration to four Moldovan schools; in March 2006 the OSCE CiO expressed concern at the situation along the Transnistrian section of the Moldovan–Ukrainian state border and instructed the Mission to pursue a solution by consulting with all relevant parties; in Jan. 2007 representatives of the OSCE, Russia and Ukraine met, with observers from the EU and USA (i.e. the so-called 5+2 negotiation format), to consider the future of the settlement process and invited chief negotiators from the Moldovan and

Transnistrian authorities to initiate mediated discussions in the following month; in Oct. the Mission organized a high-level seminar on confidence- and security-building measures, in support of peace negotiations between Moldova and Transnistria, and in April 2008 the Mission organized a seminar on economic and environmental confidence-building measures, held in Odesa, Ukraine; in Feb. 2009 a Special Representative of the CiO for Protracted Conflicts visited Moldova to promote a resumption of the Transnistrian peace negotiations; an agreement to revive the process was signed by leaders of both sides, meeting in Moscow, Russia, in March; in April the Head of Mission condemned violent demonstrations that occurred following legislative elections; the Mission and the OSCE CiO convened a seminar in June on confidence- and security-building measures in Moldova, with participation by experts and 5+2 process participants; a Trial Monitoring Programme was conducted by the Mission with ODIHR, between March 2006 and Dec. 2009, to observe and enhance Moldova's compliance with OSCE commitments and international legal standards; in June 2010 the Mission signed a Memorandum of Understanding with the Moldovan Government to implement a four-year social integration project for ex-military personnel from the Transniestrian region; the initiative commenced in Sept; in Feb. 2011 an informal meeting of participants in the 5+2 settlement process agreed a work plan for that year, which included greater bilateral contact, pursuing other confidence-building measures, and resolving outstanding problems of freedom of movement; a further informal round of consultations was held in June, in Moscow; a limited OSCE/ODIHR election observation team was dispatched in May to monitor local elections conducted in the following month; in Sept. an agreement was concluded to restart official talks between the political leaders within the 5+2 framework, which were then initiated, at a meeting in Vilnius, Lithuania, in Nov.; formal meetings (concerned with the principles and procedures for the negotiating process) were subsequently convened in Dublin, Ireland, in Feb. 2012, and in Vienna, Austria, in April; in Rottach-Egern, Germany, in June; and a further meeting was to be held in July, again in Vienna; Mission offices opened in Tiraspol, in Feb. 1995, and in Bender, in May 2003; Head of Mission JENNIFER LEIGH BRUSH (USA).

OSCE Office in Baku: 1005 Baku, Nizami küç 96, The Landmark III, Azerbaijan; tel. (12) 497-23-73; fax (12) 497-23-77; e-mail office-az@osce.org; internet www.osce.org/baku/; f. Nov. 1999 (began operations in July 2000) to undertake activities concerned with democratization, human rights, economy and the environment, and media; supports a police assistance programme, including a police training school; supports the training of legal professionals and monitors court proceedings and conditions in prisons; during 2010 the Office worked to secure democratic principles in the preparation of legislative elections, held in Nov., including initiatives to promote political dialogue, media impartiality, and public confidence in the electoral process; workshops and seminars organized by the Office in the first half of 2012 were concerned with community policing, countering money laundering and financing of terrorism, training detention facility officers, and the prevention of domestic violence; Head of Office KORAY TARGAY (Turkey).

OSCE Office in Tajikistan: 734017 Dushanbe, Zikrullo Khojaev 12, Tajikistan; tel. (372) 24-33-38; fax (372) 24-91-59; e-mail cid-tj@osce.org; internet www.osce.org/tajikistan/; f. June 2008, as successor to the OSCE Centre in Dushanbe, with an expanded mandate to support the country in efforts to promote the implementation of OSCE principles and commitments, to maintain peace and security, to counter crime, to undertake economic and environmental activities and to develop democratic political and legal institutions, incorporating respect for human rights; a Task Force Meeting, comprising OSCE officials, and representatives of the Tajik Government and civil society, convenes annually to consider the strategic partnership between the OSCE and Tajikistan; the Office implements a Mine Action Programme, initiated in 2004, and in April 2010 inaugurated a new integrated landmine clearance project along the border with Afghanistan; the Office supported the establishment of a human rights ombudsman, and hosts monthly inter-agency human rights sector meetings and an annual Human Dimension Implementation Meeting, attended by representatives of Government and civil society; a counter-terrorism and police unit assists the local law enforcement agencies to combat organized crime, including drugs-trafficking, and terrorism; in May 2009 an OSCE Border Management Staff College (BMSC) was established in Dushanbe to train border security managers and to promote co-operation between OSCE member states and partner countries; in April 2012 the BMSC organized a training course on the implementation of UN Security Council Resolution 1540 concerning the non-proliferation of weapons of mass destruction; in March 2010 the Office signed a Memorandum of Understanding with Tajikistan's Ministry of Economic Development and Trade establishing a Co-ordination Council on Free Economic Zones; the Office facilitates a Dialogue on Human Trafficking, which during 2010, developed a National Action Plan to Combat Human Trafficking; in Sept. 2011 the Office conducted a training course for election observers; Head of Office IVAR VIKKI (Norway).

OSCE Office in Yerevan: 0009 Yerevan, ul. Terian 89, Armenia; tel. (10) 54-58-45; fax (10) 54-10-61; e-mail yerevan-am@osce.org; internet www.osce.org/yerevan/; f. July 1999 (began operations in Feb. 2000); the Office works independently of the Minsk Group to promote OSCE principles within the country in order to support political and economic stability, the development of democratic institutions and the strengthening of civil society; a police assistance programme was initiated in 2004, which oversaw the renovation of a police training centre; promotes awareness of human rights, assists the Human Rights Defender's Office and supports Public Monitoring Groups concerned with detention centres; other areas of activity concern legislative reform and good governance, freedom of the media, gender issues and counter-terrorism and money-laundering; in May 2009 the Office, with other partners, organized a high-level forum concerned with discussing Armenian economic policy and addressing the local impact of the global financial crisis; during 2011 the Office, *inter alia*, supported electoral reform, the development of a new criminal procedure code, upholding human rights in the armed forces, and the process of transferring to digital broadcasting; in March 2012 the Head of Office signed a Memorandum of Understanding with Yerevan State University on establishing a Sustainable Development Centre within the University, to support Armenia in implementing UN declarations on sustainable development; Head of Office ANDREY SOROKIN (Russia).

OSCE Project Co-ordinator in Ukraine: 01054 Kyiv, vul. Striletska 16; tel. (44) 492-03-82; fax (44) 492-03-83; internet www.osce.org/ukraine/; f. June 1999, as a successor to the OSCE Mission to Ukraine (which had been established in Nov. 1994); responsible for pursuing co-operation between Ukraine and the OSCE and providing technical assistance in areas including legal and electoral reform, freedom of the media, trafficking in human beings, and the work of the human rights Ombudsman; the Project Co-ordinator has developed a Cross-Dimensional Economic-Environmental/Politico-Military Programme, in co-operation with the Ukrainian authorities, in support of the country's objectives of closer integration into European structures; the Programme incorporates activities such as strengthening border security, enhancing national capacity to combat illegal trans-boundary transportation of hazardous waste, promoting the sustainable management of the Dniestr River basin, and supporting the retraining and integration into civil society of military personnel; a new draft unified Election Code, developed with the support of the Project Co-ordinator, was presented to the Ukrainian parliament in April 2010; convenes an annual round-table meeting (most recently in Dec. 2011) aimed at promoting joint efforts in combating human trafficking between the Ukrainian authorities and diplomatic missions based in Kyiv; Project Co-ordinator LUBOMÍR KOPAJ (Slovakia).

OSCE Project Co-ordinator in Uzbekistan: 100000 Tashkent, Afrosiab ko'ch 12B, 4th Floor; tel. (71) 140-04-70; fax (71) 140-04-66; e-mail osce-cit@osce.org; internet www.osce.org/tashkent/; f. July 2006; works to assist the Government to uphold security and stability, to strengthen socio-economic development and protection of the environment, and to implement other OSCE principles; in Feb. 2011 the Project Co-ordinator formally provided the Uzbek authorities with equipment to implement improvements to the national passport system; training courses and seminars organized by the Project Co-ordinator in the first half of 2012 were concerned with the development of entrepreneurship, efforts to eliminate trafficking in human beings, combating the illegal trade in narcotics, access to information, and building ministerial press services; Project Co-ordinator GYÖRGY SZABÓ (Hungary).

Personal Representative of the OSCE Chairperson-in-Office on the Conflict Dealt with by the OSCE Minsk Conference (Nagornyi Karabakh): Tbilisi, Zovreti 15, Georgia; tel. (32) 37-61-61; fax (32) 98-85-66; e-mail persrep@access.sanet.ge; appointed in August 1995 to represent the CiO in the 11-nation Minsk Group process concerned with the conflict between Armenia and Azerbaijan in relation to the Nagornyi Karabakh region; in 2005–06 the Minsk Group undertook intensive negotiations to formulate a set of basic principles for a peaceful settlement of the conflict, including proposals for the redeployment of Armenian troops, demilitarization of formally occupied territories and a popular referendum to determine the final legal status of the region; in Nov. 2007 the Co-Chairs of the Minsk Group presented a Document of Basic Principles for the Peaceful Settlement of the Nagornyi Karabakh Conflict, which has been the basis of subsequent discussions with both sides; in Sept. 2011 the Minsk Group Co-Chairs announced a work plan focused on delineating ongoing differences concerning the basic principles; and drafting additional measures aimed at strengthening implementation of the cease-fire implemented since May 1994 in Nagornyi Karabakh; the Personal Representative is mandated to assist a High Level Planning Group, which was established in Vienna, Austria, to develop a plan for a multinational OSCE peace-keeping operation in the disputed region; Field Assistants of the Personal Representative have been deployed to Baku, Yerevan and Stepanakert/Khankendi; Personal Rep. ANDRZEJ KASPRZYK (Poland).

Finance

All activities of the institutions, negotiations, ad hoc meetings and missions are financed by contributions from member states. The unified budget for 2012 amounted to €148.1m.

Publications

Annual Report of the Secretary-General.

The Caucasus: In Defence of the Future.

Decision Manual (annually).

OSCE Handbook.

OSCE Highlights (regular electronic newsletter).

OSCE Newsletter (quarterly, in English and Russian).

Factsheets on OSCE missions, institutions and other structures are published regularly.

Summary of the Final Act of the Helsinki Conference on Security and Co-operation in Europe

(1 August 1975)

Note: The substantive articles relating to defence and security in Europe are contained in the first part of the Final Act. Other chapters incorporate provisions relating to Co-operation in the field of economics, science and technology, and the environment, Questions relating to security and co-operation in the Mediterranean, and Co-operation in humanitarian and other fields (including human contacts, information, culture and education).

Motivated by the political will, in the interest of peoples, to improve and intensify their relations and to contribute in Europe to peace, security, justice and co-operation as well as to rapprochement among themselves and with the other States of the world;

Determined, in consequence, to give full effect to the results of the Conference and to assure, among their States and throughout Europe, the benefits deriving from those results and thus to broaden, deepen and make continuing and lasting the process of détente;

The High Representatives of the participating States have solemnly adopted the following:

QUESTIONS RELATING TO SECURITY IN EUROPE

The States participating in the Conference on Security and Co-operation in Europe

Reaffirming their objective of promoting better relations among themselves and ensuring conditions in which their people can live in true and lasting peace free from any threat to or attempt against their security;

Convinced of the need to exert efforts to make détente both a continuing and an increasingly viable and comprehensive process, universal in scope, and that the implementation of the results of the Conference on Security and Co-operation in Europe will be a major contribution to this process;

Considering that solidarity among peoples, as well as the common purpose of the participating States in achieving the aims as set forth by the Conference on Security and Co-operation in Europe, should lead to the development of better and closer relations among them in all fields and thus to overcoming the confrontation stemming from the character of their past relations, and to better mutual understanding;

Mindful of their common history and recognizing that the existence of elements common to their traditions and values can assist them in developing their relations, and desiring to search, fully taking into account the individuality and diversity of their positions and views, for possibilities of joining their efforts with a view to overcoming distrust and increasing confidence, solving the problems that separate them and co-operating in the interest of mankind;

Recognizing the indivisibility of security in Europe as well as their common interest in the development of co-operation throughout Europe and among selves and expressing their intention to pursue efforts accordingly;

Recognizing the close link between peace and security in Europe and in the world as a whole and conscious of the need for each of them to make its contribution to the strengthening of world peace and security and to the promotion of fundamental rights, economic and social progress and well-being for all peoples;

Have adopted the following:

1. (a) Declaration on Principles Guiding Relations between Participating States

The participating States

Reaffirming their commitment to peace, security and justice and the continuing development of friendly relations and co-operation;

Declare their determination to respect and put into practice, each of them in its relations with all other participating States, irrespective of their political, economic or social systems as well as of their size, geographical location or level of economic development, the following principles, which all are of primary significance, guiding their mutual relations:

I. Sovereign equality, respect for the rights inherent in sovereignty.

The participating States will respect each other's sovereign equality and individuality as well as all the rights inherent in and encompassed by its sovereignty, including in particular the right of every State to juridical equality, to territorial integrity and to freedom and political independence. They will also respect each other's right freely to choose and develop its political, social, economic and cultural systems as well as its right to determine its laws and regulations.

Within the framework of international law, all the participating States have equal rights and duties. They will respect each other's right to define and conduct as it wishes its relations with other States in accordance with international law and in the spirit of the present Declaration. They consider that their frontiers can be changed, in accordance with international law, by peaceful means and by agreement. They also have the right to belong or not to belong to international organizations, to be or not to be a party to bilateral or multilateral treaties including the right to be or not to be a party to treaties of alliance; they also have the right to neutrality.

II. Refraining from the threat or use of force.

The participating States will refrain in their mutual relations, as well as in their international relations in general, from the threat or use of force against the territorial integrity or political independence of any State, or in any other manner inconsistent with the purposes of the United Nations and with the present Declaration. No consideration may be invoked to serve to warrant resort to the threat or use of force in contravention of this principle.

Accordingly, the participating States will refrain from any acts constituting a threat of force or direct or indirect use of force against another participating State.

Likewise they will refrain from any manifestation of force for the purpose of inducing another participating State to renounce the full exercise of its sovereign right. Likewise they will also refrain in their mutual relations from any act of reprisal by force.

No such threat or use of force will be employed as a means of settling disputes, or questions likely to give rise to disputes, between them.

III. Inviolability of frontiers.

The participating States regard as inviolable all one another's frontiers as well as the frontiers of all States in Europe and therefore they will refrain now and in the future from assaulting these frontiers.

Accordingly, they will also refrain from any demand for, or act of, seizure and usurpation of part or all of the territory of any participating State.

IV. Territorial integrity of States.

The participating States will respect the territorial integrity of each of the participating States.

Accordingly, they will refrain from any action inconsistent with the purposes and principles of the Charter of the United Nations against the territorial integrity, political independence or the unity of any participating State, and in particular from any such action constituting a threat or use of force.

The participating States will likewise refrain from making each other's territory the object of military occupation or other direct or indirect measures of force in contravention of international law, or the object of acquisition by means of such measures or the threat of them. No such occupation or acquisition will be recognized as legal.

V. Peaceful settlement of disputes.

The participating States will settle disputes among them by peaceful means in such a manner as not to endanger international peace and security, and justice.

They will endeavour in good faith and a spirit of co-operation to reach a rapid and equitable solution on the basis of international law.

For this purpose they will use such means as negotiation, enquiry, mediation, conciliation, arbitration, judicial settlement or other peaceful means of their own choice including any settlement procedure agreed to in advance of disputes to which they are parties.

In the event of failure to reach a solution by any of the above peaceful means, the parties to a dispute will continue to seek a mutually agreed way to settle the dispute peacefully.

Participating States, parties to a dispute among them, as well as other participating States, will refrain from any action which might aggravate the situation to such a degree as to endanger the maintenance of international peace and security and thereby make a peaceful settlement of the dispute more difficult.

VI. Non-intervention in internal affairs.

The participating States will refrain from any intervention, direct or indirect, individual or collective, in the internal or external affairs falling within the domestic jurisdiction of another participating State, regardless of their mutual relations.

They will accordingly refrain from any form of armed intervention or threat of such intervention against another participating State.

They will likewise in all circumstances refrain from any other act of military, or of political, economic or other coercion designed to subordinate to their own interest the exercise by another participating State of the rights inherent in its sovereignty and thus to secure advantages of any kind.

Accordingly, they will, *inter alia*, refrain from direct or indirect assistance to terrorist activities, or to subversive or other activities directed towards the violent overthrow of the regime of another participating State.

VII. Respect for human rights and fundamental freedoms, including the freedom of thought, conscience, religion or belief.

The participating States will respect human rights and fundamental freedoms, including the freedom of thought, conscience, religion or belief, for all without distinction as to race, sex, language or religion.

They will promote and encourage the effective exercise of civil, political, economic, social, cultural and other rights and freedoms all of which derive from the inherent dignity of the human person and are essential for his free and full development.

Within this framework the participating States will recognize and respect the freedom of the individual to profess and practice, alone or in community with others, religion or belief acting in accordance with the dictates of his own conscience.

The participating States on whose territory national minorities exist will respect the right of persons belonging to such minorities to equality before the law, will afford them the full opportunity for the actual enjoyment of human rights and fundamental freedoms and will, in this manner, protect their legitimate interests in this sphere.

The participating States recognize the universal significance of human rights and fundamental freedoms, respect for which is an essential factor for the peace, justice and well-being necessary to ensure the development of friendly relations and co-operation among themselves as among all States.

They will constantly respect these rights and freedoms in their mutual relations and will endeavour jointly and separately, including in co-operation with the United Nations, to promote universal and effective respect for them.

They confirm the right of the individual to know and act upon his rights and duties in this field.

In the field of human rights and fundamental freedoms, the participating State will act in conformity with the purposes and principles of the Charter of the United Nations and with the Universal Declaration of Human Rights. They will also fulfil their obligations as set forth in the international declarations and agreements in this field, including, *inter alia*, the International Covenants on Human Rights, by which they may be bound.

VIII. Equal rights and self-determination of peoples.

The participating States will respect the equal rights of peoples and their right to self-determination, acting at all times in conformity with the purposes and principles of the Charter of the United Nations and with the relevant norms of international law, including those relating to territorial integrity of states.

By virtue of the principle of equal rights and self-determination of peoples, all peoples always have the right, in full freedom, to determine, when and as they wish, their internal and external political status, without external interference, and to pursue as they wish their political, economic, social and cultural development.

The participating States reaffirm the universal significance of respect for and effective exercise of equal rights and self-determination of peoples for the development of friendly relations among themselves as among all States; they also recall the importance of the elimination of any form of violation of this principle.

IX. Co-operation among States.

The participating States will develop their co-operation with one another and with all States in all fields in accordance with the purposes and principles of the Charter of the United Nations. In developing their co-operation the participating States will place special emphasis on the fields as set forth within the framework of the Conference on Security and Co-operation in Europe, with each of them making its contribution in conditions of full equality.

They will endeavour, in developing their co-operation as equals, to promote mutual understanding and confidence, friendly and good-neighbourly relations among themselves, international peace, security and justice. They will equally endeavour, in developing their co-operation, to improve the well-being of peoples and contribute to the fulfilment of their aspirations through, *inter alia*, the benefits resulting from increased mutual knowledge and from progress and achievement in the economic, scientific, technological, social, cultural and humanitarian fields. They will take steps to promote conditions favourable to making these benefits available to all; they will take into account the interest of all in the narrowing of differences in the levels of economic development, and in particular the interest of developing countries throughout the world.

They confirm that governments, institutions, organizations and persons have a relevant and positive role to play in contributing toward the achievement of these aims of their co-operation.

They will strive, in increasing their co-operation as set forth above, to develop closer relations among themselves on an improved and more enduring basis for the benefit of peoples.

X. Fulfilment in good faith of obligations under international law.

The participating States will fulfil in good faith their obligations under international law, both those obligations arising from the generally recognized principles and rules of international law and those obligations arising from treaties or other agreements, in conformity with international law, to which they are parties.

In exercising their sovereign rights, including the right to determine their laws and regulations, they will conform, with their legal obligations under international law; they will furthermore pay due regard to and implement the provisions in the Final Act of the Conference on Security and Co-operation in Europe.

The participating States confirm that in the event of a conflict between the obligations of the members of the United Nations under the Charter of the United Nations and their obligations under any treaty or other international agreement, their obligations under the Charter will prevail, in accordance with Article 103 of the Charter of the United Nations.

All the principles set forth above are of primary significance and, accordingly, they will be equally and unreservedly applied, each of them being interpreted taking into account the others.

The participating States express their determination fully to respect and apply these principles, as set forth in the present Declaration, in all aspects, to their mutual relations and co-operation in order to ensure to each participating State the benefits resulting from the respect and application of these principles by all.

The participating States, paying due regard to the principles above and, in particular, to the first sentence of the tenth principle, 'Fulfilment in good faith of obligations under international law', note that the present Declaration does not affect their rights and obligations, nor the corresponding treaties and other agreements and arrangements.

The participating States express the conviction that respect for these principles will encourage the development of normal and friendly relations and the progress of co-operation among them in all fields. They also express the conviction that respect for these principles will encourage the development of political contacts among them which in time would contribute to better mutual understanding of their positions and views.

The participating States declare their intention to conduct their relations with all other States in the spirit of the principles contained in the present Declaration.

1. (b) Matters related to giving effect to certain of the above Principles

(i) The participating States:

Reaffirming that they will respect and give effect to refraining from the threat or use of force and convinced of the necessity to make it an effective norm of international life;

Declare that they are resolved to respect and carry out, in their relations with one another, *inter alia*, the following provisions which are in conformity with the Declaration on Principles Guiding Relations between Participating States:

To give effect and expression, by all the ways and forms which they consider appropriate, to the duty to refrain from the threat or use of force in their relations with one another.

To refrain from any use of armed forces inconsistent with the purposes and principles of the Charter of the United Nations and the provisions of the Declaration on Principles Guiding Relations between Participating States, against another participating State, in particular from invasion of or attack on its territory.

To refrain from any manifestation of force for the purpose of inducing another participating State to renounce the full exercise of its sovereign rights.

To refrain from any act of economic coercion designed to subordinate to their own interest the exercise by another participating State of the rights inherent in its sovereignty and thus to secure advantages of any kind.

To take effective measures which by their scope and by their nature constitute steps towards the ultimate achievement of general and complete disarmament under strict and effective international control.

To promote, by all means which each of them considers appropriate, a climate of confidence and respect among peoples consonant with their duty to refrain from propaganda for wars of aggression or for any threat or use of force inconsistent with the purposes of the United Nations and with the Declaration on Principles Guiding Relations between Participating States, against another participating State.

To make every effort to settle exclusively by peaceful means any dispute between them, the continuance of which is likely to endanger the maintenance of international peace and security in Europe, and to seek, first of all, a solution through the peaceful means set forth in Article 33 of the United Nations Charter.

To refrain from any action which could hinder the peaceful settlement of disputes between the participating States.

(ii) The participating States:

Reaffirming their determination to settle their disputes as set forth in the Principle of Peaceful Settlement of Disputes;

Convinced that the peaceful settlement of disputes is a complement to refraining from the threat or use of force, both being essential though not exclusive factors for the maintenance and consolidation of peace and security;

Desiring to reinforce and to improve the methods at their disposal for the peaceful settlement of disputes;

1. Are resolved to pursue the examination and elaboration of a generally acceptable method for the peaceful settlement of disputes aimed at complementing existing methods, and to continue to this end to work upon the 'Draft Convention on a European System for the Peaceful Settlement of Disputes' submitted by Switzerland during the second stage of the Conference on Security and Co-operation in Europe, as well as other proposals relating to it and directed towards the elaboration of such a method.

2. Decide that, on the invitation of Switzerland, a meeting of experts of all the participating States will be convoked in order to fulfil the mandate described in paragraph 1 above within the framework and under the procedures of the follow-up to the Conference laid down in the chapter 'Follow-up to the Conference'.

3. This meeting of experts will take place after the meeting of the representatives appointed by the Ministers of Foreign Affairs of the participating States, scheduled according to the chapter 'Follow-up to the Conference' for 1977; the results of the work of this meeting of experts will be submitted to Governments.

2. Document on confidence-building measures and certain aspects of security and disarmament

The participating States:

Desirous of eliminating the causes of tension that may exist among them and thus of contributing to the strengthening of peace and security in the world;

Determined to strengthen confidence among them and thus to contribute to increasing stability and security in Europe;

Determined further to refrain in their mutual relations, as well as in their international relations in general, from the threat or use of force against the territorial integrity or political independence of any State, or in any other manner inconsistent with the purposes of the United Nations and with the Declaration on Principles Guiding Relations between Participating States as adopted in this Final Act;

Recognizing the need to contribute to reducing the dangers of armed conflict and of misunderstanding or miscalculation of military activities which could give rise to apprehension, particularly in a situation where the participating States lack clear and timely information about the nature of such activities;

Taking into account considerations relevant to efforts aimed at lessening tension and promoting disarmament;

Recognizing that the exchange of observers by invitation at military manoeuvres will help to promote contacts and mutual understanding;

Having studied the question of prior notification of major military movements in the context of confidence-building;

Recognizing that there are other ways in which individual States can contribute further to their common objectives;

Convinced of the political importance of prior notification of major military manoeuvres for the promotion of mutual understanding and the strengthening of confidence, stability and security;

Accepting the responsibility of each of them to promote these objectives and to implement this measure, in accordance with the accepted criteria and modalities, as essentials for the realization of these objectives;

Recognizing that this measure deriving from political decision rests upon a voluntary basis;

Have adopted the following:

I. Prior notification of major military manoeuvres.

They will notify their major military manoeuvres to all other participating States through usual diplomatic channels in accordance with the following provisions:

Notification will be given of major military manoeuvres exceeding a total of 25,000 troops, independently or combined with any possible air or naval components (in this context the word 'troops' includes amphibious and airborne troops). In the case of independent manoeuvres of amphibious or airborne troops, or of combined manoeuvres involving them, these troops will be included in this total. Furthermore, in the case of combined manoeuvres which do not reach the above total but which involve land forces together with significant numbers of either amphibious or airborne troops, or both, notification can also be given.

Notification will be given of major military manoeuvres which take place on the territory, in Europe, of any participating State as well as, if applicable, in the adjoining sea area and air space.

In the case of a participating State whose territory extends beyond Europe, prior notification need be given only of manoeuvres which take place in an area within 250km from its frontier facing or shared with any other European participating State, the participating State need not, however, give notification in cases in which that area is also contiguous to the participating State's frontier facing or shared with a non-European non-participating State.

Notification will be given 21 days or more in advance of the start of the manoeuvre or in the case of a manoeuvre arranged at shorter notice at the earliest possible opportunity prior to its starting date.

Notification will contain information of the designation, if any, the general purpose of and the States involved in the manoeuvre, the type or types and numerical strength of the forces engaged, the area and estimated time-frame of its conduct. The participating States will also, if possible, provide additional relevant information, particularly that related to the components of the forces engaged and the period of involvement of these form.

Prior notification of other military manoeuvres.

The participating States recognize that they can contribute further to strengthening confidence and increasing security and stability, and to this end may also notify smaller-scale military manoeuvres to other participating States, with special regard for those near the area of such manoeuvres.

To the same end, the participating States also recognize that they may notify other military manoeuvres conducted by them.

Exchange of observers.

The participating States will invite other participating States, voluntarily and on a bilateral basis, in a spirit of reciprocity and goodwill towards all participating States, to send observers to attend military manoeuvres.

The inviting State will determine in each case the number of observers, the procedures and conditions of their participation, and give other information which it may consider useful. It will provide appropriate facilities and hospitality.

The invitation will be given as far ahead as is conveniently possible through usual diplomatic channels.

Prior notification of major military movements.

In accordance with the Final Recommendations of the Helsinki Consultations the participating States studied the question of prior-notification of major military movements as a measure to strengthen confidence.

Accordingly, the participating States recognize that they may, at their own discretion and with a view to contributing to confidence-building, notify their major military movements.

In the same spirit, further consideration will be given by the States participating in the Conference on Security and Co-operation in Europe to the question of prior notification of major military movements, bearing in mind, in particular, the experience gained by the implementation of the measures which are set forth in this document.

Other confidence-building measures.

The participating States recognize that there are other means by which their common objectives can be promoted.

In particular, they will, with due regard to reciprocity and with a view to better mutual understanding, promote exchanges by invitation among their military delegations.

In order to make a fuller contribution to their common objective of confidence-building, the participating States, when conducting their military activities in the area covered by the provisions for the prior notification of major military manoeuvres, will duly take into account and respect this objective.

They also recognize that the experience gained by the implementation of the provisions set forth above, together with further efforts, could lead to developing and enlarging measures aimed at strengthening confidence.

II. Questions relating to disarmament.

The participating States recognize the interest of all of them in efforts aimed at lessening military confrontation and promoting disarmament which are designed to complement political détente in Europe and to strengthen their security. They are convinced of the necessity to take effective measures in these fields which by their scope and by their nature constitute steps towards the ultimate achievement of general and complete disarmament under strict and effective international control, and which should result in strengthening peace and security throughout the world.

III. General considerations.

Having considered the views expressed on various subjects related to the strengthening of security in Europe through joint efforts aimed at promoting détente and disarmament, the participating States, when engaged in such efforts, will, in this context, proceed, in particular, from the following essential considerations:

The complementary nature of the political and military aspects of security;

The interrelation between the security of each participating State and security in Europe as a whole and the relationship which exists, in the broader context of world security, between security in Europe and security in the Mediterranean area;

Respect for the security interests of all States participating in the Conference on Security and Co-operation in Europe inherent in their sovereign equality;

The importance that participants in negotiating fora see to it that information about relevant developments, progress and results is provided on an appropriate basis to other States participating in the Conference on Security and Co-operation in Europe and, in return, the justified interest of any of those States in having their views considered.

Lisbon Declaration on a Common and Comprehensive Security Model for Europe for the Twenty-first Century

(December 1996)

1. We, the Heads of State or Government of the States participating in the OSCE and meeting in Lisbon, believe that history has offered us an unprecedented opportunity. Freedom, democracy and co-operation among our nations and peoples are now the foundation for our common security. We are determined to learn from the tragedies of the past and to translate our vision of a co-operative future into reality by creating a common security space free of dividing lines in which all States are equal partners.

2. We face serious challenges, but we face them together. They concern the security and sovereignty of States as well as the stability of our societies. Human rights are not fully respected in all OSCE States. Ethnic tension, aggressive nationalism, violations of the rights of persons belonging to national minorities, as well as serious difficulties of economic transition, can threaten stability and may also spread to other States. Terrorism, organized crime, drug and arms trafficking, uncontrolled migration and environmental damage are of increasing concern to the entire OSCE community.

3. Drawing strength from our diversity, we shall meet these challenges together, through the OSCE and in partnership with other international organizations. Our approach is one of co-operative security based on democracy, respect for human rights, fundamental freedoms and the rule of law, market economy and social justice. It excludes any quest for domination. It implies mutual confidence and the peaceful settlement of disputes.

4. The OSCE plays a central role in achieving our goal of a common security space. Its fundamental elements—the comprehensiveness and indivisibility of security and the allegiance to shared values, commitments and norms of behaviour—inspire our vision of empowering governments and individuals to build a better and more secure future.

5. We recognize that, within the OSCE, States are accountable to their citizens and responsible to each other for their implementation of OSCE commitments.

6. We jointly commit ourselves:

to act in solidarity to promote full implementation of the principles and commitments of the OSCE enshrined in the Helsinki Final Act, the Charter of Paris and other CSCE/OSCE documents;

to consult promptly—in conformity with our OSCE responsibilities and making full use of the OSCE's procedures and instruments—with a participating State whose security is threatened and to consider jointly actions that may have to be undertaken in defence of our common values;

not to support participating States that threaten or use force in violation of international law against the territorial integrity or political independence of any participating State;

to attach importance to security concerns of all participating States irrespective of whether they belong to military structures or arrangements.

7. We reaffirm the inherent right of each and every participating State to be free to choose or change its security arrangements, including treaties of alliance, as they evolve. Each participating State will respect the rights of all others in this regard. They will not strengthen their security at the expense of the security of other States. Within the OSCE, no State, organization or grouping can have any superior responsibility for maintaining peace and stability in the OSCE region, or regard any part of the OSCE region as its sphere of influence.

8. We shall ensure that the presence of foreign troops on the territory of a participating State is in conformity with international law, the freely expressed consent of the host State, or a relevant decision of the United Nations Security Council.

9. We are committed to transparency in our actions and in our relations with one another. All our States participating in security arrangements will take into consideration that such arrangements should be of a public nature, predictable and open, and should correspond to the needs of individual and collective security. These arrangements must not infringe upon the sovereign rights of other States and will take into account their legitimate security concerns.

We may use the OSCE as a repository for declarations and agreements in regard to our security arrangements.

10. Based on these foundations, our task now is to enhance our co-operation for the future. To this end:

We encourage bilateral or regional initiatives aimed at developing relations of good neighbourliness and co-operation. In this context, the OSCE could explore a menu of confidence- and security-building measures in support of regional security processes. We shall continue to follow the implementation of the Pact on Stability in Europe. Regional round tables can be a useful means of preventive diplomacy.

As an important contribution to security we reaffirm our determination to fully respect and implement all our commitments relating to the rights of persons belonging to national minorities. We reaffirm our will to co-operate fully with the High Commissioner on National Minorities. We are ready to respond to a request by any participating State seeking solutions to minority issues on its territory.

We value our co-operation with regions adjacent to the OSCE region, giving particular attention to the Mediterranean area.

We commit ourselves to the continuation of the arms control process as a central security issue in the OSCE region.

The further strengthening of stability through conventional arms control will be decisive for future European security. We reaffirm the importance of the CFE Treaty and welcome the decision of the CFE States Parties to adapt it to a changing security environment in Europe so as to contribute to common and indivisible security.

We welcome the decisions on the 'Framework for Arms Control' and on the 'Development of the Agenda of the Forum for Security Co-operation' adopted by the Forum for Security Co-operation. We are determined to make further efforts in this Forum in order to jointly address common security concerns of participating States and to pursue the OSCE's comprehensive and co-operative concept of indivisible security.

In this context, we reaffirm that we shall maintain only such military capabilities as are commensurate with individual or collective legitimate security needs, taking into account rights and obligations under international law. We shall determine our military capabilities on the basis of national democratic procedures, in a transparent manner, bearing in mind the legitimate security concerns of other States as well as the need to contribute to international security and stability.

We reaffirm that European security requires the widest co-operation and co-ordination among participating States and European and transatlantic organizations. The OSCE is the inclusive and comprehensive organization for consultation, decision-making and co-operation in its region and a regional arrangement under Chapter VIII of the United Nations Charter. As such it is particularly well suited as a forum to enhance co-operation and complementarity among such organizations and institutions. The OSCE will act in partnership with them, in order to respond effectively to threats and challenges in its area.

In exceptional circumstances the participating States may jointly decide to refer a matter to the United Nations Security Council on behalf of the OSCE whenever, in their judgement, action by the Security Council may be required under the relevant provision of Chapter VII of the Charter of the United Nations.

The OSCE will strengthen co-operation with other security organizations which are transparent and predictable in their actions, whose members individually and collectively adhere to

OSCE principles and commitments, and whose membership is based on open and voluntary commitments.

11. Our work on the Security Model is well under way and will actively continue. We instruct our representatives to work energetically on the Security Model and invite the Chairperson-in-Office to report to the next Ministerial Council in Copenhagen. The agenda for their work will include the following:

continuing review of the observance of OSCE principles and implementation of commitments to ensure progress toward the goals of the OSCE and towards the work outlined in this agenda;

enhancing instruments of joint co-operative action within the OSCE framework in the event of non-compliance with the OSCE commitments by a participating State;

defining in a Platform for Co-operative Security modalities for co-operation between the OSCE and other security organizations as set out above;

based on the experience of OSCE instruments for preventive diplomacy and conflict prevention, refining the existing tools and developing additional ones in order to encourage participating States to make greater use of the OSCE in advancing their security;

enhancing co-operation among participating States to develop further the concepts and principles included in this Declaration and to improve our ability to meet specific risks and challenges to security;

recommending any new commitments, structures or arrangements within the OSCE framework which would reinforce security and stability in Europe.

Drawing on this work, remaining committed to the Helsinki Final Act and recalling the Charter of Paris, we will consider developing a Charter on European Security which can serve the needs of our peoples in the new century.

12. Our goal is to transform our search for greater security into a mutual effort to achieve the aspirations and improve the lives of all our citizens. This quest, grounded in pragmatic achievements as well as ideals, will draw on the flexible and dynamic nature of the OSCE and its central role in ensuring security and stability.

ORGANIZATION OF AMERICAN STATES—OAS

(ORGANIZACIÓN DE LOS ESTADOS AMERICANOS—OEA)

Address: 17th St and Constitution Ave, NW, Washington, DC 20006, USA.

Telephone: (202) 458-3000; **fax:** (202) 458-6319; **e-mail:** pi@oas.org; **internet:** www.oas.org.

The ninth International Conference of American States (held in Bogotá, Colombia, in 1948) adopted the Charter of the Organization of American States; the OAS succeeded the Commercial Bureau of American Republics, founded in 1890, and the Pan-American Union. The Charter was subsequently amended by the Protocol of Buenos Aires (creating the annual General Assembly), signed in 1967 and enacted in 1970; by the Protocol of Cartagena de Indias, which was signed in 1985 and enacted in 1988; and by the Protocol of Washington, signed in 1992 and enacted in 1997. The purpose of the OAS is to strengthen the peace and security of the continent; to promote human rights and to promote and consolidate representative democracy, with due respect for the principle of non-intervention; to prevent possible causes of difficulties and to ensure the peaceful settlement of disputes that may arise among the member states; to provide for common action in the event of aggression; to seek the solution of political, juridical and economic problems that may arise among the member states; to promote, by co-operative action, their economic, social and cultural development; to achieve an effective limitation of conventional weapons; to devote the largest amount of resources to the economic and social development of the member states; and to confront shared problems such as poverty, terrorism, the trade in illegal drugs, and corruption. The OAS is the principal regional multilateral forum. It plays a leading role in implementing mandates established by the hemisphere's leaders through the Summits of the Americas.

MEMBERS

Antigua and Barbuda	Guyana
Argentina	Haiti
Bahamas	Honduras
Barbados	Jamaica
Belize	Mexico
Bolivia	Nicaragua
Brazil	Panama
Canada	Paraguay
Chile	Peru
Colombia	Saint Christopher and Nevis
Costa Rica	Saint Lucia
Cuba*	Saint Vincent and the Grenadines
Dominica	Suriname
Dominican Republic	Trinidad and Tobago
Ecuador	USA
El Salvador	Uruguay
Grenada	Venezuela
Guatemala	

* The Cuban Government was suspended from OAS activities in 1962; the suspension was revoked by the OAS General Assembly in June 2009, although Cuba's participation in the organization was to be subject to further review.

Permanent Observers: Albania, Algeria, Angola, Armenia, Austria, Azerbaijan, Belgium, Benin, Bosnia and Herzegovina, Bulgaria, People's Republic of China, Croatia, Cyprus, Czech Republic, Denmark, Egypt, Equatorial Guinea, Estonia, Finland, France, Georgia, Germany, Ghana, Greece, Holy See, Hungary, Iceland, India, Ireland, Israel, Italy, Japan, Kazakhstan, Republic of Korea, Latvia, Lebanon, Lithuania, Luxembourg, Monaco, Morocco, Netherlands, Nigeria, Norway, Pakistan, Philippines, Poland, Portugal, Qatar, Romania, Russia, Saudi Arabia, Serbia, Slovakia, Slovenia, Spain, Sri Lanka, Sweden, Switzerland, Thailand, Tunisia, Turkey, Ukraine, United Kingdom, Yemen and the European Union.

Organization

(June 2012)

GENERAL ASSEMBLY

The Assembly meets annually and may also hold special sessions when convoked by the Permanent Council. As the highest decision-making body of the OAS, it decides general action and policy. The 42nd General Assembly was held in Cochabamba, Bolivia, in June 2012.

MEETINGS OF CONSULTATION OF MINISTERS OF FOREIGN AFFAIRS

Meetings are convened, at the request of any member state, to consider problems of an urgent nature and of common interest to member states, or to serve as an organ of consultation in cases of armed attack or other threats to international peace and security. The Permanent Council determines whether a meeting should be convened and acts as a provisional organ of consultation until ministers are able to assemble.

PERMANENT COUNCIL

The Council meets regularly throughout the year at OAS headquarters. It is composed of one representative of each member state with the rank of ambassador; each government may accredit alternate representatives and advisers and when necessary appoint an interim representative. The office of Chairman is held in turn by each of the representatives, following alphabetical order according to the names of the countries in Spanish. The Vice-Chairman is determined in the same way, following reverse alphabetical order. Their terms of office are three months.

The Council guides ongoing policies and actions and oversees the maintenance of friendly relations between members. It supervises the work of the OAS and promotes co-operation with a variety of other international bodies including the United Nations. It comprises a General Committee and Committees on Juridical and Political Affairs, Hemispheric Security, Inter-American Summits Management and Civil Society Participation in OAS Activities, and Administrative and Budgetary Affairs. There are also ad hoc working groups. The official languages are English, French, Portuguese and Spanish.

In January 2012 the Secretary-General presented to the Permanent Council 'A Strategic Vision of the OAS', proposing a refocusing of the Organization's core tasks, prioritizing mandates in accordance with the principal strategic objectives, and a rationalization of the Organization's use of its financial resources.

INTER-AMERICAN COUNCIL FOR INTEGRAL DEVELOPMENT (CIDI)

The Council was established in 1996, replacing the Inter-American Economic and Social Council and the Inter-American Council for Education, Science and Culture. Its aim is to promote co-operation among the countries of the region, in order to accelerate economic and social development. An Executive Secretariat for Integral Development provides CIDI with technical and secretarial services and co-ordinates a Special Multilateral Fund of CICI (FEMCIDI), the New Programming Approaches programme, a Hemispheric Integral Development Program, a Universal Civil Identity Program in the Americas, and Migration and Development Innovative Programs. Technical co-operation and training programmes are managed by a subsidiary body of the Council, the Inter-American Agency for Co-operation and Development, which was established in 1999.

Executive Secretary: MAURICIO EDUARDO CORTÉS COSTA.

INTER-AMERICAN JURIDICAL COMMITTEE (IAJC)

The Committee's purposes are to serve as an advisory body to the OAS on juridical matters; to promote the progressive development and codification of international law; and to study juridical problems relating to the integration of the developing countries in the hemisphere, and, in so far as may appear desirable, the possibility of attaining uniformity in legislation. It comprises 11 jurists, nationals of different member states, elected for a period of four years, with the possibility of re-election.

Chairman: GUILLERMO FERNÁNDEZ DE SOTO (Colombia); Av. Marechal Floriano 196, 3° andar, Palácio Itamaraty, Centro, 20080-002, Rio de Janeiro, Brazil; tel. (21) 2206-9903; fax (21) 2203-2090; e-mail cjioea.trp@terra.com.br.

INTER-AMERICAN COMMISSION ON HUMAN RIGHTS

The Commission was established in 1960 to promote the observance and protection of human rights in the member states of the OAS. It examines and reports on the human rights situation in member countries and considers individual petitions relating to alleged human rights violations by member states. A Special Rapporteurship on the Rights of People of Afro-Descendants, and against Racial Discrimination was established in 2005. Other rapporteurs analyse and report on the rights of children, women, indigenous peoples, migrant workers, prisoners and displaced persons, and on freedom of expression.

Executive Secretary: SANTIAGO A. CANTON; 1889F St, NW, Washington, DC 20006, USA; tel. (202) 458-6002; fax (202) 458-3992; e-mail cidhoea@oas.org; internet www.cidh.oas.org.

GENERAL SECRETARIAT

The Secretariat, the central and permanent organ of the Organization, performs the duties entrusted to it by the General Assembly, Meetings of Consultation of Ministers of Foreign Affairs and the Councils. There is an Administrative Tribunal, comprising six elected members, to settle staffing disputes.

Secretary-General: JOSÉ MIGUEL INSULZA (Chile).

Assistant Secretary-General: ALBERT R. RAMDIN (Suriname).

INTER-AMERICAN COMMITTEES AND COMMISSIONS

Inter-American Committee Against Terrorism (Comité Interamericano Contra el Terrorismo—CICTE): 1889 F St, NW, Washington, DC 20006, USA; tel. (202) 458-6960; fax (202) 458-3857; e-mail cicte@oas.org; internet www.cicte.oas .org; f. 1999 to enhance the exchange of information via national authorities, formulate proposals to assist member states in drafting counter-terrorism legislation in all states, compile bilateral, sub-regional, regional and multilateral treaties and agreements signed by member states and promote universal adherence to international counter-terrorism conventions, strengthen border co-operation and travel documentation security measures, and develop activities for training and crisis management; Exec. Sec. GORDON DUGUID (USA).

Inter-American Committee on Ports (Comisión Interamericana de Puertos—CIP): 1889 F St, NW, Washington, DC 20006, USA; tel. (202) 458-3871; fax (202) 458-3517; e-mail cip@oas.org; internet www.oas.org/cip; f. 1998; serves as the permanent inter-American forum to strengthen co-operation on port-related issues among the member states, with the active participation of the private sector; the Committee, comprising 34 mem. states, meets every two years; its Executive Board, which executes policy decisions, meets annually; four technical advisory groups have been established to advise on logistics and competition (formerly port operations), port security, navigation control, and environmental protection; Sec. CARLOS M. GALLEGOS.

Inter-American Court of Human Rights (IACHR) (Corte Interamericana de Derechos Humanos): Ave 10, St 45-47 Los Yoses, San Pedro, San José; Postal 6906-1000, San José, Costa Rica; tel. (506) 2234-0581; fax (506) 2234-0584; e-mail corteidh@corteidh.or.cr; internet www.corteidh.or.cr; f. 1979 as an autonomous judicial institution whose purpose is to apply and interpret the American Convention on Human Rights (which entered into force in 1978); comprises seven jurists from OAS member states; Pres. DIEGO GARCÍA SAYÁN (Peru); Exec. Sec. PABLO SAAVEDRA ALESSANDRI (Chile); publ. *Annual Report*.

Inter-American Defense Board (Junta Interamericana de Defensa—JID): 2600 16th St, NW, Washington, DC 20441, USA; tel. (202) 939-6041; fax (202) 387-2880; e-mail iadc-registrar@jid.org; internet www.jid.org; promotes co-operative security interests in the Western Hemisphere; new statutes adopted in 2006 formally designated the Board as an OAS agency; works on issues such as disaster assistance and confidence-building measures directly supporting the hemispheric security goals of the OAS and of regional ministers of defence; also provides a senior-level academic programme in security studies for military, national police and civilian leaders at the Inter-American Defense College; Dir-Gen. Maj.-Gen. JUAREZ APARECIDO DE PAULA CUNHA (Brazil).

Inter-American Drug Abuse Control Commission (Comisión Interamericana para el Control del Abuso de Drogas—CICAD): 1889 F St, NW, Washington, DC 20006, USA; tel. (202) 458-3178; fax (202) 458-3658; e-mail oidcicad@oas.org; internet www.cicad.oas.org; f. 1986 by the OAS to promote and facilitate multilateral co-operation in the control and prevention of the trafficking, production and use of illegal drugs, and related crimes; reports regularly, through the Multilateral Evaluation Mechanism, on progress against illegal drugs in each member state and region-wide; mems: 34 countries; Exec. Sec. PAUL E. SIMONS; publs *Statistical Survey* (annually), *Directory of Governmental Institutions Charged with the Fight Against the Illicit Production, Trafficking, Use and Abuse of Narcotic Drugs and Psychotropic Substances*, *Evaluation of Progress in Drug Control*, *Progress Report on Drug Control—Implementation and Recommendations* (2 a year).

Inter-American Telecommunication Commission (Comisión Interamericana de Telecomunicaciones—CITEL): 1889 F St, NW, Washington, DC 20006, USA; tel. (202) 458-3004; fax (202) 458-6854; e-mail citel@oas.org; internet www.citel.oas .org; f. 1993 to promote the development and harmonization of telecommunications in the region, in co-operation with governments and the private sector; CITEL has more than 200 associate members representing private associations or companies, permanent observers, and international organizations; under its Permanent Executive Committee specialized consultative committees focus on telecommunication standardization and radiocommunication, including broadcasting; mems: 35 countries; Exec. Sec. CLOVIS JOSÉ BAPTISTA NETO.

Activities

STRENGTHENING DEMOCRACY

The OAS promotes and supports good governance in its member states through various activities, including electoral observations, crisis-prevention missions, and programmes to strengthen government institutions and to support a regional culture of democracy. In September 2001 the member states adopted the Inter-American Democratic Charter, which details the essential elements of representative democracy, including free and fair elections; respect for human rights and fundamental freedoms; the exercise of power in accordance with the rule of law; a pluralistic political party system; and the separation and independence of the branches of government. Transparency and responsible administration by governments, respect for social rights, freedom of expression and citizen participation are among other elements deemed by the Charter to define democracy. The 41st General Assembly, held in June 2011, in San Salvador, El Salvador, approved a final Declaration on Citizen Security in the Americas, which incorporated a request to ministers to draft a hemispheric plan of action for consideration the following year.

The observation of elections is one of the most important tasks of the OAS. Depending on the specific situation and the particular needs of each country, missions vary from a few technical experts sent for a limited time to a large country-wide team of monitors dispatched to observe the full electoral process for an extended period commencing with the political parties' campaigns. The missions present their observations to the OAS Permanent Council, along with recommendations for how each country's electoral process might be strengthened. In August 2010 a joint electoral observation mission (JEOM), with representatives from CARICOM, was deployed to oversee the presidential and legislative electoral processes in Haiti, where polling was scheduled to take place in November. The mission remained in the country after the elections to monitor the second round of voting in the presidential poll, which took place in late March 2011. The JEOM was reinforced in December 2010 by two expert missions, which were dispatched, following disputed preliminary first round results, to verify statistical procedures and to strengthen legal technical assistance. Other electoral observation missions in 2011 were dispatched to Peru, to oversee voting in presidential and legislative elections, which were conducted in April and June, to Ecuador to observe a national referendum, conducted in May, to Saint Christopher and Nevis, for legislative elections conducted in July, to Guatemala, to monitor voting in a general election, conducted in September, to Nicaragua, in November, to monitor presidential and legislative elections, to St Lucia and Guyana, also in November, to oversee legislative elections, and to Jamaica, in December, to monitor legislative elections. In the first half of 2012 OAS observer teams monitored legislative elections held in Belize and in El Salvador (in March); and parliamentary elections in the Bahamas and a presidential poll in Dominican Republic (in May). A team was to be dispatched to monitor legislative elections to be held in Mexico, in July.

The OAS has responded to numerous political crises in the region. In some cases, at the request of member states, it has sent special missions to provide critical support to the democratic process. During 2005–06 the OAS was particularly active in Nicaragua. In June 2005, responding to issues raised by the Government of President Enrique Bolaños, the OAS General Assembly expressed concern about developments that posed a threat to the separation and independence of branches of government. Citing the Inter-American Democratic Charter and the OAS Charter, the General Assembly authorized an OAS mission to help establish a broad national dialogue in that country; accordingly, the OAS Secretary-General led a high-level mission to Nicaragua to support efforts to find democratic solutions to the situation, and also appointed a special envoy to facilitate dialogue there. In 2006 the OAS Special Mission to Accompany the Democratic and Electoral Process in Nicaragua monitored regional elections, conducted in March, and a general election in November. In a subsequent report to the OAS Permanent Council, the Chief of Mission noted that Nicaragua had made significant steps forward in its democratic development and that its elections were 'increasingly clean and competitive'.

In 2005, following an institutional crisis in Ecuador, the OAS offered support for the establishment of an impartial, independent Supreme Court of Justice. The OAS Secretary-General appointed two distinguished jurists as his special representatives to observe the selection process; members of Ecuador's new Supreme Court were sworn in during November. The OAS also played a role in Bolivia in 2005, following the resignation in June of President Carlos Mesa. The OAS Secretary-General appointed a special representative to facilitate political dialogue and to head the OAS observation mission on the electoral process that resulted in Evo Morales winning the presidency.

In August 2000 the OAS Secretary-General undertook the first of several high-level missions to negotiate with the authorities in Haiti in order to resolve the political crisis resulting from a disputed general election in May. In January 2001, following a meeting with the Haitian Prime Minister, the Assistant Secretary-General recommended that the OAS renew its efforts to establish a dialogue between the Government, opposition parties and representatives of civil society in that country. In May and June the OAS and the Caribbean Community and Common Market (CARICOM) undertook joint missions to Haiti in order to assess and promote prospects for a democratic resolution to the political uncertainties. Following political and social unrest in Haiti in December, the OAS and CARICOM pledged to conduct an independent investigation into the violence, and in March 2002 an agreement to establish a Special OAS Mission for Strengthening Democracy in Haiti was signed in the capital, Port-au-Prince. The independent commission of inquiry reported to the OAS at the beginning of July, and listed a set of recommendations relating to law reform, security and other confidence-building measures to help to secure democracy in Haiti. In January 2004 the OAS Special Mission condemned the escalation of political violence in Haiti and in February took a lead in drafting a plan of action to implement a CARICOM-brokered action plan to resolve the crisis. In late February the Permanent Council met in special session, and urged the UN to take necessary and appropriate action to address the deteriorating situation in Haiti. On 29 February President Jean-Bertrand Aristide resigned and left the country; amid ongoing civil unrest, a provisional leader was sworn in. The OAS Mission continued to attempt to maintain law and order, in co-operation with a UN-authorized Multinational Interim Force, and facilitated political discussions on the establishment of a transitional government. From March the Special Mission participated in the process to develop an Interim Co-operation Framework, identifying the urgent and medium-term needs of Haiti, which was presented to a meeting of international donors held in July. In June the OAS General Assembly adopted a resolution instructing the Permanent Council to undertake all necessary diplomatic initiatives to foster the restoration of democracy in Haiti, and called upon the Special Mission to work with the new UN Stabilization Mission in Haiti in preparing, organizing and monitoring future elections. During 2005 OAS technical experts, together with UN counterparts, assisted Haiti's Provisional Electoral Council (PEC) with the process of voter registration for legislative and presidential elections, initially scheduled for later in that year, as well as to formulate an electronic vote tabulation system, which was to serve as the basis for a permanent civil registry. In January 2006 the OAS Permanent Council declared its grave concern at a further postponement of the elections. In the following month, however, the Council expressed its satisfaction that polling had taken place in a free and fair manner. The Secretary-General visited Haiti to meet with officials and offer his support for the declared President-elect, Réné Préval. The OAS has continued to extend support to the country and to co-ordinate international assistance, mainly through its Haiti Task Force, chaired by the Assistant Secretary-General. In February 2008 a special mission of the Permanent Council visited Haiti to assess priorities for future support. In July the Assistant Secretary-General announced the establishment of an OAS Haiti Fund to support the organization's mandate and priorities in that country. In September the Assistant Secretary-General, visiting Haiti after it had been struck by a series of tropical cyclones, reiterated OAS commitment to Haiti's socio-economic development and stability. In early 2009 the OAS pledged to support the electoral process in Haiti, and to monitor the forthcoming senate elections.

In April 2002 a special session of the General Assembly was convened to discuss the ongoing political instability in Venezuela. The Assembly applied its authority granted under the Inter-American Democratic Charter to condemn the alteration of the constitutional order in Venezuela which forced the temporary eviction of President Hugo Chávez from office. In January 2003 the OAS announced the establishment of a Group of Friends, composed of representatives from Brazil, Chile, Mexico, Spain, Portugal and the USA, to support its efforts to resolve the ongoing crisis in Venezuela. In March the OAS Secretary-General was invited by Venezuelan opposition groupings to mediate negotiations with the Government. The talks culminated in May with the signing of an OAS-brokered agreement which, it was hoped, would lead to mid-term referendums on elected officials, including the presidency. The OAS, with the Carter Center, subsequently oversaw and verified the collection of signatures to determine whether referendums should be held. Following the staging of a recall referendum on the Venezuelan presidency in August 2004, OAS member states urged that there should be a process of reconciliation in that country.

In June 2009 the OAS Secretary-General and Permanent Council condemned the forced expulsion from power of President José Manuel Zelaya of Honduras by members of that country's armed forces. A special session of the General Assembly was convened, which urged the Secretary-General to pursue diplomatic efforts to restore constitutional order and the rule of law. When this was not achieved within the required 72 hour period, the Assembly, on 4 July, resolved to suspend the membership rights of Honduras to participate in the organization. President Oscar Arias of Costa Rica agreed to lead efforts on behalf of the OAS to mediate with the new authorities in Honduras in order to resolve the crisis. In August the OAS organized a delegation of ministers of foreign affairs to visit Honduras and promote a settlement based on the San José Accord formulated by President Arias, which envisaged Zelaya returning to the country as head of a government of national unity, and the holding of a general election a month earlier than scheduled, in late October. Political amnesty was to be offered to all sides under the proposed agreement. The interim authorities permitted the delegation's visit conditional on the OAS Secretary-General participating only as an observer. The opposing leaders signed an accord in October, although it was soon rejected by Zelaya after he was excluded from an interim national unity government. A special session of the Permanent Council was convened in December to consider the political situation in Honduras following a general election conducted in late November. The Council urged the newly elected leader, Porfirio Lobo, fully to re-establish respect for human rights, to end 'persecution' of Zelaya, and to establish a national unity government to serve until the original presidential term ended in January 2010. In June the OAS General Assembly determined to establish a high-level commission to assess the political and human rights situation in Honduras. The commission's report, issued in late July, included the following recommendations: the termination of legal proceedings initiated against former President Zelaya; support for Zelaya's application for membership of the Central American Parliament with the status of a former constitutional president; continued investigation into alleged human rights violations; and implementation, by the new government, of further measures to protect activists, journalists, judges and others who had opposed the *coup d'etat*. The suspension of Honduras' OAS membership was removed in June 2011.

In special situations, when both or all member states involved in a dispute ask for its assistance, the OAS plays a longer-term role in supporting countries to resolve bilateral or multilateral issues. In September 2005 Belize and Guatemala signed an agreement at the OAS establishing a framework for negotiations and confidence-building measures to help to maintain good bilateral relations while they sought a permanent solution to a long-standing territorial dispute. Following a series of negotiations under OAS auspices, both sides signed a Special Agreement to resolve the dispute in December 2008. In April 2006 another OAS-supported effort was concluded successfully when El Salvador and Honduras signed an accord settling differences over the demarcation of their common border. In March 2008 a Meeting of Consultation of OAS ministers of foreign affairs was convened following an escalation of diplomatic tension between Colombia and Ecuador resulting from a violation of Ecuador's borders by Colombian soldiers in pursuit of opposition insurgents. The meeting approved a resolution to establish a Good Offices Mission to restore confidence between the two countries and to negotiate an appropriate settlement to the dispute. A Verification Commission of the Good Offices Mission presented a report in July 2009, which included proposals to strengthen bilateral relations. In November 2010 a special meeting of the Permanent Council was convened, at the request of the Costa Rican government, to consider a border dispute with Nicaragua in the San Juan river area. The Council adopted a resolution in support of recommendations of the OAS Secretary-General, who had recently visited the area, to implement various confidence-building measures, including the resumption of bilateral talks on boundary demarcation, the convening of a Binational Committee and strengthening collaborative mechanisms to counter organized crime and arms- and drugs-trafficking.

The OAS places a high priority on combating corruption in recognition of the undermining effect this has on democratic institutions. In 1996 the OAS member states adopted the Inter-American Convention against Corruption, which by 2012 had been ratified or acceded to by 33 member states. In 2002 the treaty's signatory states initiated a peer review process to examine their compliance with the treaty's key provisions. The Follow-Up Mechanism for the Implementation of the Inter-American Convention against Corruption assesses progress and recommends concrete measures that the states parties can implement to improve compliance. Representatives of civil society organizations are also given the opportunity to meet with experts and present information for their consideration. A second round of the review process commenced in 2006 and was concluded in December 2008, at which time 28 country reports had been adopted. All participating countries have been assessed at least once and the completed progress reports are available to the public. The OAS has also held seminars and training sessions in the region on such matters as improving transparency in government and drafting model anti-corruption legislation. In May 2010 the Follow-up Mechanism organized a Conference on the Progress and Challenges in Hemispheric Co-operation against Corruption, held in Lima, Peru. A second conference was convened in Cali, Colombia, in June 2011.

In recent years, the OAS has expanded its outreach to civil society. More than 200 non-governmental organizations (NGOs) are registered to take part in OAS activities. Civil society groups are encouraged to participate in workshops and round tables in advance of the OAS General Assembly to prepare proposals and recommendations to present to the member states. This is also the case with Summits of the Americas and the periodic ministerial meetings, such as those on education, labour, culture, and science and technology. NGOs contributed ideas to the development of the Inter-American Democratic Charter and have participated in follow-up work on hemispheric treaties against corruption and terrorism.

The OAS has also focused on strengthening ties with the private sector. In 2006 it concluded a co-operation agreement with the business forum Private Sector of the Americas which aimed to promote dialogue and to support public–private alliances with a view to creating jobs, combating poverty and strengthening development. Business leaders from the region develop proposals and recommendations to present to the OAS General Assembly and to the Summits of the Americas.

Under the Democratic Charter a 'respect for human rights and fundamental freedoms' is deemed to be an essential element of a democracy. The Inter-American Commission on Human Rights and the Inter-American Court of Human Rights are the pillars of a system designed to protect individuals in the Americas who have suffered violations of their rights. A key function of the Commission is to consider petitions from individuals who claim that a state has violated a protected right and that they have been unable to find justice. The Commission brings together the petitioner and the state to explore a 'friendly settlement'. If such an outcome is not possible, the Commission may recommend specific measures to be carried out by the state to remedy the violation. If a state does not follow the recommendations the Commission has the option to publish its report or take the case to the Inter-American Court of Human Rights, as long as the state involved has accepted the Court's compulsory jurisdiction. The Commission convenes for six weeks each year.

In addition to hearing cases the Court may exercise its advisory jurisdiction to interpret the human rights treaties in effect in the region. The Commission, for its part, may conduct an on-site visit to a country, at the invitation of its Government, to analyse and report on the human rights situation. The Commission has also created rapporteurships focusing on particular human rights issues. In 2005 it created a rapporteurship on the rights of persons of African descent and against racial discrimination. Other rapporteurs analyse and report on the rights of children, women, indigenous peoples migrant workers, prisoners and displaced persons, and on freedom of expression. The Commission also has a special unit on human rights defenders. The OAS also works beyond the inter-American human rights system to promote the rights of vulnerable groups. The member states are in the process of negotiating the draft American Declaration on the Rights of Indigenous Peoples, which is intended to promote and protect a range of rights covering such areas as family, spirituality, work, culture, health, the environment, and systems of knowledge, language and communication. A special fund was established for voluntary contributions by member states and permanent observers in order to help cover the costs involved in broadening indigenous participation. The OAS also works to promote and protect women's rights. The Inter-American Commission of Women (CIM), established in 1928, has had an impact on shaping laws and policies in many countries. One of its key initiatives led to the adoption of the Inter-American Convention on the Prevention, Punishment and Eradication of Violence against Women, also known as the Convention of Belém do Pará, which was adopted in 1994 by the OAS General Assembly and, by June 2012, had been ratified by 32 OAS member states. Since 2005 parties to the Belém do Pará Convention have participated in a follow-up mechanism designed to determine how the countries are complying with the treaty and progress achieved in preventing and punishing violence against women. In 2006 the CIM also initiated an examination of strategies for reversing the spread of HIV/AIDS among women in the region. The Commission has urged greater efforts to integrate a gender perspective into every aspect of the OAS agenda. An Inter-American Year of Women was inaugurated in February 2010.

SOCIAL AND ECONOMIC DEVELOPMENT

Combating poverty and promoting social equity and economic development are priority concerns of the OAS. In June 2012 the 42nd OAS General Assembly adopted a new Social Charter of the Americas. The OAS works on a number of fronts to combat poverty and promote development, in partnership with regional and global agencies, the private sector and the international community. In 2006 the OAS General Assembly approved a new Strategic Plan for Partnership for Integral Development 2006–09, which was to guide OAS actions in this area. (The Plan has subsequently been extended, most recently—in June 2012, by the 42nd General Assembly—until December 2013.) OAS development policies and priorities are determined by the organization's political bodies, including the General Assembly, the Permanent Council and the Inter-American Council for Integral Development (CIDI), with direction from the Summits of the Americas. The OAS Executive Secretariat for Integral Development (SEDI) implements the policies through projects and programmes. Specialized departments within SEDI focus on education, culture, science and technology; sustainable development; trade, tourism and competitiveness; and social development and employment. SEDI also supports the regional ministerial meetings on topics such as culture, education, labour and sustainable development that are held periodically as part of the Summit of the Americas process. These regional meetings foster dialogue and strengthen co-operation in specific sectors and ensure that Summit policies are implemented at the national level. The OAS convenes the ministerial meetings, prepares documents for discussion and tracks the implementation of Summit mandates. In June 2009 the General Assembly adopted a resolution committing members to strengthening co-operation to control the spread of communicable diseases, in particular the outbreak of the swine influenza variant pandemic (H1N1), through greater surveillance and other disease control methods.

In June 2008 a technical secretariat was established in Panama City, Panama, to co-ordinate the implementation of an action plan in support of the Decade of the Americas for the Rights and Dignity of Persons with Disabilities (2006–16). The theme of the Decade, which had been inaugurated in Santo Domingo, Dominican Republic, was 'Equality, Dignity, and Participation'. In July 2008 the first Meeting of Ministers and High Authorities of Social Development, within the framework of CIDI, was convened in Valparaiso, Chile.

The OAS Department of Sustainable Development assists member states with formulating policies and executing projects that are aimed at integrating environmental protection with rural development and poverty alleviation, and that ensure high levels of transparency, public participation and gender equity. Its projects, which receive substantial external funding, focus on several key areas. In December 2006 regional ministers of the environment met in Santa Cruz de la Sierra, Bolivia, to define strategies and goals related to sustainable development, environmental protection, the management of resources and the mitigation of natural disasters. Water resource management projects include initiatives that support member states in managing transboundary water resources in the major river basins of South and Central America, in partnership with UNEP, the World Bank and the Global Environment Facility (GEF). The OAS is also active in various international fora that address water-related issues.

Projects focusing on natural disasters and climate adaptation include a new programme, launched in April 2006, which is aimed at assisting member countries to reduce the risk of natural disasters, particularly those related to climatic variations that have been linked to rises in sea levels. The OAS also works with CARICOM on the Mainstreaming Adaptation to Climate Change project. Activities include incorporating risk reduction into development and economic planning; supporting good governance in such areas as the use of appropriate building codes and standards for public and residential buildings; supporting innovative financial instruments related to risk transfer; and supporting regional collaboration with different agencies and organizations.

The OAS serves as the technical secretariat for the Renewable Energy in the Americas initiative, which offers governments access to information on renewable energy and energy-efficient technologies, and facilitates contacts between the private sector and state energy entities in the Americas. The OAS also provides technical assistance for developing renewable energy projects and facilitating their funding.

Various OAS-supported activities help member countries to improve the management of biological diversity. The Inter-American Biodiversity Information Network (IABIN), which has been supported since 2004 by the GEF, the World Bank and other sources, is a principal focus of OAS biodiversity efforts. The Department of Sustainable Development also supports the work of national conservation authorities in areas such as migratory species and biodiversity corridors. It co-operates with the private sector to support innovative financing through payment for ecological services, and maintains a unique online portal regarding land tenure and land title, which is used throughout the Americas.

In the areas of environmental law, policy and economics the OAS conducts environmental and sustainability assessments to help member states to identify key environmental issues that impact trade. Efforts include working with countries to develop priorities for capacity building in such areas as domestic laws, regulations and standards affecting market access of goods and services. Other initiatives include supporting countries in water and renewable energy legislation; supporting efforts towards the more effective enforcement of domestic laws; and facilitating natural disaster risk reduction and relief.

In mid-2006 the OAS launched a programme aimed at supporting countries with managing pesticides and industrial chemicals. The programme was to co-ordinate its work closely with UNEP Chemicals, the UN Stockholm Convention and other entities.

The OAS supports member states at national, bilateral and multilateral level to cope with trade expansion and economic integration. Through its Department of Trade, Tourism and Competitiveness the OAS General Secretariat provides support in strengthening human and institutional capacities; and in enhancing trade opportunities and competitiveness, particularly for micro, small and medium-sized enterprises. One of the Department's key responsibilities is to help member states (especially smaller economies) to develop the capacity they need to negotiate, implement and administer trade agreements and to take advantage of the benefits offered by free trade and expanded markets. Many member states seek assistance from the OAS to meet successfully the challenges posed by increasing globalization and the need to pursue multiple trade agendas. The OAS also administers an Inter-American Foreign Trade Information System (SICE), which acts as a repository for information about trade and trade-related issues in the region, including the texts of trade agreements, information on trade disciplines, data, and national legislation. In October 2008 a meeting of Ministers and High Authorities on Science and Technology, convened in Mexico City, Mexico, declared their commitment to co-ordinating activities to promote and enhance policies relating to science, technology, engineering and innovation as tools of development, increasing productivity, and sustainable natural resource management.

The OAS provided support to the Free Trade Area of the Americas (FTAA) process, endorsed by the First Summit of the Americas, held in December 1994 (see below), as well as supporting sub-regional and bilateral trade agreements. A trade unit was established in 1995 in order to strengthen the organization's involvement in trade issues and the process of economic integration, which became a priority area following the First Summit of the Americas. The trade unit provided technical assistance in support of the establishment of the FTAA and co-ordinated activities between regional and sub-regional integration organizations. At the Special Summit of the Americas, held in January 2004 in Monterrey, Mexico, the leaders failed to specify a completion date for the negotiations, although they adopted a declaration committing themselves to its eventual establishment. Negotiations on the FTAA subsequently stalled. The unit also supports a Hemispheric Co-operation Programme, which was established by ministers of trade of the Americas, meeting in November 2002, to assist smaller economies to gain greater access to resources and technical assistance.

The 42nd General Assembly meeting, held in Cochabamba, Bolivia, in June 2012, adopted the Declaration of Cochabamba on Food Security with Sovereignty in the Americas, committing, *inter alia*, to promote agricultural development, eradicate hunger and malnutrition, and support inter-American and regional efforts to advance a common agenda on food and nutrition security.

MULTIDIMENSIONAL SECURITY

The promotion of hemispheric security is a fundamental purpose of the OAS. In October 2003, at a Special Conference on Security convened in Mexico City, Mexico, the member states established a 'multidimensional' approach that recognized both traditional security concerns and newer threats such as international terrorism, drugs-trafficking, money-laundering, illegal arms dealing, trafficking in persons, institutional corruption and organized crime. In some countries problems such as poverty, disease, environmental degradation and natural disasters increase vulnerability and undermine human security. In March 2006, during a special session of the OAS General Assembly, the member states determined to enhance co-operation on defence issues by formally designating the Inter-American Defense Board (IADB) as an OAS agency. Under its new mandate the operations and structure of the IADB were to be in keeping with the OAS Charter and the Inter-American Democratic Charter, including 'the principles of civilian oversight and the subordination of military institutions to civilian authority'. The IADB provides technical and educational advice and consultancy services to the OAS and its member states on military and defence matters. The OAS Secretary-General chairs the Inter-American Committee on Natural Disaster Reduction, which was established in 1999 comprising the principal officers of regional and international organizations concerned with the prevention and mitigation of natural disasters. In January 2010 the OAS established an emergency committee to help to co-ordinate relief efforts for Haiti, which had suffered extensive damage and loss of life as a result of a massive earthquake. A joint mission of the OAS and representatives of four inter-American institutions visited Haiti at the end of that month to assess its immediate relief and reconstruction needs. In March the OAS hosted a Haiti Diaspora Meeting, with the collaboration of the Haitian Government, which made recommendations, in particular concerning nation-building, recovery and development, for the forthcoming International Donors' Conference, held in New York, USA, at the end of that month.

Following the 11 September 2001 terrorist attacks perpetrated against targets in the USA, the OAS member states strengthened their co-operation against the threat of terrorism. The Inter-American Convention against Terrorism, which seeks to prevent the financing of terrorist activities, strengthen border controls and increase co-operation among law enforcement authorities in different countries, was opened for signature in June 2002 and entered into force in July 2003. At mid-2012 it had been signed by all 34 active member states and ratified or acceded to by 24. The Inter-American Committee against Terrorism (CICTE) offers technical assistance and specialized training in key counter-terrorism areas including port security, airport security, customs and border security, and legislation and legal assistance. In 2006 CICTE provided training to security officials in the Caribbean countries that were preparing to host the 2007 Cricket World Cup. Through CICTE member countries have also improved co-operation in improving the quality of identification and travel documents, strengthening cyber-security and adopting financial controls to prevent money-laundering and the funding of terrorist activities. In October 2008 the first meeting of ministers responsible for public security in the Americas was convened, in Mexico City. In June 2009 the General Assembly, meeting in Honduras, adopted the Declaration of San Pedro Sula, promoting the theme 'Towards a Culture of Non-violence'.

The Inter-American Drug Abuse Control Commission (CICAD) seeks to reduce the supply of and demand for illegal drugs, building on the 1996 Anti-Drug Strategy in the Hemisphere. The CICAD Executive Secretariat implements programmes aimed at preventing and treating substance abuse; reducing the supply and availability of illicit drugs; strengthening national drug control institutions; improving practices to control firearms and money-laundering; developing alternate sources of income for growers of coca, poppy and marijuana; and helping member governments to improve the gathering and analysis of data. The Multilateral Evaluation Mechanism (MEM) measures drug control progress in the member states and the hemisphere as a whole, based on a series of objective indicators. The national reports on the third evaluation round, completed in 2006, included 506 specific recommendations designed to help countries strengthen their policies to combat drugs-related activities, and to increase multilateral co-operation. Following each evaluation round the MEM process examines how countries are carrying out the recommendations. In June 2009 the OAS General Assembly agreed to initiate a review of the organization's anti-drug strategy and its instruments to counter drugs-trafficking and abuse.

In 1997 the member states adopted the Inter-American Convention against the Illicit Manufacturing of and Trafficking in Firearms, Ammunition, Explosives, and other Related Materials (known as CIFTA), which, by mid-2012, had been ratified by 30 member states. These countries have strengthened co-operation and information sharing on CIFTA-related issues. In 2005 the OAS convened the first meeting of national authorities that make operational decisions on granting export, import and transit licenses for firearms, with a view to creating an information-exchange network to prevent illegal manufacturing and trafficking. In June 1999 20 member states signed an Inter-American Convention on Transparency in Conventional Weapons Acquisition; it had been ratified by 15 members by mid-2012.

Since the 1990s the OAS has co-ordinated a comprehensive international programme to remove many thousands of anti-personnel landmines posing a threat to civilians in countries that have been affected by conflict. The OAS co-ordinates activities, identifying, obtaining and delivering the necessary resources, including funds, equipment and personnel; the IADB oversees technical demining operations, working with field supervisors from various countries; and the actual demining is executed by teams of trained soldiers, security forces or other personnel from the affected country. In addition to supporting landmine clearance the OAS Program for Comprehensive Action against Anti-personnel Mines helps with mine risk education; victim assistance and the socio-economic reintegration of formerly mined zones; the establishment of a mine action database; and support for a ban on the production, use, sale, transfer and stockpiling of anti-personnel landmines. It has also helped to destroy more than 1m. stockpiled mines in Argentina, Colombia, Chile, Ecuador, Honduras, Nicaragua and Peru. By mid-2009 Costa Rica, El Salvador, Guatemala, Honduras and Suriname had declared their territory to be clear of anti-personnel landmines. Nicaragua was officially declared to be free of landmines in June 2010.

The OAS Trafficking in Persons Section organizes seminars and training workshops for law enforcement officials and others to raise awareness on human trafficking, which includes human exploitation, smuggling and other human rights violations. In March 2006 the Venezuelan Government hosted the first Meeting of National Authorities on Trafficking in Persons in order to study ways to strengthen co-operation and to develop regional policies and strategies to prevent human trafficking. Gang violence is another growing public security concern in the region. A second Meeting was convened in Buenos Aires, Argentina, in March 2009.

In June 2010 the 40th meeting of the OAS General Assembly, meeting in Lima, Peru, adopted the Declaration of Lima, aimed at strengthening collective commitment to peace, security and co-operation, as the principal means of confronting threats to the region.

In June 2012 the 42nd OAS General Assembly issued a Declaration on the Question of the Status of the Islas Malvinas (Falkland Islands), and determined to examine that issue at subsequent sessions.

SUMMITS OF THE AMERICAS

Since December 1994, when the First Summit of the Americas was convened in Miami, USA (see below), the leaders of the region's 34 democracies have met periodically to examine political, economic and social development priorities and to determine common goals and forge a common agenda. This process has increasingly shaped OAS policies and priorities and many OAS achievements, for example the adoption of the Inter-American Democratic Charter and the creation of mechanisms to measure progress against illicit drugs and corruption, have been attained as a result of Summit mandates. The Summits of the Americas have provided direction for the OAS in the areas of human rights, hemispheric security, trade, poverty reduction, gender equity and greater civil society participation. The OAS serves as the institutional memory and technical secretariat to the Summit process. It supports the countries in follow-up and planning, and provides technical, logistical and administrative support. The OAS Summits Secretariat co-ordinates the implementation of mandates assigned to the OAS and chairs the Joint Summit Working Group, which includes the institutions of the inter-American system. The OAS also has responsibility for strengthening outreach to civil society to ensure that NGOs, academic institutions, the private sector and other interests can contribute ideas and help to monitor and implement Summit initiatives.

In December 1994 the First Summit of the Americas was convened in Miami, USA. The meeting endorsed the concept of a Free Trade Area of the Americas, and also approved a Plan of Action to strengthen democracy, eradicate poverty and promote sustainable development throughout the region. The OAS subsequently embarked on an extensive process of reform and modernization to strengthen its capacity to undertake a lead role in implementing the Plan. The organization realigned its priorities in order to respond to the mandates emerging from the Summit and developed a new institutional framework for technical assistance and co-operation, although many activities continued to be undertaken by the specialized or associated organizations of the OAS (see below). In 1996 the OAS member states participated in the interim Summit of the Americas on Sustainable Development, convened in Santa Cruz de la Sierra, Bolivia, which established sustainable development goals that incorporated economic, social and environmental concerns. The Second Summit of the Americas, which took place in 1998 in Santiago, Chile, focused on education, as well as such issues as strengthening democracy, justice and human rights; promoting integration and free trade; and eradicating poverty and discrimination. In 1998, following the Second Summit, the OAS established an Office of Summit Follow-Up, in order to strengthen its servicing of the meetings, and to co-ordinate tasks assigned to it. The Third Summit, convened in Québec, Canada, in April 2001, reaffirmed the central role of the OAS in implementing decisions of the summit meetings and instructed the organization to pursue the process of reform in order to enhance its operational capabilities, in particular in the areas of human rights, combating trade in illegal drugs, and enforcement of democratic values. The Summit declaration stated that commitment to democracy was a requirement for a country's participation in the summit process. The Third Summit urged the development of an Inter-American Democratic Charter to reinforce OAS instruments for defending and promoting democracy; the Democratic Charter was adopted in September of that year. The Third Summit also determined that the OAS was to be the technical secretariat for the summit process, assuming many of the responsibilities previously incumbent on the host country. Further to its mandate, the OAS established a Summits of the Americas Secretariat, which assists countries in planning and follow-up and provides technical, logistical and administrative support for the Summit Implementation Review Group and the summit process. An interim Special Summit of the Americas was held in January 2004, in Monterrey, Mexico, to reaffirm commitment to the process. The Fourth Summit of the Americas was convened in Mar del Plata, Argentina, in November 2005, on the theme 'Creating jobs to fight poverty and strengthen democracy'. The meeting approved a plan of action to achieve employment growth and security. The Fifth Summit was held in Port of Spain, Trinidad and Tobago, in April 2009, focusing on the theme 'Securing our citizens' future by promoting human prosperity, energy security and environmental sustainability'. All governments determined to enhance co-operation to restore global economic growth and to reduce social inequalities. The meeting mandated the OAS to pursue various objectives, including the establishment of an Inter-American Social Protection Network, to facilitate the exchange of information with regard to policies, programmes and best practices; the convening of a Conference on Development; organizing regional consultations on climate change; and strengthening the leadership of the Joint Summit Working Group. A Summits of the Americas follow-up and implementation system was inaugurated in January 2010. The Sixth Summit was held in Cartagena, Colombia, in April 2012, on the theme 'Connecting the Americas: Partners for Prosperity'. The meeting mandated the OAS to review its strategies to counter the trafficking of illegal drugs. However, no unanimity was reached on the admission of Cuba to the next summit, scheduled to be convened in Panama, in 2015.

TOURISM AND CULTURE

A specialized unit for tourism was established in 1996 in order to strengthen and co-ordinate activities for the sustainable development of the tourism industry in the Americas. The unit supports regional and sub-regional conferences and workshops, as well as the Inter-American Travel Congress, which serves as a forum to consider and formulate region-wide tourism policies. The unit also undertakes research and analysis of the industry. In April 2006 the OAS, the Caribbean Tourism Organization and the Caribbean Hotel Association signed an agreement on the provision of training and assistance aimed at improving the capacity of the Caribbean tourism industry. In June 2011 a draft regional strategy for sustainable tourism development was formulated at a preparatory meeting for the 19th Inter-American Travel Congress, which was convened in San Salvador, El Salvador, in late September. The Travel Congress adopted, by consensus, the 'Declaration of San Salvador for Sustainable Tourism Development in the Americas', recognizing the contribution of the tourism sector towards national efforts to reduce poverty and inequality, to advance standards of living in host communities, and to promote sustainable economic development. The Congress approved the establishment of a Hemispheric Tourism Fund, which was to support poor communities in developing their tourism potential.

In 1998 the OAS approved an Inter-American Programme of Culture to support efforts being undertaken by member states and to promote co-operation in areas such as cultural diversity; protection of cultural heritage; training and dissemination of information; and the promotion of cultural tourism. The OAS also assists with the preparation of national and multilateral cultural projects, and co-operates with the private sector to protect and promote cultural assets and events in the region. In July 2002 the first Inter-American meeting of ministers of culture approved the establishment of an Inter-American Committee on Culture, within the framework of CIDI, to co-ordinate high-level dialogue and co-operation on cultural issues. In November 2006 regional ministers of culture met in Montréal, Canada, to address the contribution of the cultural sector towards promoting development and combating poverty. In 2009 the General Assembly declared 2011 as the Inter-American Year of Culture.

Finance

The OAS regular budget for 2012, approved by the General Assembly in October 2011, amounted to US $85.4m.

Publications

(in English and Spanish)

Américas (6 a year).

Annual Report.

Numerous cultural, legal and scientific reports and studies.

Specialized Organizations and Associated Agencies

Inter-American Children's Institute (Instituto Americano del Niño, la Niña y Adolescentes—IIN): Avda 8 de Octubre 2904, POB 16212, Montevideo 11600, Uruguay; tel. (2) 487-2150; fax (2) 487-3242; e-mail iin@oas.org; internet www.iin.oea.org; f. 1927; promotes the regional implementation of the Convention on the Rights of the Child, assists in the development of child-oriented public policies; promotes co-operation between states; and aims to develop awareness of problems affecting children and young people in the region. The Institute organizes workshops, seminars, courses, training programmes and conferences on issues relating to children, including, for example, the rights of children, children with disabilities, and the child welfare system. It also provides advisory services, statistical data and other relevant information to authorities and experts throughout the region. The 20th Pan American Child Congress was convened in Lima, Peru, in September 2009; Dir-Gen. MARÍA DE LOS DOLORES AGUILAR MARMOLEJO; publ. *iinfancia* (annually).

Inter-American Commission of Women (Comisión Interamericana de Mujeres—CIM): 1889 F St, NW, Suite 350 Washington, DC 20006, USA; tel. (202) 458-6084; fax (202) 458-6094; e-mail spcim@oas.org; internet www.oas.org/cim; f. 1928 as the first ever official intergovernmental agency created expressly to ensure recognition of the civil and political rights of women; the CIM is the principal forum for generating hemispheric policy to advance women's rights and gender equality; comprises 34 principal delegates; the Assembly of Delegates, convened every two years, is the highest authority of the Commission, establishing policies and a plan of action for each biennium and electing the seven-member Executive Committee; Pres. MARÍA DEL ROCÍO GARCÍA GAYTÁN (Mexico); Exec. Sec. CARMEN MORENO TOSCANO (Mexico).

Inter-American Indigenous Institute (Instituto Indigenista Interamericano—III): Avda de las Fuentes 106, Col. Jardines del Pedregal, Delegación Álvaro Obregón, 01900 México, DF, Mexico; tel. (55) 5595-8410; fax (55) 5595-4324; e-mail ininin@data.net.mx; internet www.indigenista.org; f. 1940; conducts research on the situation of the indigenous peoples of America; assists the exchange of information; promotes indigenous policies in member states aimed at the elimination of poverty and development within Indian communities, and to secure their position as ethnic groups within a democratic society; Hon. Dir Dr GUILLERMO ESPINOSA VELASCO (Mexico); publs *América Indígena* (quarterly), *Anuario Indigenista*.

Inter-American Institute for Co-operation on Agriculture (IICA) (Instituto Interamericano de Cooperación para la Agricultura): Apdo Postal 55–2200, San Isidro de Coronado, San José, Costa Rica; tel. (506) 216-0222; fax (506) 216-0233; e-mail iicahq@iica.ac.cr; internet www.iica.int; f. 1942 (as the Inter-American Institute of Agricultural Sciences, present name adopted 1980); supports the efforts of member states to improve agricultural development and rural well-being; encourages co-operation between regional organizations, and provides a forum for the exchange of experience; Dir-Gen. VÍCTOR M. VILLALOBOS (Mexico).

Justice Studies Center of the Americas (Centro de Estudios de Justicia de las Américas): Rodó 1950, Providencia, Santiago, Chile; tel. (2) 2742933; fax (2) 3415769; e-mail info@cejamericas.org; internet www.cejamericas.org; f. 1999; aims to support the modernization of justice systems in the region; Exec. Dir CRISTIÁN RIEGO RAMÍREZ (Chile).

Pan American Development Foundation (PADF) (Fundación Panamericana para el Desarrollo): 1889 F St, NW, Washington, DC 20006, USA; tel. (202) 458-3969; fax (202) 458-6316; e-mail padf-dc@padf.org; internet www.padf.org; f. 1962 to promote and facilitate economic and social development in Latin America and the Caribbean by means of innovative partnerships and integrated involvement of the public and private sectors; provides low-interest credit for small-scale entrepreneurs, vocational training, improved health care, agricultural development and reafforestation, and strengthening local non-governmental organizations; provides emergency disaster relief and reconstruction assistance; Exec. Dir JOHN A. SANBRAILO.

Pan American Health Organization (PAHO) (Organización Panamericana de la Salud): 525 23rd St, NW, Washington, DC 20037, USA; tel. (202) 974-3000; fax (202) 974-3663; e-mail webmaster@paho.org; internet www.paho.org; f. 1902; co-ordinates regional efforts to improve health; maintains close relations with national health organizations and serves as the Regional Office for the Americas of the World Health Organization; Dir Dr MIRTA ROSES PERIAGO (Argentina).

Pan American Institute of Geography and History (PAIGH) (Instituto Panamericano de Geografía e Historia–IPGH): Ex-Arzobispado 29, 11860 México, DF, Mexico; tel. (55) 5277-5888; fax (55) 5271-6172; e-mail secretariageneral@ipgh.org; internet www.ipgh.org.mx; f. 1928; co-ordinates and promotes the study of cartography, geophysics, geography and history; provides technical assistance, conducts training at research centres, distributes publications, and organizes technical meetings; Sec.-Gen. SANTIAGO BORRERO MUTIS (Colombia); Publs *Revista Cartográfica* (2 a year), *Revista Geográfica* (2 a year), *Revista de Historia de América* (2 a year), *Revista Geofísica* (2 a year), *Revista de Arqueología Americana* (annually), *Folklore Americano* (annually), *Boletín de Antropología Americana* (annually).

Summary of the Charter of the Organization of American States

(adopted 30 April 1948, as amended by the 'Protocol of Buenos Aires', signed on 27 February 1967, at the Third Special Inter-American Conference, the 'Protocol of Cartagena de Indias', approved on 5 December 1985, at the 14th Special Session of the General Assembly, the 'Protocol of Washington', approved on 14 December 1992, at the 16th Special Session of the General Assembly, and by the 'Protocol of Managua', adopted on 10 June 1993, at the 19th Special Session of the General Assembly)

Note: The principal aims and activities of the Organization are contained in Part One of the Charter, and are detailed below. Part Two of the Charter is concerned with the Organs of the Organization, and Part Three General and other Miscellaneous and Transitory Provisions.

In the name of their peoples, the States represented at the Ninth International Conference of American States:

Convinced that the historic mission of America is to offer to man a land of liberty and a favorable environment for the development of his personality and the realization of his just aspirations;

Conscious that that mission has already inspired numerous agreements, whose essential value lies in the desire of the American peoples to live together in peace and, through their mutual understanding and respect for the sovereignty of each one, to provide for the betterment of all, in independence, in equality and under law;

Convinced that representative democracy is an indispensable condition for the stability, peace and development of the region;

Confident that the true significance of American solidarity and good neighborliness can only mean the consolidation on this continent, within the framework of democratic institutions, of a system of individual liberty and social justice based on respect for the essential rights of man;

Persuaded that their welfare and their contribution to the progress and the civilization of the world will increasingly require intensive continental co-operation;

Resolved to persevere in the noble undertaking that humanity has conferred upon the United Nations, whose principles and purposes they solemnly reaffirm;

Convinced that juridical organization is a necessary condition for security and peace founded on moral order and on justice; and

In accordance with Resolution IX of the Inter-American Conference on Problems of War and Peace, held in Mexico City, have agreed upon the following.

PART ONE

I. Nature and Purposes

Article 1

The American States establish by this Charter the international organization that they have developed to achieve an order of peace and justice, to promote their solidarity, to strengthen their collaboration, and to defend their sovereignty, their territorial integrity, and their independence. Within the United Nations, the Organization of American States is a regional agency.

The Organization of American States has no powers other than those expressly conferred upon it by this Charter, none of whose provisions authorizes it to intervene in matters that are within the internal jurisdiction of the Member States.

Article 2

The Organization of American States, in order to put into practice the principles on which it is founded and to fulfill its regional obligations under the Charter of the United Nations, proclaims the following essential purposes:

(a) To strengthen the peace and security of the continent;

(b) To promote and consolidate representative democracy, with due respect for the principle of non-intervention;

(c) To prevent possible causes of difficulties and to ensure the pacific settlement of disputes that may arise among the Member States;

(d) To provide for common action on the part of those States in the event of aggression;

(e) To seek the solution of political, juridical, and economic problems that may arise among them;

(f) To promote, by co-operative action, their economic, social, and cultural development;

(g) To eradicate extreme poverty, which constitutes an obstacle to the full democratic development of the peoples of the hemisphere; and

(h) To achieve an effective limitation of conventional weapons that will make it possible to devote the largest amount of resources to the economic and social development of the Member States.

II. PRINCIPLES

Article 3

The American States reaffirm the following principles:

(a) International law is the standard of conduct of States in their reciprocal relations;

(b) International order consists essentially of respect for the personality, sovereignty, and independence of States, and the faithful fulfillment of obligations derived from treaties and other sources of international law;

(c) Good faith shall govern the relations between States;

(d) The solidarity of the American States and the high aims which are sought through it require the political organization of those States on the basis of the effective exercise of representative democracy;

(e) Every State has the right to choose, without external interference, its political, economic, and social system and to organize itself in the way best suited to it, and has the duty to abstain from intervening in the affairs of another State. Subject to the foregoing, the American States shall co-operate fully among themselves, independently of the nature of their political, economic, and social systems;

(f) The elimination of extreme poverty is an essential part of the promotion and consolidation of representative democracy and is the common and shared responsibility of the American States;

(g) The American States condemn war of aggression: victory does not give rights;

(h) An act of aggression against one American State is an act of aggression against all the other American States;

(i) Controversies of an international character arising between two or more American States shall be settled by peaceful procedures;

(j) Social justice and social security are bases of lasting peace;

(k) Economic co-operation is essential to the common welfare and prosperity of the peoples of the continent;

(l) The American States proclaim the fundamental rights of the individual without distinction as to race, nationality, creed, or sex;

(m) The spiritual unity of the continent is based on respect for the cultural values of the American countries and requires their close co-operation for the high purposes of civilization;

(n) The education of peoples should be directed toward justice, freedom, and peace.

III. MEMBERS

Article 4

All American States that ratify the present Charter are Members of the Organization.

Article 5

Any new political entity that arises from the union of several Member States and that, as such, ratifies the present Charter, shall become a Member of the Organization. The entry of the new political entity into the Organization shall result in the loss of membership of each one of the States which constitute it.

Article 6

Any other independent American State that desires to become a Member of the Organization should so indicate by means of a note addressed to the Secretary General, in which it declares that it is willing to sign and ratify the Charter of the Organization and to accept all the obligations inherent in membership, especially those relating to collective security expressly set forth in Articles 28 and 29 of the Charter.

Article 7

The General Assembly, upon the recommendation of the Permanent Council of the Organization, shall determine whether it is appropriate that the Secretary General be authorized to permit the applicant State to sign the Charter and to accept the deposit of the corresponding instrument of ratification. Both the recommendation of the Permanent Council and the decision of the General Assembly shall require the affirmative vote of two thirds of the Member States.

Article 8

Membership in the Organization shall be confined to independent States of the Hemisphere that were Members of the United Nations as of 10 December 1985, and the non-autonomous territories mentioned in [the OAS] document of 5 November 1985, when they become independent.

Article 9

A Member of the Organization whose democratically constituted government has been overthrown by force may be suspended from the exercise of the right to participate in the sessions of the General Assembly, the Meeting of Consultation, the Councils of the Organization and the Specialized Conferences as well as in the commissions, working groups and any other bodies established.

(a) The power to suspend shall be exercised only when such diplomatic initiatives undertaken by the Organization for the purpose of promoting the restoration of representative democracy in the affected Member State have been unsuccessful;

(b) The decision to suspend shall be adopted at a special session of the General Assembly by an affirmative vote of two-thirds of the Member States;

(c) The suspension shall take effect immediately following its approval by the General Assembly;

(d) The suspension notwithstanding, the Organization shall endeavour to undertake additional diplomatic initiatives to contribute to the re-establishment of representative democracy in the affected Member State;

(e) The Member which has been subject to suspension shall continue to fulfill its obligations to the Organization;

(f) The General Assembly may lift the suspension by a decision adopted with the approval of two-thirds of the Member States;

(g) The powers referred to in this article shall be exercised in accordance with this Charter.

IV. FUNDAMENTAL RIGHTS AND DUTIES OF STATES

Article 10

States are juridically equal, enjoy equal rights and equal capacity to exercise these rights, and have equal duties. The rights of each State depend not upon its power to ensure the exercise thereof, but upon the mere fact of its existence as a person under international law.

Article 11

Every American State has the duty to respect the rights enjoyed by every other State in accordance with international law.

Article 12

The fundamental rights of States may not be impaired in any manner whatsoever.

Article 13

The political existence of the State is independent of recognition by other States. Even before being recognized, the State has the right to defend its integrity and independence, to provide for its preservation and prosperity, and consequently to organize itself as it sees fit, to legislate concerning its interests, to administer its services, and to determine the jurisdiction and competence of its courts. The exercise of these rights is limited only by the exercise of the rights of other States in accordance with international law.

Article 14

Recognition implies that the State granting it accepts the personality of the new State, with all the rights and duties that international law prescribes for the two States.

Article 15

The right of each State to protect itself and to live its own life does not authorize it to commit unjust acts against another State.

Article 16

The jurisdiction of States within the limits of their national territory is exercised equally over all the inhabitants, whether nationals or aliens.

Article 17

Each State has the right to develop its cultural, political, and economic life freely and naturally. In this free development, the State shall respect the rights of the individual and the principles of universal morality.

Article 18

Respect for and the faithful observance of treaties constitute standards for the development of peaceful relations among States. International treaties and agreements should be public.

Article 19

No State or group of States has the right to intervene, directly or indirectly, for any reason whatever, in the internal or external affairs of any other State. The foregoing principle prohibits not only armed force but also any other form of interference or attempted threat against the personality of the State or against its political, economic, and cultural elements.

Article 20

No State may use or encourage the use of coercive measures of an economic or political character in order to force the sovereign will of another State and obtain from it advantages of any kind.

Article 21

The territory of a State is inviolable; it may not be the object, even temporarily, of military occupation or of other measures of force taken by another State, directly or indirectly, on any grounds whatever. No territorial acquisitions or special advantages obtained either by force or by other means of coercion shall be recognized.

Article 22

The American States bind themselves in their international relations not to have recourse to the use of force, except in the case of self-defense in accordance with existing treaties or in fulfillment thereof.

Article 23

Measures adopted for the maintenance of peace and security in accordance with existing treaties do not constitute a violation of the principles set forth in Articles 19 and 21.

V. PACIFIC SETTLEMENT OF DISPUTES

Article 24

International disputes between Member States shall be submitted to the peaceful procedures set forth in this Charter.

This provision shall not be interpreted as an impairment of the rights and obligations of the Member States under Articles 34 and 35 of the Charter of the United Nations.

Article 25

The following are peaceful procedures: direct negotiation, good offices, mediation, investigation and conciliation, judicial settlement, arbitration, and those which the parties to the dispute may especially agree upon at any time.

Article 26

In the event that a dispute arises between two or more American States which, in the opinion of one of them, cannot be settled through the usual diplomatic channels, the parties shall agree on some other peaceful procedure that will enable them to reach a solution.

Article 27

A special treaty will establish adequate means for the settlement of disputes and will determine pertinent procedures for each peaceful means such that no dispute between American States may remain without definitive settlement within a reasonable period of time.

VI. COLLECTIVE SECURITY

Article 28

Every act of aggression by a State against the territorial integrity or the inviolability of the territory or against the sovereignty or political independence of an American State shall be considered an act of aggression against the other American States.

Article 29

If the inviolability or the integrity of the territory or the sovereignty or political independence of any American State should be affected by an armed attack or by an act of aggression that is not an armed attack, or by an extracontinental conflict, or by a conflict between two or more American States, or by any other fact or situation that might endanger the peace of America, the American States, in furtherance of the principles of continental solidarity or collective self-defense, shall apply the measures and procedures established in the special treaties on the subject.

VII. INTEGRAL DEVELOPMENT

Article 30

The Member States, inspired by the principles of inter-American solidarity and co-operation, pledge themselves to a united effort to ensure international social justice in their relations and integral development for their peoples, as conditions essential to peace and security. Integral development encompasses the economic, social, educational, cultural, scientific, and technological fields through which the goals that each country sets for accomplishing it should be achieved.

Article 31

Inter-American co-operation for integral development is the common and joint responsibility of the Member States, within the framework of the democratic principles and the institutions of the inter-American system. It should include the economic, social, educational, cultural, scientific, and technological fields, support the achievement of national objectives of the Member States, and respect the priorities established by each country in its development plans, without political ties or conditions.

Article 32

Inter-American co-operation for integral development should be continuous and preferably channelled through multilateral organizations, without prejudice to bilateral co-operation between Member States.

The Member States shall contribute to inter-American co-operation for integral development in accordance with their resources and capabilities and in conformity with their laws.

Article 33

Development is a primary responsibility of each country and should constitute an integral and continuous process for the establishment of a more just economic and social order that will make possible and contribute to the fulfillment of the individual.

Article 34

The Member States agree that equality of opportunity, the elimination of extreme poverty, equitable distribution of wealth and income and the full participation of their peoples in decisions relating to their own development are, among others, basic objectives of integral development. To achieve them, they likewise agree to devote their utmost efforts to accomplishing the following basic goals:

(a) Substantial and self-sustained increase of per capita national product;

(b) Equitable distribution of national income;

(c) Adequate and equitable systems of taxation;

(d) Modernization of rural life and reforms leading to equitable and efficient land-tenure systems, increased agricultural productivity, expanded use of land, diversification of production and improved processing and marketing systems for agricultural products; and the strengthening and expansion of the means to attain these ends;

(e) Accelerated and diversified industrialization, especially of capital and intermediate goods;

(f) Stability of domestic price levels, compatible with sustained economic development and the attainment of social justice;

(g) Fair wages, employment opportunities, and acceptable working conditions for all;

(h) Rapid eradication of illiteracy and expansion of educational opportunities for all;

(i) Protection of man's potential through the extension and application of modern medical science;

(j) Proper nutrition, especially through the acceleration of national efforts to increase the production and availability of food;

(k) Adequate housing for all sectors of the population;

(l) Urban conditions that offer the opportunity for a healthful, productive, and full life;

(m) Promotion of private initiative and investment in harmony with action in the public sector; and

(n) Expansion and diversification of exports.

Article 35

The Member States should refrain from practising policies and adopting actions or measures that have serious adverse effects on the development of other Member States.

Article 36

Transnational enterprises and foreign private investment shall be subject to the legislation of the host countries and to the jurisdiction of their competent courts and to the international treaties and agreements to which said countries are parties, and should conform to the development policies of the recipient countries.

Article 37

The Member States agree to join together in seeking a solution to urgent or critical problems that may arise whenever the economic development or stability of any Member State is seriously affected by conditions that cannot be remedied through the efforts of that State.

Article 38

The Member States shall extend among themselves the benefits of science and technology by encouraging the exchange and utilization of scientific and technical knowledge in accordance with existing treaties and national laws.

Article 39

The Member States, recognizing the close interdependence between foreign trade and economic and social development, should make individual and united efforts to bring about the following:

(a) Favorable conditions of access to world markets for the products of the developing countries of the region, particularly through the reduction or elimination, by importing countries, of tariff and non-tariff barriers that affect the exports of the Member States of the Organization, except when such barriers are applied in order to diversify the economic structure, to speed up the development of the less-developed Member States, and intensify their process of economic integration, or when they are related to national security or to the needs of economic balance;

(b) Continuity in their economic and social development by means of:

(i) Improved conditions for trade in basic commodities through international agreements, where appropriate; orderly marketing procedures that avoid the disruption of markets, and other measures designed to promote the expansion of markets and to obtain dependable incomes for producers, adequate and dependable supplies for consumers, and stable prices that are both remunerative to producers and fair to consumers;

(ii) Improved international financial co-operation and the adoption of other means for lessening the adverse impact of sharp fluctuations in export earnings experienced by the countries exporting basic commodities;

(iii) Diversification of exports and expansion of export opportunities for manufactured and semi-manufactured products from the developing countries; and

(iv) Conditions conducive to increasing the real export earnings of the Member States, particularly the developing countries of the region, and to increasing their participation in international trade.

Article 40

The Member States reaffirm the principle that when the more developed countries grant concessions in international trade agreements that lower or eliminate tariffs or other barriers to foreign trade so that they benefit the less-developed countries, they should not expect reciprocal concessions from those countries that are incompatible with their economic development, financial, and trade needs.

Article 41

The Member States, in order to accelerate their economic development, regional integration, and the expansion and improvement of the conditions of their commerce, shall promote improvement and co-ordination of transportation and communication in the developing countries and among the Member States.

Article 42

The Member States recognize that integration of the developing countries of the Hemisphere is one of the objectives of the inter-American system and, therefore, shall orient their efforts and take the necessary measures to accelerate the integration process, with a view to establishing a Latin American common market in the shortest possible time.

Article 43

In order to strengthen and accelerate integration in all its aspects, the Member States agree to give adequate priority to the preparation and carrying out of multinational projects and to their financing, as well as to encourage economic and financial institutions of the inter-American system to continue giving their broadest support to regional integration institutions and programs.

Article 44

The Member States agree that technical and financial co-operation that seeks to promote regional economic integration should be based on the principle of harmonious, balanced, and efficient development, with particular attention to the relatively less-developed countries, so that it may be a decisive factor that will enable them to promote, with their own efforts, the improved development of their infrastructure programs, new lines of production, and export diversification.

Article 45

The Member States, convinced that man can only achieve the full realization of his aspirations within a just social order, along with economic development and true peace, agree to dedicate every effort to the application of the following principles and mechanisms:

(a) All human beings, without distinction as to race, sex, nationality, creed, or social condition, have a right to material well-being and to their spiritual development, under circumstances of liberty, dignity, equality of opportunity, and economic security;

(b) Work is a right and a social duty, it gives dignity to the one who performs it, and it should be performed under conditions, including a system of fair wages, that ensure life, health, and a decent standard of living for the worker and his family, both during his working years and in his old age, or when any circumstance deprives him of the possibility of working;

(c) Employers and workers, both rural and urban, have the right to associate themselves freely for the defense and promotion of their interests, including the right to collective bargaining and the workers' right to strike, and recognition of the juridical personality of associations and the protection of their freedom and independence, all in accordance with applicable laws;

(d) Fair and efficient systems and procedures for consultation and collaboration among the sectors of production, with due regard for safeguarding the interests of the entire society;

(e) The operation of systems of public administration, banking and credit, enterprise, and distribution and sales, in such a way, in harmony with the private sector, as to meet the requirements and interests of the community;

(f) The incorporation and increasing participation of the marginal sectors of the population, in both rural and urban areas, in the economic, social, civic, cultural, and political life of the nation, in order to achieve the full integration of the national community, acceleration of the process of social mobility, and the consolidation of the democratic system. The encouragement of all efforts of popular promotion and co-operation that have as their purpose the development and progress of the community;

(g) Recognition of the importance of the contribution of organizations such as labor unions, co-operatives, and cultural, professional, business, neighborhood, and community associations to the life of the society and to the development process;

(h) Development of an efficient social security policy; and

(i) Adequate provision for all persons to have due legal aid in order to secure their rights.

Article 46

The Member States recognize that, in order to facilitate the process of Latin American regional integration, it is necessary to harmonize the social legislation of the developing countries, especially in the labor and social security fields, so that the rights of the workers shall be equally protected, and they agree to make the greatest efforts possible to achieve this goal.

Article 47

The Member States will give primary importance within their development plans to the encouragement of education, science, technology, and culture, oriented toward the overall improvement of the individual, and as a foundation for democracy, social justice, and progress.

Article 48

The Member States will co-operate with one another to meet their educational needs, to promote scientific research, and to encourage technological progress for their integral development. They will consider themselves individually and jointly bound to preserve and enrich the cultural heritage of the American peoples.

Article 49

The Member States will exert the greatest efforts, in accordance with their constitutional processes, to ensure the effective exercise of the right to education, on the following bases:

(a) Elementary education, compulsory for children of school age, shall also be offered to all others who can benefit from it. When provided by the State it shall be without charge;

(b) Middle-level education shall be extended progressively to as much of the population as possible, with a view to social improvement. It shall be diversified in such a way that it meets the development needs of each country without prejudice to providing a general education; and

(c) Higher education shall be available to all, provided that, in order to maintain its high level, the corresponding regulatory or academic standards are met.

Article 50

The Member States will give special attention to the eradication of illiteracy, will strengthen adult and vocational education systems, and will ensure that the benefits of culture will be available to the entire population. They will promote the use of all information media to fulfill these aims.

Article 51

The Member States will develop science and technology through educational, research, and technological development activities and information and dissemination programs. They will stimulate activities in the field of technology for the purpose of adapting it to the needs of their integral development. They will organize their co-operation in these fields efficiently and will substantially increase exchange of knowledge, in accordance with national objectives and laws and with treaties in force.

Article 52

The Member States, with due respect for the individuality of each of them, agree to promote cultural exchange as an effective means of consolidating inter-American understanding; and they recognize that regional integration programs should be strengthened by close ties in the fields of education, science, and culture.

ORGANIZATION OF ARAB PETROLEUM EXPORTING COUNTRIES—OAPEC

Address: POB 20501, Safat 13066, Kuwait.

Telephone: 24959000; **fax:** 24959755; **e-mail:** oapec@oapecorg.org; **internet:** www.oapecorg.org.

OAPEC was established in 1968 to safeguard the interests of members and to determine ways and means for their co-operation in various forms of economic activity in the petroleum industry. In 2009 OAPEC member states contributed 28.4% of total world petroleum production and 13.2% of total global marketed natural gas. At end-2009 OAPEC member states accounted for an estimated 56.6% of total global oil reserves and 28.1% of total global reserves of natural gas.

MEMBERS

Algeria	Kuwait	Saudi Arabia
Bahrain	Libya	Syria
Egypt	Qatar	United Arab Emirates
Iraq		

Organization

(June 2012)

MINISTERIAL COUNCIL

The Council consists normally of the ministers of petroleum of the member states, and forms the supreme authority of the Organization, responsible for drawing up its general policy, directing its activities and laying down its governing rules. It meets twice yearly, and may hold extraordinary sessions. Chairmanship is on an annual rotating basis.

EXECUTIVE BUREAU

Assists the Council to direct the management of the Organization, approves staff regulations, reviews the budget, and refers it to the Council, considers matters relating to the Organization's agreements and activities and draws up the agenda for the Council. The Bureau comprises one senior official from each member state. Chairmanship is by rotation on an annual basis, following the same order as the Ministerial Council chairmanship. The Bureau convenes at least three times a year.

GENERAL SECRETARIAT

Secretary-General: Abbas Ali Naqi (Kuwait).

Besides the Office of the Secretary-General, there are four departments: Finance and Administrative Affairs; Information and Library; Technical Affairs; and Economics. The last two form the Arab Centre for Energy Studies (which was established in 1983).

JUDICIAL TRIBUNAL

The Tribunal comprises seven judges from Arab countries. Its task is to settle differences in interpretation and application of the OAPEC Agreement, arising between members and also between OAPEC and its affiliates; disputes among member countries on petroleum activities falling within OAPEC's jurisdiction and not under the sovereignty of member countries; and disputes that the Ministerial Council decides to submit to the Tribunal.

President: Dr Moustafa Abdul Hayy al-Sayed.

Activities

OAPEC co-ordinates different aspects of the Arab petroleum industry through the joint undertakings described below. It co-operates with the League of Arab States and other Arab organizations, and attempts to link petroleum research institutes in the Arab states. It organizes or participates in conferences and seminars, many of which are held jointly with non-Arab organizations in order to enhance Arab and international co-operation. OAPEC collaborates with the Arab Fund for Economic and Social Development (AFESD), the Arab Monetary Fund and the League of Arab States in compiling the annual *Joint Arab Economic Report*, which is issued by the Arab Monetary Fund.

OAPEC provides training in technical matters and in documentation and information. The General Secretariat also conducts technical and feasibility studies and carries out market reviews. It provides information through a library, databank and the publications listed below.

In association with AFESD, OAPEC organizes the Arab Energy Conference every four years. The conference is attended by OAPEC ministers of petroleum and energy, senior officials from other Arab states, and representatives of invited institutions and organizations concerned with energy issues. The ninth Arab Energy Conference, focusing on the theme 'Energy and Arab Co-operation', was held in Doha, Qatar, in May 2010. The 10th was scheduled to take place in early 2014, in Beirut, Lebanon. OAPEC, with other Arab organizations, participates in the Higher Co-ordination Committee for Higher Arab Action.

Finance

The combined General Secretariat and Judicial Tribunal budget for 2010 was 2.1m. Kuwaiti dinars.

Publications

Annual Statistical Report.

Energy Resources Monitor (quarterly, Arabic).

OAPEC Monthly Bulletin (Arabic and English editions).

Oil and Arab Co-operation (quarterly, Arabic).

Secretary-General's Annual Report (Arabic and English editions).

Papers, studies, conference proceedings.

OAPEC-Sponsored Ventures

Arab Maritime Petroleum Transport Company (AMPTC): POB 22525, Safat 13086, Kuwait; tel. 24959400; fax 24842996; e-mail amptc.kuwait@amptc.net; internet www.amptc.net; f. 1973 to undertake transport of crude petroleum, gas, refined products and petro-chemicals, and thus to increase Arab participation in the tanker transport industry; owns and operates a fleet of oil tankers and other carriers; also maintains an operations office in Giza, Egypt; auth. cap. US $200m.; Gen. Man. Sulayman al-Bassam.

Arab Petroleum Investments Corporation (APICORP): POB 9599, Dammam 31423, Saudi Arabia; tel. (3) 847-0444; fax (3) 847-0022; e-mail apicorp@apicorp-arabia.com; internet www.apicorp-arabia.com; f. 1975 to finance investments in petroleum and petrochemicals projects and related industries in the Arab world and in developing countries, with priority being given to Arab joint ventures; projects financed include gas liquefaction plants, petrochemicals, tankers, oil refineries, pipelines, exploration, detergents, fertilizers and process control instrumentation; auth. cap. US $1,200m.; paid-up cap. $550m.; shareholders: Kuwait, Saudi Arabia and United Arab Emirates (17% each), Libya (15%), Iraq and Qatar (10% each), Algeria (5%), Bahrain, Egypt and Syria (3% each); CEO and Gen. Man. Ahmad Bin Hamad al-Nuaimi.

Arab Detergent Chemicals Company (ARADET): POB 27064, el-Monsour, Baghdad, Iraq; tel. (1) 541-9893; fax (1) 543-0265; e-mail info@aradetco.com; internet www.aradetco.com; f. 1981; produces and markets linear alkyl benzene; construction of a sodium multiphosphate plant is under way;

APICORP holds 32% of shares in the co; auth. cap. 72m. Iraqi dinars; subs. cap. 60m. Iraqi dinars.

Arab Petroleum Services Company (APSCO): POB 12925, Tripoli, Libya; tel. (21) 4445860; fax (21) 3335816; e-mail info@apsco.com.ly; internet apsco.com.ly; f. 1977 to provide petroleum services through the establishment of companies specializing in various activities, and to train specialized personnel; auth. cap. 100m. Libyan dinars; subs. cap. 15m. Libyan dinars.

Arab Drilling and Workover Company: POB 680, Suani Rd, km 3.5, Tripoli, Libya; tel. (21) 48004854; fax (21) 4804998; e-mail info@adwoc.com; internet www.adwoc.com; f. 1980; 40% owned by APSCO; auth. cap. 12m. Libyan dinars; Gen. Man. Omran Abukraa.

Arab Geophysical Exploration Services Company (AGESCO): POB 84224, Tripoli, Libya; tel. (21) 4804863; fax (21) 4803199; e-mail agesco@agesco-ly.com; internet agesco-ly.com; f. 1985; 40% owned by APSCO; auth. cap. 12m. Libyan dinars; subs. cap. 4m. Libyan dinars; Gen. Man. Ahmed Essed.

Arab Well Logging Company (AWLCO): POB 6225, Baghdad, Iraq; tel. (1) 541-8259; f. 1983 to provide well-logging services and data interpretation; wholly owned subsidiary of APSCO; auth. cap. 7m. Iraqi dinars.

Arab Petroleum Training Institute (APTI): POB 6037, Al-Tajeyat, Baghdad, Iraq; tel. (1) 523-4100; fax (1) 521-0526; f. 1978 to provide instruction in many technical and managerial aspects of the oil industry.

Arab Shipbuilding and Repair Yard Company (ASRY): POB 50110, Hidd, Bahrain; tel. 17671111; fax 17670236; e-mail asryco@batelco.com.bh; internet www.asry.net; f. 1974 to undertake repairs and servicing of vessels; operates a 500,000-dwt dry dock in Bahrain; two floating docks operational since 1992, and two slipways became operational in 2008; has recently diversified its activities, e.g. into building specialized service boats and upgrading oil rigs; cap. (auth. and subsidized) US $170m.; CEO Chris Potter (United Kingdom); Gen. Man. Ralf Eriksson (Sweden).

ORGANIZATION OF THE BLACK SEA ECONOMIC COOPERATION—BSEC

Address: Sakıp Sabancı Cad., Müşir Fuad Paşa Yalısı, Eski Tersane 34460 İstinye-İstanbul, Turkey.

Telephone: (212) 229-63-30; **fax:** (212) 229-63-36; **e-mail:** info@bsec-organization.org; **internet:** www.bsec-organization .org.

The Black Sea Economic Cooperation (BSEC) was established in 1992 to strengthen regional co-operation, particularly in the field of economic development. In June 1998, at a summit meeting held in Yalta, Ukraine, participating countries signed the BSEC Charter, thereby officially elevating BSEC to regional organization status. The Charter entered into force on 1 May 1999, at which time BSEC formally became the Organization of the Black Sea Economic Co-operation, retaining the same acronym.

MEMBERS

Albania	Georgia	Russia
Armenia	Greece	Serbia
Azerbaijan	Moldova	Turkey
Bulgaria	Romania	Ukraine

Note: Observer status has been granted to Austria, Belarus, Croatia, the Czech Republic, Egypt, France, Germany, Israel, Italy, Poland, Slovakia, Tunisia and the USA. The Black Sea Commission, the BSEC Business Council, the Energy Charter Conference, the European Commission, and the International Black Sea Club also have observer status. Sectoral Dialogue Partnership status has been granted to: Hungary, Iran, Japan, Jordan, Montenegro, Slovenia, the United Kingdom, and seven intergovernmental organizations.

Organization

(June 2012)

PRESIDENTIAL SUMMIT

The Presidential Summit, comprising heads of state or government of member states, represents the highest authority of the body. A 20th anniversary summit was convened in Istanbul, Turkey, in late June 2012.

COUNCIL

The Council of Ministers of Foreign Affairs is BSEC's principal decision-making organ. Ministers meet twice a year to review progress and to define new objectives. Chairmanship of the Council rotates among members every six months (1 July–31 December 2012: Turkey); the Chairman-in-Office co-ordinates the activities undertaken by BSEC. The Council is supported by a Committee of Senior Officials. Upon request of the Chairman-in-Office a Troika, comprising the current, most recent and next Chairman-in-Office, or their representatives, is convened to consider BSEC's ongoing and planned activities.

PERMANENT INTERNATIONAL SECRETARIAT

The Secretariat's tasks are, primarily, of an administrative and technical nature, and include the maintenance of archives, and the preparation and distribution of documentation. Much of the organization's activities are undertaken by 15 working groups, each headed by an Executive Manager, and by various ad hoc groups and meetings of experts.

Secretary-General: VICTOR TVIRCUN (Moldova).

Activities

In June 1992, at a summit meeting held in Istanbul, heads of state and of government signed the summit declaration on BSEC, and adopted the Bosphorus statement, which established a regional structure for economic co-operation. The grouping attained regional organization status in May 1999 (see above). The Organization's main areas of co-operation include transport; communications; trade and economic development; banking and finance; energy; tourism; agriculture and agro-industry; health care and pharmaceuticals; environmental protection; science and technology; the exchange of statistical data and economic information; collaboration between customs authorities; and combating organized crime, drugs-trafficking, trade in illegal weapons and radioactive materials, and terrorism. In order to promote regional co-operation, BSEC also aims to strengthen the business environment by providing support for small and medium-sized enterprises; facilitating closer contacts between businesses in member countries; progressively eliminating obstacles to the expansion of trade; creating appropriate conditions for investment and industrial co-operation, in particular through the avoidance of double taxation and the promotion and protection of investments; encouraging the dissemination of information concerning international tenders organized by member states; and promoting economic co-operation in free trade zones. A Working Group on Culture was established in November 2006 to promote and protect the cultural identity of the region.

A BSEC Business Council was established in Istanbul in December 1992 by the business communities of member states. It has observer status at the BSEC, and aims to identify private and public investment projects, maintain business contacts and develop programmes in various sectors. A Black Sea Trade and Development Bank has been established, in Thessaloníki, Greece, as the Organization's main funding institution, to finance and implement joint regional projects. It began operations in July 1999 (see below). A BSEC Coordination Center for the Exchange of Statistical Data and Economic Information is located in Ankara, Turkey. An International Centre for Black Sea Studies (ICBSS) was established in Athens, Greece, in March 1998, in order to undertake research concerning the BSEC, in the fields of economics, industry and technology.

In recent years BSEC has undergone a process of reform aimed at developing a more project-based orientation. In April 2001 the Council adopted the so-called BSEC Economic Agenda for the Future Towards a More Consolidated, Effective and Viable BSEC Partnership, which provided a roadmap for charting the implementation of the Organization's goals. Meeting in June 2011 the Council established an Ad Hoc Group of Experts, with a mandate to revise and update the document. In June 2012 the Council adopted a new BSEC Economic Agenda, which reflected new challenges and opportunities in the global and regional economic environment and outlined 17 priority areas of action.

In 2002 a Project Development Fund (PDF) was established and a regional programme of governance and institutional renewal was launched. A project aimed at developing renewable energy sources, and a project entitled 'Introducing climate change in the environmental strategy for the protection of the Black Sea' (ICEBS) were approved for PDF funding in 2010. Under the new orientation the roles of BSEC's Committee of Senior Officials and network of country co-ordinators were to be enhanced. In April 2008 the BSEC Council inaugurated a new €2m. BSEC Hellenic Development Fund to support regional co-operation; guidelines for the operation of the Fund were adopted at a meeting of the Council in late October. The Council also adopted the modalities for BSEC fast-track co-operation, aimed at enabling sub-groups of member states to proceed with policies that other member states were unwilling or unable to pursue. The October 2008 meeting of the Council adopted new guidelines on improving the efficiency of the grouping.

BSEC aims to foster relations with other international and regional organizations, and has been granted observer status at the UN General Assembly. BSEC supports the Stability Pact for South-Eastern Europe, initiated in June 1999 as a collaborative plan of action by the European Union (EU), the Group of Seven industrialized nations and Russia (the G8), regional governments and other organizations concerned with the stability of the region. In 1999 BSEC agreed upon a platform of co-operation for future structured relations with the EU. The main areas in which BSEC determined to develop co-operation with the EU were transport, energy and telecommunications infrastructure; trade and the promotion of foreign direct investment; sustainable development and environmental protection, including nuclear safety; science and technology; and combating terrorism and organized crime. The Declaration issued by BSEC's decennial anniversary summit, held in Istanbul in June 2002, urged that collaboration with the EU should be enhanced. In April 2005 representatives of BSEC and the EU met in Brussels, Belgium, to address possibilities for such co-operation, focusing in particular on the EU's policy in the Black Sea region and on the development of regional transport and energy networks (see Alexandroupolis Declaration, below). In June 2007 BSEC heads of state confirmed their commitment to an enhanced relationship with the EU, based on a communication of the European Commission, published in April, entitled 'Black Sea Synergy—a New Regional Cooperation Initiative'. In February 2008 a special meeting of the BSEC Council adopted a Declaration on a BSEC-EU Enhanced Relationship. Consideration of the prospects of enhanced interaction between the two organizations was pursued at a round-table discussion hosted by the European Policy Centre (and jointly organized with the BSEC International Secretariat and the International Centre for Black Sea Studies) in April 2009. A BSEC-EU Black Sea Regional Strategy was prepared, promoting BSEC-EU interaction during 2010–13. In March 2010 a Black Sea Environmental Partnership was launched by the EU, to support its efforts, and those of regional partners, including BSEC, to find co-operative approaches towards addressing environmental challenges in areas such as biodiversity conservation, integrated coastal zone and river basin management, and sources of pollution, and towards promoting environmental integration, monitoring and research.

BSEC has supported implementation of the Bucharest Convention on the Protection of the Black Sea Against Pollution, adopted by Bulgaria, Georgia, Romania, Russia, Turkey and Ukraine in April 1992. In October 1996 those countries adopted the Strategic Action Plan for the Rehabilitation and Protection of the Black Sea (BSSAP), to be implemented by the Commission of the Bucharest Convention. In March 2001 the ministers of transport of BSEC member states adopted a Transport Action Plan, which envisaged reducing the disparities in regional transport systems and integrating the BSEC regional transport infrastructure with wider international networks and projects. In November 2006 BSEC signed a Memorandum of Understanding (MOU) with the International Road Federation. In April 2007 BSEC governments signed an agreement for the co-ordinated development of a 7,100 km-long Black Sea Ring Highway (BSRH). An MOU relating to the development of 'Motorways of the Sea' was also signed. Both accords entered into effect in late 2008. In March 2005 ministers of BSEC member states responsible for energy adopted the Alexandroupolis Declaration, approving a common framework for future collaboration on the creation of a regional energy market, and urging the liberalization of electricity and natural gas markets in accordance with EU directives as a basis for this.

In April 2009 a BSEC Working Group on Banking and Finance convened in Yerevan, Armenia, to consider how the global financial and economic crisis had affected banking and finance sectors in the region and to review national stabilization measures and other efforts being undertaken to contain the crisis. The meeting preceded a regular meeting of the Council which also discussed the implications for the region of the instability of the world's financial markets and the economic downturn.

Finance

BSEC is financed by annual contributions from member states on the following scale: Greece, Russia, Turkey and Ukraine each contribute 15% of the budget; Bulgaria, Romania and Serbia contribute 7.5%; the remaining members each contribute 3.5%.

Publication

Black Sea News (quarterly).

Related Bodies

Parliamentary Assembly of the Black Sea: 1 Hareket Kösku, Dolmabahçe Sarayi, Besiktas, 80680 İstanbul, Turkey; tel. (212) 227-6070; fax (212) 227-6080; e-mail pabsec@pabsec.org; internet www.pabsec.org; f. 1993; the Assembly, consisting of the representatives of the national parliaments of member states, aims to provide a legal basis for the implementation of decisions within the BSEC framework; comprises three committees concerning economic, commercial, technological and environmental affairs; legal and political affairs; and cultural, educational and social affairs; the presidency rotates every six months; Sec.-Gen. KYRYLO TRETIAK (Ukraine).

Black Sea Trade and Development Bank: 1 Komninon str., 54624 Thessaloníki, Greece; tel. (2310) 290400; fax (2310) 221796; e-mail info@bstdb.org; internet www.bstdb.org; f. 1999; the Bank supports economic development and regional co-operation by providing trade and project financing, guarantees, and equity for development projects supporting both public and private enterprises in its member countries, in sectors including energy, infrastructure, finance, manufacturing, transport, and telecommunications; by 31 Dec. 2011 the Bank had approved 265 approved operations with funding exceeding €2,000m; auth. cap. SDR 3,000m. (March 2012); Pres. ANDREY KONDAKOV (Russia); Sec.-Gen. ORSALIA KALANTZOPOULOS (Greece).

BSEC Business Council: Müsir Fuad Pasa Yalisi, Eski Tersane, 80860 Istinye, İstanbul, Turkey; tel. (212) 229-1144; fax (212) 229-0332; e-mail info@bsec-business.org; internet www.bsec-business.org; f. 1992; aims to secure greater economic integration and to promote investment in the region; Sec.-Gen. EFTYCHIA BACOPOULOU.

International Centre for Black Sea Studies: 4 Xenophontos Str., 10557 Athens, Greece; tel. (210) 3242321; fax (210) 3242244; e-mail icbss@icbss.org; internet www.icbss.org; f. 1998; aims to foster co-operation among BSEC member states and with international partners through applied research and advocacy; hosts the International Black Sea Symposium, an Annual Lecture and other events; Dir-Gen. Dr ZEFI DIMADAMA (Greece); publs *Xenophon Paper* series, Policy Briefs, *Black Sea Monitor* (quarterly).

ORGANIZATION OF ISLAMIC COOPERATION—OIC

Address: Medina Rd, Sary St, POB 178, Jeddah 21411, Saudi Arabia.

Telephone: (2) 690-0001; **fax:** (2) 275-1953; **e-mail:** info@oic-oci.org; **internet:** www.oic-oci.org.

The Organization was formally established, as the Organization of the Islamic Conference, at the first conference of Muslim heads of state convened in Rabat, Morocco, in September 1969; the first conference of Muslim foreign ministers, held in Jeddah in March 1970, established the General Secretariat; the latter became operational in May 1971. In June 2011 the 38th ministerial conference agreed to change the name of the Organization, with immediate effect, to the Organization of Islamic Cooperation (abbreviated, as hitherto, to OIC).

MEMBERS

Afghanistan	Indonesia	Qatar
Albania	Iran	Saudi Arabia
Algeria	Iraq	Senegal
Azerbaijan	Jordan	Sierra Leone
Bahrain	Kazakhstan	Somalia
Bangladesh	Kuwait	Sudan
Benin	Kyrgyzstan	Suriname
Brunei	Lebanon	Syria
Burkina Faso	Libya	Tajikistan
Cameroon	Malaysia	Togo
Chad	Maldives	Tunisia
Comoros	Mali	Turkey
Côte d'Ivoire	Mauritania	Turkmenistan
Djibouti	Morocco	Uganda
Egypt	Mozambique	United Arab Emirates
Gabon	Niger	Uzbekistan
The Gambia	Nigeria	Yemen
Guinea	Oman	
Guinea-Bissau	Pakistan	
Guyana	Palestine	

Note: Observer status has been granted to Bosnia and Herzegovina, the Central African Republic, Russia, Thailand, the Muslim community of the 'Turkish Republic of Northern Cyprus', the Moro National Liberation Front (MNLF) of the southern Philippines, the UN, the African Union, the Non-Aligned Movement, the League of Arab States, the Economic Cooperation Organization, the Union of the Arab Maghreb and the Cooperation Council for the Arab States of the Gulf. The revised OIC Charter, endorsed in March 2008, made future applications for OIC membership and observer status conditional upon Muslim demographic majority and membership of the UN.

Organization

(June 2012)

SUMMIT CONFERENCES

The supreme body of the Organization is the Conference of Heads of State ('Islamic summit'), which met in 1969 in Rabat, Morocco, in 1974 in Lahore, Pakistan, and in January 1981 in Mecca, Saudi Arabia, when it was decided that ordinary summit conferences would normally be held every three years in future. An extraordinary summit conference was convened in Doha, Qatar, in March 2003, to consider the situation in Iraq. A further extraordinary conference, held in December 2005, in Mecca, determined to restructure the OIC. The 11th ordinary Islamic summit was convened in Dakar, Senegal, in March 2008. The summit conference troika comprises member countries equally representing the OIC's African, Arab and Asian membership.

CONFERENCE OF MINISTERS OF FOREIGN AFFAIRS

Conferences take place annually, to consider the means of implementing the general policy of the Organization, although they may also be convened for extraordinary sessions. The ministerial conference troika comprises member countries equally representing the OIC's African, Arab and Asian membership.

SECRETARIAT

The executive organ of the organization, headed by a Secretary-General (who is elected by the Conference of Ministers of Foreign Affairs for a five-year term, renewable only once) and four Assistant Secretaries-General (similarly appointed).

Secretary-General: Prof. Dr EKMELEDDIN IHSANOGLU (Turkey).

At the summit conference in January 1981 it was decided that an International Islamic Court of Justice should be established to adjudicate in disputes between Muslim countries. Experts met in January 1983 to draw up a constitution for the court; however, by 2012 it was not yet in operation.

EXECUTIVE COMMITTEE

The third extraordinary conference of the OIC, convened in Mecca, Saudi Arabia, in December 2005, mandated the establishment of the Executive Committee, comprising the summit conference and ministerial conference troikas, the OIC host country, and the OIC Secretariat, as a mechanism for following up resolutions of the Conference.

STANDING COMMITTEES

Al-Quds Committee: f. 1975 to implement the resolutions of the Islamic Conference on the status of Jerusalem (Al-Quds); it meets at the level of foreign ministers; maintains the Al-Quds Fund; Chair. King MUHAMMAD VI OF MOROCCO.

Standing Committee for Economic and Commercial Co-operation (COMCEC): f. 1981; Chair. ABDULLAH GÜL (Pres. of Turkey).

Standing Committee for Information and Cultural Affairs (COMIAC): f. 1981; Chair. MACKY SALL (Pres. of Senegal).

Standing Committee for Scientific and Technological Co-operation (COMSTECH): f. 1981; Chair. ASIF ALI ZARDARI (Pres. of Pakistan).

Other committees comprise the Islamic Peace Committee, the Permanent Finance Committee, the Committee of Islamic Solidarity with the Peoples of the Sahel, the Eight-Member Committee on the Situation of Muslims in the Philippines, the Six-Member Committee on Palestine, the Committee on UN reform, and the ad hoc Committee on Afghanistan. In addition, there is an Islamic Commission for Economic, Cultural and Social Affairs, and there are OIC contact groups on Bosnia and Herzegovina, Iraq, Kosovo, Jammu and Kashmir, Sierra Leone, and Somalia. A Commission of Eminent Persons was inaugurated in 2005.

Activities

The Organization's aims, as proclaimed in the Charter (adopted in 1972, with revisions endorsed in 1990 and 2008), are:

(i) To promote Islamic solidarity among member states;

(ii) To consolidate co-operation among member states in the economic, social, cultural, scientific and other vital fields, and to arrange consultations among member states belonging to international organizations;

(iii) To endeavour to eliminate racial segregation and discrimination and to eradicate colonialism in all its forms;

(iv) To take necessary measures to support international peace and security founded on justice;

(v) To co-ordinate all efforts for the safeguard of the Holy Places and support of the struggle of the people of Palestine, and help them to regain their rights and liberate their land;

(vi) To strengthen the struggle of all Muslim people with a view to safeguarding their dignity, independence and national rights;

(vii) To create a suitable atmosphere for the promotion of co-operation and understanding among member states and other countries.

The first summit conference of Islamic leaders (representing 24 states) took place in 1969 following the burning of the al-Aqsa Mosque in Jerusalem. At this conference it was decided that Islamic governments should 'consult together with a view to promoting close co-operation and mutual assistance in the economic, scientific, cultural and spiritual fields, inspired by the immortal teachings of Islam'. Thereafter the foreign ministers of the countries concerned met annually, and adopted the Charter of the Organization of the Islamic Conference in 1972.

At the second Islamic summit conference (Lahore, Pakistan, 1974), the Islamic Solidarity Fund was established, together with a committee of representatives that later evolved into the Islamic Commission for Economic, Cultural and Social Affairs. Subsequently, numerous other subsidiary bodies have been set up (see below).

ECONOMIC CO-OPERATION

A general agreement on economic, technical and commercial co-operation came into force in 1981, providing for the establishment of joint investment projects and trade co-ordination. This was followed by an agreement on promotion, protection and guarantee of investments among member states. A plan of action to strengthen economic co-operation was adopted at the third Islamic summit conference in 1981, aiming to promote collective self-reliance and the development of joint ventures in all sectors. The fifth summit conference, held in 1987, approved proposals for joint development of modern technology, and for improving scientific and technical skills in the less developed Islamic countries. In 1994 the 1981 plan of action was revised to place greater emphasis on private sector participation in its implementation. In October 2003 a meeting of COMCEC endorsed measures aimed at accelerating the hitherto slow implementation of the plan of action. A 10-year plan of action for fostering member states' development and strengthening economic and trade co-operation was launched in December 2005.

In 1991 22 OIC member states signed a Framework Agreement on a Trade Preferential System among the OIC Member States (TPS-OIC); this entered into force in 2003, following the requisite ratification by more than 10 member states, and was envisaged as representing the first step towards the eventual establishment of an Islamic common market. A Trade Negotiating Committee (TNC) was established following the entry into force of the Framework Agreement. The first round of trade negotiations on the establishment of the TPS-OIC, concerning finalizing tariff-reduction modalities and an implementation schedule for the Agreement, was held during April 2004–April 2005, and resulted in the conclusion of a Protocol on the Preferential Tariff Scheme for TPS-OIC (PRETAS). In November 2006, at the launch of the second round of negotiations, ministers adopted a roadmap towards establishing the TPS-OIC; the second round of negotiations ended in September 2007 with the adoption of rules of origin for the TPS-OIC. PRETAS entered into force in February 2010. By mid-2012 the Framework Agreement had been ratified by 28 OIC member states, and PRETAS had 15 ratifications.

In March 2008 the summit adopted a five-year Special Programme for the Development of Africa, covering the period 2008–12, which aimed to promote the economic development of OIC African member states and to support these countries in achieving the UN Millennium Development Goals.

The first OIC Anti-Corruption and Enhancing Integrity Forum was convened in August 2006 in Kuala Lumpur, Malaysia. The 13th Trade Fair of the OIC member states was staged in Sharjah, Saudi Arabia, in April 2011. The second OIC Tourism Fair was to take place in Cairo, Egypt, in December 2012. The seventh World Islamic Economic Forum was convened in Astana, Kazakhstan, in June 2011. In November 2009 a COMCEC Business Forum was held, in Istanbul, Turkey. An International Islamic Business and Finance Summit has been organized annually since 2009, in Kazan, Russia, by the OIC and the Russian Government; 'KAZANSUMMIT 2012' was convened in May 2012.

In March 2012 OIC ministers responsible for water approved the OIC Water Vision 2025, providing a framework for co-operation in maximizing the productive use of, and minimizing the destructive impact of, members' water resources. In May 2012 the fifth Islamic Conference of Environment Ministers, convened in Astana, adopted an Islamic Declaration on Sustainable Development. An OIC Green Technology Blue Print was under development in 2012.

CULTURAL AND TECHNICAL CO-OPERATION

The Organization supports education in Muslim communities throughout the world, and was instrumental in the establishment of Islamic universities in Niger and Uganda. It organizes seminars on various aspects of Islam, and encourages dialogue with the other monotheistic religions. Support is given to publications on Islam both in Muslim and Western countries. In June 1999 an OIC Parliamentary Union was inaugurated; its founding conference was convened in Tehran, Iran. An inaugural Conference of Muslim Women Parliamentarians was convened in January 2012, in Palembang, Indonesia.

The OIC organizes meetings at ministerial level to consider aspects of information policy and new technologies. An OIC Digital Solidarity Fund was inaugurated in May 2005. Participation by OIC member states in the Fund was promoted at the 11th OIC summit meeting in March 2008, and the meeting also requested each member state to establish a board to monitor national implementation of the Tunis Declaration on the Information Society, adopted by the November 2005 second phase of the World Summit on the Information Society. The first OIC Conference on Women was held in November 2006, on the theme 'The role of women in the development of OIC member states'. In January 2009 the OIC and the League of Arab States signed an agreement providing for the strengthening of co-operation and co-ordination in the areas of politics, media, the economy, and in the social and scientific spheres. In August 2011 the OIC organized a Decorative Arts and Calligraphy Exhibition, at its headquarters in Jeddah.

HUMANITARIAN ASSISTANCE

Assistance is given to Muslim communities affected by violent conflict and natural disasters, in co-operation with UN organizations, particularly UNCHR. The OIC has established trust funds to assist vulnerable people in Afghanistan, Bosnia and Herzegovina, and Sierra Leone. Humanitarian assistance provided by OIC member states has included aid to the Muslim population affected by the conflict in Chechnya; to victims of conflict in Darfur, southern Sudan; to Indonesia following the tsunami disaster in December 2004; and to Pakistan following the major earthquake there in October 2005. In October 2009 an OIC humanitarian mission was sent to support survivors of the earthquake that struck Padang, Indonesia, at the end of September. In mid-August 2010, at the request of the Pakistan Government, the OIC organized an emergency meeting to review the ongoing humanitarian relief operation supporting survivors of the severe floods that had devastated northern and central areas of Pakistan during that month (seriously adversely affecting at least 15m. people, of whom 8m. were believed to be at high risk of contracting waterborne diseases, and including 2m. people who had been displaced from their homes). By the end of August OIC member countries had pledged US $1,000m. in support of the flood-affected communities. It was announced at that time that an OIC Emergency Fund for Natural Disasters would be established, to assist survivors of any natural disaster occurring in future in a Muslim country. The countries of the Sahel region (Burkina Faso, Cape Verde, Chad, The Gambia, Guinea, Guinea-Bissau, Mali, Mauritania, Niger and Senegal) receive particular attention as victims of drought. In mid-March 2012 a joint OIC-UN team of technical experts was dispatched to Syria to assess the humanitarian impact of the ongoing unrest there and to prepare an evaluation of the level of humanitarian aid required; in early April, having considered the findings of the assessment team, the OIC Secretary-General stated that some $70m. in funding was required to assist at least 1m. Syrians.

In March 2008 the OIC launched a humanitarian support operation for Palestinians in Gaza; an initial 'assistance caravan' transported medical supplies and equipment to the area. An expanded extraordinary meeting of the Executive Committee, convened, at the level of ministers of foreign affairs, in January 2009 to address the ongoing intensive bombardment of the Gaza

Strip that was initiated by Israeli forces in late December 2008 with the stated aim of ending rocket attacks launched by Hamas and other militant groups on Israeli targets, requested the OIC Secretariat to co-ordinate with member states' civil society organizations to provide urgent humanitarian relief to the Palestinian people. OIC convoys of humanitarian aid, including medical supplies, food and clothing, were subsequently dispatched to Gaza.

In August 2011 OIC governments pledged US $350m. in aid to combat famine in Somalia, where some 3.7m. people were reported at that time to be at risk of starvation. The OIC Secretary-General urged donor nations to help to rehabilitate Somalia's infrastructure and agricultural production with a view to improving the long-term prospects for food security. In early October 2011 the OIC convened a conference on the theme 'Water for Life in Somalia', with participation by 32 non-governmental humanitarian relief agencies; the conference adopted a declaration pledging to drill 682 boreholes in 11 provinces of Somalia, with a view to alleviating the acute shortage of water that had contributed to the famine.

The first conference of Islamic humanitarian organizations was convened by the OIC in March 2008, and a second conference, bringing together 32 organizations, took place in April 2009. The third conference of Islamic humanitarian organizations, held in March 2010, established a working group to draft a plan aimed at strengthening co-operation between the OIC and other humanitarian organizations active in Afghanistan, Gaza, Darfur, Iraq, Niger, Somalia, and Sudan; and also approved the formation of a joint commission which was to study the structure and mechanism of co-operation and co-ordination between humanitarian organizations. The fourth conference was convened in June 2011, with the theme 'Civil Society Organizations in the Muslim World: Responsibilities and Roles'. In May 2012 the first Conference on Refugees in the Muslim World was convened by the OIC, UNHCR and the Turkmen Government, in Aşgabat, Turkmenistan.

POLITICAL CO-OPERATION

In June 2011 OIC foreign ministers adopted the Astana Declaration on Peace, Co-operation and Development, in which they recognized emerging challenges presented by unfolding significant political developments in the Middle East and North Africa (the so-called 'Arab Spring') and appealed for engagement in constructive dialogue towards peaceful solutions. The Declaration expressed grave concern at the then ongoing conflict in Libya, and at the humanitarian consequences thereof. The foreign ministers also adopted the OIC Action Plan for Cooperation with Central Asia, which aimed to establish centres of excellence with a view to encouraging scientific innovation; and to promote job training and public-private partnership; to promote a reduction in the incidence of HIV/AIDS, polio, malaria and TB in the region; to build cultural understanding; and to combat trafficking in human beings and in illegal drugs. The OIC gives support to member countries in regaining or maintaining political stability. During 2011, for example, it participated in International Contact Groups on Afghanistan, Libya, and Somalia, co-operating with the UN and other international organizations and national governments in supporting efforts to restore constitutional rule in those countries. In December 2011 the OIC Executive Committee convened a ministerial open-ended meeting on the ongoing unrest in Syria; the OIC Secretary-General strongly condemned mass killings of civilians in that country perpetrated by security forces in late May and early June 2012. A new OIC Independent Human Rights Commission (IPHRC), comprising 18 commissioners representing Africa, Asia and the Middle East, was inaugurated in February 2012. In early April the OIC Secretary-General expressed 'total rejection' of the proclamation by militants in northern Mali of an independent homeland of 'Azawad'. A delegation of the OIC was dispatched to observe legislative elections held in Algeria, in May of that year. In June 2012 the Secretary-General strongly condemned bomb attacks perpetrated by the Islamist group Boko Haram against churches in northern Nigeria, and subsequent reprisal attacks against Muslims and mosques, which had resulted in dozens of fatalities, and appealed for calm and restraint in the region.

Israel/Palestine: Since its inception the OIC has called for the vacation of Arab territories by Israel, recognition of the rights of Palestinians and of the Palestine Liberation Organization (PLO) as their sole legitimate representative, and the restoration of Jerusalem to Arab rule. The 1981 summit conference called for a *jihad* (holy war—though not necessarily in a military sense) 'for the liberation of Jerusalem and the occupied territories'; this was to include an Islamic economic boycott of Israel. In 1982 Islamic ministers of foreign affairs decided to establish Islamic offices for boycotting Israel and for military co-operation with the PLO. In view of the significant deterioration in relations between Israel and the Palestinian (National) Authority (PA) during late 2000, in December of that year the ninth summit conference of heads of state and of government, held in Doha, Qatar, issued a Declaration pledging solidarity with the Palestinian cause and accusing the Israeli authorities of implementing large-scale systematic violations of human rights against Palestinians. In June 2002 OIC ministers of foreign affairs endorsed the peace plan for the region that had been adopted by the summit meeting of the League of Arab States in March. In early January 2009 an expanded extraordinary meeting of the Executive Committee, at the level of ministers of foreign affairs, convened to address the ongoing intensive bombardment of the Gaza Strip that was initiated by Israeli forces in late December 2008 with the stated aim of ending rocket attacks launched by Hamas and other militant groups on Israeli targets. The meeting strongly condemned the Israeli attacks and ensuing destruction and loss of civilian life, and requested the OIC Secretariat to co-ordinate with member states' civil society organizations to provide urgent humanitarian relief to the Palestinian people. In March 2009, while visiting the affected area, the OIC Secretary-General urged the reconciliation of the different Palestinian political factions. In June 2010 an expanded extraordinary ministerial meeting of the Executive Committee condemned the attack by Israeli security forces, at the end of May, against a flotilla of vessels carrying humanitarian aid to Gaza, which had resulted in nine civilian deaths and caused injuries to at least 40 people. The OIC rejected a UN-commissioned report on the flotilla incident, released in September 2011, which—while concluding that the Israeli army had used 'excessive and unreasonable' force—also found the Israeli naval blockade of Gaza to have been imposed as a 'legitimate security measure' to prevent weapons from reaching Gaza by sea, and found that the flotilla had acted recklessly in attempting to breach the naval blockade. The OIC Secretary-General supported efforts to bring the issue of the blockade of Gaza before competent international legal authorities. In late September the OIC Secretary-General condemned a decision by Israel to build 1,100 new housing units in occupied East Jerusalem. During that month the OIC expressed support for the formal request by the Executive President of the Palestinian Authority for Palestine's admission to the UN, and recognition of its independent statehood.

Iraq: In August 1990 a majority of OIC member states' ministers of foreign affairs condemned Iraq's recent invasion of Kuwait, and demanded the withdrawal of Iraqi forces. The sixth summit conference, held in Senegal in December 1991, reflected the divisions in the Arab world that resulted from Iraq's invasion of Kuwait and the ensuing war. Twelve heads of state did not attend, reportedly to register protest at the presence of Jordan and the PLO at the conference, both of which had given support to Iraq. In December 1994 OIC heads of state supported the decision by Iraq to recognize Kuwait. In December 1998 the OIC appealed for a diplomatic solution to the tensions arising from Iraq's withdrawal of co-operation with UN weapons inspectors, and criticized subsequent military air-strikes, led by the USA, as having been conducted without renewed UN authority. An extraordinary summit conference of Islamic leaders convened in Doha, in early March 2003, to consider the ongoing Iraq crisis, welcomed the Saddam Hussain regime's acceptance of UN Security Council Resolution 1441 and consequent co-operation with UN weapons inspectors, and emphatically rejected military action against Iraq or threats to the security of any other Islamic state. The conference also urged progress towards the elimination of all weapons of mass destruction in the Middle East, including those held by Israel. In mid-May 2004 the OIC Secretary-General urged combat forces in Iraq to respect the inviolability of that country's holy places. In December 2005 he appealed to the people of Iraq to participate peacefully in the legislative elections that took place later in that month. In October 2006 a meeting of Iraqi Islamic scholars from all denominations issued a declaration on the Iraqi situation, in which they urged unity between different Islamic factions in that country. During 2008–11 the OIC Secretary-General repeatedly appealed for an end to sectarian strife in Iraq, and in October 2008 he condemned the persecution of Christians in northern Iraq.

Afghanistan: In October 2001 OIC ministers of foreign affairs established a fund to assist Afghan civilians, following US-led military attacks on targets in Afghanistan. In mid-2010 the OIC determined to appoint a permanent representative for Afghanistan, to be based in an OIC office in Kabul, the Afghan capital. The OIC Kabul office was inaugurated in January 2011. In March the OIC Secretary-General, addressing the International Contact Group on Afghanistan, stressed OIC support for the High Peace Council, established in Afghanistan in 2010 as a platform for dialogue between the Afghan administration and the Taliban, and stated the willingness of the Organization to contribute to peace in that country. In December 2011, attending the International Conference on Afghanistan, convened in Bonn, Germany, the OIC Secretary-General emphasized that the Organization would continue to support Afghanistan beyond 2014, when NATO forces were scheduled to leave the country.

Combating Terrorism: In December 1994 OIC heads of state adopted a Code of Conduct for Combating International Terrorism, in an attempt to control Muslim extremist groups. The code commits states to ensuring that militant groups do not use their territory for planning or executing terrorist activity against other states, in addition to states refraining from direct support or participation in acts of terrorism. An OIC Convention on Combating International Terrorism was adopted in 1998. In September 2001 the OIC Secretary-General strongly condemned major terrorist attacks perpetrated against targets in the USA. Soon afterwards the US authorities rejected a proposal by the Taliban regime that an OIC observer mission be deployed to monitor the activities of the Saudi Arabian-born exiled militant Islamist fundamentalist leader Osama bin Laden, who was accused by the US Government of having co-ordinated the attacks from alleged terrorist bases in the Taliban-administered area of Afghanistan. An extraordinary meeting of OIC ministers of foreign affairs, convened in early October, in Doha, Qatar, to consider the implications of the terrorist atrocities, condemned the attacks and declared its support for combating all manifestations of terrorism within the framework of a proposed collective initiative co-ordinated under the auspices of the UN. The meeting, which did not pronounce directly on the recently-initiated US-led military retaliation against targets in Afghanistan, urged that no Arab or Muslim state should be targeted under the pretext of eliminating terrorism. In February 2002 the Secretary-General expressed concern at statements of the US administration describing Iran and Iraq (as well as the Democratic People's Republic of Korea) as belonging to an 'axis of evil' involved in international terrorism and the development of weapons of mass destruction. In April OIC ministers of foreign affairs convened an extraordinary session on terrorism, in Kuala Lumpur, Malaysia. The meeting issued the Kuala Lumpur Declaration, which reiterated member states' collective resolve to combat terrorism, recalling the organization's 1994 code of conduct and 1998 convention to this effect; condemned attempts to associate terrorist activities with Islam or any other particular creed, civilization or nationality, and rejected attempts to associate Islamic states or the Palestinian struggle with terrorism; rejected the implementation of international action against any Muslim state on the pretext of combating terrorism; urged the organization of a global conference on international terrorism; and urged an examination of the root causes of international terrorism. The meeting adopted a plan of action on addressing the issues raised in the declaration. Its implementation was to be co-ordinated by a 13-member committee on international terrorism. Member states were encouraged to sign and ratify the Convention on Combating International Terrorism in order to accelerate its implementation. In June 2002 ministers of foreign affairs issued a declaration reiterating the OIC call for an international conference to be convened, under UN auspices, in order clearly to define terrorism and to agree on the international procedures and mechanisms for combating terrorism through the UN. In May 2003 the 30th session of the Conference of Ministers of Foreign Affairs, entitled 'Unity and Dignity', issued the Tehran Declaration, in which it resolved to combat terrorism and to contribute to preserving peace and security in Islamic countries. The Declaration also pledged its full support for the Palestinian cause and rejected the labelling as 'terrorist' of those Muslim states deemed to be resisting foreign aggression and occupation.

Supporting Muslim Minorities and Combating Anti-Islamic Feeling: In December 1995 OIC ministers of foreign affairs determined that an intergovernmental group of experts should be established to address the situation of minority Muslim communities residing in non-OIC states. The OIC committee of experts responsible for formulating a plan of action for safeguarding the rights of Muslim communities and minorities met for the first time in 1998. In June 2001 the OIC condemned attacks and ongoing discrimination against the Muslim community in Myanmar. In October 2005 the OIC Secretary-General expressed concern at the treatment of Muslims in the southern provinces of Thailand. The first tripartite meeting between the OIC, the Government of the Philippines and Muslim separatists based in the southern Philippines took place in November 2007, and in April 2009 the OIC Secretary-General announced the appointment of an OIC special envoy to assist in negotiating a peaceful solution to the conflict in the southern Philippines.

In January 2006 the OIC strongly condemned the publication in a Norwegian newspaper of a series of caricatures of the Prophet Muhammad that had originally appeared in a Danish publication in September 2005 and had caused considerable offence to many Muslims. An Islamic Observatory on Islamophobia was established in September 2006; in April 2011 the Observatory released its fourth annual report on Islamophobia. In December 2007 the OIC organized the first International Conference on Islamophobia, aimed at addressing concerns that alleged instances of defamation of Islam appeared to be increasing world-wide (particularly in Europe). Responding to a reported rise in anti-Islamic attacks on Western nations, OIC leaders denounced stereotyping and discrimination, and urged the promotion of Islam by Islamic states as a 'moderate, peaceful and tolerant religion'. In June 2011 the OIC Secretary-General issued a statement strongly condemning 'attacks on Islam and insult and vilification of the Prophet Muhummad and his wives' by the right-wing Dutch politician Geert Wilders. The Secretary-General stated in June 2012 that Islamophobia was being exploited in electoral campaigns in Europe, citing the campaigns for the French presidential election held in April–May.

Reform of the OIC: In March 1997, at an extraordinary meeting of heads of state and of government, held in Islamabad, Pakistan, an Islamabad Declaration was adopted, which pledged to increase co-operation between members of the OIC. In November 2000 OIC heads of state attended the ninth summit conference, held in Doha, Qatar, and issued the Doha Declaration, which reaffirmed commitment to the OIC Charter and undertook to modernize the organization. The 10th OIC summit meeting, held in October 2003, in Putrajaya, Malaysia, issued the Putrajaya Declaration, in which Islamic leaders resolved to enhance Islamic states' role and influence in international affairs. The leaders adopted a plan of action that entailed: reviewing and strengthening OIC positions on international issues; enhancing dialogue among Muslim thinkers and policy-makers through relevant OIC insitutions; promoting constructive dialogue with other cultures and civilizations; completing an ongoing review of the structure and efficacy of the OIC Secretariat; establishing a working group to address means of enhancing the role of Islamic education; promoting among member states the development of science and technology, discussion of ecological issues, and the role of information communication technology in development; improving mechanisms to assist member states in post-conflict situations; and advancing trade and investment through data-sharing and encouraging access to markets for products from poorer member states. In January 2005 the inaugural meeting of an OIC Commission of Eminent Persons was convened in Putrajaya. The Commission was mandated to make recommendations in the following areas: the preparation of a strategy and plan of action enabling the Islamic community to meet the challenges of the 21st century; the preparation of a comprehensive plan for promoting enlightened moderation, both within

Islamic societies and universally; and the preparation of proposals for the future reform and restructuring of the OIC system. In December the third extraordinary OIC summit, convened in Mecca, Saudi Arabia, adopted a Ten-Year Programme of Action to Meet the Challenges Facing the Ummah (the Islamic world) in the 21st Century, a related Mecca Declaration and a report by the Commission of Eminent Persons. The summit determined to restructure the OIC, and mandated the establishment of an Executive Committee, comprising the summit conference and ministerial conference troikas (equally reflecting the African, Arab and Asian member states), the OIC host country, and the OIC Secretariat, to implement Conference resolutions.

The 11th OIC heads of state summit meeting, held in Dakar, Senegal, in March 2008, endorsed a revised OIC Charter.

Finance

The OIC's activities are financed by mandatory contributions from member states.

Subsidiary Organs

Islamic Centre for the Development of Trade: Complexe Commercial des Habous, ave des FAR, BP 13545, Casablanca, Morocco; tel. (522) 314974; fax (522) 310110; e-mail icdt@icdt-oic.org; internet www.icdt-oic.org; f. 1983 to encourage regular commercial contacts, harmonize policies and promote investments among OIC mems; Dir-Gen. Dr EL HASSANE HZAINE; publs *Tijaris: International and Inter-Islamic Trade Magazine* (bi-monthly), *Inter-Islamic Trade Report* (annually).

Islamic Jurisprudence (Fiqh) Academy: POB 13917, Jeddah, Saudi Arabia; tel. (2) 667-1664; fax (2) 667-0873; internet www.fiqhacademy.org.sa; f. 1982; Gen. Sec. MAULANA KHALID SAIFULLAH RAHMANI.

Islamic Solidarity Fund: c/o OIC Secretariat, POB 1997, Jeddah 21411, Saudi Arabia; tel. (2) 698-1296; fax (2) 256-8185; e-mail info@isf-fsi.org; internet www.isf-fsi.org; f. 1974 to meet the needs of Islamic communities by providing emergency aid and the finance to build mosques, Islamic centres, hospitals, schools and universities; Exec. Dir IBRAHIM BIN ABDALLAH AL-KHOZAIM.

Islamic University in Uganda: POB 2555, Mbale, Uganda; tel. (35) 2512100; fax (45) 433502; e-mail info@iuiu.ac.ug; internet www.iuiu.ac.ug/; f. 1988 to meet the educational needs of Muslim populations in English-speaking African countries; second campus in Kampala; mainly financed by OIC; Rector Dr AHMAD KAWESA SENGENDO.

Islamic University of Niger: BP 11507, Niamey, Niger; tel. 20-72-39-03; fax 20-73-37-96; e-mail unislam@intnet.ne; internet www.universite_say.ne/; f. 1984; provides courses of study in *Shari'a* (Islamic law) and Arabic language and literature; also offers courses in pedagogy and teacher training; receives grants from Islamic Solidarity Fund and contributions from OIC member states; Rector Prof. ABDELJAOUAD SEKKAT.

Islamic University of Technology (IUT): Board Bazar, Gazipur 1704, Dhaka, Bangladesh; tel. (2) 9291250; fax (2) 9291260; e-mail vc@iut-dhaka.edu; internet www.iutoic-dhaka.edu; f. 1981 as the Islamic Centre for Technical and Vocational Training and Resources, named changed to Islamic Institute of Technology in 1994, current name adopted in 2001; aims to develop human resources in OIC mem. states, with special reference to engineering, technology, and technical education; 145 staff and 800 students; library of 30,450 vols; Vice-Chancellor Prof. Dr M. IMTIAZ HOSSAIN; publs *Journal of Engineering and Technology* (2 a year), *News Bulletin* (annually), *News Letter* (6 a year), annual calendar and announcement for admission, reports, human resources development series.

Research Centre for Islamic History, Art and Culture (IRCICA): POB 24, Beşiktaş 34354, İstanbul, Turkey; tel. (212) 2591742; fax (212) 2584365; e-mail ircica@ircica.org; internet www.ircica.org; f. 1980; library of 60,000 vols; Dir-Gen. Prof. Dr HALIT EREN; publs *Newsletter* (3 a year), monographical studies.

Statistical, Economic and Social Research and Training Centre for Islamic Countries (SESRIC): Attar Sokak No. 4, GOP 06700, Ankara, Turkey; tel. (312) 4686172; fax (312) 4673458; e-mail oicankara@sesric.org; internet www.sesric.org; became operational in 1978; has a three-fold mandate: to collate, process and disseminate socio-economic statistics and information on, and for the utilization of, its member countries; to study and assess economic and social developments in member countries with the aim of helping to generate proposals for advancing co-operation; and to organize training programmes in selected areas; the Centre also acts as a focal point for technical co-operation activities between the OIC system and related UN agencies; and prepares economic and social reports and background documentation for OIC meetings; Dir-Gen. Dr SAVAŞ ALPAY (Turkey); publs *Annual Economic Report on the OIC Countries*, *Journal of Economic Cooperation and Development* (quarterly), *Economic Cooperation and Development Review* (semi-annually), *InfoReport* (quarterly), *Statistical Yearbook* (annually), *Basic Facts and Figures on OIC Member Countries* (annually).

Specialized Institutions

International Islamic News Agency (IINA): King Khalid Palace, Madinah Rd, POB 5054, Jeddah 21422, Saudi Arabia; tel. (2) 665-8561; fax (2) 665-9358; e-mail iina@islamicnews.org; internet www.iina.me; f. 1972; distributes news and reports daily on events in the Islamic world, in Arabic, English and French; Dir-Gen. ERDEM KOK.

Islamic Educational, Scientific and Cultural Organization (ISESCO): BP 2275 Rabat 10104, Morocco; tel. (37) 772433; fax (37) 772058; e-mail cid@isesco.org.ma; internet www.isesco.org.ma; f. 1982; Dir-Gen. Dr ABDULAZIZ BIN OTHMAN ALTWAIJRI; publs *ISESCO Newsletter* (quarterly), *Islam Today* (2 a year), *ISESCO Triennial*.

Islamic Broadcasting Union (IBU): POB 6351, Jeddah 21442, Saudi Arabia; tel. (2) 672-1121; fax (2) 672-2269; e-mail ibu@ibuj.org; internet www.ibuj.org; f. 1975; Gen. Man. ZAINAL ABIDIN IBERAHIM (Malaysia).

Affiliated Institutions

International Association of Islamic Banks (IAIB): King Abdulaziz St, Queen's Bldg, 23rd Floor, Al-Balad Dist, POB 9707, Jeddah 21423, Saudi Arabia; tel. (2) 651-6900; fax (2) 651-6552; f. 1977 to link financial institutions operating on Islamic banking principles; activities include training and research; mems: 192 banks and other financial institutions in 34 countries.

Islamic Chamber of Commerce and Industry: POB 3831, Clifton, Karachi 75600, Pakistan; tel. (21) 5874910; fax (21) 5870765; e-mail icci@icci-oic.org; internet www.iccionline.net/en/icci-en/index.aspx; f. 1979 to promote trade and industry among member states; comprises nat. chambers or feds of chambers of commerce and industry; Sec.-Gen. Dr BASSEM AWADALLAH.

Islamic Committee for the International Crescent: POB 17434, Benghazi, Libya; tel. (61) 9095824; fax (61) 9095823; e-mail info@icic-oic.org; internet www.icic-oic.org; f. 1979 to attempt to alleviate the suffering caused by natural disasters and war; Pres. ALI MAHMOUD BUHEDMA.

Islamic Solidarity Sports Federation: POB 5844, Riyadh 11442, Saudi Arabia; tel. (1) 480-9253; fax (1) 482-2145; e-mail issf@awalnet.net.sa; internet issf-fssi.org; f. 1981; organizes the Islamic Solidarity Games (2005: Jeddah, Saudi Arabia, in April; the next Games were to have been held in April 2010, in Tehran, Iran, but were postponed); Sec.-Gen. Dr MOHAMMAD SALEH QAZDAR.

Organization of Islamic Capitals and Cities (OICC): POB 13621, Jeddah 21414, Saudi Arabia; tel. (2) 698-1953; fax (2)

698-1053; e-mail webmaster@oicc.org; internet www.oicc.org; f. 1980; aims to preserve the identity and the heritage of Islamic capitals and cities; to achieve and enhance sustainable development in member capitals and cities; to establish and develop comprehensive urban norms, systems and plans to serve the growth and prosperity of Islamic capitals and cities and to enhance their cultural, environmental, urban, economic and social conditions; to advance municipal services and facilities in the member capitals and cities; to support member cities' capacity-building programmes; and to consolidate fellowship and co-ordinate the scope of co-operation between members; comprises 157 capitals and cities as active members, eight observer members and 18 associate members, in Asia, Africa, Europe and South America; Sec.-Gen. OMAR KADI.

Organization of the Islamic Shipowners' Association: POB 14900, Jeddah 21434, Saudi Arabia; tel. (2) 663-7882; fax (2) 660-4920; e-mail mail@oisaonline.com; internet www.oisaonline.com; f. 1981 to promote co-operation among maritime cos in Islamic countries; in 1998 mems approved the establishment of a new commercial venture, the Bakkah Shipping Company, to enhance sea transport in the region; Sec.-Gen. Dr ABDULLATIF A. SULTAN.

World Federation of Arab-Islamic Schools: 2 Wadi el-Nile St, Maadi, Cairo, Egypt; tel. (2) 358-3278; internet www.wfais.org; f. 1976; supports Arab-Islamic schools world-wide and encourages co-operation between the institutions; promotes the dissemination of the Arabic language and Islamic culture; supports the training of personnel.

ORGANIZATION OF THE PETROLEUM EXPORTING COUNTRIES—OPEC

Address: Helferstorferstrasse 17, 1010 Vienna, Austria.

Telephone: (1) 211-12-0; **fax:** (1) 216-43-20; **e-mail:** prid@opec.org; **internet:** www.opec.org.

OPEC was established in 1960 to link countries whose main source of export earnings is petroleum; it aims to unify and co-ordinate members' petroleum policies and to safeguard their interests generally. In 1976 OPEC member states established the OPEC Fund for International Development.

OPEC's share of world petroleum production was 41.8% in 2010 (compared with 54.7% in 1974). OPEC members were estimated to possess 81.3% of the world's known reserves of crude petroleum in 2010. In that year OPEC members also possessed about 49% of known reserves of natural gas, and accounted for 18% of total production of marketed natural gas.

MEMBERS

Algeria	Iraq	Qatar
Angola	Kuwait	Saudi Arabia
Ecuador	Libya	United Arab Emirates
Iran	Nigeria	Venezuela

Organization

(June 2012)

CONFERENCE

The Conference is the supreme authority of the Organization, responsible for the formulation of its general policy. It consists of representatives of member countries, who examine reports and recommendations submitted by the Board of Governors. It approves the appointment of Governors from each country and elects the Chairman of the Board of Governors. It works on the unanimity principle, and meets at least twice a year. In September 2000 the Conference agreed that regular meetings of heads of state or government should be convened every five years.

BOARD OF GOVERNORS

The Board directs the management of the Organization; it implements resolutions of the Conference and draws up an annual budget. It consists of one governor for each member country, and meets at least twice a year.

MINISTERIAL MONITORING COMMITTEE

The Committee (f. 1982) is responsible for monitoring price evolution and ensuring the stability of the world petroleum market. As such, it is charged with the preparation of long-term strategies, including the allocation of quotas to be presented to the Conference. The Committee consists of all national representatives, and is normally convened four times a year. A Ministerial Monitoring Sub-committee, reporting to the Committee on production and supply figures, was established in 1993.

ECONOMIC COMMISSION

A specialized body operating within the framework of the Secretariat, with a view to assisting the Organization in promoting stability in international prices for petroleum at equitable levels; consists of a Board, national representatives and a commission staff; meets at least twice a year.

SECRETARIAT

Secretary-General: ABDALLA SALEM EL-BADRI (Libya).

Legal Office: Provides legal advice, supervises the Secretariat's legal commitments, evaluates legal issues of concern to the Organization and member countries, and recommends appropriate action; General Legal Counsel ASMA MUTTAWA.

Office of the Secretary-General: provides the Secretary-General with executive assistance in maintaining contacts with governments, organizations and delegations, in matters of protocol and in the preparation for and co-ordination of meetings; Head ABDULLAH AL-SHAMERI.

Research Division: comprises the Data Services Department; the Energy Studies Department; and the Petroleum Market Analysis Department; Dir Dr HASAN M. QABAZARD.

Support Services Division: responsible for providing the required infrastructure and services to the whole Secretariat, in support of its programmes; has three departments: Administration and IT Services; Finance and Human Resources; and Public Relations and Information; Dir. (vacant).

Activities

OPEC's principal objectives, according to its Statute, are to co-ordinate and unify the petroleum policies of member countries and to determine the best means for safeguarding their individual and collective interests; to seek ways and means of ensuring the stabilization of prices in international oil markets, with a view to eliminating harmful and unnecessary fluctuations; and to provide a steady income to the producing countries, an efficient, economic and regular supply of petroleum to consuming nations, and a fair return on capital to those investing in the petroleum industry.

The first OPEC conference was held in Baghdad, Iraq, in September 1960. It was attended by representatives from Iran, Iraq, Kuwait, Saudi Arabia and Venezuela, the founder members. These were joined by Qatar in the following year, when a Board of Governors was formed and statutes agreed. Indonesia and Libya were admitted to membership in 1962, Abu Dhabi in 1967, Algeria in 1969, Nigeria in 1971, Ecuador in 1973 and Gabon in 1975; Abu Dhabi's membership was transferred to the United Arab Emirates (UAE) in 1974. Ecuador resigned from OPEC in 1992 and Gabon did so in 1996. Angola became a member in 2007, and Ecuador rejoined the organization in the same year. Indonesia withdrew from OPEC in 2009.

PRICES AND PRODUCTION

OPEC's five original members first met following the imposition of price reductions by petroleum companies in the previous month (August 1960). During the 1960s members sought to assert their rights in an international petroleum market that was dominated by multinational companies. Between 1965 and 1967 a two-year joint production programme limited annual growth in output so as to secure adequate prices. During the 1970s member states increased their control over their domestic petroleum industries, and over the pricing of crude petroleum on world markets. In 1971 the five-year Tehran Agreement on pricing was concluded between the six producing countries from the Arabian Gulf region and 23 petroleum companies. In January 1972 petroleum companies agreed to adjust the petroleum revenues of the largest producers after changes in currency exchange rates (Geneva Agreement), and in 1973 OPEC and the petroleum companies agreed to raise posted prices of crude petroleum by 11.9% and installed a mechanism to make monthly adjustments to prices in future (Second Geneva Agreement). In October of that year a pricing crisis occurred when Arab member states refused to supply petroleum to nations that had supported Israel in its conflict with Egypt and Syria earlier in that month. Negotiations on the revision of the Tehran Agreement failed in the same month, and the Gulf states unilaterally declared increases of 70% in posted prices, from US $3.01 to $5.11 per barrel. In December the OPEC Conference decided to increase the posted price to $11.65 per barrel from the beginning of 1974 (despite Saudi Arabian opposition). OPEC's first summit meeting of heads of state or government was held in March 1975, and in September a ministerial meeting agreed to increase prices by 10% for the period to June 1976. During 1976 and 1977 disagreements between 'moderate' members (principally Saudi

Arabia and Iran) and 'radical' members (led by Algeria, Iraq and Libya) caused discrepancies in pricing: a 10% increase was agreed by 11 member states as of 1 January 1977, but Saudi Arabia and the UAE decided to limit their increase to 5%. A further increase of 5% by Saudi Arabia and the UAE in July restored a single level of pricing, but in December the Conference was unable to agree on a new increase, and prices remained stable until the end of 1978, when it was agreed that during 1979 prices should increase by an average of 10% in four instalments over the year, to compensate for the effects of the depreciation of the US dollar. The overthrow of the Iranian Government in early 1979, however, led to a new steep increase in petroleum prices.

In June 1980 the Conference decided to set the price for a 'marker' crude at US $32 per barrel. Prices continued to vary, however, and in May 1981 Saudi Arabia refused to increase its price of $32 per barrel unless the higher prices charged by other members were lowered. Members agreed to reduce surplus production during the year, and in October the marker price was increased to $34 per barrel, with a 'ceiling' price of $38 per barrel. In March 1982 an emergency meeting of ministers of petroleum agreed (for the first time in OPEC's history) to defend the Organization's price structure by imposing an overall production ceiling of 18m. barrels per day (b/d), reducing this to 17.5m. b/d at the beginning of 1983, although ministers initially failed to agree on production quotas for individual members, or on adjustments to the differentials in prices charged for the high-quality crude petroleum produced by Algeria, Libya and Nigeria compared with that produced by the Gulf States. In February 1983 Nigeria reduced its price to $30 per barrel, and to avoid a 'price war' OPEC set the official price of marker crude at $29 per barrel. Quotas were allocated for each member country except Saudi Arabia, which was to act as a 'swing producer' to supply the balancing quantities to meet market requirements. In October 1984 the production ceiling was lowered to 16m. b/d, and in December price differentials for light (more expensive) and heavy (cheaper) crudes were altered in an attempt to counteract price-cutting by non-OPEC producers, particularly Norway and the United Kingdom. During 1985, however, most members effectively abandoned the marker price system, and production in excess of quotas, unofficial discounts and barter deals by members, and price cuts by non-members (such as Mexico, which had hitherto kept its prices in line with those of OPEC) contributed to a weakening of the market. During the first half of 1986 petroleum prices dropped to below $10 per barrel. Discussions were held with non-member producing countries (Angola, Egypt, Malaysia, Mexico and Oman) which agreed to co-operate in limiting production, although the United Kingdom declined. In August all members except Iraq agreed upon a return to production quotas (Iraq declined to co-operate after its request to be allocated the same quota as Iran had been refused): total production was to be limited to 14.8m. b/d (16.8m. b/d including Iraq). This measure resulted in an increase in prices to about $15 per barrel. In December members (except Iraq) agreed to return to a fixed pricing system, at a level of $18 per barrel as the OPEC Reference Basket (ORB) price (based on a 'basket' of seven crudes, not, as hitherto, on a 'marker' crude, Arabian Light) with effect from 1 February 1987, setting a total production limit of 15.8m. b/d for the first half of the year. OPEC's role of actually setting crude oil prices had come to an end, however, and from the late 1980s prices were determined by movements in the international markets, with OPEC's role being to increase or restrain production in order to prevent harmful fluctuations in prices. In June 1987, with prices having stabilized, the Conference decided to limit production to 16.6m. b/d (including Iraq's output) for the rest of the year. In April 1988, following a further reduction in prices below $15 per barrel, non-OPEC producers offered to reduce the volume of their petroleum exports by 5% if OPEC members would do the same. Saudi Arabia insisted that existing quotas should be more strictly observed before it would reduce its production. The production limit was increased to 18.5m. b/d for the first half of 1989 and, after prices had recovered to about $18 per barrel, to 19.5m. b/d for the second half of 1989, and to 22m. b/d for the first half of 1990.

In May 1990 members resolved to adhere more strictly to the agreed production quotas, in response to a decline in prices, which stood at about US $14 per barrel in June. In August Iraq invaded Kuwait (which it had accused, among other grievances, of violating production quotas). Petroleum exports by the two countries were halted by an international embargo, and petroleum prices immediately increased to exceed $25 per barrel. OPEC ministers promptly allowed a temporary increase in production by other members, of between 3m. and 3.5m. b/d (mostly by Saudi Arabia, the UAE and Venezuela), to stabilize prices, and notwithstanding some fluctuations later in the year, this was achieved. During 1991 and 1992 ministers attempted to reach a minimum ORB price of $21 per barrel by imposing production limits that varied between 22.3m. b/d and 24.2m. b/d. Kuwait, which resumed production in 1992 after extensive damage had been inflicted on its oil wells during the conflict with Iraq, was granted a special dispensation to produce without a fixed quota until the following year. Ecuador withdrew from OPEC in November 1992, citing the high cost of membership and the organization's refusal to increase Ecuador's production quota. In 1993 a Ministerial Monitoring Sub-committee was established to supervise compliance with quotas, because of members' persistent over-production. A production ceiling of 24.46m. b/d was set for the first quarter of 1993 and was reduced to 23.5m. b/d from 1 March (including a fixed quota for Kuwait for the first time since the Iraqi invasion). In July discussions between Iraq and the UN on the possible supervised resumption of Iraqi petroleum exports depressed petroleum prices to below $16 per barrel, and at the end of the year prices fell below $14, after the Conference rejected any further reduction in the current limit (imposed from 1 October) of 24.52m. b/d, which remained in force during 1994 and 1995, although actual output continued to be well in excess of quotas. In March 1996 prices reached $21 per barrel (largely owing to unusually cold weather in the northern hemisphere). In May the UN and Iraq concluded an agreement allowing Iraq to resume exports of petroleum in order to fund humanitarian relief efforts within Iraq, and OPEC's overall production ceiling was accordingly raised to 25.03m. b/d from June, remaining at this level until the end of 1997. Gabon withdrew from OPEC in June 1996, citing difficulties in meeting its budgetary contribution. Prices declined during the first half of 1997, falling to a low point of $16.7 per barrel in April, owing to the resumption of Iraqi exports, depressed world demand and continuing over-production: an escalation in political tension in the Gulf region, however, and in particular Iraq's reluctance to co-operate with UN weapons inspectors, prompted a price increase to about $21.2 per barrel in October. The overall production ceiling was raised by about 10%, to 27.5m. b/d, with effect from the beginning of 1998, but during that year prices declined, falling below $12 per barrel from August (demand having been affected by the current economic difficulties in South-East Asia), and OPEC imposed a succession of reductions in output, down to 24.387m. b/d from 1 July. Non-member countries (chiefly Mexico) also concluded agreements with OPEC to limit their production in that year, and in March 1999 Mexico, Norway, Oman and Russia agreed to decrease production by a total of 388,000 b/d, while OPEC's own production limit was reduced to 22.976m. b/d. Evidence of almost 90% compliance with the new production quotas contributed to market confidence that stockpiles of petroleum would be reduced, and resulted in sustained price increases during the second half of the year: the ORB price for petroleum rose above $24 per barrel in September.

By March 2000 petroleum prices had reached their highest level since 1990, briefly exceeding US $34 per barrel. In that month OPEC ministers agreed to raise output by 1.45m. b/d, in order to ease supply shortages, and introduced an informal price band mechanism that was to signal the need for adjustments in production should prices deviate for more than 20 days from an average bracket of $22–$28 per barrel. Further increases in production, totalling 1.8m. b/d, took effect in the second half of the year (with five non-OPEC members, Angola, Mexico, Norway, Oman and Russia, also agreeing to raise their output), but prices remained high and there was intense international pressure on OPEC to resolve the situation: in September both the Group of Seven industrialized countries (G7) and the IMF issued warnings about the potential economic and social consequences of sustained high petroleum prices. In that month OPEC heads of state and government, convened in their first summit meeting since 1975, responded by issuing the Caracas Declaration, in which they resolved (among other things) to promote market stability through their policies on pricing and production, to increase co-operation with other petroleum exporters, and to improve communication with consumer countries. During the first half of 2001, with a view to stabilizing prices that by January had fallen back to around $25 per barrel, the Conference agreed to implement reductions in output totalling 2.5m. b/d, thereby limiting overall production to 24.2m. b/d, with a further reduction of 1m. b/d from 1 September. Terrorist attacks on targets in the USA in September gave rise to market uncertainty, and prices declined further, averaging $17–$18 per barrel in November and December. In September the Conference announced the establishment of a working group of experts from OPEC and non-OPEC petroleum-producing countries, to evaluate future market developments and advance dialogue and co-operation. In December the Conference announced a further reduction in output by 1.5m. b/d (to 21.7m. b/d) from 1 January 2002, provided that non-OPEC producers also reduced their output, which they agreed to do by 462,500 b/d. This output limit was maintained throughout 2002, and the ORB price averaged $24.4 per barrel during the year, with temporary increases caused partly by a one-month suspension of Iraq's exports in April (in protest at Israeli military intervention in Palestinian-controlled areas), and by a strike in the Venezuelan petroleum industry. From 1 January 2003 the production ceiling was raised to 23m. b/d, but stricter compliance with individual quotas meant a reduction in actual output, and prices rose above the target range, with the ORB price reaching $32 per barrel in February, as a result of the continued interruption of the Venezuelan supply, together with the market's reaction to the likelihood of US-led military action against Iraq. In January the Conference agreed to raise the production ceiling to 24.5m. b/d from 1 February, and in March (when Venezuelan production had resumed) members agreed to make up from their available excess capacities any shortfall that might result following military action against Iraq. In the event, the war on Iraq that commenced later in that month led to such a rapid overthrow of Saddam Hussain's regime that there were fears that a petroleum surplus, driving down prices, would result, and a production ceiling of 25.4m. b/d was set with effect from the beginning of June: although higher than the previous limit, it represented a 2m. b/d reduction in actual output at that time. The production ceiling of 24.5m. b/d was reinstated from 1 November, in view of the gradual revival of Iraqi exports. The ORB price averaged $28.1 per barrel in 2003. In 2004, however, petroleum prices increased considerably, with the ORB price averaging $36 per barrel over the year, despite OPEC's raising its production ceiling (excluding Iraq's output), in several stages, from the 23.5m. b/d limit imposed from 1 April to 27m. b/d with effect from 1 November. In January 2005 the Conference suspended the $22–$28 price band mechanism, acknowledging this to be unrealistic at the present time. The production ceiling was increased to 27.5m. b/d in March and to 28m. b/d in June, but the ORB price nevertheless averaged $50.6 per barrel over the year. The March Conference attributed the continuing rise in prices to expectations of strong demand, speculation on the futures markets, and geopolitical tensions; it expressed particular concern that a shortage of effective global refining capacity was also contributing to higher prices by causing 'bottlenecks' in the downstream sector, and announced that members had accelerated the implementation of existing capacity expansion plans. In June the Conference approved an increase in the composition of the ORB from seven to 12 crudes, representing the main export crudes of all member countries, weighted according to production and exports to the main markets: the new composition was intended to reflect more accurately the average quality of crude petroleum in OPEC's member states. In September the Conference adopted a first Long-Term Strategy for OPEC, setting objectives concerning members' long-term petroleum revenues, fair and stable prices, the role of petroleum in meeting future energy demand, the stability of the world oil market, and the security of regular supplies to consumers. During 2006 petroleum prices continued to rise, with the ORB price averaging $61.08 per barrel for the year. The rise was partly attributable to uncertainty about Iran's future output (since there was speculation that international sanctions might be imposed on that country as a penalty for continuing its nuclear development programme), and to a reduction in Nigeria's production as a result of internal unrest. Existing production targets were maintained until November, when the production ceiling was lowered to 26.3m. b/d, and a further reduction of 500,000 b/d was announced in December. In March 2007 the Conference agreed to maintain the current level of production. Concern over fuel supplies and distribution contributed to steadily rising prices, in spite of OPEC's statements estimating that there were sufficient stock levels to meet demand. In November the ORB price reached a monthly average of $88.99 per barrel, despite an increase in OPEC's output by 500,000 b/d from the start of that month (agreed by the Conference in September). In October OPEC's Secretary-General reiterated that the market was well supplied, and attributed the rising prices chiefly to market speculators, with persistent refinery bottlenecks, seasonal maintenance work, ongoing geopolitical problems in the Middle East and fluctuations in the US dollar also continuing to play a role in driving oil prices higher. In November the third OPEC summit meeting of heads of state and government agreed on principles concerning the stability of global energy markets, the role of energy in sustainable development, and the relationship between energy and environmental concerns. In December the Conference observed that, despite the current volatility of prices, the petroleum market continued to be well supplied, and decided to leave the production ceiling unchanged for the time being.

Meeting in March 2008, the Conference again determined to maintain the current production ceiling and in September, once again, the Conference resolved to maintain the production allocations agreed in September 2007 (with an adjustment to include the admission to the Organization in late 2007 of both Angola and Ecuador while excluding Indonesia, whose membership was being terminated, resulting in an overall production ceiling of 28.8m. b/d). At 11 July 2008 the ORB price reached a record high of US $147.27 per barrel, although by late October it had fallen below $60 per barrel. An extraordinary meeting of the Conference, convened at that time, observed that the ongoing global financial crisis was suppressing demand for petroleum. The Conference determined to decrease the production ceiling by 1.5m. b/d, with effect from 1 November. A subsequent extraordinary Conference meeting, held in mid-December, agreed to reduce production further, by 4.7m. b/d from the actual total production in September (29.0m. b/d), with effect from 1 January 2009. By 24 December 2008 the ORB price had fallen to $33.36 per barrel.

The ORB price stabilized in early 2009, fluctuating at around US $40 per barrel during January–mid-March (when a meeting of the Conference determined to maintain current production levels, but urged member states' full compliance with them: this had stood at 79% in February), and rising to around $50 per barrel during mid-March–early May. By mid-June the ORB price had risen to $70.89 per barrel. Meeting in late May the Conference noted that the impact of the ongoing global economic crisis had resulted in a reduction in the global demand for petroleum, this having declined during the second half of 2008 for the first time since the early 1980s. The Conference welcomed the positive effect of recent production decisions in redressing the balance of supply and demand, and decided to maintain current production levels. Reviewing the situation at the next meeting, convened in early September 2009, the Conference observed that the global economic situation continued to be very fragile and that the petroleum market remained over-supplied, and determined once more to maintain existing production levels. When convened again, in December, the Conference expressed concern at the gravity of the global economic contraction, noting that the world-wide demand for petroleum had now declined for two successive years. Production levels were kept unchanged, and remained unaltered by the next (March 2010) gathering of the Conference. The March 2010 Conference observed some improvement in the global economy, and projected marginal improvements in global demand for petroleum, but observed, also, that serious threats remained to the economic situation, and that, owing to a forecast increase in petroleum supplies from non-OPEC sources, a third successive year of declining demand for the Organization's crude oil was envisaged. The next ordinary meeting of the Conference, held in October, adopted a second Long-Term Strategy for the Organization, setting objectives relating to member countries' long-term petroleum revenues; fair and stable prices; future energy demand and OPEC's share in world oil supply; stability of the global oil market; security of regular supply to consumers, and of global demand; and enhancing the collective interests of member states in global negotiations and future multilateral agreements. An extraordinary meeting of the Conference, convened in December, observed that the global economic outlook remained fragile, and, on that basis, agreed to maintain current oil production levels. The next ordinary meeting of the Conference, held in June 2011—following, in the first half of that year, the unforeseen eruption of unrest and uncertainty in several Middle Eastern and North African countries, including Libya (where a significant decline in production was recorded), and a sharp increase in petroleum prices—failed to reach consensus on a proposed agreement to raise output. In December OPEC ministers agreed to maintain the production ceiling at current output levels (some 30m. b/d). Ministers attending the ordinary conference in mid-June 2012 agreed to maintain the production ceiling, despite marked over production by some member states and a fall in prices from $122.97 per barrel in mid-March, to $96.02 (on 15 June).

ENERGY DIALOGUES

Annual 'workshops' are convened jointly by OPEC, the International Energy Agency and the International Energy Forum, bringing together experts, analysts and government officials to discuss aspects of energy supply and demand. A workshop was staged by the three organizations in November 2010 on the theme 'Understanding the new dynamic: how the physical and financial markets for energy interact', alongside a forum on 'Energy market regulation: clarity and co-ordination'; and, in January 2011, they organized a symposium on energy outlooks.

The first annual formal ministerial meeting of the European Union (EU)-OPEC Energy Dialogue took place in June 2005, with the aim of exchanging views on energy issues of common interest, including petroleum market developments, and thus contributing to stability, transparency and predictability in the market. A round-table meeting was held in November to discuss recent petroleum market developments and future prospects, and a conference was held in 2006 to discuss energy technologies, with a particular focus on carbon capture and storage. The fifth EU-OPEC Energy Dialogue ministerial meeting, convened in June 2008, agreed to hold a round table on carbon capture and storage (this took place in October); to finalize a joint study on the impacts of financial markets on oil prices and market volatility, to be followed by an international workshop; to undertake a feasibility study on the establishment of an EU-OPEC Energy Technology Centre; and to prepare terms of reference for a joint study on the impacts of biofuels on oil refining. The sixth ministerial Dialogue, convened in June 2009, agreed to implement the joint study on the impacts of biofuels on oil refining and to conduct a workshop to review the findings of the study; to organize a round table on the impacts on the petroleum sector of the ongoing financial crisis; and to finalize the planned feasibility study on the proposed EU-OPEC Energy Technology Centre. In June 2010 a summary of the conclusions of the feasibility study was presented to the seventh ministerial Dialogue. The June 2010 Dialogue meeting determined, in 2011, to commission a study to explore the potential of technological advances in transportation, and to assess their impact on demand for petroleum; and also to arrange a round table to examine the causes of an ongoing shortage of skilled labour shortage in the energy and oil industries. The June 2011 Dialogue decided to organize, during 2011–12, a joint workshop to discuss the findings of the study on technological advances in the road transportation sector; to complete preparations for the proposed Energy Technology Centre; and to hold a round-table on the key challenges confronting oil and gas exploration and production activities.

Russia (a major producer of petroleum) was given OPEC observer status in 1992, and was subsequently represented at a number of ministerial and other meetings. A formal Energy Dialogue was established in December 2005, providing for annual ministerial meetings, together with technical exchanges, seminars and joint research, on such subjects as petroleum market developments and prospects, data flow, investments across the supply chain, and energy policies.

In March 2005 the Chinese Government proposed the creation of an official dialogue between OPEC and the People's Republic of China (a major customer of OPEC members) and this was formally established in December, with the aim of exchanging views on energy issues, particularly security of supply and demand, through annual ministerial meetings, technical exchanges and energy round-tables.

ENVIRONMENTAL CONCERNS

OPEC has frequently expressed its concern that any measures adopted to avert climate change by reducing the emission of carbon dioxide caused by the consumption of fossil fuels would seriously affect its members' income. In 1998, for example, OPEC representatives attending a conference of the parties to the UN Framework Convention on Climate Change warned that OPEC would claim compensation for any lost revenue resulting from initiatives to limit petroleum consumption, and at subsequent sessions, while expressing support for the fundamental principles of the Convention, OPEC urged that developing countries whose economies were dependent on the export of fossil fuels should not be unfairly treated. In June 2007 OPEC's Secretary-General criticized the industrialized nations' efforts to increase production of biofuel (derived from agricultural commodities) in order to reduce consumption of fossil fuels: he warned that OPEC might reduce its future investment in petroleum production accordingly. In November the third summit meeting of OPEC heads of state and government acknowledged the long-term challenge of climate change, but emphasized the continuing need for stable petroleum supplies to support global economic growth and development, and urged that policies aimed at combating climate change should be balanced, taking into account their impact on developing countries, including countries heavily dependent on the production and export of fossil fuels. The meeting stressed the importance of cleaner and more efficient petroleum technologies, and the development of technologies such as carbon capture and storage.

Finance

OPEC has an annual budget of about €25m.

Publications

Annual Report.
Annual Statistical Bulletin.
Environmental Newsletter (quarterly).
Monthly Oil Market Report.
OPEC Bulletin (10 a year).
OPEC Review (quarterly).
World Oil Outlook (annually).
Reports, information papers, press releases.

OPEC FUND FOR INTERNATIONAL DEVELOPMENT

Address: POB 995, 1011 Vienna, Austria.

Telephone: (1) 515-64-0; **fax:** (1) 513-92-38; **e-mail:** info@ofid.org; **internet:** www.ofid.org.

The OPEC Fund for International Development (initially referred to as 'the Fund', more recently as 'OFID') was established 1976 by OPEC member countries, in order to assist developing countries and to promote South-South co-operation. A revised agreement to establish the Fund as a permanent international agency was signed in May 1980.

MEMBERS

Algeria	Iraq	Qatar
Gabon	Kuwait	Saudi Arabia
Indonesia	Libya	United Arab Emirates
Iran	Nigeria	Venezuela

Organization

(June 2012)

ADMINISTRATION

OFID is administered by a Ministerial Council and a Governing Board. Each member country is represented on the Council by its minister of finance. The Board consists of one representative and one alternate for each member country.

Chairman, Ministerial Council: YOUSEF HUSSAIN KAMAL (Qatar).

Chairman, Governing Board: JAMAL NASSER LOOTAH (UAE).

Director-General of the Fund: SULEIMAN JASIR AL-HERBISH (Saudi Arabia).

FINANCIAL STRUCTURE

The resources of OFID, whose unit of account is the US dollar, consist of contributions by OPEC member countries, and income received from operations or otherwise accruing to the Fund.

The initial endowment of OFID amounted to US $800m. Its resources have been replenished three times, and have been further increased by the profits accruing to seven OPEC member countries through the sales of gold held by the International Monetary Fund (IMF). The total pledged contributions by member countries amounted to $3,435.0m. at the end of 2010, and paid-in contributions totalled some $3,050.0m.

Activities

The OPEC Fund for International Development (OFID) is a multilateral agency for financial co-operation and assistance. Its objective is to reinforce financial co-operation between OPEC member countries and other developing countries through the provision of financial support to the latter on appropriate terms, to assist them in their economic and social development. OFID was conceived as a collective financial facility which would consolidate the assistance extended by its member countries; its resources are additional to those already made available through other bilateral and multilateral aid agencies of OPEC members. It is empowered to:

(i) Provide concessional loans for balance of payments support;

(ii) Provide concessional loans for the implementation of development projects and programmes;

(iii) Contribute to the resources of other international development agencies;

(iv) Finance technical assistance, research, food aid and humanitarian emergency relief through grants; and

(v) Participate in the financing of private sector activities in developing countries.

The eligible beneficiaries of OFID's assistance are the governments of developing countries other than OPEC member countries, and international development agencies whose beneficiaries are developing countries. OFID gives priority to the countries with the lowest income.

OFID may undertake technical, economic and financial appraisal of a project submitted to it, or entrust such an appraisal to an appropriate international development agency, the executing national agency of a member country, or any other qualified agency. Most projects financed by the organization have been co-financed by other development finance agencies. In each such case, one of the co-financing agencies may be appointed to administer the loan in association with its own. This practice has enabled OFID to extend its lending activities to more than 100 countries over a short period of time and in a simple way, with the aim of avoiding duplication and complications. As its experience grew, OFID increasingly resorted to parallel, rather than joint financing, taking up separate project components to be financed according to its rules and policies. In addition, it started to finance some projects completely on its own. These trends necessitated the issuance in 1982 of guidelines for the procurement of goods and services under the Fund's loans, allowing for a margin of preference for goods and services of local origin or originating in other developing countries: the general principle of competitive bidding is, however, followed by OFID. The loans are not tied to procurement from OFID member countries or from any other countries. The margin of preference for goods and services obtainable in developing countries is allowed on the request of the borrower and within defined limits. OFID assistance in the form of programme loans has a broader coverage than project lending. Programme loans are used to stimulate an economic sector or sub-sector, and assist recipient countries in obtaining inputs, equipment and spare parts. In 2004 a supplementary lending mechanism, a Blend Facility, was established to make available additional resources at higher rates than the standard concessional lending terms. Besides extending loans for project and programme financing and balance of payments support, OFID also undertakes other operations, including grants in support of technical assistance and other activities (mainly research), emergency relief and humanitarian aid, and financial contributions to other international institutions. In 1998 the Fund began to extend lines of credit to support private sector activities in beneficiary countries. The so-called Private Sector Facility aims to encourage the growth of private enterprises, in particular small and medium-sized enterprises, and to support the development of local capital markets. A new Trade Finance Facility, to provide loans, lines of credit and guarantees in support of international trade operations in developing countries, was launched in December 2006.

In March 2009 OFID participated in a meeting of international finance institutions and development banks to discuss closer co-operation in order to respond more effectively to the global financial and economic crisis. OFID agreed to provide US $30m. to an African sub-fund of the International Finance Corporation's Recapitalization Fund, which aimed to support banks in developing countries. It also participated in a Microfinance Enhancement Facility and, though its Trade Finance Facility, in the World Bank's Global Trade Liquidity Programme. During 2010 OFID continued to work to alleviate the impact of the crisis on low-income developing countries, and to refocus efforts on achieving the UN Millennium Development Goals. In October OFID signed a Memorandum of Understanding (MOU) with the World Bank Group in order to strengthen their joint efforts to meet new development challenges, with a particular focus on the need to counter energy poverty, to improve the management of natural resources, to facilitate trade and to strengthen financial institutions. In May 2011 OFID signed an MOU with the Asian Development Bank, in order to enhance co-operation between the two organizations, and in July signed an MOU with the Arab Bank for Economic Development in Africa. In December of that year OFID's Director-General, addressing the 20th World Petroleum Congress, convened in Doha, Qatar, recommended that the Fund might act as a hub for efforts by the petroleum sector to promote the global Sustainable Energy for All by 2030 initiative that had been launched by the UN Secretary-General in September 2011.

By the end of December 2010 OFID had approved a total of US $13,056.1m. since operations began in 1976, of which $8,595.5m. was for public sector loans. Included in the public sector lending is the Fund's contribution to the Heavily Indebted Poor Countries (HIPC) initiative (see World Bank), which by the end of 2010 amounted to $155m. Private sector financing totalled $1,383.1m. committed in the same period, while loans committed under the Trade Finance Facility, amounted to $963.8m. At that time cumulative disbursements of all loans and operations amounted to $7,966.1m.

Direct loans are supplemented by grants to support technical assistance, food aid and research. By the end of December 2010 grants amounting to US $504.0m., had been committed since operations commenced, including $20m. as a special contribution to the International Fund for Agricultural Development (IFAD) and a further $20.0m. approved under a new Food Aid Special Grant Account, which was established in 2003 to combat famine in Africa. In addition, by the end of 2010 OFID had committed $1,021.8m. to the resources of IFAD, an IMF Trust Fund and the IMF's Poverty Reduction and Growth Facility (PRGF) Trust.

During the year ending 31 December 2010 the Fund's total commitments amounted to US $1,374.3m. (compared with $1,382.4m. in the previous year). These commitments included public sector loans, amounting to $637.9m., supporting 45 projects in 38 countries. The largest proportion of loans (33% of the total) was for transportation projects, for example the construction or rehabilitation of roads (in Albania, Grenada, Kenya and Niger), construction of a light rail system in Turkey, and the rehabilitation of a ship yard in Cameroon. The energy sector accounted for 24% of the total for projects including the improvement of electricity generation, transmission and distributions in Cuba, Ethiopia, Tanzania and Uganda, and the construction of a gas turbine power plant in Egypt. Public sector loans for the water supply and sewerage sector, amounting to 19% of the total, financed projects to improve water supply infrastructure in Belize, Côte d'Ivoire, Nepal, Sierra Leone and Swaziland, sewerage facilities in Panama and irrigation infrastructure in Cambodia. Health sector loans (10%) included projects to construct new health centres or hospitals in Burkina Faso, Ghana, the Maldives and Viet Nam. Agriculture and agro-industry loans (9%) financed irrigation schemes (in Egypt, Lebanon and Mali), other food security efforts (in Niger), and market access initiatives (in Cuba and Guatemala). Three loans (4%), were allocated to education projects (in The Gambia, Grenada and Yemen), while one loan (1%) was for the development of the industry sector in Lesotho.

Private sector operations approved during 2010 amounted to US $227.3m., which funded projects in the infrastructure, industry and telecommunications sectors and to the financial sector in order to enhance the availability of credit for small and medium-sized enterprises. During that year the Bank aimed to expand its trade financing activities in order to counter the effects on beneficiary countries of the global financial crisis. Approvals under the Trade Financing Facility amounted to $481.0m. in 2010 (compared with $364.0m. in 2009). Risk-sharing guarantee arrangements totalling $225.0m. were also concluded during 2010 ($480.0m. in the previous year).

During 2010 OFID approved US $28.1m. in grants for 45 projects. Of the total $10.3m. was committed from the Special Grant Account for Palestine to improve living conditions in the poorest communities and to support the work of some 65 local organizations to deliver essential social services. A further $9.4m. was approved from the HIV/AIDS Special Account to support regional or global partnership initiatives, $4.7m. for technical assistance projects, $2.0m. to provide emergency humanitarian aid (to Burkina Faso, Chile, Egypt, Haiti, Mongolia, Niger and Pakistan), and $1.8m. to fund research projects and other related activities.

Publications

Annual Report (in Arabic, English, French and Spanish).

OFID Quarterly.

Pamphlet series, author papers, books and other documents.

Statistics

TOTAL APPROVALS IN 2010, BY SECTOR AND REGION
(US $ million)

	Financing approved	%
Sector:		
Agriculture	186.2	13.5
Education	27.6	2.0
Energy	324.2	23.6
Finance	251.6	18.3
Health	73.5	5.3
Industry	90.8	6.6
Telecommunications	32.7	2.4
Transportation	257.0	18.7
Water supply	118.6	8.6
Palestine and emergency grants	12.3	0.9
Total	1,374.3	100.0
Region:		
Africa	737.0	53.6
Asia	261.3	19.0
Latin America and the Caribbean	342.7	24.9
Europe and multi-regional	33.3	2.4

Source: OFID, *Annual Report 2010*.

PACIFIC COMMUNITY

Address: BP D5, 98848 Nouméa, New Caledonia.

Telephone: 26-20-00; **fax:** 26-38-18; **e-mail:** spc@spc.int; **internet:** www.spc.int.

In February 1947 the Governments of Australia, France, the Netherlands, New Zealand, the United Kingdom, and the USA signed the Canberra Agreement establishing the South Pacific Commission, which came into effect in July 1948. (The Netherlands withdrew from the Commission in 1962, when it ceased to administer the former colony of Dutch New Guinea, now Papua, formerly known as Irian Jaya, part of Indonesia.) In October 1997 the 37th South Pacific Conference, convened in Canberra, Australia, agreed to rename the organization the Pacific Community, with effect from 6 February 1998. The Secretariat of the Pacific Community (SPC) services the Community, and provides research, technical advice, training and assistance in economic, social and cultural development to 22 countries and territories of the Pacific region. It serves a population of about 6.8m., scattered over some 30m. sq km, more than 98% of which is sea.

MEMBERS

American Samoa
Australia
Cook Islands
Fiji
France
French Polynesia
Guam
Kiribati
Marshall Islands
Federated States of Micronesia
Nauru
New Caledonia
New Zealand
Niue
Northern Mariana Islands
Palau
Papua New Guinea
Pitcairn Islands
Samoa
Solomon Islands
Tokelau
Tonga
Tuvalu
USA
Vanuatu
Wallis and Futuna Islands

Organization

(June 2012)

CONFERENCE OF THE PACIFIC COMMUNITY

The Conference is the governing body of the Community (replacing the former South Pacific Conference) and is composed of representatives of all member countries and territories. The main responsibilities of the Conference, which meets every two years, are to appoint the Director-General, to determine major national or regional policy issues in the areas of competence of the organization and to note changes to the Financial and Staff Regulations approved by the Committee of Representatives of Governments and Administrations (CRGA). The sixth Conference of the Pacific Community was convened in Majuro, Marshall Islands, in November 2011.

COMMITTEE OF REPRESENTATIVES OF GOVERNMENTS AND ADMINISTRATIONS (CRGA)

The CRGA comprises representatives of all member states and territories, having equal voting rights. It meets annually to consider the work programme evaluation conducted by the Secretariat and to discuss any changes proposed by the Secretariat in the context of regional priorities; to consider and approve any policy issues for the organization presented by the Secretariat or by member countries and territories; to consider applicants and make recommendations for the post of Director-General; to approve the administrative and work programme budgets; to approve amendments to the Financial and Staff Regulations; and to conduct annual performance evaluations of the Director-General.

SECRETARIAT

The Secretariat of the Pacific Community (SPC) is headed by a Director-General, a Senior Deputy Director-General and a Deputy Director-General, based in Suva, Fiji. In October 2009 the CRGA approved a reorganization which was completed by January 2011 and included the transfer to SPC of activities from the Pacific Islands Applied Geoscience Commission (SOPAC), with a view to making SPC the lead co-ordinating agency for the Pacific regional energy sector. The reorganization provided for Secretariat divisions of Applied Geoscience and Technology; Economic Development; Education, Training and Human Develoment; Fisheries, Aquaculture and Marine Ecosystems; Land Resources; Public Health; and Statistics for Development. A Strategic Engagement Policy and Planning Facility (SEPPF), established in 1998 and expanded in 2007, provides country and programme support; and covers areas including regional co-operation and strategic positioning initiatives; policy analysis, research and mainstreaming of cross-cutting issues; and monitoring and evaluation. The Secretariat provides information services, including library facilities, publications, translation and computer services. During February–April 2012 a review of SPC's role in regional development was undertaken.

Director-General: Dr JIMMIE RODGERS (Solomon Islands).

Deputy Directors-General: FEKITAMOELOA KATOA 'UTOIKAMANU (Tonga), RICHARD MANN (Germany).

North Pacific Regional Office: POB 2299, Botanical Garden 2, Kolonia, Pohnpei, Federated States of Micronesia; tel. 320-7523; fax 320-5854; e-mail amenay@spc.int.

Suva Regional Office: Private Mail Bag, Suva, Fiji; tel. 3370733; fax 3370021; e-mail spcsuva@spc.org.fj.

Activities

SPC provides, on request of its member countries, technical assistance, advisory services, information and clearing house services aimed at developing the technical, professional, scientific, research, planning and management capabilities of the regional population. SPC also conducts regional conferences and technical meetings, as well as training courses, workshops and seminars at the regional or country level. It provides small grants-in-aid and awards to meet specific requests and needs of members. In November 1996 the Conference agreed to establish a specific Small Islands States (SIS) fund to provide technical services, training and other relevant activities. The Pacific Community oversees the maritime programme and telecommunications policy activities of the Pacific Islands Forum Secretariat.

The 1999 Conference, held in Tahiti in December, adopted the Déclaration de Tahiti Nui, a mandate that detailed the operational policies and mechanisms of the Pacific Community, taking into account operational changes not covered by the founding Canberra Agreement. The Declaration was regarded as a 'living document' that would be periodically revised to record subsequent modifications of operational policy.

SPC has signed memoranda of understanding with the World Health Organization (WHO), the Forum Fisheries Agency, the South Pacific Regional Environment Programme (SPREP), and several other partners. The organization participates in meetings of the Council of Regional Organizations in the Pacific (CROP). Representatives of SPC and SPREP have in recent years convened periodic meetings to develop regional technical co-operation and harmonization of work programmes.

SPC aims to develop joint country strategies with each of the Pacific Community's member countries and territories, detailing the full scope of its assistance over a defined period.

APPLIED GEOSCIENCE AND TECHNOLOGY

The reorganization of SPC implemented during 2010 provided for the core work programme of SOPAC (see above) to be absorbed into SPC as a new Applied Geoscience and Technology Division. The Division has responsibility for ensuring the productive regional utilization of earth sciences (geology, geophysics, oceanography and hydrology), and comprises the following three technical work programmes: ocean and islands; water and sanitation; and disaster reduction.

In June 2012 SPC and SPREP signed a letter of agreement detailing arrangements for the joint development, by 2015, of an Integrated Regional Strategy for Disaster Risk Management and Climate Change, which was to replace both the Pacific Disaster Risk Reduction and Disaster Management Framework for Action 2005–15 and the Pacific Islands Framework for Action on Climate Change 2006–15. A roadmap on achieving the Integrated Regional Strategy had been formulated by Pacific countries and territories during a series of meetings organized in 2011.

ECONOMIC DEVELOPMENT

The Economic Development Division (EDD) has the following four pillars: programmes in the areas of Transport, Energy, Infrastructure and Information and Communications Technology (ICT). An inaugural Regional Meeting of Ministers for Energy, ICT and Transport was held in April 2011, on the theme of 'strategic engagement for economic development'.

The Transport Programme comprises the work of the former Regional Maritime Programme (RMP—amalgamated into the main Transport Programme in mid-2011), as well as research and advisory services relating to specific capacity in aviation, and research into transport research. In 2002 the RMP launched the model Pacific Islands Maritime Legislation and Regulations as a framework for the development of national maritime legislation. Since 2006 the Transport programme has provided the secretariat of the Pacific Maritime Transport Alliance. The inaugural regional meeting of ministers responsible for maritime transport was convened in April 2007. In April 2011 SPEC transport ministers adopted a Framework for Action on Transport Services (FATS) to support all Pacific Islands and Territories (PICTs) to provide regular, safe and affordable air and sea transport services

The Energy Programme comprises related activities transferred from SOPAC (see above), including its advisory functions and activities relating to petroleum data and information. The Programme co-ordinates and leads work on: energy policy, planning, legislation and regulation; petroleum, including procurement, transport, storage and pricing mechanisms; renewable energy production; energy efficiency and conservation; and support for the Pacific Power Association and other relevant bodies regarding to power generation and electric utilities. In April 2011 ministers responsible for energy adopted a Framework for Action on Energy Security in the Pacific (FAESP) and an implementation plan.

The Pacific ICT Outreach (PICTO) Programme, established in January 2010, implements the 'Framework for Action on ICT for Development in the Pacific', endorsed in June 2010 by ministers responsible for ICT; and takes into account initiatives such as the Pacific Regional Infrastructure facility; to implement the Pacific Plan Digital Strategy; to take over work on ICT policy and regulations hitherto undertaken by the Pacific Islands Forum Secretariat; to continue ongoing SPC work relating to submarine cable and satellite communication technology; and to support the ongoing Oceania 'one laptop per child' (OLPC) initiative. In October SPC launched the e-Pacific Island Countries (e-PIC), an online portal providing access to information including country profiles; downloadable documents relating to policy, legal and regulatory matters, publications, news and research materials; a regional forum; and a register of ICT professionals and policy makers. In April 2011 SPC hosted a Pacific ICT Ministerial Forum, and signed an agreement with the International Telecommunications Union to enhance co-operation between the two organizations and facilitate the implementation of ICT and cyber protection programmes throughout the region. A Pacific Regional Workshop on Cybercrime, was held in Nukúalofa, Tonga, in May.

With other regional partners, including the Pacific Islands Forum and Asian Development Bank, SPC supported the Pacific Conference on the Human Face of the Global Economic Crisis, hosted by the Vanuatu Government in February 2010, in Port Vila.

In 2012 SPC was supporting a Tonga Government project, being implemented in connection with the Australian Government's Pacific Adaptation Strategy Assistance Program (PASAP), to assess vulnerability and adaptation to sea level rises on the small island of Lifuka.

EDUCATION, TRAINING AND HUMAN DEVELOPMENT

The Division comprises the he South Pacific Board for Educational Assessment (SPBEA), the Community Education Training Centre (CETC), the Human Development Programme (HDP), the Regional Media Centre, and the Regional Rights Resource Team.

In January 2010, under the reorganization of SPC implemented in that year, the SPBEA (established in 1980 to develop procedures for assessing national and regional secondary education certificates) was merged into the Community. The SPC regional office in Fiji administers the CETC, which conducts a seven-month training course for up to 40 female community workers annually, with the objective of training women in methods of community development so that they can help others to achieve better living conditions for island families and communities.

The HDP focuses on the areas of gender; youth; and culture. The HDP's Pacific Women's Bureau (PWB) aims to promote the social, economic and cultural advancement of women in the region by assisting governments and regional organizations to include women in the development planning process. The PWB also provides technical and advisory services, advocacy and management support training to groups concerned with women in development and gender and development, and administers the Pacific Women's Information Network (PACWIN). A new adviser for gender equality was appointed in September 2008. SPC hosted the 11th Triennial Conference of Pacific Women, at its Nouméa, New Caledonia headquarters, in August 2010. The Pacific Youth Bureau (PYB) co-ordinates the implementation of the Pacific Youth Strategy (PYS), which is updated at five-yearly intervals, most recently to cover the period 2011–15, and aims to develop opportunities for young people to play an active role in society. The PYB provides non-formal education and support for youth, community workers and young adults in community development subjects and provides grants to help young people find employment. It also advises and assists the Pacific Youth Council in promoting a regional youth identity. At the first Pacific Youth Festival, held in Tahiti in July 2006, a Pacific Youth Charter was formulated, to be incorporated into the PYS. A Pacific Youth Mapping Exercise (PYME) was undertaken in 2007, with the aim of establishing a complete picture of youth programmes being implemented across the region. The second Pacific Youth Festival, held in Suva, Fiji, in July 2009, included discussions on the following issues: promoting healthy living; Pacific identity; adaptation to climate change; and governance, peace and security. In September 2011 the Community published a *State of Pacific Youth Report*, which had been prepared with the Pacific Office of the UN Children's Fund.

The HDP works to preserve and promote the cultural heritage of the Pacific Islands. The Programme assists with the training of librarians, archivists and researchers and promotes instruction in local languages, history and art at schools in the PICTs. SPC acts as the secretariat of the Council of Pacific Arts, which organizes the Festival of Pacific Arts on a four-yearly basis. The 11th Festival was to be held in July 2012, in Solomon Islands, on the theme 'Culture in Harmony with Nature'. In March 2010 representatives of cultural interests from PICTs met to consider means of strengthening the profile of Pacific culture, including developing a regional cultural strategy, incorporating culture into educational programmes, establishing partnerships at national, regional and international level, and accessing funding for cultural projects. In November 2006 the HDP published *Guidelines for developing national legislation for the protection of traditional knowledge and expressions of culture*, with the aim of protecting indigenous Pacific knowledge and cultures.

The Regional Media Centre provides training, technical assistance and production materials in all areas of the media for member countries and territories, community work programmes, donor projects and regional non-governmental organizations. The Centre comprises a radio broadcast unit, a graphic design and publication unit and a TV and video unit.

The Regional Rights Resource Team provides training, technical support, and policy and advocacy services specifically tailored towards the Pacific region.

FISHERIES, AQUACULTURE AND MARINE ECOSYSTEMS

The Fisheries, Aquaculture and Marine Ecosystems (FAME) Division aims to support and co-ordinate the sustainable development and management of inshore fisheries resources in the region, to undertake scientific research in order to provide member governments with relevant information for the sustainable development and management of tuna and billfish resources in and adjacent to the South Pacific region, and to provide data and analytical services to national fisheries departments. The principal programmes under FAME are the Coastal Fisheries Programme (CFP) and the Oceanic Fisheries Programme (OFP). The development and advisory activities of the CFP are focused within the near territorial and archipelagic waters of the PICTs. The CFP is divided into the following sections: the Reef Fisheries Observatory; sustainable fisheries development; fisheries management; fisheries training; and aqualculture. SPC administers the Pacific Island Aquaculture Network, a forum for promoting regional aquaculture development. During 2007 a Pacific Regional Aquatic Biosecurity Initiative was initiated. In contrast to the CFP, the OFP focuses it activities within 200-mile exclusive economic zones and surrounding waters, and is mandated to equip PICTs with the necessary scientific information and advice for rationally managing and exploiting the regional resources of tuna, billfish and related species. The OFP consists of the following three sections: statistics and monitoring; tuna ecology and biology; and stock assessment and modelling. The statistics and monitoring section maintains a database of industrial tuna fisheries in the region. The OFP contributed research and statistical information for the formulation of the Convention for the Conservation and Management of Highly Migratory Fish Stocks in the Western and Central Pacific, which entered into force in June 2004 and aims to establish a regime for the sustainable management of tuna reserves. In March 2002 SPC and European Commission launched a Pacific Regional Oceanic and Coastal Fisheries Project (PROCFISH). The oceanic component of the project aimed to assist the OFP with advancing knowledge of tuna fisheries ecosystems, while the coastal element was to produce the first comparative regional baseline assessment of reef fisheries. Since 2006 the OFP has organized annual tuna Stock Assessment Workshops (SAW) with participation by senior regional fishery officers; some 30 officials from 23 Pacific countries attended in 2011. The theme of the fifth Pacific Community Conference, convened in November 2007, was 'The future of Pacific fisheries'; a set of recommendations on managing the regional fisheries was endorsed by the Conference.

SPC hosts the Pacific Office of the WorldFish Center (the International Centre for Living Aquatic Resources Management—ICLARM); SPC and the WorldFish Center have jointly implemented a number of projects. SPC also hosts the Co-ordination Unit of the Coral Reef Initiative for the South Pacific (CRISP), which was launched in January 2005 to address the protection and management of the region's coral reefs.

LAND RESOURCES

The Land Resources Division (LRD) comprises three major programmes: the sustainable management of integrated forest and agriculture systems programme; the biosecurity and trade support programme; and the food security and health programme. In September 2008 ministers of agriculture and forestry of Pacific Island countries, convened in Apia, Samoa, approved a second LRD strategic plan, following on from a first strategic plan that had been implemented during 2005–08. The second plan, covering the period 2009–12, emphasized three primary objectives: strengthened regional food and nutritional security (identified in view of recently soaring global food prices); integrated and sustainable agriculture and forestry resource management and development; and improved biosecurity and increased trade in agriculture and forestry products. The LRD has increasingly decentralized the delivery of its services, which are co-ordinated at the country level by personnel within national agricultural systems. The LRD aims to develop the capacity of PICTs in initiatives such as policy analysis and advice, and support for agricultural science and technology. In December 2011 a regional meeting on biosecurity urged increased surveillance concerning alien pest and disease invasion, which at once can derive from international trade, and also risks undermining trade. In February 2012 the LRD organized a workshop aimed at supporting PICTs in strengthening crop production through improved pest management methods, and, at that time, a new regional project on building capacities to develop integrated crop management strategies was launched. SPC hosts the Centre for Pacific Crops and Trees (CePaCT, known prior to 2007 as the Regional Germplasm Centre), which assists PICTs in efforts to conserve and access regional genetic resources. In 2001 the Pacific Community endorsed the Pacific Agricultural Plant Genetic Resources Network (PAPGREN), which is implemented by the LRD and other partners. The Pacific Animal Health Information System (PAHIS) provides data on regional livestock numbers and the regional status of animal diseases, and the Pacific Islands Pest List Database provides a register of regional agriculture, forestry and environmental pests. In 2003 a European Union-funded Development of Sustainable Agriculture in the Pacific (DSAP) project was initiated to assist 10 member countries to implement sustainable agriculture measures and to improve food production and security. A further six Pacific countries joined the programme in 2004. The LRD co-ordinates the development of organic agriculture in the Pacific region. In 2008 it adopted the Pacific Organic Standard, and it supports the Pacific Organic and Ethical Trade Community (POETCom), which was launched in 2009 to replace a previous Regional Organic Task Force (established in 2006). In December 2009 a POETCom technical experts' group met to finalize a farmers' version of the Pacific Organic Standard. POETCom, which was to manage Pacific organic certification, met in May 2012 to formalize its governance framework and to establish an inclusive membership structure. IFAD and the International Federation of Organic Agricultural Movement (IFOAM) contributed to the development of the Pacific Regional Organic Strategic Plan for 2009–13. In September 2009 SPC organized a meeting of heads of forestry agencies in the Pacific, on the theme 'Forests, Climate Change and Markets'; the meeting recommended that SPC support the formulation of a policy framework aimed at facilitating the access of PICTs to funding support offered in the context of REDD+ activities undertaken through the UN Collaborative Programme on Reducing Emissions from Deforestation and Forest Degradation in Developing Countries (UN-REDD), with a view to promoting better conservation and sustainable management of regional forestry resources. Consequently, representatives of PICTs and regional organizations met in April 2012 to consider a new draft Pacific Regional Policy Framework that had been prepared in this respect. In October 2010 a multi-agency Food Secure Pacific (FSP) working group, established in 2008 by SPC, Pacific Islands Forum Secretariat, FAO, UNICEF and WHO, began implementing a new Framework for Action on Food Security in the Pacific, which had been endorsed by a Pacific Food Summit, convened in April 2010, in Port Vila, Vanuatu. The seventh Conference of the Pacific Community was held, in November 2011, on the theme 'Climate change and food security: Managing risks for sustainable development'.

PUBLIC HEALTH

The Public Health Division aims to implement health promotion programmes; to assist regional authorities to strengthen health information systems and to promote the use of new technology for health information development and disease control; to promote efficient health services management; and to help all Pacific Islanders to attain a level of health and quality of life that will enable them to contribute to the development of their communities. The three main areas of focus of the Public Health Division are: noncommunicable diseases (such as heart disease, cerebrovascular disease and diabetes, which are prevalent in parts of the region); communicable diseases (such as HIV/AIDS, other sexually tranmitted infections—STIs, TB, and vector-borne diseases such as malaria and dengue fever); and public health policy. A Healthy Pacific Lifestyle section aims to assist member countries to improve and sustain health, in particular through advice on nutrition, physical activity and the damaging effects of alcohol and tobacco. The Public Health Surveillance and Communicable Disease Control section is the focal point of the Pacific Public Health Surveillance Network (PPHSN), a regional framework established in 1996 jointly by SPC and WHO, with the aim of sustainably advancing regional public health surveillance and response. SPC operates a project (mainly funded by Australia and New Zealand), to prevent AIDS and STIs among young people through peer education and awareness. SPC is the lead regional agency for co-ordinating and monitoring the implementation of the Pacific Regional Strategy on HIV/AIDS and other STIs, endorsed by both the Community and the Pacific Islands Forum, and covering the period 2009–13. In March 2007 the Pacific Community launched the Oceania Society for Sexual Health and HIV Medicine, a new Pacific network aimed at ensuring access to best practice prevention, treatment, care and support services in the area of sexual health and HIV/AIDS. SPC and WHO jointly organize regular meetings aimed at strengthening TB control in the region. In February 2006 SPC established a Pacific Regional Infection Control Network, based in Fiji, to improve communication and access to expert technical advice on all aspects of infectious diseases and control. During 2006 SPC, in partnership with FAO, WHO and the World Organisation for Animal Health, established the Pacific Regional Influenza Pandemic Preparedness Project (PRIPPP), with the aim of supporting the PICTs in elaborating plans to prepare for outbreaks of avian influenza or other rapidly contagious diseases. A Pacific Community Pandemic Task Force, established under the PRIPPP and comprising human and animal health experts from Pacific governments and international and regional organizations, met for the first time in March 2007 at the Pacific Community headquarters. In July 2009 Pacific ministers of health met to discuss issues including the development of strategies to control and prevent escalating diseases in the region, and the impact on regional nutrition and health of reduced household incomes in view of the global economic crisis. A Pacific Non-communicable Disease (NCD) Forum, held in Nadi, Fiji, in August, agreed recommendations on action to address the increasing regional prevalence of NCDs (also referred to as 'lifestyle diseases'). In June 2011 SPC, with WHO, organized the ninth meeting of Pacific Island ministers of health, at which it was acknowledged that the escalation in incidence of NCDs remained a priority for all regional governments.

STATISTICS FOR DEVELOPMENT PROGRAMME

The Statistics Programme assists governments and administrations in the region to provide effective and efficient national statistical services through the provision of training activities, a statistical information service and other advisory services. The Programme has three working groups, on Data Collection; Statistical Analysis; and Data Dissemination. A Regional Meeting of Heads of Statistics facilitates the integration and co-ordination of statistical services throughout the region, while the Pacific Regional Information System (PRISM), initiated by the National Statistics Office of the Pacific Islands and developed with British funding, provides statistical information about member countries and territories. Pacific demographic and health surveys (covering areas including fertility, family planning, maternal and child health, nutrition, and diseases, including HIV/AIDS and malaria), and household income and expenditure surveys are undertaken. The first regional meeting concerned with cultural statistics was convened in May 2011.

Finance

SPC has an annual budget of around US $65m., to be funded jointly by Community member states and international donors.

Publications

Annual Report.

Fisheries Newsletter (quarterly).

Pacific Aids Alert Bulletin (quarterly).

Pacific Island NCDs.

Pacific Island Nutrition (quarterly).

Regional Tuna Bulletin (quarterly).

Report of the Conference of the Pacific Community.

Women's Newsletter (quarterly).

Technical publications, statistical bulletins, advisory leaflets and reports.

PACIFIC ISLANDS FORUM

Address: Private Mail Bag, Suva, Fiji.

Telephone: 3312600; **fax:** 3301102; **e-mail:** info@forumsec.org.fj; **internet:** www.forumsec.org.

The Pacific Islands Forum (which in October 2000 changed its name from South Pacific Forum, in order to reflect the expansion of its membership since its establishment) was founded as the gathering of Heads of Government of the independent and self-governing states of the South Pacific; the first annual Forum meeting was held on 5 August 1971, in Wellington, New Zealand. The Pacific Islands Forum Secretariat was established (as the South Pacific Bureau for Economic Co-operation—SPEC) by an agreement signed on 17 April 1973, at the third Forum meeting, in Apia, Western Samoa (now Samoa). SPEC was redesignated as the South Pacific Forum Secretariat in 1988, and the present name was adopted in October 2000. The Secretariat aims to enhance the economic and social well-being of the Pacific Islands peoples, in support of the efforts of national governments. In October 2005 the 36th Forum adopted an Agreement Establishing the Pacific Islands Forum, which aimed to formalize the grouping's status as a full intergovernmental organization.

Members

Australia
Cook Islands
Fiji*
Kiribati
Marshall Islands
Federated States of Micronesia
Nauru
New Zealand
Niue
Palau
Papua New Guinea
Samoa
Solomon Islands
Tonga
Tuvalu
Vanuatu

*In May 2009 Fiji was suspended from participation in the Forum.

Note: French Polynesia and New Caledonia were admitted to the Forum as associate members in 2006. The Asian Development Bank, the Commonwealth, the UN, Timor-Leste, Tokelau, Wallis and Futuna, the Western and Central Pacific Fisheries Commission, and the World Bank are observers. In September 2011 the 42nd Forum offered observer status to the ACP Group.

Organization

(June 2012)

FORUM OFFICIALS COMMITTEE

The Forum Officials Committee is the Secretariat's executive board, overseeing its activities. It comprises representatives and senior officials from all member countries. It meets twice a year, immediately before the meetings of the Pacific Islands Forum and at the end of the year, to discuss in detail the Secretariat's work programme and annual budget.

FORUM MEETING

Each annual leaders' Forum is chaired by the Head of Government of the country hosting the meeting, who remains as Forum Chairperson until the next Forum. The Forum has no written constitution or international agreement governing its activities nor any formal rules relating to its purpose, membership or conduct of meeting. Decisions are always reached by consensus, it never having been found necessary or desirable to vote formally on issues. In October 1994 the Forum was granted observer status by the General Assembly of the United Nations. The 42nd Forum was convened in Auckland, New Zealand, in September 2011. The 43rd Forum was to be held in August 2012, in Rarotonga, Cook Islands.

DIALOGUE PLENARY MEETING

From 1989–2006 each annual Pacific Islands Forum meeting was followed by individual dialogues with representatives of selected countries considered to have a long-term interest in the region. A review of the post-Forum dialogues, undertaken in August 2006, recommended that the individual dialogues should be replaced by a new single Post-Forum Dialogue Plenary Meeting, to enable structured communication at ministerial level between Forum and Dialogue countries; and that 'core' dialogue partners, with a special engagement in and commitment to the region, should be identified. The findings of the review were approved in October 2006 by the 37th Forum meeting, and the new post-Forum dialogue structure was initiated following the 38th Forum. In 2012 Canada, the People's Republic of China, France, India, Indonesia, Italy, Japan, the Republic of Korea, Malaysia, Philippines, Thailand, the United Kingdom, the USA, and the European Union (EU) had dialogue partner status. A separate post-Forum session is convened between the Republic of China (Taiwan) and six of the Forum member states. In August 2010 leaders attending the 41st Forum determined to establish a review process to reassess the status of Post-Forum Dialogue partners; it was announced in September 2011 that implementation would begin during 2012.

SECRETARIAT

The Secretariat acts as the administrative arm of the Forum. It is headed by a Secretary-General, assisted by two Deputy Secretaries-General, and has a staff of some 70 people drawn from the member countries. The Secretariat comprises the following four Divisions: Corporate Services; Development and Economic Policy; Trade and Investment; and Political, International and Legal Affairs. The Secretariat's Pacific Plan Office services the Pacific Plan Action Committee and supports the overall implementation of the Pacific Plan. A Pacific ACP/EU Co-operation unit assists member states and regional organizations with submitting projects to the EU. A Smaller Island States (SIS) unit was established within the Secretariat in 2006. The Secretariat chairs the Council of Regional Organizations in the Pacific (CROP), an ad hoc committee comprising the heads of 10 regional organizations, which aims to discuss and co-ordinate the policies and work programmes of the various agencies in order to avoid duplication of or omissions in their services to member countries.

Secretary-General: TUILOMA NERONI SLADE (Samoa).

Deputy Secretary-General (Strategic Partnership and Co-ordination): FELETI PENITALA TEO (Tuvalu).

Deputy Secretary-General (Economic Governance and Security: ANDIE FONG TOY (New Zealand).

Activities

The Pacific Islands Forum provides an opportunity for informal discussions to be held on a wide range of common issues and problems and meets annually or when issues require urgent attention.

The Pacific Islands Forum Secretariat organizes Forum-related events, implements decisions by the Leaders, facilitates the delivery of development assistance to member states, and undertakes the political and legal mandates of Forum meetings.

In February 2007 a Regional Institutional Framework (RIF) Taskforce, comprising representatives of the member states of the Council of Regional Organizations in the Pacific agencies, convened for the first time, under Secretariat auspices. The RIF Taskforce was mandated by the October 2006 Forum to develop an appropriate institutional framework for supporting the implementation of the Pacific Plan. It was envisaged that the Pacific regional institutions would be reorganized under the following three 'pillars': a political and general policy institution; an activity sector-focused technical institution; and academic/training organizations. Lourdes Pangelinan, a former Director-

General of the Pacific Community, was given responsibility for overseeing the development of the RIF.

In December 2008 the Forum Officials Committee approved a Forum corporate plan, covering the period 2008–12, and focusing on the following strategic areas: economic governance; political governance and security; regional co-ordination; and corporate services.

PACIFIC PLAN

In August 2003 regional leaders attending the 34th Forum, held in Auckland, New Zealand, authorized the establishment of an Eminent Persons Group to consider the future activities and development of the Forum. In April 2004 a Special Leaders' Retreat, also convened in Auckland, in order to review a report prepared by the Group, mandated the development of a new Pacific Plan on Strengthening Regional Co-operation and Integration as a means of addressing the challenges confronting the Pacific Island states. Consequently a Pacific Plan Task Force, managed by the Forum Secretary-General in consultation with a core leaders' group, undertook work to formulate the document. The finalized Pacific Plan, which was endorsed by the October 2005 Forum, incorporates development initiatives that are focused around the four 'pillars' of economic growth, sustainable development, good governance, and regional security and partnerships. It also recognizes the specific needs of SIS. The Pacific Plan is regarded as a 'living document', which can be amended and updated continuously to accommodate emerging priorities. The Pacific Plan Action Committee (PPAC), comprising representatives of the Forum member states and chaired by the Forum Chairperson, has met regularly since January 2006. Regional organizations, working in partnership with national governments and other partners, are responsible for co-ordinating the implementation of—and compiling reports on—many of the specific Pacific Plan initiatives. The 37th Forum leaders' meeting in October 2006 adopted the Nadi Decisions on the Pacific Plan, prioritizing several key commitments in the four pillar areas; these were consequently incorporated into the ('living') Plan during 2007. In October 2007 the 38th Forum adopted a further set of key commitments, the Vava'U Decisions on the Pacific Plan. More key commitments and priority areas, to advance the Pacific Plan over the period 2010–13, were adopted by the 40th Forum, in August 2009. The five main themes of the Plan during 2010–13 were: fostering economic development and promoting opportunities for broad-based growth; improving the livelihoods and the well-being of the Pacific peoples; addressing the impacts of climate change; achieving stronger national development through better governance; and ensuring improved social, political and legal conditions to enable future stability, safety and security.

POLITICAL AND SOCIAL AFFAIRS AND REGIONAL SECURITY

The Political, International and Legal Affairs Division of the Secretariat organizes and services the meetings of the Forum, disseminates its views, administers the Forum's observer office at the United Nations, and aims to strengthen relations with other regional and international organizations, in particular APEC and ASEAN. The Division's other main concern is to promote regional co-operation in law enforcement and legal affairs, and it provides technical support for the drafting of legal documents and for law enforcement capacity building.

In recent years the Forum Secretariat has been concerned with assessing the legislative reforms and other commitments needed to ensure implementation of the 1992 Honiara Declaration on Law Enforcement Co-operation. The Secretariat assists member countries to ratify and implement the 1988 UN Convention against Illicit Trafficking in Narcotic Drugs and Psychotropic Substances. At the end of 2001 a conference of Forum immigration ministers expressed concern at rising levels of human-trafficking and illegal immigration in the region, and recommended that member states become parties to the 2000 UN Convention Against Transnational Organized Crime. A Pacific Transnational Crime Co-ordination Centre was established in Suva, Fiji, in 2004, to enhance and gather law enforcement intelligence. In September 2006 the Forum, in co-operation with the USA and the UN Global Programme Against Money Laundering (administered by the UN Office on Drugs and Crime), launched the Pacific Anti-Money Laundering Programme (PALP). PALP provides technical assistance to member states for the development of their national anti-money laundering and counter-terrorism financing regimes, in accordance with the Pacific Plan's development priority of regional security. Under the Pacific Plan, the Forum Secretariat requested the establishment of a Pacific Islands Regional Security Technical Co-operation Unit to support legislative efforts regarding, *inter alia*, transnational organized crime, counter-terrorism and financial intelligence.

In July 1995, following a decision of the French Government to resume testing of nuclear weapons in French Polynesia, members of the Forum resolved to increase diplomatic pressure on the Governments of France, the United Kingdom, and the USA to accede to the 1986 South Pacific Nuclear-Free Zone Treaty (Treaty of Rarotonga), prohibiting the acquisition, stationing or testing of nuclear weapons in the region. Following France's decision, announced in January 1996, to end the programme four months earlier than scheduled, representatives of the Governments of the three countries signed the Treaty in March.

Since 2001 the Forum has sent election observer groups to monitor elections taking place in member states, and, since 2004, joint election observer missions have been undertaken with the Commonwealth.

In September 2008 the first Pacific Islands-EU troika ministerial meeting was convened, in Brussels, Belgium, under a new Forum-EU enhanced political dialogue framework, which was to cover areas including regional security and governance, development co-operation, economic stability and growth, the environment and trade.

In October 2000 leaders attending the 31st Forum, convened in Tarawa, Kiribati, adopted the Biketawa Declaration, which outlined a mechanism for responding to any security crises that might occur in the region, while also urging members to undertake efforts to address the fundamental causes of potential instability. In August 2003 regional leaders convened at the 34th Forum commended the swift response by member countries and territories in deploying a Regional Assistance Mission in Solomon Islands (RAMSI), which had been approved by Forum ministers of foreign affairs at a meeting held in Sydney, Australia, in June, in accordance with the Biketawa Declaration. In December 2011 the Solomon Islands Government agreed to lead a process under which RAMSI would be phased out. In March 2008 a Pacific Islands Forum Ministerial Contact Group (MCG) on Fiji, comprising the foreign ministers of Australia, New Zealand, Papua New Guinea, Samoa, Tonga and Tuvalu, was established to facilitate the restoration of democracy and rule of law in that country, where the legitimate Government had been overthrown by the military in December 2006. In January 2009 Forum heads of state and government convened a Special Leaders' Retreat, in Port Moresby, Papua New Guinea, to consider the political situation in Fiji. The meeting resolved to suspend Fiji from the Forum if no date for democratic elections had been set by the interim authorities in that country by 1 May. Fiji's suspension was confirmed in May. Visiting Fiji in early May 2012 the MCG concluded that the ongoing process leading to planned elections in 2014 was encouraging.

The 33rd Forum, held in Suva, Fiji, in August 2002, adopted the Nasonini Declaration on Regional Security, which recognized the need for immediate and sustained regional action to combat international terrorism and transnational crime, in view of the perceived increased threat to global and regional security following the major terrorist attacks perpetrated against targets in the USA in September 2001. In October 2007 the 37th Forum determined to develop a Regional Co-operation for Counter-Terrorism Assistance and Response model.

In August 2003 regional leaders attending the 34th Forum adopted a set of Forum Principles of Good Leadership, establishing key requirements for good governance, including respect for law and the system of government, and respect for cultural values, customs and traditions, and for freedom of religion.

In December 2009 the Forum Secretariat and the World Intellectual Property Organization launched a Traditional Knowledge Action Plan for Forum Island Countries, which sought to protect Pacific traditional knowledge from misuse without compensation to its owners.

In October 2005 the 36th Forum urged the adoption of national and regional avian influenza preparedness measures and considered a proposal to establish a Pacific Health Fund to address issues such as avian influenza, HIV/AIDS, malaria, and non-communicable diseases. In June 2011 regional ministers of health issued the Honiara Communiqué on the Pacific NCD Crisis, highlighting the impact of a rapid increase in non-communicable diseases (NCDs) in the region (the estimated cause of three-quarters of adult deaths). In September 2011 the 42nd Forum issued a Leaders' Statement on Non-Communicable Diseases.

In August 2010 the 41st Forum welcomed the outcome of the Pacific Conference on the Human Face of the Global Economic Crisis, which had been convened in February of that year, with participation by policy-makers and civil society and private sector delegates from 16 Pacific Island countries, as well as development partners and representatives of UN agencies and regional organizations, including the Forum Secretariat.

In October 2010 a multi-agency Food Secure Pacific (FSP) working group, established in 2008 by the Forum Secretariat, the Secretariat of the Pacific Community, FAO, UNICEF and WHO, began implementing a new Framework for Action on Food Security in the Pacific, which had been endorsed by a Pacific Food Summit, convened in April 2010, in Port Vila, Vanuatu.

TRADE, ECONOMIC CO-OPERATION AND SUSTAINABLE DEVELOPMENT

The Secretariat's Trade and Investment Division extends advice and technical assistance to member countries in policy, development, export marketing, and information dissemination. Trade policy activities are mainly concerned with improving private sector policies, for example investment promotion, assisting integration into the world economy (including the provision of information and technical assistance to member states on WTO-related matters and supporting Pacific Island ACP states with preparations for negotiations on trade partnership with the EU under the Cotonou Agreement), and the development of businesses. During 2004–09 the Secretariat was supported in these activities through PACREIP (see below). The Secretariat aims to assist both island governments and private sector companies to enhance their capacity in the development and exploitation of export markets, product identification and product development. A regional trade and investment database is being developed. The Secretariat co-ordinates the activities of the regional trade offices located in Australia, New Zealand and Japan (see below). A representative trade office in Beijing, China, opened in January 2002. A Forum office was opened in Geneva, Switzerland, in 2004 to represent member countries at the WTO. In April 2005 the Pacific Islands Private Sector Organisation (PIPSO), representing regional private sector interests, was established. The PIPSO Secretariat, hosted by the Forum Secretariat, was inaugurated in April 2007. In August of that year PIPSO organized the first Pacific Islands Business Forum, convened in Nadi, Fiji.

In 1981 the South Pacific Regional Trade and Economic Co-operation Agreement (SPARTECA) came into force. SPARTECA aimed to redress the trade deficit of the Pacific Island countries with Australia and New Zealand. It is a non-reciprocal trade agreement under which Australia and New Zealand offer duty-free and unrestricted access or concessional access for specified products originating from the developing island member countries of the Forum. In 1985 Australia agreed to further liberalization of trade by abolishing (from the beginning of 1987) duties and quotas on all Pacific products except steel, cars, sugar, footwear and garments. In August 1994 New Zealand expanded its import criteria under the agreement by reducing the rule of origin requirement for garment products from 50% to 45% of local content. In response to requests from Fiji, Australia agreed to widen its interpretation of the agreement by accepting as being of local content manufactured products that consist of goods and components of 50% Australian content. A new Fiji/Australia Trade and Economic Relations Agreement (AFTERA) was concluded in March 1999 to complement SPARTECA and compensate for certain trade benefits that were in the process of being withdrawn.

Two major regional trade accords signed by Forum heads of state in August 2001 entered into force in April 2003 and October 2002, respectively: the Pacific Island Countries Trade Agreement (PICTA), providing for the establishment of a Pacific Island free trade area (FTA); and the related Pacific Agreement on Closer Economic Relations (PACER), incorporating trade and economic co-operation measures and envisaging the phased establishment of a regional single market comprising the PICTA FTA and Australia and New Zealand. The FTA was to be implemented over a period of eight years for developing member countries and 10 years for SIS and least developed countries. It was envisaged that negotiations on free trade agreements between Pacific Island states and Australia and New Zealand, with a view to establishing the larger regional single market envisaged by PACER, would commence within eight years of PICTA's entry into force. SPARTECA (see above) would remain operative pending the establishment of the larger single market, into which it would be subsumed. Under the provisions of PACER, Australia and New Zealand were to provide technical and financial assistance to PICTA signatory states in pursuing the objectives of PACER. In August 2003 regional leaders attending the 34th Forum agreed, in principle, that the USA and France should become parties to both PICTA and PACER. In September 2004 Forum trade officials adopted a Regional Trade Facilitation Programme (RTFP), within the framework of PACER, which included measures concerned with customs procedures, quarantine, standards and other activities to harmonize and facilitate trade between Pacific Island states and Australia and New Zealand, as well as with other international trading partners. It was announced in August 2007 that a review of the RTFP was to be undertaken. In March 2008 negotiations commenced on expanding PICTA to include provisions for trade in services as well as trade in goods; the seventh round of negotiations was convened in February 2012. In August leaders attending the 40th Forum, convened in Cairns, Australia, endorsed the Cairns Compact on Strengthening Development Co-ordination in the Pacific, aimed at improving regional economic and development progress despite the ongoing global economic crisis; and agreed that negotiations on a new regional trade and economic integration agreement (PACER-Plus) should commence forthwith. The participants in the PACER-Plus negotiations (which were ongoing in 2012) are Australia, the Cook Islands, Kiribati, the Marshall Islands, the Federated States of Micronesia, Nauru, New Zealand, Niue, Palau, Papua New Guinea, Samoa, the Solomon Islands, Tonga, Tuvalu and Vanuatu. A meeting of Forum ministers of trade, convened in April 2010, proposed that a shared 10-year strategy for trade and investment promotion should be developed. The April 2010 meeting established a new umbrella body, Pacific Islands Trade and Invest, to cover and develop a co-ordinated corporate strategy for the former Pacific Islands Trade and Investment Commissions, based in Auckland, New Zealand and Sydney, Australia; and trade offices in Beijing, China and Tokyo, Japan.

In April 2001 the Secretariat convened a meeting of seven member island states—the Cook Islands, the Marshall Islands, Nauru, Niue, Samoa, Tonga and Vanuatu—as well as representatives from Australia and New Zealand, to address the regional implications of the OECD's Harmful Tax Competition Initiative. (OECD had identified the Cook Islands, the Marshall Islands, Nauru and Niue as so-called 'tax havens' lacking financial transparency and had demanded that they impose stricter legislation to address the incidence of international money-laundering on their territories.) The meeting requested the OECD to engage in conciliatory negotiations with the listed Pacific Island states. The August 2001 Forum reiterated this stance, proclaiming the sovereign right of nations to establish individual tax regimes, and supporting the development of a new co-operative framework to address financial transparency concerns.

The Development and Economic Policy Division of the Secretariat aims to co-ordinate and promote co-operation in development activities and programmes throughout the region. The Division administers a Short Term Advisory Service, which provides consultancy services to help member countries meet economic development priorities, and a Fellowship Scheme to provide practical training in a range of technical and income-generating activities. A Small Island Development Fund aims to assist the economic development of the SIS sub-group of member countries (see below) through project financing. A separate fellowship has also been established to provide training to the

Kanak population of New Caledonia, to assist in their social, economic and political development. During 2004–09 a Pacific Regional Assistance to Nauru (PRAN) initiative was implemented. The Division aims to assist regional organizations to identify development priorities and to provide advice to national governments on economic analysis, planning and structural reforms.

In November 2008 the Forum and the EU approved a Pacific Regional Strategy Paper (RSP) and Regional Indicative Programme (RIP), representing the framework for co-operation between the Pacific ACP States and European Commission over the period 2008–13.

In August 2008 the 39th Forum welcomed a new Pacific Region Infrastructure Facility initiated by the World Bank, Asian Development Bank and Governments of Australia and New Zealand.

ENVIRONMENT

The Forum actively promotes the development of effective international legislation to reduce emissions by industrialized countries of so-called 'greenhouse gases'. Such gases contribute to the warming of the earth's atmosphere (the 'greenhouse effect') and to related increases in global sea levels, and have therefore been regarded as a major threat to low-lying islands in the region. The Secretariat has played an active role in supporting regional participation at meetings of the Conference of the Parties to the UN Framework Convention on Climate Change (UNFCCC), and helps to co-ordinate Forum policy on the environment. With support from the Australian Government, it administers a network of stations to monitor sea levels and climate change throughout the Pacific region. The 29th Forum, held in Pohnpei, Federated States of Micronesia, in August 1998, adopted a Statement on Climate Change, which urged all countries to ratify and implement the gas emission reductions agreed upon by UN member states in December 1997 (the so-called Kyoto Protocol of the UNFCCC), and emphasized the Forum's commitment to further measures for verifying and enforcing emission limitation. In October 2005 the 36th Forum approved the Pacific Islands Framework for Action on Climate Change 2006–15, and noted the need to implement national action plans to address climate change issues. In October 2007 leaders attending the 38th Forum reiterated deep concern over the economic, social and environmental impact of climate change, noting the recent findings of the IPCC's *Fourth Assessment Report* and the importance of negotiating a comprehensive international framework to tackle climate change after the expiry of the Kyoto Protocol. In August 2008 the 39th Forum, held in Alofi, Niue, endorsed the Niue Declaration on Climate Change, which urged international partners to undertake immediate and effective measures to reduce emissions, to use cleaner fuels, and to increase use of renewable energy sources, and directed the Forum Secretariat to work with relevant agencies and member countries and territories in support of a number of commitments, including examining the potential for regional climate change insurance arrangements, and advancing regional expertise in the development and deployment of adaptation technologies. In November 2008 the EU and the Forum Secretariat adopted a joint declaration on co-operating in combating the challenges posed by climate change. The 40th Forum, in August 2009, adopted the Pacific Leaders Call for Action on Climate Change. A mid-term review of the Pacific Islands Framework for Action on Climate Change was undertaken in 2010.

In August 2002 regional leaders attending the 33rd Forum approved a Pacific Island Regional Ocean Policy, which aimed to ensure the future sustainable use of the ocean and its resources by Pacific Island communities and external partners. A Declaration on Deep Sea Bottom Trawling to Protect Biodiversity on the High Seas was adopted in October 2005 by the 36th Forum. In October 2007 leaders attending the 38th Forum urged increased efforts among Forum members to foster a long-term strategic approach to ensuring the effective management of fish stocks, with a particular focus on tuna, and adopted a related Declaration on Pacific Fisheries Resources. In August 2010 the 41st Forum endorsed both a new Regional Monitoring Control and Surveillance Strategy, adopted by Forum ministers responsible for fisheries in July, as the overarching framework to support regional fisheries management, and also endorsed a new Framework for a Pacific Oceanscape, aimed at ensuring the long-term, co-operative sustainable development, management and conservation of the Pacific.

In September 1995 the 26th Forum adopted the Waigani Convention, banning the import into the region of all radioactive and other hazardous wastes, and providing controls for the transboundary movement and management of these wastes. Forum leaders have frequently reiterated protests against the shipment of radioactive materials through the region.

In January 2005, meeting on the fringes of the fifth Summit of the Alliance of Small Island States, in Port Louis, Mauritius, the Secretaries-General of the Pacific Islands Forum Secretariat, the Commonwealth, CARICOM, and the Indian Ocean Commission determined to take collective action to strengthen the disaster preparedness and response capacities of their member countries in the Pacific, Caribbean and Indian Ocean areas. In October 2005 the 36th Forum endorsed the Pacific Disaster Risk Reduction and Disaster Management Framework for Action 2005–15.

TRANSPORT

The Forum established the Pacific Forum Line and the Association of South Pacific Airlines (see below), as part of its efforts to promote co-operation in regional transport. In May 1998 ministers responsible for aviation in member states approved a new regional civil aviation policy, which envisaged liberalization of air services, common safety and security standards and provisions for shared revenue. The Pacific Islands Air Services Agreement (PIASA) was opened for signature in August 2003, and entered into effect in October 2007, having been ratified by six Pacific Island countries. In August 2004 the Pacific Islands Civil Aviation and Security Treaty (PICASST) was opened for signature, and, in June 2005 PICASST entered into force, establishing a Port Vila, Vanuatu-based Pacific Aviation Security Office. In accordance with the Principles on Regional Transport Services, which were adopted by Forum Leaders in August 2004, the Secretariat was to support efforts to enhance air and shipping services, as well as develop a regional digital strategy.

In August 2004 the 35th Forum adopted a set of Principles on Regional Transport Services, based on the results of a study requested by the 34th Forum, 'to improve the efficiency, effectiveness and sustainability of air and shipping services'.

SMALLER ISLAND STATES

In 1990 the Cook Islands, Kiribati, Nauru, Niue and Tuvalu, among the Forum's smallest island member states, formed the Forum SIS economic sub-group, which convenes an annual summit meeting to address their specific smaller island concerns. These include, in particular, economic disadvantages resulting from a poor resource base, absence of a skilled work-force and lack of involvement in world markets. Small island member states have also been particularly concerned about the phenomenon of global warming and its potentially damaging effects on the region. In September 1997 the Marshall Islands was admitted as the sixth member of SIS, and Palau was subsequently admitted as the seventh member. In February 1998 senior Forum officials, for the first time, met with representatives of the Caribbean Community and the Indian Ocean Commission, as well as other major international organizations, to discuss means to enhance consideration and promotion of the interests of small island states. An SIS unit, established within the Forum Secretariat in 2006, aims to enable high-profile representation of the SIS perspective, particularly in the development of the Pacific Plan, and to enable the small island member states to benefit fully from the implementation of the Plan. In August 2010 the 41st Forum welcomed the outcome of a Pacific High Level Dialogue (convened in February of that year) on the five-year review conference of the 2005 Mauritius Strategy for the further Implementation of the 1994 Barbados Programme of Action for the Sustainable Development of SIS, which was convened in September 2010. The UN Conference on Sustainable Development, convened in June 2012, in Rio de Janeiro, Brazil, called for a third international conference on SIS to be convened during 2014.

Recent Meetings of the Pacific Islands Forum

The 41st Forum, which took place in Port Vila, Vanuatu, in August 2010, endorsed the Port Vila Declaration on Accelerating Progress on the Achievement of the UN Millennium Development Goals; endorsed a new Regional Monitoring Control and Surveillance Strategy for fisheries (see above); stated strong support for the Pacific Regional Strategy on Disability covering 2010–15, which had been approved by Forum disability ministers in October 2009; endorsed a Framework for Action on Energy Security in the Pacific; and endorsed the Framework for a Pacific Oceanscape (see above).

In early September 2011 the 42nd Forum, held in Auckland, New Zealand, endorsed the Waiheke Declaration on Sustainable Economic Development—recognizing the importance of focusing regional efforts on sectors such as tourism, fisheries and agriculture, in which there is comparative advantage; and a Forum Leaders' Statement on Non-Communicable Diseases (NCDs). Leaders emphasized maximizing the economic benefit from fisheries, expressed concern at the effect of illegal, unreported and unregulated fishing, and stressed the importance of transport links and secure access to energy. The leaders recalled the Honiara Communiqué on the Pacific NCD Crisis, issued by regional health ministers in June 2011, which highlighted the impact of a rapid increase in NCDs in the region (the estimated cause of three-quarters of adult deaths). Leaders undertook to support the Marshall Islands in raising the profile of the issue of international contaminants at international fora.

Finance

The Governments of Australia and New Zealand each contribute some one-third of the annual budget and the remaining amount is shared by the other member Governments. Extra-budgetary funding is contributed mainly by Australia, New Zealand, Japan, the EU and France. The Forum's 2010 budget amounted to $F43.5m. Following a decision of the 36th Forum a Pacific Fund was established to support the implementation of the Pacific Plan, under the management of the Pacific Plan Action Committee.

Publications

Annual Report.
Forum News (quarterly).
Forum Trends.
Forum Secretariat Directory of Aid Agencies.
Pacific Plan Progress Report.
South Pacific Trade Directory.
SPARTECA (guide for Pacific island exporters).
Reports of meetings; profiles of Forum member countries.

Overseas Agencies and Affiliated Organizations

Association of South Pacific Airlines (ASPA): POB 9817, Nadi Airport, Nadi, Fiji; tel. 6723526; fax 6720196; e-mail georgefaktaufon@aspa.aero; internet aspa.aero/index.php; f. 1979 at a meeting of airlines in the South Pacific, convened to promote co-operation among the member airlines for the development of regular, safe and economical commercial aviation within, to and from the South Pacific; mems: 16 regional airlines, two associates; Chair. Didier Tappero; New Caledonia.; Sec.-Gen. Dr Lee Kwon.

Forum Fisheries Agency (FFA): POB 629, Honiara, Solomon Islands; tel. (677) 21124; fax (677) 23995; e-mail info@ffa.int; internet www.ffa.int; f. 1979 to promote co-operation in fisheries among coastal states in the region; collects and disseminates information and advice on the living marine resources of the region, including the management, exploitation and development of these resources; provides assistance in the areas of law (treaty negotiations, drafting legislation, and co-ordinating surveillance and enforcement), fisheries development, research, economics, computers, and information management; implements a Vessel Monitoring System, to provide automated data collection and analysis of fishing vessel activities throughout the region; on behalf of its 16 member countries, the FFA administers a multilateral fisheries treaty, under which vessels from the USA operate in the region, in exchange for an annual payment; the FFA is implementing the FFA Strategic Plan 2005–20, detailing the medium-term direction of the Agency; Dir Su'a N. F. Tanielu; publs *FFA News Digest* (every two months), *FFA Reports*, *MCS Newsletter* (quarterly), *Tuna Market Newsletter* (monthly).

Pacific Forum Line: POB 105-612, Auckland 1143, New Zealand; tel. (9) 356-2333; fax (9) 356-2330; e-mail info@pflnz.co.nz; internet www.pflnz.co.nz; f. 1977 as a joint venture by South Pacific countries, to provide shipping services to meet the special requirements of the region; operates three container vessels; conducts shipping agency services in Australia, Fiji, New Zealand and Samoa, and stevedoring in Samoa; CEO Henning Hansen.

Pacific Islands Centre (PIC): Meiji University, 1-1 Kanda-Surugadai, Chiyoda-ku, Tokyo 101-8301, Japan; tel. (3) 3296-4545; e-mail info@pic.or.jp; internet www.pic.or.jp; f. 1996 to promote and to facilitate trade, investment and tourism among Forum members and Japan; Dir K. Sohma.

Pacific Islands Forum Trade Office: 5-1-3-1 Tayuan Diplomatic Compound, 1 Xin Dong Lu, Chaoyang District, Beijing 100600, People's Republic of China; tel. (10) 6532-6622; fax (10) 6532-6360; e-mail answers@pifto.org.cn; internet www.pifto.org.cn; f. 2001.

Pacific Islands Private Sector Organization (PIPSO): c/o Pacific Islands Forum Secretariat, Private Mail Bag, Suva, Fiji; tel. 3312600; fax 3301102; e-mail info@pipso.org.fj; internet www.pipso.org; f. 2005 to represent regional private sector interests; organizes Pacific Islands Business Forum; Chair. Hafiz Khan (Fiji).

Pacific Islands Trade and Invest (Sydney): Level 11, 171 Clarence St, Sydney, NSW 20010, Australia; tel. (2) 9290-2133; fax (2) 9299-2151; e-mail info@pitic.org.au; internet www.pitic.org.au; f. 1979 as Pacific Islands Trade and Investment Commission (Sydney), current name adopted 2010; assists Pacific Island Governments and business communities to identify market opportunities in Australia and promotes investment in the Pacific Island countries.

Pacific Islands Trade and Invest (New Zealand): POB 109-395, 5 Short St, Level 3, Newmarket, Auckland, New Zealand; tel. (9) 5295165; fax (9) 5231284; e-mail info@pitic.org.nz; internet www.pacifictradeinvest.com; f. 1988 as Pacific Islands Trade and Investment Commission (New Zealand), current name adopted 2010.

SOUTH ASIAN ASSOCIATION FOR REGIONAL COOPERATION—SAARC

Address: POB 4222, Tridevi Marg, Kathmandu, Nepal.
Telephone: (1) 4221785; **fax:** (1) 4227033; **e-mail:** saarc@saarc-sec.org; **internet:** www.saarc-sec.org.

The South Asian Association for Regional Cooperation (SAARC) was formally established in 1985 in order to strengthen and accelerate regional co-operation, particularly in economic development.

MEMBERS

Afghanistan	Maldives
Bangladesh	Nepal
Bhutan	Pakistan
India	Sri Lanka

Observers: People's Republic of China, Iran, Japan, the Republic of Korea, the European Union.

Organization

(June 2012)

SUMMIT MEETING

Heads of state and of government of member states represent the body's highest authority, and a summit meeting is normally held annually. The 17th summit was held in Addu City, Maldives, in November 2011, and the 18th summit was to convene in Nepal in 2013.

COUNCIL OF MINISTERS

The Council of Ministers comprises the ministers of foreign affairs of member countries, who meet twice a year. The Council may also meet in extraordinary session at the request of member states. The responsibilities of the Council include formulation of policies, assessing progress and confirming new areas of co-operation.

STANDING COMMITTEE

The Committee consists of the ministers of foreign affairs of member states. It has overall responsibility for the monitoring and co-ordination of programmes and financing, and determines priorities, mobilizes resources and identifies areas of co-operation. It usually meets twice a year, and submits its reports to the Council of Ministers. The Committee is supported by an ad hoc Programming Committee made up of senior officials, who meet to examine the budget of the Secretariat, confirm the Calendar of Activities and resolve matters assigned to it by the Standing Committee.

TECHNICAL COMMITTEES

SAARC's six Technical Committees cover: Agriculture and rural development; Environment; Health and population activities; Science and technology; Transport; and Women, Youth and Children; and are responsible for forming, co-ordinating, implementing and monitoring programmes in their respective areas of focus. Each committee comprises representatives of member states and meets annually.

SECRETARIAT

The Secretariat comprises the Secretary-General and eight Directors, from each member country, responsible for the following working divisions: Media and Integration of Afghanistan; Agriculture and Rural Development; Environment and Science and Technology; Economic, Trade and Finance; Social Affairs; Information and Publications; Administration, Energy and Tourism; and Human Resource Development, Transport and the SAARC Charter. The Secretary-General is appointed by the Council of Ministers, after being nominated by a member state, and serves a three-year term of office.

Secretary-General: AHMED SALEEM (Maldives).

Activities

The first summit meeting of SAARC heads of state and government, held in Dhaka, Bangladesh, in December 1985, resulted in the signing of the Charter of the South Asian Association for Regional Cooperation. The SAARC Charter stipulates that decisions should be made unanimously, and that 'bilateral and contentious issues' should not be discussed. In August 1993 ministers of foreign affairs of seven countries, meeting in New Delhi, India, adopted a Declaration on South Asian Regional Cooperation. In April 2010 the 16th SAARC summit meeting noted the need to develop a SAARC 'Vision Statement', and determined to organize a South Asia Forum in which to exchange ideas on future regional development. In April 2011 a steering committee for the establishment of the South Asia Forum finalized the 'Objectives, Scope and Guidelines' for the Forum. The 16th summit also directed SAARC to establish a working group to organize the creation of a Conclave of SAARC Parliamentarians, and determined to focus more strongly on people-centric development, preservation of environment and better governance. The 17th SAARC summit, convened in November 2011, in Addu City, Maldives, adopted the Addu Declaration on 'Building Bridges', urging, *inter alia*, the promotion of the region in terms of trade and tourism as 'Destination South Asia'; the elimination of terrorism and combating of maritime piracy in the region; the establishment of a regional mechanism to ensure the empowerment of women and gender equality in the region; the finalization of work to elaborate a new SAARC Regional Convention on Preventing and Combating Trafficking in Women and Children for Prostitution; the commemoration of a new SAARC Media Day and staging of a Regional Conference on Media; and the promotion of regional co-operation in other areas including trade, transport, and energy.

A priority objective is the eradication of poverty in the region, and in 1993 SAARC endorsed a conceptual framework to help achieve this. The 11th SAARC summit meeting, held in Kathmandu, Nepal, in January 2002, adopted a convention on regional arrangements for the promotion of child welfare in South Asia. The 11th summit also determined to reinvigorate regional poverty reduction activities in the context of the UN General Assembly's Millennium Development Goal of halving extreme poverty by 2015, and of other internationally agreed commitments. The meeting reconstituted the Independent South Asian Commission on Poverty Alleviation—ISACPA, which had been established in 1991. ISACPA reported to the 12th summit meeting of heads of state, held in Islamabad, Pakistan, in January 2004. The 12th summit meeting declared poverty alleviation to be the overarching goal of all SAARC activities and requested ISACPA to continue its work in an advocacy role and to prepare a set of SAARC Development Goals (SDGs). At the meeting heads of state endorsed a Plan of Action on Poverty Alleviation, and also adopted a SAARC Social Charter that had been drafted with assistance from representatives of civil society, academia, non-governmental organizations and government, under the auspices of an intergovernmental expert group, and incorporated objectives in areas including poverty alleviation, promotion of health and nutrition, food security, water supply and sanitation, children's development and rights, participation by women, and human resources development. The 13th SAARC summit meeting, held in Dhaka, in November 2005, declared the SAARC Decade of Poverty Alleviation covering the period 2006–15 and determined to replace SAARC's Three-tier Mechanism on Poverty Alleviation (established in 1995) with a Two-tier Mechanism on Poverty Alleviation, comprising ministers and secretaries responsible for poverty alleviation at national level.

The 14th summit meeting, held in New Delhi, in April 2007, acknowledged ISACPA's efforts in elaborating the SDGs and entrusted the Two-tier Mechanism with monitoring progress towards the achievement of these. The 16th summit, held in Thimphu, Bhutan, in April 2010, urged the mainstreaming of the SDGs into member states' national processes.

An agreement establishing a Food Security Reserve to meet emergency food requirements was signed in November 1987, and entered into force in August 1988. In 2004 the 12th summit meeting determined to establish a Food Bank, incorporating a Food Reserve of wheat and/or rice; the Food Bank was to act as a regional food security reserve during times of normal food shortages as well as during emergencies. The Intergovernmental Agreement establishing the SAARC Food Bank (SFB) was signed by leaders attending the 14th summit meeting in April 2007. A meeting of the SFB executive board, convened in October 2010, determined to raise the SFB's then authorized total reserve of 241,580 metric tons of food grains to 400,000 metric tons, in view of ongoing acute regional food insecurity. SAARC's 15th summit meeting, held in Colombo, Sri Lanka, in August 2008, issued the 'Colombo Statement on Food Security', urging the region—in response to the ongoing global crisis of reduced food availability and rising food prices—to forge greater co-operation with the international community to ensure regional food availability and nutrition security. An extraordinary meeting of SAARC ministers of agriculture, convened in November 2008, adopted a guiding 'SAARC Agriculture Vision 2020', and a roadmap for its achievement. In November 2011 the 17th SAARC summit adopted an agreement on the establishment of a SAARC Seed Bank, aimed at enhancing regional agricultural productivity.

The eighth SAARC summit meeting, held in New Delhi in May 1996, established a South Asian Development Fund, comprising a Fund for Regional Projects, a Regional Fund and a fund for social development and infrastructure building. A meeting of SAARC financial experts, held in September 2005, submitted for further consideration by the Association proposals that the South Asian Development Fund should be replaced by a new SAARC Development Fund (SDF), comprising a Social Window (to finance poverty alleviation projects), an Infrastructure Window (for infrastructure development) and an Economic Window (for non-infrastructure commercial programmes). The meeting also considered the possibility of establishing a South Asian Development Bank. A roadmap for the establishment of the SDF was endorsed by the SAARC Council of Ministers in August 2006, and the Fund was eventually launched in April 2010; its secretariat was to be based in Thimphu, Bhutan. In October 2010 the Japanese Government suspended new financing to a SAARC-Japan Special Fund, established in September 1993, through which funds (cumulatively totalling US $4.73m. by 2010) had been channelled to support SAARC symposia and expert meetings on socio-economic matters, especially relating to energy and disaster reduction; the Fund was to terminate operations following the allocation of some $100,000 that remained deposited at that time.

In April 2003 SAARC ministers of health convened an emergency meeting to consider the regional implications of the spread of Severe Acute Respiratory Syndrome (SARS), a previously unknown atypical pneumonia. In November of that year SAARC ministers of health determined to establish a regional surveillance and rapid reaction system for managing health crises and natural disasters; the August 2008 summit meeting approved the development of a Natural Disaster Rapid Response Mechanism. In November 2011 ministers of foreign affairsattending the 17th SAARC summit signed a regional Agreement on Rapid Response to Natural Disasters. A SAARC Regional Strategy on HIV/AIDS aims to combat the spread of the infection.

A Committee on Economic Cooperation (CEC), comprising senior trade officials of member states, was established in July 1991 to monitor progress concerning trade and economic co-operation issues. In the same year the summit meeting approved the creation of an inter-governmental group to establish a framework for the promotion of specific trade liberalization measures. A SAARC Chamber of Commerce (SCCI) became operational in 1992. In April 1993 ministers signed a SAARC Preferential Trading Arrangement (SAPTA), which came into effect in December 1995. In December 1995 the Council resolved that the ultimate objective for member states should be the establishment of a South Asian Free Trade Area (SAFTA), superseding SAPTA. An Agreement on SAFTA was signed in January 2004, at the 12th summit, and on 1 January 2006 it entered into force, providing for the phased elimination of tariffs: these were to be reduced to 30% in least developed member countries and to 20% in the others over an initial two-year period, and subsequently to 0%–5% over a period of five years. The Agreement established a mechanism for administering SAFTA and for settling disputes at ministerial level. In August 2008 the 15th summit adopted a protocol on Afghanistan's admission to SAFTA. In February 2009 the Council of Ministers issued a Statement on the Global Economic Crisis. In November 2011 the 17th SAARC summit urged the intensification of efforts to implement SAFTA effectively, and also directed SAARC finance ministers to draft a proposal on means of facilitating greater regional flow of financial capital and intra-regional long-term investment.

In January 1996 the first SAARC Trade Fair was held, in New Delhi, to promote intra-SAARC commerce. At the same time SAARC ministers of commerce convened for their first meeting to discuss regional economic co-operation. The 11th SAARC Trade Fair and Tourism Mart was held, in Dhaka, in March–April 2012, and the 12th Trade Fair and Tourism Mart was to be held in Kulhudhuffushi, Maldives, later in 2012.

Since 2007 a SAARC Youth Camp has been periodically convened (2007: Bangladesh; 2008: Sri Lanka; 2010–11: the Maldives). A Youth Awards Scheme to reward, annually, outstanding achievements by young people has been operational since 1996. Under the SAARC Agenda for Culture, approved in April 2007, the online promotion of regional culture, a SAARC website on culture, and a SAARC exchange programme on culture were to be developed. SAARC film festivals have been convened. The SAARC Consortium of Open and Distance Learning was established in 2000. A Visa Exemption Scheme, exempting (in 2012) 24 specified categories of person from visa requirements, with the aim of promoting closer regional contact, became operational in March 1992. In February 2011 a meeting of SAARC foreign ministers agreed to introduce long-term multi-entry visas for certain business people, sports people and journalists. A SAARC citizens forum promotes interaction among the people of South Asia. In addition, SAARC operates a fellowships, scholarships and chairs scheme and a scheme for the promotion of organized tourism.

In June 2005 SAARC ministers of the environment met in special session to consider the impact of the devastating earthquake and subsequent massive ocean movements, or tsunamis, that struck in the Indian Ocean at the end of 2004. The meeting reviewed an assessment of the extent of loss and damage in each country, and of the relief and rehabilitation measures being undertaken. Ministers resolved to strengthen early warning and disaster management capabilities in the region, and determined to support the rehabilitation of members' economies, in particular through the promotion of the tourism sector. In July 2008 SAARC ministers of the environment, meeting to discuss climate change, adopted a SAARC Action Plan and 'Dhaka Declaration on Climate Change', urging close co-operation in developing projects and raising mass awareness of climate change. In April 2010 leaders attending the 16th SAARC summit meeting issued the 'Thimphu Statement on Climate Change', in which they determined to review the implementation of the 2008 SAARC Action Plan and Dhaka Declaration, and agreed, *inter alia*, to establish an Inter-governmental Expert Group on Climate Change, with the aim of developing clear policy direction and guidelines for regional co-operation; to direct the Secretary-General to commission a study on 'Climate risks in the region: ways comprehensively to address the related social, economic and environmental challenges'; to implement advocacy and awareness programmes on climate change; to organize for 10m. trees to be planted in the region during 2010–15; to formulate national plans, and, when appropriate, regional projects, aimed at protecting and safeguarding the SAARC region's archeological and historical infrastructure from the adverse effects of climate change; to commission SAARC intergovernmental initiatives on the marine and mountain ecosystems, and on evolving monsoon patterns; and to organize a SAARC Inter-governmental Climate-related Disasters Initiative, aimed at integrating climate change adaptation and disaster risk reduction planning mechanisms.

From October 2004 SAARC implemented, under supervision from the Asian Development Bank (ADB), a Regional Multimodal Transport Study; this was extended in 2007 to cover Afghanistan. The first South Asia Energy dialogue was convened in March 2007 in New Delhi. The November 2011 SAARC summit urged the conclusion of a new Regional Railways Agreement; and also the conclusion of an Inter-governmental Framework Agreement for Energy Cooperation, and of a Study on Regional Power Exchange.

At the third SAARC summit, held in Kathmandu, in November 1987, member states signed a regional convention on measures to counteract terrorism. The convention, which entered into force in August 1988, commits signatory countries to the extradition or prosecution of alleged terrorists and to the implementation of preventative measures to combat terrorism. A convention on narcotic drugs and psychotropic substances was signed during the fifth SAARC summit meeting, held in Malé, Maldives, in 1990, and entered into force in September 1993. It is implemented by a co-ordination group of drug law enforcement agencies. At the 11th SAARC summit member states adopted a convention on the prevention of trafficking of women and children for prostitution. The 12th summit adopted an Additional Protocol on Suppression of Terrorism with a view to preventing the financing of terrorist activities. In February 2009 the Council of Ministers issued a Declaration on Cooperation in Combating Terrorism.

There is a wide network of SAARC Regional Centres. In 1998 an Agricultural Information Centre was established, in Dhaka, to serve as a central institution for the dissemination of knowledge and information in the agricultural sector. It maintains a network of centres in each member state, which provide for the efficient exchange of technical information and for strengthening agricultural research. Other regional centres include the SAARC Tuberculosis and HIV/AIDS Centre (inaugurated in November 2007, replacing the former SAARC Tuberculosis Centre, which had been established in 1992); a SAARC Documentation Centre, established in New Delhi in 1994; a SAARC Meteorological Research Centre, which opened in Dhaka in 1995; a Human Resources Development Centre, established in Islamabad, Pakistan in 1999; a SAARC Coastal Zone Management Centre, established in 2005 in the Maldives; a SAARC Information Centre, inaugurated in Nepal in 2005; and a SAARC Cultural Centre, which opened in Colombo, in 2009. In July 2005 the Council of Ministers approved the establishment of additional regional centres for forestry, to be based in Bhutan, and for energy, to be located in Pakistan. In January 2008 a new SAARC database on gender data (the SAARC 'Genderbase') was launched. A SAARC University was inaugurated in August 2010, based at a temporary campus in New Delhi, India; construction of a permanent campus was to commence in 2012.

SAARC has signed Memoranda of Understanding (MOUs) with UNICEF and UNCTAD (in 1993); ESCAP (1994); the Asia Pacific Telecommunity (1994); UNDP (1995); the UN Drug Programme (1995); the European Commission (1996); the International Telecommunication Union (1997); the Canadian International Development Agency (1997); WHO (2000); the ADB, FAO, the Joint UN Programme on HIV/AIDS and the UN Population Fund (2004); UNEP and UNESCO (2007); and the UN International Strategy for Disaster Reduction (2008). An informal dialogue at ministerial level has been conducted with ASEAN and the European Union since 1998. SAARC and the WTO hold regular consultations. SAARC's Secretary-General participates in regular consultative meetings of executive heads of sub-regional organizations (including ESCAP, ASEAN, the Economic Cooperation Organization, and the Pacific Islands Forum).

Finance

The national budgets of member countries provide the resources to finance SAARC activities. The Secretariat's annual budget is shared among member states according to a specified formula.

Publications

SAARC News (quarterly).

Other official documents, regional studies, reports.

Regional Apex Bodies

Association of Persons of the Legal Communities of the SAARC Countries (SAARCLAW): 495 HSIDC, Udyog Vihar Phase V, N. H. 8, Gurgaon 122016, National Capital Region, India; tel. (124) 4040193; fax (124) 4040194; e-mail info@saarclaw.com; internet www.saarclaw.com; f. 1991; recognized as a SAARC regional apex body in July 1994; aims to enhance exchanges and co-operation among the legal communities of the sub-region and to promote the development of law; Pres. SONAM TOBGYE; Sec.-Gen. HERMANT K. BATRA.

SAARC Chamber of Commerce and Industry (SCCI): House 397, St 64, I-8/3, Islamabad, Pakistan; tel. (51) 4860611; fax (51) 4860610; e-mail info@saarcchamber.org; internet www.saarcchamber.org; f. 1992; promotes economic and trade co-operation throughout the sub-region and greater interaction between the business communities of member countries; organizes SAARC Economic Cooperation Conferences and Trade Fairs; Pres. SHRI VIKRAMJIT S. SAHNEY; Sec.-Gen. MUHAMMAD IQBAL TABISH.

South Asian Federation of Accountants (SAFA): c/o Institute of Chartered Accountants of India, ICAI Bhavan, POB 7100, Indraprastha Marg, New Delhi 110002, India; tel. (11) 23370195; fax (11) 23379334; e-mail safa@icai.org; internet www.esafa.org; f. 1984; recognized as a SAARC regional apex body in Jan. 2002; aims to develop regional co-ordination for the accountancy profession; Pres. Muhammad RAFI; Sec. T. KARTHIKEYAN.

Other recognized regional bodies include the South Asian Association for Regional Cooperation of Architects, the Association of Management Development Institutions, the SAARC Federation of University Women, the SAARC Association of Town Planners, the SAARC Cardiac Society, the Association of SAARC Speakers and Parliamentarians, the Federation of State Insurance Organizations of SAARC Countries, the Federation of State Insurance Organizations of SAARC Countries, the SAARC Diploma Engineers Forum, the Radiological Society of SAARC Countries, the South Asia Initiative to End Violence Against Children (SAIEVAC), the SAARC Teachers' Federation, the SAARC Surgical Care Society and the Foundation of SAARC Writers and Literature.

SOUTHERN AFRICAN DEVELOPMENT COMMUNITY—SADC

Address: SADC HQ, Plot No. 54385, Private Bag 0095, Gaborone, Botswana.

Telephone: 3951863; **fax:** 3972848; **e-mail:** registry@sadc.int; **internet:** www.sadc.int.

The first Southern African Development Co-ordination Conference (SADCC) was held at Arusha, Tanzania, in July 1979, to harmonize development plans and to reduce the region's economic dependence on South Africa. In August 1992 the 10 member countries of the SADCC signed the Treaty establishing the Southern African Development Community (SADC), which replaced SADCC upon its entry into force in October 1993. The Treaty places binding obligations on member countries, with the aim of promoting economic integration towards a fully developed common market. The Community Tribunal, envisaged in the Treaty, was inaugurated in 2005. The Protocol on Politics, Defence and Security Co-operation, regulating the structure, operations and functions of the Organ on Politics, Defence and Security, established in June 1996 (see under Regional Security), entered into force in March 2004. A troika system, comprising the current, incoming and outgoing SADC chairpersonship, operates at the level of the summit, Council of Ministers and Standing Committee of Officials, and co-ordinates the Organ on Politics, Defence and Security. Other member states may be co-opted into the troika as required. A system of SADC national committees, comprising representatives of government, civil society and the private sector, oversees the implementation of regional programmes at country level and helps to formulate new regional strategies. In recent years SADC institutions have undergone a process of intensive restructuring.

MEMBERS

Angola	Malawi	South Africa
Botswana	Mauritius	Swaziland
Congo, Democratic Republic	Mozambique	Tanzania
Lesotho	Namibia	Zambia
Madagascar*	Seychelles	Zimbabwe

* In March 2009 Madagascar was suspended from meetings of SADC, pending its return to constitutional normalcy, following the forced resignation of the elected President and transfer of power to the military.

Organization

(June 2012)

SUMMIT MEETING

The meeting is held at least once a year and is attended by heads of state and government or their representatives. It is the supreme policy-making organ of SADC and is responsible for the appointment of the Executive Secretary. A report on the restructuring of SADC, adopted by an extraordinary summit held in Windhoek, Namibia, in March 2001, recommended that biannual summit meetings should be convened. The 2011 regular SADC summit meeting was convened in Luanda, Angola, in August. An extraordinary summit meeting was held in June 2012, in Luanda, Angola.

COUNCIL OF MINISTERS

Representatives of SADC member countries at ministerial level meet at least once a year.

INTEGRATED COMMITTEE OF MINISTERS

The Integrated Committee of Ministers (ICM), which is responsible to the Council of Ministers, meets at least once a year and comprises at least two ministers from each member state. The ICM facilitates the co-ordination and harmonization of cross-sectoral areas of regional integration; oversees the activities of the Community Directorates; and provides policy guidance to the Secretariat. The ICM formulated and supervises the implementation of the Regional Indicative Strategic Development Plan (RISDP—see below).

STANDING COMMITTEE OF OFFICIALS

The Committee, comprising senior officials, usually from the ministry responsible for economic planning or finance, acts as the technical advisory body to the Council. It meets at least once a year. Members of the Committee also act as a national contact point for matters relating to SADC.

SECRETARIAT

Executive Secretary: TOMÁS AUGUSTO SALOMÃO (Mozambique).

The Secretariat comprises permanently staffed Directorates covering the following priority areas of regional integration: Trade, Industry, Finance and Investment; Infrastructure and Services; Food, Agriculture and Natural Resources; Social and Human Development and Special Programmes; and Policy, Planning and Resource Mobilization.

SADC TRIBUNAL

The establishment of the SADC Tribunal was provided for under the Treaty establishing the SADC and facilitated by a protocol adopted in 2000. The Windhoek, Namibia-based 10-member Tribunal was inaugurated in November 2005 and is mandated to arbitrate in the case of disputes between member states arising from the Treaty.

Activities

In July 1979 the first Southern African Development Co-ordination Conference (SADCC) was attended by delegations from Angola, Botswana, Mozambique, Tanzania and Zambia, with participation by representatives from donor governments and international agencies. In April 1980 a regional economic summit conference was held in Lusaka, Zambia, and the Lusaka Declaration, a statement of strategy entitled 'Southern Africa: Towards Economic Liberation', was approved, with the aim of reducing regional economic dependence on South Africa, then in its apartheid period. The 1986 SADCC summit meeting recommended the adoption of economic sanctions against South Africa but failed to establish a timetable for doing so.

In January 1992 a meeting of the SADCC Council of Ministers approved proposals to transform the organization (by then expanded to include Lesotho, Malawi, Namibia and Swaziland) into a fully integrated economic community, and in August the Treaty establishing SADC was signed. Post-apartheid South Africa became a member of SADC in August 1994, thus strengthening the objective of regional co-operation and economic integration. Mauritius became a member in August 1995. In September 1997 SADC heads of state agreed to admit the Democratic Republic of the Congo (DRC) and Seychelles as members of the Community; Seychelles withdrew, however, in July 2004. In August 2005 Madagascar was admitted as a member.

A task force to co-ordinate a programme of co-operation between SADC and the Common Market for Eastern and Southern Africa (COMESA) was established in 2001, and in 2005 the East African Community (EAC) became incorporated into the process, which was led thereafter by the COMESA-EAC-SADC Task Force. In October 2008 the first tripartite COMESA-EAC-SADC summit was convened, in Kampala, Uganda, to discuss the harmonization of policy and programme work by the three regional economic communities (RECs). The Kampala summit approved a roadmap towards the formation of a single free trade area and the eventual establishment of a single African Economic Community (a long-term objective of African Union (AU) co-operation). At the second tripartite summit, held in June 2011, in Johannesburg, South Africa, negotiations were initiated on the establishment of the proposed COMESA-EAC-SADC Tripartite Free Trade Area. In January 2012 AU leaders endorsed a new Framework, Roadmap and Architecture for Fast Tracking the Establishment of a Continental FTA (referred to as CFTA), and an Action Plan for Boosting Intra-African Trade, which planned for the consolidation of the COMESA-EAC-SADC Tripartite FTA with other regional FTAs into the CFTA initiative during 2015–16; and the establishment of an operational CFTA by 2017. In July 2010 the SADC, COMESA and the EAC adopted a tripartite five-year Programme on Climate Change Adaptation and Mitigation in the COMESA-EAC-SADC region.

In September 1994 the first conference of ministers of foreign affairs of SADC and the European Union (EU) was held in Berlin, Germany, instigating the so-called Berlin Initiative on SADC-EU Dialogue. The participants agreed to establish working groups to promote closer trade, political, regional and economic co-operation. In particular, a declaration issued from the meeting specified joint objectives, including a reduction of exports of weapons to southern Africa and of the arms trade within the region, promotion of investment in the region's manufacturing sector and support for democracy at all levels. A second SADC-EU ministerial conference, held in Namibia in October 1996, endorsed a Regional Indicative Programme (RIP) to enhance co-operation between the two organizations over the next five years. The third ministerial conference under the Berlin Initiative took place in Vienna, Austria, in November 1998. In September 1999 SADC signed a co-operation agreement with the US Government, which incorporated measures to promote US investment in the region, and commitments to support HIV/AIDS assessment and prevention programmes and to assist member states to develop environmental protection capabilities. The fourth SADC–EU ministerial conference, convened in Gaborone, in November 2000, adopted a joint declaration on the control of small arms and light weapons in the SADC region. The fifth SADC-EU ministerial conference was held in Maputo, Mozambique, in November 2002. In July SADC and the EU approved a roadmap to guide future co-operation, and in October of that year an EU-SADC ministerial 'double troika' meeting took place in The Hague, Netherlands, to mark 10 years of dialogue between the two organizations under the Berlin Initiative. At the meeting both SADC and the EU reaffirmed their commitment to reinforcing co-operation with regard to peace and security in Africa. In November 2006, at an EU-SADC double troika meeting held in Maseru, Lesotho, SADC representatives agreed to the development of institutional support to the member states through the establishment of a Human Rights Commission and a new SADC Electoral Advisory Council (SEAC). SEAC became operational in April 2011. The 14th SADC-EU double troika ministerial conference under the Berlin initiative, convened in Brussels, Belgium, in November 2008, discussed, *inter alia*, the ongoing global financial crisis and means of addressing volatility in commodity prices and food insecurity in southern Africa. The ongoing EU-SADC Investment Promotion Programme (ESIPP) aims to mobilize foreign capital and technical investment in southern Africa. SADC has co-operated with other sub-regional organizations to finalize a common position on co-operation between African ACP countries and the EU under the Cotonou Agreement (concluded in June 2000, see chapter on the EU).

In July 1996 the SADC Parliamentary Forum was inaugurated, with the aim of promoting democracy, human rights and good governance throughout the region. In September 1997 SADC heads of state endorsed the establishment of the Forum as an autonomous institution. A regional women's parliamentary caucus was inaugurated in April 2002.

The August 2004 summit meeting of heads of state and government, held in Grand Baie, Mauritius, adopted a new Protocol on Principles and Guidelines Governing Democratic Elections, which advocated: full participation by citizens in the political process; freedom of association; political tolerance; elections at regular intervals; equal access to the state media for all political parties; equal opportunity to exercise the right to vote and be voted for; independence of the judiciary; impartiality of the electoral institutions; the right to voter education; the respect of election results proclaimed to be free and fair by a competent national electoral authority; and the right to challenge election results as provided for in the law. Regional elections are monitored by SADC Election Observation Missions (SEOMs); in May 2012 a SEOM was dispatched to oversee legislative elections in Lesotho.

At the summit meeting of heads of state and government held in Maseru, Lesotho, in August 2006, a new Protocol on Finance and Investment was adopted. Amendments to SADC protocols on the Tribunal, trade, immunities and privileges, transport, communications and meteorology, energy and mining, combating illicit drugs and education and training were also approved at the meeting. The summit emphasized the need to scale up implementation of SADC's agenda for integration, identifying the RISDP (see below) and the Strategic Indicative Plan for the Organ (SIPO) as the principal instruments for achieving this objective. In pursuit of this aim, the summit established a task force—comprising ministers responsible for finance, investment, economic development, trade and industry—charged with defining the measures necessary for the eradication of poverty and how their implementation might be accelerated.

In accordance with a decision of an extraordinary summit meeting convened in March 2001, SADC's institutions were extensively restructured during 2001–03, with a view to facilitating the more efficient and effective application of the objectives of the organization's founding Treaty and of the SPA. The March 2001 summit meeting endorsed a Common Agenda for the organization, which covered the promotion of poverty reduction measures and of sustainable and equitable socio-economic development, promotion of democratic political values and systems, and the consolidation of peace and security. Furthermore, the establishment of an integrated committee of ministers was authorized; this was mandated to formulate and oversee a Regional Indicative Strategic Development Plan (RISDP), intended as the key policy framework for managing, over a period of 15 years, the SADC Common Agenda. A draft RISDP was approved by the summit meeting convened in Dar es Salaam, Tanzania, in August 2003. In April 2006 SADC adopted the Windhoek Declaration on a new relationship between the Community and its international co-operating partners. The declaration provides a framework for co-operation and dialogue between SADC and international partners, facilitating the implementation of the SADC Common Agenda. A Consultative Conference on Poverty and Development, organized by SADC and attended by its international co-operating partners, was convened in April 2008, in Port Louis, Mauritius.

A high-level meeting concerned with integrating the objectives of the New Partnership for Africa's Development (NEPAD) into SADC's regional programme activities was convened in August 2004. SADC and NEPAD determined in late 2008 to launch a joint business hub, aimed at consolidating regional private sector investment.

An SADC Vision 2050 was under development in 2012.

REGIONAL SECURITY

In November 1994 SADC ministers of defence, meeting in Arusha, Tanzania, approved the establishment of a regional rapid-deployment peace-keeping force, which could be used to contain regional conflicts or civil unrest in member states. An SADC Mine Action Committee is maintained to monitor and co-ordinate the process of removing anti-personnel land devices from countries in the region. The summit meeting of heads of state and government held in August 2007 authorized the establishment of the SADC Standby Brigade (SADCBRIG), with the aim of ensuring collective regional security and stability. SADCBRIG is a pillar of the African Union's African Standby Force (ASF). SADC's Regional Peacekeeping Training Centre (SADC-RPTC) was established in June 1999 and since August 2005 has been directed by the SADC Secretariat.

In June 1996 SADC heads of state and government, meeting in Gaborone, Botswana, inaugurated an Organ on Politics, Defence and Security (OPDS), with the aim of enhancing co-ordination of national policies and activities in these areas. The stated objectives of the body were, *inter alia*, to safeguard the people and development of the region against instability arising from civil disorder, inter-state conflict and external aggression; to undertake conflict prevention, management and resolution activities, by mediating in inter-state and intra-state disputes and conflicts, pre-empting conflicts through an early warning system and using diplomacy and peace-keeping to achieve sustainable peace; to promote the development of a common foreign policy, in areas of mutual interest, and the evolution of common political institutions; to develop close co-operation between the police and security services of the region; and to encourage the observance of universal human rights, as provided for in the charters of the UN and the Organization of African Unity (OAU—now AU). The extraordinary summit held in March 2001 determined to develop the OPDS as a substructure of SADC, with subdivisions for defence and international diplomacy, to be chaired by a member country's head of state, working within a troika system. A Protocol on Politics, Defence and Security Co-operation—to be implemented by an Inter-state Politics and Diplomacy Committee—regulating the structure, operations and functions of the Organ, was adopted and opened for signature in August 2001 and entered into force in March 2004.

The March 2001 extraordinary SADC summit adopted a Declaration on Small Arms, promoting the curtailment of the proliferation of and illicit trafficking in light weapons in the region. A Protocol on the Control of Firearms, Ammunition and Other Related Materials was adopted in August of that year. In July SADC ministers of defence approved a draft regional defence pact, providing for a mechanism to prevent conflict involving member countries and for member countries to unite against outside aggression. In January 2002 an extraordinary summit of SADC heads of state, held in Blantyre, Malawi, adopted a Declaration against Terrorism.

An extraordinary SADC summit meeting convened in March 2007, in Dar es Salaam, Tanzania, mandated the OPDS to assess the political and security situations in the DRC and Lesotho (see below). The ministerial committee of the OPDS troika stressed to the summit the need for SADC support to the ongoing post-conflict reconstruction process in the DRC. An extraordinary meeting of the ministerial committee of the OPDS troika convened in October of that year resolved to mobilize humanitarian assistance for eastern areas of the DRC in view of an escalation in the violent unrest there, with a particular focus on assisting internally displaced civilians. In November 2008 SADC convoked an extraordinary summit of heads of state or government in response to mounting insecurity in eastern areas of the DRC. The summit determined to assist the government of the DRC, if necessary by sending a regional peace-keeping force to the province of North Kivu. In February 2009 it was reported that SADCBRIG was ready to intervene if required in the DRC situation. A large team of SADC observers, comprising more than 200 representatives of Community member states, was sent to monitor the presidential and legislative elections that were held in the DRC in November 2011.

In August 2001 SADC established a task force, comprising representatives of five member countries, to address the ongoing political crisis in Zimbabwe. The Community sent two separate observer teams to monitor the controversial presidential election held in Zimbabwe in March 2002; the SADC Council of Ministers team found the election to have been conducted freely and fairly, while the Parliamentary Forum group was reluctant to endorse the poll. Having evaluated both reports, the Community approved the election. An SADC Council of Ministers group was convened to observe the parliamentary elections held in Zimbabwe in March 2005; however, the Zimbabwean Government refused to invite a delegation from the SADC Parliamentary Forum. The Zimbabwean Government claimed to have enacted electoral legislation in accordance with the provisions of the August 2004 SADC Protocol on Principles and Guidelines Governing Democratic Elections (see above). The extraordinary summit meeting of SADC heads of state and government, convened in Dar es Salaam, Tanzania, in March 2007, to address the political, economic, and security situation in the region, declared 'solidarity with the government and people of Zimbabwe' and mandated then President Thabo Mbeki of South Africa to facilitate dialogue between the Zimbabwean government and opposition. Mbeki reported to the ordinary SADC summit held in August of that year that restoring Zimbabwe's capacity to generate foreign exchange through balance of payments support would be of pivotal importance in promoting economic recovery and that SADC should assist Zimbabwe with addressing the issue of international sanctions.

In early March 2008 an SADC election observer team was sent to monitor preparations for and the conduct of presidential and national and local legislative elections that were staged in Zimbabwe at the end of that month. In mid-April, at which time the Zimbabwe Electoral Commission had failed to declare the results of the presidental election, prompting widespread international criticism, SADC convened an extraordinary summit to address the electoral outcome. The OPDS presented to the summit a report by the observer team on the presidential and legislative elections which claimed that the electoral process had been acceptable to all parties. The summit urged the Zimbabwe Electoral Commission to verify and release the results of the elections without further delay and requested President Mbeki of South Africa to continue in his role as Facilitator of the Zimbabwe Political Dialogue. In June an emergency meeting of the OPDS troika, at the level of heads of state, was convened following an announcement by the main opposition candidate, Morgan Tsvangirai, that he was withdrawing from a forthcoming second round of voting in the presidential election owing to an escalation of violence against opposition supporters in that country. In July Mugabe and the leaders of the two main opposition parties signed a Memorandum of Understanding, brokered by President Mbeki, confirming their commitment to pursuing dialogue and forming an inclusive government. An agreement (the Global Political Agreement—GPA) to share executive responsibilities in a government of national unity was concluded and signed in September. In December 2008 SADC launched a new Zimbabwe Humanitarian and Development Assistance Framework (ZHDAF), and in January 2009 it established an All Stakeholders Working Committee to implement the ZHDAF. The extraordinary SADC summit convened in March commended political progress recently achieved in Zimbabwe, and established a committee to co-ordinate SADC support, and to mobilize international support for, Zimbabwe's recovery process. The SADC summit held in September urged the termination of all forms of international sanctions against Zimbabwe. It was reported in that month that Zimbabwe had withdrawn from participation in the SADC Tribunal. Responsibility for managing the ZHDAF was transferred to the Zimbabwe Government in December 2009. The June 2012 emergency SADC summit meeting urged President Zuma of South Africa, the current SADC Facilitator of the Zimbabwe Political Dialogue, and the parties to the GPA, to develop an implementation mechanism and establish a schedule for the implementation of a 'Road Map to Zimbabwe Elections' which had been agreed by Zimbabwean stakeholders in April 2011.

The March 2009 extraordinary summit strongly condemned the unconstitutional actions that led to the forced resignation during that month of the elected President of Madagascar, Mark Ravalomanana, and ensuing transfer of power to the military in that country; the summit suspended Madagascar from participation in the activities of the Community and urged the immediate restoration of constitutional order. In June SADC appointed the former President of Mozambique, Joachim Chissano, as the Community's mediator in the Madagascar consitutional crisis. Negotiations subsequently facilitated by Chissano, under SADC auspices, in Maputo, Mozambique, led, in August, to the conclusion of an agreement on the establishment of a power-sharing administration in Madagascar; the power-sharing accord was not, however, subsequently implemented. In March 2011 SADC mediators proposed a new 'Roadmap Out of the Crisis' for Madagascar, again envisaging a power-sharing interim government; this was approved by SADC heads of state and government at a summit convened in June 2011, and was signed by 10 of 11 Malagasy stakeholders in September. An SADC Liaison Office in Madagascar was established in November to support the implementation of the Roadmap, and was reported to be fully operational by mid-2012. The extraordinary SADC summit convened in June 2012 mandated the Community's mediator and the OPDS troika to facilitate dialogue between the main Malagasy stakeholders as a matter of urgency in order to ensure the full implementation of the Roadmap.

TRADE, INDUSTRY AND INVESTMENT

Under the Treaty establishing SADC, efforts were to be undertaken to achieve regional economic integration. The Directorate of Trade, Industry, Finance and Investment aims to facilitate such integration, and poverty eradication, through the creation of an enabling investment and trade environment in SADC countries. Objectives include the establishment of a single regional market; the progressive removal of barriers to the movement of goods, services and people; and the promotion of cross-border investment. SADC supports programmes for industrial research and development and standardization and quality assurance, and aims to mobilize industrial investment resources and to co-ordinate economic policies and the development of the financial sector. In August 1996, at a summit meeting held in Lesotho, SADC member states signed the Protocol on Trade, providing for the establishment of a regional free trade area (FTA), through the gradual elimination of tariff barriers. (Angola and the DRC are not yet signatories to the Protocol.) In October 1999 representatives of the private sector in SADC member states established the Association of SADC Chambers of Commerce, based in Mauritius. The Protocol on Trade entered into force in January 2000, and an Amendment Protocol on Trade came into force in August, incorporating renegotiated technical details on the gradual elimination of tariffs, rules of origin, customs co-operation, special industry arrangements and dispute settlement procedures. The implementation phase of the Protocol on Trade commenced in September. In accordance with a revised schedule, some 85% of intra-SADC trade tariffs were withdrawn by 1 January 2008. (The remaining intra-SADC trade tariffs were to be removed by 2012.) The SADC Free Trade Area was formally inaugurated, under the theme 'SADC FTA for Growth, Development and Wealth Creation', at the meeting of heads of state and government, held in Sandton, South Africa, in August 2008; Angola, the DRC, Malawi and Seychelles, however, had not implemented all requirements of the Protocol on Trade and were not yet participating in the FTA. According to the schedule, reaffirmed at the EU–SADC ministerial meeting in 2006, an SADC customs union was to be implemented by 2010 (however, this deadline was not achieved), a common market by 2015, monetary union by 2016, and a single currency was to be introduced by 2018. Annual meetings are convened to review the work of expert teams in the areas of standards, quality, assurance, accreditation and metrology. At an SADC Extraordinary Summit convened in October 2006 it was determined that a draft roadmap was to be developed to facilitate the process of establishing a customs union. In November 2007 the Ministerial Task Force on Regional Economic Integration approved the establishment of technical working groups to facilitate the development of policy frameworks in legal and institutional arrangements; revenue collection, sharing and distribution; policy harmonization; and a common external tariff. A strategic forum of the Ministerial Task Force, to review the regional economic integration agenda, was convened in February 2010, in Johannesburg, South Africa, immediately prior the Task Force's ninth meeting.

The mining sector contributes about 10% of the SADC region's annual GDP. The principal objective of SADC's programme of action on mining is to stimulate increased local and foreign investment in the sector, through the assimilation and dissemination of data, prospecting activities, and participation in promotional fora. In December 1994 SADC held a mining forum, jointly with the EU, in Lusaka, Zambia, with the aim of demonstrating to potential investors and promoters the possibilities of mining exploration in the region. A second mining investment forum was held in Lusaka in December 1998; and a third ('Mines 2000'), also in Lusaka, in October 2000. In April 2006 SADC and the EU launched a new initiative, in the framework of the EU-SADC Investment Promotion Programme, to facilitate European investment in some 100 mining projects in southern Africa. Other objectives of the mining sector are the improvement of industry training, increasing the contribution of small-scale mining, reducing the illicit trade in gemstones and gold, increasing co-operation in mineral exploration and processing, and minimizing the adverse impact of mining operations on the environment. In February 2000 a Protocol on Mining entered into force, providing for the harmonization of policies and programmes relating to the development and exploitation of mineral resources in the region. SADC supports the Kimberley Process Certification Scheme aimed at preventing illicit trade in illegally mined rough diamonds. (The illicit trade in so-called 'conflict diamonds' and other minerals is believed to have motivated and financed many incidences of rebel activity in the continent, for example in Angola and the DRC.)

In July 1998 a Banking Association was officially constituted by representatives of SADC member states. The Association was to establish international banking standards and regional payments systems, organize training and harmonize banking legislation in the region. In April 1999 governors of SADC central banks determined to strengthen and harmonize banking procedures and technology in order to facilitate the financial integration of the region. Efforts to harmonize stock exchanges in the region were also initiated in 1999.

The summit meeting of heads of state and government held in Maseru, Lesotho, in August 2006 adopted a new Protocol on Finance and Investment. The document, regarded as constituting the main framework for economic integration in southern Africa, outlined, *inter alia*, how the region intended to proceed towards monetary union, and was intended to complement the ongoing implementation of the SADC Protocol on Trade and targets contained in the RISDP.

INFRASTRUCTURE AND SERVICES

The Directorate of Infrastructure and Services focuses on transport, communications and meteorology, energy, tourism and water. At SADC's inception transport was regarded as the most important area to be developed, on the grounds that, as the Lusaka Declaration noted, without the establishment of an adequate regional transport and communications system, other areas of co-operation become impractical. The SADC Protocol on Transport, Communications and Meteorology, adopted in August 1996, provides, *inter alia*, for an integrated regional transport policy, an SADC Regional Trunk Road Network (RTRN), and harmonized regional policies relating to maritime and inland waterway transport; civil aviation; regional telecommunications; postal services; and meterology. An Integrated Transport Committee, and other sub-committees representing the sectors covered by the Protocol, have been established. In January 1997 the Southern African Telecommunications Regional Authority (SATRA), a regulatory authority, was established. In March 2001 the Association of Southern African National Road Agencies (ASANRA) was created to foster the development of an integrated regional road transportation system.

SADC development projects have aimed to address missing links and over-stretched sections of the regional network, as well as to improve efficiency, operational co-ordination and human resource development, such as management training projects. Other objectives have been to ensure the compatibility of technical systems within the region and to promote the harmonization of regulations relating to intra-regional traffic and trade. SADC's road network, whose length totals more than 1m. km, constitutes the regions's principal mode of transport for both freight and passengers and is thus vital to the economy. Unsurfaced, low-volume roads account for a substantial proportion of the network and many of these are being upgraded to a sealed standard as part of a wider strategy that focuses on the alleviation of poverty and the pursuit of economic growth and development. In July 1999 a 317-km rail link between Bulawayo, Zimbabwe, and the border town of Beitbridge, administered by SADC as its first build-operate-transfer project, was opened.

SADC policy guidelines on 'making information and communications technology a priority in turning SADC into an information-based economy' were adopted in November 2001. Policy guidelines and model regulations on tariffs for telecommunications services have also been adopted. An SADC Regional Information Infrastructure (SRII) was adopted in December 1999, with the aim of linking member states by means of high capacity digital land and submarine routes. In May 2010 SADC ministers responsible for telecommunications, postal services and ICT adopted a regional e-SADC Strategy Framework, which aimed to utilize ICT for regional socio-economic development and integration. Proposed priorities for the period 2011–12 under the e-SADC initiative included creating national and regional internet exchange points; harmonizing cyber security regulatory frameworks in member countries; and implementing a regional project aimed at improving interconnection of the electronic, physical and financial postal networks. In September 2011 SADC endorsed the inaugural Southern Africa Internet Governance Forum (SAIGF), hosted by the South African Government, in Pretoria, and jointly convened by NEPAD and other agencies.

The SADC Drought Monitoring Centre organizes an annual Southern African Regional Climate Outlook Forum (SARCOF), which assesses seasonal weather prospects. SARCOF-15 was convened in Windhoek, Namibia, in August 2011.

Areas of activity in the energy sector include: joint petroleum exploration, training programmes for the petroleum sector and studies for strategic fuel storage facilities; promotion of the use of coal; development of hydroelectric power and the co-ordination of SADC generation and transmission capacities; new and renewable sources of energy, including pilot projects in solar energy; assessment of the environmental and socio-economic impact of wood-fuel scarcity and relevant education programmes; and energy conservation. In July 1995 SADC energy ministers approved the establishment of the Southern African Power Pool (SAPP), whereby all member states were to be linked into a single electricity grid. Utilities participating in SAPP aim to provide to consumers in the region an economical and reliable electricity supply. SADC and COMESA have the joint objective of eventually linking SAPP and COMESA's Eastern Africa Power Pool. In July 1995 ministers also endorsed a protocol to promote greater co-operation in energy development within SADC, providing for the establishment of an Energy Commission, responsible for 'demand-side' management, pricing, ensuring private sector involvement and competition, training and research, collecting information, etc.; the protocol entered into force in September 1998. In September 1997 heads of state endorsed an Energy Action Plan to proceed with the implementation of co-operative policies and strategies in four key areas of energy: trade; information exchange; training and organizational capacity building; and investment and financing. There are two major energy supply projects in the region: utilities from Angola, Botswana, the DRC, Namibia and South Africa participate in the Western Power Corridor project, approved in October 2002, while a Zambia–Tanzania Inter-connector project was under development in 2012. In July 2007 it was announced that a Regional Petroleum and Gas Association (REPGA) would be established, with the aim of promoting a common investment destination with harmonized environmental standards.

The tourism sector operates within the context of national and regional socio-economic development objectives. It comprises four components: tourism product development; tourism marketing and research; tourism services; and human resources development and training. SADC has promoted tourism for the region through trade fairs and investment fora. In September 1997 the legal charter for the establishment of the Regional Tourism Organization for Southern Africa (RETOSA), administered jointly by SADC regional national tourism authorities and private sector operators, was signed by ministers of tourism. RETOSA assists member states to formulate tourism promotion policies and strategies. The development is under way of a region-wide common visa (UNI-VISA) system, aimed at facilitating tourism.

In June 2005 the SADC Council of Ministers endorsed the Transfrontier Conservation Area (TFCA) 2010 Development Strategy, aimed at establishing and promoting TFCAs, conservation parks straddling international borders, as premier regional tourist and investment destinations. Phase 1 of the Strategy, up to 2010, focused on the following TFCAs: Ais/Richtersveld (in Namibia and South Africa), Kgalagadi (Botswana, Namibia and South Africa), Limpopo-Shashe (Botswana, South Africa, Zimbabwe), the Great Limpopo Transfrontier Park (GLTP) (Mozambique, South Africa, Zimbabwe), Lubombo (Mozambique, South Africa, Swaziland), Maloti-Drakensburg (Lesotho, South Africa), and Kavango-Zambezi (envisaged as the largest conservation area in the world, straddling the borders of Angola, Botswana, Namibia, Zambia and Zimbabwe); while Phase 2 ('Beyond 2010') focused on Iona-Skeleton Coast (Angola, Namibia), Liuwa Plain-Kamela (Zambia, Angola), Lower Zambezi-Mana Pools (Zambia, Zimbabwe), Malawi-Zambia, Niassa-Selous (a woodland ecosystem) (Mozambique and Tanzania), Mnazi Bay-Quirimbas (Mozambique and Tanzania), and Chimanimani (Zimbabwe, Mozambique).

SADC aims to promote equitable distribution and effective management of the region's water resources, around 70% of which are shared across international borders. A Protocol on Shared Watercourse Systems entered into force in April 1998, and a Revised Protocol on Shared Watercourses came into force in September 2003. An SADC Regional Water Policy was adopted in August 2005 as a framework for providing the sustainable and integrated development, protection and utilization of national and transboundary water resources.

A first Regional Strategic Action Plan (RASP I) on Integrated Water Resources Development and Management was implemented during 1999–2004; RASP II was undertaken in 2005–10; and RASP III was ongoing during 2011–15, covering three strategic areas: water governance; infrastructure development; and water management.

FOOD, AGRICULTURE AND NATURAL RESOURCES

The Directorate of Food, Agriculture and Natural Resources aims to develop, co-ordinate and harmonize policies and programmes on agriculture and natural resources with a focus on sustainability. The Directorate covers the following sectors: agricultural research and training; inland fisheries; forestry; wildlife; marine fisheries and resources; food security; livestock production and animal disease control; and environment and land management. According to SADC figures, agriculture contributes one-third of the region's gross national product (GNP), accounts for about one-quarter of total earnings of foreign exchange and employs some 80% of the labour force. The principal objectives in this field are regional food security, agricultural development and natural resource development.

The Southern African Centre for Co-operation in Agricultural Research (SACCAR), was established in Gaborone, in 1985. It aims to strengthen national agricultural research systems, in order to improve management, increase productivity, promote the development and transfer of technology to assist local farmers, and improve training. Examples of activity include: a sorghum and millet improvement programme; a land and water management research programme; a root crop research network; agroforestry research, implemented in Malawi, Tanzania, Zambia and Zimbabwe; and a grain legume improvement programme, comprising separate research units for groundnuts, beans and cowpeas. SADC's Plant Genetic Resources Centre, based near Lusaka, Zambia, aims to collect, conserve and utilize indigenous and exotic plant genetic resources and to develop appropriate management practices. In November 2009 scientists from SADC member states urged the Community to strengthen and support regional capacity to screen for and detect genetically modified organisms (GMOs), with a view to preventing the uncontrolled influx into the region of GMO products; the results of a survey conducted across the region, released in February 2011, concluded that most Southern African countries lacked sufficient technological capacity to screen for and detect GMOs.

SADC aims to promote inland and marine fisheries as an important, sustainable source of animal protein. Marine fisheries are also considered to be a potential source of income of foreign exchange. In May 1993 the first formal meeting of SADC ministers of marine fisheries convened in Namibia, and it was agreed to hold annual meetings. Meeting in May 2002 ministers of marine fisheries expressed concern about alleged ongoing illegal, unregulated and unreported (IUU) fisheries activities in regional waters. The development of fresh water fisheries is focused on aquaculture projects, and their integration into rural community activities. The SADC Fisheries Protocol entered into force in September 2003. Environment and land management activities have an emphasis on sustainability as an essential quality of development. SADC aims to protect and improve the health, environment and livelihoods of people living in the southern African region; to preserve the natural heritage and biodiversity of the region; and to support regional economic development on a sustainable basis. There is also a focus on capacity building, training, regional co-operation and the exchange of information in all areas related to the environment and land management. SADC operates an Environmental Exchange Network and implements a Land Degradation and Desertification Control Programme. Projects on the conservation and sustainable development of forestry and wildlife are under implementation. An SADC Protocol on Forestry was signed in October 2002, and in November 2003 the Protocol on Wildlife Conservation and Law Enforcement entered into force.

Under the food security programme, the Regional Early Warning System (REWS) aims to anticipate and prevent food shortages through the provision of information relating to the food security situation in member states. As a result of frequent drought crises, SADC member states have agreed to inform the food security sector of their food and non-food requirements on a regular basis, in order to assess the needs of the region as a whole. A programme on irrigation development and water management aims to reduce regional dependency on rain-fed agricultural production, while a programme on the promotion of agricultural trade and food safety aims to increase intra-regional and inter-regional trade with a view to improving agriculture growth and rural incomes. An SADC extraordinary summit on agriculture and food security, held in May 2004 in Dar es Salaam, Tanzania, considered strategies for accelerating development in the agricultural sector and thereby securing food security and reducing poverty in the region. In July 2008 the inaugural meeting was convened of a Task Force of ministers of trade, finance and agriculture, which was established by SADC heads of government earlier in that year in response to rising food prices and production costs. The Task Force agreed upon several measures to improve the food security situation of the SADC region, including increased investment in agriculture and the establishment of a Regional Food Reserve Facility. It also directed the SADC secretariat to develop a regional policy on the production of biofuels. The first Food, Agriculture and Natural Resources cluster ministerial meeting was held in November 2008, in Gaborone, to assess the regional food security situation in view of the ongoing global food security crisis.

The Livestock Sector Unit of the Directorate of Food, Agriculture and Natural Resource co-ordinates activities related to regional livestock development, and implements the Promotion of Regional INTegration (PRINT) livestock sector capacity-strengthening programme; the SADC foot-and-mouth disease (FMD) Programme; and the SADC Transboundary Animal Diseases (TADs) project, which aims to strengthen capacity (with a special focus on Angola, Malawi, Mozambique, Tanzania, and Zambia) to control TADs such as FMD, rinderpest, contagious bovine pleuropneumonia, African swine fever, Newcastle disease, avian influenza, Rift Valley Fever, and lumpy skin disease.

In early June 2012 SADC member states, meeting in Gaborone, Botswana, adopted common regional priorities and policy in the areas of environment and development in advance of the UN Conference on Sustainable Development (Rio+20), which was convened in Rio de Janeiro, Brazil, later in that month.

SOCIAL AND HUMAN DEVELOPMENT AND SPECIAL PROGRAMMES

SADC helps to supply the region's requirements in skilled manpower by providing training in the following categories: high-level managerial personnel; agricultural managers; high- and medium-level technicians; artisans; and instructors. Human resources development activities focus on determining active labour market information systems and institutions in the region, improving education policy analysis and formulation, and addressing issues of teaching and learning materials in the region. SADC administers an Intra-regional Skills Development Programme, and the Community has initiated a programme of distance education to enable greater access to education, as well as operating a scholarship and training awards programme. In July 2000 a Protocol on Education and Training, which was to provide a legal framework for co-operation in this sector entered into force. In September 1997 SADC heads of state, meeting in Blantyre, Malawi, endorsed the establishment of a Gender Department within the Secretariat to promote the advancement and education of women. A Declaration on Gender and Development was adopted. SADC leaders adopted an SADC Protocol on Gender Equality in August 2008.

An SADC Protocol on Combating Illicit Drugs entered into force in March 1999. In October 2000 an SADC Epidemiological Network on Drug Use was established to enable the systematic collection of narcotics-related data. SADC operates a regional drugs control programme, funded by the EU.

In August 1999 an SADC Protocol on Health was adopted. In December 1999 a multisectoral sub-committee on HIV/AIDS (which are endemic in the region) was established. In August 2000 the Community adopted a set of guidelines to underpin any future negotiations with major pharmaceutical companies on improving access to and reducing the cost of drugs to combat HIV/AIDS. In July 2003 an SADC special summit on HIV/AIDS, convened in Maseru, Lesotho, and attended by representatives of the World Bank, UNAIDS and WHO, issued the Maseru Declaration on HIV/AIDS, identifying priority areas for action, including prevention, access to testing and treatment, and social mobilization. The implementation of the priority areas outlined in the Maseru Declaration is co-ordinated through an SADC Business Plan on HIV/AIDS (currently in a phase covering the period 2010–15), with a focus on harmonizing regional guidelines on mother-to-child transmission and anti-retroviral therapy; and on issues relating to access to affordable essential drugs, including bulk procurement and regional production. The SADC summit held in September 2009 urged member states to intensify their efforts to implement the Maseru Declaration. An SADC Model Law on HIV/AIDS was adopted by the SADC Parliamentary Forum in 2008; the Forum is implementing a Strategic Framework for HIV/AIDS during 2010–15. The SADC aims to achieve, by 2015, an 'HIV-Free Generation' and no new infections. Since 2008 SADC has celebrated an annual Healthy Lifestyles Day, during the last week in February (25 February in 2012). SADC is implementing a Strategic Plan for the Control of TB In the SADC Region, 2007–15, which aims to address challenges posed by the emergence of Multidrug Resistant TB (MDR-TB) and Extensive Drug Resistant TB (XDR-TB) strains. SADC supports the Southern Africa Roll Back Malaria Network (SARN), which was established in November 2007. SADC member states met in October 2011 to address the elimination of malaria from the region by 2015.

SADC seeks to promote employment and harmonize legislation concerning labour and social protection. Activities include: the implementation of International Labour Standards; the improvement of health and safety standards in the workplace; combating child labour; and the establishment of a statistical database for employment and labour issues. In February 2007 a task force was mandated to investigate measures for improving employment conditions in member countries.

Following the ratification of the Treaty establishing the Community, regional socio-cultural development was emphasized as part of the process of greater integration. Public education initiatives have been undertaken to encourage the involvement of people in the process of regional integration and development, as well as to promote democratic and human rights' values. Two SADC Artists AIDS Festivals have been organized, the first in Bulawayo, Zimbabwe, in August 2007; and the second in Lilongwe, Malawi, in December 2009. The first SADC Poetry Festival was convened in November 2009, in Windhoek, Namibia, with the second held in August 2010, in Gaborone. The creation of an SADC Culture Trust Fund is planned.

Finance

SADC's administrative budget for 2012–13 amounted to US $78.4m., to be financed by contributions from member states (45%) and by international co-operating partners (55%). Madagascar, suspended from meetings of the SADC in 2009 pending its return to constitutional normalcy, has subsequently entered into arrears (owing contributions of $1.8m. in 2012).

Publications

SACCAR Newsletter (quarterly).

SADC Annual Report.

SADC Energy Bulletin.

SADC Food Security Update (monthly).

SADC Today (six a year).

Associated Bodies

Regional Tourism Organisation of Southern Africa (RETOSA): POB 7381, Halfway House, 1685 Midrand, South Africa; tel. (11) 3152420; fax (11) 3152422; e-mail retosa@iafrica.com; internet www.retosa.co.za; f. 1997 to assist SADC member states with formulating tourism promotion policies and strategies; the establishment of a regional tourist visa (UNIVISA) system aimed at facilitating the the movement of international visitors through the region; RETOSA is administered by a Board comprising representatives of national tourism authorities in SADC member states and private sector umbrella bodies in the region.

SADC Parliamentary Forum: 578 Love St, off Robert Mugabe Ave, Windhoek, Namibia; tel. (61) 2870000; fax (61) 254642; e-mail info@sadcpf.org; f. 1996 to promote democracy, human rights and good governance throughout the SADC region, ensuring fair representation for women; endorsed in Sept. 1997 by SADC heads of state as an autonomous institution; a training arm of the Forum, the SADC Parliamentary Leadership Centre, was established in 2005; the Forum frequently deploys missions to monitor parliamentary and presidential elections in the region (most recently to observe legislative elections held in Lesotho in May 2012); adopted, in March 2001, Electoral Norms and Standards for the SADC Region; from the 2000s expanded the scope of its electoral activities beyond observation to guiding the pre- and post-election phases; under the Forum's third Strategic Plan, covering 2011–15, a review of election observation activities and of the 2001 Norms and Standards was to be implemented; programmes are also undertaken in the areas of democracy and governance; HIV/AIDS and public health; regional development and integration; gender equality and empowerment; ICTs; and parliamentary capacity development; the Forum is funded by member parliaments, governments and charitable and international organizations; mems: national parliaments of SADC countries, representing more than 3,500 parliamentarians; Sec.-Gen. Dr Esau Chiviya.

SOUTHERN COMMON MARKET—MERCOSUR/ MERCOSUL

(MERCADO COMÚN DEL SUR/MERCADO COMUM DO SUL)

Address: Edif. Mercosur, Luis Piera 1992, 1°, 11200 Montevideo, Uruguay.

Telephone: 2412-9024; **fax:** 2418-0557; **e-mail:** secretaria@mercosur.org.uy; **internet:** www.mercosur.int.

Mercosur (known as Mercosul in Portuguese) was established in March 1991 by the heads of state of Argentina, Brazil, Paraguay and Uruguay with the signature of the Treaty of Asunción. The primary objective of the Treaty is to achieve the economic integration of member states by means of a free flow of goods and services between member states, the establishment of a common external tariff, the adoption of common commercial policy, and the co-ordination of macroeconomic and sectoral policies. The Ouro Preto Protocol, which was signed in December 1994, conferred on Mercosur the status of an international legal entity with the authority to sign agreements with third countries, groups of countries and international organizations.

MEMBERS

Argentina Brazil Paraguay Uruguay

Note: Venezuela was admitted as a full member of Mercosur in July 2006, pending ratification by each country's legislature. At June 2012 ratification by the Paraguayan Congress remained outstanding; at the end of that month, however, a summit meeting determined to incorporate Venezuela as a full member with effect from 31 July, and to suspend Paraguay's membership owing to the recent removal from power of its president. Bolivia, Chile, Colombia, Ecuador and Peru are associate members.

Organization

(June 2012)

COMMON MARKET COUNCIL

The Common Market Council (Consejo del Mercado Común) is the highest organ of Mercosur and is responsible for leading the integration process and for taking decisions in order to achieve the objectives of the Treaty of Asunción. In December 2010 the Council decided to establish the position of High Representative, with a three-year term-in-office, in order to support the integration process, to promote trade and investment and to represent the grouping internationally. The first High Representative, Samuel Pinheiro Guimaraes, took office on 1 February 2011; he resigned from the position in late June 2012 owing to lack of political consensus within the grouping.

High Representative: (vacant).

COMMON MARKET GROUP

The Common Market Group (Grupo Mercado Común) is the executive body of Mercosur and is responsible for implementing concrete measures to further the integration process.

TRADE COMMISSION

The Trade Commission (Comisión de Comercio del Mercosur) has competence for the area of joint commercial policy and, in particular, is responsible for monitoring the operation of the common external tariff (see below). The Brasília Protocol may be referred to for the resolution of trade disputes between member states.

CONSULTATIVE ECONOMIC AND SOCIAL FORUM

The Consultative Economic and Social Forum (Foro Consultivo Económico-Social) comprises representatives from the business community and trade unions in the member countries and has a consultative role in relation to Mercosur.

PARLIAMENT

Parlamento del Mercosur: Pablo de María 827, 11200 Montevideo, Uruguay; tel. 2410-9797; e-mail secadministrativa@parlamentodelmercosur.org; internet www.parlamentodelmercosur.org; f. 2005, as successor to the Joint Parliamentary Commission (Comisión Parlamentaria Conjunta); aims to facilitate implementation of Mercosur decisions and regional co-operation.

ADMINISTRATIVE SECRETARIAT

Director: Dr Agustín Colombo Sierra (Argentina).

Activities

Mercosur's free trade zone entered into effect on 1 January 1995, with tariffs removed from 85% of intra-regional trade. A regime of gradual removal of duties on a list of special products was agreed, with Argentina and Brazil given four years to complete this process while Paraguay and Uruguay were allowed five years. Regimes governing intra-zonal trade in the automobile and sugar sectors remained to be negotiated. Mercosur's customs union also came into force at the start of 1995, comprising a common external tariff (CET) of 0%–20%. A list of exceptions from the CET was also agreed; these products were to lose their special status and were to be subject to the general tariff system concerning foreign goods by 2006.

In December 1995 Mercosur presidents affirmed the consolidation of free trade as Mercosur's 'permanent and most urgent goal'. To this end they agreed to prepare norms of application for Mercosur's customs code, accelerate paper procedures and increase the connections between national computerized systems. It was also agreed to increase co-operation in the areas of agriculture, industry, mining, energy, communications, transport and tourism, and finance. At this meeting Argentina and Brazil reached an accord aimed at overcoming their dispute regarding the trade in automobiles between the two countries. They agreed that cars should have a minimum of 60% domestic components and that Argentina should be allowed to complete its balance of exports of cars to Brazil, which had earlier imposed a unilateral quota on the import of Argentine cars. In June 1995 Mercosur ministers responsible for the environment agreed to harmonize environmental legislation and to form a permanent sub-group of Mercosur.

In May 1996 Mercosur parliamentarians met with the aim of harmonizing legislation on patents in member countries. In December Mercosur heads of state, meeting in Fortaleza, Brazil, approved agreements on harmonizing competition practices (by 2001), integrating educational opportunities for postgraduates and human resources training, standardizing trading safeguards applied against third country products (by 2001) and providing for intra-regional cultural exchanges. An Accord on Sub-regional Air Services was signed at the meeting (including by the heads of state of Bolivia and Chile) to liberalize civil transport throughout the region. In addition, the heads of state endorsed texts on consumer rights that were to be incorporated into a Mercosur Consumers' Defence Code.

In June 1996 Mercosur heads of state, meeting in San Luis de Mendoza, Argentina, endorsed a 'Democratic Guarantee Clause', whereby a country would be prevented from participation in Mercosur unless democratic, accountable institutions were in place. At the summit meeting, the presidents approved the entry into Mercosur of Bolivia and Chile as associate members. An Economic Complementation Accord with Bolivia, which includes Bolivia in Mercosur's free trade zone, but not in the customs union, was signed in December 1995 and was to come into force on 1 January 1997, later extended until 30 April 1997. Measures of the free trade agreement, which was signed in October 1996, were to be implemented over a transitional period commencing on 28 February 1997 (revised from 1 January). Chile's Economic Complementation Accord with Mercosur entered into effect on 1 October 1996, with duties on most products to be removed over a 10-year period (Chile's most sensitive products were given 18 years for complete tariff elimination). Chile was also to remain outside the customs union, but was to be involved in other integration projects, in particular infrastructure projects designed to give Mercosur countries access to both the Atlantic and Pacific Oceans (Chile's Pacific coast was regarded as Mercosur's potential link to the economies of the Far East).

In June 1997 the first meeting of tax administrators and customs officials of Mercosur member countries was held, with the aim of enhancing information exchange and promoting joint customs inspections. During 1997 Mercosur's efforts towards regional economic integration were threatened by Brazil's adverse external trade balance and its Government's measures to counter the deficit, which included the imposition of import duties on certain products. In November the Brazilian Government announced that it was to increase its import tariff by 3%, in a further effort to improve its external balance. The measure was endorsed by Argentina as a means of maintaining regional fiscal stability. The new external tariff, which was to remain in effect until 31 December 2000, was formally adopted by Mercosur heads of state at a meeting held in Montevideo, in December 1997. At the summit meeting a separate Protocol was signed providing for the liberalization of trade in services and government purchases over a 10-year period. In order to strengthen economic integration throughout the region, Mercosur leaders agreed that Chile, while still not a full member of the organization, should be integrated into the Mercosur political structure, with equal voting rights. In December 1998 Mercosur heads of state agreed on the establishment of an arbitration mechanism for disputes between members, and on measures to standardize human, animal and plant health and safety regulations throughout the grouping. In March 1998 the ministers of the interior of Mercosur countries, together with representatives of the Governments of Chile and Bolivia, agreed to implement a joint security arrangement for the border region linking Argentina, Paraguay and Brazil. In particular, the initiative aimed to counter drugs-trafficking, money-laundering and other illegal activities in the area.

Tensions within Mercosur were compounded in January 1999 owing to economic instability in Brazil and its Government's decision effectively to devalue the national currency, the real. In March the grouping's efforts at integration were further undermined by political instability in Paraguay. Argentina imposed tariffs on imports of Brazilian steel and demanded some form of temporary safeguards on certain products as compensation for their perceived loss of competitiveness resulting from the devalued real. An extraordinary meeting of the Common Market Council was convened, at Brazil's request, in August, in order to discuss the dispute, as well as measures to mitigate the effects of economic recession throughout the sub-region. However, little progress was made and the bilateral trade dispute continued to undermine Mercosur's integration objectives. Argentina imposed new restrictions on textiles and footwear, while, in September, Brazil withdrew all automatic import licences for Argentine products, which were consequently to be subject to the same quality control, sanitary measures and accounting checks applied to imports from non-Mercosur countries. In January 2000, however, the Argentine and Brazilian Governments agreed to refrain from adopting potentially divisive unilateral measures and resolved to accelerate negotiations on the resolution of ongoing differences. In March Mercosur determined to promote and monitor private accords to cover the various areas of contention, and also established a timetable for executing a convergence of regional macroeconomic policies. In June Argentina and Brazil signed a bilateral automobile agreement. The motor vehicle agreement, incorporating new tariffs and a nationalization index, was endorsed by all Mercosur leaders at a meeting convened in Florianópolis, Brazil, in December. (In July 2002 the summit meeting, convened in Buenos Aires, Argentina, adopted an agreement providing for reduced tariffs and increased quotas in the grouping's automotive sector, with a view to establishing a fully liberalized automotive market by 2006.) The summit meeting held in December 2000 approved criteria, formulated by Mercosur finance ministers and central bank governors, determining monetary and fiscal targets which aimed to achieve economic convergence, to promote economic stability throughout the region, and to reduce competitive disparities affecting the unity of the grouping. The Florianópolis summit meeting also recommended the formulation of social indicators to facilitate achieving targets in the reduction of poverty and the elimination of child labour. However, political debate surrounding the meeting was dominated by the Chilean Government's announcement that it had initiated bilateral free trade discussions with the USA, which was considered, in particular by the Brazilian authorities, to undermine Mercosur's unified position at multilateral free trade negotiations. Procedures to incorporate Chile as a full member of Mercosur were suspended. (Chile and the USA concluded negotiations on a bilateral free trade agreement in December 2002.) In July 2008 Mercosur and Chile concluded a protocol on trade in services.

In early 2001 Argentina imposed several emergency measures to strengthen its domestic economy, in contradiction of Mercosur's external tariffs. In March Brazil was reported to have accepted the measures, which included an elimination of tariffs on capital goods and an increase in import duties on consumer goods, as an exceptional temporary trade regime; this position was reversed by mid-2001 following Argentina's decision to exempt certain countries from import tariffs. In February 2002, at a third extraordinary meeting of the Common Market Council, held in Buenos Aires, Mercosur heads of state expressed their support for Argentina's application to receive international financial assistance, in the wake of that country's economic crisis. Although there were fears that the crisis might curb trade and stall economic growth across the region, Argentina's adoption of a floating currency made the prospect of currency harmonization between Mercosur member countries appear more viable. In December Mercosur ministers of justice signed an agreement permitting citizens of Mercosur member and associate member states to reside in any other Mercosur state, initially for a two-year period. At a summit convened in June 2003, in Asunción, Paraguay, heads of state of the four member countries agreed to strengthen integration of the bloc and to harmonize all import tariffs by 2006, thus creating the basis for a single market. They also agreed to establish a directly elected Mercosur legislature, as a successor to the Joint Parliamentary Commission. The July 2004 summit of Mercosur heads of state announced that an Asunción-based five-member tribunal (comprising one legal representative from each of Mercosur's four member countries, plus one 'consensus' member) responsible for ruling on appeals in cases of disputes between member countries was to become operational in the following month. In September 2006 the tribunal criticized the Argentine Government for allowing blockades of international bridges across the River Uruguay by protesters opposing the construction of two pulp mills on the Uruguayan side of the river. (In April 2010 the International Court of Justice delivered a judgment supporting the ongoing operations of the mills; both sides subsequently agreed to co-operate in the implementation of environmental protection measures to limit pollution of the River Uruguay.)

In June 2005 Mercosur heads of state announced a US $100m. structural convergence fund to support education, job creation and infrastructure projects in the poorest regions, in particular in Paraguay and Uruguay, in order to remove some economic disparities within the grouping. The meeting also endorsed a multilateral energy project to link gasfields in Camisea, Peru, to existing supply pipelines in Argentina, Brazil and Uruguay, via Tocopilla, Chile. In July 2008 Mercosur heads of state considered the impact of escalating food costs and the production of biofuels. In December a summit meeting, convened in Bahia, Brazil, agreed to establish a $100m. guarantee fund to facilitate access to credit for small and medium-sized businesses operating in the common market in order to alleviate the impact of the global financial crisis. In August 2010 Mercosur heads of state, meeting in San Juan, Argentina, endorsed a new common customs code, incorporating agreements on the redistribution of external customs revenue and elimination of the double taxation on goods imported from outside the group. In December Mercosur heads of state, meeting in Foz do Iguaçú, Brazil, concluded further agreements to accelerate regional integration. These included the appointment of a new High Representative, a Customs Union Consolidation Program, a Strategic Social Action Plan, which aimed to support the eradication of poverty and greater social equality, and a roadmap for the formation of a Mercosur citizenship statute in order to facilitate the free movement of persons throughout the region. A common Mercosur vehicle license plate was endorsed by the summit meeting.

In May 2007 the Mercosur parliament, the so-called Parlasur, which initially was to serve as an advisory committee, held its inaugural session in Montevideo. In April 2009 a new agreement was concluded providing for representation in the parliament to be proportionally allocated based on each country's population and introduced in two stages, in 2010 and in 2014. Thus the distribution of seats was envisaged as 36 (75 in 2014) for Brazil, 26 (43) for Argentina and 18 each for Paraguay and Uruguay. The accord required ratification by the Common Market Council. In July final consideration of the proposal was postponed owing to a demand by the Paraguayan authorities that it should be conditional on a parallel approval to establish a supranational justice tribunal to adjudicate on trade disputes.

EXTERNAL RELATIONS

During 1997 negotiations to establish a free trade accord with the Andean Community were hindered by differences regarding schedules for tariff elimination and Mercosur's insistence on a local content of 60% to qualify for rules of origin preferences. However, in April 1998 the two groupings signed an accord that committed them to the establishment of a free trade area by January 2000. Negotiations in early 1999 failed to conclude an agreement on preferential tariffs between the two blocs, and the existing arrangements were extended on a bilateral basis. In March the Andean Community agreed to initiate free trade negotiations with Brazil; a preferential tariff agreement was concluded in July. In August 2000 a similar agreement between the Community and Argentina entered into force. In September leaders of Mercosur and the Andean Community, meeting at a summit of Latin American heads of state, determined to relaunch negotiations. The establishment of a mechanism to support political dialogue and co-ordination between the two groupings, was approved at the first joint meeting of ministers of foreign affairs in July 2001. In April 2004 Mercosur and the Andean Community signed a free trade accord, providing for tariffs on 80% of trade between the two groupings to be phased out by 2014, and for tariffs to be removed from the remaining 20% of, initially protected, products by 2019. The entry into force of the accord, scheduled for 1 July 2004, was postponed owing to delays in drafting the tariff reduction schedule. Peru became an associate member of Mercosur in December 2003, and Colombia and Ecuador were granted associate membership in December 2004. In July 2004 Mexico was invited to attend all meetings of the organization with a view to future accession to associate membership. Bilateral negotiations on a free trade agreement between Mexico and Mercosur were initiated in 2001. In 2005 Mercosur and the Andean Community formulated a reciprocal association agreement, to extend associate membership to all member states of both groupings. In February 2010 foreign ministers agreed to establish an Andean Community-Mercosur Mixed Commission to facilitate and strengthen co-operation between member countries of both organizations. In December 2005 Bolivia was invited to join as a full member. At the summit meeting of heads of state held in January 2007 in Rio de Janeiro, Brazil, Bolivia stated two conditions on which its membership would be dependent: continued membership of the Andean Community and exemption from Mercosur's CET. Also in December 2005 Mercosur heads of state agreed to a request by Venezuela (which had been granted associate membership in December 2004) to become a member with full voting rights. The leaders signed a protocol, in July 2006, formally to admit Venezuela to the group. The accord, however, required ratification by each country's legislature. In August 2010 Mercosur heads of state urged a quick conclusion to Venezuela's incorporation into the organization in order to enhance regional integration. By June 2012 the Paraguayan parliament had yet to endorse the protocol, as it was blocked by the country's senate.

In December 1995 Mercosur and the European Union (EU) signed a framework agreement for commercial and economic co-operation, which provided for co-operation in the economic, trade, industrial, scientific, institutional and cultural fields and the promotion of wider political dialogue on issues of mutual interest. In June 1997 Mercosur heads of state, convened in Asunción, Paraguay, reaffirmed the group's intention to pursue trade negotiations with the EU, Mexico and the Andean Community, as well as to negotiate as a single economic bloc in discussions with regard to the establishment of a Free Trade Area of the Americas (FTAA). Chile and Bolivia were to be incorporated into these negotiations. Negotiations between Mercosur and the EU on the conclusion of an Interregional Association Agreement commenced in 1999. Specific discussion of tariff reductions and market access commenced at the fifth round of negotiations, held in July 2001, at which the EU proposed a gradual elimination of tariffs on industrial imports over a 10-year period and an extension of access quotas for agricultural products; however, negotiations stalled in 2005 owing to differences regarding farm subsidies. In July 2008 Mercosur heads of state condemned a new EU immigration policy that would permit the detention and forcible return of illegal immigrants. Leaders attending a Mercosur-EU summit meeting, convened in Madrid, Spain, in May 2010, determined to restart promptly the Association Agreement negotiations. The first discussions took place in Buenos Aires, in July, and subsequently at regular intervals. The seventh round of discussions was held in Montevideo, in November 2011, the eighth was convened in Brussels, Belgium, in March 2012, and a ninth round was to take place in July 2012, in Brazil. A cooling of relations between Argentina and Spain following a decision announced in April 2012 by the Argentine Government to renationalize the petroleum company YPF, of which the Spanish company Repsol had hitherto been the majority shareholder, was expected to impact negatively on the Mercosur–EU negotiations process. In late May the EU filed a complaint with the WTO contesting restrictions on imports imposed (since 2005) by Argentina.

In March 2003 Argentina and Brazil, with the support of other Mercosur member states, formed the Southern Agricultural Council (CAS), which was to represent the interests of the grouping as a whole in negotiations with third countries. In December 2004 leaders from 12 Latin American countries (excluding Argentina, Ecuador, Paraguay and Uruguay) attending a pan-South American summit, convened in Cusco, Peru, approved in principle the creation of a new South American Community of Nations (SACN). It was envisaged that negotiations on the formation of the new Community, which was to entail the merger of Mercosur, the Andean Community and the Latin American Integration Association (ALADI), would be completed within 15 years. In April 2005 a region-wide meeting of ministers of foreign affairs was convened within the framework of establishing the SACN. A joint SACN communiqué was released, expressing concern at the deterioration of constitutional rule and democratic institutions in Ecuador, and announcing its intention to send a ministerial mission to that country. The first SACN summit meeting was convened in September, in Brasília, Brazil. In April 2007, at the first South American Energy Summit, convened on Margarita Island, Venezuela, heads of state endorsed the establishment of a Union of South American Nations (UNASUR), to replace SACN as the lead organization for regional integration. UNASUR was to have political decision-making functions, supported by a small permanent secretariat, to be located in Quito, Ecuador, and was to co-ordinate economic and trade matters with Mercosur, the Andean Community and ALADI. A summit meeting formally to inaugurate UNASUR, scheduled to be convened in December, was postponed. A rescheduled meeting, to be convened in March 2008, was also postponed, owing to a diplomatic dispute between Ecuador and Colombia. It was later convened in May, in Brasília, Brazil, when the constitutional document formally establishing UNASUR was signed. In December Brazil hosted a Latin American and Caribbean Summit on Integration and Development, which aimed to strengthen the commitment in the region to support sustainable development. It issued the Salvador Declaration, which pledged support to strengthen co-operation among the regional and sub-regional groupings, to pursue further consultation and joint efforts to counter the effects of the global financial crisis on the region, and to promote closer collaboration on a range of issues including energy, food security, social development, physical infrastructure and natural disaster management. In February 2010 a summit meeting of the Rio Group, convened in Cancún, Mexico, approved in principle the establishment of a new Community of Latin American and Caribbean States, excluding Canada and the USA, to strengthen regional co-operation. The Community was formally established at a summit meeting held in Caracas, Venezuela, in December 2011 (post-poned from July, owing to the Venezuelan president's ill health).

In March 1998 ministers of trade of 34 countries agreed a detailed framework for negotiations on the establishment of the FTAA. Mercosur secured support for its request that a separate negotiating group be established to consider issues relating to agriculture, as one of nine key sectors to be discussed. The FTAA negotiating process was formally initiated by heads of state of the 34 countries meeting in Santiago, Chile, in April 1998. In June Mercosur and Canada signed a Trade and Investment Co-operation Arrangement, which aimed to remove obstacles to trade and to increase economic co-operation between the two signatories. The summit meeting held in December 2000 was attended by the President of South Africa, and it was agreed that Mercosur would initiate free trade negotiations with that country. (These commenced in October 2001.) In June 2001 Mercosur leaders agreed to pursue efforts to conclude a bilateral trade agreement with the USA, an objective previously opposed by the Brazilian authorities, while reaffirming their commitment to the FTAA process. Leaders attending a special summit of the Americas, convened in January 2004 in Monterrey, Mexico, failed to specify a completion date for the FTAA process, although they adopted a declaration committing themselves to its eventual establishment. Negotiations were suspended in March, and remained stalled in 2012. Regional integration and co-operation were the principal focus of the sixth summit of the Americas, held in Catagena, Colombia, in April, on the theme 'Connecting the Americas: Partners for Prosperity'.

In December 2007 Mercosur signed a free trade accord with Israel, which entered into effect in January 2010. At the meeting of heads of state, held in San Miguel de Tucumán, Argentina, in July 2008, a preferential trade agreement was signed with the Southern African Customs Union. Framework agreements on the preparation of free trade accords were also signed with Turkey and Jordan. In June 2009 a preferential trade agreement with India entered into force. A framework agreement on trade with Morocco entered into effect in April 2010. In August Mercosur signed a free trade agreement with Egypt, and in December Mercosur signed a trade and economic co-operation agreement with the Palestinian National Authority and a framework agree-ment to establish a free trade agreement with Syria. Agreements to establish mechanisms for political dialogue and co-operation were signed with Cuba and Turkey at that time.

In July 2009 Mercosur heads of state, meeting in Asunción, issued a joint statement condemning the removal by military force of President Manuel Zelaya of Honduras, demanding the immediate restoration of democratic and constitutional order, and refusing to recognize the legitimacy of the interim authorities in that country.

Finance

The annual budget for the secretariat is contributed by the four full member states.

Publication

Boletín Oficial del Mercosur (quarterly).

WORLD COUNCIL OF CHURCHES—WCC

Address: 150 route de Ferney, POB 2100, 1211 Geneva 2, Switzerland.

Telephone: 227916111; **fax:** 227910361; **e-mail:** infowcc@wcc-coe.org; **internet:** www.oikoumene.org.

The Council was founded in 1948 to promote co-operation between Christian Churches and to prepare for a clearer manifestation of the unity of the Church.

MEMBERS

There are 349 member Churches in more than 110 countries. Chief denominations: Anglican; Baptist; Congregational; Lutheran; Methodist; Moravian; Old Catholic; Orthodox; Presbyterian; Reformed; and Society of Friends. The Roman Catholic Church is not a member but sends official observers to meetings.

Organization

(June 2012)

ASSEMBLY

The governing body of the World Council, consisting of delegates of the member Churches, it meets every seven years to frame policy and consider some main themes. It elects the Presidents of the Council, who serve as members of the Central Committee. The ninth Assembly was held in Porto Alegre, Brazil, in February 2006; the 10th Assembly was scheduled to be held in Busan, Republic of Korea, in October–November 2013, on the theme 'God of life, lead us to justice and peace'.

Presidium: Archbishop Dr ANASTASIOS OF TIRANA AND ALL ALBANIA, JOHN TAROANUI DOOM (French Polynesia), Rev. Dr SIMON DOSSOU (Benin), Rev. Dr SORITUA NABABAN (Indonesia), Rev. Dr OFELIA ORTEGA (Cuba), ABUNE PAULOS (Ethiopia), Rev. Dr BERNICE POWELL JACKSON (USA), Dr MARY TANNER (United Kingdom).

CENTRAL COMMITTEE

Appointed by the Assembly to carry out its policies and decisions, the Committee consists of 150 members chosen from Assembly delegates. It meets every 12 to 18 months.

The Central Committee comprises the Programme Committee and the Finance Committee. Within the Programme Committee there are advisory groups on issues relating to communication, women, justice, peace and creation, youth, ecumenical relations, and inter-religious relations. There are also five commissions and boards.

Moderator: Rev. Dr WALTER ALTMANN (Armenian Apostolic Church, Lebanon).

Vice-Moderators: Prof. Dr GENNADIOS OF SASSIMA (Turkey), Rev. Dr MARGARETHA M. HENDRIKS-RIRIMASSE (Indonesia).

EXECUTIVE COMMITTEE

Consists of the Presidents, the Officers and 20 members chosen by the Central Committee from its membership to prepare its agenda, expedite its decisions and supervise the work of the Council between meetings of the Central Committee. Meets every six months.

CONSULTATIVE BODIES

Various bodies, including advisory groups, commissions and reference groups, comprising members from WCC governing bodies and member churches, advise the secretariat on policy direction, implementation and evaluation. The main bodies are the Commissions on Faith and Order (plenary and standing bodies), on World Mission and Evangelism, on Education and Ecumenical Formation, of the Churches on International Affairs, and the Echos Commission on Youth in the Ecumenical Movement.

GENERAL SECRETARIAT

The General Secretariat implements the policies laid down by the WCC and co-ordinates the Council's work. The General Secretariat is also responsible for an Ecumenical Institute, at Bossey, Switzerland, which provides training in ecumenical leadership.

General Secretary: Rev. Dr OLAV FYKSE TVEIT (Norway).

Activities

The ninth WCC Assembly, held in February 2006, approved a reorganization of the WCC's work programme, based on six key areas of activity.

THE WCC AND THE ECUMENICAL MOVEMENT IN THE 21ST CENTURY

The WCC aims to support co-operation among member churches and their involvement in the activities of the organization. It also works to enhance partnerships with other regional and international ecumenical organizations to support the ecumenical movement as a whole, and aims to facilitate communication and consultation among relevant bodies with regard to the future of the ecumenical movement. The WCC supported the development of a Global Christian Forum, which initiated regional consultations among churches in 2004 and convened its first global meeting in November 2007. Within this work programme was a commitment to promote the active participation of young adults in the life of churches and the ecumenical movement, for example through an internship programme at the WCC secretariat, and to ensure that women are and specific issues concerning them are fully considered and represented.

UNITY, MISSION, EVANGELISM AND SPIRITUALITY

This work programme is directed and supported by the Commissions on Faith and Order and on World Mission and Evangelism. It aims to promote a 'visible unity' among member churches and to encourage them to address potentially divisive issues and develop mutually acceptable positions. The WCC produces materials to share among churches information on worship and spiritual life practices and to co-ordinate and promote the annual Week of Prayer for Christian Unity. Other activities aim to confront and overcome any discrimination against ethnic minorities, people with disabilities or other excluded groups within the church and society as a whole. A project to study how to hold commitment to unity together with mission and evangelism was being undertaken within the work programme.

PUBLIC WITNESS: ADDRESSING POWER, AFFIRMING PEACE

The Public Witness programme aims to ensure that the Council's concerns relating to violence, war, human rights, economic injustice, poverty and exclusion are raised and addressed at an international level, including at meetings of UN or other intergovernmental bodies. At a regional and local level the Council aims to accompany churches in critical situations in their efforts to defend human rights and dignity, overcome impunity, achieve accountability and build just and peaceful societies. An Ecumenical Accompaniment Programme in Palestine and Israel (EAPPI) was inaugurated in August 2002 to provide for individuals to support and protect vulnerable groups in the Occupied Territories and to accompany the Israeli Peace movement. The WCC has established an Israeli/Palestine Ecumenical Forum to bring together churches in the region to develop unified policy positions in support of peace and justice. The WCC supported a range of activities within the framework of its Decade to Overcome Violence (2001–10); the Decade culminated in an International Ecumenical Peace Convocation, held in May 2011, in Kingston, Jamaica. An International Day of Prayer for Peace is held each year on 21 September.

JUSTICE, *DIAKONIA* AND RESPONSIBILITY FOR CREATION

The Council supports its members efforts to combat injustice and meet human needs. It aims to strengthen churches' organizational capacities and to strengthen and monitor accountability (and greater understanding) between donors and recipients of resources. It is also committed to strengthening the role of churches in the fields of health and healing, in particular in HIV/AIDS and mental health-related issues. The Council undertakes networking and advocacy activities at an international level and promotes dialogue among church health networks and those of civil society. In 2002 the Council inaugurated the Ecumenical HIV and AIDS Initiative in Africa (EHAIA) to inform and assist churches in Africa in their efforts to support communities affected by HIV/AIDS. The WCC participated in the first Summit of High Level Religious Leaders on HIV and AIDS, which was convened in Den Dolder, Netherlands, in late March 2010. A WCC Ecumenical Solidarity Fund (ESF) provides grants in support of capacity-building efforts, activities to combat racism and other strategic initiatives. The Council aims to strengthen activities relating to migration and racism and to develop new advocacy strategies. The Council provides a forum for discussion and exchange of information on the use of science and new technologies, for example genetically modified seeds and stem cell research. As part of a wider concern for challenges facing the planet, the WCC has formulated a public campaign to raise awareness of climate change, its impact and the need to address the related problems. It hosts the secretariat of the Ecumenical Water Network, which aims to highlight issues relating to the scarcity of water resources in many parts of the work and to advocate community-based initiatives to manage resources more effectively.

EDUCATION AND ECUMENICAL FORMATION

The WCC is committed to supporting ecumenical and faith formation, as well as providing educational opportunities itself. The Ecumenical Institute, in Bossey, Switzerland, offers academic courses, research opportunities and residential programmes, including one for the promotion of inter-faith dialogue. The WCC organizes seminars and workshops to promote good practices in ecumenical formation and leadership training. The Council aims to strengthen theological education through accreditation standards, exchange programmes and modifying curricula. It administers a sponsorship programme to provide opportunities for ecumenical learning in different cultures. In September 2011 the WCC, with Globethics.net, launched the Global Digital Library on Theology and Ecumenism (GlobeTheoLib, accessible at www.globethics.net/gtl), a multi-lingual theological resource providing access to research materials in theology and related disciplines.

INTER-RELIGIOUS DIALOGUE AND CO-OPERATION

This work programme aims to promote the peaceful co-existence of different faiths and communities within society. It supports inter-faith dialogue and opportunities to develop mutual trust and respect, in particular among women and young people of different faiths. It promotes best practices in inter-religious dialogue and co-operation. The Council encourages reflection on Christianity in an inter-faith society. In 2006 it inaugurated, with the Roman Catholic Church, a process of consultations on religious freedom, to result in the definition of a code of conduct on religious conversion. The Council supports churches in conflict situations to counter religious intolerance or discrimination. It undertakes research, field visits, advocacy work and capacity building in support of churches or communities affected by conflict.

Finance

The main contributors to the WCC's budget are the churches and their agencies, with funds for certain projects contributed by other organizations. The 2011 budget amounted to 30.9m. Swiss francs.

Publications

Annual Review.

Current Dialogue (2 a year).

Ecumenical News International (weekly).

Ecumenical Review (quarterly).

International Review of Mission (quarterly).

WCC e-news (electronic publication).

Catalogue of periodicals, books and audio-visuals.

WORLD FEDERATION OF TRADE UNIONS—WFTU

Address: 40 Zan Moreas St, 11745 Athens, Greece.

Telephone: (21) 09236700; **fax:** (21) 09214517; **e-mail:** info@wftucentral.org; **internet:** www.wftucentral.org.

The Federation was founded in 1945, on a world-wide basis. A number of members withdrew from the Federation in 1949 to establish the International Confederation of Free Trade Unions (now the International Trade Union Confederation).

MEMBERS

Affiliated or associated national federations (including the Trade Unions Internationals) in 126 countries representing some 135m. individuals.

Organization

(June 2012)

WORLD TRADE UNION CONGRESS

The Congress meets every five years. It reviews WFTU's work, endorses reports from the executives, and elects the General Council. The size of the delegations is based on the total membership of national federations. The Congress is also open to participation by non-affiliated organizations. The 16th Congress was held in Athens, Greece, in April 2011.

GENERAL COUNCIL

The General Council meets three times between Congresses, and comprises members and deputies elected by Congress from nominees of national federations. Every affiliated or associated organization and Trade Unions International has one member and one deputy member.

The Council receives reports from the Presidential Council, approves the plan and budget and elects officers.

PRESIDENTIAL COUNCIL

The Presidential Council meets twice a year and conducts most of the executive work of WFTU. It comprises a President, elected each year from among its members, the General Secretary and 18 Vice-Presidents.

SECRETARIAT

The Secretariat consists of the General Secretary, and six Deputy General Secretaries. It is appointed by the General Council and is responsible for general co-ordination, regional activities, national trade union liaison, press and information, administration and finance.

WFTU has regional offices in New Delhi, India (for the Asia-Pacific region); Havana, Cuba (covering the Americas); Dakar, Senegal (for Africa); Damascus, Syria (for the Middle East); Nicosia, Cyprus (for Europe); and in Moscow, Russia (covering the CIS countries).

General Secretary: GEORGE MAVRIKOS (Greece).

Activities

The April 2011 World Trade Union Congress adopted the Athens Pact, concerning the impact on the 'international working class' of the global economic crisis from 2008, regarded by the Congress as a 'deep and multifaceted crisis of the capitalist system', burdening the global labouring class most. In February 2012, meeting in Johannesburg, South Africa, the Presidential Council adopted an action plan for 2012, aiming: to address unemployment by combating anti-labour policies and urging governments and public institutions to support the survival of unemployed workers and their families, respecting their needs for affordable food, housing, clean water, and free health care and education; to organize on 3 October WFTU's annual militant International Action Day; to promote trade union education; to promote WFTU in Africa; and to support working youth and women.

Finance

Income is derived from affiliation dues, which are based on the number of members in each trade union federation.

Publication

Comments.

Flashes from WFTU.

From the World (electronic news).

Reflects.

Trade Unions Internationals

The following autonomous Trade Unions Internationals (TUIs) are associated with WFTU:

Trade Unions International of Public and Allied Employees: off 10A Shankharitola St, Kolkata 700014, India; tel. (33) 2217-7721; fax (33) 2265-9450; e-mail aisgef@dataone.in; internet www.tradeunionindia.org; f. 1949; mems: 34m. in 50 unions in 54 countries; Branch Commissions: State, Municipal, Postal and Telecommunications, Health, Banks and Insurance; Pres. LULAMILE SOTAKA (South Africa); Gen. Sec. SUKOMAL SEN (India); publ. *Information Bulletin* (in three languages).

Trade Unions International of Transport Workers (TUI-Transport): Rua Serra do Japi 31, 03309–000 São Paulo, Brazil; tel. (11) 209-536-05; fax (11) 229-633-03; e-mail info@tui-transport.org; f. 1949; holds International Trade Conference (every 4 years; 2011: Cyprus) and General Council (annually); mems: 95 unions from 37 countries; publ. *TUI Reporter* (every 2 months, in English and Spanish).

Trade Unions International of Workers of the Building, Wood and Building Materials Industries (Union Internationale des Syndicats des Travailleurs du Bâtiment, du Bois et des Matériaux de Construction—UITBB): POB 281, 00101 Helsinki, Finland; tel. (9) 693-1130; fax (9) 693-1020; e-mail rguitbb@kaapeli.fi; internet www.uitbb.org; f. 1949; mems: unions in 60 countries, grouping 2.5m. workers; Pres. ANTONIO LOPÉS DE CARBALHO (Brazil); Gen. Sec. DEBANJAN CHAKRABARTI (India); publ. *Bulletin*.

Trade Unions International of Workers in the Energy, Chemical, Oil and Related Industries (TUI-Energy): c/o 3A Calle Maestro Antonio Caso 45, Col. Tabacalera, 06470 Mexico City, Mexico; tel. and fax (55) 5546-3200; e-mail uis-temqpia@sme.org; f. 1998; Pres. SWADESH DEV ROYE; Gen. Sec. MARTIN ESPARZA FLORES (Mexico); publ. *Bulletin*.

Trade Union International Union of Workers in the Mining, the Metallurgy and the Metal industries (TUI-Metal): f. 2008; Sec.-Gen. JESÚS GETE OLARRA (Mexico); publ. *Bulletin*.

World Federation of Teachers' Unions: 6/6 Kalicharan Ghosh Rd, Kolkata 700 050, India; tel. (33) 2528-4786; fax (33) 2557-1293; f. 1946; mems: 132 national unions of teachers and educational and scientific workers in 78 countries, representing over 24m. individuals; Pres. LESTURUGE ARIYAWANSA (Sri Lanka); Gen. Sec. MRINMOY BHATTACHARYYA (India); publ. *Teachers of the World* (quarterly, in English).

The foundation congress of a new TUI for Tourism and Hotels (TUI-HOTUR) was held in December 2009, in Athens. The establishment of a new TUI representing retired workers, to be headquartered in Spain, was pending in 2012.

WORLD TRADE ORGANIZATION—WTO

Address: Centre William Rappard, 154 rue de Lausanne, 1211 Geneva, Switzerland.

Telephone: 227395111; **fax:** 227314206; **e-mail:** enquiries@wto.org; **internet:** www.wto.org.

The WTO is the legal and institutional foundation of the multilateral trading system. It was established on 1 January 1995, as the successor to the General Agreement on Tariffs and Trade (GATT). WTO oversees negotiations on trade agreements, monitors the implementation of trade agreements, undertakes dispute procedures, and works to build the trade capacity of developing states.

MEMBERS*

Albania
Angola
Antigua and Barbuda
Argentina
Armenia
Australia
Austria
Bahrain
Bangladesh
Barbados
Belgium
Belize
Benin
Bolivia
Botswana
Brazil
Brunei
Bulgaria
Burkina Faso
Burundi
Cambodia
Cameroon
Canada
Cape Verde
Central African Republic
Chad
Chile
China, People's Republic
China, Republic†
Colombia
Congo, Democratic Republic
Congo, Republic
Costa Rica
Côte d'Ivoire
Croatia
Cuba
Cyprus
Czech Republic
Denmark
Djibouti
Dominica
Dominican Republic
Ecuador
Egypt
El Salvador
Estonia
Fiji
Finland
France
Gabon
The Gambia
Georgia
Germany
Ghana
Greece
Grenada
Guatemala
Guinea
Guinea-Bissau
Guyana
Haiti
Honduras
Hong Kong
Hungary
Iceland
India
Indonesia
Ireland
Israel
Italy
Jamaica
Japan
Jordan
Kenya
Korea, Republic
Kuwait
Kyrgyzstan
Latvia
Lesotho
Liechtenstein
Lithuania
Luxembourg
Macao
Macedonia, former Yugoslav republic
Madagascar
Malawi
Malaysia
Maldives
Mali
Malta
Mauritania
Mauritius
Mexico
Moldova
Mongolia
Montenegro
Morocco
Mozambique
Myanmar
Namibia
Nepal
Netherlands
New Zealand
Nicaragua
Niger
Nigeria
Norway
Oman
Pakistan
Panama
Papua New Guinea
Paraguay
Peru
Philippines
Poland
Portugal
Qatar
Romania
Rwanda
Saint Christopher and Nevis
Saint Lucia
Saint Vincent and the Grenadines
Samoa
Saudi Arabia
Senegal
Sierra Leone
Singapore
Slovakia
Slovenia
Solomon Islands
South Africa
Spain
Sri Lanka
Suriname
Swaziland
Sweden
Switzerland
Tanzania
Thailand
Togo
Tonga
Trinidad and Tobago
Tunisia
Turkey
Uganda
Ukraine
United Arab Emirates
United Kingdom
USA
Uruguay
Venezuela
Viet Nam
Zambia
Zimbabwe

* The European Union also has membership status, and negotiates and acts within the WTO as a single body on behalf of its 27 member states, which are individually members of the WTO.

† Admitted as the Separate Customs Territory of Taiwan, Penghu, Kinmen and Matsu (referred to as Chinese Taipei).

Note: At June 2012 26 applications to join the WTO were either under consideration or awaiting consideration by accession working parties. The General Council formally approved the terms of entry of Vanuatu in October 2011. In December the eighth Ministerial Conference approved the terms of entry of Montenegro, Russia and Samoa; Montenegro and Samoa became full members of the WTO in, respectively, April and May 2012.

At June 2012 31 WTO member states were officially classified as Least Developed Countries; LDC accession guidelines, in force since 2002, were being revised in 2012.

Organization

(June 2012)

MINISTERIAL CONFERENCE

The Ministerial Conference is the highest authority of the WTO. It is composed of representatives of all WTO members at ministerial level, and may take decisions on all matters under any of the multilateral trade agreements. The Conference is normally required to meet at least every two years. The eighth Conference was convened in December 2011, in Geneva, Switzerland, on the themes 'Importance of the Multilateral Trading System and the WTO', 'Trade and Development' and 'the Doha Development Agenda'.

GENERAL COUNCIL

The General Council, which is also composed of representatives of all WTO members, is required to report to the Ministerial Conference and conducts much of the day-to-day work of the WTO. The Council convenes as the Dispute Settlement Body, to oversee the trade dispute settlement procedures, and as the Trade Policy Review Body, to conduct regular reviews of the trade policies of WTO members. The Council delegates responsibility to three other major Councils: the Intellectual Property Council (for trade-related aspects of intellectual property rights), the Goods Council (for trade in goods) and the Services Council (trade in services).

TRADE NEGOTIATIONS COMMITTEE

The Committee was established in November 2001 by the Declaration of the fourth Ministerial Conference, held in Doha, Qatar, to supervise the agreed agenda of trade negotiations. It operates under the authority of the General Council and was mandated to establish negotiating mechanisms and subsidiary bodies for each subject under consideration. A structure of negotiating groups and a declaration of principles and practices for the negotiations were formulated by the Committee in February 2002.

SECRETARIAT

The WTO Secretariat comprised some 629 staff in 2012. Its responsibilities include the servicing of WTO delegate bodies, with respect to negotiations and the implementation of agreements, undertaking accession negotiations for new members and providing technical support and expertise to developing countries.

The WTO Institute for Training and Technical Co-operation, based at the Secretariat, offers courses on trade policy; introduction to the WTO for least developed countries; WTO dispute settlement rules and procedures; and other specialized topics. Other programmes include training-of-trainers schemes and distance-learning services.

Director-General: Pascal Lamy (France).

Deputy Directors-General: Alejandro Jara (Chile), Valentine Sendanyoye Rugwabiza (Rwanda), Harsha Vardhana Singh (India), Rufus Yerxa (USA).

Activities

The Final Act of the Uruguay Round of GATT multilateral trade negotiations, which were concluded in December 1993, provided for extensive trade liberalization measures and for the establishment of a permanent structure to oversee international trading procedures. The Final Act was signed in April 1994, in Marrakesh, Morocco. At the same time a separate accord, the Marrakesh Declaration, was signed by the majority of GATT contracting states, endorsing the establishment of the WTO. The essential functions of the WTO are: to administer and facilitate the implementation of the results of the Uruguay Round; to provide a forum for multilateral trade negotiations; to administer the trade dispute settlement procedures; to review national trade policies; and to co-operate with other international institutions, in particular the IMF and the World Bank, in order to achieve greater coherence in global economic policy-making.

The WTO Agreement contains some 29 individual legal texts and more than 25 additional Ministerial declarations, decisions and understandings, which cover obligations and commitments for member states. All these instruments are based on a few fundamental principles, which form the basis of the WTO Agreement. An integral part of the Agreement is 'GATT 1994', an amended and updated version of the original GATT Agreement of 1947, which was formally concluded at the end of 1995. Under the 'most-favoured nation' (MFN) clause, members are bound to grant to each other's products treatment no less favourable than that accorded to the products of any third parties. A number of exceptions apply, principally for customs unions and free trade areas and for measures in favour of and among developing countries. The principle of 'national treatment' requires goods, having entered a market, to be treated no less favourably than the equivalent domestically produced goods. Secure and predictable market access, to encourage trade, investment and job creation, may be determined by 'binding' tariffs, or customs duties. This process means that a tariff level for a particular product becomes a commitment by a member state, and cannot be increased without compensation negotiations with its main trading partners. Other WTO agreements also contribute to predictable trading conditions by demanding commitments from member countries and greater transparency of domestic laws and national trade policies. By permitting tariffs, while adhering to the guidelines of being non-discriminatory, the WTO aims to promote open, fair and undistorted competition.

The WTO aims to encourage development and economic reform among the increasing number of developing countries and countries with economies in transition participating in the international trading system. These countries, particularly the least developed states, have been granted transition periods and greater flexibility to implement certain WTO provisions. Industrial member countries are encouraged to assist developing nations by their trading conditions and by not expecting reciprocity in trade concession negotiations. In addition, the WTO operates a limited number of technical assistance programmes, mostly relating to training (including online courses) and the provision of information technology.

Finally, the WTO Agreement recognizes the need to protect the environment and to promote sustainable development. A Committee on Trade and Environment examines the relationship between trade policies, environmental measures and sustainable development and to recommend any appropriate modifications of the multilateral trading provisions.

With the planned accession of Russia to the WTO in 2012, all members of the so-called BRICS informal grouping of large emerging economies, comprising Brazil, Russia, India, People's Republic of China, and South Africa (which together accounted for some 20% of global GDP in 2011), were to be members of the Organization. BRICS (known as BRIC prior to the accession of South Africa in December 2010) convened an inaugural summit of heads or states and government in June 2009, in Yekaterinburg, Russia, at which principles for future co-operation and development were adopted; a second summit was held in April 2010, in Brasília, Brazil; a third in Sanya, China, in April 2011, which adopted the Sanya Declaration, outlining the future deepening of co-operation in areas including trade, energy, finance and industry; and a fourth in New Delhi, India, in March 2012. The fourth summit directed member state finance ministers to examine the feasibility of establishing a new Development Bank to mobilize resources in support of infrastructure and sustainable development projects in BRICS economies, other emerging economies, and developing countries, with the aim of supplementing the existing efforts of multilateral and regional financial institutions.

At the 1996 Conference representatives of some 29 countries signed an Information Technology Agreement (ITA), which aimed to eliminate tariffs on the significant global trade in IT products by 2000. By February 1997 some 39 countries, then representing the required 90% share of the world's IT trade, had consented to implement the ITA. It was signed in March, and was to cover the following main product categories: computers; telecommunications products; semiconductors or manufacturing equipment; software; and scientific instruments. Tariff reductions in these sectors were to be undertaken in four stages, commencing in July, and subsequently on 1 January each year, providing for the elimination of all tariffs by the start of 2000. By June 2012 there were 75 participants in the ITA, representing some 97% of world trade in IT products. Informal negotiations on expanding the product coverage of the ITA were initiated in May 2012. In February 1999 the WTO announced plans to investigate methods of removing non-tariff barriers to trade in IT products, such as those resulting from non-standardization of technical regulations. A work programme on non-tariff measures was approved by the Committee of Participants on the Expansion of Trade in IT Products in November 2000.

At the end of the Uruguay Round a 'built-in' programme of work for the WTO was developed. In addition, the Ministerial Conferences in December 1996 and May 1998 addressed a range of issues. The final declaration issued from the Ministerial Conference in December 1996 incorporated a text on the contentious issue of core labour standards, although it was emphasized that the relationship between trade and labour standards was not part of the WTO agenda. The text recognized the International Labour Organization's competence in establishing and dealing with core labour standards and endorsed future WTO/ILO co-operation. The declaration also included a plan of action on measures in favour of the world's least developed countries, to assist these countries in enhancing their trading opportunities. The second Conference, convened in May 1998, decided against imposing customs duties on international electronic transactions, and agreed to establish a comprehensive work programme to address the issues of electronic commerce. The Conference also supported the creation of a framework of international rules to protect intellectual property rights and provide security and privacy in transactions. Developing countries were assured that their needs in this area would be taken into account. Members agreed to begin preparations for the launch of comprehensive talks on global trade liberalization. In addition, following repeated mass public demonstrations against free trade, it was agreed to try to increase the transparency of the WTO and improve public understanding of the benefits of open global markets.

Formal negotiations on the agenda of a new multilateral trade 'round', which was initially scheduled to be launched at the third Ministerial Conference, to be held in Seattle, USA, in late November–December 1999, commenced in September 1998. While it was confirmed that further liberalization of agriculture and services was to be considered, no consensus was reached (in particular between the Cairns Group of countries and the USA, and the European Union—EU, supported by Japan) on the terms of reference or procedures for these negotiations prior to the start of the Conference. In addition, developing countries criticized renewed efforts, mainly by the USA, to link trade and labour standards and to incorporate environmental considerations into the discussions. Efforts by the EU to broaden the talks to include investment and competition policy were also resisted by the USA. The conduct of the Ministerial Conference was severely disrupted by public demonstrations by a diverse range of interest groups concerned with the impact of WTO accords on the environment, workers' rights and developing countries. The differences between member states with regard to a formal agenda failed to be resolved during extensive negotiations, and the Conference was suspended. At a meeting of the General Council, convened later in December, member countries reached an informal understanding that any agreements concluding on

31 December would be extended. Meanwhile, the Director-General attempted to maintain a momentum for proceeding with a new round of trade negotiations. In February 2000 the General Council agreed to resume talks with regard to agriculture and services, and to consider difficulties in implementing the Uruguay Accord, which was a main concern of developing member states. The Council also urged industrialized nations to pursue an earlier initiative to grant duty-free access to the exports of least developed countries. In May the Council resolved to initiate a series of Special Sessions to consider implementation of existing trade agreements, and approved more flexible provisions for implementation of TRIPS (see below), as part of ongoing efforts to address the needs of developing member states and strengthen their confidence in the multilateral trading system.

During 2001 negotiations were undertaken to reach agreement on further trade liberalization. A draft accord was approved by the General Council in October. The fourth Ministerial Conference, held in Doha, Qatar, in November, adopted a final declaration providing a mandate for a three-year agenda for negotiations on a range of subjects, commencing on 1 January 2002. Most of the negotiations were initially scheduled to be concluded, on 1 January 2005, as a single undertaking, i.e. requiring universal agreement on all matters under consideration. (The deadline was subsequently advanced to end-2006, and in July 2006 was postponed indefinitely—see below.) A new Trade Negotiations Committee (TNC) was established to supervise the process, referred to as the Doha Development Round. Several aspects of existing agreements were to be negotiated, while new issues included WTO rules, such as subsidies, regional trade agreements and anti-dumping measures, and market access. The Declaration incorporated a commitment to negotiate issues relating to trade and the environment, including fisheries subsidies, environmental labelling requirements, and the relationship between trade obligations of multilateral environment agreements and WTO rules. The Conference approved a separate decision on implementation-related issues, to address the concerns of developing countries in meeting their WTO commitments. Several implementation issues were agreed at the meeting, while others were incorporated into the Development Agenda. Specific reference was made in the Declaration to providing greater technical co-operation and capacity-building assistance to WTO developing country members. A Doha Development Agenda Global Trust Fund was established in late 2001, with a core budget of CHF 15m., to help finance technical support for trade liberalization in less developed member states. In July 2011 Spain donated €350,000 to the Fund. In September 2002 the WTO Director-General announced that, in support of the ongoing trade negotiations, the following four 'pillars' of the organization should be strengthened: beneficial use of the legal framework binding together the multilateral system; technical and capacity-building assistance to least developed and developing countries; greater coherence in international economic policy-making; and the WTO's functioning as an institution.

The fifth Ministerial Conference, convened in Cancún, Mexico, in September 2003 to advance the Doha Development Round, failed to achieve consensus on a number of issues, in particular investment and competition policy. Senior officials from member states met in December to discuss the future of the Doha Round, but no major breakthrough was achieved. Members did, however, indicate their willingness to recommence work in negotiating groups, which had been suspended after the Cancún conference. The General Council, meanwhile, was to continue working to explore the possibilities of agreements on a multilateral approach on trade facilitation and transparency in government procurement.

In July 2004 the General Council presented for consideration and revision by WTO member states a new draft Doha Agenda Work Programme (the so-called 'July Package' of framework trade agreements) aimed at reviving the stalled Doha Development Round. Following intensive negotiations, the finalized July Package was adopted by the General Council at the beginning of August. The Package included an interim accord on agricultural subsidies that established guidelines for future Doha Round negotiations, entailing a key commitment by rich developed nations eventually to eliminate all agricultural export subsidies. Although no deadline was set for the completion of this process, it was agreed that maximum permitted subsidies would be reduced by 20% in the first year of the implementation of the new regime. The EU would remove some US $360m. of annual export subsidies, with similar concessions also to be made by the USA. The EU's subsidies to its milk and sugar producers and the USA's subsidies to its cotton farmers were withdrawn from the Package and were to be addressed by separate negotiations. Under the July Package all countries were to be required to reduce tariffs on agricultural imports, but the poorest countries would be set lower reduction targets and longer periods for their implementation.

The sixth Ministerial Conference, convened in Hong Kong, in December 2005, set a deadline of 30 April 2006 for finalizing details of the methods of reducing tariffs and subsidies (the 'modalities') in agriculture and industrial goods, with a view to concluding the Doha Round at the end of 2006. It was also agreed that duty- and quota-free access for at least 97% of least developed countries' exports should be achieved by 2008. However, in July 2006 the Doha Development Round of negotiations was suspended across all sectors, with all related deadlines postponed, owing to failure by the participating countries to reach a satisfactory final agreement on agricultural trade, and, in particular, deadlock on the issues of reductions in market access restrictions and domestic support mechanisms in the agriculture sector. Participants were urged by the WTO Director-General to reconsider their negotiating positions. In February 2007 the Director-General announced that negotiations across all sectors had been resumed. In June discussions between the EU, USA, India and Brazil, which were aimed at bridging the gaps in their negotiating positions and had been regarded as a basis for advancing the wider negotiations, failed to reach any agreement on the main areas of dispute i.e. farm subsidies and market access. In July the WTO Director-General endorsed compromise texts that had been negotiated for trade in agriculture and for non-agricultural market access.

The 2005 Ministerial Conference launched the Aid for Trade initiative, which provides a platform for developing countries to build the supply capacity and trade-related infrastructure necessary for implementing and benefiting from WTO agreements. In December 2011 the eighth Ministerial Conference determined to maintain, beyond 2011, Aid for Trade levels reflecting the average of the period 2006-08, and to pursue efforts with development banks to ensure the availability of trade finance to low-income states. In February 2012 WTO organized a workshop on Aid for Trade, sustainable development and the green economy.

Addressing the IMF in April 2008, the WTO Director-General urged WTO member governments to agree at ministerial level by the end of May a framework for cutting agricultural tariffs, agricultural subsidies and industrial tariffs. He emphasized the role of the WTO's rules-based trading system as a source of economic stability for governments, businesses and consumers, and indicated that the prompt finalization of the Doha Round would provide reassurance to international markets given the emerging climate of increased global financial uncertainty. Revised negotiating texts for trade in agriculture and non-agricultural market access were presented in May and two further revisions of the documents was released in July, prior to a formal meeting of the TNC held at end of that month. The Committee meeting failed, however, to reach agreement on the formal establishment of modalities in agriculture and non-agricultural market access, although the WTO Director-General reported that positions had converged in 18 of the 20 areas under discussion. Positions on the development of a special safeguard mechanism on farm products for developing countries reportedly remained in conflict. The seventh (Geneva) Ministerial Conference, held in late November–early December 2009, agreed that progress in the Doha Round should be assessed in the first quarter of 2010; accordingly, the TNC oversaw a phase of 'stocktaking' discussions in March. The eighth Ministerial Conference, held in Geneva in December 2011, acknowledged that, despite strong engagement to conclude the Doha Round, the negotiations remained at an *impasse*, and urged a refocusing of the discussions.

In October 2008 a task force was established within the WTO secretariat to address the effects of the ongoing global financial crisis. In January 2009 the WTO Director-General announced that WTO was to issue periodic reports on trends in global trade, and was to organize future meetings on trade finance, in order to support members with dealing with the global situation. During that month the WTO launched a database on regional trade agreements; a database on non-reciprocal preferential schemes was launched in July 2011. WTO, with UNCTAD, jointly lead an initiative on promoting trade—through combating protectionism, including through the conclusion of the Doha round, and by strengthening aid-for-trade financing-for-trade initiatives—the third of nine activities that were launched in April 2009 by the UN System Chief Executives Board for Co-ordination (CEB), with the aim of alleviating the impact on poor and vulnerable populations of the global crisis. From early 2009 WTO contributed, with the ILO, the IMF, the World Bank, and OECD (the co-ordinating agency), to the compilation of *A 'Global Charter'/ 'Legal Standard', Inventory of Possible Policy Instruments*, which aimed to stocktake the current range of financial policy instruments, as part of a united response to the financial crisis that involved establishing a shared 'global standard' of propriety and transparency for the future development of the global economic framework. The five organizations contributing to the *Inventory* had been invited by the G8 summit held in Hokkaido, Japan, in June 2008, to enhance their co-operation. In November–December 2009 the seventh WTO Ministerial Conference addressed the impact of the global financial crisis on least developed countries (numbering 49 at that time, of which 32 were WTO member states). In September 2011 WTO and the ILO jointly issued a publication entitled *Making Globalization Socially Sustainable*. In March 2012 WTO and OECD agreed to develop statistics on trade in 'value added'; accordingly, both organizations were to produce a publicly accessible database of trade flows estimated in value-added terms.

AGRICULTURE

The Final Act of the Uruguay Round extended previous GATT arrangements for trade in agricultural products through new rules and commitments to ensure more predictable and fair competition in the sector. All quantitive measures limiting market access for agricultural products were to be replaced by tariffs (i.e. a process of 'tariffication'), enabling more equal protection and access opportunities. All tariffs on agricultural items were to be reduced by 36% by developed countries, over a period of six years, and by 24% by developing countries (excluding least developed member states) over 10 years. A special treatment clause applied to 'sensitive' products (mainly rice) in four countries, for which limited import restrictions could be maintained. Efforts to reduce domestic support measures for agricultural products were to be based on calculations of total aggregate measurements of support (Total AMS) by each member state. A 20% reduction in Total AMS was required by developed countries over six years, and 13% over 10 years by developing countries. No reduction was required of least developed countries. Developed member countries were required to reduce the value and quantity of direct export subsidies by 36% and 21% respectively (on 1986–90 levels) over six years. For developing countries these reductions were to be two-thirds those of developed nations, over 10 years. A specific concern of least developed and net-food importing developing countries, which had previously relied on subsidized food products, was to be addressed through other food aid mechanisms and assistance for agricultural development. The situation was to be monitored by WTO's Committee on Agriculture. Negotiations on the further liberalization of agricultural markets were part of the WTO 'built-in' programme for 2000 or earlier, but remained a major area of contention. In March 2000 negotiations on market access in the agricultural sector commenced, under an interim chairman owing to a disagreement among participating states. The Doha Declaration, approved in that month, established a timetable for further negotiations on agriculture, which were initially scheduled to be concluded as part of the single undertaking on 1 January 2005. (The deadline was subsequently postponed indefinitely.) A compromise agreement was reached with the EU to commit to a reduction in export subsidies, with a view to phasing them out (without a firm deadline for their elimination). Member states agreed to aim for further reductions in market access restrictions and domestic support mechanisms, and to incorporate non-trade concerns, including environmental protection, food security and rural development, into the negotiations. In December 2005 the sixth Ministerial Conference set a deadline of 2013 for the elimination of agricultural export subsidies; a deadline of end-2006 was established for the elimination of export subsidies for cotton by developed countries. The Doha Round of negotiations and all associated deadlines have, however, subsequently been subject to delay (see above).

TEXTILES AND CLOTHING

From 1974–94 the former Multi-Fibre Arrangement (MFA) provided the basis of international trade concerning textiles and clothing, enabling the major importers to establish quotas and protect their domestic industries, through bilateral agreements, against more competitive low-cost goods from developing countries. MFA restrictions that were in place on 31 December 1994 were carried over into a new transitional 10-year Agreement on Textiles and Clothing (ATC) and were phased out through integration into GATT 1994, in four planned stages: products accounting for 16% of the total volume of textiles and clothing imports (at 1990 levels) to be integrated from 1 January 1995; a further 17% on 1 January 1998; not less than a further 18% on 1 January 2002; and all remaining products by 1 January 2005. Since the expiry on that date of the ATC, international trade in clothing and textiles has, as envisaged, been governed by general rules and disciplines embodied in the multilateral trading system.

TRADE IN SERVICES

The General Agreement on Trade in Services (GATS), which was negotiated during the GATT Uruguay Round, is the first set of multilaterally agreed and legally enforceable rules and disciplines ever negotiated to cover international trade in services. The GATS comprises a framework of general rules and disciplines, annexes addressing special conditions relating to individual sectors and national schedules of market access commitments. A Council for Trade in Services oversees the operation of the agreement.

The GATS framework consists of 29 articles, including the following set of basic obligations: total coverage of all internationally traded services; national treatment, i.e. according services and service suppliers of other members no less favourable treatment than that accorded to domestic services and suppliers; MFN treatment (see above), with any specific exemptions to be recorded prior to the implementation of the GATS, with a limit of 10 years' duration; transparency, requiring publication of all relevant national laws and legislations; bilateral agreements on recognition of standards and qualifications to be open to other members who wish to negotiate accession; no restrictions on international payments and transfers; progressive liberalization to be pursued; and market access and national treatment commitments to be bound and recorded in national schedules. These schedules, which include exemptions to the MFN principles, contain the negotiated and guaranteed conditions under which trade in services is conducted and are an integral part of the GATS.

Annexes to the GATS cover the movement of natural persons, permitting governments to negotiate specific commitments regarding the temporary stay of people for the purpose of providing a service; the right of governments to take measures in order to ensure the integrity and stability of the financial system; the role of telecommunications as a distinct sector of economic activity and as a means of supplying other economic activities; and air transport services, excluding certain activities relating to traffic rights.

At the end of the Uruguay Round governments agreed to continue negotiations in the following areas: basic telecommunications; maritime transport; movement of natural persons; and financial services. The Protocol to the GATS relating to movement of natural persons was concluded in July 1995. In May 1996 the USA withdrew from negotiations to conclude an agreement on maritime transport services. At the end of June the participating countries agreed to suspend the discussions and to recommence negotiations in 2000 (see below).

In July 1995 some 29 members signed an interim agreement to grant greater access to the banking, insurance, investment and securities sectors from August 1996. Negotiations to strengthen the agreement and to extend it to new signatories (including the USA, which had declined to sign the agreement, claiming lack of reciprocity by some Asian countries) commenced in April 1997. A final agreement was successfully concluded in December: 102 countries endorsed the elimination of restrictions on access to the financial services sectors from 1 March 1999, and agreed to subject those services to legally binding rules and disciplines. In late January 1999 some 35 signatory states had yet to ratify the financial services agreement, and its entry into force was postponed. Negotiations on trade in basic telecommunications began in May 1994 and were scheduled to conclude in April 1996. Before the final deadline, however, the negotiations were suspended, owing to US concerns, which included greater access to satellite telecommunications markets in Asia and greater control over foreign companies operating from the domestic markets. An agreement was finally concluded by the new deadline of 15 February 1997. Accordingly the largest telecommunications markets, i.e. the USA, the EU and Japan, were to eliminate all remaining restrictions on domestic and foreign competition in the industry by 1 January 1998 (although delays were granted to Spain, until December 1998, Ireland, until 2000, and Greece and Portugal, until 2003). The majority of the signatories to the accord also agreed on common rules to ensure that fair competition could be enforced by the WTO disputes settlement mechanism, and pledged their commitment to establishing a regulatory system for the telecommunications sector and guaranteeing transparency in government licensing. The agreement eventually entered into force in February 1998.

The negotiations to liberalize trade in services, suspended in 1996, were formally reopened in January 2000, with new guidelines and procedures for the negotiations approved in March 2001. The negotiations were incorporated into the Doha Agenda and were to be concluded as part of a single undertaking, initially by 1 January 2005, although the deadline was subsequently postponed.

INTELLECTUAL PROPERTY RIGHTS

The WTO Agreement on Trade-Related Aspects of Intellectual Property Rights (TRIPS), which entered into force on 1 January 1995, recognizes that widely varying standards in the protection and enforcement of intellectual property rights and the lack of multilateral disciplines dealing with international trade in counterfeit goods have been a growing source of tension in international economic relations. The TRIPS agreement aims to ensure that nationals of member states receive equally favourable treatment with regard to the protection of intellectual property and that adequate standards of intellectual property protection exist in all WTO member countries. These standards are largely based on the obligations of the Paris and Berne Conventions of WIPO, however, and the agreement aims to expand and enhance these where necessary, for example: computer programmes, to be protected as literary works for copyright purposes; definition of trade marks eligible for protection; stricter rules of geographical indications of consumer products; a 10-year protection period for industrial designs; a 20-year patent protection available for all inventions; tighter protection of layout design of integrated circuits; and protection for trade secrets and 'know-how' with a commercial value.

Under the agreement member governments are obliged to provide procedures and remedies to ensure the effective enforcement of intellectual property rights. Civil and administrative procedures outlined in the TRIPS include provisions on evidence, injunctions, judicial authority to order the disposal of infringing goods, and criminal procedures and penalties, in particular for trademark counterfeiting and copyright piracy. A one-year period from TRIPS' entry into force was envisaged for developed countries to bring their legislation and practices into conformity with the agreement. Developing countries were to do so in five years (or 10 years if an area of technology did not already have patent protection) and least developed countries in 11 years. A Council for Trade-Related Property Rights monitors the compliance of governments with the agreement and its operation. During 2000 the implementation of TRIPS was one the key areas of contention among WTO members. In November WTO initiated a review of TRIPS, although this was expected to consider alteration of the regime rather than of its implementation. At that time some 70 developing countries were failing to apply TRIPS rules. In November 2001 the Doha Ministerial Conference sought to resolve the ongoing dispute regarding the implementation of TRIPS in respect of pharmaceutical patents in developing countries. A separate declaration aimed to clarify a flexible interpretation of TRIPS in order for governments to meet urgent public health priorities. The deadline for some of the poorest countries to apply provisions on pharmaceutical patents was extended to 1 January 2016. The TRIPS Council was mandated to undertake further consideration of problems concerning compulsory licensing. The Doha Declaration also committed the Council to concluding, by the next (2003) Ministerial Conference, negotiations on a multilateral registration system for geographical indications for wines and spirits; however, this deadline was not achieved, and was subsequently postponed indefinitely. In November 2005 the original deadline of 1 January 2006 for least developed countries to bring their legislation and practices into conformity with TRIPS was extended by the Council for Trade-Related Property Rights to 1 July 2013; the Council also determined that technical assistance to support the application of the agreement in those member countries should be enhanced.

LEGAL FRAMEWORK

In addition to the binding agreements mentioned above, WTO aims to provide a comprehensive legal framework for the international trading system. Under GATT 1994 'anti-dumping' measures were permitted against imports of a product with an export price below its normal value, if these imports were likely to cause damage to a domestic industry. The WTO agreement provides for greater clarity and more detailed rules determining the application of these measures and determines settlement procedures in disputes relating to anti-dumping actions taken by WTO members. In general, anti-dumping measures were to be limited to five years. WTO's Agreement on Subsidies and Countervailing Measures is intended to expand on existing GATT agreements. It classifies subsidies into three categories: prohibited, which may be determined by the Dispute Settlement Body and must be immediately withdrawn; actionable, which must be withdrawn or altered if the subsidy is found to cause adverse effects on the interests of other members; and non-actionable, for example subsidies involving assistance to industrial research, assistance to disadvantaged regions or adaptation of facilities to meet new environmental requirements; non-actionable subsidies, however, were terminated in 1999. The Agreement also contains provisions on the use of duties to offset the effect of a subsidy (so-called countervailing measures) and establishes procedures for the initiation and conduct of investigations into this action. Countervailing measures must generally be terminated within five years of their imposition. Least developed countries, and developing countries with gross national product per capita of less than US $1,000, are exempt from disciplines on prohibited export subsidies; however, it was envisaged that these would be eliminated by 2003 in all other developing countries and by 2002 in countries with economies in transition. In November 2001 the Doha Ministerial Conference agreed to permit developing countries individually to request an extension of the interim period prior to elimination; consequently, a number of such member countries were granted extensions.

WTO members may take safeguard actions to protect a specific domestic industry from a damaging increase of imported products. However, the WTO agreement aims to clarify criteria for imposing safeguards, their duration (normally to be no longer than four years, which may be extended to eight years) and consultations on trade compensation for the exporting countries. Safeguard measures are not applicable to products from developing countries as long as their share of imports of the product concerned does not exceed 3%.

Further legal arrangements act to ensure the following: that technical regulations and standards (including testing and certification procedures) do not create unnecessary obstacles to trade; that import licensing procedures are transparent and predictable; that the valuation of goods for customs purposes are fair and uniform; that GATT principles and obligations apply to import preshipment inspection activities; the fair and transparent administration of rules of origin; and that no investment measures which may restrict or distort trade may be applied. A Working Group on Notification Obligations and Procedures aims to ensure that members fulfil their notification requirements, which facilitate the transparency and surveillance of the trading rules.

PLURILATERAL AGREEMENT

The majority of GATT agreements became multilateral obligations when the WTO became operational in 1995; however, four agreements, which had a selective group of signatories, remained in effect. These so-called plurilateral agreements, the Agreement on Trade in Civil Aircraft, the Agreement on Government Procurement, the International Dairy Agreement and the International Bovine Meat Agreement, aimed to increase international co-operation and fair and open trade and competition in these areas. The bovine meat and dairy agreements were terminated in 1997. The remaining two plurilateral agreements establish their own management bodies, which are required to report to the General Council.

TRADE POLICY REVIEW MECHANISM

The mechanism, which was established provisionally in 1989, was given a permanent role in the WTO. Through regular monitoring and surveillance of national trade policies the mechanism aims to increase the transparency and understanding of trade policies and practices and to enable assessment of the effects of policies on the world trading system. In addition, it records efforts made by governments to bring domestic trade legislation into conformity with WTO provisions and to implement WTO commitments. Reviews are conducted in the Trade Policy Review Body on the basis of a policy statement of the government under review and an independent report prepared by the WTO Secretariat. Under the mechanism the world's four largest traders, the EU, the USA, Japan and Canada, were to be reviewed every two years. Special groups were established to examine new regional free trade arrangements and the trade policies of acceding countries. In February 1996 a single Committee on Regional Trade Agreements was established, superseding these separate working parties. The Committee aimed to ensure that these groupings contributed to the process of global trade liberalization and to study the implications of these arrangements on the multilateral system. By the end of 2011 more than 500 regional trade agreements amongst WTO member states had been notified to the Organization; 25 new notifications were made in 2011.

SETTLEMENT OF DISPUTES

A separate annex to the WTO agreement determines a unified set of rules and procedures to govern the settlement of all WTO disputes, substantially reinforcing the GATT procedures. WTO members are committed not to undertake unilateral action against perceived violations of the trade rules, but to seek recourse in the dispute settlement mechanism and abide by its findings.

The agreements that may be cited in the bilateral consultations (first stage, see below) of the disputes process relate to: Establishing the WTO (cited in 44 cases by June 2012); Agriculture (cited in 68 cases by June 2012); Anti-dumping (Article VI of GATT 1994) (90 cases); Civil Aircraft (no citations); Customs Valuation (Article VII of GATT 1994) (cited in 15 cases); Dispute Settlement Understanding (15 cases); GATT 1947 (one case); GATT 1994 (349 cases); Government Procurement (four cases); Import Licensing (35 cases); Intellectual Property (TRIPS) (31 cases); Preshipment Inspection (no citations); Rules of Origin (seven cases); Safeguards (40 cases); Sanitary and Phytosanitary Measures (SPS) (38 cases); Services (GATS) (22 cases); Subsidies and Countervailing Measures (91 cases); Technical Barriers to Trade (TBT) (43 cases); Textiles and Clothing (16 cases); Trade-Related Investment Measures (TRIMs) (29 cases); Protocol of Accession (24 cases).

The first stage of the process requires bilateral consultations between the members concerned in an attempt to conclude a mutually acceptable solution to the issue. These may be undertaken through the good offices and mediation efforts of the Director-General. Only after a consultation period of 60 days may the complainant ask the General Council, convened as the Dispute Settlement Body (DSB), to establish an independent panel to examine the case, which then does so within the terms of reference of the agreement cited. Each party to the dispute submits its arguments and then presents its case before the panel. Third parties which notify their interest in the dispute may also present views at the first substantive meeting of the panel. At this stage an expert review group may be appointed to provide specific scientific or technical advice. The panel submits sections and then a full interim report of its findings to the parties, who may then request a further review involving additional meetings. A final report should be submitted to the parties by the panel within six months of its establishment, or within three months in cases of urgency, including those related to perishable goods. Final reports are normally adopted by the DSB within 60 days of issuance. In the case of a measure being found to be inconsistent with the relevant WTO agreement, the panel recommends ways in which the member may bring the measure into conformity with the agreement. However, under the WTO mechanism either party has the right to appeal against the decision and must notify the DSB of its intentions before adoption of the final report. Appeal proceedings, which are limited to issues of law and the legal interpretation covered by the panel report, are undertaken by three members of the Appellate Body within a maximum period of 90 days. The report of the Appellate Body must be unconditionally accepted by the parties to the dispute (unless there is a consensus within the DSB against its adoption). If the recommendations of the panel or appeal report are not implemented immediately, or within a 'reasonable period' as determined by the DSB, the parties are obliged to negotiate mutually acceptable compensation pending full implementation. Failure to agree compensation may result in the DSB authorizing the complainant to suspend concessions or obligations against the other party. In any case the DSB monitors the implementation of adopted recommendations or rulings, while any outstanding cases remain on its agenda until the issue is resolved.

By June 2012 438 trade complaints had been notified to the DSB since 1995. The DSB established nine new panels in 2011, to adjudicate 13 new cases, and nine appeals of Panel Reports were filed with the Appellate Body. During 1995–2011 the Appellate Body circulated 108 final reports. Since the early 2000s a rising proportion of disputes have been filed by developing and emerging economies. By the end of 2011 some 98 disputes had been filed by the USA; 85 by the EU; 33 by Canada; 25 by Brazil; 21 by Mexico; and 19 by India. The largest case yet to be raised in the dispute settlement system was filed in October 2004 by the USA, concerning subsidies provided by the EU to the aircraft manufacturer Airbus SAS; the EU, meanwhile, filed a similar case in June 2005 regarding US government assistance to Boeing. The Appellate Body adjudicated in May 2011 that some EU subsidies to Airbus had been illegal, and in March 2012 it ruled that subsidies granted to Boeing by the US Government were also illegitimate.

In late 1997 the DSB initiated a review of the WTO's understanding on dispute settlement, as required by the Marrakesh Agreement. The Doha Declaration, adopted in November 2001, mandated further that negotiations to be conducted on the review and on additional proposals to amend the dispute procedure as a separate undertaking from the rest of the work programme.

The Agreement on the Application of Sanitary and Phytosanitary Measures aims to regulate world-wide standards of food safety and animal and plant health in order to encourage the mutual recognition of standards and conformity, so as to facilitate trade in these products. The Agreement includes provisions on control inspection and approval procedures. In September 1997, in the first case to be brought under the Agreement, a dispute panel of the WTO ruled that the EU's ban on imports of hormone-treated beef and beef products from the USA and Canada was in breach of international trading rules. In January 1998 the Appellate Body upheld the panel's ruling, but expressed its support for restrictions to ensure food standards if there was adequate scientific evidence of risks to human health. The EU maintained the ban, against resistance from the USA, while it carried out scientific risk assessments.

In December 2009 representatives of the EU and Latin American countries initialled the EU-Latin America Bananas Agreement, under which (with a view to ending a 15-year dispute) the EU was gradually to reduce its import tariff on bananas from Latin American countries, from €176 to €114 per metric ton, by 2017. On their side, Latin American banana-producing countries undertook not to demand further tariff reductions; and to withdraw several related cases against the EU pending at the WTO. In response to the Agreement, the US authorities determined to settle a parallel dispute with the EU at the WTO relating to bananas.

CO-OPERATION WITH OTHER ORGANIZATIONS

WTO is mandated to pursue co-operation with the IMF and the World Bank, as well as with other multilateral organizations, in order to achieve greater coherence in global economic policy-making. In November 1994 the preparatory committee of the WTO resolved not to incorporate the new organization into the UN structure as a specialized agency. Instead, co-operation arrangements with the IMF and the World Bank were to be developed. In addition, efforts were pursued to enhance co-operation with UNCTAD in research, trade and technical issues. The Directors-General of the two organizations agreed to meet at least twice a year in order to develop the working relationship. In particular, co-operation was to be undertaken in WTO's special programme of activities for Africa, which aimed to help African countries expand and diversify their trade and benefit from the global trading system. Since 1997 WTO has co-operated with the IMF, ITC, UNCTAD, UNDP and the World Bank in an Integrated Framework for trade-related technical assistance to least developed countries. An enhanced Integrated Framework (EIF) was adopted in May 2007. Annually (most recently in March 2012) WTO, the IMF, the World Bank, UNCTAD and ECOSOC participate in high-level consultations.

From early 2009 WTO, the ILO, the IMF, the World Bank, and OECD entered into co-operation on the establishment of a new global standard for future economic development, in response to the ongoing global financial crisis (see above); it was announced in April 2010 that the inter-agency collaboration would be intensified. In June 2009 WTO and UNEP jointly issued a report entitled *Trade and Climate Change*, reviewing the intersections between trade and climate change from the perspectives of: the science of climate change; economics; multilateral efforts to combat climate change; and the effects on trade of national climate change policies.

In July 2010 WTO, WIPO and WHO organized a symposium to initiate a process of co-operation in addressing means of improving the access of poorer populations to necessary medicines.

International Trade Centre (UNCTAD/WTO): Palais des Nations, 1211 Geneva 10, Switzerland; tel. 227300111; fax 227334439; e-mail itcreg@intracen.org; internet www.intracen.org; f. 1964 by GATT; jointly operated with the UN (through UNCTAD) since 1968; ITC works with developing countries in product and market development, the development of trade support services, trade information, human resource development, international purchasing and supply management, and needs assessment and programme design for trade promotion; allocated US $41.3m. under the proposed UN budget for 2012–13; publs *International Trade Forum* (quarterly), market studies, handbooks, etc.

Executive Director: PATRICIA R. FRANCIS (Jamaica).

Finance

The WTO's 2012 budget amounted to 196m. Swiss francs, financed mainly by contributions from members in proportion to their share of total trading conducted by WTO members.

Publications

Annual Report (2 volumes).
Annual Report of the Appellate Body.
International Trade Statistics (annually).
World Trade Report (annually).
World Trade Review (3 a year).
World Trade Report (annually).
WTO Focus (monthly).

PART FOUR

Other International Organizations

OTHER INTERNATIONAL ORGANIZATIONS

Agriculture, Food, Forestry and Fisheries

(for organizations concerned with agricultural commodities, see Commodities)

African Agricultural Technology Foundation: POB 30709, Nairobi 00100, Kenya; tel. (20) 4223700; fax (20) 4223701; e-mail aatf@aatf-africa.org; internet www.aatf-africa.org; f. 2002; aims to facilitate and promote public/private partnerships for the access and delivery of agricultural technologies for use by resource poor smallholder farmers; Exec. Dir DENIS TUMWESIGYE KYETERE (Uganda).

African Feed Resources Network (AFRINET): c/o ASARECA, POB 765, Entebbe, Uganda; tel. (41) 320212; fax (41) 321126; e-mail asareca@imul.com; f. 1991 by merger of two African livestock fodder and one animal nutrition research networks; aims to co-ordinate research in all aspects of animal feeding and to strengthen national programmes to develop solutions for inadequate livestock food supplies and poor quality feeds; mems: in 34 countries; publ. *AFRINET Newsletter* (quarterly).

African Timber Organization (ATO): BP 1077, Libreville, Gabon; tel. 732928; fax 734030; e-mail oab-gabon@internetgabon.com; f. 1976 to enable members to study and co-ordinate ways of ensuring the optimum utilization and conservation of their forests; mems: 13 African countries; publs *ATO Information Bulletin* (quarterly), *International Magazine of African Timber* (2 a year).

Arab Authority for Agricultural Investment and Development (AAAID): POB 2102, Khartoum, Sudan; tel. (18) 7096100; fax (18) 7096295; e-mail info@aaaid.org; internet www.aaaid.org; f. 1976 to accelerate agricultural development in the Arab world and to ensure food security; acts principally by equity participation in agricultural projects in member countries; AAAID has adopted new programmes to help raise productivity of food agricultural products and introduced zero-tillage farming technology for developing the rain-fed sector, which achieved a substantial increase in the yields of grown crops, including sorghum, cotton, sesame, and sunflower; mems: 20 countries; Pres. and Chair. ALI BIN SAEED AL-SHARHAN; publs *Journal of Agricultural Investment* (English and Arabic), *Extension and Investment Bulletins*, *Annual Report* (Arabic and English), *AAAID Newsletter* (quarterly).

Association for the Advancement of Agricultural Science in Africa (AAASA): POB 30087, Addis Ababa, Ethiopia; tel. (1) 44-3536; f. 1968 to promote the development and application of agricultural sciences and the exchange of ideas; to encourage Africans to enter training; holds several seminars each year in different African countries; mems: individual agricultural scientists, research institutes in 63 countries; publs *Journal* (2 a year), *Newsletter* (quarterly).

Association of Agricultural Research Institutions in the Near East and North Africa: POB 950764, 11195 Amman, Jordan; tel. (6) 5525750; fax (6) 5525930; e-mail icarda-jordan@cgiar.org; internet www.aarinena.org; f. 1985; aims to strengthen co-operation among national, regional and international research institutions; operates the internet-based Near East and North Africa Rural and Agricultural Knowledge and Information Network (NERAKIN); Exec. Sec. IBRAHIM YUSUF HAMDAN (Jordan).

AVRDC—the World Vegetable Center: POB 42, Shanhua, Tainan 74199, Taiwan; tel. (6) 5837801; fax (6) 5830009; e-mail info@worldveg.org; internet www.avrdc.org; f. 1971 as the Asian Vegetable Research and Development Center; aims to enhance the nutritional well-being and raise the incomes of the poor in rural and urban areas of developing countries, through improved varieties and methods of vegetable production, marketing and distribution; runs an experimental farm, laboratories, gene-bank, greenhouses, quarantine house, insectarium, library and weather station; provides training for research and production specialists in tropical vegetables; exchanges and disseminates vegetable germplasm through regional offices in the developing world; serves as a clearing-house for vegetable research information; and undertakes scientific publishing; mems: Japan, Republic of Korea, Philippines, Taiwan, Thailand, USA; Dir-Gen. Dr DYNO KEATINGE; publs *Annual Report*, *Technical Bulletin*, *Proceedings*.

CAB International (CABI): Nosworthy Way, Wallingford, Oxon, OX10 8DE, United Kingdom; tel. (1491) 832111; fax (1491) 829292; e-mail enquiries@cabi.org; internet www.cabi.org; f. 1929 as the Imperial Agricultural Bureaux (later Commonwealth Agricultural Bureaux), current name adopted in 1985; aims to improve human welfare world-wide through the generation, dissemination and application of scientific knowledge in support of sustainable development; places particular emphasis on sustainable agriculture, forestry, human health and the management of natural resources, with priority given to the needs of developing countries; a separate microbiology centre, in Egham, Surrey (UK), undertakes research, consultancy, training, capacity-building and institutional development measures in sustainable pest management, biosystematics and molecular biology, ecological applications and environmental and industrial microbiology; compiles and publishes extensive information (in a variety of print and electronic forms) on aspects of agriculture, forestry, veterinary medicine, the environment and natural resources, and Third World rural development; maintains regional centres in the People's Republic of China, India, Kenya, Malaysia, Pakistan, Switzerland, Trinidad and Tobago, and the USA; mems: 45 countries and territories; Chair. JOHN RIPLEY (United Kingdom); CEO Dr TREVOR NICHOLLS (United Kingdom).

Collaborative International Pesticides Analytical Council Ltd (CIPAC): c/o Dr Ralf Hänel, Referat 206, Messeweg 11/12 38104, Braunschweig, Germany; tel. (531) 2993506; fax (531) 2993002; e-mail cipac@acw.admin.ch; internet www.cipac.org; f. 1957 to organize international collaborative work on methods of analysis for pesticides used in crop protection; 25 mems, 8 hon. life mems; Chair. Dr RALF HÄNEL (Germany); Sec. Dr LÁZLÓ BURA (Hungary).

Commission for the Conservation of Southern Bluefin Tuna: Unit 1, J.A.A. House, 19 Napier Close, Deakin, Canberra, ACT 2600, Australia; tel. (2) 6282-8396; fax (2) 6282-8407; e-mail sec@ccsbt.org; internet www.ccsbt.org; f. 1994 when the Convention for the Conservation of Southern Bluefin Tuna (signed in May 1993) entered into force; aims to promote sustainable management and conservation of the southern bluefin tuna; holds an annual meeting and annual scientific meeting; collates relevant research, scientific information and data; encourages non-member countries and bodies to co-operate in the conservation and optimum utilization of Southern Bluefin Tuna through accession to the Convention or adherence to the Commission's management arrangements; mems: Australia, Japan, Republic of Korea, New Zealand; co-operating non-mems: Philippines, South Africa, European Community; Exec. Sec. ROBERT (BOB) KENNEDY.

Desert Locust Control Organization for Eastern Africa (DLCOEA): POB 4255, Addis Ababa, Ethiopia; tel. (1) 461477; fax (1) 460296; e-mail dlc@ethionet.et; internet www.dlcoea.org.et; f. 1962 to promote effective control of desert locust in the region and to conduct research into the locust's environment and behaviour; also assists member states in the monitoring, forecasting and extermination of other migratory pests; mems: Djibouti, Eritrea, Ethiopia, Kenya, Somalia, Sudan, Tanzania, Uganda; Dir GASPAR ATTMAN MALLYA; Co-ordinator JAMES M. GATIMU; publs *Desert Locust Situation Reports* (monthly), *Annual Report*, technical reports.

European and Mediterranean Plant Protection Organization (EPPO): 21 blvd Richard Lenoir, 75011 Paris, France; tel. 1-45-20-77-94; fax 1-70-76-65-47; e-mail hq@eppo.fr; internet www.eppo.org; f. 1951, present name adopted in 1955; aims to promote international co-operation between government plant protection services to prevent the introduction and spread of pests and diseases of plants and plant products; mems: govts of 50 countries and territories; Dir-Gen. RINGOLDS ARNITIS; publs

EPPO Bulletin, Data Sheets on Quarantine Organisms, Guidelines for the Efficacy Evaluation of Pesticides, Crop Growth Stage Keys, Summary of the Phytosanitary Regulations of EPPO Member Countries, Reporting Service.

European Association for Animal Production (EAAP) (Fédération européenne de zootechnie): Via G. Tomassetti 3 A/ 1, 00161 Rome, Italy; tel. (06) 44202639; fax (06) 44266798; e-mail eaap@eaap.org; internet www.eaap.org; f. 1949 to help improve the conditions of animal production and meet consumer demand; holds annual meetings; mems: asscns in 41 countries; Sec.-Gen. ANDREA ROSATI (Italy); publs *Animal* (International Journal of Animal Biosciences), *EAAP News*.

European Association for Research on Plant Breeding (EUCARPIA): c/o Agricultural Research Institute of the Hungarian Academy of Sciences, 2462 Martonvásár, Brunszvik u2, Hungary; tel. (22) 569550; fax (22) 460213; e-mail eucarpia@mgki.hu; internet www.eucarpia.org; f. 1956 to promote scientific and technical co-operation in the plant breeding field; mems: 1,100 individuals, 65 corporate mems; Pres. Dr ZOLTÁN BEDŐ (Hungary); Sec.-Gen. Dr LÁSZLÓ LÁNG (Hungary); publ. *EUCARPIA Bulletin*.

European Grassland Federation (EGF): Dr Willy Kessler, c/o Agroscope Reckenholz-Tänikon Research Station ART, Reckenholzstr. 191, 8046, Zürich, Switzerland; tel. 443777376; fax 443770201; e-mail fedsecretary@europeangrassland.org; internet www.europeangrassland.org; f. 1963 to facilitate and maintain liaison between European grassland organizations and to promote the interchange of scientific and practical knowledge and experience; holds General Meeting every two years and a Symposium in the intervening year; mems: 31 full and 4 corresponding member countries in Europe; Pres. Prof. Dr PIOTR STYPINSKI; Sec. Dr WILLY KESSLER (Switzerland); publ. *Grassland Science in Europe*.

European Livestock and Meat Trading Union (UECBV): 81A rue de la Loi, 4th floor, 1040 Brussels, Belgium; tel. (2) 230-46-03; fax (2) 230-94-00; e-mail info@uecbv.eu; internet www.uecbv.eu; f. 1952 to study problems of the European livestock and meat trade and inform members of all relevant legislation; acts as an international arbitration commission; conducts research on agricultural markets, quality of livestock, and veterinary regulations; incorporates the European Association of Livestock Markets and the Young European Meat Committee; mems: 50 national orgs in 31 countries, representing some 20,000 companies; Pres. LAURENT SPANGHERO NUTRINAT; Sec.-Gen. JEAN-LUC MERIAUX.

European Society for Sugar Technology (ESST): Lückhoffstr. 16, 14129 Berlin, Germany; tel. (30) 8035678; fax (30) 8032049; e-mail mail@esst-sugar.org; internet www.esst-sugar.org; Pres. DENIS BOURÉE (France); Sec. Dr JÜRGEN BRUHNS (Germany).

Indian Ocean Tuna Commission (IOTC): POB 1011, Victoria, Mahé, Seychelles; tel. 4225494; fax 4224364; e-mail iotc.secretary@iotc.org; internet www.iotc.org; f. 1996 as a regional fisheries organization with a mandate for the conservation and management of tuna and tuna-like species in the Indian Ocean; mems: Australia, Belize, People's Republic of China, the Comoros, European Union, Eritrea, France, Guinea, India, Indonesia, Iran, Japan, Kenya, Republic of Korea, Madagascar, Malaysia, Maldives, Mauritius, Mozambique, Oman, Pakistan, Philippines, Seychelles, Sudan, Sri Lanka, Tanzania, Thailand, United Kingdom, Vanuatu; co-operating non-contracting parties: Senegal, South Africa; Exec. Sec. ALEJANDRO ANGANUZZI (Argentina).

Inter-American Association of Agricultural Librarians, Documentalists and Information Specialists (Asociación Interamericana de Bibliotecarios, Documentalistas y Especialistas en Información Agrícolas—AIBDA): c/o IICA-CIDIA, Apdo 55-2200 Coronado, Costa Rica; tel. 2216-0222; fax 2216-0291; e-mail info@aibda.com; internet www.aibda.com; f. 1953 to promote professional improvement through technical publications and meetings, and to promote improvement of library services in agricultural sciences; mems: 653 in 31 countries and territories; Pres. RUBÉN URBIZAGÁSTEGUI (Peru); publ. *Revista AIBDA* (2 a year).

Inter-American Tropical Tuna Commission (IATTC): 8604 La Jolla Shores Drive, La Jolla, CA 92037-1508, USA; tel. (858) 546-7100; fax (858) 546-7133; e-mail info@iattc.org; internet www.iattc.org; f. 1950; administers two programmes, the Tuna-Billfish Programme and the Tuna-Dolphin Programme. The principal responsibilities of the Tuna-Billfish Programme are: to study the biology of the tunas and related species of the eastern Pacific Ocean to estimate the effects of fishing and natural factors on their abundance; to recommend appropriate conservation measures in order to maintain stocks at levels which will afford maximum sustainable catches; and to collect information on compliance with Commission resolutions. The principal functions of the Tuna-Dolphin Programme are: to monitor the abundance of dolphins and their mortality incidental to purse-seine fishing in the eastern Pacific Ocean; to study the causes of mortality of dolphins during fishing operations and promote the use of fishing techniques and equipment that minimize these mortalities; to study the effects of different fishing methods on the various fish and other animals of the pelagic ecosystem; and to provide a secretariat for the International Dolphin Conservation Programme; mems: Belize, Canada, People's Republic of China, Colombia, Costa Rica, Ecuador, El Salvador, European Union, France, Guatemala, Japan, Kiribati, Republic of Korea, Mexico, Nicaragua, Panama, Peru, Chinese Taipei (Taiwan), USA, Vanuatu, Venezuela; co-operating non-contracting party: Cook Islands; Dir GUILLERMO A. COMPEÁN; publs *Bulletin* (irregular), *Annual Report*, *Fishery Status Report*, *Stock Assessment Report* (annually), *Special Report* (irregular).

International Association for Cereal Science and Technology (ICC): Marxergasse 2, 1030 Vienna, Austria; tel. (1) 707-72-020; fax (1) 707-72-040; e-mail office@icc.or.at; internet www.icc.or.at; f. 1955 (as the International Association for Cereal Chemistry, name changed 1986); aims to promote international co-operation in the field of cereal science and technology through the dissemination of information and the development of standard methods of testing and analysing products; mems: 49 mem. and 6 observer mem. states; Pres. Prof. MARINA CARCEA (Italy) (2011–12); Pres. Elect JOEL ABECASSIS (France) (2013–14); Sec.-Gen. and CEO Dr ROLAND POMS (Austria).

International Association for Vegetation Science (IAVS): c/o Nina A.C. Smits, IAVS Administration, Wes Beekhuizenweg 3, 6871 VJ Renkum, Netherlands; tel. (317) 477914; fax (317) 424988; e-mail admin@iavs.org; internet www.iavs.org; f. 1938; mems: 1,500 in 70 countries; Pres. MARTIN DIEKMANN (Germany); Sec. SUSAN WISER (New Zealand); publs *Journal of Vegetation Science*, *Applied Vegetation Science*.

International Association of Agricultural Economists (IAAE): 555 East Wells St, Suite 1100, Milwaukee, WI 53202, USA; tel. (414) 918-3199; fax (414) 276-3349; e-mail iaae@execinc.com; internet www.iaae-agecon.org; f. 1929 to foster development of agricultural economic sciences; aims to further the application of research into agricultural processes; works to improve economic and social conditions for agricultural and rural life; mems: in 83 countries; Pres. KEIJIRO OTSUKA (Japan); Pres. Elect Prof. JOHAN SWINNEN (Belgium); Sec. and Treas. WALTER J. ARMBRUSTER (USA); publs *Agricultural Economics* (8 a year), *IAAE Newsletter* (2 a year).

International Association of Agricultural Information Specialists: c/o Toni Greider, POB 63, Lexington, KY 40588-0063, USA; fax (859) 257-8379; e-mail info@iaald.org; internet www.iaald.org; f. 1955 to provide educational and networking opportunities for agricultural information professionals worldwide; aims to enable its members to create, capture, access and disseminate information to achieve a more productive and sustainable use of the world's land, water, and renewable natural resources and to contribute to improved livelihoods of rural communities through educational programmes, conferences, and networking opportunities; affiliated to INFITA; mems: 400 in 84 countries; Pres. FREDERICO SANCHO (Costa Rica); Sec.-Treas. TONI GREIDER (USA); publ. *Agricultural Information Worldwide*.

International Association of Horticultural Producers: Oude Herenweg 10, 2215 RZ Voorhout, Netherlands; e-mail sg@aiph.org; internet www.aiph.org; f. 1948; represents the common interests of commercial horticultural producers in the international field; authorizes international horticultural exhibitions; mems: national asscns in 25 countries; Pres. DOEKE FABER (Netherlands); Sec.-Gen. SJAAK LANGESLAG (Netherlands); publ. *Statistical Yearbook*.

International Bee Research Association (IBRA): 16 North Rd, Cardiff, CF10 3DY, United Kingdom; tel. (29) 2037-2409; fax (56) 0113-5640; e-mail mail@ibra.org.uk; internet www.ibra.org.uk; f. 1949 to further bee research and provide an information service for bee scientists and beekeepers world-wide; mems: 1,200 in 130 countries; Exec. Dir SARAH JONES (United Kingdom); publs *Apicultural Abstracts* (quarterly), *Journal of Apicultural Research* (quarterly), *Bee World* (quarterly).

International Centre for Agricultural Research in the Dry Areas (ICARDA): POB 5466, Aleppo, Syria; tel. (21) 2213433; fax (21) 2213490; e-mail icarda@cgiar.org; internet www.icarda.org; f. 1977; aims to improve the production of lentils, barley and fava beans throughout the developing world; supports the improvement of on-farm water-use efficiency, rangeland and small-ruminant production in all dry-area developing countries; within the West and Central Asia and North Africa region promotes the improvement of bread and durum wheat and chickpea production and of farming systems; undertakes research, training and dissemination of information, in co-operation with national, regional and international research institutes, universities and ministries of agriculture, in order to enhance production, alleviate poverty and promote sustainable natural resource management practices; member of the network of 15 agricultural research centres supported by the Consultative Group on International Agricultural Research (CGIAR); Dir-Gen. Dr MAHMOUD MOHAMED BASHIR EL-SOLH; publs *Annual Report*, *Caravan Newsletter* (2 a year).

International Centre for Tropical Agriculture (Centro Internacional de Agricultura Tropical—CIAT): Apdo Aéreo 6713, Cali, Colombia; tel. (2) 445-0000; fax (2) 445-0073; e-mail ciat@cgiar.org; internet www.ciat.cgiar.org; f. 1967 to contribute to the alleviation of hunger and poverty in tropical developing countries by using new techniques in agriculture research and training; focuses on production problems in field beans, cassava, rice and tropical pastures in the tropics; Dir-Gen. RUBEN G. ECHEVERRÍA; publs *Annual Report*, *Growing Affinities* (2 a year), *Pasturas Tropicales* (3 a year), catalogue of publications.

International Commission for the Conservation of Atlantic Tunas (ICCAT): Calle Corazón de María 8, 28002 Madrid, Spain; tel. (91) 4165600; fax (91) 4152612; e-mail info@iccat.es; internet www.iccat.int; f. 1969 under the provisions of the International Convention for the Conservation of Atlantic Tunas (1966) to maintain the populations of tuna and tuna-like species in the Atlantic Ocean and adjacent seas at levels that permit the maximum sustainable catch; collects statistics; conducts studies; mems: 48 contracting parties; Chair. M. MIYAHARA (Japan); Exec. Sec. DRISS MESKI (Morocco); publs *ICCAT Biennial Report*, *ICCAT Collective Vol. of Scientific Papers*, *Statistical Bulletin* (annually), *Data Record* (annually).

International Committee for Animal Recording (ICAR): Via Tomassetti 3-1/A, 00161, Rome, Italy; tel. (06) 44202639; fax (06) 44266798; e-mail icar@icar.org; internet www.icar.org; f. 1951 to extend and improve the work of recording and to standardize methods; mems: in 58 countries; Pres. UFFE LAURITSEN (Denmark); Sec. REINHARD REENTS (Germany).

International Crops Research Institute for the Semi-Arid Tropics (ICRISAT): Patancheru, Andhra Pradesh 502 324, India; tel. (40) 30713071; fax (40) 30713074; e-mail icrisat@cgiar.org; internet www.icrisat.org; f. 1972 to promote the genetic improvement of crops and for research on the management of resources in the world's semi-arid tropics, with the aim of reducing poverty and protecting the environment; research covers all physical and socio-economic aspects of improving farming systems on unirrigated land; maintains regional centres in Nairobi, Kenya (for eastern and southern Africa) and in Niamey, Niger (for western and central Africa); Dir-Gen. Dr WILLIAM D. DAR (Philippines); publs *ICRISAT Report* (annually), *Journal of Semi-Arid Tropical Agricultural Research* (2 a year), information and research bulletins.

International Dairy Federation (IDF): 70B blvd Auguste Reyers, 1030 Brussels, Belgium; tel. (2) 733-98-88; fax (2) 733-04-13; e-mail info@fil-idf.org; internet www.fil-idf.org; f. 1903 to link all dairy asscns, in order to encourage the solution of scientific, technical and economic problems affecting the dairy industry; holds annual World Dairy Summit (2012: Cape Town, South Africa, in Nov.); mems: national cttees in 53 countries; Pres. RICHARD DOYLE; publs *Bulletin of IDF*, *IDF-ISO Standard Methods of Analysis*.

International Federation of Agricultural Producers (IFAP): 60 rue St-Lazare, 75009 Paris, France; tel. 1-45-26-05-53; fax 1-48-74-72-12; e-mail ifap@ifap.org; internet www.ifap.org; f. 1946 to represent, in the international field, the interests of agricultural producers; encourages the exchange of information and ideas; works to develop understanding of world problems and their effects upon agricultural producers; encourages sustainable patterns of agricultural development; holds conference every two years; mems: national farmers' orgs and agricultural co-operatives of 83 countries; Pres. AJAY VASHEE (Zambia); Sec.-Gen. DAVID KING; publs *The World Farmer* (monthly), *Proceedings of General Conferences*.

International Federation of Beekeepers' Associations (APIMONDIA): Corso Vittorio Emanuele II 101, 00186 Rome, Italy; tel. (06) 6852286; fax (06) 6852287; e-mail apimondia@mclink.it; internet www.apimondia.com; f. 1949; collects and brings up to date documentation on international beekeeping; carries out studies into the particular problems of beekeeping; organizes international congresses, seminars, symposia and meetings; co-operates with other international organizations interested in beekeeping, in particular, with the FAO; mems: 112 asscns from 75 countries; Pres. GILLES RATIA (France); Sec.-Gen. RICCARDO JANNONI-SEBASTIANINI (Italy); publs *Dictionary of Beekeeping Terms*, *AGROVOC* (thesaurus of agricultural terms), studies.

International Food Policy Research Institute (IFPRI): 2033 K St, NW, Washington, DC 20006, USA; tel. (202) 862-5600; fax (202) 467-4439; e-mail ifpri@cgiar.org; internet www.ifpri.org; f. 1975; co-operates with academic and other institutions in further research; develops policies for cutting hunger and malnutrition; committed to increasing public awareness of food policies; Dir-Gen. SHENGGEN FAN (People's Republic of China).

International Service for National Agricultural Research (ISNAR): IFPRI, ISNAR Division, ILRI, POB 5689, Addis Ababa, Ethiopia; tel. (11) 646-3215; fax (11) 646-2927; e-mail ifpri-addisababa@cgiar.org; fmrly based in The Hague, Netherlands, the ISNAR Program relocated to Addis Ababa in 2004, under the governance of IFPRI; Dir Dr WILBERFORCE KISAMBA-MUGERWA.

International Hop Growers' Convention: Malgajeva 18, 3000 Celje, Slovenia; tel. (3) 712-16-00; fax (3) 712-16-20; e-mail martin.pavlovic@guest.arnes.si; internet www.ihgc.org; f. 1950; acts as a centre for the collection of national reports and global data on hop production and information management on the hop industry among member countries, estimates the world crop and promotes scientific research; mems: national hop producers' asscns and hop trading companies in 19 countries world-wide; Sec.-Gen. Dr MARTIN PAVLOVIČ.

International Institute for Beet Research (IIRB): 40 rue Washington, 1050 Brussels, Belgium; Holtenser Landstr. 77, 37079 Göttingen, Germany; tel. (551) 500-65-84; fax (551) 500-65-85; e-mail mail@iirb.org; internet www.iirb.org; f. 1932 to promote research and the exchange of information; organizes congresses and study group meetings; mems: 400 in 28 countries; Sec.-Gen. STEPHANIE KLUTH (Germany).

International Institute of Tropical Agriculture (IITA): Oyo Rd, PMB 5320, Ibadan, Oyo State, Nigeria; tel. (2) 7517472; fax (2) 2412221; e-mail iita@cgiar.org; internet www.iita.org; f. 1967; principal financing arranged by the Consultative Group on International Agricultural Research—CGIAR and several NGOs for special projects; research programmes comprise crop management, improvement of crops and plant protection and health; conducts a training programme for researchers in tropical agriculture; maintains a virtual library and an image database; administers Research Stations, Research Sites, and Regional Administrative Hubs in 41 African countries; Dir-Gen. Dr NTERANYA SANGINGA (Democratic Repub. of the Congo); publs *Annual Report*, *R4DReview*, *MTP Fact Sheets*, *BOT Newsletter* (quarterly), technical bulletins, research reports.

International Livestock Research Institute (ILRI): POB 30709, Nairobi 00100, Kenya; tel. (20) 4223000; fax (20) 4223001; e-mail ilri-kenya@cgiar.org; internet www.ilri.org; f. 1995 to supersede the International Laboratory for Research on Animal Diseases and the International Livestock Centre for Africa; conducts laboratory and field research on animal health and other livestock issues, focusing on the following global livestock development challenges: developing vaccine and diagnostic technologies; conservation and reproductive technologies; adaptation to and mitigation of climate change; addressing emerging diseases; broadening market access for the poor; sustainable intensification of smallholder crop-livestock systems; reducing the vulnerability of marginal systems and communities; carries out training programmes for scientists and technicians; maintains a specialized science library; Dir-Gen. JIMMY SMITH (Guyana); publs *Annual Report*, *Livestock Research for Development* (newsletter, 2 a year).

International Maize and Wheat Improvement Centre (CIMMYT): Apdo Postal 6-641, 06600 México, DF, Mexico; tel. (55) 5804-7502; fax (55) 5804-7558; e-mail cimmyt@cgiar.org; internet www.cimmyt.org; conducts world-wide research programme for sustainable maize and wheat cropping systems to help the poor in developing countries; Dir-Gen. Dr THOMAS A. LUMPKIN (USA).

International Organization for Biological Control of Noxious Animals and Plants: c/o Prof. Dr Joop C. van Lenteren, Laboratory of Entomology, Wageningen University, POB 8031, 6700 EH Wageningen, The Netherlands; e-mail Joop.vanLenteren@wur.nl; internet www.iobc-global.org; f. 1955 to promote and co-ordinate research on the more effective biological control of harmful organisms; reorganized in 1971 as a central council with world-wide affiliations and six largely autonomous regional sections; Pres. Prof. Dr JACQUES BRODEUR (Canada); Gen. Sec. Prof. Dr JOOP C. VAN LENTEREN (Netherlands); publs *BioControl*, *Newsletter*.

International Organization of Citrus Virologists (IOCV): c/o C. N. Roistacher, Dept of Plant Pathology, University of California, Riverside, CA 92521-0122, USA; tel. (909) 684-0934; fax (909) 684-4324; e-mail iocvsecretary@gmail.com; internet www.ivia.es/iocv/; f. 1957 to promote research on citrus virus diseases at international level by standardizing diagnostic techniques and exchanging information; mems: 250; Chair. NURIA DURAN-VILA; Sec. GIORGIOS VIDALAKIS.

International Red Locust Control Organization for Central and Southern Africa (IRLCO-CSA): POB 240252, Ndola, Zambia; tel. (2) 651251; fax (2) 650117; e-mail locust@zamnet.zm; f. 1971 to control locusts in eastern, central and southern Africa; also assists in the control of African army-worm and quelea-quelea; mems: 6 countries; Dir MOSES M. OKHOBA; publs *Annual Report*, *Quarterly Report*, *Monthly Report*, scientific reports.

International Rice Research Institute (IRRI): Los Baños, Laguna, DAPO Box 7777, Metro Manila, Philippines; tel. (2) 5805600; fax (2) 5805699; e-mail irri@cgiar.org; internet www.irri.org; f. 1960; conducts research on rice, with the aim of developing technologies of environmental, social and economic benefit; works to enhance national rice research systems and offers training; operates Riceworld, a museum and learning centre about rice; maintains a library of technical rice literature; organizes international conferences and workshops (third International Rice Congress held in Hanoi, Viet Nam, in Nov. 2010; sixth International Hybrid Rice Symposium: Sept. 2012, Hyderabad, India; seventh Rice Genetics Symposium: 2013, Philippines); Dir-Gen. Dr ROBERT S. ZEIGLER; publs *Rice Literature Update*, *Rice Today* (quarterly), *Hotline*, *Facts about IRRI*, *News about Rice and People*, *International Rice Research Notes*.

International Scientific Council for Trypanosomiasis Research and Control: c/o AU Interafrican Bureau for Animal Resources, POB 30786, Nairobi, Kenya; tel. (20) 338544; fax (20) 332046; e-mail ibar.office@au-ibar.org; internet www.au-ibar.org; f. 1949 to review the work on tsetse and trypanosomiasis problems carried out by organizations and workers concerned in laboratories and in the field; to stimulate further research and discussion and to promote co-ordination between research workers and organizations in the different countries in Africa, and to provide a regular opportunity for the discussion of particular problems and for the exposition of new experiments and discoveries; Sec. Dr JAMES WABACHA.

International Seed Testing Association (ISTA): Zürichstr. 50, 8303 Bassersdorf, Switzerland; tel. 448386000; fax 448386001; e-mail ista.office@ista.ch; internet www.seedtest.org; f. 1924 to promote uniformity and accurate methods of seed testing and evaluation in order to facilitate efficiency in production, processing, distribution and utilization of seeds; organizes meetings, workshops, symposia, training courses and triennial congresses; mems: 76 countries; Pres. JOËL LÉCHAPPÉ (France); Sec.-Gen. Dr MICHAEL MUSCHICK; publs *Seed Science and Technology* (3 a year), *Seed Testing International (ISTA News Bulletin)* (2 a year), *International Rules for Seed Testing* (annually).

International Sericultural Commission (ISC): 26 rue Bellecordière, 69002 Lyon, France; tel. 4-78-50-41-98; fax 4-78-86-09-57; e-mail info@inserco.org; internet www.inserco.org; f. 1948 to encourage the development of silk production; mems: 13 states; Sec.-Gen. CHRISTIAN FRESQUET (France); publ. *Sericologia* (quarterly).

International Society for Horticultural Science (ISHS): Corbeekhoeve Pastoriestraat 2, 3360 Korbeek-Lo, Belgium; POB 500, 3001 Leuven 1, Belgium; tel. (16) 22-94-27; fax (16) 22-94-50; e-mail info@ishs.org; internet www.ishs.org; f. 1959 to promote co-operation in horticultural science research; mems: 54 countries, 300 orgs, 6,000 individuals; Pres. Dr ANTÓNIO A. MONTEIRO (Portugal); Exec. Dir JOZEF VAN ASSCHE (Belgium); publs *Chronica Horticulturae* (quarterly), *Acta Horticulturae*, *Horticultural Research International*.

International Union for the Protection of New Varieties of Plant (Union internationale pour la protection des obtentions végétales—UPOV): 34 chemin des Colombettes, 1211 Geneva 20, Switzerland; tel. 223389111; fax 227330336; e-mail upov.mail@upov.int; internet www.upov.int; f. 1961 by the International Convention for the Protection of New Varieties of Plants (entered into force 1968, revised in 1972, 1978 and 1991); aims to encourage the development of new plant varieties and provide an effective system of intellectual property protection for plant breeders. Admin. support provided by the World Intellectual Property Organization; mems: 70 states; Pres. of the Council KEUN-JIN CHOI; Sec.-Gen. FRANCIS GURRY.

International Union of Forest Research Organizations (IUFRO): Mariabrunn (BFW), Hauptstr. 7, 1140 Vienna, Austria; tel. (1) 877-01-51-0; fax (1) 877-01-51-50; e-mail office@iufro.org; internet www.iufro.org; f. 1892; aims to promote global co-operation in forest-related research and enhance the understanding of the ecological, economic and social aspects of forests and trees; disseminates scientific knowledge to stakeholders and decision-makers and aims to contribute to forest policy and on-the-ground forest management; mems: more than 600 orgs in more than 100 countries, involving some 15,000 scientists; Pres. NIELS ELERS KOCH (Denmark); Exec. Dir Dr ALEXANDER BUCK (Austria); publs *Annual Report*, *IUFRO News* (10 a year, electronic format only), *IUFRO World Series*, *IUFRO Occasional Paper Series*, *IUFRO Research Series*.

International Water Management Institute (IWMI): 127 Sunil Mawatha, Pelawatte, Battaramulla, Sri Lanka; tel. (11) 2880000; fax (11) 2786854; e-mail iwmi@cgiar.org; internet www.iwmi.org; f. 1984 as International Irrigation Management Institute; aims to improve the management of land and water resources in support of food, livelihoods and nature; addresses water and land management challenges confronting poor communities in developing countries; research agenda organized around four priority themes: basin water management; land, water and livelihoods; agriculture, water and cities; and water management and environment; cross-cutting activities include: assessment of land and water productivity, and their relationship to poverty; identifying interventions that improve productivity and access to/sustainability of natural resources; and assessment of the impacts of interventions; works through collaborative research with partners world-wide and targets policy makers, development agencies, individual farmers and private-sector organizations; Dir-Gen. COLIN CHARTRES (Australia).

International Whaling Commission (IWC): The Red House, 135 Station Rd, Impington, Cambridge, CB24 9NP, United Kingdom; tel. (1223) 233971; fax (1223) 232876; e-mail secretariat@iwcoffice.com; internet www.iwcoffice.org; f. 1946 under the International Convention for the Regulation of Whaling, for the conservation of world whale stocks; reviews the regulations covering whaling operations; encourages research; collects, analyses and disseminates statistical and other information on whaling. A ban on commercial whaling was passed by the Commission in July 1982, to take effect three years subsequently (in some cases, a phased reduction of commercial operations was not completed until 1988). A revised whale-management procedure was adopted in 1994, to be implemented after the development of a complete whale management scheme; mems: 88 countries; Sec. Dr SIMON BROCKINGTON; publs *Annual Report*, *Journal of Cetacean Research and Management*.

Network of Aquaculture Centres in Asia and the Pacific (NACA): POB 1040, Kasetsart University Post Office, Bangkok 10903, Thailand; tel. (2) 561-1728; fax (2) 561-1727; e-mail sena.desilva@enaca.org; internet www.enaca.org; f. 1990; promotes the development of aquaculture in the Asia and Pacific region through development planning, interdisciplinary research, regional training and information; mems: Australia, Bangladesh, Cambodia, People's Republic of China, Hong Kong SAR, India, Indonesia, Iran, Democratic People's Republic of Korea, Laos, Malaysia, Myanmar, Nepal, Pakistan, Philippines, Sri Lanka, Thailand and Viet Nam; Dir-Gen. Dr AMBEKAR E. EKNATH; publs *NACA Newsletter* (quarterly), *Aquaculture Asia* (quarterly).

North Pacific Anadromous Fish Commission: 889 W. Pender St, Suite 502, Vancouver, BC V6C 3B2, Canada; tel. (604) 775-5550; fax (604) 775-5577; e-mail secretariat@npafc.org; internet www.npafc.org; f. 1993; mems: Canada, Japan, Republic of Korea, Russia, USA; Exec. Dir VLADIMIR FEDORENKO; publs *Annual Report*, *Newsletter* (2 a year), *Statistical Yearbook*, *Scientific Bulletin*, *Technical Report*.

Northwest Atlantic Fisheries Organization (NAFO): 2 Morris Drive, POB 638, Dartmouth, NS B2Y 3Y9, Canada; tel. (902) 468-5590; fax (902) 468-5538; e-mail info@nafo.int; internet www.nafo.int; f. 1979 (fmrly International Commission for the Northwest Atlantic Fisheries); aims at optimum use, management and conservation of resources; an amended Convention, adopted in 2007, was being ratified in 2012; promotes research and compiles statistics; Pres. VERONIKA VEITS; Exec. Sec. Dr VLADIMIR SHIBANOV; publs *Annual Report*, *Statistical Bulletin* (electronic format only), *Journal of Northwest Atlantic Fishery Science* (in electronic and print formats), *Scientific Council Reports*, *Scientific Council Studies*, *Sampling Yearbook*, *Meeting Proceedings*.

South Pacific Regional Fisheries Management Organization: Interim Secretariat, L4, ASB Bank House, POB 3797, Wellington 6140, New Zealand; tel. (4) 499-9889; fax (4) 473-9579; e-mail interim.secretariat@southpacificrfmo.org; internet www.southpacificrfmo.org; international negotiations on the establishment of a South Pacific regional fisheries management body commenced in 2005, led by New Zealand, Australia and Chile; the negotiations were concluded at the 8th international meeting on the establishment of the org., held in Auckland, New Zealand, in Nov. 2009 and the Convention was adopted unanimously; Chair. BILL MANSFIELD; Exec. Sec. Dr ROBIN ALLEN.

Western and Central Pacific Fisheries Commission: Kaselehie St, POB 2356, Kolonia, Pohnpei State 96941, Federated States of Micronesia; tel. 3201992; fax 3201108; e-mail wcpfc@wcpfc.int; internet www.wcpfc.int; f. 2004 under the Convention for the Conservation and Management of Highly Migratory Fish Stocks in the Western and Central Pacific, which entered into force in June of that year, six months after the deposit of the 13th ratification; inaugural session convened in December, in Pohnpei, Federated States of Micronesia; mems: 31 countries and the European Community; Exec. Dir Prof. GLENN HURRY; publs *Secretariat Quarterly Report*, *Newsletter*.

World Association for Animal Production (WAAP): Via Tomassetti 3A/1, 00161 Rome, Italy; tel. (06) 44202639; fax (06) 86329263; e-mail waap@waap.it; internet www.waap.it; f. 1965; holds world conference on animal production every five years; encourages, sponsors and participates in regional meetings, seminars and symposia; mems: 17 mem. orgs; Pres. NORMAN H. CASEY (South Africa); Sec.-Gen. ANDREA ROSATI (Italy); publ. *WAAP Newsletter*.

WorldFish Center (International Centre for Living Aquatic Resources Management—ICLARM): Jalan Batu Maung, Batu Maung, 11960 Bayan Lepas, Penang, Malaysia; POB 500, GPO, 10670 Penang; tel. (4) 626-1606; fax (4) 626-5530; e-mail worldfishcenter@cgiar.org; internet www.worldfishcenter.org; f. 1973; became a mem. of the Consultative Group on International Agricultural Research (CGIAR) in 1992; aims to contribute to food security and poverty eradication in developing countries through the sustainable development and use of living aquatic resources; carries out research and promotes partnerships; Dir-Gen. Dr STEPHEN J. HALL.

World Organisation of Animal Health: 12 rue de Prony, 75017 Paris, France; tel. 1-44-15-18-88; fax 1-42-67-09-87; e-mail oie@oie.int; internet www.oie.int; f. 1924 as Office International des Epizooties (OIE); objectives include promoting international transparency of animal diseases; collecting, analysing and disseminating scientific veterinary information; providing expertise and promoting international co-operation in the control of animal diseases; promoting veterinary services; providing new scientific guidelines on animal production, food safety and animal welfare; launched in May 2005, jointly with FAO and WHO, a Global Strategy for the Progressive Control of Highly Pathogenic Avian Influenza (H5N1), and, in partnership with other organizations, has convened conferences on avian influenza; experts in a network of 156 collaborating centres and reference laboratories; mems: 178; Dir-Gen. BERNARD VALLAT (France); publs *Disease Information* (weekly), *World Animal Health* (annually), *Scientific and Technical Review* (3 a year), other manuals, codes, etc.

World Ploughing Organization (WPO): Grolweg 2, 6964 BL Hall, Netherlands; tel. (313) 619634; fax (313) 619735; e-mail hans.spieker@worldploughing.org; internet www.worldploughing.org; f. 1952 to promote the World Ploughing Contest in a different country each year, to improve techniques and promote better understanding of soil cultivation practices through research and practical demonstrations; arranges tillage clinics world-wide; mems: affiliates in 30 countries; Gen. Sec. HANS SPIEKER; publ. *WPO Handbook* (annually).

World Veterinary Association: 1B rue Defacqz, 1000 Brussels, Belgium; tel. (2) 533-70-22; fax (2) 537-28-28; e-mail secretariat@worldvet.org; internet www.worldvet.org; f. 1959 as a continuation of the International Veterinary Congresses (f. 1863); organizes congress every three years (2011: Cape Town, South Africa); mems: orgs in more than 80 countries, 19 orgs of veterinary specialists as assoc. mems; Pres. Dr FAOUZI KECHRID (Tunisia); Exec. Sec. JAN VAARTEN; publ. *WVA Newsletter* (every 2 months).

World's Poultry Science Association (WPSA): c/o Dr Roel Mulder, POB 31, 7360 AA Beekbergen, Netherlands; tel. (55) 506-3250; fax (55) 506-4858; e-mail roel.mulder@wpsa.com; internet www.wpsa.com; f. 1912 (as the International Asscn of Poultry Instructors); aims to advance and exchange knowledge relating to poultry science and the poultry industry; organizes World Poultry Congress every four years (2012: Salvador, Brazil, in Aug.); mems: 7,500 individuals in more than 100 countries, branches in 77 countries; Pres. Dr BOB PYM (Australia); Sec. Dr ROEL MULDER (Netherlands); publ. *The World's Poultry Science Journal* (quarterly).

Arts and Culture

Afro-Asian Writers' Association: 18 Ismail Abou el-Fotouh St, Veiny Sq., in front of Misr International Hospital, Dokki, Cairo, Egypt; tel. (2) 37600549; fax (2) 37600548; f. 1958; mems: writers' orgs in 51 countries; Chair. MOHAMED MAGDY MORGAN; publs *Lotus Magazine of Afro-Asian Writings* (quarterly in English, French and Arabic), *Afro-Asian Literature Series* (in English, French and Arabic).

Association of Baltic Academies of Music: c/o Musikhochschule Lübeck, Grosse Petersgrube 21, 23552 Lübeck, Germany; tel. (451) 1505303; fax (451) 15050; e-mail info@mh-luebeck.de; internet www.abamusic.org; f. 1995 as a regional network of music academies in the Baltic Sea region; organizes annual summer campuses, orchestral seminars, other regular seminars and festivals; Pres. JÖRG LINOWITZKI (Germany).

Europa Nostra—Pan-European Federation for Cultural Heritage: Lange Voorhout 35, 2514 EC The Hague, Netherlands; tel. (70) 3024051; fax (70) 3617865; e-mail info@europanostra.org; internet www.europanostra.org; f. 1963; groups, organizations and individuals concerned with the protection and enhancement of the European architectural and natural heritage and of the European environment; has consultative status with the Council of Europe; mems: some 250 mem. orgs, around 170 supporting bodies, more than 1,200 individual mems; Pres. PLÁCIDO DOMINGO (Spain); Exec. Pres. DENIS DE KERGORLAY (France); Sec.-Gen. SNESKA QUAEDVLIEG-MIHAILOVIĆ.

European Association of Conservatoires, Music Academies and Music High Schools: POB 805, 3500 AV Utrecht, Netherlands; tel. (30) 2361242; fax (30) 2361290; e-mail aecinfo@aecinfo.org; internet www.aecinfo.org; f. 1953; aims to establish and foster contacts and exchanges between and represent the interests of members; initiates and supports international collaboration through research projects, congresses and seminars; mems: 273 institutions in 55 countries; Pres. PASCALE DE GROOTE (Belgium); Sec.-Gen. JÖRG LINOWITZKI (Germany); publs e-mail newsletters (2–3 a year), project newsletters (3 a year), conference proceedings, research findings, various other publs and websites.

European Cultural Foundation: Jan van Goyenkade 5, 1075 HN Amsterdam, Netherlands; tel. (20) 5733868; fax (20) 6752231; e-mail eurocult@eurocult.org; internet www.eurocult.org; f. 1954 as a non-governmental organization, supported by private sources, to promote cultural co-operation in Europe; aims to give culture a stronger voice and presence in local communities and on the European political stage; supports closer ties among Europe's richly diverse population through joint artistic and cultural exploration; promotes good cultural policy-making that improves peoples' quality of life across Europe and its neighbouring regions; Chair. Dr WOLFGANG PETRITSCH (Austria); Dir KATHERINE WATSON; publs *Annual Report*, *electronic newsletter* (7 a year).

European Society of Culture: 10 rue de la Science, 1000 Brussels, Belgium; tel. (2) 534-40-02; fax (2) 534-11-50; e-mail advocate@cultureactioneurope.org; internet www.cultureactioneurope.org; f. 1950 to unite artists, poets, scientists, philosophers and others through mutual interests and friendship in order to safeguard and improve the conditions required for creative activity; maintains a library of 10,000 volumes; mems: national and local centres, and 1,500 individuals, in 60 countries; Pres. MERCEDES GIOVINAZZO (Italy); Gen. Sec. LUCA BERGAMO.

International Association of Art Critics: 32 rue Yves Toudic, 75010 Paris, France; tel. 1-47-70-17-42; e-mail aica.office@gmail.com; internet www.aica-int.org; f. 1949 to increase co-operation in plastic arts, promote international cultural exchanges and protect the interests of mems; mems: 4,600 in 70 countries; Pres. MAREK BARTELIK (USA); Sec.-Gen. BRANE KOVIC (Slovenia); publs *Annuaire*, *Newsletter* (quarterly).

International Association of Bibliophiles: Réserve des livres rares, Quai François Mauriac, 75706 Cedex 13, France; tel. 1-53-79-54-52; fax 1-53-79-54-60; f. 1963 to create contacts between bibliophiles and encourage book-collecting in different countries; organizes and encourages congresses, meetings, exhibitions and the award of scholarships; mems: 450; Sec.-Gen. JEAN-MARC CHATELAIN (France); publs *Le Bulletin du Bibliophile* (2 a year), yearbooks.

International Association of Film and Television Schools (Centre international de liaison des écoles de cinéma et de television—CILECT): c/o Stanislav Semerdjiev, 1000 Sofia, ul. Rakosky 108A, Bulgaria; tel. (88) 7-64-63-70 (mobile); fax (2) 989-73-89; e-mail executive.director@cilect.org; internet www.cilect.org; f. 1955 to link higher teaching and research institutes and improve education of makers of films and television programmes; organizes conferences and student film festivals; runs a training programme for developing countries; mems: 122 institutions in 56 countries; Pres. Dr MARIA DORA MOURÃO (Brazil); Exec. Dir. Dr STANISLAV SEMERDJIEV (Bulgaria); publ. *Newsletter*.

International Board on Books for Young People (IBBY): Nonnenweg 12, Postfach, 4003 Basel, Switzerland; tel. 612722917; fax 612722757; e-mail ibby@ibby.org; internet www.ibby.org; f. 1953 to support and link bodies in all countries connected with children's book work; encourages the distribution of good children's books; promotes scientific investigation into problems of juvenile books; presents the Hans Christian Andersen Award every two years to a living author and a living illustrator whose work is an outstanding contribution to juvenile literature; presents the IBBY-Asahi Reading Promotion Award (every two years) to an organization that has made a significant contribution towards the encouragement of reading; sponsors International Children's Book Day (2 April); mems: national sections and individuals in more than 70 countries; Pres. AHMAD REDZA AHMAD KHAIRUDDIN (Malaysia); Exec. Dir LIZ PAGE; publs *Bookbird* (quarterly, in English), *Congress Papers*, *IBBY Honour List* (every 2 years), special bibliographies.

International Centre for the Study of the Preservation and Restoration of Cultural Property (ICCROM): Via di San Michele 13, 00153 Rome, Italy; tel. (06) 585531; fax (06) 58553349; e-mail iccrom@iccrom.org; internet www.iccrom.org; f. 1959; assembles documents on the preservation and restoration of cultural property; stimulates research and proffers advice; organizes missions of experts; undertakes training of specialists; mems: 117 countries; Dir-Gen. STEFANO DE CARO (Italy); publ. *Newsletter* (annually, in Arabic, English, French and Spanish).

International Centre of Films for Children and Young People (Centre international du film pour l'enfance et la jeunesse—CIFEJ): CIFEJ, End of Seif St, phase 3, Shahrak-e Gharb, Tehran 1466893311, Iran; tel. (21) 88087870; fax (21) 88085847; e-mail info@cifej.com; internet www.cifej.com; f. 1955; serves as a clearing house for information about: films for children and young people, the influence of films on the young, and the regulations in force for the protection and education of young people; promotes production and distribution of suitable films and their appreciation; awards the CIFEJ prize at selected film festivals; mems: 150 mems in 55 countries; Pres. FIRDOZE BULBULIA; Exec. Dir MARYAM BAFEKRPOUR; publ. *CIFEJ Info* (every 3 months).

International Comparative Literature Association (ICLA) (Association Internationale de Littérature Comparée): Brigham Young University, 3168 JFSB, Provo, UT 84602, USA; tel. (801) 422-5598; e-mail ailc.icla@gmail.com; internet www.ailc-icla.org/site/; f. 1954 to work for the development of the comparative study of literature in modern languages; mems: 35 regional asscns; Pres. STEVEN SONDRUP.

International Confederation of Societies of Authors and Composers—World Copyright Summit: 20–26 blvd du Parc, 92200 Neuilly-sur-Seine, France; tel. 1-55-62-08-50; fax 1-55-62-08-60; e-mail cisac@cisac.org; internet www.cisac.org; f. 1926 to protect the rights of authors and composers; organizes biennial summit; mems: 232 mem. societies from 121 countries; Pres. ROBIN GIBB; Dir Gen. OLIVIER HINNEWINKEL.

International Council of Museums (ICOM): Maison de l'UNESCO, 1 rue Miollis, 75732 Paris Cedex 15, France; tel. 1-47-34-05-00; fax 1-43-06-78-62; e-mail secretariat@icom.museum; internet icom.museum; f. 1946; committed to the conservation and communication to society of the world's natural and cultural heritage; achieves its major objectives through its 30 international committees, each devoted to the study of a particular type of museum or to a specific museum-related discipline; maintains with UNESCO the organization's documentation centre; mems: 26,000 individuals and institutions in 140 countries; Pres. HANS-MARTIN HINZ (Germany); Gen. Dir JULIEN ANFRUNS (France); publ. *ICOM News—Nouvelles de l'ICOM—Noticias del ICOM* (quarterly).

International Committee of Museums and Collections of Arms and Military History (ICOMAM): Parc du Cinquantenaire 3, 1000 Brussels, Belgium; tel. (2) 737-79-00; e-mail chairman@icomam.icom.museum; internet www.icomam.icom.museum; f. 1957 as International Association of Museums of Arms and Military History (IAMAM); present name assumed in 2004; links museums and other scientific institutions with public collections of arms and armour and military equipment, uniforms, etc; holds triennial conferences and occasional specialist symposia; mems: over 260 institutions in more than 60 countries; Chair. PIET DE GRYSE (Belgium); Sec.-Gen. MATHIEU WILLEMSEN (Netherlands); publs *The Mohonk Courier*, *The Magazine* (online).

International Council on Monuments and Sites (ICOMOS): 49–51 rue de la Fédération, 75015 Paris, France; tel. 1-45-67-67-70; fax 1-45-66-06-22; e-mail secretariat@icomos.org; internet www.international.icomos.org; f. 1965 to promote the study and preservation of monuments and sites and to arouse and cultivate the interest of public authorities and people of every country in their cultural heritage; disseminates the results of research into the technical, social and administrative problems connected with the conservation of architectural heritage; holds triennial General Assembly and Symposium; mems: 24 international cttees, 116 national cttees; Pres. GUSTAVO ARAOZ (USA); Sec.-Gen. KIRSTI KOVANEN (Finland); publs *ICOMOS Newsletter* (quarterly), *Scientific Journal* (quarterly).

International Federation for Theatre Research (IFTR) (Fédération Internationale pour la Recherche Théâtrale): c/o Jan Clarke, School of Modern Languages and Culture, University of Durham, Durham, DH1 3JT, United Kingdom; e-mail jan.clarke@durham.ac.uk; internet www.firt-iftr.org; f. 1955 by 21 countries at the International Conference on Theatre History, London; Pres. CHRISTOPHER BALME (Germany); Joint Secs-Gen. Prof. JAN CLARKE (United Kingdom), PAUL MURPHY (United Kingdom).

International Federation of Film Archives (Fédération Internationale des Archives du Film—FIAF): 1 rue Defacqz, 1000 Brussels, Belgium; tel. (2) 538-30-65; fax (2) 534-47-74; e-mail info@fiafnet.org; internet www.fiafnet.org; f. 1938 to encourage the creation of audio-visual archives for the collection and conservation of the moving image heritage of every country; facilitates co-operation and exchanges between film archives; promotes public interest in the art of the cinema; aids and conducts research; compiles new documentation; holds annual congress; mems: c. 150 archives in 77 countries; Pres. ERIC LE ROY (France); Sec.-Gen. MEG LABRUM (Australia); publs *Journal of Film Preservation* (2 a year), *FIAF International Film Archive Database* (2 a year).

International Federation of Film Producers' Associations (Fédération Internationale des associations de Producteurs de Films—FIAPF): 9 rue de l'Echelle, 75001 Paris, France; tel. 1-44-77-97-50; fax 1-42-56-16-55; e-mail info@fiapf.org; internet www.fiapf.org; f. 1933 to represent film production internationally, to defend its general interests and promote its development; studies all cultural, legal, economic, technical and social problems related to film production; mems: 26 producers' orgs in 23 countries; Pres. LUIS ALBERTO SCALELLA.

International Institute for Children's Literature and Reading Research (Internationales Institut für Jugendliteratur und Leseforschung): Mayerhofgasse 6, 1040 Vienna, Austria; tel. (1) 505-03-59; fax (1) 50503-5917; e-mail office@jugendliteratur.net; internet www.jugendliteratur.net; f. 1965 as an international documentation, research and advisory centre of juvenile literature and reading; maintains specialized library; arranges conferences and exhibitions; compiles recommendation lists; mems: individual and group members in 28 countries; Pres. Prof. RENATE WELSH; Dir KARIN HALLER; publ. *1000 & 1 Buch* (quarterly).

International Institute for Conservation of Historic and Artistic Works: 3 Birdcage Walk, Westminster, London, SW1H 9JJ, United Kingdom; tel. (20) 7799-5500; fax (20) 7799-4961; e-mail iic@iiconservation.org; internet www.iiconservation.org; f. 1950; mems: 2,400 individual, 400 institutional mems; Pres. JERRY PODANY (USA); Sec.-Gen. JOSEPHINE KIRBY; publs *Studies in Conservation* (quarterly), *Reviews in Conservation* (annually), *News in Conservation* (every 2 months), *Congress Preprints* (every 2 years).

International Music Council (IMC): Maison de l'UNESCO, 1 rue Miollis, 75732 Paris Cedex 15, France; tel. 1-45-68-48-50; fax 1-43-06-87-98; e-mail info@imc-cim.org; internet www.imc-cim.org; f. 1949; mems: regional music councils, international music orgs, national and specialized orgs in some 150 countries; Pres. FRANS DE RUITER; Sec.-Gen. SILJA FISCHER.

Members of IMC include:

European Festivals Association: Kasteel Borluut, Kleine Gentstraat 46, 9051 Ghent, Belgium; tel. (9) 241-80-80; fax (9) 241-80-89; e-mail info@efa-aef.eu; internet www.efa-aef.eu; f. 1952 to maintain high artistic standards and the representative character of art festivals; holds annual General Assembly; mems: more than 100 regular international performing arts festivals in 38 countries; Pres. DARKO BRLEK; Sec.-Gen. KATHRIN DEVENTER; publ. *Festivals* (annually).

International Association of Music Libraries, Archives and Documentation Centres (IAML): c/o Music and Drama Library, Göteborg University Library, POB 201, SE 405 30 Göteborg, Sweden; tel. (31) 786-40-57; fax (31) 786-40-59; e-mail secretary@iaml.info; internet www.iaml.info; f. 1951; mems: 1,742 institutions and individuals in 49 countries; Pres. ROGER FLURY (New Zealand); Sec.-Gen. PIA SHEKHTER (Sweden); publ. *Fontes artis musicae* (quarterly).

International Council for Traditional Music (ICTM): Dept of Musicology, Faculty of Arts, University of Ljubljana, 1000 Ljubljana, Slovenia; tel. (2) 6125-1449; e-mail secretariat@ictmusic.org; internet www.ictmusic.org; f. 1947 (as International Folk Music Council) to further the study, practice, documentation, preservation and dissemination of traditional music of all countries; holds ICTM World Conference every two years; mems: 1,885; Pres. Dr ADRIENNE L. KAEPPLER (USA); Sec.-Gen. Dr SVANIBOR PETTAN (Slovenia); publs *Yearbook for Traditional Music*, *ICTM Bulletin* (2 a year).

International Federation of Musicians: 21 bis rue Victor Massé, 75009 Paris, France; tel. 1-45-26-31-23; fax 1-45-26-31-57; e-mail office@fim-musicians.com; internet www.fim-musicians.com/; f. 1948 to promote and protect the interests of musicians in affiliated unions; mems: 75 unions in 64 countries; Pres. JOHN F. SMITH (United Kingdom); Gen. Sec. BENOÎT MACHUEL (France).

International Music and Media Centre (Internationales Musik + Medienzentrum): Stiftgasse 29, 1070 Vienna, Austria; tel. (1) 889 03-15; fax (1) 889 03-1577; e-mail office@imz.at; internet www.imz.at; f. 1961 for the study and dissemination of music through technical media (film, television, radio, gramophone); organizes congresses, seminars and screenings on music in audio-visual media; holds courses and competitions designed to strengthen the relationship between performing artists and audio-visual media; mems: 180 ordinary mems and 30 associate mems in 35 countries, including 50 broadcasting orgs; Pres. CHRIS HUNT (United Kingdom); Sec.-Gen. FRANZ A. PATAY (Austria).

International Society for Contemporary Music (ISCM): c/o Muziek Centrum Nederland, Rokin 111, 1012 KN Amsterdam, Netherlands; tel. (20) 3446060; e-mail info@iscm.org; internet www.iscm.org; f. 1922 to promote the development of contemporary music; organizes annual World Music Day; mems: orgs in 50 countries; Pres. JOHN DAVIS; Sec.-Gen. ARTHUR VAN DER DRIFT.

Jeunesses Musicales International (JMI): 1 rue Defacqz, 1000 Brussels, Belgium; tel. (2) 513-97-74; fax (2) 514-47-55; e-mail mail@jmi.net; internet www.jmi.net; f. 1945 to enable young people to develop, through music, and to stimulate contacts between member countries; mems: orgs in 40 countries; Sec.-Gen. BLASKO SMILEVSKI; publ. *JMI News* (6 a year).

World Federation of International Music Competitions (WFIMC): 104 rue de Carouge, 1205 Geneva, Switzerland; tel. 223213620; fax 227811418; e-mail fmcim@fmcim.org; internet www.wfimc.org; f. 1957 to co-ordinate the arrangements for affiliated competitions and to exchange experience; holds General Assembly annually; mems: 129 international music competitions; Pres. GLEN KWOK (USA); Sec.-Gen. LOTTIE CHALUT.

International PEN (World Association of Writers): Brownlow House, 50–51 High Holborn, London, WC1V 6ER, United Kingdom; tel. (20) 7405-0338; fax (20) 7405-0339; e-mail info@pen-international.org; internet www.internationalpen.org.uk; f. 1921 to promote co-operation between writers; mems: 144 centres in 102 countries; International Pres. JOHN RALSTON SAUL; Exec. Dir LAURA MCVEIGH; publ. *PEN International* (2 a year, in English, French and Spanish, with the assistance of UNESCO).

International Theatre Institute (ITI): Maison de l'UNESCO, 1 rue Miollis, 75732 Paris Cedex 15, France; tel. 1-45-68-48-80; fax 1-45-66-50-40; e-mail iti@iti-worldwide.org; internet iti-worldwide.org; f. 1948 to facilitate cultural exchanges and international understanding in the domain of the theatre and performing arts; promotes performing arts/theatre on a national and international level and facilitates international collaboration; mems: around 100 national centres and co-operating mems world-wide; Pres. RAMENDU MAJUMDAR (Bangladesh); Sec.-Gen. TOBIAS BIANCONE (Switzerland); publs *ITI News* (3 times a year in English and French), *World Theatre Directory* (every 2 years), *The World of Theatre* (every 2 years).

Nordic Cultural Fund (Nordisk Kulturfond): Ved Stranden 18, 1061 Copenhagen K, Denmark; tel. 3396-0200; fax 3332-5636; e-mail kulturfonden@norden.org; internet www .nordiskkulturfond.org; f. 1967; aims to support a broad spectrum of Nordic cultural co-operation activities; awards around 28m. Danish kroner annually towards cultural projects being implemented in the Nordic Region, and Nordic projects being undertaken outside the region; projects are designated by the Fund as 'Nordic' if a minimum of three Nordic countries (Denmark, Iceland, Finland, Norway and Sweden) or self-governing areas (Faroe Islands, Greenland, and the Åland Islands) are involved, either as participants, organizers, or as the project subject area; Dir KAREN BUE.

Organization of World Heritage Cities: 15 rue Saint-Nicolas, Québec, QC G1K 1M8, Canada; tel. (418) 692-0000; fax (418) 692-5558; e-mail secretariat@ovpm.org; internet www.ovpm .org; f. 1993 to assist cities inscribed on the UNESCO World Heritage List to implement the Convention concerning the Protection of the World Cultural and Natural Heritage (1972); promotes co-operation between city authorities, in particular in the management and sustainable development of historic sites; holds an annual General Assembly, comprising the mayors of member cities; mems: 238 cities world-wide; Sec.-Gen. DENIS RICARD; publ. *OWHC Newsletter* (2 a year, in English, French and Spanish).

Pan-African Writers' Association (PAWA): PAWA House, Roman Ridge, POB C456, Cantonments, Accra, Ghana; tel. (21) 773062; fax (21) 773042; e-mail pawahouse@gmail.com; f. 1989 to link African creative writers, defend the rights of authors and promote awareness of literature; mems: 52 national writers' associations on the continent; Sec.-Gen. ATUKWEI OKAI (Ghana).

Royal Asiatic Society of Great Britain and Ireland: 14 Stephenson Way, London, NW1 2HD, United Kingdom; tel. (20) 7388-4539; fax (20) 7391-9429; e-mail info@ royalasiaticsociety.org; internet www.royalasiaticsociety.org; f. 1823 for the study of history and cultures of the East; mems: c. 700, branch societies in Asia; Pres. Prof. GORDON JOHNSON; Dir ALISON OHTA; publ. *Journal* (3 a year).

World Crafts Council International (WCC): 98A Dr. Radhakrishnan Salai, Chennai 600004, India; tel. (44) 28478500; fax (44) 28478509; e-mail wcc.sect.in@gmail.com; internet www.worldcraftscouncil.org; f. 1964; aims to strengthen the status of crafts as a vital part of cultural and economic life, to link crafts people around the world, and to foster wider recognition of their work; mems: national orgs in more than 89 countries; Pres. USHA KRISHNA (India).

Commodities

Africa Rice Center (AfricaRice): 01 BP 2031, Cotonou, Benin; tel. 21-35-01-88; fax 21-35-05-56; e-mail AfricaRice@ cgiar.org; internet www.africarice.org/; f. 1971 (as the West Africa Rice Development Association—WARDA, present name adopted in 2009); participates in the network of agricultural research centres supported by the Consultative Group on International Agricultural Research (CGIAR); aims to contribute to food security and poverty eradication in poor rural and urban populations, through research, partnerships, capacity strengthening and policy support on rice-based systems; promotes sustainable agricultural development based on environmentally sound management of natural resources; maintains research stations in Nigeria and Senegal; provides training and consulting services; from 2007 expanded scope of membership and activities from West African to pan-African; mems: 24 African countries; Dir-Gen. Dr PAPA ABDOULAYE SECK (Senegal); publs *Program Report* (annually), *Participatory Varietal Selection* (annually), *Rice Interspecific Hybridization Project Research Highlights* (annually), *Inland Valley Newsletter*, *ROCARIZ Newsletter*, training series, proceedings, leaflets.

African Groundnut Council (AGC): C43, Wase Satellite Town, Rjiyar Zaki, Kano, Kano State, Nigeria; tel. (1) 8970605; e-mail info@afgroundnutcouncil.org; internet www .afgroundnutcouncil.org; f. 1964 to advise producing countries on marketing policies; mems: The Gambia, Mali, Niger, Nigeria, Senegal, Sudan; Exec. Sec. ELHADJ MOUR MAMADOU SAMB (Senegal); publ. *Groundnut Review*.

African Oil Palm Development Association (AFOPDA): 15 BP 341, Abidjan 15, Côte d'Ivoire; tel. 21-25-15-18; fax 20-25-47-00; f. 1985; seeks to increase production of, and investment in, palm oil; mems: Benin, Cameroon, Democratic Republic of the Congo, Côte d'Ivoire, Ghana, Guinea, Nigeria, Togo.

African Petroleum Producers' Association (APPA): POB 1097, Brazzaville, Republic of the Congo; tel. 665-38-57; fax 669-99-13; e-mail appa@appa.int; f. 1987 by African petroleum-producing countries to reinforce co-operation among regional producers and to stabilize prices; council of ministers responsible for the hydrocarbons sector meets twice a year; holds regular Congress and Exhibition: March 2010, Kinshasa, Democratic Republic of the Congo; mems: Algeria, Angola, Benin, Cameroon, Democratic Republic of the Congo, Republic of the Congo, Côte d'Ivoire, Egypt, Equatorial Guinea, Gabon, Libya, Nigeria; Exec. Sec. GABRIEL DANSOU LOKOSSOU; publ. *APPA Bulletin* (2 a year).

Asian and Pacific Coconut Community (APCC): 3rd Floor, Lina Bldg, Jalan H. R. Rasuna Said Kav. B7, Kuningan, Jakarta 12920, Indonesia; POB 1343, Jakarta 10013; tel. (21) 5221712; fax (21) 5221714; e-mail apcc@indo.net.id; internet www .apccsec.org; f. 1969 to promote and co-ordinate all activities of the coconut industry, to achieve higher production and better processing, marketing and research; organizes annual Coconut Technical Meeting (COCOTECH); mems: Fiji, India, Indonesia, Kiribati, Malaysia, Marshall Islands, Federated States of Micronesia, Papua New Guinea, Philippines, Samoa, Solomon Islands, Sri Lanka, Thailand, Vanuatu, Viet Nam; Exec. Dir ROMULO N. ARANCON, Jr; publs *Cocomunity* (monthly), *CORD* (2 a year), *CocoInfo International* (2 a year), *Coconut Statistical Yearbook*, guidelines and other ad hoc publications.

Association of Natural Rubber Producing Countries (ANRPC): Bangunan Getah Asli, 148 Jalan Ampang, 7th Floor, 50450 Kuala Lumpur, Malaysia; tel. (3) 21611900; fax (3) 21613014; e-mail anrpc.secretariat@gmail.com; internet www .anrpc.org; f. 1970 to co-ordinate the production and marketing of natural rubber, to promote technical co-operation among members and to bring about fair and stable prices for natural rubber; holds seminars, meetings and training courses on technical and statistical subjects; a joint regional marketing system has been agreed in principle; mems: Cambodia, People's Republic of China, India, Indonesia, Malaysia, Papua New Guinea, Philippines, Singapore, Sri Lanka, Thailand, Viet Nam; Sec.-Gen. Dr KAMARUL BAHARAIN BIN BASIR; publs *NR Trends & Statistics* (monthly), *Qtrly NR Market Review*, *Market and Industry Update*.

Cocoa Producers' Alliance (CPA): National Assembly Complex, Tafawa Balewa Sq., POB 1718, Lagos, Nigeria; tel. (9) 8141735; fax (9) 8141734; e-mail info@copal-cpa.org; internet www.copal-cpa.org; f. 1962 to exchange technical and scientific information, to discuss problems of mutual concern to producers, to ensure adequate supplies at remunerative prices and to promote consumption; mems: Brazil, Cameroon, Côte d'Ivoire, Dominican Republic, Gabon, Ghana, Malaysia, Nigeria, São Tomé and Príncipe, Togo; Sec.-Gen. HOPE SONA EBAI.

Common Fund for Commodities (CFC): POB 74656, 1070 BR, Amsterdam, Netherlands; tel. (20) 5754949; fax (20) 6760231; e-mail managing.director@common-fund.org; internet www.common-fund.org; f. 1989 as the result of an UNCTAD negotiation conference; finances commodity development measures including research, marketing, productivity improvements and vertical diversification, with the aim of increasing the long-term competitiveness of particular commodities; paid-in capital US $181m.; mems: 105 countries and 10 institutional members; Man. Dir (also Chief Exec.) ALI MCHUMO.

East Africa Tea Trade Association: Tea Trade Centre, Nyerere Ave, Mombasa, Kenya; tel. (41) 2228460; fax (41) 2225823; e-mail info@eatta.com; internet www.eatta.com; f. 1957; brings together producers, brokers, buyers and packers; Chair. FRANCIS KIRAGU.

European Aluminium Association (EAA): 12 ave de Broqueville, 1150 Brussels, Belgium; tel. (2) 775-63-50; fax (2) 779-05-31; e-mail eaa@eaa.be; internet www.eaa.net; f. 1981 to encourage studies, research and technical co-operation, to make representations to international bodies and to assist national asscns in dealing with national authorities; mems: individual producers of primary aluminium, 18 national groups for wrought producers, the Organization of European Aluminium Smelters, representing producers of recycled aluminium, and the European Aluminium Foil Association, representing foil rollers and converters; Sec.-Gen. PATRICK DE SCHRYNMAKERS; publs *Annual Report*, *EAA Quarterly Report*.

European Association for the Trade in Jute and Related Products: POB 93002, 2509 AA The Hague, Netherlands; tel. (70) 3490750; fax (70) 3490775; e-mail info@eurojute.com; internet www.eurojute.com; f. 1970 to maintain contacts between national asscns, permit the exchange of information and represent the interests of the trade; carries out scientific research; mems: enterprises in 9 European countries.

European Committee of Sugar Manufacturers (CEFS): 182 ave de Tervuren, 1150 Brussels, Belgium; tel. (2) 762-07-60; fax (2) 771-00-26; e-mail cefs@cefs.org; internet www.cefs.org; f. 1954 to collect statistics and information, conduct research and promote co-operation between national organizations; mems: national asscns in 22 European countries and other associate members world-wide; Pres. JOHANN MARIHART; Dir-Gen. MARIE-CHRISTINE RIBERA.

Gas Exporting Countries Forum: POB 23753, 47-48th Floors, Tornado Tower, West Bay, Doha, Qatar; tel. 44048410; fax 44048416; e-mail gecfsg@gmail.com; internet www.gecf.org; f. 2001 to represent and promote the mutual interests of gas exporting countries; aims to increase the level of co-ordination among member countries and to promote dialogue between gas producers and consumers; a ministerial meeting is convened annually; the seventh ministerial meeting, convened in Moscow, Russia, in Dec. 2008, agreed on a charter and a permanent structure for the grouping; mems: Algeria, Bolivia, Egypt, Equatorial Guinea, Iran, Libya, Nigeria, Oman, Qatar, Russia, Trinidad and Tobago, Venezuela; observers: Kazakhstan, Netherlands, Norway.

Inter-African Coffee Organization (IACO) (Organisation InterAfricaine du Café—OIAC): BP V210, Abidjan, Côte d'Ivoire; tel. 20-21-61-31; fax 20-21-62-12; e-mail sg@iaco-oiac.org; internet www.iaco-oiac.org; f. 1960 to adopt a common policy on the marketing and consumption of coffee; aims to foster greater collaboration in research technology transfer through the African Coffee Research Network (ACRN); seeks to improve the quality of coffee exports, and implement poverty reduction programmes focusing on value added product (VAP) and the manufacturing of green coffee; mems: 25 coffee-producing countries in Africa; Sec.-Gen. JOSEFA LEONEL CORREIA SACKO (Angola).

International Cadmium Association: 168 ave Tervueren, 1150 Brussels, Belgium; tel. (2) 777-05-60; fax (2) 777-05-65; e-mail info@cadmium.org; internet www.cadmium.org; f. 1976; covers all aspects of the production and use of cadmium and its compounds; includes almost all producers and users of cadmium; Exec. Dir MICHAEL TAYLOR.

International Cocoa Organization (ICCO): Commonwealth House, 1–19 New Oxford St, London, WC1A 1NU, United Kingdom; tel. (20) 7400-5050; fax (20) 7421-5500; e-mail info@icco.org; internet www.icco.org; f. 1973 under the first International Cocoa Agreement, 1972; the ICCO supervises the implementation of the agreements, and provides member governments with up-to-date information on the world cocoa economy; the sixth International Cocoa Agreement (2001) entered into force in October 2003; the seventh International Cocoa Agreement was signed in June 2010 and was to enter into force in October 2012; mems: 13 exporting countries and 28 importing countries; and the EU; Exec. Dir a.i. Dr JEAN-MARC ANGA (Côte d'Ivoire); publs *Quarterly Bulletin of Cocoa Statistics*, *Annual Report*, *World Cocoa Directory*, *Cocoa Newsletter*, studies on the world cocoa economy.

International Coffee Organization (ICO): 22 Berners St, London, W1T 3DD, United Kingdom; tel. (20) 7612-0600; fax (20) 7612-0630; e-mail info@ico.org; internet www.ico.org; f. 1963 under the International Coffee Agreement, 1962, which was renegotiated in 1968, 1976, 1983, 1994 (extended in 1999), 2001 and 2007; aims to improve international co-operation and provide a forum for intergovernmental consultations on coffee matters; to facilitate international trade in coffee by the collection, analysis and dissemination of statistics; to act as a centre for the collection, exchange and publication of coffee information; to promote studies in the field of coffee; and to encourage an increase in coffee consumption; mems: 33 exporting countries and six importing countries, plus the European Union; Chair. of Council HENRY NGABIRANO (Uganda); Exec. Dir ROBÉRIO SILVA (Brazil).

International Confederation of European Beet Growers (Confédération internationale des betteraviers européens—CIBE): 111/9 blvd Anspachlaan, 1000 Brussels, Belgium; tel. (2) 504-60-90; fax (2) 504-60-99; e-mail cibeoffice@cibe-europe.eu; internet www.cibe-europe.eu; f. 1927 to act as a centre for the co-ordination and dissemination of information about beet sugar production; to represent the interests of beet growers at an international level; mems in Austria, Belgium, Czech Republic, Denmark, Finland, France, Germany, Greece, Hungary, Italy, Netherlands, Poland, Romania, Slovakia, Sweden, Switzerland, Turkey, United Kingdom; Pres. JOS VAN CAMPEN (Netherlands); Gen. Sec. ELISABETH LACOSTE (France).

International Cotton Advisory Committee (ICAC): 1629 K St, NW, Suite 702, Washington, DC 20006-1636, USA; tel. (202) 463-6660; fax (202) 463-6950; e-mail secretariat@icac.org; internet www.icac.org; f. 1939 to observe developments in world cotton; to collect and disseminate statistics; to suggest measures for the furtherance of international collaboration in maintaining and developing a sound world cotton economy; and to provide a forum for international discussions on cotton prices; mems: 44 countries; Exec. Dir Dr TERRY TOWNSEND (USA); publs *Cotton This Week!* (internet/e-mail only), *Cotton This Month*, *Cotton: Review of the World Situation* (every 2 months), *Cotton: World Statistics* (annually), *The ICAC Recorder*, *World Textile Demand* (annually), other surveys, studies, trade analyses and technical publications.

International Energy Forum (IEF): POB 94736, Diplomatic Quarter, Riyadh-11614, Saudi Arabia; tel. (1) 4810022; fax (1) 4810055; e-mail info@ief.org; internet www.ief.org; f. 1991; annual gathering of ministers responsible for energy affairs from states accounting for about 90% of global oil and gas supply and demand; the IEF is an intergovernmental arrangement aimed at promoting dialogue on global energy matters among its membership; the annual IEF is preceded by a meeting of the International Business Energy Forum (IEBF), comprising energy ministers and CEOs of leading energy companies; 13th IEF and fifth IEBF: March 2012, Kuwait; mems: 87 states, including the mems of OPEC and the International Energy Agency; Sec.-Gen. ALDO FLORES-QUIROGA.

International Gas Union (IGU): c/o Statoil, 0246 Oslo, Norway; tel. 51-99-00-00; fax 22-53-43-40; e-mail secrigu@statoil.com; internet www.igu.org; f. 1931; represents the gas industry world-wide; organizes World Gas Conference every three years (2012: Kuala Lumpur, Malaysia); mems: 75 Charter mems, 35 Associate mems; Pres. ABDUL RAHIM HASHIM (Malaysia); Sec.-Gen. TORSTEIN INDREBØ (Norway).

International Grains Council (IGC): 1 Canada Sq., Canary Wharf, London, E14 5AE, United Kingdom; tel. (20) 7513-1122; fax (20) 7513-0630; e-mail igc@igc.int; internet www.igc.int; f. 1949 as International Wheat Council, present name adopted in 1995; responsible for the administration of the International Grains Agreement, 1995, comprising the Grains Trade Convention (GTC) and the Food Aid Convention (FAC, under which donors pledge specified minimum annual amounts of food aid for developing countries in the form of grain and other eligible products); aims to further international co-operation in all aspects of trade in grains, to promote international trade in grains, and to achieve a free flow of this trade, particularly in developing member countries; seeks to contribute to the stability of the international grain market; acts as a forum for consultations between members; provides comprehensive information on the international grain market (with effect from 1 July 2009 the definition of 'grain' was extended to include rice); mems: 26 countries and the EU; Exec. Dir ETSUO KITAHARA; publs *World Grain Statistics* (annually), *Wheat and Coarse Grain Shipments* (annually), *Report for the Fiscal Year* (annually), *Grain Market Report* (monthly), *IGC Grain Market Indicators* (weekly), *Rice Market Bulletin* (weekly).

International Jute Study Group (IJSG): 145 Monipuriparu, Tejgaon, Dhaka 1215, Bangladesh; tel. (2) 9125581; fax (2) 9125248; e-mail info@jute.org; internet www.jute.org; f. 2002 as successor to International Jute Organization (f. 1984 in accordance with an agreement made by 48 producing and consuming countries in 1982, under the auspices of UNCTAD); aims to improve the jute economy and the quality of jute and jute products through research and development projects and market promotion; Sec.-Gen BHUPENDRA SINGH (India).

International Lead and Zinc Study Group (ILZSG): Rua Almirante Barroso 38, 5th Floor, Lisbon 1000-013, Portugal; tel. (21) 3592420; fax (21) 3592429; e-mail root@ilzsg.org; internet www.ilzsg.org; f. 1959 for intergovernmental consultation on world trade in lead and zinc; conducts studies and provides information on trends in supply and demand; mems: 29 countries accounting for more than 85% of world production and usage of lead and zinc; Sec.-Gen. DON SMALE; publ. *Lead and Zinc Statistics* (monthly).

International Lead Association (also, International Lead Association—Europe): 17A Welbeck Way, London, W1G 9YJ, United Kingdom; tel. (20) 7499-8422; fax (20) 7493-1555; e-mail enq@ila-lead.org; internet www.ila-lead.org; f. 1956 as Lead Development Asscn International; provides authoritative information on the use of lead and its compounds; financed by lead producers and users in the United Kingdom, Europe and elsewhere; Dir (ILA) Dr DAVID WILSON (United Kingdom); Dir (ILA—Europe) Dr ANDY BUSH (United Kingdom).

International Molybdenum Association (IMOA): 4 Heathfield Terrace, London, W4 4JE, United Kingdom; tel. (20) 7871-1580; fax (2) 8994-6067; e-mail info@imoa.info; internet www.imoa.info; f. 1989; collates statistics; promotes the use of molybdenum; monitors health and environmental issues in the molybdenum industry; mems: 70; Pres. VICTOR PEREZ; Sec.-Gen. TIM OUTTERIDGE.

International Olive Council: Príncipe de Vergara 154, 28002 Madrid, Spain; tel. (91) 5903638; fax (91) 5631263; e-mail iooc@internationaloliveoil.org; internet www.internationaloliveoil.org; f. 1959 to administer the International Agreement on Olive Oil and Table Olives, which aims to promote international co-operation in connection with problems of the world economy for olive products; works to prevent unfair competition, to encourage the production and consumption of olive products, and their international trade, and to reduce the disadvantages caused by fluctuations of supplies on the market; also takes action to foster a better understanding of the nutritional, therapeutic and other properties of olive products, to foster international co-operation for the integrated, sustainable development of world olive growing, to encourage research and development, to foster the transfer of technology and training activities in the olive products sector, and to improve the interaction between olive growing and the environment; mems: of the International Agreement on Olive Oil and Table Olives, 2005 (fifth Agreement, in force until 31 Dec. 2014): 14 countries, and the European Union; Exec. Dir JEAN-LOUIS BARJOL; publ. *OLIVAE* (2 a year, in Arabic, English, French, Italian and Spanish).

International Organisation of Vine and Wine (Organisation Internationale de la Vigne et du Vin—OIV): 18 rue d'Aguesseau, 75008 Paris, France; tel. 1-44-94-80-80; fax 1-42-66-90-63; e-mail contact@oiv.int; internet www.oiv.int; f. 2001 (agreement establishing an International Wine Office signed Nov. 1924, name changed to International Vine and Wine Office in 1958); researches vine and vine product issues in the scientific, technical, economic and social areas, disseminates knowledge, and facilitates contacts between researchers; mems: 45 countries, 9 orgs and 1 territory had observer status, as at May 2012; Dir-Gen. FEDERICO CASTELLUCCI (Italy); publs *Bulletin de l'OIV* (every 2 months), *Lexique de la Vigne et du Vin*, *Recueil des méthodes internationales d'analyse des vins*, *Code international des Pratiques oenologiques*, *Codex oenologique international*, numerous scientific publications.

International Organization of Spice Trading Associations (IOSTA): c/o American Spice Trade Association, 2025 M St, NW, Suite 800, Washington, DC 20036, USA; tel. (202) 367-1127; fax (202) 367-2127; e-mail info@astaspice.org; internet www.astaspice.org; f. 1999; mems: 8 national and regional spice orgs.

International Pepper Community (IPC): 4th Floor, Lina Bldg, Jalan H. R. Rasuna Said, Kav. B7, Kuningan, Jakarta 12920, Indonesia; tel. (21) 5224902; fax (21) 5224905; e-mail mail@ipcnet.org; internet www.ipcnet.org; f. 1972 for promoting, co-ordinating and harmonizing all activities relating to the pepper economy; mems: Brazil, India, Indonesia, Malaysia, Sri Lanka, Viet Nam; Exec. Dir SUBRAMANIAM KANNAN; publs *Pepper Statistical Yearbook*, *International Pepper News Bulletin* (quarterly), *Directory of Pepper Exporters*, *Directory of Pepper Importers*, *Weekly Prices Bulletin*, *Pepper Market Review*.

International Platinum Group Metals Association (IPA): Schiess-Staett-Str. 30, Munich, 80339 Germany; tel. (89) 51996770; fax (89) 51996719; e-mail info@ipa-news.com; internet www.ipa-news.com/index.php; links principal producers and fabricators of platinum; Pres. WILLIAM SANDFORD; Man. Dir GABRIELE RANDLSHOFER.

International Rubber Study Group: 111 North Bridge Rd, 23-06 Peninsula Plaza, Singapore 179098; tel. 68372411; fax 63394369; e-mail irsg@rubberstudy.com; internet www.rubberstudy.com; f. 1944 to provide a forum for the discussion of problems affecting synthetic and natural rubber and to provide statistical and other general information on rubber; mems: 16 governments and the EU; Sec.-Gen. Dr STEPHEN V. EVANS; publs *Rubber Statistical Bulletin* (every 2 months), *Rubber Industry Report* (every 2 months), *Proceedings of International Rubber Forums* (annually), *World Rubber Statistics Handbook*, *Key Rubber Indicators*, *Rubber Statistics Yearbook*, *Outlook for Elastomers* (annually).

International Sugar Organization: 1 Canada Sq., Canary Wharf, London, E14 5AA, United Kingdom; tel. (20) 7513-1144; fax (20) 7513-1146; e-mail exdir@isosugar.org; internet www.isosugar.org; administers the International Sugar Agreement (1992), with the objectives of stimulating co-operation, facilitating trade and encouraging demand; aims to improve conditions in the sugar market through debate, analysis and studies; serves as a forum for discussion; holds annual seminars and workshops; sponsors projects from developing countries; mems: 84 countries producing some 83% of total world sugar; Exec. Dir Dr PETER BARON; publs *Sugar Year Book*, *Monthly Statistical Bulletin*, *Market Report and Press Summary*, *Quarterly Market Outlook*, seminar proceedings.

International Tea Committee Ltd (ITC): 1 Carlton House Terrace, London, SW1Y 5DB, United Kingdom; tel. (20) 7839-5090; e-mail info@inttea.com; internet www.inttea.com; f. 1933 to administer the International Tea Agreement; now serves as a statistical and information centre; in 1979 membership was extended to include consuming countries; producer mems: national tea boards or asscns in Bangladesh, People's Republic of China, India, Indonesia, Kenya, Malawi, Sri Lanka and Tanzania; consumer mems: Tea Asscn of the USA Inc., Irish Tea Trade Asscn, and the Tea Asscn of Canada; assoc. mems: Netherlands Ministry of Agriculture, Nature and Food Quality and United Kingdom Dept for Environment Food and Rural Affairs, and national tea boards/asscns in 10 producing and 4 consuming countries; Chief Exec. MANUJA PEIRIS; publs *Annual Bulletin of Statistics*, *Monthly Statistical Summary*.

International Tobacco Growers' Association (ITGA): Av. Gen. Humberto Delgado 30A, 6001-081 Castelo Branco, Portugal; tel. (272) 325901; fax (272) 325906; e-mail itga@tobaccoleaf.org; internet www.tobaccoleaf.org; f. 1984 to provide a forum for the exchange of views and information of interest to tobacco producers; holds annual meeting; mems: 23 countries producing over 80% of the world's internationally traded tobacco; Chief Exec. ANTÓNIO ABRUNHOSA (Portugal); publs *Tobacco Courier* (quarterly), *Tobacco Briefing*.

International Tropical Timber Organization (ITTO): International Organizations Center, 5th Floor, Pacifico-Yokohama, 1-1-1, Minato-Mirai, Nishi-ku, Yokohama 220-0012, Japan; tel. (45) 223-1110; fax (45) 223-1111; e-mail itto@itto.or.jp; internet www.itto.int; f. 1985 under the International Tropical Timber Agreement (1983); subsequently a new treaty, ITTA 1994, came into force in 1997, and this was replaced by ITTA 2006, which entered into force in Dec. 2011; provides a forum for consultation and co-operation between countries that produce and consume tropical timber, and is dedicated to the sustainable development and conservation of tropical forests; facilitates progress towards 'Objective 2000', which aims to move as rapidly as possible towards achieving exports of tropical timber and timber products from sustainably managed resources; encourages, through policy and project work, forest management, conservation and restoration, the further processing of tropical timber in producing countries, and the gathering and analysis of market intelligence and economic information; mems: 25 producing and 36 consuming countries and the EU; Exec. Dir EMMANUEL ZE MEKA (Cameroon); publs *Annual Review and Assessment of the World Timber Situation*, *Tropical Timber Market Information Service* (every 2 weeks), *Tropical Forest Update* (quarterly).

International Tungsten Industry Association (ITIA): 4 Heathfield Terrace, London, W4 4JE, United Kingdom; tel. (20) 8996-2221; fax (20) 8994-8728; e-mail info@itia.info; internet www.itia.info; f. 1988 (fmrly Primary Tungsten Asscn, f. 1975); promotes use of tungsten; collates statistics; prepares market reports; monitors health and environmental issues in the tungsten industry; mems from 18 countries; Pres. STEPHEN LEAHY; Sec.-Gen. BURGHARD ZEILER.

International Zinc Association (IZA): 168 ave de Tervueren, Boîte 4, 1150 Brussels, Belgium; tel. (2) 776-00-70; fax (2) 776-00-89; e-mail contact@zinc.org; internet www.zinc.org; f. 1990 to represent the world zinc industry; provide a forum for senior executives to address global issues requiring industry-wide action; consider new applications for zinc and zinc products; foster understanding of zinc's role in the environment; build a sustainable development policy; mems: 33 zinc-producing countries; Exec. Dir STEPHEN R. WILKINSON; publ. *Zinc Protects* (quarterly).

Kimberley Process (KP): internet www.kimberleyprocess.com; launched following a meeting of southern African diamond-producing states, held in May 2000 in Kimberley, South Africa, to address means of halting the trade in 'conflict diamonds' and of ensuring that revenue derived from diamond sales would henceforth not be used to fund rebel movements aiming to undermine legitimate governments; in Dec. of that year a landmark UN General Assembly resolution was adopted supporting the creation of an international certification scheme for rough diamonds; accordingly, the Kimberley Process Certification Scheme (KPCS), detailing requirements for controlling production of and trade in 'conflict-free' rough diamonds, entered into force on 1 Jan. 2003; it was estimated in 2012 that participating states accounted for 99.8% of global rough diamond production; a review of the core objectives and definitions of the Process was being undertaken during 2012–13; participating countries, with industry and civil society observers, meet twice a year; working groups and committees also convene frequently; implementation of the KPCS is monitored through 'review visits', annual reports, and through ongoing exchange and analysis of statistical data; mems: 49 participating states and the EU; the following 3 participating states were (in 2012) inactive mems: Côte d'Ivoire (barred by UN sanctions from trading in rough diamonds), Taiwan (yet to achieve the minimum requirements set by the KPCS), and Venezuela (voluntary suspension of exports and imports of rough diamonds in place); trade in diamonds from the Republic of the Congo was suspended from the KPCS during 2004–07; observers incl. the World Diamond Council; chaired, on a rotating basis, by participating states (2012: USA).

Petrocaribe: internet www.petrocaribe.org; f. June 2005; an initiative of the Venezuelan Government to enhance the access of countries in the Caribbean region to petroleum on preferential payment terms; aims to co-ordinate the development of energy policies and plans regarding natural resources among signatory countries; sixthh summit held in Saint Christopher and Nevis in June 2009; mems: Antigua and Barbuda, Bahamas, Belize, Cuba, Dominica, Dominican Republic, Grenada, Guatemala, Guyana, Haiti, Honduras, Jamaica, Nicaragua, Saint Christopher and Nevis, Saint Lucia, Saint Vincent and the Grenadines, Suriname, Venezuela.

Regional Association of Oil and Natural Gas Companies in Latin America and the Caribbean (Asociación Regional de Empresas de Petróleo y Gas Natural en Latinoamérica y el Caribe—ARPEL): Javier de Viana 2345, Casilla de correo 1006, 11200 Montevideo, Uruguay; tel. 2410 6993; fax 2410 9207; e-mail arpel@arpel.org.uy; internet www.arpel.org; f. 1965 as the Mutual Assistance of the Latin American Oil Companies; aims to initiate and implement activities for the development of the oil and natural gas industry in Latin America and the Caribbean; promotes the expansion of business opportunities and the improvement of the competitive advantages of its members; promotes guidelines in support of competition in the sector; and supports the efficient and sustainable exploitation of hydrocarbon resources and the supply of products and services. Works in co-operation with international organizations, governments, regulatory agencies, technical institutions, universities and non-governmental organizations; mems: 28 state-owned enterprises, representing more than 90% of regional operations, in Argentina, Bolivia, Brazil, Canada, Chile, Colombia, Costa Rica, Cuba, Ecuador, Jamaica, Mexico, Nicaragua, Paraguay, Peru, Suriname, Trinidad and Tobago, Uruguay, Venezuela; Exec. Sec. CÉSAR GONZALEZ NEWMAN; publ. *Boletín Técnico*.

Sugar Association of the Caribbean (Inc.): c/o Caroni, Brechin Castle, Trinidad and Tobago; f. 1942; administers the West Indies Central Sugar Cane Breeding Station (in Barbados) and the West Indies Sugarcane Breeding and Evaluation Network; mems: national sugar cos of Barbados, Belize, Guyana, Jamaica and Trinidad and Tobago, and Sugar Asscn of St Kitts–Nevis–Anguilla; publs *SAC Handbook*, *SAC Annual Report*, *Proceedings of Meetings of WI Sugar Technologists*.

West Indian Sea Island Cotton Association (Inc.): c/o Barbados Agricultural Development Corporation, Fairy Valley, Christ Church, Barbados; mems: organizations in Antigua and Barbuda, Barbados, Jamaica, Montserrat and Saint Christopher and Nevis; Pres. LEROY ROACH; Sec. MICHAEL I. EDGHILL.

World Association of Beet and Cane Growers (WABCG): c/o IFAP, 60 rue St Lazare, 75009 Paris, France; tel. 1-45-26-05-53; fax 1-48-74-72-12; e-mail wabcg@ifap.org; internet www.ifap.org/wabcg; f. 1983 (formal adoption of Constitution, 1984); groups national organizations of independent sugar beet and cane growers; aims to boost the economic, technical and social development of the beet- and cane-growing sector; works to strengthen professional representation in international and national fora; serves as a forum for discussion and exchange of information; mems: 21 beet-growing organizations, 14 cane-growing organizations, from 30 countries; Pres. ROGER STEWART (South Africa); Sec. DAVID LOUIS JOHN KING; publs *World Sugar Farmer News* (quarterly), *World Sugar Farmer Fax Sheet*, *WABCG InfoFlash*, study reports.

World Diamond Council: 580 Fifth Ave, 28th Floor, New York, NY 10036, USA; tel. (212) 575-8848; fax (212) 840-0496; e-mail worlddiamondcouncil@gmail.com; internet www.worlddiamondcouncil.com; f. 2000, by a resolution passed at the World Diamond Congress, convened in July by the World Federation of Diamond Bourses, with the aim of promoting responsibility within the diamond industry towards its stakeholders; lobbied for the creation of a certification scheme to prevent trade in 'conflict diamonds', and became an observer on the ensuing Kimberley Process Certification Scheme, launched in January 2003; has participated in review visits to Kimberley Process participating countries; in Oct. 2002 approved—and maintains—a voluntary System of Warranties, enabling dealers, jewellery manufacturers and retailers to pass on assurances that polished diamonds derive from certified 'conflict-free' rough diamonds, with the aim of extending the effectiveness of the Kimberley Process beyond the export and import phase; meets annually; mems: more than 50 diamond and jewellery industry orgs; Pres. ELI IZHAKOFF.

World Federation of Diamond Bourses (WFDB): 62 Pelikaanstraat, 2018 Antwerp, Belgium; tel. (3) 234-91-21; fax (3) 226-40-73; e-mail info@worldfed.com; internet www

.worldfed.com; f. 1947 to protect the interests of affiliated bourses and their individual members and to settle disputes through international arbitration; holds bienniel World Diamond Congress (2012: Mumbai, India; 2014: Singapore); mems: 25 bourses world-wide; Pres. AVI PAZ (South Africa); Sec.-Gen. RONY UNTERMAN (acting).

World Gold Council (WGC): 55 Old Broad St, London, EC2M 1RX, United Kingdom; tel. (20) 7826-4700; fax (20) 7826-4799; e-mail info@gold.org; internet www.gold.org; f. 1987 as world-wide international asscn of gold producers, to promote the demand for gold; Chair. IAN TELFER; Chief Exec. ADAM SHISHMANIAN.

World Petroleum Council (WPC): 1 Duchess St, 4th Floor, Suite 1, London, W1W 6AN, United Kingdom; tel. (20) 7637-4958; fax (20) 7637-4965; e-mail info@world-petroleum.org; internet www.world-petroleum.org; f. 1933 to serve as a forum for petroleum science, technology, economics and management; undertakes related information and liaison activities; 20th Congress: Doha, Qatar, Dec. 2011; mems: Council includes 66 mem. countries; Pres. Dr RENATO BERTANI (Brazil); Dir-Gen. Dr PIERCE W. F. RIEMER (United Kingdom).

World Sugar Research Organisation (WSRO): 70 Collingwood House, Dolphin Sq., London, SW1V 3LX, United Kingdom; tel. (20) 7821-6800; fax (20) 7834-4137; e-mail wsro@wsro.org; internet www.wsro.org; an alliance of sugar producers, processors, marketers and users; monitors and communicates research on role of sugar and other carbohydrates in nutrition and health; organizes conferences and symposia; operates a database of information; serves as a forum for exchange of views; mems: 67 orgs in 30 countries; Dir-Gen. Dr RICHARD COTTRELL; publs *WSRO Research Bulletin* (online, monthly), *WSRO Newsletter*, papers and conference proceedings.

Development and Economic Co-operation

African Capacity Building Foundation (ACBF): ZB Life Towers, 7th Floor, cnr Jason Moyo Ave/Sam Nujoma St, POB 1562, Harare, Zimbabwe; tel. (4) 702931; fax (4) 702915; e-mail root@acbf-pact.org; internet www.acbf-pact.org; f. 1991 by the World Bank, UNDP, the African Development Bank, African governments and bilateral donors; aims to build sustainable human and institutional capacity for sustainable growth, poverty reduction and good governance in Africa; mems: 44 African and non-African govts, the World Bank, UNDP, AfDB, the IMF; Exec. Sec. Dr FRANNIE A. LÉAUTIER.

African Training and Research Centre in Administration for Development (Centre Africain de Formation et de Recherche Administratives pour le Développement—CAFRAD): POB 1796, Tangier, 90001 Morocco; tel. (661) 307269; fax (539) 325785; e-mail cafrad@cafrad.org; internet www.cafrad.org; f. 1964 by agreement between Morocco and UNESCO; undertakes research into administrative problems in Africa and documents results; provides a consultation service for governments and organizations; holds workshops to train senior civil servants; prepares the Biennial Pan-African Conference of Ministers of the Civil Service; mems: 37 African countries; Chair. MOHAMED SAÂD EL-ALAMI; Dir-Gen. Dr SIMON MAMOSI LELO; publs *African Administrative Studies* (2 a year), *Research Studies*, *Newsletter* (internet), *Collection: Etudes et Documents*, *Répertoires des Consultants et des institutions de formation en Afrique*.

Afro-Asian Rural Development Organization (AARDO): No. 2, State Guest Houses Complex, Chanakyapuri, New Delhi 110 021, India; tel. (11) 24100475; fax (11) 24672045; e-mail aardohq@nde.vsnl.net.in; internet www.aardo.org; f. 1962 to act as a catalyst for the co-operative restructuring of rural life in Africa and Asia and to explore opportunities for the co-ordination of efforts to promote rural welfare and to eradicate hunger, thirst, disease, illiteracy and poverty; carries out collaborative research on development issues; organizes training; encourages the exchange of information; holds international conferences and seminars; awards 150 individual training fellowships at 12 institutes in Bangladesh, Egypt, India, Japan, the Republic of Korea, Malaysia, Nigeria, Taiwan and Zambia; mems: 15 African countries, 14 Asian countries, 1 African associate; Sec.-Gen. WASSFI HASSAN EL-SREIHIN (Jordan); publs *Afro-Asian Journal of Rural Development* (2 a year), *Annual Report*, *AARDO Newsletter* (2 a year).

Agadir Agreement: Fifth Circle, Hanna Qa'war St, Bldg 3, POB 830487, 11183 Amman, Jordan; tel. (6) 5935305; fax (6) 5935306; e-mail atu@agadiragreement.org; internet www.agadiragreement.org; a Declaration made in Agadir, in May 2001, by the governments of Egypt, Jordan, Morocco and Tunisia on the establishment of a common free trade area was followed, in Feb. 2004, by the adoption of the Agadir Agreement on the establishment of a Free Trade Zone between the Arabic Mediterranean Nations, as a means of implementing the Agadir Declaration; the Agadir Agreement entered into force in July 2006 and its implementation commenced in March 2007; mems: Egypt, Jordan, Morocco, Tunisia; Technical Unit Exec. Pres. WALID ELNOZAHY.

Amazon Co-operation Treaty Organization: SHIS-QI 05, Conjunto 16, casa 21, Lago Sul, Brasília, DF 71615-160, Brazil; tel. (61) 3248-4119; fax (61) 3248-4238; internet www.otca.org.br; f. 1978, permanent secretariat established 1995; aims to promote the co-ordinated and sustainable development of the Amazonian territories; there are regular meetings of ministers of foreign affairs; there are specialized co-ordinators of environment, health, science technology and education, infrastructure, tourism, transport and communications, and of indigenous affairs; mems: Bolivia, Brazil, Colombia, Ecuador, Guyana, Peru, Suriname, Venezuela; Sec.-Gen. ALEJANDRO A. GORDILLO (Peru); Exec. Dir. MAURICIO DORFLER.

Arab Gulf Programme for the United Nations Development Organizations (AGFUND): POB 18371, Riyadh 11415, Saudi Arabia; tel. (1) 4418888; fax (1) 4412962; e-mail info@agfund.org; internet www.agfund.org; f. 1981 to provide grants for projects in mother and child care carried out by UN organizations, Arab non-governmental organizations and other international bodies, and to co-ordinate assistance by the nations of the Gulf; financing comes mainly from member states, all of which are members of OPEC; mems: Bahrain, Kuwait, Oman, Qatar, Saudi Arabia, UAE; Pres. HRH Prince TALAL BIN ABDAL-AZIZ.

Arctic Council: c/o Fram Centre, 9296 Tromsø, Norway; tel. 77-75-01-40; fax 77-75-05-01; e-mail ac-chair@arctic-council.org; internet www.arctic-council.org; f. 1996 to promote co-ordination of activities in the Arctic region, in particular in the areas of education, development and environmental protection; working groups, supported by scientific and technical expert groups, focus on the following six areas: action on Arctic contaminants; Arctic monitoring and assessment; conservation of Arctic flora and fauna; emergency prevention, preparedness and response; protection of the Arctic marine environment; and sustainable development; ministerial meetings are normally convened at two-year intervals, most recently in Nuuk, Greenland, in May 2011; Senior Arctic Officials meet annually; mems: Canada, Denmark, Finland, Iceland, Norway, Russia, Sweden, USA; in addition the following 6 orgs representing Arctic indigenous peoples have Permanent Participant status: the Arctic Athabaskan Council, Aleut International Association, Gwich'in Council International, Inuit Circumpolar Council, Russian Arctic Indigenous Peoples of the North, and Saami Council, these are supported by an Indigenous People's Secretariat, based in Copenhagen, Denmark; chairmanship of the Council rotates on a 2-yearly basis (2011–13: Sweden); Chair. of Senior Arctic Officials GUSTAF LIND; Head of Secretariat NINA BUVANG VAAJA.

Asian and Pacific Development Centre: Pesiaran Duta, POB 12224, 50770 Kuala Lumpur, Malaysia; tel. (3) 6511088; fax (3) 6510316; internet www.apdc.org; f. 1980; undertakes research and training, acts as clearing-house for information on development and offers consultancy services, in co-operation with national institutions; current programme includes assistance regarding the implementation of national development strategies; the Centre aims to promote economic co-operation among developing countries of the region for their mutual benefit; mems: 19 countries and 2 associate members; CEO Dr FRANKLIN P. KIM; publs *Annual Report*, *Newsletter* (2 a year),

Asia-Pacific Development Monitor (quarterly), studies, reports, monographs.

Association of Caribbean States (ACS): 5–7 Sweet Briar Rd, St Clair, POB 660, Port of Spain, Trinidad and Tobago; tel. 622-9575; fax 622-1653; e-mail mail@acs-aec.org; internet www.acs-aec.org; f. 1994 by the Governments of the 13 CARICOM countries and Colombia, Costa Rica, Cuba, Dominican Republic, El Salvador, Guatemala, Haiti, Honduras, Mexico, Nicaragua, Suriname and Venezuela; aims to promote economic integration, sustainable development and co-operation in the region; to preserve the environmental integrity of the Caribbean Sea which is regarded as the common patrimony of the peoples of the region; to undertake concerted action to protect the environment, particularly the Caribbean Sea; and to co-operate in the areas of trade, transport, sustainable tourism, and natural disasters. Policy is determined by a Ministerial Council and implemented by a Secretariat based in Port of Spain. In December 2001 a third Summit of Heads of State and Government was convened in Venezuela, where a Plan of Action focusing on issues of sustainable tourism, trade, transport and natural disasters was agreed. The fourth ACS Summit was held in Panama, in July 2005. A final Declaration included resolutions to strengthen co-operation mechanisms with the EU and to promote a strategy for the Caribbean Sea Zone to be recognized as a special area for the purposes of sustainable development programmes, support for a strengthened social agenda and efforts to achieve the Millennium Development Goals, and calls for member states to sign or ratify the following accords: an ACS Agreement for Regional Co-operation in the area of Natural Disasters; a Convention Establishing the Sustainable Tourism Zone of the Caribbean; and an ACS Air Transport Agreement; mems: 25 signatory states, 5 associate mems, 19 observers, 6 founding observer countries; Sec.-Gen. ALFONSO MUÑERA CAVADÍA (Colombia).

Association of Development Financing Institutions in Asia and the Pacific (ADFIAP): Skyland Plaza, 2nd Floor, Sen. Gil J. Puyat Ave, Makati City, Metro Manila, 1200 Philippines; tel. (2) 8161672; fax (2) 8176498; e-mail info@adfiap.org; internet www.adfiap.org; f. 1976 to promote the interests and economic development of the respective countries of its member institutions, through development financing; mems: 113 institutions in 42 countries; Chair. NIHAL FONSEKA (Sri Lanka); Sec.-Gen. OCTAVIO B. PERALTA; publs *Asian Banking Digest*, *Journal of Development Finance* (2 a year), *ADFIAP Newsletter*, *ADFIAP Accompli*, *DevTrade Finance*.

Barents Euro-Arctic Council: International Secretariat, POB, 9915, Rådhusgt. 8, Kirkenes, Norway; tel. 78-97-08-70; fax 78-97-70-79; e-mail ibs@beac.st; internet www.beac.st; f. 1993 as a forum for Barents regional intergovernmental co-operation; mems: Denmark, Finland, Iceland, Norway, Russia, Sweden, European Commission; chairmanship of the Council rotates on a 2-yearly basis between the member states (2011–13:Norway); Head of Int. Secretariat ARI SIRÉN.

Benelux Economic Union: 39 rue de la Régence, 1000 Brussels, Belgium; tel. (2) 519-38-11; fax (2) 513-42-06; e-mail info@benelux.int; internet www.benelux.int; f. 1960 to bring about the economic union of Belgium, Luxembourg and the Netherlands; in June 2008 a new Benelux Treaty was adopted to enter into force upon the expiry in 2010 of the treaty establishing the Union; under the new legal framework cross-border co-operation between the member states and co-operation within a broader European context were to be advanced and the name of the organization was to be changed to Benelux Union; the Union aims to introduce common policies in the field of cross-border co-operation and harmonize standards and intellectual property legislation; structure comprises: Committee of Ministers; Council; Court of Justice; Consultative Inter-Parliamentary Council; the Economic and Social Advisory Council; the General Secretariat; a Benelux Organisation for Intellectual Property was established in Sept. 2006; Sec.-Gen. Dr J. P. R. M. VAN LAARHOVEN (Netherlands); publs *Benelux Newsletter*, *Bulletin Benelux*.

Caribbean-Britain Business Council: 2 Belgrave Sq., London, SW1X 8PJ, United Kingdom; tel. (20) 7235-9484; fax (20) 7823-1370; e-mail david.jessop@caribbean-council.org; internet www.caribbean-council.org; f. 2001; promotes trade and investment development between the United Kingdom, the Caribbean and the EU; Man. Dir DAVID JESSOP; publs *Caribbean Insight* (weekly), *Cuba Briefing* (weekly).

Central Asia Regional Economic Co-operation (CAREC): CAREC Unit, 6 ADB Ave, Mandaluyong City, 1550 Metro Manila, Philippines; tel. (2) 6326134; fax (2) 6362387; e-mail rabutiong@adb.org; internet www.carecprogram.org; f. 1997; a sub-regional alliance supported by several multilateral institutions (ADB, EBRD, the IMF, IDB, UNDP, and the World Bank) to promote economic co-operation and development; supports projects in the following priority areas: transport, energy, trade policy, trade facilitation; a Cross-Border Transport Agreement was signed by Kyrgyzstan and Tajikistan in Oct. 2010 (an agreement for Afghanistan to accede to the Agreement was concluded in Aug. 2011); mems: Afghanistan, Azerbaijan, Kazakhstan, Kyrgyzstan, Mongolia, Tajikistan, Uzbekistan, Xinjiang Uygur Autonomous Region (of the People's Republic of China); Unit Head RONALD ANTONIO Q. BUTIONG.

Central European Free Trade Association: 12–16 rue Joseph II, 1000 Brussels, Belgium; tel. (2) 229-10-11; fax (2) 229-10-19; e-mail cefta@cefta.int; internet www.cefta2006.com; f. 1992, Central European Free Trade Agreement (CEFTA) entered into force 1993; enlarged CEFTA signed 19 Dec. 2006; agreement to expand trade and foster investment by monitoring regulation between parties concerned, establishing free trade areas with the recommendation of the EU; mems: Albania, Bosnia and Herzegovina, Croatia, former Yugoslav republic of Macedonia, Moldova, Montenegro, Serbia, Kosovo; Dir. RENATA VITEZ.

Centre on Integrated Rural Development for Africa (CIRDAFRICA): Nigeria; f. 1979 (operational 1982) to promote integrated rural development through a network of national institutions; to improve the production, income and living conditions of small-scale farmers and other rural groups; to provide tech. support; and to foster the exchange of ideas and experience; financed by mem. states and donor agencies; mems: 17 African countries; Dir Dr ABDELMONEIM M. ELSHEIKH; publ. *CIRDAfrica Rural Tribune* (2 a year).

Centre on Integrated Rural Development for Asia and the Pacific (CIRDAP): Chameli House, 17 Topkhana Rd; GPO Box 2883, Dhaka 1000, Bangladesh; tel. (2) 9558751; fax (2) 9562035; e-mail infocom@cirdap.org; internet www.cirdap.org.sg; f. 1979 to support integrated rural development; promotes regional co-operation; mems: Afghanistan, Bangladesh, Fiji, India, Indonesia, Iran, Laos, Malaysia, Myanmar, Nepal, Pakistan, Philippines, Sri Lanka, Thailand, Viet Nam; Dir Dr DURGA PRASAD PAUDYAL.

Coalition for Dialogue on Africa (CoDA): POB 3001, Addis Ababa, Ethiopia; tel. (11) 15443277; e-mail coda@uneca.org; internet www.uneca.org/coda; f. 2009; brings together African stakeholders and policy-makers; policy-oriented, working in collaboration with regional and international organizations to address issues relating to security, peace, governance and development; sponsored by, but not a programme of, the AU Commission, the UN Economic Commission for Africa and the AfDB; Chair. FESTUS MOGAE.

Colombo Plan: POB 596, 31 Wijerama Rd, Colombo 7, Sri Lanka; tel. (11) 2684188; fax (11) 2684386; e-mail info@colomboplan.org; internet www.colombo-plan.org; f. 1950, as the Colombo Plan for Co-operative Economic and Social Development in Asia and the Pacific, by seven Commonwealth countries, to encourage economic and social development in that region, based on principles of partnership and collective effort; the Plan comprises four training programmes: the Drug Advisory Programme, to enhance the capabilities of officials, in government and non-governmental organizations, involved in drug abuse prevention and control; the Programme for Public Administration, to develop human capital in the public sector; the Programme for Private Sector Development, which implements skill development programmes in the area of small and medium-sized enterprises and related issues; and the Staff College for Technician Education (see below); all training programmes are voluntarily funded, while administrative costs of the organization are shared equally by all member countries; developing countries are encouraged to become donors and to participate in economic and technical co-operation activities; mems: 26 countries; Sec.-Gen. ADAM MANIKU (Maldives); publs

Annual Report, *Colombo Plan Focus* (quarterly), *Consultative Committee Proceedings and Conclusions* (every 2 years).

Colombo Plan Staff College for Technician Education: blk C, DepEd Complex, Meralco Ave, Pasig City 1600, Metro Manila, Philippines; tel. (2) 6310991; fax (2) 6310996; e-mail cpsc@cpsctech.org; internet www.cpsctech.org; f. 1973 with the support of member governments of the Colombo Plan; aims to enhance the development of technician education systems in developing mem. countries; Dir MOHAMMAD NAIM BIN YAAKUB (Malaysia); publ. *CPSC Quarterly*.

COMESA-EAC-SADC Tripartite Secretariat: 1st Floor Bldg 41, CSIR Campus, Meiring Naude Rd, Brummeria, Pretoria, 0001 South Africa; e-mail info@comesa-eac-sadc-tripartite.org; internet www.comesa-eac-sadc-tripartite.org; tripartite COMESA -EAC-SADC co-operation, aiming to advance regional integration through the harmonization of the trade and infrastructure development programmes of these AU regional economic communities (RECs), was initiated in 2005 (a COMESA-SADC task force having been active during 2001–05); a Tripartite Task Force—led by the Secretaries-General of COMESA and the EAC, and the Executive Secretary of SADC—has convened regularly thereafter; a five-year Tripartite Programme on Climate Change Adaptation and Mitigation was adopted in July 2010; the first Tripartite Summit, organized in October 2008, in Kampala, Uganda, approved a roadmap towards the formation of a single free trade area (FTA) and the eventual establishment of a single African Economic Community; at the second Tripartite summit, held in June 2011, in Johannesburg, South Africa, negotiations were initiated on the establishment of the proposed COMESA-EAC-SADC Tripartite FTA; in accordance with a Framework, Roadmap and Architecture for Fast Tracking the Establishment of a Continental FTA (referred to as CFTA), and an Action Plan for Boosting Intra-African Trade, adopted by AU leaders in January 2012, the COMESA-EAC-SADC Tripartite FTA was to be finalized by 2014 and, during 2015–16, consolidated with other regional FTAs into the CFTA initiative, with the aim of establishing by 2017 an operational CFTA.

Communauté économique des états de l'Afrique centrale (CEEAC) (Economic Community of Central African States): BP 2112, Libreville, Gabon; tel. (241) 44-47-31; fax (241) 44-47-32; e-mail secretariat@ceeac-eccas.org; internet www.ceeac-eccas.org; f. 1983, operational 1 January 1985; aims to promote co-operation between member states by abolishing trade restrictions, establishing a common external customs tariff, linking commercial banks, and setting up a development fund, over a period of 12 years; works to combat drug abuse and to promote regional security; has since July 2008 deployed the Mission for the Consolidation of Peace in the CAR—MICOPAX; a CEEAC Parliament was inaugurated in Malabo, Equatorial Guinea, in April 2010; mems: 10 African countries; Sec.-Gen. NASSOUR GUELENGDOUSKSIA OUAIDO.

Community of Sahel-Saharan States (Communauté des états Sahelo-Sahariens—CEN-SAD): Place d'Algeria, POB 4041, Tripoli, Libya; tel. (21) 361-4832; fax (21) 334-3670; e-mail info@cen-sad.org; internet www.uneca.org/cen-sad; f. 1998; fmrly known as COMESSA; aims to strengthen co-operation between signatory states in order to promote their economic, social and cultural integration and to facilitate conflict resolution and poverty alleviation; partnership agreements concluded with many orgs, including the AU, UN and ECOWAS; mems: Benin, Burkina Faso, Central African Republic, Chad, Côte d'Ivoire, Djibouti, Egypt, Eritrea, The Gambia, Ghana, Guinea-Bissau, Liberia, Libya, Mali, Morocco, Niger, Nigeria, Senegal, Sierra Leone, Somalia, Sudan, Togo, Tunisia; Sec.-Gen. Dr MOHAMMED AL-MADANI AL-AZHARI (Libya).

Conseil de l'Entente (Entente Council): 01 BP 3734, angle ave Verdier/rue de Tessières, Abidjan 01, Côte d'Ivoire; tel. 20-33-28-35; fax 20-33-11-49; e-mail fegece@conseil-entente.org; f. 1959 to promote economic development in the region; the Council's Mutual Aid and Loan Guarantee Fund (Fonds d' entraide et de garantie des emprunts) finances development projects, including agricultural projects, support for small and medium-sized enterprises, vocational training centres, research into new sources of energy and building of hotels to encourage tourism; a Convention of Assistance and Co-operation was signed in Feb. 1996; holds annual summit; mems: Benin, Burkina Faso, Côte d'Ivoire, Niger, Togo; publ. *Rapport d'activité* (annually).

Council of American Development Foundations (Consejo de Fundaciones Americanas de Desarrollo—SOLIDARIOS): Calle 6 No. 10 Paraíso, Apdo Postal 620, Santo Domingo, Dominican Republic; tel. 549-5111; fax 544-0550; e-mail solidarios@claro.net.do; internet www.redsolidarios.org; f. 1972; exchanges information and experience, arranges technical assistance, raises funds to organize training programmes and scholarships; administers development fund to finance programmes carried out by members through a loan guarantee programme; provides consultancy services. Mem. foundations provide technical and financial assistance to low-income groups for rural, housing and microenterprise development projects; mems: 18 institutional mems in 9 Latin American and Caribbean countries; Pres. Dr CESAR ALARCÓN COSTTA; Sec.-Gen. ZULEMA BREA DE VILLAMÁN; publs *Solidarios* (quarterly), *Annual Report*.

Council of Regional Organizations in the Pacific (CROP): c/o Private Mail Bag, Suva, Fiji; tel. 3312600; fax 3305573; f. 1988 as South Pacific Organizations' Co-ordinating Committee; renamed 1999; aims to co-ordinate work programmes in the region and improve the efficiency of aid resources; holds annual meetings; chairmanship alternates between the participating organizations; first meeting of subcommittee on information technologies convened in 1998; mems: Pacific Islands Development Programme, Secretariat of the Pacific Community (SPC), Pacific Islands Forum Secretariat, Secretariat of the Pacific Regional Environment Programme, Pacific Islands Forum Fisheries Agency, the South Pacific Tourism Organization (south-pacific.travel), the Fiji School of Medicine, the Pacific Aviation Safety Office, the Pacific Power Association, and the University of the South Pacific.

Developing Eight (D-8): Maya Aka Center, Buyukdere Cad. 100–102, Esentepe, 34390, Istanbul, Turkey; tel. (212) 3561823; fax (212) 3561829; e-mail secretariat@developing8.org; internet www.developing8.org; inaugurated at a meeting of heads of state in June 1997; aims to foster economic co-operation between member states and to strengthen the role of developing countries in the global economy; project areas include trade (with Egypt as the co-ordinating member state), agriculture (Pakistan), human resources (Indonesia), communication and information (Iran), rural development (Bangladesh), finance and banking (Malaysia), energy (Nigeria), and industry, and health (Turkey); seventh Summit meeting: convened in Abuja, Nigeria, July 2010; mems: Bangladesh, Egypt, Indonesia, Iran, Malaysia, Nigeria, Pakistan, Turkey; Sec.-Gen. Dr WIDI PRATIKTO (Indonesia).

Earth Council Alliance: 1250 24th St, NW Suite 300, Washington, DC 20037, USA; tel. (202) 467-2786; e-mail admin@earthcouncilalliance.org; internet www.earthcouncilalliance.org; f. 1992, as the Earth Council, in preparation for the UN Conference on Environment and Development; supported the establishment of National Councils for Sustainable Development (NCSDs) and administers a programme to promote co-operation and dialogue and to facilitate capacity-building and training, with NCSDs; works, with other partner organizations, to generate support for an Earth Charter (adopted in 2000); since 2002 supports other Earth Councils world-wide to promote and support sustainable development; Chair. MAURICE STRONG (Canada); Pres. Dr MARCELO CARVALHO DE ANDRADE (Brazil).

East African Community (EAC): AICC Bldg, Kilimanjaro Wing, 5th Floor, POB 1096, Arusha, Tanzania; tel. (27) 2504253; fax (27) 2504255; e-mail eac@eachq.org; internet www.eac.int; f. 2001, following the adoption of a treaty on political and economic integration (signed in November 1999) by the heads of state of Kenya, Tanzania and Uganda, replacing the Permanent Tripartite Commission for East African Co-operation (f. 1993) and reviving the former East African Community (f. 1967; dissolved 1977); initial areas for co-operation were to be trade and industry, security, immigration, transport and communications, and promotion of investment; further objectives were the elimination of trade barriers and ensuring the free movement of people and capital within the grouping; a customs union came into effect on 1 Jan. 2005; a Court of Justice and a

Legislative Assembly have been established; in April 2006 heads of state agreed that negotiations on a common market would commence in July; the Protocol on the Establishment of the EAC Common Market entered into force on 1 July 2010; Rwanda and Burundi formally became members of the Community on 1 July 2007; an East African Legislative Assembly and an East African Court of Justice were both inaugurated in 2001; has participated, since 2005, to advance regional co-operation through the COMESA-EAC-SADC Tripartite, with a view to advancing regional co-operationUganda; Sec.-Gen. RICHARD SEZIBERA (Rwanda).

Economic Community of the Great Lakes Countries (Communauté économique des pays des Grands Lacs—CEPGL): POB 58, Gisenyi, Rwanda; tel. 61309; fax 61319; f. 1976 main organs: annual Conference of Heads of State, Council of Ministers of Foreign Affairs, Permanent Executive Secretariat, Consultative Commission, Security Commission, three Specialized Technical Commissions; there are four specialized agencies: a development bank, the Banque de Développement des Etats des Grands Lacs (BDEGL) at Goma, Democratic Republic of the Congo; an energy centre at Bujumbura, Burundi; the Institute of Agronomic and Zootechnical Research, Gitega, Burundi; and a regional electricity company (SINELAC) at Bukavu, Democratic Republic of the Congo; mems: Burundi, Democratic Republic of the Congo, Rwanda; Exec. Sec. HERMAN TUYAGA (Burundi); publs *Grands Lacs* (quarterly review), *Journal* (annually).

Economic Research Forum: POB 12311, 21 al-Sad al-Aaly St, Dokki, Cairo, Egypt; tel. (2) 33318600; fax (2) 33318604; e-mail erf@erf.org.eg; internet www.erf.org.eg; f. 1993 to conduct in-depth economic research, compile an economic database for the Arab countries, Iran and Turkey, and to provide training to contribute to sustainable development in the region; Man. Dir AHMED GALAL; publ. *ERF Newsletter* (quarterly).

Eurasian Economic Community (EurAsEC): 105066 Moscow, 1-i Basmannyi per. 6/4, Russia; tel. (495) 223-90-00; fax (495) 223-90-23; e-mail evrazes@evrazes.ru; internet www.evrazes.com; f. 2000; formerly a Customs Union agreed between Belarus, Kazakhstan, Kyrgyzstan, Russia and Tajikistan in 1999; the merger of EurAsEC with the Central Asian Co-operation Organization (CACO) was agreed in Oct. 2005, and achieved in Jan. 2006 with the accession to EurAsEC of Uzbekistan, which had hitherto been the only mem. of CACO that did not also belong to EurAsEC; aims to create a Common Economic Space (CES) with a single currency; a free trade zone was established at the end of 2002; in Oct. 2007 EurAsEC leaders approved the legal basis for establishing a new customs union, initially to comprise Belarus, Kazakhstan and Russia, with Kyrgyzstan, Tajikistan and Uzbekistan expected to join subsequently; the customs union entered into formal existence on 1 Jan. 2010; in Dec. 2010 the heads of state of Belarus, Kazakhstan and Russia signed several agreements aimed at finalizing the establishment of the planned CES, and, in Nov. 2011, they signed a declaration on Eurasian economic integration and adopted a roadmap outlining integration processes aimed at creating a Eurasian Economic Union, to be established by 1 Jan. 2015, and to be based on the Customs Union and CES; in March 2012 the Russian President urged the EurAsEC observer states to join the ongoing economic integration process; mems co-operate on issues including customs tariff harmonization, migration, border security and negotiating admission to the WTO; Uzbekistan announced the suspension of its membership of EurAsEC in Nov. 2008; Armenia, Moldova and Ukraine have observer status; Sec.-Gen. TAIR A. MANSUROV.

European Free Trade Association (EFTA): 9–11 rue de Varembé, 1211 Geneva 20, Switzerland; tel. 223322600; fax 223322677; e-mail mail.gva@efta.int; internet www.efta.int; f. 1960 to bring about free trade in industrial goods and to contribute to the liberalization and expansion of world trade; EFTA states (except Switzerland) participate in the European Economic Area (EEA) with the 27 member countries of the European Union; has concluded free trade agreements with, *inter alia*, Canada, Chile, Colombia, Croatia, Egypt, Israel, Jordan, Republic of Korea, Lebanon, Macedonia, Mexico, Morocco, Palestinian Authority, Singapore, Southern African Customs Union (SACU), Tunisia and Turkey; mems: Iceland, Liechtenstein, Norway, Switzerland; Sec.-Gen. KÅRE BRYN (Norway); publs *EFTA Annual Report*, *EFTA Bulletin*.

Food Aid Committee: c/o International Grains Council, 1 Canada Sq., Canary Wharf, London, E14 5AE, United Kingdom; tel. (20) 7513-1122; fax (20) 7513-0630; e-mail fac@foodaidconvention.org; internet www.foodaidconvention.org; f. 1967; responsible for administration of the Food Aid Convention—FAC (1999), a constituent element of the International Grains Agreement (1995); aims to make appropriate levels of food aid available on a consistent basis to maximize the impact and effectiveness of such assistance; provides a framework for co-operation, co-ordination and information-sharing among members on matters related to food aid. The 23 donor members pledge to supply a minimum of 5m. metric tons of food annually to developing countries and territories, mostly as gifts: in practice aid has usually exceeded 8m. tons annually. Secretariat support is provided by the International Grains Council; Chair. LESLIE NORTON; publ. *Report on shipments* (annually).

Foundation for the Peoples of the South Pacific, International (FSPI): POB 18006, 49 Gladstone Rd, Suva, Fiji; tel. 3312250; fax 3312298; e-mail admin@fspi.org.fj; internet www.fspi.org.fj; f. 1965; provides training and technical assistance for self-help community development groups and co-operatives; implements long-term programmes in sustainable forestry and agriculture, the environment, education, nutrition, women in development, child survival, and fisheries; mems: non-governmental affiliates operating in Australia, Fiji, Kiribati, Papua New Guinea, Samoa, Solomon Islands, Tonga, Tuvalu, United Kingdom, USA, Vanuatu; Exec. Dir REX S. HOROI; publs *Annual Report*, *News* (quarterly), technical reports (e.g. on intermediate technology, nutrition, teaching aids).

G-20 (Doha Round negotiating group): e-mail g-20@mre.gov.br; f. 2003 with the aim of defending the interests of developing countries in the negotiations on agriculture under the WTO's Doha Development Round and meets regularly to address WTO-related agricultural trade issues; now comprises 23 developing countries; mems: Argentina, Bolivia, Brazil, Chile, People's Republic of China, Cuba, Ecuador, Egypt, Guatemala, India, Indonesia, Mexico, Nigeria, Pakistan, Paraguay, Peru, Philippines, South Africa, Tanzania, Thailand, Uruguay, Venezuela, Zimbabwe.

Gambia River Basin Development Organization (Organisation pour la mise en valeur du fleuve Gambie—OMVG): BP 2353, 13 passage Leblanc, Dakar, Senegal; tel. 822-31-59; fax 822-59-26; e-mail omvg@omvg.sn; f. 1978 by Senegal and The Gambia; Guinea joined in 1981 and Guinea-Bissau in 1983. A masterplan for the integrated development of the Kayanga/Geba and Koliba/Corubal river basins has been developed, encompassing a projected natural resources management project; a hydraulic development plan for the Gambia river was formulated during 1996–98; a pre-feasibility study on connecting the national electric grids of the four member states has been completed, and a feasibility study for the construction of the proposed Sambangalou hydroelectric dam, was undertaken in the early 2000s; maintains documentation centre; Exec. Sec. JUSTINO VIEIRA.

Group of Three (G-3): c/o Secretaría de Relaciones Exteriores, 1 Tlatelolco, Del. Cuauhtémoc, 06995 México, DF, Mexico; e-mail gtres@sre.gob.mx; f. 1990 by Colombia, Mexico and Venezuela to remove restrictions on trade between the three countries; in November 2004 Panama joined the Group, which briefly became the Group of Four until Venezuela's withdrawal in November 2006; the trade agreement covers market access, rules of origin, intellectual property, trade in services, and government purchases, and entered into force in early 1994. Tariffs on trade between member states were to be removed on a phased basis. Co-operation was also envisaged in employment creation, the energy sector and the fight against cholera. The secretariat function rotates between the member countries on a two-yearly basis; mems: Colombia, Mexico and Panama.

Group of 15 (G15): G15 Technical Support Facility, 1 route des Morillons, CP 2100, 1218 Grand Saconnex, Geneva, Switzerland; tel. 227916701; fax 227916169; e-mail tsf@g15.org; internet www.g15.org; f. 1989 by 15 developing nations during the ninth summit of the Non-Aligned Movement; retains its original name although current membership totals 17; convenes biennial summits to address the global economic and political situation and to promote economic development through South-South co-operation and North-South dialogue; mems: Algeria, Argentina, Brazil, Chile, Egypt, India, Indonesia, Iran, Jamaica, Kenya, Malaysia, Mexico, Nigeria, Senegal, Sri Lanka, Venezuela, Zimbabwe; Head of Office AUDU A. KADIRI.

Group of 77 (G77): c/o UN Headquarters, Rm NL-2077, New York, NY 10017, USA; tel. (212) 963-0192; fax (212) 963-1753; e-mail secretariat@g77.org; internet www.g77.org; f. 1964 by the 77 signatory states of the 'Joint Declaration of the Seventy-Seven Countries' (the G77 retains its original name, owing to its historic significance, although its membership has expanded since inception); first ministerial meeting, held in Algiers, Algeria, in Oct. 1967, adopted the Charter of Algiers as a basis for G77 co-operation; subsequently G77 Chapters were established with liaison offices in Geneva (UNCTAD), Nairobi (UNEP), Paris (UNESCO), Rome (FAO/IFAD), Vienna (UNIDO), and the Group of 24 (G24) in Washington, DC (IMF and World Bank); as the largest intergovernmental organization of developing states in the United Nations the G77 aims to enable developing nations to articulate and promote their collective economic interests and to improve their negotiating capacity with regard to global economic issues within the United Nations system; in Sept. 2006 G77 ministers of foreign affairs, and the People's Republic of China, endorsed the establishment of a new Consortium on Science, Technology and Innovation for the South (COSTIS); a chairperson, who also acts as spokesperson, co-ordinates the G77's activities in each Chapter; the chairmanship rotates on a regional basis between Africa, Asia, and Latin America and the Caribbean; the supreme decision-making body of the G77 is the South Summit, normally convened at five-yearly intervals (2005: Doha, Qatar; the third Summit was scheduled to be convened in Africa, during 2012); the annual meeting of G77 ministers of foreign affairs is convened at the start (in September) of the regular session of the UN General Assembly; periodic sectoral ministerial meetings are organized in preparation for UNCTAD sessions and prior to the UNIDO and UNESCO General Conferences, and with the aim of promoting South-South co-operation; other special ministerial meetings are also convened from time to time; the first G77 Ministerial Forum on Water Resources was convened in February 2009, in Muscat, Oman; mems: 132 developing countries.

Indian Ocean Commission (IOC) (Commission de l'Océan Indien—COI): Q4, Ave Sir Guy Forget, BP 7, Quatre Bornes, Mauritius; tel. 427-3366; fax 425-2709; e-mail secretariat@coi-ioc.org; internet www.coi-ioc.org; f. 1982 to promote regional co-operation, particularly in economic development; projects include tuna-fishing development, protection and management of environmental resources and strengthening of meteorological services; tariff reduction is also envisaged; organizes an annual regional trade fair; mems: the Comoros, France (representing the French Overseas Department of Réunion), Madagascar, Mauritius, Seychelles; Sec.-Gen. CALLIXTE D'OFFAY; publ. *La Lettre de l'Océan Indien*.

Indian Ocean Rim Association for Regional Co-operation (IOR–ARC): Nexteracom Tower 1, 3rd Floor, Ebene, Mauritius; tel. 454-1717; fax 468-1161; e-mail iorarcsec@iorarc.org; internet www.iorarc.org; the first intergovernmental meeting of countries in the region to promote an Indian Ocean Rim initiative was convened in March 1995; charter to establish the Asscn was signed at a ministerial meeting in March 1997; aims to promote the sustained growth and balanced devt of the region and of its mem. states and to create common ground for regional economic co-operation, *inter alia* through trade, investment, infrastructure, tourism, and science and technology; 10th meeting of Council of Ministers held in San'a, Yemen, Aug. 2010; mems: Australia, Bangladesh, India, Indonesia, Iran, Kenya, Madagascar, Malaysia, Mauritius, Mozambique, Oman, Singapore, South Africa, Sri Lanka, Tanzania, Thailand, United Arab Emirates and Yemen. Dialogue Partner countries: People's Republic of China, Egypt, France, Japan, United Kingdom. Observers: Indian Ocean Research Group (IORG) Inc., Indian Ocean Tourism Org; Sec.-Gen. K. V. BHAGIRATH.

Inter-American Planning Society (Sociedad Interamericana de Planificación—SIAP): c/o Revista Interamericana de Planificación, Casilla 01-05-1978, Cuenca, Ecuador; tel. (7) 823860; fax (7) 823949; e-mail siap1@siap.org.ec; f. 1956 to promote development of comprehensive planning; mems: institutions and individuals in 46 countries; Exec. Sec. LUIS E. CAMACHO (Colombia); publs *Correo Informativo* (quarterly), *Inter-American Journal of Planning* (quarterly).

International Centre for Integrated Mountain Development (ICIMOD): GPO Box 3226, Khumaltur, Kathmandu, Nepal; tel. (1) 5003222; fax (1) 5003299; e-mail info@icimod.org; internet www.icimod.org; f. 1983; an autonomous organization sponsored by regional member countries and by the governments of Nepal, Germany, Switzerland, Austria, Netherlands and Denmark, to help promote an economically and environmentally sound ecosystem and to improve the living standards of the population in the Hindu Kush-Himalaya; aims to serve as a focal point for multi-disciplinary documentation, training and applied research, and as a consultative centre in scientific and practical matters pertaining to mountain development; participating countries: Afghanistan, Bangladesh, Bhutan, People's Republic of China, India, Myanmar, Nepal, Pakistan; Dir-Gen. DAVID MOLDEN (USA).

International Co-operation for Development and Solidarity (Co-opération Internationale pour le Développement et la Solidarité—CIDSE): 16 rue Stévin, 1000 Brussels, Belgium; tel. (2) 230-77-22; fax (2) 230-70-82; e-mail postmaster@cidse.org; internet www.cidse.org; f. 1967; an international alliance of Catholic development agencies, whose members share a common strategy in their efforts to eradicate poverty and establish global justice. CIDSE's advocacy work covers trade and food security, climate change, resources for development, global governance, and EU development policy; promotes co-operation and the development of common strategies on advocacy work, development projects and programmes and development education; mems: 16 Catholic agencies in 15 countries and territories; Pres. CHRIS BAIN; Sec.-Gen. BERND NILLES.

Inuit Circumpolar Council: Aqqusinersuaq 3A, 1st Floor, POB 204, 3900 Nuuk Greenland; tel. 323632; fax 323001; e-mail iccgreenland@inuit.org; internet www.inuit.org; f. 1977 (as the Inuit Circumpolar Conference, name changed 2006) to protect the indigenous culture, environment and rights of the Inuit people, and to encourage co-operation among the Inuit; has adopted a Circumpolar Inuit Declaration on Sovereignty in the Arctic (in April 2009), and a Circumpolar Inuit Declaration on Resource Development Principles in Inuit Nunaat (May 2011); the Nuuk Declaration, adopted in June 2010 by the 11th General Assembly, directed the Council, *inter alia*, to implement a 2010–14 Circumpolar Inuit Health Strategy; to keep environmental stewardship of the Inuit homeland as a priority activity during 2010–14; to organize an Inuit leaders' summit on resource development; to continue to participate in international bodies to defend and promote the right of the Inuit to harvest marine mammals and to trade their products on a sustainable basis; and instructed the Council to organize a pan-Arctic Inuit leaders' summit during 2012; General Assemblies held every four years (2010: Nuuk, Greenland, in June); mems: Inuit communities in Canada, Greenland, Alaska and Russia; Chair. AQQALUK LYNGE; Exec. Dir ALFRED JAKOBSEN; publ. *Silarjualiriniq*.

Lake Chad Basin Commission (LCBC): BP 727, N'Djamena, Chad; tel. 52-41-45; fax 52-41-37; e-mail lcbc@intnet.td; internet www.cblt.org; f. 1964 to encourage co-operation in developing the Lake Chad region and to promote the settlement of regional disputes; work programmes emphasize the regulation of the utilization of water and other natural resources in the basin; the co-ordination of natural resources development projects and research; holds annual summit of heads of state; mems: Cameroon, Central African Republic, Chad, Niger, Nigeria; Exec. Sec. MUHAMMAD SANI ADAMU; publ. *Bibliographie générale de la CBLT* (2 a year).

Latin American Association of Development Financing Institutions (Asociación Latinoamericana de Instituciones Financieras para el Desarrollo—ALIDE): Apdo Postal 3988, Paseo de la República 3211, Lima 27, Peru; tel. (1) 4422400; fax (1) 4428105; e-mail sg@alide.org.pe; internet www.alide.org.pe; f. 1968 to promote co-operation among regional development financing bodies; programmes: technical assistance; training; studies and research; technical meetings; information; projects and investment promotion; mems: more than 70 active, 3 assoc.

and 5 collaborating (banks and financing institutions and development organizations in 22 Latin American countries, Canada, Germany and Spain); Pres. RODRIGO SÁNCHEZ MÚJICA; Sec.-Gen. ROMMEL ACEVEDO; publs *ALIDE Bulletin* (6 a year), *ALIDENOTICIAS Newsletter* (monthly), *Annual Report, Latin American Directory of Development Financing Institutions*.

Latin American Economic System (Sistema Económico Latinoamericano—SELA): Torre Europa, 4°, Urb. Campo Alegre, Avda Francisco de Miranda, Caracas 1060, Venezuela; Apdo 17035, Caracas 1010-A, Venezuela; tel. (212) 955-7111; fax (212) 951-5292; e-mail sela@sela.org; internet www.sela.org; f. 1975 in accordance with the Panama Convention; aims to foster co-operation and integration among the countries of Latin America and the Caribbean, and to provide a permanent system of consultation and co-ordination in economic and social matters; conducts studies and other analysis and research; extends technical assistance to sub-regional and regional co-ordination bodies; provides library, information service and databases on regional co-operation. The Latin American Council, the principal decision-making body of the System, meets annually at ministerial level and high-level regional consultation and co-ordination meetings are held; acts as the Executive Secretariat of the Working Group on Trade and Competition in Latin America and the Caribbean; mems: 28 countries; Perm. Sec. JOSÉ RIVERA BANUET (Mexico); publs *Capítulos del SELA* (3 a year), *Bulletin on Latin America and Caribbean Integration* (monthly), *SELA Antenna in the United States* (quarterly).

Liptako-Gourma Integrated Development Authority (LGA): POB 619, ave M. Thevenond, Ouagadougou, Burkina Faso; tel. (3) 30-61-48; f. 1970; scope of activities includes water infrastructure, telecommunications and construction of roads and railways; in 1986 undertook study on development of water resources in the basin of the Niger river (for hydroelectricity and irrigation); mems: Burkina Faso, Mali, Niger; Chair. SEYDOU BOUDA (Mali).

Mano River Union: Private Mail Bag 133, Delco House, Lightfoot Boston St, Freetown, Sierra Leone; tel. (22) 226883; e-mail sg@manoriveruniononline.org; internet www.manoriveruniononline.org; f. 1973 to establish a customs and economic union between member states to accelerate development via integration; a common external tariff was instituted in 1977. Intra-union free trade was officially introduced in May 1981, as the first stage in progress towards a customs union. A non-aggression treaty was signed by heads of state in 1986. The Union was inactive for three years until mid-1994, owing to regional conflict and disagreements regarding funding. In Jan. 1995 a Mano River Centre for Peace and Development was established, to provide a permanent mechanism for conflict prevention and resolution, and monitoring of human rights violations, and to promote sustainable peace and development. A new security structure was approved in 2000. In Aug. 2001 ministers of foreign affairs, security, internal affairs, and justice, meeting as the Joint Security Committee, resolved to deploy joint border security and confidence-building units, and to work to re-establish the free movement of people and goods; implements programmes in the following areas: institutional revitalisation, restructuring and development; peace and security; economic development and regional integration; and social development; mems: Guinea, Liberia, Sierra Leone; Sec.-Gen. Dr HADJA SARAN DARABA KABBA.

Mekong River Commission (MRC): POB 6101, Unit 18 Ban Sithane Neua, Sikhottabong District, Vientiane, Laos 01000; tel. (21) 263263; fax (21) 263264; e-mail mrcs@mrcmekong.org; internet www.mrcmekong.org; f. 1995 as successor to the Committee for Co-ordination of Investigations of the Lower Mekong Basin ('Mekong Committee' f. 1957); aims to promote and co-ordinate the sustainable development and use of the water and related resources of the Mekong River Basin for navigational and non-navigational purposes, in order to assist the social and economic development of member states and preserve the ecological balance of the basin; provides scientific information and policy advice; supports the implementation of strategic programmes and activities; organizes an annual donor consultative group meeting; maintains regular dialogue with Myanmar and the People's Republic of China; the first meeting of heads of government was convened in Hua Hin, Thailand, in April 2010; mems: Cambodia, Laos, Thailand, Viet Nam; CEO HANS GUTTMAN; publs *Annual Report, Catch and Culture* (3 a year), *Mekong News* (quarterly).

Mesoamerican Integration and Development Project (Proyecto de Integración y Desarrollo de Mesoamérica): Torre Roble, 8°, San Salvador, El Salvador; tel. 2261-5444; fax 2260-9176; e-mail e.whyte@proyectomesoamerica.org; internet www.proyectomesoamerica.org; f. 2001 as the Puebla-Panamá Plan (PPP); relaunched with formal institutionalized structure in 2004; current name and mandate approved in June 2008 by the Tuxtla summit meeting; aims to promote economic development and reduce poverty in member countries; eight key areas of activity: energy, transport, telecommunications, tourism, trade environment and competitiveness, human development, sustainable development, prevention and mitigation of natural disasters; administers the Mesoamerica Biological Corridor initiative to enhance the management of the region's biodiversity; mems: Belize, Colombia, Costa Rica, El Salvador, Guatemala, Honduras, Mexico, Nicaragua, Panama; Exec. Dir ELAYNE WHYTE GÓMEZ.

Niger Basin Authority (Autorité du Bassin du Niger): BP 729, Niamey, Niger; tel. 20724395; fax 20724208; e-mail sec-executif@abn.ne; internet www.abn.ne; f. 1964 (as River Niger Commission; name changed 1980) to harmonize national programmes concerned with the River Niger Basin and to execute an integrated development plan; compiles statistics; regulates navigation; runs projects on hydrological forecasting, environmental control; infrastructure and agro-pastoral development; mems: Benin, Burkina Faso, Cameroon, Chad, Côte d'Ivoire, Guinea, Mali, Niger, Nigeria; Exec. Sec. MOHAMMED BELLO TUGA (Nigeria); publ. *NBA-INFO* (quarterly).

Nile Basin Initiative: POB 192, Entebbe, Uganda; tel. (41) 321329; fax (41) 320971; e-mail nbisec@nilebasin.org; internet www.nilebasin.org; f. 1999; aims to achieve sustainable socio-economic development through the equitable use and benefits of the Nile Basin water resources and to create an enabling environment for the implementation of programmes with a shared vision. Highest authority is the Nile Basin Council of Ministers (Nile-COM); other activities undertaken by a Nile Basin Technical Advisory Committee (Nile-TAC); mems: Burundi, Democratic Republic of the Congo, Egypt, Eritrea, Ethiopia, Kenya, Rwanda, Sudan, Tanzania, Uganda; Chair. CHARITY K. NGILU.

Nordic Development Fund: POB 185, 00171 Helsinki, Finland; tel. (10) 618-002; fax (9) 622-1491; e-mail info.ndf@ndf.fi; internet www.ndf.fi; f. 1989; supports activities by national administrations for overseas development, with resources amounting to €330m; Man. Dir HELGE SEMB.

Organization for the Development of the Senegal River (Organisation pour la mise en valeur du fleuve Sénégal—OMVS): c/o Haut-Commissariat, 46 rue Carnot, BP 3152, Dakar, Senegal; tel. 859-81-81; fax 864-01-63; e-mail omvssphc@omvs.org; internet www.omvs.org; f. 1972 to promote the use of the Senegal river for hydroelectricity, irrigation and navigation; the Djama dam in Senegal provides a barrage to prevent salt water from moving upstream, and the Manantali dam in Mali is intended to provide a reservoir for irrigation of about 375,000 ha of land and for production of hydroelectricity and provision of year-round navigation for ocean-going vessels. In 1997 two companies were formed to manage the dams: Société de gestion de l'énergie de Manantali (SOGEM) and Société de gestion et d'exploitation du barrage de Djama (SOGED); mems: Guinea, Mali, Mauritania, Senegal; High Commissioner MOHAMED SALEM OULD MERZOUG (Mauritania).

Organization for the Management and Development of the Kagera River Basin (Organisation pour l'aménagement et le développement du bassin de la rivière Kagera—OBK): BP 297, Kigali, Rwanda; tel. (7) 84665; fax (7) 82172; f. 1978; envisages joint development and management of resources, including the construction of an 80-MW hydroelectric dam at Rusumo Falls, on the Rwanda-Tanzania border, a 2,000-km railway network between the four member countries, road construction (914 km), and a telecommunications network between member states; mems: Burundi, Rwanda, Tanzania, Uganda.

Organization of the Co-operatives of America (Organización de las Cooperativas de América): Apdo Postal 241263,

Carrera 11, No 86-32, Of. 101, Bogotá, Colombia; tel. (1) 6103296; fax (1) 6101912; f. 1963 for improving socio-economic, cultural and moral conditions through the use of the co-operatives system; works in every country of the continent; regional offices sponsor plans and activities based on the most pressing needs and special conditions of individual countries; mems: national or local orgs in 23 countries and territories; Exec. Sec. Dr CARLOS JULIO PINEDA SUÁREZ; publs *América Cooperativa* (monthly), *OCA News* (monthly).

Pacific Alliance: f. 2012; in June 2012 the Presidents of Chile, Colombia, Mexico and Peru, meeting in Antofagasta, Chile, signed a framework agreement establishing the Alliance; it was envisaged that Costa Rica and Panama, which participated in the meeting as observers, would join the Alliance subsequently; the inaugural meeting of the Alliance determined to finalize the establishment of a pan-Latin American stock exchange; to bring about the elimination of visa restrictions for citizens of member countries; to open joint export promotion offices in Asian countries; to establish a joint university system; and to seek to eliminate by end-2012 import duties and country-of-origin rules between member states.

Pacific Basin Economic Council (PBEC): 2803–04, 28/F, Harbour Centre, 25 Harbour Rd Wanchai, Hong Kong SAR; tel. 2815-6550; fax 2545-0499; e-mail info@pbec.org; internet www.pbec.org; f. 1967; an asscn of business representatives aiming to promote business opportunities in the region, in order to enhance overall economic development; advises governments and serves as a liaison between business leaders and government officials; encourages business relationships and co-operation among members; holds business symposia; mems: 20 economies (Australia, Canada, Chile, People's Republic of China, Colombia, Ecuador, Hong Kong SAR, Indonesia, Japan, Republic of Korea, Malaysia, Mexico, New Zealand, Peru, Philippines, Russia, Singapore, Taiwan, Thailand, USA); Chair. WILFRED WONG YING-WAI; publs *PBEC Update* (quarterly), *Executive Summary* (annual conference report).

Pacific Economic Cooperation Council (PECC): 29 Heng Mui Keng Terrace, Singapore 119620; tel. 67379823; fax 67379824; e-mail info@pecc.org; internet www.pecc.org; f. 1980; an independent, policy-orientated organization of senior research, government and business representatives from 26 economies in the Asia-Pacific region; aims to foster economic development in the region by providing a forum for discussion and co-operation in a wide range of economic areas; PECC is an official observer to APEC; holds a General Meeting annually; mems: Australia, Brunei, Canada, Chile, the People's Republic of China, Colombia, Ecuador, Hong Kong, Indonesia, Japan, the Republic of Korea, Malaysia, Mexico, Mongolia, New Zealand, Peru, Philippines, Singapore, Taiwan, Thailand, USA, Viet Nam and the Pacific Islands Forum; assoc. mem.: France (Pacific Territories); Sec.-Gen. EDUARDO PEDROSA; publs *Issues PECC* (quarterly), *Pacific Economic Outlook* (annually), *Pacific Food Outlook* (annually).

Pacific Islands Development Program: East-West Centre, 1601 East-West Rd, Honolulu, HI 96848-1601, USA; tel. (808) 944-7111; fax (808) 944-7376; e-mail pidp@eastwestcenter.org; f. 1980; promotes regional development by means of education, research and training; serves as the secretariat of the Pacific Islands Conference of Leaders; mems: 22 Pacific islands; Dirs Dr SITIVENI HALAPUA, Dr GERARD FININ; publ. *Pacific Islands Report*.

Pacific Trade and Development Forum (PAFTAD): PAFTAD International Secr., John Crawford Bldg, Asia Pacific School of Economics and Government, Australian National University, Canberra, ACT 0200, Australia; tel. (2) 6125-5539; e-mail paftad.sec@anu.edu.au; internet www.paftad.org; f. 1968; holds annual conference for discussion of regional trade policy issues by senior economists and experts; Head of Secretariat Prof. PETER DRYSDALE; Exec. Officer LUKE HURST.

Pan-African Institute for Development (PAID): BP 1756, Ouagadougou 01, Burkina Faso; tel. 5036-4807; fax 5036-4730; e-mail ipdaos@fasonet.bf; internet www.ipd-aos.org; f. 1964; gives training to people from African countries involved with development at grassroots, intermediate and senior levels; emphasis is given to: development management and financing; agriculture and rural development; issues of gender and development; promotion of small and medium-sized enterprises; training policies and systems; environment, health and community development; research, support and consultancy services; and specialized training. There are four regional institutes: Central Africa (Douala, Cameroon), Sahel (Ouagadougou, Burkina Faso), West Africa (Buéa, Cameroon), Eastern and Southern Africa (Kabwe, Zambia) and a European office in Geneva; publs *Newsletter* (2 a year), *Annual Progress Report, PAID Report* (quarterly).

Partners in Population and Development (PPD): IPH Bldg, 2nd Floor, Mohakhali, Dhaka 1212, Bangladesh; tel. (2) 988-1882; fax (2) 882-9387; e-mail partners@ppdsec.org; internet www.partners-popdev.org; f. 1994; aims to implement the decisions of the International Conference on Population and Development, held in Cairo, Egypt in 1994, in order to expand and improve South-South collaboration in the fields of family planning and reproductive health; administers a Visionary Leadership Programme, a Global Leadership Programme, and other training and technical advisory services; mems: 24 developing countries; Exec. Dir Dr JOE THOMAS.

Permanent Interstate Committee on Drought Control in the Sahel (Comité permanent inter états de lutte contre la sécheresse au Sahel—CILSS): POB 7049, Ouagadougou 03, Burkina Faso; tel. 50-37-41-25; fax 50-37-41-32; e-mail cilss.se@cilss.bf; internet www.cilss.bf; f. 1973; works in co-operation with UNDP Drylands Development Centre; aims to combat the effects of chronic drought in the Sahel region, by improving irrigation and food production, halting deforestation and creating food reserves; initiated a series of projects to improve food security and to counter poverty, entitled Sahel 21; the heads of state of all members had signed a convention for the establishment of a Fondation pour le Développement Durable du Sahel; maintains Institut du Sahel at Bamako (Mali) and centre at Niamey (Niger); mems: Burkina Faso, Cape Verde, Chad, The Gambia, Guinea-Bissau, Mali, Mauritania, Niger, Senegal; Pres. BA MAMADOU MBARE (Mauritania); Exec. Sec. ALHOUSSEÏNI BRETAUDEAU (The Gambia); publ. *Reflets Sahéliens* (quarterly).

Population Council: 1 Dag Hammarskjöld Plaza, New York, NY 10017, USA; tel. (212) 339-0500; fax (212) 755-6052; e-mail pubinfo@popcouncil.org; internet www.popcouncil.org; f. 1952; the council is organized into three programmes: HIV and AIDS; Poverty, Gender, and Youth; and Reproductive Health; aims to improve reproductive health and achieve a balance between people and resources; analyses demographic trends; conducts biomedical research to develop new contraceptives; works with private and public agencies to improve the quality and scope of family planning and reproductive health services; helps governments to design and implement population policies; communicates results of research. Four regional offices, in India, Mexico, Egypt and Ghana, and 18 country offices in the developing world, with programmes in more than 65 countries. Additional office in Washington, DC, USA, carries out worldwide operational research and activities for reproductive health and the prevention of HIV and AIDS; Pres. PETER J. DONALDSON; publs *Momentum* (2 a year), *Studies in Family Planning* (quarterly), *Population and Development Review* (quarterly), *Population Briefs* (3 a year).

Society for International Development: Via Panisperna 207, 00184 Rome, Italy; tel. (06) 4872172; fax (06) 4872170; e-mail info@sidint.org; internet www.sidint.net; f. 1957; a global network of individuals and institutions wishing to promote participative, pluralistic and sustainable development; builds partnerships with civil society groups and other sectors; fosters local initiatives and new forms of social experimentation; mems: 3,000 individual mems and 55 institutional mems in 125 countries, 65 local chapters; Pres. JUMA V. MWAPACHU (Tanzania); Man. Dir STEFANO PRATO (Italy); publ. *Development* (quarterly).

South Centre: 17–19 Chemin du Champ-d'Anier, CP 228, 1211 Geneva 19, Switzerland; tel. 227918050; fax 227988531; e-mail south@southcentre.org; internet www.southcentre.org; f. 1990 as a follow-up mechanism of the South Commission (f. 1987); in 1995 established as an intergovernmental body to promote South-South solidarity and co-operation by generating ideas and action-oriented proposals on major policy issues; mems: 50 mem. countries; Chair. BENJAMIN WILLIAM MKAPA

(Tanzania); Exec. Dir MARIN KHOR (Malaysia); publs *South Bulletin* (every 2 weeks), *Policy Brief* (monthly).

Southeast European Co-operative Initiative (SECI): Heldenplatz 1, Vienna 1010, Austria; tel. (1) 514-36-64-22; fax (1) 531-37-420; e-mail seci2@osce.org; internet www.secinet.info; f. 1996 in order to encourage co-operation among countries of the sub-region and to facilitate their integration into European structures; receives technical support from the ECE and OSCE; ad hoc Project Groups have been established to undertake preparations for the following selected projects: commercial arbitration and mediation; co-operation between the Danube countries (particularly in the areas of policy harmonization, transport, energy, culture and education); electricity grids; energy efficiency; environmental recovery; combating organized crime; regional road transport; securities markets; trade and transport facilitation; and transport infrastructure; activities are overseen by a SECI Agenda Committee, a SECI Business Advisory Council (based in Thessaloniki, Greece) and a SECI Regional Centre for Combating Transborder Crime (based in Bucharest, Romania); mems: Albania, Bosnia and Herzegovina, Bulgaria, Croatia, Greece, Hungary, former Yugoslav republic of Macedonia, Moldova, Romania, Serbia, Slovenia, Turkey; Co-ordinator ERHARD BUSEK.

Trans-Pacific Strategic Economic Partnership Agreement (P4): c/o Ministry of Foreign Affairs and Trade, Private Bag 18901, Wellington, New Zealand; tel. (4) 439-8345; e-mail tpp@mfat.govt.nz; f. 2006 upon entry into force of agreement signed by the four founding mems; eliminated some 90% of tariffs on trade between mems; negotiations on financial services and investment commenced in March 2008; negotiations on an expanded partnership agreement, to include Australia, Malaysia, Peru, the USA and Viet Nam, commenced in March 2010 (11th round held: March 2012); mems: Brunei, Chile, New Zealand, Singapore.

Union of the Arab Maghreb (Union du Maghreb arabe—UMA): 73 rue Tensift, Agdal, Rabat, Morocco; tel. (53) 7681371; fax (53) 7681377; e-mail sg.uma@maghrebarabe.org; internet www.maghrebarabe.org; f. 1989; aims to encourage joint ventures and to create a single market; structure comprises a council of heads of state (meeting annually), a council of ministers of foreign affairs, a follow-up committee, a consultative council of 30 delegates from each country, a UMA judicial court, and four specialized ministerial commissions. Chairmanship rotates annually between heads of state. A Maghreb Investment and Foreign Trade Bank, funding joint agricultural and industrial projects, has been established and a customs union created; mems: Algeria, Mauritania, Morocco, Tunisia; Sec.-Gen. HABIB BEN YAHIA (Tunisia).

United Nations African Institute for Economic Development and Planning (IDEP) (Institut africain de développement économique et de planification): rue du 18 Juin, BP 3186, Dakar, Senegal; tel. 823-10-20; fax 822-29-64; e-mail unidep@unidep.org; internet www.unidep.org; f. 1963 by UN ECA to train economic development planners, conduct research and provide advisory services; has library of books, journals and documents; mems: 53 mem. states; Dir ADEBAYO OLUKOSHI.

US-Pacific Island Nations Joint Commercial Commission: c/o Pacific Islands Development Program, 1601 East-West Rd, Honolulu, HI 96848, USA; tel. (808) 944-7721; fax (808) 944-7670; e-mail kroekers@eastwestcenter.org; internet pidp.eastwestcenter.org/jcc; f. 1993 to promote mutually beneficial commercial and economic relations between the independent Pacific island nations and the USA; mems: Cook Islands, Fiji, Kiribati, Marshall Islands, Federated States of Micronesia, Nauru, Niue, Papua New Guinea, Samoa, Solomon Islands, Tonga, Tuvalu, USA and Vanuatu.

Vienna Institute for International Dialogue and Co-operation (Wiener Institut für internationalen Dialog und Zusammenarbeit): Möllwaldplatz 5/3, 1040 Vienna, Austria; tel. (1) 713-35-94; fax (1) 713-35-73; e-mail office@vidc.org; internet www.vidc.org; f. 1987 (as Vienna Institute for Development and Co-operation; fmrly Vienna Institute for Development, f. 1964); manages development policy research on sectoral, regional and cross-cutting issues (for example, gender issues); arranges cultural exchanges between Austria and countries from Africa, Asia and Latin America; deals with conception and organization of anti-racist and integrative measures in sport, in particular football; Pres. BARBARA PRAMMER; Dir WALTER POSCH; publs *Report Series*, *Echo*.

World Economic Forum: 91–93 route de la Capite, 1223 Cologny/Geneva, Switzerland; tel. 228691212; fax 227862744; e-mail contact@weforum.org; internet www.weforum.org; f. 1971; the Forum comprises commercial interests gathered on a non-partisan basis, under the stewardship of the Swiss Government, with the aim of improving society through economic development; convenes an annual meeting in Davos, Switzerland; organizes the following programmes: Technology Pioneers; Women Leaders; and Young Global Leaders; and aims to mobilize the resources of the global business community in the implementation of the following initiatives: the Global Health Initiative; the Disaster Relief Network; the West-Islamic World Dialogue; and the G20/International Monetary Reform Project; the Forum is governed by a guiding Foundation Board; an advisory International Business Council; and an administrative Managing Board; regular mems: representatives of 1,000 leading commercial companies in 56 countries world-wide; selected mem. companies taking a leading role in the movement's activities are known as 'partners'; Chair. KLAUS SCHWAB.

Economics and Finance

Accounting and Auditing Organization for Islamic Financial Institutions (AAOIFI): POB 1176, Manama, Bahrain; tel. 244496; fax 250194; e-mail aaoifi@batelco.com.bh; internet www.aaoifi.com; f. 1990; aims to develop accounting, auditing and banking practices and to harmonize standards among member institutions; Sec.-Gen. Dr KHALED AL-FAKIH.

African Insurance Organization (AIO): 30 ave de Gaulle, BP 5860, Douala, Cameroon; tel. 33-42-01-63; fax 33-43-20-08; e-mail info@africaninsurance.net; internet www.african-insurance.org; f. 1972 to promote the expansion of the insurance and reinsurance industry in Africa, and to increase regional co-operation; holds annual conference, periodic seminars and workshops, and arranges meetings for reinsurers, brokers, consultant and regulators in Africa; has established African insurance 'pools' for aviation, petroleum and fire risks, and created asscns of African insurance educators, supervisory authorities and insurance brokers and consultants; Sec.-Gen. P. M. G. SOARES; publ. *African Insurance Annual Review*.

African Reinsurance Corporation (Africa-Re): Africa Re House, Plot 1679, Karimu Kotun St, Victoria Island, PMB 12765, Lagos, Nigeria; tel. (1) 2626660; fax (1) 2663282; e-mail info@africa-re.com; internet www.africa-re.com; f. 1976; its purpose is to foster the development of the insurance and reinsurance industry in Africa and to promote the growth of national and regional underwriting capacities; auth. cap. US $100m., of which the African Development Bank holds 10%; mems: 41 countries, 5 development finance institutions, and some 110 insurance and reinsurance companies; Chair. MUSA AL-NAAS; Man. Dir and CEO CORNEILLE KAREKEZI; publ. *The African Reinsurer* (annually).

African Rural and Agricultural Credit Association (AFRACA): ACK Garden House, 2nd Floor, POB 41378–00100, Nairobi, Kenya; tel. (20) 2717911; fax (20) 2710082; e-mail afraca@africaonline.co.ke; internet www.afraca.org; f. 1977 to develop the rural finance environment by adopting and promoting policy frameworks and assisting sustainable financial institutions to increase outreach; 86 mems in 27 African countries, including central, commercial and agricultural banks, micro-finance institutions, and national programmes working in the area of agricultural and rural finance in the continent; Chair. JEAN MARIE EMUNGU; publ. *Afraca Workshop Reports*, *Rural Finance Reports*.

Arab Society of Certified Accountants (ASCA): POB 921100, Amman 11192, Jordan; tel. (6) 5100900; fax (6) 5100901; e-mail info@ascasociety.org; internet www.ascasociety.org; f. 1984 as a professional body to supervise qualifications for Arab accountants and to maintain standards; mems in 21 countries; Chair. TALAL ABU-GHAZALEH (Jordan); Gen. Sec. SAMAR AL-LABBAD (Egypt); publs *Arab Certified*

Accountant (monthly), *ASCA Bulletin* (monthly), *International Accountancy Standards, International Audit Standards, Abu-Ghazaleh Dictionary of Accountancy*.

Asian Clearing Union (ACU): Pasdaran Ave, POB 15875-7177, 16646 Tehran, Iran; tel. (21) 22842076; fax (21) 22847677; e-mail acusecret@cbi.ir; internet www.asianclearingunion.org; f. 1974; provides a facility to settle payments, on a multilateral basis, for international transactions among participating central banks, thereby contributing to the expansion of trade and economic activity among ESCAP countries; the Central Bank of Iran is the agent for the Union; units of account are, with effect from 1 Jan. 2009, denominated as the ACU dollar and the ACU euro; mems: central banks of Bangladesh, Bhutan, India, Iran, Myanmar, Nepal, Pakistan, Sri Lanka; Chair. Dr D. SUBBARAO; Sec.-Gen. LIDA BORHAN-AZAD; publs *Annual Report, Monthly Newsletter*.

Asian Reinsurance Corporation: 17th Floor, Tower B, Chamnan Phenjati Business Center, 65 Rama 9 Rd, Huaykwang, Bangkok 10320, Thailand; tel. (2) 245-2169; fax (2) 248-1377; e-mail asianre@asianrecorp.com; internet www.asianrecorp.com; f. 1979 under ESCAP auspices; aims to operate as a professional reinsurer serving the needs of the Asia Pacific region; also aims to provide technical assistance to national insurance markets; cap. (auth.) US $100m., (subscribed and p.u.) $30.2m. (Dec. 2010); mems: Afghanistan, Bangladesh, Bhutan, People's Republic of China, India, Iran, Republic of Korea, Philippines, Sri Lanka, Thailand; Pres. and CEO S. A. KUMAR.

Association of African Central Banks (AACB): Ave Abdoulaye Fadiga, BP 3108, Dakar, Senegal; tel. 839-05-00; fax 839-08-01; e-mail akangni@bceao.int; internet www.aacb.org; f. 1968 to promote contacts in the monetary and financial sphere, in order to increase co-operation and trade among member states; aims to strengthen monetary and financial stability on the African continent; since 2002 administers an African Monetary Co-operation Programme; mems: 40 African central banks representing 47 states; Chair. Dr PERKS LIGOYA; Exec. Sec. SAMUEL MÉANGO.

Association of African Development Finance Institutions (AADFI): Immeuble AIAFD, blvd Latrille, rue J61, Cocody Deux Plateaux, Abidjan 0, Côte d'Ivoire; tel. 22-52-33-89; fax 22-52-25-84; e-mail info@adfi-ci.org; internet www.aadfi.org; f. 1975; aims to promote co-operation among financial institutions in the region in matters relating to economic and social development, research, project design, financing and the exchange of information; mems: 92 in 43 African and non-African countries; Chair. PETER M. NONI; Sec.-Gen. JOSEPH AMIHERE; publs *Annual Report, AADFI Information Bulletin* (quarterly), *Finance and Development in Africa* (2 a year).

Association of Asian Confederations of Credit Unions (AACCU): U Tower Bldg 411, 8th Floor, Srinakarin Rd, Suanluang, Bangkok 10250, Thailand; tel. (2) 704-4253; fax (2) 704-4255; e-mail accu@aaccu.coop; internet www.aaccu.asia; links and promotes credit unions and co-operatives in Asia, provides research facilities and training programmes; mems: in credit union leagues and federations in 24 Asian countries; CEO RANJITH HETTIARACHCHI (Thailand); publs *ACCU News* (every 3 months), *Annual Report, ACCU Directory*.

Association of European Institutes of Economic Research (AIECE) (Association d'instituts européens de conjoncture économique): 3 pl. Montesquieu, 1348 Louvain-la-Neuve, Belgium; tel. (10) 47-34-26; fax (10) 47-39-45; e-mail olbrechts@aiece.org; internet www.aiece.org; f. 1957; provides a means of contact between member institutes; organizes two meetings annually, at which discussions are held on the economic situation and on a special theoretical subject; mems: 43 institutes in 20 European countries and 5 int. orgs; Admin. Sec. PAUL OLBRECHTS.

Banco del Sur (South American Bank): Caracas, Venezuela; f. Dec. 2007; formal agreement establishing the bank signed in Sept. 2009; aims to provide financing for social and investment projects in South America; auth. cap. US $20,000m.; mems: Argentina, Brazil, Bolivia, Ecuador, Paraguay, Uruguay, Venezuela.

Centre for Latin American Monetary Studies (Centro de Estudios Monetarios Latinoamericanos—CEMLA): Durango 54, Col. Roma, Del. Cuauhtémoc, 06700 México, DF, Mexico; tel. (55) 5061-6640; fax (55) 5061-6695; e-mail cemla@cemla.org; internet www.cemla.org; f. 1952; organizes technical training programmes on monetary policy, development finance, etc; runs applied research programmes on monetary and central banking policies and procedures; holds regional meetings of banking officials; mems: 30 assoc. mems (Central Banks of Latin America and the Caribbean), 23 co-operating mems (supervisory institutions of the region and non-Latin American Central Banks); Dir-Gen. JAVIER GUZMÁN CALAFELL; publs *Bulletin* (every 2 months), *Monetaria* (quarterly), *Money Affairs* (2 a year).

East African Development Bank: 4 Nile Ave, POB 7128, Kampala, Uganda; tel. (417) 112900; fax (41) 259763; e-mail info@eadb.org; internet www.eadb.org; f. 1967 by the former East African Community to promote regional development within Kenya, Tanzania and Uganda, which each hold 24.07% of the equity capital; Kenya, Tanzania and Uganda each hold 27.2% of the equity capital; the remaining equity is held by the African Development Bank (6.8%), Rwanda (4.3%) and other institutional investors; Dir-Gen. VIVIENNE YEDA APOPO.

Eastern Caribbean Central Bank (ECCB): POB 89, Basseterre, St Christopher and Nevis; tel. 465-2537; fax 465-9562; e-mail info@eccb-centralbank.org; internet www.eccb-centralbank.org; f. 1983 by OECS governments; maintains regional currency (Eastern Caribbean dollar) and advises on the economic development of member states; mems: Anguilla, Antigua and Barbuda, Dominica, Grenada, Montserrat, Saint Christopher and Nevis, Saint Lucia, Saint Vincent and the Grenadines; Gov. Sir K. DWIGHT VENNER; Man. Dir JENNIFER NERO.

Econometric Society: Dept of Economics, New York University, 19 West Fourth St, 6th Floor, New York, NY 10012, USA; tel. (212) 998-3820; fax (212) 995-4487; e-mail sashi@econometricsociety.org; internet www.econometricsociety.org; f. 1930 to promote studies aiming at a unification of the theoretical-quantitative and the empirical-quantitative approaches to economic problems; mems: c. 7,000; Pres. BENGT HOLMSTRÖM; Chair. OLIVER HART; publ. *Econometrica* (6 a year).

Equator Principles Association: tel. (1621) 853-900; fax (1621) 731-483; e-mail secretariat@equator-principles.com; internet www.equator-principles.com; f. July 2010; aims to administer and develop further the Equator Principles, first adopted in 2003, with the support of the International Finance Corporation, as a set of industry standards for the management of environmental and social risk in project financing; a Strategic Review conference was convened in Beijing, People's Republic of China, in Dec. 2010; 70 signed-up Equator Principles Financial Institutions (EPFIs); Administrators JOANNA CLARK, SAMANTHA HOSKINS.

Eurasian Development Bank: 050051 Almatı, ul. Dostık 51, Kazakhstan; tel. (727) 244-40-44; fax (727) 250-81-58; e-mail info@eabr.org; internet www.eabr.org; f. 2006; aims to facilitate the economic development of the region through investment and the promotion of trade; mems: Armenia, Belarus, Kazakhstan, Kyrgyzstan, Russia; Chair. IGOR FINOGENOV.

European Federation of Finance House Associations (Euro-finas): 87 blvd Louis Schmidt, 1040 Brussels, Belgium; tel. (2) 778-05-60; fax (2) 778-05-78; e-mail i.vermeersch@eurofinas.org; internet www.eurofinas.org; f. 1959 to study the development of instalment credit financing in Europe, to collate and publish instalment credit statistics, and to promote research into instalment credit practice; mems: finance houses and professional asscns in 17 European countries; Chair. PEDRO GUIJARRO; Dir-Gen. TANGUY VAN DE WERVE; publs *Eurofinas Newsletter* (monthly), *Annual Report, Study Reports*.

European Federation of Financial Analysts Societies (EFFAS): Mainzer Landstr. 47A, Frankfurt-am-Main, Germany; tel. (69) 264848300; fax (69) 264848335; e-mail claudia.stinnes@effas.com; internet www.effas.com; f. 1962 to co-ordinate the activities of European asscns of financial analysts; aims to raise the standard of financial analysis and improve the quality of information given to investors; encourages unification of national rules and draws up rules of profession; holds biennial congress; mems: asscns in 25 European countries; Chair. GIAMPAOLO TRASI; Gen. Sec. CLAUDIA STINNES.

European Financial Management and Marketing Association (EFMA): 8 rue Bayen, 75017 Paris, France; tel. 1-47-42-52-72; fax 1-47-42-56-76; e-mail info@efma.com; internet www.efma.com; f. 1971 to link financial institutions by organizing seminars, conferences and training sessions and an annual Congress and World Convention, and by providing information services; mems: more than 3,000 financial institutions world-wide; Chair. ROBERTO NICASTRO; Sec.-Gen. PATRICK DESMARÈS; publ. *Newsletter*.

European Private Equity and Venture Capital Association (EVCA): Bastion Tower, 5 pl. du Champ de Mars, 1050 Brussels, Belgium; tel. (2) 715-00-20; fax (2) 725-07-04; e-mail info@evca.eu; internet www.evca.eu; f. 1983 to link private equity and venture capital companies within Europe; mems: over 950; Sec.-Gen. DÖRTE HÖPPNER (Germany); publs *Yearbook*, research and special papers, legal documents, industry guidelines.

Financial Action Task Force (FATF) (Groupe d'action financière—GAFI): 2 rue André-Pascal, 75775 Paris Cedex 16, France; tel. 1-45-24-79-45; fax 1-44-30-61-37; e-mail contact@fatf-gafi.org; internet www.fatf-gafi.org; f. 1989, on the recommendation of the Group of Seven industrialized nations (G7), to develop and promote policies to combat money laundering and the financing of terrorism; formulated a set of recommendations (40+9) for countries world-wide to implement; established partnerships with regional task forces in the Caribbean, Asia-Pacific, Central Asia, Europe, East and South Africa, the Middle East and North Africa and South America; mems: 34 state jurisdictions, the European Commission, and the Cooperation Council for the Arab States of the Gulf; observers: India, Basel Committee on Banking Supervision, Eurasian Group (EAG) on combating money laundering and financing of terrorism; Pres. GIANCARLO DEL BUFALO (Italy); Exec. Sec. RICK MCDONELL; publs *Annual Report*, *e-Bulletin*.

Financial Stability Board: c/o BIS, Centralbahnplatz 2, 4002 Basel, Switzerland; tel. 612808298; fax 612809100; e-mail fsb@bis.org; internet www.financialstabilityboard.org; f. 1999 as the Financial Stability Forum, name changed in April 2009; brings together senior representatives of national financial authorities, international financial institutions, international regulatory and supervisory groupings and committees of central bank experts and the European Central Bank; aims to promote international financial stability and strengthen the functioning of the financial markets; in March 2009 agreed to expand its membership to include all Group of 20 (G20) economies, as well as Spain and the European Commission; in April 2009 the meeting of G20 heads of state and government determined to re-establish the then Forum as the Financial Stability Board, strengthen its institutional structure (to include a plenary body, a steering committee and three standing committees concerned with Vulnerabilities Assessment; Supervisory and Regulatory Co-operation; and Standards Implementation) and expand its mandate to enhance its effectiveness as an international mechanism to promote financial stability; the Board was to strengthen its collaboration with the International Monetary Fund, and conduct joint 'early warning exercises'; in Dec. 2009 the Board initiated a peer review of implementation of the Principles and Standards for Sound Compensation Practices; in Nov. 2010 determined to establish six FSB regional consultative groups; Chair. MARK CARNEY (Canada).

Fonds Africain de Garantie et de Co-opération Economique (FAGACE) (African Guarantee and Economic Co-operation Fund): 01 BP 2045 RP, Cotonou, Benin; tel. 30-03-76; fax 30-02-84; e-mail fagace_dg@yahoo.fr; internet www.le-fagace.org; commenced operations in 1981; guarantees loans for development projects, provides loans and grants for specific operations and supports national and regional enterprises; mems: 13 African countries; Dir-Gen. HENRI MARIE JEANNENEY DONDRA.

Group of Seven (G7): f. 1975 as an informal framework of co-operation; despite the formation in 1998 of the Group of Eight (G8), incorporating Russia, and the inclusion of Russia in all G8 sectoral areas from 2003, the Group of Seven major industrialized countries (G7) remains a forum for regular discussion (at the level of ministers of finance and central bank governors) of developments in the global economy and of economic policy; a meeting was held in June 2012 with a focus on the sovereign debt crisis, and resolving banking instability, in the euro area; the IMF Managing Director is normally invited to participate in G7 meetings; mems: ministers of finance and central bank governors of Canada, France, Germany, Italy, Japan, United Kingdom and the USA; European Union representation.

Group of 20 (G20): internet www.g20.org; f. Sept. 1999 as an informal deliberative forum of finance ministers and central bank governors representing both industrialized and 'systemically important' emerging market nations; aims to strengthen the international financial architecture and to foster sustainable economic growth and development; in 2004 participating countries adopted the G20 Accord for Sustained Growth and stated a commitment to high standards of transparency and fiscal governance; the IMF Managing Director and IBRD President participate in G20 annual meetings; an extraordinary Summit on Financial Markets and the World Economy was convened in Washington, DC, USA, in Nov. 2008, attended by heads of state or government of G20 member economies; a second summit meeting, held in London, United Kingdom, in April 2009, issued as its final communiqué a *Global Plan for Recovery and Reform* outlining commitments to restore economic confidence, growth and jobs, to strengthen financial supervision and regulation, to reform and strengthen global financial institutions, to promote global trade and investment and to ensure a fair and sustainable economic recovery; detailed declarations were also issued on measures agreed to deliver substantial resources (of some US $850,000m.) through international financial institutions and on reforms to be implemented in order to strengthen the financial system; as a follow-up to the London summit, G20 heads of state met in Pittsburgh, USA, in Sept. 2009; the meeting adopted a *Framework for Strong, Sustainable, and Balanced Growth* and resolved to expand the role of the G20 to be at the centre of future international economic policymaking; summit meetings were held in June 2010, in Canada (at the G8 summit), and in Seoul, Republic of Korea, in Nov; the sixth G20 summit, held in Cannes, France, in Nov. 2011, concluded an *Action Plan for Growth and Jobs* but was dominated by discussion of measures to secure financial stability in the euro area countries; the seventh summit, convened in Los Cabos, Baja California Sur, Mexico, in June 2012, further considered means of stabilizing the euro area, with a particular focus on reducing the borrowing costs of highly indebted member countries; mems: Argentina, Australia, Brazil, Canada, People's Republic of China, France, Germany, India, Indonesia, Italy, Japan, Republic of Korea, Mexico, Russia, Saudi Arabia, South Africa, Turkey, United Kingdom, USA and the European Union; observers: Netherlands, Spain.

Insurance Europe: 51 rue Montoyer, 1000 Brussels, Belgium; tel. (2) 894-30-00; fax (2) 894-30-01; e-mail info@insuranceeurope.eu; internet www.insuranceeurope.eu; f. 1953 as the CEA (Comité Européen de Assurances) to represent the interests of European insurers, to encourage co-operation between members, to allow the exchange of information and to conduct studies; mems: national insurance asscns of 33 full mems, Russia and Ukraine observers; Pres. SERGIO BALBINOT (Italy); Dir-Gen. MICHAELA KOLLER (Germany); publs *European Insurance in Figures* (annually), *Indirect Taxation on Insurance Contracts* (annually).

Insurance Institute for Asia and the Pacific: 26/F Ayala Life-FGU Center, 6811 Ayala Ave, Makati City, Metro Manila, Philippines; tel. (2) 8877444; fax (2) 8877443; e-mail education@iiap.com.ph; internet www.iiap.com/ph; f. 1974 to provide insurance management training and conduct research in subjects connected with the insurance industry; Chair. MELECIO C. MALLILLIN; publ. *IIAP Journal* (quarterly).

Intergovernmental Group of 24 (G24) on International Monetary Affairs and Development: 700 19th St, NW, Rm 3-600 Washington, DC 20431, USA; tel. (202) 623-6101; fax (202) 623-6000; e-mail g24@g24.org; internet www.g24.org; f. 1971; aims to co-ordinate the position of developing countries on monetary and development finance issues; operates at the political level of ministers of finance and governors of central banks, and also at the level of government officials; mems (Africa): Algeria, Côte d'Ivoire, DRC, Egypt, Ethiopia, Gabon, Ghana, Nigeria, South Africa; (Latin America and the Caribbean): Argentina, Brazil, Colombia, Guatemala, Mexico, Peru, Trinidad and Tobago and Venezuela; (Asia and the Middle

East): India, Iran, Lebanon, Pakistan, Philippines, Sri Lanka and Syrian Arab Republic; the People's Republic of China has the status of special invitee at G24 meetings; G77 participant states may attend G24 meetings as observers.

International Accounting Standards Board (IASB): 30 Cannon St, London, EC4M 6XH, United Kingdom; tel. (20) 7246-6410; fax (20) 7246-6411; e-mail info@ifrs.org; internet www.iasb.org.uk; f. 1973 as International Accounting Standards Committee, reorganized and present name adopted 2001; aims to develop, in the public interest, a single set of high-quality, uniform, clear and enforceable global accounting standards requiring the submission of high-quality, transparent and comparable information in financial statements and other financial reporting, in order to assist participants in world-wide capital markets and other end-users to make informed decisions on economic matters; aims also to promote the use and rigorous application of these global accounting standards, and to bring about the convergence of these with national accounting standards; Chair. and CEO HANS HOOGERVORST; publs *IASB Insight* (quarterly), *Bound Volume of International Accounting Standards* (annually), *Interpretations of International Accounting Standards*.

International Association for Research in Income and Wealth: 151 Slater St, Suite 710, Ottawa, Ontario, K1P 5H3, Canada; tel. (613) 233-8891; fax (613) 233-8250; e-mail info@iariw.org; internet www.iariw.org; f. 1947 to further research in the general field of national income and wealth and related topics by the organization of biennial conferences and other means; mems: approx. 400; Chair. PETER VAN DE VEN (Netherlands); Exec. Dir ANDREW SHARPE (Canada); publ. *Review of Income and Wealth* (quarterly).

International Association of Deposit Insurers: c/o BIS, Centralbahnplatz 2, 4002 Basel, Switzerland; tel. 612809933; fax 612809554; e-mail service.iadi@bis.org; internet www.iadi.org; f. 2002; aims to contribute to the stability of the international financial system by promoting co-operation among deposit insurers and establishing effective systems; mems: 64 orgs, 8 assoc. and 12 partners; Acting Chair. MARTIN J. GRUENBERG; Sec.-Gen. CARLOS ISOARD.

International Association of Insurance Supervisors: c/o BIS, Centralbahnplatz 2, 4002 Basel, Switzerland; tel. 612257300; fax 612809151; e-mail iais@bis.org; internet www.iaisweb.org; f. 1994 to improve supervision of the insurance industry and promote global financial stability; Sec.-Gen. YOSHIHIRO KAWAI.

International Bank for Economic Co-operation (IBEC): 107996 Moscow, ul. M. Poryvayevoi 11, Russia; tel. (495) 604-71-07; fax (495) 632-95-80; e-mail info@ibec.int; internet www.ibec.int; f. 1963; provides credit and settlement facilities for member states, and also acts as an international commercial bank, offering services to commercial banks and enterprises; auth. cap. €400m., paid-up cap. €143.5m.; mems: Bulgaria, Cuba, Czech Republic, Mongolia, Poland, Romania, Russia and Slovakia, Viet Nam; Chair. VLADIMIR BELY (Russia).

International Bureau of Fiscal Documentation (IBFD): H. J. E. Wenckebachweg 210, 1096 AS Amsterdam, Netherlands; tel. (20) 5540100; fax (20) 6228658; e-mail info@ibfd.org; internet www.ibfd.org; f. 1938 to supply information on fiscal law and its application; maintains library on international taxation; Chair. S. R. B. VAN DER FELTZ; publs *Bulletin for International Fiscal Documentation*, *Asia Pacific Tax Bulletin*, *Derivatives and Financial Instruments*, *European Taxation*, *International VAT Monitor*, *International Transfer Pricing Journal*, *Supplementary Service to European Taxation* (all monthly), *Tax News Service* (weekly); studies, databases, regional tax guides.

International Capital Market Association (ICMA): Talacker 29, 8001 Zürich, Switzerland; tel. 443634222; fax 443637772; e-mail info@icma-group.org; internet www.icma-group.org; f. 2005 by merger of International Primary Market Association (IPMA) and International Securities Association (ISMA), f. 1969; maintains and develops an efficient and cost-effective market for capital; mems: 400 banks and major financial institutions in 47 countries; Chair. MARTIN SCHECK; publs reports and market surveys.

International Centre for Local Credit: Tour Dexia 2, 92919 La Défense, France; tel. 1-58-58-75-69; fax 1-58-58-87-40; e-mail estelle.ricque-mathien@dexia.com; internet www.iclc.eu; f. 1958 to promote local authority credit by gathering, exchanging and distributing information and advice on member institutions and on local authority credit and related subjects; studies important subjects in the field of local authority credit; mems: 14 financial institutions; Gen. Sec. PIERRE MARIANI (France); publs *Bulletin*, *Newsletter* (quarterly).

International Economic Association: c/o Instituto de Análisis Económico, Campus de la UAB, 08193 Barcelona, Spain; tel. (93) 5806612; fax (93) 5805214; e-mail iea@iea-world.org; internet www.iea-world.com; f. 1949 to promote international collaboration for the advancement of economic knowledge and develop personal contacts between economists, and to encourage the provision of means for the dissemination of economic knowledge; mems: asscns in 59 countries; Pres. JOSEPH STIGLITZ; Sec.-Gen. JOAN ESTEBAN.

International Federation of Accountants: 529 Fifth Ave, 6th Floor, New York, NY 10017, USA; tel. (212) 286-9344; fax (212) 286-9570; e-mail communications@ifac.org; internet www.ifac.org; f. 1977 to develop a co-ordinated world-wide accounting profession with harmonized standards; mems: 167 accountancy bodies in 127 countries; Pres. GÖRAN TIDSTRÖM (Sweden); Chief Exec. IAN BALL.

International Fiscal Association (IFA): World Trade Center, POB 30215, 3001 DE Rotterdam, Netherlands; tel. (10) 4052990; fax (10) 4055031; e-mail a.gensecr@ifa.nl; internet www.ifa.nl; f. 1938 to study international and comparative public finance and fiscal law, especially taxation; holds annual congresses; mems in 106 countries and branches in 62 countries; Pres. M. E. TRON (Mexico); Sec.-Gen. Prof. H. A. KOGELS (Netherlands); publs *Cahiers de Droit Fiscal International*, *Yearbook of the International Fiscal Association*, *IFA Congress Seminar Series*.

International Institute of Public Finance e.V.: POB 860446, 81631 Munich, Germany; tel. (89) 9224-1281; fax (89) 907795-2281; e-mail info@iipf.org; internet www.iipf.org; f. 1937; a private scientific organization aiming to establish contacts between people of every nationality, whose main or supplementary activity consists in the study of public finance; holds annual congress devoted to a specific scientific subject; 800 mems; Pres. ROBIN BOADWAY (Canada).

International Investment Bank: 107078 Moscow, ul. M. Poryvayevoi 7, Russia; tel. (495) 604-72-00; fax (495) 975-20-70; e-mail if@iibbank.org; internet www.iibbank.org; f. 1970; regional development bank focusing on project financing and providing credit facilities for construction and modernization projects and other activities; following the decision in 1989–91 of most member states to adopt a market economy, the Bank conducted its transactions (from 1 Jan. 1991) in convertible currencies, rather than in transferable roubles; auth. cap. €1,300m.; mems: Bulgaria, Cuba, Czech Republic, Mongolia, Romania, Russia, Slovakia and Viet Nam; Chair. VASILY KIRPICHEV (Russia).

International Organization of Securities Commissions (IOSCO): Calle Oquendo 12, 28006 Madrid, Spain; tel. (91) 417-5549; fax (91) 555-9368; e-mail mail@iosco.org; internet www.iosco.org; f. 1983 to facilitate co-operation between securities and futures regulatory bodies at the international level; in 1998 adopted the Objectives and Principles of Securities Regulation (the IOSCO Principles); mems: 188 agencies; Chair. JANE DIPLOCK (New Zealand); Sec.-Gen. DAVID WRIGHT; publs *Annual Report*, *IOSCO News* (3 a year).

International Union for Housing Finance (IUHF): 71 ave de Cortenbergh, 8th Floor, 1000 Brussels, Belgium; tel. (2) 285-40-30; fax (2) 285-40-31; e-mail info@housingfinance.org; internet www.housingfinance.org; f. 1914 to foster world-wide interest in savings and home ownership and co-operation among members; encourages comparative study of methods and practice in housing finance; promotes development of appropriate legislation on housing finance; mems: 108 in over 49 countries; Sec.-Gen. ANNIK LAMBERT (Belgium); publ. *Housing Finance International* (quarterly).

Islamic Financial Services Board: Level 5, Sasana Kijang, Bank Negara Malaysia, 2 Jalan Dato Onn, 50840 Kuala Lumpur, Malaysia; tel. (3) 91951400; fax (3) 91951405; e-mail ifsb_sec@

ifsb.org; internet www.ifsb.org; f. 2002; aims to formulate standards and guiding principles for regulatory and supervisory agencies working within the Islamic financial services industry; mems: 27 full mems (incl. Islamic Development Bank), 26 assoc. mems (incl. Asian Development Bank, the Bank for International Settlements, the IMF and the World Bank), and 136 observer mems; Sec.-Gen. JASEEM AHMED.

Latin American Banking Federation (Federación Latinoamericana de Bancos—FELABAN): Cra 11A No. 93-67 Of. 202 A.A 091959, Bogotá, Colombia; tel. (1) 6215848; fax (1) 6217659; e-mail mangarita@felaban.com; internet www.felaban.com; f. 1965 to co-ordinate efforts towards wide and accelerated economic development in Latin American countries; mems: 19 Latin American national banking asscns, representing more than 500 banks and financial institutions; Pres. OSCAR RIVERA (Peru); Sec.-Gen. GIORGIO TRETTENERO CASTRO (Peru).

Nordic Investment Bank (NIB) (Nordiska Investeringsbanken): Fabianinkatu 34, POB 249, 00171 Helsinki, Finland; tel. (10) 618001; fax (10) 6180725; e-mail info@nib.int; internet www.nib.int; f. 1975; provides long-term loans and guarantees for both public and private projects in and outside its member countries; main focus areas of the Bank are energy, environment, transport, logistics, communications, and innovation; mems: Governments of Denmark, Estonia, Finland, Iceland, Latvia, Lithuania, Norway and Sweden; Pres. and CEO HENRIK NORMANN.

Nordic Project Fund (Nopef): POB 241, 00171 Helsinki, Finland; tel. (9) 6840570; fax (9) 650113; e-mail ib.sonnerstad@nopef.com; internet www.nopef.com; f. 1982; aims to strengthen the international competitiveness of Nordic exporting cos, and to promote industrial co-operation in international projects (e.g. in environmental protection); grants loans to Nordic cos for feasibility expenses relating to projects; with effect from 1 Jan. 2008 Nopef's geographical target area expanded to include Bulgaria, Romania and countries outside the EU and EFTA; Chair. BO JERLSTRÖM; Man. Dir IB SØNNERSTAD.

Union of Arab Banks (UAB): POB 11-2416, Riad El-Solh 1107 2210, Beirut, Lebanon; tel. (1) 377800; fax (1) 364927; e-mail uab@uabonline.org; internet www.uabonline.org; f. 1972; aims to foster co-operation between Arab banks and to increase their efficiency; prepares feasibility studies for projects; 2007 Arab Banking Conference: Tripoli, Libya; mems: more than 300 Arab banks and financial institutions; Chair. ADNAN YOUSSIF (Bahrain); Sec.-Gen. WISSAM HASSAN FATTOUH (Lebanon).

Union of Arab Stock Exchanges and Securities Commissions: POB 22235, Safat 13083, Kuwait; tel. 22412991; fax 22420778; f. 1982 to develop capital markets in the Arab world.

West African Bankers' Association (WABA): 11–13 Ecowas St, PM Bag 1012, Freetown, Sierra Leone; tel. (22) 226752; fax (22) 229024; e-mail aabosi@waba-abao.org; internet www.wabaonline.org; f. 1981; aims to strengthen links between banks in West Africa, to enable exchange of information, and to contribute to regional economic development; holds annual general assembly; mems: 217 commercial banks in 15 West African countries; Sec.-Gen. AGBAI ABOSI; publ. *West African Banking Almanac.*

World Council of Credit Unions (WOCCU): POB 2982, 5710 Mineral Point Rd, Madison, WI 53705-4493, USA; tel. (608) 395-2000; fax (608) 395-2001; e-mail mail@woccu.org; internet www.woccu.org; f. 1970 to link credit unions and similar co-operative financial institutions and assist them in expanding and improving their services; provides technical and financial assistance to credit union asscns in developing countries; mems: 54,000 credit unions in 97 countries; Pres. and CEO BRIAN BRANCH; publs *WOCCU Annual Report*, *Credit Union World* (3 a year), *Spotlights On Development*; technical monographs and brochures.

World Federation of Exchanges: 176 rue de Rivoli, 75001 Paris, France; tel. 1-58-62-54-00; fax 1-58-62-50-48; e-mail secretariat@world-exchanges.org; internet www.world-exchanges.org; f. 1961; fmrly Fédération Internationale des Bourses de Valeurs—FIBV; central reference point for the securities industry; offers member exchanges guidance in business strategies, and improvement and harmonization of management practices; works with public financial authorities to promote increased use of regulated securities and derivatives exchanges; mems: 54 full mems, 5 associates, 13 affiliates and 32 corresponding exchanges; Chair. RONALDI ARCULLI; Sec.-Gen. HÜSEYIN ERKAN (Turkey).

World Savings Banks Institute: 11 rue Marie Thérèse, 1000 Brussels, Belgium; tel. (2) 211-11-11; fax (2) 211-11-99; e-mail info@savings-banks.com; internet www.wsbi.org; f. 1924 as International Savings Banks Institute, present name and structure adopted in 1994; promotes co-operation among members and the development of savings banks world-wide; mems: 104 banks and asscns in 86 countries; Pres. and Chair. JOSÉ ANTONIO OLAVARRIETA ARCOS (Spain); Man. Dir CHRIS DE NOOSE; publs *Annual Report*, *International Savings Banks Directory*, *Perspectives* (4–5 a year).

Education

Agence Universitaire de la Francophonie (AUF): Case postale du Musée, CP 49714, Montréal, QC H3T 2A5, Canada; tel. (514) 343-6630; fax (514) 343-2107; e-mail rectorat@auf.org; internet www.auf.org; f. 1961; aims to develop a francophone university community, through building partnerships with students, teachers, institutions and governments; mems: 67 institutions in 40 countries; Pres. YVON FONTAINE (Canada); Exec. Dir. BERNARD CERQUIGLINI; publ. *Le Français à l'Université* (quarterly).

Alliance israélite universelle: 45 rue La Bruyère, 75009 Paris Cedex 09, France; tel. 1-53-32-88-55; fax 1-48-74-51-33; e-mail info@aiu.org; internet www.aiu.org; f. 1860 to work for the emancipation and moral progress of the Jews; maintains 40 schools in France, theMediterranean area and Canada; library of 150,000 vols; mems: 8,000 in 16 countries; Pres. MARC EISENBERG; Dir-Gen. JO TOLÉDANO; publs *Les Cahiers du Judaïsme* (quarterly), *Les Éditions du Nadir.*

AMSE-AMCE-WAER (Association mondiale des sciences de l'éducation) (Asociación mundial de ciencias de la educación) (World Association for Educational Research): c/o Yves Lenoir, Faculty of Education, Sherbrooke University, 2500 blvd de l'Université Sherbrooke, QC J1K 2R1, Canada; tel. (819) 821-8000; fax (819) 829-5343; e-mail wera@aera.net; internet www.weraonline.org; f. 1953, present title adopted 2004; aims to encourage research in educational sciences by organizing congresses, issuing publications and supporting the exchange of information; mems: 27 research associations; Pres. YIN CHEONG CHENG (1 July 2012–30 June 2014); Sec.-Gen. FELICE LEVINE; publ. *Educational Research around the World.*

Arab Bureau of Education for the Gulf States: POB 94693, Riyadh 11614, Saudi Arabia; tel. (1) 480-0555; fax (1) 480-2839; e-mail abegs@abegs.org; internet www.abegs.org; f. 1975; co-ordinates and promotes co-operation and integration among member countries in the fields of education, culture and science; aims to unify the educational systems of all Gulf Arab states; specialized organs: Gulf Arab States' Educational Research Center (POB 25566, Safat, Kuwait), Council of Higher Education, Arabian Gulf University (opened in Bahrain in 1982); mems: Governments of Bahrain, Kuwait, Oman, Qatar, Saudi Arabia, United Arab Emirates and Yemen; Dir-Gen. Dr ALI AL-KARNI; publs *Risalat Ul-Khaleej al-Arabi* (quarterly), *Arab Gulf Journal of Scientific Research* (2 a year).

Asian Institute of Technology (AIT): POB 4, Klong Luang, Pathumthani 12120, Thailand; tel. (2) 516-0144; fax (2) 516-2126; e-mail president@ait.ac.th; internet www.ait.ac.th; f. 1959; Master's, Doctor's and Diploma programmes are offered in four schools: Advanced Technologies, Civil Engineering, Environment, Resources and Development, and Management; specialized training is provided by the Center for Library and Information Resources (CLAIR), the Continuing Education Center, the Center for Language and Educational Technology, the Regional Computer Center, the AIT Center in Viet Nam (based in Hanoi) and the Swiss-AIT-Viet Nam Management Development Program (in Ho Chi Minh City); other research and outpost centres are the Asian Center for Engineering Computations and Software, the Asian Center for Research on Remote Sensing, the Regional Environmental Management

Center, the Asian Center for Soil Improvement and Geosynthetics and the Urban Environmental Outreach Center; there are four specialized information centres (on ferro-cement, geotechnical engineering, renewable energy resources, environmental sanitation) under CLAIR; the Management of Technology Information Center conducts short-term courses in the management of technology and international business; Pres. Prof. SAID IRANDOUST; publs *AIT Annual Report*, *Annual Report on Research and Activities*, *AIT Review* (3 a year), *Prospectus*, other specialized publs.

Asian South Pacific Bureau of Adult Education (ASPBAE): c/o MAAPL, Eucharistic Congress Bldg No. 3, 9th Floor, 5 Convent St, Colaba, Mumbai 400 039, India; tel. (22) 22021391; fax (22) 22832217; e-mail aspbae@vsnl.com; internet www.aspbae.org; f. 1964 to assist non-formal education and adult literacy; organizes training courses and seminars; provides material and advice relating to adult education; mems in 31 countries and territories; Sec.-Gen. MARIA-LOURDES ALMAZAN-KHAN; publ. *ASPBAE News* (3 a year).

Association for Childhood Education International: 17904 Georgia Ave, Suite 215, Olney, MD 20832, USA; tel. (301) 570-2111; fax (301) 570-2212; e-mail headquarters@acei.org; internet www.acei.org; f. 1892 to work for the education of children (from infancy through early adolescence) by promoting desirable conditions in schools, raising the standard of teaching, co-operating with all groups concerned with children, informing the public of the needs of children; mems: 12,000; Pres. DEBORAH WISNESKI; Exec. Dir DIANE WHITEHEAD; publs *Childhood Education* (6 a year), *Professional Focus Newsletters*, *Journal of Research in Childhood Education* (quarterly), books on current educational subjects.

Association for the Development of Education in Africa: c/o Temporary Relocation Agency, 13 ave du Ghana, BP 323, 1002 Tunis, Tunisia; tel. 71-10-39-00; e-mail adea@afdb.org; internet www.adeanet.org; f. 1988 as Donors to African Education, adopted present name in 1995; aims to enhance collaboration in the support of African education; promotes policy dialogue and undertakes research, advocacy and capacity-building in areas of education in sub-Saharan Africa through programmes and working groups comprising representatives of donor countries and African ministries of education; Exec. Sec. AHLIN BYLL-CATARIA.

Association Montessori Internationale: Koninginneweg 161, 1075 CN Amsterdam, Netherlands; tel. (20) 6798932; fax (20) 6767341; e-mail info@montessori-ami.org; internet www.montessori-ami.org; f. 1929 to propagate the ideals and educational methods of Dr Maria Montessori on child development, without racial, religious or political prejudice; organizes training courses for teachers in 18 countries; world congress held every four years (2013: Portland, OR, USA, in July–Aug.); Pres. ANDRÉ ROBERFROID (Belgium); Exec. Dir LYNNE LAWRENCE (United Kingdom); publs *Communications* (2 a year), *AMI Bulletin*.

Association of African Universities (AAU) (Association des universités africaines): POB 5744, Accra-North, Ghana; tel. (21) 774495; fax (21) 774821; e-mail info@aau.org; internet www.aau.org; f. 1967 to promote exchanges, contact and co-operation among African university institutions and to collect and disseminate information on research and higher education in Africa; mems: 270 in 46 countries; Acting Pres. GEORGE ALBERT MAGOHA (Kenya); Sec.-Gen. Prof. OLUGBEMIRO JEGEDE (Nigeria); publs *AAU Newsletter* (3 a year), *Directory of African Universities* (every 2 years).

Association of Arab Universities: POB 2000, Amman, Jordan 13110; tel. (6) 5345131; fax (6) 5332994; e-mail secgen@aaru.edu.jo; internet www.aaru.edu.jo; f. 1964; a scientific conference is held every three years; council meetings held annually; mems: 163 universities; Sec.-Gen. Prof. Dr SALEH HASHEM; publ. *AARU Bulletin* (annually and quarterly, in Arabic).

Association of Caribbean University and Research Institutional Libraries (ACURIL): Apdo postal 21609, San Juan 00931-1906, Puerto Rico; tel. 763-6199; e-mail executivesecretariat@acuril.org; internet www.acuril.uprrp.edu; f. 1968 to foster contact and collaboration between mem. universities and institutes; holds conferences, meetings and seminars; circulates information through newsletters and bulletins; facilitates co-operation and the pooling of resources in research; encourages exchange of staff and students; mems: 250; Pres. FRANCOISE THYBULLE; Exec.-Sec. LUISA VIGO-CEPEDA; publ. *Cybernotes*.

Association of South-East Asian Institutions of Higher Learning (ASAIHL): Secretariat, Rm 113, Jamjuree 1 Bldg, Chulalongkorn University, Phyathai Rd, Bangkok 10330, Thailand; tel. (2) 251-6966; fax (2) 253-7909; e-mail ninnat.o@chula.ac.th; internet www.seameo.org/asaihl; f. 1956 to promote the economic, cultural and social welfare of the people of South-East Asia by means of educational co-operation and research programmes; and to cultivate a sense of regional identity and interdependence; collects and disseminates information, organizes discussions; mems: 170 univ. institutions in 20 countries; Pres. NARCISO ERGUIZA; Sec.-Gen. Dr NINNAT OLANVORAVUTH; publs *Newsletter*, *Handbook* (every 3 years).

Catholic International Education Office: 718 ave Houba de Strooper, 1020 Brussels, Belgium; tel. (2) 230-72-52; fax (2) 230-97-45; e-mail info@infoiec.org; internet www.infoiec.org; f. 1952 for the study of the problems of Catholic education throughout the world; co-ordinates the activities of members; represents Catholic education at international bodies; mems: 102 countries, 18 assoc. mems, 13 collaborating mems, 6 corresponding mems; Pres. Mgr CARLOS PELLEGRIN; Sec.-Gen. ÁNGEL ASTORGANO; publs *OIEC Bulletin* (every 3 months, in English, French and Spanish), *OIEC Tracts on Education*.

Comparative Education Society in Europe (CESE): European University of Cyprus, POB 22006, 6 Diogenes Street, 1516 Nicosia, Cyprus; e-mail e.klerides@euc.ac.cy; internet www.cese-europe.org; f. 1961 to promote teaching and research in comparative and international education; organizes conferences and promotes literature; mems: in 49 countries; Pres. MIGUEL PEREYRA (Spain); Sec. and Treas. ELEFTHERIOS KLERIDES (Cyprus); publ. *Newsletter* (quarterly).

Council of Legal Education (CLE): c/o Registrar, POB 323, Tunapuna, Trinidad and Tobago; tel. 662-5860; fax 662-0927; f. 1971; responsible for the training of members of the legal profession; mems: govts of 12 countries and territories.

Education Action International: 14 Dufferin St, London, EC1Y 8PD, United Kingdom; tel. (20) 7426 5800; e-mail international@education-action.org; f. 1920, as European Student Relief; focuses on improving the lives of people in conflict-affected countries and fragile states and refugees from war living in the UK through education.

European Association for Education of Adults (EAEA): 40 rue d'Arlon, 1000 Brussels, Belgium; tel. (2) 234-37-63; fax (2) 235-05-39; e-mail eaea-info@eaea.org; internet www.eaea.org; f. 1953; aims to create a 'learning society' by encouraging demand for learning, particularly from women and excluded sectors of society; seeks to improve response of providers of learning opportunities and authorities and agencies; mems: 127 orgs in 43 countries; Pres. SUSAN WADDINGTON; Gen. Sec. GINA EBNER; publs *EAEA Monograph Series*, newsletter.

European Federation for Catholic Adult Education (Federation Européene pour l'Éducation Catholique des Adultes—FEECA): Joachimstr. 1, 53113 Bonn, Germany; tel. (228) 9024710; fax (228) 9024729; e-mail hoffmeier@kbe-bonn.de; internet www.feeca.org; f. 1963 to strengthen international contact between mems and to assist with international research and practical projects in adult education; holds conference every two years; Vice-Pres. ANDREA HOFFMEIER (Germany).

European Foundation for Management Development (EFMD): 88 rue Gachard, 1050 Brussels, Belgium; tel. (2) 629-08-10; fax (2) 629-08-11; e-mail info@efmd.org; internet www.efmd.org; f. 1971 through merger of European Association of Management Training Centres and International University Contact for Management Education; aims to help improve the quality of management development, disseminate information within the economic, social and cultural context of Europe and promote international co-operation; mems: over 500 institutions in 65 countries world-wide (28 in Europe); Pres. ALAIN DOMINQUE PERRIN; Dir-Gen. ERIC CORNUEL; publs *Forum* (3 a year), *The Bulletin* (3 a year), *Guide to European Business Schools and Management Centres* (annually).

European Union of Arabic and Islamic Scholars (Union Européenne des Arabisants et Islamisants—UEAI): c/o Bernadette Martel-Thoumian, Université de Grenoble, BP 47, 38040 Grenoble, Cedex 9, France; e-mail info@ueai.eu; internet www.ueai.eu; f. 1962 to organize congresses of Arabic and Islamic Studies; holds congress every two years; mems: 300 in 28 countries; Pres. SEBASTIAN GÜNTHER (Germany); Sec.-Gen. Prof. BERNADETTE MARTEL-THOUMIAN (France).

European University Association (EUA): 24 ave de l'Yser, 1040 Brussels, Belgium; tel. (2) 230-55-44; fax (2) 230-57-51; e-mail info@eua.be; internet www.eua.be; f. 2001 by merger of the Association of European Universities and the Confederation of EU Rectors' Conferences; represents European universities and national rectors' conferences; promotes the development of a coherent system of European higher education and research through projects and membership services; provides support and guidance to mems; mems: more than 850 in 47 countries; Pres. Prof. MARIA HELENA NAZARÉ; Sec.-Gen. LESLEY WILSON; publs *Thema*, *Directory*, *Annual Report*.

Graduate Institute of International and Development Studies (Institut universitaire de hautes études internationales—HEI): POB 136, 132 rue de Lausanne, 1211 Geneva 21, Switzerland; tel. 229085700; fax 229085710; e-mail info@graduateinstitute.ch; internet graduateinstitute.ch; f. 1927, as the Graduate Institute of International Studies, to establish a centre for advanced studies in international relations of the present day; merged with the Graduate Institute of Development Studies in 2008; maintains a library of 147,000 vols; Dir Prof. PHILIPPE BURRIN.

Inter-American Centre for Research and Documentation on Vocational Training (Centro Interamericano de Investigación y Documentación sobre Formación Profesional—CINTERFOR): Avda Uruguay 1238, Casilla de correo 1761, Montevideo, Uruguay; tel. 2902 0557; fax 2902 1305; e-mail oitcinterfor@oitcinterfor.org; internet wwww.oitcinterfor.org; f. 1964 by the International Labour Organization for mutual help among the Latin American and Caribbean countries in planning vocational training; services are provided in documentation, research, exchange of experience; holds seminars and courses; Dir MARTHA PACHECA; publs *Bulletin CINTERFOR/OIT Heramientas para la transformación*, *Trazos de la formación*, studies, monographs and technical papers.

Inter-American Confederation for Catholic Education (Confederación Interamericana de Educación Católica—CIEC): Carrera 24, No. 34, Bogotá 37 DC, Colombia; tel. (1) 2871036; e-mail asistente@ciec.edu.co; internet www.ciec.edu.co; f. 1945 to defend and extend the principles and rules of Catholic education, freedom of education, and human rights; organizes congress every three years (2010: Santo Domingo, Dominican Republic); Sec.-Gen. PADRE JOSÉ LEONARDO RINCÓN CONTRERAS (Colombia); publ. *Educación Hoy*.

Inter-American Organization for Higher Education (IOHE): 475 rue du Parvis, bureau 1338, Québec, QC G1K 9H7, Canada; tel. (418) 657-4350; fax (418) 657-4150; e-mail sec.general@oui-iohe.org; internet www.oui-iohe.org; f. 1980 to promote co-operation among universities of the Americas and the development of higher education; mems: some 265 institutions and 34 national and regional higher education asscns; Exec. Dir PATRICIA GUDIÑO.

International Anti-Corruption Academy (IACA): Muenchendorfer Str. 2, 2361 Laxenburg, Austria; tel. (2236) 710-71-81-00; fax (2236) 710-71-83-11; e-mail mail@iaca.int; internet www.iaca.int; f. March 2011, as a joint initiative by the United Nations Office on Drugs and Crime (UNODC), the European Anti-Fraud Office (OLAF) and others; aims to expand existing knowledge and practice in the field of anti-corruption; Pres. EUGENIO M. CURIA (Argentina); Exec. Sec. MARTIN KREUTNER.

International Association for Educational and Vocational Guidance (IAEVG): 119 Ross Ave, Suite 202, Ottawa, ON K1Y 0N6, Canada; tel. (613) 729-6164; fax (613) 729-3515; e-mail membership@iaevg.org; internet www.iaevg.org; f. 1951 to contribute to the development of vocational guidance and promote contact between persons associated with it; mems: over 22,000 individuals; Pres. LESTER OAKES (New Zealand); Sec.-Gen. SUZANNE BULTHEEL (France); publs *IAEVG Journal* (2 a year), *Newsletter* (3 a year).

International Association for the Development of Documentation, Libraries and Archives in Africa: Villa 2547 Dieuppeul II, BP 375, Dakar, Senegal; tel. 824-09-54; f. 1957 to organize and develop documentation and archives in all African countries; mems: national asscns, institutions and individuals in 48 countries; Sec.-Gen. ZACHEUS SUNDAY ALI (Nigeria).

International Association of Educators for World Peace: POB 3282, Mastin Lake Station, Huntsville, AL 35810-0282, USA; tel. (256) 534-5501; fax (256) 536-1018; e-mail mercieca@knology.net; internet www.iaewp.org; f. 1969 to develop education designed to contribute to the promotion of peaceful relations at personal, community and international levels; aims to communicate and clarify controversial views in order to achieve maximum understanding; organizes annual World Peace Congress; helps put into practice the Universal Declaration of Human Rights; mems: 55,000 in 80 countries; Pres. Dr CHARLES MERCIECA (USA); Sec.-Gen. NENAD JAVORNIK (Croatia); publs *Diplomacy Journal* (every 3 months), *Peace Education Journal* (annually), other articles and irregular publications.

International Association of Papyrologists (Association Internationale de Papyrologues): Association Egyptologique Reine Elisabeth, Parc du Cinquantenaire 10, 1000 Brussels, Belgium; tel. (2) 741-73-64; e-mail amartin@ulb.ac.be; internet www.ulb.ac.be/assoc/aip; f. 1947; links all those interested in Graeco-Roman Egypt, especially Greek texts; mem. of the International Federation of the Societies of Classical Studies; mems: about 400; Pres. Prof. ROGER S. BAGNALL (USA); Sec./Treas. Prof. ALAIN MARTIN (Belgium).

International Association of Physical Education in Higher Education (Association Internationale des Écoles Supérieures d'Éducation Physique—AIESEP): Department of Sport Sciences, University of Liège, Allée des Sports, 4 Bât B-21 B-4000 Liège, Belgium; tel. (4) 366-38-80; fax (4) 366-29-01; e-mail marc.cloes@ulg.ac.be; internet www.aiesep.org; f. 1962; organizes congresses, exchanges, and research in physical education; mems: institutions in 51 countries; Sec.-Gen. Dr MARC CLOES.

International Association of Universities (IAU): 1 rue Miollis, 75732 Paris Cedex 15, France; tel. 1-45-68-48-00; fax 1-47-34-76-05; e-mail iau@iau-aiu.net; internet www.iau-aiu.net; f. 1948 to allow co-operation at the international level among universities and other institutions and organizations of higher education; provides clearing-house services and operates the joint IAU/UNESCO Information Centre on Higher Education; brings together institutions and organizations from some 160 countries for reflection and action on common concerns, and collaborates with various international, regional and national bodies active in higher education; incorporates the International Universities Bureau (IUB); mems: more than 600 institutions of higher education and other organizations concerned with higher education in some 160 countries; Pres. JUAN RAMON DE LA FUENTE (Mexico); Sec.-Gen. and Exec. Dir EVA EGRON-POLAK; *Higher Education Policy* (quarterly), *IAU Horizons* (3 a year), *International Handbook of Universities* (annually), *World Higher Education Database (WHED) CD-ROM* (annually).

International Association of University Professors and Lecturers (IAUPL) (Association Internationale des Professeurs et Maîtres de Conférence Universitaires): c/o Prof. Michel Gay, 4 rue de Trévise, 75009, Paris, France; tel. 1-44-90-01-01; fax 1-46-59-01-23; e-mail migay@laposte.net; f. 1945 for the development of academic fraternity among university teachers and research workers; the protection of independence and freedom of teaching and research; the furtherance of the interests of all university teachers; and the consideration of academic problems; mems: federations in 13 countries and territories.

International Baccalaureate Organization (IBO): 15 route des Morillons, Grand-Saconnex 1218, Geneva, Switzerland; tel. 227917740; fax 227910277; e-mail ibhq@ibo.org; internet www.ibo.org; f. 1968 to plan curricula and an international university entrance examination, the International Baccalaureate diploma, recognized by major universities world-wide; offers the Primary Years Programme for children aged 3–12, the Middle Years Programme for students in the 11–16 age range, and the Diploma Programme for 17–18-year-olds; mems: 2,217 participating schools in 125 countries; Pres. of Bd of Governors MONIQUE SEEFRIED (France/USA); Dir-Gen. JEFFREY BEARD.

International Catholic Federation for Physical and Sports Education (Fédération Internationale Catholique d'Education Physique et Sportive—FICEP): 22 rue Oberkampf, 75011 Paris, France; tel. 1-513-77-14; fax 1-513-40-36; e-mail info@ficep.org; internet www.ficep.org; f. 1911 to group Catholic asscns for physical education and sport of different countries and to develop the principles and precepts of Christian morality by fostering meetings, study and international co-operation; mems: 14 affiliated national federations representing about 3.5m. members; Pres. GERHARD HAUER; Sec.-Gen. ANNE CORDIER.

International Centre for Minority Studies and Inter-Cultural Relations (IMIR): 1303 Sofia, ul. I Antim 55, Bulgaria; tel. (2) 832-31-12; fax (2) 931-05-83; e-mail marko@imir-bg.org; internet www.imir-bg.org; f. 1992 to carry out scientific research and humanitarian work with minority communities in Bulgaria; works with experts in the study of ethnic relations and religious issues in the wider Balkan region; Chair. ANTONINA ZHELYAZKOVA; publs research, analyses, forecasts and policy recommendations.

International Council for Adult Education (ICAE): Ave. 18 de Julio 2095/301, CP 11200, Montevideo, Uruguay; tel. and fax 2409 7982; e-mail secretariat@icae.org.uy; internet www.icae2.org; f. 1973 as a partnership of adult learners, teachers and organizations; General Assembly meets every four years; mems: 7 regional orgs and over 700 literacy, adult and lifelong learning asscns in more than 50 countries; Pres. ALAN TUCKETT; Sec.-Gen. CELITA ECCHER; publs *Convergence*, *ICAE News*.

International Council for Open and Distance Education (ICDE): Lilleakerveien 23, 0283 Oslo, Norway; tel. 22-06-26-30; fax 22-06-26-31; e-mail icde@icde.no; internet www.icde.org; f. 1938 (name changed 1982); furthers distance education by promoting research, encouraging regional links, providing information and organizing conferences; mems: institutions, corporations and individuals world-wide; Pres. TIAN BELAWATI (Indonesia); Sec.-Gen. GARD TITLESTAD (Norway); publ. *Open Praxis* (online, at www.openpraxis.com).

International Federation for Parent Education (IFPE) (Fédération internationale pour l'éducation des parents—FIEP): 1 ave Léon Journault, 92318 Sèvres Cedex, France; tel. 4-77-21-67-43; fax 1-46-26-69-27; e-mail fiep.ifpe@gmail.com; internet www.fiep-ifpe.fr; f. 1964 to gather in congresses and colloquia experts from different scientific fields and those responsible for family education in their own countries and to encourage the establishment of family education where it does not exist; mems: 60 nat. and local mem. orgs, 35 individual mems and 4 int. or regional orgs; Sec.-Gen. HABIB ABDENNEBI; publ. *Lettre de la FIEP* (2 a year).

International Federation of Catholic Universities (Fédération internationale d'universités catholiques—FIUC): 21 rue d'Assas, 75270 Paris Cedex 06, France; tel. 1-44-39-52-26; fax 1-44-39-52-28; e-mail sgfiuc@bureau.fiuc.org; internet www.fiuc.org; f. 1948; aims to ensure a strong bond of mutual assistance among all Catholic universities in the search for truth; to help to solve problems of growth and development, and to co-operate with other international organizations; mems: some 200 in 53 countries; Pres. ANTHONY J. CERNERA (USA); Sec.-Gen. GUY-RÉAL THIVIERGE (Canada); publ. *Monthly Newsletter*.

International Federation of Library Associations and Institutions (IFLA): POB 95312, 2509 CH The Hague, Netherlands; tel. (70) 3140884; fax (70) 3834827; e-mail ifla@ifla.org; internet www.ifla.org; f. 1927 to promote international co-operation in librarianship and bibliography; mems: over 1,700 members in 150 countries; Pres. (2011-13) INGRID PARENT (Canada); Sec.-Gen. JENNEFER NICHOLSON (Australia); publs *IFLA Annual Report*, *IFLA Directory*, *IFLA Journal*, *International Cataloguing and Bibliographic Control* (quarterly), *IFLA Professional Reports*.

International Federation of Physical Education (Fédération internationale d'éducation physique—FIEP): Foz do Iguaçu, PR, Brazil; tel. (45) 3574-1949; fax (45) 3525-1272; e-mail fiep.brasil@uol.com.br; internet www.fiep.net; f. 1923; studies physical education on scientific, pedagogic and aesthetic bases, with the aim of stimulating health, harmonious development or preservation, healthy recreation, and the best adaptation of the individual to the general needs of social life; organizes international congresses and courses; awards research prize; mems: from 112 countries; Sec. ALMIR GRUHN; publ. *FIEP Bulletin* (3 a year, in English, French, and Spanish).

International Federation of Teachers of Modern Languages (Fédération des Professeurs de Langues Vivantes): POB 216, Belgrave 3160, Australia; tel. (6139) 754-4714; fax (6139) 416-9899; e-mail djc@netspace.net.au; internet www.fiplv.org; f. 1931; holds meetings on every aspect of foreign-language teaching; has consultative status with UNESCO; mems: 28 national and regional language asscns and 9 international unilingual asscns (teachers of Arabic, English, Esperanto, French, German, Portuguese, Russian); Pres. TERRY LAMB; Sec.-Gen. DENIS CUNNINGHAM.

International Federation of University Women (IFUW): 10 rue du Lac, 1207 Geneva, Switzerland; e-mail ifuw@ifuw.org; internet www.ifuw.org; f. 1919; to promote life-long learning; to work for improvement of the status of women and girls; to encourage and enable women as leaders and decision-makers; Affiliates: 63 national asscns and feds; Pres. MARIANNE HASLEGRAVE.

International Federation of Workers' Education Associations: c/o Labour Research Service, POB 376, Woodstock 7915, Cape Town, South Africa; tel. (21) 447-1677; fax (21) 447-9244; e-mail ifweasecretariat@lrs.org.za; internet www.ifwea.org; f. 1947 to promote co-operation between non-governmental bodies concerned with workers' education; organizes clearing house services; promotes exchange of information; holds international seminars, conferences and summer schools; Pres. SUE SCHURMAN (USA); Gen. Sec. SAHRA RYKLIEF (South Africa); publ. *Worker's Education* (quarterly).

International Institute of Iberoamerican Literature (Instituto Internacional de Literatura Iberoamericana): 1312 CL, University of Pittsburgh, PA 15260, USA; tel. (412) 624-3359; fax (412) 624-0829; e-mail iili@pitt.edu; internet www.pitt.edu/~hispan/iili; f. 1938 to advance the study of Iberoamerican literature, and intensify cultural relations among the peoples of the Americas; mems: scholars and artists in 37 countries; publs *Revista Iberoamericana*, *Memorias*.

International Institute of Philosophy (IIP) (Institut international de philosophie): 8 rue Jean-Calvin, 75005 Paris, France; tel. 1-43-36-39-11; e-mail inst.intern.philo@wanadoo.fr; f. 1937 to clarify fundamental issues of contemporary philosophy and to promote mutual understanding among thinkers of different backgrounds and traditions; mems: 107 in 45 countries; Pres. ENRICO BERTI (Italy); Sec.-Gen. BERNARD BOURGEOIS (France); publs *Bibliography of Philosophy* (quarterly), *Proceedings of annual meetings*, *Chroniques*, *Philosophy and World Community* (series), *Philosophical Problems Today*, *Open Problems*, *Philosophy of Education*.

International Reading Association: 800 Barksdale Rd, POB 8139, Newark, DE 19714-8139, USA; tel. (302) 731-1600; fax (302) 731-1057; e-mail pubinfo@reading.org; internet www.reading.org; f. 1956 to improve the quality of reading instruction at all levels, to promote the habit of lifelong reading, and to develop every reader's proficiency; mems: 85,000 in 118 countries; Pres. VICTORIA J. RISKO (USA); Exec. Dir. MARCIE CRAIG POST; publs *The Reading Teacher* (8 a year), *Journal of Adolescent and Adult Literacy* (8 a year), *Reading Research Quarterly*, *Lectura y Vida* (quarterly), *Reading Today* (6 a year).

International Schools Association (ISA): 10333 Diego Drive South, Boca Raton, FL 33428, USA; tel. (561) 883-3854; fax (561) 483-2004; e-mail info@isaschools.org; internet www.isaschools.org; f. 1951 to co-ordinate work in international schools and to promote their development; convenes biennial Conferences and annual Youth Leadership Seminars on topics of global concern, and organizes specialist seminars on internationalism and international-mindedness; has consultative status at ECOSOC; mems: 100 schools world-wide; Chair. LUIS MARTINEZ ZORZO.

International Society for Business Education (Société Internationale pour l'Enseignement Commercial—SIEC): 6302 Mineral Point Rd, 100 Madison, WI 53705, USA; tel. (608) 273-8467; e-mail secretary@siec-isbe.org; internet www.siec-isbe.org; f. 1901; encourages international exchange of information; organizes international courses and congresses on business education; mems: 2,200 national orgs and individuals in 23 countries; Pres. Dr TAMRA S. DAVIS (USA); Gen. Sec. Dr JUDITH OLSON-SUTTON (USA); publ. *International Review for Business Education*.

International Society for Education through Art (INSEA): e-mail secretary@insea.org; internet www.insea.org; f. 1951 to unite art teachers throughout the world, to exchange information and to co-ordinate research into art education; organizes international congresses and exhibitions of children's art; Pres. RITA IRWIN (Canada); Sec. GRAHAM NASH (Australia); publ. *International Journal for Education through Art* (3 a year).

International Society for Music Education (ISME): POB 909, Nedlands, WA 6909, Australia; tel. (8) 9386-2654; fax (8) 9386-2658; e-mail isme@isme.org; internet www.isme.org; f. 1953 to organize international conferences, seminars and publications on matters pertaining to music education; acts as advisory body to UNESCO in matters of music education; mems: national committees and individuals in more than 70 countries; Pres. YASUHARU TAKAHAGI (Japan); Sec.-Gen. JUDY THÖNELL (Australia); publs *ISME Newsletter*, *International Journal of Music Education*.

International Society for the Study of Medieval Philosophy (SIEPM): Albert-Ludwigs-Universität Freiburg, Philosophisches Seminar, Platz der Universität 3, 79085 Freiburg, Germany; tel. (10) 47-48-07; fax (10) 47-82-85; internet www.siepm.uni-freiburg.de; f. 1958 to promote the study of medieval thought and the collaboration between individuals and institutions in this field; organizes International Congress of Medieval Philosophy every five years; mems: 700; Sec. Prof. MAARTEN J. F. M. HOENEN; publ. *Bulletin de Philosophie Médiévale* (annually).

International Union for Oriental and Asian Studies: c/o Közraktar u. 12a 11/2, 1093 Budapest, Hungary; f. 1951 by the 22nd International Congress of Orientalists under the auspices of UNESCO, to promote contacts between orientalists throughout the world, and to organize congresses, research and publications; mems: in 24 countries; Sec.-Gen. Prof. GYÖRGY HAZAI.

International Youth Library (Internationale Jugendbibliothek): Schloss Blutenburg, 81247 Munich, Germany; tel. (89) 8912110; fax (89) 8117553; e-mail info@ijb.de; internet www.ijb.de; f. 1949, since 1953 an associated project of UNESCO; promotes the international exchange of children's literature; provides study opportunities for specialists in childrens' books; maintains a library of 600,000 volumes in about 130 languages; Dir Dr CHRISTIANE RAABE; publs *The White Ravens*, *Das Buecherschloss*, catalogues.

Islamic World Academy of Sciences: POB 830036 Zahran, Amman 11183, Jordan; tel. (6) 5522104; fax (6) 5511803; e-mail ias@go.com.jo; internet www.ias-worldwide.org; f. 1986; serves as a consultative organization of the Islamic *Ummah* in the field of science and technology; convenes international scientific conferences; organizes and supports capacity-building workshops in basic sciences in developing countries; provides experts and consultants in science and technology to developing countries upon request; Sec.-Gen. MOHAMED H A HASSAN; publs *IAS Newsletter* (quarterly), science journals, conference proceedings.

Italian-Latin American Institute: Via Giovanni Paisiello 24, 00198 Rome, Italy; tel. (06) 684921; fax (06) 6872834; e-mail info@iila.org; internet www.iila.org; f. 1966; aims to promote Italian culture in Latin America; awarded observer status at the UN General Assembly in 2007; Dir-Gen. SIMONETTA CAVALIERI; Sec.-Gen. GIORGIO MALFATTI DI MONTE TRETTO.

LIBER (Association of European Research Libraries) (Ligue des Bibliothèques Européennes de Recherche): National Library of the Netherlands, POB 90407, 2509 LK, The Hague, Netherlands; tel. (70) 3140767; fax (70) 3140197; e-mail liber@kb.nl; internet www.libereurope.eu; f. 1971 to encourage collaboration between the general research libraries of Europe, and national and university libraries in particular; gives assistance in finding practical ways of improving the quality of the services provided; mems: 400 libraries, library orgs and individuals in 40 countries; Pres. PAUL AYRIS; Sec.-Gen. ANN MATHESON; publ. *LIBER Quarterly*.

Organization of Ibero-American States for Education, Science and Culture (Organización de Estados Iberoamericanos para la Educación, la Ciencia y la Cultura—OEI): Centro de Recursos Documentales e Informáticos, Calle Bravo Murillo 38, 28015 Madrid, Spain; tel. (91) 5944382; fax (91) 5944622; internet www.oei.es; f. 1949 (as the Ibero-American Bureau of Education); promotes peace and solidarity between member countries, through education, science, technology and culture; provides information, encourages exchanges and organizes training courses; the General Assembly (at ministerial level) meets every four years; mems: govts of 20 countries; Sec.-Gen. ÁLVARO MARCHESI ULLASTRES; publ. *Revista Iberoamericana de Educación* (quarterly).

Organization of the Catholic Universities of Latin America (Organización de Universidades Católicas de América Latina—ODUCAL): Av. Libertador Bernardo O'Higgins 340, Of. 242, 2° piso, Santiago, Chile; tel. and fax (2) 354-1866; e-mail oducal@uc.cl; internet www.oducal.uc.cl; f. 1953 to assist the social, economic and cultural development of Latin America through the promotion of Catholic higher education in the continent; mems: 43 Catholic univs in 15 Latin American countries; Pres. Dr PEDRO PABLO ROSSO; Sec.-Gen. ANTONIO DAHER HECHEM; publs *Anuario*, *Sapientia*, *Universitas*.

Pan-African Association for Literacy and Adult Education: Rue 10, Bldg. 306, POB 21783, Ponty, Dakar, Senegal; tel. 825-48-50; fax 824-44-13; e-mail anafa@sentoo.sn; f. 2000 to succeed African Asscn for Literacy and Adult Education (f. 1984); Co-ordinator Dr LAMINE KANE.

Southeast Asian Ministers of Education Organization (SEAMEO): M. L. Pin Malakul Bldg, 920 Sukhumvit Rd, Bangkok 10110, Thailand; tel. (2) 391-0144; fax (2) 381-2587; e-mail secretariat@seameo.org; internet www.seameo.org; f. 1965 to promote co-operation among the Southeast Asian nations through projects in education, science and culture; SEAMEO has 19 regional centres including: BIOTROP for tropical biology, in Bogor, Indonesia; INNOTECH for educational innovation and technology, in Philippines; SEAMOLEC, an open-learning centre, in Indonesia; RECSAM for education in science and mathematics, in Penang, Malaysia; RELC for languages, in Singapore; RIHED for higher education development, in Bangkok, Thailand; SEARCA for graduate study and research in agriculture, in Los Baños, Philippines; SPAFA for archaeology and fine arts, in Bangkok, Thailand; TROPMED for tropical medicine and public health, with regional centres in Indonesia, Malaysia, Philippines and Thailand and a central office in Bangkok; VOCTECH for vocational and technical education; QITEPs, regional centres for quality improvement of teachers and education personnel, for language, based in Jakarta, Indonesia, for mathematics, in Yogyakarta, Indonesia, and for science, in Bandung, Indonesia; RETRAC, a training centre, in Ho Chi Minh City, Viet Nam; and the SEAMEO Regional Centre for History and Tradition (CHAT) in Yangon, Myanmar; mems: Brunei, Cambodia, Indonesia, Laos, Malaysia, Philippines, Singapore, Thailand, Timor-Leste and Viet Nam; assoc. mems: Australia, Canada, France, Germany, Netherlands, New Zealand, Norway and Spain; Dir Dr WITAYA JERADECHAKUL (Thailand); publs *Annual Report*, *SEAMEO Education Agenda*.

Southern and Eastern Africa Consortium for Monitoring Educational Quality: e-mail info@sacmeq.org; internet www.sacmeq.org; f. 1995; aims to undertake integrated research and training activities in order to develop the capacities of education planners to enhance the evaluation and monitoring of the condition of schools and the quality of education; receives technical assistance from UNESCO International Institute for Educational Planning (IIEP); mems: Ministries of Education in 15 countries of the region; Dir a.i. Dr DEMUS MAKUWA.

Union of Arab Historians: POB 6378, al-Naqabat St, Tarablus Quarter, Baghdad, Iraq; tel. (1) 537-8691; fax (1) 537-2516; f. 1974; mems: historians in 22 countries of the region; Sec.-Gen. Dr MUHAMMAD JASSIM AL-MASHHADANI; publ. *Arab Historian*.

Union of Universities of Latin America and the Caribbean (Unión de Universidades de América Latina y el Caribe—UDUAL): Edificio UDUAL, Apdo postal 70-232, Ciudad Universitaria, Del. Coyoacán, 04510 México, DF, Mexico; tel. (55) 5616-2386; fax (55) 5622-0092; e-mail contacto@udual.org; internet www.udual.org; f. 1949 to organize exchanges between professors, students, research fellows and graduates and generally encourage good relations between the Latin American universities; arranges conferences; conducts statistical research;

maintains centre for university documentation; mems: 180 univs and 8 univ. networks; Pres. Dr GUSTAVO GARCÍA DE PAREDES (Panama); Sec.-Gen. Dr ROBERTO ESCALANTE SEMERENA (Mexico); publs *Universidades* (2 a year), *Gaceta UDUAL* (quarterly), *Censo* (every 2 years).

Universal Esperanto Association (Universala Esperanto-Asocio): Nieuwe Binnenweg 176, 3015 BJ Rotterdam, Netherlands; tel. (10) 4361044; fax (10) 4361751; e-mail info@co.uea.org; internet www.uea.org; f. 1908 to assist the spread of the international language, Esperanto, and to facilitate the practical use of the language; organizes World Congresses (2012: Hanoi, Viet Nam); mems: 70 affiliated national asscns and 15,800 individuals in 118 countries; Pres. PROBAL DASGUPTA (India); Dir-Gen. OSMO BULLER (Finland); publs *Esperanto* (monthly), *Kontakto* (every 2 months), *Jarlibro* (annually).

University of the South Pacific: University of the South Pacific, Laucala Campus, Suva, Fiji; tel. 3231000; fax 3231551; e-mail webmaster@usp.ac.fj; internet www.usp.ac.fj; f. 1968; comprises three main campuses (in Fiji, Samoa and Vanuatu), 11 regional campuses and three faculties (arts and law; business and economics; and science, technology and environment); mems: Cook Islands, Fiji, Kiribati, Marshall Islands, Nauru, Niue, Samoa, Solomon Islands, Tokelau, Tonga, Tuvalu, Vanuatu; Pres. and Vice-Chancellor RAJESH CHANDRA; publs *USP Annual Report*, *USP Beat* (monthly), *USP Calendar* (annually), *Oceanian Wave* (quarterly).

West African Examinations Council (WAEC) (Conseil des examens de l'Afrique orientale): POB GP125, Accra, Ghana; tel. (30) 2248967; fax (30) 2222905; e-mail waechqrs@africaonline.com.gh; internet www.waecheadquartersgh.org; f. 1952; administers prescribed examinations in mem. countries; aims to harmonize examinations procedures and standards. Offices in each mem. country and in London, United Kingdom; mems: The Gambia, Ghana, Liberia, Nigeria, Sierra Leone; Chair. Prof. JONAS A. S. REDWOOD-SAWYERR; Registrar MULIKAT A. BELLO.

World Education Fellowship: 54 Fox Lane, London, N13 4AL, United Kingdom; tel. (20) 8245-4561; e-mail generalsecretary@wef-international.org; internet www.wef-international.org; f. 1921 to promote education for international understanding, and the exchange and practice of ideas, together with research into progressive educational theories and methods; mems: sections and groups in 20 countries; Pres. Prof. SHINJO OKUDA (Japan); Gen. Sec. GUADALUPE G. DE TURNER; publ. *The New Era in Education* (3 a year).

World Union of Catholic Teachers (Union mondiale des enseignants catholiques—UMEC): Palazzo San Calisto 16, 00120 Vatican City, Vatican; tel. (06) 69887286; fax (06) 69887207; e-mail umec@org.va; f. 1951; encourages the grouping of Catholic teachers for the greater effectiveness of Catholic schools, distributes documentation on Catholic doctrine with regard to education, and facilitates personal contacts through congresses, and seminars, etc; nationally and internationally; mems: 32 orgs in 29 countries; Pres. MARK PHILPOT; publ. *Nouvelles de l'UMEC*.

Environmental Conservation

Baltic Marine Environment Protection Commission (Helsinki Commission)—HELCOM: Katajanokanlaituri 6B, 00160 Helsinki, Finland; tel. (20) 7412649; fax (20) 7412645; e-mail monika.stankiewicz@helcom.fi; internet www.helcom.fi; f. 1980 to combat regional pollution; governing body of the Convention on the Protection of the Marine Environment of the Baltic Sea Area; responsibilities include the prevention of airborne, sea and land-based pollution; a new Convention was signed in 1992 and entered into force in 2000; in November 2007 adopted a Baltic Sea Action Plan to reduce pollution in the area by 2021; mems: Denmark, Estonia, European Community, Finland, Germany, Latvia, Lithuania, Poland, Russia and Sweden; Chair. GABRIELLA LINDHOLM (Sweden); Exec. Sec. MONIKA STANKIEWICZ; publ. *Baltic Sea Environment Proceedings*.

BirdLife International: Wellbrook Ct, Girton Rd, Cambridge, CB3 0NA, United Kingdom; tel. (1223) 277318; fax (1223) 277200; e-mail birdlife@birdlife.org; internet www.birdlife.org; f. 1922 as the International Council for Bird Preservation; a global partnership of organizations that determines status of bird species throughout the world and compiles data on all endangered species; identifies conservation problems and priorities; initiates and co-ordinates conservation projects and international conventions; mems: partners or representatives in more than 100 countries; Chair. PETER JOHAN SCHEI; Dir Dr MARCO LAMBERTINI (Italy); publs *Bird Red Data Book*, *World Birdwatch* (quarterly), *Bird Conservation Series*, study reports.

Caribbean Conservation Association: Chelford Bush Hill, St Michael, Barbados; tel. 426-5373; fax 429-8483; e-mail admin@caribbeanconservation.org; internet www.caribbeanconservation.org; f. 1967; aims to conserve the environment and cultural heritage of the region through education, legislation, and management of museums and sites; mems: 17 govts, 60 NGOs and 130 associates; Pres. ATHERTON MARTIN (Dominica); Exec. Dir LESLIE JOHN WALLING; publ. *Caribbean Conservation News* (quarterly).

Carpathian Ecoregion Initiative (CERI): c/o Daphne Institute of Applied Ecology, Podunajska 24, 821 06 Bratislava, Slovakia; tel. (2) 4552-4019; fax (2) 4564-0201; e-mail jansef@daphne.sk; internet www.carpates.org; f. 1999 as a project of the WWF Danube-Carpathian Programme to work for the protection and sustainable development of the Carpathian region; since 2004, functions independently; mems: 45 orgs in 7 countries.

Caspian Environment Programme (CEP-PMCU): c/o Kazhydromet Bldg, 7th Floor, Orynbor St, Astana, 010000 Kazakhstan; tel. (7172) 798317; e-mail msgp.meg@undp.org; internet www.caspianenvironment.org; f. 1998 by Azerbaijan, Iran, Kazakhstan, Russia and Turkmenistan with the aim of halting the deterioration of environmental conditions in the area of the Caspian Sea and also with a view to promoting sustainable development in the region; supported the efforts of the Caspian states to negotiate and conclude, in 2003, a Framework Convention for the Protection of the Marine Environment of the Caspian Sea (the Tehran Convention); Project Man. PARVIN FARSHCHI.

Coalition Clean Baltic (CCB): Östra Ågatan 53, SE-753 22 Uppsala, Sweden; tel. (18) 71-11-55; fax (18) 71-11-75; e-mail secretariat@ccb.se; internet www.ccb.se; f. 1990, network of environmental non-governmental organizations from countries bordering the Baltic Sea; Exec. Sec. GUNNAR NORÉN.

Commission for the Conservation of Antarctic Marine Living Resources (CCAMLR): POB 213, North Hobart, Tasmania 7002, Australia; tel. (3) 6210-1111; fax (3) 6224-8744; e-mail ccamlr@ccamlr.org; internet www.ccamlr.org; established under the 1982 Convention on the Conservation of Antarctic Marine Living Resources to manage marine resources in the Antarctic region; Exec. Sec. ANDREW WRIGHT.

Commission on the Protection of the Black Sea Against Pollution: Fatih Orman Kampüsü, Büyükdere Cad. 265, 34398 Maslak Şişli, Istanbul, Turkey; tel. (212) 2992940; fax (212) 2992944; e-mail secretariat@blacksea-commission.org; internet www.blacksea-commission.org; established under the 1992 Convention on the Protection of the Black Sea Against Pollution (Bucharest Convention) to implement the Convention and its Protocols; also oversees the 1996 Strategic Action Plan for the Rehabilitation and Protection of the Black Sea; Exec. Dir Prof. HALIL IBRAHIM SUR.

Conservation International: 2011 Crystal Drive, Suite 500, Arlington, VA 22202, USA; tel. (703) 341-2400; internet www.conservation.org; f. 1987; aims to demonstrate to governments, institutions and corporations that sustainable global development is necessary for human well-being, and provides strategic, technical and financial support to partners at local, national and regional level to facilitate balancing conservation actions with development objectives and economic interests; focuses on the following priority areas: biodiversity hotspots (34 threatened habitats: 13 in Asia and the Pacific; eight in Africa; five in South America; four in North and Central America and the Caribbean; and four in Europe and Central Asia) that cover just 2.3% of the Earth's surface and yet hold at least 50% of plant species and some 42% of terrestrial vertebrate species); high biodiversity wilderness areas (five areas retaining at least 70% of their original vegetation: Amazonia; the Congo Basin; New Guinea; North American deserts—covering northern parts of Mexico and southwestern areas of the USA; and the Miomo-Mopane woodlands and savannas of southern Africa); and oceans and seascapes; organized Summit for Sustainability in Africa in May 2012, in Gaborone, Botswana; maintains offices in more than 30 countries world-wide; partners: governments, businesses, local communities, nonprofit organizations and universities world-wide; Chair. and CEO PETER SELIGMANN.

Consortium for Ocean Leadership: 1201 New York Ave, NW, Suite 420, Washington, DC 20005, USA; tel. (202) 232-3900; fax (202) 462-8754; e-mail info@oceanleadership.org; internet www.oceanleadership.org; f. 2007, following the merger of the Consortium for Oceanographic Research and Education (CORE, f. 1999) and the Joint Oceanographic Institutions (JOI); aims to promote, support and advance the science of oceanography; Pres. ROBERT B. GAGOSIAN.

Environment and Security Initiative (ENVSEC): c/o UNEP Regional Office for Europe, 11–13 chemin des Anémones, 1219 Châtelaine, Geneva, Switzerland; tel. 229178779; fax 229178024; e-mail marika.palosaari@unep; internet www.envsec.org; a partnership comprising UNEP, UNDP, the UN Economic Commission for Europe, NATO, OSCE, and the Regional Environment Centre for Central and Eastern Europe; the partner agencies aim to use their specialized and complementary mandates and expertise to strengthen co-operation to contribute to the reduction of environmental and security risks in Central Asia, Eastern Europe, Southern Caucasus, and South-Eastern Europe; the ENVSEC process involves assessing the situation on the ground and mapping problem areas ('hotspots'); drawing the attention of politicians to such hotspots; developing related work programmes and project portfolios; and supporting concrete actions to address security concerns on the ground; ENVSEC undertakes vulnerability assessments, and early warning and monitoring of environmental and security risks; supports national institutions in capacity building for strengthening environmental and security policies; provides technical expertise and mobilizes financial resources for environmental clean up activities; and aims to raise awareness about linkages between environment and security risks; Co-ordination Officer MARIKA POLOSAARI.

Environmental Partnership for Sustainable Development (EPSD): Krátká 26, 100 00 Prague 10, Czech Republic; tel. and fax 274816727; e-mail david.murphy@ecn.cz; internet www.environmentalpartnership.org/regionalceg; f. 1991; a consortium of six national bodies in Bulgaria, the Czech Republic, Hungary, Poland, Romania and Slovakia, which aims to mobilize citizens to improve their local communities and environment, through some 8,000 local-level initiatives; manages the Central and Eastern European Greenways programme, establishing 'greenways' (multifunctional trails for non-motorized users, which connect communities and natural and cultural heritage sites, with a view to promoting a healthy environment) in the six ESPD countries as well as in Austria, Belarus, Serbia and Ukraine; Dir. DAVID MURPHY.

Forest Stewardship Council (FSC): Charles de Gaulle Str. 5, 53113 Bonn, Germany; tel. (228) 367660; fax (228) 3676630; e-mail fsc@fsc.org; internet www.fsc.org; f. 1994 to promote sustainable and socially aware practices in forest management while ensuring economic viability in the utilization of forest resources; certifies forest areas based on these criteria; mems: in 80 countries; Exec. Dir ANDRE GIACINI DE FREITAS (Brazil).

Friends of the Earth International: POB 19199, 1000 GD, Amsterdam, Netherlands; tel. (20) 6221369; fax (20) 6392181; internet www.foei.org; f. 1971 to promote the conservation, restoration and rational use of the environment and natural resources through public education and campaigning; mems: 77 national groups; Chair. NNIMMO BASSEY (Nigeria); publ. *Link* (quarterly).

Global Coral Reef Monitoring Network: POB 772, Townsville MC 4810, Australia; tel. (7) 4721-2699; fax (7) 4772-2808; e-mail clive.wilkinson@rrrc.org.au; internet www.gcrmn.org; f. 1994, as an operating unit of the International Coral Reef Initiative; active in more than 80 countries; aims include improving the management and sustainable conservation of coral reefs, strengthening links between regional organizations and ecological and socioeconomic monitoring networks, and disseminating information to assist the formulation of conservation plans; Global Co-ordinator Dr CLIVE WILKINSON (Australia); publ. *Status of Coral Reefs of the World*.

Global Wind Energy Council: Wind Power House, 80 rue d'Arlon, 1040 Brussels, Belgium; tel. (2) 213-18-97; fax (2) 213-18-90; e-mail info@gwec.net; internet www.gwec.net; represents the main national, regional and international institutions, companies and asscns related to wind power; aims to promote the development and growth of wind as a major source of energy; organizes a Global Wind Power Conference every two years (2011: India); Chair. KLAUS RAVE; Sec.-Gen. STEVE SAWYER; publs *Global Wind Energy Outlook*, *Wind Force 12*, other reports, surveys.

GLOBE International: 11 Dartmouth St, Westminster, London, SW1H 9BN, United Kingdom; tel. (20) 722-6955; fax (20) 7222-6959; e-mail adam.matthews@globeinternational; internet www.globeinternational.info; f. 1989 by legislators from the European Parliament, Japanese Diet, Russian State Duma, and US Congress, with the aim of co-ordinating national policy measures in response to environmental challenges; since 2005 GLOBE International has comprised 100 legislators from the parliaments of G8 and European Parliament countries, as well as from the parliaments of Brazil, the People's Republic of China, India, Mexico and South Africa; from 1992 GLOBE International urged industrialised countries to adopt fiscal instruments aimed at promoting energy efficiency in order to reduce CO2 emissions; holds biannual policy dialogues on four priority policy areas: climate change; natural capital; forestry; and marine environment; convened the first World Summit of Legislators in Rio de Janiero, Brazil, in mid-June 2012, with participation by Presidents and Speakers of world-wide legislatures, and with the aim of placing national legislation, natural capital and scrutiny at the core of the agenda of the UN Conference on Sustainable Development (UNCSD), which took place in Rio de Janeiro immediately afterwards; Sec.-Gen. ADAM C. T. MATTHEWS.

Greencross International: 160A route de Florissant, 1231 Conches/Geneva, Switzerland; tel. 227891662; fax 227891695; e-mail gcinternational@gcint.org; internet www.greencrossinternational.net; f. 1993; aims to promote Earth Charter, to mitigate the environmental legacy of conflicts, to deter conflict in water-stressed regions, to combat desertification, to promote new energy consumption patterns, and to promote international conferences on and awareness of environmental issues; Chair. JAN KULCZYK (Poland); Pres. ALEXANDER LIKHOTAL (Russia).

Greenpeace International: Ottho Heldringstraat 5, 1066 AZ Amsterdam, Netherlands; tel. (20) 718-2000; fax (20) 718-2002; e-mail supporter.services.int@greenpeace.org; internet www.greenpeace.org; f. 1971 to campaign for the protection of the environment through non-violent direct action, and to offer solutions for positive change; aims to change attitudes and behaviour, to protect and conserve the environment, to promote peace by working for solutions for positive change; to maintain its independence Greenpeace does not accept donations from governments or corporations but relies on contributions from individual supporters and foundation grants; mems: representation in more than 40 countries across Europe, the Americas, Africa, Asia and the Pacific; Chair. Bd of Dirs ANA TONI (Brazil); Exec. Dir KUMI NAIDOO (South Africa).

International Commission for the Protection of the Rhine: Postfach 200253, 56002 Koblenz; Hohenzollernstr. 18, 56068 Koblenz, Germany; tel. (261) 94252; fax (261) 9425252; e-mail sekretariat@iksr.de; internet www.iksr.org; f. 1950; prepares and commissions research on the nature of the pollution of the Rhine; proposes protection, ecological rehabilitation and flood prevention measures; mems: 23 delegates from France, Germany, Luxembourg, Netherlands, Switzerland and the EU; Chair. ANDRÉ WEIDENHAUPT; Sec.-Gen. BEN VAN DE WETERING; publ. *Annual Report*.

International Coral Reef Initiative: c/o Australia/Great Barrier Reef Marine Park Authority (GBRMPA), 2–68 Flinders St, POB 1379, Townsville, QLD, 4810, Australia; e-mail icri@gbrmpa.gov.au; internet www.icriforum.org; f. 1994 at the first Conference of the Parties of the Convention on Biological Diversity; a partnership of governments, non-governmental organizations, scientific bodies and the private sector; aims to highlight the degradation of coral reefs and provide a focus for action to ensure the sustainable management and conservation of these and related marine ecosystems; in 1995 issued a Call to Action and a Framework for Action; the Secretariat is co-chaired by a developed and a developing country, on a rotational basis among mem. states (2012–13, Australia and Belize); Co-Chair. MARGARET JOHNSON (Australia), BEVERLEY WADE (Belize).

International Emissions Trading Association: 24 rue Merle d'Aubigné, 1207 Geneva, Switzerland; tel. 227370500; fax 227370508; e-mail secretariat@ieta.org; internet www.ieta.org; f. 1999 to establish a functional international framework for trading greenhouse gas emissions, in accordance with the objectives of the UN Framework Convention on Climate Change; serves as a specialized information centre on emissions trading and the greenhouse gas market; mems: 179 int. cos; Pres. and CEO HENRY DERWENT.

International Fund for Saving the Aral Sea: 050020 Almatı, Dostyk Av. 280, Kazakhstan; tel. (727) 387-34-31; fax (727) 387-34-33; e-mail mail@ec-ifas.org; internet www.ec-ifas.org/russian_version/about.html; f. 1993 by Central Asian heads of state; incorporates an Intergovernmental Sustainable Development Commission and an Interstate Commission for Water Co-ordination; granted observer status at the UN General Assembly in Nov. 2008; in Oct. 2011 organized a conference, in Kyzylorda, southern Kazakhstan, on biodiversity conservation, climate change response, sustainable development and comprehensive integrated water resources management in the Aral Sea Basin Area; aims to incorporate the Syrdarya River Delta Wetlands into the Ramsar List of Wetlands of International Importance; mems: Kazakhstan, Kyrgyzstan, Tajikistan, Turkmenistan, Uzbekistan; Chair. SAGHIT IBATULLIN.

International Renewable Energy Agency: C67 Office Bldg, Khalidiyah (32nd) St, POB 236, Abu Dhabi, United Arab Emirates; tel. (2) 4179000; internet www.irena.org; f. 2009 at a conference held in Bonn, Germany; aims to promote the development and application of renewable sources of energy; to act as a forum for the exchange of information and technology transfer; and to organize training seminars and other educational activities; inaugural Assembly convened in April 2011; mems: 94 states and the EU; at June 2012 a further 63 countries had signed but not yet ratified the founding agreement to become full mems; Dir-Gen. ADNAN AMIN (Kenya).

IUCN—International Union for Conservation of Nature: 28 rue Mauverney, 1196 Gland, Switzerland; tel. 229990000; fax 229990002; e-mail press@iucn.org; internet www.iucn.org; f. 1948, as the International Union for Conservation of Nature and Natural Resources; supports partnerships and practical field activities to promote the conservation of natural resources, to secure the conservation of biological diversity as an essential foundation for the future; to ensure wise use of the earth's natural resources in an equitable and sustainable way; and to guide the development of human communities towards ways of life in enduring harmony with other components of the biosphere, developing programmes to protect and sustain the most important and threatened species and eco-systems and assisting governments to devise and carry out national conservation strategies; incorporates the Species Survival Commission (SSC), a science-based network of volunteer experts aiming to ensure conservation of present levels of biodiversity; compiles annually updated Red List of Threatened Species, comprising in 2011 some 59,508 species, of which 19,265 were threatened with extinction; maintains a conservation library and documentation centre and units for monitoring traffic in wildlife; mems: more than 1,000 states, government agencies, non-governmental organizations and affiliates in some 140 countries; Pres. ASHOK KHOSLA (India); Dir-Gen. JULIA MARTON-LEFÈVRE (USA); publs *World Conservation Strategy*, *Caring for the Earth*, *Red List of Threatened Plants*, *Red List of Threatened Species*, *United Nations List of National Parks and Protected Areas*, *World Conservation* (quarterly), *IUCN Today*.

Nordic Environment Finance Corporation (NEFCO): Fabianinkatu 34, POB 249, 00171 Helsinki, Finland; tel. (10) 618003; fax (9) 630976; e-mail info@nefco.fi; internet www.nefco.org; f. 1990; finances environmentally beneficial projects in Central and Eastern Europe with transboundary effects that also benefit the Nordic region; Man. Dir MAGNUS RYSTEDT.

Permanent Commission of the South Pacific (Comisión Permanente del Pacífico Sur): Av. Carlos Julio Arosemena, Km 3 Edificio Inmaral, Guayaquil, Ecuador; tel. (4) 222-1202; fax (4) 222-1201; e-mail sgeneral@cpps-int.org; internet www.cpps-int.org; f. 1952 to consolidate the presence of the zonal coastal states; Sec.-Gen. HÉCTOR SOLDI SOLDI (Peru).

Regional Environmental Centre for Central and Eastern Europe: 2000 Szentendre, Ady Endre ut. 9–11, Hungary; tel. (26) 504-000; fax (26) 311-294; e-mail zsbauer@rec.org; internet www.rec.org; f. 1990; aims to assist in the solution of environmental problems in Central and Eastern Europe through the promotion of co-operation between non-governmental organizations, governments and businesses, the free exchange of information and public participation in decision-making; provides grants and training and facilitates networking; 17 local offices; Exec. Dir MARTA SZIGETI BONIFERT.

Secretariat of the Antarctic Treaty: Maipú 757, piso 4, C1006ACI Buenos Aires, Argentina; tel. (11) 4320-4250; fax (11) 4320-4253; e-mail ats@ats.aq; internet www.ats.aq; f. 2004 to administer the Antarctic Treaty (signed in 1959); has developed an Electronic Information Exchange System; organizes annual Consultative Meeting (2012: Hobart, Australia, in June); mems: 49 states party to the Treaty; Exec. Sec. MANFRED REINKE.

Secretariat of the Pacific Regional Environment Programme (SPREP): POB 240, Apia, Samoa; tel. 21929; fax 20231; e-mail sprep@sprep.org; internet www.sprep.org; f. 1978 by the South Pacific Commission (where it was based, now Pacific Community), the South Pacific (now Pacific Islands) Forum, ESCAP and UNEP; formally established as an independent institution in 1993; SPREP's mandate is to promote co-operation in the Pacific islands region and to provide assistance in order to protect and improve the environment and to ensure sustainable development for present and future generations; has the following four strategic priorities: Bio-diversity and Ecosystems Management, Climate Change, Environmental Monitoring and Governance, Waste Management and Pollution Control; in March 2010 letters of agreement were signed relating to the transfer and integration to SPREP from the Pacific Islands Applied Geoscience Commission of the following functions: the Pacific Islands Global Ocean Observing System (PI-GOOS); the Islands Climate Update (ICU); the Climate and Meteorological Databases (CMD); and climate change-associated energy activities; mems: 21 Pacific islands, Australia, France, New Zealand, USA; Dir DAVID SHEPPARD (Australia).

South Asia Co-operative Environment Programme (SACEP): 10 Anderson Rd, Colombo 05, Sri Lanka; tel. (11) 2589787; fax (11) 2589369; e-mail info@sacep.org; internet www.sacep.org; f. 1982; aims to promote regional co-operation in the protection and management of the environment, in particular in the context of sustainable economic and social development; works closely with governmental and non-governmental national, regional and international institutions in conservation and management efforts; Governing Council meets regularly; working to establish a South Asia Biodiversity Clearing House Mechanism; also actively developing specific projects: the conservation and integrated management of marine turtles and their habitats in the South Asia Seas region; reef-based corals management; accelerated penetration of cost effective renewable energy technologies; the establishment of a Basel Convention Sub-regional Centre for South Asia; protected areas management of world heritage sites and implementation of the Ramsar Strategic Plan at a sub-regional level; mems: Afghanistan, Bangladesh, Bhutan, India, Maldives, Nepal, Pakistan, Sri Lanka; Officiating Dir-Gen. JACINTHA S. TISSERA; publs *SACEP Newsletter*, *South Asia Environmental and Education Action Plan*, other reports.

Wetlands International: POB 471, 6700 AL Wageningen, Netherlands; tel. (318) 660910; fax (318) 660950; e-mail post@wetlands.org; internet www.wetlands.org; f. 1995 by merger of several regional wetlands organizations; aims to protect and restore wetlands, their resources and biodiversity through research, information exchange and conservation activities; promotes implementation of the 1971 Ramsar Convention on Wetlands; Chair. JAN ERNST DE GROOT (Netherlands); CEO JANE MADGWICK.

World Association of Zoos and Aquariums (WAZA): IUCN Conservation Centre, 28 rue Mauverney, 1196 Gland, Switzerland; tel. 229990790; fax 229990791; e-mail secretariat@waza.org; internet www.waza.org; f. 1946, current name adopted 2000; aims to provide leadership and support for zoos and aquariums and to promote biodiversity, environmental education, and global sustainability; adopted WAZA Code of Ethics and Animal Welfare, and a Consensus Document on Responsible Reproductive Management, in 2003; in 2005 WAZA launched a World Zoo and Aquarium Conservation Strategy, adopted Research Guidelines, and participated for the first time in Conferences of the Parties to the Ramsar Convention and the Convention of Migratory Species; mems: leading zoos and aquariums and related regional and national asscn; affiliate conservation orgs; Pres. JORG JUNHOLD; Exec. Dir GERALD DICK.

World Ocean Observatory: 1 Oak St, Boothbay Harbor, Maine 04538, USA; e-mail info@thew2o.net; internet www.thew2o.net; f. 2004; recommendation of the final report of the Independent World Commission on the Oceans; serves as a focal point for ocean-related information from governments, non-governmental organizations and other networks; aims to enhance public awareness of the importance of oceans and facilitate the dissemination of information; maintains an online radio station and organizes other online events; Dir PETER NEILL; publ. *World Ocean Observer* (monthly).

World Rainforest Movement (WRM): Maldonado 1858, Montevideo 11200, Uruguay; tel. 2413 2989; fax 2410 0985; e-mail wrm@wrm.org.uy; internet www.wrm.org.uy; f. 1986; aims to secure the lands and livelihoods of rainforest peoples and supports their efforts to defend rainforests from activities including commercial logging, mining, the construction of dams, the development of plantations, and shrimp farming; issued the Penang Declaration in 1989 setting out the shared vision of an alternative model of rainforest development based on securing the lands and livelihoods of forest inhabitants; released in 1998 the Montevideo Declaration, campaigning against large-scale monocrop plantations, for example of pulpwood, oil palm and rubber; and issued the Mount Tamalpais Declaration in 2000, urging governments not to include tree plantations as carbon sinks in international action against climate change; Co-ordinator WINFRIDUS OVERBEEK; publ. *WRM Bulletin* (monthly).

World Society for the Protection of Animals (WSPA): 222 Grays Inn Rd, London, WC1X 8HB, United Kingdom; tel. (20) 7239-0500; fax (20) 7793-0208; e-mail wspa@wspa.org; internet www.wspa-international.org; f. 1981, incorporating the World Federation for the Protection of Animals (f. 1950) and the International Society for the Protection of Animals (f. 1959); promotes animal welfare and conservation by humane education, practical field projects, international lobbying and legislative work; mems: over 850 member societies in 150 countries; Pres. HANJA MAIJ-WEGGEN; Dir-Gen. MICHAEL BAKER.

World Water Council: Espace Gaymard, 2–4 pl. d'Arvieux, 13002 Marseille, France; tel. 4-91-99-41-00; fax 4-91-99-41-01; internet www.worldwatercouncil.org; f. 1996; aims to facilitate the efficient conservation, protection, development, planning, management and use of water resources on an environmentally sustainable basis; organizes a World Water Forum held every three years since 1997 (2012: Marseilles, France, in March); Pres. LOÏC FAUCHON; Gen. Dir (vacant).

World Water Organization: 1350 Ave of the Americas, 2nd Floor, New York, NY 10019, USA; tel. (212) 759-1639; fax (646) 666-4349; e-mail info@theworldwater.org; internet www.theworldwater.org; organizes conferences and special projects to highlight issues related to water security and to seek means of protecting the global water infrastructure; arranged High-Level Symposium on Water Security at UN headquarters, New York, in Oct. 2010; mems: experts from government, business, medical, and academic backgrounds; Chair. HAROLD HYUNSUK OH; Exec. Dir Dr ELAINE VALDOV.

WWF International: 27 ave du Mont-Blanc, 1196 Gland, Switzerland; tel. 223649111; fax 223648836; e-mail info@wwfint.org; internet www.wwf.panda.org; f. 1961 (as World Wildlife Fund), name changed to World Wide Fund for Nature in 1986, current nomenclature adopted 2001; aims to stop the degradation of natural environments, conserve bio-diversity, ensure the sustainable use of renewable resources, and promote the reduction of both pollution and wasteful consumption; addresses six priority issues: forests, freshwater, marine, species, climate change, and toxics; has identified, and focuses its activities in, 200 'ecoregions' (the 'Global 200'), believed to contain the best part of the world's remaining biological diversity; actively supports and operates conservation programmes in more than 90 countries; mems: 54 offices, 5 associate orgs, c. 5m. individual mems world-wide; Pres. YOLANDA KAKABADSE (Ecuador); Dir-Gen. JAMES P. LEAPE; publs *Annual Report*, *Living Planet Report*.

Government and Politics

Accord de Non-agression et d'Assistance en Matière de Défence (ANAD) (Non-Aggression and Defence Aid Agreement): 08 BP 2065, Abidjan 08, Côte d'Ivoire; tel. 20-21-88-33; fax 20-33-86-13; e-mail colpape@aviso.ci; f. 1977 to serve as a framework for sub-regional co-operation in conflict prevention and resolution; adopted a draft protocol for the establishment of a regional peace-keeping force and a fund to promote peace and security in April 1999; mems: Benin, Burkina Faso, Côte d'Ivoire, Mali, Mauritania, Niger, Senegal, Togo.

African Association for Public Administration and Management (AAPAM): Britak Centre, Ragati and Mara Rds, POB 48677, 00100 GPO, Nairobi, Kenya; tel. (20) 2730555; fax (22) 310102; e-mail aapam@aapam.org; internet www.aapam.org; f. 1971 to promote good practices, excellence and professionalism in public administration through training, seminars, research, publications; convenes regular conferences to share learning experiences among members, and an annual Roundtable Conference; funded by membership contributions, government and donor grants; mems: 500 individual, 50 corporate; Pres. ABDON AGAW JOK NHIAL (South Sudan); Sec.-Gen. Dr YOLAMU R. BARONGO (Uganda); publs *Newsletter* (quarterly), *Annual Seminar Report*, *African Journal of Public Administration and Management* (2 a year), books.

African Parliamentary Union: BP V314, Abidjan, Côte d'Ivoire; tel. 20-30-39-70; fax 20-30-44-05; e-mail upa1@aviso.ci; internet www.african-pu.org; f. 1976 (as Union of African Parliaments); holds annual conference (2012: Kigali, Rwanda, in Nov.); mems: 40 parliaments; Chair, ANGEL SERAFIN SERICHE DOUGAN MALABO (Equatorial Guinea); Sec.-Gen. N'ZI KOFFI.

Afro-Asian Peoples' Solidarity Organization (AAPSO): 89 Abdel Aziz Al-Saoud St, POB 11559-61 Manial El-Roda, Cairo, Egypt; tel. (2) 3636081; fax (2) 3637361; e-mail aapso@idsc.net.eg; internet www.aapsorg.org; f. 1958; acts among and for the peoples of Africa and Asia in their struggle for genuine independence, sovereignty, socio-economic development, peace and disarmament; mems: national committees and affiliated organizations in 66 countries and territories, assoc. mems in 15 European countries; Sec.-Gen. NOURI ABDEL RAZZAK HUSSEIN (Iraq); publs *Solidarity Bulletin* (monthly), *Socio-Economic Development* (3 a year).

Agency for the Prohibition of Nuclear Weapons in Latin America and the Caribbean (Organismo para la Proscripción de las Armas Nucleares en la América Latina y el Caribe—OPANAL): Schiller 326, 5°, Col. Chapultepec Morales, 11570 México, DF, Mexico; tel. (55) 5255-2914; fax (55) 5255-3748; e-mail info@opanal.org; internet www.opanal.org; f. 1969 to ensure compliance with the Treaty for the Prohibition of Nuclear Weapons in Latin America (Treaty of Tlatelolco), 1967; to ensure the absence of all nuclear weapons in the application zone of the Treaty; to contribute to the movement against proliferation of nuclear weapons; to promote general and complete disarmament; to prohibit all testing, use, manufacture, acquisition, storage, installation and any form of possession, by any means, of nuclear weapons; the organs of the Agency comprise the General Conference, meeting every two years, the Council, meeting every two months, and the secretariat; a General Conference is held every two years; mems: 33 states that have fully ratified the Treaty; the Treaty has two additional Protocols: the first signed and ratified by France, the Netherlands, the United Kingdom and the USA, the second signed and ratified by People's Republic of China, the USA, France, the United Kingdom and Russia; Sec.-Gen. GIOCONDA UBEDA RIVERA (until 31 Dec. 2013).

Alliance of Small Island States (AOSIS): c/o 800 Second Ave, Suite 400K, New York, NY 10017, USA; tel. (212) 599-0301; fax (212) 599-1540; e-mail grenada@un.int; internet www.aosis.info; f. 1990 as an ad hoc intergovernmental grouping to focus on the special problems of small islands and low-lying coastal developing states; mems: 42 island nations and observers; Chair. MARLENE MOSES (Nauru); publ. *Small Islands, Big Issues*.

ANZUS: c/o Dept of Foreign Affairs and Trade, R. G. Casey Bldg, John McEwen Crescent, Barton, ACT 0221, Australia; tel. (2) 6261-1111; fax (2) 6271-3111; internet www.dfat.gov.au; the ANZUS Security Treaty was signed in 1951 by Australia, New Zealand and the USA, and ratified in 1952 to co-ordinate partners' efforts for collective defence for the preservation of peace and security in the Pacific area, through the exchange of technical information and strategic intelligence, and a programme of exercises, exchanges and visits. In 1984 New Zealand refused to allow visits by US naval vessels that were either nuclear-propelled or potentially nuclear-armed, and this led to the cancellation of joint ANZUS military exercises: in 1986 the USA formally announced the suspension of its security commitment to New Zealand under ANZUS. Instead of the annual ANZUS Council meetings, ministerial consultations (AUSMIN) were subsequently held every year between Australia and the USA on policy and political-military issues. ANZUS continued to govern security relations between Australia and the USA, and between Australia and New Zealand; security relations between New Zealand and the USA were the only aspect of the treaty to be suspended. Senior-level contacts between New Zealand and the USA resumed in 1994. The Australian Govt invoked the ANZUS Security Treaty for the first time following the international terrorist attacks against targets in the USA that were perpetrated in September 2001.

Arab Inter-Parliamentary Union (Union Interparlementaire Arabe): POB 4130, AIPU Headquarters, Damascus, Syria; tel. (11) 3324045; fax (11) 2246495; e-mail info@arab-ipu.org; internet www.arab-ipu.org; f. 1974; aims to strengthen contacts and promote dialogue between Arab parliamentarians, to co-ordinate activities at international forums, to enhance democratic concepts and values in the Arab countries, to co-ordinate and unify Arab legislations, and to strengthen Arab solidarity; mems from 22 countries; Pres. MAHMOOD EL MASHHADANI; Sec.-Gen. NOUREDDINE BOUCHKOUJ.

Association of North East Asia Regional Governments (NEAR): Pohang, Gyeongsangbuk-do, Republic of Korea; tel. (54) 223-2318; fax (54) 223-2309; e-mail jaykim51@yahoo.co.kr; internet www.neargov.org; f. 1996 to promote co-operation among local governments in support of sub-regional economic development; mems: 69 local govts in six countries (People's Republic of China, Japan, Mongolia, Democratic People's Republic of Korea, Republic of Korea, Russia; Sec.-Gen. KIM JAE HYO; Gen. Dir KIM JONG-HAK.

Association of Pacific Islands Legislatures (APIL): Carl Rose Bldg, Suite 207, 181 E. Marine Corps Drive, Hagatna, Guam; tel. (671) 477-2719; fax (671) 473-3004; e-mail apil@guam.net; internet www.apilpacific.com; f. 1981 to provide a permanent structure of mutual assistance for representatives of the people of the Pacific Islands; comprises legislative representatives from 12 Pacific Island Govts; Pres. REBLUUD KESOLEI (Palau).

Association of Secretaries General of Parliaments: c/o Committee Office, House of Commons, London, SW1, United Kingdom; tel. (20) 7219-3498; fax (20) 7219-2681; e-mail asgp@parliament.uk; internet www.asgp.info; f. 1938; studies the law, practice and working methods of different Parliaments; proposes measures for improving those methods and for securing co-operation between the services of different Parliaments; operates as a consultative body to the Inter-Parliamentary Union, and assists the Union on subjects within the scope of the Association; mems: c. 200 representing 145 countries; 5 assoc. institutions; Pres. MARC BOSC (Canada); Jt Secs STEVEN MARK (United Kingdom), AGATHE LE NAHÉNEC (France); publ. *Constitutional and Parliamentary Information* (2 a year).

Atlantic Treaty Association: Quartier Prince Albert, 20 rue des Petits Carmes, 1000 Brussels, Belgium; tel. (2) 502-31-60; fax (2) 502-48-77; e-mail info@ata-sec.org; internet www.ata-sec.org; f. 1954 to inform public opinion on the North Atlantic Alliance and to promote the solidarity of the peoples of the North Atlantic; holds annual assemblies, seminars, study conferences for teachers and young politicians; mems: national asscns in 28 member countries of NATO; 12 assoc. mems from Central and Eastern Europe, 2 observer mems; Pres. Dr KARL A. LAMERS (Germany); Sec.-Gen. TROELS FRØLING (Denmark).

Baltic Assembly: Citadeles St 2-616, Rīga 1010, Latvia; tel. 722-5178; fax 722-5366; e-mail baltasam@baltasam.org; internet www.baltasam.org; f. 1991 to develop co-operation among the parliaments of Estonia, Latvia and Lithuania; comprises 20 parliamentarians from each country, who participate in seven working committees: budget and audit; legal; social and economic affairs; environment and energy; communications and informatics; education, science and culture; and security and foreign affairs; holds twice-yearly sessions; in 1994 the Assembly and the Baltic Council of Ministers formed the Baltic Council, as an institution of co-operation; from 1996 also holds joint sessions with the Nordic Council (comprising Denmark, Finland, Iceland, Norway and Sweden) to promote co-operation in Northern Europe; Pres. PAULIUS SAUDARGAS; Sec.-Gen Dr MARIKA LAIZĀNE-JURKĀNE.

Baltic Council: f. 1993 by the Baltic Assembly, comprising 60 parliamentarians from Estonia, Latvia and Lithuania; the Council of Ministers of the member countries co-ordinates policy in the areas of foreign policy, justice, the environment, education and science.

Bolivarian Alliance for the Americas (Alianza Bolivariana para las Américas—ALBA): internet www.alianzabolivariana.org; f. 2002 (as the Bolivarian Alternative for the Americas) by the President of Venezuela, Hugo Chávez, to promote an alternative model of political, economic and social co-operation and integration between Caribbean and Latin American countries sharing geographic, historical and cultural bonds; aims to reduce disparities in development between countries in the region and to combat poverty and social exclusion; in June 2007 ministers of foreign affairs convened for the inaugural meeting of ALBA's Council of Ministers agreed to the establishment of joint enterprises, as an alternative to transnational corporations, a joint bank to finance projects supported by the grouping and to develop bilateral agreements; the establishment of a Bank of ALBA was endorsed at the 6th summit meeting of heads of state, convened in January 2008; an emergency summit meeting was convened in April to consider the global food crisis; summit meeting convened in Caracas, Venezuela, in Feb. 2012; mems: Antigua and Barbuda, Bolivia, Cuba, Dominica, Ecuador, Nicaragua, Saint Vincent and the Grenadines, Venezuela.

Celtic League: c/o Mark Lockerby, 12 Magherdonnag, Ponyfields, Port Erin IM9 6BY, United Kingdom; internet www.celticleague.net; f. 1961 to foster co-operation between the six Celtic nations (Ireland, Scotland, Isle of Man, Wales, Cornwall and Brittany), especially those actively working for political autonomy by non-violent means; campaigns politically on issues affecting the Celtic countries; monitors military activity in the Celtic countries; co-operates with national cultural organizations to promote the languages and culture of the Celts; mems: approx. 1,400 individuals in the Celtic communities and elsewhere; Gen. Sec. RHISIART TAL-E-BOT; publ. *Carn* (quarterly).

Central European Initiative (CEI): CEI Executive Secretariat, Via Genova 9, 34121 Trieste, Italy; tel. (040) 7786777; fax (040) 7786766; e-mail cei@cei.int; internet www.ceinet.org; f. 1989 as 'Quadragonal' co-operation between Austria, Italy, Hungary and Yugoslavia, became 'Pentagonal' in 1990 with the admission of Czechoslovakia, and 'Hexagonal' with the admission of Poland in 1991, present name adopted in 1992, when Bosnia and Herzegovina, Croatia and Slovenia were admitted; the Czech Republic and Slovakia became separate mems in January 1993, and Macedonia also joined in that year; Albania, Belarus, Bulgaria, Romania and Ukraine joined the CEI in 1995 and Moldova in 1996; the Federal Republic of Yugoslavia (now the separate sovereign states of Montenegro and Serbia) admitted in 2000; encourages regional political and economic co-operation with a focus on the following nine areas of activity: climate, environment and sustainable energy; enterprise development (incl. tourism); human resource development; information society and media; intercultural co-operation (incl. minorities); multimodal transport; science and technology; sustainable agriculture; interregional and cross-border co-operation; economic forum held annually since 1998; Sec.-Gen. GERHARD PFANZELTER; publ. *Newsletter* (monthly).

Centrist Democrat International: 10 rue du Commerce, 1000 Brussels, Belgium; tel. (2) 285-41-45; fax (2) 300-80-13; e-mail idc@cdi-idc.org; internet www.cdi-idc.com; f. 1961 (as Christian Democrat and Peoples' Parties International); serves as an asscn of political groups adhering to Christian humanist and democratic theology; mems: parties in 64 countries (of which 47 in Europe); Pres. PIER FERDINANDO CASINI (Italy); Exec. Sec. ANTONIO LÓPEZ ISTÚRIZ (Spain); publs *DC-Info* (quarterly), *Human Rights* (5 a year), *Documents* (quarterly).

Club of Madrid: Carrera de San Jerónimo 15, 3A planta, 28014 Madrid, Spain; tel. (91) 1548230; fax (91) 1548240; e-mail clubmadrid@clubmadrid.org; internet www.clubmadrid.org; f. 2001, following Conference on Democratic Transition and Consolidation; forum of former Presidents and Prime Ministers; aims to strengthen democratic values and leadership; maintains office in Brussels, Belgium; 87 mems. from 60 countries; Pres. WIM KOK (Netherlands); Sec.-Gen. CARLOS WESTENDORP (Spain).

Collective Security Treaty Organization (CSTO): 103012 Moscow, Varvarka 7, Russia; tel. (495) 606-97-71; fax (495) 625-76-20; e-mail odkb@gov.ru; internet www.dkb.gov.ru; f. 2003 by signatories to the Treaty on Collective Security (signed Tashkent, Uzbekistan, May 1992); aims to co-ordinate and strengthen military and political co-operation and to promote regional and national security; maintains a joint rapid deployment force; the Oct. 2007 leaders' summit endorsed documents enabling the establishment of CSTO joint peace-keeping forces and the creation of a co-ordination council for the heads of member states' emergency response agencies; the leaders' summit convened in Sept. 2008 issued a joint declaration stating that conflicts should be settled preferably through political and diplomatic means in line with international law and stating the following as immediate priorities: strengthening efforts to promote nuclear non-proliferation; to combat terrorism, drugs-trafficking and weapon-smuggling; to expand co-operation with international bodies; and to promote international efforts to establish 'anti-drug and financial security belts' around Afghanistan; the CSTO became an observer in the UN General Assembly in 2004; in April 2006 it signed a protocol with the UN Office on Drugs and Crime to develop joint projects to combat drugs-trafficking, terrorism and transborder crime; in Feb. 2009 agreed to establish a rapid reaction force and conducted a joint military exercise (without the participation of Uzbekistan) in Aug.–Oct; mems: Armenia, Belarus, Kazakhstan, Kyrgyzstan, Russia, Tajikistan, Uzbekistan; Sec.-Gen. NIKOLAY BORDYUZHA.

Community of Latin American and Caribbean States (CELAC) (Comunidad de Estados de América Latina y el Caribe): 3841 NE 2nd Ave, Suite 203A, Miami, FL 33137, USA; e-mail cumbre.calc@mppre.gob.ve; internet www.celac.gob.ve; f. 2010; aim to build regional co-operation on political, cultural, social and economic issues in the countries of Latin America and the Caribbean; inaugural summit held in Dec. 2011 (2012 summit to be hosted by Chile); 32 Latin American and Caribbean states; Interim Pres. SEBASTIÁN PIÑERA (Chile).

Comunidade dos Países de Língua Portuguesa (CPLP) (Community of Portuguese-Speaking Countries): rua de S. Mamede (ao Caldas) 21, 1100-533 Lisbon, Portugal; tel. (21) 392-8560; fax (21) 392-8588; e-mail comunicacao@cplp.org; internet www.cplp.org; f. 1996; aims to produce close political, economic, diplomatic and cultural links between Portuguese-speaking countries and to strengthen the influence of the Lusophone Commonwealth within the international community; deployed an observer mission to oversee presidential elections held in Timor-Leste in May 2007; in Nov. 2010 adopted, jointly with ECOWAS, the CPLP-ECOWAS road map on reform of the defence and security sector in Guinea-Bissau; mems: Angola, Brazil, Cape Verde, Guinea-Bissau, Mozambique, Portugal, São Tomé and Príncipe, Timor-Leste; assoc. observers: Equatorial Guinea, Mauritius, Senegal; Exec. Sec. DOMINGOS SIMÕES PEREIRA (Guinea-Bissau).

Conference on Interaction and Confidence-building Measures in Asia: 050000, Almatı, Aiteke Bi 65, Kazakhstan; tel. (727) 272-01-08; fax (727) 272-40-96; e-mail s-cica@s-cica.kz; internet www.s-cica.org; f. 1999 at first meeting of 16 Asian ministers for foreign affairs, convened in Almatı; aims to provide a structure to enhance co-operation, with the objectives of promoting peace, security and stability throughout the region; first meeting of heads of state held in June 2002, adopted the Almatı Act; activities focused on a catalogue of confidence-building measures grouped into five areas: economic dimension; environmental dimension; human dimension; fight against new challenges and threats; and military-political dimension; mems: Afghanistan, Azerbaijan, People's Republic of China, Egypt, India, Iran, Israel, Jordan, Kazakhstan, Republic of Korea, Kyrgyzstan, Mongolia, Pakistan, Palestine, Russia, Tajikistan, Thailand, Turkey, United Arab Emirates, Uzbekistan; observers: Indonesia, Japan, Malaysia, Qatar, Viet Nam, Ukraine, USA, and the UN, OSCE and League of Arab States; Exec. Dir DULAT BAKISHEV.

Eastern Regional Organization for Public Administration (EROPA): National College of Public Administration, Univ. of the Philippines, Diliman, Quezon City 1101, Philippines; tel. and fax (2) 9297789; e-mail eropa@eropa.org.ph; internet www.eropa.org.ph; f. 1960 to promote regional co-operation in improving knowledge, systems and practices of governmental administration, to help accelerate economic and social development; organizes regional conferences, seminars, special studies, surveys and training programmes; accredited, in 2000, as an online regional centre of the UN Public Administration Network for the Asia and Pacific region; there are three regional centres: Training Centre (New Delhi), Local Government Centre (Tokyo), Development Management Centre (Seoul); mems: 10 countries, 63 groups, 266 individuals; Sec.-Gen. ORLANDO S. MERCADO (Philippines); publs *EROPA Bulletin* (quarterly), *Asian Review of Public Administration* (2 a year).

The Elders: c/o POB 60837, London, W6 6GS, United Kingdom; e-mail info@theelders.org; internet www.theelders.org; f. 2001; aims to alleviate human suffering world-wide by offering a catalyst for the peaceful resolution of conflicts, seeking new approaches to unresolved global issues, and sharing wisdom; comprises: Martti Ahtisaari (Finland), Kofi Annan (Ghana), Ela Bhatt (India), Lakhdar Brahimi (Algeria), Gro Brundtland (Norway), Jimmy Carter (USA), Fernando H Cardoso (Brazil), Graça Machel (Mozambique), Desmond Tutu (South Africa), Mary Robinson (Ireland); Honorary Elders: Aung San Suu Kyi (Myanmar), Nelson Mandela (South Africa); Interim Chair. BETHUEL KIPLAGAT (Kenya).

European Movement: 25 sq. de Meeûs, 1000 Brussels, Belgium; tel. (2) 508-30-88; fax (2) 508-30-89; e-mail communication@europeanmovement.eu; internet www.europeanmovement.eu; f. 1947 by a liaison committee of representatives from European organizations, to study the political, economic and technical problems of a European Union and suggest how they could be solved and to inform and lead public opinion in the promotion of integration; Conferences have led to the creation of the Council of Europe, College of Europe, etc; mems: national councils and committees in 42 European countries, and several international social and economic orgs, 32 assoc. mems; Sec.-Gen. DIOGO PINTO.

European Union of Women (EUW): Blenheim House, Henry St, Bath, BA1 1JR, United Kingdom; tel. (20) 79244124; e-mail euw@euw-uk.co.uk; internet www.euw-uk.co.uk; f. 1953 to increase the influence of women in the political and civic life of their country and of Europe; mems: national organizations in 21 countries; Chair. LYNNE FAULKNER.

Group of Eight (G8): an informal meeting of developed nations, originally comprising France, Germany, Italy, Japan, United Kingdom and the USA, first convened in Nov. 1975, at Rambouillet, France, at the level of heads of state and government; Canada became a permanent participant in 1976, forming the Group of Seven major industrialized countries—G7; from 1991 Russia was invited to participate in the then G7 summit outside the formal framework of co-operation; from 1994 Russia contributed more fully to the G7 political dialogue and from 1997 Russia became a participant in nearly all of the summit process scheduled meetings, excepting those related to finance and the global economy; from 1998 the name of the co-operation framework was changed to Group of Eight—G8, and since 2003

Russia has participated fully in all scheduled summit meetings, including those on the global economy; the EU is also represented at G8 meetings, although it may not chair fora; G8 heads of government and the President of the European Commission and President of the European Council convene an annual summit meeting, the chairmanship and venue of which are rotated in the following order: France, USA, United Kingdom, Russia, Germany, Japan, Italy, Canada; G8 summit meetings address and seek consensus, published in a final declaration, on social and economic issues confronting the international community; heads of state or government of non member countries, and representatives of selected intergovernmental organizations, have been invited to participate in meetings; dialogue commenced in 2005 in the 'G8+5' format, including the leaders of the five largest emerging economies: Brazil, People's Republic of China, India, Mexico and South Africa; G8 sectoral ministerial meetings (covering areas such as energy, environment, finance and foreign affairs) are held on the fringes of the annual summit, and further G8 sectoral ministerial meetings are convened through the year; the 2011 G8 summit meeting, convened in May, in Deauville, France, established the Deauville Partnership, aimed at supporting political and economic reforms being undertaken by several countries in North Africa and the Middle East; the 2012 summit meeting, held in May, at Camp David, Maryland, USA, without participation by the Russian President, reaffirmed the imperative of creating global growth and jobs, and—in response to the protracted euro area sovereign debt crisis, exacerbated by recent inconclusive legislative elections in Greece amid a climate of popular resistance to the social impact of economic austerity measures—agreed on the relevance for global stability of promoting a strong euro area, and welcomed ongoing discussion within the EU on means of stimulating economic growth while continuing to implement policies aimed at achieving fiscal consolidation; the participating G8 leaders also gave consideration to, *inter alia*, energy and climate change, Afghanistan's economic transition, food security, and the ongoing Deauville Partnership; and indicated readiness to request the International Energy Agency to release emergency petroleum stocks should international sanctions imposed on Iran result in disruption to global supply; mems: Canada, France, Germany, Italy, Japan, Russia, United Kingdom and the USA; European Union representation.

Gulf of Guinea Commission (Commission du Golfe de Guinée—CGG): f. 2001 to promote co-operation among mem. countries, and the peaceful and sustainable development of natural resources in the sub-region; mems: Angola, Cameroon, the Republic of the Congo, Equatorial Guinea, Gabon, Nigeria, São Tomé and Príncipe; in 2012 plans were under way to formulate, in partnership with ECOWAS and CEEAC, a regional strategy aimed at curbing piracy in the Gulf of Guinea, building on a UN assessment mission undertaken in Nov. 2011; Exec. Sec. MIGUEL TROVOADA (São Tomé and Príncipe).

Hansard Society: 40–43 Chancery Lane, London, WC2A 1JA, United Kingdom; tel. (20) 7438-1222; fax (20) 7438-1229; e-mail contact@hansardsociety.org.uk; internet www.hansardsociety.org.uk; f. 1944 as Hansard Society for Parliamentary Government; aims to promote political education and research and the informed discussion of all aspects of modern parliamentary government; presidency is held jointly by the incumbent Speakers of the United Kingdom House of Commons and House of Lords; Co-Pres JOHN BERCOW, Baroness FRANCES D'SOUZA; CEO FIONA BOOTH; publ. *Parliamentary Affairs* (quarterly).

Ibero-American General Secretariat (Secretaría General Iberoamericana—SEGIB): Paseo de Recoletos 8, 28001 Madrid, Spain; tel. (91) 5901980; e-mail info@segib.org; internet www.segib.org; f. 2003; aims to provide institutional and technical support to the annual Iberoamerican summit meetings, to monitor programmes agreed at the meetings and to strengthen the Ibero-American community; meetings of Ibero-American heads of state and government (the first of which was convened in Guadalajara, Mexico in 1991, and the 21st in Oct. 2011, in Asunción, Paraguay) aim to promote political, economic and cultural co-operation among the 19 Spanish- and Portuguese-speaking Latin American countries and three European countries; Sec.-Gen. ENRIQUE IGLESIAS (Uruguay).

International Alliance of Women (Alliance Internationale des Femmes): Aaloekken 11, 5250 Odense, Denmark; tel. 65-96-08-68; e-mail iawsec@womenalliance.org; internet www.womenalliance.org; f. 1904 to obtain equality for women in all fields and to encourage women to assume decision-making responsibilities at all levels of society; lobbies at international organizations; mems: 58 national affiliates and associates; Pres. ROSY WEISS; Sec.-Gen. LENE PIND; publs *International Women's News* (3 a year), electronic newsletter (monthly).

International Association for Community Development (IACD): The Stables, Falkland, Fife, KY15 7AF, United Kingdom; e-mail info@iacdglobal.org; internet www.iacdglobal.org; f. 1952; promotes community development across international policies and programmes, supports community development practitioners and encourages the exchange of research and information; membership open to individuals and organizations working in or supporting community development across eight world regions; organizes annual international colloquium for community-based organizations; Pres. Dr INGRID BURKETT; publs *IACD Newsletter* (2 a year), monthly e-bulletins.

International Commission for the History of Representative and Parliamentary Institutions (ICHRPI): c/o Lothar Höbelt, Department of History, University of Vienna, Universitaetsring 1, 1010 Vienna, Austria; fax (1) 4277 40821; e-mail lothar.hoebelt@univie.ac.at; internet www.ichrpi.com; f. 1936; promotes research into the origin and development of representative and parliamentary institutions world-wide; encourages wide and comparative study of such institutions, both current and historical; facilitates the exchange of information; 63rd Conference to be held in Cádiz, Spain (Sept. 2012); mems: 300 individuals in 31 countries; Pres. MARIA SOFIA CORCIULO (Italy); Sec.-Gen. Prof. LOTHAR HÖBELT (Austria); publs *Parliaments, Estates and Representation* (annually), studies.

International Conference on the Great Lakes Region, (ICGLR) (Conference Internationale sur la region des grands lacs): POB 7076, Bujumbura, Burundi; e-mail secretariat@icglr.org; internet www.icglr.org; f. 2006 following the signing of the Security, Stability and Development Pact for the Great Lakes Region at the second summit meeting of the International Conference on the Great Lakes Region, held in December, in Nairobi, Kenya; the UN Security Council proposed in 2000 the organization of a Great Lakes Conference to initiate a process that would bring together regional leaders to pursue agreement on a set of principles and to articulate programmes of action to help end the cycle of regional conflict and establish durable peace, stability, security, democracy and development in the whole region; runs the Special Fund for Reconstruction and Development (SFRD) which is hosted and managed by the African Development Bank (AfDB); the first summit meeting of the Conference was convened in Dar es Salaam, Tanzania, in November 2004; executive secretariat created in May 2007; mems: Angola, Burundi, Central African Republic, Democratic Republic of the Congo, Republic of the Congo, Kenya, Rwanda, Sudan, Tanzania, Uganda, Zambia; Exec. Sec. Prof. ALPHONSE LUMU NTUMBA LUABA.

International Democrat Union: POB 1536, Vika, 0117 Oslo, Norway; tel. 22-82-90-00; fax 22-82-90-80; e-mail secretariat@idu.org; internet www.idu.org; f. 1983 as a group of centre and centre-right political parties; facilitates the exchange of information and views; promotes networking; organizes campaigning seminars for politicians and party workers; holds Party Leaders' meetings every three years, also executive meetings and a Young Leaders' Forum; mems: political parties in some 60 countries, 46 assoc. mems in regions; Exec. Sec. EIRIK MOEN.

International Federation of Resistance Fighters (FIR): Franz Mehring Platz 1, 10243 Berlin, Germany; tel. (30) 29784174; fax (30) 29784179; e-mail office@fir.at; internet www.fir.at; f. 1951; supports the medical and social welfare of former victims of fascism; works for peace, disarmament and human rights, and against fascism and neo-fascism; mems: 76 national orgs; Pres. VILMOS HANTI (Hungary); Sec.-Gen. Dr ULRICH SCHNEIDER (Germany).

International Institute for Democracy and Electoral Assistance (IDEA): Strömsborg, 103 34 Stockholm, Sweden; tel. (8) 698-3700; fax (8) 20-2422; e-mail info@idea.int; internet www.idea.int; f. 1995; aims to promote sustainable democracy in new and established democracies; works with practitioners and institutions promoting democracy in Africa, Asia, Arab states and Latin America; 27 mem. states and one observer; Sec.-Gen. VIDAR HELGESEN (Norway).

International Institute for Peace: Möllwaldplatz 5/2, 1040 Vienna, Austria; tel. (1) 504-64-37; fax (1) 505-32-36; e-mail secretariat@iip.at; internet www.iip.at; f. 1957; non-governmental organization with consultative status at ECOSOC and UNESCO; studies conflict prevention; new structures in international law; security issues in Europe and world-wide; mems: individuals and corporate bodies invited by the executive board; Pres. Dr PETER SCHIEDER (Austria); Dir PETER STANIA (Austria); Sec.-Gen. Dr GRIGORI LOKSHIN; publ. *Peace and Security* (quarterly).

International Institute for Strategic Studies (IISS): Arundel House, 13–15 Arundel St, London, WC2R 3DX, United Kingdom; tel. (20) 7379-7676; fax (20) 7836-3108; e-mail iiss@iiss.org; internet www.iiss.org; f. 1958 as an independent institution concerned with the study of the role of force in international relations, including problems of international strategy, the ethnic, political and social sources of conflict, disarmament and arms control, peace-keeping and intervention, defence economics, etc.; mems: c. 3,000; Dir-Gen. Dr JOHN M. W. CHIPMAN; Chair. FLEUR DE VILLIERS; publs *Survival* (quarterly), *The Military Balance* (annually), *Strategic Survey* (annually), *Adelphi Papers* (10 a year), *Strategic Comments* (10 a year).

International Lesbian and Gay Association (ILGA): 17 rue de la Charité, 1020 Brussels, Belgium; tel. and fax (2) 502-24-71; fax (2) 223-48-20; e-mail information@ilga.org; internet www.ilga.org; f. 1978; works to abolish legal, social and economic discrimination against homosexual and bisexual women and men, and transexuals, throughout the world; co-ordinates political action at an international level; co-operates with other supportive movements; 2012 world conference: Stockholm. Sweden; mems: 750 national and regional asscns in 110 countries; Co-Secs-Gen. GLORIA CAREAGA, RENATO SABBADINI; publs *ILGA Bulletin* (quarterly), *GBLT Human Rights Annual Report*.

International Peace Bureau (IPB): 41 rue de Zürich, 1201 Geneva, Switzerland; tel. 227316429; fax 227389419; e-mail mailbox@ipb.org; internet www.ipb.org; f. 1891; promotes international co-operation for general and complete disarmament and the non-violent solution of international conflicts; co-ordinates and represents peace movements at the UN; conducts projects on Disarmament for Development and the abolition of nuclear weapons; mems: 300 peace orgs and 150 individual mems in 70 countries; Co-Pres TOMAS MAGNUSSON, INGEBORG BREINES; Sec.-Gen. COLIN ARCHER (United Kingdom); publs *IPB News* (every 2 weeks, by e-mail), *IPB Geneva News*.

International Political Science Association (IPSA) (Association Internationale de Science Politique—AISP): c/o Concordia University, 331 ave Docteur Penfield, Montréal, QC H3G 1C5, Canada; tel. (514) 848-8717; fax (514) 848-4095; e-mail info@ipsa.org; internet www.ipsa.org; f. 1949; aims to promote the development of political science; organizes Annual International Congress of Political Science (2012: Belfast, Ireland); mems: 41 national asscns, 100 institutions, 1,350 individual mems; Pres. LEONARDO MORLINO (Italy); Sec.-Gen. GUY LACHAPELLE (Canada); publs *Participation* (3 a year), *International Political Science Abstracts* (6 a year), *International Political Science Review* (quarterly).

Jewish Agency for Israel (JAFI): POB 92, 48 King George St, Jerusalem 91000 Israel; tel. (2) 6202251; fax (2) 6202577; e-mail barbaram@jafi.org; internet www.jafi.org.il; f. 1929; reconstituted 1971 as an instrument through which world Jewry can work to develop a national home; constituents are: World Zionist Organization, United Israel Appeal, Inc. (USA), and Keren Hayesod; Chair. Exec. NATAN SHARANSKY; Chair. of the Bd JAMES TISCH; Dir-Gen. ALAN HOFFMANN.

Latin American Parliament (Parlamento Latinoamericano): Casilla 1527, Edif. 1111-1113, Apdo 4, ave. Principal de Amador, Panama; tel. 512-8500; e-mail secgeneral@parlatino.org; internet www.parlatino.org; f. 1965; permanent democratic institution, representative of all existing political trends within the national legislative bodies of Latin America; aims to promote the movement towards economic, political and cultural integration of the Latin American republics, and to uphold human rights, peace and security; Pres. ELÍAS ARIEL CASTILLO GONZÁLEZ; Sec.-Gen. SONIA ESCUDERO; publs *Acuerdos, Resoluciones de las Asambleas Ordinarias* (annually), *Parlamento Latinoamericano–Actividades de los Órganos, Revista Patria Grande* (annually), statements and agreements.

Liberal International: 1 Whitehall Pl., London, SW1A 2HD, United Kingdom; tel. (20) 7839-5905; fax (20) 7925-2685; e-mail all@liberal-international.org; internet www.liberal-international.org; f. 1947; co-ordinates foreign policy work of member parties, and promotes freedom, tolerance, democracy, international understanding, protection of human rights and market-based economics; has consultative status at ECOSOC of United Nations and the Council of Europe; mems: 101 mem. parties and 10 co-operating orgs in 63 countries; Pres. HANS VAN BAALEN; Sec.-Gen. EMIL KIRJAS; publ. *Liberal Aerogramme* (quarterly).

Melanesian Spearhead Group (MSG): MSG Secretariat, Port Vila, Vanuatu; tel. 27750; fax 27832; internet www.mgsec.info; f. 1986 to promote political and cultural co-operation among the Melanesian peoples; supports independence process in New Caledonia; first Melanesian arts festival held in 1991; in July 1993 a free-trade agreement was signed, awarding each member country most-favoured nation status for all trade; heads of state or of government meet every two years; regular meetings of Group trade and economic officials are also held; a permanent constitution was adopted by the Group in March 2007; mems: Fiji, Papua New Guinea, Solomon Islands, Vanuatu; Front de Libération Nationale Kanake Socialiste (New Caledonia); Dir-Gen. RIVA RAVUSIRO.

NATO Parliamentary Assembly: 3 pl. du Petit Sablon, 1000 Brussels, Belgium; tel. (2) 513-28-65; fax (2) 514-18-47; internet www.nato-pa.int; f. 1955 as the NATO Parliamentarians' Conference; name changed 1966 to North Atlantic Assembly; renamed as above 1999; the inter-parliamentary assembly of the North Atlantic Alliance; holds two plenary sessions a year and meetings of committees (Political, Defence and Security, Economics and Security, Civil Dimension of Security, Science and Technology) to facilitate parliamentary awareness and understanding of key Alliance security issues, to provide the Alliance governments with a collective parliamentary voice, to contribute to a greater degree of transparency of NATO policies, and to strengthen the transatlantic dialogue; Pres. Dr KARL A. LAMERS (Germany); Sec.-Gen. DAVID HOBBS (United Kingdom).

Non-aligned Movement (NAM): c/o Ministry of Foreign Affairs, Arab Republic of Egypt, Corniche el-Nil, Cairo, Egypt; tel. (2) 25749820; fax (2) 25748822; e-mail namsummit@mfa.gov.eg; internet www.namegypt.org; f. 1961 by a meeting of 25 heads of state, with the aim of linking countries that had refused to adhere to the main East/West military and political blocs; co-ordination bureau established in 1973; works for the establishment of a new international economic order, and especially for better terms for countries producing raw materials; maintains special funds for agricultural development, improvement of food production and the financing of buffer stocks; South Commission promotes co-operation between developing countries; seeks changes at the United Nations to give developing countries greater decision-making power; holds summit conference every three years (2012: Iran); a 50th anniversary conference was convened in Bali, Indonesia, in May 2011; mems: 118 countries, 16 observer countries and 9 observer orgs.

Nordic Council: Ved Stranden 18, 1061 Copenhagen, Denmark; tel. 33-96-04-00; fax 33-11-18-70; e-mail nordisk-rad@norden.org; internet www.norden.org; f. 1952 to facilitate co-operation between Nordic parliaments and governments; 87 elected mems; Pres. KIMMO SASI (Finland); Sec.-Gen. JAN-ERIK ENESTAM (Finland); publs *Norden the Top of Europe* (monthly newsletter in English and Russian), *Norden this week* (weekly newsletter).

Nordic Council of Ministers: Ved Stranden 18, 1061, Copenhagen, Denmark; tel. 33-96-020-0; e-mail nmr@norden.org; internet www.norden.org; the Nordic Council of Ministers co-ordinates the activities of the governments of the Nordic countries when decisions are to be implemented; co-operation with adjacent areas includes the Baltic States, where Nordic governments are committed to furthering democracy, security and sustainable development, to contribute to peace, security and stability in Europe; the Nordic–Baltic Scholarship Scheme awards grants to students, teachers, scientists, civil servants and parliamentarians; Sec.-Gen. HALLDÓR ÁSGRÍMSSON (Iceland).

Northern Forum: 716 W 4th Ave, Suite 100, Anchorage, Alaska, USA; tel. (907) 561-3280; fax (907) 561-6645; e-mail nForum@northernforum.org; internet www.northernforum.org; f. 1991; aims to improve the quality of life of Northern peoples through support for sustainable development and socio-economic co-operation throughout the region; Exec. Dir PRISCILLA P. WOHL.

Organisation for the Prohibition of Chemical Weapons (OPCW): Johan de Wittlaan 32, 2517JR The Hague, Netherlands; tel. (70) 4163300; fax (70) 3063535; e-mail media@opcw.org; internet www.opcw.org; f. April 1997, on the entry into force of the Chemical Weapons Convention (CWC)—an international, multilateral disarmament treaty banning the development, production, stockpiling, transfer and use of chemical weapons—to oversee its implementation; verifies the irreversible destruction of declared chemical weapons stockpiles, as well as the elimination of all declared chemical weapons production facilities; OPCW member states undertake to provide protection and assistance if chemical weapons have been used against a state party, or if such weapons threaten a state party, and, together with OPCW inspectors, monitor the non-diversion of chemicals for activities prohibited under the CWC and verify the consistency of industrial chemical declarations; CWC states parties are obligated to declare any chemical weapons-related activities, to secure and destroy any stockpiles of chemical weapons within the stipulated deadlines, as well as to inactivate and eliminate any chemical weapons production capacity within their jurisdiction; mems: states party to the Convention (188 at June 2012); 2012 budget: €71m.; Dir-Gen. AHMET ÜZÜMCÜ (Turkey).

Organisation Internationale de la Francophonie (La Francophonie): 19-21 ave Bosquet, 75007 Paris, France; tel. 1-44-11-12-50; fax 1-44-11-12-80; e-mail oif@francophonie.org; internet www.francophonie.org; f. 1970 as l'Agence de coopération culturelle et technique; promotes co-operation among French-speaking countries in the areas of education, culture, peace and democracy, and technology; implements decisions of the Sommet francophone; technical and financial assistance has been given to projects in every member country, mainly to aid rural people; mems: 56 states and govts; 19 countries with observer status; Sec.-Gen. ABDOU DIOUF (Senegal); publ. *Journal de l'Agence de la Francophonie* (quarterly).

Organisation of Eastern Caribbean States (OECS): Morne Fortune, POB 179, Castries, Saint Lucia; tel. 455-6327; fax 453-1628; e-mail oecss@oecs.org; internet www.oecs.org; f. 1981 by the seven states which formerly belonged to the West Indies Associated States (f. 1966); aims to promote the harmonized development of trade and industry in member states; single market created on 1 Jan. 1988; principal institutions are: the Authority of Heads of Government (the supreme policy-making body), the Foreign Affairs Committee, the Defence and Security Committee, and the Economic Affairs Committee; other functional divisions include an Export Development and Agricultural Diversification Unit (EDADU, based in Dominica), a Pharmaceutical Procurement Service (PPS), a Regional Integration Unit, a Regional E-Government Unit and an HIV/AIDS Project Unit; an OECS Technical Mission to the World Trade Organization in Geneva, Switzerland, was inaugurated in June 2005; in Aug. 2008 heads of government determined to achieve economic union by 2011 and political union by 2013; an agreement to establish an economic union was signed in Dec. 2009; a Revised Treaty of Basseterre Establishing the OECS Economic Union was signed by heads of government of six member states (Antigua and Barbuda, Grenada, Dominica, Saint Christopher and Nevis, Saint Vincent and the Grenadines and Saint Lucia) in June 2010; the Treaty envisaged a new governance structure, in which an OECS Commission was to be established as a supranational executive institution; the Revised Treaty entered into force in Feb. 2011, having been ratified by four of the signatory states; in June 2012 the inauguration of the OECS Assembly was postponed; mems: Antigua and Barbuda, Dominica, Grenada, Montserrat, Saint Christopher and Nevis, Saint Lucia, Saint Vincent and the Grenadines; assoc. mems: Anguilla, British Virgin Islands; Dir-Gen. Dr LEN ISHMAEL.

Organization for Democracy and Economic Development (GUAM): 01001 Kyiv, str. Sofievska 2, Ukraine; tel. (44) 2063737; fax (44) 2063006; e-mail secretariat@guam-organization.org; internet www.guam-organization.org; f. 1997 as a consultative alliance of Georgia, Ukraine, Azerbaijan and Moldova (GUAM); Uzbekistan joined the grouping in April 1999, when it became known as GUUAM, but withdrew in May 2005, causing the grouping's name to revert to GUAM; formally inaugurated as a full international organization and current name adopted by heads of state at a summit held in Kyiv in May 2006; objectives include the promotion of a regional space of democracy, security, and stable economic and social development; strengthening relations with the EU and NATO; developing a database on terrorism, organized crime, drugs-trafficking, and related activities; establishing a GUAM energy security council; creating the GUAM Free-Trade Zone, in accordance with an agreement signed by heads of state at a meeting in Yalta, Ukraine, in July 2002; further economic development, including the creation of an East–West trade corridor and transportation routes for petroleum; and participation in conflict resolution and peace-keeping activities, with the establishment of peace-keeping forces and civilian police units under consideration; Sec.-Gen. VALERI CHECHELASHVILI (Georgia).

Organization of Solidarity of the Peoples of Africa, Asia and Latin America (OSPAAAL) (Organización de Solidaridad de los Pueblos de Africa, Asia y América Latina): Calle C No 670 esq. 29, Vedado, Havana 10400, Cuba; tel. (7) 830-5136; fax (7) 833-3985; e-mail secretario.general@tricontinental.cu; internet www.tricontinental.cu; f. 1966 at the first Conference of Solidarity of the Peoples of Africa, Asia and Latin America, to unite, co-ordinate and encourage national liberation movements in the three continents, to oppose foreign intervention in the affairs of sovereign states, colonial and neo-colonial practices, and to fight against racialism and all forms of racial discrimination; favours the establishment of a new international economic order; mems: 76 orgs in 46 countries; Sec.-Gen. ALFONSO FRAGA; publ. *Tricontinental* (quarterly).

Parliamentary Association for Euro-Arab Co-operation (PAEAC) (Institut européen de recherche sur la coopération euro-rabe): 24 Sq. de Meeus, 5th Floor, 1000 Brussels, Belgium; tel. (2) 231-13-00; fax (2) 231-06-46; e-mail secretariat@medeainstitute.org; internet www.medea.be; f. 1974 as an asscn of 650 parliamentarians of all parties from the national parliaments of the Council of Europe countries and from the European Parliament, to promote friendship and co-operation between Europe and the Arab world; Executive Committee holds annual joint meetings with Arab Inter-Parliamentary Union; represented in Council of Europe and European Parliament; works for the progress of the Euro-Arab Dialogue and a settlement in the Middle East that takes into account the national rights of the Palestinian people; Pres. FRANÇOIS-XAVIER DE DONNEA; Sec.-Gen. CHARLES KLEINERMANN; publs *Information Bulletin* (quarterly), *Euro-Arab and Mediterranean Political Fact Sheets* (2 a year), conference notes.

Party of European Socialists (PES): 98 rue du Trône, 1050 Brussels, Belgium; tel. (2) 548-90-80; fax (2) 230-17-66; e-mail info@pes.org; internet www.pes.org; f. 1992 to replace the Confederation of the Socialist Parties of the EC (f. 1974); affiliated to Socialist International; mems: 33 parties, 11 associate parties and 5 observer parties; 5 mem. orgs, 3 associate orgs and 10 observer orgs; Interim Pres. SERGEI STANISHEV; Sec.-Gen. PHILIP CORDERY; publs various, including *The New Social Europe*, *The EU on the international scene: Promoting sustainable peace*, statutes, manifestos and Congress documents.

Polynesian Leaders Group (PLG): c/o Govt of Samoa, POB L 1861, Apia, Samoa; tel. 24799; e-mail presssecretariat@samoa.ws; f. 2011 in Apia with the MOU signed by 8 states; to represent the collective interests of the Polynesian islands; first formal meeting to be held in the Cook Islands in Aug. 2012; mems: American Samoa, Cook Islands, French Polynesia, Niue, Samoa, Tokelau, Tonga and Tuvalu; Chair. TUILA'EPA SAILELE MALIELEGAOI (Samoa).

Regional Co-operation Council: 71000 Sarajevo, Trg Bosne i Hercegovine 1/V, Bosnia and Herzegovina; tel. (33) 561700; fax

(33) 561701; e-mail rcc@rcc.int; internet www.rcc.int; f. 2008, as successor to the Stability Pact for South Eastern Europe; serves as a focus for co-operation in the region; its six priority areas of activity cover: economic and social development, energy and infrastructure, justice and home affairs, security co-operation, and building human capital, with parliamentary co-operation as an overarching theme; maintains a Liaison Office in Brussels, Belgium; 50 mem. countries and orgs; Sec.-Gen. HIDO BIŠČEVIĆ.

Rio Group: f. 1987 at a meeting in Acapulco, Mexico, of eight Latin American government leaders, who agreed to establish a 'permanent mechanism for joint political action'; additional countries subsequently joined the Group; holds annual summit meetings at presidential level. At the ninth presidential summit (Quito, Ecuador, September 1995) a 'Declaration of Quito' was adopted, which set out joint political objectives, including the strengthening of democracy; combating corruption, drugs-production and -trafficking and money-laundering; and the creation of a Latin American and Caribbean free trade area (supporting the efforts of the various regional groupings). Opposes US legislation (the 'Helms-Burton' Act), which provides for sanctions against foreign companies that trade with Cuba; admitted Cuba as a member in Nov. 2008; also concerned with promoting sustainable development in the region, the elimination of poverty, and economic and financial stability. The Rio Group holds regular ministerial conferences with the EU; summit meeting in Cancún, Mexico, in Feb. 2010, determined to establish a new regional grouping, the Community of Latin American and Caribbean States (inaugurated in Dec. 2011, q.v.); mems: Argentina, Belize, Bolivia, Brazil, Chile, Colombia, Costa Rica, Cuba, Dominican Republic, Ecuador, El Salvador, Guatemala, Guyana, Haiti, Honduras, Jamaica, Mexico, Nicaragua, Panama, Paraguay, Peru, Suriname, Uruguay, Venezuela.

Shanghai Cooperation Organization (SCO): 41 Liangmaqiao Rd, Chaoyang District, Beijing, People's Republic of China; tel. (10) 65329806; fax (10) 65329808; e-mail sco@sectsco.org; internet www.sectsco.org; f. 2001, replacing the Shanghai Five (f. 1996 to address border disputes); aims to achieve security through mutual co-operation: promotes economic co-operation and measures to eliminate terrorism and drugs-trafficking; agreement on combating terrorism signed June 2001; a Convention on the Fight against Terrorism, Separatism and Extremism signed June 2002; Treaty on Long-term Good Neighbourliness, Friendship and Co-operation was signed August 2007; maintains an SCO anti-terrorism centre in Tashkent, Uzbekistan; holds annual summit meeting (2012: China); mems: People's Republic of China, Kazakhstan, Kyrgyzstan, Russia, Tajikistan and Uzbekistan; Sec.-Gen. MURATBEK IMANALIEV (Kyrgyzstan).

Socialist International: Maritime House, Clapham, London, SW4 0JW, United Kingdom; tel. (20) 7627-4449; fax (20) 7720-4448; e-mail secretariat@socialistinternational.org; internet www.socialistinternational.org; f. 1864; re-established in 1951; the world's oldest and largest asscn of political parties, grouping democratic socialist, labour and social democratic parties from every continent; provides a forum for political action, policy discussion and the exchange of ideas; works with many international orgs and trades unions (particularly members of ITUC; established a Commission for a Sustainable World Society in Nov. 2006; holds Congress every three–four years (24th Congress: Cape Town, South Africa, Aug.–Sept. 2012); the Council meets twice a year, and regular conferences and meetings of party leaders are also held; committees and councils on a variety of subjects and in different regions meet frequently; mems: 115 full member, 37 consultative and 18 observer parties in 122 countries; there are 3 fraternal orgs and 9 associated orgs, including: the Party of European Socialists (PES), the Group of the PES at the European Parliament and the International Federation of the Socialist and Democratic Press; Pres. GEORGE A. PAPANDREOU (Greece); Gen. Sec. LUIS AYALA (Chile); publ. *Socialist Affairs* (quarterly).

International Falcon Movement—Socialist Educational International: 98 rue du Trône, 2nd Floor, 1050 Brussels, Belgium; tel. (2) 215-79-27; fax (2) 245-00-83; e-mail contact@ifm-sei.org; internet www.ifm-sei.org; f. 1924 to help children and adolescents develop international understanding and a sense of social responsibility and to prepare them for democratic life; co-operates with several institutions concerned with children, youth and education; mems: 62 mems worldwide; Pres. TIM SCHOLZ (Germany); Sec.-Gen. TAMSIN PEARCE (United Kingdom); publs *IFM-SEI Newsletter* (quarterly), *IFM-SEI World News*, *EFN Newsletter* (6 a year), *Asian Regional Bulletin*, *Latin American Regional Bulletin*.

International Union of Socialist Youth (IUSY): Amtshausgasse 4, 1050 Vienna, Austria; tel. (1) 523-12-67; fax (1) 523-12-679; e-mail iusy@iusy.org; internet www.iusy.org; f. 1907 as Socialist Youth International (present name adopted 1946), to educate young people in the principles of free and democratic socialism and further the co-operation of democratic socialist youth orgs; conducts international meetings, symposia, etc; mems: 150 youth and student orgs in 100 countries; Pres. VIVIANA PIÑEIRO; Sec.-Gen. BEATRIZ TALEGÓN; publ. *IUSY Newsletter*.

Stockholm International Peace Research Institute (SIPRI): Signalistgatan 9, 169 70 Solna, Sweden; tel. (8) 655-97-00; fax (8) 655-97-33; e-mail sipri@sipri.org; internet www.sipri.org; f. 1966; researches regional and global security, armed conflict and conflict management, military spending, armaments, arms control, disarmament and non-proliferation; provides data, analysis and recommendations to policy-makers, researchers, the media, and the interested public; has recently established programmes on China and Global Security and on Global Health and Security; maintains a number of databases on international arms transfers, military expenditure, multilateral peace operations, and international arms embargoes; mems: about 50 staff mems, about 30 of whom are researchers; Dir Dr GILL BATES (USA); publs *SIPRI Yearbook: Armaments, Disarmament and International Security*, monographs and research reports.

Transparency International: Alt Moabit 96, 10559 Berlin, Germany; tel. (30) 3438200; fax (30) 34703912; e-mail ti@transparency.org; internet www.transparency.org; f. 1993; aims to promote governmental adoption of anti-corruption practices and accountability at all levels of the public sector; works to ensure that international business transactions are conducted with integrity and without resort to corrupt practices; raises awareness of the damaging effects of corruption; produces an annual Corruption Perceptions Index, a Bribe Payers Index, a Global Corruption Barometer and an annual Global Corruption Report; holds International Anti-Corruption Conference every two years; some 90 chapters world-wide; Chair. Dr HUGUETTE LABELLE.

Trilateral Commission: 1156 15th St, NW, Washington, DC 20005, USA; tel. (202) 467-5410; fax (202) 467-5415; e-mail contactus@trilateral.org; internet www.trilateral.org; also offices in Paris and Tokyo; f. 1973 by private citizens of western Europe, Japan and North America, to encourage closer co-operation among these regions on matters of common concern; through analysis of major issues the Commission seeks to improve public understanding of problems, to develop and support proposals for handling them jointly, and to nurture the habit of working together in the 'trilateral' area. The Commission issues 'task force' reports on such subjects as monetary affairs, political co-operation, trade issues, the energy crisis and reform of international institutions; mems: about 335 individuals eminent in academic life, industry, finance, labour, etc.;; those currently engaged as senior government officials are excluded; Chair. YOTARO KOBYASHI, JOSEPH S. NYE, Jr ; Dirs MICHAEL J. O'NEIL, PAUL RÉVAY, TADASHI YAMAMOTO; publs *Task Force Reports*, *Triangle Papers*.

Union for the Mediterranean Secretariat (UfMS): Palacio de Pedralbes, Pere Duran Farell, 11, 08034 Barcelona, Spain; tel. (93) 5214100; fax (93) 5214102; e-mail info@ufmsecretariat.org; internet www.ufmsecretariat.org; f. 2008 as a continuation of the Euro-Mediterranean Partnership ('Barcelona Process'), which had been launched in 1995; the statutes of the UfMS were adopted in March 2010; the UfMS's mandate is defined by the July 2008 'Paris Declaration' of the Euro-Mediterranean summit, and by the subsequent 'Marseilles Declaration', adopted in Nov. of that year; the Union was established as a framework for advancing relations (political, economic and social) between the EU and countries of the Southern and Eastern Mediterranean, in accordance with the goals detailed in the 1995 Barcelona Declaration: i.e. working to create an area of stability and shared economic prosperity, underpinned by full respect for democratic principles, human rights and fundamental freedoms; mems: 27 EU member states, the European Commission and 16 Mediterranean countries; Sec.-Gen. FATHALLAH SIJILMASSI (Morocco).

Union of International Associations (UIA): 40 rue Washington, 1050 Brussels, Belgium; tel. (2) 640-18-08; fax (2) 643-61-99; e-mail uia@uia.org; internet www.uia.org; f. 1907, present title adopted 1910; aims to facilitate the evolution of the activities of the world-wide network of non-profit orgs, especially non-governmental and voluntary asscns; collects and disseminates information on such orgs; promotes research on the legal, administrative and other problems common to these asscns; mems: 115 individuals in 28 countries and 71 assoc. corp. bodies or individuals; Sec.-Gen. JACQUES DE MÉVIUS; publs *International Congress Calendar* (quarterly), *Yearbook of International orgs*, *International Organization Participation* (annually), *Global Action Network* (annually), *Encyclopedia of World Problems and Human Potential*, *Documents for the Study of International Non-Governmental Relations*, *International Congress Science* series, *International Association Statutes* series, *Who's Who in International Organizations*.

Union of South American Nations (UNASUR): Avda 6 de Diciembre, Quito, Ecuador; tel. (2) 2554034; e-mail secretaria .general@unasursg.org; internet www.unasursg.org; in Dec. 2004 leaders from 12 Latin American countries attending a pan-South American summit, convened in Cusco, Peru, approved in principle the creation of a new South American Community of Nations (SACN), to entail the merger of the Andean Community, Mercosur and Aladi (with the participation of Chile, Guyana and Suriname); the first South American Community meeting of heads of state was held in September, in Brasília, Brazil; in April 2007, at the first South American Energy Summit, convened in Margarita Island, Venezuela, heads of state endorsed the establishment of a Union of South American Nations (UNASUR), to replace SACN as the lead organization for regional integration; it was envisaged that UNASUR would have political decision-making functions, supported by a small permanent secretariat, to be located in Quito, and would co-ordinate on economic and trade matters with the Andean Community, Mercosur and Aladi; a regional parliament was to be established in Cochabamba, Bolivia; summit meetings formally to inaugurate UNASUR were scheduled to be held in December 2007, then March 2008; both were postponed; the constituent treaty to establish UNASUR was signed by heads of state meeting in Brasília, Brazil, in May; a South American Defence Council (Consejo de Defensa Suramericano—CDS) was inaugurated in Santiago, Chile, in March 2009; in April 2009 UNASUR ministers of health approved the establishment of a South American Council on Health; the third ordinary summit meeting of heads of state was held in Quito, in August, followed by an extraordinary summit at the end of that month, in Bariloche, Argentina, to consider a military agreement between Colombia and the USA; a summit meeting in May 2010 elected the organization's first Secretary-General (deceased Oct. 2010); the fourth summit meeting was held in Georgetown, Guyana, in November; the constituent treaty entered into force on 11 March 2011, having received the required nine ratifications; in May a UNASUR centre for strategic defence studies (Centro de Estudios Estratégicos de la Defensa—CEED) was inaugurated in Buenos Aires, Argentina; the first meeting of a South American Economic and Financial Council, comprising UNASUR ministers of finance and central bank officials, was held in Buenos Aires, in Aug; Sec.-Gen. ALÍ RODRÍGUEZ ARAQUE (Venezuela).

United Cities and Local Governments (UCLG): Carrer Avinyó 15, 08002 Barcelona, Spain; tel. (93) 3428750; fax (93) 3428760; e-mail info@cities-localgovernments.org; internet www .cities-localgovernments.org; f. 2004 by merger of the Int. Union of Local Authorities and the World Federation of United Cities; aims to increase the role and influence of local governments, promotes democratic local governance, and facilitates partnerships and networks among cities and local authorities; initiated a Millennium Towns and Cities Campaign to encourage civic authorities to support implementation of the Millennium Development Goals; launched the Global Observatory on Local Democracy and Decentralisation (GOLD) to provide information on the situation and evolution of decentralisation, self-government and local government across the world; mems: 112 local government asscns, more than 1,000 mem. cities in 95 countries; Pres. KADIR TOPBAS (Turkey); Sec.-Gen. ELISABETH GATEAU; publ. *Global Report on Decentralisation and Local Democracy*.

Unrepresented Nations and Peoples Organization (UNPO): Laan van Meerdervoort 70, 2517 AN, The Hague, Netherlands; tel. (70) 3646504; fax (70) 3646608; e-mail unpo@ unpo.org; internet www.unpo.org; f. 1991; an international, non-violent, and democratic membership organization representing indigenous peoples, minorities, and unrecognised or occupied territories united in the aim of protecting and promoting their human and cultural rights, preserving their environments, and finding non-violent solutions to conflicts that affect them; mems: 60 orgs representing occupied nations, indigenous peoples and minorities; Pres. NGAWANG CHOEPHEL; Gen. Sec. MARINO BUSDACHIN; publ. *UNPO Yearbook*.

War Resisters' International: 5 Caledonian Rd, London, N1 9DX, United Kingdom; tel. (20) 7278-4040; fax (20) 7278-0444; e-mail info@wri-irg.org; internet www.wri-irg.org; f. 1921; encourages refusal to participate in or support wars or military service, collaborates with movements that work for peace and non-violent social change; mems: approx. 150,000; Chair. HOWARD CLARK; Treasurer DOMINIC SAILLARD (Spain); publs *The Broken Rifle* (quarterly), *warprofiteers-news* (every 2 months) *co-update* (monthly).

Women's International Democratic Federation (WIDF): Guimarães Passos 422, Vila Mariana, São Paulo, SP, Brazil, 04107-031; tel. (11) 2892-3087; e-mail fdim.sec@terra.com.br; internet www.fdim-widf.org; f. 1945 to unite women regardless of nationality, race, religion or political opinion; to enable them to work together to win and defend their rights as citizens, mothers and workers; to protect children; and to ensure peace and progress, democracy and national independence; structure: Congress, Secretariat and Executive Committee; mems: 660 affiliated orgs in 160 countries; Pres. MARCIA CAMPOS (Brazil); publs *Women of the Whole World* (6 a year), *Newsletter*.

World Disarmament Campaign: POB 28209, Edinburgh, EH9 1ZR, United Kingdom; tel. (20) 7377-2111; fax (20) 7377-2999; e-mail editor.worlddisarm@ntlworld.com; internet www .world-disarm.org.uk; f. 1980 to encourage governments to take decisive action to reduce armaments and military expenditure; promotes measures for disarmament, to secure peace and security in a great and sustainable global community; encourages inter-faith work for world peace; acts on the four main commitments called for in the Final Document of the UN's First Special Session on Disarmament; Co-ordinator Rev. BRIAN G. COOPER; publ. *World Disarm!* (quarterly).

World Federalist Movement (WFM): 708 Third Ave, 24th Floor, New York, NY 10017, USA; tel. (212) 599-1320; fax (212) 599-1332; e-mail info@wfm-igp.org; internet www .wfm-igp.org; f. 1947; aims to acquire for the UN the authority to make and enforce laws for the peaceful settlement of disputes, and to raise revenue under limited taxing powers; to establish better international co-operation in the areas of environment, development and disarmament; and to promote federalism throughout the world; an Institute for Global Policy was established in 1983 as the research and policy analysis mechanism of the WFM; Congress meetings held every five years (July 2012: Winnipeg, Canada); mems: 20 mem. orgs and 16 assoc. orgs; Pres. LLOYD AXWORTHY; Exec. Dir WILLIAM R. PACE; publs *World Federalist News* (quarterly), *International Criminal Court Monitor* (quarterly).

World Federation of United Nations Associations (WFUNA) (Fédération Mondiale des Associations Pour les Nations Unies—FMANU): 1 United Nations Plaza, Rm 1177, New York, NY 10017, USA; tel. (212) 963-0569 (temporary); e-mail info@wfuna.org; internet www.wfuna.org; f. 1946 to encourage popular interest and participation in United Nations programmes, discussion of the role and future of the UN, and education for international understanding; Plenary Assembly meets every three years; mems: national asscns in more than 100 countries; Pres. PARK SOO-GIL (Republic of Korea); Sec.-Gen. BONIAN GOLMOHAMMADI (Sweden); publ. *WFUNA News*.

World Peace Council: Othonos 10, Athens 10557, Greece; tel. (210) 331-6326; fax (210) 322-4302; e-mail info@wpc-in.org; internet www.wpc-in.org; f. 1950 at the Second World Peace

Congress, Warsaw; principles: the prevention of nuclear war; the peaceful co-existence of the various socio-economic systems in the world; settlement of differences between nations by negotiation and agreement; complete disarmament; elimination of colonialism and racial discrimination; and respect for the right of peoples to sovereignty and independence; mems: representatives of national orgs, groups and individuals from 140 countries, and of 30 international orgs; Executive Committee of 40 mems elected by world assembly held every three years; Pres. SOCORRO GOMES; Exec. Sec. THANASSIS PAFILIS; publ. *Peace Courier* (monthly).

World Winter Cities Association for Mayors (WWCAM): Kita 1 Nishi 2, Chuo-ku, Sapporo 060-8611, Japan; tel. (11) 222-4894; fax (11) 221-4894; internet http://www.city.sapporo.jp/somu/kokusai/wwcam; f. 1981 as the Intercity Conference of Mayors, present name adopted in 2004; aims to promote close co-operation among northern cities and enable the sharing of information on city-development and winter technologies; holds a biennial Mayors Conference (2012: Ulan Bator, Mongolia, in Jan.); mems: 19 cities from 9 countries; Pres. FUMIO UEDA.

Youth of the European People's Party (YEPP): 10 rue du Commerce, 1000 Brussels, Belgium; tel. (2) 285-41-63; fax (2) 285-41-65; e-mail yepp@epp.eu; internet www.yepp-online.net; f. 1997 to unite national youth orgs of member parties of European Young Christian Democrats and Democrat Youth Community of Europe; aims to develop contacts between youth movements and advance general political debate among young people; mems: 56 orgs in some 38 European countries; Pres. CSABA DÖMÖTÖR (Hungary); Sec.-Gen. JUHA-PEKKA NURVALA (Finland).

Industrial and Professional Relations

African Regional Organization of ITUC (ITUC-Africa): route Internationale d'Atakpamé, POB 44101, Lomé, Togo; tel. and fax 225-61-13; e-mail info@ituc-africa.org; internet www.ituc-africa.org; f. 2007; mems: 13m. workers in 44 countries; Pres. MODY GUIRO; Gen. Sec. KWASI ADU-AMANKWAH.

Association of Mutual Insurers and Insurance Co-operatives in Europe (AMICE): 98 rue de Trone, 1050 Brussels, Belgium; tel. (2) 503-38-78; fax (2) 503-30-55; e-mail secretariat@amice-eu.org; internet www.amice-eu.org; f. 2008 through the merger of the International Association of Mutual Insurance Companies (AISAM) and the Association of European Co-operative and Mutual Insurers (ACME), to raise the profile of the mutual and co-operative insurance sector in Europe; convenes congress every two years (2012: Gdańsk, Poland); mems: 100 direct mems and 1,600 indirect mems, representing one-third of the insurance companies in Europe; Pres. ASMO KALPALA (Finland); Sec.-Gen. GREGOR POZNIAK; publs *Annual Report*, *Newsletter*.

Caribbean Congress of Labour: NUPW Bldg, Dalkeith Rd, POB 90 B, St Michael, Barbados; tel. 427-5067; fax 427-2496; e-mail cclres@caribsurf.com; internet caribbeancongressoflabour.org; f. 1960; fights for the recognition of trade union organizations; to build and strengthen the ties between the free trade unions of the Caribbean and the rest of the world; supports the work of the International Trade Union Confederation; encourages the formation of national groupings and centres; mems: 30 unions in 17 countries; Pres. JACQUELINE JACK (Trinidad and Tobago); Gen.-Sec. LINCOLN LEWIS (Guyana).

European Association for Personnel Management: c/o CIPD, 151 The Broadway, Wimbledon, London, SW19 1JQ, United Kingdom; tel. (20) 8612-6000; fax (20) 8612-6201; e-mail eapmsecretary@cipd.co.uk; internet www.eapm.org; f. 1962 to disseminate knowledge and information concerning the personnel function of management, to establish and maintain professional standards, to define the specific nature of personnel management within industry, commerce and the public services, and to assist in the development of national asscns; mems: 27 national asscns; Pres. FILIPPO ABRAMO (Italy); Sec.-Gen. EILEEN PEVREALL (United Kingdom).

European Cities Marketing: 29D rue de Talant, 21000 Dijon, France; tel. 3-80-56-02-04; fax 3-80-56-02-05; e-mail headoffice@europeancitiesmarketing.com; internet www.europeancitiesmarketing.com; European Cities Marketing is the network of City Tourist Offices and Convention Bureaus; aims to strengthen city tourism by providing sales and marketing opportunities, communicating information, sharing knowledge and expertise, educating and working together on an operational level; Pres. DIETER HARDT-STREMAYR.

European Civil Service Federation (ECSF) (Fédération de la Fonction Publique Européenne—FFPE): 200 rue de la Loi, L 102 6/14,1049 Brussels, Belgium; tel. (2) 295-00-12; fax (2) 298-17-21; e-mail secretariat.politique@ffpe.org; internet www.ffpe-bxl.eu; f. 1962 to foster the idea of a European civil service of staff of international organizations operating in western Europe or pursuing regional objectives; upholds the interests of civil service members; mems: local cttees in 12 European countries and individuals in 66 countries; Pres. BACRI PIERRE-PHILIPPE; Political Sec. TOSON MYRIAM; publ. *Eurechos*.

European Construction Industry Federation (Fédération de l'Industrie Européenne de la Construction—FIEC): 225 ave Louise, 1050 Brussels, Belgium; tel. (2) 514-55-35; fax (2) 511-02-76; e-mail info@fiec.eu; internet www.fiec.org; f. 1905 as International European Construction Federation, present name adopted 1999; mems: 33 national employers' orgs in 27 countries; Pres. LUISA TODINI (Italy); Dir-Gen. ULRICH PAETZOLD; publs *FIEC News* (2 a year), *Annual Report*, *Construction Activity in Europe*.

European Industrial Research Management Association (EIRMA): 46 rue Lauriston, 75116 Paris, France; tel. 1-53-23-83-10; fax 1-47-20-05-30; e-mail info@eirma.asso.fr; internet www.eirma.asso.fr; f. 1966 under auspices of the OECD; a permanent body in which European science and technology firms meet to consider approaches to industrial innovation, support research and development, and take joint action to improve performance in their various fields; mems: 120 in 20 countries; Pres. LEOPOLD DEMIDDELEER; Sec.-Gen. MICHEL JUDKIEWICZ; publs *Annual Report*, *Conference Reports*, *Working Group Reports*, *Workshop Reports*.

European Trade Union Confederation (ETUC) (Conféderation européenne des syndicats): 5 blvd du Roi Albert II, 1210 Brussels, Belgium; tel. (2) 224-04-11; fax (2) 224-04-54; e-mail etuc@etuc.org; internet www.etuc.org; f. 1973; comprises 85 national trade union confederations and 12 European industrial federations in 36 European countries, representing 60m. workers; co-operates closely with the International Trade Union Confederation; Pres. IGNACIO FERNÁNDEZ TOXO (Spain); Gen. Sec. BERNADETTE SÉGOL.

Federation of International Civil Servants' Associations (FICSA): Palais des Nations, Office BOC 74, 1211 Geneva 10, Switzerland; tel. 229173150; fax 229170660; e-mail ficsagensec@unog.ch; internet www.ficsa.org; f. 1952 to co-ordinate policies and activities of member asscns and unions, to represent staff interests before inter-agency and legislative organs of the UN and to promote the development of an international civil service; mems: 30 asscns and unions consisting of staff of UN orgs, 9 associate mems from non-UN orgs, 16 consultative asscns and 21 inter-organizational federations with observer status; Pres. MAURO PACE; Gen. Sec. MARIE-THÉRÈSE CONILH DE BEYSSAC; publs *Annual Report*, *FICSA Newsletter*, *FICSA Update*, *FICSA circulars*.

General Confederation of Trade Unions (GCTU): 119119 Moscow, 42 Leninskii Prospekt, Russia; tel. (495) 938-01-12; fax (495) 938-21-55; e-mail mail@vkp.ru; internet www.vkp.ru; f. 1992; congress convenes every five years (6th congress: Moscow, Russia, Sept. 2007); mems: 40 trade union organizations from CIS countries, comprising about 50m. workers; Pres. MIKHAIL SHMAKOV; Gen. Sec. VLADIMIR SCHERBAKOV.

INSOL International: 6–7 Queen St, London, EC4N 1SP, United Kingdom; tel. (20) 7248-3333; fax (20) 7248-3384; e-mail heather@insol.ision.co.uk; internet www.insol.org; f. 1982 as International Federation of Insolvency Professionals; comprises national asscns of accountants and lawyers specializing in corporate turnaround and insolvency; holds seminars, an annual conference and congress every four years; mems: 36 asscns, with more than 9,500 individual members in 60 countries; Pres.

GORDON STEWART (United Kingdom); Exec. Dir CLAIRE BROUGHTON; publs *INSOL World* (quarterly newsletter), *International Insolvency Review* (2 a year).

International Association of Conference Interpreters: 46 ave Blanc, 1202 Geneva, Switzerland; tel. 229081540; fax 227324151; e-mail info@aiic.net; internet www.aiic.net; f. 1953 to represent professional conference interpreters, ensure the highest possible standards and protect the legitimate interests of mems; establishes criteria designed to improve the standards of training; recognizes schools meeting the required standards; has consultative status with the UN and several of its agencies; mems: 3,004 in more than 105 countries; Pres. LINDA FITCHETT; publs *Code of Professional Conduct*, *Yearbook* (listing interpreters), etc.

International Association of Conference Translators: 15 route des Morillons, 1218 Le Grand-Saconnex, Geneva, Switzerland; tel. 227910666; fax 227885644; e-mail secretariat@aitc.ch; internet www.aitc.ch; f. 1962; represents revisers, translators, précis writers and editors working for international conferences and organizations; aims to protect the interests of those in the profession and help maintain high standards; establishes links with international organizations and conference organizers; mems: c. 450 in 33 countries; Pres. MICHEL BOUSSOMMIER; Exec. Sec. CORALIE GOURDON; publs *Directory*, *Bulletin*.

International Confederation of Arab Trade Unions (ICATU): POB 3225, Samat at-Tahir, Damascus, Syria; tel. (11) 4459544; fax (11) 4420323; e-mail icatu@net.sy; internet www.icatu56.org; f. 1956; holds General Congress every five years; mems: trade unions in 18 countries, and 11 affiliate international federations; Sec.-Gen. RAJAB MAATOUK; publ. *Al-Oummal al-Arab* (every 2 months).

International Confederation of Energy Regulators: e-mail office@icer-regulators.net; internet www.iern.net; f. 2009; mems: 11 regional energy regulatory asscns, representing more than 200 regulatory authorities world-wide; Interim Pres. JEAN-MICHEL GLACHANT.

International Federation of Actors (Fédération internationale des acteurs—FIA): 31 rue de l'Hôpital, 1000 Brussels, Belgium; tel. (2) 234-56-53; fax (2) 235-08-61; e-mail office@fia-actors.com; internet www.fia-actors.com; f. 1952; Exec. Cttee meets annually, Congress convened every four years; mems: 97 performers' unions in 71 countries; Pres. AGNETE HAALAND (Norway); Gen. Sec. DOMINICK LUQUER.

International Federation of Air Line Pilots' Associations (IFALPA): Interpilot House, Gogmore Lane, Chertsey, Surrey, KT16 9AP, United Kingdom; tel. (1932) 571711; fax (1932) 570920; e-mail ifalpa@ifalpa.org; internet www.ifalpa.org; f. 1948 to represent pilots world-wide; aims to promote the highest level of aviation safety world-wide and to provide services, support and representation to all its Member Associations; mems: 102 asscns, representing more than 100,000 pilots; Pres. Capt. DON WYKOFF; publs *Interpilot* (6 a year), safety bulletins and news-sheets.

International Federation of Biomedical Laboratory Science (IFBLS): POB 2830, Hamilton, Ontario, ON L8N 3N8, Canada; tel. (905) 667-8695; fax (905) 528-4968; e-mail communications@ifbls.org; internet www.ifbls.org; f. 1954 to allow discussion of matters of common professional interest; fmrly the International Association of Medical Laboratory Technologists (f. 1954); aims to promote globally the highest standards in the delivery of care, of professional training, and ethical and professional practices; develops and promotes active professional partnerships in health care at the international level; promotes and encourages participation of members in international activities; holds international congress every second year; mems: 180,000 in 37 countries; Pres. VINCENT GALLICCHIO (USA); publ. *Biomedical Laboratory Science International* (quarterly).

International Federation of Business and Professional Women (BPW International): BPW International, POB 2040, Fitzroy, Victoria 3065, Australia; e-mail presidents.office@bpw-international.org; internet www.bpw-international.org; f. 1930 to promote interests of business and professional women and secure combined action by such women; mems: national federations, associate clubs and individual associates, totalling more than 100,000 mems in over 100 countries; Pres. FREDA MIRIKLIS (Australia); Exec. Sec. Dr YASMIN DARWICH (Mexico); publ. *BPW News International* (every 2 months).

International Labour and Employment Relations Association (ILERA): c/o International Labour Office, 1211 Geneva 22, Switzerland; tel. 227997371; fax 227998749; e-mail ilera@ilo.org; internet www.ilo.org/ilera; f. 1966 as the International Industrial Relations Association (IIRA); to encourage development of national asscns of specialists, facilitate the spread of information, organize conferences, and promote internationally planned research, through study groups and regional meetings; a World Congress is held every three years; mems: 39 asscns, 47 institutions and 1,100 individuals; Pres. Prof. JANICE BELLACE (USA); Sec. MOUSSA OUMAROU (Niger); publs *IIRA Bulletin* (3 a year), *IIRA Membership Directory*, *IIRA Congress proceedings*.

International Organisation of Employers (IOE): 26 chemin de Joinville, BP 68, 1216 Cointrin/Geneva, Switzerland; tel. 229290000; fax 229290001; e-mail ioe@ioe-emp.org; internet www.ioe-emp.org; f. 1920; aims to establish and maintain contacts between mems and to represent their interests at the international level; works to promote free enterprise; joined in 2008 the Green Jobs Initiative, a partnership launched in 2007 by UNEP, the ILO and the International Confederation of Trade Unions; and to assist the development of employers' organizations; General Council meets annually; there is a Management Board and a General Secretariat; mems: 150 federations in 143 countries; Pres. Dato' AZMAN SHAH SERI HARON (Malaysia); Acting Sec.-Gen. BRENT WILTON; publ. *IOE.net*.

International Organization of Experts (ORDINEX): 19 blvd Sébastopol, 75001 Paris, France; tel. 1-40-28-06-06; fax 1-40-28-03-13; e-mail contact@ordinex.net; internet www.ordinex.net; f. 1961 to establish co-operation between experts on an international level; mems: 600; Sec.-Gen. PIERRE ROYER (France); publ. *General Yearbook*.

International Public Relations Association (IPRA): POB 6945, London W1A 6US, United Kingdom; tel. (1903) 744442; e-mail info@ipra.org; internet www.ipra.org; f. 1955 to provide an exchange of ideas, technical knowledge and professional experience among those engaged in public relations, and to foster the highest standards of professional competence; mems: 700 in 80 countries; Pres. JOHANNA MCDOWELL (South Africa); publs *Frontline* (every 2 months), *Directory of Members* (annually).

International Society of City and Regional Planners (ISOCARP): POB 983, 2501 CZ, The Hague, Netherlands; tel. (70) 3462654; fax (70) 3617909; e-mail isocarp@isocarp.org; internet www.isocarp.org; f. 1965 to promote better planning practice through the exchange of professional knowledge; holds annual world congress (Sept. 2012: Perm, Russia); mems: 653 in 87 countries; Pres. ISMAEL FERNÁNDEZ MEJÍA (Mexico); Sec.-Gen. ALEX MACGREGOR (United Kingdom); publs *Newsletter* (3 a year), *ISoCaRP REVIEW* (annually), seminar and congress reports.

International Trade Union Confederation-Asian Pacific (ITUC-AP): One Marina Blvd, NTUC Centre, 9th Floor, Singapore 018989; tel. 63273590; fax 63273576; e-mail gs@ituc-ap.org; internet www.ituc-ap.org; f. 2007 by merger of ICFTU-APRO (f. 1951) and Brotherhood of Asian Trade Unionists (f. 1963); mems: 68 affiliate orgs in 29 countries; Pres. G. SANJEEVA REDDY (India); Gen. Sec. NORIYUKI SUZUKI (Japan); publs *Asian and Pacific Labour* (monthly), *ICFTU-APRO Labour Flash* (2 a week).

International Union of Architects (Union internationale des architectes—UIA): Tour Maine Montparnasse, BP 158, 33 ave du Maine, 75755 Paris Cedex 15, France; tel. 1-45-24-36-88; fax 1-45-24-02-78; e-mail uia@uia-architectes.org; internet www.uia-architectes.org; f. 1948; holds triennial congress (2011: Tokyo, Japan); mems: professional orgs in 124 countries; Pres. ALBERT DUBLER (France); Gen. Sec. MICHEL BARMAKI (Lebanon); publ. *Lettre d'informations* (monthly).

Latin American Confederation of Trade Unions (Central Latinoamericano de Trabajadores—CLAT): Apdo 6681, Caracas 1010A, Venezuela; tel. (212) 372-1549; fax (212) 372-0463; e-mail clat@telcel.net.ve; f. 1954; affiliated to the World Confederation of Labour; mems: over 50 national and regional orgs in Latin America and the Caribbean; Sec.-Gen. EDUARDO GARCÍA MOURE.

Latin American Federation of Agricultural Workers (Federación Latinoamericana de Trabajadores Agrícolas, Pecuarios y Afines—FELTRA): Antiguo Local Conadi, B° La Granja, Comayaguela, Tegucigalpa, Honduras; tel. 2252526; fax 2252525; e-mail feltra@123.hn; f. 1999 by reorganization of FELTACA (f. 1961) to represent the interests of workers in agricultural and related industries in Latin America; mems: national unions in 28 countries and territories; Sec.-Gen. MARCIAL REYES CABALLERO; publ. *Boletín Luchemos* (quarterly).

Nordic Innovation (Nordisk InnovationsCenter): Stensberggt. 25, 0170 Oslo, Norway; tel. 47-61-44-00; fax 22-56-55-65; e-mail info@nordicinnovation.org; internet www.nordicinnovation.org; f. 1973; provides grants, subsidies and loans for industrial research and development projects of interest to Nordic countries; Chair. KARIN WIKMAN; Man. Dir KARI WINQUIST.

Organisation of African Trade Union Unity (OATUU): POB M386, Accra, Ghana; tel. (21) 508855; fax (21) 508851; e-mail oatuu@ighmail.com; f. 1973 as a single continental trade union org., independent of international trade union organizations; has affiliates from all African trade unions. Congress, the supreme policy-making body, is composed of four delegates per country from affiliated national trade union centres, and meets at least every four years; the General Council, composed of one representative from each affiliated trade union, meets annually to implement Congress decisions and to approve the annual budget; mems: trade union movements in 53 independent African countries; Sec.-Gen. Gen. HASSAN A. SUNMONU (Nigeria); publ. *The African Worker*.

Pan-African Employers' Confederation (PEC): c/o Mauritius Employers' Federation (MEF), Ebene Cyber City Ebene, Mauritius; tel. 466-3600; fax 465-8200; e-mail mefmim@intnet.mu; internet www.pec-online.org; f. 1986 to link African employers' organizations and represent them at the AU, UN and the ILO; mems: representation in 39 countries on the continent; Pres. THABO MAKEKA; Sec.-Gen. AZAD JEETUN (Mauritius).

Society of European Affairs Professionals (SEAP): Brussels, Belgium; tel. 478996025; e-mail secretariat@seap.be; internet www.seap.be; f. 1997; aims to establish an open non-profit making organization of European affairs professionals dealing with European institutions; Pres. SUSANNA DI FELICIANTONIO; Sec.-Gen. GARY HILLS.

Trade Union Confederation of the Americas (TUCA-CSA) (Confederación Sindical de los Trabajadores y Trabajadoras de las Americas): Rua Formosa 367, 4to. Andar, Cjto. 450 Centros, Sao Paulo, Brazil; tel. (11) 21040750; fax (11) 21040751; e-mail sede@csa-csi.org; internet www.csa-csi.org; f. 2008 as successor to the regional organization of the International Confederation of Free Trade Unions (f. 1951); sponsors training; mems: trade unions in 29 countries (including Canada and the USA) with over 45m. individuals; Pres. LINDA CHAVEZ-THOMPSON; Gen. Sec. VICTOR BÁEZ MOSQUEIRA.

World Federation of Scientific Workers (WFSW) (Fédération mondiale des travailleurs scientifiques—FMTS): Case 404, 263 rue de Paris, 93516 Montreuil Cedex, France; tel. 1-48-18-81-75; fax 1-48-18-80-03; e-mail fmts@fmts-wfsw.org; internet www.fmts-wfsw.org; f. 1946 to improve the position of science and scientists, to assist in promoting international scientific co-operation and to promote the use of science for beneficial ends; studies and publicizes problems of general, nuclear, biological and chemical disarmament; surveys the position and activities of scientists; mems: orgs in 28 countries; Pres. JEAN-PAUL LAINÉ (France); Sec.-Gen. PASCAL JANOTS (France).

World Movement of Christian Workers (WMCW): 124 blvd du Jubilé, 1080 Brussels, Belgium; tel. (2) 421-58-40; fax (2) 421-58-49; e-mail info@mmtc-infor.com; internet www.mmtc-infor.com; f. 1961 to unite national movements that advance the spiritual and collective well-being of workers; holds General Assembly every four years; mems: more than 50 affiliated movements in 39 countries; Sec.-Gen. PAUL EDWARDS; publ. *Infor-WMCW*.

World Union of Professions (Union mondiale des professions libérales): 46 blvd de la Tour-Maubourg, 75007 Paris, France; tel. 1-44-05-90-15; fax 1-44-05-90-17; e-mail info@umpl.org; internet www.umpl.com; f. 1987 to represent and link members of the liberal professions; mems: 27 national inter-professional orgs, 2 regional groups and 12 international federations; Chair. FRANCISCO ANTÔNIO FEIJO; Sec.-Gen. DR GÉRARD GOUPIL.

Law

African Intellectual Property Organization (Organisation Africaine de la Propriété Intellectuelle—OAPI): 158 pl. de la prefecture, Yaoundé, Cameroon; tel. 22-20-57-00; fax 22-20-57-00; e-mail oapi@oapi.int; internet www.oapi.int; f. 1962; supports the technological development of member states and promotes the application of patent rights; mems: 16 African states; Dir-Gen. PAULIN EDOU EDOU.

African Society of International and Comparative Law (ASICL): Private Bag 520, Kairaba Ave, KSMD, Banjul, The Gambia; tel. 375476; fax 375469; e-mail asicl_un@freesurf.ch; f. 1986; promotes public education on law and civil liberties; aims to provide a legal aid and advice system in each African country, and to facilitate the exchange of information on civil liberties in Africa; Sec. EMILE YAKPO (Ghana); publs *Newsletter* (every 2 months), *African Journal of International and Comparative Law* (quarterly).

Arab Organization for Human Rights: 91 al-Marghany St, Heliopolis, Cairo, Egypt; tel. (2) 4181396; fax (2) 4185346; e-mail aohr@link.net; internet www.aohr.net; f. 1983 to defend fundamental freedoms of citizens of the Arab states; assists political prisoners and their families; has consultative status with UN Economic and Social Council; General Assembly convened every three years; mems in 31 countries; Sec.-Gen. MOHSEN AWAD; publs *Newsletter* (monthly), *Annual Report*, *The State of Human Rights in the Arab World*, *Nadwat Fikria* (series).

Asian-African Legal Consultative Organization (AALCO): 29-C, Rizal Marg, Diplomatic Enclave, Chanakyapuri, New Delhi 110057, India; tel. (11) 24197000; fax (11) 26117640; e-mail mail@aalco.int; internet www.aalco.int; f. 1956 to consider legal problems referred to it by member countries and to serve as a forum for Afro-Asian co-operation in international law, including international trade law, and economic relations; provides background material for conferences, prepares standard/model contract forms suited to the needs of the region; promotes arbitration as a means of settling international commercial disputes; trains officers of member states; has permanent UN observer status; has established four International Commercial Arbitration Centres in Kuala Lumpur, Malaysia; Cairo, Egypt; Lagos, Nigeria; and Tehran, Iran; mems: 47 countries; Sec.-Gen. Prof. Dr RAHMAT BIN MOHAMAD (Malaysia).

Coalition for the International Criminal Court: Bezuidenhoutseweg 99A, 2594 AC The Hague, Netherlands; tel. (70) 3111080; fax (70) 3640259; e-mail cicc@coalitionfortheicc.org; internet www.iccnow.org; f. 1995 to support the activities of the International Criminal Court and to ensure that the Court functions fairly, transparently and independently; aims to promote stronger national laws to assist victims of war crimes, humanitarian conflict and genocide; mems: 2,500 civil society orgs in 150 countries; Convenor WILLIAM R. PACE.

Centre for International Environmental Law (CIEL): 1350 Connecticut Ave, NW, Suite 1100, Washington, DC 20036, USA; tel. (202) 785-8700; fax (202) 785-8701; e-mail info@ciel.org; internet www.ciel.org; f. 1989; aims to solve environmental problems and promote sustainable societies through use of law; works to strengthen international and comparative environmental law and policy and to incorporate fundamental ecological principles into international law; provides a range of environmental legal services; educates and trains environmental lawyers; Pres. and CEO CARROLL MUFFETT.

Comité maritime international (CMI): Everdijstraat 43, 2000 Antwerp, Belgium; tel. (3) 203-45-00; fax (3) 203-45-01; e-mail admin@cmi-imc.org; internet www.comitemaritime.org; f. 1897 to contribute to the unification of maritime law and to encourage the creation of national asscns; work includes drafting of conventions on collisions at sea, salvage and assistance at sea, limitation of shipowners' liability, maritime mortgages, etc;

mems: national asscns in more than 59 countries; Pres. KARL-JOHAN GOMBRII; Sec.-Gen. NIGEL FRAWLEY (Canada); publs *CMI Newsletter, Year Book*.

Council of the Bars and Law Societies of Europe (CCBE): 1–5 ave de la Joyeuse Entrée, 1040 Brussels, Belgium; tel. (2) 234-65-10; fax (2) 234-65-11; e-mail ccbe@ccbe.eu; internet www.ccbe.eu; f. 1960; the officially recognized representative organization for the legal profession in the European Union and European Economic Area; liaises between the bars and law societies of member states and represents them before the European institutions; also maintains contact with other international organizations of lawyers; principal objective is to study all questions affecting the legal profession in member states and to harmonize professional practice; mems: 31 delegations (representing some 1m. European lawyers), and observer/associate delegations from 11 countries; Pres. JOSÉ MARÍA DAVÓ FERNÁNDEZ; Sec.-Gen. JONATHAN GOLDSMITH.

East African Court of Justice: AICC Bldg, Kilimanjaro Wing, 6th Floor, POB 1096, Arusha, Tanzania; tel. (27) 2504253; fax (27) 2504255; e-mail eacj@eachq.org; internet www.eacj.org/index.php; f. 2001; organ of the East African Community (EAC), established under the Treaty for the Establishment of the EAC with responsibility for ensuring compliance with the Treaty; Registrar Dr JOHN RUHANGISA.

East African Legislative Assembly: POB 1096, AICC Bldg, Arusha, Tanzania; tel. (27) 2504253; internet www.eala.org; f. 2001; established under the EAC's founding Treaty as the legislative organ of the Community; Speaker MARGARET NANTONGO ZZIWA (Uganda).

Eastern Caribbean Supreme Court: Heraldine Rock Bldg, Block B, Waterfront, POB 1093, Castries; tel. 457-3600; fax 457-3601; e-mail offices@eccourts.org; internet www.eccourts.org; f. 1967 as the West Indies Associated States Supreme Court, in 1974 as the Supreme Court of Grenada and the West Indies Associated States, present name adopted in 1979; composed of the High Court of Justice and the Court of Appeal, High Court is composed of the Chief Justice and 16 High Court Judges. The Court of Appeal is itinerant and presided over by the Chief Justice and three other Justices of Appeal; jurisdiction of the court extends to fundamental rights and freedoms, membership of the parliaments, and matters concerning the interpretation of constitutions; Chief Justice HUGH ANTHONY RAWLINS.

Hague Conference on Private International Law: Scheveningseweg 6, 2517 KT, The Hague, Netherlands; tel. (70) 3633303; fax (70) 3604867; e-mail secretariat@hcch.net; internet www.hcch.net; f. 1893 to work for the unification of the rules of private international law; Permanent Bureau f. 1955; mems: 72 (incl. the European Union); Sec.-Gen. J. H. A. VAN LOON; publs *Proceedings of Diplomatic Sessions* (every 4 years), *Collection of Conventions, The Judges' Newsletter on International Child Protection*.

Institute of International Law (Institut de Droit international): 132 rue de Lausanne, CP 136, 1211 Geneva 21, Switzerland; tel. 229085720; fax 229086277; e-mail joe.verhoeven@uclouvain.be; internet www.idi-iil.org; f. 1873 to promote the development of international law through the formulation of general principles, in accordance with civilized ethical standards; provides assistance for the gradual and progressive codification of international law; mems: limited to 132 members and associates world-wide; Pres. EMMANUEL ROUCOUNAS; Sec.-Gen. JOE VERHOEVEN (Belgium); publ. *Annuaire de l'Institut de Droit international*.

Inter-African Union of Lawyers (IAUL) (Union interafricaine des avocats): BP14409, Libreville, Gabon; tel. 76-41-44; fax 74-54-01; f. 1980; holds congress every three years; publ. *L'avocat africain* (2 a year).

Inter-American Bar Association (IABA): 1211 Connecticut Ave, NW, Suite 202, Washington, DC 20036, USA; tel. (202) 466-5944; fax (202) 466-5946; e-mail iaba@iaba.org; internet www.iaba.org; f. 1940 to promote the rule of law and to establish and maintain relations between asscns and organizations of lawyers in the Americas; mems: 90 asscns and 3,500 individuals in 27 countries; Pres. BEATRIZ MARTORELLO; Sec.-Gen. HUGO CHAVIANO; publs *Newsletter* (quarterly), *Conference Proceedings*.

Intergovernmental Committee of the Universal Copyright Convention: Section for the Diversity of Cultural Expressions, UNESCO, 1 rue Miollis, 75700 Paris, France; tel. 1-45-68-47-45; fax 1-45-68-55-89; e-mail convention2005@unesco.org; established to study the application and operation of the Universal Copyright Convention and to make preparations for periodic revisions of this Convention; studies other problems concerning the international protection of copyright, in co-operation with various international organizations; mems: 24 states; Dir GALIA SAOUMA-FORERO; publ. *Copyright Bulletin* (quarterly: digital format in English, French and Spanish; print format in Chinese and Russian).

International Association for the Protection of Industrial Property (AIPPI): Tödistr. 16, 8027 Zürich 27, Switzerland; tel. 442805880; fax 442805885; e-mail mail@aippi.org; internet www.aippi.org; f. 1897 to encourage the development of legislation on the international protection of industrial property and the development and extension of international conventions, and to make comparative studies of existing legislation with a view to its improvement and unification; holds triennial congress; mems: 8,200 (national and regional groups and individual mems) in 108 countries; Pres. YOON BAE KIM; Sec.-Gen. STEPHAN FREISCHEM; publs *Yearbook*, reports.

International Association of Chiefs of Police (IACP): 515 North Washington St, Alexandria, VA, 22314, USA; tel. (703) 836-6767; fax (703) 836-4543; e-mail rosenblatt@theiacp.org; internet www.theiacp.org; f. 1893 to advance the science and art of police services; Pres. MARK A. MARSHALL; Exec. Dir DANIEL N. ROSENBLATT.

International Association of Democratic Lawyers: 21 rue Brialmont, 1210 Brussels, Belgium; tel. and fax (2) 223-33-10; e-mail jsharma@vsnl.com; internet www.iadllaw.org; f. 1946 to facilitate contacts and exchange between lawyers, encourage study of legal science and international law and support the democratic principles favourable to the maintenance of peace and co-operation between nations; promotes the preservation of the environment; conducts research on labour law, private international law, agrarian law, etc; has consultative status with UN; mems: in 96 countries; Pres. JEANNE MIRER (USA); Sec.-Gen. OSAMU NIIKURA (Japan); publ. *International Review of Contemporary Law* (2 a year, in French, English and Spanish).

International Association of Jewish Lawyers and Jurists: 10 Daniel Frisch St, Tel Aviv 64731, Israel; tel. (3) 691-0673; fax (3) 695-3855; e-mail iajlj@goldmail.net.il; internet www.intjewishlawyers.org; f. 1969; promotes human rights and international co-operation based on the rule of law; works to combat anti-Semitism and Holocaust denial; holds international congresses; Pres. IRIT KOHN; Exec. Dir. RONIT GIDRON-ZEMACH; publ. *Justice*.

International Association of Law Libraries (IALL): POB 5709, Washington, DC 20016-1309, USA; e-mail xtl5d@virginia.edu; internet www.iall.org; f. 1959 to encourage and facilitate the work of librarians and others concerned with the bibliographic processing and administration of legal materials; mems: over 600 from more than 50 countries (personal and institutional); Pres. PETAL KINDER (Australia); Sec. BARBARA GARVAGLIA (USA); publ. *International Journal of Legal Information* (3 a year).

International Association of Legal Sciences (IALS) (Association internationale des sciences juridiques): c/o CISS, 1 rue Miollis, 75015 Paris, France; tel. 1-45-68-25-59; fax 1-45-66-76-03; e-mail info@aisj-ials.org; internet aisj-ials.org; f. 1950 to promote the mutual knowledge and understanding of nations and the increase of learning by encouraging throughout the world the study of foreign legal systems and the use of the comparative method in legal science; governed by a president and an executive committee of 11 members known as the International Committee of Comparative Law; sponsored by UNESCO; mems: national cttees in 47 countries; Pres. ERGUN ÖSZUNAY (Turkey); Sec.-Gen. M. LEKER (Israel).

International Association of Penal Law: 15 rue Charles Fourier, 75013 Paris, France; tel. 1-45-88-72-42; fax 1-55-04-92-89; e-mail secretariat@penal.org; internet www.penal.org; f. 1924 to promote collaboration between those from different countries working in penal law, studying criminology, or promoting the theoretical and practical development of international penal law; mems: 1,800; Pres. Prof. José Luis de la Cuesta (Spain); Sec.-Gen. Katalin Ligeti (Luxembourg); publs *Revue Internationale de Droit Pénal* (2 a year), *Nouvelles Etudes Penales*.

International Association of Youth and Family Judges and Magistrates (IAYFJM): Lagergasse 6–8, 1030 Vienna, Austria; tel. (1) 713-18-25; e-mail nesrinlushta@yahoo.com; internet www.judgesandmagistrates.org; f. 1928 to support the protection of youth and family, and criminal behaviour and juvenile maladjustment; members exercise functions as juvenile and family court judges or within professional services linked to youth and family justice and welfare; organizes study groups, meetings and an international congress every four years (April 2010: Tunis, Tunisia); mems: 12 national asscns and mems in more than 80 countries; Pres. Renate Winter (Austria); Sec.-Gen. Nesrin Lushta (Kosovo).

International Bar Association (IBA): 1 Stephen St, 10th Floor, London, W1T 1AT, United Kingdom; tel. (20) 7691-6868; fax (20) 7691-6544; e-mail iba@int-bar.org; internet www.ibanet.org; f. 1947; a non-political federation of national bar asscns and law societies; aims to discuss problems of professional organization and status; to advance the science of jurisprudence; to promote uniformity and definition in appropriate fields of law; to promote administration of justice under law among peoples of the world; to promote in their legal aspects the principles and aims of the UN; mems: 198 orgs in 194 countries, 30,000 individual members; Pres. Akira Kawamura (Japan); Exec. Dir Mark Ellis; publs *Business Law International* (3 a year), *International Bar News* (6 a year), *Competition Law International* (2 a year), *Journal of Energy and Natural Resources Law* (quarterly).

International Commission of Jurists (ICJ): POB 91, 33 rue des Bains, 1211 Geneva 8, Switzerland; tel. 229793800; fax 229793801; e-mail info@icj.org; internet www.icj.org; f. 1952 to promote the implementation of international law and principles that advance human rights; provides legal expertise to ensure that developments in international law adhere to human rights principles and that international standards are implemented at the national level; disseminates reports and other legal documents through the ICJ Legal Resource Centre; maintains Centre for the Independence of Judges and Lawyers (f. 1978); in Oct. 2005 established an Eminent Jurists' Panel on Terrorism, Counter-terrorism and Human Rights; mems: 82 sections and affiliated orgs in 62 countries; Pres. Mary Robinson (Ireland); Sec.-Gen. Wilder Tayler (Uruguay); publs special reports.

International Commission on Civil Status: 3 pl. Arnold, 67000 Strasbourg, France; e-mail ciec-sg@ciec1.org; internet www.ciec1.org; f. 1950 for the establishment and presentation of legislative documentation relating to the rights of individuals; carries out research on means of simplifying the judicial and technical administration with respect to civil status; mems: governments of Belgium, Croatia, France, Germany, Greece, Hungary, Italy, Luxembourg, Mexico, Netherlands, Poland, Portugal, Spain, Switzerland, Turkey, United Kingdom; Pres. Duncan Macniven; Sec.-Gen. Walter Pintens; publs *Guide pratique international de l'état civil* (available online), various studies on civil status.

International Copyright Society (Internationale Gesellschaft für Urheberrecht e.V.—INTERGU): Rosenheimer Str. 11, 81667 Munich, Germany; tel. (89) 48003-00; fax (89) 48003-969; f. 1954 to enquire scientifically into the natural rights of the author and to put the knowledge obtained to practical application world-wide, in particular in the field of legislation; mems: 187 individuals and corresponding orgs in 37 countries; CEO Dr Harald Heker; publs *Schriftenreihe* (61 vols), *Yearbook*.

International Council for Commercial Arbitration (ICCA): c/o International Centre for Settlement of Investment Disputes, 1818 H St, NW, Washington, DC 20433, USA; tel. (202) 744-8801; fax (202) 522-2615; e-mail arparra@earthlink.net; internet www.arbitration-icca.org; promotes international arbitration and other forms of dispute resolution; convenes Congresses and Conferences for discussion and the presentation of papers; mems: 42 mems, 17 advisory mems; Pres. Prof. Jan Paulsson (USA); Sec.-Gen. Kap-You (Kevin) Kim (Republic of Korea); publs *Yearbook on Commercial Arbitration*, *International Handbook on Commercial Arbitration*, *ICCA Congress Series*.

International Council of Environmental Law (ICEL): Godesberger Allee 108–112, 53175 Bonn, Germany; tel. (228) 2692-240; fax (228) 2692-251; e-mail icel@intlawpol.org; internet www.i-c-e-l.org; f. 1969 to promote the exchange of information and expertise on legal, administrative and policy aspects of environmental conservation and sustainable development; in has consultative status with the ECOSOC; Exec. Governors Dr Wolfgang E. Burhenne (Germany), Amado Tolentino, Jr (Philippines); publs *Directory*, *References*, *Environmental Policy and Law*, *International Environmental Law—Multilateral Treaties*, etc.

International Criminal Police Organization (INTERPOL): 200 quai Charles de Gaulle, 69006 Lyon, France; tel. 4-72-44-70-00; fax 4-72-44-71-63; e-mail info@interpol.int; internet www.interpol.int; f. 1923, reconstituted 1946; aims to promote and ensure mutual assistance between police forces in different countries; co-ordinates activities of police authorities of member states in international affairs; works to establish and develop institutions with the aim of preventing transnational crimes; centralizes records and information on international criminals; operates a global police communications network linking all member countries; maintains a Global Database on Maritime Piracy; holds General Assembly annually; mems: 190 countries; Sec.-Gen. Ronald K. Noble (USA); publ. *Annual Report*.

International Development Law Organization (IDLO): Viale Vaticano, 106 00165 Rome, Italy; tel. (06) 40403200; fax (06) 404032327; e-mail idlo@idlo.int; internet www.idlo.int; f. 1983; aims to promote the rule of law and good governance in developing countries, transition economies and nations emerging from conflict and to assist countries to establish effective infrastructure to achieve sustainable economic growth, security and access to justice; activities include Policy Dialogues, Technical Assistance, Global Network of Alumni and Partners, Training Programs, Research and Publications; maintains Regional Offices in Cairo, Egypt, covering Arabic-speaking countries and in Sydney, Australia, covering the Asia Pacific area; also operates Project Offices in Afghanistan, Indonesia, Sudan and Kyrgyzstan; mems: 22 mems (21 states and OPEC Fund for International Development); Dir-Gen. Antonio Badini (Italy).

International Federation for European Law (Fédération Internationale pour le Droit Européen—FIDE): 113 ave Louise, 1050 Brussels, Belgium; tel. (2) 534-71-63; fax (2) 534-28-58; e-mail fide2008@jku.at; f. 1961 to advance studies on European law among members of the European Community by co-ordinating activities of member societies; organizes conferences every two years; mems: 12 national asscns; Pres. Gil Carlos Rodríguez Rodríguez Iglesias (Spain); Sec.-Gen. Luis Ortiz Blanco (Spain).

International Federation of Senior Police Officers (Federation Internationale des Fonctionnaires Superieures de Police—FIFSP): FIFSP, Ministère de l'Intérieur, 127 rue Faubourg Saint Honoré, 75008 Paris, France; tel. 1-49-27-40-67; fax 1-45-62-48-52; f. 1950 to unite policemen of different nationalities, adopting the general principle that prevention should prevail over repression, and that the citizen should be convinced of the protective role of the police; established International Centre of Crime and Accident Prevention, 1976 and International Association against Counterfeiting, 1994; mems: 34 national orgs; Pres. Juan García Llovera; Sec.-Gen. Jean-Pierre Havrin (France); publ. *International Police Information* (quarterly, in English, French and German).

International Humanitarian Fact-Finding Commission (IHFFC): Fed. Palace N, 3003 Bern, Switzerland; tel. 313250768; fax 313250767; e-mail info@ihffc.org; internet www.ihffc.org; f. 1992 in response to the First Additional Protocol (1977) of the Geneva Conventions, to establish an autonomous body to address the enforcement of int. humanitarian law; operates through a declaration of recognition, signed by 71 states; first constitutional meeting convened in March 1992; organizes annual meetings (2012: Geneva, Switzerland); mems: 15 individuals elected by state parties; Pres. Michael Bothe.

International Institute for the Unification of Private Law (UNIDROIT): Via Panisperna 28, 00184 Rome, Italy; tel. (06) 696211; fax (06) 69941394; e-mail info@unidroit.org; internet www.unidroit.org; f. 1926 to undertake studies of comparative law, to prepare for the establishment of uniform legislation, to prepare drafts of international agreements on private law and to organize conferences and publish works on such subjects; holds international congresses on private law and meetings of organizations concerned with the unification of law; maintains a library of 215,000 vols; mems: govts of 63 countries; Pres. Prof. BERARDINO LIBONATI (Italy); Sec.-Gen. JOSÉ ANGELO ESTRELLA FARIA; publs *Uniform Law Review* (quarterly), *Digest of Legal Activities of International Organizations*, etc.

International Institute of Space Law (IISL): 8–10 rue Mario Nikis, 75015 Paris, France; tel. 1-45-67-42-60; fax 1-42-73-21-20; e-mail president@iafastro-iisl.com; internet www.iafastro-iisl.com; f. 1959 at the XI Congress of the International Astronautical Federation; organizes annual Space Law colloquium; studies juridical and sociological aspects of astronautics; makes awards; Pres. Dr NANDASIRI JASENTULIYANA (USA); publs *Proceedings of Annual Colloquium on Space Law*, *Survey of Teaching of Space Law in the World*.

International Juridical Institute (IJI): Permanent Office for the Supply of International Legal Information, Spui 186, 2511 BW, The Hague, Netherlands; tel. (70) 3460974; fax (70) 3625235; e-mail info@iji.nl; internet www.iji.nl; f. 1918 to supply information on any non-secret matter of international interest, respecting international, municipal and foreign law and the application thereof; Pres. E M. WESSELING VAN GENT; Dir J M J. KELTJENS.

International Law Association (ILA): Charles Clore House, 17 Russell Sq., London, WC1B 5DR, United Kingdom; tel. (20) 7323-2978; fax (20) 7323-3580; e-mail info@ila-hq.org; internet www.ila-hq.org; f. 1873 for the study and advancement of international law, both public and private and the promotion of international understanding and goodwill; mems: 3,700 in 50 regional branches; 25 international cttees; Pres. EDUARDO GREBLER (Brazil); Chair. Exec. Council Lord MANCE (United Kingdom); Sec.-Gen. DAVID J. C. WYLD (United Kingdom).

International Nuclear Law Association (INLA): 29 sq. de Meeûs, 1000 Brussels, Belgium; tel. (2) 547-58-41; fax (2) 503-04-40; e-mail info@aidn-inla.be; internet www.aidn-inla.be; f. 1972 to promote international studies of legal problems related to the peaceful use of nuclear energy; holds conference every two years; mems: 650 in 40 countries; Sec.-Gen. PATRICK REYNERS; publ. *Congress reports*.

International Penal and Penitentiary Foundation (IPPF) (Fondation internationale pénale et pénitentiaire—FIPP): c/o Prof. van Kempen, Radboud University, 6500 Nijmegen, Netherlands; tel. (24) 3615538; fax (24) 3612185; e-mail info@InternationalPenalandPenitentiaryFoundation.org; internet fondationinternationalepenaleetpenitentiaire.org/; f. 1951 to encourage studies in the field of prevention of crime and treatment of delinquents; mems in 23 countries (membership limited to 3 people from each country) and corresponding mems and fellows in another 20 countries; Pres. PHILLIP RAPOZA (USA); Sec.-Gen. PIET HEIN VAN KEMPEN (Netherlands).

International Police Association (IPA): Arthur Troop House, 1 Fox Rd, West Bridgford, Nottingham, NG2 6AJ, United Kingdom; tel. (115) 945-5985; fax (115) 982-2578; e-mail isg@ipa-iac.org; internet www.ipa-iac.org; f. 1950 to permit the exchange of professional information, create ties of friendship between all sections of the police service and organize group travel and studies; mems: 375,000 in more than 63 countries; International Pres. MICHAEL ODYSSEOS (Cyprus); International Sec.-Gen. GEORGIOS KATSAROPOULOS (Greece).

International Society for Labour and Social Security Law (ISLSSL): CP 500, CH-1211 Geneva 22, Switzerland; tel. 227996961; fax 227998749; e-mail sidtss@ilo.org; internet www.asociacion.org.ar/ISLLSS; f. 1958 to encourage collaboration between labour law and social security specialists; holds World Congress every three years, as well as irregular regional congresses (Europe, Africa, Asia and Americas); mems: 66 national asscns of labour law officers; Pres. MICHAL SEWERYNSKI (Poland); Sec.-Gen. ARTURO BRONSTEIN (Argentina).

International Union of Latin Notaries (Union Internationale du Notariat Latin—UINL): Alsina 2280, 2°, 1090 Buenos Aires, Argentina; tel. (11) 4952-8848; fax (11) 4952-7094; e-mail onpiuinl@onpi.org.ar; internet www.uinl.org; f. 1948 to study and standardize notarial legislation and promote the progress, stability and advancement of the Latin notarial system; mems: organizations and individuals in 81 countries; Pres. Dr EDUARDO GALLINO; publs *Revista Internacional del Notariado* (quarterly), *Notarius International*.

Law Association for Asia and the Pacific (LAWASIA): LAWASIA Secretariat, GPO Box 980, Brisbane, Qld 4001, Australia; tel. (7) 3222-5888; fax (7) 3222-5850; e-mail lawasia@lawasia.asn.au; internet www.lawasia.asn.au; f. 1966; provides an international, professional network for lawyers to update, reform and develop law within the region; comprises six Sections and 21 Standing Committees in Business Law and General Practice areas, which organize speciality conferences; also holds an annual conference (2012: Singapore, in May); mems: national orgs in 23 countries; 1,500 mems in 55 countries; CEO JANET NEVILLE; publs *Directory* (annually), *Journal* (annually), *LAWASIA Update* (3 a year).

Permanent Court of Arbitration: Peace Palace, Carnegieplein 2, 2517 KJ, The Hague, Netherlands; tel. (70) 3024165; fax (70) 3024167; e-mail bureau@pca-cpa.org; internet www.pca-cpa.org; f. 1899 (by the Convention for the Pacific Settlement of International Disputes); provides for the resolution of disputes involving combinations of states, private parties and intergovernmental organizations, under its own rules of procedure, by means of arbitration, conciliation and fact-finding; operates a secretariat, the International Bureau, which provides registry services and legal support to ad hoc tribunals and commissions; mems: governments of 110 countries; Sec.-Gen. CHRISTIAAN M. J. KRÖNER (Netherlands).

SECI Center: calea 13 Septembrie 3–5, Sector 5, 050711 Bucharest, Romania; tel. (21) 303-60-09; fax (21) 303-60-77; internet www.secicenter.org; f. 2000 by the Southeast European Co-operative Initiative; an operative collaboration of customs and police officials working under the guidance of recommendations and directives from INTERPOL and the World Customs Organization; Task Force on Illegal Human Beings Trafficking established May 2000, Task Force on Illegal Drugs Trafficking established July 2000, Task Force on Commercial Fraud established February 2001; the Center was to be transformed into the Southeast European Law Enforcement Co-operation Centre (SELEC) upon ratification by two-thirds of member states of a Convention establishing SELEC, signed in Dec. 2009; mems: Albania, Bosnia and Herzegovina, Bulgaria, Croatia, Greece, Hungary, former Yugoslav Republic of Macedonia, Moldova, Romania, Serbia, Slovenia, Turkey; Dir-Gen. GÜRBÜZ BAHADIR.

Society of Comparative Legislation: 28 rue Saint-Guillaume, 75007 Paris, France; tel. 1-44-39-86-23; fax 1-44-39-86-28; e-mail slc@legiscompare.com; internet www.legiscompare.com; f. 1869 to study and compare laws of different countries, and to investigate practical means of improving the various branches of legislation; mems: 600 in 48 countries; Pres. EMMANUEL PIWNICA (France); Sec.-Gen. BÉNÉDICTE FAUVARQUE-COSSON (France); publ. *Revue Internationale de Droit Comparé* (quarterly).

Union Internationale des Avocats (International Association of Lawyers): 25 rue du Jour, 75001 Paris, France; tel. 1-33-88-55-66; fax 1-33-88-55-77; e-mail uiacentre@uianet.org; internet www.uianet.org; f. 1927 to promote the independence and freedom of lawyers, and defend their ethical and material interests on an international level; aims to contribute to the development of international order based on law; mems: over 200 asscns and 3,000 lawyers in over 110 countries; Pres. PASCAL MAURER; Exec. Dir MARIE-PIERRE RICHARD.

Union of Arab Jurists (UAJ): POB 6026, Al-Mansour, Baghdad, Iraq; tel. (1) 537-2371; fax (1) 537-2369; f. 1975 to facilitate contacts between Arab lawyers, to safeguard the Arab legislative and judicial heritage, to encourage the study of Islamic jurisprudence; and to defend human rights; mems: national jurists asscns in 15 countries; Sec.-Gen. SHIBIB LAZIM AL-MALIKI; publ. *Al-Hukuki al-Arabi* (Arab Jurist).

West African Bar Association: Abuja, Nigeria; fax (229) 21305271; e-mail info@wabalaw.org; internet wabalaw.org; f. 2004; Sec.-Gen. OLAWOLE FAPOHUNDA.

World Jurist Association (WJA): 7910 Woodmont Ave, Suite 1440, Bethesda, Maryland 20814, USA; tel. (202) 466-5428; fax

(202) 452-8540; e-mail wja@worldjurist.org; internet www.worldjurist.org; f. 1963; promotes the continued development of international law and the legal maintenance of world order; holds biennial world conferences, World Law Day and demonstration trials; organizes research programmes; mems: lawyers, jurists and legal scholars in 155 countries; Pres. VALERIY YEVDOKYMOV (Ukraine); Exec. Vice-Pres. MARGARETHA M. HENNEBERRY (USA); publs *The World Jurist* (6 a year), Research Reports, *Law and Judicial Systems of Nations*, 4th revised edn (directory), *World Legal Directory*, *Law/Technology* (quarterly), *World Law Review* Vols I–V (World Conference Proceedings), *The Chief Justices and Judges of the Supreme Courts of Nations* (directory), work papers, newsletters and journals.

World Association of Judges: 7910 Woodmont Ave, Suite 1440, Bethesda, Maryland 20814, USA; tel. (202) 466-5428; fax (202) 452-8540; e-mail wja@worldjurist.org; f. 1966 to advance the administration of judicial justice through co-operation and communication among ranking jurists of all countries; Pres. Prince BOLA AJIBOLA (Nigeria).

World Association of Law Professors (WALP): 7910 Woodmont Ave, Suite 1440, Bethesda, Maryland 20814, USA; tel. (202) 466-5428; fax (202) 452-8540; e-mail wja@worldjurist.org; internet www.worldjurist.org; f. 1975 to improve scholarship and education in matters related to international law; Pres. HILARIO G. DAVIDE, Jr (Philippines).

World Association of Lawyers (WAL): 7910 Woodmont Ave, Suite 1440, Bethesda, Maryland 20814, USA; tel. (202) 466-5428; fax (202) 452-8540; e-mail wja@worldjurist.org; internet www.worldjurist.org; f. 1975 to develop international law and improve lawyers' effectiveness in this field; Pres. ALEXANDER BELOHLAVEK (Czech Republic).

Medicine and Health

Aerospace Medical Association (AsMA): 320 S. Henry St, Alexandria, VA 22314-3579, USA; tel. (703) 739-2240; fax (703) 739-9652; e-mail inquiries@asma.org; internet www.asma.org; f. 1929 as Aero Medical Association; aims to advance the science and art of aviation and space medicine; establishes and maintains co-operation between medical and allied sciences concerned with aerospace medicine; works to promote, protect, and maintain safety in aviation and astronautics; mems: individual, constituent and corporate in 75 countries; Pres. FANANCY L. ANZALONE; Exec. Dir JEFFREY SVENTEK; publ. *Aviation Space and Environmental Medicine* (monthly).

Asia Pacific Academy of Ophthalmology (APAO): c/o Dept of Ophthalmology and Visual Sciences, Chinese University of Hong Kong, 3/F 147 K Argyle St, Kowloon, Hong Kong, SAR; tel. 27623040; fax 27159490; e-mail secretariat@apaophth.org; internet www.apaophth.org; f. 1956; holds Congress annually since 2006 (previously every two years); mems: 17 mem. orgs; Pres. FRANK MARTIN; Sec.-Gen and CEO DENNIS LAM.

Asia Pacific Dental Federation (APDF): c/o 242 Tanjong Katong Rd, Singapore 437030; tel. 6345-3125; fax 6344-2116; e-mail droliver@singnet.com.sg; internet www.apdfederation.com; f. 1955 to establish closer relationships among dental asscns in Asia Pacific countries and to encourage research on dental health in the region; administers the International College of Continuing Dental Education (ICCDE); holds congress every year; mems: 27 national dental asscns; Sec.-Gen. Dr OLIVER HENNEDIGE.

Association of National European and Mediterranean Societies of Gastroenterology (ASNEMGE): Wienerbergstr. 11/12A, 1100 Vienna, Austria; tel. and fax (1) 997-16-43; fax (1) 997-16-39; e-mail info@asnemge.org; internet www.asnemge.org; f. 1947 to facilitate the exchange of ideas between gastroenterologists and to disseminate knowledge; organizes International Congress of Gastroenterology every four years; mems: in 43 countries, national societies and sections of national medical societies; Pres. MARK HULL (United Kingdom); Gen. Sec. JOOST DRENTH (Netherlands).

Council for International Organizations of Medical Sciences (CIOMS): c/o WHO, ave Appia, 1211 Geneva 27, Switzerland; tel. 227913413; fax 227914286; e-mail cioms@who.int; internet www.cioms.ch; f. 1949 to serve the scientific interests of the international biomedical community; aims to facilitate and promote activities in biomedical sciences; runs long-term programmes on bioethics, health policy, ethics and values, drug development and use, and the international nomenclature of diseases; maintains collaborative relations with the UN; holds a general assembly every three years; mems: 66 orgs; Pres. Prof. J. J. M. VAN DELDEN; Sec.-Gen. Dr GUNILLA SJÖLIN-FORSBERG; publs *Bioethics and Health Policy' Reports on Drug Development and Use*, *Proceedings of CIOMS Conferences*, *International Nomenclature of Diseases*.

Cystic Fibrosis Worldwide: 210 Park Ave, Suite 267, Worcester, MA 01609, USA; tel. (508) 762-4232; e-mail information@cfww.org; internet www.cfww.org; f. 2003 by merger of the International Association of Cystic Fibrosis Adults and International Cystic Fibrosis (Muscoviscidosis) Association (f. 1964); promotes the development of lay organizations and the advancement of knowledge among medical, scientific and health professionals in underdeveloped areas; convenes annual conference; Pres. MITCH MESSER (Australia); Exec. Dir CHRISTINE NOKE (USA); publs *Annual Report*, *CFW Newsletter* (quarterly), *Joseph Levy Lecture*, booklet on physiotherapy.

European Association for Cancer Research (EACR): c/o Pharmacy School Bldg, University of Nottingham, University Park, Nottingham, NG7 2RD, United Kingdom; tel. (115) 9515116; fax (115) 9515115; e-mail eacr@nottingham.ac.uk; internet www.eacr.org; f. 1968 to facilitate contact between cancer research workers and to organize scientific meetings in Europe; operates a number of fellowship and award programmes; mems: more than 8,000 in 76 countries world-wide, incl. 10 affiliated mem. societies in Croatia, France, Germany, Hungary, Ireland, Israel, Italy, Spain, Turkey and United Kingdom; Pres. JULIO CELIS; Sec.-Gen. RICHARD MARAIS (United Kingdom).

European Association for Paediatric Education (EAPE) (Association Européene pour l'Enseignement de la Pédatrie): c/o Dr Claude Billeaud, Dept Néonatal Médicine, Hôpital des Enfants-CHU Pellegrin, 33076 Bordeaux Cedex, France; tel. 5-56-79-56-35; fax 5-57-82-02-48; e-mail claude.billeaud@chu-bordeaux.fr; internet www.aeep.asso.fr; f. 1970 to promote research and practice in educational methodology in paediatrics; mems: 120 in 20 European countries; Pres. Dr CLAUDE BILLEAUD (France); Sec.-Gen. ELIE SALIBA (France).

European Association for Palliative Care (EAPC Onlus): National Cancer Institute Milano Via Venezian 1, 20133 Milan, Italy; e-mail amelia.giordano@istitutotumori.mi.it; internet www.eapcnet.eu; f. 1988; aims to promote palliative care in Europe and to act as a focus for all of those who work, or have an interest, in the field of palliative care at the scientific, clinical and social levels; 12th Congress: May 2011, Lisbon, Portugal; mems: 47 national asscns in 29 countries, individual mems from 48 countries world-wide; Pres. SHEILA PAYNE (United Kingdom); Chief Exec. HEIDI BLUMHUBER; publs *European Journal of Palliative Care*, *Palliative Medicine*.

European Association for the Study of Diabetes (EASD): Rheindorfer Weg 3, 40591 Düsseldorf, Germany; tel. (211) 7584690; fax (211) 75846929; e-mail secretariat@easd.org; internet www.easd.org; f. 1965 to support research in the field of diabetes, to promote the rapid diffusion of acquired knowledge and its application; holds annual scientific meetings within Europe; mems: approx. 6,000 in 101 European and other countries; Pres. A. BOLTON (United Kingdom); Exec. Dir Dr VIKTOR JÖRGENS (Germany); publ. *Diabetologia* (13 a year).

European Brain and Behaviour Society (EBBS): Einsteinweg 55, 2333 CC, Leiden, Netherlands; tel. (71) 5276289; fax (71) 5274277; e-mail vjb@st-and.ac.uk; internet www.ebbs-science.org; f. 1968; holds an annual conference and organizes workshops; Pres. CARMEN SANDI (Switzerland); Sec.-Gen. VERITY BROWN (United Kingdom); publ. *Newsletter* (annually).

European Federation of Internal Medicine (EFIM): 287 ave. Louise, 4th Floor, 1050 Brussels, Belgium; tel. (2) 643-20-40; fax (2) 645-26-71; e-mail info@efim.org; internet www.efim.org; f. 1969 as European Asscn of Internal Medicine (present name adopted 1996); aims to bring together European specialists, and establish communication between them, to promote internal medicine; organizes congresses and meetings; provides information; mems: 34 European societies of internal medicine; Pres. RAMON PUJOL FARRIOLS (Spain); Sec. Dr JAN WILLEM F. ELTE (Netherlands); publ. *European Journal of Internal Medicine* (8 a year).

European Health Management Association (EHMA): rue Belliar 15–17, 6th Floor, 1040 Brussels, Belgium; tel. (2) 502-65-25; fax (2) 503-10-07; e-mail info@ehma.org; internet www.ehma.org; f. 1966; aims to improve health care in Europe by raising standards of managerial performance in the health sector; fosters co-operation between managers, academia, policy-makers and educators to understand health management in different European contexts and to influence both service delivery and the policy agenda in Europe; mems: more than 160 institutions in 30 countries; Pres. Prof. AAD DE ROO; Dir JENNIFER BREMNER; publs *Newsletter*, *Eurobriefing* (quarterly).

European League against Rheumatism (EULAR): Seestr. 240, 8802 Kilchberg-Zürich, Switzerland; tel. 447163030; fax 447163039; e-mail eular@eular.org; internet www.eular.org; f. 1947 to co-ordinate research and treatment of rheumatic complaints; holds an annual Congress in Rheumatology; mems: in 41 countries; Pres. Prof. MAXIME DOUGADOS (France); Exec. Dir HEINZ MARCHESI; publ. *Annals of the Rheumatic Diseases*.

European Organization for Caries Research (ORCA): c/o Academic Centre for Dentistry Amsterdam (ACTA), Gustav Mahlerlaan 3004, 1081 LA Amsterdam, Netherlands; tel. (20) 5980437; e-mail m.vd.veen@acta.nl; internet www.orca-caries-research.org; f. 1953 to promote and undertake research on dental health, encourage international contacts, and make the public aware of the importance of care of the teeth; mems: research workers in 23 countries; Pres. Prof. CAROLINA GANSS (Germany); Sec.-Gen. Dr M. H. VAN DER VEEN (Netherlands); publ. *Caries Research*.

European Orthodontic Society (EOS): Flat 20, 49 Hallam St, London, W1W 6JN, United Kingdom; tel. (20) 7637-0367; fax (20) 7323-0410; e-mail eoslondon@aol.com; internet www.eoseurope.org; f. 1907 (name changed in 1935), to advance the science of orthodontics and its relations with the collateral arts and sciences; mems: more than 2,500 in 85 countries; Pres. DAVID SUÁREZ QUINTANILLA (Spain); publ. *European Journal of Orthodontics* (6 a year).

European Society of Radiology: c/o ESR Office, Neutorgasse 9/2A, Vienna, Austria; tel. (1) 533-40-64-0; fax (1) 533-40-64-44-8; e-mail communications@myesr.org; internet www.myesr.org; f. 2005 by merger of European Society of Radiology (f. 1962) and European Congress of Radiology; aims to harmonize and improve training programmes throughout Europe and develop a new research institute; organizes an Annual Congress; mems: some 29,300 individual mems; Pres. GABRIEL P. KRESTIN (Netherlands).

European Union of Medical Specialists (Union Européenne des Médecins Spécialistes—UEMS): 20 ave de la Couronne, Kroonlaan, 1050 Brussels, Belgium; tel. (2) 649-51-64; fax (2) 640-37-30; e-mail sg@uems.net; internet www.uems.net; f. 1958 to harmonize and improve the quality of medical specialist practices in the EU and safeguard the interests of medical specialists; seeks formulation of common training policy; mems: 27 full mems, 7 assoc. mems; Pres. Dr ZLATKO FRAS (Slovenia); Sec.-Gen. Dr BERNARD MAILLET (Belgium).

Eurotransplant International Foundation: POB 2304, 2301 CH Leiden, Netherlands; tel. (71) 5795700; fax (71) 5790057; e-mail secretariat@eurotransplant.org; internet www.eurotransplant.org; f. 1967; co-ordinates the exchange of donor organs for transplants in Austria, Belgium, Croatia, Germany, Luxembourg, Netherlands and Slovenia; keeps register of c. 16,000 patients with all necessary information for matching with suitable donors in the shortest possible time; organizes transport and transplantation of the donor organ; collaborates with similar orgs in western and eastern Europe; Pres. Dr BRUNO MEISER; Dirs ARIE OOSTERLEE, AXEL RAHMEL.

FDI World Dental Federation: Tour de Cointrin, 84 ave Louis Casaï, CP 3, 1216 Genève-Cointrin, Switzerland; tel. 225608150; fax 225608140; e-mail info@fdiworldental.org; internet www.fdiworldental.org; f. 1900; aims to bring together the world of dentistry, to represent the dental profession of the world and to stimulate and facilitate the exchange of information; mems: about 200 national dental asscns and groups; Pres. Dr ROBERTO VIANNA (Brazil); Exec. Dir JEAN-LUC EISELÉ; publs *International Dental Journal*, *Developing Dentistry*, *European Journal of Prosthodontics and Restorative Dentistry*.

Federation of the European Dental Industry (Fédération de l'Industrie Dentaire en Europe—FIDE): Aachener Str. 1053–1055, 50858 Cologne, Germany; tel. (221) 50068723; fax (221) 50068721; e-mail m.heibach@fide-online.org; internet www.fide-online.org; f. 1957 to promote the interests of dental industry manufacturers; mems: almost 550 dental manufacturers and national asscns in 13 European countries; Pres. and Chair. Dr JÜRGEN EBERLEIN (Germany); Sec.-Gen. Dr MARKUS HEIBACH (Germany).

Global Fund to Fight AIDS, Tuberculosis and Malaria: 8 chemin de Blandonnet, 1214 Vernier-Geneva, Switzerland; tel. 587911700; fax 587911701; e-mail info@theglobalfund.org; internet www.theglobalfund.org; f. 2002 as a partnership between governments, civil society, private sector interests, UN bodies (including WHO, UNAIDS, the IBRD and UNDP), and other agencies to raise resources for combating AIDS, tuberculosis and malaria; the Fund supports but does not implement assistance programmes; US $11,700m. was pledged by international donors at a conference convened in Oct. 2010 to replenish the Fund during 2011–13; by Dec. 2011, US $22,900m. had been approved for over 1,000 grants in 150 countries; Gen. Man. GABRIEL JARAMILLO (Colombia/Brazil).

Inter-American Association of Sanitary and Environmental Engineering (Asociación Interamericana de Ingeniería Sanitaria y Ambiental—AIDIS): Av. Angélica 2355, 01227-200 São Paulo, SP, Brazil; tel. (11) 3812-4080; fax (11) 3814-2441; e-mail aidis@aidis.org.br; internet www.aidis.org.br; f. 1948 to assist in the development of water supply and sanitation; aims to generate awareness on environmental, health and sanitary problems and assist in finding solutions; mems: 32 countries; Pres. RAFAEL DAUTANT (Venezuela); Sec.-Gen. CÉLIA G. CASTELLÓ (Brazil); publs *Revista Ingeniería Sanitaria* (quarterly), *Desafío* (quarterly).

International Academy of Aviation and Space Medicine (IAASM): c/o Dr C. Thibeault, 502-8500 rue St Charles, Brossard, QC J4X2Z8, Canada; tel. (450) 923-6826; fax (450) 923-1236; e-mail ctebo@videotron.ca; internet www.iaasm.org; f. 1955 to facilitate international co-operation in research and teaching in the fields of aviation and space medicine; mems: in 45 countries; Pres. Prof. ANTHONY BATCHELOR (United Kingdom); Sec.-Gen. Dr CLAUDE THIBEAULT (Canada).

International Academy of Cytology: POB 1347, Burgunderstr. 1, 79013 Freiburg, Germany; tel. (761) 292-3801; fax (761) 292-3802; e-mail centraloffice@cytology-iac.org; internet www.cytology-iac.org; f. 1957 to facilitate the international exchange of information on specialized problems of clinical cytology, to stimulate research and to standardize terminology; mems: 2,400; Pres. Prof. DIANE SOLOMON (USA); publs *Acta Cytologica*, *Analytical and Quantitative Cytology and Histology* (both every 2 months).

International Agency for the Prevention of Blindness (IAPB): c/o London School of Hygiene & Tropical Medicine, Keppel St, London, WC1E 7HT, United Kingdom; e-mail cgarms@iapb.org; internet www.iapb.org; f. 1975; promotes advocacy and information sharing on the prevention of blindness; aims to encourage the formation of national prevention of blindness committees and programmes; with WHO launched VISION 2020 initiative to eliminate the main causes of avoidable blindness by 2020; Pres. CHRISTIAN G. GARMS; CEO PETER ACKLAND; publ. *IAPB News*.

International Association for Child and Adolescent Psychiatry and Allied Professions (IACAPAP): c/o Daniel Fung, Duke-NUS Graduate Medical School and Division of Psychology, Nanyang Technological University, Singapore; tel. 63892309; e-mail daniel_fung@imh.com.sg; internet www.iacapap.org; f. 1937; aims to promote the study, treatment, care and prevention of mental and emotional disorders and disabilities of children, adolescents and their families. The emphasis is on practice and research through collaboration between child psychiatrists and the allied professions of psychology, social work, pediatrics, public health, nursing, education, social sciences and other relevant fields; IACAPAP developed the guidelines and principles of Ethics in Child and Adolescent Mental Health; IACAPAP also develops and adopts other Declarations, Statements and Position Papers of help to mental health professionals in their work; mems: national asscns and individuals in 45 countries; Pres. Dr Olayinka Omigbodun (Nigeria); Sec.-Gen. Dr Daniel Fung (Singapore); publs *The Child in the Family* (Yearbook of the IACAPAP), *Newsletter (IACAPAP Bulletin)*, Monographs.

International Association for Dental Research (IADR): 1619 Duke St, Alexandria, VA 22314-3406, USA; tel. (703) 548-0066; fax (703) 548-1883; e-mail research@iadr.org; internet www.dentalresearch.org; f. 1920; aims to advance research and increase knowledge for the improvement of oral health worldwide; holds annual meetings, triennial conferences and divisional meetings; Pres. Dr Dianne Rekow; Exec. Dir Dr Christopher H. Fox.

International Association for Group Psychotherapy and Group Processes (IAGP): IAGP, rua Sergipe 401 conjunto 808, São Paulo, SP CEP 01243-906, Brazil; tel. and fax (11) 31591653; e-mail office@iagp.com; internet www.iagp.com; f. 1973; holds a congress every three years and regional congresses at more frequent intervals; mems: in 49 countries; Pres. Jorge Burmeister (Switzerland/Spain); Sec. Ivan Urlic (Croatia); publs *Forum* (annually), *Globeletter* (2 a year).

International Association for the Study of Obesity (IASO): Charles Darwin House, 12 Roger St, London, WCIN 2JU, United Kingdom; tel. (20) 7685-2580; fax (20) 7685-2581; e-mail enquiries@iaso.org; internet www.iaso.org; f. 1986; supports research into the prevention and management of obesity throughout the world and disseminates information regarding disease and accompanying health and social issues; incorporates the International Obesity Task Force; international congress every four years (2010: Stockholm, Sweden); mems: 52 asscns representing 56 countries; Pres. Philip James; Exec. Dir Christine Trimmer.

International Association of Agricultural Medicine and Rural Health (IAAMRH): Pravara Medical Trust, Loni-413736, Maharashtra State, India; tel. and fax (24) 2273600; fax (24) 2273413; e-mail contact@pmtpims.org; internet www.iaamrh.org; f. 1961 to study the problems of medicine in agriculture in all countries and to prevent the diseases caused by the conditions of work in agriculture; mems: 405 in 51 countries; Pres. Dr Ashok Patil (India); Gen. Sec. Dr Syusuke Natsukawa (Japan).

International Association of Applied Psychology (IAAP): c/o Prof. José M. Prieto, Colegio Oficial de Psicólogos, Cuesta de San Vicente 4–5, 28008 Madrid, Spain; tel. (91) 3943236; fax (91) 3510091; e-mail iaap@psy.ulaval.ca; internet www.iaapsy.org; f. 1920, present title adopted in 1955; aims to establish contacts between those carrying out scientific work on applied psychology, to promote research and to encourage the adoption of measures contributing to this work; organizes International Congress of Applied Psychology every four years (2010: Melbourne, Australia, in July) and co-sponsors International Congress of Psychology (2008: Berlin, Germany) and European Congress of Psychology (2009: Oslo, Norway); mems: 2,200 in 94 countries; Pres. Prof. José Maria Péiro (Spain); Sec.-Gen. Prof. Janel Gauthier (Canada); publ. *Applied Psychology: An International Review* (quarterly).

International Association of Asthmology (INTERASMA): (no permanent secretariat); internet www.interasma.org; f. 1954 to advance medical knowledge of bronchial asthma and allied disorders; mems: 1,100 in 54 countries; Pres. Kim You-Young (Republic of Korea); Sec.-Gen. Carlos Nuñes (Portugal); publs *Interasma News, Journal of Investigative Allergology and Clinical Immunology* (every 2 months), *Allergy and Clinical Immunology International* (every 2 months).

International Association of Bioethics: POB 280, University of the Philippines, Diliman, Quezon City 1101, Philippines; tel. and fax (2) 426-9590; e-mail secretariat@bioethics-international.org; internet www.bioethics-international.org; f. 1992; aims to facilitate contact and to promote exchange of information among people working in the bioethics field; aims to promote the development of research and training in bioethics; organizes international conferences every two years (11th World Congress of Bioethics: June 2012, Rotterdam, Netherlands); mems: over 1,000 individuals and institutions in more than 40 countries; Pres. Prof. Nikola Biller-Andorno (Switzerland); Sec. Prof. Leonardo de Castro (Philippines); publ. *Bioethics Journal*.

International Association of Gerontology and Geriatrics (IAGG): c/o Faculté de Médecine, Institut du Vieillissement, 37 Allées Jules Guesde, 31000 Toulouse, France; tel. 5-61-14-56-39; fax 5-61-14-56-40; e-mail contact@iagg.info; internet www.iagg.info; f. 1950 as the International Association of Gerontological Societies to promote research and training in all fields of gerontology and to protect the interests of gerontological societies and institutions; assumed current name in 2005, with the aim of promoting and developing Geriatrics as a medical specialism; holds World Congress every four years; mems: more than 40,000 in some 60 countries; Pres. Prof. Bruno Vellas (France); Sec.-Gen./Vice-Pres. Alain Franco (France); publ. *IAGG Newsletter* (quarterly).

International Association of Logopedics and Phoniatrics (IALP): c/o Robbin King, University of Illinois, 1206 S Fourth St, Champaign, IL 61820, USA; tel. (217) 333-2129; fax (217) 333-0404; e-mail office@ialp.info; internet www.ialp.info; f. 1924 to promote standards of training and research in human communication disorders, to establish information centres and communicate with kindred organizations; 28th International Congress on Logopedics and Phoniatrics: Athens, Greece, in Aug. 2010; mems: 125,000 in 56 societies from 30 countries; Pres. Dr Tanya Gallagher; publ. *Folia Phoniatrica et Logopedica* (6 a year).

International Association of Medicine and Biology of the Environment (IAMBE): c/o 115 rue de la Pompe, 75116 Paris, France; tel. 1-45-53-45-04; fax 1-45-53-41-75; e-mail aimbe.world@free.fr; f. 1971 with assistance from the UN Environment Programme; aims to contribute to the solution of problems caused by human influence on the environment; structure includes 13 technical commissions; mems: individuals and orgs in 79 countries; Pres. Céline Abbou.

International Association of Oral and Maxillofacial Surgeons (IAOMS): 17 W 220, 22nd St, Suite 420, Oakbrook Terrace, IL 60181, USA; tel. (630) 833-0945; fax (630) 833-1382; e-mail info@iaoms.org; internet www.iaoms.org; f. 1962 to advance the science and art of oral and maxillofacial surgery; organizes biennial international conference; mems: over 5,000; Pres. Dr Larry Nissen (USA); Exec. Dir Dr John F. Helfrick (USA); publs *International Journal of Oral and Maxillofacial Surgery* (2 a year), *Newsletter*.

International Brain Research Organization (IBRO): 255 rue St Honoré, 75001 Paris, France; tel. 1-46-47-92-92; fax 1-45-20-60-06; e-mail stephanie@ibro.info; internet www.ibro.org; f. 1960 to further all aspects of brain research; Exec. Dir Stephanie de la Rochefoucauld; publs *IBRO News*, *Neuroscience* (every 2 months).

International Bronchoesophagological Society (IBES): Mayo Clinic Arizona, 13400 E. Shea Blvd, Scottsdale, AZ 85259, USA; tel. (480) 301-9692; fax (480) 301-9088; e-mail hillard.julie@mayo.edu; internet www.ibesociety.org; f. 1951 to promote the progress of bronchoesophagology and to provide a forum for discussion among bronchoesophagologists with various medical and surgical specialities; holds Congress every two years; mems: over 700 in 30 countries; Exec. Sec./Treas. Paul F. Castellanos.

International Bureau for Epilepsy (IBE): 11 Priory Hall, Stillorgan, Blackrock, Co Dublin, Ireland; tel. (1) 2108850; fax (1) 2108450; e-mail ibedublin@eircom.net; internet www.ibe-epilepsy.org; f. 1961; collects and disseminates information about social and medical care for people with epilepsy; organizes international and regional meetings; advises and answers questions on social aspects of epilepsy; has special consultative status with ECOSOC; mems: 126 national epilepsy orgs; Pres. Mike Glynn; Exec. Dir Dr Carlos Acevedo; publ. *International Epilepsy News* (quarterly).

International Catholic Committee of Nurses and Medico-Social Assistants (Comité International Catholique des Infirmières et Assistantes Médico-Sociales—CICIAMS): St. Mary's Bloomfield Ave, Donnybrook, Dublin 4, Ireland; tel. (1) 668-9150; e-mail ciciams@eircom.net; internet www.ciciams.org; f. 1933 to group professional Catholic nursing asscns; to represent Christian thought in the general professional field at international level; to co-operate in the general development of the profession and to promote social welfare; mems: 30 full, 10 corresponding mems; Pres. MARYLEE MEEHAN; Acting Sec. JOSEPHINE BARTLEY; publ. *Nouvelles/News/Nachrichten* (3 a year).

International Cell Research Organization (ICRO) (Organisation Internationale de Recherche sur la Cellule): c/o UNESCO, SC/BES/LSC, 1 rue Miollis, 75732 Paris, France; fax 1-45-68-58-16; e-mail icro@unesco.org; internet www.unesco.org/icro; f. 1962 to create, encourage and promote co-operation between scientists of different disciplines throughout the world for the advancement of fundamental knowledge of the cell, normal and abnormal; organizes international laboratory courses on modern topics of cell and molecular biology and biotechnology for young research scientists; mems: 400; Pres. Prof. QI-SHUI LIN (People's Republic of China); Exec. Sec. Prof. GEORGES N. COHEN (France).

International Centre for Diarrhoeal Disease Research, Bangladesh, B: Centre for Health and Population Research (ICDDR,B): GPO Box 128, Dhaka 1000, Bangladesh; tel. (2) 8860523; fax (2) 8823116; e-mail communications@icddrb.org; internet www.icddrb.org; f. 1960 as Pakistan-SEATO Cholera Research Laboratory, international health research institute since 1978; undertakes research, training and information dissemination on diarrhoeal diseases, child health, nutrition, emerging infectious diseases, environmental health, sexually transmitted diseases, HIV/AIDS, poverty and health, vaccine evaluation and case management, with particular reference to developing countries; supported by 55 governments and international orgs; Exec. Dir Dr ALEJANDRO CRAVIOTO; publs *Annual Report*, *Journal of Health, Population and Nutrition* (quarterly), *Glimpse* (quarterly), *Shasthya Sanglap* (3 a year), *Health and Science Bulletin* (quarterly), *SUZY* (newsletter, 2 a year), scientific reports, working papers, monographs, special publications.

International Chiropractors' Association: 6400 Arlington Blvd, Suite 800, Falls Church, VA 22042, USA; tel. (703) 528-5000; fax (703) 528-5023; e-mail chiro@chiropractic.org; internet www.chiropractic.org; f. 1926 to promote advancement of the art and science of chiropractors; mems: 7,000 individuals, and affiliated asscns; Pres. Dr GARY WALSEMANN; Int. Dir PINCHAS NOYMAN; publs *International Review of Chiropractic* (every 2 months), *ICA Today* (every 2 months), *The Chiropractic Choice*.

International College of Angiology: 161 Morin Dr., Jay, VT 05859-9283, USA; tel. (802) 988-4065; fax (802) 988-4066; e-mail denisemrossignol@cs.com; internet www.intlcollegeofangiology.org; f. 1958, as an association of scientists working in the field of vascular medicine and surgery; aims to encourage, support, and facilitate research and education in the problems of vascular disease; Chair. JOHN B. CHANG (USA); Exec. Dir DENISE M. ROSSIGNOL (USA); publ.*International Journal of Angiology*.

International College of Surgeons (ICS): 1516 N. Lake Shore Drive, Chicago, IL 60610, USA; tel. (312) 642-3555; fax (312) 787-1624; e-mail info@icsglobal.org; internet www.icsglobal.org; f. 1935, as a world-wide federation of surgeons and surgical specialists for the advancement of the art and science of surgery; aims to create a common bond among the surgeons of all nations and promote the highest standards of surgery, without regard to nationality, creed, or colour; sends teams of surgeons to developing countries to teach local surgeons; provides research and scholarship grants, organizes surgical congresses around the world; manages the International Museum of Surgical Science in Chicago; mems: c. 8,000 in 100 countries and regions; Pres. Dr. SAID A. DAEE (USA); Exec. Dir MAX C. DOWNHAM (USA); publ. *International Surgery* (every 2 months).

International Commission on Occupational Health (ICOH): Via Fontana Candida 1, 1-00040 Monteporzio Catone (Rome), Italy; tel. (06) 94181407; fax (06) 94181556; e-mail icoh@ispesl.it; internet www.icohweb.org; f. 1906, present name adopted 1985; aims to study and prevent pathological conditions arising from industrial work; arranges congresses on occupational medicine and the protection of workers' health; provides information for public authorities and learned societies; mems: 1,800 in 94 countries; Pres. Dr KAZUTAKA KOGI (Japan); Sec.-Gen. Dr SERGIO IAVICOLI (Italy); publ. *Newsletter* (electronic version).

International Commission on Radiological Protection (ICRP): POB 1046, Station B, 280 Slater St, Ottawa, Ontario, Canada, K1P 5S9; tel. (613) 947-9750; fax (613) 944-1920; e-mail sci.sec@icrp.org; internet www.icrp.org; f. 1928 to provide technical guidance and promote international co-operation in the field of radiation protection; committees on Radiation Effects, Doses from Radiation Exposure, Protection in Medicine, Application of Recommendations, and Radiological Protection of the Environment; mems: c. 85; Exec. Sec. LYNNE LEMAIRE; Scientific Sec. Dr CHRISTOPHER CLEMENT (Canada); publ. *Annals of the ICRP*.

International Committee of Military Medicine (ICMM) (Comité international de médecine militaire—CIMM): Hôpital Militaire Reine Astrid, rue Bruyn, 1120 Brussels, Belgium; tel. (2) 264-43-48; fax (2) 264-43-67; e-mail info@cimm-icmm.org; internet www.cimm-icmm.org; f. 1921 as Permanent Committee of the International Congresses of Military Medicine and Pharmacy; name changed 1990; aims to increase co-operation and promote activities in the field of military medicine; considers issues relating to mass medicine, dentistry, military pharmacy, veterinary sciences and the administration and organization of medical care missions, among others; mems: official delegates from 110 countries; Chair. Brig.-Gen. Dr HILARY M. A. AGADA (Nigeria); Sec.-Gen. Maj.-Gen. Dr ROGER VAN HOOF (Belgium); publ. *International Review of the Armed Forces Medical Services* (quarterly).

International Council for Laboratory Animal Science (ICLAS): c/o School of Veterinary Medicine, University of Pennsylvania, 3800 Spruce St, Philadelphia, PA 19104, USA; tel. (215) 728-2525; fax (215) 214-4040; e-mail rozmiar@pobox.upenn.edu; internet www.iclas.org; f. 1956; promotes the ethical care and use of laboratory animals in research, with the aim of advancing human and animal health; establishes standards and provides support resources; encourages international collaboration to develop knowledge; Pres. Dr PATRI VERGARA (Spain); Sec.-Gen. Dr HARRY ROZMIAREK (USA).

International Council for Physical Activity and Fitness Research (ICPAFR): c/o Prof. F. G. Viviani, Faculty of Psychology, University of Padua, via Venezia 8, 35131 Padua, Italy; tel. (049) 880-4668; fax (049) 827-6600; e-mail franco.viviani@unipd.it; internet icpafr.psy.unipd.it; f. 1964 to construct international standardized physical fitness tests, to encourage research based upon the standardized tests and to enhance participation in physical activity; organizes biennial symposiums on topics related to physical activity and fitness; mems: 34 countries; Pres. Prof. FRANCO G. VIVIANI (Italy); Sec./Treas. ALISON MACMANUS; publs *International Guide to Fitness and Health*, biennial proceedings of seminars and symposia, other fitness and health publs.

International Council of Nurses (ICN): 3 pl. Jean-Marteau, 1201 Geneva, Switzerland; tel. 229080100; fax 229080101; e-mail icn@icn.ch; internet www.icn.ch; f. 1899 to allow national asscns of nurses to work together to develop the contribution of nursing to the promotion of health; holds quadrennial Congresses; mems: more than 130 national nurses' asscns; Pres. ROSEMARY BRYANT (Australia); CEO DAVID BENTON; publ. *The International Nursing Review* (quarterly).

International Council of Ophthalmology: 945 Green St, San Francisco, CA 94133, USA; tel. (415) 409-8410; fax (415) 409-8403; e-mail info@icoph.org; internet www.icoph.org; f. 1927; works to support and develop ophthalmology, especially in developing countries; carries out education and assessment programmes; promotes clinical standards; holds World Ophthalmology Congress every two years (2014: Tokyo, Japan, in April); Pres. Dr BRUCE E. SPIVEY; Sec.-Gen. JEAN-JACQUES DE LAEY (France).

International Diabetes Federation (IDF): 166 Chaussée de la Hulpe, 1170 Brussels, Belgium; tel. (2) 538-55-11; fax (2) 538-51-14; e-mail info@idf.org; internet www.idf.org; f. 1949 to help in the collection and dissemination of information on diabetes and to improve the welfare of people suffering from diabetes; mems: more than 200 asscns in more 160 countries; Pres. JEAN CLAUDE MBANYA (Cameroon); Exec. Dir ANN KEELING; publs *Diabetes Voice*, *Bulletin of the IDF* (quarterly).

International Epidemiological Association (IEA): 1500 Sunday Dr., Suite 102, Raleigh, NC 27607, USA; tel. (919) 861-5586; fax (919) 787-4916; e-mail nshore@firstpointresources.com; internet www.ieaweb.org; f. 1954; mems: 1,500; promotes epidemiology and organizes international scientific meetings and region-specific meetings; Pres. Dr CESAR VICTORA (Brazil); Sec. Dr MATHIAS EGGER; publ. *International Journal of Epidemiology* (6 a year).

International Federation for Medical and Biological Engineering (IFMBE): 10000 Zagreb, Unska 3, Faculty of Electrical Engineering and Computing, University of Zagreb, Croatia; tel. (1) 6129938; fax (1) 6129652; e-mail office@ifmbe.org; internet www.ifmbe.org; f. 1959; mems: 58 societies; Pres. HERBERT F. VOIGT; Sec.-Gen. Prof. RATKO MAGJAREVIC (Croatia).

International Federation for Psychotherapy: c/o Cornelia Erpenbeck, Department of Psychiatry, University Hospital Zurich. Culmannstr. 8, 8091 Zürich, Switzerland; tel. 442555251; fax 442554408; e-mail secretariat@ifp.name; internet www.ifp.name; f. 1935 (as General Medical Society for Psychotherapy); aims to further research and teaching of psychotherapy; encourages and supports development within psychotherapy; organizes international congresses; mems: c. 6,000 psychotherapists from around 40 countries, 36 societies; Pres. Prof. FRANZ CASPAR (Switzerland); publ. *Newsletter*, *Psychotherapy and Psychosomatics*.

International Federation of Association of Anatomists: c/o Friedrich P. Paulsen, Dept of Anatomy and Cell Biology, Martin Luther University of Halle-Wittenberg, Grosse Steinstr. 52, 06097 Germany; e-mail friedrich.paulsen@medizin.uni-halle.de; internet www.ifaa.net; f. 1903 as the Federative International Anatomical Congress; 18th Conference: Beijing, People's Republic of China, 2014; Pres. BERNARD MOXHAM (United Kingdom); Sec.-Gen. FRIEDRICH P. PAULSEN (Germany); publ. *Plexus* (2 a year).

International Federation of Clinical Chemistry and Laboratory Medicine (IFCC): via Carlo Farini 81, 20159 Milan, Italy; tel. (02) 6680-9912; fax (02) 6078-1846; e-mail ifcc@ifcc.org; internet www.ifcc.org; f. 1952; mems: 86 national societies (about 35,000 individuals) and 46 corporate mems; Pres. Dr GRAHAM BEASTALL (United Kingdom); Sec. Dr SERGIO BERNARDINI (Italy); publs *IFCC eNews*, *eIFCC* (electronic journal), *Annual Report*.

International Federation of Clinical Neurophysiology: c/o Venue West Conference Services Ltd, 100–873 Beatty St, Vancouver, BC, Canada, V6B 2M6; tel. (604) 681-5226; fax (604) 681-2503; e-mail sstevenson@venuewest.com; internet www.ifcn.info; f. 1949 to attain the highest level of knowledge in the field of electro-encephalography and clinical neurophysiology in all the countries of the world; mems in 58 countries; Pres. Prof. PAOLO M. ROSSINI; Sec. Prof. REINHARD DENGLER (Germany); publs *Clinical Neurophysiology* (monthly), *Evoked Potentials* (every 2 months), *EMG and Motor Control* (every 2 months).

International Federation of Fertility Societies (IFFS): 19 Mantua Rd, Mount Royal, NJ 08061, USA; tel. (856) 423-7222; fax (856) 423-3420; e-mail secretariat@iffs-reproduction.org; internet www.iffs-reproduction.org; f. 1951 to study problems of fertility and sterility; mems: approx. 40,000 world-wide; Pres. Prof. DAVID HEALY (Australia); Sec.-Gen. RICHARD KENNEDY (United Kingdom); publ. *Newsletter* (2 a year).

International Federation of Gynecology and Obstetrics (FIGO): FIGO House, Suite 3, Waterloo Court, 10 Theed St, London, SE1 8ST, United Kingdom; tel. (20) 7928-1166; fax (20) 7928-7099; e-mail figo@figo.org; internet www.figo.org; f. 1954; aims to improve standards in gynaecology and obstetrics, promote better health care for women, facilitate the exchange of information, and perfect methods of teaching; mems in 124 countries and territories; Pres. Prof. GAMAL SEROUR (Egypt); CEO Prof. HAMID RISHWAN; publ. *International Journal of Obstetrics and Gynecology*.

International Federation of Oto-Rhino-Laryngological Societies (IFOS): Antolská 11, 851 07, Bratislava Slovakia; e-mail info@ifosworld.org; internet www.ifosworld.org; f. 1965 to initiate and support programmes to protect hearing and prevent hearing impairment; holds Congresses every four years; mems: societies in 120 countries; Pres. Dr PAULO PONTES (Brazil); Gen. Sec. MILAN PROFANT (Slovakia); publ. *IFOS Newsletter* (quarterly).

International Federation of Surgical Colleges: c/o Royal College of Surgeons in Ireland, 123 St Stephen's Green, Dublin 2, Ireland; tel. (1) 4022707; fax (1) 4022230; e-mail ifsc@rcsi.ie; internet www.ifsc-net.org; f. 1958 to encourage high standards in surgical training; accepts volunteers to serve as surgical teachers in developing countries and co-operates with WHO in these countries; provides journals and text books for needy medical schools; conducts international symposia; offers grants; mems: colleges or asscns in 77 countries, 420 individual associates; Pres. Prof. PETER MCLEAN (Ireland); Hon. Sec. Prof. S. WILLIAM. A. GUNN (Switzerland); publ. *IFSC News*.

International Hospital Federation (IHF) (Fédération Internationale des Hôpitaux—FIH): Hôpital de Löex, 151 route de Löex, 1233 Bern, Switzerland; tel. 228509420; fax 227571016; e-mail info@ihf-fih.org; internet www.ihf-fih.org; f. 1947 for information exchange and education in hospital and health service matters; represents institutional health care in discussions with WHO; conducts conferences and courses on management and policy issues; mems in three categories: national hospital and health service organizations; assoc. mems, regional organizations and individual hospitals; honorary mems; Pres. THOMAS C. DOLAN (USA); CEO Dr ERIC DE ROODENBEKE; publs *World Hospitals and Health Services Journal* (quarterly), *IHF e-Newsletter* (5 a year).

International League against Epilepsy (ILAE): 342 North Main St, West Hartford, CT 06117-2507, USA; tel. (860) 586-7547; fax (860) 586-7550; internet www.ilae-epilepsy.org; f. 1909 to link national professional asscns and to encourage research, including classification and the development of anti-epileptic drugs; collaborates with the International Bureau for Epilepsy and with WHO; mems: 103 chapters; Pres. SOLOMON MOSHE; Sec.-Gen. SAMUEL WIEBE.

International League of Associations for Rheumatology (ILAR): All India Institute of Medical Sciences, Ansari Nagar, New Delhi 110029, India; e-mail ilar@rheumatology.org; internet www.ilar.org; f. 1927 to promote international co-operation for the study and control of rheumatic diseases; to encourage the foundation of national leagues against rheumatism; to organize regular international congresses and to act as a connecting link between national leagues and international organizations; mems: 13,000; Chair. ROHINI HANDA (India); publs *Annals of the Rheumatic Diseases* (in the United Kingdom), *Revue du Rhumatisme* (in France), *Reumatismo* (in Italy), *Arthritis and Rheumatism* (in the USA), etc.

International Leprosy Association (ILA): c/o Diana N. J. Lockwood, Dept of Clinical Sciences, London School of Hygiene and Tropical Medicine, Keppel St, London WC1E 7HT, United Kingdom; e-mail diana.lockwood@lshtm.ac.uk; internet www.leprosy-ila.org; f. 1931 to promote international co-operation in work on leprosy; holds congress every five years (2008: Hyderabad, India); Pres. Dr MARCOS VIRMOND (Brazil); Sec. Dr INDIRA NATH (India); publ. *The International Journal of Leprosy and Other Mycobacterial Diseases* (quarterly).

International Narcotics Control Board (INCB): Vienna International Centre, Rm E-1339, 1400 Vienna, POB 500, Austria; tel. (1) 260-60-0; fax (1) 260-60-58-67; e-mail raechelle.newman@incb.org; internet www.incb.org; f. 1961 by the Single Convention on Narcotic Drugs, to supervise implementation of drug control treaties by governments; mems: 13 individuals; Pres. RAYMOND YANS; publ. *Annual Report* (with 3 technical supplements).

International Opticians' Association: c/o Association of British Dispensing Opticians, 199 Gloucester Terrace, London, W2 6LD, United Kingdom; tel. (20) 7298-5100; fax (20) 7298-5111; e-mail bdoris@abdo.org.uk; internet www.abdo.org.uk; f. 1951 to promote the science of opthalmic dispensing, and to maintain and advance standards and effect co-operation in optical dispensing; Pres. JENNIFER BROWER; Gen. Sec. Sir ANTHONY GARRETT.

International Organization for Medical Physics (IOMP): Fairmount House, 230 Tadcaster Rd, York, YO24 1ES, United Kingdom; tel. (0) 7787563913; e-mail nuesslin@lrz

.tu-muenchen.de; internet www.iomp.org; f. 1963; aims to advance medical physics practice world-wide by disseminating scientific and technical information, fostering the educational and professional development of medical physicists, and promoting the highest quality medical services for patients; mems: represents more than 16,000 medical physicists world-wide and 75 adhering national orgs of medical physics; Pres. Prof. FRIDTJOF NÜSSLIN (Germany); Sec.-Gen. Dr MADAN REHANI (United Kingdom); publ. *Medical Physics World*.

International Pediatric Association (IPA): 1–3 rue de Chantepoulet, POB 1726,1211 Geneva 1, Switzerland; tel. 229069152; fax 227322852; e-mail adminoffice@ipa-world.org; internet www.ipa-world.org; f. 1912; holds triennial congresses and regional and national workshops; mems: national paediatric societies in 136 countries, 10 regional affiliate societies, 11 paediatric specialty societies; Pres. SERGIO AUGUSTO CABRAL (Brazil); Exec. Dir Dr WILLIAM J. KEENAN (USA); publ. *International Child Health* (quarterly).

International Pharmaceutical Federation (Fédération Internationale Pharmaceutique—FIP): POB 84200, 2508 AE, The Hague, Netherlands; tel. (70) 3021970; fax (70) 3021999; e-mail fip@fip.org; internet www.fip.org; f. 1912; aims to represent and serve pharmacy and pharmaceutical sciences world-wide and to improve access to medicines; holds World Congress of Pharmacy and Pharmaceutical Sciences annually; mems: 86 national pharmaceutical orgs in 62 countries, 55 associate, supportive and collective mems, 4,000 individuals; Gen. Sec. and CEO A. J. M. (TON) HOEK (Netherlands); Exec. Sec. RACHEL VAN KESTEREN; publ. *International Pharmacy Journal* (2 a year).

International Psychoanalytical Association (IPA): Broomhills, Woodside Lane, London, N12 8UD, United Kingdom; tel. (20) 8446-8324; fax (20) 8445-4729; e-mail ipa@ipa.org.uk; internet www.ipa.org.uk; f. 1908; aims to assure the continued vigour and development of psychoanalysis; acts as a forum for scientific discussions; controls and regulates training; contributes to the interdisciplinary area common to the behavioural sciences; mems: 11,500 in 34 countries; Pres. Prof. CHARLES M. T. HANLY; Sec.-Gen. H. GUNTHER PERDIGAO; publs *Bulletin*, *Newsletter*.

International Rhinologic Society: c/o Prof. Dr Metin Önerci, Hacettepe University Faculty of Medicine, Dept of Otorhinolaryngology, 06100 Hacettepe, Ankara, Turkey; tel. (532) 393-8668; fax (312) 311-3500; e-mail metin@tr.net; f. 1965; holds congress every two years; Pres. HIROSHI MORIYAMA; Gen. Sec. METIN ÖNERCI (Turkey); publ. *Rhinology*.

International Society for the Psychopathology of Expression and Art Therapy (SIPE): Hôpital La Grave-Casselardit, 170 ave de Casselardit, TSA 40031, 31059 Toulouse Cedex 9, France; tel. 4-90-03-92-12; fax 4-90-03-92-25; e-mail contact@sipe-art-therapy.com; internet www.sipe-art-therapy.com; f. 1959 to bring together specialists interested in the problems of expression and artistic activities in connection with psychiatric, sociological and psychological research; mems: 625; Pres. LAURENT SCHMITT (France); Sec.-Gen. JEAN-LUC SUDRES (France); publ. *Newsletter* (quarterly).

International Society for Vascular Surgery: 11 Scott Drive, Smithtown, NY 11787, USA; tel. (631) 979-3780; e-mail info@isvs.com; internet www.isvs.com; f. 1950 as the International Society for Cardiovascular Surgery (ISCVS) to stimulate research on the diagnosis and therapy of cardiovascular diseases and to exchange ideas on an international basis; present name adopted in 2005; Pres. Dr ENRICO ASCHER (USA); Sec. Dr TIMUR SARAC (USA).

International Society of Audiology: 121 Anchor Drive, Halifax, Nova Scotia, B3N 3B9 Canada; tel. (902) 477-5360; e-mail info@isa-audiology.org; internet www.isa-audiology.org; f. 1952 to facilitate the knowledge, protection and rehabilitation of human hearing and to represent the interests of audiology professionals and of the hearing-impaired; organizes biannual Congress and workshops and seminars; mems: 500 individuals; Pres. JOSÉ JUAN BARAJAS DE PRAT (Spain); Gen. Sec. Dr GEORGE MENCHER; publ. *International Journal of Audiology* (monthly).

International Society of Blood Transfusion (ISBT): Marnixstraat 317, 1016 TB Amsterdam, Netherlands; tel. and fax (20) 7601761; e-mail office@isbtweb.org; internet www.isbtweb.org; f. 1935; mems: c. 2,000 in over 97 countries; Pres. SILVANO WENDEL (Germany); Sec.-Gen. GEOFF DANIELS; publ. *Transfusion Today* (quarterly).

International Society of Developmental Biologists (ISDB): c/o Marianne Bronner, Biology Div., California Institute of Technology, 1200 E. California Blvd, Pasadena, CA 91125, USA; tel. (626) 395-4952; fax (626) 449-0756; e-mail mbronner@caltech.edu; internet www.developmental-biology.org; f. 1911 as International Institute of Embryology; aims to promote the study of developmental biology and to encourage international co-operation among investigators in the field; mems: 850 in 33 countries; Pres. CLAUDIO STERN (United Kingdom); International Sec. MARIANNE BRONNER-FRASER (USA); publs *Mechanisms of Development* (monthly), *Gene Expression Patterns* (6 a year).

International Society of Internal Medicine (ISIM): Dept of Internal Medicine, RSZ-Bern Hospitals, Zieglerspital, Morillonstr. 75-91, 3001 Bern, Switzerland; tel. 319707178; fax 319707763; e-mail hanspeter.kohler@spitalnetzbern.ch; internet www.acponline.org/isim; f. 1948 to encourage research and education in internal medicine; mems: 61 national societies; Pres. Prof. WILLIAM J. HALL (USA); Sec.-Gen. Prof. HANS-PETER KOHLER (Switzerland).

International Society of Lymphology: POB 245066, Tucson, AZ 85724-5066, USA; tel. (520) 626-6118; e-mail lymph@u.arizona.edu; internet www.u.arizona.edu/~witte/ISL.htm; f. 1966 to further progress in lymphology through personal contacts and the exchange of ideas; mems: 375 in 42 countries; Pres. R. BAUMEISTER (Germany); Sec.-Gen. MARYLS H. WITTE (USA); publ. *Lymphology* (quarterly).

International Society of Neuropathology: c/o David Hilton, Dept of Neuropathology, Derriford Hospital, Plymouth, PL6 8DH, United Kingdom; fax (117) 9753765; e-mail davidhilton@nhs.net; internet www.intsocneuropathol.com; f. 1950 as International Committee of Neuropathology; renamed as above in 1967; Pres. Dr HERBERT BUDKA (Austria); Sec.-Gen. Dr DAVID HILTON (United Kingdom); publ. *Brain Pathology* (quarterly).

International Society of Orthopaedic Surgery and Traumatology (Société Internationale de Chirurgie Orthopédique et de Traumatologie): 40 rue Washington, bte 9, 1050 Brussels, Belgium; tel. (2) 648-68-23; fax (2) 649-86-01; e-mail hq@sicot.org; internet www.sicot.org; f. 1929; organizes Triennial World Congresses, Annual International Conferences and Trainees' Meetings; mems: 3,000 mems in 102 countries; Pres. Prof. MAURICE HINSENKAMP; Sec.-Gen. JOCHEN EULERT; publ. *International Orthopaedics* (scientific journal), *Newsletter* (quarterly), *e-Newsletter* (monthly).

International Society of Physical and Rehabilitation Medicine (ISPRM): ISPRM Central Office, Werner van Cleemputte, Medicongress, Kloosterstraat 5, 9960 Assenede, Belgium; tel. (9) 344-39-59; fax (9) 344-40-10; e-mail info@isprm.org; internet www.isprm.org; f. 1999 by merger of International Federation of Physical Medicine and Rehabilitation (f. 1952) and International Rehabilitation Medicine Association (f. 1968); sixth international congress: San Juan, Puerto Rico (June 2011); mems: in 68 countries; Pres. GEROLD STUCKI; Sec. JORGE LAINS; publs *Newsletter*, *Disability and Rehabilitation*, Journal of Rehabilitation Medicine.

International Society of Radiology (ISR): 7910 Woodmont Ave, Suite 400, Bethesda, Maryland 20814, USA; tel. (301) 657-2652 (ext. 22); fax (301) 907-8768; e-mail director@intsocradiology.org; internet www.isradiology.org; f. 1953 to promote radiology world-wide; International Commissions on Radiation Units and Measurements (ICRUM), on Radiation Protection (ICRP), and on Radiological Education (ICRE); organizes biannual International Congress of Radiology; collaborates with WHO and IAEA; mems: more than 80 national radiological societies; Pres. JAN LABASCAGNE (Australia); Sec.-Gen. LUIS DONOSO BACH (Spain); Exec. Dir OTHA W. LINTON; publ. *Newsletter*.

International Society of Surgery (ISS): Seltisbergerstr. 16, 4419 Lupsingen, Switzerland; tel. 618159666; fax 618114775; e-mail surgery@iss-sic.ch; internet www.iss-sic.com; f. 1902 to promote understanding between surgical disciplines; groups surgeons to address issues of interest to all surgical specialists; supports general surgery as a training base for abdominal surgery,

surgery with integuments and endocrine surgery; organizes congresses (2011 World Congress of Surgery: Yokohama, Japan, Aug.–Sept.); mems: 4,000; Pres. GÖRAN AKERSTRÖM; Sec.-Gen. Prof. JEAN-CLAUDE GIVEL; publ. *World Journal of Surgery* (monthly).

International Society of Veterinary Dermatopathology (ISVD): c/o Sonja Bettenay, Tierdermatologie Deisenhofen, Schaeftlarner Weg 1A, Deisenhofen 82041, Germany; e-mail s-bettena@t-online.de; internet www.isvd.org; f. 1958; aims to advance veterinary and comparative dermatopathology, to group individuals with a professional interest in the histologic interpretation of animal skin diseases, to assist with and co-ordinate the adaptation and implementation of emerging technologies for the morphologic diagnosis of skin diseases in animals, and to provide an affiliation with physician dermatopathologists in order to exchange information on comparative dermatopathology; promotes professional training; Pres. Dr JUDITH NIMMO (Australia); Sec. SONJA BETTENAY (Germany).

International Spinal Cord Society (ISCoS): National Spinal Injuries Centre, Stoke Mandeville Hospital, Aylesbury, Bucks, HP21 8AL, United Kingdom; tel. (1296) 315866; fax (1296) 315870; e-mail admin@iscos.org.uk; internet www.iscos.org.uk; f. 1961; formerly the International Medical Society of Paraplegia (f. 1961); studies all problems relating to traumatic and non-traumatic lesions of the spinal cord, including causes, prevention, research and rehabilitation; promotes the exchange of information; assists in efforts to guide and co-ordinate research; Pres. FIN BIERING-SORENSEN (Denmark); Hon. Sec. SHINSUKE KATOH (Japan); publ. *Spinal Cord*.

International Union against Tuberculosis and Lung Disease (The Union): 68 blvd St Michel, 75006 Paris, France; tel. 1-44-32-03-60; fax 1-43-29-90-87; e-mail union@iuatld.org; internet www.theunion.org; f. 1920 to co-ordinate the efforts of anti-tuberculosis and respiratory disease asscns, to mobilize public interest, to assist control programmes and research around the world, to collaborate with governments and WHO and to promote conferences; mems: asscns in 145 countries, 10,000 individual mems; Pres. Dr JANE CARTER (USA); Sec.-Gen. Prof. CAMILO ROA, Jr (Philippines); publs *The International Journal of Tuberculosis and Lung Disease* (monthly), *Newsletter*.

International Union for Health Promotion and Education (IUHPE): 42 blvd de la Libération, 93203 St Denis Cedex, France; tel. 1-48-13-71-20; fax 1-48-09-17-67; e-mail iuhpe@iuhpe.org; internet www.iuhpe.org; f. 1951; provides an international network for the exchange of practical information on developments in health promotion and education; promotes research; encourages professional training for health workers, teachers, social workers and others; holds a World Conference on Health Promotion and Health Education every three years; organizes regional conferences and seminars; mems: in more than 90 countries; Pres. MICHAEL SPARKS (Australia); Exec. Dir MARIE-CLAUDE LAMARRE (France); publs *Health Promotion International*, *Promotion and Education* (quarterly, in English, French and Spanish).

Latin American Odontological Federation (Federación Odontológica Latinoamericana): c/o Federación Odontológica Colombiana, Calle 71 No 11-10, Of. 1101, Apdo Aéreo 52925, Bogotá, Colombia; e-mail arn@codetel.net.do; internet www.folaoral.com; f. 1917; linked to FDI World Dental Federation; mems: national orgs in 12 countries; Pres. Dr ADOLFO RODRÍGUEZ; Sec. Dr MARCOS ALVALLERO.

Medical Women's International Association (MWIA): 7555 Morley Drive, Burnaby, BC, V5E 3Y2, Canada; tel. (604) 522-1960; fax (604) 439-8994; e-mail secretariat@mwia.net; internet www.mwia.net; f. 1919 to facilitate contacts between women in medicine and to encourage co-operation in matters connected with international health problems; mems: national asscns in 48 countries, and individuals; Pres. Prof. AFUA HESSE (Japan); Sec.-Gen. Dr SHELLEY ROSS (Canada); publ. *MWIA UPDATE* (3 a year).

Multiple Sclerosis International Federation (MSIF): Skyline House, 3rd Floor, 200 Union St, London, SE1 0LX, United Kingdom; tel. (20) 7620-1911; fax (20) 7620-1922; e-mail info@msif.org; internet www.msif.org; f. 1967; promotes shared scientific research into multiple sclerosis and related neurological diseases; stimulates the active exchange of information; provides support for new and existing multiple sclerosis organizations; Pres. and Chair. WEYMAN JOHNSON (USA); CEO PEER BANEKE; publs *MSIF Annual Review*, *MS in Focus* (2 a year).

Organisation panafricaine de lutte contre le SIDA (OPALS): 15–21 rue de L'Ecole de Médecine, 75006 Paris, France; tel. 1-43-26-72-28; fax 1-43-29-70-93; internet www.opals.asso.fr; f. 1988; disseminates information relating to the treatment and prevention of AIDS; provides training of medical personnel; promotes co-operation between African medical centres and specialized centres in the USA and Europe; Pres. Prof. MARC GENTILINI; Sec.-Gen. Prof. DOMINIQUE RICHARD-LENOBLE; publ. *OPALS Liaison*.

Organization for Co-ordination in the Struggle against Endemic Diseases in Central Africa (Organisation de coordination pour la lutte contre les endémies en Afrique Centrale—OCEAC): BP 288, Yaoundé, Cameroon; tel. 23-22-32; fax 23-00-61; e-mail contact@oceac.org; internet www.oceac.org; f. 1965 to standardize methods of controlling endemic diseases, to co-ordinate national action, and to negotiate programmes of assistance and training on a regional scale; mems: Cameroon, Central African Republic, Chad, Republic of the Congo, Equatorial Guinea, Gabon; Exec. Sec. Dr JEAN JACQUES MOKA; publ. *Bulletin de Liaison et de Documentation* (quarterly).

Pan-American Association of Ophthalmology (PAAO): 1301 South Bowen Rd, Suite 450, Arlington, TX 76013, USA; tel. (817) 275-7553; fax (817) 275-3961; e-mail info@paao.org; internet www.paao.org; f. 1939 to promote friendship within the profession and the dissemination of scientific information; holds Congress every two years (2011: Buenos Aires, Argentina); mems: national ophthalmological societies and other bodies in 39 countries; Pres. MARK MANNIS; Exec. Dir TERESA BRADSHAW; publ. *Vision Panamerica* (quarterly).

Pan-American Medical Association (Asociación Médica Panamericana): c/o Pan-American Medical Association of Central Florida, POB 536488, Orlando, Florida 32853-6488, USA; tel. (212) 753-6033; internet www.pamacfl.org; f. 1925; holds inter-American congresses, conducts seminars and grants post graduate scholarships to Latin American physicians; Pres. Dr RODRIGO NEHGME; Sec. Dr MANUEL PEREZ-IZQUIERDO; mems: 6,000 in 30 countries.

Pan Caribbean Partnership against HIV and AIDS: POB 10827, Georgetown, Guyana; tel. 222-0001; fax 222-0203; e-mail pancap@caricom.org; internet www.pancap.org; f. 2001 by heads of state and government of CARICOM; aims to co-ordinate efforts by national, regional and international agencies to counter the spread of HIV/AIDS and mitigate its impact throughout the region; Dir JULIET BYNOE-SUTHERLAND (Barbados).

Pan-Pacific Surgical Association: 1212 Punahou St, Suite 3506, Honolulu, HI 96826, Hawaii, USA; tel. (808) 941-1010; fax (808) 951-7004; e-mail ppsa.info@panpacificsurgical.org; internet www.panpacificsurgical.org; f. 1929 to bring together surgeons to exchange scientific knowledge relating to surgery and medicine, and to promote the improvement and standardization of hospitals and their services and facilities; congresses are held every two years; mems: 2,716 regular, associate and senior mems from 44 countries; Pres. Dr JEROME C. GOLDSTEIN.

Rehabilitation International: 25 East 21st St, 4th Floor, New York, NY 10010, USA; tel. (212) 420-1500; fax (212) 505-0871; e-mail ri@riglobal.org; internet www.riglobal.org; f. 1922 to improve the lives of people with disabilities through the exchange of information and research on equipment and methods of assistance; functions as a global network of disabled people, service providers, researchers and government agencies; advocates promoting and implementing the rights, inclusion and rehabilitation of people with disabilities; organizes international conferences and co-operates with UN agencies and other international organizations; mems: 700 orgs in more than 90 countries; Pres. ANNE HAWKER; Sec.-Gen. VENUS ILAGAN; publs *International Rehabilitation Review* (annually), *Rehabilitación* (2 or 3 a year).

Society of French-speaking Neuro-Surgeons (Société de neuro-chirurgie de langue française—SNCLF): Cabinet de Neurochirurgie, 4 ave de Vaudagne, 1217 Geneva, Switzerland;

tel. 227830304; fax 227830308; e-mail daniel.may@bluewin.ch; internet www.snclf.com; f. 1949; holds annual convention and congress; mems: 700; Pres. FRANÇOIS-XAVIER ROUX (France); Sec.-Gen. DANIEL MAY; publ. *Neurochirurgie* (6 a year).

Transplantation Society (Société de Transplantation): 1255 University St, Suite 325, Montréal, QC, H3B 3B4 Canada; tel. (514) 874-1717; fax (514) 874-1716; e-mail info@tts.org; internet www.transplantation-soc.org; f. 1966; aims to provide a focus for development of the science and clinical practice of transplantations, scientific communication, education, and guidance on ethics; mems: more than 3,000 in 65 countries; Pres. GERHARD OPELZ.

Union for International Cancer Control (Union internationale contre le cancer—UICC): 62 route de Frontenex, 1207 Geneva, Switzerland; tel. 228091811; fax 228091810; e-mail info@uicc.org; internet www.uicc.org; f. 1933 to promote the campaign to prevent and control cancer on an international level; aims to connect, mobilize and support organizations, leading experts, key stakeholders and volunteers in a community working together to eliminate cancer as a life-threatening disease for future generations; works closely with its member orgs and partners to implement a comprehensive strategy that includes: organizing the World Cancer Congress; promoting the World Cancer Declaration; raising awareness through the World Cancer Campaign; co-ordinating World Cancer Day annually, on 4 February; reviewing and disseminating the TNM (tumour-node-metastasis) classification of malignant tumours; developing effective cancer control programmes especially in low- and middle-income countries; changing cancer-related beliefs and behaviour through information and education; creating special initiatives in prevention, early detection, access to treatment and supportive care; awarding international cancer fellowships; producing scientific publications; mems: 470 orgs in 124 countries; Pres. Dr EDUARDO CAZAP (Argentina); CEO CARY ADAMS (United Kingdom); publs *International Journal of Cancer* (24 a year), *UICC News* (quarterly).

World Allergy Organization (IAACI): 555 East Wells St, Suite 1100, Milwaukee, WI 53202-3823, USA; tel. (414) 276-1791; fax (414) 276-3349; e-mail info@worldallergy.org; internet www.worldallergy.org; f. 1945, as International Association of Allergology and Clinical Immunology, to further work in the educational, research and practical medical aspects of allergic and immunological diseases; World Congresses held every two years (Dec. 2011: Cancún, Mexico); mems: 77 national and regional societies; Pres. RUBY PAWANKAR (India/Japan); Sec.-Gen. Prof. MARIO SÁNCHEZ BORGES (Venezuela); publ. *Allergy and Clinical Immunology International* (6 a year).

World Association for Disaster and Emergency Medicine (WADEM): International Office, POB 55158, Madison, WI 53705-8958, USA; tel. (608) 819-6604; fax (608) 819-6055; e-mail info@wadem.org; internet www.wadem.org; f. 1976; aims to improve prehospital and emergency health care, public health, and disaster health and preparedness; became a full partner in the Global Health Cluster of the UN Inter-Agency Standing Committee in April 2008; mems: 600 in 55 countries; Pres. PAUL ARBON (Australia); Sec. DARREN WALTER (United Kingdom); publs *International Disaster Nursing*, *Prehospital and Disaster Medicine*.

World Association of Societies of Pathology and Laboratory Medicine (WASPaLM): 2/F UI Bldg, 2-2 Kanda Ogawamachi, Chiyoda-ku, Tokyo, 101-0052, Japan; tel. (3) 3295-0353; fax (3) 3295-0352; e-mail info@waspalm.org; internet www.waspalm.org; f. 1947 to link national societies and co-ordinate their scientific and technical means of action; promotes the development of anatomic and clinical pathology, especially by convening conferences, congresses and meetings, and through the interchange of publications and personnel; mems: 54 national asscns; Chair. Dr HENRY TRAVERS (USA); Exec. Dir. Dr MASSAMI MURAKAMI (Japan); publ. *Newsletter* (quarterly).

World Confederation for Physical Therapy (WCPT): Victoria Charity Centre, 11 Belgrave Rd, London, SW1V 1RB, United Kingdom; tel. (20) 7931-6465; fax (20) 7931-6494; e-mail info@wcpt.org; internet www.wcpt.org; f. 1951; represents physical therapy internationally; encourages high standards of physical therapy education and practice; promotes exchange of information among members, and the development of a scientific professional base through research; aims to contribute to the development of informed public opinion regarding physical therapy; holds seminars and workshops and quadrennial scientific congress showcasing advancements in physical therapy research, practice and education (2011: Amsterdam, Netherlands, in June; 2015: Singapore, in May); mems: 106 national physical therapy orgs; Pres. MARILYN MOFFAT; Sec.-Gen. BRENDA J. MYERS; publ. *WCPT News* (quarterly).

World Council of Optometry (WCO): 42 Craven St, London, WC2N 5NG, United Kingdom; tel. (20) 7839-6000; fax (20) 7839-6800; e-mail enquiries@worldoptometry.org; internet www.worldoptometry.org; f. 1927 to co-ordinate efforts to provide a good standard of ophthalmic optical (optometric) care throughout the world; enables exchange of ideas between different countries; focuses on optometric education; gives advice on standards of qualification; considers optometry legislation throughout the world; mems: 94 optometric orgs in 45 countries; Pres. TONE GARAAS-MAURDALEN (Norway).

World Federation for Medical Education (WFME) (Fédération mondiale pour l'enseignement de la medicine): University of Copenhagen, Faculty of Health Sciences, Blegdamsvej 3, 2200 Copenhagen N, Denmark; tel. (353) 27103; fax (353) 27070; e-mail wfme@wfme.org; internet www.wfme.org; f. 1972; aims to promote and integrate medical education world-wide; links regional and international asscns; has official relations with WHO, UNICEF, UNESCO, UNDP and the World Bank; Pres. Prof. STEFAN LINDGREN; Sec. ANNA IVERSEN.

World Federation for Mental Health (WFMH): POB 807, Occoquan, VA 22125, USA; fax (703) 490-6926; e-mail info@wfmh.com; internet www.wfmh.org; f. 1948 to promote the highest standards of mental health; works with agencies of the UN in promoting global mental health needs; assists grassroots efforts to improve mental health services, treatment and stigma; voting, affiliate and individual members in more than 100 countries; Pres. DEBORAH WAN (Hong Kong SAR); Sec.-Gen. VIJAY GANJU; publs *Newsletter* (quarterly), *Annual Report*.

World Federation for Ultrasound in Medicine and Biology: 14750 Sweitzer Ln, Suite 100, Laurel, MD 20707-5906, USA; e-mail admin@wfumb.org; internet www.wfumb.org; f. 1973; Pres. MASATOSHI KUDO; Sec. DAVID EVANS; publs *Ultrasound in Medicine and Biology* (monthly), *Echoes* (2 a year).

World Federation of Associations of Paediatric Surgeons (WOFAPS): c/o Prof. J. Boix-Ochoa, Clinica Infantil 'Vall d'Hebron', Departamento de Cirugía Pediátrica, Valle de Hebron 119–129, Barcelona 08035, Spain; e-mail jboix99@hotmail.com; internet www.wofaps.org; f. 1974; World Congress (2010: New Delhi, India); mems: 80 asscns; Pres. Prof. PREM PURI; Sec.-Gen./Treas. Prof. PEPE BOIX-OCHOA.

World Federation of Hydrotherapy and Climatotherapy: Cattedra di Terapia Med. E Medic. Termal, Università degli Studi, via Cicognara 7, 20129 Milan, Italy; tel. (02) 50318458; fax (02) 50318461; e-mail crbbmn@unimi.it; internet www.femteconline.org; f. 1947 as International Federation of Thermalism and Climatism; recognized by WHO in 1986; present name adopted 1999; mems: in 44 countries; Pres. M. NIKOLAI A. STOROZHENKO (Russia); Gen. Sec. Prof. UMBERTO SOLIMENE (Italy).

World Federation of Neurology (WFN): Hill House, Heron Sq., Richmond, Surrey, TW9 1EP, United Kingdom; tel. (20) 8439-9556; fax (20) 8439-9499; e-mail info@wfneurology.org; internet www.wfneurology.org; f. 1955 as International Neurological Congress, present title adopted 1957; aims to assemble members of various congresses associated with neurology and promote co-operation among neurological researchers; organizes Congress every four years; mems: 23,000 in 102 countries; Pres. VLADIMIR HACHINSKI (Canada); Sec.-Treas. Dr RAAD SHAKIR (United Kingdom); publs *Journal of the Neurological Sciences*, *World Neurology* (quarterly).

World Federation of Neurosurgical Societies (WFNS): 5 rue du Marché, 1260 Nyon Vaud, Switzerland; tel. 223624303; fax 223624352; e-mail teresachen@wfns.ch; internet www.wfns.org; f. 1957 to assist in the development of neurosurgery and to help the formation of asscns; facilitates the exchange of information and encourages research; mems: 116 societies; Pres. PETER M. BLACK; Sec. Dr HILDO AZEVEDO-FILHO.

World Federation of Occupational Therapists (WFOT): POB 30, Forrestfield, Western Australia 6058, Australia; fax (8) 9453-9746; e-mail admin@wfot.org.au; internet www.wfot.org; f. 1952 to further the rehabilitation of the physically and mentally disabled by promoting the development of occupational therapy in all countries; facilitates the exchange of information and publications; promotes research in occupational therapy; holds international congresses every four years; mems: national professional asscns in 69 countries, with total membership of c. 300,000; Pres. SHARON BRINTNELL (Canada); Exec. Dir MARILYN PATTISON (Australia); publ. *Bulletin* (2 a year).

World Federation of Public Health Associations: Office of the Secretariat, c/o Institute for Social and Preventive Medicine, University of Geneva CMU, 1 rue Michel Servet, 1211 Geneva 4, Switzerland; tel. 223970466; fax 223970452; e-mail bettina .borisch@unige.ch; internet www.wfpha.org; f. 1967; brings together researchers, teachers, health service providers and workers in a multidisciplinary environment of professional exchange, studies and action; endeavours to influence policies and to set priorities to prevent disease and promote health; holds a Congress every three years: 2012, Addis Ababa, Ethiopia, in April; mems: 68 national public health asscns and 5 regional asscns; Pres. JIM CHAUVIN (Canada); publs *WFPHA Report* (in English), occasional technical papers.

World Federation of Societies of Anaesthesiologists (WFSA): 21 Portland Pl., London, W1B 1PY, United Kingdom; tel. (20) 7631-8880; fax (20) 7631-8882; e-mail wfsahq@ anaesthesiologists.org; internet www.anaesthesiologists.org; f. 1955; aims to make available the highest standards of anaesthesia, pain treatment, trauma management and resuscitation to all peoples of the world; mems: 122 national societies; Pres. Dr DAVID WILKINSON (United Kingdom); Sec. Dr GONZALO BARREIRO (Uruguay); publs *Update in Anaesthesia* (2 a year), *Annual Report*.

World Gastroenterology Organization (WGO): 555 East Wells St, Suite 1100, Milwaukee, WI 53202, USA; tel. (414) 918-9798; fax (414) 276-3349; e-mail info@ worldgastroenterology.org; internet www.worldgastroenterology .org; f. 1958 as Organisation mondiale de gastro-entérologie—OMGE, to promote clinical and academic gastroenterological practice throughout the world, and to ensure high ethical standards; focuses on the improvement of standards in gastroenterology training and education on a global scale; renamed as above in 2007; a WGO Foundation, incorporated in 2007, is dedicated to raising funds to support WGO educational programs and activities; mems: 103 national societies, 4 regional asscns; Pres. Prof. HENRY COHEN (Uruguay); Sec.-Gen. Prof. CIHAN YURDAYDIN (Turkey).

World Heart Federation: 7 rue des Battoir, 1211 Geneva 4, Switzerland; tel. 228070320; fax 228070339; e-mail admin@ worldheart.org; internet www.world-heart-federation.org; f. 1978 as International Society and Federation of Cardiology, name changed as above 1998; aims to help people to achieve a longer and better life through prevention and control of heart disease and stroke, with a focus on low- and middle-income countries; mems: 197 orgs in more than 100 countries; Pres. Dr SIDNEY C. SMITH, Jr (USA); Sec. JOHANNA RALSTON (Switzerland); publs *Nature Clinical Practice Cardiovascular Journal*, *Global Heart*.

World Medical Association (WMA): 13 chemin du Levant, CIB-Bâtiment A, 01210 Ferney-Voltaire, France; tel. 4-50-40-75-75; fax 4-50-40-59-37; e-mail wma@wma.net; internet www .wma.net; f. 1947 to achieve the highest international standards in all aspects of medical education and practice, to promote closer ties among doctors and national medical asscns by personal contact and all other means, to study problems confronting the medical profession, and to present its views to appropriate bodies; holds an annual General Assembly; mems: 83 national medical asscns; Pres. Dr JOSÉ LUIZ GOMES (Brazil); Sec.-Gen. Dr OTMAR KLOIBER (Germany); publ. *The World Medical Journal* (quarterly).

World Psychiatric Association (WPA): Psychiatric Hospital, 2 chemin du Petit-Bel-Air 1225, Chêne-Bourg, Switzerland; tel. 223055737; fax 223055735; e-mail wpasecretariat@wpanet.org; internet www.wpanet.org; f. 1961; aims to increase knowledge and skills necessary for work in the field of mental health and the care for the mentally ill; organizes World Psychiatric Congresses and regional and interregional scientific meetings; mems: 135 national psychiatric societies, representing some 200,000 psychiatrists, in 117 countries; Pres. PEDRO RUIZ (USA); Sec.-Gen. LEVENT KUEY (Turkey).

World Self-Medication Industry (WSMI): 13 chemin du Levant, 01210 Ferney-Voltaire, France; tel. 4-50-28-47-28; fax 4-50-28-40-24; e-mail admin@wsmi.org; internet www.wsmi .org; f. 1970; aims to promote understanding and development of responsible self-medication; Chair. ZHENYU GUO (People's Republic of China); Dir-Gen. Dr DAVID E. WEBBER.

Posts and Telecommunications

Arab Permanent Postal Commission: c/o Arab League Bldg, Tahrir Sq., Cairo, Egypt; tel. (2) 5750511; fax (2) 5779546; f. 1952; aims to establish stricter postal relations between the Arab countries than those laid down by the Universal Postal Union, and to pursue the development and modernization of postal services in member countries; publs *APU Bulletin* (monthly), *APU Review* (quarterly), *APU News* (annually).

Asia-Pacific Telecommunity (APT): No. 12/49, Soi 5, Chaengwattana Rd, Thungsonghong, Bangkok 10210, Thailand; tel. (2) 573-0044; fax (2) 573-7479; e-mail aptmail@apt.int; internet www.aptsec.org; f. 1979 to cover all matters relating to telecommunications in the region; serves as the focal organization for ICT in the Asia-Pacific region; contributes, through its various programmes and activities, to the growth of the ICT sector in the region and assists members in their preparation for global telecommunications conferences, as well as promoting regional harmonization for such events; mems: Afghanistan, Australia, Bangladesh, Bhutan, Brunei, Cambodia, People's Republic of China, Fiji, India, Indonesia, Iran, Japan, Democratic Republic of Korea, Republic of Korea, Laos, Malaysia, Maldives, Marshall Islands, Federated States of Micronesia, Mongolia, Myanmar, Nauru, Nepal, New Zealand, Pakistan, Palau, Papua New Guinea, Philippines, Samoa, Singapore, Sri Lanka, Thailand, Tonga, Tuvalu, Vanuatu, Viet Nam; assoc. mems: Cook Islands, Hong Kong, Macao, Niue; 130 affiliated mems; Sec.-Gen. TOSHIYUKI YAMADA.

Asian-Pacific Postal Union (APPU): APPU Bureau, POB 1, Laksi Post Office, 111 Chaeng Wattana Rd, Bangkok 10210, Thailand; tel. (2) 573-7282; fax (2) 573-1161; e-mail admin@ appu-bureau.org; internet www.appu-bureau.org; f. 1962 to extend, facilitate and improve the postal relations between the member countries and to promote co-operation in the field of postal services; holds Congress every four years (2013: India); mems: postal administrations in 32 countries; Dir SOMCHAI REOPANICHKUL; publs *Annual Report*, *Exchange Program of Postal Officials*, *APPU Newsletter*.

European Conference of Postal and Telecommunications Administrations: Penblingehus, Nansensgade 19-3, 1366 Copenhagen, Denmark; tel. 33-89-63-00; fax 33-89-63-30; e-mail ceptpresidency@cept.org; internet www.cept.org; f. 1959 to strengthen relations between member administrations and to harmonize and improve their technical services; set up Eurodata Foundation, for research and publishing; supported by a separate European Communications Office (ECO); mems: 48 countries; Joint Chair. THOMAS EWERS, ULRICH DAMMANN, ANDERS JÖNSSON; Dir ECO MARK THOMAS (United Kingdom); publ. *Bulletin*.

European Telecommunications Satellite Organization (EUTELSAT): 33 ave du Maine, 75755 Paris, France; tel. 1-44-10-41-10; fax 1-44-10-41-11; e-mail secigo@eutelsat.fr; internet www.eutelsatigo.int; f. 1977 to operate satellites for fixed and mobile communications in Europe; EUTELSAT's in-orbit resource comprises 18 satellites; commercialises capacity in three satellites operated by other companies; mems: public and private telecommunications operations in 49 countries; Exec. Sec. CHRISTIAN ROISSE.

International Mobile Satellite Organization (IMSO): 99 City Rd, London, EC1Y 1AX, United Kingdom; tel. (20) 7728-1249; fax (20) 7728-1172; e-mail info@imso.org; internet www .imso.org; f. 1979, as the International Maritime Satellite Organization (name changed in 1994) to provide (from Feb.

1982) global communications for shipping via satellites on a commercial basis; in 1985 the operating agreement was amended to include aeronautical communications, and in 1988 amendments were approved which allowed provision of global land mobile communications; in April 1999 the commercial functions of the organization became the limited company INMARSAT Ltd (the first intergovernmental org. to be transferred to the private sector); IMSO was maintained, initially to monitor, under a Public Services Agreement adopted in 1999, INMARSAT Ltd's public service obligations in respect of the Global Maritime Distress and Safety System (GMDSS); following amendments adopted in 2008 to the IMSO Convention, IMSO's oversight functions were extended to all satellite operators approved to provide GMDSS services, and IMSO was also mandated to oversee long range tracking and identification of ships (LRIT); mems: 97 states party to the founding Convention; Dir-Gen. Capt. ESTEBAN PACHA-VICENTE.

International Multinational Partnership against Cyber Threats (IMPACT): Jalan IMPACT, 63000 Cyberjaya, Malaysia; tel. (3) 83132020; fax (3) 83192020; e-mail contactus@impact-alliance.org; internet www.impact-alliance.org; f. 2006 as a global public-private partnership; aims to promote collaboration in order strengthen the capability of the international community and individual partner countries to prevent, defend against and respond to cyber threats; signed a Memorandum of Understanding with the ITU in Sept. 2008 to administer the Global Cyber Agenda; Chair. Datuk MOHD NOOR AMIN.

International Telecommunications Satellite Organization (ITSO): 3400 International Drive, NW, Washington, DC 20008-3098, USA; tel. (202) 243-5096; fax (202) 243-5018; internet www.itso.int; f. 1964 to establish a global commercial satellite communications system; Assembly of Parties attended by representatives of member governments, meets every two years to consider policy and long-term aims and matters of interest to members as sovereign states; meeting of Signatories to the Operating Agreement held annually; 24 INTELSAT satellites in geosynchronous orbit provide a global communications service; provides most of the world's overseas traffic; in 1998 INTELSAT agreed to establish a private enterprise, incorporated in the Netherlands, to administer six satellite services; mems: 150 govts; Dir-Gen. JOSÉ TOSCANO (USA).

Internet Corporation for Assigned Names and Numbers (ICANN): 4676 Admiralty Way, Suite 330, Marina del Rey, CA 90292-6601, USA; tel. (310) 823-9358; fax (310) 823-8649; e-mail icann@icann.org; internet www.icann.org; f. 1998; non-profit, private sector body; aims to co-ordinate the technical management and policy development of the Internet in relation to addresses, domain names and protocol; supported by an At-Large Advisory Committee (representing individual users of the Internet), a Country Code Names Supporting Organization (ccNSO), a Governmental Advisory Committee, a Generic Names Supporting Organization (GNSO), and a Security and Stability Advisory Committee; through its Internet Assigned Numbers Authority (IANA) department ICANN manages the global co-ordination of domain name system roots and Internet protocol addressing; at 30 June 2011 there were 310 top-level domains (TLDs), 30 of which were in non-Latin scripts, and the most common of which were generic TLDs (gTLDs) (such as .org or .com) and country code TLDs (ccTLDs); in June 2011 ICANN adopted an expanded gTLD programme, under which applications were to be accepted from 2012 from qualified orgs wishing to register domain names of their choosing, including the possibility of Internationalized Domain Names (IDNs) incorporating non-Latin character sets (Arabic, Chinese and Cyrillic), with a view to making the Internet more globally inclusive; details of the first 1,930 filed applications were published in June 2012 ('app' being the most popular), in advance of a seven-month objection period; the International Chamber of Commerce International Centre for Expertise ('the Centre') was to administer the objections process; Pres. and CEO ROD BECKSTROM (USA).

Pacific Islands Telecommunications Association (PITA): Level 8, Dominion House, Edward St, Suva, Fiji; tel. 3311638; fax 3308750; e-mail pita@connect.com.fj; internet www.pita.org.fj; represents the interests in the area of telecommunications of Pacific region small island nations; PITA was to organize a Pacific Forum on Broadband Access and Application in June 2012, and a Pacific Internet Business Forum in July 2012; mems: telecommunication entities in the Pacific region; Pres. IVAN FONG; Man. FRED CHRISTOPHER.

Pacific Telecommunications Council (PTC): 914 Coolidge St, Honolulu, HI 96826-3085, USA; tel. (808) 941-3789; fax (808) 944-4874; e-mail info@ptc.org; internet www.ptc.org; f. 1978 to facilitate the adoption of telecommunications and advanced information technologies throughout the Asia-Pacific region; enables the exchange of ideas and commerce through its annual conference each Jan; mems: 3,000 mem. representatives from more than 50 countries; Pres. RICHARD TAYLOR (USA); CEO SHARON NAKAMA.

Postal Union of the Americas, Spain and Portugal (PUASP) (Unión Postal de las Américas, España y Portugal): Cebollatí 1468/70, 1°, Casilla de Correos 20.042, Montevideo, Uruguay; tel. 2410 0070; fax 2410 5046; e-mail secretaria@upaep.com.uy; internet www.upaep.com.uy; f. 1911 to extend, facilitate and study the postal relationships of member countries; mems: 27 countries; Sec.-Gen. SERRANA BASSINI CASCO.

Regional African Satellite Communications System (RASCOM): 2 ave Thomasset, BP 3528, Abidjan 01, Côte d'Ivoire; tel. (225) 20223683; fax (225) 20223676; e-mail rascomps@rascom.org; internet www.rascom.org; f. 1992; aims to provide telecommunications facilities to African countries and supports a regional satellite communication system; mems: 45 countries; Dir-Gen. JONES A. KILLIMBE.

Press, Radio and Television

African Union of Broadcasting (AUB): 101 rue Carnot, BP 3237, Dakar, Senegal; tel. 821-16-25; fax 822-51-13; internet www.aub-uar.org/eng/; f. 1962 as Union of National Radio and Television Organizations of Africa (URTNA), new org. f. Nov. 2006; co-ordinates radio and television services, including monitoring and frequency allocation, the exchange of information and coverage of national and international events among African countries; mems: 48 orgs and 6 assoc. members; Pres. TEWFIK KHELLADI (Algeria), LAWRENCE ADDO-YAO ATIASE (Ghana).

Asia-Pacific Broadcasting Union (ABU): POB 1164, Lorong Maarof, 59000 Kuala Lumpur, Malaysia; tel. and fax (3) 22823592; e-mail info@abu.org.my; internet www.abu.org.my; f. 1964 to foster and co-ordinate the development of broadcasting in the Asia-Pacific area, to develop means of establishing closer collaboration and co-operation among broadcasting orgs, and to serve the professional needs of broadcasters in Asia and the Pacific; holds annual General Assembly; mems: more than 200 in 58 countries and territories; Pres. Dr KIM IN-KYU (Republic of Korea); Sec.-Gen. Dr JAVAD MOTTAGHI (Iran); publs *ABU News* (every 2 months), *ABU Technical Review* (every 2 months).

Association for the Promotion of International Press Distribution (DISTRIPRESS): Seefeldstr. 35, 8008 Zürich, Switzerland; tel. 442024121; fax 442021025; e-mail info@distripress.net; internet www.distripress.net; f. 1955 to assist in the promotion of the freedom of the press throughout the world, supporting and aiding UNESCO in promoting the free flow of ideas; organizes meetings of publishers and distributors of newspapers, periodicals and paperback books, to promote the exchange of information and experience among members; mems: 470 in 95 countries; Pres. TONY JASHANMAL (UAE); Man. Dir DAVID OWEN (United Kingdom); publs *Distripress Gazette*, *Who's Who*.

Association of European Journalists (AEJ): 145 ave Baron Albert d'Huart, 1950 Kraainem, Belgium; tel. (478) 291985; e-mail npkramer@skynet.be; internet www.aej.org; f. 1963 to participate actively in the development of a European consciousness; to promote deeper knowledge of European problems and secure appreciation by the general public of the work of European institutions; to facilitate members' access to sources of European information; and to defend freedom of the press; mems: 2,100 individuals and national asscns in 25 countries; Pres. EILEEN DUNNE (Ireland); Sec.-Gen. N. PETER KRAMER (Belgium).

Cable Europe: 41 ave des Arts, 1040 Brussels, Belgium; tel. (2) 521-17-63; fax (2) 521-79-76; e-mail info@cable-europe.eu; internet www.cable-europe.eu; f. 1955 as European Cable Communications Associations (name changed in 2006); promotes the interests of the European cable industry and fosters co-operation among companies and national asscns; Pres. MANUEL KOHNSTAMM (Netherlands).

Confederation of ASEAN Journalists: Gedung Dewan Pers, 4th Floor, 34 Jalan Kebon Sirih, Jakarta 10110, Indonesia; tel. (21) 3453131; fax (21) 3453175; e-mail aseanjour@cbn.net.id; f. 1975; holds General Assembly every two years, Press Convention, workshops; mems: journalists' asscns in Brunei, Indonesia, Laos, Malaysia, Philippines, Singapore, Thailand and Viet Nam; observers: journalists' asscns in Cambodia and Myanmar; Perm. Sec. MUHAMMAD SAIFUL HADI; publs *The ASEAN Journalist* (quarterly), *CAJ Yearbook*.

European Alliance of News Agencies: Norrbackagatan 23, 11341 Stockholm, Sweden; tel. and fax (8) 301-324; e-mail erik-n@telia.com; internet www.newsalliance.org; f. 1957 as European Alliance of Press Agencies (name changed 2002); aims to promote co-operation among members and to study and protect their common interests; annual assembly; mems: in 30 countries; Sec.-Gen. ERIK NYLÉN.

European Broadcasting Union (EBU): CP 45, 17A Ancienne-Route, 1218 Grand-Saconnex, Geneva, Switzerland; tel. 227172111; fax 227474000; e-mail ebu@ebu.ch; internet www.ebu.ch; f. 1950 in succession to the International Broadcasting Union; a professional asscn of broadcasting organizations, supporting the interests of members and assisting the development of broadcasting in all its forms; activities include the Eurovision news and programme exchanges and the Euroradio music exchanges; mems: 85 active in 56 countries, 37 assoc. mems; Pres. JEAN-PAUL PHILIPPOT (Belgium); Dir-Gen. INGRID DELTENRE; publs *EBU Technical Review* (annually), *Dossiers* (2 a year).

Federation of African Journalists (FAJ): c/o East African Journalists' Association Secretariat, BP 4099, Djibouti; e-mail omar@nusoj.org; f. 2008; defends the freedom of the press, and addresses professional issues affecting journalists; supports a network encompassing the West African Journalists Association, the Southern African Journalists Association, the Eastern African Journalists Association, the Association of Media Professionals Unions of Central Africa, and the Network of North African Journalists; Pres. OMAR FARUK OSMAN NUR (Somalia).

Inter-American Press Association (IAPA) (Sociedad Interamericana de Prensa): Jules Dubois Bldg, 1801 SW 3rd Ave, Miami, FL 33129, USA; tel. (305) 634-2465; fax (305) 635-2272; e-mail info@sipiapa.org; internet www.sipiapa.org; f. 1942 to guard the freedom of the press in the Americas; to promote and maintain the dignity, rights and responsibilities of the profession of journalism; to foster a wider knowledge and greater interchange among the peoples of the Americas; mems: 1,400; Exec. Dir JULIO E. MUÑOZ; publ. *IAPA News* (monthly).

International Amateur Radio Union: POB 310905, Newington, CT 06131-0905, USA; tel. (860) 594-0200; fax (860) 594-0259; e-mail iaru@iaru.org; internet www.iaru.org; f. 1925 to link national amateur radio societies and represent the interests of two-way amateur radio communication; mems: 161 national amateur radio societies; Pres. TIMOTHY ELLAM (Canada); Sec. RODNEY STAFFORD.

International Association of Broadcasting (Asociación Internacional de Radiodifusión—AIR): Carlos Quijano 1264, 1110 Montevideo, Uruguay; tel. (2) 9011319; fax (2) 9080458; e-mail mail@airiab.com; internet www.airiab.com; f. 1946 (as the Interamerican Association of Broadcasting) to preserve free and private broadcasting; to promote co-operation between the corporations and public authorities; to defend freedom of expression; mems: national asscns of broadcasters; Pres. LUIS PARDO SAINZ (Chile); Dir-Gen. Dr HÉCTOR OSCAR AMENGUAL; publ. *La Gaceta de AIR* (every 2 months).

International Association of Sound and Audiovisual Archives: c/o Ilse Assmann, Radio Broadcast Facilities, SABC, POB 931, Auckland Park 2006, Johannesburg, South Africa; tel. (11) 714-4041; fax (11) 714-4419; e-mail assmanni@sabc.co.za; internet www.iasa-web.org; f. 1969; supports the professional exchange of sound and audiovisual documents, and fosters international co-operation between audiovisual archives in all fields, in particular in the areas of acquisition, documentation, access, exploitation, copyright, and preservation; holds annual conference; mems: 400 individuals and institutions in 64 countries; Pres. JACQUELINE VON ARB (Norway) (2011–14); Sec.-Gen. LYNN JOHNSON (South Africa); publs *IASA Journal* (2 a year), *IASA Information Bulletin* (2 a year), *eBulletin* (2 a year).

International Association of Women in Radio and Television (IAWRT): 3/F GIF Medical Bldg, 510C Raymundo Ave, Caniogan, Pasig City 1606, Philippines; tel. and fax (2) 6434583; e-mail secretariat@iawrt.org; internet www.iawrt.org; f. 1951; Pres. RACHEAL NAKITARE (Kenya); Sec. VIOLET GONDA (Zimbabwe).

International Catholics Organisation of the Media (ICOM) (World Forum of Professionals and Institutions in Secular and Religious Journalism): 37–39 rue de Vermont, CP 197, 1211 Geneva 20, Switzerland; tel. 227340017; fax 227340053; e-mail icom@bluewin.ch; internet www.icomworld.info; f. 2011, as a successor organization to the International Catholic Union of the Press (f. 1927); focuses on inspiring and encouraging all media professionals world-wide, irrespective of differences, and on promoting the rights to information and freedom of opinion, and supports journalistic ethics; World Congress to be held in 2013, in Panama; mems: in 172 countries.

International Council for Film, Television and Audiovisual Communication (Conseil international du cinema de la television et de la communication audiovisuelle): 1 rue Miollis, 75732 Paris Cedex 15, France; tel. 1-45-68-48-55; fax 1-45-67-28-40; e-mail secretariat@cict-unesco.org; internet www.unesco.org/iftc; f. 1958 to support collaboration between UNESCO and professionals engaged in cinema, television and audiovisual communications; mems: 36 international film and television organizations; Pres. HISANORI ISOMURA; Sec.-Gen. LOLA POGGI GOUJON; publ. *Letter of Information* (monthly).

International Council of French-speaking Radio and Television Organizations (Conseil international des radios-télévisions d'expression française): 52 blvd Auguste-Reyers, 1044 Brussels, Belgium; tel. (2) 732-45-85; fax (2) 732-62-40; e-mail cirtef@rtbf.be; internet www.cirtef.org; f. 1978 to establish links between French-speaking radio and television organizations; mems: 46 orgs; Sec.-Gen. GUILA THIAM (Senegal).

International Federation of Film Critics (Fédération Internationale de la Presse Cinématographique—FIPRESCI): Schleissheimerstr. 83, 80797 Munich, Germany; tel. (89) 182303; fax (89) 184766; e-mail info@fipresci.org; internet www.fipresci.org; f. 1930 to develop the cinematographic press and promote cinema as an art; organizes international meetings and juries in film festivals; mems: national orgs or corresponding mems in 68 countries; Pres. JEAN ROY (France); Gen. Sec. KLAUS EDER (Germany).

International Federation of Press Cutting Agencies (FIBEP) (Fédération Internationale des Bureaux D'Extraits de Presse): Chaussée de Wavre 1945, 1160 Brussels, Belgium; tel. (2) 508-17-13; fax (2) 513-82-18; internet www.fibep.info; f. 1953 to improve the standing of the profession, prevent infringements, illegal practices and unfair competition; and to develop business and friendly relations among press cuttings agencies throughout the world; Congress held every 18 months, Oct. 2012: Krakow, Poland; mems: 90 agencies in more than 40 countries; Pres. NOGUEIRA FRESCO; Gen. Sec. JOACHIM VON BEUST (Belgium).

International Federation of the Periodical Press (FIPP): Queen's House, 55/56 Lincoln's Inn Fields, London, WC2A 3LJ, United Kingdom; tel. (20) 7404-4169; fax (20) 7404-4170; e-mail info@fipp.com; internet www.fipp.com; f. 1925; works for the benefit of magazine publishers around the world by promoting the common editorial, cultural and economic interests of consumer and business-to-business publishers, both in print and electronic media; fosters formal and informal alliances between magazine publishers and industry suppliers; mems: 52 national asscns, 470 publishing cos, 180 assoc. mems and 6 individual mems; Pres. and CEO CHRIS LLEWELYN; publ. *Magazine World* (quarterly).

International Institute of Communications: 2 Printers Yard, 90A The Broadway, London, SW19 1RD, United Kingdom; tel. (20) 8417-0600; fax (20) 8417-0800; e-mail enquiries@iicom.org; internet www.iicom.org; f. 1969 (as the International Broadcast Institute) to link all working in the field of communications, including policy makers, broadcasters, industrialists and engineers; holds local, regional and international meetings; undertakes research; mems: over 1,000 corporate, institutional and individual; Pres. FABIO COLASANTI; Dir-Gen. ANDREA MILLWOOD HARGRAVE; publ. *Intermedia* (5 a year).

International Maritime Radio Association: South Bank House, Black Prince Rd, London, SE1 7SJ, United Kingdom; tel. (20) 7587-1245; fax (20) 7793-2329; e-mail secgen@cirm.org; internet www.cirm.org; f. 1928 to study and develop means of improving marine radio communications and radio aids to marine navigation; mems: some 75 orgs and companies from 21 maritime nations involved in marine electronics in the areas of radio communications and navigation; Pres. HANS RASMUSSEN; Sec.-Gen. MICHAEL RAMBAUT.

International Press Institute (IPI): Spiegelgasse 2, 1010 Vienna, Austria; tel. (1) 5129011; fax (1) 5129014; e-mail ipi@freemedia.at; internet www.freemedia.at; f. 1951 as a non-governmental organization of editors, publishers and news broadcasters supporting the principles of a free and responsible press; aims to defend press freedom; conducts research; maintains a library; holds regional meetings and an annual World Congress; mems: about 2,000 from 120 countries; Chair. CARL-EUGEN EBERLE (Germany); Exec. Dir ALISON BETHEL MCKENZIE (USA); publs *IPI Congress Report* (annually), *World Press Freedom Review* (annually).

International Press Telecommunications Council (IPTC): 20 Garrick St, London, WC2E 9BT, United Kingdom; tel. (20) 3178-4922; fax (20) 7664-7878; e-mail office@iptc.org; internet www.iptc.org; f. 1965 to safeguard the telecommunications interests of the world press; acts as the news industry's formal standards body; meets three times a year and maintains three committees and four working parties; mems: 65 news agencies, newspapers, news websites and industry vendors; Chair. VINCENT BABY; Man. Dir MICHAEL STEIDL; publs *IPTC Spectrum* (annually), *IPTC Mirror* (6 a year).

Organization of Asia-Pacific News Agencies (OANA): c/o Anadolu Ajansi, Gazi Mustafa Kemal Bulvari 128/c, Tandogan, Ankara, Turkey; tel. (312) 2317000; fax (231) 2312174; e-mail oana@aa.com.tr; internet www.oananews.org; f. 1961 to promote co-operation in professional matters and mutual exchange of news, features, etc. among the news agencies of Asia and the Pacific via the Asia-Pacific News Network (ANN); 14th General Assembly: Istanbul, Turkey, Nov. 2010; mems: 43 news agencies in 34 countries; Pres. KEMAL ÖZTÜRK (Turkey); Sec.-Gen. ERCAN GÖÇER (Turkey).

Pacific Islands News Association (PINA): Damodar Centre, 46 Gordon St, PMB, Suva, Fiji; tel. 3303623; fax 3317055; e-mail pina@connect.com.fj; internet www.pina.com.fj; f. 1991; regional press asscn; defends freedom of information and expression, promotes professional co-operation, provides training and education; mems: media orgs in 23 countries and territories; Man. MATAI AKAUOLA.

Pasifika Media Association (PasiMA): Apia, Samoa; internet www.pacific-media.org; f. 2010; Chair. SAVEA SANO MALIFA (Samoa); Sec./Treas. JOHN WOODS (New Zealand).

Reporters sans Frontières: 47 rue Vivienne, 75002 Paris, France; tel. 1-44-83-84-84; fax 1-45-23-11-51; e-mail rsf@rsf.org; internet www.rsf.org; f. 1985 to defend press freedom throughout the world; generates awareness of violations of press freedoms and supports journalists under threat or imprisoned as a result of their work; mems in 77 countries; Sec.-Gen. OLIVIER BASILLE; publs *Annual Report*, *La Lettre de Reporters sans Frontières* (6 a year).

Southern African Broadcasting Association (SABA): Postnet Suite 210, P/Bag X9, Melville 2109, Johannesburg, South Africa; tel. (11) 7144918; fax (11) 7144868; e-mail sabasg@telkomsa.net; f. 1993; promotes quality public broadcasting; facilitates training of broadcasters at all levels; co-ordinates broadcasting activities in the SADC region; organizes radio news exchange service; produces television and radio programmes; mems: corpns in more than 20 countries; Sec.-Gen. ARLINDO LOPES (Mozambique).

World Association for Christian Communication (WACC): 308 Main St, Toronto, ON M4C 4X7, Canada; tel. (416) 691-1999; fax (416) 691-1997; e-mail wacc@waccglobal.org; internet www.waccglobal.org; f. 1975 to promote human dignity, justice and peace through freedom of expression and the democratization of communication; offers professional guidance on communication policies; interprets developments in and the consequences of global communication methods; works towards the empowerment of women; assists the training of Christian communicators; mems: corporate and personal mems in 120 countries, organized in 8 regional asscns; Pres. Dr DENNIS SMITH; Gen. Sec. Rev. Dr KARIN ACHTELSTETTER (Germany); publs *Action*, *Newsletter* (10 a year), *Media Development* (quarterly), *Communication Resource*, *Media and Gender Monitor* (both occasional).

World Association of Newspapers and News Publishers (WAN-IFRA): Washingtonplatz 1, 64287 Darmstadt, Germany; tel. (6151) 7336; fax (6151) 733800; e-mail info@wan-ifra.org; internet www.wan-ifra.org; f. 2009 by merger of World Association of Newspapers (f. 1948) and IFRA (f. 1961); WAN-IFRA is the world-wide service and representative org of newspapers and the entire news publishing industry; aims to support this industry, as well as its technology and service; mems: more than 3,000 companies in 120 countries; Pres. JACOB MATHEW (India); CEO ANDREAS MUSIELAK (Germany); publ. *WAN-IFRA Magazine* (every 2 months, and online).

World Catholic Association for Communication (SIGNIS): 310 rue Royale, 1210 Brussels, Belgium; tel. (2) 734-97-08; fax (2) 734-70-18; e-mail sg@signis.net; internet www.signis.net; f. 2001; brings together professionals working in radio, television, cinema, video, media education, internet, and new technology; Sec.-Gen. ALVITO DE SOUZA.

Religion

ACER–MJO (l'Action Chrétienne des Etudiants Russes—Mouvement de Jeunesse Orthodoxe): 91 rue Olivier de Serres, 75015 Paris, France; tel. 1-42-50-53-46; fax 1-42-50-19-08; e-mail secretariat@acer-mjo.org; internet www.acer-mjo.org; f. 1923; incorporated, since 1961, an active section Aid to Believers in the Soviet Union; in 1995 adopted a new Charter to reflect a broader membership to include all Orthodox religions; supports Christianity, in particular the Russian Orthodox Church, in the countries of the former USSR; organizes a summer camp.

Agudath Israel World Organisation: Hacherut Sq., POB 326, Jerusalem 91002, Israel; tel. (2) 5384357; fax (2) 5383634; f. 1912 to help solve the problems facing Jewish people all over the world in the spirit of the Jewish tradition; holds World Congress (every five years) and an annual Central Council; mems: over 500,000 in 25 countries; Secs Rabbi MOSHE GEWIRTZ, Rabbi CHAIM WEINSTOCK; publs *Hamodia* (Jerusalem, daily, in Hebrew; New York, daily, in English; Paris, weekly, in French), *Jedion* (Hebrew, monthly), *Jewish Tribune* (London, weekly), *Jewish Observer* (New York, monthly), *Dos Yiddishe Vort* (New York, monthly), *Coalition* (New York), *Perspectives* (Toronto, monthly), *La Voz Judia* (Buenos Aires, monthly), *Jüdische Stimme* (Zürich, weekly).

All Africa Conference of Churches (AACC): Waiyaki Way, POB 14205, 00800 Westlands, Nairobi, Kenya; tel. (20) 4441483; fax (20) 4443241; e-mail secretariat@aacc-ceta.org; internet www.aacc-ceta.org; f. 1963; an organ of co-operation and continuing fellowship among Protestant, Orthodox and independent churches and Christian Councils in Africa; 10th Assembly: Kampala, Uganda, in June 2013; mems: 173 churches and affiliated Christian councils in 40 African countries; Pres. Archbishop VALENTINE MOKIWA (Tanzania); Gen. Sec. Rev. Dr ANDRÉ KARAMAGA (Rwanda); publs *ACIS/APS Bulletin*, *Tam Tam*.

Bahá'í International Community: Bahá'í World Centre, POB 155, 31001 Haifa, Israel; tel. (4) 8358394; fax (4) 8313312; e-mail opi@bwc.org; internet www.bahai.org; f. 1844; promotes and applies the principles of the Bahá'í Faith, i.e. the abandonment of all forms of prejudice, the equality of women and men, recognition of the oneness of religion, the elimination of extremes of poverty and wealth, the realization of universal education and recognition that true religion is in harmony with reason and the pursuit of scientific knowledge, in order to contribute to the development of a peaceful, just, and sustainable society, and the resolution of the challenges currently facing humanity; Baha'is undertake to strengthen the moral and spiritual character of communities, for example by conducting classes that address the development of children and channel the energies of young people, and initiating study groups that enable people of varied backgrounds to explore the application of the Bahá'í teachings to their individual and collective lives; in some communities there is an annual election of a local council to administer affairs at that level; at the national level, there elected governing councils; the head of the Baha'i Faith is the Universal House of Justice, a body of nine members elected by the 186 National Spiritual Assemblies; has more than 5m. followers, living in more than 100,000 localities; 186 national governing councils; Sec.-Gen. ALBERT LINCOLN (USA); publs *Bahá'í World News Service* (online), *One Country* (quarterly, in 6 languages).

Baptist World Alliance: 405 North Washington St, Falls Church, VA 22046, USA; tel. (703) 790-8980; fax (703) 893-5160; e-mail bwa@bwanet.org; internet www.bwanet.org; f. 1905; aims to unite Baptists, lead in evangelism, respond to people in need, defend human rights, and promote theological reflection; mems: 37m. individuals and more than 200 Baptist unions and conventions representing about 105m. people worldwide; Pres. JOHN UPTON (USA); Gen. Sec. NEVILLE CALLAM (Jamaica); publ. *The Baptist World* (quarterly).

Caribbean Conference of Churches: POB 876, Port of Spain, Trinidad and Tobago; tel. 662-3064; fax 662-1303; e-mail ccchq@tstt.net.tt; internet www.ccc-caribe.org; f. 1973; governed by a General Assembly which meets every five years and appoints a 15-member Continuation Committee (board of management) to establish policies and direct the work of the organization between Assemblies; maintains two sub-regional offices in Antigua, Jamaica and Trinidad with responsibility for programme implementation in various territories; mems: 33 member churches in 34 territories in the Dutch-, English-, French-, and Spanish-speaking territories of the region; Gen. Sec. GERARD GRANADO; publ. *Ecuscope Caribbean*.

Christian Conference of Asia (CCA): c/o Payap Univ. Muang, Chiang Mai 50000, Thailand; tel. (53) 243906; fax (53) 247303; e-mail cca@cca.org.hk; internet www.cca.org.hk; f. 1957 (present name adopted 1973) to promote co-operation and joint study in matters of common concern among the Churches of the region and to encourage interaction with other regional Conferences and the World Council of Churches; mems: nearly 100 national churches, and 17 national councils in 21 countries; Gen. Sec. HENRIETTE HUTABARAT LEBANG (Indonesia); publ. *CCA News* (quarterly), *CTC Bulletin* (occasional).

Christian Peace Conference: POB 136, Prokopova 4, 130 00 Prague 3, Czech Republic; tel. 222781800; fax 222781801; e-mail christianpeace@volny.cz; internet www.volny.cz/christianpeace; f. 1958 as an international movement of theologians, clergy and lay people, aiming to bring Christendom to recognize its share of guilt in both world wars and to dedicate itself to the service of friendship, reconciliation and peaceful co-operation of nations, to concentrate on united action for peace and justice, and to co-ordinate peace groups in individual churches and facilitate their effective participation in the peaceful development of society; works through five continental asscns, regional groups and member churches in many countries; Moderator Dr SERGIO ARCE MARTÍNEZ; Co-ordinator Rev. BRIAN G. COOPER; publs *CPC Information* (8 a year, in English and German), occasional *Study Volume*.

Conference of European Churches (CEC): POB 2100, 150 route de Ferney, 1211 Geneva 2, Switzerland; tel. 227916228; fax 227916227; e-mail cec@cec-kek.org; internet www.ceceurope.org; f. 1959 as a regional ecumenical organization for Europe and a meeting-place for European churches, including members and non-members of the World Council of Churches; holds a General Assembly every six years; mems: 120 Protestant, Anglican, Orthodox and Old Catholic churches in all European countries; Gen. Sec. a.i. Rev. Dr GUY LIAGRE; publs *Monitor* (quarterly), CEC communiqués, reports.

Consultative Council of Jewish Organizations (CCJO): 420 Lexington Ave, New York, NY 10170, USA; tel. (212) 808-5437; f. 1946 to co-operate and consult with the UN and other international bodies directly concerned with human rights and to defend the cultural, political and religious rights of Jews throughout the world; Sec.-Gen. WARREN GREEN (USA).

European Baptist Federation (EBF): Nad Habrovkou 3, Jeneralka, 164 00 Prague 6, Czech Republic; tel. 296392250; fax 296392254; e-mail office@ebf.org; internet www.ebf.org; f. 1949 to promote fellowship and co-operation among Baptists in Europe; to further the aims and objects of the Baptist World Alliance; to stimulate and co-ordinate evangelism in Europe; to provide for consultation and planning of missionary work in Europe and elsewhere in the world; mems: 57 Baptist Unions in European countries and the Middle East; Pres. VALERIU GHILETCHI (Moldova); Gen. Sec. TONY PECK (United Kingdom).

European Evangelical Alliance: Hoofdstraat 51A, 3971 KB Driebergen, Netherlands; tel. (343) 513693; fax (343) 531488; e-mail office@europeanea.org; internet www.europeanea.org; f. 1953 to promote understanding and co-operation among evangelical Christians in Europe and to stimulate evangelism; mems: 15m. in 36 European countries; Gen. Sec. NIEK M. TRAMPER.

Federation of Jewish Communities of the CIS: 127055 Moscow, 2-i Vysheslavtsev per. 5A, Russia; tel. (495) 737-82-75; fax (495) 783-84-71; e-mail info@fjc.ru; internet www.fjc.ru; f. 1998 to restore Jewish society, culture and religion throughout the countries of the fmr Soviet Union through the provision of professional assistance, educational support and funding to member communities; Pres. LEV LEVAYEV.

Friends World Committee for Consultation: 173 Euston Rd, London, NW1 2AX, United Kingdom; tel. (20) 7663-1199; fax (20) 7663-1189; e-mail world@friendsworldoffice.org; internet www.fwccworld.org; f. 1937 to encourage and strengthen the spiritual life within the Religious Society of Friends (Quakers); to help Friends to a better understanding of their vocation in the world; and to promote consultation among Friends of all countries; representation at the United Nations as a non-governmental organization with general consultative status; mems: appointed representatives and individuals from 70 countries; Gen. Sec. NANCY IRVING; publs *Friends World News* (2 a year), *Calendar of Yearly Meetings* (annually), *Quakers around the World* (handbook).

Global Christian Forum: POB 306, 1290 Versoix, Switzerland; tel. 227554546; fax 227550108; e-mail gcforum@sunrise.ch; internet www.globalchristianforum.org; f. 1998 by the World Council of Churches, with an autonomous Continuation Committee, to provide opportunities for representatives of all the main Christian traditions to meet, foster mutual respect and address common challenges; a series of regional meetings was held during 2004–07 and the first Global Forum was convened in November 2007 in Limuru, near Nairobi, Kenya; Sec.-Gen. HUBERT VAN BEEK.

International Association for Religious Freedom (IARF): 3-8-21 Sangenya-Nishi, Taisho-ku, Osaka 551-0001, Japan; tel. (6) 7503-5602; e-mail hq@iarf.net; internet www.iarf.net; f. 1900 as a world community of religions, subscribing to the principle of openness and upholding the UN's Universal Declaration on freedom of religion or belief; conducts religious freedom programmes, focusing on inter-religious harmony; holds regional conferences and triennial congress; mems: 100 groups in 25 countries; Pres. MITSUO MIYAKE (Japan); Treas. JEFFREY TEAGLE (United Kingdom).

International Association of Buddhist Studies (IABS): c/o Prof. T. J. F. Tillemans, Section des langues et civilisations orientales, Université de Lausanne, 1015 Lausanne, Switzerland; fax 216923045; e-mail mail@iabsinfo.org; internet www.iabsinfo.net; f. 1976; supports studies of Buddhist religion, philosophy and literature; holds international conference every three or four years (16th Congress: Jinshan, Republic of China, June 2011); Pres. CRISTINA SCHERRER-SCHAUB (France); Gen. Sec. ULRICH PAGEL (Germany); publ. *Journal* (2 a year).

International Council of Christians and Jews (ICCJ): Martin Buber House, POB 1129, 64629 Heppenheim, Germany; tel. (6252) 6896810; fax (6252) 68331; e-mail info@iccj.org; internet www.iccj.org; f. 1947 to promote mutual respect and co-operation; holds annual international colloquium, seminars, meetings for young people and for women; maintains a forum for Jewish–Christian–Muslim relations; mems: 38 national councils world-wide; Pres. Dr DEBORAH WEISMAN; publs *ICCJ History*, *ICCJ Brochure*, conference documents.

International Council of Jewish Women: 5655 Silver Creek Valley Rd, 480 San Jose, CA 95138, USA; tel. (408) 274-8020; fax (408) 274-0807; e-mail president@icjw.org; internet www.icjw.org; f. 1912 to promote friendly relations and understanding among Jewish women throughout the world; campaigns for human and women's rights, exchanges information on community welfare activities, promotes volunteer leadership, sponsors field work in social welfare, co-sponsors the International Jewish Women's Human Rights Watch and fosters Jewish education; mems: over 2m. in 52 orgs across 47 countries; Pres. SHARON SCOTT GUSTAFSON; Sec. VERA KRONENBERG; publs *Newsletter*, *Links around the World* (2 a year, English and Spanish), *International Jewish Women's Human Rights Watch* (2 a year).

International Fellowship of Reconciliation (IFOR): Spoorstraat 38, 1815 BK Alkmaar, Netherlands; tel. (72) 512-30-14; fax (72) 515-11-02; e-mail office@ifor.org; internet www.ifor-mir.org; f. 1919; international, spiritually based movement committed to active non-violence as a way of life and as a means of building a culture of peace and non-violence; maintains over 81 branches, affiliates and groups in more than 48 countries; Pres. HANS ULRICH GERBER (Netherlands); Int. Co-ordinator FRANCESCO CANDELARI; publs *IFOR in Action* (quarterly), *Patterns in Reconciliation*(2 a year), *International Reconciliation* (3–4 times a year), *Cross the Lines* (3 a year, in Arabic, English, French, Russian and Spanish), occasional paper series.

International Humanist and Ethical Union (IHEU): 1 Gower St, London, WC1E 6HD, United Kingdom; tel. and fax (20) 7636-4797; e-mail office-iheu@iheu.org; internet www.iheu.org; f. 1952 to bring into asscn all those interested in promoting ethical and scientific humanism and human rights; mems: national orgs and individuals in 40 countries; Pres. SONJA EGGERICKX; Int. Dir BABU GOGINENI; publ. *International Humanist News* (quarterly).

International Organization for the Study of the Old Testament: Dolnicarjeva 1, 1000 Ljubljana, Slovenia; tel. (1) 4340198; fax (1) 4330405; f. 1950; holds triennial congresses (20th Congress: Helskini, Finland, Aug. 2010); publ. *Vetus Testamentum* (quarterly).

Latin American Council of Churches (Consejo Latinoamericano de Iglesias—CLAI): Casilla 17-08-8522, Calle Inglaterra N.32–113 y Mariana de Jesús, Quito, Ecuador; tel. (2) 250-4377; fax (2) 256-8373; e-mail nilton@clailatino.org; internet www.clailatino.org; f. 1982; mems: some 150 churches in 21 countries; Pres. Rev. JULIO MURRAY (Panama); Gen. Sec. Rev. NILTON GUISE (Brazil); publs *Nuevo Siglo* (monthly, in Spanish), *Latin American Ecumenical News* (quarterly), *Signos de Vida* (quarterly), other newsletters.

Latin American Episcopal Council (Consejo Episcopal Latinoamericano—CELAM): Carrera 5A 118–31, Apartado Aéreo 51086, Bogotá, Colombia; tel. (1) 5879710; fax (1) 5879117; e-mail celam@celam.org; internet www.celam.org; f. 1955 to co-ordinate Church activities in and with the Latin American and the Caribbean Catholic Bishops' Conferences; mems: 22 Episcopal Conferences of Central and South America and the Caribbean; Pres. Archbishop RAYMUNDO DAMASCENO ASSIS (Brazil); publ. *Boletín* (6 a year).

Lutheran World Federation: 150 route de Ferney, POB 2100, 1211 Geneva 2, Switzerland; tel. 227916111; fax 227916630; e-mail info@lutheranworld.org; internet www.lutheranworld.org; f. 1947; provides inter-church aid and relief work in various areas of the globe; gives service to refugees, including resettlement; carries out theological research, advocates for human rights, organizes conferences and exchanges; grants scholarship aid in various fields of church life; conducts inter-confessional dialogue and conversation with the Anglican, Baptist, Methodist, Orthodox, Reformed, Roman Catholic and Seventh-day Adventist churches; mems: 70.3m. world-wide; groups 145 Lutheran Churches in 79 countries; Pres. Rev. MUNIB A. YOUNAN (Jordan); Gen. Sec. Rev. MARTIN JUNGE (Chile); publs *Lutheran World Information* (English and German, daily e-mail news service, online and monthly print edition), *LWF Annual Report*, *LWF Documentation* (in English and German).

Middle East Council of Churches: POB 5376, Beirut, Lebanon; tel. (1) 344896; fax (1) 344894; e-mail mecc@cyberia.net.lb; internet www.mec-churches.org; f. 1974; mems: 28 churches; Pres Catholicose ARAM I, Patriarch THEOPHILOS III, Archbishop BOULOS MATAR, Rev. Dr SAFWAT AL-BAYADI; Gen. Sec. GUIRGIS IBRAHIM SALEH; publs *MECC News Report* (monthly), *Al Montada News Bulletin* (quarterly, in Arabic), *Courrier oecuménique du Moyen-Orient* (quarterly), *MECC Perspectives* (3 a year).

Muslim World League (MWL) (Rabitat al-Alam al-Islami): POB 537, Makkah, Saudi Arabia; tel. (2) 5600919; fax (2) 5601319; e-mail mymwlsite@hotmail.com; internet www.muslimworldleague.org; f. 1962; aims to advance Islamic unity and solidarity, and to promote world peace and respect for human rights; provides financial assistance for education, medical care and relief work; has 45 offices throughout the world; Sec.-Gen. Prof. Dr ABDULLAH BIN ABDUL MOHSIN AL-TURKI; publs *Al-Aalam al Islami* (weekly, Arabic), *Dawat al-Haq* (monthly, Arabic), *Muslim World League Journal* (monthly, English), *Muslim World League Journal* (quarterly, Arabic).

Opus Dei (Prelature of the Holy Cross and Opus Dei): Viale Bruno Buozzi 73, 00197 Rome, Italy; tel. (06) 808961; e-mail info@opusdei.org; internet www.opusdei.org; f. 1928 by St Josemaría Escrivá de Balaguer to spread, at every level of society, an increased awareness of the universal call to sanctity and apostolate in the exercise of one's work; mems: 87,564 Catholic laypeople and 1,996 priests; Prelate Most Rev. JAVIER ECHEVARRÍA; publ. *Romana (Bulletin of the Prelature)* (2 a year).

Pacific Conference of Churches: POB 208, 4 Thurston St, Suva, Fiji; tel. 3311277; fax 3303205; e-mail pacific@pcc.org.fj; internet www.pcc.org.fj; f. 1961; organizes assembly every five years, as well as regular workshops, meetings and training seminars throughout the region; mems: 36 churches and councils; Moderator Bishop APIMELEKI QILIHO; Gen. Sec. FE'ILOAKITAU TEVI.

Pax Romana International Catholic Movement for Intellectual and Cultural Affairs (ICMICA); and International Movement of Catholic Students (IMCS): 3 rue de Varembé, 4th Floor, POB 161, 1211 Geneva 20, Switzerland; tel. 228230707; fax 228230708; e-mail international_secretariat@paxromana.org; internet www.icmica-miic.org; f. 1921 (IMCS), 1947 (ICMICA), to encourage in members an awareness of their responsibilities as people and Christians in the student and intellectual milieux; to promote contacts between students and graduates throughout the world and co-ordinate the contribution of Catholic intellectual circles to international life; mems: 80 student and 60 intellectual orgs in 80 countries; ICMICA—Pres. JAVIER MARÍA IGUIÑIZ ECHEVERRIA (Peru); Gen. Sec. LAURENCE KWARK (France); IMCS—Pres. MEHULBHAI KANTIBHAI DABHI; Sec.-Gen. CHRISTOPHER DERIGE MALANO.

Salvation Army: International HQ, 101 Queen Victoria St, London, EC4V 4EH, United Kingdom; tel. (20) 7332-0101; fax (20) 7236-4981; e-mail ihq-website@salvationarmy.org; internet www.salvationarmy.org; f. 1865 to spread the Christian gospel and relieve poverty; emphasis for members is placed on the need for personal Christian discipleship; to enhance the effectiveness of its evangelism and non-discriminatory practical ministry it has adopted a quasi-military form of organization; social, medical, educational and emergency relief activities are also performed in the 124 countries where the Army operates; Gen. LINDA BOND; Chief of Staff Commissioner BARRY SWANSON; publs *All the World*, *Revive*, *The Officer*, *The Yearbook of the Salvation Army*, *Words of Life*, various other publs, including the Army's *Handbook of Doctrine*, are published under its Salvation Books label.

Slavic Gospel Association: 6151 Commonwealth Dr., Loves Park, IL 61111, USA; tel. (815) 282-8900; fax (815) 282-8901; e-mail info@sga.org; internet www.sga.org; f. 1934; runs Regional Ministry Centres in Belarus, Russia and Ukraine; sponsors bible and ministry training to church pastors and workers in CIS countries; provides Russian-language bibles and Christian literature; sponsors national church-planting missionaries and workers with children; Pres. Dr ROBERT W. PROVOST; publs *Insight* (monthly newsletter), *Prayer and Praise* (calendar).

Theosophical Society: Adyar, Chennai 600 020, India; tel. (44) 24912474; fax (44) 4902706; e-mail intl.hq@ts-adyar.org; internet www.ts-adyar.org; f. 1875; aims at universal brotherhood, without distinction of race, creed, sex, caste or colour; study of comparative religion, philosophy and science; investigation of unexplained laws of nature and powers latent in man; mems: 32,000 in 70 countries; Pres. RADHA S. BURNIER; Int. Sec. MARY ANDERSON; publs *The Theosophist* (monthly), *Adyar News Letter* (quarterly), *Brahmavidya* (annually), *Wake Up India* (quarterly).

Union of Councils of Soviet Jews: POB 11676, Cleveland Park, Washington, DC 20008, USA; tel. (202) 237-8262; fax (202) 237-2236; e-mail mnaftalin@ucsj.com; internet www.ucsj.com; f. 1970; supports the Jewish community in the former USSR through eight bureaux in Moscow, St Petersburg, Almatı, Bishkek, Lviv, Rīga, Tbilisi and Minsk; co-ordinates the Yad L'Yad partnership programme, linking Jewish communities in the former USSR with participating schools and synagogues in the USA; Pres. LAWRENCE LERNER; Sec. (vacant).

United Bible Societies: World Service Centre, Reading Bridge House, Reading, RG1 8PJ, United Kingdom; tel. (118) 950-0200; fax (118) 950-0857; e-mail comms@ubs-wsc.org; internet www.unitedbiblesocieties.org; f. 1946; co-ordinates the translation, production and distribution of the Bible by Bible Societies world-wide; works with national Bible Societies to develop religious programmes; mems: 145 Bible Societies in more than 200 countries; Pres. Rev. Dr Robert CUNVILLE (India); Gen. Sec. MICHAEL PERREAU (United Kingdom); publs *The Bible Translator* (quarterly), *Publishing World* (3 a year), *Prayer Booklet* (annually).

Watch Tower Bible and Tract Society: 25 Columbia Heights, Brooklyn, NY 11201–2483, USA; tel. (718) 560-5600; fax (718) 560-5619; internet www.watchtower.org; f. 1881; 98 branches; serves as legal agency for Jehovah's Witnesses; publ. *The Watchtower* (in 188 languages).

World Alliance of Reformed Churches (Presbyterian and Congregational): Box 2100, 150 route de Ferney, 1211 Geneva 2, Switzerland; tel. 227916240; fax 227916505; e-mail warc@warc.ch; internet www.warc.ch; f. 1970 by merger of WARC (Presbyterian) (f. 1875) with International Congregational Council (f. 1891) to promote fellowship among Reformed, Presbyterian and Congregational churches; mems: 216 churches in 107 countries; Pres. CLIFTON KIRKPATRICK (USA); Gen. Sec. Rev. Dr SETRI NYOMI (Ghana); publs *Reformed World* (quarterly), *Up-Date*.

World Christian Life Community: Borgo Santo Spirito 8, 00193 Rome, Italy; tel. (06) 6869844; fax (06) 68132497; e-mail exsec@cvx-clc.net; internet www.cvx-clc.net; f. 1953 as World Federation of the Sodalities of our Lady (first group f. 1563) as a lay organization based on the teachings of Ignatius Loyola, to integrate Christian faith and daily living; mems: groups in 60 countries representing about 100,000 individuals; Pres. DANIELA FRANK; Exec. Sec. FRANKLIN IBAÑEZ; publ. *Progressio* (in English, French and Spanish).

World Conference of Religions for Peace: 777 United Nations Plaza, New York, NY 10017, USA; tel. (212) 687-2163; fax (212) 983-0098; e-mail info@wcrp.org; internet www.religionsforpeace.org; f. 1970 to co-ordinate action of various world religions for world peace; mems: more than 80 inter-religious councils in Africa, Asia, Europe and Latin America; Sec.-Gen. Dr WILLIAM VENDLEY.

World Congress of Faiths: London Inter Faith Centre, 125 Salusbury Rd, London, NW6 6RG, United Kingdom; tel. (20) 8959-3129; fax (20) 7604-3052; e-mail enquiries@worldfaiths.org; internet www.worldfaiths.org; f. 1936 to promote a spirit of fellowship among mankind through an understanding of one another's religions, to bring together people of all nationalities, backgrounds and creeds in mutual respect and tolerance, to encourage the study and understanding of issues arising out of multi-faith societies, and to promote welfare and peace; sponsors lectures, conferences, retreats, etc; works with other interfaith organizations; mems: about 400; Pres. Rev. MARCUS BRAYBROOKE; Chair. Rabbi JACQUELINE TABICK; publs *Interreligious Insight* (quarterly), *One Family*.

World Evangelical Alliance: 600 Alden Rd, Suite 300, Markham, ON L3R 0E7, Canada; tel. (905) 752-2164; fax (905) 479-4742; e-mail info@worldevangelical.org; internet www.worldevangelical.org; f. 1951 as World Evangelical Fellowship, on reorganization of World Evangelical Alliance (f. 1846), reverted to original name Jan. 2002; an int. grouping of national and regional bodies of evangelical Christians; encourages the organization of national fellowships and assists national mems in planning their activities; mems: 7 regional asscns and 128 national evangelical asscns; Int. Dir GEOFF TUNNICLIFFE; publs *Evangelical World* (monthly), *Evangelical Review of Theology* (quarterly).

World Fellowship of Buddhists (WFB): 616 Benjasiri Pk, Soi Medhinivet off Soi Sukhumvit 24, Bangkok 10110, Thailand; tel. (2) 661-1284-7; fax (2) 661-0555; e-mail wfb_hq@truemail.co.th; internet www.wfb-hq.org; f. 1950 to promote strict observance and practice of the teachings of the Buddha; holds General Conference every two years; 170 regional centres in 38 countries; Pres. PHAN WANNAMETHEE; Sec.-Gen. PHALLOP THAIARRY; publs *WFB Journal* (quarterly), *WFB Review* (quarterly), *WFB Newsletter* (monthly), documents, booklets.

World Hindu Federation: POB 20418, Kathmandu, Nepal; tel. (1) 470182; fax (1) 470131; e-mail whfintl@wlink.com.np; internet www.worldhindufederation; f. 1981 to promote and preserve Hindu philosophy and culture and to protect the rights of Hindus, particularly the right to worship; executive board meets annually; mems: in 45 countries and territories; Int. Pres. HEM BAHADUR KARKI; Sec.-Gen. Dr BINOD RAJBHANDARI (Nepal); publ. *Vishwa Hindu* (monthly).

World Jewish Congress: 501 Madison Ave, New York, NY 10022, USA; tel. (212) 755-5770; fax (212) 755-5883; e-mail info@worldjewishcongress.org; internet www.worldjewishcongress.org; f. 1936 as a voluntary asscn of representative Jewish communities and organizations throughout the world; aims to foster the unity of the Jewish people and ensure the continuity and development of their heritage; mems: Jewish communities in 100 countries; Pres. RONALD LAUDER (USA); Sec.-Gen. DANIEL DIKER; publs *Dispatches*, *Jerusalem Review*, regular updates, policy studies.

World Methodist Council: International Headquarters, POB 518, Lake Junaluska, NC 28745, USA; tel. (828) 456-9432; fax (828) 456-9433; e-mail georgefreeman@mindspring.com; internet www.worldmethodistcouncil.org; f. 1881 to deepen the fellowship of the Methodist peoples, encourage evangelism, foster Methodist participation in the ecumenical movement and promote the unity of Methodist witness and service; mems: 76 churches in 132 countries, comprising 38m. individuals; Gen. Sec. GEORGE H. FREEMAN (USA); publ. *World Parish* (quarterly).

World Sephardi Federation: 13 rue Marignac, 1206 Geneva, Switzerland; tel. 223473313; fax 223472839; e-mail office@wsf.org.il; internet www.jafi.org.il/wsf; f. 1951 to strengthen the unity of Jewry and Judaism among Sephardi and Oriental Jews, to defend and foster religious and cultural activities of all Sephardi and Oriental Jewish communities and preserve their spiritual heritage, to provide moral and material assistance where necessary and to co-operate with other similar organizations; mems: 50 communities and orgs in 33 countries; Pres. NESSIM D. GAON; Sec.-Gen. AVI SHLUSH.

World Student Christian Federation (WSCF): Ecumenical Centre, POB 2100, 1211 Geneva 2, Switzerland; tel. 227916358; fax 227916152; e-mail wscf@wscf.ch; internet www.wscfglobal.org; f. 1895; aims to proclaim Jesus Christ as Lord and Saviour in the academic community, and to present students with the claims of the Christian faith over their whole life; has consultative status with the UN and advisory status at the World Council of Churches; holds General Assembly every four years; mems: more than 100 national Student Christian Movements, and 6 regional officers; Chair. HORACIO MESONES (Uruguay); Gen. Sec. CHRISTINE HOUSEL (USA).

World Union for Progressive Judaism: 13 King David St, Jerusalem 94101, Israel; tel. (2) 6203447; fax (2) 6203525; e-mail wupj@wupj.org.il; internet www.wupj.org; f. 1926; promotes and co-ordinates efforts of Reform, Liberal, Progressive and Reconstructionist congregations throughout the world; supports new congregations; assigns and employs rabbis; sponsors seminaries and schools; organizes international conferences;

maintains a youth section; mems: orgs and individuals in around 45 countries; Chair. MICHAEL GRABINER; Chief Operating Officer SHAI PINTO; publs *News Updates*, *International Conference Reports*, *European Judaism*.

World Union of Catholic Women's Organisations: 37 rue Notre-Dame-des-Champs, 75006 Paris, France; tel. 1-45-44-27-65; fax 1-42-84-04-80; e-mail wucwosecgen@gmail.com; internet www.wucwo.org; f. 1910 to promote and co-ordinate the contribution of Catholic women in international life, in social, civic, cultural and religious matters; General Assembly held every four or five years (2010: Jerusalem, Israel, in Oct.); mems: some 100 orgs representing 5m. women; Pres. MARIA GIOVANNA RUGGIERI (Italy); Sec.-Gen. LILIANE STEVENSON; publ. *Women's Voice* (quarterly, in 4 languages).

Science

Association for the Taxonomic Study of the Flora of Tropical Africa (Association pour l'Etude Taxonomique de la Flore d'Afrique Tropicale—AETFAT): c/o Herbarium, Royal Botanic Gardens, Kew, Surrey, TW9 3AR, United Kingdom; e-mail aetfat-sec@kew.org; internet www.kew.org/aetfat/index.html; f. 1951 to facilitate co-operation and liaison between botanists engaged in the study of the flora of tropical Africa south of the Sahara including Madagascar; holds Congress every three years (April 2010: Antananarivo, Madagascar); maintains a library; mems: c. 800 botanists in 63 countries; Sec.-Gen. Dr SYLVAIN RAZAFIMANDIMBISON; publs *AETFAT Bulletin* (annually), *Proceedings*.

Association of Geoscientists for International Development (AGID): c/o Geological Survey of Bangladesh, Segunbagicha, Dhaka 1000, Bangladesh; tel. (2) 8358144; e-mail afia@dhaka.agni.com; internet www.bgs.ac.uk/agid; f. 1974 to encourage communication and the exchange of knowledge between those interested in the application of the geosciences to international development; contributes to the funding of geoscience development projects; provides postgraduate scholarships; mems: 500 individual and institutional mems in 70 countries; Pres. AFIA AKHTAR (Bangladesh) (2009–12); Sec. Dr A. J. REEDMAN (United Kingdom); publ. *Geoscience and Development* (annually), *Geoscience Newsletter* (quarterly).

CIESM—The Mediterranean Science Commission (Commission internationale pour l'exploration scientifique de la mer Méditerranée): Villa Girasole, 16 blvd de Suisse, 98000 Monaco; tel. 93-30-38-79; fax 92-16-11-95; e-mail contact@ciesm.org; internet www.ciesm.org; f. 1919 for scientific exploration of the Mediterranean Sea; organizes multilateral research investigations, workshops, congresses; includes six permanent scientific committees; mems: 23 member countries, 4,300 scientists; Pres. HSH Prince ALBERT II of MONACO; Dir-Gen. Prof. FREDERIC BRIAND; publs White Papers, Congress reports.

Co-ordinating Committee for Geoscience Programmes in East and Southeast Asia (CCOP): CCOP Building, 75/10 Rama VI Rd, Phayathai, Ratchathewi, Bangkok 10400, Thailand; tel. (2) 644-5468; fax (2) 644-5429; e-mail ccopts@ccop.or.th; internet www.ccop.or.th; f. 1966 as a regional intergovernmental organization, to promote and co-ordinate geoscientific programmes concerning the exploration of mineral and hydrocarbon resources and environmentally sound coastal zone management in the offshore and coastal areas of member nations; fmrly the Co-ordinating Committee for Coastal and Offshore Geoscience Programmes in East and Southeast Asia, current name adopted in 2002; works in partnership with developed nations which have provided geologists and geophysicists as technical advisers; receives aid from co-operating countries, and other sources; mems: Cambodia, People's Republic of China, Indonesia, Japan, Republic of Korea, Malaysia, Papua New Guinea, Philippines, Singapore, Thailand, Viet Nam; Chair. Steering Cttee Dato' YUNUS ABDUL RAZAK (Malaysia); Dir Technical Secretariat Dr HE QINGCHENG (People's Republic of China); publs *CCOP Newsletter* (quarterly), *CCOP Geo-Resources E-News*, *Technical Bulletin*, *Technical Publication*, *CCOP Map Series*, *Proceedings of Annual Session*, digital dataset/CD-ROM series, other technical reports.

Council for the International Congress of Entomology: c/o CSIRO Entomology, Private Bag No 5, PO Wembley, WA 6913, Australia; e-mail james.ridsdill-smith@csiro.au; f. 1910 to act as a link between quadrennial congresses and to arrange the venue for each congress held every four years (2012: Daegou, Republic of Korea); the Council is also the entomology section of the International Union of Biological Sciences; Chair. Dr HARI SHARMA (India); Sec. JAMES RIDSDILL-SMITH (Australia).

Council of Managers of National Antarctic Programs: Private Bag 4800, Gateway Antarctica, University of Canterbury, Ilam Rd, Christchurch, New Zealand; tel. (3) 364-2273; fax (3) 364-2297; e-mail sec@comnap.aq; internet www.comnap.aq; f. 1988; brings together National Antarctic Programs, developed by signatories to the Antarctic Treaty, with the aim of developing and promoting best practice in managing the support of scientific research in Antarctica; Chair. JOSÉ RETAMALES (Chile); Exec. Sec. MICHELLE ROGAN-FINNEMORE.

European Association of Geoscientists and Engineers (EAGE): De Molen 42, POB 59, 3990 DB Houten, Netherlands; tel. (30) 6354055; fax (30) 6343524; e-mail eage@eage.org; internet www.eage.org; f. 1997 by merger of European Asscn of Exploration Geophysicists and Engineers (f. 1951) and the European Asscn of Petroleum Geoscientists and Engineers (f. 1988); these two organizations have become, respectively, the Geophysical and the Petroleum Divisions of the EAGE; aims to promote the applications of geoscience and related subjects and to foster co-operation between those working or studying in the fields; organizes conferences, workshops, education programmes and exhibitions; seeks global co-operation with organizations with similar objectives; mems: approx. 8,500 in more than 100 countries; Pres. DAVIDE CALCAGNI; Exec. Dir ANTON VAN GERWEN; publs *Geophysical Prospecting* (6 a year), *First Break* (monthly), *Petroleum Geoscience* (quarterly).

European Atomic Forum (FORATOM): 65 rue Belliard, 1040 Brussels, Belgium; tel. (2) 502-45-95; fax (2) 502-39-02; e-mail foratom@foratom.org; internet www.foratom.org; f. 1960; promotes the peaceful use of nuclear energy; provides information on nuclear energy issues to the EU, the media and the public; represents the nuclear energy industry within the EU institutions; holds periodical conferences; mems: national nuclear asscns in 17 countries; Pres. Dr RALF GÜLDNER; Dir-Gen. SANTIAGO SAN ANTONIO.

European Molecular Biology Organization (EMBO): Meyerhofstr. 1, Postfach 1022.40, 69012 Heidelberg, Germany; tel. (6221) 8891-0; fax (6221) 8891-200; e-mail embo@embo.org; internet www.embo.org; f. 1962 to promote collaboration in the field of molecular biology and to establish fellowships for training and research; has established the European Molecular Biology Laboratory where a majority of the disciplines comprising the subject are represented; mems: 1,300 elected mems in Europe, 80 assoc. mems world-wide; Dir HERMANN BUJARD; publs *Annual Report*, *The EMBO Journal* (24 a year), *EMBO Reports* (monthly), *EMBO Molecular Medicine*, *Molecular Systems Biology*, *EMBO Encounters*.

European Organization for Nuclear Research (CERN): 1211 Geneva 23, Switzerland; tel. 227676111; fax 227676555; e-mail press.office@cern.ch; internet www.cern.ch; f. 1954 to provide for collaboration among European states in nuclear research of a pure scientific and fundamental character, for peaceful purposes only; Council comprises two representatives of each member state; major experimental facilities: Proton Synchrotron (of 25–28 GeV), Super Proton Synchrotron (of 450 GeV), and LHC (of 14 TeV); mems: 20 European countries; observers: India, Japan, Russia, Turkey, USA, European Commission, UNESCO; Dir-Gen. ROLF-DIETER HEUER; publs *CERN Courier* (monthly), *Annual Report*, *Scientific Reports*.

European-Mediterranean Seismological Centre (EMSC): c/o CEA, Bt. Sâbles Centre DAM, Ile de France, Bruyères le Châtel, 91297 Arpajon Cedex, France; fax 1-69-26-70-00; e-mail contact@emsc-csem.org; internet www.emsc-csem.org; f. 1976 for rapid determination of seismic hypocentres in the region; maintains database; mems: institutions in 45 countries; Pres. CHRIS BROWITT (United Kingdom); Sec.-Gen. RÉMY BOSSU (France); publ. *Newsletter* (2 a year).

Federation of Asian Scientific Academies and Societies (FASAS): c/o Australian Academy of Science, POB 783,

Canberra ACT 2601, Australia; tel. (2) 6201-9456; fax (2) 6201-9494; e-mail fasas@science.org.au; internet www.fasas.org.au; f. 1984 to stimulate regional co-operation and promote national and regional self-reliance in science and technology, by organizing meetings, training and research programmes and encouraging the exchange of scientists and of scientific information; mems: 16 national scientific academies and societies from Afghanistan, Australia, Bangladesh, People's Republic of China, India, Republic of Korea, Malaysia, Nepal, New Zealand, Pakistan, Philippines, Singapore, Sri Lanka, Thailand; Pres. Tan Sri Datuk Dr OMAR ABDUL RAHMAN (Malaysia); Sec. Dato' IR LEE YEE CHEONG (Malaysia).

Federation of European Biochemical Societies: c/o Dept of Immunology, The Weizmann Institute of Science, POB 26, Rehovot 76100, Israel; tel. (8) 9344019; fax (8) 9465264; e-mail febs@weizmann.ac.il; internet www.febs.org; f. 1964 to promote the science of biochemistry through meetings of European biochemists, advanced courses and the provision of fellowships; mems: approx. 40,000 in 36 societies; Chair. Prof. WINNIE ESKILD (Norway); Sec.-Gen. ISRAEL PECHT (Israel); publs *The FEBS Journal*, *FEBS News*, *FEBS Letters*, *FEBS Newsletter*.

Foundation for International Scientific Co-ordination (Fondation 'Pour la science', Centre international de synthèse): Caphés-CNRS ENS, 45 rue d'Ulm, 75005 Paris, France; tel. 1-44-32-26-54; fax 1-44-32-26-56; e-mail revuedesynthese@ens.fr; internet www.ehess.fr/acta/synthese; f. 1925; Dir ERIC BRIAN; publs *Revue de Synthèse*, *Revue d'Histoire des Sciences*, *Semaines de Synthèse*, *L'Evolution de l'Humanité*.

Institute of General Semantics: 3000 A Landers St, Fort Worth, TX 76107, USA; tel. (817) 922-9950; fax (817) 922-9903; e-mail isgs@time-binding.org; internet time-binding.org; f. 1943 as the International Society for General Semantics to advance knowledge of and inquiry into non-Aristotelian systems and general semantics; merged with Institute of General Semantics (f. 1938) in 2004; mems: approx. 700 (100 int.); Pres. MARTIN H. LEVINSON (USA); Exec. Dir LANCE STRATE (USA).

Intergovernmental Oceanographic Commission: UNESCO, 1 rue Miollis, 75732 Paris Cedex 15, France; tel. 1-45-68-39-84; fax 1-45-68-58-12; e-mail ioc.secretariat@unesco.org; internet ioc.unesco.org; f. 1960 to promote scientific investigation of the nature and resources of the oceans through the concerted action of its members; mems: 129 govts; Chair. JAVIER A. VALLADARES (Argentina); Exec. Sec. WENDY WATSON-WRIGHT; publs *IOC Technical Series* (irregular), IOC *Manuals* and *Guides* (irregular), *IOC Workshop Reports* (irregular) and *IOC Training Course Reports* (irregular), annual reports.

International Academy of Astronautics (IAA): 6 rue Galilee, POB 1268-16, 75766 Paris Cedex 16, France; tel. 1-47-23-82-15; fax 1-47-23-82-16; e-mail sgeneral@iaamail.org; internet iaaweb.org; f. 1960; fosters the development of astronautics for peaceful purposes, holds scientific meetings and makes scientific studies, reports, awards and book awards; maintains 19 scientific cttees and a multilingual terminology database (20 languages); mems: 1,213 active mems, 5 hon. mems, in 75 countries; Pres. Dr MADHAVAN G. NAIR (India); Sec.-Gen. Dr JEAN-MICHEL CONTANT (France); publ. *Acta Astronautica* (monthly).

International Association for Biologicals (IABS): 79 ave Louis-Casaï, 1216 Geneva, Switzerland; tel. 223011036; fax 223011037; e-mail iabs@iabs.org; internet www.iabs.org; f. 1955 to connect producers and controllers of immunological products (sera, vaccines, etc.), for the study and development of methods of standardization; supports international organizations in their efforts to solve problems of standardization; mems: c. 400; Pres. and Sec. DANIEL GAUDRY (France); publs *Newsletter* (quarterly), *Biologicals* (6 a year).

International Association for Earthquake Engineering: Ken chiku-kaikan Bldg, 3rd Floor, 5-26-20, Shiba, Minato-ku, Tokyo 108-0014, Japan; tel. (3) 3453-1281; fax (3) 3453-0428; e-mail secretary@iaee.or.jp; internet www.iaee.or.jp; f. 1963 to promote international co-operation among scientists and engineers in the field of earthquake engineering through exchange of knowledge, ideas and results of research and practical experience; mems: national cttees in 49 countries; Pres. Prof. POLAT GÜLKAN (Turkey); Sec.-Gen. MANABU YOSHIMURA (Japan).

International Association for Ecology (INTECOL): c/o College of Forest Science, Department of Forest Resources, Kookmin University, Songbuk-gu, Seoul 136-702, Republic of Korea; tel. (10) 3785-4814; fax (2) 910-4809; e-mail kimeuns@kookmin.ac.kr; internet www.intecol.org; f. 1967 to provide opportunities for communication among ecologists world-wide; to co-operate with organizations and individuals having related aims and interests; to encourage studies in the different fields of ecology; affiliated to the International Union of Biological Sciences; mems: 35 national and international ecological societies, and 2,000 individuals; Pres. ALAN COVICH (USA); Sec.-Gen. EUN-SHIK KIM (Republic of Korea).

International Association for Mathematical Geology (IAMG): 5868 Westheimer Rd. Suite 537, Houston, TX 77057, USA; tel. (832) 380-8833; e-mail office@iamg.org; internet www.iamg.org; f. 1968 for the preparation and elaboration of mathematical models of geological processes; the introduction of mathematical methods in geological sciences and technology; assistance in the development of mathematical investigation in geological sciences; the organization of international collaboration in mathematical geology through various forums and publications; educational programmes for mathematical geology; affiliated to the International Union of Geological Sciences; mems: c. 600; Pres. VERA PAWLOWSKY GLAHN (Spain); Sec.-Gen. DANIEL M. TETZLAFF (USA); publs *Mathematical Geology* (8 a year), *Computers and Geosciences* (10 a year), *Natural Resources Research* (quarterly), *Newsletter* (2 a year).

International Association for Mathematics and Computers in Simulation: c/o Free University of Brussels, Automatic Control, CP 165/84, 50 ave F. D. Roosevelt, 1050 Brussels, Belgium; tel. (2) 650-20-85; fax (2) 650-45-34; e-mail Robert.Beauwens@ulb.ac.be; internet www.research.rutgers.edu/~imacs/; f. 1955 to further the study of mathematical tools and computer software and hardware, analogue, digital or hybrid computers for simulation of soft or hard systems; mems: 1,100 and 27 assoc. mems; Pres. ROBERT BEAUWENS (Belgium); Treas. ERNEST H. MUND; publs *Mathematics and Computers in Simulation* (6 a year), *Applied Numerical Mathematics* (6 a year), *Journal of Computational Acoustics*.

International Association for Plant Physiology (IAPP): c/o Dr D. Graham, Div. of Food Science and Technology, CSIRO, POB 52, North Ryde, NSW, Australia 2113; tel. (2) 9490-8333; fax (2) 9490-3107; e-mail douglasgraham@dfst.csiro.au; f. 1955 to promote the development of plant physiology at the international level through congresses, symposia and workshops, by maintaining communication with national societies and by encouraging interaction between plant physiologists in developing and developed countries; affiliated to the International Union of Biological Sciences; Pres. Prof. S. MIYACHI; Sec.-Treas. Dr D. GRAHAM.

International Association for Plant Taxonomy (IAPT): Institute of Botany, University of Vienna, Rennweg 14, 1030 Vienna, Austria; tel. (1) 4277-54098; fax (1) 4277-54099; e-mail office@iapt-taxon.org; internet www.botanik.univie.ac.at/iapt; f. 1950 to promote the development of plant taxonomy and encourage contacts between people and institutes interested in this work; maintains the International Bureau for Plant Taxonomy and Nomenclature; affiliated to the International Union of Biological Sciences; mems: institutes and individuals in 85 countries; Exec. Sec. Dr ALESSANDRA RICCIUTI LAMONEA; publs *Taxon* (quarterly), *Regnum vegetabile* (irregular).

International Association for the Physical Sciences of the Oceans (IAPSO): Johan Rodhe, POB 460, 40530 Göteborg, Sweden; e-mail johan.rodhe@gu.se; internet iapso.iugg.org; f. 1919 to promote the study of scientific problems relating to the oceans and interactions occurring at its boundaries, chiefly in so far as such study may be carried out by the aid of mathematics, physics and chemistry; to initiate, facilitate and co-ordinate oceanic research; and to provide for discussion, comparison and publication; affiliated to the International Union of Geodesy and Geophysics (IUGG); mems: 65 states; Pres. Dr EUGENE MOROZOV; Sec.-Gen. Prof JOHAN RODHE (Sweden).

International Association of Botanic Gardens (IABG): c/o Prof. J. E. Hernández-Bermejo, Córdoba Botanic Garden, Apdo 3048, 14071 Córdoba, Spain; tel. (957) 200355; fax (957) 295333; e-mail jardinbotcord@retemail.es; internet www.bgci

.org/global/iabg; f. 1954 to promote co-operation between scientific collections of living plants, including the exchange of information and specimens; to promote the study of the taxonomy of cultivated plants; and to encourage the conservation of rare plants and their habitats; affiliated to the International Union of Biological Sciences; Pres. Prof. HE SHANAN (People's Republic of China); Sec. Prof. J. ESTEBAN HERNÁNDEZ-BERMEJO (Spain).

International Association of Geodesy: Deutsches Geodaetisches Forschungsinstitut (DGFI), Alfons-Goppel-Str. 11, 80539 Munich, Germany; tel. (89) 23031-1107; fax (89) 23031-1240; e-mail iag@dgfi.badw.de; internet www.iag-aig.org; f. 1922 to promote the study of all scientific problems of geodesy and encourage geodetic research; to promote and co-ordinate international co-operation in this field; to publish results; affiliated to the International Union of Geodesy and Geophysics; mems: national cttees in 73 countries; Pres. MICHAEL SIDERIS (Canada); Sec.-Gen. HERMANN DREWES (Germany); publs *Journal of Geodesy*, *Travaux de l'AIG*.

International Association of Geomagnetism and Aeronomy (IAGA): c/o Mioara Mandea, 50 blvd St Marcel, 75005 Paris, France; tel. 1-57-27-84-84; fax 1-57-27-84-82; e-mail iaga_sg@gfz-potsdam.de; f. 1919 for the study of questions relating to geomagnetism and aeronomy and the encouragement of research; holds General and Scientific Assemblies every two years; affiliated to the International Union of Geodesy and Geophysics; mems: countries that adhere to the IUGG; Pres. EIGEL FRIIS-CHRISTENSEN (Denmark); Sec.-Gen. MIOARA MANDEA (France); publs *IAGA Bulletin*, *IAGA News*, *IAGA Guides*.

International Association of Hydrological Sciences: Agrocampus Ouest, 65 rue de Saint-Brieuc, 35042 Rennes, France; tel. 2-23-48-55-58; e-mail cudennec@agrocampus-ouest.fr; internet iahs.info; f. 1922 to promote co-operation in the study of hydrology and water resources; Pres. Prof. GORDON YOUNG (Canada); Sec.-Gen. Prof. CHRISTOPHE CUDENNEC (France).

International Association of Meteorology and Atmospheric Sciences (IAMAS): Institut für Physik der Atmosphäre (IPA), Deutsches Zentrum für Luft und Raumfahrt, DLR-Oberpfaffenhofen, 82234 Wessling, Germany; tel. (8153) 282570; fax (8153) 281841; e-mail Hans.Volkert@dlr.de; internet www.iamas.org; f. 1919; maintains permanent commissions on atmospheric ozone, radiation, atmospheric chemistry and global pollution, dynamic meteorology, polar meteorology, clouds and precipitation, climate, atmospheric electricity, planetary atmospheres and their evolution, and meteorology of the upper atmosphere; holds general assemblies every four years, special assemblies between general assemblies; affiliated to the International Union of Geodesy and Geophysics; Pres. Dr GUOXIONG WU (People's Republic of China); Sec.-Gen. Dr HANS VOLKERT (Germany).

International Association of Sedimentologists: c/o Prof. Vincenzo Pascucci, Dipartimento di Scienze Botaniche, Ecologiche e Geologiche, Università di Sassari, Via Piandanna 4, Sassari, Italy; tel. (079) 228685; fax (079) 233600; e-mail pascucci@uniss.it; internet www.sedimentologists.org; f. 1952; affiliated to the International Union of Geological Sciences; mems: 2,200; Pres. POPPE DE BOER (Netherlands); Gen. Sec. VINCENZO PASCUCCI (Italy); publ. *Sedimentology* (every 2 months).

International Association of Volcanology and Chemistry of the Earth's Interior (IAVCEI): Institute of Earth Sciences 'Jaume Almera', CSIC, Lluis Sole Sabaris s/n, 08028 Barcelona, Spain; tel. (93) 4095410; fax (93) 4110012; e-mail joan.marti@ictja.csic.es; internet www.iavcei.org; f. 1919 to examine scientifically all aspects of volcanology; affiliated to the International Union of Geodesy and Geophysics; Pres. Prof. RAY CAS (Australia); Sec.-Gen. Prof. JOAN MARTI (Spain); publs *Bulletin of Volcanology*, *Catalogue of the Active Volcanoes of the World*, *Proceedings in Volcanology*.

International Association of Wood Anatomists: c/o Netherlands Centre for Biodiversity Naturalis, POB 9514, 2300 RA Leiden, Netherlands; tel. (71) 5273570; e-mail lens@nhn.leidenuniv.nl; internet www.iawa-website.org; f. 1931 for the purpose of study, documentation and exchange of information on the structure of wood; holds annual conference; mems: 650 in 68 countries; Exec. Sec. FREDERIC LENS; publ. *IAWA Journal*.

International Astronautical Federation (IAF): 94 bis ave du Suffren, 75015 Paris, France; tel. 1-45-67-42-60; fax 1-42-73-21-20; e-mail secretariat.iaf@iafastro.org; internet www.iafastro.org; f. 1950; fosters the development of astronautics for peaceful purposes at national and international levels, encourages the advancement of knowledge about space and the development and application of space assets for the benefit of humanity; organizes an annual International Astronautical Congress in conjunction with its associates, the International Academy of Astronautics (IAA) and the International Institute of Space Law (IISL); mems: 227; Pres. BERNDT FEUERBACHER; Exec. Dir CHRISTIAN FEICHTINGER.

International Astronomical Union (IAU): 98 bis blvd d'Arago, 75014 Paris, France; tel. 1-43-25-83-58; fax 1-43-25-26-16; e-mail iau@iap.fr; internet www.iau.org; f. 1919 to facilitate co-operation between the astronomers of various countries and to further the study of astronomy in all its branches; organizes colloquia every two months; mems: orgs in 65 countries, and 9,000 individual mems; Pres. ROBERT WILLIAMS (USA); Gen. Sec. IAN F. CORBETT; publs *IAU Information Bulletin* (2 a year), *Symposia Series* (6 a year), *Highlights* (every 3 years).

International Biometric Society: International Business Office, 1444 I St, NW, Suite 700, Washington, DC 20005, USA; tel. (202) 712-9049; fax (202) 216-9646; e-mail ibs@tibs.org; internet www.tibs.org; f. 1947 for the advancement of quantitative biological science through the development of quantitative theories and the application, development and dissemination of effective mathematical and statistical techniques; the Society has 16 regional organizations and 17 national groups, is affiliated with the International Statistical Institute and WHO, and constitutes the Section of Biometry of the International Union of Biological Sciences; mems: over 6,000 in more than 70 countries; Pres. KAYE E. BASFORD; Exec. Dir DEE ANN WALKER; publs *Biometrics* (quarterly), *Biometric Bulletin* (quarterly), *Journal of Agricultural, Biological and Environmental Statistics* (quarterly).

International Botanical Congress: c/o Congress Secretariat, ICMS Australasia, GPO Box 5005, Melbourne, Victoria 3205, Australia; tel. (3) 9682-0500; fax (3) 9682-0344; e-mail info@ibc2011.com; internet www.ibc2011.com; f. 1864 to inform botanists of recent progress in the plant sciences; the Nomenclature Section of the Congress attempts to provide a uniform terminology and methodology for the naming of plants; other Divisions deal with developmental, metabolic, structural, systematic and evolutionary, ecological botany; genetics and plant breeding; 2011 Congress: Melbourne, Australia; affiliated to the International Union of Biological Sciences; Pres. Dr JUDY WEST; Sec.-Gen. KAREN WILSON.

International Bureau of Weights and Measures (Bureau international des poids et mesures—BIPM): Pavillon de Breteuil, 92312 Sèvres Cedex, France; tel. 1-45-07-70-70; fax 1-45-34-20-21; e-mail info@bipm.org; internet www.bipm.org; f. 1875; works to ensure the international unification of measurements and their traceability to the International System of Unification; carries out research and calibration; organizes international comparisons of national measurement standards; mems: 51 member states and 10 associates; Pres. J. KOVALEVSKY (France); Prof. A. J. WALLARD; publs *Le Système International d'Unités* (in English and French), *Metrologia* (6 a year), scientific articles, reports and monographs, committee reports.

International Cartographic Association (ICA) (Association Cartographique Internationale—ACI): c/o Eotvos University, Dept of Cartography and Geoinformatics, H-1117 Budapest, Pazmany Peter setany 1/A, Hungary; tel. (1) 372-2975; fax (1) 372-2951; e-mail lzentai@caesar.elte.hu; internet www.icaci.org; f. 1959 for the advancement, instigation and co-ordination of cartographic research involving co-operation between different nations; particularly concerned with furtherance of training in cartography, study of source material, compilation, graphic design, digital presentation of maps as artefacts communicating geographic information; organizes international conferences, symposia, meetings, exhibitions; mems: 80 countries; Pres. GEORG GARTNER (Austria); Sec.-Gen./Treas. LASZLO ZENTAI (Hungary); publ. *ICA Newsletter* (2 a year).

International Centre of Insect Physiology and Ecology: POB 30772-00100, Nairobi, Kenya; tel. (20) 8632000; fax (20) 8632001; e-mail icipe@icipe.org; internet www.icipe.org; f. 1970; aims to alleviate poverty, ensure food security and improve the overall health status of peoples of the tropics through developing and extending tools and strategies for managing harmful and useful arthropods, while preserving the natural resource base through research and capacity building; Dir-Gen. Prof. CHRISTIAN BORGEMEISTER (Germany); publs *International Journal of Tropical Insect Science* (quarterly), *Biennial Report*, training manuals, technical bulletins, newsletter.

International Commission for Optics (ICO): c/o Angela M. Guzman, Physics Dept, Florida Atlantic University, 777 Glades Rd, Boca Raton, FL 33431, USA; tel. (561) 297-1310; fax (561) 297-2662; e-mail angela.guzman@fau.edu; internet www.ico-optics.org; f. 1948; aims to contribute, on an international basis, to the progress and diffusion of knowledge in the field of optics; co-ordinates the dissemination and advancement of scientific and technical knowledge relating to optics; holds Gen. Assembly every three years; mems: cttees in 52 territories, and 6 int. societies; Pres. Prof. MARIA L. CALVO (Spain); Sec.-Gen. Prof. ANGELA M. GUZMAN; publ. *ICO Newsletter*.

International Commission for Plant-Bee Relationships (ICPBR): Hassellstr. 23, 29223 Celle, Germany; e-mail icpbr@uoguelph.ca; internet www.uoguelph.ca/icpbr; f. 1950 to promote research and its application in the field of bee botany, and collect and spread information; to organize meetings, etc., and collaborate with scientific organizations; affiliated to the International Union of Biological Sciences; mems: 240 in 41 countries; Pres. Dr PETER KEVAN; Sec. Dr JOB VAN PRAAGH.

International Commission on Physics Education: e-mail elm@physics.unoquelph.ca; internet web.phys.ksu.edu/icpe/; f. 1960 to encourage and develop international collaboration in the improvement and extension of the methods and scope of physics education at all levels; collaborates with UNESCO and organizes international conferences; mems: appointed triennially by the International Union of Pure and Applied Physics; Chair. PRATIBHA JOLLY; Sec. DEAN ZOLLMAN.

International Commission on Radiation Units and Measurements, Inc (ICRU): 7910 Woodmont Ave, Suite 400, Bethesda, MD 20814-3095, USA; tel. (301) 657-2652; fax (301) 907-8768; e-mail icru@icru.org; internet www.icru.org; f. 1925 to develop internationally acceptable recommendations regarding: quantities and units of radiation and radioactivity, procedures suitable for the measurement and application of these quantities in clinical radiology and radiobiology, and physical data needed in the application of these procedures; makes recommendations on quantities and units for radiation protection; mems: from about 18 countries; Chair. HANS-GEORG MENZEL (acting); Exec. Sec. PATRICIA RUSSELL; publs reports.

International Commission on Zoological Nomenclature: c/o Natural History Museum, Cromwell Rd, London, SW7 5BD, United Kingdom; tel. (20) 7942-5653; e-mail iczn@nhm.ac.uk; internet www.iczn.org; f. 1895; has judicial powers to determine all matters relating to the interpretation of the International Code of Zoological Nomenclature and also plenary powers to suspend the operation of the Code where the strict application of the Code would lead to confusion and instability of nomenclature; also responsible for maintaining and developing the Official Lists and Official Indexes of Names and Works in Zoology; affiliated to the International Union of Biological Sciences; Pres. Dr JAN VAN TOL (Netherlands); Exec. Sec. Dr ELLINOR MICHEL (United Kingdom); publs *Bulletin of Zoological Nomenclature* (quarterly), *International Code of Zoological Nomenclature*, *Official Lists and Indexes of Names and Works in Zoology*, *Towards Stability in the Names of Animals*.

International Council for Science (ICSU): 5 rue Auguste Vacquerie, 75116 Paris, France; tel. 1-45-25-03-29; fax 1-42-88-94-31; e-mail secretariat@icsu.org; internet www.icsu.org; f. 1919 as International Research Council; present name adopted 1998; revised statutes adopted 2011; incorporates national scientific bodies and International Scientific Unions, as well as 19 Interdisciplinary Bodies (international scientific networks established to address specific areas of investigation); through its global network co-ordinates interdisciplinary research to address major issues of relevance to both science and society; advocates for freedom in the conduct of science, promotes equitable access to scientific data and information, and facilitates science education and capacity-building; General Assembly of representatives of national and scientific members meets every three years to formulate policy. Interdisciplinary Bodies and Joint Initiatives: Future Earth; Urban Health and Well-being; Committee on Space Research (COSPAR); Scientific Committee on Antarctic Research (SCAR); Scientific Committee on Oceanic Research (SCOR); Scientific Committee on Solar-Terrestrial Physics (SCOSTEP); Integrated Research on Disaster Risk (IRDR); Programme on Ecosystem Change and Society (PECS); DIVERSITAS; International Geosphere-Biosphere Programme (IGBP); International Human Dimensions Programme on Global Environmental Change (IHDP); World Climate Research Programme (WCRP); Global Climate Observing System (GCOS); Global Ocean Observing System (GOOS); Global Terrestrial Observing System (GTOS); Committee on Data for Science and Technology (CODATA); International Network for the Availability of Scientific Publications (INASP); Scientific Committee on Frequency Allocations for Radio Astronomy and Space Science (IUCAF); World Data System (WDS); mems: 120 national mems from 140 countries, 31 Int. Scientific Unions; Pres. LEE YUAN-TSEH (Taiwan); publs *Insight* (quarterly), *Annual Report*.

International Council for Scientific and Technical Information: 5 rue Ambroise Thomas, 75009 Paris, France; tel. 1-45-25-65-92; fax 1-42-15-12-62; e-mail icsti@icsti.org; internet www.icsti.org; f. 1984 as the successor to the International Council of Scientific Unions Abstracting Board (f. 1952); aims to increase accessibility to scientific and technical information; fosters communication and interaction among all participants in the information transfer chain; mems: 48 orgs; Pres. ROBERTA SHAFFER (USA); Gen. Sec. WENDY WARR (United Kingdom).

International Council for the Exploration of the Sea (ICES): H. C. Andersens Blvd 44–46, 1553 Copenhagen V, Denmark; tel. 33-38-67-00; fax 33-93-42-15; e-mail info@ices.dk; internet www.ices.dk; f. 1902 to encourage and facilitate research on the utilization and conservation of living resources and the environment in the North Atlantic Ocean and its adjacent seas; publishes and disseminates results of research; advises member countries and regulatory commissions; mems: 20 mem. countries, 5 affiliated institutes, 2 non-governmental orgs with observer status; Pres. MICHAEL SINCLAIR; Gen. Sec. ANNE CHRISTINE BRUSENDORFF; publs *ICES Journal of Marine Science*, *ICES Marine Science Symposia*, *ICES Fisheries Statistics*, *ICES Cooperative Research Reports*, *ICES Insight*, *ICES Techniques in Marine Environmental Sciences*, *ICES Identification Leaflets for Plankton*, *ICES Identification Leaflets for Diseases and Parasites of Fish and Shellfish*.

International Council of Psychologists: c/o Life Sq, Teshirogi A-101Matsushiro, 4-9-10 Tsukuba Science City, 305-0035 Japan; e-mail neditt33@yahoo.com; internet icpweb.org; f. 1941 to advance psychology and the application of its scientific findings throughout the world; holds annual conventions; mems: 1,200 qualified psychologists; Pres. ANN O'ROARK (USA); Sec.-Gen. Dr EDIT NAGY-TANAKA (Japan); publs *International Psychologist* (quarterly), *World Psychology* (quarterly).

International Council of the Aeronautical Sciences: c/o FOI, SE-16490 Stockholm, Sweden; tel. (8) 55503151; e-mail secr.exec@icas.org; internet www.icas.org; f. 1957 to encourage free interchange of information on aeronautical science and technology; holds biennial Congresses (2012: Brisbane, Australia; 2014: St Petersburg, Russia); mems: national asscns in more than 30 countries; Pres. IAN POLL (United Kingdom); Exec. Sec. ANDERS GUSTAFSSON (Sweden).

International Earth Rotation and Reference Systems Service: Central Bureau, c/o Bundesamt für Kartographie und Geodäsie (BKG), Richard-Strauss-Allee 11, 60598 Frankfurt am Main, Germany; tel. (69) 6333273; fax (69) 6333425; e-mail central_bureau@iers.org; internet www.iers.org; f. 1988 (fmrly International Polar Motion Service and Bureau International de l'Heure); maintained by the International Astronomical Union and the International Union of Geodesy and Geophysics; defines and maintains the international terrestrial and celestial reference systems; determines earth orientation parameters (terrestrial and celestial co-ordinates of the pole and universal time) connecting these systems; monitors global geophysical fluids; organizes collection, analysis and dissemination of data; Chair. of Directing Bd Prof. CHOPO MA; Dir BERND RICHTER (Germany).

International Federation of Cell Biology (IFCB): c/o Dr Denys Wheatley, Leggat House, Keithhall, Inverurie, Aberdeen, AB51 0LX, United Kingdom; tel. and fax (1467) 670280; e-mail wheatley@abdn.ac.uk; internet www.ifcbiol.org; f. 1972 to foster international co-operation, and organize conferences; mems: some 30 full member societies, 20 associated and affiliated societies; Pres. Prof. DENYS WHEATLEY (United Kingdom); Sec.-Gen. Prof. HERNANDES CARVALHO (Brazil); publs *Cell Biology International* (monthly), reports.

International Federation of Operational Research Societies (IFORS): c/o Mary Magrogan, 7240 Parkway Drive, Suite 300 Hanover, MD 21076, USA; tel. (443) 757-3534; fax (443) 757-3535; e-mail secretary@ifors.org; internet www.ifors.org; f. 1959 for development of operational research as a unified science and its advancement in all nations of the world; mems: c. 30,000 individuals, 48 national societies, 5 kindred societies; Pres. DOMINIQUE DE WERRA; Sec. MARY MAGROGAN; publs *International Abstracts in Operational Research, IFORS News, International Transactions in Operational Research.*

International Federation of Societies for Microscopy (IFSM): c/o Centre for Microscopy and Microanalysis, University of Western Australia, 35 Stirling Hwy, Perth, WA 6008, Australia; tel. (8) 6488-2739; fax (8) 6488-1087; e-mail bjg@cmm.uwa.edu.au; internet www.ifsm.uconn.edu; f. 1955 to contribute to the advancement of all aspects of electron microscopy; promotes and co-ordinates research; sponsors meetings and conferences; holds International Congress every four years; mems: representative orgs of 40 countries; Pres. Prof. C. BARRY CARTER (USA); Gen. Sec. BRENDAN GRIFFIN (Australia).

International Food Information Service (IFIS): Lane End House, Shinfield Rd, Shinfield, Reading, RG2 9BB, United Kingdom; tel. (118) 988-3895; fax (118) 988-5065; e-mail ifis@ifis.org; internet www.ifis.org; f. 1968; board of governors comprises two members each from CAB-International (United Kingdom), Bundesministerium für Landwirtschaft, Ernährung und Forsten (represented by Deutsche Landwirtschafts-Gesellschaft e.V.) (Germany), and the Institute of Food Technologists (USA); collects and disseminates information on all disciplines relevant to food science, food technology and nutrition; Man. Dir RICHARD HOLLINGSWORTH; publ. *Food Science and Technology Abstracts* (monthly, also available online).

International Foundation of the High-Altitude Research Stations Jungfraujoch and Gornergrat: Sidlerstr. 5, 3012 Bern, Switzerland; tel. 316314052; fax 316314405; e-mail louise.wilson@space.unibe.ch; internet www.ifjungo.ch; f. 1931; international research centre which enables scientists from many scientific fields to carry out experiments at high altitudes. Six countries contribute to support the station: Austria, Belgium, Germany, Italy, Switzerland, United Kingdom; Pres. Dr ERWIN FLÜCKIGER; Dir Prof. MARKUS LEUENBERGER.

International Geographical Union (IGU): University of Cape Town, Department of Geographical and Environmental Science, Rondebosch 7701, South Africa; tel. (21) 6502873; fax (21) 6503456; e-mail mmeadows@mweb.co.za; internet www.igu-net.org; f. 1922 to encourage the study of problems relating to geography, to promote and co-ordinate research requiring international co-operation, and to organize international congresses and commissions; mems: 83 countries, 11 associates; Pres. RONALD F. ABLER (USA); Sec.-Gen. Prof. MICHAEL MEADOWS (South Africa); publ. *IGU Bulletin* (annually).

International Glaciological Society: Scott Polar Research Institute, Lensfield Rd, Cambridge, CB2 1ER, United Kingdom; tel. (1223) 355974; fax (1223) 354931; e-mail igsoc@igsoc.org; internet www.igsoc.org; f. 1936; aims to stimulate interest in and encourage research into the scientific and technical problems associated with snow and ice; mems: 850 in 30 countries; Pres. Dr ERIC BRUN; Sec.-Gen. MAGNÚS MÁR MAGNÚSSON; publs *Journal of Glaciology* (3 a year), *ICE* (News Bulletin, 3 a year), *Annals of Glaciology*.

International Hydrographic Organization (IHO): 4 quai Antoine 1er, BP 445, 98000 Monaco; tel. 93-10-81-00; fax 93-10-81-40; e-mail info@ihb.mc; internet www.iho.int; f. 1921 to link the hydrographic offices of member governments and co-ordinate their work, with a view to rendering navigation easier and safer; seeks to obtain, as far as possible, uniformity in charts and hydrographic documents; fosters the development of electronic chart navigation; encourages adoption of the best methods of conducting hydrographic surveys; encourages surveying in those parts of the world where accurate charts are lacking; provides IHO Data Centre for Digital Bathymetry; and organizes quinquennial conference; mems: 80 states; Directing Committee: Pres. Vice Adm. A. MARATOS (Greece); Dirs Capt. R. WARD (Australia), Capt. H. GORZIGLIA (Chile); publs *International Hydrographic Bulletin, IHO Yearbook*, other documents (available on the IHO website).

International Institute of Refrigeration: 177 blvd Malesherbes, 75017 Paris, France; tel. 1-42-27-32-35; fax 1-47-63-17-98; e-mail iif-iir@iifiir.org; internet www.iifiir.org; f. 1908 to further the science of refrigeration and its applications on a world-wide scale; to investigate, discuss and recommend any aspects leading to improvements in the field of refrigeration; mems: 60 nat., 1,200 associates; Pres. Prof. E. JOACHIM PAUL; Dir DIDIER COULOMB (France); publs *International Journal of Refrigeration* (8 a year), *Newsletter* (quarterly), books, proceedings, recommendations.

International Mathematical Union (IMU): Markgrafenstr. 32, 10117 Berlin, Germany; fax (30) 20372-439; e-mail office@mathunion.org; internet www.mathunion.org; f. 1952 to support and assist the International Congress of Mathematicians and other international scientific meetings or conferences and to encourage and support other international mathematical activities considered likely to contribute to the development of mathematical science—pure, applied or educational; mems: 78 countries; Pres. INGRID DAUBECHIES (USA); Sec.-Gen. MARTIN GRÖTSCHEL (Germany); publ. *IMU-Net Newsletter.*

International Mineralogical Association: c/o Robert Downs, Dept of Geosciences, Gould-Simpson Bldg 522, University of Arizona, 1040 E 4th St. Tucson, AZ 8572-10077, USA; tel. (520) 626-8092; fax (520) 621-2672; e-mail downs@geo.arizona.edu; internet www.ima-mineralogy.org; f. 1958 to further international co-operation in the science of mineralogy; affiliated to the International Union of Geological Sciences; mems: national societies in 39 countries; Pres. Prof. EKKEHART TILLMANNS (Austria); Sec. RICHARD GÖD.

International Organization of Legal Metrology: 11 rue Turgot, 75009 Paris, France; tel. 1-48-78-12-82; fax 1-42-82-17-27; e-mail biml@oiml.org; internet www.oiml.org; f. 1955 to serve as documentation and information centre on the verification, checking, construction and use of measuring instruments, to determine characteristics and standards to which measuring instruments must conform for their use to be recommended internationally, and to determine the general principles of legal metrology; mems: govts of 59 countries; Pres. ALAN E. JOHNSTON (Canada); Dir JEAN-FRANÇOIS MAGAÑA; publ. *Bulletin* (quarterly).

International Palaeontological Association: c/o Paleontological Institute, 1475 Jayhawk Blvd, Rm 121, Lindley Hall, University of Kansas, Lawrence, KS 66045, USA; tel. (785) 864-3338; fax (785) 864-5276; e-mail rmaddocks@uh.edu; internet ipa.geo.ku.edu; f. 1933; affiliated to the International Union of Geological Sciences and the International Union of Biological Sciences; Pres. Dr MICHAEL BENTON (United Kingdom); Sec.-Gen. Prof. ROSALIE F. MADDOCKS (USA); publs *Lethaia* (quarterly), *Directory of Paleontologists of the World, Directory of Fossil Collectors of the World.*

International Peat Society: Vapaudenkatu 12, 40100 Jyväskylä, Finland; tel. (14) 3385440; fax (14) 3385410; e-mail ips@peatsociety.org; internet www.peatsociety.org; f. 1968 to encourage co-operation in the study and use of mires, peatlands, peat and related material, through international meetings, research groups and the exchange of information; mems: 21 National Cttees, research institutes and other orgs, and individuals from 37 countries; Pres. DONAL CLARKE (Ireland); Sec.-Gen. JAAKKO SILPOLA (Finland); publs *Peat News* (monthly electronic newsletter), *International Peat Journal* (annually), *Peatlands International* (2 a year).

International Permafrost Association: c/o Dr Hugues Lantuit, Alfred Wegener Institute for Polar and Marine Research,

Telefrafenberg A43, 14473 Potsdam, Germany; tel. (331) 288-2162; fax (331) 288-2188; e-mail contact@ipa-permafrost.org; internet ipa.arcticportal.org; f. 1983; aims to foster dissemination and exchange of knowledge concerning permafrost and to promote co-operation among persons and organizations involved in scientific investigation and engineering work in permafrost; organizes the International Conference on Permafrost, held generally every five years (2012: Salekhard, Russia, in June); mems: Adhering Bodies from 26 countries; Pres. Prof. HANS-W. HUBBERTEN; Sec. Dr HUGUES LANTUIT; publs *Frozen Ground* (annually), conference proceedings, other scientific reports and assessments, reports in *Permafrost and Periglacial Process* (2 a year).

International Phonetic Association: Department of Theoretical and Applied Linguistics, School of English, Aristotle University of Thessaloniki, Thessaloniki 54124, Greece; tel. (2310) 997429; fax (2310) 997432; e-mail knicol@enl.auth.gr; internet www.langsci.ucl.ac.uk/ipa/l; f. 1886 to promote the scientific study of phonetics and its applications; organizes International Congress of Phonetic Sciences every four years (2011: Hong Kong, SAR, in Aug.); mems: 550; Sec. Dr KATERINA NICOLAIDIS; publs *Journal of the International Phonetic Association* (3 a year), *Handbook of the International Phonetic Association*.

International Phycological Society: c/o University of Adelaide School of Earth and Environmental Sciences, 112 Darling Bldg, Adelaide, SA 5005, Australia; tel. (8) 8222-9291; fax (8) 8222-9456; e-mail carlos.gurgel@adelaide.edu.au; internet www.intphycsoc.org; f. 1960 to promote the study of algae, the distribution of information, and international co-operation in this field; mems: about 1,000; Pres. JOE ZUCCARELLO (New Zealand); Sec. CARLOS F. GURGEL; publ. *Phycologia* (every 2 months).

International Primatological Society: c/o California State University San Marcos, San Marcos, CA 92096, USA; tel. (760) 750-4145; fax (760) 750-3418; e-mail ncaine@csusm.edu; internet www.internationalprimatologicalsociety.org; f. 1964 to promote primatological science in all fields; Congress held every two years (2012: Cancún, Mexico; 2014: Hanoi, Viet Nam); mems: about 1,500; Pres. JUICHI YAMAGIWA (Japan); Sec.-Gen. NANCY CAINE; publs *IPS Bulletin*, *International Journal of Primatology*, *Codes of Practice*.

International Radiation Protection Association (IRPA): c/o Jacques Lochard, CEPN, 28 rue de la Redoute, Fontenay-aux-Roses 92260, France; tel. 1-55-52-19-20; fax 1-55-52-19-21; e-mail irpa.exof@irpa.net; internet www.irpa.net; f. 1966 to link individuals and societies throughout the world concerned with protection against ionizing radiations and allied effects, and to represent doctors, health physicists, radiological protection officers and others engaged in radiological protection, radiation safety, nuclear safety, legal, medical and veterinary aspects and in radiation research and other allied activities; mems: 16,000 in 42 societies; Pres. KENNETH R. KASE (USA); Exec. Officer JACQUES LOCHARD (France); publ. *IRPA Bulletin*.

International Society for Human and Animal Mycology (ISHAM): c/o Dept of Haematology, Radboud University, Nijmegen Medical Centre & Nijmegen Institute for Infection, Inflammation and Immunity, Geert Grooteplein Zuid 8, 6525 GA Nijmegen, Netherlands; tel. (24) 361-9987; fax (24) 354-2080; e-mail p.donnelly@usa.net; internet www.isham.org; f. 1954 to pursue the study of fungi pathogenic for man and animals; holds congresses (2012: Berlin, Germany); mems: 1,100 in 70 countries; Pres. Prof. DAVID ELLIS (Australia); Gen. Sec. Dr PETER DONNELLY (Netherlands); publ. *Medical Mycology* (6 a year).

International Society for Rock Mechanics: c/o Laboratório Nacional de Engenharia Civil, 101 Av. do Brasil, 1700-066 Lisboa, Portugal; tel. (21) 8443419; fax (21) 8443021; e-mail secretariat.isrm@lnec.pt; internet www.isrm.net; f. 1962 to encourage and co-ordinate international co-operation in the science of rock mechanics; assists individuals and local organizations in forming national bodies; maintains liaison with organizations representing related sciences, including geology, geophysics, soil mechanics, mining engineering, petroleum engineering and civil engineering; organizes international meetings; encourages the publication of research; mems: c. 5,000 mems and 46 nat. groups; Pres. Prof. JOHN A. HUDSON; Sec.-Gen. Dr LUÍS LAMAS; publ. *News Journal* (3 a year).

International Society for Stereology: c/o Prof. Eric Pirard, Universite de Liege, GeMMe—Genie Mineral, Materiaux & Environnement, Sart Tilman B52, 4000 Liege, Belgium; fax (4) 366-91-98; e-mail mail@stereologysociety.org; internet www.stereologysociety.org; f. 1961; an interdisciplinary society gathering scientists from metallurgy, geology, mineralogy and biology to exchange ideas on three-dimensional interpretation of two-dimensional samples (sections, projections) of their material by means of stereological principles; mems: 300; Pres. Prof. JENS R. NYENGAARD (Denmark); Treas./Sec. Prof. ERIC PIRARD (Belgium); publs *Journal of Microscopy, Image Analysis & Stereology* (fmrly Acta Stereologica).

International Society for Tropical Ecology: c/o Botany Dept, Banaras Hindu University, Varanasi, 221 005 India; tel. (542) 2368399; fax (542) 2368174; e-mail singh.js1@gmail.com; internet www.tropecol.com; f. 1956 to promote and develop the science of ecology in the tropics in the service of humanity; to publish a journal to aid ecologists in the tropics in communication of their findings; and to hold symposia from time to time to summarize the state of knowledge in particular or general fields of tropical ecology; mems: 500; Sec. Prof. J. S. SINGH (India); publ. *Tropical Ecology* (3 a year).

International Society of Biometeorology: c/o Dept of Geography, Bolton 410, POB 413, University of Wisconsin-Milwaukee, Milwaukee, WI 53201-0413, USA; tel. (414) 229-3740; fax (414) 229-3981; e-mail mds@uwm.edu; internet www.biometeorology.org; f. 1956 to unite all biometeorologists working in the fields of agricultural, botanical, cosmic, entomological, forest, human, medical, veterinarian, zoological and other branches of biometeorology; mems: 250 individuals, nationals of 46 countries; Pres. PAUL BEGGS (Australia); Sec. MARK D. SCHWARTZ (USA); publs *Biometeorology* (Proceedings of the Congress of ISB), *International Journal of Biometeorology* (quarterly), *Biometeorology Bulletin*.

International Society of Criminology (ISC) (Société internationale de criminologie): 12 rue Charles Fourier, 75013 Paris, France; tel. 1-45-88-00-23; fax 1-45-88-96-40; e-mail crim.sic@wanadoo.fr; f. 1934 to promote the development of the sciences in their application to the criminal phenomenon; mems: in 63 countries; Pres. TONY PETERS (Belgium); Sec.-Gen. RACHIDA TOUAHRIA (France); publ. *Annales internationales de Criminologie*.

International Society of Limnology (Societas Internationalis Limnologiae—SIL): University of North Carolina at Chapel Hill, SPH, ESE, CB 7431, Rosenau Hall, Chapel Hill, NC 27599-7431, USA; tel. (336) 376-9362; fax (336) 376-8825; e-mail msondergaard@bi.ku.dk; internet www.limnology.org; f. 1922 (as the International Asscn of Theoretical and Applied Limnology, name changed 2007) for the study of physical, chemical and biological phenomena of lakes and rivers; affiliated to the International Union of Biological Sciences; mems: c. 3,200; Pres. Dr BRIAN MOSS (United Kingdom); Gen. Sec. and Treas. Dr MORTEN SØNDERGAARD (Denmark).

International Union for Physical and Engineering Sciences in Medicine (IUPESM): c/o Dr Heikki Terio, Karolinska University Hospital, Dept of Biomedical Engineering, 14186 Stockholm, Sweden; tel. (8) 58580852; fax (8) 58586290; e-mail heikki.terio@karolinska.se; internet www.iupesm.org; f. 1980 by its two constituent orgs (International Federation for Medical and Biological Engineering, and International Organization for Medical Physics); promotes international co-operation in health care science and technology and represents the professional interests of members; organizes seminars, workshops, scientific conferences; holds World Congress every three years (2012: Beijing, People's Republic of China, in May); Pres. Prof. BARRY ALLEN (Australia); Sec.-Gen. Dr HEIKKI TERIO (Sweden); publs *IUPESM Newsletter* (2 a year), Congress proceedings.

International Union for Pure and Applied Biophysics (IUPAB): Bosch Institute, Anderson Stuart F13, The University of Sydney, Sydney, 2006 Australia; tel. (2) 9351-3209; fax (2) 9351-6546; e-mail dosremedios@iupab.org; internet www.iupab.org; f. 1961 to organize international co-operation in biophysics and promote communication between biophysics and allied subjects, to encourage national co-operation between biophysical societies, and to contribute to the advancement of biophysical knowledge; mems: 50 adhering bodies; Pres. KUNIAKI NAGAYAMA (Japan); Sec.-Gen. Prof. CRISTOBAL G. DOS REMEDIOS (Australia); publ. *Quarterly Reviews of Biophysics*.

International Union for Quaternary Research (INQUA): Dept of Geography, Museum Building, Trinity College, Dublin 2, Ireland; tel. (1) 6081213; e-mail pcoxon@tcd.ie; internet www.inqua.tcd.ie; f. 1928 to co-ordinate research on the Quaternary geological era throughout the world; holds congress every four years (2011: Bern, Switzerland); mems: in 48 countries and states; Pres. Prof. ALLAN R. CHIVAS (Australia); Sec.-Gen. Prof. PETER COXON (Ireland); publs *Quaternary International*, *Quaternary Perspectives*.

International Union of Biochemistry and Molecular Biology (IUBMB): c/o Dept of Biochemistry & Molecular Biology, University of Calgary, Faculty of Medicine, 3330 Hospital Drive, NW Calgary, Alberta, T2N 4N1 Canada; tel. (403) 220-3021; fax (403) 270-2211; e-mail walsh@ucalgary.ca; internet www.iubmb.org; f. 1955 to sponsor the International Congresses of Biochemistry, to co-ordinate research and discussion, to organize co-operation between the societies of biochemistry and molecular biology, to promote high standards of biochemistry and molecular biology throughout the world and to contribute to the advancement of biochemistry and molecular biology in all its international aspects; mems: 76 bodies; Pres. Prof. ANGELO AZZI (USA); Gen. Sec. Prof. MICHAEL WALSH (Canada).

International Union of Biological Sciences (IUBS): Bâtiment 442, Université Paris-Sud 11, 91405 Orsay Cedex, France; tel. 1-69-15-50-27; fax 1-69-15-79-47; e-mail secretariat@iubs.org; internet www.iubs.org; f. 1919; serves as an international forum for the promotion of biology; administers scientific programmes on biodiversity, integrative biology (of ageing, bioenergy, and climate change), biological education, bioethics, bio-energy, and Darwin 200; carries out international collaborative research programmes; convenes General Assembly every three years; mems: 44 national bodies, 80 scientific bodies; Pres. Dr GIORGIO BERNARDI (Italy); Exec. Dir Dr NATHALIE FOMPROIX; publs *Biology International* (quarterly), *IUBS Monographs*, *IUBS Methodology*, *Manual Series*.

International Union of Crystallography: c/o M. H. Dacombe, 2 Abbey Sq., Chester, CH1 2HU, United Kingdom; tel. (1244) 345431; fax (1244) 344843; internet www.iucr.org; f. 1947 to facilitate the international standardization of methods, units, nomenclature and symbols used in crystallography; and to form a focus for the relations of crystallography to other sciences; mems: in 40 countries; Pres. Prof. G. R. DESIRAJU (India); Gen. Sec. L. VAN MEERWELT (Belgium); publs *IUCR Newsletter*, *Acta Crystallographica*, *Journal of Applied Crystallography*, *Journal of Synchroton Radiation*, *International Tables for Crystallography*, *World Directory of Crystallographers*, *IUCr/OUP Crystallographic Symposia*, *IUCr/OUP Monographs on Crystallography*, *IUCr/OUP Texts on Crystallography*.

International Union of Food Science and Technology (IUFoST): POB 61021, 511 Maplegrove Rd, Oakville, ON L6J 6X0, Canada; tel. (905) 815-1926; fax (905) 815-1574; e-mail secretariat@iufost.org; internet www.iufost.org; f. 1970; sponsors international symposia and congresses; mems: 60 national groups; Pres. GEOFFREY CAMPBELL-PLATT (United Kingdom); Sec.-Gen./Treas. JUDITH MEECH (Canada); publs *IUFOST Newsline* (3 a year), *International Review of Food Science and Technology*.

International Union of Geodesy and Geophysics (IUGG): IUGG Secretariat, Karlsruhe Institute of Technology (KIT), Geophysical Institute, Hertzstr. 16, 76187 Karlsruhe, Germany; tel. (721) 6084494; e-mail secretariat@iugg.org; internet www.iugg.org; f. 1919; federation of eight asscns representing Cryospheric Sciences, Geodesy, Geomagnetism and Aeronomy, Hydrological Sciences, Meteorology and Atmospheric Physics, Seismology and Physics of the Earth's Interior, Physical Sciences of the Ocean, and Volcanology and Chemistry of the Earth's Interior, which meet in committees and at the General Assemblies of the Union; organizes scientific meetings and sponsors various permanent services to collect, analyse and publish geophysical data; mems: 65 countries; Pres. Dr HARSH GUPTA (India); Sec.-Gen. Dr ALIK ISMAIL-ZADEH (Germany); publs *IUGG Yearbook*, *Journal of Geodesy* (quarterly), *IASPEI Newsletter* (irregular), *Bulletin of Volcanology* (8 a year), *Hydrological Sciences Journal* (6 a year), *IAMAS Newsletter* (irregular).

International Union of Geological Sciences (IUGS): c/o Richard Calnan, MS-917, US Geological Survey, Reston, VA 20192, USA; tel. (703) 648-6050; fax (703) 648-4227; e-mail IUGS@usgs.gov; internet www.iugs.org; f. 1961; aims to encourage the study of geoscientific problems, to facilitate international and inter-disciplinary co-operation in geology and related sciences, and to support the quadrennial International Geological Congress; organizes international meetings and co-sponsors joint programmes, including the International Geological Correlation Programme (with UNESCO); mems: in 121 countries; Pres. Prof. ALBERTO C. RICCARDI (Argentina); Sec.-Gen. Dr PETER T. BOBROWSKY (Canada).

International Union of Immunological Societies (IUIS): IUIS Central Office, c/o Vienna Academy of Postgraduate Medical Education and Research, Alser Str. 4, 1090 Vienna, Austria; tel. (1) 405-13-83-18; fax (1) 407-82-87; e-mail iuis-central-office@medacad.org; internet www.iuisonline.org; f. 1969; holds triennial international congress; mems: national societies in 65 countries and territories; Pres. STEFAN H. E. KAUFMANN (Germany); Sec.-Gen. Dr SEPPO MERI (Finland); Exec. Man. GERLINDE JAHN.

International Union of Microbiological Societies (IUMS): c/o Dr Robert A. Samson, Centraalbureau voor Schimmelcultures Fungal Biodiversity Centre, POB 85167, 3508 AD, Utrecht, Netherlands; tel. (30) 2122600; fax (30) 2512097; e-mail samson@cbs.knaw.nl; internet www.iums.org; f. 1930; mems: 106 national microbiological societies; Pres. DANIEL O. SORDELLI (Argentina); Sec.-Gen. ROBERT A. SAMSON (Netherlands); publs *International Journal of Systematic Bacteriology* (quarterly), *International Journal of Food Microbiology* (every 2 months), *Advances in Microbial Ecology* (annually), *Archives of Virology*.

International Union of Nutritional Sciences (IUNS): c/o Dr Galal, UCLA School of Public Health, Community Health Sciences, POB 951772, Los Angeles, CA 90095-1772, USA; tel. (310) 206-9639; fax (310) 794-1805; e-mail info@iuns.org; internet www.iuns.org; f. 1946 to promote advancement in nutrition science, research and development through international co-operation at the global level; aims to encourage communication and collaboration among nutrition scientists as well as to disseminate information in nutritional sciences through modern communication technology; mems: 80 adhering bodies; Pres. Dr IBRAHIM ELMADFA (Austria); Sec.-Gen. Prof. REKIA BELAHSEN (Morocco); publs *Annual Report*, *IUNS Directory*, *Newsletter*.

International Union of Pharmacology: c/o Lindsay Hart, Dept of Pharmacology, College of Medicine, University of California, Irvine, CA 92697, USA; tel. (949) 824-1178; fax (949) 824-4855; e-mail l.hart@iuphar.org; internet www.iuphar.org; f. 1963 to promote co-ordination of research, discussion and publication in the field of pharmacology, including clinical pharmacology, drug metabolism and toxicology; co-operates with WHO in all matters concerning drugs and drug research; holds international congresses; mems: 54 national societies, 12 assoc. mem. societies, 3 corporate mems; Pres. PAUL M. VANHOUTTE (France); Sec.-Gen. Prof. SUE PIPER DUCKLES; publ. *PI (Pharmacology International)*.

International Union of Photobiology: c/o Dept of Dermatology, Medical University of Vienna, AKH-E07 Waehringer Guertel 18-20m, 1090 Vienna, Austria; tel. (1) 40400-7702; fax (1) 40400-7699; e-mail herbert.hoenigsmann@meduniwien.ac.at; internet www.pol-us.net/iupb/index.html; f. 1928 (frmly International Photobiology Asscn); stimulation of scientific research concerning the physics, chemistry and climatology of non-ionizing radiations (ultra-violet, visible and infra-red) in relation to their biological effects and their applications in biology and medicine; 18 national cttees represented; affiliated to the International Union of Biological Sciences. International Congresses held every four years; Pres. HENRY LIM (USA); Sec.-Gen./Treas. HERBERT HÖNIGSMANN (Austria).

International Union of Physiological Sciences (IUPS): IUPS Secretariat, LGN, Bâtiment CERVI, Hôpital de la Pitié-Salpêtrière, 83 blvd de l'Hôpital, 75013 Paris, France; tel. 1-42-17-75-37; fax 1-42-17-75-75; e-mail iups@case.edu; internet www.iups.org; f. 1955; mems: 51 national, 14 asscn, 4 regional, 2 affiliated mems; Pres. Prof. DENIS NOBLE; Sec.-Gen. WALTER BORON.

International Union of Psychological Science: c/o Prof. P. L.-J. Ritchie, Ecole de psychologie, Université d'Ottawa, 145 Jean-Jacques-Lussier, CP 450, Succ. A, Ottawa, ON KIN 6N5, Canada; tel. (613) 562-5800; fax (613) 562-5169; e-mail pritchie@uottawa.ca; internet www.iupsys.org; f. 1951 to contribute to the development of intellectual exchange and scientific relations between psychologists of different countries; mems: 68 national and 12 affiliate orgs; Pres. Prof. REINER SILBEREISEN (Germany); Sec.-Gen. Prof. P. L.-J. RITCHIE (Canada); publs *International Journal of Psychology* (quarterly), *The IUPsyS Directory* (irregular), *Psychology CD Rom Resource File* (annually).

International Union of Pure and Applied Chemistry (IUPAC): POB 13757, 104 T. W. Alexander Dr., Bldg 19, Research Triangle Park, NC 27709-3757, USA; tel. (919) 485-8700; fax (919) 485-8706; e-mail secretariat@iupac.org; internet www.iupac.org; f. 1919 to organize permanent co-operation between chemical asscns in the member countries, to study topics of international importance requiring standardization or codification, to co-operate with other international organizations in the field of chemistry and to contribute to the advancement of all aspects of chemistry; holds a biennial General Assembly; mems: in 56 countries; Pres. Prof. NICOLE MOREAU (France); Sec.-Gen. Dr DAVID BLACK (Australia).

International Union of Pure and Applied Physics (IUPAP): c/o Institute of Physics, 76 Portland Pl., London, W1B 1NT, United Kingdom; tel. (20) 7470-4849; fax (20) 7470-4861; e-mail admin.iupap@iop.org; internet www.iupap.org; f. 1922 to promote and encourage international co-operation in physics and facilitate the world-wide development of science; hosts a General Assembly every three years; mems: in 60 countries; Pres. CECILIA JARLSKOG (Sweden); Sec.-Gen. ROBERT KIRBY-HARRIS (United Kingdom).

International Union of Radio Science: c/o INTEC, Ghent University, Sint-Pietersnieuwstraat 41, 9000 Ghent, Belgium; tel. (9) 264-3320; fax (9) 264-4288; e-mail info@ursi.org; internet www.ursi.org; f. 1919 to stimulate and co-ordinate, on an international basis, studies, research, applications, scientific exchange and communication in the field of radio science; aims to encourage the adoption of common methods of measurement and the standardization of measuring instruments used in scientific work; represents radio science at national and international levels; mems: 44 national cttees; Pres. Dr PHIL WILKINSON (Australia); Sec.-Gen. Prof. PAUL LAGASSE (Belgium); publs *The Radio Science Bulletin* (quarterly), *Records of General Assemblies* (every 3 years).

International Union of Soil Sciences: c/o Dept of Soil Science, University of Wisconsin-Madison, Madison, WI 53706, USA; tel. (608) 263-4947; e-mail hartemink@wisc.edu; internet www.iuss.org; f. 1924; mems: national academies or national soil science societies from 143 countries; Pres. Prof. JAE YANG (Republic of Korea); Sec.-Gen. Prof. ALFRED HARTEMINK (USA); publ. *Bulletin* (2 a year).

International Union of the History and Philosophy of Science: Division of the History of Science and Technology (DHST): National Hellenic Research Foundation, 48 Vas. Constantinou av., 11635 Athens, Greece; e-mail e.nicolaidis@dhstweb.org; Division of the History of Logic, Methodology and Philosophy of Science (DLMPS): 161 rue Ada, 34392 Montpellier, France; f. 1956 to promote research into the history and philosophy of science; DHST has 50 national committees and DLMPS has 35 committees; DHST: Pres. Prof. DUN LIU (People's Republic of China); Sec.-Gen. Prof. EFTHYMIOS NICOLAÏDES (Greece); DLMPS Council: Pres. Prof. WILFRID HODGES; Sec.-Gen. Prof. PETER CLARK.

International Union of Theoretical and Applied Mechanics (IUTAM): IUTAM-Secretariat, Centre de Mathématiques et de Leurs Applications, Ecole Normale Supérieure de Cachan, 94235 Cachan, France; tel. 1-47-40-59-00; fax 1-47-40-59-01; e-mail sg@iutam.net; internet www.iutam.net; f. 1947 to form links between those engaged in scientific work (theoretical or experimental) in mechanics or related sciences; organizes international congresses of theoretical and applied mechanics, through a standing Congress Committee, and other international meetings; engages in other activities designed to promote the development of mechanics as a science; mems: from 49 countries; Pres. Prof. TIMOTHY PEDLEY (United Kingdom); Sec.-Gen. Prof. FREDERIC DIAS (France); publs *Annual Report*, *Newsletter*.

International Union of Toxicology: IUTOX Headquarters, 1821 Michael Faraday Dr., Suite 300, Reston, VA 20190, USA; tel. (703) 438-3103; fax (703) 438-3113; e-mail iutoxhq@iutox.org; internet www.iutox.org; f. 1980 to foster international co-operation among toxicologists and promote world-wide acquisition, dissemination and utilization of knowledge in the field; sponsors International Congresses and other education programmes; mems: 47 national societies; Pres. Dr DANIEL ACOSTA, Jr; Sec.-Gen. Prof. ELAINE FAUSTMAN; publs *IUTOX Newsletter*, Congress proceedings.

International Water Association (IWA): Alliance House, 12 Caxton St, London, SW1H OQS, United Kingdom; tel. (20) 7654-5500; fax (20) 7654-5555; e-mail water@iwahq.org.uk; internet www.iwahq.org; f. 1999 by merger of the International Water Services Association and the International Association on Water Quality; aims to encourage international communication, co-operative effort, and exchange of information on water quality management, through conferences, electronic media and publication of research reports; mems: c. 9,000 in 130 countries; Pres. Dr GLEN DAIGGER; Exec. Dir PAUL REITER; publs *Water Research* (monthly), *Water Science and Technology* (24 a year), *Water 21* (6 a year), *Yearbook*, *Scientific and Technical Reports*.

Nuclear Threat Initiative: 1747 Pennsylvania Ave NW, 7th Floor, Washington, DC 20006, USA; tel. (202) 296-4810; fax (202) 296-4810; e-mail contact@nti.org; internet www.nti.org; f. 2001 to help strengthen global security by reducing the risk of use of and preventing the spread of nuclear, biological and chemical weapons; promotes the objectives of the Nuclear Non-Proliferation Treaty; Co-Chair. R. E. (TED) TURNER; Co-Chair. and CEO SAM NUNN; Pres. and Chief Operating Officer JOAN ROHLFING.

Pacific Science Association: 1525 Bernice St, Honolulu, HI 96817, USA; tel. (808) 848-4124; fax (808) 847-8252; e-mail info@pacificscience.org; internet www.pacificscience.org; f. 1920; a regional non-governmental organization that seeks to advance science, technology, and sustainable development in and of the Asia-Pacific region, by actively promoting interdisciplinary and international research and collaboration; sponsors Pacific Science Congresses and Inter-Congresses and scientific working groups and facilitates research initiatives on critical emerging issues for the region; 12th Inter-Congress: Suva, Fiji, in July, on the theme: 'Human Security in the Pacific'; 22nd Congress: Kuala Lumpur, Malaysia, June 2011; mems: institutional representatives from 35 areas, scientific societies, individual scientists; Pres. Prof. NANCY D. LEWIS (USA); Sec-Gen. MAKOTO TSUCHIYA (Japan); publs *Pacific Science* (quarterly), *Information Bulletin* (2 a year).

Pan-African Union of Science and Technology: POB 641, Brazzaville, Republic of the Congo; tel. 832265; fax 832185; f. 1987 to promote the use of science and technology in furthering the development of Africa; organizes triennial congress; Sec.-Gen. Prof. LÉVY MAKANY.

Pugwash Conferences on Science and World Affairs: Ground Floor Flat, 63A Great Russell St, London, WC1B 3BJ, United Kingdom; tel. (20) 7405-6661; fax (20) 7831-5651; e-mail pugwash@mac.com; internet www.pugwash.org; f. 1957 to organize international conferences of scientists to discuss problems arising from the development of science, particularly the dangers to mankind from weapons of mass destruction; mems: national Pugwash groups in 38 countries; Pres. JAYANTHA DHENAPALA; Sec.-Gen. Prof. PAOLO COTTA-RAMUSINO; publs *Pugwash Newsletter* (2 a year), occasional papers, monographs.

Scientific, Technical and Research Commission of African Unity (OAU/STRC): Nigerian Ports Authority Bldg, PMB 2359, Marina, Lagos, Nigeria; tel. (1) 2633359; fax (1) 2636093; e-mail oaustrcl@hyperia.com; f. 1965 to succeed the Commission for Technical Co-operation in Africa (f. 1954); implements priority programmes of the African Union relating to science and technology for development; supervises the Inter-African Bureau for Animal Resources (Nairobi, Kenya), the Inter-African Bureau for Soils (Lagos, Nigeria) and the Inter-African Phytosanitary Commission (Yaoundé, Cameroon) and several joint research projects; provides training in agricultural management, and conducts pest control programmes; services various inter-African committees of experts, including the Scientific Council for Africa; publishes and distributes specialized scientific books and documents of original value to Africa; organizes training courses, seminars, symposia, workshops and technical meetings; Exec. Sec. Dr MBAYE NDOYE.

Southern and Eastern African Mineral Centre (SEAMIC): POB 9573, Dar es Salaam, Tanzania; tel. (22) 2650-347; fax (22) 2650-319; e-mail seamic@seamic.org; internet www.seamic.org; f. 1977 to promote socio-economic and environmentally responsible mineral sector development in the region; sponsored by mem. states; provides advisory and consultancy services in exploration geology, geophysics, geochemistry, mining and mineral processing; archives and processes geoinformation data; organizes training courses in the areas of geoinformatics; provides minerals related specialized laboratory services; mems: Angola, Comoros, Ethiopia, Kenya, Mozambique, Tanzania, Sudan, Uganda (membership limited to eastern and southern African countries until May 2007; subsequently opened to all African countries); Dir-Gen. KETEMA TADESSE; publ. *Seamic Newsletter* (2 a year).

Unitas Malacologica (Malacological Union): c/o Dr Jackie Van Goethem, Royal Belgian Institute of Natural Sciences, Vautierstraat 29, 1000 Brussels, Belgium; tel. (2) 627-43-43; fax (2) 627-41-41; e-mail jackie.vangoethem@naturalsciences.be; internet www.unitasmalacologica.org; f. 1962 to further the study of molluscs world-wide; affiliated to the International Union of Biological Sciences; holds triennial world congress; mems: 400 in more than 35 countries; Pres. ANTÓNIO DE FRIAS MARTINS (Portugal); Sec. JESÚS TRONCOSO (Spain); publ. *UM Newsletter* (2 a year).

United Nations University Institute for Natural Resources in Africa (UNU/INRA): ISSER Bldg Complex, Botanical Gardens Rd, University of Ghana, Legon; Private Mail Bag, Kotoka International Airport, Accra, Ghana; tel. (21) 500396; fax (21) 500792; e-mail unuinra@yahoo.com; internet inra.unu.edu; f. 1986 as a research and training centre of the United Nations University (Tokyo, Japan); operational since 1990; aims at human resource development and institutional capacity building through co-ordination with African universities and research institutes in advanced research, training and dissemination of knowledge and information on the conservation and management of Africa's natural resources and their rational utilization for sustainable devt; Dir. Dr ELIAS TAKOR AYUK; INRA has a mineral resources unit (MRU) at the University of Zambia in Lusaka; MRU Co-ordinator Prof. STEPHEN SIMUKANGA.

World Institute for Nuclear Security (WINS): Graben 19 Vienna, 1010 Austria; tel. (1) 230-606-088; fax (1) 230-606-089; e-mail info@wins.org; internet www.wins.org; f. 2008; aims to strengthen the physical protection and security of nuclear materials and facilities world-wide; Exec. Dir Dr ROGER HOWSLEY (United Kingdom).

World Organisation of Systems and Cybernetics (WOSC): c/o Prof Raul Espejo, 3 North Pl., 30 Nettleham Rd, Lincoln, LN2 1RE, United Kingdom; tel. and fax (1522) 589252; e-mail r.espejo@syncho.org; internet www.wosc.co; f. 1969 to act as clearing-house for all societies concerned with cybernetics and systems, to aim for the recognition of cybernetics as fundamental science, to organize and sponsor international exhibitions of automation and computer equipment, congresses and symposia, and to promote and co-ordinate research in systems and cybernetics; sponsors an honorary fellowship and awards a Norbert Wiener memorial gold medal; mems: dirs. from 16 countries belonging to nat. and int. societies in 30 countries; Pres. Prof. R. VALLÉE (France); Dir-Gen. Prof. RAUL ESPEJO; publs *Kybernetes, International Journal of Cybernetics and Systems*.

Social Sciences

African Centre for Applied Research and Training in Social Development (ACARTSOD): Africa Centre, Wahda Quarter, Zawia Rd, POB 80606, Tripoli, Libya; tel. (21) 4835103; fax (21) 4835066; e-mail info@acartsod.net; internet www.acartsod.net; f. 1977 under the joint auspices of the ECA and OAU (now AU) to promote and co-ordinate applied research and training in social devt, and to assist in formulating nat. development strategies; Exec. Dir Dr AHMED SAID FITURI.

African Social and Environmental Studies Programme: Box 4477, Nairobi, Kenya; tel. (20) 747960; fax (20) 747960; f. 1968; develops and disseminates educational material on social and environmental studies in eastern and southern Africa; mems: 18 African countries; Chair. Prof. WILLIAM SENTEZA-KAJUBI; Exec. Dir Prof. PETER MUYANDA MUTEBI; publs *African Social and Environmental Studies Forum* (2 a year), teaching guides.

Arab Towns Organization (ATO): POB 68160, Kaifan 71962, Kuwait; tel. 24849705; fax 24849319; e-mail ato@ato.net; internet www.ato.net; f. 1967; works to preserve the identity and heritage of Arab towns; to support the development and modernization of municipal and local authorities in member towns; to improve services and utilities in member towns; to support development schemes in member towns through the provision of loans and other assistance; to support planning and the co-ordination of development activities and services; to facilitate the exchange of service-related expertise among member towns; to co-ordinate efforts to modernize and standardize municipal regulations and codes among member towns; to promote co-operation in all matters related to Arab towns; manages the Arab Towns Development Fund, the Arab Institute for Urban Development, the Arab Towns Organization Award, the Arab Urban Environment Centre, the Arab Forum on Information Systems, and the Heritage and Arab Historic City Foundation; mems: 413 towns; Sec.-Gen. ABD AL-AZIZ Y. AL-ADASANI; publ. *Al-Madinah Al-Arabiyah* (every 2 months).

Association for the Study of the World Refugee Problem (AWR): POB 1241, 97201 Höchberg, Germany; e-mail awr_int_forschungsg@yahoo.de; internet www.awr-int.de; f. 1951 to promote and co-ordinate scholarly research on refugee problems; Pres. RAINER WIESTNER (Italy); Gen. Sec. Prof. MARKUS BABO; publs *AWR Bulletin* (quarterly, in English, French, Italian and German), treatises on refugee problems (17 vols).

Council for Research in Values and Philosophy (CRVP): 620 Michigan Ave, NE, Washington, DC 20064, USA; tel. and fax (202) 319-6089; e-mail cua-rvp@cua.edu; internet www.crvp.org; f. 1983; organizes conferences and an annual 10-week seminar; mems: 70 teams from 60 countries; Pres. Prof. KENNETH L. SCHMITZ (Canada); Sec.-Treas. Prof. GEORGE F. MCLEAN (USA); publs *Cultural Heritage and Contemporary Change* series (220 titles).

Council for the Development of Social Science Research in Africa (CODESRIA): Ave Cheikh, Anta Diop X Canal IV, BP 3304, CP 18524, Dakar, Senegal; tel. 825-98-22; fax 825-12-89; internet www.codesria.org; f. 1973; promotes research, organizes conferences, working groups and information services; mems: research institutes and university faculties and researchers in African countries; Exec. Sec. Dr EBRIMA SALL; publs *Africa Development* (quarterly), *CODESRIA Bulletin* (quarterly), *Index of African Social Science Periodical Articles* (annually), *African Journal of International Affairs* (2 a year), *African Sociological Review* (2 a year), *Afrika Zamani* (annually), *Identity, Culture and Politics* (2 a year), *Afro Arab Selections for Social Sciences* (annually), directories of research.

Eastern Regional Organisation for Planning and Housing: Ministry of Housing and Local Government, Aras 4, Block B (North), Pusat Bandar Damansara, Kuala Lumpur, Malaysia; tel. (3) 20925217; fax (3) 20924217; e-mail secretariat@earoph.info; internet www.earoph.info; f. 1956 to promote and co-ordinate the study and practice of housing and regional town and country planning; maintains offices in Japan, India and Indonesia; mems: 57 orgs and 213 individuals in 28 countries; Pres. MICHAEL HARBISON (Australia); Sec.-Gen. NORLIZA HASHIM (Malaysia); publs *EAROPH News and Notes* (monthly), *Town and Country Planning* (bibliography).

English-Speaking Union: Dartmouth House, 37 Charles St, Berkeley Sq., London, W1J 5ED, United Kingdom; tel. (20) 7529-1550; fax (20) 7495-6108; e-mail esu@esu.org; internet www.esu.org; f. 1918 to promote international understanding through the use of the English language; mems: 37 United

Kingdom branches; 50 international affiliates; Chair. Dame Mary Richardson; Dir-Gen. Peter Kyle.

European and Mediterranean Network of the Social Sciences: c/o Foundation for International Studies, St Paul St, Valletta VLT07, Malta; tel. 237547; fax 230551; e-mail aspiteri@arts.um.edu.mt; established as successor to the European Co-ordination Centre for Research and Documentation in Social Sciences; aims to provide a forum for discussion and exchange of research towards greater understanding of issues affecting the well-being of the region's peoples; publ. *Mediterranean Social Sciences Review.*

European Association for Population Studies (EAPS): POB 11676, 2502 AR The Hague, Netherlands; Lange Houtst. 19, 2511 CV The Hague, Netherlands; tel. (70) 3565200; fax (70) 3647187; e-mail contact@eaps.nl; internet www.eaps.nl; f. 1983 to foster research and provide information on European population problems; organizes conferences, seminars and workshops; mems: demographers from 40 countries; Exec. Sec. Helga de Valk; publ. *European Journal of Population/Revue Européenne de Démographie* (quarterly).

European Society for Rural Sociology: c/o M. Lehtola, Swedish School of Social Science, POB 16, University of Helsinki, Finland; tel. (9) 19128483; fax (9) 19128485; e-mail minna.lehtola@helsinki.fi; internet www.ruralsociology.eu; f. 1957 to further research in, and co-ordination of, rural sociology and provide a centre for documentation of information; also involved in the study of agriculture and fisheries, food production and consumption, nature and environmental care, etc; mems: 300 individuals, institutions and asscns in 29 European countries and 9 countries outside Europe; Pres. Dr Jo Little (United Kingdom); Sec. Minna Lehtola (Finland); publ. *Sociologia Ruralis* (quarterly).

Federation EIL: 70 Landmark Hill, Suite 204, Brattleboro, VT 05301 USA; tel. (802) 246-1154; fax (802) 246-1154; e-mail federation@experiment.org; internet www.experiment.org; f. 1932 as Experiment in International Living; an international federation of non-profit educational and cultural exchange institutions; works to create mutual understanding and respect among people of different nations, as a means of furthering peace; mems: orgs in more than 20 countries; Dir Ilene Todd.

Fédération internationale des associations vexillologiques (International Federation of Vexillological Associations): 504 Branard St, Houston, TX 77006-5018, USA; tel. (713) 529-2545; e-mail sec.gen@fiav.org; internet www.fiav.org; f. 1969; unites associations and institutions throughout the world whose object is the pursuit of vexillology, i.e. the creation and development of a body of knowledge about flags of all types, their forms and functions, and of scientific theories and principles based on that knowledge; sponsors International Congresses of Vexillology every two years (2013: Rotterdam, Netherlands); mems: 52 institutions and asscns world-wide; Pres. Prof. Michel Lupant (Belgium); Sec.-Gen. Charles A. Spain, Jr (USA); publs *Info FIAV* (annually), *Proceedings of the International Congresses of Vexillology* (every 2 years).

International African Institute (IAI): School of Oriental and African Studies, Thornhaugh St, Russell Sq., London, WC1H 0XG, United Kingdom; tel. (20) 7898-4420; fax (20) 7898-4419; e-mail iai@soas.ac.uk; internet www.internationalafricaninstitute.org; f. 1926 to promote the study of African peoples, their languages, cultures and social life in their traditional and modern settings; organizes an international seminar programme bringing together scholars from Africa and elsewhere; links scholars in order to facilitate research projects, especially in the social sciences; Chair. Prof. V. Y. Mudimbe; Hon. Dir Prof. Philip Burnham; publs *Africa* (quarterly), *Africa Bibliography* (annually).

International Association for Media and Communication Research: c/o Annabelle Sreberny, Centre for Media and Film Studies, School of Oriental and African Studies, University of London, Russell Square, London, WC1 0XG, United Kingdom; tel. (20) 7898-4422; internet www.iamcr.org; f. 1957 (fmrly International Asscn for Mass Communication Research) to stimulate interest in mass communication research and the dissemination of information about research and research needs, to improve communication practice, policy and research and training for journalism, and to provide a forum for researchers and others involved in mass communication to meet and exchange information; mems: over 2,300 in c. 70 countries; Pres. Prof. Annabelle Sreberny; publ. *Newsletter.*

International Association for the History of Religions (IAHR): c/o Prof. Tim Jensen, Institute of Philosophy, Education and the Study of Religion, Dept of the Study of Religions, University of Southern Denmark, Odense, Campusvej 55, 5230 Odense M, Denmark; tel. 65-50-33-15; fax 65-50-26-68; e-mail t.jensen@ifpr.sdu.dk; internet www.iahr.dk; f. 1950 to promote international collaboration of scholars, to organize congresses and to stimulate research; mems: 37 nat. and 5 regional asscns; Pres. Prof. Rosalind I. J. Hackett; Gen. Sec. Prof. Tim Jensen; publ. *Numen: International Review for the History of Religions* (annually).

International Association of Applied Linguistics (Association internationale de linguistique appliquée—AILA): Theaterstr. 15, 8401 Winterthur, Switzerland; tel. 589346060; e-mail secretariat@aila.info; internet www.aila.info; f. 1964; organizes seminars on applied linguistics, and a World Congress every three years (2011: Beijing, People's Republic of China, in Aug.; 2014: Brisbane, Australia, in April); mems: more than 8,000; Pres. Prof. Bernd Rueschoff (Germany); Sec.-Gen. Prof. Daniel Perrin (Switzerland); publ. *AILA Review* (annually).

International Association of Metropolitan City Libraries (INTAMEL): c/o Frans Meijer, Bibliotheek Rotterdam, Hoogstraat 110, 3011 PV Rotterdam, Netherlands; tel. (10) 2816140; fax (10) 2816221; e-mail f.meijer@bibliotheek.rotterdam.nl; f. 1966; serves as a platform for libraries in cities of over 400,000 inhabitants or serving a wide and diverse geographical area; promotes the exchange of ideas and information on a range of topics including library networks, automation, press relations and research; mems: 98 libraries in 28 countries; Pres. Frans Meijer (Netherlands).

International Committee for Social Sciences Information and Documentation: c/o Clacso, Callao 875, 3rd Floor, Buenos Aires 1023, Argentina; e-mail saugy@clacso.edu.ar; internet www.unesco.org/most/icssd.htm; f. 1950 to collect and disseminate information on documentation services in social sciences, to help improve documentation, to advise societies on problems of documentation and to draw up rules likely to improve the presentation of documents; mems: from international asscns specializing in social sciences or in documentation, and from other specialized fields; Pres. Krishana G. Tyagi; Sec.-Gen. Catalina Saugy (Argentina); publs *International Bibliography of the Social Sciences* (annually), *Newsletter* (2 a year).

International Committee for the History of Art: c/o Prof. Dr P. J. Schneemann, Institut für Kunstgeschichte, Hodlerstr. 8, 3011 Bern, Switzerland; tel. 316314741; fax 316318669; e-mail ciha@unam.mx; internet www.esteticas.unam.mx/ciha; f. 1930 by the 12th International Congress on the History of Art, for collaboration in the scientific study of the history of art; holds international congress every four years, and at least two colloquia between congresses; mems: National Committees in 34 countries; Sec. Prof. Dr Peter Johannes Schneemann (Switzerland); publ. *Bibliographie d'Histoire de l'Art—Bibliography of the History of Art* (quarterly).

International Committee of Historical Sciences (Comité International des Sciences Historiques — CISH): Département d'histoire, UQAM, CP 8888, Succursale Centre-ville, Montréal, QC H3C 3P8, Canada; e-mail cish@uqam.ca; internet www.cish.org; f. 1926 to work for the advancement of historical sciences by means of international co-ordination; holds international congress every five years, 2010: Amsterdam, Netherlands; mems: 53 national cttees, 28 affiliated international orgs and 12 internal commissions; Pres. Prof. Marjatta Hietala (Finland); Sec.-Gen. Prof. Robert Frank (France); publ. *Bulletin d'Information du CISH.*

International Council for Philosophy and Humanistic Studies (ICPHS): Maison de l'UNESCO, 1 rue Miollis, 75732 Paris Cedex 15, France; tel. 1-45-68-48-85; fax 1-40-65-94-80; e-mail cipsh@unesco.org; internet www.unesco.org/cipsh; f. 1949 under the auspices of UNESCO to encourage respect for cultural autonomy by the comparative study of civilization and to contribute towards international understanding through a better knowledge of humanity; works to develop international co-operation in philosophy, humanistic and kindred studies; encourages the setting up of international organizations; promotes the dissemination of information in these fields; sponsors works of learning, etc; mems: 13 orgs representing 145 countries; Pres. IN SUK CHA; Sec.-Gen. MAURICE AYMARD; publs *Bulletin of Information* (biennially), *Diogenes* (quarterly).

International Council on Archives (ICA): 60 rue des Francs-Bourgeois, 75003 Paris, France; tel. 1-40-27-63-06; fax 1-42-72-20-65; e-mail ica@ica.org; internet www.ica.org; f. 1948 to develop relationships between archivists in different countries; aims to protect and enhance archives, to ensure preservation of archival heritage; facilitates training of archivists and conservators; promotes implementation of a professional code of conduct; encourages ease of access to archives; has 13 regional branches; mems: more than 1,465 in 198 countries; Pres. MARTIN BERENDSE (Netherlands); Sec.-Gen. DAVID LEITCH; publs *Comma* (2 a year), *Flash Newsletter* (2 a year), annual CD-Rom.

International Ergonomics Association (IEA): 1515 Engineering Drive, 3126 Engineering Centers Building, Madison, WI 53706, USA; tel. (608) 265-0503; fax (608) 263-1425; e-mail carayon@engr.wisc.edu; internet www.iea.cc; f. 1957 to bring together organizations and persons interested in the scientific study of human work and its environment; to establish international contacts among those specializing in this field, to co-operate with employers' asscns and trade unions in order to encourage the practical application of ergonomic sciences in industries, and to promote scientific research in this field; mems: 42 federated societies; Pres. ANDREW S. IMADA (USA); Sec.-Gen. Prof. Dr ERIC MIN-YANG WANG; publ. *Ergonomics* (monthly).

International Federation for Housing and Planning (IFHP): Binckhorstlaan 36, 2516 CG The Hague, Netherlands; tel. (70) 3244557; fax (70) 3282085; e-mail info@ifhp.org; internet www.ifhp.org; f. 1913 to study and promote the improvement of housing and the theory and practice of town planning; holds an annual World Congress (2012: Göteburg, Sweden, in Sept.); mems: 200 orgs and 300 individuals in 65 countries; Pres. JOHN ZETTER (United Kingdom); Sec.-Gen. DEREK MARTIN; publ. *Newsletter* (quarterly).

International Federation for Modern Languages and Literatures: c/o A. Pettersson, Dept of Culture and Media Studies, Umea University, 901 87 Umea, Sweden; tel. (90) 139-556; e-mail anders.pettersson@littvet.umu.se; internet www.fillm.ulg.ac.be; f. 1928 to establish permanent contact between historians of literature, to develop or perfect facilities for their work and to promote the study of modern languages and literature; holds Congress every three years; mems: 19 asscns, with individual mems in 98 countries; Pres. ROGER D. SELL (Finland); Sec.-Gen. ANDERS PETTERSSON (Sweden).

International Federation of Philosophical Societies (FISP): c/o Human Rights Centre, Maltepe University, 34857 Maltepe, Istanbul, Turkey; tel. (216) 6261132; fax (216) 6261125; e-mail kemp@dpu.dk; internet www.fisp.org; f. 1948 under the auspices of UNESCO, to encourage international co-operation in the field of philosophy; holds World Congress of Philosophy every five years (2008: Seoul, Republic of Korea); mems: 114 societies from 52 countries; 27 international societies; Pres. WILLIAM MCBRIDE (USA); Sec.-Gen. LUCA SCARANTINO (Italy); publs *Newsletter*, *International Bibliography of Philosophy*, *Chroniques de Philosophie*, *Contemporary Philosophy*, *Philosophical Problems Today*, *Philosophy and Cultural Development*, *Ideas Underlying World Problems*, *The Idea of Values*.

International Federation of Social Science Organizations (IFSSO): 245/69 Baromtrilokanart Rd, Muang District, Phitsanulok 65000, Thailand; tel. and fax (55) 244-240; e-mail sudakarn_p@yahoo.com; f. 1979 to assist research and teaching in the social sciences, and to facilitate co-operation and enlist mutual assistance in the planning and evaluation of programmes of major importance to members; mems: 31 national councils or academies in 29 countries; Sec.-Gen. Dr NESTOR CASTRO; publs *IFSSO Newsletter* (2 a year), *International Directory of Social Science Organizations*.

International Federation of Societies of Classical Studies: c/o Prof. P. Schubert, 7 rue des Beaux-Arts, 2000 Neuchatel, Switzerland; tel. 223797035; fax 223797932; e-mail paul.schubert@unige.ch; internet www.fiecnet.org; f. 1948 under the auspices of UNESCO; mems: 80 societies in 44 countries; Pres. Dame AVERIL CAMERON (United Kingdom); Sec.-Gen. Prof. PAUL SCHUBERT (Switzerland); publs *L'Année Philologique*, *Thesaurus linguae Latinae*.

International Institute for Ligurian Studies: Via Romana 39, 18012 Bordighera, Italy; tel. (0184) 263601; fax (0184) 266421; e-mail istituto@usl.it; f. 1947 to conduct research on ancient monuments and regional traditions in the north-west arc of the Mediterranean (France and Italy); maintains library of 80,000 vols; mems: in France, Italy, Spain, Switzerland; Dir Prof. CARLO VARALDO (Italy).

International Institute of Administrative Sciences (IIAS): 1 rue Defacqz, 1000 Brussels, Belgium; tel. (2) 536-08-80; fax (2) 537-97-02; e-mail iias@iias-iisa.org; internet www.iias-iisa.org; f. 1930 for the comparative examination of administrative experience; carries out research and programmes designed to improve administrative law and practices; has consultative status with UN, UNESCO and ILO; organizes international congresses, annual conferences, working groups; mems: 27 mem. states, 31 national sections, 3 int. governmental orgs, 36 corporate mems; Pres. KIM PAN-SUK (Republic of Korea); Dir-Gen. ROLET LORETAN (Switzerland); publs *International Review of Administrative Sciences* (quarterly), *Newsletter* (3 a year).

International Institute of Sociology (IIS): c/o The Swedish Collegium for Advanced Study, Thunbergsvägen 2, 75238 Uppsala, Sweden; tel. (18) 55-70-85; e-mail info@iisoc.org; internet www.iisoc.org; f. 1893 to enable sociologists to meet and to study sociological questions; mems: c. 300 in 47 countries; Pres. BJÖRN WITTROCK (Sweden); Sec.-Gen. PETER HEDSTRÖM; publ. *The Annals of the IIS*.

International Musicological Society (IMS): POB 1561, CH-4001 Basel, Switzerland; tel. 449231022; fax 449231027; e-mail dorothea.baumann@ims-online.ch; internet www.ims-online.ch; f. 1927; holds international congresses every five years (2012: Rome, Italy); mems: c. 1,000 in 53 countries; Pres. DINKO FABRIS (Italy); Sec.-Gen. Dr DOROTHEA BAUMANN (Switzerland); publ. *Acta Musicologica* (2 a year).

International Numismatic Council (Conseil international de numismatique): Kunsthistorisches Museum, Coin Cabinet, Burgring 5, 1010 Vienna, Austria; tel. (1) 525-24-42-01; fax (1) 525-24-42-99; e-mail michael.alram@khm.at; internet www.inc-cin.org; f. 1934 as International Numismatic Commission; name changed to present in 2009; facilitates co-operation between scholars studying coins and medals; mems: 160 in 38 countries; Pres. Dr CARMEN ARNOLD-BIUCCHI; Sec. MICHAEL ALRAM.

International Peace Institute: 777 United Nations Plaza, New York, NY 10017-3521, USA; tel. (212) 687-4300; fax (212) 983-8246; e-mail ipi@ipinst.org; internet www.ipacademy.org; f. 1970 (as the International Peace Academy) to promote the prevention and settlement of armed conflicts between and within states through policy research and development; educates government officials in the procedures needed for conflict resolution, peace-keeping, mediation and negotiation, through international training seminars and publications; off-the-record meetings are also conducted to gain complete understanding of a specific conflict; Chair. RITA E. HAUSER; Pres. TERJE ROD-LARSEN.

International Peace Research Association (IPRA): University of Leuven, Van Evenstraat 2B, Leuven, Belgium; tel. (16) 32-32-41; fax (16) 32-30-88; e-mail luc.reychler@soc.kuleuven.ac.be; internet www.human.mie-u.ac.jp/~peace/; f. 1964 to encourage interdisciplinary research on the conditions of peace and the causes of war; mems: 150 corporate, 5 regional branches, 1,000 individuals, in 93 countries; Sec.-Gen. LUC REYCHLER (Belgium); publ. *IPRA Newsletter* (quarterly).

International Social Science Council (ISSC): Maison de l'UNESCO, 1 rue Miollis, 75732 Paris Cedex 15, France; tel. 1-45-68-48-60; fax 1-45-66-76-03; e-mail issc@unesco.org; internet www.unesco.org/ngo/issc; f. 1952; aims to promote the advancement of the social sciences throughout the world and their application to the major problems of the world; encourages co-operation at an international level between specialists in the social sciences; comprises programmes on International Human Dimensions of Global Environmental Change (IHDP), Gender, Globalization and Democratization, and Comparative Research on Poverty (CROP); mems: International Association of Legal Sciences, International Economic Association, International

Federation of Social Science Organizations, International Geographical Union, International Institute of Administrative Sciences, International Peace Research Association, International Political Science Association, International Sociological Association, International Union for the Scientific Study of Population, International Union of Anthropological and Ethnological Sciences, International Union of Psychological Science, World Association for Public Opinion Research, World Federation for Mental Health; 28 national orgs; 16 associate members; Pres. Prof. GUDMUND HERNES (Norway); Sec.-Gen. Dr HEIDE HACKMANN (France).

International Society of Social Defence and Humane Criminal Policy (ISSD): c/o Centro nazionale di prevenzione e difesa sociale, Piazza Castello 3, 20121 Milan, Italy; tel. (02) 86460714; fax (02) 72008431; e-mail cnpds.ispac@cnpds.it; internet www.cnpds.it; f. 1945 to combat crime, to protect society and to prevent citizens from being tempted to commit criminal actions; mems: in 43 countries; Sec.-Gen. EDMONDO BRUTI LIBERATI (Italy); publ. *Cahiers de défense sociale* (annually).

International Sociological Association: c/o Faculty of Political Sciences and Sociology, Universidad Complutense, 28223 Madrid, Spain; tel. (91) 3527650; fax (91) 3524945; e-mail isa@isa-sociology.org; internet www.isa-sociology.org; f. 1949 to promote sociological knowledge, facilitate contacts between sociologists, encourage the dissemination and exchange of information and facilities and stimulate research; has 55 research committees on various aspects of sociology; holds World Congresses every four years (18th Congress: Yokohama, Japan, July 2014); Exec. Sec. IZABELA BARLINSKA; publs *Current Sociology* (6 a year), *International Sociology* (6 a year), *Sage Studies in International Sociology* (based on World Congress).

International Statistical Institute (ISI): POB 24070, 2490 AB The Hague, Netherlands; tel. (70) 3375737; fax (70) 3860025; e-mail isi@cbs.nl; internet www.isi-web.org; f. 1885; devoted to the development and improvement of statistical methods and their application throughout the world; executes international research programmes; mems: 2,000 ordinary mems, 11 hon. mems, 166 *ex officio* mems, 69 corporate mems, 45 affiliated orgs, 32 national statistical societies; Pres. LEE JAE-CHANG (Republic of Korea); Dir Permanent Office ADA VAN KRIMPEN; publs *Bulletin of the International Statistical Institute* (proceedings of biennial sessions), *International Statistical Review* (3 a year), *Short Book Reviews* (3 a year), *Statistical Theory and Method Abstracts–Z* (available on CD-Rom and online), *ISI Newsletter* (3 a year), *Membership Directory* (available online).

International Studies Association (ISA): Social Science 324, Univ. of Arizona, Tucson, AZ 85721, USA; tel. (520) 621-7715; fax (520) 621-5780; e-mail isa@u.arizona.edu; internet www.isanet.org; f. 1959; links those whose professional concerns extend beyond their own national boundaries (government officials, representatives of business and industry, and scholars); mems: 3,500 in 60 countries; Pres. THOMAS WEISS (USA); Exec. Dir THOMAS J. VOLGY; publs *International Studies Quarterly*, *International Studies Perspectives*, *International Studies Review*, *ISA Newsletter*.

International Union for Oriental and Asian Studies: Közraktar u. 12A 11/2, 1093 Budapest, Hungary; f. 1951 by the 22nd International Congress of Orientalists (now the International Congress of Asian and North African Studies) under the auspices of UNESCO, to promote contacts between orientalists throughout the world, and to organize congresses, research and publications; mems: in 24 countries; Sec.-Gen. Prof. GEORG HAZAI; publs *Philologiae Turcicae Fundamenta*, *Materalien zum Sumerischen Lexikon*, *Sanskrit Dictionary*, *Corpus Inscriptionum Iranicarum*, *Linguistic Atlas of Iran*, *Matériels des parlers iraniens*, *Turcology Annual*, *Bibliographieegyptologique*.

International Union for the Scientific Study of Population (IUSSP): 3–5 rue Nicolas, 75980 Paris Cedex 20, France; tel. 1-56-06-21-73; fax 1-56-06-22-04; e-mail iussp@iussp.org; internet www.iussp.org; f. 1928 to advance the progress of quantitative and qualitative demography as a science (reconstituted in 1947); organizes International Population Conference every four years (27th Conference: Busan, Republic of Korea, Aug. 2013); mems: 1,917 in 121 countries; Pres. PETER MCDONALD (Australia); Sec.-Gen./Treas. EMILY GRUNDY (United Kingdom); publs *IUSSP Bulletin* and books on population.

International Union of Academies (IUA) (Union académique internationale—UAI): Palais des Académies, 1 rue Ducale, 1000 Brussels, Belgium; tel. (2) 550-22-00; fax (2) 550-22-05; e-mail info@uai-iua.org; internet www.uai-iua.org; f. 1919 to promote international co-operation through collective research in philology, archaeology, art history, history and social sciences; mems: academic institutions in 61 countries; Sec.-Gen. HERVÉ HASQUIN.

International Union of Anthropological and Ethnological Sciences (IUAES): Dept of Anthropology, Faculty of Human Sciences, Osaka University, 1–2 Yamadaoka, Suita, Osaka 565-0871, Japan; tel. (6) 6879-7002; e-mail iuaes@glocol.osaka-u.ac.jp; internet www.glocol.osaka-u.ac.jp/iuaes; f. 1948 under the auspices of UNESCO, to enhance exchange and communication between scientists and institutions in the fields of anthropology and ethnology; aims to promote harmony between nature and culture; organizes 22 international research commissions; mems: institutions and individuals in 100 countries; Pres. Dr PETER J. M. NAS (Netherlands); Sec.-Gen. JUNJI KOIZUMI (Japan); publ. *IUAES Newsletter* (3 a year).

International Union of Prehistoric and Protohistoric Sciences: GRI, Inst Politécnico de Tomar, ave Dr Cândido Madueira, 2300-531 Tomar, Portugal; tel. (249) 346363; fax (249) 346366; e-mail uispp@ipt.pt; internet www.uispp.ipt.pt; f. 1931 to promote congresses and scientific work in the fields of pre- and proto-history; mems: 120 countries; Sec.-Gen. LUIZ OOSTERBEEK.

Mensa International: c/o British Mensa, St John's House, St. John's Sq., Wolverhampton, WV2 4AH, United Kingdom; tel. (1902) 772771; fax (1902) 392500; e-mail enquiries@mensa.org; internet www.mensa.org; f. 1946 to identify and foster intelligence for the benefit of humanity; mems: individuals who score higher than 98% of people in general in a recognized intelligence test may become mems; there are 100,000 mems world-wide; Exec. Dir MICHAEL FEENAN (United Kingdom); publ. *Mensa International Journal* (monthly).

Permanent International Committee of Linguists: Postbus 3023, 2301 DA Leiden, Netherlands; tel. (71) 5211552; e-mail cipl.secretary-general@planet.nl; internet www.ciplnet.com; f. 1928; aims to further linguistic research, to co-ordinate activities undertaken for the advancement of linguistics, and to make the results of linguistic research known internationally; holds Congress every five years; mems: 34 countries and 2 int. linguistic orgs; Pres. F. KIEFER (Hungary); Sec.-Gen. P. G. J. VAN STERKENBURG (Netherlands); publ. *Linguistic Bibliography* (annually).

Southern African Research and Documentation Centre (SARDC): POB 5690, Harare, Zimbabwe; tel. (4) 791141; fax (4) 791271; e-mail sardc@sardc.net; internet www.sardc.net; f. 1987; aims to enhance and disseminate information on political, economic, cultural and social developments in southern Africa; Exec. Dir PHYLLIS JOHNSON.

Third World Forum: 39 Dokki St, POB 43, Orman Giza, Cairo, Egypt; tel. (2) 7488092; fax (2) 7480668; e-mail 20sabry2@gega.net; internet www.forumtiersmonde.net; f. 1975 to link social scientists and others from the developing countries, to discuss alternative development policies and encourage research; maintains regional offices in Egypt, Mexico, Senegal and Sri Lanka; mems: individuals in more than 50 countries.

World Association for Public Opinion Research: c/o University of Nebraska-Lincoln, UNL Gallup Research Center, 201 N 13th St, Lincoln, NE 68588-0242, USA; tel. (402) 472-7720; fax (402) 472-7727; e-mail renae@wapor.org; internet www.wapor.org; f. 1947 to establish and promote contacts between persons in the field of survey research on opinions, attitudes and behaviour of people in the various countries of the world; works to further the use of objective, scientific survey research in national and international affairs; mems: 450 from 72 countries; Pres. Dr TOM W. SMITH; Gen. Sec. Prof. Dr ALLAN MCCUTCHEON; publs *WAPOR Newsletter* (quarterly), *International Journal of Public Opinion* (quarterly).

World Society for Ekistics: c/o Athens Center of Ekistics, 23 Strat. Syndesmou St, 106 73 Athens, Greece; tel. (210) 3623216;

fax (210) 3629337; e-mail ekistics@otenet.gr; internet www.ekistics.org; f. 1965; aims to promote knowledge and ideas concerning human settlements through research, publications and conferences; encourages the development and expansion of education in ekistics; aims to recognize the benefits and necessity of an inter-disciplinary approach to the needs of human settlements; mems: 233 individuals; Pres. CALOGERO MUSCARA; Sec.-Gen. P. PSOMOPOULOS.

Social Welfare and Human Rights

African Commission on Human and Peoples' Rights: 31 Bijilo Annex Layout, POB 673, Banjul, The Gambia; tel. 4410505; fax 4410504; e-mail au-banjul@africa-union.org; internet www.achpr.org; f. 1987; mandated to monitor compliance with the African Charter on Human and People's Rights (ratified in 1986); investigates claims of human rights abuses perpetrated by govts that have ratified the Charter (claims may be brought by other African govts, the victims themselves, or by a third party); meets twice a year for 15 days in March and Oct; mems: 11; Exec. Sec. Dr MARY MABOREKE.

African Union of Mutuals: Rabat, Morocco; internet www.unionafricainemutualite.org; f. 2007; promotes co-operation among African companies concerned with health care and social insurance; Pres. MOHAMEN EL FARRAH (Morocco); Sec.-Gen. CLARISSE KAYE (Côte d'Ivoire).

Aid to Displaced Persons (L'Aide aux Personnes Déplacées): 33 rue du Marché, 4500 Huy, Belgium; tel. (85) 21-34-81; fax (85) 23-01-47; e-mail aidepersdepl.huy@skynet.be; internet www.aideauxpersonnesdeplacees.be; f. 1949; aims to provide aid and support for refugees.

Amnesty International: 1 Easton St, London, WC1X ODW, United Kingdom; tel. (20) 7413-5500; fax (20) 7956-1157; e-mail amnestyis@amnesty.org; internet www.amnesty.org; f. 1961; an independent, democratic, self-governing world-wide movement of people who campaign for internationally recognized human rights, such as those enshrined in the Universal Declaration of Human Rights; undertakes research and action focused on preventing and ending grave abuses of the rights to physical and mental integrity, freedom of conscience and expression, and freedom from discrimination, within the context of its work impartially to promote and protect all human rights; mems: more than 2.2m. represented by 7,800 local, youth, student and other specialist groups, in more than 150 countries and territories; nationally organized sections in 58 countries and pre-section co-ordinating structures in another 22 countries; major policy decisions are taken by an International Council comprising representatives from all national sections; financed by donations; no funds are sought or accepted from governments; Sec.-Gen. SALIL SHETTY (India); publs *International Newsletter* (monthly), *Annual Report*, other country reports.

Anti-Slavery International: Thomas Clarkson House, The Stableyard, Broomgrove Rd, London, SW9 9TL, United Kingdom; tel. (20) 7501-8920; fax (20) 7738-4110; e-mail info@antislavery.org; internet www.antislavery.org; f. 1839; aims to eliminate all forms of slavery by exposing manifestations of it around the world and campaigning against it; supports initiatives by local organizations to release people from slavery, and develops rehabilitation programmes aimed at preventing people from re-entering slavery; pressures governments to implement international laws prohibiting slavery and to develop and enforce similar national legislation; maintains digital collection of 18th- and 19th-century documentation on the Transatlantic Slave Trade at www.recoveredhistories.org; mems: c. 2,000 world-wide; Dir AIDAN MCQUADE; publs *Annual Review* (quarterly), *Reporter* (quarterly), special reports and research documentation.

Article 19: 60 Farringdon Rd, London, EC1R 3GA, United Kingdom; tel. (20) 7324-2500; e-mail info@article19.org; internet www.article19.org; f. 1987; an international human rights org., in particular dedicated to defending and promoting freedom of expression and of information; Exec. Dir Dr AGNÈS CALLAMARD.

Associated Country Women of the World (ACWW): Mary Sumner House, 24 Tufton St, London, SW1P 3RB, United Kingdom; tel. (20) 7799-3875; fax (20) 7340-9950; e-mail info@acww.org.uk; internet www.acww.org.uk; f. 1933; aims to aid the economic and social development of countrywomen and home-makers of all nations, to promote international goodwill and understanding, to work to alleviate poverty, and promote good health and education; Pres MAY KIDD; Gen. Sec. JO ELLEN ALMOND; publ. *The Countrywoman* (quarterly).

Association Internationale de la Mutualité (AIM) (International Association of Mutual Health Funds): 50 rue d'Arlon, 5th Floor, 1000 Brussels, Belgium; tel. (2) 234-57-00; fax (2) 234-57-08; e-mail aim.secretariat@aim-mutual.org; internet www.aim-mutual.org; f. 1950 as a grouping of autonomous health insurance and social protection bodies; aims to promote and reinforce access to health care by developing the sound management of mutualities; serves as a forum for exchange of information and debate; mems: 45 national federations in 28 countries; Pres. WILLI BUDDE (Germany); publs *AIMS* (newsletter), reports on health issues.

Aviation sans Frontières (ASF): Orly Fret 768, 94398 Orly Aérogare Cedex, France; tel. 1-49-75-74-37; fax 1-49-75-74-33; e-mail asfparis@asf-fr.org; internet www.asf-fr.org; f. 1983 to make available the resources of the aviation industry to humanitarian organizations, for carrying supplies and equipment at minimum cost, both on long-distance flights and locally; Pres. HUGUES GENDRE; Gen. Sec. PATRICK SAUMONT.

Caritas Internationalis (International Confederation of Catholic Organizations for charitable and social action): Palazzo San Calisto, 00120 Città del Vaticano; tel. (06) 6987-9799; fax (06) 6988-7237; e-mail caritas.internationalis@caritas.va; internet www.caritas.org; f. 1950 to study problems arising from poverty, their causes and possible solutions; national mem. organizations undertake assistance and development activities. The Confederation co-ordinates emergency relief and development projects, and represents mems at international level; mems: 162 national orgs; Pres. Cardinal OSCAR RODRIGUEZ MARADIAGA (Honduras); Sec.-Gen. MICHEL ROY (France); publs *Caritas Matters* (quarterly), *Emergency Calling* (2 a year).

CISV International Ltd: Mea House, Ellison Pl., Newcastle upon Tyne, NE1 8XS, United Kingdom; tel. (191) 232-4998; fax (191) 261-4710; e-mail international@cisv.org; internet www.cisv.org; f. 1950 as the International Association of Children's International Summer Villages to promote peace, education and cross-cultural friendship; conducts International Camps for children and young people mainly between the ages of 11 and 19; mems: c. 49,000; International Pres. ARNE-CHRISTIAN HAUKELAND; Sec.-Gen. GABRIELLE MANDELL.

CIVICUS (World Alliance for Citizen Participation): POB 933, Southdale, Johannesburg 2135, South Africa; tel. (11) 833-5959; fax (11) 833-7997; e-mail info@civicus.org; internet www.civicus.org; f. 1993; aims to protect and strengthen citizen action and civil society throughout the world, in particular in areas where participatory democracy and citizen freedoms are threatened; convenes a World Assembly every two years (2012: Montréal, Canada, in Sept.); mems: 450 orgs in 110 countries; Acting Sec.-Gen. KATSUJI IMATA (Japan).

Co-ordinating Committee for International Voluntary Service (CCIVS): Maison de l'UNESCO, 1 rue Miollis, 75732 Paris Cedex 15, France; tel. 1-45-68-49-36; fax 1-42-73-05-21; e-mail secretariat@ccivs.org; internet www.ccivs.org; f. 1948 to co-ordinate youth voluntary service organizations world-wide; organizes seminars and conferences; publishes relevant literature; undertakes planning and execution of projects in collaboration with UNESCO, the UN, the EU, etc; affiliated mems: 220 orgs in more than 100 countries; Pres. JINSU YOM; Dir FRANCESCO VOLPINI; publs *News from CCIVS* (3 a year), *The Volunteer's Handbook*, other guides, handbooks and directories.

Co-ordinator of the Indigenous Organizations of the Amazon Basin (COICA): Calle Sevilla 24–358 y Guipuzcoa, La Floresta, Quito, Ecuador; e-mail com@coica.org.ec; internet www.coica.org.ec; f. 1984; aims to co-ordinate the activities of national organizations concerned with the indigenous people and environment of the Amazon basin, and promotes respect for human rights and the self-determination of the indigenous populations; mems: 9 orgs; Co-ordinator-Gen. EDWIN VÁSQUEZ

CAMPOS; publ. *Nuestra Amazonia* (quarterly, in English, Spanish, French and Portuguese).

EIRENE (International Christian Service for Peace): Postfach 1322, 56503 Neuwied, Germany; tel. (2631) 83790; fax (2631) 837990; e-mail eirene-int@eirene.org; internet www.eirene.org; f. 1957; carries out professional training, apprenticeship programmes, agricultural work and work to support co-operatives in Africa and Latin America; runs volunteer programmes in co-operation with peace groups in Europe and the USA; Gen. Sec. ANGELA KÖNIG.

European Federation of Older Persons (EURAG): Mozartgasse 14A, 8010 Graz, Austria; tel. (316) 380-29-64; fax (316) 380-92-12; e-mail dana_stein@volny.cz; internet eurageurope.org; f. 1962 as the European Federation for the Welfare of the Elderly (present name adopted 2002); serves as a forum for the exchange of experience and practical co-operation among member organizations; represents the interests of members before international organizations; promotes understanding and co-operation in matters of social welfare; draws attention to the problems of old age; mems: 148 orgs in 33 countries; Pres. Dr EVELINE HÖNIGSPERGER; Sec.-Gen. DANA STEINOVA (Czech Republic); publ. (in English, French, German and Italian) *EURAG Information* (monthly).

Federation of Asia-Pacific Women's Associations (FAWA): 962 Josefa Llanes Escoda St, Ermita, Manila, Philippines; tel. (2) 741-1675; e-mail nfwcp@yahoo.com; internet fawainternational.org; f. 1959 to provide closer relations, and bring about joint efforts among Asians, particularly women, through mutual appreciation of cultural, moral and socio-economic values; mems: 415,000; Pres. KRISTAL KOGA (USA); Sec. REBECCA STEPHENSON (USA); publ. *FAWA News Bulletin* (quarterly).

Global Migration Group: c/o UNICEF, 3 United Nations Plaza, New York, NY 10017, USA; tel. and fax (212) 906-5001; internet www.globalmigrationgroup.org; f. 2003, as the Geneva Migration Group; renamed as above in 2006; mems: ILO, IOM, UNCTAD, UNDP, United Nations Department of Economic and Social Affairs (UNDESA), UNFPA, OHCHR, UNHCR, UNODC, and the World Bank; holds regular meetings to discuss issues relating to int. migration, chaired by mem. orgs on a six-month rotational basis.

Inclusion Europe: Galeries de la Toison d'Or, 29 ch. d'Ixelles, bte 393/32, 1050 Brussels, Belgium; tel. (2) 502-28-15; fax (2) 502-80-10; e-mail secretariat@inclusion-europe.org; internet www.inclusion-europe.org; f. 1988 to advance the human rights and defend the interests of people with learning or intellectual disabilities, and their families, in Europe; mems: 46 societies in 34 European countries; Pres. MAUREEN PIGGOT (United Kingdom); publs *INCLUDE* (in English and French), *Information Letter* (weekly online, in English and French), *Human Rights Observer* (in English and French), *Enlargement Update* (online every 2 weeks, in English and French), other papers and publs.

Initiatives of Change International: 1 rue de Varembé, 1202 Geneva, Switzerland; tel. 227491620; fax 227330267; e-mail iofc-international@iofc.org; internet www.iofc.org; f. 1921; name changed from the Moral Rearmament Movement in 2001; an international network specializing in conflict resolution that is open to people of all cultures, nationalities, religions and beliefs, and works towards change, both locally and globally, commencing at the personal level; has special consultative status with ECOSOC and participatory status with the Council of Europe; supports and publicizes the grassroots work of the National Societies of Initiatives of Change; works in 60 countries; Pres. OMNIA MARZOUK; publs *Changer International* (French, 6 a year), *For a Change* (English, 6 a year), *Caux Information* (German, monthly).

Inter-American Conference on Social Security (Conferencia Interamericano de Seguridad Social—CISS): c/o F. Flores, Instituto Mexicano del Seguro Social, Paseo de la Reforma 476, 1°, Col. Juarez, Del. Cuauhtemoc, CP 06600, México, DF, Mexico; tel. (55) 5211-4853; fax (55) 5211-2623; e-mail ciss@ciss.org.mx; internet www.ciss.org.mx; f. 1942 to contribute to the development of social security in the countries of the Americas and to co-operate with social security institutions; CISS bodies are: the General Assembly, the Permanent Inter-American Committee on Social Security, the Secretariat General, six American Commissions of Social Security and the Inter-American Center for Social Security Studies; mems: 66 social security institutions in 36 countries; Pres. DANIEL KARAM TOUMEH (Mexico); Sec.-Gen. Dr GABRIEL MARTÍNEZ GONZÁLEZ (Mexico); publs *Social Security Journal/Seguridad Social* (every 2 months), *The Americas Social Security Report* (annually), *Social Security Bulleting* (monthly, online), monographs, study series.

International Association for Suicide Prevention: IASP Central Administrative Office, Sognsvannsveien 21, Bygg 12, 0372 Oslo, Norway; tel. 22-92-37-15; fax 22-92-39-58; e-mail office@iasp.info; internet www.iasp.info; f. 1960; serves as a common platform for interchange of acquired experience, literature and information about suicide; disseminates information; arranges special training; encourages and carries out research; organizes the Biennial International Congress for Suicide Prevention (Sept. 2013: Oslo, Norway); mems: 340 individuals and societies, in 55 countries of all continents; Pres. Dr LANNY BERMAN; publ. *Crisis* (quarterly).

International Association of Schools of Social Work: c/o A. Tasse, Graduate School of Social Work, University of Addis Ababa, POB 1176, Ethiopia; tel. (1) 231084; fax (1) 239768; e-mail abye.tasse@ids.fr; internet www.iassw-aiets.org; f. 1928 to provide international leadership and encourage high standards in social work education; mems: 1,600 schools of social work in 70 countries, and 25 national asscns of schools; Pres. Prof. Dr ANGELINA YUEN (Hong Kong, SAR); Sec. HELLE STRAUSS; publs *Newsletters* (in English, French and Spanish), *Directory of Schools of Social Work*, *Journal of International Social Work*, reports and case studies.

International Association of Social Educators (AIEJI): Galgebakken Soender 5-4, DK-2620 Albertslund, Denmark; tel. 72486841; e-mail dee@sl.dk; internet www.aieji.net; f. 1951 (as International Asscn of Workers for Troubled Children and Youth); provides a centre of information about child welfare; encourages co-operation between members; 2013 Congress: Luxembourg, in April; mems: national and regional public or private asscns from 22 countries and individual members in many other countries; Pres. BENNY ANDERSEN (Denmark); Gen. Sec. LARS STEINOV (Denmark).

International Catholic Migration Commission (ICMC): 37–39 rue de Vermont, CP 96, 1211 Geneva 20, Switzerland; tel. 229191020; fax 229191048; e-mail info@icmc.net; internet www.icmc.net; f. 1951; serves and protects uprooted people (refugees, internationally displaced persons and migrants), regardless of faith, race, ethnicity or nationality; maintains staff and programmes in more than 40 countries; advocates for rights-based policies and durable solutions; Pres. JOHN KLINK (USA); Sec.-Gen. JOHAN KETELERS (Belgium).

International Civil Defence Organization (ICDO) (Organisation internationale de protection civile—OIPC): POB 172, 10–12 chemin de Surville, 1213 Petit-Lancy 2, Geneva, Switzerland; tel. 228796969; fax 228796979; e-mail icdo@icdo.org; internet www.icdo.org; f. 1931, present statutes in force 1972; aims to contribute to the development of structures ensuring the protection of populations and the safeguarding of property and the environment in the face of natural and man-made disasters; promotes co-operation between civil defence organizations in member countries; Sec.-Gen. NAWAF B. S. AL SLEIBI (Jordan); publ. *International Civil Defence Journal* (quarterly, in Arabic, English, French, Russian and Chinese).

International Commission for the Prevention of Alcoholism and Drug Dependency: 12501 Old Columbia Pike, Silver Spring, MD 20904-6600, USA; tel. (301) 680-6719; fax (301) 680-6707; e-mail the_icpa@hotmail.com; f. 1952 to encourage scientific research on intoxication by alcohol, its physiological, mental and moral effects on the individual, and its effect on the community; mems: individuals in 120 countries; Exec. Dir Dr PETER N. LANDLESS; publ. *ICPA Reporter*.

International Council of Voluntary Agencies (ICVA): 26–28 ave Guiseppe Motta, 1202 Geneva, Switzerland; tel. 229509600; fax 229509609; e-mail secretariat@icva.ch; internet www.icva.ch; f. 1962 as a global network of human rights and humanitarian non-governmental organizations; focuses on information exchange and advocacy, primarily in the areas of humanitarian affairs and refugee issues; mems: 74 non-governmental orgs; Chair. PAUL O'BRIEN; Co-ordinator ED

SCHENKENBERG VAN MIEROP; publ. *Talk Back* (newsletter, available online).

International Council of Women (ICW) (Conseil International des Femmes—CIF): 13 rue Caumartin, 75009 Paris, France; tel. 1-47-42-19-40; fax 1-42-66-26-23; e-mail icw-cif@wanadoo.fr; internet www.icw-cif.org; f. 1888 to bring together in international affiliation Nat. Councils of Women from all continents, for consultation and joint action; promotes equal rights for men and women and the integration of women in development and decision-making; has five standing committees; mems: 65 national councils; Pres. COSIMA SCHENK; Sec.-Gen. RADOSVETA BRUZAUD; publ. *Newsletter*.

International Council on Alcohol and Addictions (ICAA): CP 189, 1001 Lausanne, Switzerland; tel. 213209865; fax 213209817; e-mail secretariat@icaa.ch; internet www.icaa.ch; f. 1907; provides an international forum for all those concerned with the prevention of harm resulting from the use of alcohol and other drugs; offers advice and guidance in development of policies and programmes; organizes training courses, congresses, symposia and seminars in different countries; mems: affiliated orgs in 74 countries, as well as individual members; Pres. Dr PETER A. VAMOS (Canada); publs *ICAA Newsflash*, *Alcoholism* (2 a year), *President's Letter*.

International Council on Social Welfare (ICSW): Berkerly Lane, Plot 4, Entebbe, POB 28957, Kampala, Uganda; tel. (414) 32-1150; e-mail dcorrell@icsw.org; internet www.icsw.org; f. 1928 to provide an international forum for the discussion of social work and related issues and to promote interest in social welfare; holds international conference every two years with the International Association of Schools of Social Work and the International Federation of Social Workers; provides documentation and information services; mems: 57 national cttees, 6 int. orgs, 34 other orgs in 87 countries; Pres. CHRISTIAN ROLLET; Exec. Dir DENYS CORRELL; publ. *Global Cooperation Newsletter Monthly*.

International Dachau Committee: 2 rue Chauchat, 75009 Paris, France; tel. 1-45-23-39-99; fax 1-48-00-06-13; e-mail info@comiteinternationaldachau.com; internet www.comiteinternationaldachau.com; f. 1958 to perpetuate the memory of the political prisoners of Dachau; to manifest the friendship and solidarity of former prisoners whatever their beliefs or nationality; to maintain the ideals of their resistance, liberty, tolerance and respect for persons and nations; and to maintain the former concentration camp at Dachau as a museum and international memorial; mems: national asscns in 20 countries; Pres. PIETER DIETZ DE LOOS; publ. *Bulletin Officiel du Comité International de Dachau* (2 a year).

International Federation for Human Rights Leagues (FIDH): 17 passage de la Main d'Or, 75011 Paris, France; tel. 1-43-55-25-18; fax 1-43-55-18-80; e-mail fidh@fidh.org; internet www.fidh.org; f. 1922; promotes the implementation of the Universal Declaration of Human Rights and other instruments of human rights protection; aims to raise awareness and alert public opinion to issues of human rights violations; undertakes investigation and observation missions; carries out training; uses its consultative and observer status to lobby international authorities; mems: 155 national leagues in over 100 countries; Pres. SOUHAYR BELHASSEN (Tunisia); Exec. Dir ANTOINE BERNARD; publs *Lettre* (2 a month), mission reports.

International Federation of Educative Communities (FICE): Vogelsbergstr. 212, 63679 Schotten, Germany; tel. (60) 4460090; fax (60) 444394; e-mail info@fice.de; internet www.fice-europe.org; f. 1948 under the auspices of UNESCO to co-ordinate the work of national asscns, and to promote the international exchange of knowledge and experience in the field of childcare; Congress held every two years; mems: national asscns from 21 European countries, Canada, India, Israel, Morocco, South Africa and the USA; Pres. MONIKA NIEDERLE (Austria); Gen. Sec. ANDREW HOSIE (United Kingdom); publ. *Bulletin* (2 a year).

International Federation of Persons with Physical Disability (FIMITIC): Rákóczi út. 36, 2600 Vác, Hungary; tel. and fax (27) 502661; e-mail fimitic@invitel.hu; internet www.fimitic.org; f. 1953; an international, humanitarian, non-profit, politically and religiously neutral non-governmental umbrella federation of persons with physical disability under the guidance of the disabled themselves; focuses activities on ensuring the equalization of opportunities and full participation of persons with physical disabilities in society and fights against any kind of discrimination against persons with disabilities; mems: national groups from 28 European countries; Pres. MIGUEL ANGEL GARCÍA OCA (Spain); publs *Bulletin*, *Nouvelles*.

International Federation of Social Workers (IFSW): POB 6875, Schwarztorstr. 22, 3001 Bern, Switzerland; tel. 225483625; fax 313808301; e-mail global@ifsw.org; internet www.ifsw.org; f. 1928 as International Permanent Secretariat of Social Workers; present name adopted 1956; aims to promote social work as a profession through international co-operation on standards, training, ethics and working conditions; organizes international conferences; represents the profession at the UN and other international bodies; supports national asscns of social workers; mems: national asscns in 90 countries; Pres. GARY BAILEY (USA); Sec.-Gen, Dr RORY G. TRUELL (New Zealand); publs *IFSW update* (available online), policy statements and manifestos.

International Federation of the Blue Cross: CP 6813, 3001 Bern, Switzerland; tel. 313005860; fax 313005869; e-mail office@ifbc.info; internet www.ifbc.info; f. 1877 to aid the victims of intemperance and drug addiction, and to take part in the general movement against alcoholism; mems: 40 orgs; Pres. GEIR GUNDERSEN (Norway); Sec.-Gen MARK MOSER.

International League against Racism and Antisemitism (La Ligue Internationale contre le Racisme et l'Antisémitisme—LICRA): 42 rue du Louvre, 75001 Paris, France; tel. 1-45-08-08-08; fax 1-45-08-18-18; e-mail licra@licra.org; internet www.licra.org; f. 1927; campaigns against all forms of racism in sport, culture, education, law, etc.; Pres. ALAIN JAKUBOWICZ.

International League for Human Rights: 352 Seventh Ave, Suite 1234, New York, NY 10001, USA; tel. (212) 661-0480; fax (212) 661-0416; e-mail info@ilhr.org; internet www.ilhr.org; f. 1942 to implement political, civil, social, economic and cultural rights contained in the Universal Declaration of Human Rights adopted by the United Nations and to support and protect defenders of human rights world-wide; maintains offices in Geneva, Switzerland, and in Freetown, Sierra Leone; mems: individuals, national affiliates and correspondents throughout the world; Pres. ROBERT ARSENAULT; Exec. Dir DAVID TAM-BARYOH; publs various human rights reports.

International Planned Parenthood Federation (IPPF): 4 Newhams Row, London, SE1 3UZ, United Kingdom; tel. (20) 7939-8200; fax (20) 7939-8300; e-mail info@ippf.org; internet www.ippf.org; f. 1952; aims to promote and support sexual and reproductive health rights and choices world-wide, with a particular focus on the needs of young people; works to bring relevant issues to the attention of the media, parliamentarians, academics, governmental and non-governmental organizations, and the general public; mobilizes financial resources to fund programmes and information materials; offers technical assistance and training; collaborates with other international organizations; the International Medical Panel of the IPPF formulates guidelines and statements on current medical and scientific advice and best practices; mems: independent family planning asscns in over 151 countries; Pres. Dr JACQUELINE SHARPE; Dir-Gen. Dr GILL GREER.

International Prisoners' Aid Association: POB 7333, Arlington, VA 22207, USA; tel. (703) 836-0024; fax (703) 836-0024; e-mail desifl@aol.com; f. 1950; works to improve prisoners' aid services, with the aim of promoting the rehabilitation of the individual and increasing the protection of society; mems: national federations in 29 countries; Pres. Dr WOLFGANG DOLEISCH (Austria); Exec. Dir Dr ELIZABETH DESIDERIO GONDLES; publ. *Newsletter* (3 a year).

International Social Security Association (ISSA): 4 route des Morillons, CP 1, 1211 Geneva 22, Switzerland; tel. 227996617; fax 227998509; e-mail issa@ilo.org; internet www.issa.int; f. 1927 to promote the development of social security throughout the world, mainly through the improvement of techniques and administration, in order to advance social and economic conditions on the basis of social justice; collects and disseminates information on social security programmes throughout the world; undertakes research and policy analysis on the social security issues and distributes their results; encourages mutual assistance between member orgs; facilitates good practice collection and exchange; co-operates with other international or regional orgs exercising activities related to the field; communicates with its constituency and media and promotes social security through advocacy and information; and forges partnerships between the ISSA and other international orgs active in the area of social security to advance common strategies, including the ILO, the OECD and the World Bank; organizes a World Social Security Forum (2013: Doha, Qatar, in Nov.) and four Regional Social Security Forums (in Africa, the Americas, Asia/Pacific and Europe); convenes topic-related technical seminars in various regions; hosts international conferences, for example on information and communication technology in social security, social security actuaries and statisticians, and international policy research; co-organizes the World Congress on Occupational Safety and Health every three years; mems: 340 institutions in 150 countries; Pres. CORAZON DE LA PAZ-BERNARDO (Philippines); Sec.-Gen. HANS-HORST KONKOLEWSKY; publs *International Social Security Review* (quarterly, in English, French, German, Spanish), *Social Security Observer* (quarterly, in English, French, German, Spanish), *Social Security Worldwide*, online Social Security Observatory and other databases.

International Social Service (Service social international—SSI): 32 quai du Seujet, 1201 Geneva, Switzerland; tel. 229067700; fax 229067701; e-mail info@iss-ssi.org; internet www.iss-ssi.org; f. 1921 to aid families and individuals whose problems require services beyond the boundaries of the country in which they live, and where the solution of these problems depends upon co-ordinated action on the part of social workers in two or more countries; studies from an international standpoint the conditions and consequences of emigration in their effect on individual, family, and social life; operates on a non-sectarian and non-political basis; mems: 13 branches, 4 affiliated bureaux, and correspondents in more than 120 countries; Pres. a.i. DOUG LEWIS; Sec.-Gen. JEAN AYOUB.

International Society for Human Rights: Borsigallee 9, 60388 Frankfurt a.M. Germany; tel. (69) 4201080; fax (69) 42010833; e-mail info@ishr.org; internet www.ishr.org; f. 1972; promotes fundamental human rights and religious freedom; mems: 30,000 in 26 countries (incl. Azerbaijan, Belarus, Moldova, Russia, Ukraine, Uzbekistan); Pres. ALEXANDER FRHR. VON BISCHOFFSHAUSEN (Germany); Dir Gen. KARL HAFEN; publs *Für die Menschenrechte* (every two months), *Newsletter* (quarterly).

International Union of Tenants: Box 7514, 10392 Stockholm, Sweden; tel. (8) 7910224; fax (8) 204344; e-mail info@iut.nu; internet www.iut.nu; f. 1955 to collaborate in safeguarding the interests of tenants; participates in activities of UN-Habitat; has working groups for EC matters, eastern Europe, developing countries and for future development; holds annual council meeting and triennial congress; mems: national tenant orgs in 29 European countries, and Australia, Benin, Canada, India, Japan, New Zealand, Nigeria, South Africa, Tanzania, Togo, Uganda, and USA; Chair. SVEN BERGENSTRÅHLE; Sec.-Gen. MAGNUS HAMMAR; publ. *The Global Tenant* (quarterly).

Inter-University European Institute on Social Welfare (IEISW): 179 rue du Débarcadère, 6001 Marcinelle, Belgium; tel. (71) 44-72-67; fax (71) 47-27-44; e-mail ieiasmayence@hotmail.com; f. 1970 to promote, carry out and publicize scientific research on social welfare and community work; Pres. JOSEPH GILLAIN; Gen. Dir SERGE MAYENCE; publ. *COMM*.

Lions Clubs International: 300 West 22nd St, Oak Brook, IL 60523-8842, USA; tel. (630) 571-5466; fax (630) 571-8890; e-mail lions@lionsclubs.org; internet www.lionsclubs.org; f. 1917 to foster understanding among people of the world; to promote principles of good government and citizenship and an interest in civic, cultural, social and moral welfare and to encourage service-minded people to serve their community without financial reward; mems: 1.35m. in over 45,000 clubs in 197 countries and geographic areas; Pres. WING-KUN TAM; publ. *The Lion* (10 a year, in 20 languages).

Médecins sans frontières (MSF): 78 rue de Lausanne, CP 116, 1211 Geneva 21, Switzerland; tel. 228498400; fax 228498404; internet www.msf.org; f. 1971; independent medical humanitarian org. composed of physicians and other members of the medical profession; aims to provide medical assistance to victims of war and natural disasters; operates longer-term programmes of nutrition, immunization, sanitation, public health, and rehabilitation of hospitals and dispensaries; awarded the Nobel Peace Prize in 1999; mems: national sections in 21 countries in Europe, Asia and North America; Pres. Dr UNNI KRISHNAN KARUNAKARA; Sec.-Gen. KRIS TORGESON; publ. *Activity Report* (annually).

Pacific Disability Forum: POB 18458, Suva, Fiji; tel. 3312008; fax 3310469; e-mail program@pacificdisability.org; internet www.pacificdisability.org; f. 2002 to foster regional co-operation in addressing issues related to disability for the benefit of affected persons; aims to build awareness and pool resources among regional orgs to work for the rights and dignity of people with disabilities; organizes a Pacific Disability Regional Conference (2013: Nouméa); mems: 44 individuals and regional orgs; CEO SETAREKI MACANAWAI.

Pan-Pacific and South East Asia Women's Association (PPSEAWA): POB 119, Nuku'alofa, Tonga; tel. 24003; fax 41404; e-mail info@ppseawa.org; internet www.ppseawa.org; f. 1928 to foster better understanding and friendship among women in the region, and to promote co-operation for the study and improvement of social conditions; holds international conference every three years (2013: Suva, Fiji, in Aug.); mems: 22 national member orgs; Pres. Dr VIOPAPA ANNANDALE; publ. *PPSEAWA Bulletin* (2 a year).

Relief International: 5455 Wilshire Blvd, Suite 1280 Los Angeles, CA 90024, USA; tel. (310) 478-1200; fax (310) 478-1212; e-mail info@ri.org; internet ri.org; f. 1990 to provide emergency relief, rehabilitation and development assistance to people suffering as a result of social conflict or natural disaster; CEO and Pres. FARSHAD RASTEGAR.

Rotary International: 1560 Sherman Ave, Evanston, IL 60201, USA; tel. (847) 866-3000; fax (847) 328-3000; e-mail ers@rotary.org; internet www.rotary.org; f. 1905 to carry out activities for the service of humanity, to promote high ethical standards in business and professions and to further international understanding, goodwill and peace; mems: 1.2m. in more than 32,000 Rotary Clubs in more than 200 countries; Pres. SAKUJI TANAKA (Japan) (from 1 July 2012); Gen. Sec. EDWIN H. FUTA (USA); publs *The Rotarian* (monthly, English), *Rotary World* (5 a year, in 9 languages).

Service Civil International (SCI): St-Jacobsmarkt 82, 2000 Antwerp, Belgium; tel. (3) 226-57-27; fax (3) 232-03-44; e-mail info@sciint.org; internet www.sciint.org; f. 1920 to promote peace and understanding through voluntary service projects; more than 3,000 volunteers participate in SCI volunteer projects world-wide each year; SCI is also active in the field of peace education and organizes seminars, training activities and meetings; mems: 43 branches world-wide; Int. Pres. MIHAI CRISAN (Romania); publ. *Action* (quarterly).

Shack/Slum Dwellers International (SDI): POB 14038, Mowbray 7705 Cape Town, South Africa; tel. (21) 689-9408; fax (21) 689-3912; e-mail sdi@courc.co.za; internet www.sdinet.co.za; f. 1996; a transnational network of local shack/slum dweller orgs; Pres. ARPUTHAM JOCKIN.

Society of Saint Vincent de Paul: 6 rue du Londres, 75009 Paris, France; tel. 1-53-45-87-53; fax 1-42-61-72-56; e-mail cgi.information@ozanet.org; internet www.ssvpglobal.org; f. 1833 to conduct charitable activities such as childcare, youth work, work with immigrants, adult literacy programmes, residential care for the sick, handicapped and elderly, social counselling and work with prisoners and the unemployed, through personal contact; mems: over 700,000 in 141 countries; Pres. MICHAEL THIO; Sec.-Gen. BRUNO MENARD; publ. *Confeder@tioNews* (quarterly, in English, French and Spanish).

SOLIDAR: 22 rue de Commerce, 1000 Brussels, Belgium; tel. (2) 500-10-20; fax (2) 500-10-30; e-mail solidar@solidar.org; internet www.solidar.org; f. 1948 (fmrly International Workers' Aid); network of non-governmental orgs working to advance social justice in Europe and world-wide; mems: 52 orgs based in 25 countries, operating in more than 90 countries; Sec.-Gen. CONNY REUTER.

Soroptimist International: 87 Glisson Rd, Cambridge, CB1 2HG, United Kingdom; tel. (1223) 311833; fax (1223) 467951; e-mail hq@soroptimistinternational.org; internet www

.soroptimistinternational.org; f. 1921; unites professional and business women in promoting a world where women and girls may achieve their individual and collective potential, attain equality, and establish strong, peaceful communities world-wide; aims, through a global network of members and international partnerships, to inspire action, and to create opportunities, that might transform the lives of women and girls; convention held every four years (2012: Porto Alegre, Brazil, in Jan., on the theme 'Capitalist Crisis, Social Justice and Environment'); mems: about 90,000 in 3,000 clubs in 124 countries and territories; International Pres. ALICE WELLS (USA) (2011–13); Exec. Officer (vacant); publ. *The International Soroptimist* (quarterly).

Women for Women International: 4455 Connecticut Ave, NW, Suite 200, Washington, DC 20008, USA; tel. (202) 737-7705; fax (202) 737-7709; e-mail general@womenforwomen.org; internet www.womenforwomen.org; f. 1993; aims to assist the recovery and rehabilitation of women in conflict and post-conflict environments, in order to promote sustainable and peaceful societies; Pres. and Chief Operating Officer ANDRÉE SIMON.

Women's Global Network for Reproductive Rights: 13 Dao St, Project 3, Quezon City, 1102 Metro Manila, Philippines; tel. and fax (2) 7093193; e-mail office@wgnrr.org; internet www.wgnrr.org; f. 1984; aims to promote and work for sexual and reproductive health, rights and justice for women and all marginalized groups; Chair. FELISTAH MBITHE (Kenya).

World Blind Union: 1929 Bayview Ave, Toronto, ON M4G 3E8, Canada; tel. (416) 486-9698; fax (416) 486-8107; e-mail info@wbuoffice.org; internet www.worldblindunion.org; f. 1984 (amalgamating the World Council for the Welfare of the Blind and the International Federation of the Blind) to work for the prevention of blindness and the welfare of blind and visually impaired people; encourages development of braille, talking book programmes and other media for the blind; organizes rehabilitation, training and employment; works on the prevention and cure of blindness in co-operation with the International Agency for the Prevention of Blindness; co-ordinates aid to the blind in developing countries; maintains the Louis Braille birthplace as an international museum; mems: in 190 countries; Pres. MARYANNE DIAMOND (Australia); Sec.-Gen. ENRIQUE PÉREZ (Spain); publ. *E-Bulletin* (quarterly).

World Family Organization (WFO): 28 pl. Saint-Georges, 75009 Paris, France; tel. 1-48-78-07-59; fax 1-42-82-95-24; e-mail info@worldfamilyorganization.org; internet www.worldfamilyorganization.org; f. 1947 as the International Union of Family Organizations (IUOF), to bring together all organizations throughout the world working for family welfare; present name adopted 1998; maintains commissions and working groups on issues including standards of living, housing, marriage guidance, rural families, etc; there are six regional organizations: the Pan-African Family Organisation (Rabat, Morocco), the North America organization (Montréal, Canada), the Arab Family Organisation (Tunis, Tunisia), the Asian Union of Family Organisations (New Delhi, India), the European regional organization (Bern, Switzerland) and the Latin American Secretariat (Curitiba, Brazil); mems: national asscns, groups and governmental departments in over 55 countries; Pres. Dr DEISI NOELI WEBER KUSZTRA (Brazil).

World Federation of the Deaf (WFD): POB 65, 00401 Helsinki, Finland; tel. (9) 5803573; fax (9) 5803572; e-mail Info@wfdeaf.org; internet www.wfdeaf.org; f. 1951 to serve the interests of deaf people and their national organizations and represent these in international fora; works towards the goal of full participation by deaf people in society; encourages deaf people to set up and run their own organizations; priority is given to the promotion of the recognition and use of national sign languages, the education of deaf people and deaf people in the developing world; mems: 133 member countries; Pres. COLIN ALLEN; publ. *WFD Newsletter* (6 a year).

World ORT: ORT House, 126 Albert St, London, NW1 7NE, United Kingdom; tel. (20) 7446-8500; fax (20) 7446-8650; e-mail wo@ort.org; internet www.ort.org; f. 1880 for the development of industrial, agricultural and artisanal skills among Jews; conducts vocational training programmes for children and adults, including instructors' and teachers' education and apprenticeship training; implements technical assistance programmes in co-operation with interested governments; manages global network of schools, colleges, training centres and programmes; has assisted more than 3m. people; mems: committees in more than 40 countries; Pres. JEAN DE GUNZBURG; Dir-Gen. ROBERT SINGER; publs *Annual Report*, *World ORT Times*.

World Social Forum (WSF): Support Office: Rua General Jardim 660, 7° andar, São Paulo, Brazil 01223-010; tel. (11) 3258-8914; fax (11) 3258-8469; e-mail fsminfo@forumsocialmundial.org.br; internet www.forumsocialmundial.org.br; f. 2001 as an annual global meeting of civil society bodies; a Charter of Principles was adopted in June 2002; the WSF is a permanent global process which aims to pursue alternatives to neo-liberal policies and commercial globalization; its objectives include the development and promotion of democratic international systems and institutions serving social justice, equality and the sovereignty of peoples, based on respect for the universal human rights of citizens of all nations and for the environment; the 10th (2011) WSF was held in Dakar, Senegal, in February; an International Council, comprising more than 150 civil society orgs and commissions, guides the Forum and considers general political questions and methodology; the Support Office in São Paulo, Brazil, provides administrative assistance to the Forum process, to the International Council and to the specific organizing committees for each biannual event; mems: civil society orgs and movements world-wide.

World Veterans Federation: 17 rue Nicolo, 75116 Paris, France; tel. 1-40-72-61-00; fax 1-40-72-80-58; e-mail wvf@wvf-fmac.org; internet www.wvf-fmac.org; f. 1950 to maintain international peace and security by the application of the San Francisco Charter and work to help implement the Universal Declaration of Human Rights and related international conventions; aims to defend the spiritual and material interests of war veterans and war victims; promotes practical international co-operation in disarmament, legislation concerning war veterans and war victims, and development of international humanitarian law, etc; maintains regional committees for Africa, Asia and the Pacific, and Europe and a Standing Committee on Women; mems: 173 national orgs in 90 countries, representing about 27m. war veterans and war victims; Pres. ABDUL HAMID IBRAHIM (Malaysia); Sec.-Gen. MOHAMMED BENJELLOUN (Morocco); publ. *WVF News*.

Zonta International: 1211 W 22nd St, Suite 900, Oak Brook, IL 60523, USA; tel. (630) 928-1400; fax (630) 928-1559; e-mail zontaintl@zonta.org; internet www.zonta.org; f. 1919; links executives in business and the professions, with the aim of advancing the status of women world-wide; carries out local and international projects; supports women's education and leadership; makes fellowship awards in various fields; mems: 30,000 in 63 countries and areas; Pres. DIANNE CURTIS; Exec. Dir JASON FRISKE; publ. *The Zontian* (quarterly).

Sport and Recreations

Badminton World Federation: Batu 3, 1/2 Jalan Cheras, 56000 Kuala Lumpur, Malaysia; tel. (3) 92837155; fax (3) 92847155; e-mail bwf@bwfbadminton.org; internet www.internationalbadminton.org; f. 1934, as International Badminton Federation, to oversee the sport of badminton world-wide; mems: affiliated national orgs in 164 countries and territories; Pres. Dr KANG YOUNG JOONG; Chief Operating Officer THOMAS LUND; publs *World Badminton* (available online), *Statute Book* (annually).

Confederation of African Football (Confédération africaine de football—CFA): 3 Abdel Khalek Sarwat St, El Hay El Motamayez, POB 23, 6th October City, Egypt; tel. (2) 38371000; fax (2) 38370006; e-mail info@cafonline.com; internet www.cafonline.com; f. 1957; promotes football in Africa; organizes inter-club competitions and Cup of Nations; General Assembly held every two years; mems: national asscns in 54 countries; Pres. ISSA HAYATOU (Cameroon); Sec.-Gen. HICHAM EL AMRANI (Morocco) (acting); publ. *CAF News* (quarterly).

European Club Association: c/o UEFA, 9 route de St-Cergue, 1260 Nyon 2, Switzerland; e-mail info@ecaeurope.com; internet www.ecaeurope.com; f. 2008; represents the interests of European football clubs; inaugural general assembly held in July 2008; mems: 103 clubs as ordinary mems, 41 clubs as associated mems; Chair. KARL-HEINZ RUMMENIGGE (Germany); Gen. Sec. MICHELE CENTENARO.

Fédération Aéronautique Internationale (FAI) (World Air Sports Federation): 24 ave Mon Repos, 1005 Lausanne, Switzerland; tel. 213451070; fax 213451077; e-mail sec@fai.org; internet www.fai.org; f. 1905 to promote all aeronautical sports; sanctions world championships; develops rules through Air Sports Commissions; endorses world aeronautical and astronautical records; mems: in 100 countries and territories; Pres. PIERRE PORTMANN; Sec.-Gen. STÉPHANE DESPREZ (France).

Fédération Internationale de Philatélie (FIP): Biberlinstr. 6, 8032 Zürich, Switzerland; tel. 444223839; fax 444223843; e-mail ats@f-i-p.ch; internet www.f-i-p.ch/; f. 1926 to promote philately internationally; also aims to establish and maintain close relations with the philatelic trade and postal administrations and to promote philatelic exhibitions; mems: 87 national federations, 3 associated mems (continental federations); Pres. JOSEPH WOLFF (Luxembourg); Sec.-Gen. ANDRÉE TROMMER (Luxembourg); publ. quarterly journal.

International Amateur Athletic Federation: 17 rue Princesse Florestine, BP 359, 98007 Monte Carlo Cedex, Monaco; tel. 93-10-88-88; fax 93-15-95-15; e-mail info@iaaf.org; internet www.iaaf.org; f. 1912 to ensure co-operation and fairness and to combat discrimination in athletics; compiles athletic competition rules and organizes championships at all levels; frames regulations for the establishment of World, Olympic and other athletic records; settles disputes between members; conducts a programme of development consisting of coaching, judging courses, etc; and affiliates national governing bodies; mems: national asscns in 213 countries and territories; Pres. LAMINE DIACK (Senegal); Gen. Sec. PIERRE WEISS (France); publs *IAAF Handbook* (every 2 years), *IAAF Review* (quarterly), *IAAF Directory* (annually), *New Studies in Athletics* (quarterly).

International Automobile Federation (Fédération Internationale de l'Automobile—FIA): 2 chemin de Blandonnet, CP 296, 1215 Geneva, Switzerland; tel. 225444400; fax 225444450; e-mail admin@fiacommunications.com; internet www.fia.com; f. 1904; manages world motor sport and organizes international championships; mems: 213 national automobile clubs and asscns in 120 countries; Pres. JEAN TODT (France); Sec.-Gen. (Sport) PIERRE DE CONINCK; Sec.-Gen. (Mobility) SUSAN PIKRALLIDAS.

International Basketball Federation (Fédération Internationale de Basketball): 53 ave Louis Casai, 1216 Cointrin/Geneva, Switzerland; tel. 225450000; fax 225450099; e-mail info@fiba.com; internet www.fiba.com; f. 1932, as International Amateur Basketball Federation (present name adopted 1989); world governing body for basketball; mems: 213 affiliated national federations; Pres. YVAN MAININI (France); Sec.-Gen. PATRICK BAUMANN (Switzerland); publ. *FIBA Assist* (monthly).

International Boxing Association (AIBA): Maison du Sport International, 54 ave de Rhodanie, 1007 Lausanne, Switzerland; tel. 213212777; fax 213212772; e-mail info@aiba.org; internet www.aiba.org; f. 1946 as the world body controlling amateur boxing for the Olympic Games, continental, regional and internation championships and tournaments in every part of the world; mems: 195 national asscns; Pres. Dr CHING-KUO WU (Republic of China); publ. *World Amateur Boxing Magazine* (quarterly).

International Canoe Federation (ICF): 54 ave de Rhodanie, 1007, Lausanne, Switzerland; tel. 216120290; fax 216120291; e-mail info@canoeicf.com; internet www.canoeicf.com; f. 1924; administers canoeing at the Olympic Games; promotes canoe/kayak activity in general; mems: 148 national federations; Pres. JOSÉ PERURENA LÓPEZ (Spain); Sec.-Gen. SIMON TOULSON.

International Council for Health, Physical Education, Recreation, Sport and Dance (ICHPERSD): 1900 Association Drive, Reston, VA 20191, USA; tel. (800) 213-7193; e-mail ichper@aaperd.org; internet www.ichpersd.org; f. 1958 to encourage the development of programmes in health, physical education, recreation, sport and dance throughout the world, by linking teaching professionals in these fields; Sec.-Gen. Dr ADEL M. ELNASHAR (Bahrain); publ. *Journal* (quarterly).

International Cricket Council: POB 500070, St 69, Dubai Sports City, Emirates Rd, Dubai, UAE; tel. (4) 382-8800; fax (4) 382-8600; e-mail enquiry@icc-cricket.com; internet www.icc-cricket.com; f. 1909 as the governing body for international cricket; holds an annual conference; mems: Australia, Bangladesh, England, India, New Zealand, Pakistan, South Africa, Sri Lanka, West Indies, Zimbabwe, and 23 associate and 13 affiliate mems; Pres. SHARAD PAWAR; CEO HAROON LORGAT.

International Cycling Union (UCI): 12 ch. de la Mêlée, 1860 Aigle, Switzerland; tel. 244685811; fax 244685812; e-mail admin@uci.ch; internet www.uci.ch; f. 1900 to develop, regulate and control all forms of cycling as a sport; mems: 160 federations; Pres. PATRICK MCQUAID (Ireland); publs *International Calendar* (annually), *Velo World* (6 a year).

International Equestrian Federation (Fédération Equestre Internationale—FEI): 37 ave Rumine, 1005 Lausanne, Switzerland; tel. 213104747; fax 213104760; e-mail info@fei.org; internet www.fei.org; f. 1921; international governing body of equestrian sport recognized by the International Olympic Committee; establishes rules and regulations for conduct of international equestrian events, including on the health and welfare of horses; mems: 135 countries; Pres. HRH Princess HAYA BINT AL HUSSEIN (Jordan); Sec.-Gen. ALEXANDER MCLIN.

International Federation of Associated Wrestling Styles: 6 rue du Château, 1804 Corsier-sur-Vevey, Switzerland; tel. 213128426; fax 213236073; e-mail fila@fila-wrestling.com; internet www.fila-wrestling.com; f. 1912 to encourage the development of amateur wrestling and promote the sport in countries where it is not yet practised and to further friendly relations between all members; mems: 168 federations; Pres. RAPHAËL MARTINETTI; Sec.-Gen. MICHEL DUSSON; publs *News Bulletin*, *Wrestling Revue*.

International Federation of Association Football (Fédération internationale de football association—FIFA): FIFA-Str. 20, POB 8044, Zürich, Switzerland; tel. 432227777; fax 432227878; e-mail media@fifa.org; internet www.fifa.com; f. 1904 to promote the game of association football and foster friendly relations among players and national asscns; to control football and uphold the laws of the game as laid down by the International Football Association Board; to prevent discrimination of any kind between players; and to provide arbitration in disputes between national asscns; organizes World Cup competition every four years (2014: Brazil); the FIFA Executive Committee—comprising the Federation's President, eight vice-presidents and 15 members—meets at least twice a year; in May 2011 FIFA provisionally suspended, with immediate effect, one of the Federation's vice-presidents and a member of the Executive Committee in relation to alleged violations of the Federation's code of ethics relating to the election to the FIFA presidency held on 1 June 2011; mems: 208 national asscns, 6 continental confederations; Pres. JOSEPH (SEPP) BLATTER (Switzerland); Gen. Sec. JÉRÔME VALCKE (France); publs *FIFA News* (monthly), *FIFA Magazine* (every 2 months) (both in English, French, German and Spanish), *FIFA Directory* (annually), *Laws of the Game* (annually), *Competitions' Regulations* and *Technical Reports* (before and after FIFA competitions).

International Federation of Park and Recreation Administration (IFPRA): Globe House, Crispin Close, Caversham, Reading, Berks, RG4 7JS, United Kingdom; tel. and fax (118) 946-1680; e-mail ifpraworld@aol.com; internet www.ifpra.org; f. 1957 to provide a world centre for members of government departments, local authorities, and all organizations concerned with recreational and environmental services to discuss relevant matters; mems: 550 in over 50 countries; Gen. Sec. ALAN SMITH (United Kingdom); publ. *IFPRA World* (monthly).

International Fencing Federation (Fédération internationale d'escrime—FIE): Maison du Sport International, 54 ave de Rhodanie, 1007 Lausanne, Switzerland; tel. 213203115; fax 213203116; e-mail info@fie.ch; internet www.fie.ch; f. 1913; promotes development and co-operation between amateur fencers; determines rules for international events; organizes World Championships; mems: 134 national federations; Pres. ALISHER USMANOV (Russia); Sec.-Gen. MAXIM PARAMONOV (Ukraine).

International Go Federation (Fédération internationale d'escrime—FIE): 4th Floor, Nihon Ki-in Kaikan, 7-2 Gobancho, Chiyoda-ku, Tokyo 102-0076, Japan; tel. (3) 3288-8727; fax (3)

3239-0899; e-mail igf@nihonkiin.or.jp; internet www.intergofed .org; f. 1982; promotes the sport of Go; organizes World Amateur Go Championships; mems: 71 national federations; Pres. CHANG ZHENMING (People's Republic of China); Sec.-Gen. YUKI SHIGENO (Japan); publ. *Ranka* (quarterly).

International Gymnastic Federation (Fédération internationale de Gymnastique—FIG): 12 ave de la Gare, 1003 Lausanne, Switzerland; tel. 213215510; fax 213215519; e-mail info@ fig-gymnastics.org; internet www.fig-gymnastics.com; f. 1881 to promote the exchange of official documents and publications on gymnastics; mems: 120 affiliated federations; Pres. BRUNO GRANDI (Italy); Gen. Sec. ANDRÉ GUEISBUHLER (Switzerland); publs *FIG Bulletin* (3 a year), *World of Gymnastics* (3 a year).

International Hockey Federation: 61 rue du Valentin, Lausanne, Switzerland; tel. 216410606; fax 216410607; e-mail info@fih.ch; internet www.fih.ch; f. 1924; mems: 127 national asscns; Pres. LEANDRO NEGRE (Spain); CEO KELLY G. FAIRWEATHER (South Africa).

International Judo Federation: Maison du Sport International, ave de Rhodanie 54, 1007 Lausanne, Switzerland; tel. 216017720; fax 216017727; e-mail office@ijf.org; internet www .ijf.org; f. 1951 to promote cordial and friendly relations between members; to protect the interests of judo throughout the world; to organize World Championships and the judo events of the Olympic Games; to develop and spread the techniques and spirit of judo throughout the world; and to establish international judo regulations; Pres. MARIUS VIZER (Hungary); Gen. Sec. JEAN-LUC ROUGE (France).

International Kung Fu Federation: 1073 Baku, 529 Block, Metbuat Ave, Azerbaijan; tel. (12) 470-14-65; e-mail office@ internationalkungfu.com; internet www.internationalkungfu .com; f. 2003; governing authority of national and international kung fu and taichi organizations world-wide; established internationally recognized rules and regulations and promotes regional and world championships; Pres. DAVUD MAHMUDZADEH (Azerbaijan).

International Paralympic Committee (IPC): Adenauerallee 212–214, 53113 Bonn, Germany; tel. (228) 2097200; fax (228) 2097209; e-mail info@paralympic.org; internet www.paralympic .org; f. 1989 as the international governing body of the Paralympic Movement; supervises and co-ordinates the Paralympic Summer and Winter Games, and other multi-disability competitions, including the World and Regional Championships; promotes paralympic sports through the paralympic sport television channel (www.ParalympicSport.TV); mems: 160 National Paralympic Committees and 4 disability-specific sport orgs and several international sports federations; Pres. Sir PHILIP CRAVEN (United Kingdom); CEO XAVIER GONZALEZ (Spain); publ. *The Paralympian* (quarterly), *IPC Newsflash* (monthly), *Annual Report*.

International Rowing Federation (Fédération internationale des sociétés d'aviron—FISA): MSI, 54 ave de Rhodanie, 1007 Lausanne, Switzerland; tel. 216178373; fax 216178375; e-mail info@fisa.org; internet www.worldrowing.com; f. 1892; serves as the world controlling body of the sport of rowing; mems: 128 national federations; Pres. DENIS OSWALD (Switzerland); Sec.-Gen. and Exec. Dir MATT SMITH (USA); publs *World Rowing Directory* (annually), *World Rowing E-Magazine* (quarterly), *FISA Bulletins* (annually).

International Rugby Board: Huguenot House, 35-38 St Stephen's Green, Dublin 2, Ireland; tel. (1) 240-9200; fax (1) 240-9201; e-mail irb@irb.com; internet www.irb.com; f. 1886; serves as the world governing and law-making body for the game of rugby union; supports education and development of the game and promotes it through regional and world tournaments; since 1987 has organized a Rugby World Cup every four years (2011: New Zealand); holds General Assembly every two years; mems: 97 national unions as full mems, 20 assoc. mems and six regional asscns; Chair. BERNARD LAPASSET; Acting CEO ROBERT BROPHY.

International Sailing Federation (ISAF): Ariadne House, Town Quay, Southampton, Hants, SO14 2AQ, United Kingdom; tel. (2380) 635111; fax (2380) 635789; e-mail secretariat@ isaf.co.uk; internet www.sailing.org; f. 1907; world governing body for the sport of sailing; establishes and amends Racing Rules of Sailing; organizes the Olympic Sailing Regatta, the ISAF Sailing World Championships, the ISAF World Cup and other events; mems: 138 member national authorities, 105 classes, 9 affiliated members; Pres. GÖRAN PETERSSON; Sec.-Gen. JEROME PELS; publ. *Making Waves* (weekly).

International Shooting Sport Federation (ISSF): 80336 Munich, Bavariaring 21, Germany; tel. (89) 5443550; fax (89) 54435544; e-mail munich@issf-sports.org; internet www .issf-sports.org; f. 1907 to promote and guide the development of amateur shooting sports; organizes World Championships and controls the organization of continental and regional championships; supervises the shooting events of the Olympic and Continental Games under the auspices of the International Olympic Committee; mems: 157 nat. federations from 137 affiliated countries; Pres. OLEGARIO VÁZQUEZ RAÑA (Mexico); Sec.-Gen. FRANZ SCHREIBER (Germany); publs *ISSF News*, *International Shooting Sport* (6 a year).

International Skating Union (ISU): 2 chemin de Primerose, 1007 Lausanne, Switzerland; tel. 216126666; fax 216126677; e-mail info@isu.ch; internet www.isu.org; f. 1892; holds regular conferences; mems: 78 national federations in 61 countries; Pres. OTTAVIO CINQUANTA (Italy); Gen. Sec. FREDI SCHMID; publs Judges' manuals, referees' handbooks, general and special regulations.

International Ski Federation (Fédération Internationale de Ski—FIS): Marc Hodler House, Blochstr. 2, 3653 Oberhofen am Thunersee, Switzerland; tel. 332446161; fax 332446171; e-mail mail@fisski.ch; internet www.fis-ski.com; f. 1924 to further the sport of skiing; to prevent discrimination in skiing matters on racial, religious or political grounds; to organize World Ski Championships and regional championships and, as supreme international skiing authority, to establish the international competition calendar and rules for all ski competitions approved by the FIS, and to arbitrate in any disputes; mems: 108 national ski asscns; Pres. GIAN FRANCO KASPER (Switzerland); Sec.-Gen. SARAH LEWIS (United Kingdom); publs *Weekly Newsflash*, *FIS Bulletin* (2 a year).

International Swimming Federation (Fédération internationale de natation—FINA): POB 4, ave de l'Avant, 1005 Lausanne, Switzerland; tel. 213104710; fax 213126610; internet www.fina .org; f. 1908 to promote amateur swimming and swimming sports internationally; administers rules for swimming sports, competitions and for establishing records; organizes world championships and FINA events; runs a development programme to increase the popularity and quality of aquatic sports; mems: 201 federations; Pres. JULIO C. MAGLIONE (Uruguay); Exec. Dir CORNEL MARCULESCU; publs *Handbook* (every 4 years), *FINA News* (monthly), *World of Swimming* (quarterly).

International Table Tennis Federation: 11 chemin de la Roche, 1020 Renens/Lausanne, Switzerland; tel. 213407090; fax 213407099; e-mail ittf@ittf.com; internet www.ittf.com; f. 1926; Pres. ADHAM SHARARA (Canada); Exec. Dir JORDI SERRA; publs *Table Tennis Illustrated*, *Table Tennis News* (both every 2 months), *Table Tennis Legends*, *Table Tennis Fascination*, *Table Tennis: The Early Years*.

International Tennis Federation: Bank Lane, Roehampton, London, SW15 5XZ, United Kingdom; tel. (20) 8878-6464; fax (20) 8878-7799; e-mail communications@itftennis.com; internet www.itftennis.com; f. 1913 to govern the game of tennis throughout the world, promote its teaching and preserve its independence of outside authority; produces the Rules of Tennis; organizes and promotes the Davis Cup Competition for men, the Fed. Cup for women, the Olympic Games Tennis Event, wheelchair tennis, 16 cups for veterans, the ITF Sunshine Cup and the ITF Continental Connelly Cup for players of 18 years old and under, the World Youth Cup for players of 16 years old and under, and the World Junior Tennis Tournament for players of 14 years old and under; organizes entry-level professional tournaments as well as junior and senior circuits, monitors equipment and technology and oversees the education and advancement of officials; mems: 145 full and 65 associate; Pres. FRANCESCO RICCI BITTI.

International Volleyball Federation (Fédération internationale de volleyball—FIVB): Château Les Tourelles, Edouard-Sandoz 2–4, Lausanne 1, Switzerland; tel. 213453535; fax 213453545; e-mail info@fivb.org; internet www.fivb.org;

f. 1947 to encourage, organize and supervise the playing of volleyball, beach volleyball, and park volley; organizes biennial congress; mems: 220 national federations; Pres. JIZHONG WEI (People's Republic of China); publs *VolleyWorld* (every 2 months), *X-Press* (monthly).

International Weightlifting Federation (IWF): 1146 Budapest, Istvanmezei út 1–3, Hungary; tel. (1) 3530530; fax (1) 3530199; e-mail iwf@iwfnet.net; internet www.iwf.net; f. 1905 to control international weightlifting; draws up technical rules; trains referees; supervises World Championships, Olympic Games, regional games and international contests of all kinds; registers world records; mems: 189 national orgs; Pres. Dr TAMÁS AJAN (Hungary); Gen. Sec. MA WENGUANG (People's Republic of China); publs *IWF Constitution and Rules* (every 4 years), *World Weightlifting* (quarterly).

International World Games Association: 10 Lake Circle, Colorado Springs, CO 80906, USA; tel. (719) 471-8096; fax (719) 471-8105; e-mail info@theworldgames.org; internet www.theworldgames.org; f. 1980; organizes World Games every four years (2013: Cali, Colombia), comprising 32 sports that are not included in the Olympic Games; Pres. RON FROEHLICH; CEO JOACHIM GOSSOW.

Olympic Council of Asia: POB 6706, Hawalli, 32042 Kuwait City, Kuwait; tel. 25734972; fax 25734973; e-mail info@ocasia.org; internet www.ocasia.org; f. 1982; organizes Asian Games and Asian Winter Games (held every four years), and Asian Indoor Games and Asian Beach Games (held every two years); mems: 45 national Olympic cttees; Dir-Gen. HUSAIN A. H. Z. AL-MUSALLAM.

SportAccord: Maison du Sport International, 54 ave de Rhodanie, 1007 Lausanne, Switzerland; tel. 216123070; fax 216123071; e-mail sportaccord@sportaccord.com; internet www.sportaccord.com; f. 1967 as the General Assembly of International Sports Federations (name changed in 1976 to General Association of International Sports Federations—GAISF, and in March 2009 renamed as above) to act as a forum for the exchange of ideas and discussion of common problems in sport; collects and circulates information; and provides secretarial, translation, documentation and consultancy services for members; mems: 104 international sports orgs; Pres. HEIN VERBRUGGEN (Netherlands); Dir NOLVENN DUFAY DE LAVALLAZ (France); publs *GAISF Calendar* (online), *Sports Insider* (weekly, electronic bulletin), *Sports Insider Magazine* (annually).

Union of Arab Olympic Committees: POB 62997, Riyadh 11595, Saudi Arabia; tel. (1) 482-4927; fax (1) 482-1944; e-mail olympiccommittees@gmail.com; f. 1976 as Arab Sports Confederation to encourage regional co-operation in sport; mems: 21 Arab national Olympic Committees, 53 Arab sports federations; Sec.-Gen. OTHMAN M. AL-SAAD; publ. *Annual Report*.

Union of European Football Associations (UEFA): 46 route de Genève, 1260 Nyon 2, Switzerland; tel. 848002727; fax 848012727; e-mail info@uefa.com; internet www.uefa.com; f. 1954; works on behalf of Europe's national football asscns to promote football; aims to foster unity and solidarity between national asscns; mems: 53 national asscns; Pres. MICHEL PLATINI (France); Gen. Sec. GIANNI INFANTINO (Italy); publ. *Magazine* (available online).

World Archery Federation (Fédération mondiale de tir à l'arc): 54 ave de Rhodanie, 1007 Lausanne, Switzerland; tel. 216143050; fax 216143055; e-mail info@archery.org; internet www.worldarchery.org; f. 1931 to promote international archery; organizes world championships, world cup events and Olympic tournaments; holds Biennial Congress; mems: national asscns in 147 countries; Pres. UGUR ERDENER; Sec.-Gen. TOM DIELEN (Switzerland); publs *World Archery News* (monthly), *The Target* (2 a year).

World Boxing Organization: First Federal Bldg, 1056 Muñoz Rivera Ave, Suite 711–714, San Juan, PR 00927, Puerto Rico; tel. (787) 765-4628; fax (787) 758-9053; e-mail boxing@wbo-int.com; internet www.wbo-int.com; f. 1962; regulates professional boxing; Pres. FRANCISCO VALCARCEL; Sec. ARNALDO SANCHEZ-RECIO.

World Bridge Federation: c/o 10 Ch. Des Charmilles, Les Roussets, 01210 Ornex, France; tel. 4-50-40-41-31; fax 4-50-40-42-57; internet www.worldbridge.org; e-mail office@worldbridge.org; f. 1958 to promote the game of contract bridge throughout the world; federates national bridge asscns in all countries; conducts world championships competitions; establishes standard bridge laws; mems: 89 countries; Pres. JOSÉ DAMIANI (France); Hon. Sec. DAN MORSE (USA); publ. *World Bridge News* (annually).

World Chess Federation (Fédération internationale des echecs—FIDE): 9 Syggrou Ave, Athens 11743, Greece; tel. (210) 9212047; fax (210) 9212859; e-mail office@fide.com; internet www.fide.com; f. 1924; controls chess competitions of world importance and awards international chess titles; mems: national orgs in more than 160 countries; Pres. KIRSAN ILYUMZHINOV; publ. *International Rating List* (2 a year).

World Curling Federation: 74 Tay St, Perth, PN2 8NP, Scotland, United Kingom; tel. (1738) 451630; fax (1738) 451641; e-mail info@worldcurling.org; internet www.worldcurling.org; f. 1991; mems: 48 mem. asscns; Sec.-Gen. COLIN GRAHAMSLAW.

World Squash Federation Ltd: 25 Russell St, Hastings, East Sussex, TN34 1QU, United Kingdom; tel. (1424) 447440; fax (1424) 430737; e-mail admin@worldsquash.org; internet www.worldsquash.org; f. 1966 to maintain quality and reputation of squash and increase its popularity; monitors rules and makes recommendations for change; trains, accredits and assesses international and world referees; sets standards for all technical aspects of squash; co-ordinates coaching training and awards; runs World Championships; mems: 147 national orgs; Pres. N. RAMACHANDRAN; Co Sec. Dr GEORGE MIERAS.

World Underwater Federation: Viale Tiziano 74, 00196 Rome, Italy; tel. (06) 32110594; fax (06) 32110595; e-mail cmas@cmas.org; internet www.cmas2000.org; f. 1959 to develop underwater activities; to form bodies to instruct in the techniques of underwater diving; to perfect existing equipment, encourage inventions and experiment with newly marketed products; and to organize international competitions; mems: orgs in 100 countries; Pres. ACHILLE FERRERO (Italy); Sec.-Gen. ALESSANDRO ZERBI; publs *International Year Book of CMAS*, *Scientific Diving: A Code of Practice*, manuals.

Technology

African Organization of Cartography and Remote Sensing: 5 route de Bedjarah, BP 102, Hussein Dey, Algiers, Algeria; tel. (21) 23-17-17; fax (21) 23-33-39; e-mail sg2@oact.dz; f. 1988 by amalgamation of African Association of Cartography and African Council for Remote Sensing; aims to encourage the development of cartography and of remote sensing by satellites; organizes conferences and other meetings, promotes establishment of training institutions; maintains four regional training centres (in Burkina Faso, Kenya, Nigeria and Tunisia); mems: national cartographic institutions of 24 African countries; Sec.-Gen. ANWER SIALA.

African Regional Centre for Technology: Imm. Fahd, 17th Floor, blvd Djilly Mbaye, BP 2435, Dakar, Senegal; tel. 823-77-12; fax 823-77-13; e-mail arct@sonatel.senet.net; f. 1977 to encourage the development of indigenous technology and to improve the terms of access to imported technology; assists the establishment of national centres; mems: govts of 31 countries; Exec. Dir. Dr OUSMANE KANE; publs *African Technodevelopment*, *Alert Africa*.

AIIM International: 1100 Wayne Ave, Suite 1100, Silver Spring, MD 20910, USA; tel. (301) 587-8202; fax (301) 587-2711; e-mail aiim@aiim.org; internet www.aiim.org; f. 1999 by merger of the Association for Information and Image Management (f. 1943) and the International Information Management Congress (f. 1962); serves as the international body of the document technologies industry; Chair. JOHN OPDYKE; Pres. JOHN F. MANCINI.

Bureau International de la Recupération et du Recyclage (Bureau of International Recycling): 24 ave Franklin Roosevelt, 1050 Brussels, Belgium; tel. (2) 627-57-70; fax (2) 627-57-73; e-mail bir@bir.org; internet www.bir.org; f. 1948 as the world federation of the reclamation and recycling industries; promotes international trade in scrap iron and steel, non-ferrous metals, paper, textiles, plastics and glass; mems: asscns in 70 countries; Pres. BJÖRN GRUFMAN (Sweden); Dir-Gen. FRANCIS VEYS (Belgium).

Ecma International: 114 rue de Rhône, 1204 Geneva, Switzerland; tel. 228496000; fax 228496001; e-mail istvan@ecma-international.org; internet www.ecma-international.org; f. 1961 to develop standards and technical reports, in co-operation with the appropriate national, European and international organizations, in order to facilitate and standardize the use of information processing and telecommunications systems; promulgates various standards applicable to the functional design and use of these systems; mems: 15 ordinary mems, 16 associate mems, 3 small and medium-sized enterprises, 32 not-for-profit mems, 3 small private company mems; Sec.-Gen. Dr ISTVAN SEBESTYEN; publs *Ecma Standards*, *Ecma Memento*, *Ecma Technical Reports*.

EURELECTRIC (Union of the Electricity Industry): 66 blvd de l'Impératrice, BP 2, 1000 Brussels, Belgium; tel. (2) 515-10-00; fax (2) 515-10-10; e-mail mdebois@euelectric.org; internet www.eurelectric.org; f. 1999 by merger of International Union of Producers and Distributors of Electrical Energy (UNIPEDE, f. 1925) and European Grouping of the Electricity Industry (EEIG, f. 1989); a sector asscn representing the common interests of the electricity industry at pan-European level; contributes to the competitiveness of the electricity industry, provides effective representation for the sector in public affairs, promotes the role of electricity both in the advancement of society and in helping tp provide solutions to the challenges of sustainable development; Pres. FULVIO CONTI; Sec.-Gen. HANS TEN BERGE; publ. *Watt's New* (newsletter).

EUREKA: 107 rue Neerveld, bte 5, 1200 Brussels, Belgium; tel. (2) 777-09-50; fax (2) 770-74-95; e-mail info@eurekanetwork.org; internet www.eurekanetwork.org; f. 1985; aims to promote industrial collaboration between member countries on non-military research and development activities; enables joint development of technology; supports innovation and systematic use of standardization in new technology sectors; administers Eurostars programme, with European Commission, to fund and support collaborative research and innovation projects; mems: 38 countries and the EC; Dir LUUK BORG; publs *Annual Report*, *Eureka Bulletin*.

European Convention for Constructional Steelwork (ECCS): 32 ave des Ombrages, bte 20, 1200 Brussels, Belgium; tel. (2) 762-04-29; fax (2) 762-09-35; e-mail eccs@steelconstruct.com; internet www.steelconstruct.com; f. 1955 for the consideration of problems involved in metallic construction; mems: 20 full mems, 6 assoc. mems, 3 int. mems and 2 supporting mems; Sec.-Gen. VÉRONIQUE BAES-DEHAN; publs Information sheets and documents, symposia reports, model codes.

European Federation of Chemical Engineering: c/o Institution of Chemical Engineers, Davis Bldg, 165–189 Railway Terrace, Rugby, Warwickshire, CV21 3HQ, United Kingdom; tel. (1788) 578214; fax (1788) 560833; e-mail dbrown@icheme.org.uk; internet www.efce.info; f. 1953 to encourage co-operation between non-profit-making scientific and technical societies, for the advancement of chemical engineering and its application in the processing industries; mems: 40 societies in 30 European countries, 15 corresponding societies in other countries; Pres. Prof. RICHARD DARTON.

European Federation of Corrosion: 1 Carlton House Terrace, London, SW1Y 5DB, United Kingdom; tel. (20) 7451-7336; fax (20) 8392-2289; e-mail info@efcweb.org; internet www.efcweb.org; f. 1955 to encourage co-operation in research on methods of combating corrosion; mems: societies in 26 countries; Pres. PHILIPPE MARCUS (France).

European Federation of National Engineering Associations (Fédération européenne d'associations nationales d'ingénieurs—FEANI): 18 ave R. Vandendriessche, 1150 Brussels, Belgium; tel. (2) 639-03-90; fax (2) 639-03-99; e-mail secretariat.general@feani.org; internet www.feani.org; f. 1951 to affirm the professional identity of the engineers of Europe and to strive for the unity of the engineering profession in Europe; mems: 32 mem. countries; Pres. LARS BYTOFT (Denmark); Sec.-Gen. DIRK BOCHAR; publs *FEANI News*, *INDEX*.

European Metal Union: 4 rue J. de Lalaing, 1040 Brussels, Belgium; tel. (2) 282-05-33; fax (2) 282-05-35; e-mail contact@emu-online.info; internet www.emu-online.info; f. 1954 as International Union of Metal; liaises between national craft organizations and small and medium-sized enterprises in the metal industry; represents members' interests at a European level; provides for the exchange of information and ideas; mems: national federations from Austria, Germany, Hungary, Luxembourg, Netherlands and Switzerland; Pres. ERWIN KOSTYRA; Sec. MARIETTE WENNMACHER (Belgium).

European Organisation for the Exploitation of Meteorological Satellites (EUMETSAT): 64295 Darmstadt, Eumetsat Allee 1, Germany; tel. (6151) 8077; fax (6151) 807555; e-mail ops@eumetsat.int; internet www.eumetsat.int; f. 1986; establishes, maintains and exploits European systems of operational meteorological satellites; projects include a second generation Meteosat programme for gathering weather data and satellite application facilities; mems: 26 European countries and 5 co-operating states; Dir-Gen. ALAIN RATIER; publs *Annual Report*, *IMAGE Newsletter* (2 a year), brochures, conference and workshop proceedings.

European Organization for Civil Aviation Equipment (EURO-CAE): 102 rue Etienne Dolet, 4th Floor, 92240 Malakoff, France; tel. 1-40-92-79-30; fax 1-46-55-62-65; e-mail eurocae@eurocae.net; internet www.eurocae.net; f. 1963; studies and advises on problems related to the equipment used in aeronautics; assists international bodies in the establishment of international standards; mems: 92 manufacturers, and regulatory and research bodies; Sec.-Gen. ABDOULAYE N'DIAYE; publs reports, documents and specifications on civil aviation equipment.

Eurospace: 15–17 ave de Ségur, 75005 Paris, France; tel. 1-44-42-00-70; fax 1-44-42-00-79; e-mail letterbox@eurospace.org; internet www.eurospace.org; f. 1961 as an asscn of European aerospace industrial companies responsible for promotion of European Space activity; carries out studies on the legal, economic, technical and financial aspects of space activity; acts as an industrial adviser to the European Space Agency, in particular with regard to future space programmes and industrial policy matters; mems: 60 in 13 European countries; Sec.-Gen. JEAN-JACQUES TORTORA.

Federation of Arab Engineers: 30 Sharia Ramses, Cairo, Egypt; tel. (2) 25775744; fax (2) 25749404; e-mail arabengs@hotmail.com; internet www.arabfedeng.org; f. 1963 as Arab Engineering Union; a regional body of the World Federation of Engineering Organizations; co-operates with the Arab League, UNESCO and the other regional engineering federations; holds a Pan-Arab conference on engineering studies every three years and annual symposia and seminars in different Arab countries; mems: engineering asscns in 15 Arab countries; Sec.-Gen. ADEL AL-HADITHI.

CIRP—International Academy for Production Engineering: 9 rue Mayran, 75009 Paris, France; tel. 1-45-26-21-80; fax 1-45-26-92-15; e-mail cirp@cirp.net; internet www.cirp.net; f. 1951, as International Institution for Production Engineering Research, to promote by scientific research the study of the mechanical processing of all solid materials; mems: 580 in 40 countries; Sec.-Gen. DIDIER DUMUR (France); publ. *Annals* (2 a year).

International Association for Bridge and Structural Engineering (IABSE): ETH—Hönggerberg, 8093 Zürich, Switzerland; tel. 446332647; fax 446331241; e-mail secretariat@iabse.org; internet www.iabse.org; f. 1929 to exchange knowledge and advance the practice of structural engineering world-wide; mems: 4,000 government departments, local authorities, universities, institutes, firms and individuals in over 100 countries; Pres. PREDRAG POPOVIC (USA); Exec. Dir UELI BRUNNER; publs *Structural Engineering International* (quarterly), *Structural Engineering Documents*, *IABSE Report*, *e-newsletter*.

International Association of Hydraulic Engineering and Research (IAHR): Paseo Bajo Virgen del Puerto 3, 28005 Madrid, Spain; tel. (91) 3357908; fax (91) 3357935; e-mail iahr@iahr.org; internet www.iahr.org; f. 1935; promotes advancement and exchange of knowledge on hydraulic engineering; holds biennial congresses and symposia; mems: 1,850 individual, 300 corporate; Pres. ROGER FALCONER; Exec. Dir

CHRISTOPHER GEORGE; publs *The International Journal of River Basin Management*, *IAHR Newsletter*, *Hydrolink*, *Journal of Hydraulic Research*, *Proceedings of Biennial Conferences*, *Fluvial Processes Monograph*, *Fluvial Processes Solutions Manual*, *Hydraulicians in Europe 1800–2000*.

International Association of Marine Aids to Navigation and Lighthouse Authorities: 20 ter rue Schnapper, 78100 St Germain en Laye, France; tel. 1-34-51-70-01; fax 1-34-51-82-05; e-mail contact@iala-aism.org; internet www.iala-aism.org; f. 1957; holds technical conference every four years; working groups study special problems and formulate technical recommendations, guidelines and manuals; mems in 80 countries; Pres. DAVID GORDON; Sec.-Gen. GARY PROSSER; publ. *Bulletin* (quarterly).

International Association of Scientific and Technological University Libraries (IATUL): c/o Paul Sheehan, Dublin City University Library, Dublin 9, Ireland; e-mail paul.sheehan@dcu.ie; internet www.iatul.org; f. 1955 to promote co-operation between member libraries and stimulate research on library problems; mems: 238 university libraries in 41 countries; Pres. AINSLIE DEWE (Australia); Sec. PAUL SHEEHAN (Ireland); publs *IATUL Proceedings*, *IATUL Newsletter* (electronic version only).

International Bridge, Tunnel and Turnpike Association: 1146 19th St, NW, Suite 800, Washington, DC 20036-3725, USA; tel. (202) 659-4620; fax (202) 659-0500; e-mail info@ibtta.org; internet www.ibtta.org; f. 1932 to serve as a forum for sharing knowledge, with the aim of promoting toll-financed transportation services; mems: 280 mems in 25 countries; Exec. Dir and CEO PATRICK D. JONES; publ. *Tollways* (monthly).

International Cargo Handling Co-ordination Association (ICHCA): Suite 2, 85 Western Rd, Romford, Essex, RM1 3LS, United Kingdom; tel. (1708) 735295; fax (1708) 735225; e-mail info@ichca.com; internet www.ichca.com; f. 1952 to foster economy and efficiency in the movement of goods from origin to destination; mems: 2,000 in 90 countries; Int. Chair. DAVID BENDALL; Exec. Dir ROSEMARY NEILSON.

International Colour Association: c/o Nick Harkness Pty Ltd, Birdcage 3.1, 65 Doody St, Alexandria, NSW 2015, Australia; e-mail nick@nhpl.com.au; internet www.aic-colour.org; f. 1967 to encourage research in colour in all its aspects, disseminate the knowledge gained from this research and promote its application to the solution of problems in the fields of science, art and industry; holds international congresses and symposia; mems: orgs in 26 countries; Pres. BERIT BERGSTRÖM (Sweden); Sec. and Treas. NICK HARKNESS (Australia); publ. *Journal of the International Colour Association* (online).

International Commission of Agricultural and Biosystems Engineering (CIGR): Research Group of Bioproduction Engineering, Research Faculty of Agriculture, Hokkaido University, N–9, W–9, Kita-ku, Sapporo, Hokkaido 060-8589, Japan; tel. (11) 706-3885; fax (11) 706-4147; e-mail cigr_gs2010@bpe.agr.hokudai.ac.jp; internet www.cigr.org; f. 1930; aims to stimulate development of science and technology in agricultural engineering; encourages education, training and mobility of professionals; facilitates exchange of research; represents profession at international level; mems: asscns from 92 countries; Pres. Prof. FEDRO ZAZUETA (USA); Sec.-Gen. Prof. TOSHINORI KIMURA (Japan); publs *Bulletin de la CIGR*, *Newsletter* (quarterly), technical reports.

International Commission on Glass: Via Molinella 17, Piombino, 35017 Padova, Italy; e-mail psimurka@stonline.sk; internet www.icglass.org; f. 1933 to co-ordinate research in glass and allied products, exchange information and organize conferences; hosts an International Congress every three years (2013: Prague, Czech Republic, in July); mems: 37 national orgs; Pres. FABIANO NICOLETTI; Exec. Sec. PETER SIMURKA.

International Commission on Illumination (CIE) (Commission internationale de l'eclairage): Kegelgasse 27, 1030 Vienna, Austria; tel. (1) 714-31-87-0; fax (1) 714-31-87-18; e-mail ciecb@cie.co.at; internet www.cie.co.at; f. 1900 as International Commission on Photometry, present name adopted 1913; aims to provide an international forum for all matters relating to the science and art of light and lighting; serves as a forum for the exchange of information; develops and publishes international standards and provides guidance in their application; mems: 40 national cttees, 12 supportive; Pres. ANN WEBB; Gen. Sec. MARTINA PAUL; publs standards, technical reports, congress organization.

International Commission on Irrigation and Drainage (ICID) (Commission Internationale des Irrigations et du Drainage): 48 Nyaya Marg, Chanakyapuri, New Delhi 110 021, India; tel. (11) 26115679; fax (11) 26115962; e-mail icid@icid.org; internet www.icid.org; f. 1950; aims to enhance the world-wide supply of food and fibre by improving the productivity of irrigated and drained lands through the appropriate management of water and application of irrigation, drainage and flood management techniques; promotes the development and application of the arts, sciences and techniques of engineering, agriculture, economics, ecological and social sciences in managing water and land resources for irrigation, drainage and flood management and for river training applications; holds triennial congresses; mems: 105 national cttees; Pres. GAO ZHANYI (People's Republic of China); Sec.-Gen. AVINASH C. TYAGI (India); publs *Ir* (quarterly), *World Irrigation*, *Multilingual Technical Dictionary*, *Historical Dams*, *Indus Basin*, *Danube Valley*, *Application of Geosynthetics in Irrigation and Drainage Projects*, technical books.

International Commission on Large Dams (ICOLD): 61 ave Kléber, 75116 Paris, France; tel. 1-47-04-17-80; fax 1-53-75-18-22; e-mail secretaire.general@icold-cigb.org; internet www.icold-cigb.org; f. 1928; mems: in 85 countries; Pres. JIA JINSHENG (People's Republic of China); Sec.-Gen. MICHEL DE VIVO; publs *Technical Bulletin* (3 or 4 a year), *World Register of Dams*, *World Register of Mine and Industrial Wastes*, *Technical Dictionary on Dams*, studies.

International Committee on Aeronautical Fatigue (ICAF): c/o Prof. O. Buxbaum, Fraunhofer-Institut für Betriebsfestigkeit LBF, 64289 Darmstadt, Bartningstr. 47, Germany; tel. (6151) 7051; fax (6151) 705214; f. 1951 for collaboration between aeronautical bodies and laboratories on questions of fatigue of aeronautical structures; organizes periodical conferences (2013: Jerusalem, Israel, in June); mems: national centres in 13 countries; Sec. Dr ANDERS BLOM (Sweden).

International Council for Research and Innovation in Building and Construction: Kruisplein 25G, POB 1837, 3000 BV Rotterdam, Netherlands; tel. (10) 4110240; fax (10) 4334372; e-mail secretariat@cibworld.nl; internet www.cibworld.nl; f. 1953 as the Conseil International du Bâtiment (International Council for Building); aims to facilitate co-operation in building research, studies and documentation in all aspects; mems: governmental and industrial orgs and qualified individuals in 70 countries; Pres. JOHN MCCARTHY (Australia); Sec.-Gen. WIM J. P. BAKENS; publs *Information Bulletin* (every 2 months), conference proceedings and technical, best practice and other reports.

International Council on Large High-Voltage Electric Systems (Conseil international des grands réseaux électriques—CIGRE): 21 rue d'Artois, 75008 Paris, France; tel. 1-53-89-12-95; fax 1-53-89-12-99; e-mail secretary-general@cigre.org; internet www.cigre.org; f. 1921 to facilitate and promote the exchange of technical knowledge and information in the general field of electrical generation and transmission at high voltages; holds general sessions (every two years) and symposia; mems: more than 11,000 in over 80 countries; Pres. ANDRÉ MERLIN (France); Sec.-Gen. FRANÇOIS MESLIER (France); publ. *Electra* (every 2 months).

International Electrotechnical Commission (IEC): 3 rue de Varembé, POB 131, 1211 Geneva 20, Switzerland; tel. 229190211; fax 229190300; e-mail info@iec.ch; internet www.iec.ch; f. 1906 as the authority for world standards for electrical and electronic engineering: its standards are used as the basis for regional and national standards, and are used in the preparation of specifications for international trade; mems: national cttees representing all branches of electrical and electronic activities in some 60 countries; Pres. KLAUS WUCHERER; Sec. KATHERINE FRAGA PEARSON; publs *International Standards and Reports*, *IEC Bulletin*, *Annual Report*, *Catalogue of Publications*.

International Federation for Information Processing (IFIP): Hofstr. 3, 2361 Laxenburg, Austria; tel. (2236) 73616; fax (2236) 736169; e-mail ifip@ifip.org; internet www.ifip.org; f. 1960 to promote information science and technology; encourages research, development and application of information processing in science and human activities; furthers the dissemination and exchange of information on information processing; mems: 49 full mems, 10 hon. mems, 4 assoc. mems and 4 *ex officio* mems; Pres. LEON STROUS (Netherlands); Sec. MARIA RAFFAI.

International Federation for the Promotion of Machine and Mechanism Science: Laboratory of Robotics and Mechatronics, University of Cassino, via di Biasio 43, 03043 Cassino, Italy; tel. (0776) 299-3663; fax (0776) 299-3711; e-mail ceccarelli@unicas.it; internet www.iftomm.org; f. 1969 to study mechanisms, robots, man-machine systems, etc.; promotes research and development in the field of machines and mechanisms by theoretical and experimental methods and practical application; Pres. M. CECCARELLI; Sec.-Gen. CARLOS LOPEZ-CAJUN; publs *Mechanism and Machine Theory*, *Problems of Mechanics*, *Journal of Gearing and Transmissions*, *Electronic Journal on Computational Kinematics*.

International Federation of Airworthiness (IFA): 14 Railway Approach, East Grinstead, West Sussex, RH19 1BP, United Kingdom; tel. (1342) 301788; fax (1342) 317808; e-mail sec@ifairworthy.com; internet www.ifairworthy.com; f. 1964 to provide a forum for the exchange of international experience in maintenance, design and operations; holds annual conference; awards international aviation scholarship annually; mems include 14 airlines, 6 regulatory authorities, 4 aerospace manufacturing companies, 8 service and repair orgs, 2 consultancies, 5 professional societies, 2 aviation insurance companies, 3 educational institutions, 1 aircraft leasing company, the Flight Safety Foundation (USA) and the Military Aviation Authority Netherlands (MAA-NLD); Exec. Dir JOHN W. SAULL (United Kingdom); publ. *IFA News* (quarterly).

International Federation of Automatic Control (IFAC): Schlosspl. 12, 2361 Laxenburg, Austria; tel. (2236) 71447; fax (2236) 72859; e-mail secretariat@ifac-control.org; internet www.ifac-control.org; f. 1957 to serve those concerned with the theory and application of automatic control and systems engineering; mems: 50 national asscns; Pres. IAN CRAIG; Sec. KURT SCHLACHER; publs *Annual Reviews in Control*, *Automatica*, *Control Engineering Practice*, *Journal of Process Control*, *Newsletter*, *Engineering Applications of AI*, IFAC journals and affiliated journals.

International Federation of Automotive Engineering Societies (Fédération Internationale des Sociétés d'Ingénieurs des Techniques de l'Automobile—FISITA): 30 Percy St, London, W1T 2DB, United Kingdom; tel. (20) 7299-6630; fax (20) 7299-6633; e-mail info@fisita.com; internet www.fisita.com; f. 1948 to promote the technical and sustainable development of all forms of automotive transportation; maintains electronic job centre for automotive engineers (www.fisitajobs.com); holds congresses every two years (2012: Beijing, People's Republic of China, in Nov.); mems: national orgs in 38 countries; Pres. J. E. ROBERTSON; Chief Exec. IAN DICKIE; publ. *AutoTechnology*.

International Federation of Consulting Engineers (Fédération internationale des ingénieurs-conseils—FIDIC): POB 311, 1215 Geneva 15, Switzerland; tel. 227994900; fax 227994901; e-mail fidic@fidic.org; internet www.fidic.org; f. 1913 to encourage international co-operation and the establishment of standards for consulting engineers; organizes World Conference (Sept. 2012: Seoul); mems: 89 national asscns, representing some 1m professionals; Pres. GEOFF FRENCH; publs *FIDIC Report*, *Annual Survey*, *Annual Review*.

International Federation of Hospital Engineering: 2 Abingdon House, Cumberland Business Centre, Northumberland Rd, Portsmouth, PO5 1DS, United Kingdom; tel. (2392) 823186; fax (2392) 815927; e-mail ifhe@iheem.org.uk; internet www.ifhe.info; f. 1970 to promote internationally standards of hospital engineering and to provide for the exchange of knowledge and experience in the areas of hospital and health care facility design, construction, engineering, commissioning, maintenance and estate management; mems: 50 in more than 30 countries; Pres. OLE RIST (Norway); Gen. Sec. GUNNAR BAEKKEN (Norway); publ. *Hospital Engineering* (quarterly).

International Institute of Seismology and Earthquake Engineering (IISEE): Building Research Institute, 1 Tatehara, Tsukuba City, Ibaraki 305-0802, Japan; tel. (298) 79-0677; fax (298) 64-6777; e-mail iisee@kenken.go.jp; internet iisee.kenken.go.jp; f. 1962 to work on seismology and earthquake engineering for the purpose of reducing earthquake damage in the world; trains seismologists and earthquake engineers from the earthquake-prone countries; undertakes surveys, research, guidance and analysis of information on earthquakes and related matters; mems: 75 countries; Dir Dr SHOICHI ANDO; publs *Bulletin* (annually), *Individual Studies* (annually).

International Institute of Welding: 90 rue des Vanesses, ZI Paris Nord II, 93420 Villepinte, France; tel. 1-49-90-36-08; fax 1-49-90-36-80; e-mail c.mayer@iiwelding.org; internet www.iiwelding.org; f. 1948; serves as the world-wide network for knowledge exchange of joining technologies; develops authorized education, training, qualification and certification programmes; mems: 53 mem. societies; Chief Exec. CÉCILE MAYER (France); publ. *Welding in the World* (6 a year).

International Measurement Confederation (IMEKO): POB 457, 1371 Budapest 5, Hungary; tel. and fax (1) 353-1562; e-mail imeko.ime@mtesz.hu; internet www.imeko.org; f. 1958 as a federation of member organizations concerned with the advancement of measurement technology; aims to promote exchange of scientific and technical information in field of measurement and instrumentation and to enhance co-operation between scientists and engineers; holds World Congress every three years (2012: Busan, Republic of Korea, in Sept.); mems: 39 orgs; Pres. Dr DAE-IM KANG (Republic of Korea); Sec.-Gen. Prof. MLADEN BORSIC (Croatia); publs *Acta IMEKO* (proceedings of World Congresses), *IMEKO TC Events Series*, *Measurement* (quarterly), *IMEKO Bulletin* (2 a year).

International Organization for Standardization: POB 56, 1 rue de de la Voie-Creuse, 1211 Geneva 20, Switzerland; tel. 227490111; fax 227333430; e-mail central@iso.org; internet www.iso.org; f. 1947 to reach international agreement on industrial and commercial standards; mems: national standards bodies of 161 countries; Pres. Dr BORIS ALESHIN (Russia); Sec.-Gen. ROBERT STEELE; publs *ISO International Standards*, *ISO Memento* (annually), *ISO Management Systems* (6 a year), *ISO Focus* (11 a year), *ISO Catalogue* (annually, updated regularly online), *ISO Annual Report*.

International Research Group on Wood Protection: Drottning Kristinas väg 33A, Stockholm, Sweden; tel. (8) 10-14-53; fax (8) 10-80-81; e-mail irg@sp.se; internet www.irg-wp.com; f. 1965 as Wood Preservation Group by OECD; independent since 1969; consists of five sections; holds plenary annual meeting; mems: 350 in 53 countries; Pres. JACK NORTON (Australia); Sec.-Gen. JÖRAN JERMER (Sweden); publs technical documents.

International Rubber Research and Development Board (IRRDB): POB 10150, 50908 Kuala Lumpur, Malaysia; tel. (3) 42521612; fax (3) 42560487; e-mail sec_gen@theirrdb.org; internet www.irrdb.com; f. 1960 following the merger of International Rubber Regulation Committee (f. 1934) and International Rubber Research Board (f. 1937); mems: 15 research institutes; Sec. Dr Datuk A. AZIZ.

International Society for Photogrammetry and Remote Sensing (ISPRS): c/o National Geomatics Centre of China, 28 Lianhuachixi Rd, Haidian District, Beijing 100830, People's Republic of China; tel. (10) 63881102; fax (10) 63881026; e-mail chenjun@nsdi.gov.cn; internet www.isprs.org; f. 1910; holds congress every four years (2012: Melbourne, Australia, in Aug.-Sept.), and technical symposia; mems: 103 countries; Pres. ORHAN ALTAN (Turkey); Sec.-Gen. CHEN JUN (People's Republic of China); publs *Journal of Photogrammetry and Remote Sensing* (6 a year), *ISPRS Highlights* (quarterly), *International Archives of Photogrammetry and Remote Sensing* (every 2 years).

International Society for Soil Mechanics and Geotechnical Engineering: City University London, Northampton Sq., London, EC1V 0HB, United Kingdom; tel. (20) 7040-8154; fax (20) 7040-8832; e-mail secretariat@issmge.org; internet www.issmge.org; f. 1936 to promote international co-operation among scientists and engineers in the field of geotechnics and its engineering applications; maintains 30 technical committees; holds quadrennial international conference, regional conferences and specialist conferences; mems: 18,000 individuals, 85 national societies, 21 corporate members; Pres. Prof. JEAN LOUIS BRIAUD; Sec.-Gen. Prof. R. N. TAYLOR; publs *ISSMGE Bulletin* (quarterly), *Lexicon of Soil Mechanics Terms* (in 8 languages).

International Solar Energy Society: Villa Tannheim, Wiesentalstr. 50, 79115 Freiburg, Germany; tel. (761) 459060; fax (761) 4590699; e-mail hq@ises.org; internet www.ises.org; f. 1954; addresses all aspects of renewable energy, including characteristics, effects and methods of use; undertakes projects in several countries on various aspects of renewable energy technology and implementation; organizes major international, regional and national congresses; mems: c. 30,000 in some 100 countries; Pres. DAVID RENNÉ (USA); publs *Solar Energy Journal* (monthly), *Renewable Energy Focus* (6 a year).

International Solid Waste Association (ISWA): Auerspergstr. 15, Top 41, 1080 Vienna, Austria; tel. 253-6001; e-mail iswa@iswa.org; internet www.iswa.org; f. 1970 to promote the exchange of information and experience in solid waste management, in order to protect human health and the environment; promotes research and development activities; provides advice; organizes conferences (World Congress, Sept. 2012: Florence, Italy); Pres. JEFF COOPER; Man. Dir. HERMANN KOLLER; publs *Waste Management World*, *Waste Management and Research* (monthly).

International Special Committee on Radio Interference (Comité International Spécial des Perturbations Radioélectriques—CISPR): 143 Jumping Brook Rd, Lincroft, NJ 07738-1442, USA; tel. (732) 741-7723; e-mail steven.leitner@us.ul.com; f. 1934; special committee of the IEC, promoting international agreement on the protection of radio reception from interference by equipment other than authorized transmitters; recommends limits of such interference and specifies equipment and methods of measurement; mems: national cttees of IEC and 7 other int. orgs; Sec. STEVEN LEITNER.

International Union for Electricity Applications: 5 rue Chante-Coq, 92808 Puteaux Cedex, France; tel. 1-41-26-56-48; fax 1-41-26-56-49; e-mail uie@uie.org; internet www.uie.org; f. 1953, present title adopted 1994; aims to study all questions relative to electricity applications, except commercial questions; links national groups and organizes international congresses on electricity applications (May 2012: St Petersburg, Russia); mems: national cttees, corporate, associated and individual mems in 18 countries; Sec. KOEN VAN REUSEL; publ. UIE proceedings.

International Union for Vacuum Science, Technique and Applications (IUVSTA): c/o Dr R. J. Reid, 84 Oldfield Drive, Vicars Cross, Chester, CH3 5LW, United Kingdom; tel. (1244) 342675; e-mail iuvsta.secretary.general@ronreid.me.uk; internet www.iuvsta.org; f. 1958; collaborates with the International Standards Organization in defining and adopting technical standards; holds triennial International Vacuum Congress, European Vacuum Conference, triennial International Conference on Thin Films, and International Conference on Solid Surfaces; administers the Welch Foundation scholarship for postgraduate research in vacuum science and technology; mems: orgs in 30 countries; Pres. Prof. JEAN-JACQUES PIREAUX; Sec.-Gen. Dr RON J. REID (United Kingdom); publ. *News Bulletins* (2 a year, electronic version).

International Union of Air Pollution Prevention and Environmental Protection Associations: Oakwood House, 11 Wingle Tye Rd, Burgess Hill, West Sussex RH15 9HR, United Kingdom; tel. (1444) 236848; e-mail secretariat@iuappa.org; internet www.iuappa.org; f. 1963; organizes triennial World Clean Air Congress and regional conferences for developing countries (several a year); undertakes policy development and research programmes on international environmental issues; World Congress: Cape Town, South Africa (Sept. 2013); Pres. HANLIE LIEBENBERG ENSLIN (South Africa); Dir-Gen. RICHARD MILLS; publ. *IUAPPA Newsletter*.

International Union of Laboratories and Experts in Construction Materials, Systems and Structures (Réunion Internationale des Laboratoires et Experts des Matériaux, systèmes de construction et ouvrages—RILEM): 157 rue des Blains, 92220 Bagneux, France; tel. 1-45-36-10-20; fax 1-45-36-63-20; e-mail sg@rilem.net; internet www.rilem.net; f. 1947 for the exchange of information and the promotion of co-operation on experimental research concerning structures and materials; promotes research with a view to improvement and standardization; mems: laboratories and individuals in 73 countries; Pres. Dr PETER RICHNER; Sec.-Gen. PASCALE DUCORNET; publs *Materials and Structures* (10 a year), *RILEM Technical Recommendations*, conference proceedings.

International Union of Technical and Engineering Associations (Union internationale des associations et organismes techniques—UATI): UNESCO House, 1 rue Miollis, 75732 Paris Cedex 15, France; tel. 1-45-68-48-29; fax 1-43-06-29-27; e-mail uati@uati.info; internet www.uati.info; f. 1951 (fmrly Union of International Technical Associations) under the auspices of UNESCO; aims to promote and co-ordinate activities of member organizations and represent their interests; facilitates relations with international organizations, notably UN agencies; receives proposals and makes recommendations on the establishment of new international technical asscns; mems: 14 orgs; Pres. PHILIPPE AUSSOURD (France); Sec.-Gen. ROGER FRANK; publ. *Convergence* (3 a year).

International Water Resources Association (IWRA): c/o Association Verseau Développement, 859 rue Jean-François Breton, 34093 Montpellier Cedex 5, France; tel. 4-4-67-61-29-45; fax 4-4-67-52-28-29; e-mail office@iwra.org; internet www.iwra.org; f. 1972 to promote collaboration in and support for international water resources programmes; holds conferences; conducts training in water resources management; Pres. JUN XIA (People's Republic of China); Exec. Dir. TOM SOO; publ. *Water International* (quarterly).

Latin American Association of Pharmaceutical Industries (Asociación Latinoamericana de Industrias Farmaceuticas—ALIFAR): Av. Libertador 602, 6°, 1001 ABT Buenos Aires, Argentina; tel. and fax (11) 903-4440; e-mail info@alifar.org.ar; internet www.cifabol.com/alifar.html; f. 1980; mems: about 400 enterprises in 15 countries; Sec.-Gen. RUBÉN ABETE.

Latin-American Energy Organization (Organización Latinoamericana de Energía—OLADE): Avda Mariscal Antonio José de Sucre, No N58–63 y Fernándes Salvador, Edif. OLADE, Sector San Carlos, POB 17-11-6413 CCI, Quito, Ecuador; tel. (2) 2598-122; fax (2) 2531-691; e-mail oladel@olade.org.ec; internet www.olade.org.ec; f. 1973 to act as an instrument of co-operation in using and conserving the energy resources of the region; mems: 26 Latin-American and Caribbean countries; Exec. Sec. VICTORIO OXILIA DAVALOS; publ. *Enerlac Magazine*.

Latin American Steel Association (Asociación Latinamericana del Acero—Alacero): Benjamín 2944, 5°, Las Condes, Santiago, Chile; tel. (2) 233-0545; fax (2) 233-0768; e-mail alacero@alacero.org; internet wwww.alacero.org; f. 1959 as the Latin American Iron and Steel Institute (ILAFA) to help achieve the harmonious development of iron and steel production, manufacture and marketing in Latin America; conducts economic surveys on the steel sector; organizes technical conventions and meetings; disseminates industrial processes suited to regional conditions; prepares and maintains statistics on production, end uses, etc., of raw materials and steel products within this area; mems: 18 hon. mems; 49 active mems; 36 assoc. mems; Chair. RAÚL MANUEL GUTIÉRREZ MUGUERZA (Mexico); Sec. ROBERTO DE ANDRACA BARBAS (Chile); publs *Industry Year Book*, *Latin American Steel Directory* (now electronic); also technical books, bulletins and manuals.

NORDTEST: Stensberggt. 25, 0170 Oslo, Norway; tel. 47-61-44-00; fax 22-56-55-65; e-mail info@nordicinnovation.org; internet www.nordtest.info; f. 1973; inter-Nordic agency for technical testing and standardization of methods and of laboratory accreditation; Man.Dir IVAR H. KRISTENSEN.

Regional Centre for Mapping of Resources for Development (RCMRD): POB 632, 00618 Ruaraka, Nairobi, Kenya; tel. (20) 8560227; fax (20) 8561673; e-mail rcmrd@rcmrd.org; internet www.rcmrd.org; f. 1975; present name adopted 1997; provides services for the professional techniques of map-making and the application of satellite and remote sensing data in resource analysis and development planning; undertakes research and provides advisory services to African governments; mems: 15 signatory and 10 non-signatory govts; Dir-Gen. Dr HUSSEIN O. FARAH.

Regional Centre for Training in Aerospace Surveys (RECTAS) (Centre Regional de Formations aux Techniques des leves aerospatiaux): PMB 5545, Ile-Ife, Nigeria; tel. (803) 384-0581; e-mail info@rectas.org; internet www.rectas.org; f. 1972; provides training, research and advisory services in aerospace surveys and geoinformatics; administered by the ECA; mems: 8 govts; Exec. Dir Prof. ISI IKHUORIA.

Union of Arab Information and Communication Technology Associations: 1st Floor, Fouad Farrah Bldg, cross rd of Masaref St and Wegan St, Beirut Central District, Beirut, Lebanon; tel. (1) 985440; internet www.ijma3.org; mems: Arab national associations; Sec.-Gen. and CEO NIZAR ZAKKA.

World Association of Industrial and Technological Research Organizations (WAITRO): c/o SIRIM Berhad, 1 Persiaran Dato' Menteri, Section 2, POB 7035, 40911 Shah Alam, Malaysia; tel. 55446635; fax 55446735; e-mail info@waitro.sirim.my; internet www.waitro.org; f. 1970 by the UN Industrial Development Organization to organize co-operation in industrial and technological research; provides financial assistance for training and joint activities; arranges international seminars; facilitates the exchange of information; mems: 168 research institutes in 77 countries; Pres. Dr R.K. KHANDAL (India); Sec.-Gen. Dr ROHANI HASHIM; publ. *WAITRO News* (quarterly).

World Association of Nuclear Operators (WANO): Cavendish Court, First Floor, 11–15 Wigmore St, London, W1U 1PF, United Kingdom; tel. (20) 7478-9200; fax (20) 7495-4502; internet www.wano.org.uk; f. 1989 by operators of nuclear power plants; aims to improve the safety and reliability of nuclear power plants through the exchange of information; operates four regional centres (in Paris, France; Tokyo, Japan; Moscow, Russia; and Atlanta, USA) and a Co-ordinating Centre in the United Kingdom; mems: in 35 countries; Pres. VLADIMIR ASMOLOV; Man. Dir GEORGE FELGATE.

World Bureau of Metal Statistics: 27A High St, Ware, Herts, SG12 9BA, United Kingdom; tel. (1920) 461274; fax (1920) 464258; e-mail enquiries@world-bureau.co.uk; internet www.world-bureau.com; f. 1947; produces statistics of production, consumption, stocks, prices and international trade in copper, lead, zinc, tin, nickel, aluminium and several other minor metals; publs *World Metal Statistics* (monthly), *World Tin Statistics* (monthly), *World Nickel Statistics* (monthly), *World Metal Statistics Yearbook*, *World Metal Statistics Quarterly Summary*, *Annual Stainless Steel Statistics* (annually), *Metallstatistik* (annually).

World Energy Council: 5th Floor, Regency House, 1–4 Warwick St, London, W1B 5LT, United Kingdom; tel. (20) 7734-5996; fax (20) 7734-5926; e-mail info@worldenergy.org; internet www.worldenergy.org; f. 1924 to link all branches of energy and resources technology and maintain liaison between world experts; holds congresses every three years; mems: cttees in over 90 countries; Chair. PIERRE GADONNEIX (France); Sec.-Gen. Dr CHRISTOPH FREI (Switzerland); publs energy supply and demand projections, resources surveys, technical assessments, reports.

World Federation of Engineering Organizations (WFEO): Maison de l'UNESCO, 1 rue Miollis, 75732 Paris, Cedex 15, France; tel. 1-45-68-48-47; fax 1-45-68-48-65; e-mail info@wfeo.net; internet www.wfeo.net; f. 1968 to advance engineering as a profession; fosters co-operation between engineering organizations throughout the world; undertakes special projects in co-operation with other international bodies; mems: 90 national mems, 9 int. mems; Pres. ADEL ALKHARAFI (Kuwait); Exec. Dir TAHANI YOUSSEF (France); publ. *WFEO Newsletter* (2 a year).

World Foundry Organization (WFO): Winton House, Lyonshall, Kington, Herefordshire, HR5 3JP, United Kingdom; tel. (121) 601-6976; fax (1544) 340-332; e-mail secretary@thewfo.com; internet www.thewfo.com; f. 1927, as International Committee of Foundry Technical Asscns; named changed to World Foundrymen Organization in 2000, and as above in 2010; Pres. XABIER GONZALES ASPIRI (Spain).

Tourism

Alliance Internationale de Tourisme (AIT): 2 Chemin de Blandonnet, CP 111, 1215 Geneva 15, Switzerland; tel. and fax 225444500; internet www.aitgva.ch; f. 1898, present title adopted 1919; represents motoring orgs and touring clubs around the world; aims to study all questions relating to automobile mobility; mems: 120 mem. asscns in 101 countries; Pres. WERNER KRAUS (Austria).

Baltic Sea Tourism Commission (BTC): Snickarbacken 2, 4-5 tr, 111 39 Stockholm, Sweden; e-mail info@balticsea.com; tel. (8) 667-25-97; internet www.balticsea.com; f. in 1983 as a non-profit organization to promote tourism to and within the Baltic Sea Region; mems: more than 80 members in 15 countries, incl. Estonia, Latvia, Lithuania and Poland; Pres. NIELS LUND (Denmark); Exec. Dir MARTIN AHLBERG.

Caribbean Hotel and Tourism Association: 2655 Le Jeune Road, Suite 910 Coral Gables, FL 33134, USA; tel. (305) 443-3040; fax (305) 443-3005; internet www.caribbeanhotelassociation.com; f. 1962 (as the Caribbean Hotel Asscn; name changed July 2008); represents and promotes the hotel and tourism industry in the Caribbean region; jointly owns and operates, with the Caribbean Tourism Organization, the Caribbean Tourism Development Co; mems: 849 hotels in 36 national hotel asscns; Pres. RICHARD DOUMENG; CEO and Dir-Gen. ALEC SANGUINETTI; publ. *CHA Weekly News*.

Caribbean Tourism Organization: One Financial Pl., Collymore Rock, St Michael, Barbados; tel. 427-5242; fax 429-3065; e-mail ctobar@caribsurf.com; internet www.onecaribbean.org; f. 1989, by merger of the Caribbean Tourism Association (f. 1951) and the Caribbean Tourism Research and Development Centre (f. 1974); aims to encourage tourism in the Caribbean region; organizes annual Caribbean Tourism Conference, Sustainable Tourism Development Conference and Tourism Investment Conference; conducts training and other workshops on request; maintains offices in New York, Canada and London; mems: 32 Caribbean govts, 400 allied mems; Sec.-Gen. HUGH RILEY; publs *Caribbean Tourism Statistical News* (quarterly), *Caribbean Tourism Statistical Report* (annually).

European Travel Commission: 61 rue du Marché aux Herbes, 1000 Brussels, Belgium; tel. (2) 548-90-00; fax (2) 514-18-43; e-mail info@visiteurope.com; internet www.etc-corporate.org; f. 1948; currently promotes and markets 'Destination Europe' around the world, through its operations groups in Canada, Brazil (for Latin America), Japan (for Asia), and the USA; mems: national tourist orgs in 33 European countries; Exec. Dir EDUARDO SANTANDER (Belgium).

International Association of Scientific Experts in Tourism: Dufourstr. 40A, 9000 St Gallen, Switzerland; tel. 712242530; fax 712242536; e-mail aiest@unisg.ch; internet www.aiest.org; f. 1949 to encourage scientific activity in tourism, to support tourist institutions of a scientific nature and to organize conventions; mems: 300 from more than 50 countries; Pres. Prof. Dr PETER KELLER (Switzerland); Gen. Sec. Prof. Dr CHRISTIAN LAESSER (Switzerland); publ. *The Tourism Review* (quarterly).

International Council of Tourism Partners: POB 208, Haleiwa, HI 96712, USA; e-mail supporters@tourismpartners.org; internet www.tourismpartners.org; f. 2012; aims to promote the sharing of resources and greater collaboration between member tourism destinations and their stakeholders; promotes the adoption of Green Growth strategies; mems: 178 in 40 countries; Pres. GEOFFREY LIPMAN.

International Hotel and Restaurant Association: 87 rue de Montbrillant, 1202 Geneva, Switzerland; tel. 227348041; fax 227348056; e-mail info@ih-ra.ch; internet www.ih-ra.com; f. 1869 to act as the authority on matters affecting the international hotel and restaurant industry, to promote its interests and to contribute to its growth, profitability and quality; membership extended to restaurants in 1996; mems: 130 national hospitality asscns, 200 national and international hotel and restaurant chains; Pres. and CEO GHASSAN AIDI; publs *Hotels* (monthly), *Yearbook and Directory* (annually).

International Tourism Trade Fairs Association: 1 Old Forge Cottage, Carrington Rd, Richmond, Surrey, TW10 5AA, United Kingdom; tel. (0777) 5571033; e-mail info@ittfa.org; internet www.ittfa.org; f. 1992 as European Tourism Trade Fairs Asscn; Chair. TOM NUTLEY (United Kingdom); Pres. ZELJKA TOMLJENOVIC (2012).

Latin-American Confederation of Tourist Organizations (Confederación de Organizaciones Turísticas de la América Latino—COTAL): Viamonte 640, 3°, 1053 Buenos Aires, Argentina; tel. (11) 4322-4003; fax (11) 5277-4176; e-mail cotal@cotal.org.ar; internet www.cotal.org.ar; f. 1957 to link Latin American national asscns of travel agents and their members with other tourist bodies around the world; mems: in 21 countries; Pres. LUIS FELIPE AQUINO; publ. *Revista COTAL* (every 2 months).

Pacific Asia Travel Association (PATA): Unit B1, 28th Floor, Siam Tower, 989 Rama 1 Rd, Pratumwan, Bangkok 10330, Thailand; tel. (2) 658-2000; fax (2) 658-2010; e-mail patabkk@pata.org; internet www.pata.org; f. 1951; aims to enhance the growth, value and quality of Pacific Asia travel and tourism for the benefit of PATA members; holds annual conference and travel fair; divisional offices in Germany (Frankfurt), Australia (Sydney), USA (Oakland, CA) and the People's Republic of China (Beijing); mems: more than 1,200 governments, carriers, tour operators, travel agents and hotels; Chair. HIRAN COORAY (Sri Lanka); CEO MARTIN CRAIGS (United Kingdom/Ireland); publs *PATA Compass* (every 2 months), *Statistical Report* (quarterly), *Forecasts Book*, research reports, directories, newsletters.

South Pacific Tourism Organization: POB 13119, Suva, Fiji; tel. 3304177; fax 3301995; e-mail tourism@spto.org; internet www.south-pacific.travel; fmrly the Tourism Council of the South Pacific; also known as south-pacific.travel; aims to foster regional co-operation in the development, marketing and promotion of tourism in the island nations of the South Pacific; receives EU funding and undertakes sustainable activities; mems: 13 govts in the South Pacific, more than 200 private sector members in 25 countries world-wide; CEO ILISONI VUIDREKETI (Fiji); publ. *Weekly Newsletter.*

United Federation of Travel Agents' Associations (UFTAA): 19 ave des Castelans, Entrée C, 98000 Monaco; tel. 92-05-28-29; fax 92-05-29-87; e-mail uftaa@uftaa.org; internet www.uftaa.org; f. 1966 to unite travel agents' asscns; represents the interests of travel agents at the international level; helps in international legal differences; issues literature on travel; mems: regional federations representing some 80 national asscns; Pres. MARIO BEVACQUA.

World Association of Travel Agencies (WATA): Tranchepied 25, 1278 La Rippe, Switzerland; tel. 792397279; fax 223620753; e-mail wata@wata.net; internet www.wata.net; f. 1949 to foster the development of tourism, to help the rational organization of tourism in all countries, to collect and disseminate information and to participate in commercial and financial operations to foster the development of tourism; mems: more than 100 individual travel agencies in some 50 countries; Pres. MARC DANS (Belgium); publ. *WATA News* (online).

World Travel and Tourism Council (WTTC): 1–2 Queen Victoria Terrace, Sovereign Court, London, E1W 3HA, United Kingdom; tel. (20) 7481-8007; fax (20) 7488-1008; e-mail enquiries@wttc.org; internet www.wttc.org; f. 1989; promotes the development of the travel/tourism industry; analyses impact of tourism on employment levels and local economies and promotes greater expenditure on tourism infrastructure; administers a 'Green Globe' certification programme to enhance environmental management throughout the industry; mems: reps from 100 cos world-wide; Pres. and CEO DAVID SCOWSILL; publs *WTTC Backgrounder*, *Travel and Tourism Review*, *Viewpoint* (quarterly), *Blueprint for New Tourism*, regional and country reports.

Trade and Industry

African Organization for Standardization (ARSO): POB 57363-00200, Nairobi, Kenya; tel. (20) 224561; fax (20) 218792; e-mail info@arso-oran.org; internet www.arso-oran.org; f. 1977 to promote standardization, quality control, certification and metrology in the African region, to formulate regional standards, and to co-ordinate participation in international standardization activities; mems: 27 African states; Pres. KIOKO MANG'ELI (Kenya); Sec.-Gen. (vacant); publs *ARSO Bulletin* (2 a year), *ARSO Catalogue of Regional Standards* (annually), *ARSO Annual Report.*

African Regional Intellectual Property Organization (ARIPO): 11 Natal Rd, POB 4228, Harare, Zimbabwe; tel. (4) 794065; fax (4) 794072; e-mail mail@aripo.org; internet www.aripo.org; f. 1976 to grant patents, register industrial designs and marks and to promote devt and harmonization of laws concerning industrial property; mems: Botswana, The Gambia, Ghana, Kenya, Lesotho, Liberia, Malawi, Mozambique, Namibia, Sierra Leone, Somalia, Sudan, Swaziland, Tanzania, Uganda, Zambia and Zimbabwe; Dir-Gen. (vacant); publs *Newsletter* (every 2 months), *Industrial Designs and Tradements Journal* (quarterly).

African Water Association (Association Africaine de l'Eau): 05 BP 1910, Abidjan 05, Côte d'Ivoire; tel. 21-24-14-43; fax 21-24-26-29; e-mail contact@afwa-hq.org; internet www.afwa-hq.org; f. 1980; facilitates co-operation between public and private bodies concerned with water supply and sewage management in Africa; promotes the study of economic, technical and scientific matters relating to the industry; congress held every two years (16th Congress: Marrakesh, Morocco, Feb. 2012); mems: 70 water and sanitation utilities in 36 countries; Sec.-Gen. SYLVAIN USHER; publ. *AFWA News Magazine* (quarterly).

Asian Productivity Organization: Hirakawacho Daiichi Seimei Bldg 2F, 1-2-10 Hirakawa-cho, Chiyoda-ku, Tokyo 102–0093, Japan; tel. (3) 5226-3920; fax (3) 5226-3950; e-mail apo@apo-tokyo.org; internet www.apo-tokyo.org; f. 1961 as non-political, non-profit-making, non-discriminatory regional inter-governmental organization with the aim of contributing to the socio-economic development of Asia and the Pacific through productivity promotion; activities cover industry, agriculture and service sectors, with the primary focus on human resources development; five key areas are incorporated into its activities: knowledge management, green productivity, strengthening small and medium enterprises, integrated community development and development of national productivity organizations; serves its members as a think tank, catalyst, regional adviser, institution builder and clearing house; mems: 20 countries; Sec.-Gen. RYUICHIRO YAMAZAKI (Japan); publs *APO News* (monthly), *Annual Report*, *APO Productivity Databook*, *Eco-products Directory*, other books and monographs.

Association of European Chambers of Commerce and Industry (EUROCHAMBRES): The Chamber House, 19A/D ave des Arts, 1000 Brussels, Belgium; tel. (2) 282-08-50; fax (2) 230-00-38; e-mail eurochambres@eurochambres.eu; internet www.eurochambres.eu; f. 1958 to promote the exchange of experience and information among its members and to bring their joint opinions to the attention of the institutions of the European Union; conducts studies and seminars; co-ordinates EU projects; mems: 45 nat. asscns of Chambers of Commerce and Industry and 1 transnational Chamber org, 2,000 regional and local Chambers and 19m. mem. enterprises in Europe; Pres. ALESSANDRO BARBERIS (Italy); Sec.-Gen. ARNALDO ABRUZZINI (Italy).

BusinessEurope: 168 ave de Cortenbergh, 1000 Brussels, Belgium; tel. (2) 237-65-11; fax (2) 231-14-45; e-mail main@businesseurope.eu; internet www.businesseurope.eu; f. 1958 as Union of Industrial and Employers' Confederations of Europe (UNICE); name changed, as above, Jan. 2007; aims to ensure that European Union policy-making takes account of the views of European business; committees and working groups develop joint positions in fields of interest to business and submit these to the Community institutions concerned; the Council of Presidents (of member federations) lays down general policy; the Executive Committee (of Directors-General of member federations) is the managing body; and the Committee of Permanent Delegates, consisting of federation representatives in Brussels, ensures permanent liaison with mems; mems: 41 industrial and employers' federations from 35 countries; Pres. JÜRGEN THUMANN (Germany); Dir. Gen. PHILIPPE DE BUCK (Belgium); publ. *BusinessEurope Newsletter* (weekly, electronic).

CAEF—The European Foundry Association: Sohnstr. 70, 40237 Düsseldorf, Germany; tel. (211) 6871217; fax (211) 6871347; e-mail info@caef.eu; internet www.caef.eu; f. 1953 to safeguard the common interests of European foundry industries and to collect and exchange information; mems: asscns in 20 countries; Sec.-Gen. MAX SCHUMACHER; publ. *The European Foundry Industry* (annually).

Cairns Group: (no permanent secretariat); e-mail agriculture.negotiations@dfat.gov.au; internet www.cairnsgroup.org;

f. 1986 by major agricultural exporting countries; aims to bring about reforms in international agricultural trade, including reductions in export subsidies, in barriers to access and in internal support measures; represents members' interests in WTO negotiations; mems: Argentina, Australia, Bolivia, Brazil, Canada, Chile, Colombia, Costa Rica, Guatemala, Indonesia, Malaysia, New Zealand, Pakistan, Paraguay, Peru, Philippines, South Africa, Thailand, Uruguay; Chair. Dr CRAIG EMERSON (Australia).

Caribbean Association of Industry and Commerce (CAIC): Ground Floor, 27A Saddle Rd, Maraval, Trinidad and Tobago; tel. 628-9859; fax 622-7810; e-mail caic.admin@gmail.com; internet www.caic.org.tt; f. 1955; aims to encourage economic development through the private sector; undertakes research and training and gives assistance to small enterprises; encourages export promotion; mems: chambers of commerce and enterprises in 20 countries and territories; Pres. CAROL EVELYN (Saint Christopher and Nevis); publ. *Caribbean Investor* (quarterly).

CEI-Bois (European Confederation of Woodworking Industries): 24 rue Montoyer, POB 20, 1000 Brussels, Belgium; tel. (2) 556-25-85; fax (2) 287-08-75; e-mail info@cei-bois.org; internet www.cei-bois.org; f. 1952 to liaise between national organizations, undertake research and defend the interests of the industry; mems: national federations in 25 European countries, 8 branch feds; Chair. MATTI MIKKOLA (Finland); Sec.-Gen. FILIP DE JAEGER; publ. *Brochure*.

CINOA—International Confederation of Art and Antique Dealers: 33 rue Ernest-Allard, 1000 Brussels, Belgium; tel. (2) 502-26-92; e-mail secretary@cinoa.org; internet www.cinoa.org; f. 1936; mems: 32 art and antique dealer asscns in 22 countries, representing 5,000 dealers; holds anuual conference (June 2012: Bruges, Belgium); Pres. JAN DE MAERE; Sec.-Gen. ERIKA BOCHEREAU.

Committee for European Construction Equipment (CECE): Diamant Bldg, 80 blvd Reyers, 1030 Brussels, Belgium; tel. (2) 706-82-26; fax (2) 706-82-10; e-mail info@cece.eu; internet www.cece.eu; f. 1959 to further contact between manufacturers, to improve market conditions and productivity and to conduct research into techniques; mems: representatives from 12 European countries; Pres. JOHANN SAILER; Sec.-Gen. RALF WEZEL.

Confederation of Asia-Pacific Chambers of Commerce and Industry (CACCI): 14/F, 3 11 Songgao Rd, Taipei 11073, Taiwan; tel. (2) 27255663; fax (2) 27255665; e-mail cacci@cacci.org.tw; internet www.cacci.org.tw; f. 1966; holds biennial conferences to examine regional co-operation, and an annual Council meeting; liaises with governments to promote laws conducive to regional co-operation; serves as a centre for compiling and disseminating trade and business information; encourages contacts between businesses; conducts training and research; mems: 29 national chambers of commerce and industry from the region, also affiliate and special mems; Pres. BENEDICTO V. YUJUICO; Dir-Gen. Dr WEBSTER KIANG; publs *CACCI Profile* (monthly), *CACCI Journal of Commerce and Industry* (2 a year).

Consumers International: 24 Highbury Cres., London, N5 1RX, United Kingdom; tel. (20) 7226-6663; fax (20) 7354-0607; e-mail consint@consint.org; internet www.consumersinternational.org; f. 1960 as International Organization of Consumers' Unions—IOCU; links consumer groups world-wide through information networks and international seminars; supports new consumer groups and represents consumers' interests at the international level; maintains four regional offices; mems: over 220 orgs in 115 countries; Dir-Gen. HELEN MCCALLUM; publs *World Consumer Rights Day Kit* (annually, English, French and Spanish), *Annual Report*, Policy Briefing Papers and Issue-specific reports.

CropLife International: 326 ave Louise, POB 35, 1050 Brussels, Belgium; tel. (2) 542-04-10; fax (2) 542-04-19; e-mail croplife@croplife.org; internet www.croplife.org; f. 1960 as European Group of National Asscns of Pesticide Manufacturers, international body since 1967, present name adopted in 2001, evolving from Global Crop Protection Federation; represents the plant science industry, with the aim of promoting sustainable agricultural methods; aims to harmonize national and international regulations concerning crop protection products and agricultural biotechnology; promotes observation of the FAO Code of Conduct on the Distribution and Use of Pesticides; holds an annual General Assembly; mems: 8 cos, regional bodies and national asscns in 91 countries; Pres. and CEO HOWARD MINIGH.

Energy Charter Conference: 56 blvd de la Woluwe, 1200 Brussels, Belgium; tel. (2) 775-98-00; fax (2) 775-98-01; e-mail info@encharter.org; internet www.encharter.org; f. 1995 under the provisions of the Energy Charter Treaty (1994); provides a legal framework for promotion of trade and investment across Eurasia in the energy industries; mems: 51 states; Sec.-Gen. URBAN RUSNÁK (Slovakia); publs *Putting a Price on Energy: International Pricing Mechanisms for Oil and Gas*, *The Energy Charter Treaty—A Reader's Guide*, reports.

ESOMAR—World Association of Opinion and Marketing Research Professionals: Eurocenter 2, 11th Floor, Barbara Strozzilaan 384, 1083 HN Amsterdam, Netherlands; tel. (20) 6642141; fax (20) 5897885; e-mail customerservice@esomar.org; internet www.esomar.org; f. 1948 (as European Society for Opinion and Marketing Research); aims to further professional interests and encourage high technical standards in the industry; creates and manages a comprehensive programme of industry-specific and thematic conferences, publications and communications, as well as actively advocating self-regulation and the world-wide code of practice; mems: over 4,500 in 100 countries; Pres. DIETER KORCZAK; publs *Research World* (monthly), *Global Market Research* (annually).

European and International Booksellers Federation (EIBF): 10 rue de la science, 1000 Brussels, Belgium; tel. (2) 223-49-40; fax (2) 223-49-38; e-mail fran@ibf-booksellers.org; internet www.ibf-booksellers.org; f. 2010 by the merger of the former European Booksellers Federation and International Booksellers Federation (f. 1956) to promote the book trade and the exchange of information, and to protect the interests of booksellers when dealing with other international orgs; addresses pricing, book market research, advertising, customs and tariffs, the problems of young booksellers, etc; mems: 200 in 25 countries; Pres. KARL PUS; Dir FRANÇOISE DUBRUILLE; publ. *IBF Newsletter* (quarterly).

European Association of Communications Agencies (EACA): 152 blvd Brand Whitlock, 1200 Brussels, Belgium; tel. (2) 740-07-10; fax (2) 740-07-17; e-mail dominic.lyle@eaca.be; internet www.eaca.eu; f. 1959 (as European Association of Advertising Agencies) to maintain and raise the standards of service of all European advertising, media and sales promotions agencies; aims to promote honest, effective advertising, high professional standards, and awareness of the contribution of advertising in a free market economy and to encourage close co-operation between agencies, advertisers and media in European advertising bodies; mems: 30 national advertising agency asscns and 17 multinational agency networks; Pres. MORAY MACLENNAN; Dir-Gen. DOMINIC LYLE.

European Association of Electrical Contractors (AIE): 1 J. Chantraineplantsoen, 3070 Kortenberg, Belgium; tel. (2) 253-42-22; fax (2) 253-67-63; e-mail info@aie.eu; internet www.aie.eu; f. 1953 (as International Association of Electrical Contractors); aims to promote improved technical standardization, efficient solutions, provide information on market trends, and represent common interests of European electrical contractors; mems: national asscns in 20 countries and territories; Pres. JANNE SKOGBERG; Gen. Sec. EVELYNE SCHELLEKENS; publ. *AIE Directory* (every 2 years).

European Association of National Productivity Centres (EANPC): c/o Prevent, 88 rue de la Gachard, 1050 Brussels, Belgium; tel. (2) 643-44-51; fax (2) 643-44-50; e-mail ingrid.dhondt@prevent.be; internet www.eanpc.eu; f. 1966 to enable members to pool knowledge about their policies and activities; mems: 15 European centres; Pres. JOHN HEAP (United Kingdom); Sec.-Gen. MARC DE GREEF (Belgium); publs *EPI* (3 a year), *Europroductivity* (3 a year).

European Brewery Convention: c/o The Brewers of Europe, 23–25 rue Caroly, 1050 Brussels, Belgium; tel. (2) 551-18-28; fax (2) 660-09-02; e-mail info@europeanbreweryconvention.org; internet www.europeanbreweryconvention.org; f. 1947; aims to promote scientific co-ordination in malting and brewing; mems: national asscns in 20 European countries; Pres. Dr STEFAN

LUSDIG; publs *Analytica, Thesaurus, Dictionary of Brewing*, monographs, conference proceedings, manuals of good practice.

European Chemical Industry Council: 4 ave E. van Nieuwenhuyse, Box 1, 1160 Brussels, Belgium; tel. (2) 676-72-11; fax (2) 676-73-00; e-mail apy@cefic.be; internet www.cefic.org; f. 1972; represents and defends the interests of the chemical industry in legal and trade policy, internal market, environmental and technical matters; liaises with intergovernmental organizations; provides secretariat for some 100 product sector groups; mems: 22 national federations, incl. 6 assoc. mem. feds; Pres. GIORGIO SQUINZI; Dir-Gen. HUBERT MANDERY.

European Committee for Standardization (Comité européen de normalisation—CEN): 17 ave Marnix, 1000 Brussels, Belgium; tel. (2) 550-08-11; fax (2) 550-08-19; e-mail infodesk@cenorm.be; internet www.cenorm.be; f. 1961 to promote European standardization; works to eliminate obstacles caused by technical requirements, in order to facilitate the exchange of goods and services; mems: 32 national standards bodies, 8 associated and 5 affiliated bodies in central and eastern Europe and 7 partnership standardization bodies; Pres. FRIEDRICH SMAXWIL; Dir. Gen. ELENA SANTIAGO CID; publs *Catalogue of European Standards* (2 a year), *CEN Networking* (newsletter, every 2 months), *Bulletin* (quarterly), *Directives and related standards* (in English, French and German), *Directions, European Standardization in a Global Context, The Benefits of Standards, Marking of Products and System Certification.*

European Committee of Associations of Manufacturers of Agricultural Machinery: 80 blvd A. Reyers, 1030 Brussels, Belgium; tel. (2) 706-82-16; e-mail info@cema-agri.org; internet www.cema-agri.org; f. 1959 to study economic and technical problems in field of agricultural machinery manufacture, to protect members' interests and to disseminate information; mems: 11 mem. countries; Pres. GILLES DRYANCOUR; Sec.-Gen. RALF WEZEL (Germany).

European Committee of Textile Machinery Manufacturers (CEMATEX): POB 248, Newcastle upon Tyne, NE7 7WY, United Kingdom; e-mail info@cematex.com; internet www.cematex.com; f. 1952; promotes general interests of the industry; mems: national asscns in 9 European countries; Pres. STEPHEN COMBES (United Kingdom); Gen. Sec. MARIA AVERY.

European Council of Paint, Printing Ink and Artists' Colours Industry: 6 ave E. van Nieuwenhuyse, 1160 Brussels, Belgium; tel. (2) 676-74-80; fax (2) 676-74-90; e-mail secretariat@cepe.org; internet www.cepe.org; f. 1951 to study questions relating to the paint and printing ink industries, to take or recommend measures for the development of these industries or to support their interests, and to exchange information; organizes an Annual Conference and General Assembly (Sept. 2012: Seville, Spain); mems: company mems of national asscns in 23 European countries; Chair. JOAO SERRENHO; Man. Dir JAN VAN DER MEULEN; publs *Annual Review*, guidance documents.

European Crop Protection Association (ECPA): 6 ave E. van Nieuwenhuyse, 1160 Brussels, Belgium; tel. (2) 663-15-50; fax (2) 663-15-60; e-mail ecpa@ecpa.eu; internet www.ecpa.eu; aims to harmonize national and international regulations concerning crop protection products, to support the development of the industry and to promote observation of the FAO Code of Conduct on the Distribution and Use of Pesticides, forms part of Croplife International; mems: in 26 countries; Pres. VINCENT GROS; Dir-Gen. Dr FRIEDHELM SCHMIDER (Germany); publs *Annual Report.*

European Federation of Associations of Insulation Enterprises: c/o Thermal Insulation Contractors Assn, TICA House, Allington Way, Darlington, DL1 4QB, United Kingdom; tel. (1325) 734140; e-mail bfa.wksb@bauindustrie.de; f. 1970; groups organizations in Europe representing insulation firms; aims to facilitate contacts between member asscns; studies problems of interest to the profession; works to safeguard the interests of the profession and represent it in international fora; mems: professional orgs in 16 European countries; Sec.-Gen. JUERGEN SCHMOLDT.

European Federation of Associations of Marketing Research Organisations (EFAMRO): Bastion Tower, 20e étage, Pl. du Champ de Mars 5, 1050 Brussels, Belgium; tel. (2) 550-35-48; fax (2) 550-35-84; e-mail info@efamro.eu; internet www.efamro.eu; f. 1965 (frmly known as FEMRA) to facilitate contacts between researchers; maintains specialist divisions on European chemical marketing research, European technological forecasting, paper and related industries, industrial materials, automotives, textiles, methodology, and information technology; mems: nat. asscns in 9 countries; Pres. ANDREW CANNON; publs *EFAMRO Monitoring Report* (weekly).

European Federation of Insurance Intermediaries (BIPAR): 40 ave Albert-Elisabeth, 1200 Brussels, Belgium; tel. (2) 735-60-48; fax (2) 732-14-18; e-mail bipar@skynet.be; internet www.bipar.eu; f. 1937; represents, promotes and defends the interests of national asscns of professional insurance agents and brokers at the European and international level; works to co-ordinate members' activities; mems: 48 asscns from 30 countries, representing approx. 250,000 brokers and agents; Chair. ALESSANDRO DE BESI; Sec.-Gen. ANDRÉ LAMOTTE; publ. *BIPAR Press* (10 a year).

European Federation of Management Consultancies' Associations: 3–5 ave des Arts, 6e étage, 1210 Brussels, Belgium; tel. (2) 250-06-50; e-mail feaco@feaco.org; internet www.feaco.org; f. 1960; aims to promote networking within the management consultancy sector and its interests and promote a high standard of professional competence, by encouraging discussions of, and research into, problems of common professional interest; mems: 17 asscns; Chair. EZIO LATTANZIO (Italy); Sec.-Gen. DAVID IFRAH; publs *FEACO Newsletter* (quarterly), *Annual Survey of the European Management Consultancy Market.*

European Federation of Materials Handling and Storage Equipment: Diamant Bldg, 80 blvd A. Reyers, 1030 Brussels, Belgium; tel. (2) 706-82-37; fax (2) 706-82-53; e-mail olivier.janin@orgalime.org; internet www.fem-eur.com; f. 1953 to represent the technical, economic and political interests of one of the largest industrial sectors of the European mechanical engineering industry; mems: national orgs in 12 European countries; Pres. JOHN MEALE; Sec.-Gen. OLIVIER JANIN.

European Federation of the Plywood Industry (FEIC): 24 rue Montoyer, 1000 Brussels, Belgium; tel. (2) 556-25-84; fax (2) 287-08-75; e-mail info@europlywood.org; internet www.europlywood.org; f. 1957 to organize co-operation between members of the industry at the international level; mems: asscns in 18 European countries and 1 assoc. mem; Pres. JONI LUKKAROINEN; Sec.-Gen. K. WŸNENDAELE.

European Furniture Manufacturers Federation (Union européenne de l'ameublement—UEA): 163 rue Royale, Koningsstraat, 1210 Brussels, Belgium; tel. (2) 218-18-89; fax (2) 219-27-01; e-mail secretariat@uea.be; internet www.ueanet.com; f. 1950 to determine and support the general interests of the European furniture industry and facilitate contacts between members of the industry; mems: orgs in 25 European countries; Pres. MARTIN ČUDKA (Czech Republic); Sec.-Gen. BART DE TURCK; publs *UEA Newsletter* (every 2 months), *Focus on Issues, Strategy Survey.*

European General Galvanizers Association (EGGA): Maybrook House, Godstone Rd, Caterham, Surrey, CR3 6RE, United Kingdom; tel. (1883) 331277; fax (1883) 331287; e-mail mail@egga.com; internet www.egga.com; f. 1955 to promote co-operation between members of the industry, especially in improving processes and finding new uses for galvanized products; mems: asscns in 16 European countries; Dir MURRAY COOK (United Kingdom); Exec. Sec. FRANCES HOLMES.

European Organization for Packaging and the Environment (EUROPEN): Le Royal Tervuren, 6 ave de l'Armée Legerlaan, 1040 Brussels, Belgium; tel. (2) 736-36-00; fax (2) 736-35-21; e-mail packaging@europen.be; internet www.europen.be; provides policy support and a forum for the exchange of industry information related to packaging and the environment; mems: 42 corporate mems and 5 national orgs; Chair JOHN SWIFT; Man. Dir. VÉRONIQUE BAGGE; publ. *EUROPEN Bulletin* (6 a year).

European Organization for Quality (EOQ): 36-38 rue Joseph II, 1000 Brussels, Belgium; tel. 474-24-08-00 (mobile); e-mail eoq@eoq-org.eu; internet www.eoq.org; f. 1956 to encourage the use and application of quality management, with the aim of improving quality, lowering costs and increasing productivity; organizes the exchange of information and documentation; mems: orgs in 34 European countries; Dir-Gen. Eric Janssens.

European Panel Federation: 24 rue Montoyer, Box 20, 1000 Brussels, Belgium; tel. (2) 556-25-89; fax (2) 287-08-75; e-mail info@europanels.org; internet www.europanels.org; f. 1958 as European Federation of Associations of Particle Board Manufacturers; present name adopted 1999; works to develop and encourage international co-operation in the particle board and MDF industry; mems: in 23 countries; Pres. L. Döry; Sec.-Gen. K. Wijnendale (Belgium); publ. *Annual Report*.

European Patent Organisation (Office européen des brevets): Erhardtstr. 27, 80469 Munich, Germany; tel. (89) 2399-1101; fax (89) 2399-2891; e-mail council_secretary@epo.org; internet www.epo.org; f. 1977, in accordance with the European Patent Convention signed in Munich in 1973; conducts searches and examination of European patent applications; grants European patents; the Organisation comprises the European Patent Office (EPO) and an Administrative Council; mems: 38 European countries; Pres Benoît Battistelli (France); Head Council Secr. Yves Grandjean.

European Photovoltaic Industry Association: 63–67 rue d'Arlon, 1040 Brussels, Belgium; tel. (2) 465-38-84; fax (2) 400-10-10; internet www.epia.org; f. 1985; promotes and represents the European photovoltaics industry and advises mems. in developing businesses within the EU and internationally; organizes annual conference (2012: Munich, Germany); mems: more than 230 cos; Pres. Dr Winfried Hoffmann; Sec.-Gen Reinhold Buttgereit; publs reports, research documents and policy recommendations.

European Steel Association (EURO-FER): Integrale Bldg, 3rd Floor, 5 ave Ariane, 1200 Brussels, Belgium; tel. (2) 738-79-37; fax (2) 738-79-60; e-mail a.katsiboubas@eurofer.be; internet www.eurofer.eu; f. 1976 as the European Confederation of Iron and Steel Industries, named changed in 2011; aims to foster co-operation between the member federations and companies and to represent their common interests to the EU and other international organizations; mems: 60 national federations and cos in 23 European countries; Gen. Dir Gordon Moffat.

European Union of the Natural Gas Industry (EUROGAS): 172 ave de Cortenbergh, Box 6, 1000 Brussels, Belgium; tel. (2) 894-48-48; fax (2) 894-48-00; e-mail eurogas@eurogas.org; internet www.eurogas.org; f. 1910; mems: 50 orgs, federations and cos in 27 European countries; Pres. Jean-François Cirelli (France); Sec.-Gen. Beate Rabbe; publs *Annual Report*, annual statistical brochures.

Fairtrade International: Bonner Talweg 177 53129 Bonn, Germany; tel. (228) 949230; fax (228) 2421713; e-mail info@fairtrade.net; internet www.fairtrade.net; f. 1997; co-ordinates Fairtrade labelling internationally, aims to set the strategic direction for Fairtrade, to produce the standards by which Fairtrade is conducted, and to support producers to gain Fairtrade certification and secure market opportunities; Producer Networks represent the interest of producers in the system while the Labelling Initiatives promote Fairtrade to business and consumers in the developed world; effective Dec. 2011, Fairtrade USA resigned its membership from the umbrella org; mems: 3 producer networks, 19 labelling initiatives, 2 marketing orgs and 1 assoc. in 25 countries; Chair. Esther Guluma; CEO Rob Cameron.

Federación de Cámaras de Comercio del Istmo Centroamericano (Federation of Central American Chambers of Commerce): 9a avda Norte y 5, Calle Poniente 333, San Salvador, El Salvador; tel. 2231-3065; e-mail aechevarria@fecamco.com; internet www.fecamco.com; f. 1961; plans and co-ordinates industrial and commercial exchanges and exhibitions; mems: Chambers of Commerce in 11 countries; Pres. Mario González; Exec. Dir Maria Eugenia Pacas.

Federation of West African Chambers of Commerce and Industry (FEWACCI): Aviation House 204, POB CT 5875, Accra, Ghana; tel. (21) 763720; internet www.fewacci.org; f. 1975 to bring together the National Chambers of Commerce of ECOWAS mem. states; Pres. Wilson Atta Krofah; CEO Cherno Sallow.

General Arab Insurance Federation: 8 Kasr en-Nil St, POB 611, 11511 Cairo, Egypt; tel. (2) 5743177; fax (2) 5762310; e-mail gaif@tedata.net.eg; internet www.gaif-1.org; f. 1964; Sec.-Gen. Abd al-Khaliq R. Khalil (Iraq).

General Union of Chambers of Commerce, Industry and Agriculture for Arab Countries (GUCCIAAC): POB 11-2837, Beirut, Lebanon; tel. (1) 826020; fax (1) 826021; e-mail uac@uac.org.lb; internet www.gucciaac.org.lb; f. 1951 to enhance Arab economic development, integration and security through the co-ordination of industrial, agricultural and trade policies and legislation; mems: chambers of commerce, industry and agriculture in 22 Arab countries; Pres. Adnan Kassar; Sec.-Gen. Dr Imad Shihab; publs *Arab Economic Report*, *Al-Omran Al-Arabi* (every 2 months), economic papers, proceedings.

Gulf Organization for Industrial Consulting (GOIC): POB 5114, Doha, Qatar; tel. 4858888; fax 4831465; e-mail goic@goic.org.qa; internet www.goic.org.qa; f. 1976 by the Gulf Arab states to encourage industrial co-operation among Gulf Arab states, to pool industrial expertise and to encourage joint development of projects; undertakes feasibility studies, market diagnosis, assistance in policy-making, legal consultancies, project promotion, promotion of small and medium industrial investment profiles and technical training; maintains industrial data bank; mems: mem. states of the Cooperation Council for the Arab States of the Gulf; Sec.-Gen. Abdulaziz bin Hamad al-Ageel; publs *GOIC Monthly Bulletin* (in Arabic), *Al Ta'awon al Sina'e* (quarterly, in Arabic and English).

Instituto Centroamericano de Administración de Empresas (INCAE) (Central American Institute for Business Administration): Apdo 960, 4050 Alajuela, Costa Rica; tel. 2443-9908; fax 2433-9983; e-mail costarica@incae.edu; internet www.incae.edu; f. 1964; provides a postgraduate programme in business administration; runs executive training programmes; carries out management research and consulting; maintains a second campus in Nicaragua; libraries of 85,000 vols; Pres. Dr Arturo Condo; publs *Alumni Journal* (in Spanish), *Bulletin* (quarterly), books and case studies.

International Advertising Association Inc: World Service Center, 275 Madison Ave, Suite 2102, New York, NY 10016, USA; tel. (212) 557-1133; fax (212) 983-0455; e-mail iaa@iaaglobal.org; internet www.iaaglobal.org; f. 1938 as a global partnership of advertisers, agencies, the media and other marketing communications professionals; aims to protect freedom of commercial speech and consumer choice; holds World Congress every two years (2012: Manama, Bahrain); mems: 4,000 individuals, 55 corporate mems and 30 orgs in 76 countries; Chair. and World Pres. Alan Rutherford (United Kingdom); Exec. Dir Michael Lee (USA); publs (electronic newsletters) *IAA EU News*, *IAA Intelligence*, *IAA Network News*, *Annual Report*.

International Agricultural Trade Research Consortium (IATRC): World Service Center, 275 Madison Ave, Suite 2102, New York, NY 10016, USA; tel. (763) 755-9143; e-mail lbipes@umn.edu; internet www.iatrcweb.org; f. 1980 as an association of agricultural trade policy researchers, promoting policy formulation and industry knowledge; mems: 200 economists in 31 countries; Chair. Munisamy Gopinath; publs. trade issues, commissioned papers and policy briefs.

International Association for Textile Professionals (American Association for Textile Chemists and Colourists): 1 Davis Dr., POB 12215, Research Triangle Park, NC 27709-2215, USA; tel. (919) 549-8141; fax (919) 549 8933; e-mail danielsj@aatcc.org; f. 1921 to establish industrial test methods, enable quality control and initiate networking between textile professionals globally; individual and corporate mems in 60 countries world-wide; Pres. R. Michael Tyndall.

International Association of Department Stores: 11-13 rue Guersant, 75017 Paris, France; tel. 1-42-94-02-02; fax 1-42-94-02-04; e-mail iads@iads.org; internet www.iads.org; f. 1928 to conduct research and exchange information and statistics on management, organization and technical problems; maintains a documentation centre; mems: large-scale retail enterprises operating department stores in 16 countries; Pres. Paul Delaoutre (France); Gen. Sec. Maarten de Groot van Embden (Netherlands).

International Association of the Soap, Detergent and Maintenance Products Industry (AISE) (Association internationale de la savonnerie, de la détergence et des produits d'entretien): 15 A ave Herrmann Debroux, 3rd Floor, 1160 Brussels, Belgium; tel. (2) 679-62-60; fax (2) 679-62-79; e-mail aise.main@aise.eu; internet www.aise.eu; f. 1952; aims to promote the manufacture and use of a wide range of cleaning products, polishes, bleaches, disinfectants and insecticides; mems: 37 national asscns in 42 countries; Dir-Gen. SUSANNE ZAENKER.

International Bureau for the Standardization of Man-Made Fibres (BISFA): 6 ave E. van Nieuwenhuyse, 1160 Brussels, Belgium; tel. (2) 676-74-55; fax (2) 676-74-54; e-mail secretariat@bisfa.org; internet www.bisfa.org; f. 1928 to examine and establish rules for the standardization, classification and naming of various categories of man-made fibres; mems: individual producers in 17 countries; Sec.-Gen. BERNARD DEFRAYE.

International Butchers' Confederation: Bte 10, 4 rue Jacques de Lalaing, 1040 Brussels, Belgium; tel. (2) 230-38-76; fax (2) 230-34-51; e-mail info@cibc.be; internet www.cibc.be; f. 1907; aims to defend the interests of small and medium-sized enterprises in the meat trading and catering industry; represents 16 asscns from the EU and EFTA; Pres. JEAN-MARIE OSWALD (Luxembourg); Sec.-Gen. MARTIN FUCHS.

International Centre for Trade and Sustainable Development (ICTSD): 7-9 chemin de Balexert, 1219 Geneva, Switzerland; tel. 229178492; fax 229178093; e-mail ictsd@ictsd.ch; internet www.ictsd.org; f. 1996 with the aim of promoting trade policy that encourages sustainable development through information services, reporting and monitoring activities; CEO RICARDO MELÉNDEZ-ORTIZ.

International Confederation for Printing and Allied Industries (INTERGRAF): 7 pl. E. Flagey, Bte 5, 1050 Brussels, Belgium; tel. (2) 230-86-46; fax (2) 231-14-64; e-mail intergraf@intergraf.eu; internet www.intergraf.org; f. 1983 to work for the common interests of the printing and related industries in mem. countries through its lobbying, informing and networking activities; mems: 22 federations in 20 countries; Pres. HAVARD GRJOTHEIM; Sec.-Gen. BEATRICE KLOSE.

International Congress and Convention Association (ICCA): Toren A, De Entree 57, 1101 BH Amsterdam, Netherlands; tel. (20) 3981919; fax (20) 6990781; e-mail icca@icca.nl; internet www.iccaworld.com; f. 1963 to establish world-wide co-operation between all involved in organizing congresses, conventions and exhibitions; mems: more than 938 in 87 countries and territories; Pres. ARNALDO NARDONE; CEO MARTIN SIRK; publs *ICCA Intelligence* (5 a year, electronic), *ICCA Statistics* (annual).

International Co-operative Alliance (ICA): 150 route de Ferney, 1211 Geneva 2, Switzerland; tel. 229298888; fax 227984122; e-mail ica@ica.coop; internet www.ica.coop; f. 1895 for the pursuit of co-operative aims; a General Assembly and four Regional Assemblies meet every two years, on an alternating basis; a 23-member ICA Board controls the affairs of the organization between meetings of the General Assembly; sectoral organisations and thematic committees have been established to promote co-operative activities in the following fields: agriculture; banking; fisheries; consumer affairs; tourism; communications; co-operative research; health; human resource development; housing; insurance; gender issues; and industrial, artisanal and worker co-operatives; mems: 267 affiliated national orgs, with a total membership of more than 1,000m. individuals in 96 countries, and 4 int. orgs; Pres. Dame PAULINE GREEN (United Kingdom); Dir-Gen. CHARLES GOULD (USA); publs *Review of International Co-operation* (quarterly), *ICA Digest* (electronic newsletter, 2 a month), *Co-op Dialogue* (2 a year).

International Council of Communication Design (Icograda): 455 St Antoine Ouest, Suite SS 10, Montréal, QC H2Z 1J1, Canada; tel. (514) 448-4949; fax (514) 448-4948; e-mail info@icograda.org; internet www.icograda.org; f. 1963; aims to raise standards of communication design; promotes the exchange of information; organizes events; maintains archive; mems: 11 int. affiliated mems, 56 professional mems, 18 promotional mems, 86 educational mems, 5 corporate mems and 2 observers; Pres. LEIMEI JULIA CHIU (Japan); Sec.-Gen. IVA BRABAJA (Croatia); publs *Iridescent* (online) *electronic Newsletter* (weekly), *Regulations and Guidelines governing International Design Competitions*, *Model Code of Professional Conduct*, other professional documents.

International Council of Societies of Industrial Design (ICSID): 455 St Antoine Ouest, Suite SS 10, Montréal, QC H2Z 1J1, Canada; tel. (514) 448-4949; fax (514) 448-4948; e-mail office@icsid.org; internet www.icsid.org; f. 1957 to encourage the development of high standards in the practice of industrial design; works to improve and expand the contribution of industrial design throughout the world; mems: 8 assoc., 28 corporate, 61 educational, 24 professional and 54 promotional mems; Pres. LEE SOON-IN (South Korea); Sec.-Gen. DILKI DE SILVA; publs *ICSID News* (6 a year), *World Directory of Design Schools*.

International Council of Tanners: Leather Trade House, Kings Park Rd, Moulton Park, Northampton, NN3 6JD, United Kingdom; tel. (1604) 679917; fax (1604) 679998; e-mail sec@tannerscouncilict.org; internet www.tannerscouncilict.org; f. 1926 to study all questions relating to the leather industry and maintain contact with national asscns; mems: national tanners' orgs in 33 countries; Pres. WOLFGANG GOERLICH (Brazil).

International Council on Mining and Metals (ICMM): 35 Portman Sq., 6th Floor, London, W1H 6LR, United Kingdom; tel. (20) 7467-5070; fax (20) 7467-5071; e-mail info@icmm.com; internet www.icmm.com; f. 1991 (as the International Council on Metals and the Environment, present name adopted 2002); aims to promote sustainable development practices and policies in the mining, use, recycling and disposal of minerals and metals; mems: 19 cos, 30 asscns; Chair. MARIUS CLOPPERS (USA); publ. *ICMM Newsletter* (quarterly).

International Customs Tariffs Bureau: 15 rue des Petits Carmes, 1000 Brussels, Belgium; tel. (2) 501-87-74; fax (2) 501-31-47; e-mail dir@bitd.org; internet www.bitd.org; f. 1890; serves as the executive instrument of the International Union for the Publication of Customs Tariffs; translates and publishes all customs tariffs in five languages—English, French, German, Italian, Spanish; mems: 50 mem. countries; Pres. DIRK ACHTEN; Dir MICHEL GODFRIND; publs *International Customs Journal*, *Annual Report*.

International Exhibitions Bureau (Bureau International des Expositions): 34 ave d'Iéna, 75116 Paris, France; tel. 1-45-00-38-63; fax 1-45-00-96-15; e-mail info@bie-paris.org; internet www.bie-paris.org; f. 1931, revised by Protocol 1972, for the authorization and registration of international exhibitions falling under the 1928 Convention; mems: 160 states; Pres. JEAN-PIERRE LAFON; Sec.-Gen. VICENTE GONZALES LOSCERTALES; publs *BIE Bulletin*.

International Federation of Pharmaceutical Manufacturers and Associations (IFPMA): 15 chemin Louis-Dunant, POB 195, 1211 Geneva 20, Switzerland; tel. 223383200; fax 223383299; e-mail admin@ifpma.org; internet www.ifpma.org; f. 1968 for the exchange of information and international co-operation in all questions of interest to the pharmaceutical industry, particularly in the field of health legislation, science and research; represents the research-based pharmaceutical, biotech and vaccine sectors; develops ethical principles and practices and co-operates with national and international orgs; mems: 27 int. cos and 45 national and regional industry asscns; Pres. DAVID BRENNAN (USA); Dir-Gen. EDUARDO PISANI (Italy); publs *IFPMA Code of Pharmaceutical Marketing Practices*, action papers, occasional publications.

International Federation of the Phonographic Industry (IFPI): 10 Piccadilly, London, W1J 0DD, United Kingdom; tel. (20) 7878-7900; fax (20) 7878-7950; e-mail info@ifpi.org; internet www.ifpi.org; f. 1933; represents the interests of record producers by campaigning for the introduction, improvement and enforcement of copyright and related rights legislation; co-ordinates the recording industry's anti-piracy activities; mems: around 1,400 in 66 countries and nat. groups in 45 countries; CEO FRANCES MOORE; publs *Digital Music Report* (annually), *Recording Industry in Numbers* (annually); reports on digital music and commercial piracy, world sales.

International Fertilizer Industry Association (IFA): 28 rue Marbeuf, 75008 Paris, France; tel. 1-53-93-05-00; fax 1-53-93-05-45; e-mail ifa@fertilizer.org; internet www.fertilizer.org;

f. 1927; represents companies involved in all aspects of the global fertilizer industry, including the production and distribution of fertilizers, their raw materials and intermediates; also represents organizations involved in agronomic research and training with regard to crop nutrition; mems: some 540 in more than 85 countries; Pres. WILLIAM J. DOYLE; Dir-Gen. LUC MAENE; publ. *Fertilizers and Agriculture*.

International Foodservice Distributors Association (IFDA): 1410 Spring Hill Rd, Suite 210, McLean, VA 22102, USA; tel. (703) 532-9400; fax (703) 538-4673; internet www.ifdaonline.org; f. 1906; mems: over 140 mems; Chair. THOMAS A ZATINA; Pres. and CEO MARK S. ALLEN.

International Fragrance Association (IFRA): 6 ave des Arts, 1210 Brussels, Belgium; tel. (2) 214-20-60; fax (2) 214-20-69; e-mail secretariat@ifraorg.org; internet www.ifraorg.org; f. 1973 to develop and advance the fragrance industry, to collect and study scientific data on fragrance materials and to make recommendations on their safe use; mems: national asscns of fragrance manufacturers in 19 countries; Chair. MICHEL BONGI; Pres. PIERRE SIVAC; publs *Code of Practice*, *Information Letters*.

International Fur Trade Federation: POB 495, Weybridge, Surrey, KT12 8WD, United Kingdom; tel. (1932) 850020; e-mail info@iftf.com; internet www.iftf.com; f. 1949 to promote and organize joint action by fur trade organizations in order to develop and protect the trade in fur skins and the processing of skins; mems: 42 orgs in 35 countries; Chair. ANDREAS LENHART.

International Meat Secretariat (Office international de la viande): 6 rue de la Victoire, 75009 Paris, France; tel. 1-45-26-68-97; fax 1-45-26-68-98; e-mail info@meat-ims.org; internet www.meat-ims.org; f. 1974; organizes World Meat Congress every two years (2012: Paris, France, in June); mems: in 28 countries; Pres. ARTURO LLAVALLOL (Argentina); Sec.-Gen. HSIN HUANG; publs *Newsletter* (fortnightly), *IMS-GIRA World Meat Facts Book* (annual).

International Organization of Motor Vehicle Manufacturers (Organisation internationale des constructeurs d'automobiles—OICA): 4 rue de Berri, 75008 Paris, France; tel. 1-43-59-00-13; fax 1-45-63-84-41; e-mail oica@oica.net; internet www.oica.net; f. 1919 to co-ordinate and further the interests of the automobile industry, to promote the study of economic and other matters affecting automobile construction, and to control automobile manufacturers' participation in international exhibitions in Europe; mems: 37 national trade asscns; Pres. PATRICK BLAIN (USA); Gen. Sec. YVES VAN DER STRAATEN; publ. *Yearbook of the World's Motor Industry*.

International Organization of the Flavour Industry (IOFI): 6 ave des Arts, 1210 Brussels, Belgium; tel. (2) 214-20-50; fax (2) 214-20-69; e-mail secretariat@iofiorg.org; internet www.iofi.org; f. 1969 to support and promote the flavour industry; active in the fields of safety evaluation and regulation of flavouring substances; mems: national asscns in 24 countries; Exec. Dir JOS STELDER; publs *Documentation Bulletin*, *Information Letters*, *Code of Practice*.

International Publishers' Association: 3 ave de Miremont, 1206 Geneva, Switzerland; tel. 227041820; fax 227041821; e-mail secretariat@internationalpublishers.org; internet www.internationalpublishers.org; f. 1896 to defend the freedom of publishers to publish, to defend publishers interests, and to foster international co-operation; promotes the international trade in books and literacy as a step to economic and social development; carries out work on international copyright; mems: 62 professional book publishers' orgs in 55 countries; Pres. YOUNGSUK CHI; Sec.-Gen. JENS BAMMEL.

International Rayon and Synthetic Fibres Committee (Comité international de la rayonne et des fibres synthétiques—CIRFS): 6 ave E. van Nieuwenhuyse, 1160 Brussels, Belgium; tel. (2) 676-74-55; fax (2) 676-74-54; e-mail info@cirfs.org; internet www.cirfs.org; f. 1950 to improve the quality and promote the use of man-made fibres and products made from fibres; mems: individual producers in 24 countries; Pres. ANDREAS EULE; Dir-Gen. FRÉDÉRIC VAN HOUTE; publs *Statistical Booklet* (annually), market reports, technical test methods.

International Shopfitting Organisation (ISO): Thornberg-Bailey AB, Torna Hällestad, 247 95 Lund, Sweden; tel. (46) 53-202; fax (46) 53-229; e-mail info@iso-shopfitting.com; internet www.iso-shopfitting.com; f. 1959 to promote the interchange of ideas between individuals and firms concerned with shopfitting; mems: national asscns and individuals in 20 countries; Pres. CARSTEN SCHEMBERG; Sec.-Gen. PREBEN BAILEY.

International Textile Manufacturers Federation (ITMF): Wiedingstr. 9, 8055 Zürich, Switzerland; tel. 442836380; fax 442836389; e-mail secretariat@itmf.org; internet www.itmf.org; f. 1904, present title adopted 1978; aims to protect and promote the interests of its members, disseminate information, and encourage co-operation; mems: national textile trade asscns and companies in some 50 countries; Pres. BASHIR H. ALI MOHAMMAD (Pakistan); Dir-Gen. Dr CHRISTIAN P. SCHINDLER (Germany); publs *Annual Conference Report*, *Cotton Contamination Survey* (2 a year), *Country Statements* (annually), *International Textile Machinery Shipment Statistics* (annually), *International Cotton Industry Statistics* (annually), *International Production Cost Comparison* (2 a year), *State of Trade Report* (quarterly), *Directory*, various statistics, sectoral reports and guidelines.

International Union of Marine Insurance (IUMI): C.F. Meyer-Str. 14, POB 4288, 8022 Zürich, Switzerland; tel. 442082874; fax 442082800; e-mail simone.hirt@svv.ch; internet www.iumi.com; f. 1873 to collect and distribute information on marine insurance on a world-wide basis; mems: 54 asscns; organizes annual conference (Sept. 2012: San Diego, USA); Pres. OLE WIKBORG; Sec.-Gen. FRITZ STABINGER.

International Wool Textile Organisation (IWTO) (Fédération lanière internationale—FLI): 4 rue de l'Industrie, 1000 Brussels, Belgium; tel. (2) 505-40-10; fax (2) 503-47-85; e-mail info@iwto.org; internet www.iwto.org; f. 1929 to link wool textile organizations in member countries and represent their interests; holds annual Congress (2012: New York, USA, in May); mems: 21 national asscns, 27 assoc. mems; Pres. PETER ACKROYD (United Kingdom); Sec.-Gen. ELISABETH VAN DELDEN; publs *Wool Statistics* (annually), *Global Wool Supplies and Wool Textile Manufacturing Activity* (annually), *Blue Book*, *Red Book*.

International Wrought Copper Council: 55 Bryanston St, London, W1H 7AJ, United Kingdom; tel. (20) 7868-8930; fax (20) 7868-8819; e-mail iwcc@coppercouncil.org; internet www.coppercouncil.org; f. 1953 to link and represent copper fabricating industries and represent the views of copper consumers to raw material producers; organizes specialist activities on technical work and the development of copper; mems: 16 national groups in Europe, Australia, Japan and Malaysia, 9 corporate mems; Chair. JIN ROY RYU; Sec.-Gen. MARK LOVEITT; publs *Annual Report*, surveys.

Orgalime (European Engineering Industries Association): Diamant Bldg, 5th Floor, 80 blvd A Reyers, 1030 Brussels, Belgium; tel. (2) 706-82-35; fax (2) 706-82-50; e-mail secretariat@orgalime.org; internet www.orgalime.org; f. 1954 to provide a permanent liaison between the mechanical, electrical and electronic engineering, and metalworking industries of member countries; mems: 33 national trade asscns in 22 European countries; Pres. RICHARD DICK; Dir. Gen. ADRIAN HARRIS.

Pacific Power Association: Private Mail Bag, Suva, Fiji; tel. 3306022; fax 3302038; e-mail ppa@ppa.org.fj; internet www.ppa.org.fj; f. 1992 to facilitate co-operation and development of regional power utilities; represents the Pacific Islands' power sector at international meetings; mems: 25 power utilities throughout the region; mems: in 18 countries; Exec. Dir ANDREW DAKA; publ. *Pacific Power* (quarterly).

South East Asia Iron and Steel Institute (SEAISI): POB 7094, 40702 Shah Alam, Selangor Darul Ehson, Malaysia; tel. (3) 55191102; fax (3) 55191159; e-mail seaisi@seaisi.org; internet www.seaisi.org; f. 1971 to further the development of the iron and steel industry in the region, encourage regional co-operation, provide advisory services and a forum for the exchange of knowledge, establish training programmes, promote standardization, collate statistics and issue publications; mems: more than 800 in 40 countries; May 2012 Conference: Bali, Indonesia; Chair. FAZWAR BUJANG; Sec.-Gen. TAN AH YONG; publs *SEAISI Quarterly Journal*, *SEAISI Directory* (annually), *Iron and Steel Statistics* (annually, for each member country), *SEASI Quarterly Journal*, *Newsletter* (monthly), country reports.

Southern African Customs Union: Private Bag 13285, Windhoek, Namibia; tel. (61) 243950; fax (61) 245611; e-mail info@sacu.int; internet www.sacu.int; f. 1969; provides common pool of customs, excise and sales duties, according to the relative volume of trade and production in each country; goods are traded within the union free of duty and quotas, subject to certain protective measures for less developed mems; the South African rand is legal tender in Lesotho, Namibia and Swaziland; the Customs Union Commission meets quarterly in each of the mems' capital cities in turn; mems: Botswana, Lesotho, Namibia, South Africa, Swaziland; Exec. Sec. TSWELOPELE CORNELIA MOREMI.

Tiles and Bricks Europe (TBE): 17 rue Montagne, 1000 Brussels, Belgium; tel. (2) 808-38-80; fax (2) 511-51-74; e-mail sykes@cerameunie.eu; internet www.tiles-bricks.eu; f. 1952 to co-ordinate research between members of the industry, improve technical knowledge and encourage professional training; mems: asscns in 24 European and East European countries; Sec.-Gen. CHRISTOPHE SYKES.

UFI (Global Association of the Exhibition Industry): 17 rue Louise Michel, 92300 Levallois-Perret, France; tel. 1-46-39-75-00; fax 1-46-39-75-01; e-mail info@ufi.org; internet www.ufi.org; f. 1925 as Union des Foires Internationales; works to increase co-operation between international trade fairs/exhibitions, safeguard their interests and extend their operations; imposes exhibition quality criteria and defines standards; approves 805 events; mems: 586 in 84 countries; Pres. ARIE BRIENAN; Man. Dir PAUL WOODWARD.

Union of European Beverages Associations (UNESDA): 79 blvd St Michel, 1040 Brussels, Belgium; tel. (2) 743-40-50; fax (2) 732-51-02; e-mail mail@unesda.org; internet www.unesda.org; f. 1958, as Confederation of International Soft Drinks Associations; aims to promote co-operation among the national asscns of non-alcoholic drinks manufacturers on all industrial and commercial matters, to stimulate the sales and consumption of soft drinks, to deal with matters of interest to all member asscns and to represent the common interests of member asscns; holds a congress every year; mems: 25 national asscns and 11 companies; Sec.-Gen. ALAIN BEAUMONT.

Union of Producers, Conveyors and Distributors of Electric Power in Africa (UPDEA): 01 BP 1345, Abidjan 01, Côte d'Ivoire; tel. 20-20-60-53; fax 20-33-12-10; e-mail secgen@updea-africa.org; internet www.updea-africa.org; f. 1970 to study tech. matters and to promote efficient devt of enterprises in this sector; operates training school in Côte d'Ivoire; mems: 53 cos in 42 countries; Pres. EDWARD NJOROGE; Sec.-Gen. ABEL DIDIER TELLA; publs *UPDEA Information* (quarterly), technical papers.

World Customs Organization (WCO): 30 rue du Marché, 1210 Brussels, Belgium; tel. (2) 209-92-11; fax (2) 209-92-62; e-mail communication@wcoomd.org; internet www.wcoomd.org; f. 1952 as Customs Co-operation Council (CCC); aims to enhance the effectiveness and efficiency of customs administrations by building capacity for more effective border enforcement, better application of international trade regulations, enhanced measures to protect society, and increased revenue security; mems: customs administrations of 177 countries and customs territories; Sec.-Gen. KUNIO MIKURIYA (Japan); publ. *WCO News* (3 a year).

World Fair Trade Organization: Prijssestraat 24, 4101 CR, Culemborg, Netherlands; tel. (34) 5535914; fax (84) 7474401; e-mail info@wfto.com; internet www.wfto.com; f. 1989 as the International Fair Trade Association; coalition of trading and producer organizations; prescribes 10 standards that fair trade organizations must follow in their day-to-day work and carries out monitoring to ensure these principles are upheld; mems: 450 alternative trade orgs from 75 countries; Pres. PAUL MYERS (USA); Sec. PAUL DEIGHTON (Australia).

World Federation of Advertisers: 120 ave Louise, Box 6, 1050 Brussels; tel. (2) 502-57-40; fax (2) 502-56-66; e-mail info@wfanet.org; internet www.wfanet.org; f. 1953; promotes and studies advertising and its related problems; mems: asscns in 56 countries and more than 60 international cos; Pres. CHRIS BURGGRAEVE; Man. Dir STEPHAN LOERKE; publ. *EU Brief* (weekly).

World Packaging Organisation: 1833 Centre Point Circle, Suite 123, Naperville IL 60563, USA; tel. (630) 596-9007; fax (630) 544-5055; e-mail wpo@kellencompany.com; internet www.worldpackaging.org; f. 1968 to provide a forum for the exchange of knowledge of packaging technology and, in general, to create conditions for the conservation, preservation and distribution of world food production; holds annual congress and competition; mems: Asian, North American, Latin American, European and African packaging federations; full mems in 44 countries, 7 affiliated mems; Pres. THOMAS SCHNEIDER (USA); Gen. Sec. KEITH PEARSON (South Africa).

World Steel Association: 120 rue Col Bourg, 1140 Brussels, Belgium; tel. (2) 702-89-00; fax (2) 702-88-99; e-mail info@worldsteel.org; internet www.worldsteel.org; f. 1967, as International Iron and Steel Institute, to promote the welfare and interests of the world's steel industries; name changed as above in 2008; undertakes research into all aspects of steel industries; serves as a forum for exchange of knowledge and discussion of problems relating to steel industries; collects, disseminates and maintains statistics and information; serves as a liaison body between international and national steel organizations; mems: in over 50 countries; Dir-Gen. EDWIN BASSON; publs *Worldsteel Newsletter*, policy statements and reports.

World Trade Centers Association: 420 Lexington Ave, Suite 518, New York, NY 10170, USA; tel. (212) 432-2626; fax (212) 488-0064; e-mail wtca@wtca.org; internet www.wtca.org; f. 1968 to promote trade through the establishment of world trade centres, including education facilities, information services and exhibition facilities; operates an electronic trading and communication system (WTC Online); mems: 322 trade centres, chambers of commerce and other orgs in more than 107 countries; Pres. GUY F. TOZZOLI; Chair. GHAZI ABU NAHL; publ. *WTCA News* (monthly), *Trade Center Profiles* (annually), *World Business Directory* (annually).

Transport

African Airlines Association: POB 20116, Nairobi 00200, Kenya; tel. (20) 604855; fax (20) 601173; e-mail afraa@afraa.org; internet www.afraa.org; f. 1968 to give African air companies expert advice in technical, financial, juridical and market matters; to improve air transport in Africa through inter-carrier co-operation; and to develop manpower resources; mems: 34 national carriers; Dir RAPHAEL KUUCHI; Sec.-Gen. ELIJAH CHINGOSHO; publs *Newsletter*, reports.

Agency for the Safety of Air Navigation in Africa and Madagascar (ASECNA) (Agence pour la Sécurité de la Navigation Aérienne en Afrique et Madagascar): 32–38 ave Jean Jaurès, BP 3144, Dakar, Senegal; tel. 849-66-00; fax 823-46-54; e-mail contact@asecna.aero; internet www.asecna.aero; f. 1959 under Article 2 of the Dakar Convention; organizes air-traffic communications in mem. states; co-ordinates meteorological forecasts; provides training for air-traffic controllers, meteorologists and airport fire-fighters; ASECNA is under the authority of a cttee comprising Ministers of Civil Aviation of mem. states; mems: Benin, Burkina Faso, Cameroon, Central African Repub., Chad, Comoros, Repub. of the Congo, Côte d'Ivoire, Equatorial Guinea, Gabon, Guinea Bissau, Madagascar, Mali, Mauritania, Niger, Senegal, Togo; Dir-Gen. AMADOU OUSMANE GUITTEYE.

Airports Council International (ACI): POB 302, 800 Rue du Sq. Victoria, Montréal, QC H4Z 1G8, Canada; tel. (514) 373-1200; fax (514) 373-1201; e-mail aci@aci.aero; internet www.aci.aero; f. 1991, following merger of Airport Operators Council International and International Civil Airports Association; aims to represent and enhance co-operation among airports of the world and promote high standards in airport development and management; organizes an annual General Assembly, Conference and Exhibition (September 2012: Calgary, Canada); mems: 577 mems operating over 1,689 airports in 179 countries and territories; Chair. Dr YIANNIS PARASCHIS (Greece); Dir-Gen. ANGELA GITTENS; publs *World Report* (6 a year), *Airport World Magazine*, *Policy Handbook*, reports.

Arab Air Carriers' Organization (AACO): POB 13-5468, Beirut, Lebanon; tel. (1) 861297; fax (1) 863168; e-mail info@aaco.org; internet www.aaco.org; f. 1965 to promote co-operation in the activities of Arab airline companies; mems: 27 Arab air carriers; Chair. GHAIDA ABDULLATIF; Sec.-Gen. ABDUL WAHAB TEFFAHA; publs bulletins, reports and research documents.

Association of Asia Pacific Airlines: Kompleks Antarabangsa, 9th Floor, Jalan Sultan Ismail, 50250 Kuala Lumpur, Malaysia; tel. (3) 21455600; fax (3) 21452500; e-mail info@aapa.org.my; internet www.aapairlines.org; f. 1966 as Orient Airlines Asscn; present name adopted in 1997; as the trade association of the region's airlines, the AAPA aims to represent their interests and to provide a forum for all members to exchange information and views on matters of common concern; maintains international representation in Brussels, Belgium, and in Washington, DC, USA; mems: 15 scheduled international airlines (carrying approx. one-fifth of global passenger traffic and one-third of global cargo traffic); Dir-Gen. ANDREW J. HERDMAN; publs *Annual Report*, *Annual Statistical Report*, *Asia Pacific Perspectives*, *Orient Aviation* (10 a year).

Association of European Airlines: 350 ave Louise, 1050 Brussels, Belgium; tel. (2) 639-89-89; fax (2) 639-89-99; e-mail aea.secretariat@aea.be; internet www.aea.be; f. 1954 to carry out research on political, commercial, economic and technical aspects of air transport; maintains statistical data bank; mems: 34 airlines; Chair. BERNARD GUSTIN; Sec.-Gen. ATHAR HUSAIN KHAN (acting).

Association of the European Rail Industry (UNIFE): 221 ave Louise, bte 11, 1050 Brussels, Belgium; tel. (2) 626-12-60; fax (2) 626-12-61; e-mail info@unife.org; internet www.unife.org; f. 1975 with the merger of ICMR (Association internationale des constructeurs de matérial roulant), AFEDEF (Association des fabricants européens d'equipements ferroviaires) and CELTE (Constructeurs européens des locomotives thermiques et electriques); represents companies concerned with the design, manufacture and maintenance of railway systems and equipment; mems: 60 cos and 18 national railway industry asscns in 14 countries; Chair. HENRI POUPART-LAFARGE; Dir-Gen. PHILIPPE CITROËN; publ. *Newsletter* (quarterly).

Baltic and International Maritime Council (BIMCO): Bagsvaerdvej 161, 2880 Bagsvaerd, Denmark; tel. 44-36-68-00; fax 44-36-68-68; e-mail mailbox@bimco.org; internet www.bimco.org; f. 1905 to unite shipowners and other persons and organizations connected with the shipping industry, to facilitate commercial operations by sharing information and training resources and to establish sound business practices; mems: 2,500 in 123 countries, representing over 65% of world merchant shipping by tonnage; Pres. YUDHISHTHIR KHATAU; Sec.-Gen. TORBEN SKAANILD; publs *BIMCO Review* (annually), *BIMCO Bulletin* (6 a year), *Vessel*, manuals.

Central Commission for the Navigation of the Rhine: Palais du Rhin, 2 Pl. de la République, 67082 Strasbourg, France; tel. 3-88-52-20-10; fax 3-88-32-10-72; e-mail ccnr@ccr-zkr.org; internet www.ccr-zkr.org; f. 1815 to ensure free movement of traffic and standard river facilities for ships of all nations; draws up navigational rules; standardizes customs regulations; arbitrates in disputes involving river traffic; approves plans for river maintenance work; there is an administrative centre for social security for boatmen; mems: Belgium, France, Germany, Netherlands, Switzerland; Sec.-Gen. JEAN-MARIE WOEHRLING (France); publs guides, rules and directives (in French and German).

Danube Commission: Benczúr utca 25, 1068 Budapest, Hungary; tel. (1) 352-1835; fax (1) 352-1839; e-mail secretariat@danubecom-intern.org; internet www.danubecommission.org; f. 1948; supervises implementation of the Belgrade Convention on the Regime of Navigation on the Danube; approves projects for river maintenance; supervises a uniform system of traffic regulations on the whole navigable portion of the Danube and on river inspection; mems: Austria, Bulgaria, Croatia, Germany, Hungary, Moldova, Romania, Russia, Serbia, Slovakia, Ukraine; Pres. DIMITAR IKONOMOV (Bulgaria); Dir-Gen. Dr ISTVÁN VALKÁR; publs *Basic Regulations for Navigation on the Danube*, *Hydrological Yearbook*, *Statistical Yearbook*, proceedings of sessions.

European Civil Aviation Conference (ECAC): 3 bis Villa Emile-Bergerat, 92522 Neuilly-sur-Seine Cedex, France; tel. 1-46-41-85-44; fax 1-46-24-18-18; e-mail secretariat@ecac-ceac.org; internet www.ecac-ceac.org; f. 1955; aims to promote the continued development of a safe, efficient and sustainable European air transport system; mems: 44 European states; Pres. CATALIN RADU; Exec. Sec. SALVATORE SCIACCHITANO.

European Organisation for the Safety of Air Navigation (EUROCONTROL): 96 rue de la Fusée, 1130 Brussels, Belgium; tel. (2) 729-90-11; fax (2) 729-90-44; e-mail infocentre@eurocontrol.int; internet www.eurocontrol.int; f. 1960; aims to develop a coherent and co-ordinated air traffic control system in Europe. A revised Convention was signed in June 1997, incorporating the following institutional structure: a General Assembly (known as the Commission in the transitional period), a Council (known as the Provisional Council) and an Agency under the supervision of the Director-General; there are directorates, covering human resources and finance matters and a general secretariat. A special organizational structure covers the management of the European Air Traffic Management Programme. EUROCONTROL also operates the Experimental Centre (at Brétigny-sur-Orge, France), the Institute of Air Navigation Services (in Luxembourg), the Central Route Charges Office, the Central Flow Management Unit (both in Brussels) and the Upper Area Control Centre (in Maastricht, Netherlands); mems: 39 states and the European Community; Dir-Gen. DAVID MCMILLAN (United Kingdom).

Forum Train Europe FTE: Mittelstr. 43, 3000 Bern 65, Switzerland; tel. 512202715; fax 512201242; e-mail mailbox@forumtraineurope.org; internet www.forumtraineurope.org; f. 1923 as the European Passenger Train Time-Table Conference to arrange international passenger connections by rail and water; since 1997 concerned also with rail freight; mems: 98 mems from 35 European countries; Pres. HANS-JÜRG SPILLMANN; Sec.-Gen. PETER JÄGGY.

Inland Waterways International: Crabtree Hall, Mill Lane, Lower Beeding, Horsham, West Sussex, RH13 6PX, United Kingdom; e-mail info@inlandwaterwaysinternational.org; internet www.inlandwaterwaysinternational.org; f. 1995; promotes the use, conservation and development of inland waterways world-wide; hosts the steering commitee to choose the venue of the annual World Canals Conference; mems: 18 countries; Pres. DAVID BALLINGER (Canada).

Intergovernmental Organization for International Carriage by Rail: Gryphenhübeliweg 30, 3006 Bern, Switzerland; tel. 313591010; fax 313591011; e-mail info@otif.org; internet www.otif.org; f. 1893 as Central Office for International Carriage by Rail, present name adopted 1985; aims to establish and develop a uniform system of law governing the international carriage of passengers and goods by rail in member states; composed of a General Assembly, an Administrative Committee, a Revision Committee, a Committee of Experts on the Transport of Dangerous Goods, a Committee of Technical Experts and a Rail Facilitation Committee; mems: 47 states in Europe, the Middle East and North Africa, and one assoc. mem (Jordan); Sec.-Gen. STEFAN SCHIMMING; publ. *Bulletin des Transports Internationaux ferroviaires* (quarterly, in English, French and German).

International Air Transport Association (IATA): 800 Pl. Victoria, POB 113, Montréal, Québec, QC H4Z 1M1, Canada; tel. (514) 874-0202; fax 2(514) 874-1753; e-mail iata@iata.org; internet www.iata.org; f. 1945 to represent and serve the airline industry; aims to promote safe, reliable and secure air services; to assist the industry to attain adequate levels of profitability while developing cost-effective operational standards; to promote the importance of the industry in global social and economic development; and to identify common concerns and represent the industry in addressing these at regional and international level; plays a leading role in aviation activities world-wide; maintains regional offices in Amman, Brussels, Dakar, London, Nairobi, Santiago, Singapore and Washington, DC; mems: c. 240 airlines; Chair. ALAN JOYCE; Dir-Gen. and CEO TONY TYLER; publ. *Airlines International* (every 2 months).

International Association of Ports and Harbors (IAPH): 7F, New Pier Takeshiba South Tower, 1-16-1, Kaigan, Minato-ku, Tokyo 105-0022, Japan; tel. (3) 5403-2770; fax (3) 5403-7651; e-mail info@iaphworldports.org; internet www.iaphworldports.org; f. 1955 to increase the efficiency of ports and harbours through the dissemination of information on port organization, management, administration, operation, development and promotion; encourages the growth of waterborne commerce; holds conference every two years; mems: 350 in 90 states; Pres. GERALDINE KNATZ (USA); Sec.-Gen. SUSUMU NARUSE (Japan); publs *Ports and Harbors* (6 a year), *Membership Directory* (annually).

International Association of Public Transport: 6 rue Sainte-Marie, Quai de Charbonnages, 1080 Brussels, Belgium; tel. (2) 673-61-00; fax (2) 660-10-72; e-mail info@uitp.org; internet www.uitp.org; f. 1885 to study all problems connected with the urban and regional public passenger transport industry; serves as an international network for public transport authorities and operators, policy decision-makers, scientific institutes and the public transport supply and service industry; mems: 3,400 in 92 countries; Pres. OUSMANE THIAM; Sec.-Gen. ALAIN FLAUSCH; publs *Public Transport International* (every 2 months), *EUExpress*, *Mobility News* (monthly, electronic), statistics reports.

International Bureau of Containers and Intermodal Transport (Bureau international des containers et du transport intermodal — BIC): 38 rue des Blancs Manteaux, 75004 Paris, France; tel. 1-47-66-03-90; fax 1-47-66-08-91; e-mail bis@bic-code.org; internet www.bic-code.org; f. 1933 as Bureau International des Containers by the International Chamber of Commerce, present name adopted in 1948 on the assumption of intermodal activities; aims to bring together representatives of all means of transport and activities concerning containers, to promote combined door-to-door transport by the successive use of several means of transport, to examine and bring into effect advances in administrative, technical and customs practice, and to centralize data on behalf of mems; mems: 1,700; Chair. MICHEL HENNEMAND; Sec.-Gen. BERTRAND GEOFFRAY; publs *Containers Bulletin*, *Containers Bic-Code* (annually).

International Chamber of Shipping: 38 St Mary Axe, London, EC3A 8BH, United Kingdom; tel. (20) 7090-1460; e-mail info@ics-shipping.org; internet www.ics-shipping.org; f. 1921 to co-ordinate the views of the international shipping industry on matters of common interest, in the policy-making, technical and legal fields of shipping operations; mems: national asscns representing free-enterprise shipowners and operators in 34 countries, representing about 80% of the world merchant fleet; Chair. SPYROS POLEMIS (Greece); Sec.-Gen. PETER HINCHLIFFE.

International Federation of Freight Forwarders Associations (FIATA): Schaffhauserstr. 104, 8152 Glattbrugg, Switzerland; tel. 432116500; fax 432116565; e-mail info@fiata.com; internet www.fiata.com; f. 1926 to represent the freight forwarding industry at an international level; has consultative status with the United Nations Economic and Social Council (*inter alia* ECE, ESCAP, ESCWA), the United Nations Conference on Trade and Development (see p.) and the United Nations Convention on International Trade Law; mems: 44,000 forwarding and logistics firms in 150 countries; Pres. JEAN-CLAUDE DELEN (Belgium); Dir MARCO A. SANGALETTI; publ. *FIATA Review* (every 2 months).

International Rail Transport Committee (Comité international des transports ferroviaires—CIT): Weltpoststr. 20, 3015 Bern, Switzerland; tel. 313500190; fax 313500199; e-mail info@cit-rail.org; internet www.cit-rail.org; f. 1902 for the development of international law relating to railway transport, on the basis of the Convention concerning International Carriage by Rail (COTIF) and its Appendices (CIV, CIM), and for the adoption of standard rules on other questions relating to international transport law; mems: 120 transport undertakings in 42 countries; Pres. JEAN-LUC DUFOURNAUD; Sec.-Gen. CESARE BRAND (Switzerland).

International Road Federation (IRF): Geneva Programme Centre: 2 chemin de Blandonnet 1214, Vernier, Geneva, Switzerland; tel. 223060260; fax 223060270; e-mail info@irfnet.org; internet www.irfnet.org; f. 1948 to encourage the development and improvement of highways and highway transportation; Programme Centres in Geneva, Switzerland, Brussels, Belgium and Washington, DC, USA; organizes IRF world and regional meetings; mems: 80 national road asscns and 500 individual firms and industrial asscns; Chair. KIRAN KAPILA; Dir-Gen. SIBYLLE RUPPRECHT; publs *World Road Statistics* (annually), *World Highways* (8 a year).

International Road Safety Organization (La prevention routière internationale—PRI): Rietgors 1, 3755 GA Eemnes, Netherlands; tel. (69) 8908758; fax (67) 1354578; e-mail contact@lapri.info; internet www.lapri.info; f. 1959 for exchange of ideas and material on road safety; organizes international action and congresses; assists non-member countries; mems: 50 national orgs; Pres. JOOP GOOS; publs *Newsletter* (6 a year), also annual reports, news, brochures, booklets and manuals.

International Road Transport Union (IRU): Centre International, 3 rue de Varembé, BP 44, 1211 Geneva 20, Switzerland; tel. 229182700; fax 229182741; e-mail iru@iru.org; internet www.iru.org; f. 1948 to study all problems of road transport, to advocate harmonisation and simplification of regulations relating to road transport, and to promote the use of road transport for passengers and goods; represents, promotes and upholds the interests of the road transport industry at an international level; asscns and assoc. mems in 73 countries; Pres. JANUSZ LACNY; Sec.-Gen. MARTIN MARMY.

International Shipping Federation: 38 St Mary Axe, London, EC3A 8BH, United Kingdom; tel. (20) 7090-1460; e-mail info@ics-shipping.org; internet www.ics-shipping.org; f. 1909 to consider all personnel questions affecting the interests of shipowners; responsible for Shipowners' Group at conferences of the International Labour Organisation; represents shipowners at the International Maritime Organization; mems: national shipowners' orgs in 32 countries; Pres. SPYROS POLEMIS (Greece); Sec.-Gen. PETER HINCHLIFFE; publs conference papers, guidelines and training records.

International Transport Forum: 2 rue André Pascal, 75775 Paris Cedex 16, France; tel. 1-45-24-97-10; fax 1-45-24-97-42; e-mail itf.contact@oecd.org; internet www.internationaltransportforum.org; f. 2006 by a decision of the European Conference of Ministers of Transport (f. 1953) to broaden membership of the org; aims to create a safe, sustainable, efficient, integrated transport system; provides an annual Forum in Liepzig, Germany (May 2012: 'Seamless Transport: Making Connections'); holds round tables, seminars and symposia; shares Secretariat staff with OECD; mems: 53 countries; Sec.-Gen. MICHAEL KLOTH (acting); publs *Annual Report*, various statistical publications and surveys.

International Union of Railways (Union internationale des chemins de fer—UIC): 16 rue Jean-Rey, 75015 Paris, France; tel. 1-44-49-20-20; fax 1-44-49-20-29; e-mail loubinoux@uic.org; internet www.uic.org; f. 1922 for the harmonization of railway operations and the development of international rail transport; aims to ensure international interoperability of the rail system; compiles information on economic, management and technical aspects of railways; co-ordinates research and collaborates with industry and the EU; organizes international conferences; mems: 196 in 92 countries; Chair. YOSHIO ISHIDA; Dir-Gen. JEAN-PIERRE LOUBINOUX; publs *International Railway Statistics* (annually), *Activities Reports*, *UIC News* (newsletter).

International Association for the Rhine Ships Register (IVR) (Internationale Vereniging het Rijnschepenregister): Vasteland 12E, 3011 BL Rotterdam (POB 23210, 3001 KE Rotterdam), Netherlands; tel. (10) 4116070; fax (10) 4129091; e-mail info@ivr.nl; internet www.ivr.nl; f. 1947 for the classification of Rhine ships, the organization and publication of a Rhine ships register, the unification of general average rules and the maintenance of European inland navigation law; provides a platform for experts in the field of shipping, insurance, maritime affairs and related sectors, and representatives of national governments; Gen. Sec. THERESIA K. HACKSTEINER; publs *IVR Report* (2 a year), *Registre de l'IVR* (annually).

Nordisk Defence Club (Nordisk Skibsrederforening): Kristinelundv. 22, POB 3033, Elisenberg, 0207 Oslo, Norway; tel. 22-13-56-00; fax 22-43-00-35; e-mail post@nordisk.no; internet www.nordisk.no; f. 1889 to assist mems in disputes over charter parties, contracts and sale and purchase; functions as a safeguard bearing the cost of all legal intervention while also providing commercial and strategic advice; mems: mainly Finnish, Swedish and Norwegian and some non-Scandinavian shipowners, representing about 2,150 ships and drilling rigs with gross tonnage of about 53m.; Man. Dir GEORGE SCHEEL; Chair. NILS P. DYVIK; publs *A Law Report of Scandinavian Maritime Cases* (annually), *Medlemsbladet (Membership Circular)* (2 a year), *Annual Report*.

Organisation for Co-operation Between Railways: Hozà 63–67, 00681 Warsaw, Poland; tel. (22) 6573600; fax (22) 6219417; e-mail osjd@osjd.org.pl; internet osjd.org; f. 1956; aims to improve standards and co-operation in railway traffic between countries of Europe and Asia; promotes co-operation on issues relating to traffic policy and economic and environmental aspects of railway traffic; ensures enforcement of a number of rail agreements; aims to elaborate and standardize general principles for international transport law. Conference of Ministers of mem. countries meets annually; Conference of Gen. Dirs of Railways meets at least once a year; mems: ministries of transport of 27 countries world-wide; Chair. TADEUSZ SZOZDA; publ. *OSShD Journal* (every 2 months, in Chinese, German and Russian), *Statistic Report on Railway Transport* (annually).

Pan American Railway Congress Association (Asociación del Congreso Panamericano de Ferrocarriles): Av. Dr José María Ramos Mejía 1302, Planta Baja, 1104 Buenos Aires, Argentina; tel. (11) 4315-3445; fax (11) 4312-3834; e-mail acpf@acpf.com.ar; internet www.acpf.com.ar; f. 1907, present title adopted 1941; aims to promote the development and progress of railways in the American continent; holds Congresses every three years; mems: govt representatives, railway enterprises and individuals in 20 countries; Pres. LORENZO PEPE; Gen. Sec. JULIO SOSA; publ. *Boletín ACPF* (5 a year).

PIANC (World Association for Waterborne Transport Infrastructure): Bât Graaf de Ferraris, 11e étage, 20 blvd Roi Albert II, bte 3, 1000 Brussels, Belgium; tel. (2) 553-71-61; fax (2) 553-71-55; e-mail info@pianc.org; internet www.pianc.org; f. 1885; fmrly Permanent International Asscn of Navigation Congresses; fosters progress in the construction, maintenance and operation of inland and maritime waterways, of inland and maritime ports and of coastal areas; holds International Navigation Congress every four years (2010: Liverpool, United Kingdom); mems: 33 govts, 3,400 others; Pres. GEOFFREY CAUDE; Sec.-Gen. LOUIS VAN SCHEL; publs *On Course* (quarterly), *Illustrated Technical Dictionary* (in 6 languages), *Sailing Ahead* (electronic newsletter), technical reports, Congress papers.

World Airlines Clubs Association (WACA): c/o IATA, 800 Pl. Victoria, POB 113, Montréal, Québec, QC H4Z 1M1, Canada; tel. (514) 874-0202; fax (514) 874-1753; e-mail info@waca.org; internet www.waca.org; f. 1966; holds a General Assembly annually, regional meetings, social programmes, international events and sports tournaments; mems: clubs in 35 countries; Pres. MAGA RAMASAMY; Sec.-Gen. ANGELA LERESCHE; publs *WACA Contact*, *WACA World News* (2 a year), *Annual Report*.

World Road Association (PIARC): La Grande Arche, Paroi Nord, Niveau 5, 92055 La Défense Cedex, France; tel. 1-47-96-81-21; fax 1-49-00-02-02; e-mail info@piarc.org; internet www.piarc.org; f. 1909 as the Permanent International Association of Road Congresses; aims to promote the construction, improvement, maintenance, use and economic development of roads; organizes technical committee and study sessions; mems: 113 govts; public bodies, orgs and private individuals in 142 countries; Pres. ANNE-MARIE LECLERC (Canada); Sec.-Gen. JEAN-FRANÇOIS CORTÉ (France); publs *Bulletin*, *Technical Dictionary*, *Lexicon*, technical reports.

Youth and Students

AIESEC International: Teilingerstraat 126, 3032 Rotterdam, Netherlands; tel. (10) 4434383; fax (10) 2651386; e-mail info@ai.aiesec.org; internet www.aiesec.org; f. 1948 as International Association of Students in Economics and Management; provides an international platform for young people to discover and develop their potential; enters into partnerships with selected organizations; mems: 60,000 students in more than 2,100 universities in c. 110 countries and territories; Pres. FLORENT MEIYI (People's Republic of China) (2012–13).

Asian Students Association: 2 Jordan Rd, Kowloon, Hong Kong, SAR; tel. 23880515; fax 27825535; e-mail asasec@netvigator.com; internet www.asianstudents.blogspot.com/; f. 1969; aims to promote students' solidarity in struggling for democracy, self-determination, peace, justice and liberation; conducts campaigns, training of activists, and workshops on human rights and other issues of importance; there are Student Commissions for Peace, Education and Human Rights; mems: 40 national or regional student unions in 25 countries and territories; publs *Movement News* (monthly), *ASA News* (quarterly).

Council on International Educational Exchange (CIEE): 300 Fore St, Portland, ME 04101, USA; tel. (207) 553-4000; fax (207) 553-4299; e-mail contact@ciee.org; internet www.ciee.org; f. 1947; issues International Student Identity Card entitling holders to discounts and basic insurance; arranges overseas work and study programmes for students; co-ordinates summer work programme in the USA for foreign students; administers programmes for teachers and other professionals and sponsors conferences on educational exchange; operates a voluntary service programme; mems: over 350 colleges, universities and international educational orgs in 22 countries; CEO JAMES P. PELLOW (USA); publs include *The Knowledge Series*, *Annual Report*, Occasional Papers in International Education.

European Law Students' Association (ELSA): 239 blvd Général Jacques, 1050 Brussels, Belgium; tel. (2) 646-26-26; fax (2) 646-29-23; e-mail elsa@elsa.org; internet www.elsa.org; f. 1981 to foster mutual understanding and promote social responsibility of law students and young laywers; mems: c. 30,000 students and lawyers in more than 300 law faculties in 42 countries; Pres. NIOUSHA NADEMI (Sweden); Sec.-Gen. JAANA SAARIJÄRVI (Finland); publs *Synergy* (2 a year), *Legal Studies in Europe*.

European Students' Forum (Association des Etats Généraux des Etudiants de l'Europe—AEGEE): 15 rue Nestor de Tière, 1030 Schaarbeek/Brussels, Belgium; tel. (2) 246-03-20; fax (2) 246-03-29; e-mail headoffice@aegee.org; internet www.aegee.org; promotes cross-border communication, co-operation and integration between students; fosters inter-cultural exchange; holds specialized conferences; mems: 13,000 students in 200 university cities in 40 countries; Sec.-Gen. ALMA MOZGOVAJA.

European Youth Forum: 120 rue Joseph II, 1000 Brussels, Belgium; tel. (2) 230-64-90; fax (2) 230-21-23; e-mail youthforum@youthforum.org; internet www.youthforum.org; f. 1996; represents and advocates for the needs and interests of all young people in Europe; promotes their active participation in democratic processes, as well as understanding and respect for human rights; consults with international organizations and governments on issues relevant to young people; mems: 98 national youth councils and international non-governmental youth orgs; Pres. PETER MATJASIC; Sec.-Gen. GIUSEPPE PORCARO.

Hostelling International: Gate House, 2nd Floor, Fretherne Rd, Welwyn Garden City, Herts., AL8 6RD, United Kingdom; tel. (1707) 324170; fax (1707) 323980; e-mail info@hihostels.com; internet www.hihostels.com; f. 1932 as International Youth Hostel Federation, present name adopted 2006; facilitates international travel by members of the various youth hostel asscns; advises and helps in the formation of youth hostel asscns in countries where no such organizations exist; records over 35m. overnight stays annually in some 4,000 youth hostels; mems: 90 national asscns with over 3.2m. national mems and 1m. international guest mems; 12 associated national orgs; CEO MIKAEL HANSSON; publs *Annual Report*, *Guidebook on World Hostels* (annually), *Manual*, *News Bulletin*.

International Association for the Exchange of Students for Technical Experience (IAESTE): POB 35-05, Belgrade, Serbia; tel. (11) 303-1677; fax (11) 303-1675; e-mail general.secretary@iaeste.org; internet www.iaeste.org; f. 1948; operates an exchange programme between students and employers; launched a web-based alumni network in 2011, accessible at alumni.iaeste.org; mems: 88 national cttees and co-operating institutions in 85 countries; Sec.-Gen. GORAN RADNOVIÇ (Serbia) (2010–14); publs *Activity Report*, *Annual Report*, *IAESTE Bulletin* (quarterly).

International Association of Dental Students (IADS): c/o FDI World Dental Federation, Tour de Cointrin, Ave Louis Casaï 84, CP 3, 1216 Genève-Cointrin, Switzerland; tel. 225608150; fax 225608140; e-mail info@fdiworldental.org; internet www.iads-web.org; f. 1951 to represent dental students and their opinions internationally, to promote dental student exchanges and international congresses; mems: 60,000 students in 45 countries, 15,000 corresponding mems; Pres. STEFÁNIA ZSUZSANNA RADÓ (Hungary); Sec. PAVEL SCARLAT (Moldova); publ. *IADS Newsletter* (2 a year).

International Federation of Medical Students' Associations (IFMSA): c/o WMA, BP 63, 01212 Ferney-Voltaire Cedex, France; fax 4-50-40-59-37; e-mail gs@ifmsa.org; internet www.ifmsa.org; f. 1951 to promote international co-operation in professional treatment and the achievement of humanitarian ideals; provides forum for medical students; maintains standing committees on professional and research exchange, medical education, public health, refugees and reproductive health, including AIDS; organizes annual General Assembly; mems: 94 asscns; Pres. CHRISTOPHER PLEYER; Gen. Sec. MIRJANA SPASOJEVIC (2011–12); publ. *IFMSA Newsletter* (quarterly).

International Pharmaceutical Students' Federation (IPSF): POB 84200, 2508 AE The Hague, Netherlands; tel. (70) 3021992; fax (70) 3021999; e-mail ipsf@ipsf.org; internet www.ipsf.org; f. 1949 to study and promote the interests of pharmaceutical students and to encourage international co-operation; mems: represents some 350,000 pharmacy students and recent graduates in 70 countries world-wide; Pres. SANNE TOFTE RASMUSSEN (Denmark); Sec.-Gen. LAERKE ARNFAST (Denmark); publ. *IPSF News Bulletin* (2 a year).

International Scout and Guide Fellowship (ISGF): 38 ave de la Porte de Hal, 1060 Brussels, Belgium; tel. and fax (2) 511-46-95; e-mail worldbureau@isgf.org; internet www.isgf.org; f. 1953 to help adult scouts and guides to keep alive the spirit of the Scout and Guide Promise and Laws in their own lives and to bring that spirit into the communities in which they live and work; promotes liaison and co-operation between national organizations for adult scouts and guides; encourages the founding of an organization in any country where no such organization exists; mems: 90,000 in 61 mem. states; Chair. of Cttee MIDÁ RODRIGUES; Sec.-Gen. FAOUZIA KCHOUK.

International Union of Students: POB 58, 17th November St, 110 01 Prague 01, Czech Republic; tel. and fax 271731257; e-mail ius@cfs-fcee.ca; internet www.stud.uni-hannover.de/gruppen/ius; f. 1946 to defend the rights and interests of students and strive for peace, disarmament, the eradication of illiteracy and of all forms of discrimination; activities include conferences, meetings, solidarity campaigns, relief projects; awards 30–40 scholarships annually; mems: 152 orgs from 114 countries; publs *World Student News* (quarterly), *IUS Newsletter*, *Student Life* (quarterly), *DE—Democratization of Education* (quarterly).

International Young Christian Workers: 4 ave G. Rodenbach, 1030 Brussels, Belgium; tel. (2) 242-18-11; fax (2) 242-48-00; e-mail joci@jociycw.net; internet www.jociycw.net; f. 1925, on the inspiration of the Priest-Cardinal Joseph Cardijn; aims to educate young workers to take on present and future responsibilities in their commitment to the working class, and to gain personal fulfilment through their actions; Pres. GEETHANI PERIES (Sri-Lanka); publs *International INFO* (3 a year), *IYCW Bulletin* (quarterly).

International Young Democrat Union: e-mail iydu@iydu.com; internet www.iydu.org; f. 1991; a global alliance of centre right political youth organizations; mems: 127 orgs from 81 countries; Chair. ARIS KALAFATIS (Greece); Sec.-Gen. JAMES MARRIOTT (United Kingdom).

Junior Chamber International (JCI), Inc.: 15645 Olive blvd, Chesterfield, MO 63017, USA; tel. (636) 449-3100; fax (636) 449-3107; e-mail news@jci.cc; internet www.jci.cc; f. 1944 to encourage and advance international understanding and goodwill; aims to solve civic problems by arousing civic consciousness; Junior Chamber organizations throughout the world provide opportunities for leadership training and for the discussion of social, economic and cultural questions; mems: 200,000 in more than 100 countries; Pres. BERTOLD DAEMS (Netherlands) (2012); publs *JCI News* (monthly in English, French and Spanish), *Leader Magazine* (2 a year).

Latin American and Caribbean Alliance of Young Men's Christian Associations (la Alianza Latinoamericana y del Caribe de Asociaciones Cristianas de Jóvenes): Rua N Pestana 125, 10° andar, Conj. 103, São Paulo 01303-010, Brazil; tel. (11) 3257-5867; fax (11) 3151-2573; e-mail secretariogeneral@lacaymca.org; internet www.lacaymca.org; f. 1914; aims to encourage the moral, spiritual, intellectual, social and physical development of young men; to strengthen the work of national Asscns and to sponsor the establishment of new Asscns; mems: affiliated YMCAs in 94 countries; Pres. GERARDO VITUREIRA (Uruguay); Gen. Sec. MAURICIO DIAZ VANDORSEE (Brazil); publs *Diecisiete/21* (bulletin), *Carta Abierta*, *Brief*, technical articles and other studies.

Pan-African Youth Union (Union pan-africaine de la jeunesse): Khartoum, Sudan; tel. 8037038097 (mobile); f. 1962; aims to encourage the participation of African youth in socio-economic and political development and democratization; organizes conferences and seminars, youth exchanges and youth festivals; 2011 Congress: Khartoum, Sudan, in Dec; mems: youth groups in 52 African countries and liberation movements; Pres. ANDILE LUNGISA (South Africa) (2012–14); publ. *MPJ News* (quarterly).

Round Table International: e-mail secretary@rtinternational.org; internet www.rtinternational.org; f. 1947 to promote international fellowship and co-operation among national Round Table groupings aimed at young business people 18–40 years of age; mems: some 2,700 clubs in 65 countries; Pres. STIJN DE FRENE (Belgium) (2011–12).

WFUNA Youth: c/o WFUNA, 1 United Nations Plaza, Room DC1-1177, New York, NY 10017, USA; tel. (212) 963-5610; fax (212) 963-0447; e-mail info@wfuna-youth.net; internet www.wfuna.org/youth; f. 1948 by the World Federation of United Nations Associations (WFUNA) as the International Youth and Student Movement for the United Nations (ISMUN), independent since 1949; an international non-governmental organization of students and young people dedicated especially to supporting the principles embodied in the United Nations Charter and Universal Declaration of Human Rights; encourages constructive action in building economic, social and cultural equality and in working for national independence, social justice and human rights on a world-wide scale; organizes periodic regional WFUNA International Model United Nations (WIMUN) conferences; maintains regional offices in Austria, France, Ghana, Panama and the USA; mems: asscns in over 100 mem. states of the UN.

World Alliance of Young Men's Christian Associations: 12 Clos. Belmont, 1208 Geneva, Switzerland; tel. 228495100; fax 228495110; e-mail office@ymca.int; internet www.ymca.int; f. 1855; organizes World Council every four years (2010: Hong Kong, SAR; 2014: Estes Park, USA); mems: federation of YMCAs in 125 countries with a membership of over 45m.; Pres. KEN COLLOTON (USA) (2010–14); Sec.-Gen. Rev. JOHAN VILHELM ELTVIK (Norway) (2010–14); publ. *YMCA World* (quarterly).

World Assembly of Youth: World Youth Complex, Lebuh Ayer Keroh, Ayer Keroh, 75450 Melaka, Malaysia; tel. (6) 2321871; fax (6) 2327271; e-mail info@way.org.my; internet www.way.org.my; f. 1949 as co-ordinating body for national youth councils and organizations; organizes conferences, training courses and practical development projects; has consultative status with the UN Economic and Social Council; mems: 120 mem. orgs; Pres. Datuk Wira IDRIS HARON; Sec.-Gen. EDIOLA PASHOLLARI; publs *WAY Information* (every 2 months), *Youth Roundup* (every 2 months), *WAY Forum* (quarterly).

World Association of Girl Guides and Girl Scouts (WAGGGS): World Bureau, Olave Centre, 12c Lyndhurst Rd, London, NW3 5PQ, United Kingdom; tel. (20) 7794-1181; fax (20) 7431-3764; e-mail wagggs@wagggsworld.org; internet www.wagggsworld.org; f. 1928 to enable girls and young women to develop their full potential as responsible citizens, and to support friendship and mutual understanding among girls and young women world-wide; operates four 'World Centres': Pax Lodge (United Kingdom), and a Sangam (India), Cabaña (Mexico), and Chalet (Switzerland), which provide residential training programmes to enable girls and young women to develop leadership skills and friendships; World Conference meets every three years; mems: about 10m. individuals in 145 orgs; Chair. World Board NADINE EL-ACHY (Lebanon); Chief Exec. MARY MCPHAIL (Ireland); publs *Triennial Review*, *Annual Report*, *Trefoil Round the World* (every 3 years), *Our World News* (quarterly).

World Federation of Democratic Youth (WFDY): 1139 Budapest, Frangepán u. 16, Hungary; tel. (1) 350-2202; fax (1) 350-1204; e-mail wfdy@wfdy.org; internet www.wfdy.org; f. 1945; promotes the unity, co-operation, organized action, solidarity and exchange of information and experiences of work and struggle among the progressive youth forces; campaigns against imperialism, fascism, colonialism, exploitation and war and for peace, internationalist solidarity, social progress and youth rights under the slogans Youth unite! and Forward for lasting peace!; mems: 152 members in 102 countries; publ. *World Youth*.

World Organization of the Scout Movement: CP 91, 1211 Geneva 4 Plainpalais, Switzerland; tel. 227051010; fax 227051020; e-mail worldbureau@world.scout.org; internet www.scout.org; f. 1922 to promote unity and understanding of scouting throughout the world; to develop good citizenship among young people by forming their characters for service, co-operation and leadership; and to provide aid and advice to members and potential member asscns. The World Scout Bureau (Geneva) has regional offices in Egypt, Kenya, Panama, the Philippines, Russia, Senegal, South Africa and Ukraine (the European Region has its offices in Brussels and Geneva); mems: over 30m. in 161 countries and territories; Sec.-Gen. LUC PANISSOD (France); publs *Worldinfo*, *Triennial Report*.

World Union of Jewish Students (WUJS): POB 39359, Tel Aviv 61392, Israel; tel. (2) 6251682; fax (2) 6251688; e-mail info@wujs.org.il; internet www.wujs.org.il; f. 1924 (with Albert Einstein as its first President); promotes dialogue and co-operation among Jewish university students world-wide; divided into six regions; organizes Congress every year; mems: 52 national unions representing over 1.5m. students; Chair. OLIVER WORTH; publs *The Student Activist Yearbook*, *Heritage and History*, *Forum*, *WUJS Report*.

World Young Women's Christian Association (World YWCA): 16 Ancienne Route, 1218 Grand-Saconnex, Geneva, Switzerland; tel. 229296040; fax 229296044; e-mail worldoffice@worldywca.org; internet www.worldywca.org; f. 1894; global movement which aims to empower women and girls to change their lives and communities; works to achieve social and economic justice through grassroots development and global advocacy; addresses critical issues affecting women, such as HIV and AIDS and violence; promotes the sharing of human and financial resources among member asscns; mems: in 106 countries; Pres. DEBORAH THOMAS-AUSTIN (Trinidad and Tobago); Gen. Sec. NYARADZAYI GUMBONZVANDA (Zimbabwe); publs *Annual Report*, *Common Concern*, *Week of Prayer* (booklet), other reports.

PART FIVE

Who's Who in International Organizations

ABDELAZIZ, Maged Abdelfattah; Egyptian; *Special Adviser to the Secretary-General on Africa, United Nations;* b. 1954; m.; one d. **Education:** Ain Shams Univ. School of Law. **Career:** joined diplomatic service 1979; served in several positions in Ministry of Foreign Affairs including International Orgs Div., Legal and Treaties Dept 1979–83 (Head 1987–89), Second and First Sec., Perm. Mission to UN, New York 1983–87, Political Counsellor in charge of Middle East, Arab-Soviet Relations, International Orgs and Disarmament, Embassy in Moscow 1989–93, Head, Specialized Agencies Dept, Multilateral Sector, Ministry of Foreign Affairs 1993–95; Political Counsellor, Office of Perm. Rep. to UN, New York 1995–97, Prin. Rep. in all disarmament issues 1997–99, Deputy Perm. Rep. to UN 1997–99, Co-ordinator, Del. during membership on Security Council 1996–97, apptd Rep. in Expert Group, UN Sec.-Gen., UN Register for Conventional Arms 1997, apptd Chair. Disarmament Comm. 1999; Diplomatic Adviser and Official Spokesman of Pres. 1999–2005; Amb. and Perm. Rep. 2005–12; Special Adviser to the Sec.-Gen. on Africa, UN 2012–. **Address:** Office of the Secretary-General, United Nations, New York, NY 10017, USA. **Telephone:** (212) 963-1234. **Fax:** (212) 963-4879. **Internet:** www.un.org.

ABRIAL, Gen. Stéphane; French; *Supreme Allied Commander Transformation, NATO;* b. 1954, Gers; m. Michaela Abrial; two c. **Education:** US Air War Coll., Montgomery, AL, Institut des hautes études de défense nationale, Paris. **Career:** began mil. service 1973, exchange programme in USAF Acad., graduated from French Air Force Acad. 1975, completed pilot training 1976, extensive experience as fighter pilot and operational commdr, served in unit of German Luftwaffe 1981–84, in unit of Greek Air Force 1988, took part in liberation of Kuwait as commdr of French Air Force's 5th Fighter Wing during Operation Desert Storm 1990–91, served at NATO Int. Mil. Staff in Brussels 1996–99, several appointments to pvt. offices of French Prime Minister and Pres., went on to serve as head of French air defence and air operations, Air Force Chief of Staff 2006–09; Supreme Allied Commdr Transformation, NATO 2009– (first European apptd permanently as head of a NATO strategic command); Grand Officier, Légion d'honneur, Commdr, US Legion of Merit, Verdienstkreuz der Bundeswehr (Silver); Hon. DSc (Old Dominion Univ.) 2011. **Address:** Allied Command Transformation, 7857 Blandy Road, Suite 100, Norfolk, VA 23551-2490, USA. **Telephone:** (757) 747-3400. **Fax:** (757) 747-3234. **E-mail:** pio@act.nato.int. **Internet:** www.act.nato.int.

ALEMÁN GURDIÁN, Juan Daniel, BLaw&SocSci, DrIntLaw; Guatemalan/Salvadorean (b. Nicaraguan); *Secretary-General, Central American Integration System (Sistema de la Integración Centroamericana—SICA);* b. 28 Aug. 1956, Leon, Nicaragua; m. Silvia Elizabeth Cáceres Vettorazzi; two s. **Education:** Universidad Rafael Landívar, Guatemala, Univ. of Navarre, Pamplona, Spain. **Career:** moved to Guatemala City and became Guatemalan citizen 1973; Pres. Law Students' Asscn 1978–79; participated in summer seminars in Univs of London, UK and Nice, France; began professional career as Tax Dept Man., Peat Marwick & Mitchell (law firm), Guatemala; began career as Univ. Lecturer in Faculty of Law, Universidad Rafael Landívar, later held Chair of Int. Public Law and Business Law; also taught Int. Econ. Law at Inst. of Int. Relations, Universidad Francisco Marroquin, Guatemala, later became its Dir; apptd Adjoint Sec.-Gen. Cen. American Econ. Integration Secr. (SIECA), Guatemala City 1991; left office in SIECA to fill Policy Secr. of Presidency of Repub. of Guatemala; granted incorporation as advocate and notary of Repub. of Nicaragua 1994; moved to San Salvador to serve as Corp. Advocate of SIGMA/Q group (Cen. American co.) 1995, served as Sec. Bd and mem. Strategic Cttee; Visiting Prof. of Business Ethics, Escuela Superior de Negocios (ESEN), El Salvador 2001; granted Salvadorean nationality 2001; authorized to practise as lawyer and notary in El Salvador 2004–; Sec. Gen. Cen. American Integration System (Sistema de la Integración Centroamericana—SICA) 2009–; mem. Chamber of Industry of Guatemala, Training Centre of Guatemala (TAYASAL); Sec. Bd Centre for Nat. Econ. Research of Guatemala (CIEN); Founding mem., Dir and Chair. Cttee of Legal Studies, Salvadoran Foundation for Econ. and Social Devt (FUSADES). **Publications:** regular contrib. to specialized publs. **Address:** Sistema de la Integración Centroamericana (SICA), Final Blv. Cancillería, Ciudad Merliot, Antiguo Cuscatlán, La Libertad, San Salvador, El Salvador. **Telephone:** 2248-8801. **Fax:** 2248-8899. **E-mail:** info.sgsica@sica.int. **Internet:** www.sica.int; www.sica.int/sgsica.

ALI, Ahmad Mohamed, BA, MA, PhD; Saudi Arabian; *Chairman of the Board of Executive Directors and President, Islamic Development Bank;* b. 13 April 1934, Medina; m. Ghada Mahmood Masri 1968; one s. three d. **Education:** Cairo Univ., Univ. of Michigan and State Univ. of New York, Albany Univ., USA. **Career:** Dir Scientific and Islamic Inst., Aden 1958–59; Deputy Rector, King Abdul Aziz Univ., Jeddah 1967–72; Deputy Minister of Educ. for Tech. Affairs 1972–75; Pres. Islamic Devt Bank 1975–93, 1995–, currently also Chair. Bd of Exec. Dirs; Sec.-Gen. Muslim World League 1993–95; mem. King Abdul Aziz Univ. Council, King Saud Univ., Oil and Minerals Univ., Islamic Univ., Imam Mohammed Ben Saud Univ.; mem. Admin. Bd Saudi Credit Bank, Saudi Fund for Devt. **Publications:** numerous articles and working papers on Islamic econs, banking and educ. **Address:** Islamic Development Bank, PO Box 5925, Jeddah 21432, Saudi Arabia. **Telephone:** (2) 6361400. **Fax:** (2) 6366871. **E-mail:** idbarchives@isdb.org. **Internet:** www.isdb.org.

ALKALAJ, Sven, BS, MS; Bosnia and Herzegovina; *Executive Secretary, United Nations Economic Commission for Europe;* b. 11 Nov. 1948, Sarajevo; m.; two c. **Education:** Univ. of Sarajevo, Harvard Business School, USA. **Career:** Commercial Man., Petrolinvest, Sarajevo 1975–85; Regional Man. for Middle and Far East Energoinvest, Sarajevo 1985–88, Man. Dir Energoinvest, Thailand 1988–94; Amb. to USA 1994–2000, to OAS 2000–04, to Belgium and Head of Perm. Mission to NATO 2004–07; Minister of Foreign Affairs 2007–12; Exec. Sec. UN ECE 2012–; mem. Party for Bosnia and Herzegovina (SBiH); Silver Badge of Petrolinvest 1994, Sarajevo City Memorial Plaque, for contribs to the City devt, Award of the Centre for Peace, Non-Violence and Human Rights, Sarajevo 2003, Sloboda Award. **Address:** UN Economic Commission for Europe, Palais des Nations, 1211 Geneva 10, Switzerland. **Telephone:** 229174444. **Fax:** 229170505. **E-mail:** info.ece@unece.org. **Internet:** www.unece.org.

ALTMANN, Rev. Walter, PhD; Brazilian; *Moderator, Central Committee, World Council of Churches;* b. 4 Feb. 1944, Porto Alegre; m. Madalena Zwetsch Altmann; four d. **Education:** studied theology in São Leopoldo, Brazil, Buenos Aires, Argentina and Univ. of Hamburg, Germany. **Career:** parish pastor, Ijui, southern Brazil 1972–74; Prof. of Systematic Theology, Theological Coll., São Leopoldo 1974–2002, 2011–, Head of Theological Coll. 1981–87; Dir Ecumenical Inst. for Postgraduate Studies 1989–94; Pres. Consejo Latinoamericano de Iglesias (Latin American Council of Churches) 1995–2001; Vice-Pres. Evangelical Church of the Lutheran Confession in Brazil 1998–2002, Pres. 2002–10; mem. Council of Lutheran World Fed. 2003–06; Moderator Cen. Cttee, WCC 2006–; Award of Merit (category: Theological Reflection), Associated Church Press (ACP) 1990. **Publications:** more than 10 books, including Der Begriff der Tradition bei Karl Rahner 1974, Luther and Liberation, A Latin American Perspective 1992, Nossa fé e suas razões: O Credo Apostólico – história, mensagem, atualidade 2004, Palavra a seu Tempo 2010, Maravilhoso Presente 2010; 180 articles on Martin Luther, Latin American theology, ethics and ecumenism. **Address:** World Council of Churches, PO Box 2100, 150 route de Ferney, 1211 Geneva 2, Switzerland. **Telephone:** 227916111. **Fax:** 227910361. **E-mail:** walteraltmann@msn.com; moderator-wcc@ieclb.org.br. **Internet:** www.oikumene.org.

ALVAREZ, Carlos Alberto (Chacho); Argentine; *Secretary-General, Latin American Integration Association;* b. 26 Dec. 1948, Balvanera; m. Liliana Chiernajowsky; one s. three d. **Education:** Mariano Acosta Coll., Univ. of Buenos Aires. **Career:** Assessor, Regional Econ. Cttee of Nat. Senate 1983–89; elected Deputy to Nat. Ass. (Partido Justicialista) for Fed. Capital 1989–93, 1997–99; left Partido Justicialista and f. Partido Movimento por la Democracia y la Justicia Social (MODEJUSO) 1990; f. Frente Grande; Pres. Frente Grande Bloc in

Nat. Constitutional Convention 1994; Founder, Leader Frente del País Solidario—FREPASO 1994–; Vice-Pres. of Argentina 1999–2000 (resgnd); Pres. Cttee of Perm. Reps, Mercosur 2005–09; Sec.-Gen. Latin American Integration Asscn 2011–. **Address:** Latin American Integration Association, Cebollatí 1461, Casilla 20.005, 11200 Montevideo, Uruguay. **Telephone:** 2410 1121. **Fax:** 2419 0649. **E-mail:** sgaladi@aladi.org. **Internet:** www.aladi.org.

AMANO, Yukiya; Japanese; *Director-General, International Atomic Energy Agency;* b. 9 May 1947, Kanagawa Pref.; m. **Education:** Tokyo Univ., Univ. of Franche-Comté, France, Univ. of Nice, France. **Career:** joined Ministry of Foreign Affairs 1972, postings include embassies in Vientiane, Washington, DC and Brussels; mem. Japanese Del. to Conf. on Disarmament, Geneva, Switzerland; Japanese Consul Gen., Marseille, France 1997; fmr Dir Science Div., Ministry of Foreign Affairs, also Dir Nuclear Energy Div., Deputy Dir-Gen. for Arms Control and Scientific Affairs, Dir-Gen. for Arms Control and Scientific Affairs 2002–04, Dir-Gen. Disarmament, Nonproliferation and Science Dept 2004–05, Perm. Rep. and Amb. to Int. Orgs, UN, Vienna 2005; mem. for Japan, Int. Atomic Energy Agency (IAEA) Bd of Govs 2005–, Chair. IAEA Bd of Govs 2005–06, Dir Gen. IAEA 2009–. **Publications:** Sea Dumping of Liquid Radioactive Waste by Russia 1994; several articles on nuclear non-proliferation and nuclear disarmament. **Address:** Office of the Director-General, International Atomic Energy Agency, PO Box 100, Wagramer Strasse 5, 1400 Vienna, Austria. **Telephone:** (1) 26000. **Fax:** (1) 26007. **E-mail:** official.mail@iaea.org. **Internet:** www.iaea.org.

AMOS, Baroness (Life Peer), cr. 1997, of Brondesbury in the London Borough of Brent; **Valerie Ann Amos,** MA; British; *Under-Secretary-General for Humanitarian Affairs and Emergency Relief Co-ordinator, United Nations;* b. 13 March 1954, Guyana. **Education:** Univs of Warwick, Birmingham and East Anglia, UK. **Career:** Race Relations Adviser, London Borough of Lambeth 1981–83; Women's Adviser, London Borough of Camden 1983–85; Head of Training and Devt, London Borough of Hackney 1985–87, Head of Man. Services 1988–89; Chief Exec. Equal Opportunities Comm. 1989–94; Dir Fraser Bernard 1994–98; Govt Whip 1998–2001; Parl. Under-Sec. of State, FCO 2001–03; Sec. of State for Int. Devt 2003; Leader House of Lords 2003–07; High Commr to Australia 2009–10; Under-Sec.-Gen. for Humanitarian Affairs and Emergency Relief Co-ordinator, UN, New York 2010–; Commr Fulbright Comm. 2009; Dir Hampstead Theatre 1992–98; Chair. Royal African Soc. 2007–; Deputy Chair. Runnymede Trust 1990–98; Fellow, Centre for Corp. Reputation, Univ. of Oxford 2007–; Dir (non-exec.) Travant Capital Partners 2007–; fmr Dir (non-exec.) Univ. Coll. London Hospitals Trust; fmr Chair. Afiya Trust, Bd of Govs, Royal Coll. of Nursing Inst.; mem. Advisory Cttee Centre for Educ. Devt Appraisal and Research, Univ. of Warwick 1991–98, Gen. Advisory Council BBC, King's Fund Coll. Cttee 1992–98, Council Inst. of Employment Studies 1993–98, Advisory Bd Global Health Group, Univ. of San Francisco; Trustee, Women's Therapy Centre 1989–; fmr Trustee, Inst. of Public Policy Research, VSO; Hon. Prof., Thames Valley Univ. 1995; Hon. LLD (Warwick) 2000, (Staffordshire) 2000, (Manchester) 2001, (Leicester) 2006, (Bradford) 2007, (Birmingham) 2008, (Stirling) 2010. **Address:** Office for the Co-ordination of Humanitarian Affairs, United Nations Plaza, New York, NY 10017, USA. **Telephone:** (212) 963-1234. **Fax:** (212) 963-1312; (212) 963-9489. **E-mail:** ochany@un.org. **Internet:** ochaonline.un.org.

ANNAN, Kofi Atta, GCMG, BA (Econs), MSc; Ghanaian; *Joint Special Envoy of the United Nations and the League of Arab States on the Syrian Crisis;* b. 8 April 1938; m. Nane Lagergren; one s. two d. **Education:** Univ. of Science and Tech., Kumasi, Macalester Coll., St Paul, Minn., USA, Institut des Hautes Etudes Internationales, Geneva, Switzerland, Massachusetts Inst. of Tech., USA. **Career:** held posts in UN ECA, Addis Ababa, UN, New York, WHO, Geneva 1962–71, Admin. Man. Officer, UN, Geneva 1972–74; Alfred P. Sloan Fellow, MIT 1971–72; Chief Civilian Personnel Officer, UNEF, Cairo 1974; Man. Dir Ghana Tourist Devt Co. 1974–76; Deputy Chief of Staff Services, Office of Personnel Services, Office of UNHCR, Geneva 1976–80, Deputy Dir Div. of Admin. and Head Personnel Service 1980–83; Dir of Admin. Man. Service, then Dir of Budget, Office of Financial Services, UN, New York 1984–87, Asst Sec.-Gen., Office of Human Resources Man. 1987–90; Controller Office of Programme Planning, Budget and Finance 1990–92; Asst Sec.-Gen. Dept of Peace-Keeping Operations 1992–93; Under-Sec.-Gen. 1993–96; UN Special Envoy (a.i.) to Fmr Yugoslavia 1995–96; Sec.-Gen. of UN 1997–2006; Jt Special Envoy of the UN and the League of Arab States on the Syrian crisis 2012–; Pres. Kofi Annan Foundation 2007–; Pres. Global Humanitarian Forum 2007–10; Chair. Alliance for a Green Revolution in Africa (AGRA) 2007–, Africa Progress Panel 2007–; Chancellor, Univ. of Ghana 2008–; Li Ka Shing Prof., Lee Kuan Yew School of Public Policy, Nat. Univ., Singapore 2009–; Chair., Prize Cttee, Mo Ibrahim Award for Excellence in African Leadership 2007–; apptd Global Fellow, Columbia Univ., USA 2009; Bd mem. UN Foundation, World Econ. Forum, Carnegie Endowment for International Peace, Carnegie Corpn of New York, Club of Madrid, World Org. Against Torture; mem. The Elders; Foreign Hon. mem., American Acad. of Arts and Sciences 2003; Companion of the Order of the Star (Ghana) 2000, Grand Cross with Collar of the Order of the Star (Romania) 2001, Grand Collar of the Order of Liberty (Portugal) 2005, Knight Grand Cross of the Order of the Lion (Netherlands) 2006, Grand Decoration of Honour in Gold with Sash for Services to the Republic of Austria (2007), Grand Cross 1st class of the Order of Merit (Germany) 2008; Dr hc (Univ. of Pennsylvania) 2005, (Universidade Nova de Lisboa) 2005, (George Washington Univ.) 2006, (Univ. of Tokyo) 2006, (Georgetown Univ.) 2006, (King's Coll., London) 2008, (Glasgow Caledonian Univ.) 2011 and several others; Kora All Africa Music Awards in the category of Lifetime Achievement 2000, Philadelphia Liberty Medal 2001, Nobel Peace Prize (jtly with UN) 2001, Profiles in Courage Award, JFK Memorial Museum 2002, James Madison Award, American Whig-Cliosophic Soc. 2002, Freedom Prize, Max Schmidheiny Foundation, Univ. of St Gallen 2003, Zayed Prize 2005, International Achievement Award, Inter Press Service 2006, Olof Palme Prize 2006, Crystal Tiger Award, Princeton Univ. 2006, MacArthur Award 2007, Peace of Westphalia Prize 2008, Gottlieb Duttweiler Prize 2008, Open Soc. Award, CEU Business School Budapest 2008. **Address:** Kofi Annan Foundation, POB 157, 1211 Geneva, Switzerland. **Telephone:** 229197520. **Fax:** 229197529. **E-mail:** info@kofiannanfoundation.org. **Internet:** www.kofiannanfoundation.org.

ANSTEY, Caroline, PhD; British; *Managing Director, World Bank Group;* b. 7 Nov. 1955, London; m. Milton W. Hudson; two s. **Education:** Univ. of Leeds, Univ. of California, Berkeley, USA, London School of Economics. **Career:** Political Asst to Prime Minister James Callaghan 1974–79; apptd Consultant in External Affairs, World Bank, Washington, DC 1995, Asst to World Bank Pres. 1996, Country Dir for the Caribbean –2007, Chief of Staff 2007–10, Vice-Pres. of External Affairs 2010–11, Man. Dir World Bank Group 2011–, fmr Dir of Media Relations and Chief Spokesperson; fmr Ed. Analysis (BBC weekly current affairs programme); fmr Secr. mem. InterAction Council. **Address:** Office of the Managing Director, World Bank Group, 1818 H St, NW, Washington, DC 20433, USA. **Telephone:** (202) 473-1000. **Fax:** (202) 477-6391. **Internet:** www.worldbank.org.

ARABY, Nabil El-, LLB, LLM, JSD; Egyptian; *Secretary-General, League of Arab States;* b. 15 March 1935, Cairo; m.; two s. one d. **Education:** Cairo Univ., New York Univ. Law School, USA. **Career:** fmr Rep. of Egypt to various UN bodies, including Gen. Ass., Security Council, ECOSOC, Comm. on Human Rights, Conf. on Disarmament; Legal Adviser to Egyptian del. to UN Middle East Peace Conf., Geneva 1973–75; Dir Legal and Treaties Dept, Ministry of Foreign Affairs 1976–78, 1983–87; Amb. to India 1981–83; led Egyptian del. to Taba talks 1986–89; Deputy Perm. Rep. to UN, New York 1978–81, Perm. Rep. 1991–99; Perm. Rep., UN Office at Geneva 1987–91; apptd by ICC as Arbitrator in a dispute concerning Suez Canal 1989; Judge, Judicial Tribunal of Org. of Arab Petroleum Exporting Countries (OAPEC) 1990–; Visiting Scholar, Robert F. Wagner Grad. School of Public Service, New York Univ. 1992–93; apptd Partner, Zaki Hashem and Partners, Cairo 1998, currently Sr Partner; Commr UN Compensation Comm., Geneva 1999–2001; Pres. Ordinary Arbitration Div., Court of Arbitration for Sport; Dir Regional Cairo Centre for Int. Commercial Arbitration 2008–; Minister of Foreign Affairs March–June 2011; Sec.-Gen. League of Arab States 2011–; fmr chair. numerous UN cttees and working groups; mem. Governing Bd Stockholm Int. Peace Research Inst. 2000–10, Egyptian Bar Asscn; mem. Int. Law Comm. 1994–2001, Int. Court of Justice 2001–06, Perm. Court of Arbitration 2005–; Kt of Italian Repub. 1962, Order of the Repub. (Egypt) 1976. **Publications include:** several articles on UN Charter, peace-keeping and various int. issues. **Address:** League of Arab States, PO Box 11642, Arab League Building, Tahrir Square, Cairo 11211, Egypt. **Telephone:** (2) 575-0511. **Fax:** (2) 574-0331. **Internet:** www.arableagueonline.org.

ARBIA, Silvana, LLD; Italian; *Registrar, International Criminal Court;* b. 19 Nov. 1952, Senise. **Education:** Univ. of Padua. **Career:** prosecutor and judge in Venice, Rome and Milan Courts of Appeal 1979–; mem. Italian Del., Diplomatic Conf. on drafting statute of Int. Criminal Court, Rome 1998; Judge, Supreme Court and Court of Cassation of Italy 1999; Sr Trial Attorney, Int. Criminal Tribunal for Rwanda 1999, becoming Acting Chief of Prosecutions and Chief of Prosecutions; Registrar, Int. Criminal Court, The Hague 2008–; Paul Harris Fellow, Rotary Int.; Premio Nicola Sole 2011. **Publications include:** Mentre il Mondo, Stava a Guardare 2011; several essays and books on human rights and children's rights. **Address:** International Criminal Court, PO Box 19519, 2500 CM The Hague, Netherlands. **Telephone:** (70) 5158515. **Fax:** (70) 5158555. **Internet:** www.icc-cpi.int.

ASHTON OF UPHOLLAND, Baroness (Life Peer), cr. 1999, of St Albans in the County of Hertfordshire; **Catherine Margaret Ashton,** PC, BSc; British; *High Representative of the Union for Foreign Affairs and Security Policy, European Union;* b. 20 March 1956, Upholland, Lancs., England; m. Peter Kellner 1988; one s. one d. three step-c. **Education:** Upholland Grammar School, Billinge Higher End, Lancs., Wigan Mining and Tech. Coll., Wigan, Bedford Coll., London (now part of Royal Holloway, Univ. of London). **Career:** Admin. Sec., Campaign for Nuclear Disarmament 1977–79; Man. Coverdale Org. 1979–81; Dir of Public Affairs, Business in the Community 1983–89; policy adviser 1989–98; Chair. Hertfordshire Health Authority 1998–2001; Parl. Under-Sec. of State and Govt Spokesperson, Dept for Educ. and Skills 2001–04, Early Years and School Standards 2001–02, Early Years and Childcare 2002, Sure Start (also Dept for Work and Pensions) 2002–04; Govt Spokesperson for Children 2003; Parl. Under-Sec. of State and Govt Spokesperson, Dept for Constitutional Affairs/Ministry of Justice 2004–07, Leader House of Lords and Lord Pres. of the Council 2007–08; Commr for Trade, EC 2008–09, High Rep. of the Union for Foreign Affairs and Security Policy, EU 2009–, also first Vice-Pres. EC 2010–; hon. degree from Univ. of East London 2005; House Magazine Minister of the Year 2005, Channel 4 Peer of the Year 2005, Stonewall Politician of the Year 2006. **Address:** BERL 12, 200 rue de la Loi-Wetstraat, 1049 Brussels, Belgium. **Telephone:** (2) 298-85-90. **Fax:** (2) 298-86-57. **E-mail:** COMM-SPP-HRVP-ASHTON@ec.europa.eu. **Internet:** eeas.europa.eu.

BACHELET JERIA, (Verónica) Michelle, MD; Chilean; *Under-Secretary-General for Gender Equality and the Empowerment of Women, United Nations;* b. 29 Sept. 1951, Santiago; m.; three c. **Education:** Universidad de Chile, Inter-American Coll. of Defense, Washington, DC, USA. **Career:** placed in Villa Grimaldi and Cuatro Alamos detention centres for father's resistance to Pinochet regime 1975; lived in Australia, then Germany 1975–80; trained as medical surgeon, podiatrist and epidemiologist, Universidad de Chile; Head of Medical Dept, PIDEE (NGO assisting the children of victims of the military regime); consultant to Panamerican Health Org. and WHO 1990; mem. Cen. Cttee Socialist Party 1995–, Political Cttee 1998–; Adviser to Under-Sec. of Health 1994–97, to Ministry of Defence 1998–99; Minister of Health 2000–02, of Nat. Defence (first woman in position) 2002–04; Pres. of Chile (first woman) 2006–10; Under-Sec.-Gen. for Gender Equality and the Empowerment of Women, UN, New York 2010–; ranked by Forbes magazine amongst 100 Most Powerful Women (17th) 2006, (27th) 2007, (25th) 2008, (22nd) 2009. **Address:** Office of the Under-Secretary-General for Gender Equality and the Empowerment of Women, United Nations, New York, NY 10017, USA. **Telephone:** (212) 963-1234. **Fax:** (212) 963-4879. **Internet:** www.un.org.

BAN, Ki-moon, BA, MPA; South Korean; *Secretary-General, United Nations;* b. 13 June 1944, Eumseong, North Chungcheong; m. Yoo Soon-taek; one s. two d. **Education:** Seoul Nat. Univ., Kennedy School of Govt, Harvard Univ., USA. **Career:** early assignments at Embassy in New Delhi, two terms at Embassy in Washington, DC, First Sec., Perm. Observer Mission to UN, New York; fmr Dir UN Div.; Amb. to Austria, also Chair. Preparatory Comm. for the Comprehensive Nuclear Test Ban Treaty Org. (CTBTO) 1999; Dir-Gen. of American Affairs 1990–92; Vice-Chair. South-North Jt Nuclear Control Comm. 1992; Deputy Minister for Policy Planning 1995–96; Nat. Security Adviser to the Pres. 1996–2000; Chef-de-Cabinet to Pres. of UN Gen. Ass. 2001; Vice-Minister 2000, then Foreign Policy Adviser to the Pres.; Minister of Foreign Affairs and Trade 2004–06; Sec.-Gen.-designate UN Oct.–Dec. 2006, Sec.-Gen. 2007–; Order of Service Merit 1975, 1986, 2006, Grand Decoration of Honour (Austria) 2001, Grand Cross of Rio Blanco (Brazil) 2002, Gran Cruz del Sol (Peru) 2006, Grand'Croix, Ordre Nat. (Burkina Faso) 2008, Grand Officier, Ordre Nat. (Côte d'Ivoire); Dr hc (Seoul Nat. Univ.) 2008, Hon. LLD (Univ. of the Philippines Coll. of Law) 2008; James A. Van Fleet Award, Korea Soc., New York 2005, ranked by Forbes magazine amongst The World's Most Powerful People (41st) 2010, (38th) 2011. **Address:** Office of the Secretary-General, United Nations, New York, NY 10017, USA. **Telephone:** (212) 963-1234. **Fax:** (212) 963-4879. **Internet:** www.un.org/sg.

BARBUT, Monique, MPhil(Econs), MA (Econs); French; *Chairperson and CEO, Global Environment Facility;* b. 22 Aug. 1956; m.; three c. **Education:** Univ. of Paris I, Grad. Inst. of Int. Studies, IHE, Paris II. **Career:** several internships in banking, including three months at Volksbank, Zürich, Switzerland 1979; Program Man. Saint-Denis La Réunion, Caisse Centrale de Cooperation Economique 1981–84, Head of Dept of sector-based policies and retrospective evaluation 1984–89, in charge of all public credit and housing cos in French Overseas Depts 1990, at Ministry of Cooperation and Devt 1990–93, in charge of Secr. of French Global Environment Fund (inter-ministerial field) 1994–96; Deputy Dir French Overseas Depts and Territories and Dir Div. in charge of Devt inside same Dept, Agence Française de Développement (AFD) 1996–2000, Exec. Dir at AFD, in charge of all activities in French Overseas Depts and Territories, and responsible for all programmes for Pacific, Indian, Caribbean Ocean Islands 2000–02; Dir Div. of Tech., Industry and Econs, UNEP 2003–06; Chair. and CEO Global Environment Facility 2006–; mem. French Govt Del., Earth Summit, Rio de Janeiro, Brazil 1992. **Address:** Global Environment Facility Secretariat, 1818 H St, NW, Washington, DC 20433, USA. **Telephone:** (202) 473-3202. **Fax:** (202) 522-3240. **E-mail:** mbarbut@thegef.org. **Internet:** www.thegef.org.

BÁRCENA IBARRA, Alicia, BSc, MSc, MPA; Mexican; *Executive Secretary, United Nations Economic Commission for Latin America and the Caribbean;* b. 5 March 1952. **Education:** Universidad Nacional Autónoma de Mexico (UNAM), Harvard Univ., USA, Instituto Miguel Angel, Mexico. **Career:** Research Asst, UNAM 1975-76, Assoc. Prof. of Botany, UNAM (Universidad Autónoma Metropolitana) 1976–78; Researcher on Ethnobotany, Instituto Nacional sobre Recursos Bióticos 1978–80; Regional Exec. Dir/Research Co-ordinator Instituto Nacional de Investigaciones sobre Recursos 1980–82; Under-Sec. of Ecology (Vice-Minister), Secretaría de Desarrollo Urbano y Ecología—SEDUE), Ministry of Urban Devt and Ecology 1982–86; consultant, IDB Aug.–Nov. 1987; Pres. Cultura Ecológica, Civil Soc. Org. in Mexico 1987–88; Dir Gen. Nat. Inst. of Fisheries, SEPESCA (Secretaría de Pesca) 1988-90; Prin. Officer, Programme Unit II, UN Conf. on Environment and Devt, Geneva, Switzerland 1990–92; Exec. Dir Earth Council Foundation, San Jose, Costa Rica 1992–95; Programme Co-ordinator Global Environmental Citizenship Programme, UNEP 1996–97; Chief Tech. Adviser on Environment and Devt, seconded by UNEP, Regional Bureau for Latin America and the Caribbean, UNDP 1998–99; Chief, Div. of Sustainable Devt and Human Settlements, ECLAC 1999–2003, Deputy Exec. Sec. 2003–06; Deputy Chef de Cabinet, UN, New York Feb.–March 2006, Acting Chef de Cabinet March 2006–07, Under-Sec.-Gen. for Man. 2007–08; Exec. Sec. ECLAC 2008–. **Publications:** The Millenium Development Goals: A Latin American and Caribbean Perspective 2005; numerous articles in professional journals. **Address:** Economic Commission for Latin America and the Caribbean, Casilla de Correo 179-D, Av. Dag Hammarskjöld, 3477 Vitacura, Santiago, Chile. **Telephone:** (2) 471-2000. **Fax:** (2) 208-0252. **E-mail:** secretaria.se@cepal.org. **Internet:** www.eclac.org.

BENJAMIN, Raymond; French; *Secretary-General, International Civil Aviation Organization.* **Career:** began career in civil aviation with French Civil Aviation Admin in 1976, with Human Resources Div. 1976–77, responsible for negotiating bilateral air transport agreements on behalf of Admin 1977–82; Air Transport Officer, European Civil Aviation Conf. 1982–83, Deputy Sec. 1983–89, Exec. Sec. 1994–2007; Chief of Aviation Security Br., ICAO 1989–94, also served as Sec. Aviation Security Panel and Group of Experts for the Detection of Plastic Explosives, Sec. Gen. ICAO 2009–; Special Adviser to Jt Aviation Authorities Training Org. (JAA/TO) and to European Aviation Security Training Inst. 2007–. **Address:** International Civil Aviation Organization, 999 University St, Montréal, PQ H3C 5H7, Canada. **Telephone:** (514) 954-8220. **Fax:** (514) 954-6376. **E-mail:** icaohq@icao.int. **Internet:** www.icao.int.

BENSOUDA, Fatou B., LLM; Gambian; *Chief Prosecutor, International Criminal Court;* b. 31 Jan. 1961, Banjul; m.; two c. **Education:** Univ. of Ife, Nigeria, Nigeria Law School, Int. Maritime Law Inst., Malta. **Career:** various roles with state prosecution service, including Public Prosecutor, Sr State Counsel and Prin. State Counsel 1987–93, Deputy Dir of Public Prosecutions 1993–97, Solicitor-Gen. and Legal Sec. 1997–98, Attorney-Gen. and Sec. of State (Minister of Justice) 1998–2000; served in pvt legal practice, Ya Sadi, Bensouda and Co. Chambers, Banjul 2000–02; Gen. Man. Int. Bank for Commerce (Gambia) Ltd Jan.–May 2002; Legal Adviser and Trial Attorney, Int. Criminal Tribunal for Rwanda, becoming Sr Legal Adviser and Head of Legal Advisory Unit, Tanzania 2002–04; Deputy Prosecutor in charge of Prosecutions Div., Int. Criminal Court (ICC) 2004–12, Chief Prosecutor 2012–; Visiting Lecturer, Univ. of Turin, Italy, Kennesaw State Univ., USA; mem. Int. Asscn of Prosecutors, Gambian Bar Asscn, Nigerian Bar Asscn; mem. Int. Advisory Council, Int. Bd of Maritime Healthcare 2000–, Professional Women's Advisory Bd 2000–, Advisory Bd African Centre For Democracy and Human Rights Studies 1998–2000; mem. Bd of Govs The Gambia High School 1992–95; Int. Jurists Award, Int. Comm. of Jurists 2009, World Peace Through Law Award, Whitney Harris World Law Inst., Washington Univ. in St Louis, USA 2011. **Address:** International Criminal Court, Maanweg 174, 2516 AB, The Hague, Netherlands. **Telephone:** (70) 5158515. **Fax:** (70) 5158555. **Internet:** www.icc-cpi.int.

BOKOVA, Irina Georgieva, MBA; Bulgarian; *Director-General, United Nations Educational, Scientific and Cultural Organization (UNESCO);* b. 12 July 1952; m.; two c. **Education:** First English Language School, Sofia, Moscow State Inst. of Int. Relations, Russia, Univ. of Maryland, John F. Kennedy School of Govt, Harvard Univ., USA. **Career:** Attaché and Third Sec., Ministry of Foreign Affairs, Sofia 1977–82, Third Sec., Perm. Mission to UN, New York 1982–84, Third, later Second Sec., UN Dept, Ministry of Foreign Affairs 1984–86, Adviser to Minister of Foreign Affairs (rank of First Sec.) 1986–90, First Sec., European Security Dept 1991–92, State Sec. on European Integration 1995–97, Minister of Foreign Affairs 1996–97, Adviser to Minister of Foreign Affairs (rank of Amb.) Feb.–Sept. 1997, Amb. to France 2005–09; mem. Constituent Nat. Ass. 1990–91; mem. Narodno Sobranie (Parl.) for Bulgarian Socialist Party 2001; Dir Gen. UNESCO 2009–; NATO Fellow, Program for Cen. and Eastern Europe on democratic insts focusing on the nat. and legal mechanism for the protection of minorities 1992–94. **Publications:** numerous articles on foreign policy and European integration issues. **Address:** Office of the Director-General, UNESCO, 7 place de Fontenoy, 75352 Paris 07 SP, France. **Telephone:** 1-45-68-10-00. **Fax:** 1-45-67-16-90. **E-mail:** bpi@unesco.org. **Internet:** www.unesco.org.

BRAMMERTZ, Serge; Belgian; *Prosecutor, International Criminal Tribunal for the former Yugoslavia (ICTY);* b. 17 Feb. 1962, Eupen. **Career:** Deputy Prosecutor, then Chief Deputy Prosecutor, Court of First Instance, Eupen 1996–97, before becoming Deputy to the Prosecutor-Gen., Liège Court of Appeal; Fed. Prosecutor of the Kingdom of Belgium 1997–2002; Scientific Asst, then Prof. of Law, Univ. of Liège –2002; Deputy Prosecutor of Int. Criminal Court in charge of Investigations Div. of Office of the Prosecutor 2003–07; Commr Int. Ind. Investigation Comm. into the murder of fmr Lebanese Prime Minister Rafiq Hariri 2006–07; Prosecutor, Int. Criminal Tribunal for the fmr Yugoslavia (ICTY) 2008–; assisted Council of Europe as expert on organized crime; also served on Justice and Internal Affairs Cttee of EC and as adviser for Int. Org. for Migration, leading major research studies on cases of cross-border corruption and trafficking in human beings in Cen. Europe and the Balkans. **Publications:** has published extensively in int. academic journals on global terrorism, organized crime and corruption. **Address:** Office of the Prosecutor, International Criminal Tribunal for the former Yugoslavia, Churchillplein 1, 2517 JW The Hague, Netherlands. **Telephone:** (70) 512-53-60. **Fax:** (70) 512-53-58. **E-mail:** brammertz@un.org. **Internet:** www.un.org/icty.

BURROW, Sharan Leslie; Australian; *General Secretary, International Trade Union Confederation;* b. 1954, Warren, NSW. **Education:** Univ. of New South Wales. **Career:** became an organizer for NSW Teachers' Fed., Bathurst; Pres. Bathurst Trades and Labour Council 1980s; fmr Sr Vice-Pres. NSW Teachers' Fed.; fmr mem. Bd Curriculum Corpn; Vice-Pres. Education International 1995–2000; Pres. Australian Educ. Union 1993–2000; Pres. Australian Council of Trade Unions (second woman) 2000–10; Pres. (first woman) Int. Confed. of Free Trade Unions (ICFTU) Asia Pacific Region Org. 2000–04, Pres. ICFTU (first woman) 2004–06, Pres. Int. Trade Union Confed. (ITUC) 2006–10, Gen. Sec. 2010–; mem. Governing Body of ILO (chaired Workers' Group of Sub-cttee on Multinational Enterprises), Stakeholder Council of Global Reporting Initiative. **Address:** International Trade Union Confederation, 5 blvd du Roi Albert II, Bte 1, 1210 Brussels, Belgium. **Telephone:** (2) 224-02-11. **Fax:** (2) 201-58-15. **E-mail:** sharan.burrow@ituc-csi.org. **Internet:** www.ituc-csi.org.

BUTTENHEIM, Lisa M.; American; *Special Representative of the Secretary-General and Head, United Nations Peace-keeping Force in Cyprus;* b. 1954; m. Jean-Claude Aimé. **Education:** Stanford Univ., Johns Hopkins Univ. School of Advanced Int. Studies. **Career:** joined UN 1983, served in various positions including in Exec. Office of Sec.-Gen., in Office of Under-Secs-Gen. for Special Political Affairs, New York and UN Truce Supervision Org., Jerusalem, Sr Political Adviser, Office of Dir-Gen., UN, Geneva 1997–2003, also assignments as Chief of Staff, Office of the Special Rep. of Sec.-Gen. UN Interim Admin Mission in Kosovo and Dir and Sr Adviser, Office of the Special Envoy for Balkans, Geneva, Dir and Head of UN Office, Belgrade 2003–04, Dir Asia and Middle East Div., Dept of Peace-keeping Operations 2004–07, Dir Asia and Pacific Div. 2008, Dir Middle East and West Asia Div., Dept of Political Affairs 2009–10, Special Rep. of UN Sec.-Gen. and Head of Mission, UN Peace-keeping Force in Cyprus (UNFICYP) 2010–. **Address:** UNFICYP Headquarters, PO Box 21642, 1590 Nicosia, Cyprus. **E-mail:** unficyp-public-information-office@un.org. **Internet:** www.unficyp.org.

CARRIER, Jean-Guy; Canadian; *Secretary-General, International Chamber of Commerce.* **Career:** various positions with Int. Inst. for Systems Analysis, Vienna, Austria, Econ. Council of Canada, CBC and with several global communications consulting firms; several sr positions with WTO 1996–2008, including Publr and Chief Ed.; Acting Sec.-Gen., ICC 2010–11, Sec.-Gen. 2011–; mem. UN Global Compact Bd. **Publications include:** My Father's House 1974, Family 1977, A Cage of Bone 1978, The Trudeau Decade (co-author) 1979, Patriots and Traitors 1992, The End of War 1992; numerous articles in nat. and int. media. **Address:** International Chamber of Commerce, 38 cours Albert 1er, 75008 Paris, France. **Telephone:** 1-49-53-28-28. **Fax:** 1-49-53-28-59. **Internet:** www.iccwbo.org.

CARUANA LACORTE, Jaime; Spanish; *General Manager, Bank for International Settlements;* b. 14 March 1952, Valencia. **Education:** Univ. Complutense Madrid. **Career:** fmr telecommunications engineer; various posts with Ministry of Trade 1979–84; Commercial attaché to the Spanish Commercial Office, New York 1984–87; Man. Dir and CEO Renta 4, SA, SVB 1987–91, Pres. 1991–96; Gen. Dir of the Treasury and Financial Policy 1996–99; mem. Bd SEPP (State Holding Co.) 1996–99; mem. EU Monetary Cttee 1996–99; Pres. SETE (Euro State Co.) 1997–99; Gen. Dir for Supervision, Banco de España 1999–2000, Gov. 2000–06; Counsellor and Dir Monetary and Capital Markets Dept, IMF 2006–09, Gen. Man. BIS 2009–; Chair. Basel Cttee for Banking Supervision 2003–06, Int. Org. of Securities Comms (IOSCO) 2004–06, Int. Asscn of Insurance Supervisors 2004–06, Jt Forum 2004–06; mem. Governing Council, European Cen. Bank 2000–, Financial Stability Forum 2003–, Group of Thirty Consultative Group on Int. Econ. and Monetary Affairs, Inc. (G-30), Washington, DC 2003–. **Publications:** numerous articles on the Spanish financial system, the financing of public admins and the man. of public debt. **Address:** Bank for International Settlements, Centralbahnplatz 2, 4002 Basel, Switzerland. **Telephone:** 612808080. **Fax:** 612809100. **E-mail:** email@bis.org. **Internet:** www.bis.org.

CAYLEY, Andrew T., QC, LLB, LLM; British; *International Co-Prosecutor, Extraordinary Chambers in the Courts of Cambodia;* b. 1964. **Education:** Brighton Coll., Univ. Coll., London, Coll. of Law, Guildford. **Career:** Asst Solicitor and Articled Clerk with Thomas Eggar, London 1987–91; Legal Officer, British Army 1991–98; Prosecuting Counsel, Office of Prosecutor, International Criminal Tribunal for the Former Yugoslavia (ICTY), The Hague 1994–2001, Sr Prosecuting Counsel 2001–05, Sr Prosecuting Counsel, International Criminal Court, The Hague 2005–07; counsel on the defence team for Charles Ghankay Taylor and also for Ivan Cermak before ICTY 2007–09; Int. Co-Prosecutor, Extraordinary Chambers in the Courts of Cambodia (Khmer Rouge Tribunal) 2009–; Assoc. Tenant, Doughty Street Chambers, London 2007–. **Address:** Office of the Co-Prosecutors, Extraordinary Chambers in the Courts of Cambodia, National Road 4, Chaom Chau Commune, Dangkao District, PO Box 71, Phnom Penh, Cambodia. **Telephone:** (23) 219814. **Fax:** (23) 219841. **E-mail:** a.cayley@doughtystreet.co.uk. **Internet:** www.eccc.gov.kh.

CHAKRABARTI, Sir Suma, Kt, KCB, BA, MA; British (b. Indian); *President, European Bank for Reconstruction and Development;* b. 1969, West Bengal, India; m.; one d. **Education:** City of London School, New Coll., Oxford, Univ. of Sussex. **Career:** started career with IMF and World Bank in 1980s; Sr Econ. Asst, British Overseas Devt Admin 1984; fmr Private Sec. to the then Minister of State for Overseas Devt Lynda Chalker; fmr Head of Aid Policy and Resources; worked with HM Treasury 1996; fmr Head of Econ. and Domestic Affairs Secr., Cabinet Office; Dir-Gen. for Regional Devt Programmes, Dept for International Development 2001–02, Perm. Sec. 2002–07; Perm. Sec., Ministry of Justice 2007–12; Pres. EBRD 2012–; mem. Advisory Council, Oxford Dept of International Development; Fellow, Overseas Development Inst.; Hon. Master of the Bench 2009; Dr hc (Univ. of East Anglia) 2010. **Address:** Office of the President, European Bank for Reconstruction and Development, 175 Bishopsgate, One Exchange Square, London, EC2A 2JN, England. **Telephone:** (20) 7338-6000. **Fax:** (20) 7338-6100. **E-mail:** generalenquiries@ebrd.com. **Internet:** www.ebrd.com.

CHAN, Margaret Fung Fu-chun, OBE, MSc, MScPH, MD, DSc, FFPHM; Chinese; *Director-General, World Health Organization;* b. 1947, Hong Kong; m.; one s. **Education:** Northcote Coll. of Educ., Hong Kong, Univ. of Western Ontario, Canada, Nat. Univ. of Singapore, Harvard Business School, USA, Tsinghua Univ., Beijing, Nat. School of Admin, Beijing. **Career:** Rotating Internship, Victoria Hosp., London, Ont. 1977–78; Medical Officer (Maternal and Child Health Services), Dept of Health, Hong Kong 1978–85, Sr Medical Officer (Family Health Services) 1985–78, Prin. Medical Officer (Health Admin) 1987–89, Asst Dir (Personal Health Services) 1989–92, Deputy Dir 1992–94, Dir Dept of Health, Hong Kong Special Admin. Region 1994–2003; Dir Dept of Protection of the Human Environment, WHO 2003–05, Asst Dir-Gen. of Communicable Diseases and Rep. of Dir-Gen. for Pandemic Influenza 2005–06, Dir-Gen. WHO 2006–, Organizer 43rd Session WHO Regional Cttee for the Western Pacific 1992, Chair. 49th Session WHO Regional Cttee for the Western Pacific 1998, WHO Guidelines on Methodologies for Research and Evaluation of Traditional Medicine 2000, WHO Int. Conf. for Drug Regulatory Authorities 2001 Planning Cttee 2000–02, Vice-Chair. WHO Working Group on Framework Convention on Tobacco Control 1999–2000, Moderator WHO Western Pacific Region Ministerial Roundtable on Social Safety Net 1999; Prince Mahidol Award in Public Health (Thailand) 1999, ranked by Forbes magazine amongst The World's 100 Most Powerful Women (37th) 2007, (84th) 2008, (38th) 2009, (68th) 2011. **Address:** World Health Organization, 20 ave Appia 20, 1211 Geneva 27, Switzerland. **Telephone:** 227912111. **Fax:** 227913111. **E-mail:** info@who.int. **Internet:** www.who.int.

CHEA, Leang, MA; Cambodian; *National Co-Prosecutor, Extraordinary Chambers in the Courts of Cambodia (ECCC).* **Education:** Martin Luther Univ., Halle-Wittenberg, Germany. **Career:** with Ministry of Justice 1996–2002, posts include Deputy, Training Office and mem. Cambodian Cttee for the Penal Code; Prosecutor, Cambodian Court of Appeals 2002–09; Prosecutor-Gen. Supreme Court 2009–; Nat. Co-Prosecutor, Extraordinary Chambers in the Courts of Cambodia 2006–. **Address:** Office of the Co-Prosecutors, Extraordinary Chambers in the Courts of Cambodia, National Road 4, Chaom Chau Commune, Dangkao District, PO Box 71, Phnom Penh, Cambodia. **Telephone:** (23) 219814. **Fax:** (23) 219841. **E-mail:** info@eccc.gov.kh. **Internet:** www.eccc.gov.kh/en.

CLARK, Rt Hon. Helen Elizabeth, ONZ, PC, MA; New Zealand; *Administrator, United Nations Development Programme (UNDP);* b. 26 Feb. 1950, Hamilton; m. Peter Davis. **Education:** Epsom Girls' Grammar School, Auckland, Auckland Univ. **Career:** Jr Lecturer, Dept of Political Studies, Auckland Univ. 1973–75, Lecturer 1977–81; MP for Mount Albert 1981–96, 1999–, for Owairaka 1996–99, mem. Foreign Affairs, Defence and Trade Cttee; Minister of Housing and Minister of Conservation 1987–89, of Health 1989–90, of Labour 1989–90; Deputy Prime Minister 1989–90, Prime Minister of New Zealand Nov. 1999–2008, also Minister for Arts, Culture and Heritage; Deputy Leader of the Opposition 1990–93, Spokesperson on Health and Labour 1990–93, Leader of the Opposition 1993–99; Leader NZ Labour Party 1993–2008; mem. Labour Party 1971–, Spokesperson on Foreign Affairs, on Arts, Culture and Heritage 2008–; Admin. UNDP 2009–, also Chair. UN Devt Group; Peace Prize, Danish Peace Foundation 1986, ranked by Forbes magazine amongst 100 Most Powerful Women (43rd) 2004, (24th) 2005, (20th) 2006, (38th) 2007, (56th) 2008, (65th) 2009, (50th) 2011. **Address:** Office of the Administrator, United Nations Development Programme, One United Nations Plaza, New York, NY 10017, USA. **Telephone:** (212) 906-5295. **Fax:** (212) 906-5364. **E-mail:** hq@undp.org. **Internet:** www.undp.org.

CLINTON, William (Bill) Jefferson, JD; American; *Special Envoy to Haiti, United Nations;* b. 19 Aug. 1946, Hope, AR; m. Hillary Rodham Clinton 1975; one d. **Education:** Hot Springs High School, AR, Georgetown Univ., Univ. Coll., Oxford, UK, Yale Law School. **Career:** Prof., Univ. of Arkansas Law School 1974–76; Democratic Nominee for US House of Reps from Third AR Dist 1974; Attorney-Gen. of AR 1977–79, Gov. of

AR 1979–81, 1983–93; mem. counsel, Wright, Lindsey & Jennings (law firm) 1981–83; Pres. of USA, Washington, DC 1993–2001; impeached by US House of Reps for perjury and obstruction of justice Dec. 1998, acquitted in US Senate on both counts Jan. 1999; suspended from practising law in US Supreme Court 2001–06; UN Special Envoy for Tsunami Recovery 2005–07, to Haiti 2009–; Chair. Nat. Constitution Center, Philadelphia 2009–; headed mission to N Korea to free US journalists 2009; Chair. Southern Growth Policies Bd 1985–86; Chair. Nat. Govs Asscn 1987, Co-Chair. Task Force on Educ. 1990–91; Vice-Chair. Democratic Govs Asscn 1987–88, Chair. (elect) 1988–89, Chair. 1989–90; Chair. Educ. Comm. of the States 1987; Chair. Democratic Party Affirmative Action 1975, Southern Growth Policies Bd 1980; Chair. Democratic Leadership Council 1990–91; mem. US Supreme Court Bar, Bd of Trustees, Southern Center for Int. Studies of Atlanta, Ga; Chair. Bd of Dirs Global Fairness Initiative; Founder William J. Clinton Foundation, New York and Clinton Presidential Center, Ark.; Hon. Co-Chair. Club of Madrid; Hon. Fellow, Univ. Coll., Oxford 1992; Hon. DCL (Oxford) 1994; Hon. DLitt (Ulster) 1995; Dr hc (Northeastern Univ.) 1993, (Pace Univ.) 2006, (Univ. of New Hampshire) 2007; co-recipient TED (Tech. Entertainment Design) Prize 2007, ranked by Forbes magazine amongst The World's Most Powerful People (31st) 2009, (50th) 2011. **Publications include:** Between Hope and History 1996, My Life (memoir) (British Book Award for Biography of the Year 2005) 2004, Giving: How Each of Us Can Change the World 2008, Back to Work: Why We Need Smart Government for a Strong Economy 2011. **Address:** William J. Clinton Foundation, 55 West 125th St, New York, NY 10027. **Internet:** www.clintonfoundation.org.

CLOS, Joan; Spanish; *Executive Director, United Nations Human Settlements Programme (UN-Habitat);* b. 29 June 1949, Parets del Vallés, Barcelona; m.; two c. **Education:** Universidad Autónoma de Barcelona, Univ. of Edinburgh, UK. **Career:** worked as anaesthetist; apptd Dir of Public Health 1979; Chair. Spanish Soc. of Epidemiology and Healthcare Admin 1981–91; City Councillor, Barcelona 1983–87, Deputy Mayor in charge of Finance and Budgeting 1990–94; elected Councillor, Barcelona Council for Socialists' Party of Catalonia 1993; Mayor of Barcelona and Chair. Metropolitan Greater Area of Barcelona 1997–2006; apptd Pres. Metropolis 1998, World Asscn of Cities and Local Authorities 2000; Chair. UN Advisory Cttee of Local Authorities 2000–07; Minister of Industry, Tourism and Trade 2006–08; Amb. to Turkey and Azerbaijan 2008–10; Exec. Dir UN Human Settlements Programme 2010–; mem. Council of European Municipalities and Regions 1997–2003; Gold Medal, RIBA 1999, Scroll of Honour Award, UN Human Settlements Programme 2002. **Address:** United Nations Human Settlements Programme (UN-Habitat), POB 30030, Nairobi, Kenya. **Telephone:** (20) 621234. **Fax:** (20) 624266. **E-mail:** infohabitat@unhabitat.org. **Internet:** www.unhabitat.org.

COLOMBO SIERRA, Agustín, M Int Pvt Law, DJur; Argentine; *Executive Director, Mercosur;* b. 1952, Buenos Aires. **Education:** Univ. of Buenos Aires, Univ. of the Sorbonne-Paris II, France, Univ. of San Andrés. **Career:** held various positions within several multinational telecommunications cos 1992–2003; Chief of Staff, Secr. of Foreign Relations, Ministry of Foreign Affairs 2003–05, Advisory Group Co-ordinator and Tech. Policy Del. to World Summit of Information Society Phase I, Geneva 2003, Phase II, Tunis 2005, Chief of Staff, Chancery 2005–06, Undersecretary for Latin American Policy 2007–10; Exec. Dir Mercosur (Spanish: Mercado Común del Sur, Portuguese: Mercado Comum do Sul, English: Southern Common Market) 2010–; mem. Bd of Educ.ar 2005–, Internet Governance Forum 2006–, Advisory Group of UN Sec.-Gen. 2006–. **Address:** Secretaría del Mercosur, Código Postal 11.200, Dr Luis Piera 1992, 1° Piso – Edificio MERCOSUR, Montevideo, Uruguay. **Telephone:** 2412 9024. **Fax:** 2418 0557. **E-mail:** secretaria@mercosur.org.uy. **Internet:** www.mercosur.int.

COOK, Sarah, PhD; British; *Director, United Nations Research Institute for Social Development.* **Education:** Univ. of Oxford, London School of Econs, Harvard Univ., USA. **Career:** has carried out int. academic research and has taught in field of devt studies; has undertaken policy and advisory work for int. governmental and non-governmental devt agencies; spent more than 12 years living in China, and has also worked in India, East Africa, Cambodia and Mongolia; with Inst. of Devt Studies, Univ. of Sussex, Brighton –2009, Ford Foundation China 2000–05; Dir UN Research Inst. for Social Devt 2009–. **Publications:** numerous articles on social policy, social protection in Asia, social welfare in China, the informalization of employment and the gender impacts of econ. reform. **Address:** United Nations Research Institute for Social Development (UNRISD), Palais des Nations, 1211 Geneva 10, Switzerland. **Telephone:** (22) 917-3060. **Fax:** (22) 917-0650. **E-mail:** director@unrisd.org. **Internet:** www.unrisd.org.

COOMARASWAMY, Radhika, BA, LLM, JD; Sri Lankan; *Special Representative of the Secretary-General for Children and Armed Conflict, United Nations.* **Education:** Yale, Columbia and Harvard Univs and UN Int. School, New York, USA. **Career:** Special Rapporteur on Violence Against Women 1994–2003; Chair. Sri Lanka Human Rights Comm. 2003–; Dir Int. Centre for Ethnic Studies, Colombo; Special Rep. of the UN Sec.-Gen. for Children and Armed Conflict 2006–; mem. Global Faculty, New York Univ. School of Law; teaches a summer course at New Coll., Oxford, UK every July; title of 'Deshamanya' conferred on her by Pres. of Sri Lanka 2005 (only female recipient); Hon. PhD (Amherst Coll., Univ. of Edinburgh, Univ. of Essex); ABA Int. Law Award, Human Rights Award, Int. Human Rights Law Group, Bruno Kreisky Award 2000, Leo Ettinger Human Rights Prize, Univ. of Oslo, Cesar Romero Award, Univ. of Dayton, William J. Butler Award, Univ. of Cincinnati, Robert S. Litvack Award, McGill Univ. **Publications:** two books on constitutional law and numerous articles on ethnic studies and the status of women. **Address:** Office of the Special Representative of the Secretary-General for Children and Armed Conflict, United Nations, Room S-3161, New York, NY 10017, USA. **Telephone:** (212) 963-3178. **Fax:** (212) 963-0807. **Internet:** www.un.org/special-rep/children-armed-conflict.

CORSEPIUS, Uwe; German; *Secretary General, Council of the European Union;* b. 9 Aug. 1960, Berlin; m.; two c. **Education:** Univ. of Erlangen-Nuremberg, Kiel Inst. for World Econs. **Career:** Research Fellow, Kiel Inst. for World Econs 1985–89; Economist, Int. Econ. Policy Div., Fed. Ministry of Econs 1990; Economist, Policy Dept, IMF, Washington, DC 1992–94; several positions with German Fed. Chancellery including Economist, Directorate for Gen. Econ. Questions 1991–92, Div. for Gen. Econ. Policy 1994–96, Private Sec. to Dir-Gen. 1995, Head of Div. for Econ. Issues relating to European Integration 1997–99, Head of Div. for G8, IMF, WTO and International Financial Market Issues 1999–2003, Head of Group for European Policy Coordination, Econ. Aspects of European Integration 2003–05, Dir-Gen., European Policy Adviser to Fed. Chancellor 2006–11, G8-Sherpa Feb.–June 2011; Sec.-Gen. Council of the EU, Brussels 2011–. **Address:** Council of the European Union, 175 rue de la Loi, 1048 Brussels, Belgium. **Telephone:** (2) 281-61-11. **Fax:** (2) 281-69-34. **Internet:** www.consilium.europa.eu.

COUSIN, Ertharin, BA, JD; American; *Executive Director, United Nations World Food Programme;* b. 1957, Chicago, Ill. **Education:** Univ. of Illinois, Chicago, Univ. of Georgia School of Law. **Career:** fmr Asst Attorney Gen., State of Illinois, Chicago; Deputy Chief of Staff, Democratic Nat. Cttee, Washington, DC 1993–94; White House liaison, US Dept of State 1994–96; Exec. Dir Pres. Clinton Re-election Campaign Team for Illinois 1997; Vice-Pres. Govt, Community and Political Affairs, Presidential Inaugural Cttee 1997; Vice-Pres. for Govt and Community Affairs, Jewel Food Stores 1997–99; Vice-Pres. of Public Affairs, Albertsons Foods 1999–2001, Sr Vice-Pres. for Public and Govt Affairs 201–04, also served as Pres. and Chair. of co.'s corp. foundation; Exec. Vice-Pres. and COO Feeding America (fmrly America's Second Harvest) 2004–06; Founder and Pres. The Polk Street Group (nat. public affairs firm), Chicago 2007–09; Sr Advisor to Obama for America 2007–08; Commr Bd for Int. Food and Agricultural Devt, USAID 1997–2001; Amb. and Perm. Rep. to UN Agencies for Food and Agric., Rome 2009–12; Exec. Dir

United Nations World Food Programme, Rome 2012–. **Address:** United Nations World Food Programme, Via C.G.Viola 68, Parco dei Medici, 00148 Rome, Italy. **Telephone:** (06) 65131. **Fax:** (06) 6590632. **Internet:** www.wfp.org.

COUVREUR, Philippe; Belgian; *Registrar, International Court of Justice;* b. 29 Nov. 1951, Schaerbeek. **Education:** Collège Jean XXIII, Brussels, Facultés Notre-Dame de la Paix, Namur, Université Catholique de Louvain, King's Coll., London, UK, Universidad Complutense de Madrid, Spain. **Career:** Intern, Legal Service, Comm. of EC 1978–79 (worked on accessions of Spain and Portugal to join EC); Special Asst in offices Registrar and Deputy-Registrar, Int. Court of Justice 1982–86, Sec. 1986–94, First Sec. 1994–95, Prin. Legal Sec. 1995–2000; Registrar Int. Court of Justice, The Hague 2000– (re-elected 2007); Asst Prof., Centre d'études européennes and in Law Faculty of Université Catholique de Louvain 1976–82; Visiting Prof. in the Law of Int. Orgs, Univ. of Ouagadougou, Burkina Faso 1980–82; Professeur extraordinaire in Law of Nations and Comparative Constitutional Law, Ecole des Hautes études commerciales Saint-Louis, Brussels 1986–96; Guest Lecturer in Public Int. Law, Université Catholique de Louvain 1997–; Corresp. mem. Spanish Royal Acad. of Moral and Political Sciences; mem. various other learned socs; Netherlands Embassy Prize 1969. **Publications:** numerous publs and articles. **Address:** International Court of Justice, Peace Palace, Carnegieplein 2, 2517 KJ The Hague, The Netherlands. **Telephone:** (70) 3022323. **Fax:** (70) 3649928. **E-mail:** info@icj-cij.org. **Internet:** www.icj-cij.org.

DAY, Catherine, MA; Irish; *Secretary-General, European Commission;* b. 16 June 1954, Dublin. **Education:** Univ. Coll., Dublin. **Career:** loan officer, Investment Bank of Ireland 1974–75; EC Information Officer, Confed. of Irish Industry 1975–79; Admin., Directorate Gen. (DG) III 1979–82, mem. Cabinet of Richard Burke, in charge of Personnel and Admin 1982–84, Cabinet of Peter Sutherland, in charge of Competition 1985–89, Cabinet of Sir Leon Brittan, in charge of Competition and External Relations 1989–95, Deputy Chef de Cabinet to Sir Leon Brittan, in charge of External Relations 1995–96, Dir DG IA (External Relations) responsible for relations with the Balkans, Turkey and Cyprus 1996–97, Dir DG IA, subsequently DG Enlargement, responsible for relations with cand. countries of Cen. and Eastern Europe 1997–2000, Deputy Dir-Gen. DG for External Relations, responsible for relations with the Western Balkans, New Ind. States (NIS), Mediterranean including the Middle East 2000–02, Dir-Gen. DG Environment 2002–05, Sec.-Gen. EC 2005–; Hon. LLD (Nat. Univ. of Ireland) 2003. **Address:** Secretariat-General, European Commission, 1049 Brussels, Belgium. **Telephone:** (2) 295-83-12. **Fax:** (2) 299-32-29. **E-mail:** catherine.day@ec.europa.eu.

DAYAN, Edouard; French; *Director-General, Universal Postal Union.* **Career:** Head of Air Transport Bureau 1984–86; held positions successively as Head Int. Mail Man. Dept, Int. Accounting Dept and Int. Partnership Strategy Dept, La Poste 1986–92, Deputy Dir of European and Int. Affairs 1993–97, Dir 1998–2005; Postal Expert, European Comm. 1992–93; Dir-Gen. UPU 2005–; Chair. European Social Dialogue Cttee 1994–; Chair. Tech. Cooperation Action Group, UPU 2001, also Chair. Quality of Service Fund Cttee and Bd of Trustees; fmr mem. Bd of Man. PostEurop; Chevalier, Légion d'honneur, Ordre nat. du Mérite. **Address:** Universal Postal Union, International Bureau, CP 13, 3000 Berne 15, Switzerland. **Telephone:** 313503111. **Fax:** 313503110. **E-mail:** edouard.dayan@upu.int. **Internet:** www.upu.int.

DE KEPPER, Christophe; Belgian; *Director-General, International Olympic Committee;* b. 1963, Uccle. **Education:** Univ. of Louvain, Univ. of Brussels. **Career:** fmr Asst to Legal Dir Belgian Olympic Cttee; Chief of Staff, Exec. Office of Pres., IOC 2002–11, Dir-Gen. IOC 2011–; fmr Dir European Olympic Cttee's liaison office with EU. **Address:** International Olympic Committee (IOC), Château de Vidy, 1007 Lausanne, Switzerland. **Telephone:** 216216111. **Fax:** 216216216. **Internet:** www.olympic.org.

DENG, Francis Mading, LLB, LLM, JSD; South Sudanese; *Special Adviser to the Secretary-General on the Prevention of Genocide, United Nations;* b. 1938. **Education:** Khartoum Univ., Yale Univ. Law School, USA, postgraduate educ. in UK. **Career:** fmr Human Rights Officer, UN Secr., New York; fmr Amb. to Canada, USA and Scandinavian countries; fmr Minister of State for Foreign Affairs; Guest Scholar, Woodrow Wilson Int. Center for Scholars 1983, later Sr Research Assoc.; Sr Fellow (non-resident), Brookings Inst., est. African Studies Br. of Foreign Policy Studies Program 1989, Co-Founder and Co-Dir (with Roberta Cohen) Brookings Project on Internal Displacement, Ralph Bunche Inst. for Int. Studies, Grad. Center, CUNY, New York 1992, Prof. of Political Science 2001; Special Rep. of Sec.-Gen. on Internally Displaced Persons, Office of the High Commr for Human Rights, Geneva 1992–2004; Research Prof. of Int. Politics, Law and Society and Dir Center for Displacement Studies, Paul H. Nitze School for Advanced Int. Studies, Johns Hopkins Univ., Washington, DC 2003–; Distinguished Visiting Scholar, Kluge Center, US Library of Congress, Washington, DC 2005–06; Wilhelm Fellow, Center for Int. Studies, MIT 2006–07; UN Sec.-Gen.'s Special Adviser on the Prevention of Genocide 2007–; Sr Fellow, US Inst. of Peace 2002–03, now Dir Sudan Peace Support Project; fmr Visiting Lecturer, Yale Univ. School of Law, New York Univ.; Acting Chair. African Leadership Forum 1996; fmr Distinguished Fellow, Rockefeller Brothers Fund; Grawemeyer Award for Ideas Improving World (with Roberta Cohen), Univ. of Lousiville 2005, Merage Foundation American Dream Leadership Award 2007. **Publications include:** Tradition and Modernization: A Challenge for Law Amongst the Dinka of the Sudan 1971, The Man Called Majok: A Biography of Power, Polygamy and Change 1986, Cry of the Owl 1989, Talking it Out: Stories in Negotiating Human Relations 2006; (as co-author): Conflict Resolution in Africa 1991, The Challenges of Famine Relief: Emergency Operations in the Sudan 1992, Protecting the Dispossessed: A Challenge for the International Community 1993, War of Visions: Conflict Identities in the Sudan 1995, Masses in Flight: The Global Crisis of Internal Displacement 1998, A Strategic Vision for Africa: The Kampala Movement 2002; (as co-ed.): Human Rights in Africa: Cross-Cultural Perspectives (co-ed.) 1990, Sovereignty as Responsibility: Conflict Management in Africa 1996, The Forsaken People: Case Studies of the Internally Displaced 1998, African Reckoning: A Quest for Good Governance 1998. **Address:** Paul H. Nitze School of Advanced International Studies (SAIS), The Johns Hopkins University, 1740 Massachusetts Ave NW, Washington, DC 20036, USA. **Telephone:** (202) 663-5871. **E-mail:** fdeng1@mail.jhuwash.jhu.edu. **Internet:** www.sais-jhu.edu.

DESAI, Nitin Dayalji, BA, MA; Indian; *Special Adviser to the Secretary-General for Internet Governance, United Nations;* b. 5 July 1941, Bombay; m. Aditi Gupta 1979; two s. **Education:** St Xavier's High School and Elphinstone Coll., Mumbai, Univ. of Bombay, London School of Econs, UK. **Career:** Lecturer in Econs, Univ. of Liverpool, UK 1965–67, Univ. of Southampton, UK 1967–70; consultant, Tata (India) Econ. Consultancy Services 1970–73; consultant/adviser, Planning Comm. Govt of India 1973–85; Sr Adviser, Brundtland Comm. 1985–87; Special Sec. Planning Comm. India 1987–88; Sec./Chief Econ. Adviser, Ministry of Finance 1988–90; Deputy Under-Sec.-Gen. UNCED, Geneva 1990–92, UN Under-Sec.-Gen. for Econ. and Social Affairs 1992–2003, Under-Sec.-Gen. of Dept for Policy Co-ordination and Sustainable Devt 1993–97, Sec.-Gen. of Johannesburg Summit 2002, Sec.-Gen.'s Special Adviser for the World Summit on the Information Society 2003–05, Special Adviser to Sec.-Gen. for Internet Governance, UN 2003–; mem. Advisory Bd IDEAcarbon; Chair. Cttee on Tech. Innovation and Venture Capital set up by Planning Comm., Govt of India 2006, Int. Working Group on Internet Governance; Co-Chair. (with Lord Chris Patten) India-UK Round Table; Finance Chair. The Poona Club Ltd; associated with Helsinki Process on Globalisation and Democracy, many academic orgs, research bodies and NGOs dealing with econ., social and environmental issues and also security and foreign policy; Distinguished Visiting Fellow, Centre for the Study of Global Governance, LSE 2003–04, Energy and Resources Inst.; fmr mem. Commonwealth Secretariat Expert Group on Climate Change; Hon. Fellow, LSE 2004. **Publications:** several articles and papers on devt planning, regional econs, industry, energy and int. econ. relations; writes a monthly column for Business Standard (economic daily published from Delhi). **Telephone:** 229174665. **Fax:** 229170092. **E-mail:** igf@unog.ch. **Internet:** www.intgovforum.org.

DIARRA, Cheick Sidi; Malian; *Special Adviser on Africa and Under-Secretary-General and High Representative for the Least Developed Countries, Landlocked Developing Countries and Small Island Developing States, United Nations;* b. 31 May 1957, Kayes; m.; two c. **Education:** Dakar Univ., Senegal. **Career:** joined civil service in 1981, assigned to Ministry of Foreign Affairs and Int. Co-operation, Legal Adviser 1987–88; First Counsellor, Perm. Mission to UN, New York 1989–93, Perm. Rep. to UN, New York 1993–2007; UN Under-Sec.-Gen. and High Rep. for the Least Developed Countries, Landlocked Developing Countries and Small Island Developing States 2007–08, Special Adviser on Africa and Under-Sec.-Gen. and High Rep. for the Least Developed Countries, Landlocked Developing Countries and Small Island Developing States Jan. 2008–; Chevalier, Ordre Nat. du Mali. **Address:** Office of the High Representative for the Least Developed Countries, Landlocked Developing Countries and Small Island Developing States, United Nations, Room S-770, New York, NY 10017, USA. **Telephone:** (212) 963-7778. **Fax:** (917) 367-3415. **E-mail:** ohrlls-unhq@un.org. **Internet:** www.unohrlls.org.

DJINNIT, Said; Algerian; *Special Representative of the Secretary-General and Head, United Nations Office for West Africa (UNOWA);* b. 7 June 1954. **Education:** Ecole Nationale d'Admin, Paris, France, Centre for Int. Relations Studies, Univ. of Brussels, Inst. of Political Affairs, Univ. of Algiers. **Career:** served on various diplomatic missions, including as Chargé d'affaires, Embassy in Brussels and Deputy Head of Mission in Addis Ababa; also served in various capacities in OAU (now African Union, AU), including as OAU Asst Sec.-Gen. for Political Affairs, also served as Chair. OAU Secr. Task Force on drafting of Constitutive Act of AU 1999–2000; Commr for Peace and Security at AU, with responsibility for issues including Darfur conflict –2008; Special Rep. of Sec.-Gen. and Head of UN Office for West Africa (UNOWA) 2008–. **Address:** UN Office for West Africa (UNOWA), 5 Avenue Carde, Immeuble Caisse de Sécurité Sociale, BP 23851, Dakar, Senegal. **Telephone:** 849-07-29. **Fax:** 842-50-95. **Internet:** www.un.org/unowa.

DORDAIN, Jean-Jacques; French; *Director-General, European Space Agency;* b. 14 April 1946. **Education:** Ecole Centrale. **Career:** researcher, Office nat. d'études et de recherches aérospatiales (ONERA) 1970–76, Co-ordinator of Space Activities 1976–86, Dir of Fundamental Physics 1983–86; Prof., Ecole Nationale Supérieure de l'Aéronautique et de l'Espace 1973–87; Sr Lecturer in Mechanical Eng, Ecole Polytechnique 1977–93; joined ESA 1986, Head of Space Station and Platforms Promotion and Utilisation Dept 1986, later Head of Microgravity and Columbus Utilization Dept, Assoc. Dir for Strategy, Planning and Int. Policy 1993–99, Dir Directorate of Strategy and Tech. Assessment 1999–2001, Dir of Launchers 2001–03, Dir-Gen. ESA 2003–; Exec. Sec. Evaluation Cttee of Japanese Space Agency 1997; mem. Académie des Technologies, Académie de l'Air et de l'Espace; Legion d'Honneur, Ordre National du Mérite. **Address:** European Space Agency, 8–10 rue Mario Nikis, 75738 Paris Cedex 15, France. **Telephone:** 1-53-69-76-54. **Fax:** 1-53-69-75-60. **Internet:** www.esa.int.

DRAGHI, Mario, PhD; Italian; *President, European Central Bank;* b. 3 Sept. 1947, Rome. **Education:** La Sapienza Univ. of Rome, Massachusetts Inst. of Tech., USA. **Career:** Prof. of Econs, Florence Univ., Italy 1981–91; Exec. Dir IBRD (World Bank), Washington, DC, USA 1984–90; Adviser to Bank of Italy 1990; Dir-Gen. Ministry of the Treasury and of the Budget 1991–2001; apptd mem. Econ. and Financial Cttee EEC (now EU) 1991 (Chair. 2000–01); Chair. Italian Cttee for Privatizations 1993; Dir ENI –2001; Vice-Chair. and Man. Dir Goldman Sachs Int., London, UK 2002–06; Gov. Banca d'Italia 2006–11; Pres. European Central Bank 2011–; Gov. for Italy, IBRD, Asian Devt Bank; Chair. Financial Stability Forum 2006–11 (renamed Financial Stability Bd 2009); mem. Group of Seven deputies 1991; mem. Group of Thirty Consultative Group on Int. Econ. and Monetary Affairs, Inc. (G-30), Washington, DC 2007; IOP Fellow, Kennedy School of Govt, Harvard Univ., USA; Trustee, Inst. for Advanced Study, Princeton, NJ, The Brookings Inst., Washington, DC 2003–; Chair. cttee that drafted legislation governing Italian financial markets ('Draghi Law'); ranked by Forbes magazine amongst The World's Most Powerful People (12th) 2011. **Publications include:** Produttività del lavoro, salari reali, e occupazione (Collana di economia: Sezione 4; 17) 1979, Public Debt Management: Theory & History (co-author) 1990, Transparency, Risk Management and International Financial Fragility: Geneva Reports on the World Economy 4 (co-author) 2004. **Address:** European Central Bank, Eurotower, Kaiserstr 29, 60311 Frankfurt am Main, Germany. **Fax:** (69) 13446000. **E-mail:** info@ecb.europa.eu. **Internet:** www.ecb.europa.eu.

DURÃO BARROSO, José Manuel, MPolSci; Portuguese; *President, European Commission;* b. 23 March 1956, Lisbon; m. Margarida Sousa Uva; three s. **Education:** Univs of Lisbon and Geneva. **Career:** mem. Maoist party after revolution in Portugal 1974; Lecturer, Faculty of Law, Univ. of Lisbon, Dept of Political Science, Univ. of Geneva; mem. Parl. 1985–; fmr Sec. of State for Home Affairs and for Foreign Affairs and Co-operation; Minister of Foreign Affairs 1992–95; mem. Nat. Council Social Democratic Party (PSD), Leader 1999–; Vice-Pres. EPP 1999–; Prime Minister of Portugal 2002–04 (resgnd); Chair. Comm. for Foreign Affairs 1995–96; Pres. European Comm. 2004–; Head, Dept of Int. Relations, Univ. Lusíada 1995–99; Visiting Scholar, Georgetown Univ., Washington, DC, Visiting Prof. 1996–98; decorations from Brazil, Germany, Japan, Morocco, Netherlands, Portugal, Spain, UK; Hon. DUniv (Rhode Island) 2005, Hon. DH (Georgetown Univ.) 2006, Hon. Dr rer. pol (Genoa Univ.) 2006, Hon. DIur (Kobe Univ.) 2006. **Publications include:** Governmental System and Party System (co-author) 1980, Le Système Politique Portugais face à l'Intégration Européenne 1983, Política de Cooperação 1990, A Política Externa Portuguesa 1992–93, A Política Externa Portuguesa 1994–95, Uma Certa Ideia de Europa 1999, Uma Ideia para Portugal 2000; several studies on political science and constitutional law in collective works, encyclopaedias and int. journals. **Address:** European Commission, 200 rue de la Loi, 1049 Brussels, Belgium. **Telephone:** (2) 298-18-00. **Fax:** (2) 295-01-38. **Internet:** europa.eu.

ECARMA, Maj.-Gen. (retd) Natalio C., III; Philippine; *Head of Mission and Force Commander, United Nations Disengagement Observer Force (UNDOF);* b. 3 June 1955, Manila; m. Dr Beverly Antonio; two s. **Education:** Philippines Mil. Acad., Marine Corp Univ., Nat. Defense Coll. of Philippines. **Career:** joined Philippine Marine Corps 1977, held several posts including Commdr of the Presidential Guards Bn, Presidential Security Group, 3rd Marine Brigade, Combat and Service Support Brigade; numerous staff appointments including Asst Chief of Staff for Intelligence, Philippine Marine Corps, Asst Supt, Marine Corps Training Center, Chief of Staff, Philippine Marine Corps, Deputy Commdt; Concurrent Commdr, Marine Forces; retd from mil. service 2011; Head of Mission and Force Commdr, UN Disengagement Observer Force (UNDOF) 2010–; Fellow, AIM TeaM Energy Center for Bridging Leadership; two Distinguished Service Stars, two Bronze Cross Medals 2001, 17 Mil. Merit Medals, six Mil. Commendation Medals. **Address:** United Nations Disengagement Observer Force (UNDOF), Department of Peace-keeping Operations, Room S-3727-B, United Nations, New York, NY 10017, USA. **Telephone:** (212) 963-8077. **Fax:** (212) 963-9222. **Internet:** .www.undof.unmissions.org.

ECHÁVARRI, Luis Enrique, MSc; Spanish; *Director-General of Nuclear Energy Agency, Organisation for Economic Co-operation and Development;* b. 17 April 1949, Bilbao; m.; two c. **Education:** Univ. of Basque Country, Univ. of Madrid. **Career:** Project Man. for Lemóniz, Sayago and Almaraz nuclear power plants, Westinghouse Electric, Madrid; Tech. Dir and Commr, Consejo de Seguridad Nuclear (Spanish nuclear regulatory comm.); Dir-Gen. OECD Nuclear Energy Agency (NEA) 1997–; rep. of Spain at int. fora on nuclear energy, including Int. Atomic Energy Agency and EU; mem. INSAG-IAEA; represents NEA at Int. Energy Agency Governing bd. **Address:** OECD Nuclear Energy Agency, Le Seine Saint-Germain, 12 boulevard des Iles, 92130 Issy-les-Moulineux, France. **Telephone:** 1-45-24-10-01. **Fax:** 1-45-24-11-15. **E-mail:** nea@nea.fr. **Internet:** www.nea.fr.

EL-BADRI, Abdalla Salem, BS; Libyan; *Secretary-General, Organization of the Petroleum Exporting Countries (OPEC);* b. 25 May 1940, Ghemmines; m.; five c. **Education:** Univ. of Southern Florida, USA. **Career:** began career at Esso-Libya 1965, Asst Accountant and Co-ordinator, Man. Information Systems, then Asst Controller; Chair. Waha Oil Co. 1980–83; Chair. Nat. Oil Corpn 1983–90, 2000, 2004–06, Sec. Gen. People's Cttee of Petroleum 1990–92, Sec. Gen. People's Cttee of Energy 1993–2000, Deputy Sec. Gen. People's Cttee for Services 2000–02, Deputy Sec. Gen. People's Cttee 2002–04; Sec.-Gen. OPEC 1994, 2007–; Pres. OPEC Conf. 1994, 1996–97; Pres. OAPEC 1998; Chair. Bd of Dirs Arab Petroleum Services Co. 1987–90; mem. Bd Libya Oil Invest (Tamoil), Chair. 2005–06; mem. Bd of Dirs Umm Al-Jawabi Oil Co. 1977–80; ranked 53rd by Forbes magazine amongst The World's Most Powerful People 2010. **Address:** Organization of the Petroleum Exporting Countries (OPEC), Helferstorferstrasse 17, 1010 Vienna, Austria. **Telephone:** (1) 211-12-0. **Fax:** (1) 216-43-20. **Internet:** www.opec.org.

ELIASSON, Jan Kenneth Glenn, MA; Swedish; *Deputy Secretary-General, United Nations;* b. 17 Sept. 1940, Göteborg; m. Kerstin Englesson 1967; one s. two d. **Education:** School of Econs, Göteborg. **Career:** entered Foreign Service 1965; Swedish OECD Del., Paris 1967; at Swedish Embassy, Bonn 1967–70; First Sec. Swedish Embassy, Washington 1970–74; Head of Section, Political Dept, Ministry for Foreign Affairs, Stockholm 1974–75; Personal Asst to the Under-Sec. of State for Foreign Affairs 1975–77; Dir Press and Information Div., Ministry for Foreign Affairs 1977–80, Asst Under-Sec., Head of Div. for Asian and African Affairs, Political Dept 1980–82; Foreign Policy Adviser, Prime Minister's Office 1982–83; Under-Sec. for Political Affairs, Stockholm 1983–87; Perm. Rep. of Sweden to UN, New York 1988–92; Chair. UN Trust Fund for SA 1988–92; Personal Rep. to UN Sec.-Gen. on Iran-Iraq 1988–92; Vice-Pres. ECOSOC 1991–92; Under-Sec.-Gen. for Humanitarian Affairs, UN 1992–94; Chair. Minsk Conf. on Nagornyi Karabakh 1994; State Sec. for Foreign Affairs 1994–2000; Amb. to USA 2000–05; Pres. 60th UN General Ass. 2005–06; Minister of Foreign Affairs April–Oct. 2006; Special Envoy of the UN Sec.-Gen. for Darfur 2006–08; Sr Visiting Scholar, US Inst. of Peace 2008–; Deputy Sec.-Gen. UN 2012–; Sec. to Swedish Foreign Policy Advisory Bd 1983–87; Expert, Royal Swedish Defence Comm. 1984–86; Dir Inst. for East–West Security Studies, New York 1989–93, Int. Peace Acad. 1989–2001; currently Visiting Prof., Uppsala Univ.; currently also Chair. WaterAid, Sweden; mem. of UN Sec.-Gen.'s Advocacy Group of the Millennium Development Goals; Dr hc (American Univ. Washington, DC) 1994, (Gothenburg) 2001, (Bethany Coll., Kansas) 2005, (Uppsala) 2006. **Address:** United Nations, New York, NY 10017, USA. **Telephone:** (212) 963-1234. **Fax:** (212) 963-4879. **Internet:** www.un.org.

FARRELL, Norman, LLM; Canadian; *Chief Prosecutor, Special Tribunal for Lebanon;* b. 23 April 1959. **Education:** Queen's Univ., Kingston, Ont., Columbia Univ., USA. **Career:** admitted to Law Society of Upper Canada, Ontario 1988; Crown Counsel (Criminal Div.) with Attorney Gen. for Province of Ont. 1988–96; held several positions in CRC, including as Del. and Co-ordinator in charge of dissemination of int. humanitarian law in Bosnia and Herzegovina, Legal Adviser on int. humanitarian law in Ethiopia, Adviser on int. criminal law and int. humanitarian law in Switzerland 1996–99; Appeals Counsel, International Criminal Tribunal for the Former Yugoslavia 1999–2002, Head of Appeals Section and Sr Appeals Counsel 2002–05, Prin. Legal Officer, Office of the Prosecutor 2005–08, Deputy Prosecutor 2008–12, Head of Appeals Section and Sr Appeals Counsel, International Criminal Tribunal for Rwanda 2002–03, Chief Prosecutor, Special Tribunal for Lebanon 2012–; Lecturer on Int. Criminal Law, Queen's Univ. 2004–11; Visiting Scholar, Int. Studies Center, Queens Univ. Law School, Herstmonceux, UK. **Address:** Special Tribunal for Lebanon, PO Box 115, 2260 AC Leidschendam, Netherlands. **Telephone:** (70) 8003400. **E-mail:** stl-pressoffice@un.org. **Internet:** www.stl-tsl.org.

FEDOTOV, Yury Victorovich; Russian; *Executive Director, United Nations Office on Drugs and Crime, and Director-General UN Office in Vienna;* b. 14 Dec. 1947, Moscow; m. Elena Fedotova; one s. one d. **Education:** Moscow State Inst. of Int. Relations. **Career:** entered diplomatic service 1971, served in various posts in Ministry of Foreign Affairs and abroad (Algeria 1974–80, India 1983–88), Deputy Head, Dept of Int. Relations, Ministry of Foreign Affairs 1991–93, Deputy Perm. Rep. and Acting First Deputy Perm. Rep. to UN, New York 1993–99, Dir Dept of Int. Orgs, Ministry of Foreign Affairs 1999–2002, Deputy Minister of Foreign Affairs 2002–05, mem. Bd of Dirs 2000–05, Amb. to UK 2005–10; Exec. Dir UN Office on Drugs and Crime (UNODC) 2010–, also Dir-Gen. UN Office in Vienna (UNOV) 2010–; Order of Friendship; Certificate of Appreciation, President of the Russian Fed. **Address:** United Nations Office on Drugs and Crime, Vienna International Centre, PO Box 500, 1400 Vienna, Austria. **Telephone:** (1) 26060-0. **Fax:** (1) 26060-5866. **E-mail:** unodc@unodc.org. **Internet:** www.unodc.org.

FERNÁNDEZ AMUNATEGUI, Mariano, LLB; Chilean; *Special Representative of the Secretary-General for Haiti, United Nations;* b. 21 April 1945, Santiago; m. María Angélica Morales: two s. one d. **Education:** Universidad Católica de Santiago, Bonn Univ., Germany. **Career:** joined Chilean Foreign Service 1967; Third Sec., Embassy in Germany 1971–74; in exile, Bonn, Germany 1974–82; Ed. Development and Cooperation (magazine) and Chief Ed. IPS-Dritte Welt Nachrichtenagentur (news agency) 1974–82; Chief Ed. Handbuch der Entwicklungshilfe 1974–76; returned to Chile 1982; Researcher and mem. Exec. Cttee Centre of Studies for Devt (CED) 1982–90; Amb. to EC 1990–92, to Italy (also accred to Malta) 1992–94, to Spain (also accred to Andorra) 2000–02, to UK 2002–06, to USA 2006–09; Under-Sec. of Foreign Affairs 1994–2000, Minister of Foreign Affairs 2009–10; Special Rep. of Sec.-Gen. for Haiti, UN 2011–; Head UN Stabilization Mission in Haiti 2011–; Pres. Int. Council of Latin-American Centre for Relations with Europe (CELARE), Santiago 1996–98; Vice-Pres. European-Latin American Relations Inst. (IRELA), Madrid, Spain 1992, Pres. 1992–94; Vice-Chair. Italian-Latin-American Inst. 1992–94; Commr Int. Whaling Comm. 2003–07; mem. Exec. Cttee Jacques Maritian Inst., Rome, Italy 1994–96; mem. Bd of Dirs Fintesa Financial Agency (Banco del Desarrollo) 1982–84, Radio Cooperativa 1982–90; mem. Editorial Bd Mensaje (magazine) 1984–86, Fortin Mapocho (newspaper) 1986–88, Apsi (magazine) 1986–89; mem. Political Science Asscn of Chile, Acad. Int. du Vin; Hon. Pres., Chilean Asscn of Sommeliers; Grand Cross (Argentina, Brazil, Colombia, Ecuador, Finland, Germany, Holy See, Italy, Mexico, Panama, Peru, Spain), Grand Officer (Croatia, Germany, Sweden). **Address:** Special Representative of United Nations Secretary-General for Haiti, United Nations, New York, NY 10017, USA. **Telephone:** (212) 963-1234. **Fax:** (212) 963-4879. **Internet:** www.un.org.

GAMBARI, Ibrahim Agboola, CFR, BSc, MA, PhD; Nigerian; *Joint Special Representative for the African Union/UN Hybrid Operation in Darfur (UNAMID), United Nations;* b. 24 Nov. 1944, Ilorin, Kwara State; m. Fatima Oniyangi 1969; two s. one d. **Education:** Kings Coll., Lagos, London School of Econs, UK, Columbia Univ., New York, USA. **Career:** Lecturer, Queen's Coll., CUNY 1969–74; Asst Prof., State Univ. of New York (Albany) 1974–77; Sr Lecturer, Ahmadu Bello Univ., Zaria 1977–80, Assoc. Prof. 1980–83, Prof. 1983–89, fmr Chair. Dept of Political Science and Founder, Undergraduate Programme in Int. Studies (first in Nigeria); Dir-Gen. Nigerian Inst. of Int. Affairs 1983–84; Minister for Foreign Affairs 1984–85; Visiting Prof., Johns Hopkins Univ. School of Advanced Int. Studies, Howard Univ., Georgetown Univ. and Brookings Inst. 1986–89; Resident Scholar, Rockefeller Foundation Bellagio Study and Conf. Centre, Italy Nov.–Dec. 1989; Perm. Rep. to UN, New York 1990–99, Chair. Special Cttee against Apartheid; UN Under-Sec.-Gen. and Special Adviser on Africa 1999–2005, Special Rep. of the Sec.-Gen. and Head of UN Mission to Angola 2002–03, Under-Sec.-Gen. for Political Affairs 2005–07, Special Adviser to the Sec.-Gen. on the Int. Compact with Iraq and Other Political Issues 2007–09, Special Envoy to Myanmar 2007–09, Jt Special Rep. to African Union/UN Hybrid Operation in Darfur (UNAMID) 2010–; Founder Savannah Centre for Diplomacy, Democracy and Devt (think-tank), Abuja, Nigeria; fmr Guest Scholar, Wilson Center for Int. Scholars, Smithsonian Inst., USA; Chair. Nat. Seminar to Commemorate 25th Anniversary of OAU, Lagos 1988; mem. Soc. of Scholars, Johns Hopkins Univ. 2002–; Hon. Prof., Chugsan Univ., Guangzhou, People's Repub. of China 1985; Commdr Fed. Repub. of Nigeria 2002; Hon. DHumLitt (Univ. of Bridgeport) 2002, (Fairleigh Dickinson Univ.) 2006; Dr hc (Chatham Univ.) 2008; Special Recognition for Int. Devt and Diplomacy award, Africa-America Inst. 2007, Distinguished Service Award 2008, Harry Edmonds Award for Lifetime Achievement 2009. **Publications:** Party Politics and Foreign Policy in Nigeria During the First Republic 1981, Theory and Reality in Foreign Policy Making: Nigeria After the Second Republic 1989, Political and Comparative Dimensions of Regional Integration: The Case of ECOWAS 1991, Report of the Security Council Mission to Rwanda 1995, United Nations 21: Better Service, Better Value, Better Management, Progress Report of the Efficiency Board to the Secretary-General (co-author) 1996. **Address:** United Nations, Room L-0331, New York, NY 10017, USA. **Telephone:** (917) 367-3670. **Fax:** (917) 367-0150. **Internet:** www.un.org/en/peacekeeping/missions/unamid.

GELETA, Bekele, BA, MEconSc; Ethiopian/Canadian; *Secretary-General, International Federation of Red Cross and Red Crescent Societies;* b. 1 July 1944; m. Tsehay Mulugeta; four s. **Education:** Addis Abba Univ., Univ. of Leeds, UK. **Career:** fmr Gen.-Man. Franco-Ethiopian Railway Co.; fmr Urban Devt Officer, Irish Concern Int.; fmr programme man. for Kenya and Somalia, Care Canada; fmr Amb. to Japan; fmr Vice-Minister of Transport and Communications; Sec.-Gen. Ethiopian Red Cross 1984–88; various positions within Int. Fed. of Red Cross and Red Crescent Socs (IFRC) 1996–2007 including Head of Africa Dept, Secr., Geneva, Deputy Head, IFRC del. to UN, New York, Head of regional del. in Bangkok, Gen.-Man. Int. Operations, Canadian Red Cross, Sec.-Gen. IFRC 2008–. **Address:** International Federation of Red Cross and Red Crescent Societies, PO Box 372, 1211 Geneva 19, Switzerland. **Telephone:** 227304222. **Fax:** 227330395. **E-mail:** info@ifrc.org. **Internet:** www.ifrc.org.

GRANDI, Filippo, BA; Italian; *Commissioner-General, United Nations Relief and Works Agency for Palestine Refugees in the Near East (UNRWA);* b. 1957. **Education:** State Univs of Venice and Milan, Gregorian Univ., Rome. **Career:** joined UNHCR 1988, served in several countries, including Sudan, Syria, Turkey and Iraq following first Gulf War, also headed several emergency operations, including in Kenya, Benin, Ghana, Liberia, the Great Lakes Region of Cen. Africa, Yemen and Afghanistan, Field Co-ordinator for UNHCR and UN humanitarian activities in Democratic Repub. of the Congo during civil war 1996–97, Special Asst, then Chief of Staff, Exec. Office of UNHCR, Geneva 1997–2001, Chief of Mission of UN High Commr for Refugees 2001–04; Deputy Special Rep. of UN Sec.-Gen. responsible for Political Affairs, UN Assistance Mission in Afghanistan 2004–05; Deputy Commr-Gen. UN Relief and Works Agency for Palestine Refugees in the Near East 2005–10, Commr-Gen. 2010–. **Address:** UNRWA Headquarters Gaza, Gamal Abdul Nasser St, Gaza City, Palestinian Autonomous Areas; PO Box 140157, Amman 11814, Jordan. **Telephone:** (8) 677-7333. **Fax:** (8) 677-7555. **E-mail:** unrwa-pio@unrwa.org. **Internet:** www.un.org/unrwa.

GRAZIANO DA SILVA, José, BA, PhD; Brazilian/Italian; *Director-General, United Nations Food and Agriculture Organization;* b. 17 Nov. 1949, Urbana, IL, USA; m. Paola Ligasacchi; two c. **Education:** Univ. of São Paulo, State Univ. of Campinas, Univ. Coll., London, UK, Univ. of California, Santa Cruz, USA. **Career:** Prof., State Univ. of Campinas 1978–, also Chair of Master's and Doctoral Program in Econ. Devt, Space, and Environment at Inst. for Econs; co-ordinated the formulation of the "Zero Hunger" Program (Fome Zero) in 2001; Extraordinary Minister for Food Security 2003–04; Special Adviser to the Presidency of the Repub. 2004–06; Prof., State Univ. of Campinas and Chair of Master's and Doctoral Program in Econ. Devt, Space and Environment; Regional Rep. for Latin America and the Caribbean and Asst Dir-Gen. FAO 2006–11, Dir-Gen. 2011–; Ordem de Rio Branco; Paulista Medal for Scientific and Technological Merit, Brazilian Soc. of Rural Econs Prêmio Sober. **Publications include:** 25 books including O que é a questão agrária (What is the Agrarian Question?), De boias frias a empregados rurais (From Bóias Frias to Rural Workers). **Address:** Food and Agriculture Organization, Viale delle Terme di Caracalla, 00153 Rome, Italy. **Telephone:** (06) 5705-1. **Fax:** (06) 5705-3152. **E-mail:** fao-hq@fao.org. **Internet:** www.fao.org; www.grazianodasilva.org.

GRYNSPAN, Rebeca, BS, MS; Costa Rican; *Under-Secretary-General and Associate Administrator, United Nations Development Programme (UNDP);* b. 1955; m.; one s. one d. **Education:** Univ. of Costa Rica, Hebrew Univ., Israel, Univ. of Sussex, UK. **Career:** fmr Prof., Univ. of Costa Rica; fmr Researcher, Instituto de Investigaciones de Ciencias Económicas de Costa Rica; various ministerial level positions 1986–94; Vice-Pres., Repub. of Costa Rica 1994–98; joined UN, becoming Dir Mexican Div., ECLAC 2001–06, Asst Admin. and Regional Dir, UNDP Latin America and Caribbean Bureau 2006–09, Under-Sec.-Gen. and Assoc. Admin., UNDP 2009–; fmr Vice-Pres. Int. Food Policy Research Inst. **Address:** United Nations Development Programme, One United Nations Plaza, New York, NY 10017, USA. **Telephone:** (212) 906-5000. **Fax:** (212) 906-5001. **E-mail:** UNDP-newsroom@undp.org. **Internet:** www.undp.org.

GURRÍA TREVIÑO, José Ángel, BA, MA; Mexican; *Secretary-General, Organisation for Economic Co-operation and Development;* b. 8 May 1950, Tampico, Tamaulipas; m. Dr Lulu Quintana; three c. **Education:** Universidad Nacional Autónoma de México, Univ. of Leeds, UK, Harvard Univ., USA. **Career:** Perm. Rep. of Mexico to Int. Coffee Org., London 1976–78; held various positions in Fed. Electricity Comm., Nat. Devt Bank (Nafinsa), Rural Devt Fund and Office of Mayor of Mexico City; at Finance Ministry 1978–92; Pres. and CEO Bancomext (export-import bank) 1992–93, Nacional Financiera (nat. devt bank) 1993–94; Minister of Foreign Affairs 1994–98, of Finance and Public Credit 1998–2000; Sec.-Gen. OECD 2006–; Chair. External Advisory Group, IDB. **Address:** OECD, 2 rue André Pascal, 75775 Paris Cedex 16, France. **Telephone:** 1-45-24-82-00. **Fax:** 1-45-24-85-00. **E-mail:** secretary.general@oecd.org. **Internet:** www.oecd.org.

GURRY, Francis, LLB, LLM, PhD; Australian; *Director-General, World Intellectual Property Organization;* b. 17 May 1951, Melbourne, Vic.; m.; three c. **Education:** Univ. of Melbourne, Univ. of Cambridge, UK. **Career:** articled clerk, then attorney-at-law, Arthur Robinson & Co., Melbourne 1974–76; admitted barrister and solicitor, Supreme Court of Vic. 1975; Sr Lecturer in Law, Univ. of Melbourne 1979–84; Visiting Prof. of Law, Univ. of Dijon, France 1982–83; attorney-at-law, Freehills, Sydney 1984; joined WIPO 1985, held various positions, including Deputy Dir Gen. 2003–08, Dir Gen. 2008–; Sec. Gen. Int. Union for the Protection of New Varieties of Plants (UPOV) 2008–; Hon. Professorial Fellow, Univ. of Melbourne 2001; Hon. Prof., Peking Univ. 2009; Dr hc (Univ. of World and Nat. Economy, Sofia, Bulgaria) 2009, Nat. Tech. Univ. of Ukraine 'Kiev Polytechnic Inst.') 2010, (Haifa Univ.) 2010, (Renmin Univ.) 2010; Yorke Prize, Univ. of Cambridge. **Publications:** Breach of Confidence 1984, International Intellectual Property System: Commentary and Materials (with Frederick Abbott and Thomas Cottier) 1999, Intellectual Property in an Integrated World Economy (with Frederick Abbot and Thomas Cottier) 2007; several book chapters and articles in professional journals. **Address:** WIPO, PO Box 18, 34 chemin des Colombettes, 1211 Geneva 20, Switzerland. **Telephone:** 223389428. **Fax:** 223388090. **E-mail:** directorgeneral@wipo.int. **Internet:** www.wipo.int.

GUTERRES, António Manuel de Oliveira; Portuguese; *High Commissioner, United Nations High Commissioner for Refugees;* b. 30 April 1949, Lisbon; m. (wife died 1998); one s. one d. **Education:** Instituto Superior Técnico, Lisbon. **Career:** trained as electrical engineer; joined Socialist Party 1974; Chief of Staff to Sec. of State for Industry 1974–75; fmr asst to several cabinet ministers; Pres. Municipal Ass. of Fundão 1979–95; Deputy to Ass. of the Repub. 1976–83, 1985–, Pres. several parl. comms, Pres. Socialist Parl. Group 1988–91; Strategic Devt Dir IPE (State Investment and Participation Agency) 1984–85; mem. Council of State 1991–; Leader of Socialist Party 1992–; Vice-Pres. Socialist Int. 1992–99, Pres. 1999–; Prime Minister of Portugal 1995–2001; High Commr, Office of the UN High Commr for Refugees 2005–; Co-ordinator Tech. Electoral Comm. 1980–87; Founder and Vice-Pres. Portuguese Asscn for the Defence of the Consumer 1973–74; mem. Asscn for Econ. and Social Devt 1970–96; ranked 64th by Forbes magazine amongst The World's Most Powerful People 2009. **Publications:** various books and articles for newspapers and magazines. **Address:** Office of the United Nations High Commissioner for Refugees, CP 2500, 1211 Geneva 2 Dépôt, Switzerland. **Telephone:** 227398254. **Fax:** 227397346. **Internet:** www.unhcr.org.

HAMAD, Abdul-Latif al-, BA; Kuwaiti; *Director-General and Chairman, Arab Fund for Economic and Social Development;* b. 1936; m.; four c. **Education:** Claremont Coll., Calif. and Harvard Univ., USA. **Career:** mem. Kuwaiti del. to UN 1962; Dir-Gen. Kuwait Fund for Arab Econ. Devt 1963–81; Dir The South & Arabian Gulf Soc. 1963–81, Assistance Authority for the Gulf and Southern Arabia 1967–81; Dir, then Man. Dir Kuwait Investment Co. 1963–71; Man. Dir Kuwait Investment Co. 1965–74; Chair. Kuwait Prefabricated Bldg Co. 1965–78, United Bank of Kuwait Ltd, London 1966–84; Exec. Dir Arab Fund for Econ. and Social Devt 1972–81, Dir Gen. and Chair. Bd of Dirs 1985–; Chair. Compagnie Arabe et Internationale d'Investissements, Luxembourg 1973–81; Chair. Devt Cttee Task Force on Multilateral Devt Banks; mem. Bd of Trustees, Corporate Property Investors, New York 1975–; mem. Governing Body Inst. of Devt Studies, Sussex, UK 1975–87; mem. Ind. Comm. on Int. Devt Issues (Brandt Comm.) 1976–79; mem. Bd Int. Inst. for Environment and Devt, London 1976–80; Minister of Finance and Planning 1981–83; Gov. for Kuwait, World Bank and IMF 1981–83; mem. UN Cttee for Devt Planning 1982–91, Chair. 1987; mem. IFC Banking Advisory Bd Group 1987–, Advisory Group on Financial Flows for Africa (UN) 1987–88, South Comm. 1987–89, Group of Ten (African Devt Bank) 1987–, World Bank's Pvt. Sector Devt Review Group 1988–, UN Panel for Public Hearings on Activities of Transnational Corpns in S Africa and Namibia 1989–92, Bd Trustees of Stockholm Environment Inst. 1989–92, Comm. on Global Governance 1992–, Int. Finance Corpn, Banking Advisory Bd Group (World Bank), Bd of Kuwait Investment Authority, Group of Thirty Consultative Group on Int. Econ. and Monetary Affairs, Inc., Washington, DC; Trustee, Arab Planning Inst. **Address:** Arab Fund for Economic and Social Development, PO Box 21923, Safat 13080, Kuwait. **Telephone:** 4844500. **Fax:** 4815760. **E-mail:** hq@arabfund.org. **Internet:** www.arabfund.org.

HAQ, Ameerah, BA, MA, MBA; Bangladeshi; *Under-Secretary-General, Department of Field Support, United Nations;*one s. one d. **Education:** Viqarun Nisa Noon School, Holy Cross Coll., Dhaka, Western Coll. for Women, Oxford, Ohio, Columbia Univ., New York Univ., USA. **Career:** Jr Professional Officer, Jakarta 1976; UNDP Asst Resident Rep., Afghanistan 1978, Co-ordinator of Round Table Meetings and Area Officer, Regional Bureau for Asia and the Pacific, Chief UNIFEM Asia and the Pacific Unit 1987–88, UN Resident Co-ordinator and UNDP Resident Rep., Laos 1991–94, Malaysia 1994–97, Assoc. Dir UN Devt Group Office –2002, Deputy Asst Admin. and Deputy Dir, UNDP Bureau for Crisis Prevention and Recovery 2002–04, Deputy Special Rep. of the UN Sec.-Gen. in Afghanistan, responsible for Recovery and Reconstruction, UN Assistance Mission for Afghanistan (UNAMA), also UN Resident Co-ordinator, Humanitarian Co-ordinator, UNDP Resident Rep. 2004–07, Deputy Special Rep. of UN Sec.-Gen. for Sudan, also UN Resident Co-ordinator and Humanitarian Co-ordinator 2007–09, Under-Sec.-Gen., Special Rep. of UN Sec.-Gen. for Timor-Leste and Head of UN Integrated Mission in Timor-Leste (UNMIT) 2009–12, Under-Sec.-Gen. Dept of Field Support 2012–. **Address:** Department of Field Support, United Nations, New York, NY 10017, USA. **Telephone:** (212) 963-1234. **Fax:** (212) 963-4879. **Internet:** www.un.org/en/peacekeeping/about/dfs.

HERBISH, Suleiman Jasir Al-, BA, MEconSc; Saudi Arabian; *Director-General, OPEC Fund for International Development;* b. 6 Nov. 1942, Ar-Rass; m. Dr May Al-Jasser; four c. **Education:** Trinity Univ., San Antonio, Tex., USA, Univ. of Cairo, Egypt. **Career:** fmr Dir Saline Water Conversion Corpn, Saudi Co. for Precious Metals; fmr Asst Deputy Minister; fmr Chair. Nat. Shipping Co. of Saudi Arabia, Saudi Arabian Oil Texaco Ltd (later renamed Saudi Arabian Chevron Co.), Arabian Drilling Co.; Gov. for Saudi Arabia, OPEC, Vienna 1990–2003; Dir-Gen. OPEC Fund for Int. Devt 2003–; head of numerous Saudi Arabian dels to int. confs and negotiations on energy-related issues; Commdr, Ordre Nat. Ivoirien (Côte d'Ivoire) 2009, Commdr, Order of Wissam Al Alaoui (Morocco) 2009; Congressional Medal of Achievement (Philippines) 2005, Prix de la Fondation, Crans Montana Forum 2007, Anania Shirakatsi Medal (Armenia) 2009. **Address:** OPEC Fund for International Development, PO Box 995, 1011 Vienna, Austria. **Telephone:** (1) 51564. **Fax:** (1) 51392-38. **E-mail:** info@ofid.org. **Internet:** www.ofid.org.

HEYZER, Noeleen, PhD; Singaporean; *Executive Secretary, Economic and Social Commission for Asia and the Pacific (ESCAP), United Nations;* m.; two d. **Education:** Univ. of Singapore, Univ. of Cambridge, UK. **Career:** Fellow and Research Officer, Inst. of Devt Studies, Univ. of Sussex, UK 1979–81; with Social Devt Div., ESCAP, Bangkok, Thailand early 1980s; Dir Gender and Devt Programme, Asian and Pacific Devt Centre, Kuala Lumpur, Malaysia 1984–94; Co-ordinator for the Asia-Pacific NGO Working Group for the UN Fourth World Conf. on Women, Beijing, People's Repub. of China; Exec. Dir UN Devt Fund for Women (UNIFEM) 1994–2007; Exec. Sec. ESCAP 2007–; Convener Int. Women's Comm. for a Just and Sustainable Palestinian-Israeli Peace; mem. Bd Pres. Ahtisaari's Crisis Man. Initiative; mem. High-Level Commonwealth Comm. on Respect and Understanding; New Millennium Distinguished Visiting Scholar, Columbia Univ.; Chair. Consortium Advisory Group, Research Programme on Women's Empowerment in Muslim Contexts; has served on bds of several humanitarian orgs including Devt Alternatives with Women for a New Era, the Global South, ISIS, Oxfam, Panos and Soc. for Int. Devt; Global Tolerance Award for Humanitarian Service, Friends of the UN 2000, Lifetime Achievement Award, Inst. for Leadership Devt 2000, Woman of Distinction Award, UN NGO Cttee 2003, Leadership Award, Mount Sinai Hosp., New York 2004, Leadership Award, UN Asscn Greater Boston 2004, Dag Hammarskjöld Medal 2004, NCRW Women Who Make a Difference Award 2005. **Publications include:** Gender, Economic Growth and Poverty, The Trade in Domestic Workers, Working Women in South-East Asia. **Address:** Economic and Social Commission for Asia and the Pacific (ESCAP), United Nations Building, Rajadamnern Nok Ave, Bangkok 10200, Thailand. **Telephone:** (2) 288-1234. **Fax:** (2) 288-1000. **E-mail:** unisbkk.unescap@un.org. **Internet:** www.unescap.org.

HITCHENS, Theresa; American; *Director, United Nations Institute for Disarmament Research (UNIDIR).* **Career:** served internships with Senator John Glenn (Democrat–Ohio) and with NATO Parl. Ass., Brussels; worked at Inside Washington Publrs on group's environmental and defence-related newsletters 1983–88; first Brussels Bureau Chief, Defense News 1989–93, Ed. Defense News 1998–2000; fmr Dir of Research, British American Security Information Council, Washington, DC and London; Dir Center for Defense Information (CDI), World Security Inst., Washington, DC –2008, led CDI's Space Security Project in co-operation with Secure World Foundation; Dir UN Inst. for Disarmament Research (UNIDIR), Geneva 2009–; mem. Editorial Bd The Bulletin of the Atomic Scientists; mem. Women in Int. Security, IISS. **Publications:** Growing Pains: The Debate on the Next Round of NATO Enlargement (with Tomas Valasek) 2002, Future Security In

Space: Charting a Cooperative Course 2004, European Military Space Capabilities: A Primer (with Tomas Valasek) 2006; numerous articles on space and nuclear arms control issues, military, defence industry and NATO affairs. **Address:** United Nations Institute for Disarmament Research, Palais des Nations, 1211 Geneva 10, Switzerland. **Telephone:** 229173186. **Fax:** 229170176. **E-mail:** unidir@unog.ch. **Internet:** www.unidir.org.

HOLLIS, Brenda Joyce, JD; American; *Chief Prosecutor, Special Court for Sierra Leone, United Nations.* **Education:** Bowling Green State Univ., Ohio, Univ. of Denver. **Career:** Sr Trial Attorney, Int. Criminal Tribunal for the Fmr Yugoslavia (ICTY) 1994–2001; Expert Legal Consultant on int. law and criminal procedure 2001–07, trained judges, prosecutors and investigators at courts and int. tribunals in Indonesia, Iraq and Cambodia, also assisted victims of int. crimes in Democratic Repub. of the Congo and in Colombia to prepare submissions requesting investigations by Int. Criminal Court in The Hague; consultant to Office of the Prosecutor 2002–03, 2006, Prin. Trial Attorney, Office of the Prosecutor 2007–, responsible for leading legal team prosecuting fmr Liberian Pres. Charles Taylor; Chief Prosecutor, Special Court for Sierra Leone, UN 2010–. **Address:** The Special Court for Sierra Leone, Jomo Kenyatta Road, New England, Freetown, Sierra Leone. **Telephone:** (22) 297000. **Fax:** (22) 297001. **E-mail:** scsl-mail@un.org. **Internet:** www.sc-sl.org.

IHSANOĞLU, Ekmeleddin, BSc, MSc, PhD; Turkish; *Secretary-General, Organization of Islamic Cooperation;* b. 26 Dec. 1943, Cairo, Egypt; m. Füsun Bilgiç 1971; three s. **Education:** Ankara Univ. **Career:** cataloger of printed and manuscript books, Dept of Oriental Studies, Cairo Nat. Library, 1962–66; Lecturer in Turkish Literature and Language, Ain Shams Univ., Cairo 1966–70, Ankara Univ., Turkey 1971–75; Research Fellow, Univ. of Exeter, UK 1975–77; Lecturer and Assoc. Prof., Faculty of Science, Ankara Univ. 1970–80; Assoc. Prof., İnönü Univ., Malatya, Turkey 1978–80; Dir-Gen. Islamic Conf. Research Centre for Islamic History, Art and Culture, Org. of the Islamic Conf. (OIC), Istanbul 1980–2004, Sec.-Gen. OIC (renamed Organization of Islamic Cooperation in 2011), Jeddah, Saudi Arabia 2005–; Sec. Islamic Conf. Org. Int. Comm. for Preservation of Islamic Cultural Heritage, Istanbul 1983–2000 (now defunct); Founder and Chair. first Dept of History of Science in Turkey, Univ. of Istanbul 1984–2000; Chair. Turkish Soc. for History of Science, Istanbul 1989–; Vice-Chair. Al Furqan Islamic Heritage Foundation, London, UK 1998–; Pres. Int. Union of History and Philosophy of Science/Div. of History of Science 2001–; mem. numerous orgs concerned with study of history of science and Islamic civilization, including Acad. Int. d'Histoire des Sciences, Paris, Cultural Centre of the Atatürk Supreme Council for Culture, Language and History, Ankara, Int. Soc. for History of Arabic and Islamic Sciences and Philosophy, Paris, Royal Acad. of Islamic Civilization Research, Jordan, Middle East and the Balkans, Research Foundation, Istanbul, Acad. of Arabic Language (Jordan, Egypt, Syria), Egyptian History Soc., Cairo, Tunisian Acad. of Sciences, Letters and Arts 'Bait al Hikma', Tunis, Int. Soc. for History of Medicine, Paris; apptd Amb.-at-Large by Govt of Bosnia-Herzegovina 1997; Visiting Prof., Ludwig Maximilians Univ., Munich, Germany 2003; Hon. Consul, The Gambia 1990–; Commdr de l'Ordre Nat. du Mérit (Senegal) 2002, Commdr de l'Ordre Nat. du Lion (Senegal) 2006; Dr hc (Mimar Sinan Univ., Istanbul) 1994, (Dowling Coll., New York) 1996, (Azerbaijan Acad. of Sciences) 2000, (Univ. of Sofia) 2001, (Univ. of Sarajevo) 2001, (Univ. of Padova) 2006, (Islamic Univ. of Islamabad) 2007, (Univ. of Exeter) 2007, (Islamic Univ., Uganda) 2008; Distinction of the First Order Medal (Egypt) 1990, Certificate of Honour and Distinction, Org. of the Islamic Conf. 1995, Independence Medal of the First Order (Jordan) 1996, Medal of Distinguished State Service (Turkey) 2000, World Prize for Book of the Year (Iran) 2000, UNESCO Avicenna Medal 2004, Medal of Glory (Russia) 2006, Medal of Glory (Azerbaijan) 2006, Int. Acad. of the History of Science Alexandre Koyre Medal 2008. **Publications:** has written, edited and translated several books on Islamic culture and science; over 70 articles and papers. **Address:** Organization of Islamic Cooperation, POB 178, Jeddah 21411, Saudi Arabia. **Fax:** (2) 2751953. **E-mail:** cabinet@oic-oci.org. **Internet:** www.oic-oci.org.

INDRAWATI, HE Sri Mulyani, BA, PhD; Indonesian; *Managing Director, World Bank Group;* b. 26 Aug. 1962, Tanjungkarang, Lampung; m.; three c. **Education:** Univ. of Indonesia, Jakarta, Univ. of Illinois at Urbana-Champaign, USA. **Career:** several positions at Inst. for Econ. and Social Research, Faculty of Econs, Univ. Indonesia (LPEM-FEUI) 1992–2004 including Assoc. Dir Research 1992–93, Assoc. Dir Educ. and Training 1993–95, Dir Program Magister, Planning and Public Policy, Grad. Program Econs 1996–99, Dir 1998–2004; Staff Expert in Policy Analysis, Overseas Training Office 1994–95; adviser, Nat. Econ. Council 1999–2001, Sec.-Gen.; consultant to USAID 2001–; Visiting Faculty mem., Andrew Young School of Policy Studies, Georgia State Univ. 2001–02; Exec. Dir IMF 2002; Minister of State and Chair. Nat. Devt Planning Agency 2004–05; Minister of Finance and State Enterprises Devt 2005–10 (resgnd), also Acting Co-ordinating Minister for Econ. Affairs 2008–09; Man. Dir responsible for Latin America and Caribbean, Middle East and North Africa and East Asia and Pacific, World Bank Group 2010–; Best Asian Finance Minister, Emerging Market 2006, ranked by Globe Asia amongst Most Influential Indonesian Woman (second) 2006, ranked by Forbes magazine amongst The World's 100 Most Powerful Women (23rd) 2008, (72nd) 2009, (65th) 2011. **Publications include:** Potential and Student Savings in DKI Jakarta 1995, Domestic Industry Preparedness for the Free Trade Era 1997, Forget CBS, Get Serious About Reform 1998. **Address:** The World Bank, 1818 H St, NW, Washington, DC 20433, USA. **Telephone:** (202) 473-1000. **Fax:** (202) 477-6391. **Internet:** web.worldbank.org.

INSULZA SALINAS, José Miguel, MA; Chilean; *Secretary-General, Organization of American States;* b. 2 June 1943; m. Georgina Núñez Reyes; three c. **Education:** St George's Coll., Santiago, Law School, Universidad de Chile, Facultad Latinoamericana de Ciencias Sociales and Univ. of Michigan, USA. **Career:** Prof. of Political Theory, Universidad de Chile, of Political Sciences, Pontificia Universidad Católica de Chile –1973; Political Adviser to Ministry of Foreign Relations, Dir Diplomatic Acad. –1973; researcher, then Dir Instituto de Estudios de Estados Unidos, Centro de Investigación y Docencia Económicas, Mexico 1981–88; Prof., Universidad Autónoma de México 1981–88; Head, Multilateral Econ. Affairs Dept, Ministry of Foreign Relations, Deputy Chair. Int. Co-operation Agency 1990–94; Under-Sec. for Foreign Affairs 1994, Minister 1994–99, Minister Sec.-Gen. Office of the Pres. 1999; Minister of the Interior (Vice-Pres. of the Repub.) 2000–; Sec.-Gen. OAS 2005–; mem. Bd of Dirs Instituto de Fomento de Desarrollo Científico y Tecnológico; mem. Consejo Chileno de Relaciones Internacionales, Consejo de Redacción, Nexos Magazine, Mexico, Corporación de Desarrollo Tecnológico Empresarial, Chilean Asscn of Political Science, Bar Asscn. **Address:** Organization of American States, 17th St and Constitution Ave, NW, Washington, DC 20006, USA; Ministry of the Interior, Palacio de la Moneda, Santiago, Chile. **Telephone:** (2) 690-4000 (Santiago); (202) 458-3000 (Washington). **Fax:** (2) 699-2165 (Santiago). **E-mail:** pi@oas.org. **Internet:** www.oas.org.

JAGLAND, Thorbjørn; Norwegian; *Secretary-General, Council of Europe;* b. 5 Nov. 1950, Drammen; m. Hanne Grotjord 1975; two c. **Education:** Univ. of Oslo. **Career:** mem. Buskerud Co. Council 1975–83; Chair. Labour Youth League (AUF), Buskerud Co. 1973–76, Chair. Norwegian Labour Youth League 1977–81, Sec. Labour Party Cttee on Disarmament 1982–, Acting Party Sec. Labour Party 1986–87, Chair. Labour Party Int. Cttee 1986–, Sec. Labour Party Programme Cttee 1986–89, Party Sec. Labour Party 1987–92, Chair. Norwegian Labour Party 1992–2002; mem. Storting for Buskerud Co. 1993–2009, Chair. Labour Party Parl. Group, Chair. Parl. EEA Consultative Cttee 2000–05, Parl. Standing Cttee on Foreign Affairs and Enlarged Foreign Affairs Cttee 2001–05, Pres. Storting 2005–09; Prime Minister 1996–97; Minister of Foreign Affairs 2000–01; Sec.-Gen. Council of Europe 2009–; mem. Norwegian del. for Relations with the European Parl. 1993–96, 1997–2000, Head of del. 2001–05; mem. Norwegian del. to Nordic Council 1993–96, 1997–2000, to NATO Parl. Ass. 2001–05; Head of Norwegian del. at Second Summit of Council of Europe, Strasbourg 1997; Chair. Socialist Int. Finance and Admin Cttee 1987–92, Vice-Pres. Socialist International 1999–2008, Chair. Middle East Cttee 2000–06; Chair. Oslo Center for Peace and Human Rights 2006–, Nobel Norwegian Cttee 2009–; mem. Int. Bd of Govs Peres Center for Peace 1997–; mem. Sharm El-Sheikh Fact-Finding Comm. ('Mitchell Comm.') 2000–01. **Publications include:** Min europeiske drøm 1990, Ny solidaritet 1993, Brev 1995, Vår sårbare verden 2002, For det blir for sent (co-author) 1982, Ti teser om EU og Norge 2003; numerous articles on defence, nat. security and disarmament. **Address:** Office of the Secretary General, Council of Europe, 67075 Strasbourg Cedex, France. **Telephone:** 3-88-41-20-00. **Fax:** 3-88-41-27-99. **E-mail:** private.office@coe.int. **Internet:** www.coe.int.

JALLOW, Hassan Bubacar, LLB, LLM; Gambian; *Chief Prosecutor, Criminal Tribunal for Rwanda;* b. 14 Aug. 1951, Bansang. **Education:** Univ. of Dar es Salaam, Tanzania, Nigerian Law School, Univ. Coll., London, UK. **Career:** State Attorney, Attorney-Gen.'s Chamber, Gambia 1976–82, Solicitor Gen. 1982–84, Attorney-Gen. and Minister of Justice 1984–94, Judge, Supreme Court 1998–2002; Judge, Appeals Chamber, Special Court for Sierra Leone 2002; Prosecutor, UN Int. Criminal Tribunal 1998–, carried out judicial evaluation for Yugoslavia, Chief Prosecutor, Int. Criminal Tribunal for Rwanda (ICTR) 2003–, also UN Under-Sec.-Gen.; legal expert for OAU and Commonwealth; Chair. Commonwealth Governmental Working Group of Experts in Human Rights; Commdr, Nat. Order of the Repub. of Gambia. **Achievements:** worked on drafting and conclusion of African Charter on Human Rights, adopted 1981. **Publications:** Law, Justice and Governance – Selected Papers 1998, The Law of Evidence in The Gambia 1998. **Address:** Office of the Prosecutor, International Criminal Tribunal for Rwanda, Arusha International Conference Centre, PO Box 6016, Arusha, Tanzania. **Telephone:** (27) 2504369/72. **Fax:** (27) 2504000/4373. **Internet:** www.ictr.org.

JARRAUD, Michel; French; *Secretary-General, World Meteorological Organization;* b. Jan. 1952, Châtillon-sur-Indre; m.; two c. **Education:** Ecole Polytechnique, Ecole de la Météorologie Nationale. **Career:** researcher, Météo-France 1976–78, Dir Weather Forecasting Dept 1986–89; researcher in numerical weather prediction, European Centre for Medium-Range Weather Forecasts (ECMWF) 1978–85, Dir Operational Dept 1990–91, Deputy Dir ECMWF 1991–95; Deputy Sec.-Gen. WMO 1995–2003, Sec.-Gen. 2004–; mem. Soc. Météorologique de France, Royal Meteorological Soc. (UK), African Meteorological Soc.; Fellow, American Meteorological Soc.; Hon. mem. Chinese Meteorological Soc., Cuban Meteorological Soc.; Commdr, Ordre nat. du Lion (Senegal) 2005, First Class Distinction, Civil Defence of Venezuela 1999; Hon. DSc (Universidad Nacional Agraria 'La Molina', Peru) 2004. **Address:** World Meteorological Organization, 7 bis, ave de la Paix, CP 2300, 1211 Geneva 2, Switzerland. **E-mail:** sgomm@wmo.int. **Internet:** www.wmo.int.

JENČA, Miroslav, DIur; Slovak; *Special Representative of the Secretary-General and Head of Regional Centre for Preventive Diplomacy for Central Asia (UNRCCA), United Nations;* b. 1965, Krompachy; m.; two c. **Education:** Comenius Univ., Bratislava, Univ. of Econs, Bratislava, Moscow State Inst. of Int. Relations, USSR, Stanford Univ., USA. **Career:** has held several positions in Ministry of Foreign Affairs, including Head of Div. for Devt Assistance and Cross-border Co-operation and Deputy Political Dir and Dir Dept for EU and NATO countries, has served in overseas missions as Counsellor and Chargé d'affaires, Embassy in Dublin and Press Sec., Embassy in Mexico, also served as Amb. and Perm. Rep. to Political and Security Cttee of EU and as Amb. to Mexico, Venezuela and Columbia, Amb. and Head of Mission to OSCE Centre, Tashkent, Uzbekistan *c.* 2005, Dir Office of Minister for Foreign Affairs –2008; Special Rep. of UN Sec.-Gen. and Head of UN Regional Centre for Preventive Diplomacy for Cen. Asia (UNRCCA), Aşgabat, Turkmenistan 2008–. **Address:** UN Regional Centre for Preventive Diplomacy for Cen. Asia (UNRCCA), 43 Archabil Shaeli, Aşgabat, Turkmenistan. **Telephone:** (12) 481612. **Fax:** (12) 481607. **E-mail:** UNRCCA-DPA@un.org. **Internet:** www.un.org.

JOHNSON, Hilde Frafjord, MA, PhD, KrF; Norwegian; *Special Representative of Secretary-General and Head of Mission in Republic of South Sudan (UNMISS), United Nations;* b. 29 Aug. 1963, Arusha, Tanzania. **Education:** Univ. of Oslo. **Career:** started career as journalist for Stavanger Aftenblad 1982, Folkets Framtid 1987; Chair. Christian Democratic Party Rogaland (CDP) 1988–89; Political Adviser to Kjell Magne Bondevik 1988–91, Minister of Foreign Affairs 1989–90; Alt. mem. of Parl. 1989–93, mem. of Parl. 1993–2001; Exec. Officer, UN Summit on Environment and Devt, Ministry of Foreign Affairs 1992–93; Minister of Int. Devt and Human Rights 1997–2000, Minister of Int. Devt 2001–05; Sr Adviser to Pres. of ADB 2006–07; Co-Chair. Global Coalition for Africa; Deputy Exec. Dir UNICEF 2007–11; Special Rep. of Sec.-Gen. and Head of UN Mission in Repub. of South Sudan, Juba 2011–; Chair. Sudan Cttee IGAD Partners Forum 1998–2000, 2001; initiator and mem. Utstein 4, 1998-2000, 2001; Order of the Two Niles First Class (Sudan); Commitment to Devt Award, Foreign Policy and Centre for Global Devt 2003. **Publication:** Waging Peace in Sudan 2011. **Address:** United Nations Mission in South Sudan, Juba, South Sudan; United Nations Mission in Republic of South Sudan (UNMISS), Department of Peacekeeping, United Nations, New York, NY 10017, USA. **Telephone:** (212) 963-8077. **Fax:** (212) 963-9222. **Internet:** www.un.org/en/peacekeeping/missions/unmiss.

JOHNSSON, Anders B., LLM; Swedish; *Secretary-General, Inter-Parliamentary Union;* b. 1948, Lund; m.; three c. **Education:** Univs of Lund and New York. **Career:** mem. staff UNHCR, posts in Honduras, Pakistan, Sudan and Viet Nam, then Prin. Legal Adviser to High Commr, Geneva 1976–91; Under-Sec.-Gen. IPU 1991–94, Deputy Sec.-Gen. and Legal Adviser 1994–98, Sec.-Gen. 1998–. **Address:** Inter-Parliamentary Union, CP 330, 1218 Le Grand-Saconnex/Geneva, Switzerland. **Telephone:** 229194150. **Fax:** 229194160. **E-mail:** postbox@mail.ipu.org. **Internet:** www.ipu.org.

KABERUKA, Donald, MPhil, PhD; Rwandan; *Executive President and Chairman, African Development Bank.* **Education:** Tanzania, Glasgow Univ., LSE, UK. **Career:** early career in banking industry; fmr State Minister for Budget and Planning; Minister of Finance and Econ. Planning 1997–2005; Exec. Pres. and Chair. African Devt Bank 2005–; Chair. Bd of Govs Africa Trade Insurance Agency (ATI) 2003–; Chair. Nat. Africa Peer Review Comm. 2004–; Chair. PTA Bank (East, Central and Southern Africa devt bank) 2001-02; Vice-Chair. Nat. AIDS Comm. 2002–03. **Address:** African Development Bank, rue Joseph Anoma, 01 BP 1387, Abidjan 01, Côte d'Ivoire. **Telephone:** 20-20-44-44. **Fax:** 20-20-49-59. **E-mail:** afdb@afdb.org. **Internet:** www.afdb.org.

KANE, Angela, MA; German; *High Representative for Disarmament Affairs, United Nations;* b. (Angela Uther), 29 Sept. 1948, Hameln; m. William P. Kane. **Education:** Univ. of Munich, Bryn Mawr Coll., PA USA, Johns Hopkins School of Advanced Int. Studies, Washington, DC. **Career:** early career includes positions at World Bank, Washington, DC and pvt. industry in Europe; staff mem. UN since 1977 with various positions including postings to Jakarta and Bangkok, Jr Officer Cabinet Sec.-Gen. Waldheim, election monitor Nicaragua and El Salvador, responsible for disarmament issues and World Disarmament Campaign, mem. negotiating team for Cen. American Peace Process 1990–91, Prin. Officer for Political Affairs, Office of Sec.-Gen. Boutros Boutros-Ghali 1991–95, Man. Library and Publ., Dept Public Information 1995–99, Dir Americas and Europe Div., Dept Political Affairs 1999–2002, Deputy Special Rep. of Sec.-Gen. to UN Mission in Ethiopia and Eritrea (UNMEE) Asmara 2003–04, Asst Sec.-Gen., Dept for Gen. Ass. and Conf. Man. (DGACM) 2004–05, Asst Sec.-Gen. for Political Affairs 2005–08, Under-Sec.-Gen. for Man. 2008–12, High Rep. for Disarmament Affairs 2012–. **Address:** Office of the High Representative for Disarmament Affairs, United Nations, Information and Outreach Branch, 220 East 42nd St, Room DN-2501, New York, NY 10017, USA. **Fax:**

(212) 963-8995. **E-mail:** angela.kane@un.org. **Internet:** www.un.org/disarmament.

KELL, Georg; German; *Executive Director, Global Compact, United Nations.* **Education:** Tech. Univ. of Berlin. **Career:** extensive experience as financial analyst in Africa and Asia; began UN career with UNCTAD in Geneva 1987–90, joined New York office of UNCTAD 1990, Head of New York Office 1993–97, Sr Officer in Exec. Office of UN Sec.-Gen. Kofi Annan 1997–2000, Exec. Dir UN Global Compact 2000–. **Address:** Global Compact Office, UN Headquarters, First Ave at 46th St, New York, NY 10017, USA. **E-mail:** wynhoven@un.org. **Internet:** www.unglobalcompact.org.

KHALAF, Rima, BA, PhD; Jordanian; *Under-Secretary-General and Executive Secretary, United Nations Economic and Social Commission for Western Asia;* b. 1953; m. Hani K. Hunaidi; two c. **Education:** American Univ. of Beirut, Portland State Univ., USA. **Career:** Lecturer, Dept of Econs, Portland State Univ. 1979; Dir-Gen. Jordan Export Devt and Commercial Centres Corpn 1990–93; Dir-Gen. for Investment Promotion Dept, Amman 1990–93; Minister for Industry and Trade 1993–95, for Planning 1995–98; Senator 1997–2000; Deputy Prime Minister 1999–2000; Asst Sec.-Gen. and Dir of Regional Bureau for Arab States, UNDP 2000–06; Under-Sec.-Gen. and Exec. Sec., UN Econ. and Social Comm. for Western Asia 2010–; Chair. Advisory Bd UN Global Democracy Fund 2006–07; Dir Center for Global Devt; CEO Mohammed bin Rashid Al Maktoum Foundation 2008–09; mem. Bd of Dirs AMIDEAST, Carnegie Middle East Advisory Council, IMF Middle East Advisory Group; mem. Bd of Trustees, American Univ. of Beirut, Nat. Center for Human Rights, Higher Educ. Council; mem. Econ. Consultative Council; participated in High-Level Comm. for Modernisation of World Bank Group Governance 2008–09; Grand Codon of the Order of Al-Kawkab Al-Urduni (Jordan) 1995; Hon. DHumLitt (American Univ. of Cairo) 2009; League of Arab States Award 2005, Prince Claus Award, King Hussein Leadership Prize 2009, listed among top fifty people who shaped the decade by Financial Times newspaper 2009. **Address:** United Nations Economic and Social Commission for Western Asia, PO Box 11-8575, Riad el-Solh Square, Beirut, Lebanon. **Telephone:** (1) 981301. **Fax:** (1) 981510. **Internet:** www.escwa.un.org.

KHARE, Atul, MB, BS, MA, MBA, FRSA; Indian; *Head of Change Management Team, United Nations;* b. 14 Aug. 1959; m. Vandna Khare. **Education:** All India Inst. of Medical Sciences, Univ. of Southern Queensland, Australia, Indian Defence School of Languages. **Career:** mem. of staff, Foreign Service 1984–2006, postings include Deputy High Commr to Mauritius, Counsellor at Perm. Mission to UN, New York and Chargé d'affaires, Embassy in Senegal (also accred to Mali, Mauritania, The Gambia, Guinea-Bissau and Cape Verde), also held posts as Chef de Cabinet of Foreign Sec. of India and Dir UN Div.; Chief of Staff, UN Mission of Support in East Timor (UNMISET) 2002–04, Deputy Special Rep. of UN Sec.-Gen. for East Timor 2004–05, Special Rep. of UN Sec.-Gen. for Timor-Leste and Head of UN Integrated Mission in Timor-Leste (UNMIT) 2006–10, Asst Sec.-Gen. for Peace-keeping Operations 2010, Head of UN Change Man. Team 2011–;. **Address:** United Nations, New York, NY 10017, USA. **Telephone:** (212) 963-1234. **Fax:** (212) 963-4879. **E-mail:** info@un.org. **Internet:** www.un.org.

KILPIÄ, Maj.-Gen. Juha; Finnish; *Head of Mission and Chief of Staff, United Nations Truce Supervision Organization (UNTSO);* b. 1953; m.; one d. **Education:** Finnish War Coll., NATO School, Germany, NATO Defense Coll., Italy. **Career:** commissioned in Army Command Finland 1977; served in several other posts in UN peace-keeping missions including Chief of Operations UN Interim Force in Lebanon (UNIFIL) 1991, UN Disengagement Observer Force (UNDOF) 1993; Bn Commdr NATO Operations Joint Endeavour (IFOR)/Operation Joint Forge (SFOR) 1996–97; Commdr Multinational Task Force in EU operation 2004–05; Mil. Rep. to EU and NATO, Brussels 2007–09; Chief of Staff, Army Command 2009–11; Head of Mission and Chief of Staff UN Truce Supervision Org. (UNTSO) 2011–. **Address:** United Nations Truce Supervision Organization, Department of Peace-keeping Operations, Room S-3727-B, United Nations, New York, NY 10017, USA. **Telephone:** (212) 963-8077. **Fax:** (212) 963-9222. **Internet:** www.un.org/en/peacekeeping/missions/untso.

KIM, Jim Yong, AB, MD, PhD; American (b. South Korean); *President, World Bank Group;* b. 1959, Seoul, South Korea; m. Younsook Lim; two c. **Education:** Brown Univ., Harvard Univ. **Career:** Founding Trustee, Partners in Health (Harvard–affiliated nonprofit org.) 1987, currently mem. Bd of Dirs; apptd by WHO to help lead int. response to drug-resistant tuberculosis by establishing pilot MDR TB treatment programs and organizing effective delivery systems for antibiotics 1999; Lecturer in Social Medicine, Dept of Social Medicine, Harvard Medical School 1993–95, Instructor in Social Medicine 1995–2000, Asst Prof. of Medical Anthropology 2000–03, Asst Prof. of Medicine, Dept of Medicine 2002–03, Assoc. Prof. of Social Medicine and Assoc. Prof. of Medicine 2003–05, Assoc. Clinical Prof. of Medicine and Assoc. Clinical Prof. of Social Medicine 2005–06, François-Xavier Bagnoud Prof. of Health and Human Rights, Harvard School of Public Health 2005–09, Prof. of Medicine and Prof. of Social Medicine, Harvard Medical School 2006–09; Co-Chief Div. of Social Medicine and Health Inequalities, Brigham and Women's Hospital, Boston 2002–03; Sr Adviser to Dir-Gen. WHO 2003–06, Dir Dept of HIV/AIDS 2004–06; Pres. Dartmouth Coll. 2009–12; Pres. World Bank Group, Washington, DC 2012–; mem. American Anthropological Asscn 1984–, Soc. for Medical Anthropology 1986–, Soc. for Latin American Anthropology 1996–, Int. Union Against Tuberculosis and Lung Disease 1997–, Critical Anthropology of Health Working Group 1999–, Inst. of Medicine of NAS 2004–, American Acad. of Arts and Sciences 2010–; John D. and Catherine T. MacArthur Foundation Genius Fellowship 2003, Treatment Action Group "Research in Action" Award 2007, William Rogers Award for Service to Soc., Brown Univ. Alumni Asscn 2008, Distinguished Leadership Award, Korean American Coalition 2008. **Publication:** Dying for Growth: Global Inequality and the Health of the Poor (co-ed.). **Address:** World Bank Group, 1818 H St, NW, Washington, DC 20433, USA. **Telephone:** (202) 473-1000. **Fax:** (202) 477-6391. **Internet:** www.worldbank.org.

KOBAYASHI, Izumi; Japanese; *Executive Vice-President, Multilateral Investment Guarantee Agency, World Bank Group.* **Education:** Seikei Univ. **Career:** joined Merrill Lynch Japan, Tokyo 1985, held several global exec. roles, Pres. and Rep. Dir Merrill Lynch Japan –2008, also served as Dir of Operations and Chief Admin. Officer; Exec. Vice-Pres. Multilateral Investment Guarantee Agency (MIGA), World Bank Group, New York, USA 2008–; mem. Bd of Dirs Keizai Doyukai (Japanese asscn of corp. execs); Business Woman of the Year Award, Veuve Clicquot 2004, featured in the Wall Street Journal's '50 Women to Watch' Oct. 2005. **Address:** Multilateral Investment Guarantee Agency, World Bank Group, 1818 H St NW, Washington, DC 20433, USA. **Telephone:** (202) 473-2503. **Fax:** (202) 522-2630. **E-mail:** ikobayashi@worldbank.org. **Internet:** www.miga.org.

KOBEH GONZÁLEZ, Roberto; Mexican; *President, Council, International Civil Aviation Organization.* **Education:** Nat. Polytechnic Inst. of Mexico. **Career:** fmr Prof. of Aeronautical Electronics, Nat. Polytechnic Inst.; 40 years of experience as public servant in Mexican Govt, occupying various posts in Civil Aeronautics Directorate, including Deputy Dir-Gen. for Admin and Air Transport, Dir-Gen. Air Navigation Services of Mexico (SENEAM) 1978–97; Rep. of Mexico on Council of ICAO, serving as First Vice-Pres., Chair. Finance Cttee, and as mem. Air Transport and Unlawful Interference Cttees 1998–2006, Pres. Council 2006–; Emilio Carranza Medal, Award for Extraordinary Service, Fed. Aviation Admin (USA), honoured by Cen. American Corpn of Aerial Navigation Services for his contrib. to devt of aviation in Cen. America. **Address:** International Civil Aviation Organization, External Relations and Public Information Office, 999 University Street, Montréal, PQ H3C 5H7, Canada. **Telephone:** (514) 954-8220; (514) 954-8221. **Fax:** (514) 954-6376. **E-mail:** icaohq@icao.int. **Internet:** www.icao.int.

KOBLER, Martin; German; *Special Representative of Secretary-General and Head, UN Assistance Mission for Iraq, United Nations;* b. 1953, Stuttgart; m.; three c. **Education:** Pajajaran Univ., Indonesia. **Career:** served as legal practitioner 1980–83; entered foreign service 1983, Deputy Head, Balkan Task Force, Foreign Ministry 1997–98; Chief of Cabinet to fmr German Foreign Minister Joschka Fischer 2000–03, fmr Dir-Gen. for Culture and Communication, Ministry of Foreign Affairs; fmr Amb. to Egypt, Iraq 2003–07; Electoral Observer with UN missions in Haiti, Nicaragua and Cambodia, Deputy Special Rep. (Political) for Afghanistan 2010–11, Special Rep. of UN Sec.-Gen. for Iraq and Head, UN Assistance Mission for Iraq (UNAMI) 2011–. **Address:** Department of Political Affairs, United Nations, New York, NY 10017, USA. **Telephone:** (212) 963-1234. **Fax:** (212) 963-4879. **E-mail:** achouri@un.org. **Internet:** www.uniraq.org.

KOENDERS, Albert (Bert) Gerard, BA, MA; Dutch; *Special Representative of the Secretary-General and Head, United Nations Operation in Côte d'Ivoire (UNOCI);* b. 28 May 1958, Arnhem. **Education:** Free Univ., Johns Hopkins Univ., USA. **Career:** personal asst to mems of House of Reps, Co-ordinating Foreign Policy Asst for Labour Party 1983–92; Adjunct Prof. of Int. Relations, Webster Univ., Leiden 1984–87; part-time consultant and European Dir of Parliamentarians for Global Action, New York 1987; European staff mem. and Political Adviser to Special Rep. of UN Sec.-Gen. working in Mozambique, South Africa and Mexico 1993–94; Prin. Admin., Policy Planning Staff, Directorate-Gen. for External Relations, Conflict Prevention and EU Enlargement, EC, Brussels –1997; mem. House of Reps 1997–2007; Minister for Devt Cooperation 2007–10; Special Rep. of the Sec.-Gen. and Head of the UN Operation in Côte d'Ivoire (UNOCI) 2011–; Visiting Prof. for Conflict Man., Johns Hopkins Univ., Bologna 2000–02; Chair. Supervisory Bd, Rutgers World Population Foundation 2011–; fmr Pres. NATO Parliamentary Ass.; fmr Deputy Chair. Netherlands Atlantic Asscn; mem. French-Dutch Cooperation Council; mem. Governing Council, Soc. for International Development; mem. Supervisory Council, Inst. for Multiparty Democracy. **Address:** United Nations Operation in Côte d'Ivoire (UNOCI), Department of Peace-keeping Operations, United Nations, New York, NY 10017, USA. **Telephone:** (212) 963-1234. **Fax:** (212) 963-4879. **Internet:** www.un.org/en/peacekeeping/missions/unoci.

KONOÉ, Tadateru, BA; Japanese; *President, International Federation of Red Cross and Red Crescent Societies;* b. 8 May 1939, brother of fmr Prime Minister Morihiro Hosokawa; m. Yasuko Konoe 1966; one s. **Education:** Gakushuin Univ., Tokyo, London School of Econs, UK. **Career:** joined Japanese Red Cross Soc. as volunteer 1964, Dir Int. Dept 1964–72, Dir-Gen. Int. Dept 1976–81, Dir Social Dept 1985–88, Dir-Gen. 1988, Vice-Pres. Japanese Red Cross Soc. 1991–2005, Pres. 2005–; seconded to Secr., Int. Fed. of Red Cross and Red Crescent Socs (IFRC), Geneva, Switzerland 1972, becoming officer, IFRC Disaster Preparedness Bureau 1972–75, Dir 1981–85, mem. IFRC Finance Comm. 1985–93, 2003–, mem. Standing Comm. 1995–2003, mem. Governing Bd 2001–05, Vice Pres. IFRC 2005–09, Pres. 2009–; Councillor, Japan Cttee for UNICEF; Adviser, Japan Campaign to Ban Landmines, Japan Center for Conflict Prevention. **Address:** International Federation of Red Cross and Red Crescent Societies, 17 Chemin des Crêts, Petit-Saconnex, CP 372, 1211 Geneva 19, Switzerland. **Telephone:** 227304333. **Fax:** 227330395. **E-mail:** secretariat@ifrc.org. **Internet:** www.ifrc.org; tadateru-konoe.com.

KOTEREC, Miloš, MSc, MBA; Slovak; *President, United Nations Economic and Social Council;* b. 1962, Partizánske; m. (divorced); two c. **Education:** Faculty of Electrotechnical Eng and Informatics, Slovak Tech. Univ., Bratislava, Faculty of Law, Commenius Univ., Bratislava. **Career:** Asst Lecturer, Faculty of Electrotechnical Eng and Informatics, Slovak Tech. Univ., Bratislava 1989–93; began career in civil service 1993, promoted to Chief of UN Section, Dept of the UN and Other Int. Orgs, Ministry of Foreign Affairs, Second Sec., Perm. Mission to UN, New York 1995–98, First Sec. and Acting Deputy Chief of Mission 1998–99, served in Dept for the OSCE, Disarmament and Council of Europe, Ministry of Foreign Affairs 1999–2000, Dir 2000–01, apptd Counsellor, Mission of Slovakia to NATO, Brussels 2001, Deputy Perm. Rep. 2001–04, Amb. and Perm. Rep. to UN, New York 2009–, apptd Chair of First Cttee (Disarmament and International Security), UN 2010, Sr Vice-Pres. UN ECOSOC 2011–12, Pres. 2012–; mem. European Parl. 2004–09. **Address:** Permanent Mission of Slovakia to the United Nations, 801 Second Ave, 12th Floor, New York, NY 10017, USA. **Telephone:** (212) 286-8880. **Fax:** (212) 286-8419. **E-mail:** un.newyork@mzv.sk. **Internet:** www.un.org/en/ecosoc.

KUBIŠ, Ján; Slovak; *Special Representative and Head, United Nations Assistance Mission in Afghanistan (UNAMA), United Nations;* b. 12 Nov. 1952, Bratislava; m.; one d. **Education:** Moscow State Inst. for Int. Affairs. **Career:** served in Dept of Int. Econ. Orgs, Ministry of Foreign Affairs (Czechoslovakia) 1976–80, Head of Security and Arms Control Section 1985–88, Dir-Gen. Euro-Atlantic Section 1991–92; served in Embassy in Addis Ababa 1980–85; First Sec. Embassy in Moscow 1989–90, Deputy Head and Head of Political Dept 1990–91; Chair. CSCE Cttee of Sr Officials and Amb.-at-Large 1992; Perm. Rep. (for Slovakia), UN Office, GATT and other Int. Orgs, Geneva 1993–94; Chief Negotiator (for Slovakia) for Pact for Stability in Europe 1994; Dir OSCE Conflict Prevention Centre 1994–98; Special Rep. of UN Sec.-Gen. for Tajikistan and Head, UN Mission of Mil. Observers 1998–99; Sec.-Gen. OSCE 1999–2005, Personal Rep. of Chair.-in-Office for Cen. Asia 2000; EU Special Rep. for Cen. Asia 2005–06; Minister of Foreign Affairs 2006–09; Under-Sec.-Gen. and Exec. Sec. UN Econ. Comm. for Europe 2009–12; Special Rep. of UN Sec.-Gen. for Afghanistan and Head, UN Assistance Mission in Afghanistan (UNAMA) 2012–; mem. UN Sec.-Gen. Sr Man. Group; OSCE Medal 1998. **Address:** United Nations Assistance Mission in Afghanistan (UNAMA), PO Box 5858, Grand Central Station, New York, NY 10163-5858, USA; United Nations Assistance Mission in Afghanistan (UNAMA), Compound B, Peace St, Kabul, Afghanistan. **E-mail:** spokesman-unama@un.org. **Internet:** unama.unmissions.org.

KURODA, Haruhiko, BA, MPhil; Japanese; *Chairman and President, Asian Development Bank;* b. 25 Oct. 1944; m. Kumiko Kuroda; two s. **Education:** Univ. of Tokyo, Univ. of Oxford, UK. **Career:** joined Ministry of Finance 1967; secondment to IMF, Washington, DC 1975–78; Dir Int. Orgs Div., Int. Finance Bureau 1987–88; Sec. to Minister of Finance 1988–89; Dir of several divs, Tax Bureau 1989–92; Deputy Vice Minister of Finance for Int. Affairs 1992–93; Commr Osaka Regional Taxation Bureau 1993–94; Deputy Dir-Gen., Int. Finance Bureau 1994–96, Dir-Gen. 1997–99; Pres. Inst. of Fiscal and Monetary Policy 1996–97; Vice Minister of Finance for Int. Affairs 1999–2003; Special Adviser to Cabinet 2003–05; Chair. Bd of Dirs and Pres. Asian Devt Bank 2005–; Prof., Grad. School of Econs, Hitotsubashi Univ. 2003–05. **Publications:** several books on monetary policy, exchange rates, int. finance policy, int. taxation and int. negotiations. **Address:** Asian Development Bank, 6 ADB Ave, Mandaluyong City 0401 Metro Manila; PO Box 789, 0980 Manila Philippines. **Telephone:** (2) 6324444. **Fax:** (2) 6362444. **E-mail:** information@adb.org. **Internet:** www.adb.org.

LADSOUS, Hervé; French; *Under-Secretary-General for Peace-keeping Operations, United Nations;* b. 12 April 1950; m.; three c. **Education:** École nationale des langues orientales. **Career:** Vice-Consul in Hong Kong 1973–75; with Econ. Affairs Div., Ministry of Foreign Affairs 1976–81; Second Counsellor, Embassy in Canberra 1981–83, Beijing 1983–86; Second Counsellor, Perm. Mission to UN, Geneva 1986–88, First Counsellor 1988–90; Asst Dir for the Americas, Ministry of Foreign Affairs 1990–92; Acting Chargé d'affaires, Embassy in Port-au-Prince 1991–92; First Counsellor, Perm. Mission to UN, New York 1992–94, Minister Counsellor 1994–97; Perm. Rep. to OSCE, Vienna 1997–2001; Amb. to Indonesia 2001–03 (also accred to E Timor 2002–03); Communications Dir Ministry of Foreign Affairs 2003–05, Dir for Asia and Oceania 2005; Amb. to People's Repub. of China 2006–10; Chief of Staff to Minister for Foreign Affairs 2010–11; Under-Sec.-Gen. for Peace-keeping Operations, UN 2011–; Chevalier, Légion d'honneur, Officier, Ordre nat. du Mérite. **Address:** Department of Peacekeeping Operations, United Nations,

Room S-3727-B, New York, NY 10017, USA. **Telephone:** (212) 963-8077. **Fax:** (212) 963-9222. **Internet:** www.un.org/en/peacekeeping.

LAGARDE, Christine Madeleine Odette, MA; French; *Madame Chairman of the Executive Board and Managing Director, International Monetary Fund;* b. 1 Jan. 1956, Paris; m. (divorced); two s.; partner Xavier Giocanti from 2006. **Education:** Lycée Claude Monet, Le Havre, Holton-Arms School, Bethesda, Md, USA, Univ. Paris X, Institut d'études politiques d'Aix-en-Provence (Sciences Po Aix). **Career:** worked as an intern at US Capitol, Washington, DC as William Cohen's congressional asst; started career as Lecturer at Univ. of Paris X; joined Baker & McKenzie LLP (law firm) 1981, apptd Partner 1987, Man. Partner 1991–95, elected to Global Exec. Cttee 1995, Chair. European Regional Council and Professional Devt Cttee 1995–98, Chair. Exec. Cttee 1999–2004, Chair. Global Policy Cttee 2004–05, f. European Law Centre, Brussels; Minister for Foreign Trade 2005–07, of Agric. 2007, of Economy, Finance and Industry 2007–11; Madame Chair. Exec. Bd and Man. Dir IMF 2011–; mem. Supervisory Bd ING Group April 2005–June 2005; mem. Int. Advisory Bd Escuela Superior de Administración y Dirección de Empresas; mem. Int. Bd of Overseers, Illinois Inst. of Tech.; mem. Bd and Sec., Execs Club of Chicago; mem. Strategic Council on Attractivity of France; Co-Chair. US-Europe-Poland Action Comm., Center for Strategic and Int. Studies; mem. Int. Business Advisory Bd, Mayor of Beijing; Chevalier, Légion d'honneur 2000; Jaume Cordelles Award, Escuela Superior de Administración y Dirección de Empresas (ESADE), Barcelona 2004, ranked by Forbes magazine amongst The World's 100 Most Powerful Women (76th) 2004, (88th) 2005, (30th) 2006, (12th) 2007, (14th) 2008, (17th) 2009, (43rd) 2010, (ninth) 2011, chosen by TIME magazine amongst the 100 Most Influential People in the World 2009, ranked by The Financial Times the Best Minister of Finance of the Eurozone 2009, ranked by Forbes magazine amongst The World's Most Powerful People (39th) 2011. **Address:** International Monetary Fund, 700 19th St NW, Washington, DC 20431, USA. **Telephone:** (202) 623-7000. **Fax:** (202) 623-6278. **E-mail:** publicaffairs@imf.org. **Internet:** www.imf.org.

LAKE, (William) Anthony (Kirsopp), PhD; American; *Executive Director, United Nations Children's Fund (UNICEF);* b. 2 April 1939, New York City, NY; m.; three c. **Education:** Harvard Coll., Trinity Coll., Cambridge, UK, Woodrow Wilson School of Public and Int. Affairs, Princeton Univ. **Career:** joined Foreign Service 1962, Special Asst to Amb. Henry Cabot Lodge, Viet Nam; aide to Nat. Security Adviser Henry Kissinger 1969–70; Head of State Dept's policy planning operation 1977–81; Prof., Amherst Coll. 1981–84, Mount Holyoke Coll. 1984–92; foreign policy adviser to fmr Pres. Clinton during presidential campaign 1992; Nat. Security Adviser 1993–97; served as US Pres.'s Special Envoy to Haiti as well as Ethiopia and Eritrea from 1997; worked with third Exec. Dir of UNICEF, James P. Grant, on org.'s presentation of the 1993 edn of its flagship publication, 'The State of the World's Children', at the White House, mem. Bd of US Fund for UNICEF 1998–2007, Chair. 2004–07, Perm. Hon. mem. 2007–, Exec. Dir UNICEF 2010–; Int. Adviser to ICRC 2000–03; Distinguished Prof. in Practice of Diplomacy, Edmund A. Walsh School of Foreign Service, Georgetown Univ. –2010; fmr Chair. Marshall Legacy Inst.; has led Int. Voluntary Services; mem. Bd Save the Children 1975–77; fmr mem. Bd Overseas Devt Council; fmr mem. Bd of Trustees, Mount Holyoke Coll.; fmr mem. Advisory Council, Princeton Inst. for Int. and Regional Studies; has served on Governance Bd of Center for the Study of Democracy at St Mary's Coll. of Maryland; co-f. journal Foreign Policy; White House Samuel Nelson Drew Award 2000. **Publications:** The 'Tar Baby' Option: American Policy Toward Southern Rhodesia 1976, Third World Radical Regimes: US Policy under Carter and Reagan 1985, Somoza Falling: A Case Study of Washington at Work 1990, Six Nightmares 2001. **Address:** UNICEF House, 3 United Nations Plaza, New York, NY 10017, USA. **Telephone:** (212) 326-7000. **Fax:** (212) 887-7465. **E-mail:** info@unicef.org. **Internet:** www.unicef.org.

LAMY, Pascal Lucien Fernand, MBA; French; *Director-General, World Trade Organization;* b. 8 April 1947, Levallois-Perret (Seine); m. Geneviève Luchaire 1972; three s. **Education:** Lycée Carnot, Paris, Ecole des Hautes Etudes Commerciales, Paris, Inst. d'Etudes Politiques, Ecole Nationale d'Admin, Paris. **Career:** Lt-Commdr (navy); served in Inspection Générale des Finances 1975–79; Sec.-Gen. Mayoux Cttee 1979; Deputy Sec.-Gen., then Sec.-Gen. Interministerial Cttee for the Remodelling of Industrial Structures (CIASI) Treasury Dept 1979–81; Tech. Adviser, then Deputy Dir Office of the Minister for Econ. and Financial Affairs 1981–82; Deputy Dir Office of the Prime Minister (Pierre Mauroy) 1983–84; Chef de Cabinet to Pres. of Comm. of EC (Jacques Delors) 1984–94; Dir Gen. and mem. Exec. Cttee Crédit Lyonnais 1994–99; Commr for Trade, European Comm. 1999–2004; Pres. Asscn 'Notre Europe' 2004–; Assoc. Prof., Institut d'Etudes Politiques, Paris 2004–; Dir Gen. WTO 2005–; Officier, Légion d'honneur 1990, Kt Commdr's Cross (Badge and Star) of the Order of Merit (Germany) 1991, Commdr Order of Merit (Luxembourg) 1995, Officer of the Order of Merit (Gabon) 2000, Order of the Aztec Eagle (Mexico) 2003, Order of Merit (Chile) 2004; Dr hc (Louvain) 2003. **Publications:** Report on Welfare Assistance for Children (co-author) 1979, Report on 'Monde-Europe' (XI Plan of the Commissariat Général au Plan) 1993, L'Europe en première ligne 2002, L'Europe de nos volontés (co-author) 2002, La démocratie monde 2004. **Address:** Office of the Director-General, World Trade Organization, Centre William Rappard, 154 rue de Lausanne, 1211 Geneva, Switzerland. **Telephone:** 227395100. **Fax:** 227395460. **E-mail:** enquiries@wto.org. **Internet:** www.wto.org.

LANDGREN, Karin, BSc, LLM; Swedish; *Special Representative of the Secretary-General and Head, Mission in Liberia (UNMIL) United Nations;* b. 13 Oct. 1957; two c. **Education:** London School of Econs, UK. **Career:** grew up in Japan; spent nearly 20 years with UNHCR, worked extensively with Afghan, Iranian and Vietnamese asylum seekers as Protection Officer for UNHCR in India and as Deputy Rep. in the Philippines 1980s, headed UNHCR office in Bosnia-Herzegovina during the war 1990s, as well as offices in Eritrea and Singapore, later Chief of Standards and Legal Advice, UNHCR, Head of Child Protection, UNICEF 1998–2008, UN Deputy Special Rep. of Sec.-Gen. for Nepal 2008–09, UN Rep. for Nepal and Head of UN Mission in Nepal (UNMIN) 2009–10, Special Rep. and Head, UN Office in Burundi (BNUB) 2010–12, Special Rep. of Sec.-Gen. and Head of UN Mission in Liberia (UNMIL) 2012–; Corresp. Ed. International Legal Materials; mem. Editorial Bd Sec.-Gen.'s Study on Violence against Children 2006; Adjunct Prof., School of Int. and Public Affairs, Columbia Univ., New York, USA. **Publications include:** has published widely on humanitarian, refugee and child protection issues. **Address:** UNMIL, PO Box 4677, Grand Central Station, New York, NY 10163-4677, USA. **Telephone:** (212) 963-9925. **Internet:** unmil.unmissions.org.

LAPOINTE, Carman L.; Canadian; *Under-Secretary-General, United Nations Office of Internal Oversight Services;* b. 1951, Virden, Manitoba; three c. **Education:** Algonquin Coll., Colorado State Univ., USA. **Career:** has held chief oversight positions in several Canadian crown corpns, including Corp. Auditor with Canada Post Corpn, Auditor of Bank of Canada, Vice-Pres. Internal Audit and Evaluation with Export Development Canada; fmr Chair. and mem. OSCE Audit Cttee; fmr mem. UNRWA Audit Cttee; Chair. Inst. of Internal Auditors 1994–95; Auditor Gen. World Bank Group 2004–09; Dir Office of Audit and Oversight, IFAD 2009–10; Under-Sec.-Gen., Office of Internal Oversight Services, UN, New York 2010–; mem. Standards Task Force, International Federation of Accountants; mem. Criteria of Control Bd, Canadian Inst. of Chartered Accountants. **Address:** Office of Internal Oversight Services, United Nations, New York, NY 10017, USA. **Telephone:** (212) 963-1234. **Fax:** (212) 963-4879. **Internet:** www.un.org/Depts/oios.

LAROCQUE, Irwin, MA; Dominican; *Secretary-General, Caribbean Community and Common Market (CARICOM);* m.; c. **Education:** Queen's Coll., New School for Social Research, New York Univ., USA. **Career:** served in numerous civil service positions for more than 18 years in Dominica including as Perm. Sec. in Ministries of Trade, Industry, Enterprise Devt, Tourism, and Foreign Affairs, also Prin. Adviser to govt on regional integration and int. trade, Sr Policy Adviser on revision of Treaty of Chaguaramas; Asst Sec.-Gen. for Trade and Econ. Integration, Caribbean Community and Common Market (CARICOM) Secr. 2005–11, Sec.-Gen. CARICOM 2011–. **Address:** Caribbean Community and Common Market (CARICOM), POB 10827, Georgetown, Guyana. **Telephone:** (2) 222-0001. **Fax:** (2) 222-0171. **E-mail:** info@caricom.org. **Internet:** www.caricom.org.

LEBEDEV, Col-Gen. Sergei Nikolayevich; Russian; *Executive Secretary, Commonwealth of Independent States;* b. 9 April 1948, Jizzax, Uzbek SSR; m. Vera Mikhailovna; two s. **Education:** Kyiv Polytechnic Inst., Ukrainian SSR, Diplomatic Acad. of USSR. **Career:** staff mem., Chernihiv br., Kyiv Polytechnic Inst. 1970; army service 1971–72; with state security bodies 1973–75, Foreign Intelligence Service 1975–78; Rep. of Foreign Intelligence Service to USA 1998–2000; Dir Fed. Foreign Intelligence Service (SVR) 2000–07; Exec. Sec. Commonwealth of Independent States (CIS) 2007–; numerous state awards. **Address:** Office of the Executive Secretary, Commonwealth of Independent States, 220000 Minsk, vul. Kirova 17, Belarus. **Telephone:** (17) 222-35-17. **Fax:** (17) 227-23-39. **E-mail:** anna@cis.minsk.by. **Internet:** www.cis.minsk.by.

LIPTON, David, BA, MA, PhD; American; *First Deputy Managing Director, International Monetary Fund.* **Education:** Wesleyan Univ., Harvard Univ. **Career:** economist, IMF, Washington, DC 1981–89; econ. advisor (with Harvard Univ. Prof. Jeffrey Sachs) to govts of Russia, Poland, Slovenia 1989–92; Fellow, Woodrow Wilson Center of Scholars 1992–93; Under-Sec. for Int. Affairs, US Treasury Dept, Washington, DC 1993–98; Man. Dir Moore Capital Strategy Group, Moore Capital Management 2000–05; Man. Dir and Head of Global Country Risk Man. Citigroup 2005–08; Special Asst to US President Obama, Sr Dir for Int. Econ. Affairs, Nat. Econ. Council and Nat. Security Council, The White House 2008–11; Special Advisor to Man. Dir, IMF July–Nov. 2011, First Deputy Man. Dir 2011–; mem. Nat. Advisory Bd, Merage Foundation for the American Dream. **Address:** International Monetary Fund, 700 19th St, NW, Washington, DC 20431, USA. **Telephone:** (202) 623-7000. **Fax:** (202) 623-4661. **Internet:** www.imf.org.

LOPES, Carlos, PhD; Guinea-Bissau; *Executive Secretary (designate), United Nations Economic Commission for Africa;* b. 7 March 1960. **Education:** Univ. of Geneva, Univ. of Paris 1 Panthéon-Sorbonne, France. **Career:** taught at univs in Lisbon, Coimbra, Zurich, Uppsala, Mexico, San Paulo and Rio de Janeiro; fmr consultant for UNESCO, Swedish Int. Devt Cooperation Agency, UN Econ. Comm. for Africa, Research and Technological Exchange Group, Ruraltec Switzerland; Devt Economist, UNDP 1988, then Deputy Dir Office of Evaluation and Strategic Planning, Resident Rep. in Zimbabwe, Deputy, then Dir Bureau for Devt Policy, Asst Admin. UNDP, UN Resident Co-ordinator and UNDP Resident Rep. in Brazil 2003–05; apptd Dir Exec. Office of Sec.-Gen. in charge of Political, Peace-keeping and Humanitarian affairs 2005; Exec. Dir UNITAR 2007–12; Exec. Sec., UN Econ. Comm. for Africa 2012–; fmr Dir UN System Staff Coll.; elected to Lisbon Acad. of Sciences, Portugal 2008; mem. Instituto Ethos, Ecôle Polytechnique Fédérale de Lausanne, King Baudouin International Development Prize Selection Committee; mem. Advisory Bd Kofi Annan Foundation, UNESCO Int. Inst. for Educational Planning, Bonn Int. Center for Conversion, Swiss Network for Int. Studies; mem. Editorial Cttee Géopolitique Africaine, African Sociological Review, African Identities, Cooperation South Journal; Dr hc (Univ. of Cândido, Brazil). **Address:** United Nations Economic Commission for Africa, PO Box 3001, Addis Ababa, Ethiopia. **Telephone:** (11) 5443336. **Fax:** (11) 5514416. **E-mail:** ecaweb@uneca.org. **Internet:** www.uneca.org.

LUCK, Edward C., BA, MA, MIA, MPhil, PhD; American; *Special Adviser to the Secretary-General, United Nations;* b. 17 Oct. 1948; m.; one d. **Education:** Dartmouth Coll., Hanover, NH, Columbia Univ., New York. **Career:** Founder and Exec. Dir Center for the Study of Int. Org. (research centre jointly est. by School of Law, New York Univ. and Woodrow Wilson School of Public and Int. Affairs, Princeton Univ.) –2001; Prof. in the Professional Practice of Int. Affairs, School of Int. and Public Affairs, Columbia Univ. and Dir Center on Int. Org. 2001– (currently on public service leave); Vice-Pres. and Dir of Studies, Int. Peace Acad. 2008–09; Sr Consultant, Dept of Admin and Man., UN 1995–97, Staff Dir Gen. Ass.'s Open-ended High-level Working Group on the Strengthening of the United Nations System 1995–97, adviser to Pres. of Gen. Ass. on proposals for Security Council reform 1995–97, fmr sr consultant to Sec.-Gen.'s Special Rep. for Children and Armed Conflict, fmr mem. Sec.-Gen.'s Policy Working Group on the UN and Terrorism, Special Adviser at Asst Sec.-Gen. level to Sec.-Gen., UN 2008–; served in several research and man. capacities, UNA of the USA 1974–84, Pres. and CEO 1984–94, Pres. Emer. 1994–98; fmr Visiting Prof., Sciences-Po, Paris; fmr consultant to numerous pvt. foundations and research centres. **Publications:** Mixed Messages: American Politics and International Organization, 1919–1999 1999, International Law and Organization: Closing the Compliance Gap (co-ed.) 2004, The UN Security Council: Practice and Promise 2006; has published numerous articles in Foreign Policy, Washington Quarterly, Current History, Disarmament, and other scholarly journals, as well as in the New York Times, Washington Post, Los Angeles Times, Christian Science Monitor, International Herald Tribune, USA Today, Newsday, and other newspapers. **Address:** Office of the Secretary-General, UN Headquarters, First Ave at 46th St, New York, NY 10017, USA. **Telephone:** (212) 854-1794. **E-mail:** info@un.org. **Internet:** www.un.org.

LUNDIN, Jan, BA; Swedish; *Director-General, Council of the Baltic Sea States Secretariat;* m.; two d. **Education:** Univ. of Uppsala, Univ. of Stockholm. **Career:** several years with Swedish Ministry of Foreign Affairs (MFA), served at Embassy in Yugoslavia 1984–86, First Sec., Embassy in Lithuania 1992–94, Counsellor, Embassy in Russian Fed. 1994–96, Counsellor and Deputy Head of Mission, Embassy in Serbia, Deputy Head of Mission and Head of Political Dept, Embassy in Germany 1996–2000, Co-ordinator, Stability Pact for SE Europe, Ministry of Foreign Affairs 1999; Researcher, Stockholm Inst. for Soviet and E European Econs and Politics, Uppsala Univ. 1987–88; European Exec. Dir Russian–European Centre for Econ. Policy 1998–99; Dir-Gen., Council of the Baltic Sea States Secr. 2010–. **Address:** Council of the Baltic Sea States Secretariat, POB 2010, Slussplan 9, 103 11 Stockholm, Sweden. **Telephone:** (8) 440-19-20. **Fax:** (8) 440-19-20. **E-mail:** cbss@cbss.org. **Internet:** www.cbss.org.

MAALIM, Mahboub M., BSc, MSc; Kenyan; *Executive Secretary, Intergovernmental Authority on Development (IGAD);* b. Garissa. **Education:** Univ. of Texas, USA. **Career:** Dist Water Engineer, Ministry of Water 1985–94; Nat. Co-ordinator Arid Lands Resource Man. Project 1996–2004; Perm. Sec. Ministry of Water and Irrigation 2006–08; Exec. Sec. IGAD 2008–; Assoc. mem. American Soc. of Civil Engineers. **Address:** Office of the Executive Secretary, IGAD Secretariat, Ave Georges Clemenceau, PO Box 2653, Djibouti, Republic of Djibouti. **Telephone:** 356452. **Fax:** 353520. **E-mail:** igad@igad.org. **Internet:** www.igad.org.

MAHIGA, Augustine Philip, BA, MA, PhD; Tanzanian; *Special Representative of the Secretary-General and Head, Political Office for Somalia, United Nations;* b. 28 Aug. 1945; m. **Education:** Univ. of East Africa, Dar-es-Salaam, Univ. of Toronto, Canada. **Career:** Sr Lecturer in Int. Affairs and Regional Co-operation, Univ. of Dar-es-Salaam 1975–77; Dir of Research and Training, Office of the Pres. of Tanzania 1977–80, Acting Dir Gen. Office of the Pres. 1980–83; High Commr to Canada 1983–89; Amb. and Perm. Rep. to UN, Geneva 1989–92; on secondment to UNHCR 1993, UNHCR Chief of Mission, Monrovia, Liberia 1992–94, Deputy Dir and Co-ordinator Great Lakes Region of Africa Refugee Emergency Operation, Geneva 1994–98, UNHCR Chief of Mission, New Delhi 1998–2002, UNHCR Rep. to Italy (also accred to Malta and San Marino) 2002–03; Amb. and Perm. Rep. to UN, New York 2003–10, Head of del. to UN Security Council 2005, also Asst

Sec.-Gen. for Peace-building Support for UN Peace-building Comm., Special Rep. for Somalia and Head of UN Political Office for Somalia (UNPOS) 2010–; Lifetime Achievement Award, Miracle Corners of the World 2007. **Address:** UN Political Office for Somalia (UNPOS), PO Box 48246-00100, Nairobi, Kenya. **Telephone:** (20) 7622131. **Fax:** (20) 7622697. **Internet:** www.un-somalia.org.

MALCORRA, Susana; Argentine; *Chef de Cabinet to the Executive Office, United Nations;* b. 1954; m.; one s. **Education:** Univ. of Rosario. **Career:** grad. trainee with IBM, eventually becoming Dir of Public Sector, later assigned to IBM's corp. HQ in USA where she oversaw relations between HQ and Mexico and the Andean region of Latin America –1993; various admin. positions with Telecom Argentina 1993–2003, COO and Exec. Dir 1995–2001, CEO 2001–02; co-f. Vectis Management 2002; Deputy Exec. Dir (Admin) WFP 2004–07 (led initial phase of operational response to tsunami emergency Dec. 2004), Deputy Exec. Dir and COO Jan.–March 2008, Under-Sec.-Gen. and Head of Dept of Field Support, UN 2008–12, Chef de Cabinet to the Exec. Office 2012–; Founding mem. Argentine chapter, Int. Women's Forum; mem. Advisory Bd of Business School of Univ. of San Andres, Buenos Aires, Advisory Bd of Equidad. **Address:** United Nations, New York, NY 10017, USA. **Telephone:** (212) 963-1234. **Fax:** (212) 963-4879. **Internet:** www.un.org.

MANNAI, Jassim Abdullah al-, PhD; Bahraini; *Director-General and Chairman, Arab Monetary Fund;* b. 1948. **Education:** Univ. of the Sorbonne, Paris, France and Harvard Business School. **Career:** Exec. Vice-Pres. Gulf Investment Corpn, Kuwait 1987–94; CEO and Chair. Arab Trade Financing Program, Abu Dhabi 1994–; Dir-Gen. and Chair. Arab Monetary Fund, Abu Dhabi 1994–; Chair. Inter Arab Rating Co. EC (mem. Fitch IBCA Group) 1995–2001. **Publications:** numerous articles on economic and financial issues in various publs. **Address:** Office of the Director-General, Arab Monetary Fund Building, Corniche Road, PO Box 2818, Abu Dhabi, United Arab Emirates. **Telephone:** (2) 6171400. **Fax:** (2) 6326454. **E-mail:** centralmail@amfad.org.ae. **Internet:** www.amf.org.ae.

MANSARAY, Binta, BA, MA; Sierra Leonean; *Registrar, Special Court for Sierra Leone, United Nations.* **Education:** Fourah Bay Coll., Univ. of Sierra Leone, Fordham Univ., USA. **Career:** fmr human rights advocate for victims and ex-combatants with several orgs; held post of Country Rep. for Women's Comm. for Refugee Women and Children in Sierra Leone, worked with Campaign for Good Governance, and served as consultant with UN Mission in Sierra Leone (UNAMSIL) and several civil soc. orgs; Outreach Co-ordinator, UN Special Court for Sierra Leone, Freetown 2003–07, Deputy Registrar, Special Court for Sierra Leone 2007–09, Acting Registrar 2009–10, Registrar 2010–. **Address:** The Special Court for Sierra Leone, PO Box 19536, 2500 CM The Hague, The Netherlands. **Telephone:** (70) 5159750. **Fax:** (70) 3222711. **Internet:** www.sc-sl.org.

MAROOFI, Mohammad Yahya; Afghan; *Secretary-General, Economic Cooperation Organization;* b. (b. Beryalai Maroofi), 5 March 1939, Kabul; m. Soraya Ludin Maroofi; one s. one d. **Education:** Kabul Univ., Fairleigh Dickson Univ., USA. **Career:** mem. Law and Treaties Dept, Ministry of Foreign Affairs 1965–66, Secr. of Minister of Foreign Affairs 1966–6, Attaché, Perm. Mission of Afghanistan to UN, New York 1969–73, mem. UN and Int. Relations Dept, Ministry of Foreign Affairs 1973–74, Deputy Dir UN Affairs and Int. Relations Dept 1974–77, Dir 1977–79; Nat. Co-ordinator of Narcotics, Govt of Afghanistan 1977–79; Regional Adviser, Regional Rep. and Diplomatic Liaison for S and Cen. Asia and Special Envoy of Dir Gen. of Int. Org. for Migration for Afghanistan, Iran and Pakistan 1984–99; Minister, Advisor on Int. Relations to Pres. of Afghanistan 2002–04; mem. Nat. Security Council 2002–04; Amb. to Norway (also accred to Denmark, Sweden, Iceland and Finland) 2004–07, to Iran 2007–09, Perm. Rep. to ECO, Tehran 2007–09, Amb. (non-resident) to Azerbaijan 2008–09; Sec.-Gen. ECO 2009–; various acknowledgements of services as Sr Govt Official, Diplomat and Int. Civil Servant; Struggle Against the Occupation of the Soviet Union. **Address:** Economic Cooperation Organization Secretariat, 1 Golobu Alley, Kamranieh, PO Box 14155-6176, Tehran, Iran. **Telephone:** (21) 22831733. **Fax:** (21) 22831732. **E-mail:** sg@ecosecretariat.org; www.ecosecretariat.org.

MARTIN, Ian; British; *Special Representative of the Secretary-General for Libya and Head, United Nations Support Mission in Libya (UNSMIL);* b. 10 Aug. 1946. **Career:** Community Relations Officer, Redbridge Community Relations Council 1973–75, Councillor, London Borough of Redbridge 1978–82; Head of Asia Research Dept, Amnesty International 1985–86, Sec.-Gen. 1986–92; Sr Assoc., Carnegie Endowment for International Peace, Washington, DC 1993; Dir of Human Rights and Deputy Exec. Dir UN Mission to Haiti 1993–95, Chief of UN Human Rights Field Operation, Rwanda 1995–96, also served in Office of High Rep. in Bosnia, Deputy High Rep. Human Rights Field Operation in Bosnia and Herzegovina 1998–99, Dir Human Rights, International Civilian Mission in Haiti, Special Rep. for East Timor Popular Consultation 1999; Deputy Special Rep. of Sec.-Gen. UN Mission in Ethiopia and Eritrea 2000–01; Vice-Pres. International Centre for Transitional Justice 2002–05; UN human rights adviser during Sri Lankan peace process 2003–05, Rep. to UN High Commr for Human Rights, Nepal 2005–06, Special Envoy for Timor-Leste 2006, Special Rep. of Sec.-Gen. in Nepal 2006–09, Head of HQ Bd of Inquiry, Gaza Strip 2009, Special Adviser to Sec.-Gen. on Post-Conflict Planning for Libya –2011, Special Rep. of the Sec.-Gen. for Libya and Head, UN Support Mission in Libya (UNSMIL) 2011–. **Publications include:** Immigration Law and Practice (co-author) 1982, Self-Determination in East Timor 2001: the United Nations, the Ballot, and International Intervention. **Address:** United Nations Support Mission in Libya (UNSMIL), Department of Political Affairs, United Nations, New York, NY 10017, USA. **Telephone:** (212) 963-1234. **Fax:** (212) 963-4879. **Internet:** unsmil.unmissions.org.

MATAKA, Elizabeth; Botswanan; *Special Envoy to the Secretary-General for HIV/AIDS in Africa, United Nations;* b. 1946, Francistown; m.; four c. **Education:** Univ. of Zambia. **Career:** several years' experience in the field of HIV/AIDS with govt insts, private sector and non-govt orgs in Zambia; Founder and Exec. Dir Family Health Trust, Lusaka 1990–2003; fmr Vice-Chair. Global Fund to Fight AIDS, Tuberculosis and Malaria; Exec. Dir Zambia Nat. AIDS Network 2003–07; Special Envoy of UN Sec.-Gen. for HIV/AIDS in Africa 2007–; mem. Advisory Bd UNESCO, North Star Foundation; mem. Reference Group, Swedish /Norwegian HIV/AIDS Team for Africa; Dir Centre for Infectious Disease Research, Zambia; Dir and Chair. Children Int. Zambia; Founder-mem. Southern African Network of AIDS Service Orgs; mem. Compact Working Group on Gender, Global Task Force on Women, Girls Gender Equality and HIV 2009–. **Address:** UNAIDS Secretariat, 20 ave Appia, 1211 Geneva 27, Switzerland. **Telephone:** 227913666. **Fax:** 227914187. **E-mail:** communications@unaids.org. **Internet:** www.specialenvoyforaidsinafrica.org.

MAURER, Peter, PhD; Swiss; *President, International Committee of the Red Cross;* b. 20 Nov. 1956, Thun; m. Doris Maurer-Scheidegger; two d. **Education:** Univ. of Bern, Univ. of Perugia, Italy. **Career:** joined Fed. Dept of Foreign Affairs 1987, served as Diplomatic Adviser, Political Secr. 1989–91, Pvt. Sec. to State Sec. for Foreign Affairs 1991–96; Deputy Perm. Observer to Observer Mission to UN, New York 1996–2000; Head, Political Affairs Div. IV (Human Security), Political Affairs Govt Directorate 2000–04; Amb. and Perm. Rep. to UN, New York 2004–10, Head of Fifth Comm. (overseeing budget and admin. matters); Sec. of State, Fed. Dept of Foreign Affairs 2010–12; Pres. International Cttee of the Red Cross 2012–. **Address:** International Committee of the Red Cross (ICRC), 19 ave de la Paix, 1202 Geneva, Switzerland. **Telephone:** 227346001. **Fax:** 227332057. **E-mail:** press.gva@icrc.org. **Internet:** www.icrc.org.

MAVRIKOS, George; Greek; *General Secretary, World Federation of Trade Unions.* **Career:** Deputy Pres. Gen. Confed. of Workers in Greece; Sec. All Workers Militant Front (PAME) (a CP of Greece-affiliated trade union); Vice-Pres. WFTU and Co-ordinator of its European Office –2005, Gen. Sec. WFTU

2005–. **Address:** World Federation of Trade Unions, 40 Zan Moreas Str., 117 45 Athens, Greece. **Telephone:** (21) 09236700. **Fax:** (21) 09214517. **E-mail:** info@wftucentral .org. **Internet:** www.wftucentral.org.

MEECE, Roger A., BS; American; *Special Representative of the Secretary General and Head, United Nations Organization Stabilization Mission in the Democratic Republic of the Congo (MONUSCO);* b. 1949, Indianapolis, IN. **Education:** Michigan State Univ., Nat. Defence Coll. of Canada, Kingston, US Foreign Service Inst., Arlington. **Career:** Peace Corps volunteer in Sierra Leone 1971, several Peace Corps staff assignments, including Assoc. Dir for Peace Corps in Niger and Cameroon, Deputy Dir for Peace Corps, Brazzaville, Repub. of the Congo, Dir Peace Corps in Gabon; joined Foreign Service 1979, served in Embassies in Cameroon and Malawi, worked in Bureau of Int. Narcotics Matters, Washington, DC, assigned to Office of Vice-Pres. of the USA 1986–88, Deputy Chief of Mission, Brazzaville, Consul-Gen., Halifax, Canada, Deputy Chief of Mission, Kinshasa 1995–98, Dir for Cen. African Affairs, State Dept 1998–2000, Amb. to Malawi 2000–03, Diplomat-in-Residence, Florida Int. Univ. 2003, served as Chargé d'affaires a.i., Embassy in Nigeria 2003, Amb. to Democratic Repub. of the Congo 2004–07, Chargé d'affaires a.i., Embassy in Ethiopia 2010; Special Rep. of the Sec.-Gen. and Head, UN Org. Stabilization Mission in the Democratic Repub. of the Congo (MONUSCO) 2010–. **Address:** UN Organization Stabilization Mission in the Democratic Republic of the Congo (MONUSCO), BP 8811, Kinshasa, Democratic Republic of the Congo. **Telephone:** (81) 8906000. **Fax:** (81) 89056208. **Internet:** www.monuc.unmissions.org.

MENKERIOS, Haile, MA; South African (b. Eritrean); *Special Envoy of the Secretary-General for Sudan and South Sudan, United Nations;* b. 1 Oct. 1946, Adi Felesti; m. Hebret Berhe 1979 (divorced); one s. one d. **Education:** Addis Ababa Univ., Brandeis and Harvard Univs, USA. **Career:** Teaching Fellow, Harvard Univ. 1971–73; guerilla fighter in Eritrean People's Liberation Army (EPLA) 1973–74; Head of Tigrigna Section, Dept of Information and Propaganda, Eritrean People's Liberation Front (EPLF) 1974–75, mem. Foreign Relations Cttee 1976–77, mem. Cen. Council 1977–2001, Deputy Head of Dept of Foreign Relations 1977–79, Head of Research Div., Political, Educ. and Culture Dept 1979–86; Dir Research and Information Centre of Eritrea 1986–87; Head, Research and Policy Div., Dept of Foreign Relations 1987–90; Gov. of East and South Zone of Eritrea 1990–91; mem. Eritrean Nat. Council 1991–2001; Rep. of Provisional Govt of Eritrea to Ethiopia 1991–93; Special Envoy of Pres. to Somalia 1991–96, to the Greater Lakes Region 1996–97; mem. High Level Horn of Africa Cttee on Somalia 1993–95; Amb. of State of Eritrea to Ethiopia and OAU 1993–96; Perm. Rep. of State of Eritrea to UN 1997–2001; Chair. UN Cttee of Experts re Sanctions on arms and terrorist camps, Afghanistan 2001; Sr Adviser to Special Envoy of Sec.-Gen. to the Inter-Congolese Dialogue 2002–03; Dir Africa Div., UN Dept of Political Affairs 2003–05; UN Sec.-Gen.'s Deputy Special Rep. for UN Mission in the Democratic Repub. of the Congo (MONUC) 2005–07; UN Asst Sec.-Gen. for Political Affairs 2007–10; UN Sec.-Gen.'s Special Rep. for the Sudan and Head of UN Mission in Sudan (UNMIS) 2010–11; Special Envoy of the Sec.-Gen. for Sudan and South Sudan, UN 2011–; mem. Advisory Bd, Conflict Prevention and Peace Forum; Fellow, Rift Valley Inst.; Medal of Honour for the fight against Genocide (Pres. of Rwanda), Medal of Recognition for support to the Liberation of Rwanda (Pres. of Rwanda). **Publications include:** various articles on African politics. **Address:** Office of the Secretary-General, United Nations, New York, NY 10017. **Telephone:** (212) 963-1234. **Fax:** (212) 963-4879. **E-mail:** menkerios@ un.org. **Internet:** www.un.org.

MOHIELDIN, Mahmoud, BS, MS, PhD; Egyptian; *Managing Director, World Bank Group;* b. 15 Jan. 1965. **Education:** Cairo Univ., Univs of Warwick, York, UK. **Career:** Prof. of Financial Economics, Cairo Univ. 1995–; held several positions in Egyptian govt, including Econ. Adviser to Minister of State for Econ. Affairs, Sr Econ. Adviser to Minister of Economy and Foreign Trade, Sr Adviser to Minister of Foreign Trade; Minister of Investment 2004–10, also served as Gov. of Egypt to World Bank, Alt. Gov. to AfDB, Alt. Gov. Islamic Development Bank; Man. Dir World Bank Group, Washington, DC 2010–; fmr mem. Bd of Dirs Central Bank of Egypt; mem. Bd of Trustees, British Univ. of Egypt; mem. Center of European Studies, Arab Soc. for Econ. Research, Comm. on Growth and Devt. **Address:** World Bank Group, 1818 H St, NW, Washington, DC 20433, USA. **Telephone:** (202) 473-1000. **Fax:** (202) 477-6391. **Internet:** www.worldbank.org.

MOOD, Maj.-Gen. Robert; Norwegian; *Chief Military Observer and Head, United Nations Supervision Mission in Syria (UNSMIS);* b. 8 Dec. 1958, Telemark; m. Eva Tverberg; one s. **Education:** United States Marine Corps Univ., NATO Defense Coll., Rome, Norwegian Army Staff Coll. **Career:** started mil. career 1977, Leader, Operations Officer, Norwegian Bn, UN Interim Force in Lebanon (UNIFIL) 1989–90, Lt Commdr, Telemark Bn 1993–94; achieved rank of Lt Colonel 1996; Operations Officer, 6th Div. –1998; Head of Telemark Bn 1999–2000, Chief of Planning Branch, High Command 2000–02, Chief of Hærens Kampvåpen 2002–04, Chief, Army Transformation and Doctrine Command (TRADOK) 2004–05, Chief of Staff 2005–09; Chief, Jt Implementation Comm., KFOR Command Group; Commanding Officer, Norwegian Army Transformation and Doctrine Command; Head of Mission and Chief of Staff, UN Truce Supervision Org. (UNTSO) 2009–11; Insp.-Gen. Veteran Affairs, Defence Veteran Services (FVT) 2011–12; Chief Mil. Observer and Head of Mission, UN Supervision Mission in Syria (UNSMIS) 2012–; Badge of Honour, Norwegian Veteran Asscn of Int. Operations; Defense Service Medal, Armed Forces Medal for Int. Operations, Army Nat. Service Medal, UN Medal for Truce Supervision Org., UN Medal for UN Interim Force in Lebanon, NATO Medal for Kosovo. **Address:** United Nations Supervision Mission in Syria (UNSMIS), Department of Peace-keeping Operations, Room S-3727-B, United Nations, New York, NY 10017, USA. **Telephone:** (212) 963-8077. **Fax:** (212) 963-9222. **Internet:** www.un.org/en/peacekeeping/ missions/unsmis.

MORENO-MEJÍA, Luis Alberto, BA, MBA; Colombian; *President, Inter-American Development Bank;* b. 3 May 1953, Philadelphia, USA; m. Gabriela Febres-Cordero 1970; one s. one d. **Education:** Florida Int. Univ., Thunderbird Univ., Phoenix, Ariz. and Harvard Univs. **Career:** Div. Man. Praco 1977–82; exec. producer of nationwide nightly news programme and other entertainment and children's programmes 1982–90; Neiman Fellow, Harvard Univ. 1990–91; Pres. Inst. de Foment Industrial 1991–92; Minister of Econ. Devt 1992–94; telecommunications adviser and pvt. consultant, Luis Carlos Sarmiento Org., Bogotá 1994–97; Pnr, Westsphere Andean Advisers 1997–98; Campaign Man. of Andrés Pastrana 1994; Amb. to USA 1998–2005; Pres. IDB, Washington, DC 2005–; Orden al Mérito Civil Ciudad de Bogotá, en el Grado de Gran Cruz, awarded by Mayor of Bogotá 1990, Orden al Mérito Industrial – José Gutiérrez Gómez, Colombian Nat. Business Asscn 2002, Orden de Boyacá en el Grado de Gran Cruz awarded by the Pres. of Colombia 2002; King of Spain Prize for journalistic excellence. **Publications include:** articles on Colombian and int. politics and econs for publs in Colombia and USA; writings have appeared in New York Times, Boston Globe, Miami Herald, El Tiempo, Foreign Affairs en Español and Semana. **Address:** Inter-American Development Bank, 1300 New York Ave, NW, Washington, DC 20577, USA. **Telephone:** (202) 623-1000. **Fax:** (202) 623-3096. **E-mail:** pic@iadb.org. **Internet:** www.iadb.org.

MOUSSA, Abou; Chadian; *Special Representative of the Secretary-General and Head, United Nations Regional Office for Central Africa (UNOCA);* b. 1950; m.; three c. **Education:** Univ. of Lagos, Nigeria, Advanced School of Journalism, France, Univ. of Paris 1 Panthéon-Sorbonne. **Career:** joined UNHCR 1980, served in several duty stations, including Democratic Repub. of Congo, Switzerland, Ethiopia, Zambia fmr Regional Dir for West Africa; Rep. of Sec.-Gen. and Head of UN Peace-building Support Office in Liberia (UNOL) 2002–03, Deputy Special Rep. of Sec.-Gen., Humanitarian Co-ordinator and UN Devt Programme Resident, Rep. for Liberia 2003–05, Prin. Deputy Rep. of Sec.-Gen. in Côte d'Ivoire 2005–11, Special Rep. of Sec.-Gen. and Head, UN Regional Office for Central Africa

(UNOCA) 2011–. **Address:** United Nations Regional Office for Central Africa (UNOCA), Department of Political Affairs, United Nations, New York, NY 10017, USA. **Telephone:** (212) 963-1234. **Fax:** (212) 963-4879. **Internet:** www.un.org/Depts/dpa.

MUTABOBA, Joseph, MPhil; Rwandan; *Special Representative of the Secretary-General for Guinea-Bissau and Head of United Nations Integrated Peace-Building Office in Guinea-Bissau (UNIOGBIS), United Nations;* b. 21 Dec. 1949; m.; three c. **Education:** North London Univ., UK. **Career:** served as Sec.-Gen. in Ministries of Foreign Affairs and of Internal Affairs, as Deputy Nat. Co-ordinator for Rwanda and Head of Peace and Security thematic group in Int. Conf. on Great Lakes Region, and as sr diplomat in Addis Ababa and Washington, DC; Perm. Rep. to UN, New York 1999–2001; Pres. of Rwanda's Special Envoy to Great Lakes Region –2009; Rep. of UN Sec.-Gen. for Guinea-Bissau and Head of UN Integrated Peace-building Office in Guinea-Bissau (UNIOGBIS) 2009–. **Address:** UNIOGBIS, Predio das Nações Unidas, Rua Rui Djassi, CP 179, PO Box 1011, Bissau, Guinea-Bissau. **Telephone:** 203618. **Fax:** 203613. **E-mail:** webmaster@uniogbis.org. **Internet:** uniogbis.unmissions.org.

NABARRO, David, BA, MA, MSc, CBE, FRCP; British; *Special Representative of the Secretary-General on Food Security and Nutrition, United Nations;* b. 26 Aug. 1949, London; m. Gillian Frances Holmes 2002; one s. one d.; two s. one d. from previous relationship. **Education:** Worcester Coll., Oxford, Univ. Coll. Hosp., Univ. of London. **Career:** began career as Medical Officer, Save the Children Fund, later postings include Relief Expedition, N Iraq 1974–75, Dist Medical Officer, Dhankuta, E Nepal 1977–79, Regional Medical Adviser, S Asia, Kathmandu, Nepal 1982–85; House Officer, later Sr House Officer with Nat. Health Service 1975–77; Lecturer in Nutrition and Public Health, London Univ. 1980–82; Sr Lecturer in Int. Health, Liverpool Univ. Medical School 1985–89, also Hon. Consultant, Mersey Regional Health Authority; Regional Health and Population Adviser, E Africa, British Govt Overseas Devt Admin (ODA) 1989–90, Chief Health and Population Adviser and Head of Health and Population Div., ODA 1990–97 (renamed British Govt Dept for Int. Devt, DFID 1997) 1997–99; Project Man., Roll Back Malaria, WHO, Geneva 1999–2000, Exec. Dir Office of the Dir-Gen., WHO 2000–02, Exec. Dir Sustainable Devt and Sr Policy Adviser to Dir-Gen. 2002–03, Rep of Dir-Gen. for Health Action in Crises 2003–05; Sr Co-ordinator for Avian and Human Influenza, UN Devt Group, New York 2005–; Deputy UN System Co-ordinator for Global Food Security Crisis 2008; Special Rep. of Sec.-Gen. on Food Security and Nutrition, UN 2009–. **Address:** Office of the Secretary-General, UN Headquarters, First Ave at 46th St, New York, NY 10017, USA. **Internet:** www.un.org.

NAMBIAR, Vijay K., MA; Indian; *Special Adviser of the Secretary General on Myanmar, United Nations;* b. Aug. 1943, Poona (now Pune); m. Malini Nambiar; two d. **Education:** Univ. of Bombay. **Career:** joined Foreign Service 1967, early years specializing in Chinese language and serving in Hong Kong and Beijing; subsequent posts included Belgrade, Yugoslavia in mid-1970s; numerous bilateral and multilateral postings in Beijing, Belgrade and New York in 1970s and 1980s, also Jt Sec. (Dir Gen.) for E Asia 1988 and multilateral affairs at New Delhi HQ 1980s; Amb. to Algeria 1985–88, to Afghanistan 1990–92, to Malaysia 1993–96, to China 1996–2000, to Pakistan 2000–01; Perm. Rep. to UN, New York 2002–04; Deputy Nat. Security Adviser (DNSA) and Head, Nat. Security Council Secr. 2005–06; Under-Sec.-Gen. and Special Adviser to UN Sec.-Gen., New York 2006–07, Chef de Cabinet (Chief of Staff), UN Sec.-Gen. 2007–12, Special Adviser of the Sec.-Gen. on Myanmar, UN 2012–; Chancellor's Gold Medal, Univ. of Bombay 1965. **Address:** Office of the Secretary-General, United Nations, New York, NY 10017, USA. **Telephone:** (212) 963-1234. **Fax:** (212) 963-4879. **Internet:** www.un.org.

NAQI, Abbas Ali, BComm; Kuwaiti; *Secretary-General, Organization of Arab Petroleum Exporting Countries;* b. 1947. **Education:** Kuwait Univ., Univ. of Southern California, USA. **Career:** Financial Accountant, State Budget, Ministry of Finance and Oil 1971–75, Controller, Oil and Gas Marketing, Ministry of Oil 1975–81, Controller, Int. Relations and Orgs Dept 1981–84, Dir Econ. Planning and Analysis Dept 1984–89, Dir Oil Accounting and Financial Analysis Dept 1989–94, Asst Under-Sec. for Econ. Affairs 1994–2007, Under-Sec. 2007–08; Sec. Gen. Org. of Arab Petroleum Exporting Countries 2008–, mem. Exec. Bd representing Kuwait 2000–08; Chair. Kuwaiti Nat. Cttee for UN Convention on Climate Change 1994–; Vice Pres. representing Asia, Second UN Convention on Climate Change 1996; Head of Jt Exec. Cttee, Aramco Overseas Co. 2000–02; mem. Bd of Dirs Arab Maritime Petroleum Transport Co. 1977–96, Kuwait Nat. Petroleum Co. 1995–98, Kuwait Oil Co. 1998–2002, Arab Petroleum Investments Corpn 1996–, Kuwait Gulf Oil Co. 2004–07, Kuwait Nat. Petroleum Corpn 2007–; mem. UN Cttee for Sustainable Devt, Kuwait Accountant Soc. **Address:** Organization of Arab Petroleum Exporting Countries, POB 20501, Safat 13066, Kuwait. **Telephone:** 24959000. **Fax:** 24959755. **E-mail:** oateefa@oapecorg.org. **Internet:** www.oapecorg.org.

NASSER, Nassir bin Abdulaziz al-; Qatari; *President, United Nations General Assembly;* b. 15 Sept. 1952, Doha; m. Muna Rihani; one s. **Career:** joined Ministry of Foreign Affairs (MFA) 1971, Attaché, Embassy in Beirut 1972–74, mem. Qatari Del. to Org. of the Islamic Conf. 1974–75, Gen. Counsellor, Embassy in Dubai 1975–81, with MFA 1981–85, Deputy Foreign Minister 1984–85, minister at Perm. Mission to UN, New York 1986–93, Amb. to Jordan 1993–98, Amb. and Perm. Rep. to UN, New York 1998–2011, Vice-Pres. UN Gen. Ass. 2002–03, Pres. Security Council Dec. 2006, Chair. Group of 77 2004, Pres. UN Gen. Ass. 2011–; mem. Bd of Advisors, New York Univ. Center for Dialogues; Hon. Fellow, Foreign Policy Asscn, New York 2009; Grand Officer, Order of Merit (Italy) 2004, Medal of Grand Commander of Order of Makarios III (Cyprus) 2007, Nat. Order of Doctor José Matias Delgado (El Salvador) 2007, Commander of Nat. Order (Côte d'Ivoire) 2008; Dr hc (Chongqing Univ.) 2007; Medal of Independence (Jordan) 1998, High Honour Awards (Italy) 2005. **Address:** Office of the President, United Nations General Assembly, New York, NY 10017, USA. **Telephone:** (212) 963-1234. **Fax:** (212) 963-4879. **Internet:** www.un.org/en/ga.

NGWENYA, Sindiso, BSc, MSc; Zimbabwean; *Secretary-General, Common Market for Eastern and Southern Africa (COMESA);* b. 16 April 1951; m.; three c. **Education:** Middlesex Polytechnic, Univ. of Birmingham, UK. **Career:** Corp. Planning Officer, Ethiopia Airlines 1979–80; Planning Officer, Nat. Railways of Zimbabwe 1980–83; Sr Transport Expert, Common Market for Eastern and Southern Africa (COMESA) 1994–98, Asst Sec. Gen., in charge of Programming 1998–2008, Sec. Gen. 2008–; mem. Interim Cttee Food, Agric. and Natural Resources Policy Analysis Network 2007. **Address:** COMESA Secretariat, PO Box 30051, Ben Bella Rd, 101101 Lusaka, Zambia. **Telephone:** (1) 229725. **Fax:** (1) 225107. **E-mail:** webmaster@comesa.int. **Internet:** www.comesa.int.

NOOR, Muhamad; Malaysian; *Executive Director, Asia-Pacific Economic Cooperation (APEC).* **Education:** Univ. of Malaya, Univ. of Wisconsin-Madison, USA, Advanced Man. Programme, Harvard Business School, USA. **Career:** Asst Sec., Int. Affairs Div., Ministry of Plantation Industry and Commodities 1974–84; Trade Commr (Commodities), Malaysian High Comm., London 1984–87; Prin. Asst Sec., Ministry of Plantation Industry and Commodities 1987–96; Head of Planning and Policy Research and Chief Information Officer, Ministry of Human Resources 1996–2001, concurrently Dir of Electronic Labour Exchange Project; Deputy Sec.-Gen., Ministry of Women, Family and Community Devt 2001–03; Amb. and Perm. Rep. to WTO 2003–09, Chair. WTO Negotiating Group on Trade Facilitation 2004–05, Chair. WTO Dispute Settlement Body 2006, Chair. Gen. Council 2007; Exec. Dir APEC 2010–; fmr Chair. Exec. Cttee Int. Rubber Study Group, Man. Bd Int. Tin Research Inst.; fmr Vice-Chair. Int. Cocoa Council; Excellent Public Service Award, Ministry of Plantation Industry and Commodities 1995, Kesatria Mangku Negara, HM King of Malaysia 1996, Darjah Indera Mahkota

Pahang (carries the title Dato'), HRH Sultan of Pahang 2006, Johan Mangku Negara, HM King of Malaysia 2006. **Address:** APEC Secretariat, 35 Heng Mui Keng Terrace, Singapore 119616, Singapore. **Telephone:** 68919600. **Fax:** 68919690. **E-mail:** info@apec.org. **Internet:** www.apec.org.

NOYER, Christian; French; *Chair., Bank for International Settlements;* b. 6 Oct. 1950, Soisy-sous-Montmorency, Val d'Oise. **Education:** Univs of Rennes and Paris, Inst. of Political Science, Ecole Nat. d'Admin. **Career:** mil. service as naval officer 1972; joined French Treasury 1976, Chief of Banking Office, then of Export Credit Office 1982–85, Deputy Dir in charge of Int. Multilateral Issues 1988–90, then of Debt Man., Monetary and Banking Issues 1990–92, Dir of Dept responsible for public holdings and public financing 1992–93, Dir of Treasury 1993–95; financial attaché, French Del. to EC, Brussels 1980–82; Econ. Adviser to Minister for Econ. Affairs and Finance, Edouard Balladur 1986–88, Chief of Staff to E. Alphandéry 1993, to Jean Arthuis 1995–97; Dir, Ministry for Econ. Affairs, Finance and Industry 1997–98; Alt. Gov., IMF and World Bank 1993–95; Vice-Pres., European Cen. Bank 1998–2002; Gov., Banque de France 2003–; Alt. mem. European Monetary Cttee 1988–90, mem. 1993–95, 1998; Alt. mem. G7 and G10 1993–95; mem. Working Party No. 3 OECD 1993–95; Chair. Paris Club of Creditor Countries 1993–97; mem. European Econ. and Financial Cttee 1999–2002; Chair. Bank for Int. Settlements, Basel, Switzerland 2010–; Officier Légion d'honneur, Chevalier Ordre nat. du Mérite, Commdr Nat. Order of the Lion (Senegal), Grand Cross, Orden del Mérito (Spain). **Publications:** Banks: The Rules of the Game 1990; various articles. **Address:** Bank for International Settlements, Centralbahnplatz 2, 4002 Basel, Switzerland. **Telephone:** 612808080. **Fax:** 612809100. **E-mail:** email@bis.org. **Internet:** www.bis.org.

NWANZE, Kanayo F., BSc, MSc, PhD; Nigerian; *President, International Fund for Agricultural Development.* **Education:** Univ. of Ibadan, Kansas State Univ., USA. **Career:** experience in poverty reduction through agric., rural devt and research world-wide since late 1970s; Dir-Gen. Africa Rice Centre (WARDA) for ten years; held sr positions at several research centres affiliated to Consultative Group on Int. Agricultural Research (CGIAR), Chair. Centre Dirs' Cttee, help establish Alliance of CGIAR Centres; Vice-Pres. IFAD, Rome, Italy 2007–09, Pres. 2009–; has served on exec. bds of various insts; mem. several scientific asscns; instrumental in introducing and promoting New Rice for Africa (NERICA), a high-yield, drought- and pest-resistant rice variety developed specifically for the African landscape; numerous prizes and awards. **Publications:** numerous publs and articles in scientific journals. **Address:** International Fund for Agricultural Development, Via Paolo di Dono 44, 00142 Rome, Italy. **Telephone:** (06) 54591. **Fax:** (06) 5043463. **E-mail:** ifad@ifad.org. **Internet:** www.ifad.org.

OBASANJO, Gen. (retd) Olusegun Mathew Okikiola Aremu; Nigerian; *Secretary-General's Special Envoy for the Great Lakes Region, United Nations;* b. 5 March 1937, Abeokuta, Ogun State; m. 1st Oluremi Akinbwon; two s. four d.; m. 2nd Stella Abebe (died 2005). **Education:** Abeokuta Baptist High School and Mons Officers' Cadet School, UK. **Career:** joined Nigerian Army 1958, commissioned 1959; served in Congo (now Democratic Repub. of the Congo) 1960; promoted Capt. 1963, Maj. 1965, Lt-Col 1967, Col 1969, Brig. 1972, Lt-Gen. 1976, Gen. 1979; Commdr Eng Corps 1963, later Commdr 2nd Div. (Rear), Ibadan; GOC 3rd Infantry Div. 1969; Commdr 3rd Marine Commando Div. during Nigerian Civil War, accepted surrender of Biafran forces Jan. 1970; Commdr Eng Corps 1970–75; Fed. Commr for Works and Housing Jan.–July 1975; Chief of Staff, Supreme HQ 1975–76; mem. Supreme Mil. Council 1975–79; Head of Fed. Mil. Govt and C-in-C of Armed Forces 1976–79; mem. Advisory Council of State 1979; farmer 1979–; arrested March 1995, interned 1995; Pres. of Nigeria and C-in-C of Armed Forces 1999–2007; Chair. Bd of Trustees, People's Democratic Party 2007–; UN Special Envoy for the Democratic Repub. of the Congo 2008, for the Great Lakes Region Dec. 2008–; fmr Chair. African Union; Fellow, Univ. of Ibadan 1979–81; mem. Ind. Comm. on Disarmament and Security 1980, mem. Exec. Cttee Inter Action Council of fmr Heads of Govt; Chair. Africa Leadership Forum and Foundation; Co-Chair. Eminent Persons Group on S Africa 1985; Grand Commdr, Order of the Fed. Repub. of Nigeria 1980; Hon. DHumLitt (Howard); Hon. LLD (Maiduguri) 1980, (Ahmadu Bello Univ., Zaria) 1985, (Ibadan) 1988. **Publications:** My Command 1980, Africa in Perspective 'Myths and Realities' 1987, Nzeogwu 1987, Africa Embattled 1988, Constitution for National Integration and Development 1989, Not My Will 1990, Elements of Development 1992, Elements of Democracy 1993, Africa: Rise to Challenge 1993, Hope for Africa 1993, This Animal Called Man 1999, Exemplary Youth in a Difficult World 2002, I See Hope 2002. **Address:** Olusegun Obasanjo Presidential Library Foundation, Presidential Boulevard, Oke-Mosan Abeokuta, Ogun, Nigeria. **Telephone:** (9) 245821; (9) 245690. **E-mail:** info@ooplibrary.org. **Internet:** www.ooplibrary.org.

O'BRIEN, Patricia, BA, MA, BL, LLB; Irish; *Under-Secretary-General for Legal Affairs and Legal Counsel, United Nations;* b. 8 Feb. 1957; m.; three c. **Education:** Trinity Coll., Dublin, Kings Inns, Dublin, Univ. of Ottawa, Canada. **Career:** lawyer, Irish Bar 1979–88; called to Bar of England and Wales 1986; fmr lawyer, Bar of BC, Canada; Lecturer, Dept of Law, Univ. of British Columbia 1989–92; fmr Sr Legal Adviser to Irish Attorney-Gen.; fmr Legal Counsellor, Irish Perm. Representation to EU, Brussels; Legal Adviser, Dept of Foreign Affairs, Dublin 2003–08; Under-Sec.-Gen. for Legal Affairs and Legal Counsel, UN 2008–; Fellow, Soc. for Advanced Legal Studies, Inst. of Advanced Legal Studies, London. **Address:** Office of Legal Affairs, United Nations Headquarters, Room No. 3427A, New York, NY 10017, USA. **Fax:** (212) 963-6430. **Internet:** untreaty.un.org/ola.

ODUNTON, Nii Allotey, MS; Ghanaian; *Secretary-General, International Seabed Authority;* b. 14 June 1951; m. Nijama Odunton; four c. **Education:** Achimeta Secondary School, Accra, Henry Krumb School of Mines, Columbia Univ., USA. **Career:** Mine Planning Officer, Bethlehem Steel Corpn, Morgantown, Pa 1974–75; Econ. Affairs Officer, Dept of Int. Econ. Social Affairs, UN Secr., New York 1980–83, held several other UN positions 1984–88 including Chief of Mineral Resources Section and Ocean Econs and Tech. Br., First Officer in Charge, UN Office for Law of the Sea, Kingston, Jamaica 1988–; Adviser to Minerals Comm. of Govt of Ghana 1984–87; Interim Dir-Gen. and Programme Co-ordinator, Int. Seabed Authority 1996–2008, Head of Office of Resources and Environmental Monitoring 2008, Deputy to Sec.-Gen. 2008, Sec.-Gen. 2009–; mem. American Inst. of Mining, Metallurgical and Petroleum Engineers, Ghana Inst. of Engineers; African Scholarship Programme of American Univs Award 1969, 1969–72, Henry Krumb Research Fellow 1972, Henry Krumb Fellow 1974–75. **Address:** International Seabed Authority, 14–20 Port Royal Street, Kingston, Jamaica. **Telephone:** 922-9105. **Fax:** 922-0195. **Internet:** www.isa.org.jm.

OSOTIMEHIN, Babatunde, BM, MBBS, MD; Nigerian; *Executive Director, United Nations Population Fund;* b. 1949, Ogun State; m.; five c. **Education:** Univ. of Ibadan, Univ. of Birmingham, UK. **Career:** Prof. of Clinical Pathology, Coll. of Medicine, Univ. of Ibadan 1980, later Head, Dept of Clinical Pathology, Provost, Coll. of Medicine 1990–94; fmr Project Man., Nigerian Nat. HIV/AIDS Programme Devt Project; Dir-Gen., Nigerian Nat. Agency for Control of AIDS 2007–08; Minister of Health 2008–10; Exec. Dir UN Population Fund (UNFPA) 2011–; Chair. Nat. Action Cttee on AIDS, Nigeria 2002–07, Cttee of Presidential Advisers of AIDS Watch Africa; Fellow, Graduate School of Medicine, Cornell Univ., New York 1979–80; Visiting Fellow, Harvard Centre for Population and Devt Studies, USA 1996–97; Fellow, Nigerian Acad. of Sciences 2006–; Distinguished Visitor, John D. and Catherine T. MacArthur Foundation, Chicago 1996; fmr Co-ordinator, Social Sciences and Reproductive Health Research Network, Ibadan; fmr Ed. African Journal of Medicine and Medical Sciences; mem. Royal Coll. of Physicians, Population Asscn of America, Int. Advisory Group, Population and Reproductive Health, John D. & Catherine T. MacArthur Foundation, Chicago, Nigerian Soc. of Endocrinology and Metabolism, Nigerian Medical Asscn, Nigerian Inst. of Man., Policy and Strategy Cttee, Global Fund for AIDS, Tuberculosis and

Malaria, Global Steering Cttee on Universal Access; Officer of the Order of the Niger 2005. **Address:** United Nations Population Fund, 605 Third Ave, New York, NY 10158, USA. **Telephone:** (212) 297-5000. **Fax:** (212) 370-0201. **E-mail:** hq@unfpa.org. **Internet:** www.unfpa.org.

OSTERWALDER, Konrad, PhD; Swiss; *Rector, United Nations University;* b. 3 June 1942, Frauenfeld, Thurgau; m.; three c. **Education:** Eidgenössische Technische Hochschule (ETH) Zürich, Univ. of Zürich, Harvard Grad. School for Higher Educ., USA. **Career:** Asst Prof. of Math. Physics, Harvard Univ. 1973–76, Assoc. Prof. 1976–78; Prof. of Math. Physics, ETH Zürich 1977–, Head Dept of Math. 1986–90, Head, Planning Cttee 1990–95, Rector 1995–2007; Guest Prof., Univ. of Austin, Tex., Univ. of Cambridge, UK, IHES, Bures-sur-Yvette, France, Max-Planck-Institut für Physik und Astrophysik, Munich, Università La Sapienza, Rome, Università di Napoli, Tokyo Univ., Weitzmann Inst., Rehovot, Israel; Rector UN Univ., Tokyo 2007–; Founder and Pres. UNITECH Int.; Chair. Univ. Council, Tech. Univ., Darmstadt, Germany; mem. Admin. Cttee, Ecole Polytechnique de France, Educ. Cttee, Ecole des Mines, Paris, Conseil d'Orientation Statégique, ParisTech, Consiglio dell'Università della Svizzera, Italy, Academic Council, Int. Council on Systems Eng; mem. Swiss Acad. of Tech. Sciences 2000; Fellow, Alfred P. Sloan Foundation 1974–78; Hon. mem. Riga Tech. Univ. 2002; Dr hc (Tech. Univ., Helsinki) 2003; J. Bauer Prize 1959, 1960, ETH Medaille, Kern Prize 1970, Matteo Ricci Award 2009. **Address:** United Nations University Centre, 53–70, Jingumae 5-chome, Shibuya-ku, Tokyo 150-8925, Japan. **Telephone:** (3) 5467-1212. **Fax:** (3) 3499-2828. **E-mail:** mbox@unu.edu. **Internet:** www.unu.edu.

OUEDRAOGO, Kadré Désiré; Burkinabè; *President, Economic Community of West African States (ECOWAS) Commission;* m. Solange Ouedraogo. **Education:** Haute Ecole, Paris, Université Paris I Sorbonne, France. **Career:** fmr Deputy Exec. Sec. Econ. Community of West African States (ECOWAS) in charge of Econ. Affairs; fmr Gov. of Cen. Bank of West African States; Prime Minister of Burkina Faso 1996–2000; Amb. to the EU (also accred to Belgium, Luxembourg, Netherlands and UK), Brussels 2001–12; Pres. ECOWAS Comm., Abuja, Nigeria 2012–; Grand Officier, Ordre Nat. du Burkina Faso 1996. **Address:** ECOWAS Executive Secretariat, 60 Yakubu Gowon Crescent, PMB 401, Asokoro, Abuja, Nigeria; 01 BP 3474, Ouagadougou 01, Burkina Faso. **Telephone:** (9) 3147647. **Fax:** (9) 3147646. **E-mail:** info@ecowas.int. **Internet:** www.ecowas.int.

PACHAURI, Rajendra Kumar, MS, DEcon, DEng; Indian; *Chairman, Intergovernmental Panel on Climate Change;* b. 20 Aug. 1940, Nainital; m. Saroj Pachauri; three d. **Education:** North Carolina State Univ., USA. **Career:** Asst Prof., North Carolina State Univ. 1974–75, Visiting Faculty mem., Dept of Econs and Business 1976–77; mem. Sr Faculty, Admin. Staff Coll. of India 1975–79, Dir Consulting and Applied Research Div. 1979–81; Dir The Energy Research Inst. (TERI), New Delhi 1982–2001, Dir-Gen. 2001–; Visiting Prof., Resource Econs, Univ. of West Virginia 1981–82; Sr Visiting Fellow, Resource Systems Inst., East-West Center, USA 1982; Visiting Fellow, Energy Dept, IBRD 1990; Pres. Int. Asscn for Energy Econs 1988, Chair. 1989–90; Pres. Asian Energy Inst. 1992–; Adviser on Energy and Sustainable Man. of Natural Resources to the Admin., UNDP 1994–99; Adviser, Int. Advisory Bd, Toyota Motor Corpn, Japan 2006–09; Vice-Chair. Intergovernmental Panel on Climate Change (IPCC) 1997, Chair. 2002–; Dir-Gen. Energy and Resources Inst., New Delhi; Chancellor TERI Univ.; Dir Yale Climate and Energy Inst.; mem. Bd of Dirs Int. Solar Energy Soc. 1991–97, Inst. for Global Environmental Strategies 1999–, Indian Oil Corpn Ltd 1999–2003, Nat. Thermal Power Corpn Ltd 2002–05, GAIL (India) Ltd 2003–04, Oil and Natural Gas Corpn Ltd 2006–09; McCluskey Fellow, Yale Univ., USA Sept.–Dec. 2000; mem. Advisory Bd, Clinton Climate Initiative, USA 2010–; mem. High Panel on Peace and Dialogue among Cultures, UNESCO, France 2009–; mem. Bd of Govs, Shriram Scientific and Industrial Research Foundation 1987–90; mem. Exec. Cttee, India Int. Centre, New Delhi, mem. Bd of Trustees 1985–; Vice-Pres. Bangalore Int. Centre; mem. Governing Council, India Habitat Centre, New Delhi 1987–, Pres. 2004–06; mem. Court of Govs, Admin. Staff Coll. of India 1979–81; mem. Advisory Bd on Energy, reporting directly to Prime Minister 1983–88, World Energy Council 1990–93, Nat. Environmental Council, under Prime Minister 1993–99, Oil Industry Restructuring Group, 'R' Group, Ministry of Petroleum and Natural Gas 1994, Econ. Advisory Council to Prime Minister 2001–04, Prime Minister's Advisory Council on Climate Change 2007–; Hon. Prof., HEC Paris 2009; Officier de la Legion d'honneur 2006, Commdr of the Order of the White Rose (Finland) 2010, Order of the Rising Sun, Gold and Silver Star (Japan) 2010; Dr hc (Ritsumeikan Univ.) 2007, (Univ. of Liege) 2008, (Univ. of Athens) 2009, Hon. DHumLitt (Yale Univ.) 2008, (Brandeis Univ.) 2009, Hon. DSc (Kumaun Univ.) 2008, (Rani Durgavati Vishwavidyalaya, Jabalpur) 2008, (Univ. of New South Wales) 2008, (Univ. of Warwick) 2009, (Univ. of Kalyani) 2009, (Illinois Univ.) 2009, (Gustavus Adolphus Coll., Minnesota) 2009, Hon. ScD (Univ. of East Anglia) 2008; Millennium Pioneer Award 2000, Padma Bhushan 2001, Intergovernmental Panel on Climate Change awarded Nobel Peace Prize (shared with Al Gore) 2007, NDTV Global Indian Award 2007, Padma Vibhushan 2008, IIFA Global Leadership Award 2008, GQ Global Indian of the Year Award 2009. **Publications include:** The Dynamics of Electrical Energy Supply and Demand 1975, Energy and Economic Development in India 1977, International Energy Studies 1980, Energy Policy for India: An Interdisciplinary Analysis 1980, National Energy Data Systems (co-author) 1984, The Political Economy of Global Energy 1985, Global Energy Interactions 1986, Global Warming and Climate Change: Perspectives from Developing Countries (co-ed.) 1990, Role of Innovative Technologies and Approaches for India (co-ed.) 1991, Global Warming: Mitigation Strategies and Perspectives from Asia and Brazil (co-ed.) 1991, Energy-Environment-Development (co-ed.) 1991, Global Warming: Collaborative Study on Strategies to Limit CO2 emissions in Asia and Brazil (co-ed.) 1992, Contemporary India 1992, Climate Change in Asia and Brazil: The Role of Technology Transfer (co-ed. with Preety Bhandari) 1994, Population, Environment and Development (ed. with Lubina F. Qureshy) 1997; Energy in the Indian Sub-Continent (co-ed. with Gurneeta Vasudeva) 2000, Directions, Innovations, and Strategies for Harnessing Action for Sustainable Development 2001, Business Unusual: Championing Corporate Social Responsibility (ed) 2004, Petroleum Pricing in India: Balancing Efficiency and Equity (co-author) 2005, The Promises and Challenges of Biofuels for the Poor in Developing Countries 2006, CITIES: Steering Towards Sustainability 2009; scientific papers and newspaper articles. **Address:** Intergovernmental Panel on Climate Change, World Meteorological Organization, 7 bis ave de la Paix, CP 2300, 1211 Geneva 2, Switzerland. **Telephone:** 227308208. **Fax:** 227308025. **E-mail:** IPCC-Sec@wmo.int. **Internet:** www.ipcc.ch.

PANITCHPAKDI, Supachai, MA, PhD; Thai; *Secretary-General, United Nations Conference on Trade and Development (UNCTAD);* b. 30 May 1946, Bangkok; m. Mrs Sasai; one s. one d. **Education:** St Gabriel's Coll. and Trium Udom School, Bangkok, Netherlands School of Econs (now Erasmus Univ.), Rotterdam, and in UK. **Career:** worked in Research Dept, Int. Finance Div., and Financial Insts Supervision Dept, Bank of Thailand 1974–86; elected mem. Thai Parl. 1986, Deputy Minister of Finance 1986–88; Dir and Adviser, then Pres. Thai Military Bank 1988–92; apptd Senator 1992, then Deputy Prime Minister of Thailand 1992–95, Deputy Prime Minister and Minister of Commerce 1997–99; Dir-Gen. WTO 2002–05; Sec.-Gen. UNCTAD 2005–; Visiting Prof., Int. Inst. for Man. Devt, Lausanne 2001; Knight Grand Cordon (Special Class) of the Most Exalted Order of the White Elephant. **Publications include:** Globalization and Trade in the New Millennium 2001, China and WTO: Changing China Changing WTO (with Mark Clifford) 2002. **Address:** United Nations Conference on Trade and Development (UNCTAD), Palais des Nations 8-14, ave de la Paix, 1211 Geneva 10, Switzerland. **Telephone:** 229175806. **Fax:** 229170042. **E-mail:** sgo@unctad.org. **Internet:** www.unctad.org.

PANSIERI, Flavia, PhD; Italian; *Executive Co-ordinator, United Nations Volunteers.* **Education:** Milan and Venice Univs. **Career:** began UN career with UNDP in China 1983, responsible for UN Volunteers (UNV) and TOKTEN programmes, as well as for projects in energy sector, continued with UNDP in Bangladesh 1987–90 and Myanmar 1990–93, posted to Laos directing UN Drug Control Programme (UNDCP) activities, served at UNDCP HQ in Vienna 1995–98, Deputy Exec. Dir UNIFEM, New York 1998–2001, took charge of Country Div. of Regional Bureau for Arab States at UNDP 2001–04, UN Resident Co-ordinator and Resident Rep. of UNDP in Yemen 2004–08, Exec. Co-ordinator UNV 2008–. **Address:** United Nations Volunteers, Postfach 260 111, 53153 Bonn, Germany. **Telephone:** (228) 815-2000. **Fax:** (228) 815-2001. **E-mail:** information@unvolunteers.org. **Internet:** www.unvolunteers.org.

PILLAY, Navanethem (Navi), BA, LLB, LLM, SJD; South African; *High Commissioner for Human Rights, United Nations Office of the High Commissioner for Human Rights;* b. 23 Sept. 1941, Durban; m. (deceased); two d. **Education:** Natal Univ., Harvard Univ., USA. **Career:** first woman to start a law practice in Natal Prov. 1967, Sr Partner 1967–95; first black woman apptd Acting Judge High Court of SA 1995; Judge, UN Int. Criminal Tribunal for Rwanda 1995–2003, Pres. 1999–2003; Judge, Int. Criminal Court 2003–08; UN High Commr for Human Rights, Geneva 2008–; Chair. Equality Now 1990–95, Hon. Chair. 1995–; Pres. Advice Desk for Abused Women 1989–99, Women Lawyers' Asscn 1995–98; Vice-Chair. of Council, Univ. of Durban-Westville 1995–98; Lecturer, Dept of Public Law, Natal Univ. 1980; Trustee, Legal Resources Centre 1995–98, Lawyers for Human Rights 1998–2001; mem. Women's Nat. Coalition 1992–93, Black Lawyers' Asscn 1995–98, UN Expert Groups on Refugees and on Gender Persecution 1997, Rules Bd for Courts 1997–98, Expert Group on African Perspectives on Universal Jurisdiction, Cairo and Arusha 2001–02; currently mem. Int. Criminal Law Network, Advisory Bd Journal of Int. Criminal Justice, Bd Harvard-South Africa Scholarship Cttee, Bd Dirs Nozala Investments (women's component of Nat. Econ. Initiative); Hon. mem. American Soc. of Int. Law; Unifem and Noel Foundation Life Award (Los Angeles), Award for Leadership in the Fight for Human Rights, California Legislative Assembly, Dr Edgar Brookes Award, Natal Univ., Award for Outstanding contrib. in Raising Awareness of Women's Rights and Domestic Violence, Advice Desk for Abused Women, Award for Dedication to Human Rights, Equality Now, New York, One Hundred Heroines Award, Washington DC, Human Rights Award, Int. Asscn of Women Judges, Award for High Achievement by a Woman in the Legal Profession, Center for Human Rights and Univ. of Pretoria; further awards from Asscn of Law Soc. of SA, Black Lawyers' Asscn, Feminist Majority Foundation, Int. Bar Asscn, Peter Gruber Foundation; ranked by Forbes magazine amongst 100 Most Powerful Women (64th) 2009. **Publications:** contrib.: Civilians in War 2001, Essays in Memory of Judge Cassese 2003. **Address:** Office of the High Commissioner for Human Rights, Palais Wilson 52 rue des Pâquis, 1201 Geneva, Switzerland. **Telephone:** 229179011. **Fax:** 229179008. **E-mail:** registry@ohchr.org. **Internet:** www.ohchr.org.

PITSUWAN, Surin, PhD; Thai; *Secretary-General, Association of Southeast Asian Nations (ASEAN);* b. 28 Oct. 1949, Nakhon Si Thammarat; m. Alisa Ariya 1983; three s. **Education:** Claremont McKenna Coll., Harvard Univ., USA. **Career:** taught at Thammasat Univ. 1975–86, Academic Asst to Dean of Faculty of Political Science and to Vice-Rector for Academic Affairs 1985–86; columnist, The Nation Review and Bangkok Post newspapers 1980–92; fmr corresp. and analyst, ASEAN Forecast; Congressional Fellow, Office of US Rep. Geraldine Ferraro and Senate Republican Conf. 1983–84; mem. Parl. from Nakhon Si Thammarat Prov. 1986–; Sec. to Speaker of House of Reps 1986; Asst Sec. to Minister of Interior 1988; Deputy Minister of Foreign Affairs 1992–95; Minister of Foreign Affairs 1997–2001; adviser to Int. Comm. on Intervention and State Sovereignty 1999–2001; mem. UN Comm. on Human Security 2001–03; served on ILO's World Comm. on the Social Dimension of Globalization 2002–04; Sec.-Gen. ASEAN 2008–31 Dec. 2012; mem. Democratic Party (fmr Deputy Leader); mem. Advisory Bd Council on Foreign Relations, New York, Int. Advisory Bd Int. Crisis Group, Advisory Bd UN Human Security Trust Fund, 'Wise Men Group' under auspices of the Henri Dunant Centre for Humanitarian Dialogue, Geneva (advising peace negotiations between Acehnese Independence Movt (GAM) and Govt of Indonesia) 2002–04, Islamic Devt Bank's 1440 AH (2020) Vision Comm. –2005; fmr mem. Nat. Reconciliation Comm.; Int. Academic Advisor, Centre for Islamic Studies, Univ. of Oxford, UK; adviser to the Leaders Project (conf. arm of the Cohen Group of fmr US Sec. of Defense William S. Cohen), Washington, DC. **Address:** ASEAN Secretariat, 70A Jalan Sisingamangaraja, PO Box 2072, Jakarta 12110, Indonesia. **Telephone:** (21) 7262991. **Fax:** (21) 7398234. **E-mail:** termsak@aseansec.org. **Internet:** www.aseansec.org.

PLUMBLY, Sir Derek John, KCMG, BA; British; *Special Co-ordinator of the Secretary-General for Lebanon, United Nations;* b. 15 May 1948, Lyndhurst, Hants.; m. Nadia Youssef Gohar 1979; one d. two s. **Education:** Brockenhurst Grammar School, Magdalen Coll., Oxford. **Career:** with VSO, Pakistan 1970–71; joined FCO 1972, Arabic language training, Middle East Centre for Arab Studies, Lebanon 1973–74, Second Sec., Embassy in Jeddah 1975–77, First Sec., Embassy in Cairo 1977–80, at FCO 1980–84, at Embassy in Washington, DC 1984–88, Counsellor, Embassy in Riyadh 1988–92, with Perm. Mission to UN, New York 1992–96, Dir Drugs and Crime Dept, FCO 1996–97, Dir Middle East and North Africa Dept 1997–2000, Amb. to Saudi Arabia 2000–03, to Egypt 2003–07; Chair. Assessment and Evaluation Comm., est. under Sudan Comprehensive Peace Agreement, Khartoum 2008–11; Special Co-ordinator of the UN Sec.-Gen. for Lebanon 2012–; Dr hc (Loughborough) 2007. **E-mail:** unscol-website@un.org. **Internet:** www.unscol.unmissions.org.

RABEE, Mohammed al-; Yemeni; *Secretary-General, Council of Arab Economic Unity.* **Career:** Asst Sec.-Gen. Council of Arab Econ. Unity (CAEU) 2005–10, Sec.-Gen. CAEU 2010–. **Address:** Council of Arab Economic Unity, 1113 Corniche en-Nil, 4th Floor, PO Box 1, 11518 Cairo, Egypt. **Telephone:** (2) 25755045. **Fax:** (2) 25754090. **E-mail:** caeu@idsc.net.eg. **Internet:** www.caeu.org.eg.

RASMUSSEN, Anders Fogh, MSc; Danish; *Secretary-General, NATO;* b. 26 Jan. 1953, Ginnerup, Jutland; m. Anne-Mette Rasmussen; three c. **Education:** Viborg Cathedral School, Univ. of Århus. **Career:** consultant to Danish Fed. of Crafts and Small Industries 1978–87; mem. Folketing (Parl.) 1978–, mem. Econ. and Political Affairs Cttee 1982–87, Vice-Chair. 1993–98; Vice-Chair. Housing Cttee 1981–86; Minister for Taxation 1987–92, also for Econ. Affairs 1990–92; Vice-Chair. Econ. and Political Affairs Cttee 1993–98; Prime Minister of Denmark 2001–09; Sec.-Gen. North Atlantic Treaty Org. (NATO) 2009–; mem. Venstre (Liberal Party), Vice-Chair. Nat. Org. Venstre 1985–98, mem. Man. Cttee Parl. Party 1984–87, 1992–2001, Spokesman for Venstre 1992–98, Vice-Chair. Foreign Policy Bd 1998–2001, Chair. Venstre 1998–2009; Grand Cross of the Portuguese Order of Merit 1992, Commdr (First Degree) of the Order of the Dannebrog 2002, Danish Gold Medal of Merit 2002, Grand Cross of the German Order of Merit 2002, Grand Cross of the Order of Merit of Poland 2003, Grand Cross of the Order of the Oak Crown of Luxembourg 2003, Grand Cross of the Order of Nicaragua 2003, Great Cross of the Pedro Joaquín Chamorro Order 2003, Ordinul Steaua României Mare Cruce 2004, Grand Cross of the Order of the Lithuanian Grand Duke Gediminas 2004, Three Star Order of Latvia 2005, Order of Stara Planina, First Class (Bulgaria) 2006, Grand Cross of the Nordstjärneorden (Sweden) 2007, Grand Cross of the Order of the South Cross (Brazil) 2007, Grand Cross of Order of Dannebrog 2009, Estonian Order of Cross of Terra Mañana 2009; Dr hc (George Washington Univ.) 2002; Hon. DIur (Hampden-Sydney Coll., VA) 2003; Hon. Alumni (Århus) 2009; Adam Smith Award 1993, Politician of the Year (Dansk Markedsfuringsforbund) 1998, Netherlands Youth Org. for Freedom and Democracy Liberal of the Year 2002, European Leader Award, Polish Leaders Forum 2003, Danish European Movt European of the Year 2003, Robert Schumann Medal

2003, Pedro Joaquin Chamorro Medal, Nicaragua 2003, Best Leader in Denmark 2005, Politician of the Year 2005, Chevalier du St-Chinian 2007. **Publications:** Opgør med skattesystemet 1979, Den truede velstand (co-author) 1980, Kampen om boligen 1982, Fra Socialstat til Minimalstat 1993, I Godvejr og storm (interviews) 2001. **Address:** North Atlantic Treaty Organization Headquarters, Blvd Léopold III, 1110 Brussels, Belgium. **Telephone:** (2) 707-41-11. **Fax:** (2) 707-45-79. **E-mail:** natodoc@hq.nato.int. **Internet:** www.nato.int.

RIFAI, Taleb, BSc, MSc, PhD; Jordanian; *Secretary-General, World Tourism Organization;* b. 1949; m.; five c. **Education:** Univ. of Cairo, Illinois Inst. of Tech., Chicago and Univ. of Pennsylvania, USA. **Career:** Prof. of Architecture, Planning and Urban Design, Univ. of Jordan 1973–93; Head of Jordan's first Econ. Mission to USA, Washington, DC 1993–95; Dir Gen. Investment Promotion Corpn 1995–97; CEO Jordan Cement Co. 1997–99; held several sr govt portfolios, as Minister of Tourism and Antiquities (Chair. Exec. Council World Tourism Org. (UNWTO) 2002–03) 1999–2003, Minister of Information and Minister of Planning and Int. Co-operation; Asst to Dir-Gen. and Regional Dir for Arab States, ILO 2003–06; Deputy Sec.-Gen. UNWTO 2006–Jan. 2009, Sec.-Gen. a.i. Jan.–Oct. 2009, Sec.-Gen. Oct. 2009–; fmr Chair. Jordan Tourism Bd; fmr Pres. Ammon School for Tourism and Hospitality. **Achievements include:** responsible for founding Jordan's first Archaeological Park in ancient city of Petra in collaboration with UNESCO and World Bank, along with other projects in Jerash, the Dead Sea and Wadi Rum. **Address:** World Tourism Organization, Capitán Haya 42, 28020 Madrid, Spain. **Telephone:** (91) 5678100. **Fax:** (91) 5713733. **E-mail:** omt@unwto.org. **Internet:** www.unwto.org.

RODGERS, Jimmie, MD; Solomon Islands; *Director-General, Secretariat of the Pacific Community.* **Career:** holds degree in health admin; Under-Sec., later Perm. Sec. for Health, Ministry of Health and Medical Services, Solomon Islands 1990–96; joined Secr. of the Pacific Community (SPC) as Dir of Programmes in 1996, later re-designated as Deputy Dir-Gen. based in Noumea, Head of SPC Suva Regional Office 1998, later Sr Deputy Dir-Gen., Dir-Gen. SPC 2005–. **Address:** Secretariat of the Pacific Community Headquarters, BP D5, 98848 Noumea Cedex, New Caledonia. **Telephone:** 26-20-00. **Fax:** 26-38-18. **E-mail:** JimmieR@spc.int. **Internet:** www.spc.int.

ROED-LARSEN, Terje, PhD; Norwegian; *Under-Secretary-General and Special Envoy for the Implementation of Security Council Resolution 1559 (on Lebanon), United Nations;* b. 22 Nov. 1947, Bergen; m. Mona Juul. **Career:** taught sociology and philosophy at Univs of Bergen and Oslo –1981; Founder and Exec. Dir Inst. of Applied Social Sciences (FAFO) 1991, Hon. Chair. Programme for Int. Co-operation and Conflict Resolution; fmr Deputy Foreign Minister; facilitated negotiations between reps of Israel's Labour Govt and Palestine Liberation Org. (PLO) leading to signing of Declaration of Principles, Washington, DC 13 Sept. 1993; Amb. and Special Adviser to Norwegian Foreign Minister for the Middle East Peace Process 1993, 1998–; UN Deputy Sec.-Gen. and Special Co-ordinator in the Occupied Territories, Gaza 1994–96; Minister of Planning 1996–98; Special Co-ordinator for the Middle East Peace Process and Personal Rep. of the UN Sec.-Gen. to the PLO and Palestinian Authority 1999–2005; Under-Sec.-Gen. and Special Envoy for the Implementation of UN Security Council Resolution 1559 (calling for Syrian withdrawal from Lebanon and disarmament of Hezbollah) 2005–; Pres. Int. Peace Acad., New York 2005–. **Address:** Executive Office of the UN Secretary-General, United Nations Plaza, New York, NY 10017, USA. **Telephone:** (212) 906-5791. **Fax:** (212) 906-5778. **Internet:** www.un.org.

ROGGE, Jacques; Belgian; *President, International Olympic Committee;* b. 1942, Ghent; m.; two c. **Career:** fmr orthopaedic surgeon and sports medicine lecturer; participated as Olympic sailing competitor 1968, 1972, 1976; Pres. Belgian Nat. Olympic Cttee 1989–92; Pres. European Olympic Cttee 1989–2001, Chef de mission, two winter and three summer Olympic Games (Chief Co-ordinator, Olympic Games 2000, 2004); mem. IOC 1991–, Pres. 2001–; UNEP Champion of the Earth Laureate 2007, ranked by Forbes magazine amongst The World's Most Powerful People (60th) 2009, (67th) 2010, (68th) 2011. **Address:** International Olympic Committee, Château de Vidy, 1007 Lausanne, Switzerland. **Telephone:** 216216111. **Fax:** 216216216. **Internet:** www.olympic.org.

RYDER, Guy, CBE; British; *Director-General, International Labour Organization;* b. 3 Jan. 1956, Liverpool. **Education:** Univ. of Cambridge. **Career:** Asst, International Dept, TUC 1981–85; Sec., Industry Trade Section, International Fed. of Commercial, Clerical, Professional and Technical Employees (FIET), Geneva, Switzerland 1985–88; Sec., Workers' Group, ILO 1993–96, 1996–98, International Labour Conf. 1994–98, Dir of Bureau for Workers' Activities 1998–99, Chief of Cabinet 1999–2001, Special Adviser to Dir-Gen. –2001, Exec. Dir Standards and Fundamental Principles and Rights at Work Sector 2010–12, Dir-Gen. 2012–; Asst Dir, then Dir ICFTU, Geneva 1988–98, Gen. Sec. 2002–06, Gen. Sec. International Trade Union Confed. (formed after merger of ICFTU with World Confed. of Labour and eight nat. trade union orgs) 2006–10. **Address:** International Labour Organization, 4 route des Morillons, 1211 Geneva 22, Switzerland. **Telephone:** 227996111. **Fax:** 227988685. **E-mail:** ilo@ilo.org. **Internet:** www.ilo.org.

SACHS, Jeffrey David, BA, MA, PhD; American; *Special Adviser to the Secretary-General on Millennium Development Goals, United Nations;* b. 5 Nov. 1954, Detroit, Mich.; m. Sonia Ehrlich; one s. two d. **Education:** Harvard Univ. **Career:** Research Assoc. Nat. Bureau of Econ. Research, Cambridge, Mass. 1980–85; Asst Prof. of Econs, Harvard Univ. 1980–82, Assoc. Prof. 1982–83, Galen L. Stone Prof. of International Trade 1984–2001, Dir Harvard Inst. for International Devt 1995–2002, Center for International Devt –2002; Quetelet Prof. of Sustainable Devt and Prof. of Health Policy and Man. and Dir The Earth Inst., Columbia Univ. 2002–; Adviser, Brookings Inst., Washington, DC 1982–; Special Adviser to UN Sec.-Gen. on Millennium Devt Goals 2002–, Dir Millennium Project 2002–06; Founder Millennium Villages Project; Founder and Co-Pres. Millennium Promise Alliance; Founder and Chair. Exec. Cttee Inst. of Econ. Analysis, Moscow 1993–; Chair. Comm. on Macroeconomics and Health, WHO 2000–01; Co-Chair. Advisory Bd The Global Competitiveness Report; mem. International Financial Insts Advisory Comm., US Congress 1999–2000; econ. adviser to various govts in Latin America, Eastern Europe, the fmr Soviet Union, Asia and Africa, Jubilee 2000 movt; fmr consultant to IMF, World Bank, OECD and UNDP; Adviser to Pres. of Bolivia 1986–90; Fellow, World Econometric Soc.; Research Assoc. Nat. Bureau of Econ. Research; syndicated newspaper column appears in more than 50 countries; mem. American Acad. of Arts and Sciences, Harvard Soc. of Fellows, Brookings Panel of Economists, Bd of Advisers, Inst. of Medicine, Fellows of the World Econometric Soc., Nat. Bureau of Econ. Research, Bd of Advisors Chinese Economists Soc., among other international orgs; Distinguished Visiting Lecturer, LSE, Univ. of Oxford, Tel-Aviv, Jakarta, Yale Univs; Hon. Prof., Universidad del Pacifico, Peru; Commdr's Cross, Order of Merit (Poland) 1999; Hon. PhD (St Gallen, Switzerland) 1990, (Universidad del Pacífico, Peru) 1997, (Lingnan Coll., Hong Kong) 1998, (Varna Econs Univ., Bulgaria) 2000, (Iona Coll., New York) 2000; hon. degrees from Pace Univ., State Univ. of New York, Kraków Univ. of Econs, Ursinus Coll., Whitman Coll., Mount Sinai School of Medicine, Ohio Wesleyan Univ., Coll. of the Atlantic, Southern Methodist Univ., Simon Fraser Univ., McGill Univ., Southern New Hampshire Univ., St John's Univ.; Frank E. Seidman Award in Political Econ. 1991, cited in New York Times Magazine as 'probably the most important economist in the world' 1993, named by TIME magazine as 'the world's best-known economist' 1994, cited by Le Nouvel Observateur magazine as 'one of the world's 50 most important leaders on globalization' 1997, Berhard Harms Prize (Germany) 2000, Distinguished Public Service Award, Sec. of State's Open Forum 2002, named by TIME magazine as one of the 100 Most Influential People in the World 2004, 2005, Sargent Shriver Award for Equal Justice 2005, named by the World Affairs Councils of America as one of the '500 Most Influential People in the Field of Foreign Policy' 2007, Padma

Bhushan, Govt of India 2007, Cardozo Journal of Conflict Resolution International Advocate for Peace Award 2007, Centennial Medal, Harvard Grad. School of Arts and Sciences for his contribs to society 2007, BBC Reith Lecturer 2007, first holder of Royal Prof. Ungku Aziz Chair in Poverty Studies, Centre for Poverty and Devt Studies, Univ. of Malaya, Kuala Lumpur, Malaysia 2007–09, ranked 98th by Vanity Fair magazine on its list of 100 members of the New Establishment 2008, gave commencement address to Lehigh Univ.'s Class of 2009. **Publications include:** Economics of Worldwide Stagflation (with Michael Bruno) 1985, Developing Country Debt and the Economic Performance (ed.) 1989, Global Linkages: Macroeconomic Interdependence and Cooperation in the World Economy (with Warwick McKibbin) 1991, Peru's Path to Recovery (with Carlos Paredes) 1991, Macroeconomics in the Global Economy (with Felipe Larrain) 1993, Poland's Jump to the Market Economy 1993, The Transition in Eastern Europe (with Olivier Blanchard and Kenneth Froot) 1994, Russia and the Market Economy (in Russian) 1995, Economic Reform and the Process of Global Integration (with A. Warner) 1995, The Collapse of the Mexican Peso: What Have We Learned? (co-author) 1995, Natural Resource Abundance and Economic Growth (with A. Warner) 1996, The Rule of Law and Economic Reform in Russia (co-ed.) 1997, Economies in Transition (co-ed.) 1997, The End of Poverty 2005, Common Wealth: Economics for a Crowded Planet 2008, The Price of Civilization 2011; more than 200 scholarly articles. **Address:** c/o The Earth Institute at Columbia University, 405 Low Library, 535 West 116th St, MC 4335, New York, NY 10027, USA. **Telephone:** (212) 854-8704. **Fax:** (212) 854-8702. **Internet:** www.earth.columbia.edu/about/director; www.un.org/millenniumgoals.

SALEEM, Ahmed; Maldivian; *Secretary-General, South Asian Association for Regional Cooperation;* b. 26 May 1949, Malé. **Career:** joined Foreign Service 1968, held several positions including Chief of Protocol and Head of Multilateral Div., served at High Comm. in Sri Lanka and Perm. Mission to UN, New York; with Ministry of Finance 1977, served as Alt. Gov. to World Bank, IDA, Asian Development Bank; apptd Dir SAARC Secr. 1990, Sec.-Gen. SAARC 2012–; mem. Human Rights Comm. of the Maldives 2003–10 (Pres. 2006–10); fmr mem. Maldivian Democratic Party. **Address:** South Asian Association for Regional Cooperation, POB 4222, Tridevi Marg, Kathmandu, Nepal. **Telephone:** (1) 4221785. **Fax:** (1) 4227033. **E-mail:** saarc@saarc-sec.org. **Internet:** www.saarc-sec.org.

SALOMÃO, Tomaz Augusto, BA MA; Mozambican; *Executive Secretary, Southern African Development Community;* b. 16 Oct. 1954, Inhambane Prov.; m. **Education:** Commercial and Industrial School Vasca da Gama-Inhambane, Commercial Inst. of Lurenco Marques, Eduardo Mondlane Univ. **Career:** expert for study unit of Montepio Savings Bank of Mozambique 1974–76; expert at Ministry of Industry and Trade 1976–78; head of production unit at CIFEL 1978–81; Sec. of State for Nat. Defence 1983–89; Lecturer, Eduardo Mondlane Univ. 1990–93; Deputy Minister of Planning and Finance 1990–94, Minister of Planning and Finance, Gov. for Mozambique at African Devt Bank, IMF, World Bank 1994–99; Chair. SADC Transport and Communications Ministers' Cttee 2000–02, Chair. SADC Ministers' Cttee on ICTs 2002–03; Chair. African Union Ministers' Cttee on ICTs 2003–04; Minister of Transport and Communications of Mozambique 2000–04; Exec. Sec. SADC 2005–; mem. Ass. of the Repub. (Parl.) 2005–. **Address:** SADC HQ, CBD 54385, Square, Private Bag 0095, Gaborone, Botswana. **Telephone:** 3951863. **Fax:** 3972848. **E-mail:** registry@sadc.int. **Internet:** www.sadc.int.

SAMPAIO, Jorge Fernando Branco de; Portuguese; *High Representative of the Secretary-General for the Alliance of Civilizations, United Nations;* b. 18 Sept. 1939; m. Maria José Ritta; one s. one d. **Education:** Univ. of Lisbon. **Career:** leader of students' union and led protests against govt as student in Lisbon 1960–61; following graduation as lawyer defended several political prisoners; fmr mem. Socialist Left Movt then joined Socialist Party (PS), elected Deputy to Nat. Parl. 1979, Pres. Parl. Bench 1986–87, Sec.-Gen. 1989–91; mem. European Comm. for Human Rights 1979–84; Mayor of Lisbon 1989–95; Pres. of Portugal 1996–2006; Special Envoy of the UN Sec.-Gen. to Stop Tuberculosis 2006–, High Rep. of the UN Sec.-Gen. for the Alliance of Civilizations 2006–; Council of Europe North–South Prize 2008. **Address:** Alliance of Civilizations, c/o United Nations, New York, NY 10017, USA. **Telephone:** (917) 367-5118. **E-mail:** ContactAOC@unops.org. **Internet:** www.unaoc.org.

SANTOS PAIS, Marta, BA, MA; Portuguese; *Special Representative of the Secretary-General on Violence against Children, United Nations;* b. 1952; m.; two c. **Education:** Univ. of Lisbon. **Career:** more than 25 years' experience on human rights issues and engagement in intergovernmental processes; Rapporteur, UN Cttee on the Rights of the Child 1991–97, served as Vice-Chair. Co-ordinating Cttee on Childhood Policies, Council of Europe; Dir of Evaluation, Policy and Planning, UNICEF 1997–2001, served as Co-Chair. UN Devt Group Working Group on Human Rights, Dir UNICEF Innocenti Research Centre, Florence, Italy 2001–09; Special Rep. on Violence against Children at level of Asst Sec.-Gen. 2009–; held several advisory positions on human rights and legal issues in Portugal; served as Special Adviser to Machel Study on children affected by armed conflict and to UN Study on Violence against Children. **Publications:** numerous studies and publs. **Address:** Office of the Secretary-General, UN Headquarters, First Ave at 46th St, New York, NY 10017, USA. **E-mail:** info@un.org. **Internet:** www.un.org.

SEKIMIZU, Koji, BS, MS; Japanese; *Secretary-General, International Maritime Organization;* b. 3 Dec. 1952, Yokohama; m.; one s. one d. **Education:** Osaka Univ. **Career:** joined Ministry of Transport 1977, Ship Inspector 1977–79, Tech. Official 1979–80, Special Tech. Researcher, Shipbuilding Research Asscn 1981–82, Deputy Dir Environment Div. 1982–84; Deputy Dir, Second Int. Orgs Div., Econ. Affairs Bureau, Ministry of Foreign Affairs 1984–86; Deputy Dir Safety Standards Div., Maritime Tech. and Safety Bureau, Ministry of Transport 1986–89; Tech. Official, Maritime Safety Div., IMO 1989–97, Sr Deputy Dir Marine Environment Div. 1997–2000, Dir Marine Environment Div. 2000–04, Dir Maritime Safety Div. 2004–12, Sec.-Gen. IMO 2012–; mem. Japan Soc. of Naval Architects and Ocean Engineers. **Address:** International Maritime Organization, 4 Albert Embankment, London, SE1 7SR, England. **Telephone:** (20) 7735-7611. **Fax:** (20) 7587-3210. **E-mail:** info@imo.org. **Internet:** www.imo.org.

SERRA, Maj.-Gen. Paolo; Italian; *Force Commander and Head, United Nations Interim Force in Lebanon (UNIFIL);* b. 1956. **Education:** Military Acad., Univ. of Turin, Army War Coll., USA. **Career:** commissioned as Alpini Lieutenant 1979, Platoon Leader and Co. Commdr, Mountain Troops 1980–82, Anti-Tank Co. Commdr, Italian Contingent, ACE Mobile Force 1983–89, Commdr Susa Alpini Bn 1994–96, Commdr 9th Alpini Regt (deployed in Kosovo in Peace Support Operations) 1999–2000; also commanded task force to support law and order against organized crime in southern Italy 1995; Exec. Officer to Army Chief of Staff, Rome 2003; Army Attaché, Embassy in Washington, DC 2004–07; Commdr of the Regional Command West, Int. Security Assistance Force (ISAF), Afghanistan 2008, Chief of Staff, NATO Rapid Deployable Corps–Italy 2009; Chief of Logistics and Land Transformation, Italian Army –2012; Head of Mission and Force Commdr of the UN Interim Force in Lebanon (UNIFIL) 2012–; Legion of Merit (US), Knighthood of the Italian Repub.; Silver Cross for Meritorious Service, Bronze Medal for Long Command, Silver Cross for Long Service, Urkunde Medal (bronze) (Germany). **Address:** United Nations Interim Force in Lebanon (UNIFIL), Department of Peace-keeping Operations, United Nations, New York, NY 10017, USA. **Telephone:** (212) 963-1234. **Fax:** (212) 963-4879. **Internet:** www.un.org/en/peacekeeping/missions/unifil.

SERRY, Robert H.; Dutch; *Special Co-ordinator for the Middle East Peace Process, Secretary-General's Personal Representative to the Palestine Liberation Organization and the Palestinian Authority, and Secretary-General's Envoy to the Quartet, United Nations;* b. 1950, Calcutta, India; m.; three c. **Education:** Univ. of

Amsterdam. **Career:** led Middle Eastern Affairs Div., Ministry of Foreign Affairs, The Hague, participated in events leading to Middle East Peace Conf., Madrid during Netherlands EC presidency 1991, diplomatic postings in Bangkok, Moscow, New York (UN) and Kyiv, also held position of Deputy Asst Sec.-Gen. for Crisis Man. and Operations, NATO, fmr Amb. to Ireland; UN Special Co-ordinator for Middle East Peace Process, Sec.-Gen.'s Personal Rep. to Palestine Liberation Org. and Palestinian Authority, and Sec.-Gen.'s Envoy to Quartet 2007–. **Publications:** Standplaats Kiev 1997; several articles on political and peace-keeping topics, ranging from the Middle East to Eastern Europe. **Address:** Office of the Secretary-General, UN Headquarters, First Ave at 46th St, New York, NY 10017, USA. **E-mail:** info@un.org. **Internet:** www.un.org.

SHA, Zukang; Chinese; *Under-Secretary-General for Economic and Social Affairs, United Nations;* b. Sept. 1947, Jiangsu prov.; m.; one s. **Education:** Nanjing Univ. **Career:** staff mem., Embassy in London 1971–74, in Sri Lanka 1974–80, Attaché and Third Sec., Embassy in Delhi 1980–85, Deputy Div. Dir and First Sec. Dept of Int. Orgs and Confs 1985–88, Adviser and Deputy Dir-Gen. 1992–95, First Sec. and Adviser, Perm. Mission to UN, New York 1988–92, Amb. for Disarmament Affairs and Deputy Perm. Rep. to UN Office and Other Int. Orgs, Geneva, Switzerland 1995–97, Dir-Gen. Dept of Arms Control 1997–2001, Perm. Rep. to UN, Geneva 2001–07; Under-Sec.-Gen. for Econ. and Social Affairs, UN, New York 2007–, Sec.-Gen. Rio+20 (UN Conf. on Sustainable Devt 2012) 2010–. **Address:** Office of the Under-Secretary-General for Economic and Social Affairs, United Nations, Room DC2-2320, New York, NY 10017, USA. **E-mail:** esa@un.org. **Internet:** www.un.org/esa/desa.

SHARMA, Kamalesh; Indian; *Secretary-General, Commonwealth;* b. 30 Sept. 1941; m. Babli Sharma; one s. one d. **Education:** St Stephen's Coll., Delhi Univ., King's Coll. Cambridge, UK. **Career:** joined Indain Foreign Service 1965; Head of Divs of Econ. Relations, Int. Orgs and Policy Planning, Foreign Office; Head of Div. Ministry of Finance; served in Bonn, Hong Kong, Saudi Arabia and Turkey; Amb. to fmr GDR, Kazakhstan, Kyrgyzstan; Amb. to UN, Geneva, also Amb. for Disarmament and Spokesman for developing countries in UNCTAD; Perm. Rep. to UN, New York 1997–2002; Special Rep. of UN Sec.-Gen. for East Timor (now Timor-Leste) and Head of UN Mission of Support in East Timor (UNMISET) 2002–04; Dir Int. Peace Acad., New York; High Commr to UK 2004–08; Sec.-Gen. Commonwealth 2008–; Chancellor, Queen's Univ. Belfast 2009–; Fellow, Weatherhead Center for Int. Affairs, Harvard Univ.; mem. US Foreign Policy Asscn; fmr mem. Bd Dirs Peace Acad., New York, Education Consultants India Ltd; Gov. Ditchley Foundation; Hon. LLD (De Montfort Univ., UK); Medal of US Foreign Policy Asscn. **Publications include:** Mille Fleurs: Poetry from Around the World (compilation of poems by diplomats and officials) (ed.), Imaging Tomorrow: Rethinking the Global Challange. **Address:** Commonwealth Secretariat, Marlborough House, Pall Mall, London, SW1Y 5HX, England. **Telephone:** (20) 7747-6500. **Fax:** (20) 7930-0827. **E-mail:** info@commonwealth.int. **Internet:** www.thecommonwealth.org.

SLADE, Tuiloma Neroni, LLB; Samoan; *Secretary-General, Pacific Islands Forum;* b. 8 April 1941; m.; two d. **Education:** Hague Acad. of Int. Law. **Career:** qualified as solicitor and barrister, worked in law practice in Wellington, NZ 1967–68; legal counsel, Office of Attorney-Gen., Wellington 1969–73; Parl. Counsel 1973–75; Head of Del. UN Conf. on the Law of the Sea 1973–76; Attorney-Gen. of Western Samoa 1976–82, also Chief Justice for periods between 1980–82; Asst Dir Legal Div. Commonwealth Secr., London 1983–93; Amb. to USA 1993–2003, also Perm. Rep. to the UN, New York and High Commr to Canada; Chair. Alliance of Small Island States 1997–2003; Leader, Samoan del. to Preparatory Comm. for Int. Criminal Court, New York 1999–2002; Distinguished Diplomat in Residence, Temple Univ., Philadelphia 2003; Judge, Int. Criminal Court 2003–06; Sec.-Gen. Pacific Islands Forum 2008–; Chair. first S Pacific Law Conf. 1986; legal consultant S Pacific Forum Fisheries Agency 1989; UNITAR Fellowship, Hague Acad. of Int. Law and UN Legal Office; Order of Samoa (Poloaiga Sili a Samoa) 2005. **Address:** Office of the Secretary General, Pacific Islands Forum Secretariat, Private Mail Bag, Suva, Fiji. **Telephone:** 3312600. **Fax:** 3220230. **E-mail:** info@forumsec.org.fj. **Internet:** www.forumsec.org.

SONG, Sang-hyun, LLM, JSD; South Korean; *President, International Criminal Court;* b. 21 Dec. 1941; m.; one s. one d. **Education:** Seoul Nat. Univ., Tulane Law School, New Orleans and Cornell Law School, Ithaca, NY, USA, Univ. of Cambridge, UK. **Career:** called to the Bar, Repub. of Korea 1964; Mil. Prosecutor then Judge, Judge Advocate Office, Korean Armed Forces 1964–67; Attorney Haight, Gardner, Poor & Havens, New York 1970–72; Prof. of Law, Seoul Nat. Univ. 1972–2007, Dean Law School 1996–98; Lecturer in Law, Nat. Police Coll., Seoul 1983–2003; Judge (Appeals Div.), Int. Criminal Court (ICC), The Hague, Netherlands 2003–, Pres. ICC 2009–; Vice-Pres. UNICEF Korea 1998–2012; Pres. Korea Childhood Leukemia Foundation 1999–2009; has lectured at Univ. of Melbourne Law School, Harvard Law School and New York Univ.; Nat. Decoration of 2nd Highest Order (Moran), Govt of Repub. of Korea 1997, Nat. Decoration of the Highest Order (Mugunghwa), Govt of Repub. of Korea 2011; Most Distinguished Alumni Medal, Cornell Univ. 1994, Legal Culture Award, Korean Fed. Bar Asscn 1998. **Publications:** books: Introduction to the Law and Legal System of Korea 1983, An Introduction to Law and Economics 1983, Korean Law in the Global Economy 1996, The Korean Civil Procedure 2004; numerous articles in professional journals. **Address:** International Criminal Court, Maanweg 174, 2516 The Hague AB, Netherlands. **Telephone:** (70) 5158208. **Fax:** (70) 5158620. **E-mail:** pio@icc-cpi.int. **Internet:** www.icc-cpi.int.

STARR, Gregory B., BSc, MSc; American; *Under-Secretary-General for Safety and Security, United Nations;* b. 3 Feb. 1953; m.; two c. **Education:** George Washington Univ. **Career:** Sr Regional Security Officer, Embassy in Tel-Aviv 1997–2000; also served as Regional Security Officer at embassies in Tunis, Dakar and Kinshasa; Dir Office of Physical Security Programs, US Dept of State, Washington, DC 2000–04, Deputy Asst Sec. of State for Countermeasures 2004–07, Acting Asst Sec. for Diplomatic Security and Acting Dir of Office of Foreign Missions 2007–08, Dir Diplomatic Security Service and Prin. Deputy Asst Sec. for Diplomatic Security 2008–09; Under-Sec.-Gen. for Safety and Security, UN 2009–. **Address:** Office of the Under-Secretary-General for Safety and Security, United Nations, New York, NY 10017, USA. **Internet:** dss.un.org/dssweb.

STAVRIDIS, Adm. James G., PhD, MALD; American; *Supreme Allied Commander, Europe, NATO;* b. S Fla; m. Laura Stavridis; two d. **Education:** US Naval Acad. (distinguished grad.), Nat. War Coll. (distinguished grad.), Fletcher School of Law and Diplomacy at Tufts Univ. **Career:** Surface Warfare Officer, commanded Destroyer USS Barry (DDG-52) 1993–95, completed UN and NATO deployments to Haiti and Bosnia, and combat cruise to the Arabian Gulf, commanded Destroyer Squadron 21 1998, deployed to Arabian Gulf, commanded Enterprise Carrier Strike Group 2002–04, conducted combat operations in Arabian Gulf in support of both Operation Iraqi Freedom and Operation Enduring Freedom, commanded US Southern Command in Miami focused on Latin America and the Caribbean 2006–09; has served as a strategic and long-range planner on staffs of Chief of Naval Operations and Chair. of Jt Chiefs of Staff; also served as Exec. Asst to the Sec. of the Navy and as Sr Mil. Asst to the Sec. of Defense; Supreme Allied Commdr, Europe, NATO 2009–; Defense Distinguished Service Medal, Defense Superior Service Medal, five awards of the Legion of Merit; Gullion Prize, Fletcher School of Law and Diplomacy 1984, USS Barry won the Battenberg Cup as the top ship in the Atlantic Fleet under his command, John Paul Jones Award for Inspirational Leadership, Navy League 1998. **Publications:** author or co-author of several books on naval ship-handling and leadership, including Command at Sea, Destroyer Captain. **Address:** Public Affairs Office, 7010 SHAPE, Belgium. **Telephone:** (65) 44-4119. **Fax:** (65) 44-3100. **E-mail:** shapepao@shape.nato.int. **Internet:** www.aco.nato.int.

STEINER, Achim, BA, MA; German; *United Nations Under-Secretary-General and Executive Director, United Nations Environment Programme;* b. 17 May 1961, Brazil; m. Liz Rihoy. **Education:** Univs of Oxford and London, UK, German Devt Inst., Berlin, Harvard Business School, USA. **Career:** Sr Policy Adviser, Global Policy Unit, Int. Union for the Conservation of Nature and Natural Resources (IUCN—The World Conservation Union), Washington, DC mid-1990s, worked in SE Asia as Chief Tech. Adviser on a programme for sustainable man. of Mekong River watersheds and community-based natural resources man., worked in IUCN's Southern Africa Regional Office, Dir-Gen. IUCN 2001–06; Sec.-Gen. World Comm. on Dams, based in SA 1998–2001; UN Under-Sec.-Gen. and Exec. Dir UNEP 2006–, also Dir-Gen. UNON (UN Office at Nairobi); Founding mem. Institut du développement durable et des relations internationales (France); mem. several int. advisory bds including China Council for Inst. Cooperation on Environment and Devt, Environmental Advisory Council (ENVAC) of EBRD, UN Sec.-Gen.'s Advisory Council for the Global Compact, Int. Advisory Cttee of Global Environmental Action (Japan), Bd of Global Public Policy Inst. (Germany); Bruno H. Schubert-Stiftung Award, Steiger Award for Environment 2007, Tallberg Award for Environmental Leadership 2010. **Address:** United Nations Environment Programme, United Nations Ave, Gigiri, PO Box 30552, 00100 Nairobi, Kenya. **Telephone:** (20) 7624001. **Fax:** (20) 7624275. **E-mail:** executiveoffice@unep.org. **Internet:** www.unep.org.

SUTHERLAND, Peter Denis, , BCL; Irish; *Special Representative of the Secretary-General for Migration, United Nations;* b. 25 April 1946; m. Maria del Pilar Cabria Valcarcel 1971; two s. one d. **Education:** Gonzaga Coll., Univ. Coll. Dublin and King's Inns. **Career:** called to Irish Bar (King's Inns), English Bar (Middle Temple) and New York Bar; admitted to Bar of the Supreme Court of the United States; practising mem. of Irish Bar 1968–81; Tutor in Law, Univ. Coll., Dublin 1968–71; apptd. Sr Counsel 1980; Attorney-Gen. 1981–82, 1982–84; mem. Strategy Cttee Fine Gael Party 1978–81, Dir Policy Programme, 1981 Gen. Election; mem. Comm. of the European Communities (responsible for Competition and Relations with the European Parl.) 1985–89; Dir-Gen. GATT (later World Trade Org.) 1993–95; Chair. Allied Irish Banks 1989–93; mem. Bd of Dirs British Petroleum Co. PLC (now BP plc), Deputy Chair. 1995–97, Chair. 1997–2009; Chair. (non-exec.) Goldman Sachs International 1995–; Chair. London School of Econs 2008–; Special Rep. of UN Sec.-Gen. for Migration, 2006–; mem. advisory group to José Manuel Barroso, Pres. of EC, on energy and climate change issues 2007–; Chair. Trilateral Comm. (Europe); Vice-Chair. European Roundtable of Industrialists; Pres., Federal Trust; mem. Foundation Bd, World Econ. Forum; mem. Advisory Council, European Policy Center; Consultor, Admin of the Patrimony of the Holy See; Goodwill Amb. UNIDO; Visiting Fellow, Kennedy School of Govt, Harvard Univ. 1989; Visiting Prof., Univ. Coll. Dublin; mem. Royal Irish Acad.; Hon. Bencher, King's Inns Dublin 1995, Hon. Fellow, London Business School 1997, Oxford Univ. Inst. of Econs, Bencher, Middle Temple 2002, Hon. KCMG, Kt Commdr of the Order of St Gregory 2008, Hon. Vice-Pres. Law Soc., Univ. Coll. Dublin 2011; Grand Cross of Civil Merit (Spain) 1989, Grand Cross of King Leopold II (Belgium) 1989, Chevalier Légion d'honneur 1993, Commdr du Wissam (Morocco) 1994, Order of Rio Branco (Brazil) 1996, Grand Cross of Order of Infante Dom Henrique (Portugal) 1998, Medal of Merit of Baden-Württemburg (Germany) 2008; Hon. LLD (St Louis, Nat. Univ. of Ireland, Coll. of Holy Cross, Bath Univ., Suffolk Univ., USA, Open Univ., Trinity Coll. (Dublin), Reading, Nottingham, Exeter, Queen's Univ. Belfast, Univ. of Notre Dame, Univ. of Sussex); Hon. DPhil (Dublin City Univ., Koc Univ., Turkey); European Person of the Year 1988, Gold Medal of European Parl. 1988, First European Law Prize Paris 1988, Irish People of the Year Award 1989, Robert Schuman Medal 1989, New Zealand Centenary Medal 1990, Consumer for World Trade Annual Award 1994, Dean's Medal, Wharton School, Univ. of Pennsylvania 1996, David Rockefeller Int. Leadership Award 1998, Lifetime Achievement Award, Ireland Chamber of Commerce 2009. **Publications include:** 1er janvier 1993–ce qui va changer en Europe 1989; and numerous articles in law journals. **Address:** Office of the Secretary-General, UN Headquarters, First Ave at 46th St, New York, NY 10017, USA. **Internet:** www.un.org.

SWING, William Lacy, BA, BD; American; *Director-General, International Organization for Migration;* b. 11 Sept. 1934, Lexington, NC; m. Yuen Cheong 1993; one s. one d. from previous m. **Education:** Catawba Coll., Yale Univ., Tübingen Univ., Harvard Univ. **Career:** Vice-Consul, Port Elizabeth, S. Africa 1963–66; int. economist, Bureau of Econ. Affairs, Dept of State 1966–68; Consul, Hamburg 1968–72; Desk Officer for FRG, Dept of State 1972–74; Deputy Chief of Mission, US Embassy, Bangui, Cen. African Repub. 1974–76; Sr Fellow, Center for Int. Affairs, Harvard Univ. 1976–77; Deputy Dir, Office of Cen. African Affairs, Dept of State 1977–79; Amb. to People's Repub. of Congo 1979–81, to Liberia 1981–85, to S Africa 1989–93, to Nigeria 1992–93, to Haiti 1993–98, to Democratic Repub. of Congo 1998–2001; Dir Office of Foreign Service Assignments and Career Devt 1985–87; Deputy Asst Sec. for Personnel 1987–89; Special Rep. of UN Sec.-Gen. for Western Sahara 2001–03, Democratic Repub. of Congo 2003–08; Dir-Gen. Int. Org. for Migration 2008–; Fellow, Harvard Univ.; Hon. LLD (Catawba Coll.) 1980; Hon. DHumLitt (Hofstra) 1994; Presidential Distinguished Service Award 1985; Distinguished Honor Award 1994, Award for Valor 1995, Presidential Meritorious Service Award 1987, 1990, 1994, 1998, Presidential Certificate of Commendation 1998. **Publications:** Education for Decision 1963, U.S. Policy Towards South Africa: Dilemmas and Priorities 1977, Liberia: The Road to Recovery 1982, Haiti: In Physical Contact with History 1994; book chapter in Challenges of Peace Implementation 2004. **Address:** International Organization for Migration, 17 route des Morillons, CP 71, 1211 Geneva 19, Switzerland. **Telephone:** 227179111. **Fax:** 227986150. **E-mail:** hq@iom.int. **Internet:** www.iom.int.

TESFAY, Lt-Gen. Tadesse Werede, MBA; Ethiopian; *Force Commander and Head, United Nations Interim Security Force for Abyei (UNISFA);* b. 13 July 1958; m.; four c. **Career:** joined Nat. Defence Forces, held several posts including Head of Jt Training Dept, Commdr Army Corps, mem. Defence Commdrs Council; Head of Mission and Force Commdr, UN Interim Security Force for Abyei (UNISFA) 2011–. **Address:** United Nations Interim Security Force for Abyei (UNISFA), Department of Peace-keeping Operations, Room S-3727-B, United Nations, New York, NY 10017, USA. **Telephone:** (212) 963-8077. **Fax:** (212) 963-9222. **Internet:** www.un.org/en/peacekeeping/missions/unisfa.

THUNELL, Lars H., PhD; Swedish; *CEO and Executive Vice-President, International Finance Corporation, World Bank Group.* **Education:** Univ. of Stockholm. **Career:** fmr Research Fellow, Harvard Univ. Center for Int. Affairs, USA; fmr CEO Trygg-Hansa insurance co.; fmr Deputy CEO Nordbanken; fmr Pres. and CEO Securum (asset man. co.), Stockholm; CEO Skandinaviska Enskilda Banken AB 1997–2005; Chair. Bd IBX Integrated Business Exchange AB; mem. or fmr mem. Bd of Dirs Svenska Cellulosa AB, Swedish Bankers Assen, Akzo Nobel NV, Mentor Foundation; worked at ABB Zurich and American Express, New York; has also held numerous non-exec. bd positions with int. cos and non-governmental orgs; CEO and Exec. Vice-Pres. IFC (mem. World Bank Group) 2006–. **Publications:** author of books and articles on risk and risk man. in int. business. **Address:** International Finance Corporation, 2121 Pennsylvania Ave, NW, Washington, DC 20433, USA. **Telephone:** (202) 473-1000. **Internet:** www.ifc.org.

TOKAYEV, Kassym-Jomart Kemeluli, DPolSci; Kazakhstani; *Director-General, United Nations, Geneva;* b. 17 May 1953, Almaty; m. Nadeyda Tokaeva (née Poznanskaya) 1983; one s. **Education:** Moscow Inst. of Int. Relations, Diplomatic Acad., USSR Ministry of Foreign Affairs, Inst. of the Chinese Language, Beijing. **Career:** with USSR Ministry of Foreign Affairs 1975; served at Embassy in Singapore 1975–79; Attaché, Third Sec., Ministry of Foreign Affairs 1979–83; Second Sec. of Dept 1984–85; Second, then First Sec., Embassy in Beijing 1985–91; attained rank of Amb. of

Kazakhstan 1994; Deputy Minister, then First Deputy Minister of Foreign Affairs Repub. of Kazakhstan 1992–94, State Sec. and Minister 1994–99; Deputy Prime Minister March–Oct. 1999, Prime Minister of Kazakhstan 1999–2002; Minister of Foreign Affairs 2002–06; Chair. (Speaker) Senat (Senate) 2007–11; Dir-Gen. UN Office, Geneva (UNOG) 2011–; Parasat (Nat. Award) 1996, Astana Medal, Independence Medal, First Pres. (Nat. Award) 2004, Friendship (Russia) 2004, Yaroslav Mudry (Ukraine) 2007. **Publications:** How it Was... Disturbance in Beijing 1993, United Nations: Half a Century of Serving for Peace 1995, Under the Banner of Independence 1997, Kazakhstani Foreign Policy in the Context of Globalisation 2000, Diplomacy of the Republic of Kazakhstan 2001, Meeting up the Challenge 2003, Light and Shadow – Essays of the Diplomat 2007. **Address:** United Nations Office at Geneva, Palais des Nations, 1211 Geneva 10, Switzerland. **Telephone:** 229171234. **Fax:** 229170123. **E-mail:** webmaster@unog.ch. **Internet:** www.unog.ch.

TOMKA, Peter, LLM, PhD; Slovak; *Judge and President, International Court of Justice;* b. 1 June 1956, Banska Bystrica; m. Zuzana Halgasová 1990; one s. one d. **Education:** Faculty of Law, Charles Univ., Prague, Faculty of Int. Law and Int. Relations, Ukraine, Law Inst. of Peace and Devt, France, Inst. of Int. Public Law and Int. Relations, Greece, Hague Acad. of Int. Law. **Career:** Asst, Faculty of Law, Charles Univ., Prague 1980–84, Lecturer 1985–86, Adjunct Lecturer 1986–91; Asst Legal Adviser, Ministry of Foreign Affairs, Czechoslovakia 1986–90, Head of Public Int. Law Div. 1990–91; Counsellor and Legal Adviser, Czechoslovakian Mission to the UN 1991–92; Deputy Perm. Rep. of Slovakia to the UN 1993–97, Perm. Rep. 1999–2003; Agent of Slovakia before the Int. Court of Justice (ICJ) 1993–2003, Judge, ICJ 2003–, Vice-Pres. 2009–12, Pres. 2012–; Legal Adviser to Slovak Ministry of Foreign Affairs 1997–99; Chair. UN Legal Cttee 1997, Cttee of Advisers on Public Int. Law, Council of Europe 2001–02; mem. Perm. Court of Arbitration, The Hague 1994–, UN Int. Law Comm. 1999–2003, American Soc. of Int. Law 2000–, European Soc. of Int. Law 2004–; Arbitrator in the Iron Rhine case (Belgium/Netherlands) 2003–05, in Kishenganga Court of Arbitration (Pakistan versus India) 2010–, in Annex VII to the UN Convention on the Law of the Sea 2004–, and in Int. Centre for Settlement of Investment Disputes 2005–; mem. Bd of Eds Právník (The Lawyer) 1990–91; Hon. Pres. Slovak Soc. of Int. Law 2003–. **Publications:** numerous articles in professional journals. **Address:** International Court of Justice, Peace Palace, Carnegieplein 2, 2517 KJ The Hague, Netherlands. **Telephone:** (70) 3022323. **Fax:** (70) 3649928. **E-mail:** p.tomka@icj-cij.org. **Internet:** www.icj-cij.org.

TOURÉ, Hamadoun, PhD; Malian; *Secretary-General, International Telecommunication Union (ITU);* b. 3 Sept. 1953; m.; four c. **Education:** Tech. Inst. of Electronics and Telecommunications of Leningrad, Univ. of Electronics, Telecommunications and Informatics, Moscow, Russia. **Career:** worked at PANAFTEL microwave terminal 1979; worked at International Switching Centre, Bamako 1980, Engineer in charge of operation and maintenance of the International Satellite earth station, Bamako 1981–84; Group Dir and Regional Dir Int. Telecommunications Satellite Org. (INTELSAT), Washington, DC 1985–96; Dir Gen. Africa Region, ICO Global Communications 1996–98; Dir Telecommunications Devt Bureau (BDT), Int. Telecommunication Union (ITU), Geneva 1998–2006, Sec.-Gen. ITU 2007–; mem. IEEE 1986–, Asscn of Satellite Professionals 1990–, Int. Telecommunications Acad. 1999–, Royal Swedish Acad. of Eng Sciences 2010–; Kt of Nat. Order of Mali, Officer, Nat. Order of Côte d'Ivoire, Grand Officer, Nat. Order of the Dominican Republic, 2009; Dr hc (tate Odessa Nat. Acad. of Telecommunications, Ukraine), (Univ. of Belarus) 2009, (Nat. Univ. of Moldova) 2010, (Russian–Armenian (Slavonic) Univ., Armenia) 2010, (Kigali Inst. of Science and Tech.) 2010, (Wroclaw Univ. of Tech., Poland) 2010. **Address:** International Telecommunication Union, Place des Nations, 1211 Geneva 20, Switzerland. **Telephone:** 227305111. **Fax:** 227337256. **E-mail:** itumail@itu.int. **Internet:** www.itu.int.

TOYBERG-FRANDZEN, Jens Anders; Danish; *Executive Representative of the Secretary-General and Head, United Nations Integrated Peace-building Office in Sierra Leone (UNIPSIL);* b. 1950; m. **Education:** Aarhus Univ. **Career:** has served as Acting UN Resident Co-ordinator, UNDP Resident Rep. in Yemen, Resident Co-ordinator and Resident Rep. in Bosnia and Herzegovina, also served with UN in Bhutan, Iraq, Nepal and Turkey; Exec. Rep. of Sec.-Gen. and Head of the UN Integrated Peace-building Office in Sierra Leone (UNIPSIL) 2012–. **Address:** United Nations Integrated Peacebuilding Office in Sierra Leone (UNIPSIL), Cabenda Hotel, 14 Signal Hill Road, PO Box 5, Freetown, Sierra Leone. **Internet:** www.unipsil.unmissions.org.

TURUNEN, Antti; Finnish; *Representative of the United Nations Secretary-General for Georgia, United Nations.* **Career:** joined Foreign Service 1985, served in Washington, DC and Moscow, and as Adviser to EU High Rep. Javier Solana, Head of Unit for Eastern Europe and Cen. Asia, Ministry of Foreign Affairs 2004–07, led EU fact-finding mission to Tashkent, Uzbekistan Aug. 2006, Head of Perm. Mission to OSCE, Vienna 2007–10, chaired Perm. Council of OSCE during the Finnish Chairmanship 2008, was involved, among others, in settlement of Georgian-Ossetian conflict; Rep. of UN Sec.-Gen. for Georgia (Jt Incident Prevention and Response Mechanism) 2010–. **Address:** Office of the Secretary-General, United Nations, New York, NY 10017, USA. **Telephone:** (212) 963-1234 (New York). **Fax:** (212) 963-4879 (New York). **E-mail:** info@unomig.org. **Internet:** www.unomig.org.

TVEIT, Olav Fykse, Cand Theol, DTheol; Norwegian; *General Secretary, World Council of Churches;* b. 24 Nov. 1960. **Education:** Norwegian School of Theology/Menighetsfakultetet, Oslo. **Career:** ordained as pastor in Church of Norway, served as parish priest in Haram, Møre Diocese 1988–91 and as army chaplain during compulsory year of nat. service 1987–88; Sec. Church of Norway Doctrinal Comm. 1999–2000, Church–State Relations 2001–02; Gen. Sec. Church of Norway Council on Ecumenical and Int. Relations 2002–09; mem. Faith and Order Plenary Comm. and Co-Chair. Palestine Israel Ecumenical Forum core group, WCC, Gen. Sec. WCC 2010–; mem. Bd of Dirs and Exec. Cttee Christian Council of Norway; Moderator of Church of Norway-Islamic Council of Norway contact group, Jewish Congregation contact group; fmr mem. Inter-Faith Council of Norway, Bd of Trustees, Norwegian Church Aid. **Publications:** Evangeliet i vår kultur (The Gospel in our Culture; co-ed.) 1995, Mutual Accountability as Ecumenical Attitude. A Study in Ecumenical Ecclesiology Based on Faith and Order Texts 1948–1998 (thesis) 2001, Ei vedkjennande kyrkje. Hovudforedrag på Kyrkjemøtet 2004, Christian Solidarity in the Cross of Christ 2012; several articles on ecumenism. **Address:** World Council of Churches, 150 route de Ferney. PO Box 2100, 1211 Geneva 2, Switzerland. **Telephone:** 227916111. **Fax:** 227910361. **E-mail:** info@oikoumene.org. **Internet:** www.oikoumene.org.

VAN DER HOEVEN, Maria Josephina Arnoldina; Dutch; *Executive Director, International Energy Agency;* b. 13 Sept. 1949, Meerssen; m. Lou Buytendijk. **Career:** teacher 1969, school counsellor 1971; Head Adult Commercial Vocational Training Centre, Maastricht –1987; Head Limburg Tech. Centre 1987–91; mem. (Christian Democratic Alliance) House of Reps, States Gen. 1991–2002; Minister of Educ., Culture and Science 2002–07, of Economic Affairs 2007–10; Exec. Dir IEA 2011–; Chair. Supervisory Bd, Alzheimer Netherlands; fmr Chair. St Nicholas Catholic Asscn of Bargees; fmr mem. Bd of Govs, Maastricht Coll. of Higher Professional Educ., Southern Dutch Opera Asscn; Officer, Order of Orange-Nassau 2010. **Address:** International Energy Agency, 9 rue de la Fédération, 75739 Paris Cedex 15, France. **Telephone:** 1-40-57-65-00. **Fax:** 1-40-57-65-09. **E-mail:** info@iea.org. **Internet:** www.iea.org.

VAN ROMPUY, Herman, BA, MA; Belgian; *President, European Council;* b. 31 Oct. 1947, Etterbeek, Brussels; m. Geertrui Windels; two s. two d. **Education:** Sint-Jan Berchmans Coll., Brussels, Catholic Univ. of Leuven. **Career:** attache study service, Nat. Bank of Belgium 1972–75; Nat. Vice-Pres. CVP (Christian Democrat Party, now CD&V—Christen-Democratisch en Vlaams) Youth, 1973–75, mem. Nat. CVP 1978, Nat. Pres. CVP 1988–93; adviser to Cabinet of Prime

Minister leo Tindemans 1975–78, to Minister of Finance 1978–80; Lecturer, Handelshogeschool Antwerpen 1980–87, Vlaamse Economische Hogeschool Brussel (VLEKHO) 1982–; Dir Centre for Political, Econ. and Social Studies 1980–88; Senator 1988–95; Sec. of State for Finance and Small and Medium-Sized Enterprises 1988–93; Deputy Prime Minister and Minister of Budget 1993–99; mem. Chamber of Reps 1995–2009, Pres. 2007–08; Minister of State 2004; Prime Minister of Belgium 2008–09; Pres. European Council 2009–; Grand Ribbon, Order of Leopold 2009; Collier du Mérite européen, European Merit Foundation (Luxembourg) 2010. **Publications:** De kentering der tijden 1979, Hopen na 1984, Het christendom. Een moderne gedachte 1990, Vernieuwing in hoofd en hart. Een tegendraadse visie 1998, De binnenkant op een kier. Avonden zonder politiek 2000, Dagboek van een vijftiger 2004, Op zoek naar wijsheid 2007, Haiku 2010, In de wereld van Herman Van Rompuy (with Kathleen Cools) 2010. **Address:** Office of the President of the European Council, Justus Lipsius Building, 175 rue de la Loi, 1048 Brussels, Belgium. **Telephone:** (2) 281-97-29. **Fax:** (2) 281-67-37. **E-mail:** ec.president@european-council.europa.eu. **Internet:** www.european-council.europa.eu.

VOGT, Margaret, BA, MA, PhD; Nigerian; *Special Representative of the Secretary-General and Head, United Nations Integrated Peace-building Office in Central African Republic (BINUCA);* b. 1950; m.; six c. **Education:** Barnard Coll., Columbia Univ., USA. **Career:** held numerous academic positions, including Dir of Studies, Command and Staff Coll. Jaji, Nigeria, Lecturer, Nigerian War Coll. and Inst. for Strategic Studies, Kuru, Nigeria, Dir Africa Programme, Int. Peace Acad., Assoc. Research Prof., Nigerian Inst. of Int. Affairs; served in African Union as Dir Office of the African Union Comm. Chair.; Acting Deputy Special Rep. of Sec.-Gen., UN Political Office for Somalia, then Deputy Dir Africa I Div., Dept of Political Affairs, UN Secr. –2011; Special Rep. of the Sec.-Gen. and Head, UN Integrated Peace-building Office in Cen. African Repub. (BINUCA) 2011–; mem. Bd of Trustees Centre for Peace Initiatives in Africa. **Publications include:** The Liberian Crisis and ECOMOG: A Bold Attempt at Regional Peace Keeping 1992, Nigerian Defence Policy: Issues and Problems, International Peacekeeping (co-ed.). **Address:** United Nations Integrated Peace-building Office in Central African Republic (BINUCA), Department of Political Affairs, United Nations, New York, NY 10017, USA. **Telephone:** (212) 963-1234. **Fax:** (212) 963-4879. **Internet:** binuca.unmissions.org.

WAHLSTRÖM, Margareta, BA; Swedish; *Assistant Secretary-General for Disaster Risk Reduction and Special Representative of the Secretary-General for the Implementation of the Hyogo Framework for Action in the Secretariat for the International Strategy for Disaster Reduction, United Nations;* b. 30 March 1950. **Education:** Univ. of Stockholm. **Career:** has held numerous positions with non-governmental orgs and pvt. cos in SE Asia, Latin America and Africa; several sr positions with Int. Fed. of the Red Cross and Red Crescent Socs, Geneva 1989–2000, including Under-Sec.-Gen. for the Response and Operations Co-ordination Div.; ind. consultant 2000–02; fmr Chief of Staff of the Special Rep. of the Sec.-Gen., UN Assistance Mission in Afghanistan (UNAMA), Deputy Special Rep. responsible for relief, reconstruction and devt –2004, Asst Sec.-Gen. for Humanitarian Affairs and Deputy Emergency Relief Co-ordinator, UN 2004–08, concurrently Special Co-ordinator of the Sec.-Gen. for Humanitarian Assistance to Tsunami-Affected Countries, Asst Sec.-Gen. for Disaster Risk Reduction and Special Rep. of the Sec.-Gen. for Implementation of Hyogo Framework for Action in Secr. for Int. Strategy for Disaster Reduction, Geneva 2008–; mem. Comm. on Climate Change and Devt. **Address:** UN International Strategy for Disaster Reduction, Palais des Nations, Geneva 10, Switzerland. **E-mail:** isdr@un.org. **Internet:** www.unisdr.org.

WILLIAMS, Michael C., BSc, MSc, PhD; British; *Special Co-ordinator for Lebanon, United Nations;* b. 11 June 1949, Bridgend, Wales; m. Isobelle Jaques; two c. **Education:** Univ. Coll., London, School of Oriental and African Studies, Univ. of London. **Career:** worked for several years with Amnesty International as Head of Asia Research; Ed., later Sr Ed. for Asia, BBC World Service 1984–91; held several sr positions with UN in 1990s, including Dir of Human Rights in UN Transitional Admin in Cambodia (UNTAC) and Dir of Information in UN Protection Force in Fmr Yugoslavia (UNPROFOR); Sr Fellow, IISS, London 1996–98; Special Adviser to UK Foreign Sec. Robin Cook 1999–2001 and Jack Straw 2001–05; fmr Dir for Asia and Pacific Div., Dept of Political Affairs, later Sec.-Gen.'s Special Adviser on Situation in Middle East, Special Co-ordinator for Middle East Peace Process and Personal Rep. to Palestine Liberation Org. and Palestinian Authority 2007–08 (also served as Sec.-Gen.'s Envoy to Quartet), UN Special Co-ordinator for Lebanon (UNSCOL) 2008–; mem. Exec. Cttee and Council of Royal Inst. for Int. Affairs (now Chatham House). **Publications:** Vietnam at the Crossroads 1992, Civil Military Relations and Peacekeeping 1998; has written widely on Asian politics, int. security and peacekeeping. **Address:** Office of the Special Co-ordinator for Lebanon (UNSCOL), UN Headquarters, First Ave at 46th St, New York, NY 10017, USA. **E-mail:** unscolwebsite@un.org. **Internet:** unscol.unmissions.org.

WORMS, Gérard Etienne; French; *Chairman, International Chamber of Commerce;* b. 1 Aug. 1936, Paris; m. Michèle Rousseau 1960; one s. one d. **Education:** Lycées Carnot and Saint-Louis, Ecole Polytechnique and Ecole Nat. Supérieure des Mines, Paris. **Career:** Engineer, Org. commune des régions sahariennes 1960–62; Head of Dept, Délégation à l'Aménagement du Territoire et à l'Action Régionale 1963–67; Tech. Adviser, Office of Olivier Guichard (Minister of Industry, later of Planning) 1967–69, Office of Jacques Chaban-Delmas (Prime Minister) 1969–71; Asst Man. Dir, Librairie Hachette 1972–75, Man. Dir 1975–81, Dir 1978–81; Prof., Ecole des Hautes Etudes Commerciales 1962–69, Supervisor of complementary courses, Faculty of Letters and Human Sciences, Paris 1963–69; Prof. Ecole Polytechnique 1974–85; Vice-Pres. Syndicat nat. de l'édition 1974–81; Exec. Vice-Pres. Rhône-Poulenc SA 1981–83; Exec. Vice-Pres. Compagnie de Suez 1984–90, Chair. and CEO 1990–95; Pres. Banque Indosuez 1994–95; Pres. Supervisory Bd Rothschild, Compagnie Banque Paris 1995–99, Man. Partner Rothschild et Cie and Rothschild et Cie Banque 1999–, Vice-Chair. Rothschild Europe; Chair. ICC France 2006–, ICC 2011–; Pres. Centre for research into econ. expansion and business Devt 1996–, Supervisory Council for health information systems 1997–2000, History channel 1997–; Hon. Chair. Nat. Technical Research Asscn, Société d'Economie Politique; mem. bd Telecom Italia 1998–2001, Publicis, Métropole Télévision; Chevalier, Ordre nat. du Mérite, Ordre du Mérite maritime, Commdr Légion d'honneur 2007. **Publications include:** Les méthodes modernes de l'économie appliquée 1965; various articles on econ. methods in specialized journals. **Address:** International Chamber of Commerce, 38 cours Albert 1er, 75008 Paris. **Telephone:** 1-49-53-28-28. **Fax:** 1-49-53-28-59. **Internet:** www.iccwbo.org.

YUMKELLA, Kandeh K., BSc, MSc, PhD; Sierra Leonean; *Director-General, United Nations Industrial Development Organization;* m.; several c. **Education:** Njala Univ. Coll., Univ. of Illinois, USA. **Career:** held several academic and research positions in USA; Minister for Trade, Industry and State Enterprises, Sierra Leone 1994–95; Special Adviser to Dir-Gen. UNIDO 1996, Dir Africa and Least Developed Countries Regional Bureau 1996–2000, UNIDO Rep. and Dir Regional Industrial Devt Centre 2000–03, Sr Adviser to Dir-Gen. 2003–05, Dir-Gen. UNIDO 2005–. **Publications:** co-author of numerous books, articles and staff papers on int. trade and devt issues. **Address:** UNIDO Headquarters, Vienna International Centre, Wagramerstr. 5, PO Box 300, 1400 Vienna, Austria. **Telephone:** (1) 26026-0. **Fax:** (1) 2633011. **E-mail:** unido@unido.org. **Internet:** www.unido.org.

ZANNIER, Lamberto, DIur; Italian; *Secretary-General, Organization for Security and Co-operation in Europe;* b. 1954; m.; two s. two d. **Education:** Univ. of Trieste, Italian Diplomatic Inst. **Career:** served with FAO Legal Office, Rome 1976–78; joined Ministry of Foreign Affairs in 1978, worked on Multilateral Econ. Co-operation Desk, Second Sec., Embassy in Abu Dhabi 1979–82 First Sec. (for Multilateral Affairs), Embassy in Vienna 1982–87, with Political Affairs Div. then Office of Sec.-Gen., Ministry of Foreign Affairs 1987–91; seconded to

NATO as Head of Disarmament, Arms Control and Cooperative Security Section 1991–97; Deputy Chief of Mission, Perm. Mission to OSCE, Vienna, Chair. for negotiations on Adaptation of the Treaty on Conventional Armed Forces in Europe 1997–2000; Rep. Exec. Council of Org. for Prohibition of Chemical Weapons 2000–02; Dir OSCE Conflict Prevention Centre 2002–06; worked on EU common foreign and security policy, Ministry of Foreign Affairs 2006–08; UN Sec.-Gen.'s Special Rep. for Kosovo and Head of Mission, UN Interim Admin. Mission in Kosovo (UNMIK) 2008–11; Sec.-Gen. OSCE 2011–. **Publications include:** numerous publs and articles on arms control, peace-keeping and security co-operation. **Address:** Organization for Security and Co-operation in Europe (OSCE), Wallnerstrasse 6, 1010 Vienna, Austria. **Telephone:** (1) 514-36-0. **Fax:** (1) 514-36-96. **E-mail:** info@osce.org. **Internet:** www.osce.org.

ZARIF, Farid; Afghan; *Special Representative of the Secretary-General for Kosovo and Head, United Nations Interim Administration Mission in Kosovo (UNMIK);* b. 9 Jan. 1951; m. Alia Zarif; two s. **Education:** Faculty of Law and Political Science, Kabul Univ., Afghan Inst. of Diplomacy, Univ. of Oxford, UK. **Career:** joined Ministry of Foreign Affairs 1974, First Sec., later Charge d'Affaires, Embassy in Havana 1979–80, Amb. and Perm. Rep. to UN, New York 1981–87, Deputy Foreign Minister 1987–89; Prin. Foreign Policy Adviser to Pres. 1989–91; Sec.-Gen. Economic Advisory Council, Chambers of Commerce and Industry 1991–92; joined UN 1993, Referendum/Elections Co-ordinator UN missions in Eritrea and South Africa 1993 and 1995, Chief Elections Officer, UN Mission in Liberia (UNMIL) 1994–96, UN Deputy Humanitarian Co-ordinator in Iraq 1997–2000, fmr Chief, then Dir Office of Iraq Programme, New York, Chief of Staff, UN Assistance Mission for Iraq (UNAMI) 2004, then Chief of Staff and Acting Deputy Special Rep. of Sec.-Gen., UN Mission in Sudan (UNMIS), Dir Europe and Latin America Div., Dept of Peace-keeping Operations (DPKO) 2010, Special Rep. of Sec.-Gen. for Kosovo and Head, UN Interim Admin Mission in Kosovo (UNMIK) 2011–. **Address:** United Nations Interim Administration Mission in Kosovo (UNMIK), Department of Peace-keeping Operations, Room S-3727-B, United Nations, New York, NY 10017, USA. **Telephone:** (212) 963-8077. **Fax:** (212) 963-9222. **Internet:** www.unmikonline.org.

ZAYANI, Lt-Gen. (retd) Abdul Latif bin Rashid al-; Bahraini; *Secretary-General, Cooperation Council of Arab States of the Gulf (GCC);* b. Muharraq. **Education:** Royal Mil. Acad., Sandhurst, UK, Air Force Inst. of Tech., Dayton, Ohio, USA, Naval Postgraduate School, Monterey, USA. **Career:** numerous positions in Bahrain Defence Force including Officer, 1st Royal Mechanized Bn, Royal Air Defence, Royal Bahraini Air Force, Dir of Planning and Org., Dir of Jt Operations, Asst Chief of Staff for Operations; Chief of Public Security, Ministry of the Interior 2004; Adviser with rank of Minister, Gen. Court of Ministry of Foreign Affairs 2010; Sec.-Gen., GCC 2011–; Chair. Jt Steering Cttee between Bahrain and UK; Chair. Devt and Regulation Cttee, Ministry of Foreign Affairs; fmr Prof. of Quantitative Methods, Univ. of Bahrain; fmr Prof. of Mathematics and Statistics, Univ. of Maryland, Bahrain; Efficiency Medal 2nd Class, Mil. Assessment Medal 1st Class, Bahrain Medal 3rd Grade, Shaikh Isa Medal 3rd Grade, Bahrain Medal 2nd Grade, Mil. Duty Medal, Hawar Medal 1st Grade, Liberation of Kuwait Medal 2nd Grade, Liberation of Kuwait Medal, Security Medal for Devotion to Duty 1st Class, Bahrain Medal 1st Grade, Sword of Honor along with title of Master Logistician from USA Army, Int. Police Leadership Award NPIA, UK 2010. **Address:** Gulf Cooperation Council Building, King Khaled Road Diplomatic Area, PO Box 7153, Riyadh 11462, Saudi Arabia. **Telephone:** (1) 482-7777. **Fax:** (1) 482-9089. **E-mail:** info@gcc-sg.org. **Internet:** www.gcc-sg.org.

ZERIHOUN, Tayé-Brook, MPhil; Ethiopian; *Assistant Secretary-General for Political Affairs, United Nations;* m.; one s. three d. **Education:** Columbia Univ., New York, USA. **Career:** joined UN 1981, worked on special assignments on decolonization, trusteeship, conflict prevention and resolution, peacemaking and peace-building, New York, Deputy Dir, then Dir Africa I Div., Dept of Political Affairs, with responsibility for countries of Horn of Africa, Great Lakes and Southern Africa regions and regional orgs including Inter-Governmental Authority on Devt and Southern African Devt Community 1995–2003, Chair. Inter-departmental Task Force for Sudan 2003–04, Sec.-Gen.'s Prin. Deputy Special Rep. in Sudan with rank of Asst Sec.-Gen. 2004–08; Special Rep. of Sec.-Gen. and Head of UN Peace-keeping Force in Cyprus (UNFICYP) 2008–10; Asst Sec.-Gen. for Political Affairs 2010–. **Address:** Department of Political Affairs, United Nations, New York, NY 10017, USA. **Telephone:** (212) 963-1234. **Fax:** (212) 963-4879. **Internet:** www.un.org/Depts/dpa.

ZEWDE, Sahle-Work; Ethiopian; *Director-General, United Nations, Nairobi;* b. 21 Feb. 1950; two s. **Education:** Univ. of Montpellier, France. **Career:** Amb. to Senegal (also accred to Mali, Cape Verde, Guinea-Bissau, Gambia and Guinea) 1989–93, Amb. to Djibouti and Perm. Rep. to IGAD 1993–2002, Amb. to France and Perm. Rep. to UNESCO (also accred to Tunisia and Morocco) 2002–06, Perm. Rep. of Ethiopia to the African Union (AU) and UN ECA 2006–09, Dir-Gen. for African Affairs, Ministry of Foreign Affairs 2006–09, has represented Ethiopia in the Peace and Security Council of the AU 2006–; Special Rep. of the UN Sec.-Gen. and Head of UN Integrated Peace-building Office in the Cen. African Repub. (BINUCA) 2009–11, Dir-Gen. UN Office in Nairobi 2011–; Co-Chair. UN Security Council-AU Peace and Security Council jt meeting, New York April 2008; has attended most IGAD meetings, as well as OAU/AU summits and led the experts group in different partnership summits with Africa (China-India-EU-France-S America-Turkey), and has led OAU observer team in parl. and presidential elections in Mali 1991 and Niger 1993, 1996. **Address:** United Nations Office at Nairobi, PO Box 67578, Nairobi 00200, Kenya. **Telephone:** (20) 7621234. **Internet:** www.unon.org.

INDEX OF INTERNATIONAL ORGANIZATIONS

(Main reference only)

A

B

C

F

O

P